ST/ESA/STAT/SER.R/47

Department of Economic and Social Affairs
Département des affaires économiques et sociales

2017
Demographic Yearbook
Annuaire démographique

Sixty-eighth issue/Soixante-huitième édition

United Nations
New York, 2018

The Department of Economic and Social Affairs of the United Nations Secretariat is a vital interface between global policies in the economic, social and environmental spheres and national action. The Department works in three main interlinked areas: (i) it compiles, generates and analyses a wide range of economic, social and environmental data and information on which Member States of the United Nations draw to review common problems and to take stock of policy options; (ii) it facilitates the negotiations of Member States in many intergovernmental bodies on joint courses of action to address ongoing or emerging global challenges; and (iii) it advises interested Governments on the ways and means of translating policy frameworks developed in United Nations conferences and summits into programmes at the country level and, through technical assistance, helps build national capacities.

Le Département des affaires économiques et sociales du Secrétariat de l'Organisation des Nations Unies sert de relais entre les orientations arrêtées au niveau international dans les domaines économiques, sociaux et environnementaux et les politiques exécutées à l'échelon national. Il intervient dans trois grands domaines liés les uns aux autres : i) il compile, produit et analyse une vaste gamme de données et d'éléments d'information sur des questions économiques, sociales et environnementales dont les États Membres de l'Organisation se servent pour examiner des problèmes communs et évaluer les options qui s'offrent à eux; ii) il facilite les négociations entre les États Membres dans de nombreux organes intergouvernementaux sur les orientations à suivre de façon collective afin de faire face aux problèmes mondiaux existants ou en voie d'apparition; iii) il conseille les gouvernements intéressés sur la façon de transposer les orientations politiques arrêtées à l'occasion des conférences et sommets des Nations Unies en programmes exécutables au niveau national et aide à renforcer les capacités nationales au moyen de programmes d'assistance technique.

NOTE

Symbols of United Nations documents are composed of capital letters combined with figures. Mention of such a symbol indicates reference to a United Nations document.

The designations employed and the presentation of material in this publication do not imply the expression of any opinion whatsoever on the part of the Secretariat of the United Nations concerning the legal status of any country, territory, city or area, or of its authorities, or concerning the delimitation of its frontiers or boundaries.

Where the designation "country or area" appears in the headings of tables, it covers countries, territories, or areas.

NOTE

Les cotes des documents de l'Organisation des Nations Unies se composent de lettres majuscules et de chiffres. La simple mention d'une cote dans un texte signifie qu'il s'agit d'un document de l'Organisation.

Les appellations employées dans cette publication et la présentation des données qui y figurent n'impliquent de la part du Secrétariat de l'Organisation des Nations Unies aucune prise de position quant au statut juridique des pays, territoires, villes ou zones, ou de leurs autorités, ni quant au tracé de leurs frontières ou limites.

L'appellation "pays ou zone" figurant dans les titres des rubriques des tableaux désigne des pays, des territoires, ou des zones.

ST/ESA/STAT/SER.R/47

UNITED NATIONS PUBLICATION
Sales number: B.19.XIII.1 H

PUBLICATION DES NATIONS UNIES
Numéro de vente: B.19.XIII.1 H

ISBN 978-92-1-148305-5
eISBN 978-92-1-047422-1
Print ISSN: 0082-8041
Online ISSN: 2412-0006

Topics of the Demographic Yearbook series: 1948 - 2017

Sujets des diverses éditions de l'Annuaire démographique : 1948 - 2017

Year Année	Sales No. - Numéro de vente	Issue - Edition	Special topic - Sujet spécial
1948	49.XIII.1	First-Première	General demography-Démographie générale
1949-50	51.XIII.1	Second-Deuxième	Natality statistics-Statistiques de la natalité
1951	52.XIII.1	Third-Trosième	Mortality statistics-Statistiques de la mortalité
1952	53.XIII.1	Fourth-Quatrième	Population distribution-Répartition de la population
1953	54.XIII.1	Fifth-Cinquième	General demography-Démographie générale
1954	55.XIII.1	Sixth-Sixième	Natality statistics -Statistiques de la natalité
1955	56.XIII.1	Seventh-Septième	Population censuses-Recensement de population
1956	57.XIII.1	Eighth-Huitième	Ethnic and economic characteristics of population-Caractéristiques ethniques et économiques de la population
1957	58.XIII.1	Ninth-Neuvième	Mortality statistics- Statistiques de la mortalité
1958	59.XIII.1	Tenth-Dixième	Marriage and divorce statistics- Statistiques de la nuptialitè et de la divortialité
1959	60.XIII.1	Eleventh-Onzième	Natality statistics- Statistiques de la natalité
1960	61.XIII.1	Twelfth-Douzième	Population trends- l' évolution de la population
1961	62.XIII.1	Thirteenth-Treizième	Mortality Statistics- Statistiques de la mortalité
1962	63.XIII.1	Fourteenth-Quatorzième	Population census statistics I- Statistiques des recensements de population I
1963	64.XIII.1	Fifteenth-Quinzième	Population census statistics II- Statistiques des recensements de population II
1964	65.XIII.1	Sixteenth-Seizième	Population census statistics III- Statistiques des recensements de population III
1965	66.XIII.1	Seventeenth-Dix-septième	Natality statistics- Statistiques de la natalité
1966	67.XIII.1	Eighteenth-Dix-huitième	Mortality statistics I- Statistiques de la mortalité I
1967	E/F.68.XIII.1	Nineteenth-Dix-neuvième	Mortality statistics II - Statistiques de la mortalité II
1968	E/F.69.XIII.1	Twentieth-Vingtième	Marriage and divorce statistics-Statistiques de la nuptialité et de la divortialité
1969	E/F.70.XIII.1	Twenty-first-Vingt et unième	Natality statistics-Statistiques de la natalité
1970	E/F.71.XIII.1	Twenty-second-Vingt-deuxième	Population trends-l' évolution de la population
1971	E/F.72.XIII.1	Twenty-third-Vingt-troisième	Population census statistics I- Statistiques de recensements de population I
1972	E/F.73.XIII.1	Twenty-fourth-Vingt-quatrième	Population census statistics II- Statistiques des recensements de population II
1973	E/F.74.XIII.1	Twenty-fifth-Vingt-cinquième	Population census statistics III- Statistiques des recensements de population III
1974	E/F.75.XIII.1	Twenty-sixth-Vingt-sixième	Mortality statistics - Statistiques de la mortalité
1975	E/F.76.XIII.1	Twenty-seventh-Vingt-septième	Natality statistics- Statistiques de la natalité
1976	E/F.77.XIII.1	Twenty-eighth-Vingt-huitième	Marriage and divorce statistics- Statistiques de la nuptialité et de la divortialité
1977	E/F.78.XIII.1	Twenty-ninth-Vingt-neuvième	International Migration Statistics- internationales
1978	E/F.79.XIII.1	Thirtieth-Trentième	General tables- Tableaux de caractère général
1978	E/F.79.XIII.8	Special issue-Edition spéciale	Historical supplement-Supplément rétrospectif
1979	E/F.80.XIII.1	Thirty-first-Trente et unième	Population census statistics-Statistiques des recensements de population
1980	E/F.81.XIII.1	Thirty-second-Trente-deuxième	Mortality statistics- Statistiques de la mortalité
1981	E/F.82.XIII.1	Thirty-third-Trente-troisième	Natality statistics-Statistiques de la natalité
1982	E/F.83.XIII.1	Thirty-fourth-Trente-quatrième	Marriage and divorce statistics-Statistiques de la nuptialité et de la divortialité
1983	E/F.84.XIII.1	Thirty fifth-Trente-cinquième	Population census statistics I-Statistiques des recensements de population I
1984	E/F.85.XIII.1	Thirty-sixth-	Population census statistics II-

Topics of the Demographic Yearbook series: 1948 - 2017

Sujets des diverses éditions de l'Annuaire démographique : 1948 - 2017

Year Année	Sales No. - Numéro de vente	Issue - Edition	Special topic - Sujet spécial
		Trente-sixième	Statistiques des recensements de population II
1985	E/F.86.XIII.1	Thirty-seventh- Trente-septième	Mortality statistics- Statistiques de la mortalité
1986	E/F.87.XIII.1	Thirty-eighth- Trente-huitième	Natality statistics- Statistiques de la natalité
1987	E/F.88.XIII.1	Thirty-ninth- Trente-neuvième	Household composition- Les éléments du ménage
1988	E/F.89.XIII.1	Fortieth- Quarantième	Population census statistics- Statistiques des recensements de population
1989	E/F.90.XIII.1	Forty-first- Quarante-et-unième	International Migration Statistics- Statistiques des migration internationales
1990	E/F.91.XIII.1	Forty-second- Quarante-deuxième	Marriage and divorce statistics- Statistiques de la nuptialité et de la divortialité
1991	E/F.92.XIII.1	Forty-third- Quarante-troisième	General tables- Tableaux de caractère général
1991	E/F.92.XIII.9	Special Issue	Population Ageing and the Situation of Elderly Persons Vieillissement de la population et situation des personnes âgées
1992	E/F.94.XIII.1	Forty-fourth- Quarante-quatrième	Fertility and mortality statistics- Statistiques de la fecondité et de la mortalité
1993	E/F.95.XIII.1	Forty-fifth- Quarante-cinquième	Population census statistics I- Statistiques des recensements de population I
1994	E/F.96.XIII.1	Forty-sixth- Quarante-sixième	Population census statistics II- Statistiques des recensements de population II
1995	E/F.97.XIII.1	Forty-seventh- Quarante-septième	Household composition-Les éléments du ménage
1996	E/F.98.XIII.1	Forty-eighth- Quarante-huitième	Mortality statistics- Statistiques de la mortalité
1997	E/F.99.XIII.1	Forty-ninth- Quarante-neuvième	General tables- Tableaux de caractère général
1997	E/F.99.XIII.12	Special issue- Edition spéciale (CD)	Historical supplement- Supplément rétrospectif
1998	E/F.00.XIII.1	Fiftieth- Cinquantième	General tables- Tableaux de caractère général
1999	E/F.01.XIII.1	Fifty-first- Cinquante-et-unième	General tables- Tableaux de caractère général
1999	E/F.02.XIII.6	Special issue- Edition spéciale (CD)	Natality Statistics- Statistiques de la natalité
2000	E/F.02.XIII.1	Fifty-second- Cinquante-deuxième	General tables- Tableaux de caractère général
2001	E/F.03.XIII.1	Fifty-third- Cinquante- troisième	General tables- Tableaux de caractère général
2002	E/F.05.XIII.1	Fifty-fourth- Cinquante-quatrième	General tables- Tableaux de caractère général
2003	E/F.06.XIII.1	Fifty-fifth- Cinquante-cinquième	General tables- Tableaux de caractère général
2004	E/F.07.XIII.1	Fifty-sixth- Cinquante-sixième	General tables- Tableaux de caractère général
2005	E/F.08.XIII.1	Fifty-seventh- Cinquante-septième	General tables- Tableaux de caractère général
2006	E/F.09.XIII.1	Fifty-eighth- Cinquante-huitième	General tables- Tableaux de caractère général
2007	E/F.10.XIII.1	Fifty-ninth- Cinquante-neuvième	General tables- Tableaux de caractère général
2008	E/F.11.XIII.1	Sixtieth- Soixantième	General tables- Tableaux de caractère général
2009 - 2010	B.12.XIII.1 H	Sixty-first Soixante-et-unième	General tables- Tableaux de caractère général
2011	B.13.XIII.1 H	Sixty-second Soixante- deuxième	General tables- Tableaux de caractère général
2012	B.14.XIII.1 H	Sixty-third Soixante- troisième	General tables- Tableaux de caractère général

Year Année	Sales No. - Numéro de vente	Issue - Edition	Special topic - Sujet spécial
2013	B.15.XIII.1 H	Sixty-fourth Soixante- quatrième	General tables- Tableaux de caractère général
2014	B.16.XIII.1 H	Sixty-fifth Soixante- cinquième	General tables and Whipple's Index, censuses,1985-2014 - Tableaux de caractère général et l'indice de Whipple, recensements, 1985-2014
2015	B.17.XIII.1 H	Sixty-sixth Soixante- sixième	General tables and Whipple's Index, censuses,1985-2015 - Tableaux de caractère général et l'indice de Whipple, recensements, 1985-2015
2016	B.18.XIII.1 H	Sixty-seventh Soixante- septième	General tables and Whipple's Index, censuses,1985-2016 - Tableaux de caractère général et l'indice de Whipple, recensements, 1985-2016
2017	B.19.XIII.1 H	Sixty-eighth Soixante- huitième	General tables and Whipple's Index, censuses,1985-2017 - Tableaux de caractère général et l'indice de Whipple, recensements, 1985-2017

CONTENTS - TABLE DES MATIERES

FERTILITY

FOETAL MORTALITY

INFANT AND MATERNAL MORTALITY

GENERAL MORTALITY

NATALITÉ

MORTALITÉ FŒTALES

MORTALITÉ INFANTILE ET MORTALITÉ LIÉE À LA MATERNITÉ

MORTALITÉ GÉNÉRALE

EXPLANATIONS OF SYMBOLS

Category not applicable ....

Data not available... ...

Magnitude zero or less than half of unit employed .... -

Provisional .... *

Data tabulated by year of registration rather than occurrence .... +

Based on less than specified minimum .... ◆

Relatively reliable data .... Roman type

Data of lesser reliability .... *Italics*

EXPLICATION DES SIGNES

Sans objet ....

Données non disponibles ....

Néant ou chiffre inférieur à la moitié de l'unité employée .... -

Données provisoires .... *

Donnée exploitées selon l'année de l'enregistrement et non l'année de l'événement   +

Rapport fondé sur un nombre inférieur à celui spécifié............................. ◆

Données relativement sûres.. Caractères romains

Données dont l'exactitude est moindre .... *Italiques*

INTRODUCTION

The *Demographic Yearbook* is an international compendium of national demographic statistics provided by national statistical authorities to the Statistics Division of the United Nations Department of Economic and Social Affairs. The *Demographic Yearbook* is part of the set of coordinated and interrelated publications issued by the United Nations and its specialized agencies, designed to supply statistical data for such users as demographers, economists, public-health workers and sociologists. Through the co-operation of national statistical services, available official demographic statistics are compiled in the *Demographic Yearbook* for more than 230 countries or areas throughout the world.

The *Demographic Yearbook 2017* is the sixty-eighth issue in a series published by the United Nations since 1948. It contains tables on a wide range of demographic statistics, including a world summary of selected demographic statistics, statistics on the size, distribution and trends in national populations, fertility, foetal mortality, infant and maternal mortality, general mortality, nuptiality and divorce. Data are shown by urban/rural residence, as available. The volume provides Technical Notes, a synoptic table, a historical index and a listing of the issues of the *Demographic Yearbook* published to date. This issue of *Demographic Yearbook* contains data as available including reference year 2017.

This edition of the *Demographic Yearbook* features also table 3a with Whipple's index by sex and urban/rural residence for the population censuses conducted worldwide since 1985. Whipple's index is an index of age preference in age reporting and can therefore serve to highlight some of the problems related to age distribution.

The Technical Notes on the Statistical Tables are provided to assist the reader in using the tables. Table A, the synoptic table, provides an overview of the completeness of data coverage of the current *Demographic Yearbook*. The cumulative historical index is a guide on content and coverage of all sixty-eight issues, and indicates, for each of the topics that have been published, the issues in which they are presented and the years covered. It also contains a list of tables published online through UNdata[1] (http://data.un.org/Explorer.aspx?d=POP). A list of the *Demographic Yearbook* issues, with their corresponding sales numbers and the special topics featured in each issue are shown on pages iii and iv. Additionally, all issues of the *Demographic Yearbook* are available online at the Statistics Division's website: https://unstats.un.org/unsd/demographic-social/products/dyb/index.cshtml.

Until the 48th issue (1996), each issue consisted of two parts, the general tables and special topic tables, published in the same volume[2]. Beginning with the 49th issue (1997), the special topic tables were being disseminated in digital format as supplements to the regular issues. Two CD-ROMs have been issued: the *Demographic Yearbook Historical Supplement*, which presents a wide panorama of basic demographic statistics for the period 1948 to 1997, and the *Demographic Yearbook: Natality Statistics*, which contains a series of detailed tables dedicated to natality and covering the period from 1980 to 1998. Later on, three volumes of *Demographic Yearbook* Special Census Topics for the 2000 round of censuses, covering the period from 1995 to 2004, were published on-line at http://unstats.un.org/unsd/demographic/products/dyb/dybcens.htm. Current *Demographic Yearbook* population and housing censuses data for the 2000, 2010 and 2020 rounds (1995 to the present) are presented at https://unstats.un.org/unsd/demographic-social/products/dyb/index.cshtml#censusdatasets. These datasets cover basic population characteristics, educational, household, ethnocultural and economic characteristics, and also foreign-born and foreign population. Special tabulations on household and economic characteristics with data based on population censuses since 1995 are available respectively at https://unstats.un.org/unsd/demographic-social/products/dyb/dyb_household/ and https://unstats.un.org/unsd/demographic-social/products/dyb/dyb_eco/.

Population statistics are not available for all countries or areas, for a variety of reasons. In an effort to provide estimates of mid-year population and of selected vital statistics for all countries and areas, two annexes are presented. Annex I presents United Nations population estimates for the period 2008-2017 and Annex II presents the medium variant estimates of crude birth and death rates, infant mortality and total fertility rates, as well as life expectancy at birth over the period 2015-2020. These data were produced by the United Nations Population Division and are published in the *2017 Revision of World Population Prospects*[3].

Demographic statistics shown in this issue of the *Demographic Yearbook* are available online at the *Demographic Yearbook* website https://unstats.un.org/unsd/demographic-social/products/dyb/index.cshtml#overview.

Information about the Statistics Division's data collection and dissemination programme is also available on the same website. Additional information can be made available by contacting the Statistics Division of the United Nations Department of Economic and Social Affairs at demostat@un.org.

TECHNICAL NOTES ON THE STATISTICAL TABLES

1. GENERAL REMARKS

1.1 Arrangement of Technical Notes

These Technical Notes are designed to provide the reader with relevant information related to the statistical tables. Information pertaining to the *Demographic Yearbook* in general is presented in the sections dealing with geographical aspects, population and vital statistics. In addition, preceding each table are notes describing the variables, remarks on the reliability and limitation of the data, countries and areas covered, and information on the presentation of earlier data. When appropriate, details on computation of rates, ratios or percentages are presented.

1.2 Arrangement of tables

The numbering of tables from one issue of *Demographic Yearbook* to the next is preserved to the extent possible. However, since for some of the tables the numbering may not correspond exactly to those in previous issues, the reader is advised to use the historical index that appears at the end of this book to find the reference to data in earlier issues.

1.3 Source of data

The statistics presented in the *Demographic Yearbook* are national data provided by official statistical authorities unless otherwise indicated. The primary source of data for the *Demographic Yearbook* is a set of questionnaires sent annually by the United Nations Statistics Division to over 230 national statistical services. Data reported on these questionnaires are supplemented, to the extent possible, with data taken from official national publications, official websites and through correspondence with national statistical services. In the interest of comparability, rates, ratios and percentages have been calculated by the Statistics Division of the United Nations, except for the life table functions, the total fertility rate, and also crude birth rate and crude death rate for some countries or areas as appropriately noted. The methods used by the Statistics Division to calculate these rates and ratios are described in the Technical Notes for each table. The population figures used for these computations are those pertaining to the corresponding years published in this or previous issues of the *Demographic Yearbook*.

In cases when data in this issue of the *Demographic Yearbook* differ from those published in earlier issues or related publications, statistics in this issue may be assumed to reflect revisions to the data received by June 2018.

2. GEOGRAPHICAL ASPECTS

2.1 Coverage

Data are shown for all individual countries or areas that provided information. Table 3 is the most comprehensive in geographical coverage, presenting data on population and surface area for all countries or areas with a population of at least 50 persons. Not all of these countries or areas appear in subsequent tables. In many cases the data required for a particular table are not available. In general, the more detailed the data required for a table, the fewer the number of countries or areas that can provide them.

In addition, rates and ratios are presented only for countries or areas reporting at least a minimum number of relevant events. The minimums are stated in the Technical Notes to individual tables.

Except for summary data shown for the world and by major areas and regions in tables 1 and 2 and data shown for capital cities and cities with a population of 100 000 or more in table 8, all data are presented at the national level. The number of countries or areas shown in each table is provided in table A, the synoptic table.

2.2 Territorial composition

To the extent possible, all data, including time series data, relate to the territory within 2017 boundaries. Exceptions are footnoted in individual tables. Relevant clarifications are specified below.

Data relating to **Denmark** exclude Faeroe Islands and Greenland, which are shown separately.

Data relating to **Finland** include Åland Islands, unless otherwise indicated by a footnote.

Data relating to **France** exclude Overseas Departments, namely, French Guiana, Guadeloupe, Martinique and Réunion, which are shown separately, unless otherwise indicated by a footnote.

Data relating to **United Kingdom of Great Britain and Northern Ireland** exclude Guernsey, Isle of Man and Jersey which are shown separately.

Data relating to **Western Sahara** comprise the Northern Region (former Saguia el Hamra) and Southern Region (former Rio de Oro).

2.3 Nomenclature

Because of space limitations, the country or area names listed in the tables are generally the commonly employed short titles currently in use[4] in the United Nations, the full titles being used only when a short form is not available. The latest version of the *Standard Country or Area Codes for Statistics Use* can be accessed at https://unstats.un.org/unsd/methodology/m49/.

2.3.1 Order of presentation

Countries or areas are listed in English alphabetical order within the following continents: Africa, North America, South America, Asia, Europe and Oceania.

The designations and presentation of the material in this publication were adopted solely for the purpose of providing a convenient geographical basis for the accompanying statistical series. The same qualification applies to all notes and explanations concerning the geographical units for which data are presented.

2.4 Surface area data

Surface area data shown in table 1 represent the land area, whereas in table 3 the total surface area unless otherwise indicated. The total surface area comprises land area and inland waters (assumed to consist of major rivers and lakes) and excluding only Polar Regions and uninhabited islands. The surface area given is the most recent estimate available. They are presented in square kilometres; a conversion factor of 2.589988 having been applied to surface areas originally reported in square miles.

2.4.1 Comparability over time

Comparability over time in surface area estimates for any given country or area may be affected by changes in the surface area estimation procedures, increases in actual land surface by reclamation, boundary changes, changes in the concept of "land surface area" used or a change in the unit of measurement used. In most cases it was possible to ascertain the reason for a revision; otherwise, the latest figures have generally been accepted as correct.

2.4.2 International comparability

Lack of international comparability between surface area estimates arises primarily from differences in definition. In particular, there is considerable variation in the treatment of coastal bays, inlets and gulfs, rivers and lakes. International comparability is also impaired by the variation in methods employed to estimate surface area. These range from surveys based on modern scientific methods to conjectures based on diverse types of information. Some estimates are recent while others may not be. Since neither the exact method of determining the surface area nor the precise definition of its composition and time reference is known for all countries or areas, the estimates in table 3 should not be considered strictly comparable from one country or area to another.

3. POPULATION

Population statistics, that is, those pertaining to the size, geographical distribution and demographic characteristics of the population, are presented in a number of tables of the *Demographic Yearbook*.

Summary estimates of the mid-year population of the world, major areas and regions for selected years and of its age and sex distribution in 2017 are set forth in tables 1 and 2, respectively.

Data for countries or areas include population census figures, estimates based on results of sample surveys (in the absence of a census), postcensal or intercensal estimates and those derived from continuous population registers. In the present issue of the *Demographic Yearbook*, the latest available census figure of the total population of each country or area and mid-year estimates for 2010 and 2017 are presented in table 3. Mid-year estimates of total population for ten years (2008-2017) are shown in table 5 and mid-year estimates of urban and total population by sex for ten years (2008-2017) are shown in table 6. The latest available data on population by age, sex and urban/rural residence are given in table 7. The latest available figures on the population of capital cities and of cities or urban agglomerations of 100 000 or more inhabitants are presented in table 8.

The statistics on total population, population by age, sex, or urban/rural distribution are used for the calculation of rates in the *Demographic Yearbook*. Vital rates by residence (urban/rural), age or sex were calculated using data presented in tables 6 or 7 in this issue or the corresponding tables of previous issues of the *Demographic Yearbook*.

3.1 Sources of variation of data

The comparability of data is affected by several factors, including (1) the definition of total population; (2) the definition used to classify the population into its urban/rural components; (3) the accuracy of age reporting; (4) the extent of over-enumeration or under-enumeration in the most recent census or other source of benchmark population statistics; and (5) the quality of population estimates. These five factors will be discussed in some detail in sections 3.1.1 to 3.1.3 below. Other relevant problems are discussed in the technical notes to the individual tables. Readers interested in more detail, relating in particular to the basic concepts of population size, distribution and characteristics as elaborated by the United Nations, should consult the *Principles and Recommendations for Population and Housing Censuses, Revision 3*[5].

3.1.1 Total population

The most important impediment to comparability of total populations is the difference between the concept of a *de facto* and *de jure* population. A *de facto* population includes all persons physically present in the country or area at the reference date. The *de jure* population, by contrast, includes all usual residents of the given country or area, whether or not they were physically present in the area at the reference date. By definition, therefore, a *de facto* total and a *de jure* total are not entirely comparable.

Comparability of even two *de facto* or *de jure* totals is often affected by the fact that strict conformity to either of these concepts is rare. For example, some so-called *de facto* counts do not include foreign military, naval and diplomatic personnel present in the country or area on official duty, and their accompanying family and household members; some do not include foreign visitors in transit through the country or area or transients on ships in harbours. On the other hand, they may include such persons as merchant seamen and fishermen who are temporarily out of the country or area working at their trade.

4

The *de jure* population figure presents even greater variations in comparability, in part because it depends in the first place on the concept of "usual residence", which varies from one country or area to another and is difficult to apply consistently in a census or survey enumeration. For example, non-national civilians temporarily in a country or area as short-term workers may officially be considered residents after a stay of a specified period of time or they may be considered as non-residents throughout the duration of their stay; at the same time, these individuals may be officially considered as residents or non-residents of the country or area from which they came, depending on the duration and/or purpose of their absence. Furthermore, regardless of the official treatment, individual respondents may apply their own interpretation of residence in responding to the inquiry. In addition, there may be considerable differences in the accuracy with which countries or areas are informed about the number of their residents temporarily out of the country or area.

The population statistics presented in the tables of the *Demographic Yearbook* refer to the *de facto* population or to the *de jure* population. In an effort to overcome, to the extent possible, the effect of the lack of strict conformity to either the *de facto* or the *de jure* concept given above, significant exceptions with respect to inclusions and exclusions of specific population groups, are footnoted when they are known.

A possible source of variation within the statistics of a single country or area may arise from the fact that some countries or areas collect information on both the *de facto* and the *de jure* population in, for example, a census, but prepare detailed tabulations for only the *de jure* population. Hence, even though the total population shown in table 3 is de facto, the figures shown in the tables presenting various characteristics of the population, for example, urban/rural distribution, age and sex distribution, may be on the *de jure* concept.

3.1.2 Urban/rural classification

International comparability of urban/rural distributions is seriously impaired by the wide variation among national definitions of the concept of "urban". The definitions used by individual countries or areas and their implications are shown at the end of technical notes for table 6.

3.1.3 Age distribution

The classification of population by age is a core element of most analyses, estimation and projection of population statistics. Unfortunately, age data are subject to a number of sources of error and non-comparability. Accordingly, the reliability of age data should be of concern to users of these statistics.

3.1.3.1 Collection and compilation of age data

Age is the estimated or calculated interval of time between the date of birth and the date of the census or survey, expressed in completed solar years[6]. There are two methods of collecting information on age. The first is to obtain the date of birth for each member of the population in a census or survey and then to calculate the completed age of the individual by subtracting the date of birth from the date of enumeration[7]. The second method is to record the individual's completed age at the time of the census or survey, that is to say, age at last birthday.

The recommended method is to calculate age at last birthday by subtracting the exact date of birth from the date of the census. Some practices, however, do not use this method but instead calculate the difference between the year of birth and the year of the census. Classifications of this type are footnoted whenever possible. They can be identified to a certain extent by a smaller than expected population under one year of age. However, an irregular number of births from one year to the next or age selective omission of infants may also obscure the expected population under one year of age.

5

3.1.3.2 Errors in age data

Errors in age data may be due to a variety of causes, including ignorance of the correct age; reporting years of age in terms of a calendar concept other than completed solar years since birth[8]; carelessness in reporting and recording age; a general tendency to state age in figures ending in certain digits (such as zero, two, five and eight); a tendency to exaggerate length of life at advanced ages; a subconscious aversion to certain numbers; and wilful misrepresentations.

These reasons for errors in reported age data are common to most investigations of age and to most countries or areas, and they may significantly impair comparability of the data.

As a result of the above-mentioned difficulties, the age-sex distribution of population in many countries or areas shows irregularities which may be summarized as follows: (1) a deficiency in the number of infants and young children; (2) a concentration at ages ending with zero and five (that is, 5, 10, 15, 20, ...); (3) heaping at even ages (for example, 10, 12, 14, ...) relative to odd ages (for example, 11, 13, 15, ...); (4) unexpectedly large differences between the frequency of males and females at certain ages; and (5) unaccountably large differences between the frequencies in adjacent age groups. Comparing of identical age-sex cohorts from successive censuses, as well as studying the age-sex composition of each census, may reveal these and other inconsistencies, some of which in varying degree are characteristic of even the most modern censuses.

This edition of the *Demographic Yearbook* features a tabulation (table 3a) with Whipple's index by sex and urban/ rural residence for the population censuses conducted worldwide since 1985. Whipple's index is an index of age preference in age reporting and can therefore serve to highlight some of the problems related to age distribution.

4. VITAL STATISTICS

For purposes of the *Demographic Yearbook*, vital statistics of concern are those of live birth, death, foetal death, marriage and divorce.

This volume of the *Demographic Yearbook* presents tables on fertility, nuptiality and divorce as well as tables on mortality referring to foetal mortality, infant and maternal mortality and general mortality.

4.1 Sources of variation of data

Most of the vital statistics data published in this *Demographic Yearbook* are sourced from national civil registration systems. The completeness and the accuracy of the data that these systems produce vary from one country or area to another.

National civil registration systems may not exist in all countries, and in some cases, the registration system covers only certain vital events. For example, in some countries or areas only births and deaths are registered. There are also differences in the effectiveness with which national laws pertaining to civil registration operate in the various countries or areas. The manner in which the law is implemented and the degree to which the public complies with the legislation determine the reliability of vital statistics obtained from the civil registers.

It should be noted that some statistics on marriage and divorce are obtained from sources other than civil registers. For example, in some countries or areas, the only source for data on marriages is church registers. Divorce statistics, on the other hand, are obtained from court records and/or civil registers according to national practice. The actual compilation of these statistics may be the responsibility of the civil registrar, the national statistical office or other government offices.

Other factors affecting international comparability of vital statistics are much the same as those that must be considered in evaluating the variations in other population statistics. Differences in statistical definitions of vital events, differences in geographical and ethnic coverage of the data and diverse tabulation procedures may also influence comparability.

In addition to vital statistics from civil registers, some vital statistics published in the *Demographic Yearbook* are official estimates. These estimates are frequently from population censuses and sample surveys. As such, their comparability may be affected by the national completeness of reporting in population censuses and household surveys, whether a *de facto* or *de jure* based census, non-sampling and sampling errors and other sources of bias.

Readers interested in more detailed information on standards for vital statistics should consult the *Principles and Recommendations for a Vital Statistics System Revision 3*[9]; *Handbook on Civil Registration and Vital Statistics Systems: Preparation of a Legal Framework*[10]; *Handbook on Civil Registration and Vital Statistics Systems: Management, Operation and Maintenance*[11]; *Handbook on Civil Registration and Vital Statistics Systems: Developing Information, Education and Communication*[12]; *Handbook on Civil Registration and Vital Statistics Systems: Policies and Protocols for the Release and Archiving of Individual Records*[13]; and *Handbook on Civil Registration and Vital Statistics Systems: Computerization*[14]. The *Handbook on the Collection of Fertility and Mortality Data*[15] provides information in collection and evaluation of data on fertility and mortality collected in population censuses and household surveys. These publications are also available on the website at https://unstats.un.org/unsd/demographic-social/Standards-and-Methods/index.cshtml.

4.1.1 Statistical definition of events

An important source of variation lies in the statistical definition of each vital event. The *Demographic Yearbook* attempts to collect data on vital events, using the standard definitions put forth in Chapter I of *Principles and Recommendations for a Vital Statistics System Revision 3*. These definitions are as follows:

LIVE BIRTH is the complete expulsion or extraction from its mother of a product of conception, irrespective of the duration of pregnancy, which after such separation breathes or shows any other evidence of life such as beating of the heart, pulsation of the umbilical cord, or definite movement of voluntary muscles, whether or not the umbilical cord has been cut or the placenta is attached; each product of such a birth is considered live-born.

DEATH is the permanent disappearance of all evidence of life at any time after the occurrence of live birth, i.e., the postnatal cessation of vital functions without capability of resuscitation. This definition excludes foetal deaths.

FOETAL DEATH is death prior to the complete expulsion or extraction from its mother of a product of conception, irrespective of the duration of the period of gestation. Death is indicated by the fact that after such separation, the foetus does not breathe or show any other evidence of life, such as beating of the heart, pulsation of the umbilical cord, or definite movement of voluntary muscles.

MARRIAGE is an act, ceremony or process by which the legal relationship of spouses is constituted. The legality of the union may be established by civil, religious or other means as recognized by the laws of each country. Countries may wish to expand the definition to cover civil unions if they are registered. In that case, registered partnership usually refers to a legal construct, entailing registration with the public authorities according to the laws of each country, that becomes the basis for legal conjugal obligations between two persons.

DIVORCE is a final legal dissolution of a marriage, that is, the separation of spouses that confers on the parties the right to remarriage under civil, religious and/or other provisions, according to the laws of each country. In the case where a country recognizes registered partnerships, a legal dissolution of a registered partnership constitutes the legal final dissolution of such a partnership, according to national laws, which confers on the parties the right to enter into another partnership or marriage.

In addition to these internationally recommended definitions, the *Demographic Yearbook* collects and presents data on abortions, defined as:

ABORTION is defined, with reference to the woman, as any interruption of pregnancy before 28 weeks of gestation with a dead foetus. There are two major categories of abortion: spontaneous and induced. Induced abortions are those initiated by deliberate action undertaken with the intention of terminating pregnancy; all other abortions are considered spontaneous.

4.1.2 Problems relating to standard definitions

A basic problem affecting international comparability of vital statistics is deviations from the standard definitions of vital events. An example of this can be seen in the cases of live births and foetal deaths. In some countries or areas, an infant must survive for at least 24 hours, to be inscribed in the live-birth register. Infants who die before the expiration of the 24-hour period are classified as late foetal deaths and, barring special tabulation procedures, they would not be counted either as live births or as deaths. Similarly, in several other countries or areas, those infants who are born alive but die before registration of their birth, are also considered late foetal deaths.

Unless special tabulation procedures are adopted in such cases, the live-birth and death statistics will both be deficient by the number of these infants, while the incidence of late foetal deaths will be increased by the same amount. Hence the infant mortality rate is underestimated. Although both components (infant deaths and live births) are deficient by the same absolute amount, the deficiency is proportionately greater in relation to the infant deaths, causing greater errors in the infant mortality rate than in the birth rate.

Moreover, the practice exaggerates the late foetal death ratios. Some countries or areas make provision for correcting this deficiency (at least in the total frequencies) at the tabulation stage. Data for which the correction has not been made are indicated by a footnote whenever possible.

The definitions used for marriage and divorce also present problems for international comparability. Unlike birth and death, which are biological events, marriage and divorce are defined only in terms of law and custom and as such are less amenable to universally applicable statistical definitions. They have therefore been defined for statistical purposes in general terms referring to the laws of individual countries or areas. Laws pertaining to marriage and particularly to divorce, vary from one country or area to another. With respect to marriage, the most widespread requirement relates to the minimum age at which persons may marry but frequently other requirements are specified.

When known the minimum legal age of men and women at which marriage can occur with or without parental consent is presented in table 24-1. Laws and regulations relating to the dissolution of marriage by divorce range from total prohibition, through a wide range of grounds upon which divorces may be granted, to the granting of divorce in response to a simple statement of desire or intention by spouses.

4.1.3 Fragmentary geographical or ethnic coverage

Ideally, vital statistics for any given country or area should cover the entire geographical area and include all ethnic groups. Fragmentary coverage is, however, not uncommon. In some countries or areas, registration is compulsory for only a small part of the population, limited to certain ethnic groups, for example. In other places there is no national provision for compulsory registration, but only municipal or state ordinances that do not cover the entire geographical area. Still others have developed a registration area that comprises only a part of the country or area, the remainder being excluded because of inaccessibility or for economic and cultural considerations that make regular registration practically impossible.

4.1.4 Tabulation procedures

4.1.4.1 By place of occurrence

Vital statistics presented at the national level relate to the de facto, that is, the present-in-area population. Thus, unless otherwise noted, vital statistics for a given country or area cover all the events that occur within its present boundaries and among all segments of the population therein. They may be presumed to include events among nomadic tribes and indigenous peoples, and among nationals and foreigners. When known, deviations from the *de facto* concept are footnoted.

Urban/rural differentials in vital rates for some countries may vary considerably depending on whether the relevant vital events were tabulated on the basis of place of occurrence or place of usual residence. For example, if a substantial number of women residing in rural areas near major urban centres travel to hospitals or maternity homes located in a city to give birth, urban fertility and neo-natal and infant mortality rates will usually be higher (and the corresponding rural rates will usually be lower) if the events are tabulated on the basis of place of occurrence rather than on the basis of place of usual residence. A similar process will affect general mortality differentials if substantial numbers of persons residing in rural areas use urban health facilities when seriously ill.

4.1.4.2 By date of occurrence versus by date of registration

To the extent possible, the vital statistics presented in the *Demographic Yearbook* refer to events that occurred during the specified year, rather than to those that were registered during that period. However, a considerable number of countries or areas tabulate their vital statistics not by date of occurrence, but by date of registration. Because such statistics can be misleading, the countries or areas known to tabulate vital statistics by date of registration are identified in the tables by a plus sign "+". Since information on the method of tabulating vital statistics is not available for all countries and areas, tabulation by date of registration may be more prevalent than the symbols on the vital statistics tables would indicate.

Because quality of data is inextricably related to the timeliness of registration, this must always be considered in conjunction with the quality code description in section 4.2.1 below. If registration of births is complete and timely (code "C"), the ill effects of tabulating by date of registration, are, for all practical purposes, nullified. Similarly, with respect to death statistics, the effect of tabulating events by date of registration may be minimized in many countries or areas in which the sanitary code requires that a death must be registered before a burial permit can be issued, and this regulation tends to make registration prompt. With respect to foetal death, registration is usually done right away or not at all. Therefore, if registration is prompt, the difference between statistics tabulated by date of occurrence and those tabulated by date of registration may be negligible. In many cases, the length of the statutory time period allowed for registering various vital events plays an important part in determining the effects of tabulation by date of registration on the comparability of data.

With respect to marriage and divorce, the practice of tabulating data by date of registration does not generally pose serious problems. In many countries or areas marriage is a civil legal contract which, to establish its legality, must be celebrated before a civil officer. It follows that for these countries or areas registration would tend to be almost automatic at the time of, or immediately following, the marriage ceremony. Because the registration of a divorce in many countries or areas is the responsibility solely of the court or the authority which granted it, and since the registration record in such cases is part of the records of the court proceedings, it follows that divorces are likely to be registered soon after the decree is granted.

On the other hand, if registration is not prompt, vital statistics by date of registration will not produce internationally comparable data. Under the best circumstances, statistics by date of registration will include primarily events that occurred in the immediately preceding year; in countries or areas with less developed systems, tabulations will include some events that occurred many years in the past. Examination of available information reveals that delays of many years are not uncommon for birth registration, though the majority is recorded between two to four years after birth.

As long as registration is not prompt, statistics by date of registration will not be internationally comparable either among themselves or with statistics by date of occurrence.

It should also be mentioned that lack of international comparability is not the only limitation introduced by date-of-registration tabulation. Even within the same country or area, comparability over time may be lost by the practice of counting registrations rather than occurrences. If the number of events registered from year to year fluctuates because of *ad hoc* incentives to stimulate registration, or to the sudden need, for example, for proof of (unregistered) birth or death to meet certain requirements, vital statistics tabulated by date of registration are not useful in measuring and analyzing demographic levels and trends. All they can give is an indication of the fluctuations in the need for a birth, death or marriage certificate and the work-load of the registrars. Therefore, statistics tabulated by date of registration may be of very limited use for either national or international studies.

4.2 Quality of published vital statistics

The quality of vital statistics can be assessed in terms of a number of factors. Most fundamental is the completeness of the civil registration system on which these statistics are based.

4.2.1 Quality code for vital statistics from registers.

In the *Demographic Yearbook* annual "Questionnaire on Vital Statistics" national statistical offices are asked to provide their own estimates of the completeness of the births, deaths, late foetal deaths, marriages and divorces recorded in their civil registers.

On the basis of information from the questionnaires, from direct correspondence and from relevant official publications, it has been possible to classify current national statistics from civil registers of birth, death, infant death, late foetal death, marriage and divorce into three broad quality categories, as follows:

C: Data estimated to be virtually complete, that is, representing at least 90 per cent of the events occurring each year.

U: Data estimated to be incomplete, that is representing less than 90 per cent of the events occurring each year.

|: Data not derived from civil registration systems but considered reliable, such as estimates derived from population and housing censuses.

...: Data for which no specific information is available regarding completeness.

These quality codes appear in the first column of the tables which show total frequencies and crude rates (or ratios) over a period of years for all tables on live births, late foetal deaths, infant deaths, deaths, marriages, and divorces. Reliability of maternal mortality statistics is provided by the World Health Organisation.

The classification of countries and areas in terms of these quality codes may not be uniform. Nevertheless, it was felt that national statistical offices were in the best position to judge the quality of their data. It was considered that even the very broad categories that could be established on the basis of the available information would provide useful indicators of the quality of the vital statistics presented in the *Demographic Yearbook*.

Among the countries or areas indicating that the registration of live births was estimated to be 90 per cent or more complete (and hence classified as "C" or "+C" in table 9), the following countries or areas provided information on the method used to evaluate the completeness estimate:

(a) Demographic analysis – Argentina, Australia, Austria, Brazil, Bulgaria, Chile, China - Hong Kong SAR, Croatia, Egypt, Estonia, Italy, Latvia, Lithuania, Malaysia, Malta, Mauritius, New Zealand, Panama, Republic of Moldova, Saudi Arabia, Seychelles, South Africa, Sweden and Venezuela (Bolivarian Republic of).

(b) Dual record check – Australia, Austria, Bahrain, Belgium, Brazil, Cuba, Cyprus, Estonia, Faeroe Islands, Greenland, Hungary, Israel, Italy, Latvia, Malaysia, Mongolia, Montserrat, New Zealand, Norway, Qatar, Republic of Korea, Saint Vincent and the Grenadines, Uruguay and Venezuela (Bolivarian Republic of).

(c) Other specified methods -- Aruba, Australia, Bolivia (Plurinational State of), Brazil, Curaçao, Denmark, France, Georgia, Germany, Guatemala, Ireland, Jordan, Kyrgyzstan, Liechtenstein, Luxembourg, Malaysia, Panama, Philippines, Poland, Puerto Rico, Romania, Singapore, Slovenia, Spain, State of Palestine, Sweden, Uzbekistan and Venezuela (Bolivarian Republic of).

Among the countries or areas indicating that the registration of late foetal-deaths was estimated to be 90 per cent or more complete (and hence classified as "C" or "+C" in table 12), the following countries or areas provided information on the method used to evaluate the completeness estimate:

(a) Demographic analysis -- Argentina, Austria, Bulgaria, Croatia, Egypt, Estonia, Italy, Latvia, Lithuania, Malta, Mauritius, Republic of Korea, Saudi Arabia, Sweden and Venezuela (Bolivarian Republic of).

(b) Dual record check -- Austria, Cuba, Estonia, Greenland, Hungary, Israel, Italy, Latvia, Lithuania, Montserrat, New Zealand and Norway.

(c) Other specified methods – Denmark, Germany, Kyrgyzstan, Luxembourg, Poland, Puerto Rico, Romania, Slovenia, Spain, Sweden and Uzbekistan.

Among the countries or areas indicating that the registration of infant deaths was estimated to be 90 per cent or more complete (and hence classified as "C" or "+C" in table 15), the following countries or areas provided information on the method used to evaluate the completeness estimate:

(a) Demographic analysis -- Argentina, Australia, Austria, Brazil, Bulgaria, Chile, China - Hong Kong SAR, Croatia, Egypt, Estonia, Israel, Italy, Latvia, Lithuania, Malta, Mauritius, New Zealand, Panama, Republic of Korea, Republic of Moldova, Saudi Arabia, Seychelles and Sweden.

(b) Dual record check -- Austria, Bahrain, Belgium, Brazil, Cuba, Cyprus, Estonia, Faeroe Islands, Greenland, Hungary, Ireland, Israel, Italy, Latvia, Lithuania, Montserrat, New Zealand, Norway and Qatar.

(c) Other specified methods -- Aruba, Brazil, Curaçao, Cayman Islands, Denmark, Germany, Kyrgyzstan, Liechtenstein, Luxembourg, Poland, Puerto Rico, Romania, Singapore, Slovenia, Spain, Sweden and Uzbekistan.

Among the countries or areas indicating that the registration of deaths was estimated to be 90 per cent or more complete (and hence classified as "C" or "+C" in table 18), the following countries or areas provided information on the method used to evaluate the completeness estimate:

(a) Demographic analysis -- Argentina, Australia, Austria, Brazil, Bulgaria, Chile, China - Hong Kong SAR, Croatia, Egypt, Estonia, Israel, Italy, Latvia, Lithuania, Malta, Mauritius, New Zealand, Panama, Republic of Korea, Republic of Moldova, Saudi Arabia, Seychelles, South Africa, Sweden, United States of America and Venezuela (Bolivarian Republic of).

(b) Dual record check -- Austria, Bahrain, Belgium, Brazil, Cuba, Cyprus, Estonia, Faeroe Islands, Greenland, Hungary, Israel, Italy, Latvia, Lithuania, Mongolia, Montserrat, New Zealand, Norway, Qatar and Venezuela (Bolivarian Republic of).

(c) Other specified methods -- Aruba, Brazil, Curaçao, Denmark, France, Germany, Kyrgyzstan, Liechtenstein, Luxembourg, Malaysia, Poland, Puerto Rico, Romania, Saint Vincent and the Grenadines, Singapore, Slovenia, Spain, Sweden, United States of America and Uzbekistan.

Among the countries or areas indicating that the registration of marriages was estimated to be 90 per cent or more complete (and hence classified as "C" or "+C" in table 23), the following countries or areas provided information on the method used to evaluate the completeness estimate:

(a) Demographic analysis -- Argentina, Australia, Austria, Bulgaria, Chile, China - Hong Kong SAR, Croatia, Egypt, Estonia, Italy, Latvia, Lithuania, Malta, Mauritius, Republic of Moldova, Saudi Arabia, Seychelles, Sweden and Venezuela (Bolivarian Republic of).

(b) Dual record check – Austria, Belgium, Cuba, Estonia, Faeroe Islands, Hungary, Israel, Italy, Latvia, New Zealand, Norway, Qatar, Republic of Korea and State of Palestine.

(c) Other specified methods -- Aruba, Curaçao, Denmark, Dominican Republic, France, Germany, Jordan, Kyrgyzstan, Liechtenstein, Luxembourg, Poland, Puerto Rico, Romania, Slovenia, Spain, Sweden, Tajikistan and Uzbekistan.

Among the countries or areas indicating that the registration of divorces was estimated to be 90 per cent or more complete (and hence classified as "C" or "+C" in table 24), the following countries or areas provided information on the method used to evaluate the completeness estimate:

(a) Demographic analysis – Austria, Bulgaria, Croatia, Dominican Republic, Egypt, Estonia, Italy, Latvia, Lithuania, Republic of Moldova, Saudi Arabia, Seychelles, Sweden and Venezuela (Bolivarian Republic of).

(b) Dual record check -- Belgium, Cuba, Estonia, Faeroe Islands, Hungary, Israel, Italy, Latvia, New Zealand, Norway, Qatar, Republic of Korea and State of Palestine.

(c) Other specified methods -- Aruba, Australia, Curaçao, Cyprus, Denmark, Jordan, Kyrgyzstan, Liechtenstein, Luxembourg, Mauritius, Poland, Puerto Rico, Romania, Slovenia, Sweden, Tajikistan and Uzbekistan.

4.2.2 Treatment of vital statistics from registers

On the basis of the quality code described above, the vital statistics shown in all tables of the *Demographic Yearbook* are treated as either reliable or unreliable. Data coded "C" are considered reliable and appear in roman type. Data coded "U" or "..." are considered unreliable and appear in *italics*.

It should be noted that the indications of reliability used for infant mortality rates, maternal mortality ratios and late foetal death ratios (all of which are calculated using the number of live births in the denominator) are determined on the basis of the quality codes for infant deaths, deaths and late foetal deaths respectively. To evaluate these rates and ratios more precisely, one would have to take into account the quality of the live-birth data used in the denominator of these rates and ratios. The quality codes for live births are shown in table 9 and described more fully in the text of the technical notes for that table.

4.2.3 Treatment of estimated vital statistics

In addition to data from vital registration systems, estimated frequencies and rates of the events, usually *ad hoc* official estimates that have been derived either from the results of a population census or sample survey or by demographic analyses, also appear in the *Demographic Yearbook*. Estimated frequencies and rates have been included in the tables because it is assumed that they provide information that is more accurate than that from existing civil registration systems. By implication, they are assumed to be reliable and as such they are set in roman type.

Estimated data are denoted by the symbol "|".

4.3 Cause of death

World Health Organization (WHO) Member States are bound by the International Nomenclature Regulations to provide the Organization with cause of death data coded in accordance with the current revision of the International Statistical Classification of Diseases and Related Health Problems (ICD). In order to promote international comparability of cause of death statistics, the World Health Organization organizes and conducts an international conference for the revision of the ICD on a regular basis in order to ensure that the Classification is kept current with the most recent clinical and statistical concepts. The data are now usually submitted to WHO at the full four-character level of detail provided by the ICD and are compiled and stored in the WHO Mortality Database at the level of detail as provided by the country. Data from the WHO Mortality Database are available in electronic format at http://www3.who.int/whosis/menu.cfm.

Although revisions provide an up-to-date version of the ICD, such revisions create several problems related to the comparability of cause of death statistics. The first is the lack of comparability over time that inevitably accompanies the use of a new classification. The second problem affects comparability between countries and areas because they may adopt a new classification at different times. The more refined the classification becomes the greater is the need for expert clinical diagnosis of cause of death. In many countries or areas, few of the deaths occur in the presence of an attendant who is medically trained, i.e., most deaths are certified by a non-medically trained attendant. Because the ICD contains many diagnoses that cannot be identified by a non-medically trained person, the ICD is not always accurately or precisely used, which affects international comparability particularly between countries and areas where the level of medical services differs widely.

The chapters of the tenth revision[16], consist of an alphanumeric coding scheme of one letter followed by three numbers at the four-character level. Chapter one contains infectious and parasitic diseases, chapter two refers to all neoplasms, chapter three to disorders of the immune mechanism including diseases of the blood and blood-forming organs; and chapter four to endocrine, nutritional and metabolic diseases. The remaining chapters group diseases according to the anatomical site affected, except for chapters that refer to mental disorders; complications of pregnancy, childbirth and the puerperium; congenital malformations; and conditions originating in the perinatal period. Finally, an entire chapter is devoted to symptoms, signs, and abnormal findings.

4.3.1 Maternal mortality

According to the tenth revision of the ICD, "Maternal death" is defined as the death of a woman while pregnant or within 42 days of termination of pregnancy, irrespective of the duration and the site of the pregnancy, from any cause related to or aggravated by the pregnancy or its management but not from accidental or incidental causes.

"Maternal deaths" should be subdivided into direct and indirect obstetric deaths. Direct obstetric deaths are those resulting from obstetric complications of the pregnant state (pregnancy, labour and puerperium), from interventions, omissions, incorrect treatment, or from a chain of events resulting from any of the above. Indirect obstetric deaths are those resulting from previous existing disease or disease that developed during pregnancy and which was not due to direct obstetric causes, but which was aggravated by physiologic effects of pregnancy.

While the denominator for the maternal mortality ratio theoretically should be the number of pregnant women, it is impossible to determine the number of pregnant women. A further recommendation by the tenth revision is therefore that maternal mortality ratios be expressed per 100,000 live births or per 100,000 total births (live births and foetal deaths). The maternal mortality ratio calculated here is expressed per 100,000 live births. Although live births do not represent an unbiased estimate of pregnant women, this figure is more reliable than other estimates. In particular, live births are more accurately registered than live births plus foetal deaths.

[1] UNdata is an internet based data service maintained by the Statistics Division of the United Nations Department of Economic and Social Affairs.

[2] There are two exceptions – the 1978 and 1991 issues, which were disseminated in separate volumes from the respective regular issues.

[3] United Nations, Department of Economic and Social Affairs, Population Division (2017). *2017 Revision of World Population Prospects* (http://esa.un.org/unpd/wpp/).

[4] ST/ESA/STAT/SER.M/49/Rev.4/WWW ; https://unstats.un.org/unsd/methodology/m49/; see also Standard Country or Area Codes for Statistical Use, Sales No. M.98.XVII.9, United Nations, New York, 1999.

[5] Sales No. E.15.XVII.10, United Nations, New York, 2015.

[6] Ibid, para. 4.151.

[7] Alternatively, if a population register is used, completed ages are calculated by subtracting the date of birth of individuals listed in the register from a reference date to which the age data pertain.

[8] A source of non-comparability may result from differences in the method of reckoning age, for example, the Western versus the Eastern or, as it is usually known, the English versus the Chinese system. By the latter, a child is considered one year old at birth and advances an additional year at each Chinese New Year. The effect of this system is most obvious at the beginning of the age span, where the frequencies in the under-one-year category are markedly understated. The effect on higher age groups is not so apparent. Distributions constructed on this basis are often adjusted before publication, but the possibility of such aberrations should not be excluded when census data by age are compared.

[9] Sales No. E.13.XVII.10, United Nations, New York, 2014.

[10] Sales No. E.98.XVII.7, United Nations, New York, 1998.

[11] Sales No. E.98.XVII.11, United Nations, New York, 1998.

[12] Sales No. E.98.XVII.4, United Nations, New York, 1998.

[13] Sales No. E.98.XVII.6, United Nations, New York, 1998.

[14] Sales No. E.98.XVII.10, United Nations, New York, 1998.

[15] Sales No. E.03.XVII.11, United Nations, New York, 2004.

[16] *International Statistical Classification of Diseases and Related Health Problems*, Tenth Revision, Volume 2, World Health Organization, Geneva, 1992.

INTRODUCTION

L'Annuaire démographique est un recueil de statistiques démographiques internationales qui est établi par la Division de statistique du Département des affaires économiques et sociales de l'Organisation des Nations Unies. Il fait partie d'un ensemble de publications complémentaires publiées par l'Organisation des Nations Unies et les institutions spécialisées, qui ont pour objet de fournir des statistiques aux démographes, aux économistes, aux spécialistes de la santé publique et aux sociologues. Grâce à la coopération des services nationaux de statistique, il a été possible de faire figurer dans la présente édition de *l'Annuaire démographique* les statistiques officielles disponibles pour plus de 230 pays ou zones du monde entier.

L'Annuaire démographique 2017 est la soixante-huitième édition d'une série que publie l'ONU depuis 1948. Le présent volume comprend un aperçu mondial des statistiques démographiques de base et des tableaux qui regroupent des statistiques sur la dimension, la répartition et les tendances de la population, la natalité, la mortalité fœtale, la mortalité infantile et la mortalité liée à la maternité, la mortalité générale, la nuptialité et la divortialité. Des données classées selon le lieu de résidence (zone urbaine ou rurale) sont présentées dans un grand nombre de tableaux. L'*Annuaire démographique* contient des notes techniques, un tableau synoptique, un index historique et une liste des éditions de *l'Annuaire démographique* publiées jusqu'à présent. Cette édition de l'*Annuaire démographique* contient les données disponibles couvrant les années de référence jusqu'à 2017.

La présente édition de *l'Annuaire démographique* comprend aussi le tableau 3a avec l'indice de Whipple selon le sexe et la résidence urbaine/rurale pour les recensements de la population effectués dans le monde entier depuis 1985. L'indice de Whipple est un indice de préférence pour certains âges dans la déclaration de l'âge et peut donc servir à mettre en évidence certaines des difficultés liées à la répartition par âge.

Les notes techniques sur les tableaux statistiques sont destinées à aider le lecteur. Le tableau A, qui correspond au tableau synoptique, donne un aperçu de l'"exhaustivité des données publiées dans la présente édition de *l'Annuaire démographique*. Un index cumulatif donne des renseignements sur les matières traitées dans chacune des 68 éditions et sur les années sur lesquelles portent les données. L'index contient aussi une liste des tableaux publiés en ligne à travers le portail UNdata[1] (http://data.un.org/Explorer.aspx?d=POP). Les numéros de vente des éditions antérieures et une liste des sujets spéciaux traités dans les différentes éditions sont indiqués aux pages iii et iv. En plus, toutes les éditions de *l'Annuaire démographique* sont disponibles en ligne sur le site web de la Division des Statistiques : https://unstats.un.org/unsd/demographic-social/products/dyb/index.cshtml

Jusqu'à la 48e édition (1996), chaque édition se composait de deux parties : les tableaux de caractère général et ceux sur des sujets spéciaux, publiés dans le même volume[2]. À partir de 49e édition (1997), les tableaux sur les sujets spéciaux ont été publiés dans un format numérique en tant que suppléments à l'*Annuaire démographique*. Deux CD-ROM ont été produits : l'*Annuaire démographique : Supplément historique*, qui présente un grand nombre de statistiques démographiques pour la période allant de 1948 à 1997, et l'*Annuaire démographique : Statistiques de la natalité*, qui contient des tableaux détaillés sur la natalité pour la période allant de 1980 à 1998. Par la suite, trois volumes concernant *l'Annuaire démographique* consacrés à des thèmes de recensement spéciaux pour le cycle de recensements de 2000 ont été publiés en ligne à l'adresse suivante : http://unstats.un.org/unsd/demographic/products/dyb/dybcens.htm. Les données actuelles sur les thèmes du recensement de l'*Annuaire démographique* pour les années de référence entre 1995 et aujourd'hui, lorsqu'elles sont disponibles, sont présentées sur https://unstats.un.org/unsd/demographic-social/products/dyb/index.cshtml#censusdatasets. Ils comprennent des données sur la population selon les principales caractéristiques démographiques, scolaires, ethnoculturelles et économiques, les caractéristiques des ménages ainsi que des données sur les étrangers dans le pays ou les personnes nées à l'étranger. Particulièrement, on a présenté sous forme de table aux adresses suivantes, les données des recensements pour les années de référence entre 1995 et aujourd'hui, qui portent sur les thèmes des caractéristiques des ménages et des caractéristiques économiques : https://unstats.un.org/unsd/demographic-social/products/dyb/dyb_household/ et https://unstats.un.org/unsd/demographic-social/products/dyb/dyb_eco/.

Les statistiques sur la population ne sont pas disponibles pour tous les pays et zones pour plusieurs raisons. Deux annexes sont présentées afin d'offrir des estimations sur la population en milieu d'année et un aperçu des statistiques de l'état civil pour chaque pays ou zone. La première porte sur des estimations concernant la population pour la période 2008-2017. La seconde présente les estimations des variantes moyennes concernant les taux bruts de natalité et de mortalité, la mortalité infantile, les indicateurs synthétiques de fécondité et l'espérance de vie à la naissance pour la période 2015-2020. Ces données ont été établies par la Division de la population de l'ONU et publiées dans les *Perspectives de la population mondiale : La révision de 2017*[3].

Les statistiques démographiques figurant dans la présente édition de l'*Annuaire démographique* sont disponibles en ligne sur les pages Web consacrées à l'*Annuaire démographique* : https://unstats.un.org/unsd/demographic-social/products/dyb/index.cshtml#overview. On trouvera également des renseignements sur le programme de collecte et de diffusion des données de la Division de statistique sur le même site. Il est possible de se procurer d'autres données en contactant la Division de statistique du Département des affaires économiques et sociales de l'Organisation des Nations Unies à l'adresse suivante : demostat@un.org.

NOTES TECHNIQUES SUR LES TABLEAUX STATISTIQUES

1. REMARQUES D'ORDRE GÉNÉRAL

1.1 Notes techniques

Les notes techniques ont pour but de donner au lecteur des informations pertinentes en lien avec les tableaux statistiques. Les renseignements qui concernent l'*Annuaire démographique* en général sont présentés dans des sections portant sur diverses considérations géographiques, sur la population et sur les statistiques de natalité et de mortalité. Les tableaux sont ensuite commentés séparément et l'on trouvera pour chacun une description des variables et des observations sur la fiabilité et les lacunes des données ainsi que sur les pays et zones visés et sur les données publiées antérieurement. Des détails sont également donnés, le cas échéant, sur le mode de calcul des taux, quotients et pourcentages.

1.2 Tableaux

Dans la mesure du possible, la numérotation des tableaux dans les éditions successives de l'*Annuaire démographique* est préservée. Comme la numérotation des tableaux ne correspond pas exactement à celle des éditions précédentes, il est recommandé de se reporter à l'index qui figure à la fin du présent ouvrage pour trouver les données publiées dans les précédentes éditions.

1.3 Origine des données

Sauf indication contraire, les statistiques présentées dans l'*Annuaire démographique* sont des données nationales fournies par les organismes de statistique officiels. Elles sont recueillies essentiellement au moyen de questionnaires qui sont envoyés tous les ans à plus de 230 services nationaux de statistique. Les données communiquées en réponse à ces questionnaires sont complétées, dans toute la mesure possible, par des données tirées de publications nationales officielles et des sites web d'organismes officiels et des renseignements communiqués par les services nationaux de statistique à la demande de l'ONU. Pour que les données soient comparables, les taux, rapports et pourcentages ont été calculés par la Division de statistique de l'ONU, à l'exception des paramètres des tables de mortalité et des indicateurs synthétiques de fécondité ainsi que des taux bruts de natalité et de mortalité pour certains pays et zones, qui ont été dûment signalés en note. Les méthodes suivies par la Division pour le calcul des taux et rapports sont décrites dans les notes techniques relatives à chaque tableau. Les chiffres de population utilisés pour ces calculs sont ceux qui figurent dans la présente édition de l'*Annuaire démographique* ou qui ont paru dans des éditions antérieures.

Chaque fois que l'on constatera des différences entre les données du présent volume et celles des éditions antérieures de l'*Annuaire démographique*, ou de certaines publications apparentées, on pourra en conclure que les statistiques publiées cette année sont des chiffres révisés communiqués à la Division de statistique avant juin 2018.

2. CONSIDÉRATIONS GÉOGRAPHIQUES

2.1 Portée

Des données sont présentées sur tous les pays ou zones qui en ont communiquées. Le tableau 3, le plus complet, contient des données sur la population et la superficie de chaque pays ou zone ayant une population d'au moins 50 habitants. Ces pays ou zones ne figurent pas tous dans les tableaux qui suivent. Dans bien des cas, les données requises pour un tableau particulier n'étaient pas disponibles. En général, les pays ou zones qui peuvent fournir des données sont d'autant moins nombreux que les données demandées sont plus détaillées.

De plus, les taux et rapports ne sont présentés que pour les pays ou zones ayant communiqué des chiffres correspondant à un nombre minimal de faits considérés. Les minimums sont indiqués dans les notes techniques relatives à chacun des tableaux.

À l'exception des données récapitulatives présentées dans les tableaux 1 et 2 pour l'ensemble du monde et les grandes zones et régions et des données relatives aux capitales et aux villes de 100 000 habitants ou plus dans le tableau 8, toutes les données se rapportent aux pays. Le nombre de pays sur lequel porte chacun des tableaux est indiqué dans le tableau A.

2.2 Composition territoriale

Autant que possible, toutes les données, y compris les séries chronologiques, se rapportent au territoire de 2017. Les exceptions à cette règle sont signalées en note à la fin des tableaux. Des clarifications importantes sont présentées ci-dessous.

Les données relatives au **Danemark** ne comprennent pas les Iles Féroé et le Groenland, qui font l'objet de rubriques distinctes.

Les données relatives à la **Finlande** comprennent les Îles d'Åland, sauf indication contraire en note de bas de page.

Les données relatives à la **France** ne comprennent pas les départements d'outre-mer, à savoir, la Guyane française, Guadeloupe, la Martinique et La Réunion, qui font l'objet de rubriques distinctes, sauf indication contraire en note de bas de page.

Les données relatives au **Royaume-Uni de Grande-Bretagne et d'Irlande du Nord** ne comprennent pas la Guernesey, l'île de Man et Jersey, qui font l'objet de rubriques distinctes.

Les données relatives au **Sahara Occidental** comprennent la région septentrionale (ancien Saguia-el-Hamra) et la région méridionale (ancien Rio de Oro).

2.3 Nomenclature

En règle générale, pour gagner de la place, on a jugé commode de désigner dans les tableaux les pays ou zones par les noms abrégés couramment utilisés par l'Organisation des Nations Unies[4], les désignations complètes n'étant utilisées que lorsqu'il n'existait pas de forme abrégée. La liste des désignations des pays ou zones est disponible à l'adresse suivante : https://unstats.un.org/unsd/methodology/m49/.

2.3.1 Ordre de présentation

Les pays ou zones sont classés dans l'ordre alphabétique anglais et regroupés par continent comme ci-après : Afrique, Amérique du Nord, Amérique du Sud, Asie, Europe et Océanie.

Les appellations employées dans la présente édition et la présentation des données qui y figurent n'ont d'autre objet que de donner un cadre géographique commode aux séries statistiques. La même observation vaut pour toutes les notes et précisions concernant les unités géographiques pour lesquelles des données sont présentées.

2.4 Superficie

Les données relatives à la superficie qui figurent dans le tableaux 1 représentent la superficie des terres alors que les données relatives à la superficie qui figurent dans le tableaux 3 représentent la superficie totale, sauf indication contraire par une note. La superficie totale englobe les terres émergées (la superficie des terres) et les eaux intérieures qui sont censées comprendre les principaux lacs et cours d'eau, mais excluent les régions polaires et les îles inhabitées. Les données relatives à la superficie correspondent aux chiffres estimatifs les plus récents. Les superficies sont toutes exprimées en kilomètres carrés ; les chiffres qui avaient été communiqués en miles carrés ont été convertis au moyen d'un coefficient de 2,589988.

2.4.1 Comparabilité dans le temps

La révision des estimations antérieures de la superficie, des augmentations effectives de la superficie terrestre due par exemple à des travaux d'assèchement, à des rectifications de frontières, à des changements d'interprétation du concept de « terres émergées » ou à l'utilisation de nouvelles unités de mesure peut avoir des incidences sur la comparabilité dans le temps des estimations relatives à la superficie d'un pays ou d'une zone donnés. Dans la plupart des cas, il a été possible de déterminer la raison de ces révisions ; toutefois, même lorsque la raison n'était pas connue, on a généralement admis que ces derniers sont exacts.

2.4.2 Comparabilité internationale

Le manque de comparabilité internationale entre les données relatives à la superficie est dû principalement à des différences de définition. En particulier, la définition des golfes, baies et criques, lacs et cours d'eau varie sensiblement d'un pays à l'autre. La diversité des méthodes employées pour estimer les superficies nuit elle aussi à la comparabilité internationale. Certaines données proviennent de levés effectués selon des méthodes scientifiques modernes ; d'autres ne représentent que des conjectures reposant sur diverses catégories de renseignements. Certains chiffres sont récents, d'autres pas. Étant donné que ni la méthode de calcul de la superficie ni la composition du territoire et la date à laquelle se rapportent les données ne sont connues avec précision pour tous les pays ou zones, les estimations figurant dans le tableau 3 ne doivent pas être considérées comme rigoureusement comparables d'un pays ou d'une zone à une autre.

3. POPULATION

Les statistiques de la population, c'est-à-dire celles qui se rapportent à la dimension, à la répartition géographique et aux caractéristiques démographiques de la population, sont présentées dans un certain nombre de tableaux de *l'Annuaire démographique*.

Les tableaux 1 et 2 présentent respectivement des estimations récapitulatives de milieu d'année de la population du monde, des grandes zones et régions, pour certaines années présélectionnées, ainsi que de sa répartition selon l'âge et le sexe pour l'année 2017.

Les données concernant les pays ou les zones représentent les résultats de recensements de population, des estimations fondées sur les résultats d'enquêtes par sondage (s'il n'y a pas eu recensement), des estimations postcensitaires ou intercensitaires, ou des estimations établies à partir de données provenant des registres permanents de population. Dans la présente édition, le tableau 3 indique pour chaque pays ou zone le chiffre le plus récent de la population totale issu du dernier recensement et des estimations établies au milieu de l'année 2010 et de l'année 2017. Le tableau 5 contient des estimations de la population totale au milieu de chaque année pendant 10 ans (2008-2017), et le tableau 6 des estimations de la population urbaine et de la population totale, par sexe, au milieu de chaque année pendant 10 ans (2008-2017). Les dernières données disponibles sur la répartition de la population selon l'âge, le sexe et le lieu de résidence (zone urbaine ou rurale) sont présentées dans le tableau 7. Les derniers chiffres disponibles sur la population des capitales et des villes de 100 000 habitants ou plus sont regroupés dans le tableau 8.

On a utilisé pour le calcul des taux les statistiques de la population totale et de la population répartie selon l'âge, le sexe ou le lieu de résidence (zone urbaine ou rurale). Les taux démographiques selon la résidence (urbaine/rurale), l'âge ou le sexe ont été calculés à partir des données présentées dans les tableaux 6 ou 7 de la présente édition ou dans les tableaux correspondants d'éditions précédentes de l'*Annuaire démographique*.

3.1 Sources de variation des données

Plusieurs facteurs influent sur la comparabilité des données : 1) la définition de la population totale ; 2) les définitions utilisées pour faire la distinction entre population urbaine et population rurale ; 3) les difficultés liées aux déclarations d'âge ; 4) l'étendue du surdénombrement ou du sous-dénombrement dans le recensement le plus récent ou dans une autre source de statistiques de référence sur la population ; 5) la qualité des estimations relatives à la population. Ces cinq facteurs sont analysés en détail aux sections 3.1.1 à 3.1.3 ci-après. D'autres questions seront traitées dans les notes techniques relatives à chaque tableau. Pour plus de précisions concernant, notamment, les notions fondamentales de dimension, de répartition et de caractéristiques de la population qui ont été élaborées par l'Organisation des Nations Unies, le lecteur est invité à se reporter aux *Principes et recommandations concernant les recensements de la population et de l'habitat, Révision 3*[5].

3.1.1 Population totale

Le principal obstacle à la comparabilité des données relatives à la population totale est la différence qui existe entre population de fait et population de droit. La population de fait comprend toutes les personnes présentes dans le pays ou la zone à la date de référence, tandis que la population de droit comprend toutes celles qui résident habituellement dans le pays ou la zone, qu'elles y aient été ou non présentes à la date de référence. Par définition, la population totale de fait et la population totale de droit ne sont donc pas rigoureusement comparables entre elles.

Même lorsque l'on veut comparer deux totaux qui se rapportent à des populations de fait ou deux totaux qui se rapportent à des populations de droit, on risque souvent de faire des erreurs pour cette raison qu'il est rare que l'une et l'autre notions soient appliquées strictement. Pour citer quelques exemples, certains chiffres qui sont censés porter sur la population de fait ne tiennent pas compte du personnel militaire, naval et diplomatique étranger en fonction dans le pays ou la zone, ni des membres de leurs familles et de leurs ménages ; d'autres ne comprennent pas les visiteurs étrangers de passage dans le pays ou la zone ni les personnes à bord de navires ancrés dans des ports. En revanche, il arrive que l'on compte des personnes, inscrits maritimes et marins pêcheurs par exemple, qui, en raison de leur activité professionnelle, se trouvent hors du pays ou de la zone de recensement.

Les risques de disparités sont encore plus grands quand il s'agit de comparer des populations de droit, car les comparaisons dépendent au premier chef de la définition que l'on donne à l'expression « lieu de résidence habituel », qui varie d'un pays ou d'une zone à l'autre et qu'il est, de toute façon, difficile d'appliquer uniformément pour le dénombrement lors d'un recensement ou d'une enquête. Par exemple, les civils étrangers qui se trouvent temporairement dans un pays ou une zone comme travailleurs à court terme peuvent officiellement être considérés comme résidents après un séjour d'une durée déterminée, mais ils peuvent aussi être considérés comme non-résidents pendant toute la durée de leur séjour ; ailleurs, ces mêmes personnes peuvent être considérées officiellement comme résidents ou comme non-résidents du pays ou de la zone d'où elles viennent, selon la durée et, éventuellement, la raison de leur absence. En plus, quel que soit son statut officiel, chacun des recensés peut, au moment de l'enquête, interpréter à sa façon la notion de résidence. De plus, les autorités nationales ou les entités responsables des zones ne savent pas toutes avec la même précision combien de leurs résidents se trouvent temporairement à l'étranger.

Les chiffres de population présentés dans les tableaux de l'*Annuaire démographique* représentent la population de fait ou la population de droit. Lorsque l'on savait que les données avaient été recueillies selon une définition de la population de fait ou de la population de droit qui s'écartait sensiblement de celle exposée plus haut, on l'a signalé en note, de manière à compenser dans toute la mesure possible les conséquences des divergences.

Il peut y avoir hétérogénéité dans les statistiques d'un même pays ou d'une même zone dans le cas des pays ou zones qui ne font une exploitation statistique détaillée des données que pour la population de droit alors qu'ils recueillent des données sur la population de droit et sur la population de fait à l'occasion d'un recensement, par exemple. Ainsi, tandis que les chiffres relatifs à la population totale qui figurent au tableau 3 se rapportent à la population de fait, ceux des tableaux qui présentent des données sur diverses caractéristiques de la population, par exemple le lieu de résidence (zone urbaine ou rurale), l'âge et le sexe, peuvent être basés sur le concept de la population de droit.

3.1.2 Lieu de résidence (zone urbaine ou rurale)

L'hétérogénéité des définitions nationales du terme « urbain » nuit considérablement à la comparabilité internationale des données concernant la répartition selon le lieu de résidence. Les définitions utilisées par les différents pays ou zones et leurs implications sont exposées à la fin des notes techniques correspondant au tableau 6.

3.1.3 Répartition par âge

La répartition de la population selon l'âge est un paramètre fondamental de la plupart des analyses, estimations et projections relatives aux statistiques de la population. Malheureusement, ces données sont sujettes à un certain nombre d'erreurs et difficilement comparables. C'est pourquoi pratiquement tous les utilisateurs de ces statistiques doivent considérer ces répartitions avec la plus grande circonspection.

3.1.3.1 Collecte et exploitation des données sur l'âge

L'âge est l'intervalle de temps déterminé par calcul ou par estimation qui sépare la date de naissance de la date du recensement et qui est exprimé en années solaires révolues[6]. Les données sur l'âge peuvent être recueillies selon deux méthodes : la première consiste à obtenir la date de naissance de chaque personne à l'occasion d'un recensement ou d'un sondage, puis à calculer l'âge en années révolues en soustrayant la date de naissance de celle du dénombrement[7]. La seconde consiste à enregistrer l'âge en années révolues au moment du recensement, c'est-à-dire l'âge au dernier anniversaire.

La méthode recommandée consiste à calculer l'âge au dernier anniversaire en soustrayant la date exacte de la naissance de la date du recensement. Toutefois, on n'a pas toujours recours à cette méthode ; certains pays ou zones calculent l'âge en faisant la différence entre l'année du recensement et l'année de la naissance. Lorsque les données sur l'âge ont été établies de cette façon, on l'a signalé chaque fois que possible par une note. On peut d'ailleurs s'en rendre compte dans une certaine mesure, car les chiffres dans la catégorie des moins d'un an sont plus faibles qu'ils ne devraient l'être. Cependant, un nombre irrégulier de naissances d'une année à l'autre ou l'omission de certains âges parmi les moins d'un an peut aussi fausser les chiffres de la population de moins d'un an.

3.1.3.2 Erreurs dans les données sur l'âge

Les causes d'erreurs dans les données sur l'âge sont diverses : on peut citer notamment l'ignorance de l'âge exact, la déclaration d'années d'âge correspondant à un calendrier différent de celui des années solaires révolues depuis la naissance[8], la négligence dans les déclarations et dans la façon dont elles sont consignées, la tendance générale à déclarer des âges se terminant par certains chiffres tels que 0, 2, 5 ou 8, la tendance pour les personnes âgées à exagérer leur âge, une aversion subconsciente pour certains nombres, et les fausses déclarations faites délibérément.

Les causes d'erreurs mentionnées ci-dessus, communes à la plupart des enquêtes sur l'âge et à la plupart des pays ou zones, peuvent nuire sensiblement à la comparabilité.

À cause des difficultés indiquées ci-dessus, les répartitions par âge et par sexe de la population d'un grand nombre de pays ou de zones font apparaître les irrégularités suivantes : 1) sous-estimation des groupes d'âge correspondant aux enfants de moins d'un an et aux jeunes enfants ; 2) polarisation des déclarations sur les âges se terminant par les chiffres 0 ou 5 (c'est-à-dire 5, 10, 15, 20...) ; 3) prépondérance des âges pairs (par exemple 10, 12, 14...) au détriment des âges impairs (par exemple 11, 13, 15...) ; 4) écart considérable et surprenant entre le rapport masculin/féminin à certains âges ; 5) différences importantes et difficilement explicables entre les données concernant des groupes d'âge voisins. En comparant les statistiques provenant de recensements successifs pour des cohortes identiques sur le plan de l'âge et de la répartition par sexe et en étudiant la répartition par âge et par sexe de la population à chaque recensement, on peut déceler l'existence de ces incohérences et de quelques autres, un certain nombre d'entre elles se retrouvant à des degrés divers même dans les recensements les plus modernes.

La présente édition de l'*Annuaire démographique* comprend le tableau 3a avec l'indice de Whipple selon le sexe et la résidence urbaine/rurale pour les recensements de la population effectués dans le monde entier depuis 1985. L'indice de Whipple est un indice de préférence pour certains âges dans la déclaration de l'âge et peut donc servir à mettre en évidence certaines des difficultés liées à la répartition par âge.

4. STATISTIQUES DE L'ÉTAT CIVIL

Aux fins de l'*Annuaire démographique*, on entend par statistiques de l'état civil les statistiques des naissances vivantes, des décès, des morts fœtales, des mariages et des divorces.

Dans le présent volume de l'*Annuaire démographique*, on a présenté des tableaux sur la natalité, la mortalité, la nuptialité et la divortialité. Les tableaux consacrés à la mortalité sont groupés sous les rubriques suivantes : mortalité fœtale, mortalité infantile, mortalité liée à la maternité et mortalité générale.

4.1 Sources de variations des données

La plupart des statistiques de l'état civil publiées dans le présent volume de l'*Annuaire démographique* émanent des systèmes nationaux d'enregistrement des faits d'état civil. Le degré d'exhaustivité et d'exactitude de ces données varie d'un pays ou d'une zone à l'autre.

Il n'existe pas partout de système national d'enregistrement des faits d'état civil et, dans quelques cas, seuls certains faits sont enregistrés. Par exemple, dans certains pays ou zones, seuls les naissances et les décès sont enregistrés. Il existe également des différences quant au degré d'efficacité avec lequel les lois relatives à l'enregistrement des faits d'état civil sont appliquées dans les divers pays ou zones. La fiabilité des statistiques provenant des registres d'état civil dépend des modalités d'application de la loi et de la mesure dans laquelle le public s'y soumet.

Il est à signaler que dans certains cas les statistiques de la nuptialité et de la divortialité sont tirées d'autres sources que les registres d'état civil. Dans certains pays ou zones, par exemple, les seules données disponibles sur la nuptialité proviennent des registres des églises. Selon la pratique suivie par chaque pays, les statistiques de la divortialité sont tirées des actes des tribunaux et/ou des registres d'état civil. L'officier de l'état civil, le service national de statistique ou d'autres services administratifs peuvent être chargés d'établir ces statistiques.

Les autres facteurs qui influent sur la comparabilité internationale des statistiques de l'état civil sont à peu près les mêmes que ceux qu'il convient de prendre en considération pour interpréter les variations observées dans les statistiques de la population. La définition des faits d'état civil aux fins de statistique, la portée des données du point de vue géographique et ethnique ainsi que les méthodes d'exploitation des données sont autant d'éléments qui peuvent influer sur la comparabilité.

En plus des statistiques tirées des registres d'état civil, l'*Annuaire démographique* présente des statistiques de l'état civil qui sont des estimations officielles nationales, fondées souvent sur les résultats de sondages ou des recensements de la population. Aussi leur comparabilité varie-t-elle en fonction du degré d'exhaustivité des déclarations recueillies lors des recensements de la population ou d'enquêtes sur les ménages, des erreurs d'échantillonnage ou autres, et des distorsions d'origines diverses.

Pour plus de détails sur les normes d'établissement des statistiques d'état civil, le lecteur pourra se reporter aux : *Principes et recommandations pour un système de statistiques de l'état civil, troisième révision*[9] ; *Manuel des systèmes d'enregistrement des faits d'état civil et de statistiques de l'état civil : Élaboration d'un cadre juridique*[10] ; *Manuel des systèmes d'enregistrement des faits d'état civil et de statistiques de l'état civil : Gestion, fonctionnement et tenue*[11]; *Manuel des systèmes d'enregistrement des faits d'état civil et de statistiques de l'état civil : Élaboration de programmes d'information, d'éducation et de communication*[12]; *Manuel des systèmes d'enregistrement des faits d'état civil et de statistiques de l'état civil : Principes et protocoles concernant la communication et l'archivage des documents individuels*[13]; *Manuel des systèmes d'enregistrement des faits d'état civil et de statistiques de l'état civil : Informatisation*[14]. Le *Manuel de collecte de données sur la fécondité et la mortalité*[15] fournit des informations ayant trait à la collecte et à l'évaluation des données sur la fécondité, sur la mortalité et sur d'autres faits d'état civil, qui ont été recueillies au cours des enquêtes sur les ménages. Ces publications sont également disponibles sur le Web à partir des adresses suivantes : https://unstats.un.org/unsd/demographic-social/Standards-and-Methods/index.cshtml

4.1.1 Définition des faits d'état civil aux fins de la statistique

Une cause importante d'hétérogénéité dans les données est le manque d'uniformité des définitions des différents faits d'état civil. Aux fins de *l'Annuaire démographique*, il est recommandé de recueillir les données relatives aux faits d'état civil en utilisant les définitions établies au Chapitre I des *Principes et recommandations pour un système de statistiques de l'état civil, troisième révision*. Ces définitions sont les suivantes :

La NAISSANCE VIVANTE est l'expulsion ou l'extraction complète du corps de la mère, indépendamment de la durée de la gestation, d'un produit de la conception qui, après cette séparation, respire ou manifeste tout autre signe de vie, tel que battement de cœur, pulsation du cordon ombilical ou contraction effective d'un muscle soumis à l'action de la volonté, que le cordon ombilical ait été coupé ou non et que le placenta soit ou non demeuré attaché ; tout produit d'une telle naissance est considéré comme « enfant né vivant ».

Le DÉCÈS est la disparition permanente de tout signe de vie à un moment quelconque postérieur à la naissance vivante (cessation des fonctions vitales après la naissance sans possibilité de réanimation). Cette définition ne comprend pas les morts fœtales.

La MORT FŒTALE est le décès d'un produit de la conception lorsque ce décès est survenu avant l'expulsion ou l'extraction complète du corps de la mère, indépendamment de la durée de la gestation. Le décès est indiqué par le fait qu'après cette séparation le fœtus ne respire ni ne manifeste aucun signe de vie, tel que battement de cœur, pulsation du cordon ombilical ou contraction effective d'un muscle soumis à l'action de la volonté.

Le MARIAGE est l'acte, la cérémonie ou la procédure qui établit un rapport légal entre les époux. L'union peut être rendue légale par une procédure civile ou religieuse, ou par toute autre procédure, conformément à la législation du pays.

Le DIVORCE est la dissolution légale et définitive des liens du mariage, c'est-à-dire la séparation des époux qui confère aux parties le droit de se remarier civilement ou religieusement, ou selon toute autre procédure, conformément à la législation du pays.

En plus de ces notions définies internationalement, l'*Annuaire démographique* recueille et met à disposition ces données sur les avortements :

Par référence à la femme, l'AVORTEMENT se définit comme toute interruption de grossesse qui est survenue avant 28 semaines de gestation et dont le produit est un fœtus mort. Il existe deux grandes catégories d'avortement : l'avortement spontané et l'avortement provoqué. L'avortement provoqué a pour origine une action délibérée entreprise en vue d'interrompre une grossesse. Tout autre avortement est considéré comme spontané.

4.1.2 Problèmes posés par les définitions établies

Les variations par rapport aux définitions établies des faits d'état civil sont le principal obstacle à la comparabilité internationale des statistiques de l'état civil. Un exemple en est fourni par le cas des naissances vivantes et celui des morts fœtales. Dans certains pays ou zones, il faut que le nouveau-né ait vécu 24 heures pour pouvoir être inscrit sur le registre des naissances vivantes. Les décès d'enfants qui surviennent avant l'expiration du délai de 24 heures sont classés parmi les morts fœtales tardives et, en l'absence de méthodes spéciales d'exploitation des données, ne sont comptés ni dans les naissances vivantes ni dans les décès. De même, dans plusieurs autres pays ou zones, les décès d'enfants nés vivants et décédés avant l'enregistrement de leur naissance sont également comptés parmi les morts fœtales tardives.

À moins que des méthodes spéciales n'aient été adoptées pour l'exploitation de ces données, les statistiques des naissances vivantes et des décès ne tiendront pas compte de ces cas, qui viendront en revanche accroître d'autant le nombre des morts fœtales tardives. Le taux de mortalité infantile sera donc sous-estimé. Bien que les éléments constitutifs du taux (décès d'enfants de moins d'un an et naissances vivantes) accusent exactement la même insuffisance en valeur absolue, les lacunes sont proportionnellement plus fortes pour les décès de moins d'un an, ce qui cause des erreurs plus importantes dans les taux de mortalité infantile.

De plus, cette pratique augmente les rapports de mortinatalité. Quelques pays ou zones effectuent les ajustements nécessaires pour corriger cette anomalie (du moins dans les fréquences totales) au moment de l'établissement des tableaux. Si aucun ajustement n'a été effectué, cela est indiqué dans les notes chaque fois que possible.

Les définitions du mariage et du divorce posent aussi un problème du point de vue de la comparabilité internationale. Contrairement à la naissance et au décès, qui sont des faits biologiques, le mariage et le divorce sont uniquement déterminés par la législation et la coutume et, de ce fait, il est moins facile d'en donner une définition statistique qui ait une application universelle. À des fins statistiques, ces notions ont donc été définies de manière générale par référence à la législation de chaque pays ou zone. La législation relative au mariage et plus particulièrement au divorce varie d'un pays ou d'une zone à l'autre. En ce qui concerne le mariage, l'âge de nubilité est la condition la plus fréquemment requise, mais il arrive souvent que d'autres conditions soient exigées.

Lorsqu'il est connu, l'âge minimum auquel le mariage peut avoir lieu avec le consentement des parents (et dans certains cas sans le consentement des parents) est indiqué au tableau 24-1. Les lois et règlements relatifs à la dissolution du mariage par le divorce vont de l'interdiction absolue, en passant par diverses conditions requises pour l'obtention du divorce, jusqu'à la simple déclaration, par l'épouse, de son désir ou de son intention de divorcer.

4.1.3 Couverture géographique ou ethnique fragmentaire

En principe, les statistiques de l'état civil devraient s'étendre à l'ensemble du pays ou de la zone auxquels elles se rapportent et englober tous les groupes ethniques. En fait, il n'est pas rare que les données soient fragmentaires. Dans certains pays ou zones, l'enregistrement n'est obligatoire que pour une petite partie de la population, par exemple pour certains groupes ethniques. Dans d'autres, il n'existe pas de disposition qui prescrive l'enregistrement obligatoire sur le plan national, mais seulement des règlements ou décrets des municipalités ou des États, qui ne s'appliquent pas à l'ensemble du territoire. Il en est encore autrement dans d'autres pays ou zones où les autorités ont institué une zone d'enregistrement comprenant seulement une partie du territoire, le reste étant exclu en raison des difficultés d'accès ou parce qu'il est pratiquement impossible, pour des raisons d'ordre économique ou culturel, d'y procéder à un enregistrement régulier.

4.1.4 Méthodes de présentation des données

4.1.4.1 Selon le lieu de l'événement

Les statistiques de l'état civil qui sont présentées pour l'ensemble du territoire national se rapportent à la population de fait ou la population présente. En conséquence, sauf indication contraire, les statistiques de l'état civil relatives à une zone ou à un pays donné portent sur tous les faits survenus dans l'ensemble de la population, à l'intérieur des frontières actuelles de la zone ou du pays considéré. On peut donc estimer qu'elles englobent les faits d'état civil survenus dans les tribus nomades et parmi les populations autochtones ainsi que parmi les ressortissants du pays et les étrangers. Des notes signalent les exceptions lorsque celles-ci sont connues.

Pour certains pays, les écarts entre les taux démographiques pour les zones urbaines et pour les zones rurales peuvent varier notablement selon que les faits d'état civil ont été exploités sur la base du lieu de l'événement ou du lieu de résidence habituel. Par exemple, si un nombre appréciable de femmes résidant dans des zones rurales proches de grands centres urbains accouchent dans les hôpitaux ou maternités d'une ville, les taux de fécondité ainsi que les taux de mortalité néo-natale et infantile seront généralement plus élevés dans les zones urbaines (et par conséquent plus faibles dans les zones rurales) si les faits sont exploités en se fondant sur le lieu de l'événement et non sur le lieu de résidence habituel. Le phénomène sera le même dans le cas de la mortalité générale si un bon nombre de personnes résidant dans des zones rurales font appel aux services de santé des villes lorsqu'elles sont gravement malades.

4.1.4.2 Selon la date de l'événement ou la date de l'enregistrement

Autant que possible, les statistiques de l'état civil figurant dans l'*Annuaire démographique* se rapportent aux faits survenus pendant l'année considérée et non aux faits enregistrés au cours de ladite année. Bon nombre de pays ou zones, toutefois, exploitent leurs statistiques de l'état civil selon la date de l'enregistrement et non selon la date de l'événement. Comme ces statistiques risquent d'induire en erreur, les pays ou zones dont on sait qu'ils établissent leurs statistiques d'après la date de l'enregistrement sont signalés dans les tableaux par un signe plus « + ». On ne dispose toutefois pas pour tous les pays ou zones de renseignements complets sur la méthode d'exploitation des statistiques de l'état civil et les données sont peut-être exploitées selon la date de l'enregistrement plus souvent que ne le laisserait supposer l'emploi des signes.

Étant donné que la qualité des données est inextricablement liée aux retards dans l'enregistrement, il faudra toujours considérer en même temps le code de qualité qui est décrit à la section 4.2.1 ci-après. Évidemment, si l'enregistrement des naissances est complet et effectué en temps voulu (code « C »), les effets perturbateurs de la méthode consistant à exploiter les données selon la date de l'enregistrement seront pratiquement annulés. De même, s'agissant des statistiques des décès, les effets pourront bien souvent être réduits au minimum dans les pays ou zones où le code sanitaire subordonne la délivrance du permis d'inhumer à l'enregistrement du décès, ce qui tend à hâter l'enregistrement. Quant aux morts fœtales, elles sont généralement déclarées immédiatement ou ne sont pas déclarées du tout. En conséquence, si l'enregistrement se fait dans un délai très court, la différence entre les statistiques établies selon la date de l'événement et celles qui sont établies selon la date de l'enregistrement peut être négligeable. Dans bien des cas, la durée des délais légaux accordés pour l'enregistrement des faits d'état civil est un facteur dont dépend dans une large mesure l'incidence sur la comparabilité de l'exploitation des données selon la date de l'enregistrement.

En ce qui concerne le mariage et le divorce, la pratique consistant à exploiter les statistiques selon la date de l'enregistrement ne pose généralement pas de graves problèmes. Le mariage étant, dans de nombreux pays ou zones, un contrat juridique civil qui, pour être légal, doit être conclu devant un officier de l'état civil, il s'ensuit que dans ces pays ou zones l'enregistrement a lieu presque systématiquement au moment de la cérémonie ou immédiatement après. De même, dans de nombreux pays ou zones, le tribunal ou l'autorité qui a prononcé le divorce est seul habilité à enregistrer cet acte, et comme l'acte d'enregistrement figure alors sur les registres du tribunal l'enregistrement suit généralement de peu le jugement.

En revanche, si l'enregistrement n'a lieu qu'avec un certain retard, les statistiques de l'état civil établies selon la date de l'enregistrement ne sont pas comparables sur le plan international. Au mieux, les statistiques par date de l'enregistrement prendront surtout en considération des faits survenus au cours de l'année précédente ; dans les pays ou zones où le système d'enregistrement n'est pas très développé, il y entrera des faits datant de plusieurs années. Il ressort des documents dont on dispose que des retards de plusieurs années dans l'enregistrement des naissances ne sont pas rares, encore que, dans la majorité des cas, les retards ne dépassent pas deux à quatre ans.

Tant que l'enregistrement se fera avec retard, les statistiques fondées sur la date d'enregistrement ne seront comparables sur le plan international ni entre elles ni avec les statistiques établies selon la date de fait d'état civil.

Il convient également de noter que l'exploitation des données selon la date de l'enregistrement ne nuit pas seulement à la comparabilité internationale des statistiques. Même à l'intérieur d'un pays ou d'une zone, le procédé qui consiste à compter les enregistrements et non les faits peut compromettre la comparabilité des chiffres sur une longue période. Si le nombre des faits d'état civil enregistrés varie d'une année à l'autre (par suite de l'application de mesures visant tout particulièrement à encourager l'enregistrement ou parce qu'il est subitement devenu nécessaire de produire le certificat d'une naissance ou d'un décès non enregistré pour l'accomplissement de certaines formalités), les statistiques de l'état civil établies d'après la date de l'enregistrement ne permettent pas de quantifier ni d'analyser l'état et l'évolution de la population. Tout au plus peuvent-elles révéler l'évolution des conditions d'exigibilité de l'acte de naissance, de décès ou de mariage et les fluctuations du volume de travail des bureaux d'état civil. Les statistiques établies selon la date de l'enregistrement peuvent donc ne présenter qu'une utilité très réduite pour des études nationales ou internationales.

4.2 La qualité des statistiques de l'état civil qui sont publiées

La qualité des statistiques de l'état civil peut être évaluée en se fondant sur plusieurs facteurs. Le facteur essentiel est la complétude du système d'enregistrement des faits d'état civil d'après lequel ces statistiques sont établies.

4.2.1 Codage qualitatif des statistiques provenant des registres de l'état civil

Dans le questionnaire relatif au mouvement de la population qui leur est envoyé chaque année dans le cadre de l'établissement de *l'Annuaire démographique*, les services nationaux de statistique sont invités à donner leur propre évaluation du degré de complétude des données sur les naissances, les décès, les décès d'enfants de moins d'un an, les morts fœtales tardives, les mariages et les divorces figurant dans leurs registres d'état civil.

D'après les renseignements directement communiqués par les gouvernements ou extraits des questionnaires ou de publications officielles pertinentes, il a été possible de classer les statistiques de l'enregistrement des faits d'état civil (naissances, décès, décès d'enfants de moins d'un an, morts fœtales tardives, mariages et divorces) en trois grandes catégories, selon leur qualité :

C : Données jugées pratiquement complètes, c'est-à-dire représentant au moins 90 % des faits d'état civil survenant chaque année.

U : Données jugées incomplètes, c'est-à-dire représentant moins de 90 % des faits survenant chaque année.

| : Données ne provenant pas des systèmes nationaux d'enregistrement des faits d'état civil, mais jugées fiables, telles que les estimations dérivées des recensements de population ou du logement.

... : Données dont le degré de complétude ne fait pas l'objet de renseignements précis.

Ces codes de qualité figurent dans la première colonne des tableaux qui présentent, pour un nombre d'années déterminé les chiffres absolus et les taux (ou rapports) bruts concernant les naissances vivantes, les morts fœtales tardives, les décès d'enfants de moins d'un an, les décès, les mariages et les divorces. Les niveaux de fiabilité des statistiques de mortalité maternelle sont transmis par l'Organisation mondiale de la santé.

La classification des pays ou zones selon ces codes de qualité peut ne pas être uniforme. On a estimé néanmoins que les services nationaux de statistique étaient les mieux placés pour juger de la qualité de leurs données. On a pensé que les catégories que l'on pouvait distinguer sur la base des renseignements disponibles, bien que très larges, permettaient cependant de se faire une idée de la qualité des statistiques de l'état civil publiées dans l'*Annuaire démographique*.

Sur les pays ou zones qui ont estimé à 90 % ou plus le degré d'exhaustivité de leur enregistrement des naissances vivantes (classé « C » ou « +C » dans le tableau 9), les pays ou zones suivants ont communiqué des renseignements concernant les bases sur lesquelles leur estimation reposait :

a) Analyse démographique : Afrique du Sud, Arabie saoudite, Argentine, Australie, Autriche, Brésil, Bulgarie, Chili, Chine - Hong Kong RAS, Croatie, Égypte, Estonie, Italie, Lettonie, Lituanie, Malaisie, Malte, Maurice, Nouvelle-Zélande, Panama, République de Moldova, Seychelles, Suède et Venezuela (République bolivarienne du).

b) Double contrôle des registres : Australie, Autriche, Bahreïn, Belgique, Brésil, Chypre, Cuba, Estonie, Groenland, Hongrie, Îles Féroé, Israël, Italie, Lettonie, Malaisie, Mongolie, Montserrat, Norvège, Nouvelle-Zélande, Qatar, République de Corée, Roumanie, Saint Vincent et les Grenadines, Uruguay et Venezuela (République bolivarienne du).

c) Autre méthode : Allemagne, Aruba, Australie, Bolivie (État plurinational de), Brésil, Curaçao, Danemark, Espagne, État de Palestine, France, Géorgie, Guatemala, Irlande, Jordanie, Kirghizstan, Liechtenstein, Luxembourg, Malaisie, Mexique, Ouzbékistan, Panama, Philippines, Pologne, Porto Rico, Roumanie, Singapour, Slovénie, Suède et Venezuela (République bolivarienne du).

Sur les pays ou zones qui ont estimé à 90 % ou plus le degré d'exhaustivité de leur enregistrement des morts fœtales tardives (classé « C » ou « +C » dans le tableau 12), les pays ou zones suivants ont communiqué des renseignements concernant les bases sur lesquelles leur estimation reposait :

a) Analyse démographique : Arabie saoudite, Argentine, Autriche, Bulgarie, Croatie, Égypte, Estonie, Italie, Lettonie, Lituanie, Malte, MauriceMexique, République de Corée, Suède et Venezuela (République bolivarienne du).

b) Double contrôle des registres : Autriche, Cuba, Estonie, Groenland, Hongrie, Israël, Italie, Leetonie, Lituanie, Montserrat, Norvège et Nouvelle-Zélande.

c) Autre méthode : Allemagne, Danemark, Espagne, Kirghizstan, Luxembourg, Ouzbékistan, Pologne, Porto Rico, Roumanie, Slovénie et Suède.

Sur les pays ou zones qui ont estimé à 90 % ou plus le degré d'exhaustivité de leur enregistrement des décès à moins d'un an (classé « C » ou « +C » dans le tableau 15), les pays ou zones suivants ont donné des indications touchant la base de cette estimation :

a) Analyse démographique : Arabie saoudite, Argentine, Australie, Autriche, Brésil, Bulgarie, Chili, Chine - Hong Kong RAS, Croatie, Égypte, Estonie, Israël, Italie, Lettonie, Lituanie, Malte, Maurice, Nouvelle-Zélande, Panama, République de Corée, République de Moldova, Seychelles et Suède.

b) Double contrôle des registres : Autriche, Bahreïn, Belgique, Brésil, Cuba, Chypre, Estonie, Groenland, Hongrie, Îles Féroé, Irlande, Israël, Italie, Lettonie, Lituanie, Montserrat, Norvège, Nouvelle-Zélande et Qatar.

c) Autre méthode : Allemagne, Aruba, Brésil, Curaçao, Danemark, Espagne, Îles Caïmans, Kirghizstan, Liechtenstein, Luxembourg, Ouzbékistan, Pologne, Porto Rico, Roumanie, Singapour, Slovénie et Suède.

Sur les pays ou zones qui ont estimé à 90 % ou plus le degré d'exhaustivité de leur enregistrement des décès (classé « C » ou « +C » dans le tableau 18), les pays ou zones suivants ont donné des indications touchant la base de cette estimation :

a) Analyse démographique : Arabie saoudite, Afrique du Sud, Argentine, Australie, Autriche, Brésil, Bulgarie, Chili, Chine - Hong Kong RAS, Croatie, Égypte, Estonie, États-Unis d'Amérique, Israël, Italie, Lettonie, Lituanie, Malte, Maurice, Nouvelle-Zélande, Panama, République de Corée, République de Moldova, Seychelles, Suède et Venezuela (République bolivarienne du).

b) Double contrôle des registres : Autriche, Bahreïn, Belgique, Brésil, Cuba, Chypre, Estonie, Groenland, Hongrie, Îles Féroé, Israël, Italie, Lettonie, Lituanie, Mongolie, Montserrat, Norvège, Nouvelle-Zélande, Qatar et Venezuela (République bolivarienne du).

c) Autre méthode : Allemagne, Aruba, Brésil, Curaçao, Danemark, Espagne, États-Unis d'Amérique, France, Kirghizstan, Liechtenstein, Luxembourg, Malaisie, Ouzbékistan, Pologne, Porto Rico, Roumanie, Saint Vincent et les Grenadines, Singapour, Slovénie et Suède.

Sur les pays ou zones qui ont estimé à 90 % ou plus le degré d'exhaustivité de leur enregistrement des mariages (classé « C » ou « +C « » dans le tableau 23), les pays ou zones suivants ont communiqué des renseignements concernant les bases sur lesquelles leur estimation reposait :

a) Analyse démographique : Arabie saoudite, Argentine, Australie, Autriche, Bulgarie, Chili, Chine - Hong Kong RAS, Croatie, Égypte, Estonie, Italie, Lettonie, Lituanie, Malte, Maurice, République de Moldova, Seychelles, Suède et Venezuela (République bolivarienne du).

b) Double contrôle des registres : Autriche, Belgique, Cuba, Estonie, État de Palestine, Hongrie, Îles Féroé, Israël, Italie, Lettonie, Norvège, Nouvelle-Zélande, Qatar et République de Corée.

c) Autre méthode : Allemagne, Aruba, Curaçao, Danemark, Espagne, France, Kirghizstan, Jordanie, Liechtenstein, Luxembourg, Ouzbékistan, Pologne, Porto Rico, République dominicaine, Roumanie, Slovénie, Suède et Tadjikistan.

Sur les pays ou zones qui ont estimé à 90 % ou plus le degré d'exhaustivité de leur enregistrement des divorces (classé « C » ou « +C » dans le tableau 24), les pays ou zones suivants ont communiqué des renseignements concernant les bases sur lesquelles leur estimation reposait :

a) Analyse démographique : Arabie saoudite, Autriche, Bulgarie, Croatie, Égypte, Estonie, Italie, Lettonie, Lituanie, République de Moldova, République dominicaine, Seychelles, Suède et Venezuela (République bolivarienne du).

b) Double contrôle des registres : Belgique, Cuba, Estonie, État de Palestine, Hongrie, Îles Féroé, Israël, Italie, Lettonie, Norvège, Nouvelle-Zélande, Qatar et République de Corée.

c) Autre méthode : Aruba, Australie, Chypre, Curaçao, Danemark, Jordanie, Kirghizstan, Liechtenstein, Luxembourg, Maurice, Ouzbékistan, Pologne, Porto Rico, Roumanie, Slovénie, Suède et Tadjikistan.

4.2.2 Traitement des statistiques tirées des registres d'état civil

Dans tous les tableaux de l'*Annuaire démographique*, on a indiqué le degré de fiabilité des statistiques de l'état civil en se fondant sur le codage qualitatif décrit ci-dessus. Les statistiques codées « C », jugées sûres, sont imprimées en caractères romains. Celles qui sont codées « U » ou « ... », jugées douteuses, sont reproduites en *italique*.

Il convient de noter que, pour les taux de mortalité infantile, les taux de mortalité maternelle et les rapports de morts fœtales tardives (calculées en utilisant au dénominateur le nombre de naissances vivantes), les indications relatives à la fiabilité sont déterminées sur la base des codes de qualité utilisés pour les décès d'enfants de moins d'un an, les décès totaux et les morts fœtales tardives, respectivement. Pour évaluer ces taux et rapports de façon plus précise, il faudrait tenir compte de la qualité des données relatives aux naissances vivantes, utilisées au dénominateur dans leur calcul. Les codes de qualité pour les naissances vivantes figurent au tableau 9 et sont décrits plus en détail dans les notes techniques se rapportant à ce tableau.

4.2.3 Traitement des estimations fondées sur les statistiques de l'état civil

En plus des données provenant des systèmes d'enregistrement des faits d'état civil, *l'Annuaire démographique* contient aussi des estimations relatives aux fréquences et aux taux. Il s'agit d'estimations officielles, généralement calculées à partir des résultats d'un recensement de la population ou d'un sondage ou par analyse démographique. Si des estimations concernant les fréquences et les taux figurent dans les tableaux, c'est parce que l'on considère qu'elles fournissent des renseignements plus exacts que les systèmes existants d'enregistrement des faits d'état civil. En conséquence, elles sont également jugées sûres et sont donc imprimées en caractères romains.

Les données estimatives sont dénotées par le «|».

4.3 Causes de décès

Les États membres de l'Organisation mondiale de la santé (OMS) sont tenus de communiquer à celle-ci les données sur les causes de décès codifiées selon la révision en vigueur de la Classification internationale des maladies et des problèmes de santé connexes (CIM). Pour assurer la comparabilité internationale des statistiques des causes de décès, l'OMS organise régulièrement des conférences internationales de révision de la Classification internationale des maladies afin de suivre, au fur et à mesure, les progrès les plus récents de la médecine clinique et de la statistique. Les données sont généralement présentées à l'OMS selon le degré de détail à tous les quatre caractères requis par la CIM et sont compilées et archivées dans la Base de données sur la mortalité de l'OMS au degré de détail présenté par le pays. Les données de la Base de données sur la mortalité de l'OMS sont disponibles sur le site Internet suivant : http://www3.who.int/whosis/menu.cfm.

Les révisions de la CIM permettent certes de disposer d'une version actualisée, mais elles posent plusieurs problèmes de comparabilité des statistiques des causes de décès. Le premier tient au manque de comparabilité dans le temps, qui accompagne inévitablement la mise en œuvre d'une classification nouvelle. Le deuxième est celui de la comparabilité entre pays ou zones, car les différents pays peuvent adopter la nouvelle classification à des époques différentes. Établir la cause des décès exige des compétences de plus en plus poussées à mesure que la classification devient plus précise. Or, dans beaucoup de pays ou zones, il est rare que les décès se produisent en présence d'un témoin possédant une formation médicale et le certificat de décès est le plus souvent établi par quelqu'un qui n'est pas qualifié sur le plan médical. Étant donné que la CIM répertorie de nombreux diagnostics qu'il est impossible d'établir si l'on n'a pas de formation en médecine, la CIM n'est pas toujours exactement ou précisément utilisée ce qui affecte la comparabilité internationale, notamment entre pays ou zones où la qualité des services médicaux est très disparate.

Les chapitres de la dixième révision[16] se fondent sur un système de codification alphanumérique à une lettre suivie de trois chiffres pour les catégories à quatre caractères. Le chapitre 1 concerne les maladies infectieuses et parasitaires et le chapitre 2 l'ensemble des néoplasmes. Le chapitre 3 a trait aux troubles du système immunitaire, aux maladies du sang et aux organes hématopoïétiques. Le chapitre 4 porte sur les maladies du système endocrinien, de la nutrition et du métabolisme. Les autres chapitres groupent les maladies selon leur site anatomique, à l'exception de ceux qui concernent les affections mentales, les complications de la grossesse, de l'accouchement et des suites de couches, les malformations congénitales et les affections de la période périnatale. Enfin, un chapitre entier est consacré aux symptômes, manifestations et résultats anormaux.

4.3.1 Mortalité liée à la maternité

D'après la dixième révision de la CIM, la « mortalité liée à la maternité » est définie comme le décès d'une femme survenu au cours de la grossesse ou dans un délai de 42 jours après sa terminaison, quelle qu'en soit la durée et la localisation, pour une cause quelconque déterminée ou aggravée par la grossesse ou les soins qu'elle a motivés, mais ni accidentelle ni fortuite.

Les « décès liés à la maternité » doivent se répartir en décès par cause obstétricale directe et indirecte. Les décès par cause obstétricale directe sont ceux qui résultent de complications obstétricales de l'état de grossesse (grossesse, travail et suites de couches), d'interventions, d'omissions, d'un traitement incorrect ou d'un enchaînement d'événements de l'un quelconque des facteurs ci-dessus. Les décès par cause obstétricale indirecte sont ceux qui résultent d'une maladie préexistante ou d'une affection apparue au cours de la grossesse, sans qu'elle soit due à des causes obstétricales directes, mais qui a été aggravée par les effets physiologiques de la grossesse.

En théorie, le nombre de femmes enceintes aurait dû être pris comme dénominateur pour le taux de mortalité maternelle, mais il est impossible de déterminer ce nombre. En conséquence, il est en outre recommandé dans la dixième révision d'exprimer les taux de mortalité maternelle sur la base de 100 000 naissances vivantes ou 100 000 naissances totales (naissances vivantes et morts fœtales). Le taux de mortalité maternelle est ici calculé par 100 000 naissances vivantes. Bien que les naissances vivantes ne permettent pas d'évaluer sans distorsion le nombre des femmes enceintes, leur nombre est plus fiable que d'autres estimations car le nombre des naissances vivantes est plus exactement enregistré que celui des naissances vivantes et des morts fœtales.

---

[1] UNdata est un service de données en ligne géré par la Division de statistique du Département des affaires économiques et sociales de l'Organisation des Nations Unies.

[2] Les éditions de 1978 et de 1991 font exception à la règle, puisque les tableaux sur des sujets spéciaux ont été publiés séparément.

[3] Organisation des Nations Unies, Département des affaires économiques et sociales, Division de la population (2017). Perspectives de la population mondiale : La révision de 2017 (http://esa.un.org/unpd/wpp/).

[4] ST/ESA/STAT/SER.M/49/Rev.4/WWW ; https://unstats.un.org/unsd/methodology/m49/ ; voir également Code standard des pays et des zones à usage statistique, numéro de vente : M.98.XVII.9, Nations Unies, New York, 1999.

[5] Numéro de vente : E.15.XVII.10, Nations Unies, New York, 2015.

[6] Ibid., par. 4.151.

[7] Lorsque l'on utilise un registre de la population, on peut également calculer l'âge en années révolues en soustrayant la date de naissance de chaque personne inscrite sur le registre de la date de référence à laquelle se rapportent les données sur l'âge.

[8] L'emploi de méthodes différentes de calcul de l'âge, par exemple la méthode occidentale et la méthode orientale, ou, comme on les désigne plus communément, la méthode anglaise et la méthode chinoise, représente une cause de non-comparabilité. Selon la méthode chinoise, on considère que l'enfant est âgé d'un an à sa naissance et qu'il avance d'un an à chaque nouvelle année chinoise. Les répercussions de cette méthode sont particulièrement apparentes dans les données pour le premier âge : les données concernant les enfants de moins d'un an sont nettement inférieures à la réalité. Les effets sur les chiffres relatifs aux groupes d'âge suivants sont moins visibles. Les séries ainsi établies sont souvent ajustées avant d'être publiées, mais il ne faut pas exclure la possibilité d'aberrations de ce genre lorsque l'on compare des données censitaires sur l'âge.

[9] Numéro de vente : E.13.XVII.10, publication des Nations Unies, New York, 2014.

[10] Numéro de vente : F. 98.XVII.7, publication des Nations Unies, New York, 1998.

[11] Numéro de vente : F.98.XVII.11, publication des Nations Unies, New York, 1998.

[12] Numéro de vente : F.98.XVII.4, publication des Nations Unies, New York, 1998.

[13] Numéro de vente : F.98.XVII.6, publication des Nations Unies, New York, 1998.

[14] Numéro de vente : F.98.XVII.10, publication des Nations Unies, New York, 1998.

[15] Numéro de vente : F.03.XVII.11, United Nations, New York, 2004.

[16] Organisation mondiale de la santé, Classification statistique internationale des maladies et problèmes de santé connexes, dixième révision, vol. 2, Genève, 1992.

Table A. Demographic Yearbook 2017 synoptic table: Availability of data by country/area, table and sex, where applicable

Tableau A. Tableau synoptique de l'Annuaire démographique 2017 : Disponibilité des données par pays ou zone, tableau et le sexe, si disponible

Table A. Demographic Yearbook 2017 synoptic table: Availability of data by country/area, table and sex, where applicable
Tableau A. Tableau synoptique de l'Annuaire démographique 2017 : Disponibilité des données par pays ou zone, tableau et le sexe, si disponible

General topic and table number - Sujet général et numéro de tableau

Continent and country or area / Continent et pays ou zone	Table totals	Summary - Aperçu 3 Total	3 M/F	4	5	Population 6 Total¹	6 M/F	7 Total	7 M/F	8 Total	8 M/F	Fertility - Natalité 9	10 Total	10 M/F	11	Foetal mortality - Mortalité foetale 12	13	14
Total number of countries or areas - Total des pays ou zones	..	240	223	177	225	229	229	218	213	207	165	166	148	126	87	91	62	51

AFRICA - AFRIQUE

Continent and country or area	Table totals	3 Total	3 M/F	4	5	6 Total¹	6 M/F	7 Total	7 M/F	8 Total	8 M/F	9	10 Total	10 M/F	11	12	13	14
Algeria - Algérie	17	•	•		•	•	•	•	•	•	...	•	...	...	...	•	...	...
Angola	11	•	•		•	•	•	•	•	...	...	•	...	...	...	...	...	...
Benin - Bénin	10	•	•	...	•	•	•	•	•	•	...	...	...	...	...	...	...	...
Botswana	19	•	•		•	•	•	•	•	•	•	•	•	•	...	...	...	...
Burkina Faso	10	•	•	...	•	•	•	•	•	•	...	...	...	...	...	...	...	...
Burundi	14	•	•		•	•	•	•	•	•	•	•	...	...	...	•	•	...
Cabo Verde	12	•	•	...	•	•	•	•	•	•	...	...	...	...	...	...	...	...
Cameroon - Cameroun	9	•	•		•	•	•	•	•	•	...	...	...	...	...	...	...	...
Central African Republic - République centrafricaine	2	•	•	...	...	...	...	...	...	...	...	...	...	...	...	...	...	...
Chad - Tchad	4	•	•	...	•	•	•	...	...	...	...	...	...	...	...	...	...	...
Comoros - Comores	2	•	•	...	•	...	...	...	...	...	...	...	...	...	...	...	...	...
Congo	8	•	•	...	•	•	•	•	•	...	...	...	...	...	...	...	...	...
Côte d'Ivoire	18	•	•	•	•	•	•	•	•	•	•	•	•	•	...	...	...	...
Democratic Republic of the Congo - République démocratique du Congo	2	•	•	...	...	...	...	...	...	...	...	...	...	...	...	...	...	...
Djibouti	7	•	•	...	•	•	•	•	•	...	...	...	...	...	...	...	...	...
Egypt - Égypte	25	•	•	•	•	•	•	•	•	•	•	•	•	•	•	•	...	...
Equatorial Guinea - Guinée équatoriale	8	•	•	...	•	•	•	•	•	•	...	...	...	...	...	...	...	...
Eritrea - Érythrée	7	•	•	...	•	•	•	•	•	...	...	...	...	...	...	...	...	...
Eswatini	9	•	•	•	•	•	•	•	•	...	...	...	...	...	...	...	...	...
Ethiopia - Éthiopie	9	•	•	...	•	•	•	•	•	•	...	•	...	...	...	...	...	...
Gabon	6	•	•	...	•	•	•	•	...	...	...	•	...	...	...	...	...	...
Gambia - Gambie	4	•	•	...	•	•	•	...	...	...	...	...	...	...	...	...	...	...
Ghana	17	•	•	•	•	•	•	•	•	•	•	•	•	•	...	...	...	...
Guinea - Guinée	18	•	•	•	•	•	•	•	•	•	•	•	•	•	...	...	...	...
Guinea-Bissau - Guinée-Bissau	10	•	•	•	•	•	•	•	•	•	...	•	...	...	...	...	...	...
Kenya	18	•	•	•	•	•	•	•	•	•	•	•	•	•	...	...	...	...
Lesotho	18	•	•	•	•	•	•	•	•	•	...	•	•	•	...	•	...	...
Liberia - Libéria	12	•	•	•	•	•	•	•	•	•	•	•	...	...	...	•	...	...
Libya - Libye	8	•	•		•	•	•	•	•	...	...	•	...	...	...	...	...	...
Madagascar	5	•	•	...	•	...	...	•	•	...	...	...	...	...	...	...	...	...
Malawi	14	•	•	...	•	•	•	•	•	•	...	•	•	...	...	...	...	...
Mali	13	•	•	...	•	•	•	•	•	•	...	•	•	...	...	...	...	...
Mauritania - Mauritanie	11	•	...	•	•	•	•	•	...	•	...	•	...	...	...	...	...	...
Mauritius - Maurice	27	•	•	•	•	•	•	•	•	•	•	•	•	•	•	•	...	...
Mayotte	15	•	•	•	•	•	•	•	•	•	...	•	•	•	...	...	...	...
Morocco - Maroc	11	•	•	•	•	•	•	•	•	...	...	•	...	...	...	...	...	...
Mozambique	12	•	•	...	•	•	•	•	•	•	...	•	•	...	...	...	...	...
Namibia - Namibie	14	•	•	...	•	•	•	•	•	•	...	•	•	•	•	...	...	...
Niger	11	•	•	...	•	•	•	•	•	•	...	•	...	...	...	...	...	...
Nigeria - Nigéria	6	•	•	...	•	•	...	...	...	...	...	...	...	...	...	...	...	...
Republic of South Sudan - République de Soudan du Sud	13	•	•	...	•	•	•	•	•	•	•	...	...	...	...	...	...	...
Reunion - Réunion	19	•	•	•	•	•	•	•	•	•	•	•	...	...	...	•	...	...
Rwanda	10	•	•	...	•	•	•	•	•	•	...	•	...	...	...	...	...	...
Saint Helena ex. dep. - Sainte-Hélène sans dép.	21	•	...	•	•	•	•	•	•	•	•	•	•	•	...	...	...	...
Saint Helena: Ascension - Sainte-Hélène: Ascension	6	•	...		•	•	•	•	...	...	...	...	...	...	...	...	...	...
Saint Helena: Tristan da Cunha - Sainte-Hélène: Tristan da Cunha	4	•	...		•	•	•	•	...	...	...	...	...	...	...	...	...	...
Sao Tome and Principe - Sao Tomé-et-Principe	15	•	•	•	•	•	•	•	•	•	...	•	•	...	...	...	...	...
Senegal - Sénégal	13	•	•	...	•	•	•	•	•	•	...	•	•	...	...	...	...	...
Seychelles	24	•	•	•	•	•	•	•	•	•	•	•	•	•	•	•	•	•
Sierra Leone	17	•	•	•	•	•	•	•	•	•	•	•	•	•	...	...	...	...
Somalia - Somalie	3	•	•	...	•	...	...	...	...	...	...	...	...	...	...	...	...	...
South Africa - Afrique du Sud	27	•	•	•	•	•	•	•	•	•	•	•	•	•	•	...	...	...
Sudan - Soudan	10	•	•	...	•	•	•	•	•	•	...	•	...	...	...	...	...	...
Togo	8	•	•	...	•	•	•	•	•	...	...	...	...	...	...	...	...	...
Tunisia - Tunisie	19	•	•	•	•	•	•	•	•	•	•	•	•	...	...	...	...	...

Table A. Demographic Yearbook 2017 synoptic table: Availability of data by country/area, table and sex, where applicable
Tableau A. Tableau synoptique de l'Annuaire démographique 2017 : Disponibilité des données par pays ou zone, tableau et le sexe, si disponible

Continent and country or area / Continent et pays ou zone	Infant and maternal mortality - Mortalité infantile et mortalité liée à la maternité				General mortality - Mortalité générale						Nuptiality and divorces - Nuptialité et divortialité		
	15	16 Total	16 M/F	17	18	19 Total	19 M/F	20	21	22	23	24	25
Total number of countries or areas - Total des pays ou zones	130	105	102	129	163	146	145	118	71	184	135	108	116

AFRICA - AFRIQUE

Continent and country or area	15	16 Total	16 M/F	17	18	19 Total	19 M/F	20	21	22	23	24	25
Algeria - Algérie	•	...	...	...	•	...	...	...	•	•	...	...	...
Angola	•	...	...	...	•	...	...	...	...	•	...	...	...
Benin - Bénin	...	...	...	...	...	...	...	...	•	...	...	...	...
Botswana	•	...	...	...	•	•	•	...	•	•	•	•	...
Burkina Faso	...	...	...	...	...	...	...	...	•	...	...	...	...
Burundi	...	...	...	...	...	...	...	...	•	...	...	...	...
Cabo Verde	...	•	...	•	...	...	...	...	...	•	...	...	...
Cameroon - Cameroun	...	...	...	...	...	...	...	...	...	•	...	...	...
Central African Republic - République centrafricaine	...	...	...	...	...	...	...	...	...	...	...	...	...
Chad - Tchad	...	...	...	...	...	...	...	...	...	...	...	...	...
Comoros - Comores	...	...	...	...	...	...	...	...	...	...	...	...	...
Congo	...	...	...	...	•	...	...	...	...	...	...	...	...
Côte d'Ivoire	•	...	...	...	•	...	...	...	•	•	...	...	•
Democratic Republic of the Congo - République démocratique du Congo	...	...	...	...	...	...	...	...	...	...	...	...	...
Djibouti	...	...	...	...	...	...	...	...	•	...	...	...	...
Egypt - Égypte	•	•	...	•	•	•	...	•	•	•	•	•	•
Equatorial Guinea - Guinée équatoriale	...	...	...	...	...	...	...	...	•	...	...	...	...
Eritrea - Érythrée	...	...	...	...	...	...	...	...	...	...	...	...	...
Eswatini	...	...	...	...	...	...	...	...	...	•	...	...	...
Ethiopia - Éthiopie	...	...	...	...	...	...	...	...	...	...	...	...	...
Gabon	...	...	...	...	...	...	...	...	...	...	...	...	...
Gambia - Gambie	...	...	...	...	...	...	...	...	...	...	...	...	...
Ghana	...	...	...	...	•	•	•	...	•	...	...	...	...
Guinea - Guinée	•	...	...	...	•	•	•	...	•	...	...	...	...
Guinea-Bissau - Guinée-Bissau	...	...	...	...	•	•	•	...	•	...	...	...	...
Kenya	•	...	...	...	•	•	•	...	•	...	...	...	...
Lesotho	...	...	...	...	•	•	•	...	•	•	•	•	•
Liberia - Libéria	...	...	...	...	•	•	•	...	•	...	...	...	...
Libya - Libye	...	...	...	...	...	...	...	...	...	...	...	...	...
Madagascar	...	...	...	...	...	...	...	...	...	...	...	...	...
Malawi	...	...	...	...	•	•	...	...	•	...	...	...	...
Mali	...	...	...	...	•	...	...	...	...	...	...	...	...
Mauritania - Mauritanie	...	...	...	...	...	...	...	...	•	...	...	...	...
Mauritius - Maurice	•	•	•	•	•	•	•	•	•	•	•	•	•
Mayotte	...	...	...	•	•	...	...	...	•	•	•	...	•
Morocco - Maroc	...	...	...	•	...	...	...	•	...	•	...	...	...
Mozambique	...	...	...	...	...	...	...	...	•	...	...	...	...
Namibia - Namibie	...	...	...	...	•	•	...	...	•	...	...	...	...
Niger	...	...	...	...	•	•	...	...	...	...	...	...	...
Nigeria - Nigéria	...	...	...	...	...	...	...	...	...	...	...	...	...
Republic of South Sudan - République de Soudan du Sud	...	...	...	...	•	•	...	•	...	•	...	...	...
Reunion - Réunion	...	...	...	•	...	...	...	•	...	•	•	...	•
Rwanda	...	...	...	...	...	...	...	...	...	...	...	...	...
Saint Helena ex. dep. - Sainte-Hélène sans dép.	•	•	•	•	•	•	•	...	•	•	...	...	•
Saint Helena: Ascension - Sainte-Hélène: Ascension	...	...	...	...	...	...	...	...	...	...	...	...	...
Saint Helena: Tristan da Cunha - Sainte-Hélène: Tristan da Cunha	...	...	...	...	...	...	...	...	...	...	...	...	...
Sao Tome and Principe - Sao Tomé-et-Principe	...	...	...	...	•	•	...	...	•	...	...	...	...
Senegal - Sénégal	...	...	...	...	•	...	...	...	•	...	...	...	...
Seychelles	•	...	...	•	•	•	•	•	•	•	•	...	•
Sierra Leone	...	...	...	...	•	•	•	...	•	...	...	...	...
Somalia - Somalie	...	...	...	...	...	...	...	...	...	...	...	...	...
South Africa - Afrique du Sud	•	•	...	•	•	•	•	...	•	•	•	...	...
Sudan - Soudan	...	...	...	...	...	...	...	...	•	...	•	•	•
Togo	...	...	...	...	...	...	...	...	...	...	...	...	...
Tunisia - Tunisie	...	...	...	•	•	...	...	•	...	•	•	...	•

31

General topic and table number - Sujet général et numéro de tableau

Continent and country or area / Continent et pays ou zone	Table totals	Summary - Apercu 3 Total	3 M/F	4	5	Population 6 Total[1]	6 M/F	7 Total	7 M/F	8 Total	8 M/F	Fertility - Natalité 9	10 Total	10 M/F	11	Foetal mortality - Mortalité foetale 12	13	14
AFRICA - AFRIQUE																		
Uganda - Ouganda	10	•	•	•	•	•	•	•	•	•	…	…	…	…	…	…	…	…
United Republic of Tanzania - République Unie de Tanzanie	10	•	•	•	•	•	•	•	•	•	…	…	…	…	…	…	…	…
Western Sahara - Sahara occidental	3	•	•	…	•	…	…	…	…	•	•	…	…	…	…	…	…	…
Zambia - Zambie	13	•	•	…	•	•	•	•	•	•	•	…	•	•	…	…	…	…
Zimbabwe	10	•	•	…	•	•	•	•	•	•	•	…	…	…	…	…	…	…
AMERICA, NORTH - AMÉRIQUE DU NORD																		
Anguilla	19	•	•	•	•	•	•	•	•	•	•	•	…	…	…	…	…	…
Antigua and Barbuda - Antigua-et-Barbuda	9	•	…	…	•	•	•	•	•	…	…	•	…	…	…	…	…	…
Aruba	25	•	•	•	•	•	•	•	•	•	•	•	•	•	•	…	…	…
Bahamas	26	•	•	•	•	•	•	•	•	•	•	•	•	•	•	•	…	…
Barbados - Barbade	14	•	•	•	•	•	•	•	•	•	•	•	…	…	…	•	…	…
Belize	22	•	•	•	•	•	•	•	•	•	•	•	•	•	…	•	…	…
Bermuda - Bermudes	28	•	•	•	•	•	•	•	•	•	•	•	•	•	…	•	•	•
British Virgin Islands - Îles Vierges britanniques	13	•	•	•	•	•	•	…	…	•	•	•	…	…	…	…	…	…
Canada	25	•	•	•	•	•	•	•	•	•	•	•	•	•	•	•	…	…
Cayman Islands - Îles Caïmanes	19	•	•	•	•	•	•	•	•	•	•	•	•	…	…	…	…	•
Costa Rica	30	•	•	•	•	•	•	•	•	•	•	•	•	•	•	•	…	•
Cuba	29	•	•	•	•	•	•	•	•	•	•	…	•	•	•	…	…	…
Curaçao	22	•	•	•	•	•	•	•	•	•	…	…	•	•	…	…	…	…
Dominica - Dominique	14	•	•	•	•	•	•	•	•	•	…	…	…	…	…	…	…	…
Dominican Republic - République dominicaine	29	•	•	•	•	•	•	•	•	•	•	•	•	•	•	•	•	…
El Salvador	25	•	•	•	•	•	•	•	•	•	•	•	•	•	…	…	…	…
Greenland - Groenland	21	•	•	•	•	•	•	•	•	•	•	•	•	•	…	…	…	…
Grenada - Grenade	23	•	•	•	•	•	•	•	•	•	…	•	•	…	…	…	…	…
Guadeloupe	17	•	•	•	•	•	•	•	•	•	•	•	•	…	…	…	…	…
Guatemala	27	•	•	•	•	•	•	•	•	•	•	•	•	•	•	…	…	…
Haiti - Haïti	9	•	•	…	•	•	•	•	•	•	•	…	…	…	…	…	…	…
Honduras	12	•	•	•	•	•	•	•	•	•	•	…	…	•	…	…	…	…
Jamaica - Jamaïque	21	•	•	•	•	•	•	•	•	•	•	•	•	•	…	…	…	…
Martinique	18	•	•	•	•	•	•	•	•	•	•	•	•	…	…	…	…	…
Mexico - Mexique	30	•	•	•	•	•	•	•	•	•	•	•	•	•	•	•	•	•
Montserrat	22	•	•	•	•	•	•	•	•	•	…	•	•	•	…	•	…	…
Nicaragua	22	•	•	•	•	•	•	•	•	•	…	•	•	•	…	…	…	…
Panama	28	•	•	•	•	•	•	•	•	•	•	•	•	•	•	…	…	…
Puerto Rico - Porto Rico	28	•	•	•	•	•	•	•	•	•	•	•	•	•	•	•	…	…
Saint Kitts and Nevis - Saint-Kitts-et-Nevis	11	•	•	•	•	•	•	•	•	•	…	…	…	•	…	•	…	…
Saint Lucia - Sainte-Lucie	12	•	•	…	•	•	•	•	•	•	…	…	…	•	…	…	…	…
Saint Pierre and Miquelon - Saint Pierre-et-Miquelon	4	•	…	•	…	…	…	…	…	•	…	…	…	…	…	…	…	…
Saint Vincent and the Grenadines - Saint-Vincent-et-les Grenadines	24	•	•	•	•	•	•	•	•	•	…	•	•	…	•	…	…	…
Saint-Barthélemy	1	•	…	…	…	…	…	…	…	…	…	…	…	…	…	…	…	…
Saint-Martin (French part) - Saint-Martin (partie française)	1	•	…	…	…	…	…	…	…	…	…	…	…	…	…	…	…	…
Sint Maarten (Dutch part) - Saint-Martin (partie néerlandaise)	13	•	•	•	•	•	•	•	•	•	…	•	…	…	…	…	…	…
Trinidad and Tobago - Trinité-et-Tobago	24	•	•	•	•	•	•	•	•	•	•	•	•	•	…	•	…	…
Turks and Caicos Islands - Îles Turques et Caïques	20	•	•	•	•	•	•	•	•	•	…	•	•	•	…	…	…	…
United States of America - États-Unis d'Amérique	27	•	•	•	•	•	•	•	•	•	…	•	•	•	•	•	•	…
United States Virgin Islands - Îles Vierges américaines	10	•	•	…	•	•	•	•	•	•	…	…	…	…	…	…	…	…

Table A. Demographic Yearbook 2017 synoptic table: Availability of data by country/area, table and sex, where applicable
Tableau A. Tableau synoptique de l'Annuaire démographique 2017 : Disponibilité des données par pays ou zone, tableau et le sexe, si disponible (continued - suite)

Continent and country or area / Continent et pays ou zone	Infant and maternal mortality - Mortalité infantile et mortalité liée à la maternité				General mortality - Mortalité générale						Nuptiality and divorces - Nuptialité et divortialité		
	15	16 Total	16 M/F	17	18	19 Total	19 M/F	20	21	22	23	24	25
AFRICA - AFRIQUE													
Uganda - Ouganda	...	...	...	...	...	...	...	...	...	•	...	...	...
United Republic of Tanzania - République Unie de Tanzanie	...	...	...	...	...	...	...	...	...	...	...	...	...
Western Sahara - Sahara occidental	...	...	...	...	...	...	...	...	...	...	...	...	...
Zambia - Zambie	...	...	...	...	...	•	•	...	...	...	...	...	...
Zimbabwe	...	...	...	...	...	...	...	...	...	•	...	...	...
AMERICA, NORTH - AMÉRIQUE DU NORD													
Anguilla	•	...	...	•	•	•	•	•	...	•	•	•	...
Antigua and Barbuda - Antigua-et-Barbuda	...	...	...	•	•	•	•	•	...	•	•	•	...
Aruba	•	•	•	•	•	•	•	•	...	•	•	•	•
Bahamas	•	•	•	•	•	•	•	•	...	•	•	•	...
Barbados - Barbade	•	•	•	•	•	•	•	•	...	•	•	•	•
Belize	•	•	•	•	•	•	•	•	...	•	•	•	•
Bermuda - Bermudes	•	•	•	•	•	•	•	•	...	•	•	•	•
British Virgin Islands - Îles Vierges britanniques	...	...	...	•	•	...	...	•	...	•	•	•	...
Canada	...	...	...	...	...	...	...	...	...	•	•	...	...
Cayman Islands - Îles Caïmanes	...	•	•	•	•	•	•	•	...	•	•	•	...
Costa Rica	•	•	•	•	•	•	•	•	•	•	•	•	...
Cuba	•	•	•	•	•	•	•	•	•	•	•	•	•
Curaçao	•	•	•	...	•	•	•	...	•	•	•	•	•
Dominica - Dominique	...	...	...	•	...	...	...	•	...	...	•	•	...
Dominican Republic - République dominicaine	•	•	•	•	•	•	•	•	...	•	•	•	:
El Salvador	•	•	•	•	•	•	•	•	...	•	•	...	...
Greenland - Groenland	•	...	...	...	•	•	•	•	...	•	•	•	...
Grenada - Grenade	•	•	•	•	•	•	•	•	...	•	•	•	...
Guadeloupe	...	•	•	•	...	•	•	...	•	•	...	•	•
Guatemala	•	•	•	•	•	•	•	...	•	•	•	•	...
Haiti - Haïti	...	...	...	...	...	...	...	•	...	...	•	...	...
Honduras	...	...	...	•	...	...	...	•	...	•	•	...	...
Jamaica - Jamaïque	...	...	...	•	...	•	•	...	...	•	•	•	...
Martinique	...	•	•	•	...	•	•	...	•	•	...	•	•
Mexico - Mexique	•	•	•	•	•	•	•	•	•	•	•	•	•
Montserrat	•	•	•	•	•	•	•	•	...	•	•	•	...
Nicaragua	...	•	•	•	•	•	•	•	...	•	•	•	...
Panama	•	•	•	•	•	•	•	•	•	•	•	•	...
Puerto Rico - Porto Rico	•	•	•	•	•	•	•	•	•	•	•	•	•
Saint Kitts and Nevis - Saint-Kitts-et-Nevis	...	...	...	•	•	...	...	•	...	•	...	...	...
Saint Lucia - Sainte-Lucie	...	...	...	•	...	...	...	•	...	•	...	...	...
Saint Pierre and Miquelon - Saint Pierre-et-Miquelon	...	...	...	•	...	...	...	...	...	...	...	...	...
Saint Vincent and the Grenadines - Saint-Vincent-et-les Grenadines	•	•	•	•	•	•	•	•	...	•	•	•	•
Saint-Barthélemy	...	...	...	...	...	...	...	...	...	...	...	...	...
Saint-Martin (French part) - Saint-Martin (partie française)	...	...	...	...	...	...	...	...	...	...	...	...	...
Sint Maarten (Dutch part) - Saint-Martin (partie néerlandaise)	...	...	...	...	•	...	...	...	...	•	•	...	...
Trinidad and Tobago - Trinité-et-Tobago	•	•	•	•	•	•	•	•	...	•	•	•	•
Turks and Caicos Islands - Îles Turques et Caïques	•	...	...	•	•	...	...	•	...	•	•	•	...
United States of America - États-Unis d'Amérique	•	•	•	•	•	•	•	•	•	•	•	...	...
United States Virgin Islands - Îles Vierges américaines	...	...	...	•	...	...	...	•	...	...	...	...	...

Table A. Demographic Yearbook 2017 synoptic table: Availability of data by country/area, table and sex, where applicable
Tableau A. Tableau synoptique de l'Annuaire démographique 2017 : Disponibilité des données par pays ou zone, tableau et le sexe, si disponible (continued - suite)

General topic and table number - Sujet général et numéro de tableau

Continent and country or area / Continent et pays ou zone	Table totals	Summary - Aperçu 3 Total	3 M/F	4	5	Population 6 Total[1]	6 M/F	7 Total	7 M/F	8 Total	8 M/F	9	Fertility - Natalité 10 Total	10 M/F	11	Foetal mortality - Mortalité foetale 12	13	14
AMERICA, SOUTH - AMÉRIQUE DU SUD																		
Argentina - Argentine	23	•	•	•	•	•	•	•	•	•	•	•	•	•	...	•	...	...
Bolivia (Plurinational State of) - Bolivie (État plurinational de)	17	•	•	•	•	•	•	•	•	•	•	...	...	...	...	...	...	...
Brazil - Brésil	26	•	•	•	•	•	•	•	•	•	...	•	•	•	•	•	•	•
Chile - Chili	27	•	•	•	•	•	•	•	•	•	•	•	•	•	•	•	•	•
Colombia - Colombie	26	•	•	•	•	•	•	•	•	•	•	•	•	•	•	•	•	•
Ecuador - Équateur	29	•	•	•	•	•	•	•	•	•	...	•	•	•	•	•	•	•
Falkland Islands (Malvinas) - Îles Falkland (Malvinas)	8	•	•	...	...	•	•	•	•	•	•	...	...	...	...	...	...	...
French Guiana - Guyane française	18	•	•	•	•	•	•	•	•	•	•	...	...	...	...	...	...	...
Guyana	14	•	•	•	•	•	•	•	•	•	•	...	...	...	...	...	•	...
Paraguay	23	•	•	•	•	•	•	•	•	•	•	•	•	•	...	...	•	...
Peru - Pérou	25	•	•	•	•	•	•	•	•	•	•	•	•	•	...	...	...	...
Suriname	22	•	•	•	•	•	•	•	•	•	•	•	•	•	...	...	...	...
Uruguay	26	•	•	•	•	•	•	•	•	•	•	•	•	•	•	•	•	•
Venezuela (Bolivarian Republic of) - Venezuela (République bolivarienne du)	24	•	•	•	•	•	•	•	•	•	...	•	•	•	•	•	•	...
ASIA - ASIE																		
Afghanistan	10	•	•	...	•	•	•	•	•	•	•	...	•	...	...	...	...	...
Armenia - Arménie	29	•	•	•	•	•	•	•	•	•	•	•	•	•	...	•	•	•
Azerbaijan - Azerbaïdjan	29	•	•	•	•	•	•	•	•	•	•	•	•	•	•	•	•	...
Bahrain - Bahreïn	28	•	•	•	•	•	•	•	•	•	•	•	•	•	•	•	•	...
Bangladesh	15	•	•	•	•	•	•	•	•	•	•	•	•	•	...	•	...	...
Bhutan - Bhoutan	10	•	•	...	•	•	•	•	•	•	•	...	•	...	...	...	...	...
Brunei Darussalam - Brunéi Darussalam	25	•	•	•	•	•	•	•	•	•	•	•	•	•	...	•	•	•
Cambodia - Cambodge	9	•	•	...	•	•	•	•	•	•	•	...	...	...	...	...	...	...
China - Chine[2]	14	•	•	•	•	•	•	•	•	•	...	•	•	...	...	...	...	...
China, Hong Kong SAR - Chine, Hong Kong RAS	30	•	•	•	•	•	•	•	•	•	•	•	•	•	•	•	•	•
China, Macao SAR - Chine, Macao RAS	26	•	•	•	•	•	•	•	•	•	•	•	•	•	...	•	•	•
Cyprus - Chypre	25	•	•	•	•	•	•	•	•	•	...	•	•	•	...	•	•	•
Democratic People's Republic of Korea - République populaire démocratique de Corée	13	•	•	•	...	•	•	•	•	•	•	•	•	•	...	•	...	...
Georgia - Géorgie	28	•	•	•	•	•	•	•	•	•	•	...	•	•	•	•	•	...
India - Inde[3]	14	•	•	•	•	•	•	•	•	•	•	...	•	...	...	•	...	...
Indonesia - Indonésie	15	•	•	...	•	•	•	•	•	•	•	...	•	...	...	•	•	•
Iran (Islamic Republic of) - Iran (République islamique d')	23	•	•	•	•	•	•	•	•	•	•	•	•	•	...	...	...	...
Iraq	13	•	•	•	•	•	•	•	•	•	•	...	•	...	...	•	•	•
Israel - Israël[4]	30	•	•	•	•	•	•	•	•	•	•	•	•	•	•	•	•	•
Japan - Japon	30	•	•	•	•	•	•	•	•	•	•	•	•	•	•	•	•	•
Jordan - Jordanie	18	•	•	•	•	•	•	•	•	•	•	...	•	...	•	•	•	...
Kazakhstan	29	•	•	•	•	•	•	•	•	•	•	•	•	•	•	•	•	...
Kuwait - Koweït	26	•	•	•	•	•	•	•	•	•	•	•	•	•	...	•	•	•
Kyrgyzstan - Kirghizstan	30	•	•	•	•	•	•	•	•	•	•	•	•	•	•	•	•	•
Lao People's Democratic Republic - République démocratique populaire lao	11	•	•	•	•	•	•	•	•	•	•	...	•	...	...	•	...	...
Lebanon - Liban	11	•	•	...	•	...	...	•	•	•	•	...	•	...	...	•	...	...
Malaysia - Malaisie	21	•	•	•	•	•	•	•	•	...	•	•	•	•	...	•	•	•
Maldives	25	•	•	•	•	•	•	•	•	•	•	•	•	•	...	•	•	•
Mongolia - Mongolie	28	•	•	•	•	•	•	•	•	•	•	•	•	•	•	•	•	...
Myanmar	21	•	•	•	•	•	•	•	•	•	•	•	•	•	...	•	•	•
Nepal - Népal	10	•	•	...	•	•	•	•	•	•	•	...	•	...	...	•	...	...
Oman	26	•	•	•	•	•	•	•	•	•	•	•	•	•	...	•	•	•
Pakistan[5]	7	•	•	•	•	•	•	•	•	•	•	...	•	...	...	...	...	...
Philippines	23	•	•	•	•	•	•	•	•	•	...	•	•	•	...	•	•	...
Qatar	27	•	•	•	•	•	•	•	•	•	•	•	•	•	...	•	•	•
Republic of Korea - République de Corée	28	•	•	•	•	•	•	•	•	•	•	•	•	•	•	•	•	•
Saudi Arabia - Arabie saoudite	20	•	•	•	•	•	•	•	•	•	•	•	•	•	...	•	•	•
Singapore - Singapour	29	•	•	•	•	•	•	•	•	•	...	•	•	•	•	•	•	•

34

Continent and country or area / Continent et pays ou zone	Infant and maternal mortality - Mortalité infantile et mortalité liée à la maternité				General mortality - Mortalité générale						Nuptiality and divorces - Nuptialité et divortialité		
	15	16 Total	16 M/F	17	18	19 Total	19 M/F	20	21	22	23	24	25

AMERICA, SOUTH - AMÉRIQUE DU SUD

Country	15	16T	16M/F	17	18	19T	19M/F	20	21	22	23	24	25
Argentina - Argentine	•	...	...	•	•	•	•	•	•	•	•	...	...
Bolivia (Plurinational State of) - Bolivie (État plurinational de)	...	...	...	...	•	...	...	•	•	•	•	•	...
Brazil - Brésil	•	•	•	...	•	•	•	•	•	•	•	•	•
Chile - Chili	•	•	•	•	•	•	•	•	•	•	•	•	...
Colombia - Colombie	•	•	•	•	•	•	•	•	•	...	•	...	...
Ecuador - Équateur	•	•	•	•	•	•	•	•	...	•	...	•	•
Falkland Islands (Malvinas) - Îles Falkland (Malvinas)	...	...	...	...	...	...	...	...	...	...	...	...	...
French Guiana - Guyane française	...	...	...	•	•	...	...	•	•	•	•	•	•
Guyana	...	...	...	•	•	...	...	•	•	•	•	•	•
Paraguay	•	...	...	•	•	•	•	...	•	•	•	•	•
Peru - Pérou	•	...	...	•	•	•	•	...	•	•	•	•	•
Suriname	•	...	...	•	•	•	•	•	•	•	•	...	•
Uruguay	•	...	...	•	•	•	•	•	•	•	•	...	...
Venezuela (Bolivarian Republic of) - Venezuela (République bolivarienne du)	•	...	...	•	•	...	...	•	•	•	•	•	•

ASIA - ASIE

Country	15	16T	16M/F	17	18	19T	19M/F	20	21	22	23	24	25
Afghanistan	...	...	...	...	...	...	...	...	...	•	...	...	...
Armenia - Arménie	•	•	•	•	•	•	•	•	•	•	•	•	...
Azerbaijan - Azerbaïdjan	•	•	•	•	•	•	•	...	•	•	•	•	•
Bahrain - Bahreïn	•	•	•	•	•	•	•	...	•	•	•	•	•
Bangladesh	•	•	•	•	•	•	•	...	•	•	...	...	...
Bhutan - Bhoutan	•	...	...	•	•	•	•	...	•	•	...	...	...
Brunei Darussalam - Brunéi Darussalam	•	...	...	•	•	•	•	...	•	•	•	...	...
Cambodia - Cambodge	...	...	...	•	•	...	...	•	•	...	...	...	...
China - Chine[2]	...	...	...	...	•	...	...	•	•	...	...	...	...
China, Hong Kong SAR - Chine, Hong Kong RAS	•	•	•	•	•	•	•	•	•	•	•	•	•
China, Macao SAR - Chine, Macao RAS	•	•	•	•	•	•	•	•	•	•	•	•	•
Cyprus - Chypre	•	•	•	•	•	•	•	...	•	•	•	•	•
Democratic People's Republic of Korea - République populaire démocratique de Corée	...	...	...	...	•	...	...	•	•	...	...	...	...
Georgia - Géorgie	•	•	•	•	•	•	•	•	•	•	•	•	•
India - Inde[3]	•	...	...	•	•	...	...	•	•	...	•	•	•
Indonesia - Indonésie	...	...	...	...	•	...	...	•	•	...	...	...	...
Iran (Islamic Republic of) - Iran (République islamique d')	...	...	...	•	•	...	...	•	•	•	•	•	•
Iraq	...	...	...	•	•	...	...	•	...	...	•	•	•
Israel - Israël[4]	•	•	•	•	•	•	•	•	•	•	•	•	•
Japan - Japon	•	•	•	•	•	•	•	•	•	•	•	•	•
Jordan - Jordanie	•	...	...	•	•	•	...	•	•	•	•	•	•
Kazakhstan	•	•	•	•	•	•	•	•	•	•	•	•	•
Kuwait - Koweït	•	•	•	•	•	•	•	...	•	•	•	•	•
Kyrgyzstan - Kirghizstan	•	•	•	•	•	•	•	•	•	•	•	•	•
Lao People's Democratic Republic - République démocratique populaire lao	...	...	...	...	...	...	...	...	...	...	...	...	...
Lebanon - Liban	...	...	...	•	•	...	...	•	•	...	...	...	•
Malaysia - Malaisie	•	•	•	•	•	•	•	•	•	•	...	...	•
Maldives	•	•	•	•	•	•	•	•	•	•	•	•	•
Mongolia - Mongolie	•	•	•	•	•	•	•	...	•	•	•	•	•
Myanmar	...	...	...	...	•	...	...	•	•	...	...	...	...
Nepal - Népal	...	...	...	...	•	...	...	•	•	...	...	...	...
Oman	•	•	•	•	•	•	•	•	•	•	•	•	•
Pakistan[5]	•	...	...	•	•	...	...	•	•	...	...	...	...
Philippines	•	•	•	•	•	•	•	•	•	•	•	•	•
Qatar	•	•	•	•	•	•	•	•	•	•	•	•	•
Republic of Korea - République de Corée	•	•	•	•	•	•	•	•	•	•	•	•	•
Saudi Arabia - Arabie saoudite	•	...	...	•	•	•	•	...	•	•	•	...	...
Singapore - Singapour	•	•	•	•	•	•	•	•	•	•	•	•	•

Table A. Demographic Yearbook 2017 synoptic table: Availability of data by country/area, table and sex, where applicable
Tableau A. Tableau synoptique de l'Annuaire démographique 2017 : Disponibilité des données par pays ou zone, tableau et le sexe, si disponible (continued - suite)

Continent and country or area / Continent et pays ou zone	Table totals	Summary - Apercu 3 Total	3 M/F	4	5	Population 6 Total¹	6 M/F	7 Total	7 M/F	8 Total	8 M/F	9	Fertility 10 Total	10 M/F	11	Foetal mortality 12	13	14
ASIA - ASIE																		
Sri Lanka	19	•	•	•	•	•	•	•	•	•	•	•	...	...	•	...	...	...
State of Palestine - État de Palestine	18	•	•	•	•	•	•	•	...	•	•	...	...	•	...	...	...	...
Syrian Arab Republic - République arabe syrienne	10	•	•	...	...	•	•	•	•	•	...	...	...	...	•	...	•	...
Tajikistan - Tadjikistan	28	•	•	•	•	•	•	•	•	•	•	•	•	...	...	•	...	...
Thailand - Thaïlande	24	•	•	•	•	•	•	•	•	•	•	•	...	...	•	...	...	...
Timor-Leste	12	•	•	•	•	•	•	•	•	•	•	...	...	...	•	...	...	...
Turkey - Turquie	27	•	•	•	•	•	•	•	•	•	•	•	•	•	•	...	...	...
Turkmenistan - Turkménistan	4	•	•	...	...	...	...	...	...	...	...	...	...	...	...	...	...	...
United Arab Emirates - Émirats arabes unis	14	•	•	•	•	•	•	•	•	•	•	•	•	•	...	...	...	...
Uzbekistan - Ouzbékistan	29	•	•	•	•	•	•	•	•	•	•	•	•	•	•	•	•	...
Viet Nam	9	•	•	•	•	•	•	•	...	...	...	...	...	...	...	...	...	...
Yemen - Yémen	12	•	•	•	•	•	•	•	...	•	...	...	...	...	...	...	...	...
EUROPE																		
Åland Islands - Îles d'Åland	27	•	•	•	•	•	•	•	•	•	•	•	•	•	•	•	•	•
Albania - Albanie	27	•	•	•	•	•	•	•	•	•	•	•	•	•	•	•	•	•
Andorra - Andorre	25	•	•	•	•	•	•	•	•	•	•	•	•	•	•	...	•	...
Austria - Autriche	28	•	•	•	•	•	•	•	•	•	•	•	•	•	•	•	•	•
Belarus - Bélarus	29	•	•	•	•	•	•	•	•	•	•	•	•	•	...	•	•	•
Belgium - Belgique	30	•	•	•	•	•	•	•	•	•	•	•	•	•	•	•	•	•
Bosnia and Herzegovina - Bosnie-Herzégovine	24	•	•	•	•	•	•	...	...	•	•	•	•	•	•	...	...	...
Bulgaria - Bulgarie	30	•	•	•	•	•	•	•	•	•	•	•	•	•	•	•	•	•
Croatia - Croatie	29	•	•	•	•	•	•	•	•	•	•	•	•	•	•	•	•	•
Czechia - Tchéquie	30	•	•	•	•	•	•	•	•	•	•	•	•	•	•	•	•	•
Denmark - Danemark	30	•	•	•	•	•	•	•	•	•	•	•	•	•	•	•	•	•
Estonia - Estonie	30	•	•	•	•	•	•	•	•	•	•	•	•	•	•	•	•	•
Faeroe Islands - Îles Féroé	28	•	•	•	•	•	•	•	•	•	•	•	•	•	•	•	•	•
Finland - Finlande	30	•	•	•	•	•	•	•	•	•	•	•	•	•	•	•	•	•
France	29	•	•	•	•	•	•	•	•	•	•	•	•	•	•	...	•	•
Germany - Allemagne	30	•	•	•	•	•	•	•	•	•	•	•	•	•	•	•	•	•
Gibraltar	18	•	•	•	•	•	•	•	•	•	•	•	•	•	...	...	•	...
Greece - Grèce	28	•	•	•	•	•	•	•	•	•	•	•	•	•	•	•	•	•
Guernsey - Guernesey	11	•	•	•	•	•	•	•	...	...	•	•	•	...	...	•	...	...
Holy See - Saint-Siège	6	•	•	...	...	•	...	...	•	•	...	...	...	...	•	...	...	...
Hungary - Hongrie	30	•	•	•	•	•	•	•	•	•	•	•	•	•	•	•	•	•
Iceland - Islande	28	•	•	•	•	•	•	•	•	•	•	•	•	•	•	•	•	•
Ireland - Irlande	27	•	•	•	•	•	•	•	•	•	•	•	•	•	•	•	...	...
Isle of Man - Île de Man	16	•	...	•	•	•	•	•	•	•	•	•	•	•	...	...	...	...
Italy - Italie	30	•	•	•	•	•	•	•	•	•	•	•	•	•	•	•	•	•
Jersey	12	•	•	•	•	•	•	•	•	•	•	•	...	...	•	•	•	•
Latvia - Lettonie	30	•	•	•	•	•	•	•	•	•	•	•	•	•	•	•	•	•
Liechtenstein	21	•	...	•	•	•	•	•	•	•	•	•	•	•	•	...	...	•
Lithuania - Lituanie	30	•	•	•	•	•	•	•	•	•	•	•	•	•	•	•	•	•
Luxembourg	28	•	•	•	•	•	•	•	•	•	•	•	•	•	...	...	•	•
Malta - Malte	28	•	•	•	•	•	•	•	•	•	•	•	•	•	•	...	•	•
Monaco	12	•	•	•	•	•	•	•	•	•	•	•	...	...	...	...	...	...
Montenegro - Monténégro	25	•	•	•	•	•	•	•	•	•	•	•	•	•	•	...	...	•
Netherlands - Pays-Bas	28	•	•	•	•	•	•	•	•	•	•	•	•	•	•	•	•	...
Norway - Norvège	29	•	•	•	•	•	•	•	•	•	•	•	•	•	•	•	•	•
Poland - Pologne	30	•	•	•	•	•	•	•	•	•	•	•	•	•	•	•	•	•
Portugal	30	•	•	•	•	•	•	•	•	•	•	•	•	•	•	•	•	•
Republic of Moldova - République de Moldova	29	•	•	•	•	•	•	•	•	•	•	•	•	•	•	...	...	•
Romania - Roumanie	30	•	•	•	•	•	•	•	•	•	•	•	•	•	•	•	•	•
Russian Federation - Fédération de Russie	28	•	•	•	•	•	•	•	•	•	•	•	•	•	•	•	•	•
San Marino - Saint-Marin	28	•	•	•	•	•	•	•	•	•	•	•	•	•	•	...	...	•
Serbia - Serbie	30	•	•	•	•	•	•	•	•	•	•	•	•	•	•	•	•	•
Slovakia - Slovaquie	30	•	•	•	•	•	•	•	•	•	•	•	•	•	•	•	•	•
Slovenia - Slovénie	30	•	•	•	•	•	•	•	•	•	•	•	•	•	•	•	•	•
Spain - Espagne	30	•	•	•	•	•	•	•	•	•	•	•	•	•	•	•	•	•

Table A. Demographic Yearbook 2017 synoptic table: Availability of data by country/area, table and sex, where applicable
Tableau A. Tableau synoptique de l'Annuaire démographique 2017 : Disponibilité des données par pays ou zone, tableau et le sexe, si disponible (continued - suite)

Continent and country or area / Continent et pays ou zone	\$\$ Infant and maternal mortality - Mortalité infantile et mortalité liée à la maternité \$\$				General mortality - Mortalité générale						Nuptiality and divorces - Nuptialité et divortialité		
	15	16 Total	16 M/F	17	18	19 Total	19 M/F	20	21	22	23	24	25

ASIA - ASIE

	15	16T	16MF	17	18	19T	19MF	20	21	22	23	24	25
Sri Lanka	•	...	...	...	•	•	•	...	...	•	•	...	...
State of Palestine - État de Palestine	•	...	...	...	•	•	•	•	•	•	•	•	•
Syrian Arab Republic - République arabe syrienne	...	...	...	•	•	...	...	...	...	•	•	...	...
Tajikistan - Tadjikistan	•	•	•	•	•	•	•	...	...	•	•	•	•
Thailand - Thaïlande	•	•	•	•	•	•	•	...	...	•	•	...	•
Timor-Leste	...	...	...	...	•	...	...	...	...	...	...	...	...
Turkey - Turquie	•	•	•	•	•	•	•	•	•	•	•	•	•
Turkmenistan - Turkménistan	...	...	...	...	•	...	...	...	...	•	•	...	...
United Arab Emirates - Émirats arabes unis	•	•	•	•	...	...	...	...	...	•	•	...	•
Uzbekistan - Ouzbékistan	•	•	•	•	•	...	...	...	•	•	•	...	•
Viet Nam	...	...	...	...	•	...	...	...	...	•	•	...	...
Yemen - Yémen	...	...	...	...	•	...	...	...	...	•	...	...	...

EUROPE

	15	16T	16MF	17	18	19T	19MF	20	21	22	23	24	25
Åland Islands - Îles d'Åland	•	•	•	•	•	•	•	...	...	•	•	•	•
Albania - Albanie	•	•	•	•	...	•	•	•	...	•	•	•	•
Andorra - Andorre	•	•	•	•	•	•	•	...	...	...	•	•	...
Austria - Autriche	•	•	•	•	•	•	•	•	•	•	•	•	•
Belarus - Bélarus	•	•	•	•	•	•	•	•	•	•	•	•	•
Belgium - Belgique	•	•	•	•	•	•	•	•	•	•	•	•	•
Bosnia and Herzegovina - Bosnie-Herzégovine	•	•	•	•	•	•	•	...	•	•	•	•	•
Bulgaria - Bulgarie	•	•	•	•	•	•	•	•	•	•	•	•	•
Croatia - Croatie	•	•	•	•	•	•	•	...	•	•	•	•	•
Czechia - Tchéquie	•	•	•	•	•	•	•	•	•	•	•	•	•
Denmark - Danemark	•	•	•	•	•	•	•	•	•	•	•	•	•
Estonia - Estonie	•	•	•	•	•	•	•	•	•	•	•	•	•
Faeroe Islands - Îles Féroé	•	•	•	...	•	•	...	•	•	•	•	•	•
Finland - Finlande	•	•	•	•	•	•	•	•	•	•	•	•	•
France	•	•	•	•	•	•	•	•	•	•	•	•	•
Germany - Allemagne	•	•	•	•	•	•	•	•	•	...	•	•	•
Gibraltar	•	...	...	...	•	...	...	...	•	•	•	...	...
Greece - Grèce	•	•	•	•	•	•	•	•	•	•	•	•	•
Guernsey - Guernesey	...	...	...	...	...	...	...	...	...	•	•	•	...
Holy See - Saint-Siège	...	...	...	...	...	...	...	...	...	...	...	...	...
Hungary - Hongrie	•	•	•	•	•	•	•	•	•	•	•	•	•
Iceland - Islande	•	•	•	•	•	•	•	•	•	...	•	...	...
Ireland - Irlande	•	...	...	•	•	•	•	•	•	•	•	•	•
Isle of Man - Île de Man	•	•	...	•	•	•	•	•	•	•	•	•	•
Italy - Italie	•	•	•	•	•	•	•	•	•	•	•	•	•
Jersey	...	...	...	•	•	...	...	...	•	•	•	•	•
Latvia - Lettonie	•	•	•	•	•	•	•	•	•	•	•	•	•
Liechtenstein	•	•	•	•	•	•	•	...	...	•	•	•	•
Lithuania - Lituanie	•	•	•	•	•	•	•	•	•	•	•	•	•
Luxembourg	•	•	•	•	•	•	•	•	•	•	•	•	•
Malta - Malte	•	•	•	•	•	•	•	•	•	•	•	•	•
Monaco	...	...	...	...	...	...	...	...	...	...	...	...	...
Montenegro - Monténégro	•	•	•	•	•	•	•	...	•	...	•	•	•
Netherlands - Pays-Bas	•	•	•	•	•	•	•	•	•	•	•	•	•
Norway - Norvège	•	•	•	•	•	•	•	•	•	•	•	•	•
Poland - Pologne	•	•	•	•	•	•	•	•	•	•	•	•	•
Portugal	•	•	•	•	•	•	•	•	•	•	•	•	•
Republic of Moldova - République de Moldova	•	•	•	•	•	•	•	•	•	•	•	•	•
Romania - Roumanie	•	•	•	•	•	•	•	•	•	•	•	•	•
Russian Federation - Fédération de Russie	...	•	•	•	•	•	•	•	•	•	•	•	•
San Marino - Saint-Marin	•	•	•	•	•	•	•	•	•	•	•	•	•
Serbia - Serbie	•	•	•	•	•	•	•	•	•	•	•	•	•
Slovakia - Slovaquie	•	•	•	•	•	•	•	•	•	•	•	•	•
Slovenia - Slovénie	•	•	•	•	•	•	•	•	•	•	•	•	•
Spain - Espagne	•	•	•	•	•	•	•	•	•	•	•	•	•

Table A. Demographic Yearbook 2017 synoptic table: Availability of data by country/area, table and sex, where applicable
Tableau A. Tableau synoptique de l'Annuaire démographique 2017 : Disponibilité des données par pays ou zone, tableau et le sexe, si disponible (continued - suite)

General topic and table number - Sujet général et numéro de tableau

Continent and country or area / Continent et pays ou zone	Table totals	Summary - Apercu				Population							Fertility - Natalité			Foetal mortality - Mortalité foetale		
		3 Total	3 M/F	4	5	6 Total[1]	6 M/F	7 Total	7 M/F	8 Total	8 M/F	9	10 Total	10 M/F	11	12	13	14
EUROPE																		
Svalbard and Jan Mayen Islands - Îles Svalbard et Jan Mayen	3	•	•	...		...	...	•		...		...	...	...	...	...	•	...
Sweden - Suède	30	•	•	•	•	•	•	•	•	•	•	•	•	•	•	•	•	•
Switzerland - Suisse	30	•	•	•	•	•	•	•	•	•	•	•	•	•	•	•	•	•
TFYR of Macedonia - L'ex-R. y. de Macédoine	29	•	•	•	•	•	•	•	•	•	•	•	•	•	•	•	•	•
Ukraine	29	•	•	•	•	•	•	•	•	•	•	•	...	•	•	•	•	•
United Kingdom of Great Britain and Northern Ireland - Royaume-Uni de Grande-Bretagne et d'Irlande du Nord	30	•	•	•	•	•	•	•	•	•	•	•	•	•	•	•	•	•
OCEANIA - OCÉANIE																		
American Samoa - Samoas américaines	18	•	•	•	•	•	•	•	•	...	•	•	•	...	•	...	...	...
Australia - Australie	28	•	•	•	•	•	•	•	•	•	•	•	•	•	•	•	•	•
Cook Islands - Îles Cook	18	•	•	•	•	•	•	•	•	•	•	•	•	...	...	•	•	...
Fiji - Fidji	21	•	•	•	•	•	•	•	•	•	•	•	...	...	•	•	•	...
French Polynesia - Polynésie française	16	•	...	•	•	•	•	•	•	•	•	•	•	•	•	•	•	...
Guam	25	•	•	•	•	•	•	•	•	•	•	•	•	•	•	•	•	•
Kiribati	12	•	•	...	•	•	•	•	•	•	...	...	...	...	•	...	...	...
Marshall Islands - Îles Marshall	9	•	•	•	•	•	•	•	...	...	...	...	...	...	•	...	...	...
Micronesia (Federated States of) - Micronésie (États fédérés de)	9	•	•	...	•	•	•	•	•	...	...	...	...	...	•	...	...	...
Nauru	15	•	•	•	•	•	•	•	•	...	•	•	•	•	•	•	•	...
New Caledonia - Nouvelle-Calédonie	22	•	•	•	•	•	•	•	•	•	•	•	•	•	•	•	•	...
New Zealand - Nouvelle-Zélande	30	•	•	•	•	•	•	•	•	•	•	•	•	•	•	•	•	•
Niue - Nioué	14	•	•	...	•	•	•	•	•	...	...	...	...	...	•	...	...	...
Norfolk Island - Île Norfolk	9	•	•	•	...	•	•	•	...	...	...	...	...	...	•	...	•	...
Northern Mariana Islands - Îles Mariannes septentrionales	14	•	•	•	•	•	•	•	•	•	•	•	•	...	•	•	...	...
Palau - Palaos	18	•	•	•	•	•	•	•	•	•	•	•	•	•	...	•	•	...
Papua New Guinea - Papouasie-Nouvelle-Guinée	9	•	•	...	•	•	•	•	...	•	•	•	...	...	...	...	...	...
Pitcairn	11	•	•	•	•	•	•	•	...	•	•	•	...	...	...	...	...	...
Samoa	16	•	...	•	•	•	•	•	•	...	•	•	•	...	...	...	...	...
Solomon Islands - Îles Salomon	9	•	•	•	•	•	•	•	•	...	•	•	•	...	...	...	...	...
Tokelau - Tokélaou	8	•	•	•	•	•	•	•	...	...	•	•	•	...	...	...	...	...
Tonga	9	•	...	...	•	•	•	•	•	...	•	•	...	...	...	...	...	...
Tuvalu	7	•	...	•	•	•	•	•	...	•	...	...	...	...	...	...	...	...
Vanuatu	9	•	...	...	•	•	•	•	•	•	...	•	...	...	...	...	...	...
Wallis and Futuna Islands - Îles Wallis et Futuna	12	•	...	...	•	•	•	•	•	•	...	•	•	...	...	...	...	...

Continent and country or area / Continent et pays ou zone	Infant and maternal mortality - Mortalité infantile et mortalité liée à la maternité				General mortality - Mortalité générale						Nuptiality and divorces - Nuptialité et divortialité		
	15	16 Total	16 M/F	17	18	19 Total	19 M/F	20	21	22	23	24	25
EUROPE													
Svalbard and Jan Mayen Islands - Îles Svalbard et Jan Mayen	…	…	…	…	…	…	…	…	…	…	…	…	…
Sweden - Suède	•	•	•	•	•	•	•	•	•	•	•	•	•
Switzerland - Suisse	•	•	•	•	•	•	•	•	•	•	•	•	•
TFYR of Macedonia - L'ex-R. y. de Macédoine	•	•	•	•	•	•	•	•	•	•	•	•	•
Ukraine	•	•	…	…	•	•	…	•	•	•	•	•	•
United Kingdom of Great Britain and Northern Ireland - Royaume-Uni de Grande-Bretagne et d'Irlande du Nord	•	•	•	•	•	•	•	•	•	•	•	•	•
OCEANIA - OCÉANIE													
American Samoa - Samoas américaines	•	…	…	…	•	•	…	…	•	…	•	…	•
Australia - Australie	•	•	•	…	•	•	•	…	…	…	•	•	•
Cook Islands - Îles Cook	•	…	…	…	•	•	…	…	…	…	•	•	•
Fiji - Fidji	•	…	…	…	•	•	…	…	…	…	•	…	…
French Polynesia - Polynésie française	•	•	…	…	•	•	…	…	…	…	•	•	…
Guam	•	…	…	…	•	•	…	…	…	…	•	…	…
Kiribati	…	…	…	…	…	…	…	…	…	…	•	…	…
Marshall Islands - Îles Marshall	…	…	…	…	•	…	…	…	…	…	•	…	…
Micronesia (Federated States of) - Micronésie (États fédérés de)	…	…	…	…	•	•	…	…	…	…	•	…	…
Nauru	…	…	…	…	•	•	…	…	…	…	•	…	…
New Caledonia - Nouvelle-Calédonie	•	•	•	…	•	•	…	…	…	…	•	…	…
New Zealand - Nouvelle-Zélande	•	•	•	•	•	•	•	•	•	•	•	•	•
Niue - Nioué	…	…	…	…	•	•	…	…	•	…	•	…	…
Norfolk Island - Île Norfolk	…	…	…	…	•	•	…	…	…	…	•	…	…
Northern Mariana Islands - Îles Mariannes septentrionales	•	…	…	…	…	…	…	…	…	…	•	…	…
Palau - Palaos	•	…	…	…	•	•	•	…	…	…	•	…	…
Papua New Guinea - Papouasie-Nouvelle-Guinée	…	…	…	…	…	…	…	…	…	…	•	…	…
Pitcairn	…	…	…	…	…	…	…	…	…	…	…	…	…
Samoa	…	…	…	…	•	•	…	…	…	…	•	…	•
Solomon Islands - Îles Salomon	…	…	…	…	…	…	…	…	…	…	•	…	…
Tokelau - Tokélaou	…	…	…	…	…	…	…	…	…	…	•	…	…
Tonga	…	…	…	…	…	…	…	…	…	…	•	…	…
Tuvalu	…	…	…	…	…	…	…	…	…	…	•	…	…
Vanuatu	…	…	…	…	•	•	…	…	…	…	•	…	…
Wallis and Futuna Islands - Îles Wallis et Futuna	…	…	…	…	•	…	…	…	…	…	•	…	…

FOOTNOTES - NOTES

* Data presented in the table. - Les données présentées dans le tableau.
… Data not available. - Données non disponibles.

[1] Including countries with data on total population by sex but without data on urban population. - Y compris les pays avec des données sur la population totale selon le sexe mais pas sur la population urbaine.

[2] For statistical purposes, the data for China do not include those for the Hong Kong Special Administrative Region (Hong Kong SAR), Macao special Administrative Region (Macao SAR) and Taiwan province of China. - Pour la présentation des statistiques, les données pour Chine ne comprennent pas la Région Administrative Spéciale de Hong Kong (Hong Kong RAS), la Région Administrative Spéciale de Macao (Macao RAS) et Taïwan province de Chine.

[3] Including data for the Indian-held part of Jammu and Kashmir, the final status of which has not yet been determined. - Y compris les données pour la partie du Jammu et du Cachemire occupée par l'Inde dont le statut définitif n'a pas encore été déterminé.

[4] Including data for East Jerusalem and Israeli residents in certain other territories under occupation by Israeli military forces since June 1967. - Y compris les données pour Jérusalem-Est et les résidents israéliens dans certains autres territoires occupés depuis 1967 par les forces armées israéliennes.

[5] Excluding data for the Pakistan-held part of Jammu and Kashmir, the final status of which has not yet been determined. - Non compris les données concernant la partie du Jammu et Cachemire occupée par le Pakistan dont le statut définitif n'a pas été déterminé.

Table 1 – Demographic Yearbook 2017

Table 1 presents for the world and major areas and regions estimates of the order of magnitude of population size, rates of population increase, crude birth and death rates, land area as well as population density.

Description of variables: Estimates of world population by major areas and by regions are presented for 1960, 1970, 1980, 1990, 2000, 2010 and 2017. Average annual percentage rates of population growth, crude birth and crude death rates are shown for the period from 2015 to 2020. Land area in square kilometers and population density estimates relate to 2017.

All population estimates and rates presented in this table were prepared by the Population Division of the United Nations Department of Economic and Social Affairs, and have been published in the *2017 Revision of World Population Prospects*[1].

The scheme of regionalization used for these estimates is described below. Although some continental totals are given, this table presents six major areas that are so drawn as to obtain greater homogeneity in sizes of population, types of demographic circumstances and accuracy of demographic statistics. Five of the major areas are subdivided into a total of 20 regions, which are arranged within the major areas; these regions together with Northern America, which is not subdivided, make a total of 21 regions.

The major areas of Northern America and Latin America and the Caribbean are distinguished, rather than the conventional continents of North America and South America, because population trends in the middle American mainland and the Caribbean region more closely resemble those of South America than those of America north of Mexico. Data for the traditional continents of North and South America can be obtained by adding Central America and Caribbean region to Northern America and deducting from Latin America. Latin America, as defined here, has somewhat wider limits than it would be if defined only to include the Spanish-speaking, French-speaking and Portuguese-speaking countries.

The average annual percentage rates of population growth are calculated by the Population Division of the United Nations using an exponential rate of increase.

Crude birth and crude death rates are expressed in terms of the average annual number of births and deaths, respectively, per 1 000 mid-year population. These rates are estimated.

The land areas of regions are estimated by the Population Division of the United Nations.

Computation: Density, calculated by the Statistics Division of the United Nations, is the number of persons in the total population of 2017 per square kilometer of the respective land area.

Reliability of data: With the exception of land area, all data are set in *italic* type to indicate their conjectural quality.

Limitations: The estimated orders of magnitude of population and land area are subject to all the basic limitations set forth in connection with table 3, and to the same qualifications set forth for population and surface area statistics in sections 3 and 2.4 of the Technical Notes, respectively.

Likewise, rates of population increase and population density are affected by the limitations of the original figures. However, it may be noted that, in compiling data for regional and major areas totals, errors in the components may tend to compensate each other and the resulting aggregates may be more reliable than the quality of the individual components would imply.

Because of their estimated character, many of the birth and death rates shown should also be considered only as orders of magnitude, and not as measures of the true level of fertility or mortality.

In interpreting the population densities, one should consider that some of the regions include large segments of land that are uninhabitable or barely habitable, and density values calculated as described make no allowance for this, nor for differences in patterns of land settlement.

Composition of major areas and regions

AFRICA

Eastern Africa
Burundi
Comoros
Djibouti
Eritrea
Ethiopia
Kenya
Madagascar
Malawi
Mauritius
Mayotte
Mozambique
Réunion
Rwanda
Seychelles
Somalia
South Sudan
Uganda
United Republic of Tanzania
Zambia
Zimbabwe

Middle Africa
Angola
Cameroon
Central African Republic
Chad
Congo
Democratic Republic of the
  Congo
Equatorial Guinea
Gabon
Sao Tome and Principe

Northern Africa
Algeria
Egypt
Libyan Arab Jamahiriya
Morocco
Sudan
Tunisia
Western Sahara

Southern Africa
Botswana
Eswatini
Lesotho
Namibia
South Africa

Western Africa
Benin
Burkina Faso
Cabo Verde
Côte d'Ivoire

Gambia
Ghana
Guinea
Guinea-Bissau
Liberia
Mali
Mauritania
Niger
Nigeria
Saint Helena
Senegal
Sierra Leone
Togo

ASIA

Eastern Asia
China
China, Hong Kong SAR
China, Macao SAR
Democratic People's
  Republic of Korea
Japan
Mongolia
Republic of Korea

South-Central Asia
Afghanistan
Bangladesh
Bhutan
India
Iran (Islamic Republic of)
Kazakhstan
Kyrgyzstan
Maldives
Nepal
Pakistan
Sri Lanka
Tajikistan
Turkmenistan
Uzbekistan

South-Eastern Asia
Brunei Darussalam
Cambodia
Indonesia
Lao People's Democratic
  Republic
Malaysia
Myanmar
Philippines
Singapore
Thailand
Timor Leste
Viet Nam

Western Asia
Armenia
Azerbaijan
Bahrain
Cyprus
Georgia
Iraq
Israel
Jordan
Kuwait
Lebanon
Oman
Qatar
Saudi Arabia
State of Palestine
Syrian Arab Republic
Turkey
United Arab Emirates
Yemen

EUROPE

Eastern Europe
Belarus
Bulgaria
Czech Republic
Hungary
Poland
Republic of Moldova
Romania
Russian Federation
Slovakia
Ukraine

Northern Europe
Åland Islands
Denmark
Estonia
Faeroe Islands
Finland
Guernsey
Iceland
Ireland
Isle of Man
Jersey
Latvia
Lithuania
Norway
Sweden
United Kingdom of Great Britain
  and Northern Ireland

Southern Europe
Albania
Andorra
Bosnia and Herzegovina

Croatia
Gibraltar
Greece
Holy See
Italy
Malta
Montenegro
Portugal
San Marino
Serbia
Slovenia
Spain
TFYR of Macedonia

Western Europe
Austria
Belgium
France
Germany
Liechtenstein
Luxembourg
Monaco
Netherlands
Switzerland

LATIN AMERICA
  ## and the CARIBBEAN

Caribbean
Anguilla
Antigua and Barbuda
Aruba
Bahamas
Barbados
Bonaire, Saba and Sint Eustatius
British Virgin Islands
Cayman Islands
Cuba
Curaçao
Dominica
Dominican Republic
Grenada
Guadaloupe

Haiti
Jamaica
Martinique
Montserrat
Puerto Rico
Saint Kitts and Nevis
Saint Lucia
Saint Vincent and the
  Grenadines
Sint Maarten (Dutch part)
Trinidad and Tobago
Turks and Caicos Islands
United States Virgin
  Islands

Central America
Belize
Costa Rica
El Salvador
Guatemala
Honduras
Mexico
Nicaragua
Panama

South America
Argentina
Bolivia (Plurinational State of)
Brazil
Chile
Colombia
Ecuador
Falkland Islands (Malvinas)
French Guiana
Guyana
Paraguay
Peru
Suriname
Uruguay
Venezuela (Bolivarian Republic of)

NORTHERN AMERICA

Bermuda
Canada
Greenland
Saint Pierre and Miquelon
United States of America

OCEANIA

Australia and New Zealand
Australia
New Zealand
Norfolk Island

Melanesia
Fiji
New Caledonia
Papua New Guinea
Solomon Islands
Vanuatu

Micronesia
Guam
Kiribati
Marshall Islands
Micronesia (Federated States of)
Nauru
Northern Mariana Islands
Palau

Polynesia
American Samoa
Cook Islands
French Polynesia
Niue
Pitcairn
Samoa
Tokelau
Tonga
Tuvalu
Wallis and Futuna Islands

[1] *United Nations, Department of Economic and Social Affairs, Population Division (2017). World Population Prospects: The 2017 Revision* (http://esa.un.org/unpd/wpp/)

Tableau 1 – *Annuaire démographique 2017*

Le tableau 1 présente, pour l'ensemble du monde et les grandes zones et régions, des estimations concernant l'ordre de grandeur de la population, les taux d'accroissement démographique, les taux bruts de natalité et de mortalité, la superficie des terres et la densité de peuplement.

Description des variables : des estimations de la population mondiale par grandes zones et régions sont présentées pour 1960, 1970, 1980, 1990, 2000 et 2010 ainsi que pour 2017. Les taux annuels moyens d'accroissement de la population et les taux bruts de natalité et de mortalité portent sur la période allant de 2015 à 2020. Les indications concernant la superficie des terres exprimée en kilomètres carrés et les estimations de la densité de population se rapportent à 2017.

Toutes les estimations de population et les taux de natalité, taux de mortalité et taux annuels d'accroissement de la population qui sont présentés dans le tableau 1 ont été établis par la Division de la population du Département des affaires économiques et sociales de l'Organisation des Nations Unies, et ont été publiés dans les *Perspectives de la population mondiale : La révision de 2017* [1].

Bien que l'on ait donné certains totaux pour les continents (tous les autres pouvant être calculés), on a réparti le monde en six grandes zones qui ont été découpées de manière à obtenir une plus grande homogénéité du point de vue des dimensions de population, des types de situations démographiques et de l'exactitude des statistiques démographiques. Cinq de ces six grandes zones ont été subdivisées en 20 régions. Avec l'Amérique septentrionale, qui n'est pas subdivisée, on arrive à un total de 21 régions.

Au lieu de faire la distinction classique entre l'Amérique du Nord et l'Amérique du Sud, on a choisi d'opérer une comparaison entre l'Amérique septentrionale et l'Amérique latine et Caraïbes, parce que les tendances démographiques dans la partie continentale de l'Amérique centrale et dans la région des Caraïbes se rapprochent davantage de celles de l'Amérique du Sud que de celles de l'Amérique au nord du Mexique. On obtient les données pour les continents traditionnels de l'Amérique du Nord et de l'Amérique du Sud en extrayant les données concernant l'Amérique centrale et les Caraïbes de celles relatives à l'Amérique latine et en les regroupant avec celles relatives à l'Amérique septentrionale. L'Amérique latine ainsi définie a par conséquent des limites plus larges que celles des pays ou zones de langues espagnole, portugaise et française qui constituent l'Amérique latine au sens le plus strict du terme.

Les taux annuels moyens d'accroissement de la population sont calculés par la Division de la population de l'Organisation des Nations Unies en appliquant un taux d'accroissement exponentiel.

Les taux bruts de natalité et de mortalité représentent respectivement le nombre annuel moyen de naissances et de décès par millier d'habitants en milieu d'année. Ces taux sont estimatifs.

La superficie des terres pour les régions a été estimée par la Division de la population de l'Organisation des Nations Unies.

Calculs : la densité, calculée par la Division de statistique de l'Organisation des Nations Unies, est égale au rapport entre l'effectif total de la population en 2017 et la superficie des terres exprimée en kilomètres carrés.

Fiabilité des données : á l'exception des données concernant la superficie des terres, toutes les données sont reproduites en *italique* pour en faire ressortir le caractère conjectural.

Insuffisance des données : les estimations concernant l'ordre de grandeur de la population et la superficie des terres reposent en partie sur les données du tableau 3 ; elles appellent donc toutes les réserves fondamentales formulées à propos de ce tableau, et celles qui ont été respectivement formulées aux sections 3 et 2.4 des Notes techniques en ce qui concerne les statistiques relatives à la population et à la superficie.

Les taux d'accroissement et les indices de densité de la population se ressentent eux aussi des insuffisances inhérentes aux données de base. Toutefois, il est à noter que, lorsque l'on additionne des données par territoire pour obtenir des totaux régionaux et par grandes zones, les erreurs qu'elles comportent arrivent parfois à s'équilibrer, de sorte que les agrégats obtenus peuvent être un peu plus exacts que chacun des éléments dont on est parti.

Vu leur caractère estimatif, nombre des taux de natalité et de mortalité du tableau 1 doivent être considérés uniquement comme des ordres de grandeur et ne sont pas censés mesurer exactement le niveau de la natalité ou de la mortalité.

Pour interpréter les valeurs de la densité de population, on se souviendra qu'il existe dans certaines des régions de vastes étendues de terres inhabitables ou à peine habitables et que les chiffres calculés selon la méthode indiquée ne tiennent compte ni de ce fait ni des différences de dispersion de la population selon le mode d'habitat.

Composition des grandes zones et régions

AFRIQUE

Afrique orientale
Burundi
Comores
Djibouti
Érythrée
Éthiopie
Kenya
Madagascar
Malawi
Maurice
Mayotte
Mozambique
Ouganda
République-Unie de Tanzanie
Réunion
Rwanda
Seychelles
Somalie
Soudan du Sud
Zambie
Zimbabwe

Afrique centrale
Angola
Cameroun
Congo
Gabon
Guinée équatoriale
République centrafricaine
République démocratique du Congo
Sao Tomé-et-Principe
Tchad

Afrique septentrionale
Algérie
Égypte
Jamahiriya arabe libyenne
Maroc
Sahara occidental
Soudan
Tunisie

Afrique australe
Afrique du Sud
Botswana
Eswatini
Lesotho
Namibie

Afrique occidentale
Bénin
Burkina Faso
Cabo Verde

Côte d'Ivoire
Gambie
Ghana
Guinée
Guinée-Bissau
Libéria
Mali
Mauritanie
Niger
Nigéria
Sainte-Hélène
Sénégal
Sierra Leone
Togo

AMÉRIQUE LATINE ET CARAÏBES

Caraïbes
Anguilla
Antigua-et-Barbuda
Aruba
Bahamas
Barbade
Bonaire, Saint-Eustache et Saba
Cuba
Curaçao
Dominique
Grenade
Guadeloupe
Haïti
Îles Caïmanes
Îles Turques et Caïques
Îles Vierges américaines
Îles Vierges britanniques
Jamaïque
Martinique
Montserrat
Porto Rico
République dominicaine
Saint-Kitts-et-Nevis
Sainte-Lucie
Saint-Martin (partie néerlandaise)
Saint-Vincent-et-les Grenadines
Trinité-et-Tobago

Amérique centrale
Belize
Costa Rica
El Salvador
Guatemala
Honduras

Mexique
Nicaragua
Panama

Amérique du Sud
Argentine
Bolivie (État plurinational de)
Brésil
Chili
Colombie
Équateur
Guyana
Guyane française
Îles Falkland (Malvinas)
Paraguay
Pérou
Suriname
Uruguay
Venezuela (République bolivarienne du)

AMÉRIQUE SEPTENTRIONALE

Bermudes
Canada
États-Unis d'Amérique
Groenland
Saint-Pierre-et-Miquelon

ASIE

Asie orientale
Chine
Chine, Région administrative spéciale de Hong Kong
Chine, Région administrative spéciale de Macao
Japon
Mongolie
République de Corée
République populaire démocratique de Corée

Asie centrale et Asie du Sud
Afghanistan
Bangladesh
Bhoutan
Inde
Iran (République Islamique d')
Kazakhstan
Kirghizistan
Maldives
Népal
Ouzbékistan

Pakistan
Sri Lanka
Tadjikistan
Turkménistan

Asie du Sud-Est
Brunéi Darussalam
Cambodge
Indonésie
Malaisie
Myanmar
Philippines
République démocratique populaire lao
Singapour
Thaïlande
Timor-Leste
Viet Nam

Asie occidentale
Arabie saoudite
Arménie
Azerbaïdjan
Bahreïn
Chypre
Émirats arabes unis
État de Palestine
Géorgie
Iraq
Israël
Jordanie
Koweït
Liban
Oman
Qatar
République arabe syrienne
Turquie
Yémen

EUROPE

Europe orientale
Bélarus
Bulgarie
Fédération de Russie
Hongrie

Pologne
République de Moldova
République tchèque
Roumanie
Slovaquie
Ukraine

Europe septentrionale
Danemark
Estonie
Finlande
Guernesey
Île de Man
Îles d'Åland
Îles Féroé
Îles Svalbard et Jan Mayen
Irlande
Islande
Jersey
Lettonie
Lituanie
Norvège
Royaume-Uni de Grande-Bretagne et d'Irlande du Nord
Suède

Europe méridionale
Albanie
Andorre
Bosnie-Herzégovine
Croatie
Espagne
Gibraltar
Grèce
Italie
L'ex-R. y. de Macédoine
Malte
Monténégro
Portugal
Saint-Marin
Saint-Siège
Serbie
Slovénie

Europe occidentale
Allemagne
Autriche
Belgique
France
Liechtenstein
Luxembourg
Monaco
Pays-Bas
Suisse

OCÉANIE

Australie et Nouvelle-Zélande
Australie
Île Norfolk
Nouvelle-Zélande

Mélanésie
Fidji
Îles Salomon
Nouvelle-Calédonie
Papouasie-Nouvelle-Guinée
Vanuatu

Micronésie
Guam
Îles Mariannes septentrionales
Îles Marshall
Kiribati
Micronésie (États fédérés de)
Nauru
Palaos

Polynésie
Îles Cook
Îles Wallis et Futuna
Nioué
Pitcairn
Polynésie française
Samoa
Samoa américaines
Tokélaou
Tonga
Tuvalu

---

[1] Organisation des Nations Unies, Département des affaires économiques et sociales, Division de la population (2017). Perspectives de la population mondiale : La révision de 2017 (http://esa.un.org/unpd/wpp/)

1. Population, rate of increase, birth and death rates, land area and density for the world, major areas and regions: selected years
Population, taux d'accroissement, taux de natalité et taux de mortalité, superficie des terres et densité pour l'ensemble du monde, les régions macro géographiques et les composantes géographiques : diverses années

Major areas and regions Régions macro géographiques et composantes	Mid-year population estimates - Estimations de population au milieu de l'année (millions)							Annual rate of increase - Taux d'accroissement annuel (%)	Crude birth rate - Taux bruts de natalité	Crude death rate - Taux bruts de mortalité	Land area (km2) - Superficie des terres (km2) (000s)	Density - Densité[1]
	1960	1970	1980	1990	2000	2010	2017	2015-2020	2015-2020	2015-2020	2017	2017
WORLD TOTAL - ENSEMBLE DU MONDE	3 033.2	3 700.6	4 458.4	5 330.9	6 145.0	6 958.2	7 550.3	1.1	19	8	130 094	58
AFRICA - AFRIQUE	285.1	366.5	480.0	634.6	817.6	1 049.4	1 256.3	2.5	34	8	29 648	42
Eastern Africa - Afrique orientale	84.2	110.3	147.5	198.6	261.1	347.0	422.0	2.7	35	7	6 667	63
Middle Africa - Afrique centrale	32.4	41.1	53.6	71.3	96.1	131.4	163.5	3.0	40	10	6 497	25
Northern Africa - Afrique septentrionale	63.7	83.1	107.7	141.2	172.6	204.3	233.6	1.8	24	6	7 769	30
Southern Africa - Afrique méridionale	19.8	25.8	33.7	42.8	52.3	59.0	65.1	1.3	21	9	2 651	25
Western Africa - Afrique occidentale	85.1	106.1	137.5	180.5	235.5	307.8	372.0	2.7	38	11	6 064	61
LATIN AMERICA AND CARIBBEAN - AMÉRIQUE LATIN ET CARAÏBES	221.1	288.1	364.3	445.9	525.8	597.6	645.6	1.0	16	6	20 139	32
Caribbean - Caraïbes	20.7	25.3	29.8	34.2	38.4	41.7	43.9	0.6	17	8	226	194
Central America - Amérique centrale	51.5	69.9	92.7	114.7	138.0	160.6	177.3	1.3	19	5	2 452	72
South America - Amérique méridionale	148.8	192.8	241.8	297.0	349.4	395.3	424.4	0.9	16	6	17 461	24
NORTHERN AMERICA - AMÉRIQUE SEPTENTRIONALE	204.8	231.1	254.4	280.3	312.8	342.9	361.2	0.7	12	8	18 652	19
ASIA - ASIE	1 700.5	2 137.8	2 642.5	3 221.3	3 730.4	4 194.4	4 504.4	0.9	16	7	31 033	145
Eastern Asia - Asie orientale	803.0	996.4	1 191.8	1 388.8	1 512.4	1 595.8	1 648.2	0.3	11	8	11 560	143
South Central Asia - Asie centrale méridionale	618.1	774.6	980.0	1 239.7	1 508.3	1 768.5	1 939.8	1.2	20	7	10 327	188
South Eastern Asia - Asie méridionale orientale	213.3	280.6	357.0	444.1	524.7	597.3	648.8	1.1	18	7	4 341	149
Western Asia - Asie occidentale	66.0	86.2	113.8	148.8	185.0	232.7	267.7	1.7	21	5	4 805	56
EUROPE	605.9	657.4	694.2	721.7	727.2	737.2	742.1	0.1	10	11	22 135	34
Eastern Europe - Europe orientale	253.6	276.2	294.8	309.9	304.0	294.5	292.5	-0.2	11	13	18 053	16
Northern Europe - Europe septentrionale	81.8	87.4	89.9	92.1	94.5	100.3	104.2	0.5	12	9	1 702	61
Southern Europe - Europe méridionale	117.9	127.7	138.8	143.8	145.7	153.9	152.0	-0.1	9	10	1 295	117
Western Europe - Europe occidentale	152.6	166.1	170.7	175.9	183.0	188.4	193.4	0.3	10	10	1 085	178
OCEANIA - OCÉANIA	15.8	19.7	23.0	27.1	31.2	36.6	40.7	1.4	16	7	8 486	5
Australia and New Zealand - Australie et Nouvelle Zélande	12.7	15.7	17.8	20.4	22.9	26.5	29.2	1.2	13	7	7 946	4
Melanesia - Melanésie	2.7	3.4	4.4	5.7	7.2	9.0	10.3	1.9	26	7	530	19
Micronesia	0.2	0.2	0.3	0.4	0.5	0.5	0.5	0.8	20	6	3	166
Polynesia - Polynésie	0.3	0.4	0.5	0.5	0.6	0.7	0.7	0.7	20	6	8	85

FOOTNOTES - NOTES

[1] Population per square kilometre of land area. Figures are estimates of population divided by land area and are not to be considered as either reflecting density in the urban sense or as indicating the supporting power of a territory's land and resources. - Habitants par kilomètre carré. Il s'agit simplement du quotient calculé en divisant la population par la superficie des terres et n'est par considéré comme indiquant la densité au sens urbain du terme ni l'effectif de population que les terres et les ressources du territoire sont capables de nourrir.

Table 2 - *Demographic Yearbook 2017*

Table 2 presents estimates of population and the percentage distribution by age group and sex as well as the sex ratio for all ages; data are presented for the world, the six major areas and the twenty regions for 2017.

Description of variables: All population estimates presented in this table are prepared by the Population Division of the United Nations Department of Economic and Social Affairs. These estimates are published (using more detailed age groups) in the *2017 Revision of World Population Prospects*[1].

The scheme of regionalization used for these estimates is discussed in detail in the technical notes for table 1. Age groups presented in this table are: 0-14 years, 15-64 years, and 65 years or over. Sex ratio refers to the number of males per 100 females of all ages.

The percentage distributions and the sex ratios that appear in this table were calculated by the Statistics Division of the United Nations Department of Economic and Social Affairs using the estimates prepared by the Population Division of the United Nations Department of Economic and Social Affairs.

Reliability of data: All data are set in *italic* type to indicate their conjectural quality.

Limitations: The data presented in this table are from the same series of estimates, prepared by the Population Division of the United Nations, presented in table 1. The estimated orders of magnitude of population are subject to all the basic limitations set forth for population statistics in section 3 of the Technical Notes. In brief, because they are estimates, these distributions by broad age groups and sex should be considered only as orders of magnitude. However, in compiling data for regional and major areas' totals, errors in the components tend to compensate each other and the resulting aggregates may be somewhat more reliable than the quality of the individual components would imply.

In addition, data in this table are limited by factors affecting data by age. These factors are described in the technical notes for table 7. Because the age groups presented in this table are broad, these problems are minimized.

---

[1] *United Nations, Department of Economic and Social Affairs, Population Division (2017). World Population Prospects: The 2017 Revision* (http://esa.un.org/unpd/wpp/)

Tableau 2 – *Annuaire démographique 2017*

Le tableau 2 présente, pour l'ensemble du monde, les six grandes zones et les vingt régions, des estimations concernant la population en 2017 ainsi que sa répartition en pourcentage selon des tranches d' âge et le sexe, et le rapport de masculinité pour tous les âges.

Description des variables : toutes les données figurant dans le tableau 2 ont été établies par la Division de la population du Département des affaires économiques et sociales de l'Organisation des Nations Unies, et ont été publiés dans les *Perspectives de la population mondiale : La révision de 2017*[1].

La classification géographique utilisée pour établir ces estimations est exposée en détail dans les notes techniques relatives au tableau 1. Les groupes d'âge présentés dans ce tableau sont définis comme suit : de 0 à 14 ans, de 15 à 64 ans et 65 ans ou plus. Le rapport de masculinité correspond au nombre d'individus de sexe masculin pour 100 individus de sexe féminin sans considération d'âge.

Les pourcentages et les rapports de masculinité qui sont présentés dans le tableau 2 ont été calculés par la Division de statistique du Département des affaires économiques et sociales de l'Organisation des Nations Unies à partir des estimations établies par la Division de la population de l'Organisation des Nations Unies.

Fiabilité des données : toutes les données figurant dans ce tableau sont reproduites en *italique* pour en faire ressortir le caractère conjectural.

Insuffisance des données : les données de ce tableau appartiennent à la même série d'estimations, établie par la Division de la population de l'Organisation des Nations Unies, que celles qui figurent au tableau 1. Les estimations concernant l'ordre de grandeur de la population appellent donc toutes les réserves fondamentales qui ont été formulées à la section 3 des Notes techniques à propos des statistiques relatives à la population. Sans entrer dans le détail, il convient de préciser que les données relatives à la répartition par grand groupe d'âge et par sexe doivent être considérées uniquement comme des ordres de grandeur en raison de leur caractère estimatif. Toutefois, il est à noter que, lorsque l'on additionne des données par territoire pour obtenir des totaux régionaux et par grandes zones, les erreurs qu'elles comportent arrivent parfois à s'équilibrer, de sorte que les agrégats obtenus peuvent être un peu plus exacts que chacun des éléments dont on est parti.

En outre, les donnés figurant dans le tableau 2 comportent certaines imprécisions en raison des facteurs influant sur les données par âge (voir à ce propos les notes techniques relatives au tableau 7). Ces imprécisions sont cependant atténuées du fait de l'étendue des groupes d'âge présentés dans le tableau 2.

---

[1] *Organisation des Nations Unies, Département des affaires économiques et sociales, Division de la population (2017). Perspectives de la population mondiale : La révision de 2017 (http://esa.un.org/unpd/wpp/)*

2. Estimates of population and its percentage distribution by age group and sex, and sex ratio, for the world, major areas and regions: 2017
Estimations de la population et pourcentage de répartition selon les tranches d'âge et le sexe, et le rapport de masculinité, pour l'ensemble du monde, les grandes régions et les régions géographiques : 2017

Major areas and regions / Grandes régions et régions	Population (millions)												Sex ratio - Rapport de masculinité[1]
	Both sexes - Les deux sexes				Male - Masculin				Female - Féminin				
	All ages - Tous âges	0-14	15-64	65+	All ages - Tous âges	0-14	15-64	65+	All ages - Tous âges	0-14	15-64	65+	
WORLD TOTAL - ENSEMBLE DU MONDE													
Number - Nombre	7 550	1 957	4 937	657	3 809	1 012	2 501	296	3 741	945	2 435	361	
Percent - Pourcentage	100.0	25.9	65.4	8.7	100.0	26.6	65.7	7.8	100.0	25.3	65.1	9.6	101.8
AFRICA - AFRIQUE													
Number - Nombre	1 256	513	699	44	627	260	348	20	629	253	352	24	
Percent - Pourcentage	100.0	40.8	55.7	3.5	100.0	41.4	55.4	3.2	100.0	40.2	55.9	3.9	99.8
Eastern Africa - Afrique orientale													
Number - Nombre	422	180	229	13	209	91	113	6	213	89	116	7	
Percent - Pourcentage	100.0	42.8	54.2	3.0	100.0	43.5	53.8	2.7	100.0	42.1	54.6	3.3	98.5
Middle Africa - Afrique centrale													
Number - Nombre	163	74	84	5	81	37	42	2	82	37	42	3	
Percent - Pourcentage	100.0	45.5	51.6	2.9	100.0	45.9	51.4	2.6	100.0	45.1	51.7	3.2	99.3
Northern Africa - Afrique septentrionale													
Number - Nombre	234	76	145	13	117	39	73	6	116	37	72	7	
Percent - Pourcentage	100.0	32.5	62.1	5.4	100.0	33.1	62.0	5.0	100.0	31.8	62.3	5.9	100.9
Southern Africa - Afrique méridionale													
Number - Nombre	65	19	42	3	32	10	21	1	33	10	22	2	
Percent - Pourcentage	100.0	29.8	65.1	5.2	100.0	30.6	65.4	4.0	100.0	29.0	64.8	6.2	96.2
Western Africa - Afrique occidentale													
Number - Nombre	372	163	199	10	187	83	100	5	185	80	99	6	
Percent - Pourcentage	100.0	43.7	53.4	2.8	100.0	44.2	53.1	2.6	100.0	43.2	53.8	3.0	101.3
LATIN AMERICA AND CARIBBEAN - AMÉRIQUE LATIN ET CARAÏBES													
Number - Nombre	646	161	433	52	319	82	214	23	327	79	219	29	
Percent - Pourcentage	100.0	24.9	67.0	8.1	100.0	25.7	67.1	7.1	100.0	24.1	67.0	9.0	97.7
Caribbean - Caraïbes													
Number - Nombre	44	11	29	4	22	5	14	2	22	5	15	2	
Percent - Pourcentage	100.0	24.5	65.7	9.8	100.0	25.3	65.7	9.0	100.0	23.7	65.7	10.6	97.9
Central America - Amérique centrale													
Number - Nombre	177	49	116	12	88	25	58	5	89	24	59	6	
Percent - Pourcentage	100.0	27.7	65.6	6.6	100.0	28.6	65.3	6.1	100.0	26.9	66.0	7.1	98.5
South America - Amérique méridionale													
Number - Nombre	424	101	288	36	209	51	142	15	215	49	145	20	
Percent - Pourcentage	100.0	23.7	67.8	8.5	100.0	24.6	68.0	7.4	100.0	23.0	67.5	9.5	97.4
NORTHERN AMERICA - AMÉRIQUE SEPTENTRIONALE													
Number - Nombre	361	67	238	56	179	34	119	25	182	33	118	31	
Percent - Pourcentage	100.0	18.6	65.8	15.6	100.0	19.2	66.7	14.1	100.0	18.0	64.9	17.1	98.1
ASIA - ASIE													
Number - Nombre	4 504	1 089	3 052	364	2 305	570	1 565	170	2 200	519	1 487	194	
Percent - Pourcentage	100.0	24.2	67.8	8.1	100.0	24.7	67.9	7.4	100.0	23.6	67.6	8.8	104.8
Eastern Asia - Asie orientale													
Number - Nombre	1 648	283	1 167	199	844	151	599	93	805	132	568	105	
Percent - Pourcentage	100.0	17.2	70.8	12.0	100.0	17.9	71.0	11.1	100.0	16.4	70.6	13.1	104.8
South Central Asia - Asie centrale méridionale													
Number - Nombre	1 940	557	1 273	110	997	291	653	53	943	266	619	57	
Percent - Pourcentage	100.0	28.7	65.6	5.7	100.0	29.2	65.5	5.3	100.0	28.2	65.7	6.1	105.8
South Eastern Asia - Asie méridionale orientale													
Number - Nombre	649	170	438	41	324	87	219	18	325	83	219	23	
Percent - Pourcentage	100.0	26.2	67.5	6.3	100.0	27.0	67.6	5.4	100.0	25.5	67.4	7.1	99.7
Western Asia - Asie occidentale													
Number - Nombre	268	79	174	15	140	40	93	6	128	38	81	8	
Percent - Pourcentage	100.0	29.4	65.2	5.4	100.0	28.8	66.6	4.6	100.0	30.0	63.6	6.3	109.5
EUROPE													
Number - Nombre	742	118	489	135	359	60	242	56	384	57	246	80	
Percent - Pourcentage	100.0	15.9	65.9	18.2	100.0	16.9	67.6	15.5	100.0	15.0	64.3	20.8	93.5
Eastern Europe - Europe orientale													
Number - Nombre	292	48	199	46	138	25	97	16	155	23	102	29	
Percent - Pourcentage	100.0	16.4	68.0	15.6	100.0	17.9	70.3	11.8	100.0	15.1	66.0	19.0	88.9
Northern Europe - Europe septentrionale													
Number - Nombre	104	18	66	19	51	9	33	9	53	9	33	11	
Percent - Pourcentage	100.0	17.6	63.8	18.6	100.0	18.3	64.8	17.0	100.0	16.9	62.9	20.2	97.3
Southern Europe - Europe méridionale													
Number - Nombre	152	22	99	31	74	11	49	14	78	11	49	18	
Percent - Pourcentage	100.0	14.3	65.1	20.6	100.0	15.1	66.7	18.2	100.0	13.6	63.5	22.9	95.5

2. Estimates of population and its percentage distribution by age group and sex, and sex ratio, for the world, major areas and regions: 2017

Estimations de la population et pourcentage de répartition selon les tranches d'âge et le sexe, et le rapport de masculinité, pour l'ensemble du monde, les grandes régions et les régions géographiques : 2017 (continued - suite)

Major areas and regions	Population (millions)												Sex ratio - Rapport de masculinité[1]
	Both sexes - Les deux sexes				Male - Masculin				Female - Féminin				
Grandes régions et régions	All ages - Tous âges	0-14	15-64	65+	All ages - Tous âges	0-14	15-64	65+	All ages - Tous âges	0-14	15-64	65+	
Western Europe - Europe occidentale													
Number - Nombre	193	30	125	39	95	15	63	17	98	15	62	22	
Percent - Pourcentage	100.0	15.4	64.4	20.2	100.0	16.1	65.9	18.1	100.0	14.8	62.9	22.3	97.1
OCEANIA - OCÉANIA													
Number - Nombre	40.69	9.56	26.11	5.02	20.36	4.92	13.09	2.34	20.33	4.64	13.01	2.68	
Percent - Pourcentage	100.0	23.5	64.2	12.3	100.0	24.2	64.3	11.5	100.0	22.8	64.0	13.2	100.1
Australia and New Zealand - Australie et Nouvelle Zélande													
Number - Nombre	29.16	5.58	19.07	4.51	14.49	2.86	9.52	2.12	14.66	2.72	9.55	2.40	
Percent - Pourcentage	100.0	19.1	65.4	15.5	100.0	19.7	65.7	14.6	100.0	18.5	65.1	16.3	98.9
Melanesia - Melanésie													
Number - Nombre	10.32	3.62	6.27	0.43	5.25	1.87	3.19	0.19	5.07	1.75	3.08	0.24	
Percent - Pourcentage	100.0	35.1	60.7	4.2	100.0	35.6	60.7	3.6	100.0	34.5	60.7	4.8	103.4
Micronesia													
Number - Nombre	0.53	0.15	0.34	0.03	0.27	0.08	0.17	0.02	0.26	0.07	0.17	0.02	
Percent - Pourcentage	100.0	29.2	64.3	6.6	100.0	29.8	64.2	6.1	100.0	28.6	64.4	7.1	101.5
Polynesia - Polynésie													
Number - Nombre	0.69	0.20	0.44	0.05	0.35	0.11	0.22	0.02	0.34	0.10	0.21	0.03	
Percent - Pourcentage	100.0	29.8	63.4	6.7	100.0	30.2	63.7	6.0	100.0	29.4	63.1	7.4	103.4

FOOTNOTES - NOTES

[1] Males per 100 females of all ages - Hommes pour 100 femmes de tous âges

Table 3 - *Demographic Yearbook 2017*

Table 3 presents for each country or area of the world the total, male and female population enumerated at the latest population census, estimates of the mid-year total population for 2010 and 2017, the average annual exponential rate of population increase (or decrease) for the period 2010 to 2017, the surface area and the population density for 2017.

Description of variables: The total, male and female population is the population enumerated at the most recent census for which data are available. The date of this census is given. Population census data are usually the results of a nation-wide gathering of individual information through full field enumeration. Alternatively, other approaches for generating reliable statistics on population and housing can be used by countries, such as the use of population registers. Data that are the result of such an alternative approach are also coded as census and are footnoted accordingly. Also, the results of sample surveys, essentially national in character, may be presented showing the appropriate code.

Mid-year population estimates refer to the population on 1 July. Otherwise, a footnote is appended. Mid-year estimates of the total population are those provided by national statistical offices.

Surface area, expressed in square kilometres, refers to the total surface area, comprising land area and inland waters (assumed to consist of major rivers and lakes) and excluding polar regions as well as uninhabited islands. Exceptions to this are noted. Surface areas, originally reported in square miles by the country or area, have been converted to square kilometres using a conversion factor of 2.589988.

Computation: The annual rate of population increase is the average annual exponential rate of population growth between 2010 and 2017, computed by the Statistics Division of the United Nations Department of Economic and Social Affairs using the unrounded mid-year estimates of 2010 and 2017. This rate is expressed as percentage.

Density is the number of persons in the 2017 total population per square kilometre of total surface area.

Reliability of data: Reliable mid-year population estimates are those that are based on a complete census (or a sample survey) and have been adjusted by a continuous population register or on the basis of the calculated balance of births, deaths and migration. Mid-year estimates of this type are considered reliable and appear in roman type. Mid-year estimates not calculated on this basis are considered less reliable and are shown in italics.

Census data and sample survey results are considered reliable and, therefore, appear in roman type.

Rates of population increase that were calculated using population estimates considered less reliable, as described above, are set in italics rather than roman type.

All surface area data are assumed to be reliable and therefore appear in roman type.

Population density data, however, are considered reliable or less reliable on the basis of the reliability of the 2017 population estimates used as the numerator.

Limitations: Statistics on the total population enumerated at the time of the census, surface area data and estimates of the mid-year total population are subject to the same qualifications as have been set forth for surface area and population data in sections 2.4 and 3 of the Technical Notes, respectively.

Regarding the limitations of census data, it should be noted that although census data are considered reliable, and therefore appear in roman type, the actual quality of census data varies widely from one country or area to another. When known, an estimate of the extent of over-enumeration or under-enumeration is given in footnotes.

Rates of population increase are subject to all the qualifications of the population estimates mentioned above. In some cases, they simply reflect the rate calculated or assumed in constructing the estimates themselves when adequate measures of natural increase and net migration were not available. Despite their shortcomings, these rates provide a useful index for studying population change and can be also useful in evaluating the accuracy of vital and migration statistics.

Population density data as shown in this table give only an indication of actual population density as they do not take account of the dispersion or concentration of population within countries or areas nor the proportion of habitable land. They should not be interpreted as reflecting density in the urban sense or as indicating the supporting power of a territory's land and resources.

Tableau 3 – *Annuaire démographique 2017*

Le tableau 3 indique pour chaque pays ou zone du monde la population totale selon le sexe d'après les derniers recensements effectués, les estimations concernant la population totale au milieu de l'année 2010 et de l'année 2017, le taux moyen d'accroissement annuel exponentiel positif ou négatif de la population pour la période allant de 2010 à 2017, ainsi que la superficie et la densité de population en 2017.

Description des variables : la population masculine et féminine totale est, la population enregistrée lors du recensement le plus récent sur lequel on dispose de données. La date de ce recensement est indiquée. Les données des recensements de la population sont habituellement le résultat d'un collecte à l'échelle nationale des données individuelles obtenues au moyen d'un dénombrement complet. Les pays peuvent recourir à d'autres moyens pour établir des statistiques fiables sur la population et le logement, tels que des registres de la population. Les données obtenues par ce moyen sont présentées comme celles d'un recensement et sont annotées en conséquence. Par ailleurs, les résultats des enquêtes par sondage, réalisées habituellement à l'échelle nationale, peuvent être présentés à l'aide du code correspondant.
Les estimations de la population en milieu d'année sont celles de la population au 1er juillet. Lorsque la date est différente, cela est signalé par une note. Les estimations de la population totale en milieu d'année sont celles qui ont été communiquées par les services nationaux de statistique.

La superficie - exprimée en kilomètres carrés - représente la superficie totale, c'est-à-dire qu'elle englobe les terres émergées et les eaux intérieures (qui sont censées comprendre les principaux lacs et cours d'eau) mais exclut les régions polaires et certaines îles inhabitées. Les exceptions à cette règle sont signalées en note. Les superficies initialement exprimées en miles carrés par les pays ou les zones ont été transformées en kilomètres carrés au moyen d'un coefficient de conversion de 2,589988.

Calculs : le taux d'accroissement annuel est le taux exponentiel annuel moyen de variation (en pourcentage) de la population entre 2010 et 2017, calculé par la Division de statistique du Département des affaires économiques et sociales de l'Organisation des Nations Unies à partir des estimations en milieu d'année non arrondies pour les années 2010 et 2017.

La densité est égale au rapport de l'effectif total de la population en 2017 à la superficie totale, exprimée en kilomètres carrés.

Fiabilité des données : les estimations en milieu d'année qui sont considérées sûres sont fondées sur un recensement complet (ou sur une enquête par sondage) et ont été ajustées en fonction des données provenant d'un registre permanent de population ou en fonction de la balance établie par le calcul des naissances, des décès et des migrations. Les estimations de ce type sont considérées comme sûres et apparaissent en caractères romains. Les estimations en milieu d'année dont le calcul n'a pas été effectué sur cette base sont considérées comme moins sûres et apparaissent en italique.

Les données de recensements ou les résultats d'enquêtes par sondage sont considérés comme sûrs et apparaissent par conséquent en caractères romains.

Les taux d'accroissement de la population, calculés à partir d'estimations jugées moins sûres d'après les normes décrites ci-dessus, sont indiqués en italique plutôt qu'en caractères romains.

Toutes les données de superficie sont présumées sûres et apparaissent par conséquent en caractères romains. En revanche, les données relatives à la densité de la population sont considérées plus ou moins sûres en fonction de la fiabilité des estimations de la population en 2017 ayant servi de numérateur.

Insuffisance des données : les statistiques portant sur la population totale dénombrée lors d'un recensement, les données de superficie et les estimations de la population totale en milieu d'année appellent les mêmes réserves que celles formulées aux sections 2.4 et 3 des Notes techniques à propos des statistiques relatives à la superficie et à la population.

S'agissant de l'insuffisance des données obtenues par recensement, il convient d'indiquer que, bien que ces données soient considérées comme sûres et apparaissent par conséquent en caractères romains, leur qualité réelle varie considérablement d'un pays ou d'une région à l'autre. Lorsque l'on possédait les renseignements voulus, on a donné une estimation du degré de sur-dénombrement ou de sous-dénombrement.
Les taux d'accroissement appellent toutes les réserves formulées plus haut à propos des estimations concernant la population. Dans certains cas, ils représentent seulement le taux calculé ou que l'on a pris

pour base pour établir les estimations elles-mêmes lorsque l'on ne disposait pas de mesures appropriées de l'accroissement naturel et des migrations nettes. Malgré leurs imperfections, ces taux fournissent des indications intéressantes pour l'étude du mouvement de la population et, utilisés avec les précautions nécessaires, ils peuvent également servir à évaluer l'exactitude des statistiques de l'état civil et des migrations.

Les données relatives à la densité de population figurant dans le tableau 3 n'ont qu'une valeur indicative en ce qui concerne la densité de population effective, car elles ne tiennent compte ni de la dispersion ou de la concentration de la population à l'intérieur des pays ou zones, ni de la proportion du territoire qui est habitable. Il ne faut donc y voir d'indication ni de la densité au sens urbain du terme ni du nombre d'habitants qui pourraient vivre sur les terres et avec les ressources naturelles du territoire considéré.

3. Population by sex, annual rate of population increase, surface area and density
Population selon le sexe, taux d'accroissement annuel de la population, superficie et densité

Continent, country or area and census date / Continent, pays ou zone et date du recensement	Census type[a]	Population at the latest available census / Population d'après le dernier recensement disponible (in units — en unités)			Estimate type[a]	Mid-year estimates / Estimations au milieu de l'année (in thousands — en milliers)		Annual rate of increase / Taux d' accrois sement annuel 2010-17	Surface area / Superficie (km²) 2017	Density / Densité 2017[b]
		Both sexes / Les deux sexes	Male / Masculin	Female / Feminin		2010	2017			

AFRICA - AFRIQUE

Algeria - Algérie										
16 IV 2008 .... DF		34 452 759[1]	17 428 500[1]	17 024 259[1]	DJ	35 978	41 696	2.1	2 381 741	18
Angola										
16 V 2014 .... DF		25 789 024	12 499 041	13 289 983	DF	17 430[2]	28 360[3]	7.0	1 246 700	23
Benin - Bénin										
11 V 2013 .... DF		10 008 749	4 887 820	5 120 929	DF	8 779[4]	...	...	114 763	...
Botswana										
9 VIII 2011 .... DF		2 024 904	988 957	1 035 947	DJ	1 823	2 267[5]	3.1	582 000	4
Burkina Faso										
9 XII 2006 .... DF		14 196 259	6 842 560	7 353 699	DJ	15 731[4]	...	...	272 967	...
Burundi										
16 VIII 2008 .... DF		7 877 728	3 838 045	4 039 683	DF	9 461	11 495	2.8	27 834	413
Cabo Verde										
16 VI 2010 .... DJ		491 683	243 403	248 280	DJ	494[4]	538[4]	1.2	4 033	133
Cameroon - Cameroun										
11 XI 2005 .... DF		17 052 134	8 408 495	8 643 639	DF	19 648[4]	23 248[4]	2.4	475 650	49
Central African Republic - République centrafricaine										
8 XII 2003 .... DF		3 151 072	1 569 446	1 581 626		...	...	...	622 984	...
Chad - Tchad										
20 V 2009 .... DJ		11 175 915	5 509 522	5 666 393		...	...	...	1 284 000	...
Comoros - Comores										
1 IX 2003 .... DF		575 660[6]	285 590[6]	290 070[6]		...	...	...	2 235	...
Congo										
28 IV 2007 .... DF		3 697 490	1 821 357	1 876 133	DF	...	4 709	...	342 000	14
Côte d'Ivoire										
15 V 2014 .... DF		22 224 509	11 441 896	10 782 613	DF	20 845[7]	24 571[8]	2.3	322 462	76
Democratic Republic of the Congo - République démocratique du Congo										
1 VII 1984 .... DF		29 916 800	14 543 800	15 373 000		...	...	...	2 344 858	...
Djibouti										
29 V 2009 .... DF		818 159	440 067	378 092	DF	841[9]	...	...	23 200	...
Egypt - Égypte										
18 IV 2017 .... DF		94 798 827	48 891 518	45 907 309	DF	78 685	95 203	2.7	1 002 000	95
Equatorial Guinea - Guinée équatoriale										
20 VI 2015 .... DF		*1 222 442	*651 820	*570 622	DF	1 622[10]	*1 309[11]	-3.1	28 051	47
Eritrea - Érythrée										
9 V 1984 .... DF		2 621 566[12]	1 309 736[12]	1 311 830[12]	DF	2 691[13]	3 212[13]	2.5	121 144	27
Eswatini										
11 III 2007 .... DF		844 223	405 868	438 355	DF	1 056	1 146	1.2	17 363	66
Ethiopia - Éthiopie										
29 V 2007 .... DF		73 750 932	37 217 130	36 533 802	DF	79 634[14]	94 352[14]	2.4	1 104 300	85
Gabon										
22 V 2013 .... DF		1 811 079	934 072	877 007		...	...	...	267 668	...
Gambia - Gambie										
15 IV 2013 .... DF		*1 882 450	*930 699	*951 751		...	...	...	11 295	...
Ghana										
26 IX 2010 .... DF		24 658 823	12 024 845	12 633 978		...	...	...	238 537	...
Guinea - Guinée										
15 III 2014 .... DJ		10 523 261	5 084 306	5 438 955	...	10 537[4]	11 555[3]	...	245 836	47
Guinea-Bissau - Guinée-Bissau										
15 III 2009 .... DF		1 497 859	725 956	771 903	DF	1 460[4]	...	...	36 125	...
Kenya										
24 VIII 2009 .... DF		38 610 097	19 192 458	19 417 639	DF	38 474[15]	46 595[15]	2.7	591 958	79
Lesotho										
10 IV 2016 .... DJ		2 007 201	982 133	1 025 068	DF	1 892[16]	...	...	30 355	...
Liberia - Libéria										
21 III 2008 .... DF		3 476 608	1 739 945	1 736 663	DF	3 627	...	...	111 369	...
Libya - Libye										
15 IV 2006 .... DF		*5 298 152[17]	*2 687 513[17]	*2 610 639[17]	DF	5 689[17]	...	...	1 676 198	...

3. Population by sex, annual rate of population increase, surface area and density
Population selon le sexe, taux d'accroissement annuel de la population, superficie et densité (continued - suite)

Continent, country or area and census date / Continent, pays ou zone et date du recensement	Census type[a]	Population at the latest available census / Population d'après le dernier recensement disponible (in units — en unités)			Estimate type[a]	Mid-year estimates Estimations au milieu de l'année (in thousands — en milliers)		Annual rate of increase Taux d'accrois sement annuel 2010-17	Surface area Superficie (km²) 2017	Density Densité 2017[b]
		Both sexes Les deux sexes	Male Masculin	Female Feminin		2010	2017			
AFRICA - AFRIQUE										
Madagascar										
1 VIII 1993 .... DF	DF	12 238 914	6 088 116	6 150 798	DF	20 142[4]	...	...	587 295	...
Malawi										
8 VI 2008 .... DF	DF	13 077 160	6 358 933	6 718 227	DF	13 948[4]	...	...	117 726	...
Mali										
1 IV 2009 .... DF	DF	14 528 662	7 204 990	7 323 672	DF	15 370[18]	...	...	1 240 192	...
Mauritania - Mauritanie										
24 III 2013 .... DF	DF	3 460 388[19]	...	...	DF	3 341[4]	...	...	1 030 700	...
Mauritius - Maurice[20]										
4 VII 2011 .... DF	DF	1 237 000	611 053	625 947	DJ	1 281[21]	1 265[22]	-0.2	1 979	639
Mayotte										
21 VIII 2012 .... DJ	DJ	212 645	103 173	109 471	DJ	...	*254[23]	...	374	680
Morocco - Maroc										
1 IX 2014 .... DJ	DJ	33 848 242	...	...	...	31 894[24]	34 852[25]	...	446 550	78
Mozambique										
1 VIII 2017 .... DF	DF	*28 861 863	*13 800 857	*15 061 006	DF	22 417[26]	27 129[26]	2.7	799 380	34
Namibia - Namibie										
28 VIII 2011 .... DF	DF	2 113 077	1 021 912	1 091 165	DF	2 143[4]	2 369[27]	1.4	824 116	3
Niger										
10 XII 2012 .... DF	DF	16 734 935	8 183 513	8 551 422	DJ	15 204[4]	...	...	1 267 000	...
Nigeria - Nigéria										
21 III 2006 .... DF	DF	140 431 790	71 345 488	69 086 302	DF	159 608[16]	...	...	923 768	...
Republic of South Sudan - République de Soudan du Sud										
21 IV 2008 .... DF	DF	8 260 490	4 287 300	3 973 190	DF	9 005[28]	11 868[28]	3.9	658 841	18
Reunion - Réunion										
1 I 2010 .... DJ	DJ	821 136	398 006	423 130	DJ	821[29]	*863[23]	0.7	2 513	344
Rwanda										
15 VIII 2012 .... DF	DF	10 393 542	4 981 197	5 412 345	DF	10 413[4]	11 809[30]	1.8	26 338	448
Saint Helena ex. dep. - Sainte-Hélène sans dép.										
7 II 2016 .... DF	DF	4 802	...	...	DF	4	...	...	122	...
Saint Helena: Ascension - Sainte-Hélène: Ascension										
7 II 2016 .... DJ	DJ	556[31]	...	...	...	...	...	...	88	...
Saint Helena: Tristan da Cunha - Sainte-Hélène: Tristan da Cunha										
9 II 2016 .... DJ	DJ	271[31]	...	...	...	...	...	...	98	...
Sao Tome and Principe - Sao Tomé-et-Principe										
13 V 2012 .... DJ	DJ	178 739	88 867	89 872	...	164	198[32]	...	964	205
Senegal - Sénégal										
19 XI 2013 .... DF	DF	13 357 492	6 658 089	6 699 403	DJ	12 509[33]	15 256[4]	2.8	196 712[34]	78
Seychelles										
26 VIII 2010 .... DF	DF	90 945	46 912	44 033	DF	90	96	0.9	457	210
Sierra Leone										
5 XII 2015 .... DF	DF	7 092 113	3 490 978	3 601 135	DF	5 747	...	...	72 300	...
Somalia - Somalie										
15 II 1987 .... DF	DF	7 114 431	3 741 664	3 372 767		...	...	...	637 657	...
South Africa - Afrique du Sud										
10 X 2011 .... DF	DF	51 770 560	25 188 791	26 581 769	DF	50 979	56 522	1.5	1 221 037	46
Sudan - Soudan										
21 IV 2008 .... DF	DF	30 894 000	15 786 677	15 107 323	DF	32 962	...	...	...	...
Togo										
6 XI 2010 .... DJ	DJ	6 191 155	3 009 095	3 182 060	DJ	6 191[4]	7 229[4]	2.2	56 785	127
Tunisia - Tunisie										
23 IV 2014 .... DF	DF	10 982 754	5 472 338	5 510 416	DF	10 566	11 446	1.1	163 610	70
Uganda - Ouganda										
27 VIII 2014 .... DF	DF	34 634 650	16 897 849	17 736 801	DF	31 785	37 674[8]	2.4	241 550	156

3. Population by sex, annual rate of population increase, surface area and density
Population selon le sexe, taux d'accroissement annuel de la population, superficie et densité (continued - suite)

Continent, country or area and census date Continent, pays ou zone et date du recensement	Census type[a]	Population at the latest available census Population d'après le dernier recensement disponible (in units — en unités)			Estimate type[a]	Mid-year estimates Estimations au milieu de l'année (in thousands — en milliers)		Annual rate of increase Taux d' accrois sement annuel 2010-17	Surface area Superficie (km²) 2017	Density Densité 2017[b]
		Both sexes Les deux sexes	Male Masculin	Female Feminin		2010	2017			
AFRICA - AFRIQUE										
United Republic of Tanzania - République Unie de Tanzanie										
26 VIII 2012 .... DF		44 928 923[35]	21 869 990[35]	23 058 933[35]	DF	43 188[36]	52 555[30]	2.8	947 303	55
Western Sahara - Sahara occidental[37]										
31 XII 1970 .... DF		76 425	43 981	32 444		...	...	...	266 000	...
Zambia - Zambie										
16 X 2010 .... DF		12 526 314	6 117 253	6 409 061	DJ	...	16 405[38]	...	752 612	22
Zimbabwe										
17 VIII 2012 .... DF		13 061 239	6 280 539	6 780 700	DF	...	14 542[32]	...	390 757	37
AMERICA, NORTH - AMÉRIQUE DU NORD										
Anguilla										
11 V 2011 .... DF		13 572	6 707	6 865	DF	16	...	...	91	...
Antigua and Barbuda - Antigua-et-Barbuda										
27 V 2011 .... DF		88 566	...	...	DF	91	...	...	442	...
Aruba										
29 IX 2010 .... DJ		101 484	48 241	53 243	DJ	102	111	1.2	180	616
Bahamas										
3 V 2010 .... DJ		351 461	170 257	181 204	DJ	352[38]	377[38]	1.0	13 940	27
Barbados - Barbade										
1 V 2010 .... DJ		277 821[39]	133 018[39]	144 803[39]	DJ	278	...	...	431	...
Belize										
12 V 2010 .... DJ		322 453	161 227	161 226	DJ	324	388	2.6	22 966	17
Bermuda - Bermudes										
20 V 2016 .... DJ		63 779	30 690	33 089	DJ	64[40]	62[40]	-0.6	54	1 134
British Virgin Islands - Îles Vierges britanniques										
12 VII 2010 .... DF		28 054	13 820	14 234	DF	28	...	...	151	...
Canada										
10 V 2016 .... DJ		35 151 730[41]	17 264 200[41]	17 887 530[41]	DJ	34 005[42]	*36 708[43]	1.1	9 984 670	4
Cayman Islands - Îles Caïmanes										
10 X 2010 .... DJ		55 036[44]	27 218[44]	27 818[44]	DJ	56	63[33]	1.9	264	240
Costa Rica										
30 V 2011 .... DJ		4 301 712	2 106 063	2 195 649	DJ	4 538[45]	4 947[46]	1.2	51 100	97
Cuba										
14 IX 2012 .... DJ		11 167 325	5 570 825	5 596 500	DJ	11 171	11 230	0.1	109 884	102
Curaçao										
26 III 2011 .... DJ		150 563	68 848	81 715	DJ	149[47]	160[3]	1.1	444	361
Dominica - Dominique										
14 V 2011 .... DF		68 913	34 973	33 940	DF	71	...	...	750	...
Dominican Republic - République dominicaine										
1 XII 2010 .... DJ		9 445 281	4 739 038	4 706 243	DJ	9 479[4]	10 169[4]	1.0	48 671	209
El Salvador										
12 V 2007 .... DJ		5 744 113	2 719 371	3 024 742	DJ	6 183[48]	6 582[48]	0.9	21 041	313
Greenland - Groenland										
1 I 2008 .... DJ		56 462[49]	29 885[49]	26 577[49]	DJ	57[49]	56[49]	-0.1	2 166 086	0
Grenada - Grenade										
12 V 2011 .... DF		106 667	53 898	52 769	DF	105	111	0.8	345	323
Guadeloupe										
1 I 2010 .... DJ		403 355[50]	187 932[50]	215 423[50]	DJ	404[50]	*392[50]	-0.4	1 705	230
Guatemala										
24 XI 2002 .... DJ		11 237 196	5 496 839	5 740 357	DJ	14 362[36]	...	...	108 889	...
Haiti - Haïti										
11 I 2003 .... DJ		8 373 750	4 039 272	4 334 478	DJ	10 085[51]	...	...	27 750	...
Honduras										
10 VIII 2013 .... DF		8 303 771	4 052 316	4 251 456	DF	8 046[52]	...	...	112 492	...

3. Population by sex, annual rate of population increase, surface area and density
Population selon le sexe, taux d'accroissement annuel de la population, superficie et densité (continued - suite)

| Continent, country or area and census date / Continent, pays ou zone et date du recensement | Census type[a] | Population at the latest available census / Population d'après le dernier recensement disponible (in units — en unités) | | | Estimate type[a] | Mid-year estimates / Estimations au milieu de l'année (in thousands — en milliers) | | Annual rate of increase / Taux d'accroissement annuel 2010-17 | Surface area / Superficie (km²) 2017 | Density / Densité 2017[b] |
		Both sexes / Les deux sexes	Male / Masculin	Female / Feminin		2010	2017			
AMERICA, NORTH - AMÉRIQUE DU NORD										
Jamaica - Jamaïque										
4 IV 2011 .... DJ	DJ	2 697 983[53]	1 334 533[53]	1 363 450[53]	DJ	2 702	2 729	0.1	10 991	248
Martinique										
1 I 2010 .... DJ	DJ	394 173	182 073	212 100	DJ	394[29]	*375[29]	-0.7	1 128	332
Mexico - Mexique										
12 VI 2010 .... DF	DF	112 336 538[54]	54 855 231[54]	57 481 307[54]	DJ	114 256[4]	123 518[4]	1.1	1 964 375	63
Montserrat										
12 V 2011 .... DJ	DJ	4 922	2 546	2 376	DF	5	...	...	103	...
Nicaragua										
4 VI 2005 .... DJ	DJ	5 142 098	2 534 491	2 607 607	DJ	5 816	6 394	1.4	130 373	49
Panama										
16 V 2010 .... DF	DF	3 405 813	1 712 584	1 693 229	DF	3 662[40]	4 098[40]	1.6	75 320	54
Puerto Rico - Porto Rico										
1 IV 2010 .... DJ	DJ	3 725 789[55]	1 785 171[55]	1 940 618[55]	DJ	3 721[56]	3 337[57]	-1.6	8 868	376
Saint Kitts and Nevis - Saint-Kitts-et-Nevis										
15 V 2011 .... DF	DF	*46 398	*22 846	*23 552	DF	*53	...	...	261	...
Saint Lucia - Sainte-Lucie										
10 V 2010 .... DJ	DJ	165 770	83 502	82 268		...	...	...	539[58]	...
Saint Pierre and Miquelon - Saint-Pierre-et-Miquelon										
1 I 2013 .... DJ	DJ	6 286	...	...		...	...	...	242	
Saint Vincent and the Grenadines - Saint-Vincent-et-les Grenadines										
12 VI 2012 .... DJ	DJ	109 991	56 419	53 572	DJ	110	...	...	389	...
Saint-Barthélemy										
1 I 2013 .... DJ	DJ	9 417	...	...		...	...	...	22	...
Saint-Martin (French part) - Saint-Martin (partie française)										
1 I 2013 .... DJ	DJ	36 457	...	...		...	...	...	53	...
Sint Maarten (Dutch part) - Saint-Martin (partie néerlandaise)										
9 IV 2011 .... DF	DF	33 609	15 868	17 741	DF	36	...	...	34	...
Trinidad and Tobago - Trinité-et-Tobago										
9 I 2011 .... DF	DF	1 332 901	...	...	DF	1 318[21]	1 357[22]	0.4	5 127	265
Turks and Caicos Islands - Îles Turques et Caïques										
25 I 2012 .... DJ	DJ	*31 458[59]	*16 037[59]	*15 421[59]	DJ	35	40	2.0	948[60]	42
United States of America - États-Unis d'Amérique										
1 IV 2010 .... DJ	DJ	308 745 538	151 781 326	156 964 212	DJ	309 348[61]	...	...	9 833 517	...
United States Virgin Islands - Îles Vierges américaines										
1 IV 2010 .... DJ	DJ	106 405[55]	50 854[55]	55 551[55]	DJ	106[62]	...	...	347	...
AMERICA, SOUTH - AMÉRIQUE DU SUD										
Argentina - Argentine										
27 X 2010 .... DF	DF	40 117 096	19 523 766	20 593 330	DF	40 788[38]	44 045[38]	1.1	2 796 427[63]	16
Bolivia (Plurinational State of) - Bolivie (État plurinational de)										
21 XI 2012 .... DF	DF	10 059 856	5 019 447	5 040 409	DF	10 031	11 146	1.5	1 098 581[64]	10
Brazil - Brésil										
31 VII 2010 .... DJ	DJ	190 755 799	93 406 990	97 348 809	DJ	195 498[65]	207 661[65]	0.9	8 515 767	24

3. Population by sex, annual rate of population increase, surface area and density
Population selon le sexe, taux d'accroissement annuel de la population, superficie et densité (continued - suite)

Continent, country or area and census date / Continent, pays ou zone et date du recensement	Census type[a]	Population at the latest available census / Population d'après le dernier recensement disponible (in units — en unités)			Estimate type[a]	Mid-year estimates / Estimations au milieu de l'année (in thousands — en milliers)		Annual rate of increase / Taux d'accrois sement annuel 2010-17	Surface area / Superficie (km²) 2017	Density / Densité 2017[b]
		Both sexes / Les deux sexes	Male / Masculin	Female / Feminin		2010	2017			
AMERICA, SOUTH - AMÉRIQUE DU SUD										
Chile - Chili										
24 IV 2002 .... DF	DF	15 116 435	7 447 695	7 668 740	DF	17 094	18 374	1.0	756 102	24
Colombia - Colombie										
22 V 2005 .... DF	DF	41 468 384	20 336 117	21 132 267	DJ	45 510[66]	49 292[66]	1.1	1 141 748	43
Ecuador - Équateur										
28 XI 2010 .... DF	DF	14 483 499	7 177 683	7 305 816	DF	15 012[67]	16 777[67]	1.6	257 217[68]	65
Falkland Islands (Malvinas) - Îles Falkland (Malvinas)[69]										
15 IV 2012 .... DF	DF	2 840[70]	1 491[70]	1 349[70]		...	...	...	12 173	...
French Guiana - Guyane française										
1 I 2013 .... DJ	DJ	244 118	121 653	122 465	DJ	229[29]	274[29]	2.6	83 534	3
Guyana										
15 IX 2012 .... DF	DF	746 955	371 805	375 150	DF	752	741	-0.2	214 969	3
Paraguay										
28 VIII 2002 .... DF	DF	5 163 198	2 603 242	2 559 956	DF	6 266[71]	6 954[71]	1.5	406 752	17
Peru - Pérou										
21 X 2007 .... DF	DF	27 412 157	13 622 640	13 789 517	DF	29 462[72]	31 826[72]	1.1	1 285 216	25
Suriname										
13 VIII 2012 .... DJ	DJ	541 638	270 629	271 009	DJ	531	...	...	163 820	...
Uruguay										
4 X 2011 .... DJ	DJ	3 286 314	1 577 725[73]	1 708 481[73]	DJ	3 397	3 493[4]	0.4	173 626	20
Venezuela (Bolivarian Republic of) - Venezuela (République bolivarienne du)										
1 IX 2011 .... DJ	DJ	27 227 930	13 549 752	13 678 178	DF	28 524	31 277	1.3	929 690	34
ASIA - ASIE										
Afghanistan										
23 VI 1979 .... DF	DF	13 051 358[74]	6 712 377[74]	6 338 981[74]	DF	24 486[75]	28 224[75]	2.0	652 864	43
Armenia - Arménie										
12 X 2011 .... DF	DF	2 871 771	1 346 729	1 525 042	DJ	3 045	2 979	-0.3	29 743	100
Azerbaijan - Azerbaïdjan										
13 IV 2009 .... DJ	DJ	8 922 447	4 414 398	4 508 049	DJ	9 054	9 850	1.2	86 600	114
Bahrain - Bahreïn										
27 IV 2010 .... DJ	DJ	1 234 571	768 414	466 157	DJ	1 229	1 501	2.9	778	1 928
Bangladesh										
15 III 2011 .... DF	DF	144 043 697	72 109 796	71 933 901	DF	148 620	161 750	1.2	147 570	1 096
Bhutan - Bhoutan										
30 V 2017 .... DF	DF	727 145	380 453	346 692	DF	696[76]	...	...	38 394	...
Brunei Darussalam - Brunéi Darussalam										
20 VI 2011 .... DJ	DJ	393 372	203 144	190 228	...	387[47]	421	...	5 765	73
Cambodia - Cambodge										
3 III 2008 .... DF	DF	13 395 682[77]	6 516 054[77]	6 879 628[77]	DF	14 303[78]	...	...	181 035	...
China - Chine										
1 XI 2010 .... DJ	DJ	1 339 724 852[79]	686 852 572[79]	652 872 280[79]	DF	1 337 700[80]	1 384 373[80]	0.5	9 600 000	144
China, Hong Kong SAR - Chine, Hong Kong RAS										
30 VI 2016 .... DJ	DJ	7 336 585[81]	3 375 362[81]	3 961 223[81]	DJ	7 024	7 392	0.7	1 106	6 683
China, Macao SAR - Chine, Macao RAS										
12 VIII 2011 .... DF	DF	625 674	305 398	320 276	DJ	537	*653	2.8	30[82]	21 770
Cyprus - Chypre										
1 X 2011 .... DJ	DJ	840 407[83]	408 780[83]	431 627[83]	DJ	829[84]	855[85]	0.4	9 251	92
Democratic People's Republic of Korea - République populaire démocratique de Corée										
1 X 2008 .... DJ	DJ	24 052 231	11 721 838	12 330 393		...	...	...	120 538	...

3. Population by sex, annual rate of population increase, surface area and density
Population selon le sexe, taux d'accroissement annuel de la population, superficie et densité (continued - suite)

| Continent, country or area and census date / Continent, pays ou zone et date du recensement | Census type[a] | Population at the latest available census / Population d'après le dernier recensement disponible (in units — en unités) | | | Estimate type[a] | Mid-year estimates Estimations au milieu de l'année (in thousands — en milliers) | | Annual rate of increase Taux d'accrois sement annuel 2010-17 | Surface area Superficie (km²) 2017 | Density Densité 2017[b] |
		Both sexes Les deux sexes	Male Masculin	Female Feminin		2010	2017			
ASIA - ASIE										
Georgia - Géorgie										
5 XI 2014 .... DJ	DJ	3 713 804	1 772 864	1 940 940	...	4 453	3 728[86]	...	69 700	53
India - Inde										
9 II 2011 .... DF	DF	1 210 854 977[87]	623 270 258[87]	587 584 719[87]	DF	1 176 742[88]	1 283 600[88]	1.2	3 287 263	390
Indonesia - Indonésie										
1 V 2010 .... DJ	DJ	237 641 326	119 630 913	118 010 413	DJ	238 519[89]	261 891[89]	1.3	1 910 931	137
Iran (Islamic Republic of) - Iran (République islamique d')										
24 IX 2016 .... DJ	DJ	79 926 270	40 498 442	39 427 828	DJ	74 340[90]	81 070[90]	1.2	1 628 762[91]	50
Iraq										
16 X 1997 .... DF	DF	19 184 543[92]	9 536 570[92]	9 647 973[92]	DF	32 211	...	...	435 052	...
Israel - Israël										
27 XII 2008 .... DF	DF	7 412 180[93]	3 663 910[93]	3 748 270[93]	DJ	7 624[94]	*8 713[94]	1.9	22 072	395
Japan - Japon										
1 X 2015 .... DJ	DJ	127 094 745[95]	61 841 738[95]	65 253 007[95]	DJ	128 070[95]	126 786[96]	-0.1	377 930[97]	335
Jordan - Jordanie										
30 XI 2015 .... DF	DF	9 531 712[98]	5 046 822[98]	4 484 890[98]	DF	6 699[99]	10 053[99]	5.8	89 318	113
Kazakhstan										
25 II 2009 .... DF	DF	16 009 597	7 712 224	8 297 373	DF	16 322[100]	18 038[100]	1.4	2 724 902	7
Kuwait - Koweït										
21 IV 2011 .... DF	DF	3 065 850	1 738 372	1 327 478	DF	2 933	4 083[29]	4.7	17 818	229
Kyrgyzstan - Kirghizstan										
24 III 2009 .... DJ	DJ	5 362 793	2 645 921	2 716 872	DJ	5 448[23]	6 198[23]	1.8	199 949	31
Lao People's Democratic Republic - République démocratique populaire lao										
1 III 2015 .... DJ	DJ	6 492 400	3 254 800	3 237 600	DJ	6 230[11]	6 901[11]	1.5	236 800	29
Lebanon - Liban										
1 X 2011 .... SDF	SDF	3 779 859[101]	1 840 940[101]	1 938 919[101]		...	...	...	10 452	...
Malaysia - Malaisie										
6 VII 2010 .... DJ	DJ	28 334 135[102]	14 562 638[102]	13 771 497[102]	DJ	28 589[103]	32 050[103]	1.6	330 345	97
Maldives										
20 IX 2014 .... DF	DF	402 071[104]	227 749[104]	174 322[104]	DF	320	492[105]	6.1	300	1 639
Mongolia - Mongolie										
11 XI 2010 .... DF	DF	2 647 199	1 314 246	1 332 953	DF	2 739	3 149	2.0	1 564 116	2
Myanmar										
29 III 2014 .... DF	DF	51 486 253[106]	24 824 586[106]	26 661 667[106]	DF	59 780[107]	53 388[108]	-1.6	676 553	79
Nepal - Népal										
22 VI 2011 .... DJ	DJ	26 494 504	12 849 041	13 645 463	DJ	28 044	28 826[27]	0.4	147 181	196
Oman										
12 XII 2010 .... DF	DF	2 773 479	1 612 408	1 161 071	DF	...	4 560[109]	...	309 500	15
Pakistan										
15 III 2017 .... DF	DF	*207 774 520[110]	*106 449 322[111]	*101 314 780[111]	DF	173 510[110]	...	...	796 095	...
Philippines										
1 VIII 2015 .... DJ	DJ	100 979 303[112]	51 069 962[112]	49 909 341[112]	DJ	93 135[40]	104 921[40]	1.7	300 000	350
Qatar										
20 IV 2015 .... DF	DF	2 404 776	1 816 981	587 795	DF	1 715	2 725	6.6	11 628	234
Republic of Korea - République de Corée										
1 XI 2015 .... DJ	DJ	51 069 375	25 608 502	25 460 873	DJ	49 554	51 446	0.5	100 339	513
Saudi Arabia - Arabie saoudite										
27 IV 2010 .... DF	DF	27 236 156	15 531 471	11 704 685	DF	27 411	32 613	2.5	2 206 714	15
Singapore - Singapour										
30 VI 2010 .... DJ	DJ	3 771 721[113]	1 861 133[113]	1 910 588[113]	DJ	5 077[114]	5 612[114]	1.4	720[115]	7 795
Sri Lanka										
20 III 2012 .... DJ	DJ	20 359 439	9 856 634	10 502 805	...	20 675	*21 444	...	65 610	327
State of Palestine - État de Palestine										
1 XII 2007 .... DF	DF	3 669 244[116]	1 862 027[116]	1 807 217[116]	DF	4 048	4 952	2.9	6 020	823
Syrian Arab Republic - République arabe syrienne										
22 IX 2004 .... DF	DF	*17 921 000[117]	*9 161 000[117]	*8 760 000[117]	DF	20 619[117]	...	...	185 180	...

3. Population by sex, annual rate of population increase, surface area and density
Population selon le sexe, taux d'accroissement annuel de la population, superficie et densité (continued - suite)

Continent, country or area and census date / Continent, pays ou zone et date du recensement	Census type[a]	Population at the latest available census / Population d'après le dernier recensement disponible (in units — en unités)			Estimate type[a]	Mid-year estimates / Estimations au milieu de l'année (in thousands — en milliers)		Annual rate of increase Taux d'accrois sement annuel 2010-17	Surface area Superficie (km²) 2017	Density Densité 2017[b]
		Both sexes Les deux sexes	Male Masculin	Female Feminin		2010	2017			
ASIA - ASIE										
Tajikistan - Tadjikistan										
21 IX 2010 .... DF	DF	7 564 502	3 817 004	3 747 498	DF	7 519	...	...	142 600	...
Thailand - Thaïlande										
1 IX 2010 .... DJ	DJ	65 981 659	32 355 032	33 626 627	DJ	63 878	65 522	0.4	513 140	128
Timor-Leste										
11 VII 2015 .... DF	DF	1 183 643	601 112	582 531	DF	...	1 242[4]	...	14 919	83
Turkey - Turquie										
3 X 2011 .... DJ	DJ	74 526 000[118]	37 431 000[118]	37 095 000[118]	DJ	73 723[119]	80 313[120]	1.2	780 004	103
Turkmenistan - Turkménistan										
10 I 1995 .... DF	DF	4 483 251	2 225 331	2 257 920		...	...	...	488 100	...
United Arab Emirates - Émirats arabes unis										
5 XII 2005 .... DF	DF	4 106 427[121]	2 806 141[121]	1 300 286[121]	DF	8 264[121]	...	...	71 024[91]	...
Uzbekistan - Ouzbékistan										
12 I 1989 .... DJ	DJ	19 810 077	9 784 156	10 025 921	DJ	28 562[122]	32 121[123]	1.7	448 969	72
Viet Nam										
1 IV 2009 .... DJ	DJ	85 846 997	42 413 143	43 433 854	DJ	86 947[124]	*93 672[124]	1.1	330 967	283
Yemen - Yémen										
16 XII 2004 .... DF	DF	19 685 161	10 036 953	9 648 208	DJ	23 154[4]	...	...	527 968	...
EUROPE										
Åland Islands - Îles d'Åland										
31 XII 2000 .... DJ	DJ	25 776[125]	12 700[125]	13 076[125]	DJ	28[49]	29[49]	0.7	1 583	19
Albania - Albanie										
1 X 2011 .... DJ	DJ	2 800 138	1 403 059	1 397 079	...	2 913	2 873	...	28 748	100
Andorra - Andorre										
31 XII 2011 .... DJ	DJ	78 115[49]	39 863[49]	38 252[49]	DJ	70[126]	...	...	468	...
Austria - Autriche										
31 X 2011 .... DJ	DJ	8 401 940	4 093 938	4 308 002	DJ	8 361	8 773[29]	0.7	83 882	105
Belarus - Bélarus										
14 X 2009 .... DJ	DJ	9 503 807	4 420 039	5 083 768	DJ	9 491	9 498	0.0	207 600	46
Belgium - Belgique										
1 I 2011 .... DJ	DJ	11 000 638	5 401 718	5 598 920	DJ	10 896	11 382	0.6	30 528	373
Bosnia and Herzegovina - Bosnie-Herzégovine										
30 IX 2013 .... DJ	DJ	3 531 159	1 732 270	1 798 889	...	3 843	*3 510[29]	...	51 209	69
Bulgaria - Bulgarie										
1 II 2011 .... DJ	DJ	7 364 570	3 586 571	3 777 999	DJ	7 534	7 076	-0.9	110 372	64
Croatia - Croatie										
1 IV 2011 .... DJ	DJ	4 284 889	2 066 335	2 218 554	DJ	4 295	4 130	-0.6	56 594	73
Czechia - Tchéquie										
25 III 2011 .... DJ	DJ	10 436 560	5 109 766	5 326 794	DJ	10 474	10 594	0.2	78 870	134
Denmark - Danemark[127]										
1 I 2011 .... DJ	DJ	5 560 628[49]	2 756 582[49]	2 804 046[49]	DJ	5 545[49]	5 761[49]	0.5	42 921	134
Estonia - Estonie										
31 XII 2011 .... DJ	DJ	1 294 455	600 526	693 929	DJ	1 331	1 317	-0.2	45 227	29
Faeroe Islands - Îles Féroé										
11 XI 2011 .... DJ	DJ	48 346	25 125	23 221	DJ	49	50	0.4	1 393	36
Finland - Finlande										
31 XII 2010 .... DJ	DJ	5 375 276	2 638 416	2 736 860	DJ	5 335[128]	5 508[49]	0.5	336 866[129]	16
France										
1 I 2006 .... DJ	DJ	61 399 541[130]	29 714 539[130]	31 685 002[130]	DJ	62 918[130]	*64 910[130]	0.4	551 500	118
Germany - Allemagne										
9 V 2011 .... DJ	DJ	80 219 695	39 145 941	41 073 754	DJ	81 757	82 522[131]	0.1	357 578	231
Gibraltar										
12 XI 2012 .... DJ	DJ	32 194[132]	16 061[132]	16 133[132]	DF	31[133]	...	...	6	...
Greece - Grèce										
9 V 2011 .... DF	DF	10 816 286	5 303 223	5 513 063	DF	11 121	10 768[29]	-0.5	131 957	82
Guernsey - Guernesey										
31 III 2015 .... DJ	DJ	62 234	30 819	31 415	DJ	62[134]	62[134]	-0.1	64	972

3. Population by sex, annual rate of population increase, surface area and density
Population selon le sexe, taux d'accroissement annuel de la population, superficie et densité (continued - suite)

Continent, country or area and census date / Continent, pays ou zone et date du recensement	Census type[a]	Population at the latest available census / Population d'après le dernier recensement disponible (in units — en unités)			Estimate type[a]	Mid-year estimates Estimations au milieu de l'année (in thousands — en milliers)		Annual rate of increase Taux d'accrois sement annuel 2010-17	Surface area Superficie (km²) 2017	Density Densité 2017[b]
		Both sexes Les deux sexes	Male Masculin	Female Feminin		2010	2017			
EUROPE										
Holy See - Saint-Siège[135]										
1 VII 2009	DF	466[136]	320	146	DF	0[137]	...	...	0[138]	...
Hungary - Hongrie										
1 X 2011	DF	9 937 628	4 718 479	5 219 149	DJ	10 000	9 788[139]	-0.3	93 022	105
Iceland - Islande										
31 XII 2011	DJ	315 556[140]	158 151[140]	157 405[140]	DJ	318[140]	343[140]	1.1	103 000	3
Ireland - Irlande										
24 IV 2016	DJ	4 761 865	2 354 428	2 407 437	DF	4 560	4 784[29]	0.7	69 825	69
Isle of Man - Île de Man										
24 IV 2016	DF	78 560	...	...	DJ	83[141]	84[141]	0.2	572	146
Italy - Italie										
9 X 2011	DJ	59 433 744	28 745 507	30 688 237	DJ	59 277	60 537	0.3	302 073	200
Jersey										
27 III 2011	DJ	97 857	48 296	49 561	DJ	97	...	...	116	...
Latvia - Lettonie										
1 III 2011	DJ	2 070 371	946 102	1 124 269	DJ	2 098	1 942	-1.1	64 573	30
Liechtenstein										
31 XII 2015	DJ	37 622	...	...	DJ	36	38	0.7	160	237
Lithuania - Lituanie										
1 III 2011	DJ	3 043 429	1 402 604	1 640 825	DJ	3 097	2 828[139]	-1.3	65 286	43
Luxembourg										
1 II 2011	DJ	512 353	254 967	257 386	DJ	507	596	2.3	2 586	231
Malta - Malte										
20 XI 2011	DF	417 432	207 625	209 807	DJ	415[142]	468[142]	1.7	315	1 486
Monaco										
7 VI 2016	DJ	37 308[143]	18 240[143]	19 068[143]	DJ	36[143]	38[144]	0.7	2	18 775
Montenegro - Monténégro										
1 IV 2011	DJ	620 029	306 236	313 793	DJ	619	622[139]	0.1	13 812	45
Netherlands - Pays-Bas										
1 I 2011	DJ	16 655 799	8 243 482	8 412 317	DJ	16 615	17 100	0.4	41 543	412
Norway - Norvège										
19 XI 2011	DJ	4 979 955[145]	2 495 777[145]	2 484 178[145]	DJ	4 889[139]	5 277[146]	1.1	323 772	16
Poland - Pologne										
31 III 2011	DJ	38 044 565	18 420 389	19 624 176	DJ	38 042[139]	37 975[146]	0.0	312 679	121
Portugal										
21 III 2011	DF	10 282 306	4 868 755	5 413 551	DJ	10 573	10 300	-0.4	92 226	112
Republic of Moldova - République de Moldova										
1 IV 2014	DJ	2 804 801[147]	1 352 099[147]	1 452 702[147]	DJ	3 562[147]	...	...	33 846	...
Romania - Roumanie										
20 X 2011	DF	20 039 141	9 736 342	10 302 799	...	20 247[139]	19 644[29]	...	238 391	82
Russian Federation - Fédération de Russie										
14 X 2010	DF	143 436 145	66 457 074	76 979 071	DJ	142 849	...	...	17 098 246	...
San Marino - Saint-Marin										
7 XI 2010	DF	*30 652	*14 791[148]	*15 818[148]	DF	33[49]	34[149]	0.4	61	560
Serbia - Serbie										
1 X 2011	DJ	7 186 862[150]	3 499 176[150]	3 687 686[150]	DJ	7 291[150]	7 021[151]	-0.5	88 417	79
Slovakia - Slovaquie										
21 V 2011	DJ	5 397 036	2 627 772	2 769 264	DJ	5 391	5 439[23]	0.1	49 035[152]	111
Slovenia - Slovénie										
1 I 2015	DJ	2 062 874	1 022 229	1 040 645	DJ	2 049	2 066[23]	0.1	20 273	102
Spain - Espagne										
1 XI 2011	DJ	46 815 915	23 104 350	23 711 560	DJ	46 562	46 549[140]	0.0	505 980	92
Svalbard and Jan Mayen Islands - Îles Svalbard et Jan Mayen										
1 XI 1960	DF	3 431[153]	2 545[153]	886[153]		...	...	...	62 422	...
Sweden - Suède										
31 XII 2011	DJ	9 482 855[49]	4 726 834[49]	4 756 021[49]	DJ	9 378[49]	10 058[154]	1.0	438 574	23
Switzerland - Suisse										
31 XII 2011	DF	8 035 391	3 973 280	4 062 111	DJ	7 825	8 420[155]	1.0	41 291	204

3. Population by sex, annual rate of population increase, surface area and density
Population selon le sexe, taux d'accroissement annuel de la population, superficie et densité (continued - suite)

Continent, country or area and census date / Continent, pays ou zone et date du recensement	Census type[a]	Population at the latest available census / Population d'après le dernier recensement disponible (in units — en unités)			Estimate type[a]	Mid-year estimates / Estimations au milieu de l'année (in thousands — en milliers)		Annual rate of increase / Taux d'accrois sement annuel 2010-17	Surface area / Superficie (km²) 2017	Density / Densité 2017[b]
		Both sexes / Les deux sexes	Male / Masculin	Female / Feminin		2010	2017			
EUROPE										
TFYR of Macedonia - L'ex-R. y. de Macédoine										
31 X 2002 .... DJ	DJ	2 022 547	1 015 377	1 007 170	DJ	2 055	2 075[23]	0.1	25 713	81
Ukraine										
5 XII 2001 .... DF	DF	48 240 902	22 316 317	25 924 585	DF	45 871	42 316[156]	-1.2	603 500	70
United Kingdom of Great Britain and Northern Ireland - Royaume-Uni de Grande-Bretagne et d'Irlande du Nord[157]										
27 III 2011 .... DF	DF	63 379 787	31 126 054	32 253 733	DJ	62 759	65 809[158]	0.7	242 495	271
OCEANIA - OCÉANIE										
American Samoa - Samoas américaines										
1 IV 2010 .... DJ	DJ	55 519[55]	28 164[55]	27 355[55]	DJ	67[55]	...	...	199	...
Australia - Australie										
9 VIII 2016 .... DF	DF	23 717 421[159]	11 686 665[159]	12 030 751[159]	DJ	22 032[160]	24 599[160]	1.6	7 692 024	3
Cook Islands - Îles Cook[161]										
1 XII 2016 .... DF	DF	*17 459	*8 597	*8 862	DF	24	...	...	236	...
Fiji - Fidji										
17 IX 2017 .... DF	DF	884 887	448 595	436 292	DF	857	...	...	18 272	...
French Polynesia - Polynésie française										
17 VIII 2017 .... DF	DF	281 674	...	...	DF	265	...	...	4 000	...
Guam										
1 IV 2010 .... DJ	DJ	159 358	81 552	77 806	DJ	...	164[55]	...	549	298
Kiribati										
7 XI 2015 .... DF	DF	110 136	54 096	56 040		...	...	...	726[162]	...
Marshall Islands - Îles Marshall										
3 IV 2011 .... DF	DF	53 158	27 243	25 915	DF	54[163]	...	...	181	...
Micronesia (Federated States of) - Micronésie (États fédérés de)										
1 IV 2010 .... DJ	DJ	102 843	52 193	50 650	DJ	108[4]	...	...	702	...
Nauru										
31 X 2011 .... DF	DF	10 084	5 105	4 979		...	...	...	21	...
New Caledonia - Nouvelle-Calédonie										
26 VIII 2014 .... DF	DF	268 767	135 542	133 225	DF	250	279[29]	1.6	19 100	15
New Zealand - Nouvelle-Zélande										
5 III 2013 .... DF	DF	4 353 198[164]	2 119 464[164]	2 233 734[164]	DJ	4 351[165]	4 794[165]	1.4	268 107	18
Niue - Nioué										
11 IX 2011 .... DF	DF	1 611	802	809	DJ	1	...	...	260	...
Norfolk Island - Île Norfolk										
9 VIII 2011 .... DF	DF	2 302	1 082	1 220		...	...	...	36	...
Northern Mariana Islands - Îles Mariannes septentrionales										
1 IV 2010 .... DF	DF	53 883	27 746	26 137	DF	48	...	...	457	...
Palau - Palaos										
13 IV 2015 .... DJ	DJ	17 661	9 433	8 228	DJ	21	18	-2.2	459	39
Papua New Guinea - Papouasie-Nouvelle-Guinée										
10 VII 2011 .... DF	DF	7 275 324	3 772 864	3 502 460		...	...	...	462 840	...
Pitcairn										
31 XII 2013 .... DJ	DJ	49	23	26		...	...	...	5	...
Samoa										
7 XI 2016 .... DF	DF	195 979	...	...	DF	184	198[166]	1.0	2 842	70

3. Population by sex, annual rate of population increase, surface area and density
Population selon le sexe, taux d'accroissement annuel de la population, superficie et densité (continued - suite)

Continent, country or area and census date / Continent, pays ou zone et date du recensement	Census type[a]	Population at the latest available census / Population d'après le dernier recensement disponible (in units — en unités)			Estimate type[a]	Mid-year estimates Estimations au milieu de l'année (in thousands — en milliers)		Annual rate of increase Taux d'accrois sement annuel 2010-17	Surface area Superficie (km²) 2017	Density Densité 2017[b]
		Both sexes Les deux sexes	Male Masculin	Female Feminin		2010	2017			

OCEANIA - OCÉANIE

Solomon Islands - Îles Salomon										
22 XI 2009 .... DF	DF	515 870[116]	264 455[116]	251 415[116]	DF	*555*[167]	*653*[167]	2.3	28 896	23
Tokelau - Tokélaou										
18 X 2016 .... DF	DF	1 285	652	633		...	...	...	12	...
Tonga										
30 XI 2016 .... DF	DF	100 266	...	...		...	...	...	747	...
Tuvalu										
4 XI 2012 .... DF	DF	10 782	...	...		...	...	...	26	...
Vanuatu										
7 XI 2016 .... DF	DF	272 459	138 265	134 194	DF	*239*	...	...	12 189	...
Wallis and Futuna Islands - Îles Wallis et Futuna										
23 VII 2018 .... DF	DF	11 562	...	...		...	...	...	142	...

FOOTNOTES - NOTES

Italics: estimates which are less reliable. - Italiques : estimations moins sûres.

* Provisional. - Données provisoires.

[a] 'Code' indicates the source of data, as follows:
DF - De facto
DJ - De jure
SDF - Sample survey, de facto
SDJ - Sample survey, de jure

Le 'Code' indique la source des données, comme suit :
DF - Population de fait
DJ - Population de droit
SDF - Enquête par sondage, population de fait
SDJ - Enquête par sondage, Population de droit

[b] Population per square kilometre of surface area. Figures are estimates of population divided by surface area and are not to be considered either as reflecting density in the urban sense or as indicating the supporting power of a territory's land and resources. - Nombre d'habitants au kilomètre carré. Il s'agit simplement d'estimations de la population divisé par celui de la superficie: il ne faut pas y voir d'indication de la densité au sens urbain du terme ni de l'effectif de population que les terres et les ressources du territoire sont capables de nourrir.

[1] Total resident population including common and collective households of nomadic population, and population counted separately. - Population résidente totale y compris les ménages ordinaires et collectifs de la population nomade, et la population comptée à part.
[2] Unrevised data that do not take into account the results of the 2014 population census. - Ces données n'ont pas été revisées et elles ne prennent pas en compte les résultats du recensement de la population de 2014.
[3] Postcensal estimates. - Estimations post censitaires.
[4] Data refer to national projections. - Les données se réfèrent aux projections nationales.
[5] Data based on the 2011 Census. - Données fondées sur le recensement de 2011.
[6] Excluding Mayotte. - Non compris Mayotte.
[7] Estimates based on the 2014 Population Census. - Estimations fondées sur le recensement de la population de 2014.
[8] Projections based on the 2014 Population Census. - Projections fondées sur le recensement de la population de 2014.
[9] Data are calculated from the results of the Population and Housing Census of 2009. - Les données sont calculées à partir des résultats du recensement de la population et de l'habitat de 2009.

[10] Data refer to projections based on the 1983 Population Census. - Les données se réfèrent aux projections basées sur le recensement de la population de 1983.
[11] Estimates based on the results of 2015 population census. - Estimations fondées sur les résultats du recensement de la population de 2015.
[12] Source: The 1984 Population and Housing Census of Ethiopia (Analytical Report at National Level). - Source : Recensement de la population et des logements de l'Éthiopie en 1984 (rapport analytique au niveau national).
[13] Projections based on the 2000 quick population count results and 1995, 2002 and 2010 Eritrea Demographic and Health Surveys. - Projections fondées sur le dénombrement rapide de la population de 2000 et sur les enquêtes érythréennes de la démographie et de la santé de 1995, 2002 et 2010.
[14] Estimates considering also the results of the 2007 Population Census. - Estimations en prennant en considération les résultats du recensement de la population de 2007.
[15] Post-censal estimates based on the 2009 Population Census. - Les estimations post-censitaire fondées sur le recensement de la population de 2009.
[16] Data are projections based on the 2006 Population Census. - Projections fondées sur le recensement de la population de 2006.
[17] Data refer to Libyan nationals only. - Les données se raportent aux nationaux libyens seulement.
[18] Projections considering also the results of the 2009 Population Census. - Projections en prennant en considération les résultats du recensement de la population de 2009.
[19] Including nomadic population. - Y compris la population nomade.
[20] Excludes the islands of St. Brandon and Agalega. - Non compris les îles St. Brandon et Agalega.
[21] Based on the results of the 2000 Population Census. - Basé sur les résultats du recencement de la population de 2000.
[22] Based on the results of the 2011 Population Census. - Basé sur les résultats du recencement de la population de 2011.
[23] Data refer to annual average population. - Les données correspondent à la population annuelle moyenne.
[24] Based on the results of the 2004 Population Census. - D'après des résultats du recensement de la population de 2004.
[25] Projections based on the results of national survey on population and health conducted between 2010 and 2011, and especially population and housing census 2014. - Des projections de la population fondées sur les résultats de l'enquête nationale de la population et de la santé réalisée entre 2010 et 2011 et, surtout, du recensement général de la population et de l'habitat de 2014.
[26] Data refer to national projections based on 2007 census. - Les données sont des projections nationales d'après les résultats du recensement de la population de 2007.
[27] Data refer to projections based on the 2011 Population Census. - Les données se réfèrent aux projections basées sur le recensement de la population de 2011.
[28] Data are projections based on the 2008 Population and Housing Census. - Projection basée sur le recensement 2008 de la population et des logements.

²⁹ Data refer to 1 January. - Données se raportent au 1 janvier.

³⁰ Projections based on the 2012 Population and Housing Census. - Projections fondées sur le recensement 2012 de la population et des logements.

³¹ Data refer to Saint Helenian resident population. - Pour la population résidante de Sainte-Hélène.

³² Projections based on the 2012 Population Census. - Projections fondées sur le recensement de la population de 2012.

³³ Data refer to 31 December. - Données se raportent au 31 décembre.

³⁴ Surface area is based on the 2002 population and housing census. - La superficie est fondée sur les données provenant du recensement de la population et du logement de 2002.

³⁵ Data have not been adjusted for underenumeration, estimated at 7 per cent. - Les données n'ont pas été ajustées pour compenser les lacunes du dénombrement, estimées à 7 p. 100.

³⁶ Projections based on the 2002 Population Census. - Projections fondées sur le recensement de la population de 2002.

³⁷ Comprising the Northern Region (former Saguia el Hamra) and Southern Region (former Rio de Oro). - Comprend la région septentrionale (ancien Saguia-el-Hamra) et la région méridionale (ancien Rio de Oro).

³⁸ Projections based on the 2010 Population and Housing Census. - Projections fondées sur le recensement 2010 de la population et des logements.

³⁹ Data refers to resident population adjusted for the undercount of 18 per cent and including the institutional population. - Les données concernent la population résidente, y compris la population des institutions, et ont été ajustées pour tenir compte du sous-dénombrement estimé à 18 p. 100.

⁴⁰ Data based on the 2010 Population Census. - Les données sont fondées sur le recensement de la population de 2010.

⁴¹ To ensure confidentiality, the values, including totals are randomly rounded either up or down to a multiple of '5' or '10.' As a result, when these data are summed or grouped, the total value may not match the individual values since totals and sub-totals are independently rounded. Similarly, percentages, which are calculated on rounded data, may not necessarily add up to 100%. - À des fins de confidentialité, les chiffres, y compris les totaux, sont aléatoirement arrondis au multiple de 5 ou de 10 inférieur ou supérieur. Par conséquent, lorsque ces chiffres sont additionnés, le total peut ne pas correspondre à la somme des valeurs individuelles, dans la mesure où les totaux et les totaux partiels sont arrondis indépendamment. De même, la somme des pourcentages, qui sont calculés à partir des données arrondies, peut ne pas correspondre à 100 %.

⁴² Adjusted for census net undercoverage (including adjustment for incompletely enumerated Indian reserves). Final intercensal estimates. - Ajusté pour la sous-estimation du recensement (y compris les réservations en Inde incomplètement énumérées). Estimations inter-censitaires definitives.

⁴³ Adjusted for census net undercoverage (including adjustment for incompletely enumerated Indian reserves). Preliminary postcensal estimates. - Ajusté pour la sous-estimation du recensement (y compris les réservations en Inde incomplètement énumérées). Estimations post censitaires préliminaires.

⁴⁴ Excluding the institutional population. - Non compris la population dans les institutions.

⁴⁵ Based on the national household surveys 2010-2014 and the 2011 population census. - D'après les données de l'enquête nationale des ménages 2010-2014 et les résultats du recensement de la population de 2011.

⁴⁶ Based on the national household survey of 2017. - D'après l'enquête nationale auprès des ménages de 2017.

⁴⁷ Intercensal estimates. - Estimations inter-censitaires.

⁴⁸ Estimates or projections based on the 2007 Population Census. - Estimations ou projections fondées sur le recensement de la population de 2007.

⁴⁹ Population statistics are compiled from registers. - Les statistiques de la population sont compilées à partir des registres.

⁵⁰ Excluding data for Saint Barthélémy and Saint Martin. - Non compris les données pour Saint Barthélémy et Saint Martin.

⁵¹ Projections produced by l'Institut Haïtien de Statistique et d'Informatique (IHSI) and the Latin American and Caribbean Demographic Centre (CELADE) - Population Division of ECLAC. - Les données sont projections produits par l'Institut Haïtien de Statistique et d'Informatique (IHSI) et le centre démographique de l'Amérique latine et les Caraïbes - Division de la population de la CEPALC.

⁵² Data refer to projections based on the 2001 Population Census. - Les données se réfèrent aux projections basées sur le recensement de la population de 2001.

⁵³ The figures represent the census counts adjusted for under-coverage. Adjustments are done by applying weights calculated (to 4 decimal places) for each sex and age group to the enumerated population when the tabulations are produced. Minor discrepancies between totals and the sum of the component parts of a table and minor discrepancies between the totals across tables are due to rounding after weights are applied. - Les chiffres représentent le dénombrement résultant du recensement ajusté pour tenir compte du sous-dénombrement. Les ajustements sont effectués en appliquant un coefficient

de pondération calculé (à la quatrième décimale) pour chaque sexe et groupe d'âges de la population dénombrée lors de l'établissement des tableaux. Les écarts mineurs entre les totaux et la somme des éléments constitutifs d'un tableau ainsi qu'entre les totaux figurant dans différents tableaux sont dus au fait que les chiffres sont arrondis après la pondération.

⁵⁴ Including an estimation of 1 334 585 persons corresponding to 448 195 housing units without information of the occupants. - Y compris une estimation de 1 334 585 personnes correspondant aux 448 195 unités d'habitation sans information sur les occupants.

⁵⁵ Including armed forces stationed in the area. - Y compris les militaires en garnison sur le territoire.

⁵⁶ Including armed forces stationed in the area. Based on the results of the 2010 Population Census. - Y compris les militaires en garnison sur le territoire. D'après le résultats du recensement de la population de 2010.

⁵⁷ Including armed forces stationed in the area. Postcensal estimates. - Y compris les militaires en garnison sur le territoire. Estimations post censitaires.

⁵⁸ Refers to habitable area. Excludes St. Lucia's Forest Reserve. - S'applique à la zone habitable. Exclut la réserve forestière de Sainte-Lucie.

⁵⁹ Excluding residents of institutions. - À l'exclusion de personnes en établissements de soins.

⁶⁰ Including low water level for all islands (area to shoreline). - Incluent le niveau de basses eaux pour toutes les îles.

⁶¹ Excluding U.S. Armed Forces overseas and civilian U.S. citizens whose usual place of residence is outside the United States. Postcensal estimates. - Non compris les militaires américains à l'étranger et les civils américains dont le lieu de résidence habituel est en dehors des États-Unis. Estimations post censitaires.

⁶² Source: U.S. National Center for Health Statistics, National Vital Statistics Reports (NVSR). Including armed forces stationed in the area. - Source : US National Center for Health Statistics, National Vital Statistics Reports (NVSR). Y compris les militaires en garnison sur le territoire.

⁶³ The total area includes continental areas and islands, and excludes Antarctic area. - La superficie totale comprend les zones continentales et les îles, mais n'inclut pas la région de l'Antarctique.

⁶⁴ Data updated according to "Superintendencia Agraria". Interior waters correspond to natural or artificial bodies of water or snow. - Données actualisées d'après la « Superintendencia Agraria ». Les eaux intérieures correspondent aux étendues d'eau naturelles ou artificielles et aux étendues neigeuses.

⁶⁵ Data refer to national projections. Data include persons in remote areas, military personnel outside the country, merchant seamen at sea, civilian seasonal workers outside the country, and other civilians outside the country, and exclude nomads, foreign military, civilian aliens temporarily in the country, transients on ships and Indian jungle population. - Les données se réfèrent aux projections nationales. Y compris les personnes vivant dans des régions éloignées, le personel militaire en dehors du pays, les marins marchands, les ouvriers saisonniers en dehors du pays, et autres civils en dehors du pays, et non compris les nomades, les militaires étrangers, les étrangers civils temporairement dans le pays, les transiteurs sur des bateaux et les Indiens de la jungle.

⁶⁶ Data are revised projections taking into consideration also the results of the 2005 census. - Les données sont des projections révisées tenant compte également des résultats du recensement de 2005.

⁶⁷ Data based on the 2010 Population Census. Excludes nomadic Indian tribes. - Les données sont fondées sur le recensement de la population de 2010. Non compris les tribus d'Indiens nomades.

⁶⁸ Excludes nomadic Indian tribes. - Non compris les tribus d'Indiens nomades.

⁶⁹ A dispute exists between the governments of Argentina and the United Kingdom of Great Britain and Northern Ireland concerning sovereignty over the Falkland Islands (Malvinas). - La souveraineté sur les îles Falkland (Malvinas) fait l'objet d'un différend entre le Gouvernement argentin et le Gouvernement du Royaume-Uni de Grande-Bretagne et d'Irlande du Nord.

⁷⁰ Excluding military personnel and their families, visitors and transients. - Non compris les militaires et leur familles, ni les visiteurs et transients.

⁷¹ Estimates or projections considering also the results of the 2012 Population Census. - Estimations ou projections en prennant en considération les résultats du recensement de la population de 2012.

⁷² Data refer to 30 June. Estimates or projections based on the 2007 Population Census. - Données se raportent au 30 juin. Estimations ou projections fondées sur le recensement de la population de 2007.

⁷³ Figures for male and female population do not add up to the figure for total population, because they exclude 108 homeless people of unknown sex. - Les chiffres relatifs à la population masculine et féminine ne correspondent pas au chiffre de la population totale, parce que l'on en a exclu 108 personnes sans toit dont le sexe n'est pas connu.

⁷⁴ Data refer to the settled population based on the 1979 Population Census and the latest household prelisting. The refugees of Afghanistan in Iran, Pakistan, and an estimated 1.5 million nomads, are not included. Excluding nomad population. - Les données se rapportent à la population stationnaire sur la base du

recensement de 1979 et du recensement préliminaire des logements le plus récent. Sont exclus les réfugiés d'Afghanistan en Iran et au Pakistan et les nomades estimés à 1,5 million. Non compris les nomades.

75 Data refer to the settled population based on the 1979 Population Census and the latest household prelisting. The refugees of Afghanistan in Iran, Pakistan, and an estimated 1.5 million nomads, are not included. - Les données se rapportent à la population stationnaire sur la base du recensement de 1979 et du recensement préliminaire des logements le plus récent. Sont exclus les réfugiés d'Afghanistan en Iran et au Pakistan et les nomades estimés à 1,5 million.

76 Data refer to projected figures based on the Population and Housing Census 2005 (district projection). - Les données se réfèrent aux projections basées sur le recensement de la population et de l'habitat de 2005 (projections locales).

77 Excluding foreign diplomatic personnel and their dependants. - Non compris le personnel diplomatique étranger et les membres de leur famille les accompagnant.

78 Excluding foreign diplomatic personnel and their dependants. Data based on the 2008 Population Census. - Non compris le personnel diplomatique étranger et les membres de leur famille les accompagnant. Données fondées sur le recensement de population de 2008.

79 Data are from Communique of the National Bureau of Statistics of the People's Republic of China on Major Figures of the 2010 Population Census (No.1). For statistical purposes, the data for China do not include those for the Hong Kong Special Administrative Region (Hong Kong SAR), Macao Special Administrative Region (Macao SAR) and Taiwan province of China. - Données issues du communiqué du Bureau national de la statistique de la République populaire de Chine sur les chiffres importants du recensement de 2010 (n° 1). Pour la présentation des statistiques, les données pour la Chine ne comprennent pas la Région Administrative Spéciale de Hong Kong (Hong Kong RAS), la Région Administrative Spéciale de Macao (Macao RAS) et Taïwan province de Chine.

80 For statistical purposes, the data for China do not include those for the Hong Kong Special Administrative Region (Hong Kong SAR), Macao Special Administrative Region (Macao SAR) and Taiwan province of China. Data have been estimated on the basis of the annual National Sample Survey on Population Changes. - Pour la présentation des statistiques, les données pour la Chine ne comprennent pas la Région Administrative Spéciale de Hong Kong (Hong Kong RAS), la Région Administrative Spéciale de Macao (Macao RAS) et Taïwan province de Chine. Les données ont été estimées sur la base de l'enquête annuelle "National Sample Survey on Population Changes".

81 Data refer to Hong Kong resident population at the census moment, which covers usual residents and mobile residents. Usual residents refer to two categories of people: (1) Hong Kong permanent residents who had stayed in Hong Kong for at least three months during the six months before or for at least three months during the six months after the census moment, regardless of whether they were in Hong Kong or not at the census moment; and (2) Hong Kong non-permanent residents who were in Hong Kong at the census moment. Mobile Residents, they are Hong Kong permanent residents who had stayed in Hong Kong for at least one month but less than three months during the six months before or for at least one month but less than three months during the six months after the census moment, regardless of whether they were in Hong Kong or not at the census moment. Data are estimates from sample enquiry. - Les données se rapportent à la population résidente à Hong Kong au moment du recensement. Cette population est composée des résidants habituels et des résidants mobiles. La population résidente est partagée en deux catégories: (1) les résidents permanents qui ont habité à Hong Kong au moins trois mois pendant les six mois précédents ou les six mois suivants le recensement; (2) les habitants non-permanents de Hong Kong qui étaient à Hong Kong au moment du recensement. La population mobile se rapporte aux résidents permanents de Hong Kong qui ont habité à Hong Kong pendant les six mois après le recensement pour une période comprise entre un mois et trois mois, indépendamment du fait qu'ils étaient à Hong Kong au moment du recensement au pays. Les données sont des chiffres estimatifs dérivés d'une enquête par sondage.

82 Inland waters include the reservoirs. - Les eaux intérieures comprennent les réservoirs.

83 Data refer to government controlled areas. - Les données se rapportent aux zones contrôlées par le Gouvernement.

84 Data refer to government controlled areas. Data refer to annual average population. - Les données se rapportent aux zones contrôlées par le Gouvernement. Les données correspondent à la population annuelle moyenne.

85 Data refer to government controlled areas. Data refer to 1 January. - Les données se rapportent aux zones contrôlées par le Gouvernement. Données se raportent au 1 janvier.

86 Based on the results of the 2014 Population Census. - D'après les résultats du recensement de la population de 2014.

87 Includes data for the Indian-held part of Jammu and Kashmir, the final status of which has not yet been determined. - Y compris les données pour la partie du

Jammu et du Cachemire occupée par l'Inde dont le statut définitif n'a pas encore été déterminé.

88 Includes data for the Indian-held part of Jammu and Kashmir, the final status of which has not yet been determined. Data refer to 1 March. Data refer to projections based on the 2001 Population Census. - Y compris les données pour la partie du Jammu et du Cachemire occupée par l'Inde dont le statut définitif n'a pas encore été déterminé. Données se raportent au 1 mars. Les données se réfèrent aux projections basées sur le recensement de la population de 2001.

89 Data are based on the publication: "Indonesia Population Projection 2010-2035" - Les données sont basées sur la publication : << Indonesia Population Projection 2010-2035 >>

90 Data refer to the Iranian Year which begins on 21 March and ends on 20 March of the following year. - Les données concernent l'année iranienne, qui commence le 21 mars et se termine le 20 mars de l'année suivante.

91 Land area only. - La superficie des terres seulement.

92 Excluding the population in three autonomous provinces in the north of the country. - La population des trois provinces autonomes dans le nord du pays est exclue.

93 Includes data for East Jerusalem and Israeli residents in certain other territories under occupation by Israeli military forces since June 1967. Data are rounded for confidentiality reasons. - Y compris les données pour Jérusalem-Est et les résidents israéliens dans certains autres territoires occupés depuis 1967 par les forces armées israéliennes. Chiffres arrondis pour des raisons de confidentialité.

94 Includes data for East Jerusalem and Israeli residents in certain other territories under occupation by Israeli military forces since June 1967. Data refer to Israeli citizens and permanent residents who are listed in the Population Register. - Y compris les données pour Jérusalem-Est et les résidents israéliens dans certains autres territoires occupés 1967 par les forces armées israéliennes. Les données se rapportent aux citoyens israéliens et aux résidents permanents qui sont répertoriés dans le registre de la population.

95 Excluding diplomatic personnel outside the country and foreign military and civilian personnel and their dependants stationed in the area. - Non compris le personnel diplomatique hors du pays ni les militaires et agents civils étrangers en poste sur le territoire et les membres de leur famille les accompagnant.

96 Excluding diplomatic personnel outside the country and foreign military and civilian personnel and their dependants stationed in the area. Estimates based on the complete counts of the 2015 Population Census. - Non compris le personnel diplomatique hors du pays ni les militaires et agents civils étrangers en poste sur le territoire et les membres de leur famille les accompagnant. Estimations basées sur le dénombrement complet du recensement de la population de 2015.

97 Data refer to 1 October 2007. - Les données se réfèrent au 1er octobre 2007.

98 Excluding data for Jordanian territory under occupation since June 1967 by Israeli military forces. - Non compris les données pour le territoire jordanien occupé depuis juin 1967 par les forces armées israéliennes.

99 Excluding data for Jordanian territory under occupation since June 1967 by Israeli military forces. Data refer to 31 December. - Non compris les données pour le territoire jordanien occupé depuis juin 1967 par les forces armées israéliennes. Données se raportent au 31 décembre.

100 Recalculated population estimates taking into account late registration of births and deaths until May 2017. Data refer to resident population. - Réestimation du nombre d'habitants compte tenu de l'enregistrement tardif des naissances et des décès jusqu'en mai 2017. Les données concernent la population résidente.

101 Source: Living conditions of household survey, October 2011 to September 2012. - Source: Enquête sur les conditions de vie des ménages, octobre 2011 à septembre 2012.

102 Data have been adjusted for underenumeration. - Les données ont été ajustées pour compenser les lacunes du dénombrement.

103 Estimates based on the adjusted results of the Population and Housing Census of 2010. - Les estimations sont fondée sur les résultats ajustées du recensement de la population et de l'habitat de 2010.

104 Data refer to resident population which includes resident Maldivians and resident foreigners. - Les données concernent la population résidente, qui comprend les Maldiviens et les étrangers.

105 Data refer to resident population which includes resident Maldivians and resident foreigners. Estimates based on the 2014 Population Census. - Les données concernent la population résidente, qui comprend les Maldiviens et les étrangers. Estimations fondées sur le recensement de la population de 2014.

106 The total for the whole country includes 1,206,353 persons estimated not to have been counted in parts of States of Rakhine, Kachin and Kayin. - Le total pour l'ensemble du pays s'élève à 1 206 353 personnes qui ne vivraient pas dans les États rakhine, kachin et kayin.

107 Data refer to 1 October. - Données se raportent au 1 octobre.

108 Data refer to 1 October. Based on the results of the 2014 Population Census. - Données se raportent au 1 octobre. D'après les résultats du recensement de la population de 2014.

109 Data refer to registered population data from Royal Oman Police. - Les données portent sur la population enregistrée par la police royale de l'Oman.

110 Excluding data for the Pakistan-held part of Jammu and Kashmir, the final status of which has not yet been determined. - Non compris les données concernant la partie du Jammu et Cachemire occupée par le Pakistan dont le statut définitif n'a pas été déterminé.

111 Excluding data for the Pakistan-held part of Jammu and Kashmir, the final status of which has not yet been determined. Figures for male and female may not add up to the total, since they do not include the category "Unknown". - Non compris les données concernant la partie du Jammu et Cachemire occupée par le Pakistan dont le statut définitif n'a pas été déterminé. La somme des chiffres indiqués pour les sexes masculin et féminin peut n'être pas égale au total parce qu'elle n'inclut pas la catégorie " inconnue ".

112 Excluding 2134 Filipinos in Philippine Embassies, Consulates and Missions Abroad. - Excepté 2134 Philippins travaillant dans les ambassades, les consulats et les missions des Philippines à l'étranger.

113 Data are based on the latest register-based population estimates for 2010. Data refer to resident population which comprises Singapore citizens and permanent residents. Urban and rural breakdown not applicable as Singapore is a city-state. - Données basées sur les estimations démographiques les plus récentes fondées sur les registres de 2010. Les données se rapportent à la population résidente composé des citoyens de Singapour et des résidents permanents. La ventilation entre zones urbaines et zones rurales ne s'applique pas à Singapour, puisqu'il s'agit d'une ville État.

114 Data refer to total population, which comprises Singapore residents and non-residents. Data refer to 30 June. Data exclude residents who have been away from Singapore for a continuous period of 12 months or longer as at the reference date. - Les données se rapportent à la population totale composé des résidents de Singapour et les non résidents. Données se rapportent au 30 juin. Non compris les résidents hors de Singapour pour une période ininterrompue de 12 mois ou plus avant de la date de référence.

115 The land area of Singapore comprises the mainland and other islands. - La superficie terrestre de Singapour comprend l'île principale et les autres îles.

116 Data have not been adjusted for underenumeration. - Les données n'ont pas été ajustées pour compenser les lacunes du dénombrement.

117 Including Palestinian refugees. - Y compris les réfugiés de Palestine.

118 Based on a sample taken at the time of census. Because of rounding, totals are not in all cases the sum of the respective components. - D'après un échantillon obtenu au moment du recensement. Les chiffres étant arrondis, les totaux ne correspondent pas toujours rigoureusement à la somme des composants respectifs.

119 Data refer to 31 December. Data based on Address Based Population Registration System. - Données se raportent au 31 décembre. Les données sont basées sur le registre national de la population basé sur l'adresse.

120 Data based on address-based population registration system. - Les données sont basées sur le registre national de la population basé sur l'adresse.

121 Data include non-national population. - Les données comprennent les non-nationaux.

122 Data refer to resident population. - Les données concernent la population résidente.

123 Data refer to resident population. Data refer to 1 January. - Les données concernent la population résidente. Données se raportent au 1 janvier.

124 Data are adjusted according to the results of the 2009 census and 2014 intercensus. - Les données ont été ajustées à partir des résultats du recensement de la population de 2009 et des données intercensitaires de 2014.

125 Statistics are compiled from registers. - Les statistiques sont compilées à partir des registres.

126 Decrease in population due to revision in administrative registers. Population statistics are compiled from registers. Data refer to 1 January. - Diminution de la population due à la révision des registres administratifs. Les statistiques de la population sont compilées à partir des registres. Données se raportent au 1 janvier.

127 Excluding Faeroe Islands and Greenland shown separately, if available. - Non compris les Iles Féroé et le Groenland, qui font l'objet de rubriques distinctes, si disponible.

128 Population statistics are compiled from registers. Excluding Åland Islands. - Les statistiques de la population sont compilées à partir des registres. Non compris les Îles d'Åland.

129 Excluding Åland Islands. - Non compris les Îles d'Åland.

130 Excluding diplomatic personnel outside the country and including members of alien armed forces not living in military camps and foreign diplomatic personnel not living in embassies or consulates. - Non compris le personnel diplomatique hors du pays et y compris les militaires étrangers ne vivant pas dans des camps militaires et le personnel diplomatique étranger ne vivant pas dans les ambassades ou les consulats.

131 Data refer to 1 January. Data based on the 2011 Census. - Données se raportent au 1 janvier. Données fondées sur le recensement de 2011.

132 Excluding military personnel, visitors and transients. - Non compris les militaires, ni les visiteurs et transients.

133 Excluding military personnel, visitors and transients. Data refer to 31 December. - Non compris les militaires, ni les visiteurs et transients. Données se raportent au 31 décembre.

134 Data refer to 31 March. - Données se raportent au 31 mars.

135 Data refer to the Vatican City State. - Les données se rapportent à l'Etat de la Cité du Vatican.

136 The population figure is 466 persons. - La population est égale à 466 personnes.

137 The population figure is 466 persons. Data refer to 6 December. - La population est égale à 466 personnes. Données se raportent au 6 décembre.

138 Surface area is 0.44 km². - Superficie: 0,44 km².

139 Data refer to usually resident population. - Les données concernent la population habituellement résidente.

140 Data refer to registered resident population. - Les données concernent la population enregistrée résidente.

141 Data refer to 30 April. - Données se raportent au 30 avril.

142 Including civilian nationals temporarily outside the country. - Y compris les civils nationaux temporairement hors du pays.

143 Data refer to resident population only. - Pour la population résidante seulement.

144 Data refer to resident population only. Data refer to 1 January. - Pour la population résidante seulement. Données se raportent au 1 janvier.

145 Including residents temporarily outside the country. Population statistics are compiled from registers. - Y compris les résidents se trouvant temporairement hors du pays. Les statistiques de la population sont compilées à partir des registres.

146 Data refer to annual average population. Data refer to usually resident population. - Les données correspondent à la population annuelle moyenne. Les données concernent la population habituellement résidente.

147 Excluding Transnistria and the municipality of Bender. - Les données ne tiennent pas compte de l'information sur la Transnistria et la municipalité de Bender.

148 Figures for male and female may not add up to the total, since they do not include the category "Unknown". - La somme des chiffres indiqués pour les sexes masculin et féminin peut n'être pas égale au total parce qu'elle n'inclut pas la catégorie " inconnue ".

149 Data refer to 1 January. Population statistics are compiled from registers. - Données se raportent au 1 janvier. Les statistiques de la population sont compilées à partir des registres.

150 Excludes data for Kosovo and Metohia. - Sans les données pour le Kosovo et Metohie.

151 Excludes data for Kosovo and Metohia. Data refer to annual average population. Based on the results of the 2011 Population Census. - Sans les données pour le Kosovo et Metohie. Les données correspondent à la population annuelle moyenne. Basé sur les résultats du recencement de la population de 2011.

152 Excluding inland water. - Exception faite des eaux intérieures.

153 Inhabited only during the winter season. The Norwegian population of these islands is included also in the de jure population of Norway. - N'est habitée que pendant la saison d'hiver. La population norvégienne de ces îles est comprise également dans la population de droit de la Norvège.

154 Population statistics are compiled from registers. Data refer to annual average population. Data refer to registered resident population. - Les statistiques de la population sont compilées à partir des registres. Les données correspondent à la population annuelle moyenne. Les données concernent la population enregistrée résidente.

155 Data refer to legal resident population. Data refer to 1 January. - Les données concernent la population légalement résidente. Données se raportent au 1 janvier.

156 Data refer to annual average population. The Government of Ukraine has informed the United Nations that it is not in a position to provide statistical data concerning the Autonomous Republic of Crimea and the city of Sevastopol. - Les données correspondent à la population annuelle moyenne. Le gouvernement Ukrainien a informé l'ONU qu'il n'est pas en mesure de fournir des données statistiques concernant la République autonome de Crimée et la ville de Sébastopol.

157 Excluding Channel Islands (Guernsey and Jersey) and Isle of Man, shown separately, if available. - Non compris les îles Anglo-Normandes (Guernesey et Jersey) et l'île de Man, qui font l'objet de rubriques distinctes, si disponible.

[158] Data refer to 1 January. Data refer to usually resident population. - Données se raportent au 1 janvier. Les données concernent la population habituellement résidente.

[159] Including population in off-shore, migratory and shipping. These data have been randomly rounded to protect confidentiality. Individual figures may not add up to totals, and values for the same data may vary in different tables. - Y compris les populations extraterritoriales, les populations nomades et les populations maritimes. Ces données ont été arrondies de façon aléatoire afin d'en préserver la confidentialité. La somme de certains chiffres peut ne pas correspondre aux totaux indiqués et les valeurs des mêmes données peuvent varier d'un tableau à un autre.

[160] Based on the results of the 2016 Population Census. - Basé sur les résultats du recencement de la population de 2016.

[161] Excluding Niue, shown separately, which is part of Cook Islands, but because of remoteness is administered separately. - Non compris Nioué, qui fait l'objet d'une rubrique distincte et qui fait partie des îles Cook, mais qui, en raison de son éloignement, est administrée séparément.

[162] Land area only. Excluding 84 square km of uninhabited islands. - La superficie des terres seulement. Exclut des îles inhabitées d'une superficie de 84 kilomètres carrés.

[163] Projections are prepared by the Secretariat of the Pacific Community based on the 1999 census of population and housing. - Les projections sont preparées par le Secrétariat de la Communauté du Pacifique à partir des résultats du recensement de la population et de l'habitat de 1999.

[164] These data have been randomly rounded to protect confidentiality. Individual figures may not add up to totals, and values for the same data may vary in different tables. Data include overseas visitors in New Zealand on census night. - Ces données ont été arrondies de façon aléatoire afin d'en préserver la confidentialité. La somme de certains chiffres peut ne pas correspondre aux totaux indiqués et les valeurs des mêmes données peuvent varier d'un tableau à un autre. Y compris les visiteurs étrangers qui se trouvaient en Nouvelle-Zélande le soir du recensement.

[165] Because of rounding, totals are not in all cases the sum of the respective components. - Les chiffres étant arrondis, les totaux ne correspondent pas toujours rigoureusement à la somme des composants respectifs.

[166] Estimates based on the 2016 Population Census. - Estimations basées sur le recensement de la population de 2016.

[167] Projections based on adjusted 2009 census counts. - Projections fondées à partir des comptes rajustés du recensement de 2009.

Table 3a presents the values of the Whipple's index by sex, urban or rural residence, for total area and both sexes combined, according to the availability of the underlying data in the *Demographic Yearbook* database.

The data used to compile these indices are the datasets of population by single years of age, sex, and urban or rural residence, of the population censuses conducted worldwide since 1985. These datasets have been reported by the National Statistical Offices to the United Nations Statistics Division via the *Demographic Yearbook* questionnaires.

The footnotes that appear at the end of this table are notes that refer to the respective dataset of population by single years of age, sex, and urban or rural residence.

Whipple's index is an index of age preference in age reporting. The way it is calculated for this table, it is meant to indicate preference or avoidance of ages ending in digits "0" (zero) or "5" (five) during age reporting for a population census.

The formula used to calculate the values of the Whipple's index for this table is:

$$\frac{P25+P30+P35+P40+P45+P50+P55+P60}{\frac{1}{5}(P23+P24+P25+\cdots+P58+P59+P60+P61+P62)}*100$$

where Px refers to the number of persons of age x in completed years. The sum in brackets in the denominator is the sum of the number of persons of every single age from 23 to 62.

The values of the Whipple's index generally vary between 100, indicating no preference for "0" or "5" (in other words no heaping in ages ending in "0" or "5"), and 500, indicating that age reporting was entirely concentrated in ages ending in digits "0" or "5". The higher than 100 the value of the index, the higher is the heaping of age reporting in ages ending in "0" or "5".

For more information about the measurement of age and digit preference, please refer to *The Methods and Materials of Demography, Second Edition* (2004), Edited by Jacob S. Siegel and David A. Swanson.

Tableau 3a – *Annuaire démographique 2017*

Le tableau 3a présente les valeurs de l'indice de Whipple par sexe, résidence urbaine ou rurale, pour la superficie totale et les sexes combinés, selon la disponibilité des données sous-jacentes dans la base de données de l'*Annuaire démographique*.

Les données utilisées pour établir ces indices sont les séries de données de la population par âge simple, sexe et résidence urbaine ou rurale, pour les recensements de la population effectués dans le monde entier depuis 1985. Ces séries de données sont communiquées par les services nationaux de statistique à la Division de statistique de l'Organisation des Nations Unies par le biais des questionnaires de l'*Annuaire démographique*.

Les notes qui figurent à la fin de ce tableau sont des notes renvoyant aux différentes séries de données de la population par âge simple, sexe et résidence urbaine ou rurale.

L'indice de Whipple est un indice de préférence de certains âges dans les déclarations de l'âge. La manière dont il est calculé pour ce tableau permet d'indiquer l'attraction ou la répulsion pour des âges se terminant par les chiffres « 0 » (zéro) ou « 5 » (cinq) lors de la déclaration de l'âge effectuée dans le cadre d'un recensement de population.

La formule utilisée pour calculer les valeurs de l'indice de Whipple pour ce tableau est la suivante:

$$\frac{P25+P30+P35+P40+P45+P50+P55+P60}{\frac{1}{5}(P23+P24+P25+\cdots+P58+P59+P60+P61+P62)} *100$$

Px étant le nombre de personnes d'âge x en années révolues. La somme entre parenthèses en dénominateur est la somme du nombre de personnes selon l'âge simple de 23 à 62 ans.

Les valeurs de l'indice de Whipple varient généralement entre 100, indication d'absence de préférence pour « 0 » ou « 5 » (en d'autres termes pas de prépondérance des âges se terminant par « 0 » ou « 5 »), et 500, indiquant que les déclarations de l'âge étaient entièrement polarisées sur les âges se terminant par les chiffres « 0 » ou « 5 ». Plus la valeur de l'indice est supérieure à 100, plus les déclarations de l'âge sont polarisées sur les âges se terminant par « 0 » ou « 5 ».

Pour en savoir plus sur la mesure de l'âge et la préférence pour les chiffres, prière de consulter l'ouvrage intitulé *The Methods and Materials of Demography, Second Edition (2004)*, publié sous la direction de Jacob S. Siegel et David A. Swanson.

3a. Whipple's Index by sex and urban/rural residence, 1985 - 2017
L'indice de Whipple par le sexe et la résidence urbaine/rurale, 1985 - 2017

Continent, country or area, date and code[a] Continent, pays ou zone, date et code[a]	Total			Urban - Urbaine			Rural - Rurale		
	Both sexes Les deux sexes	Male Masculin	Female Féminin	Both sexes Les deux sexes	Male Masculin	Female Féminin	Both sexes Les deux sexes	Male Masculin	Female Féminin
AFRICA - AFRIQUE									
Algeria - Algérie[1]									
16 IV 2008 (CDJC)	100.7	100.5	100.9	100.7	100.5	100.9	100.7	100.6	100.8
Angola									
16 V 2014 (CDFC)	106.1	105.3	106.8	104.9	104.5	105.4	108.2	107.1	109.1
Benin - Bénin									
15 II 1992 (CDFC)	216.1	205.6	224.6	185.4	171.6	197.9	234.6	228	239.6
11 II 2002 (CDJC)	229.1	218.9	237.8	190.4	180.1	200	257.5	250	263.5
Botswana									
21 VIII 1991 (CDFC)	104.8	106.6	103.3	102.4	103.6	101.4	107.7	110.8	105.3
17 VIII 2001 (CDFC)	100.9	101.8	100.2	...	...	...	...	...	...
9 VIII 2011 (CDFC)	100.8	101.3	100.3	101.7	101.8	101.6	99	100.5	97.5
Burkina Faso									
10 XII 1985 (CDJC)	193	173.8	208.4	153.1	140.9	166.7	198.6	179.4	213.2
10 XII 1996 (CDJC)	162.6[2]	144[2]	177.5[2]	99.5[3]	99.6[3]	99.5[3]	99.6[3]	99.7[3]	99.5[3]
9 XII 2006 (CDJC)	145.1	133.8	154.5	131.1	130.5	131.8	150.2	135.3	161.5
Burundi									
16 VIII 1990 (CDJC)	152.9	141.7	163	...	...	...	...	...	...
16 VIII 2008 (CDJC)	156.8	149.4	164.4	137.2	136.5	138.3	159.4	151.5	167.1
Cabo Verde									
23 VI 1990 (CDFC)	111.9	110.7	112.8	108	107.7	108.3	115.3	113.7	116.4
16 VI 2010 (CDJC)	105.8	105.7	105.9	105.3	105.1	105.6	106.7	106.8	106.5
Cameroon - Cameroun									
11 XI 2005 (CDJC)	173.5	165.1	181.4	...	...	...	...	...	...
Central African Republic - République centrafricaine									
8 XII 1988 (CDFC)	139.4	132	146.1	129.9	125.2	134.3	144.5	135.8	152.3
Congo									
1 I 1985 (CDJC)	107.3	107.5	107.1	...	...	...	...	...	...
28 IV 2007 (CDFC)	103.5	103.1	103.8	...	...	...	...	...	...
Côte d'Ivoire									
1 III 1988 (CDFC)	126.3	117.3	136.2	116.4	112.7	121	132.7	120.5	145
15 V 2014 (CDJC)	116.5	114.3	118.9	112.3	111.8	112.9	121.2	117.1	125.6
Egypt - Égypte									
21 XI 2006 (CDFC)	196.5	175.3	218.2	177.1	162.7	191.9	213.5	186.4	241.4
Eswatini									
25 VIII 1986 (CDFC)	125.9	125.4	126.3	118.3	118.2	118.5	129.3	130.1	128.8
11 V 1997 (CDFC)	120.6	121.5	119.7	116.9	117.9	115.8	122.3	123.7	121.2
11 V 2007 (CDJC)	99.8	101.2	98.6	99	100.7	97.4	100.1	101.5	99.1
Ethiopia - Éthiopie									
11 X 1994 (CDFC)	272.3	258.9	285	248.7	232.6	264	276.5	263.7	288.7
29 V 2007 (CDFC)	252.1	241	262.9	232.3	222.5	242.4	256.7	245.4	267.5
Gabon									
31 VII 1993 (CDFC)	116.6	115.9	117.4	...	...	...	...	...	...
Gambia - Gambie									
15 IV 1993 (CDFC)	229.8	215.2	244.5	191.2	183.2	201.2	256.2	241.6	268.9
Ghana									
26 III 2000 (CDFC)	184	175.8	191.6	159.7	154.7	164.5	205.6	195.2	215.3
26 IX 2010 (CDFC)	159.1	155.2	162.5	138.3	136.6	139.8	184.7	178.2	190.6
Guinea - Guinée									
15 III 2014 (CDJC)	200.7	185	214	166.2	160.8	171.9	221.1	202.1	235.4
Guinea-Bissau - Guinée-Bissau[4]									
15 III 2009 (CDJC)	137.8	128.9	145.7	...	...	...	...	...	...
Kenya									
24 VIII 1989 (CDJC)	147.8	142.6	152.8	144.1	140.8	149.4	148.9	143.3	153.5
24 VIII 1999 (CDJC)	148.3	143.2	153.2	...	...	...	...	...	...
24 VIII 2009 (CDJC)	146.4	144.6	148.2	141.1	141.1	141.2	149.8	147.1	152.2
Lesotho									
13 IV 2006 (CDJC)	105.3	105.8	104.9	...	...	...	...	...	...
Liberia - Libéria									
21 III 2008 (CDFC)	142.2	136.3	148.1	...	...	...	...	...	...
Malawi									
1 IX 1987 (CDFC)	138.5	137.9	139.1	...	...	...	...	...	...
1 IX 1998 (CDFC)	147.7	149.2	146.4	142.6	146.5	137.3	148.7	149.7	147.7
8 VI 2008 (CDFC)	120.6	121	120.2	113	114.7	111	122.2	122.5	121.9
Mali									
1 IV 1987 (CDJC)	184.5	171.4	195.9	163.7	154.1	173	190.4	176.7	202
1 IV 1998 (CDJC)	180.1	166.8	192.3	166.5	158	175.2	185.6	170.7	198.6

3a. Whipple's Index by sex and urban/rural residence, 1985 - 2017
L'indice de Whipple par le sexe et la résidence urbaine/rurale, 1985 - 2017 (continued - suite)

Continent, country or area, date and code[a] / Continent, pays ou zone, date et code[a]	Total			Urban - Urbaine			Rural - Rurale		
	Both sexes Les deux sexes	Male Masculin	Female Féminin	Both sexes Les deux sexes	Male Masculin	Female Féminin	Both sexes Les deux sexes	Male Masculin	Female Féminin
AFRICA - AFRIQUE									
1 IV 2009 (CDFC).............	156.5	145.7	166.6	142.7	139.1	146.8	161.1	148.2	172.5
Mauritius - Maurice[5]									
1 VII 1990 (CDFC).............	103.4	102.4	104.3	...	...	...	...	...	...
2 VII 2000 (CDJC).............	102.4	102.1	102.7	102.3	102	102.7	102.5	102.2	102.7
4 VII 2011 (CDJC).............	100.6	101	100.3	100.8	101.2	100.3	100.5	100.9	100.2
Mayotte									
31 VII 2007 (CDJC).............	124.4	126.9	122.3	...	...	...	...	...	...
21 VIII 2012 (CDJC).............	101.1	102.9	99.6	...	...	...	...	...	...
Morocco - Maroc									
1 IX 2004 (CDFC).............	113.4	108.4	118	110.1	107.5	112.5	118.2	109.8	126.2
Mozambique									
1 VIII 1997 (CDJC).............	118.6	117.9	119.3	111.7	110.9	112.4	121.5	121	121.9
1 VIII 2007 (CDFC).............	126	126.2	125.9	...	...	...	...	...	...
Namibia - Namibie									
21 X 1991 (CDFC).............	105.8	104.9	106.5	103.5	102.9	104.2	107.1	106.4	107.6
27 VIII 2001 (CDFC).............	103.9	103.2	104.5	103.6	102.9	104.4	104.1	103.5	104.6
28 VIII 2011 (CDFC).............	103.9	103.8	104	104.3	103.6	105	103.4	104.1	102.9
Niger									
20 V 2001 (CDJC).............	270.1	254.7	285.2	...	...	...	...	...	...
10 XII 2012 (CDJC).............	105.1	104.7	105.4	...	...	...	...	...	...
Nigeria - Nigéria									
26 XI 1991 (CDFC).............	293.5	279.8	307.1	...	...	...	...	...	...
Republic of South Sudan - République de Soudan du Sud									
21 IV 2008 (CDFC).............	183.1	178.4	187.9	...	...	...	...	...	...
Reunion - Réunion									
15 III 1990 (CDFC).............	99.9	99.8	100.1	...	...	...	...	...	...
8 III 1999 (CDJC).............	100	100.3	99.7	...	...	...	...	...	...
Rwanda									
16 VIII 2002 (CDJC).............	106.3	106.6	106.1	107.4	108.3	106.2	106	106	106.1
15 VIII 2012 (CDJC).............	110.2	110.4	109.9	108.3	109.3	107.1	110.6	110.7	110.5
Saint Helena ex. dep. - Sainte-Hélène sans dép.									
8 III 1998 (CDJC).............	101	98.8	103.3	...	...	...	...	...	...
10 II 2008 (CDJC)[6].............	98.8	99.9	97.8	...	...	...	...	...	...
7 II 2016 (CDJC)[7].............	103.9	99.4	109	...	...	...	...	...	...
Saint Helena: Ascension - Sainte-Hélène: Ascension									
8 III 1998 (CDJC).............	117.5	111	130.7	...	...	...	...	...	...
Sao Tome and Principe - Sao Tomé-et-Principe									
4 VIII 1991 (CDFC).............	102.7	101.5	103.8	...	...	...	...	...	...
25 VIII 2001 (CDJC).............	105.7	106.2	105.3	...	...	...	...	...	...
13 V 2012 (CDJC).............	104.1	103.2	105	...	...	...	...	...	...
Seychelles									
17 VIII 1987 (CDFC).............	100.9	102.8	99	...	...	...	...	...	...
26 VIII 1994 (CDFC).............	100.9	99.9	102	...	...	...	...	...	...
29 VIII 1997 (CDFC).............	101.6	100.8	102.5	...	...	...	...	...	...
26 VIII 2002 (CDJC).............	100.8	99.2	102.5	...	...	...	...	...	...
26 VIII 2010 (CDFC).............	101.3	101.7	101	...	...	...	...	...	...
South Africa - Afrique du Sud									
5 III 1985 (CDFC).............	124.3	120.9	127.7	...	...	...	...	...	...
7 III 1991 (CDFC).............	113.1	111.5	114.7	...	...	...	...	...	...
10 X 1996 (CDFC)[8].............	100.5	100.3	100.7	99.3	99.5	99.1	102.5	101.7	103.1
Tunisia - Tunisie									
20 IV 1994 (CDFC).............	102.4	102.4	102.4	102.4	102.4	102.4	102.4	102.3	102.4
Uganda - Ouganda									
12 I 1991 (CDFC).............	168	154.8	180.5	158.6	150.8	167.3	169.4	155.5	182.2
12 IX 2002 (CDFC).............	134.2	129.6	138.4	128.2	128.5	128	135.2	129.7	140
27 VIII 2014 (CDFC).............	131.5	129	133.7	130.6	132.2	129	131.8	127.7	135.4
United Republic of Tanzania - République Unie de Tanzanie									
28 VIII 1988 (CDFC).............	189.2	175.1	201.8	173.7	167.3	180.7	193.3	177.4	206.7
26 VIII 2012 (CDFC).............	154.4	152.6	156.1	139.5	141.5	137.7	162.3	158.8	165.5
Zambia - Zambie									
20 VIII 1990 (CDFC).............	120.7	121.9	119.6	117.2	119.8	114.2	123.1	123.5	122.7
25 X 2000 (CDFC).............	127.6	128.9	126.3	123.9	125.3	122.4	129.9	131.4	128.5

Continent, country or area, date and code[a] Continent, pays ou zone, date et code[a]	Total			Urban - Urbaine			Rural - Rurale		
	Both sexes Les deux sexes	Male Masculin	Female Féminin	Both sexes Les deux sexes	Male Masculin	Female Féminin	Both sexes Les deux sexes	Male Masculin	Female Féminin
AFRICA - AFRIQUE									
16 X 2010 (CDJC)	123.8	126.8	120.7	122.3	125.2	119.3	124.9	128.2	121.8
Zimbabwe									
18 VIII 1992 (CDFC)	120.6	122.2	119.2	115.9	119.5	111.4	123.7	124.6	123
17 VIII 2002 (CDFC)	115.1	115.2	115	109.7	110.9	108.4	119	119	119.1
17 VIII 2012 (CDFC)	110.8	110.8	110.8	...	...	...	...	...	...
AMERICA, NORTH - AMÉRIQUE DU NORD									
Anguilla									
13 IV 1992 (CDFC)	104.8	109	100.4	...	...	...	...	...	...
9 V 2001 (CDFC)	104.4	105.6	103.2	...	...	...	...	...	...
Antigua and Barbuda - Antigua-et-Barbuda									
28 V 2001 (CDFC)	104.3	103.1	105.4	...	...	...	...	...	...
Aruba									
6 X 1991 (CDJC)	99.3	99.4	99.3	...	...	...	...	...	...
14 X 2000 (CDJC)	103.9[9]	103.3	104.5	...	...	...	...	...	...
29 IX 2010 (CDJC)[9]	103.4	103.6	103.3	...	...	...	...	...	...
Bahamas									
1 V 1990 (CDFC)	103.4	102.3	104.5	...	...	...	...	...	...
1 V 2000 (CDFC)	101.5	100.4	102.5	...	...	...	...	...	...
3 V 2010 (CDJC)	101.3	101.6	101.1	...	...	...	...	...	...
Barbados - Barbade									
1 V 2000 (CDFC)	103.8	104.4	103.3	...	...	...	...	...	...
Belize									
12 V 1991 (CDFC)	103.5	103.2	103.8	...	...	...	...	...	...
12 V 2010 (CDJC)	104.2	103.9	104.5	...	...	...	...	...	...
Bermuda - Bermudes									
20 V 1991 (CDJC)	99	97.9	100	...	...	...	...	...	...
20 V 2000 (CDJC)[10]	100.2	100	100.3	...	...	...	...	...	...
20 V 2010 (CDJC)[11]	100.9	101.1	100.8	100.9	101.1	100.8	...	...	...
20 V 2016 (CDJC)	101.2	100.5	101.8	...	...	...	...	...	...
British Virgin Islands - Îles Vierges britanniques									
12 V 1991 (CDJC)	102.6	104.5	100.5	...	...	...	...	...	...
Canada									
4 VI 1991 (CDJC)[12]	99.6	99.6	99.6	99.6	99.6	99.7	99.6	99.6	99.5
14 V 1996 (CDJC)[12]	99.7	99.7	99.7	...	...	...	...	...	...
15 V 2001 (CDJC)[12]	99.7	99.7	99.8	99.8	99.8	99.8	99.6	99.5	99.8
16 V 2006 (CDJC)[13]	99.9	100	99.9	100	100	100	99.6	99.6	99.7
2 V 2011 (CDJC)[12]	100.8	101	100.7	100.9	101.1	100.8	100.4	100.6	100.3
10 V 2016 (CDJC)[14]	100.8	101	100.7	100.9	101	100.7	100.7	100.7	100.7
Cayman Islands - Îles Caïmanes									
15 X 1989 (CDFC)	104.1	102.7	105.5	...	...	...	...	...	...
10 X 2010 (CDJC)[10]	102.3	102.8	101.8	102.3	102.8	101.8	...	...	...
Costa Rica									
26 VI 2000 (CDJC)	109.1	109.8	108.4	108.6	108.9	108.3	109.9	111.1	108.6
30 V 2011 (CDJC)	104	104.2	103.9	103.8	103.8	103.9	104.6	105.2	103.9
Cuba									
7 IX 2002 (CDJC)	102.2	102.5	101.9	102.5	102.7	102.2	101.5	102	100.9
14 IX 2012 (CDJC)	101.5	101.6	101.3	...	...	...	...	...	...
Dominican Republic - République dominicaine									
24 IX 1993 (CDJC)	116.5	114.9	118	111.5	109.9	113	123.5	121.4	125.5
18 X 2002 (CDJC)	108	108.9	107.1	105.8	106.3	105.4	112.1	113.5	110.7
1 XII 2010 (CDJC)	111.5	113.8	109.2	109.9	111.9	108.1	116.5	119.3	113.1
El Salvador									
27 IX 1992 (CDFC)	126	127.5	124.6	119.9	119.7	120	133.5	136.6	130.7
12 V 2007 (CDJC)	105.9	107.1	105	105.3	106.3	104.5	107.3	108.7	106.2
Guadeloupe									
8 III 1999 (CDJC)	100.5	100.5	100.4	...	...	...	...	...	...
Honduras									
11 V 1988 (CDFC)	104.1	104.5	103.6	102.4	102.5	102.3	105.3	105.9	104.8
28 VII 2001 (CDJC)	121.8	123.3	120.4	118.5	118.8	118.3	125.1	127.5	122.7
10 VIII 2013 (CDFC)	119.7	121.6	118.1	120	120.9	119.1	119.4	122.4	116.6

3a. Whipple's Index by sex and urban/rural residence, 1985 - 2017
L'indice de Whipple par le sexe et la résidence urbaine/rurale, 1985 - 2017 (continued - suite)

Continent, country or area, date and code[a] Continent, pays ou zone, date et code[a]	Total			Urban - Urbaine			Rural - Rurale		
	Both sexes Les deux sexes	Male Masculin	Female Féminin	Both sexes Les deux sexes	Male Masculin	Female Féminin	Both sexes Les deux sexes	Male Masculin	Female Féminin
AMERICA, NORTH - AMÉRIQUE DU NORD									
Jamaica - Jamaïque									
7 IV 1991 (CDJC)	107.6	108.8	106.5	...	...	...	...	...	...
10 IX 2001 (CDJC)[15]	107.4	108.7	106.1	106.9	107.5	106.4	107.9	110	105.7
4 IV 2011 (CDJC)	103.3	103.4	103.1	103.6	103.6	103.6	102.8	103.2	102.5
Martinique									
15 III 1990 (CDJC)	104.4	104.1	104.6	...	...	...	...	...	...
Mexico - Mexique									
12 III 1990 (CDJC)	125.2	123.5	126.8	...	...	...	...	...	...
14 II 2000 (CDJC)	116.7	116.5	116.9	114.8	114.3	115.3	123.4	124.3	122.7
17 X 2005 (CDJC)	118.8	118.7	118.9	117.5	117	117.9	123.8	124.8	122.8
12 VI 2010 (CDFC)[16]	114	114.1	113.9	113.7	113.6	113.9	115.1	116.2	114.1
Montserrat									
12 V 2011 (CDJC)	101.9	95.9	108.4	...	...	...	...	...	...
Nicaragua									
4 VI 2005 (CDJC)	111.6	112.8	110.5	108.5	109.2	107.8	116.4	117.8	115.1
Panama									
13 V 1990 (CDFC)	109.3	109.2	109.3	104.6	104.5	104.8	115.6	115	116.3
14 V 2000 (CDFC)	103.2	103.3	103.2	...	...	...	...	...	...
Puerto Rico - Porto Rico									
1 IV 1990 (CDJC)	105.6	106.1	105.1	...	...	...	...	...	...
1 IV 2000 (CDJC)	101.7	102	101.6	...	...	...	...	...	...
1 IV 2010 (CDJC)[17]	102	102	102	...	...	...	...	...	...
Saint Lucia - Sainte-Lucie									
12 V 1991 (CDFC)	110.5	110.5	110.4	...	...	...	...	...	...
22 V 2001 (CDFC)	105.5	105.8	105.2	104	100.5	107.3	106.2	108	104.4
Saint Pierre and Miquelon - Saint Pierre-et-Miquelon									
8 III 1999 (CDFC)	100.5	104.6	96.1	...	...	...	...	...	...
Saint Vincent and the Grenadines - Saint-Vincent-et-les Grenadines									
12 V 1991 (CDFC)	106.6	105.2	107.9	...	...	...	...	...	...
12 VI 2001 (CDFC)	105.3	105.3	105.3	105.6	106.8	104.4	105.1	104.1	106.1
Sint Maarten (Dutch part) - Saint-Martin (partie néerlandaise)									
9 IV 2011 (CDFC)	100.7	100.2	101.2	...	...	...	...	...	...
Trinidad and Tobago - Trinité-et-Tobago									
9 I 2011 (CDJC)	106.6	107.2	105.9	...	...	...	...	...	...
Turks and Caicos Islands - Îles Turques et Caïques									
10 IX 2001 (CDFC)	104.2	100.1	108.6	...	...	...	...	...	...
United States of America - États-Unis d'Amérique									
1 IV 1990 (CDJC)	104.5	104.8	104.2	...	...	...	...	...	...
1 IV 2000 (CDJC)[18]	101.8	102.1	101.5	102.1	102.4	101.7	100.8	101	100.5
1 IV 2010 (CDJC)	102.2	102.5	102	102.4	102.7	102.2	101.5	101.7	101.2
AMERICA, SOUTH - AMÉRIQUE DU SUD									
Argentina - Argentine									
15 V 1991 (CDFC)	104.2	103.3	105.2	...	...	...	...	...	...
18 XI 2001 (CDFC)	102.4	101.8	103	...	...	...	...	...	...
27 X 2010 (CDFC)	102.6	102.5	102.7	102.6	102.5	102.7	102.5	102.9	102
Bolivia (Plurinational State of) - Bolivie (État plurinational de)									
3 VI 1992 (CDFC)	125.4	121.1	129.5	111.4	108	114.4	146.1	139.4	152.7
5 IX 2001 (CDFC)	114.6	113.1	116	109.1	108	110.2	124.6	121.9	127.6
21 XI 2012 (CDFC)	110.4	110.5	110.3	108	108.1	108	115.7	115.4	116.1
Brazil - Brésil									
1 IX 1991 (CDJC)	103.3	103.3	103.3	102.3	102.3	102.2	107.2	106.9	107.4
1 VIII 2000 (CDJC)[19]	104.2	104.3	104	103.6	103.7	103.5	107.1	107.3	107
31 VII 2010 (CDJC)	104.8	105.6	104.1	104.7	105.4	104	105.6	106.6	104.4
Chile - Chili									
22 IV 1992 (CDFC)	100.3	98.9	101.7	100.2	98.6	101.7	101	100.2	101.9

74

Continent, country or area, date and code[a] / Continent, pays ou zone, date et code[a]	Total			Urban - Urbaine			Rural - Rurale		
	Both sexes Les deux sexes	Male Masculin	Female Féminin	Both sexes Les deux sexes	Male Masculin	Female Féminin	Both sexes Les deux sexes	Male Masculin	Female Féminin
AMERICA, SOUTH - AMÉRIQUE DU SUD									
24 IV 2002 (CDFC)	99.5	98.5	100.5	99.4	98.2	100.5	100.2	100	100.4
Colombia - Colombie									
15 X 1985 (CDFC)	147.9	146.5	149.2	139.8	136.8	142.4	166.9	166.5	167.3
24 X 1993 (CDFC)	118.9	117.7	120	111.7	108.9	114.1	139.6	139.9	139.4
22 V 2005 (CDFC)	103.5	104.2	102.9	102.1	102.4	101.8	108.6	109.8	107.3
22 V 2005 (CDJC)	103.5	104.2	102.9	102.1	102.4	101.8	108.7	109.9	107.3
Ecuador - Équateur									
25 XI 1990 (CDFC)[20]	132.5	131.2	133.8	122.9	121	124.7	146.6	145.4	147.9
25 XI 2001 (CDFC)[20]	112.1	111.8	112.4	107.9	107	108.7	119.9	120.4	119.4
28 XI 2010 (CDFC)	103.7	104.1	103.3	103	103.4	102.7	104.9	105.4	104.4
French Guiana - Guyane française									
15 III 1990 (CDJC)	106.2	105.7	106.7	...	...	...	...	...	...
8 III 1999 (CDJC)	101.1	100.9	101.3	...	...	...	...	...	...
Paraguay									
26 VIII 1992 (CDFC)	108.6	107.9	109.3	105.7	104.3	107	112	111.8	112.3
28 VIII 2002 (CDFC)	104.8	104.3	105.2	103.2	102.6	103.7	107.1	106.5	107.8
Peru - Pérou									
21 X 2007 (CDFC)	109.4	109.1	109.6	106.9	106.5	107.3	118.8	118.5	119.1
Suriname									
2 VIII 2004 (CDJC)	101.1	100.4	102	102.4[21]	101.4[21]	103.5[21]	98.3[21]	98.2[21]	98.4[21]
13 VIII 2012 (CDJC)	101.7	101.8	101.7	...	...	...	...	...	...
Uruguay									
23 X 1985 (CDFC)	106.2	104.9	107.4	106.2	104.7	107.5	106.3	106.1	106.5
22 V 1996 (CDFC)	103.3	102.8	103.8	103.2	102.5	103.8	104	104.5	103.3
1 VI 2004 (CDFC)[22]	106	105.9	106.2	106.1	105.9	106.3	105.4	105.7	105
4 X 2011 (CDJC)	101.8	101.9	101.7	101.8	101.9	101.7	101.8	101.6	102
Venezuela (Bolivarian Republic of) - Venezuela (République bolivarienne du)									
20 X 1990 (CDFC)[23]	106.4	106.5	106.3	105	104.8	105.3	114.9	116.1	113.4
1 IX 2011 (CDJC)	101.3	101.6	101	101.3[24]	101.6[24]	101[24]	101.4[24]	102[24]	100.7[24]
ASIA - ASIE									
Armenia - Arménie									
10 X 2001 (CDJC)	103	102.8	103.3	103.7	103.7	103.8	101.6	101.1	102.1
12 X 2011 (CDJC)	101.8	101.5	102	102.4	102.3	102.6	100.6	100.2	101
Azerbaijan - Azerbaïdjan									
27 I 1999 (CDJC)	100.4	99.8	101	100.3	99.8	100.8	100.5	99.7	101.2
13 IV 2009 (CDJC)	100.4	100.1	100.7	100.8	100.3	101.3	99.9	99.7	100.1
Bahrain - Bahreïn									
16 XI 1991 (CDFC)	96.6	98.3	93.6	...	...	...	...	...	...
7 IV 2001 (CDJC)	100.2	99.9	100.9	...	...	...	...	...	...
27 IV 2010 (CDJC)	100.2	99.3	101.9	...	...	...	...	...	...
Bangladesh[25]									
22 I 2001 (CDFC)	299.5	295.8	303.4	283.1	277.9	289.8	305	302.6	307.4
Bhutan - Bhoutan									
30 V 2005 (CDFC)	116.4	117.7	114.9	118.7	119.6	117.4	115.4	116.8	113.9
30 V 2017 (CDFC)	108.1	110.4	105.4	...	...	...	...	...	...
Brunei Darussalam - Brunéi Darussalam									
7 VIII 1991 (CDFC)	98.8	98.7	98.8	...	...	...	...	...	...
20 VI 2011 (CDJC)	100.9	101.6	100.2	100.6	101.3	99.8	102	102.3	101.6
Cambodia - Cambodge									
3 III 1998 (CDFC)	118.1	116.2	119.6	119.8	117.6	121.8	117.6	115.9	119.1
3 III 2008 (CDFC)[26]	109.9	108.2	111.3	109.7	108.5	110.8	109.9	108.1	111.5
China - Chine									
1 VII 1990 (CDFC)	101	101.1	100.9	101.9	102	101.8	100.6	100.7	100.5
1 XI 2000 (CDJC)	101.7	101.7	101.6	101.6	101.8	101.4	101.7	101.7	101.7
1 XI 2010 (CDJC)[27]	98.8	98.9	98.8	98.7	98.9	98.6	98.9	98.9	99
China, Hong Kong SAR - Chine, Hong Kong RAS									
11 III 1986 (CDFC)	101.7	101.4	102.1	101.7	101.3	102.1	102.1	102.5	101.7
15 III 1996 (CDFC)	99.7	99.8	99.7	...	...	...	...	...	...
14 III 2001 (CDJC)[28]	100.2	100.3	100.1	...	...	...	...	...	...

3a. Whipple's Index by sex and urban/rural residence, 1985 - 2017
L'indice de Whipple par le sexe et la résidence urbaine/rurale, 1985 - 2017 (continued - suite)

Continent, country or area, date and code[a] / Continent, pays ou zone, date et code[a]	Total			Urban - Urbaine			Rural - Rurale		
	Both sexes Les deux sexes	Male Masculin	Female Féminin	Both sexes Les deux sexes	Male Masculin	Female Féminin	Both sexes Les deux sexes	Male Masculin	Female Féminin
ASIA - ASIE									
14 VII 2006 (CDJC)[29]	98.3	98.4	98.3	...	...	...	...	...	...
30 VI 2011 (CDJC)[28]	99.4	100	98.9	...	...	...	...	...	...
30 VI 2016 (CDJC)[29]	99.9	99.9	99.8	...	...	...	...	...	...
China, Macao SAR - Chine, Macao RAS									
30 VIII 1991 (CDJC)	100.8	101.4	100.3	...	...	...	...	...	...
23 VIII 2001 (CDJC)	95.5	94.7	96.2	...	...	...	...	...	...
12 VIII 2011 (CDJC)	98.9	97.6	100	...	...	...	...	...	...
Cyprus - Chypre									
1 X 1992 (CDJC)	98.7	98.3	99	98.8	98.4	99.3	98.4	98.3	98.5
1 X 2001 (CDJC)[30]	100.7	100.7	100.6	100.9	101.4	100.4	100.1	99.1	101.1
1 X 2011 (CDJC)[30]	105.4	106.6	104.4	...	...	...	...	...	...
Democratic People's Republic of Korea - République populaire démocratique de Corée									
31 XII 1993 (CDJC)	105	105.2	104.7	104.4	104.6	104.2	105.8	106.2	105.5
1 X 2008 (CDJC)	101	100.6	101.3	...	...	...	...	...	...
Georgia - Géorgie									
17 I 2002 (CDJC)	101.4	101.7	101.1	101.6	102	101.3	101.1	101.4	100.8
5 XI 2014 (CDJC)	99.9	99.9	99.8	99.8	99.6	99.9	100	100.4	99.7
India - Inde									
1 III 1991 (CDFC)[31]	290.3	292.6	287.9	258.7	253.8	264.3	302.1	307.7	296.2
1 III 2001 (CDFC)[32]	230	241	218.4	217.2	216.8	217.8	235.5	252	218.7
9 II 2011 (CDFC)[33]	171	174.6	167.4	152.9	151	154.9	180.5	187.1	173.8
Indonesia - Indonésie									
31 X 1990 (CDFC)	163.3	160.2	166.3	139.7	135.8	143.7	174.2	171.7	176.5
30 VI 2000 (CDJC)[34]	152.2	151.3	153.1	136.8	136.4	137.2	164.2	163.1	165.2
1 V 2010 (CDJC)	114.5	114.2	114.9	110.2	110.2	110.2	119	118.4	119.7
Iran (Islamic Republic of) - Iran (République islamique d')									
22 IX 1986 (CDFC)	122.6	121.1	124.1	114.4	113.4	115.5	133.1	131.3	134.8
11 IX 1991 (CDJC)	128.7	127	130.4	122.5	121.3	123.9	138.5	136.4	140.6
11 IX 1994 (CDJC)	107.4	106.8	108.1	107.1	108	106.2	107.8	104.5	111.2
23 X 1996 (CDJC)	108.8	108.6	109	105.7	105.6	105.8	114.1	114	114.3
28 X 2006 (CDJC)[35]	111.6	110.4	112.8	109.3	108.5	110.1	117.2	115.2	119.2
24 X 2011 (CDJC)	103.7	103.8	103.5	103.6	103.8	103.5	103.7[36]	103.8[36]	103.6[36]
24 IX 2016 (CDJC)	104.1	104.2	104	104[35]	104.1[35]	103.9[35]	104.5[35]	104.6[35]	104.3[35]
Iraq									
16 X 1997 (CDFC)	106.2	105.6	106.8	105.5	104.9	106.1	108	107.6	108.5
Israel - Israël									
4 XI 1995 (CDFC)[37]	101.4	101.8	101	101.3	101.8	100.9	101.9	101.5	102.3
4 XI 1995 (CDJC)	101.1	101.1	101.1	101	101	101	101.5	101.6	101.4
27 XII 2008 (CDFC)[38]	98.9	99	98.9	99	99.1	98.9	98.6	98.3	99
Japan - Japon									
1 X 1985 (CDFC)	98.4	98.4	98.3	98.3	98.4	98.2	98.7	98.5	98.8
1 X 1990 (CDFC)	98.9	98.9	98.9	98.9	99	98.8	98.8	98.6	99
1 X 1995 (CDFC)	99	99	99	99	99.1	99	98.8	98.6	98.9
1 X 2000 (CDJC)	99.1	99.1	99	99.1	99.2	99	99	98.8	99.2
1 X 2005 (CDJC)[39]	99.1	99.2	99.1	99.2	99.2	99.1	99	98.8	99.1
1 X 2010 (CDJC)[39]	100.9	100.9	100.9	100.9	100.9	100.8	101	100.9	101.1
1 X 2015 (CDJC)[39]	100.8	100.7	100.8	100.8	100.7	100.8	100.8	100.7	100.9
Jordan - Jordanie									
1 X 2004 (CDFC)[40]	100.8	100.4	101.3	...	...	...	...	...	...
30 XI 2015 (CDFC)[41]	111.4	112.3	110.3	...	...	...	...	...	...
Kazakhstan									
12 I 1989 (CDFC)	98.9	98.8	99	98.7	98.6	98.8	99.2	99	99.4
26 II 1999 (CDJC)[42]	99.9	99.8	99.9	100.1	100	100.2	99.5	99.5	99.4
Kuwait - Koweït									
20 IV 1985 (CDFC)	139.5	142.6	133.9	...	...	...	...	...	...
21 IV 2011 (CDFC)	102.2	102.6	101.7	102.2	102.6	101.7	...	...	...
Kyrgyzstan - Kirghizstan									
12 I 1989 (CDJC)	99.3	99.1	99.5	98.4	98	98.8	99.9	99.8	100.1
24 III 1999 (CDJC)	99.4	99.2	99.6	99.2	98.9	99.5	99.5	99.3	99.7
24 III 2009 (CDJC)	100.6	100.5	100.8	...	...	...	...	...	...

Continent, country or area, date and code[a] Continent, pays ou zone, date et code[a]	Total			Urban - Urbaine			Rural - Rurale		
	Both sexes Les deux sexes	Male Masculin	Female Féminin	Both sexes Les deux sexes	Male Masculin	Female Féminin	Both sexes Les deux sexes	Male Masculin	Female Féminin
ASIA - ASIE									
Lao People's Democratic Republic - République démocratique populaire lao									
1 III 2005 (CDJC)	138.3	136.4	140.2	120.8[43]	120.9[43]	120.6[43]	146[43]	143.3[43]	148.5[43]
1 III 2015 (CDJC)	129.3	128.4	130.2	...	...	...	...	...	...
Malaysia - Malaisie									
14 VIII 1991 (CDFC)	114.2	113.8	114.6	110.3	110.2	110.3	118.8	117.9	119.7
6 VII 2010 (CDJC)	120.4	120.7	120	120.6	120.7	120.5	119.7	120.6	118.7
6 VII 2010 (CDJC)[44]	120.7	121.1	120.3	...	...	...	...	...	...
Maldives									
25 III 1985 (CDFC)	176.7	175.3	178.4	166.3	170.9	159.4	180.7	177.2	184.2
8 III 1990 (CDFC)	156.4	159.9	152.7	149.3	154.5	142.6	159.2	162.4	156.1
25 III 1995 (CDFC)	143.1	144.5	141.7	137.3	137.9	136.7	145.5	147.5	143.5
31 III 2000 (CDFC)	106.9	109.5	104.3	...	...	...	...	...	...
21 III 2006 (CDFC)[45]	103.8	104.9	102.8	104	105.5	102.5	103.7	104.5	102.9
20 IX 2014 (CDFC)[46]	105.4	109.8	99.1	106.1	110.5	100.1	105	109.4	98.3
Mongolia - Mongolie									
5 I 2000 (CDFC)	99.9	99.6	100.2	99.9	99.7	100.1	99.9	99.5	100.2
11 XI 2010 (CDJC)	101.6	101.3	101.9	101.7	101.4	102	101.5	101.3	101.7
Myanmar[47]									
29 III 2014 (CDFC)	123.3	124	122.6	115.8	116	115.6	126.7	127.6	125.8
Nepal - Népal									
22 VI 1991 (CDJC)	202.4	195.6	209	186.2	179.2	193.9	204.2	197.6	210.5
22 VI 2001 (CDJC)	206.1	205.7	206.6	...	...	...	...	...	...
22 VI 2011 (CDJC)	188.6	191.3	186.2	169.9	167.8	172	193.1	197.5	189.3
Oman									
7 XII 2003 (CDFC)	158.5	165.6	146.9	154.9	163.1	141.1	170.2	174.1	164.4
Philippines									
1 IX 1995 (CDJC)	115.7	116.5	114.9	...	...	...	...	...	...
1 V 2000 (CDJC)	110.8	111.6	110	...	...	...	...	...	...
1 VIII 2007 (CDJC)	104.8	104.9	104.7	...	...	...	...	...	...
1 V 2010 (CDJC)[48]	108.5	109.1	107.9	...	...	...	...	...	...
1 VIII 2015 (CDJC)[49]	106.8	107.2	106.3	...	...	...	...	...	...
Qatar									
16 III 1986 (CDFC)	149.1	151.9	140.2	...	...	...	...	...	...
Republic of Korea - République de Corée									
1 XI 1985 (CDFC)	99.4	98.9	99.8	99.6	99.4	99.8	98.8	97.9	99.6
1 XI 1990 (CDFC)	99.5	99.2	99.8	99.6	99.4	99.8	99.1	98.5	99.7
1 XI 1995 (CDJC)	99.9	99.7	100.1	100	99.8	100.2	99.4	99.2	99.6
1 XI 2000 (CDJC)[50]	100	99.8	100.2	100.2	100	100.4	99.2	98.9	99.4
1 XI 2005 (CDJC)[50]	100.4	100.2	100.6	100.6	100.4	100.8	99.4	99.2	99.7
1 XI 2015 (CDJC)	101.8	101.3	102.3	101.8	101.3	102.2	101.8	101.2	102.5
Singapore - Singapour									
30 VI 2000 (CDJC)	98.2	98.1	98.3	...	...	...	...	...	...
30 VI 2010 (CDJC)[51]	99.7	99.7	99.7	...	...	...	...	...	...
Sri Lanka									
17 VII 2001 (CDFC)[52]	97	97.5	96.4	98.2	98.5	97.8	96.8[53]	97.3[53]	96.2[53]
20 III 2012 (CDJC)	100.2	100.3	100	100.3	100.7	100	100.1	100.2	100.1
State of Palestine - État de Palestine									
9 XII 1997 (CDFC)[54]	109.1	103	115.3	...	...	...	...	...	...
1 XII 2007 (CDFC)[34]	103.8	102.6	104.9	104.4[55]	103.2[55]	105.7[55]	100.8	100	101.6
Syrian Arab Republic - République arabe syrienne[56]									
3 IX 1994 (CDFC)	111.8	109.9	113.8	111.9	110.4	113.5	111.7	109.2	114.1
Tajikistan - Tadjikistan									
12 I 1989 (CDJC)	99	98.9	99.1	97.6	97.1	98	99.9	100	99.9
20 I 2000 (CDFC)	99.3	99.2	99.4	100.1	100	100.1	99	98.9	99.1
21 IX 2010 (CDFC)	103.6	103.9	103.4	105.8	106.6	105	102.8	102.9	102.7
Thailand - Thaïlande									
1 IV 2000 (CDJC)[57]	104.7	104.7	104.8	108.1	108.1	108.1	103	103	103
1 IX 2010 (CDJC)	110.6	111.1	110.1	115.6	116.2	115	106.3	106.8	105.8
Timor-Leste									
11 VII 2010 (CDFC)	130.3	128.9	131.7	126	125.6	126.5	132.3	130.6	134
Turkey - Turquie									
20 X 1985 (CDFC)	149.4	133.8	165.3	...	...	...	...	...	...
21 X 1990 (CDFC)	139.7	128.9	150.8	...	...	...	...	...	...

Continent, country or area, date and code[a] / Continent, pays ou zone, date et code[a]	Total			Urban - Urbaine			Rural - Rurale		
	Both sexes Les deux sexes	Male Masculin	Female Féminin	Both sexes Les deux sexes	Male Masculin	Female Féminin	Both sexes Les deux sexes	Male Masculin	Female Féminin
ASIA - ASIE									
22 X 2000 (CDFC)............................	125.7	123.2	128.3	122.7	121.3	124.2	131.7	127.2	136.4
3 X 2011 (CDJC)[58]	101.2	101.7	100.8	101.4	101.7	101.1	100.8	101.5	99.9
Viet Nam									
1 IV 1989 (CDJC)	98.5	98.1	98.8	98.3	97.8	98.8	98.4	98	98.7
1 IV 1999 (CDJC)	99.2	98.8	99.6	99.1	98.6	99.6	99.3	98.8	99.7
1 IV 2009 (CDJC)	100.4	99.8	100.9	100.6	100	101.1	100.3	99.8	100.8
Yemen - Yémen									
16 XII 1994 (CDFC)........................	293.9	282.6	304.9	245	229.6	265	311.7	305.8	316.8
EUROPE									
Åland Islands - Îles d'Åland[59]									
31 XII 2000 (CDJC)	100.7	101.5	99.8	102.9	101.9	103.8	99	101.2	96.7
Austria - Autriche									
15 V 1991 (CDJC)	97.9	97.9	97.9	97.8	97.9	97.7	98.2	98.1	98.2
15 V 2001 (CDJC)	97.4	97.5	97.3	97.3	97.5	97.2	97.5	97.3	97.6
31 X 2011 (CDJC)	100	100.1	100	100.2	100.2	100.2	99.7	99.8	99.7
Belarus - Bélarus									
12 I 1989 (CDJC)	99.4	99.3	99.5	98.9	98.8	99.1	100.3	100.3	100.2
16 II 1999 (CDJC)	99.6	99.4	99.8	99.7	99.6	99.9	99.2	98.9	99.5
14 X 2009 (CDJC)	101.5	101.6	101.5	101.7	101.6	101.7	101	101.3	100.7
Belgium - Belgique									
1 X 2001 (CDJC)	99.5	99.4	99.7	99.5	99.4	99.7	99.2	98.9	99.4
1 I 2011 (CDJC)	100	99.9	100.1	100	99.9	100.1	100.3	99.1	101.6
Bosnia and Herzegovina - Bosnie-Herzégovine									
31 III 1991 (CDJC)	100.4	100.5	100.2	...	...	...	...	...	...
30 IX 2013 (CDJC)	100.1	99.8	100.3	...	...	...	...	...	...
Bulgaria - Bulgarie									
1 II 2011 (CDJC).............................	101.2	101	101.4	101.1	100.9	101.3	101.4	101.4	101.4
Croatia - Croatie									
31 III 1991 (CDFC)	99.1	99.2	99.1	99	99.3	98.8	99.2	99.1	99.4
31 III 2001 (CDJC)	98.2	98.4	98.1	98.3	98.6	98.1	98.1	98.1	98.2
1 IV 2011 (CDJC)	100.3	100.5	100.2	100.3	100.4	100.2	100.4	100.5	100.2
Czechia - Tchéquie									
3 III 1991 (CDJC)	99	98.8	99.1	...	...	...	...	...	...
1 III 2001 (CDJC)	99.2	99.1	99.3	99	98.9	99.1	99.8	99.8	99.9
25 III 2011 (CDJC)..........................	99.6	99.6	99.7	99.5	99.4	99.6	99.9	100.1	99.8
Denmark - Danemark[60]									
1 I 1991 (CDJC)	100.5	100.6	100.5	...	...	...	...	...	...
Estonia - Estonie									
31 III 2000 (CDJC)	100	99.7	100.3	100.2	100	100.4	99.7	99.1	100.2
31 XII 2011 (CDJC)	100	100	100.1	100.1	100	100.1	100	99.9	100.2
Finland - Finlande									
17 XI 1985 (CDJC)	99.8	99.9	99.6	...	...	...	...	...	...
31 XII 1990 (CDJC)	99.5	99.6	99.5	...	...	...	...	...	...
31 XII 2000 (CDJC)	99.5	99.6	99.4	99.9	100.1	99.7	98.9	98.9	98.8
31 XII 2010 (CDJC)	100.1	100.1	100	100	100.1	99.8	100.3	100	100.5
France									
5 III 1990 (CDJC)	99.2	99	99.3	99.5	99.4	99.6	98.2	98.1	98.4
8 III 1999 (CDJC)[61]	100.5	100.5	100.5	100.5	100.5	100.5	100.8	100.7	100.8
Germany - Allemagne									
9 V 2011 (CDJC)	100	100	100.1	100	100	100.1	100.1	100.1	100.1
Gibraltar									
14 X 1991 (CDFC)...........................	105.7	104.9	106.6	...	...	...	...	...	...
12 XI 2001 (CDFC)[62]	98	98.6	97.5	...	...	...	...	...	...
12 XI 2012 (CDJC)[63]	99.5	100.3	98.7	...	...	...	...	...	...
Greece - Grèce									
17 III 1991 (CDFC)	108.8	107.4	110.1	108.5	107.3	109.7	109.1	107.6	110.7
18 III 2001 (CDJC)[64]......................	105	104.9	105.1	104.8	104.6	104.9	105.8	105.7	106
9 V 2011 (CDFC)	101.4	101.8	101.1	101.3	101.6	101.1	101.8	102.3	101.2
Guernsey - Guernesey									
23 III 1986 (CDJC)	96.1	96.1	96	...	...	...	...	...	...
13 III 1996 (CDJC)	97.5	98.5	96.6	...	...	...	...	...	...
29 IV 2001 (CDJC)	97.2	97.4	96.9	...	...	...	...	...	...
31 III 2015 (CDJC)	101.4	102.4	100.3	...	...	...	...	...	...

3a. Whipple's Index by sex and urban/rural residence, 1985 - 2017
L'indice de Whipple par le sexe et la résidence urbaine/rurale, 1985 - 2017 (continued - suite)

Continent, country or area, date and code[a] / Continent, pays ou zone, date et code[a]	Total			Urban - Urbaine			Rural - Rurale		
	Both sexes Les deux sexes	Male Masculin	Female Féminin	Both sexes Les deux sexes	Male Masculin	Female Féminin	Both sexes Les deux sexes	Male Masculin	Female Féminin
EUROPE									
Hungary - Hongrie									
1 I 1990 (CDFC)	102.1	102.5	101.8	102.4	102.8	102	101.7	101.9	101.5
1 II 2001 (CDFC)	101.6	101.8	101.5	101.9	102.2	101.6	101.2	101.2	101.2
1 X 2011 (CDFC)	100.2	100.2	100.2	100.1	100.2	100.1	100.4	100.3	100.5
Ireland - Irlande									
21 IV 1991 (CDFC)	100.5	100.5	100.4	...	...	...	...	...	...
28 IV 1996 (CDFC)	100.2	100.2	100.1	100.3	100.5	100.2	99.9	99.7	100
28 IV 2002 (CDFC)	99.5	99.8	99.2	99.7	99.9	99.4	99.3	99.5	99
23 IV 2006 (CDFC)	100.9	101	100.8	101	101.2	100.8	100.8	100.7	100.8
10 IV 2011 (CDFC)[65]	100.7	101	100.5	100.9	101.2	100.5	100.5	100.5	100.4
Isle of Man - Île de Man									
6 IV 1986 (CDJC)	99.2	98.6	99.8	...	...	...	...	...	...
14 IV 1991 (CDJC)	97.7	98.1	97.3	...	...	...	...	...	...
14 IV 1996 (CDJC)	97.9	98.9	97	...	...	...	...	...	...
29 IV 2001 (CDJC)	97.8	98	97.5	...	...	...	...	...	...
23 IV 2006 (CDJC)	98.3	98.4	98.3	...	...	...	...	...	...
27 III 2011 (CDJC)	99.3	100.4	98.2	...	...	...	...	...	...
24 IV 2016 (CDJC)	99	99.3	98.7	...	...	...	...	...	...
Italy - Italie									
21 X 2001 (CDJC)	101.1	101	101.1	...	...	...	...	...	...
9 X 2011 (CDJC)	99.8	99.8	99.8	...	...	...	...	...	...
Jersey									
23 III 1986 (CDFC)	98	98	98	...	...	...	...	...	...
10 III 1991 (CDJC)	99.2	100.6	97.8	...	...	...	...	...	...
10 III 1996 (CDJC)	99.4	100.7	98.1	...	...	...	...	...	...
11 III 2001 (CDJC)	98.9	99.6	98.3	...	...	...	...	...	...
27 III 2011 (CDJC)	100	100.7	99.3	...	...	...	...	...	...
Latvia - Lettonie									
31 III 2000 (CDJC)[66]	100.5	100.2	100.7	100.4	100.4	100.4	100.6	99.8	101.5
1 III 2011 (CDJC)	99.4	99.6	99.3	99.5	99.7	99.3	99.3	99.3	99.4
Liechtenstein									
31 XII 2010 (CDJC)	100.5	102.1	99	...	...	...	...	...	...
Lithuania - Lituanie									
12 I 1989 (CDJC)	100.6	100.5	100.7	100.7	100.6	100.8	100.3	100.2	100.4
6 IV 2001 (CDJC)	99.8	99.7	99.9	99.4	99	99.7	100.8	101.1	100.5
1 III 2011 (CDJC)	100	100.1	99.9	100	100.2	99.8	100	99.9	100
Luxembourg									
15 II 2001 (CDJC)	99.2	98.9	99.6	...	...	...	...	...	...
1 II 2011 (CDJC)	99.7	99	100.4	...	...	...	...	...	...
Malta - Malte									
26 XI 1995 (CDJC)	101.2	101.2	101.2	101.2	101.2	101.2	125.7	107.6	138.4
27 XI 2005 (CDJC)	101.3	101.9	100.6	101.2	102	100.5	114.3	100	127.3
20 XI 2011 (CDFC)	99.4	100	98.9	99.4	99.9	98.9	100.3	102.3	98.1
Monaco									
21 VI 2000 (CDJC)	100.9	99.9	101.9	...	...	...	...	...	...
Montenegro - Monténégro									
31 X 2003 (CDJC)	100.2	99.9	100.5	100.2	99.6	100.8	100.2	100.3	100
1 IV 2011 (CDJC)	100	99.7	100.3	99.9	99.3	100.5	100.1	100.2	99.9
Netherlands - Pays-Bas									
1 I 2002 (CDJC)	101.2	101.3	101	101.3	101.5	101.1	101	101.1	101
1 I 2011 (CDJC)	100.2	100.2	100.2	...	...	...	...	...	...
Norway - Norvège									
3 XI 1990 (CDJC)	99.9	99.9	99.9	99.9	99.9	100	99.9	100	99.8
3 XI 2001 (CDJC)[67]	100.1	100.1	100.1	100.1	100.1	100.2	99.7	99.9	99.6
19 XI 2011 (CDJC)[67]	99.8	99.8	99.7	99.7[68]	99.6[68]	99.7[68]	100.1[68]	100.4[68]	99.8[68]
Poland - Pologne									
6 XII 1988 (CDFC)	100.5	100.6	100.4	100.5	100.6	100.4	100.5	100.6	100.5
20 V 2002 (CDJC)[69]	100.7	100.7	100.7	100.9	100.8	100.9	100.4	100.5	100.2
31 III 2011 (CDJC)	100.1	100.1	100.1	100.1	100.1	100.1	100.1	100.1	100
Portugal									
15 IV 1991 (CDFC)	101.4	101.7	101.1	101.4	101.7	101.2	101.3	101.6	101.1
21 III 2011 (CDJC)	100.7	100.8	100.5	100.8	101	100.7	100.4	100.4	100.3
Republic of Moldova - République de Moldova									
12 I 1989 (CDJC)	100.5	100.4	100.5	100.2	99.9	100.4	100.7	100.8	100.6
5 X 2004 (CDFC)[70]	103.2	103.3	103.2	102.9	102.9	102.9	103.5	103.5	103.5

3a. Whipple's Index by sex and urban/rural residence, 1985 - 2017
L'indice de Whipple par le sexe et la résidence urbaine/rurale, 1985 - 2017 (continued - suite)

Continent, country or area, date and code[a] / Continent, pays ou zone, date et code[a]	Total			Urban - Urbaine			Rural - Rurale		
	Both sexes Les deux sexes	Male Masculin	Female Féminin	Both sexes Les deux sexes	Male Masculin	Female Féminin	Both sexes Les deux sexes	Male Masculin	Female Féminin
EUROPE									
Romania - Roumanie									
7 I 1992 (CDJC)	96.2	96.2	96.2	95.6	95.8	95.4	97.1	96.8	97.4
18 III 2002 (CDJC)	95.8	95.9	95.8	95.3	95.5	95.2	96.5	96.3	96.7
20 X 2011 (CDJC)	96.6	96.6	96.6	96.4	96.5	96.3	96.8	96.7	96.9
Russian Federation - Fédération de Russie									
12 I 1989 (CDJC)	97.8	97.7	97.9	97.7	97.6	97.7	98.3	98.2	98.4
14 X 2010 (CDJC)	103	103	103	103.5	103.5	103.5	101.7	101.6	101.7
Serbia - Serbie[71]									
31 III 2002 (CDJC)	99.9	99.9	100	100.4	100.4	100.5	99.2	99.3	99.2
1 X 2011 (CDJC)	99.4	99.2	99.5	99.7	99.3	100	98.9	99.1	98.7
Slovakia - Slovaquie									
3 III 1991 (CDJC)	100	99.8	100.2	...	...	...	...	...	...
25 V 2001 (CDJC)	99.5	99.5	99.6	99.7	99.6	99.8	99.3	99.3	99.3
21 V 2011 (CDJC)	100.2	100.2	100.3	100.3	100.2	100.4	100.2	100.2	100.1
Slovenia - Slovénie									
31 III 1991 (CDJC)	99	99.1	98.9	99.7	99.7	99.6	98.4	98.6	98.1
31 III 2002 (CDJC)	101.9	102.1	101.8	102.2	102.3	102.2	101.6	101.9	101.3
1 I 2011 (CDJC)	100.6	100.1	101.3	100.7	100.1	101.3	100.6	100	101.3
1 I 2015 (CDJC)	99.3	99.5	99	99.3	99.6	99.1	99.2	99.4	99
Spain - Espagne									
1 III 1991 (CDJC)	102.4	102.4	102.3	...	...	...	...	...	...
1 XI 2001 (CDFC)[72]	99	99	99	99	99	98.9	99.1	99	99.1
1 XI 2011 (CDJC)	98.3	98.6	98.1	...	...	...	...	...	...
Sweden - Suède									
1 XI 1990 (CDJC)	99.7	99.8	99.6	...	...	...	...	...	...
31 XII 2003 (CDJC)	100	100	100.1	...	...	...	...	...	...
31 XII 2011 (CDJC)	99.7	99.8	99.6	...	...	...	...	...	...
Switzerland - Suisse									
4 XII 1990 (CDJC)	100.6	100.9	100.2	100.7	100.9	100.5	100.2	100.7	99.7
5 XII 2000 (CDFC)	99.7	99.9	99.5	99.7	99.9	99.6	99.5	99.9	99.1
31 XII 2011 (CDJC)	99.9	99.9	99.9	99.9	99.9	99.8	100	99.9	100.1
TFYR of Macedonia - L'ex-R. y. de Macédoine									
20 VI 1994 (CDJC)	100.2	100.2	100.2	100	100.1	99.8	100.6	100.5	100.8
31 X 2002 (CDJC)	100.3	100.3	100.3	...	...	...	...	...	...
Ukraine									
5 XII 2001 (CDFC)	102.7	102.7	102.7	103.1	103.1	103.2	101.7	101.8	101.5
United Kingdom of Great Britain and Northern Ireland - Royaume-Uni de Grande-Bretagne et d'Irlande du Nord[73]									
21 IV 1991 (CDFC)[74]	98	98	98	...	...	...	...	...	...
29 IV 2001 (CDFC)[75]	98.1	98	98.1	98.2	98.2	98.2	97.6	97.5	97.7
27 III 2011 (CDJC)	100.2	100.3	100.2	100.3	100.3	100.3	99.8	99.8	99.8
OCEANIA - OCÉANIE									
Australia - Australie									
30 VI 1986 (CDFC)	101.6	101.7	101.5	101.6	101.6	101.5	101.8	102	101.6
6 VIII 1991 (CDFC)	101.7	101.4	102.1	...	...	...	...	...	...
9 VIII 1996 (CDFC)	101.6	101.5	101.7	...	...	...	...	...	...
7 VIII 2001 (CDJC)	101.4	101.3	101.5	101.4	101.3	101.5	101.3	101.4	101.3
8 VIII 2006 (CDJC)[76]	100.2[77]	100.3[77]	100.2[77]	100.2	100.2	100.1	100.4	100.5	100.3
9 VIII 2011 (CDJC)[76]	100.8[77]	100.8[77]	100.7[77]	100.7	100.7	100.7	101.3	101.3	101.3
9 VIII 2016 (CDJC)[76]	101.1[77]	101.1[77]	101[77]	101	101	101	101.8	102	101.6
Cook Islands - Îles Cook[78]									
1 XII 1996 (CDJC)	99.1	97.2	101.1	...	...	...	...	...	...
Fiji - Fidji									
31 VIII 1986 (CDFC)	105.4	105	105.7	...	...	...	...	...	...
25 VIII 1996 (CDFC)	100.2	100.6	99.8	99.8	99.9	99.7	100.6	101.3	99.9
French Polynesia - Polynésie française									
3 IX 1996 (CDFC)	98.6	97.8	99.5	...	...	...	...	...	...
20 VIII 2007 (CDFC)	102.8	103.2	102.4	...	...	...	...	...	...

3a. Whipple's Index by sex and urban/rural residence, 1985 - 2017
L'indice de Whipple par le sexe et la résidence urbaine/rurale, 1985 - 2017 (continued - suite)

Continent, country or area, date and code[a] / Continent, pays ou zone, date et code[a]	Total			Urban - Urbaine			Rural - Rurale		
	Both sexes Les deux sexes	Male Masculin	Female Féminin	Both sexes Les deux sexes	Male Masculin	Female Féminin	Both sexes Les deux sexes	Male Masculin	Female Féminin
OCEANIA - OCÉANIE									
Guam									
1 IV 1990 (CDJC)	107.1	106.2	108.2	107	105.5	108.7	107.2	106.6	107.8
1 IV 2000 (CDJC)[17]	100.3	100.4	100.3	...	...	...	...	...	...
Kiribati									
10 X 2010 (CDFC)	104.7	103.3	105.9	106	106	106.1	103.3	100.7	105.7
7 XI 2015 (CDFC)	105.8	107.1	104.5	107.5	110.9	104.5	103.9	103.1	104.6
Marshall Islands - Îles Marshall									
13 XI 1988 (CDFC)	101.2	103.3	98.9	...	...	...	...	...	...
1 VI 1999 (CDFC)	104	106.2	101.7	...	...	...	...	...	...
New Caledonia - Nouvelle-Calédonie									
4 IV 1989 (CDFC)	99.5	99.4	99.6	...	...	...	...	...	...
New Zealand - Nouvelle-Zélande									
4 III 1986 (CDJC)	100.7	100.6	100.7	100.7	100.7	100.8	100.2	99.9	100.6
5 III 1991 (CDFC)	100.3	100.4	100.3	100.5	100.6	100.4	99.7	99.3	100
5 III 1996 (CDJC)	100	100	100	100.1	100.1	100.1	99.5	99.5	99.5
6 III 2001 (CDJC)[76]	100	99.9	100	100.2	100.1	100.2	99	99	99.1
7 III 2006 (CDFC)[76]	99.7	...	...	...	...	...	...	...	...
7 III 2006 (CDJC)[76]	99.6	99.7	99.6	99.7	99.8	99.7	99.1	99.3	98.9
5 III 2013 (CDJC)[76]	100.3	100	100.5	100.3	100.1	100.5	100.2	100	100.4
Niue - Nioué									
29 IX 1986 (CDFC)	105.8	106	105.6	...	...	...	...	...	...
7 IX 2001 (CDFC)	98.5	93.8	103.4	...	...	...	...	...	...
Northern Mariana Islands - Îles Mariannes septentrionales									
1 IV 1990 (CDFC)	108	108.4	107.4	111.7	111.2	112.1	106.6	107.5	105.3
Palau - Palaos									
15 IV 2000 (CDJC)	103.4	105.5	100.5	...	...	...	...	...	...
Papua New Guinea - Papouasie-Nouvelle-Guinée									
11 VII 1990 (CDFC)	139	140.1	137.7	...	...	...	...	...	...
9 VII 2000 (CDFC)	134	134.2	133.8	131	133.4	128	134.5	134.4	134.7
Pitcairn									
31 XII 1991 (CDFC)	96.2	90.9	100	...	...	...	...	...	...
Samoa									
5 XI 2001 (CDFC)	96.4	95.9	97	...	...	...	...	...	...
Tokelau - Tokélaou									
18 X 2011 (CDFC)	102.7	104.3	101.2	...	...	...	...	...	...
18 X 2011 (CDJC)[79]	105.7	109.6	102	...	...	...	...	...	...
Tonga									
28 XI 1986 (CDJC)	98.2	99	97.4	...	...	...	...	...	...
30 XI 1996 (CDFC)[80]	100.7	101.7	99.6	...	...	...	...	...	...
30 XI 2006 (CDJC)	98.6	97.8	99.4	95.2	93.3	97.2	99.7	99.3	100.1
30 XI 2016 (CDJC)	99.6	99.7	99.4	96	97.1	95	100.7	100.6	100.9
Tuvalu									
1 XI 2002 (CDFC)	98.5	100.8	96.4	...	...	...	...	...	...
Vanuatu									
16 V 1989 (CDJC)	106.9	104.8	109	102.4	98.1	107.8	108.1	106.8	109.3
16 XI 2009 (CDFC)	110.5	111.3	109.7	...	...	...	...	...	...
7 XI 2016 (CDFC)	112.2	112.9	111.6	...	...	...	...	...	...
Wallis and Futuna Islands - Îles Wallis et Futuna									
3 X 1996 (CDFC)	96	97.8	94.3	...	...	...	...	...	...

FOOTNOTES - NOTES

Italics: estimates which are less reliable. - Italiques : estimations moins sûres.

* Provisional. - Données provisoires.

[a] 'Code' indicates the source of data, as follows:
CDFC - Census, de facto, complete tabulation
CDJC - Census, de jure, complete tabulation

Le 'Code' indique la source des données, comme suit :
CDFC - Recensement, population de fait, tabulation complète

CDJC - Recensement, population de droit, tabulation complète

[1] Data refer to population in housing units and collective living quarters only. - Correspond aux personnes qui vivent dans des unités d'habitation et dans des logements collectifs seulement.

[2] Data for urban and rural do not add up to the total; reason for discrepancy not ascertained. - La somme des données pour la résidence urbaine et rurale n'est pas égale au total; on ne sait pas comment s'explique la divergence.

[3] Urban and rural data were reported in different years and do not add up to the total. - Les données concernant la population urbaine et la population rurale portent sur des années différentes et leur somme ne correspond pas au total cité.

[4] Excludes collective living quarters. - Exclut les logements collectifs.

5 Excludes the islands of St. Brandon and Agalega. - Non compris les îles St. Brandon et Agalega.

6 Data refer to Saint Helenian resident population. - Pour la population résidente de Sainte-Hélène.

7 Data refer to total resident population, Saint Helenian and other nationalities. - Les données concernent la population résidente totale, originaire de Sainte-Hélène ou possédant une autre nationalité.

8 Data have been adjusted for underenumeration, estimated at 6.8 per cent. - Les données ont été ajustées pour compenser les lacunes du dénombrement estimées à 6,8 p. 100.

9 Because of rounding, totals are not in all cases the sum of the respective components. - Les chiffres étant arrondis, les totaux ne correspondent pas toujours rigoureusement à la somme des composants respectifs.

10 Excluding the institutional population. - Non compris la population dans les institutions.

11 Bermuda is 100 per cent urban. - 100 pour cent de la population des Bermudes est urbaine.

12 Adjusted for census net undercoverage (including adjustment for incompletely enumerated Indian reserves). - Ajusté pour la sous-estimation du recensement (y compris les réservations en Inde incomplètement énumérées).

13 Because of rounding, totals are not in all cases the sum of the respective components. Adjusted for census net undercoverage (including adjustment for incompletely enumerated Indian reserves). - Les chiffres étant arrondis, les totaux ne correspondent pas toujours rigoureusement à la somme des composants respectifs. Ajusté pour la sous-estimation du recensement (y compris les réservations en Inde incomplètement énumérées).

14 To ensure confidentiality, the values, including totals are randomly rounded either up or down to a multiple of '5' or '10.' As a result, when these data are summed or grouped, the total value may not match the individual values since totals and sub-totals are independently rounded. Similarly, percentages, which are calculated on rounded data, may not necessarily add up to 100%. - À des fins de confidentialité, les chiffres, y compris les totaux, sont aléatoirement arrondis au multiple de 5 ou de 10 inférieur ou supérieur. Par conséquent, lorsque ces chiffres sont additionnés, le total peut ne pas correspondre à la somme des valeurs individuelles, dans la mesure où les totaux et les totaux partiels sont arrondis indépendamment. De même, la somme des pourcentages, qui sont calculés à partir des données arrondies, peut ne pas correspondre à 100 %.

15 Total represents population in private dwellings, the non-institutional population and persons found on the streets between the hours of 5am and 7am on September 26, 2001; the figures represent the census counts adjusted for under-coverage. - Le total représente la population vivant dans des logements privés et les personnes trouvées dans la rue entre 5 et 7 heures du matin le 26 septembre 2001, mais ne tient pas compte des personnes vivant dans des établissements; les chiffres sont ceux du recensement corrigés pour tenir compte du sous-dénombrement.

16 Including an estimation of 1 334 585 persons corresponding to 448 195 housing units without information of the occupants. - Y compris une estimation de 1 334 585 personnes correspondant aux 448 195 unités d'habitation sans information sur les occupants.

17 Including armed forces stationed in the area. - Y compris les militaires en garnison sur le territoire.

18 Excluding U.S. Armed Forces overseas and civilian U.S. citizens whose usual place of residence is outside the United States. - Non compris les militaires américains à l'étranger et les civils américains dont le lieu de résidence habituel est en dehors des États-Unis.

19 Data include persons in remote areas, military personnel outside the country, merchant seamen at sea, civilian seasonal workers outside the country, and other civilians outside the country, and exclude nomads, foreign military, civilian aliens temporarily in the country, transients on ships and Indian jungle population. - Y compris les personnes vivant dans des régions éloignées, le personel militaire en dehors du pays, les marins marchands, les ouvriers saisonniers en dehors du pays, et autres civils en dehors du pays, et non compris les nomades, les militaires étrangers, les étrangers civils temporairement dans le pays, les transiteurs sur des bateaux et les Indiens de la jungle.

20 Excludes nomadic Indian tribes. - Non compris les tribus d'Indiens nomades.

21 The districts of Paramaribo and Wanica are considered urban areas, whereas all other districts are considered more or less rural areas. - Les districts de Paramaribo et de Wanica sont considérés comme des zones urbaines, les autres districts étant considérés comme des zones rurales à divers degrés.

22 Unrevised data. Data refer to resident population in Uruguay according to Census Phase 1, carried out between the months of June and July 2004. - Les données n'ont pas été révisées. Les données se rapportent à la population résidente en Uruguay d'après la phase 1 du recensement, qui a eu lieu entre juin et juillet 2004.

23 Excluding Indian jungle population. - Non compris les Indiens de la jungle.

24 For operational purposes, population centers with 2,500 and more inhabitants are considered as urban area and less than 2,500 are considered as rural area. - À des fins opérationnelles, les centres de population comptant 2 500 habitants ou plus sont considérés comme zones urbaines, ceux qui en comptent moins de 2 500 comme zones rurales.

25 Data have not been adjusted for underenumeration, estimated at 4.96 per cent. - Les données n'ont pas été ajustées pour compenser les lacunes du dénombrement, estimées à 4,96 p.100.

26 Excluding foreign diplomatic personnel and their dependants. - Non compris le personnel diplomatique étranger et les membres de leur famille les accompagnant.

27 For statistical purposes, the data for China do not include those for the Hong Kong Special Administrative Region (Hong Kong SAR), Macao Special Administrative Region (Macao SAR) and Taiwan province of China. Data exclude 2.3 million servicemen, 4.65 million persons with permanent resident status difficult to define, and 0.12 per cent undercount based on the post enumeration survey. - Pour la présentation des statistiques, les données pour la Chine ne comprennent pas la Région Administrative Spéciale de Hong Kong (Hong Kong RAS), la Région Administrative Spéciale de Macao (Macao RAS) et Taïwan province de Chine. Les données ne comprennent pas 2,3 millions de militaires, 4,65 millions de personnes ayant le statut de résident permanent mais difficiles à définir, et des lacunes estimées à 0,12 pour cent sur la base de l'enquête de vérification du recensement.

28 Data refer to Hong Kong resident population at the census moment, which covers usual residents and mobile residents. Usual residents refer to two categories of people: (1) Hong Kong permanent residents who had stayed in Hong Kong for at least three months during the six months before or for at least three months during the six months after the census moment, regardless of whether they were in Hong Kong or not at the census moment; and (2) Hong Kong non-permanent residents who were in Hong Kong at the census moment. Mobile Residents, they are Hong Kong permanent residents who had stayed in Hong Kong for at least one month but less than three months during the six months before or for at least one month but less than three months during the six months after the census moment, regardless of whether they were in Hong Kong or not at the census moment. - Les données se rapportent à la population résidente à Hong Kong au moment du recensement. Cette population est composée des résidants habituels et des résidants mobiles. La population résidente est partagée en deux catégories: (1) les résidents permanents qui ont habité à Hong Kong au moins trois mois pendant les six mois précédents ou les six mois suivants le recensement; (2) les habitants non-permanents de Hong Kong qui étaient à Hong Kong au moment du recensement. La population mobile se rapporte aux résidents permanents de Hong Kong qui ont habité à Hong Kong pendant les six mois après le recensement pour une période comprise entre un mois et trois mois, indépendamment du fait qu'ils étaient à Hong Kong au moment du recensement au pays.

29 Data refer to Hong Kong resident population at the census moment, which covers usual residents and mobile residents. Usual residents refer to two categories of people: (1) Hong Kong permanent residents who had stayed in Hong Kong for at least three months during the six months before or for at least three months during the six months after the census moment, regardless of whether they were in Hong Kong or not at the census moment; and (2) Hong Kong non-permanent residents who were in Hong Kong at the census moment. Mobile Residents, they are Hong Kong permanent residents who had stayed in Hong Kong for at least one month but less than three months during the six months before or for at least one month but less than three months during the six months after the census moment, regardless of whether they were in Hong Kong or not at the census moment. Data are estimates from sample enquiry. - Les données se rapportent à la population résidente à Hong Kong au moment du recensement. Cette population est composée des résidants habituels et des résidants mobiles. La population résidente est partagée en deux catégories: (1) les résidents permanents qui ont habité à Hong Kong au moins trois mois pendant les six mois précédents ou les six mois suivants le recensement; (2) les habitants non-permanents de Hong Kong qui étaient à Hong Kong au moment du recensement. La population mobile se rapporte aux résidents permanents de Hong Kong qui ont habité à Hong Kong pendant les six mois après le recensement pour une période comprise entre un mois et trois mois, indépendamment du fait qu'ils étaient à Hong Kong au moment du recensement au pays. Les données sont des chiffres estimatifs dérivés d'une enquête par sondage.

30 Data refer to government controlled areas. - Les données se rapportent aux zones contrôlées par le Gouvernement.

31 Excluding data for Jammu and Kashmir. - Non compris les données concernant la partie du Jammu et Cachemire.

32 Includes data for the Indian-held part of Jammu and Kashmir, the final status of which has not yet been determined. Excluding Mao-Maram, Paomata and Purul sub-divisions of Senapati district of Manipur. The population of Manipur including the estimated population of the three sub-divisions of Senapati district is

2,291,125 (Males 1,161,173 and females 1,129,952). - Y compris les données pour la partie du Jammu et du Cachemire occupée par l'Inde dont le statut définitif n'a pas encore été déterminé. Non compris les subdivisions Mao-Maram Paomata et Purul du district de Senapati dans l'État du Manipur. Cet État compte 2 291 125 habitants (1 161 173 hommes et 1 129 952 femmes), y compris la population estimative des trois subdivisions du district de Senapati.

[33] Includes data for the Indian-held part of Jammu and Kashmir, the final status of which has not yet been determined. - Y compris les données pour la partie du Jammu et du Cachemire occupée par l'Inde dont le statut définitif n'a pas encore été déterminé.

[34] Data have not been adjusted for underenumeration. - Les données n'ont pas été ajustées pour compenser les lacunes du dénombrement.

[35] Differences between the total country figures and sum of urban and rural areas are due to the inclusion of unsettled population. - Les différences entre les chiffres pour l'ensemble du pays et la somme des zones urbaines et rurales s'expliquent par l'inclusion de la population non sédentaire.

[36] Including unsettled population. - Y compris la population non sédentaire.

[37] The data is from the census sample. - Données extraites de l'échantillon de recensement.

[38] Because of rounding, totals are not in all cases the sum of the respective components. Includes data for East Jerusalem and Israeli residents in certain other territories under occupation by Israeli military forces since June 1967. Data are rounded for confidentiality reasons. - Les chiffres étant arrondis, les totaux ne correspondent pas toujours rigoureusement à la somme des composants respectifs. Y compris les données pour Jérusalem-Est et les résidents israéliens dans certains autres territoires occupés depuis 1967 par les forces armées israéliennes. Chiffres arrondis pour des raisons de confidentialité.

[39] Excluding diplomatic personnel outside the country and foreign military and civilian personnel and their dependants stationed in the area. - Non compris le personnel diplomatique hors du pays ni les militaires et agents civils étrangers en poste sur le territoire et les membres de leur famille les accompagnant.

[40] Excluding data for Jordanian territory under occupation since June 1967 by Israeli military forces. Including registered Palestinian refugees and Jordanians abroad. - Non compris les données pour le territoire jordanien occupé depuis juin 1967 par les forces armées israéliennes. Y compris les réfugiés palestiniens enregistrés et les Jordaniens à l'étranger.

[41] Excluding data for Jordanian territory under occupation since June 1967 by Israeli military forces. - Non compris les données pour le territoire jordanien occupé depuis juin 1967 par les forces armées israéliennes.

[42] Unrevised data. - Les données n'ont pas été révisées.

[43] Excluding usual residents not in the country at the time of census. - À l'exclusion des résidents habituels qui ne sont pas dans le pays au moment du recensement.

[44] Data have been adjusted for underenumeration. - Les données ont été ajustées pour compenser les lacunes du dénombrement.

[45] Total population is taken as de facto and de jure together. - Population totale considérée comme de fait et de droit.

[46] Data refer to resident population which includes resident Maldivians and resident foreigners. - Les données concernent la population résidente, qui comprend les Maldiviens et les étrangers.

[47] Data refer to enumerated population. The total for the whole country excludes 1,206,353 persons estimated not to have been counted in parts of States of Rakhine, Kachin and Kayin. - Les données se rapportent à la population dénombrée. L' effectif de la population pour le pays ne comprend pas les personnes qui ne sont pas dénombrées dans certaines régions des États de Rakhine, Kachin et Kayin estimées à un chiffre de 1 206 353 personnes.

[48] Excluding 2739 Filipinos in Philippine Embassies, Consulates and Missions Abroad. - Excepté 2739 Philippins travaillant dans les ambassades, les consulats et les missions des Philippines à l'étranger.

[49] Excluding 2134 Filipinos in Philippine Embassies, Consulates and Missions Abroad. - Excepté 2134 Philippins travaillant dans les ambassades, les consulats et les missions des Philippines à l'étranger.

[50] Excluding foreigners. - Non compris les étrangers.

[51] Data are based on the latest register-based population estimates for 2010. Data refer to resident population which comprises Singapore citizens and permanent residents. - Données basées sur les estimations démographiques les plus récentes fondées sur les registres de 2010. Les données se rapportent à la population résidente composé des citoyens de Singapour et des résidents permanents.

[52] The Population and Housing Census 2001 did not cover the whole area of the country due to the security problems; data refer to the 18 districts for which the census was completed only (in three districts it was not possible to conduct the census at all and in four districts it was partially conducted). Unrevised data. - Le recensement de la population et du logement de 2001 n'a pas été réalisé sur la superficie totale du pays à cause de problèmes de sécurité; les données ne concernent que les 18 districts entièrement recensés (3 districts n'ont pas été

recensés du tout, et 4 ont été recensés en partie). Les données n'ont pas été révisées.

[53] Data for rural areas include data of estate sectors consist of all plantations which are 20 acres or more in extent and with ten or more resident labourers. - Les données pour les zones rurales comprennent celles pour les domaines, dont l'ensemble des plantations de plus de 10 hectares comptant au moins 10 travailleurs résidents.

[54] Total population does not include Palestinian population living in those parts of Jerusalem governorate which were annexed by Israel in 1967, amounting to 210 209 persons. Likewise, the results does not include the estimates of not enumerated population based on the findings of the post enumeration study, i.e 83 805 persons. - Les données relatives à la population totale ne comprennent pas la population palestinienne -équivalent à 210 209 personnes - habitant dans les territoires du gouvernorat de Jérusalem qui ont été annexés par Israël en 1967. Egalement, les données ne tiennent pas compte des estimations de la population calculée sur la base des résultats de l'enquête postcensitaire, équivalent à 83 805 personnes.

[55] Data for urban include population in refugee camps. - Les données pour la population urbaine comprennent la population dans les camps réfugiés.

[56] Including Palestinian refugees. - Y compris les réfugiés de Palestine.

[57] All persons falling within the scope of the census were enumerated on a de jure basis, except students who were enumerated on a de facto basis. - Toutes les personnes englobées dans le recensement ont été dénombrées comme population de droit, à l'exception des étudiants qui ont été dénombrés comme population de fait.

[58] Based on a sample taken at the time of census. Because of rounding, totals are not in all cases the sum of the respective components. The figures were calculated by dividing and rounding to thousand. Therefore, "0" may indicate value of less than 500. - D'après un échantillon obtenu au moment du recensement. Les chiffres étant arrondis, les totaux ne correspondent pas toujours rigoureusement à la somme des composants respectifs. Les chiffres ont été calculés en divisant et en arrondissant au millier. Par conséquent, "0" peut indiquer une valeur inférieure à 500.

[59] Statistics are compiled from registers. - Les statistiques sont compilées à partir des registres.

[60] Excluding Faeroe Islands and Greenland shown separately, if available. - Non compris les Iles Féroé et le Groenland, qui font l'objet de rubriques distinctes, si disponible.

[61] Data include Overseas Departments. - Y compris les données des départements d'outre-mer.

[62] Excluding families of military personnel, visitors and transients. - Non compris les familles des militaires, ni les visiteurs et transients.

[63] Excluding military personnel, visitors and transients. - Non compris les militaires, ni les visiteurs et transients.

[64] Including armed forces stationed outside the country and alien armed forces in the area. - Y compris les militaires nationaux hors du pays et les militaires étrangers en garnison sur le territoire.

[65] The figures refer to usual residents in private households and persons present in communal establishments during the 2011 census. - Données se rapportant aux résidents habituels membres de ménages privés et aux personnes recensées dans des établissements collectifs au recensement de 2011.

[66] Age classification is based on the difference between the year of birth and the year of the census, rather than on completed years of age. - La classification par âge est fondée sur la différence entre l'année de naissance et l'année de recensement,et non sur l'âge en années révolues.

[67] Including residents temporarily outside the country. Population statistics are compiled from registers. - Y compris les résidents se trouvant temporairement hors du pays. Les statistiques de la population sont compilées à partir des registres.

[68] The total number may include 'Unknown residence', but the categories urban and rural do not. - Le nombre total peut inclure les personnes dont la résidence n'est pas connue, à l'inverse des catégories de population urbaine et rurale.

[69] Excluding civilian aliens within the country, but including civilian nationals temporarily outside the country. - Non compris les civils étrangers dans le pays, mais y compris les civils nationaux temporairement hors du pays.

[70] Excluding Transnistria and the municipality of Bender. Excluding non-residents present in country at time of census. - Les données ne tiennent pas compte de l'information sur la Transnistria et la municipalité de Bender. Non compris les non-résidents présents dans le pays au moment du recensement.

[71] Excludes data for Kosovo and Metohia. - Sans les données pour le Kosovo et Metohie.

[72] Excluding transients visitors. - Non compris les visiteurs en transit.

[73] Excluding Channel Islands (Guernsey and Jersey) and Isle of Man, shown separately, if available. - Non compris les îles Anglo-Normandes (Guernesey et Jersey) et l'île de Man, qui font l'objet de rubriques distinctes, si disponible.

[74] Counts for the 1991 Census are taken from 'Key Statistics for Urban and Rural Areas: Great Britain 1991' published volume based on the usually resident population. - Les chiffres du recensement de 1991 sont extraits de l'ouvrage « Key Statistics for Urban Areas: Great Britain 1991 » et sont fondés sur la notion de résidence habituelle.

[75] Counts for the 2001 Census are taken from 'Key Statistics table 1 for the Urban/Rural classification: England and Wales' available on CD based on the usually resident population. - Les chiffres du recensement de 2001 proviennent du tableau intitulé « Key Statistics table 1 for the Urban/Rural classification: England and Wales » disponible sur CD-ROM et sont fondés sur la notion de résidence habituelle.

[76] These data have been randomly rounded to protect confidentiality. Individual figures may not add up to totals, and values for the same data may vary in different tables. - Ces données ont été arrondies de façon aléatoire afin d'en préserver la confidentialité. La somme de certains chiffres peut ne pas correspondre aux totaux indiqués et les valeurs des mêmes données peuvent varier d'un tableau à un autre.

[77] Including population in off-shore, migratory and shipping. - Y compris les populations extraterritoriales, les populations nomades et les populations maritimes.

[78] Excluding Niue, shown separately, which is part of Cook Islands, but because of remoteness is administered separately. - Non compris Nioué, qui fait l'objet d'une rubrique distincte et qui fait partie des îles Cook, mais qui, en raison de son éloignement, est administrée séparément.

[79] Data includes Tokelaun Public Service employees and their immediate families based in Apia but excludes non-residents present at the time of the census. - Les données comprennent les agents de la fonction publique des Tokélaou et leur famille directe basés à Apia mais excluent les non-résidents présents au moment du recensement.

[80] Data refer to Tongans and part-Tongans only. - Les données ne concernent que la population tongane et partie-Tongans seulement.

Table 4 - *Demographic Yearbook 2017*

Table 4 presents, for each country or area of the world, basic vital statistics for the period 2013 - 2017: live births, crude birth rate, deaths, crude death rate, rate of natural increase, infant deaths, infant mortality rate, life expectancy at birth by sex and total fertility rate.

Description of variables: The vital events and rates shown in this table are defined as follows[1]:

Live birth is the complete expulsion or extraction from its mother of a product of conception, irrespective of the duration of pregnancy, which after such separation breathes or shows any other evidence of life such as beating of the heart, pulsation of the umbilical cord, definite movement of voluntary muscles, whether or not the umbilical cord has been cut or the placenta is attached; each product of such a birth is considered live born.

Death is the permanent disappearance of all evidence of life at any time after live birth has taken place (post-natal cessation of vital functions without capability of resuscitation).

Infant deaths are deaths of live born infants under one year of age.

Life expectancy at birth is defined as the average number of years of life for males and females if they continued to be subject to the same mortality experienced in the year(s) to which these life expectancies refer.

The total fertility rate is the average number of children that would be born alive to a hypothetical cohort of women if, throughout their reproductive years, the age-specific fertility rates remained unchanged. The standard method of calculating the total fertility rate is the sum of the age-specific fertility rates.

Crude birth rates and crude death rates presented in this table are calculated using the number of live births and the number of deaths obtained from civil registers. These civil registration data are used only if they are considered reliable (estimated completeness of 90 per cent or more).

Similarly, infant mortality rates presented in this table are calculated using the number of live births and the number of infant deaths obtained from civil registers. If, however, the registration of births or infant deaths for any given country or area is estimated to be less than 90 per cent complete, the rates are not calculated.

For some countries, the data and rates presented in this table are based on vital statistics data sourced from censuses or demographic surveys.

Rate computation: The crude birth and death rates are the annual number of each of these vital events per 1 000 mid-year population. Infant mortality rate is the annual number of deaths of infants under one year of age per 1 000 live births in the same year.

Rates of natural increase are the difference between the crude birth rate and the crude death rate. It should be noted that the rates of natural increase presented here may differ from the population growth rates presented in table 3 as rates of natural increase do not take net international migration into account while the population growth rates do.

Crude birth rates, crude death rates and infant mortality rates that appear in this table have been calculated by the United Nations Statistics Division, unless otherwise noted. Exceptions include official estimated rates for India, which were based on the sample registration system. Rates calculated by the United Nations Statistics Division presented in this table have been limited to those countries or areas having a minimum number of 30 events (for live births, deaths or infant deaths) in a given year.

Reliability of data: Rates calculated on the basis of registered vital statistics which are considered unreliable (estimated to be less than 90 per cent complete) are not calculated. Estimated rates, prepared by individual countries or areas, are presented whenever applicable.

The designation of vital statistics as being either reliable or unreliable is discussed in general in section 4.2 of the Technical Notes. The technical notes for tables 9, 15 and 18 provide specific information on reliability of statistics on live births, infant deaths, and deaths, respectively.

The values shown for life expectancy in this table come from official life tables. It is assumed that, if necessary, the basic data (population and deaths classified by age and sex) have been adjusted for deficiencies before their use in constructing the life tables.

Limitations: Statistics on births, deaths and infant deaths are subject to the same qualifications as have been set forth for vital statistics, in general, in section 4 of the Technical Notes and in the technical notes for individual tables presenting detailed data on these events (table 9, live births; table 15, infant deaths; table 18, deaths).

In assessing comparability, it is important to take into account the reliability of the data used to calculate the rates, as discussed above.

The problem of obtaining precise correspondence between numerator (births and deaths) and denominator (population for crude birth and death rates) as regards the inclusion or exclusion of armed forces, refugees, displaced persons and other special groups is particularly difficult where vital rates are concerned.

It should also be noted that crude rates are particularly affected by the age-sex structure of the population. Infant mortality rates, and to a much lesser extent crude birth rates and crude death rates, are affected by the variation in the definition of a live birth and tabulation procedures.

NOTES

[1] *Principles and Recommendations for a Vital Statistics System Revision 3,* Sales No. E.13.XVII.10, United Nations, New York, 2014.

Tableau 4 – *Annuaire démographique 2017*

Le tableau 4 présente, pour chaque pays ou zone du monde, des statistiques de base de l'état civil pour les années 2013 – 2017 : les naissances vivantes, le taux brut de natalité, les décès, le taux brut de mortalité et le taux d'accroissement naturel de la population, les décès d'enfants de moins d'un an et le taux de mortalité infantile, l'espérance de vie à la naissance par sexe et l'indice synthétique de fécondité.

Description des variables : les faits d'état civil utilisés aux fins du calcul des taux présentés dans le tableau 4 sont définis comme suit[1] :

La naissance vivante est l'expulsion ou l'extraction complète du corps de la mère, indépendamment de la duré de la gestation, d'un produit de la conception qui après cette séparation, respire ou manifeste tout autre signe de vie, tel que battement de cœur, pulsation du cordon ombilical ou contraction effective d'un muscle soumis à l'action de la volonté, que le cordon ombilical ait été coupé ou non et que le placenta soit ou non demeuré attaché ; tout produit d'une telle naissance est considéré comme « enfant né vivant ».

Le décès est la disparition permanente de tout signe de vie à un moment quelconque postérieur à la naissance vivante (cessation des fonctions vitales après la naissance sans possibilité de réanimation).

Il convient de préciser que les chiffres relatifs aux décès d'enfants de moins d'un an se rapportent aux naissances vivantes.

L'espérance de vie à la naissance est le nombre moyen d'années que vivraient les individus de sexe masculin et de sexe féminin s'ils continuaient d'être soumis aux mêmes conditions de mortalité que celles qui existaient pendant les années auxquelles se rapportent les valeurs indiquées.

L'indice synthétique de fécondité représente le nombre moyen d'enfants que mettrait au monde une cohorte hypothétique de femmes qui seraient soumises, tout au long de leur vie, aux mêmes conditions de fécondité par âge que celles auxquelles sont soumises les femmes, dans chaque groupe d'âge, au cours d'une année ou d'une période donnée. La méthode standard pour calculer l'indice synthétique de fécondité consiste à additionner les taux de fécondité par âge simple.

Les taux bruts de natalité et de mortalité ont été établis sur la base du nombre de naissances vivantes et du nombre de décès inscrits sur les registres de l'état civil. Ces données n'ont été utilisées que lorsqu'elles étaient considérées comme sûres (degré estimatif de complétude égal ou supérieur à 90 p. 100).

De même, les taux de mortalité infantile présentés dans le tableau 4 ont été établis à partir du nombre de naissances vivantes et du nombre de décès d'enfants de moins d'un an inscrits sur les registres de l'état civil. Toutefois, lorsque les données relatives aux naissances ou aux décès d'enfants de moins d'un an pour un pays ou zone quelconque n'étaient pas considérées complètes à 90 p. 100 au moins, les indices n'ont pas été calculés.

Pour quelques pays, les données et les taux présentés dans ce tableau ont été extraites des recensements de la population ou des enquêtes démographiques.

Calcul des taux : les taux bruts de natalité et de mortalité, représentent le nombre annuel de chacun de ces faits d'état civil pour 1 000 habitants au milieu de l'année considérée. Les taux de mortalité infantile correspondent au nombre annuel de décès d'enfants de moins d'un an pour 1 000 naissances vivantes survenues pendant la même année.

Le taux d'accroissement naturel est égal à la différence entre le taux brut de natalité et le taux brut de mortalité. Il y a lieu de noter que les taux d'accroissement naturel indiqués dans le tableau 4 peuvent différer des taux d'accroissement de la population figurant dans le tableau 3, les taux d'accroissement naturel ne tenant pas compte des taux nets de migration internationale, alors que ceux-ci sont inclus dans les taux d'accroissement de la population.

Sauf indication contraire, les taux bruts de natalité et de mortalité, et les taux de mortalité infantile figurant dans le tableau 4, ont été calculés par la Division des statistiques de l'Organisation des Nations Unies. Les exceptions comprennent l'Inde, pour laquelle les taux estimatifs officiels ont été fournis sur la base d'un système d'enregistrement par échantillonnage. Les taux calculés par la Division des statistiques de l'Organisation des Nations Unies qui sont présentés dans le tableau 4 se rapportent aux pays ou zones où l'on a enregistré au moins 30 événements (pour les naissances vivantes, les décès ou pour les décès d'enfants de moins d'un an) au cours d'une année donnée.

Fiabilité des données : les taux n'ont pas été calculés lorsque les statistiques de l'état civil issues de systèmes d'enregistrement d'état civil étaient jugées douteuses (degré estimatif de complétude inférieur à 90 p.100) et des taux estimatifs, calculés par les pays ou zones, ont été présentés lorsqu'ils étaient disponibles.

On trouve à la section 4.2 des Notes techniques des explications générales concernant la façon dont les statistiques de l'état civil ont été classées selon leur degré de fiabilité. Les notes techniques relatives aux tableaux 9, 15 et 18 ont trait respectivement à la fiabilité des statistiques des naissances vivantes, des décès d'enfants de moins d'un an et des décès.

Les valeurs relatives à l'espérance de vie figurant dans le tableau 4 proviennent de tables officielles de mortalité. On présume que les données de base (la population et les décès par sexe et âge) ont été rectifiées d'éventuelles insuffisances avant d'être utilisées pour construire les tables de mortalité.

Insuffisance des données : les statistiques des naissances, décès et décès d'enfants de moins d'un an appellent toutes les réserves qui ont été formulées à propos des statistiques de l'état civil en général à la section 4 des Notes techniques et dans les notes techniques relatives aux différents tableaux présentant des données détaillées sur ces événements [tableau 9 (naissances vivantes), tableau 15 (décès d'enfants de moins d'un an) et tableau 18 (décès)].

Pour évaluer la comparabilité des divers taux, il importe de tenir compte de la fiabilité des données utilisées pour calculer ces taux, comme il a été indiqué précédemment.

Le calcul des taux est particulièrement affecté par la difficulté à obtenir une correspondance parfaite entre le numérateur (naissances et décès) et le dénominateur (population, pour les taux bruts de natalité et de mortalité) en raison de l'inclusion ou non dans la population des forces armées, des réfugiés, des personnes déplacées ou d'autres groupes sociaux.

Il y a lieu de noter que la structure par âge et par sexe de la population influe de façon particulière sur les taux bruts. Le manque d'uniformité dans la définition des naissances vivantes et dans les procédures de mise en tableaux a une incidence sur les taux de mortalité infantile et, à un moindre degré, sur les taux bruts de natalité et les taux bruts de mortalité.

NOTE

[1] *Principles and Recommendations for a Vital Statistics System Revision 3*, Sales No. E.13.XVII.10, United Nations, New York, 2014

4. Vital statistics summary and life expectancy at birth: 2013 - 2017
Aperçu des statistiques de l'état civil et de l'espérance de vie à la naissance : 2013 - 2017

Continent, country or area and year / Continent, pays ou zone et année	Code[a]	Live births Naissances vivantes — Number Nombre	Crude birth rate Taux brut de natalité	Code[a]	Deaths Décès — Number Nombre	Crude death rate Taux brut de mortalité	Rate of natural increase Taux d'accroissement naturel	Code[a]	Infant deaths Décès d'enfants de moins d'un an — Number Nombre	Rate (per 1000 births) Taux (par 1000 naissances)	Life expectancy at birth Espérance de vie à la naissance — Male[b] Masculin[b]	Female[b] Féminin[b]	Total fertility rate L'indice synthétique de fécondité
AFRICA - AFRIQUE													
Algeria - Algérie													
2013	C	962 722[1]	25.1	U	168 136[1]	...	...	U	21 586[1]	...	76.5[2]	77.6[2]	2.930
2014	C	1 014 248[1]	25.9	U	173 781[1]	...	...	U	22 282[1]	...	76.6[2]	77.8[2]	3.030
2015	C	1 040 285[1]	26.0	U	182 570[1]	...	...	U	23 150[1]	...	76.4[2]	77.8[2]	3.100
2016	C	1 066 823[1]	26.1	U	180 404[1]	...	...	U	22 271[1]	...	77.1[2]	78.2[2]	3.100
Angola[3]													
2014	I	1 152 490	44.5	I	239 252	9.2	35.3	I	45 627	39.6	...	...	...
Botswana													
2013	U	44 794[4]	...	U	11 967[4]	...	...	U	960[4]	...	...	...	...
2014	U	41 741[4]	...	U	12 177[4]	...	...	U	1 045[4]	...	...	...	...
2015	U	46 765[4]	...	U	13 030[4]	...	...	U	1 012[4]	...	...	...	...
2016	U	49 984[4]	...	U	12 825[4]	...	...	U	1 041[4]	...	64.9[5]	65.9[5]	...
Burundi													
2013	+U	248 395[6]	...		...	...	...		...	...	...	...	5.840
2014	+U	253 698[6]	...		...	...	...		...	...	56.5	60.6	6.140
2015	+U	266 820[6]	...		...	...	...		...	...	...	...	5.700
2016		...	...		...	...	...		...	...	56.3	60.5	5.500[7]
2017		...	...		...	...	...		...	...	56.9	61.3	4.340
Côte d'Ivoire													
2014	I	841 081[3]	37.0	I	248 930[3]	11.0	26.1	I	44 530[3]	52.9	...	...	4.790
2016		...	...		...	...	...		...	...	54.9	57.5	...
Egypt - Égypte													
2013	+C	2 621 902	31.0	C	511 183	6.0	24.9	C	38 753	14.8	...	...	3.000
2014	+C	2 720 495	31.3	C	531 864	6.1	25.2	C	39 679	14.6	...	...	3.500
2015	+C	2 685 276	30.2	C	573 879	6.5	23.7	C	42 050	15.7	...	...	3.500
2016	+C	2 600 173	28.6	C	556 148	6.1	22.5	C	39 301	15.1	70.5	73.3	3.500
2017	+C	2 557 440	26.9	C	547 208	5.7	21.1	C	38 685	15.1	...	...	...
Eswatini													
2013		...	...		...	...	...		...	...	...	...	3.600
2014		...	...		...	...	...		...	...	...	...	3.600
2015		...	...		...	...	...		...	...	...	...	3.500
Ghana													
2013	+U	463 409[8]	...	+U	51 466[9]	...	...		...	...	...	...	...
Guinea - Guinée													
2013	+U	205 658	...		...	...	...		...	...	...	...	...
2014	I	440 340[10]	41.5	I	119 969[11]	11.3	30.2	I	30 907[12]	70.2	57.4[13]	60.4[13]	5.200[14]
2015		...	...		...	...	...		...	...	...	...	5.000[14]
2016		...	...		...	...	...		...	...	...	...	4.800[14]
2017		...	...		...	...	...		...	...	58.4	61.4	4.745[14]
Guinea-Bissau - Guinée-Bissau													
2014		...	...		...	...	...		...	...	51.2	53.6	...
Kenya													
2013	U	870 599	...	U	194 332	...	...	U	20 888	...	...	...	...
2014	U	954 254	...	U	198 611	...	...	U	18 672	...	...	...	...
2015	U	950 224	...	U	200 205	...	...	U	15 861	...	...	...	...
2016	U	948 351	...	U	189 930	...	...	U	13 839	...	...	...	...
Lesotho													
2016	+U	9 655	...	+U	13 768	...	...		...	...	...	...	...
Liberia - Libéria													
2013		...	...		...	...	...		...	...	...	...	4.700
2014		...	...		...	...	...		...	...	...	...	4.600
Mauritania - Mauritanie													
2013	I	114 420[15]	32.3		...	...	...		...	...	58.3	61.8	...
Mauritius - Maurice[16]													
2013	+C	13 488	10.7	+C	9 440	7.5	3.2	+C	165	12.2	...	...	1.438
2014	+C	13 283	10.5	+C	9 682	7.7	2.9	+C	194	14.6	III71.0	77.6	1.424
2015	+C	12 640	10.0	+C	9 747	7.7	2.3	+C	173	13.7	III71.1	77.8	1.362

4. Vital statistics summary and life expectancy at birth: 2013 - 2017
Aperçu des statistiques de l'état civil et de l'espérance de vie à la naissance : 2013 - 2017 (continued - suite)

Continent, country or area and year / Continent, pays ou zone et année	Live births / Naissances vivantes Code[a]	Number Nombre	Crude birth rate Taux brut de natalité	Deaths / Décès Code[a]	Number Nombre	Crude death rate Taux brut de mortalité	Rate of natural increase Taux d'accrois-sement naturel	Infant deaths / Décès d'enfants de moins d'un an Code[a]	Number Nombre	Rate (per 1000 births) Taux (par 1000 naiss-ances)	Life expectancy at birth / Espérance de vie à la naissance Male[b] Masculin[b]	Female[b] Féminin[b]	Total fertility rate L'indice synthétique de fécondité
AFRICA - AFRIQUE													
Mauritius - Maurice[16]													
2016	+C	12 948	10.2	+C	10 174	8.1	2.2	+C	154	11.9	[III]71.2	77.8	1.399
2017	+C	13 385	10.6	+C	10 140	8.0	2.6	+C	164	12.3	[III]71.3	77.9	1.449
Mayotte													
2014	C	7 306	32.4	C	590	2.6	29.8	...	...		74.7	77.9	...
2015	C	8 997	38.3	C	636	2.7	35.6	...	...		75.3	77.2	...
2016	C	9 496	38.9	C	705	2.9	36.0	...	...		...	...	...
2017	C	9 762	38.4	C	735	2.9	35.5	...	...		...	...	...
Morocco - Maroc													
2013		...	...		...	...	...		...	...	72.4	75.1	...
Mozambique													
2013	U	746 185[17]	...		...	...	...		...	...	...	...	5.400
2014	U	794 718[17]	...		...	...	...		...	...	50.2	55.4	...
2015		...	...		...	...	...		...	...	51.7	55.9	...
2016		...	...		...	...	...		...	...	52.0	56.2	...
Reunion - Réunion													
2014	C	14 095[18]	16.6	C	4 355	5.1	11.5	...	...		77.1	83.7	...
2015	C	14 011[18]	16.4	C	4 531	5.3	11.1	...	...		77.1	83.6	...
2016	C	13 742[18]	16.0	C	4 689	5.5	10.5	...	...		...	...	...
2017	C	13 708[18]	15.9	C	4 673	5.4	10.5	...	...		...	...	...
Saint Helena ex. dep. - Sainte-Hélène sans dép.													
2013	C	35	8.3	C	55	13.1	-4.7	C	-	...	...	...	...
2014	C	48	10.9	C	61	13.9	-3.0	C	1	...	...	...	...
2015	C	40	8.9	C	55	12.3	-3.4		...	...	...	...	...
2016	C	35	7.5	C	45	9.7	-2.1		...	...	...	...	...
2017	C	36	...	C	58	...	...		...	...	...	...	...
Sao Tome and Principe - Sao Tomé-et-Principe													
2013	C	4 856	26.6	C	1 267	6.9	19.7	...	...		...	...	...
2014	C	4 939	26.6	C	1 243	6.7	19.9	...	...		...	...	...
2015	C	5 022	26.5	C	1 226	6.5	20.0	...	...		...	...	...
2016	C	5 105	26.4	C	1 212	6.3	20.1	...	...		...	...	...
2017	C	5 190	26.3	C	1 202	6.1	20.2	...	...		...	...	...
Senegal - Sénégal													
2013	I	478 898[19]	35.5	I	136 460[19]	10.1	25.3	...	...		63.2[20]	66.5[20]	...
Seychelles													
2013	+C	1 566	17.4	+C	717	8.0	9.4	+C	29	...	69.9	76.5	2.370
2014	+C	1 557	17.0	+C	725	7.9	9.1	+C	17	...	68.4	78.3	2.340
2015	+C	1 592	17.0	+C	703	7.5	9.5	+C	17	...	...	...	...
2016	+C	1 645	17.4	+C	747	7.9	9.5		...	...	...	...	...
2017	+C	1 651	17.2	+C	748	7.8	9.4	+C	18	...	70.3	78.5	...
Sierra Leone[21]													
2013	+U	229 947	...	+U	19 403	...	...	+U	2 276	...	...	...	...
South Africa - Afrique du Sud													
2013	U	1 012 808	...	U	477 163	...	...	U	26 841	...	...	...	2.540
2014	U	1 008 740	...	U	476 891	...	...	U	26 785	...	59.1	63.1	2.510
2015	U	952 242	...	U	473 266	...	...	U	24 994	...	...	...	2.480
2016	C	876 435	15.7	U	456 612	...	...	U	20 649	...	...	...	2.430
2017		...	...		...	...	...		...	...	...	...	2.420
Tunisia - Tunisie													
2013	C	222 962	20.5	U	61 730	...	...		...	...	...	...	...
2014	C	225 887	20.5	U	62 785	...	...		...	...	...	...	...
2015	C	222 534	20.0	U	65 743	...	...		...	...	74.5	77.8	...
2016	C	219 441	19.4	U	62 601	...	...		...	...	...	...	...
2017	C	209 236	18.3	U	67 447	...	...		...	...	...	...	...

4. Vital statistics summary and life expectancy at birth: 2013 - 2017
Aperçu des statistiques de l'état civil et de l'espérance de vie à la naissance : 2013 - 2017 (continued - suite)

Continent, country or area and year / Continent, pays ou zone et année	Code[a]	Number Nombre	Crude birth rate Taux brut de natalité	Code[a]	Number Nombre	Crude death rate Taux brut de mortalité	Rate of natural increase Taux d'accroissement naturel	Code[a]	Number Nombre	Rate (per 1000 births) Taux (par 1000 naissances)	Male[b] Masculin[b]	Female[b] Féminin[b]	Total fertility rate L'indice synthétique de fécondité
AFRICA - AFRIQUE													
Uganda - Ouganda[22]													
2014		...	...		...	...	...		...	...	62.2	64.2	...
United Republic of Tanzania - République Unie de Tanzanie[23]													
2013		...	...		...	...	...		...	...	...	...	5.300
2014		...	...		...	...	...		...	...	...	...	5.300
2015		...	...		...	...	...		...	...	...	...	5.200
2016		...	...		...	...	...		...	...	...	...	5.200
2017		...	...		...	...	...		...	...	...	...	5.100
AMERICA, NORTH - AMÉRIQUE DU NORD													
Anguilla													
2013	+C	165	11.9	+C	68[24]	4.9	7.0	+C	3	...	...	...	...
2014	+C	151	10.6	+C	59[24]	4.1	6.5		...	...	...	...	...
2015	+C	165	11.2	+C	61[24]	4.1	7.1		...	...	...	...	...
2016	+C	135	9.0	+C*	83[24]	5.5	3.4		...	...	...	...	...
2017	+C	145	...		...	...	...		...	...	...	...	...
Aruba													
2013	C	1 346	12.7	C	560	5.3	7.4	+C	5	...	...	...	2.032
2014	C	1 376	12.8	C	643	6.0	6.8	+C	5	...	...	...	2.041
2015	C	1 244	11.4	C	679	6.2	5.2	+C	6	...	...	...	1.821
2016	C	1 259	11.4	C	781	7.1	4.3	+C	5	...	...	...	1.821
2017	C	1 202	10.8	C	707	6.4	4.5	+C	6	...	...	...	1.746
Bahamas													
2013	+U	4 330	...	+C	2 065	5.7	...	+C	51	...	...	...	1.725
2014	+U*	4 155	...	+C*	2 132	5.9	...	+C*	85	...	...	...	1.475*
2015	+U*	4 253	...	+C*	2 243	6.1	...	+C*	82	...	...	...	...
2016	+U*	4 093	...	+C*	2 288	6.1	...	+C*	70	...	...	...	...
2017	+U*	4 017	...	+C*	2 372	6.3	...	+C*	72	...	...	...	...
Barbados - Barbade													
2013	+C	3 020	10.9	+C	2 276	8.2	2.7		...	...	...	...	...
2014	+C	2 902	10.5	+C	2 580	9.3	1.2		...	...	...	...	...
Belize													
2013	U	7 264	...	U	1 637	...	...	U	129	...	...	...	2.394
2014	U	7 318	...	U	1 620	...	...	U	91	...	...	...	2.353
2015	U	7 456	...	U	1 772	...	...	U	127	...	...	...	2.347
2016	U	7 200	...	U	1 796	...	...	U	103	...	...	...	2.195
Bermuda - Bermudes													
2013	C	648[25]	10.5	C	471[25]	7.6	2.9	C	1	...	76.9	84.5	1.594
2014	C	574[25]	9.3	C	480[25]	7.8	1.5	C	2	...	77.1	84.7	1.420
2015	C	583[25]	9.4	C	478[25]	7.7	1.7	C	2	...	77.3	84.9	1.450
2016	C	591[25]	9.6	C	492[25]	8.0	1.6	C	2	...	77.5	85.1	1.496
2017	C*	576[25]	9.3	C*	481[25]	7.8	1.5		...	...	77.7	85.4	...
British Virgin Islands - Îles Vierges britanniques													
2013	C	277	9.7	C	113	4.0	5.8		...	...	...	...	...
2014	C	280	...	C	111	...	...		...	...	...	...	...
2015	C	266	9.1	C	136	4.7	4.5		...	...	...	...	...
Canada													
2013	C	380 323[26]	10.8	C	252 338[26]	7.2	3.6	C	1 884[26]	5.0	...	...	1.587
2014	C	384 100[26]	10.8	C	258 821[26]	7.3	3.5	C	1 794[26]	4.7	...	...	1.582
2015	C	382 392[26]	10.7	C	264 333[26]	7.4	3.3	C	1 737[26]	4.5	III79.9	84.0	1.563
2016	C	383 102[26]	10.6	C	267 213[26]	7.4	3.2	C	1 741[26]	4.5	...	...	1.543
2017	C	376 291[26]	10.3	C	...	...	...		...	...	...	...	...

4. Vital statistics summary and life expectancy at birth: 2013 - 2017
Aperçu des statistiques de l'état civil et de l'espérance de vie à la naissance : 2013 - 2017 (continued - suite)

Continent, country or area and year / Continent, pays ou zone et année	Live births / Naissances vivantes Code[a]	Number Nombre	Crude birth rate Taux brut de natalité	Deaths / Décès Code[a]	Number Nombre	Crude death rate Taux brut de mortalité	Rate of natural increase Taux d'accrois-sement naturel	Infant deaths / Décès d'enfants de moins d'un an Code[a]	Number Nombre	Rate (per 1000 births) Taux (par 1000 naiss-ances)	Life expectancy at birth / Espérance de vie à la naissance Male[b] Masculin[b]	Female[b] Féminin[b]	Total fertility rate L'indice synthétique de fécondité
AMERICA, NORTH - AMÉRIQUE DU NORD													
Cayman Islands - Îles Caïmanes													
2013	C	705	12.5	C	182[27]	3.2	9.3		...	...	...	...	...
2014	C	711	12.5	C	163[27]	2.9	9.6		...	...	...	...	...
2015	C	649	11.0	C	170[27]	2.9	8.1		...	...	...	...	...
2016	C	660	10.8	C	193[27]	3.2	7.7		...	...	...	...	...
2017	C	625	9.9	C	216[27]	3.4	6.4		...	...	...	...	...
Costa Rica													
2013	C	70 550	15.0	C	19 647	4.2	10.8	C	612	8.7	...	...	1.760
2014	C	71 793[28]	15.0	C	20 553	4.3	10.7	C	575	8.0	77.2	82.3	1.860
2015	C	71 819	14.9	C	21 039	4.4	10.5	C	557	7.8	77.4	82.4	1.750
2016	C	70 004	14.3	C	22 603	4.6	9.7	C	555	7.9	...	...	1.700*
2017	C*	68 816	13.9	C*	23 251	4.7	9.2	C*	548	8.0	77.6	82.7	1.671*
Cuba													
2013	C	125 880	11.2	C	92 273	8.2	3.0	C	525	4.2	III76.5	80.5	1.714
2014	C	122 643	10.9	C	96 330	8.6	2.3	C	514	4.2	...	...	1.681
2015	C	125 064	11.1	C	99 691	8.9	2.3	C	535	4.3	...	...	1.721
2016	C	116 872	10.4	C	99 388	8.8	1.6	C	497	4.3	...	...	1.626
2017	C	114 971	10.2	C	106 941	9.5	0.7	C	465	4.0	...	...	...
Curaçao													
2013	C	1 962	12.8	C	1 250	8.1	4.6	C	15	...	...	...	2.100
2014	C	1 963	12.6	C	1 370	8.8	3.8	C	24	...	IV74.0	81.2	2.000
2015	C	1 877	11.9	C	1 398	8.8	3.0	C	20	...	...	...	1.900
2016	C	1 789	11.2	C	1 482	9.3	1.9	C	20	...	74.9	81.0	1.700
2017	C	1 548	9.7	C	1 420	8.9	0.8	C	16	...	III74.7	81.5	1.500
Dominica - Dominique													
2013	+C	931	13.1	+C	630	8.8	4.2		...	...	...	...	...
2014	+C	858	12.0	+C	590	8.2	3.7		...	...	...	...	...
Dominican Republic - République dominicaine													
2013	U	159 785[29]	...	U	36 025	...	...	U	659	...	...	...	2.391
2014	U	161 306[29]	...	U	40 466	...	...	U	844	...	...	...	2.364
2015	U	157 422[29]	...	U	40 948	...	...	U	926	...	VI70.0	74.8	2.336
2016	U	139 583[29]	...	U	42 199	...	...	U	800	...	...	...	2.310[30]
2017		...	...		...	...	...		...	...	...	...	2.286[30]
El Salvador													
2013	C	109 617[31]	17.4	C	34 212	5.4	12.0	C	859[32]	7.8	...	...	2.200
2014	C	108 903[31]	17.2	C	37 461	5.9	11.3	C	876[32]	8.0	...	...	...
2015	C	109 617[31]	17.0		...	...	...		...	...	...	...	...
Greenland - Groenland													
2013	C	820	14.5	C	444	7.9	6.7	C	7	...	V68.5	73.7	2.051
2014	C	805	14.3	C	461	8.2	6.1	C	6	...	V69.1	73.7	1.995
2015	C	854	15.2	C	472	8.4	6.8	C	9	...	...	...	2.131
2016	C	830	14.8	C	487	8.7	6.1	C	6	...	...	...	...
2017	C	853	15.2	C	499	8.9	6.3	C	6	...	...	...	...
Grenada - Grenade													
2013	+C	1 838	16.9	+C	822	7.6	9.4	+C	32	17.4	...	...	...
2014	+C	1 750	16.0	+C	958	8.8	7.2	+C	33	18.9	...	...	...
Guadeloupe													
2013	C	5 069[18]	12.6	C	2 951[18]	7.4	5.3		...	...	...	...	...
2014	C	5 001[18]	12.5	C	3 290[18]	8.2	4.3		...	...	76.1	83.4	...
2015	C	4 714[18]	11.9	C	2 906[18]	7.3	4.6		...	...	77.0	84.8	...
2016	C	4 653[18]	11.8	C	3 227[18]	8.2	3.6		...	...	...	...	...
2017	C	4 126[18]	10.5	C	3 121[18]	8.0	2.6		...	...	...	...	...
Guatemala													
2013	C	387 342	25.1	C	76 639	5.0	20.1	C	7 221	18.6	...	...	...
2014	C	386 195	24.4	C	77 807	4.9	19.5	C	7 342	19.0	...	...	...

4. Vital statistics summary and life expectancy at birth: 2013 - 2017
Aperçu des statistiques de l'état civil et de l'espérance de vie à la naissance : 2013 - 2017 (continued - suite)

Continent, country or area and year / Continent, pays ou zone et année	Code[a]	Live births / Naissances vivantes Number Nombre	Crude birth rate Taux brut de natalité	Code[a]	Deaths / Décès Number Nombre	Crude death rate Taux brut de mortalité	Rate of natural increase Taux d'accrois-sement naturel	Code[a]	Infant deaths / Décès d'enfants de moins d'un an Number Nombre	Rate (per 1000 births) Taux (par 1000 naiss-ances)	Life expectancy at birth / Espérance de vie à la naissance Male[b] Masculin[b]	Female[b] Féminin[b]	Total fertility rate L'indice synthétique de fécondité
AMERICA, NORTH - AMÉRIQUE DU NORD													
Guatemala													
2015	C	391 425	24.2	C	80 876	5.0	19.2	C	8 202	21.0	VI67.9	75.0	...
2016	C	390 382	...	C	82 565	...	...	C	8 366	21.4	...	...	...
Jamaica - Jamaïque													
2013	C	36 746	13.5	U	17 350[33]	...	...	...	...	...	...	...	...
2014	C	36 996	13.6	U	18 320	...	...	...	...	...	...	...	...
2015	C	37 900	13.9	U	19 249	...	...	...	...	...	...	...	...
2016	C	36 160	13.3	U	19 761	...	...	...	...	...	...	...	...
2017	C	34 169	12.5	U	18 879	...	...	...	...	...	...	...	...
Martinique													
2013	C	4 130[18]	10.7		...	...	...		...	...	...	...	1.900
2014	C	4 367[18]	11.4	C	3 319[18]	8.6	2.7		...	...	78.1	83.9	...
2015	C	3 972[18]	10.4	C	3 057[18]	8.0	2.4		...	...	79.4	84.7	...
2016	C	3 782[18]	10.0	C	3 284[18]	8.7	1.3		...	...	...	...	...
2017	C	3 640[18]	9.7	C	3 217[18]	8.6	1.1		...	...	...	...	...
Mexico - Mexique													
2013	C	2 168 933[34]	18.3	+C	622 495[35]	5.3	13.1	+C	27 802[35]	12.8	71.7	77.4	...
2014	C	2 129 825[34]	17.8	+C	632 587[35]	5.3	12.5	+C	26 385[35]	12.4	72.1	77.6	...
2015	C	2 096 274[34]	17.3	+C	654 593[35]	5.4	11.9	+C	26 045[35]	12.4	72.3	77.7	...
2016	C*	2 293 708	18.8	+C	684 437[35]	5.6	13.2	+C	24 722[35]	10.8	...	...	...
Montserrat													
2013	C	41	8.3	C	45	9.1	-0.8	C	-	...	...	...	...
2014	C	50	10.0	C	32	6.4	3.6	C	-	...	...	...	...
2015	C	48	9.6	C	49	9.8	-0.2	C	3	...	...	...	...
2016	C	46	9.1	C	43	8.5	0.6	C	-	...	...	...	...
Nicaragua													
2016	+U	137 772	...	+U	23 205	...	...						
Panama													
2013	C	73 804	19.2	U	17 767	...	...	U	1 106	...	74.4[36]	80.5[36]	2.400
2014	C	75 183	19.2	C	18 171	4.6	14.6	C	1 036	13.8	74.6[36]	80.7[36]	2.400
2015	C*	75 901	19.1	C	18 182	4.6	14.5	C	935	12.3	74.8[36]	80.9[36]	2.400
2016	C*	75 184	18.6	C*	18 882	4.7	13.9	C*	1 046	13.9	75.0[36]	81.1[36]	2.400
2017	C*	74 832	18.3	C*	18 388	4.5	13.8		...	...	...	...	...
Puerto Rico - Porto Rico													
2013	C	36 580	10.2	C	29 416	8.2	2.0	C	270	7.4	...	...	1.470
2014	C	34 503	9.8	C	30 333	8.6	1.2	C	242	7.0	...	...	1.434
2015	C	31 241	9.0	C	28 409	8.2	0.8	C	222	7.1	III76.4	84.0	1.339
2016	C	28 344	8.3	C	29 649	8.7	-0.4	C	222	7.8	III76.6	84.1	1.246
2017	C	24 370	7.3	C	30 977	9.3	-2.0	C	172	7.1	III76.6	84.4	...
Saint Kitts and Nevis - Saint-Kitts-et-Nevis													
2013	+C	547	...	+C	348	...	...		...	...	...	...	...
2014	+C	641	...	+C	411	...	...		...	...	...	...	...
Saint Vincent and the Grenadines - Saint-Vincent-et-les Grenadines													
2013	C	1 738	15.8	C	926	8.4	7.4	C	32	18.4	...	...	2.090
2014	C	1 841	16.7	C	1 006	9.1	7.6	C	29	...	68.4	74.6	2.211
2016		...	...		...	...	...		...	...	71.0	75.2	...
Sint Maarten (Dutch part) - Saint-Martin (partie néerlandaise)[37]													
2013	+C	511	14.0	+C	171	4.7	9.3		...	...	...	...	...
Trinidad and Tobago - Trinité-et-Tobago													
2013	C*	18 823	14.0	C*	10 661	8.0	6.1	C*	326	17.3	...	...	...
2014	C*	18 729	13.9	C*	11 461	8.5	5.4		...	...	...	...	...
2015	C*	18 062	13.4	C*	11 240	8.3	5.1		...	...	...	...	...

4. Vital statistics summary and life expectancy at birth: 2013 - 2017
Aperçu des statistiques de l'état civil et de l'espérance de vie à la naissance : 2013 - 2017 (continued - suite)

Continent, country or area and year / Continent, pays ou zone et année	Code[a] / Code[a]	Live births - Naissances vivantes / Number Nombre	Live births / Crude birth rate Taux brut de natalité	Code[a] / Code[a]	Deaths - Décès / Number Nombre	Deaths / Crude death rate Taux brut de mortalité	Rate of natural increase Taux d'accroissement naturel	Code[a] / Code[a]	Infant deaths - Décès d'enfants de moins d'un an / Number Nombre	Infant deaths / Rate (per 1000 births) Taux (par 1000 naissances)	Life expectancy at birth - Espérance de vie à la naissance / Male[b] Masculin[b]	Life expectancy / Female[b] Féminin[b]	Total fertility rate L'indice synthétique de fécondité
AMERICA, NORTH - AMÉRIQUE DU NORD													
Turks and Caicos Islands - Îles Turques et Caïques													
2013	C	502	14.9	C	101[38]	3.0	11.9	C	12	...	...	...	...
2014	C	437	12.4	C	76[38]	2.2	10.3	C	2	...	...	...	...
2015	C	437	11.9		...	...	...		...	...	...	...	...
2016	C	518	13.7		...	...	...		...	...	...	...	...
United States of America - États-Unis d'Amérique													
2013	C	3 932 181	12.4	C	2 596 993	8.2	4.2	C	23 440	6.0	76.4	81.2	1.857
2014	C	3 988 076	12.5	C	2 626 418	8.2	4.3	C	23 215	5.8	76.4	81.2	1.863
2015	C	3 978 497	12.4	C	2 712 630	8.5	3.9	C	23 455	5.9	76.3	81.2	1.844
AMERICA, SOUTH - AMÉRIQUE DU SUD													
Argentina - Argentine													
2013	C	754 603	17.9	C	326 197	7.7	10.2	C	8 174	10.8	...	...	2.335
2014	C	777 012	18.2	C	325 539	7.6	10.6	C	8 202	10.6	...	...	2.309
2015	C	770 040	17.9	C	333 407	7.7	10.1	C	7 445	9.7	73.7[30]	80.3[30]	2.282
2016	C	728 035	16.7	C	352 992	8.1	8.6	C	7 093	9.7	...	...	2.263
2017		...	...		...	...	...		...	...	...	...	2.243
Bolivia (Plurinational State of) - Bolivie (État plurinational de)													
2013	U	149 832	...		...	...	...		...	...	...	...	...
2014	U	153 016	...		...	...	...		...	...	...	...	...
2015	+U	277 498	...		...	...	...		...	...	VI25.3	28.0	...
2016		...	...		...	...	...		...	...	II68.6[39]	75.3[39]	...
2017		...	...		...	...	...		...	...	II69.1[40]	75.9[40]	...
Brazil - Brésil													
2013	U	2 832 590[41]	...	U	1 180 796[42]	...	...	U	31 944[43]	...	71.3[36]	78.5[36]	1.770[44]
2014	U	2 913 121[41]	...	+C	1 194 164[42]	5.9	...	U	31 679[43]	...	71.6[36]	78.8[36]	1.742[44]
2015	+C	2 952 969	14.4	+C	1 231 400[42]	6.0	8.4	+C	31 238	10.6	71.9	79.1	1.716[44]
2016	+C	2 903 933	14.1	+C	1 274 630[42]	6.2	7.9	+C	30 541	10.5	...	...	1.692[44]
Chile - Chili													
2013	C	242 005	13.8	C	99 770	5.7	8.1	C	1 692	7.0	76.3	81.4	1.790
2014	C	250 997	14.1	C	101 960	5.7	8.4	C	1 825	7.3	76.8	82.5	1.850
2015	C	244 670	13.6	C	103 327	5.7	7.8	C	1 683	6.9	77.1	82.7	1.790
2016	C*	232 616	12.8	C*	104 026	5.7	7.1		...	...	...	...	...
Colombia - Colombie													
2013	U	658 835	...	U	203 071	...	...	U	7 618	...	...	...	...
2014	U	669 137	...	U	210 051	...	...	U	7 589	...	...	...	...
2015	U	660 999	...	U	219 472	...	...	U	7 244	...	VI72.1	78.5	...
2016	U	647 521	...	U	223 078	...	...	U	7 220	...	...	...	...
2017		...	...		...	...	...		...	...	...	...	2.289[45]
Ecuador - Équateur[46]													
2013	U	277 620	...	U	63 104	...	...	U	2 928	...	...	...	2.634[47]
2014	U	278 460	...	U	62 981	...	...	U	2 821	...	73.2[30]	78.6[30]	2.587[47]
2015	U	283 313	...	U	64 790	...	...	U	2 979	...	VI73.2[47]	78.8[47]	2.542[47]
2016	U*	266 464	...	U	67 506	...	...	U	3 042	...	73.7[47]	79.3[47]	2.499[47]
2017		...	...		...	...	...		...	...	VIII73.9[47]	79.5[47]	2.459[47]
French Guiana - Guyane française													
2013	C	6 474[18]	26.5	C	767[18]	3.1	23.4		...	...	...	...	...
2014	C	6 591[18]	26.1	C	786[18]	3.1	23.0		...	...	76.7	83.1	...
2015	C	6 806[18]	26.4	C	834[18]	3.2	23.2		...	...	76.4	82.0	...

Continent, country or area and year / Continent, pays ou zone et année	Live births / Naissances vivantes			Deaths / Décès			Rate of natural increase Taux d'accrois-sement naturel	Infant deaths / Décès d'enfants de moins d'un an			Life expectancy at birth / Espérance de vie à la naissance		Total fertility rate / L'indice synthétique de fécondité
	Code[a]	Number Nombre	Crude birth rate Taux brut de natalité	Code[a]	Number Nombre	Crude death rate Taux brut de mortalité		Code[a]	Number Nombre	Rate (per 1000 births) Taux (par 1000 naiss-ances)	Male[b] Masculin[b]	Female[b] Féminin[b]	
AMERICA, SOUTH - AMÉRIQUE DU SUD													
French Guiana - Guyane française													
2016	C	7 270[18]	27.7	C	901[18]	3.4	24.3	...	...	...	...	...	...
2017	C	8 057[18]	29.4	C	964[18]	3.5	25.9	...	...	...	...	...	...
Guyana													
2013		...	...	+C	5 195	7.0	...	...	...	...	...	...	...
2014		...	...	+C	5 268	7.1	...	...	...	...	...	...	...
2015		...	...	+C	4 922	6.6	...	...	...	...	...	...	...
2016		...	...	+C	5 109	6.9	...	...	...	...	...	...	...
2017		...	...	+C	4 909	6.6	...	...	...	...	...	...	...
Paraguay													
2013	+U	114 619	...	+U	24 193	...	...	...	...	...	...	...	...
2014	+U	116 592	...	+U	22 625	...	...	+U	468	...	...	...	...
2015	+U	132 241	...	+U	24 885	...	...	...	...	...	...	...	...
2016	+U	128 117	...	+U	27 243	...	...	+U	485	...	...	...	...
Peru - Pérou													
2013	+U	475 349[48]	...	+U	94 394[48]	...	...	+U	4 548[48]	...	...	...	2.364[30]
2014	+U	492 008[48]	...	+U	96 460[48]	...	...	+U	4 243[48]	...	...	...	2.328[30]
2015	+U	529 029[48]	...	+U	96 240[48]	...	...	+U	3 852[48]	...	VI71.5	76.8	2.294[30]
2016	+U*	522 269[48]	...	+U*	97 897[48]	...	...	+U*	3 616[48]	...	...	...	2.263[30]
2017	+U*	482 914[48]	...		...	...	...	...	...	...	...	...	2.233[30]
Suriname													
2013	C	10 012	18.2	C	3 557	6.5	11.7	C	168	16.8	III69.3	75.1	2.323
2014	C	10 407	18.6	C	3 738	6.7	11.9	C	163	15.7	...	...	2.370
2015	C	10 148	17.9	C	3 663	6.5	11.4	C	149	14.7	III70.1	75.3	2.330
2016	C	9 910	17.2	C	3 591	6.2	11.0	C	170	17.2	...	...	2.230
Uruguay													
2013	C	48 681	14.2	C	32 698	9.5	4.6	C	430	8.8	...	...	1.957
2014	C	48 368	14.0	C	32 122	9.3	4.7	C	376	7.8	...	...	1.936
2015	C	48 926	14.1	C	32 967	9.5	4.6	C	367	7.5	...	...	...
2016	C	47 058	13.5	C	34 273	9.8	3.7	C	376	8.0	73.8	80.6	...
Venezuela (Bolivarian Republic of) - Venezuela (République bolivarienne du)													
2013	U	597 902	...	C	147 901	5.0	...	C	7 630	...	...	...	2.427[49]
2014	U	597 773	...	C	159 239	5.3	...	C	8 396	...	...	...	2.410[49]
2015	U	600 875	...	C	163 712	5.4	...	C	9 276	...	...	...	...
2016	U	642 644	...	C	185 697	6.0	...	C	11 783	...	72.3[50]	78.4[50]	...
2017	U*	561 603	...	C	181 297	5.8	...	C	11 082	...	...	...	...
ASIA - ASIE													
Armenia - Arménie													
2013	C*	41 790	13.8	C*	27 196[51]	9.0	4.8		...	...	...	...	1.600
2014	C	43 031	14.3	C	27 714[51]	9.2	5.1	C	376[51]	8.7	...	...	1.700
2015	C	41 763	13.9	C	27 878[51]	9.3	4.6	C	370[51]	8.9	II71.7	78.2	1.600
2016	C	40 592	13.6	C	28 226[51]	9.4	4.1	C	352[51]	8.7	II2.9	2.5	...
2017	C	37 700	12.7	C	27 157[51]	9.1	3.5		...	...	...	...	...
Azerbaijan - Azerbaïdjan													
2013	+C	172 671[51]	18.3	+C	54 383[51]	5.8	12.6	+C	1 862[51]	10.8	71.6	76.8	2.200
2014	+C	170 503[51]	17.9	+C	55 648[51]	5.8	12.0	+C	1 655[51]	9.7	72.2	77.3	2.200
2015	+C	166 210[51]	17.2	+C	54 697[51]	5.7	11.6	+C	2 033[51]	12.2	72.7	77.6	2.100
2016	+C	159 464[51]	16.3	+C	56 648[51]	5.8	10.5	+C	1 666[51]	10.4	72.8	77.5	2.000
Bahrain - Bahreïn													
2013	C	19 995[52]	16.0	C	2 588[52]	2.1	13.9	C	141[53]	7.1	...	...	2.157
2014	C	20 931[52]	15.9	C	2 805[52]	2.1	13.8	C	218[53]	10.4	...	...	2.173

4. Vital statistics summary and life expectancy at birth: 2013 - 2017
Aperçu des statistiques de l'état civil et de l'espérance de vie à la naissance : 2013 - 2017 (continued - suite)

Continent, country or area and year / Continent, pays ou zone et année	Code[a]	Live births / Naissances vivantes — Number Nombre	Crude birth rate Taux brut de natalité	Code[a]	Deaths / Décès — Number Nombre	Crude death rate Taux brut de mortalité	Rate of natural increase Taux d'accroissement naturel	Code[a]	Infant deaths / Décès d'enfants de moins d'un an — Number Nombre	Rate (per 1000 births) Taux (par 1000 naissances)	Life expectancy at birth — Male[b] Masculin[b]	Female[b] Féminin[b]	Total fertility rate L'indice synthétique de fécondité
ASIA - ASIE													
Bahrain - Bahreïn													
2015	C	20 983[52]	15.3	C	2 787[52]	2.0	13.3	C	156[53]	7.4	VI75.8	77.4	...
2016	C	20 714[52]	14.5	C	2 858[52]	2.0	12.5	C	109[53]	5.3	...	...	...
Bangladesh													
2013		...	...		...	...	...		...	...	68.8	71.4	2.110
2016		...	...		...	...	...		...	...	70.3[54]	72.9[54]	
Brunei Darussalam - Brunéi Darussalam													
2013	+C	6 680	16.6	+C	1 398	3.5	13.1	+C	51	7.6	...	...	1.900
2014	+C	6 891	16.9	+C	1 470	3.6	13.3	+C	51	7.4	75.9	78.8	1.900
2015	+C	6 699	16.2	+C	1 547	3.8	12.5	+C	58	8.7	...	...	1.900
2016	+C	6 437	15.4	+C	1 632	3.9	11.5	+C	52	8.1	80.5	80.8	1.900
China - Chine[55]													
2013	I	16 400 000	12.1	I	9 720 000	7.2	4.9		...	...	...	...	...
2014	I	16 870 000	12.4	I	9 770 000	7.2	5.2		...	...	...	...	...
2015	I	16 550 000	12.1	I	9 750 000	7.1	5.0		...	...	...	...	...
China, Hong Kong SAR - Chine, Hong Kong RAS													
2013	C	57 084	8.0	C	43 397	6.0	1.9	C	100	1.8	81.1	86.7	1.125[56]
2014	C	62 305	8.6	C	45 087	6.2	2.4	C	103	1.7	81.2	86.9	1.235[56]
2015	C	59 878	8.2	C	46 108	6.3	1.9	C	85	1.4	42.1	47.8	1.196[56]
2016	C	60 856	8.3	C	46 905	6.4	1.9	C	109	1.8	81.3	87.3	1.205[56]
2017	C	56 548	7.7	C	46 829	6.3	1.3	C	97	1.7	81.9	87.6	1.125
China, Macao SAR - Chine, Macao RAS													
2013	C	6 571	11.1	C	1 920	3.2	7.9	C	13	...	...	...	1.150
2014	C	7 360	11.8	C	1 939	3.1	8.7	C	15	...	IV79.6	86.0	1.224
2015	C	7 055	11.0	C	2 002	3.1	7.9	C	11	...	IV79.9	86.3	1.142
2016	C	7 146	11.1	C	2 248	3.5	7.6	I	12[57]	...	IV80.3	86.4	...
2017	C	6 529	10.0	C	2 120	3.2	6.8		...	...	...	...	...
Cyprus - Chypre[58]													
2013	C	9 341	10.8	C	5 141[59]	6.0	4.9	C	15	...	80.0	84.8	1.300
2014	C	9 258	10.9	C	5 424[59]	6.4	4.5	C	19	...	80.2	84.2	1.310
2015	C	9 170	10.8	C	5 859[59]	6.9	3.9	C	25	...	79.8	83.5	1.320
2016	C	9 455	11.1	C	5 471[59]	6.4	4.7	C	25	...	80.3	84.7	...
2017	C*	9 229	10.7	C*	5 997[59]	7.0	3.8		...	...	...	...	...
Georgia - Géorgie													
2013	C	57 878	12.9	C	48 553[51]	10.8	2.1	C	640[51]	11.1	...	...	1.700
2014	C	60 635	16.3	C	49 087[51]	13.2	3.1	C	578[51]	9.5	...	...	2.200
2015	C	59 249	15.9	C	49 121[51]	13.2	2.7	C	507[51]	8.6	68.6	77.2	2.300
2016	C	56 569	15.2	C	50 771[51]	13.7	1.6	C	507[51]	9.0	68.2	77.1	2.200
2017	C	53 293	14.3	C	47 822[51]	12.8	1.5	C	512[51]	9.6	...	...	...
India - Inde[60]													
2013	I	...	21.4[61]	I	...	7.0[61]	...	I	...	40.0[61]	...	...	2.300
2014	I	...	21.0[61]	I	...	6.7[61]	...	I	...	39.0[61]	...	...	2.300
2015	I	...	20.8[61]	I	...	6.5[61]	...	I	...	37.0[61]	...	...	2.300
2016	I	...	20.4[61]	I	...	6.4[61]	...	I	...	34.0[61]	V67.4	70.2	2.300
Iran (Islamic Republic of) - Iran (République islamique d')													
2013	+C	1 471 834[62]	19.1	+C	372 279[62]	4.8	14.3	+C	8 015[62]	5.4	...	...	...
2014	+C	1 534 362[62]	19.7	+C	446 333[62]	5.7	14.0	+C	7 430[62]	4.8	...	...	...
2015	+C	1 570 219[62]	19.9	+C	374 827[62]	4.8	15.2		...	...	...	...	...
2016	+C	1 528 053[62]	19.2	+C	369 751[62]	4.6	14.5	+C	8 261[62]	5.4	72.5[62]	75.5[62]	2.113
Iraq													
2013	U*	1 077 645	...	U*	189 118	...	...		...	...	...	...	...
Israel - Israël[63]													
2013	C	171 444	21.3	C	41 683[64]	5.2	16.1	C	539[64]	3.1	80.3	83.9	3.030
2014	C	176 427	21.5	C	42 457[64]	5.2	16.3	C	548[64]	3.1	80.3	84.1	3.085

4. Vital statistics summary and life expectancy at birth: 2013 - 2017
Aperçu des statistiques de l'état civil et de l'espérance de vie à la naissance : 2013 - 2017 (continued - suite)

Continent, country or area and year / Continent, pays ou zone et année	Code[a]	Live births Naissances vivantes — Number Nombre	Crude birth rate Taux brut de natalité	Code[a]	Deaths Décès — Number Nombre	Crude death rate Taux brut de mortalité	Rate of natural increase Taux d'accrois-sement naturel	Code[a]	Infant deaths Décès d'enfants de moins d'un an — Number Nombre	Rate (per 1000 births) Taux (par 1000 naiss-ances)	Life expectancy at birth — Male[b] Masculin[b]	Female[b] Féminin[b]	Total fertility rate L'indice synthétique de fécondité
ASIA - ASIE													
Israel - Israël[63]													
2015	C	178 723	21.3	C	44 507[64]	5.3	16.0	C	563[64]	3.2	80.1	84.1	3.093
2016	C	181 405	21.2	C	44 204[64]	5.2	16.1	C	568[64]	3.1	80.7	84.2	3.108
2017	C*	183 656	21.1	C	44 423[64]	5.1	16.0	C	553[64]	3.0	...	...	...
Japan - Japon[65]													
2013	C	1 029 816[29]	8.1	C	1 268 436[29]	10.0	-1.9	C	2 185[29]	2.1	80.2	86.6	1.427[66]
2014	C	1 003 539[29]	7.9	C	1 273 004[29]	10.0	-2.1	C	2 080[29]	2.1	80.5	86.8	1.422[66]
2015	C	1 005 677[29]	7.9	C	1 290 444[29]	10.1	-2.2	C	1 916[29]	1.9	80.8	87.1	1.450[66]
2016	C	976 978[29]	7.7	C	1 307 748[29]	10.3	-2.6	C	1 928[29]	2.0	81.0	87.1	1.441[66]
2017	C*	946 060	7.5	C*	1 340 433	10.6	-3.1	...	...	...	...	...	...
Jordan - Jordanie[67]													
2013	C	178 143	22.0	U	23 898	...	...	...	...	...	...	...	...
2014	C	188 902	21.5	U	25 782	...	...	...	...	...	...	...	...
2015	C	198 018	20.7	U	26 640	...	...	...	...	...	...	...	...
2016	C	197 789	20.2	U	27 608	...	...	...	...	...	72.8	74.2	3.380
2017		...	...	U	27 516	...	...	...	...	...	...	...	...
Kazakhstan													
2013	C	387 256	22.7	U	136 368	...	...	C	4 400	11.4	7.8	9.6	2.644
2014	C	399 309	23.1	U	132 287	...	...	C	3 907	9.8	66.9	75.8	2.730
2015	C	398 458	22.7	U	130 811	...	...	C	3 751	9.4	67.5	76.3	2.739
2016	C	400 694	22.5	U	131 231	...	...	C	3 438	8.6	68.0	76.6	2.775
2017	C	390 262	21.6	U	129 009	...	...	C	3 109	8.0	68.7	76.9	2.732
Kuwait - Koweït													
2013	C	59 426	17.3	C	5 909	1.7	15.6	C	453	7.6	77.3	81.9	1.720
2014	C	61 313	16.3	C	6 031	1.6	14.7	C	456	7.4	78.7	80.2	1.900
2015	C	59 271	14.9	C	6 481	1.6	13.3	C	456	7.7	79.1	80.0	...
2016	C	58 797	14.4	C	6 338	1.6	12.9	C	448	7.6	81.0	80.5	...
Kyrgyzstan - Kirghizstan													
2013	C	155 520	27.2	C	34 880	6.1	21.1	C	3 093	19.9	60.1	67.9	3.109
2014	C	161 813	27.7	C	35 564	6.1	21.6	C	3 268	20.2	66.5	74.5	3.186
2015	C	163 452	27.4	C	34 808	5.8	21.6	C	2 945	18.0	66.8	74.8	3.189
2016	C	158 160	26.0	C	33 475	5.5	20.5	C	2 621	16.6	67.0	75.1	3.059
2017	C	153 620	24.8	C	33 166	5.4	19.4	C	2 401	15.6	...	...	2.953
Lao People's Democratic Republic - République démocratique populaire lao													
2013		...	...		...	...	...		...	...	...	...	3.200
2014		...	...		...	...	...		...	...	...	...	3.060
2015		...	...		...	...	...		...	...	61.8[68]	65.2[68]	3.200
Lebanon - Liban													
2013	C	95 246	...	C	24 013	...	...		...	...	...	...	...
2014	C	104 872	...	C	27 020	...	...		...	...	...	...	...
Malaysia - Malaisie													
2013	C	503 914	16.7	C	142 202	4.7	12.0	C	3 199	6.3	...	...	2.022
2014	C	528 612	17.2	C	150 318	4.9	12.3	C	3 543	6.7	...	...	2.072
2015	C	521 136	16.7	C	155 786	5.0	11.7	C	3 582	6.9	...	...	2.002
2016	C	508 203	16.1	C	162 201	5.1	10.9	C	3 390	6.7	72.6	77.2	1.918
2017		...	...		...	...	...		...	...	72.7	77.4	...
Maldives													
2013	C	7 153[69]	21.3	C	1 120[69]	3.3	17.9	C	46[69]	6.4	...	...	...
2014	C	7 245[69]	21.2	C	1 143[69]	3.3	17.9	C	59[69]	8.1	73.1	74.8	2.460
2015	C	6 986[69]	20.3	C	1 130[69]	3.3	17.0	C	63[69]	9.0	73.1	74.6	...
2016	C	6 756[69]	19.3	C	1 226[69]	3.5	15.8	C	53[69]	7.8	73.0	74.7	...
Mongolia - Mongolie													
2013	+C	79 780	27.5	+C	17 247	5.9	21.6	+C	1 166	14.6	65.4	75.0	3.000
2014	+C	82 839	28.0	+C	16 521	5.6	22.4	+C	1 251	15.1	65.9	75.5	3.100
2015	+C	82 130	27.1	+C	17 620	5.8	21.3	+C	1 234	15.0	ˣ65.3	74.8	3.100
2016	+C	79 920	25.9	+C	17 763	5.8	20.1	+C	1 315	16.5	...	...	3.000
2017	+C	75 321	23.9	+C	17 357	5.5	18.4	+C	1 009	13.4	65.9	15.3	2.800

Continent, country or area and year / Continent, pays ou zone et année	Live births / Naissances vivantes			Deaths / Décès			Rate of natural increase / Taux d'accroissement naturel	Infant deaths / Décès d'enfants de moins d'un an			Life expectancy at birth / Espérance de vie à la naissance		Total fertility rate / L'indice synthétique de fécondité
	Code[a]	Number / Nombre	Crude birth rate / Taux brut de natalité	Code[a]	Number / Nombre	Crude death rate / Taux brut de mortalité		Code[a]	Number / Nombre	Rate (per 1000 births) / Taux (par 1000 naissances)	Male[b] / Masculin[b]	Female[b] / Féminin[b]	
ASIA - ASIE													
Myanmar													
2013	+U	835 595[70]	...	+U	257 216[70]	...	...	+U	11 516[70]	...	65.5	69.1	2.222
2014	+U	736 369[71]	...	+U	213 085[71]	...	...	+U	9 386[71]	...	61.0[72]	68.6[72]	2.505
2015	+U	739 152[71]	...	+U	225 526[71]	...	...	+U	9 849[71]	...	59.7[72]	69.3[72]	2.483
Oman													
2013	U	79 417[73]	...	U	7 669[73]	...	...	U	772[73]	...	74.8	78.5	2.900
2014	U	82 981[73]	...	U	7 819[73]	...	...	U	645[73]	...	74.8	78.5	2.900
2015	U	86 286[73]	...	U	8 167[73]	...	...	U	818[73]	...	74.2[74]	78.8[74]	2.900
2016	U	88 346[73]	...	U	8 196[73]	...	...	U	816[73]	...	...	...	2.900
2017	C	90 371	19.8	U	8 861	...	...	C	850	9.4	74.8[74]	79.2[74]	2.896
Philippines													
2013	C	1 761 602	17.9	C	531 280	5.4	12.5	C	21 992	12.5	...	...	...
2014	C	1 748 857	17.5	C	551 716	5.5	12.0	C	21 572	12.3	...	...	...
2015	C	1 744 767	17.2	C	560 605	5.5	11.7	C	20 750	11.9	...	...	...
2016	C	1 731 289	16.8	C	582 183	5.6	11.1	C	21 874	12.6	...	...	...
Qatar													
2013	C	23 708	11.8	C	2 133	1.1	10.8	C	158	6.7	...	...	2.000
2014	C	25 443	11.5	C	2 366	1.1	10.4	C	168	6.6	...	...	2.000
2015	C	26 622	10.9	C	2 317	1.0	10.0	C	197	7.4	77.5	82.1	2.000
2016	C	26 816	10.2	C	2 347	0.9	9.3	C	161	6.0	78.9	82.3	1.850
2017	C*	25 906	9.5	C*	2 294	0.8	8.7		...	...	...	...	...
Republic of Korea - République de Corée													
2013	C	436 455[75]	8.6	C	266 257[76]	5.3	3.4	C	1 305[76]	3.0	78.1	84.6	1.187[76]
2014	C	435 435[75]	8.6	C	267 692[76]	5.3	3.3	C	1 305[76]	3.0	78.6	85.0	1.205[76]
2015	C	438 420[75]	8.6	C	275 895[76]	5.4	3.2	C	1 190[76]	2.7	79.0	85.2	1.239[76]
2016	C	406 243[75]	7.9	C	280 827[76]	5.5	2.5		...	...	79.3	85.4	...
2017	C	357 771[75]	7.0	C	285 534[76]	5.6	1.4	C	1 000[76]	2.8	...	...	...
Saudi Arabia - Arabie saoudite													
2013	I	501 583[77]	16.9	...	106 521[78]	...	...		...	...	...	...	2.810[79]
2014	I	514 325[77]	17.0		...	...	...		...	...	...	...	2.750[79]
2015	I	449 149[77]	14.5	I	69 206[80]	2.2	12.2		...	...	73.1[79]	75.7[79]	2.690[79]
2016	I	447 040[77]	14.1	I	58 097[77]	1.8	12.2	I	5 084[77]	11.4	73.5[81]	74.8[81]	2.360[77]
2017	I	404 909[77]	12.4	I	58 915[77]	1.8	10.6		...	...	...	...	2.340[77]
Singapore - Singapour													
2013	C	39 720	10.3	+C	18 938	4.9	5.4	+C	94	2.4	80.1[82]	84.5[82]	1.190[83]
2014	C	42 232	10.9	+C	19 393	5.0	5.9	+C	83	2.0	80.3[82]	84.8[82]	1.250[83]
2015	C	42 185	10.8	+C	19 862	5.1	5.7	+C	84	2.0	80.5[82]	85.1[82]	1.240[83]
2016	C	41 251	10.5	+C	20 017	5.1	5.4	+C	101	2.4	80.7[82]	85.1[82]	1.200[83]
2017	C	39 615	10.0	+C	20 905	5.3	4.7	+C	94	2.4	80.7[84]	85.2[84]	1.160[83]
Sri Lanka													
2013	+C	365 762	17.8	+C	127 183	6.2	11.6	+C	3 043	8.3	...	...	2.263
2014	+C*	349 715	16.8	+C*	127 758	6.2	10.7	+C	2 799	8.0	...	...	...
2015	+C*	334 821	16.0	+C*	131 614	6.3	9.7	+C	2 845	8.5	...	...	...
2016	+C	331 073	15.6	+C	130 765	6.2	9.4		...	...	...	...	...
2017	+C	326 052	15.2	+C	139 822	6.5	8.7		...	...	...	...	...
State of Palestine - État de Palestine													
2013	U	127 454[85]	...	U	11 188[85]	...	...	U	845[85]	...	71.5	74.4	4.100[86]
2014	U	128 073[85]	...	U	13 390[85]	...	...	U	800[85]	...	71.8	74.7	...
2015	U	124 331[85]	...	U	11 908[85]	...	...	U	852[85]	...	72.0	75.0	...
2016		...	...		...	...	...		...	...	72.1	75.2	...
Tajikistan - Tadjikistan													
2013	U	209 417[87]	...	U	31 706[51]	...	...	U	3 622[51]	...	...	...	2.616
2014	U	229 460[87]	...	U	32 879[51]	...	...	U	3 273[51]	...	71.6	75.4	2.980
2015	U	237 541[87]	...	U	33 563[51]	...	...	U	3 082[51]	...	...	...	3.064
2016	U	230 044[87]	...	U	34 134[51]	...	...	U	2 725[51]	...	71.9	75.7	2.930

Continent, country or area and year / Continent, pays ou zone et année	Live births / Naissances vivantes			Deaths / Décès			Rate of natural increase Taux d'accroissement naturel	Infant deaths / Décès d'enfants de moins d'un an			Life expectancy at birth / Espérance de vie à la naissance		Total fertility rate / L'indice synthétique de fécondité
	Code[a]	Number Nombre	Crude birth rate Taux brut de natalité	Code[a]	Number Nombre	Crude death rate Taux brut de mortalité		Code[a]	Number Nombre	Rate (per 1000 births) Taux (par 1000 naissances)	Male[b] Masculin[b]	Female[b] Féminin[b]	
ASIA - ASIE													
Thailand - Thaïlande													
2013	+U	782 129	...	+U	438 648	...	...	+U	4 755	...	...	...	...
2014	+U	776 370	...	+U	448 601	...	...	+U	4 615	...	...	...	...
2015	+U	738 930	...	+U	456 391	...	...	+U	4 221	...	...	...	...
2016	+U	704 058	...	+U	480 434	...	...	+U	4 233	...	...	...	...
2017		...	...	+U	468 911	...	...		...	...	...	...	...
Timor-Leste[88]													
2015	I	36 202	30.6	I	9 209	7.8	22.8		...	...	...	...	...
Turkey - Turquie													
2013	C	1 295 987	16.9	C	373 041[89]	4.9	12.0	C	14 027[89]	10.8	75.3	80.7	2.104
2014	C	1 348 413	17.4	C	390 944[89]	5.0	12.3	C	14 938[89]	11.1	75.3	80.7	2.182
2015	C	1 333 329	16.9	C	405 202[89]	5.1	11.8	C	13 654[89]	10.2	III75.3	80.7	2.151
2016	C	1 309 771	16.4	C	422 135[89]	5.3	11.1	C	13 036[89]	10.0	III75.3	80.7	2.105
2017	C*	1 291 055	16.1	C*	425 781	5.3	10.8		...	...	...	...	...
United Arab Emirates - Émirats arabes unis[90]													
2013	...	93 539	...	...	8 015	...	...	...	...	...	...	...	...
2014	...	95 860	...	...	8 265	...	...	...	...	...	...	...	...
2015	...	97 328	...	...	8 755	...	...	...	...	...	...	...	...
Uzbekistan - Ouzbékistan													
2013	+C	679 519	22.5	+C	145 672[51]	4.8	17.7	+C	6 569[51]	9.7	...	...	2.350
2014	+C	718 036	23.3	+C	149 761[51]	4.9	18.5	+C	7 688[51]	10.7	71.1	75.8	2.457
2015	+C	734 141	23.5	+C	152 035[51]	4.9	18.6	+C	8 320[51]	11.3	71.2	76.0	2.491
2016	+C	726 170	23.0	+C	154 791[51]	4.9	18.1		...	...	71.4	76.2	...
2017	+C	715 519	22.3	+C	160 723[51]	5.0	17.3		...	...	71.3	76.1	...
Viet Nam													
2013		...	...		...	...	...		...	...	70.5	75.8	2.100
2014		...	...		...	...	...		...	...	70.6	76.0	2.090
2015		...	...		...	...	...		...	...	70.7	76.1	2.100
2016		...	...		...	...	...		...	...	70.8	76.1	2.090
Yemen - Yémen													
2013	U	425 165[91]	...	U	35 066[92]	...	...		...	...	...	...	...
EUROPE													
Åland Islands - Îles d'Åland													
2013	C	287	10.0	C	269	9.4	0.6	C	-	...	79.0	85.9	1.800
2014	C	282	9.8	C	251	8.7	1.1	C	-	...	80.9	84.3	1.783
2015	C	275	9.5	C	285	9.8	-0.3	C	-	...	80.6	84.0	1.690
2016	C	293	10.1	C	297	10.2	-0.1	C	1	...	78.5	83.6	1.790
2017	C*	282	9.6	C*	251	8.6	1.1		...	...	...	...	...
Albania - Albanie													
2013	C	35 750	12.3	C	20 442	7.1	5.3	C	282	7.9	76.0	80.3	...
2014	C	35 760	12.4	C	20 656	7.1	5.2	C	281	7.9	...	...	...
2015	C	33 221	11.5	C	22 422	7.8	3.7	C	233	7.0	...	...	...
2016	C	31 733	11.0	C	21 388	7.4	3.6	C	277	8.7	77.0	80.1	...
2017	C	30 869	10.7	C	22 232	7.7	3.0		...	...	...	...	...
Andorra - Andorre													
2013	C	637	9.1	C	239	3.4	5.7	C	1	...	...	...	...
2014	C	639	9.1	C	276	3.9	5.2	C	2	...	...	...	...
2015	C	659	9.3	C	282	4.0	5.3	C	-	...	...	...	...
2016	C	634	8.8	C	310	4.3	4.5		...	...	...	...	...
Austria - Autriche													
2013	C	79 330	9.4	C	79 526[93]	9.4	0.0	C	245	3.1	78.5	83.6	1.437
2014	C	81 722	9.6	C	78 252[93]	9.2	0.4	C	249	3.0	79.1	84.0	1.465
2015	C	84 381[94]	9.8	C	83 073[93]	9.6	0.2	C	259	3.1	78.6	83.6	1.494
2016	C	87 675[94]	10.0	C	80 669[93]	9.2	0.8	C	269	3.1	79.1	84.0	1.529
2017	C*	87 633[94]	10.0	C*	83 270[93]	9.5	0.5		...	...	...	...	...

Continent, country or area and year — Continent, pays ou zone et année	Live births — Naissances vivantes			Deaths — Décès			Rate of natural increase — Taux d'accrois-sement naturel	Infant deaths — Décès d'enfants de moins d'un an			Life expectancy at birth — Espérance de vie à la naissance		Total fertility rate — L'indice synthétique de fécondité
	Code[a]	Number Nombre	Crude birth rate Taux brut de natalité	Code[a]	Number Nombre	Crude death rate Taux brut de mortalité		Code[a]	Number Nombre	Rate (per 1000 births) Taux (par 1000 naiss-ances)	Male[b] Masculin[b]	Female[b] Féminin[b]	
EUROPE													
Belarus - Bélarus													
2013	C	117 997	12.5	C	125 326	13.2	-0.8	C	407	3.4	67.3	77.9	1.668
2014	C	118 534	12.5	C	121 542	12.8	-0.3	C	409	3.5	67.8	78.6	1.696
2015	C	119 028	12.5	C	120 026	12.6	-0.1	C	352	3.0	68.6	78.9	...
2016	C	117 779	12.4	C	119 379	12.6	-0.2	C	373	3.2	68.9	79.0	...
2017	C	102 556	10.8	C	119 311	12.6	-1.8		...	...	...	...	...
Belgium - Belgique													
2013	C	125 606[95]	11.2	C	109 334[95]	9.8	1.5	C	436[95]	3.5	77.9	82.9	...
2014	C	125 014[95]	11.1	C	104 755[95]	9.3	1.8	C	423[95]	3.4	78.6	83.5	...
2015	C	122 274[95]	10.8	C	110 541[95]	9.8	1.0	C	400[95]	3.3	78.5[96]	83.1[96]	...
2016	C	121 896[95]	10.8	C	108 097[95]	9.5	1.2	C	387[95]	3.2	...	...	...
2017	C	119 690[95]	10.5	C	109 666[95]	9.6	0.9		...	...	...	...	...
Bosnia and Herzegovina - Bosnie-Herzégovine													
2013	C	31 103	8.8	C	35 837	10.1	-1.3	C	161	5.2	...	...	...
2014	C	29 247	8.3	C	34 824	9.9	-1.6	C	140	4.8	...	...	...
2015	C	28 906	8.2	C	37 070	10.5	-2.3	C	174	6.0	...	...	...
2016	C	29 276	8.3	C	35 530	10.1	-1.8	C	152	5.2	...	...	...
2017	C	29 158	8.3	C	36 336	10.4	-2.0	C	183	6.3	...	...	...
Bulgaria - Bulgarie													
2013	C	66 578	9.2	C	104 345	14.4	-5.2	C	489	7.3	...	...	1.484
2014	C	67 585	9.4	C	108 952	15.1	-5.7	C	517	7.6	71.1	78.0	1.523
2015	C	65 950	9.2	C	110 117	15.3	-6.2	C	434	6.6	III71.1	78.0	1.529
2016	C	64 984	9.1	C	107 580	15.1	-6.0	C	423	6.5	III3.1	3.6	1.542
2017	C	63 955	9.0	C	109 791	15.5	-6.5		...	...	...	...	...
Croatia - Croatie													
2013	C	39 939	9.4	C	50 386	11.8	-2.5	C	162	4.1	...	...	...
2014	C	39 566	9.3	C	50 839	12.0	-2.7	C	199	5.0	74.7	81.0	...
2015	C	37 503	8.9	C	54 205	12.9	-4.0	C	154	4.1	...	...	...
2016	C	37 537	9.0	C	51 542	12.3	-3.4	C	161	4.3	...	...	...
2017	C	36 556	8.9	C	53 477	12.9	-4.1		...	...	...	...	...
Czechia - Tchéquie													
2013	C	106 751	10.2	C	109 160	10.4	-0.2	C	265	2.5	75.2	81.1	1.456
2014	C	109 860	10.4	C	105 665	10.0	0.4	C	263	2.4	75.8	81.7	1.528
2015	C	110 764	10.5	C	111 173	10.5	0.0	C	272	2.5	6.6	7.1	1.570
2016	C	112 663	10.7	C	107 750	10.2	0.5	C	317	2.8	76.2	82.1	1.630
2017	C	114 405	10.8	C	111 443	10.5	0.3		...	...	...	...	...
Denmark - Danemark[97]													
2013	C	55 873	10.0	C	52 471	9.4	0.6	C	195	3.5	II78.0	81.9	1.669
2014	C	56 870	10.1	C	51 340	9.1	1.0	C	229	4.0	78.5	82.7	1.691
2015	C	58 205	10.3	C	52 555	9.3	1.0	C	216	3.7	II78.6	82.5	1.714
2016	C	61 614	10.8	C	52 824	9.2	1.5	C	194	3.1	II78.8	82.8	1.785
2017	C	61 397	10.7	C	53 261	9.2	1.4		...	...	...	...	...
Estonia - Estonie													
2013	C	13 531	10.3	C	15 244	11.6	-1.3	C	28	...	72.7	81.4	1.520
2014	C	13 551	10.3	C	15 484	11.8	-1.5	C	36	2.7	72.3	81.5	1.540
2015	C	13 907	10.6	C	15 243	11.6	-1.0	C	35	2.5	73.1	81.8	1.580
2016	C	14 053	10.7	C	15 392	11.7	-1.0	C	33	2.3	73.2	81.9	1.600
2017	C	13 784	10.5	C	15 543	11.8	-1.3		...	...	...	...	...
Faeroe Islands - Îles Féroé													
2013	C	624	12.9	C	361	7.5	5.4	C	-	...	...	...	2.537
2014	C	636	13.1	C	394	8.1	5.0	C	4	...	...	...	2.563
2015	C	605	12.4	C	376	7.7	4.7	C	-	...	II66.8	71.8	2.427
2016	C	676	13.7	C	381	7.7	6.0	C	3	...	...	...	2.624
2017	C	655	13.0	C	446	8.9	4.2	C	6	...	II80.9	83.7	2.470
Finland - Finlande													
2013	C	57 847[98]	10.7	C	51 203[98]	9.5	1.2	C	102[98]	1.8	...	...	1.750
2014	C	56 950[98]	10.5	C	51 935[98]	9.6	0.9	C	124[98]	2.2	78.2[98]	83.9[98]	1.710
2015	C	55 197[98]	10.1	C	52 207[98]	9.6	0.5	C	97[98]	1.8	78.5[98]	84.1[98]	1.650

Continent, country or area and year / Continent, pays ou zone et année	Co-de[a]	Live births Naissances vivantes		Co-de[a]	Deaths Décès		Rate of natural increase Taux d'accrois-sement naturel	Co-de[a]	Infant deaths Décès d'enfants de moins d'un an		Life expectancy at birth Espérance de vie à la naissance		Total fertility rate L'indice synthétique de fécondité
		Number Nombre	Crude birth rate Taux brut de natalité		Number Nombre	Crude death rate Taux brut de mortalité			Number Nombre	Rate (per 1000 births) Taux (par 1000 naiss-ances)	Male[b] Masculin[b]	Female[b] Féminin[b]	
EUROPE													
Finland - Finlande													
2016	C	52 521[98]	9.6	C	53 626[98]	9.8	-0.2	C	99[98]	1.9	78.4[98]	84.1[98]	1.570
2017	C	50 321	9.1	C	53 722	9.8	-0.6		...	...	...	...	...
France													
2013	C	781 621	12.2	C	558 408	8.7	3.5	C	2 710	3.5	III78.6[96]	85.0[96]	1.973
2014	C	781 167	12.2	C	547 003	8.5	3.6	C	2 598	3.3	III78.9[96]	85.1[96]	1.974[96]
2015	C	760 421	11.8	C	581 770	9.0	2.8	C	2 655	3.5	IV79.1[96]	85.1[96]	1.924[96]
2016	C	744 697	11.5	C	581 073	9.0	2.5	C	2 577	3.5	...	...	1.894[96]
2017	C*	730 700	11.3	C*	593 400	9.1	2.1		...	...	...	...	...
Germany - Allemagne													
2013	C	682 069	8.5	C	893 825	11.1	-2.6	C	2 250	3.3	...	...	1.420
2014	C	714 927	8.8	C	868 356	10.7	-1.9	C	2 284	3.2	78.7	83.6	1.470
2015	C	737 575	9.0	C	925 200	11.3	-2.3	C	2 405	3.3	III78.2	83.1	1.500
2016	C	792 137	9.6	C	910 902	11.1	-1.4	C	2 700	3.4	...	...	...
2017	C*	785 234	9.5	C*	933 000	11.3	-1.8		...	...	...	...	...
Gibraltar													
2013	+C	426[99]	13.0	+C	230[100]	7.0	6.0	+C	-	...	...	...	...
2014	+C	488[99]	14.7	+C	248[100]	7.5	7.2		...	...	...	...	...
2015	+C	492[99]	14.7	+C	235[100]	7.0	7.7		...	...	...	...	...
Greece - Grèce													
2013	C	94 134	8.6	C	111 794	10.2	-1.6	C	347	3.7	...	...	...
2014	C	92 149	8.5	C	113 740	10.4	-2.0	C	346	3.8	78.5	83.5	...
2015	C	91 847	8.5	C	121 183	11.2	-2.7	C	364	4.0	78.1	83.2	...
2016	C	92 898	8.6	C	118 785	11.0	-2.4	C	387	4.2	78.4	83.4	...
2017	C*	88 523	8.2	C	124 530	11.6	-3.3		...	...	...	...	...
Guernsey - Guernesey													
2013	C	667	10.6	C	556	8.9	1.8		...	...	...	...	...
2014	C	627	10.1	C	526	8.4	1.6		...	...	...	...	...
2015	C	620	10.0	C	560	9.0	1.0		...	...	...	...	...
2016	C	654	10.5	C	536	8.6	1.9		...	...	...	...	...
Hungary - Hongrie													
2013	C	89 524[101]	9.0	C	126 677[102]	12.8	-3.8	C	448[103]	5.0	72.0	78.7	1.350
2014	C	93 281[104]	9.5	C	126 294[105]	12.8	-3.3	C	418[106]	4.5	72.1	78.9	1.440
2015	C	92 135[104]	9.4	C	131 575[105]	13.4	-4.0	C	383[106]	4.2	72.1	78.6	...
2016	C	95 361[104]	9.7	C	127 098[105]	13.0	-3.2	C	368[106]	3.9	72.4	79.2	...
2017	C	94 646[104]	9.7	C	131 877[105]	13.5	-3.8	C	332[106]	3.5	...	...	...
Iceland - Islande													
2013	C	4 326	13.4	C	2 154	6.7	6.7	C	8	...	II80.8	83.7	1.932
2014	C	4 375	13.4	C	2 049	6.3	7.1	C	9	...	II80.6	83.6	1.932
2015	C	4 129	12.5	C	2 178	6.6	5.9	C	9	...	II81.0	83.6	1.805
2016	C	4 034	12.0	C	2 309	6.9	5.1	C	3	...	II3.0	3.6	1.745
2017	C	4 071	11.9	C	2 239	6.5	5.3	C	11	...	...	...	...
Ireland - Irlande													
2013	+C	68 930	14.9	+C	30 018	6.5	8.4	+C	243	3.5	...	...	1.960
2014	+C	67 285	14.4	+C	29 188	6.3	8.2	+C	224	3.3	79.3[96]	83.5[96]	1.950
2015	+C	65 537	13.9	+C	30 064	6.4	7.5	+C	224	3.4	...	...	1.940
2016	+C	63 836	13.4	+C	30 390	6.4	7.0	+C	208	3.3	...	...	...
2017	+C	62 084	12.9	+C	30 484	6.3	6.6	+C	174	2.8	...	...	...
Isle of Man - Île de Man													
2013	+C	859	10.0	+C	792	9.2	0.8		...	...	...	...	...
2014	+C	805	9.3	+C	787	9.1	0.2		...	...	...	...	...
2015	+C	785	9.0		...	...	...		...	...	...	...	...
2016	+C	758	8.9	+C	852	10.0	-1.1	I	2[107]	...	...	...	1.683
2017	+C	753	9.0	+C	837	10.0	-1.0		...	...	...	...	...
Italy - Italie													
2013	+C	514 308	8.5	C	600 744	10.0	-1.4	C	1 493	2.9	79.8	84.6	1.390
2014	C	502 596	8.3	C	598 364	9.8	-1.6	C	1 523	3.0	80.3	85.0	1.370
2015	C	485 780	8.0	C	647 571	10.7	-2.7	C	1 398	2.9	...	...	1.350

4. Vital statistics summary and life expectancy at birth: 2013 - 2017
Aperçu des statistiques de l'état civil et de l'espérance de vie à la naissance : 2013 - 2017 (continued - suite)

Continent, country or area and year / Continent, pays ou zone et année	Code[a]	Number Nombre (Live births)	Crude birth rate Taux brut de natalité	Code[a]	Number Nombre (Deaths)	Crude death rate Taux brut de mortalité	Rate of natural increase Taux d'accroissement naturel	Code[a]	Number Nombre (Infant deaths)	Rate (per 1000 births) Taux (par 1000 naissances)	Male[b] Masculin[b]	Female[b] Féminin[b]	Total fertility rate L'indice synthétique de fécondité
EUROPE													
Italy - Italie													
2016	C	473 438	7.8	C	615 261	10.1	-2.3	C	1 427	3.0	80.6	85.0	...
2017	C	458 151	7.6	C	649 061	10.7	-3.2		...	...	...	...	...
Jersey													
2013	+C	1 029[34]	...	+C	717	...	...		...	...	...	...	...
2014	+C	985[34]	9.8	+C	700	6.9	2.8		...	...	...	...	...
2015	+C	1 021[34]	9.9	+C	756	7.4	2.6		...	...	...	...	...
Latvia - Lettonie													
2013	C	20 596	10.2	C	28 691	14.3	-4.0	C	91	4.4	69.5	79.0	1.531
2014	C	21 746	10.9	C	28 466	14.3	-3.4	C	83	3.8	69.3	79.5	1.654
2015	C	21 979	11.1	C	28 478	14.4	-3.3	C	90	4.1	69.7	79.3	1.707
2016	C	21 968	11.2	C	28 580	14.6	-3.4	C	81	3.7	69.8	79.4	1.743
2017	C	20 828	10.7	C	28 757	14.8	-4.1		...	...	...	...	...
Liechtenstein													
2013	C	339	9.2	C	246	6.7	2.5	C	2	...	...	...	...
2014	C	372	10.0	C	268	7.2	2.8	C	1	...	...	...	...
2015	C	325	8.7	C	252	6.7	1.9	C	2	...	...	...	...
2016	C	378	10.0	C	271	7.2	2.8	C	1	...	...	...	1.610
2017	C*	338	8.9	C*	249	6.6	2.3		...	...	...	...	...
Lithuania - Lituanie													
2013	C	29 885	10.1	C	41 511	14.0	-3.9	C	110	3.7	68.5	79.4	...
2014	C	30 369	10.4	C	40 252	13.7	-3.4	C	118	3.9	69.1	79.9	...
2015	C	31 475	10.8	C	41 776	14.4	-3.5	C	132	4.2	69.1	79.6	...
2016	C	30 623	10.7	C	41 106	14.3	-3.7	C	139	4.5	67.8	78.4	...
2017	C	28 696	10.1	C	40 142	14.2	-4.0		...	...	...	...	...
Luxembourg													
2013	C	6 115	11.3	C	3 822	7.0	4.2	C	24	...	III26.2	30.8	...
2014	C	6 070	10.9	C	3 841	6.9	4.0	C	17	...	III79.3	84.0	...
2015	C	6 115	10.7	C	3 983	7.0	3.7	C	17	...	...	...	...
2016	C	6 050	10.4	C	3 967	6.8	3.6	C	23	...	III80.7	85.4	...
2017	C	6 174	10.4	C	4 263	7.1	3.2	C	20	...	...	...	...
Malta - Malte													
2013	C	4 032	9.5	C	3 236	7.6	1.9	C	27	...	79.6	84.0	1.370
2014	C	4 191	9.8	C	3 270	7.7	2.2	C	21	...	79.8	84.3	1.420
2015	C	4 325	10.0	C	3 442	8.0	2.0	C	25	...	79.7	84.0	...
2016	C	4 476	9.8	C	3 342	7.3	2.5	C	33	7.4	80.6	84.4	...
2017	C	4 319	9.2	C	3 571	7.6	1.6		...	...	...	...	...
Monaco													
2013	C	992[108]	26.8	C	567[109]	15.3	11.5		...	...	...	...	...
2014	C	974[108]	26.4	C	524[109]	14.2	12.2		...	...	...	...	...
2015	C	1 067[108]	28.4	C	595[109]	15.8	12.6		...	...	...	...	...
2016	C	938[108]	24.6	C	503[109]	13.2	11.4		...	...	...	...	...
Montenegro - Monténégro													
2013	C	7 475	12.0	C	5 917	9.5	2.5	C	33	4.4	...	...	...
2014	C	7 529	12.1	C	6 014	9.7	2.4	C	37	4.9	...	...	...
2015	C	7 386	11.9	C	6 329	10.2	1.7	C	16	...	...	...	...
2016	C	7 569	12.2	C	6 464	10.4	1.8	C	26	...	...	...	...
2017	C	7 432	11.9	C	6 523	10.5	1.5		...	...	...	...	...
Netherlands - Pays-Bas													
2013	C	171 341[110]	10.2	C	141 245[110]	8.4	1.8	C	645[110]	3.8	...	...	...
2014	C	175 181[110]	10.4	C	139 223[110]	8.3	2.1	C	630[110]	3.6	80.0	83.5	...
2015	C	170 510[110]	10.1	C	147 134[110]	8.7	1.4	C	561[110]	3.3	...	...	...
2016	C	172 520[110]	10.1	C	148 997[110]	8.7	1.4	C	597[110]	3.5	...	...	...
2017	C*	169 200[110]	9.9	C*	150 027[110]	8.8	1.1		...	...	...	...	...
Norway - Norvège													
2013	C	58 878	11.6	C	41 131[111]	8.1	3.5	C	140[111]	2.4	...	...	1.780
2014	C	58 976	11.5	C	40 369[111]	7.9	3.6	C	139[111]	2.4	80.1	84.2	1.760
2015	C	58 815	11.3	C	40 676[111]	7.8	3.5	C	133[111]	2.3	...	...	1.730

Continent, country or area and year / Continent, pays ou zone et année	Live births Naissances vivantes			Deaths Décès			Rate of natural increase Taux d'accrois-sement naturel	Infant deaths Décès d'enfants de moins d'un an			Life expectancy at birth Espérance de vie à la naissance		Total fertility rate L'indice synthétique de fécondité
	Code[a]	Number Nombre	Crude birth rate Taux brut de natalité	Code[a]	Number Nombre	Crude death rate Taux brut de mortalité		Code[a]	Number Nombre	Rate (per 1000 births) Taux (par 1000 naiss-ances)	Male[b] Masculin[b]	Female[b] Féminin[b]	
EUROPE													
Norway - Norvège													
2016	C	58 890	11.3	C	40 726[111]	7.8	3.5	C	128[111]	2.2	...	...	1.710
2017	C	56 633	10.7	C	40 774[111]	7.7	3.0		...	...	...	...	...
Poland - Pologne													
2013	C	369 576	9.7	C	387 312	10.2	-0.5	C	1 684	4.6	...	...	1.256
2014	C	375 160	9.9	C	376 467	9.9	0.0	C	1 583	4.2	73.7	81.7	1.290
2015	C	369 308	9.7	C	394 921	10.4	-0.7	C	1 476	4.0	73.6	81.6	1.289
2016	C	382 257	10.1	C	388 009	10.2	-0.2	C	1 522	4.0	73.9	81.9	1.357
2017	C	401 982	10.6	C	402 852	10.6	0.0		...	...	...	...	...
Portugal													
2013	C	82 787[34]	7.9	C	106 554[112]	10.2	-2.3	C	243[112]	2.9	III76.9	82.8	1.210
2014	C	82 367[34]	7.9	C	104 843[112]	10.1	-2.2	C	236[112]	2.9	III77.2	83.0	1.230
2015	C	85 500[34]	8.3	C	108 539[112]	10.5	-2.2	C	250[112]	2.9	III77.4	83.2	1.300
2016	C	87 126[34]	8.4	C	110 573[112]	10.7	-2.3	C	282[112]	3.2	III77.6	83.3	1.360
2017	C	86 154[34]	8.4	C	109 586[112]	10.6	-2.3		...	...	...	...	...
Republic of Moldova - République de Moldova													
2013	C	37 871[113]	10.6	C	38 060[113]	10.7	-0.1	C	359[113]	9.5	...	...	1.240
2014	C	38 616[113]	12.9	C	39 494[113]	13.2	-0.3	C	372[113]	9.6	...	...	1.280
2015	C	38 610[113]	...	C	39 906[113]	...	...	C	375[113]	9.7	...	...	1.300
2016	C	37 394[113]	...	C	38 489[113]	...	...	C	353[113]	9.4	...	...	1.280
2017	C	34 060[113]	...	C	36 768[113]	...	...	C	330[113]	9.7	...	...	1.190[113]
Romania - Roumanie													
2013	C	182 313	9.1	C	246 967	12.4	-3.2	C	1 677	9.2	III71.2	78.3	1.400[114]
2014	C	198 740	10.0	C	254 965	12.8	-2.8	C	1 632	8.2	III72.0	78.9	...
2015	C	197 491	10.0	C	261 294	13.2	-3.2	C	1 500	7.6	III71.9	78.9	...
2016	C	200 009	10.1	C	257 215	13.1	-2.9	C	1 398	7.0	...	...	...
2017	C*	189 474	9.7	C*	260 599	13.3	-3.6		...	...	...	...	...
Russian Federation - Fédération de Russie[51]													
2013	C	1 895 822	13.2	C	1 871 809	13.0	0.2		...	...	...	...	...
San Marino - Saint-Marin													
2013	C	320	9.6	C	247	7.4	2.2	C	1	...	81.7	86.4	...
2014	C	296	8.8	C	252	7.5	1.3	C	1	...	...	...	...
2015	C	269	8.0	C	235	6.9	1.0	C	-	...	...	...	...
2016	C	262	7.7	C	253	7.4	0.3	C	1	...	...	...	...
2017	C	228	6.6	C	278	8.1	-1.5	C	-	...	1.8	2.2	...
Serbia - Serbie[115]													
2013	+C	65 554	9.1	+C	100 300	14.0	-4.8	+C	413	6.3	72.5	77.7	1.429
2014	+C	66 461	9.3	+C	101 247	14.2	-4.9	+C	381	5.7	72.6	77.7	1.465
2015	+C	65 657	9.3	+C	103 678	14.6	-5.4	+C	346	5.3	72.6	77.7	1.464
2016	+C	64 734	9.2	+C	100 834	14.3	-5.1	+C	348	5.4	72.7	77.8	1.460
2017	+C	64 894	9.2	+C	103 722	14.8	-5.5		...	...	...	...	...
Slovakia - Slovaquie													
2013	C	54 823	10.1	C	52 089	9.6	0.5	C	301	5.5	72.9	79.6	1.339
2014	C	55 033	10.2	C	51 346	9.5	0.7	C	318	5.8	73.2	80.0	1.367
2015	C	55 602	10.3	C	53 826	9.9	0.3	C	285	5.1	73.0	79.7	1.400
2016	C	57 557	10.6	C	52 351	9.6	1.0	C	311	5.4	73.7	80.4	...
2017	C	57 969	10.7	C	53 914	9.9	0.7		...	...	...	...	...
Slovenia - Slovénie													
2013	C	21 111	10.3	C	19 334	9.4	0.9	C	62	2.9	77.0	83.2	1.550
2014	C	21 165	10.3	C	18 886	9.2	1.1	C	39	1.8	78.0	83.7	1.580
2015	C	20 641	10.0	C	19 834	9.6	0.4	C	33	1.6	...	...	1.570
2016	C	20 345	9.9	C	19 689	9.5	0.3	C	41	2.0	II77.6	83.5	...
2017	C	20 241	9.8	C	20 509	9.9	-0.1		...	...	...	...	...
Spain - Espagne													
2013	C	424 440	9.1	C	388 600	8.3	0.8	C	1 149	2.7	80.0	85.6	1.270
2014	C	426 076	9.2	C	393 734	8.5	0.7	C	1 202	2.8	80.4	86.2	1.320
2015	C	418 432	9.0	C	420 408	9.1	0.0	C	1 117	2.7	...	...	1.330

Continent, country or area and year / Continent, pays ou zone et année	Live births / Naissances vivantes			Deaths / Décès			Rate of natural increase / Taux d'accrois-sement naturel	Infant deaths / Décès d'enfants de moins d'un an			Life expectancy at birth / Espérance de vie à la naissance		Total fertility rate / L'indice synthétique de fécondité
	Code[a]	Number / Nombre	Crude birth rate / Taux brut de natalité	Code[a]	Number / Nombre	Crude death rate / Taux brut de mortalité		Code[a]	Number / Nombre	Rate (per 1000 births) / Taux (par 1000 naissances)	Male[b] / Masculin[b]	Female[b] / Féminin[b]	
EUROPE													
Spain - Espagne													
2016	C	408 734	8.8	C	408 231	8.8	0.0	C	1 097	2.7	80.3	85.8	1.330
2017	C*	390 024	8.4	C*	421 269	9.1	-0.7		...	...	...	...	...
Sweden - Suède													
2013	C	113 593	11.8	C	90 402	9.4	2.4	C	306	2.7	...	...	1.890
2014	C	114 907	11.9	C	88 976	9.2	2.7	C	251	2.2	80.4	84.2	1.880
2015	C	114 870	11.7	C	90 907	9.3	2.4	C	282	2.5	...	...	1.850
2016	C	117 425	11.8	C	90 982	9.2	2.7	C	292	2.5	...	...	1.850
2017	C*	115 416	11.5	C*	91 972	9.1	2.3		...	...	...	...	...
Switzerland - Suisse													
2013	C	82 731	10.2	C	64 961	8.0	2.2	C	320	3.9	...	...	1.520
2014	C	85 287	10.4	C	63 938	7.8	2.6	C	331	3.9	[II]80.7	84.9	1.540
2015	C	86 559	10.5	C	67 606	8.2	2.3	C	340	3.9	[II]2.6	2.9	1.540
2016	C	87 883	10.5	C	64 964	7.8	2.7	C	316	3.6	[II]81.1	85.0	1.550
2017	C	87 381	10.3	C	66 971	7.9	2.4		...	...	...	...	...
TFYR of Macedonia - L'ex-R. y. de Macédoine													
2013	C	23 138	11.2	C	19 208	9.3	1.9	C	237	10.2	...	...	1.500
2014	C	23 596	11.4	C	19 718	9.5	1.9	C	233	9.9	73.5	77.4	1.500
2015	C	23 075	11.1	C	20 461	9.9	1.3	C	198	8.6	11.2	12.4	1.500
2016	C	23 002	11.1	C	20 417	9.9	1.2	C	273	11.9	...	...	1.500
2017	C	21 754	10.5	C	20 318	9.8	0.7		...	...	...	...	...
Ukraine													
2013	+C	503 657[116]	11.1	+C	662 368[117]	14.6	-3.5	+C	4 030[117]	8.0	66.3	76.2	1.506
2014	+C	465 882[118]	10.8	+C	632 296[119]	14.7	-3.9	+C	3 656[119]	7.8	...	...	...
2015	+C	411 781[118]	9.6	+C	594 796[119]	13.9	-4.3	+C	3 318[119]	8.1	...	...	...
2016	+C	397 037[118]	9.3	+C	583 631[119]	13.7	-4.4	+C	2 955[119]	7.4	66.7[120]	76.5[120]	...
2017	+C	363 987[118]	8.6	+C	574 123[119]	13.6	-5.0		...	...	...	...	...
United Kingdom of Great Britain and Northern Ireland - Royaume-Uni de Grande-Bretagne et d'Irlande du Nord[121]													
2013	C	778 358[122]	12.1	+C	574 945	9.0	3.2	+C	3 030	3.9	...	...	1.830
2014	C	775 908[122]	12.0	+C	568 840	8.8	3.2	+C	2 990	3.9	...	...	1.820
2015	C	776 746[122]	11.9	+C	601 272	9.2	2.7	+C	3 005	3.9	...	...	...
2016	C	774 386[122]	11.8	+C	595 655	9.1	2.7	+C	2 976	3.8	[III]79.2	82.9	...
2017	C*	755 043[122]	11.4	+C*	607 172	9.2	2.2		...	...	...	...	...
OCEANIA - OCÉANIE													
American Samoa - Samoas américaines													
2013	C	1 161	18.5	C	270	4.3	14.2	C	5	...	...	...	...
2014	C	1 084	17.5	C	259	4.2	13.3	C	9	...	...	...	...
Australia - Australie													
2013	C	308 065	13.3	C	147 678	6.4	6.9	C	1 094	3.6	[III]80.1	84.3	1.878
2014	C	299 697	12.8	C	153 580	6.5	6.2	C	1 012	3.4	[III]80.3	84.4	1.791
2015	C	305 377	12.8	C	159 052	6.7	6.1	C	991	3.2	[III]80.4	84.5	1.790
2016	C	311 104	12.8	C	158 504	6.5	6.3	C	970	3.1	[III]80.5	84.6	1.789
Cook Islands - Îles Cook[123]													
2013	+C	256	13.8	+C	115	6.2	7.6	+C	-	...	...	...	...
2014	+C	204	11.0	+C	113	6.1	4.9	+C	-	...	...	...	...
2015	+C*	205	11.0	+C*	102	5.5	5.5	+C	-	...	...	...	...
Fiji - Fidji													
2013	+C	18 633	21.6	+C	6 488	7.5	14.1	+C	353	18.9	...	...	...
2014	+C	18 251	21.1	+C	5 801	6.7	14.4	+C	141	7.7	...	...	...

Continent, country or area and year / Continent, pays ou zone et année	Live births / Naissances vivantes			Deaths / Décès			Rate of natural increase / Taux d'accroissement naturel	Infant deaths / Décès d'enfants de moins d'un an			Life expectancy at birth / Espérance de vie à la naissance		Total fertility rate / L'indice synthétique de fécondité
	Code[a]	Number Nombre	Crude birth rate Taux brut de natalité	Code[a]	Number Nombre	Crude death rate Taux brut de mortalité		Code[a]	Number Nombre	Rate (per 1000 births) Taux (par 1000 naissances)	Male[b] Masculin[b]	Female[b] Féminin[b]	
OCEANIA - OCÉANIE													
French Polynesia - Polynésie française													
2013	C	4 203	15.6	C	1 441	5.3	10.2	C	37	8.8	72.9	77.4	1.980
2014	C	4 161	15.3	C	1 427	5.3	10.1	C	28	...	73.8	78.0	1.960
2015	C	3 888	14.3	C	1 394	5.1	9.2	C	29	...	74.4	78.1	...
Guam													
2013	C	3 329[124]	20.8	C	904[124]	5.6	15.1	C	31[124]	9.3	75.6	81.9	2.410
2014	C	3 396[124]	21.1	C	952[124]	5.9	15.2	C	28[124]	...	75.8	82.1	2.380
2015	C	3 367[124]	20.8	C	1 009[124]	6.2	14.6	C	47[124]	14.0	75.9	82.2	...
2016	C	3 433[124]	21.1	C	1 022[124]	6.3	14.8	C	37[124]	10.8	...	...	...
2017	C	3 292[124]	20.1	C	1 008[124]	6.2	13.9	C	28[124]	...	73.6	78.6	2.800
Nauru													
2013	C	320	...	C	95	...	...		...	...	...	...	...
New Caledonia - Nouvelle-Calédonie													
2013	C	4 373	16.6	C	1 374	5.2	11.4	C	19	...	...	...	...
2014	C	4 370	16.3	C	1 406	5.2	11.1	C	23	...	...	...	...
2015	C	4 191	15.4	C	1 465	5.4	10.0	C	25	...	...	...	...
2016	C	4 234	15.4	C	1 580	5.8	9.7		...	...	...	...	...
New Zealand - Nouvelle-Zélande													
2013	+C	58 716[125]	13.2	+C	29 568[125]	6.7	6.6	+C	261[125]	4.4	[III]79.7	83.2	2.007
2014	+C	57 243[125]	12.7	+C	31 065[125]	6.9	5.8	+C	327[125]	5.7	[III]79.6	83.3	1.924
2015	+C	61 038[125]	13.3	+C	31 608[125]	6.9	6.4	+C	249[125]	4.1	...	...	1.994
2016	+C	59 427[126]	12.7	+C	31 179[127]	6.6	6.0	+C	213[127]	3.6	...	...	1.875
2017	+C	59 610[126]	12.4	+C	33 339[127]	7.0	5.5	+C	228[127]	3.8	...	...	1.811
Norfolk Island - Île Norfolk[128]													
2013		...	...	+C	11	...	...		...	...	...	...	...
2014		...	...	+C	13	...	...		...	...	...	...	...
2015		...	...	+C	11	...	...		...	...	...	...	...
Northern Mariana Islands - Îles Mariannes septentrionales													
2013	U	1 057[129]	...	U	200[129]	...	...	U	8[130]	...	...	...	...
2014	U	1 057[129]	...	U	220[129]	...	...	U	7[130]	...	...	...	...
Palau - Palaos													
2013	C	229	13.0	C	192	10.9	2.1	C	7	...	...	...	...
2014	C	241	13.7	C	167	9.5	4.2	C	3	...	...	...	...
2015	C	242	13.7	C	136	7.7	6.0	C	4	...	...	...	...
2016	C	213	12.0	C	175	9.9	2.1	C	-	...	...	...	...
2017	C	221	12.4	C	183	10.3	2.1	C	5	...	...	...	...
Pitcairn													
2013	C	-	...		...	...	...		...	...	...	...	...
Samoa													
2013	+U	4 631	...	+U	876	...	...		...	...	...	...	...
2014	+U	8 493	...	+U	884	...	...		...	...	...	...	4.400
2015	+U	8 207	...	+U	1 124	...	...		...	...	...	...	...
2016	+U	9 379	...	+U	2 034	...	...		...	...	...	...	...

FOOTNOTES - NOTES

Italics: data from civil registers which are incomplete or of unknown completeness. - Italiques : données incomplètes ou dont le degré d'exactitude n'est pas connu, provenant des registres de l'état civil.

[*] Provisional. - Données provisoires.

[a] 'Code' indicates the source of data, as follows:
C - Civil registration, estimated over 90% complete

U - Civil registration, estimated less than 90% complete
| - Other source, estimated reliable
+ - Data tabulated by date of registration rather than occurence
... - Information not available

Le 'Code' indique la source des données, comme suit :
C - Registres de l'état civil considérés complets à 90 p. 100 au moins
U - Registres de l'état civil qui ne sont pas considérés complets à 90 p. 100 au moins
| - Autre source, considérée fiable

+ - Données exploitées selon la date de l'enregistrement et non la date de l'événement

... - Information non disponible

[b] A Roman number in front of the data for males specifies the range of the reference period of life expectancy for males and females presented on the row. For example, a reference year of 2005 and a range of V years means that the reference period for the life expectancy is 2001 - 2005. The absence of a Roman number means the reference period is one year and the reference period therefore coincides with the reference year. - Un chiffre romain devant la donnée relative aux hommes indique l'étendue de la période de référence concernant l'espérance de vie des hommes et des femmes présentée dans la ligne. Par exemple, une année de référence 2005 et une étendue de V signifie que la période de référence pour l'espérance de vie est 2001-2005. L'absence de chiffre romain signifie que la période de référence est d'un an et donc coïncide avec l'année de référence.

[1] Excluding live-born infants who died before their birth was registered. Data refer to Algerian population only. - Non compris les enfants nés vivants décédés avant l'enregistrement de leur naissance. Les données ne concernent que la population algérienne.

[2] Data refer to Algerian population only. - Les données ne concernent que la population algérienne.

[3] Data refer to the 12 months preceding the census in May. - Les données se rapportent aux 12 mois précédant le recensement de mai.

[4] Source: Vital Statistics Report 2016. - Source: Vital Statistics Report 2016.

[5] Source: Botswana Population Projections 2011-2026. - Source: Botswana Population Projections 2011-2026.

[6] Data refer only to events recorded in hospitals and health centres. - Ces données ne concernent que les faits d'état civil enregistrés dans les hôpitaux et les centres de santé uniquement.

[7] The calculation of the total fertility rate is based on the number of live births during the three year period prior to the survey. - L' indice synthétique de fécondité a été calculé sur bases des enfants nés sur la période des trois années précédant l'enquête.

[8] The coverage of registration is estimated at 66 per cent. - Le degré de complétude de l'enregistrement est évalué à 66 pour cent.

[9] The coverage of registration is estimated at 26 per cent. - Le degré de complétude de l'enregistrement est évalué à 26 pour cent.

[10] Adjusted number of births in households referring to the 12 months preceding the census in March. - Le nombre ajusté de naissances vivantes des ménages ordinaires se rapportent aux 12 mois précédant le recensement de mars.

[11] Adjusted number of deaths in households referring to the 12 months preceding the census in March. - Le nombre ajusté de décès des ménages ordinaires se rapportent aux 12 mois précédant le recensement de mars.

[12] Adjusted number of infant deaths in households referring to the 12 months preceding the census in March. - Le nombre ajusté de décès d'enfants des ménages ordinaires se rapportent aux 12 mois précédant le recensement de mars.

[13] Based on underlying data of the Population and Housing Census 2014. - Données fondées sur le recensement de la population de 2014.

[14] Based on underlying data of the Population and Housing Census 2014 and Multiple Indicator Cluster Survey 2016. - Estimations basées sur le Récensement Général de la Population et de l'Habitation 2014 et Enquête par Grappes à Indicateurs Multiples 2016.

[15] Data refer to the 12 months preceding the census in March. Including nomadic population. - Les données se rapportent aux 12 mois précédant le recensement de mars. Y compris la population nomade.

[16] Excludes the islands of St. Brandon and Agalega. - Non compris les îles St. Brandon et Agalega.

[17] Source: Ministry of Health, National Directorate of Planning and Cooperation. - Source : Ministère de la santé, Direction nationale de la planification et de la coopération.

[18] Excluding live-born infants who died before their birth was registered. - Non compris les enfants nés vivants décédés avant l'enregistrement de leur naissance.

[19] Based on estimates and projections from 'Agence Nationale de la Statistique et de la Démographie'. - Données fondées sur des estimations et des projections provenant de l'Agence Nationale de la Statistique et de la Démographie.

[20] Data refer to the 12 months preceding the census in November. - Données se rapportant aux 12 mois précédant le recensement de novembre.

[21] Source: National Office of Births and Deaths. - Source : Le bureau national des naissances et des décès.

[22] Based on the results of the 2014 Population Census. Provisional data. - D'après les résultats du recensement de la population de 2014. Données provisoires.

[23] Source: Demographic and Health Survey. - Source : Demographic and Health Survey (enquête démographique et sanitaire).

[24] Excluding visitors. - Ne comprend pas les visiteurs.

[25] Excluding non-residents and foreign service personnel and their dependants. - À l'exclusion des non-résidents et du personnel diplomatique et de leurs charges de famille.

[26] Including Canadian residents temporarily in the United States, but excluding United States residents temporarily in Canada. - Y compris les résidents canadiens se trouvant temporairement aux Etats-Unis, mais ne comprenant pas les résidents des Etats-Unis se trouvant temporairement au Canada.

[27] Total includes resident deaths outside of the islands but buried in the islands. - Le total comprend les décès de résidents hors des îles mais inhumés dans les îles.

[28] Definition of urban and rural distribution changed from the year 2014. - La définition de la répartition urbaine et rurale a changé depuis 2014.

[29] The total number may include 'Unknown residence', but the categories urban and rural do not. - Le nombre total peut inclure les personnes dont la résidence n'est pas connue, à l'inverse des catégories de population urbaine et rurale.

[30] Data refer to national projections. - Les données se réfèrent aux projections nationales.

[31] Excluding children born in the country of non-resident mothers. - Exceptés les enfants nés dans le pays des mères non-résidentes.

[32] Excluding infant deaths to mothers living abroad. - Exception faite des décès d'enfants en bas âge survenus lorsque la mère résidait à l'étranger.

[33] Data have been adjusted for undercoverage of infant deaths and sudden and violent deaths. - Ajusté pour la sous-estimation de la mortalité infantile, du nombre de morts soudaines et de morts violentes.

[34] Data refer to births to resident mothers. - Ces données concernent les enfants nés de mères résidentes.

[35] Data refer to resident population only. - Pour la population résidante seulement.

[36] Excluding Indian jungle population. - Non compris les Indiens de la jungle.

[37] Source: Population Registry and STAT/CBS estimates. - Source: Le registre de la population et les estimations du STAT/CBS.

[38] Excluding deaths of persons living abroad. - Exception faite des personnes décédées à l'étranger.

[39] Data refer to the 12 months from 30 June 2015 to 30 June 2016. - Les données font référence aux douze mois de 30 juin 2015 à 30 juin 2016.

[40] Data refer to the 12 months from 30 June 2016 to 30 June 2017. - Les données font référence aux douze mois de 30 juin 2016 à 30 juin 2017.

[41] Including births abroad and births of unknown residence of mother. - Y compris les naissances à l'étranger et les naissances pour lesquelles le lieu de résidence de la mère est inconnu.

[42] Including deaths abroad and deaths of unknown place of residence. - Y compris décès à l'étranger et décès dont le lieu de résidence n'est pas connu.

[43] Including deaths abroad and deaths of unknown residence of mother. - Y compris décès à l'étranger et décès de nourrissons nés de mères dont le lieu de résidence n'est pas connu.

[44] Projected value based on the results of 2000 and 2010 censuses, statistics from civil registration and reporting of live births in the ministry of health system. - Projection basée sur les résultats des recensements de 2000 et 2010, des statistiques d'état civil et les registres des naissances vivantes du Ministère de la santé.

[45] Estimate for 2015 – 2020. - Estimation pour la période 2015-2020.

[46] Excludes nomadic Indian tribes. - Non compris les tribus d'Indiens nomades.

[47] Data based on the 2010 Population Census. - Les données sont fondées sur le recensement de la population de 2010.

[48] Source: Reports of the Ministry of Health. - Source : Rapports du Ministère de la Santé.

[49] Indicators based on projected or estimated fertility from the 2001 Population Census. - Les indicateurs sont fondés sur la fécondité projetée ou estimée à partir du recensement de population de 2001.

[50] Based on the results of the 2011 Population Census. - Basé sur les résultats du recencement de la population de 2011.

[51] Excluding infants born alive of less than 28 weeks' gestation, of less than 1 000 g in weight and 35 cm in length, who die within seven days of birth. - Non compris les enfants nés vivants après moins de 28 semaines de gestations, pesant moins de 1 000 g, mesurant moins de 35 cm et décédés dans les sept jours qui ont suivi leur naissance.

[52] Sources: Births and Deaths National Registration System database, and medical records of government hospitals. - Les sources: Les bases de données des << Births and Deaths National Registration System >> et les dossiers médicaux des hôpitaux du gouvernement.

[53] Deaths include deaths among some visitors. Sources: Births and Deaths National Registration System database, and medical records of government hospitals. - Les décès comprennent des décès parmi certains visiteurs. Les

sources: Les bases de données des << Births and Deaths National Registration System >> et les dossiers médicaux des hôpitaux du gouvernement.

[54] Source: Sample vital registration system of Bangladesh - Source : << Sample Vital Registration System >> du Bangladesh.

[55] Data have been estimated on the basis of the annual National Sample Survey on Population Changes. For statistical purposes, the data for China do not include those for the Hong Kong Special Administrative Region (Hong Kong SAR), Macao Special Administrative Region (Macao SAR) and Taiwan province of China. - Les données ont été estimées sur la base de l'enquête annuelle "National Sample Survey on Population Changes". Pour la présentation des statistiques, les données pour la Chine ne comprennent pas la Région Administrative Spéciale de Hong Kong (Hong Kong RAS), la Région Administrative Spéciale de Macao (Macao RAS) et Taïwan province de Chine.

[56] The fertility rates have been compiled using a population denominator which has excluded female foreign domestic helpers. - Les taux de fécondité ont été compilés pour une population (en dénominateur) ne comprenant pas les domestiques étrangères.

[57] Data refer to the 12 months preceding the census in August. - Les données se rapportent aux 12 mois précédant le recensement d'août.

[58] Data refer to government controlled areas. - Les données se rapportent aux zones contrôlées par le Gouvernement.

[59] Data refer to deaths of residents only. - Les données renvoient aux décès de résidents uniquement.

[60] Includes data for the Indian-held part of Jammu and Kashmir, the final status of which has not yet been determined. - Y compris les données pour la partie du Jammu et du Cachemire occupée par l'Inde dont le statut définitif n'a pas encore été déterminé.

[61] Rates were obtained by the Sample Registration System of India, which is a large demographic survey. - Les taux ont été obtenus par le Système de l'enregistrement par échantillon de l'Inde qui est une large enquête démographique.

[62] Data refer to the Iranian Year which begins on 21 March and ends on 20 March of the following year. - Les données concernent l'année iranienne, qui commence le 21 mars et se termine le 20 mars de l'année suivante.

[63] Includes data for East Jerusalem and Israeli residents in certain other territories under occupation by Israeli military forces since June 1967. - Y compris les données pour Jérusalem-Est et les résidents israéliens dans certains autres territoires occupés depuis 1967 par les forces armées israéliennes.

[64] Including deaths abroad of Israeli residents who were out of the country for less than a year. - Y compris les décès à l'étranger de résidents israéliens qui ont quitté le pays depuis moins d'un an.

[65] Data refer to Japanese nationals in Japan only. - Les données se raportent aux nationaux japonais au Japon seulement.

[66] Total fertility rate computed as the sum of the age-specific fertility rates from age 15 to 49 years old. - Le taux de fécondité cumulé est calculé comme somme des taux de fécondité par âge de 15 à 49 ans.

[67] Excluding data for Jordanian territory under occupation since June 1967 by Israeli military forces. Excluding foreigners, including registered Palestinian refugees. - Non compris les données pour le territoire jordanien occupé depuis juin 1967 par les forces armées israéliennes. Non compris les étrangers, mais y compris les réfugiés de Palestine enregistrés.

[68] Based on underlying data of the 2015 census. - Données fondées sur celles extraites du recensement de 2015.

[69] Data do not include foreigners. - Les données sur les etrangers ne sont pas inclus.

[70] Source: "Department of Public Health" - Source : << Le Service de la santé publique >>

[71] Data are from Vital Registration System (VRS). - Les données proviennent du système d'enregistrement des faits d'état civil.

[72] Based on Vital Registration System (VRS). - Système d'enregistrement des faits d'état civil.

[73] Data from Births and Deaths Notification System (Ministry of Health and all health care providers). - Les données proviennent du système de notification des naissances et des décès (Ministère de la santé et tous prestataires de soins de santé).

[74] Data refer to Omani citizen only. - Les données concernent les citoyens d'Oman uniquement.

[75] Data refer to residence of child. Excluding alien armed forces, civilian aliens employed by armed forces, and foreign diplomatic personnel and their dependants. - Les données correspondent à la résidence de l'enfant. Non compris les militaires étrangers, les civils étrangers employés par les forces armées ni le personnel diplomatique étranger et les membres de leur famille les accompagnant.

[76] Excluding alien armed forces, civilian aliens employed by armed forces, and foreign diplomatic personnel and their dependants. - Non compris les militaires étrangers, les civils étrangers employés par les forces armées ni le personnel diplomatique étranger et les membres de leur famille les accompagnant.

[77] Data refer to Saudi Arabian nationals only. Survey based estimates. - Les données ne concernent que les ressortissants saoudiens. Estimations basées sur des enquêtes.

[78] Projections based on the final results of the 2004 Population and Housing Census. - Projections basées sur les résultats définitifs du recensement de la population et de l'habitat de 2004.

[79] Projections based on the 2010 Population and Housing Census. - Projections fondées sur le recensement 2010 de la population et des logements.

[80] Data refer to Saudi Arabian nationals only. Based on 2010 population census and 2016 demographic survey. - Les données ne concernent que les ressortissants saoudiens. D'après le recensement de la population de 2010 et l'enquête démographique de 2016.

[81] Data refer to Saudi Arabian nationals only. - Les données ne concernent que les ressortissants saoudiens.

[82] Data refer to resident population which comprises Singapore citizens and permanent residents. - Les données se rapportent à la population résidente composé des citoyens de Singapour et des résidents permanents.

[83] Data refer to resident total fertility rate. - Les données se rapportent aux indices synthétique de fécondité de la population résidante.

[84] Provisional data. Data refer to resident population which comprises Singapore citizens and permanent residents. - Données provisoires. Les données se rapportent à la population résidente composé des citoyens de Singapour et des résidents permanents.

[85] Source: Palestinian Central Bureau of Statistics, Population Register, updated version 22/02/2016. - Source: Bureau central de statistique palestinien, registre de la population, version actualisée jusqu'au 22/02/2016.

[86] Source: Palestinian Multiple Indicator Cluster Survey 2014. - Source: Enquête palestinienne par grappes à indicateurs multiples, 2014.

[87] Data have been adjusted for under-registration. Excluding infants born alive of less than 28 weeks' gestation, of less than 1 000 g in weight and 35 cm in length, who die within seven days of birth. - Y compris un ajustement pour sous-enregistrement. Non compris les enfants nés vivants après moins de 28 semaines de gestations, pesant moins de 1 000 g, mesurant moins de 35 cm et décédés dans les sept jours qui ont suivi leur naissance.

[88] Data refer to the 12 months preceding the census in July. - Les données se rapportent aux 12 mois précédant le recensement de juillet.

[89] Data from MERNIS (Central Population Administrative System). - Données de MERNIS (Système central de données démographiques).

[90] The registration of births and deaths is conducted by the Ministry of Health. An estimate of completeness is not provided. - L'enregistrement des naissances et des décès est mené par le Ministère de la Santé. Le degré estimatif de complétude n'est pas fourni.

[91] Including Non-Yemeni births. - Y compris les naissances non-yéménites.

[92] Including Non-Yemeni deaths. - Y compris les décès non-yéménites.

[93] Including deaths of nationals abroad. - Y compris les décès des nationaux survenus à l'étranger.

[94] Including births occurring abroad of mothers with residence in Austria. - Y compris les naissances survenues à l'étranger des mères avec résidence en Autriche.

[95] Including armed forces stationed outside the country, but excluding alien armed forces stationed in the area. - Y compris les militaires nationaux hors du pays, mais non compris les militaires étrangers en garnison sur le territoire.

[96] Provisional data. - Données provisoires.

[97] Excluding Faeroe Islands and Greenland shown separately, if available. - Non compris les Iles Féréo et le Groenland, qui font l'objet de rubriques distinctes, si disponible.

[98] Excluding Åland Islands. - Non compris les Îles d'Åland.

[99] Including live births by military personnel and their dependants. - Y compris les naissances vivantes parmi les membres du personnel militaire et leurs personnes à charge.

[100] Excluding armed forces. - Non compris les militaires en garnison.

[101] Data include the live births of women with unknown residence and homeless. Till 2012 data refer to all live births occurred in Hungary. From 2013 data include the live births of women with Hungarian usual residence regardless of whether the live birth occurred in Hungary or in a foreign country, and do not include the live births of women with foreign country usual residence. - Les données incluent les enfants nés vivants de femmes dont la résidence n'est pas connue et de femmes sans domicile fixe. Jusqu'en 2012 les données concernent toutes les naissances vivantes survenues en Hongrie. À partir de 2013, les données concernent les enfants nés vivants de femmes dont la résidence habituelle est en Hongrie, que la naissance vivante ait eu lieu en Hongrie ou dans un pays étranger, et ne comprennent pas les enfants nés vivants de femmes dont la résidence habituelle est dans un pays étranger.

[102] Till 2012 data refer to all deaths occurred in Hungary. From 2013 data include the deceased persons with Hungarian usual residence regardless of whether the death occurred in Hungary or in a foreign country, and do not include the deceased persons with foreign country usual residence. - Jusqu'en 2012 les

données concernent tous les décès survenus en Hongrie. À partir de 2013, les données comprennent les décès de personnes dont la résidence habituelle était en Hongrie, que le décès ait eu lieu en Hongrie ou dans un pays étranger, et ne comprennent pas les décès de personnes dont la residence habituelle était dans un pays étranger.

[103] Till 2012 data refer to all infant deaths occurred in Hungary. From 2013 data include the deceased infants with Hungarian usual residence regardless of whether the death occurred in Hungary or in a foreign country, and do not include the deceased infants with foreign country usual residence. - Jusqu'en 2012 les données concernent tous les décès de nourrissons survenus en Hongrie. À partir de 2013, les données comprennent les nourrissons décédés alors que leur résidence habituelle était en Hongrie, que le décès ait eu lieu en Hongrie ou dans un pays étranger, et ne comprennent pas les nourrissons décédés dont la résidence habituelle était dans un pays étranger.

[104] Data include the live births of women with unknown residence and homeless. Data include the live births of women with Hungarian usual residence regardless of whether the live birth occurred in Hungary or in a foreign country, and do not include the live births of women with foreign country usual residence. - Les données incluent les enfants nés vivants de femmes dont la résidence n'est pas connue et de femmes sans domicile fixe. Les données concernent les enfants nés vivants de femmes dont la résidence habituelle est en Hongrie, que la naissance vivante ait eu lieu en Hongrie ou dans un pays étranger, et ne comprennent pas les enfants nés vivants de femmes dont la résidence habituelle est dans un pays étranger.

[105] Data include the deceased persons with Hungarian usual residence regardless of whether the death occurred in Hungary or in a foreign country, and do not include the deceased persons with foreign country usual residence. - Les données comprennent tous les décès survenus alors que leur résidence habituelle était en Hongrie, que le décès ait eu lieu en Hongrie ou dans un pays étranger, et ne comprennent pas les décès des personnes dont la residence habituelle était dans un pays étranger.

[106] Data include the deceased infants with Hungarian usual residence regardless of whether the death occurred in Hungary or in a foreign country, and do not include the deceased infants with foreign country usual residence. - Les données comprennent les nourrissons décédés alors que leur résidence habituelle était en Hongrie, que le décès ait eu lieu en Hongrie ou dans un pays étranger, et ne comprennent pas les nourrissons décédés dont la residence habituelle était dans un pays étranger.

[107] Data refer to the 12 months preceding the census in April. - Les données se rapportent aux douze mois précédant le recensement d'avril.

[108] Source: City Hall, Civil Status Registry Office, resident and non-resident births. - Source : La mairie, Bureau de l'État Civil, toutes les naissances.

[109] Source: City Hall, Civil Status Registry Office, resident and non-resident deaths. Including still births. - Source : La mairie, Bureau de l'État Civil, toutes les décès. Les données comprennent les mortinaissances.

[110] Including residents outside the country if listed in a Netherlands population register. - Englobe les résidents se trouvant à l'étranger à condition qu'ils soient inscrits sur le registre de population des Pays-Bas.

[111] Including residents temporarily outside the country. - Y compris les résidents se trouvant temporairement hors du pays.

[112] Data refer to usually resident population. - Les données concernent la population habituellement résidente.

[113] Excluding Transnistria and the municipality of Bender. - Les données ne tiennent pas compte de l'information sur la Transnistria et la municipalité de Bender.

[114] Live births that occured outside of the country were not included in the calculation of the fertility rate. - Les naissances vivantes survenues en dehors du pays ne sont pas prises en compte dans les calculs de l'indice syntetique de fécondité.

[115] Excludes data for Kosovo and Metohia. - Sans les données pour le Kosovo et Metohie.

[116] Data refer to births with weight 500g and more (if weight is unknown - with length 25 centimeters and more, or with gestation during 22 weeks or more). - Données concernant les nouveau-nés de 500 grammes ou plus (si le poids est inconnu – de 25 centimètres de long ou plus, ou après une grossesse de 22 semaines ou plus).

[117] Data includes deaths resulting from births with weight 500 g and more (if weight is unknown - with length 25 cm and more, or with gestation during 22 weeks or more). - Y compris les décès de nouveau-nés de 500 g ou plus (si le poids est inconnu – de 25 cm de long ou plus, ou après une grossesse de 22 semaines ou plus).

[118] Data refer to births with weight 500g and more (if weight is unknown - with length 25 centimeters and more, or with gestation during 22 weeks or more). The Government of Ukraine has informed the United Nations that it is not in a position to provide statistical data concerning the Autonomous Republic of Crimea and the city of Sevastopol. - Données concernant les nouveau-nés de 500 grammes ou plus (si le poids est inconnu – de 25 centimètres de long ou plus, ou après une

grossesse de 22 semaines ou plus). Le gouvernement Ukrainien a informé l'ONU qu'il n'est pas en mesure de fournir des données statistiques concernant la République autonome de Crimée et la ville de Sébastopol.

[119] The Government of Ukraine has informed the United Nations that it is not in a position to provide statistical data concerning the Autonomous Republic of Crimea and the city of Sevastopol. Data includes deaths resulting from births with weight 500 g and more (if weight is unknown - with length 25 cm and more, or with gestation during 22 weeks or more). - Le gouvernement Ukrainien a informé l'ONU qu'il n'est pas en mesure de fournir des données statistiques concernant la République autonome de Crimée et la ville de Sébastopol. Y compris les décès de nouveau-nés de 500 g ou plus (si le poids est inconnu – de 25 cm de long ou plus, ou après une grossesse de 22 semaines ou plus).

[120] The Government of Ukraine has informed the United Nations that it is not in a position to provide statistical data concerning the Autonomous Republic of Crimea and the city of Sevastopol. - Le gouvernement Ukrainien a informé l'ONU qu'il n'est pas en mesure de fournir des données statistiques concernant la République autonome de Crimée et la ville de Sébastopol.

[121] Excluding Channel Islands (Guernsey and Jersey) and Isle of Man, shown separately, if available. - Non compris les îles Anglo-Normandes (Guernesey et Jersey) et l'île de Man, qui font l'objet de rubriques distinctes, si disponible.

[122] Data tabulated by date of occurrence for England and Wales, and by date of registration for Northern Ireland and Scotland. - Données exploitées selon la date de l'événement pour l'Angleterre et le pays de Galles, et selon la date de l'enregistrement pour l'Irlande du Nord et l'Ecosse.

[123] Excluding Niue, shown separately, which is part of Cook Islands, but because of remoteness is administered separately. - Non compris Nioué, qui fait l'objet d'une rubrique distincte et qui fait partie des îles Cook, mais qui, en raison de son éloignement, est administrée séparément.

[124] Including United States military personnel, their dependants and contract employees. - Y compris les militaires des Etats-Unis, les membres de leur famille les accompagnant et les agents contractuels des Etats-Unis.

[125] Random rounding to base 3 is applied in this table as a confidentiality measure. - Les chiffres sont arrondis à la base 3 de manière aléatoire, pour des raisons de confidentialité.

[126] Random rounding to base 3 is applied in this table as a confidentiality measure. Data refers to births registered in the country to mothers resident in the country. - Les chiffres sont arrondis à la base 3 de manière aléatoire, pour des raisons de confidentialité. Les données se rapportent aux naissances enregistrées dans le pays pour lesquelles la mère réside dans le pays.

[127] Random rounding to base 3 is applied in this table as a confidentiality measure. Data refer to deaths of residents only. - Les chiffres sont arrondis à la base 3 de manière aléatoire, pour des raisons de confidentialité. Les données renvoient aux décès de résidents uniquement.

[128] Data cover the period from 1 July of the previous year to 30 June of the present year. - Pour la période allant du 1er juillet de l'année précédente au 30 juin de l'année en cours.

[129] Source: Commonwealth Health Center - Vital Statistics Office - Source : Centre de Santé du Commonwealth - Bureau des statistiques d'État civil

[130] Source: U.S. National Center for Health Statistics, National Vital Statistics Reports (NVSR). - Source : US National Center for Health Statistics, National Vital Statistics Reports (NVSR).

Table 5 - *Demographic Yearbook 2017*

Table 5 presents national estimates of mid-year population for all available years between 2008 and 2017.

Description of variables: Mid-year estimates of the total population are those provided by national statistical offices. They refer to the *de facto* or *de jure* population on 1 July of the reference year. Exceptions to this are footnoted accordingly. The data are presented in thousands, rounded by the Statistics Division of the United Nations Department of Economic and Social Affairs.

For some countries or areas the figures presented in this table and the figures used to calculate rates in subsequent tables are not the same, as these countries have provided a reference population for vital events that is different than the total population.

Unless otherwise indicated, all estimates relate to the population within present geographical boundaries. Major exceptions to this principle are explained in footnotes.

Reliability of data: Reliable mid-year population estimates are those that are based on a complete census (or on a sample survey) and have been adjusted on a basis of a continuous population register or on the balance of births, deaths and migration. Reliable mid-year estimates appear in roman type. Mid-year estimates that are not calculated on this basis are considered less reliable and are shown in *italics*.

Limitations: Statistics on estimates of the mid-year total population are subject to the same qualifications as have been set forth for population statistics in general in section 3 of the Technical Notes.

International comparability of mid-year population estimates is also affected by the fact that some of these estimates refer to the *de jure*, and not the *de facto*, population. These are indicated in the column titled "Code". The difference between the *de facto* and the *de jure* population is discussed in section 3.1.1 of the Technical Notes.

Earlier data: Estimates of mid-year population have been shown in previous issues of the *Demographic Yearbook*. Information on the years and specific topics covered is presented in the Historical Index.

Tableau 5 – *Annuaire démographique 2017*

Le tableau 5 présente des estimations nationales de la population en milieu d'année pour le plus grand nombre possible d'années entre 2008 et 2017.

Description des variables : les estimations de la population totale en milieu d'année sont celles qui ont été communiquées par les services nationaux de statistique. Elles correspondent à la population de fait ou se réfèrent à la population de droit, au 1er juillet de l'année de référence. Lorsque la date est différente, cela est signalé par une note. Sauf indication contraire, tous les chiffres sont exprimés en milliers. Les données ont été arrondies par la Division de statistique du Département des affaires économiques et sociales de l'Organisation des Nations Unies.

Pour certains pays ou territoires, les données présentées dans ce tableau sont différentes des données utilisées pour calculer les taux dans les tableaux suivants, parce que ces pays ont fourni une population de référence pour les événements démographiques différente de la population totale.

Sauf indication contraire, toutes les estimations se rapportent à la population présente sur le territoire actuel des pays ou zones considérés. Les principales exceptions à cette règle sont expliquées en note.

Fiabilité des données : les estimations de la population en milieu d'année sont considérées sûres quand elles sont fondées sur un recensement complet (ou sur une enquête par sondage) et ont été ajustées en fonction des données provenant d'un registre permanent de population ou en fonction des naissances, décès et mouvements migratoires qui ont eu lieu pendant la période. Les estimations considérées comme sûres apparaissent en caractères romains. Les estimations dont le calcul n'a pas été effectué sur cette base sont considérées comme moins sûres et apparaissent en italique.

Insuffisance des données : les statistiques concernant les estimations de la population totale en milieu d'année appellent toutes les réserves qui ont été formulées à la section 3 des Notes techniques à propos des statistiques de la population en général.

Le fait que certaines des estimations concernant la population en milieu d'année se réfèrent à la population de droit et non à la population de fait influe sur la comparabilité internationale. Ces cas ont été signalés dans la colonne « Code ». La différence entre la population de fait et la population de droit est expliquée à la section 3.1.1 des Notes techniques.

Données publiées antérieurement : des estimations de la population en milieu d'année ont été publiées dans des éditions antérieures de l'*Annuaire démographique*. Pour plus de précisions concernant les années et les sujets pour lesquels des données ont été publiées, se reporter à l'index.

5. Estimates of mid-year population: 2008 - 2017
Estimations de la population au milieu de l'année : 2008 - 2017

Continent and country or area / Continent et pays ou zone	Code[a]	2008	2009	2010	2011	2012	2013	2014	2015	2016	2017
AFRICA - AFRIQUE											
Algeria - Algérie	DJ	34 591	35 268	35 978	36 717	37 495	38 297	39 114	39 963	40 836	41 696
Angola	DF	16 368[1]	16 889[1]	17 430[1]	17 992[1]	18 577[1]	19 184[1]	25 901[2]	26 682[2]	27 504[2]	28 360[2]
Benin - Bénin	DF	8 225[3]	8 498[3]	8 779[3]	9 067[3]	9 365[3]	...	10 293[4]	10 585[4]	10 883[4]	...
Botswana	DJ	1 755	1 776	1 823	1 850	2 071[5]	2 115[5]	2 156[5]	2 195[5]	2 231[5]	2 267[5]
Burkina Faso[3]	DJ	14 731	15 225	15 731	16 249	16 779	17 323	17 880	18 450	...	...
Burundi	DF	...	...	9 461	9 771	10 073	10 367	10 654	10 933	11 215	11 495
Cabo Verde	DF	500	509	...	...	...	...	...	...	...	...
	DJ	...	...	494[3]	500[3]	506[3]	512[3]	518[3]	525[3]	531[3]	538[3]
Cameroon - Cameroun[3]	DF	18 691	19 166	19 648	20 139	20 637	21 143	21 657	22 180	22 710	23 248
Congo	DF	3 741	3 838	...	...	...	4 278	...	...	...	4 709
Côte d'Ivoire	DF	19 932[6]	20 389[6]	20 845[6]	21 302[6]	21 758[6]	22 215[6]	22 723[7]	23 334[7]	23 950[7]	24 571[7]
Djibouti[8]	DF	797	...	841	865	...	...	...	...	...	...
Egypt - Égypte	DF	75 194	76 925	78 685	80 530	82 550	84 629	86 811	88 958	91 023	95 203
Equatorial Guinea - Guinée équatoriale	DF	1 508[9]	1 566[9]	1 622[9]	...	...	...	...	...	1 265[10]	*1 309[10]
Eritrea - Érythrée[11]	DF	2 565	2 627	2 691	2 759	2 829	2 901	2 976	3 052	3 131	3 212
Eswatini	DF	1 032	1 044	1 056	1 068	1 080	1 093	1 106	1 119	1 133	1 146
Ethiopia - Éthiopie[12]	DF	75 719	77 651	79 634	81 668	83 741	85 837	87 952	90 075	92 205	94 352
Ghana	DF	22 901	23 417	...	25 235[13]	25 825[13]	26 428[13]	27 043[13]	27 670[13]	28 308[13]	...
Guinea - Guinée	DF	10 183[3]	10 218[3]	10 537[3]	10 864[3]	...	...	...	...	...	...
	DJ	...	...	...	...	...	...	10 600[2]	10 918[2]	11 233[2]	11 555[2]
Guinea-Bissau - Guinée-Bissau[3]	DF	...	...	1 460	1 472	1 485	1 499	1 514	1 531	1 548	...
Kenya	DF	38 278	37 725[14]	38 474[14]	39 545[14]	40 657[14]	41 788[14]	42 961[14]	44 157[14]	45 389[14]	46 595[14]
Lesotho[15]	DF	1 884	1 887	1 892	1 897	1 903	1 909	1 917	1 924	...	...
Liberia - Libéria	DF	...	3 551	3 627	3 705	3 784	3 865	3 946	...	...	...
Libya - Libye[16]	DF	5 490	5 589	5 689	5 791	5 892	5 994	6 096	6 162	...	...
Madagascar[3]	DF	19 072	19 601	20 142	20 696	21 263	21 842	22 434	...	...	...
Malawi[3]	DF	13 630	13 520	13 948	14 389	14 845	15 317	15 805	16 310	16 833	...
Mali[17]	DF	14 161	14 671	15 370	15 843	16 312	16 808	17 319	17 819	18 341	...
Mauritania - Mauritanie[3]	DF	3 162	3 251	3 341	3 297	3 378	3 537	3 637	3 720	3 783	...
Mauritius - Maurice[18]	DJ	1 269[19]	1 275[19]	1 281[19]	1 252[20]	1 256[20]	1 259[20]	1 261[20]	1 263[20]	1 263[20]	1 265[20]
Mayotte	DJ	...	...	...	...	...	...	225[21]	230[22]	*244[21]	*254[21]
Morocco - Maroc	DF	31 195[23]	31 543[23]	31 894[23]	32 245[23]	32 597[23]	32 950[23]	...	...	...	...
	DJ	...	...	...	...	...	...	33 770[24]	34 125[24]	34 487[24]	34 852[24]
Mozambique[25]	DF	21 208	21 803	22 417	23 050	23 701	24 366	25 042	25 728	26 424	27 129
Namibia - Namibie	DF	2 065[3]	2 104[3]	2 143[3]	2 116[26]	2 155[26]	2 196[26]	2 238[26]	2 281[26]	2 324[26]	2 369[26]
Niger	DJ	14 198[3]	14 693[3]	15 204[3]	15 731[3]	16 994[27]	17 680[27]	18 389[27]	19 125[27]	19 865[27]	...
Nigeria - Nigéria[15]	DF	149 713	154 582	159 608	164 798	170 157	175 690	181 403	187 302	193 393	...
Republic of South Sudan - République de Soudan du Sud[28]	DF	8 368	8 685	9 005	9 389	9 783	10 182	10 585	11 000	11 425	11 868
Reunion - Réunion	DJ	808[22]	816[22]	821[22]	829[22]	834[22]	839[21]	847[21]	851[22]	*858[21]	*863[21]
Rwanda	DF	9 832[3]	10 117[3]	10 413[3]	10 718[3]	10 483[27]	10 737[27]	10 997[27]	11 263[27]	11 533[27]	11 809[27]
Saint Helena ex. dep. - Sainte-Hélène sans dép.	DF	4	4	4	4	4	4[29]	4	4	5	...
Saint Helena: Ascension - Sainte-Hélène: Ascension	DJ	1	...	...	...	...	...	...	...	...	...
Saint Helena: Tristan da Cunha - Sainte-Hélène: Tristan da Cunha[30]	DF	0	0	...	...	...	...	...	...	...	...
Sao Tome and Principe - Sao Tomé-et-Principe	DF	158	161	164	167	...					
	DJ	...	...	...	...	...	182[31]	186[31]	190[31]	194[31]	198[31]
Senegal - Sénégal	DJ	11 841[29]	12 171[29]	12 509[29]	12 842[29]	13 208[3]	13 509[3]	13 926[3]	14 357[3]	14 800[3]	15 256[3]
Seychelles	DF	87	87	90	87	88	90	91	93	95	96
Sierra Leone	DF	5 474	5 608	5 747	5 890	6 038	...	...	...	...	...
South Africa - Afrique du Sud	DF	49 558	50 256	50 979	51 729	52 507	53 312	54 147	55 012	55 909	56 522
Sudan - Soudan	DF	30 979	31 957	32 962	33 998	35 064	36 163	37 292	38 454	39 648	...
Togo	DF	5 596	5 731	...							
	DJ	...	...	6 191[3]	6 338[3]	6 491[3]	6 648[3]	6 809[3]	6 974[3]	7 143[3]	7 229[3]
Tunisia - Tunisie	DF	10 352	10 458	10 566	10 674	10 784	10 895	11 007	11 154	11 304	11 446
Uganda - Ouganda	DF	29 593	30 661	31 785	32 940	34 131	...	34 141[7]	35 492[7]	36 561[7]	37 674[7]
United Republic of Tanzania - République Unie de Tanzanie	DF	40 668[32]	41 916[32]	43 188[32]	44 485[32]	45 798[32]	46 356[27]	47 831[27]	49 359[27]	50 942[27]	52 555[27]
Zambia - Zambie	DF	12 526[3]	12 897[3]								
	DJ	...	...	13 719[33]	14 145[33]	14 580[33]	15 023[33]	15 474[33]	15 934[33]	16 405[33]	
Zimbabwe	DF	12 150[32]	13 668[32]	...	...	...	13 369[31]	13 652[31]	13 943[31]	14 240[31]	14 542[31]

Continent and country or area / Continent et pays ou zone	Code[a]	Population estimates (in thousands) - Estimations (en milliers)									
		2008	2009	2010	2011	2012	2013	2014	2015	2016	2017
AMERICA, NORTH - AMÉRIQUE DU NORD											
Anguilla	DF	16	16	16	...	14	14	14	15	15	...
Antigua and Barbuda - Antigua-et-Barbuda	DF	88	89	91	...	...	...	...	...	...	...
Aruba	DJ	101	102	102	103	105	106	108	109	110	111
Bahamas	DF	338[34]	342[34]	...	...	...	...	...	...	...	...
	DJ	...	...	352[33]	355[33]	359[33]	362[33]	366[33]	370[33]	373[33]	377[33]
Barbados - Barbade	DF	275	275	...	...	...	...	...	...	...	...
	DJ	...	...	278	278	278	277	277	275	...	...
Belize	DF	307	315	...	...	...	...	...	...	...	...
	DJ	...	...	324	332	341	350	359	368	378	388
Bermuda - Bermudes	DJ	64[34]	64[34]	64[13]	63[13]	62[13]	62[13]	62[13]	62[13]	62[13]	62[13]
British Virgin Islands - Îles Vierges britanniques	DF	28	28	28	28	28	29	...	29	...	...
Canada[35]	DJ	33 246[36]	33 629[36]	34 005[36]	34 343[37]	34 751[37]	35 152[37]	35 535[38]	35 833[38]	36 265[38]	*36 708[39]
Cayman Islands - Îles Caïmanes	DJ	56	57	56	55	56	56	57	59	61	63[29]
Costa Rica	DJ	4 533[40]	4 620[40]	4 538[41]	4 592[41]	4 651[41]	4 712[41]	4 772[41]	4 834[42]	4 890[43]	4 947[44]
Cuba	DJ	11 181	11 174	11 171	11 172	11 174	11 192	11 224	11 239	11 239	11 230
Curaçao	DJ	146[45]	147[45]	149[45]	151[45]	152[2]	154[2]	156[2]	158[2]	160[2]	160[2]
Dominica - Dominique	DF	71	71	71	71	71	71	72	...	...	...
Dominican Republic - République dominicaine	DJ	9 280	9 380	9 479[3]	9 580[3]	9 681[3]	9 785[3]	9 883[3]	9 980[3]	10 075[3]	10 169[3]
El Salvador[46]	DJ	6 125	6 153	6 183	6 216	6 251	6 289	6 328	6 460	6 521	6 582
Greenland - Groenland[47]	DJ	56	56	57	57	57	56	56	56	56	56
Grenada - Grenade	DF	105	105	105	107	108	109	109	110	111	111
Guadeloupe[48]	DJ	402	402	404	404	403	401	399	397	395	*392
Guatemala[32]	DJ	13 678	14 017	14 362	14 714	15 073	15 438	15 807	16 176	...	...
Haiti - Haïti[49]	DJ	9 762	9 923	10 085	10 248	10 413	10 579	10 746	10 912	...	...
Honduras	DF	7 707[50]	7 877[50]	8 046[50]	8 215[50]	8 385[50]	...	8 432[4]	8 577[4]	...	...
Jamaica - Jamaïque	DJ	2 687	2 696	2 702	2 700	2 708	2 715	2 721	2 725	2 728	2 729
Martinique[22]	DJ	398	396	394	392	388	386	384	381	*378	*375
Mexico - Mexique	DJ	111 299	112 853	114 256[3]	115 683[3]	117 054[3]	118 395[3]	119 713[3]	121 006[3]	122 273[3]	123 518[3]
Montserrat	DF	5	5	5	...	...	...	...	...	...	...
	DJ	...	...	...	5	5	5	5	5	5	...
Nicaragua	DJ	5 669	5 742	5 816	5 997	6 071	6 134	6 198	6 263	6 328	6 394
Panama	DF	3 538[51]	3 600[51]	3 662[13]	3 724[13]	3 788[13]	3 851[13]	3 913[13]	3 975[13]	4 037[13]	4 098[13]
Puerto Rico - Porto Rico[52]	DJ	3 761[45]	3 740[45]	3 721[53]	3 679[2]	3 634[2]	3 593[2]	3 535[2]	3 473[2]	3 411[2]	3 337[2]
Saint Kitts and Nevis - Saint-Kitts-et-Nevis	DF	*51	*52	*53	...	...	...	...	...	...	...
Saint Lucia - Sainte-Lucie	DF	170	172	...	167	169	171	173	173	...	...
Saint Pierre and Miquelon - Saint-Pierre-et-Miquelon[22]	DJ	...	...	...	6	6	...	...	...	...	...
Saint Vincent and the Grenadines - Saint-Vincent-et-les Grenadines	DJ	110	110	110	110	...	110	110	110	...	...
Sint Maarten (Dutch part) - Saint-Martin (partie néerlandaise)	DF	40	39	36	33	35	37	37[22]	...	...	...
Trinidad and Tobago - Trinité-et-Tobago	DF	1 309[19]	1 310[19]	1 318[19]	...	1 335[20]	1 341[20]	1 345[20]	1 350[20]	1 354[20]	1 357[20]
Turks and Caicos Islands - Îles Turques et Caïques	DJ	37	36	35	34	32	34	35	37	38	40
United States of America - États-Unis d'Amérique[54]	DJ	304 094[45]	306 772[45]	309 348[2]	311 663[2]	313 998[2]	316 205[2]	318 563[2]	320 897[2]	323 128[2]	...
United States Virgin Islands - Îles Vierges américaines[52]	DJ	110	110[55]	106[55]	106[55]	105[55]	105[55]	104[55]	...	...	...
AMERICA, SOUTH - AMÉRIQUE DU SUD											
Argentina - Argentine	DF	39 746	40 134	40 788[33]	41 261[33]	41 733[33]	42 203[33]	42 670[33]	43 132[33]	43 590[33]	44 045[33]
Bolivia (Plurinational State of) - Bolivie (État plurinational de)	DF	9 710	9 870	10 031	10 191	10 351	10 508	10 666	10 825	10 985	11 146
Brazil - Brésil[56]	DJ	191 532	193 544	195 498	197 397	199 242	201 033	202 769	204 451	206 081	207 661

5. Estimates of mid-year population: 2008 - 2017
Estimations de la population au milieu de l'année : 2008 - 2017 (continued - suite)

Continent and country or area / Continent et pays ou zone	Code[a]	Population estimates (in thousands) - Estimations (en milliers)									
		2008	2009	2010	2011	2012	2013	2014	2015	2016	2017
AMERICA, SOUTH - AMÉRIQUE DU SUD											
Chile - Chili	DF	16 763	16 929	17 094	17 248	17 403	17 557	17 819	18 006	18 192	18 374
Colombia - Colombie[57]	DJ	44 451	44 979	45 510	46 045	46 582	47 121	47 662	48 203	48 748	49 292
Ecuador - Équateur[58]	DF	14 473	14 738	15 012	15 266	15 521	15 775	16 027	16 279	16 529	16 777
French Guiana - Guyane française[22]	DJ	219	224	229	238	240	244	252	257	263	274
Guyana	DF	774	753	752	751	747	746	746	745	743	741
Paraguay[59]	DF	6 072	6 169	6 266	6 363	6 461	6 559	6 657	6 756	6 855	6 954
Peru - Pérou[60]	DF	28 807	29 132	29 462	29 798	30 136	30 475	30 814	31 152	31 489	31 826
Suriname	DJ	517	524	531	540	...	550	559	567	576	...
Uruguay	DJ	3 363	3 378	3 397	3 413	3 426[3]	3 440[3]	3 454[3]	3 467[3]	3 480[3]	3 493[3]
Venezuela (Bolivarian Republic of) - Venezuela (République bolivarienne du)	DF	27 689	28 106	28 524	28 811	29 231	29 650	30 070	30 489	30 883	31 277
ASIA - ASIE											
Afghanistan[61]	DF	23 511	23 994	24 486	24 988	25 500	26 023	26 557	27 101	27 657	28 224
Armenia - Arménie	DJ	3 087	3 066	3 045	3 028	3 024	3 022	3 014	3 005	2 992	2 979
Azerbaijan - Azerbaïdjan	DJ	8 839	8 947	9 054	9 173	9 296	9 417	9 535	9 649	9 758	9 850
Bahrain - Bahreïn	DJ	1 103	1 178	1 229	1 195	1 209	1 253	1 315	1 370	1 424	1 501
Bangladesh	DF	144 500	146 600	148 620	150 611	152 700	154 790	156 880	158 900	160 800	161 750
Bhutan - Bhoutan[62]	DF	671	683	696	708	721	733	745	757	769	...
Brunei Darussalam - Brunéi Darussalam	DF / DJ	375[45]	380[45]	387[45]	...	...	399 / 403	408	412	417[63]	421
Cambodia - Cambodge[64]	DF	13 868	14 085	14 303	14 521	14 741	14 963	15 184	15 405	...	...
China - Chine[65]	DF	1 324 700[66]	1 331 300[66]	1 337 700[66]	1 344 100[67]	1 350 695[67]	1 357 380[66]	1 364 270[66]	1 371 220[66]	1 378 665[66]	1 384 373[66]
China, Hong Kong SAR - Chine, Hong Kong RAS	DJ	6 958	6 973	7 024	7 072	7 150	7 179	7 230	7 291	7 337	7 392
China, Macao SAR - Chine, Macao RAS	DJ	541	535	537	550	568	592	622	643	*645	*653
Cyprus - Chypre[68]	DJ	787[21]	808[21]	829[21]	851[21]	864[21]	862[21]	853[21]	848[21]	852[21]	855[22]
Georgia - Géorgie	DF / DJ	4 384	4 411	4 453	4 483	4 491	4 487	3 727[69]	3 717[69]	3 719[69]	3 728[69]
India - Inde[70]	DF	1 150 196	1 160 813[71]	1 176 742[71]	1 192 506[71]	1 208 116[71]	1 223 581[71]	1 238 887[71]	1 254 019[71]	1 268 961[71]	1 283 600[71]
Indonesia - Indonésie	DJ	228 523[72]	231 370[72]	238 519[73]	241 991[73]	245 425[73]	248 818[73]	252 165[73]	255 462[73]	258 705[73]	261 891[73]
Iran (Islamic Republic of) - Iran (République islamique d')[74]	DJ	72 182	73 202	74 340	...	76 038	76 942	77 856	78 773	79 686	81 070
Iraq	DF	30 315	31 393	32 211	33 052	33 913	34 794	35 736	36 659	...	...
Israel - Israël[75]	DJ	7 309	7 486[76]	7 624[76]	7 766[76]	7 911[76]	8 059[76]	8 216[76]	8 380[76]	8 546[76]	*8 713[76]
Japan - Japon[77]	DJ	128 063	128 047	128 070	127 833[78]	127 629[78]	127 445[78]	127 276[78]	127 141[79]	126 995[79]	126 786[78]
Jordan - Jordanie[80]	DF	6 293	6 490	6 699	6 993	7 427	8 114	8 804	9 559	9 798	10 053
Kazakhstan[81]	DF	15 982	16 093[82]	16 322[82]	16 557[82]	16 792[82]	17 036[82]	17 288[82]	17 543[82]	17 794[82]	18 038[82]
Kuwait - Koweït	DF	2 632	2 778	2 933	3 107	3 247	3 428	3 767	3 971	4 079	4 083[22]
Kyrgyzstan - Kirghizstan[21]	DJ	5 319	5 383	5 448	5 515	5 608	5 720	5 836	5 957	6 080	6 198
Lao People's Democratic Republic - République démocratique populaire lao[10]	DJ	5 990	6 111	6 230	6 349	6 466	6 581	6 693	6 672	6 787	6 901
Malaysia - Malaisie	DJ	27 568[83]	28 081[83]	28 589[84]	29 062[84]	29 510[84]	30 214[84]	30 709[84]	31 186[84]	31 634[84]	32 050[84]
Maldives	DF	310	315	320	325	331	336	438[85]	454[85]	472[85]	492[85]
Mongolia - Mongolie	DF	2 643	2 691	2 739	2 786	2 840	2 899	2 963	3 027	3 089	3 149
Myanmar[86]	DF	58 377	59 130	59 780	50 149[69]	50 667[69]	51 184[69]	51 991[69]	52 451[69]	52 917[69]	53 388[69]
Nepal - Népal	DJ	26 967	27 504	28 044	28 585	26 873[26]	27 257[26]	27 646[26]	28 038[26]	28 431[26]	28 826[26]
Oman	DF	2 867	3 174	...	3 295[87]	3 623[87]	3 855[87]	3 993[87]	4 159[87]	4 414[87]	4 560[87]
Pakistan[88]	DF	166 410	169 940	173 510	177 100	...	184 350	188 020	191 710	...	...
Philippines	DJ	90 457[34]	92 227[34]	93 135[13]	94 824[13]	96 511[13]	98 197[13]	99 880[13]	101 562[13]	103 243[13]	104 921[13]
Qatar	DF	1 448	1 639	1 715	1 733	1 833	2 004	2 216	2 438	2 618	2 725
Republic of Korea - République de Corée	DJ	49 055	49 308	49 554	49 937	50 200	50 429	50 747	51 015	51 246	51 446
Saudi Arabia - Arabie saoudite	DF	25 744	26 576	27 411	28 173	28 897	29 613	30 340	31 062	31 788	32 613
Singapore - Singapour[89]	DJ	4 839	4 988	5 077	5 184	5 312	5 399	5 470	5 535	5 607	5 612
Sri Lanka	DF / DJ	20 246	20 476	20 675	20 892	20 425	20 585	*20 771	*20 966	*21 203	*21 444
State of Palestine - État de Palestine	DF	3 826	3 935	4 048	4 169	4 293	4 421	4 550	4 682	4 817	4 952

113

5. Estimates of mid-year population: 2008 - 2017
Estimations de la population au milieu de l'année : 2008 - 2017 (continued - suite)

Continent and country or area / Continent et pays ou zone	Code[a]	Population estimates (in thousands) - Estimations (en milliers)									
		2008	2009	2010	2011	2012	2013	2014	2015	2016	2017
ASIA - ASIE											
Syrian Arab Republic - République arabe syrienne[90]..	DF	19 644	20 125	20 619	21 124	...	...	...	...	...	...
Tajikistan - Tadjikistan................	DF	7 295	7 334	7 519	7 714	7 897	8 074	8 257	8 452	8 647	...
Thailand - Thaïlande	DJ	63 390	63 525	63 878	64 076	64 266	64 621	64 955	65 027	65 013	65 522
Timor-Leste[3]	DF	1 081	1 115	...	...	...	1 180	1 212	...	...	1 242
Turkey - Turquie	DJ	71 517[91]	72 561[91]	73 723[91]	74 724[91]	75 627[91]	76 668[91]	77 696[91]	78 741[91]	79 815[91]	80 313[92]
United Arab Emirates - Émirats arabes unis[93]	DF	8 074[29]	8 200[29]	8 264	...	...	...	...	...	9 121[29]	...
Uzbekistan - Ouzbékistan[81].......	DJ	27 303	27 767	28 562	29 339	29 774	30 243	30 758	31 299	31 575[22]	32 121[22]
Viet Nam[94]	DF	85 119	...	...	...	...	...	...	...	...	...
	DJ	...	86 025	86 947	87 860	88 809	89 760	90 729	91 710	*92 695	*93 672
Yemen - Yémen........................	DF	22 198[29]	...	...	...	...	...	...	...	...	...
	DJ	...	22 492[3]	23 154[3]	23 833[3]	24 527[3]	25 235[3]	25 956[3]	...	...	...
EUROPE											
Åland Islands - Îles d'Åland[47]	DJ	27	28	28	28	28	29	29	29	29	29
Albania - Albanie	DF	2 947	2 928	2 913	...	...	...	...	...	...	...
	DJ	...	...	...	2 905	2 900	2 895	2 889	2 881	2 876	2 873
Andorra - Andorre[47]	DJ	84	85	70[95]	70[22]	70[22]	70	70	71	72	...
Austria - Autriche	DJ	8 322	8 341	8 361	8 389	8 426	8 477	8 544	8 629	8 740	8 773[22]
Belarus - Bélarus....................	DJ	9 528	9 507	9 491	9 473	9 464	9 466	9 475	9 490	9 502[21]	9 498
Belgium - Belgique	DJ	10 710	10 796	10 896	11 044	11 128	11 183	11 231	11 285[21]	11 331[21]	11 382
Bosnia and Herzegovina - Bosnie-Herzégovine	DF	3 842	3 843	3 843	3 841	3 837	...	...	...	...	...
	DJ	...	...	...	...	...	3 531	3 526	3 518	3 511	*3 510[21]
Bulgaria - Bulgarie	DJ	7 623	7 585	7 534	7 348	7 306	7 264	7 224	7 178	7 128[21]	7 076
Croatia - Croatie	DJ	4 310	4 305	4 295	4 281	4 268	4 256	4 238	4 204	4 174	4 130
Czechia - Tchéquie	DJ	10 385	10 444	10 474	10 496	10 511	10 511	10 525	10 543	10 565	10 594
Denmark - Danemark[96]	DJ	5 489	5 519	5 545	5 567	5 587	5 609	5 640	5 678	5 724	5 761
Estonia - Estonie	DJ	1 337	1 335	1 331	1 327	1 323	1 318	1 315	1 315	1 316[21]	1 317
Faeroe Islands - Îles Féroé	DJ	49	49	49	49	48	48	48	49	49	50
Finland - Finlande[47]	DJ	5 286[97]	5 311[97]	5 335[97]	5 360[97]	5 386[97]	5 410[97]	5 433[97]	5 451[97]	5 466[97]	5 508
France[98]	DJ	62 300	62 615	62 918	63 223	63 537	63 863	64 164	*64 430	*64 680	*64 910
Germany - Allemagne	DJ	82 120	81 875	81 757	80 275[5]	80 426[5]	80 646[5]	80 983[5]	81 687[5]	82 349[99]	82 522[100]
Gibraltar[101]	DF	30	31	31	32	33	33	33	34	...	...
Greece - Grèce......................	DF	11 078	11 107	11 121	11 105	11 045	10 965	10 892	10 821	10 776	10 768[22]
Guernsey - Guernesey[102]	DJ	62	62	62	63	63	63	62	...	62	62
Holy See - Saint-Siège[103].........	DF	...	...	0[104]	...	0[105]	...	...	...	...	...
Hungary - Hongrie	DJ	10 038	10 023	10 000	9 972	9 920	9 893	9 866[106]	9 843[106]	9 814[106]	9 788[106]
Iceland - Islande[107].................	DJ	319	319	318	319	321	324	327	331	335	343
Ireland - Irlande	DF	4 426	4 459	4 560	4 580	4 600	4 624	4 658	4 702	4 755	4 784[22]
Isle of Man - Île de Man[108]........	DJ	82	82	83	...	85	86	86	87	86	84
Italy - Italie............................	DJ	58 827	59 095	59 277	59 379	59 540	60 234	60 789	60 731	60 627	60 537
Jersey	DJ	95	96	97	98	99	...	101	103	104	...
Latvia - Lettonie	DJ	2 177	2 142	2 098	2 060	2 034	2 013	1 994	1 978	1 960	1 942
Liechtenstein	DJ	35	36	36	36	37	37	37	37	38	38
Lithuania - Lituanie	DJ	3 198	3 163	3 097	3 028	2 988	2 958	2 932[106]	2 905[106]	2 868[106]	2 828[106]
Luxembourg	DJ	489	498	507	518	531	543	556	570	583	596
Malta - Malte[109]	DJ	409	413	415	416	420	423	427	432	455	468
Monaco[110]	DJ	...	35	36	36	36	37	37[22]	38[22]	38[22]	38[22]
Montenegro - Monténégro........	DJ	616	632	619	620	621	621	622[106]	622[106]	622[106]	622[106]
Netherlands - Pays-Bas	DJ	16 446	16 530	16 615	16 693	16 755	16 804	16 865	16 940	17 030	17 100
Norway - Norvège[106]	DJ	4 768	4 829	4 889	4 953	5 019	5 080	5 137	5 189	5 235[21]	5 277[21]
Poland - Pologne....................	DJ	38 116[111]	38 153[111]	38 042[106]	38 051[106]	38 059[106]	38 032[106]	38 006[106]	37 982[106]	37 957[106]	37 975[112]
Portugal	DJ	10 558	10 568	10 573	10 558	10 515	10 457	10 401	10 358	10 325	10 300
Republic of Moldova - République de Moldova[113]......	DJ	3 570	3 566	3 562	3 560	3 560	3 559	2 998	...	...	...
Romania - Roumanie	DF	...	...	...	...	...	19 989	19 916	19 820	19 707	19 644[22]
	DJ	20 538[106]	20 367[106]	20 247[106]	20 148[106]	20 060[106]	...	...	...	...	...
Russian Federation - Fédération de Russie	DJ	142 742	142 785	142 849	142 961	143 202	*143 507	...	...	...	...
San Marino - Saint-Marin[47].......	DF	32	33	33	33	34	33	34	34[22]	34[22]	34[22]
Serbia - Serbie[114]	DJ	7 350	7 321	7 291	7 237[20]	7 201[20]	7 167[20]	7 132[20]	7 095[20]	7 058[20]	7 021[115]
Slovakia - Slovaquie................	DJ	5 379	5 386	5 391	5 398	5 408	5 413	5 419	5 424	5 431	5 439[21]
Slovenia - Slovénie..................	DJ	2 023	2 042	2 049	2 052	2 056	2 059	2 062	2 063	2 064	2 066[21]

Continent and country or area / Continent et pays ou zone	Code[a]	Population estimates (in thousands) - Estimations (en milliers)									
		2008	2009	2010	2011	2012	2013	2014	2015	2016	2017
EUROPE											
Spain - Espagne	DJ	45 983	46 368	46 562	46 736	46 766	46 593	46 481[107]	46 448[107]	46 450[107]	46 549[107]
Svalbard and Jan Mayen Islands - Îles Svalbard et Jan Mayen[116]	DF	2	...	...	...	...	...	...	...	...	...
Sweden - Suède[47]	DJ	9 220	9 299	9 378	9 449	9 519	9 600[107]	9 696[107]	9 799[107]	9 923[117]	10 058[117]
Switzerland - Suisse	DJ	7 648	7 744	7 825	7 912	7 997	8 089	8 189[118]	8 282[118]	8 373[118]	8 420[119]
TFYR of Macedonia - L'ex-R. y. de Macédoine	DJ	2 047	2 051	2 055	2 059	2 061	2 064	2 067	2 070	2 072	2 075[21]
Ukraine	DF	46 258	46 053	45 871	45 706	45 593	45 553[22]	45 426[22]	42 675[120]	42 503[120]	42 316[120]
United Kingdom of Great Britain and Northern Ireland - Royaume-Uni de Grande-Bretagne et d'Irlande du Nord[121]	DJ	61 824	62 260	62 759	63 285	63 705	64 106[106]	64 597[106]	65 110[106]	65 596[112]	65 809[122]
OCEANIA - OCÉANIE											
American Samoa - Samoas américaines[52]	DJ	69	70	67	64	64	63	62	61	...	...
Australia - Australie[123]	DJ	21 249	21 692	22 032	22 340	22 742	23 146	23 504	23 851	24 211	24 599
Cook Islands - Îles Cook[124]	DF	22	23	24	19	20	*19	*19	*19	*20	...
Fiji - Fidji	DF	841	843	857	854	858	862	866	867[125]	871	...
French Polynesia - Polynésie française	DF	261	263	265	267	268	270	271	272	...	...
Guam[52]	DJ	159	159	...	160	160	160	161	162	163	164
Kiribati[125]	DF	...	...	...	...	...	109	...	...	...	...
Marshall Islands - Îles Marshall	DF	53[126]	54[126]	54[126]	...	...	54[125]	...	...	...	...
Micronesia (Federated States of) - Micronésie (États fédérés de)[3]	DJ	108	108	108	108	107	107	106	106	...	...
Nauru[3]	DF	...	...	...	...	10	...	...	11	...	...
New Caledonia - Nouvelle-Calédonie	DF	243	246	250	254	259	264	268	272	275[22]	279[22]
New Zealand - Nouvelle-Zélande[127]	DJ	4 260	4 303	4 351	4 384	4 408	4 442	4 510	4 596	4 693	4 794
Niue - Nioué	DJ	...	2	1	1	...	...	...	...	...	...
Northern Mariana Islands - Îles Mariannes septentrionales	DF	55	51	48	46	51[55]	51[55]	51[55]	...	...	...
Palau - Palaos	DJ	20	21	21	21	21	18	18	...	18	18
Papua New Guinea - Papouasie-Nouvelle-Guinée[128]	DF	...	...	...	...	...	...	...	...	8 151	...
Pitcairn[129]	DF	0	...	...	...	...	...	...	...	...	...
Samoa	DF	182	183	184	185	189[130]	191[130]	192[130]	193[130]	...	198[131]
Solomon Islands - Îles Salomon	DF	507[3]	518[3]	555[132]	570[132]	584[132]	598[132]	612[132]	625[132]	639[132]	653[132]
Tokelau - Tokélaou[133]	DF	...	...	...	...	...	1	...	...	...	...
Tonga[134]	DF	104	...	...	...	...	...	...	...	...	...
Tuvalu	DF	...	...	...	11	...	11	...	...	10[128]	...
Vanuatu	DF	...	...	239	245	250	265	271	...	...	...
Wallis and Futuna Islands - Îles Wallis et Futuna[128]	DF	...	...	...	...	...	...	...	...	12	...

FOOTNOTES - NOTES

Italics: estimates which are less reliable. - Italiques : estimations moins sûres.

* Provisional. - Données provisoires.

a 'Code' indicates source of data, as follows: - Le 'Code' indique la source des données, comme suit :
DF: Population de facto - Population de fait
DJ : Population de jure - Population de droit

1 Unrevised data that do not take into account the results of the 2014 population census. - Ces données n'ont pas été revisées et elles ne prennent pas en compte les résultats du recensement de la population de 2014.

2 Postcensal estimates. - Estimations post censitaires.

3 Data refer to national projections. - Les données se réfèrent aux projections nationales.

4 Projections based on the 2013 Population Census. - Projections fondées sur le recensement de la population de 2013.

5 Data based on the 2011 Census. - Données fondées sur le recensement de 2011.

6 Estimates based on the 2014 Population Census. - Estimations fondées sur le recensement de la population de 2014.

7 Projections based on the 2014 Population Census. - Projections fondées sur le recensement de la population de 2014.

8 Data are calculated from the results of the Population and Housing Census of 2009. - Les données sont calculées à partir des résultats du recensement de la population et de l'habitat de 2009.

9 Data refer to projections based on the 1983 Population Census. - Les données se réfèrent aux projections basées sur le recensement de la population de 1983.

10 Estimates based on the results of 2015 population census. - Estimations fondées sur les résultats du recensement de la population de 2015.

11 Projections based on the 2000 quick population count results and 1995, 2002 and 2010 Eritrea Demographic and Health Surveys. - Projections fondées sur le dénombrement rapide de la population de 2000 et sur les enquêtes érythréennes de la démographie et de la santé de 1995, 2002 et 2010.

12 Estimates considering also the results of the 2007 Population Census. - Estimations en prennant en considération les résultats du recensement de la population de 2007.

13 Data based on the 2010 Population Census. - Les données sont fondées sur le recensement de la population de 2010.

14 Post-censal estimates based on the 2009 Population Census. - Les estimations post-censitaire fondées sur le recensement de la population de 2009.

15 Data are projections based on the 2006 Population Census. - Projections fondées sur le recensement de la population de 2006.

16 Data refer to Libyan nationals only. - Les données se raportent aux nationaux libyens seulement.

17 Projections considering also the results of the 2009 Population Census. - Projections en prennant en considération les résultats du recensement de la population de 2009.

18 Excludes the islands of St. Brandon and Agalega. - Non compris les îles St. Brandon et Agalega.

19 Based on the results of the 2000 Population Census. - Basé sur les résultats du recencement de la population de 2000.

20 Based on the results of the 2011 Population Census. - Basé sur les résultats du recencement de la population de 2011.

21 Data refer to annual average population. - Les données correspondent à la population annuelle moyenne.

22 Data refer to 1 January. - Données se raportent au 1 janvier.

23 Based on the results of the 2004 Population Census. - D'après des résultats du recensement de la population de 2004.

24 Projections based on the results of national survey on population and health conducted between 2010 and 2011, and especially population and housing census 2014. - Des projections de la population fondées sur les résultats de l'enquête nationale de la population et de la santé réalisée entre 2010 et 2011 et, surtout, du recensement général de la population et de l'habitat de 2014.

25 Data refer to national projections based on 2007 census. - Les données sont des projections nationales d'après les résultats du recensement de la population de 2007.

26 Data refer to projections based on the 2011 Population Census. - Les données se réfèrent aux projections basées sur le recensement de la population de 2011.

27 Projections based on the 2012 Population and Housing Census. - Projections fondées sur le recensement 2012 de la population et des logements.

28 Data are projections based on the 2008 Population and Housing Census. - Projection basée sur le recensement 2008 de la population et des logements.

29 Data refer to 31 December. - Données se raportent au 31 décembre.

30 Data refer to 31 December. Based on the results of a population count. The population figures are 264, 263 and 262 persons for 2007, 2008 and 2009 respectively. - Données se raportent au 31 décembre. D'après les résultats d'un comptage de la population. La population est respectivement égale à 264, 263 et 262 personnes pour les années 2007, 2008 et 2009.

31 Projections based on the 2012 Population Census. - Projections fondées sur le recensement de la population de 2012.

32 Projections based on the 2002 Population Census. - Projections fondées sur le recensement de la population de 2002.

33 Projections based on the 2010 Population and Housing Census. - Projections fondées sur le recensement 2010 de la population et des logements.

34 Data refer to projections based on the 2000 Population Census. - Les données se réfèrent aux projections basées sur le recensement de la population de 2000.

35 Adjusted for census net undercoverage (including adjustment for incompletely enumerated Indian reserves). - Ajusté pour la sous-estimation du recensement (y compris les réservations en Inde incomplètement énumérées).

36 Final intercensal estimates. - Estimations inter-censitaires definitives.

37 Final postcensal estimates. - Estimations postcensitaires definitives.

38 Updated postcensal estimates. - Estimations post censitaires mises à jour.

39 Preliminary postcensal estimates. - Estimations post censitaires préliminaires.

40 The source of data is the national household survey. - La source des données est l'enquête nationale des ménages.

41 Based on the national household surveys 2010-2014 and the 2011 population census. - D'après les données de l'enquête nationale des ménages 2010-2014 et les résultats du recensement de la population de 2011.

42 Based on the national household survey of 2015. - Basée sur l' enquête nationale auprès des ménages de 2015.

43 Based on the national household survey of 2016. - D'après l'enquête nationale auprès des ménages de 2016.

44 Based on the national household survey of 2017. - D'après l'enquête nationale auprès des ménages de 2017.

45 Intercensal estimates. - Estimations inter-censitaires.

46 Estimates or projections based on the 2007 Population Census. - Estimations ou projections fondées sur le recensement de la population de 2007.

47 Population statistics are compiled from registers. - Les statistiques de la population sont compilées à partir des registres.

48 Excluding data for Saint Barthélémy and Saint Martin. - Non compris les données pour Saint Barthélémy et Saint Martin.

49 Projections produced by l'Institut Haïtien de Statistique et d'Informatique (IHSI) and the Latin American and Caribbean Demographic Centre (CELADE) - Population Division of ECLAC. - Les données sont projections produits par l'Institut Haïtien de Statistique et d'Informatique (IHSI) et le centre démographique de l'Amérique latine et les Caraïbes - Division de la population de la CEPALC.

50 Data refer to projections based on the 2001 Population Census. - Les données se réfèrent aux projections basées sur le recensement de la population de 2001.

51 Estimates based on the 2010 Population Census. - Estimations basées sur le recensement de la population de 2010.

52 Including armed forces stationed in the area. - Y compris les militaires en garnison sur le territoire.

53 Based on the results of the 2010 Population Census. - D'après le résultats du recensement de la population de 2010.

54 Excluding U.S. Armed Forces overseas and civilian U.S. citizens whose usual place of residence is outside the United States. - Non compris les militaires américains à l'étranger et les civils américains dont le lieu de résidence habituel est en dehors des États-Unis.

55 Source: U.S. National Center for Health Statistics, National Vital Statistics Reports (NVSR). - Source : US National Center for Health Statistics, National Vital Statistics Reports (NVSR).

56 Data include persons in remote areas, military personnel outside the country, merchant seamen at sea, civilian seasonal workers outside the country, and other civilians outside the country, and exclude nomads, foreign military, civilian aliens temporarily in the country, transients on ships and Indian jungle population. Data refer to national projections. - Y compris les personnes vivant dans des régions éloignées, le personel militaire en dehors du pays, les marins marchands, les ouvriers saisonniers en dehors du pays, et autres civils en dehors du pays, et non compris les nomades, les militaires étrangers, les étrangers civils temporairement dans le pays, les transiteurs sur des bateaux et les Indiens de la jungle. Les données se réfèrent aux projections nationales.

57 Data are revised projections taking into consideration also the results of the 2005 census. - Les données sont des projections révisées tenant compte également des résultats du recensement de 2005.

58 Excludes nomadic Indian tribes. Data based on the 2010 Population Census. - Non compris les tribus d'Indiens nomades. Les données sont fondées sur le recensement de la population de 2010.

59 Estimates or projections considering also the results of the 2012 Population Census. - Estimations ou projections en prennant en considération les résultats du recensement de la population de 2012.

60 Data refer to 30 June. Estimates or projections based on the 2007 Population Census. - Données se raportent au 30 juin. Estimations ou projections fondées sur le recensement de la population de 2007.

61 Data refer to the settled population based on the 1979 Population Census and the latest household prelisting. The refugees of Afghanistan in Iran, Pakistan, and an estimated 1.5 million nomads, are not included. - Les données se rapportent à la population stationnaire sur la base du recensement de 1979 et du recensement préliminaire des logements le plus récent. Sont exclus les réfugiés d'Afghanistan en Iran et au Pakistan et les nomades estimés à 1,5 million.

62 Data refer to projected figures based on the Population and Housing Census 2005 (district projection). - Les données se réfèrent aux projections basées sur le recensement de la population et de l'habitat de 2005 (projections locales).

63 Source: 2016 Population and Housing Census Update. - Source : Révision des chiffres du recensement de la population et des logements de 2016.

64 Excluding foreign diplomatic personnel and their dependants. Data based on the 2008 Population Census. - Non compris le personnel diplomatique étranger et les membres de leur famille les accompagnant. Données fondées sur le recensement de population de 2008.

65 For statistical purposes, the data for China do not include those for the Hong Kong Special Administrative Region (Hong Kong SAR), Macao Special Administrative Region (Macao SAR) and Taiwan province of China. - Pour la présentation des statistiques, les données pour la Chine ne comprennent pas la Région Administrative Spéciale de Hong Kong (Hong Kong RAS), la Région Administrative Spéciale de Macao (Macao RAS) et Taïwan province de Chine.

66 Data have been estimated on the basis of the annual National Sample Survey on Population Changes. - Les données ont été estimées sur la base de l'enquête annuelle "National Sample Survey on Population Changes".

67 Data have been adjusted on the basis of the Population Census of 2010. - Les données ont été ajustées à partir des résultats du recensement de la population de 2010.

68 Data refer to government controlled areas. - Les données se rapportent aux zones contrôlées par le Gouvernement.

69 Based on the results of the 2014 Population Census. - D'après les résultats du recensement de la population de 2014.

70 Includes data for the Indian-held part of Jammu and Kashmir, the final status of which has not yet been determined. Data refer to projections based on the 2001 Population Census. - Y compris les données pour la partie du Jammu et du Cachemire occupée par l'Inde dont le statut définitif n'a pas encore été déterminé. Les données se réfèrent aux projections basées sur le recensement de la population de 2001.

71 Data refer to 1 March. - Données se raportent au 1 mars.

72 Data are based on the publication: "Indonesia Population Projection 2005-2015" - Les données sont basées sur la publication : << Indonesia Population Projection 2005-2015 >>

73 Data are based on the publication: "Indonesia Population Projection 2010-2035" - Les données sont basées sur la publication : << Indonesia Population Projection 2010-2035 >>

74 Data refer to the Iranian Year which begins on 21 March and ends on 20 March of the following year. - Les données concernent l'année iranienne, qui commence le 21 mars et se termine le 20 mars de l'année suivante.

75 Includes data for East Jerusalem and Israeli residents in certain other territories under occupation by Israeli military forces since June 1967. - Y compris les données pour Jérusalem-Est et les résidents israéliens dans certains autres territoires occupés depuis 1967 par les forces armées israéliennes.

76 Data refer to Israeli citizens and permanent residents who are listed in the Population Register. - Les données se rapportent aux citoyens israéliens et aux résidents permanents qui sont répertoriés dans le registre de la population.

77 Excluding diplomatic personnel outside the country and foreign military and civilian personnel and their dependants stationed in the area. - Non compris le personnel diplomatique hors du pays ni les militaires et agents civils étrangers en poste sur le territoire et les membres de leur famille les accompagnant.

78 Estimates based on the complete counts of the 2015 Population Census. - Estimations basées sur le dénombrement complet du recensement de la population de 2015.

79 Because of rounding, totals are not in all cases the sum of the respective components. Estimates based on the complete counts of the 2015 Population Census. - Les chiffres étant arrondis, les totaux ne correspondent pas toujours rigoureusement à la somme des composants respectifs. Estimations basées sur le dénombrement complet du recensement de la population de 2015.

80 Data refer to 31 December. Excluding data for Jordanian territory under occupation since June 1967 by Israeli military forces. - Données se raportent au 31 décembre. Non compris les données pour le territoire jordanien occupé depuis juin 1967 par les forces armées israéliennes.

81 Data refer to resident population. - Les données concernent la population résidente.

82 Recalculated population estimates taking into account late registration of births and deaths until May 2017. - Réestimation du nombre d'habitants compte tenu de l'enregistrement tardif des naissances et des décès jusqu'en mai 2017.

83 Intercensal Mid-Year Population Estimates based on the adjusted Population and Housing Census of 2000 and 2010. - Les estimations inter-censitaires au milieu de l'année sont fondée sur les résultats ajustées des recensements de la population et de l'habitat de 2000 et 2010.

84 Estimates based on the adjusted results of the Population and Housing Census of 2010. - Les estimations sont fondée sur les résultats ajustées du recensement de la population et de l'habitat de 2010.

85 Data refer to resident population which includes resident Maldivians and resident foreigners. Estimates based on the 2014 Population Census. - Les données concernent la population résidente, qui comprend les Maldiviens et les étrangers. Estimations fondées sur le recensement de la population de 2014.

86 Data refer to 1 October. - Données se raportent au 1 octobre.

87 Data refer to registered population data from Royal Oman Police. - Les données portent sur la population enregistrée par la police royale de l'Oman.

88 Excluding data for the Pakistan-held part of Jammu and Kashmir, the final status of which has not yet been determined. - Non compris les données concernant la partie du Jammu et Cachemire occupée par le Pakistan dont le statut définitif n'a pas été déterminé.

89 Data refer to 30 June. Data refer to total population, which comprises Singapore residents and non-residents. Data exclude residents who have been away from Singapore for a continuous period of 12 months or longer as at the reference date. - Données se raportent au 30 juin. Les données se rapportent à la population totale composé des résidents de Singapour et les non résidents. Non compris les résidents hors de Singapour pour une période ininterrompue de 12 mois ou plus avant de la date de référence.

90 Including Palestinian refugees. - Y compris les réfugiés de Palestine.

91 Data refer to 31 December. Data based on Address Based Population Registration System. - Données se raportent au 31 décembre. Les données sont basées sur le registre national de la population basé sur l'adresse.

92 Data based on address-based population registration system. - Les données sont basées sur le registre national de la population basé sur l'adresse.

93 Data include non-national population. - Les données comprennent les non-nationaux.

94 Data are adjusted according to the results of the 2009 census and 2014 intercensus. - Les données ont été ajustées à partir des résultats du recensement de la population de 2009 et des données intercensitaires de 2014.

95 Data refer to 1 January. Decrease in population due to revision in administrative registers. - Données se raportent au 1 janvier. Diminution de la population due à la révision des registres administratifs.

96 Excluding Faeroe Islands and Greenland shown separately, if available. Population statistics are compiled from registers. - Non compris les Iles Féroé et le Groenland, qui font l'objet de rubriques distinctes, si disponible. Les statistiques de la population sont compilées à partir des registres.

97 Excluding Åland Islands. - Non compris les Îles d'Åland.

98 Excluding diplomatic personnel outside the country and including members of alien armed forces not living in military camps and foreign diplomatic personnel not living in embassies or consulates. - Non compris le personnel diplomatique hors du pays et y compris les militaires étrangers ne vivant pas dans des camps militaires et le personnel diplomatique étranger ne vivant pas dans les ambassades ou les consulats.

99 Data refer to annual average population. Data based on the 2011 Census. - Les données correspondent à la population annuelle moyenne. Données fondées sur le recensement de 2011.

100 Data refer to 1 January. Data based on the 2011 Census. - Données se raportent au 1 janvier. Données fondées sur le recensement de 2011.

101 Data refer to 31 December. Excluding military personnel, visitors and transients. - Données se raportent au 31 décembre. Non compris les militaires, ni les visiteurs et transients.

102 Data refer to 31 March. - Données se raportent au 31 mars.

103 Data refer to the Vatican City State. - Les données se rapportent à l'Etat de la Cité du Vatican.

104 Data refer to 26 February. The population figure is 460 persons. - Données se raportent au 26 février. La population est égale à 460 personnes.

105 Data refer to 21 June. The population figure is 451 persons. - Données se raportent au 21 juin. La population est égale à 451 personnes.

106 Data refer to usually resident population. - Les données concernent la population habituellement résidente.

107 Data refer to registered resident population. - Les données concernent la population enregistrée résidente.

108 Data refer to 30 April. - Données se raportent au 30 avril.

109 Including civilian nationals temporarily outside the country. - Y compris les civils nationaux temporairement hors du pays.

110 Data refer to resident population only. - Pour la population résidante seulement.

111 Excluding civilian aliens within the country, but including civilian nationals temporarily outside the country. - Non compris les civils étrangers dans le pays, mais y compris les civils nationaux temporairement hors du pays.

112 Data refer to annual average population. Data refer to usually resident population. - Les données correspondent à la population annuelle moyenne. Les données concernent la population habituellement résidente.

113 Excluding Transnistria and the municipality of Bender. - Les données ne tiennent pas compte de l'information sur la Transnistria et la municipalité de Bender.

114 Excludes data for Kosovo and Metohia. - Sans les données pour le Kosovo et Metohie.

115 Data refer to annual average population. Based on the results of the 2011 Population Census. - Les données correspondent à la population annuelle moyenne. Basé sur les résultats du recensement de la population de 2011.

116 Data refer to 1 January. Data refer to Svalbard only. - Données se raportent au 1 janvier. Données ne concernant que le Svalbard.

[117] Data refer to annual average population. Data refer to registered resident population. - Les données correspondent à la population annuelle moyenne. Les données concernent la population enregistrée résidente.

[118] Data refer to legal resident population. - Les données concernent la population légalement résidente.

[119] Data refer to 1 January. Data refer to legal resident population. - Données se raportent au 1 janvier. Les données concernent la population légalement résidente.

[120] Data refer to annual average population. The Government of Ukraine has informed the United Nations that it is not in a position to provide statistical data concerning the Autonomous Republic of Crimea and the city of Sevastopol. - Les données correspondent à la population annuelle moyenne. Le gouvernement Ukrainien a informé l'ONU qu'il n'est pas en mesure de fournir des données statistiques concernant la République autonome de Crimée et la ville de Sébastopol.

[121] Excluding Channel Islands (Guernsey and Jersey) and Isle of Man, shown separately, if available. - Non compris les îles Anglo-Normandes (Guernesey et Jersey) et l'île de Man, qui font l'objet de rubriques distinctes, si disponible.

[122] Data refer to 1 January. Data refer to usually resident population. - Données se raportent au 1 janvier. Les données concernent la population habituellement résidente.

[123] Based on the results of the 2016 Population Census. - Basé sur les résultats du recencement de la population de 2016.

[124] Excluding Niue, shown separately, which is part of Cook Islands, but because of remoteness is administered separately. - Non compris Nioué, qui fait l'objet d'une rubrique distincte et qui fait partie des îles Cook, mais qui, en raison de son éloignement, est administrée séparément.

[125] Projections are prepared by the Secretariat of the Pacific Community based on the 2011 census of population and housing. - Les projections sont preparées par le Secrétariat de la Communauté du Pacifique à partir des résultats du recensement de la population et de l'habitat de 2011.

[126] Projections are prepared by the Secretariat of the Pacific Community based on the 1999 census of population and housing. - Les projections sont preparées par le Secrétariat de la Communauté du Pacifique à partir des résultats du recensement de la population et de l'habitat de 1999.

[127] Because of rounding, totals are not in all cases the sum of the respective components. - Les chiffres étant arrondis, les totaux ne correspondent pas toujours rigoureusement à la somme des composants respectifs.

[128] Estimates are prepared by the Secretariat of the Pacific Community based on the last population and housing census. - Les estimations sont preparées par le Secrétariat de la Communauté du Pacifique à partir des résultats du dernier recensement de la population et de l'habitat.

[129] Data refer to 31 December. The population figures are 64 and 58 persons for 2007 and 2008 respectively. - Données se raportent au 31 décembre. La population est respectivement égale à 64 et 58 personnes pour les années 2007 et 2008.

[130] Estimates based on the 2011 Population Census. - Estimations basées sur le recensement de la population de 2011.

[131] Estimates based on the 2016 Population Census. - Estimations basées sur le recensement de la population de 2016.

[132] Projections based on adjusted 2009 census counts. - Projections fondées à partir des comptes rajustés du recensement de 2009.

[133] Data refer to 1 December. - Données se raportent au 1 décembre.

[134] Data refer to national projections. Based on the results of the 1996 population census. - Les données se réfèrent aux projections nationales. À partir des résultats du recensement de la population de 1996.

Table 6 - Demographic Yearbook 2017

Table 6 presents total population by sex for as many years as possible between 2008 and 2017, as well as urban population as available.

Description of variables: Data are from nation-wide population censuses or are estimates, some of which are based on sample surveys of population carried out among all segments of the population. This characteristic of the data is indicated in the column "Code". The codes used are explained at the end of the table.

Urban is defined according to the national census definition. The definitions for each country, as available, are provided as part of this technical note.

Percentage computation: Urban percentages are the number of persons residing in an area defined as "urban" per 100 total population. They are calculated by the Statistics Division of the United Nations Department of Economic and Social Affairs. In very few cases the data for total population have been revised whereas the data for the urban and rural population have not been revised. These data are footnoted accordingly. In these cases, particular caution should be used in interpreting the figures for the percentages urban.

Reliability of data: Estimates that are believed to be less reliable are set in *italics* rather than in roman type. Classification in terms of reliability is based on the method of construction of the total population estimate discussed in the technical notes for table 3.

Limitations: Statistics on urban population by sex are subject to the same qualifications as have been set forth for population statistics in general, as discussed in section 3 of the Technical Notes.

The basic limitations imposed by variations in the definition of the total population and in the degree of under-enumeration are perhaps more important in relation to urban/rural than to any other distributions. The classification by urban and rural is affected by variations in defining usual residence for purposes of sub-national tabulations. Likewise, the geographical differentials in the degree of under-enumeration in censuses affect the comparability of these categories throughout the table. The distinction between *de facto* and *de jure* population is also very important with respect to urban/rural distributions. The difference between the *de facto* and the *de jure* population is discussed at length in section 3.1.1 of the Technical Notes.

A most important and specific limitation, however, lies in the national differences in the definition of urban. Because the distinction between urban and rural areas is made in so many different ways, the definitions have been included at the end of this table. The definitions are necessarily brief and, where the classification of urban involves administrative civil divisions, they are often given in the terminology of the particular country or area. As a result of variations in terminology, it may appear that differences between countries or areas are greater than they actually are. On the other hand, similar or identical terms (for example, town, village, district) as used in different countries or areas may have quite different meanings.

The definition of urban/rural areas is based on both qualitative and quantitative criteria that may include any combination of the following: size of population, population density, distance between built-up areas, predominant type of economic activity, conformity to legal or administrative status and urban characteristics such as specific services and facilities[1].   Although statistics classified by urban/rural areas are widely available, no international standard definition appears to be possible at this time since the meaning differs from one country or area to another. The urban/rural classification of population used here is reported according to the national definition.

Earlier data: Urban and total population by sex have been shown in previous issues of the Demographic Yearbook. For information on specific years covered, readers should consult the Historical Index.

DEFINITION OF "URBAN"

AFRICA

Algeria: The urban/rural delimitation is performed after the census operation based on the classification of built-up areas. Groupings of 100 or more constructions, distant less than 200 metres from one another are considered urban.
Botswana: Agglomeration of 5 000 or more inhabitants where 75 per cent of the economic activity is non-agricultural.

Burundi: Commune of Bujumbura.

Burkina Faso: All administrative centres of provinces (total of 45) plus 4 medium-sized towns are considered as urban areas.

Comoros: Every locality or administrative centre of an island, region or prefecture that has the following facilities: asphalted roads, electricity, a medical centre, telephone services, etc.

Egypt: Governorates of Cairo, Alexandria, Port Said, Ismailia, Suez, frontier governorates and capitals of other governorates, as well as district capitals (Markaz). The definition of urban areas for the 2006 Census is "shiakha", a part of a district.

Equatorial Guinea: District centres and localities with 300 dwellings and/or 1 500 inhabitants or more.

Ethiopia: Localities of 2 000 or more inhabitants.

Guinea: Administrative centres of prefectures and the capital city (Conakry).

Kenya: Areas having a population of 2 000 or more inhabitants that have transport systems, build-up areas, industrial/manufacturing structures and other developed structures.

Lesotho: All administrative headquarters and settlements of rapid growth.

Liberia: Localities of 2 000 or more inhabitants.

Malawi: All townships and town planning areas and all district centres.

Mauritius: The five Municipal Council Areas which are subdivided into twenty Municipal Wards defined according to proclaimed boundaries.

Namibia: Proclaimed urban areas for which cadastral data is available and other unplanned squatter areas.

Niger: Capital city, capitals of the departments and districts.

Rwanda: All administrative areas recognized as urban by the law. These are all administrative centres of provinces, and the cities of Kigali, Nyanza, Ruhango and Rwamagana.

Senegal: Agglomerations of 10 000 or more inhabitants.

South Africa: Places with some form of local authority.

Sudan: Localities of administrative and/or commercial importance or with population of 5 000 or more inhabitants.

Swaziland: A geographical area constituting of a city or town, characterized by higher population density and vast human features in comparison to areas surrounding it.

Tunisia: Population living in communes.

Uganda: Gazettes, cities, municipalities and towns.

United Republic of Tanzania: Areas legally recognized (gazetted) as urban and all areas recognized by local government authorities as urban.

Zambia: Localities of 5 000 or more inhabitants, the majority of whom all depend on non-agricultural activities.

AMERICA, NORTH

Bermuda: The country is considered 100 per cent urban.

Canada: Places of 1 000 or more inhabitants, having a population density of 400 or more per square kilometre.

Costa Rica: Administrative centres of cantons.

Cuba: Localities with 2 000 or more inhabitants; or localities with more than 1 000 inhabitants having half or more of economically active population engaged in non-agricultural activities.

Dominican Republic: Administrative centres of municipalities and municipal districts, some of which include suburban zones of rural character.

El Salvador: Administrative centres of municipalities.

Greenland: Localities of 200 or more inhabitants.

Guatemala: Municipality of Guatemala Department and officially recognized centres of other departments and municipalities.

Haiti: Administrative centres of communes.

Honduras: Localities of 2 000 or more inhabitants, having essentially urban characteristics.

Jamaica: Localities of 2 000 or more inhabitants, having urban characteristics.

Mexico: Localities of 2 500 or more inhabitants.

Nicaragua: Administrative centres of municipalities and localities of 1 000 or more inhabitants or with more than 150 dwellings, with streets, electric light, water service, school and health centre.

Panama: Localities of 1 500 or more inhabitants having essentially urban characteristics. Beginning 1970, localities of 1 500 or more inhabitants with such urban characteristics as streets, water supply systems, sewerage systems and electric light.

Puerto Rico: Agglomerations of 2 500 or more inhabitants, generally having population densities of 1 000 persons per square mile or more. Two types of urban areas: urbanized areas of 50 000 or more inhabitants and urban clusters of at least 2 500 and less than 50 000 inhabitants.

United States of America: Agglomerations of 2 500 or more inhabitants, generally having population densities of 1 000 persons per square mile or more. Two types of urban areas: urbanized areas of 50 000 or more inhabitants and urban clusters of at least 2 500 and less than 50 000 inhabitants.

United States Virgin Islands: Agglomerations of 2 500 or more inhabitants, generally having population densities of 1 000 persons per square mile or more. Two types of urban areas: urbanized areas of 50 000 or more inhabitants and urban clusters of at least 2 500 and less than 50 000 inhabitants. (As of the 2000 Census, no urbanized areas are identified in the United States Virgin Islands.)

AMERICA, SOUTH

Argentina: Populated centres with 2 000 or more inhabitants.
Bolivia: Localities of 2 000 or more inhabitants.
Brazil: Area inside the urban perimeter of a city or town, defined by municipal law.
Chile: Areas of concentrated housing units with more than 2 000 inhabitants, or between 1 001 and 2 000 inhabitants having 50 per cent or more of its economically active population doing secondary or tertiary activities. As an exception, centres of tourism and recreation with more than 250 housing units that do not satisfy the population requirement are nevertheless considered urban.
Colombia: Areas with a city hall, defined by an urban perimeter established by municipal agreements.
Ecuador: Capitals of provinces and cantons.
Falkland Islands (Malvinas): Town of Stanley.
Paraguay: Cities, towns and administrative centres of departments and districts.
Peru: Populated centres with 100 or more dwellings.
Suriname: The districts of Paramaribo and Wanica.
Uruguay: Cities, villages, towns and other populated areas as defined by the Law of Population Centers.
Venezuela (Bolivarian Republic of): Centres with a population of 2 500 or more inhabitants.

ASIA

Armenia: Cities and urban-type localities, officially designated as such, usually according to the criteria of number of inhabitants and predominance of agricultural, or number of non-agricultural workers and their families.
Azerbaijan: An administrative division which covers more than 15 000 population, engaging mainly in industrial and other economic and social activities and which include administrative and cultural centers.
Brunei Darussalam: Municipality areas of Bandar Seri Begawan, Kuala Belait, Seria, Pekan Tutong and Pekan Bangar; and heavily populated areas with urban characteristics.
Bahrain: Communes or villages of 2 500 or more inhabitants.
Cambodia: Areas at the commune level satisfying the following three conditions: (1) Population Density exceeding 200 per square Km, (2) Percentage of male employed in agriculture below 50 per cent, (3) Total population of the commune exceeds 2 000 inhabitants.
China: According to the Regulation on the Classification of Urban/Rural Residence for Statistical Purposes.
Cyprus: As determined by the Department of Town Planning and Housing of the Ministry of Interior.
Georgia: Cities and urban-type localities, officially designated as such, usually according to the criteria of number of inhabitants and predominance of agricultural, or number of non-agricultural workers and their families.
India: Towns (places with municipal corporation, municipal area committee, town committee, notified area committee or cantonment board); also, all places having 5 000 or more inhabitants, a density of not less than 1 000 persons per square mile or 400 per square kilometre, pronounced urban characteristics and at least three fourths of the adult male population employed in pursuits other than agriculture.
Indonesia: Area which satisfies certain criteria in terms of population density, percentage of agricultural households, access to urban facilities, existence of additional facilities, and percentage of built up area not for housing.
Iran (Islamic Republic of): Every district with a municipality.
Israel: Localities with 2 000 or more residents.
Japan: City (shi) having 50 000 or more inhabitants with 60 per cent or more of the houses located in the main built-up areas and 60 per cent or more of the population (including their dependants) engaged in manufacturing, trade or other urban type of business.
Jordan: Localities of 5 000 or more inhabitants.
Kazakhstan: Cities of Republican status (population centres of special national importance or with a population of usually more than one million), Oblast status (population centres that are major economic and cultural centres with developed industrial and social infrastructure and a population of more than 50,000, the country has 40 Oblast status cities), Raion status and settlements located under their administrative jurisdiction.
Kuwait: All localities in Kuwait are urban.
Kyrgyzstan: Cities and urban-type localities, officially designated as such, usually according to the criteria of number of inhabitants and predominance of agricultural, or number of non-agricultural workers and their families.
Lao People's Democratic Republic: Areas or villages that satisfy at least three of the following five conditions: located in metropolitan areas of district or province, there is access to road in dry and rainy seasons, about 70 per cent or 2/3 of the population has access to piped water, about 70 per cent or 2/3 of the population has access to public electricity, there is a market operating every day.

Malaysia: Gazetted areas with their adjoining built-up areas which have a combined population of 10 000 or more. Built-up areas are defined as areas contiguous to a gazetted area and have at least 60 per cent of their population (aged 15 years and over) engaged in non-agricultural activities. The definition of urban areas also takes into account the special development area which is not gazetted and can be indentified and separated from the gazetted area or built-up area of more than 5km and a population of at least 10 000 with 60 per cent of the population (aged 15 years and over) engaged in non-agricultural activities.

Maldives: Malé, the capital.

Mongolia: Capital (Ulaanbaatar), provincial centers and towns.

Myanmar: Areas classified by the General Administration Department as wards. Generally, these areas have an increased density of building structures, population and better infrastructure development.

Nepal: As declared by the government municipalities.

Pakistan: Places with municipal corporation, town committee or cantonment.

Philippines: Cities and municipalities and their central districts with a population density of at least 500 persons per square km. Urban areas are considered other districts regardless of population size that have streets, at least six establishments (commercial, manufacturing, recreational and/or personal services), and at least three public structures such as town hall, church, public park, school, hospital, library, etc.

Republic of Korea: For estimates: Localities with 50 000 or more inhabitants. For census: the figures are composed in the basis of the minor administrative divisions such as Dongs (mostly urban areas) and Eups or Myeons (rural areas).

Saudi Arabia: Localities with more than 5 000 inhabitants.

Singapore: Singapore is a city-state.

Sri Lanka: All areas administered by municipal and urban councils.

State of Palestine: Any locality where the population amounts to 10 000 persons or more. This applies to all governorates/districts regardless of their size, and to all localities whose populations vary from 4 000 to 9 999 persons provided they have at least four of the following elements: public electricity network, public water network, post office, health center with a full time physician and a school offering a general secondary education certificate.

Syrian Arab Republic: Cities, Mohafaza centres and Mantika centres, and communities with 20 000 or more inhabitants.

Tajikistan: Cities and urban-type localities, officially designated as such, usually according to the criteria of number of inhabitants and predominance of agricultural, or number of non-agricultural workers and their families.

Thailand: Municipal areas.

Turkey: Localities with 20 000 inhabitants or more.

Turkmenistan: Cities and urban-type localities, officially designated as such, usually according to the criteria of number of inhabitants and predominance of agricultural, or number of non-agricultural workers and their families.

Uzbekistan: Cities and urban-type localities, officially designated as such, usually according to the criteria of number of inhabitants and predominance of agricultural, or number of non-agricultural workers and their families.

Viet Nam: Urban areas include inside urban districts of cities, urban quarters and towns. All other local administrative units (communes) belong to rural areas.

EUROPE

Albania: Towns and other industrial centres of more than 400 inhabitants.

Austria: Urban areas are localities with 2 000 or more inhabitants. The delineation of localities goes back to 1991.

Belarus: Urban settlements are settlements authorized under the law as towns, urban-type settlements, workers settlements and health resort areas.

Belgium: All the communes which are not part of the list of rural communes are considered as urban communes. There are 33 communes which are considered rural: Alveringem, Amblève, Bertogne, Bièvre, Bullange, Burg-Reuland, Clavier, Erezée, Fauvillers, Frasnes-lez-Anvaing, Froidchapelle, Gedinne, Gouvy, Havelange, Herstappe, Heuvelland, Houffalize, Houyet, Langemark-Poelkapelle, Léglise, Lierneux, Lo-Reninge, Manhay, Momignies, Ravels, Sainte-Ode, Sint-Laureins, Sivry-Rance, Stoumont, Tenneville, Vaux-sur-Sûre, Vleteren and Vresse-sur-Semois.

Bulgaria: All towns and cities according to the Territorial and Administrative-Territorial Division of the country.

Czech Republic: Localities with 2 000 or more inhabitants.

Estonia: Urban settlements include cities, cities without municipal status and towns.

Finland: Urban communes including those municipalities in which at least 90 per cent of the population lives in urban settlements or in which the population of the largest urban settlement is at least 15 000.

France: Communes containing an agglomeration of more than 2 000 inhabitants living in contiguous houses or with not more than 200 metres between houses, also communes of which the major portion of the population is part of a multi-communal agglomeration of this nature.

Greece: Urban is considered every municipal or communal department of which the largest locality has 2 000 inhabitants and over.

Hungary: Localities recognized by the President of the Republic with the title of town, on the basis of specific (economic, commercial, institutional, cultural etc.) criteria.

Iceland: Localities of 200 or more inhabitants.

Ireland: Cities and towns including suburbs of 1 500 or more inhabitants.

Latvia: Cities and urban-type localities, officially designated as such, usually according to the criteria of number of inhabitants and predominance of agricultural, or number of non-agricultural workers and their families.

Lithuania: Urban population refers to persons who live in cities and towns, i.e., the population areas with closely built permanent dwellings and with the resident population of more than 3 000 of which 2/3 of employees work in industry, social infrastructure and business. In a number of towns the population may be less than 3 000 since these areas had already the status of "town" before the law was enforced (July 1994).

Malta: Grid cells of 1 square km with a density of at least 300 inhabitants per square km and a minimum population of 5 000, and densely populated areas (i.e. areas with a density superior to 500 inhabitants per square km).

Montenegro: According to the current law of territorial division of Montenegro, which conveys to each local community the obligation to decide which settlements are urban and which are rural.

Netherlands: Urban: Municipalities with a population of 2 000 and more inhabitants. Semi-urban: Municipalities with a population of less than 2 000 but with not more than 20 per cent of their economically active male population engaged in agriculture, and specific residential municipalities of commuters.

Norway: A hub of buildings inhabited by at least 200 people and where the distance between the buildings does not exceed 50 metres. The boundaries are dynamic and may be changed due to developments and population changes.

Poland: All areas which have town rights or the status of a town with provisions of separate laws.

Portugal: Localities with 2 000 or more inhabitants.

Republic of Moldova: Cities and urban-type localities, officially designated as such, usually according to the criteria of number of inhabitants and predominance of agricultural, or number of non-agricultural workers and their families.

Romania: Localities in which the majority of the resources are employed in non-agricultural activities with a diversified level of endowment, having a constant and significant socio-economic influence on the whole area.

Russian Federation: Cities and urban-type localities, officially designated as such, usually according to the criteria of number of inhabitants and predominance of agricultural, or number of non-agricultural   workers and their families.

Serbia: Municipalities, cities and the city of Belgrade.

Slovakia: Municipalities with the status of towns, according to the following criteria: 1) it is an economic, administrative, cultural or tourism centre; 2) provides services for other municipalities; 3) has urban character (at least partly); and 4) has 5 000 inhabitants or more.

Slovenia: Settlements of 3 000 or more inhabitants, settlements that serve as seats of municipalities with at least 1 400 inhabitants, and sub-urban areas that are being gradually integrated with an urban settlement of 5 000 or more inhabitants.

Spain: For the purposes of publishing comparable results at the European level, Eurostat proposes to consider as urban, intermediate and rural, areas formed by municipalities with respectively a population over 10 000 inhabitants, 2 001 to 10 000 inhabitants, and 2 000 or less inhabitants.

Switzerland: Agglomerations and isolated towns (towns not attached to a cluster with at least 10,000 inhabitants) are the urban space.

TFYR Macedonia: A city is a populated place that has more than 3000 inhabitants, has a developed industrial and social infrastructure, and over 51% of employees work outside the primary activities.

Ukraine: Cities and urban-type localities officially designated as such, usually according to the criteria of number of inhabitants and predominance of agricultural, or number of non-agricultural workers and their families.

United Kingdom of Great Britain and Northern Ireland: For England and Wales, the built-up areas of 10 000 or more inhabitants; for Scotland, the settlements of 3 000 or more inhabitants; and for Northern Ireland, the settlements of 5 000 or more inhabitants.

OCEANIA

Australia: Urban are considered all Significant Urban Areas, as defined by the 2011 Australian Statistical Geography Standard. Significant Urban Areas represent concentrations of urban development with population of 10,000 people or more.

American Samoa: Agglomerations of 2 500 or more inhabitants, generally having population densities of 1 000 persons per square mile or more. Two types of urban areas: urbanized areas of 50 000 or more inhabitants and urban clusters of at least 2 500 and less than 50 000 inhabitants. (As of Census 2000, no urbanized areas are identified in American Samoa.)

Cook Islands: Raratonga, the most populous island.

Guam: Agglomerations of 2 500 or more inhabitants, generally having population densities of 1 000 persons per square mile or more, referred to as "urban clusters".

New Caledonia: Nouméa and communes of Païta, Nouvel Dumbéa and Mont-Dore.

New Zealand: All cities, plus boroughs, town districts, townships and country towns with a population of 1 000 or more usual residents.

Northern Mariana Islands: Agglomerations of 2 500 or more inhabitants, generally having population densities of 1 000 persons per square mile or more. Two types of urban areas: urbanized areas of 50 000 or more inhabitants and urban clusters of at least 2 500 and less than 50 000 inhabitants.

Palau: States with 2 500 inhabitants or more (the only state which satisfies this condition is Koror state).
Tokelau: All of Tokelau's population is considered to be rural.
Tonga: Nuku'alofa.
Vanuatu: Luganville centre and Port Vila.

NOTES

[1] For further information, see *Social and Demographic Statistics: Classifications of Size and Type of Locality and Urban/Rural Areas*. E/CN.3/551, United Nations, New York, 1980.

Tableau 6 – *Annuaire démographique 2017*

Le tableau 6 présente des données sur la population totale selon le sexe pour le plus grand nombre possible d'années entre 2008 et 2017, ainsi que la population urbaine si disponible.

Description des variables : les données proviennent de recensements de la population ou sont des estimations fondées, dans certains cas, sur des enquêtes par sondage portant sur toute la population. Le code qui figure dans la colonne « Code » du tableau indique comment les données ont été obtenues. Les codes utilisés sont expliqués à la fin du tableau.

Le sens donné au terme « urbain » est conforme aux définitions utilisées dans les recensements nationaux. Les définitions pour chaque pays, si disponible, font partie de ce note technique.

Calcul des pourcentages : les pourcentages de la population urbaine sont calculés par la Division de statistique du Département des affaires économiques et sociales de l'Organisation des Nations Unies et représentent le nombre de personnes qui vivent dans des régions considérées comme urbaines pour 100 personnes de la population totale. Dans de très rares cas, les données pour la population totale ont été révisées mais les données pour la population urbaine et la population rurale ne l'ont pas été. Ces données sont indiquées en note. Dans ces cas, les proportions de population urbaine ou rurale sont à interpréter avec précaution.

Fiabilité des données : les estimations considérées comme moins sûres sont indiquées en italique plutôt qu'en caractères romains. Le classement du point de vue de la fiabilité est fondé sur la méthode utilisée pour établir l'estimation de la population totale qui figure au tableau 3 (voir les explications dans les notes techniques relatives à ce même tableau).

Insuffisance des données : les statistiques de la population urbaine selon le sexe appellent toutes les réserves qui ont été formulées à la section 3 des Notes techniques à propos des statistiques de la population en général.

Les limitations fondamentales imposées par les variations de la définition de la population totale et par les lacunes du recensement se font peut-être sentir davantage dans la répartition de la population en population urbaine et population rurale que dans sa répartition suivant toute autre caractéristique. De fait, des différences dans la définition du lieu de résidence habituel utilisée pour l'exploitation des données à l'échelon sous-national influent sur la classification en population urbaine et en population rurale. De même, les différences de degré de sous-dénombrement suivant la zone, à l'occasion des recensements, ont une incidence sur la comparabilité de ces deux catégories dans l'ensemble du tableau. La distinction entre population de fait et population de droit est également très importante du point de vue de la répartition de la population en population urbaine et en population rurale. Cette distinction est expliquée en détail à la section 3.1.1 des Notes techniques.

Toutefois, la difficulté la plus importante tient aux différences de définition du terme « urbain » selon le pays. Les distinctions faites entre « zone urbaine » et « zone rurale » varient tellement que les définitions utilisées ont été reproduites à la fin de ces notes techniques. Les définitions sont forcément brèves et, lorsque le classement en « zone urbaine » repose sur des divisions administratives, on a souvent désigné celles-ci par le nom qu'elles portent dans la zone ou le pays considéré. Par suite des variations dans la terminologie, les différences entre pays ou zones peuvent sembler plus grandes qu'elles ne le sont réellement. Il se peut aussi que des termes similaires ou identiques, tels que ville, village ou district, aient des significations très différentes selon les pays ou zones.

La distinction entre « zone urbaine » et « zone rurale » repose sur une série de critères qualitatifs aussi bien que quantitatifs, notamment l'effectif de la population, la densité de peuplement, la distance entre îlots d'habitations, le type prédominant d'activité économique, le statut juridique ou administratif, et les caractéristiques d'une agglomération urbaine, c'est-à-dire l'existence de services publics et d'équipements collectifs[1]. Bien que les statistiques différenciant les zones urbaines des zones rurales soient très répandues, il ne paraît pas possible pour le moment d'adopter une classification internationale type de ces zones, vu la diversité des interprétations nationales. La classification de la population en population urbaine et population rurale retenue ici est celle qui correspond aux définitions nationales.

Données publiées antérieurement : des statistiques concernant la population urbaine et la population totale selon le sexe ont été publiées dans des éditions antérieures de l'*Annuaire démographique*. Pour plus de précisions concernant les années pour lesquelles ces données ont été publiées, se reporter à l'index historique.

DÉFINITIONS DU TERME « URBAIN »

AFRIQUE

Algérie : La délimitation des zones urbaines et rurales se font après l'opération du recensement sur la base de la classification des agglomérations. Regroupement de 100 constructions ou plus distantes l'une à l'autre de moins de 200m ont été considérées comme zones urbaines.

Afrique du Sud : Zones dotées d'une administration locale.

Botswana : Agglomération de 5 000 habitants ou plus dont 75 p. 100 de l'activité économique n'est pas de type agricole.

Burkina Faso : Tous les chefs-lieux de province (45 au total) plus 4 villes moyennes ont été considérées comme zones urbaines.

Burundi : Commune de Bujumbura.

Comores : Toute localité ou chef-lieu d'une île, région/préfecture disposant des infrastructures suivantes : route bitumée, électricité, centre hospitalier, téléphone, etc.

Égypte : Chefs-lieux des gouvernorats du Caire, d'Alexandrie, de Port Saïd, d'Ismaïlia, de Suez ; chefs-lieux des gouvernorats frontaliers, autres chefs-lieux de gouvernorat et chefs-lieux de district (Markaz). La définition des zones urbaines pour le recensement de 2006 est celle de « shiakha », une partie d'un district.

Éthiopie : Localités de 2 000 habitants ou plus.

Guinée : Centres administratifs des préfectures et la ville capitale (Conakry).

Guinée équatoriale : Chefs-lieux de district et localités comprenant 300 habitations et/ou 1 500 habitants ou plus.

Kenya : Zone ayant une population de 2 000 habitants ou plus qui dispose de réseaux de transport, comporte des zones bâties, des structures industrielles ou manufacturières et d'autres équipements modernes.

Lesotho : Tous les chefs-lieux administratifs et établissements en forte croissance.

Libéria : Localités de 2 000 habitants ou plus.

Malawi : Toutes les villes et zones urbanisées et tous les chefs-lieux de district.

Maurice : Les cinq circonscriptions municipales, divisées en vingt arrondissements municipaux dont les limites ont été officiellement définies.

Namibie : Zones urbaines déclarées pour lesquelles il existe des données cadastrales et autres zones d'habitat non planifié.

Niger : Ville capital, villes capitales de départements ou de districts.

Ouganda : « Gazettes », villes, municipalités et bourgs.

République-Unie de Tanzanie : Toutes les zones érigées en communes et les zones reconnues par les autorités gouvernementales comme urbaines.

Rwanda : Toutes les zones administratives reconnues comme urbaines par la loi. Il s'agit de tous les chefs-lieux des provinces, de la ville de Kigali ainsi que des villes de Nyanza, Ruhango et Rwamagana.

Sénégal : Agglomérations de 10 000 habitants ou plus.

Soudan : Centres administratifs et/ou commerciaux ou localités ayant une population de 5 000 habitants ou plus.

Swaziland : Zone géographique qui constitue une ville et se caractérise par une densité de population et de constructions humaines plus élevée que dans les zones qui l'entourent.

Tunisie : Population vivant dans les communes.

Zambie : Localités de 5 000 habitants ou plus dont l'activité économique prédominant n'est pas de type agricole.

AMÉRIQUE DU NORD

Bermudes : Le pays est considéré entièrement urbain.

Canada : Agglomérations de 1 000 habitants ou plus ayant une densité de population d'au moins 400 habitants au kilomètre carré.

Costa Rica : Chefs-lieux de canton.

Cuba : Localités ayant une population supérieure à 2 000 habitants ; ou une population supérieure à 1 000 habitants dont la moitié de la population économiquement active s'occupe des activités non-agricoles.

El Salvador : Chefs-lieux des municipalités.

États-Unis d'Amérique : Agglomérations de 2 500 habitants ou plus ayant généralement une densité de population d'au moins 1 000 habitants au mile carré. Deux types de zones urbaines : zones urbanisées de 50 000 habitants ou plus et groupements urbains comptant au moins 2 500 habitants mais moins de 50 000.

Groenland : Localités d'au moins 200 habitants.

Guatemala : Municipalité du département de Guatemala et centres administratifs officiels d'autres départements et municipalités.

Haïti : Chefs-lieux de communes.

Honduras : Localités d'au moins 2 000 habitants ayant des caractéristiques essentiellement urbaines.

Îles Vierges américaines : Agglomérations de 2 500 habitants ou plus ayant généralement une densité de population d'au moins 1 000 habitants au mile carré. Deux types de zones urbaines : zones urbanisées de 50 000 habitants ou plus et groupements urbains comptant au moins 2 500 habitants mais moins de 50 000. (D'après les résultats du recensement de 2 000, les Îles Vierges américaines ne comptent aucune zone urbanisée.)

Jamaïque : Localités de 2 000 habitants ou plus ayant des caractéristiques urbaines.

Mexique : Localités d'au moins 2 500 habitants.

Nicaragua : Centres administratifs des municipalités et localités d'au moins 1 000 habitants ou d'au moins 150 logements, possédant des rues, un éclairage électrique, un réseau de distribution d'eau, une école et un dispensaire.

Panama : Localités d'au moins 1 500 habitants ayant des caractéristiques essentiellement urbaines. À partir de 1970, localités de 1 500 habitants ou plus présentant des caractéristiques urbaines, telles que rues, éclairage électrique, systèmes d'approvisionnement en eau et réseaux d'égouts.

Porto Rico : Agglomérations de 2 500 habitants ou plus ayant généralement une densité de population d'au moins 1 000 habitants au mile carré. Deux types de zones urbaines : zones urbanisées de 50 000 habitants ou plus et groupements urbains comptant au moins 2 500 habitants mais moins de 50 000.

République dominicaine : Chefs-lieux des municipalités et districts municipaux, dont certains comprennent des zones suburbaines ayant des caractéristiques rurales.

AMÉRIQUE DU SUD

Argentine : Centres comptant au moins 2 000 habitants.

Bolivie : Localités de 2 000 habitants ou plus.

Brésil : Zone à l'intérieur du périmètre urbain d'une ville, définie par la législation municipale.

Chili : Zones d'habitat concentré comptant 2 000 habitants ou plus, ou comptant entre 1 001 et 2 000 habitants dont 50 pour cent au moins de la population active s'occupe d'une activité secondaire ou tertiaire. Par dérogation, les centres qui ont une fonction touristique ou récréative et plus de 250 unités de logement mais n'atteignent pas le critère de population sont néanmoins considérés comme zones urbaines.

Colombie : Zone avec une mairie, définie par un périmètre urbain qui est établie par des accords municipaux.

Équateur : Capitales des provinces et chefs-lieux de canton.

Îles Falkland (Malvinas) : Ville de Stanley.

Paraguay : Grandes villes, villes et chefs-lieux des départements et des districts.

Pérou : Centres de peuplement comptant plus de 100 logements.

Suriname : Les districts de Paramaribo et de Wanica.

Uruguay : Les villes, villages et autres zones habitées répondant aux définitions de la loi sur les agglomérations.

Venezuela (République bolivarienne du) : Centres de 2 500 habitants ou plus.

ASIE

Arabie saoudite : Localités de plus de 5 000 habitants.

Arménie : Grandes villes et localités de type urbain, officiellement désignées comme telles, généralement sur la base du nombre d'habitants et de la prédominance des travailleurs agricoles ou non agricoles avec leur famille.

Azerbaïdjan : Division administrative regroupant plus de 15 000 habitants se livrant principalement à des activités industrielles et autres activités économiques et sociales et comprenant des centres administratifs et culturels.

Bahreïn : Communes ou villages comptant au moins 2 500 habitants.

Brunéi Darussalam : Les communes de Bandar, Seri Begawan, Kuala Belait, Seria, Pekan Tutong and Pekan Bangar; et les zones densement peuplé qui possèdent des caractéristiques urbaines.

Cambodge : Zones au niveau de la commune répondant aux trois conditions suivantes : 1) Densité démographique supérieure à 200 habitants au km carré, 2) pourcentage d'hommes travaillant dans l'agriculture inférieur à 50 pour cent, 3) population totale de la commune supérieure à 2 000 habitants.

Chine : Suivant la Réglementation sur la classification de la résidence urbaine/rurale à des fins de statistiques.

Chypre : Selon la définition du Département de l'urbanisme et du logement du Ministère de l'intérieur.

État de Palestine : Localités peuplées de plus de 10 000 personnes. L'expression désigne tous les gouvernorats (districts), quelle qu'en soit la taille, ainsi que toutes les villes dont la population est comprise entre 4 000 et 9 999 personnes qui disposent d'au moins quatre des éléments suivants : réseau public de distribution d'électricité, réseau public de distribution d'eau, bureau de poste, centre médical doté d'un médecin à temps plein et école préparant les élèves au certificat général de l'enseignement secondaire.

Géorgie : Grandes villes et localités de type urbain, officiellement désignées comme telles, généralement sur la base du nombre d'habitants et de la prédominance des travailleurs agricoles ou non agricoles avec leur famille.

Inde : Villes [localités dotées d'une charte municipale, d'un comité de zone municipale, d'un comité de zone déclarée urbaine ou d'un comité de zone de regroupement (cantonnement)] ; également toutes les localités qui ont une population de 5 000 habitants au moins, une densité de population d'au moins 1 000 habitants au mile carré ou 400 au kilomètre carré, des caractéristiques urbaines prononcées et où les trois quarts au moins des adultes de sexe masculin ont une occupation non agricole.

Indonésie : Les zones urbaines sont celles qui répondent à certains critères : densité de population, pourcentage de ménages agricoles, accès aux équipements urbains, existence d'équipements supplémentaires, et pourcentage de superficie bâtie à usage autre que l'habitation.

Iran (République islamique d') : Tous les districts comptant une municipalité.

Israël : Tous les lieux comptant au moins 2 000 résidents.

Japon : Villes (shi), comptant au moins 50 000 habitants, où 60 p. 100 au moins des logements sont situés dans les principales zones bâties, et dont 60 p. 100 au moins de population (y compris les personnes à charge) exercent un métier dans l'industrie, le commerce et d'autres branches d'activités essentiellement urbaines.

Jordanie : Localités comptant 5 000 habitants ou plus.

Kazakhstan : Villes ayant statut républicain (centres de population présentant une importance nationale spéciale ou comptant une population généralement de plus d'un million d'habitants), statut régional (Oblast') (centres de population qui sont de grands centres économiques et culturels, dotés d'une infrastructure industrielle et sociale développée et comptant une population de plus 50 000 habitants, le pays compte 40 villes ayant statut régional), statut départemental, et agglomérations relevant de leur juridiction administrative.

Kirghizistan : Grandes villes et localités de type urbain, officiellement désignées comme telles, généralement sur la base du nombre d'habitants et de la prédominance des travailleurs agricoles ou non agricoles avec leur famille.

Koweït : Toutes les localités sont urbaines au Koweït.

Malaisie : Zone ayant le statut de centre urbain et dont la population totale dépasse 10 000 habitants. On nomme périphérie toute zone contiguë à un centre urbain dont au moins 60 % de la population (âgée de 15 ans et plus) a une activité non agricole. La définition des zones urbaines couvre également les zones spéciales de développement qui n'ont pas officiellement le statut de centre urbain, se trouvent à 5 kilomètres ou plus d'un tel centre ou de sa périphérie et comptent au moins 10 000 habitants dont 60 % (parmi les plus de 15 ans) ont une activité non agricole.

Maldives : Malé (la capitale).

Mongolie : Ulaanbaatar (la capitale), les chefs-lieux des provinces et les villes.

Myanmar : Les zones reconnues par les autorités gouvernementales comme urbaines. Ces zones se caractérisent par une densité de population et de constructions humaines plus élevée et disposent de meilleures infrastructures.

Népal : Zones déclarées telles par les municipalités.

Ouzbékistan : Grandes villes et localités de type urbain, officiellement désignées comme telles, généralement sur la base du nombre d'habitants et de la prédominance des travailleurs agricoles ou non agricoles avec leur famille.

Pakistan : Localités dotées d'une charte municipale ou d'un comité municipal et regroupements (cantonments).

Philippines : Villes et municipalités et leurs quartiers centraux dont la densité démographique est d'au moins 500 habitants au km carré. Sont considérés comme zones urbaines les autres quartiers quelle que soit leur population qui sont équipés de routes et possèdent au moins six établissements (commerce, industrie manufacturière, équipements récréatifs ou services aux personnes), et au moins trois équipements publics tels que hôtel de ville, église, parc public, école, hôpital, bibliothèque, etc.

République arabe syrienne : Villes, chefs-lieux de district (Mohafaza) et chefs-lieux de sous district (Mantika), et communes d'au moins 20 000 habitants.

République de Corée : Pour les estimations : localités de 50 000 habitants ou plus. Pour recensements, les données sont établies sont la base des divisions administratives mineures comme les Dongs (principalement en zone urbaines) et des Eups ou Myeons (en zones rurales).

République démocratique populaire lao : Zones ou villages répondant à au moins trois des cinq conditions suivantes: situés dans l'aire métropolitaine du district ou de la province, accessibles par la route en toute saison, quelque 70 pour cent ou deux tiers de la population ayant accès à de l'eau distribuée par canalisation, quelque 70 pour cent ou deux tiers de la population ayant accès au réseau d'électricité et existence d'un marché ouvert tous les jours.

Singapour : Le pays consiste seulement d'une ville.

Sri Lanka : Toutes les zones administrées par les conseils municipaux et urbains.

Tadjikistan : Grandes villes et localités de type urbain, officiellement désignées comme telles, généralement sur la base du nombre d'habitants et de la prédominance des travailleurs agricoles ou non agricoles avec leur famille.

Thaïlande : Zones municipales.

Turkménistan : Grandes villes et localités de type urbain, officiellement désignées comme telles, généralement sur la base du nombre d'habitants et de la prédominance des travailleurs agricoles ou non agricoles avec leur famille.

Turquie : Localités comptant 20 000 habitants ou plus.

Viet Nam : Zones urbaines comprises à l'intérieur des districts urbains des villes ainsi que des quartiers urbains et des localités. Toutes les autres unités administratives locales (communes) sont considérées comme zones rurales.

EUROPE

Albanie : Villes et autres centres industriels de plus de 400 habitants.

Autriche : Les zones urbaines sont les localités comptant 2 000 habitants ou plus. Leur délimitation remonte à 1991.

Bélarus : Les établissements urbains sont des établissements autorisés en vertu de la loi comme les villes, les agglomérations de type urbain, les cités ouvrières et les zones de villégiature de santé.

Belgique : Toutes les communes qui ne sont pas dans la liste des communes rurales sont considérées comme des communes urbaines. Il y a 33 communes qui sont considérées comme rurales: Alveringem, Amblève, Bertogne, Bièvre, Bullange, Burg-Reuland, Clavier, Erezée, Fauvillers, Frasnes-lez-Anvaing, Froidchapelle, Gedinne, Gouvy, Havelange, Herstappe, Heuvelland, Houffalize, Houyet, Langemark-Poelkapelle, Léglise, Lierneux, Lo-Reninge, Manhay, Momignies, Ravels, Sainte-Ode, Sint-Laureins, Sivry-Rance, Stoumont, Tenneville, Vaux-sur-Sûre, Vleteren et Vresse-sur-Semois.

Bulgarie : Toutes les zones considérées comme villes et bourgs selon la Division territoriale et administrative du pays.

Espagne : Aux fins de la publication de résultats qui soient comparables au niveau européen, Eurostat propose de considérer comme zones urbaines, intermédiaires et rurales les communes comptant respectivement plus de 10 000 habitants, de 2 001 à 10 000 habitants et moins de 2 000 habitants.

Estonie : Les établissements urbains comprennent les villes et les agglomérations n'ayant pas de statut municipal.

Fédération de Russie : Grandes villes et localités de type urbain, officiellement désignées comme telles, généralement sur la base du nombre d'habitants et de la prédominance des travailleurs agricoles ou non agricoles avec leur famille.

Finlande : Communes urbaines (communes où au moins 90 % de la population vit en milieu urbain ou dont le plus grand centre urbain compte au moins 15 000 habitants).

France : Communes comprenant une agglomération de plus de 2 000 habitants vivant dans des habitations contiguës ou qui ne sont pas distantes les unes des autres de plus de 200 mètres et communes où la majeure partie de la population vit dans une agglomération regroupant plusieurs communes de cette nature.

Grèce : Est considérée comme zone urbaine toute municipalité ou commune dont la plus grande localité compte 2 000 habitants ou plus.

Hongrie : Localités dont le statut de ville a été reconnu par le Président de la République compte tenu de critères spécifiques (économiques, commerciaux, institutionnels, culturels, etc.).

Irlande : Localités, y compris leur banlieues, comptant 1 500 habitants ou plus.

Islande : Localités de 200 habitants ou plus.

L'ex-R. y. de Macédoine : Villes sont les localités comptant au moins 3 000 habitants, dotés d'une infrastructure industrielle et sociale développée, dont plus de 51 pour cent de la population active s'occupe des activités qui ne sont pas primaires.

Lettonie : Grandes villes et localités de type urbain, officiellement désignées comme telles, généralement sur la base du nombre d'habitants et de la prédominance des travailleurs agricoles ou non agricoles avec leur famille.

Lituanie : Par population urbaine, on entend les personnes qui vivent dans des villes ou des localités, à savoir les zones habitées comportant des logements permanents proches les uns des autres et dont la population est d'au moins 3 000 habitants, les deux tiers desquels étant employés dans le secteur industriel, l'infrastructure sociale ou le commerce. Un certain nombre de villes peuvent compter moins de 3 000 habitants dans la mesure où elles avaient acquis le statut de ville avant l'entrée en vigueur de la nouvelle loi en juillet 1994.

Malte : Zones de 1 kilomètre carré avec une densité minimum de 300 au kilomètre carré et un minimum de 5 000 habitants, et zones à forte densité de population (supérieure à 500 habitants au kilomètre carré).

Monténégro : D'après la législation actuelle relative à l'organisation territoriale du Monténégro, qui oblige chaque collectivité à déterminer quelles sont ses zones urbaines et rurales.

Norvège : Ensemble construit habité par au moins 200 personnes, où les bâtiments ne sont pas éloignés de plus de 50 mètres les uns des autres. Les limites en sont évolutives et peuvent être redéfinies pour tenir compte de l'urbanisation et de l'évolution de la population.

Pays Bas : Zones urbaines : municipalités comptant au moins 2 000 habitants. Zones semi-urbaines : municipalités comptant moins de 2 000 habitants, mais où 20 p. 100 au maximum de la population active de sexe masculin pratiquent l'agriculture, et certaines municipalités de caractère résidentiel dont les habitants travaillent ailleurs.

Pologne : Toutes les zones qui ont les droits d'une ville ou le statut d'une ville avec dispositions de lois distinctes.

Portugal : Localités comptant 2 000 habitants ou davantage.

République de Moldova : Grandes villes et localités de type urbain, officiellement désignées comme telles, généralement sur la base du nombre d'habitants et de la prédominance des travailleurs agricoles ou non agricoles avec leur famille.

République tchèque : Localités d'au moins 2 000 habitants.

Roumanie : Localités où la majorité des ressources en main-d'œuvre est employée dans des activités non agricoles avec un niveau diversifié de ressources, exerçant une influence socioéconomique constante et importante sur l'ensemble de la zone.

Royaume-Uni de Grande-Bretagne et d'Irlande du Nord : Pour l'Angleterre et le Pays de Galles, les zones bâties comptant 10 000 habitants ou plus ; pour l'Écosse, les établissements humains comptant 3 000 habitants ou davantage et pour l'Irlande du Nord, les établissements comptant 5 000 habitants.

Serbie : Municipalités, villes et Belgrade.

Slovaquie : Municipalités avec statut de ville, conformément aux critères : 1) est un centre économique, administratif, culturel ou touristique ; 2) fournit des services pour d'autres municipalités ; 3) a un caractère urbain, au moins en partie ; et 4) compte 5 000 habitants ou plus.

Slovénie : Établissements de 3 000 habitants ou plus, chefs-lieux de municipalités comptant au moins 1 400 habitants, et quartiers suburbains qui s'intègrent progressivement dans une ville de 5 000 habitants ou plus.

Suisse : L'espace urbain comprend les agglomérations et les villes isolées (n'appartenant pas à une agglomération et comptant au moins 10 000 habitants à elles seules).

Ukraine : Grandes villes et localités de type urbain, officiellement désignées comme telles, généralement sur la base du nombre d'habitants et de la prédominance des travailleurs agricoles ou non agricoles avec leur famille.

OCÉANIE

Australie : Sont considérées comme urbaines toutes les « zones urbaines importantes » (Significant Urban Areas), telles que définies dans la Norme géographique australienne de statistique de 2011. Il s'agit de concentrations urbanisées comptant 10 000 habitants ou plus.

Guam : Agglomérations de 2 500 habitants ou plus ayant généralement une densité de population d'au moins 1 000 habitants au mile carré et considérées comme étant des groupements urbains.

Îles Cook : Rarotonga, île la plus peuplée.

Îles Mariannes septentrionales : Agglomérations de 2 500 habitants ou plus ayant généralement une densité de population d'au moins 1 000 habitants au mile carré. Deux types de zones urbaines : zones urbanisées de 50 000 habitants ou plus et groupements urbains comptant au moins 2 500 habitants mais moins de 50 000.

Nouvelle-Calédonie : Nouméa et communes de Païta, Dumbéa et Mont-Dore.

Nouvelle-Zélande : Toutes les villes et les quartiers, districts et bourgs ayant 1 000 habitants permanents ou plus.

Palaos : États comptant 2 500 habitants ou plus (le seul État qui remplit cette condition est l'État de Koror).

Samoa américaines : Agglomérations de 2 500 habitants ou plus ayant généralement une densité de population d'au moins 1 000 habitants au mile carré. Deux types de zones urbaines : zones urbanisées de 50 000 habitants ou plus et groupements urbains comptant au moins 2 500 habitants mais moins de 50 000. (D'après les résultats du recensement de 2000, les Samoa américaines ne comptent aucune zone urbanisée.)

Tokélaou : L'ensemble de la population est considéré comme vivant en milieu rural.

Tonga : Nuku'alofa.

Vanuatu : Centre de Luganville et Port-Vila.

NOTES

[1] Pour plus de précisions, voir *Social and Demographic Statistics : Classifications of Size and Type of Locality and Urban/Rural Areas*, E/CN.3/551, publication des Nations Unies, New York, 1980.

6. Total and urban population by sex: 2008 - 2017
Population totale et population urbaine selon le sexe : 2008 - 2017

Continent, country or area, and date / Continent, pays ou zone et date — Code[a]	Both sexes - Les deux sexes			Male - Masculin			Female - Féminin		
	Total	Urban - Urbaine Number Nombre	Urban - Urbaine Percent P.100	Total	Urban - Urbaine Number Nombre	Urban - Urbaine Percent P.100	Total	Urban - Urbaine Number Nombre	Urban - Urbaine Percent P.100
AFRICA - AFRIQUE									
Algeria - Algérie									
16 IV 2008[1] ....CDFC	34 452 759	...	...	17 428 500	...	...	17 024 259	...	...
1 VII 2008 ....ESDJ	34 591 000	22 808 000	65.9	17 493 000	...	...	17 098 000	...	...
1 VII 2009 ....ESDJ	35 268 000	...	...	17 846 000	...	...	17 422 000	...	...
1 VII 2010 ....ESDJ	35 978 000	...	...	18 205 000	...	...	17 773 000	...	...
1 VII 2011 ....ESDJ	36 717 000	...	...	18 579 000	...	...	18 138 000	...	...
1 VII 2012 ....ESDJ	37 495 000	...	...	18 976 000	...	...	18 519 000	...	...
1 VII 2013 ....ESDJ	38 297 000	...	...	19 383 000	...	...	18 914 000	...	...
1 VII 2014 ....ESDJ	39 114 275	...	...	19 801 163	...	...	19 313 112	...	...
1 VII 2015 ....ESDJ	39 963 249	...	...	20 235 204	...	...	19 728 045	...	...
1 VII 2016 ....ESDJ	40 835 602	...	...	20 680 271	...	...	20 155 331	...	...
1 VII 2017 ....ESDJ	41 695 626	...	...	21 118 894	...	...	20 576 732	...	...
Angola									
1 VII 2008[2] ....ESDF	16 368 000	...	...	7 899 000	...	...	8 469 000	...	...
1 VII 2009[2] ....ESDF	16 888 858	...	...	8 158 550	...	...	8 730 308	...	...
1 VII 2010[2] ....ESDF	17 429 637	...	...	8 427 802	...	...	9 001 835	...	...
1 VII 2011[2] ....ESDF	17 992 033	...	...	8 707 868	...	...	9 284 165	...	...
1 VII 2012[2] ....ESDF	18 576 568	...	...	8 999 074	...	...	9 577 494	...	...
1 VII 2013[2] ....ESDF	19 183 590	...	...	9 301 632	...	...	9 881 958	...	...
16 V 2014 ....CDFC	25 789 024	16 153 987	62.6	12 499 041	7 860 614	62.9	13 289 983	8 293 373	62.4
1 VII 2014[3] ....ESDF	25 901 182	16 235 542	62.7	12 553 707	7 900 523	62.9	13 347 475	8 335 019	62.4
1 VII 2015[3] ....ESDF	26 681 590	16 761 094	62.8	12 943 812	8 165 438	63.1	13 737 778	8 595 656	62.6
1 VII 2016[3] ....ESDF	27 503 526	17 310 474	62.9	13 355 101	8 442 190	63.2	14 148 425	8 868 284	62.7
1 VII 2017[3] ....ESDF	28 359 634	17 881 283	63.1	13 783 460	8 729 543	63.3	14 576 174	9 151 740	62.8
Benin - Bénin									
1 VII 2008[4] ....ESDF	8 224 642	3 499 506	42.5	4 021 094	1 716 411	42.7	4 203 548	1 783 095	42.4
1 VII 2009[4] ....ESDF	8 497 827	3 682 496	43.3	4 159 291	1 808 057	43.5	4 338 536	1 874 439	43.2
1 VII 2010[4] ....ESDF	8 778 648	3 873 462	44.1	4 301 224	1 903 683	44.3	4 477 424	1 969 779	44.0
1 VII 2011[4] ....ESDF	9 067 076	4 072 574	44.9	4 446 877	2 003 366	45.1	4 620 199	2 069 208	44.8
1 VII 2012[4] ....ESDF	9 364 619	4 280 693	45.7	4 597 122	...	...	4 767 497	...	...
11 V 2013 ....CDFC	10 008 749	4 460 503	44.6	4 887 820	...	...	5 120 929	...	...
1 VII 2014[5] ....ESDF	10 293 235	...	...	5 033 372	...	...	5 259 863	...	...
1 VII 2015[5] ....ESDF	10 584 935	...	...	5 182 478	...	...	5 402 457	...	...
1 VII 2016[5] ....ESDF	10 882 953	...	...	5 334 603	...	...	5 548 350	...	...
Botswana									
1 VII 2008 ....ESDJ	1 755 246	...	...	859 167	...	...	896 079	...	...
1 VII 2009 ....ESDJ	1 776 494	...	...	871 964	...	...	904 530	...	...
1 VII 2010 ....ESDJ	1 822 859	...	...	895 007	...	...	927 852	...	...
1 VII 2011 ....ESDJ	1 849 692	...	...	910 404	...	...	939 288	...	...
9 VIII 2011 ....CDFC	2 024 904	1 297 287	64.1	988 957	619 472	62.6	1 035 947	677 815	65.4
1 VII 2012[6] ....ESDJ	2 070 984	1 361 699	65.8	1 010 236	664 243	65.8	1 060 748	697 456	65.8
1 VII 2013[6] ....ESDJ	2 114 890	1 411 436	66.7	1 031 654	688 505	66.7	1 083 236	722 931	66.7
1 VII 2014[6] ....ESDJ	2 156 366	1 460 383	67.7	1 051 886	712 382	67.7	1 104 480	748 001	67.7
1 VII 2015[6] ....ESDJ	2 195 134	1 508 277	68.7	1 070 797	735 745	68.7	1 124 337	772 532	68.7
1 VII 2016[6] ....ESDJ	2 230 905	1 554 836	69.7	1 088 246	758 457	69.7	1 142 659	796 379	69.7
1 VII 2017[6] ....ESDJ	2 266 857	1 602 216	70.7	1 110 760	785 086	70.7	1 156 097	817 130	70.7
Burkina Faso[4]									
1 VII 2008 ....ESDJ	14 731 167	...	...	7 110 097	...	...	7 621 070	...	...
1 VII 2009 ....ESDJ	15 224 780	...	...	7 346 835	...	...	7 877 945	...	...
1 VII 2010 ....ESDJ	15 730 977	...	...	7 590 133	...	...	8 140 844	...	...
1 VII 2011 ....ESDJ	16 248 558	...	...	7 839 350	...	...	8 409 208	...	...
1 VII 2012 ....ESDJ	16 779 206	...	...	8 095 324	...	...	8 683 882	...	...
1 VII 2013 ....ESDJ	17 322 796	...	...	8 357 967	...	...	8 964 829	...	...
1 VII 2014 ....ESDJ	17 880 386	...	...	8 627 830	...	...	9 252 556	...	...
1 VII 2015 ....ESDJ	18 450 494	...	...	8 904 256	...	...	9 546 238	...	...
Burundi									
16 VIII 2008 ....CDFC	7 877 728	799 802	10.2	3 838 045	432 442	11.3	4 039 683	367 360	9.1
1 VII 2010 ....ESDF	9 461 117	...	...	4 667 414	...	...	4 793 703	...	...
1 VII 2011 ....ESDF	9 770 964	...	...	4 821 918	...	...	4 949 047	...	...
1 VII 2012 ....ESDF	10 072 586	...	...	4 972 344	...	...	5 100 243	...	...
1 VII 2013 ....ESDF	10 367 162	...	...	5 119 079	...	...	5 248 084	...	...
1 VII 2014 ....ESDF	10 654 123	...	...	5 261 798	...	...	5 392 325	...	...
1 VII 2015 ....ESDF	10 933 343	...	...	5 400 272	...	...	5 533 071	...	...
1 VII 2016 ....ESDF	11 215 019	...	...	5 539 821	...	...	5 675 198	...	...
1 VII 2017 ....ESDF	11 495 438	...	...	5 678 569	...	...	5 816 869	...	...

Continent, country or area, and date / Continent, pays ou zone et date	Code[a]	Both sexes - Les deux sexes Total	Urban - Urbaine Number Nombre	Urban - Urbaine Percent P.100	Male - Masculin Total	Urban - Urbaine Number Nombre	Urban - Urbaine Percent P.100	Female - Féminin Total	Urban - Urbaine Number Nombre	Urban - Urbaine Percent P.100
AFRICA - AFRIQUE										
Cabo Verde										
1 VII 2008	ESDF	499 796	303 512	60.7	241 914	...	...	257 882	...	...
1 VII 2009	ESDF	508 633	310 958	61.1	246 219	...	...	262 414	...	...
16 VI 2010	CDJC	491 683	303 673	61.8	243 403	151 219	62.1	248 280	152 454	61.4
1 VII 2010[4]	ESDJ	494 040	...	...	244 338	...	...	249 702	...	...
1 VII 2011[4]	ESDJ	499 929	...	...	247 814	...	...	252 115	...	...
1 VII 2012[4]	ESDJ	505 983	...	...	251 384	...	...	254 599	...	...
1 VII 2013[4]	ESDJ	512 173	...	...	255 033	...	...	257 140	...	...
1 VII 2014[4]	ESDJ	518 467	...	...	258 744	...	...	259 723	...	...
1 VII 2015[4]	ESDJ	524 833	...	...	262 501	...	...	262 331	...	...
1 VII 2016[4]	ESDJ	531 239	...	...	266 287	...	...	264 951	...	...
1 VII 2017[4]	ESDJ	537 661	...	...	270 091	...	...	267 570	...	...
Cameroon - Cameroun[4]										
1 VII 2008	ESDF	18 691 490	...	...	9 237 549	...	...	9 453 941	...	...
1 VII 2009	ESDF	19 165 905	...	...	9 472 009	...	...	9 693 896	...	...
1 VII 2010	ESDF	19 648 287	...	...	9 707 318	...	...	9 940 969	...	...
1 VII 2011	ESDF	20 138 637	...	...	9 949 573	...	...	10 189 064	...	...
1 VII 2012	ESDF	20 636 954	...	...	10 195 770	...	...	10 441 184	...	...
1 VII 2013	ESDF	21 143 237	...	...	10 445 903	...	...	10 697 334	...	...
1 VII 2014	ESDF	21 657 488	...	...	10 699 969	...	...	10 957 519	...	...
1 VII 2015	ESDF	22 179 707	...	...	10 955 014	...	...	11 224 693	...	...
1 VII 2016	ESDF	22 709 892	...	...	11 216 886	...	...	11 493 006	...	...
1 VII 2017	ESDF	23 248 044	...	...	11 482 685	...	...	11 765 359	...	...
Chad - Tchad										
20 V 2009	CDJC	11 175 915	...	...	5 509 522	...	...	5 666 393	...	...
Congo										
1 VII 2008	ESDF	3 740 851	...	...	1 841 589	...	...	1 899 262	...	...
1 VII 2009	ESDF	3 838 238	...	...	1 891 558	...	...	1 946 680	...	...
Côte d'Ivoire										
1 VII 2008[7]	ESDF	19 932 082	...	...	10 259 383	...	...	9 672 699	...	...
1 VII 2009[7]	ESDF	20 388 627	...	...	10 500 861	...	...	9 887 766	...	...
1 VII 2010[7]	ESDF	20 845 167	...	...	10 742 336	...	...	10 102 831	...	...
1 VII 2011[7]	ESDF	21 301 704	...	...	10 983 811	...	...	10 317 893	...	...
1 VII 2012[7]	ESDF	21 758 244	...	...	11 225 286	...	...	10 532 958	...	...
1 VII 2013[7]	ESDF	22 214 787	...	...	11 466 762	...	...	10 748 025	...	...
15 V 2014	CDFC	22 224 509	10 881 387	49.0	11 441 896	5 495 438	48.0	10 782 613	5 385 949	50.0
1 VII 2014[8]	ESDF	22 723 460	11 444 572	50.4	11 734 076	5 834 493	49.7	10 989 384	5 610 079	51.0
1 VII 2015[8]	ESDF	23 334 439	11 830 560	50.7	12 036 040	6 102 272	50.7	11 298 398	5 728 288	50.7
1 VII 2016[8]	ESDF	23 950 475	12 262 643	51.2	12 340 861	6 318 521	51.2	11 609 614	5 944 122	51.2
1 VII 2017[8]	ESDF	24 571 044	12 678 659	51.6	12 648 124	6 526 432	51.6	11 922 920	6 152 227	51.6
Djibouti										
29 V 2009	CDFC	818 159	577 933	70.6	440 067	322 796	73.4	378 092	255 137	67.5
Egypt - Égypte										
1 VII 2008	ESDF	75 193 567	32 248 476	42.9	38 413 404	16 437 464	42.8	36 780 163	15 811 012	43.0
1 VII 2009	ESDF	76 925 139	33 082 770	43.0	39 327 098	16 887 176	42.9	37 598 041	16 195 594	43.1
1 VII 2010	ESDF	78 684 622	33 804 181	43.0	40 228 119	17 255 735	42.9	38 456 503	16 548 446	43.0
1 VII 2011	ESDF	80 529 566	34 495 468	42.8	41 152 525	17 596 284	42.8	39 377 041	16 899 184	42.9
1 VII 2012	ESDF	82 549 976	35 372 982	42.9	42 167 660	18 031 407	42.8	40 382 316	17 341 575	42.9
1 VII 2013	ESDF	84 628 982	36 213 473	42.8	43 217 105	18 470 748	42.7	41 411 877	17 742 725	42.8
1 VII 2014	ESDF	86 811 192	37 098 131	42.7	44 300 565	18 894 134	42.6	42 510 627	18 203 997	42.8
1 VII 2015	ESDF	88 957 833	37 999 018	42.7	45 378 728	19 347 041	42.6	43 579 105	18 651 977	42.8
1 VII 2016	ESDF	91 023 393	38 895 815	42.7	46 413 993	19 787 083	42.6	44 609 400	19 108 732	42.8
18 IV 2017	CDFC	94 798 827	...	...	48 891 518	...	...	45 907 309	...	...
1 VII 2017	ESDF	95 202 532	40 432 110	42.5	49 095 021	20 818 309	42.4	46 107 511	19 613 801	42.5
Equatorial Guinea - Guinée équatoriale										
20 VI 2015*	CDFC	1 222 442	863 313	70.6	651 820	...	...	570 622	...	...
Eritrea - Érythrée[9]										
1 VII 2008	ESDF	2 565 350	910 435	35.5	1 267 564	436 365	34.4	1 297 786	474 070	36.5
1 VII 2009	ESDF	2 626 931	934 510	35.6	1 297 153	447 525	34.5	1 329 778	486 984	36.6
1 VII 2010	ESDF	2 691 414	959 076	35.6	1 328 220	458 920	34.6	1 363 194	500 156	36.7
1 VII 2011	ESDF	2 758 710	984 049	35.7	1 360 721	470 508	34.6	1 397 989	513 542	36.7
1 VII 2012	ESDF	2 828 680	1 009 342	35.7	1 394 589	482 248	34.6	1 434 091	527 093	36.8
1 VII 2013	ESDF	2 901 138	1 034 874	35.7	1 429 730	494 104	34.6	1 471 407	540 771	36.8
1 VII 2014	ESDF	2 975 851	1 060 585	35.6	1 466 026	506 044	34.5	1 509 825	554 541	36.7

Continent, country or area, and date / Continent, pays ou zone et date	Code[a]	Both sexes - Les deux sexes			Male - Masculin			Female - Féminin		
		Total	Urban - Urbaine		Total	Urban - Urbaine		Total	Urban - Urbaine	
			Number Nombre	Percent P.100		Number Nombre	Percent P.100		Number Nombre	Percent P.100
AFRICA - AFRIQUE										
Eritrea - Érythrée[9]										
1 VII 2015	ESDF	3 052 498	1 086 415	35.6	1 503 313	518 040	34.5	1 549 185	568 375	36.7
1 VII 2016	ESDF	3 131 148	1 112 354	35.5	1 541 625	530 088	34.4	1 589 523	582 266	36.6
1 VII 2017	ESDF	3 211 946	1 138 401	35.4	1 581 036	542 187	34.3	1 630 910	596 213	36.6
Eswatini										
1 VII 2008	ESDF	1 031 747	229 516	22.2	488 132	109 937	22.5	543 615	119 579	22.0
1 VII 2009	ESDF	1 043 509	233 504	22.4	494 061	111 704	22.6	549 448	121 800	22.2
1 VII 2010	ESDF	1 055 506	237 641	22.5	500 070	113 554	22.7	555 436	124 087	22.3
1 VII 2011	ESDF	1 067 773	241 947	22.7	506 186	115 493	22.8	561 587	126 454	22.5
1 VII 2012	ESDF	1 080 337	246 441	22.8	512 432	117 528	22.9	567 905	128 913	22.7
1 VII 2013	ESDF	1 093 158	251 122	23.0	518 788	119 658	23.1	574 370	131 464	22.9
1 VII 2014	ESDF	1 106 189	255 986	23.1	525 232	121 881	23.2	580 957	134 105	23.1
1 VII 2015	ESDF	1 119 375	261 028	23.3	531 737	124 195	23.4	587 638	136 833	23.3
1 VII 2016	ESDF	1 132 657	266 230	23.5	538 274	126 593	23.5	594 383	139 637	23.5
1 VII 2017	ESDF	1 145 970	271 873	23.7	544 811	...	...	601 159	...	...
Ethiopia - Éthiopie[10]										
1 VII 2008	ESDF	75 719 000	12 716 000	16.8	38 215 000	6 353 000	16.6	37 504 000	6 363 000	17.0
1 VII 2009	ESDF	77 651 000	13 318 000	17.2	39 155 000	6 649 000	17.0	38 496 000	6 669 000	17.3
1 VII 2010	ESDF	79 634 000	13 931 000	17.5	40 123 000	6 950 000	17.3	39 511 000	6 981 000	17.7
1 VII 2011	ESDF	81 668 000	14 589 000	17.9	41 119 000	7 274 000	17.7	40 549 000	7 315 000	18.0
1 VII 2012	ESDF	83 741 000	15 246 000	18.2	42 135 000	7 598 000	18.0	41 606 000	7 648 000	18.4
1 VII 2013	ESDF	85 837 000	15 979 000	18.6	43 164 000	7 960 000	18.4	42 673 000	8 019 000	18.8
1 VII 2014	ESDF	87 952 000	16 734 000	19.0	44 204 000	8 332 000	18.8	43 748 000	8 402 000	19.2
1 VII 2015	ESDF	90 075 000	17 521 000	19.5	45 250 000	8 721 000	19.3	44 825 000	8 800 000	19.6
1 VII 2016	ESDF	92 205 000	18 327 000	19.9	46 303 000	9 120 000	19.7	45 902 000	9 207 000	20.1
1 VII 2017	ESDF	94 352 138	19 161 490	20.3	47 364 992	9 534 811	20.1	46 987 146	9 626 679	20.5
Gabon										
22 V 2013	CDFC	1 811 079	1 577 646	87.1	934 072	813 098	87.0	877 007	764 548	87.2
Gambia - Gambie										
15 IV 2013*	CDFC	1 882 450	...	...	930 699	...	...	951 751	...	...
Ghana										
1 VII 2008	ESDF	22 900 927	...	...	11 343 581	...	...	11 557 346	...	...
1 VII 2009	ESDF	23 416 518	10 243 312	43.7	11 600 326	5 006 198	43.2	11 816 192	5 237 114	44.3
26 IX 2010	CDFC	24 658 823	12 545 229	50.9	12 024 845	6 016 059	50.0	12 633 978	6 529 170	51.7
1 VII 2011[11]	ESDF	25 235 268	12 844 745	50.9	12 319 770	6 270 758	50.9	12 915 498	6 573 987	50.9
1 VII 2012[11]	ESDF	25 824 920	13 144 879	50.9	12 621 125	6 424 150	50.9	13 203 795	6 720 729	50.9
1 VII 2013[11]	ESDF	26 427 760	13 451 714	50.9	12 928 916	6 580 808	50.9	13 498 844	6 870 906	50.9
1 VII 2014[11]	ESDF	27 043 093	13 764 931	50.9	13 242 709	6 740 539	50.9	13 800 384	7 024 392	50.9
1 VII 2015[11]	ESDF	27 670 174	13 817 894	49.9	13 562 093	6 903 107	50.9	14 108 081	6 914 787	49.0
1 VII 2016[11]	ESDF	28 308 301	...	...	13 886 734	...	...	14 421 567	...	...
Guinea - Guinée										
1 VII 2008[4]	ESDF	10 182 926	2 851 219	28.0	...	...	...	...	...	...
1 VII 2009[4]	ESDF	10 217 591	...	...	5 038 823	...	...	5 178 768	...	...
1 VII 2010[4]	ESDF	10 537 234	...	...	5 200 608	...	...	5 336 626	...	...
1 VII 2011[4]	ESDF	10 863 888	...	...	5 309 110	...	...	5 554 778	...	...
15 III 2014	CDJC	10 523 261	3 657 122	34.8	5 084 306	1 821 369	35.8	5 438 955	1 835 753	33.8
1 VII 2014[3]	ESDJ	10 599 848	3 684 996	34.8	5 115 365	1 832 976	35.8	5 484 483	1 852 020	33.8
1 VII 2015[3]	ESDJ	10 917 710	3 825 273	35.0	5 273 425	1 847 667	35.0	5 644 286	1 977 606	35.0
1 VII 2016[3]	ESDJ	11 233 037	3 966 389	35.3	5 430 371	1 917 466	35.3	5 802 667	2 048 923	35.3
1 VII 2017[3]	ESDJ	11 555 061	4 111 607	35.6	5 590 797	1 989 359	35.6	5 964 265	2 122 248	35.6
Guinea-Bissau - Guinée-Bissau										
15 III 2009	CDFC	1 497 859	...	...	725 956	...	...	771 903	...	...
1 VII 2010[4]	ESDF	1 460 221	584 228	40.0	709 482	283 859	40.0	750 739	300 369	40.0
1 VII 2011[4]	ESDF	1 472 233	595 358	40.4	716 622	289 796	40.4	755 611	305 562	40.4
1 VII 2012[4]	ESDF	1 485 189	606 976	40.9	724 208	295 974	40.9	760 981	311 002	40.9
1 VII 2013[4]	ESDF	1 499 277	619 166	41.3	732 337	302 438	41.3	766 940	316 728	41.3
1 VII 2014[4]	ESDF	1 514 451	631 938	41.7	740 981	309 191	41.7	773 470	322 747	41.7
1 VII 2015[4]	ESDF	1 530 673	645 283	42.2	750 119	316 226	42.2	780 554	329 057	42.2
1 VII 2016[4]	ESDF	1 547 777	659 138	42.6	759 666	323 512	42.6	788 111	335 626	42.6
Kenya										
1 VII 2008	ESDF	38 277 856	...	...	18 743 686	...	...	19 534 170	...	...
1 VII 2009[12]	ESDF	37 724 850	12 200 486	32.3	18 674 184	6 109 258	32.7	19 050 666	6 091 229	32.0
24 VIII 2009	CDFC	38 610 097	12 487 375	32.3	19 192 458	6 278 811	32.7	19 417 639	6 208 564	32.0
1 VII 2010[12]	ESDF	38 473 893	...	...	19 047 448	...	...	19 426 445	...	...

Continent, country or area, and date / Continent, pays ou zone et date	Code[a]	Both sexes - Les deux sexes			Male - Masculin			Female - Féminin		
		Total	Urban - Urbaine		Total	Urban - Urbaine		Total	Urban - Urbaine	
			Number Nombre	Percent P.100		Number Nombre	Percent P.100		Number Nombre	Percent P.100
AFRICA - AFRIQUE										
Kenya										
1 VII 2011[12]	ESDF	39 545 118	...	...	19 583 833	...	...	19 961 285	...	...
1 VII 2012[12]	ESDF	40 656 572	...	...	20 137 201	...	...	20 519 371	...	...
1 VII 2013[12]	ESDF	41 787 735	...	...	20 707 136	...	...	21 080 599	...	...
1 VII 2014[12]	ESDF	42 961 187	...	...	21 289 752	...	...	21 671 435	...	...
1 VII 2015[12]	ESDF	44 156 577	14 280 766	32.3	21 886 677	7 160 225	32.7	22 269 900	7 120 541	32.0
1 VII 2016[12]	ESDF	45 389 112	14 679 464	32.3	22 508 628	7 363 696	32.7	22 880 484	7 315 769	32.0
1 VII 2017[12]	ESDF	46 595 199	15 069 937	32.3	23 117 881	...	...	23 477 319	...	...
Lesotho										
1 VII 2008[13]	ESDF	1 883 595	...	...	912 711	...	...	970 884	...	...
1 VII 2009[13]	ESDF	1 887 479	...	...	912 760	...	...	974 719	...	...
1 VII 2010[13]	ESDF	1 891 830	...	...	913 030	...	...	978 800	...	...
1 VII 2011[13]	ESDF	1 896 833	...	...	913 701	...	...	983 132	...	...
1 VII 2012[13]	ESDF	1 902 707	...	...	914 954	...	...	987 753	...	...
1 VII 2013[13]	ESDF	1 909 321	...	...	916 722	...	...	992 599	...	...
1 VII 2014[13]	ESDF	1 916 573	...	...	918 944	...	...	997 629	...	...
1 VII 2015[13]	ESDF	1 924 381	...	...	921 565	...	...	1 002 816	...	...
10 IV 2016	CDJC	2 007 201	685 938	34.2	982 133	...	...	1 025 068	...	...
Liberia - Libéria										
21 III 2008	CDFC	3 476 608	1 633 719	47.0	1 739 945	802 092	46.1	1 736 663	831 627	47.9
1 VII 2009	ESDF	3 551 078	1 682 364	47.4	1 776 406	823 978	46.4	1 774 672	858 386	48.4
1 VII 2010	ESDF	3 627 144	1 732 457	47.8	1 813 631	846 461	46.7	1 813 513	885 996	48.9
1 VII 2011	ESDF	3 704 838	1 784 042	48.2	1 851 636	869 557	47.0	1 853 202	914 485	49.3
1 VII 2012	ESDF	3 784 197	1 837 163	48.5	1 890 438	893 283	47.3	1 893 759	943 880	49.8
1 VII 2013	ESDF	3 865 256	1 891 865	48.9	1 930 053	917 657	47.5	1 935 203	974 208	50.3
1 VII 2014	ESDF	3 946 311	1 946 567	49.3	1 969 668	942 031	47.8	1 976 643	1 004 536	50.8
Libya - Libye[14]										
1 VII 2008	ESDF	5 490 478	4 839 715	88.1	2 784 122	2 457 272	88.3	2 706 356	2 382 443	88.0
1 VII 2009	ESDF	5 589 289	4 926 097	88.1	2 833 691	2 500 626	88.2	2 755 598	2 425 471	88.0
1 VII 2010	ESDF	5 689 419	5 013 386	88.1	2 883 880	2 544 388	88.2	2 805 538	2 468 998	88.0
1 VII 2011	ESDF	5 790 518	5 101 275	88.1	2 934 512	2 588 402	88.2	2 856 006	2 512 874	88.0
1 VII 2012	ESDF	5 892 239	5 189 460	88.1	2 985 408	2 632 510	88.2	2 906 831	2 556 950	88.0
1 VII 2013	ESDF	5 994 241	5 277 638	88.0	3 036 393	2 676 558	88.1	2 957 849	2 601 081	87.9
1 VII 2014	ESDF	6 096 208	5 365 529	88.0	3 087 301	2 720 398	88.1	3 008 907	2 645 131	87.9
1 VII 2015	ESDF	6 162 356	5 411 529	87.8	3 129 260	2 707 215	86.5	3 033 156	2 704 314	89.2
Malawi										
8 VI 2008	CDFC	13 077 160	2 003 309	15.3	6 358 933	1 014 477	16.0	6 718 227	988 832	14.7
1 VII 2008[4]	ESDF	13 630 164	...	...	6 711 263	...	...	6 918 901	...	...
1 VII 2009[4]	ESDF	13 520 098	...	...	6 585 786	...	...	6 934 312	...	...
1 VII 2010[4]	ESDF	13 947 592	...	...	6 804 310	...	...	7 143 282	...	...
1 VII 2011[4]	ESDF	14 388 550	...	...	7 029 149	...	...	7 359 401	...	...
1 VII 2012[4]	ESDF	14 844 822	...	...	7 261 499	...	...	7 583 323	...	...
1 VII 2013[4]	ESDF	15 316 860	...	...	7 501 653	...	...	7 815 207	...	...
1 VII 2014[4]	ESDF	15 805 239	...	...	7 749 963	...	...	8 055 276	...	...
1 VII 2015[4]	ESDF	16 310 431	...	...	8 006 715	...	...	8 303 716	...	...
1 VII 2016[4]	ESDF	16 832 910	...	...	8 272 152	...	...	8 560 758	...	...
Mali										
1 IV 2009	CDFC	14 528 662	3 274 727	22.5	7 204 990	1 643 671	22.8	7 323 672	1 631 056	22.3
1 VII 2010[15]	ESDF	15 370 000	...	...	7 679 000	...	...	7 691 000	...	...
1 VII 2011[15]	ESDF	15 843 000	...	...	7 919 000	...	...	7 924 000	...	...
1 VII 2012[15]	ESDF	16 312 000	...	...	8 159 000	...	...	8 153 000	...	...
1 VII 2013[15]	ESDF	16 808 000	...	...	8 411 000	...	...	8 397 000	...	...
1 VII 2014[15]	ESDF	17 319 000	...	...	8 671 000	...	...	8 648 000	...	...
1 VII 2015[15]	ESDF	17 819 000	...	...	8 838 000	...	...	8 981 000	...	...
1 VII 2016[15]	ESDF	18 341 000	...	...	9 244 000	...	...	9 097 000	...	...
Mauritania - Mauritanie										
1 VII 2008[4]	ESDF	3 162 338	...	...	1 584 913	...	...	1 577 425	...	...
1 VII 2010[4]	ESDF	3 340 627	...	...	1 678 324	...	...	1 662 303	...	...
1 VII 2011[4]	ESDF	3 296 958	...	...	1 644 572	...	...	1 652 386	...	...
24 III 2013	CDFC	3 460 388[16]	1 697 792	49.1	...	...	...	...	...	...
1 VII 2013[4]	ESDF	3 537 368	...	...	1 743 074	...	...	1 794 294	...	...
1 VII 2015[4]	ESDF	3 720 125	...	...	1 834 735	...	...	1 885 390	...	...
1 VII 2016[4]	ESDF	3 782 701	...	...	1 864 664	...	...	1 918 037	...	...

6. Total and urban population by sex: 2008 - 2017
Population totale et population urbaine selon le sexe : 2008 - 2017 (continued - suite)

Continent, country or area, and date / Continent, pays ou zone et date	Code[a]	Both sexes - Les deux sexes			Male - Masculin			Female - Féminin		
		Total	Urban - Urbaine		Total	Urban - Urbaine		Total	Urban - Urbaine	
			Number Nombre	Percent P.100		Number Nombre	Percent P.100		Number Nombre	Percent P.100
AFRICA - AFRIQUE										
Mauritius - Maurice[17]										
1 VII 2008[18]	ESDJ	1 268 565	531 097	41.9	626 556	260 675	41.6	642 009	270 422	42.1
1 VII 2009[18]	ESDJ	1 275 032	532 591	41.8	629 157	261 041	41.5	645 875	271 550	42.0
1 VII 2010[18]	ESDJ	1 280 924	533 771	41.7	631 692	261 489	41.4	649 232	272 282	41.9
1 VII 2011[19]	ESDJ	1 252 404	509 229	40.7	619 591	249 439	40.3	632 813	259 790	41.1
4 VII 2011	CDFC	1 237 000	496 841	40.2	611 053	243 629	39.9	625 947	253 212	40.5
1 VII 2012[19]	ESDJ	1 255 882	509 177	40.5	621 297	249 422	40.1	634 585	259 755	40.9
1 VII 2013[19]	ESDJ	1 258 653	519 306	41.3	622 861	254 605	40.9	635 792	264 701	41.6
1 VII 2014[19]	ESDJ	1 260 934	518 370	41.1	624 002	254 204	40.7	636 932	264 166	41.5
1 VII 2015[19]	ESDJ	1 262 605	517 482	41.0	624 769	253 796	40.6	637 836	263 686	41.3
1 VII 2016[19]	ESDJ	1 263 473	516 160	40.9	625 206	253 181	40.5	638 267	262 979	41.2
1 VII 2017[19]	ESDJ	1 264 613	514 937	40.7	625 727	252 588	40.4	638 886	262 349	41.1
Mayotte										
21 VIII 2012	CDJC	212 645	...	...	103 173	...	...	109 471	...	...
1 VII 2014[20]	ESDJ	225 308	...	...	109 307	...	...	116 001	...	...
1 I 2015	ESDJ	230 315	...	...	111 736	...	...	118 579	...	...
1 VII 2016*[20]	ESDJ	244 343	...	...	118 536	...	...	125 807	...	...
1 VII 2017*[20]	ESDJ	254 154	...	...	123 297	...	...	130 857	...	...
Morocco - Maroc										
1 VII 2008[21]	ESDF	31 195 000	17 753 000	56.9	15 484 000	8 734 000	56.4	15 711 000	9 019 000	57.4
1 VII 2009[21]	ESDF	31 543 000	18 097 000	57.4	15 657 000	8 891 000	56.8	15 886 000	9 205 000	57.9
1 VII 2010[21]	ESDF	31 894 046	18 446 241	57.8	15 831 463	9 051 145	57.2	16 062 583	9 395 096	58.5
1 VII 2011[21]	ESDF	32 245 120	18 802 208	58.3	16 010 979	9 212 763	57.5	16 234 141	9 589 444	59.1
1 VII 2012[21]	ESDF	32 596 997	19 157 539	58.8	16 190 815	9 373 546	57.9	16 406 182	9 783 993	59.6
1 VII 2013[21]	ESDF	32 950 445	19 512 904	59.2	16 371 475	9 533 742	58.2	16 578 971	9 979 162	60.2
1 VII 2014[22]	ESDJ	33 769 512	20 352 799	60.3	16 825 793	10 068 187	59.8	16 943 719	10 284 612	60.7
1 IX 2014	CDJC	33 848 242	20 432 439	60.4	...	...	...	...	...	...
1 VII 2015[22]	ESDJ	34 124 870	20 751 800	60.8	17 001 717	10 255 722	60.3	17 123 153	10 496 078	61.3
1 VII 2016[22]	ESDJ	34 486 536	21 154 782	61.3	17 180 879	10 445 229	60.8	17 305 657	10 709 553	61.9
1 VII 2017[22]	ESDJ	34 852 121	21 560 585	61.9	17 361 992	10 636 101	61.3	17 490 129	10 924 484	62.5
Mozambique										
1 VII 2008[23]	ESDF	21 207 929	6 472 214	30.5	10 210 267	3 176 209	31.1	10 997 662	3 296 005	30.0
1 VII 2009[23]	ESDF	21 802 866	6 685 108	30.7	10 499 954	3 277 805	31.2	11 302 912	3 407 303	30.1
1 VII 2010[23]	ESDF	22 416 881	6 908 291	30.8	10 799 284	3 384 605	31.3	11 617 597	3 523 686	30.3
1 VII 2011[23]	ESDF	23 049 621	7 141 715	31.0	11 108 128	3 496 582	31.5	11 941 493	3 645 133	30.5
1 VII 2012[23]	ESDF	23 700 715	7 385 294	31.2	11 426 321	3 613 684	31.6	12 274 394	3 771 610	30.7
1 VII 2013[23]	ESDF	24 366 112	7 639 557	31.4	11 751 849	3 736 166	31.8	12 614 263	3 903 391	30.9
1 VII 2014[23]	ESDF	25 041 922	7 905 004	31.6	12 082 782	3 864 267	32.0	12 959 140	4 040 737	31.2
1 VII 2015[23]	ESDF	25 727 911	8 181 475	31.8	12 419 014	3 997 895	32.2	13 308 897	4 183 580	31.4
1 VII 2016[23]	ESDF	26 423 623	8 468 799	32.1	12 760 324	4 136 950	32.4	13 663 299	4 331 849	31.7
1 VII 2017[23]	ESDF	27 128 530	8 766 777	32.3	13 106 447	4 281 319	32.7	14 022 083	4 485 458	32.0
1 VIII 2017*	CDFC	28 861 863	...	...	13 800 857	...	...	15 061 006	...	...
Namibia - Namibie										
1 VII 2008[4]	ESDF	2 065 226	...	...	1 008 115	...	...	1 057 111	...	...
1 VII 2009[4]	ESDF	2 103 761	...	...	1 027 736	...	...	1 076 025	...	...
1 VII 2010[4]	ESDF	2 143 410	...	...	1 047 900	...	...	1 095 510	...	...
1 VII 2011[24]	ESDF	2 116 077	900 163	42.5	1 026 911	439 993	42.8	1 089 166	460 170	42.2
28 VIII 2011	CDFC	2 113 077	903 434	42.8	1 021 912	440 334	43.1	1 091 165	463 100	42.4
1 VII 2012[24]	ESDF	2 155 440	940 825	43.6	1 046 434	459 668	43.9	1 109 006	481 157	43.4
1 VII 2013[24]	ESDF	2 196 086	982 519	44.7	1 066 541	479 844	45.0	1 129 545	502 675	44.5
1 VII 2014[24]	ESDF	2 237 894	1 025 147	45.8	1 087 178	500 469	46.0	1 150 716	524 678	45.6
1 VII 2015[24]	ESDF	2 280 716	1 068 625	46.9	1 108 276	521 496	47.1	1 172 440	547 129	46.7
1 VII 2016[24]	ESDF	2 324 388	1 112 868	47.9	1 129 754	542 893	48.1	1 194 634	569 975	47.7
1 VII 2017[24]	ESDF	2 368 747	1 157 806	48.9	1 151 533	564 615	49.0	1 217 214	593 191	48.7
Niger										
1 VII 2008[4]	ESDJ	14 197 601	2 728 541	19.2	7 088 858	1 366 304	19.3	7 108 743	1 362 237	19.2
1 VII 2009[4]	ESDJ	14 693 113	2 911 006	19.8	7 337 909	1 457 958	19.9	7 355 203	1 453 048	19.8
1 VII 2010[4]	ESDJ	15 203 820	3 104 574	20.4	7 594 624	1 555 201	20.5	7 609 198	1 549 372	20.4
1 VII 2011[4]	ESDJ	15 730 756	3 309 954	21.0	7 859 534	1 658 395	21.1	7 871 221	1 651 559	21.0
1 VII 2012[25]	ESDJ	16 993 563	2 750 279	16.2	8 446 540	1 366 889	16.2	8 547 023	1 383 390	16.2
10 XII 2012	CDFC	16 734 935	...	...	8 183 513	...	...	8 551 422	...	...
1 VII 2013[25]	ESDJ	17 679 758	2 899 523	16.4	8 792 478	1 441 063	16.4	8 887 281	1 458 460	16.4
1 VII 2014[25]	ESDJ	18 389 162	3 010 567	16.4	9 150 266	1 496 252	16.4	9 238 897	1 514 315	16.4

Continent, country or area, and date / Continent, pays ou zone et date	Code[a]	Both sexes - Les deux sexes			Male - Masculin			Female - Féminin		
		Total	Urban - Urbaine		Total	Urban - Urbaine		Total	Urban - Urbaine	
			Number Nombre	Percent P.100		Number Nombre	Percent P.100		Number Nombre	Percent P.100
AFRICA - AFRIQUE										
Niger										
1 VII 2015[25]	ESDJ	19 124 882	3 125 234	16.3	9 521 427	1 553 241	16.3	9 603 456	1 571 993	16.4
1 VII 2016[25]	ESDJ	19 865 066	3 242 161	16.3	9 898 628	1 611 354	16.3	9 966 438	1 630 807	16.4
Nigeria - Nigéria[13]										
1 VII 2008	ESDF	149 713 264	...	...	76 353 765	...	...	73 359 499	...	...
1 VII 2009	ESDF	154 581 566	...	...	78 836 599	...	...	75 744 967	...	...
1 VII 2010	ESDF	159 608 173	...	...	81 400 168	...	...	78 208 005	...	...
1 VII 2011	ESDF	164 798 232	...	...	84 047 098	...	...	80 751 134	...	...
1 VII 2012	ESDF	170 157 060	...	...	86 780 100	...	...	83 376 959	...	...
1 VII 2013	ESDF	175 690 143	...	...	89 601 973	...	...	86 088 170	...	...
1 VII 2014	ESDF	181 403 148	...	...	92 515 605	...	...	88 887 542	...	...
1 VII 2015	ESDF	187 301 926	...	...	95 523 982	...	...	91 777 944	...	...
1 VII 2016	ESDF	193 392 517	...	...	98 630 184	...	...	94 762 333	...	...
Republic of South Sudan - République de Soudan du Sud										
21 IV 2008	CDFC	8 260 490	1 405 186	17.0	4 287 300	754 086	17.6	3 973 190	651 100	16.4
1 VII 2008[26]	ESDF	8 367 688	...	...	4 340 674	...	...	4 027 014	...	...
1 VII 2009[26]	ESDF	8 684 963	...	...	4 495 511	...	...	4 189 452	...	...
1 VII 2010[26]	ESDF	9 005 261	...	...	4 652 459	...	...	4 352 803	...	...
1 VII 2011[26]	ESDF	9 389 376	...	...	4 844 597	...	...	4 544 780	...	...
1 VII 2012[26]	ESDF	9 782 927	...	...	5 041 284	...	...	4 741 642	...	...
1 VII 2013[26]	ESDF	10 182 291	...	...	5 240 881	...	...	4 941 410	...	...
1 VII 2014[26]	ESDF	10 585 044	...	...	5 442 151	...	...	5 142 892	...	...
1 VII 2015[26]	ESDF	11 000 128	...	...	5 649 689	...	...	5 350 439	...	...
1 VII 2016[26]	ESDF	11 425 377	...	...	5 862 347	...	...	5 563 030	...	...
1 VII 2017[26]	ESDF	11 868 209	...	...	6 083 876	...	...	5 784 333	...	...
Reunion - Réunion										
1 I 2008	ESDJ	808 250	...	...	392 041	...	...	416 209	...	...
1 I 2009	ESDJ	816 364	...	...	395 688	...	...	420 676	...	...
1 I 2010	CDJC	821 136	808 540	98.5	398 006	391 623	98.4	423 130	416 917	98.5
1 I 2010	ESDJ	821 136	...	...	397 953	...	...	423 183	...	...
1 I 2011	ESDJ	828 581	...	...	401 139	...	...	427 442	...	...
1 I 2012	ESDJ	833 944	...	...	403 504	...	...	430 440	...	...
1 VII 2013[20]	ESDJ	838 935	...	...	405 519	...	...	433 416	...	...
1 VII 2014[20]	ESDJ	846 747	...	...	409 035	...	...	437 713	...	...
1 I 2015	ESDJ	850 727	...	...	410 762	...	...	439 965	...	...
1 VII 2016*[20]	ESDJ	858 404	...	...	413 922	...	...	444 482	...	...
1 VII 2017*[20]	ESDJ	863 321	...	...	415 947	...	...	447 374	...	...
Rwanda										
1 VII 2008[4]	ESDF	9 831 501	...	...	4 736 104	...	...	5 095 397	...	...
1 VII 2009[4]	ESDF	10 117 029	...	...	4 880 233	...	...	5 236 796	...	...
1 VII 2010[4]	ESDF	10 412 820	1 541 097	14.8	5 029 450	...	...	5 383 371	...	...
1 VII 2011[4]	ESDF	10 718 379	1 564 883	14.6	5 183 505	...	...	5 534 874	...	...
1 VII 2012[25]	ESDF	10 482 641	1 732 175	16.5	5 049 164	889 118	17.6	5 433 477	843 057	15.5
15 VIII 2012	CDFC	10 393 542	1 760 994	16.9	4 981 197	902 501	18.1	5 412 345	858 493	15.9
1 VII 2013[25]	ESDF	10 736 771	1 844 040	17.2	5 178 354	889 382	17.2	5 558 417	954 658	17.2
1 VII 2014[25]	ESDF	10 996 891	1 962 945	17.8	5 310 430	947 912	17.9	5 686 461	1 015 033	17.8
1 VII 2015[25]	ESDF	11 262 564	2 086 390	18.5	5 445 206	1 008 724	18.5	5 817 359	1 077 666	18.5
1 VII 2016[25]	ESDF	11 533 445	2 214 421	19.2	5 582 519	1 071 844	19.2	5 950 925	1 142 578	19.2
1 VII 2017[25]	ESDF	11 809 300	2 347 098	19.9	5 722 258	1 137 299	19.9	6 087 041	1 209 799	19.9
Saint Helena ex. dep. - Sainte-Hélène sans dép.										
10 II 2008	CDFC	4 257	...	...	2 165	...	...	2 092	...	...
1 VII 2008	ESDF	3 981	...	...	2 022	...	...	1 959	...	...
1 VII 2012	ESDF	4 123	...	...	2 094	...	...	2 029	...	...
31 XII 2013	ESDF	4 211	...	...	2 139	...	...	2 072	...	...
7 II 2016[27]	CDJC	4 534	...	...	2 396	...	...	2 138	...	...

6. Total and urban population by sex: 2008 - 2017
Population totale et population urbaine selon le sexe : 2008 - 2017 (continued - suite)

Continent, country or area, and date / Continent, pays ou zone et date	Code[a]	Both sexes - Les deux sexes Total	Urban - Urbaine Number Nombre	Urban - Urbaine Percent P.100	Male - Masculin Total	Urban - Urbaine Number Nombre	Urban - Urbaine Percent P.100	Female - Féminin Total	Urban - Urbaine Number Nombre	Urban - Urbaine Percent P.100
AFRICA - AFRIQUE										
Saint Helena: Ascension - Sainte-Hélène: Ascension										
1 VII 2008 ....ESDJ		702	...	...	397	...	...	305	...	...
Saint Helena: Tristan da Cunha - Sainte-Hélène: Tristan da Cunha[28]										
31 XII 2009 ....ESDF		262[29]	...	...	123	...	...	139	...	...
Sao Tome and Principe - Sao Tomé-et-Principe										
1 VII 2008 ....ESDF		157 847	...	...	77 641	...	...	80 206	...	...
1 VII 2009 ....ESDF		160 820	...	...	79 027	...	...	81 794	...	...
1 VII 2010 ....ESDF		163 783	...	...	80 409	...	...	83 375	...	...
1 VII 2011 ....ESDF		166 728	...	...	81 783	...	...	84 945	...	...
13 V 2012 ....CDJC		178 739	119 781	67.0	88 867	58 710	66.1	89 872	61 071	68.0
1 VII 2013[30] ....ESDJ		182 328	122 398	67.1	90 577	60 805	67.1	91 751	61 593	67.1
1 VII 2014[30] ....ESDJ		186 024	125 121	67.3	92 347	62 113	67.3	93 677	63 008	67.3
1 VII 2015[30] ....ESDJ		189 819	127 922	67.4	94 173	63 464	67.4	95 646	64 457	67.4
1 VII 2016[30] ....ESDJ		193 712	130 798	67.5	96 053	64 857	67.5	97 659	65 941	67.5
1 VII 2017[30] ....ESDJ		197 700	133 748	67.7	97 988	66 291	67.7	99 712	67 457	67.7
Senegal - Sénégal										
31 XII 2008 ....ESDJ		11 841 137	4 815 214	40.7	5 828 711	2 387 209	41.0	6 012 426	2 428 005	40.4
31 XII 2009 ....ESDJ		12 171 264	4 949 461	40.7	5 991 214	2 453 764	41.0	6 180 050	2 495 697	40.4
31 XII 2010 ....ESDJ		12 509 434	5 086 978	40.7	6 157 675	2 521 940	41.0	6 351 759	2 565 038	40.4
31 XII 2011 ....ESDJ		12 841 702	6 086 966	47.4	6 350 673	3 010 218	47.4	6 491 029	3 076 748	47.4
1 VII 2013[4] ....ESDJ		13 508 715	...	...	6 735 420	...	...	6 773 295	...	...
19 XI 2013 ....CDFC		13 357 492	...	...	6 658 089	...	...	6 699 403	...	...
1 VII 2014[4] ....ESDJ		13 926 253	...	...	6 941 357	...	...	6 961 847	...	...
1 VII 2015[4] ....ESDJ		14 356 575	...	...	7 153 656	...	...	7 202 919	...	...
1 VII 2016[4] ....ESDJ		14 799 859	...	...	7 372 487	...	...	7 427 372	...	...
1 VII 2017[4] ....ESDJ		15 256 346	...	...	7 597 938	...	...	7 658 408	...	...
Seychelles										
1 VII 2008 ....ESDF		86 956	...	...	44 999	...	...	41 957	...	...
1 VII 2009 ....ESDF		87 298	...	...	45 022	...	...	42 276	...	...
1 VII 2010 ....ESDF		89 770	...	...	45 907	...	...	43 863	...	...
26 VIII 2010 ....CDFC		90 945	...	...	46 912	...	...	44 033	...	...
1 VII 2011 ....ESDF		87 441	...	...	43 127	...	...	44 314	...	...
1 VII 2012 ....ESDF		88 303	...	...	43 313	...	...	44 990	...	...
1 VII 2013 ....ESDF		89 949	...	...	44 735	...	...	45 214	...	...
1 VII 2014 ....ESDF		91 359	...	...	45 278	...	...	46 081	...	...
1 VII 2015 ....ESDF		93 419	...	...	46 322	...	...	47 097	...	...
1 VII 2016 ....ESDF		94 677	...	...	47 343	...	...	47 334	...	...
1 VII 2017 ....ESDF		95 843	...	...	48 793	...	...	47 050	...	...
Sierra Leone										
1 VII 2008 ....ESDF		5 473 530	2 142 918	39.2	2 653 490	1 058 523	39.9	2 820 040	1 084 395	38.5
1 VII 2009 ....ESDF		5 607 930	2 221 331	39.6	2 719 034	1 097 256	40.4	2 888 896	1 124 075	38.9
1 VII 2010 ....ESDF		5 746 800	2 304 955	40.1	2 786 577	1 138 563	40.9	2 960 045	1 166 392	39.4
1 VII 2011 ....ESDF		5 890 080	2 394 041	40.6	2 856 755	1 182 568	41.4	3 033 325	1 211 473	39.9
1 VII 2012 ....ESDF		6 037 660	2 489 123	41.2	2 928 862	1 229 535	42.0	3 108 798	1 259 588	40.5
5 XII 2015 ....CDFC		7 092 113	2 905 097	41.0	3 490 978	1 438 591	41.2	3 601 135	1 466 506	40.7
South Africa - Afrique du Sud										
1 VII 2008 ....ESDF		49 557 573	...	...	24 078 593	...	...	25 478 980	...	...
1 VII 2009 ....ESDF		50 255 813	...	...	24 449 834	...	...	25 805 979	...	...
1 VII 2010 ....ESDF		50 979 432	...	...	24 832 080	...	...	26 147 353	...	...
1 VII 2011 ....ESDF		51 729 345	...	...	25 225 720	...	...	26 503 626	...	...
10 X 2011 ....CDFC		51 770 560	32 559 331	62.9	25 188 791	...	...	26 581 769	...	...
1 VII 2012 ....ESDF		52 506 515	...	...	25 631 161	...	...	26 875 354	...	...
1 VII 2013 ....ESDF		53 311 956	...	...	26 048 829	...	...	27 263 126	...	...
1 VII 2014 ....ESDF		54 146 735	...	...	26 479 167	...	...	27 667 567	...	...
1 VII 2015 ....ESDF		55 011 977	...	...	26 922 639	...	...	28 089 338	...	...
1 VII 2016 ....ESDF		55 908 865	...	...	27 379 728	...	...	28 529 137	...	...
1 VII 2017 ....ESDF		56 521 948	...	...	27 620 642	...	...	28 901 306	...	...

Continent, country or area, and date / Continent, pays ou zone et date	Code[a]	Both sexes - Les deux sexes			Male - Masculin			Female - Féminin		
		Total	Urban - Urbaine		Total	Urban - Urbaine		Total	Urban - Urbaine	
			Number Nombre	Percent P.100		Number Nombre	Percent P.100		Number Nombre	Percent P.100
AFRICA - AFRIQUE										
Sudan - Soudan										
21 IV 2008	CDFC	30 894 000	...	...	15 786 677	...	...	15 107 323	...	...
1 VII 2008	ESDF	30 978 758	10 314 730	33.3	15 790 134	5 350 451	33.9	15 188 624	4 964 279	32.7
1 VII 2009	ESDF	31 956 791	10 860 950	34.0	16 275 239	5 531 361	34.0	15 681 552	5 329 589	34.0
1 VII 2010	ESDF	32 961 966	11 296 966	34.3	16 774 288	5 749 007	34.3	16 187 678	5 547 959	34.3
1 VII 2011	ESDF	33 997 538	11 749 240	34.6	17 289 105	5 974 957	34.6	16 708 434	5 774 283	34.6
1 VII 2012	ESDF	35 064 299	12 218 313	34.8	17 820 009	6 209 462	34.8	17 244 290	6 008 851	34.8
1 VII 2013	ESDF	36 162 516	12 704 550	35.1	18 367 086	6 452 691	35.1	17 795 430	6 251 858	35.1
1 VII 2014	ESDF	37 292 376	13 208 281	35.4	18 930 385	6 704 798	35.4	18 361 991	6 503 483	35.4
1 VII 2015	ESDF	38 454 040	13 729 842	35.7	19 509 961	6 965 944	35.7	18 944 080	6 763 898	35.7
1 VII 2016	ESDF	39 647 621	14 269 540	36.0	20 105 842	7 236 276	36.0	19 541 779	7 033 264	36.0
Togo										
6 XI 2010	CDJC	6 191 155	2 334 495	37.7	3 009 095	1 131 533	37.6	3 182 060	1 202 962	37.8
Tunisia - Tunisie										
1 VII 2008	ESDF	10 351 582	6 836 588	66.0	5 156 280[31]	...	...	5 172 580[31]	...	...
1 VII 2009	ESDF	10 458 095	6 937 505	66.3	5 224 946	...	...	5 233 149	...	...
1 VII 2010	ESDF	10 565 704	7 039 718	66.6	5 275 893	...	...	5 289 811	...	...
1 VII 2011	ESDF	10 674 420	7 084 742	66.4	5 327 337	...	...	5 347 083	...	...
1 VII 2012	ESDF	10 784 255	7 248 086	67.2	5 379 282	...	...	5 404 972	...	...
1 VII 2013	ESDF	10 895 219	7 354 268	67.5	5 431 735	...	...	5 463 485	...	...
23 IV 2014	CDFC	10 982 754	7 437 671	67.7	5 472 338	3 713 527	67.9	5 510 416	3 724 144	67.6
1 VII 2014	ESDF	11 007 326	7 461 796	67.8	5 484 581	...	...	5 522 745	...	...
1 VII 2015	ESDF	11 154 372	7 574 564	67.9	5 557 966	...	...	5 596 404	...	...
1 VII 2016	ESDF	11 304 482	7 671 696[32]	67.9	5 620 629	...	...	5 683 853	...	...
1 VII 2017	ESDF	11 446 316	7 797 248	68.1	...	...	...	...	...	...
Uganda - Ouganda										
1 VII 2008	ESDF	29 592 600	4 372 000	14.8	14 383 200	2 095 700	14.6	15 209 400	2 276 300	15.0
1 VII 2009	ESDF	30 661 300	4 524 900	14.8	14 933 900	2 171 400	14.5	15 727 400	2 353 500	15.0
1 VII 2010	ESDF	31 784 600	...	...	15 516 600	...	...	16 268 000	...	...
1 VII 2011	ESDF	32 939 800	...	...	16 118 600	...	...	16 821 200	...	...
1 VII 2012	ESDF	34 131 400	...	...	16 741 400	...	...	17 390 000	...	...
1 VII 2014[8]	ESDF	34 141 299	...	...	16 594 490	...	...	17 546 809	...	...
27 VIII 2014	CDFC	34 634 650	8 438 009	24.4	16 897 849	4 042 324	23.9	17 736 801	4 395 685	24.8
1 VII 2015[8]	ESDF	35 492 100	...	...	17 337 600	...	...	18 154 500	...	...
1 VII 2016[8]	ESDF	36 560 700	...	...	17 882 300	...	...	18 678 400	...	...
1 VII 2017[8]	ESDF	37 673 800	...	...	18 449 000	...	...	19 224 800	...	...
United Republic of Tanzania - République Unie de Tanzanie										
1 VII 2008[33]	ESDF	40 667 794	10 419 287	25.6	19 970 944	5 139 187	25.7	20 696 850	5 280 100	25.5
1 VII 2009[33]	ESDF	41 915 880	10 892 350	26.0	20 604 730	5 375 260	26.1	21 311 150	5 517 090	25.9
1 VII 2010[33]	ESDF	43 187 823	11 378 015	26.3	21 252 423	5 618 133	26.4	21 935 400	5 759 882	26.3
1 VII 2011[33]	ESDF	44 484 857	11 875 395	26.7	21 914 229	5 867 287	26.8	22 570 628	6 008 108	26.6
1 VII 2012[33]	ESDF	45 798 475	12 386 841	27.0	22 585 634	6 123 839	27.1	23 212 841	6 263 002	27.0
26 VIII 2012[34]	CDFC	44 928 923	13 305 004	29.6	21 869 990	6 407 396	29.3	23 058 933	6 897 608	29.9
1 VII 2013[25]	ESDF	46 356 279	...	...	22 585 059	...	...	23 771 220	...	...
1 VII 2014[25]	ESDF	47 831 361	...	...	23 323 466	...	...	24 507 895	...	...
1 VII 2015[25]	ESDF	49 359 408	...	...	24 088 086	...	...	25 271 322	...	...
1 VII 2016[25]	ESDF	50 941 672	...	...	24 879 894	...	...	26 061 778	...	...
1 VII 2017[25]	ESDF	52 554 628	...	...	25 687 154	...	...	26 867 474	...	...
Zambia - Zambie										
16 X 2010	CDFC	12 526 314	5 021 022	40.1	6 117 253	2 452 904	40.1	6 409 061	2 568 118	40.1
1 VII 2011[35]	ESDJ	13 718 722	5 563 212	40.6	6 786 799	2 757 061	40.6	6 931 923	2 806 151	40.5
1 VII 2012[35]	ESDJ	14 145 327	5 780 936	40.9	6 997 492	2 863 581	40.9	7 147 835	2 917 355	40.8
1 VII 2013[35]	ESDJ	14 580 290	6 005 218	41.2	7 212 648	2 973 485	41.2	7 367 642	3 031 733	41.1
1 VII 2014[35]	ESDJ	15 023 315	6 235 786	41.5	7 432 123	3 086 651	41.5	7 591 192	3 149 135	41.5
1 VII 2015[35]	ESDJ	15 473 905	6 472 258	41.8	7 655 669	3 202 882	41.8	7 818 236	3 269 376	41.8
1 VII 2016[35]	ESDJ	15 933 883	6 715 149	42.1	7 884 009	3 322 364	42.1	8 049 874	3 392 785	42.1
1 VII 2017[35]	ESDJ	16 405 229	6 964 965	42.5	8 117 939	3 445 261	42.4	8 287 290	3 519 704	42.5
Zimbabwe										
1 VII 2008[33]	ESDF	12 150 000	3 495 205	28.8	5 885 184	1 691 434	28.7	6 264 816	1 803 752	28.8
1 VII 2009[33]	ESDF	13 667 894	...	...	6 642 551	...	...	7 025 344	...	...
17 VIII 2012	CDFC	13 061 239	4 284 145	32.8	6 280 539	2 039 224	32.5	6 780 700	2 244 921	33.1
1 VII 2013[30]	ESDF	13 368 620	4 424 783[32]	33.1	6 428 233	2 108 204[32]	32.8	6 940 389	2 316 578[32]	33.4
1 VII 2014[30]	ESDF	13 652 297	4 535 793[32]	33.2	6 564 085	2 162 369[32]	32.9	7 088 214	2 373 427[32]	33.5

Continent, country or area, and date / Continent, pays ou zone et date	Code[a]	Both sexes - Les deux sexes			Male - Masculin			Female - Féminin		
			Urban - Urbaine			Urban - Urbaine			Urban - Urbaine	
		Total	Number Nombre	Percent P.100	Total	Number Nombre	Percent P.100	Total	Number Nombre	Percent P.100
Zimbabwe										
1 VII 2015[30] .... ESDF		13 943 242	4 648 970[32]	33.3	6 703 559	2 217 591[32]	33.1	7 239 681	2 431 379[32]	33.6
1 VII 2016[30] .... ESDF		14 240 168	4 763 408[32]	33.5	6 846 020	2 273 413[32]	33.2	7 394 149	2 489 990[32]	33.7
1 VII 2017[30] .... ESDF		14 542 235	4 878 395[32]	33.5	6 991 066	2 329 497[32]	33.3	7 551 172	2 548 898[32]	33.8
AMERICA, NORTH - AMÉRIQUE DU NORD										
Anguilla										
11 V 2011 .... CDFC		13 572	...	...	6 707	...	...	6 865	...	...
Antigua and Barbuda - Antigua-et-Barbuda										
27 V 2011 .... CDJC		85 567	...	...	40 986	...	...	44 581	...	...
Aruba										
1 VII 2008 .... ESDJ		100 916	...	...	47 890			53 027	...	...
1 VII 2009 .... ESDJ		101 604	...	...	48 291	...	...	53 312	...	...
1 VII 2010 .... ESDJ		101 873	...	...	48 419	...	...	53 454	...	...
29 IX 2010 .... CDJC		101 484	...	...	48 241	...	...	53 243	...	...
1 VII 2011 .... ESDJ		102 809	...	...	48 801	...	...	54 008	...	...
1 VII 2012 .... ESDJ		104 574	...	...	49 558	...	...	55 016	...	...
1 VII 2013 .... ESDJ		106 380	...	...	50 329	...	...	56 051	...	...
1 VII 2014 .... ESDJ		107 820	...	...	50 990	...	...	56 830	...	...
1 VII 2015 .... ESDJ		109 222	...	...	51 682	...	...	57 540	...	...
1 VII 2016 .... ESDJ		110 352	...	...	52 251	...	...	58 101	...	...
1 VII 2017 .... ESDJ		110 848	...	...	52 544	...	...	58 304	...	...
Bahamas										
1 VII 2008[36] .... ESDF		338 300	...	...	164 800	...	...	173 500	...	...
1 VII 2009[36] .... ESDF		342 400	...	...	166 800	...	...	175 600	...	...
3 V 2010 .... CDJC		351 461	...	...	170 257	...	...	181 204	...	...
1 VII 2010[35] .... ESDJ		351 500	...	...	170 200	...	...	181 300	...	...
1 VII 2011[35] .... ESDJ		355 020	...	...	171 810	...	...	183 210	...	...
1 VII 2012[35] .... ESDJ		358 600	...	...	173 460	...	...	185 140	...	...
1 VII 2013[35] .... ESDJ		362 230	...	...	175 120	...	...	187 110	...	...
1 VII 2014[35] .... ESDJ		365 920	...	...	176 810	...	...	189 110	...	...
1 VII 2015[35] .... ESDJ		369 670	...	...	178 530	...	...	191 140	...	...
1 VII 2016[35] .... ESDJ		373 480	...	...	180 280	...	...	193 200	...	...
1 VII 2017[35] .... ESDJ		377 360	...	...	182 300	...	...	195 060	...	...
Barbados - Barbade										
1 VII 2008 .... ESDF		274 848	...	...	132 786	...	...	142 062	...	...
1 VII 2009 .... ESDF		275 441	...	...	133 133	...	...	142 308	...	...
1 V 2010[37] .... CDJC		277 821	...	...	133 018	...	...	144 803	...	...
1 VII 2010 .... ESDJ		277 758	...	...	133 018	...	...	144 740	...	...
1 VII 2011 .... ESDJ		277 622	...	...	133 119	...	...	144 503	...	...
1 VII 2012 .... ESDJ		277 668	...	...	133 355	...	...	144 313	...	...
1 VII 2013 .... ESDJ		277 492	...	...	133 369	...	...	144 123	...	...
1 VII 2014 .... ESDJ		277 199	...	...	133 343	...	...	143 856	...	...
1 VII 2015 .... ESDJ		274 633	...	...	131 146	...	...	143 487	...	...
Belize										
1 VII 2008 .... ESDF		306 809	138 716	45.2	153 570	67 647	44.0	153 239	71 069	46.4
1 VII 2009 .... ESDF		315 082	142 447	45.2	157 622	69 450	44.1	157 460	72 997	46.4
12 V 2010 .... CDJC		322 453	145 832	45.2	161 227	71 087	44.1	161 226	74 745	46.4
1 VII 2010 .... ESDJ		323 598	146 323	45.2	161 800	71 328	44.1	161 798	74 995	46.4
1 VII 2011 .... ESDJ		332 084	149 955	45.2	166 043	73 110	44.0	166 041	76 845	46.3
1 VII 2012 .... ESDJ		340 792	153 683	45.1	170 397	74 938	44.0	170 395	78 745	46.2
1 VII 2013 .... ESDJ		349 728	157 508	45.0	174 865	76 815	43.9	174 863	80 693	46.1
1 VII 2014 .... ESDJ		358 899	161 434	45.0	179 451	78 740	43.9	179 448	82 694	46.1
1 VII 2015 .... ESDJ		368 310	165 463	44.9	184 157	80 717	43.8	184 153	84 746	46.0
1 VII 2016 .... ESDJ		377 968	169 598	44.9	188 986	82 746	43.8	188 982	86 852	46.0
1 VII 2017 .... ESDJ		387 879	173 841	44.8	193 942	84 827	43.7	193 937	89 014	45.9
Bermuda - Bermudes										
1 VII 2008[36] .... ESDJ		64 209	...	...	30 644	...	...	33 565	...	...
1 VII 2009[36] .... ESDJ		64 395	...	...	30 704	...	...	33 691	...	...
20 V 2010[38] .... CDJC		64 237	64 237	100.0	30 858	30 858	100.0	33 379	33 379	100.0
1 VII 2010[11] .... ESDJ		64 129	...	...	30 792	...	...	33 337	...	...
1 VII 2011[11] .... ESDJ		63 193	...	...	30 218	...	...	32 975	...	...
1 VII 2012[11] .... ESDJ		62 408	...	...	29 819	...	...	32 589	...	...
1 VII 2013[11] .... ESDJ		61 954	...	...	29 587	...	...	32 367	...	...
1 VII 2014[11] .... ESDJ		61 777	...	...	29 499	...	...	32 278	...	...

Continent, country or area, and date / Continent, pays ou zone et date	Code[a]	Both sexes - Les deux sexes Total	Urban - Urbaine Number Nombre	Urban - Urbaine Percent P.100	Male - Masculin Total	Urban - Urbaine Number Nombre	Urban - Urbaine Percent P.100	Female - Féminin Total	Urban - Urbaine Number Nombre	Urban - Urbaine Percent P.100
AMERICA, NORTH - AMÉRIQUE DU NORD										
Bermuda - Bermudes										
1 VII 2015[11]	ESDJ	61 735	...	...	29 480	...	...	32 255	...	...
20 V 2016	CDJC	63 779	63 779	100.0	30 690	30 690	100.0	33 089	33 089	100.0
1 VII 2016[11]	ESDJ	61 695	...	...	29 463	...	...	32 232	...	...
1 VII 2017[11]	ESDJ	61 658	...	...	29 447	...	...	32 211	...	...
British Virgin Islands - Îles Vierges britanniques										
12 VII 2010	CDFC	28 054	...	...	13 820	...	...	14 234	...	...
Canada										
1 VII 2008[39]	ESDJ	33 245 773	...	...	16 473 545	...	...	16 772 228	...	...
1 VII 2009[39]	ESDJ	33 628 571	...	...	16 663 222	...	...	16 965 349	...	...
1 VII 2010[39]	ESDJ	34 005 274	...	...	16 847 961	...	...	17 157 313	...	...
2 V 2011	CDJC	33 476 690	27 147 190	81.1	16 414 225	13 190 225	80.4	17 062 455	13 956 960	81.8
1 VII 2011[40]	ESDJ	34 342 780	...	...	17 015 959	...	...	17 326 821	...	...
1 VII 2012[40]	ESDJ	34 750 545	...	...	17 227 368	...	...	17 523 177	...	...
1 VII 2013[40]	ESDJ	35 152 370	...	...	17 430 375	...	...	17 721 995	...	...
1 VII 2014[41]	ESDJ	35 535 348	...	...	17 623 557	...	...	17 911 791	...	...
1 VII 2015[41]	ESDJ	35 832 513	...	...	17 767 811	...	...	18 064 702	...	...
10 V 2016[42]	CDJC	35 151 730	28 575 665	81.3	17 264 200	13 912 045	80.6	17 887 530	14 663 615	82.0
1 VII 2016[41]	ESDJ	36 264 604	...	...	17 984 435	...	...	18 280 169	...	...
1 VII 2017*[43]	ESDJ	36 708 083	...	...	18 207 841	...	...	18 500 242	...	...
Cayman Islands - Îles Caïmanes										
31 XII 2008	ESDJ	57 009	...	...	28 264	...	...	28 745	...	...
31 XII 2009	ESDJ	56 005	...	...	27 840	...	...	28 165	...	...
10 X 2010[44]	CDJC	55 036	55 036	100.0	27 218	27 218	100.0	27 818	27 818	100.0
31 XII 2010	ESDJ	55 036	...	...	27 219	...	...	27 817	...	...
31 XII 2011	ESDJ	55 517	...	...	27 454	...	...	28 063	...	...
31 XII 2012	ESDJ	56 732	...	...	27 753	...	...	28 979	...	...
31 XII 2013	ESDJ	55 747	...	...	27 133	...	...	28 614	...	...
31 XII 2014	ESDJ	58 238	...	...	28 322	...	...	29 916	...	...
31 XII 2015	ESDJ	60 413	...	...	30 264	...	...	30 149	...	...
31 XII 2017	ESDJ	63 415	...	...	32 212	...	...	31 203	...	...
Costa Rica										
1 VII 2008[45]	ESDJ	4 533 162	2 671 667	58.9	2 246 474	1 299 940	57.9	2 286 688	1 371 727	60.0
1 VII 2009[45]	ESDJ	4 620 482	2 722 273	58.9	2 291 886	1 325 468	57.8	2 328 596	1 396 805	60.0
1 VII 2010[46]	ESDJ	4 538 307	3 304 248[47]	72.8	2 206 526	1 579 816[47]	71.6	2 331 781	1 724 432[47]	74.0
30 V 2011	CDJC	4 301 712	3 130 871	72.8	2 106 063	1 509 161	71.7	2 195 649	1 621 710	73.9
1 VII 2011[46]	ESDJ	4 592 346	3 343 241	72.8	2 238 615	1 603 354	71.6	2 353 731	1 739 887	73.9
1 VII 2012[46]	ESDJ	4 651 166	3 384 925	72.8	2 266 220	1 621 617	71.6	2 384 946	1 763 308	73.9
1 VII 2013[46]	ESDJ	4 711 986	3 427 548	72.7	2 276 708	1 624 941	71.4	2 435 278	1 802 607	74.0
1 VII 2014[46]	ESDJ	4 772 098	3 469 802	72.7	2 325 438	1 662 288	71.5	2 446 660	1 807 514	73.9
1 VII 2015[48]	ESDJ	4 833 752	3 512 683	72.7	2 350 223	1 683 770	71.6	2 483 529	1 828 913	73.6
1 VII 2016[49]	ESDJ	4 889 762	3 551 728	72.6	2 373 531	1 703 473	71.8	2 516 231	1 848 255	73.5
1 VII 2017[50]	ESDJ	4 946 700	3 592 070	72.6	2 405 636	1 722 499	71.6	2 541 064	1 869 571	73.6
Cuba										
1 VII 2008	ESDJ	11 181 012	8 426 393	75.4	5 597 673	4 146 862	74.1	5 583 339	4 279 531	76.6
1 VII 2009	ESDJ	11 174 474	8 420 630	75.4	5 594 504	4 145 111	74.1	5 579 971	4 275 519	76.6
1 VII 2010	ESDJ	11 171 443	8 416 524	75.3	5 592 729	4 143 388	74.1	5 578 714	4 273 136	76.6
1 VII 2011	ESDJ	11 171 679	8 409 543	75.3	5 592 332	4 140 377	74.0	5 579 347	4 269 166	76.5
1 VII 2012	ESDJ	11 174 287	8 494 128	76.0	5 583 306	4 159 342	74.5	5 590 981	4 334 786	77.5
14 IX 2012	CDJC	11 167 325	8 575 189	76.8	5 570 825	4 177 485	75.0	5 596 500	4 397 704	78.6
1 VII 2013	ESDJ	11 191 608	8 596 991	76.8	5 580 810	4 186 436	75.0	5 610 798	4 410 555	78.6
1 VII 2014	ESDJ	11 224 190	8 625 144	76.8	5 595 379	4 199 578	75.1	5 628 811	4 425 566	78.6
1 VII 2015	ESDJ	11 238 661	8 639 191	76.9	5 600 904	4 205 871	75.1	5 637 757	4 433 320	78.6
1 VII 2016	ESDJ	11 239 114	8 644 181	76.9	5 599 279	4 207 382	75.1	5 639 835	4 436 798	78.7
1 VII 2017	ESDJ	11 230 142	8 642 754	77.0	5 591 525	4 204 316	75.2	5 638 617	4 438 438	78.7
Curaçao										
1 VII 2008[51]	ESDJ	145 882	...	...	66 746	...	...	79 136	...	...
1 VII 2009[51]	ESDJ	146 833	...	...	67 237	...	...	79 596	...	...
1 VII 2010[51]	ESDJ	148 703	...	...	68 065	...	...	80 639	...	...
26 III 2011	CDJC	150 563	...	...	68 848	...	...	81 715	...	...
1 VII 2011[51]	ESDJ	150 831	...	...	68 910	...	...	81 921	...	...

Continent, country or area, and date / Continent, pays ou zone et date	Code[a]	Both sexes - Les deux sexes			Male - Masculin			Female - Féminin		
		Total	Urban - Urbaine		Total	Urban - Urbaine		Total	Urban - Urbaine	
			Number Nombre	Percent P.100		Number Nombre	Percent P.100		Number Nombre	Percent P.100
AMERICA, NORTH - AMÉRIQUE DU NORD										
Curaçao										
1 VII 2012[3]	ESDJ	152 088	...	...	69 490	...	...	82 598	...	...
1 VII 2013[3]	ESDJ	153 822	...	...	70 342	...	...	83 480	...	...
1 VII 2014[3]	ESDJ	155 909	...	...	71 269	...	...	84 640	...	...
1 VII 2015[3]	ESDJ	157 980	...	...	72 187	...	...	85 794	...	...
1 VII 2016[3]	ESDJ	159 663	...	...	72 990	...	...	86 674	...	...
1 VII 2017[3]	ESDJ	160 175	...	...	73 246	...	...	86 929	...	...
Dominica - Dominique										
1 VII 2008	ESDF	70 726	...	...	35 602	...	...	35 124	...	...
1 VII 2009	ESDF	70 747	...	...	35 811	...	...	34 936	...	...
1 VII 2010	ESDF	70 730	...	...	35 604	...	...	35 126	...	...
14 V 2011	CDFC	68 913	...	...	34 973	...	...	33 940	...	...
1 VII 2011	ESDF	70 755	...	...	35 762	...	...	34 992	...	...
1 VII 2012	ESDF	71 042	...	...	36 053	...	...	34 989	...	...
1 VII 2013	ESDF	71 221	...	...	36 144	...	...	35 077	...	...
1 VII 2014	ESDF	71 575	...	...	36 324	...	...	35 251	...	...
Dominican Republic - République dominicaine										
1 VII 2008	ESDJ	9 279 602	6 594 497	71.1	4 649 902	3 235 238	69.6	4 629 700	3 359 259	72.6
1 VII 2009	ESDJ	9 380 152	6 788 782	72.4	4 699 042	3 331 179	70.9	4 681 110	3 457 603	73.9
1 VII 2010[4]	ESDJ	9 478 612	6 992 189	73.8	4 747 103	3 431 480	72.3	4 731 509	3 560 709	75.3
1 XII 2010	CDJC	9 445 281	7 013 575	74.3	4 739 038	3 449 122	72.8	4 706 243	3 564 453	75.7
1 VII 2011[4]	ESDJ	9 580 139	7 172 502	74.9	4 796 628	3 520 702	73.4	4 783 511	3 651 800	76.3
1 VII 2012[4]	ESDJ	9 680 963	7 348 975	75.9	4 845 755	3 608 025	74.5	4 835 208	3 740 950	77.4
1 VII 2013[4]	ESDJ	9 784 680	7 524 149	76.9	4 896 319	3 694 713	75.5	4 888 361	3 829 436	78.3
1 VII 2014[4]	ESDJ	9 883 486	7 691 885	77.8	4 944 386	3 777 718	76.4	4 939 100	3 914 167	79.2
1 VII 2015[4]	ESDJ	9 980 243	7 854 203	78.7	4 991 398	3 858 029	77.3	4 988 845	3 996 174	80.1
1 VII 2016[4]	ESDJ	10 075 045	8 011 084	79.5	5 037 329	3 935 569	78.1	5 037 716	4 075 515	80.9
1 VII 2017[4]	ESDJ	10 169 172	8 163 504	80.3	5 082 876	4 010 852	78.9	5 086 296	4 152 652	81.6
El Salvador[52]										
1 VII 2008	ESDJ	6 124 705	3 828 004	62.5	2 895 210	1 779 210	61.5	3 229 495	2 048 794	63.4
1 VII 2009	ESDJ	6 152 558	3 890 523	63.2	2 903 737	1 806 310	62.2	3 248 821	2 084 213	64.2
1 VII 2010	ESDJ	6 183 002	3 954 803	64.0	2 913 743	1 834 400	63.0	3 269 259	2 120 404	64.9
1 VII 2011	ESDJ	6 216 143	4 019 742	64.7	2 925 284	1 862 924	63.7	3 290 858	2 156 818	65.5
1 VII 2012	ESDJ	6 251 495	4 086 880	65.4	2 938 123	1 892 642	64.4	3 313 372	2 194 238	66.2
1 VII 2013	ESDJ	6 288 899	4 156 007	66.1	2 952 174	1 923 447	65.2	3 336 726	2 232 560	66.9
1 VII 2014	ESDJ	6 328 196	...	...	2 967 351	...	...	3 360 845	...	...
1 VII 2015	ESDJ	6 460 271	4 502 693	69.7	3 042 036	2 119 867	69.7	3 418 235	2 382 826	69.7
1 VII 2016	ESDJ	6 520 675	4 590 491	70.4	3 070 065	2 161 168	70.4	3 450 610	2 429 323	70.4
1 VII 2017	ESDJ	6 581 940	4 678 816	71.1	3 098 633	2 202 778	71.1	3 483 307	2 476 038	71.1
Greenland - Groenland[53]										
1 I 2008	CDJC	56 462	...	...	29 885	...	...	26 577	...	...
1 VII 2008	ESDJ	56 328	47 103	83.6	29 847	24 790	83.1	26 481	22 313	84.3
1 VII 2009	ESDJ	56 323	47 230	83.9	29 873	24 865	83.2	26 451	22 366	84.6
1 VII 2010	ESDJ	56 534	47 646	84.3	29 939	25 045	83.7	26 595	22 601	85.0
1 VII 2011	ESDJ	56 682	48 045	84.8	29 992	25 233	84.1	26 690	22 812	85.5
1 VII 2012	ESDJ	56 810	48 224	84.9	30 105	25 331	84.1	26 705	22 893	85.7
1 VII 2013	ESDJ	56 483	48 221	85.4	29 867	25 333	84.8	26 616	22 888	86.0
1 VII 2014	ESDJ	56 295	48 232	85.7	29 742	25 320	85.1	26 553	22 912	86.3
1 VII 2015	ESDJ	56 114	48 284	86.0	29 634	25 329	85.5	26 480	22 955	86.7
1 VII 2016	ESDJ	56 186	48 447	86.2	29 701	25 436	85.6	26 485	23 011	86.9
1 VII 2017	ESDJ	56 171	48 527	86.4	29 651	25 435	85.8	26 520	23 092	87.1
Grenada - Grenade										
1 VII 2008	ESDF	105 298	...	...	52 655	...	...	52 643	...	...
1 VII 2009	ESDF	105 175	...	...	52 720	...	...	52 455	...	...
1 VII 2010	ESDF	105 038	...	...	52 788	...	...	52 250	...	...
12 V 2011	CDFC	106 667	...	...	53 898	...	...	52 769	...	...
1 VII 2011	ESDF	106 667	...	...	53 898	...	...	52 769	...	...
1 VII 2012	ESDF	107 599	...	...	54 435	...	...	53 164	...	...
1 VII 2013	ESDF	108 580	...	...	54 926	...	...	53 654	...	...
1 VII 2014	ESDF	109 374	...	...	55 185	...	...	54 189	...	...
1 VII 2015	ESDF	110 096	...	...	55 543	...	...	54 553	...	...

Continent, country or area, and date / Continent, pays ou zone et date	Code[a]	Both sexes - Les deux sexes			Male - Masculin			Female - Féminin		
		Total	Urban - Urbaine		Total	Urban - Urbaine		Total	Urban - Urbaine	
			Number Nombre	Percent P.100		Number Nombre	Percent P.100		Number Nombre	Percent P.100
AMERICA, NORTH - AMÉRIQUE DU NORD										
Grenada - Grenade										
1 VII 2016	ESDF	110 910	...	...	55 955	...	...	54 955	...	...
1 VII 2017	ESDF	111 467	...	...	56 222	...	...	55 245	...	...
Guadeloupe[54]										
1 VII 2008	ESDJ	401 669	...	...	188 128	...	...	213 541	...	...
1 VII 2009	ESDJ	402 455	...	...	187 890	...	...	214 565	...	...
1 I 2010	CDJC	403 355	397 070	98.4	187 932	184 752	98.3	215 423	212 318	98.6
1 VII 2010	ESDJ	403 995	...	...	187 847	...	...	216 148	...	...
1 VII 2011	ESDJ	403 975	...	...	187 410	...	...	216 565	...	...
1 VII 2012	ESDJ	402 717	...	...	186 558	...	...	216 159	...	...
1 VII 2013	ESDJ	401 153	...	...	185 375	...	...	215 778	...	...
1 VII 2014	ESDJ	399 088	...	...	183 941	...	...	215 147	...	...
1 VII 2015	ESDJ	397 001	...	...	182 561	...	...	214 440	...	...
1 VII 2016	ESDJ	394 826	...	...	181 161	...	...	213 666	...	...
1 VII 2017*	ESDJ	392 172	...	...	179 512	...	...	212 661	...	...
Guatemala[33]										
1 VII 2008	ESDJ	13 677 815	...	...	6 673 533	...	...	7 004 282	...	...
1 VII 2009	ESDJ	14 017 057	...	...	6 836 849	...	...	7 180 208	...	...
1 VII 2010	ESDJ	14 361 666	...	...	7 003 337	...	...	7 358 328	...	...
1 VII 2011	ESDJ	14 713 763	...	...	7 173 966	...	...	7 539 797	...	...
1 VII 2012	ESDJ	15 073 375	...	...	7 352 869	...	...	7 720 506	...	...
1 VII 2013	ESDJ	15 438 384	...	...	7 903 145	...	...	7 535 238	...	...
1 VII 2014	ESDJ	15 806 675	...	...	8 087 279	...	...	7 719 396	...	...
1 VII 2015	ESDJ	16 176 133	...	...	8 272 469	...	...	7 903 664	...	...
Haiti - Haïti[55]										
1 VII 2008	ESDJ	9 761 927	...	...	4 831 621	...	...	4 930 306	...	...
1 VII 2009	ESDJ	9 923 243	...	...	4 912 515	...	...	5 010 728	...	...
1 VII 2010	ESDJ	10 085 214	4 817 666	47.8	4 993 731	2 321 608	46.5	5 091 483	2 496 059	49.0
1 VII 2011	ESDJ	10 248 306	...	...	5 075 517	...	...	5 172 789	...	...
1 VII 2012	ESDJ	10 413 211	5 154 940	49.5	5 158 254	2 495 108	48.4	5 254 957	2 659 832	50.6
1 VII 2013	ESDJ	10 579 230	...	...	5 241 572	...	...	5 337 658	...	...
1 VII 2014	ESDJ	10 745 665	...	...	5 325 099	...	...	5 420 566	...	...
1 VII 2015	ESDJ	10 911 819	...	...	5 408 465	...	...	5 503 354	...	...
Honduras										
1 VII 2008[56]	ESDF	7 706 907	...	...	3 800 300	...	...	3 906 607	...	...
1 VII 2009[56]	ESDF	7 876 662	...	...	3 882 957	...	...	3 993 705	...	...
1 VII 2010[56]	ESDF	8 045 990	...	...	3 965 430	...	...	4 080 560	...	...
10 VIII 2013	CDFC	8 303 771	4 480 746	54.0	4 052 316	2 116 113	52.2	4 251 456	2 364 633	55.6
1 VII 2014[5]	ESDF	8 432 153	...	...	4 113 061	...	...	4 319 092	...	...
1 VII 2015[5]	ESDF	8 576 532	...	...	4 181 657	...	...	4 394 875	...	...
Jamaica - Jamaïque										
1 VII 2008	ESDJ	2 687 241	1 396 470	52.0	1 324 277	666 761	50.3	1 362 964	729 709	53.5
1 VII 2009	ESDJ	2 695 583	...	...	1 328 124	...	...	1 367 460	...	...
1 VII 2010	ESDJ	2 702 314	...	...	1 324 134	...	...	1 378 180	...	...
4 IV 2011[57]	CDJC	2 697 983	1 454 153	53.9	1 334 533	700 957	52.5	1 363 450	753 196	55.2
1 VII 2011	ESDJ	2 699 838	...	...	1 335 466	...	...	1 364 372	...	...
1 VII 2012	ESDJ	2 707 805	...	...	1 339 740	...	...	1 368 065	...	...
1 VII 2013	ESDJ	2 714 669	...	...	1 343 798	...	...	1 370 871	...	...
1 VII 2014	ESDJ	2 720 554	...	...	1 346 711	...	...	1 373 843	...	...
1 VII 2015	ESDJ	2 725 288	...	...	1 349 294	...	...	1 375 994	...	...
1 VII 2016	ESDJ	2 728 151	...	...	1 350 950	...	...	1 377 201	...	...
1 VII 2017	ESDJ	2 728 915	...	...	1 351 375	...	...	1 377 540	...	...
Martinique										
1 I 2008	ESDJ	397 693	...	...	184 437	...	...	213 256	...	...
1 I 2009	ESDJ	396 404	...	...	183 655	...	...	212 749	...	...
1 I 2010	CDJC	394 173	380 973	96.7	182 073	175 573	96.4	212 100	205 400	96.8
1 I 2010	ESDJ	394 173	...	...	182 110	...	...	212 063	...	...
1 I 2011	ESDJ	392 291	...	...	180 676	...	...	211 615	...	...
1 I 2012	ESDJ	388 364	...	...	178 824	...	...	209 540	...	...
1 I 2013	ESDJ	385 551	...	...	177 955	...	...	207 596	...	...
1 I 2014	ESDJ	383 911	...	...	177 502	...	...	206 409	...	...
1 I 2015	ESDJ	380 877	...	...	176 077	...	...	204 800	...	...
1 I 2016*	ESDJ	378 043	...	...	174 799	...	...	203 244	...	...
1 I 2017*	ESDJ	374 780	...	...	173 293	...	...	201 487	...	...

Continent, country or area, and date / Continent, pays ou zone et date	Code[a]	Both sexes - Les deux sexes			Male - Masculin			Female - Féminin		
		Total	Urban - Urbaine		Total	Urban - Urbaine		Total	Urban - Urbaine	
			Number Nombre	Percent P.100		Number Nombre	Percent P.100		Number Nombre	Percent P.100

AMERICA, NORTH - AMÉRIQUE DU NORD

Mexico - Mexique

1 VII 2008 .... ESDJ		111 299 015	...	...	54 373 653	...	...	56 925 362	...	...
1 VII 2009 .... ESDJ		112 852 594	...	...	55 144 845	...	...	57 707 749	...	...
12 VI 2010[58] ..... CDFC		112 336 538	86 287 410	76.8	54 855 231	41 946 540	76.5	57 481 307	44 340 870	77.1
1 VII 2010[4] .... ESDJ		114 255 555	82 629 456	72.3	55 801 919	...	...	58 453 636	...	...
1 VII 2011[4] .... ESDJ		115 682 868	83 726 767	72.4	56 519 798	...	...	59 163 070	...	...
1 VII 2012[4] .... ESDJ		117 053 750	84 776 446	72.4	57 174 268	...	...	59 879 482	...	...
1 VII 2013[4] .... ESDJ		118 395 054	85 792 843	72.5	57 810 955	...	...	60 584 099	...	...
1 VII 2014[4] .... ESDJ		119 713 204	86 782 031	72.5	58 435 900	...	...	61 277 304	...	...
1 VII 2015[4] .... ESDJ		121 005 816	87 743 091	72.5	59 046 837	...	...	61 958 979	...	...
1 VII 2016[4] .... ESDJ		122 273 473	88 677 252	72.5	59 644 308	...	...	62 629 165	...	...
1 VII 2017[4] .... ESDJ		123 518 270	89 586 802	72.5	60 230 241	...	...	63 288 029	...	...

Montserrat

12 V 2011 .... CDJC		4 922	...	...	2 546	...	...	2 376	...	...
1 VII 2016 .... ESDJ		5 045	...	...	2 596	...	...	2 449	...	...

Nicaragua

1 VII 2008 .... ESDJ		5 668 866	3 206 205	56.6	2 809 918	1 542 386	54.9	2 858 948	1 663 819	58.2
1 VII 2009 .... ESDJ		5 742 316	3 259 955	56.8	2 844 244	1 569 555	55.2	2 898 072	1 690 400	58.3
1 VII 2010 .... ESDJ		5 815 524	...	...	2 878 523	...	...	2 937 001	...	...
1 VII 2011 .... ESDJ		5 996 619	...	...	2 966 111	...	...	3 030 508	...	...
1 VII 2012 .... ESDJ		6 071 045	...	...	3 000 778	...	...	3 070 267	...	...
1 VII 2013 .... ESDJ		6 134 270	...	...	3 029 990	...	...	3 104 280	...	...
1 VII 2014 .... ESDJ		6 198 154	...	...	3 059 810	...	...	3 138 344	...	...
1 VII 2015 .... ESDJ		6 262 703	3 630 420	58.0	3 090 448	1 755 776	56.8	3 172 255	1 874 644	59.1
1 VII 2016 .... ESDJ		6 327 927	3 676 119	58.1	3 122 048	1 776 327	56.9	3 205 879	1 899 792	59.3
1 VII 2017 .... ESDJ		6 393 824	3 722 549	58.2	3 154 465	1 797 179	57.0	3 239 359	1 925 370	59.4

Panama

1 VII 2008[59] ..... ESDF		3 537 986	...	...	1 780 140	...	...	1 757 846	...	...
1 VII 2009[59] ..... ESDF		3 600 000	...	...	1 810 794	...	...	1 789 206	...	...
16 V 2010 .... CDFC		3 405 813	...	...	1 712 584	...	...	1 693 229	...	...
1 VII 2010[11] ..... ESDF		3 661 835	2 385 445	65.1	1 841 305	1 171 489	63.6	1 820 530	1 213 956	66.7
1 VII 2011[11] ..... ESDF		3 723 821	2 449 917	65.8	1 871 749	1 203 430	64.3	1 852 072	1 246 487	67.3
1 VII 2012[11] ..... ESDF		3 787 511	2 514 402	66.4	1 903 085	1 235 377	64.9	1 884 426	1 279 025	67.9
1 VII 2013[11] ..... ESDF		3 850 735	2 578 868	67.0	1 934 264	1 267 319	65.5	1 916 471	1 311 549	68.4
1 VII 2014[11] ..... ESDF		3 913 275	2 643 353	67.5	1 965 087	1 299 262	66.1	1 948 188	1 344 091	69.0
1 VII 2015[11] ..... ESDF		3 975 404	2 707 838	68.1	1 995 695	1 331 207	66.7	1 979 709	1 376 631	69.5
1 VII 2016[11] ..... ESDF		4 037 043	2 772 324	68.7	2 026 044	1 363 153	67.3	2 010 999	1 409 171	70.1
1 VII 2017[11] ..... ESDF		4 098 135	2 836 794	69.2	2 056 085	1 395 090	67.9	2 042 050	1 441 704	70.6

Puerto Rico - Porto Rico[60]

1 VII 2008[51] ..... ESDJ		3 760 866	...	...	1 803 341	...	...	1 957 525	...	...
1 VII 2009[51] ..... ESDJ		3 740 410	...	...	1 793 049	...	...	1 947 361	...	...
1 IV 2010 .... CDJC		3 725 789	3 493 256	93.8	1 785 171	...	...	1 940 618	...	...
1 VII 2010[61] ..... ESDJ		3 721 208	...	...	1 782 619	...	...	1 938 589	...	...
1 VII 2011[3] ...... ESDJ		3 678 732	...	...	1 763 441	...	...	1 915 291	...	...
1 VII 2012[3] ...... ESDJ		3 634 488	...	...	1 739 072	...	...	1 895 416	...	...
1 VII 2013[3] ...... ESDJ		3 593 077	...	...	1 720 280	...	...	1 872 797	...	...
1 VII 2014[3] ...... ESDJ		3 534 874	...	...	1 688 886	...	...	1 845 988	...	...
1 VII 2015[3] ...... ESDJ		3 473 181	...	...	1 656 338	...	...	1 816 843	...	...
1 VII 2016[3] ...... ESDJ		3 411 307	...	...	1 623 672	...	...	1 787 635	...	...

Saint Kitts and Nevis - Saint-Kitts-et-Nevis

1 VII 2008* .... ESDF		51 300	...	...	25 085	...	...	26 215	...	...
1 VII 2009* .... ESDF		51 970	...	...	25 415	...	...	26 555	...	...
1 VII 2010* .... ESDF		52 650	...	...	25 750	...	...	26 900	...	...
15 V 2011* .... CDFC		46 398	...	...	22 846	...	...	23 552	...	...

Saint Lucia - Sainte-Lucie

1 VII 2008 .... ESDF		170 331	...	...	83 478	...	...	86 853	...	...
1 VII 2009 .... ESDF		172 370	...	...	84 465	...	...	87 905	...	...
10 V 2010 .... CDJC		165 770	...	...	83 502	...	...	82 268	...	...
1 VII 2011 .... ESDF		167 366	...	...	82 925	...	...	84 441	...	...
1 VII 2012 .... ESDF		169 170	...	...	83 861	...	...	85 309	...	...

Continent, country or area, and date Continent, pays ou zone et date	Code[a]	Both sexes - Les deux sexes			Male - Masculin			Female - Féminin		
		Total	Urban - Urbaine		Total	Urban - Urbaine		Total	Urban - Urbaine	
			Number Nombre	Percent P.100		Number Nombre	Percent P.100		Number Nombre	Percent P.100
AMERICA, NORTH - **AMÉRIQUE DU NORD**										
Saint Lucia - Sainte-Lucie										
1 VII 2013 ....ESDF	ESDF	170 925	...	...	84 768	...	...	86 158	...	...
1 VII 2014 ....ESDF	ESDF	172 623	...	...	85 639	...	...	86 984	...	...
Saint Vincent and the Grenadines - Saint-Vincent-et-les Grenadines										
1 VII 2008 ....ESDJ	ESDJ	109 639	49 870	45.5	55 770	...	...	53 869	...	...
1 VII 2009 ....ESDJ	ESDJ	109 727	49 911	45.5	55 814	...	...	53 912	...	...
1 VII 2010 ....ESDJ	ESDJ	109 815	49 951	45.5	55 859	...	...	53 956	...	...
1 VII 2011 ....ESDJ	ESDJ	109 903	49 991	45.5	55 904	...	...	53 999	...	...
12 VI 2012 ....CDJC	CDJC	109 991	50 926	46.3	56 419	...	...	53 572	...	...
1 VII 2013 ....ESDJ	ESDJ	110 079	50 967	46.3	56 464	...	...	53 615	...	...
1 VII 2014 ....ESDJ	ESDJ	110 167	51 008	46.3	56 509	...	...	53 658	...	...
1 VII 2015 ....ESDJ	ESDJ	110 255	51 048	46.3	56 555	...	...	53 701	...	...
Sint Maarten (Dutch part) - Saint-Martin (partie néerlandaise)										
1 VII 2008 ....ESDF	ESDF	40 461	...	...	19 632	...	...	20 829	...	...
1 VII 2009 ....ESDF	ESDF	39 172	...	...	18 918	...	...	20 254	...	...
1 VII 2010 ....ESDF	ESDF	35 526	...	...	16 927	...	...	18 600	...	...
9 IV 2011 ....CDFC	CDFC	33 609	...	...	15 868	...	...	17 741	...	...
1 VII 2011 ....ESDF	ESDF	33 436	...	...	15 772	...	...	17 656	...	...
1 VII 2012 ....ESDF	ESDF	34 670	...	...	16 656	...	...	18 005	...	...
1 VII 2013 ....ESDF	ESDF	36 611	...	...	17 910	...	...	18 701	...	...
1 I 2014 ....ESDF	ESDF	37 132	...	...	18 159	...	...	18 973	...	...
Trinidad and Tobago - Trinité-et-Tobago										
1 VII 2008[18] ....ESDF	ESDF	1 308 587	...	...	656 257	...	...	652 330	...	...
1 VII 2009[18] ....ESDF	ESDF	1 310 106	...	...	657 018	...	...	653 088	...	...
1 VII 2010[18] ....ESDF	ESDF	1 317 714	...	...	660 822	...	...	656 892	...	...
9 I 2011 ....CDJC	CDJC	1 328 019	...	...	666 305	...	...	661 714	...	...
1 VII 2012[19] ....ESDF	ESDF	1 335 194	...	...	669 905	...	...	665 289	...	...
1 VII 2013[19] ....ESDF	ESDF	1 340 557	...	...	672 596	...	...	667 961	...	...
1 VII 2014[19] ....ESDF	ESDF	1 345 343	...	...	674 997	...	...	670 346	...	...
1 VII 2015[19] ....ESDF	ESDF	1 349 667	...	...	677 166	...	...	672 501	...	...
1 VII 2016[19] ....ESDF	ESDF	1 353 895	...	...	679 288	...	...	674 607	...	...
1 VII 2017[19] ....ESDF	ESDF	1 356 633	...	...	680 661	...	...	675 972	...	...
Turks and Caicos Islands - Îles Turques et Caïques										
1 VII 2009 ....ESDJ	ESDJ	*36 000*	...	...	*18 810*	...	...	*17 190*	...	...
1 VII 2010 ....ESDJ	ESDJ	*34 500*	...	...	*17 810*	...	...	*16 690*	...	...
1 VII 2011 ....ESDJ	ESDJ	*33 500*	...	...	*17 160*	...	...	*16 340*	...	...
25 I 2012*[62] ....CDJC	CDJC	31 458	...	...	16 037	...	...	15 421	...	...
1 VII 2012 ....ESDJ	ESDJ	*32 199*	...	...	*16 365*	...	...	*15 834*	...	...
1 VII 2013 ....ESDJ	ESDJ	*33 677*	...	...	*17 132*	...	...	*16 545*	...	...
1 VII 2014 ....ESDJ	ESDJ	*35 168*	...	...	*17 907*	...	...	*17 261*	...	...
1 VII 2015 ....ESDJ	ESDJ	*36 689*	...	...	*18 689*	...	...	*18 000*	...	...
1 VII 2016 ....ESDJ	ESDJ	*37 910*	...	...	*19 169*	...	...	*18 741*	...	...
1 VII 2017 ....ESDJ	ESDJ	*39 792*	...	...	*20 296*	...	...	*19 496*	...	...
United States of America - États-Unis d'Amérique										
1 VII 2008[63] ....ESDJ	ESDJ	304 093 966	...	...	149 489 951	...	...	154 604 015	...	...
1 VII 2009[63] ....ESDJ	ESDJ	306 771 529	...	...	150 807 454	...	...	155 964 075	...	...
1 IV 2010 ....CDJC	CDJC	308 745 538	249 253 271	80.7	151 781 326	121 698 595	80.2	156 964 212	127 554 676	81.3
1 VII 2010[64] ....ESDJ	ESDJ	309 348 193	...	...	152 088 743	...	...	157 259 450	...	...
1 VII 2011[64] ....ESDJ	ESDJ	311 663 358	...	...	153 263 360	...	...	158 399 998	...	...
1 VII 2012[64] ....ESDJ	ESDJ	313 998 379	...	...	154 467 180	...	...	159 531 199	...	...
1 VII 2013[64] ....ESDJ	ESDJ	316 204 908	...	...	155 589 564	...	...	160 615 344	...	...
1 VII 2014[64] ....ESDJ	ESDJ	318 563 456	...	...	156 780 062	...	...	161 783 394	...	...
1 VII 2015[64] ....ESDJ	ESDJ	320 896 618	...	...	157 960 035	...	...	162 936 583	...	...
1 VII 2016[64] ....ESDJ	ESDJ	323 127 513	...	...	159 078 923	...	...	164 048 590	...	...

Continent, country or area, and date / Continent, pays ou zone et date	Code[a]	Both sexes - Les deux sexes			Male - Masculin			Female - Féminin		
		Total	Urban - Urbaine		Total	Urban - Urbaine		Total	Urban - Urbaine	
			Number Nombre	Percent P.100		Number Nombre	Percent P.100		Number Nombre	Percent P.100
AMERICA, NORTH - AMÉRIQUE DU NORD										
United States Virgin Islands - Îles Vierges américaines[60]										
1 VII 2008 ....ESDJ		109 840	...	...	52 045	...	...	57 795	...	...
1 IV 2010 ....CDJC		106 405	...	...	50 854	...	...	55 551	...	...
AMERICA, SOUTH - AMÉRIQUE DU SUD										
Argentina - Argentine										
1 VII 2008 ....ESDF		39 745 613	36 137 648	90.9	19 465 305	17 597 280	90.4	20 280 308	18 540 368	91.4
1 VII 2009 ....ESDF		40 134 425	36 553 965	91.1	19 657 086	17 810 843	90.6	20 477 339	18 743 122	91.5
1 VII 2010[35] ....ESDF		40 788 453	37 126 653	91.0	19 940 704	17 996 224	90.2	20 847 749	19 130 429	91.8
27 X 2010 ....CDFC		40 117 096	36 467 245	90.9	19 523 766	17 596 022	90.1	20 593 330	18 871 223	91.6
1 VII 2011[35] ....ESDF		41 261 490	37 600 508	91.1	20 180 791	18 236 611	90.4	21 080 699	19 363 897	91.9
1 VII 2012[35] ....ESDF		41 733 271	38 073 305	91.2	20 420 391	18 476 577	90.5	21 312 880	19 596 728	91.9
1 VII 2013[35] ....ESDF		42 202 935	38 544 203	91.3	20 659 037	18 715 667	90.6	21 543 898	19 828 536	92.0
1 VII 2014[35] ....ESDF		42 669 500	39 021 268	91.5	20 896 203	18 958 322	90.7	21 773 297	20 062 946	92.1
1 VII 2015[35] ....ESDF		43 131 966	39 487 935	91.6	21 131 346	19 195 446	90.8	22 000 620	20 292 489	92.2
1 VII 2016[35] ....ESDF		43 590 368	39 951 022	91.7	21 364 470	19 430 772	90.9	22 225 898	20 520 250	92.3
1 VII 2017[35] ....ESDF		44 044 811	40 410 715	91.7	21 595 623	19 664 392	91.1	22 449 188	20 746 323	92.4
Bolivia (Plurinational State of) - Bolivie (État plurinational de)										
1 VII 2008 ....ESDF		9 709 958	...	...	4 889 348	...	...	4 820 610	...	...
1 VII 2009 ....ESDF		9 870 229	...	...	4 973 094	...	...	4 897 135	...	...
1 VII 2010 ....ESDF		10 030 501	...	...	5 056 056	...	...	4 974 445	...	...
1 VII 2011 ....ESDF		10 190 775	...	...	5 138 206	...	...	5 052 569	...	...
1 VII 2012 ....ESDF		10 351 118	6 965 568	67.3	5 219 006	3 437 451	65.9	5 132 112	3 528 117	68.7
21 XI 2012 ....CDFC		10 059 856	6 788 962	67.5	5 019 447	3 314 824	66.0	5 040 409	3 474 138	68.9
1 VII 2013 ....ESDF		10 507 789	7 110 575	67.7	5 297 727	3 511 796	66.3	5 210 062	3 598 779	69.1
1 VII 2014 ....ESDF		10 665 841	7 256 749	68.0	5 376 880	3 586 449	66.7	5 288 961	3 670 300	69.4
1 VII 2015 ....ESDF		10 825 013	7 403 841	68.4	5 456 332	3 661 290	67.1	5 368 681	3 742 551	69.7
1 VII 2016 ....ESDF		10 985 059	7 551 625	68.7	5 535 975	3 736 216	67.5	5 449 084	3 815 409	70.0
1 VII 2017 ....ESDF		11 145 770	7 699 908	69.1	5 615 713	3 811 135	67.9	5 530 057	3 888 773	70.3
Brazil - Brésil										
1 VII 2008[65] ....ESDJ		191 532 439	160 383 924	83.7	94 816 963	...	...	96 715 476	...	...
1 VII 2009[65] ....ESDJ		193 543 969	162 670 274	84.0	95 776 055	...	...	97 767 914	...	...
1 VII 2010[65] ....ESDJ		195 497 797	164 920 459	84.4	96 706 703	...	...	98 791 094	...	...
31 VII 2010 ....CDJC		190 755 799	160 925 804	84.4	93 406 990	77 710 179	83.2	97 348 809	83 215 625	85.5
1 VII 2011[65] ....ESDJ		197 397 018	167 096 245	84.6	97 610 297	...	...	99 786 721	...	...
1 VII 2012[65] ....ESDJ		199 242 462	169 230 105	84.9	98 487 258	...	...	100 755 204	...	...
1 VII 2013[65] ....ESDJ		201 032 714	171 317 079	85.2	99 336 858	...	...	101 695 856	...	...
1 VII 2014[65] ....ESDJ		202 768 562	173 358 764	85.5	100 159 507	...	...	102 609 055	...	...
1 VII 2015[65] ....ESDJ		204 450 649	175 355 103	85.8	100 955 522	...	...	103 495 127	...	...
1 VII 2016[65] ....ESDJ		206 081 432	177 309 126	86.0	101 726 102	...	...	104 355 330	...	...
1 VII 2017[65] ....ESDJ		207 660 929	179 217 279	86.3	102 471 274	...	...	105 189 655	...	...
Chile - Chili										
1 VII 2008 ....ESDF		16 763 470	14 570 311	86.9	8 297 819	7 131 097	85.9	8 465 651	7 439 214	87.9
1 VII 2009 ....ESDF		16 928 873	14 719 246	86.9	8 379 571	7 204 720	86.0	8 549 302	7 514 526	87.9
1 VII 2010 ....ESDF		17 094 275	14 868 172	87.0	8 461 327	7 278 342	86.0	8 632 948	7 589 830	87.9
1 VII 2011 ....ESDF		17 248 450	15 006 226	87.0	8 536 904	7 346 185	86.1	8 711 546	7 660 041	87.9
1 VII 2012 ....ESDF		17 402 630	15 144 277	87.0	8 612 483	7 414 026	86.1	8 790 147	7 730 251	87.9
1 VII 2013 ....ESDF		17 556 815	15 282 334	87.0	8 688 067	7 481 874	86.1	8 868 748	7 800 460	88.0
1 VII 2014 ....ESDF		17 819 054	15 559 039	87.3	8 819 725	7 628 149	86.5	8 999 329	7 930 890	88.1
1 VII 2015 ....ESDF		18 006 407	15 729 803	87.4	8 911 940	7 714 356	86.6	9 094 467	8 015 447	88.1
1 VII 2016 ....ESDF		18 191 884	15 898 145	87.4	9 003 254	7 799 463	86.6	9 188 630	8 098 682	88.1
1 VII 2017 ....ESDF		18 373 917	16 063 564	87.4	9 092 950	7 883 072	86.7	9 280 967	8 180 492	88.1
Colombia - Colombie[66]										
1 VII 2008 ....ESDJ		44 451 147	33 396 380	75.1	21 942 355	16 100 320	73.4	22 508 792	17 296 060	76.8
1 VII 2009 ....ESDJ		44 978 832	33 892 634	75.4	22 203 708	16 343 820	73.6	22 775 124	17 548 814	77.1
1 VII 2010 ....ESDJ		45 509 584	34 388 013	75.6	22 466 660	16 587 100	73.8	23 042 924	17 800 913	77.3
1 VII 2011 ....ESDJ		46 044 601	34 883 399	75.8	22 731 299	16 830 795	74.0	23 313 302	18 052 604	77.4

6. Total and urban population by sex: 2008 - 2017
Population totale et population urbaine selon le sexe : 2008 - 2017 (continued - suite)

Continent, country or area, and date / Continent, pays ou zone et date	Code[a]	Both sexes - Les deux sexes			Male - Masculin			Female - Féminin		
		Total	Urban - Urbaine		Total	Urban - Urbaine		Total	Urban - Urbaine	
			Number Nombre	Percent P.100		Number Nombre	Percent P.100		Number Nombre	Percent P.100
AMERICA, SOUTH - AMÉRIQUE DU SUD										
Colombia - Colombie[66]										
1 VII 2012 ....ESDJ		46 581 823	35 377 138	75.9	22 997 087	17 073 806	74.2	23 584 736	18 303 332	77.6
1 VII 2013 ....ESDJ		47 121 089	35 869 246	76.1	23 264 039	17 315 981	74.4	23 857 050	18 553 265	77.8
1 VII 2014 ....ESDJ		47 661 787	36 359 268	76.3	23 531 670	17 556 826	74.6	24 130 117	18 802 442	77.9
1 VII 2015 ....ESDJ		48 203 405	36 846 935	76.4	23 799 679	17 796 724	74.8	24 403 726	19 050 211	78.1
1 VII 2016 ....ESDJ		48 747 708	37 332 955	76.6	24 069 035	18 035 960	74.9	24 678 673	19 296 995	78.2
1 VII 2017 ....ESDJ		49 291 609	37 816 051	76.7	24 337 747	18 273 530	75.1	24 953 862	19 542 521	78.3
Ecuador - Équateur										
1 VII 2008[67] ....ESDF		14 472 881	9 064 267	62.6	7 192 128	4 449 107	61.9	7 280 753	4 615 160	63.4
1 VII 2009[67] ....ESDF		14 738 472	9 236 112	62.7	7 316 020	4 528 987	61.9	7 422 452	4 707 125	63.4
1 VII 2010[67] ....ESDF		15 012 228	9 412 612	62.7	7 443 875	4 611 039	61.9	7 568 353	4 801 573	63.4
28 XI 2010 ....CDFC		14 483 499	9 090 786	62.8	7 177 683	4 451 434	62.0	7 305 816	4 639 352	63.5
1 VII 2011[67] ....ESDF		15 266 431	9 596 628	62.9	7 567 676	4 700 620	62.1	7 698 755	4 896 008	63.6
1 VII 2012[67] ....ESDF		15 520 973	9 780 650	63.0	7 691 912	4 790 437	62.3	7 829 061	4 990 213	63.7
1 VII 2013[67] ....ESDF		15 774 749	9 963 884	63.2	7 815 935	4 880 045	62.4	7 958 814	5 083 839	63.9
1 VII 2014[67] ....ESDF		16 027 466	10 145 875	63.3	7 939 552	4 969 197	62.6	8 087 914	5 176 678	64.0
1 VII 2015[67] ....ESDF		16 278 844	10 326 384	63.4	8 062 610	5 057 750	62.7	8 216 234	5 268 634	64.1
1 VII 2016[67] ....ESDF		16 528 730	10 505 180	63.6	8 184 970	5 145 594	62.9	8 343 760	5 359 586	64.2
1 VII 2017[67] ....ESDF		16 776 977	10 682 148	63.7	8 306 557	5 232 565	63.0	8 470 420	5 449 583	64.3
Falkland Islands (Malvinas) - Îles Falkland (Malvinas)[68]										
15 IV 2012 ....CDFC		2 840	...	...	1 491	...	...	1 349	...	...
French Guiana - Guyane française										
1 I 2008 ....ESDJ		219 266	...	...	108 673	...	...	110 593	...	...
1 I 2009 ....ESDJ		224 469	...	...	111 201	...	...	113 268	...	...
1 I 2010 ....CDJC		229 040	201 042	87.8	113 599	98 933	87.1	115 441	102 109	88.5
1 I 2010 ....ESDJ		229 040	201 042	87.8	113 599	98 933	87.1	115 441	102 109	88.5
1 I 2011 ....ESDJ		237 549	...	...	117 732	...	...	119 817	...	...
1 I 2012 ....ESDJ		239 648	...	...	119 538	...	...	120 110	...	...
1 I 2013 ....CDJC		244 118	...	...	121 653	...	...	122 465	...	...
1 I 2013 ....ESDJ		244 118	...	...	121 653	...	...	122 465	...	...
1 I 2014 ....ESDJ		252 338	...	...	125 189	...	...	127 149	...	...
1 I 2015 ....ESDJ		257 348	...	...	127 840	...	...	129 508	...	...
1 I 2016 ....ESDJ		262 527	...	...	130 596	...	...	131 931	...	...
1 I 2017 ....ESDJ		274 153	...	...	136 093	...	...	138 060	...	...
Guyana										
1 VII 2008 ....ESDF		774 443	...	...	387 649	...	...	386 794	...	...
1 VII 2009 ....ESDF		753 227	...	...	377 759	...	...	375 468	...	...
1 VII 2010 ....ESDF		752 113	...	...	377 267	...	...	374 846	...	...
1 VII 2011 ....ESDF		750 663	...	...	376 596	...	...	374 067	...	...
1 VII 2012 ....ESDF		746 724	...	...	371 731	...	...	374 993	...	...
15 IX 2012 ....CDFC		746 955	...	...	371 805	...	...	375 150	...	...
1 VII 2013 ....ESDF		746 263	...	...	371 609	...	...	374 654	...	...
1 VII 2014 ....ESDF		745 873	...	...	371 519	...	...	374 355	...	...
1 VII 2015 ....ESDF		744 945	...	...	371 149	...	...	373 796	...	...
1 VII 2016 ....ESDF		743 458	...	...	370 491	...	...	372 967	...	...
1 VII 2017 ....ESDF		741 365	...	...	369 520	...	...	371 845	...	...
Paraguay[69]										
1 VII 2008 ....ESDF		6 071 781	3 486 807	57.4	3 068 356	1 704 209	55.5	3 003 425	1 782 599	59.4
1 VII 2009 ....ESDF		6 168 757	3 569 718	57.9	3 116 847	1 744 890	56.0	3 051 910	1 824 828	59.8
1 VII 2010 ....ESDF		6 265 877	3 652 713	58.3	3 165 316	1 785 556	56.4	3 100 561	1 867 157	60.2
1 VII 2011 ....ESDF		6 363 276	3 738 905	58.8	3 213 839	1 827 856	56.9	3 149 438	1 911 049	60.7
1 VII 2012 ....ESDF		6 461 041	3 825 311	59.2	3 262 466	1 870 215	57.3	3 198 575	1 955 096	61.1
1 VII 2013 ....ESDF		6 559 027	3 911 850	59.6	3 311 123	1 912 591	57.8	3 247 904	1 999 259	61.6
1 VII 2014 ....ESDF		6 657 232	3 998 524	60.1	3 359 806	1 954 982	58.2	3 297 426	2 043 541	62.0
1 VII 2015 ....ESDF		6 755 756	4 085 396	60.5	3 408 566	1 997 419	58.6	3 347 190	2 087 977	62.4
1 VII 2016 ....ESDF		6 854 536	4 174 834	60.9	3 457 365	2 041 139	59.0	3 397 170	2 133 695	62.8
1 VII 2017 ....ESDF		6 953 646	4 264 473	61.3	3 506 242	2 084 904	59.5	3 447 404	2 179 568	63.2
Peru - Pérou[52]										
30 VI 2008 ....ESDF		28 807 034	20 995 699	72.9	14 443 858	10 386 799	71.9	14 363 176	10 608 900	73.9
30 VI 2009 ....ESDF		29 132 013	21 398 222	73.5	14 605 206	10 584 348	72.5	14 526 807	10 813 874	74.4
30 VI 2010 ....ESDF		29 461 933	21 805 837	74.0	14 768 901	10 784 345	73.0	14 693 032	11 021 492	75.0

Continent, country or area, and date / Continent, pays ou zone et date	Code[a]	Both sexes - Les deux sexes			Male - Masculin			Female - Féminin		
		Total	Urban - Urbaine		Total	Urban - Urbaine		Total	Urban - Urbaine	
			Number Nombre	Percent P.100		Number Nombre	Percent P.100		Number Nombre	Percent P.100
AMERICA, SOUTH - AMÉRIQUE DU SUD										
Peru - Pérou[52]										
30 VI 2011 ...... ESDF		29 797 694	22 219 201	74.6	14 935 396	10 987 090	73.6	14 862 298	11 232 111	75.6
30 VI 2012 ...... ESDF		30 135 875	22 635 742	75.1	15 103 003	11 191 332	74.1	15 032 872	11 444 410	76.1
30 VI 2013 ...... ESDF		30 475 144	23 054 394	75.6	15 271 062	11 396 589	74.6	15 204 082	11 657 805	76.7
30 VI 2014 ...... ESDF		30 814 175	23 474 069	76.2	15 438 887	11 602 321	75.1	15 375 288	11 871 748	77.2
30 VI 2015 ...... ESDF		31 151 643	23 893 654	76.7	15 605 814	11 808 006	75.7	15 545 829	12 085 648	77.7
30 VI 2016 ...... ESDF		31 488 625	24 313 862	77.2	15 772 385	12 013 953	76.2	15 716 240	12 299 909	78.3
30 VI 2017 ...... ESDF		31 826 018	24 735 295	77.7	15 939 059	12 220 551	76.7	15 886 959	12 514 744	78.8
Suriname										
1 VII 2008 ...... ESDJ		517 052	...	...	260 898	...	...	256 154	...	...
13 VIII 2012 ...... CDJC		541 638	359 146	66.3	270 629	177 215	65.5	271 009	181 931	67.1
1 VII 2013 ...... ESDJ		550 222	...	...	274 859	...	...	275 363	...	...
1 VII 2014 ...... ESDJ		558 773	...	...	279 071	...	...	279 702	...	...
1 VII 2015 ...... ESDJ		567 291	...	...	283 259	...	...	284 032	...	...
1 VII 2016 ...... ESDJ		575 763	...	...	287 422	...	...	288 341	...	...
Uruguay										
1 VII 2008 ...... ESDJ		3 363 060	3 169 767	94.3	1 624 932	1 515 980	93.3	1 738 128	1 653 786	95.1
1 VII 2009 ...... ESDJ		3 378 083	3 191 384	94.5	1 632 052	1 527 146	93.6	1 746 031	1 664 238	95.3
1 VII 2010 ...... ESDJ		3 396 706	3 216 519	94.7	1 640 886	1 539 959	93.8	1 755 820	1 676 560	95.5
1 VII 2011 ...... ESDJ		3 412 636	3 238 644	94.9	1 648 466	1 551 366	94.1	1 764 170	1 687 279	95.6
4 X 2011 ...... CDJC		3 286 314	3 110 701	94.7	1 577 725[70]	1 478 967[70]	93.7	1 708 481[70]	1 631 626[70]	95.5
1 VII 2012[4] ...... ESDJ		3 426 466	3 253 370	94.9	1 655 693	1 559 292	94.2	1 770 774	1 694 078	95.7
1 VII 2013[4] ...... ESDJ		3 440 157	3 268 281	95.0	1 662 884	1 567 325	94.3	1 777 273	1 700 956	95.7
1 VII 2014[4] ...... ESDJ		3 453 691	3 283 177	95.1	1 670 026	1 575 363	94.3	1 783 665	1 707 813	95.7
1 VII 2015[4] ...... ESDJ		3 467 054	3 297 948	95.1	1 677 118	1 583 363	94.4	1 789 936	1 714 585	95.8
1 VII 2016[4] ...... ESDJ		3 480 222	3 312 523	95.2	1 684 140	1 591 280	94.5	1 796 082	1 721 243	95.8
1 VII 2017[4] ...... ESDJ		3 493 205	3 326 886	95.2	1 691 102	1 599 115	94.6	1 802 103	1 727 772	95.9
Venezuela (Bolivarian Republic of) - Venezuela (République bolivarienne du)										
1 VII 2008 ...... ESDF		27 688 638	24 384 883	88.1	13 889 561	12 109 269	87.2	13 799 077	12 275 614	89.0
1 VII 2009 ...... ESDF		28 105 913	24 758 144	88.1	14 097 305	12 295 131	87.2	14 008 608	12 463 013	89.0
1 VII 2010 ...... ESDF		28 524 411	25 131 837	88.1	14 305 797	12 481 264	87.2	14 218 614	12 650 573	89.0
1 VII 2011 ...... ESDF		28 810 899	...	...	14 443 172	...	...	14 367 727	...	...
1 IX 2011 ...... CDJC		27 227 930	24 182 998[71]	88.8	13 549 752	11 902 155[71]	87.8	13 678 178	12 280 843[71]	89.8
1 VII 2012 ...... ESDF		29 230 592	...	...	14 654 181	...	...	14 576 411	...	...
1 VII 2013 ...... ESDF		29 650 188	...	...	14 865 265	...	...	14 784 923	...	...
1 VII 2014 ...... ESDF		30 069 829	...	...	15 075 999	...	...	14 993 830	...	...
1 VII 2015 ...... ESDF		30 489 354	...	...	15 283 762	...	...	15 205 592	...	...
1 VII 2016 ...... ESDF		30 883 254	...	...	15 488 512	...	...	15 394 742	...	...
1 VII 2017 ...... ESDF		31 277 130	...	...	15 690 386	...	...	15 586 744	...	...
ASIA - ASIE										
Afghanistan[72]										
1 VII 2008 ...... ESDF		23 511 400	5 330 200	22.7	12 025 700	2 744 400	22.8	11 485 700	2 585 800	22.5
1 VII 2009 ...... ESDF		23 993 500	5 507 300	23.0	12 272 900	2 835 900	23.1	11 720 600	2 671 400	22.8
1 VII 2010 ...... ESDF		24 485 600	5 690 300	23.2	12 524 700	2 929 900	23.4	11 960 900	2 760 400	23.1
1 VII 2011 ...... ESDF		24 987 700	5 879 200	23.5	12 782 600	3 027 400	23.7	12 205 700	2 851 800	23.4
1 VII 2012 ...... ESDF		25 500 100	6 074 200	23.8	13 044 000	3 127 700	24.0	12 455 700	2 946 500	23.7
1 VII 2013 ...... ESDF		26 023 100	6 275 600	24.1	13 312 400	3 231 600	24.3	12 710 700	3 044 000	23.9
1 VII 2014 ...... ESDF		26 556 754	6 483 434	24.4	13 585 933	3 338 764	24.6	12 970 821	3 144 670	24.2
1 VII 2015 ...... ESDF		27 101 365	6 698 033	24.7	13 865 015	3 449 379	24.9	13 236 350	3 248 654	24.5
1 VII 2016 ...... ESDF		27 657 145	6 919 560	25.0	14 149 838	3 563 570	25.2	13 507 307	3 355 990	24.8
1 VII 2017 ...... ESDF		28 224 323	7 148 224	25.3	14 438 456	3 631 353	25.2	13 785 867	3 516 871	25.5
Armenia - Arménie										
1 VII 2008 ...... ESDJ		3 087 119	1 967 259	63.7	1 481 408	924 337	62.4	1 605 711	1 042 922	65.0
1 VII 2009 ...... ESDJ		3 066 045	1 950 215	63.6	1 471 121	915 610	62.2	1 594 924	1 034 605	64.9
1 VII 2010 ...... ESDJ		3 044 868	1 933 144	63.5	1 460 773	906 766	62.1	1 584 095	1 026 378	64.8
1 VII 2011 ...... ESDJ		3 027 938	1 918 721	63.4	1 452 588	899 253	61.9	1 575 350	1 019 468	64.7
12 X 2011 ...... CDFC		2 871 771	1 847 124	64.3	1 346 729	851 475	63.2	1 525 042	995 649	65.3
1 VII 2012 ...... ESDJ		3 024 127	1 915 060	63.3	1 450 560	897 133	61.8	1 573 567	1 017 927	64.7

Continent, country or area, and date / Continent, pays ou zone et date	Code[a]	Both sexes - Les deux sexes			Male - Masculin			Female - Féminin		
		Total	Urban - Urbaine		Total	Urban - Urbaine		Total	Urban - Urbaine	
			Number Nombre	Percent P.100		Number Nombre	Percent P.100		Number Nombre	Percent P.100
ASIA - ASIE										
Armenia - Arménie										
1 VII 2013	ESDJ	3 021 979	1 915 758	63.4	1 447 572	896 463	61.9	1 574 407	1 019 295	64.7
1 VII 2014	ESDJ	3 013 839	1 913 481	63.5	1 441 323	894 594	62.1	1 572 516	1 018 887	64.8
1 VII 2015	ESDJ	3 004 588	1 909 960	63.6	1 434 095	891 769	62.2	1 570 493	1 018 191	64.8
1 VII 2016	ESDJ	2 992 364	1 904 230	63.6	1 423 906	886 581	62.3	1 568 458	1 017 649	64.9
1 I 2017	ESDJ	2 986 151	...	...	1 418 771	...	...	1 567 380	...	...
Azerbaijan - Azerbaïdjan										
1 VII 2008	ESDJ	8 838 500	4 690 000	53.1	4 368 600	2 304 800	52.8	4 469 900	2 385 200	53.4
13 IV 2009	CDJC	8 922 447	4 739 123	53.1	4 414 398	2 330 527	52.8	4 508 049	2 408 596	53.4
1 VII 2009	ESDJ	8 947 300	4 751 400	53.1	4 427 900	2 337 100	52.8	4 519 400	2 414 300	53.4
1 VII 2010	ESDJ	9 054 300	4 802 200	53.0	4 486 300	2 364 400	52.7	4 568 000	2 437 800	53.4
1 VII 2011	ESDJ	9 173 100	4 859 100	53.0	4 550 300	2 394 700	52.6	4 622 800	2 464 400	53.3
1 VII 2012	ESDJ	9 295 800	4 936 900	53.1	4 616 200	2 435 200	52.8	4 679 600	2 501 700	53.5
1 VII 2013	ESDJ	9 416 800	5 016 000	53.3	4 681 200	2 476 300	52.9	4 735 600	2 539 700	53.6
1 VII 2014	ESDJ	9 535 100	5 072 100	53.2	4 744 700	2 505 700	52.8	4 790 400	2 566 400	53.6
1 VII 2015	ESDJ	9 649 300	5 126 300	53.1	4 805 700	2 534 000	52.7	4 843 600	2 592 300	53.5
1 VII 2016	ESDJ	9 757 800	5 175 700	53.0	4 863 400	2 559 600	52.6	4 894 400	2 616 100	53.5
1 VII 2017	ESDJ	9 850 100	5 224 600	53.0	4 909 400	2 583 800	52.6	4 940 700	2 640 800	53.4
Bahrain - Bahreïn										
1 VII 2008	ESDJ	1 103 496	...	...	676 590	...	...	426 906	...	...
1 VII 2009	ESDJ	1 178 415	...	...	731 997	...	...	446 418	...	...
27 IV 2010	CDJC	1 234 571	1 234 571	100.0	768 414	768 414	100.0	466 157	466 157	100.0
1 VII 2010	ESDJ	1 228 543	...	...	764 357	...	...	464 186	...	...
1 VII 2011	ESDJ	1 195 020	...	...	741 483	...	...	453 537	...	...
1 VII 2012	ESDJ	1 208 964	...	...	760 449	...	...	448 515	...	...
1 VII 2013	ESDJ	1 253 191	...	...	788 381	...	...	464 810	...	...
1 VII 2014	ESDJ	1 314 562	...	...	806 487	...	...	508 075	...	...
1 VII 2015	ESDJ	1 370 322	...	...	846 365	...	...	523 957	...	...
1 VII 2016	ESDJ	1 423 726	...	...	888 389	...	...	535 337	...	...
1 VII 2017	ESDJ	1 501 116	...	...	951 312	...	...	549 804	...	...
Bangladesh										
1 VII 2008	ESDF	144 500 000	36 700 000	25.4	74 000 000	...	...	70 500 000	...	...
1 VII 2010	ESDF	148 620 000	38 540 000	25.9	76 120 000	20 427 000	26.8	72 500 000	18 113 000	25.0
15 III 2011[73]	CDFC	149 772 364	...	...	74 980 386	...	...	74 791 978	...	...
1 VII 2011	ESDF	150 611 000	39 000 000	25.9	77 101 062	20 560 587	26.7	73 509 938	18 439 413	25.1
1 VII 2012	ESDF	152 700 000	41 100 000	26.9	78 200 000	...	...	74 500 000	...	...
1 VII 2013	ESDF	154 790 000	42 580 000	27.5	77 510 000	...	...	77 280 000	...	...
1 VII 2014	ESDF	156 880 000	44 110 000	28.1	78 560 000	...	...	78 320 000	...	...
1 VII 2015	ESDF	158 900 000	45 700 000	28.8	79 600 000	...	...	79 300 000	...	...
1 VII 2016	ESDF	160 800 000	47 400 000	29.5	80 500 000	...	...	80 300 000	...	...
1 VII 2017	ESDF	161 750 000	...	...	81 000 000	...	...	80 750 000	...	...
Bhutan - Bhoutan										
1 VII 2008[74]	ESDF	671 083	222 753	33.2	351 269	119 342	34.0	319 814	103 411	32.3
1 VII 2009[74]	ESDF	683 407	232 232	34.0	357 305	124 246	34.8	326 102	107 986	33.1
1 VII 2010[74]	ESDF	695 823	242 001	34.8	363 384	129 298	35.6	332 439	112 703	33.9
1 VII 2011[74]	ESDF	708 265	252 038	35.6	369 476	134 484	36.4	338 789	117 554	34.7
1 VII 2012[74]	ESDF	720 679	262 325	36.4	375 554	139 798	37.2	345 125	122 530	35.5
1 VII 2013[74]	ESDF	733 004	272 839	37.2	381 582	145 219	38.1	351 421	127 619	36.3
1 VII 2014[74]	ESDF	745 153	283 543	38.1	387 520	150 737	38.9	357 633	132 806	37.1
1 VII 2015[74]	ESDF	757 042	294 402	38.9	393 324	156 328	39.7	363 718	138 074	38.0
1 VII 2016[74]	ESDF	768 577	...	...	398 948	...	...	369 629	...	...
30 V 2017	CDFC	727 145	274 316	37.7	380 453	143 313	37.7	346 692	131 003	37.8
Brunei Darussalam - Brunéi Darussalam										
1 VII 2008[51]	ESDF	375 000	...	...	193 700	...	...	181 300	...	...
1 VII 2009[51]	ESDF	380 100	...	...	196 300	...	...	183 800	...	...
1 VII 2010[51]	ESDF	386 800	...	...	199 800	...	...	187 000	...	...
20 VI 2011	CDJC	393 372	296 257	75.3	203 144	151 663	74.7	190 228	144 594	76.0
1 VII 2012	ESDJ	398 700	...	...	205 800	...	...	192 900	...	...
1 VII 2013	ESDJ	403 300	...	...	207 900	...	...	195 400	...	...
1 VII 2014	ESDJ	407 600	...	...	209 700	...	...	197 900	...	...
1 VII 2015	ESDJ	412 400	...	...	211 900	...	...	200 500	...	...
1 VII 2016[75]	ESDJ	417 256	312 448	74.9	214 104	160 061	74.8	203 152	152 387	75.0
1 VII 2017	ESDJ	421 300	...	...	216 400	...	...	204 900	...	...

6. Total and urban population by sex: 2008 - 2017
Population totale et population urbaine selon le sexe : 2008 - 2017 (continued - suite)

Continent, country or area, and date / Continent, pays ou zone et date	Code[a]	Both sexes - Les deux sexes			Male - Masculin			Female - Féminin		
		Total	Urban - Urbaine		Total	Urban - Urbaine		Total	Urban - Urbaine	
			Number Nombre	Percent P.100		Number Nombre	Percent P.100		Number Nombre	Percent P.100

ASIA - ASIE

Cambodia - Cambodge

3 III 2008[76]	CDFC	13 395 682	2 614 027	19.5	6 516 054	1 255 570	19.3	6 879 628	1 358 457	19.7
1 VII 2008[77]	ESDF	13 868 227	2 707 240	19.5	6 745 592	1 299 799	19.3	7 122 635	1 407 441	19.8
1 VII 2009[77]	ESDF	14 085 324	2 814 943	20.0	6 859 756	1 351 939	19.7	7 225 568	1 463 004	20.2
1 VII 2010[77]	ESDF	14 302 779	2 926 810	20.5	6 973 994	1 406 183	20.2	7 328 785	1 520 627	20.7
1 VII 2011[77]	ESDF	14 521 275	3 042 794	21.0	7 088 691	1 462 518	20.6	7 432 584	1 580 276	21.3
1 VII 2012[77]	ESDF	14 741 414	3 165 683	21.5	7 204 166	1 520 722	21.1	7 537 248	1 644 961	21.8
3 III 2013[78]	SSDF	14 676 591	3 146 212	21.4	7 121 508	1 527 479	21.4	7 555 083	1 618 734	21.4
1 VII 2013[77]	ESDF	14 962 591	3 285 951	22.0	7 320 112	1 580 866	21.6	7 642 479	1 705 085	22.3
1 VII 2014[77]	ESDF	15 184 116	3 412 183	22.5	7 436 178	1 642 397	22.1	7 747 938	1 769 786	22.8
1 VII 2015[77]	ESDF	15 405 157	3 540 575	23.0	7 551 944	1 705 018	22.6	7 853 213	1 835 557	23.4

China - Chine[79]

1 VII 2008[80]	ESDF	1 324 700 000	624 030 000[82]	47.1	683 570 000[81]	...	...	644 450 000[81]	...	...
1 VII 2009[80]	ESDF	1 331 300 000	645 120 000[82]	48.5	686 470 000[81]	...	...	648 030 000[81]	...	...
1 VII 2010[80]	ESDF	1 337 700 000	669 780 000[82]	50.1	687 480 000[81]	...	...	653 430 000[81]	...	...
1 XI 2010[83]	CDJC	1 339 724 852	665 575 306	49.7	686 852 572	...	...	652 872 280	...	...
1 VII 2011[84]	ESDF	1 344 100 000	691 000 000[82]	51.4	691 000 000[81]	...	...	657 000 000[81]	...	...
1 VII 2012[84]	ESDF	1 350 695 000	701 305 000[85]	51.9	692 315 000	...	...	658 380 000	...	...
1 VII 2013[80]	ESDF	1 357 380 000	721 465 000[85]	53.2	695 615 000	...	...	661 765 000	...	...
1 VII 2014[80]	ESDF	1 364 270 000	740 135 000[85]	54.3	699 035 000	...	...	665 235 000	...	...
1 VII 2015[80]	ESDF	1 371 220 000	760 160 000[85]	55.4	702 465 000	...	...	668 755 000	...	...
1 VII 2016[80]	ESDF	1 378 665 000	782 070 000[85]	56.7	706 145 000	...	...	672 520 000	...	...

China, Hong Kong SAR - Chine, Hong Kong RAS

1 VII 2008	ESDJ	6 957 800	...	...	3 290 200	...	...	3 667 600	...	...
1 VII 2009	ESDJ	6 972 800	...	...	3 284 800	...	...	3 688 000	...	...
1 VII 2010	ESDJ	7 024 200	...	...	3 294 300	...	...	3 729 900	...	...
30 VI 2011[86]	CDJC	7 071 576	...	...	3 303 015	...	...	3 768 561	...	...
1 VII 2011	ESDJ	7 071 600	...	...	3 303 000	...	...	3 768 600	...	...
1 VII 2012	ESDJ	7 150 100	...	...	3 327 300	...	...	3 822 800	...	...
1 VII 2013	ESDJ	7 178 900	...	...	3 329 900	...	...	3 849 000	...	...
1 VII 2014	ESDJ	7 229 500	...	...	3 344 500	...	...	3 885 000	...	...
1 VII 2015	ESDJ	7 291 300	...	...	3 365 600	...	...	3 925 700	...	...
30 VI 2016[87]	CDJC	7 336 585	...	...	3 375 362	...	...	3 961 223	...	...
1 VII 2016	ESDJ	7 336 600	...	...	3 375 400	...	...	3 961 200	...	...
1 VII 2017	ESDJ	7 391 700	...	...	3 392 500	...	...	3 999 200	...	...

China, Macao SAR - Chine, Macao RAS

1 VII 2008	ESDJ	540 700	...	...	264 900	...	...	275 800	...	...
1 VII 2009	ESDJ	535 000	...	...	257 900[81]	...	...	277 200[81]	...	...
1 VII 2010	ESDJ	537 000	...	...	257 200[81]	...	...	279 700[81]	...	...
1 VII 2011	ESDJ	549 600	...	...	263 500	...	...	286 100	...	...
12 VIII 2011	CDFC	625 674	...	...	305 398	...	...	320 276	...	...
1 VII 2012	ESDJ	567 900	...	...	274 300	...	...	293 600	...	...
1 VII 2013	ESDJ	591 900	...	...	285 700	...	...	306 200	...	...
1 VII 2014	ESDJ	621 700	...	...	305 500	...	...	316 200	...	...
1 VII 2015	ESDJ	642 900	...	...	317 500	...	...	325 400	...	...
7 VIII 2016[88]	SSDJ	650 834	...	...	314 018	...	...	336 816	...	...

Cyprus - Chypre[89]

1 VII 2008[20]	ESDJ	786 632	...	...	385 192	...	...	401 440	...	...
1 VII 2009[20]	ESDJ	808 035	...	...	394 766	...	...	413 270	...	...
1 VII 2010[20]	ESDJ	829 446	...	...	404 182	...	...	425 264	...	...
1 VII 2011[20]	ESDJ	850 881	...	...	413 876	...	...	437 006	...	...
1 X 2011	CDJC	840 407	566 191	67.4	408 780	273 065	66.8	431 627	293 126	67.9
1 VII 2012[20]	ESDJ	863 945	...	...	420 015	...	...	443 930	...	...
1 VII 2013[20]	ESDJ	861 930	...	...	419 183	...	...	442 747	...	...
1 VII 2014[20]	ESDJ	852 504	...	...	414 682	...	...	437 823	...	...
1 VII 2015[20]	ESDJ	847 700	...	...	412 300	...	...	435 400	...	...
1 VII 2016[20]	ESDJ	851 600	...	...	414 700	...	...	436 900	...	...
1 I 2017	ESDJ	854 802	...	...	416 663	...	...	438 139	...	...

6. Total and urban population by sex: 2008 - 2017
Population totale et population urbaine selon le sexe : 2008 - 2017 (continued - suite)

Continent, country or area, and date / Continent, pays ou zone et date	Code[a]	Both sexes - Les deux sexes Total	Urban - Urbaine Number Nombre	Urban - Urbaine Percent P.100	Male - Masculin Total	Urban - Urbaine Number Nombre	Urban - Urbaine Percent P.100	Female - Féminin Total	Urban - Urbaine Number Nombre	Urban - Urbaine Percent P.100
ASIA - ASIE										
Democratic People's Republic of Korea - République populaire démocratique de Corée										
1 X 2008 ....CDJC		24 052 231	...	...	11 721 838	...	...	12 330 393	...	...
Georgia - Géorgie										
1 VII 2008 ....ESDF		4 383 800	2 306 500	52.6	2 079 600	...	...	2 304 200	...	...
1 VII 2009 ....ESDF		4 410 900	2 332 700	52.9	2 094 800	...	...	2 316 100	...	...
1 VII 2010 ....ESDF		4 452 800	2 360 900	53.0	2 118 100	...	...	2 334 700	...	...
1 VII 2011 ....ESDF		4 483 400	2 381 500	53.1	2 135 600	...	...	2 347 800	...	...
1 VII 2012 ....ESDF		4 490 700	...	...	2 141 300	...	...	2 349 400	...	...
1 VII 2013 ....ESDF		4 487 150	...	...	2 140 100	...	...	2 347 050	...	...
5 XI 2014 ....CDJC		3 713 804	2 122 623	57.2	1 772 864	980 985	55.3	1 940 940	1 141 638	58.8
1 VII 2015[90] ....ESDJ		3 717 100	2 125 700	57.2	1 776 300	...	...	1 940 800	...	...
1 VII 2016[90] ....ESDJ		3 719 300	2 128 500	57.2	1 780 500	...	...	1 938 800	...	...
1 I 2017[90] ....ESDJ		3 718 200	...	...	1 781 500	...	...	1 936 700	...	...
India - Inde[91]										
1 VII 2008[92] ....ESDF		*1 150 196 000*	*338 356 000*	*29.4*	*595 291 000*	*178 041 000*	*29.9*	*554 905 000*	*160 315 000*	*28.9*
1 III 2009[92] ....ESDF		*1 160 813 000*	...	...	*600 816 000*	...	...	*889 997 000*	...	...
1 III 2010[92] ....ESDF		*1 176 742 000*	...	...	*609 107 000*	...	...	*567 634 000*	...	...
9 II 2011 ....CDFC		*1 210 854 977*	*377 106 125*	*31.1*	*623 270 258*	*195 489 200*	*31.4*	*587 584 719*	*181 616 925*	*30.9*
1 III 2011[92] ....ESDF		*1 192 506 000*	...	...	*617 316 000*	...	...	*575 191 000*	...	...
1 III 2012[92] ....ESDF		*1 208 116 000*	...	...	*625 446 000*	...	...	*582 670 000*	...	...
1 III 2013[92] ....ESDF		*1 223 581 000*	...	...	*633 505 000*	...	...	*590 076 000*	...	...
1 III 2014[92] ....ESDF		*1 238 887 000*	...	...	*641 484 000*	...	...	*597 403 000*	...	...
1 III 2015[92] ....ESDF		*1 254 019 000*	...	...	*649 374 000*	...	...	*604 644 000*	...	...
1 III 2016[92] ....ESDF		*1 268 961 000*	...	...	*657 168 000*	...	...	*611 793 000*	...	...
1 III 2017[92] ....ESDF		*1 283 600 000*	...	...	*664 802 000*	...	...	*618 799 000*	...	...
Indonesia - Indonésie										
1 VII 2008[93] ....ESDJ		*228 523 300*	...	...	*114 399 200*	...	...	*114 124 100*	...	...
1 VII 2009[93] ....ESDJ		*231 369 500*	...	...	*115 817 900*	...	...	*115 551 600*	...	...
1 V 2010 ....CDJC		*237 641 326*	*118 320 256*	*49.8*	*119 630 913*	*59 559 622*	*49.8*	*118 010 413*	*58 760 634*	*49.8*
1 VII 2010[94] ....ESDJ		*238 518 787*	*118 803 981*	*49.8*	*119 852 718*	*59 698 817*	*49.8*	*118 666 069*	*59 105 164*	*49.8*
1 VII 2011[94] ....ESDJ		*241 990 736*	*122 164 186*	*50.5*	*121 602 475*	*61 382 741*	*50.5*	*120 388 261*	*60 781 445*	*50.5*
1 VII 2012[94] ....ESDJ		*245 425 244*	*125 558 071*	*51.2*	*123 331 006*	*63 081 616*	*51.1*	*122 094 238*	*62 476 455*	*51.2*
1 VII 2013[94] ....ESDJ		*248 818 090*	*128 964 283*	*51.8*	*125 036 002*	*64 785 519*	*51.8*	*123 782 088*	*64 178 764*	*51.8*
1 VII 2014[94] ....ESDJ		*252 164 786*	*132 387 038*	*52.5*	*126 715 188*	*66 493 813*	*52.5*	*125 449 598*	*65 893 225*	*52.5*
1 VII 2015[94] ....ESDJ		*255 461 686*	*135 823 286*	*53.2*	*128 366 718*	*68 214 177*	*53.1*	*127 094 968*	*67 609 109*	*53.2*
1 VII 2016[94] ....ESDJ		*258 704 986*	*139 240 964*	*53.8*	*129 988 690*	*69 924 467*	*53.8*	*128 716 296*	*69 316 497*	*53.9*
1 VII 2017[94] ....ESDJ		*261 890 900*	...	...	*131 579 200*	...	...	*130 311 700*	...	...
Iran (Islamic Republic of) - Iran (République islamique d')										
1 VII 2008[95] ....ESDJ		*72 181 632*	*49 576 146*	*68.7*	*36 691 780*	*25 253 132*	*68.8*	*35 489 488*	*24 323 014*	*68.5*
1 VII 2009[95] ....ESDJ		*73 202 096*	*50 365 184*	*68.8*	*37 198 776*	*25 660 500*	*69.0*	*36 003 320*	*24 704 684*	*68.6*
1 VII 2010[95] ....ESDJ		*74 339 576*	*51 242 546*	*68.9*	*37 767 220*	*26 114 342*	*69.1*	*36 572 356*	*25 128 204*	*68.7*
24 X 2011 ....CDJC		*75 149 669*	*53 646 661*	*71.4*	*37 905 669*	*27 023 638*	*71.3*	*37 244 000*	*26 623 023*	*71.5*
1 VII 2012[95] ....ESDJ		*76 037 535*	*54 611 776[96]*	*71.8*	*38 336 983*	*27 547 622[96]*	*71.9*	*37 700 552*	*27 064 154[96]*	*71.8*
1 VII 2013[95] ....ESDJ		*76 942 276*	*55 506 192[96]*	*72.1*	*38 777 566*	*27 988 342[96]*	*72.2*	*38 164 710*	*27 517 850[96]*	*72.1*
1 VII 2014[95] ....ESDJ		*77 856 411*	*56 412 837*	*72.5*	*39 224 036*	*28 435 933*	*72.5*	*38 632 375*	*27 976 904*	*72.4*
1 VII 2015[95] ....ESDJ		*78 773 093*	*57 326 841*	*72.8*	*39 672 171*	*28 887 379*	*72.8*	*39 100 922*	*28 439 462*	*72.7*
1 VII 2016[95] ....ESDJ		*79 685 926*	*58 224 240*	*73.1*	*40 118 657*	*29 330 524*	*73.1*	*39 567 269*	*28 893 716*	*73.0*
24 IX 2016 ....CDJC		*79 926 270*	*59 146 847[97]*	*74.0*	*40 498 442*	*29 841 414[97]*	*73.7*	*39 427 828*	*29 305 433[97]*	*74.3*
1 VII 2017[95] ....ESDJ		*81 070 480*	*60 281 499*	*74.4*	*41 048 740*	*30 517 645*	*74.3*	*40 021 740*	*29 763 854*	*74.4*
Iraq										
1 VII 2008 ....ESDF		*30 315 243*	...	...	*15 261 719*	...	...	*15 053 524*	...	...
1 VII 2009 ....ESDF		*31 392 903*	...	...	*16 010 232*	...	...	*15 382 671*	...	...
1 VII 2010 ....ESDF		*32 210 813*	...	...	*16 418 691*	...	...	*15 792 122*	...	...
1 VII 2011 ....ESDF		*33 051 526*	...	...	*16 839 048*	...	...	*16 212 479*	...	...
1 VII 2012 ....ESDF		*33 913 305*	*23 475 543*	*69.2*	*17 270 036*	*11 954 703*	*69.2*	*16 643 269*	*11 520 840*	*69.2*
1 VII 2013 ....ESDF		*34 794 194*	*24 162 634*	*69.4*	*17 710 750*	*12 299 131*	*69.4*	*17 083 444*	*11 863 502*	*69.4*
1 VII 2014 ....ESDF		*35 736 260*	*24 896 261*	*69.7*	*18 182 503*	*12 667 144*	*69.7*	*17 553 757*	*12 229 117*	*69.7*
1 VII 2015 ....ESDF		*36 658 503*	*25 631 821*	*69.9*	*18 520 532*	*12 935 587*	*69.8*	*18 137 971*	*12 696 234*	*70.0*

Continent, country or area, and date / Continent, pays ou zone et date	Code[a]	Both sexes - Les deux sexes			Male - Masculin			Female - Féminin		
		Total	Urban - Urbaine		Total	Urban - Urbaine		Total	Urban - Urbaine	
			Number Nombre	Percent P.100		Number Nombre	Percent P.100		Number Nombre	Percent P.100
ASIA - ASIE										
Israel - Israël[98]										
1 VII 2008	ESDJ	7 308 795	6 701 217[99]	91.7	3 614 125	3 303 732[99]	91.4	3 694 671	3 397 485[99]	92.0
27 XII 2008[100]	CDFC	7 412 180	6 799 340[81]	91.7	3 663 910	3 350 610[81]	91.4	3 748 270	3 448 730[81]	92.0
1 VII 2009[101]	ESDJ	7 485 565	6 864 957[81]	91.7	3 701 159	3 384 295[81]	91.4	3 784 406	3 480 662[81]	92.0
1 VII 2010[101]	ESDJ	7 623 561	6 987 615[81]	91.7	3 771 020	3 446 730[81]	91.4	3 852 541	3 540 885[81]	91.9
1 VII 2011[101]	ESDJ	7 765 832	7 111 015[81]	91.6	3 843 068	3 509 308[81]	91.3	3 922 764	3 601 706[81]	91.8
1 VII 2012[101]	ESDJ	7 910 525	7 235 231[81]	91.5	3 916 125	3 572 531[81]	91.2	3 994 400	3 662 700[81]	91.7
1 VII 2013[101]	ESDJ	8 059 456	7 369 053[81]	91.4	3 991 347	3 640 471[81]	91.2	4 068 109	3 728 581[81]	91.7
1 VII 2014[101]	ESDJ	8 215 668	7 502 325[81]	91.3	4 070 269	3 707 183[81]	91.1	4 145 398	3 795 142[81]	91.6
1 VII 2015[101]	ESDJ	8 380 149	7 643 990[81]	91.2	4 153 233	3 778 276[81]	91.0	4 226 916	3 865 714[81]	91.5
1 VII 2016[101]	ESDJ	8 546 009	7 795 761[81]	91.2	4 237 229	3 855 306[81]	91.0	4 308 780	3 940 455[81]	91.5
Japan - Japon[102]										
1 VII 2008	ESDJ	128 063 000	...	...	62 409 000	...	...	65 654 000	...	...
1 VII 2009	ESDJ	128 047 000	...	...	62 354 000	...	...	65 693 000	...	...
1 VII 2010	ESDJ	128 070 000	...	...	62 330 000	...	...	65 740 000	...	...
1 X 2010	CDJC	128 057 352	116 156 631	90.7	62 327 737	56 569 051	90.8	65 729 615	59 587 580	90.7
1 VII 2011[103]	ESDJ	127 833 000	...	...	62 202 000	...	...	65 631 000	...	...
1 VII 2012[103]	ESDJ	127 629 000	...	...	62 085 000	...	...	65 544 000	...	...
1 VII 2013[103]	ESDJ	127 445 000	...	...	61 987 000	...	...	65 458 000	...	...
1 VII 2014[103]	ESDJ	127 276 000	...	...	61 906 000	...	...	65 370 000	...	...
1 VII 2015[104]	ESDJ	127 141 000	...	...	61 848 000	...	...	65 294 000	...	...
1 X 2015	CDJC	127 094 745	116 137 232	91.4	61 841 738	56 532 149	91.4	65 253 007	59 605 083	91.3
1 VII 2016[104]	ESDJ	126 995 000	...	...	61 781 000	...	...	65 213 000	...	...
1 VII 2017[103]	ESDJ	126 786 000	...	...	61 681 000	...	...	65 105 000	...	...
Jordan - Jordanie[105]										
31 XII 2008	ESDF	6 293 000	5 685 000	90.3	3 243 000	...	...	3 050 000	...	...
31 XII 2009	ESDF	6 490 000	5 863 000	90.3	3 340 000	...	...	3 150 000	...	...
31 XII 2010	ESDF	6 699 000	6 051 000	90.3	3 448 000	...	...	3 250 000	...	...
31 XII 2011	ESDF	6 993 000	6 318 000	90.3	3 704 852	...	...	3 288 148	...	...
31 XII 2012	ESDF	7 427 000	6 710 000	90.3	3 934 783	...	...	3 492 217	...	...
31 XII 2013	ESDF	8 114 000	7 331 000	90.4	4 298 752	...	...	3 815 248	...	...
31 XII 2014	ESDF	8 804 000	7 954 000	90.3	4 664 310	...	...	4 139 690	...	...
30 XI 2015	CDFC	9 531 712	...	...	5 046 822	...	...	4 484 890	...	...
31 XII 2015	ESDF	9 559 000	8 636 000	90.3	5 061 000	...	...	4 498 000	...	...
31 XII 2016	ESDF	9 798 000	8 852 000	90.3	5 188 000	...	...	4 610 000	...	...
31 XII 2017	ESDF	10 053 000	9 082 000	90.3	5 323 000	...	...	4 730 000	...	...
Kazakhstan										
1 VII 2008[106]	ESDF	15 982 370	8 662 919	54.2	7 698 875	4 056 041	52.7	8 283 495	4 606 878	55.6
25 II 2009	CDFC	16 009 597	8 662 432	54.1	7 712 224	4 055 341	52.6	8 297 373	4 607 091	55.5
1 VII 2009[107]	ESDF	16 092 822	8 741 269	54.3	7 753 418	4 092 781	52.8	8 339 404	4 648 488	55.7
1 VII 2010[107]	ESDF	16 321 872	8 896 771	54.5	7 866 461	4 165 677	53.0	8 455 411	4 731 094	56.0
1 VII 2011[107]	ESDF	16 557 201	9 050 732	54.7	7 983 365	4 237 915	53.1	8 573 836	4 812 817	56.1
1 VII 2012[107]	ESDF	16 792 089	9 202 707	54.8	8 100 335	4 309 949	53.2	8 691 754	4 892 758	56.3
1 VII 2013[107]	ESDF	17 035 550	9 355 723	54.9	8 221 757	4 383 901	53.3	8 813 793	4 971 822	56.4
1 VII 2014[107]	ESDF	17 288 285	9 635 300	55.7	8 348 857	4 523 126	54.2	8 939 428	5 112 174	57.2
1 VII 2015[107]	ESDF	17 542 806	9 936 301	56.6	8 477 451	4 672 945	55.1	9 065 355	5 263 356	58.1
1 VII 2016[107]	ESDF	17 794 055	10 142 840	57.0	8 605 139	4 774 020	55.5	9 188 916	5 368 820	58.4
1 VII 2017[107]	ESDF	18 037 776	10 336 836	57.3	8 729 888	4 868 292	55.8	9 307 888	5 468 544	58.8
Kuwait - Koweït										
1 VII 2008	ESDF	2 631 963	...	...	1 525 129	...	...	1 106 834	...	...
1 VII 2009	ESDF	2 777 861	...	...	1 597 843	...	...	1 180 018	...	...
1 VII 2010	ESDF	2 933 268	...	...	1 674 156	...	...	1 259 112	...	...
21 IV 2011	CDFC	3 065 850	3 065 850	100.0	1 738 372	1 738 372	100.0	1 327 478	1 327 478	100.0
1 VII 2011	ESDF	3 106 676	...	...	1 767 685	...	...	1 338 991	...	...
1 VII 2012	ESDF	3 246 622	...	...	1 856 265	...	...	1 390 357	...	...
1 VII 2013	ESDF	3 427 595	...	...	1 968 382	...	...	1 459 213	...	...
1 VII 2014	ESDF	3 767 415	...	...	2 161 594	...	...	1 605 821	...	...
1 I 2015	ESDF	3 743 660	...	...	2 185 298	...	...	1 558 362	...	...
1 VII 2016	ESDF	4 079 305	...	...	2 505 012	...	...	1 574 293	...	...
1 I 2017	ESDF	4 082 704	...	...	2 455 424	...	...	1 627 280	...	...
Kyrgyzstan - Kirghizstan										
1 VII 2008[20]	ESDJ	5 318 729	1 816 886	34.2	2 623 575	857 874	32.7	2 695 154	959 012	35.6
24 III 2009	CDJC	5 362 793	1 827 136	34.1	2 645 921	863 002	32.6	2 716 872	964 134	35.5
1 VII 2009[20]	ESDJ	5 383 277	1 835 028	34.1	2 656 660	866 718	32.6	2 726 617	968 310	35.5

6. Total and urban population by sex: 2008 - 2017
Population totale et population urbaine selon le sexe : 2008 - 2017 (continued - suite)

Continent, country or area, and date / Continent, pays ou zone et date	Code[a]	Both sexes - Les deux sexes			Male - Masculin			Female - Féminin		
		Total	Urban - Urbaine		Total	Urban - Urbaine		Total	Urban - Urbaine	
			Number Nombre	Percent P.100		Number Nombre	Percent P.100		Number Nombre	Percent P.100

ASIA - ASIE

Kyrgyzstan - Kirghizstan

1 VII 2010[20] ....ESDJ		5 447 960	1 854 245	34.0	2 689 231	876 120	32.6	2 758 729	978 125	35.5
1 VII 2011[20] ....ESDJ		5 514 754	1 873 047	34.0	2 722 714	885 117	32.5	2 792 040	987 930	35.4
1 VII 2012[20] ....ESDJ		5 607 511	1 878 643	33.5	2 770 269	887 727	32.0	2 837 242	990 916	34.9
1 VII 2013[20] ....ESDJ		5 719 852	1 921 936	33.6	2 827 672	909 216	32.2	2 892 180	1 012 720	35.0
1 VII 2014[20] ....ESDJ		5 835 816	1 965 159	33.7	2 886 758	930 751	32.2	2 949 058	1 034 408	35.1
1 VII 2015[20] ....ESDJ		5 957 271	2 008 148	33.7	2 948 932	952 329	32.3	3 008 339	1 055 819	35.1
1 VII 2016[20] ....ESDJ		6 079 840	2 051 748	33.7	3 011 702	973 955	32.3	3 068 138	1 077 793	35.1
1 VII 2017[20] ....ESDJ		6 198 465	2 097 487	33.8	3 072 164	996 210	32.4	3 126 301	1 101 277	35.2

Lao People's Democratic Republic - République démocratique populaire lao

1 VII 2008[108] ....ESDJ		*5 990 100*	*...*	*...*	*2 985 800*	*...*	*...*	*3 004 300*	*...*	*...*
1 VII 2009[108] ....ESDJ		*6 110 600*	*...*	*...*	*3 046 400*	*...*	*...*	*3 064 200*	*...*	*...*
1 VII 2010[108] ....ESDJ		*6 230 200*	*...*	*...*	*3 106 600*	*...*	*...*	*3 123 700*	*...*	*...*
1 VII 2011[108] ....ESDJ		*6 348 800*	*...*	*...*	*3 166 300*	*...*	*...*	*3 182 500*	*...*	*...*
1 VII 2012[108] ....ESDJ		*6 465 800*	*...*	*...*	*3 225 200*	*...*	*...*	*3 240 600*	*...*	*...*
1 VII 2013[108] ....ESDJ		*6 580 800*	*...*	*...*	*3 283 200*	*...*	*...*	*3 297 600*	*...*	*...*
1 VII 2014[108] ....ESDJ		*6 693 300*	*...*	*...*	*3 339 800*	*...*	*...*	*3 353 400*	*...*	*...*
1 III 2015 ....CDJC		6 492 400	*...*	*...*	3 254 800	*...*	*...*	3 237 600	*...*	*...*
1 VII 2015[108] ....ESDJ		*6 671 680*	*...*	*...*	*3 342 462*	*...*	*...*	*3 329 218*	*...*	*...*
1 VII 2016[108] ....ESDJ		*6 787 007*	*...*	*...*	*3 400 453*	*...*	*...*	*3 386 554*	*...*	*...*
1 VII 2017[108] ....ESDJ		*6 900 846*	*...*	*...*	*3 457 542*	*...*	*...*	*3 443 304*	*...*	*...*

Lebanon - Liban[109]

1 X 2011 ....SSDF		3 779 859	*...*	*...*	1 840 940	*...*	*...*	1 938 919	*...*	*...*

Malaysia - Malaisie

1 VII 2008[110] ....ESDJ		27 567 636	19 068 738	69.2	14 179 117	9 767 066	68.9	13 388 519	9 301 672	69.5
1 VII 2009[110] ....ESDJ		28 081 497	19 675 872	70.1	14 456 940	10 085 459	69.8	13 624 557	9 590 413	70.4
1 VII 2010[111] ....ESDJ		28 588 637	20 290 864	71.0	14 730 542	10 404 757	70.6	13 858 095	9 886 107	71.3
6 VII 2010[73] ....CDJC		28 334 135	20 124 970	71.0	14 562 638	10 298 698	70.7	13 771 497	9 826 272	71.4
1 VII 2011[111] ....ESDJ		29 062 036	20 826 580	71.7	14 980 010	10 684 359	71.3	14 082 026	10 142 221	72.0
1 VII 2012[111] ....ESDJ		29 510 022	21 355 255	72.4	15 215 309	10 965 006	72.1	14 294 713	10 390 249	72.7
1 VII 2013[111] ....ESDJ		30 213 664	22 041 500	73.0	15 604 813	11 330 984	72.6	14 608 851	10 710 516	73.3
1 VII 2014[111] ....ESDJ		30 708 527	22 597 286	73.6	15 867 796	11 624 061	73.3	14 840 731	10 973 225	73.9
1 VII 2015[111] ....ESDJ		31 186 135	23 173 701	74.3	16 112 125	11 925 089	74.0	15 074 010	11 248 612	74.6
1 VII 2016[111] ....ESDJ		31 633 518	23 677 030	74.8	16 346 281	12 186 777	74.6	15 287 237	11 490 253	75.2
1 VII 2017[111] ....ESDJ		32 049 740	24 182 507	75.5	16 561 112	12 448 465	75.2	15 488 628	11 734 042	75.8

Maldives

1 VII 2008 ....ESDF		309 575	*...*	*...*	156 714	*...*	*...*	152 861	*...*	*...*
1 VII 2009 ....ESDF		314 542	*...*	*...*	159 159	*...*	*...*	155 383	*...*	*...*
1 VII 2010 ....ESDF		319 738	*...*	*...*	161 708	*...*	*...*	158 030	*...*	*...*
1 VII 2011 ....ESDF		325 135	*...*	*...*	164 349	*...*	*...*	160 786	*...*	*...*
1 VII 2012 ....ESDF		330 655	*...*	*...*	167 058	*...*	*...*	163 597	*...*	*...*
1 VII 2013 ....ESDF		336 224	*...*	*...*	169 800	*...*	*...*	166 424	*...*	*...*
1 VII 2014[112] ....ESDF		437 535	171 165	39.1	261 709	101 744	38.9	175 826	69 422	39.5
20 IX 2014[113] ....CDFC		402 071	153 904	38.3	227 749	85 438	37.5	174 322	68 466	39.3
1 VII 2015[112] ....ESDF		454 434	180 019	39.6	274 607	107 894	39.3	179 827	72 125	40.1
1 VII 2016[112] ....ESDF		472 426	189 458	40.1	288 502	114 514	39.7	183 924	74 944	40.7
1 VII 2017[112] ....ESDF		491 589	199 523	40.6	303 478	121 647	40.1	188 111	77 876	41.4

Mongolia - Mongolie

1 VII 2008 ....ESDF		2 643 201	1 684 282	63.7	1 289 282	811 224	62.9	1 353 919	873 058	64.5
1 VII 2009 ....ESDF		2 691 115	1 743 008	64.8	1 314 729	840 520	63.9	1 376 386	902 488	65.6
1 VII 2010 ....ESDF		2 738 622	1 799 648	65.7	1 335 111	863 536	64.7	1 403 511	936 112	66.7
11 XI 2010 ....CDFC		2 647 199	1 797 338	67.9	1 314 246	869 827	66.2	1 332 953	927 511	69.6
1 VII 2011 ....ESDF		2 786 322	1 856 224	66.6	1 354 472	886 139	65.4	1 431 850	970 085	67.8
1 VII 2012 ....ESDF		2 839 711	1 911 462	67.3	1 379 091	910 746	66.0	1 460 620	1 000 716	68.5
1 VII 2013 ....ESDF		2 899 011	1 961 169	67.6	1 409 648	936 682	66.4	1 489 363	1 024 487	68.8
1 VII 2014 ....ESDF		2 963 113	1 993 017	67.3	1 446 149	955 833	66.1	1 516 964	1 037 184	68.4
1 VII 2015 ....ESDF		3 026 864	2 043 251	67.5	1 485 034	985 919	66.4	1 541 830	1 057 332	68.6
1 VII 2016 ....ESDF		3 088 856	2 122 131	68.7	1 518 797	1 027 311	67.6	1 570 059	1 094 820	69.7
1 VII 2017 ....ESDF		3 148 917	2 139 269	67.9	1 548 177	1 034 384	66.8	1 600 740	1 104 885	69.0

Myanmar

1 X 2008 ....ESDF		*58 376 839*	*17 894 194*	*30.7*	*29 025 480*	*8 798 657*	*30.3*	*29 351 359*	*9 095 537*	*31.0*
1 X 2009 ....ESDF		*59 129 900*	*18 133 654*	*30.7*	*29 399 744*	*8 888 838*	*30.2*	*29 730 156*	*9 244 816*	*31.1*

Continent, country or area, and date / Continent, pays ou zone et date	Code[a]	Both sexes - Les deux sexes			Male - Masculin			Female - Féminin		
		Total	Urban - Urbaine		Total	Urban - Urbaine		Total	Urban - Urbaine	
			Number Nombre	Percent P.100		Number Nombre	Percent P.100		Number Nombre	Percent P.100
ASIA - ASIE										
Myanmar										
1 X 2010	ESDF	59 780 329	18 342 824	30.7	29 723 184	8 992 226	30.3	30 057 145	9 350 598	31.1
1 X 2011[90]	ESDF	50 149 496	14 650 579	29.2	24 185 705	7 009 280	29.0	25 963 791	7 641 299	29.4
1 X 2012[90]	ESDF	50 666 887	14 824 883	29.3	24 435 871	7 092 798	29.0	26 231 016	7 732 085	29.5
1 X 2013[90]	ESDF	51 184 273	14 999 184	29.3	24 686 034	7 176 313	29.1	26 498 239	7 822 871	29.5
29 III 2014[114]	CDFC	50 279 900	14 877 943	29.6	24 228 714	7 114 224	29.4	26 051 186	7 763 719	29.8
1 X 2014[90]	ESDF	51 991 031	15 173 838	29.2	25 066 439	7 256 002	28.9	26 924 592	7 917 836	29.4
1 X 2015[90]	ESDF	52 450 516	15 363 901	29.3	25 256 187	7 331 696	29.0	27 194 329	8 032 205	29.5
1 X 2016[90]	ESDF	52 916 691	15 560 352	29.4	25 450 309	7 411 120	29.1	27 466 382	8 149 232	29.7
1 X 2017[90]	ESDF	53 387 948	15 762 776	29.5	25 647 847	7 494 003	29.2	27 740 101	8 268 773	29.8
Nepal - Népal										
1 VII 2008	ESDJ	26 966 581	...	...	13 515 938	...	...	13 450 643	...	...
1 VII 2009	ESDJ	27 504 280	...	...	13 790 836	...	...	13 713 444	...	...
1 VII 2010	ESDJ	28 043 744	...	...	14 066 638	...	...	13 977 106	...	...
22 VI 2011	CDJC	26 494 504	4 523 820	17.1	12 849 041	2 306 049	17.9	13 645 463	2 217 771	16.3
1 VII 2011	ESDJ	28 584 975	...	...	14 343 343	...	...	14 241 632	...	...
1 VII 2012[24]	ESDJ	26 873 066	...	...	13 030 795	...	...	13 842 271	...	...
1 VII 2013[24]	ESDJ	27 257 347	...	...	13 215 791	...	...	14 041 556	...	...
1 VII 2014[24]	ESDJ	27 646 053	...	...	13 403 432	...	...	14 242 621	...	...
1 VII 2015[24]	ESDJ	28 037 904	...	...	13 593 069	...	...	14 444 835	...	...
1 VII 2016[24]	ESDJ	28 431 494	...	...	13 784 009	...	...	14 647 486	...	...
1 VII 2017[24]	ESDJ	28 825 709	...	...	13 975 678	...	...	14 850 032	...	...
Oman										
1 VII 2008	ESDF	2 867 428	2 077 862	72.5	1 687 414	1 238 527	73.4	1 180 014	839 335	71.1
1 VII 2009	ESDF	3 173 917	2 314 865	72.9	1 971 115	1 457 197	73.9	1 202 802	857 668	71.3
12 XII 2010	CDFC	2 773 479	2 091 320	75.4	1 612 408	1 227 680	76.1	1 161 071	863 640	74.4
1 VII 2011	ESDF	3 295 298[115]	2 484 794[116]	75.4	2 090 883[115]	1 591 989[116]	76.1	1 204 415[115]	895 881[116]	74.4
1 VII 2012	ESDF	3 623 001[115]	2 731 895[116]	75.4	2 332 687[115]	1 776 097[116]	76.1	1 290 314[115]	959 775[116]	74.4
1 VII 2013	ESDF	3 855 206[115]	2 906 988[116]	75.4	2 502 235[115]	1 905 190[116]	76.1	1 352 971[115]	1 006 381[116]	74.4
1 VII 2014	ESDF	3 992 893[115]	3 010 810[116]	75.4	2 579 811[115]	1 964 256[116]	76.1	1 413 082[115]	1 051 093[116]	74.4
1 VII 2015	ESDF	4 159 102[115]	3 136 138[116]	75.4	2 684 844[115]	2 044 228[116]	76.1	1 474 258[115]	1 096 598[116]	74.4
1 VII 2016	ESDF	4 414 051[115]	3 432 019[117]	77.8	2 886 083[115]	2 296 140[117]	79.6	1 527 968[115]	1 133 279[117]	74.2
1 VII 2017	ESDF	4 559 963[115]	3 542 940[117]	77.7	2 984 404[115]	2 374 363[117]	79.6	1 575 559[115]	1 168 577[117]	74.2
Pakistan[118]										
1 VII 2008	ESDF	166 410 000	...	...	86 130 000	...	...	80 280 000	...	...
1 VII 2009	ESDF	169 940 000	...	...	87 940 000	...	...	82 010 000	...	...
1 VII 2010	ESDF	173 510 000	...	...	89 760 000	...	...	83 750 000	...	...
1 VII 2011	ESDF	177 100 000	...	...	91 590 000	...	...	85 510 000	...	...
15 III 2017*	CDFC	207 774 520	75 584 989	36.4	106 449 322[31]	39 149 151[31]	36.8	101 314 780[31]	36 428 187[31]	36.0
Philippines										
1 VII 2008[36]	ESDJ	90 457 200	...	...	45 483 100	...	...	44 974 100	...	...
1 VII 2009[36]	ESDJ	92 226 600	...	...	46 368 900	...	...	45 857 700	...	...
1 V 2010[119]	CDJC	92 335 113	41 855 571	45.3	46 634 257	20 840 798	44.7	45 700 856	21 014 773	46.0
1 VII 2010[11]	ESDJ	93 135 100	...	...	46 980 200	...	...	46 154 900	...	...
1 VII 2011[11]	ESDJ	94 823 800	...	...	47 832 400	...	...	46 991 400	...	...
1 VII 2012[11]	ESDJ	96 510 900	...	...	48 684 200	...	...	47 826 700	...	...
1 VII 2013[11]	ESDJ	98 196 500	...	...	49 535 100	...	...	48 661 400	...	...
1 VII 2014[11]	ESDJ	99 880 300	...	...	50 385 100	...	...	49 495 200	...	...
1 VII 2015[11]	ESDJ	101 562 300	...	...	51 234 200	...	...	50 328 100	...	...
1 VIII 2015[120]	CDJC	100 979 303	...	...	51 069 962	...	...	49 909 341	...	...
1 VII 2016[11]	ESDJ	103 242 900	...	...	52 081 400	...	...	51 161 500	...	...
1 VII 2017[11]	ESDJ	104 921 400	...	...	52 927 400	...	...	51 994 000	...	...
Qatar										
1 VII 2008	ESDF	1 448 479	...	...	1 111 176	...	...	337 303	...	...
1 VII 2009	ESDF	1 638 626	1 638 626	100.0	1 265 146	1 265 146	100.0	373 480	373 480	100.0
21 IV 2010	CDFC	1 699 435	...	...	1 284 739	...	...	414 696	...	...
1 VII 2010	ESDF	1 715 098	1 715 098	100.0	1 296 110	1 296 110	100.0	418 988	418 988	100.0
1 VII 2011	ESDF	1 732 717	1 732 717	100.0	1 288 590	1 288 590	100.0	444 127	444 127	100.0
1 VII 2012	ESDF	1 832 903	1 832 903	100.0	1 355 199	1 355 199	100.0	477 704	477 704	100.0
1 VII 2013	ESDF	2 003 700	2 003 700	100.0	1 477 632	1 477 632	100.0	526 068	526 068	100.0
1 VII 2014	ESDF	2 216 180	2 216 180	100.0	1 652 037	1 652 037	100.0	564 143	564 143	100.0
20 IV 2015	CDFC	2 404 776	...	...	1 816 981	...	...	587 795	...	...
1 VII 2015	ESDF	2 437 790	2 437 790	100.0	1 840 643	1 840 643	100.0	597 147	597 147	100.0

6. Total and urban population by sex: 2008 - 2017
Population totale et population urbaine selon le sexe : 2008 - 2017 (continued - suite)

Continent, country or area, and date / Continent, pays ou zone et date	Code[a]	Both sexes - Les deux sexes			Male - Masculin			Female - Féminin		
		Total	Urban - Urbaine		Total	Urban - Urbaine		Total	Urban - Urbaine	
			Number Nombre	Percent P.100		Number Nombre	Percent P.100		Number Nombre	Percent P.100
ASIA - ASIE										
Qatar										
1 VII 2016 ....ESDF		2 617 634	2 617 634	100.0	1 975 536	1 975 536	100.0	642 098	642 098	100.0
1 VII 2017 ....ESDF		2 724 606	2 724 606	100.0	2 046 047	2 046 047	100.0	678 559	678 559	100.0
Republic of Korea - République de Corée										
1 VII 2008 ....ESDJ		49 054 708	...	...	24 671 648	...	...	24 383 060	...	...
1 VII 2009 ....ESDJ		49 307 835	...	...	24 774 341	...	...	24 533 494	...	...
1 VII 2010 ....ESDJ		49 554 112	...	...	24 881 114	...	...	24 672 998	...	...
1 XI 2010[121] ....CDJC		48 580 293	39 822 647	82.0	24 167 098	19 798 739	81.9	24 413 195	20 023 908	82.0
1 VII 2011 ....ESDJ		49 936 638	...	...	25 069 867	...	...	24 866 771	...	...
1 VII 2012 ....ESDJ		50 199 853	...	...	25 187 380	...	...	25 012 473	...	...
1 VII 2013 ....ESDJ		50 428 893	...	...	25 285 319	...	...	25 143 574	...	...
1 VII 2014 ....ESDJ		50 746 659	...	...	25 445 077	...	...	25 301 582	...	...
1 VII 2015 ....ESDJ		51 014 947	...	...	25 585 894	...	...	25 429 053	...	...
1 XI 2015 ....CDJC		51 069 375	41 677 695	81.6	25 608 502	20 791 896	81.2	25 460 873	20 885 799	82.0
1 VII 2016 ....ESDJ		51 245 707	...	...	25 693 983	...	...	25 551 724	...	...
1 VII 2017 ....ESDJ		51 446 201	...	...	25 790 240	...	...	25 655 961	...	...
Saudi Arabia - Arabie saoudite										
1 VII 2008 ....ESDF		25 743 895	...	...	14 530 844	...	...	11 213 051	...	...
1 VII 2009 ....ESDF		26 576 321	...	...	15 074 067	...	...	11 502 254	...	...
27 IV 2010 ....CDFC		27 236 156	...	...	15 531 471	...	...	11 704 685	...	...
1 VII 2010 ....ESDF		27 410 508	...	...	15 643 804	...	...	11 766 704	...	...
1 VII 2011 ....ESDF		28 173 195	...	...	16 124 760	...	...	12 048 435	...	...
1 VII 2012 ....ESDF		28 896 840	...	...	16 566 096	...	...	12 330 744	...	...
1 VII 2013 ....ESDF		29 613 064	...	...	16 974 234	...	...	12 638 830	...	...
1 VII 2014 ....ESDF		30 339 795	...	...	17 393 435	...	...	12 946 360	...	...
1 VII 2015 ....ESDF		31 062 069	...	...	17 818 656	...	...	13 243 413	...	...
1 VII 2016 ....ESDF		31 787 580	...	...	18 259 719	...	...	13 527 861	...	...
1 VII 2017 ....ESDF		32 612 846	...	...	18 746 422	...	...	13 866 424	...	...
Singapore - Singapour[122]										
30 VI 2008[123] ....ESDJ		3 642 659	...	...	1 802 992	...	...	1 839 667	...	...
30 VI 2009[123] ....ESDJ		3 733 876	...	...	1 844 732	...	...	1 889 144	...	...
30 VI 2010[124] ....CDJC		3 771 721	...	...	1 861 133	...	...	1 910 588	...	...
30 VI 2010[123] ....ESDJ		3 771 721	...	...	1 861 133	...	...	1 910 588	...	...
30 VI 2011[123] ....ESDJ		3 789 251	...	...	1 868 170	...	...	1 921 081	...	...
30 VI 2012[123] ....ESDJ		3 818 205	...	...	1 880 046	...	...	1 938 159	...	...
30 VI 2013[123] ....ESDJ		3 844 751	...	...	1 891 504	...	...	1 953 247	...	...
30 VI 2014[123] ....ESDJ		3 870 739	...	...	1 902 410	...	...	1 968 329	...	...
30 VI 2015[123] ....ESDJ		3 902 690	...	...	1 916 628	...	...	1 986 062	...	...
30 VI 2016[123] ....ESDJ		3 933 559	...	...	1 929 526	...	...	2 004 033	...	...
30 VI 2017[123] ....ESDJ		3 965 796	...	...	1 943 545	...	...	2 022 251	...	...
Sri Lanka										
1 VII 2008 ....ESDF		20 246 000	...	...	10 060 000	...	...	10 186 000	...	...
1 VII 2009 ....ESDF		20 476 000	...	...	10 174 000	...	...	10 302 000	...	...
1 VII 2010 ....ESDF		20 675 000	...	...	10 273 000	...	...	10 402 000	...	...
1 VII 2011 ....ESDF		20 892 000	...	...	10 381 000	...	...	10 511 000	...	...
20 III 2012 ....CDJC		20 359 439	3 704 470	18.2	9 856 634	1 800 327	18.3	10 502 805	1 904 143	18.1
1 VII 2012 ....ESDJ		20 425 000	...	...	9 888 000	...	...	10 537 000	...	...
1 VII 2013 ....ESDJ		20 585 000	...	...	9 966 000	...	...	10 619 000	...	...
1 VII 2014* ....ESDJ		20 771 000	...	...	10 056 000	...	...	10 715 000	...	...
1 VII 2015* ....ESDJ		20 966 000	...	...	10 151 000	...	...	10 815 000	...	...
1 VII 2016* ....ESDJ		21 203 000	...	...	10 265 460	...	...	10 937 540	...	...
1 VII 2017* ....ESDJ		21 444 350	...	...	10 382 372	...	...	11 061 978	...	...
State of Palestine - État de Palestine										
1 VII 2008 ....ESDF		3 825 512	3 175 546[125]	83.0	1 941 742	...	...	1 883 770	...	...
1 VII 2009 ....ESDF		3 935 249	3 267 977[125]	83.0	1 997 625	...	...	1 937 624	...	...
1 VII 2010 ....ESDF		4 048 403	3 363 385[125]	83.1	2 055 211	...	...	1 993 192	...	...
1 VII 2011 ....ESDF		4 168 860	3 465 483[125]	83.1	2 116 782	...	...	2 052 078	...	...
1 VII 2012 ....ESDF		4 293 313	3 571 037[125]	83.2	2 180 386	...	...	2 112 927	...	...
1 VII 2013 ....ESDF		4 420 549	3 679 034[125]	83.2	2 245 400	...	...	2 175 149	...	...
1 VII 2014 ....ESDF		4 550 368	3 789 308[125]	83.3	2 311 721	...	...	2 238 647	...	...
1 VII 2015 ....ESDF		4 682 467	3 901 606[125]	83.3	2 379 184	...	...	2 303 283	...	...

Continent, country or area, and date / Continent, pays ou zone et date	Code[a]	Both sexes - Les deux sexes Total	Urban - Urbaine Number Nombre	Urban - Urbaine Percent P.100	Male - Masculin Total	Urban - Urbaine Number Nombre	Urban - Urbaine Percent P.100	Female - Féminin Total	Urban - Urbaine Number Nombre	Urban - Urbaine Percent P.100
ASIA - ASIE										
State of Palestine - État de Palestine										
1 VII 2016	ESDF	4 816 503	4 015 645[125]	83.4	2 447 616	...	...	2 368 887	...	...
1 VII 2017	ESDF	4 952 168	...	...	2 516 852	...	...	2 435 316	...	...
Syrian Arab Republic - République arabe syrienne[126]										
1 VII 2008	ESDF	19 644 000	10 511 000	53.5	10 042 000	5 394 000	53.7	9 602 000	5 117 000	53.3
1 VII 2009	ESDF	20 125 000	10 769 000	53.5	10 287 000	5 526 000	53.7	9 838 000	5 243 000	53.3
1 VII 2010	ESDF	20 619 000	11 033 000	53.5	10 539 000	5 661 000	53.7	10 080 000	5 372 000	53.3
1 VII 2011	ESDF	21 124 000	11 297 000	53.5	10 794 000	5 795 000	53.7	10 330 000	5 502 000	53.3
Tajikistan - Tadjikistan										
1 VII 2008	ESDF	7 294 747	1 918 996	26.3	3 659 238	965 220	26.4	3 635 510	953 776	26.2
1 VII 2009	ESDF	7 334 083	1 944 038	26.5	3 699 641	979 510	26.5	3 634 442	964 528	26.5
1 VII 2010	ESDF	7 519 280	1 996 961	26.6	3 794 467	1 007 796	26.6	3 724 813	989 165	26.6
21 IX 2010	CDFC	7 564 502	2 006 605	26.5	3 817 004	1 012 642	26.5	3 747 498	993 963	26.5
1 VII 2011	ESDF	7 714 198	2 042 660	26.5	3 893 798	1 032 106	26.5	3 820 401	1 010 554	26.5
1 VII 2012	ESDF	7 897 313	2 085 698	26.4	3 987 517	1 054 904	26.5	3 909 796	1 030 794	26.4
1 VII 2013	ESDF	8 074 266	2 138 737	26.5	4 078 857	1 083 119	26.6	3 995 409	1 055 618	26.4
1 VII 2014	ESDF	8 256 572	2 193 224	26.6	4 174 269	1 112 352	26.6	4 082 303	1 080 873	26.5
1 VII 2015	ESDF	8 451 630	2 237 893	26.5	4 276 777	1 136 493	26.6	4 174 854	1 101 401	26.4
1 VII 2016	ESDF	8 646 973	2 280 367	26.4	4 379 342	1 159 476	26.5	4 267 631	1 120 891	26.3
Thailand - Thaïlande										
1 VII 2008	ESDJ	63 389 730	...	...	31 255 869	...	...	32 133 861	...	...
1 VII 2009	ESDJ	63 525 062	...	...	31 293 096	...	...	32 231 966	...	...
1 VII 2010	ESDJ	63 878 267	...	...	31 451 801	...	...	32 426 466	...	...
1 IX 2010	CDJC	65 981 659	29 133 829	44.2	32 355 032	14 120 842	43.6	33 626 627	15 012 987	44.6
1 VII 2011	ESDJ	64 076 033	...	...	31 529 148	...	...	32 546 885	...	...
1 VII 2012	ESDJ	64 266 365	...	...	31 614 938	...	...	32 651 427	...	...
1 VII 2013	ESDJ	64 621 302	...	...	31 773 349	...	...	32 847 953	...	...
1 VII 2014	ESDJ	64 955 313	...	...	31 922 490	...	...	33 032 823	...	...
1 VII 2015	ESDJ	65 027 401	...	...	31 932 092	...	...	33 095 309	...	...
1 VII 2016	ESDJ	65 013 495	...	...	31 894 480	...	...	33 119 015	...	...
1 VII 2017	ESDJ	65 521 660	32 257 097	49.2	31 807 391	15 626 525	49.1	33 714 269	16 630 572	49.3
Timor-Leste										
1 VII 2008[4]	ESDF	1 080 742	...	...	549 000[81]	...	...	532 000[81]	...	...
11 VII 2010	CDFC	1 066 409	316 086	29.6	544 198	166 163	30.5	522 211	149 923	28.7
1 VII 2013[4]	ESDF	1 180 069	...	...	602 526	...	...	577 544	...	...
1 VII 2014[4]	ESDF	1 212 107	...	...	618 789	...	...	593 318	...	...
11 VII 2015	CDFC	1 183 643	349 208	29.5	601 112	179 565	29.9	582 531	169 643	29.1
1 VII 2017[4]	ESDF	1 241 506	...	...	633 197	...	...	608 309	...	...
Turkey - Turquie										
31 XII 2008[127]	CDJC	71 517 100	...	...	35 901 154	...	...	35 615 946	...	...
31 XII 2008[127]	ESDJ	71 517 100	49 514 530	69.2	35 901 154	24 865 097	69.3	35 615 946	24 649 433	69.2
31 XII 2009[127]	ESDJ	72 561 312	50 872 734	70.1	36 462 470	25 607 137	70.2	36 098 842	25 265 597	70.0
31 XII 2010[127]	ESDJ	73 722 988	52 340 830	71.0	37 043 182	26 348 394	71.1	36 679 806	25 992 436	70.9
3 X 2011[128]	CDJC	74 526 000	53 321 000	71.5	37 431 000	26 777 000	71.5	37 095 000	26 544 000	71.6
31 XII 2011[127]	ESDJ	74 724 269	53 630 845	71.8	37 532 954	26 947 983	71.8	37 191 315	26 682 862	71.7
31 XII 2012[127]	ESDJ	75 627 384	54 705 188	72.3	37 956 168	27 442 260	72.3	37 671 216	27 262 928	72.4
31 XII 2013[127]	ESDJ	76 667 864	66 488 105[129]	86.7	38 473 360	33 344 846[129]	86.7	38 194 504	33 143 259[129]	86.8
31 XII 2014[127]	ESDJ	77 695 904	67 720 318	87.2	38 984 302	33 954 681	87.1	38 711 602	33 765 637	87.2
31 XII 2015[127]	ESDJ	78 741 053	69 004 143	87.6	39 511 191	34 598 184	87.6	39 229 862	34 405 959	87.7
31 XII 2016[127]	ESDJ	79 814 871	70 165 359	87.9	40 043 650	35 162 317	87.8	39 771 221	35 003 042	88.0
United Arab Emirates - Émirats arabes unis[130]										
31 XII 2008	ESDF	8 073 626	...	...	6 039 971	...	...	2 033 655	...	...
31 XII 2009	ESDF	8 199 996	...	...	6 120 885	...	...	2 079 111	...	...
1 VII 2010	ESDF	8 264 070	...	...	6 161 820	...	...	2 102 250	...	...
31 XII 2016	ESDF	9 121 167	...	...	6 298 294	...	...	2 822 873	...	...
Uzbekistan - Ouzbékistan[106]										
1 VII 2008	ESDJ	27 302 782	14 141 300	51.8	13 653 947	7 037 900	51.5	13 648 835	7 103 400	52.0
1 VII 2009	ESDJ	27 767 408	14 330 900	51.6	13 893 825	7 129 600	51.3	13 873 583	7 201 300	51.9
1 VII 2010	ESDJ	28 562 405	14 661 700	51.3	14 291 711	7 295 300	51.0	14 270 694	7 366 400	51.6
1 VII 2011	ESDJ	29 339 368	15 062 700	51.3	14 680 424	7 496 500	51.1	14 658 944	7 566 200	51.6

Continent, country or area, and date / Continent, pays ou zone et date	Code[a]	Both sexes - Les deux sexes			Male - Masculin			Female - Féminin		
		Total	Urban - Urbaine		Total	Urban - Urbaine		Total	Urban - Urbaine	
			Number Nombre	Percent P.100		Number Nombre	Percent P.100		Number Nombre	Percent P.100
ASIA - ASIE										
Uzbekistan - Ouzbékistan[106]										
1 VII 2012 .... ESDJ	ESDJ	29 774 448	15 285 000	51.3	14 905 603	7 613 400	51.1	14 868 845	7 671 600	51.6
1 VII 2013 .... ESDJ	ESDJ	30 243 172	15 462 637	51.1	15 148 116	7 707 450	50.9	15 095 056	7 755 187	51.4
1 VII 2014 .... ESDJ	ESDJ	30 757 669	15 651 614	50.9	15 414 846	7 809 449	50.7	15 342 823	7 842 165	51.1
1 VII 2015 .... ESDJ	ESDJ	31 298 929	15 855 953	50.7	15 695 568	7 919 014	50.5	15 603 361	7 936 939	50.9
1 I 2016 .... ESDJ	ESDJ	31 575 300	15 963 900	50.6	...	...	...	...	...	...
1 I 2017 .... ESDJ	ESDJ	32 120 500	16 250 800	50.6	...	...	...	...	...	...
Viet Nam										
1 VII 2008[131] .... ESDF	ESDF	85 118 704	24 673 136	29.0	41 956 098	...	...	43 162 606	...	...
1 IV 2009 .... CDJC	CDJC	85 846 997	25 436 896	29.6	42 413 143	12 349 995	29.1	43 433 854	13 086 901	30.1
1 VII 2009[131] .... ESDJ	ESDJ	86 024 979	25 584 740	29.7	42 523 416	...	...	43 501 563	...	...
1 VII 2010[131] .... ESDJ	ESDJ	86 947 439	26 515 900	30.5	42 993 487	...	...	43 953 952	...	...
1 VII 2011[131] .... ESDJ	ESDJ	87 860 387	27 719 300	31.5	43 446 781	...	...	44 413 606	...	...
1 VII 2012[131] .... ESDJ	ESDJ	88 809 279	28 269 200	31.8	43 908 201	...	...	44 901 078	...	...
1 VII 2013[131] .... ESDJ	ESDJ	89 759 538	28 874 900	32.2	44 364 894	...	...	45 394 644	...	...
1 VII 2014[131] .... ESDJ	ESDJ	90 728 941	30 035 405	33.1	44 758 132	...	...	45 970 809	...	...
1 VII 2015[131] .... ESDJ	ESDJ	91 709 825	31 067 492	33.9	45 224 031	...	...	46 485 794	...	...
1 VII 2016*[131] .... ESDJ	ESDJ	92 695 121	31 985 992	34.5	45 705 601	...	...	46 989 520	...	...
Yemen - Yémen[4]										
1 VII 2008 .... ESDJ	ESDJ	21 843 554	6 281 475	28.8	11 127 218	...	...	10 716 336	...	...
1 VII 2009 .... ESDJ	ESDJ	22 492 035	6 475 802	28.8	11 454 963	...	...	11 037 072	...	...
1 VII 2010 .... ESDJ	ESDJ	23 153 982	6 673 916	28.8	11 789 814	...	...	11 364 168	...	...
1 VII 2011 .... ESDJ	ESDJ	23 832 569	6 875 789	28.9	12 133 362	...	...	11 699 207	...	...
1 VII 2012 .... ESDJ	ESDJ	24 526 703	7 075 639	28.8	12 485 039	...	...	12 041 664	...	...
1 VII 2013 .... ESDJ	ESDJ	25 235 079	7 280 367	28.9	12 844 169	...	...	12 390 910	...	...
EUROPE										
Åland Islands - Îles d'Åland[53]										
1 VII 2008 .... ESDJ	ESDJ	27 305	10 954	40.1	13 552	5 189	38.3	13 753	5 765	41.9
1 VII 2009 .... ESDJ	ESDJ	27 595	11 064	40.1	13 724	5 264	38.4	13 871	5 800	41.8
1 VII 2010 .... ESDJ	ESDJ	27 871	11 157	40.0	13 880	5 327	38.4	13 991	5 830	41.7
1 VII 2011 .... ESDJ	ESDJ	28 181	11 227	39.8	14 045	5 364	38.2	14 137	5 863	41.5
1 VII 2012 .... ESDJ	ESDJ	28 429	11 305	39.8	14 172	5 408	38.2	14 257	5 897	41.4
1 VII 2013 .... ESDJ	ESDJ	28 585	11 370	39.8	14 255	5 445	38.2	14 330	5 925	41.3
1 VII 2014 .... ESDJ	ESDJ	28 792	11 437	39.7	14 375	5 490	38.2	14 417	5 947	41.2
1 VII 2015 .... ESDJ	ESDJ	28 950	11 471	39.6	14 466	5 521	38.2	14 484	5 950	41.1
1 VII 2016 .... ESDJ	ESDJ	29 099	11 513	39.6	14 526	5 538	38.1	14 573	5 975	41.0
1 VII 2017 .... ESDJ	ESDJ	29 352	11 621	39.6	14 644	5 583	38.1	14 708	6 038	41.1
Albania - Albanie										
1 VII 2008 .... ESDF	ESDF	2 947 314	1 495 552	50.7	1 472 660	740 747	50.3	1 474 654	754 805	51.2
1 VII 2009 .... ESDF	ESDF	2 927 519	1 518 397	51.9	1 463 537	752 178	51.4	1 463 982	766 219	52.3
1 VII 2010 .... ESDF	ESDF	2 913 021	1 541 310	52.9	1 457 661	763 780	52.4	1 455 360	777 530	53.4
1 VII 2011 .... ESDJ	ESDJ	2 904 780	1 564 139	53.8	1 455 074	775 313	53.3	1 449 706	788 826	54.4
1 X 2011 .... CDJC	CDJC	2 800 138	1 498 508	53.5	1 403 059	742 671	52.9	1 397 079	755 837	54.1
1 VII 2012 .... ESDJ	ESDJ	2 900 401	...	...	1 459 681	...	...	1 440 720	...	...
1 VII 2013 .... ESDJ	ESDJ	2 895 092	...	...	1 461 076	...	...	1 434 016	...	...
1 VII 2014 .... ESDJ	ESDJ	2 889 104	...	...	1 461 389	...	...	1 427 715	...	...
1 VII 2015 .... ESDJ	ESDJ	2 880 703	...	...	1 459 831	...	...	1 420 872	...	...
1 VII 2016 .... ESDJ	ESDJ	2 876 101	...	...	1 456 000	...	...	1 420 101	...	...
1 I 2017 .... ESDJ	ESDJ	2 876 591	...	...	1 453 541	...	...	1 423 050	...	...
Andorra - Andorre[53]										
1 VII 2008 .... ESDJ	ESDJ	83 884	...	...	43 911	...	...	39 973	...	...
1 VII 2009 .... ESDJ	ESDJ	85 116	...	...	44 444	...	...	40 672	...	...
1 I 2010[132] .... ESDJ	ESDJ	70 290	...	...	35 592	...	...	34 698	...	...
1 I 2011 .... ESDJ	ESDJ	69 772	...	...	35 204	...	...	34 568	...	...
31 XII 2011 .... CDJC	CDJC	78 115	...	...	39 863	...	...	38 252	...	...
1 I 2012 .... CDJC	CDJC	69 758	...	...	35 147	...	...	34 611	...	...
1 VII 2013 .... ESDJ	ESDJ	69 929	...	...	35 206	...	...	34 723	...	...
1 VII 2014 .... ESDJ	ESDJ	70 155	...	...	35 364	...	...	34 791	...	...
1 VII 2015 .... ESDJ	ESDJ	70 901	...	...	35 741	...	...	35 160	...	...
1 VII 2016 .... ESDJ	ESDJ	72 358	...	...	36 590	...	...	35 768	...	...

6. Total and urban population by sex: 2008 - 2017
Population totale et population urbaine selon le sexe : 2008 - 2017 (continued - suite)

Continent, country or area, and date / Continent, pays ou zone et date	Code[a]	Both sexes - Les deux sexes — Total	Urban - Urbaine Number Nombre	Urban - Urbaine Percent P.100	Male - Masculin — Total	Urban - Urbaine Number Nombre	Urban - Urbaine Percent P.100	Female - Féminin — Total	Urban - Urbaine Number Nombre	Urban - Urbaine Percent P.100
EUROPE										
Austria - Autriche										
1 VII 2008	ESDJ	8 321 541	...	...	4 050 215	...	...	4 271 326	...	...
1 VII 2009	ESDJ	8 341 483	...	...	4 061 195	...	...	4 280 288	...	...
1 VII 2010	ESDJ	8 361 069	...	...	4 071 773	...	...	4 289 296	...	...
1 VII 2011	ESDJ	8 388 534	...	...	4 087 188	...	...	4 301 346	...	...
31 X 2011	CDJC	8 401 940	5 643 239	67.2	4 093 938	2 713 930	66.3	4 308 002	2 929 309	68.0
1 VII 2012	ESDJ	8 426 311	...	...	4 109 431	...	...	4 316 880	...	...
1 VII 2013	ESDJ	8 477 230	...	...	4 138 693	...	...	4 338 537	...	...
1 VII 2014	ESDJ	8 543 975	...	...	4 176 554	...	...	4 367 421	...	...
1 VII 2015	ESDJ	8 629 496	...	...	4 229 064	...	...	4 400 432	...	...
1 VII 2016	ESDJ	8 739 806	...	...	4 295 164	...	...	4 444 642	...	...
1 I 2017	ESDJ	8 772 865	...	...	4 312 441	...	...	4 460 424	...	...
Belarus - Bélarus										
1 VII 2008	ESDJ	9 527 985	7 008 135	73.6	4 433 031	3 249 263	73.3	5 094 954	3 758 872	73.8
1 VII 2009	ESDJ	9 506 765	7 052 045	74.2	4 421 789	3 266 240	73.9	5 084 976	3 785 805	74.5
14 X 2009	CDJC	9 503 807	7 064 529	74.3	4 420 039	3 271 014	74.0	5 083 768	3 793 515	74.6
1 VII 2010	ESDJ	9 490 583	7 100 147	74.8	4 413 225	3 285 104	74.4	5 077 358	3 815 043	75.1
1 VII 2011	ESDJ	9 473 172	7 148 636	75.5	4 403 227	3 303 932	75.0	5 069 945	3 844 704	75.8
1 VII 2012	ESDJ	9 464 495	7 198 575	76.1	4 397 910	3 324 299	75.6	5 066 585	3 874 276	76.5
1 VII 2013	ESDJ	9 465 997	7 247 854	76.6	4 399 369	3 345 878	76.1	5 066 628	3 901 976	77.0
1 VII 2014	ESDJ	9 474 511	7 299 878	77.0	4 405 204	3 369 054	76.5	5 069 307	3 930 824	77.5
1 VII 2015	ESDJ	9 489 616	7 347 512	77.4	4 415 020	3 390 465	76.8	5 074 596	3 957 047	78.0
1 VII 2016[20]	ESDJ	9 501 534	7 385 438	77.7	4 423 680	3 407 394	77.0	5 077 854	3 978 044	78.3
1 I 2017	ESDJ	9 504 704	7 400 832	77.9	4 426 519	3 414 000	77.1	5 078 185	3 986 832	78.5
Belgium - Belgique										
1 VII 2008	ESDJ	10 709 973	10 555 681	98.6	5 246 480	5 169 223	98.5	5 463 493	5 386 458	98.6
1 VII 2009	ESDJ	10 796 493	10 641 089	98.6	5 290 436	5 212 557	98.5	5 506 057	5 428 532	98.6
1 VII 2010	ESDJ	10 895 638	10 739 291	98.6	5 341 252	5 262 796	98.5	5 554 386	5 476 495	98.6
1 I 2011	CDJC	11 000 638	10 842 520	98.6	5 401 718	5 322 172	98.5	5 598 920	5 520 348	98.6
1 VII 2011	ESDJ	11 043 788	10 884 939	98.6	5 425 814	5 345 964	98.5	5 617 974	5 538 975	98.6
1 VII 2012	ESDJ	11 128 246	...	...	5 469 608	...	...	5 658 638	...	...
1 VII 2013	ESDJ	11 182 817	...	...	5 497 753	...	...	5 685 065	...	...
1 VII 2014	ESDJ	11 231 213	...	...	5 522 163	...	...	5 709 051	...	...
1 VII 2015[20]	ESDJ	11 284 776	...	...	5 552 760	...	...	5 732 016	...	...
1 VII 2016[20]	ESDJ	11 331 422	...	...	5 579 268	...	...	5 752 154	...	...
1 I 2017	ESDJ	11 351 727	...	...	5 589 272	...	...	5 762 455	...	...
Bosnia and Herzegovina - Bosnie-Herzégovine										
1 VII 2008	ESDF	3 842 265	...	...	1 877 165	...	...	1 965 100	...	...
1 VII 2009	ESDF	3 842 566	...	...	1 877 312	...	...	1 965 254	...	...
1 VII 2010	ESDF	3 843 126	...	...	1 877 587	...	...	1 965 539	...	...
1 VII 2011	ESDF	3 841 224	...	...	1 876 546	...	...	1 964 678	...	...
1 VII 2012	ESDF	3 837 455	...	...	1 874 608	...	...	1 962 848	...	...
30 IX 2013	CDJC	3 531 159	...	...	1 732 270	...	...	1 798 889	...	...
Bulgaria - Bulgarie										
1 VII 2008	ESDJ	7 623 395	5 405 147	70.9	3 690 485	2 597 929	70.4	3 932 910	2 807 218	71.4
1 VII 2009	ESDJ	7 585 131	5 408 330	71.3	3 670 296	2 598 442	70.8	3 914 835	2 809 888	71.8
1 VII 2010	ESDJ	7 534 289	5 388 142	71.5	3 644 560	2 587 844	71.0	3 889 729	2 800 298	72.0
1 II 2011	CDJC	7 364 570	5 338 261	72.5	3 586 571	2 580 734	72.0	3 777 999	2 757 527	73.0
1 VII 2011	ESDJ	7 348 328	5 336 366	72.6	3 577 847	2 579 205	72.1	3 770 481	2 757 161	73.1
1 VII 2012	ESDJ	7 305 888	5 316 384	72.8	3 555 920	2 568 535	72.2	3 749 968	2 747 849	73.3
1 VII 2013	ESDJ	7 263 859	...	...	3 534 276	...	...	3 729 584	...	...
1 VII 2014	ESDJ	7 223 937	5 279 577	73.1	3 513 480	2 548 437	72.5	3 710 457	2 731 140	73.6
1 VII 2015	ESDJ	7 177 991	5 247 331	73.1	3 489 596	2 530 439	72.5	3 688 395	2 716 892	73.7
1 VII 2016[20]	ESDJ	7 127 822	5 215 784	73.2	3 463 578	2 512 987	72.6	3 664 244	2 702 797	73.8
1 I 2017	ESDJ	7 101 859	5 204 385	73.3	3 449 978	2 506 628	72.7	3 651 881	2 697 757	73.9
Croatia - Croatie										
1 VII 2008	ESDJ	4 309 705	...	...	2 076 517	...	...	2 233 188	...	...
1 VII 2009	ESDJ	4 305 181	...	...	2 075 321	...	...	2 229 860	...	...
1 VII 2010	ESDJ	4 295 427	...	...	2 071 195	...	...	2 224 232	...	...
1 IV 2011	CDJC	4 284 889	2 368 506	55.3	2 066 335	1 121 328	54.3	2 218 554	1 247 178	56.2
1 VII 2011	ESDJ	4 280 622	...	...	2 064 314	...	...	2 216 308	...	...
1 VII 2012	ESDJ	4 267 558	...	...	2 058 701	...	...	2 208 857	...	...
1 VII 2013	ESDJ	4 255 689	...	...	2 053 788	...	...	2 201 901	...	...
1 VII 2014	ESDJ	4 238 389	...	...	2 045 801	...	...	2 192 588	...	...
1 VII 2015	ESDJ	4 203 604	...	...	2 028 640	...	...	2 174 964	...	...

Continent, country or area, and date / Continent, pays ou zone et date	Code[a]	Both sexes - Les deux sexes Total	Urban - Urbaine Number Nombre	Urban - Urbaine Percent P.100	Male - Masculin Total	Urban - Urbaine Number Nombre	Urban - Urbaine Percent P.100	Female - Féminin Total	Urban - Urbaine Number Nombre	Urban - Urbaine Percent P.100
EUROPE										
Croatia - Croatie										
1 VII 2016	ESDJ	4 174 349	...	...	2 014 837	...	...	2 159 512	...	...
1 I 2017	ESDJ	4 154 213	...	...	2 005 210	...	...	2 149 003	...	...
Czechia - Tchéquie										
1 VII 2008	ESDJ	10 384 603	...	...	5 090 898	...	...	5 293 705	...	...
1 VII 2009	ESDJ	10 443 936	...	...	5 126 422	...	...	5 317 514	...	...
1 VII 2010	ESDJ	10 474 410	...	...	5 141 699	...	...	5 332 711	...	...
25 III 2011	CDJC	10 436 560	7 650 450	73.3	5 109 766	3 712 348	72.7	5 326 794	3 938 102	73.9
1 VII 2011	ESDJ	10 496 088	...	...	5 152 721	...	...	5 343 368	...	...
1 VII 2012	ESDJ	10 510 786	...	...	5 161 280	...	...	5 349 506	...	...
1 VII 2013	ESDJ	10 510 719	7 683 793	73.1	5 161 617	3 740 790	72.5	5 349 102	3 943 003	73.7
1 VII 2014	ESDJ	10 524 783	7 693 352	73.1	5 169 146	3 744 873	72.4	5 355 637	3 948 479	73.7
1 VII 2015	ESDJ	10 542 942	7 702 624	73.1	5 180 242	3 749 901	72.4	5 362 700	3 952 723	73.7
1 VII 2016	ESDJ	10 565 284	7 725 090	73.1	5 193 012	3 761 862	72.4	5 372 272	3 963 228	73.8
1 I 2017	ESDJ	10 578 820	7 731 256	73.1	5 200 687	3 765 692	72.4	5 378 133	3 965 564	73.7
Denmark - Danemark[133]										
1 VII 2008	ESDJ	5 489 022	...	...	2 720 016	...	...	2 769 006	...	...
1 VII 2009	ESDJ	5 519 441	...	...	2 735 983	...	...	2 783 458	...	...
1 VII 2010	ESDJ	5 545 039	...	...	2 748 439	...	...	2 796 600	...	...
1 I 2011	CDJC	5 560 628	...	...	2 756 582	...	...	2 804 046	...	...
1 VII 2011	ESDJ	5 566 856	...	...	2 760 140	...	...	2 806 716	...	...
1 VII 2012	ESDJ	5 587 085	...	...	2 771 208	...	...	2 815 877	...	...
1 VII 2013	ESDJ	5 608 784	...	...	2 782 661	...	...	2 826 123	...	...
1 VII 2014	ESDJ	5 639 719	...	...	2 799 895	...	...	2 839 824	...	...
1 VII 2015	ESDJ	5 678 348	...	...	2 822 535	...	...	2 855 813	...	...
1 VII 2016	ESDJ	5 724 456	...	...	2 848 030	...	...	2 876 426	...	...
1 VII 2017	ESDJ	5 760 694	...	...	2 866 952	...	...	2 893 742	...	...
Estonia - Estonie										
1 VII 2008	ESDJ	1 337 090	911 285	68.2	621 685	411 555	66.2	715 405	499 730	69.9
1 VII 2009	ESDJ	1 334 515	907 675	68.0	621 060	410 130	66.0	713 455	497 545	69.7
1 VII 2010	ESDJ	1 331 475	904 365	67.9	620 250	408 720	65.9	711 225	495 645	69.7
1 VII 2011	ESDJ	1 327 439	903 066	68.0	618 919	408 988	66.1	708 520	494 078	69.7
31 XII 2011	CDJC	1 294 455	879 157	67.9	600 526	396 719	66.1	693 929	482 438	69.5
1 VII 2012	ESDJ	1 322 696	902 743	68.3	617 153	409 784	66.4	705 543	492 959	69.9
1 VII 2013	ESDJ	1 317 997	900 071	68.3	615 543	408 564	66.4	702 454	491 507	70.0
1 VII 2014	ESDJ	1 314 545	897 901	68.3	614 654	407 677	66.3	699 891	490 224	70.0
1 VII 2015	ESDJ	1 314 608	899 288[96]	68.4	615 549	406 894[96]	66.1	699 059	492 395[96]	70.4
1 VII 2016[20]	ESDJ	1 315 790	900 266[96]	68.4	617 123	406 142[96]	65.8	698 667	494 124[96]	70.7
1 I 2017	ESDJ	1 315 635	899 283[96]	68.4	617 538	406 016[96]	65.7	698 097	493 267[96]	70.7
Faeroe Islands - Îles Féroé										
1 I 2008[53]	CDJC	48 433	...	...	25 174	...	...	23 259	...	...
1 VII 2008	ESDJ	48 555	17 707	36.5	25 218	8 966	35.6	23 337	8 741	37.5
1 VII 2009	ESDJ	48 798	18 001	36.9	25 345	9 117	36.0	23 453	8 884	37.9
1 VII 2010	ESDJ	48 669	18 131	37.3	25 276	9 195	36.4	23 393	8 936	38.2
1 VII 2011	ESDJ	48 563	18 110	37.3	25 179	9 120	36.2	23 384	8 990	38.4
11 XI 2011	CDJC	48 346	...	...	25 125	...	...	23 221	...	...
1 VII 2012	ESDJ	48 319	18 033	37.3	25 074	9 072	36.2	23 245	8 961	38.6
1 VII 2013	ESDJ	48 286	18 220	37.7	25 014	9 147	36.6	23 272	9 073	39.0
1 VII 2014	ESDJ	48 462	18 373	37.9	25 048	9 207	36.8	23 414	9 166	39.1
1 VII 2015	ESDJ	48 929	18 663	38.1	25 312	9 381	37.1	23 617	9 282	39.3
1 VII 2016	ESDJ	49 497	18 964	38.3	25 546	9 514	37.2	23 951	9 450	39.5
1 VII 2017	ESDJ	50 216	19 249	38.3	25 886	9 672	37.4	24 330	9 577	39.4
Finland - Finlande										
1 VII 2008[134]	ESDJ	5 286 095	3 586 744	67.9	2 590 669	1 737 294	67.1	2 695 426	1 849 450	68.6
1 VII 2009[134]	ESDJ	5 311 276	3 615 933	68.1	2 604 636	1 753 169	67.3	2 706 640	1 862 764	68.8
1 VII 2010[134]	ESDJ	5 335 481	3 643 170	68.3	2 617 862	1 767 855	67.5	2 717 620	1 875 315	69.0
31 XII 2010	CDJC	5 375 276	3 662 915	68.1	2 638 416	1 777 697	67.4	2 736 860	1 885 218	68.9
1 VII 2011[134]	ESDJ	5 360 091	3 671 777	68.5	2 631 431	1 783 058	67.8	2 728 660	1 888 719	69.2
1 VII 2012[134]	ESDJ	5 385 543	3 701 923	68.7	2 645 408	1 799 025	68.0	2 740 136	1 902 898	69.4
1 VII 2013[134]	ESDJ	5 410 389	3 732 928	69.0	2 659 239	1 815 818	68.3	2 751 150	1 917 110	69.7
1 VII 2014[134]	ESDJ	5 432 721	3 762 906	69.3	2 671 740	1 831 826	68.6	2 760 981	1 931 080	69.9
1 VII 2015[134]	ESDJ	5 450 581	3 849 116	70.6	2 682 211	1 875 949	69.9	2 768 370	1 973 167	71.3
1 VII 2016[134]	ESDJ	5 466 204	3 880 555	71.0	2 692 383	1 893 551	70.3	2 773 822	1 987 004	71.6
1 I 2017[53]	ESDJ	5 503 297	...	...	2 712 327	...	...	2 790 970	...	...

Continent, country or area, and date / Continent, pays ou zone et date	Code[a]	Both sexes - Les deux sexes Total	Both sexes Urban - Urbaine Number Nombre	Both sexes Urban - Urbaine Percent P.100	Male - Masculin Total	Male Urban - Urbaine Number Nombre	Male Urban - Urbaine Percent P.100	Female - Féminin Total	Female Urban - Urbaine Number Nombre	Female Urban - Urbaine Percent P.100
EUROPE										
France[135]										
1 VII 2008 ....ESDJ		62 300 288	...	...	30 166 091	...	...	32 134 197	...	...
1 VII 2009 ....ESDJ		62 615 472	...	...	30 322 692	...	...	32 292 780	...	...
1 I 2010 ....CDJS		62 765 235	48 387 303	77.1	30 393 079	23 208 841	76.4	32 372 156	25 178 462	77.8
1 VII 2010 ....ESDJ		62 917 790	...	...	30 475 789	...	...	32 442 001	...	...
1 VII 2011 ....ESDJ		63 223 158	...	...	30 626 399	...	...	32 596 759	...	...
1 VII 2012 ....ESDJ		63 536 918	...	...	30 782 589	...	...	32 754 329	...	...
1 VII 2013 ....ESDJ		63 862 912	...	...	30 945 467	...	...	32 917 445	...	...
1 VII 2014 ....ESDJ		64 164 390	...	...	31 086 155	...	...	33 078 235	...	...
1 VII 2015* ....ESDJ		64 429 647	...	...	31 210 477	...	...	33 219 170	...	...
1 VII 2016* ....ESDJ		64 679 784	...	...	31 332 989	...	...	33 346 795	...	...
1 VII 2017* ....ESDJ		64 909 596	...	...	31 446 345	...	...	33 463 251	...	...
Germany - Allemagne										
1 VII 2008 ....ESDJ		82 119 776	...	...	40 238 595	...	...	41 881 181	...	...
1 VII 2009 ....ESDJ		81 874 770	...	...	40 133 270	...	...	41 741 500	...	...
1 VII 2010 ....ESDJ		81 757 471	...	...	40 099 871	...	...	41 657 600	...	...
9 V 2011 ....CDJC		80 219 695	64 444 232	80.3	39 145 941	31 227 832	79.8	41 073 754	33 216 400	80.9
1 VII 2011[6] ....ESDJ		80 274 983		...	39 177 274		...	41 097 709		...
1 VII 2012[6] ....ESDJ		80 425 823	...	...	39 305 462	...	...	41 120 362	...	...
1 VII 2013[6] ....ESDJ		80 645 605	...	...	39 468 950	...	...	41 176 655	...	...
1 VII 2014[6] ....ESDJ		80 982 500	...	...	39 696 190	...	...	41 286 310	...	...
1 VII 2015[6] ....ESDJ		81 686 663	...	...	40 174 816	...	...	41 511 847	...	...
1 VII 2016[136] ....ESDJ		82 348 669	...	...	40 605 621	...	...	41 743 048	...	...
1 I 2017[6] ....ESDJ		82 521 653	...	...	40 697 118	...	...	41 824 535	...	...
Gibraltar[137]										
31 XII 2008 ....ESDF		30 496	...	...	15 113	...	...	15 383	...	...
31 XII 2009 ....ESDF		30 963	...	...	15 378	...	...	15 585	...	...
31 XII 2010 ....ESDF		31 465	...	...	15 666	...	...	15 799	...	...
31 XII 2011 ....ESDF		32 003	...	...	15 977	...	...	16 026	...	...
12 XI 2012 ....CDJC		32 194	...	...	16 061	...	...	16 133	...	...
31 XII 2012 ....ESDF		32 577	...	...	16 311	...	...	16 266	...	...
31 XII 2013 ....ESDF		32 734	...	...	16 460	...	...	16 274	...	...
31 XII 2014 ....ESDF		33 140	...	...	16 694	...	...	16 446	...	...
31 XII 2015 ....ESDF		33 573	...	...	16 938	...	...	16 635	...	...
Greece - Grèce										
1 VII 2008 ....ESDF		11 077 863	...	...	5 452 027	...	...	5 625 836	...	...
1 VII 2009 ....ESDF		11 107 024	...	...	5 458 449	...	...	5 648 575	...	...
1 VII 2010 ....ESDF		11 121 383	...	...	5 457 186	...	...	5 664 197	...	...
9 V 2011 ....CDFC		10 816 286	8 285 259	76.6	5 303 223	4 022 889	75.9	5 513 063	4 262 370	77.3
1 VII 2011 ....ESDF		11 104 995	...	...	5 438 712	...	...	5 666 283	...	...
1 VII 2012 ....ESDF		11 045 040	...	...	5 395 104	...	...	5 649 936	...	...
1 VII 2013 ....ESDF		10 965 241	...	...	5 339 750	...	...	5 625 491	...	...
1 VII 2014 ....ESDF		10 892 369	...	...	5 290 797	...	...	5 601 572	...	...
1 VII 2015 ....ESDF		10 820 964	...	...	5 246 345	...	...	5 574 619	...	...
1 VII 2016 ....ESDF		10 775 989	...	...	5 222 749	...	...	5 553 240	...	...
1 I 2017 ....ESDF		10 768 193	...	...	5 221 277	...	...	5 546 916	...	...
Guernsey - Guernesey										
31 III 2008 ....ESDJ		61 726	...	...	30 405	...	...	31 321	...	...
31 III 2009 ....ESDJ		62 274	...	...	30 777	...	...	31 497	...	...
31 III 2010 ....ESDJ		62 431	...	...	30 695	...	...	31 736	...	...
31 III 2011 ....ESDJ		62 915	...	...	31 025	...	...	31 890	...	...
31 III 2012 ....ESDJ		62 904	...	...	30 966	...	...	31 938	...	...
31 III 2013 ....ESDJ		62 732	...	...	31 081	...	...	31 651	...	...
31 III 2014 ....ESDJ		62 341	...	...	30 804	...	...	31 537	...	...
31 III 2015 ....CDJC		62 234	...	...	30 819	...	...	31 415	...	...
31 III 2016 ....ESDJ		62 266	...	...	30 851	...	...	31 415	...	...
31 III 2017 ....ESDJ		62 193	...	...	30 799	...	...	31 394	...	...
Holy See - Saint-Siège[138]										
1 VII 2009 ....CDFC		466[139]	...	...	320	...	...	146	...	...
Hungary - Hongrie										
1 VII 2008 ....ESDJ		10 038 188	6 810 173	67.8	4 766 306	3 191 030	66.9	5 271 882	3 619 143	68.6
1 VII 2009 ....ESDJ		10 022 650	6 861 432	68.5	4 759 975	3 215 749	67.6	5 262 675	3 645 683	69.3
1 VII 2010 ....ESDJ		10 000 023	6 953 071	69.5	4 750 401	3 260 344	68.6	5 249 623	3 692 727	70.3
1 VII 2011 ....ESDJ		9 971 727	6 945 873	69.7	4 737 813	3 256 796	68.7	5 233 914	3 689 077	70.5
1 X 2011 ....CDFC		9 937 628	6 903 858	69.5	4 718 479	3 241 911	68.7	5 219 149	3 661 947	70.2

6. Total and urban population by sex: 2008 - 2017
Population totale et population urbaine selon le sexe : 2008 - 2017 (continued - suite)

Continent, country or area, and date / Continent, pays ou zone et date	Code[a]	Both sexes - Les deux sexes			Male - Masculin			Female - Féminin		
		Total	Urban - Urbaine		Total	Urban - Urbaine		Total	Urban - Urbaine	
			Number Nombre	Percent P.100		Number Nombre	Percent P.100		Number Nombre	Percent P.100
EUROPE										
Hungary - Hongrie										
1 VII 2012	ESDJ	9 920 362	6 877 231	69.3	4 720 310	3 234 447	68.5	5 200 052	3 642 785	70.1
1 VII 2013	ESDJ	9 893 082	6 864 757	69.4	4 709 672	3 229 480	68.6	5 183 410	3 635 277	70.1
1 VII 2014[140]	ESDJ	9 866 468	6 950 391	70.4	4 699 585	3 272 050	69.6	5 166 883	3 678 342	71.2
1 VII 2015[140]	ESDJ	9 843 028	6 937 836	70.5	4 692 149	3 267 756	69.6	5 150 879	3 670 081	71.3
1 VII 2016[140]	ESDJ	9 814 023	6 916 274	70.5	4 681 905	3 259 506	69.6	5 132 118	3 656 768	71.3
1 VII 2017[140]	ESDJ	9 787 966	...	...	4 673 447	...	...	5 114 519	...	...
Iceland - Islande[141]										
1 VII 2008	ESDJ	319 355	298 024	93.3	163 176	151 378	92.8	156 179	146 646	93.9
1 VII 2009	ESDJ	319 246	298 890	93.6	161 548	150 604	93.2	157 698	148 286	94.0
1 VII 2010	ESDJ	318 006	297 432	93.5	159 838	148 901	93.2	158 168	148 531	93.9
1 VII 2011	ESDJ	319 014	300 395	94.2	160 185	...	...	158 829	...	...
31 XII 2011	CDJC	315 556	295 874	93.8	158 151	147 681	93.4	157 405	148 193	94.1
1 VII 2012	ESDJ	320 716	300 237	93.6	160 901	150 074	93.3	159 815	150 163	94.0
1 VII 2013	ESDJ	323 764	303 136	93.6	162 378	151 471	93.3	161 386	151 665	94.0
1 VII 2014	ESDJ	327 386	306 633	93.7	164 252	153 265	93.3	163 134	153 368	94.0
1 VII 2015	ESDJ	330 815	309 868	93.7	166 228	155 146	93.3	164 587	154 723	94.0
1 VII 2016	ESDJ	335 439	314 123	93.6	169 152	157 819	93.3	166 288	156 304	94.0
1 I 2017	ESDJ	338 349	...	...	171 033	...	...	167 316	...	...
Ireland - Irlande										
1 VII 2008	ESDF	4 425 683	...	...	2 206 165	...	...	2 219 518	...	...
1 VII 2009	ESDF	4 458 942	...	...	2 215 646	...	...	2 243 297	...	...
1 VII 2010	ESDF	4 560 155	...	...	2 265 200	...	...	2 294 955	...	...
10 IV 2011	CDFC	4 588 252	2 846 882	62.0	2 272 699	1 389 160	61.1	2 315 553	1 457 722	63.0
1 VII 2011	ESDF	4 580 084	...	...	2 271 713	...	...	2 308 372	...	...
1 VII 2012	ESDF	4 599 533	...	...	2 278 731	...	...	2 320 803	...	...
1 VII 2013	ESDF	4 623 816	...	...	2 289 656	...	...	2 334 160	...	...
1 VII 2014	ESDF	4 657 740	...	...	2 304 596	...	...	2 353 144	...	...
1 VII 2015	ESDF	4 701 957	...	...	2 326 242	...	...	2 375 715	...	...
24 IV 2016	CDJC	4 761 865	...	...	2 354 428	...	...	2 407 437	...	...
1 VII 2016	ESDF	4 755 335	...	...	2 353 530	...	...	2 401 805	...	...
1 I 2017	ESDF	4 784 383	...	...	2 367 918	...	...	2 416 465	...	...
Isle of Man - Île de Man										
30 IV 2008	ESDJ	81 722	...	...	40 472	...	...	41 250	...	...
30 IV 2009	ESDJ	82 371	...	...	40 849	...	...	41 522	...	...
30 IV 2010	ESDJ	82 691	...	...	41 053	...	...	41 638	...	...
27 III 2011	CDJC	84 497	...	...	41 971	...	...	42 526	...	...
30 IV 2012	ESDJ	85 047	...	...	42 273	...	...	42 775	...	...
30 IV 2013	ESDJ	85 682	...	...	42 622	...	...	43 060	...	...
30 IV 2014	ESDJ	86 322	...	...	42 971	...	...	43 352	...	...
30 IV 2015	ESDJ	86 963	...	...	43 319	...	...	43 644	...	...
24 IV 2016	CDJC	83 314	...	...	41 269	...	...	42 045	...	...
30 IV 2016	ESDJ	85 619	...	...	42 665	...	...	42 954	...	...
Italy - Italie										
1 VII 2008	ESDJ	58 826 731	...	...	28 490 625	...	...	30 336 106	...	...
1 VII 2009	ESDJ	59 095 365	...	...	28 609 696	...	...	30 485 669	...	...
1 VII 2010	ESDJ	59 277 417	...	...	28 682 321	...	...	30 595 096	...	...
1 VII 2011	ESDJ	59 379 449	...	...	28 720 928	...	...	30 658 521	...	...
9 X 2011	CDJC	59 433 744	...	...	28 745 507	...	...	30 688 237	...	...
1 VII 2012	ESDJ	59 539 717	...	...	28 808 098	...	...	30 731 619	...	...
1 VII 2013	ESDJ	60 233 948	...	...	29 187 081	...	...	31 046 867	...	...
1 VII 2014	ESDJ	60 789 140	...	...	29 493 077	...	...	31 296 063	...	...
1 VII 2015	ESDJ	60 730 582	...	...	29 478 956	...	...	31 251 626	...	...
1 VII 2016	ESDJ	60 627 498	...	...	29 451 031	...	...	31 176 467	...	...
1 I 2017	ESDJ	60 589 445	...	...	29 445 741	...	...	31 143 704	...	...
Jersey										
27 III 2011	CDJC	97 857	...	...	48 296	...	...	49 561	...	...
Latvia - Lettonie										
1 VII 2008	ESDJ	2 177 322	1 478 831	67.9	999 845	663 658	66.4	1 177 477	815 173	69.2
1 VII 2009	ESDJ	2 141 669	1 453 570	67.9	981 789	650 486	66.3	1 159 880	803 084	69.2
1 VII 2010	ESDJ	2 097 555	1 422 675	67.8	959 435	634 393	66.1	1 138 120	788 282	69.3
1 III 2011	CDJC	2 070 371	1 404 251	67.8	946 102	625 150	66.1	1 124 269	779 101	69.3
1 VII 2011	ESDJ	2 059 709	1 394 429	67.7	941 375	620 484	65.9	1 118 334	773 945	69.2
1 VII 2012	ESDJ	2 034 319	1 374 215	67.6	930 696	611 604	65.7	1 103 623	762 611	69.1
1 VII 2013	ESDJ	2 012 647	1 362 004	67.7	921 813	606 624	65.8	1 090 834	755 380	69.2

6. Total and urban population by sex: 2008 - 2017
Population totale et population urbaine selon le sexe : 2008 - 2017 (continued - suite)

Continent, country or area, and date / Continent, pays ou zone et date	Code[a]	Both sexes - Les deux sexes			Male - Masculin			Female - Féminin		
		Total	Urban - Urbaine		Total	Urban - Urbaine		Total	Urban - Urbaine	
			Number Nombre	Percent P.100		Number Nombre	Percent P.100		Number Nombre	Percent P.100
EUROPE										
Latvia - Lettonie										
1 VII 2014	ESDJ	1 993 782	1 353 269	67.9	914 126	603 112	66.0	1 079 656	750 157	69.5
1 VII 2015	ESDJ	1 977 527	1 344 291	68.0	907 753	599 629	66.1	1 069 774	744 662	69.6
1 VII 2016	ESDJ	1 959 537	1 336 137	68.2	899 991	596 307	66.3	1 059 546	739 830	69.8
1 I 2017	ESDJ	1 950 116	...	...	895 683	...	...	1 054 433	...	...
Liechtenstein										
1 VII 2008	ESDJ	35 446	...	...	17 508	...	...	17 938	...	...
1 VII 2009	ESDJ	35 789	...	...	17 716	...	...	18 073	...	...
1 VII 2010	ESDJ	36 010	...	...	17 817	...	...	18 193	...	...
31 XII 2010	CDJC	36 149	...	...	17 886	...	...	18 263	...	...
1 VII 2011	ESDJ	36 281	...	...	17 950	...	...	18 331	...	...
1 VII 2012	ESDJ	36 636	...	...	18 123	...	...	18 513	...	...
1 VII 2013	ESDJ	36 942	...	...	18 314	...	...	18 628	...	...
1 VII 2014	ESDJ	37 215	...	...	18 458	...	...	18 757	...	...
1 VII 2015	ESDJ	37 468	...	...	18 580	...	...	18 888	...	...
1 VII 2016	ESDJ	37 686	...	...	18 673	...	...	19 013	...	...
1 VII 2017	ESDJ	37 877	...	...	18 768	...	...	19 109	...	...
Lithuania - Lituanie										
1 VII 2008	ESDJ	3 198 231	2 134 908	66.8	1 480 386	966 638	65.3	1 717 845	1 168 270	68.0
1 VII 2009	ESDJ	3 162 916	2 112 248	66.8	1 461 776	953 885	65.3	1 701 140	1 158 363	68.1
1 VII 2010	ESDJ	3 097 282	2 068 095	66.8	1 428 711	931 128	65.2	1 668 571	1 136 967	68.1
1 III 2011	CDJC	3 043 429	2 031 211	66.7	1 402 604	912 943	65.1	1 640 825	1 118 268	68.2
1 VII 2011	ESDJ	3 028 115	2 021 365	66.8	1 395 367	907 995	65.1	1 632 748	1 113 370	68.2
1 VII 2012	ESDJ	2 987 773	1 997 436	66.9	1 376 201	896 102	65.1	1 611 572	1 101 334	68.3
1 VII 2013	ESDJ	2 957 689	1 981 924	67.0	1 362 443	888 578	65.2	1 595 246	1 093 346	68.5
1 VII 2014[140]	ESDJ	2 932 367	1 968 596	67.1	1 351 126	881 978	65.3	1 581 241	1 086 618	68.7
1 VII 2015[140]	ESDJ	2 904 910	1 952 920	67.2	1 337 932	873 571	65.3	1 566 978	1 079 349	68.9
1 VII 2016[140]	ESDJ	2 868 231	1 927 148	67.2	1 320 897	860 905	65.2	1 547 334	1 066 243	68.9
1 I 2017[140]	ESDJ	2 847 904	...	...	1 312 186	...	...	1 535 718	...	...
Luxembourg										
1 VII 2008	ESDJ	488 650	...	...	242 221	...	...	246 429	...	...
1 VII 2009	ESDJ	497 782	...	...	247 120	...	...	250 662	...	...
1 VII 2010	ESDJ	506 953	...	...	252 013	...	...	254 941	...	...
1 II 2011	CDJC	512 353	...	...	254 967	...	...	257 386	...	...
1 VII 2011	ESDJ	518 347	...	...	258 220	...	...	260 127	...	...
1 VII 2012	ESDJ	530 946	...	...	265 116	...	...	265 830	...	...
1 VII 2013	ESDJ	543 360	...	...	271 765	...	...	271 595	...	...
1 VII 2014	ESDJ	556 319	...	...	278 544	...	...	277 775	...	...
1 VII 2015	ESDJ	569 604	...	...	285 583	...	...	284 021	...	...
1 VII 2016	ESDJ	583 458	...	...	292 917	...	...	290 541	...	...
1 I 2017	ESDJ	590 667	...	...	296 641	...	...	294 026	...	...
Malta - Malte										
1 VII 2008[142]	ESDJ	409 429	...	...	203 696	...	...	205 733	...	...
1 VII 2009[142]	ESDJ	412 530	...	...	205 432	...	...	207 098	...	...
1 VII 2010[142]	ESDJ	414 562	...	...	206 333	...	...	208 229	...	...
1 VII 2011[142]	ESDJ	416 318	...	...	207 072	...	...	209 246	...	...
20 XI 2011	CDFC	417 432	400 557	96.0	207 625	199 151	95.9	209 807	201 406	96.0
1 VII 2012[142]	ESDJ	419 507	...	...	208 811	...	...	210 696	...	...
1 VII 2013[142]	ESDJ	423 431	...	...	211 182	...	...	212 249	...	...
1 VII 2014[142]	ESDJ	427 421	...	...	213 607	...	...	213 814	...	...
1 VII 2015[142]	ESDJ	431 936	...	...	216 185	...	...	215 751	...	...
1 VII 2016[142]	ESDJ	455 410	...	...	229 058	...	...	226 352	...	...
1 I 2017[142]	ESDJ	460 297	...	...	231 663	...	...	228 634	...	...
Monaco[143]										
9 VI 2008	CDJC	31 109	...	...	15 076[144]	...	...	15 914[144]	...	...
7 VI 2016	CDJC	37 308	...	...	18 240	...	...	19 068	...	...
Montenegro - Monténégro										
1 VII 2008	ESDJ	616 350	397 747	64.5	303 641	193 393	63.7	312 709	204 354	65.3
1 VII 2009	ESDJ	631 532	400 928	63.5	311 258	195 088	62.7	320 278	205 840	64.3
1 VII 2010	ESDJ	619 426	...	...	305 674	...	...	313 752	...	...
1 IV 2011	CDJC	620 029	399 264	64.4	306 236	193 691	63.2	313 793	205 573	65.5
1 VII 2011	ESDJ	620 079	...	...	306 242	...	...	313 837	...	...
1 VII 2012	ESDJ	620 601	...	...	306 580	...	...	314 021	...	...
1 VII 2013	ESDJ	621 207	...	...	306 978	...	...	314 229	...	...

6. Total and urban population by sex: 2008 - 2017
Population totale et population urbaine selon le sexe : 2008 - 2017 (continued - suite)

Continent, country or area, and date / Continent, pays ou zone et date	Code[a]	Both sexes - Les deux sexes			Male - Masculin			Female - Féminin		
		Total	Urban - Urbaine		Total	Urban - Urbaine		Total	Urban - Urbaine	
			Number Nombre	Percent P.100		Number Nombre	Percent P.100		Number Nombre	Percent P.100
EUROPE										
Montenegro - Monténégro										
1 VII 2014[140] .... ESDJ		621 810	...	...	307 339	...	...	314 471	...	...
1 VII 2015[140] .... ESDJ		622 159	...	...	307 628	...	...	314 531	...	...
1 VII 2016[140] .... ESDJ		622 303	...	...	307 743	...	...	314 560	...	...
1 I 2017[140] .... ESDJ		622 387	...	...	307 752	...	...	314 635	...	...
Netherlands - Pays-Bas										
1 VII 2008 .... ESDJ		16 445 593	10 877 858	66.1	8 134 235	5 350 572	65.8	8 311 359	5 527 286	66.5
1 VII 2009 .... ESDJ		16 530 388	10 938 780	66.2	8 179 936	5 383 776	65.8	8 350 452	5 555 004	66.5
1 VII 2010 .... ESDJ		16 615 394	11 096 288	66.8	8 223 479	5 464 083	66.4	8 391 915	5 632 205	67.1
1 I 2011 .... CDJC		16 655 799	11 124 721	66.8	8 243 482	5 478 213	66.5	8 412 317	5 646 508	67.1
1 VII 2011 .... ESDJ		16 693 074	...	...	8 263 177	...	...	8 429 897	...	...
1 VII 2012 .... ESDJ		16 754 962	...	...	8 295 105	...	...	8 459 857	...	...
1 VII 2013 .... ESDJ		16 804 432	...	...	8 320 862	...	...	8 483 570	...	...
1 VII 2014 .... ESDJ		16 865 007	...	...	8 353 621	...	...	8 511 386	...	...
1 VII 2015 .... ESDJ		16 939 923	...	...	8 394 997	...	...	8 544 926	...	...
1 VII 2016 .... ESDJ		17 030 314	...	...	8 445 119	...	...	8 585 195	...	...
1 I 2017 .... ESDJ		17 081 507	...	...	8 475 102	...	...	8 606 405	...	...
Norway - Norvège										
1 VII 2008[140] .... ESDJ		4 768 212	...	...	2 377 372	...	...	2 390 840	...	...
1 VII 2009[140] .... ESDJ		4 828 726	...	...	2 410 903	...	...	2 417 823	...	...
1 VII 2010[140] .... ESDJ		4 889 252	...	...	2 443 801	...	...	2 445 452	...	...
1 VII 2011[140] .... ESDJ		4 953 088	...	...	2 479 860	...	...	2 473 228	...	...
19 XI 2011[145] .... CDJC		4 979 955	3 951 427[96]	79.3	2 495 777	1 959 424[96]	78.5	2 484 178	1 992 003[96]	80.2
1 VII 2012[140] .... ESDJ		5 018 573	...	...	2 517 390	...	...	2 501 183	...	...
1 VII 2013[140] .... ESDJ		5 079 623	...	...	2 551 458	...	...	2 528 165	...	...
1 VII 2014[140] .... ESDJ		5 137 232	...	...	2 583 105	...	...	2 554 127	...	...
1 VII 2015[140] .... ESDJ		5 188 607	...	...	2 611 414	...	...	2 577 194	...	...
1 VII 2016[146] .... ESDJ		5 234 519	...	...	2 636 378	...	...	2 598 142	...	...
1 I 2017[140] .... ESDJ		5 258 317	...	...	2 649 130	...	...	2 609 187	...	...
Poland - Pologne										
1 VII 2008[147] .... ESDJ		38 115 909	23 305 018	61.1	18 408 405	11 041 359	60.0	19 707 504	12 263 659	62.2
1 VII 2009[147] .... ESDJ		38 153 389	23 293 906	61.1	18 423 343	11 032 562	59.9	19 730 046	12 261 344	62.1
1 VII 2010[140] .... ESDJ		38 042 403	23 156 309	60.9	18 422 344	11 000 170	59.7	19 620 059	12 156 139	62.0
31 III 2011 .... CDJC		38 044 565	23 116 673	60.8	18 420 389	10 977 424	59.6	19 624 176	12 139 249	61.9
1 VII 2011[140] .... ESDJ		38 051 032	23 111 377	60.7	18 422 837	10 973 937	59.6	19 628 195	12 137 440	61.8
1 VII 2012[140] .... ESDJ		38 059 134	23 066 408	60.6	18 424 160	10 948 639	59.4	19 634 974	12 117 769	61.7
1 VII 2013[140] .... ESDJ		38 031 632	23 000 324	60.5	18 411 126	10 915 023	59.3	19 620 506	12 085 301	61.6
1 VII 2014[140] .... ESDJ		38 006 154	22 951 357	60.4	18 397 470	10 888 729	59.2	19 608 684	12 062 628	61.5
1 VII 2015[140] .... ESDJ		37 981 588	22 916 634	60.3	18 384 771	10 869 587	59.1	19 596 817	12 047 047	61.5
1 VII 2016[140] .... ESDJ		37 956 779	22 872 493	60.3	18 370 677	10 846 647	59.0	19 586 102	12 025 846	61.4
1 I 2017[140] .... ESDJ		37 972 964	...	...	18 377 837	...	...	19 595 127	...	...
Portugal										
1 VII 2008 .... ESDJ		10 558 177	...	...	5 067 993	...	...	5 490 184	...	...
1 VII 2009 .... ESDJ		10 568 247	...	...	5 064 992	...	...	5 503 255	...	...
1 VII 2010 .... ESDJ		10 573 100	...	...	5 058 644	...	...	5 514 456	...	...
21 III 2011 .... CDFC		10 282 306	6 286 712	61.1	4 868 755	2 949 862	60.6	5 413 551	3 336 850	61.6
1 VII 2011 .... ESDJ		10 557 560	...	...	5 041 990	...	...	5 515 570	...	...
1 VII 2012 .... ESDJ		10 514 844	...	...	5 013 067	...	...	5 501 777	...	...
1 VII 2013 .... ESDJ		10 457 295	...	...	4 976 859	...	...	5 480 437	...	...
1 VII 2014 .... ESDJ		10 401 062	...	...	4 940 843	...	...	5 460 219	...	...
1 VII 2015 .... ESDJ		10 358 076	...	...	4 912 588	...	...	5 445 489	...	...
1 VII 2016 .... ESDJ		10 325 452	...	...	4 891 983	...	...	5 433 469	...	...
1 I 2017 .... ESDJ		10 309 573	...	...	4 882 456	...	...	5 427 117	...	...
Republic of Moldova - République de Moldova[148]										
1 VII 2008 .... ESDJ		3 570 108	1 475 609	41.3	1 716 195	693 550	40.4	1 853 913	782 059	42.2
1 VII 2009 .... ESDJ		3 565 604	1 476 390	41.4	1 714 209	694 134	40.5	1 851 395	782 257	42.3
1 VII 2010 .... ESDJ		3 562 045	1 479 196	41.5	1 712 783	695 603	40.6	1 849 262	783 593	42.4
1 VII 2011 .... ESDJ		3 559 986	1 483 731	41.7	1 711 916	697 492	40.7	1 848 070	786 239	42.5
1 VII 2012 .... ESDJ		3 559 520	1 488 966	41.8	1 712 036	699 880	40.9	1 847 484	789 086	42.7
1 IV 2014 .... CDJC		2 804 801	950 994	33.9	1 352 099	...	...	1 452 702	...	...
1 VII 2014 .... ESDJ		2 998 235	1 144 428	38.2	...	...	...	...	...	...

Continent, country or area, and date / Continent, pays ou zone et date	Code[a]	Both sexes - Les deux sexes			Male - Masculin			Female - Féminin		
		Total	Urban - Urbaine		Total	Urban - Urbaine		Total	Urban - Urbaine	
			Number Nombre	Percent P.100		Number Nombre	Percent P.100		Number Nombre	Percent P.100

EUROPE

Romania - Roumanie

1 VII 2008[140] .... ESDJ		20 537 848	11 102 802	54.1	10 000 515	5 314 752	53.1	10 537 333	5 788 050	54.9
1 VII 2009[140] .... ESDJ		20 367 437	10 976 558	53.9	9 916 107	5 249 975	52.9	10 451 330	5 726 583	54.8
1 VII 2010[140] .... ESDJ		20 246 798	10 922 169	53.9	9 856 669	5 223 471	53.0	10 390 129	5 698 698	54.8
1 VII 2011[140] .... ESDJ		20 147 657	10 878 099	54.0	9 805 108	5 198 460	53.0	10 342 549	5 679 639	54.9
20 X 2011 .... CDFC		20 039 141	10 858 790	54.2	9 736 342	5 185 636	53.3	10 302 799	5 673 154	55.1
1 VII 2012[140] .... ESDJ		20 060 182	10 823 218	54.0	9 770 353	5 170 875	52.9	10 289 829	5 652 343	54.9
1 VII 2013 .... ESDF		19 988 694	10 772 678	53.9	9 756 310	5 153 631	52.8	10 232 384	5 619 047	54.9
1 VII 2014 .... ESDF		19 916 451	10 728 929	53.9	9 730 258	5 134 314	52.8	10 186 193	5 594 615	54.9
1 VII 2015 .... ESDF		19 819 697	10 669 579	53.8	9 680 537	5 098 318	52.7	10 139 160	5 571 261	54.9
1 VII 2016 .... ESDF		19 706 529	10 585 664	53.7	9 628 271	5 053 625	52.5	10 078 258	5 532 039	54.9
1 I 2017 .... ESDF		19 644 350	...	...	9 602 578	...	...	10 041 772	...	...

Russian Federation - Fédération de Russie

1 VII 2008 .... ESDJ		142 742 366	104 890 297	73.5	65 968 338	47 938 815	72.7	76 774 028	56 951 482	74.2
1 VII 2009 .... ESDJ		142 785 349	104 988 448	73.5	65 988 356	47 969 474	72.7	76 796 993	57 018 974	74.2
1 VII 2010 .... ESDJ		142 849 468	105 241 319	73.7	66 033 070	48 081 267	72.8	76 816 398	57 160 052	74.4
14 X 2010 .... CDFC		143 436 145	...	...	66 457 074	...	...	76 979 071	...	...
1 VII 2011 .... ESDJ		142 960 908	105 581 615	73.9	66 113 269	48 243 019	73.0	76 847 639	57 338 596	74.6
1 VII 2012 .... ESDJ		143 201 730	105 930 122	74.0	66 264 910	48 419 208	73.1	76 936 820	57 510 914	74.8

San Marino - Saint-Marin

1 VII 2008[53] .... ESDF		31 662	...	...	15 874	...	...	15 788	...	...
1 VII 2009[53] .... ESDF		33 066	...	...	16 088	...	...	16 978	...	...
1 VII 2010[53] .... ESDF		33 270	...	...	16 171	...	...	17 099	...	...
7 XI 2010* .... CDFC		30 652	...	...	14 791[31]	...	...	15 818[31]	...	...
1 VII 2011[53] .... ESDF		33 389	...	...	16 221	...	...	17 169	...	...
1 VII 2012[53] .... ESDF		33 518	...	...	16 296	...	...	17 222	...	...
1 VII 2013[53] .... ESDF		33 469	...	...	16 280	...	...	17 189	...	...
1 VII 2014[53] .... ESDF		33 648	...	...	16 396	...	...	17 252	...	...
1 I 2015[53] .... ESDF		33 738	...	...	16 425	...	...	17 313	...	...
1 I 2016[53] .... ESDF		34 006	...	...	16 560	...	...	17 446	...	...
1 I 2017[53] .... ESDF		34 267	...	...	16 677	...	...	17 590	...	...

Serbia - Serbie[149]

1 VII 2008 .... ESDJ		7 350 222	4 275 245	58.2	3 573 814	2 038 642	57.0	3 776 408	2 236 603	59.2
1 VII 2009 .... ESDJ		7 320 807	4 279 035	58.5	3 560 048	2 039 934	57.3	3 760 759	2 239 101	59.5
1 VII 2010 .... ESDJ		7 291 436	4 283 985	58.8	3 546 374	2 041 975	57.6	3 745 062	2 242 010	59.9
1 VII 2011[19] .... ESDJ		7 236 519	4 275 178	59.1	3 523 911	2 041 228	57.9	3 712 608	2 233 950	60.2
1 X 2011 .... CDJC		7 186 862	4 271 872	59.4	3 499 176	2 039 105	58.3	3 687 686	2 232 767	60.5
1 VII 2012[19] .... ESDJ		7 201 497	4 273 861	59.3	3 506 947	2 039 649	58.2	3 694 550	2 234 212	60.5
1 VII 2013[19] .... ESDJ		7 166 552	4 272 061	59.6	3 489 683	2 037 554	58.4	3 676 869	2 234 507	60.8
1 VII 2014[19] .... ESDJ		7 131 787	4 270 367	59.9	3 472 746	2 035 772	58.6	3 659 041	2 234 595	61.1
1 VII 2015[19] .... ESDJ		7 095 383	4 267 079	60.1	3 455 335	2 033 446	58.8	3 640 048	2 233 633	61.4
1 VII 2016[19] .... ESDJ		7 058 322	4 262 256	60.4	3 437 630	2 030 532	59.1	3 620 692	2 231 724	61.6
1 I 2017[19] .... ESDJ		7 040 272	...	...	3 429 027	...	...	3 611 245	...	...

Slovakia - Slovaquie

1 VII 2008 .... ESDJ		5 379 233	...	...	2 616 013	...	...	2 763 220	...	...
1 VII 2009 .... ESDJ		5 386 406	...	...	2 620 942	...	...	2 765 464	...	...
1 VII 2010 .... ESDJ		5 391 428	...	...	2 624 360	...	...	2 767 069	...	...
21 V 2011 .... CDJC		5 397 036	2 937 735	54.4	2 627 772	1 412 818	53.8	2 769 264	1 524 917	55.1
1 VII 2011 .... ESDJ		5 398 384	2 938 053	54.4	2 628 463	1 412 966	53.8	2 769 922	1 525 087	55.1
1 VII 2012 .... ESDJ		5 407 579	2 935 710	54.3	2 633 866	1 411 738	53.6	2 773 714	1 523 972	54.9
1 VII 2013 .... ESDJ		5 413 393	2 931 444	54.2	2 637 520	1 409 503	53.4	2 775 873	1 521 941	54.8
1 VII 2014 .... ESDJ		5 418 649	2 925 291	54.0	2 640 694	1 406 300	53.3	2 777 955	1 518 991	54.7
1 VII 2015 .... ESDJ		5 423 801	2 919 718	53.8	2 644 205	1 403 692	53.1	2 779 596	1 516 027	54.5
1 VII 2016 .... ESDJ		5 430 798	2 925 475	53.9	2 648 883	1 406 787	53.1	2 781 915	1 518 688	54.6
1 I 2017 .... ESDJ		5 435 343	...	...	2 651 684	...	...	2 783 659	...	...

Slovenia - Slovénie

1 VII 2008 .... ESDJ		2 022 629	1 012 477	50.1	996 969	491 605	49.3	1 025 660	520 872	50.8
1 VII 2009 .... ESDJ		2 042 335	1 024 087	50.1	1 011 767	500 253	49.4	1 030 568	523 834	50.8
1 VII 2010 .... ESDJ		2 049 261	1 024 812	50.0	1 014 716	500 063	49.3	1 034 545	524 749	50.7
1 I 2011 .... CDFC		2 058 051	1 030 172	50.1	1 019 826	503 083	49.3	1 038 225	527 089	50.8
1 VII 2011 .... ESDJ		2 052 496	1 023 650	49.9	1 015 430	498 490	49.1	1 037 066	525 160	50.6
1 VII 2012 .... ESDJ		2 056 262	1 023 236	49.8	1 017 414	498 297	49.0	1 038 848	524 939	50.5
1 VII 2013 .... ESDJ		2 059 114	1 047 560	50.9	1 019 658	513 084	50.3	1 039 456	534 476	51.4
1 VII 2014 .... ESDJ		2 061 623	1 051 087	51.0	1 021 419	514 828	50.4	1 040 204	536 259	51.6

Continent, country or area, and date / Continent, pays ou zone et date	Code[a]	Both sexes - Les deux sexes			Male - Masculin			Female - Féminin		
		Total	Urban - Urbaine		Total	Urban - Urbaine		Total	Urban - Urbaine	
			Number Nombre	Percent P.100		Number Nombre	Percent P.100		Number Nombre	Percent P.100
EUROPE										
Slovenia - Slovénie										
1 I 2015	CDJC	2 062 874	1 107 064	53.7	1 022 229	542 636	53.1	1 040 645	564 428	54.2
1 VII 2015	ESDJ	2 063 077	1 106 955	53.7	1 022 554	542 847	53.1	1 040 523	564 108	54.2
1 VII 2016	ESDJ	2 064 241	1 107 409	53.6	1 023 872	543 571	53.1	1 040 369	563 838	54.2
1 I 2017	ESDJ	2 065 895	...	...	1 025 125	...	...	1 040 770	...	...
Spain - Espagne										
1 VII 2008	ESDJ	45 983 167	...	...	22 756 861	...	...	23 226 306	...	...
1 VII 2009	ESDJ	46 367 545	...	...	22 934 497	...	...	23 433 048	...	...
1 VII 2010	ESDJ	46 562 486	...	...	23 008 587	...	...	23 553 899	...	...
1 VII 2011	ESDJ	46 736 255	...	...	23 073 274	...	...	23 662 981	...	...
1 XI 2011	CDJC	46 815 915	...	...	23 104 350	...	...	23 711 560	...	...
1 VII 2012	ESDJ	46 766 399	...	...	23 055 715	...	...	23 710 684	...	...
1 VII 2013	ESDJ	46 593 236	...	...	22 933 751	...	...	23 659 485	...	...
1 VII 2014[141]	ESDJ	46 480 882	...	...	22 852 004	...	...	23 628 879	...	...
1 VII 2015[141]	ESDJ	46 447 697	...	...	22 817 983	...	...	23 629 714	...	...
1 VII 2016[141]	ESDJ	46 450 439	...	...	22 805 443	...	...	23 644 996	...	...
1 VII 2017[141]	ESDJ	46 549 045	...	...	22 838 035	...	...	23 711 009	...	...
Sweden - Suède[53]										
1 VII 2008	ESDJ	9 219 637	...	...	4 583 816	...	...	4 635 822	...	...
1 VII 2009	ESDJ	9 298 515	...	...	4 626 362	...	...	4 672 153	...	...
1 VII 2010	ESDJ	9 378 126	...	...	4 669 629	...	...	4 708 497	...	...
1 VII 2011	ESDJ	9 449 213	...	...	4 708 539	...	...	4 740 674	...	...
31 XII 2011	CDJC	9 482 855	...	...	4 726 834	...	...	4 756 021	...	...
1 VII 2012	ESDJ	9 519 375	...	...	4 746 370	...	...	4 773 005	...	...
1 VII 2013[141]	ESDJ	9 600 379	...	...	4 790 131	...	...	4 810 248	...	...
1 VII 2014[141]	ESDJ	9 696 110	...	...	4 843 299	...	...	4 852 811	...	...
1 VII 2015[141]	ESDJ	9 799 186	...	...	4 901 603	...	...	4 897 583	...	...
1 VII 2016[150]	ESDJ	9 923 085	...	...	4 972 157	...	...	4 950 929	...	...
1 I 2017[141]	ESDJ	9 995 153	...	...	5 013 347	...	...	4 981 806	...	...
Switzerland - Suisse										
1 VII 2008	ESDJ	7 647 675	5 622 042	73.5	3 756 845	2 744 671	73.1	3 890 831	2 877 371	74.0
1 VII 2009	ESDJ	7 743 832	5 699 003	73.6	3 808 621	2 786 186	73.2	3 935 211	2 912 817	74.0
1 VII 2010	ESDJ	7 824 909	...	...	3 851 028	...	...	3 973 882	...	...
1 VII 2011	ESDJ	7 912 398	5 823 816	73.6	3 899 840	2 853 440	73.2	4 012 559	2 970 376	74.0
31 XII 2011	CDFC	8 035 391	5 920 706	73.7	3 973 280	2 909 793	73.2	4 062 111	3 010 913	74.1
1 VII 2012	ESDJ	7 996 861	5 887 939	73.6	3 945 389	2 887 886	73.2	4 051 473	3 000 053	74.0
1 VII 2013	ESDJ	8 089 346	5 958 174	73.7	3 995 308	2 925 500	73.2	4 094 038	3 032 674	74.1
1 VII 2014[151]	ESDJ	8 188 649	6 033 396	73.7	4 047 986	2 964 948	73.2	4 140 663	3 068 448	74.1
1 VII 2015[151]	ESDJ	8 282 396	6 997 929[152]	84.5	4 097 676	3 451 374[152]	84.2	4 184 721	3 546 555[152]	84.8
1 VII 2016[151]	ESDJ	8 373 338	7 078 247	84.5	4 147 454	3 494 909	84.3	4 225 884	3 583 339	84.8
1 I 2017[151]	ESDJ	8 419 550	7 119 751	84.6	4 173 437	3 517 940	84.3	4 246 113	3 601 811	84.8
TFYR of Macedonia - L'ex-R. y. de Macédoine										
1 VII 2008	ESDJ	2 046 898	...	...	1 026 022	...	...	1 020 876	...	...
1 VII 2009	ESDJ	2 050 671	...	...	1 027 810	...	...	1 022 861	...	...
1 VII 2010	ESDJ	2 055 004	...	...	1 029 848	...	...	1 025 156	...	...
1 VII 2011	ESDJ	2 058 539	...	...	1 031 403	...	...	1 027 136	...	...
1 VII 2012	ESDJ	2 061 044	...	...	1 032 532	...	...	1 028 512	...	...
1 VII 2013	ESDJ	2 064 032	...	...	1 033 990	...	...	1 030 042	...	...
1 VII 2014	ESDJ	2 067 471	...	...	1 035 680	...	...	1 031 791	...	...
1 VII 2015	ESDJ	2 070 225	...	...	1 037 060	...	...	1 033 166	...	...
1 VII 2016	ESDJ	2 072 490	...	...	1 038 107	...	...	1 034 383	...	...
1 I 2017	ESDJ	2 073 702	...	...	1 038 613	...	...	1 035 089	...	...
Ukraine										
1 VII 2008	ESDF	46 258 189	31 627 980	68.4	21 347 279	14 512 344	68.0	24 910 910	17 115 637	68.7
1 VII 2009	ESDF	46 053 307	31 556 002	68.5	...	...	...	...	...	...
1 VII 2010	ESDF	45 870 741	31 483 222	68.6	21 175 816	14 436 554	68.2	24 694 925	17 046 668	69.0
1 VII 2011	ESDF	45 706 086	31 411 262	68.7	21 110 638	14 401 999	68.2	24 595 448	17 009 263	69.2
1 VII 2012	ESDF	45 593 342	31 379 757	68.8	21 075 702	14 392 490	68.3	24 517 640	16 987 267	69.3
1 I 2013	ESDF	45 553 047	31 378 639	68.9	21 068 718	14 397 904	68.3	24 484 329	16 980 735	69.4
1 I 2014	ESDF	45 426 249	31 336 623	69.0	21 024 262	14 382 728	68.4	24 401 987	16 953 895	69.5
1 VII 2015[153]	ESDF	42 675 270	...	...	19 752 854	...	...	22 922 417	...	...
1 VII 2016[153]	ESDF	42 502 892	...	...	19 681 231	...	...	22 821 662	...	...
1 I 2017[154]	ESDF	42 584 542	29 482 313	69.2	19 743 710	13 547 487	68.6	22 840 832	15 934 826	69.8

Continent, country or area, and date / Continent, pays ou zone et date	Code[a]	Both sexes - Les deux sexes Total	Urban - Urbaine Number Nombre	Urban - Urbaine Percent P.100	Male - Masculin Total	Urban - Urbaine Number Nombre	Urban - Urbaine Percent P.100	Female - Féminin Total	Urban - Urbaine Number Nombre	Urban - Urbaine Percent P.100
EUROPE										
United Kingdom of Great Britain and Northern Ireland - Royaume-Uni de Grande-Bretagne et d'Irlande du Nord[155]										
1 VII 2008	ESDJ	61 823 772	...	...	30 300 623	...	...	31 523 149	...	...
1 VII 2009	ESDJ	62 260 486	...	...	30 532 212	...	...	31 728 274	...	...
1 VII 2010	ESDJ	62 759 456	...	...	30 805 493	...	...	31 953 963	...	...
27 III 2011	CDFC	63 379 787	51 399 714	81.1	31 126 054	25 214 631	81.0	32 253 733	26 185 083	81.2
1 VII 2011	ESDJ	63 285 145	...	...	31 097 259	...	...	32 187 886	...	...
1 VII 2012	ESDJ	63 705 000	...	...	31 315 200	...	...	32 389 800	...	...
1 VII 2013[140]	ESDJ	64 105 700	...	...	31 533 000	...	...	32 572 600	...	...
1 VII 2014[140]	ESDJ	64 596 800	...	...	31 793 800	...	...	32 803 000	...	...
1 VII 2015[140]	ESDJ	65 110 000	...	...	32 074 400	...	...	33 035 600	...	...
1 VII 2016[146]	ESDJ	65 595 565	...	...	32 345 297	...	...	33 250 268	...	...
1 I 2017[140]	ESDJ	65 808 573	...	...	32 466 065	...	...	33 342 508	...	...
OCEANIA - OCÉANIE										
American Samoa - Samoas américaines[60]										
1 IV 2010	CDJC	55 519	...		28 164	...	...	27 355	...	...
Australia - Australie										
1 VII 2008[156]	ESDJ	21 249 199	18 170 662	85.5	10 572 045	8 993 280	85.1	10 677 154	9 177 382	86.0
1 VII 2009[156]	ESDJ	21 691 653	18 574 681	85.6	10 800 797	9 201 882	85.2	10 890 856	9 372 799	86.1
1 VII 2010[156]	ESDJ	22 031 750	18 886 173	85.7	10 967 831	9 354 529	85.3	11 063 919	9 531 644	86.2
1 VII 2011[156]	ESDJ	22 340 024	19 172 952	85.8	11 118 234	9 494 673	85.4	11 221 790	9 678 279	86.2
9 VIII 2011[157]	CDFC	21 727 158[158]	19 312 642	88.9	10 737 148[158]	9 471 918	88.2	10 990 010[158]	9 840 724	89.5
1 VII 2012[156]	ESDJ	22 742 475	19 544 674	85.9	11 316 375	9 678 605	85.5	11 426 100	9 866 069	86.3
1 VII 2013[156]	ESDJ	23 145 901	19 919 750	86.1	11 512 700	9 861 755	85.7	11 633 201	10 057 995	86.5
1 VII 2014[156]	ESDJ	23 504 138	20 260 961	86.2	11 679 392	10 023 075	85.8	11 824 746	10 237 886	86.6
1 VII 2015[156]	ESDJ	23 850 784	20 597 118	86.4	11 840 827	10 182 740	86.0	12 009 957	10 414 378	86.7
1 VII 2016[156]	ESDJ	24 210 809	20 944 131	86.5	12 011 846	10 350 638	86.2	12 198 963	10 593 493	86.8
9 VIII 2016[157]	CDFC	23 717 421[158]	21 806 740	91.9	11 686 665[158]	10 676 368	91.4	12 030 751[158]	11 130 367	92.5
1 VII 2017[156]	ESDJ	24 598 933	...	...	12 204 419	...	...	12 394 514	...	...
Cook Islands - Îles Cook[159]										
1 XII 2011	CDFC	17 794	...	...	8 815	...	...	8 979	...	...
1 XII 2016*	CDFC	17 459	...	...	8 597	...	...	8 862	...	...
Fiji - Fidji										
1 VII 2008	ESDF	841 351	426 931	50.7	...	...	...	...	...	...
1 VII 2010	ESDF	857 000	446 000	52.0	...	...	...	...	...	...
17 IX 2017	CDFC	884 887	494 252	55.9	448 595	245 928	54.8	436 292	248 324	56.9
French Polynesia - Polynésie française										
1 I 2009	ESDF	264 000	...	...	135 200	...	...	128 800	...	...
1 I 2011	ESDF	269 989	...	...	138 127	...	...	131 862	...	...
22 VIII 2012	CDFC	268 207	...	...	136 996	...	...	131 211	...	...
1 I 2015	ESDF	271 796	...	...	138 447	...	...	133 349	...	...
Guam										
1 VII 2008[60]	ESDJ	159 169	...	...	80 982	...	...	78 187	...	...
1 VII 2009[60]	ESDJ	159 323	...	...	81 010	...	...	78 313	...	...
1 IV 2010	CDJC	159 358	149 918	94.1	81 552	...	...	77 806	...	...
1 VII 2011[60]	ESDJ	159 600	...	...	81 053	...	...	78 547	...	...
1 VII 2012[60]	ESDJ	159 914	...	...	81 165	...	...	78 749	...	...
1 VII 2013[60]	ESDJ	160 378	...	...	81 354	...	...	79 024	...	...
1 VII 2014[60]	ESDJ	161 001	...	...	81 625	...	...	79 376	...	...
1 VII 2015[60]	ESDJ	161 785	...	...	81 978	...	...	79 807	...	...
1 VII 2016[60]	ESDJ	162 742	...	...	82 420	...	...	80 322	...	...
1 VII 2017[60]	ESDJ	163 875	...	...	82 951	...	...	80 924	...	...
Kiribati										
10 X 2010	CDFC	103 058	...	...	50 796	...	...	52 262	...	...
7 XI 2015	CDFC	110 136	56 388	51.2	54 096	27 159	50.2	56 040	29 229	52.2

Continent, country or area, and date / Continent, pays ou zone et date	Code[a]	Both sexes - Les deux sexes			Male - Masculin			Female - Féminin		
		Total	Urban - Urbaine		Total	Urban - Urbaine		Total	Urban - Urbaine	
			Number Nombre	Percent P.100		Number Nombre	Percent P.100		Number Nombre	Percent P.100
OCEANIA - OCÉANIE										
Marshall Islands - Îles Marshall										
1 VII 2008[160]	ESDF	53 236	...	...	27 297	...	...	25 939	...	...
1 VII 2009[160]	ESDF	53 763	...	...	27 567	...	...	26 196	...	...
1 VII 2010[160]	ESDF	54 305	...	...	27 843	...	...	26 462	...	...
3 IV 2011	CDFC	53 158	...	...	27 243	...	...	25 915	...	...
Micronesia (Federated States of) - Micronésie (États fédérés de)										
1 VII 2008[4]	ESDJ	108 026	...	...	54 350	...	...	53 676	...	...
1 VII 2009[4]	ESDJ	107 973	...	...	54 275	...	...	53 698	...	...
1 IV 2010	CDJC	102 843	22 924	22.3	52 193	...	...	50 650	...	...
1 VII 2010[4]	ESDJ	107 839	...	...	54 158	...	...	53 681	...	...
1 VII 2011[4]	ESDJ	107 581	...	...	53 975	...	...	53 606	...	...
1 VII 2012[4]	ESDJ	107 249	...	...	53 749	...	...	53 500	...	...
1 VII 2013[4]	ESDJ	106 841	...	...	53 488	...	...	53 353	...	...
1 VII 2014[4]	ESDJ	106 374	...	...	53 200	...	...	53 174	...	...
1 VII 2015[4]	ESDJ	105 830	...	...	52 883	...	...	52 947	...	...
Nauru										
31 X 2011	CDFC	10 084	...	...	5 105	...	...	4 979	...	...
1 VII 2012[4]	ESDF	10 376	...	...	5 126	...	...	5 250	...	...
1 VII 2015[4]	ESDF	11 288	...	...	5 701	...	...	5 587	...	...
New Caledonia - Nouvelle-Calédonie										
26 VIII 2014	CDFC	268 767	...	...	135 542	...	...	133 225	...	...
1 I 2016	ESDF	274 579	...	...	138 197	...	...	136 382	...	...
1 I 2017	ESDF	278 495	...	...	140 000	...	...	138 495	...	...
New Zealand - Nouvelle-Zélande										
1 VII 2008[81]	ESDJ	4 259 800	3 669 100[161]	86.1	2 083 400	1 780 600[161]	85.5	2 176 300	1 888 600[161]	86.8
1 VII 2009[81]	ESDJ	4 302 600	3 703 800[161]	86.1	2 104 700	1 797 800[161]	85.4	2 197 900	1 906 000[161]	86.7
1 VII 2010[81]	ESDJ	4 350 700	3 743 300[161]	86.0	2 127 700	1 816 700[161]	85.4	2 222 900	1 926 600[161]	86.7
1 VII 2011[81]	ESDJ	4 384 000	3 765 400[161]	85.9	2 143 600	1 826 900[161]	85.2	2 240 400	1 938 500[161]	86.5
1 VII 2012[81]	ESDJ	4 408 100	3 784 600[161]	85.9	2 155 000	1 836 200[161]	85.2	2 253 100	1 948 500[161]	86.5
5 III 2013[162]	CDFC	4 353 198	3 732 537	85.7	2 119 464	1 801 341	85.0	2 233 734	1 931 199	86.5
1 VII 2013[81]	ESDJ	4 442 100	3 818 300[161]	86.0	2 172 200	1 853 100[161]	85.3	2 269 900	1 965 200[161]	86.6
1 VII 2014[81]	ESDJ	4 509 700	3 884 000[161]	86.1	2 209 600	1 889 100[161]	85.5	2 300 200	1 995 000[161]	86.7
1 VII 2015[81]	ESDJ	4 595 700	3 959 200[161]	86.2	2 257 200	1 931 800[161]	85.6	2 338 500	2 027 400[161]	86.7
1 VII 2016[81]	ESDJ	4 693 200	4 056 200[161]	86.4	2 309 100	1 983 600[161]	85.9	2 384 100	2 072 600[161]	86.9
1 VII 2017[81]	ESDJ	4 793 900	4 144 300[161]	86.4	2 361 100	2 029 700[161]	86.0	2 432 800	2 114 600[161]	86.9
Niue - Nioué										
1 VII 2010	ESDJ	1 496	...	...	754	...	...	740	...	...
11 IX 2011	CDFC	1 611	...	...	802	...	...	809	...	...
Norfolk Island - Île Norfolk										
9 VIII 2011	CDFC	2 302	...	...	1 082	...	...	1 220	...	...
Northern Mariana Islands - Îles Mariannes septentrionales										
1 VII 2008	ESDF	55 244	...	...	26 524	...	...	28 720	...	...
1 VII 2009	ESDF	51 484	...	...	24 738	...	...	26 746	...	...
1 IV 2010	CDFC	53 883	...	...	27 746	...	...	26 137	...	...
1 VII 2010	ESDF	48 317	...	...	23 231	...	...	25 086	...	...
1 VII 2011	ESDF	46 050	...	...	22 153	...	...	23 897	...	...
Palau - Palaos										
1 XII 2012	CDJC	17 501	14 202	81.1	9 217	7 506	81.4	8 284	6 696	80.8
13 IV 2015	CDJC	17 661	14 209	80.5	9 433	7 620	80.8	8 228	6 589	80.1
Papua New Guinea - Papouasie-Nouvelle-Guinée										
10 VII 2011	CDFC	7 275 324	...	...	3 772 864	...	...	3 502 460	...	...
1 VII 2016[163]	ESDF	8 151 300	...	...	4 205 000	...	...	3 946 300	...	...

Continent, country or area, and date / Continent, pays ou zone et date	Code[a]	Both sexes - Les deux sexes			Male - Masculin			Female - Féminin		
		Total	Urban - Urbaine		Total	Urban - Urbaine		Total	Urban - Urbaine	
			Number Nombre	Percent P.100		Number Nombre	Percent P.100		Number Nombre	Percent P.100

OCEANIA - OCÉANIE

Pitcairn										
31 XII 2008	ESDF	58[164]	...	...	30	...	...	28	...	...
10 VIII 2012	CDJC	48	...	...	22	...	...	26	...	...
31 XII 2013	CDJC	49	...	...	23	...	...	26	...	...
Samoa										
1 VII 2008	ESDF	182 379	38 050	20.9	94 526	19 293	20.4	87 853	18 756	21.3
1 VII 2009	ESDF	183 204	38 222	20.9	94 953	19 381	20.4	88 250	18 841	21.3
1 VII 2010	ESDF	184 032	38 395	20.9	95 383	19 468	20.4	88 649	18 926	21.3
1 VII 2011	ESDF	184 864	38 568	20.9	95 814	19 556	20.4	89 050	19 012	21.3
7 XI 2011	CDFC	187 820	36 735	19.6	96 990	18 485	19.1	90 830	18 250	20.1
1 VII 2012[165]	ESDF	189 236	36 540	19.3	...	...	...	...	...	...
1 VII 2013[165]	ESDF	190 652	36 346	19.1	...	...	...	...	...	...
1 VII 2014[165]	ESDF	192 067	36 151	18.8	...	...	...	...	...	...
1 VII 2015[165]	ESDF	193 483	35 957	18.6	...	...	...	...	...	...
7 XI 2016	CDFC	195 979	37 391	19.1	...	...	...	...	...	...
1 VII 2017[166]	ESDF	197 611	37 522	19.0	...	...	...	...	...	...
Solomon Islands - Îles Salomon										
1 VII 2008[4]	ESDF	506 992	...	...	261 214	...	...	245 778	...	...
1 VII 2009[4]	ESDF	518 321	...	...	267 704	...	...	250 617	...	...
22 XI 2009[167]	CDFC	515 870	102 030	19.8	264 455	53 596	20.3	251 415	48 434	19.3
1 VII 2010[168]	ESDF	555 447	...	...	285 040	...	...	270 408	...	...
1 VII 2011[168]	ESDF	569 600	...	...	292 105	...	...	277 495	...	...
1 VII 2012[168]	ESDF	583 672	...	...	299 131	...	...	284 541	...	...
1 VII 2013[168]	ESDF	597 653	...	...	306 112	...	...	291 541	...	...
1 VII 2014[168]	ESDF	611 538	...	...	313 044	...	...	298 494	...	...
1 VII 2015[168]	ESDF	625 374	...	...	319 954	...	...	305 420	...	...
1 VII 2016[168]	ESDF	639 157	...	...	326 837	...	...	312 321	...	...
1 VII 2017[168]	ESDF	652 886	...	...	333 693	...	...	319 193	...	...
Tokelau - Tokélaou										
18 X 2011	CDFC	1 205	...	...	600	...	...	605	...	...
1 XII 2013	ESDF	1 383	...	...	683	...	...	700	...	...
18 X 2016	CDFC	1 285	...	...	652	...	...	633	...	...
Tonga										
1 VII 2008[169]	ESDF	103 647	...	...	52 972	...	...	50 673	...	...
30 XI 2011	CDJC	103 252	24 229	23.5	51 979	12 156	23.4	51 273	12 073	23.5
30 XI 2016	CDJC	100 651	23 221	23.1	50 255	...	...	50 396	...	...
Tuvalu										
1 VII 2011	ESDF	11 206	...	...	5 582	...	...	5 625	...	...
1 VII 2013	ESDF	10 900	...	...	5 600	...	...	5 400	...	...
1 VII 2016[163]	ESDF	10 100	...	...	5 100	...	...	5 000	...	...
Vanuatu										
16 XI 2009	CDFC	234 023	57 195	24.4	119 091	29 618	24.9	114 932	27 577	24.0
1 VII 2010	ESDF	239 374	59 199	24.7	121 726	...	...	117 648	...	...
1 VII 2011	ESDF	244 847	61 277	25.0	124 420	...	...	120 427	...	...
1 VII 2012	ESDF	250 445	63 432	25.3	127 173	...	...	123 273	...	...
1 VII 2013	ESDF	264 652	...	...	135 170	...	...	129 483	...	...
1 VII 2014	ESDF	271 087	...	...	138 474	...	...	132 613	...	...
7 XI 2016	CDFC	272 459	67 749	24.9	138 265	34 506	25.0	134 194	33 243	24.8
Wallis and Futuna Islands - Îles Wallis et Futuna										
21 VII 2008	CDFC	13 445	...	...	6 669	...	...	6 776	...	...
22 VII 2013	CDFC	12 197	...	...	5 927	...	...	6 270	...	...
1 VII 2016[163]	ESDF	11 800	...	...	5 700	...	...	6 100	...	...

FOOTNOTES - NOTES

Italics: estimates which are less reliable. - Italiques : estimations moins sûres.

* Provisional. - Données provisoires.

[a] 'Code' indicates the source of data, as follows:
CDFC - Census, de facto, complete tabulation

CDFS - Census, de facto, sample tabulation
CDJC - Census, de jure, complete tabulation
CDJS - Census, de jure, sample tabulation
SSDF - Sample survey, de facto
SSDJ - Sample survey, de jure
ESDF - Estimates, de facto
ESDJ - Estimates, de jure

Le 'Code' indique la source des données, comme suit :
CDFC - Recensement, population de fait, tabulation complète
CDFS - Recensement, population de fait, tabulation par sondage
CDJC - Recensement, population de droit, tabulation complète
CDJS - Recensement, population de droit, tabulation par sondage
SSDF - Enquête par sondage, population de fait
SSDJ - Enquête par sondage, population de droit
ESDF - Estimations, population de fait
ESDJ - Estimations, population de droit

[1] Total resident population including common and collective households of nomadic population, and population counted separately. - Population résidente totale y compris les ménages ordinaires et collectifs de la population nomade, et la population comptée à part.

[2] Unrevised data that do not take into account the results of the 2014 population census. - Ces données n'ont pas été revisées et elles ne prennent pas en compte les résultats du recensement de la population de 2014.

[3] Postcensal estimates. - Estimations post censitaires.

[4] Data refer to national projections. - Les données se réfèrent aux projections nationales.

[5] Projections based on the 2013 Population Census. - Projections fondées sur le recensement de la population de 2013.

[6] Data based on the 2011 Census. - Données fondées sur le recensement de 2011.

[7] Estimates based on the 2014 Population Census. - Estimations fondées sur le recensement de la population de 2014.

[8] Projections based on the 2014 Population Census. - Projections fondées sur le recensement de la population de 2014.

[9] Projections based on the 2000 quick population count results and 1995, 2002 and 2010 Eritrea Demographic and Health Surveys. - Projections fondées sur le dénombrement rapide de la population de 2000 et sur les enquêtes érythréennes de la démographie et de la santé de 1995, 2002 et 2010.

[10] Estimates considering also the results of the 2007 Population Census. - Estimations en prennant en considération les résultats du recensement de la population de 2007.

[11] Data based on the 2010 Population Census. - Les données sont fondées sur le recensement de la population de 2010.

[12] Post-censal estimates based on the 2009 Population Census. - Les estimations post-censitaire fondées sur le recensement de la population de 2009.

[13] Data are projections based on the 2006 Population Census. - Projections fondées sur le recensement de la population de 2006.

[14] Data refer to Libyan nationals only. - Les données se raportent aux nationaux libyens seulement.

[15] Projections considering also the results of the 2009 Population Census. - Projections en prennant en considération les résultats du recensement de la population de 2009.

[16] Including nomadic population. - Y compris la population nomade.

[17] Excludes the islands of St. Brandon and Agalega. - Non compris les îles St. Brandon et Agalega.

[18] Based on the results of the 2000 Population Census. - Basé sur les résultats du rencement de la population de 2000.

[19] Based on the results of the 2011 Population Census. - Basé sur les résultats du rencement de la population de 2011.

[20] Data refer to annual average population. - Les données correspondent à la population annuelle moyenne.

[21] Based on the results of the 2004 Population Census. - D'après des résultats du recensement de la population de 2004.

[22] Projections based on the results of national survey on population and health conducted between 2010 and 2011, and especially population and housing census 2014. - Des projections de la population fondées sur les résultats de l'enquête nationale de la population et de la santé réalisée entre 2010 et 2011 et, surtout, du recensement général de la population et de l'habitat de 2014.

[23] Data refer to national projections based on 2007 census. - Les données sont des projections nationales d'après les résultats du recensement de la population de 2007.

[24] Data refer to projections based on the 2011 Population Census. - Les données se réfèrent aux projections basées sur le recensement de la population de 2011.

[25] Projections based on the 2012 Population and Housing Census. - Projections fondées sur le recensement 2012 de la population et des logements.

[26] Data are projections based on the 2008 Population and Housing Census. - Projection basée sur le recensement 2008 de la population et des logements.

[27] Data refer to total resident population, Saint Helenian and other nationalities. - Les données concernent la population résidente totale, originaire de Sainte-Hélène ou possédant une autre nationalité.

[28] Based on the results of a population count. - D'après les résultats d'un comptage de la population.

[29] The population figures are 264, 263 and 262 persons for 2007, 2008 and 2009 respectively. - La population est respectivement égale à 264, 263 et 262 personnes pour les années 2007, 2008 et 2009.

[30] Projections based on the 2012 Population Census. - Projections fondées sur le recensement de la population de 2012.

[31] Figures for male and female may not add up to the total, since they do not include the category "Unknown". - La somme des chiffres indiqués pour les sexes masculin et féminin peut n'être pas égale au total parce qu'elle n'inclut pas la catégorie " inconnue ".

[32] Data for urban and rural do not add up to the total; reason for discrepancy not ascertained. - La somme des données pour la résidence urbaine et rurale n'est pas égale au total; on ne sait pas comment s'explique la divergence.

[33] Projections based on the 2002 Population Census. - Projections fondées sur le recensement de la population de 2002.

[34] Data have not been adjusted for underenumeration, estimated at 7 per cent. - Les données n'ont pas été ajustées pour compenser les lacunes du dénombrement, estimées à 7 p. 100.

[35] Projections based on the 2010 Population and Housing Census. - Projections fondées sur le recensement 2010 de la population et des logements.

[36] Data refer to projections based on the 2000 Population Census. - Les données se réfèrent aux projections basées sur le recensement de la population de 2000.

[37] Data refers to resident population adjusted for the undercount of 18 per cent and including the institutional population. - Les données concernent la population résidente, y compris la population des institutions, et ont été ajustées pour tenir compte du sous-dénombrement estimé à 18 p. 100.

[38] Bermuda is 100 per cent urban. - 100 pour cent de la population des Bermudes est urbaine.

[39] Adjusted for census net undercoverage (including adjustment for incompletely enumerated Indian reserves). Final intercensal estimates. - Ajusté pour la sous-estimation du recensement (y compris les réservations en Inde incomplètement énumérées). Estimations inter-censitaires definitives.

[40] Adjusted for census net undercoverage (including adjustment for incompletely enumerated Indian reserves). Final postcensal estimates. - Ajusté pour la sous-estimation du recensement (y compris les réservations en Inde incomplètement énumérées). Estimations postcensitaires definitives.

[41] Updated postcensal estimates. Adjusted for census net undercoverage (including adjustment for incompletely enumerated Indian reserves). - Estimations post censitaires mises à jour. Ajusté pour la sous-estimation du recensement (y compris les réservations en Inde incomplètement énumérées).

[42] To ensure confidentiality, the values, including totals are randomly rounded either up or down to a multiple of '5' or '10.' As a result, when these data are summed or grouped, the total value may not match the individual values since totals and sub-totals are independently rounded. Similarly, percentages, which are calculated on rounded data, may not necessarily add up to 100%. - À des fins de confidentialité, les chiffres, y compris les totaux, sont aléatoirement arrondis au multiple de 5 ou de 10 inférieur ou supérieur. Par conséquent, lorsque ces chiffres sont additionnés, le total peut ne pas correspondre à la somme des valeurs individuelles, dans la mesure où les totaux et les totaux partiels sont arrondis indépendamment. De même, la somme des pourcentages, qui sont calculés à partir des données arrondies, peut ne pas correspondre à 100 %.

[43] Adjusted for census net undercoverage (including adjustment for incompletely enumerated Indian reserves). Preliminary postcensal estimates. - Ajusté pour la sous-estimation du recensement (y compris les réservations en Inde incomplètement énumérées). Estimations post censitaires préliminaires.

[44] Excluding the institutional population. - Non compris la population dans les institutions.

[45] The source of data is the national household survey. - La source des données est l'enquête nationale des ménages.

[46] Based on the national household surveys 2010-2014 and the 2011 population census. - D'après les données de l'enquête nationale des ménages 2010-2014 et les résultats du recensement de la population de 2011.

[47] Definition of urban and rural distribution changed from the year 2010. - La définition des régions urbaines et rurales a changée depuis 2010.

[48] Based on the national household survey of 2015. - Basée sur l' enquête nationale auprès des ménages de 2015.

[49] Based on the national household survey of 2016. - D'après l'enquête nationale auprès des ménages de 2016.

[50] Based on the national household survey of 2017. - D'après l'enquête nationale auprès des ménages de 2017.

[51] Intercensal estimates. - Estimations inter-censitaires.

[52] Estimates or projections based on the 2007 Population Census. - Estimations ou projections fondées sur le recensement de la population de 2007.

⁵³ Population statistics are compiled from registers. - Les statistiques de la population sont compilées à partir des registres.

⁵⁴ Excluding data for Saint Barthélémy and Saint Martin. - Non compris les données pour Saint Barthélémy et Saint Martin.

⁵⁵ Projections produced by l'Institut Haïtien de Statistique et d'Informatique (IHSI) and the Latin American and Caribbean Demographic Centre (CELADE) - Population Division of ECLAC. - Les données sont projections produits par l'Institut Haïtien de Statistique et d'Informatique (IHSI) et le centre démographique de l'Amérique latine et les Caraïbes - Division de la population de la CEPALC.

⁵⁶ Data refer to projections based on the 2001 Population Census. - Les données se réfèrent aux projections basées sur le recensement de la population de 2001.

⁵⁷ The figures represent the census counts adjusted for under-coverage. Adjustments are done by applying weights calculated (to 4 decimal places) for each sex and age group to the enumerated population when the tabulations are produced. Minor discrepancies between totals and the sum of the component parts of a table and minor discrepancies between the totals across tables are due to rounding after weights are applied. - Les chiffres représentent le dénombrement résultant du recensement ajusté pour tenir compte du sous-dénombrement. Les ajustements sont effectués en appliquant un coefficient de pondération calculé (à la quatrième décimale) pour chaque sexe et groupe d'âges de la population dénombrée lors de l'établissement des tableaux. Les écarts mineurs entre les totaux et la somme des éléments constitutifs d'un tableau ainsi qu'entre les totaux figurant dans différents tableaux sont dus au fait que les chiffres sont arrondis après la pondération.

⁵⁸ Including an estimation of 1 334 585 persons corresponding to 448 195 housing units without information of the occupants. - Y compris une estimation de 1 334 585 personnes correspondant aux 448 195 unités d'habitation sans information sur les occupants.

⁵⁹ Estimates based on the 2010 Population Census. - Estimations basées sur le recensement de la population de 2010.

⁶⁰ Including armed forces stationed in the area. - Y compris les militaires en garnison sur le territoire.

⁶¹ Based on the results of the 2010 Population Census. - D'après le résultats du recensement de la population de 2010.

⁶² Excluding residents of institutions. - À l'exclusion de personnes en établissements de soins.

⁶³ Excluding U.S. Armed Forces overseas and civilian U.S. citizens whose usual place of residence is outside the United States. Intercensal estimates. - Non compris les militaires américains à l'étranger et les civils américains dont le lieu de résidence habituel est en dehors des États-Unis. Estimations inter-censitaires.

⁶⁴ Postcensal estimates. Excluding U.S. Armed Forces overseas and civilian U.S. citizens whose usual place of residence is outside the United States. - Estimations post censitaires. Non compris les militaires américains à l'étranger et les civils américains dont le lieu de résidence habituel est en dehors des États-Unis.

⁶⁵ Data include persons in remote areas, military personnel outside the country, merchant seamen at sea, civilian seasonal workers outside the country, and other civilians outside the country, and exclude nomads, foreign military, civilian aliens temporarily in the country, transients on ships and Indian jungle population. Data refer to national projections. - Y compris les personnes vivant dans des régions éloignées, le personel militaire en dehors du pays, les marins marchands, les ouvriers saisonniers en dehors du pays, et autres civils en dehors du pays, et non compris les nomades, les militaires étrangers, les étrangers civils temporairement dans le pays, les transiteurs sur des bateaux et les Indiens de la jungle. Les données se réfèrent aux projections nationales.

⁶⁶ Data are revised projections taking into consideration also the results of the 2005 census. - Les données sont des projections révisées tenant compte également des résultats du recensement de 2005.

⁶⁷ Data based on the 2010 Population Census. Excludes nomadic Indian tribes. - Les données sont fondées sur le recensement de la population de 2010. Non compris les tribus d'Indiens nomades.

⁶⁸ A dispute exists between the governments of Argentina and the United Kingdom of Great Britain and Northern Ireland concerning sovereignty over the Falkland Islands (Malvinas). Excluding military personnel and their families, visitors and transients. - La souveraineté sur les îles Falkland (Malvinas) fait l'objet d'un différend entre le Gouvernement argentin et le Gouvernement du Royaume-Uni de Grande-Bretagne et d'Irlande du Nord. Non compris les militaires et leur familles, ni les visiteurs et transients.

⁶⁹ Estimates or projections considering also the results of the 2012 Population Census. - Estimations ou projections en prennent en considération les résultats du recensement de la population de 2012.

⁷⁰ Figures for male and female population do not add up to the figure for total population, because they exclude 108 homeless people of unknown sex. - Les chiffres relatifs à la population masculine et féminine ne correspondent pas au chiffre de la population totale, parce que l'on en a exclu 108 personnes sans toit dont le sexe n'est pas connu.

⁷¹ For operational purposes, population centers with 2,500 and more inhabitants are considered as urban area and less than 2,500 are considered as rural area. - À des fins opérationnelles, les centres de population comptant 2 500 habitants ou plus sont considérés comme zones urbaines, ceux qui en comptent moins de 2 500 comme zones rurales.

⁷² Data refer to the settled population based on the 1979 Population Census and the latest household prelisting. The refugees of Afghanistan in Iran, Pakistan, and an estimated 1.5 million nomads, are not included. - Les données se rapportent à la population stationnaire sur la base du recensement de 1979 et du recensement préliminaire des logements le plus récent. Sont exclus les réfugiés d'Afghanistan en Iran et au Pakistan et les nomades estimés à 1,5 million.

⁷³ Data have been adjusted for underenumeration. - Les données ont été ajustées pour compenser les lacunes du dénombrement.

⁷⁴ Data refer to projected figures based on the Population and Housing Census 2005 (district projection). - Les données se réfèrent aux projections basées sur le recensement de la population et de l'habitat de 2005 (projections locales).

⁷⁵ Source: 2016 Population and Housing Census Update. - Source : Révision des chiffres du recensement de la population et des logements de 2016.

⁷⁶ Excluding foreign diplomatic personnel and their dependants. - Non compris le personnel diplomatique étranger et les membres de leur famille les accompagnant.

⁷⁷ Excluding foreign diplomatic personnel and their dependants. Data based on the 2008 Population Census. - Non compris le personnel diplomatique étranger et les membres de leur famille les accompagnant. Données fondées sur le recensement de population de 2008.

⁷⁸ Based on the results of the Cambodia Intercensal Population Survey. Data exclude foreign diplomatic personnel and their dependants. - Sur la base de l'enquête intercensitaire de la population de Cambodge. Non compris le personnel diplomatique étranger et les membres de leur famille les accompagnant.

⁷⁹ For statistical purposes, the data for China do not include those for the Hong Kong Special Administrative Region (Hong Kong SAR), Macao Special Administrative Region (Macao SAR) and Taiwan province of China. - Pour la présentation des statistiques, les données pour la Chine ne comprennent pas la Région Administrative Spéciale de Hong Kong (Hong Kong RAS), la Région Administrative Spéciale de Macao (Macao RAS) et Taïwan province de Chine.

⁸⁰ Data have been estimated on the basis of the annual National Sample Survey on Population Changes. - Les données ont été estimées sur la base de l'enquête annuelle "National Sample Survey on Population Changes".

⁸¹ Because of rounding, totals are not in all cases the sum of the respective components. - Les chiffres étant arrondis, les totaux ne correspondent pas toujours rigoureusement à la somme des composants respectifs.

⁸² Because of rounding, totals are not in all cases the sum of the respective components. The military personnel are classified as urban population. - Les chiffres étant arrondis, les totaux ne correspondent pas toujours rigoureusement à la somme des composants respectifs. Le personnel militaire est classé dans la population urbaine.

⁸³ Data are from Communique of the National Bureau of Statistics of the People's Republic of China on Major Figures of the 2010 Population Census (No.1). - Données issues du communiqué du Bureau national de la statistique de la République populaire de Chine sur les chiffres importants du recensement de 2010 (n° 1).

⁸⁴ Data have been adjusted on the basis of the Population Census of 2010. - Les données ont été ajustées à partir des résultats du recensement de la population de 2010.

⁸⁵ The military personnel are classified as urban population. - Le personnel militaire est classé dans la population urbaine.

⁸⁶ Data refer to Hong Kong resident population at the census moment, which covers usual residents and mobile residents. Usual residents refer to two categories of people: (1) Hong Kong permanent residents who had stayed in Hong Kong for at least three months during the six months before or for at least three months during the six months after the census moment, regardless of whether they were in Hong Kong or not at the census moment; and (2) Hong Kong non-permanent residents who were in Hong Kong at the census moment. Mobile Residents, they are Hong Kong permanent residents who had stayed in Hong Kong for at least one month but less than three months during the six months before or for at least one month but less than three months during the six months after the census moment, regardless of whether they were in Hong Kong or not at the census moment. - Les données se rapportent à la population résidente à Hong Kong au moment du recensement. Cette population est composée des résidants habituels et des résidants mobiles. La population résidente est partagée en deux catégories: (1) les résidents permanents qui ont habité à Hong Kong au moins trois mois pendant les six mois précédents ou les six mois suivants le recensement; (2) les habitants non-permanents de Hong Kong qui étaient à Hong Kong au moment du recensement. La population mobile

se rapporte aux résidents permanents de Hong Kong qui ont habité à Hong Kong pendant les six mois après le recensement pour une période comprise entre un mois et trois mois, indépendamment du fait qu'ils étaient à Hong Kong au moment du recensement au pays.

[87] Data refer to Hong Kong resident population at the census moment, which covers usual residents and mobile residents. Usual residents refer to two categories of people: (1) Hong Kong permanent residents who had stayed in Hong Kong for at least three months during the six months before or for at least three months during the six months after the census moment, regardless of whether they were in Hong Kong or not at the census moment; and (2) Hong Kong non-permanent residents who were in Hong Kong at the census moment. Mobile Residents, they are Hong Kong permanent residents who had stayed in Hong Kong for at least one month but less than three months during the six months before or for at least one month but less than three months during the six months after the census moment, regardless of whether they were in Hong Kong or not at the census moment. Data are estimates from sample enquiry. - Les données se rapportent à la population résidente à Hong Kong au moment du recensement. Cette population est composée des résidants habituels et des résidants mobiles. La population résidente est partagée en deux catégories: (1) les résidants permanents qui ont habité à Hong Kong au moins trois mois pendant les six mois précédents ou les six mois suivants le recensement; (2) les habitants non-permanents de Hong Kong qui étaient à Hong Kong au moment du recensement. La population mobile se rapporte aux résidents permanents de Hong Kong qui ont habité à Hong Kong pendant les six mois après le recensement pour une période comprise entre un mois et trois mois, indépendamment du fait qu'ils étaient à Hong Kong au moment du recensement au pays. Les données sont des chiffres estimatifs dérivés d'une enquête par sondage.

[88] Population by-census is conducted between two population censuses, adopting a sampling method to select 29,421 housing units in Macao for enumeration, with the unit of observation being the individuals residing in the selected housing units. - Aux fins du recensement partiel de la population, conduit entre deux recensements, la méthode d'échantillonnage adoptée a permis de sélectionner 29 421 unités d'habitation à Macao, l'unité d'observation étant les personnes qui y résident.

[89] Data refer to government controlled areas. - Les données se rapportent aux zones contrôlées par le Gouvernement.

[90] Based on the results of the 2014 Population Census. - D'après les résultats du recensement de la population de 2014.

[91] Includes data for the Indian-held part of Jammu and Kashmir, the final status of which has not yet been determined. - Y compris les données pour la partie du Jammu et du Cachemire occupée par l'Inde dont le statut définitif n'a pas encore été déterminé.

[92] Data refer to projections based on the 2001 Population Census. - Les données se réfèrent aux projections basées sur le recensement de la population de 2001.

[93] Data are based on the publication: "Indonesia Population Projection 2005-2015" - Les données sont basées sur la publication : << Indonesia Population Projection 2005-2015 >>

[94] Data are based on the publication: "Indonesia Population Projection 2010-2035" - Les données sont basées sur la publication : << Indonesia Population Projection 2010-2035 >>

[95] Data refer to the Iranian Year which begins on 21 March and ends on 20 March of the following year. - Les données concernent l'année iranienne, qui commence le 21 mars et se termine le 20 mars de l'année suivante.

[96] The total number may include 'Unknown residence', but the categories urban and rural do not. - Le nombre total peut inclure les personnes dont la résidence n'est pas connue, à l'inverse des catégories de population urbaine et rurale.

[97] Differences between the total country figures and sum of urban and rural areas are due to the inclusion of unsettled population. - Les différences entre les chiffres pour l'ensemble du pays et la somme des zones urbaines et rurales s'expliquent par l'inclusion de la population non sédentaire.

[98] Includes data for East Jerusalem and Israeli residents in certain other territories under occupation by Israeli military forces since June 1967. - Y compris les données pour Jérusalem-Est et les résidents israéliens dans certains autres territoires occupés depuis 1967 par les forces armées israéliennes.

[99] Excluding residents who had been registered in the Israeli localities (the Jewish localities) in the Gaza Area and northern Samaria, which were evacuated in August 2005, but did not notify the Ministry of Interior of their new address. These residents are included in total. - Hors résidents enregistrés dans les localités d'Israel (localités juives) de la Bande de Gaza (verfify) et du nord de la Samarie, qui ont été évacués en Août 2005, mais qui n'ont pas notifié leur nouvelle adresse au ministère de l'intérieur. Ces résidents sont inclus dans le total.

[100] Data are rounded for confidentiality reasons. - Chiffres arrondis pour des raisons de confidentialité.

[101] Data refer to Israeli citizens and permanent residents who are listed in the Population Register. - Les données se rapportent aux citoyens israéliens et aux résidents permanents qui sont répertoriés dans le registre de la population.

[102] Excluding diplomatic personnel outside the country and foreign military and civilian personnel and their dependants stationed in the area. - Non compris le personnel diplomatique hors du pays ni les militaires et agents civils étrangers en poste sur le territoire et les membres de leur famille les accompagnant.

[103] Estimates based on the complete counts of the 2015 Population Census. - Estimations basées sur le dénombrement complet du recensement de la population de 2015.

[104] Estimates based on the complete counts of the 2015 Population Census. Because of rounding, totals are not in all cases the sum of the respective components. - Estimations basées sur le dénombrement complet du recensement de la population de 2015. Les chiffres étant arrondis, les totaux ne correspondent pas toujours rigoureusement à la somme des composants respectifs.

[105] Excluding data for Jordanian territory under occupation since June 1967 by Israeli military forces. - Non compris les données pour le territoire jordanien occupé depuis juin 1967 par les forces armées israéliennes.

[106] Data refer to resident population. - Les données concernent la population résidente.

[107] Data refer to resident population. Recalculated population estimates taking into account late registration of births and deaths until May 2017. - Les données concernent la population résidente. Réestimation du nombre d'habitants compte tenu de l'enregistrement tardif des naissances et des décès jusqu'en mai 2017.

[108] Estimates based on the results of 2015 population census. - Estimations fondées sur les résultats du recensement de la population de 2015.

[109] Source: Living conditions of household survey, October 2011 to September 2012. - Source: Enquête sur les conditions de vie des ménages, octobre 2011 à septembre 2012.

[110] Intercensal Mid-Year Population Estimates based on the adjusted Population and Housing Census of 2000 and 2010. - Les estimations inter-censitaires au milieu de l'année sont fondée sur les résultats ajustées des recensements de la population et de l'habitat de 2000 et 2010.

[111] Estimates based on the adjusted results of the Population and Housing Census of 2010. - Les estimations sont fondée sur les résultats ajustées du recensement de la population et de l'habitat de 2010.

[112] Data refer to resident population which includes resident Maldivians and resident foreigners. Estimates based on the 2014 Population Census. - Les données concernent la population résidente, qui comprend les Maldiviens et les étrangers. Estimations fondées sur le recensement de la population de 2014.

[113] Data refer to resident population which includes resident Maldivians and resident foreigners. - Les données concernent la population résidente, qui comprend les Maldiviens et les étrangers.

[114] Data refer to enumerated population. The total for the whole country excludes 1,206,353 persons estimated not to have been counted in parts of States of Rakhine, Kachin and Kayin. - Les données se rapportent à la population dénombrée. L' effectif de la population pour le pays ne comprend pas les personnes qui ne sont pas dénombrées dans certaines régions des États de Rakhine, Kachin et Kayin estimées à un chiffre de 1 206 353 personnes.

[115] Data refer to registered population data from Royal Oman Police. - Les données portent sur la population enregistrée par la police royale de l'Oman.

[116] Data for the urban and rural population are based on the percentage distribution according to the 2010 census. - Les données de la population urbaine et rurale sont fondées sur la répartition des pourcentages d'après le recensement de 2010.

[117] Data for the urban and rural population are based on percentage distribution according to the 2016 survey. - Les données de la population urbaine et rurale sont fondées sur la répartition des pourcentages d'après l'enquête de 2016.

[118] Excluding data for the Pakistan-held part of Jammu and Kashmir, the final status of which has not yet been determined. - Non compris les données concernant la partie du Jammu et Cachemire occupée par le Pakistan dont le statut définitif n'a pas été déterminé.

[119] Excluding 2739 Filipinos in Philippine Embassies, Consulates and Missions Abroad. - Excepté 2739 Philippins travaillant dans les ambassades, les consulats et les missions des Philippines à l'étranger.

[120] Excluding 2134 Filipinos in Philippine Embassies, Consulates and Missions Abroad. - Excepté 2134 Philippins travaillant dans les ambassades, les consulats et les missions des Philippines à l'étranger.

[121] Excluding usual residents not in the country at the time of census. - À l'exclusion des résidents habituels qui ne sont pas dans le pays au moment du recensement.

[122] Data refer to resident population which comprises Singapore citizens and permanent residents. - Les données se rapportent à la population résidente composé des citoyens de Singapour et des résidents permanents.

123 Data exclude residents who have been away from Singapore for a continuous period of 12 months or longer as at the reference date. - Non compris les résidents hors de Singapour pour une période ininterrompue de 12 mois ou plus avant de la date de référence.

124 Data are based on the latest register-based population estimates for 2010. Urban and rural breakdown not applicable as Singapore is a city-state. - Données basées sur les estimations démographiques les plus récentes fondées sur les registres de 2010. La ventilation entre zones urbaines et zones rurales ne s'applique pas à Singapour, puisqu'il s'agit d'une ville État.

125 Data for urban include population in refugee camps. - Les données pour la population urbaine comprennent la population dans les camps réfugiés.

126 Including Palestinian refugees. - Y compris les réfugiés de Palestine.

127 Data based on Address Based Population Registration System. - Les données sont basées sur le registre national de la population basé sur l'adresse.

128 Because of rounding, totals are not in all cases the sum of the respective components. Based on a sample taken at the time of census. - Les chiffres étant arrondis, les totaux ne correspondent pas toujours rigoureusement à la somme des composants respectifs. D'après un échantillon obtenu au moment du recensement.

129 The reason for the differences in the urban-rural population from the previous years is the changes in administrative attachment, legal entity and borders, regulated by related laws. - La raison des différences dans la population urbaine-rurale par rapport aux années précédentes est la modification de l'attachement administratif, de l'entité juridique et des frontières, réglementée par des lois connexes.

130 Data include non-national population. - Les données comprennent les non-nationaux.

131 Data are adjusted according to the results of the 2009 census and 2014 intercensus. - Les données ont été ajustées à partir des résultats du recensement de la population de 2009 et des données intercensitaires de 2014.

132 Decrease in population due to revision in administrative registers. - Diminution de la population due à la révision des registres administratifs.

133 Excluding Faeroe Islands and Greenland shown separately, if available. Population statistics are compiled from registers. - Non compris les îles Féroé et le Groenland, qui font l'objet de rubriques distinctes, si disponible. Les statistiques de la population sont compilées à partir des registres.

134 Population statistics are compiled from registers. Excluding Åland Islands. - Les statistiques de la population sont compilées à partir des registres. Non compris les Îles d'Åland.

135 Excluding diplomatic personnel outside the country and including members of alien armed forces not living in military camps and foreign diplomatic personnel not living in embassies or consulates. - Non compris le personnel diplomatique hors du pays et y compris les militaires étrangers ne vivant pas dans des camps militaires et le personnel diplomatique étranger ne vivant pas dans les ambassades ou les consulats.

136 Data refer to annual average population. Data based on the 2011 Census. - Les données correspondent à la population annuelle moyenne. Données fondées sur le recensement de 2011.

137 Excluding military personnel, visitors and transients. - Non compris les militaires, ni les visiteurs et transients.

138 Data refer to the Vatican City State. - Les données se rapportent à l'Etat de la Cité du Vatican.

139 The population figure is 466 persons. - La population est égale à 466 personnes.

140 Data refer to usually resident population. - Les données concernent la population habituellement résidente.

141 Data refer to registered resident population. - Les données concernent la population enregistrée résidente.

142 Including civilian nationals temporarily outside the country. - Y compris les civils nationaux temporairement hors du pays.

143 Data refer to resident population only. - Pour la population résidante seulement.

144 Figures for male and female population do not add up to the figure for total population, because they exclude 119 persons of unknown sex. - Les chiffres relatifs à la population masculine et féminine ne correspondent pas au chiffre de la population totale, parce que l'on en a exclu 119 personnes de sexe inconnu.

145 Population statistics are compiled from registers. Including residents temporarily outside the country. - Les statistiques de la population sont compilées à partir des registres. Y compris les résidents se trouvant temporairement hors du pays.

146 Data refer to usually resident population. Data refer to annual average population. - Les données concernent la population habituellement résidente. Les données correspondent à la population annuelle moyenne.

147 Excluding civilian aliens within the country, but including civilian nationals temporarily outside the country. - Non compris les civils étrangers dans le pays, mais y compris les civils nationaux temporairement hors du pays.

148 Excluding Transnistria and the municipality of Bender. - Les données ne tiennent pas compte de l'information sur la Transnistria et la municipalité de Bender.

149 Excludes data for Kosovo and Metohia. - Sans les données pour le Kosovo et Metohia.

150 Data refer to annual average population. Data refer to registered resident population. - Les données correspondent à la population annuelle moyenne. Les données concernent la population enregistrée résidente.

151 Data refer to legal resident population. - Les données concernent la population légalement résidente.

152 From 2015, urban refers to urban centers and areas under the influence of urban centers. - A partir de 2015, le territoire urbain inclut l'espace des centres urbains ainsi que l'espace sous influence des centres urbains.

153 The Government of Ukraine has informed the United Nations that it is not in a position to provide statistical data concerning the Autonomous Republic of Crimea and the city of Sevastopol. Data refer to annual average population. - Le gouvernement Ukrainien a informé l'ONU qu'il n'est pas en mesure de fournir des données statistiques concernant la République autonome de Crimée et la ville de Sébastopol. Les données correspondent à la population annuelle moyenne.

154 The Government of Ukraine has informed the United Nations that it is not in a position to provide statistical data concerning the Autonomous Republic of Crimea and the city of Sevastopol. - Le gouvernement Ukrainien a informé l'ONU qu'il n'est pas en mesure de fournir des données statistiques concernant la République autonome de Crimée et la ville de Sébastopol.

155 Excluding Channel Islands (Guernsey and Jersey) and Isle of Man, shown separately, if available. - Non compris les îles Anglo-Normandes (Guernesey et Jersey) et l'île de Man, qui font l'objet de rubriques distinctes, si disponible.

156 Based on the results of the 2016 Population Census. - Basé sur les résultats du recensement de la population de 2016.

157 These data have been randomly rounded to protect confidentiality. Individual figures may not add up to totals, and values for the same data may vary in different tables. - Ces données ont été arrondies de façon aléatoire afin d'en préserver la confidentialité. La somme de certains chiffres peut ne pas correspondre aux totaux indiqués et les valeurs des mêmes données peuvent varier d'un tableau à un autre.

158 Including population in off-shore, migratory and shipping. - Y compris les populations extraterritoriales, les populations nomades et les populations maritimes.

159 Excluding Niue, shown separately, which is part of Cook Islands, but because of remoteness is administered separately. - Non compris Nioué, qui fait l'objet d'une rubrique distincte et qui fait partie des îles Cook, mais qui, en raison de son éloignement, est administrée séparément.

160 Projections are prepared by the Secretariat of the Pacific Community based on the 1999 census of population and housing. - Les projections sont préparées par le Secrétariat de la Communauté du Pacifique à partir des résultats du recensement de la population et de l'habitat de 1999.

161 Population estimates by urban/rural residence exclude inland waters and oceanic areas. - Les estimations de la population par lieu de résidence urbaine ou rurale excluent les eaux intérieures et les zones océaniques.

162 These data have been randomly rounded to protect confidentiality. Individual figures may not add up to totals, and values for the same data may vary in different tables. Data include overseas visitors in New Zealand on census night. - Ces données ont été arrondies de façon aléatoire afin d'en préserver la confidentialité. La somme de certains chiffres peut ne pas correspondre aux totaux indiqués et les valeurs des mêmes données peuvent varier d'un tableau à un autre. Y compris les visiteurs étrangers qui se trouvaient en Nouvelle-Zélande le soir du recensement.

163 Estimates are prepared by the Secretariat of the Pacific Community based on the last population and housing census. - Les estimations sont préparées par le Secrétariat de la Communauté du Pacifique à partir des résultats du dernier recensement de la population et de l'habitat.

164 The population figures are 64 and 58 persons for 2007 and 2008 respectively. - La population est respectivement égale à 64 et 58 personnes pour les années 2007 et 2008.

165 Estimates based on the 2011 Population Census. - Estimations basées sur le recensement de la population de 2011.

166 Estimates based on the 2016 Population Census. - Estimations basées sur le recensement de la population de 2016.

167 Data have not been adjusted for underenumeration. - Les données n'ont pas été ajustées pour compenser les lacunes du dénombrement.

168 Projections based on adjusted 2009 census counts. - Projections fondées à partir des comptes rajustés du recensement de 2009.

169 Based on the results of the 1996 population census. Data refer to national projections. - À partir des résultats du recensement de la population de 1996. Les données se réfèrent aux projections nationales.

Table 7 - *Demographic Yearbook 2017*

Table 7 presents population by age, sex and urban/rural residence for the latest available year between 2008 and 2017.

Description of variables: Data in this table are either population census figures or estimates, some of which are based on sample surveys. The source of data is indicated by the 'code' explained at the end of the table.

The reference date of the census or estimate appears in the left-most column of the table. In general, the estimates refer to mid-year, i.e. 1 July.

Age is defined as age at last birthday, that is, the difference between the date of birth and the reference date of the age distribution expressed in completed solar years. The age classification used in this table is the following: under 1 year, 1-4 years, 5-year groups through 95-99 years, and 100 years or over.

Statistics are presented for one year, the most recent available. However, if more complete disaggregation is available for an earlier year, both are displayed.

The urban/rural classification of population is that provided by each country or area; it is presumed to be based on the national census definitions of urban population that have been set forth at the end of the technical notes to table 6.

Reliability of data: Estimates which are believed to be less reliable are set in *italics* rather than in roman type.

Limitations: Statistics on population by age and sex are subject to the same qualifications as have been set forth for population statistics in general and age distributions in particular, as discussed in sections 3 and 3.1.3, respectively, of the Technical Notes.

Comparability of population data classified by age and sex is limited by variations in the definition of total population, discussed in detail in section 3 of the Technical Notes, and by the accuracy of the original enumeration. Both factors are more important in relation to certain age groups than to others. For example, under-enumeration is known to be more prevalent among infants and young children than among older persons. Similarly, the exclusion from the total population of certain groups that tend to be of selected ages (such as the armed forces) can markedly affect the age structure and its comparability with that for other countries or areas. Consideration should be given to the implications of these basic limitations in using the data.

In addition to these general qualifications are the special problems of comparability that arise in relation to age statistics in particular. Age distributions of population are known to suffer from certain deficiencies that have their origin in irregularities in age reporting. Although some of the irregularities tend to be obscured or eliminated when data are tabulated in five-year age groups rather than by single years, precision still continues to be affected, though the degree of distortion is not always readily seen.

Another factor limiting comparability is the age classification employed by the various countries or areas. Age may be based on the year of birth rather than the age at last birthday, in other words, calculated using the day, month and year of birth. Distributions based only on the year of birth are footnoted when known.

The absence of data in the unknown age group does not necessarily indicate completely accurate reporting and tabulation of the age item. The unknowns may have been eliminated by assigning ages to them before tabulation, or by proportionately distributing the unknown category across the age groups after tabulation.

As noted in connection with table 5, intercensal estimates of total population are usually revised to accord with the results of a census of population if inexplicable discontinuities appear to exist. Intercensal age-sex distributions, however, are less likely to be revised in this way. When it is known that a total population estimate for a given year has been revised and the corresponding age distribution has not been revised, a note is provided. Distributions of this type should be used with caution when studying trends over a period of years, though their utility for studying age structure for the specified year is probably unimpaired.

The comparability of data by urban/rural residence is affected by the national definitions of urban and rural used in tabulating these data. When known, the definitions of urban used in national population censuses are presented at the end of the technical notes for table 6. As discussed in detail in the technical notes for table 6, these definitions vary considerably from one country or area to another.

Earlier data: Population by age, sex and urban/rural residence has been shown in previous issues of the *Demographic Yearbook*. For more information on specific topics, and years for which data are reported, readers should consult the Historical Index. In addition, population data by single years of age, sex and urban/rural residence, for censuses conducted since 1995, are shown in the *Demographic Yearbook* webpage https://unstats.un.org/unsd/demographic-social/products/dyb/index.cshtml#censusdatasets.

Tableau 7 – Annuaire démographique 2017

Le tableau 7 présente les données les plus récentes disponibles pour la période 2008-2017 sur la population selon l'âge, le sexe et le lieu de résidence (zone urbaine ou rurale).

Description des variables : les données de ce tableau proviennent de recensements de la population ou correspondent à des estimations, fondées dans certains cas, sur des enquêtes par sondage. Le 'code' indique comment les données ont été obtenues. Les codes utilisés sont expliqués à la fin du tableau.

La date du recensement ou de l'estimation figure dans la colonne de gauche du tableau. En général, les estimations se rapportent au milieu de l'année (1er juillet).

L'âge désigne l'âge au dernier anniversaire, c'est-à-dire la différence entre la date de naissance et la date de référence de la répartition par âge exprimée en années solaires révolues. La classification par âge utilisée dans ce tableau est la suivante : moins d'un an, 1 à 4 ans, groupes quinquennaux jusqu'à 95-99 ans et 100 ans ou plus.

Les statistiques portent sur une année, qui correspond à celle pour laquelle on dispose des statistiques les plus récentes. Toutefois, si l'on dispose de répartitions plus complètes pour des années antérieures, les statistiques sont alors présentées pour les deux années.

La classification par zones urbaines et rurales de la population est celle qui est communiquée par chaque pays ou zone ; on part du principe qu'elle repose sur les définitions de la population urbaine utilisées pour les recensements de la population nationaux telles qu'elles sont reproduites à la fin des notes techniques du tableau 6.

Fiabilité des données : les estimations considérées comme moins sûres sont indiquées en italique plutôt qu'en caractères romains.

Insuffisance des données : les statistiques de la population selon l'âge et le sexe appellent les mêmes réserves que celles qui ont été formulées aux sections 3 et 3.1.3 des Notes techniques à propos des statistiques de la population en général et des répartitions par âge en particulier.

La comparabilité des statistiques de la population selon l'âge et le sexe pâtit du manque d'uniformité dans la définition de la population totale (voir la section 3 des Notes techniques) et des lacunes des dénombrements. L'influence de ces deux facteurs varie selon les groupes d'âge. Ainsi, le dénombrement des enfants de moins d'un an et des jeunes enfants comporte souvent plus de lacunes que celui des personnes plus âgées. De même, le fait que certains groupes de personnes appartenant souvent à des groupes d'âge déterminés, par exemple les militaires, ne soient pas pris en compte dans la population totale peut influer sensiblement sur la structure par âge et sur la comparabilité des données avec celles d'autres pays ou zones. Il conviendra de tenir compte de ces facteurs fondamentaux lorsque l'on utilisera les données du tableau.

Outre ces difficultés d'ordre général, la comparabilité pose des problèmes particuliers lorsqu'il s'agit des données par âge. On sait que les répartitions de la population selon l'âge présentent certaines imperfections dues à l'inexactitude des déclarations d'âge. Certaines de ces anomalies ont tendance à s'estomper ou à disparaître lorsque l'on classe les données par groupes d'âge quinquennaux et non par années d'âge, mais une certaine imprécision subsiste, même s'il n'est pas toujours facile de voir à quel point il y a distorsion.

Le degré de comparabilité dépend également de la classification par âge employée dans les divers pays ou zones. L'âge retenu peut être défini par date exacte (jour, mois et année) de naissance ou par celle du dernier anniversaire. Lorsqu'elles étaient connues, les répartitions établies seulement d'après l'année de la naissance ont été signalées en note à la fin du tableau.

Si aucun nombre ne figure dans la rangée réservée aux âges inconnus, cela ne signifie pas nécessairement que les déclarations d'âge et l'exploitation des données par âge aient été tout à fait exactes. C'est souvent une indication que l'on a attribué un âge aux personnes d'âge inconnu avant l'exploitation des données ou qu'elles ont été réparties proportionnellement entre les différents groupes après cette opération.

Comme on l'a indiqué à propos du tableau 5, les estimations intercensitaires de la population totale sont d'ordinaire rectifiées d'après les résultats des recensements de population si l'on constate des discontinuités inexplicables. Les données intercensitaires concernant la répartition de la population par âge et par sexe ont toutefois moins de chance d'être rectifiées de cette manière. Lorsque l'on savait qu'une estimation de la population totale pour une année donnée avait été rectifiée sans qu'il en soit de même pour la répartition par âge correspondante, cela a été indiquée dans une note. Les répartitions de ce type doivent être utilisées avec prudence lorsque l'on étudie les tendances sur un certain nombre d'années, quoique leur utilité pour l'étude de la structure par âge de la population pour l'année visée reste probablement entière.

La comparabilité des données selon le lieu de résidence (zone urbaine ou rurale) peut être limitée par les définitions nationales des termes « urbain » et « rural » utilisées pour la mise en tableaux de ces données. Les définitions du terme « urbain » utilisées pour les recensements nationaux de population ont été présentées à la fin des notes techniques du tableau 6 lorsqu'elles étaient connues. Comme on l'a précisé dans les notes techniques relatives au tableau 6, ces définitions varient considérablement d'un pays ou d'une zone à l'autre.

Données publiées antérieurement : des statistiques concernant la population selon l'âge, le sexe et le lieu de résidence (zone urbaine ou rurale) ont été présentées dans des éditions antérieures de l'*Annuaire démographique*. Pour plus de précisions concernant les années et les sujets pour lesquels des données ont été publiées, se reporter à l'index historique. En plus, des statistiques disponibles concernant la « Population selon chaque année d'âge, le sexe et la résidence urbaine/rurale », pour les recensements depuis 1995, ont été présentées dans la page internet suivante de l'*Annuaire démographique* https://unstats.un.org/unsd/demographic-social/products/dyb/index.cshtml#censusdatasets.

7. Population by age, sex and urban/rural residence: latest available year, 2008 - 2017
Population selon l'âge, le sexe et la résidence, urbaine/rurale : dernière année disponible, 2008 - 2017

Continent, country or area, date, code[a] and age (in years) Continent, pays ou zone, date, code[a] et âge (en années)	Total			Urban - Urbaine			Rural - Rurale		
	Both sexes Les deux sexes	Male Masculin	Female Féminin	Both sexes Les deux sexes	Male Masculin	Female Féminin	Both sexes Les deux sexes	Male Masculin	Female Féminin
AFRICA - AFRIQUE									
Algeria - Algérie									
16 IV 2008 (CDJC)[1]									
Total	34 080 030	17 232 753	16 847 277	22 413 189	11 288 724	11 124 466	11 666 841	5 944 029	5 722 812
0 - 4	3 404 918	1 750 097	1 654 821	2 242 705	1 151 239	1 091 466	1 162 213	598 858	563 355
5 - 9	2 888 376	1 475 674	1 412 702	1 888 091	963 262	924 829	1 000 285	512 412	487 873
10 - 14	3 258 773	1 662 262	1 596 511	2 096 819	1 067 727	1 029 092	1 161 954	594 535	567 419
15 - 19	3 635 171	1 847 312	1 787 859	2 309 568	1 169 541	1 140 028	1 325 603	677 772	647 831
20 - 24	3 763 504	1 895 703	1 867 801	2 378 019	1 188 465	1 189 553	1 385 485	707 238	678 247
25 - 29	3 422 377	1 730 411	1 691 966	2 186 560	1 096 016	1 090 545	1 235 816	634 395	601 421
30 - 34	2 740 996	1 379 085	1 361 910	1 802 265	901 021	901 245	938 730	478 064	460 666
35 - 39	2 342 779	1 167 250	1 175 529	1 601 928	793 133	808 795	740 852	374 118	366 734
40 - 44	2 018 327	1 007 683	1 010 644	1 414 371	705 266	709 105	603 956	302 417	301 539
45 - 49	1 629 436	817 005	812 432	1 132 297	570 706	561 591	497 140	246 299	250 841
50 - 54	1 346 695	682 358	664 336	927 655	474 005	453 650	419 040	208 353	210 687
55 - 59	1 062 578	547 180	515 398	720 761	371 528	349 233	341 817	175 652	166 165
60 - 64	711 482	354 694	356 788	479 760	236 949	242 811	231 722	117 745	113 977
65 - 69	631 303	314 958	316 345	420 685	207 760	212 925	210 618	107 198	103 420
70 - 74	504 926	248 672	256 254	336 819	164 109	172 710	168 107	84 563	83 544
75 - 79	363 843	181 478	182 364	240 563	118 362	122 201	123 280	63 116	60 164
80 - 84	187 130	93 472	93 657	121 942	59 267	62 675	65 187	34 205	30 982
85 - 89	89 722	43 307	46 416	58 550	27 171	31 379	31 172	16 136	15 037
90 - 94	29 672	13 575	16 097	19 375	8 488	10 887	10 297	5 087	5 210
95 - 99	10 028	4 178	5 851	6 647	2 638	4 009	3 382	1 540	1 842
100 +	650	252	398	445	170	274	205	82	123
Unknown - Inconnu	37 347	16 146	21 200	27 365	11 901	15 464	9 981	4 245	5 736
1 VII 2017 (ESDJ)									
Total	41 695 626	21 118 894	20 576 732	...	...	...	...	...	...
0	1 021 058	524 107	496 951	...	...	...	...	...	...
1 - 4	3 916 677	2 013 103	1 903 574	...	...	...	...	...	...
5 - 9	4 189 528	2 155 222	2 034 306	...	...	...	...	...	...
10 - 14	3 256 178	1 672 925	1 583 253	...	...	...	...	...	...
15 - 19	2 963 876	1 513 910	1 449 966	...	...	...	...	...	...
20 - 24	3 391 633	1 728 672	1 662 960	...	...	...	...	...	...
25 - 29	3 725 030	1 887 412	1 837 618	...	...	...	...	...	...
30 - 34	3 759 980	1 891 310	1 868 670	...	...	...	...	...	...
35 - 39	3 310 996	1 672 000	1 638 996	...	...	...	...	...	...
40 - 44	2 637 762	1 322 807	1 314 955	...	...	...	...	...	...
45 - 49	2 270 354	1 128 564	1 141 789	...	...	...	...	...	...
50 - 54	1 921 129	957 002	964 127	...	...	...	...	...	...
55 - 59	1 529 628	764 232	765 395	...	...	...	...	...	...
60 - 64	1 237 817	623 980	613 837	...	...	...	...	...	...
65 - 69	917 624	464 950	452 674	...	...	...	...	...	...
70 - 74	592 925	288 205	304 720	...	...	...	...	...	...
75 - 79	489 454	237 094	252 360	...	...	...	...	...	...
80 - 84	327 360	156 185	171 174	...	...	...	...	...	...
85 +	236 619	117 213	119 406	...	...	...	...	...	...
Angola									
16 V 2014 (CDFC)									
Total	25 789 024	12 499 041	13 289 983	16 153 987	7 860 614	8 293 373	9 635 037	4 638 427	4 996 610
0 - 4	4 998 148	2 484 582	2 513 566	2 912 064	1 450 139	1 461 924	2 086 085	1 034 443	1 051 642
5 - 9	4 160 174	2 062 888	2 097 287	2 559 781	1 258 439	1 301 342	1 600 393	804 448	795 945
10 - 14	3 038 173	1 504 180	1 533 993	1 975 562	953 924	1 021 638	1 062 612	550 256	512 355
15 - 19	2 510 436	1 222 700	1 287 736	1 677 783	809 594	868 189	832 653	413 106	419 547
20 - 24	2 174 501	1 020 699	1 153 802	1 477 330	696 023	781 307	697 171	324 676	372 496
25 - 29	1 945 050	913 726	1 031 323	1 338 058	640 293	697 765	606 992	273 433	333 559
30 - 34	1 503 520	714 239	789 281	1 026 351	498 258	528 093	477 169	215 982	261 188
35 - 39	1 382 959	654 408	728 550	902 362	439 369	462 993	480 597	215 040	265 558
40 - 44	1 050 085	510 344	539 742	660 913	332 669	328 245	389 172	177 675	211 497
45 - 49	864 904	417 953	446 951	525 157	266 263	258 894	339 747	151 690	188 057
50 - 54	709 169	332 638	376 532	400 902	195 727	205 174	308 268	136 910	171 357
55 - 59	483 319	229 641	253 678	264 296	131 985	132 310	219 023	97 656	121 367
60 - 64	356 154	165 937	190 217	174 161	82 701	91 460	181 993	83 236	98 757
65 - 69	215 387	95 614	119 773	96 774	42 538	54 236	118 613	53 077	65 536
70 - 74	180 167	78 673	101 494	73 334	30 023	43 311	106 833	48 650	58 183
75 - 79	92 944	39 257	53 687	38 891	14 759	24 133	54 052	24 498	29 554

Continent, country or area, date, code[a] and age (in years) / Continent, pays ou zone, date, code[a] et âge (en années)	Total			Urban - Urbaine			Rural - Rurale		
	Both sexes Les deux sexes	Male Masculin	Female Féminin	Both sexes Les deux sexes	Male Masculin	Female Féminin	Both sexes Les deux sexes	Male Masculin	Female Féminin
AFRICA - AFRIQUE									
Angola									
16 V 2014 (CDFC)									
80 - 84	66 792	28 351	38 441	25 743	9 211	16 532	41 049	19 140	21 909
85 - 89	24 828	9 967	14 861	10 546	3 575	6 972	14 281	6 392	7 889
90 - 94	18 175	7 603	10 572	7 058	2 483	4 576	11 117	5 121	5 996
95 +	14 138	5 640	8 498	6 921	2 641	4 280	7 217	2 999	4 218
Benin - Bénin									
1 VII 2011 (ESDF)[2]									
Total	9 067 076	4 446 877	4 620 199	4 072 574	2 003 366	2 069 208	4 994 502	2 443 511	2 550 991
0 - 4	1 629 512	828 064	801 448	633 629	321 667	311 962	995 883	506 397	489 486
0	350 292	178 565	171 727	...	...	...	...	...	...
1 - 4	1 279 220	649 499	629 721	...	...	...	...	...	...
5 - 9	1 335 166	675 912	659 254	511 822	251 283	260 539	823 344	424 629	398 715
10 - 14	1 137 068	572 756	564 312	517 373	244 437	272 936	619 695	328 319	291 376
15 - 19	1 081 199	553 241	527 958	550 694	279 420	271 274	530 505	273 821	256 684
20 - 24	767 946	398 920	369 026	406 496	224 092	182 404	361 450	174 828	186 622
25 - 29	609 489	291 598	317 891	303 896	153 731	150 165	305 593	137 867	167 726
30 - 34	537 893	227 400	310 493	264 521	117 596	146 925	273 372	109 804	163 568
35 - 39	494 619	213 385	281 234	236 804	106 800	130 004	257 815	106 585	151 230
40 - 44	378 111	175 956	202 155	178 115	86 225	91 890	199 996	89 731	110 265
45 - 49	308 866	142 056	166 810	145 334	68 351	76 983	163 532	73 705	89 827
50 - 54	232 650	110 074	122 576	101 866	48 831	53 035	130 784	61 243	69 541
55 - 59	171 970	82 190	89 780	77 819	37 319	40 500	94 151	44 871	49 280
60 - 64	135 768	64 968	70 800	52 261	24 642	27 619	83 507	40 326	43 181
65 - 69	75 534	35 915	39 619	31 238	14 546	16 692	44 296	21 369	22 927
70 - 74	82 740	36 511	46 229	30 032	12 558	17 474	52 708	23 953	28 755
75 - 79	36 453	15 591	20 862	14 064	5 573	8 491	22 389	10 018	12 371
80 +	52 092	22 340	29 752	16 610	6 295	10 315	35 482	16 045	19 437
1 VII 2016 (ESDF)[3]									
Total	10 882 953	5 334 603	5 548 350	...	...	...	...	...	...
0 - 4	1 724 707	876 597	848 110	...	...	...	...	...	...
5 - 9	1 690 244	853 324	836 920	...	...	...	...	...	...
10 - 14	1 530 148	780 536	749 612	...	...	...	...	...	...
15 - 19	1 163 229	600 456	562 773	...	...	...	...	...	...
20 - 24	936 421	456 779	479 642	...	...	...	...	...	...
25 - 29	818 147	356 225	461 922	...	...	...	...	...	...
30 - 34	722 299	314 616	407 683	...	...	...	...	...	...
35 - 39	588 013	272 972	315 041	...	...	...	...	...	...
40 - 44	466 547	224 131	242 416	...	...	...	...	...	...
45 - 49	344 261	171 500	172 761	...	...	...	...	...	...
50 - 54	259 141	126 844	132 297	...	...	...	...	...	...
55 - 59	202 796	99 128	103 668	...	...	...	...	...	...
60 - 64	129 272	63 241	66 031	...	...	...	...	...	...
65 - 69	122 941	57 543	65 398	...	...	...	...	...	...
70 - 74	64 104	29 468	34 636	...	...	...	...	...	...
75 - 79	57 572	25 240	32 332	...	...	...	...	...	...
80 +	63 111	26 003	37 108	...	...	...	...	...	...
Botswana[4]									
1 VII 2017 (ESDJ)									
Total	2 266 990	1 107 191	1 159 799	1 452 383	693 532	758 851	814 607	413 658	400 948
0 - 4	61 940	31 397	30 544	37 124	18 879	18 245	24 816	12 518	12 298
5 - 9	203 745	102 949	100 797	116 405	58 772	57 632	87 341	44 176	43 164
10 - 14	240 886	121 521	119 365	141 315	70 695	70 619	99 571	50 826	48 745
15 - 19	232 077	116 903	115 174	140 422	69 995	70 428	91 655	46 908	44 746
20 - 24	235 942	117 349	118 592	161 551	77 071	84 479	74 391	40 278	34 113
25 - 29	224 303	108 876	115 427	158 279	74 123	84 156	66 023	34 752	31 271
30 - 34	232 702	113 292	119 409	165 346	77 884	87 462	67 356	35 408	31 948
35 - 39	190 931	94 619	96 312	136 536	65 716	70 821	54 395	28 904	25 491
40 - 44	151 385	76 617	74 768	105 606	51 881	53 725	45 779	24 735	21 043
45 - 49	111 168	54 597	56 571	75 396	36 406	38 991	35 772	18 192	17 580
50 - 54	92 096	42 410	49 686	59 159	27 007	32 152	32 936	15 403	17 533
55 - 59	74 296	33 298	40 998	45 078	20 249	24 828	29 218	13 048	16 170
60 - 64	60 511	27 281	33 229	34 113	15 217	18 896	26 398	12 064	14 334
65 - 69	42 077	19 418	22 660	21 535	9 303	12 231	20 543	10 114	10 429
70 - 74	31 064	13 707	17 358	15 223	6 191	9 031	15 842	7 516	8 326

7. Population by age, sex and urban/rural residence: latest available year, 2008 - 2017
Population selon l'âge, le sexe et la résidence, urbaine/rurale : dernière année disponible, 2008 - 2017 (continued - suite)

Continent, country or area, date, code[a] and age (in years) Continent, pays ou zone, date, code[a] et âge (en années)	Total			Urban - Urbaine			Rural - Rurale		
	Both sexes Les deux sexes	Male Masculin	Female Féminin	Both sexes Les deux sexes	Male Masculin	Female Féminin	Both sexes Les deux sexes	Male Masculin	Female Féminin

AFRICA - AFRIQUE

Botswana[4]
1 VII 2017 (ESDJ)

75 - 79	24 922	10 595	14 327	11 975	4 485	7 490	12 948	6 111	6 837
80 - 84	20 031	7 801	12 230	9 604	3 262	6 341	10 428	4 539	5 889
85 - 89	14 799	5 458	9 342	6 843	2 171	4 672	7 957	3 287	4 670
90 - 94	9 233	3 163	6 070	4 418	1 362	3 055	4 815	1 800	3 015
95 - 99	4 390	1 542	2 848	2 062	669	1 393	2 328	872	1 455
100 +	8 492	4 400	4 092	4 394	2 192	2 202	4 098	2 208	1 890

Burkina Faso[2]
1 VII 2015 (ESDJ)

Total	18 450 494	8 904 256	9 546 238	...	...	...	...	...	...
0 - 4	3 382 595	1 727 798	1 654 797	...	...	...	...	...	...
5 - 9	2 908 754	1 495 367	1 413 387	...	...	...	...	...	...
10 - 14	2 486 098	1 279 388	1 206 710	...	...	...	...	...	...
15 - 19	2 019 668	1 007 291	1 012 377	...	...	...	...	...	...
20 - 24	1 570 287	747 367	822 920	...	...	...	...	...	...
25 - 29	1 285 878	548 045	737 833	...	...	...	...	...	...
30 - 34	1 028 499	426 955	601 544	...	...	...	...	...	...
35 - 39	882 336	377 591	504 745	...	...	...	...	...	...
40 - 44	677 094	300 004	377 090	...	...	...	...	...	...
45 - 49	581 242	255 406	325 836	...	...	...	...	...	...
50 - 54	449 604	200 660	248 944	...	...	...	...	...	...
55 - 59	366 471	161 682	204 789	...	...	...	...	...	...
60 - 64	265 938	123 614	142 324	...	...	...	...	...	...
65 - 69	221 400	101 732	119 668	...	...	...	...	...	...
70 - 74	141 840	67 215	74 625	...	...	...	...	...	...
75 - 79	98 034	45 504	52 530	...	...	...	...	...	...
80 +	84 756	38 637	46 119	...	...	...	...	...	...

Burundi
1 VII 2015 (ESDF)[5]

Total	9 823 828	4 822 838	5 000 990	1 473 574	723 426	750 148	8 350 254	4 099 412	4 250 842
0 - 4	1 712 483	856 714	855 769	220 830	99 976	120 854	1 491 653	756 738	734 915
5 - 9	1 379 000	679 740	699 260	172 229	76 843	95 386	1 206 771	602 897	603 874
10 - 14	1 234 086	604 457	629 629	154 449	67 431	87 018	1 079 637	537 026	542 611
15 - 19	1 021 915	496 353	525 562	161 685	74 964	86 721	860 230	421 389	438 841
20 - 24	974 645	467 123	507 522	176 946	89 742	87 204	797 699	377 381	420 318
25 - 29	843 366	397 323	446 043	174 840	90 183	84 657	668 526	307 140	361 386
30 - 34	659 106	321 348	337 758	140 254	76 414	63 840	518 852	244 934	273 918
35 - 39	466 561	236 115	230 446	82 657	46 719	35 938	383 904	189 396	194 508
40 - 44	366 466	182 701	183 765	57 283	33 163	24 120	309 183	149 538	159 645
45 - 49	310 594	153 796	156 798	40 803	22 094	18 709	269 791	131 702	138 089
50 - 54	265 180	134 933	130 247	30 364	16 749	13 615	234 816	118 184	116 632
55 - 59	225 278	113 470	111 808	25 692	13 147	12 545	199 586	100 323	99 263
60 - 64	145 211	74 556	70 655	14 954	7 579	7 375	130 257	66 977	63 280
65 - 69	90 785	44 744	46 041	9 023	4 024	4 999	81 762	40 720	41 042
70 - 74	54 548	25 722	28 826	4 874	2 027	2 847	49 674	23 695	25 979
75 - 79	36 220	16 056	20 164	3 504	1 175	2 329	32 716	14 881	17 835
80 +	38 384	17 687	20 697	3 187	1 196	1 991	35 197	16 491	18 706

1 VII 2017 (ESDF)

Total	11 495 438	5 678 569	5 816 869	...	...	...	...	...	...
0	365 297	184 470	180 827	...	...	...	...	...	...
1 - 4	1 400 229	703 374	696 855	...	...	...	...	...	...
5 - 9	1 720 903	861 082	859 822	...	...	...	...	...	...
10 - 14	1 439 441	716 240	723 201	...	...	...	...	...	...
15 - 19	1 159 625	572 344	587 281	...	...	...	...	...	...
20 - 24	1 057 909	516 750	541 158	...	...	...	...	...	...
25 - 29	985 828	474 667	511 161	...	...	...	...	...	...
30 - 34	831 629	402 522	429 107	...	...	...	...	...	...
35 - 39	624 386	310 238	314 149	...	...	...	...	...	...
40 - 44	444 109	221 310	222 799	...	...	...	...	...	...
45 - 49	359 975	176 371	183 604	...	...	...	...	...	...
50 - 54	314 777	155 695	159 082	...	...	...	...	...	...
55 - 59	272 063	135 229	136 834	...	...	...	...	...	...
60 - 64	214 857	106 219	108 637	...	...	...	...	...	...
65 - 69	133 190	64 843	68 347	...	...	...	...	...	...

7. Population by age, sex and urban/rural residence: latest available year, 2008 - 2017
Population selon l'âge, le sexe et la résidence, urbaine/rurale : dernière année disponible, 2008 - 2017 (continued - suite)

Continent, country or area, date, code[a] and age (in years) / Continent, pays ou zone, date, code[a] et âge (en années)	Total			Urban - Urbaine			Rural - Rurale		
	Both sexes Les deux sexes	Male Masculin	Female Féminin	Both sexes Les deux sexes	Male Masculin	Female Féminin	Both sexes Les deux sexes	Male Masculin	Female Féminin
AFRICA - AFRIQUE									
Burundi									
1 VII 2017 (ESDF)									
70 - 74	80 263	37 484	42 779	...	...	...	...	...	...
75 - 79	50 827	22 743	28 085	...	...	...	...	...	...
80 +	40 129	16 988	23 141	...	...	...	...	...	...
Cabo Verde									
16 VI 2010 (CDJC)									
Total	491 683	243 403	248 280	303 673	151 219	152 454	188 010	92 184	95 826
0 - 4	50 200	25 131	25 069	30 842	15 542	15 300	19 358	9 589	9 769
5 - 9	50 208	25 168	25 040	29 705	14 799	14 906	20 503	10 369	10 134
10 - 14	55 225	27 864	27 361	30 408	15 260	15 148	24 817	12 604	12 213
15 - 19	59 060	29 655	29 405	33 772	16 678	17 094	25 288	12 977	12 311
20 - 24	52 905	27 327	25 578	34 402	17 504	16 898	18 503	9 823	8 680
25 - 29	44 341	23 336	21 005	30 990	16 055	14 935	13 351	7 281	6 070
30 - 34	34 504	18 165	16 339	24 684	13 012	11 672	9 820	5 153	4 667
35 - 39	27 236	14 106	13 130	18 641	9 726	8 915	8 595	4 380	4 215
40 - 44	26 291	12 988	13 303	17 086	8 680	8 406	9 205	4 308	4 897
45 - 49	23 512	11 347	12 165	15 227	7 625	7 602	8 285	3 722	4 563
50 - 54	18 161	8 162	9 999	11 243	5 392	5 851	6 918	2 770	4 148
55 - 59	12 143	4 947	7 196	7 183	3 229	3 954	4 960	1 718	3 242
60 - 64	6 193	2 613	3 580	3 656	1 663	1 993	2 537	950	1 587
65 - 69	6 215	2 499	3 716	3 420	1 411	2 009	2 795	1 088	1 707
70 - 74	8 666	3 437	5 229	4 237	1 656	2 581	4 429	1 781	2 648
75 - 79	7 433	2 980	4 453	3 602	1 377	2 225	3 831	1 603	2 228
80 - 84	5 277	2 092	3 185	2 485	891	1 594	2 792	1 201	1 591
85 - 89	2 185	827	1 358	1 058	331	727	1 127	496	631
90 - 94	1 073	377	696	520	171	349	553	206	347
95 +	497	172	325	248	65	183	249	107	142
Unknown - Inconnu	358	210	148	264	152	112	94	58	36
1 VII 2017 (ESDJ)[2]									
Total	537 661	270 091	267 570	...	...	...	...	...	...
0	10 525	5 386	5 140	...	...	...	...	...	...
1 - 4	41 681	21 317	20 364	...	...	...	...	...	...
5 - 9	50 192	25 290	24 902	...	...	...	...	...	...
10 - 14	51 381	25 628	25 753	...	...	...	...	...	...
15 - 19	48 805	24 777	24 028	...	...	...	...	...	...
20 - 24	51 597	26 257	25 339	...	...	...	...	...	...
25 - 29	54 609	28 535	26 074	...	...	...	...	...	...
30 - 34	48 587	25 927	22 660	...	...	...	...	...	...
35 - 39	38 506	20 995	17 511	...	...	...	...	...	...
40 - 44	29 856	15 774	14 082	...	...	...	...	...	...
45 - 49	25 964	13 153	12 811	...	...	...	...	...	...
50 - 54	24 531	11 796	12 735	...	...	...	...	...	...
55 - 59	19 062	8 773	10 289	...	...	...	...	...	...
60 - 64	12 781	5 140	7 641	...	...	...	...	...	...
65 - 69	7 171	2 901	4 269	...	...	...	...	...	...
70 - 74	5 418	2 143	3 275	...	...	...	...	...	...
75 - 79	5 656	2 118	3 537	...	...	...	...	...	...
80 - 84	5 566	2 078	3 489	...	...	...	...	...	...
85 - 89	3 695	1 443	2 252	...	...	...	...	...	...
90 - 94	1 471	523	949	...	...	...	...	...	...
95 +	607	137	469	...	...	...	...	...	...
Cameroon - Cameroun[2]									
1 I 2010 (ESDJ)									
Total	19 406 100	9 599 224	9 806 876	...	...	...	...	...	...
0 - 4	3 287 234	1 662 298	1 624 936	...	...	...	...	...	...
5 - 9	2 783 459	1 412 467	1 370 992	...	...	...	...	...	...
10 - 14	2 394 671	1 227 470	1 167 201	...	...	...	...	...	...
15 - 19	2 170 035	1 068 509	1 101 526	...	...	...	...	...	...
20 - 24	1 837 289	855 334	981 955	...	...	...	...	...	...
25 - 29	1 525 816	712 550	813 266	...	...	...	...	...	...
30 - 34	1 209 607	588 210	621 397	...	...	...	...	...	...
35 - 39	942 713	460 394	482 319	...	...	...	...	...	...
40 - 44	793 846	388 539	405 307	...	...	...	...	...	...
45 - 49	640 247	323 507	316 740	...	...	...	...	...	...

Continent, country or area, date, code[a] and age (in years) / Continent, pays ou zone, date, code[a] et âge (en années)	Total			Urban - Urbaine			Rural - Rurale		
	Both sexes Les deux sexes	Male Masculin	Female Féminin	Both sexes Les deux sexes	Male Masculin	Female Féminin	Both sexes Les deux sexes	Male Masculin	Female Féminin
AFRICA - AFRIQUE									
Cameroon - Cameroun[2]									
1 I 2010 (ESDJ)									
50 - 54	521 910	261 626	260 284	...	...	...	...	...	...
55 - 59	337 988	178 876	159 112	...	...	...	...	...	...
60 - 64	315 879	155 208	160 671	...	...	...	...	...	...
65 - 69	227 290	110 645	116 645	...	...	...	...	...	...
70 - 74	189 571	88 969	100 602	...	...	...	...	...	...
75 - 79	98 078	47 173	50 905	...	...	...	...	...	...
80 - 84	71 585	31 609	39 976	...	...	...	...	...	...
85 - 89	26 564	12 109	14 455	...	...	...	...	...	...
90 - 94	15 715	6 942	8 773	...	...	...	...	...	...
95 +	16 603	6 789	9 814	...	...	...	...	...	...
Congo									
1 VII 2009 (ESDF)									
Total	3 838 238	1 891 558	1 946 680	...	...	...	...	...	...
0 - 4	586 578	294 305	292 273	...	...	...	...	...	...
5 - 9	475 864	238 682	237 182	...	...	...	...	...	...
10 - 14	417 074	208 162	208 912	...	...	...	...	...	...
15 - 19	382 673	186 405	196 268	...	...	...	...	...	...
20 - 24	358 745	167 519	191 226	...	...	...	...	...	...
25 - 29	339 133	160 897	178 236	...	...	...	...	...	...
30 - 34	304 009	152 642	151 367	...	...	...	...	...	...
35 - 39	254 997	131 794	123 203	...	...	...	...	...	...
40 - 44	198 594	103 248	95 346	...	...	...	...	...	...
45 - 49	148 798	76 921	71 877	...	...	...	...	...	...
50 - 54	111 812	54 925	56 887	...	...	...	...	...	...
55 - 59	80 842	38 051	42 791	...	...	...	...	...	...
60 - 64	59 601	27 592	32 009	...	...	...	...	...	...
65 - 69	46 706	20 879	25 827	...	...	...	...	...	...
70 - 74	34 961	14 954	20 007	...	...	...	...	...	...
75 - 79	21 868	8 820	13 048	...	...	...	...	...	...
80 +	15 983	5 762	10 221	...	...	...	...	...	...
Côte d'Ivoire[6]									
1 VII 2017 (ESDF)									
Total	24 571 044	12 648 124	11 922 920	12 678 659	6 526 432	6 152 227	11 892 385	6 121 692	5 770 693
0	830 679	422 830	407 849	371 171	190 700	180 471	459 508	232 130	227 378
1 - 4	3 054 526	1 566 438	1 488 088	1 364 848	706 478	658 370	1 689 678	859 959	829 697
5 - 9	3 502 451	1 804 903	1 697 548	1 583 344	809 635	773 709	1 919 107	995 268	923 839
10 - 14	2 942 549	1 535 496	1 407 053	1 556 643	785 508	771 135	1 385 906	749 988	635 918
15 - 19	2 380 938	1 250 881	1 130 057	1 427 256	740 842	686 414	953 682	510 039	443 643
20 - 24	2 052 959	1 020 756	1 032 203	1 177 474	590 233	587 241	875 484	430 523	444 961
25 - 29	2 083 203	1 005 785	1 077 418	1 154 531	555 762	598 769	928 671	450 022	478 649
30 - 34	1 938 494	959 503	978 991	1 061 166	528 354	532 812	877 327	431 148	446 179
35 - 39	1 584 277	835 508	748 769	872 829	468 853	403 976	711 448	366 655	344 793
40 - 44	1 174 597	650 422	524 175	624 850	353 876	270 974	549 748	296 547	253 201
45 - 49	868 173	475 047	393 126	441 488	243 974	197 514	426 684	231 072	195 612
50 - 54	689 484	362 925	326 559	348 864	185 197	163 667	340 620	177 728	162 892
55 - 59	524 814	274 600	250 214	267 036	142 470	124 566	257 778	132 130	125 648
60 - 64	354 683	189 578	165 105	173 791	96 277	77 514	180 893	93 301	87 592
65 - 69	250 087	130 570	119 517	114 005	61 409	52 596	136 082	69 161	66 921
70 - 74	156 528	76 914	79 614	66 327	32 729	33 598	90 201	44 185	46 016
75 - 79	93 253	44 218	49 035	38 231	18 011	20 220	55 022	26 207	28 815
80 +	89 350	41 751	47 599	34 807	16 123	18 684	54 543	25 628	28 915
Egypt - Égypte									
1 VII 2017 (ESDF)									
Total	95 202 532	49 095 021	46 107 511	40 432 110	20 818 309	19 613 801	54 770 422	28 276 712	26 493 710
0	2 604 364	1 340 651	1 263 713	934 031	473 768	460 263	1 670 333	866 883	803 450
1 - 4	10 352 766	5 280 771	5 071 995	3 872 575	1 963 511	1 909 064	6 480 191	3 317 260	3 162 931
5 - 9	10 559 696	5 486 224	5 073 472	4 045 161	2 106 489	1 938 672	6 514 535	3 379 735	3 134 800
10 - 14	9 069 349	4 726 389	4 342 960	3 587 893	1 867 598	1 720 295	5 481 456	2 858 791	2 622 665
15 - 19	9 044 869	4 696 773	4 348 096	3 734 537	1 933 404	1 801 133	5 310 332	2 763 369	2 546 963
20 - 24	8 267 301	4 253 791	4 013 510	3 607 768	1 848 902	1 758 866	4 659 533	2 404 889	2 254 644
25 - 29	8 202 489	4 051 915	4 150 574	3 536 449	1 747 768	1 788 681	4 666 040	2 304 147	2 361 893
30 - 34	7 375 339	3 780 810	3 594 529	3 259 822	1 655 921	1 603 901	4 115 517	2 124 889	1 990 628
35 - 39	6 513 735	3 351 872	3 161 863	2 900 909	1 494 296	1 406 613	3 612 826	1 857 576	1 755 250

Continent, country or area, date, code[a] and age (in years) / Continent, pays ou zone, date, code[a] et âge (en annèes)	Total			Urban - Urbaine			Rural - Rurale		
	Both sexes Les deux sexes	Male Masculin	Female Féminin	Both sexes Les deux sexes	Male Masculin	Female Féminin	Both sexes Les deux sexes	Male Masculin	Female Féminin
AFRICA - AFRIQUE									
Egypt - Égypte									
1 VII 2017 (ESDF)									
40 - 44	5 174 335	2 669 248	2 505 087	2 395 770	1 213 443	1 182 327	2 778 565	1 455 805	1 322 760
45 - 49	4 410 937	2 294 763	2 116 174	2 044 042	1 062 483	981 559	2 366 895	1 232 280	1 134 615
50 - 54	4 014 843	2 059 345	1 955 498	1 899 979	975 961	924 018	2 114 864	1 083 384	1 031 480
55 - 59	3 274 033	1 721 545	1 552 488	1 573 984	824 365	749 619	1 700 049	897 180	802 869
60 - 64	2 660 463	1 422 382	1 238 081	1 324 139	713 579	610 560	1 336 324	708 803	627 521
65 - 69	1 727 385	946 457	780 928	841 168	469 707	371 461	886 217	476 750	409 467
70 - 74	1 020 205	533 228	486 977	477 882	256 111	221 771	542 323	277 117	265 206
75 +	930 423	478 857	451 566	396 001	211 003	184 998	534 422	267 854	266 568
Eritrea - Érythrée[7]									
1 VII 2017 (ESDF)									
Total	3 211 946	1 581 036	1 630 910	1 138 401	542 187	596 213	2 073 545	1 038 848	1 034 697
0	104 506	52 126	52 381	29 368	13 963	15 405	75 139	38 163	36 976
1 - 4	384 581	191 192	193 389	112 894	53 597	59 296	271 687	137 595	134 092
5 - 9	414 782	205 698	209 083	130 007	61 674	68 333	284 774	144 024	140 750
10 - 14	341 230	169 008	172 222	112 238	53 329	58 909	228 992	115 679	113 313
15 - 19	273 982	138 671	135 311	92 031	44 578	47 452	181 952	94 093	87 859
20 - 24	322 780	166 414	156 366	103 659	53 838	49 821	219 121	112 576	106 545
25 - 29	308 539	155 109	153 430	106 355	52 209	54 146	202 184	102 899	99 284
30 - 34	240 229	119 989	120 240	98 769	46 603	52 166	141 460	73 386	68 074
35 - 39	160 566	76 336	84 230	74 844	34 341	40 503	85 722	41 995	43 727
40 - 44	139 393	60 518	78 875	65 615	28 947	36 669	73 777	31 571	42 206
45 - 49	119 891	54 415	65 476	53 197	24 726	28 471	66 694	29 689	37 005
50 - 54	96 519	43 409	53 109	38 981	17 828	21 153	57 537	25 581	31 956
55 - 59	81 259	38 500	42 759	31 506	15 162	16 344	49 753	23 338	26 415
60 - 64	64 778	32 936	31 841	25 350	12 906	12 444	39 428	20 030	19 398
65 - 69	56 346	28 129	28 216	23 193	10 668	12 525	33 152	17 461	15 691
70 - 74	45 680	21 054	24 627	18 214	7 619	10 595	27 467	13 435	14 032
75 - 79	31 422	14 257	17 165	11 882	5 181	6 701	19 540	9 076	10 464
80 - 84	16 648	8 380	8 267	6 444	3 104	3 340	10 204	5 277	4 928
85 +	8 816	4 894	3 922	3 854	1 913	1 940	4 962	2 980	1 982
Eswatini									
1 VII 2017 (ESDF)									
Total	1 145 970	544 811	601 159	271 573	129 068	142 505	874 397	415 743	458 654
0 - 4	152 127	77 478	74 649	28 212	14 355	13 857	123 915	63 123	60 792
5 - 9	139 135	71 216	67 919	23 317	11 872	11 445	115 818	59 344	56 474
10 - 14	125 977	63 854	62 123	20 173	9 992	10 181	105 804	53 862	51 942
15 - 19	127 374	63 188	64 186	21 159	9 507	11 652	106 215	53 681	52 534
20 - 24	121 764	59 293	62 471	27 316	11 793	15 523	94 448	47 500	46 948
25 - 29	106 346	50 075	56 271	34 291	15 621	18 670	72 055	34 454	37 601
30 - 34	88 190	38 866	49 324	34 784	16 705	18 079	53 406	22 161	31 245
35 - 39	71 287	29 674	41 613	26 498	12 947	13 551	44 789	16 727	28 062
40 - 44	53 935	21 745	32 190	18 862	9 173	9 689	35 073	12 572	22 501
45 - 49	42 820	17 287	25 533	13 927	6 669	7 258	28 893	10 618	18 275
50 - 54	32 823	13 684	19 139	9 126	4 442	4 684	23 697	9 242	14 455
55 - 59	25 604	10 988	14 616	6 214	2 985	3 229	19 390	8 003	11 387
60 - 64	19 571	8 647	10 924	3 686	1 628	2 058	15 885	7 019	8 866
65 - 69	14 735	6 803	7 932	1 953	754	1 199	12 782	6 049	6 733
70 - 74	10 670	5 148	5 522	994	322	672	9 676	4 826	4 850
75 - 79	6 839	3 459	3 380	589	192	397	6 250	3 267	2 983
80 +	6 773	3 406	3 367	472	111	361	6 301	3 295	3 006
Ethiopia - Éthiopie[8]									
1 VII 2017 (ESDF)									
Total	94 352 138	47 364 992	46 987 146	19 161 490	9 534 811	9 626 679	75 190 648	37 830 181	37 360 467
0 - 4	13 528 590	6 876 421	6 652 169	1 811 130	916 366	894 764	11 717 460	5 960 055	5 757 405
5 - 9	12 448 401	6 301 867	6 146 534	1 997 393	994 561	1 002 832	10 451 008	5 307 306	5 143 702
10 - 14	11 359 359	5 747 959	5 611 400	2 116 099	1 045 113	1 070 986	9 243 260	4 702 846	4 540 414
15 - 19	10 500 705	5 336 198	5 164 507	2 205 114	1 094 367	1 110 747	8 295 591	4 241 831	4 053 760
20 - 24	9 322 415	4 725 170	4 597 245	2 201 754	1 099 832	1 101 922	7 120 661	3 625 338	3 495 323
25 - 29	8 110 849	4 047 502	4 063 347	2 114 464	1 035 202	1 079 262	5 996 385	3 012 300	2 984 085
30 - 34	6 687 272	3 281 910	3 405 362	1 754 863	878 820	876 043	4 932 409	2 403 090	2 529 319
35 - 39	5 518 185	2 692 328	2 825 857	1 422 837	722 152	700 685	4 095 348	1 970 176	2 125 172
40 - 44	4 257 426	2 070 519	2 186 907	977 335	503 594	473 741	3 280 091	1 566 925	1 713 166
45 - 49	3 413 015	1 658 680	1 754 335	746 608	379 131	367 477	2 666 407	1 279 549	1 386 858

Continent, country or area, date, code[a] and age (in years) / Continent, pays ou zone, date, code[a] et âge (en années)	Total			Urban - Urbaine			Rural - Rurale		
	Both sexes Les deux sexes	Male Masculin	Female Féminin	Both sexes Les deux sexes	Male Masculin	Female Féminin	Both sexes Les deux sexes	Male Masculin	Female Féminin
AFRICA - AFRIQUE									
Ethiopia - Éthiopie[8]									
1 VII 2017 (ESDF)									
50 - 54	2 660 564	1 320 044	1 340 520	535 794	271 036	264 758	2 124 770	1 049 008	1 075 762
55 - 59	2 093 237	1 042 645	1 050 592	414 152	201 275	212 877	1 679 085	841 370	837 715
60 - 64	1 569 090	786 289	782 801	309 257	143 766	165 491	1 259 833	642 523	617 310
65 - 69	1 152 886	582 858	570 028	218 632	100 563	118 069	934 254	482 295	451 959
70 - 74	804 281	409 104	395 177	156 165	70 226	85 939	648 116	338 878	309 238
75 - 79	500 836	256 264	244 572	99 355	44 448	54 907	401 481	211 816	189 665
80 +	425 027	229 234	195 793	80 538	34 359	46 179	344 489	194 875	149 614
Ghana[9]									
1 VII 2015 (ESDF)									
Total	27 670 174	13 562 093	14 108 081	13 817 894	6 903 107	6 914 787	13 852 280	6 658 986	7 193 294
0	841 301	425 611	415 690	403 605	195 150	208 455	437 696	230 461	207 235
1 - 4	3 158 109	1 595 165	1 562 944	1 513 925	731 409	782 516	1 644 184	863 756	780 428
5 - 9	3 312 878	1 688 452	1 624 426	1 579 799	755 911	823 888	1 733 079	932 541	800 538
10 - 14	3 097 352	1 567 043	1 530 309	1 538 503	749 266	789 237	1 558 849	817 777	741 072
15 - 19	2 825 578	1 414 987	1 410 591	1 458 024	735 981	722 043	1 367 554	679 006	688 548
20 - 24	2 537 799	1 251 759	1 286 040	1 377 177	736 425	640 752	1 160 622	515 334	645 288
25 - 29	2 252 493	1 083 877	1 168 616	1 211 633	636 338	575 295	1 040 860	447 539	593 321
30 - 34	1 967 166	935 947	1 031 219	1 014 879	537 402	477 477	952 287	398 545	553 742
35 - 39	1 665 237	785 200	880 037	840 000	437 656	402 344	825 237	347 544	477 693
40 - 44	1 404 309	661 789	742 520	703 098	362 522	340 576	701 211	299 267	401 944
45 - 49	1 145 932	546 030	599 902	560 013	275 131	284 882	585 919	270 899	315 020
50 - 54	933 268	445 531	487 737	477 984	238 760	239 224	455 284	206 771	248 513
55 - 59	728 002	348 118	379 884	337 828	159 376	178 452	390 174	188 742	201 432
60 - 64	570 616	270 642	299 974	271 174	129 651	141 523	299 442	140 991	158 451
65 - 69	419 501	196 219	223 282	178 422	73 727	104 695	241 079	122 492	118 587
70 - 74	313 256	142 378	170 878	149 542	68 333	81 209	163 714	74 045	89 669
75 - 79	223 087	96 514	126 573	90 638	36 406	54 232	132 449	60 108	72 341
80 +	274 290	106 831	167 459	111 650	43 663	67 987	162 640	63 168	99 472
Guinea - Guinée[10]									
1 VII 2017 (ESDJ)									
Total	11 555 061	5 590 798	5 964 265	4 111 607	1 989 358	2 122 248	7 443 455	3 601 439	3 842 016
0	418 779	211 196	207 583	82 819	38 725	44 094	335 960	172 471	163 489
1 - 4	1 577 927	799 784	778 143	463 733	226 967	236 766	1 114 194	572 817	541 377
5 - 9	1 758 536	891 818	866 717	560 477	268 350	292 126	1 198 059	623 468	574 591
10 - 14	1 453 705	728 066	725 640	549 929	258 271	291 657	903 777	469 794	433 982
15 - 19	1 185 586	580 541	605 045	495 761	235 284	260 476	689 826	345 257	344 569
20 - 24	1 003 008	466 078	536 930	461 184	227 566	233 618	541 824	238 512	303 312
25 - 29	851 753	371 649	480 104	387 440	185 820	201 621	464 312	185 829	278 484
30 - 34	701 388	304 120	397 267	272 365	129 357	143 008	429 022	174 763	254 259
35 - 39	567 539	249 375	318 164	204 572	98 540	106 032	362 967	150 835	212 132
40 - 44	467 711	210 719	256 992	162 914	80 049	82 865	304 797	130 670	174 127
45 - 49	381 951	179 092	202 860	127 970	64 641	63 328	253 982	114 450	139 531
50 - 54	310 521	151 513	159 008	100 989	51 453	49 537	209 532	100 060	109 472
55 - 59	248 560	126 908	121 653	77 469	40 881	36 587	171 091	86 026	85 065
60 - 64	199 936	103 462	96 474	58 164	31 428	26 735	141 772	72 034	69 738
65 - 69	155 855	80 757	75 099	42 636	22 873	19 763	113 220	57 884	55 336
70 - 74	114 316	58 795	55 521	28 799	14 886	13 913	85 518	43 909	41 608
75 - 79	74 742	37 283	37 459	16 484	7 377	9 107	58 258	29 906	28 352
80 +	83 248	39 642	43 606	17 903	6 890	11 014	65 344	32 752	32 592
Guinea-Bissau - Guinée-Bissau[2]									
1 VII 2016 (ESDF)									
Total	1 547 777	759 666	788 111	659 138	323 512	335 626	888 639	436 154	452 485
0 - 4	269 444	137 948	131 496	94 949	47 138	47 811	174 495	90 810	83 685
5 - 9	215 817	109 491	106 326	79 346	37 773	41 573	136 471	71 718	64 753
10 - 14	187 811	94 320	93 491	80 604	37 519	43 085	107 207	56 801	50 406
15 - 19	162 179	81 815	80 364	78 714	38 866	39 848	83 465	42 949	40 516
20 - 24	148 027	73 767	74 260	76 552	39 614	36 938	71 475	34 153	37 322
25 - 29	131 987	63 514	68 473	64 453	32 944	31 509	67 534	30 570	36 964
30 - 34	115 408	53 601	61 807	55 985	27 603	28 382	59 423	25 998	33 425
35 - 39	84 460	39 105	45 355	37 434	18 349	19 085	47 026	20 756	26 270
40 - 44	63 176	29 175	34 001	28 544	14 067	14 477	34 632	15 108	19 524
45 - 49	48 276	22 161	26 115	20 566	10 031	10 535	27 710	12 130	15 580

Continent, country or area, date, code[a] and age (in years) Continent, pays ou zone, date, code[a] et âge (en années)	Total			Urban - Urbaine			Rural - Rurale		
	Both sexes Les deux sexes	Male Masculin	Female Féminin	Both sexes Les deux sexes	Male Masculin	Female Féminin	Both sexes Les deux sexes	Male Masculin	Female Féminin
AFRICA - AFRIQUE									
Guinea-Bissau - Guinée-Bissau[2]									
1 VII 2016 (ESDF)									
50 - 54	38 825	17 920	20 905	15 837	7 929	7 908	22 988	9 991	12 997
55 - 59	29 961	13 484	16 477	11 184	5 190	5 994	18 777	8 294	10 483
60 - 64	19 202	9 020	10 182	6 158	2 965	3 193	13 044	6 055	6 989
65 - 69	14 036	6 641	7 395	4 173	1 901	2 272	9 863	4 740	5 123
70 - 74	9 043	3 909	5 134	2 419	971	1 448	6 624	2 938	3 686
75 - 79	5 038	1 967	3 071	1 196	383	813	3 842	1 584	2 258
80 +	5 087	1 828	3 259	1 024	269	755	4 063	1 559	2 504
Kenya									
24 VIII 2009 (CDFC)									
Total	38 610 097	19 192 458	19 417 639	12 487 375	6 278 811	6 208 564	26 122 722	12 913 647	13 209 075
0	1 221 937	616 843	605 094	388 883	195 861	193 022	833 054	420 982	412 072
1 - 4	4 717 369	2 383 596	2 333 773	1 350 368	679 969	670 399	3 367 001	1 703 627	1 663 374
5 - 9	5 597 716	2 832 669	2 765 047	1 484 285	742 473	741 812	4 113 431	2 090 196	2 023 235
10 - 14	5 034 855	2 565 313	2 469 542	1 312 671	650 438	662 233	3 722 184	1 914 875	1 807 309
15 - 19	4 169 543	2 123 653	2 045 890	1 244 054	587 384	656 670	2 925 489	1 536 269	1 389 220
20 - 24	3 775 103	1 754 105	2 020 998	1 572 026	708 458	863 568	2 203 077	1 045 647	1 157 430
25 - 29	3 201 226	1 529 116	1 672 110	1 442 798	715 957	726 841	1 758 428	813 159	945 269
30 - 34	2 519 506	1 257 035	1 262 471	1 056 483	568 615	487 868	1 463 023	688 420	774 603
35 - 39	2 008 632	1 004 361	1 004 271	785 390	431 054	354 336	1 223 242	573 307	649 935
40 - 44	1 476 169	743 594	732 575	533 174	297 202	235 972	942 995	446 392	496 603
45 - 49	1 272 745	635 276	637 469	422 941	235 467	187 474	849 804	399 809	449 995
50 - 54	956 206	478 346	477 860	286 074	159 814	126 260	670 132	318 532	351 600
55 - 59	711 953	359 466	352 497	187 793	103 563	84 230	524 160	255 903	268 257
60 - 64	593 778	295 197	298 581	139 271	73 800	65 471	454 507	221 397	233 110
65 - 69	390 763	183 151	207 612	83 728	41 299	42 429	307 035	141 852	165 183
70 - 74	339 301	160 301	179 000	68 868	32 691	36 177	270 433	127 610	142 823
75 - 79	218 508	99 833	118 675	42 247	19 276	22 971	176 261	80 557	95 704
80 +	383 701	159 125	224 576	77 003	30 335	46 668	306 698	128 790	177 908
Unknown - Inconnu	21 086	11 478	9 608	9 318	5 155	4 163	11 768	6 323	5 445
1 VII 2017 (ESDF)[11]									
Total	46 595 199	23 117 881	23 477 319	...	...	...	...	...	...
0	1 479 846	749 229	730 617	...	...	...	...	...	...
1 - 4	5 649 697	2 848 841	2 800 856	...	...	...	...	...	...
5 - 9	6 409 780	3 233 878	3 175 902	...	...	...	...	...	...
10 - 14	5 668 486	2 867 168	2 801 317	...	...	...	...	...	...
15 - 19	4 948 884	2 510 323	2 438 561	...	...	...	...	...	...
20 - 24	4 335 111	2 139 798	2 195 314	...	...	...	...	...	...
25 - 29	3 909 855	1 871 462	2 038 393	...	...	...	...	...	...
30 - 34	3 366 938	1 587 480	1 779 458	...	...	...	...	...	...
35 - 39	2 696 724	1 306 876	1 389 848	...	...	...	...	...	...
40 - 44	2 057 867	1 032 134	1 025 733	...	...	...	...	...	...
45 - 49	1 631 976	818 166	813 809	...	...	...	...	...	...
50 - 54	1 240 344	618 971	621 373	...	...	...	...	...	...
55 - 59	949 533	472 914	476 619	...	...	...	...	...	...
60 - 64	728 997	358 931	370 066	...	...	...	...	...	...
65 - 69	521 927	251 108	270 819	...	...	...	...	...	...
70 - 74	391 353	184 500	206 853	...	...	...	...	...	...
75 - 79	254 042	116 739	137 303	...	...	...	...	...	...
80 +	353 840	149 363	204 477	...	...	...	...	...	...
Lesotho									
10 IV 2016 (CDJC)									
Total	2 007 201	982 133	1 025 068	...	...	...	...	...	...
0 - 4	200 155	100 793	99 362	...	...	...	...	...	...
5 - 9	221 476	109 953	111 523	...	...	...	...	...	...
10 - 14	215 813	107 879	107 934	...	...	...	...	...	...
15 - 19	209 866	106 214	103 652	...	...	...	...	...	...
20 - 24	199 267	98 827	100 440	...	...	...	...	...	...
25 - 29	188 943	95 802	93 141	...	...	...	...	...	...
30 - 34	168 145	86 956	81 189	...	...	...	...	...	...
35 - 39	130 381	68 246	62 135	...	...	...	...	...	...
40 - 44	96 295	48 665	47 630	...	...	...	...	...	...
45 - 49	74 887	36 425	38 462	...	...	...	...	...	...

Continent, country or area, date, code[a] and age (in years) / Continent, pays ou zone, date, code[a] et âge (en annèes)	Total			Urban - Urbaine			Rural - Rurale		
	Both sexes Les deux sexes	Male Masculin	Female Féminin	Both sexes Les deux sexes	Male Masculin	Female Féminin	Both sexes Les deux sexes	Male Masculin	Female Féminin
AFRICA - AFRIQUE									
Lesotho									
10 IV 2016 (CDJC)									
50 - 54	70 359	31 785	38 574	...	...	...	...	...	...
55 - 59	59 817	25 759	34 058	...	...	...	...	...	...
60 - 64	49 221	20 770	28 451	...	...	...	...	...	...
65 - 69	37 358	15 311	22 047	...	...	...	...	...	...
70 - 74	30 808	12 017	18 791	...	...	...	...	...	...
75 - 79	24 174	8 467	15 707	...	...	...	...	...	...
80 - 84	18 621	5 424	13 197	...	...	...	...	...	...
85 - 89	7 074	1 873	5 201	...	...	...	...	...	...
90 - 94	2 789	662	2 127	...	...	...	...	...	...
95 +	1 752	305	1 447	...	...	...	...	...	...
Liberia - Libéria									
21 III 2008 (CDFC)									
Total	3 476 608	1 739 945	1 736 663	...	...	...	...	...	...
0 - 4	534 475	270 564	263 911	...	...	...	...	...	...
5 - 9	501 931	251 411	250 520	...	...	...	...	...	...
10 - 14	421 666	214 859	206 807	...	...	...	...	...	...
15 - 19	375 695	189 407	186 288	...	...	...	...	...	...
20 - 24	342 930	161 951	180 979	...	...	...	...	...	...
25 - 29	291 858	141 006	150 852	...	...	...	...	...	...
30 - 34	219 632	107 326	112 306	...	...	...	...	...	...
35 - 39	203 536	99 136	104 400	...	...	...	...	...	...
40 - 44	155 737	81 670	74 067	...	...	...	...	...	...
45 - 49	118 807	63 827	54 980	...	...	...	...	...	...
50 - 54	82 940	44 870	38 070	...	...	...	...	...	...
55 - 59	56 460	30 975	25 485	...	...	...	...	...	...
60 - 64	52 830	25 473	27 357	...	...	...	...	...	...
65 - 69	39 807	19 250	20 557	...	...	...	...	...	...
70 - 74	25 746	12 343	13 403	...	...	...	...	...	...
75 - 79	22 913	11 580	11 333	...	...	...	...	...	...
80 - 84	12 007	5 408	6 599	...	...	...	...	...	...
85 +	17 638	8 889	8 749	...	...	...	...	...	...
Libya - Libye[12]									
1 VII 2015 (ESDF)									
Total	6 162 247	3 129 026	3 033 221	...	...	...	...	...	...
0 - 4	615 556	316 497	299 059	...	...	...	...	...	...
5 - 9	577 905	297 303	280 602	...	...	...	...	...	...
10 - 14	555 149	284 318	270 831	...	...	...	...	...	...
15 - 19	525 115	268 106	257 009	...	...	...	...	...	...
20 - 24	546 408	278 875	267 533	...	...	...	...	...	...
25 - 29	571 230	289 113	282 117	...	...	...	...	...	...
30 - 34	568 834	287 480	281 354	...	...	...	...	...	...
35 - 39	551 606	279 699	271 907	...	...	...	...	...	...
40 - 44	466 373	235 088	231 285	...	...	...	...	...	...
45 - 49	360 825	180 029	180 796	...	...	...	...	...	...
50 - 54	253 647	126 799	126 848	...	...	...	...	...	...
55 - 59	173 760	87 135	86 625	...	...	...	...	...	...
60 - 64	116 033	56 199	59 834	...	...	...	...	...	...
65 - 69	102 645	51 782	50 863	...	...	...	...	...	...
70 - 74	72 486	38 750	33 736	...	...	...	...	...	...
75 - 79	52 558	26 942	25 616	...	...	...	...	...	...
80 - 84	30 271	15 038	15 233	...	...	...	...	...	...
85 +	21 846	9 873	11 973	...	...	...	...	...	...
Malawi									
8 VI 2008 (CDFC)									
Total	13 077 160	6 358 933	6 718 227	2 003 309	1 014 477	988 832	11 073 851	5 344 456	5 729 395
0	503 385	247 809	255 576	67 264	33 375	33 889	436 121	214 434	221 687
1 - 4	1 866 626	922 138	944 488	248 703	122 976	125 727	1 617 923	799 162	818 761
5 - 9	1 968 299	972 307	995 992	261 838	127 930	133 908	1 706 461	844 377	862 084
10 - 14	1 670 391	826 076	844 315	232 203	110 545	121 658	1 438 188	715 531	722 657
15 - 19	1 276 692	625 664	651 028	218 307	105 746	112 561	1 058 385	519 918	538 467
20 - 24	1 240 329	554 799	685 530	248 790	117 648	131 142	991 539	437 151	554 388
25 - 29	1 102 976	530 103	572 873	236 512	122 761	113 751	866 464	407 342	459 122
30 - 34	827 547	417 599	409 948	162 061	91 637	70 424	665 486	325 962	339 524

Continent, country or area, date, code[a] and age (in years) / Continent, pays ou zone, date, code[a] et âge (en années)	Total			Urban - Urbaine			Rural - Rurale		
	Both sexes Les deux sexes	Male Masculin	Female Féminin	Both sexes Les deux sexes	Male Masculin	Female Féminin	Both sexes Les deux sexes	Male Masculin	Female Féminin
AFRICA - AFRIQUE									
Malawi									
8 VI 2008 (CDFC)									
35 - 39	623 330	323 643	299 687	105 572	61 564	44 008	517 758	262 079	255 679
40 - 44	441 231	218 546	222 685	67 267	37 061	30 206	373 964	181 485	192 479
45 - 49	343 190	167 285	175 905	47 706	25 811	21 895	295 484	141 474	154 010
50 - 54	269 634	126 778	142 856	33 849	18 400	15 449	235 785	108 378	127 407
55 - 59	258 214	122 616	135 598	26 253	14 525	11 728	231 961	108 091	123 870
60 - 64	184 679	87 008	97 671	16 622	9 256	7 366	168 057	77 752	90 305
65 - 69	153 829	72 038	81 791	11 298	6 217	5 081	142 531	65 821	76 710
70 - 74	106 020	46 481	59 539	6 992	3 573	3 419	99 028	42 908	56 120
75 - 79	106 769	46 003	60 766	5 629	2 769	2 860	101 140	43 234	57 906
80 - 84	55 970	21 945	34 025	2 926	1 262	1 664	53 044	20 683	32 361
85 - 89	40 784	16 680	24 104	1 895	818	1 077	38 889	15 862	23 027
90 - 94	18 739	6 967	11 772	780	323	457	17 959	6 644	11 315
95 +	18 526	6 448	12 078	842	280	562	17 684	6 168	11 516
1 VII 2016 (ESDF)[2]									
Total	16 832 910	8 272 152	8 560 758	...	...	...	...	...	...
0	671 720	340 496	331 224	...	...	...	...	...	...
1 - 4	2 422 973	1 230 512	1 192 461	...	...	...	...	...	...
5 - 9	2 552 762	1 281 823	1 270 939	...	...	...	...	...	...
10 - 14	2 143 289	1 057 905	1 085 384	...	...	...	...	...	...
15 - 19	1 811 043	888 033	923 010	...	...	...	...	...	...
20 - 24	1 495 820	729 550	766 270	...	...	...	...	...	...
25 - 29	1 253 796	607 734	646 062	...	...	...	...	...	...
30 - 34	1 039 216	499 637	539 579	...	...	...	...	...	...
35 - 39	841 126	405 449	435 677	...	...	...	...	...	...
40 - 44	669 608	323 674	345 934	...	...	...	...	...	...
45 - 49	515 517	248 311	267 206	...	...	...	...	...	...
50 - 54	380 651	183 468	197 183	...	...	...	...	...	...
55 - 59	296 075	140 581	155 494	...	...	...	...	...	...
60 - 64	226 409	104 599	121 810	...	...	...	...	...	...
65 - 69	173 220	78 337	94 883	...	...	...	...	...	...
70 - 74	129 016	57 500	71 516	...	...	...	...	...	...
75 - 79	91 842	39 462	52 380	...	...	...	...	...	...
80 +	118 827	55 081	63 746	...	...	...	...	...	...
Mali									
1 IV 2009 (CDFC)									
Total	14 528 662	7 204 990	7 323 672	3 274 727	1 643 671	1 631 056	11 253 935	5 561 319	5 692 616
0 - 4	2 623 385	1 328 871	1 294 514	501 628	253 735	247 893	2 121 757	1 075 136	1 046 621
5 - 9	2 357 823	1 202 875	1 154 948	438 784	220 467	218 317	1 919 039	982 408	936 631
10 - 14	1 784 004	918 866	865 138	382 494	183 203	199 291	1 401 510	735 663	665 847
15 - 19	1 516 146	732 526	783 620	427 554	194 158	233 396	1 088 592	538 368	550 224
20 - 24	1 141 903	529 535	612 368	341 272	171 703	169 569	800 631	357 832	442 799
25 - 29	995 702	449 099	546 603	267 899	132 127	135 772	727 803	316 972	410 831
30 - 34	812 798	385 003	427 795	206 544	109 060	97 484	606 254	275 943	330 311
35 - 39	651 949	325 055	326 894	164 783	89 830	74 953	487 166	235 225	251 941
40 - 44	546 603	271 239	275 364	128 845	70 127	58 718	417 758	201 112	216 646
45 - 49	445 887	228 626	217 261	103 042	56 502	46 540	342 845	172 124	170 721
50 - 54	381 806	189 424	192 382	82 013	44 826	37 187	299 793	144 598	155 195
55 - 59	282 677	148 594	134 083	57 960	31 957	26 003	224 717	116 637	108 080
60 - 64	251 018	127 557	123 461	46 442	23 790	22 652	204 576	103 767	100 809
65 - 69	165 374	88 292	77 082	30 159	15 641	14 518	135 215	72 651	62 564
70 - 74	133 382	67 319	66 063	23 729	11 518	12 211	109 653	55 801	53 852
75 - 79	77 101	40 904	36 197	12 871	6 306	6 565	64 230	34 598	29 632
80 +	85 594	41 992	43 602	14 246	6 009	8 237	71 348	35 983	35 365
Unknown - Inconnu	275 510	129 213	146 297	44 462	22 712	21 750	231 048	106 501	124 547
1 VII 2016 (ESDF)[13]									
Total	18 341 000	9 244 000	9 097 000	...	...	...	...	...	...
0 - 4	3 475 000	1 751 000	1 724 000	...	...	...	...	...	...
5 - 9	2 821 000	1 422 000	1 399 000	...	...	...	...	...	...
10 - 14	2 353 000	1 186 000	1 167 000	...	...	...	...	...	...
15 - 19	1 957 000	986 000	971 000	...	...	...	...	...	...
20 - 24	1 661 000	837 000	824 000	...	...	...	...	...	...
25 - 29	1 411 000	711 000	700 000	...	...	...	...	...	...
30 - 34	1 159 000	584 000	575 000	...	...	...	...	...	...

7. Population by age, sex and urban/rural residence: latest available year, 2008 - 2017
Population selon l'âge, le sexe et la résidence, urbaine/rurale : dernière année disponible, 2008 - 2017 (continued - suite)

Continent, country or area, date, code[a] and age (in years) Continent, pays ou zone, date, code[a] et âge (en années)	Total			Urban - Urbaine			Rural - Rurale		
	Both sexes Les deux sexes	Male Masculin	Female Féminin	Both sexes Les deux sexes	Male Masculin	Female Féminin	Both sexes Les deux sexes	Male Masculin	Female Féminin
AFRICA - AFRIQUE									
Mali									
1 VII 2016 (ESDF)[13]									
35 - 39	917 000	462 000	455 000	...	...	...	...	...	...
40 - 44	693 000	349 000	344 000	...	...	...	...	...	...
45 - 49	516 000	260 000	256 000	...	...	...	...	...	...
50 - 54	403 000	203 000	200 000	...	...	...	...	...	...
55 - 59	329 000	166 000	163 000	...	...	...	...	...	...
60 - 64	244 000	123 000	121 000	...	...	...	...	...	...
65 - 69	196 000	99 000	97 000	...	...	...	...	...	...
70 - 74	115 000	58 000	57 000	...	...	...	...	...	...
75 - 79	61 000	31 000	30 000	...	...	...	...	...	...
80 +	30 000	15 000	15 000	...	...	...	...	...	...
Mauritania - Mauritanie[2]									
1 VII 2016 (ESDF)									
Total	3 782 701	...	...	...	...	...	...	...	...
0 - 4	579 832	...	...	...	...	...	...	...	...
5 - 9	567 643	...	...	...	...	...	...	...	...
10 - 14	478 293	...	...	...	...	...	...	...	...
15 - 19	396 650	...	...	...	...	...	...	...	...
20 - 24	333 473	...	...	...	...	...	...	...	...
25 - 29	280 531	...	...	...	...	...	...	...	...
30 - 34	236 864	...	...	...	...	...	...	...	...
35 - 39	196 168	...	...	...	...	...	...	...	...
40 - 44	164 707	...	...	...	...	...	...	...	...
45 - 49	137 439	...	...	...	...	...	...	...	...
50 - 54	111 936	...	...	...	...	...	...	...	...
55 - 59	90 008	...	...	...	...	...	...	...	...
60 - 64	68 836	...	...	...	...	...	...	...	...
65 - 69	50 266	...	...	...	...	...	...	...	...
70 - 74	36 188	...	...	...	...	...	...	...	...
75 - 79	24 540	...	...	...	...	...	...	...	...
80 +	29 328	...	...	...	...	...	...	...	...
Mauritius - Maurice[14]									
4 VII 2011 (CDJC)									
Total	1 236 817	610 848	625 969	499 349	244 688	254 661	737 468	366 160	371 308
0 - 4	73 078	36 702	36 376	26 297	13 220	13 077	46 781	23 482	23 299
5 - 9	89 015	44 947	44 068	32 036	16 177	15 859	56 979	28 770	28 209
10 - 14	93 639	47 302	46 337	35 028	17 523	17 505	58 611	29 779	28 832
15 - 19	101 008	50 715	50 293	39 403	19 725	19 678	61 605	30 990	30 615
20 - 24	92 671	46 871	45 800	37 224	18 836	18 388	55 447	28 035	27 412
25 - 29	90 937	45 589	45 348	35 908	17 899	18 009	55 029	27 690	27 339
30 - 34	103 429	52 182	51 247	39 099	19 805	19 294	64 330	32 377	31 953
35 - 39	87 797	44 241	43 556	32 781	16 142	16 639	55 016	28 099	26 917
40 - 44	89 386	45 150	44 236	34 449	17 010	17 439	54 937	28 140	26 797
45 - 49	99 341	49 800	49 541	41 705	20 637	21 068	57 636	29 163	28 473
50 - 54	86 337	42 996	43 341	37 429	18 627	18 802	48 908	24 369	24 539
55 - 59	73 054	35 713	37 341	32 421	15 983	16 438	40 633	19 730	20 903
60 - 64	57 342	27 143	30 199	25 449	12 058	13 391	31 893	15 085	16 808
65 - 69	35 439	15 846	19 593	16 700	7 527	9 173	18 739	8 319	10 420
70 - 74	25 375	10 986	14 389	12 872	5 661	7 211	12 503	5 325	7 178
75 - 79	18 044	7 349	10 695	9 320	3 851	5 469	8 724	3 498	5 226
80 - 84	11 369	4 176	7 193	6 028	2 253	3 775	5 341	1 923	3 418
85 - 89	6 368	2 135	4 233	3 427	1 179	2 248	2 941	956	1 985
90 - 94	1 982	512	1 470	1 046	275	771	936	237	699
95 - 99	491	107	384	297	60	237	194	47	147
100 +	96	13	83	55	7	48	41	6	35
Unknown - Inconnu	619	373	246	375	233	142	244	140	104
1 VII 2017 (ESDJ)[15]									
Total	1 264 613	625 727	638 886	...	...	...	...	...	...
0	12 907	6 614	6 293	...	...	...	...	...	...
1 - 4	52 988	27 057	25 931	...	...	...	...	...	...
5 - 9	76 042	38 317	37 725	...	...	...	...	...	...
10 - 14	91 854	46 766	45 088	...	...	...	...	...	...
15 - 19	97 662	49 751	47 911	...	...	...	...	...	...
20 - 24	98 502	49 411	49 091	...	...	...	...	...	...

Continent, country or area, date, code[a] and age (in years) / Continent, pays ou zone, date, code[a] et âge (en années)	Total			Urban - Urbaine			Rural - Rurale		
	Both sexes Les deux sexes	Male Masculin	Female Féminin	Both sexes Les deux sexes	Male Masculin	Female Féminin	Both sexes Les deux sexes	Male Masculin	Female Féminin
AFRICA - AFRIQUE									
Mauritius - Maurice[14]									
1 VII 2017 (ESDJ)[15]									
25 - 29	93 947	47 722	46 225	...	...	...	...	...	...
30 - 34	84 833	42 775	42 058	...	...	...	...	...	...
35 - 39	100 887	51 115	49 772	...	...	...	...	...	...
40 - 44	87 289	44 269	43 020	...	...	...	...	...	...
45 - 49	84 579	42 641	41 938	...	...	...	...	...	...
50 - 54	94 652	47 214	47 438	...	...	...	...	...	...
55 - 59	84 568	41 320	43 248	...	...	...	...	...	...
60 - 64	71 214	34 242	36 972	...	...	...	...	...	...
65 - 69	55 416	25 586	29 830	...	...	...	...	...	...
70 - 74	32 787	14 175	18 612	...	...	...	...	...	...
75 - 79	20 686	8 501	12 185	...	...	...	...	...	...
80 - 84	13 643	5 134	8 509	...	...	...	...	...	...
85 +	10 157	3 117	7 040	...	...	...	...	...	...
Mayotte									
1 I 2017* (ESDJ)									
Total	249 154	120 866	128 288	...	...	...	...	...	...
0 - 4	39 315	19 795	19 520	...	...	...	...	...	...
5 - 9	37 568	18 811	18 757	...	...	...	...	...	...
10 - 14	33 071	16 348	16 723	...	...	...	...	...	...
15 - 19	25 744	12 578	13 166	...	...	...	...	...	...
20 - 24	15 215	6 805	8 410	...	...	...	...	...	...
25 - 29	17 212	6 880	10 332	...	...	...	...	...	...
30 - 34	18 177	7 740	10 437	...	...	...	...	...	...
35 - 39	16 911	7 760	9 151	...	...	...	...	...	...
40 - 44	13 630	7 201	6 429	...	...	...	...	...	...
45 - 49	9 023	4 705	4 318	...	...	...	...	...	...
50 - 54	7 296	3 838	3 458	...	...	...	...	...	...
55 - 59	5 598	3 053	2 545	...	...	...	...	...	...
60 - 64	3 885	2 156	1 729	...	...	...	...	...	...
65 - 69	2 384	1 215	1 169	...	...	...	...	...	...
70 - 74	1 782	887	895	...	...	...	...	...	...
75 - 79	1 074	547	527	...	...	...	...	...	...
80 - 84	710	305	405	...	...	...	...	...	...
85 - 89	292	127	165	...	...	...	...	...	...
90 - 94	188	87	101	...	...	...	...	...	...
95 +	79	28	51	...	...	...	...	...	...
Morocco - Maroc[16]									
1 VII 2016 (ESDF)									
Total	34 486 536	17 180 879	17 305 657	21 154 782	10 445 229	10 709 553	13 331 754	6 735 650	6 596 104
0 - 4	3 290 297	1 682 558	1 607 739	1 872 220	957 156	915 064	1 418 077	725 402	692 675
5 - 9	3 135 807	1 600 430	1 535 377	1 770 389	903 588	866 801	1 365 418	696 842	668 576
10 - 14	3 032 113	1 549 765	1 482 348	1 700 125	867 499	832 626	1 331 988	682 266	649 722
15 - 19	3 006 335	1 520 962	1 485 373	1 725 696	867 861	857 835	1 280 639	653 101	627 538
20 - 24	3 039 330	1 511 786	1 527 544	1 861 811	910 251	951 560	1 177 519	601 535	575 984
25 - 29	2 904 798	1 431 657	1 473 141	1 838 585	889 373	949 212	1 066 213	542 284	523 929
30 - 34	2 693 230	1 321 224	1 372 006	1 722 385	833 754	888 631	970 845	487 470	483 375
35 - 39	2 458 449	1 195 261	1 263 188	1 582 198	755 607	826 591	876 251	439 654	436 597
40 - 44	2 237 586	1 089 022	1 148 564	1 462 406	700 306	762 100	775 180	388 716	386 464
45 - 49	1 930 384	940 143	990 241	1 289 997	620 288	669 709	640 387	319 855	320 532
50 - 54	1 813 238	884 733	928 505	1 212 980	590 094	622 886	600 258	294 639	305 619
55 - 59	1 534 387	774 866	759 521	1 023 245	518 325	504 920	511 142	256 541	254 601
60 - 64	1 219 656	626 965	592 691	789 956	411 050	378 906	429 700	215 915	213 785
65 - 69	790 533	397 367	393 166	491 866	249 139	242 727	298 667	148 228	150 439
70 - 74	569 081	266 366	302 715	334 043	154 527	179 516	235 038	111 839	123 199
75 - 79	363 321	175 054	188 267	215 963	101 115	114 848	147 358	73 939	73 419
80 +	467 991	212 720	255 271	260 917	115 296	145 621	207 074	97 424	109 650
Mozambique[17]									
1 VII 2017 (ESDF)									
Total	27 128 530	13 106 447	14 022 083	8 766 777	4 281 319	4 485 458	18 361 753	8 825 128	9 536 625
0 - 4	4 557 840	2 277 526	2 280 314	1 163 788	580 924	582 864	3 394 052	1 696 602	1 697 450
5 - 9	3 997 583	1 992 967	2 004 616	1 108 187	552 191	555 996	2 889 396	1 440 776	1 448 620
10 - 14	3 519 245	1 749 479	1 769 766	1 092 175	539 751	552 424	2 427 070	1 209 728	1 217 342
15 - 19	2 946 806	1 473 812	1 472 994	1 044 149	515 419	528 730	1 902 657	958 393	944 264

7. Population by age, sex and urban/rural residence: latest available year, 2008 - 2017
Population selon l'âge, le sexe et la résidence, urbaine/rurale : dernière année disponible, 2008 - 2017 (continued - suite)

Continent, country or area, date, code[a] and age (in years) / Continent, pays ou zone, date, code[a] et âge (en années)	Total			Urban - Urbaine			Rural - Rurale		
	Both sexes Les deux sexes	Male Masculin	Female Féminin	Both sexes Les deux sexes	Male Masculin	Female Féminin	Both sexes Les deux sexes	Male Masculin	Female Féminin
AFRICA - AFRIQUE									
Mozambique[17]									
1 VII 2017 (ESDF)									
20 - 24	2 470 502	1 179 270	1 291 232	965 641	476 936	488 705	1 504 861	702 334	802 527
25 - 29	2 035 518	914 196	1 121 322	807 851	387 340	420 511	1 227 667	526 856	700 811
30 - 34	1 692 760	752 742	940 018	640 494	297 453	343 041	1 052 266	455 289	596 977
35 - 39	1 362 667	634 117	728 550	502 245	237 161	265 084	860 422	396 956	463 466
40 - 44	1 123 344	528 397	594 947	396 939	191 051	205 888	726 405	337 346	389 059
45 - 49	918 912	430 645	488 267	314 503	152 578	161 925	604 409	278 067	326 342
50 - 54	696 087	342 800	353 287	222 907	112 234	110 673	473 180	230 566	242 614
55 - 59	550 481	264 269	286 212	170 928	84 738	86 190	379 553	179 531	200 022
60 - 64	428 657	194 900	233 757	123 516	59 143	64 373	305 141	135 757	169 384
65 - 69	319 540	145 236	174 304	88 321	41 584	46 737	231 219	103 652	127 567
70 - 74	225 428	102 256	123 172	57 447	25 630	31 817	167 981	76 626	91 355
75 - 79	146 194	65 188	81 006	35 638	15 096	20 542	110 556	50 092	60 464
80 +	136 966	58 647	78 319	32 048	12 090	19 958	104 918	46 557	58 361
Namibia - Namibie[18]									
1 VII 2017 (ESDF)									
Total	2 368 747	1 151 533	1 217 214	1 157 806	564 615	593 191	1 210 941	586 918	624 023
0	67 299	34 071	33 228	33 858	17 138	16 720	33 441	16 933	16 508
1 - 4	258 125	130 473	127 652	123 479	62 401	61 078	134 646	68 072	66 574
5 - 9	294 131	148 296	145 835	113 340	56 995	56 345	180 791	91 301	89 490
10 - 14	243 963	122 704	121 259	86 993	42 941	44 052	156 970	79 763	77 207
15 - 19	241 207	119 817	121 390	93 438	43 897	49 541	147 769	75 920	71 849
20 - 24	236 333	115 924	120 409	109 392	50 012	59 380	126 941	65 912	61 029
25 - 29	213 992	104 922	109 070	139 804	67 312	72 492	74 188	37 610	36 578
30 - 34	174 795	84 908	89 887	123 304	60 848	62 456	51 491	24 060	27 431
35 - 39	143 442	69 508	73 934	93 748	46 684	47 064	49 694	22 824	26 870
40 - 44	119 844	57 389	62 455	71 414	35 463	35 951	48 430	21 926	26 504
45 - 49	93 983	43 969	50 014	52 942	26 202	26 740	41 041	17 767	23 274
50 - 54	76 299	34 592	41 707	39 792	20 053	19 739	36 507	14 539	21 968
55 - 59	58 439	25 155	33 284	28 498	13 855	14 643	29 941	11 300	18 641
60 - 64	43 666	18 552	25 114	18 718	8 914	9 804	24 948	9 638	15 310
65 - 69	35 584	15 397	20 187	11 651	5 097	6 554	23 933	10 300	13 633
70 - 74	25 931	10 579	15 352	7 141	2 962	4 179	18 790	7 617	11 173
75 - 79	17 375	6 929	10 446	4 748	1 868	2 880	12 627	5 061	7 566
80 +	24 339	8 348	15 991	5 546	1 973	3 573	18 793	6 375	12 418
Niger[19]									
1 VII 2016 (ESDJ)									
Total	19 865 067	9 898 628	9 966 439	3 242 161	1 617 882	1 624 278	16 622 906	8 280 747	8 342 160
0 - 4	3 966 109	2 009 845	1 956 264	560 061	281 015	279 046	3 406 048	1 728 830	1 677 218
5 - 9	3 533 085	1 810 213	1 722 872	514 367	259 502	254 565	3 018 718	1 550 412	1 468 306
10 - 14	2 790 727	1 418 659	1 372 068	450 479	223 341	227 137	2 340 248	1 195 317	1 144 931
15 - 19	2 021 025	1 010 216	1 010 809	344 569	173 980	170 589	1 676 456	836 236	840 220
20 - 24	1 619 917	777 760	842 157	316 826	159 697	157 130	1 303 090	618 063	685 027
25 - 29	1 236 640	592 643	643 996	220 452	107 039	113 413	1 016 188	485 605	530 583
30 - 34	1 013 696	493 232	520 464	186 768	91 960	94 808	826 927	401 271	425 656
35 - 39	845 916	404 801	441 115	153 624	74 733	78 891	692 293	330 068	362 225
40 - 44	679 710	326 886	352 824	123 978	61 940	62 037	555 732	264 946	290 786
45 - 49	544 473	267 053	277 420	98 818	50 233	48 585	445 656	216 820	228 836
50 - 54	460 236	223 786	236 450	81 307	40 036	41 271	378 929	183 750	195 179
55 - 59	351 487	174 412	177 075	62 257	30 864	31 393	289 230	143 548	145 681
60 - 64	264 109	129 848	134 261	45 097	22 523	22 574	219 012	107 324	111 687
65 - 69	192 038	94 284	97 754	31 661	15 974	15 688	160 376	78 310	82 066
70 - 74	145 168	69 830	75 338	22 937	11 136	11 801	122 231	58 694	63 537
75 - 79	99 975	48 349	51 626	15 105	7 379	7 725	84 870	40 970	43 900
80 +	100 757	46 811	53 946	13 855	6 229	7 626	86 902	40 582	46 320
Nigeria - Nigéria[20]									
1 VII 2016 (ESDF)									
Total	193 392 517	...	...	...	...	...	...	...	...
0 - 4	31 116 156	...	...	...	...	...	...	...	...
5 - 9	27 549 964	...	...	...	...	...	...	...	...
10 - 14	22 221 265	...	...	...	...	...	...	...	...
15 - 19	20 518 404	...	...	...	...	...	...	...	...
20 - 24	18 501 820	...	...	...	...	...	...	...	...
25 - 29	16 816 694	...	...	...	...	...	...	...	...

7. Population by age, sex and urban/rural residence: latest available year, 2008 - 2017
Population selon l'âge, le sexe et la résidence, urbaine/rurale : dernière année disponible, 2008 - 2017 (continued - suite)

Continent, country or area, date, code[a] and age (in years) / Continent, pays ou zone, date, code[a] et âge (en années)	Total			Urban - Urbaine			Rural - Rurale		
	Both sexes Les deux sexes	Male Masculin	Female Féminin	Both sexes Les deux sexes	Male Masculin	Female Féminin	Both sexes Les deux sexes	Male Masculin	Female Féminin

AFRICA - AFRIQUE

Nigeria - Nigéria[20]
1 VII 2016 (ESDF)

30 - 34	13 038 009	...	...	...	...	...	...	...	...
35 - 39	10 096 763	...	...	...	...	...	...	...	...
40 - 44	8 891 384	...	...	...	...	...	...	...	...
45 - 49	6 322 797	...	...	...	...	...	...	...	...
50 - 54	5 851 717	...	...	...	...	...	...	...	...
55 - 59	2 845 486	...	...	...	...	...	...	...	...
60 - 64	3 374 357	...	...	...	...	...	...	...	...
65 - 69	1 585 140	...	...	...	...	...	...	...	...
70 - 74	1 832 402	...	...	...	...	...	...	...	...
75 - 79	798 511	...	...	...	...	...	...	...	...
80 - 84	1 046 690	...	...	...	...	...	...	...	...
85 +	984 956	...	...	...	...	...	...	...	...

Republic of South Sudan - République de Soudan du Sud
21 IV 2008 (CDFC)

Total	8 260 490	4 287 300	3 973 190	1 405 186	754 086	651 100	6 855 304	3 533 214	3 322 090
0	231 146	121 882	109 264	43 300	22 617	20 683	187 846	99 265	88 581
1 - 4	1 072 985	567 545	505 440	174 976	91 509	83 467	898 009	476 036	421 973
5 - 9	1 297 816	688 385	609 431	196 136	101 760	94 376	1 101 680	586 625	515 055
10 - 14	1 057 390	569 537	487 853	160 054	84 981	75 073	897 336	484 556	412 780
15 - 19	889 829	462 902	426 927	153 683	81 602	72 081	736 146	381 300	354 846
20 - 24	739 006	360 788	378 218	148 237	78 336	69 901	590 769	282 452	308 317
25 - 29	698 011	335 398	362 613	141 623	76 445	65 178	556 388	258 953	297 435
30 - 34	536 915	258 531	278 384	101 597	56 705	44 892	435 318	201 826	233 492
35 - 39	475 813	238 985	236 828	87 844	49 346	38 498	387 969	189 639	198 330
40 - 44	339 704	173 493	166 211	58 645	33 444	25 201	281 059	140 049	141 010
45 - 49	276 100	149 941	126 159	45 605	26 316	19 289	230 495	123 625	106 870
50 - 54	197 265	104 812	92 453	31 870	17 548	14 322	165 395	87 264	78 131
55 - 59	121 795	67 845	53 950	18 520	10 557	7 963	103 275	57 288	45 987
60 - 64	115 631	64 236	51 395	16 523	8 849	7 674	99 108	55 387	43 721
65 - 69	73 155	41 455	31 700	9 750	5 239	4 511	63 405	36 216	27 189
70 - 74	59 287	34 785	24 502	7 756	4 087	3 669	51 531	30 698	20 833
75 - 79	28 919	17 424	11 495	3 522	1 898	1 624	25 397	15 526	9 871
80 - 84	24 514	14 314	10 200	2 867	1 497	1 370	21 647	12 817	8 830
85 - 89	10 982	6 731	4 251	1 121	550	571	9 861	6 181	3 680
90 - 94	7 361	4 477	2 884	873	472	401	6 488	4 005	2 483
95 +	6 866	3 834	3 032	684	328	356	6 182	3 506	2 676

1 VII 2017 (ESDF)[21]

Total	11 868 210	6 083 876	5 784 333	...	...	...	...	...	...
0 - 4	2 513 999	1 266 004	1 247 995	...	...	...	...	...	...
5 - 9	1 862 651	939 611	923 040	...	...	...	...	...	...
10 - 14	1 279 536	675 473	604 062	...	...	...	...	...	...
15 - 19	1 333 547	710 668	622 880	...	...	...	...	...	...
20 - 24	937 525	504 484	433 041	...	...	...	...	...	...
25 - 29	917 392	461 759	455 633	...	...	...	...	...	...
30 - 34	632 490	309 065	323 425	...	...	...	...	...	...
35 - 39	708 283	334 134	374 149	...	...	...	...	...	...
40 - 44	417 605	210 102	207 503	...	...	...	...	...	...
45 - 49	454 991	226 756	228 235	...	...	...	...	...	...
50 - 54	258 042	138 080	119 961	...	...	...	...	...	...
55 - 59	230 130	123 768	106 362	...	...	...	...	...	...
60 - 64	108 851	60 676	48 175	...	...	...	...	...	...
65 - 69	108 859	61 030	47 829	...	...	...	...	...	...
70 - 74	51 017	29 780	21 237	...	...	...	...	...	...
75 - 79	35 070	20 771	14 299	...	...	...	...	...	...
80 - 84	12 971	8 307	4 664	...	...	...	...	...	...
85 - 89	4 278	2 769	1 509	...	...	...	...	...	...
90 - 94	937	613	324	...	...	...	...	...	...
95 +	36	26	10	...	...	...	...	...	...

7. Population by age, sex and urban/rural residence: latest available year, 2008 - 2017
Population selon l'âge, le sexe et la résidence, urbaine/rurale : dernière année disponible, 2008 - 2017 (continued - suite)

Continent, country or area, date, code[a] and age (in years) / Continent, pays ou zone, date, code[a] et âge (en années)	Total			Urban - Urbaine			Rural - Rurale		
	Both sexes Les deux sexes	Male Masculin	Female Féminin	Both sexes Les deux sexes	Male Masculin	Female Féminin	Both sexes Les deux sexes	Male Masculin	Female Féminin
AFRICA - AFRIQUE									
Reunion - Réunion									
1 I 2017* (ESDJ)									
Total	860 815	414 911	445 904	...	...	...	...	...	...
0 - 4	62 821	31 872	30 949	...	...	...	...	...	...
5 - 9	68 358	35 163	33 195	...	...	...	...	...	...
10 - 14	71 209	36 576	34 633	...	...	...	...	...	...
15 - 19	68 406	35 211	33 195	...	...	...	...	...	...
20 - 24	52 754	26 370	26 384	...	...	...	...	...	...
25 - 29	50 931	23 495	27 436	...	...	...	...	...	...
30 - 34	52 196	23 800	28 396	...	...	...	...	...	...
35 - 39	54 451	24 822	29 629	...	...	...	...	...	...
40 - 44	58 757	27 355	31 402	...	...	...	...	...	...
45 - 49	63 105	30 283	32 822	...	...	...	...	...	...
50 - 54	64 689	31 532	33 157	...	...	...	...	...	...
55 - 59	53 612	25 795	27 817	...	...	...	...	...	...
60 - 64	45 659	21 911	23 748	...	...	...	...	...	...
65 - 69	32 734	15 547	17 187	...	...	...	...	...	...
70 - 74	23 024	10 599	12 425	...	...	...	...	...	...
75 - 79	17 180	7 301	9 879	...	...	...	...	...	...
80 - 84	11 460	4 396	7 064	...	...	...	...	...	...
85 - 89	6 024	1 976	4 048	...	...	...	...	...	...
90 - 94	2 655	711	1 944	...	...	...	...	...	...
95 +	790	196	594	...	...	...	...	...	...
Rwanda[19]									
1 VII 2017 (ESDF)									
Total	11 809 300	5 722 258	6 087 041	2 347 098	1 137 299	1 209 799	9 462 201	4 584 959	4 877 242
0 - 4	1 623 164	819 331	803 832	289 098	137 035	152 063	1 334 065	682 296	651 769
5 - 9	1 503 836	748 810	755 026	241 500	112 901	128 599	1 262 335	635 909	626 427
10 - 14	1 506 822	748 820	758 002	255 798	117 766	138 032	1 251 024	631 054	619 970
15 - 19	1 252 138	616 454	635 684	258 914	112 934	145 980	993 224	503 520	489 704
20 - 24	1 096 983	537 619	559 365	286 194	139 054	147 140	810 789	398 565	412 225
25 - 29	1 010 566	489 394	521 172	270 753	137 567	133 186	739 813	351 826	387 987
30 - 34	911 301	447 177	464 124	226 960	120 107	106 854	684 341	327 070	357 270
35 - 39	746 438	359 941	386 497	173 935	92 121	81 814	572 503	267 820	304 684
40 - 44	497 634	226 688	270 947	102 422	52 564	49 857	395 213	174 123	221 090
45 - 49	403 926	184 948	218 978	71 776	37 099	34 677	332 149	147 848	184 301
50 - 54	328 161	148 945	179 216	48 660	24 701	23 959	279 501	124 244	155 257
55 - 59	321 430	143 136	178 294	43 487	21 243	22 244	277 943	121 893	156 050
60 - 64	224 720	98 454	126 266	29 059	13 645	15 414	195 661	84 809	110 852
65 - 69	157 644	67 407	90 237	20 517	8 889	11 628	137 127	58 518	78 609
70 - 74	85 889	33 017	52 872	10 521	3 940	6 581	75 368	29 077	46 291
75 - 79	68 908	25 730	43 179	8 731	3 017	5 714	60 177	22 713	37 464
80 +	69 739	26 388	43 351	8 773	2 715	6 058	60 966	23 673	37 294
Saint Helena ex. dep. - Sainte-Hélène sans dép.[22]									
7 II 2016 (CDJC)									
Total	4 534	2 396	2 138	...	...	...	...	...	...
0 - 4	213	107	106	...	...	...	...	...	...
5 - 9	209	116	93	...	...	...	...	...	...
10 - 14	191	98	93	...	...	...	...	...	...
15 - 19	236	123	113	...	...	...	...	...	...
20 - 24	203	122	81	...	...	...	...	...	...
25 - 29	235	128	107	...	...	...	...	...	...
30 - 34	288	141	147	...	...	...	...	...	...
35 - 39	249	130	119	...	...	...	...	...	...
40 - 44	334	184	150	...	...	...	...	...	...
45 - 49	403	222	181	...	...	...	...	...	...
50 - 54	357	182	175	...	...	...	...	...	...
55 - 59	365	188	177	...	...	...	...	...	...
60 - 64	314	176	138	...	...	...	...	...	...
65 - 69	343	178	165	...	...	...	...	...	...
70 - 74	269	159	110	...	...	...	...	...	...
75 - 79	152	74	78	...	...	...	...	...	...
80 +	173	68	105	...	...	...	...	...	...

7. Population by age, sex and urban/rural residence: latest available year, 2008 - 2017
Population selon l'âge, le sexe et la résidence, urbaine/rurale : dernière année disponible, 2008 - 2017 (continued - suite)

Continent, country or area, date, code[a] and age (in years) / Continent, pays ou zone, date, code[a] et âge (en années)	Total			Urban - Urbaine			Rural - Rurale		
	Both sexes Les deux sexes	Male Masculin	Female Féminin	Both sexes Les deux sexes	Male Masculin	Female Féminin	Both sexes Les deux sexes	Male Masculin	Female Féminin
AFRICA - AFRIQUE									
Saint Helena: Ascension - Sainte-Hélène: Ascension									
1 VII 2008 (ESDJ)									
Total	702	397	305	...	...	...	...	...	...
0 - 4	32	16	16	...	...	...	...	...	...
5 - 9	19	9	10	...	...	...	...	...	...
10 - 14	41	20	21	...	...	...	...	...	...
15 - 19	30	19	11	...	...	...	...	...	...
20 - 24	63	29	34	...	...	...	...	...	...
25 - 29	73	42	31	...	...	...	...	...	...
30 - 34	76	41	35	...	...	...	...	...	...
35 - 39	92	58	34	...	...	...	...	...	...
40 - 44	85	42	43	...	...	...	...	...	...
45 - 49	65	36	29	...	...	...	...	...	...
50 - 54	51	32	19	...	...	...	...	...	...
55 - 59	43	29	14	...	...	...	...	...	...
60 - 64	21	15	6	...	...	...	...	...	...
65 - 69	10	9	1	...	...	...	...	...	...
70 - 74	-	-	-	...	...	...	...	...	...
75 - 79	-	-	-	...	...	...	...	...	...
80 +	1	-	1	...	...	...	...	...	...
Sao Tome and Principe - Sao Tomé-et-Principe[23]									
1 VII 2017 (ESDJ)									
Total	197 700	97 988	99 712	133 748	66 291	67 457	63 952	31 697	32 255
0 - 4	24 133	12 031	12 102	16 249	8 217	8 032	7 883	3 814	4 070
5 - 9	27 500	13 833	13 667	18 273	9 375	8 898	9 227	4 458	4 769
10 - 14	25 390	12 677	12 714	17 054	8 509	8 546	8 336	4 168	4 168
15 - 19	21 345	10 673	10 672	14 430	7 149	7 281	6 915	3 524	3 391
20 - 24	18 341	9 278	9 062	12 555	6 298	6 257	5 786	2 981	2 805
25 - 29	15 841	7 895	7 946	11 026	5 460	5 566	4 815	2 435	2 380
30 - 34	14 665	7 276	7 389	10 078	4 984	5 094	4 587	2 292	2 295
35 - 39	12 358	6 105	6 252	8 237	4 046	4 191	4 120	2 059	2 061
40 - 44	9 546	4 762	4 784	6 404	3 155	3 249	3 142	1 607	1 535
45 - 49	7 654	3 831	3 822	5 256	2 618	2 638	2 398	1 214	1 184
50 - 54	6 033	2 880	3 153	4 200	2 000	2 200	1 833	881	953
55 - 59	5 004	2 384	2 620	3 518	1 690	1 827	1 486	694	792
60 - 64	3 431	1 573	1 858	2 326	1 054	1 272	1 105	519	586
65 - 69	2 249	1 076	1 173	1 477	689	787	772	386	385
70 - 74	1 500	665	835	932	400	532	568	265	303
75 - 79	1 313	535	777	796	320	477	516	216	301
80 +	1 400	514	886	938	329	609	463	185	277
Senegal - Sénégal[2]									
1 VII 2016 (ESDJ)									
Total	14 799 859	7 372 487	7 427 372	...	...	...	...	...	...
0 - 4	2 384 522	1 212 846	1 171 676	...	...	...	...	...	...
5 - 9	2 016 277	1 037 276	979 001	...	...	...	...	...	...
10 - 14	1 784 725	918 849	865 876	...	...	...	...	...	...
15 - 19	1 560 123	797 927	762 196	...	...	...	...	...	...
20 - 24	1 359 140	675 294	683 846	...	...	...	...	...	...
25 - 29	1 166 100	559 321	606 779	...	...	...	...	...	...
30 - 34	973 530	466 740	506 790	...	...	...	...	...	...
35 - 39	795 699	384 264	411 435	...	...	...	...	...	...
40 - 44	645 123	307 640	337 483	...	...	...	...	...	...
45 - 49	511 410	240 118	271 292	...	...	...	...	...	...
50 - 54	430 078	204 461	225 617	...	...	...	...	...	...
55 - 59	360 730	174 948	185 782	...	...	...	...	...	...
60 - 64	276 702	135 025	141 677	...	...	...	...	...	...
65 - 69	198 778	97 438	101 340	...	...	...	...	...	...
70 - 74	141 928	69 235	72 693	...	...	...	...	...	...
75 - 79	90 654	43 423	47 231	...	...	...	...	...	...
80 +	104 340	47 682	56 658	...	...	...	...	...	...

7. Population by age, sex and urban/rural residence: latest available year, 2008 - 2017
Population selon l'âge, le sexe et la résidence, urbaine/rurale : dernière année disponible, 2008 - 2017 (continued - suite)

Continent, country or area, date, code[a] and age (in years) / Continent, pays ou zone, date, code[a] et âge (en annèes)	Total			Urban - Urbaine			Rural - Rurale		
	Both sexes Les deux sexes	Male Masculin	Female Féminin	Both sexes Les deux sexes	Male Masculin	Female Féminin	Both sexes Les deux sexes	Male Masculin	Female Féminin
AFRICA - AFRIQUE									
Seychelles									
1 VII 2017 (ESDF)									
Total	95 843	48 793	47 050	...	...	...	...	...	...
0 - 4	7 682	3 971	3 711	...	...	...	...	...	...
5 - 9	6 336	3 225	3 111	...	...	...	...	...	...
10 - 14	5 218	2 629	2 589	...	...	...	...	...	...
15 - 19	4 012	1 980	2 032	...	...	...	...	...	...
20 - 24	3 694	2 202	1 492	...	...	...	...	...	...
25 - 29	5 958	3 368	2 590	...	...	...	...	...	...
30 - 34	7 990	4 680	3 310	...	...	...	...	...	...
35 - 39	9 323	4 814	4 509	...	...	...	...	...	...
40 - 44	6 859	3 529	3 330	...	...	...	...	...	...
45 - 49	8 439	4 333	4 106	...	...	...	...	...	...
50 - 54	6 856	2 991	3 865	...	...	...	...	...	...
55 - 59	8 424	4 177	4 247	...	...	...	...	...	...
60 - 64	5 812	2 901	2 911	...	...	...	...	...	...
65 - 69	3 863	1 924	1 939	...	...	...	...	...	...
70 - 74	2 086	995	1 091	...	...	...	...	...	...
75 - 79	1 528	603	925	...	...	...	...	...	...
80 - 84	994	315	679	...	...	...	...	...	...
85 - 89	540	116	424	...	...	...	...	...	...
90 +	229	40	189	...	...	...	...	...	...
Sierra Leone									
1 VII 2010 (ESDF)									
Total	5 746 800	2 786 797	2 960 003	2 304 955	1 138 563	1 166 392	3 441 845	1 648 234	1 793 611
0 - 4	878 231	437 908	440 323	297 865	147 565	150 300	580 366	290 343	290 023
5 - 9	856 605	424 222	432 383	307 007	145 641	161 366	549 598	278 581	271 017
10 - 14	662 651	338 453	324 198	303 094	148 401	154 693	359 557	190 052	169 505
15 - 19	637 914	308 982	328 932	287 597	141 564	146 033	350 317	167 418	182 899
20 - 24	488 054	221 932	266 122	241 599	119 622	121 977	246 455	102 310	144 145
25 - 29	473 952	210 004	263 948	205 137	102 492	102 645	268 815	107 512	161 303
30 - 34	356 727	160 822	195 905	149 414	73 308	76 106	207 313	87 514	119 799
35 - 39	341 470	160 326	181 144	133 461	66 104	67 357	208 009	94 222	113 787
40 - 44	247 978	123 279	124 699	97 102	51 623	45 479	150 876	71 656	79 220
45 - 49	201 708	107 932	93 776	76 536	41 832	34 704	125 172	66 100	59 072
50 - 54	149 167	77 236	71 931	55 139	30 564	24 575	94 028	46 672	47 356
55 - 59	96 801	51 344	45 457	37 477	21 157	16 320	59 324	30 187	29 137
60 - 64	99 394	44 873	54 521	31 058	14 915	16 143	68 336	29 958	38 378
65 - 69	71 174	34 054	37 120	24 423	11 420	13 003	46 751	22 634	24 117
70 - 74	61 847	28 198	33 649	18 941	8 268	10 673	42 906	19 930	22 976
75 - 79	41 728	21 586	20 142	12 876	6 356	6 520	28 852	15 230	13 622
80 +	81 399	35 646	45 753	26 229	7 731	18 498	55 170	27 915	27 255
5 XII 2015 (CDFC)									
Total	7 092 113	3 490 978	3 601 135	...	...	...	...	...	...
0 - 4	938 453	469 092	469 361	...	...	...	...	...	...
5 - 9	1 108 715	555 292	553 423	...	...	...	...	...	...
10 - 14	847 292	431 588	415 704	...	...	...	...	...	...
15 - 19	873 620	430 792	442 828	...	...	...	...	...	...
20 - 24	662 819	308 135	354 684	...	...	...	...	...	...
25 - 29	607 983	277 618	330 365	...	...	...	...	...	...
30 - 34	434 203	199 964	234 239	...	...	...	...	...	...
35 - 39	421 172	201 459	219 713	...	...	...	...	...	...
40 - 44	299 215	154 121	145 094	...	...	...	...	...	...
45 - 49	242 188	133 783	108 405	...	...	...	...	...	...
50 - 54	186 793	99 050	87 743	...	...	...	...	...	...
55 - 59	110 449	59 261	51 188	...	...	...	...	...	...
60 - 64	112 682	53 987	58 695	...	...	...	...	...	...
65 - 69	73 722	36 414	37 308	...	...	...	...	...	...
70 - 74	65 568	30 606	34 962	...	...	...	...	...	...
75 - 79	39 728	20 044	19 684	...	...	...	...	...	...
80 - 84	31 359	13 177	18 182	...	...	...	...	...	...
85 - 89	15 888	7 258	8 630	...	...	...	...	...	...
90 - 94	9 984	4 430	5 554	...	...	...	...	...	...
95 +	10 280	4 907	5 373	...	...	...	...	...	...

Continent, country or area, date, code[a] and age (in years) / Continent, pays ou zone, date, code[a] et âge (en annèes)	Total			Urban - Urbaine			Rural - Rurale		
	Both sexes Les deux sexes	Male Masculin	Female Féminin	Both sexes Les deux sexes	Male Masculin	Female Féminin	Both sexes Les deux sexes	Male Masculin	Female Féminin
AFRICA - AFRIQUE									
South Africa - Afrique du Sud									
1 VII 2017 (ESDF)									
Total	56 521 948	27 620 642	28 901 306	...	...	...	...	...	...
0 - 4	5 866 573	2 946 312	2 920 261	...	...	...	...	...	...
5 - 9	5 764 576	2 888 925	2 875 651	...	...	...	...	...	...
10 - 14	5 093 681	2 547 260	2 546 421	...	...	...	...	...	...
15 - 19	4 592 001	2 287 717	2 304 284	...	...	...	...	...	...
20 - 24	5 031 271	2 504 334	2 526 937	...	...	...	...	...	...
25 - 29	5 518 305	2 751 293	2 767 012	...	...	...	...	...	...
30 - 34	5 253 733	2 635 257	2 618 476	...	...	...	...	...	...
35 - 39	4 243 537	2 142 780	2 100 757	...	...	...	...	...	...
40 - 44	3 392 431	1 725 089	1 667 342	...	...	...	...	...	...
45 - 49	2 787 590	1 355 592	1 431 998	...	...	...	...	...	...
50 - 54	2 376 586	1 085 068	1 291 518	...	...	...	...	...	...
55 - 59	2 005 845	905 701	1 100 144	...	...	...	...	...	...
60 - 64	1 604 739	702 660	902 079	...	...	...	...	...	...
65 - 69	1 190 825	499 711	691 114	...	...	...	...	...	...
70 - 74	793 616	314 644	478 972	...	...	...	...	...	...
75 - 79	513 955	187 084	326 871	...	...	...	...	...	...
80 +	492 684	141 215	351 469	...	...	...	...	...	...
Sudan - Soudan									
1 VII 2016 (ESDF)									
Total	39 647 621	20 105 842	19 541 779	14 269 540	7 236 276	7 033 264	25 378 082	12 869 567	12 508 515
0	1 495 606	762 197	733 409	454 208	223 675	230 524	1 041 398	538 523	502 885
1 - 4	5 388 576	2 744 131	2 644 444	1 636 483	805 294	831 198	3 752 093	1 938 838	1 813 247
5 - 9	5 479 254	2 801 266	2 677 988	1 758 182	874 065	884 117	3 721 072	1 927 201	1 793 872
10 - 14	4 522 096	2 325 624	2 196 472	1 542 867	777 406	765 461	2 979 229	1 548 218	1 431 011
15 - 19	4 025 611	2 073 006	1 952 605	1 447 819	739 848	707 970	2 577 793	1 333 158	1 244 635
20 - 24	3 537 491	1 816 041	1 721 450	1 363 235	711 648	651 587	2 174 256	1 104 393	1 069 863
25 - 29	3 067 006	1 547 613	1 519 393	1 222 270	635 394	586 876	1 844 735	912 219	932 517
30 - 34	2 625 594	1 295 965	1 329 629	1 066 750	549 164	517 585	1 558 844	746 801	812 043
35 - 39	2 221 636	1 085 101	1 136 535	908 234	463 534	444 700	1 313 401	621 567	691 835
40 - 44	1 840 327	891 195	949 131	741 484	371 028	370 456	1 098 843	520 167	578 675
45 - 49	1 494 962	732 711	762 251	600 105	301 816	298 289	894 857	430 895	463 963
50 - 54	1 175 703	589 400	586 304	472 806	241 174	231 632	702 897	348 225	354 672
55 - 59	899 359	458 118	441 240	358 957	184 543	174 414	540 402	273 575	266 827
60 - 64	654 915	340 396	314 518	256 819	133 591	123 228	398 096	206 805	191 290
65 - 69	474 001	248 570	225 431	181 190	93 976	87 214	292 812	154 595	138 217
70 - 74	322 506	170 069	152 437	118 162	60 482	57 680	204 344	109 588	94 757
75 - 79	206 936	109 224	97 712	70 332	34 777	35 555	136 604	74 447	62 157
80 +	216 042	115 214	100 828	69 638	34 862	34 776	146 405	80 353	66 052
Togo									
6 XI 2010 (CDJC)									
Total	6 191 155	3 009 095	3 182 060	...	...	...	...	...	...
0	190 136	96 043	94 093	...	...	...	...	...	...
1 - 4	711 135	360 481	350 654	...	...	...	...	...	...
5 - 9	951 700	482 501	469 199	...	...	...	...	...	...
10 - 14	747 726	390 477	357 249	...	...	...	...	...	...
15 - 19	606 401	313 257	293 144	...	...	...	...	...	...
20 - 24	545 245	252 807	292 438	...	...	...	...	...	...
25 - 29	496 822	214 803	282 019	...	...	...	...	...	...
30 - 34	424 380	199 636	224 744	...	...	...	...	...	...
35 - 39	352 008	166 528	185 480	...	...	...	...	...	...
40 - 44	291 584	139 731	151 853	...	...	...	...	...	...
45 - 49	228 446	112 191	116 255	...	...	...	...	...	...
50 - 54	178 233	82 969	95 264	...	...	...	...	...	...
55 - 59	115 950	54 936	61 014	...	...	...	...	...	...
60 - 64	102 694	44 431	58 263	...	...	...	...	...	...
65 - 69	66 324	26 700	39 624	...	...	...	...	...	...
70 - 74	61 756	24 127	37 629	...	...	...	...	...	...
75 - 79	33 574	13 250	20 324	...	...	...	...	...	...
80 +	73 591	27 960	45 631	...	...	...	...	...	...
Unknown - Inconnu	13 450	6 267	7 183	...	...	...	...	...	...

7. Population by age, sex and urban/rural residence: latest available year, 2008 - 2017
Population selon l'âge, le sexe et la résidence, urbaine/rurale : dernière année disponible, 2008 - 2017 (continued - suite)

Continent, country or area, date, code[a] and age (in years) Continent, pays ou zone, date, code[a] et âge (en années)	Total			Urban - Urbaine			Rural - Rurale		
	Both sexes Les deux sexes	Male Masculin	Female Féminin	Both sexes Les deux sexes	Male Masculin	Female Féminin	Both sexes Les deux sexes	Male Masculin	Female Féminin
AFRICA - AFRIQUE									
Tunisia - Tunisie									
1 VII 2016 (ESDF)									
Total	11 304 483	5 620 629	5 683 853	...	...	...	...	...	...
0 - 4	1 057 906	...	...	...	...	...	...	...	...
5 - 9	893 438	...	...	...	...	...	...	...	...
10 - 14	805 398	...	...	...	...	...	...	...	...
15 - 19	801 924	...	...	...	...	...	...	...	...
20 - 24	887 393	...	...	...	...	...	...	...	...
25 - 29	920 248	...	...	...	...	...	...	...	...
30 - 34	970 488	...	...	...	...	...	...	...	...
35 - 39	886 447	...	...	...	...	...	...	...	...
40 - 44	751 607	...	...	...	...	...	...	...	...
45 - 49	694 780	...	...	...	...	...	...	...	...
50 - 54	666 469	...	...	...	...	...	...	...	...
55 - 59	579 393	...	...	...	...	...	...	...	...
60 - 64	466 135	...	...	...	...	...	...	...	...
65 - 69	311 467	...	...	...	...	...	...	...	...
70 - 74	219 781	...	...	...	...	...	...	...	...
75 - 79	170 737	...	...	...	...	...	...	...	...
80 +	220 872	...	...	...	...	...	...	...	...
Uganda - Ouganda									
27 VIII 2014 (CDFC)									
Total	34 634 650	16 897 849	17 736 801	8 438 009	4 042 324	4 395 685	26 196 641	12 855 525	13 341 116
0 - 4	6 131 028	3 173 950	2 957 078	1 342 058	699 470	642 588	4 788 970	2 474 480	2 314 490
5 - 9	5 551 678	2 834 456	2 717 222	1 135 262	575 893	559 369	4 416 416	2 258 563	2 157 853
10 - 14	4 920 443	2 462 789	2 457 654	1 017 614	487 602	530 012	3 902 829	1 975 187	1 927 642
15 - 19	3 956 633	1 917 797	2 038 836	1 015 017	449 250	565 767	2 941 616	1 468 547	1 473 069
20 - 24	3 188 611	1 444 438	1 744 173	1 024 995	444 919	580 076	2 163 616	999 519	1 164 097
25 - 29	2 486 176	1 143 467	1 342 709	825 746	377 888	447 858	1 660 430	765 579	894 851
30 - 34	1 951 739	908 447	1 043 292	584 396	280 869	303 527	1 367 343	627 578	739 765
35 - 39	1 535 837	726 355	809 482	434 901	214 481	220 420	1 100 936	511 874	589 062
40 - 44	1 272 417	617 034	655 383	316 293	162 345	153 948	956 124	454 689	501 435
45 - 49	921 124	452 081	469 043	217 719	112 768	104 951	703 405	339 313	364 092
50 - 54	808 103	371 126	436 977	172 367	81 867	90 500	635 736	289 259	346 477
55 - 59	480 284	224 765	255 519	97 541	46 042	51 499	382 743	178 723	204 020
60 - 64	440 053	195 283	244 770	81 233	36 927	44 306	358 820	158 356	200 464
65 - 69	301 150	136 107	165 043	50 965	22 770	28 195	250 185	113 337	136 848
70 - 74	277 236	115 862	161 374	46 835	19 032	27 803	230 401	96 830	133 571
75 - 79	150 473	69 095	81 378	25 771	11 009	14 762	124 702	58 086	66 616
80 - 84	131 269	51 871	79 398	23 763	9 044	14 719	107 506	42 827	64 679
85 - 89	51 776	21 572	30 204	9 925	3 912	6 013	41 851	17 660	24 191
90 - 94	37 171	15 125	22 046	8 116	3 484	4 632	29 055	11 641	17 414
95 +	41 449	16 229	25 220	7 492	2 752	4 740	33 957	13 477	20 480
1 VII 2017 (ESDF)[6]									
Total	37 673 800	...	...	...	...	...	...	...	...
0	1 503 800	...	...	...	...	...	...	...	...
1 - 4	5 168 600	...	...	...	...	...	...	...	...
5 - 9	5 746 800	...	...	...	...	...	...	...	...
10 - 14	5 176 800	...	...	...	...	...	...	...	...
15 - 19	4 471 200	...	...	...	...	...	...	...	...
20 - 24	3 621 900	...	...	...	...	...	...	...	...
25 - 29	2 810 500	...	...	...	...	...	...	...	...
30 - 34	2 217 700	...	...	...	...	...	...	...	...
35 - 39	1 707 200	...	...	...	...	...	...	...	...
40 - 44	1 355 700	...	...	...	...	...	...	...	...
45 - 49	1 067 200	...	...	...	...	...	...	...	...
50 - 54	818 300	...	...	...	...	...	...	...	...
55 - 59	608 500	...	...	...	...	...	...	...	...
60 - 64	454 500	...	...	...	...	...	...	...	...
65 - 69	327 900	...	...	...	...	...	...	...	...
70 - 74	237 000	...	...	...	...	...	...	...	...
75 - 79	162 500	...	...	...	...	...	...	...	...
80 +	217 700	...	...	...	...	...	...	...	...

Continent, country or area, date, code[a] and age (in years) / Continent, pays ou zone, date, code[a] et âge (en années)	Total			Urban - Urbaine			Rural - Rurale		
	Both sexes Les deux sexes	Male Masculin	Female Féminin	Both sexes Les deux sexes	Male Masculin	Female Féminin	Both sexes Les deux sexes	Male Masculin	Female Féminin
AFRICA - AFRIQUE									
United Republic of Tanzania - République Unie de Tanzanie[24]									
1 VII 2013 (ESDF)									
Total	47 132 580	23 267 957	23 864 623	12 909 536	6 386 303	6 523 233	34 223 044	16 881 654	17 341 390
0	1 776 107	895 971	880 136	403 952	203 710	200 242	1 372 155	692 261	679 894
1 - 4	6 536 000	3 295 033	3 240 967	1 521 372	766 466	754 906	5 014 628	2 528 567	2 486 061
5 - 9	7 160 846	3 608 891	3 551 955	1 723 220	857 109	866 111	5 437 626	2 751 782	2 685 844
10 - 14	5 464 181	2 735 494	2 728 687	1 364 854	661 195	703 659	4 099 327	2 074 299	2 025 028
15 - 19	4 985 943	2 494 983	2 490 960	1 427 786	682 734	745 052	3 558 157	1 812 249	1 745 908
20 - 24	4 340 143	2 179 173	2 160 970	1 333 476	672 789	660 687	3 006 667	1 506 384	1 500 283
25 - 29	3 484 607	1 730 600	1 754 007	1 134 814	563 796	571 018	2 349 793	1 166 804	1 182 989
30 - 34	2 852 197	1 289 114	1 563 083	974 580	450 823	523 757	1 877 617	838 291	1 039 326
35 - 39	2 601 610	1 207 182	1 394 428	867 422	418 436	448 986	1 734 188	788 746	945 442
40 - 44	2 121 302	1 032 605	1 088 697	672 984	346 836	326 148	1 448 318	685 769	762 549
45 - 49	1 568 017	770 149	797 868	469 417	248 681	220 736	1 098 600	521 468	577 132
50 - 54	1 234 201	604 621	629 580	339 138	180 385	158 753	895 063	424 236	470 827
55 - 59	881 484	422 141	459 343	223 562	117 172	106 390	657 922	304 969	352 953
60 - 64	734 938	347 604	387 334	172 297	88 004	84 293	562 641	259 600	303 041
65 - 69	466 882	223 365	243 517	100 337	50 363	49 974	366 545	173 002	193 543
70 - 74	387 755	179 960	207 795	78 544	35 541	43 003	309 211	144 419	164 792
75 - 79	245 872	115 076	130 796	46 843	20 380	26 463	199 029	94 696	104 333
80 +	290 495	135 995	154 500	54 938	21 883	33 055	235 557	114 112	121 445
Zambia - Zambie[25]									
1 VII 2017 (ESDJ)									
Total	16 405 229	8 117 939	8 287 290	6 964 965	3 445 261	3 519 704	9 440 264	4 672 678	4 767 586
0 - 4	2 947 208	1 485 740	1 461 468	1 149 443	581 738	567 705	1 797 765	904 002	893 763
0	640 430	323 807	316 623	...	...	...	...	...	...
1 - 4	2 306 778	1 161 933	1 144 845	...	...	...	...	...	...
5 - 9	2 510 922	1 260 542	1 250 380	921 125	464 323	456 802	1 589 797	796 219	793 578
10 - 14	2 071 369	1 039 287	1 032 082	804 426	404 098	400 328	1 266 943	635 189	631 754
15 - 19	1 793 158	892 277	900 881	760 266	364 125	396 141	1 032 892	528 152	504 740
20 - 24	1 572 512	774 663	797 849	736 162	348 738	387 424	836 350	425 925	410 425
25 - 29	1 236 588	584 304	652 284	634 118	299 342	334 776	602 470	284 962	317 508
30 - 34	1 016 079	468 785	547 294	524 903	247 100	277 803	491 176	221 685	269 491
35 - 39	836 241	407 906	428 335	422 209	211 324	210 885	414 032	196 582	217 450
40 - 44	667 380	342 467	324 913	321 271	171 861	149 410	346 109	170 606	175 503
45 - 49	489 035	254 732	234 303	218 811	119 295	99 516	270 224	135 437	134 787
50 - 54	359 090	181 102	177 988	149 084	77 286	71 798	210 006	103 816	106 190
55 - 59	282 628	135 523	147 105	113 367	55 302	58 065	169 261	80 221	89 040
60 - 64	192 958	92 913	100 045	77 697	38 506	39 191	115 261	54 407	60 854
65 - 69	146 665	68 231	78 434	52 954	26 283	26 671	93 711	41 948	51 763
70 - 74	110 972	49 386	61 586	34 464	16 321	18 143	76 508	33 065	43 443
75 - 79	74 684	33 561	41 123	20 885	9 507	11 378	53 799	24 054	29 745
80 +	97 740	46 520	51 220	23 780	10 112	13 668	73 960	36 408	37 552
Zimbabwe[26]									
1 VII 2017 (ESDF)									
Total	14 542 235	6 991 066	7 551 172	4 878 395	2 329 497	2 548 898	9 748 347	4 704 677	5 043 669
0 - 4	1 954 985	961 158	993 827	700 296	346 728	353 567	1 344 814	659 343	685 472
5 - 9	1 934 227	958 717	975 510	594 710	294 988	299 722	1 344 013	665 985	678 027
10 - 14	1 682 929	835 617	847 313	441 731	215 243	226 488	1 239 623	619 544	620 079
15 - 19	1 680 999	840 341	840 657	433 657	205 019	228 638	1 246 110	634 650	611 460
20 - 24	1 393 592	687 479	706 113	460 574	196 246	264 328	932 200	490 748	441 451
25 - 29	1 176 434	531 805	644 630	485 164	210 651	274 513	690 957	321 100	369 857
30 - 34	1 111 742	508 024	603 719	480 172	220 677	259 495	631 378	287 431	343 948
35 - 39	902 493	432 576	469 918	381 361	188 220	193 140	520 930	244 433	276 497
40 - 44	719 195	352 058	367 136	287 418	148 562	138 856	431 522	203 526	227 996
45 - 49	509 284	259 088	250 196	203 269	109 895	93 374	305 837	149 225	156 612
50 - 54	334 484	153 529	180 955	124 175	61 489	62 686	210 114	92 017	118 097
55 - 59	332 315	129 731	202 584	100 343	46 208	54 135	231 142	83 414	147 728
60 - 64	261 490	110 039	151 451	74 378	36 129	38 249	186 818	73 735	113 083
65 - 69	201 054	84 012	117 042	46 738	21 905	24 833	153 563	61 794	91 768
70 - 74	137 852	58 662	79 191	28 600	12 720	15 881	108 419	45 554	62 865
75 - 79	100 317	43 763	56 554	18 464	7 888	10 577	80 905	35 386	45 519
80 +	108 843	44 467	64 376	17 345	6 929	10 416	90 002	36 792	53 210

Continent, country or area, date, code[a] and age (in years) / Continent, pays ou zone, date, code[a] et âge (en années)	Total			Urban - Urbaine			Rural - Rurale		
	Both sexes Les deux sexes	Male Masculin	Female Féminin	Both sexes Les deux sexes	Male Masculin	Female Féminin	Both sexes Les deux sexes	Male Masculin	Female Féminin
AMERICA, NORTH - AMÉRIQUE DU NORD									
Anguilla									
11 V 2011 (CDFC)									
Total	13 572	6 707	6 865	...	...	...	...	...	...
0	245	130	115	...	...	...	...	...	...
1 - 4	813	416	397	...	...	...	...	...	...
5 - 9	1 056	529	527	...	...	...	...	...	...
10 - 14	1 069	530	539	...	...	...	...	...	...
15 - 19	916	466	450	...	...	...	...	...	...
20 - 24	917	466	451	...	...	...	...	...	...
25 - 29	1 120	533	587	...	...	...	...	...	...
30 - 34	1 016	480	536	...	...	...	...	...	...
35 - 39	1 145	569	576	...	...	...	...	...	...
40 - 44	1 138	567	571	...	...	...	...	...	...
45 - 49	1 089	538	551	...	...	...	...	...	...
50 - 54	878	425	453	...	...	...	...	...	...
55 - 59	694	347	347	...	...	...	...	...	...
60 - 64	453	228	225	...	...	...	...	...	...
65 - 69	323	161	162	...	...	...	...	...	...
70 - 74	250	118	132	...	...	...	...	...	...
75 +	450	204	246	...	...	...	...	...	...
Antigua and Barbuda - Antigua-et-Barbuda									
27 V 2011 (CDJC)									
Total	85 567	40 986	44 581	...	...	...	...	...	...
0 - 4	6 623	3 361	3 262	...	...	...	...	...	...
5 - 9	6 460	3 272	3 188	...	...	...	...	...	...
10 - 14	7 329	3 690	3 638	...	...	...	...	...	...
15 - 19	7 073	3 554	3 519	...	...	...	...	...	...
20 - 24	6 624	3 206	3 418	...	...	...	...	...	...
25 - 29	6 647	3 135	3 512	...	...	...	...	...	...
30 - 34	6 617	3 101	3 516	...	...	...	...	...	...
35 - 39	6 748	3 049	3 699	...	...	...	...	...	...
40 - 44	6 712	3 124	3 588	...	...	...	...	...	...
45 - 49	6 241	2 893	3 348	...	...	...	...	...	...
50 - 54	5 110	2 416	2 694	...	...	...	...	...	...
55 - 59	3 721	1 763	1 957	...	...	...	...	...	...
60 - 64	2 968	1 398	1 569	...	...	...	...	...	...
65 - 69	2 238	1 066	1 172	...	...	...	...	...	...
70 - 74	1 500	690	810	...	...	...	...	...	...
75 - 79	1 181	527	654	...	...	...	...	...	...
80 - 84	850	331	520	...	...	...	...	...	...
85 - 89	512	214	298	...	...	...	...	...	...
90 - 94	193	72	122	...	...	...	...	...	...
95 +	84	27	57	...	...	...	...	...	...
Unknown - Inconnu	136	96	40	...	...	...	...	...	...
Aruba									
1 VII 2017 (ESDJ)									
Total	110 848	52 544	58 304	...	...	...	...	...	...
0	1 245	661	584	...	...	...	...	...	...
1 - 4	5 422	2 795	2 627	...	...	...	...	...	...
5 - 9	6 707	3 404	3 303	...	...	...	...	...	...
10 - 14	7 115	3 638	3 477	...	...	...	...	...	...
15 - 19	7 271	3 665	3 605	...	...	...	...	...	...
20 - 24	6 566	3 365	3 201	...	...	...	...	...	...
25 - 29	6 532	3 282	3 251	...	...	...	...	...	...
30 - 34	6 790	3 200	3 590	...	...	...	...	...	...
35 - 39	7 303	3 346	3 957	...	...	...	...	...	...
40 - 44	7 532	3 478	4 054	...	...	...	...	...	...
45 - 49	8 721	3 997	4 723	...	...	...	...	...	...
50 - 54	9 086	4 198	4 888	...	...	...	...	...	...
55 - 59	8 810	4 092	4 718	...	...	...	...	...	...
60 - 64	7 191	3 261	3 931	...	...	...	...	...	...
65 - 69	5 389	2 441	2 948	...	...	...	...	...	...
70 - 74	3 754	1 617	2 137	...	...	...	...	...	...

7. Population by age, sex and urban/rural residence: latest available year, 2008 - 2017
Population selon l'âge, le sexe et la résidence, urbaine/rurale : dernière année disponible, 2008 - 2017 (continued - suite)

Continent, country or area, date, code[a] and age (in years) / Continent, pays ou zone, date, code[a] et âge (en annèes)	Total			Urban - Urbaine			Rural - Rurale		
	Both sexes Les deux sexes	Male Masculin	Female Féminin	Both sexes Les deux sexes	Male Masculin	Female Féminin	Both sexes Les deux sexes	Male Masculin	Female Féminin
AMERICA, NORTH - AMÉRIQUE DU NORD									
Aruba									
1 VII 2017 (ESDJ)									
75 - 79	2 620	1 117	1 503	...	...	...	...	...	...
80 - 84	1 618	585	1 034	...	...	...	...	...	...
85 - 89	832	308	525	...	...	...	...	...	...
90 - 94	251	69	183	...	...	...	...	...	...
95 +	91	26	65	...	...	...	...	...	...
Bahamas[27]									
1 VII 2016* (ESDF)									
Total	373 480	180 280	193 200	...	...	...	...	...	...
0	5 170	2 630	2 540	...	...	...	...	...	...
1 - 4	22 400	11 230	11 170	...	...	...	...	...	...
5 - 9	30 550	15 130	15 420	...	...	...	...	...	...
10 - 14	32 010	15 780	16 230	...	...	...	...	...	...
15 - 19	31 940	15 870	16 070	...	...	...	...	...	...
20 - 24	31 400	15 800	15 600	...	...	...	...	...	...
25 - 29	27 160	13 490	13 670	...	...	...	...	...	...
30 - 34	26 750	12 650	14 100	...	...	...	...	...	...
35 - 39	27 480	13 080	14 400	...	...	...	...	...	...
40 - 44	29 250	13 920	15 330	...	...	...	...	...	...
45 - 49	26 580	12 700	13 880	...	...	...	...	...	...
50 - 54	24 820	11 900	12 920	...	...	...	...	...	...
55 - 59	19 580	9 110	10 470	...	...	...	...	...	...
60 - 64	13 560	6 240	7 320	...	...	...	...	...	...
65 - 69	9 380	4 290	5 090	...	...	...	...	...	...
70 - 74	6 870	3 000	3 870	...	...	...	...	...	...
75 - 79	4 500	1 890	2 610	...	...	...	...	...	...
80 +	4 080	1 570	2 510	...	...	...	...	...	...
Barbados - Barbade[28]									
1 V 2010 (CDJC)									
Total	277 821	133 018	144 803	...	...	...	...	...	...
0 - 4	17 352	8 873	8 479	...	...	...	...	...	...
5 - 9	18 838	9 683	9 155	...	...	...	...	...	...
10 - 14	18 567	9 445	9 122	...	...	...	...	...	...
15 - 19	18 870	9 452	9 418	...	...	...	...	...	...
20 - 24	18 169	9 061	9 108	...	...	...	...	...	...
25 - 29	19 088	9 313	9 775	...	...	...	...	...	...
30 - 34	18 785	9 150	9 635	...	...	...	...	...	...
35 - 39	20 516	9 884	10 632	...	...	...	...	...	...
40 - 44	20 113	9 663	10 450	...	...	...	...	...	...
45 - 49	21 365	10 062	11 303	...	...	...	...	...	...
50 - 54	20 050	9 411	10 639	...	...	...	...	...	...
55 - 59	16 653	7 871	8 782	...	...	...	...	...	...
60 - 64	13 486	6 326	7 160	...	...	...	...	...	...
65 - 69	10 151	4 511	5 640	...	...	...	...	...	...
70 - 74	8 680	3 804	4 876	...	...	...	...	...	...
75 - 79	6 937	2 863	4 074	...	...	...	...	...	...
80 - 84	5 153	1 986	3 167	...	...	...	...	...	...
85 +	5 048	1 660	3 388	...	...	...	...	...	...
Belize									
1 VII 2017 (ESDJ)									
Total	*387 879*	*193 942*	*193 937*	...	...	...	...	...	...
0	*8 739*	*4 490*	*4 248*	...	...	...	...	...	...
1 - 4	*36 591*	*18 673*	*17 918*	...	...	...	...	...	...
5 - 9	*47 195*	*23 771*	*23 424*	...	...	...	...	...	...
10 - 14	*45 352*	*22 693*	*22 659*	...	...	...	...	...	...
15 - 19	*41 681*	*20 850*	*20 831*	...	...	...	...	...	...
20 - 24	*36 741*	*18 046*	*18 695*	...	...	...	...	...	...
25 - 29	*31 885*	*15 427*	*16 458*	...	...	...	...	...	...
30 - 34	*27 472*	*13 335*	*14 137*	...	...	...	...	...	...
35 - 39	*24 876*	*12 144*	*12 732*	...	...	...	...	...	...
40 - 44	*20 862*	*10 367*	*10 495*	...	...	...	...	...	...
45 - 49	*17 989*	*9 187*	*8 802*	...	...	...	...	...	...
50 - 54	*14 101*	*7 152*	*6 949*	...	...	...	...	...	...

7. Population by age, sex and urban/rural residence: latest available year, 2008 - 2017
Population selon l'âge, le sexe et la résidence, urbaine/rurale : dernière année disponible, 2008 - 2017 (continued - suite)

Continent, country or area, date, code[a] and age (in years) Continent, pays ou zone, date, code[a] et âge (en années)	Total			Urban - Urbaine			Rural - Rurale		
	Both sexes Les deux sexes	Male Masculin	Female Féminin	Both sexes Les deux sexes	Male Masculin	Female Féminin	Both sexes Les deux sexes	Male Masculin	Female Féminin
AMERICA, NORTH - AMÉRIQUE DU NORD									
Belize									
1 VII 2017 (ESDJ)									
55 - 59	10 392	5 416	4 976	...	...	...	...	...	...
60 - 64	7 484	3 957	3 527	...	...	...	...	...	...
65 - 69	5 288	2 814	2 474	...	...	...	...	...	...
70 - 74	4 205	2 230	1 975	...	...	...	...	...	...
75 - 79	3 082	1 564	1 518	...	...	...	...	...	...
80 +	3 770	1 776	1 994	...	...	...	...	...	...
Bermuda - Bermudes									
20 V 2010 (CDJC)[29]									
Total	64 237	30 858	33 379	64 237	30 858	33 379	-	-	-
0	709	372	337	709	372	337	-	-	-
1 - 4	2 858	1 479	1 379	2 858	1 479	1 379	-	-	-
5 - 9	3 456	1 759	1 697	3 456	1 759	1 697	-	-	-
10 - 14	3 481	1 706	1 775	3 481	1 706	1 775	-	-	-
15 - 19	3 431	1 682	1 749	3 431	1 682	1 749	-	-	-
20 - 24	3 342	1 608	1 734	3 342	1 608	1 734	-	-	-
25 - 29	4 076	1 947	2 129	4 076	1 947	2 129	-	-	-
30 - 34	4 645	2 259	2 386	4 645	2 259	2 386	-	-	-
35 - 39	5 050	2 572	2 478	5 050	2 572	2 478	-	-	-
40 - 44	5 158	2 588	2 570	5 158	2 588	2 570	-	-	-
45 - 49	5 731	2 811	2 920	5 731	2 811	2 920	-	-	-
50 - 54	5 427	2 531	2 896	5 427	2 531	2 896	-	-	-
55 - 59	4 498	2 146	2 352	4 498	2 146	2 352	-	-	-
60 - 64	3 692	1 733	1 959	3 692	1 733	1 959	-	-	-
65 - 69	2 807	1 290	1 517	2 807	1 290	1 517	-	-	-
70 - 74	2 163	961	1 202	2 163	961	1 202	-	-	-
75 - 79	1 768	747	1 021	1 768	747	1 021	-	-	-
80 - 84	1 120	432	688	1 120	432	688	-	-	-
85 - 89	584	185	399	584	185	399	-	-	-
90 - 94	187	41	146	187	41	146	-	-	-
95 - 99	48	8	40	48	8	40	-	-	-
100 +	6	1	5	6	1	5	-	-	-
1 VII 2017 (ESDJ)[9]									
Total	61 658	29 447	32 211	...	...	...	...	...	...
0	613	310	303	...	...	...	...	...	...
1 - 4	2 447	1 215	1 232	...	...	...	...	...	...
5 - 9	3 172	1 593	1 579	...	...	...	...	...	...
10 - 14	2 869	1 489	1 380	...	...	...	...	...	...
15 - 19	2 843	1 404	1 439	...	...	...	...	...	...
20 - 24	2 963	1 405	1 558	...	...	...	...	...	...
25 - 29	3 622	1 713	1 909	...	...	...	...	...	...
30 - 34	4 024	1 954	2 070	...	...	...	...	...	...
35 - 39	4 222	2 123	2 099	...	...	...	...	...	...
40 - 44	4 285	2 148	2 137	...	...	...	...	...	...
45 - 49	4 692	2 341	2 351	...	...	...	...	...	...
50 - 54	5 316	2 645	2 671	...	...	...	...	...	...
55 - 59	5 223	2 383	2 840	...	...	...	...	...	...
60 - 64	4 440	2 035	2 405	...	...	...	...	...	...
65 - 69	3 556	1 643	1 913	...	...	...	...	...	...
70 - 74	2 858	1 295	1 563	...	...	...	...	...	...
75 - 79	1 932	831	1 101	...	...	...	...	...	...
80 - 84	1 425	569	856	...	...	...	...	...	...
85 +	1 156	351	805	...	...	...	...	...	...
British Virgin Islands - Îles Vierges britanniques									
12 VII 2010 (CDFC)									
Total	28 054	13 820	14 234	...	...	...	...	...	...
0 - 4	2 134	1 126	1 008	...	...	...	...	...	...
5 - 9	2 090	1 065	1 025	...	...	...	...	...	...
10 - 14	2 044	1 032	1 012	...	...	...	...	...	...
15 - 19	1 767	867	900	...	...	...	...	...	...
20 - 24	1 720	789	931	...	...	...	...	...	...
25 - 29	2 316	1 126	1 190	...	...	...	...	...	...

Continent, country or area, date, code[a] and age (in years) / Continent, pays ou zone, date, code[a] et âge (en années)	Total			Urban - Urbaine			Rural - Rurale		
	Both sexes Les deux sexes	Male Masculin	Female Féminin	Both sexes Les deux sexes	Male Masculin	Female Féminin	Both sexes Les deux sexes	Male Masculin	Female Féminin
AMERICA, NORTH - AMÉRIQUE DU NORD									
British Virgin Islands - Îles Vierges britanniques									
12 VII 2010 (CDFC)									
30 - 34	2 537	1 165	1 372	...	...	...	...	...	...
35 - 39	2 599	1 226	1 373	...	...	...	...	...	...
40 - 44	2 559	1 236	1 323	...	...	...	...	...	...
45 - 49	2 338	1 193	1 145	...	...	...	...	...	...
50 - 54	1 842	962	880	...	...	...	...	...	...
55 - 59	1 387	680	707	...	...	...	...	...	...
60 - 64	1 028	541	487	...	...	...	...	...	...
65 - 69	670	350	320	...	...	...	...	...	...
70 - 74	415	204	211	...	...	...	...	...	...
75 - 79	230	98	132	...	...	...	...	...	...
80 - 84	216	91	125	...	...	...	...	...	...
85 - 89	84	39	45	...	...	...	...	...	...
90 +	78	30	48	...	...	...	...	...	...
Canada									
10 V 2016 (CDJC)[30]									
Total	35 151 730	17 264 200	17 887 530	28 575 665	13 912 050	14 663 615	6 576 065	3 352 150	3 223 910
0	369 735	189 085	180 645	303 795	155 030	148 765	65 935	34 055	31 880
1 - 4	1 529 060	783 945	745 115	1 248 230	639 935	608 295	280 830	144 010	136 820
5 - 9	2 018 130	1 034 685	983 445	1 633 720	836 950	796 770	384 410	197 740	186 670
10 - 14	1 922 645	985 200	937 445	1 546 225	791 500	754 730	376 420	193 700	182 720
15 - 19	2 026 160	1 039 215	986 940	1 641 330	839 980	801 345	384 830	199 235	185 595
20 - 24	2 242 695	1 144 495	1 098 200	1 907 165	967 775	939 390	335 525	176 715	158 805
25 - 29	2 285 990	1 144 475	1 141 515	1 976 755	986 505	990 255	309 235	157 970	151 265
30 - 34	2 329 400	1 148 290	1 181 105	1 989 865	978 690	1 011 170	339 535	169 605	169 935
35 - 39	2 288 365	1 118 635	1 169 730	1 924 280	935 630	988 645	364 085	183 000	181 085
40 - 44	2 255 135	1 104 445	1 150 690	1 871 860	910 205	961 655	383 280	194 240	189 035
45 - 49	2 359 965	1 157 755	1 202 205	1 925 635	939 350	986 290	434 325	218 410	215 915
50 - 54	2 678 070	1 318 755	1 359 320	2 120 605	1 038 360	1 082 250	557 465	280 395	277 070
55 - 59	2 620 240	1 285 190	1 335 050	2 029 030	986 135	1 042 895	591 210	299 055	292 155
60 - 64	2 290 510	1 114 880	1 175 630	1 745 665	835 295	910 375	544 850	279 585	265 260
65 - 69	1 972 475	953 070	1 019 405	1 506 495	710 615	795 875	465 985	242 455	223 535
70 - 74	1 420 875	677 975	742 900	1 097 395	507 680	589 710	323 480	170 290	153 190
75 - 79	1 021 850	469 550	552 305	817 520	363 230	454 285	204 335	106 315	98 020
80 - 84	749 645	325 760	423 885	622 775	262 700	360 075	126 875	63 065	63 810
85 - 89	482 525	185 535	296 985	413 945	155 020	258 925	68 575	30 510	38 065
90 - 94	223 505	68 675	154 835	196 075	58 750	137 325	27 435	9 920	17 510
95 - 99	56 525	13 245	43 280	49 945	11 535	38 410	6 585	1 705	4 870
100 +	8 230	1 340	6 895	7 355	1 175	6 180	875	160	710
1 VII 2017* (ESDJ)[31]									
Total	36 708 083	18 207 841	18 500 242	...	...	...	...	...	...
0	388 800	199 416	189 384	...	...	...	...	...	...
1 - 4	1 564 240	802 626	761 614	...	...	...	...	...	...
5 - 9	2 003 143	1 026 129	977 014	...	...	...	...	...	...
10 - 14	1 920 898	985 050	935 848	...	...	...	...	...	...
15 - 19	2 056 445	1 058 325	998 120	...	...	...	...	...	...
20 - 24	2 476 338	1 275 995	1 200 343	...	...	...	...	...	...
25 - 29	2 574 384	1 295 885	1 278 499	...	...	...	...	...	...
30 - 34	2 553 635	1 272 577	1 281 058	...	...	...	...	...	...
35 - 39	2 506 165	1 249 393	1 256 772	...	...	...	...	...	...
40 - 44	2 364 959	1 178 674	1 186 285	...	...	...	...	...	...
45 - 49	2 405 165	1 202 547	1 202 618	...	...	...	...	...	...
50 - 54	2 640 429	1 324 561	1 315 868	...	...	...	...	...	...
55 - 59	2 683 302	1 338 117	1 345 185	...	...	...	...	...	...
60 - 64	2 374 636	1 172 908	1 201 728	...	...	...	...	...	...
65 - 69	1 997 090	974 624	1 022 466	...	...	...	...	...	...
70 - 74	1 547 668	740 352	807 316	...	...	...	...	...	...
75 - 79	1 077 431	494 332	583 099	...	...	...	...	...	...
80 - 84	763 413	331 080	432 333	...	...	...	...	...	...
85 - 89	504 232	195 547	308 685	...	...	...	...	...	...
90 - 94	236 012	74 138	161 874	...	...	...	...	...	...

Continent, country or area, date, code[a] and age (in years) / Continent, pays ou zone, date, code[a] et âge (en années)	Total			Urban - Urbaine			Rural - Rurale		
	Both sexes Les deux sexes	Male Masculin	Female Féminin	Both sexes Les deux sexes	Male Masculin	Female Féminin	Both sexes Les deux sexes	Male Masculin	Female Féminin
AMERICA, NORTH - AMÉRIQUE DU NORD									
Canada									
1 VII 2017* (ESDJ)[31]									
95 - 99	63 078	14 822	48 256	...	...	...	...	...	...
100 +	6 620	743	5 877	...	...	...	...	...	...
Cayman Islands - Îles Caïmanes									
31 XII 2017 (ESDJ)									
Total	63 415	32 212	31 203	...	...	...	...	...	...
0 - 14	10 643	5 745	4 898	...	...	...	...	...	...
15 - 24	5 922	3 332	2 590	...	...	...	...	...	...
25 - 34	11 059	5 806	5 253	...	...	...	...	...	...
35 - 44	12 637	6 266	6 372	...	...	...	...	...	...
45 - 54	11 848	5 743	6 106	...	...	...	...	...	...
55 - 64	6 003	2 946	3 057	...	...	...	...	...	...
65 +	5 162	2 329	2 833	...	...	...	...	...	...
Unknown - Inconnu	140	47	93	...	...	...	...	...	...
Costa Rica[32]									
1 VII 2017 (ESDJ)									
Total	4 946 700	2 405 636	2 541 064	3 592 070	1 722 499	1 869 571	1 354 630	683 137	671 493
0 - 4	306 949	153 647	153 302	214 442	108 334	106 108	92 507	45 313	47 194
5 - 9	360 212	180 403	179 809	250 531	125 054	125 477	109 681	55 349	54 332
10 - 14	374 944	200 123	174 821	256 361	134 902	121 459	118 583	65 221	53 362
15 - 19	427 853	216 776	211 077	308 577	155 907	152 670	119 276	60 869	58 407
20 - 24	420 889	215 301	205 588	306 411	155 599	150 812	114 478	59 702	54 776
25 - 29	387 604	188 815	198 789	284 834	139 304	145 530	102 770	49 511	53 259
30 - 34	373 541	176 356	197 185	276 431	133 882	142 549	97 110	42 474	54 636
35 - 39	336 139	161 288	174 851	249 839	117 883	131 956	86 300	43 405	42 895
40 - 44	310 102	145 430	164 672	228 842	107 360	121 482	81 260	38 070	43 190
45 - 49	300 003	136 591	163 412	212 240	94 072	118 168	87 763	42 519	45 244
50 - 54	314 660	146 253	168 407	225 177	101 114	124 063	89 483	45 139	44 344
55 - 59	278 642	133 924	144 718	205 897	96 114	109 783	72 745	37 810	34 935
60 - 64	234 485	108 422	126 063	178 383	78 724	99 659	56 102	29 698	26 404
65 - 69	175 473	83 152	92 321	135 927	62 869	73 058	39 546	20 283	19 263
70 - 74	130 593	55 495	75 098	100 171	39 917	60 254	30 422	15 578	14 844
75 - 79	96 313	50 799	45 514	70 404	34 731	35 673	25 909	16 068	9 841
80 - 84	59 302	28 176	31 126	44 325	20 913	23 412	14 977	7 263	7 714
85 - 89	36 935	16 164	20 771	27 564	11 207	16 357	9 371	4 957	4 414
90 - 94	16 347	6 159	10 188	11 610	3 491	8 119	4 737	2 668	2 069
95 +	5 714	2 362	3 352	4 104	1 122	2 982	1 610	1 240	370
Cuba									
1 VII 2017 (ESDJ)									
Total	11 230 142	5 591 525	5 638 617	8 642 754	4 204 316	4 438 438	2 587 389	1 387 210	1 200 179
0	115 444	60 044	55 400	93 708	48 715	44 993	21 736	11 329	10 407
1 - 4	492 361	254 910	237 451	389 472	201 897	187 576	102 889	53 013	49 876
5 - 9	609 721	313 515	296 206	454 429	233 432	220 997	155 292	80 083	75 210
10 - 14	604 447	310 925	293 523	453 537	232 515	221 022	150 911	78 410	72 501
15 - 19	701 528	361 278	340 250	536 592	274 817	261 776	164 936	86 462	78 474
20 - 24	703 345	363 326	340 019	537 392	274 468	262 924	165 953	88 858	77 095
25 - 29	815 236	420 495	394 742	626 975	317 233	309 742	188 261	103 262	85 000
30 - 34	733 969	375 886	358 083	564 260	283 018	281 242	169 709	92 868	76 841
35 - 39	620 510	315 219	305 291	466 840	231 724	235 116	153 670	83 495	70 176
40 - 44	863 483	432 219	431 264	645 195	314 730	330 465	218 288	117 489	100 799
45 - 49	998 786	494 150	504 637	754 026	361 857	392 169	244 761	132 293	112 468
50 - 54	1 015 326	496 212	519 114	795 250	377 850	417 401	220 076	118 363	101 714
55 - 59	720 133	348 839	371 295	564 643	265 510	299 133	155 491	83 329	72 162
60 - 64	594 872	284 945	309 928	466 798	216 032	250 766	128 075	68 913	59 162
65 - 69	524 160	250 785	273 375	416 115	192 245	223 870	108 045	58 540	49 505
70 - 74	426 148	199 531	226 618	337 604	152 103	185 502	88 544	47 428	41 116
75 - 79	312 848	144 867	167 981	246 953	108 631	138 322	65 896	36 236	29 660
80 - 84	196 108	88 163	107 945	152 991	64 198	88 793	43 117	23 965	19 152
85 +	181 722	76 221	105 501	139 979	53 344	86 635	41 744	22 877	18 867

Continent, country or area, date, code[a] and age (in years) Continent, pays ou zone, date, code[a] et âge (en années)	Total			Urban - Urbaine			Rural - Rurale		
	Both sexes Les deux sexes	Male Masculin	Female Féminin	Both sexes Les deux sexes	Male Masculin	Female Féminin	Both sexes Les deux sexes	Male Masculin	Female Féminin
AMERICA, NORTH - AMÉRIQUE DU NORD									
Curaçao[10]									
1 VII 2017 (ESDJ)									
Total...................	160 175	73 246	86 929	...	...	...	...	...	...
0	1 657	839	818	...	...	...	...	...	...
1 - 4	7 823	3 989	3 834	...	...	...	...	...	...
5 - 9	9 830	5 064	4 766	...	...	...	...	...	...
10 - 14	9 862	4 996	4 867	...	...	...	...	...	...
15 - 19	10 249	5 305	4 944	...	...	...	...	...	...
20 - 24	9 332	4 681	4 651	...	...	...	...	...	...
25 - 29	9 017	4 180	4 838	...	...	...	...	...	...
30 - 34	9 479	4 216	5 263	...	...	...	...	...	...
35 - 39	9 237	3 951	5 286	...	...	...	...	...	...
40 - 44	10 088	4 422	5 666	...	...	...	...	...	...
45 - 49	11 888	5 316	6 573	...	...	...	...	...	...
50 - 54	12 709	5 603	7 106	...	...	...	...	...	...
55 - 59	12 382	5 334	7 048	...	...	...	...	...	...
60 - 64	10 441	4 551	5 890	...	...	...	...	...	...
65 - 69	8 997	3 973	5 024	...	...	...	...	...	...
70 - 74	6 935	2 900	4 035	...	...	...	...	...	...
75 - 79	4 589	1 880	2 709	...	...	...	...	...	...
80 - 84	3 151	1 229	1 923	...	...	...	...	...	...
85 - 89	1 629	578	1 052	...	...	...	...	...	...
90 - 94	661	198	463	...	...	...	...	...	...
95 - 99	186	35	151	...	...	...	...	...	...
100 + ...	40	12	28	...	...	...	...	...	...
Dominica - Dominique									
14 V 2011 (CDFC)									
Total...................	68 913	34 973	33 940	...	...	...	...	...	...
0 - 4	6 380	3 240	3 140	...	...	...	...	...	...
5 - 9	5 096	2 601	2 495	...	...	...	...	...	...
10 - 14	5 822	2 946	2 876	...	...	...	...	...	...
15 - 19	6 297	3 237	3 060	...	...	...	...	...	...
20 - 24	5 258	2 691	2 567	...	...	...	...	...	...
25 - 29	4 861	2 389	2 472	...	...	...	...	...	...
30 - 34	4 029	2 118	1 911	...	...	...	...	...	...
35 - 39	4 507	2 271	2 236	...	...	...	...	...	...
40 - 44	4 953	2 544	2 409	...	...	...	...	...	...
45 - 49	4 472	2 337	2 135	...	...	...	...	...	...
50 - 54	3 946	2 162	1 784	...	...	...	...	...	...
55 - 59	3 093	1 682	1 411	...	...	...	...	...	...
60 - 64	2 493	1 281	1 212	...	...	...	...	...	...
65 - 69	2 159	1 054	1 105	...	...	...	...	...	...
70 - 74	1 867	884	983	...	...	...	...	...	...
75 - 79	1 587	724	863	...	...	...	...	...	...
80 - 84	1 102	467	635	...	...	...	...	...	...
85 - 89	599	212	387	...	...	...	...	...	...
90 - 94	274	101	173	...	...	...	...	...	...
95 + ...	118	32	86	...	...	...	...	...	...
Dominican Republic - République dominicaine[2]									
1 VII 2017 (ESDJ)									
Total...................	10 169 172	5 082 876	5 086 296	8 163 504	4 010 852	4 152 652	2 005 668	1 072 024	933 644
0 - 4	965 628	492 808	472 820	772 173	392 468	379 705	193 455	100 340	93 115
0	192 216	98 634	93 582	...	...	...	...	...	...
1 - 4	773 412	394 174	379 238	...	...	...	...	...	...
5 - 9	967 050	492 702	474 348	767 897	388 780	379 117	199 153	103 922	95 231
10 - 14	969 552	492 107	477 445	769 898	386 714	383 184	199 654	105 393	94 261
15 - 19	951 536	480 035	471 501	762 290	378 678	383 612	189 246	101 357	87 889
20 - 24	908 884	455 440	453 444	736 462	362 329	374 133	172 422	93 111	79 311
25 - 29	844 097	420 715	423 382	689 010	337 215	351 795	155 087	83 500	71 587
30 - 34	763 030	377 850	385 180	622 770	303 203	319 567	140 260	74 647	65 613
35 - 39	688 020	339 877	348 143	559 839	271 761	288 078	128 181	68 116	60 065
40 - 44	619 955	306 097	313 858	503 136	243 768	259 368	116 819	62 329	54 490
45 - 49	557 593	275 488	282 105	451 222	218 086	233 136	106 371	57 402	48 969

Continent, country or area, date, code[a] and age (in years) / Continent, pays ou zone, date, code[a] et âge (en années)	Total			Urban - Urbaine			Rural - Rurale		
	Both sexes Les deux sexes	Male Masculin	Female Féminin	Both sexes Les deux sexes	Male Masculin	Female Féminin	Both sexes Les deux sexes	Male Masculin	Female Féminin
AMERICA, NORTH - AMÉRIQUE DU NORD									
Dominican Republic - République dominicaine[2]									
1 VII 2017 (ESDJ)									
50 - 54	495 065	245 299	249 766	399 183	193 089	206 094	95 882	52 210	43 672
55 - 59	416 445	206 257	210 188	332 567	160 275	172 292	83 878	45 982	37 896
60 - 64	331 015	162 912	168 103	261 568	124 880	136 688	69 447	38 032	31 415
65 - 69	248 523	121 894	126 629	193 769	91 820	101 949	54 754	30 074	24 680
70 - 74	177 500	86 739	90 761	137 449	64 639	72 810	40 051	22 100	17 951
75 - 79	126 407	61 133	65 274	97 318	45 037	52 281	29 089	16 096	12 993
80 +	138 872	65 523	73 349	106 953	48 110	58 843	31 919	17 413	14 506
El Salvador[33]									
1 VII 2017 (ESDJ)									
Total	6 581 940	3 098 633	3 483 307	...	...	...	...	...	...
0	111 299	56 941	54 358	...	...	...	...	...	...
1 - 4	446 740	228 345	218 395	...	...	...	...	...	...
5 - 9	567 307	289 964	277 343	...	...	...	...	...	...
10 - 14	614 163	314 135	300 028	...	...	...	...	...	...
15 - 19	682 932	347 360	335 572	...	...	...	...	...	...
20 - 24	703 384	351 669	351 715	...	...	...	...	...	...
25 - 29	597 142	284 515	312 627	...	...	...	...	...	...
30 - 34	474 137	210 535	263 602	...	...	...	...	...	...
35 - 39	406 945	173 276	233 669	...	...	...	...	...	...
40 - 44	376 093	159 892	216 201	...	...	...	...	...	...
45 - 49	340 258	145 527	194 731	...	...	...	...	...	...
50 - 54	291 141	124 103	167 038	...	...	...	...	...	...
55 - 59	242 500	103 228	139 272	...	...	...	...	...	...
60 - 64	203 360	87 005	116 355	...	...	...	...	...	...
65 - 69	167 862	71 983	95 879	...	...	...	...	...	...
70 - 74	132 816	56 878	75 938	...	...	...	...	...	...
75 - 79	100 621	42 776	57 845	...	...	...	...	...	...
80 - 84	67 398	28 096	39 302	...	...	...	...	...	...
85 +	55 842	22 405	33 437	...	...	...	...	...	...
Greenland - Groenland[34]									
1 VII 2017 (ESDJ)									
Total	56 171	29 651	26 520	48 527	25 435	23 092	7 644	4 216	3 428
0	841	442	399	695	365	330	146	77	69
1 - 4	3 172	1 650	1 522	2 736	1 422	1 314	436	228	208
5 - 9	3 897	2 030	1 867	3 342	1 743	1 599	555	287	268
10 - 14	3 887	1 976	1 911	3 308	1 675	1 633	579	301	278
15 - 19	3 801	1 903	1 898	3 228	1 617	1 611	573	286	287
20 - 24	4 333	2 199	2 134	3 745	1 889	1 856	588	310	278
25 - 29	4 639	2 385	2 254	4 038	2 071	1 967	601	314	287
30 - 34	4 110	2 104	2 006	3 652	1 833	1 819	458	271	187
35 - 39	3 560	1 867	1 693	3 142	1 635	1 507	418	232	186
40 - 44	2 986	1 663	1 323	2 607	1 448	1 159	379	215	164
45 - 49	3 891	2 093	1 798	3 353	1 806	1 547	538	287	251
50 - 54	5 132	2 762	2 370	4 450	2 359	2 091	682	403	279
55 - 59	4 337	2 419	1 918	3 736	2 057	1 679	601	362	239
60 - 64	3 032	1 696	1 336	2 570	1 423	1 147	462	273	189
65 - 69	1 861	1 100	761	1 598	933	665	263	167	96
70 - 74	1 353	753	600	1 162	638	524	191	115	76
75 - 79	786	390	396	682	334	348	104	56	48
80 - 84	365	159	206	312	134	178	53	25	28
85 - 89	156	50	106	141	43	98	15	7	8
90 - 94	29	9	20	27	9	18	2	-	2
95 +	3	1	2	3	1	2	-	-	-
Grenada - Grenade									
1 VII 2017 (ESDF)									
Total	111 467	56 222	55 245	...	...	...	...	...	...
0	1 375	735	640	...	...	...	...	...	...
1 - 4	6 779	3 547	3 232	...	...	...	...	...	...
5 - 9	7 427	3 793	3 634	...	...	...	...	...	...
10 - 14	8 668	4 392	4 276	...	...	...	...	...	...
15 - 19	9 687	4 869	4 818	...	...	...	...	...	...

7. Population by age, sex and urban/rural residence: latest available year, 2008 - 2017
Population selon l'âge, le sexe et la résidence, urbaine/rurale : dernière année disponible, 2008 - 2017 (continued - suite)

Continent, country or area, date, code[a] and age (in years) / Continent, pays ou zone, date, code[a] et âge (en années)	Total			Urban - Urbaine			Rural - Rurale		
	Both sexes Les deux sexes	Male Masculin	Female Féminin	Both sexes Les deux sexes	Male Masculin	Female Féminin	Both sexes Les deux sexes	Male Masculin	Female Féminin
AMERICA, NORTH - AMÉRIQUE DU NORD									
Grenada - Grenade									
1 VII 2017 (ESDF)									
20 - 24	9 824	5 027	4 797	...	...	...	...	...	...
25 - 29	9 480	4 758	4 722	...	...	...	...	...	...
30 - 34	7 110	3 596	3 514	...	...	...	...	...	...
35 - 39	6 554	3 424	3 130	...	...	...	...	...	...
40 - 44	6 024	3 120	2 904	...	...	...	...	...	...
45 - 49	6 614	3 416	3 198	...	...	...	...	...	...
50 - 54	6 374	3 179	3 195	...	...	...	...	...	...
55 - 59	4 686	2 455	2 231	...	...	...	...	...	...
60 - 64	3 571	1 806	1 765	...	...	...	...	...	...
65 - 69	2 758	1 261	1 497	...	...	...	...	...	...
70 - 74	2 393	1 106	1 287	...	...	...	...	...	...
75 - 79	1 731	732	999	...	...	...	...	...	...
80 - 84	1 112	417	695	...	...	...	...	...	...
85 - 89	527	168	359	...	...	...	...	...	...
90 +	275	78	197	...	...	...	...	...	...
Guadeloupe[35]									
1 I 2017* (ESDJ)									
Total	393 640	180 409	213 231	...	...	...	...	...	...
0 - 4	22 013	11 198	10 815	...	...	...	...	...	...
5 - 9	25 177	12 836	12 341	...	...	...	...	...	...
10 - 14	29 003	14 532	14 471	...	...	...	...	...	...
15 - 19	27 718	14 081	13 637	...	...	...	...	...	...
20 - 24	19 002	9 706	9 296	...	...	...	...	...	...
25 - 29	18 485	8 184	10 301	...	...	...	...	...	...
30 - 34	18 437	7 559	10 878	...	...	...	...	...	...
35 - 39	20 100	8 150	11 950	...	...	...	...	...	...
40 - 44	27 185	11 371	15 814	...	...	...	...	...	...
45 - 49	30 071	13 087	16 984	...	...	...	...	...	...
50 - 54	32 443	14 678	17 765	...	...	...	...	...	...
55 - 59	29 053	13 567	15 486	...	...	...	...	...	...
60 - 64	25 526	11 744	13 782	...	...	...	...	...	...
65 - 69	22 133	10 120	12 013	...	...	...	...	...	...
70 - 74	16 521	7 450	9 071	...	...	...	...	...	...
75 - 79	12 158	5 271	6 887	...	...	...	...	...	...
80 - 84	9 368	3 804	5 564	...	...	...	...	...	...
85 - 89	5 435	1 839	3 596	...	...	...	...	...	...
90 - 94	2 804	913	1 891	...	...	...	...	...	...
95 +	1 008	319	689	...	...	...	...	...	...
Guatemala[24]									
1 VII 2015 (ESDJ)									
Total	16 176 133	7 903 664	8 272 469	...	...	...	...	...	...
0 - 4	2 262 514	1 153 297	1 109 217	...	...	...	...	...	...
5 - 9	2 142 308	1 090 294	1 052 014	...	...	...	...	...	...
10 - 14	1 988 541	1 008 018	980 523	...	...	...	...	...	...
15 - 19	1 776 352	893 687	882 665	...	...	...	...	...	...
20 - 24	1 553 450	771 615	781 835	...	...	...	...	...	...
25 - 29	1 286 639	624 841	661 798	...	...	...	...	...	...
30 - 34	1 099 039	517 919	581 120	...	...	...	...	...	...
35 - 39	889 673	403 769	485 904	...	...	...	...	...	...
40 - 44	707 191	311 703	395 488	...	...	...	...	...	...
45 - 49	563 431	248 840	314 591	...	...	...	...	...	...
50 - 54	459 432	206 306	253 126	...	...	...	...	...	...
55 - 59	377 242	173 501	203 741	...	...	...	...	...	...
60 - 64	330 803	155 222	175 581	...	...	...	...	...	...
65 +	739 518	344 652	394 866	...	...	...	...	...	...
Haiti - Haïti[36]									
1 VII 2010 (ESDJ)									
Total	10 085 214	4 993 731	5 091 483	4 817 666	2 321 608	2 496 059	5 267 548	2 672 123	2 595 424
0 - 4	1 263 322	644 550	618 772	532 352	274 597	257 755	730 970	369 953	361 017
5 - 9	1 195 479	608 495	586 984	493 368	249 982	243 386	702 111	358 513	343 598
10 - 14	1 158 478	588 618	569 860	532 573	255 002	277 571	625 905	333 616	292 289
15 - 19	1 092 364	551 467	540 897	583 183	276 258	306 925	509 181	275 209	233 972

Continent, country or area, date, code[a] and age (in years) Continent, pays ou zone, date, code[a] et âge (en années)	Total			Urban - Urbaine			Rural - Rurale		
	Both sexes Les deux sexes	Male Masculin	Female Féminin	Both sexes Les deux sexes	Male Masculin	Female Féminin	Both sexes Les deux sexes	Male Masculin	Female Féminin
AMERICA, NORTH - AMÉRIQUE DU NORD									
Haiti - Haïti[36]									
1 VII 2010 (ESDJ)									
20 - 24	1 019 589	509 042	510 547	600 175	296 233	303 943	419 414	212 809	206 604
25 - 29	919 636	454 123	465 513	537 063	267 198	269 865	382 573	186 925	195 648
30 - 34	702 596	340 518	362 078	390 054	189 432	200 622	312 542	151 086	161 456
35 - 39	548 004	261 157	286 847	272 855	128 575	144 280	275 149	132 582	142 567
40 - 44	488 482	235 182	253 300	225 057	106 072	118 985	263 425	129 110	134 315
45 - 49	423 377	204 077	219 300	179 712	81 240	98 472	243 665	122 837	120 828
50 - 54	342 913	166 418	176 495	138 580	61 854	76 726	204 333	104 564	99 769
55 - 59	284 731	136 034	148 697	107 391	46 062	61 329	177 340	89 972	87 368
60 - 64	206 835	95 939	110 896	73 562	29 974	43 588	133 273	65 965	67 308
65 - 69	175 898	81 854	94 044	61 671	24 975	36 696	114 227	56 879	57 348
70 - 74	129 436	58 181	71 255	44 448	17 100	27 347	84 988	41 081	43 908
75 - 79	80 898	35 538	45 360	27 630	10 473	17 158	53 268	25 065	28 202
80 +	53 176	22 538	30 638	17 992	6 581	11 412	35 184	15 957	19 226
1 VII 2015 (ESDJ)									
Total	10 911 819	5 408 465	5 503 354	...	...	...	...	...	...
0 - 4	1 288 122	657 439	630 683	...	...	...	...	...	...
5 - 9	1 229 531	626 512	603 019	...	...	...	...	...	...
10 - 14	1 176 046	597 528	578 518	...	...	...	...	...	...
15 - 19	1 134 999	574 685	560 314	...	...	...	...	...	...
20 - 24	1 061 190	531 790	529 400	...	...	...	...	...	...
25 - 29	985 754	489 910	495 844	...	...	...	...	...	...
30 - 34	888 731	437 789	450 942	...	...	...	...	...	...
35 - 39	676 720	327 116	349 604	...	...	...	...	...	...
40 - 44	526 642	250 559	276 083	...	...	...	...	...	...
45 - 49	467 790	224 321	243 469	...	...	...	...	...	...
50 - 54	403 336	193 540	209 796	...	...	...	...	...	...
55 - 59	322 085	155 116	166 969	...	...	...	...	...	...
60 - 64	261 216	123 379	137 837	...	...	...	...	...	...
65 - 69	182 089	83 131	98 958	...	...	...	...	...	...
70 - 74	144 907	66 031	78 876	...	...	...	...	...	...
75 - 79	96 066	41 905	54 161	...	...	...	...	...	...
80 +	66 595	27 714	38 881	...	...	...	...	...	...
Honduras									
10 VIII 2013 (CDFC)									
Total	8 303 771	4 052 316	4 251 456	4 480 746	2 116 113	2 364 633	3 823 025	1 936 203	1 886 823
0 - 4	971 015	494 034	476 980	485 103	247 341	237 762	485 911	246 693	239 218
5 - 9	958 543	489 821	468 723	472 721	240 952	231 769	485 823	248 868	236 954
10 - 14	1 020 406	520 842	499 564	499 521	251 358	248 163	520 885	269 485	251 400
15 - 19	982 164	487 949	494 215	523 989	248 745	275 244	458 175	239 204	218 971
20 - 24	840 800	398 093	442 708	483 289	219 539	263 750	357 511	178 554	178 957
25 - 29	656 443	303 379	353 065	384 221	171 360	212 861	272 222	132 019	140 203
30 - 34	567 367	262 951	304 416	329 661	147 590	182 072	237 705	115 361	122 344
35 - 39	484 740	224 965	259 775	277 833	124 524	153 309	206 907	100 441	106 465
40 - 44	399 555	190 323	209 232	231 557	106 187	125 370	167 998	84 135	83 862
45 - 49	318 026	150 635	167 391	183 503	84 007	99 495	134 524	66 628	67 896
50 - 54	293 256	141 174	152 082	167 798	77 351	90 447	125 458	63 823	61 636
55 - 59	210 708	101 062	109 646	116 409	53 286	63 124	94 299	47 777	46 522
60 - 64	189 636	91 291	98 345	103 821	47 002	56 819	85 815	44 290	41 526
65 - 69	135 709	64 441	71 267	72 921	32 263	40 657	62 788	32 178	30 610
70 - 74	106 566	51 803	54 762	57 407	25 756	31 650	49 159	26 047	23 112
75 - 79	78 407	38 419	39 988	41 388	18 486	22 902	37 019	19 933	17 086
80 - 84	48 965	22 977	25 988	26 407	11 230	15 177	22 558	11 748	10 810
85 - 89	29 532	13 681	15 851	16 153	6 682	9 471	13 380	7 000	6 380
90 - 94	8 241	3 162	5 079	4 867	1 717	3 150	3 374	1 445	1 929
95 +	3 692	1 313	2 379	2 177	738	1 439	1 515	575	940
Jamaica - Jamaïque									
4 IV 2011 (CDJC)									
Total	2 697 983	1 334 533	1 363 450	1 454 151	700 957	753 194	1 243 832	633 576	610 256
0 - 4	209 871	106 107	103 764	109 121	55 157	53 965	100 750	50 950	49 799
5 - 9	226 378	114 792	111 586	114 520	57 817	56 703	111 858	56 975	54 883
10 - 14	266 586	136 183	130 403	138 596	70 428	68 168	127 990	65 755	62 235
15 - 19	274 658	139 777	134 881	143 644	72 173	71 471	131 014	67 604	63 410

Continent, country or area, date, code[a] and age (in years) / Continent, pays ou zone, date, code[a] et âge (en années)	Total			Urban - Urbaine			Rural - Rurale		
	Both sexes Les deux sexes	Male Masculin	Female Féminin	Both sexes Les deux sexes	Male Masculin	Female Féminin	Both sexes Les deux sexes	Male Masculin	Female Féminin
AMERICA, NORTH - AMÉRIQUE DU NORD									
Jamaica - Jamaïque									
4 IV 2011 (CDJC)									
20 - 24	250 711	125 243	125 468	140 770	68 692	72 078	109 941	56 551	53 390
25 - 29	226 120	109 919	116 201	129 961	61 980	67 981	96 159	47 939	48 220
30 - 34	185 495	87 810	97 685	106 228	49 452	56 776	79 267	38 358	40 909
35 - 39	183 756	86 647	97 109	103 560	47 408	56 152	80 196	39 239	40 957
40 - 44	173 924	85 656	88 268	97 069	46 377	50 693	76 855	39 279	37 575
45 - 49	155 389	79 201	76 188	88 044	41 385	46 658	67 345	37 816	29 530
50 - 54	137 895	67 297	70 598	74 271	34 341	39 930	63 624	32 956	30 668
55 - 59	100 798	50 717	50 081	54 090	26 020	28 070	46 708	24 697	22 011
60 - 64	88 057	44 407	43 650	46 868	22 549	24 319	41 189	21 858	19 331
65 - 69	65 164	32 543	32 621	33 182	15 691	17 491	31 982	16 852	15 130
70 - 74	51 276	24 627	26 649	25 354	11 785	13 569	25 922	12 842	13 080
75 - 79	42 762	19 847	22 915	20 542	9 085	11 458	22 220	10 762	11 457
80 - 84	30 738	13 258	17 480	14 941	6 132	8 809	15 797	7 126	8 671
85 - 89	18 457	7 267	11 190	8 789	3 151	5 638	9 668	4 116	5 552
90 - 94	6 921	2 303	4 618	3 238	957	2 281	3 683	1 346	2 337
95 - 99	2 503	808	1 695	1 119	326	793	1 384	482	902
100 +	524	124	400	243	53	190	281	71	210
1 VII 2017 (ESDJ)									
Total	2 728 915	1 351 375	1 377 540	...	...	...	...	...	...
0 - 4	180 672	92 151	88 521	...	...	...	...	...	...
5 - 9	200 295	101 561	98 734	...	...	...	...	...	...
10 - 14	215 272	108 949	106 323	...	...	...	...	...	...
15 - 19	247 511	126 151	121 360	...	...	...	...	...	...
20 - 24	271 136	137 643	133 493	...	...	...	...	...	...
25 - 29	243 420	121 867	121 553	...	...	...	...	...	...
30 - 34	217 119	105 767	111 352	...	...	...	...	...	...
35 - 39	183 616	87 269	96 347	...	...	...	...	...	...
40 - 44	172 149	80 997	91 152	...	...	...	...	...	...
45 - 49	171 811	82 738	89 073	...	...	...	...	...	...
50 - 54	153 454	77 004	76 450	...	...	...	...	...	...
55 - 59	133 003	66 170	66 833	...	...	...	...	...	...
60 - 64	99 197	49 379	49 818	...	...	...	...	...	...
65 - 69	80 133	40 443	39 690	...	...	...	...	...	...
70 - 74	59 150	29 002	30 148	...	...	...	...	...	...
75 +	100 977	44 284	56 693	...	...	...	...	...	...
Martinique									
1 I 2017* (ESDJ)									
Total	374 780	173 293	201 487	...	...	...	...	...	...
0 - 4	18 526	9 457	9 069	...	...	...	...	...	...
5 - 9	21 964	11 264	10 700	...	...	...	...	...	...
10 - 14	24 061	12 219	11 842	...	...	...	...	...	...
15 - 19	23 980	12 519	11 461	...	...	...	...	...	...
20 - 24	17 552	8 991	8 561	...	...	...	...	...	...
25 - 29	17 063	7 867	9 196	...	...	...	...	...	...
30 - 34	17 625	7 523	10 102	...	...	...	...	...	...
35 - 39	18 086	7 720	10 366	...	...	...	...	...	...
40 - 44	23 443	10 022	13 421	...	...	...	...	...	...
45 - 49	29 641	13 170	16 471	...	...	...	...	...	...
50 - 54	33 113	14 950	18 163	...	...	...	...	...	...
55 - 59	29 928	13 964	15 964	...	...	...	...	...	...
60 - 64	25 957	11 916	14 041	...	...	...	...	...	...
65 - 69	22 031	9 948	12 083	...	...	...	...	...	...
70 - 74	16 867	7 669	9 198	...	...	...	...	...	...
75 - 79	13 670	6 061	7 609	...	...	...	...	...	...
80 - 84	10 371	4 361	6 010	...	...	...	...	...	...
85 - 89	6 389	2 417	3 972	...	...	...	...	...	...
90 - 94	3 067	921	2 146	...	...	...	...	...	...
95 +	1 446	334	1 112	...	...	...	...	...	...
Mexico - Mexique									
12 VI 2010 (CDFC)[37]									
Total	112 336 538	54 855 231	57 481 307	86 287 410	41 946 540	44 340 870	26 049 128	12 908 691	13 140 437
0 - 4	10 528 322	5 346 943	5 181 379	7 766 149	3 945 636	3 820 513	2 762 173	1 401 307	1 360 866

7. Population by age, sex and urban/rural residence: latest available year, 2008 - 2017
Population selon l'âge, le sexe et la résidence, urbaine/rurale : dernière année disponible, 2008 - 2017 (continued - suite)

Continent, country or area, date, code[a] and age (in years) / Continent, pays ou zone, date, code[a] et âge (en années)	Total			Urban - Urbaine			Rural - Rurale		
	Both sexes Les deux sexes	Male Masculin	Female Féminin	Both sexes Les deux sexes	Male Masculin	Female Féminin	Both sexes Les deux sexes	Male Masculin	Female Féminin
AMERICA, NORTH - AMÉRIQUE DU NORD									
Mexico - Mexique									
12 VI 2010 (CDFC)[37]									
5 - 9	11 047 537	5 604 175	5 443 362	8 124 337	4 124 524	3 999 813	2 923 200	1 479 651	1 443 549
10 - 14	10 939 937	5 547 613	5 392 324	7 974 649	4 041 649	3 933 000	2 965 288	1 505 964	1 459 324
15 - 19	11 026 112	5 520 121	5 505 991	8 191 229	4 097 876	4 093 353	2 834 883	1 422 245	1 412 638
20 - 24	9 892 271	4 813 204	5 079 067	7 725 598	3 775 245	3 950 353	2 166 673	1 037 959	1 128 714
25 - 29	8 788 177	4 205 975	4 582 202	6 985 279	3 354 569	3 630 710	1 802 898	851 406	951 492
30 - 34	8 470 798	4 026 031	4 444 767	6 719 047	3 188 789	3 530 258	1 751 751	837 242	914 509
35 - 39	8 292 987	3 964 738	4 328 249	6 642 253	3 160 713	3 481 540	1 650 734	804 025	846 709
40 - 44	7 009 226	3 350 322	3 658 904	5 633 205	2 676 230	2 956 975	1 376 021	674 092	701 929
45 - 49	5 928 730	2 824 364	3 104 366	4 739 911	2 241 753	2 498 158	1 188 819	582 611	606 208
50 - 54	5 064 291	2 402 451	2 661 840	4 051 487	1 904 317	2 147 170	1 012 804	498 134	514 670
55 - 59	3 895 365	1 869 537	2 025 828	3 043 924	1 443 868	1 600 056	851 441	425 669	425 772
60 - 64	3 116 466	1 476 667	1 639 799	2 403 645	1 119 077	1 284 568	712 821	357 590	355 231
65 - 69	2 317 265	1 095 273	1 221 992	1 719 078	794 137	924 941	598 187	301 136	297 051
70 - 74	1 873 934	873 893	1 000 041	1 338 906	603 945	734 961	535 028	269 948	265 080
75 - 79	1 245 483	579 689	665 794	892 237	399 026	493 211	353 246	180 663	172 583
80 - 84	798 936	355 277	443 659	576 855	244 082	332 773	222 081	111 195	110 886
85 - 89	454 164	197 461	256 703	322 844	132 826	190 018	131 320	64 635	66 685
90 - 94	164 924	68 130	96 794	116 950	45 123	71 827	47 974	23 007	24 967
95 - 99	65 732	25 920	39 812	44 084	16 122	27 962	21 648	9 798	11 850
100 +	18 475	7 228	11 247	10 451	3 753	6 698	8 024	3 475	4 549
Unknown - Inconnu	1 397 406	700 219	697 187	1 265 292	633 280	632 012	132 114	66 939	65 175
1 VII 2017 (ESDJ)[2]									
Total	123 518 266	60 230 241	63 288 029	89 586 802	...	...	33 931 468	...	...
0	2 211 684	1 131 511	1 080 173	...	...	...	...	...	...
1 - 4	8 825 526	4 515 316	4 310 209	...	...	...	...	...	...
5 - 9	11 094 537	5 679 630	5 414 908	...	...	...	...	...	...
10 - 14	11 172 801	5 703 157	5 469 645	...	...	...	...	...	...
15 - 19	11 095 657	5 616 454	5 479 202	...	...	...	...	...	...
20 - 24	10 793 624	5 362 015	5 431 609	...	...	...	...	...	...
25 - 29	10 018 405	4 853 193	5 165 211	...	...	...	...	...	...
30 - 34	9 236 136	4 386 709	4 849 427	...	...	...	...	...	...
35 - 39	8 796 453	4 136 259	4 660 195	...	...	...	...	...	...
40 - 44	8 278 291	3 896 244	4 382 047	...	...	...	...	...	...
45 - 49	7 474 662	3 530 718	3 943 945	...	...	...	...	...	...
50 - 54	6 338 862	2 992 143	3 346 719	...	...	...	...	...	...
55 - 59	5 208 219	2 449 810	2 758 409	...	...	...	...	...	...
60 - 64	4 141 037	1 946 394	2 194 643	...	...	...	...	...	...
65 - 69	3 092 655	1 447 131	1 645 525	...	...	...	...	...	...
70 - 74	2 245 132	1 037 257	1 207 874	...	...	...	...	...	...
75 - 79	1 561 646	709 012	852 634	...	...	...	...	...	...
80 - 84	1 007 596	448 122	559 474	...	...	...	...	...	...
85 - 89	568 186	244 679	323 508	...	...	...	...	...	...
90 - 94	252 963	104 139	148 823	...	...	...	...	...	...
95 - 99	83 499	32 687	50 812	...	...	...	...	...	...
100 +	20 695	7 659	13 036	...	...	...	...	...	...
Montserrat									
12 V 2011 (CDJC)									
Total	4 922	2 546	2 376	...	...	...	...	...	...
0 - 4	301	157	144	...	...	...	...	...	...
5 - 9	311	146	165	...	...	...	...	...	...
10 - 14	359	187	172	...	...	...	...	...	...
15 - 19	319	179	140	...	...	...	...	...	...
20 - 24	269	152	117	...	...	...	...	...	...
25 - 29	299	154	145	...	...	...	...	...	...
30 - 34	298	138	160	...	...	...	...	...	...
35 - 39	368	172	196	...	...	...	...	...	...
40 - 44	406	189	217	...	...	...	...	...	...
45 - 49	381	196	185	...	...	...	...	...	...
50 - 54	331	183	148	...	...	...	...	...	...
55 - 59	314	181	133	...	...	...	...	...	...
60 - 64	275	165	110	...	...	...	...	...	...
65 - 69	231	130	101	...	...	...	...	...	...

7. Population by age, sex and urban/rural residence: latest available year, 2008 - 2017
Population selon l'âge, le sexe et la résidence, urbaine/rurale : dernière année disponible, 2008 - 2017 (continued - suite)

Continent, country or area, date, code[a] and age (in years) / Continent, pays ou zone, date, code[a] et âge (en années)	Total			Urban - Urbaine			Rural - Rurale		
	Both sexes Les deux sexes	Male Masculin	Female Féminin	Both sexes Les deux sexes	Male Masculin	Female Féminin	Both sexes Les deux sexes	Male Masculin	Female Féminin
AMERICA, NORTH - AMÉRIQUE DU NORD									
Montserrat									
12 V 2011 (CDJC)									
70 - 74	145	75	70	...	...	...	...	...	...
75 - 79	116	61	55	...	...	...	...	...	...
80 - 84	94	44	50	...	...	...	...	...	...
85 +	105	37	68	...	...	...	...	...	...
Nicaragua									
1 VII 2017 (ESDJ)									
Total	6 393 824	3 154 465	3 239 359	3 722 549	1 797 179	1 925 370	2 671 275	1 357 286	1 313 989
0 - 4	679 444	347 128	332 316	335 461	174 369	161 092	343 983	172 759	171 224
5 - 9	678 786	346 271	332 515	355 520	182 519	173 001	323 266	163 752	159 514
10 - 14	648 245	330 132	318 113	349 081	177 414	171 667	299 164	152 718	146 446
15 - 19	630 345	319 935	310 410	348 231	174 655	173 576	282 114	145 280	136 834
20 - 24	627 690	314 266	313 424	362 183	177 082	185 101	265 507	137 184	128 323
25 - 29	570 080	280 857	289 223	339 353	162 817	176 536	230 727	118 040	112 687
30 - 34	508 427	247 440	260 987	312 277	147 292	164 985	196 150	100 148	96 002
35 - 39	439 523	209 400	230 123	277 999	127 747	150 252	161 524	81 653	79 871
40 - 44	359 194	169 454	189 740	232 818	108 016	124 802	126 376	61 438	64 938
45 - 49	292 467	139 449	153 018	190 838	89 414	101 424	101 629	50 035	51 594
50 - 54	245 700	117 462	128 238	159 264	73 630	85 634	86 436	43 832	42 604
55 - 59	215 887	101 958	113 929	139 688	63 182	76 506	76 199	38 776	37 423
60 - 64	176 700	83 162	93 538	112 726	50 503	62 223	63 974	32 659	31 315
65 - 69	110 334	51 986	58 348	69 975	31 080	38 895	40 359	20 906	19 453
70 - 74	79 732	37 489	42 243	50 788	22 300	28 488	28 944	15 189	13 755
75 - 79	63 811	29 534	34 277	41 831	18 060	23 771	21 980	11 474	10 506
80 +	67 459	28 542	38 917	44 516	17 099	27 417	22 943	11 443	11 500
Panama[9]									
1 VII 2017 (ESDF)									
Total	4 098 135	2 056 085	2 042 050	2 836 794	1 395 090	1 441 704	1 261 341	660 995	600 346
0	74 312	37 978	36 334	46 421	23 764	22 657	27 891	14 214	13 677
1 - 4	296 363	151 405	144 958	183 730	94 033	89 697	112 633	57 372	55 261
5 - 9	364 928	186 352	178 576	225 722	115 347	110 375	139 206	71 005	68 201
10 - 14	361 445	184 455	176 990	223 516	113 625	109 891	137 929	70 830	67 099
15 - 19	353 511	180 161	173 350	225 567	113 359	112 208	127 944	66 802	61 142
20 - 24	332 785	168 919	163 866	225 526	112 566	112 960	107 259	56 353	50 906
25 - 29	315 804	159 462	156 342	217 241	107 423	109 818	98 563	52 039	46 524
30 - 34	304 663	153 577	151 086	220 888	108 957	111 931	83 775	44 620	39 155
35 - 39	291 349	146 853	144 496	220 975	109 946	111 029	70 374	36 907	33 467
40 - 44	277 685	139 448	138 237	215 662	106 848	108 814	62 023	32 600	29 423
45 - 49	254 145	126 988	127 157	197 746	96 332	101 414	56 399	30 656	25 743
50 - 54	218 331	108 463	109 868	169 062	81 844	87 218	49 269	26 619	22 650
55 - 59	182 878	90 057	92 821	138 211	66 100	72 111	44 667	23 957	20 710
60 - 64	142 517	69 349	73 168	104 251	48 476	55 775	38 266	20 873	17 393
65 - 69	109 387	52 542	56 845	75 474	34 200	41 274	33 913	18 342	15 571
70 - 74	82 527	39 046	43 481	54 943	24 234	30 709	27 584	14 812	12 772
75 - 79	59 263	27 478	31 785	38 542	16 588	21 954	20 721	10 890	9 831
80 - 84	38 925	17 574	21 351	26 356	10 817	15 539	12 569	6 757	5 812
85 +	37 317	15 978	21 339	26 961	10 631	16 330	10 356	5 347	5 009
85 - 89	22 406	9 787	12 619	...	...	...	...	...	...
90 - 94	10 553	4 437	6 116	...	...	...	...	...	...
95 - 99	3 663	1 481	2 182	...	...	...	...	...	...
100 +	695	273	422	...	...	...	...	...	...
Puerto Rico - Porto Rico[38]									
1 VII 2016 (ESDJ)									
Total	3 411 307	1 623 672	1 787 635	...	...	...	...	...	...
0	30 122	15 458	14 664	...	...	...	...	...	...
1 - 4	131 392	67 401	63 991	...	...	...	...	...	...
5 - 9	188 163	95 805	92 358	...	...	...	...	...	...
10 - 14	206 604	106 372	100 232	...	...	...	...	...	...
15 - 19	234 298	119 826	114 472	...	...	...	...	...	...
20 - 24	240 621	121 579	119 042	...	...	...	...	...	...
25 - 29	225 720	111 318	114 402	...	...	...	...	...	...
30 - 34	198 834	94 823	104 011	...	...	...	...	...	...
35 - 39	215 572	101 801	113 771	...	...	...	...	...	...

7. Population by age, sex and urban/rural residence: latest available year, 2008 - 2017
Population selon l'âge, le sexe et la résidence, urbaine/rurale : dernière année disponible, 2008 - 2017 (continued - suite)

Continent, country or area, date, code[a] and age (in years) / Continent, pays ou zone, date, code[a] et âge (en années)	Total			Urban - Urbaine			Rural - Rurale		
	Both sexes Les deux sexes	Male Masculin	Female Féminin	Both sexes Les deux sexes	Male Masculin	Female Féminin	Both sexes Les deux sexes	Male Masculin	Female Féminin
AMERICA, NORTH - AMÉRIQUE DU NORD									
Puerto Rico - Porto Rico[38]									
1 VII 2016 (ESDJ)									
40 - 44	213 188	101 315	111 873	...	...	...	...	...	...
45 - 49	219 701	104 318	115 383	...	...	...	...	...	...
50 - 54	228 911	105 712	123 199	...	...	...	...	...	...
55 - 59	222 473	102 248	120 225	...	...	...	...	...	...
60 - 64	209 821	95 407	114 414	...	...	...	...	...	...
65 - 69	199 167	89 977	109 190	...	...	...	...	...	...
70 - 74	165 601	74 072	91 529	...	...	...	...	...	...
75 - 79	119 272	52 531	66 741	...	...	...	...	...	...
80 - 84	81 594	33 887	47 707	...	...	...	...	...	...
85 +	80 253	29 822	50 431	...	...	...	...	...	...
Saint Lucia - Sainte-Lucie[39]									
10 V 2010* (CDJC)									
Total	165 594	81 919	83 675	...	...	...	...	...	...
0 - 4	11 810	5 979	5 831	...	...	...	...	...	...
5 - 9	13 150	6 678	6 472	...	...	...	...	...	...
10 - 14	14 918	7 479	7 439	...	...	...	...	...	...
15 - 19	15 921	8 116	7 805	...	...	...	...	...	...
20 - 24	13 620	6 744	6 876	...	...	...	...	...	...
25 - 29	13 289	6 553	6 736	...	...	...	...	...	...
30 - 34	12 253	6 150	6 103	...	...	...	...	...	...
35 - 39	12 285	5 952	6 333	...	...	...	...	...	...
40 - 44	12 218	6 043	6 175	...	...	...	...	...	...
45 - 49	10 963	5 496	5 467	...	...	...	...	...	...
50 - 54	8 926	4 447	4 479	...	...	...	...	...	...
55 - 59	6 490	3 177	3 313	...	...	...	...	...	...
60 - 64	5 484	2 687	2 797	...	...	...	...	...	...
65 - 69	4 380	2 087	2 293	...	...	...	...	...	...
70 - 74	3 591	1 722	1 869	...	...	...	...	...	...
75 - 79	2 565	1 145	1 420	...	...	...	...	...	...
80 - 84	1 904	796	1 108	...	...	...	...	...	...
85 - 89	1 170	428	742	...	...	...	...	...	...
90 - 94	445	163	282	...	...	...	...	...	...
95 - 99	176	69	107	...	...	...	...	...	...
100 +	36	8	28	...	...	...	...	...	...
Saint Vincent and the Grenadines - Saint-Vincent-et-les Grenadines[39]									
1 VII 2015 (ESDF)									
Total	109 557	55 739	53 818	...	...	...	...	...	...
0	1 570	786	785	...	...	...	...	...	...
1 - 4	7 104	3 543	3 561	...	...	...	...	...	...
5 - 9	8 549	4 323	4 226	...	...	...	...	...	...
10 - 14	9 793	5 059	4 734	...	...	...	...	...	...
15 - 19	9 945	5 070	4 875	...	...	...	...	...	...
20 - 24	8 636	4 369	4 267	...	...	...	...	...	...
25 - 29	8 345	4 242	4 103	...	...	...	...	...	...
30 - 34	7 890	3 900	3 989	...	...	...	...	...	...
35 - 39	7 579	3 852	3 727	...	...	...	...	...	...
40 - 44	7 179	3 785	3 394	...	...	...	...	...	...
45 - 49	7 491	3 874	3 617	...	...	...	...	...	...
50 - 54	6 570	3 448	3 123	...	...	...	...	...	...
55 - 59	5 048	2 651	2 397	...	...	...	...	...	...
60 - 64	3 834	1 977	1 857	...	...	...	...	...	...
65 - 69	2 851	1 462	1 389	...	...	...	...	...	...
70 - 74	2 545	1 286	1 258	...	...	...	...	...	...
75 - 79	1 985	966	1 018	...	...	...	...	...	...
80 - 84	1 448	665	783	...	...	...	...	...	...
85 +	1 196	482	714	...	...	...	...	...	...

7. Population by age, sex and urban/rural residence: latest available year, 2008 - 2017
Population selon l'âge, le sexe et la résidence, urbaine/rurale : dernière année disponible, 2008 - 2017 (continued - suite)

Continent, country or area, date, code[a] and age (in years) Continent, pays ou zone, date, code[a] et âge (en annèes)	Total			Urban - Urbaine			Rural - Rurale		
	Both sexes Les deux sexes	Male Masculin	Female Féminin	Both sexes Les deux sexes	Male Masculin	Female Féminin	Both sexes Les deux sexes	Male Masculin	Female Féminin
AMERICA, NORTH - AMÉRIQUE DU NORD									
Sint Maarten (Dutch part) - Saint-Martin (partie néerlandaise)									
1 I 2013 (ESDF)									
Total	36 090	17 661	18 429	...	...	...	...	...	...
0 - 4	2 352	1 235	1 117	...	...	...	...	...	...
5 - 9	2 531	1 289	1 242	...	...	...	...	...	...
10 - 14	2 692	1 348	1 344	...	...	...	...	...	...
15 - 19	2 469	1 302	1 167	...	...	...	...	...	...
20 - 24	2 161	1 047	1 114	...	...	...	...	...	...
25 - 29	2 462	1 161	1 300	...	...	...	...	...	...
30 - 34	2 816	1 290	1 526	...	...	...	...	...	...
35 - 39	3 142	1 452	1 689	...	...	...	...	...	...
40 - 44	3 259	1 556	1 703	...	...	...	...	...	...
45 - 49	3 360	1 693	1 667	...	...	...	...	...	...
50 - 54	2 790	1 345	1 445	...	...	...	...	...	...
55 - 59	2 295	1 127	1 167	...	...	...	...	...	...
60 - 64	1 690	835	854	...	...	...	...	...	...
65 - 69	990	490	500	...	...	...	...	...	...
70 - 74	516	258	258	...	...	...	...	...	...
75 - 79	289	143	147	...	...	...	...	...	...
80 - 84	146	51	95	...	...	...	...	...	...
85 +	130	37	93	...	...	...	...	...	...
Trinidad and Tobago - Trinité-et-Tobago[15]									
1 VII 2017 (ESDF)									
Total	1 356 633	680 661	675 972	...	...	...	...	...	...
0	17 131	8 820	8 311	...	...	...	...	...	...
1 - 4	79 018	40 058	38 960	...	...	...	...	...	...
5 - 9	93 299	47 378	45 921	...	...	...	...	...	...
10 - 14	89 858	45 922	43 937	...	...	...	...	...	...
15 - 19	100 499	50 780	49 719	...	...	...	...	...	...
20 - 24	116 701	58 644	58 058	...	...	...	...	...	...
25 - 29	126 179	63 610	62 570	...	...	...	...	...	...
30 - 34	107 855	55 058	52 797	...	...	...	...	...	...
35 - 39	94 533	47 872	46 661	...	...	...	...	...	...
40 - 44	88 020	44 428	43 591	...	...	...	...	...	...
45 - 49	98 185	49 734	48 451	...	...	...	...	...	...
50 - 54	89 062	44 929	44 134	...	...	...	...	...	...
55 - 59	74 793	37 510	37 282	...	...	...	...	...	...
60 - 64	59 911	30 284	29 627	...	...	...	...	...	...
65 - 69	45 600	22 048	23 552	...	...	...	...	...	...
70 - 74	30 941	14 515	16 425	...	...	...	...	...	...
75 - 79	21 196	9 486	11 710	...	...	...	...	...	...
80 +	23 853	9 586	14 267	...	...	...	...	...	...
Turks and Caicos Islands - Îles Turques et Caïques									
1 VII 2017 (ESDJ)									
Total	39 792	20 296	19 496	...	...	...	...	...	...
0 - 4	2 824	1 426	1 398	...	...	...	...	...	...
5 - 9	2 499	1 270	1 229	...	...	...	...	...	...
10 - 14	2 303	1 146	1 157	...	...	...	...	...	...
15 - 19	2 266	1 111	1 155	...	...	...	...	...	...
20 - 24	2 671	1 306	1 365	...	...	...	...	...	...
25 - 29	3 232	1 582	1 650	...	...	...	...	...	...
30 - 34	3 774	1 889	1 885	...	...	...	...	...	...
35 - 39	4 388	2 248	2 140	...	...	...	...	...	...
40 - 44	4 172	2 162	2 010	...	...	...	...	...	...
45 - 49	3 718	1 948	1 770	...	...	...	...	...	...
50 - 54	2 949	1 553	1 396	...	...	...	...	...	...
55 - 59	1 983	1 050	933	...	...	...	...	...	...
60 - 64	1 366	730	636	...	...	...	...	...	...
65 - 69	820	445	375	...	...	...	...	...	...
70 - 74	471	258	213	...	...	...	...	...	...

Continent, country or area, date, code[a] and age (in years) Continent, pays ou zone, date, code[a] et âge (en années)	Total			Urban - Urbaine			Rural - Rurale		
	Both sexes Les deux sexes	Male Masculin	Female Féminin	Both sexes Les deux sexes	Male Masculin	Female Féminin	Both sexes Les deux sexes	Male Masculin	Female Féminin
AMERICA, NORTH - AMÉRIQUE DU NORD									
Turks and Caicos Islands - Îles Turques et Caïques									
1 VII 2017 (ESDJ)									
75 - 79	206	112	94	...	...	...	...	...	...
80 +	150	60	90	...	...	...	...	...	...
United States of America - États-Unis d'Amérique									
1 IV 2010 (CDJC)									
Total	308 745 538	151 781 326	156 964 212	249 253 271	121 698 595	127 554 676	59 492 267	30 082 731	29 409 536
0 - 4	20 201 362	10 319 427	9 881 935	16 838 001	8 597 234	8 240 767	3 363 361	1 722 193	1 641 168
5 - 9	20 348 657	10 389 638	9 959 019	16 597 127	8 464 939	8 132 188	3 751 530	1 924 699	1 826 831
10 - 14	20 677 194	10 579 862	10 097 332	16 576 171	8 466 809	8 109 362	4 101 023	2 113 053	1 987 970
15 - 19	22 040 343	11 303 666	10 736 677	17 946 265	9 149 187	8 797 078	4 094 078	2 154 479	1 939 599
20 - 24	21 585 999	11 014 176	10 571 823	18 653 468	9 450 066	9 203 402	2 932 531	1 564 110	1 368 421
25 - 29	21 101 849	10 635 591	10 466 258	18 163 244	9 110 029	9 053 215	2 938 605	1 525 562	1 413 043
30 - 34	19 962 099	9 996 500	9 965 599	16 857 801	8 409 694	8 448 107	3 104 298	1 586 806	1 517 492
35 - 39	20 179 642	10 042 022	10 137 620	16 629 937	8 249 301	8 380 636	3 549 705	1 792 721	1 756 984
40 - 44	20 890 964	10 393 977	10 496 987	16 837 761	8 347 894	8 489 867	4 053 203	2 046 083	2 007 120
45 - 49	22 708 591	11 209 085	11 499 506	17 847 074	8 760 812	9 086 262	4 861 517	2 448 273	2 413 244
50 - 54	22 298 125	10 933 274	11 364 851	17 279 058	8 401 091	8 877 967	5 019 067	2 532 183	2 486 884
55 - 59	19 664 805	9 523 648	10 141 157	15 060 179	7 204 444	7 855 735	4 604 626	2 319 204	2 285 422
60 - 64	16 817 924	8 077 500	8 740 424	12 750 365	6 020 393	6 729 972	4 067 559	2 057 107	2 010 452
65 - 69	12 435 263	5 852 547	6 582 716	9 299 030	4 275 616	5 023 414	3 136 233	1 576 931	1 559 302
70 - 74	9 278 166	4 243 972	5 034 194	7 011 129	3 115 814	3 895 315	2 267 037	1 128 158	1 138 879
75 - 79	7 317 795	3 182 388	4 135 407	5 693 807	2 409 946	3 283 861	1 623 988	772 442	851 546
80 - 84	5 743 327	2 294 374	3 448 953	4 629 581	1 800 531	2 829 050	1 113 746	493 843	619 903
85 - 89	3 620 459	1 273 867	2 346 592	3 005 285	1 036 583	1 968 702	615 174	237 284	377 890
90 - 94	1 448 366	424 387	1 023 979	1 216 647	351 491	865 156	231 719	72 896	158 823
95 - 99	371 244	82 263	288 981	315 589	69 008	246 581	55 655	13 255	42 400
100 +	53 364	9 162	44 202	45 752	7 713	38 039	7 612	1 449	6 163
1 VII 2016 (ESDJ)[40]									
Total	323 127 513	159 078 923	164 048 590	...	...	...	...	...	...
0	3 970 145	2 030 478	1 939 667	...	...	...	...	...	...
1 - 4	15 956 892	8 156 375	7 800 517	...	...	...	...	...	...
5 - 9	20 429 799	10 429 923	9 999 876	...	...	...	...	...	...
10 - 14	20 618 233	10 518 732	10 099 501	...	...	...	...	...	...
15 - 19	21 129 999	10 801 846	10 328 153	...	...	...	...	...	...
20 - 24	22 381 028	11 491 065	10 889 963	...	...	...	...	...	...
25 - 29	22 890 884	11 631 474	11 259 410	...	...	...	...	...	...
30 - 34	21 786 359	10 968 264	10 818 095	...	...	...	...	...	...
35 - 39	20 773 905	10 376 442	10 397 463	...	...	...	...	...	...
40 - 44	19 696 251	9 776 321	9 919 930	...	...	...	...	...	...
45 - 49	20 947 623	10 375 955	10 571 668	...	...	...	...	...	...
50 - 54	21 839 056	10 730 184	11 108 872	...	...	...	...	...	...
55 - 59	21 980 108	10 683 406	11 296 702	...	...	...	...	...	...
60 - 64	19 483 036	9 315 632	10 167 404	...	...	...	...	...	...
65 - 69	16 820 083	7 936 919	8 883 164	...	...	...	...	...	...
70 - 74	11 810 247	5 454 190	6 356 057	...	...	...	...	...	...
75 - 79	8 367 895	3 723 619	4 644 276	...	...	...	...	...	...
80 - 84	5 865 639	2 453 255	3 412 384	...	...	...	...	...	...
85 - 89	3 885 222	1 463 286	2 421 936	...	...	...	...	...	...
90 - 94	1 882 830	604 835	1 277 995	...	...	...	...	...	...
95 - 99	530 383	140 380	390 003	...	...	...	...	...	...
100 +	81 896	16 342	65 554	...	...	...	...	...	...
United States Virgin Islands - Îles Vierges américaines[41]									
1 IV 2010 (CDJC)									
Total	106 405	50 854	55 551	...	...	...	...	...	...
0 - 4	7 500	3 736	3 764	...	...	...	...	...	...
5 - 9	7 150	3 694	3 456	...	...	...	...	...	...
10 - 14	7 484	3 849	3 635	...	...	...	...	...	...
15 - 19	7 560	3 765	3 795	...	...	...	...	...	...
20 - 24	5 894	2 707	3 187	...	...	...	...	...	...
25 - 29	5 969	2 695	3 274	...	...	...	...	...	...

7. Population by age, sex and urban/rural residence: latest available year, 2008 - 2017
Population selon l'âge, le sexe et la résidence, urbaine/rurale : dernière année disponible, 2008 - 2017 (continued - suite)

Continent, country or area, date, code[a] and age (in years) / Continent, pays ou zone, date, code[a] et âge (en années)	Total			Urban - Urbaine			Rural - Rurale		
	Both sexes Les deux sexes	Male Masculin	Female Féminin	Both sexes Les deux sexes	Male Masculin	Female Féminin	Both sexes Les deux sexes	Male Masculin	Female Féminin
AMERICA, NORTH - AMÉRIQUE DU NORD									
United States Virgin Islands - Îles Vierges américaines[41]									
1 IV 2010 (CDJC)									
30 - 34	6 137	2 825	3 312	...	...	...	...	...	...
35 - 39	6 675	3 133	3 542	...	...	...	...	...	...
40 - 44	7 450	3 506	3 944	...	...	...	...	...	...
45 - 49	7 743	3 680	4 063	...	...	...	...	...	...
50 - 54	7 900	3 800	4 100	...	...	...	...	...	...
55 - 59	7 192	3 341	3 851	...	...	...	...	...	...
60 - 64	7 367	3 510	3 857	...	...	...	...	...	...
65 - 69	5 853	2 883	2 970	...	...	...	...	...	...
70 - 74	3 717	1 739	1 978	...	...	...	...	...	...
75 - 79	2 328	1 043	1 285	...	...	...	...	...	...
80 - 84	1 332	568	764	...	...	...	...	...	...
85 +	1 154	380	774	...	...	...	...	...	...
AMERICA, SOUTH - AMÉRIQUE DU SUD									
Argentina - Argentine[25]									
1 VII 2017 (ESDF)									
Total	44 044 811	21 595 623	22 449 188	40 410 715	19 664 392	20 746 323	3 634 096	1 931 231	1 702 865
0 - 4	3 748 846	1 928 846	1 820 000	3 367 999	1 731 865	1 636 134	380 847	196 981	183 866
0	746 338	384 064	362 274	...	...	...	...	...	...
1 - 4	3 002 508	1 544 782	1 457 726	...	...	...	...	...	...
5 - 9	3 669 575	1 889 493	1 780 082	3 300 366	1 695 977	1 604 389	369 209	193 516	175 693
10 - 14	3 513 167	1 801 584	1 711 583	3 198 722	1 637 299	1 561 423	314 445	164 285	150 160
15 - 19	3 519 280	1 793 078	1 726 202	3 181 393	1 615 335	1 566 058	337 887	177 743	160 144
20 - 24	3 569 502	1 803 625	1 765 877	3 228 707	1 620 235	1 608 472	340 795	183 390	157 405
25 - 29	3 439 542	1 721 706	1 717 836	3 166 598	1 572 575	1 594 023	272 944	149 131	123 813
30 - 34	3 205 836	1 593 874	1 611 962	2 972 996	1 470 872	1 502 124	232 840	123 002	109 838
35 - 39	3 142 130	1 554 318	1 587 812	2 919 045	1 439 550	1 479 495	223 085	114 768	108 317
40 - 44	2 871 282	1 412 178	1 459 104	2 674 020	1 308 686	1 365 334	197 262	103 492	93 770
45 - 49	2 429 989	1 187 120	1 242 869	2 255 491	1 091 864	1 163 627	174 498	95 256	79 242
50 - 54	2 198 619	1 064 970	1 133 649	2 038 227	975 020	1 063 207	160 392	89 950	70 442
55 - 59	2 041 236	976 710	1 064 526	1 893 080	893 941	999 139	148 156	82 769	65 387
60 - 64	1 832 328	861 250	971 078	1 696 222	785 006	911 216	136 106	76 244	59 862
65 - 69	1 573 449	718 924	854 525	1 457 797	654 843	802 954	115 652	64 081	51 571
70 - 74	1 232 878	538 648	694 230	1 142 540	489 104	653 436	90 338	49 544	40 794
75 - 79	893 988	362 996	530 992	828 777	328 690	500 087	65 211	34 306	30 905
80 - 84	606 633	221 851	384 782	565 228	201 814	363 414	41 405	20 037	21 368
85 - 89	352 861	111 904	240 957	330 758	102 750	228 008	22 103	9 154	12 949
90 - 94	154 738	41 676	113 062	146 178	38 738	107 440	8 560	2 938	5 622
95 - 99	42 057	9 634	32 423	40 087	9 073	31 014	1 970	561	1 409
100 +	6 875	1 238	5 637	6 484	1 155	5 329	391	83	308
Bolivia (Plurinational State of) - Bolivie (État plurinational de)									
1 VII 2017 (ESDF)									
Total	11 145 770	5 615 713	5 530 057	7 699 908	3 811 135	3 888 773	3 445 862	1 804 578	1 641 284
0	243 110	123 532	119 578	163 169	82 905	80 264	79 941	40 627	39 314
1 - 4	971 491	493 171	478 320	653 137	331 538	321 599	318 354	161 633	156 721
5 - 9	1 212 188	618 611	593 577	808 949	411 287	397 662	403 239	207 324	195 915
10 - 14	1 185 221	604 137	581 084	794 674	401 853	392 821	390 547	202 284	188 263
15 - 19	1 108 915	564 837	544 078	760 717	382 035	378 682	348 198	182 802	165 396
20 - 24	1 012 154	514 446	497 708	724 080	360 079	364 001	288 074	154 367	133 707
25 - 29	913 555	462 878	450 677	667 794	328 802	338 992	245 761	134 076	111 685
30 - 34	837 729	423 570	414 159	616 472	303 425	313 047	221 257	120 145	101 112
35 - 39	735 969	371 605	364 364	537 457	263 912	273 545	198 512	107 693	90 819
40 - 44	620 129	312 647	307 482	446 061	218 067	227 994	174 068	94 580	79 488
45 - 49	516 335	259 305	257 030	362 197	176 262	185 935	154 138	83 043	71 095
50 - 54	432 015	216 234	215 781	298 532	145 455	153 077	133 483	70 779	62 704
55 - 59	360 544	179 477	181 067	241 041	116 825	124 216	119 503	62 652	56 851

Continent, country or area, date, code[a] and age (in years) Continent, pays ou zone, date, code[a] et âge (en années)	Total			Urban - Urbaine			Rural - Rurale		
	Both sexes Les deux sexes	Male Masculin	Female Féminin	Both sexes Les deux sexes	Male Masculin	Female Féminin	Both sexes Les deux sexes	Male Masculin	Female Féminin
AMERICA, SOUTH - **AMÉRIQUE DU SUD**									
Bolivia (Plurinational State of) - Bolivie (État plurinational de)									
1 VII 2017 (ESDF)									
60 - 64	298 734	147 344	151 390	192 169	92 114	100 055	106 565	55 230	51 335
65 - 69	235 279	114 673	120 606	149 289	70 735	78 554	85 990	43 938	42 052
70 - 74	181 839	87 297	94 542	114 569	53 322	61 247	67 270	33 975	33 295
75 - 79	123 806	57 271	66 535	77 189	34 771	42 418	46 617	22 500	24 117
80 - 84	82 961	36 032	46 929	50 222	21 374	28 848	32 739	14 658	18 081
85 - 89	48 508	19 750	28 758	28 104	11 317	16 787	20 404	8 433	11 971
90 - 94	19 984	7 343	12 641	11 240	4 166	7 074	8 744	3 177	5 567
95 +	5 304	1 553	3 751	2 846	891	1 955	2 458	662	1 796
Brazil - Brésil									
31 VII 2010 (CDJC)									
Total	190 755 799	93 406 990	97 348 809	160 925 804	77 710 179	83 215 625	29 829 995	15 696 811	14 133 184
0	2 713 244	1 378 532	1 334 712	2 246 034	1 141 784	1 104 250	467 210	236 748	230 462
1 - 4	11 082 914	5 638 455	5 444 459	9 055 114	4 603 340	4 451 774	2 027 800	1 035 115	992 685
5 - 9	14 969 375	7 624 144	7 345 231	12 135 285	6 169 531	5 965 754	2 834 090	1 454 613	1 379 477
10 - 14	17 166 761	8 725 413	8 441 348	13 956 987	7 062 057	6 894 930	3 209 774	1 663 356	1 546 418
15 - 19	16 990 872	8 558 868	8 432 004	14 039 001	6 998 102	7 040 899	2 951 871	1 560 766	1 391 105
20 - 24	17 245 192	8 630 229	8 614 963	14 706 068	7 276 963	7 429 105	2 539 124	1 353 266	1 185 858
25 - 29	17 104 414	8 460 995	8 643 419	14 772 957	7 225 732	7 547 225	2 331 457	1 235 263	1 096 194
30 - 34	15 744 512	7 717 658	8 026 854	13 611 921	6 586 877	7 025 044	2 132 591	1 130 781	1 001 810
35 - 39	13 888 579	6 766 664	7 121 915	11 975 407	5 750 498	6 224 909	1 913 172	1 016 166	897 006
40 - 44	13 009 364	6 320 568	6 688 796	11 187 429	5 344 982	5 842 447	1 821 935	975 586	846 349
45 - 49	11 833 352	5 692 014	6 141 338	10 181 394	4 806 322	5 375 072	1 651 958	885 692	766 266
50 - 54	10 140 402	4 834 995	5 305 407	8 708 339	4 074 679	4 633 660	1 432 063	760 316	671 747
55 - 59	8 276 221	3 902 344	4 373 877	7 025 474	3 238 531	3 786 943	1 250 747	663 813	586 934
60 - 64	6 509 120	3 041 035	3 468 085	5 474 944	2 479 882	2 995 062	1 034 176	561 153	473 023
65 - 69	4 840 810	2 224 065	2 616 745	4 040 016	1 792 798	2 247 218	800 794	431 267	369 527
70 - 74	3 741 636	1 667 372	2 074 264	3 142 173	1 349 329	1 792 844	599 463	318 043	281 420
75 - 79	2 563 447	1 090 517	1 472 930	2 174 038	889 908	1 284 130	389 409	200 609	188 800
80 - 84	1 666 972	668 623	998 349	1 423 603	546 865	876 738	243 369	121 758	121 611
85 - 89	819 483	310 759	508 724	695 385	251 112	444 273	124 098	59 647	64 451
90 - 94	326 558	114 964	211 594	273 348	90 960	182 388	53 210	24 004	29 206
95 - 99	98 335	31 529	66 806	81 121	24 365	56 756	17 214	7 164	10 050
100 +	24 236	7 247	16 989	19 766	5 562	14 204	4 470	1 685	2 785
1 VII 2017 (ESDJ)[42]									
Total	207 660 929	102 471 274	105 189 655	...	...	...	...	...	...
0	2 807 954	1 437 041	1 370 913	...	...	...	...	...	...
1 - 4	11 552 824	5 909 371	5 643 453	...	...	...	...	...	...
5 - 9	15 329 961	7 836 274	7 493 687	...	...	...	...	...	...
10 - 14	16 447 927	8 395 463	8 052 464	...	...	...	...	...	...
15 - 19	17 150 098	8 722 384	8 427 714	...	...	...	...	...	...
20 - 24	17 034 257	8 615 332	8 418 925	...	...	...	...	...	...
25 - 29	17 003 793	8 551 296	8 452 497	...	...	...	...	...	...
30 - 34	17 563 875	8 783 049	8 780 826	...	...	...	...	...	...
35 - 39	16 652 990	8 280 489	8 372 501	...	...	...	...	...	...
40 - 44	14 554 024	7 189 428	7 364 596	...	...	...	...	...	...
45 - 49	13 096 707	6 416 042	6 680 665	...	...	...	...	...	...
50 - 54	12 064 747	5 848 101	6 216 646	...	...	...	...	...	...
55 - 59	10 437 153	4 988 727	5 448 426	...	...	...	...	...	...
60 - 64	8 397 098	3 940 598	4 456 500	...	...	...	...	...	...
65 - 69	6 389 645	2 926 875	3 462 770	...	...	...	...	...	...
70 - 74	4 473 931	1 975 674	2 498 257	...	...	...	...	...	...
75 - 79	3 084 038	1 294 881	1 789 157	...	...	...	...	...	...
80 - 84	1 954 490	773 558	1 180 932	...	...	...	...	...	...
85 - 89	1 049 081	388 325	660 756	...	...	...	...	...	...
90 +	616 336	198 366	417 970	...	...	...	...	...	...
Chile - Chili									
1 VII 2017 (ESDF)									
Total	18 373 917	9 092 950	9 280 967	16 063 564	7 883 072	8 180 492	2 310 353	1 209 878	1 100 475
0	248 757	126 615	122 142	217 937	111 035	106 902	30 820	15 580	15 240
1 - 4	993 489	505 570	487 919	879 781	448 127	431 654	113 708	57 443	56 265

Continent, country or area, date, code[a] and age (in years) / Continent, pays ou zone, date, code[a] et âge (en années)	Total Both sexes Les deux sexes	Total Male Masculin	Total Female Féminin	Urban - Urbaine Both sexes Les deux sexes	Urban - Urbaine Male Masculin	Urban - Urbaine Female Féminin	Rural - Rurale Both sexes Les deux sexes	Rural - Rurale Male Masculin	Rural - Rurale Female Féminin
AMERICA, SOUTH - AMÉRIQUE DU SUD									
Chile - Chili									
1 VII 2017 (ESDF)									
5 - 9	1 250 349	637 268	613 081	1 129 437	576 008	553 429	120 912	61 260	59 652
10 - 14	1 188 428	606 498	581 930	1 055 583	538 993	516 590	132 845	67 505	65 340
15 - 19	1 279 420	652 915	626 505	1 112 375	567 504	544 871	167 045	85 411	81 634
20 - 24	1 413 548	720 988	692 560	1 223 280	623 094	600 186	190 268	97 894	92 374
25 - 29	1 525 562	772 009	753 553	1 322 712	666 743	655 969	202 850	105 266	97 584
30 - 34	1 434 151	722 580	711 571	1 265 666	630 926	634 740	168 485	91 654	76 831
35 - 39	1 275 801	639 592	636 209	1 135 605	564 714	570 891	140 196	74 878	65 318
40 - 44	1 244 604	620 626	623 978	1 100 227	544 747	555 480	144 377	75 879	68 498
45 - 49	1 249 640	619 872	629 768	1 090 659	536 170	554 489	158 981	83 702	75 279
50 - 54	1 245 803	613 999	631 804	1 082 110	525 157	556 953	163 693	88 842	74 851
55 - 59	1 124 744	550 183	574 561	980 076	470 211	509 865	144 668	79 972	64 696
60 - 64	895 319	433 067	462 252	779 561	369 141	410 420	115 758	63 926	51 832
65 - 69	690 220	326 286	363 934	596 912	275 670	321 242	93 308	50 616	42 692
70 - 74	528 300	239 709	288 591	450 942	199 072	251 870	77 358	40 637	36 721
75 - 79	368 781	157 818	210 963	308 818	127 152	181 666	59 963	30 666	29 297
80 +	417 001	147 355	269 646	331 883	108 608	223 275	85 118	38 747	46 371
Colombia - Colombie[43]									
1 VII 2017 (ESDJ)									
Total	49 291 609	24 337 747	24 953 862	37 816 051	18 273 530	19 542 521	11 475 558	6 064 217	5 411 341
0	878 602	449 714	428 888	621 359	317 702	303 657	257 243	132 012	125 231
1 - 4	3 469 474	1 775 309	1 694 165	2 477 837	1 266 575	1 211 262	991 637	508 734	482 903
5 - 9	4 270 908	2 184 229	2 086 679	3 101 932	1 582 163	1 519 769	1 168 976	602 066	566 910
10 - 14	4 256 204	2 175 150	2 081 054	3 144 602	1 594 727	1 549 875	1 111 602	580 423	531 179
15 - 19	4 299 236	2 194 279	2 104 957	3 229 760	1 620 578	1 609 182	1 069 476	573 701	495 775
20 - 24	4 307 133	2 201 266	2 105 867	3 290 933	1 653 618	1 637 315	1 016 200	547 648	468 552
25 - 29	4 083 624	2 080 552	2 003 072	3 165 261	1 586 871	1 578 390	918 363	493 681	424 682
30 - 34	3 676 508	1 824 409	1 852 099	2 905 295	1 414 199	1 491 096	771 213	410 210	361 003
35 - 39	3 318 380	1 613 457	1 704 923	2 648 342	1 258 624	1 389 718	670 038	354 833	315 205
40 - 44	2 961 657	1 429 577	1 532 080	2 356 190	1 109 197	1 246 993	605 467	320 380	285 087
45 - 49	2 856 190	1 363 549	1 492 641	2 268 294	1 051 228	1 217 066	587 896	312 321	275 575
50 - 54	2 773 926	1 318 127	1 455 799	2 220 892	1 020 998	1 199 894	553 034	297 129	255 905
55 - 59	2 386 809	1 125 784	1 261 025	1 901 444	864 122	1 037 322	485 365	261 662	223 703
60 - 64	1 876 548	878 207	998 341	1 480 844	663 866	816 978	395 704	214 341	181 363
65 - 69	1 420 127	658 313	761 814	1 108 423	491 115	617 308	311 704	167 198	144 506
70 - 74	1 013 539	459 560	553 979	781 111	337 617	443 494	232 428	121 943	110 485
75 - 79	711 175	308 208	402 967	544 709	222 356	322 353	166 466	85 852	80 614
80 +	731 569	298 057	433 512	568 823	217 974	350 849	162 746	80 083	82 663
Ecuador - Équateur[44]									
1 VII 2017 (ESDF)									
Total	16 776 977	8 306 557	8 470 420	10 682 148	5 232 565	5 449 583	6 094 829	3 073 992	3 020 837
0	333 325	170 406	162 919	199 218	102 346	96 872	134 107	68 060	66 047
1 - 4	1 337 525	683 569	653 956	800 879	410 047	390 832	536 646	273 522	263 124
5 - 9	1 688 923	863 498	825 425	1 011 089	516 914	494 175	677 834	346 584	331 250
10 - 14	1 656 326	846 765	809 561	1 004 109	511 824	492 285	652 217	334 941	317 276
15 - 19	1 571 587	800 288	771 299	986 880	498 864	488 016	584 707	301 424	283 283
20 - 24	1 455 114	734 190	720 924	949 240	474 466	474 774	505 874	259 724	246 150
25 - 29	1 333 918	664 950	668 968	888 136	439 024	449 112	445 782	225 926	219 856
30 - 34	1 230 770	604 154	626 616	822 311	400 134	422 177	408 459	204 020	204 439
35 - 39	1 126 901	543 723	583 178	753 048	359 059	393 989	373 853	184 664	189 189
40 - 44	1 005 358	480 568	524 790	675 825	318 088	357 737	329 533	162 480	167 053
45 - 49	885 641	423 308	462 333	597 908	281 178	316 730	287 733	142 130	145 603
50 - 54	775 775	371 255	404 520	519 872	245 006	274 866	255 903	126 249	129 654
55 - 59	659 812	315 855	343 957	432 956	203 718	229 238	226 856	112 137	114 719
60 - 64	535 058	255 520	279 538	338 873	158 317	180 556	196 185	97 203	98 982
65 - 69	416 270	197 097	219 173	252 712	116 187	136 525	163 558	80 910	82 648
70 - 74	310 756	144 718	166 038	182 731	81 779	100 952	128 025	62 939	65 086
75 - 79	216 192	98 800	117 392	125 457	54 693	70 764	90 735	44 107	46 628
80 - 84	133 411	60 481	72 930	77 869	33 654	44 215	55 542	26 827	28 715
85 - 89	68 508	31 155	37 353	40 830	17 706	23 124	27 678	13 449	14 229
90 - 94	27 529	12 537	14 992	16 945	7 327	9 618	10 584	5 210	5 374
95 - 99	7 937	3 562	4 375	5 039	2 136	2 903	2 898	1 426	1 472
100 +	341	158	183	221	98	123	120	60	60

Continent, country or area, date, code[a] and age (in years) / Continent, pays ou zone, date, code[a] et âge (en années)	Total			Urban - Urbaine			Rural - Rurale		
	Both sexes Les deux sexes	Male Masculin	Female Féminin	Both sexes Les deux sexes	Male Masculin	Female Féminin	Both sexes Les deux sexes	Male Masculin	Female Féminin
AMERICA, SOUTH - AMÉRIQUE DU SUD									
Falkland Islands (Malvinas) - Îles Falkland (Malvinas)[45]									
15 IV 2012 (CDFC)									
Total	2 840	1 491	1 349	...	...	...	...	...	...
0 - 4	152	72	80	...	...	...	...	...	...
5 - 9	161	69	92	...	...	...	...	...	...
10 - 14	152	68	84	...	...	...	...	...	...
15 - 19	143	68	75	...	...	...	...	...	...
20 - 24	165	89	76	...	...	...	...	...	...
25 - 29	203	88	115	...	...	...	...	...	...
30 - 34	217	115	102	...	...	...	...	...	...
35 - 39	256	132	124	...	...	...	...	...	...
40 - 44	266	158	108	...	...	...	...	...	...
45 - 49	225	130	95	...	...	...	...	...	...
50 - 54	235	127	108	...	...	...	...	...	...
55 - 59	189	109	80	...	...	...	...	...	...
60 - 64	145	89	56	...	...	...	...	...	...
65 - 69	109	55	54	...	...	...	...	...	...
70 - 74	72	42	30	...	...	...	...	...	...
75 - 79	62	30	32	...	...	...	...	...	...
80 +	58	29	29	...	...	...	...	...	...
Unknown - Inconnu	30	21	9	...	...	...	...	...	...
French Guiana - Guyane française									
1 I 2016 (ESDJ)									
Total	262 527	130 596	131 931	...	...	...	...	...	...
0 - 4	29 702	15 281	14 421	...	...	...	...	...	...
5 - 9	29 783	15 217	14 566	...	...	...	...	...	...
10 - 14	28 367	14 154	14 213	...	...	...	...	...	...
15 - 19	24 291	12 347	11 944	...	...	...	...	...	...
20 - 24	17 903	8 907	8 996	...	...	...	...	...	...
25 - 29	18 210	8 751	9 459	...	...	...	...	...	...
30 - 34	18 810	8 809	10 001	...	...	...	...	...	...
35 - 39	18 508	8 968	9 540	...	...	...	...	...	...
40 - 44	17 569	8 656	8 913	...	...	...	...	...	...
45 - 49	15 611	7 970	7 641	...	...	...	...	...	...
50 - 54	12 606	6 135	6 471	...	...	...	...	...	...
55 - 59	10 319	5 203	5 116	...	...	...	...	...	...
60 - 64	7 894	4 152	3 742	...	...	...	...	...	...
65 - 69	5 438	2 714	2 724	...	...	...	...	...	...
70 - 74	3 132	1 560	1 572	...	...	...	...	...	...
75 - 79	1 885	859	1 026	...	...	...	...	...	...
80 - 84	1 262	512	750	...	...	...	...	...	...
85 - 89	735	275	460	...	...	...	...	...	...
90 - 94	349	64	285	...	...	...	...	...	...
95 +	153	62	91	...	...	...	...	...	...
Guyana									
15 IX 2012 (CDFC)									
Total	746 955	371 805	375 150	...	...	...	...	...	...
0 - 4	70 440	35 876	34 564	...	...	...	...	...	...
5 - 9	71 268	35 954	35 314	...	...	...	...	...	...
10 - 14	83 139	42 302	40 837	...	...	...	...	...	...
15 - 19	84 798	42 749	42 049	...	...	...	...	...	...
20 - 24	63 282	31 350	31 932	...	...	...	...	...	...
25 - 29	52 061	25 487	26 574	...	...	...	...	...	...
30 - 34	53 099	26 103	26 996	...	...	...	...	...	...
35 - 39	51 479	25 457	26 022	...	...	...	...	...	...
40 - 44	47 955	24 212	23 743	...	...	...	...	...	...
45 - 49	43 115	21 573	21 542	...	...	...	...	...	...
50 - 54	37 444	18 878	18 566	...	...	...	...	...	...
55 - 59	29 043	14 045	14 998	...	...	...	...	...	...
60 - 64	21 513	10 479	11 034	...	...	...	...	...	...
65 - 69	13 835	6 638	7 197	...	...	...	...	...	...
70 - 74	10 339	4 817	5 522	...	...	...	...	...	...

Continent, country or area, date, code[a] and age (in years) / Continent, pays ou zone, date, code[a] et âge (en années)	Total			Urban - Urbaine			Rural - Rurale		
	Both sexes Les deux sexes	Male Masculin	Female Féminin	Both sexes Les deux sexes	Male Masculin	Female Féminin	Both sexes Les deux sexes	Male Masculin	Female Féminin
AMERICA, SOUTH - AMÉRIQUE DU SUD									
Guyana									
15 IX 2012 (CDFC)									
75 - 79	6 908	3 037	3 871	...	...	...	...	...	...
80 - 84	4 079	1 714	2 365	...	...	...	...	...	...
85 +	3 158	1 134	2 024	...	...	...	...	...	...
Paraguay[46]									
1 VII 2016 (ESDF)									
Total	6 854 536	3 457 365	3 397 170	4 174 834	2 041 139	2 133 695	2 679 702	1 416 226	1 263 476
0 - 4	702 082	358 151	343 930	398 012	203 198	194 814	304 070	154 954	149 116
0	141 537	72 268	69 269	...	...	...	...	...	...
1 - 4	560 544	285 883	274 661	...	...	...	...	...	...
5 - 9	691 901	352 576	339 325	390 221	196 151	194 070	301 680	156 425	145 255
10 - 14	683 516	347 937	335 579	390 252	193 879	196 374	293 263	154 058	139 205
15 - 19	672 867	342 993	329 874	405 622	200 837	204 785	267 245	142 156	125 089
20 - 24	641 263	326 861	314 403	409 703	202 663	207 041	231 560	124 198	107 362
25 - 29	600 414	304 844	295 570	395 319	194 698	200 621	205 095	110 146	94 949
30 - 34	534 718	269 735	264 982	348 434	170 244	178 190	186 283	99 491	86 792
35 - 39	437 936	218 332	219 604	279 314	134 520	144 794	158 622	83 812	74 809
40 - 44	381 358	190 079	191 279	239 963	115 207	124 756	141 396	74 872	66 523
45 - 49	339 976	169 955	170 021	211 545	101 587	109 958	128 431	68 368	60 063
50 - 54	295 002	147 946	147 056	181 799	87 310	94 489	113 203	60 636	52 567
55 - 59	253 974	128 857	125 118	154 665	74 768	79 897	99 309	54 088	45 221
60 - 64	206 424	104 679	101 745	124 312	59 641	64 671	82 112	45 038	37 074
65 - 69	148 797	74 454	74 343	88 717	41 583	47 134	60 080	32 871	27 209
70 - 74	105 964	51 654	54 309	62 824	28 359	34 464	43 140	23 295	19 845
75 - 79	72 546	33 577	38 969	42 954	18 111	24 843	29 593	15 466	14 127
80 +	85 799	34 734	51 065	51 178	18 384	32 794	34 621	16 350	18 271
Peru - Pérou[33]									
30 VI 2017 (ESDF)									
Total	31 826 018	15 939 059	15 886 959	24 735 295	12 220 551	12 514 744	7 090 723	3 718 508	3 372 215
0 - 4	2 831 055	1 445 122	1 385 933	2 012 262	1 030 934	981 328	818 793	414 188	404 605
0	563 692	288 039	275 653	...	...	...	...	...	...
1 - 4	2 267 363	1 157 083	1 110 280	...	...	...	...	...	...
5 - 9	2 891 287	1 473 968	1 417 319	2 083 528	1 060 753	1 022 775	807 759	413 215	394 544
10 - 14	2 913 810	1 483 727	1 430 083	2 134 348	1 080 190	1 054 158	779 462	403 537	375 925
15 - 19	2 886 546	1 466 289	1 420 257	2 192 316	1 100 104	1 092 212	694 230	366 185	328 045
20 - 24	2 839 017	1 438 000	1 401 017	2 266 319	1 130 373	1 135 946	572 698	307 627	265 071
25 - 29	2 715 239	1 371 191	1 344 048	2 166 604	1 074 955	1 091 649	548 635	296 236	252 399
30 - 34	2 485 122	1 251 238	1 233 884	1 973 796	973 128	1 000 668	511 326	278 110	233 216
35 - 39	2 302 392	1 156 915	1 145 477	1 855 332	910 341	944 991	447 060	246 574	200 486
40 - 44	2 072 765	1 038 422	1 034 343	1 676 124	818 448	857 676	396 641	219 974	176 667
45 - 49	1 803 078	899 326	903 752	1 466 802	715 726	751 076	336 276	183 600	152 676
50 - 54	1 562 831	774 590	788 241	1 289 156	629 725	659 431	273 675	144 865	128 810
55 - 59	1 293 000	634 510	658 490	1 060 345	513 851	546 494	232 655	120 659	111 996
60 - 64	1 034 068	501 128	532 940	826 764	396 877	429 887	207 304	104 251	103 053
65 - 69	794 999	379 352	415 647	626 907	297 020	329 887	168 092	82 332	85 760
70 - 74	582 918	271 687	311 231	455 242	210 615	244 627	127 676	61 072	66 604
75 - 79	416 026	186 805	229 221	324 814	143 682	181 132	91 212	43 123	48 089
80 +	401 865	166 789	235 076	324 636	133 829	190 807	77 229	32 960	44 269
Suriname									
13 VIII 2012 (CDJC)									
Total	541 638	270 629	271 009	359 146	177 215	181 931	182 492	93 414	89 078
0 - 4	50 548	25 968	24 580	30 755	15 787	14 968	19 793	10 181	9 612
5 - 9	47 735	24 549	23 186	28 390	14 549	13 841	19 345	10 000	9 345
10 - 14	50 484	26 166	24 318	31 147	16 037	15 110	19 338	10 130	9 208
15 - 19	45 108	22 772	22 336	30 010	15 040	14 970	15 097	7 731	7 366
20 - 24	43 762	21 656	22 106	31 096	15 201	15 895	12 666	6 455	6 211
25 - 29	43 946	21 761	22 185	30 679	15 107	15 572	13 267	6 654	6 613
30 - 34	39 051	19 355	19 696	26 819	13 234	13 585	12 232	6 121	6 111
35 - 39	36 429	18 316	18 113	24 050	11 860	12 190	12 379	6 456	5 923
40 - 44	37 383	18 763	18 620	24 796	12 167	12 629	12 587	6 596	5 991
45 - 49	36 031	18 083	17 948	24 438	12 032	12 406	11 593	6 051	5 542
50 - 54	30 651	15 313	15 338	21 072	10 258	10 814	9 579	5 055	4 525
55 - 59	22 588	10 929	11 659	15 699	7 417	8 282	6 889	3 512	3 377

Continent, country or area, date, code[a] and age (in years) / Continent, pays ou zone, date, code[a] et âge (en années)	Total			Urban - Urbaine			Rural - Rurale		
	Both sexes Les deux sexes	Male Masculin	Female Féminin	Both sexes Les deux sexes	Male Masculin	Female Féminin	Both sexes Les deux sexes	Male Masculin	Female Féminin
AMERICA, SOUTH - AMÉRIQUE DU SUD									
Suriname									
13 VIII 2012 (CDJC)									
60 - 64	16 497	7 734	8 763	11 475	5 304	6 171	5 022	2 430	2 592
65 - 69	13 008	5 951	7 057	9 134	4 166	4 968	3 874	1 785	2 089
70 - 74	10 133	4 619	5 514	6 983	3 211	3 772	3 150	1 408	1 742
75 - 79	7 556	3 393	4 163	5 149	2 296	2 853	2 407	1 097	1 310
80 - 84	4 433	1 934	2 499	3 019	1 308	1 711	1 414	626	788
85 +	2 900	1 081	1 819	2 088	758	1 330	812	323	489
85 - 89	1 978	743	1 235	...	...	...	...	...	...
90 - 94	712	274	438	...	...	...	...	...	...
95 +	210	64	146	...	...	...	...	...	...
Unknown - Inconnu	3 395	2 286	1 109	2 347	1 483	864	1 048	803	245
1 VII 2016 (ESDJ)									
Total	575 763	287 422	288 341	...	...	...	...	...	...
0	9 910	5 167	4 743	...	...	...	...	...	...
1 - 4	43 043	21 845	21 198	...	...	...	...	...	...
5 - 9	49 856	25 722	24 134	...	...	...	...	...	...
10 - 14	49 275	25 294	23 981	...	...	...	...	...	...
15 - 19	48 202	24 592	23 610	...	...	...	...	...	...
20 - 24	46 617	23 594	23 023	...	...	...	...	...	...
25 - 29	44 826	22 478	22 348	...	...	...	...	...	...
30 - 34	42 795	21 406	21 389	...	...	...	...	...	...
35 - 39	40 564	20 261	20 303	...	...	...	...	...	...
40 - 44	38 305	19 124	19 181	...	...	...	...	...	...
45 - 49	36 310	18 147	18 163	...	...	...	...	...	...
50 - 54	32 184	15 957	16 227	...	...	...	...	...	...
55 - 59	27 453	13 428	14 025	...	...	...	...	...	...
60 - 64	22 067	10 589	11 478	...	...	...	...	...	...
65 - 69	16 364	7 611	8 753	...	...	...	...	...	...
70 - 74	12 009	5 432	6 577	...	...	...	...	...	...
75 - 79	8 031	3 505	4 526	...	...	...	...	...	...
80 +	7 952	3 270	4 682	...	...	...	...	...	...
Uruguay[2]									
1 VII 2017 (ESDJ)									
Total	3 493 205	1 691 102	1 802 103	3 326 886	1 599 115	1 727 772	166 319	91 987	74 332
0	45 583	23 330	22 252	43 794	22 413	21 382	1 788	918	871
1 - 4	183 617	93 968	89 649	176 099	90 093	86 006	7 518	3 875	3 643
5 - 9	234 308	119 819	114 490	223 999	114 466	109 533	10 310	5 353	4 957
10 - 14	246 452	125 924	120 528	234 953	119 935	115 019	11 499	5 990	5 509
15 - 19	263 151	134 287	128 864	252 152	128 417	123 735	10 999	5 870	5 129
20 - 24	270 014	136 951	133 064	259 285	130 945	128 340	10 729	6 006	4 724
25 - 29	253 103	127 506	125 598	242 615	121 534	121 080	10 488	5 971	4 517
30 - 34	240 722	120 598	120 124	229 942	114 616	115 325	10 780	5 982	4 799
35 - 39	240 765	118 871	121 895	229 061	112 308	116 753	11 705	6 563	5 142
40 - 44	234 051	115 285	118 766	222 197	108 548	113 649	11 854	6 737	5 117
45 - 49	212 448	103 327	109 122	201 157	96 992	104 165	11 291	6 334	4 957
50 - 54	203 670	97 797	105 873	192 654	91 500	101 154	11 016	6 297	4 719
55 - 59	197 027	93 752	103 275	186 273	87 619	98 654	10 754	6 132	4 622
60 - 64	173 860	81 127	92 733	164 071	75 498	88 573	9 789	5 629	4 160
65 - 69	143 615	64 759	78 856	135 033	59 768	75 265	8 582	4 991	3 591
70 - 74	119 708	51 364	68 344	112 956	47 468	65 487	6 752	3 895	2 857
75 - 79	94 131	37 512	56 618	89 320	34 806	54 514	4 811	2 706	2 104
80 - 84	69 480	24 859	44 620	66 341	23 232	43 109	3 139	1 628	1 512
85 - 89	44 084	13 850	30 234	42 389	13 082	29 307	1 695	767	928
90 +	23 415	6 216	17 199	22 595	5 873	16 721	820	343	477
Venezuela (Bolivarian Republic of) - Venezuela (République bolivarienne du)									
1 IX 2011 (CDJC)									
Total	27 227 930	13 549 752	13 678 178	24 180 964[47]	11 900 242[47]	12 280 722[47]	3 046 966[47]	1 649 510[47]	1 397 456[47]
0 - 4	2 437 631	1 254 208	1 183 423	2 130 561[47]	1 095 625[47]	1 034 936[47]	307 070[47]	158 583[47]	148 487[47]
5 - 9	2 402 364	1 236 217	1 166 147	2 083 248[47]	1 071 223[47]	1 012 025[47]	319 116[47]	164 994[47]	154 122[47]
10 - 14	2 516 779	1 298 191	1 218 588	2 179 907[47]	1 121 671[47]	1 058 236[47]	336 872[47]	176 520[47]	160 352[47]
15 - 19	2 641 320	1 336 159	1 305 161	2 317 888[47]	1 164 992[47]	1 152 896[47]	323 432[47]	171 167[47]	152 265[47]

Continent, country or area, date, code[a] and age (in years) / Continent, pays ou zone, date, code[a] et âge (en années)	Total			Urban - Urbaine			Rural - Rurale		
	Both sexes Les deux sexes	Male Masculin	Female Féminin	Both sexes Les deux sexes	Male Masculin	Female Féminin	Both sexes Les deux sexes	Male Masculin	Female Féminin
AMERICA, SOUTH - AMÉRIQUE DU SUD									
Venezuela (Bolivarian Republic of) - Venezuela (République bolivarienne du)									
1 IX 2011 (CDJC)									
20 - 24	2 560 649	1 280 125	1 280 524	2 289 728[47]	1 134 290[47]	1 155 438[47]	270 921[47]	145 835[47]	125 086[47]
25 - 29	2 344 332	1 159 400	1 184 932	2 104 335[47]	1 030 636[47]	1 073 699[47]	239 997[47]	128 764[47]	111 233[47]
30 - 34	2 219 741	1 105 617	1 114 124	1 994 628[47]	982 139[47]	1 012 489[47]	225 113[47]	123 478[47]	101 635[47]
35 - 39	1 905 253	942 311	962 942	1 708 084[47]	833 596[47]	874 488[47]	197 169[47]	108 715[47]	88 454[47]
40 - 44	1 755 490	873 509	881 981	1 578 118[47]	772 872[47]	805 246[47]	177 372[47]	100 637[47]	76 735[47]
45 - 49	1 528 781	747 704	781 077	1 377 721[47]	662 225[47]	715 496[47]	151 060[47]	85 479[47]	65 581[47]
50 - 54	1 337 934	651 255	686 679	1 208 133[47]	576 212[47]	631 921[47]	129 801[47]	75 043[47]	54 758[47]
55 - 59	1 108 799	530 935	577 864	1 002 491[47]	469 613[47]	532 878[47]	106 308[47]	61 322[47]	44 986[47]
60 - 64	848 358	407 656	440 702	763 622[47]	358 620[47]	405 002[47]	84 736[47]	49 036[47]	35 700[47]
65 - 69	568 688	267 691	300 997	507 772[47]	232 506[47]	275 266[47]	60 916[47]	35 185[47]	25 731[47]
70 - 74	410 455	189 285	221 170	364 425[47]	163 019[47]	201 406[47]	46 030[47]	26 266[47]	19 764[47]
75 - 79	292 992	130 126	162 866	259 357[47]	111 084[47]	148 273[47]	33 635[47]	19 042[47]	14 593[47]
80 - 84	188 895	78 996	109 899	168 413[47]	68 078[47]	100 335[47]	20 482[47]	10 918[47]	9 564[47]
85 - 89	104 141	40 560	63 581	93 151[47]	34 885[47]	58 266[47]	10 990[47]	5 675[47]	5 315[47]
90 - 94	40 370	14 875	25 495	36 160[47]	12 804[47]	23 356[47]	4 210[47]	2 071[47]	2 139[47]
95 +	14 958	4 932	10 026	13 222[47]	4 152[47]	9 070[47]	1 736[47]	780[47]	956[47]
1 VII 2017 (ESDF)									
Total	31 277 130	15 690 386	15 586 744	...	...	...	...	...	...
0	539 368	278 383	260 985	...	...	...	...	...	...
1 - 4	2 175 595	1 121 996	1 053 599	...	...	...	...	...	...
5 - 9	2 766 913	1 426 010	1 340 903	...	...	...	...	...	...
10 - 14	2 793 296	1 438 957	1 354 339	...	...	...	...	...	...
15 - 19	2 746 372	1 412 197	1 334 175	...	...	...	...	...	...
20 - 24	2 653 986	1 356 814	1 297 172	...	...	...	...	...	...
25 - 29	2 598 204	1 316 385	1 281 819	...	...	...	...	...	...
30 - 34	2 514 973	1 264 123	1 250 850	...	...	...	...	...	...
35 - 39	2 254 154	1 126 743	1 127 411	...	...	...	...	...	...
40 - 44	2 014 537	1 002 297	1 012 240	...	...	...	...	...	...
45 - 49	1 865 747	924 525	941 222	...	...	...	...	...	...
50 - 54	1 713 036	844 658	868 378	...	...	...	...	...	...
55 - 59	1 420 756	695 010	725 746	...	...	...	...	...	...
60 - 64	1 081 541	523 731	557 810	...	...	...	...	...	...
65 - 69	783 836	372 696	411 140	...	...	...	...	...	...
70 - 74	556 705	258 636	298 069	...	...	...	...	...	...
75 - 79	369 089	165 860	203 229	...	...	...	...	...	...
80 - 84	222 870	94 047	128 823	...	...	...	...	...	...
85 - 89	120 541	44 727	75 814	...	...	...	...	...	...
90 - 94	57 401	16 833	40 568	...	...	...	...	...	...
95 - 99	22 656	4 746	17 910	...	...	...	...	...	...
100 +	5 554	1 012	4 542	...	...	...	...	...	...
ASIA - ASIE									
Afghanistan[48]									
1 VII 2017 (ESDF)									
Total	28 224 323	14 438 456	13 785 867	7 148 224	3 631 353	3 516 871	21 076 099	10 807 104	10 268 995
0 - 4	4 808 437	2 428 976	2 379 461	1 015 897	520 969	494 928	3 792 540	1 908 007	1 884 533
5 - 9	4 539 772	2 360 084	2 179 688	985 757	506 032	479 725	3 554 015	1 854 052	1 699 963
10 - 14	3 970 838	2 126 274	1 844 564	1 039 616	551 669	487 947	2 931 221	1 574 605	1 356 617
15 - 19	3 208 826	1 628 746	1 580 080	952 546	469 972	482 574	2 256 281	1 158 774	1 097 506
20 - 24	2 509 764	1 252 034	1 257 729	738 398	377 352	361 046	1 771 366	874 682	896 684
25 - 29	1 942 657	952 973	989 685	491 787	240 181	251 605	1 450 870	712 791	738 079
30 - 34	1 349 144	682 575	666 569	332 073	164 557	167 516	1 017 072	518 019	499 053
35 - 39	1 217 040	566 658	650 382	328 050	151 690	176 360	888 990	414 968	474 022
40 - 44	1 059 371	520 509	538 862	274 716	132 425	142 291	784 655	388 084	396 571
45 - 49	928 922	446 228	482 695	244 178	125 988	118 190	684 745	320 240	364 504
50 - 54	890 307	431 148	459 159	231 440	99 341	132 099	658 866	331 807	327 059
55 - 59	521 418	274 507	246 911	144 671	76 050	68 621	376 747	198 457	178 290

Continent, country or area, date, code[a] and age (in years) Continent, pays ou zone, date, code[a] et âge (en années)	Total			Urban - Urbaine			Rural - Rurale		
	Both sexes Les deux sexes	Male Masculin	Female Féminin	Both sexes Les deux sexes	Male Masculin	Female Féminin	Both sexes Les deux sexes	Male Masculin	Female Féminin
ASIA - ASIE									
Afghanistan[48]									
1 VII 2017 (ESDF)									
60 - 64	*542 981*	*303 005*	*239 977*	*144 642*	*81 143*	*63 499*	*398 340*	*221 862*	*176 478*
65 +	*734 845*	*464 740*	*270 105*	*224 454*	*133 985*	*90 469*	*510 391*	*330 755*	*179 636*
Armenia - Arménie									
1 VII 2016 (ESDJ)									
Total	2 992 364	1 423 906	1 568 458	1 904 230	886 581	1 017 649	1 088 134	537 325	550 809
0	40 865	21 604	19 261	26 611	13 937	12 674	14 254	7 667	6 587
1 - 4	167 380	88 991	78 389	107 070	56 492	50 578	60 310	32 499	27 811
5 - 9	206 210	109 809	96 401	127 163	67 193	59 970	79 047	42 616	36 431
10 - 14	177 876	95 215	82 661	109 166	57 729	51 437	68 710	37 486	31 224
15 - 19	175 328	92 647	82 681	103 551	54 468	49 083	71 777	38 179	33 598
20 - 24	222 314	109 573	112 741	129 970	63 226	66 744	92 344	46 347	45 997
25 - 29	275 140	132 544	142 596	167 353	78 168	89 185	107 787	54 376	53 411
30 - 34	257 977	123 121	134 856	165 577	76 542	89 035	92 400	46 579	45 821
35 - 39	211 454	100 745	110 709	141 788	66 967	74 821	69 666	33 778	35 888
40 - 44	178 253	82 846	95 407	118 182	54 690	63 492	60 071	28 156	31 915
45 - 49	168 059	76 513	91 546	103 980	45 949	58 031	64 079	30 564	33 515
50 - 54	200 976	90 529	110 447	121 603	51 881	69 722	79 373	38 648	40 725
55 - 59	217 085	97 877	119 208	140 333	60 216	80 117	76 752	37 661	39 091
60 - 64	161 477	70 629	90 848	112 906	47 871	65 035	48 571	22 758	25 813
65 - 69	111 317	46 574	64 743	82 400	34 157	48 243	28 917	12 417	16 500
70 - 74	56 283	22 733	33 550	41 135	16 731	24 404	15 148	6 002	9 146
75 - 79	86 795	33 120	53 675	57 185	22 174	35 011	29 610	10 946	18 664
80 - 84	50 094	19 116	30 978	31 892	12 269	19 623	18 202	6 847	11 355
85 +	27 481	9 720	17 761	16 365	5 921	10 444	11 116	3 799	7 317
1 I 2017 (ESDJ)									
Total	2 986 151	1 418 771	1 567 380	...	...	...	...	...	...
0	40 285	21 256	19 029	...	...	...	...	...	...
1 - 4	167 642	89 082	78 560	...	...	...	...	...	...
5 - 9	207 626	110 525	97 101	...	...	...	...	...	...
10 - 14	180 259	96 473	83 786	...	...	...	...	...	...
15 - 19	170 952	90 511	80 441	...	...	...	...	...	...
20 - 24	211 638	104 716	106 922	...	...	...	...	...	...
25 - 29	273 419	131 318	142 101	...	...	...	...	...	...
30 - 34	260 102	123 718	136 384	...	...	...	...	...	...
35 - 39	215 155	102 521	112 634	...	...	...	...	...	...
40 - 44	179 297	83 206	96 091	...	...	...	...	...	...
45 - 49	165 819	75 295	90 524	...	...	...	...	...	...
50 - 54	194 365	87 178	107 187	...	...	...	...	...	...
55 - 59	219 156	98 506	120 650	...	...	...	...	...	...
60 - 64	164 829	71 886	92 943	...	...	...	...	...	...
65 - 69	115 128	48 172	66 956	...	...	...	...	...	...
70 - 74	55 882	22 520	33 362	...	...	...	...	...	...
75 - 79	85 397	32 556	52 841	...	...	...	...	...	...
80 - 84	51 720	19 458	32 262	...	...	...	...	...	...
85 +	27 480	9 874	17 606	...	...	...	...	...	...
Azerbaijan - Azerbaïdjan									
1 VII 2016 (ESDJ)									
Total	9 757 812	4 863 426	4 894 386	5 175 695	2 559 578	2 616 117	4 582 117	2 303 848	2 278 269
0	162 837	86 662	76 175	79 052	41 856	37 196	83 785	44 806	38 979
1 - 4	680 857	364 527	316 330	332 888	177 009	155 879	347 969	187 518	160 451
5 - 9	735 568	395 033	340 535	366 637	195 914	170 723	368 931	199 119	169 812
10 - 14	623 993	332 690	291 303	314 868	167 976	146 892	309 125	164 714	144 411
15 - 19	678 282	358 230	320 052	336 771	179 021	157 750	341 511	179 209	162 302
20 - 24	857 738	443 081	414 657	430 560	223 176	207 384	427 178	219 905	207 273
25 - 29	942 759	469 267	473 492	500 204	246 705	253 499	442 555	222 562	219 993
30 - 34	855 082	421 070	434 012	472 008	229 658	242 350	383 074	191 412	191 662
35 - 39	721 124	358 773	362 351	402 828	199 508	203 320	318 296	159 265	159 031
40 - 44	617 829	299 591	318 238	332 281	158 090	174 191	285 548	141 501	144 047
45 - 49	650 864	311 080	339 784	345 415	161 581	183 834	305 449	149 499	155 950
50 - 54	659 014	312 039	346 975	358 665	166 663	192 002	300 349	145 376	154 973
55 - 59	594 792	283 611	311 181	339 911	162 516	177 395	254 881	121 095	133 786
60 - 64	367 994	170 893	197 101	219 377	102 089	117 288	148 617	68 804	79 813
65 - 69	232 306	103 905	128 401	143 362	64 915	78 447	88 944	38 990	49 954

Continent, country or area, date, code[a] and age (in years) Continent, pays ou zone, date, code[a] et âge (en années)	Total			Urban - Urbaine			Rural - Rurale		
	Both sexes Les deux sexes	Male Masculin	Female Féminin	Both sexes Les deux sexes	Male Masculin	Female Féminin	Both sexes Les deux sexes	Male Masculin	Female Féminin
ASIA - ASIE									
Azerbaijan - Azerbaïdjan									
1 VII 2016 (ESDJ)									
70 - 74	105 306	44 558	60 748	64 461	27 261	37 200	40 845	17 297	23 548
75 - 79	146 461	59 399	87 062	77 629	32 009	45 620	68 832	27 390	41 442
80 - 84	80 934	32 335	48 599	38 706	15 431	23 275	42 228	16 904	25 324
85 - 89	32 723	12 873	19 850	15 295	6 300	8 995	17 428	6 573	10 855
90 - 94	8 013	2 915	5 098	3 611	1 436	2 175	4 402	1 479	2 923
95 - 99	2 682	772	1 910	960	417	543	1 722	355	1 367
100 +	654	122	532	206	47	159	448	75	373
1 I 2017 (ESDJ)									
Total	9 809 981	4 891 210	4 918 771	...	...	...	...	...	...
0	159 464	84 909	74 555	...	...	...	...	...	...
1 - 4	676 012	361 389	314 623	...	...	...	...	...	...
5 - 9	761 883	409 524	352 359	...	...	...	...	...	...
10 - 14	622 310	331 632	290 678	...	...	...	...	...	...
15 - 19	663 536	351 320	312 216	...	...	...	...	...	...
20 - 24	842 193	435 951	406 242	...	...	...	...	...	...
25 - 29	941 928	470 445	471 483	...	...	...	...	...	...
30 - 34	870 114	427 849	442 265	...	...	...	...	...	...
35 - 39	732 920	365 041	367 879	...	...	...	...	...	...
40 - 44	621 874	302 116	319 758	...	...	...	...	...	...
45 - 49	646 017	309 112	336 905	...	...	...	...	...	...
50 - 54	657 361	310 771	346 590	...	...	...	...	...	...
55 - 59	608 829	290 229	318 600	...	...	...	...	...	...
60 - 64	384 923	178 755	206 168	...	...	...	...	...	...
65 - 69	242 333	108 484	133 849	...	...	...	...	...	...
70 - 74	106 558	45 257	61 301	...	...	...	...	...	...
75 - 79	141 935	57 502	84 433	...	...	...	...	...	...
80 - 84	85 532	33 932	51 600	...	...	...	...	...	...
85 - 89	32 439	12 882	19 557	...	...	...	...	...	...
90 - 94	8 382	3 100	5 282	...	...	...	...	...	...
95 - 99	2 755	862	1 893	...	...	...	...	...	...
100 +	683	148	535	...	...	...	...	...	...
Bahrain - Bahreïn									
1 VII 2017 (ESDJ)									
Total	1 501 116	951 312	549 804	...	...	...	...	...	...
0 - 4	109 092	55 654	53 438	...	...	...	...	...	...
5 - 9	99 642	50 901	48 741	...	...	...	...	...	...
10 - 14	87 927	44 789	43 138	...	...	...	...	...	...
15 - 19	76 992	40 082	36 910	...	...	...	...	...	...
20 - 24	109 179	65 637	43 542	...	...	...	...	...	...
25 - 29	209 489	148 268	61 221	...	...	...	...	...	...
30 - 34	215 996	156 455	59 541	...	...	...	...	...	...
35 - 39	169 616	118 758	50 858	...	...	...	...	...	...
40 - 44	127 900	86 853	41 047	...	...	...	...	...	...
45 - 49	97 952	65 842	32 110	...	...	...	...	...	...
50 - 54	73 569	46 027	27 542	...	...	...	...	...	...
55 - 59	54 118	33 189	20 929	...	...	...	...	...	...
60 - 64	31 489	18 604	12 885	...	...	...	...	...	...
65 - 69	16 877	9 750	7 127	...	...	...	...	...	...
70 - 74	8 921	4 633	4 288	...	...	...	...	...	...
75 - 79	6 308	3 064	3 244	...	...	...	...	...	...
80 - 84	3 297	1 524	1 773	...	...	...	...	...	...
85 +	2 752	1 282	1 470	...	...	...	...	...	...
Bangladesh									
15 III 2011 (CDFC)									
Total	144 043 697	72 109 796	71 933 901	33 563 183[49]	17 529 792[49]	16 033 391[49]	110 480 514	54 580 004	55 900 510
0 - 4	15 061 970	7 638 523	7 423 447	3 015 500[49]	1 534 508[49]	1 480 992[49]	12 046 470	6 104 015	5 942 455
5 - 9	18 173 229	9 322 514	8 850 715	3 520 080[49]	1 810 786[49]	1 709 294[49]	14 653 149	7 511 728	7 141 421
10 - 14	16 646 615	8 614 889	8 031 726	3 609 866[49]	1 868 428[49]	1 741 438[49]	13 036 749	6 746 461	6 290 288
15 - 19	12 861 890	6 509 492	6 352 398	3 417 088[49]	1 735 931[49]	1 681 157[49]	9 444 802	4 773 561	4 671 241
20 - 24	13 299 789	5 777 370	7 522 419	3 750 754[49]	1 803 092[49]	1 947 662[49]	9 549 035	3 974 278	5 574 757
25 - 29	13 479 508	6 225 252	7 254 256	3 638 634[49]	1 846 338[49]	1 792 296[49]	9 840 874	4 378 914	5 461 960
30 - 34	10 499 765	5 079 106	5 420 659	2 757 615[49]	1 460 253[49]	1 297 362[49]	7 742 150	3 618 853	4 123 297
35 - 39	9 556 428	4 697 349	4 859 079	2 424 331[49]	1 291 114[49]	1 133 217[49]	7 132 097	3 406 235	3 725 862

Continent, country or area, date, code[a] and age (in years) Continent, pays ou zone, date, code[a] et âge (en annèes)	Total			Urban - Urbaine			Rural - Rurale		
	Both sexes Les deux sexes	Male Masculin	Female Féminin	Both sexes Les deux sexes	Male Masculin	Female Féminin	Both sexes Les deux sexes	Male Masculin	Female Féminin
ASIA - ASIE									
Bangladesh									
15 III 2011 (CDFC)									
40 - 44	8 261 662	4 280 923	3 980 739	2 014 738[49]	1 124 193[49]	890 545[49]	6 246 924	3 156 730	3 090 194
45 - 49	6 380 073	3 363 273	3 016 800	1 504 983[49]	849 659[49]	655 324[49]	4 875 090	2 513 614	2 361 476
50 - 54	5 552 271	2 952 596	2 599 675	1 225 174[49]	703 282[49]	521 892[49]	4 327 097	2 249 314	2 077 783
55 - 59	3 500 997	1 923 534	1 577 463	758 757[49]	448 673[49]	310 084[49]	2 742 240	1 474 861	1 267 379
60 - 64	3 934 014	2 081 306	1 852 708	759 025[49]	425 996[49]	333 029[49]	3 174 989	1 655 310	1 519 679
65 - 69	2 113 490	1 149 569	963 921	386 330[49]	217 634[49]	168 696[49]	1 727 160	931 935	795 225
70 - 74	2 231 712	1 206 398	1 025 314	379 459[49]	207 611[49]	171 848[49]	1 852 253	998 787	853 466
75 - 79	874 727	488 338	386 389	146 831[49]	80 832[49]	65 999[49]	727 896	407 506	320 390
80 - 84	880 079	443 239	436 840	138 128[49]	68 117[49]	70 011[49]	741 951	375 122	366 829
85 - 89	262 611	138 268	124 343	42 824[49]	21 933[49]	20 891[49]	219 787	116 335	103 452
90 - 94	250 189	116 916	133 273	38 679[49]	16 945[49]	21 734[49]	211 510	99 971	111 539
95 +	222 678	100 941	121 737	34 387[49]	14 467[49]	19 920[49]	188 291	86 474	101 817
1 VII 2016 (ESDF)									
Total	160 800 000	80 500 000	80 300 000	...	...	...	...	...	...
0	2 882 946	1 262 898	1 620 048	...	...	...	...	...	...
1 - 4	11 132 126	5 596 094	5 536 032	...	...	...	...	...	...
5 - 9	16 758 940	8 512 307	8 246 633	...	...	...	...	...	...
10 - 14	18 767 445	9 514 032	9 253 413	...	...	...	...	...	...
15 - 19	15 614 548	8 246 602	7 367 946	...	...	...	...	...	...
20 - 24	14 365 508	6 490 899	7 874 610	...	...	...	...	...	...
25 - 29	13 957 754	6 339 834	7 617 920	...	...	...	...	...	...
30 - 34	13 104 942	6 225 025	6 879 917	...	...	...	...	...	...
35 - 39	11 304 360	5 661 891	5 642 469	...	...	...	...	...	...
40 - 44	9 746 887	5 001 069	4 745 818	...	...	...	...	...	...
45 - 49	8 160 344	4 482 247	3 678 097	...	...	...	...	...	...
50 - 54	7 819 673	3 804 471	4 015 201	...	...	...	...	...	...
55 - 59	5 202 764	2 829 099	2 373 664	...	...	...	...	...	...
60 - 64	4 606 009	2 504 982	2 101 026	...	...	...	...	...	...
65 - 69	2 882 045	1 594 568	1 287 477	...	...	...	...	...	...
70 - 74	2 200 014	1 229 160	970 854	...	...	...	...	...	...
75 - 79	1 002 308	572 366	429 942	...	...	...	...	...	...
80 - 84	709 229	354 665	354 564	...	...	...	...	...	...
85 - 89	269 757	143 343	126 414	...	...	...	...	...	...
90 - 94	169 881	76 204	93 677	...	...	...	...	...	...
95 +	142 520	58 244	84 276	...	...	...	...	...	...
Bhutan - Bhoutan									
30 V 2017 (CDFC)									
Total	727 145	380 453	346 692	274 316	143 313	131 003	452 829	237 140	215 689
0 - 4	57 474	29 176	28 298	21 453	11 059	10 394	36 021	18 117	17 904
5 - 9	62 991	32 035	30 956	22 567	11 429	11 138	40 424	20 606	19 818
10 - 14	68 952	34 656	34 296	24 285	12 129	12 156	44 667	22 527	22 140
15 - 19	68 286	34 679	33 607	30 378	15 058	15 320	37 908	19 621	18 287
20 - 24	75 415	41 075	34 340	35 689	18 941	16 748	39 726	22 134	17 592
25 - 29	79 280	42 802	36 478	35 586	18 698	16 888	43 694	24 104	19 590
30 - 34	65 180	35 059	30 121	27 753	14 698	13 055	37 427	20 361	17 066
35 - 39	55 549	29 689	25 860	22 460	12 039	10 421	33 089	17 650	15 439
40 - 44	41 495	22 274	19 221	14 868	8 387	6 481	26 627	13 887	12 740
45 - 49	35 533	18 865	16 668	11 938	6 810	5 128	23 595	12 055	11 540
50 - 54	29 317	15 456	13 861	8 334	4 706	3 628	20 983	10 750	10 233
55 - 59	23 898	12 379	11 519	5 494	2 895	2 599	18 404	9 484	8 920
60 - 64	20 711	10 498	10 213	4 321	2 150	2 171	16 390	8 348	8 042
65 - 69	14 654	7 585	7 069	2 998	1 481	1 517	11 656	6 104	5 552
70 - 74	11 468	5 876	5 592	2 401	1 069	1 332	9 067	4 807	4 260
75 - 79	7 871	3 965	3 906	1 715	802	913	6 156	3 163	2 993
80 - 84	5 397	2 651	2 746	1 172	542	630	4 225	2 109	2 116
85 +	3 674	1 733	1 941	904	420	484	2 770	1 313	1 457
Brunei Darussalam - Brunéi Darussalam									
1 VII 2016 (ESDJ)[50]									
Total	417 256	214 104	203 152	312 448	160 061	152 387	104 808	54 043	50 765
0	3 878	2 075	1 803	2 945	1 582	1 363	933	493	440
1 - 4	24 549	12 789	11 760	18 534	9 661	8 873	6 015	3 128	2 887

Continent, country or area, date, code[a] and age (in years) Continent, pays ou zone, date, code[a] et âge (en années)	Total			Urban - Urbaine			Rural - Rurale		
	Both sexes Les deux sexes	Male Masculin	Female Féminin	Both sexes Les deux sexes	Male Masculin	Female Féminin	Both sexes Les deux sexes	Male Masculin	Female Féminin
ASIA - ASIE									
Brunei Darussalam - Brunéi Darussalam									
1 VII 2016 (ESDJ)[50]									
5 - 9	30 426	15 673	14 753	23 168	11 918	11 250	7 258	3 755	3 503
10 - 14	34 306	17 663	16 643	25 904	13 378	12 526	8 402	4 285	4 117
15 - 19	36 417	18 949	17 468	27 115	14 167	12 948	9 302	4 782	4 520
20 - 24	39 027	20 544	18 483	28 741	15 067	13 674	10 286	5 477	4 809
25 - 29	39 812	21 416	18 396	29 722	15 861	13 861	10 090	5 555	4 535
30 - 34	36 895	19 313	17 582	27 970	14 506	13 464	8 925	4 807	4 118
35 - 39	34 492	17 815	16 677	26 642	13 749	12 893	7 850	4 066	3 784
40 - 44	31 164	15 743	15 421	23 783	11 945	11 838	7 381	3 798	3 583
45 - 49	27 701	13 682	14 019	20 748	10 264	10 484	6 953	3 418	3 535
50 - 54	23 160	11 651	11 509	17 466	8 819	8 647	5 694	2 832	2 862
55 - 59	19 239	9 462	9 777	14 213	7 049	7 164	5 026	2 413	2 613
60 - 64	14 591	7 068	7 523	10 457	5 061	5 396	4 134	2 007	2 127
65 - 69	8 958	4 257	4 701	6 337	3 053	3 284	2 621	1 204	1 417
70 - 74	5 095	2 537	2 558	3 564	1 735	1 829	1 531	802	729
75 - 79	3 780	1 737	2 043	2 625	1 142	1 483	1 155	595	560
80 - 84	2 206	974	1 232	1 491	637	854	715	337	378
85 - 89	1 015	498	517	679	314	365	336	184	152
90 - 94	396	184	212	254	105	149	142	79	63
95 - 99	124	64	60	75	40	35	49	24	25
100 +	25	10	15	15	8	7	10	2	8
1 VII 2017 (ESDJ)									
Total	421 300	216 400	204 900	...	...	...	...	...	...
0 - 4	28 400	14 900	13 500	...	...	...	...	...	...
5 - 9	30 600	16 000	14 600	...	...	...	...	...	...
10 - 14	32 700	16 900	15 800	...	...	...	...	...	...
15 - 19	36 800	19 100	17 700	...	...	...	...	...	...
20 - 24	38 400	20 100	18 300	...	...	...	...	...	...
25 - 29	39 600	21 300	18 300	...	...	...	...	...	...
30 - 34	37 500	19 600	17 900	...	...	...	...	...	...
35 - 39	35 300	18 300	17 000	...	...	...	...	...	...
40 - 44	31 700	16 100	15 600	...	...	...	...	...	...
45 - 49	28 800	14 100	14 700	...	...	...	...	...	...
50 - 54	23 200	11 600	11 600	...	...	...	...	...	...
55 - 59	20 500	10 200	10 300	...	...	...	...	...	...
60 - 64	15 200	7 400	7 800	...	...	...	...	...	...
65 - 69	9 800	4 900	4 900	...	...	...	...	...	...
70 - 74	5 400	2 600	2 800	...	...	...	...	...	...
75 - 79	4 200	1 900	2 300	...	...	...	...	...	...
80 - 84	2 000	900	1 100	...	...	...	...	...	...
85 +	1 200	500	700	...	...	...	...	...	...
Cambodia - Cambodge[51]									
1 VII 2015 (ESDF)									
Total	15 405 157	7 551 944	7 853 213	3 540 575	1 705 018	1 835 557	11 864 582	5 846 926	6 017 656
0	343 968	175 388	168 580	86 946	44 740	42 206	257 022	130 648	126 374
1 - 4	1 256 559	639 680	616 879	287 909	146 676	141 233	968 650	493 004	475 646
5 - 9	1 478 056	751 537	726 519	266 331	135 468	130 863	1 211 725	616 069	595 656
10 - 14	1 424 533	727 116	697 417	222 335	114 171	108 164	1 202 198	612 945	589 253
15 - 19	1 637 111	838 821	798 290	273 601	136 051	137 550	1 363 510	702 770	660 740
20 - 24	1 698 824	877 158	821 666	407 469	188 296	219 173	1 291 355	688 862	602 493
25 - 29	1 478 710	737 077	741 633	484 549	223 014	261 535	994 161	514 063	480 098
30 - 34	1 333 262	649 670	683 592	427 395	205 047	222 348	905 867	444 623	461 244
35 - 39	879 004	427 791	451 213	237 471	117 764	119 707	641 533	310 027	331 506
40 - 44	761 990	367 586	394 404	177 884	89 396	88 488	584 106	278 190	305 916
45 - 49	793 754	374 975	418 779	175 105	87 482	87 623	618 649	287 493	331 156
50 - 54	677 057	312 718	364 339	144 559	70 342	74 217	532 498	242 376	290 122
55 - 59	533 368	224 272	309 096	119 460	52 954	66 506	413 908	171 318	242 590
60 - 64	398 784	159 105	239 679	89 373	37 736	51 637	309 411	121 369	188 042
65 - 69	282 114	117 449	164 665	58 973	24 909	34 064	223 141	92 540	130 601
70 - 74	191 298	79 144	112 154	36 584	14 784	21 800	154 714	64 360	90 354
75 - 79	126 227	50 567	75 660	23 103	8 844	14 259	103 124	41 723	61 401
80 +	110 538	41 890	68 648	21 528	7 344	14 184	89 010	34 546	54 464

Continent, country or area, date, code[a] and age (in years) Continent, pays ou zone, date, code[a] et âge (en années)	Total			Urban - Urbaine			Rural - Rurale		
	Both sexes Les deux sexes	Male Masculin	Female Féminin	Both sexes Les deux sexes	Male Masculin	Female Féminin	Both sexes Les deux sexes	Male Masculin	Female Féminin
ASIA - ASIE									
China - Chine[53]									
1 XI 2010 (CDJC)[54]									
Total	1332810869	682 329 104	650 481 765	670 005 546	343 040 783	326 964 763	662 805 323	339 288 321	323 517 002
0 - 4	75 532 610	41 062 566	34 470 044	30 936 470	16 749 729	14 186 741	44 596 140	24 312 837	20 283 303
5 - 9	70 881 549	38 464 665	32 416 884	30 565 659	16 580 910	13 984 749	40 315 890	21 883 755	18 432 135
10 - 14	74 908 462	40 267 277	34 641 185	32 807 526	17 664 790	15 142 736	42 100 936	22 602 487	19 498 449
15 - 19	99 889 114	51 904 830	47 984 284	53 589 992	27 603 777	25 986 215	46 299 122	24 301 053	21 998 069
20 - 24	127 412 518	64 008 573	63 403 945	71 058 518	36 041 784	35 016 734	56 354 000	27 966 789	28 387 211
25 - 29	101 013 852	50 837 038	50 176 814	57 679 956	28 973 516	28 706 440	43 333 896	21 863 522	21 470 374
30 - 34	97 138 203	49 521 822	47 616 381	56 010 957	28 432 073	27 578 884	41 127 246	21 089 749	20 037 497
35 - 39	118 025 959	60 391 104	57 634 855	65 025 365	33 349 280	31 676 085	53 000 594	27 041 824	25 958 770
40 - 44	124 753 964	63 608 678	61 145 286	63 786 496	32 845 769	30 940 727	60 967 468	30 762 909	30 204 559
45 - 49	105 594 553	53 776 418	51 818 135	53 629 541	27 723 132	25 906 409	51 965 012	26 053 286	25 911 726
50 - 54	78 753 171	40 363 234	38 389 937	39 186 388	20 130 395	19 055 993	39 566 783	20 232 839	19 333 944
55 - 59	81 312 474	41 082 938	40 229 536	37 437 535	18 762 887	18 674 648	43 874 939	22 320 051	21 554 888
60 - 64	58 667 282	29 834 426	28 832 856	26 036 917	13 067 045	12 969 872	32 630 365	16 767 381	15 862 984
65 - 69	41 113 282	20 748 471	20 364 811	17 910 329	8 866 594	9 043 735	23 202 953	11 881 877	11 321 076
70 - 74	32 972 397	16 403 453	16 568 944	14 777 260	7 241 891	7 535 369	18 195 137	9 161 562	9 033 575
75 - 79	23 852 133	11 278 859	12 573 274	10 531 503	5 048 471	5 483 032	13 320 630	6 230 388	7 090 242
80 - 84	13 373 198	5 917 502	7 455 696	5 762 828	2 665 218	3 097 610	7 610 370	3 252 284	4 358 086
85 - 89	5 631 928	2 199 810	3 432 118	2 392 190	982 284	1 409 906	3 239 738	1 217 526	2 022 212
90 - 94	1 578 307	530 872	1 047 435	687 763	246 031	441 732	890 544	284 841	605 703
95 - 99	369 979	117 716	252 263	176 542	60 991	115 551	193 437	56 725	136 712
100 +	35 934	8 852	27 082	15 811	4 216	11 595	20 123	4 636	15 487
31 XII 2011 (ESDF)[55]									
Total	1347304706	690 634 118	656 670 588	...	...	...	...	...	...
0 - 4	76 270 588	41 467 059	34 803 529	...	...	...	...	...	...
5 - 9	72 092 941	39 108 235	32 984 706	...	...	...	...	...	...
10 - 14	73 507 059	39 657 647	33 849 412	...	...	...	...	...	...
15 - 19	94 574 118	49 489 412	45 084 706	...	...	...	...	...	...
20 - 24	127 725 882	64 991 765	62 732 941	...	...	...	...	...	...
25 - 29	105 010 588	52 912 941	52 096 471	...	...	...	...	...	...
30 - 34	96 644 706	49 303 529	47 341 176	...	...	...	...	...	...
35 - 39	113 994 118	58 317 647	55 676 471	...	...	...	...	...	...
40 - 44	126 342 353	64 477 647	61 864 706	...	...	...	...	...	...
45 - 49	118 650 588	60 510 588	58 140 000	...	...	...	...	...	...
50 - 54	73 181 176	37 436 471	35 744 706	...	...	...	...	...	...
55 - 59	84 314 118	42 603 529	41 709 412	...	...	...	...	...	...
60 - 64	62 009 412	31 397 647	30 611 765	...	...	...	...	...	...
65 - 69	42 416 471	21 251 765	21 164 706	...	...	...	...	...	...
70 - 74	33 912 941	16 934 118	16 978 824	...	...	...	...	...	...
75 - 79	24 910 588	11 716 471	13 195 294	...	...	...	...	...	...
80 - 84	14 075 294	6 263 529	7 811 765	...	...	...	...	...	...
85 - 89	5 642 353	2 182 353	3 460 000	...	...	...	...	...	...
90 - 94	1 690 588	524 706	1 165 882	...	...	...	...	...	...
95 +	341 176	85 882	254 118	...	...	...	...	...	...
China, Hong Kong SAR - Chine, Hong Kong RAS									
1 VII 2017 (ESDJ)									
Total	7 391 700	3 392 500	3 999 200	...	...	...	...	...	...
0	53 400	27 600	25 800	...	...	...	...	...	...
1 - 4	223 600	115 700	107 900	...	...	...	...	...	...
5 - 9	304 800	158 500	146 300	...	...	...	...	...	...
10 - 14	263 000	134 300	128 700	...	...	...	...	...	...
15 - 19	315 800	163 500	152 300	...	...	...	...	...	...
20 - 24	441 600	217 900	223 700	...	...	...	...	...	...
25 - 29	505 600	230 100	275 500	...	...	...	...	...	...
30 - 34	570 200	229 000	341 200	...	...	...	...	...	...
35 - 39	582 400	230 600	351 800	...	...	...	...	...	...
40 - 44	571 000	233 500	337 500	...	...	...	...	...	...
45 - 49	569 900	239 000	330 900	...	...	...	...	...	...
50 - 54	626 000	281 600	344 400	...	...	...	...	...	...
55 - 59	627 600	306 900	320 700	...	...	...	...	...	...
60 - 64	522 200	257 600	264 600	...	...	...	...	...	...
65 - 69	412 300	204 000	208 300	...	...	...	...	...	...

Continent, country or area, date, code[a] and age (in years) / Continent, pays ou zone, date, code[a] et âge (en années)	Total			Urban - Urbaine			Rural - Rurale		
	Both sexes Les deux sexes	Male Masculin	Female Féminin	Both sexes Les deux sexes	Male Masculin	Female Féminin	Both sexes Les deux sexes	Male Masculin	Female Féminin
ASIA - ASIE									
China, Hong Kong SAR - Chine, Hong Kong RAS									
1 VII 2017 (ESDJ)									
70 - 74	249 700	124 900	124 800	...	...	...	...	...	...
75 - 79	198 100	97 900	100 200	...	...	...	...	...	...
80 - 84	171 400	76 500	94 900	...	...	...	...	...	...
85 +	183 100	63 400	119 700	...	...	...	...	...	...
China, Macao SAR - Chine, Macao RAS[52]									
7 VIII 2016 (SSDJ)									
Total	650 834	314 018	336 816	...	...	...	...	...	...
0 - 4	30 999	16 318	14 681	...	...	...	...	...	...
5 - 9	25 932	13 391	12 541	...	...	...	...	...	...
10 - 14	20 916	10 672	10 244	...	...	...	...	...	...
15 - 19	32 689	15 762	16 927	...	...	...	...	...	...
20 - 24	52 773	25 613	27 160	...	...	...	...	...	...
25 - 29	71 139	35 421	35 718	...	...	...	...	...	...
30 - 34	63 877	31 900	31 977	...	...	...	...	...	...
35 - 39	50 042	24 570	25 472	...	...	...	...	...	...
40 - 44	51 495	23 797	27 698	...	...	...	...	...	...
45 - 49	50 630	22 077	28 553	...	...	...	...	...	...
50 - 54	53 376	23 451	29 925	...	...	...	...	...	...
55 - 59	49 272	24 205	25 067	...	...	...	...	...	...
60 - 64	38 311	18 674	19 637	...	...	...	...	...	...
65 - 69	26 349	13 599	12 750	...	...	...	...	...	...
70 - 74	12 127	6 045	6 082	...	...	...	...	...	...
75 - 79	7 918	3 858	4 060	...	...	...	...	...	...
80 - 84	6 358	2 535	3 823	...	...	...	...	...	...
85 +	6 631	2 130	4 501	...	...	...	...	...	...
Cyprus - Chypre[56]									
1 X 2011 (CDJC)									
Total	840 407	408 780	431 627	566 191	273 065	293 126	274 216	135 715	138 501
0 - 4	45 015	23 061	21 954	29 726	15 202	14 524	15 289	7 859	7 430
5 - 9	42 635	21 921	20 714	28 050	14 386	13 664	14 585	7 535	7 050
10 - 14	47 298	24 179	23 119	30 926	15 730	15 196	16 372	8 449	7 923
15 - 19	55 818	28 683	27 135	36 345	18 593	17 752	19 473	10 090	9 383
20 - 24	66 073	33 891	32 182	44 948	22 847	22 101	21 125	11 044	10 081
25 - 29	74 114	36 992	37 122	51 855	25 842	26 013	22 259	11 150	11 109
30 - 34	69 834	33 149	36 685	48 938	23 133	25 805	20 896	10 016	10 880
35 - 39	61 862	27 754	34 108	43 232	19 204	24 028	18 630	8 550	10 080
40 - 44	59 728	27 031	32 697	41 295	18 416	22 879	18 433	8 615	9 818
45 - 49	57 240	27 059	30 181	39 233	18 225	21 008	18 007	8 834	9 173
50 - 54	56 128	27 517	28 611	38 287	18 499	19 788	17 841	9 018	8 823
55 - 59	47 762	23 771	23 991	31 716	15 541	16 175	16 046	8 230	7 816
60 - 64	45 034	22 057	22 977	29 704	14 438	15 266	15 330	7 619	7 711
65 - 69	36 328	17 656	18 672	23 459	11 295	12 164	12 869	6 361	6 508
70 - 74	29 433	14 044	15 389	18 991	9 048	9 943	10 442	4 996	5 446
75 - 79	21 058	9 647	11 411	13 545	6 239	7 306	7 513	3 408	4 105
80 +	24 948	10 342	14 606	15 853	6 408	9 445	9 095	3 934	5 161
Unknown - Inconnu	99	26	73	88	19	69	11	7	4
1 I 2017 (ESDJ)									
Total	854 802	416 663	438 139	...	...	...	...	...	...
0	9 357	4 784	4 573	...	...	...	...	...	...
1 - 4	37 730	19 583	18 147	...	...	...	...	...	...
5 - 9	47 997	24 556	23 441	...	...	...	...	...	...
10 - 14	44 223	22 594	21 629	...	...	...	...	...	...
15 - 19	50 442	25 525	24 917	...	...	...	...	...	...
20 - 24	66 350	32 953	33 397	...	...	...	...	...	...
25 - 29	71 603	35 636	35 967	...	...	...	...	...	...
30 - 34	68 689	33 031	35 658	...	...	...	...	...	...
35 - 39	62 976	29 911	33 065	...	...	...	...	...	...
40 - 44	55 288	25 864	29 424	...	...	...	...	...	...
45 - 49	53 119	25 385	27 734	...	...	...	...	...	...
50 - 54	54 670	26 550	28 120	...	...	...	...	...	...
55 - 59	52 993	26 080	26 913	...	...	...	...	...	...

Continent, country or area, date, code[a] and age (in years) / Continent, pays ou zone, date, code[a] et âge (en années)	Total			Urban - Urbaine			Rural - Rurale		
	Both sexes Les deux sexes	Male Masculin	Female Féminin	Both sexes Les deux sexes	Male Masculin	Female Féminin	Both sexes Les deux sexes	Male Masculin	Female Féminin
ASIA - ASIE									
Cyprus - Chypre[56]									
1 I 2017 (ESDJ)									
60 - 64	46 322	22 815	23 507	...	...	...	...	...	...
65 - 69	44 737	21 753	22 984	...	...	...	...	...	...
70 - 74	32 757	15 464	17 293	...	...	...	...	...	...
75 - 79	26 270	12 176	14 094	...	...	...	...	...	...
80 - 84	16 892	7 199	9 693	...	...	...	...	...	...
85 - 89	8 975	3 487	5 488	...	...	...	...	...	...
90 - 94	2 938	1 085	1 853	...	...	...	...	...	...
95 - 99	405	181	224	...	...	...	...	...	...
100 +	69	51	18	...	...	...	...	...	...
Democratic People's Republic of Korea - République populaire démocratique de Corée									
1 X 2008 (CDJC)									
Total	24 052 231	11 721 838	12 330 393	...	...	...	...	...	...
0 - 4	1 710 039	872 173	837 866	...	...	...	...	...	...
5 - 9	1 846 785	943 048	903 737	...	...	...	...	...	...
10 - 14	2 021 350	1 035 282	986 068	...	...	...	...	...	...
15 - 19	2 052 342	1 050 113	1 002 229	...	...	...	...	...	...
20 - 24	1 841 400	941 017	900 383	...	...	...	...	...	...
25 - 29	1 737 185	887 573	849 612	...	...	...	...	...	...
30 - 34	1 680 272	853 276	826 996	...	...	...	...	...	...
35 - 39	2 214 929	1 118 391	1 096 538	...	...	...	...	...	...
40 - 44	2 015 514	1 005 140	1 010 374	...	...	...	...	...	...
45 - 49	1 559 527	766 054	793 473	...	...	...	...	...	...
50 - 54	1 315 101	637 737	677 364	...	...	...	...	...	...
55 - 59	902 876	423 625	479 251	...	...	...	...	...	...
60 - 64	1 058 263	476 727	581 536	...	...	...	...	...	...
65 - 69	913 304	379 456	533 848	...	...	...	...	...	...
70 - 74	662 627	228 286	434 341	...	...	...	...	...	...
75 - 79	335 467	79 231	256 236	...	...	...	...	...	...
80 - 84	132 149	18 884	113 265	...	...	...	...	...	...
85 - 89	42 760	4 930	37 830	...	...	...	...	...	...
90 - 94	8 634	809	7 825	...	...	...	...	...	...
95 - 99	1 643	86	1 557	...	...	...	...	...	...
100 +	64	-	64	...	...	...	...	...	...
Georgia - Géorgie									
5 XI 2014 (CDJC)									
Total	3 713 804	1 772 864	1 940 940	2 122 623	980 985	1 141 638	1 591 181	791 879	799 302
0 - 4	255 089	132 700	122 389	152 766	78 799	73 967	102 323	53 901	48 422
5 - 9	230 024	121 245	108 779	139 301	72 526	66 775	90 723	48 719	42 004
10 - 14	206 216	109 481	96 735	119 287	62 645	56 642	86 929	46 836	40 093
15 - 19	226 022	118 877	107 145	130 446	66 924	63 522	95 576	51 953	43 623
20 - 24	266 125	135 305	130 820	162 336	79 100	83 236	103 789	56 205	47 584
25 - 29	278 662	139 945	138 717	168 601	80 608	87 993	110 061	59 337	50 724
30 - 34	262 060	129 921	132 139	160 622	76 264	84 358	101 438	53 657	47 781
35 - 39	248 549	121 943	126 606	150 707	71 177	79 530	97 842	50 766	47 076
40 - 44	243 281	118 318	124 963	143 846	67 326	76 520	99 435	50 992	48 443
45 - 49	239 407	114 036	125 371	133 670	60 443	73 227	105 737	53 593	52 144
50 - 54	271 386	126 710	144 676	150 014	66 843	83 171	121 372	59 867	61 505
55 - 59	245 391	111 641	133 750	133 348	57 828	75 520	112 043	53 813	58 230
60 - 64	211 385	92 412	118 973	114 908	47 738	67 170	96 477	44 674	51 803
65 - 69	155 702	64 889	90 813	84 433	33 489	50 944	71 269	31 400	39 869
70 - 74	123 605	48 483	75 122	61 257	22 399	38 858	62 348	26 084	36 264
75 - 79	135 764	49 895	85 869	64 993	21 828	43 165	70 771	28 067	42 704
80 - 84	71 675	25 100	46 575	32 119	10 106	22 013	39 556	14 994	24 562
85 - 89	34 508	10 166	24 342	15 957	4 154	11 803	18 551	6 012	12 539
90 - 94	7 495	1 620	5 875	3 473	712	2 761	4 022	908	3 114
95 - 99	1 171	163	1 008	456	69	387	715	94	621
100 +	287	14	273	83	7	76	204	7	197
1 I 2017 (ESDJ)[57]									
Total	3 718 200	1 781 500	1 936 700	...	...	...	...	...	...
0	56 300	28 700	27 600	...	...	...	...	...	...

Continent, country or area, date, code[a] and age (in years) / Continent, pays ou zone, date, code[a] et âge (en années)	Total			Urban - Urbaine			Rural - Rurale		
	Both sexes Les deux sexes	Male Masculin	Female Féminin	Both sexes Les deux sexes	Male Masculin	Female Féminin	Both sexes Les deux sexes	Male Masculin	Female Féminin
ASIA - ASIE									
Georgia - Géorgie									
1 I 2017 (ESDJ)[57]									
1 - 4	210 300	109 400	100 900	...	...	...	...	...	...
5 - 9	251 100	131 400	119 700	...	...	...	...	...	...
10 - 14	206 400	109 400	97 000	...	...	...	...	...	...
15 - 19	214 500	113 500	101 000	...	...	...	...	...	...
20 - 24	231 300	119 300	112 000	...	...	...	...	...	...
25 - 29	278 300	139 900	138 400	...	...	...	...	...	...
30 - 34	271 800	135 700	136 100	...	...	...	...	...	...
35 - 39	249 700	123 500	126 200	...	...	...	...	...	...
40 - 44	242 300	119 200	123 100	...	...	...	...	...	...
45 - 49	236 700	114 500	122 200	...	...	...	...	...	...
50 - 54	253 900	119 600	134 300	...	...	...	...	...	...
55 - 59	258 000	118 300	139 700	...	...	...	...	...	...
60 - 64	220 200	96 700	123 500	...	...	...	...	...	...
65 - 69	180 800	75 300	105 500	...	...	...	...	...	...
70 - 74	99 700	38 900	60 800	...	...	...	...	...	...
75 - 79	137 500	49 600	87 900	...	...	...	...	...	...
80 - 84	74 500	25 900	48 600	...	...	...	...	...	...
85 +	44 900	12 700	32 200	...	...	...	...	...	...
India - Inde[58]									
9 II 2011 (CDFC)									
Total	1210854977	623 270 258	587 584 719	377 106 125	195 489 200	181 616 925	833 748 852	427 781 058	405 967 794
0 - 4	112 806 778	58 632 074	54 174 704	29 820 118	15 595 697	14 224 421	82 986 660	43 036 377	39 950 283
5 - 9	126 928 126	66 300 466	60 627 660	33 120 514	17 475 207	15 645 307	93 807 612	48 825 259	44 982 353
10 - 14	132 709 212	69 418 835	63 290 377	35 904 718	18 930 677	16 974 041	96 804 494	50 488 158	46 316 336
15 - 19	120 526 449	63 982 396	56 544 053	36 623 977	19 411 839	17 212 138	83 902 472	44 570 557	39 331 915
20 - 24	111 424 222	57 584 693	53 839 529	37 589 176	19 446 031	18 143 145	73 835 046	38 138 662	35 696 384
25 - 29	101 413 965	51 344 208	50 069 757	35 345 695	17 968 219	17 377 476	66 068 270	33 375 989	32 692 281
30 - 34	88 594 951	44 660 674	43 934 277	30 683 172	15 726 482	14 956 690	57 911 779	28 934 192	28 977 587
35 - 39	85 140 684	42 919 381	42 221 303	29 077 977	14 793 820	14 284 157	56 062 707	28 125 561	27 937 146
40 - 44	72 438 112	37 545 386	34 892 726	24 857 104	12 980 151	11 876 953	47 581 008	24 565 235	23 015 773
45 - 49	62 318 327	32 138 114	30 180 213	21 630 099	11 273 844	10 356 255	40 688 228	20 864 270	19 823 958
50 - 54	49 069 254	25 843 266	23 225 988	17 037 466	9 053 719	7 983 747	32 031 788	16 789 547	15 242 241
55 - 59	39 146 055	19 456 012	19 690 043	13 284 541	6 919 483	6 365 058	25 861 514	12 536 529	13 324 985
60 - 64	37 663 707	18 701 749	18 961 958	11 372 462	5 770 157	5 602 305	26 291 245	12 931 592	13 359 653
65 - 69	26 454 983	12 944 326	13 510 657	7 538 713	3 736 015	3 802 698	18 916 270	9 208 311	9 707 959
70 - 74	19 208 842	9 651 499	9 557 343	5 401 242	2 673 320	2 727 922	13 807 600	6 978 179	6 829 421
75 - 79	9 232 503	4 490 603	4 741 900	2 848 786	1 377 179	1 471 607	6 383 717	3 113 424	3 270 293
80 - 84	6 220 229	2 927 040	3 293 189	1 800 347	807 610	992 737	4 419 882	2 119 430	2 300 452
85 - 89	2 383 167	1 120 106	1 263 061	785 179	349 809	435 370	1 597 988	770 297	827 691
90 - 94	1 446 534	652 465	794 069	422 547	180 500	242 047	1 023 987	471 965	552 022
95 - 99	633 297	294 759	338 538	187 628	84 120	103 508	445 669	210 639	235 030
100 +	605 778	289 325	316 453	198 314	95 860	102 454	407 464	193 465	213 999
Unknown - Inconnu	4 489 802	2 372 881	2 116 921	1 576 350	839 461	736 889	2 913 452	1 533 420	1 380 032
Indonesia - Indonésie[59]									
1 VII 2015 (ESDJ)[60]									
Total	255 182 144	128 231 889	126 950 255	135 613 086	68 118 678	67 494 408	119 569 058	60 113 211	59 455 847
0	4 129 206	2 086 586	2 042 620	2 203 413	1 109 637	1 093 776	1 925 793	976 949	948 844
1 - 4	18 649 805	9 556 167	9 093 638	9 674 406	4 940 927	4 733 479	8 975 399	4 615 240	4 360 159
5 - 9	24 564 098	12 588 393	11 975 705	12 624 775	6 489 085	6 135 690	11 939 323	6 099 308	5 840 015
10 - 14	23 496 807	12 029 572	11 467 235	11 975 376	6 101 228	5 874 148	11 521 431	5 928 344	5 593 087
15 - 19	21 110 721	10 788 401	10 322 320	11 183 002	5 651 624	5 531 378	9 927 719	5 136 777	4 790 942
20 - 24	20 950 475	10 634 769	10 315 706	11 993 749	6 046 995	5 946 754	8 956 726	4 587 774	4 368 952
25 - 29	21 172 507	10 585 769	10 586 738	11 618 534	5 839 754	5 778 780	9 553 973	4 746 015	4 807 958
30 - 34	20 336 001	10 150 408	10 185 593	11 135 834	5 589 237	5 546 597	9 200 167	4 561 171	4 638 996
35 - 39	19 987 441	9 936 043	10 051 398	11 017 643	5 476 010	5 541 633	8 969 798	4 460 033	4 509 765
40 - 44	18 009 072	9 063 867	8 945 205	9 612 758	4 880 339	4 732 419	8 396 314	4 183 528	4 212 786
45 - 49	16 474 327	8 247 350	8 226 977	8 891 443	4 423 750	4 467 693	7 582 884	3 823 600	3 759 284
50 - 54	13 119 231	6 638 517	6 480 714	7 064 986	3 515 250	3 549 736	6 054 245	3 123 267	2 930 978
55 - 59	11 572 736	5 729 185	5 843 551	5 887 496	2 988 434	2 899 062	5 685 240	2 740 751	2 944 489
60 - 64	8 297 601	4 206 906	4 090 695	4 245 745	2 143 629	2 102 116	4 051 856	2 063 277	1 988 579
65 - 69	5 101 072	2 427 508	2 673 564	2 500 758	1 203 349	1 297 409	2 600 314	1 224 159	1 376 155
70 - 74	3 954 635	1 772 393	2 182 242	1 949 235	874 108	1 075 127	2 005 400	898 285	1 107 115
75 +	4 256 409	1 790 055	2 466 354	2 033 933	845 322	1 188 611	2 222 476	944 733	1 277 743

Continent, country or area, date, code[a] and age (in years) / Continent, pays ou zone, date, code[a] et âge (en années)	Total			Urban - Urbaine			Rural - Rurale		
	Both sexes Les deux sexes	Male Masculin	Female Féminin	Both sexes Les deux sexes	Male Masculin	Female Féminin	Both sexes Les deux sexes	Male Masculin	Female Féminin
ASIA - ASIE									
Indonesia - Indonésie[59]									
1 VII 2017 (ESDJ)									
Total	261 890 900	131 579 200	130 311 700	...	...	...	...	...	...
0 - 4	23 848 400	12 166 000	11 682 400	...	...	...	...	...	...
5 - 9	23 733 900	12 144 900	11 589 000	...	...	...	...	...	...
10 - 14	22 713 100	11 639 900	11 073 200	...	...	...	...	...	...
15 - 19	22 212 900	11 365 600	10 847 300	...	...	...	...	...	...
20 - 24	21 703 600	11 007 900	10 695 700	...	...	...	...	...	...
25 - 29	21 022 200	10 571 600	10 450 600	...	...	...	...	...	...
30 - 34	20 509 100	10 239 600	10 269 500	...	...	...	...	...	...
35 - 39	20 072 500	9 979 500	10 093 000	...	...	...	...	...	...
40 - 44	18 884 200	9 475 300	9 408 900	...	...	...	...	...	...
45 - 49	17 028 000	8 542 500	8 485 500	...	...	...	...	...	...
50 - 54	14 601 500	7 274 200	7 327 300	...	...	...	...	...	...
55 - 59	11 903 300	5 932 400	5 970 900	...	...	...	...	...	...
60 - 64	8 870 500	4 472 100	4 398 400	...	...	...	...	...	...
65 - 69	6 035 400	2 950 700	3 084 700	...	...	...	...	...	...
70 - 74	4 082 200	1 873 800	2 208 400	...	...	...	...	...	...
75 +	4 670 100	1 943 200	2 726 900	...	...	...	...	...	...
Iran (Islamic Republic of) - Iran (République islamique d')[61]									
1 VII 2017 (ESDJ)									
Total	81 070 480	41 048 740	40 021 740	60 281 499	30 517 645	29 763 854	20 788 981	10 531 095	10 257 886
0 - 4	7 270 867	3 731 847	3 539 020	5 154 499	2 652 710	2 501 789	2 116 368	1 079 137	1 037 231
5 - 9	6 631 576	3 400 895	3 230 681	4 725 138	2 432 091	2 293 047	1 906 438	968 804	937 634
10 - 14	5 807 622	2 973 032	2 834 590	4 161 329	2 137 487	2 023 842	1 646 293	835 545	810 748
15 - 19	5 420 188	2 768 536	2 651 652	3 943 134	2 006 548	1 936 586	1 477 054	761 988	715 066
20 - 24	6 097 247	3 090 546	3 006 701	4 391 482	2 180 379	2 211 103	1 705 765	910 167	795 598
25 - 29	7 888 242	3 985 977	3 902 265	5 887 695	2 930 628	2 957 067	2 000 547	1 055 349	945 198
30 - 34	8 687 421	4 382 592	4 304 829	6 716 907	3 373 200	3 343 707	1 970 514	1 009 392	961 122
35 - 39	7 395 181	3 748 081	3 647 100	5 692 581	2 885 178	2 807 403	1 702 600	862 903	839 697
40 - 44	5 745 778	2 928 126	2 817 652	4 380 585	2 241 094	2 139 491	1 365 193	687 032	678 161
45 - 49	4 953 484	2 517 814	2 435 670	3 836 620	1 964 903	1 871 717	1 116 864	552 911	563 953
50 - 54	4 070 042	2 050 375	2 019 667	3 175 143	1 616 466	1 558 677	894 899	433 909	460 990
55 - 59	3 444 247	1 716 450	1 727 797	2 638 350	1 332 387	1 305 963	805 897	384 063	421 834
60 - 64	2 680 099	1 321 772	1 358 327	2 021 922	1 020 515	1 001 407	658 177	301 257	356 920
65 - 69	1 819 162	861 913	957 249	1 337 889	649 982	687 907	481 273	211 931	269 342
70 - 74	1 217 943	581 431	636 512	882 585	426 848	455 737	335 358	154 583	180 775
75 - 79	855 091	425 911	429 180	600 281	297 607	302 674	254 810	128 304	126 506
80 +	1 086 290	563 442	522 848	735 359	369 622	365 737	350 931	193 820	157 111
Iraq									
1 VII 2015 (ESDF)									
Total	36 658 503	18 520 532	18 137 971	25 631 821	12 935 587	12 696 234	11 026 682	5 584 945	5 441 737
0	1 137 967	584 535	553 432	752 979	386 080	366 899	384 988	198 455	186 533
1 - 4	4 331 718	2 225 935	2 105 783	2 876 835	1 475 521	1 401 314	1 454 883	750 414	704 469
5 - 9	4 910 887	2 527 175	2 383 712	3 286 086	1 687 351	1 598 735	1 624 801	839 824	784 977
10 - 14	4 359 943	2 246 489	2 113 454	2 947 957	1 515 198	1 432 759	1 411 986	731 291	680 695
15 - 19	3 848 199	1 978 743	1 869 456	2 637 780	1 353 470	1 284 310	1 210 419	625 273	585 146
20 - 24	3 328 277	1 703 854	1 624 423	2 331 929	1 192 710	1 139 219	996 348	511 144	485 204
25 - 29	2 895 690	1 471 180	1 424 510	2 057 867	1 045 789	1 012 078	837 823	425 391	412 432
30 - 34	2 486 941	1 245 726	1 241 215	1 791 620	899 685	891 935	695 321	346 041	349 280
35 - 39	2 133 553	1 058 276	1 075 277	1 551 758	772 320	779 438	581 795	285 956	295 839
40 - 44	1 807 120	887 149	919 971	1 322 951	651 530	671 421	484 169	235 619	248 550
45 - 49	1 494 733	727 670	767 063	1 104 497	539 556	564 941	390 236	188 114	202 122
50 - 54	1 171 634	564 478	607 156	880 319	425 836	454 483	291 315	138 642	152 673
55 - 59	915 225	438 062	477 163	694 340	333 828	360 512	220 885	104 234	116 651
60 - 64	675 377	321 617	353 760	515 990	246 884	269 106	159 387	74 733	84 654
65 - 69	480 527	228 559	251 968	369 196	176 457	192 739	111 331	52 102	59 229
70 - 74	304 637	145 516	159 121	235 201	112 862	122 339	69 436	32 654	36 782
75 - 79	147 670	72 473	75 197	113 997	56 096	57 901	33 673	16 377	17 296
80 +	228 407	93 096	135 311	160 521	64 415	96 106	67 886	28 681	39 205

Continent, country or area, date, code[a] and age (in years) / Continent, pays ou zone, date, code[a] et âge (en années)	Total			Urban - Urbaine			Rural - Rurale		
	Both sexes Les deux sexes	Male Masculin	Female Féminin	Both sexes Les deux sexes	Male Masculin	Female Féminin	Both sexes Les deux sexes	Male Masculin	Female Féminin
ASIA - ASIE									
Israel - Israël[62]									
1 VII 2016 (ESDJ)									
Total	8 546 009	4 237 229	4 308 780	7 795 761	3 855 306	3 940 455	750 248	381 924	368 325
0	179 536	92 345	87 190	163 225	83 966	79 260	16 311	8 380	7 931
1 - 4	698 646	358 625	340 021	631 975	324 385	307 589	66 671	34 240	32 431
5 - 9	806 950	413 368	393 582	724 294	370 633	353 661	82 656	42 735	39 921
10 - 14	730 466	374 197	356 270	658 807	337 078	321 730	71 659	37 119	34 540
15 - 19	669 259	342 658	326 601	601 864	306 844	295 020	67 395	35 815	31 580
20 - 24	615 920	313 916	302 004	564 134	286 516	277 618	51 786	27 400	24 386
25 - 29	596 047	300 631	295 417	550 337	277 009	273 327	45 711	23 621	22 089
30 - 34	584 735	292 334	292 402	538 267	269 461	268 806	46 469	22 873	23 596
35 - 39	558 751	277 596	281 156	509 042	253 368	255 674	49 709	24 228	25 482
40 - 44	532 786	264 081	268 705	482 477	239 261	243 215	50 309	24 820	25 489
45 - 49	454 137	224 286	229 851	412 453	203 046	209 407	41 684	21 240	20 444
50 - 54	404 113	197 874	206 239	370 539	180 562	189 977	33 574	17 312	16 261
55 - 59	386 670	185 715	200 955	355 698	170 010	185 688	30 972	15 704	15 268
60 - 64	369 329	175 270	194 059	340 604	160 584	180 020	28 725	14 686	14 039
65 - 69	335 407	157 052	178 355	311 331	144 732	166 599	24 076	12 320	11 756
70 - 74	206 358	95 238	111 120	191 089	87 692	103 397	15 269	7 546	7 723
75 - 79	173 343	75 657	97 686	162 608	70 483	92 124	10 736	5 174	5 562
80 - 84	122 044	50 804	71 240	113 994	47 260	66 734	8 049	3 544	4 505
85 - 89	75 525	28 942	46 583	70 394	26 999	43 396	5 130	1 943	3 187
90 - 94	34 876	12 229	22 647	32 366	11 292	21 073	2 510	936	1 574
95 - 99	8 026	3 099	4 927	7 421	2 878	4 542	605	220	385
100 +	3 085	1 314	1 771	2 843	1 246	1 597	242	67	174
Japan - Japon[63]									
1 X 2015 (CDJC)									
Total	127 094 745	61 841 738	65 253 007	116 137 232	56 532 149	59 605 083	10 957 513	5 309 589	5 647 924
0 - 4	4 987 706	2 550 921	2 436 785	4 585 047	2 344 645	2 240 402	402 659	206 276	196 383
5 - 9	5 299 787	2 714 591	2 585 196	4 842 315	2 480 103	2 362 212	457 472	234 488	222 984
10 - 14	5 599 317	2 868 024	2 731 293	5 098 044	2 611 161	2 486 883	501 273	256 863	244 410
15 - 19	6 008 388	3 085 416	2 922 972	5 512 237	2 829 307	2 682 930	496 151	256 109	240 042
20 - 24	5 968 127	3 046 392	2 921 735	5 557 062	2 834 296	2 722 766	411 065	212 096	198 969
25 - 29	6 409 612	3 255 717	3 153 895	5 947 621	3 016 085	2 931 536	461 991	239 632	222 359
30 - 34	7 290 878	3 684 747	3 606 131	6 748 938	3 407 192	3 341 746	541 940	277 555	264 385
35 - 39	8 316 157	4 204 202	4 111 955	7 682 014	3 879 376	3 802 638	634 143	324 826	309 317
40 - 44	9 732 218	4 914 018	4 818 200	9 002 172	4 540 962	4 461 210	730 046	373 056	356 990
45 - 49	8 662 804	4 354 877	4 307 927	8 008 263	4 026 225	3 982 038	654 541	328 652	325 889
50 - 54	7 930 296	3 968 311	3 961 985	7 266 826	3 636 156	3 630 670	663 470	332 155	331 315
55 - 59	7 515 246	3 729 523	3 785 723	6 791 248	3 368 519	3 422 729	723 998	361 004	362 994
60 - 64	8 455 010	4 151 119	4 303 891	7 593 671	3 722 143	3 871 528	861 339	428 976	432 363
65 - 69	9 643 867	4 659 662	4 984 205	8 719 913	4 203 013	4 516 900	923 954	456 649	467 305
70 - 74	7 695 811	3 582 440	4 113 371	6 983 090	3 247 479	3 735 611	712 721	334 961	377 760
75 - 79	6 276 856	2 787 417	3 489 439	5 654 811	2 511 652	3 143 159	622 045	275 765	346 280
80 - 84	4 961 420	1 994 326	2 967 094	4 425 840	1 779 702	2 646 138	535 580	214 624	320 956
85 - 89	3 117 257	1 056 641	2 060 616	2 749 324	932 310	1 817 014	367 933	124 331	243 602
90 - 94	1 349 120	333 335	1 015 785	1 183 214	292 810	890 404	165 906	40 525	125 381
95 - 99	359 347	63 265	296 082	314 841	55 450	259 391	44 506	7 815	36 691
100 +	61 763	8 383	53 380	54 031	7 351	46 680	7 732	1 032	6 700
Unknown - Inconnu	1 453 758	828 411	625 347	1 416 710	806 212	610 498	37 048	22 199	14 849
1 VII 2017 (ESDJ)[64]									
Total	126 786 000	61 681 000	65 105 000	...	...	...	...	...	...
0 - 4	4 931 000	2 524 000	2 407 000	...	...	...	...	...	...
5 - 9	5 272 000	2 701 000	2 571 000	...	...	...	...	...	...
10 - 14	5 462 000	2 796 000	2 666 000	...	...	...	...	...	...
15 - 19	6 023 000	3 092 000	2 930 000	...	...	...	...	...	...
20 - 24	6 220 000	3 198 000	3 021 000	...	...	...	...	...	...
25 - 29	6 316 000	3 234 000	3 083 000	...	...	...	...	...	...
30 - 34	7 167 000	3 641 000	3 526 000	...	...	...	...	...	...
35 - 39	7 937 000	4 022 000	3 915 000	...	...	...	...	...	...
40 - 44	9 516 000	4 818 000	4 698 000	...	...	...	...	...	...
45 - 49	9 403 000	4 746 000	4 656 000	...	...	...	...	...	...
50 - 54	8 075 000	4 054 000	4 020 000	...	...	...	...	...	...
55 - 59	7 564 000	3 770 000	3 794 000	...	...	...	...	...	...
60 - 64	7 886 000	3 885 000	4 000 000	...	...	...	...	...	...

7. Population by age, sex and urban/rural residence: latest available year, 2008 - 2017
Population selon l'âge, le sexe et la résidence, urbaine/rurale : dernière année disponible, 2008 - 2017 (continued - suite)

Continent, country or area, date, code[a] and age (in years) / Continent, pays ou zone, date, code[a] et âge (en années)	Total			Urban - Urbaine			Rural - Rurale		
	Both sexes Les deux sexes	Male Masculin	Female Féminin	Both sexes Les deux sexes	Male Masculin	Female Féminin	Both sexes Les deux sexes	Male Masculin	Female Féminin
ASIA - ASIE									
Japan - Japon[63]									
1 VII 2017 (ESDJ)[64]									
65 - 69	10 071 000	4 870 000	5 201 000	...	...	...	...	...	...
70 - 74	7 594 000	3 552 000	4 042 000	...	...	...	...	...	...
75 - 79	6 691 000	2 986 000	3 705 000	...	...	...	...	...	...
80 - 84	5 263 000	2 141 000	3 122 000	...	...	...	...	...	...
85 - 89	3 362 000	1 160 000	2 203 000	...	...	...	...	...	...
90 - 94	1 563 000	410 000	1 153 000	...	...	...	...	...	...
95 - 99	403 000	70 000	333 000	...	...	...	...	...	...
100 +	68 000	9 000	59 000	...	...	...	...	...	...
Jordan - Jordanie[65]									
30 XI 2015 (CDFC)									
Total	9 531 712	5 046 824	4 484 888	8 611 323	4 561 944	4 049 379	920 389	484 880	435 509
0	208 691	107 002	101 689	186 255	95 466	90 789	22 436	11 536	10 900
1 - 4	885 507	454 278	431 229	792 037	406 308	385 729	93 470	47 970	45 500
5 - 9	1 169 491	597 975	571 516	1 050 857	537 071	513 786	118 634	60 904	57 730
10 - 14	1 010 398	519 876	490 522	910 848	468 508	442 340	99 550	51 368	48 182
15 - 19	947 821	498 519	449 302	854 544	449 845	404 699	93 277	48 674	44 603
20 - 24	945 975	519 140	426 835	856 226	470 218	386 008	89 749	48 922	40 827
25 - 29	830 606	459 841	370 765	750 184	414 978	335 206	80 422	44 863	35 559
30 - 34	734 400	395 939	338 461	663 266	357 518	305 748	71 134	38 421	32 713
35 - 39	651 190	352 691	298 499	589 773	319 919	269 854	61 417	32 772	28 645
40 - 44	560 931	304 330	256 601	508 054	276 252	231 802	52 877	28 078	24 799
45 - 49	473 409	258 567	214 842	431 427	236 137	195 290	41 982	22 430	19 552
50 - 54	349 837	187 189	162 648	320 505	171 594	148 911	29 332	15 595	13 737
55 - 59	244 699	127 359	117 340	225 052	117 524	107 528	19 647	9 835	9 812
60 - 64	167 078	86 254	80 824	152 320	78 409	73 911	14 758	7 845	6 913
65 - 69	135 653	67 492	68 161	124 292	62 013	62 279	11 361	5 479	5 882
70 - 74	99 792	52 668	47 124	91 281	48 326	42 955	8 511	4 342	4 169
75 - 79	64 187	32 428	31 759	58 154	29 476	28 678	6 033	2 952	3 081
80 +	52 047	25 276	26 771	46 248	22 382	23 866	5 799	2 894	2 905
80 - 84	30 957	15 324	15 633	...	...	...	...	...	...
85 - 89	13 738	6 387	7 351	...	...	...	...	...	...
90 - 94	4 035	1 797	2 238	...	...	...	...	...	...
95 +	3 317	1 768	1 549	...	...	...	...	...	...
Kazakhstan[66]									
1 VII 2017 (ESDF)									
Total	18 037 776	8 729 888	9 307 888	10 336 836	4 868 292	5 468 544	7 700 940	3 861 596	3 839 344
0	392 547	202 800	189 747	224 755	116 034	108 721	167 792	86 766	81 026
1 - 4	1 554 067	800 022	754 045	873 057	449 948	423 109	681 010	350 074	330 936
5 - 9	1 756 140	901 972	854 168	949 720	488 701	461 019	806 420	413 271	393 149
10 - 14	1 333 587	685 049	648 538	676 886	348 281	328 605	656 701	336 768	319 933
15 - 19	1 112 290	568 860	543 430	568 489	290 205	278 284	543 801	278 655	265 146
20 - 24	1 320 911	672 380	648 531	733 433	361 963	371 470	587 478	310 417	277 061
25 - 29	1 607 999	796 885	811 114	1 023 305	484 763	538 542	584 694	312 122	272 572
30 - 34	1 490 747	737 634	753 113	905 691	436 191	469 500	585 056	301 443	283 613
35 - 39	1 255 389	617 782	637 607	747 717	358 830	388 887	507 672	258 952	248 720
40 - 44	1 147 696	553 751	593 945	667 491	310 189	357 302	480 205	243 562	236 643
45 - 49	1 061 598	507 517	554 081	614 676	282 690	331 986	446 922	224 827	222 095
50 - 54	1 024 485	479 343	545 142	586 756	263 127	323 629	437 729	216 216	221 513
55 - 59	966 868	438 366	528 502	561 332	243 933	317 399	405 536	194 433	211 103
60 - 64	709 547	303 022	406 525	415 658	168 630	247 028	293 889	134 392	159 497
65 - 69	524 707	207 121	317 586	317 531	118 860	198 671	207 176	88 261	118 915
70 - 74	250 769	93 089	157 680	150 410	52 957	97 453	100 359	40 132	60 227
75 - 79	297 050	97 150	199 900	177 976	54 413	123 563	119 074	42 737	76 337
80 - 84	145 977	44 322	101 655	89 375	25 373	64 002	56 602	18 949	37 653
85 - 89	62 568	16 393	46 175	39 353	9 789	29 564	23 215	6 604	16 611
90 - 94	18 878	4 904	13 974	11 214	2 648	8 566	7 664	2 256	5 408
95 - 99	3 166	1 127	2 039	1 628	583	1 045	1 538	544	994
100 +	790	399	391	383	184	199	407	215	192
Kuwait - Koweït									
1 I 2017 (ESDF)									
Total	4 082 704	2 455 424	1 627 280	...	...	...	...	...	...
0	57 853	30 049	27 804	...	...	...	...	...	...
1 - 4	252 192	133 756	118 436	...	...	...	...	...	...

Continent, country or area, date, code[a] and age (in years) Continent, pays ou zone, date, code[a] et âge (en années)	Total			Urban - Urbaine			Rural - Rurale		
	Both sexes Les deux sexes	Male Masculin	Female Féminin	Both sexes Les deux sexes	Male Masculin	Female Féminin	Both sexes Les deux sexes	Male Masculin	Female Féminin
ASIA - ASIE									
Kuwait - Koweït									
1 I 2017 (ESDF)									
5 - 9	308 883	168 392	140 491	...	...	...	...	...	...
10 - 14	259 120	140 045	119 075	...	...	...	...	...	...
15 - 19	223 426	119 735	103 691	...	...	...	...	...	...
20 - 24	209 581	114 412	95 169	...	...	...	...	...	...
25 - 29	260 340	139 004	121 336	...	...	...	...	...	...
30 - 34	455 011	267 482	187 529	...	...	...	...	...	...
35 - 39	516 150	336 700	179 450	...	...	...	...	...	...
40 - 44	511 531	333 537	177 994	...	...	...	...	...	...
45 - 49	375 847	246 804	129 043	...	...	...	...	...	...
50 - 54	261 516	171 651	89 865	...	...	...	...	...	...
55 - 59	172 684	115 652	57 032	...	...	...	...	...	...
60 - 64	106 017	71 016	35 001	...	...	...	...	...	...
65 - 69	55 382	35 093	20 289	...	...	...	...	...	...
70 - 74	28 369	16 150	12 219	...	...	...	...	...	...
75 - 79	15 494	8 750	6 744	...	...	...	...	...	...
80 +	13 308	7 196	6 112	...	...	...	...	...	...
Kyrgyzstan - Kirghizstan[67]									
1 VII 2017 (ESDJ)									
Total	6 198 465	3 072 164	3 126 301	2 097 487	996 210	1 101 277	4 100 978	2 075 954	2 025 024
0	153 674	78 878	74 796	50 790	26 021	24 769	102 884	52 857	50 027
1 - 4	624 235	321 049	303 186	207 427	106 993	100 434	416 808	214 056	202 752
5 - 9	673 907	344 573	329 334	217 396	111 126	106 270	456 511	233 447	223 064
10 - 14	543 470	276 917	266 553	157 585	79 774	77 811	385 885	197 143	188 742
15 - 19	497 079	253 073	244 006	139 125	70 665	68 460	357 954	182 408	175 546
20 - 24	556 096	283 536	272 560	162 667	80 353	82 314	393 429	203 183	190 246
25 - 29	580 904	292 693	288 211	227 567	105 940	121 627	353 337	186 753	166 584
30 - 34	502 049	251 984	250 065	186 909	87 950	98 959	315 140	164 034	151 106
35 - 39	391 950	196 453	195 497	143 343	67 797	75 546	248 607	128 656	119 951
40 - 44	340 627	167 218	173 409	121 854	55 533	66 321	218 773	111 685	107 088
45 - 49	319 033	154 326	164 707	117 362	52 751	64 611	201 671	101 575	100 096
50 - 54	291 181	138 139	153 042	103 823	46 607	57 216	187 358	91 532	95 826
55 - 59	264 854	123 125	141 729	94 203	41 445	52 758	170 651	81 680	88 971
60 - 64	178 026	79 396	98 630	63 155	26 243	36 912	114 871	53 153	61 718
65 - 69	117 727	49 495	68 232	44 195	17 150	27 045	73 532	32 345	41 187
70 - 74	49 872	20 066	29 806	19 795	7 161	12 634	30 077	12 905	17 172
75 - 79	55 296	20 911	34 385	20 717	6 905	13 812	34 579	14 006	20 573
80 - 84	32 500	11 258	21 242	11 394	3 408	7 986	21 106	7 850	13 256
85 - 89	17 356	5 815	11 541	5 597	1 574	4 023	11 759	4 241	7 518
90 - 94	6 687	2 619	4 068	2 027	649	1 378	4 660	1 970	2 690
95 - 99	1 596	505	1 091	434	129	305	1 162	376	786
100 +	346	135	211	122	36	86	224	99	125
Lao People's Democratic Republic - République démocratique populaire lao[68]									
1 VII 2017 (ESDJ)									
Total	6 900 846	3 457 542	3 443 304	...	...	...	...	...	...
0 - 4	791 701	401 628	390 073	...	...	...	...	...	...
5 - 9	761 355	384 813	376 542	...	...	...	...	...	...
10 - 14	713 475	361 521	351 954	...	...	...	...	...	...
15 - 19	697 259	351 951	345 308	...	...	...	...	...	...
20 - 24	675 227	339 282	335 945	...	...	...	...	...	...
25 - 29	618 772	310 058	308 714	...	...	...	...	...	...
30 - 34	543 680	273 208	270 473	...	...	...	...	...	...
35 - 39	454 633	228 761	225 872	...	...	...	...	...	...
40 - 44	375 829	189 063	186 766	...	...	...	...	...	...
45 - 49	319 560	158 650	160 910	...	...	...	...	...	...
50 - 54	269 670	132 574	137 096	...	...	...	...	...	...
55 - 59	219 894	107 504	112 390	...	...	...	...	...	...
60 - 64	163 744	80 295	83 449	...	...	...	...	...	...
65 - 69	114 436	55 823	58 614	...	...	...	...	...	...
70 - 74	76 415	36 027	40 388	...	...	...	...	...	...
75 - 79	53 876	24 302	29 574	...	...	...	...	...	...
80 +	51 318	22 083	29 235	...	...	...	...	...	...

Continent, country or area, date, code[a] and age (in years) / Continent, pays ou zone, date, code[a] et âge (en années)	Total			Urban - Urbaine			Rural - Rurale		
	Both sexes Les deux sexes	Male Masculin	Female Féminin	Both sexes Les deux sexes	Male Masculin	Female Féminin	Both sexes Les deux sexes	Male Masculin	Female Féminin
ASIA - ASIE									
Malaysia - Malaisie[69]									
1 VII 2017 (ESDJ)									
Total	32 049 740	16 561 112	15 488 628	24 182 507	12 448 465	11 734 042	7 867 233	4 112 647	3 754 586
0	516 032	266 613	249 419	381 884	197 573	184 311	134 148	69 040	65 108
1 - 4	2 104 899	1 087 786	1 017 113	1 552 815	804 604	748 211	552 084	283 182	268 902
5 - 9	2 532 621	1 307 235	1 225 386	1 867 422	964 665	902 757	665 199	342 570	322 629
10 - 14	2 579 390	1 324 214	1 255 176	1 904 115	977 108	927 007	675 275	347 106	328 169
15 - 19	2 873 033	1 488 928	1 384 105	2 053 695	1 062 678	991 017	819 338	426 250	393 088
20 - 24	3 251 119	1 711 520	1 539 599	2 357 437	1 237 179	1 120 258	893 682	474 341	419 341
25 - 29	3 245 174	1 735 521	1 509 653	2 488 178	1 308 525	1 179 653	756 996	427 196	329 800
30 - 34	2 845 266	1 496 286	1 348 980	2 243 247	1 158 432	1 084 815	602 019	337 854	264 165
35 - 39	2 336 876	1 227 668	1 109 208	1 863 225	966 143	897 082	473 651	261 525	212 126
40 - 44	1 934 605	1 000 295	934 310	1 533 979	787 910	746 069	400 626	212 385	188 241
45 - 49	1 755 612	881 666	873 946	1 374 957	687 755	687 202	380 655	193 911	186 744
50 - 54	1 604 110	814 142	789 968	1 241 540	631 786	609 754	362 570	182 356	180 214
55 - 59	1 383 373	705 658	677 715	1 056 926	545 927	510 999	326 447	159 731	166 716
60 - 64	1 084 841	543 863	540 978	812 723	411 005	401 718	272 118	132 858	139 260
65 - 69	815 961	403 109	412 852	604 112	300 058	304 054	211 849	103 051	108 798
70 - 74	528 090	255 647	272 443	384 937	187 267	197 670	143 153	68 380	74 773
75 - 79	334 964	158 107	176 857	240 898	115 033	125 865	94 066	43 074	50 992
80 +	323 774	152 654	171 120	220 417	104 817	115 600	103 357	47 837	55 520
Maldives[70]									
1 VII 2017 (ESDF)									
Total	491 589	303 478	188 111	199 523	121 647	77 876	292 066	181 831	110 235
0 - 4	37 675	19 708	17 966	14 099	7 327	6 772	23 576	12 381	11 195
5 - 9	36 569	19 061	17 508	12 814	6 676	6 138	23 755	12 385	11 370
10 - 14	27 990	14 400	13 590	9 345	4 772	4 573	18 645	9 628	9 018
15 - 19	30 811	17 161	13 650	10 309	5 694	4 615	20 502	11 466	9 035
20 - 24	58 457	40 585	17 872	27 852	18 477	9 375	30 604	22 108	8 497
25 - 29	75 542	53 842	21 700	33 182	23 259	9 923	42 360	30 583	11 777
30 - 34	63 002	42 280	20 722	26 596	17 252	9 344	36 405	25 027	11 378
35 - 39	44 219	28 825	15 394	19 098	11 942	7 156	25 121	16 882	8 239
40 - 44	31 842	20 250	11 592	13 645	8 511	5 134	18 196	11 739	6 458
45 - 49	25 239	14 945	10 294	10 584	6 231	4 353	14 655	8 714	5 941
50 - 54	18 653	10 426	8 227	7 530	4 128	3 403	11 122	6 298	4 824
55 - 59	15 230	8 104	7 125	5 704	2 951	2 753	9 526	5 154	4 372
60 - 64	9 043	4 833	4 210	3 323	1 736	1 587	5 721	3 098	2 623
65 - 69	5 432	2 807	2 625	2 049	1 036	1 014	3 382	1 771	1 612
70 - 74	4 368	2 169	2 198	1 432	674	759	2 935	1 496	1 440
75 - 79	3 919	2 039	1 880	1 101	533	568	2 817	1 505	1 312
80 +	3 602	2 044	1 559	859	447	412	2 743	1 597	1 147
Mongolia - Mongolie									
11 XI 2010 (CDJC)									
Total	2 647 545	1 313 968	1 333 577	1 798 147	872 989	925 158	849 398	440 979	408 419
0 - 4	288 497	146 516	141 981	188 882	95 671	93 211	99 615	50 845	48 770
5 - 9	216 214	110 117	106 097	133 740	68 119	65 621	82 474	41 998	40 476
10 - 14	236 865	120 064	116 801	143 846	72 244	71 602	93 019	47 820	45 199
15 - 19	257 645	130 560	127 085	188 334	92 124	96 210	69 311	38 436	30 875
20 - 24	292 183	147 472	144 711	221 784	107 751	114 033	70 399	39 721	30 678
25 - 29	247 983	124 490	123 493	171 685	83 922	87 763	76 298	40 568	35 730
30 - 34	222 522	111 976	110 546	149 461	73 525	75 936	73 061	38 451	34 610
35 - 39	202 383	100 819	101 564	136 034	66 149	69 885	66 349	34 670	31 679
40 - 44	179 267	88 273	90 994	120 105	57 388	62 717	59 162	30 885	28 277
45 - 49	158 756	77 475	81 281	108 736	51 528	57 208	50 020	25 947	24 073
50 - 54	122 082	58 009	64 073	83 084	38 547	44 537	38 998	19 462	19 536
55 - 59	71 989	33 384	38 605	49 342	22 373	26 969	22 647	11 011	11 636
60 - 64	49 453	22 106	27 347	34 724	15 234	19 490	14 729	6 872	7 857
65 - 69	38 232	17 262	20 970	26 004	11 578	14 426	12 228	5 684	6 544
70 - 74	29 332	13 081	16 251	19 556	8 594	10 962	9 776	4 487	5 289
75 - 79	18 617	7 252	11 365	12 384	4 742	7 642	6 233	2 510	3 723
80 - 84	9 166	3 258	5 908	6 234	2 225	4 009	2 932	1 033	1 899
85 - 89	4 415	1 378	3 037	2 948	945	2 003	1 467	433	1 034
90 - 94	1 459	383	1 076	962	274	688	497	109	388
95 - 99	402	80	322	251	47	204	151	33	118
100 +	83	13	70	51	9	42	32	4	28

Continent, country or area, date, code[a] and age (in years) / Continent, pays ou zone, date, code[a] et âge (en années)	Total			Urban - Urbaine			Rural - Rurale		
	Both sexes Les deux sexes	Male Masculin	Female Féminin	Both sexes Les deux sexes	Male Masculin	Female Féminin	Both sexes Les deux sexes	Male Masculin	Female Féminin
ASIA - ASIE									
Mongolia - Mongolie									
1 VII 2017 (ESDF)									
Total	3 148 917	1 548 177	1 600 740	...	...	...	...	...	...
0	77 621	39 996	37 625	...	...	...	...	...	...
1 - 4	316 628	162 113	154 515	...	...	...	...	...	...
5 - 9	331 943	169 536	162 407	...	...	...	...	...	...
10 - 14	226 515	115 614	110 901	...	...	...	...	...	...
15 - 19	234 700	119 187	115 513	...	...	...	...	...	...
20 - 24	250 062	126 289	123 773	...	...	...	...	...	...
25 - 29	312 635	156 710	155 925	...	...	...	...	...	...
30 - 34	278 678	138 448	140 230	...	...	...	...	...	...
35 - 39	238 964	117 639	121 325	...	...	...	...	...	...
40 - 44	215 822	104 436	111 386	...	...	...	...	...	...
45 - 49	184 085	87 455	96 630	...	...	...	...	...	...
50 - 54	160 046	74 434	85 612	...	...	...	...	...	...
55 - 59	124 314	55 757	68 557	...	...	...	...	...	...
60 - 64	76 898	33 240	43 658	...	...	...	...	...	...
65 - 69	45 518	18 624	26 894	...	...	...	...	...	...
70 - 74	31 073	12 672	18 401	...	...	...	...	...	...
75 - 79	23 187	9 474	13 713	...	...	...	...	...	...
80 - 84	12 382	4 367	8 015	...	...	...	...	...	...
85 - 89	5 577	1 654	3 923	...	...	...	...	...	...
90 - 94	1 718	445	1 273	...	...	...	...	...	...
95 - 99	472	75	397	...	...	...	...	...	...
100 +	79	12	67	...	...	...	...	...	...
Myanmar[57]									
1 X 2017 (ESDF)									
Total	53 387 948	25 647 847	27 740 101	15 762 776	7 494 003	8 268 773	37 625 172	18 153 844	19 471 328
0 - 4	4 976 052	2 519 158	2 456 894	1 228 076	622 974	605 102	3 747 976	1 896 184	1 851 792
0	1 016 426	515 842	500 584	...	...	...	...	...	...
1 - 4	3 959 626	2 003 316	1 956 310	...	...	...	...	...	...
5 - 9	4 796 228	2 422 612	2 373 616	1 159 473	588 421	571 052	3 636 755	1 834 191	1 802 564
10 - 14	5 167 389	2 631 932	2 535 457	1 255 580	646 827	608 753	3 911 809	1 985 105	1 926 704
15 - 19	4 922 623	2 475 632	2 446 991	1 481 305	756 613	724 692	3 441 318	1 719 019	1 722 299
20 - 24	4 525 132	2 208 387	2 316 745	1 589 286	786 362	802 924	2 935 846	1 422 025	1 513 821
25 - 29	4 243 777	2 023 654	2 220 123	1 450 427	697 463	752 964	2 793 350	1 326 191	1 467 159
30 - 34	4 077 296	1 948 154	2 129 142	1 288 277	618 802	669 475	2 789 019	1 329 352	1 459 667
35 - 39	3 787 706	1 809 401	1 978 305	1 175 358	559 562	615 796	2 612 348	1 249 839	1 362 509
40 - 44	3 469 555	1 635 403	1 834 152	1 049 930	485 650	564 280	2 419 625	1 149 753	1 269 872
45 - 49	3 177 031	1 475 651	1 701 380	982 898	442 328	540 570	2 194 133	1 033 323	1 160 810
50 - 54	2 816 955	1 293 372	1 523 583	858 548	375 920	482 628	1 958 407	917 452	1 040 955
55 - 59	2 368 894	1 071 490	1 297 404	713 199	304 127	409 072	1 655 695	767 363	888 332
60 - 64	1 832 616	812 518	1 020 098	550 822	229 559	321 263	1 281 794	582 959	698 835
65 - 69	1 318 350	570 066	748 284	395 822	160 804	235 018	922 528	409 262	513 266
70 - 74	819 006	336 523	482 483	253 991	99 190	154 801	565 015	237 333	327 682
75 - 79	525 308	207 034	318 274	155 745	58 910	96 835	369 563	148 124	221 439
80 - 84	351 627	133 659	217 968	106 766	38 739	68 027	244 861	94 920	149 941
85 - 89	151 698	53 349	98 349	46 608	15 300	31 308	105 090	38 049	67 041
90 +	60 705	19 852	40 853	20 665	6 452	14 213	40 040	13 400	26 640
Nepal - Népal									
22 VI 2011 (CDJC)									
Total	26 494 504	12 849 041	13 645 463	4 523 820	2 306 049	2 217 771	21 970 684	10 542 992	11 427 692
0 - 4	2 567 963	1 314 957	1 253 006	327 100	172 598	154 502	2 240 863	1 142 359	1 098 504
5 - 9	3 204 859	1 635 176	1 569 683	431 121	227 618	203 503	2 773 738	1 407 558	1 366 180
10 - 14	3 475 424	1 764 630	1 710 794	507 618	266 722	240 896	2 967 806	1 497 908	1 469 898
15 - 19	2 931 980	1 443 191	1 488 789	520 714	273 601	247 113	2 411 266	1 169 590	1 241 676
20 - 24	2 358 071	1 043 981	1 314 090	520 546	260 529	260 017	1 837 525	783 452	1 054 073
25 - 29	2 079 354	917 243	1 162 111	452 256	220 230	232 026	1 627 098	697 013	930 085
30 - 34	1 735 305	770 577	964 728	372 219	181 542	190 677	1 363 086	589 035	774 051
35 - 39	1 604 319	740 200	864 119	324 965	161 347	163 618	1 279 354	578 853	700 501
40 - 44	1 386 121	660 290	725 831	263 008	136 600	126 408	1 123 113	523 690	599 423
45 - 49	1 172 959	575 101	597 858	205 833	106 627	99 206	967 126	468 474	498 652
50 - 54	1 005 476	505 864	499 612	165 685	86 471	79 214	839 791	419 393	420 398
55 - 59	818 263	412 892	405 371	123 667	63 841	59 826	694 596	349 051	345 545
60 - 64	756 827	368 451	388 376	105 862	52 258	53 604	650 965	316 193	334 772

7. Population by age, sex and urban/rural residence: latest available year, 2008 - 2017
Population selon l'âge, le sexe et la résidence, urbaine/rurale : dernière année disponible, 2008 - 2017 (continued - suite)

Continent, country or area, date, code[a] and age (in years) / Continent, pays ou zone, date, code[a] et âge (en années)	Total			Urban - Urbaine			Rural - Rurale		
	Both sexes Les deux sexes	Male Masculin	Female Féminin	Both sexes Les deux sexes	Male Masculin	Female Féminin	Both sexes Les deux sexes	Male Masculin	Female Féminin
ASIA - ASIE									
Nepal - Népal									
22 VI 2011 (CDJC)									
65 - 69	554 449	277 782	276 667	76 074	37 256	38 818	478 375	240 526	237 849
70 - 74	395 153	199 610	195 543	55 001	26 400	28 601	340 152	173 210	166 942
75 - 79	235 135	117 358	117 777	35 764	16 538	19 226	199 371	100 820	98 551
80 - 84	128 777	62 787	65 990	21 053	9 435	11 618	107 724	53 352	54 372
85 - 89	52 526	25 810	26 716	9 857	4 350	5 507	42 669	21 460	21 209
90 - 94	20 335	8 940	11 395	3 788	1 474	2 314	16 547	7 466	9 081
95 +	11 208	4 201	7 007	1 689	612	1 077	9 519	3 589	5 930
1 VII 2016 (ESDJ)[18]									
Total	28 431 494	13 784 009	14 647 486	...	...	...	...	...	...
0 - 4	2 950 167	1 525 630	1 424 537	...	...	...	...	...	...
5 - 9	2 674 278	1 368 495	1 305 783	...	...	...	...	...	...
10 - 14	3 062 865	1 564 080	1 498 784	...	...	...	...	...	...
15 - 19	3 317 315	1 680 525	1 636 790	...	...	...	...	...	...
20 - 24	3 021 919	1 476 611	1 545 309	...	...	...	...	...	...
25 - 29	2 340 931	1 033 222	1 307 709	...	...	...	...	...	...
30 - 34	1 998 816	860 512	1 138 303	...	...	...	...	...	...
35 - 39	1 740 784	771 970	968 815	...	...	...	...	...	...
40 - 44	1 521 989	691 192	830 797	...	...	...	...	...	...
45 - 49	1 334 086	632 128	701 958	...	...	...	...	...	...
50 - 54	1 140 179	552 834	587 346	...	...	...	...	...	...
55 - 59	930 950	462 675	468 275	...	...	...	...	...	...
60 - 64	770 098	382 738	387 360	...	...	...	...	...	...
65 - 69	627 821	303 255	324 567	...	...	...	...	...	...
70 - 74	482 949	231 131	251 818	...	...	...	...	...	...
75 - 79	339 914	162 123	177 791	...	...	...	...	...	...
80 +	176 432	84 889	91 543	...	...	...	...	...	...
Oman									
1 VII 2009 (ESDF)									
Total	3 173 917	1 971 115	1 202 802	2 314 865	1 457 197	857 668	859 049	513 917	345 132
0 - 4	272 144	139 614	132 530	184 595	94 803	89 792	87 549	44 811	42 738
5 - 9	245 026	124 776	120 250	162 307	82 954	79 353	82 718	41 821	40 897
10 - 14	254 610	129 964	124 646	168 924	86 326	82 598	85 685	43 638	42 047
15 - 19	284 826	145 215	139 611	194 123	99 854	94 269	90 703	45 361	45 342
20 - 24	387 448	238 483	148 965	285 594	176 341	109 253	101 854	62 142	39 712
25 - 29	475 403	327 686	147 717	362 531	249 782	112 749	112 871	77 904	34 967
30 - 34	367 536	247 107	120 429	288 055	192 969	95 086	79 481	54 138	25 343
35 - 39	272 100	192 483	79 617	212 145	150 865	61 280	59 955	41 618	18 337
40 - 44	207 202	149 090	58 112	161 282	117 670	43 612	45 920	31 420	14 500
45 - 49	145 430	103 908	41 522	111 077	81 065	30 012	34 353	22 843	11 510
50 - 54	113 587	83 057	30 530	84 975	63 752	21 223	28 612	19 305	9 307
55 - 59	59 890	40 488	19 402	42 674	29 489	13 185	17 216	10 999	6 217
60 - 64	39 730	23 538	16 192	26 050	15 494	10 556	13 680	8 044	5 636
65 - 69	20 811	11 811	9 000	13 363	7 537	5 826	7 448	4 274	3 174
70 - 74	14 933	7 721	7 212	9 224	4 703	4 521	5 709	3 018	2 691
75 - 79	6 817	3 303	3 514	4 201	1 981	2 220	2 616	1 322	1 294
80 +	6 424	2 871	3 553	3 745	1 612	2 133	2 679	1 259	1 420
1 VII 2017 (ESDF)[71]									
Total	4 559 963	2 984 404	1 575 559	...	...	...	...	...	...
0	76 660	39 062	37 598	...	...	...	...	...	...
1 - 4	339 131	172 974	166 157	...	...	...	...	...	...
5 - 9	335 194	170 548	164 646	...	...	...	...	...	...
10 - 14	256 730	130 860	125 870	...	...	...	...	...	...
15 - 19	234 879	119 775	115 104	...	...	...	...	...	...
20 - 24	402 377	260 950	141 427	...	...	...	...	...	...
25 - 29	727 009	539 984	187 025	...	...	...	...	...	...
30 - 34	682 507	505 362	177 145	...	...	...	...	...	...
35 - 39	499 408	362 836	136 572	...	...	...	...	...	...
40 - 44	331 047	236 887	94 160	...	...	...	...	...	...
45 - 49	228 738	167 237	61 501	...	...	...	...	...	...
50 - 54	152 741	106 418	46 323	...	...	...	...	...	...
55 - 59	111 329	73 357	37 972	...	...	...	...	...	...
60 - 64	66 416	39 704	26 712	...	...	...	...	...	...
65 - 69	39 565	20 402	19 163	...	...	...	...	...	...

7. Population by age, sex and urban/rural residence: latest available year, 2008 - 2017
Population selon l'âge, le sexe et la résidence, urbaine/rurale : dernière année disponible, 2008 - 2017 (continued - suite)

Continent, country or area, date, code[a] and age (in years) / Continent, pays ou zone, date, code[a] et âge (en années)	Total			Urban - Urbaine			Rural - Rurale		
	Both sexes Les deux sexes	Male Masculin	Female Féminin	Both sexes Les deux sexes	Male Masculin	Female Féminin	Both sexes Les deux sexes	Male Masculin	Female Féminin
ASIA - ASIE									
Oman									
1 VII 2017 (ESDF)[71]									
70 - 74	27 629	13 518	14 111	...	...	...	...	...	...
75 - 79	21 611	10 817	10 794	...	...	...	...	...	...
80 - 84	12 879	6 743	6 136	...	...	...	...	...	...
85 - 89	7 622	3 740	3 882	...	...	...	...	...	...
90 - 94	3 554	1 776	1 778	...	...	...	...	...	...
95 - 99	1 911	920	991	...	...	...	...	...	...
100 +	1 026	534	492	...	...	...	...	...	...
Philippines									
1 V 2010 (CDJC)[72]									
Total	92 335 113	46 634 257	45 700 856	41 855 571	20 840 798	21 014 773	50 479 542	25 793 459	24 686 083
0	1 968 131	1 018 386	949 745	873 792	453 065	420 727	1 094 339	565 321	529 018
1 - 4	8 265 653	4 274 825	3 990 828	3 571 743	1 850 296	1 721 447	4 693 910	2 424 529	2 269 381
5 - 9	10 321 543	5 332 287	4 989 256	4 384 024	2 267 726	2 116 298	5 937 519	3 064 561	2 872 958
10 - 14	10 179 610	5 237 006	4 942 604	4 286 862	2 195 115	2 091 747	5 892 748	3 041 891	2 850 857
15 - 19	9 705 354	4 931 506	4 773 848	4 301 712	2 120 800	2 180 912	5 403 642	2 810 706	2 592 936
20 - 24	8 408 656	4 256 999	4 151 657	4 050 916	1 989 031	2 061 885	4 357 740	2 267 968	2 089 772
25 - 29	7 423 723	3 746 311	3 677 412	3 693 442	1 821 972	1 871 470	3 730 281	1 924 339	1 805 942
30 - 34	6 772 929	3 443 582	3 329 347	3 353 327	1 676 968	1 676 359	3 419 602	1 766 614	1 652 988
35 - 39	6 013 953	3 057 323	2 956 630	2 886 723	1 448 968	1 437 755	3 127 230	1 608 355	1 518 875
40 - 44	5 471 588	2 778 661	2 692 927	2 588 569	1 292 882	1 295 687	2 883 019	1 485 779	1 397 240
45 - 49	4 680 649	2 367 809	2 312 840	2 180 936	1 082 303	1 098 633	2 499 713	1 285 506	1 214 207
50 - 54	3 894 850	1 953 952	1 940 898	1 808 298	890 919	917 379	2 086 552	1 063 033	1 023 519
55 - 59	2 987 148	1 475 861	1 511 287	1 358 685	660 616	698 069	1 628 463	815 245	813 218
60 - 64	2 228 399	1 064 116	1 164 283	979 510	461 508	518 002	1 248 889	602 608	646 281
65 - 69	1 497 557	680 227	817 330	593 219	263 603	329 616	904 338	416 624	487 714
70 - 74	1 142 562	492 152	650 410	437 280	181 972	255 308	705 282	310 180	395 102
75 - 79	707 115	286 079	421 036	265 280	102 308	162 972	441 835	183 771	258 064
80 - 84	394 188	145 937	248 251	145 081	50 979	94 102	249 107	94 958	154 149
85 - 89	188 511	64 125	124 386	67 310	21 250	46 060	121 201	42 875	78 326
90 - 94	60 102	19 598	40 504	21 070	6 202	14 868	39 032	13 396	25 636
95 - 99	18 099	5 684	12 415	6 223	1 753	4 470	11 876	3 931	7 945
100 +	4 793	1 831	2 962	1 569	562	1 007	3 224	1 269	1 955
1 VII 2017 (ESDJ)[9]									
Total	104 921 400	52 927 400	51 994 000	...	...	...	...	...	...
0	2 313 698	1 195 048	1 118 650	...	...	...	...	...	...
1 - 4	9 087 958	4 665 382	4 422 576	...	...	...	...	...	...
5 - 9	10 902 400	5 582 800	5 319 600	...	...	...	...	...	...
10 - 14	10 421 300	5 358 600	5 062 700	...	...	...	...	...	...
15 - 19	10 180 000	5 241 700	4 938 300	...	...	...	...	...	...
20 - 24	9 811 900	5 013 600	4 798 300	...	...	...	...	...	...
25 - 29	8 806 400	4 472 200	4 334 200	...	...	...	...	...	...
30 - 34	7 692 100	3 886 300	3 805 800	...	...	...	...	...	...
35 - 39	6 907 000	3 492 800	3 414 200	...	...	...	...	...	...
40 - 44	6 176 600	3 126 800	3 049 800	...	...	...	...	...	...
45 - 49	5 526 000	2 789 300	2 736 700	...	...	...	...	...	...
50 - 54	4 787 400	2 400 000	2 387 400	...	...	...	...	...	...
55 - 59	3 944 100	1 950 800	1 993 300	...	...	...	...	...	...
60 - 64	3 029 000	1 464 600	1 564 400	...	...	...	...	...	...
65 - 69	2 170 000	1 006 600	1 163 400	...	...	...	...	...	...
70 - 74	1 410 800	613 400	797 400	...	...	...	...	...	...
75 - 79	908 300	365 200	543 100	...	...	...	...	...	...
80 +	846 500	302 300	544 200	...	...	...	...	...	...
Qatar									
1 VII 2017 (ESDF)									
Total	2 724 606	2 046 047	678 559	...	...	...	...	...	...
0	27 553	13 992	13 561	...	...	...	...	...	...
1 - 4	116 320	58 875	57 445	...	...	...	...	...	...
5 - 9	127 987	64 510	63 477	...	...	...	...	...	...
10 - 14	100 500	50 830	49 670	...	...	...	...	...	...
15 - 19	92 557	56 516	36 041	...	...	...	...	...	...
20 - 24	284 380	237 357	47 023	...	...	...	...	...	...
25 - 29	481 993	389 213	92 780	...	...	...	...	...	...
30 - 34	457 113	361 510	95 603	...	...	...	...	...	...

Continent, country or area, date, code[a] and age (in years) / Continent, pays ou zone, date, code[a] et âge (en années)	Total			Urban - Urbaine			Rural - Rurale		
	Both sexes Les deux sexes	Male Masculin	Female Féminin	Both sexes Les deux sexes	Male Masculin	Female Féminin	Both sexes Les deux sexes	Male Masculin	Female Féminin
ASIA - ASIE									
Qatar									
1 VII 2017 (ESDF)									
35 - 39	347 715	271 350	76 365	...	...	...	...	...	...
40 - 44	257 362	204 770	52 592	...	...	...	...	...	...
45 - 49	179 486	144 520	34 966	...	...	...	...	...	...
50 - 54	113 169	89 760	23 409	...	...	...	...	...	...
55 - 59	73 572	58 221	15 351	...	...	...	...	...	...
60 - 64	34 468	25 299	9 169	...	...	...	...	...	...
65 - 69	15 570	10 862	4 708	...	...	...	...	...	...
70 - 74	7 436	4 452	2 984	...	...	...	...	...	...
75 - 79	3 780	2 141	1 639	...	...	...	...	...	...
80 +	3 645	1 869	1 776	...	...	...	...	...	...
Republic of Korea - République de Corée									
1 XI 2015 (CDJC)									
Total	51 069 375	25 608 502	25 460 873	41 677 695	20 791 896	20 885 799	9 391 680	4 816 606	4 575 074
0	422 337	216 797	205 540	353 330	181 250	172 080	69 007	35 547	33 460
1 - 4	1 836 333	942 214	894 119	1 529 774	784 742	745 032	306 559	157 472	149 087
5 - 9	2 267 851	1 169 770	1 098 081	1 893 768	976 334	917 434	374 083	193 436	180 647
10 - 14	2 427 792	1 262 770	1 165 022	2 042 651	1 060 734	981 917	385 141	202 036	183 105
15 - 19	3 194 079	1 668 683	1 525 396	2 679 885	1 395 027	1 284 858	514 194	273 656	240 538
20 - 24	3 531 108	1 887 776	1 643 332	2 980 057	1 568 333	1 411 724	551 051	319 443	231 608
25 - 29	3 265 288	1 728 888	1 536 400	2 757 203	1 428 161	1 329 042	508 085	300 727	207 358
30 - 34	3 811 610	1 986 796	1 824 814	3 221 411	1 651 851	1 569 560	590 199	334 945	255 254
35 - 39	3 926 862	2 022 466	1 904 396	3 306 159	1 678 522	1 627 637	620 703	343 944	276 759
40 - 44	4 338 827	2 218 442	2 120 385	3 656 010	1 837 640	1 818 370	682 817	380 802	302 015
45 - 49	4 388 157	2 217 013	2 171 144	3 677 944	1 829 471	1 848 473	710 213	387 542	322 671
50 - 54	4 263 447	2 153 186	2 110 261	3 506 520	1 751 909	1 754 611	756 927	401 277	355 650
55 - 59	3 956 849	1 969 232	1 987 617	3 182 242	1 572 740	1 609 502	774 607	396 492	378 115
60 - 64	2 821 457	1 379 694	1 441 763	2 210 398	1 077 319	1 133 079	611 059	302 375	308 684
65 - 69	2 144 023	1 028 129	1 115 894	1 629 723	778 383	851 340	514 300	249 746	264 554
70 - 74	1 770 741	793 855	976 886	1 273 733	578 485	695 248	497 008	215 370	281 638
75 - 79	1 362 669	553 178	809 491	913 754	375 959	537 795	448 915	177 219	271 696
80 - 84	814 222	276 627	537 595	523 437	179 372	344 065	290 785	97 255	193 530
85 - 89	372 987	98 855	274 132	240 935	63 626	177 309	132 052	35 229	96 823
90 - 94	124 723	28 759	95 964	80 613	18 467	62 146	44 110	10 292	33 818
95 - 99	24 796	4 923	19 873	16 059	3 271	12 788	8 737	1 652	7 085
100 +	3 217	449	2 768	2 089	300	1 789	1 128	149	979
1 VII 2017 (ESDJ)									
Total	51 446 201	25 790 240	25 655 961	...	...	...	...	...	...
0	410 949	210 764	200 185	...	...	...	...	...	...
1 - 4	1 758 229	901 030	857 199	...	...	...	...	...	...
5 - 9	2 315 416	1 192 239	1 123 177	...	...	...	...	...	...
10 - 14	2 266 449	1 174 811	1 091 638	...	...	...	...	...	...
15 - 19	2 978 019	1 552 681	1 425 338	...	...	...	...	...	...
20 - 24	3 525 627	1 878 484	1 647 143	...	...	...	...	...	...
25 - 29	3 376 535	1 798 846	1 577 689	...	...	...	...	...	...
30 - 34	3 498 845	1 830 845	1 668 000	...	...	...	...	...	...
35 - 39	4 062 933	2 096 427	1 966 506	...	...	...	...	...	...
40 - 44	4 086 502	2 089 384	1 997 118	...	...	...	...	...	...
45 - 49	4 515 970	2 285 324	2 230 646	...	...	...	...	...	...
50 - 54	4 173 106	2 112 972	2 060 134	...	...	...	...	...	...
55 - 59	4 232 916	2 106 396	2 126 520	...	...	...	...	...	...
60 - 64	3 169 187	1 554 147	1 615 040	...	...	...	...	...	...
65 - 69	2 289 256	1 099 994	1 189 262	...	...	...	...	...	...
70 - 74	1 758 803	801 164	957 639	...	...	...	...	...	...
75 - 79	1 495 014	621 058	873 956	...	...	...	...	...	...
80 - 84	931 356	329 093	602 263	...	...	...	...	...	...
85 - 89	426 825	116 401	310 424	...	...	...	...	...	...
90 - 94	139 616	31 404	108 212	...	...	...	...	...	...
95 - 99	31 097	6 271	24 826	...	...	...	...	...	...
100 +	3 551	505	3 046	...	...	...	...	...	...

Continent, country or area, date, code[a] and age (in years) / Continent, pays ou zone, date, code[a] et âge (en années)	Total			Urban - Urbaine			Rural - Rurale		
	Both sexes Les deux sexes	Male Masculin	Female Féminin	Both sexes Les deux sexes	Male Masculin	Female Féminin	Both sexes Les deux sexes	Male Masculin	Female Féminin
ASIA - ASIE									
Saudi Arabia - Arabie saoudite									
1 VII 2017 (ESDF)									
Total	32 612 641	18 745 846	13 866 795	...	...	...	...	...	...
0 - 4	2 734 316	1 393 704	1 340 612	...	...	...	...	...	...
5 - 9	2 835 657	1 444 212	1 391 445	...	...	...	...	...	...
10 - 14	2 483 984	1 263 267	1 220 717	...	...	...	...	...	...
15 - 19	2 265 472	1 156 356	1 109 116	...	...	...	...	...	...
20 - 24	2 526 143	1 344 232	1 181 911	...	...	...	...	...	...
25 - 29	3 111 770	1 715 996	1 395 774	...	...	...	...	...	...
30 - 34	3 147 830	1 846 029	1 301 801	...	...	...	...	...	...
35 - 39	3 503 179	2 189 173	1 314 006	...	...	...	...	...	...
40 - 44	3 132 169	1 991 685	1 140 484	...	...	...	...	...	...
45 - 49	2 327 996	1 533 512	794 484	...	...	...	...	...	...
50 - 54	1 626 211	1 108 410	517 801	...	...	...	...	...	...
55 - 59	1 124 497	742 885	381 612	...	...	...	...	...	...
60 - 64	742 511	462 413	280 098	...	...	...	...	...	...
65 - 69	414 534	225 283	189 251	...	...	...	...	...	...
70 - 74	276 103	144 120	131 983	...	...	...	...	...	...
75 - 79	164 237	86 688	77 549	...	...	...	...	...	...
80 +	196 032	97 881	98 151	...	...	...	...	...	...
Singapore - Singapour[73]									
30 VI 2017 (ESDJ)									
Total	3 965 796	1 943 545	2 022 251	...	...	...	...	...	...
0 - 4	187 653	96 041	91 612	...	...	...	...	...	...
5 - 9	200 575	102 010	98 565	...	...	...	...	...	...
10 - 14	206 253	104 885	101 368	...	...	...	...	...	...
15 - 19	232 973	119 500	113 473	...	...	...	...	...	...
20 - 24	259 072	131 825	127 247	...	...	...	...	...	...
25 - 29	290 198	142 427	147 771	...	...	...	...	...	...
30 - 34	279 340	132 378	146 962	...	...	...	...	...	...
35 - 39	300 956	142 776	158 180	...	...	...	...	...	...
40 - 44	311 484	150 641	160 843	...	...	...	...	...	...
45 - 49	303 457	148 095	155 362	...	...	...	...	...	...
50 - 54	312 814	156 386	156 428	...	...	...	...	...	...
55 - 59	301 678	151 320	150 358	...	...	...	...	...	...
60 - 64	262 651	130 589	132 062	...	...	...	...	...	...
65 - 69	203 969	99 351	104 618	...	...	...	...	...	...
70 - 74	119 494	56 463	63 031	...	...	...	...	...	...
75 - 79	91 953	40 524	51 429	...	...	...	...	...	...
80 - 84	54 341	22 400	31 941	...	...	...	...	...	...
85 +	46 935	15 934	31 001	...	...	...	...	...	...
Sri Lanka									
20 III 2012 (CDJC)									
Total	20 359 439	9 856 634	10 502 805	3 704 470	1 800 327	1 904 143	16 654 969	8 056 307	8 598 662
0 - 4	1 743 862	879 223	864 639	281 707	142 039	139 668	1 462 155	737 184	724 971
5 - 9	1 747 752	882 108	865 644	292 480	147 539	144 941	1 455 272	734 569	720 703
10 - 14	1 640 052	829 069	810 983	286 653	145 640	141 013	1 353 399	683 429	669 970
15 - 19	1 644 249	819 927	824 322	306 654	155 546	151 108	1 337 595	664 381	673 214
20 - 24	1 532 883	742 316	790 567	308 605	151 666	156 939	1 224 278	590 650	633 628
25 - 29	1 552 848	743 510	809 338	290 825	142 387	148 438	1 262 023	601 123	660 900
30 - 34	1 639 415	796 866	842 549	294 944	145 860	149 084	1 344 471	651 006	693 465
35 - 39	1 409 077	686 037	723 040	260 479	127 396	133 083	1 148 598	558 641	589 957
40 - 44	1 359 209	661 623	697 586	253 831	124 363	129 468	1 105 378	537 260	568 118
45 - 49	1 285 830	618 140	667 690	237 646	113 675	123 971	1 048 184	504 465	543 719
50 - 54	1 219 460	581 293	638 167	223 940	106 249	117 691	995 520	475 044	520 476
55 - 59	1 064 229	500 871	563 358	192 715	90 444	102 271	871 514	410 427	461 087
60 - 64	917 910	425 428	492 482	169 167	78 370	90 797	748 743	347 058	401 685
65 - 69	633 289	283 764	349 525	121 751	54 401	67 350	511 538	229 363	282 175
70 - 74	412 414	181 846	230 568	77 909	33 807	44 102	334 505	148 039	186 466
75 - 79	283 186	116 389	166 797	52 087	21 036	31 051	231 099	95 353	135 746
80 - 84	159 379	64 250	95 129	30 707	11 775	18 932	128 672	52 475	76 197
85 - 89	73 441	28 293	45 148	14 121	5 097	9 024	59 320	23 196	36 124
90 - 94	24 258	9 293	14 965	4 932	1 790	3 142	19 326	7 503	11 823
95 +	16 696	6 388	10 308	3 317	1 247	2 070	13 379	5 141	8 238

7. Population by age, sex and urban/rural residence: latest available year, 2008 - 2017
Population selon l'âge, le sexe et la résidence, urbaine/rurale : dernière année disponible, 2008 - 2017 (continued - suite)

Continent, country or area, date, code[a] and age (in years) / Continent, pays ou zone, date, code[a] et âge (en années)	Total			Urban - Urbaine			Rural - Rurale		
	Both sexes Les deux sexes	Male Masculin	Female Féminin	Both sexes Les deux sexes	Male Masculin	Female Féminin	Both sexes Les deux sexes	Male Masculin	Female Féminin
ASIA - ASIE									
Sri Lanka									
1 VII 2017* (ESDJ)									
Total	21 444 350	10 382 372	11 061 978	...	...	...	...	...	...
0 - 4	1 839 188	927 284	911 904	...	...	...	...	...	...
5 - 9	1 842 646	929 982	912 664	...	...	...	...	...	...
10 - 14	1 728 952	873 968	854 984	...	...	...	...	...	...
15 - 19	1 733 148	864 163	868 985	...	...	...	...	...	...
20 - 24	1 614 555	781 763	832 792	...	...	...	...	...	...
25 - 29	1 635 890	783 157	852 733	...	...	...	...	...	...
30 - 34	1 726 790	839 276	887 514	...	...	...	...	...	...
35 - 39	1 483 827	722 435	761 392	...	...	...	...	...	...
40 - 44	1 431 052	696 615	734 437	...	...	...	...	...	...
45 - 49	1 354 017	650 971	703 046	...	...	...	...	...	...
50 - 54	1 283 895	612 093	671 802	...	...	...	...	...	...
55 - 59	1 120 160	527 286	592 874	...	...	...	...	...	...
60 - 64	965 685	447 659	518 026	...	...	...	...	...	...
65 - 69	665 807	298 390	367 417	...	...	...	...	...	...
70 - 74	433 536	191 216	242 320	...	...	...	...	...	...
75 - 79	297 641	122 380	175 261	...	...	...	...	...	...
80 +	287 561	113 734	173 827	...	...	...	...	...	...
State of Palestine - État de Palestine									
1 VII 2016 (ESDF)									
Total	4 816 503	2 447 616	2 368 887	...	...	...	...	...	...
0	148 776	76 075	72 701	...	...	...	...	...	...
1 - 4	569 313	291 039	278 274	...	...	...	...	...	...
5 - 9	609 503	310 845	298 658	...	...	...	...	...	...
10 - 14	559 144	285 511	273 633	...	...	...	...	...	...
15 - 19	530 322	270 712	259 610	...	...	...	...	...	...
20 - 24	495 035	252 377	242 658	...	...	...	...	...	...
25 - 29	414 334	211 305	203 029	...	...	...	...	...	...
30 - 34	320 463	163 780	156 683	...	...	...	...	...	...
35 - 39	265 799	135 413	130 386	...	...	...	...	...	...
40 - 44	224 673	113 626	111 047	...	...	...	...	...	...
45 - 49	188 061	95 886	92 175	...	...	...	...	...	...
50 - 54	155 661	80 634	75 027	...	...	...	...	...	...
55 - 59	116 766	60 064	56 702	...	...	...	...	...	...
60 - 64	78 511	39 334	39 177	...	...	...	...	...	...
65 - 69	54 985	25 996	28 989	...	...	...	...	...	...
70 - 74	37 786	16 226	21 560	...	...	...	...	...	...
75 - 79	24 430	9 844	14 586	...	...	...	...	...	...
80 +	22 941	8 949	13 992	...	...	...	...	...	...
Syrian Arab Republic - République arabe syrienne[74]									
1 VII 2011 (ESDF)									
Total	21 124 000	10 794 000	10 330 000	11 297 000	5 795 000	5 502 000	9 827 000	4 999 000	4 828 000
0 - 4	2 775 000	1 428 000	1 347 000	1 384 000	713 000	671 000	1 391 000	715 000	676 000
5 - 9	2 654 000	1 384 000	1 270 000	1 357 000	719 000	638 000	1 297 000	665 000	632 000
10 - 14	2 430 000	1 232 000	1 198 000	1 270 000	637 000	633 000	1 160 000	595 000	565 000
15 - 19	2 279 000	1 191 000	1 088 000	1 193 000	626 000	567 000	1 086 000	565 000	521 000
20 - 24	1 979 000	1 035 000	944 000	1 045 000	545 000	500 000	934 000	490 000	444 000
25 - 29	1 737 000	864 000	873 000	937 000	475 000	462 000	800 000	389 000	411 000
30 - 34	1 371 000	674 000	697 000	733 000	359 000	374 000	638 000	315 000	323 000
35 - 39	1 229 000	601 000	628 000	694 000	336 000	358 000	535 000	265 000	270 000
40 - 44	1 096 000	545 000	551 000	644 000	325 000	319 000	452 000	220 000	232 000
45 - 49	870 000	437 000	433 000	536 000	272 000	264 000	334 000	165 000	169 000
50 - 54	792 000	387 000	405 000	458 000	232 000	226 000	334 000	155 000	179 000
55 - 59	573 000	293 000	280 000	322 000	168 000	154 000	251 000	125 000	126 000
60 - 64	481 000	254 000	227 000	260 000	139 000	121 000	221 000	115 000	106 000
65 +	858 000	469 000	389 000	464 000	249 000	215 000	394 000	220 000	174 000
Tajikistan - Tadjikistan									
1 VII 2016 (ESDF)									
Total	8 646 973	4 379 342	4 267 631	2 280 367	1 159 476	1 120 891	6 366 605	3 219 866	3 146 739
0	231 472	122 055	109 417	50 631	26 825	23 806	180 840	95 229	85 611
1 - 4	872 364	456 206	416 158	207 973	108 972	99 001	664 390	347 233	317 157

Continent, country or area, date, code[a] and age (in years) Continent, pays ou zone, date, code[a] et âge (en années)	Total			Urban - Urbaine			Rural - Rurale		
	Both sexes Les deux sexes	Male Masculin	Female Féminin	Both sexes Les deux sexes	Male Masculin	Female Féminin	Both sexes Les deux sexes	Male Masculin	Female Féminin
ASIA - ASIE									
Tajikistan - Tadjikistan 1 VII 2016 (ESDF)									
5 - 9	1 036 435	533 763	502 672	245 857	126 508	119 349	790 578	407 255	383 323
10 - 14	833 962	428 190	405 772	207 892	107 015	100 877	626 070	321 175	304 895
15 - 19	863 941	442 007	421 934	228 650	119 077	109 573	635 291	322 929	312 362
20 - 24	851 536	431 968	419 568	241 846	131 159	110 687	609 690	300 809	308 881
25 - 29	840 806	422 421	418 385	232 834	124 549	108 285	607 972	297 872	310 100
30 - 34	671 292	338 507	332 785	169 351	84 581	84 770	501 941	253 926	248 015
35 - 39	509 888	257 221	252 662	138 011	66 970	71 041	371 871	190 251	181 620
40 - 44	438 802	217 224	221 578	126 381	59 245	67 136	312 421	157 979	154 442
45 - 49	396 381	194 806	201 575	119 334	57 205	62 129	277 047	137 601	139 446
50 - 54	357 781	174 969	182 812	104 952	50 230	54 722	252 829	124 739	128 090
55 - 59	288 861	141 542	147 318	83 316	40 060	43 256	205 545	101 483	104 062
60 - 64	178 110	86 053	92 057	51 065	23 939	27 126	127 045	62 114	64 931
65 - 69	107 680	52 098	55 582	31 127	14 560	16 567	76 553	37 538	39 015
70 - 74	57 258	29 469	27 789	15 962	7 635	8 327	41 296	21 835	19 461
75 - 79	58 073	27 642	30 431	14 624	6 552	8 072	43 449	21 089	22 360
80 - 84	31 661	13 975	17 685	6 852	2 856	3 996	24 809	11 119	13 690
85 - 89	14 860	6 888	7 972	2 637	1 109	1 528	12 222	5 779	6 443
90 - 94	4 813	1 956	2 857	889	326	563	3 924	1 630	2 294
95 - 99	845	309	537	138	69	69	707	240	467
100 +	159	73	86	45	33	12	114	40	74
Thailand - Thaïlande 1 VII 2017 (ESDJ)									
Total	65 521 660	31 807 391	33 714 269	32 257 097	15 626 525	16 630 572	33 264 563	16 180 866	17 083 697
0 - 4	3 661 555	1 872 247	1 789 308	1 792 273	916 261	876 012	1 869 282	955 986	913 295
0	721 683	369 306	352 378	...	...	...	...	...	...
1 - 4	2 939 871	1 502 941	1 436 930	...	...	...	...	...	...
5 - 9	3 760 113	1 923 678	1 836 435	1 757 747	899 422	858 325	2 002 366	1 024 256	978 110
10 - 14	4 071 457	2 079 375	1 992 082	1 842 247	943 055	899 193	2 229 210	1 136 320	1 092 890
15 - 19	4 416 067	2 244 537	2 171 529	2 022 351	1 027 332	995 019	2 393 716	1 217 206	1 176 510
20 - 24	4 584 174	2 311 801	2 272 373	2 195 601	1 107 445	1 088 156	2 388 573	1 204 355	1 184 218
25 - 29	4 395 408	2 198 898	2 196 511	2 355 102	1 165 928	1 189 174	2 040 307	1 032 970	1 007 337
30 - 34	4 383 056	2 168 363	2 214 693	2 375 033	1 159 442	1 215 590	2 008 023	1 008 920	999 103
35 - 39	4 861 798	2 371 586	2 490 211	2 607 031	1 268 687	1 338 344	2 254 767	1 102 900	1 151 867
40 - 44	5 148 705	2 486 553	2 662 152	2 640 455	1 278 511	1 361 944	2 508 250	1 208 042	1 300 208
45 - 49	5 352 661	2 561 963	2 790 698	2 688 918	1 290 530	1 398 388	2 663 743	1 271 433	1 392 310
50 - 54	5 173 034	2 456 951	2 716 083	2 526 279	1 200 024	1 326 254	2 646 756	1 256 927	1 389 829
55 - 59	4 487 810	2 115 271	2 372 538	2 180 384	1 026 584	1 153 800	2 307 426	1 088 687	1 218 739
60 - 64	3 704 169	1 728 447	1 975 722	1 765 250	819 775	945 474	1 938 920	908 672	1 030 248
65 - 69	2 726 809	1 254 515	1 472 293	1 286 193	588 071	698 122	1 440 616	666 444	774 172
70 - 74	1 914 155	858 054	1 056 101	886 843	394 210	492 633	1 027 312	463 844	563 468
75 - 79	1 346 901	579 113	767 789	625 254	266 341	358 914	721 647	312 772	408 875
80 - 84	897 021	361 369	535 653	413 590	166 331	247 258	483 432	195 037	288 394
85 - 89	458 484	173 302	285 182	212 460	79 776	132 685	246 024	93 526	152 498
90 - 94	144 430	50 880	93 551	68 041	23 872	44 169	76 389	27 007	49 382
95 +	...	...	...	16 046	4 927	11 118	17 806	5 561	12 245
95 - 99	29 621	9 336	20 285	...	...	...	...	...	...
100 +	4 231	1 153	3 078	...	...	...	...	...	...
Timor-Leste 11 VII 2010 (CDFC)									
Total	1 066 409	544 198	522 211	316 086	166 163	149 923	750 323	378 035	372 288
0 - 4	153 334	79 169	74 165	40 622	20 978	19 644	112 712	58 191	54 521
5 - 9	153 108	78 980	74 128	39 668	20 480	19 188	113 440	58 500	54 940
10 - 14	135 464	70 513	64 951	33 309	17 369	15 940	102 155	53 144	49 011
15 - 19	116 535	58 754	57 781	42 791	21 249	21 542	73 744	37 505	36 239
20 - 24	94 427	47 336	47 091	41 612	22 175	19 437	52 815	25 161	27 654
25 - 29	76 836	38 269	38 567	31 190	16 578	14 612	45 646	21 691	23 955
30 - 34	51 911	25 805	26 106	19 454	10 623	8 831	32 457	15 182	17 275
35 - 39	57 508	29 961	27 547	18 377	10 284	8 093	39 131	19 677	19 454
40 - 44	48 372	25 407	22 965	13 599	7 748	5 851	34 773	17 659	17 114
45 - 49	38 917	20 430	18 487	9 971	5 692	4 279	28 946	14 738	14 208
50 - 54	30 084	15 539	14 545	7 205	3 954	3 251	22 879	11 585	11 294
55 - 59	22 346	11 796	10 550	5 007	2 725	2 282	17 339	9 071	8 268
60 - 64	37 333	17 419	19 914	5 419	2 596	2 823	31 914	14 823	17 091

7. Population by age, sex and urban/rural residence: latest available year, 2008 - 2017
Population selon l'âge, le sexe et la résidence, urbaine/rurale : dernière année disponible, 2008 - 2017 (continued - suite)

Continent, country or area, date, code[a] and age (in years) / Continent, pays ou zone, date, code[a] et âge (en années)	Total			Urban - Urbaine			Rural - Rurale		
	Both sexes Les deux sexes	Male Masculin	Female Féminin	Both sexes Les deux sexes	Male Masculin	Female Féminin	Both sexes Les deux sexes	Male Masculin	Female Féminin
ASIA - ASIE									
Timor-Leste									
11 VII 2010 (CDFC)									
65 - 69	23 106	11 573	11 533	3 407	1 638	1 769	19 699	9 935	9 764
70 - 74	12 705	6 285	6 420	2 079	991	1 088	10 626	5 294	5 332
75 - 79	7 125	3 404	3 721	1 127	508	619	5 998	2 896	3 102
80 - 84	3 755	1 818	1 937	614	275	339	3 141	1 543	1 598
85 +	3 543	1 740	1 803	635	300	335	2 908	1 440	1 468
Turkey - Turquie[75]									
31 XII 2016 (ESDJ)									
Total	79 814 871	40 043 650	39 771 221	70 165 359	35 162 317	35 003 042	9 649 512	4 881 333	4 768 179
0	1 257 621	645 189	612 432	1 130 150	579 619	550 531	127 471	65 570	61 901
1 - 4	5 201 674	2 669 353	2 532 321	4 663 143	2 393 043	2 270 100	538 531	276 310	262 221
5 - 9	6 337 444	3 253 345	3 084 099	5 652 023	2 902 020	2 750 003	685 421	351 325	334 096
10 - 14	6 129 043	3 147 133	2 981 910	5 389 905	2 768 455	2 621 450	739 138	378 678	360 460
15 - 19	6 623 319	3 400 443	3 222 876	5 800 098	2 974 076	2 826 022	823 221	426 367	396 854
20 - 24	6 365 723	3 247 764	3 117 959	5 627 511	2 838 374	2 789 137	738 212	409 390	328 822
25 - 29	6 246 041	3 169 360	3 076 681	5 632 462	2 834 163	2 798 299	613 579	335 197	278 382
30 - 34	6 310 411	3 196 645	3 113 766	5 744 868	2 895 078	2 849 790	565 543	301 567	263 976
35 - 39	6 494 333	3 275 175	3 219 158	5 890 373	2 962 766	2 927 607	603 960	312 409	291 551
40 - 44	5 634 317	2 833 655	2 800 662	5 068 027	2 545 869	2 522 158	566 290	287 786	278 504
45 - 49	4 748 514	2 412 875	2 335 639	4 221 574	2 141 667	2 079 907	526 940	271 208	255 732
50 - 54	4 756 244	2 381 640	2 374 604	4 140 755	2 073 974	2 066 781	615 489	307 666	307 823
55 - 59	3 715 736	1 855 171	1 860 565	3 184 498	1 590 376	1 594 122	531 238	264 795	266 443
60 - 64	3 342 948	1 636 510	1 706 438	2 778 159	1 364 247	1 413 912	564 789	272 263	292 526
65 - 69	2 412 537	1 132 464	1 280 073	1 954 497	920 907	1 033 590	458 040	211 557	246 483
70 - 74	1 680 492	763 121	917 371	1 323 989	602 259	721 730	356 503	160 862	195 641
75 - 79	1 202 050	512 607	689 443	926 470	393 352	533 118	275 580	119 255	156 325
80 - 84	809 325	336 206	473 119	616 881	250 671	366 210	192 444	85 535	106 909
85 - 89	401 758	136 238	265 520	306 417	101 762	204 655	95 341	34 476	60 865
90 - 94	121 771	34 280	87 491	94 888	26 104	68 784	26 883	8 176	18 707
95 - 99	18 338	3 802	14 536	14 596	3 005	11 591	3 742	797	2 945
100 +	5 232	674	4 558	4 075	530	3 545	1 157	144	1 013
Uzbekistan - Ouzbékistan[76]									
1 VII 2015 (ESDJ)									
Total	31 298 929	15 695 568	15 603 361	15 855 953	7 919 014	7 936 939	15 442 976	7 776 554	7 666 422
0	700 155	364 308	335 847	314 693	163 697	150 996	385 462	200 611	184 851
1 - 4	2 569 021	1 331 960	1 237 061	1 171 852	607 940	563 912	1 397 169	724 020	673 149
5 - 9	3 015 258	1 551 922	1 463 336	1 371 477	703 840	667 637	1 643 781	848 082	795 699
10 - 14	2 569 558	1 318 964	1 250 594	1 259 615	645 426	614 189	1 309 943	673 538	636 405
15 - 19	2 841 508	1 453 864	1 387 644	1 402 806	716 934	685 872	1 438 702	736 930	701 772
20 - 24	3 238 160	1 648 485	1 589 675	1 583 875	812 193	771 682	1 654 285	836 292	817 993
25 - 29	3 085 365	1 561 037	1 524 328	1 544 612	787 618	756 994	1 540 753	773 419	767 334
30 - 34	2 581 117	1 294 280	1 286 837	1 331 499	669 183	662 316	1 249 618	625 097	624 521
35 - 39	2 152 092	1 075 561	1 076 531	1 131 979	562 901	569 078	1 020 113	512 660	507 453
40 - 44	1 923 930	957 647	966 283	1 051 285	523 195	528 090	872 645	434 452	438 193
45 - 49	1 650 639	801 329	849 310	910 665	449 528	461 137	739 974	351 801	388 173
50 - 54	1 584 938	764 588	820 350	857 095	411 311	445 784	727 843	353 277	374 566
55 - 59	1 273 308	614 125	659 183	704 226	334 974	369 252	569 082	279 151	289 931
60 - 64	835 627	396 007	439 620	478 698	222 129	256 569	356 929	173 878	183 051
65 - 69	466 332	216 263	250 069	278 318	124 941	153 377	188 014	91 322	96 692
70 - 74	277 898	129 852	148 046	157 652	69 591	88 061	120 246	60 261	59 985
75 - 79	275 297	119 011	156 286	157 297	62 680	94 617	118 000	56 331	61 669
80 - 84	128 512	49 173	79 339	71 787	24 793	46 994	56 725	24 380	32 345
85 +	130 214	47 192	83 022	76 522	26 140	50 382	53 692	21 052	32 640
Viet Nam									
1 IV 2009 (CDJC)									
Total	85 846 997	42 413 143	43 433 854	25 436 896	12 349 995	13 086 901	60 410 101	30 063 148	30 346 953
0 - 4	7 034 144	3 662 889	3 371 255	1 949 105	1 019 547	929 558	5 085 039	2 643 342	2 441 697
5 - 9	6 710 737	3 458 159	3 252 578	1 757 679	910 339	847 340	4 953 058	2 547 820	2 405 238
10 - 14	7 248 378	3 725 369	3 523 009	1 761 650	904 731	856 919	5 486 728	2 820 638	2 666 090
15 - 17	5 236 771	2 681 653	2 555 118	1 311 350	662 369	648 981	3 925 421	2 019 284	1 906 137
18 - 19	3 727 131	1 896 261	1 830 870	1 188 578	562 169	626 409	2 538 553	1 334 092	1 204 461
20 - 24	8 432 867	4 253 618	4 179 249	2 759 456	1 305 436	1 454 020	5 673 411	2 948 182	2 725 229
25 - 29	7 790 003	3 904 730	3 885 273	2 519 920	1 205 518	1 314 402	5 270 083	2 699 212	2 570 871
30 - 34	6 868 158	3 462 905	3 405 253	2 164 824	1 062 838	1 101 986	4 703 334	2 400 067	2 303 267

Continent, country or area, date, code[a] and age (in years) / Continent, pays ou zone, date, code[a] et âge (en années)	Total			Urban - Urbaine			Rural - Rurale		
	Both sexes Les deux sexes	Male Masculin	Female Féminin	Both sexes Les deux sexes	Male Masculin	Female Féminin	Both sexes Les deux sexes	Male Masculin	Female Féminin
ASIA - ASIE									
Viet Nam									
1 IV 2009 (CDJC)									
35 - 39	6 531 607	3 298 266	3 233 341	2 059 356	1 027 075	1 032 281	4 472 251	2 271 191	2 201 060
40 - 44	5 966 856	2 967 934	2 998 922	1 818 188	896 290	921 898	4 148 668	2 071 644	2 077 024
45 - 49	5 450 928	2 642 466	2 808 462	1 728 008	840 047	887 961	3 722 920	1 802 419	1 920 501
50 - 54	4 412 051	2 082 098	2 329 953	1 435 970	683 749	752 221	2 976 081	1 398 349	1 577 732
55 - 59	2 984 619	1 364 319	1 620 300	931 382	421 296	510 086	2 053 237	943 023	1 110 214
60 - 64	1 937 948	861 897	1 076 051	590 161	259 193	330 968	1 347 787	602 704	745 083
65 - 69	1 554 678	653 287	901 391	453 756	195 857	257 899	1 100 922	457 430	643 492
70 - 74	1 412 538	568 312	844 226	378 105	155 224	222 881	1 034 433	413 088	621 345
75 - 79	1 198 893	480 088	718 805	306 226	125 948	180 278	892 667	354 140	538 527
80 - 84	725 985	264 997	460 988	182 550	69 573	112 977	543 435	195 424	348 011
85 +	622 705	183 895	438 810	140 632	42 796	97 836	482 073	141 099	340 974
1 VII 2016* (ESDJ)									
Total	92 695 100	45 705 600	46 989 500	31 986 000	...	...	60 709 100	...	...
0 - 4	7 712 700	4 065 400	3 647 300	2 461 800	...	...	5 250 800	...	...
5 - 9	7 339 000	3 828 100	3 510 900	2 376 200	...	...	4 962 900	...	...
10 - 14	7 032 800	3 620 000	3 412 800	2 200 300	...	...	4 832 500	...	...
15 - 19	6 371 000	3 248 300	3 122 600	1 993 600	...	...	4 377 400	...	...
20 - 24	6 899 200	3 527 900	3 371 300	2 437 100	...	...	4 462 100	...	...
25 - 29	7 424 200	3 766 900	3 657 300	2 621 400	...	...	4 802 800	...	...
30 - 34	7 450 700	3 676 700	3 773 900	2 735 800	...	...	4 714 800	...	...
35 - 39	6 885 800	3 412 600	3 473 200	2 474 300	...	...	4 411 500	...	...
40 - 44	6 693 500	3 314 300	3 379 300	2 387 700	...	...	4 305 800	...	...
45 - 49	6 291 700	3 162 300	3 129 500	2 243 900	...	...	4 047 900	...	...
50 - 54	6 247 300	2 963 000	3 284 200	2 239 800	...	...	4 007 500	...	...
55 - 59	5 301 000	2 465 000	2 836 000	2 000 700	...	...	3 300 300	...	...
60 - 64	3 651 900	1 669 600	1 982 300	1 317 200	...	...	2 334 700	...	...
65 - 69	2 484 100	1 091 400	1 392 700	901 400	...	...	1 582 700	...	...
70 - 74	1 524 600	628 000	896 600	542 800	...	...	981 800	...	...
75 - 79	1 379 000	545 200	833 800	449 400	...	...	929 600	...	...
80 +	2 006 800	720 800	1 286 000	602 600	...	...	1 404 200	...	...
Yemen - Yémen[2]									
1 VII 2013 (ESDJ)									
Total	25 235 079	12 844 169	12 390 910	...	...	...	...	...	...
0	867 766	442 297	425 470	...	...	...	...	...	...
1 - 4	3 183 851	1 627 558	1 556 293	...	...	...	...	...	...
5 - 9	3 377 146	1 723 755	1 653 391	...	...	...	...	...	...
10 - 14	3 007 245	1 539 447	1 467 798	...	...	...	...	...	...
15 - 19	2 954 657	1 530 854	1 423 803	...	...	...	...	...	...
20 - 24	2 738 574	1 426 490	1 312 083	...	...	...	...	...	...
25 - 29	2 226 915	1 146 775	1 080 140	...	...	...	...	...	...
30 - 34	1 688 248	851 154	837 094	...	...	...	...	...	...
35 - 39	1 276 748	635 492	641 256	...	...	...	...	...	...
40 - 44	916 385	448 186	468 200	...	...	...	...	...	...
45 - 49	758 743	366 733	392 010	...	...	...	...	...	...
50 - 54	644 689	310 025	334 665	...	...	...	...	...	...
55 - 59	488 859	238 877	249 982	...	...	...	...	...	...
60 - 64	352 671	178 041	174 631	...	...	...	...	...	...
65 - 69	266 902	135 090	131 812	...	...	...	...	...	...
70 - 74	195 287	98 257	97 029	...	...	...	...	...	...
75 - 79	133 347	66 656	66 691	...	...	...	...	...	...
80 +	157 047	78 482	78 565	...	...	...	...	...	...
EUROPE									
Åland Islands - Îles d'Åland[34]									
1 VII 2017 (ESDJ)									
Total	29 352	14 644	14 708	11 621	5 583	6 038	17 731	9 061	8 670
0	292	149	143	114	59	56	178	90	88
1 - 4	1 250	636	615	431	220	211	820	416	404
5 - 9	1 633	829	804	552	273	279	1 081	556	525
10 - 14	1 637	850	787	559	274	285	1 078	576	502
15 - 19	1 576	835	741	627	318	309	949	517	432

Continent, country or area, date, code[a] and age (in years) / Continent, pays ou zone, date, code[a] et âge (en années)	Total			Urban - Urbaine			Rural - Rurale		
	Both sexes Les deux sexes	Male Masculin	Female Féminin	Both sexes Les deux sexes	Male Masculin	Female Féminin	Both sexes Les deux sexes	Male Masculin	Female Féminin
EUROPE									
Åland Islands - Îles d'Åland[34]									
1 VII 2017 (ESDJ)									
20 - 24	1 381	737	644	686	372	315	695	365	330
25 - 29	1 776	953	823	842	462	381	934	491	443
30 - 34	1 738	877	861	737	382	355	1 001	495	506
35 - 39	1 811	940	871	712	367	346	1 099	574	525
40 - 44	1 875	952	923	694	342	352	1 181	610	571
45 - 49	2 028	1 011	1 017	767	359	409	1 261	652	609
50 - 54	2 124	1 046	1 078	777	361	416	1 347	685	662
55 - 59	1 944	939	1 005	724	322	402	1 221	617	604
60 - 64	2 007	956	1 051	794	356	439	1 213	601	613
65 - 69	1 933	936	997	774	338	436	1 159	598	561
70 - 74	1 700	846	854	716	325	391	985	522	463
75 - 79	1 103	554	549	455	217	238	648	337	311
80 - 84	783	336	447	342	137	206	441	199	242
85 - 89	471	193	278	196	78	118	276	116	160
90 - 94	236	62	174	102	23	79	134	39	95
95 - 99	56	10	46	22	3	19	35	8	27
100 +	4	2	3	2	1	1	2	1	2
Albania - Albanie									
1 VII 2013 (ESDJ)[5]									
Total	2 897 364	1 458 648	1 438 716	1 633 617	798 615	835 002	1 263 747	660 033	603 714
0 - 4	173 349	90 068	83 281	75 341	39 381	35 960	98 008	50 687	47 321
0	35 445	18 414	17 031	...	...	...	...	...	...
1 - 4	137 903	71 653	66 250	...	...	...	...	...	...
5 - 9	171 833	90 701	81 132	100 478	52 421	48 057	71 355	38 280	33 075
10 - 14	220 582	114 164	106 418	117 500	60 576	56 924	103 082	53 587	49 494
15 - 19	261 669	132 810	128 859	134 718	67 303	67 414	126 952	65 507	61 445
20 - 24	235 615	126 936	108 680	153 986	75 706	78 280	81 630	51 230	30 400
25 - 29	209 075	112 236	96 839	136 959	65 999	70 960	72 116	46 237	25 879
30 - 34	187 077	92 149	94 928	95 098	44 074	51 024	91 979	48 075	43 904
35 - 39	173 587	82 445	91 142	89 169	40 432	48 737	84 418	42 013	42 405
40 - 44	189 099	89 772	99 327	106 471	50 381	56 091	82 627	39 391	43 236
45 - 49	197 020	95 657	101 363	113 719	55 342	58 377	83 301	40 315	42 986
50 - 54	209 575	104 084	105 490	121 293	60 655	60 638	88 282	43 430	44 852
55 - 59	184 593	92 037	92 556	105 093	51 906	53 188	79 500	40 131	39 369
60 - 64	141 532	71 276	70 256	83 065	40 768	42 296	58 467	30 508	27 960
65 - 69	106 945	54 278	52 666	60 973	29 333	31 640	45 971	24 945	21 026
70 - 74	102 875	49 827	53 048	55 109	26 020	29 089	47 766	23 807	23 959
75 - 79	71 589	35 241	36 348	41 911	19 956	21 955	29 678	15 285	14 393
80 - 84	38 203	16 977	21 226	25 030	11 374	13 656	13 174	5 603	7 570
85 +	23 147	7 992	15 155	17 705	6 988	10 717	5 443	1 004	4 438
1 I 2017 (ESDJ)									
Total	2 876 591	1 453 541	1 423 050	...	...	...	...	...	...
0	31 733	16 401	15 332	...	...	...	...	...	...
1 - 4	134 872	69 837	65 035	...	...	...	...	...	...
5 - 9	164 309	85 561	78 748	...	...	...	...	...	...
10 - 14	191 196	99 423	91 773	...	...	...	...	...	...
15 - 19	220 937	112 793	108 144	...	...	...	...	...	...
20 - 24	254 172	130 180	123 992	...	...	...	...	...	...
25 - 29	230 218	123 096	107 122	...	...	...	...	...	...
30 - 34	189 712	101 216	88 496	...	...	...	...	...	...
35 - 39	163 850	82 229	81 621	...	...	...	...	...	...
40 - 44	166 499	80 792	85 707	...	...	...	...	...	...
45 - 49	187 034	90 193	96 841	...	...	...	...	...	...
50 - 54	198 530	97 914	100 616	...	...	...	...	...	...
55 - 59	200 892	99 865	101 027	...	...	...	...	...	...
60 - 64	164 686	81 437	83 249	...	...	...	...	...	...
65 - 69	127 474	62 763	64 711	...	...	...	...	...	...
70 - 74	97 129	48 162	48 967	...	...	...	...	...	...
75 - 79	84 156	40 302	43 854	...	...	...	...	...	...
80 - 84	46 901	22 165	24 736	...	...	...	...	...	...
85 +	22 291	9 212	13 079	...	...	...	...	...	...

Continent, country or area, date, code[a] and age (in years) / Continent, pays ou zone, date, code[a] et âge (en années)	Total			Urban - Urbaine			Rural - Rurale		
	Both sexes Les deux sexes	Male Masculin	Female Féminin	Both sexes Les deux sexes	Male Masculin	Female Féminin	Both sexes Les deux sexes	Male Masculin	Female Féminin
EUROPE									
Andorra - Andorre[34]									
1 I 2016 (ESDJ)									
Total	71 732	36 229	35 503	...	...	...	...	...	...
0	516	260	256	...	...	...	...	...	...
1 - 4	2 671	1 340	1 331	...	...	...	...	...	...
5 - 9	3 918	1 987	1 931	...	...	...	...	...	...
10 - 14	3 813	1 996	1 817	...	...	...	...	...	...
15 - 19	3 908	2 060	1 848	...	...	...	...	...	...
20 - 24	3 642	1 923	1 719	...	...	...	...	...	...
25 - 29	4 087	2 075	2 012	...	...	...	...	...	...
30 - 34	5 337	2 624	2 713	...	...	...	...	...	...
35 - 39	6 345	3 132	3 213	...	...	...	...	...	...
40 - 44	6 937	3 476	3 461	...	...	...	...	...	...
45 - 49	6 540	3 325	3 215	...	...	...	...	...	...
50 - 54	6 131	3 142	2 989	...	...	...	...	...	...
55 - 59	4 949	2 556	2 393	...	...	...	...	...	...
60 - 64	3 700	1 920	1 780	...	...	...	...	...	...
65 - 69	2 999	1 550	1 449	...	...	...	...	...	...
70 - 74	2 228	1 138	1 090	...	...	...	...	...	...
75 - 79	1 520	704	816	...	...	...	...	...	...
80 - 84	1 162	532	630	...	...	...	...	...	...
85 - 89	861	316	545	...	...	...	...	...	...
90 - 94	341	129	212	...	...	...	...	...	...
95 - 99	103	36	67	...	...	...	...	...	...
100 +	24	8	16	...	...	...	...	...	...
Austria - Autriche									
31 X 2011 (CDJC)									
Total	8 401 940	4 093 938	4 308 002	5 643 239	2 713 930	2 929 309	2 758 701	1 380 008	1 378 693
0 - 4	394 706	202 637	192 069	267 743	137 645	130 098	126 963	64 992	61 971
5 - 9	406 027	207 779	198 248	268 770	137 636	131 134	137 257	70 143	67 114
10 - 14	426 957	218 499	208 458	276 347	141 429	134 918	150 610	77 070	73 540
15 - 19	488 818	251 251	237 567	313 792	160 620	153 172	175 026	90 631	84 395
20 - 24	527 675	267 651	260 024	364 267	181 574	182 693	163 408	86 077	77 331
25 - 29	552 783	277 236	275 547	390 454	193 719	196 735	162 329	83 517	78 812
30 - 34	538 307	270 267	268 040	375 886	187 248	188 638	162 421	83 019	79 402
35 - 39	564 817	280 207	284 610	383 183	187 902	195 281	181 634	92 305	89 329
40 - 44	675 242	338 455	336 787	453 188	224 449	228 739	222 054	114 006	108 048
45 - 49	710 388	358 163	352 225	470 749	234 757	235 992	239 639	123 406	116 233
50 - 54	626 162	312 890	313 272	409 191	200 993	208 198	216 971	111 897	105 074
55 - 59	517 280	253 019	264 261	339 245	161 747	177 498	178 035	91 272	86 763
60 - 64	480 665	231 598	249 067	322 367	151 726	170 641	158 298	79 872	78 426
65 - 69	402 829	189 221	213 608	283 946	130 760	153 186	118 883	58 461	60 422
70 - 74	410 314	187 956	222 358	273 352	123 395	149 957	136 962	64 561	72 401
75 - 79	262 203	110 870	151 333	165 864	68 812	97 052	96 339	42 058	54 281
80 - 84	218 133	83 066	135 067	142 903	52 895	90 008	75 230	30 171	45 059
85 - 89	141 772	40 153	101 619	99 777	27 332	72 445	41 995	12 821	29 174
90 - 94	46 362	10 997	35 365	34 057	7 767	26 290	12 305	3 230	9 075
95 - 99	9 388	1 836	7 552	7 274	1 377	5 897	2 114	459	1 655
100 +	1 112	187	925	884	147	737	228	40	188
1 I 2017 (ESDJ)									
Total	8 772 865	4 312 441	4 460 424	...	...	...	...	...	...
0	86 851	44 661	42 190	...	...	...	...	...	...
1 - 4	338 800	174 912	163 888	...	...	...	...	...	...
5 - 9	414 639	213 075	201 564	...	...	...	...	...	...
10 - 14	423 450	217 224	206 226	...	...	...	...	...	...
15 - 19	453 985	237 103	216 882	...	...	...	...	...	...
20 - 24	553 007	285 134	267 873	...	...	...	...	...	...
25 - 29	598 504	305 726	292 778	...	...	...	...	...	...
30 - 34	598 686	303 131	295 555	...	...	...	...	...	...
35 - 39	572 365	288 962	283 403	...	...	...	...	...	...
40 - 44	582 792	289 729	293 063	...	...	...	...	...	...
45 - 49	684 053	342 559	341 494	...	...	...	...	...	...
50 - 54	712 250	357 863	354 387	...	...	...	...	...	...
55 - 59	622 986	309 458	313 528	...	...	...	...	...	...
60 - 64	504 980	243 935	261 045	...	...	...	...	...	...

Continent, country or area, date, code[a] and age (in years) / Continent, pays ou zone, date, code[a] et âge (en années)	Total			Urban - Urbaine			Rural - Rurale		
	Both sexes Les deux sexes	Male Masculin	Female Féminin	Both sexes Les deux sexes	Male Masculin	Female Féminin	Both sexes Les deux sexes	Male Masculin	Female Féminin
EUROPE									
Austria - Autriche									
1 I 2017 (ESDJ)									
65 - 69	452 914	213 857	239 057	...	...	...	...	...	...
70 - 74	370 922	169 449	201 473	...	...	...	...	...	...
75 - 79	368 181	162 458	205 723	...	...	...	...	...	...
80 - 84	210 561	83 888	126 673	...	...	...	...	...	...
85 - 89	143 700	50 091	93 609	...	...	...	...	...	...
90 - 94	65 044	16 503	48 541	...	...	...	...	...	...
95 - 99	13 047	2 556	10 491	...	...	...	...	...	...
100 - 104	1 087	160	927	...	...	...	...	...	...
105 - 109	60	7	53	...	...	...	...	...	...
110 +	1	-	1	...	...	...	...	...	...
Belarus - Bélarus									
1 I 2017 (ESDJ)									
Total	9 504 704	4 426 519	5 078 185	7 400 832	3 414 000	3 986 832	2 103 872	1 012 519	1 091 353
0	118 071	60 795	57 276	91 721	47 140	44 581	26 350	13 655	12 695
1 - 4	476 026	245 418	230 608	374 072	192 849	181 223	101 954	52 569	49 385
5 - 9	537 904	276 916	260 988	424 565	218 308	206 257	113 339	58 608	54 731
10 - 14	447 276	229 454	217 822	346 288	178 064	168 224	100 988	51 390	49 598
15 - 19	453 289	232 830	220 459	373 566	188 786	184 780	79 723	44 044	35 679
20 - 24	553 605	284 005	269 600	478 101	238 550	239 551	75 504	45 455	30 049
25 - 29	737 917	378 443	359 474	634 660	317 490	317 170	103 257	60 953	42 304
30 - 34	774 280	392 703	381 577	650 488	324 408	326 080	123 792	68 295	55 497
35 - 39	690 002	343 605	346 397	567 725	279 301	288 424	122 277	64 304	57 973
40 - 44	654 338	317 951	336 387	511 435	244 583	266 852	142 903	73 368	69 535
45 - 49	635 870	302 278	333 592	476 164	220 033	256 131	159 706	82 245	77 461
50 - 54	686 973	320 000	366 973	511 816	229 134	282 682	175 157	90 866	84 291
55 - 59	742 446	335 665	406 781	557 223	240 219	317 004	185 223	95 446	89 777
60 - 64	601 179	253 863	347 316	456 060	184 632	271 428	145 119	69 231	75 888
65 - 69	483 764	189 766	293 998	364 031	138 829	225 202	119 733	50 937	68 796
70 - 74	252 237	88 281	163 956	174 714	61 783	112 931	77 523	26 498	51 025
75 - 79	311 219	92 527	218 692	202 769	61 214	141 555	108 450	31 313	77 137
80 - 84	196 951	50 049	146 902	112 452	29 201	83 251	84 499	20 848	63 651
85 - 89	110 982	24 758	86 224	63 924	14 337	49 587	47 058	10 421	36 637
90 - 94	34 807	6 297	28 510	23 946	4 347	19 599	10 861	1 950	8 911
95 - 99	4 649	777	3 872	4 224	660	3 564	425	117	308
100 +	919	138	781	888	132	756	31	6	25
Belgium - Belgique									
1 I 2011 (CDJC)									
Total	11 000 638	5 401 718	5 598 920	10 842 520	5 322 172	5 520 348	158 118	79 546	78 572
0 - 4	645 512	330 184	315 328	636 217	325 336	310 881	9 295	4 848	4 447
5 - 9	607 325	310 560	296 765	597 723	305 654	292 069	9 602	4 906	4 696
10 - 14	614 460	313 738	300 722	604 574	308 723	295 851	9 886	5 015	4 871
15 - 19	649 018	331 790	317 228	638 725	326 452	312 273	10 293	5 338	4 955
20 - 24	684 093	344 647	339 446	674 173	339 520	334 653	9 920	5 127	4 793
25 - 29	700 373	351 045	349 328	691 593	346 539	345 054	8 780	4 506	4 274
30 - 34	722 936	364 728	358 208	713 667	360 044	353 623	9 269	4 684	4 585
35 - 39	741 204	375 815	365 389	730 809	370 490	360 319	10 395	5 325	5 070
40 - 44	789 895	401 530	388 365	778 159	395 446	382 713	11 736	6 084	5 652
45 - 49	828 167	418 827	409 340	816 018	412 531	403 487	12 149	6 296	5 853
50 - 54	781 240	391 809	389 431	770 016	385 999	384 017	11 224	5 810	5 414
55 - 59	702 331	349 489	352 842	692 496	344 347	348 149	9 835	5 142	4 693
60 - 64	650 904	320 714	330 190	641 771	316 010	325 761	9 133	4 704	4 429
65 - 69	480 199	230 217	249 982	473 668	226 987	246 681	6 531	3 230	3 301
70 - 74	448 374	205 382	242 992	441 884	202 344	239 540	6 490	3 038	3 452
75 - 79	401 594	171 538	230 056	395 900	168 962	226 938	5 694	2 576	3 118
80 - 84	304 788	115 591	189 197	300 342	113 821	186 521	4 446	1 770	2 676
85 - 89	180 495	57 963	122 532	177 932	57 048	120 884	2 563	915	1 648
90 - 94	52 708	13 541	39 167	52 007	13 341	38 666	701	200	501
95 - 99	13 392	2 412	10 980	13 233	2 381	10 852	159	31	128
100 +	1 630	198	1 432	1 613	197	1 416	17	1	16
1 I 2017 (ESDJ)									
Total	11 351 727	5 589 272	5 762 455	...	...	...	...	...	...
0	121 779	62 345	59 434	...	...	...	...	...	...
1 - 4	509 358	260 647	248 711	...	...	...	...	...	...

7. Population by age, sex and urban/rural residence: latest available year, 2008 - 2017
Population selon l'âge, le sexe et la résidence, urbaine/rurale : dernière année disponible, 2008 - 2017 (continued - suite)

Continent, country or area, date, code[a] and age (in years) / Continent, pays ou zone, date, code[a] et âge (en années)	Total			Urban - Urbaine			Rural - Rurale		
	Both sexes Les deux sexes	Male Masculin	Female Féminin	Both sexes Les deux sexes	Male Masculin	Female Féminin	Both sexes Les deux sexes	Male Masculin	Female Féminin
EUROPE									
Belgium - Belgique									
1 I 2017 (ESDJ)									
5 - 9	666 986	341 304	325 682	...	...	...	...	...	...
10 - 14	629 697	322 222	307 475	...	...	...	...	...	...
15 - 19	632 988	324 580	308 408	...	...	...	...	...	...
20 - 24	681 140	346 753	334 387	...	...	...	...	...	...
25 - 29	738 490	370 223	368 267	...	...	...	...	...	...
30 - 34	727 461	364 079	363 382	...	...	...	...	...	...
35 - 39	746 788	375 095	371 693	...	...	...	...	...	...
40 - 44	737 199	372 835	364 364	...	...	...	...	...	...
45 - 49	786 509	398 366	388 143	...	...	...	...	...	...
50 - 54	817 724	413 181	404 543	...	...	...	...	...	...
55 - 59	773 690	385 904	387 786	...	...	...	...	...	...
60 - 64	686 675	337 865	348 810	...	...	...	...	...	...
65 - 69	609 072	294 783	314 289	...	...	...	...	...	...
70 - 74	478 946	224 318	254 628	...	...	...	...	...	...
75 - 79	379 378	167 200	212 178	...	...	...	...	...	...
80 - 84	316 652	127 667	188 985	...	...	...	...	...	...
85 - 89	206 628	71 888	134 740	...	...	...	...	...	...
90 - 94	85 487	23 980	61 507	...	...	...	...	...	...
95 - 99	17 324	3 781	13 543	...	...	...	...	...	...
100 - 104	1 653	247	1 406	...	...	...	...	...	...
105 - 109	101	9	92	...	...	...	...	...	...
110 +	2	-	2	...	...	...	...	...	...
Bosnia and Herzegovina - Bosnie-Herzégovine									
30 IX 2013 (CDJC)									
Total	3 531 159	1 732 270	1 798 889	...	...	...	...	...	...
0 - 4	174 064	89 442	84 622	...	...	...	...	...	...
5 - 9	176 980	90 881	86 099	...	...	...	...	...	...
10 - 14	192 675	98 653	94 022	...	...	...	...	...	...
15 - 19	242 742	124 900	117 842	...	...	...	...	...	...
20 - 24	228 056	116 883	111 173	...	...	...	...	...	...
25 - 29	252 318	129 248	123 070	...	...	...	...	...	...
30 - 34	252 633	128 593	124 040	...	...	...	...	...	...
35 - 39	249 266	126 145	123 121	...	...	...	...	...	...
40 - 44	241 138	121 595	119 543	...	...	...	810	...	...
45 - 49	260 928	130 087	130 841	...	...	...	...	...	...
50 - 54	276 575	136 153	140 422	...	...	...	...	...	...
55 - 59	258 537	125 576	132 961	...	...	...	...	...	...
60 - 64	223 251	104 970	118 281	...	...	...	...	...	...
65 - 69	153 569	69 066	84 503	...	...	...	...	...	...
70 - 74	140 455	59 854	80 601	...	...	...	...	...	...
75 - 79	117 267	47 403	69 864	...	...	...	...	...	...
80 - 84	62 636	23 769	38 867	...	...	...	...	...	...
85 +	28 069	9 052	19 017	...	...	...	...	...	...
Bulgaria - Bulgarie									
1 I 2017 (ESDJ)									
Total	7 101 859	3 449 978	3 651 881	5 204 385	2 506 628	2 697 757	1 897 474	943 350	954 124
0	64 665	33 172	31 493	48 645	24 869	23 776	16 020	8 303	7 717
1 - 4	265 610	136 543	129 067	201 218	103 434	97 784	64 392	33 109	31 283
5 - 9	349 350	179 593	169 757	262 424	134 911	127 513	86 926	44 682	42 244
10 - 14	321 394	165 601	155 793	234 703	120 696	114 007	86 691	44 905	41 786
15 - 19	309 596	159 294	150 302	226 530	116 235	110 295	83 066	43 059	40 007
20 - 24	350 006	180 552	169 454	261 326	133 426	127 900	88 680	47 126	41 554
25 - 29	465 523	239 641	225 882	362 133	183 202	178 931	103 390	56 439	46 951
30 - 34	481 875	250 016	231 859	375 184	191 748	183 436	106 691	58 268	48 423
35 - 39	513 551	265 779	247 772	400 230	204 307	195 923	113 321	61 472	51 849
40 - 44	542 793	279 190	263 603	421 156	213 790	207 366	121 637	65 400	56 237
45 - 49	512 792	262 394	250 398	386 130	193 930	192 200	126 662	68 464	58 198
50 - 54	470 548	236 270	234 278	346 405	169 881	176 524	124 143	66 389	57 754
55 - 59	488 734	238 596	250 138	357 619	170 054	187 565	131 115	68 542	62 573
60 - 64	493 306	229 793	263 513	355 463	161 939	193 524	137 843	67 854	69 989
65 - 69	483 221	212 058	271 163	335 168	144 939	190 229	148 053	67 119	80 934
70 - 74	377 433	156 417	221 016	246 496	101 500	144 996	130 937	54 917	76 020

Continent, country or area, date, code[a] and age (in years) / Continent, pays ou zone, date, code[a] et âge (en années)	Total			Urban - Urbaine			Rural - Rurale		
	Both sexes Les deux sexes	Male Masculin	Female Féminin	Both sexes Les deux sexes	Male Masculin	Female Féminin	Both sexes Les deux sexes	Male Masculin	Female Féminin
EUROPE									
Bulgaria - Bulgarie									
1 I 2017 (ESDJ)									
75 - 79	273 709	105 731	167 978	170 653	64 635	106 018	103 056	41 096	61 960
80 - 84	206 692	75 010	131 682	128 268	44 946	83 322	78 424	30 064	48 360
85 - 89	97 420	33 737	63 683	62 865	21 294	41 571	34 555	12 443	22 112
90 - 94	29 618	9 391	20 227	19 203	6 092	13 111	10 415	3 299	7 116
95 - 99	3 769	1 127	2 642	2 407	746	1 661	1 362	381	981
100 +	254	73	181	159	54	105	95	19	76
100 - 104	234	66	168	...	...	...	...	...	...
105 - 109	20	7	13	...	...	...	...	...	...
110 +	-	-	-	...	...	...	...	...	...
Croatia - Croatie									
1 IV 2011 (CDJC)									
Total	4 284 889	2 066 335	2 218 554	2 368 506	1 121 328	1 247 178	1 916 383	945 007	971 376
0 - 4	212 709	109 251	103 458	116 367	59 768	56 599	96 342	49 483	46 859
5 - 9	204 317	104 841	99 476	108 481	55 715	52 766	95 836	49 126	46 710
10 - 14	235 402	120 633	114 769	124 241	63 763	60 478	111 161	56 870	54 291
15 - 19	244 177	124 918	119 259	130 369	66 506	63 863	113 808	58 412	55 396
20 - 24	261 658	133 455	128 203	142 681	72 037	70 644	118 977	61 418	57 559
25 - 29	289 066	147 416	141 650	164 754	82 466	82 288	124 312	64 950	59 362
30 - 34	294 619	149 998	144 621	173 166	86 363	86 803	121 453	63 635	57 818
35 - 39	284 754	143 984	140 770	165 450	81 745	83 705	119 304	62 239	57 065
40 - 44	286 933	143 603	143 330	161 295	78 845	82 450	125 638	64 758	60 880
45 - 49	307 561	152 446	155 115	167 593	80 182	87 411	139 968	72 264	67 704
50 - 54	320 502	157 981	162 521	174 963	81 945	93 018	145 539	76 036	69 503
55 - 59	311 818	153 750	158 068	174 376	81 746	92 630	137 442	72 004	65 438
60 - 64	272 740	127 851	144 889	154 706	69 577	85 129	118 034	58 274	59 760
65 - 69	202 002	89 364	112 638	114 109	49 018	65 091	87 893	40 346	47 547
70 - 74	212 401	88 912	123 489	113 737	47 978	65 759	98 664	40 934	57 730
75 - 79	175 526	66 456	109 070	91 966	35 801	56 165	83 560	30 655	52 905
80 - 84	108 104	35 999	72 105	56 658	19 022	37 636	51 446	16 977	34 469
85 - 89	47 641	12 415	35 226	26 213	7 045	19 168	21 428	5 370	16 058
90 - 94	10 758	2 580	8 178	6 081	1 517	4 564	4 677	1 063	3 614
95 - 99	2 003	446	1 557	1 181	270	911	822	176	646
100 +	198	36	162	119	19	100	79	17	62
1 I 2017 (ESDJ)									
Total	4 154 213	2 005 210	2 149 003	...	...	...	...	...	...
0	37 398	18 996	18 402	...	...	...	...	...	...
1 - 4	156 604	80 984	75 620	...	...	...	...	...	...
5 - 9	208 924	107 129	101 795	...	...	...	...	...	...
10 - 14	200 524	103 067	97 457	...	...	...	...	...	...
15 - 19	224 781	115 093	109 688	...	...	...	...	...	...
20 - 24	241 706	123 744	117 962	...	...	...	...	...	...
25 - 29	254 011	129 474	124 537	...	...	...	...	...	...
30 - 34	278 209	141 220	136 989	...	...	...	...	...	...
35 - 39	288 189	146 548	141 641	...	...	...	...	...	...
40 - 44	276 363	139 298	137 065	...	...	...	...	...	...
45 - 49	274 327	136 807	137 520	...	...	...	...	...	...
50 - 54	295 726	145 389	150 337	...	...	...	...	...	...
55 - 59	304 126	147 432	156 694	...	...	...	...	...	...
60 - 64	299 063	143 847	155 216	...	...	...	...	...	...
65 - 69	251 335	114 522	136 813	...	...	...	...	...	...
70 - 74	181 592	76 653	104 939	...	...	...	...	...	...
75 - 79	172 911	67 826	105 085	...	...	...	...	...	...
80 - 84	126 413	43 986	82 427	...	...	...	...	...	...
85 - 89	61 264	18 502	42 762	...	...	...	...	...	...
90 - 94	17 900	4 124	13 776	...	...	...	...	...	...
95 - 99	2 684	536	2 148	...	...	...	...	...	...
100 - 104	150	32	118	...	...	...	...	...	...
105 - 109	13	1	12	...	...	...	...	...	...
110 +	-	-	-	...	...	...	...	...	...
Czechia - Tchéquie									
1 I 2017 (ESDJ)									
Total	10 578 820	5 200 687	5 378 133	7 731 256	3 765 692	3 965 564	2 847 564	1 434 995	1 412 569
0	112 544	57 757	54 787	82 440	42 394	40 046	30 104	15 363	14 741

Continent, country or area, date, code[a] and age (in years) Continent, pays ou zone, date, code[a] et âge (en années)	Total			Urban - Urbaine			Rural - Rurale		
	Both sexes Les deux sexes	Male Masculin	Female Féminin	Both sexes Les deux sexes	Male Masculin	Female Féminin	Both sexes Les deux sexes	Male Masculin	Female Féminin
EUROPE									
Czechia - Tchéquie									
1 I 2017 (ESDJ)									
1 - 4	442 290	226 643	215 647	322 352	165 070	157 282	119 938	61 573	58 365
5 - 9	593 168	303 559	289 609	427 418	218 516	208 902	165 750	85 043	80 707
10 - 14	499 273	256 689	242 584	355 079	182 490	172 589	144 194	74 199	69 995
15 - 19	458 673	235 431	223 242	324 370	166 097	158 273	134 303	69 334	64 969
20 - 24	553 701	283 208	270 493	396 417	201 497	194 920	157 284	81 711	75 573
25 - 29	685 593	350 383	335 210	508 803	258 796	250 007	176 790	91 587	85 203
30 - 34	730 407	376 224	354 183	544 902	280 447	264 455	185 505	95 777	89 728
35 - 39	848 689	436 905	411 784	620 229	318 356	301 873	228 460	118 549	109 911
40 - 44	914 338	469 722	444 616	661 499	336 354	325 145	252 839	133 368	119 471
45 - 49	713 002	365 300	347 702	517 981	261 687	256 294	195 021	103 613	91 408
50 - 54	694 843	352 551	342 292	509 326	254 649	254 677	185 517	97 902	87 615
55 - 59	631 422	314 173	317 249	458 444	224 711	233 733	172 978	89 462	83 516
60 - 64	711 955	342 397	369 558	518 302	245 287	273 015	193 653	97 110	96 543
65 - 69	691 356	319 288	372 068	505 130	228 475	276 655	186 226	90 813	95 413
70 - 74	532 653	232 026	300 627	400 918	171 340	229 578	131 735	60 686	71 049
75 - 79	340 072	137 596	202 476	256 335	103 004	153 331	83 737	34 592	49 145
80 - 84	229 227	83 098	146 129	172 312	62 378	109 934	56 915	20 720	36 195
85 - 89	138 667	43 637	95 030	105 187	33 230	71 957	33 480	10 407	23 073
90 - 94	48 997	12 443	36 554	37 674	9 634	28 040	11 323	2 809	8 514
95 - 99	7 255	1 491	5 764	5 619	1 152	4 467	1 636	339	1 297
100 +	695	166	529	519	128	391	176	38	138
100 - 104	588	125	463	...	...	...	...	...	...
105 - 109	107	41	66	...	...	...	...	...	...
110 +	-	-	-	...	...	...	...	...	...
Denmark - Danemark[77]									
1 VII 2017 (ESDJ)									
Total	5 760 694	2 866 952	2 893 742	...	...	...	...	...	...
0	62 143	32 001	30 142	...	...	...	...	...	...
1 - 4	236 943	121 664	115 279	...	...	...	...	...	...
5 - 9	326 098	167 325	158 773	...	...	...	...	...	...
10 - 14	335 179	171 820	163 359	...	...	...	...	...	...
15 - 19	346 025	177 162	168 863	...	...	...	...	...	...
20 - 24	389 288	199 351	189 937	...	...	...	...	...	...
25 - 29	380 096	193 985	186 111	...	...	...	...	...	...
30 - 34	334 050	170 626	163 424	...	...	...	...	...	...
35 - 39	341 094	171 651	169 443	...	...	...	...	...	...
40 - 44	382 269	191 369	190 900	...	...	...	...	...	...
45 - 49	392 600	197 925	194 675	...	...	...	...	...	...
50 - 54	423 077	213 582	209 495	...	...	...	...	...	...
55 - 59	365 147	182 601	182 546	...	...	...	...	...	...
60 - 64	340 822	168 662	172 160	...	...	...	...	...	...
65 - 69	326 319	159 537	166 782	...	...	...	...	...	...
70 - 74	320 620	154 538	166 082	...	...	...	...	...	...
75 - 79	205 833	95 164	110 669	...	...	...	...	...	...
80 - 84	133 147	57 250	75 897	...	...	...	...	...	...
85 - 89	75 517	28 504	47 013	...	...	...	...	...	...
90 - 94	34 392	10 149	24 243	...	...	...	...	...	...
95 - 99	8 940	1 936	7 004	...	...	...	...	...	...
100 +	1 095	150	945	...	...	...	...	...	...
Estonia - Estonie									
1 I 2017 (ESDJ)									
Total	1 315 635	617 538	698 097	899 283[78]	406 016[78]	493 267[78]	415 180[78]	210 954[78]	204 226[78]
0	14 075	7 375	6 700	9 511[78]	4 976[78]	4 535[78]	4 562[78]	2 398[78]	2 164[78]
1 - 4	56 114	28 705	27 409	38 161[78]	19 449[78]	18 712[78]	17 949[78]	9 253[78]	8 696[78]
5 - 9	76 861	39 431	37 430	51 568[78]	26 346[78]	25 222[78]	25 286[78]	13 083[78]	12 203[78]
10 - 14	66 559	34 149	32 410	44 161[78]	22 438[78]	21 723[78]	22 384[78]	11 704[78]	10 680[78]
15 - 19	59 546	30 730	28 816	38 779[78]	19 934[78]	18 845[78]	20 736[78]	10 779[78]	9 957[78]
20 - 24	70 389	36 013	34 376	47 669[78]	23 579[78]	24 090[78]	22 680[78]	12 414[78]	10 266[78]
25 - 29	96 576	50 529	46 047	67 702[78]	34 187[78]	33 515[78]	28 821[78]	16 307[78]	12 514[78]
30 - 34	95 273	49 228	46 045	67 336[78]	33 680[78]	33 656[78]	27 864[78]	15 496[78]	12 368[78]
35 - 39	90 052	46 297	43 755	61 797[78]	30 507[78]	31 290[78]	28 148[78]	15 722[78]	12 426[78]
40 - 44	90 416	45 878	44 538	60 811[78]	29 456[78]	31 355[78]	29 504[78]	16 348[78]	13 156[78]

7. Population by age, sex and urban/rural residence: latest available year, 2008 - 2017
Population selon l'âge, le sexe et la résidence, urbaine/rurale : dernière année disponible, 2008 - 2017 (continued - suite)

Continent, country or area, date, code[a] and age (in years) / Continent, pays ou zone, date, code[a] et âge (en annèes)	Total Both sexes Les deux sexes	Total Male Masculin	Total Female Féminin	Urban - Urbaine Both sexes Les deux sexes	Urban Male Masculin	Urban Female Féminin	Rural - Rurale Both sexes Les deux sexes	Rural Male Masculin	Rural Female Féminin
EUROPE									
Estonia - Estonie 1 I 2017 (ESDJ)									
45 - 49	87 871	43 563	44 308	57 358[78]	27 046[78]	30 312[78]	30 406[78]	16 451[78]	13 955[78]
50 - 54	84 678	41 056	43 622	55 969[78]	25 755[78]	30 214[78]	28 608[78]	15 250[78]	13 358[78]
55 - 59	89 106	41 279	47 827	60 492[78]	26 353[78]	34 139[78]	28 515[78]	14 872[78]	13 643[78]
60 - 64	83 645	36 759	46 886	58 246[78]	24 125[78]	34 121[78]	25 327[78]	12 609[78]	12 718[78]
65 - 69	75 851	30 840	45 011	53 310[78]	20 423[78]	32 887[78]	22 401[78]	10 371[78]	12 030[78]
70 - 74	52 762	19 800	32 962	35 773[78]	12 641[78]	23 132[78]	16 915[78]	7 139[78]	9 776[78]
75 - 79	56 572	18 367	38 205	40 724[78]	12 646[78]	28 078[78]	15 775[78]	5 708[78]	10 067[78]
80 - 84	37 131	10 461	26 670	26 507[78]	7 293[78]	19 214[78]	10 583[78]	3 158[78]	7 425[78]
85 - 89	22 858	5 470	17 388	16 742[78]	4 005[78]	12 737[78]	6 090[78]	1 462[78]	4 628[78]
90 - 94	7 983	1 435	6 548	5 760[78]	1 052[78]	4 708[78]	2 216[78]	382[78]	1 834[78]
95 - 99	1 192	159	1 033	826[78]	114[78]	712[78]	366[78]	45[78]	321[78]
100 +	125	14	111	81[78]	11[78]	70[78]	44[78]	3[78]	41[78]
100 - 104	118	12	106	...	...	...	...	...	...
105 - 109	7	2	5	...	...	...	...	...	...
110 +	-	-	-	...	...	...	...	...	...
Faeroe Islands - Îles Féroé 1 VII 2017 (ESDJ)									
Total	50 216	25 886	24 330	19 249	9 672	9 577	30 967	16 214	14 753
0	695	332	363	263	144	119	432	188	244
1 - 4	2 703	1 355	1 348	1 057	520	537	1 646	835	811
5 - 9	3 455	1 790	1 665	1 344	668	676	2 111	1 122	989
10 - 14	3 705	1 888	1 817	1 408	693	715	2 297	1 195	1 102
15 - 19	3 514	1 839	1 675	1 348	688	660	2 166	1 151	1 015
20 - 24	3 034	1 644	1 390	1 209	630	579	1 825	1 014	811
25 - 29	2 850	1 561	1 289	1 086	586	500	1 764	975	789
30 - 34	2 707	1 441	1 266	1 029	522	507	1 678	919	759
35 - 39	3 002	1 535	1 467	1 149	585	564	1 853	950	903
40 - 44	3 197	1 716	1 481	1 237	647	590	1 960	1 069	891
45 - 49	3 260	1 700	1 560	1 300	639	661	1 960	1 061	899
50 - 54	3 458	1 829	1 629	1 510	795	715	1 948	1 034	914
55 - 59	3 099	1 572	1 527	1 169	594	575	1 930	978	952
60 - 64	2 846	1 472	1 374	1 102	534	568	1 744	938	806
65 - 69	2 742	1 395	1 347	1 004	502	502	1 738	893	845
70 - 74	2 195	1 165	1 030	756	388	368	1 439	777	662
75 - 79	1 574	780	794	551	257	294	1 023	523	500
80 - 84	1 062	484	578	334	150	184	728	334	394
85 - 89	718	281	437	244	89	155	474	192	282
90 - 94	324	88	236	117	33	84	207	55	152
95 - 99	65	17	48	27	7	20	38	10	28
100 +	11	2	9	5	1	4	6	1	5
Finland - Finlande[34] 1 VII 2016 (ESDJ)[79]									
Total	5 466 204	2 692 383	2 773 822	3 880 555	1 893 551	1 987 004	1 585 650	798 832	786 818
0	54 070	27 609	26 461	39 824	20 322	19 502	14 246	7 287	6 959
1 - 4	235 372	120 438	114 935	169 220	86 622	82 598	66 152	33 816	32 337
5 - 9	306 676	156 819	149 857	215 093	109 900	105 193	91 584	46 919	44 665
10 - 14	294 248	150 269	143 979	201 777	103 111	98 666	92 471	47 158	45 313
15 - 19	298 328	152 778	145 550	209 072	105 404	103 668	89 256	47 374	41 883
20 - 24	335 677	171 784	163 893	273 641	136 854	136 787	62 036	34 930	27 106
25 - 29	343 460	176 137	167 323	278 271	141 860	136 411	65 189	34 277	30 912
30 - 34	355 018	183 088	171 931	275 157	141 983	133 174	79 862	41 105	38 757
35 - 39	344 442	177 141	167 301	259 101	133 153	125 948	85 342	43 989	41 353
40 - 44	319 418	163 867	155 552	233 654	119 821	113 834	85 764	44 046	41 718
45 - 49	343 018	173 589	169 429	244 229	122 731	121 498	98 789	50 858	47 932
50 - 54	371 562	186 724	184 838	257 588	127 775	129 814	113 974	58 949	55 025
55 - 59	364 828	180 910	183 918	245 017	119 199	125 819	119 811	61 712	58 100
60 - 64	369 647	180 431	189 217	243 286	114 934	128 353	126 361	65 497	60 864
65 - 69	376 276	180 890	195 386	247 937	115 249	132 688	128 340	65 642	62 698
70 - 74	266 464	123 768	142 697	177 395	79 929	97 466	89 070	43 839	45 231
75 - 79	203 427	87 994	115 433	131 659	55 266	76 394	71 768	32 729	39 040
80 - 84	143 962	56 462	87 501	91 263	34 519	56 744	52 699	21 943	30 757
85 - 89	94 115	30 658	63 457	58 712	18 398	40 314	35 403	12 260	23 143

Continent, country or area, date, code[a] and age (in years) / Continent, pays ou zone, date, code[a] et âge (en années)	Total			Urban - Urbaine			Rural - Rurale		
	Both sexes Les deux sexes	Male Masculin	Female Féminin	Both sexes Les deux sexes	Male Masculin	Female Féminin	Both sexes Les deux sexes	Male Masculin	Female Féminin
EUROPE									
Finland - Finlande[34]									
1 VII 2016 (ESDJ)[79]									
90 - 94	37 841	9 490	28 351	23 379	5 600	17 779	14 463	3 890	10 573
95 - 99	7 577	1 420	6 157	4 775	857	3 918	2 802	563	2 239
100 +	782	122	660	511	68	443	272	54	218
1 I 2017 (ESDJ)									
Total	5 503 297	2 712 327	2 790 970	...	...	...	...	...	...
0	53 155	26 996	26 159	...	...	...	...	...	...
1 - 4	234 382	120 045	114 337	...	...	...	...	...	...
5 - 9	308 897	157 910	150 987	...	...	...	...	...	...
10 - 14	297 744	152 119	145 625	...	...	...	...	...	...
15 - 19	298 664	153 194	145 470	...	...	...	...	...	...
20 - 24	335 040	171 797	163 243	...	...	...	...	...	...
25 - 29	347 839	178 544	169 295	...	...	...	...	...	...
30 - 34	356 563	184 004	172 559	...	...	...	...	...	...
35 - 39	346 604	178 273	168 331	...	...	...	...	...	...
40 - 44	324 746	166 845	157 901	...	...	...	...	...	...
45 - 49	339 818	171 965	167 853	...	...	...	...	...	...
50 - 54	372 735	187 364	185 371	...	...	...	...	...	...
55 - 59	365 424	181 217	184 207	...	...	...	...	...	...
60 - 64	371 711	181 384	190 327	...	...	...	...	...	...
65 - 69	375 219	180 472	194 747	...	...	...	...	...	...
70 - 74	274 915	128 014	146 901	...	...	...	...	...	...
75 - 79	211 742	92 022	119 720	...	...	...	...	...	...
80 - 84	145 222	57 201	88 021	...	...	...	...	...	...
85 - 89	95 460	31 507	63 953	...	...	...	...	...	...
90 - 94	38 716	9 850	28 866	...	...	...	...	...	...
95 - 99	7 886	1 469	6 417	...	...	...	...	...	...
100 - 104	790	131	659	...	...	...	...	...	...
105 - 109	24	4	20	...	...	...	...	...	...
110 +	1	-	1	...	...	...	...	...	...
France[80]									
1 VII 2017* (ESDJ)									
Total	64 909 596	32 454 484	32 455 113	...	...	...	...	...	...
0 - 4	3 676 342	1 837 192	1 839 150	...	...	...	...	...	...
5 - 9	4 011 136	2 006 192	2 004 945	...	...	...	...	...	...
10 - 14	4 015 997	2 007 807	2 008 191	...	...	...	...	...	...
15 - 19	3 985 671	1 992 769	1 992 902	...	...	...	...	...	...
20 - 24	3 647 353	1 823 825	1 823 528	...	...	...	...	...	...
25 - 29	3 786 794	1 895 043	1 891 752	...	...	...	...	...	...
30 - 34	3 950 148	1 974 403	1 975 746	...	...	...	...	...	...
35 - 39	4 083 849	2 038 566	2 045 283	...	...	...	...	...	...
40 - 44	4 137 562	2 068 389	2 069 174	...	...	...	...	...	...
45 - 49	4 391 252	2 196 584	2 194 669	...	...	...	...	...	...
50 - 54	4 362 009	2 181 927	2 180 082	...	...	...	...	...	...
55 - 59	4 166 151	2 084 454	2 081 697	...	...	...	...	...	...
60 - 64	3 959 614	1 979 290	1 980 324	...	...	...	...	...	...
65 - 69	3 867 221	1 931 434	1 935 787	...	...	...	...	...	...
70 - 74	2 853 608	1 422 627	1 430 981	...	...	...	...	...	...
75 - 79	2 096 518	1 051 854	1 044 664	...	...	...	...	...	...
80 - 84	1 836 938	922 916	914 022	...	...	...	...	...	...
85 - 89	1 293 014	646 540	646 475	...	...	...	...	...	...
90 - 94	615 273	308 337	306 936	...	...	...	...	...	...
95 +	173 150	84 340	88 810	...	...	...	...	...	...
Germany - Allemagne									
9 V 2011 (CDJC)									
Total	80 219 695	39 145 941	41 073 754	64 444 232	31 227 832	33 216 400	15 775 463	7 918 109	7 857 354
0 - 4	3 338 895	1 714 872	1 624 023	2 712 601	1 393 763	1 318 838	626 294	321 109	305 185
5 - 9	3 525 830	1 809 024	1 716 806	2 798 622	1 435 745	1 362 877	727 208	373 279	353 929
10 - 14	3 940 566	2 021 305	1 919 261	3 074 610	1 575 684	1 498 926	865 956	445 621	420 335
15 - 19	4 013 880	2 057 155	1 956 725	3 144 832	1 606 068	1 538 764	869 048	451 087	417 961
20 - 24	4 835 639	2 463 932	2 371 707	3 993 247	2 003 582	1 989 665	842 392	460 350	382 042
25 - 29	4 872 533	2 455 885	2 416 648	4 113 697	2 057 507	2 056 190	758 836	398 378	360 458
30 - 34	4 751 911	2 385 305	2 366 606	3 942 747	1 977 628	1 965 119	809 164	407 677	401 487
35 - 39	4 742 893	2 378 055	2 364 838	3 833 417	1 920 448	1 912 969	909 476	457 607	451 869

7. Population by age, sex and urban/rural residence: latest available year, 2008 - 2017
Population selon l'âge, le sexe et la résidence, urbaine/rurale : dernière année disponible, 2008 - 2017 (continued - suite)

Continent, country or area, date, code[a] and age (in years) / Continent, pays ou zone, date, code[a] et âge (en années)	Total			Urban - Urbaine			Rural - Rurale		
	Both sexes Les deux sexes	Male Masculin	Female Féminin	Both sexes Les deux sexes	Male Masculin	Female Féminin	Both sexes Les deux sexes	Male Masculin	Female Féminin
EUROPE									
Germany - Allemagne									
9 V 2011 (CDJC)									
40 - 44	6 351 189	3 209 481	3 141 708	5 029 918	2 540 433	2 489 485	1 321 271	669 048	652 223
45 - 49	6 999 679	3 547 254	3 452 425	5 488 622	2 771 239	2 717 383	1 511 057	776 015	735 042
50 - 54	6 206 294	3 113 463	3 092 831	4 845 747	2 413 038	2 432 709	1 360 547	700 425	660 122
55 - 59	5 419 450	2 668 976	2 750 474	4 252 008	2 066 178	2 185 830	1 167 442	602 798	564 644
60 - 64	4 702 815	2 298 903	2 403 912	3 753 504	1 808 314	1 945 190	949 311	490 589	458 722
65 - 69	4 173 351	1 999 287	2 174 064	3 423 376	1 624 839	1 798 537	749 975	374 448	375 527
70 - 74	4 861 239	2 247 196	2 614 043	3 931 373	1 801 914	2 129 459	929 866	445 282	484 584
75 - 79	3 270 283	1 413 881	1 856 402	2 633 648	1 128 379	1 505 269	636 635	285 502	351 133
80 - 84	2 328 083	878 797	1 449 286	1 890 025	704 565	1 185 460	438 058	174 232	263 826
85 - 89	1 335 076	369 029	966 047	1 108 944	302 059	806 885	226 132	66 970	159 162
90 - 94	430 600	95 074	335 526	368 116	79 884	288 232	62 484	15 190	47 294
95 - 99	106 044	17 388	88 656	93 152	15 094	78 058	12 892	2 294	10 598
100 +	13 445	1 679	11 766	12 026	1 471	10 555	1 419	208	1 211
1 I 2017 (ESDJ)[4]									
Total	82 521 653	40 697 118	41 824 535	...	...	...	...	...	...
0	788 299	403 564	384 735	...	...	...	...	...	...
1 - 4	2 968 147	1 525 024	1 443 123	...	...	...	...	...	...
5 - 9	3 613 927	1 857 190	1 756 737	...	...	...	...	...	...
10 - 14	3 678 195	1 893 522	1 784 673	...	...	...	...	...	...
15 - 19	4 172 869	2 187 398	1 985 471	...	...	...	...	...	...
20 - 24	4 574 031	2 395 930	2 178 101	...	...	...	...	...	...
25 - 29	5 366 756	2 787 105	2 579 651	...	...	...	...	...	...
30 - 34	5 221 075	2 676 180	2 544 895	...	...	...	...	...	...
35 - 39	5 058 038	2 557 606	2 500 432	...	...	...	...	...	...
40 - 44	4 821 986	2 428 357	2 393 629	...	...	...	...	...	...
45 - 49	6 259 912	3 162 743	3 097 169	...	...	...	...	...	...
50 - 54	6 984 307	3 526 252	3 458 055	...	...	...	...	...	...
55 - 59	6 223 126	3 104 747	3 118 379	...	...	...	...	...	...
60 - 64	5 281 280	2 573 457	2 707 823	...	...	...	...	...	...
65 - 69	4 563 301	2 186 608	2 376 693	...	...	...	...	...	...
70 - 74	3 654 937	1 703 714	1 951 223	...	...	...	...	...	...
75 - 79	4 349 557	1 930 680	2 418 877	...	...	...	...	...	...
80 - 84	2 694 971	1 099 541	1 595 430	...	...	...	...	...	...
85 - 89	1 497 342	519 702	977 640	...	...	...	...	...	...
90 - 94	606 407	151 582	454 825	...	...	...	...	...	...
95 - 99	127 981	23 789	104 192	...	...	...	...	...	...
100 - 104	13 479	2 046	11 433	...	...	...	...	...	...
105 - 109	1 491	287	1 204	...	...	...	...	...	...
110 +	239	94	145	...	...	...	...	...	...
Gibraltar[81]									
12 XI 2012 (CDJC)									
Total	32 194	16 061	16 133	...	...	...	...	...	...
0 - 4	1 952	982	970	...	...	...	...	...	...
5 - 9	1 894	967	927	...	...	...	...	...	...
10 - 14	1 987	1 050	937	...	...	...	...	...	...
15 - 19	1 997	1 038	959	...	...	...	...	...	...
20 - 24	2 028	1 042	986	...	...	...	...	...	...
25 - 29	1 985	999	986	...	...	...	...	...	...
30 - 34	2 154	1 107	1 047	...	...	...	...	...	...
35 - 39	2 217	1 080	1 137	...	...	...	...	...	...
40 - 44	2 198	1 076	1 122	...	...	...	...	...	...
45 - 49	2 384	1 203	1 181	...	...	...	...	...	...
50 - 54	2 158	1 072	1 086	...	...	...	...	...	...
55 - 59	2 041	1 054	987	...	...	...	...	...	...
60 - 64	1 954	1 034	920	...	...	...	...	...	...
65 - 69	1 655	853	802	...	...	...	...	...	...
70 - 74	1 176	563	613	...	...	...	...	...	...
75 - 79	1 021	456	565	...	...	...	...	...	...
80 - 84	732	297	435	...	...	...	...	...	...
85 - 89	437	141	296	...	...	...	...	...	...
90 - 94	180	37	143	...	...	...	...	...	...
95 - 99	39	10	29	...	...	...	...	...	...
100 +	5	-	5	...	...	...	...	...	...

7. Population by age, sex and urban/rural residence: latest available year, 2008 - 2017
Population selon l'âge, le sexe et la résidence, urbaine/rurale : dernière année disponible, 2008 - 2017 (continued - suite)

Continent, country or area, date, codeᵃ and age (in years) / Continent, pays ou zone, date, codeᵃ et âge (en années)	Total			Urban - Urbaine			Rural - Rurale		
	Both sexes Les deux sexes	Male Masculin	Female Féminin	Both sexes Les deux sexes	Male Masculin	Female Féminin	Both sexes Les deux sexes	Male Masculin	Female Féminin
EUROPE									
Greece - Grèce									
9 V 2011 (CDFC)									
Total	10 816 286	5 303 223	5 513 063	8 285 259	4 022 889	4 262 370	2 531 027	1 280 334	1 250 693
0 - 4	537 243	274 788	262 455	431 611	220 917	210 694	105 632	53 871	51 761
5 - 9	512 596	262 432	250 164	405 436	207 479	197 957	107 160	54 953	52 207
10 - 14	519 429	265 787	253 642	406 962	208 070	198 892	112 467	57 717	54 750
15 - 19	553 276	286 386	266 890	440 869	226 682	214 187	112 407	59 704	52 703
20 - 24	627 097	325 127	301 970	510 067	259 795	250 272	117 030	65 332	51 698
25 - 29	723 771	371 617	352 154	583 506	295 880	287 626	140 265	75 737	64 528
30 - 34	822 475	417 861	404 614	666 145	334 794	331 351	156 330	83 067	73 263
35 - 39	812 829	409 681	403 148	651 826	323 821	328 005	161 003	85 860	75 143
40 - 44	832 666	414 026	418 640	663 331	323 632	339 699	169 335	90 394	78 941
45 - 49	748 429	367 086	381 343	590 034	283 391	306 643	158 395	83 695	74 700
50 - 54	731 486	355 552	375 934	565 986	268 882	297 104	165 500	86 670	78 830
55 - 59	660 368	321 466	338 902	501 507	240 725	260 782	158 861	80 741	78 120
60 - 64	625 769	301 589	324 180	459 249	219 165	240 084	166 520	82 424	84 096
65 - 69	508 276	241 832	266 444	356 701	167 557	189 144	151 575	74 275	77 300
70 - 74	542 165	246 264	295 901	363 133	162 560	200 573	179 032	83 704	95 328
75 - 79	475 077	209 983	265 094	309 622	134 691	174 931	165 455	75 292	90 163
80 - 84	352 373	146 455	205 918	229 214	91 916	137 298	123 159	54 539	68 620
85 - 89	159 841	60 933	98 908	104 058	37 922	66 136	55 783	23 011	32 772
90 - 94	53 445	18 760	34 685	34 608	11 513	23 095	18 837	7 247	11 590
95 - 99	15 187	4 948	10 239	9 822	3 081	6 741	5 365	1 867	3 498
100 +	2 488	650	1 838	1 572	416	1 156	916	234	682
1 I 2017 (ESDF)									
Total	10 768 193	5 221 277	5 546 916	...	...	...	...	...	...
0	93 927	48 359	45 568	...	...	...	...	...	...
1 - 4	381 632	196 237	185 395	...	...	...	...	...	...
5 - 9	547 020	280 191	266 829	...	...	...	...	...	...
10 - 14	532 090	273 144	258 946	...	...	...	...	...	...
15 - 19	538 027	275 824	262 203	...	...	...	...	...	...
20 - 24	551 499	282 307	269 192	...	...	...	...	...	...
25 - 29	586 211	293 909	292 302	...	...	...	...	...	...
30 - 34	671 552	337 784	333 768	...	...	...	...	...	...
35 - 39	797 374	398 648	398 726	...	...	...	...	...	...
40 - 44	807 139	398 915	408 224	...	...	...	...	...	...
45 - 49	825 444	400 874	424 570	...	...	...	...	...	...
50 - 54	748 206	358 241	389 965	...	...	...	...	...	...
55 - 59	715 104	337 815	377 289	...	...	...	...	...	...
60 - 64	653 227	310 338	342 889	...	...	...	...	...	...
65 - 69	610 017	286 853	323 164	...	...	...	...	...	...
70 - 74	517 499	239 299	278 200	...	...	...	...	...	...
75 - 79	468 764	205 680	263 084	...	...	...	...	...	...
80 - 84	387 417	161 774	225 643	...	...	...	...	...	...
85 - 89	224 670	91 664	133 006	...	...	...	...	...	...
90 - 94	83 804	32 524	51 280	...	...	...	...	...	...
95 - 99	20 470	8 292	12 178	...	...	...	...	...	...
100 - 104	5 020	1 886	3 134	...	...	...	...	...	...
105 - 109	1 526	529	997	...	...	...	...	...	...
110 +	554	190	364	...	...	...	...	...	...
Guernsey - Guernesey									
31 III 2017 (ESDJ)									
Total	62 193	30 799	31 394	...	...	...	...	...	...
0	575	298	277	...	...	...	...	...	...
1 - 4	2 483	1 271	1 212	...	...	...	...	...	...
5 - 9	3 245	1 698	1 547	...	...	...	...	...	...
10 - 14	3 047	1 569	1 478	...	...	...	...	...	...
15 - 19	3 347	1 716	1 631	...	...	...	...	...	...
20 - 24	3 664	1 900	1 764	...	...	...	...	...	...
25 - 29	4 027	2 060	1 967	...	...	...	...	...	...
30 - 34	3 836	1 975	1 861	...	...	...	...	...	...
35 - 39	3 803	1 931	1 872	...	...	...	...	...	...
40 - 44	3 950	1 927	2 023	...	...	...	...	...	...
45 - 49	4 792	2 320	2 472	...	...	...	...	...	...
50 - 54	5 024	2 482	2 542	...	...	...	...	...	...

Continent, country or area, date, code[a] and age (in years) / Continent, pays ou zone, date, code[a] et âge (en années)	Total			Urban - Urbaine			Rural - Rurale		
	Both sexes Les deux sexes	Male Masculin	Female Féminin	Both sexes Les deux sexes	Male Masculin	Female Féminin	Both sexes Les deux sexes	Male Masculin	Female Féminin
EUROPE									
Guernsey - Guernesey									
31 III 2017 (ESDJ)									
55 - 59	4 515	2 194	2 321	...	...	...	...	...	...
60 - 64	3 795	1 947	1 848	...	...	...	...	...	...
65 - 69	3 601	1 738	1 863	...	...	...	...	...	...
70 - 74	2 982	1 448	1 534	...	...	...	...	...	...
75 - 79	2 200	1 052	1 148	...	...	...	...	...	...
80 - 84	1 646	705	941	...	...	...	...	...	...
85 - 89	1 037	385	652	...	...	...	...	...	...
90 - 94	472	150	322	...	...	...	...	...	...
95 - 99	131	31	100	...	...	...	...	...	...
100 +	21	2	19	...	...	...	...	...	...
Hungary - Hongrie[82]									
1 VII 2016 (ESDJ)									
Total	9 814 023	4 681 905	5 132 118	6 916 274	3 259 506	3 656 768	2 897 750	1 422 399	1 475 351
0	93 300	47 913	45 387	65 094	33 479	31 615	28 206	14 434	13 772
1 - 4	365 004	187 674	177 330	260 663	134 270	126 393	104 342	53 405	50 937
5 - 9	481 302	246 483	234 819	337 560	172 797	164 763	143 742	73 687	70 056
10 - 14	484 052	248 761	235 291	326 279	167 506	158 773	157 773	81 255	76 518
15 - 19	499 131	256 789	242 342	341 549	174 300	167 249	157 583	82 489	75 094
20 - 24	605 799	311 276	294 523	415 603	211 698	203 906	190 196	99 578	90 618
25 - 29	618 394	318 847	299 547	436 213	221 839	214 374	182 181	97 008	85 174
30 - 34	617 505	314 268	303 238	446 222	223 613	222 610	171 283	90 655	80 628
35 - 39	775 151	391 622	383 530	564 738	281 404	283 334	210 414	110 218	100 196
40 - 44	804 544	406 765	397 779	576 659	287 806	288 853	227 885	118 959	108 927
45 - 49	703 778	352 593	351 185	492 342	243 340	249 003	211 436	109 253	102 183
50 - 54	588 047	288 126	299 921	401 050	192 855	208 195	186 997	95 271	91 726
55 - 59	637 378	299 741	337 637	433 384	198 228	235 157	203 994	101 514	102 480
60 - 64	728 240	328 954	399 286	515 231	226 657	288 574	213 009	102 297	110 712
65 - 69	587 756	252 464	335 292	421 121	177 416	243 705	166 636	75 049	91 587
70 - 74	457 187	183 196	273 991	332 630	132 996	199 634	124 557	50 201	74 357
75 - 79	344 352	121 751	222 602	245 244	87 779	157 466	99 108	33 972	65 136
80 - 84	235 276	74 326	160 950	167 217	53 986	113 232	68 059	20 341	47 718
85 - 89	129 837	36 425	93 412	94 515	27 155	67 360	35 323	9 270	26 053
90 - 94	47 394	11 323	36 071	35 055	8 434	26 621	12 339	2 890	9 450
95 - 99	9 045	2 128	6 917	6 752	1 600	5 152	2 294	529	1 765
100 +	1 557	484	1 073	1 159	355	804	399	130	269
1 I 2017 (ESDJ)									
Total	9 797 561	4 675 291	5 122 270	...	...	...	...	...	...
0	94 858	48 700	46 158	...	...	...	...	...	...
1 - 4	366 881	188 634	178 247	...	...	...	...	...	...
5 - 9	474 702	243 160	231 542	...	...	...	...	...	...
10 - 14	486 424	249 863	236 561	...	...	...	...	...	...
15 - 19	493 069	253 732	239 337	...	...	...	...	...	...
20 - 24	596 660	306 587	290 073	...	...	...	...	...	...
25 - 29	620 563	320 288	300 275	...	...	...	...	...	...
30 - 34	610 309	311 254	299 055	...	...	...	...	...	...
35 - 39	755 139	381 187	373 952	...	...	...	...	...	...
40 - 44	819 308	414 419	404 889	...	...	...	...	...	...
45 - 49	710 839	356 343	354 496	...	...	...	...	...	...
50 - 54	589 143	289 295	299 848	...	...	...	...	...	...
55 - 59	620 066	292 174	327 892	...	...	...	...	...	...
60 - 64	731 374	330 778	400 596	...	...	...	...	...	...
65 - 69	597 868	256 411	341 457	...	...	...	...	...	...
70 - 74	457 173	183 521	273 652	...	...	...	...	...	...
75 - 79	347 900	123 968	223 932	...	...	...	...	...	...
80 - 84	235 120	73 906	161 214	...	...	...	...	...	...
85 - 89	130 695	36 817	93 878	...	...	...	...	...	...
90 - 94	47 959	11 433	36 526	...	...	...	...	...	...
95 - 99	9 931	2 317	7 614	...	...	...	...	...	...
100 - 104	1 266	345	921	...	...	...	...	...	...
105 - 109	290	144	146	...	...	...	...	...	...
110 +	24	15	9	...	...	...	...	...	...

Continent, country or area, date, code[a] and age (in years) / Continent, pays ou zone, date, code[a] et âge (en années)	Total			Urban - Urbaine			Rural - Rurale		
	Both sexes Les deux sexes	Male Masculin	Female Féminin	Both sexes Les deux sexes	Male Masculin	Female Féminin	Both sexes Les deux sexes	Male Masculin	Female Féminin
EUROPE									
Iceland - Islande[83]									
1 VII 2016 (ESDJ)									
Total	335 439	169 152	166 288	314 123	157 819	156 304	21 317	11 333	9 984
0	4 081	2 082	1 999	3 880	1 978	1 902	202	104	98
1 - 4	17 590	8 914	8 676	16 713	8 484	8 229	877	430	447
5 - 9	23 507	12 105	11 402	22 332	11 474	10 858	1 176	631	545
10 - 14	21 500	10 935	10 565	20 294	10 315	9 979	1 207	621	586
15 - 19	22 032	11 198	10 835	20 556	10 441	10 115	1 477	757	720
20 - 24	25 036	12 901	12 136	23 332	12 040	11 292	1 705	861	844
25 - 29	25 036	13 039	11 997	23 496	12 189	11 307	1 540	850	690
30 - 34	23 225	11 990	11 236	22 070	11 358	10 712	1 156	632	524
35 - 39	22 805	11 654	11 151	21 711	11 080	10 631	1 094	574	520
40 - 44	22 009	11 218	10 792	20 830	10 599	10 231	1 180	619	561
45 - 49	20 557	10 319	10 239	19 202	9 597	9 605	1 356	722	634
50 - 54	21 866	10 833	11 034	20 211	9 959	10 252	1 656	874	782
55 - 59	21 095	10 620	10 475	19 455	9 732	9 723	1 640	888	752
60 - 64	18 345	9 211	9 134	16 904	8 408	8 496	1 441	803	638
65 - 69	15 306	7 776	7 531	14 114	7 116	6 998	1 192	660	533
70 - 74	11 463	5 640	5 823	10 546	5 126	5 420	917	514	404
75 - 79	7 774	3 691	4 083	7 165	3 361	3 804	609	330	280
80 - 84	6 139	2 753	3 386	5 669	2 504	3 165	470	249	221
85 - 89	4 086	1 648	2 438	3 791	1 492	2 299	295	156	140
90 - 94	1 619	526	1 094	1 522	482	1 040	97	44	54
95 - 99	334	92	243	302	76	226	32	16	17
100 +	38	14	25	36	12	24	3	2	1
1 I 2017 (ESDJ)									
Total	338 349	171 033	167 316	...	...	...	...	...	...
0	4 049	2 053	1 996	...	...	...	...	...	...
1 - 4	17 448	8 837	8 611	...	...	...	...	...	...
5 - 9	23 606	12 146	11 460	...	...	...	...	...	...
10 - 14	21 713	11 056	10 657	...	...	...	...	...	...
15 - 19	21 943	11 134	10 809	...	...	...	...	...	...
20 - 24	25 186	13 009	12 177	...	...	...	...	...	...
25 - 29	25 701	13 495	12 206	...	...	...	...	...	...
30 - 34	23 341	12 109	11 232	...	...	...	...	...	...
35 - 39	23 178	11 905	11 273	...	...	...	...	...	...
40 - 44	22 297	11 416	10 881	...	...	...	...	...	...
45 - 49	20 547	10 386	10 161	...	...	...	...	...	...
50 - 54	22 083	10 955	11 128	...	...	...	...	...	...
55 - 59	21 159	10 669	10 490	...	...	...	...	...	...
60 - 64	18 657	9 402	9 255	...	...	...	...	...	...
65 - 69	15 567	7 865	7 702	...	...	...	...	...	...
70 - 74	11 774	5 826	5 948	...	...	...	...	...	...
75 - 79	7 829	3 735	4 094	...	...	...	...	...	...
80 - 84	6 124	2 733	3 391	...	...	...	...	...	...
85 - 89	4 116	1 661	2 455	...	...	...	...	...	...
90 - 94	1 636	533	1 103	...	...	...	...	...	...
95 - 99	356	94	262	...	...	...	...	...	...
100 - 104	36	13	23	...	...	...	...	...	...
105 - 109	3	1	2	...	...	...	...	...	...
110 +	-	-	-	...	...	...	...	...	...
Ireland - Irlande									
10 IV 2011 (CDFC)[84]									
Total	4 588 252	2 272 699	2 315 553	2 846 882	1 389 160	1 457 722	1 741 370	883 539	857 831
0 - 4	356 329	182 076	174 253	224 004	114 284	109 720	132 325	67 792	64 533
5 - 9	320 770	164 037	156 733	188 818	96 160	92 658	131 952	67 877	64 075
10 - 14	302 491	155 076	147 415	172 930	88 433	84 497	129 561	66 643	62 918
15 - 19	283 019	144 262	138 757	170 523	86 129	84 394	112 496	58 133	54 363
20 - 24	297 231	146 636	150 595	208 146	100 226	107 920	89 085	46 410	42 675
25 - 29	361 122	173 714	187 408	266 457	126 362	140 095	94 665	47 352	47 313
30 - 34	393 945	194 774	199 171	278 935	137 689	141 246	115 010	57 085	57 925
35 - 39	364 261	182 237	182 024	233 417	116 912	116 505	130 844	65 325	65 519
40 - 44	330 812	166 330	164 482	198 432	99 162	99 270	132 380	67 168	65 212
45 - 49	305 185	151 516	153 669	178 630	87 087	91 543	126 555	64 429	62 126
50 - 54	274 386	136 737	137 649	158 031	77 106	80 925	116 355	59 631	56 724

Continent, country or area, date, code[a] and age (in years) / Continent, pays ou zone, date, code[a] et âge (en années)	Total			Urban - Urbaine			Rural - Rurale		
	Both sexes Les deux sexes	Male Masculin	Female Féminin	Both sexes Les deux sexes	Male Masculin	Female Féminin	Both sexes Les deux sexes	Male Masculin	Female Féminin
EUROPE									
Ireland - Irlande									
10 IV 2011 (CDFC)[84]									
55 - 59	244 522	122 121	122 401	137 973	66 919	71 054	106 549	55 202	51 347
60 - 64	218 786	109 869	108 917	122 606	59 521	63 085	96 180	50 348	45 832
65 - 69	173 638	86 298	87 340	97 999	46 741	51 258	75 639	39 557	36 082
70 - 74	131 190	63 476	67 714	76 683	35 378	41 305	54 507	28 098	26 409
75 - 79	102 036	46 631	55 405	59 519	25 708	33 811	42 517	20 923	21 594
80 - 84	70 113	28 423	41 690	40 585	15 449	25 136	29 528	12 974	16 554
85 - 89	39 887	13 591	26 296	22 742	7 303	15 439	17 145	6 288	10 857
90 - 94	14 877	4 155	10 722	8 363	2 200	6 163	6 514	1 955	4 559
95 - 99	3 263	682	2 581	1 884	360	1 524	1 379	322	1 057
100 +	389	58	331	205	31	174	184	27	157
1 I 2017 (ESDF)									
Total	4 784 383	2 367 918	2 416 465	...	...	...	...	...	...
0	63 094	32 193	30 901	...	...	...	...	...	...
1 - 4	263 470	134 990	128 480	...	...	...	...	...	...
5 - 9	359 156	183 247	175 909	...	...	...	...	...	...
10 - 14	322 735	165 236	157 499	...	...	...	...	...	...
15 - 19	307 218	157 108	150 110	...	...	...	...	...	...
20 - 24	276 208	140 409	135 799	...	...	...	...	...	...
25 - 29	293 702	144 336	149 366	...	...	...	...	...	...
30 - 34	351 326	167 872	183 454	...	...	...	...	...	...
35 - 39	393 295	191 928	201 367	...	...	...	...	...	...
40 - 44	362 163	179 653	182 510	...	...	...	...	...	...
45 - 49	330 641	164 907	165 734	...	...	...	...	...	...
50 - 54	301 675	149 287	152 388	...	...	...	...	...	...
55 - 59	272 468	135 175	137 293	...	...	...	...	...	...
60 - 64	240 715	119 814	120 901	...	...	...	...	...	...
65 - 69	210 434	104 533	105 901	...	...	...	...	...	...
70 - 74	167 212	82 095	85 117	...	...	...	...	...	...
75 - 79	116 332	54 779	61 553	...	...	...	...	...	...
80 - 84	82 610	36 045	46 565	...	...	...	...	...	...
85 - 89	46 024	17 417	28 607	...	...	...	...	...	...
90 - 94	18 395	5 528	12 867	...	...	...	...	...	...
95 - 99	4 893	1 244	3 649	...	...	...	...	...	...
100 - 104	579	118	461	...	...	...	...	...	...
105 - 109	38	4	34	...	...	...	...	...	...
110 +	-	-	-	...	...	...	...	...	...
Isle of Man - Île de Man									
24 IV 2016 (CDJC)									
Total	83 314	41 269	42 045	...	...	...	...	...	...
0 - 4	4 144	2 186	1 958	...	...	...	...	...	...
5 - 9	4 733	2 436	2 297	...	...	...	...	...	...
10 - 14	4 469	2 346	2 123	...	...	...	...	...	...
15 - 19	4 789	2 506	2 283	...	...	...	...	...	...
20 - 24	4 422	2 252	2 170	...	...	...	...	...	...
25 - 29	4 326	2 131	2 195	...	...	...	...	...	...
30 - 34	4 506	2 148	2 358	...	...	...	...	...	...
35 - 39	4 873	2 371	2 502	...	...	...	...	...	...
40 - 44	5 612	2 715	2 897	...	...	...	...	...	...
45 - 49	6 497	3 255	3 242	...	...	...	...	...	...
50 - 54	6 681	3 359	3 322	...	...	...	...	...	...
55 - 59	5 887	2 889	2 998	...	...	...	...	...	...
60 - 64	5 170	2 612	2 558	...	...	...	...	...	...
65 - 69	5 441	2 715	2 726	...	...	...	...	...	...
70 - 74	4 212	2 074	2 138	...	...	...	...	...	...
75 - 79	3 155	1 529	1 626	...	...	...	...	...	...
80 - 84	2 129	958	1 171	...	...	...	...	...	...
85 - 89	1 380	522	858	...	...	...	...	...	...
90 - 94	675	202	473	...	...	...	...	...	...
95 - 99	188	53	135	...	...	...	...	...	...
100 +	25	10	15	...	...	...	...	...	...

Continent, country or area, date, code^a and age (in years) Continent, pays ou zone, date, code^a et âge (en annèes)	Total			Urban - Urbaine			Rural - Rurale		
	Both sexes Les deux sexes	Male Masculin	Female Féminin	Both sexes Les deux sexes	Male Masculin	Female Féminin	Both sexes Les deux sexes	Male Masculin	Female Féminin
EUROPE									
Italy - Italie									
1 I 2017 (ESDJ)									
Total	60 589 445	29 445 741	31 143 704	...	...	...	...	...	...
0	467 657	240 100	227 557	...	...	...	...	...	...
1 - 4	2 033 798	1 045 540	988 258	...	...	...	...	...	...
5 - 9	2 824 345	1 453 249	1 371 096	...	...	...	...	...	...
10 - 14	2 856 784	1 471 182	1 385 602	...	...	...	...	...	...
15 - 19	2 888 804	1 496 090	1 392 714	...	...	...	...	...	...
20 - 24	3 006 549	1 556 761	1 449 788	...	...	...	...	...	...
25 - 29	3 249 766	1 654 258	1 595 508	...	...	...	...	...	...
30 - 34	3 462 938	1 742 861	1 720 077	...	...	...	...	...	...
35 - 39	3 930 724	1 969 070	1 961 654	...	...	...	...	...	...
40 - 44	4 684 706	2 335 028	2 349 678	...	...	...	...	...	...
45 - 49	4 901 028	2 425 228	2 475 800	...	...	...	...	...	...
50 - 54	4 849 951	2 386 722	2 463 229	...	...	...	...	...	...
55 - 59	4 199 045	2 038 234	2 160 811	...	...	...	...	...	...
60 - 64	3 704 800	1 782 536	1 922 264	...	...	...	...	...	...
65 - 69	3 618 837	1 725 034	1 893 803	...	...	...	...	...	...
70 - 74	2 977 579	1 384 021	1 593 558	...	...	...	...	...	...
75 - 79	2 799 480	1 240 926	1 558 554	...	...	...	...	...	...
80 - 84	2 070 988	840 924	1 230 064	...	...	...	...	...	...
85 - 89	1 338 502	467 008	871 494	...	...	...	...	...	...
90 - 94	578 009	160 306	417 703	...	...	...	...	...	...
95 - 99	127 525	27 752	99 773	...	...	...	...	...	...
100 - 104	16 645	2 790	13 855	...	...	...	...	...	...
105 - 109	967	119	848	...	...	...	...	...	...
110 +	18	2	16	...	...	...	...	...	...
Jersey									
27 III 2011 (CDJC)									
Total	97 857	48 296	49 561	...	...	...	...	...	...
0 - 4	5 015	2 466	2 549	...	...	...	...	...	...
5 - 9	4 852	2 470	2 382	...	...	...	...	...	...
10 - 14	5 302	2 729	2 573	...	...	...	...	...	...
15 - 19	5 495	2 863	2 632	...	...	...	...	...	...
20 - 24	5 944	3 006	2 938	...	...	...	...	...	...
25 - 29	6 705	3 351	3 354	...	...	...	...	...	...
30 - 34	7 236	3 670	3 566	...	...	...	...	...	...
35 - 39	7 225	3 615	3 610	...	...	...	...	...	...
40 - 44	8 363	4 183	4 180	...	...	...	...	...	...
45 - 49	8 357	4 187	4 170	...	...	...	...	...	...
50 - 54	7 198	3 536	3 662	...	...	...	...	...	...
55 - 59	6 042	2 955	3 087	...	...	...	...	...	...
60 - 64	5 650	2 832	2 818	...	...	...	...	...	...
65 - 69	4 048	1 938	2 110	...	...	...	...	...	...
70 - 74	3 632	1 732	1 900	...	...	...	...	...	...
75 - 79	2 893	1 343	1 550	...	...	...	...	...	...
80 - 84	2 005	822	1 183	...	...	...	...	...	...
85 - 89	1 225	446	779	...	...	...	...	...	...
90 - 94	483	115	368	...	...	...	...	...	...
95 +	187	37	150	...	...	...	...	...	...
Latvia - Lettonie									
1 VII 2016 (ESDJ)									
Total	1 959 537	899 991	1 059 546	1 336 137	596 307	739 830	623 400	303 684	319 716
0	21 862	11 375	10 487	15 128	7 862	7 266	6 734	3 513	3 221
1 - 4	83 435	43 079	40 356	57 725	29 817	27 908	25 710	13 262	12 448
5 - 9	102 737	52 678	50 059	70 039	35 932	34 107	32 698	16 746	15 952
10 - 14	93 885	48 229	45 656	62 023	31 728	30 295	31 862	16 501	15 361
15 - 19	86 040	44 068	41 972	54 592	27 737	26 855	31 448	16 331	15 117
20 - 24	107 920	55 523	52 397	68 115	34 444	33 671	39 805	21 079	18 726
25 - 29	139 666	71 761	67 905	95 361	47 369	47 992	44 305	24 392	19 913
30 - 34	137 934	70 565	67 369	98 291	48 969	49 322	39 643	21 596	18 047
35 - 39	125 928	62 980	62 948	88 773	43 377	45 396	37 155	19 603	17 552
40 - 44	133 846	65 912	67 934	91 759	44 000	47 759	42 087	21 912	20 175
45 - 49	133 735	64 329	69 406	89 498	41 652	47 846	44 237	22 677	21 560
50 - 54	138 363	65 060	73 303	91 862	41 410	50 452	46 501	23 650	22 851

Continent, country or area, date, code[a] and age (in years) / Continent, pays ou zone, date, code[a] et âge (en années)	Total			Urban - Urbaine			Rural - Rurale		
	Both sexes Les deux sexes	Male Masculin	Female Féminin	Both sexes Les deux sexes	Male Masculin	Female Féminin	Both sexes Les deux sexes	Male Masculin	Female Féminin
EUROPE									
Latvia - Lettonie									
1 VII 2016 (ESDJ)									
55 - 59	143 978	65 279	78 699	97 149	41 737	55 412	46 829	23 542	23 287
60 - 64	122 950	52 283	70 667	85 906	34 662	51 244	37 044	17 621	19 423
65 - 69	109 026	42 901	66 125	77 236	28 839	48 397	31 790	14 062	17 728
70 - 74	89 057	31 300	57 757	60 164	20 350	39 814	28 893	10 950	17 943
75 - 79	89 509	28 288	61 221	62 659	19 344	43 315	26 850	8 944	17 906
80 - 84	55 226	14 931	40 295	38 121	10 209	27 912	17 105	4 722	12 383
85 - 89	32 298	7 488	24 810	23 088	5 422	17 666	9 210	2 066	7 144
90 - 94	10 571	1 712	8 859	7 523	1 261	6 262	3 048	451	2 597
95 - 99	1 413	229	1 184	1 018	177	841	395	52	343
100 +	158	21	137	107	9	98	51	12	39
1 I 2017 (ESDJ)									
Total	1 950 116	895 683	1 054 433	...	...	...	...	...	...
0	21 841	11 358	10 483	...	...	...	...	...	...
1 - 4	85 132	44 043	41 089	...	...	...	...	...	...
5 - 9	101 634	52 147	49 487	...	...	...	...	...	...
10 - 14	94 980	48 802	46 178	...	...	...	...	...	...
15 - 19	85 799	43 851	41 948	...	...	...	...	...	...
20 - 24	102 510	52 732	49 778	...	...	...	...	...	...
25 - 29	137 155	70 433	66 722	...	...	...	...	...	...
30 - 34	138 635	70 883	67 752	...	...	...	...	...	...
35 - 39	125 024	62 589	62 435	...	...	...	...	...	...
40 - 44	132 105	65 103	67 002	...	...	...	...	...	...
45 - 49	133 550	64 266	69 284	...	...	...	...	...	...
50 - 54	135 855	63 918	71 937	...	...	...	...	...	...
55 - 59	144 574	65 686	78 888	...	...	...	...	...	...
60 - 64	123 413	52 609	70 804	...	...	...	...	...	...
65 - 69	110 632	43 615	67 017	...	...	...	...	...	...
70 - 74	86 241	30 274	55 967	...	...	...	...	...	...
75 - 79	90 133	28 599	61 534	...	...	...	...	...	...
80 - 84	55 838	15 115	40 723	...	...	...	...	...	...
85 - 89	32 474	7 659	24 815	...	...	...	...	...	...
90 - 94	10 940	1 743	9 197	...	...	...	...	...	...
95 - 99	1 499	240	1 259	...	...	...	...	...	...
100 - 104	140	18	122	...	...	...	...	...	...
105 - 109	12	-	12	...	...	...	...	...	...
110 +	-	-	-	...	...	...	...	...	...
Liechtenstein									
1 I 2017 (ESDJ)									
Total	37 810	18 746	19 064	...	...	...	...	...	...
0	381	195	186	...	...	...	...	...	...
1 - 4	1 440	779	661	...	...	...	...	...	...
5 - 9	1 898	1 009	889	...	...	...	...	...	...
10 - 14	1 905	960	945	...	...	...	...	...	...
15 - 19	2 086	1 038	1 048	...	...	...	...	...	...
20 - 24	2 216	1 117	1 099	...	...	...	...	...	...
25 - 29	2 287	1 176	1 111	...	...	...	...	...	...
30 - 34	2 326	1 143	1 183	...	...	...	...	...	...
35 - 39	2 477	1 272	1 205	...	...	...	...	...	...
40 - 44	2 687	1 312	1 375	...	...	...	...	...	...
45 - 49	3 200	1 601	1 599	...	...	...	...	...	...
50 - 54	3 178	1 569	1 609	...	...	...	...	...	...
55 - 59	2 912	1 428	1 484	...	...	...	...	...	...
60 - 64	2 405	1 183	1 222	...	...	...	...	...	...
65 - 69	2 134	1 083	1 051	...	...	...	...	...	...
70 - 74	1 743	857	886	...	...	...	...	...	...
75 - 79	1 208	554	654	...	...	...	...	...	...
80 - 84	722	283	439	...	...	...	...	...	...
85 - 89	386	136	250	...	...	...	...	...	...
90 - 94	183	40	143	...	...	...	...	...	...
95 - 99	32	9	23	...	...	...	...	...	...
100 +	4	2	2	...	...	...	...	...	...

Continent, country or area, date, code[a] and age (in years) / Continent, pays ou zone, date, code[a] et âge (en années)	Total			Urban - Urbaine			Rural - Rurale		
	Both sexes Les deux sexes	Male Masculin	Female Féminin	Both sexes Les deux sexes	Male Masculin	Female Féminin	Both sexes Les deux sexes	Male Masculin	Female Féminin
EUROPE									
Lithuania - Lituanie[82]									
1 VII 2016 (ESDJ)									
Total	2 868 231	1 320 897	1 547 334	1 927 148	860 905	1 066 243	941 083	459 992	481 091
0	30 936	15 959	14 977	21 389	11 096	10 293	9 547	4 863	4 684
1 - 4	120 145	61 548	58 597	84 167	43 084	41 083	35 978	18 464	17 514
5 - 9	141 385	72 451	68 934	97 840	50 156	47 684	43 545	22 295	21 250
10 - 14	130 469	66 827	63 642	83 481	42 752	40 729	46 988	24 075	22 913
15 - 19	157 596	81 035	76 561	97 632	49 942	47 690	59 964	31 093	28 871
20 - 24	189 209	96 853	92 356	118 740	59 393	59 347	70 469	37 460	33 009
25 - 29	194 637	100 254	94 383	137 572	66 938	70 634	57 065	33 316	23 749
30 - 34	179 341	91 092	88 249	134 591	65 740	68 851	44 750	25 352	19 398
35 - 39	170 574	84 845	85 729	121 041	58 768	62 273	49 533	26 077	23 456
40 - 44	189 921	91 787	98 134	127 596	59 903	67 693	62 325	31 884	30 441
45 - 49	205 552	97 939	107 613	132 810	60 816	71 994	72 742	37 123	35 619
50 - 54	216 891	102 118	114 773	141 317	62 991	78 326	75 574	39 127	36 447
55 - 59	219 939	99 625	120 314	147 591	63 173	84 418	72 348	36 452	35 896
60 - 64	172 273	73 748	98 525	116 814	47 052	69 762	55 459	26 696	28 763
65 - 69	148 853	58 819	90 034	101 032	37 684	63 348	47 821	21 135	26 686
70 - 74	127 083	45 571	81 512	84 055	29 029	55 026	43 028	16 542	26 486
75 - 79	119 542	39 230	80 312	79 361	25 498	53 863	40 181	13 732	26 449
80 - 84	87 091	25 177	61 914	55 824	16 127	39 697	31 267	9 050	22 217
85 - 89	48 504	12 491	36 013	31 725	8 374	23 351	16 779	4 117	12 662
90 - 94	15 709	3 051	12 658	10 595	2 062	8 533	5 114	989	4 125
95 - 99	2 262	400	1 862	1 686	269	1 417	576	131	445
100 +	319	77	242	289	58	231	30	19	11
1 I 2017 (ESDJ)									
Total	2 847 904	1 312 186	1 535 718	...	...	...	...	...	...
0	30 409	15 738	14 671	...	...	...	...	...	...
1 - 4	120 262	61 536	58 726	...	...	...	...	...	...
5 - 9	142 254	73 048	69 206	...	...	...	...	...	...
10 - 14	129 197	66 139	63 058	...	...	...	...	...	...
15 - 19	153 051	78 744	74 307	...	...	...	...	...	...
20 - 24	182 556	93 525	89 031	...	...	...	...	...	...
25 - 29	193 381	99 841	93 540	...	...	...	...	...	...
30 - 34	179 798	91 550	88 248	...	...	...	...	...	...
35 - 39	167 640	83 683	83 957	...	...	...	...	...	...
40 - 44	185 756	89 967	95 789	...	...	...	...	...	...
45 - 49	204 487	97 593	106 894	...	...	...	...	...	...
50 - 54	212 589	100 260	112 329	...	...	...	...	...	...
55 - 59	223 136	101 239	121 897	...	...	...	...	...	...
60 - 64	173 191	74 221	98 970	...	...	...	...	...	...
65 - 69	151 223	59 803	91 420	...	...	...	...	...	...
70 - 74	124 160	44 496	79 664	...	...	...	...	...	...
75 - 79	118 918	39 018	79 900	...	...	...	...	...	...
80 - 84	88 073	25 492	62 581	...	...	...	...	...	...
85 - 89	49 014	12 667	36 347	...	...	...	...	...	...
90 - 94	16 096	3 139	12 957	...	...	...	...	...	...
95 - 99	2 425	411	2 014	...	...	...	...	...	...
100 - 104	234	59	175	...	...	...	...	...	...
105 - 109	49	14	35	...	...	...	...	...	...
110 +	5	3	2	...	...	...	...	...	...
Luxembourg									
1 I 2017 (ESDJ)									
Total	590 667	296 641	294 026	...	...	...	...	...	...
0	6 128	3 108	3 020	...	...	...	...	...	...
1 - 4	25 935	13 311	12 624	...	...	...	...	...	...
5 - 9	32 255	16 551	15 704	...	...	...	...	...	...
10 - 14	31 605	16 442	15 163	...	...	...	...	...	...
15 - 19	33 248	17 004	16 244	...	...	...	...	...	...
20 - 24	37 040	18 912	18 128	...	...	...	...	...	...
25 - 29	43 165	22 000	21 165	...	...	...	...	...	...
30 - 34	45 453	22 805	22 648	...	...	...	...	...	...
35 - 39	46 106	23 165	22 941	...	...	...	...	...	...
40 - 44	44 376	22 610	21 766	...	...	...	...	...	...
45 - 49	46 294	23 850	22 444	...	...	...	...	...	...

Continent, country or area, date, code[a] and age (in years) / Continent, pays ou zone, date, code[a] et âge (en années)	Total			Urban - Urbaine			Rural - Rurale		
	Both sexes Les deux sexes	Male Masculin	Female Féminin	Both sexes Les deux sexes	Male Masculin	Female Féminin	Both sexes Les deux sexes	Male Masculin	Female Féminin
EUROPE									
Luxembourg									
1 I 2017 (ESDJ)									
50 - 54	45 103	23 604	21 499	...	...	...	...	...	...
55 - 59	38 415	19 810	18 605	...	...	...	...	...	...
60 - 64	31 413	15 763	15 650	...	...	...	...	...	...
65 - 69	25 572	12 799	12 773	...	...	...	...	...	...
70 - 74	19 527	9 464	10 063	...	...	...	...	...	...
75 - 79	15 855	6 970	8 885	...	...	...	...	...	...
80 - 84	11 812	4 823	6 989	...	...	...	...	...	...
85 - 89	7 904	2 820	5 084	...	...	...	...	...	...
90 - 94	2 819	684	2 135	...	...	...	...	...	...
95 - 99	568	138	430	...	...	...	...	...	...
100 - 104	67	7	60	...	...	...	...	...	...
105 - 109	7	1	6	...	...	...	...	...	...
110 +	-	-	-	...	...	...	...	...	...
Malta - Malte									
20 XI 2011 (CDFC)									
Total	417 432	207 625	209 807	400 557	199 151	201 406	16 875	8 474	8 401
0 - 4	20 061	10 347	9 714	19 247	9 926	9 321	814	421	393
5 - 9	19 419	9 971	9 448	18 602	9 562	9 040	817	409	408
10 - 14	22 248	11 355	10 893	21 218	10 854	10 364	1 030	501	529
15 - 19	26 182	13 509	12 673	25 026	12 907	12 119	1 156	602	554
20 - 24	29 450	15 062	14 388	28 269	14 475	13 794	1 181	587	594
25 - 29	30 320	15 722	14 598	29 154	15 110	14 044	1 166	612	554
30 - 34	30 194	15 641	14 553	29 141	15 074	14 067	1 053	567	486
35 - 39	28 799	14 757	14 042	27 712	14 202	13 510	1 087	555	532
40 - 44	25 236	12 840	12 396	24 151	12 293	11 858	1 085	547	538
45 - 49	26 895	13 574	13 321	25 716	12 972	12 744	1 179	602	577
50 - 54	30 596	15 292	15 304	29 293	14 628	14 665	1 303	664	639
55 - 59	29 246	14 655	14 591	28 127	14 052	14 075	1 119	603	516
60 - 64	30 595	15 130	15 465	29 452	14 551	14 901	1 143	579	564
65 - 69	23 728	11 429	12 299	22 791	10 986	11 805	937	443	494
70 - 74	16 205	7 389	8 816	15 572	7 106	8 466	633	283	350
75 - 79	13 287	5 579	7 708	12 749	5 332	7 417	538	247	291
80 - 84	8 494	3 181	5 313	8 121	3 036	5 085	373	145	228
85 - 89	4 567	1 622	2 945	4 371	1 546	2 825	196	76	120
90 - 94	1 583	480	1 103	1 532	455	1 077	51	25	26
95 - 99	296	82	214	284	77	207	12	5	7
100 +	31	8	23	29	7	22	2	1	1
1 I 2017 (ESDJ)[85]									
Total	460 297	231 663	228 634	...	...	...	...	...	...
0	4 621	2 442	2 179	...	...	...	...	...	...
1 - 4	18 079	9 406	8 673	...	...	...	...	...	...
5 - 9	21 818	11 224	10 594	...	...	...	...	...	...
10 - 14	20 566	10 597	9 969	...	...	...	...	...	...
15 - 19	23 374	12 007	11 367	...	...	...	...	...	...
20 - 24	30 574	16 005	14 569	...	...	...	...	...	...
25 - 29	36 940	19 111	17 829	...	...	...	...	...	...
30 - 34	36 129	18 994	17 135	...	...	...	...	...	...
35 - 39	34 220	17 906	16 314	...	...	...	...	...	...
40 - 44	31 300	16 143	15 157	...	...	...	...	...	...
45 - 49	27 220	14 037	13 183	...	...	...	...	...	...
50 - 54	28 170	14 291	13 879	...	...	...	...	...	...
55 - 59	31 277	15 656	15 621	...	...	...	...	...	...
60 - 64	29 430	14 732	14 698	...	...	...	...	...	...
65 - 69	29 921	14 658	15 263	...	...	...	...	...	...
70 - 74	23 154	11 007	12 147	...	...	...	...	...	...
75 - 79	14 485	6 393	8 092	...	...	...	...	...	...
80 - 84	10 756	4 332	6 424	...	...	...	...	...	...
85 - 89	5 598	1 914	3 684	...	...	...	...	...	...
90 - 94	2 117	662	1 455	...	...	...	...	...	...
95 - 99	482	127	355	...	...	...	...	...	...
100 - 104	61	16	45	...	...	...	...	...	...
105 - 109	5	3	2	...	...	...	...	...	...
110 +	-	-	-	...	...	...	...	...	...

Continent, country or area, date, code[a] and age (in years) / Continent, pays ou zone, date, code[a] et âge (en années)	Total			Urban - Urbaine			Rural - Rurale		
	Both sexes Les deux sexes	Male Masculin	Female Féminin	Both sexes Les deux sexes	Male Masculin	Female Féminin	Both sexes Les deux sexes	Male Masculin	Female Féminin
EUROPE									
Monaco[86]									
9 VI 2008 (CDJC)									
Total	31 109[87]	15 076	15 914	...	...	...	...	...	...
0 - 4	1 134	577	557	...	...	...	...	...	...
5 - 9	1 430	706	724	...	...	...	...	...	...
10 - 14	1 401	727	674	...	...	...	...	...	...
15 - 19	1 398	724	674	...	...	...	...	...	...
20 - 24	1 248	647	601	...	...	...	...	...	...
25 - 29	1 305	638	667	...	...	...	...	...	...
30 - 34	1 514	751	766	...	...	...	...	...	...
35 - 39	2 122	1 003	1 119	...	...	...	...	...	...
40 - 44	2 342	1 163	1 179	...	...	...	...	...	...
45 - 64	2 359	1 194	1 165	...	...	...	...	...	...
50 - 54	2 218	1 128	1 090	...	...	...	...	...	...
55 - 59	2 217	1 120	1 097	...	...	...	...	...	...
60 - 64	2 337	1 134	1 203	...	...	...	...	...	...
65 - 69	1 960	945	1 015	...	...	...	...	...	...
70 - 74	1 648	801	847	...	...	...	...	...	...
75 +	3 758	1 530	2 228	...	...	...	...	...	...
Unknown - Inconnu	715[87]	288	308	...	...	...	...	...	...
Montenegro - Monténégro									
1 IV 2011 (CDJC)									
Total	620 029	306 236	313 793	399 264	193 691	205 573	220 765	112 545	108 220
0 - 4	38 950	20 361	18 589	25 277	13 247	12 030	13 673	7 114	6 559
5 - 9	38 430	20 016	18 414	24 781	12 973	11 808	13 649	7 043	6 606
10 - 14	41 371	21 389	19 982	26 526	13 698	12 828	14 845	7 691	7 154
15 - 19	44 093	22 815	21 278	28 376	14 654	13 722	15 717	8 161	7 556
20 - 24	42 816	22 084	20 732	28 218	14 347	13 871	14 598	7 737	6 861
25 - 29	45 793	23 299	22 494	31 083	15 290	15 793	14 710	8 009	6 701
30 - 34	44 495	22 188	22 307	30 133	14 495	15 638	14 362	7 693	6 669
35 - 39	41 879	20 523	21 356	27 869	13 311	14 558	14 010	7 212	6 798
40 - 44	40 496	20 136	20 360	26 265	12 539	13 726	14 231	7 597	6 634
45 - 49	43 089	21 401	21 688	28 332	13 444	14 888	14 757	7 957	6 800
50 - 54	43 613	21 817	21 796	28 705	13 851	14 854	14 908	7 966	6 942
55 - 59	41 223	20 509	20 714	27 021	13 143	13 878	14 202	7 366	6 836
60 - 64	34 196	15 941	18 255	21 738	9 981	11 757	12 458	5 960	6 498
65 - 69	22 121	9 774	12 347	12 692	5 522	7 170	9 429	4 252	5 177
70 - 74	25 141	10 909	14 232	14 441	6 116	8 325	10 700	4 793	5 907
75 - 79	17 184	7 251	9 933	9 665	4 041	5 624	7 519	3 210	4 309
80 - 84	10 021	4 050	5 971	5 375	2 112	3 263	4 646	1 938	2 708
85 - 89	3 739	1 324	2 415	2 038	699	1 339	1 701	625	1 076
90 - 94	885	283	602	453	130	323	432	153	279
95 - 99	202	61	141	103	30	73	99	31	68
100 +	44	13	31	23	7	16	21	6	15
Unknown - Inconnu	248	92	156	150	61	89	98	31	67
1 I 2017 (ESDJ)[82]									
Total	622 387	307 752	314 635	...	...	...	...	...	...
0	7 634	3 886	3 748	...	...	...	...	...	...
1 - 4	29 594	15 433	14 161	...	...	...	...	...	...
5 - 9	38 071	19 873	18 198	...	...	...	...	...	...
10 - 14	38 003	19 842	18 161	...	...	...	...	...	...
15 - 19	41 096	21 243	19 853	...	...	...	...	...	...
20 - 24	40 937	21 180	19 757	...	...	...	...	...	...
25 - 29	40 985	21 034	19 951	...	...	...	...	...	...
30 - 34	46 354	23 711	22 643	...	...	...	...	...	...
35 - 39	44 099	22 015	22 084	...	...	...	...	...	...
40 - 44	41 710	20 343	21 367	...	...	...	...	...	...
45 - 49	39 917	19 711	20 206	...	...	...	...	...	...
50 - 54	41 863	20 687	21 176	...	...	...	...	...	...
55 - 59	42 228	20 787	21 441	...	...	...	...	...	...
60 - 64	40 107	19 593	20 514	...	...	...	...	...	...
65 - 69	32 351	14 788	17 563	...	...	...	...	...	...
70 - 74	19 088	8 009	11 079	...	...	...	...	...	...
75 - 79	19 170	7 990	11 180	...	...	...	...	...	...
80 - 84	11 929	4 747	7 182	...	...	...	...	...	...

7. Population by age, sex and urban/rural residence: latest available year, 2008 - 2017
Population selon l'âge, le sexe et la résidence, urbaine/rurale : dernière année disponible, 2008 - 2017 (continued - suite)

Continent, country or area, date, code[a] and age (in years) / Continent, pays ou zone, date, code[a] et âge (en années)	Total			Urban - Urbaine			Rural - Rurale		
	Both sexes Les deux sexes	Male Masculin	Female Féminin	Both sexes Les deux sexes	Male Masculin	Female Féminin	Both sexes Les deux sexes	Male Masculin	Female Féminin
EUROPE									
Montenegro - Monténégro									
1 I 2017 (ESDJ)[82]									
85 - 89	5 390	2 187	3 203	...	...	...	...	...	...
90 - 94	1 558	603	955	...	...	...	...	...	...
95 - 99	300	87	213	...	...	...	...	...	...
100 - 104	-	-	-	...	...	...	...	...	...
105 - 109	3	-	3	...	...	...	...	...	...
110 +	-	-	-	...	...	...	...	...	...
Netherlands - Pays-Bas									
1 I 2011 (CDJC)									
Total	16 655 799	8 243 482	8 412 317	11 124 721	5 478 213	5 646 508	5 531 078	2 765 269	2 765 809
0 - 4	923 106	472 308	450 798	633 381	323 854	309 527	289 725	148 454	141 271
0	184 007	93 892	90 115	...	...	...	...	...	...
1 - 4	739 099	378 416	360 683	...	...	...	...	...	...
5 - 9	985 229	503 882	481 347	640 541	327 757	312 784	344 688	176 125	168 563
10 - 14	998 740	510 974	487 766	633 115	323 581	309 534	365 625	187 393	178 232
15 - 19	1 006 744	514 830	491 914	658 458	333 676	324 782	348 286	181 154	167 132
20 - 24	1 034 729	522 667	512 062	757 280	373 366	383 914	277 449	149 301	128 148
25 - 29	1 001 538	504 117	497 421	749 880	373 340	376 540	251 658	130 777	120 881
30 - 34	1 004 744	503 323	501 441	736 350	368 630	367 720	268 414	134 693	133 721
35 - 39	1 121 568	560 289	561 279	779 994	391 390	388 604	341 574	168 899	172 675
40 - 44	1 295 925	653 664	642 261	861 292	436 235	425 057	434 633	217 429	217 204
45 - 49	1 298 292	655 302	642 990	850 566	428 796	421 770	447 726	226 506	221 220
50 - 54	1 196 319	601 040	595 279	776 285	388 221	388 064	420 034	212 819	207 215
55 - 59	1 090 247	546 952	543 295	700 036	348 502	351 534	390 211	198 450	191 761
60 - 64	1 103 652	553 446	550 206	700 926	349 188	351 738	402 726	204 258	198 468
65 - 69	790 560	390 725	399 835	488 433	238 792	249 641	302 127	151 933	150 194
70 - 74	637 518	302 542	334 976	401 165	187 850	213 315	236 353	114 692	121 661
75 - 79	499 321	219 108	280 213	316 949	136 949	180 000	182 372	82 159	100 213
80 - 84	360 828	139 348	221 480	234 884	89 412	145 472	125 944	49 936	76 008
85 - 89	212 056	66 949	145 107	141 532	44 184	97 348	70 524	22 765	47 759
90 - 94	76 191	18 812	57 379	51 102	12 438	38 664	25 089	6 374	18 715
95 +	18 472	3 204	15 268	12 552	2 052	10 500	5 920	1 152	4 768
1 I 2017 (ESDJ)									
Total	17 081 507	8 475 102	8 606 405	...	...	...	...	...	...
0	172 288	88 427	83 861	...	...	...	...	...	...
1 - 4	700 001	358 725	341 276	...	...	...	...	...	...
5 - 9	929 180	475 593	453 587	...	...	...	...	...	...
10 - 14	980 299	501 845	478 454	...	...	...	...	...	...
15 - 19	1 035 405	530 288	505 117	...	...	...	...	...	...
20 - 24	1 066 243	542 404	523 839	...	...	...	...	...	...
25 - 29	1 090 087	552 023	538 064	...	...	...	...	...	...
30 - 34	1 032 122	519 664	512 458	...	...	...	...	...	...
35 - 39	1 018 187	508 665	509 522	...	...	...	...	...	...
40 - 44	1 073 880	534 389	539 491	...	...	...	...	...	...
45 - 49	1 282 591	643 263	639 328	...	...	...	...	...	...
50 - 54	1 281 617	644 905	636 712	...	...	...	...	...	...
55 - 59	1 191 605	596 070	595 535	...	...	...	...	...	...
60 - 64	1 068 342	532 366	535 976	...	...	...	...	...	...
65 - 69	1 015 641	503 756	511 885	...	...	...	...	...	...
70 - 74	807 859	392 865	414 994	...	...	...	...	...	...
75 - 79	571 885	264 275	307 610	...	...	...	...	...	...
80 - 84	402 119	168 051	234 068	...	...	...	...	...	...
85 - 89	239 804	85 084	154 720	...	...	...	...	...	...
90 - 94	98 476	27 597	70 879	...	...	...	...	...	...
95 - 99	21 651	4 527	17 124	...	...	...	...	...	...
100 - 104	2 125	312	1 813	...	...	...	...	...	...
105 - 109	98	8	90	...	...	...	...	...	...
110 +	2	-	2	...	...	...	...	...	...
Norway - Norvège									
19 XI 2011 (CDJC)[88]									
Total	4 979 955	2 495 777	2 484 178	3 951 427[78]	1 959 424[78]	1 992 003[78]	1 011 071[78]	524 519[78]	486 552[78]
0 - 4	310 523	159 582	150 941	252 348[78]	129 655[78]	122 693[78]	57 552[78]	29 590[78]	27 962[78]
5 - 9	300 625	153 598	147 027	239 702[78]	122 174[78]	117 528[78]	60 262[78]	31 070[78]	29 192[78]
10 - 14	312 618	160 122	152 496	245 562[78]	125 764[78]	119 798[78]	66 422[78]	34 008[78]	32 414[78]

Continent, country or area, date, code[a] and age (in years) / Continent, pays ou zone, date, code[a] et âge (en années)	Total			Urban - Urbaine			Rural - Rurale		
	Both sexes Les deux sexes	Male Masculin	Female Féminin	Both sexes Les deux sexes	Male Masculin	Female Féminin	Both sexes Les deux sexes	Male Masculin	Female Féminin
EUROPE									
Norway - Norvège									
19 XI 2011 (CDJC)[88]									
15 - 19	324 682	167 701	156 981	254 774[78]	131 385[78]	123 389[78]	69 376[78]	36 049[78]	33 327[78]
20 - 24	329 537	167 828	161 709	268 150[78]	135 424[78]	132 726[78]	60 351[78]	31 776[78]	28 575[78]
25 - 29	321 171	163 754	157 417	268 356[78]	135 940[78]	132 416[78]	51 166[78]	26 654[78]	24 512[78]
30 - 34	325 241	166 578	158 663	269 924[78]	137 478[78]	132 446[78]	53 565[78]	27 843[78]	25 722[78]
35 - 39	352 008	180 904	171 104	286 185[78]	146 143[78]	140 042[78]	64 091[78]	33 501[78]	30 590[78]
40 - 44	373 191	191 483	181 708	297 629[78]	151 231[78]	146 398[78]	73 666[78]	38 863[78]	34 803[78]
45 - 49	350 537	180 834	169 703	275 817[78]	140 624[78]	135 193[78]	73 001[78]	38 909[78]	34 092[78]
50 - 54	322 729	165 233	157 496	250 381[78]	126 209[78]	124 172[78]	70 881[78]	37 897[78]	32 984[78]
55 - 59	304 335	154 029	150 306	233 724[78]	116 035[78]	117 689[78]	69 504[78]	37 194[78]	32 310[78]
60 - 64	286 319	144 699	141 620	218 480[78]	108 289[78]	110 191[78]	67 016[78]	35 823[78]	31 193[78]
65 - 69	247 451	122 740	124 711	188 932[78]	91 896[78]	97 036[78]	57 895[78]	30 414[78]	27 481[78]
70 - 74	166 680	78 850	87 830	126 640[78]	58 122[78]	68 518[78]	39 687[78]	20 517[78]	19 170[78]
75 - 79	130 209	58 013	72 196	99 673[78]	42 842[78]	56 831[78]	30 271[78]	15 028[78]	15 243[78]
80 - 84	108 243	44 024	64 219	84 440[78]	32 980[78]	51 460[78]	23 582[78]	10 955[78]	12 627[78]
85 - 89	74 057	25 608	48 449	58 579[78]	19 436[78]	39 143[78]	15 272[78]	6 085[78]	9 187[78]
90 - 94	32 243	8 769	23 474	25 938[78]	6 706[78]	19 232[78]	6 185[78]	2 017[78]	4 168[78]
95 - 99	6 825	1 310	5 515	5 593[78]	1 001[78]	4 592[78]	1 199[78]	300[78]	899[78]
100 +	731	118	613	600[78]	90[78]	510[78]	127[78]	26[78]	101[78]
1 I 2017 (ESDJ)[82]									
Total	5 258 317	2 649 130	2 609 187	...	...	...	...	...	...
0	59 335	30 650	28 685	...	...	...	...	...	...
1 - 4	244 158	125 207	118 951	...	...	...	...	...	...
5 - 9	322 811	165 749	157 062	...	...	...	...	...	...
10 - 14	311 406	159 157	152 249	...	...	...	...	...	...
15 - 19	325 020	167 960	157 060	...	...	...	...	...	...
20 - 24	343 302	177 559	165 743	...	...	...	...	...	...
25 - 29	367 938	187 079	180 859	...	...	...	...	...	...
30 - 34	354 883	182 649	172 234	...	...	...	...	...	...
35 - 39	345 142	178 077	167 065	...	...	...	...	...	...
40 - 44	363 010	186 902	176 108	...	...	...	...	...	...
45 - 49	378 720	194 302	184 418	...	...	...	...	...	...
50 - 54	351 522	180 770	170 752	...	...	...	...	...	...
55 - 59	319 031	162 575	156 456	...	...	...	...	...	...
60 - 64	297 217	149 114	148 103	...	...	...	...	...	...
65 - 69	273 454	136 705	136 749	...	...	...	...	...	...
70 - 74	232 059	113 064	118 995	...	...	...	...	...	...
75 - 79	148 329	68 252	80 077	...	...	...	...	...	...
80 - 84	104 602	44 336	60 266	...	...	...	...	...	...
85 - 89	71 769	26 497	45 272	...	...	...	...	...	...
90 - 94	34 737	10 480	24 257	...	...	...	...	...	...
95 - 99	8 927	1 896	7 031	...	...	...	...	...	...
100 - 104	890	139	751	...	...	...	...	...	...
105 - 109	51	10	41	...	...	...	...	...	...
110 +	4	1	3	...	...	...	...	...	...
Poland - Pologne[82]									
1 VII 2016 (ESDJ)									
Total	37 956 779	18 370 677	19 586 102	22 872 493	10 846 647	12 025 846	15 084 286	7 524 030	7 560 256
0	365 869	187 864	178 005	216 408	111 093	105 315	149 461	76 771	72 690
1 - 4	1 513 396	777 778	735 618	879 303	451 990	427 313	634 093	325 788	308 305
5 - 9	2 050 010	1 051 689	998 321	1 164 288	597 196	567 092	885 722	454 493	431 229
10 - 14	1 780 890	913 619	867 271	969 581	497 234	472 347	811 309	416 385	394 924
15 - 19	1 933 855	990 799	943 056	1 029 089	525 591	503 498	904 766	465 208	439 558
20 - 24	2 339 453	1 192 516	1 146 937	1 248 434	633 498	614 936	1 091 019	559 018	532 001
25 - 29	2 758 936	1 407 155	1 351 781	1 621 297	813 811	807 486	1 137 639	593 344	544 295
30 - 34	3 142 548	1 600 183	1 542 365	1 960 315	985 623	974 692	1 182 233	614 560	567 673
35 - 39	3 019 054	1 531 339	1 487 715	1 882 014	943 735	938 279	1 137 040	587 604	549 436
40 - 44	2 726 685	1 378 153	1 348 532	1 640 377	818 331	822 046	1 086 308	559 822	526 486
45 - 49	2 312 294	1 159 725	1 152 569	1 348 269	661 999	686 270	964 025	497 726	466 299
50 - 54	2 345 949	1 161 430	1 184 519	1 381 562	659 773	721 789	964 387	501 657	462 730
55 - 59	2 756 875	1 329 545	1 427 330	1 716 069	791 034	925 035	1 040 806	538 511	502 295
60 - 64	2 725 138	1 270 621	1 454 517	1 789 526	799 290	990 236	935 612	471 331	464 281
65 - 69	2 213 178	984 423	1 228 755	1 479 140	638 322	840 818	734 038	346 101	387 937

Continent, country or area, date, code[a] and age (in years) / Continent, pays ou zone, date, code[a] et âge (en années)	Total			Urban - Urbaine			Rural - Rurale		
	Both sexes Les deux sexes	Male Masculin	Female Féminin	Both sexes Les deux sexes	Male Masculin	Female Féminin	Both sexes Les deux sexes	Male Masculin	Female Féminin
EUROPE									
Poland - Pologne[82]									
1 VII 2016 (ESDJ)									
70 - 74	1 251 396	519 715	731 681	828 680	339 180	489 500	422 716	180 535	242 181
75 - 79	1 129 881	424 113	705 768	726 020	269 231	456 789	403 861	154 882	248 979
80 - 84	865 829	290 778	575 051	546 657	184 627	362 030	319 172	106 151	213 021
85 - 89	510 376	148 823	361 553	312 351	93 404	218 947	198 025	55 419	142 606
90 - 94	181 706	43 262	138 444	112 240	27 175	85 065	69 466	16 087	53 379
95 - 99	28 305	6 095	22 210	17 314	3 784	13 530	10 991	2 311	8 680
100 +	5 156	1 052	4 104	3 559	726	2 833	1 597	326	1 271
1 I 2017 (ESDJ)									
Total	37 972 964	18 377 837	19 595 127	...	...	...	...	...	...
0	375 509	192 679	182 830	...	...	...	...	...	...
1 - 4	1 505 958	773 931	732 027	...	...	...	...	...	...
5 - 9	2 055 401	1 054 423	1 000 978	...	...	...	...	...	...
10 - 14	1 795 455	921 101	874 354	...	...	...	...	...	...
15 - 19	1 905 208	976 207	929 001	...	...	...	...	...	...
20 - 24	2 289 902	1 166 978	1 122 924	...	...	...	...	...	...
25 - 29	2 732 215	1 393 916	1 338 299	...	...	...	...	...	...
30 - 34	3 131 458	1 595 062	1 536 396	...	...	...	...	...	...
35 - 39	3 026 097	1 535 198	1 490 899	...	...	...	...	...	...
40 - 44	2 776 151	1 403 189	1 372 962	...	...	...	...	...	...
45 - 49	2 333 383	1 170 323	1 163 060	...	...	...	...	...	...
50 - 54	2 319 007	1 148 776	1 170 231	...	...	...	...	...	...
55 - 59	2 710 407	1 307 965	1 402 442	...	...	...	...	...	...
60 - 64	2 733 162	1 276 249	1 456 913	...	...	...	...	...	...
65 - 69	2 263 567	1 007 541	1 256 026	...	...	...	...	...	...
70 - 74	1 296 343	539 442	756 901	...	...	...	...	...	...
75 - 79	1 116 102	419 557	696 545	...	...	...	...	...	...
80 - 84	867 151	291 250	575 901	...	...	...	...	...	...
85 - 89	517 986	152 088	365 898	...	...	...	...	...	...
90 - 94	186 515	44 257	142 258	...	...	...	...	...	...
95 - 99	30 712	6 635	24 077	...	...	...	...	...	...
100 - 104	4 445	859	3 586	...	...	...	...	...	...
105 - 109	719	181	538	...	...	...	...	...	...
110 +	111	30	81	...	...	...	...	...	...
Portugal									
21 III 2011 (CDJC)									
Total	10 562 178	5 046 600	5 515 578	6 438 593	3 047 968	3 390 625	4 123 585	1 998 632	2 124 953
0 - 4	482 647	246 396	236 251	316 068	161 365	154 703	166 579	85 031	81 548
5 - 9	525 087	268 965	256 122	329 692	168 925	160 767	195 395	100 040	95 355
10 - 14	564 595	288 638	275 957	344 809	176 287	168 522	219 786	112 351	107 435
15 - 19	565 250	288 525	276 725	342 328	174 252	168 076	222 922	114 273	108 649
20 - 24	582 065	293 023	289 042	358 412	178 982	179 430	223 653	114 041	109 612
25 - 29	656 076	324 848	331 228	425 629	208 104	217 525	230 447	116 744	113 703
30 - 34	773 567	378 734	394 833	508 225	247 125	261 100	265 342	131 609	133 733
35 - 39	824 683	402 307	422 376	529 287	255 858	273 429	295 396	146 449	148 947
40 - 44	773 098	374 962	398 136	478 840	228 255	250 585	294 258	146 707	147 551
45 - 49	770 294	370 989	399 305	466 564	219 783	246 781	303 730	151 206	152 524
50 - 54	722 360	346 248	376 112	435 982	203 867	232 115	286 378	142 381	143 997
55 - 59	677 651	322 095	355 556	410 020	190 860	219 160	267 631	131 235	136 396
60 - 64	634 741	298 546	336 195	382 547	177 485	205 062	252 194	121 061	131 133
65 - 69	551 701	253 004	298 697	319 398	146 189	173 209	232 303	106 815	125 488
70 - 74	496 438	220 461	275 977	273 513	119 844	153 669	222 925	100 617	122 308
75 - 79	429 706	180 131	249 575	231 208	94 394	136 814	198 498	85 737	112 761
80 - 84	297 888	113 325	184 563	159 578	57 948	101 630	138 310	55 377	82 933
85 - 89	164 356	55 635	108 721	88 444	28 423	60 021	75 912	27 212	48 700
90 - 94	53 847	15 679	38 168	29 038	7 847	21 191	24 809	7 832	16 977
95 - 99	14 602	3 816	10 786	8 158	2 029	6 129	6 444	1 787	4 657
100 +	1 526	273	1 253	853	146	707	673	127	546
1 I 2017 (ESDJ)									
Total	10 309 573	4 882 456	5 427 117	...	...	...	...	...	...
0	87 075	44 759	42 316	...	...	...	...	...	...
1 - 4	341 169	174 957	166 212	...	...	...	...	...	...
5 - 9	490 004	250 319	239 685	...	...	...	...	...	...
10 - 14	524 168	268 357	255 811	...	...	...	...	...	...

Continent, country or area, date, code[a] and age (in years) / Continent, pays ou zone, date, code[a] et âge (en années)	Total			Urban - Urbaine			Rural - Rurale		
	Both sexes Les deux sexes	Male Masculin	Female Féminin	Both sexes Les deux sexes	Male Masculin	Female Féminin	Both sexes Les deux sexes	Male Masculin	Female Féminin
EUROPE									
Portugal									
1 I 2017 (ESDJ)									
15 - 19	558 165	285 028	273 137	...	...	...	...	...	...
20 - 24	538 556	272 947	265 609	...	...	...	...	...	...
25 - 29	551 919	276 452	275 467	...	...	...	...	...	...
30 - 34	614 838	300 227	314 611	...	...	...	...	...	...
35 - 39	731 253	350 696	380 557	...	...	...	...	...	...
40 - 44	811 722	387 780	423 942	...	...	...	...	...	...
45 - 49	758 984	362 673	396 311	...	...	...	...	...	...
50 - 54	756 882	358 709	398 173	...	...	...	...	...	...
55 - 59	714 805	337 798	377 007	...	...	...	...	...	...
60 - 64	653 393	304 151	349 242	...	...	...	...	...	...
65 - 69	606 795	279 324	327 471	...	...	...	...	...	...
70 - 74	510 244	223 647	286 597	...	...	...	...	...	...
75 - 79	426 680	178 883	247 797	...	...	...	...	...	...
80 - 84	347 305	134 204	213 101	...	...	...	...	...	...
85 - 89	196 899	66 841	130 058	...	...	...	...	...	...
90 - 94	68 559	18 908	49 651	...	...	...	...	...	...
95 - 99	15 876	4 207	11 669	...	...	...	...	...	...
100 - 104	3 703	1 392	2 311	...	...	...	...	...	...
105 - 109	571	189	382	...	...	...	...	...	...
110 +	8	8	-	...	...	...	...	...	...
Republic of Moldova - République de Moldova[89]									
1 VII 2012 (ESDJ)									
Total	3 559 519	1 712 036	1 847 484	1 488 966	699 880	789 086	2 070 554	1 012 156	1 058 398
0	38 856	20 015	18 842	14 501	7 501	7 000	24 356	12 514	11 842
1 - 4	155 545	80 386	75 159	57 044	29 740	27 305	98 501	50 646	47 855
5 - 9	185 646	95 525	90 121	67 697	35 209	32 489	117 949	60 317	57 632
10 - 14	194 993	100 101	94 893	66 615	34 473	32 142	128 379	65 628	62 751
15 - 19	257 790	131 414	126 376	88 575	45 309	43 267	169 215	86 106	83 110
20 - 24	333 714	169 543	164 171	138 548	69 044	69 505	195 166	100 499	94 667
25 - 29	343 489	174 869	168 620	174 571	84 151	90 420	168 918	90 718	78 200
30 - 34	289 604	146 740	142 864	133 836	65 353	68 483	155 769	81 387	74 382
35 - 39	251 655	124 669	126 986	111 448	54 088	57 360	140 207	70 581	69 627
40 - 44	225 706	109 887	115 819	97 757	46 129	51 629	127 949	63 758	64 191
45 - 49	237 350	112 506	124 844	102 616	46 409	56 207	134 735	66 097	68 638
50 - 54	274 163	127 681	146 482	119 669	52 882	66 787	154 495	74 799	79 696
55 - 59	235 036	106 431	128 605	104 053	44 876	59 177	130 983	61 555	69 428
60 - 64	182 091	79 587	102 504	79 353	34 316	45 038	102 738	45 272	57 467
65 - 69	105 809	44 763	61 046	43 360	18 966	24 394	62 449	25 797	36 652
70 - 74	100 565	38 142	62 423	39 059	15 111	23 948	61 506	23 031	38 475
75 - 79	72 497	25 841	46 656	24 995	8 598	16 397	47 502	17 243	30 259
80 - 84	47 586	15 881	31 706	15 963	5 051	10 912	31 624	10 830	20 794
85 - 89	20 400	5 920	14 480	6 963	1 957	5 006	13 437	3 963	9 474
90 - 94	5 438	1 597	3 841	1 780	526	1 254	3 658	1 071	2 588
95 - 99	1 163	395	768	391	150	241	772	245	527
100 +	429	148	282	177	45	132	253	103	150
Romania - Roumanie									
1 VII 2016 (ESDF)									
Total	19 706 529	9 628 271	10 078 258	10 585 664	5 053 625	5 532 039	9 120 865	4 574 646	4 546 219
0	196 665	101 050	95 615	108 010	55 579	52 431	88 655	45 471	43 184
1 - 4	766 081	393 971	372 110	412 643	212 529	200 114	353 438	181 442	171 996
5 - 9	1 049 007	538 742	510 265	536 074	275 843	260 231	512 933	262 899	250 034
10 - 14	1 049 871	539 539	510 332	495 480	254 129	241 351	554 391	285 410	268 981
15 - 19	1 079 165	554 009	525 156	488 471	248 353	240 118	590 694	305 656	285 038
20 - 24	1 063 780	547 629	516 151	540 328	268 664	271 664	523 452	278 965	244 487
25 - 29	1 324 645	687 957	636 688	787 955	392 060	395 895	536 690	295 897	240 793
30 - 34	1 299 178	671 221	627 957	777 565	393 633	383 932	521 613	277 588	244 025
35 - 39	1 519 624	774 102	745 522	874 304	436 372	437 932	645 320	337 730	307 590
40 - 44	1 516 890	777 807	739 083	820 425	406 552	413 873	696 465	371 255	325 210
45 - 49	1 677 370	860 446	816 924	943 073	456 520	486 553	734 297	403 926	330 371
50 - 54	1 054 891	533 213	521 678	603 624	285 511	318 113	451 267	247 702	203 565
55 - 59	1 290 765	625 034	665 731	763 753	351 239	412 514	527 012	273 795	253 217
60 - 64	1 351 064	625 320	725 744	789 896	360 183	429 713	561 168	265 137	296 031

Continent, country or area, date, code[a] and age (in years) / Continent, pays ou zone, date, code[a] et âge (en années)	Total			Urban - Urbaine			Rural - Rurale		
	Both sexes Les deux sexes	Male Masculin	Female Féminin	Both sexes Les deux sexes	Male Masculin	Female Féminin	Both sexes Les deux sexes	Male Masculin	Female Féminin
EUROPE									
Romania - Roumanie									
1 VII 2016 (ESDF)									
65 - 69	1 123 956	498 539	625 417	590 429	260 700	329 729	533 527	237 839	295 688
70 - 74	765 871	319 854	446 017	361 629	148 988	212 641	404 242	170 866	233 376
75 - 79	726 662	279 034	447 628	324 621	122 646	201 975	402 041	156 388	245 653
80 - 84	500 629	182 292	318 337	214 048	75 271	138 777	286 581	107 021	179 560
85 - 89	250 853	86 478	164 375	108 879	35 582	73 297	141 974	50 896	91 078
90 - 94	83 108	27 164	55 944	36 682	11 226	25 456	46 426	15 938	30 488
95 - 99	14 762	4 373	10 389	6 928	1 834	5 094	7 834	2 539	5 295
100 +	1 692	497	1 195	847	211	636	845	286	559
1 I 2017 (ESDF)									
Total	19 644 350	9 602 578	10 041 772	...	...	...	...	...	...
0	198 022	101 421	96 601	...	...	...	...	...	...
1 - 4	773 164	397 608	375 556	...	...	...	...	...	...
5 - 9	1 035 636	532 361	503 275	...	...	...	...	...	...
10 - 14	1 050 202	539 224	510 978	...	...	...	...	...	...
15 - 19	1 074 830	552 981	521 849	...	...	...	...	...	...
20 - 24	1 047 512	536 128	511 384	...	...	...	...	...	...
25 - 29	1 291 607	673 853	617 754	...	...	...	...	...	...
30 - 34	1 292 242	670 354	621 888	...	...	...	...	...	...
35 - 39	1 499 719	764 677	735 042	...	...	...	...	...	...
40 - 44	1 518 003	777 730	740 273	...	...	...	...	...	...
45 - 49	1 719 145	882 317	836 828	...	...	...	...	...	...
50 - 54	1 037 392	525 874	511 518	...	...	...	...	...	...
55 - 59	1 254 632	609 309	645 323	...	...	...	...	...	...
60 - 64	1 356 615	628 866	727 749	...	...	...	...	...	...
65 - 69	1 143 539	506 929	636 610	...	...	...	...	...	...
70 - 74	772 964	323 631	449 333	...	...	...	...	...	...
75 - 79	713 431	273 968	439 463	...	...	...	...	...	...
80 - 84	507 899	184 412	323 487	...	...	...	...	...	...
85 - 89	253 971	87 472	166 499	...	...	...	...	...	...
90 - 94	84 954	27 869	57 085	...	...	...	...	...	...
95 - 99	17 155	5 085	12 070	...	...	...	...	...	...
100 - 104	1 697	500	1 197	...	...	...	...	...	...
105 - 109	19	9	10	...	...	...	...	...	...
110 +	-	-	-	...	...	...	...	...	...
Russian Federation - Fédération de Russie									
1 VII 2012 (ESDJ)									
Total	143 201 730	66 264 910	76 936 820	105 930 122	48 419 208	57 510 914	37 271 608	17 845 702	19 425 906
0	1 837 406	944 299	893 107	1 299 253	668 312	630 941	538 153	275 987	262 166
1 - 4	6 695 802	3 433 227	3 262 575	4 714 200	2 419 141	2 295 059	1 981 602	1 014 086	967 516
5 - 9	7 350 838	3 762 806	3 588 032	5 189 787	2 657 166	2 532 621	2 161 051	1 105 640	1 055 411
10 - 14	6 628 125	3 396 364	3 231 761	4 584 611	2 348 219	2 236 392	2 043 514	1 048 145	995 369
15 - 19	7 391 866	3 776 026	3 615 840	5 367 803	2 718 897	2 648 906	2 024 063	1 057 129	966 934
20 - 24	11 223 730	5 708 187	5 515 543	8 636 085	4 330 536	4 305 549	2 587 645	1 377 651	1 209 994
25 - 29	12 442 007	6 262 379	6 179 628	9 541 009	4 744 648	4 796 361	2 900 998	1 517 731	1 383 267
30 - 34	11 231 149	5 583 513	5 647 636	8 675 785	4 272 864	4 402 921	2 555 364	1 310 649	1 244 715
35 - 39	10 419 383	5 087 565	5 331 818	7 966 185	3 854 320	4 111 865	2 453 198	1 233 245	1 219 953
40 - 44	9 451 487	4 589 504	4 861 983	7 068 002	3 394 309	3 673 693	2 383 485	1 195 195	1 188 290
45 - 49	9 784 092	4 632 279	5 151 813	7 108 256	3 298 718	3 809 538	2 675 836	1 333 561	1 342 275
50 - 54	11 498 441	5 279 364	6 219 077	8 339 186	3 721 713	4 617 473	3 159 255	1 557 651	1 601 604
55 - 59	10 298 414	4 480 855	5 817 559	7 573 444	3 197 844	4 375 600	2 724 970	1 283 011	1 441 959
60 - 64	8 534 857	3 523 990	5 010 867	6 428 296	2 585 856	3 842 440	2 106 561	938 134	1 168 427
65 - 69	4 174 510	1 602 839	2 571 671	3 204 644	1 214 486	1 990 158	969 866	388 353	581 513
70 - 74	5 965 072	1 989 724	3 975 348	4 331 090	1 428 165	2 902 925	1 633 982	561 559	1 072 423
75 - 79	3 888 860	1 179 476	2 709 384	2 762 682	822 673	1 940 009	1 126 178	356 803	769 375
80 - 84	2 795 954	722 151	2 073 803	1 965 242	501 515	1 463 727	830 712	220 636	610 076
85 - 89	1 261 655	253 028	1 008 627	927 939	193 530	734 409	333 716	59 498	274 218
90 - 94	266 163	46 736	219 427	200 155	37 401	162 754	66 008	9 335	56 673
95 - 99	52 622	8 634	43 988	39 307	7 154	32 153	13 315	1 480	11 835
100 +	9 297	1 964	7 333	7 161	1 741	5 420	2 136	223	1 913

Continent, country or area, date, code[a] and age (in years) Continent, pays ou zone, date, code[a] et âge (en années)	Total			Urban - Urbaine			Rural - Rurale		
	Both sexes Les deux sexes	Male Masculin	Female Féminin	Both sexes Les deux sexes	Male Masculin	Female Féminin	Both sexes Les deux sexes	Male Masculin	Female Féminin
EUROPE									
San Marino - Saint-Marin[34]									
1 I 2017 (ESDF)									
Total	34 267	16 677	17 590	...	...	...	...	...	...
0	263	132	131	...	...	...	...	...	...
1 - 4	1 246	646	600	...	...	...	...	...	...
5 - 9	1 780	891	889	...	...	...	...	...	...
10 - 14	1 670	917	753	...	...	...	...	...	...
15 - 19	1 725	893	832	...	...	...	...	...	...
20 - 24	1 546	809	737	...	...	...	...	...	...
25 - 29	1 615	803	812	...	...	...	...	...	...
30 - 34	1 875	914	961	...	...	...	...	...	...
35 - 39	2 353	1 112	1 241	...	...	...	...	...	...
40 - 44	2 958	1 408	1 550	...	...	...	...	...	...
45 - 49	3 123	1 520	1 603	...	...	...	...	...	...
50 - 54	3 106	1 506	1 600	...	...	...	...	...	...
55 - 59	2 478	1 218	1 260	...	...	...	...	...	...
60 - 64	2 041	975	1 066	...	...	...	...	...	...
65 - 69	1 821	881	940	...	...	...	...	...	...
70 - 74	1 528	734	794	...	...	...	...	...	...
75 - 79	1 230	585	645	...	...	...	...	...	...
80 - 84	918	405	513	...	...	...	...	...	...
85 - 89	646	230	416	...	...	...	...	...	...
90 - 94	262	81	181	...	...	...	...	...	...
95 - 99	75	17	58	...	...	...	...	...	...
100 +	8	-	8	...	...	...	...	...	...
Serbia - Serbie[90]									
1 VII 2016 (ESDJ)									
Total	7 058 322	3 437 630	3 620 692	4 262 256	2 030 532	2 231 724	2 796 066	1 407 098	1 388 968
0	64 838	33 532	31 306	44 747	23 205	21 542	20 091	10 327	9 764
1 - 4	263 241	135 609	127 632	181 191	93 262	87 929	82 050	42 347	39 703
5 - 9	332 767	171 535	161 232	208 304	107 358	100 946	124 463	64 177	60 286
10 - 14	355 733	182 763	172 970	211 578	108 552	103 026	144 155	74 211	69 944
15 - 19	353 422	181 779	171 643	206 542	106 087	100 455	146 880	75 692	71 188
20 - 24	408 693	210 151	198 542	242 715	123 171	119 544	165 978	86 980	78 998
25 - 29	445 416	227 890	217 526	277 684	137 618	140 066	167 732	90 272	77 460
30 - 34	484 256	246 587	237 669	315 678	155 582	160 096	168 578	91 005	77 573
35 - 39	497 774	252 683	245 091	325 744	161 170	164 574	172 030	91 513	80 517
40 - 44	491 408	246 654	244 754	309 267	151 174	158 093	182 141	95 480	86 661
45 - 49	466 992	231 566	235 426	281 851	135 617	146 234	185 141	95 949	89 192
50 - 54	476 688	232 873	243 815	283 078	133 051	150 027	193 610	99 822	93 788
55 - 59	505 367	243 436	261 931	297 569	136 988	160 581	207 798	106 448	101 350
60 - 64	558 779	264 939	293 840	325 546	147 640	177 906	233 233	117 299	115 934
65 - 69	476 171	217 734	258 437	278 212	121 943	156 269	197 959	95 791	102 168
70 - 74	293 228	127 392	165 836	162 407	68 503	93 904	130 821	58 889	71 932
75 - 79	278 149	114 859	163 290	150 922	60 605	90 317	127 227	54 254	72 973
80 - 84	191 608	74 876	116 732	100 551	38 910	61 641	91 057	35 966	55 091
85 - 89	86 060	31 526	54 534	43 550	15 165	28 385	42 510	16 361	26 149
90 - 94	23 225	7 791	15 434	12 687	4 195	8 492	10 538	3 596	6 942
95 - 99	4 078	1 313	2 765	2 212	676	1 536	1 866	637	1 229
100 +	429	142	287	221	60	161	208	82	126
1 I 2017 (ESDJ)									
Total	7 040 272	3 429 027	3 611 245	...	...	...	...	...	...
0	64 386	33 267	31 119	...	...	...	...	...	...
1 - 4	263 216	135 619	127 597	...	...	...	...	...	...
5 - 9	331 287	170 928	160 359	...	...	...	...	...	...
10 - 14	353 592	181 616	171 976	...	...	...	...	...	...
15 - 19	351 171	180 540	170 631	...	...	...	...	...	...
20 - 24	404 028	207 955	196 073	...	...	...	...	...	...
25 - 29	442 158	226 252	215 906	...	...	...	...	...	...
30 - 34	481 621	245 358	236 263	...	...	...	...	...	...
35 - 39	495 251	251 491	243 760	...	...	...	...	...	...
40 - 44	494 139	248 101	246 038	...	...	...	...	...	...
45 - 49	467 191	232 022	235 169	...	...	...	...	...	...
50 - 54	471 622	230 576	241 046	...	...	...	...	...	...
55 - 59	499 395	240 389	259 006	...	...	...	...	...	...

Continent, country or area, date, code[a] and age (in years) / Continent, pays ou zone, date, code[a] et âge (en annèes)	Total			Urban - Urbaine			Rural - Rurale		
	Both sexes Les deux sexes	Male Masculin	Female Féminin	Both sexes Les deux sexes	Male Masculin	Female Féminin	Both sexes Les deux sexes	Male Masculin	Female Féminin
EUROPE									
Serbia - Serbie[90]									
1 I 2017 (ESDJ)									
60 - 64	558 753	264 636	294 117	...	...	...	...	...	...
65 - 69	483 260	220 946	262 314	...	...	...	...	...	...
70 - 74	294 987	128 372	166 615	...	...	...	...	...	...
75 - 79	275 174	113 658	161 516	...	...	...	...	...	...
80 - 84	192 198	75 137	117 061	...	...	...	...	...	...
85 - 89	87 333	32 240	55 093	...	...	...	...	...	...
90 - 94	24 330	8 219	16 111	...	...	...	...	...	...
95 - 99	4 672	1 538	3 134	...	...	...	...	...	...
100 +	508	167	341	...	...	...	...	...	...
Slovakia - Slovaquie									
1 VII 2016 (ESDJ)									
Total	5 430 798	2 648 883	2 781 915	2 925 475	1 406 787	1 518 688	2 505 323	1 242 096	1 263 227
0	57 194	29 357	27 837	29 853	15 297	14 556	27 340	14 059	13 280
1 - 4	228 247	117 040	111 207	117 684	60 249	57 435	110 563	56 791	53 773
5 - 9	287 112	147 072	140 040	143 401	73 425	69 977	143 711	73 647	70 064
10 - 14	263 584	135 443	128 142	127 450	65 558	61 893	136 134	69 885	66 249
15 - 19	281 862	144 660	137 202	133 634	68 614	65 021	148 228	76 046	72 182
20 - 24	341 360	174 458	166 902	169 457	86 327	83 130	171 903	88 131	83 772
25 - 29	400 312	203 962	196 350	217 565	110 300	107 266	182 747	93 663	89 085
30 - 34	434 684	223 114	211 570	244 166	124 660	119 506	190 518	98 454	92 064
35 - 39	455 530	234 529	221 001	254 113	129 976	124 137	201 417	104 553	96 864
40 - 44	426 682	217 883	208 800	230 675	116 082	114 593	196 008	101 801	94 207
45 - 49	354 250	178 607	175 643	189 098	92 227	96 871	165 153	86 380	78 773
50 - 54	365 921	181 625	184 296	201 855	95 897	105 958	164 066	85 728	78 338
55 - 59	369 836	179 861	189 975	211 236	98 458	112 779	158 600	81 403	77 197
60 - 64	364 930	170 695	194 235	213 049	96 859	116 190	151 882	73 836	78 046
65 - 69	288 223	127 670	160 553	166 180	72 324	93 856	122 044	55 346	66 698
70 - 74	194 760	78 379	116 382	108 722	43 569	65 154	86 038	34 810	51 228
75 - 79	143 803	52 081	91 722	76 691	28 231	48 460	67 112	23 850	43 263
80 - 84	97 566	31 619	65 947	51 286	17 293	33 993	46 280	14 326	31 954
85 - 89	52 542	15 008	37 534	27 465	8 200	19 265	25 078	6 809	18 269
90 - 94	18 379	4 662	13 718	9 665	2 574	7 092	8 714	2 088	6 626
95 - 99	3 195	866	2 329	1 710	483	1 228	1 485	383	1 102
100 +	831	300	532	524	189	335	308	111	197
1 I 2017 (ESDJ)									
Total	5 435 343	2 651 684	2 783 659	...	...	...	...	...	...
0	58 277	29 808	28 469	...	...	...	...	...	...
1 - 4	226 328	116 188	110 140	...	...	...	...	...	...
5 - 9	290 886	148 912	141 974	...	...	...	...	...	...
10 - 14	264 737	135 958	128 779	...	...	...	...	...	...
15 - 19	277 754	142 564	135 190	...	...	...	...	...	...
20 - 24	332 754	170 276	162 478	...	...	...	...	...	...
25 - 29	396 907	202 208	194 699	...	...	...	...	...	...
30 - 34	432 619	222 075	210 544	...	...	...	...	...	...
35 - 39	453 287	233 239	220 048	...	...	...	...	...	...
40 - 44	434 461	222 224	212 237	...	...	...	...	...	...
45 - 49	355 840	179 698	176 142	...	...	...	...	...	...
50 - 54	363 869	180 720	183 149	...	...	...	...	...	...
55 - 59	366 397	178 482	187 915	...	...	...	...	...	...
60 - 64	366 568	171 581	194 987	...	...	...	...	...	...
65 - 69	297 613	132 158	165 455	...	...	...	...	...	...
70 - 74	196 756	79 454	117 302	...	...	...	...	...	...
75 - 79	146 356	53 214	93 142	...	...	...	...	...	...
80 - 84	97 487	31 621	65 866	...	...	...	...	...	...
85 - 89	53 429	15 328	38 101	...	...	...	...	...	...
90 - 94	18 602	4 706	13 896	...	...	...	...	...	...
95 - 99	3 524	943	2 581	...	...	...	...	...	...
100 - 104	735	268	467	...	...	...	...	...	...
105 - 109	137	54	83	...	...	...	...	...	...
110 +	20	5	15	...	...	...	...	...	...

7. Population by age, sex and urban/rural residence: latest available year, 2008 - 2017

Population selon l'âge, le sexe et la résidence, urbaine/rurale : dernière année disponible, 2008 - 2017 (continued - suite)

Continent, country or area, date, code[a] and age (in years) / Continent, pays ou zone, date, code[a] et âge (en années)	Total			Urban - Urbaine			Rural - Rurale		
	Both sexes Les deux sexes	Male Masculin	Female Féminin	Both sexes Les deux sexes	Male Masculin	Female Féminin	Both sexes Les deux sexes	Male Masculin	Female Féminin
EUROPE									
Slovenia - Slovénie									
1 VII 2016 (ESDJ)									
Total	2 064 241	1 023 872	1 040 369	1 107 409	543 571	563 838	956 832	480 301	476 531
0	20 412	10 463	9 949	10 751	5 540	5 211	9 661	4 923	4 738
1 - 4	86 058	44 239	41 819	46 111	23 681	22 430	39 947	20 558	19 389
5 - 9	108 822	56 051	52 771	57 832	29 831	28 001	50 990	26 220	24 770
10 - 14	92 088	47 422	44 666	47 654	24 556	23 098	44 434	22 866	21 568
15 - 19	94 096	48 592	45 504	48 395	25 127	23 268	45 701	23 465	22 236
20 - 24	102 894	52 896	49 998	59 244	29 399	29 845	43 650	23 497	20 153
25 - 29	126 359	65 460	60 899	67 981	34 935	33 046	58 378	30 525	27 853
30 - 34	142 579	74 566	68 013	77 659	40 489	37 170	64 920	34 077	30 843
35 - 39	157 116	82 583	74 533	85 856	44 871	40 985	71 260	37 712	33 548
40 - 44	151 701	79 105	72 596	81 134	42 123	39 011	70 567	36 982	33 585
45 - 49	147 540	75 693	71 847	77 439	39 424	38 015	70 101	36 269	33 832
50 - 54	154 697	78 506	76 191	81 465	40 857	40 608	73 232	37 649	35 583
55 - 59	149 119	75 011	74 108	78 116	38 511	39 605	71 003	36 500	34 503
60 - 64	145 188	72 625	72 563	77 699	37 874	39 825	67 489	34 751	32 738
65 - 69	120 038	57 838	62 200	65 206	30 401	34 805	54 832	27 437	27 395
70 - 74	85 053	38 072	46 981	46 256	20 272	25 984	38 797	17 800	20 997
75 - 79	76 609	31 964	44 645	41 657	17 366	24 291	34 952	14 598	20 354
80 - 84	56 730	20 296	36 434	30 877	11 251	19 626	25 853	9 045	16 808
85 - 89	33 102	9 583	23 519	18 118	5 322	12 796	14 984	4 261	10 723
90 - 94	11 968	2 534	9 434	6 764	1 520	5 244	5 204	1 014	4 190
95 - 99	1 863	342	1 521	1 071	199	872	792	143	649
100 +	209	31	178	124	22	102	85	9	76
1 I 2017 (ESDJ)									
Total	2 065 895	1 025 125	1 040 770	...	...	...	...	...	...
0	20 324	10 357	9 967	...	...	...	...	...	...
1 - 4	85 132	43 817	41 315	...	...	...	...	...	...
5 - 9	110 092	56 604	53 488	...	...	...	...	...	...
10 - 14	93 046	47 888	45 158	...	...	...	...	...	...
15 - 19	93 598	48 371	45 227	...	...	...	...	...	...
20 - 24	102 222	52 637	49 585	...	...	...	...	...	...
25 - 29	123 848	64 210	59 638	...	...	...	...	...	...
30 - 34	140 803	73 592	67 211	...	...	...	...	...	...
35 - 39	156 809	82 624	74 185	...	...	...	...	...	...
40 - 44	152 605	79 484	73 121	...	...	...	...	...	...
45 - 49	146 679	75 371	71 308	...	...	...	...	...	...
50 - 54	155 160	78 796	76 364	...	...	...	...	...	...
55 - 59	148 636	74 773	73 863	...	...	...	...	...	...
60 - 64	146 515	73 377	73 138	...	...	...	...	...	...
65 - 69	121 360	58 547	62 813	...	...	...	...	...	...
70 - 74	86 507	38 793	47 714	...	...	...	...	...	...
75 - 79	76 767	32 199	44 568	...	...	...	...	...	...
80 - 84	57 504	20 774	36 730	...	...	...	...	...	...
85 - 89	33 643	9 842	23 801	...	...	...	...	...	...
90 - 94	12 360	2 634	9 726	...	...	...	...	...	...
95 - 99	2 064	399	1 665	...	...	...	...	...	...
100 - 104	207	30	177	...	...	...	...	...	...
105 - 109	14	6	8	...	...	...	...	...	...
110 +	-	-	-	...	...	...	...	...	...
Spain - Espagne[83]									
1 VII 2017 (ESDJ)									
Total	46 549 045	22 838 035	23 711 009	...	...	...	...	...	...
0	393 112	202 106	191 005	...	...	...	...	...	...
1 - 4	1 725 627	888 802	836 825	...	...	...	...	...	...
5 - 9	2 439 004	1 258 758	1 180 245	...	...	...	...	...	...
10 - 14	2 420 260	1 246 260	1 174 001	...	...	...	...	...	...
15 - 19	2 241 216	1 155 039	1 086 177	...	...	...	...	...	...
20 - 24	2 256 184	1 151 190	1 104 994	...	...	...	...	...	...
25 - 29	2 509 327	1 261 713	1 247 613	...	...	...	...	...	...
30 - 34	2 903 733	1 446 341	1 457 391	...	...	...	...	...	...
35 - 39	3 645 297	1 834 948	1 810 349	...	...	...	...	...	...
40 - 44	3 965 000	2 013 657	1 951 343	...	...	...	...	...	...
45 - 49	3 754 261	1 895 885	1 858 375	...	...	...	...	...	...

Continent, country or area, date, code[a] and age (in years) Continent, pays ou zone, date, code[a] et âge (en années)	Total			Urban - Urbaine			Rural - Rurale		
	Both sexes Les deux sexes	Male Masculin	Female Féminin	Both sexes Les deux sexes	Male Masculin	Female Féminin	Both sexes Les deux sexes	Male Masculin	Female Féminin
EUROPE									
Spain - Espagne[83]									
1 VII 2017 (ESDJ)									
50 - 54	3 557 835	1 774 860	1 782 975	...	...	...	...	...	...
55 - 59	3 178 469	1 565 388	1 613 081	...	...	...	...	...	...
60 - 64	2 675 308	1 299 143	1 376 165	...	...	...	...	...	...
65 - 69	2 387 950	1 137 913	1 250 037	...	...	...	...	...	...
70 - 74	2 090 936	966 762	1 124 174	...	...	...	...	...	...
75 - 79	1 535 059	675 826	859 234	...	...	...	...	...	...
80 - 84	1 433 440	579 917	853 523	...	...	...	...	...	...
85 - 89	933 478	337 013	596 466	...	...	...	...	...	...
90 - 94	394 530	119 862	274 668	...	...	...	...	...	...
95 - 99	96 138	24 119	72 018	...	...	...	...	...	...
100 +	12 881	2 532	10 349	...	...	...	...	...	...
Sweden - Suède[91]									
1 I 2017 (ESDJ)									
Total	9 995 153	5 013 347	4 981 806	...	...	...	...	...	...
0	119 023	61 005	58 018	...	...	...	...	...	...
1 - 4	478 018	246 387	231 631	...	...	...	...	...	...
5 - 9	600 853	309 001	291 852	...	...	...	...	...	...
10 - 14	563 100	289 269	273 831	...	...	...	...	...	...
15 - 19	529 612	276 575	253 037	...	...	...	...	...	...
20 - 24	640 179	331 021	309 158	...	...	...	...	...	...
25 - 29	711 687	365 217	346 470	...	...	...	...	...	...
30 - 34	641 176	330 321	310 855	...	...	...	...	...	...
35 - 39	617 317	315 589	301 728	...	...	...	...	...	...
40 - 44	647 816	329 405	318 411	...	...	...	...	...	...
45 - 49	658 991	334 272	324 719	...	...	...	...	...	...
50 - 54	666 684	338 866	327 818	...	...	...	...	...	...
55 - 59	581 418	292 812	288 606	...	...	...	...	...	...
60 - 64	562 422	281 162	281 260	...	...	...	...	...	...
65 - 69	573 266	282 774	290 492	...	...	...	...	...	...
70 - 74	539 911	264 573	275 338	...	...	...	...	...	...
75 - 79	356 786	167 768	189 018	...	...	...	...	...	...
80 - 84	247 030	106 917	140 113	...	...	...	...	...	...
85 - 89	162 745	61 441	101 304	...	...	...	...	...	...
90 - 94	75 564	23 869	51 695	...	...	...	...	...	...
95 - 99	19 574	4 771	14 803	...	...	...	...	...	...
100 - 104	1 883	322	1 561	...	...	...	...	...	...
105 - 109	92	9	83	...	...	...	...	...	...
110 +	6	1	5	...	...	...	...	...	...
Switzerland - Suisse[92]									
1 I 2017 (ESDJ)									
Total	8 419 550	4 173 437	4 246 113	7 119 751	3 517 940	3 601 811	1 299 799	655 497	644 302
0	86 296	44 165	42 131	73 838	37 733	36 105	12 458	6 432	6 026
1 - 4	343 819	177 139	166 680	291 265	150 063	141 202	52 554	27 076	25 478
5 - 9	420 456	215 898	204 558	353 970	181 744	172 226	66 486	34 154	32 332
10 - 14	404 420	207 439	196 981	338 838	173 854	164 984	65 582	33 585	31 997
15 - 19	436 475	225 978	210 497	363 205	188 046	175 159	73 270	37 932	35 338
20 - 24	495 535	254 086	241 449	415 613	212 261	203 352	79 922	41 825	38 097
25 - 29	568 581	288 343	280 238	489 566	246 909	242 657	79 015	41 434	37 581
30 - 34	596 100	301 290	294 810	517 297	260 960	256 337	78 803	40 330	38 473
35 - 39	590 339	298 142	292 197	509 525	257 082	252 443	80 814	41 060	39 754
40 - 44	584 230	294 236	289 994	500 571	251 682	248 889	83 659	42 554	41 105
45 - 49	644 679	324 274	320 405	544 505	273 479	271 026	100 174	50 795	49 379
50 - 54	669 041	339 192	329 849	562 030	284 215	277 815	107 011	54 977	52 034
55 - 59	575 812	290 114	285 698	479 611	240 961	238 650	96 201	49 153	47 048
60 - 64	480 708	238 531	242 177	399 734	196 809	202 925	80 974	41 722	39 252
65 - 69	430 368	208 092	222 276	358 402	171 346	187 056	71 966	36 746	35 220
70 - 74	384 240	182 193	202 047	323 031	151 811	171 220	61 209	30 382	30 827
75 - 79	281 899	126 025	155 874	238 137	105 749	132 388	43 762	20 276	23 486
80 - 84	214 971	88 581	126 390	181 496	74 467	107 029	33 475	14 114	19 361
85 - 89	136 470	48 707	87 763	115 391	41 021	74 370	21 079	7 686	13 393
90 - 94	59 878	17 517	42 361	50 774	14 794	35 980	9 104	2 723	6 381
95 - 99	13 687	3 232	10 455	11 638	2 728	8 910	2 049	504	1 545
100 +	1 546	263	1 283	1 314	226	1 088	232	37	195

7. Population by age, sex and urban/rural residence: latest available year, 2008 - 2017
Population selon l'âge, le sexe et la résidence, urbaine/rurale : dernière année disponible, 2008 - 2017 (continued - suite)

Continent, country or area, date, code[a] and age (in years) / Continent, pays ou zone, date, code[a] et âge (en années)	Total			Urban - Urbaine			Rural - Rurale		
	Both sexes Les deux sexes	Male Masculin	Female Féminin	Both sexes Les deux sexes	Male Masculin	Female Féminin	Both sexes Les deux sexes	Male Masculin	Female Féminin
EUROPE									
Switzerland - Suisse[92]									
1 I 2017 (ESDJ)									
100 - 104	1 467	253	1 214	...	...	...	...	...	...
105 - 109	75	8	67	...	...	...	...	...	...
110 +	4	2	2	...	...	...	...	...	...
TFYR of Macedonia - L'ex-R. y. de Macédoine									
1 I 2017 (ESDJ)									
Total	2 073 702	1 038 613	1 035 089	...	...	...	...	...	...
0	22 745	11 740	11 005	...	...	...	...	...	...
1 - 4	92 381	47 913	44 468	...	...	...	...	...	...
5 - 9	114 932	59 501	55 431	...	...	...	...	...	...
10 - 14	113 261	58 315	54 946	...	...	...	...	...	...
15 - 19	124 973	64 484	60 489	...	...	...	...	...	...
20 - 24	146 511	75 291	71 220	...	...	...	...	...	...
25 - 29	160 662	82 651	78 011	...	...	...	...	...	...
30 - 34	163 775	83 644	80 131	...	...	...	...	...	...
35 - 39	157 758	81 054	76 704	...	...	...	...	...	...
40 - 44	150 632	76 278	74 354	...	...	...	...	...	...
45 - 49	144 456	72 793	71 663	...	...	...	...	...	...
50 - 54	143 086	72 152	70 934	...	...	...	...	...	...
55 - 59	137 305	68 626	68 679	...	...	...	...	...	...
60 - 64	126 040	61 952	64 088	...	...	...	...	...	...
65 - 69	102 419	47 565	54 854	...	...	...	...	...	...
70 - 74	69 791	31 347	38 444	...	...	...	...	...	...
75 - 79	52 526	22 953	29 573	...	...	...	...	...	...
80 - 84	34 380	14 413	19 967	...	...	...	...	...	...
85 - 89	12 075	4 612	7 463	...	...	...	...	...	...
90 - 94	2 704	988	1 716	...	...	...	...	...	...
95 +	1 071	305	766	...	...	...	...	...	...
Unknown - Inconnu	219	36	183	...	...	...	...	...	...
Ukraine[93]									
1 I 2017 (ESDJ)									
Total	42 414 905	19 644 580	22 770 325	29 243 516	13 418 650	15 824 866	13 171 389	6 225 930	6 945 459
0	394 626	203 793	190 833	256 862	132 607	124 255	137 764	71 186	66 578
1 - 4	1 829 449	942 977	886 472	1 199 180	618 702	580 478	630 269	324 275	305 994
5 - 9	2 334 380	1 202 669	1 131 711	1 555 638	802 108	753 530	778 742	400 561	378 181
10 - 14	1 977 081	1 016 111	960 970	1 316 135	676 605	639 530	660 946	339 506	321 440
15 - 19	1 881 631	965 479	916 152	1 216 242	621 262	594 980	665 389	344 217	321 172
20 - 24	2 451 572	1 260 866	1 190 706	1 621 769	834 339	787 430	829 803	426 527	403 276
25 - 29	3 212 459	1 641 657	1 570 802	2 189 032	1 105 147	1 083 885	1 023 427	536 510	486 917
30 - 34	3 619 265	1 833 344	1 785 921	2 692 769	1 350 499	1 342 270	926 496	482 845	443 651
35 - 39	3 186 012	1 584 916	1 601 096	2 326 837	1 142 052	1 184 785	859 175	442 864	416 311
40 - 44	3 062 265	1 490 192	1 572 073	2 168 205	1 043 764	1 124 441	894 060	446 428	447 632
45 - 49	2 840 642	1 356 894	1 483 748	1 951 549	910 301	1 041 248	889 093	446 593	442 500
50 - 54	2 925 578	1 344 355	1 581 223	2 024 977	901 297	1 123 680	900 601	443 058	457 543
55 - 59	3 154 026	1 392 753	1 761 273	2 224 269	951 947	1 272 322	929 757	440 806	488 951
60 - 64	2 678 385	1 110 294	1 568 091	1 923 723	775 669	1 148 054	754 662	334 625	420 037
65 - 69	2 269 745	882 024	1 387 721	1 631 346	623 783	1 007 563	638 399	258 241	380 158
70 - 74	1 299 459	446 878	852 581	868 976	301 443	567 533	430 483	145 435	285 048
75 - 79	1 751 144	545 123	1 206 021	1 145 683	360 897	784 786	605 461	184 226	421 235
80 - 84	835 982	245 597	590 385	511 603	155 066	356 537	324 379	90 531	233 848
85 - 89	509 241	130 214	379 027	300 181	80 446	219 735	209 060	49 768	159 292
90 - 94	164 668	37 531	127 137	93 689	23 015	70 674	70 979	14 516	56 463
95 - 99	30 456	8 842	21 614	19 552	6 126	13 426	10 904	2 716	8 188
100 +	6 839	2 071	4 768	5 299	1 575	3 724	1 540	496	1 044
United Kingdom of Great Britain and Northern Ireland - Royaume-Uni de Grande-Bretagne et d'Irlande du Nord[94]									
27 III 2011 (CDJC)									
Total	63 182 178	31 028 143	32 154 035	51 217 521	25 124 237	26 093 284	11 964 657	5 903 906	6 060 751
0 - 4	3 913 953	2 002 494	1 911 459	3 302 119	1 689 719	1 612 400	611 834	312 775	299 059
5 - 9	3 516 615	1 799 999	1 716 616	2 878 114	1 472 489	1 405 625	638 501	327 510	310 991

Continent, country or area, date, code[a] and age (in years) Continent, pays ou zone, date, code[a] et âge (en années)	Total			Urban - Urbaine			Rural - Rurale		
	Both sexes Les deux sexes	Male Masculin	Female Féminin	Both sexes Les deux sexes	Male Masculin	Female Féminin	Both sexes Les deux sexes	Male Masculin	Female Féminin

EUROPE

United Kingdom of Great Britain and Northern Ireland - Royaume-Uni de Grande-Bretagne et d'Irlande du Nord[94]

27 III 2011 (CDJC)

10 - 14	3 669 326	1 878 838	1 790 488	2 951 079	1 509 796	1 441 283	718 247	369 042	349 205
15 - 19	3 996 452	2 040 725	1 955 727	3 277 414	1 667 480	1 609 934	719 038	373 245	345 793
20 - 24	4 297 198	2 164 141	2 133 057	3 737 543	1 863 922	1 873 621	559 655	300 219	259 436
25 - 29	4 306 340	2 145 054	2 161 286	3 781 906	1 876 471	1 905 435	524 434	268 583	255 851
30 - 34	4 125 449	2 059 312	2 066 137	3 573 410	1 789 511	1 783 899	552 039	269 801	282 238
35 - 39	4 194 477	2 082 310	2 112 167	3 495 390	1 745 563	1 749 827	699 087	336 747	362 340
40 - 44	4 625 635	2 283 902	2 341 733	3 734 709	1 851 446	1 883 263	890 926	432 456	458 470
45 - 49	4 643 100	2 293 572	2 349 528	3 683 527	1 821 257	1 862 270	959 573	472 315	487 258
50 - 54	4 094 454	2 028 748	2 065 706	3 216 769	1 593 822	1 622 947	877 685	434 926	442 759
55 - 59	3 614 078	1 785 598	1 828 480	2 790 096	1 378 906	1 411 190	823 982	406 692	417 290
60 - 64	3 807 974	1 868 912	1 939 062	2 869 025	1 404 882	1 464 143	938 949	464 030	474 919
65 - 69	3 017 480	1 463 355	1 554 125	2 248 845	1 082 105	1 166 740	768 635	381 250	387 385
70 - 74	2 462 745	1 162 621	1 300 124	1 874 997	873 593	1 001 404	587 748	289 028	298 720
75 - 79	2 006 019	903 433	1 102 586	1 549 014	686 269	862 745	457 005	217 164	239 841
80 - 84	1 498 896	615 163	883 733	1 166 619	470 552	696 067	332 277	144 611	187 666
85 - 89	918 343	324 063	594 280	717 808	249 645	468 163	200 535	74 418	126 117
90 - 94	368 425	104 072	264 353	287 454	80 165	207 289	80 971	23 907	57 064
95 - 99	92 951	19 756	73 195	72 117	15 038	57 079	20 834	4 718	16 116
100 +	12 268	2 075	10 193	9 566	1 606	7 960	2 702	469	2 233
1 I 2017 (ESDJ)[82]									
Total	65 808 573	32 466 065	33 342 508	...	...	...	...	...	...
0	771 346	395 452	375 894	...	...	...	...	...	...
1 - 4	3 212 295	1 646 702	1 565 593	...	...	...	...	...	...
5 - 9	4 073 281	2 084 912	1 988 369	...	...	...	...	...	...
10 - 14	3 676 570	1 883 216	1 793 354	...	...	...	...	...	...
15 - 19	3 735 882	1 917 632	1 818 250	...	...	...	...	...	...
20 - 24	4 233 444	2 169 380	2 064 064	...	...	...	...	...	...
25 - 29	4 528 517	2 287 511	2 241 006	...	...	...	...	...	...
30 - 34	4 415 686	2 203 457	2 212 229	...	...	...	...	...	...
35 - 39	4 227 655	2 101 989	2 125 666	...	...	...	...	...	...
40 - 44	4 112 720	2 039 013	2 073 707	...	...	...	...	...	...
45 - 49	4 593 867	2 264 442	2 329 425	...	...	...	...	...	...
50 - 54	4 646 892	2 288 673	2 358 219	...	...	...	...	...	...
55 - 59	4 122 577	2 034 306	2 088 271	...	...	...	...	...	...
60 - 64	3 564 318	1 746 238	1 818 080	...	...	...	...	...	...
65 - 69	3 553 580	1 722 591	1 830 989	...	...	...	...	...	...
70 - 74	2 979 444	1 422 927	1 556 517	...	...	...	...	...	...
75 - 79	2 165 151	995 092	1 170 059	...	...	...	...	...	...
80 - 84	1 620 096	702 080	918 016	...	...	...	...	...	...
85 - 89	1 002 000	386 207	615 793	...	...	...	...	...	...
90 - 94	444 842	144 066	300 776	...	...	...	...	...	...
95 - 99	113 488	27 724	85 764	...	...	...	...	...	...
100 - 104	14 047	2 353	11 694	...	...	...	...	...	...
105 - 109	843	99	744	...	...	...	...	...	...
110 +	32	3	29	...	...	...	...	...	...

OCEANIA - OCÉANIE

American Samoa - Samoas américaines[41]

1 IV 2010 (CDJC)

Total	55 519	28 164	27 355	...	...	...	...	...	...
0 - 4	6 611	3 417	3 194	...	...	...	...	...	...
5 - 9	6 535	3 470	3 065	...	...	...	...	...	...
10 - 14	6 279	3 214	3 065	...	...	...	...	...	...
15 - 19	6 296	3 218	3 078	...	...	...	...	...	...
20 - 24	3 891	1 944	1 947	...	...	...	...	...	...
25 - 29	3 324	1 670	1 654	...	...	...	...	...	...

Continent, country or area, date, code[a] and age (in years) / Continent, pays ou zone, date, code[a] et âge (en années)	Total			Urban - Urbaine			Rural - Rurale		
	Both sexes Les deux sexes	Male Masculin	Female Féminin	Both sexes Les deux sexes	Male Masculin	Female Féminin	Both sexes Les deux sexes	Male Masculin	Female Féminin
OCEANIA - OCÉANIE									
American Samoa - Samoas américaines[41]									
1 IV 2010 (CDJC)									
30 - 34	3 510	1 726	1 784	...	...	...	...	...	...
35 - 39	3 609	1 845	1 764	...	...	...	...	...	...
40 - 44	3 600	1 793	1 807	...	...	...	...	...	...
45 - 49	3 389	1 673	1 716	...	...	...	...	...	...
50 - 54	2 679	1 335	1 344	...	...	...	...	...	...
55 - 59	2 049	1 011	1 038	...	...	...	...	...	...
60 - 64	1 480	755	725	...	...	...	...	...	...
65 - 69	960	500	460	...	...	...	...	...	...
70 - 74	654	321	333	...	...	...	...	...	...
75 - 79	337	155	182	...	...	...	...	...	...
80 - 84	206	76	130	...	...	...	...	...	...
85 +	110	41	69	...	...	...	...	...	...
Australia - Australie									
9 VIII 2016 (CDJC)[95]									
Total	23 401 892[96]	11 546 638[96]	11 855 248[96]	20 947 027	10 272 706	10 674 324	2 408 494	1 247 068	1 161 434
0 - 4	1 464 779[96]	752 142[96]	712 638[96]	1 336 616	685 952	650 669	126 709	65 397	61 311
5 - 9	1 502 646[96]	771 055[96]	731 592[96]	1 344 588	689 488	655 097	156 982	81 048	75 936
10 - 14	1 397 183[96]	717 629[96]	679 553[96]	1 235 225	634 353	600 867	161 197	82 899	78 303
15 - 19	1 421 595[96]	727 677[96]	693 915[96]	1 271 620	648 915	622 703	148 214	77 831	70 379
20 - 24	1 566 793[96]	795 423[96]	771 369[96]	1 450 806	733 001	717 808	111 412	60 023	51 392
25 - 29	1 664 602[96]	824 084[96]	840 525[96]	1 552 207	765 000	787 204	106 999	56 028	50 964
30 - 34	1 703 847[96]	839 821[96]	864 026[96]	1 581 611	777 789	803 827	117 953	59 416	58 529
35 - 39	1 561 679[96]	773 132[96]	788 548[96]	1 430 249	706 810	723 443	127 958	64 090	63 861
40 - 44	1 583 257[96]	777 702[96]	805 551[96]	1 421 315	696 143	725 169	158 552	79 305	79 246
45 - 49	1 581 455[96]	773 170[96]	808 282[96]	1 396 196	679 375	716 817	181 989	91 702	90 287
50 - 54	1 523 551[96]	748 954[96]	774 601[96]	1 325 563	647 826	677 740	194 496	99 006	95 491
55 - 59	1 454 332[96]	709 115[96]	745 214[96]	1 250 479	604 527	645 952	200 381	102 735	97 653
60 - 64	1 299 397[96]	632 357[96]	667 048[96]	1 109 118	532 463	576 659	186 649	97 951	88 698
65 - 69	1 188 999[96]	581 230[96]	607 766[96]	1 017 067	488 734	528 335	168 592	90 566	78 027
70 - 74	887 716[96]	431 325[96]	456 390[96]	768 955	366 287	402 666	117 045	63 987	53 056
75 - 79	652 657[96]	307 441[96]	345 217[96]	580 146	267 655	312 494	71 759	39 344	32 415
80 - 84	460 549[96]	204 026[96]	256 529[96]	420 294	182 666	237 628	39 967	21 194	18 775
85 - 89	308 960[96]	123 502[96]	185 463[96]	287 180	112 867	174 313	21 646	10 569	11 073
90 - 94	140 398[96]	46 828[96]	93 570[96]	132 505	43 595	88 911	7 829	3 211	4 616
95 - 99	33 920[96]	9 244[96]	24 672[96]	31 991	8 576	23 418	1 915	662	1 247
100 +	3 569[96]	777[96]	2 788[96]	3 301	687	2 607	264	87	181
1 VII 2017 (ESDJ)[97]									
Total	24 598 933	12 204 419	12 394 514	...	...	...	...	...	...
0	302 388	155 366	147 022	...	...	...	...	...	...
1 - 4	1 269 536	651 671	617 865	...	...	...	...	...	...
5 - 9	1 588 146	814 761	773 385	...	...	...	...	...	...
10 - 14	1 471 962	756 495	715 467	...	...	...	...	...	...
15 - 19	1 484 110	759 892	724 218	...	...	...	...	...	...
20 - 24	1 719 169	876 414	842 755	...	...	...	...	...	...
25 - 29	1 845 982	924 491	921 491	...	...	...	...	...	...
30 - 34	1 833 716	909 473	924 243	...	...	...	...	...	...
35 - 39	1 658 227	827 284	830 943	...	...	...	...	...	...
40 - 44	1 604 762	798 823	805 939	...	...	...	...	...	...
45 - 49	1 646 919	806 733	840 186	...	...	...	...	...	...
50 - 54	1 539 231	756 419	782 812	...	...	...	...	...	...
55 - 59	1 506 920	739 161	767 759	...	...	...	...	...	...
60 - 64	1 333 065	650 170	682 895	...	...	...	...	...	...
65 - 69	1 196 026	588 288	607 738	...	...	...	...	...	...
70 - 74	958 190	470 790	487 400	...	...	...	...	...	...
75 - 79	677 834	322 218	355 616	...	...	...	...	...	...
80 - 84	468 431	209 613	258 818	...	...	...	...	...	...
85 - 89	306 771	124 636	182 135	...	...	...	...	...	...
90 - 94	145 332	49 846	95 486	...	...	...	...	...	...
95 - 99	38 138	10 898	27 240	...	...	...	...	...	...
100 +	4 078	977	3 101	...	...	...	...	...	...

7. Population by age, sex and urban/rural residence: latest available year, 2008 - 2017
Population selon l'âge, le sexe et la résidence, urbaine/rurale : dernière année disponible, 2008 - 2017 (continued - suite)

Continent, country or area, date, code[a] and age (in years) Continent, pays ou zone, date, code[a] et âge (en années)	Total			Urban - Urbaine			Rural - Rurale		
	Both sexes Les deux sexes	Male Masculin	Female Féminin	Both sexes Les deux sexes	Male Masculin	Female Féminin	Both sexes Les deux sexes	Male Masculin	Female Féminin
OCEANIA - OCÉANIE									
Cook Islands - Îles Cook[98]									
1 XII 2011 (CDFC)									
Total............................	17 794	8 815	8 979	...	...	...	...	...	...
0 - 4	1 584	806	778	...	...	...	...	...	...
5 - 9	1 539	768	771	...	...	...	...	...	...
10 - 14	1 504	794	710	...	...	...	...	...	...
15 - 19	1 495	768	727	...	...	...	...	...	...
20 - 24	1 273	611	662	...	...	...	...	...	...
25 - 29	1 263	590	673	...	...	...	...	...	...
30 - 34	1 122	534	588	...	...	...	...	...	...
35 - 39	1 179	543	636	...	...	...	...	...	...
40 - 44	1 252	605	647	...	...	...	...	...	...
45 - 49	1 282	636	646	...	...	...	...	...	...
50 - 54	1 059	534	525	...	...	...	...	...	...
55 - 59	863	430	433	...	...	...	...	...	...
60 - 64	749	394	355	...	...	...	...	...	...
65 - 69	649	333	316	...	...	...	...	...	...
70 - 74	496	251	245	...	...	...	...	...	...
75 - 79	285	130	155	...	...	...	...	...	...
80 + ...	200	88	112	...	...	...	...	...	...
Fiji - Fidji									
17 IX 2017 (CDFC)									
Total............................	884 887	448 595	436 292	494 252	245 928	248 324	390 635	202 667	187 968
0 - 4	91 897	47 195	44 702	47 904	24 614	23 290	43 993	22 581	21 412
5 - 9	88 295	45 243	43 052	45 436	23 231	22 205	42 859	22 012	20 847
10 - 14	79 596	40 715	38 881	40 784	20 676	20 108	38 812	20 039	18 773
15 - 19	74 088	38 032	36 056	42 045	20 713	21 332	32 043	17 319	14 724
20 - 24	73 616	37 464	36 152	46 942	23 397	23 545	26 674	14 067	12 607
25 - 29	69 308	35 253	34 055	41 756	21 030	20 726	27 552	14 223	13 329
30 - 34	68 818	35 266	33 552	40 741	20 609	20 132	28 077	14 657	13 420
35 - 39	65 150	33 382	31 768	37 684	18 904	18 780	27 466	14 478	12 988
40 - 44	53 514	27 697	25 817	30 590	15 476	15 114	22 924	12 221	10 703
45 - 49	49 504	25 314	24 190	27 872	13 998	13 874	21 632	11 316	10 316
50 - 54	48 610	24 649	23 961	26 585	13 241	13 344	22 025	11 408	10 617
55 - 59	42 008	21 263	20 745	23 113	11 249	11 864	18 895	10 014	8 881
60 - 64	30 615	14 891	15 724	16 744	7 805	8 939	13 871	7 086	6 785
65 - 69	21 328	10 076	11 252	11 469	5 138	6 331	9 859	4 938	4 921
70 - 74	14 148	6 367	7 781	7 342	3 131	4 211	6 806	3 236	3 570
75 + ...	14 392	5 788	8 604	7 245	2 716	4 529	7 147	3 072	4 075
French Polynesia - Polynésie française									
1 I 2015 (ESDF)									
Total............................	271 796	138 447	133 349	...	...	...	...	...	...
0 - 4	21 691	10 938	10 753	...	...	...	...	...	...
5 - 9	21 973	11 252	10 721	...	...	...	...	...	...
10 - 14	22 896	11 732	11 164	...	...	...	...	...	...
15 - 19	22 653	11 795	10 858	...	...	...	...	...	...
20 - 24	22 850	11 623	11 227	...	...	...	...	...	...
25 - 29	21 204	10 534	10 670	...	...	...	...	...	...
30 - 34	20 789	10 380	10 409	...	...	...	...	...	...
35 - 39	19 482	9 864	9 618	...	...	...	...	...	...
40 - 44	20 216	10 302	9 914	...	...	...	...	...	...
45 - 49	19 623	10 189	9 434	...	...	...	...	...	...
50 - 54	16 540	8 602	7 938	...	...	...	...	...	...
55 - 59	13 167	6 942	6 225	...	...	...	...	...	...
60 - 64	9 849	5 079	4 770	...	...	...	...	...	...
65 - 69	7 193	3 653	3 540	...	...	...	...	...	...
70 - 74	5 309	2 699	2 610	...	...	...	...	...	...
75 - 79	3 346	1 565	1 781	...	...	...	...	...	...
80 + ...	3 015	1 298	1 717	...	...	...	...	...	...
Guam[41]									
1 VII 2017 (ESDJ)									
Total............................	163 875	82 951	80 924	...	...	...	...	...	...
0	2 695	1 386	1 309	...	...	...	...	...	...
1 - 4	10 717	5 512	5 205	...	...	...	...	...	...

Continent, country or area, date, code[a] and age (in years) Continent, pays ou zone, date, code[a] et âge (en années)	Total			Urban - Urbaine			Rural - Rurale		
	Both sexes Les deux sexes	Male Masculin	Female Féminin	Both sexes Les deux sexes	Male Masculin	Female Féminin	Both sexes Les deux sexes	Male Masculin	Female Féminin
OCEANIA - OCÉANIE									
Guam[41]									
1 VII 2017 (ESDJ)									
5 - 9	13 410	6 895	6 515	...	...	...	...	...	...
10 - 14	13 445	6 915	6 530	...	...	...	...	...	...
15 - 19	14 402	7 508	6 894	...	...	...	...	...	...
20 - 24	13 515	6 963	6 552	...	...	...	...	...	...
25 - 29	12 411	6 289	6 122	...	...	...	...	...	...
30 - 34	10 858	5 499	5 359	...	...	...	...	...	...
35 - 39	9 696	4 838	4 858	...	...	...	...	...	...
40 - 44	9 961	5 049	4 912	...	...	...	...	...	...
45 - 49	10 597	5 415	5 182	...	...	...	...	...	...
50 - 54	10 352	5 374	4 978	...	...	...	...	...	...
55 - 59	8 976	4 605	4 371	...	...	...	...	...	...
60 - 64	7 158	3 568	3 590	...	...	...	...	...	...
65 - 69	5 910	2 899	3 011	...	...	...	...	...	...
70 - 74	3 891	1 845	2 046	...	...	...	...	...	...
75 - 79	2 785	1 232	1 553	...	...	...	...	...	...
80 - 84	1 850	728	1 122	...	...	...	...	...	...
85 - 89	863	319	544	...	...	...	...	...	...
90 - 94	303	94	209	...	...	...	...	...	...
95 - 99	72	17	55	...	...	...	...	...	...
100 +	8	1	7	...	...	...	...	...	...
Kiribati									
7 XI 2015 (CDFC)									
Total	110 136	54 096	56 040	56 388	27 159	29 229	53 748	26 937	26 811
0 - 4	14 393	7 546	6 847	7 140	3 724	3 416	7 253	3 822	3 431
5 - 9	13 600	6 903	6 697	6 470	3 313	3 157	7 130	3 590	3 540
10 - 14	10 445	5 309	5 136	4 700	2 327	2 373	5 745	2 982	2 763
15 - 19	11 676	5 851	5 825	6 290	2 988	3 302	5 386	2 863	2 523
20 - 24	10 319	5 199	5 120	6 137	3 015	3 122	4 182	2 184	1 998
25 - 29	9 672	4 682	4 990	5 468	2 603	2 865	4 204	2 079	2 125
30 - 34	8 012	3 838	4 174	4 356	2 052	2 304	3 656	1 786	1 870
35 - 39	6 584	3 161	3 423	3 422	1 661	1 761	3 162	1 500	1 662
40 - 44	5 091	2 433	2 658	2 555	1 198	1 357	2 536	1 235	1 301
45 - 49	5 707	2 676	3 031	2 724	1 227	1 497	2 983	1 449	1 534
50 - 54	4 905	2 372	2 533	2 483	1 182	1 301	2 422	1 190	1 232
55 - 59	3 321	1 548	1 773	1 694	743	951	1 627	805	822
60 - 64	2 406	1 051	1 355	1 174	494	680	1 232	557	675
65 - 69	1 748	731	1 017	815	322	493	933	409	524
70 - 74	1 238	460	778	551	183	368	687	277	410
75 - 79	608	217	391	241	86	155	367	131	236
80 - 84	267	80	187	109	30	79	158	50	108
85 - 89	109	30	79	42	6	36	67	24	43
90 - 94	24	7	17	10	3	7	14	4	10
95 - 99	11	2	9	7	2	5	4	-	4
100 +	-	-	-	-	-	-	-	-	-
Marshall Islands - Îles Marshall[99]									
1 VII 2010 (ESDF)									
Total	54 305	27 843	26 462	...	...	...	...	...	...
0 - 4	7 899	4 053	3 846	...	...	...	...	...	...
5 - 9	7 131	3 660	3 470	...	...	...	...	...	...
10 - 14	7 207	3 732	3 475	...	...	...	...	...	...
15 - 19	6 120	3 126	2 993	...	...	...	...	...	...
20 - 24	6 347	3 310	3 038	...	...	...	...	...	...
25 - 29	4 808	2 478	2 330	...	...	...	...	...	...
30 - 34	2 761	1 389	1 372	...	...	...	...	...	...
35 - 39	2 128	1 071	1 058	...	...	...	...	...	...
40 - 44	2 039	1 043	996	...	...	...	...	...	...
45 - 49	2 023	1 025	998	...	...	...	...	...	...
50 - 54	1 814	878	936	...	...	...	...	...	...
55 - 59	1 592	854	737	...	...	...	...	...	...
60 - 64	1 089	573	516	...	...	...	...	...	...
65 - 69	572	299	273	...	...	...	...	...	...

Continent, country or area, date, code[a] and age (in years) / Continent, pays ou zone, date, code[a] et âge (en années)	Total			Urban - Urbaine			Rural - Rurale		
	Both sexes Les deux sexes	Male Masculin	Female Féminin	Both sexes Les deux sexes	Male Masculin	Female Féminin	Both sexes Les deux sexes	Male Masculin	Female Féminin
OCEANIA - OCÉANIE									
Marshall Islands - Îles Marshall[99]									
1 VII 2010 (ESDF)									
70 - 74	361	165	196	...	...	...	...	...	...
75 +	412	184	228	...	...	...	...	...	...
Micronesia (Federated States of) - Micronésie (États fédérés de)[2]									
1 VII 2015 (ESDJ)									
Total	105 830	52 883	52 947	...	...	...	...	...	...
0 - 4	11 865	6 079	5 786	...	...	...	...	...	...
5 - 9	12 365	6 323	6 042	...	...	...	...	...	...
10 - 14	12 243	6 248	5 995	...	...	...	...	...	...
15 - 19	10 782	5 471	5 311	...	...	...	...	...	...
20 - 24	8 344	4 194	4 150	...	...	...	...	...	...
25 - 29	6 945	3 590	3 355	...	...	...	...	...	...
30 - 34	6 753	3 291	3 462	...	...	...	...	...	...
35 - 39	5 731	2 841	2 890	...	...	...	...	...	...
40 - 44	5 911	2 754	3 157	...	...	...	...	...	...
45 - 49	5 485	2 554	2 931	...	...	...	...	...	...
50 - 54	5 242	2 576	2 666	...	...	...	...	...	...
55 - 59	4 823	2 415	2 408	...	...	...	...	...	...
60 - 64	3 887	1 978	1 909	...	...	...	...	...	...
65 - 69	2 492	1 253	1 239	...	...	...	...	...	...
70 - 74	1 285	580	705	...	...	...	...	...	...
75 +	1 677	736	941	...	...	...	...	...	...
Nauru									
31 X 2011 (CDFC)									
Total	10 084	5 105	4 979	...	...	...	...	...	...
0 - 14	3 813	1 984	1 829	...	...	...	...	...	...
15 - 24	1 948	993	955	...	...	...	...	...	...
25 - 59	4 035	2 005	2 030	...	...	...	...	...	...
60 +	287	122	165	...	...	...	...	...	...
New Caledonia - Nouvelle-Calédonie									
1 I 2017 (ESDF)									
Total	278 495	140 000	138 495	...	...	...	...	...	...
0 - 4	20 587	10 481	10 106	...	...	...	...	...	...
5 - 9	21 295	11 009	10 286	...	...	...	...	...	...
10 - 14	21 505	10 922	10 583	...	...	...	...	...	...
15 - 19	22 963	11 621	11 342	...	...	...	...	...	...
20 - 24	19 937	10 329	9 608	...	...	...	...	...	...
25 - 29	20 738	10 338	10 400	...	...	...	...	...	...
30 - 34	21 487	10 760	10 727	...	...	...	...	...	...
35 - 39	20 717	10 255	10 462	...	...	...	...	...	...
40 - 44	21 555	10 853	10 702	...	...	...	...	...	...
45 - 49	19 744	9 795	9 949	...	...	...	...	...	...
50 - 54	17 719	8 939	8 780	...	...	...	...	...	...
55 - 59	13 955	7 010	6 945	...	...	...	...	...	...
60 - 64	11 230	5 722	5 508	...	...	...	...	...	...
65 - 69	8 877	4 516	4 361	...	...	...	...	...	...
70 - 74	6 650	3 339	3 311	...	...	...	...	...	...
75 - 79	4 642	2 157	2 485	...	...	...	...	...	...
80 - 84	2 793	1 198	1 595	...	...	...	...	...	...
85 - 89	1 538	607	931	...	...	...	...	...	...
90 - 94	436	119	317	...	...	...	...	...	...
95 +	127	30	97	...	...	...	...	...	...
New Zealand - Nouvelle-Zélande[100]									
1 VII 2017 (ESDJ)									
Total	4 793 900	2 361 100	2 462 800	4 144 300	2 029 700	2 114 600	648 800	331 000	317 800
0	60 570	30 880	29 690	52 890	26 920	25 970	7 680	3 960	3 720
1 - 4	245 410	126 200	119 200	213 890	110 010	103 870	31 520	16 190	15 330
5 - 9	326 350	167 580	158 770	279 570	143 600	135 970	46 760	23 970	22 790
10 - 14	301 360	154 320	147 040	254 780	130 410	124 370	46 570	23 910	22 660

7. Population by age, sex and urban/rural residence: latest available year, 2008 - 2017
Population selon l'âge, le sexe et la résidence, urbaine/rurale : dernière année disponible, 2008 - 2017 (continued - suite)

Continent, country or area, date, code[a] and age (in years) / Continent, pays ou zone, date, code[a] et âge (en années)	Total			Urban - Urbaine			Rural - Rurale		
	Both sexes Les deux sexes	Male Masculin	Female Féminin	Both sexes Les deux sexes	Male Masculin	Female Féminin	Both sexes Les deux sexes	Male Masculin	Female Féminin
OCEANIA - OCÉANIE									
New Zealand - Nouvelle-Zélande[100]									
1 VII 2017 (ESDJ)									
15 - 19	316 510	162 480	154 030	275 740	140 910	134 830	40 740	21 560	19 190
20 - 24	355 830	185 620	170 200	322 420	167 090	155 330	33 390	18 530	14 870
25 - 29	361 860	183 060	178 800	329 580	166 330	163 250	32 260	16 720	15 540
30 - 34	314 080	153 310	160 770	283 460	138 010	145 440	30 600	15 280	15 320
35 - 39	286 610	137 820	148 790	253 850	121 860	131 990	32 720	15 940	16 780
40 - 44	295 710	141 580	154 130	255 210	121 760	133 450	40 470	19 800	20 670
45 - 49	322 620	154 250	168 370	273 670	130 300	143 370	48 900	23 920	24 980
50 - 54	314 550	151 690	162 860	262 600	125 960	136 640	51 880	25 690	26 190
55 - 59	304 500	147 130	157 370	250 650	120 260	130 400	53 760	26 810	26 950
60 - 64	264 850	128 250	136 600	216 900	103 680	113 210	47 850	24 500	23 340
65 - 69	235 050	114 570	120 490	193 560	93 010	100 550	41 400	21 510	19 900
70 - 74	181 270	87 580	93 690	151 950	72 050	79 900	29 250	15 490	13 760
75 - 79	135 280	63 460	71 830	117 120	53 830	63 290	18 140	9 610	8 530
80 - 84	86 230	38 650	47 590	77 370	33 990	43 370	8 850	4 640	4 210
85 +	85 220	32 680	52 540	79 120	29 690	49 430	6 090	2 980	3 110
85 - 89	55 140	22 770	32 370	...	...	...	...	...	...
90 +	30 080	9 910	20 170	...	...	...	...	...	...
Niue - Nioué[101]									
1 VII 2010 (ESDJ)									
Total	1 496	754	740	...	...	...	...	...	...
0 - 4	135	69	64	...	...	...	...	...	...
5 - 9	134	58	76	...	...	...	...	...	...
10 - 14	116	60	56	...	...	...	...	...	...
15 - 19	124	79	45	...	...	...	...	...	...
20 - 24	100	50	50	...	...	...	...	...	...
25 - 29	90	38	52	...	...	...	...	...	...
30 - 34	71	39	32	...	...	...	...	...	...
35 - 39	85	45	40	...	...	...	...	...	...
40 - 44	101	55	46	...	...	...	...	...	...
45 - 49	92	42	50	...	...	...	...	...	...
50 - 54	107	58	49	...	...	...	...	...	...
55 - 59	89	42	47	...	...	...	...	...	...
60 - 64	70	34	36	...	...	...	...	...	...
65 - 69	75	37	38	...	...	...	...	...	...
70 - 74	53	23	30	...	...	...	...	...	...
75 +	54	25	29	...	...	...	...	...	...
Norfolk Island - Île Norfolk									
9 VIII 2011 (CDFC)									
Total	2 302	1 082	1 220	...	...	...	...	...	...
0 - 4	106	53	53	...	...	...	...	...	...
5 - 9	123	63	60	...	...	...	...	...	...
10 - 14	132	69	63	...	...	...	...	...	...
15 - 19	73	35	38	...	...	...	...	...	...
20 - 24	41	20	21	...	...	...	...	...	...
25 - 29	60	19	41	...	...	...	...	...	...
30 - 34	100	48	52	...	...	...	...	...	...
35 - 39	127	56	71	...	...	...	...	...	...
40 - 44	146	64	82	...	...	...	...	...	...
45 - 49	167	81	86	...	...	...	...	...	...
50 - 54	180	86	94	...	...	...	...	...	...
55 - 59	232	103	129	...	...	...	...	...	...
60 - 64	262	120	142	...	...	...	...	...	...
65 - 69	205	99	106	...	...	...	...	...	...
70 - 74	142	70	72	...	...	...	...	...	...
75 - 79	96	49	47	...	...	...	...	...	...
80 - 84	58	24	34	...	...	...	...	...	...
85 +	52	23	29	...	...	...	...	...	...

7. Population by age, sex and urban/rural residence: latest available year, 2008 - 2017
Population selon l'âge, le sexe et la résidence, urbaine/rurale : dernière année disponible, 2008 - 2017 (continued - suite)

Continent, country or area, date, code[a] and age (in years) Continent, pays ou zone, date, code[a] et âge (en années)	Total			Urban - Urbaine			Rural - Rurale		
	Both sexes Les deux sexes	Male Masculin	Female Féminin	Both sexes Les deux sexes	Male Masculin	Female Féminin	Both sexes Les deux sexes	Male Masculin	Female Féminin
OCEANIA - OCÉANIE									
Northern Mariana Islands - Îles Mariannes septentrionales									
1 VII 2011 (ESDF)									
Total................................	46 050	22 153	23 897	...	...	...	...	...	...
0 - 4	4 852	2 495	2 357	...	...	...	...	...	...
5 - 9	3 622	1 883	1 739	...	...	...	...	...	...
10 - 14	3 500	1 971	1 529	...	...	...	...	...	...
15 - 19	3 802	2 121	1 681	...	...	...	...	...	...
20 - 24	3 398	1 607	1 791	...	...	...	...	...	...
25 - 29	3 831	1 050	2 781	...	...	...	...	...	...
30 - 34	3 696	1 008	2 688	...	...	...	...	...	...
35 - 39	3 211	1 550	1 661	...	...	...	...	...	...
40 - 44	3 584	1 858	1 726	...	...	...	...	...	...
45 - 49	3 738	1 967	1 771	...	...	...	...	...	...
50 - 54	3 441	1 824	1 617	...	...	...	...	...	...
55 - 59	2 270	1 260	1 010	...	...	...	...	...	...
60 - 64	1 440	769	671	...	...	...	...	...	...
65 - 69	794	366	428	...	...	...	...	...	...
70 - 74	416	248	168	...	...	...	...	...	...
75 - 79	239	101	138	...	...	...	...	...	...
80 - 84	147	54	93	...	...	...	...	...	...
85 - 89	53	17	36	...	...	...	...	...	...
90 - 94	14	3	11	...	...	...	...	...	...
95 - 99	1	1	-	...	...	...	...	...	...
100 + ...	1	-	1	...	...	...	...	...	...
Palau - Palaos									
13 IV 2015 (CDJC)									
Total................................	17 661	9 433	8 228	14 209	7 620	6 589	3 452	1 813	1 639
0 - 4	1 200	653	547	962	528	434	238	125	113
5 - 9	1 219	614	605	932	483	449	287	131	156
10 - 14	1 209	636	573	916	489	427	293	147	146
15 - 19	1 201	624	577	975	495	480	226	129	97
20 - 24	1 195	687	508	1 018	587	431	177	100	77
25 - 29	1 217	694	523	1 041	581	460	176	113	63
30 - 34	1 338	759	579	1 163	661	502	175	98	77
35 - 39	1 420	813	607	1 215	701	514	205	112	93
40 - 44	1 501	861	640	1 235	715	520	266	146	120
45 - 49	1 538	820	718	1 248	657	591	290	163	127
50 - 54	1 363	708	655	1 067	549	518	296	159	137
55 - 59	1 126	605	521	856	459	397	270	146	124
60 - 64	851	432	419	641	318	323	210	114	96
65 - 69	554	271	283	414	202	212	140	69	71
70 - 74	314	137	177	233	106	127	81	31	50
75 + ...	415	119	296	293	89	204	122	30	92
Papua New Guinea - Papouasie-Nouvelle-Guinée[102]									
1 VII 2016 (ESDF)									
Total................................	8 151 300	...	...	...	...	...	...	...	...
0 - 14	2 970 800	...	...	...	...	...	...	...	...
15 - 24	1 641 400	...	...	...	...	...	...	...	...
25 - 59	3 177 700	...	...	...	...	...	...	...	...
60 + ...	361 400	...	...	...	...	...	...	...	...
Pitcairn									
31 XII 2013 (CDJC)									
Total................................	49	23	26	...	...	...	...	...	...
0 - 17	8	3	5	...	...	...	...	...	...
18 - 40	7	4	3	...	...	...	...	...	...
41 - 64	24	13	11	...	...	...	...	...	...
65 + ...	10	3	7	...	...	...	...	...	...
Samoa									
7 XI 2016 (CDFC)									
Total................................	195 979	...	...	...	...	...	...	...	...
0 - 4	28 159	...	...	...	...	...	...	...	...

7. Population by age, sex and urban/rural residence: latest available year, 2008 - 2017
Population selon l'âge, le sexe et la résidence, urbaine/rurale : dernière année disponible, 2008 - 2017 (continued - suite)

Continent, country or area, date, code[a] and age (in years) / Continent, pays ou zone, date, code[a] et âge (en années)	Total			Urban - Urbaine			Rural - Rurale		
	Both sexes Les deux sexes	Male Masculin	Female Féminin	Both sexes Les deux sexes	Male Masculin	Female Féminin	Both sexes Les deux sexes	Male Masculin	Female Féminin
OCEANIA - OCÉANIE									
Samoa									
7 XI 2016 (CDFC)									
5 - 9	25 019	...	...	...	...	...	...	...	...
10 - 14	21 438	...	...	...	...	...	...	...	...
15 - 19	18 952	...	...	...	...	...	...	...	...
20 - 24	15 919	...	...	...	...	...	...	...	...
25 - 29	13 332	...	...	...	...	...	...	...	...
30 - 34	11 916	...	...	...	...	...	...	...	...
35 - 39	10 799	...	...	...	...	...	...	...	...
40 - 44	10 252	...	...	...	...	...	...	...	...
45 - 49	9 774	...	...	...	...	...	...	...	...
50 - 54	8 448	...	...	...	...	...	...	...	...
55 - 59	7 010	...	...	...	...	...	...	...	...
60 - 64	5 225	...	...	...	...	...	...	...	...
65 - 69	3 475	...	...	...	...	...	...	...	...
70 - 74	2 688	...	...	...	...	...	...	...	...
75 +	3 429	...	...	...	...	...	...	...	...
Unknown - Inconnu	144	...	...	...	...	...	...	...	...
Solomon Islands - Îles Salomon									
22 XI 2009 (CDFC)									
Total	515 870	264 455	251 415	102 030	53 596	48 434	413 840	210 859	202 981
0 - 4	76 227	39 728	36 499	12 500	6 573	5 927	63 727	33 155	30 572
5 - 9	71 126	36 974	34 152	11 328	5 853	5 475	59 798	31 121	28 677
10 - 14	61 931	32 562	29 369	10 354	5 382	4 972	51 577	27 180	24 397
15 - 19	51 212	26 189	25 023	10 995	5 525	5 470	40 217	20 664	19 553
20 - 24	45 419	22 399	23 020	12 344	6 360	5 984	33 075	16 039	17 036
25 - 29	42 674	20 794	21 880	11 160	5 696	5 464	31 514	15 098	16 416
30 - 34	37 592	18 807	18 785	8 817	4 568	4 249	28 775	14 239	14 536
35 - 39	33 151	17 010	16 141	7 447	4 000	3 447	25 704	13 010	12 694
40 - 44	23 638	12 070	11 568	5 161	2 808	2 353	18 477	9 262	9 215
45 - 49	19 713	10 189	9 524	4 064	2 265	1 799	15 649	7 924	7 725
50 - 54	14 339	7 498	6 841	2 818	1 650	1 168	11 521	5 848	5 673
55 - 59	11 787	6 111	5 676	2 011	1 198	813	9 776	4 913	4 863
60 - 64	8 916	4 535	4 381	1 272	726	546	7 644	3 809	3 835
65 - 69	7 021	3 693	3 328	822	466	356	6 199	3 227	2 972
70 - 74	4 698	2 402	2 296	478	259	219	4 220	2 143	2 077
75 - 79	3 374	1 784	1 590	279	160	119	3 095	1 624	1 471
80 - 84	1 525	800	725	102	58	44	1 423	742	681
85 - 89	894	512	382	58	34	24	836	478	358
90 - 94	301	170	131	8	4	4	293	166	127
95 - 99	332	228	104	12	11	1	320	217	103
1 VII 2017 (ESDF)[103]									
Total	652 886	333 693	319 193	...	...	...	...	...	...
0 - 4	82 614	42 673	39 941	...	...	...	...	...	...
5 - 9	81 769	42 029	39 741	...	...	...	...	...	...
10 - 14	78 993	40 671	38 321	...	...	...	...	...	...
15 - 19	69 113	35 696	33 417	...	...	...	...	...	...
20 - 24	57 042	29 535	27 507	...	...	...	...	...	...
25 - 29	51 108	26 441	24 667	...	...	...	...	...	...
30 - 34	47 447	24 412	23 035	...	...	...	...	...	...
35 - 39	41 278	20 759	20 520	...	...	...	...	...	...
40 - 44	36 348	17 934	18 414	...	...	...	...	...	...
45 - 49	29 600	14 743	14 857	...	...	...	...	...	...
50 - 54	22 070	11 093	10 977	...	...	...	...	...	...
55 - 59	17 250	8 706	8 544	...	...	...	...	...	...
60 - 64	12 637	6 398	6 239	...	...	...	...	...	...
65 - 69	9 947	4 884	5 063	...	...	...	...	...	...
70 - 74	7 036	3 434	3 602	...	...	...	...	...	...
75 - 79	4 646	2 312	2 333	...	...	...	...	...	...
80 +	3 987	1 972	2 014	...	...	...	...	...	...
Tokelau - Tokélaou									
18 X 2016 (CDFC)									
Total	1 285	652	633	...	...	...	...	...	...
0 - 4	139	74	65	...	...	...	...	...	...

Continent, country or area, date, code[a] and age (in years) / Continent, pays ou zone, date, code[a] et âge (en années)	Total			Urban - Urbaine			Rural - Rurale		
	Both sexes Les deux sexes	Male Masculin	Female Féminin	Both sexes Les deux sexes	Male Masculin	Female Féminin	Both sexes Les deux sexes	Male Masculin	Female Féminin
OCEANIA - OCÉANIE									
Tokelau - Tokélaou									
18 X 2016 (CDFC)									
5 - 9	150	75	75	...	...	...	...	...	...
10 - 14	137	72	65	...	...	...	...	...	...
15 - 19	116	63	53	...	...	...	...	...	...
20 - 24	93	54	39	...	...	...	...	...	...
25 - 29	86	39	47	...	...	...	...	...	...
30 - 34	79	36	43	...	...	...	...	...	...
35 - 39	62	35	27	...	...	...	...	...	...
40 - 44	75	35	40	...	...	...	...	...	...
45 - 49	81	41	40	...	...	...	...	...	...
50 - 54	63	27	36	...	...	...	...	...	...
55 - 59	53	33	20	...	...	...	...	...	...
60 - 64	54	31	23	...	...	...	...	...	...
65 - 69	37	14	23	...	...	...	...	...	...
70 - 74	25	14	11	...	...	...	...	...	...
75 +	35	9	26	...	...	...	...	...	...
Tonga									
30 XI 2016 (CDJC)									
Total	100 651	50 255	50 396	23 221	11 529	11 692	77 430	38 726	38 704
0 - 4	12 499	6 440	6 059	2 648	1 357	1 291	9 851	5 083	4 768
5 - 9	12 153	6 417	5 736	2 557	1 351	1 206	9 596	5 066	4 530
10 - 14	11 882	6 139	5 743	2 518	1 244	1 274	9 364	4 895	4 469
15 - 19	10 502	5 449	5 053	2 374	1 246	1 128	8 128	4 203	3 925
20 - 24	8 234	4 106	4 128	2 070	1 029	1 041	6 164	3 077	3 087
25 - 29	6 629	3 162	3 467	1 762	888	874	4 867	2 274	2 593
30 - 34	6 521	2 994	3 527	1 641	790	851	4 880	2 204	2 676
35 - 39	5 645	2 704	2 941	1 368	641	727	4 277	2 063	2 214
40 - 44	5 189	2 473	2 716	1 209	577	632	3 980	1 896	2 084
45 - 49	5 181	2 600	2 581	1 220	605	615	3 961	1 995	1 966
50 - 54	4 150	2 129	2 021	1 012	519	493	3 138	1 610	1 528
55 - 59	3 254	1 571	1 683	803	369	434	2 451	1 202	1 249
60 - 64	2 696	1 297	1 399	628	301	327	2 068	996	1 072
65 - 69	2 030	968	1 062	474	215	259	1 556	753	803
70 - 74	1 601	735	866	345	154	191	1 256	581	675
75 - 79	1 250	575	675	269	121	148	981	454	527
80 - 84	725	315	410	175	70	105	550	245	305
85 - 89	358	127	231	78	23	55	280	104	176
90 - 94	99	25	74	27	5	22	72	20	52
95 +	12	6	6	2	1	1	10	5	5
Unknown - Inconnu	41	23	18	41	23	18	-	-	-
Tuvalu[102]									
1 VII 2016 (ESDF)									
Total	*10 100*	...	...	...	...	...	...	...	...
0 - 14	*3 200*	...	...	...	...	...	...	...	...
15 - 24	*1 900*	...	...	...	...	...	...	...	...
25 - 59	*4 100*	...	...	...	...	...	...	...	...
60 +	*1 000*	...	...	...	...	...	...	...	...
Vanuatu									
16 XI 2009 (CDFC)									
Total	234 023	119 091	114 932	57 195	29 618	27 577	176 828	89 473	87 355
0 - 4	33 367	17 310	16 057	7 224	3 828	3 396	26 143	13 482	12 661
5 - 9	29 685	15 455	14 230	5 591	2 850	2 741	24 094	12 605	11 489
10 - 14	27 921	14 762	13 159	5 250	2 755	2 495	22 671	12 007	10 664
15 - 19	23 882	12 027	11 855	6 460	3 122	3 338	17 422	8 905	8 517
20 - 24	21 541	10 415	11 126	7 186	3 606	3 580	14 355	6 809	7 546
25 - 29	18 415	9 124	9 291	5 542	2 937	2 605	12 873	6 187	6 686
30 - 34	15 693	7 790	7 903	4 517	2 300	2 217	11 176	5 490	5 686
35 - 39	14 171	7 076	7 095	3 844	1 965	1 879	10 327	5 111	5 216
40 - 44	11 523	5 814	5 709	3 242	1 710	1 532	8 281	4 104	4 177
45 - 49	10 241	5 066	5 175	2 817	1 474	1 343	7 424	3 592	3 832
50 - 54	7 415	3 789	3 626	1 923	1 036	887	5 492	2 753	2 739
55 - 59	6 363	3 261	3 102	1 495	845	650	4 868	2 416	2 452
60 - 64	4 319	2 192	2 127	826	455	371	3 493	1 737	1 756

Continent, country or area, date, code[a] and age (in years) Continent, pays ou zone, date, code[a] et âge (en années)	Total			Urban - Urbaine			Rural - Rurale		
	Both sexes Les deux sexes	Male Masculin	Female Féminin	Both sexes Les deux sexes	Male Masculin	Female Féminin	Both sexes Les deux sexes	Male Masculin	Female Féminin
OCEANIA - OCÉANIE									
Vanuatu									
16 XI 2009 (CDFC)									
65 - 69	3 826	2 054	1 772	590	355	235	3 236	1 699	1 537
70 + ...	5 661	2 956	2 705	688	380	308	4 973	2 576	2 397
7 XI 2016 (CDFC)									
Total..............................	272 459	138 265	134 194	...	...	...	...	...	...
0 - 4	38 936	20 172	18 764	...	...	...	...	...	...
5 - 9	37 148	19 276	17 872	...	...	...	...	...	...
10 - 14	29 846	15 560	14 286	...	...	...	...	...	...
15 - 19	25 902	13 207	12 695	...	...	...	...	...	...
20 - 24	24 862	11 738	13 124	...	...	...	...	...	...
25 - 29	23 031	10 986	12 045	...	...	...	...	...	...
30 - 34	18 067	8 909	9 158	...	...	...	...	...	...
35 - 39	16 233	8 148	8 085	...	...	...	...	...	...
40 - 44	13 251	6 726	6 525	...	...	...	...	...	...
45 - 49	11 833	6 125	5 708	...	...	...	...	...	...
50 - 54	9 329	4 756	4 573	...	...	...	...	...	...
55 - 59	7 227	3 792	3 435	...	...	...	...	...	...
60 - 64	5 357	2 832	2 525	...	...	...	...	...	...
65 - 69	4 010	2 089	1 921	...	...	...	...	...	...
70 + ...	7 225	3 838	3 387	...	...	...	...	...	...
Unknown - Inconnu	202	111	91	...	...	...	...	...	...
Wallis and Futuna Islands - Îles Wallis et Futuna									
22 VII 2013 (CDFC)									
Total..............................	12 197	5 927	6 270	...	...	...	...	...	...
0 - 4	997	507	490	...	...	...	...	...	...
5 - 9	1 136	560	576	...	...	...	...	...	...
10 - 14	1 297	687	610	...	...	...	...	...	...
15 - 19	1 168	615	553	...	...	...	...	...	...
20 - 24	583	257	326	...	...	...	...	...	...
25 - 29	600	266	334	...	...	...	...	...	...
30 - 34	719	315	404	...	...	...	...	...	...
35 - 39	864	398	466	...	...	...	...	...	...
40 - 44	922	434	488	...	...	...	...	...	...
45 - 49	762	354	408	...	...	...	...	...	...
50 - 54	761	344	417	...	...	...	...	...	...
55 - 59	669	352	317	...	...	...	...	...	...
60 - 64	571	310	261	...	...	...	...	...	...
65 - 69	462	238	224	...	...	...	...	...	...
70 - 74	309	153	156	...	...	...	...	...	...
75 - 79	201	82	119	...	...	...	...	...	...
80 - 84	111	35	76	...	...	...	...	...	...
85 - 89	50	17	33	...	...	...	...	...	...
90 - 94	15	3	12	...	...	...	...	...	...
95 + ...	-	-	-	...	...	...	...	...	...

FOOTNOTES - NOTES

Italics: estimates which are less reliable. - Italiques : estimations moins sûres.

* Provisional. - Données provisoires.

[a] 'Code' indicates the source of data, as follows:
CDFC - Census, de facto, complete tabulation
CDFS - Census, de facto, sample tabulation
CDJC - Census, de jure, complete tabulation
CDJS - Census, de jure, sample tabulation
SSDF - Sample survey, de facto
SSDJ - Sample survey, de jure
ESDF - Estimates, de facto
ESDJ - Estimates, de jure

Le 'Code' indique la source des données, comme suit :

CDFC - Recensement, population de fait, tabulation complète
CDFS - Recensement, population de fait, tabulation par sondage
CDJC - Recensement, population de droit, tabulation complète
CDJS - Recensement, population de droit, tabulation par sondage
SSDF - Enquête par sondage, population de fait
SSDJ - Enquête par sondage, population de droit
ESDF - Estimations, population de fait
ESDJ - Estimations, population de droit

[1] Data refer to population in housing units and collective living quarters only. - Correspond aux personnes qui vivent dans des unités d'habitation et dans des logements collectifs seulement.
[2] Data refer to national projections. - Les données se réfèrent aux projections nationales.
[3] Projections based on the 2013 Population Census. - Projections fondées sur le recensement de la population de 2013.

4 Data based on the 2011 Census. - Données fondées sur le recensement de 2011.

5 Unrevised data. - Les données n'ont pas été révisées.

6 Projections based on the 2014 Population Census. - Projections fondées sur le recensement de la population de 2014.

7 Projections based on the 2000 quick population count results and 1995, 2002 and 2010 Eritrea Demographic and Health Surveys. - Projections fondées sur le dénombrement rapide de la population de 2000 et sur les enquêtes érythréennes de la démographie et de la santé de 1995, 2002 et 2010.

8 Estimates considering also the results of the 2007 Population Census. - Estimations en prennant en considération les résultats du recensement de la population de 2007.

9 Data based on the 2010 Population Census. - Les données sont fondées sur le recensement de la population de 2010.

10 Postcensal estimates. - Estimations post censitaires.

11 Post-censal estimates based on the 2009 Population Census. - Les estimations post-censitaire fondées sur le recensement de la population de 2009.

12 Data refer to Libyan nationals only. - Les données se raportent aux nationaux libyens seulement.

13 Projections considering also the results of the 2009 Population Census. - Projections en prennant en considération les résultats du recensement de la population de 2009.

14 Excludes the islands of St. Brandon and Agalega. - Non compris les îles St. Brandon et Agalega.

15 Based on the results of the 2011 Population Census. - Basé sur les résultats du recencement de la population de 2011.

16 Projections based on the results of national survey on population and health conducted between 2010 and 2011, and especially population and housing census 2014. - Des projections de la population fondées sur les résultats de l'enquête nationale de la population et de la santé réalisée entre 2010 et 2011 et, surtout, du recensement général de la population et de l'habitat de 2014.

17 Data refer to national projections based on 2007 census. - Les données sont des projections nationales d'après les résultats du recensement de la population de 2007.

18 Data refer to projections based on the 2011 Population Census. - Les données se réfèrent aux projections basées sur le recensement de la population de 2011.

19 Projections based on the 2012 Population and Housing Census. - Projections fondées sur le recensement 2012 de la population et des logements.

20 Data are projections based on the 2006 Population Census. - Projections fondées sur le recensement de la population de 2006.

21 Data are projections based on the 2008 Population and Housing Census. - Projection basée sur le recensement 2008 de la population et des logements.

22 Data refer to total resident population, Saint Helenian and other nationalities. - Les données concernent la population résidente totale, originaire de Sainte-Hélène ou possédant une autre nationalité.

23 Projections based on the 2012 Population Census. - Projections fondées sur le recensement de la population de 2012.

24 Projections based on the 2002 Population Census. - Projections fondées sur le recensement de la population de 2002.

25 Projections based on the 2010 Population and Housing Census. - Projections fondées sur le recensement 2010 de la population et des logements.

26 Projections based on the 2012 Population Census. Data for urban and rural do not add up to the total; reason for discrepancy not ascertained. - Projections fondées sur le recensement de la population de 2012. La somme des données pour la résidence urbaine et rurale n'est pas égale au total; on ne sait pas comment s'explique la divergence.

27 Data refer to national projections. Projections based on the 2010 Population and Housing Census. - Les données se réfèrent aux projections nationales. Projections fondées sur le recensement 2010 de la population et des logements.

28 Data refers to resident population adjusted for the undercount of 18 per cent and including the institutional population. - Les données concernent la population résidente, y compris la population des institutions, et ont été ajustées pour tenir compte du sous-dénombrement estimé à 18 p. 100.

29 Bermuda is 100 per cent urban. - 100 pour cent de la population des Bermudes est urbaine.

30 To ensure confidentiality, the values, including totals are randomly rounded either up or down to a multiple of '5' or '10.' As a result, when these data are summed or grouped, the total value may not match the individual values since totals and sub-totals are independently rounded. Similarly, percentages, which are calculated on rounded data, may not necessarily add up to 100%. - À des fins de confidentialité, les chiffres, y compris les totaux, sont aléatoirement arrondis au multiple de 5 ou 10 inférieur ou supérieur. Par conséquent, lorsque ces chiffres sont additionnés, le total peut ne pas correspondre à la somme des valeurs individuelles, dans la mesure où les totaux et les totaux partiels sont arrondis indépendamment. De même, la somme des pourcentages, qui sont calculés à partir des données arrondies, peut ne pas correspondre à 100 %.

31 Adjusted for census net undercoverage (including adjustment for incompletely enumerated Indian reserves). Preliminary postcensal estimates. - Ajusté pour la sous-estimation du recensement (y compris les réservations en Inde incomplètement énumérées). Estimations post censitaires préliminaires.

32 Based on the national household survey of 2017. - D'après l'enquête nationale auprès des ménages de 2017.

33 Estimates or projections based on the 2007 Population Census. - Estimations ou projections fondées sur le recensement de la population de 2007.

34 Population statistics are compiled from registers. - Les statistiques de la population sont compilées à partir des registres.

35 Excluding data for Saint Barthélémy and Saint Martin. - Non compris les données pour Saint Barthélémy et Saint Martin.

36 Projections produced by l'Institut Haïtien de Statistique et d'Informatique (IHSI) and the Latin American and Caribbean Demographic Centre (CELADE) - Population Division of ECLAC. - Les données sont projections produits par l'Institut Haïtien de Statistique et d'Informatique (IHSI) et le centre démographique de l'Amérique latine et les Caraïbes - Division de la population de la CEPALC.

37 Including an estimation of 1 334 585 persons corresponding to 448 195 housing units without information of the occupants. - Y compris une estimation de 1 334 585 personnes correspondant aux 448 195 unités d'habitation sans information sur les occupants.

38 Including armed forces stationed in the area. Postcensal estimates. - Y compris les militaires en garnison sur le territoire. Estimations post censitaires.

39 Population in households only. - Population dans les ménages seulement.

40 Excluding U.S. Armed Forces overseas and civilian U.S. citizens whose usual place of residence is outside the United States. Postcensal estimates. - Non compris les militaires américains à l'étranger et les civils américains dont le lieu de résidence habituel est en dehors des États-Unis. Estimations post censitaires.

41 Including armed forces stationed in the area. - Y compris les militaires en garnison sur le territoire.

42 Data refer to national projections. Data include persons in remote areas, military personnel outside the country, merchant seamen at sea, civilian seasonal workers outside the country, and other civilians outside the country, and exclude nomads, foreign military, civilian aliens temporarily in the country, transients on ships and Indian jungle population. - Les données se réfèrent aux projections nationales. Y compris les personnes vivant dans des régions éloignées, le personel militaire en dehors du pays, les marins marchands, les ouvriers saisonniers en dehors du pays, et autres civils en dehors du pays, et non compris les nomades, les militaires étrangers, les étrangers civils temporairement dans le pays, les transiteurs sur des bateaux et les Indiens de la jungle.

43 Data are revised projections taking into consideration also the results of the 2005 census. - Les données sont des projections révisées tenant compte également des résultats du recensement de 2005.

44 Data based on the 2010 Population Census. Excludes nomadic Indian tribes. - Les données sont fondées sur le recensement de la population de 2010. Non compris les tribus d'Indiens nomades.

45 A dispute exists between the governments of Argentina and the United Kingdom of Great Britain and Northern Ireland concerning sovereignty over the Falkland Islands (Malvinas). Excluding military personnel and their families, visitors and transients. - La souveraineté sur les îles Falkland (Malvinas) fait l'objet d'un différend entre le Gouvernement argentin et le Gouvernement du Royaume-Uni de Grande-Bretagne et d'Irlande du Nord. Non compris les militaires et leur familles, ni les visiteurs et transients.

46 Estimates or projections considering also the results of the 2012 Population Census. - Estimations ou projections en prennant en considération les résultats du recensement de la population de 2012.

47 For operational purposes, population centers with 2,500 and more inhabitants are considered as urban area and less than 2,500 are considered as rural area. - À des fins opérationnelles, les centres de population comptant 2 500 habitants ou plus sont considérés comme zones urbaines, ceux qui en comptent moins de 2 500 comme zones rurales.

48 Data refer to the settled population based on the 1979 Population Census and the latest household prelisting. The refugees of Afghanistan in Iran, Pakistan, and an estimated 1.5 million nomads, are not included. - Les données se rapportent à la population stationnaire sur la base du recensement de 1979 et du recensement préliminaire des logements le plus récent. Sont exclus les réfugiés d'Afghanistan en Iran et au Pakistan et les nomades estimés à 1,5 million.

49 Including "Other Urban" (Total of Both Sexes-6094394, Male-3127003, Female-29673941). - Y compris "Autres citadins" (total des deux sexes 6 094 394; hommes : 3 127 003; femmes: 2 967 391).

50 Source: 2016 Population and Housing Census Update. - Source : Révision des chiffres du recensement de la population et des logements de 2016.

51 Data based on the 2008 Population Census. Excluding foreign diplomatic personnel and their dependants. - Données fondées sur le recensement de population de 2008. Non compris le personnel diplomatique étranger et les membres de leur famille les accompagnant.

52 Population by-census is conducted between two population censuses, adopting a sampling method to select 29,421 housing units in Macao for enumeration, with the unit of observation being the individuals residing in the selected housing units. - Aux fins du recensement partiel de la population, conduit entre deux recensements, la méthode d'échantillonnage adoptée a permis de sélectionner 29 421 unités d'habitation à Macao, l'unité d'observation étant les personnes qui y résident.

53 For statistical purposes, the data for China do not include those for the Hong Kong Special Administrative Region (Hong Kong SAR), Macao Special Administrative Region (Macao SAR) and Taiwan province of China. - Pour la présentation des statistiques, les données pour la Chine ne comprennent pas la Région Administrative Spéciale de Hong Kong (Hong Kong RAS), la Région Administrative Spéciale de Macao (Macao RAS) et Taïwan province de Chine.

54 Data exclude 2.3 million servicemen, 4.65 million persons with permanent resident status difficult to define, and 0.12 per cent undercount based on the post enumeration survey. - Les données ne comprennent pas 2,3 millions de militaires, 4,65 millions de personnes ayant le statut de résident permanent mais difficiles à définir, et des lacunes estimées à 0,12 pour cent sur la base de l'enquête de vérification du recensement.

55 Data have been adjusted on the basis of the Population Census of 2010. Because of rounding, totals are not in all cases the sum of the respective components. - Les données ont été ajustées à partir des résultats du recensement de la population de 2010. Les chiffres étant arrondis, les totaux ne correspondent pas toujours rigoureusement à la somme des composants respectifs.

56 Data refer to government controlled areas. - Les données se rapportent aux zones contrôlées par le Gouvernement.

57 Based on the results of the 2014 Population Census. - D'après les résultats du recensement de la population de 2014.

58 Includes data for the Indian-held part of Jammu and Kashmir, the final status of which has not yet been determined. - Y compris les données pour la partie du Jammu et du Cachemire occupée par l'Inde dont le statut définitif n'a pas encore été déterminé.

59 Data are based on the publication: "Indonesia Population Projection 2010-2035" - Les données sont basées sur la publication : << Indonesia Population Projection 2010-2035 >>

60 Data refer to the 2015 Intercensal Survey. - Les données concernent l'enquête intercensitaire de 2015.

61 Data refer to the Iranian Year which begins on 21 March and ends on 20 March of the following year. - Les données concernent l'année iranienne, qui commence le 21 mars et se termine le 20 mars de l'année suivante.

62 Includes data for East Jerusalem and Israeli residents in certain other territories under occupation by Israeli military forces since June 1967. Because of rounding, totals are not in all cases the sum of the respective components. Data refer to Israeli citizens and permanent residents who are listed in the Population Register. - Y compris les données pour Jérusalem-Est et les résidents israéliens dans certains autres territoires occupés depuis 1967 par les forces armées israéliennes. Les chiffres étant arrondis, les totaux ne correspondent pas toujours rigoureusement à la somme des composants respectifs. Les données se rapportent aux citoyens israéliens et aux résidents permanents qui sont répertoriés dans le registre de la population.

63 Excluding diplomatic personnel outside the country and foreign military and civilian personnel and their dependants stationed in the area. - Non compris le personnel diplomatique hors du pays ni les militaires et agents civils étrangers en poste sur le territoire et les membres de leur famille les accompagnant.

64 Because of rounding, totals are not in all cases the sum of the respective components. Estimates based on the complete counts of the 2015 Population Census. - Les chiffres étant arrondis, les totaux ne correspondent pas toujours rigoureusement à la somme des composants respectifs. Estimations basées sur le dénombrement complet du recensement de la population de 2015.

65 Excluding data for Jordanian territory under occupation since June 1967 by Israeli military forces. - Non compris les données pour le territoire jordanien occupé depuis juin 1967 par les forces armées israéliennes.

66 Data refer to resident population. Recalculated population estimates taking into account late registration of births and deaths until May 2017. - Les données concernent la population résidente. Réestimation du nombre d'habitants compte tenu de l'enregistrement tardif des naissances et des décès jusqu'en mai 2017.

67 Data refer to annual average population. - Les données correspondent à la population annuelle moyenne.

68 Because of rounding, totals are not in all cases the sum of the respective components. Estimates based on the results of 2015 population census. - Les chiffres étant arrondis, les totaux ne correspondent pas toujours rigoureusement à la somme des composants respectifs. Estimations fondées sur les résultats du recensement de la population de 2015.

69 Estimates based on the adjusted results of the Population and Housing Census of 2010. - Les estimations sont fondée sur les résultats ajustées du recensement de la population et de l'habitat de 2010.

70 Data refer to resident population which includes resident Maldivians and resident foreigners. Estimates based on the 2014 Population Census. - Les données concernent la population résidente, qui comprend les Maldiviens et les étrangers. Estimations fondées sur le recensement de la population de 2014.

71 Data refer to registered population data from Royal Oman Police. - Les données portent sur la population enregistrée par la police royale de l'Oman.

72 Excluding 2739 Filipinos in Philippine Embassies, Consulates and Missions Abroad. - Excepté 2739 Philippins travaillant dans les ambassades, les consulats et les missions des Philippines à l'étranger.

73 Data refer to resident population which comprises Singapore citizens and permanent residents. Data exclude residents who have been away from Singapore for a continuous period of 12 months or longer as at the reference date. - Les données se rapportent à la population résidente composé des citoyens de Singapour et des résidents permanents. Non compris les résidents hors de Singapour pour une période ininterrompue de 12 mois ou plus avant de la date de référence.

74 Including Palestinian refugees. - Y compris les réfugiés de Palestine.

75 Data based on Address Based Population Registration System. - Les données sont basées sur le registre national de la population basé sur l'adresse.

76 Data refer to resident population. - Les données concernent la population résidente.

77 Excluding Faeroe Islands and Greenland shown separately, if available. Population statistics are compiled from registers. - Non compris les Iles Féroé et le Groenland, qui font l'objet de rubriques distinctes, si disponible. Les statistiques de la population sont compilées à partir des registres.

78 The total number may include 'Unknown residence', but the categories urban and rural do not. - Le nombre total peut inclure les personnes dont la résidence n'est pas connue, à l'inverse des catégories de population urbaine et rurale.

79 Excluding Åland Islands. - Non compris les Îles d'Åland.

80 Data refer to annual average population. Excluding diplomatic personnel outside the country and including members of alien armed forces not living in military camps and foreign diplomatic personnel not living in embassies or consulates. - Les données correspondent à la population annuelle moyenne. Non compris le personnel diplomatique hors du pays et y compris les militaires étrangers ne vivant pas dans des camps militaires et le personnel diplomatique étranger ne vivant pas dans les ambassades ou les consulats.

81 Excluding military personnel, visitors and transients. - Non compris les militaires, ni les visiteurs et transients.

82 Data refer to usually resident population. - Les données concernent la population habituellement résidente.

83 Data refer to registered resident population. - Les données concernent la population enregistrée résidente.

84 The figures refer to usual residents in private households and persons present in communal establishments during the 2011 census. - Données se rapportant aux résidents habituels membres de ménages privés et aux personnes recensées dans des établissements collectifs au recensement de 2011.

85 Including civilian nationals temporarily outside the country. - Y compris les civils nationaux temporairement hors du pays.

86 Data refer to resident population only. - Pour la population résidante seulement.

87 Figures for male and female population do not add up to the figure for total population, because they exclude 119 persons of unknown sex. - Les chiffres relatifs à la population masculine et féminine ne correspondent pas au chiffre de la population totale, parce que l'on en a exclu 119 personnes de sexe inconnu.

88 Population statistics are compiled from registers. Including residents temporarily outside the country. - Les statistiques de la population sont compilées à partir des registres. Y compris les résidents se trouvant temporairement hors du pays.

89 Excluding Transnistria and the municipality of Bender. - Les données ne tiennent pas compte de l'information sur la Transnistria et la municipalité de Bender.

90 Excludes data for Kosovo and Metohia. Based on the results of the 2011 Population Census. - Sans les données pour le Kosovo et Metohie. Basé sur les résultats du recensement de la population de 2011.

91 Data refer to registered resident population. Population statistics are compiled from registers. - Les données concernent la population enregistrée résidente. Les statistiques de la population sont compilées à partir des registres.

92 Data refer to legal resident population. - Les données concernent la population légalement résidente.

93 The Government of Ukraine has informed the United Nations that it is not in a position to provide statistical data concerning the Autonomous Republic of Crimea and the city of Sevastopol. - Le gouvernement Ukrainien a informé l'ONU qu'il n'est pas en mesure de fournir des données statistiques concernant la République autonome de Crimée et la ville de Sébastopol.

94 Excluding Channel Islands (Guernsey and Jersey) and Isle of Man, shown separately, if available. - Non compris les îles Anglo-Normandes (Guernesey et Jersey) et l'île de Man, qui font l'objet de rubriques distinctes, si disponible.

95 These data have been randomly rounded to protect confidentiality. Individual figures may not add up to totals, and values for the same data may vary in different tables. - Ces données ont été arrondies de façon aléatoire afin d'en préserver la confidentialité. La somme de certains chiffres peut ne pas correspondre aux totaux indiqués et les valeurs des mêmes données peuvent varier d'un tableau à un autre.

96 Including population in off-shore, migratory and shipping. - Y compris les populations extraterritoriales, les populations nomades et les populations maritimes.

97 Based on the results of the 2016 Population Census. - Basé sur les résultats du recencement de la population de 2016.

98 Excluding Niue, shown separately, which is part of Cook Islands, but because of remoteness is administered separately. - Non compris Nioué, qui fait l'objet d'une rubrique distincte et qui fait partie des îles Cook, mais qui, en raison de son éloignement, est administrée séparément.

99 Projections are prepared by the Secretariat of the Pacific Community based on the 1999 census of population and housing. - Les projections sont preparées par le Secrétariat de la Communauté du Pacifique à partir des résultats du recensement de la population et de l'habitat de 1999.

100 Population estimates by urban/rural residence exclude inland waters and oceanic areas. Because of rounding, totals are not in all cases the sum of the respective components. - Les estimations de la population par lieu de résidence urbaine ou rurale excluent les eaux intérieures et les zones océaniques. Les chiffres étant arrondis, les totaux ne correspondent pas toujours rigoureusement à la somme des composants respectifs.

101 Figures for male and female may not add up to the total, since they do not include the category "Unknown". - La somme des chiffres indiqués pour les sexes masculin et féminin peut n'être pas égale au total parce qu'elle n'inclut pas la catégorie " inconnue ".

102 Estimates are prepared by the Secretariat of the Pacific Community based on the last population and housing census. - Les estimations sont preparées par le Secrétariat de la Communauté du Pacifique à partir des résultats du dernier recensement de la population et de l'habitat.

103 Projections based on adjusted 2009 census counts. - Projections fondées à partir des comptes rajustés du recensement de 2009.

Table 8 - Demographic Yearbook 2017

Table 8 presents population of capital cities and cities of 100 000 or more inhabitants for the latest available year between 1998 and 2017.

Description of variables: Since the way in which cities are delimited differs from one country or area to another, the table not only presents data for the so-called city proper, but also for the urban agglomeration, if available.

City proper is defined as a locality with legally fixed boundaries and an administratively recognized urban status, usually characterized by some form of local government.

Urban agglomeration has been defined as comprising the city or town proper and also the suburban fringe or densely settled territory lying outside of, but adjacent to, the city boundaries.

For some countries or areas, however, the data relate to entire administrative divisions known, for example, as shi or municipalities (municipios) which are composed of a populated centre and adjoining territory, some of which may contain other, often separate urban localities or may be distinctively rural in character. For this group of countries or areas the type of civil division is given in a footnote.

The surface area of the city or urban agglomeration is presented, when available.

City names are presented in the original language of the country or area in which the cities are located. In cases where the original names are not in the Roman alphabet, they have been romanized. Cities are listed in English alphabetical order.

Capital cities are shown in the table regardless of their population size. The names of the capital cities are printed in capital letters. The designation of any specific city as a capital city is as reported by the country or area.

The table also covers cities whose urban agglomeration's population exceeds 100 000; that is, while the urban agglomeration should have a population of 100 000 or more to be included in the table, the city proper may be of a smaller population size.

The reference date of each population figure appears in the left-most column of the table. Estimates based on results of sample surveys and city censuses or from other sources are explained by the 'code' also appearing in the left-most column of the table. The codes are explained at the end of the table.

Reliability of data: Specific information is generally not available on the reliability of the estimates of the population of cities or urban agglomerations presented in this table.

In the absence of such quality assessment, data from population censuses, sample surveys and city censuses are considered reliable and, therefore, set in Roman type. Other estimates are considered reliable if they are based on a complete census (or a sample survey), and have been adjusted by a continuous population register or adjusted on the basis of the calculated balance of births, deaths, and migration.

Limitations: Statistics on the population of capital cities and cities of 100 000 or more inhabitants are subject to the same qualifications as have been set forth for population statistics in general as discussed in section 3 of the Technical Notes.

International comparability of data on city population is limited by variations in national concepts and definitions. Although an effort is made to reduce the sources of non-comparability somewhat by presenting the data for both city proper and urban agglomeration, many serious problems of comparability remain.

Data presented in the "city proper" column for some countries represent an urban administrative area legally distinguished from surrounding rural territory, while for other countries these data represent a commune or an equally small administrative unit. In still other countries, the administrative units may be relatively extensive and thereby include considerable territories beyond the urban centre itself.

City data are also especially affected by whether the data refer to *de facto* or *de jure* population, as well as variations among countries in how each of these concepts is applied. With reference to the total population, the difference between the *de facto* and *de jure* population is discussed at length in section 3.1.1 of the Technical Notes.

Data on city populations based on intercensal estimates present additional problems: comparability is impaired by the different methods used in making the estimates, and by the loss of precision in applying to selected segments of the population methods best suited for the whole population. For example, it is far more difficult to apply the component method of estimating population growth to cities than it is to the entire country.

Births and deaths occurring in the cities do not all originate in the population present in or resident of that area. Therefore, the use of natural increase to estimate the probable size of the city population is a potential source of error. Internal migration is another component of population change that cannot be measured with accuracy in many areas.   Because of these factors, estimates in this table may be less valuable in general and in particular limited for purposes of international comparison.

City data, even when set in Roman type, are often not as reliable as estimates for the total population of the country or area. Furthermore, because the sources of these data include censuses (national or city), surveys and estimates, the years to which they refer vary widely. In addition, because city boundaries may alter over time, comparisons covering different years should be carried out with caution.

Earlier data: Population of capital cities and cities with a population of 100 000 or more have been shown in previous issues of the *Demographic Yearbook*. For more information on specific topics and years for which data are reported, readers should consult the Historical Index.

283

Tableau 8 – *Annuaire démographique 2017*

Le tableau 8 présente les données les plus récentes disponibles pour la période 1998 – 2017 sur la population des capitales et des villes de 100 000 habitants ou plus.

Description des variables : étant donné que les villes ne sont pas délimitées de la même manière dans tous les pays ou zones, on s'est efforcé de donner, dans ce tableau, des chiffres correspondant non seulement aux villes proprement dites, mais aussi, le cas échéant, aux agglomérations urbaines.

On entend par villes proprement dites les localités qui ont des limites juridiquement définies et sont administrativement considérées comme villes, ce qui se caractérise généralement par l'existence d'une autorité locale.

L'agglomération urbaine comprend, par définition, la ville proprement dite ainsi que la proche banlieue, c'est-à-dire la zone fortement peuplée qui est extérieure, mais contiguë aux limites de la ville.

En outre, dans certains pays ou zones, les données se rapportent à des divisions administratives entières, connues par exemple sous le nom de shi ou de municipios, qui comportent une agglomération et le territoire avoisinant, lequel peut englober d'autres agglomérations urbaines tout à fait distinctes ou être à caractère essentiellement rural. Pour ce groupe de pays ou zones, le type de division administrative est indiqué en note.

On trouvera en plus la superficie des villes ou des agglomérations urbaines chaque fois que possible.

Les noms des villes sont indiqués dans la langue du pays ou zone où ces villes sont situées. Les noms de villes qui ne sont pas à l'origine libellés en caractères latins ont été romanisés. Les villes sont énumérées dans l'ordre alphabétique anglais.

Les capitales figurent dans le tableau quel que soit le chiffre de leur population et leur nom a été imprimé en lettres majuscules. Ne sont indiquées comme capitales que les villes ainsi désignées par le pays ou zone intéressé.

En ce qui concerne les autres villes, le tableau indique celles dont la population est égale ou supérieure à 100 000 habitants. Ce chiffre limite s'applique à l'agglomération urbaine et non à la ville proprement dite, dont la population peut être moindre.

La date à laquelle se réfère le chiffre correspondant, figure dans la colonne de gauche du tableau. Le 'code' aussi figurant dans la colonne de gauche du tableau, permet de savoir si les estimations sont fondées sur les résultats d'enquêtes par sondage ou de recensements municipaux ou sont tirées d'autres sources. Les codes utilisés sont expliqués à la fin du tableau.

Fiabilité des données : on ne possède généralement pas de renseignements précis sur la fiabilité des estimations de la population des villes ou agglomérations urbaines présentées dans ce tableau.

Les données provenant de recensements de la population, d'enquêtes par sondage ou de recensements municipaux sont jugées sûres et figurent par conséquent en caractères romains. D'autres estimations sont considérées comme sûres si elles sont fondées sur un recensement complet (ou une enquête par sondage) et ont été ajustées en fonction des données provenant d'un registre permanent de population ou en fonction de la balance, établie par le calcul des naissances, des décès et des migrations.

Insuffisance des données : les statistiques portant sur la population des capitales et des villes de 100 000 habitants ou plus appellent toutes les réserves qui ont été formulées à la section 3 des Notes techniques à propos des statistiques de la population en général.

La comparabilité internationale des données portant sur la population des villes est compromise par la diversité des définitions nationales. Bien que l'on se soit efforcé de réduire les facteurs de non-comparabilité en présentant à la fois dans le tableau les données relatives aux villes proprement dites et celles concernant les agglomérations urbaines, de graves problèmes de comparabilité n'en subsistent pas moins.

Pour certains pays, les données figurant dans la colonne intitulée « Ville proprement dite » correspondent à une zone administrative urbaine juridiquement distincte du territoire rural environnant, tandis que pour d'autres pays ces données correspondent à une commune ou petite unité administrative analogue. Pour d'autres encore, les unités administratives en cause peuvent être relativement étendues et englober par conséquent un vaste territoire au-delà du centre urbain lui-même.

L'emploi de données se rapportant tantôt à la population de fait, tantôt à la population de droit, ainsi que les différences de traitement de ces deux notions d'un pays à l'autre influent particulièrement sur les statistiques urbaines. En ce qui concerne la population totale, la différence entre population de fait et population de droit est expliquée en détail à la section 3.1.1 des Notes techniques.

Les statistiques relatives à la population urbaine qui sont fondées sur des estimations intercensitaires posent encore plus de problèmes que les données issues de recensement. Leur comparabilité est compromise par la diversité des méthodes employées pour établir les estimations, et par l'imprécision qui résulte de l'application de certaines méthodes qui sont conçues pour être appliquées à l'ensemble de la population. La méthode des composantes, par exemple, est beaucoup plus difficile à appliquer en vue de l'estimation de l'accroissement de la population lorsqu'il s'agit de villes que lorsqu'il s'agit d'un pays tout entier.

Les naissances et décès qui surviennent dans les villes ne correspondent pas tous à la population présente ou résidente. En conséquence, des erreurs peuvent se produire si l'on établit pour les villes des estimations fondées sur l'accroissement naturel de la population. Les migrations intérieures constituent un second élément d'estimation que, dans bien des régions, on ne peut pas toujours mesurer avec exactitude. Pour ces raisons, les estimations présentées dans ce tableau risquent dans l'ensemble d'être peu fiables et leur valeur est particulièrement limitée du point de vue des comparaisons internationales.

Même lorsqu'elles figurent en caractères romains, il arrive souvent que les statistiques urbaines ne soient pas aussi fiables que les estimations concernant la population totale de la zone ou du pays considéré. De surcroît, comme ces statistiques proviennent aussi bien de recensements (nationaux ou municipaux) que d'enquêtes ou d'estimations, les années auxquelles elles se rapportent sont extrêmement variables. Enfin, comme les limites urbaines varient parfois d'une époque à une autre, il y a lieu d'être prudent lorsque l'on compare des données se rapportant à des années différentes.

Données publiées antérieurement : des statistiques concernant la population des capitales et des villes de 100 000 habitants ou plus ont été présentées dans des éditions antérieures de l'*Annuaire démographique*. Pour plus de précisions concernant les années et les sujets pour lesquels des données ont été publiées, se reporter à l'index historique.

8. Population of capital cities and cities of 100 000 or more inhabitants: latest available year, 1998 - 2017
Population des capitales et des villes de 100 000 habitants ou plus : dernière année disponible, 1998 - 2017

Continent, country or area, date, code[a] and city / Continent, pays ou zone, date, code[a] et ville	City proper - Ville proprement dite				Urban agglomeration - Agglomération urbaine			
	Population			Surface area - Superficie (km²)	Population			Surface area - Superficie (km²)
	Both sexes - Les deux sexes	Male - Masculin	Female - Féminin		Both sexes - Les deux sexes	Male - Masculin	Female - Féminin	

AFRICA - AFRIQUE

Algeria - Algérie
16 IV 2008 (CDJC)

Adrar	200 834	...	...	...	...	...	...	...
Ain Defla	450 280	...	...	...	...	...	...	...
Ain Temouchent	299 341	...	...	...	...	...	...	...
ALGIERS (EL DJAZAIR)	2 712 944	...	...	...	...	...	...	...
Annaba	442 230	...	...	...	...	...	...	...
Batna	768 444	...	...	...	...	...	...	...
Béchar	236 213	...	...	...	...	...	...	...
Bejaïa	559 981	...	...	...	...	...	...	...
Beskra (Biskra)	563 245	...	...	...	...	...	...	...
Bordj Bou Arreridj	422 986	...	...	...	...	...	...	...
Bouira	372 196	...	...	...	...	...	...	...
Boumerdes	459 250	...	...	...	...	...	...	...
Chlef	521 070	...	...	...	...	...	...	...
El Bayadh	192 958	...	...	...	...	...	...	...
El Boulaïda (Blida)	719 515	...	...	...	...	...	...	...
El Djelfa	825 411	...	...	...	...	...	...	...
El Oued	495 573	...	...	...	...	...	...	...
El Tarf	230 157	...	...	...	...	...	...	...
Ghardaïa	355 701	...	...	...	...	...	...	...
Ghilizane (Relizane)	432 386	...	...	...	...	...	...	...
Guelma	363 716	...	...	...	...	...	...	...
Jijel	391 096	...	...	...	...	...	...	...
Khenchela	288 849	...	...	...	...	...	...	...
Laghouat	371 204	...	...	...	...	...	...	...
Lemdiyya (Médéa)	519 383	...	...	...	...	...	...	...
Mestghanem (Mostaganem)	338 143	...	...	...	...	...	...	...
Mila	440 735	...	...	...	...	...	...	...
Mouaskar (Mascara)	513 432	...	...	...	...	...	...	...
M'Sila	666 848	...	...	...	...	...	...	...
Naama	160 381	...	...	...	...	...	...	...
Oum El Bouaghi	467 997	...	...	...	...	...	...	...
Qacentina (Constantine)	717 646	...	...	...	...	...	...	...
Saïda	248 939	...	...	...	...	...	...	...
Sidi-bel-Abbès	517 836	...	...	...	...	...	...	...
Skikda	543 402	...	...	...	...	...	...	...
Souq Ahras	308 319	...	...	...	...	...	...	...
Stif (Sétif)	856 457	...	...	...	...	...	...	...
Tamanrasset	136 822	...	...	...	...	...	...	...
Tbessa (Tébessa)	515 786	...	...	...	...	...	...	...
Tihert (Tiaret)	637 991	...	...	...	...	...	...	...
Tilimsen (Tlemcen)	672 490	...	...	...	...	...	...	...
Tipaza	343 838	...	...	...	...	...	...	...
Tissemsilt	193 011	...	...	...	...	...	...	...
Tizi Ouzou	585 775	...	...	...	...	...	...	...
Wahran (Oran)	1 165 687	...	...	...	...	...	...	...
Wargla (Ouargla)	473 543	...	...	...	...	...	...	...

Benin - Bénin
11 V 2013 (CDFC)

Cotonou	679 012	325 872	353 140	...	...	...	...	...
Parakou	255 478	127 328	128 150	...	...	...	...	...
PORTO-NOVO	264 320	126 016	138 304	...	...	...	...	...

Botswana
1 VII 2017 (ESDJ)

Francistown	110 077[1]	...	...	199	...	...	...	...
GABORONE	264 311[1]	...	...	198	...	...	...	...

Burkina Faso
9 XII 2006 (CDFC)

Banfora	75 917	38 399	37 518	...	109 824	54 581	55 243	...
Bobo Dioulasso	489 967	244 136	245 831	...	554 042	275 703	278 339	...
Dori	21 078	10 431	10 647	...	106 808	52 992	53 816	...
Fada N'gourma	41 785	21 220	20 565	...	124 577	62 193	62 384	...
Gorom-Gorom	8 882	4 509	4 373	...	106 346	53 129	53 217	...
Kaya	54 365	26 989	27 376	...	117 122	56 209	60 913	...

8. Population of capital cities and cities of 100 000 or more inhabitants: latest available year, 1998 - 2017
Population des capitales et des villes de 100 000 habitants ou plus : dernière année disponible, 1998 - 2017 (continued - suite)

Continent, country or area, date, code[a] and city / Continent, pays ou zone, date, code[a] et ville	City proper - Ville proprement dite				Urban agglomeration - Agglomération urbaine			
	Population			Surface area - Superficie (km²)	Population			Surface area - Superficie (km²)
	Both sexes - Les deux sexes	Male - Masculin	Female - Féminin		Both sexes - Les deux sexes	Male - Masculin	Female - Féminin	
AFRICA - AFRIQUE								
Burkina Faso								
9 XII 2006 (CDFC)								
Koudougou	88 184	42 803	45 381	...	138 209	64 362	73 847	...
OUAGADOUGOU	1 475 223	745 289	729 934	...	1 475 223	745 289	729 934	...
Ouahigouya	73 153	36 370	36 783	...	125 030	61 002	64 028	...
Solenzo	16 850	8 557	8 293	...	121 819	59 892	61 927	...
Tenkodogo	44 491	21 476	23 015	...	124 985	58 003	66 982	...
Burundi								
16 VIII 2008 (CDJC)								
BUJUMBURA	497 169	274 979	222 190	...	...	...	...	...
Cabo Verde[2]								
1 VII 2011 (ESDF)								
PRAIA	...	...	...	...	133 863	65 412	68 451	...
Cameroon - Cameroun[2]								
1 VII 2016 (ESDF)								
Douala	2 948 464	1 488 593	1 459 871	...	...	...	...	...
YAOUNDE	2 873 567	1 450 087	1 423 480	...	...	...	...	...
Côte d'Ivoire								
15 V 2014 (CDJC)								
Abengourou	100 910	51 153	49 757	...	...	...	...	...
Abidjan	4 395 243	2 180 526	2 214 717	...	...	...	...	...
Anyama	103 297	52 169	51 128	...	...	...	...	...
Bouake	536 719	273 502	263 217	...	...	...	...	...
Daloa	245 360	128 922	116 438	...	...	...	...	...
Divo	105 397	54 614	50 783	...	...	...	...	...
Gagnoa	160 465	82 615	77 850	...	...	...	...	...
Korhogo	243 048	126 493	116 555	...	...	...	...	...
Man	148 945	77 005	71 940	...	...	...	...	...
San Pédro	164 944	85 168	79 776	...	...	...	...	...
Soubre	101 196	53 799	47 397	...	...	...	...	...
YAMOUSSOUKRO	212 670	107 871	104 799	...	...	...	...	...
Djibouti								
29 V 2009 (CDFC)								
DJIBOUTI	475 322	...	...	...	...	...	...	...
Egypt - Égypte[3]								
18 IV 2017 (CDFC)								
Alexandria	...	...	...	...	5 163 750	2 654 824	2 508 926	...
CAIRO	...	...	...	...	9 539 673	4 960 625	4 579 048	...
Port Said	...	...	...	...	749 371	385 129	364 242	...
Suez	...	...	...	...	728 180	374 399	353 781	...
Equatorial Guinea - Guinée équatoriale								
1 VII 2001 (ESDF)								
MALABO	...	...	...	...	211 276	106 923	104 353	...
Ethiopia - Éthiopie								
1 VII 2017 (ESDF)								
ADDIS ABABA	4 215 965	2 097 591	2 118 375	...	...	...	...	...
Awassa	241 825	120 317	121 509	...	...	...	...	...
Bahir Dar	239 192	119 006	120 186	...	...	...	...	...
Debre Zeit	153 782	76 512	77 270	...	...	...	...	...
Dessie	184 817	91 953	92 864	...	...	...	...	...
Dire Dawa	358 914	178 572	180 342	...	...	...	...	...
Gondar	318 625	158 527	160 098	...	...	...	...	...
Harar	152 920	76 083	76 837	...	...	...	...	...
Jimma	186 148	92 615	93 533	...	...	...	...	...
Mekele	471 545	234 610	236 935	...	...	...	...	...
Nazareth	338 890	168 610	170 280	...	...	...	...	...
Gabon								
22 V 2013 (CDFC)								
Franceville	...	...	...	...	110 568	63 518	47 050	...
LIBREVILLE	...	...	...	...	703 939	360 012	343 927	...
Port-Gentil	...	...	...	...	136 462	69 978	66 484	...
Ghana								
26 IX 2010 (CDFC)								
ACCRA	1 594 419	763 870	830 549	...	...	...	...	...
Ashiaman	190 972	93 727	97 245	...	...	...	...	...

8. Population of capital cities and cities of 100 000 or more inhabitants: latest available year, 1998 - 2017
Population des capitales et des villes de 100 000 habitants ou plus : dernière année disponible, 1998 - 2017 (continued - suite)

Continent, country or area, date, code[a] and city / Continent, pays ou zone, date, code[a] et ville	City proper - Ville proprement dite				Urban agglomeration - Agglomération urbaine			
	Population			Surface area - Superficie (km²)	Population			Surface area - Superficie (km²)
	Both sexes - Les deux sexes	Male - Masculin	Female - Féminin		Both sexes - Les deux sexes	Male - Masculin	Female - Féminin	
AFRICA - AFRIQUE								
Ghana								
26 IX 2010 (CDFC)								
Koforidua	122 300	59 056	63 244	...	...	...	...	...
Kumasi	1 730 249	826 479	903 770	...	...	...	...	...
Madina	111 926	54 271	57 655	...	...	...	...	...
Obuasi	168 641	81 015	87 626	...	...	...	...	...
Tamale	223 252	111 109	112 143	...	...	...	...	...
Tema	292 773	139 958	152 815	...	...	...	...	...
Guinea - Guinée[4]								
15 III 2014 (CDJC)								
Boke	185 548	94 132	91 416	...	...	...	...	...
CONAKRY	1 659 785	832 734	827 051	...	1 879 695	942 184	937 511	...
Coyah	216 928	103 627	113 301	...	...	...	...	...
Dubreka	157 017	79 041	77 976	...	...	...	...	...
Kankan	190 722	96 574	94 148	...	...	...	...	...
Kindia	138 695	67 746	70 949	...	...	...	...	...
Nzérékoré	195 027	97 286	97 741	...	...	...	...	...
Siguiri	127 492	65 562	61 930	...	...	...	...	...
Guinea-Bissau - Guinée-Bissau								
15 III 2009 (CDFC)								
BISSAU	387 909	...	...	...	...	...	...	...
Kenya								
1 VII 2010 (ESDF)								
Eldoret	247 500	...	...	...	312 351[5]	...	...	...
Garissa	109 224	...	...	...	115 744[5]	...	...	...
Kangundo	13 119	...	...	...	205 603[5]	...	...	...
Karuri	107 754	...	...	...	115 731[5]	...	...	...
Kikuyu	200 285	...	...	...	264 714[5]	...	...	...
Kisumu	254 016	...	...	...	383 444[5]	...	...	...
Machakos	40 819	...	...	...	109 648[5]	...	...	...
Mavoko/AthiRiver	108 924	...	...	...	135 571[5]	...	...	...
Mombasa	905 627	...	...	...	925 137[5]	...	...	...
NAIROBI	3 109 861	1 590 658	1 519 203	695	...	...	...	...
Nakuru	343 395	...	...	...	367 183[5]	...	...	...
Ngong	103 927	...	...	...	107 042[5]	...	...	...
Ruiru	238 329	...	...	...	240 226[5]	...	...	...
Thika	136 386	...	...	...	151 225[5]	...	...	...
Lesotho[6]								
10 IV 2016 (CDJC)								
MASERU	330 760	...	...	...	...	...	...	...
Liberia - Libéria[7]								
21 III 2008 (CDFC)								
MONROVIA	...	...	...	...	970 824	476 473	494 351	...
Madagascar								
1 VII 2005 (ESDF)								
ANTANANARIVO[8]	1 015 140	495 393	519 747	...	...	...	...	...
Antsirabe	...	...	...	...	180 180	87 691	92 489	...
Fianarantsoa	...	...	...	...	165 220	80 410	84 810	...
Mahajanga	...	...	...	...	152 785	74 359	78 426	...
Toamasina	...	...	...	...	203 469	99 026	104 443	...
Toliara	...	...	...	...	113 993	55 479	58 514	...
Malawi								
1 VII 2016 (ESDF)								
Blantyre City	920 226[2]	464 649[2]	455 577[2]	220	...	...	...	...
LILONGWE	1 098 167[2]	559 741[2]	538 426[2]	456	...	...	...	...
Mzuzu City	239 008[2]	119 374[2]	119 634[2]	48	...	...	...	...
Zomba City	147 131[2]	73 250[2]	73 881[2]	39	...	...	...	...
Mali								
1 IV 2009 (CDFC)								
BAMAKO[9]	...	...	...	...	1 810 366	907 643	902 723	...
Kayes	...	...	...	...	149 129	76 470	72 659	...
Koutiala	...	...	...	...	141 444	70 905	70 539	...
Mopti	...	...	...	...	120 786	60 080	60 706	...

8. Population of capital cities and cities of 100 000 or more inhabitants: latest available year, 1998 - 2017
Population des capitales et des villes de 100 000 habitants ou plus : dernière année disponible, 1998 - 2017 (continued - suite)

Continent, country or area, date, code[a] and city / Continent, pays ou zone, date, code[a] et ville	City proper - Ville proprement dite				Urban agglomeration - Agglomération urbaine			
	Population			Surface area - Superficie (km²)	Population			Surface area - Superficie (km²)
	Both sexes - Les deux sexes	Male - Masculin	Female - Féminin		Both sexes - Les deux sexes	Male - Masculin	Female - Féminin	

AFRICA - AFRIQUE

Mali
1 IV 2009 (CDFC)

Ségou	...	...	...	...	133 501	66 819	66 682	...
Sikasso	...	...	...	...	226 618	114 171	112 447	...

Mauritania - Mauritanie[10]
24 III 2013 (CDJC)

Nouadhibou	118 167	67 275	50 892	...	...	...	...	...
NOUAKCHOTT	958 399	494 885	463 514	...	...	...	...	...

Mauritius - Maurice[11]
1 VII 2017 (ESDJ)

Beau Bassin - Rose Hill	104 389	51 752	52 637	...	...	...	...	...
PORT LOUIS	148 147	74 016	74 131	...	...	...	...	...
Vacoas - Phoenix	106 183	51 270	54 913	...	...	...	...	...

Morocco - Maroc
1 VII 2014 (ESDF)

Agadir	505 765	...	...	...	598 484	...	...	...
Al Hoceima	137 024	...	...	...	399 586	...	...	...
Azilal	100 327	...	...	...	553 121	...	...	...
Béni-Mellal	325 405	...	...	...	549 559	...	...	...
Benslimane	113 341	...	...	...	232 509	...	...	...
Berkane	182 203	...	...	...	288 807	...	...	...
Berrechid	272 356	...	...	...	482 119	...	...	...
Casablanca (Dar-el-Beida)	3 352 399	...	...	...	3 352 399	...	...	...
Chtouka-Ait Baha	111 522	...	...	...	369 706	...	...	...
El Hajeb	121 226	...	...	...	246 461	...	...	...
El Kelâa des Sraghna	152 900	...	...	...	536 191	...	...	...
El-Jadida	311 038	...	...	...	784 432	...	...	...
Errachidia	193 748	...	...	...	418 069	...	...	...
Essaouira	106 319	...	...	...	450 569	...	...	...
Fès	1 126 551	...	...	...	1 146 967	...	...	...
Fquih Ben Salah	204 732	...	...	...	502 021	...	...	...
Guelmim	138 788	...	...	...	187 428	...	...	...
Inezgane ait Melloul	511 209	...	...	...	538 786	...	...	...
Kénitra	604 206	...	...	...	1 058 359	...	...	...
Khemisset	279 890	...	...	...	541 868	...	...	...
Khénifra	228 509	...	...	...	370 952	...	...	...
Khouribga	376 829	...	...	...	541 365	...	...	...
Laayoune	234 870	...	...	...	237 384	...	...	...
Larache	264 802	...	...	...	496 264	...	...	...
Marrakech	978 045	...	...	...	1 325 571	...	...	...
M'Diq-Fnideq	196 586	...	...	...	208 337	...	...	...
Médiouna	119 054	...	...	...	171 684	...	...	...
Meknès	685 408	...	...	...	833 456	...	...	...
Midelt	124 684	...	...	...	288 757	...	...	...
Mohammedia	288 131	...	...	...	403 087	...	...	...
Nador	390 913	...	...	...	564 354	...	...	...
Nouaceur	271 052	...	...	...	331 651	...	...	...
Ouarzazate	113 230	...	...	...	297 018	...	...	...
Oued Ed-Dahab	105 193	...	...	...	125 747	...	...	...
Oujda	504 480	...	...	...	550 406	...	...	...
RABAT	578 644	...	...	...	578 644	...	...	...
Rehamna	102 715	...	...	...	314 605	...	...	...
Safi	345 595	...	...	...	691 128	...	...	...
Salé	912 957	...	...	...	979 228	...	...	...
Sefrou	154 973	...	...	...	286 009	...	...	...
Settat	215 665	...	...	...	633 500	...	...	...
Sidi Kacem	168 302	...	...	...	521 694	...	...	...
Sidi Slimane	130 576	...	...	...	319 528	...	...	...
Skhirate-Témara	512 867	...	...	...	570 855	...	...	...
Tanger	998 972	...	...	...	1 059 562	...	...	...
Taourirt	149 604	...	...	...	232 712	...	...	...
Taroudannt	247 428	...	...	...	837 797	...	...	...
Taza	207 719	...	...	...	528 917	...	...	...
Tétouan	396 806	...	...	...	549 062	...	...	...
Youssoufia	100 617	...	...	...	251 692	...	...	...

8. Population of capital cities and cities of 100 000 or more inhabitants: latest available year, 1998 - 2017
Population des capitales et des villes de 100 000 habitants ou plus : dernière année disponible, 1998 - 2017 (continued - suite)

Continent, country or area, date, code[a] and city / Continent, pays ou zone, date, code[a] et ville	City proper - Ville proprement dite				Urban agglomeration - Agglomération urbaine			
	Population			Surface area - Superficie (km²)	Population			Surface area - Superficie (km²)
	Both sexes - Les deux sexes	Male - Masculin	Female - Féminin		Both sexes - Les deux sexes	Male - Masculin	Female - Féminin	
AFRICA - AFRIQUE								
Mozambique								
1 VII 2015 (ESDF)								
Beira	460 904	231 684	229 220	633	...	...	...	...
Chimoio	314 751	158 700	156 051	174	...	...	...	...
Lichinga	214 614	108 147	106 467	290	...	...	...	...
MAPUTO	1 241 702	597 109	644 593	300	...	...	...	...
Matola	927 123	447 365	479 759	375	...	...	...	...
Maxixe	127 372	57 145	70 227	282	...	...	...	...
Nacala	241 066	118 325	122 741	340	...	...	...	...
Nampula	622 423	313 343	309 080	320	...	...	...	...
Pemba	199 457	99 447	100 010	194	...	...	...	...
Quelimane	241 077	121 599	119 478	117	...	...	...	...
Tete	213 406	107 128	106 278	286	...	...	...	...
Xai-Xai	128 946	59 452	69 494	135	...	...	...	...
Namibia - Namibie								
28 VIII 2011 (CDFC)								
WINDHOEK	325 858	160 730	165 128	...	...	...	...	...
Niger								
10 XII 2012 (CDJC)								
Maradi	267 249	137 051	130 198	...	...	...	...	...
NIAMEY	1 026 848	511 166	515 682	...	...	...	...	...
Tahoua	149 498	74 096	75 402	...	...	...	...	...
Zinder	322 935	162 705	160 230	...	...	...	...	...
Republic of South Sudan - République de Soudan du Sud								
21 IV 2008 (CDFC)								
JUBA	230 195	129 427	100 768	56	...	...	...	...
Malakal	114 528	60 440	54 088	25	...	...	...	...
Wau	118 331	63 777	54 554	75	...	...	...	...
Reunion - Réunion								
1 I 2010 (CDJC)								
SAINT-DENIS	145 022	68 075	76 947	142.8	174 973	82 815	92 158	230
Saint-Paul	103 346	51 327	52 019	241.3	172 137	84 793	87 344	376
Rwanda								
15 VIII 2012 (CDJC)								
KIGALI	859 332	451 673	407 659	...	...	...	...	...
Saint Helena ex. dep. - Sainte-Hélène sans dép.[12]								
7 II 2016 (CDJC)								
JAMESTOWN	629	...	...	...	...	...	...	...
Sao Tome and Principe - Sao Tomé-et-Principe								
25 VIII 2001 (CDJC)								
SAO TOME	...	...	...	...	49 957	24 003	25 954	...
Senegal - Sénégal[13]								
31 XII 2011 (ESDJ)								
DAKAR	1 056 009	526 299	529 710	...	...	...	...	...
Diourbel	279 667	136 961	142 706	...	...	...	...	...
Guediawaye	317 464	157 992	159 472	...	...	...	...	...
Kaolack	410 577	199 057	211 520	...	...	...	...	...
Mbour	605 346	307 461	297 885	...	...	...	...	...
Pikine	941 245	472 868	468 377	...	...	...	...	...
Rufisque	333 032	167 942	165 090	...	...	...	...	...
Saint Louis	277 245	136 957	140 289	...	...	...	...	...
Thiès	618 436	304 087	314 349	...	...	...	...	...
Ziguinchor	337 295	167 048	170 247	...	...	...	...	...
Seychelles[14]								
26 VIII 2010 (CDFC)								
VICTORIA	...	...	...	...	26 450	...	...	...
Sierra Leone								
5 XII 2015 (CDFC)								
Bo	174 369	83 998	90 371	...	...	...	...	...
FREETOWN	1 055 964	528 207	527 757	...	...	...	...	...
Kenema	200 443	97 818	102 625	...	...	...	...	...
Makeni	124 634	61 494	63 140	...	...	...	...	...

8. Population of capital cities and cities of 100 000 or more inhabitants: latest available year, 1998 - 2017
Population des capitales et des villes de 100 000 habitants ou plus : dernière année disponible, 1998 - 2017 (continued - suite)

Continent, country or area, date, code[a] and city / Continent, pays ou zone, date, code[a] et ville	City proper - Ville proprement dite				Urban agglomeration - Agglomération urbaine			
	Population			Surface area - Superficie (km²)	Population			Surface area - Superficie (km²)
	Both sexes - Les deux sexes	Male - Masculin	Female - Féminin		Both sexes - Les deux sexes	Male - Masculin	Female - Féminin	
AFRICA - AFRIQUE								
Somalia - Somalie								
1 VII 2001 (ESDF)								
MOGADISHU	*1 212 000*	...	...	...	...	...	...	...
South Africa - Afrique du Sud								
10 X 2011 (CDFC)								
CAPE TOWN[15]	433 688	209 082	224 607	...	...	...	...	...
Durban	595 061	288 871	306 189	...	...	...	...	...
Johannesburg	957 441	484 293	473 148	...	...	...	...	...
PRETORIA[15]	741 651	359 139	382 512	...	...	...	...	...
Togo[2]								
1 VII 2015 (ESDF)								
Kara	*104 400*	...	...	...	...	...	...	...
LOME	...	...	...	...	*1 788 600*	...	...	...
Sokode	*101 900*	...	...	...	...	...	...	...
Tunisia - Tunisie[16]								
23 IV 2014 (CDFC)								
Monastir	...	...	...	...	548 828	274 215	274 613	...
TUNIS	...	...	...	...	1 056 247	528 145	528 102	...
Uganda - Ouganda								
27 VIII 2014 (CDFC)								
Gulu[17]	...	...	...	...	149 802	...	...	...
Hoima[17]	...	...	...	...	100 126	...	...	...
KAMPALA	1 507 114	...	...	...	...	...	...	...
Kasese[17]	...	...	...	...	101 557	...	...	...
Kira[17]	...	...	...	...	317 428	...	...	...
Lugazi[17]	...	...	...	...	114 163	...	...	...
Makindye Ssabagabo[17]	...	...	...	...	282 664	...	...	...
Masaka[17]	...	...	...	...	103 293	...	...	...
Mbarara[17]	...	...	...	...	195 160	...	...	...
Mukono[17]	...	...	...	...	162 744	...	...	...
Nansana[17]	...	...	...	...	365 857	...	...	...
United Republic of Tanzania - République Unie de Tanzanie								
26 VIII 2012 (CDFC)								
Dar es Salaam	4 364 541	2 125 786	2 238 755	...	...	...	...	...
DODOMA	2 083 588	1 014 974	1 068 614	...	...	...	...	...
Mwanza	2 772 509	1 360 381	1 412 128	...	...	...	...	...
Zanzibar	1 303 569	630 677	672 892	...	...	...	...	...
Western Sahara - Sahara occidental[18]								
1 VII 1999 (ESDF)								
EL AAIUN	*169 000*	...	...	...	...	...	...	...
Zambia - Zambie								
16 X 2010 (CDJC)								
Chingola	216 626	108 464	108 162	...	...	...	...	...
Chipata	455 783	224 934	230 849	...	...	...	...	...
Kabwe	202 360	98 781	103 579	...	...	...	...	...
Kasama	231 824	114 208	117 616	...	...	...	...	...
Kitwe	517 543	256 740	260 803	...	...	...	...	...
Livingstone	139 509	68 763	70 746	...	...	...	...	...
Luanshya	156 059	77 368	78 691	...	...	...	...	...
LUSAKA	1 747 152	860 424	886 728	...	...	...	...	...
Mufulira	162 889	81 355	81 534	...	...	...	...	...
Ndola	451 246	223 020	228 226	...	...	...	...	...
Zimbabwe								
17 VIII 2012 (CDFC)								
Bulawayo	653 337	303 346	349 991	...	...	...	...	...
Chitungwiza	356 840	168 600	188 240	...	...	...	...	...
HARARE	1 485 231	716 595	768 636	...	...	...	...	...
Mutare	262 124	125 850	136 274	...	...	...	...	...

8. Population of capital cities and cities of 100 000 or more inhabitants: latest available year, 1998 - 2017
Population des capitales et des villes de 100 000 habitants ou plus : dernière année disponible, 1998 - 2017 (continued - suite)

Continent, country or area, date, code[a] and city / Continent, pays ou zone, date, code[a] et ville	City proper - Ville proprement dite				Urban agglomeration - Agglomération urbaine			
	Population			Surface area - Superficie (km²)	Population			Surface area - Superficie (km²)
	Both sexes - Les deux sexes	Male - Masculin	Female - Féminin		Both sexes - Les deux sexes	Male - Masculin	Female - Féminin	
AMERICA, NORTH - AMÉRIQUE DU NORD								
Anguilla								
11 V 2011 (CDFC)								
THE VALLEY	2 812	...	...	...	...	...	...	...
Aruba								
29 IX 2010 (CDJC)								
ORANJESTAD	28 295	13 139	15 156	...	...	...	...	...
Bahamas								
1 VII 2016* (ESDF)								
NASSAU	266 100	128 100	138 000	...	...	...	...	...
Belize								
1 VII 2017 (ESDF)								
BELMOPAN	*21 814*	*10 715*	*11 099*	...	...	...	...	...
Bermuda - Bermudes								
20 V 2016 (CDJC)								
HAMILTON	854	480	374	...	...	...	...	...
Canada[19]								
1 VII 2017* (ESDJ)								
Abbotsford[20]	149 928	74 782	75 146	...	...	...	...	...
Abbotsford-Mission	...	...	...	...	190 714[20]	95 665[20]	95 049[20]	605.2
Ajax	121 780[20]	59 272[20]	62 508[20]	67.1	...	...	...	...
Barrie	153 356[20]	75 074[20]	78 282[20]	77.4	209 081[20]	103 926[20]	105 155[20]	897.8
Brampton	603 346[20]	299 363[20]	303 983[20]	266.3	...	...	...	...
Brantford	102 159[20]	49 779[20]	52 380[20]	72.5	147 489[20]	72 490[20]	74 999[20]	1073.1
Burlington	205 960[20]	99 743[20]	106 217[20]	185.7	...	...	...	...
Burnaby	249 197[20]	123 468[20]	125 729[20]	90.6	...	...	...	...
Calgary	1 336 274[20]	673 246[20]	663 028[20]	825.3	1 488 841[20]	751 009[20]	737 832[20]	5107.5
Cambridge	140 099[20]	69 495[20]	70 604[20]	113	...	...	...	...
Chatham-Kent	105 529[20]	51 865[20]	53 664[20]	2458.1	...	...	...	...
Coquitlam	140 028[20]	69 557[20]	70 471[20]	122.3	...	...	...	...
Delta	110 848[20]	54 976[20]	55 872[20]	180.1	...	...	...	...
Edmonton	981 280[20]	494 654[20]	486 626[20]	684.4	1 411 945[20]	712 386[20]	699 559[20]	9426.7
Gatineau	284 557[20]	139 578[20]	144 979[20]	343	336 670[20]	166 629[20]	170 041[20]	...
Greater Sudbury / Grand Sudbury	164 926[20]	81 438[20]	83 488[20]	3227.4	165 270[20]	81 579[20]	83 691[20]	3410.6
Guelph	135 474[20]	66 037[20]	69 437[20]	87.2	159 988[20]	78 471[20]	81 517[20]	593.5
Halifax	431 479[20]	212 515[20]	218 964[20]	5490.3	431 701[20]	212 627[20]	219 074[20]	5495.7
Hamilton	579 200[20]	286 129[20]	293 071[20]	1117.2	787 195[20]	386 670[20]	400 525[20]	1371.9
Kelowna	132 084[20]	64 365[20]	67 719[20]	211.8	202 208[20]	99 483[20]	102 725[20]	2904.9
Kingston	136 685[20]	67 261[20]	69 424[20]	451.2	173 862[20]	86 447[20]	87 415[20]	1938.9
Kitchener	242 368[20]	120 405[20]	121 963[20]	136.8	...	...	...	...
Kitchener-Cambridge-Waterloo	...	...	...	...	527 765[20]	262 674[20]	265 091[20]	827.4
Langley	143 224[20]	70 563[20]	72 661[20]	308	...	...	...	...
Laval	437 413[20]	214 800[20]	222 613[20]	247.1	...	...	...	...
Lévis V	145 584[20]	71 820[20]	73 764[20]	449.3	...	...	...	...
London	404 699[20]	197 182[20]	207 517[20]	420.6	521 756[20]	255 323[20]	266 433[20]	2665.6
Longueuil	246 855[20]	121 293[20]	125 562[20]	115.6	...	...	...	...
Markham	342 970[20]	168 170[20]	174 800[20]	212.6	...	...	...	...
Mississauga	828 854[20]	407 791[20]	421 063[20]	292.4	...	...	...	...
Moncton	85 198[20]	42 120[20]	43 078[20]	141.2	152 169[20]	75 456[20]	76 713[20]	2406.3
Montréal	1 779 726[20]	880 796[20]	898 930[20]	365.1	4 138 254[20]	2 045 363[20]	2 092 891[20]	4258.3
Oakville	211 382[20]	103 002[20]	108 380[20]	138.9	...	...	...	...
Oshawa	170 071[20]	83 340[20]	86 731[20]	145.7	402 399[20]	198 175[20]	204 224[20]	903.5
OTTAWA	994 837[20]	487 147[20]	507 690[20]	2790.2	1 040 346[20]	509 439[20]	530 907[20]	...
Ottawa - Gatineau	...	...	...	...	1 377 016[20]	676 068[20]	700 948[20]	6287
Peterborough	84 230[20]	39 802[20]	44 428[20]	63.8	126 291[20]	60 851[20]	65 440[20]	1506.9
Québec	542 298[20]	265 266[20]	277 032[20]	454.1	812 205[20]	400 338[20]	411 867[20]	3349.1
Red Deer	103 588[20]	51 784[20]	51 804[20]	104.3	...	...	...	...
Regina	228 928[20]	113 923[20]	115 005[20]	145.5	253 220[20]	126 619[20]	126 601[20]	3408.3
Richmond	216 288[20]	105 004[20]	111 284[20]	129.3	...	...	...	...
Richmond Hill	208 370[20]	101 825[20]	106 545[20]	100.9	...	...	...	...
Saanich	119 229[20]	58 440[20]	60 789[20]	103.8	...	...	...	...
Saguenay	145 965[20]	72 668[20]	73 297[20]	1126.5	159 258[20]	79 680[20]	79 578[20]	2564
Saint John	70 785[20]	34 125[20]	36 660[20]	315.8	128 541[20]	62 691[20]	65 850[20]	3362.9

8. Population of capital cities and cities of 100 000 or more inhabitants: latest available year, 1998 - 2017
Population des capitales et des villes de 100 000 habitants ou plus : dernière année disponible, 1998 - 2017 (continued - suite)

Continent, country or area, date, code[a] and city / Continent, pays ou zone, date, code[a] et ville	City proper - Ville proprement dite				Urban agglomeration - Agglomération urbaine			
	Population			Surface area - Superficie (km²)	Population			Surface area - Superficie (km²)
	Both sexes - Les deux sexes	Male - Masculin	Female - Féminin		Both sexes - Les deux sexes	Male - Masculin	Female - Féminin	
AMERICA, NORTH - AMÉRIQUE DU NORD								
Canada[19]								
1 VII 2017* (ESDJ)								
Saskatoon	273 010[20]	136 443[20]	136 567[20]	209.6	323 809[20]	162 475[20]	161 334[20]	5214.5
Sherbrooke	167 162[20]	82 279[20]	84 883[20]	353.5	218 633[20]	107 903[20]	110 730[20]	1459.6
St. Catharines[20]	140 370	67 548	72 822	...				
St. Catharines-Niagara	...	...	...		416 539[20]	203 176[20]	213 363[20]	1397.5
St. John's	113 948[20]	55 337[20]	58 611[20]	446.1	219 207[20]	108 065[20]	111 142[20]	804.7
Surrey	518 467[20]	258 981[20]	259 486[20]	316.4	...	...	...	...
Terrebonne	116 319[20]	58 033[20]	58 286[20]	154.7	...	...	...	...
Thunder Bay	110 172[20]	53 840[20]	56 332[20]	328.2	124 164[20]	61 128[20]	63 036[20]	2556.4
Toronto	2 929 886[20]	1 426 359[20]	1 503 527[20]	630.2	6 346 088[20]	3 107 520[20]	3 238 568[20]	5905.7
Trois-Rivières	137 188[20]	66 904[20]	70 284[20]	288.9	158 942[20]	77 971[20]	80 971[20]	1041.2
Vancouver	675 218[20]	333 943[20]	341 275[20]	115	2 571 262[20]	1 270 374[20]	1 300 888[20]	2882.5
Vaughan	323 281[20]	158 554[20]	164 727[20]	273.5	...	...	...	...
Victoria	92 141[20]	44 130[20]	48 011[20]	19.5	377 414[20]	184 123[20]	193 291[20]	696.1
Waterloo	113 520[20]	56 780[20]	56 740[20]	64	...	...	...	...
Whitby	135 566[20]	66 520[20]	69 046[20]	146.5	...	...	...	...
Windsor	233 763[20]	114 223[20]	119 540[20]	146.3	344 747[20]	169 684[20]	175 063[20]	1022.3
Winnipeg	749 534[20]	370 495[20]	379 039[20]	464.1	825 713[20]	409 303[20]	416 410[20]	5303.1
Cayman Islands - Îles Caïmanes[21]								
10 X 2010 (CDJC)								
GEORGE TOWN	28 089	14 253	13 836	...	...	...	...	...
Costa Rica[22]								
1 VII 2017 (ESDJ)								
Alajuela	302 074	153 271	148 803	388.4	...	...	...	...
Cartago	160 457	80 593	79 864	287.8	...	...	...	...
Desamparados	238 312	118 840	119 472	118.3	...	...	...	...
Goicoechea	134 855	66 498	68 357	31.5	...	...	...	...
Heredia	138 562	68 164	70 398	282.6	...	...	...	...
La Unión	108 990	54 724	54 266	44.8	...	...	...	...
Pérez Zeledón	142 550	71 159	71 391	1905.5	...	...	...	...
Pococí	144 339	74 936	69 403	2403.5	...	...	...	...
Puntarenas	134 400	68 897	65 503	1842.3	...	...	...	...
San Carlos	191 126	98 205	92 921	3348	...	...	...	...
SAN JOSÉ	339 581	168 055	171 526	44.6	...	...	...	...
Cuba								
31 XII 2017 (ESDJ)								
Bayamo	159 629	...	...	27[23]	...	...	...	...
Camagüey	306 152	...	...	82[23]	...	...	...	...
Ciego de Ávila	119 859	...	...	21[23]	...	...	...	...
Cienfuegos	150 736	...	...	46[23]	...	...	...	...
Guantánamo	215 691	...	...	34[23]	...	...	...	...
Holguín	294 965	...	...	58[23]	...	...	...	...
LA HABANA	2 129 553	...	...	721[23]	...	...	...	...
Las Tunas	169 711	...	...	31[23]	...	...	...	...
Matanzas	140 545	...	...	44[23]	...	...	...	...
Pinar del Río	143 012	...	...	32[23]	...	...	...	...
Sancti Spíritus	108 482	...	...	23[23]	...	...	...	...
Santa Clara	216 142	...	...	44[23]	...	...	...	...
Santiago de Cuba	433 498	...	...	70[23]	...	...	...	...
Dominican Republic - République dominicaine								
1 VII 2011 (ESDJ)								
Azua	102 339[2]	51 620[2]	50 719[2]	155	...	...	...	...
Bajos de Haina	143 807[2]	71 130[2]	72 677[2]	40	...	...	...	...
Baní	177 588[2]	88 818[2]	88 770[2]	740	...	...	...	...
Boca Chica	122 216[2]	61 317[2]	60 899[2]	142	...	...	...	...
Bonao	148 857[2]	73 877[2]	74 980[2]	674	...	...	...	...
Higüey	211 453[2]	106 575[2]	104 878[2]	2026	...	...	...	...
La Romana	152 454[2]	73 291[2]	79 163[2]	263	...	...	...	...
La Vega	273 547[2]	137 511[2]	136 036[2]	641	...	...	...	...
Los Alcarrizos	249 595[2]	126 001[2]	123 594[2]	46	...	...	...	...
Moca	182 767[2]	91 506[2]	91 261[2]	337	...	...	...	...

8. Population of capital cities and cities of 100 000 or more inhabitants: latest available year, 1998 - 2017
Population des capitales et des villes de 100 000 habitants ou plus : dernière année disponible, 1998 - 2017 (continued - suite)

Continent, country or area, date, code[a] and city / Continent, pays ou zone, date, code[a] et ville	City proper - Ville proprement dite				Urban agglomeration - Agglomération urbaine			
	Population			Surface area - Superficie (km²)	Population			Surface area - Superficie (km²)
	Both sexes - Les deux sexes	Male - Masculin	Female - Féminin		Both sexes - Les deux sexes	Male - Masculin	Female - Féminin	
AMERICA, NORTH - AMÉRIQUE DU NORD								
Dominican Republic - République dominicaine								
1 VII 2011 (ESDJ)								
Puerto Plata	156 123[2]	76 741[2]	79 382[2]	496	...	...	...	...
San Cristóbal	278 767[2]	138 614[2]	140 153[2]	214	...	...	...	...
San Francisco de Macorís	185 925[2]	92 282[2]	93 643[2]	760	...	...	...	...
San Juan de la Maguana	137 881[2]	70 406[2]	67 475[2]	1722	...	...	...	...
San Pedro de Macorís	233 255[2]	113 249[2]	120 006[2]	146	...	...	...	...
Santiago de los Caballeros	757 933[2]	372 332[2]	385 601[2]	529	...	...	...	...
SANTO DOMINGO	1 126 306[2]	537 506[2]	588 800[2]	91	1 126 306[2]	537 506[2]	588 800[2]	91
Santo Domingo East - Santo Domingo Este	966 393[2]	468 484[2]	497 909[2]	169	...	...	...	...
Santo Domingo North - Santo Domingo Norte	453 046[2]	228 840[2]	224 206[2]	388	...	...	...	...
Santo Domingo West - Santo Domingo Oeste	349 175[2]	170 849[2]	178 326[2]	54	...	...	...	...
El Salvador								
1 VII 2017 (ESDJ)								
Ahuachapán	129 750	61 829	67 921	244.8	...	...	...	...
Apopa	185 073	84 297	100 776	51.8	...	...	...	...
Ciudad Delgado	128 012	59 141	68 871	33.4	...	...	...	...
Ilopango	135 703	61 394	74 309	34.6	...	...	...	...
Mejicanos	144 872	65 747	79 125	22.1	...	...	...	...
San Martin	103 245	47 568	55 677	55.8	...	...	...	...
San Miguel	265 921	123 506	142 415	594	...	...	...	...
SAN SALVADOR	238 244	108 919	129 325	72.3	...	...	...	...
Santa Ana	272 554	129 805	142 749	400.1	...	...	...	...
Santa Tecla	138 695	62 884	75 811	112.2	...	...	...	...
Soyapango	283 223	128 956	154 267	29.7	...	...	...	...
Greenland - Groenland[24]								
1 VII 2017 (ESDJ)								
NUUK (GODTHAB)	17 635	9 317	8 318	...	...	...	...	...
Grenada - Grenade								
12 V 2011* (CDFC)								
ST. GEORGE'S	36 823	...	...	...	...	...	...	...
Guadeloupe								
8 III 1999 (CDJC)								
BASSE-TERRE	12 377	5 687	6 690	...	44 747	21 252	23 495	...
Pointe-à-Pitre	...	...	...	...	171 773	...	...	...
Guatemala								
24 XI 2002 (CDJC)								
CUIDAD DE GUATEMALA	942 348	444 429	497 919	...	...	...	...	...
Haiti - Haïti								
1 VII 1999 (ESDJ)								
Cap-Haitien	113 555	50 064	63 491	10	...	...	...	...
Carrefour	336 222	146 838	189 384	23	...	...	...	...
Delmas	284 079	124 774	159 305	26	...	...	...	...
PORT-AU-PRINCE	990 558	436 170	554 388	21	...	...	...	...
Honduras								
10 VIII 2013 (CDFC)								
Catacamas	117 493	57 796	59 697	...	...	...	...	...
Choloma	231 669	111 124	120 545	...	...	...	...	...
Choluteca	152 519	73 637	78 882	...	...	...	...	...
Comayagua	144 785	69 290	75 495	...	...	...	...	...
Danlí	195 916	97 441	98 474	...	...	...	...	...
El Progreso	188 366	89 734	98 633	...	...	...	...	...
Juticalpa	124 828	59 944	64 885	...	...	...	...	...
La Ceiba	197 267	93 209	104 058	...	...	...	...	...
Olanchito	104 609	50 858	53 750	...	...	...	...	...
Puerto Cortés	122 426	59 113	63 313	...	...	...	...	...
San Pedro Sula	719 064	343 111	375 953	...	...	...	...	...
TEGUCIGALPA	1 157 509	544 099	613 410	...	...	...	...	...
Villanueva	149 977	72 504	77 474	...	...	...	...	...
Jamaica - Jamaïque								
4 IV 2011 (CDJC)								
KINGSTON[25]	...	...	...	...	592 291	285 509	306 782	149
Montego Bay	...	...	...	...	111 037	53 601	57 436	76.7

8. Population of capital cities and cities of 100 000 or more inhabitants: latest available year, 1998 - 2017
Population des capitales et des villes de 100 000 habitants ou plus : dernière année disponible, 1998 - 2017 (continued - suite)

Continent, country or area, date, code[a] and city / Continent, pays ou zone, date, code[a] et ville	City proper - Ville proprement dite				Urban agglomeration - Agglomération urbaine			
	Population			Surface area - Superficie (km²)	Population			Surface area - Superficie (km²)
	Both sexes - Les deux sexes	Male - Masculin	Female - Féminin		Both sexes - Les deux sexes	Male - Masculin	Female - Féminin	

AMERICA, NORTH - AMÉRIQUE DU NORD

Jamaica - Jamaïque
4 IV 2011 (CDJC)

Portmore	...	...	...	...	182 800	85 380	97 420	182.1
Spanish Town	...	...	...	...	149 479	72 885	76 594	64.6

Martinique
1 I 2006 (CDJC)

FORT-DE-FRANCE	90 347	40 128	50 219	...	133 281	59 945	73 336	...

Mexico - Mexique[2]
1 VII 2017 (ESDJ)

Acapulco	...	...	...	...	930 744	448 895	481 850	...
Acayucan	...	...	...	...	121 298	58 397	62 902	...
Aguascalientes	...	...	...	...	1 043 618	507 577	536 042	...
Apatzingán de la Constitución	...	...	...	...	102 370	...	...	...
Campeche	...	...	...	...	170 685		...	...
Cancún	...	...	...	...	256 911	...	...	...
Cárdenas	...	...	...	...	847 144	427 387	419 757	...
Celaya	...	...	...	...	105 133	...	...	...
Chalco de Diaz Covarrubias	...	...	...	...	650 872	310 953	339 919	...
Chetumal	...	...	...	...	189 421	...	...	...
Chihuahua	...	...	...	...	970 211	470 431	499 780	...
Chilpacingo de los Bravo	...	...	...	...	217 441	...	...	...
Ciudad Acuña	...	...	...	...	146 195	...	...	...
Ciudad Del Carmen	...	...	...	...	192 071	...	...	...
Ciudad Guzmán	...	...	...	...	104 719	...	...	...
Ciudad Lázaro Cárdenas	...	...	...	...	144 818	...	...	...
Ciudad Obregón	...	...	...	...	343 292	...	...	...
Ciudad Valles	...	...	...	...	134 940	...	...	...
Ciudad Victoria	...	...	...	...	340 140	...	...	...
Coatzacoalcos	...	...	...	...	376 890	182 791	194 100	...
Colima-Villa de Álvarez	...	...	...	...	382 739	186 072	196 667	...
Comitán de Domínguez	...	...	...	...	112 730	...	...	...
Córdoba	...	...	...	...	338 704	160 377	178 327	...
Cuauhtemoc	...	...	...	...	132 959	...	...	...
Cuautla	...	...	...	...	485 999	234 503	251 496	...
Cuernavaca	...	...	...	...	1 020 959	490 525	530 434	...
Culiacán Rosales	...	...	...	...	775 082	...	...	...
Delicias	...	...	...	...	133 706	...	...	...
Ensenada	...	...	...	...	308 995	...	...	...
Fresnillo	...	...	...	...	135 377	...	...	...
Guadalajara	...	...	...	...	4 909 287	2 400 431	2 508 857	...
Guanajuato	...	...	...	...	115 086	...	...	...
Guaymas	...	...	...	...	228 454	113 767	114 687	...
Hermosillo	...	...	...	...	809 376	...	...	...
Heroica Nogales	...	...	...	...	242 584	...	...	...
Hidalgo del Parral	...	...	...	...	115 181	...	...	...
Iguala de la Independencia	...	...	...	...	122 924	...	...	...
Irapuato	...	...	...	...	419 065	...	...	...
Juárez	...	...	...	...	1 448 859	715 356	733 503	...
La Laguna	...	...	...	...	1 342 139	657 372	684 767	...
La Paz	...	...	...	...	255 294	...	...	...
La Piedad-Pénjamo	...	...	...	...	264 944	125 669	139 275	...
Lagos de Moreno	...	...	...	...	108 046	...	...	...
León	...	...	...	...	1 743 903	845 750	898 152	...
Los Mochis	...	...	...	...	291 195	...	...	...
Manzanillo	...	...	...	...	163 102	...	...	...
Matamoros	...	...	...	...	536 685	265 219	271 465	...
Mazatlán	...	...	...	...	424 522	...	...	...
Mérida	...	...	...	...	1 092 242	531 506	560 736	...
Mexicali	...	...	...	...	1 052 657	528 857	523 799	...
MEXICO, CIUDAD DE	...	...	...	...	21 650 668	10 478 042	11 172 625	...
Minatitlán	...	...	...	...	384 208	185 650	198 558	...
Monclova-Frontera	...	...	...	...	345 617	171 445	174 172	...
Monterrey	...	...	...	...	4 603 254	2 285 795	2 317 459	...
Morelia	...	...	...	...	901 782	430 392	471 390	...
Moroleón Uriangato - Moroleón-Uriangato	...	...	...	...	115 184	54 615	60 569	...

8. Population of capital cities and cities of 100 000 or more inhabitants: latest available year, 1998 - 2017
Population des capitales et des villes de 100 000 habitants ou plus : dernière année disponible, 1998 - 2017 (continued - suite)

Continent, country or area, date, code[a] and city / Continent, pays ou zone, date, code[a] et ville	City proper - Ville proprement dite				Urban agglomeration - Agglomération urbaine			
	Population			Surface area - Superficie (km²)	Population			Surface area - Superficie (km²)
	Both sexes - Les deux sexes	Male - Masculin	Female - Féminin		Both sexes - Les deux sexes	Male - Masculin	Female - Féminin	

AMERICA, NORTH - AMÉRIQUE DU NORD

Mexico - Mexique[2]
1 VII 2017 (ESDJ)

Navojoa	...	...	...	...	128 708	...	...	...
Nuevo Laredo	...	...	...	...	424 098	209 637	214 461	...
Oaxaca	...	...	...	...	665 644	312 970	352 674	...
Ocotlán	...	...	...	...	152 549	74 574	77 975	...
Orizaba	...	...	...	...	457 541	217 274	240 267	...
Pachuca	...	...	...	...	587 255	280 436	306 818	...
Piedras Negras	...	...	...	...	195 299	97 843	97 456	...
Playa del Carmen	...	...	...	...	208 096	...	...	...
Poza Rica	...	...	...	...	545 486	263 247	282 239	...
Puebla-Tlaxcala	...	...	...	...	3 017 463	1 446 389	1 571 074	...
Puerto Vallarta	...	...	...	...	461 213	231 196	230 017	...
Querétaro	...	...	...	...	1 250 429	606 901	643 529	...
Reynosa-Río Bravo	...	...	...	...	832 911	413 338	419 573	...
Rioverde-Ciudad Fernández	...	...	...	...	145 830	71 184	74 647	...
Salamanca	...	...	...	...	172 739	...	...	...
Saltillo	...	...	...	...	924 348	458 095	466 253	...
San Cristóbal de las Casas	...	...	...	...	177 696	...	...	...
San Francisco del Rincón	...	...	...	...	198 649	96 784	101 865	...
San José del Cabo	...	...	...	...	126 977	...	...	...
San Juan Bautista Tuxtepec	...	...	...	...	113 476	...	...	...
San Juan del Río	...	...	...	...	155 688	...	...	...
San Luis Potosí-Soledad de Graciano Sánchez	...	...	...	...	1 149 729	553 968	595 761	...
San Luis Rio Colorado	...	...	...	...	179 768	...	...	...
Tampico	...	...	...	...	946 517	459 434	487 083	...
Tapachula de Cordova y Ordoñez	...	...	...	...	235 336	...	...	...
Tecomán	...	...	...	...	161 942	81 085	80 857	...
Tehuacán	...	...	...	...	325 728	153 973	171 755	...
Tehuantepec	...	...	...	...	171 763	82 795	88 968	...
Tepatitlán De Morelos	...	...	...	...	101 992	...	...	...
Tepic	...	...	...	...	503 330	244 428	258 902	...
Teziutlán	...	...	...	...	133 781	63 541	70 240	...
Tianguistenco	...	...	...	...	185 558	90 217	95 341	...
Tijuana	...	...	...	...	1 996 587	999 493	997 094	...
Tlaxcala	...	...	...	...	561 014	269 667	291 347	...
Toluca	...	...	...	...	2 260 149	1 103 257	1 156 892	...
Tula	...	...	...	...	224 998	109 441	115 556	...
Tulancingo	...	...	...	...	268 873	127 476	141 398	...
Túxpan de Rodríguez Cano	...	...	...	...	117 843	...	...	...
Tuxtla Gutiérrez	...	...	...	...	782 703	375 446	407 257	...
Uruapan	...	...	...	...	299 965	...	...	...
Veracruz	...	...	...	...	876 738	416 470	460 268	...
Victoria de Durango	...	...	...	...	586 904	...	...	...
Villahermosa	...	...	...	...	843 392	411 005	432 387	...
Xalapa	...	...	...	...	732 835	346 805	386 030	...
Zacatecas-Guadalupe	...	...	...	...	345 581	165 680	179 901	...
Zamora-Jacona	...	...	...	...	265 316	127 690	137 626	...
Nicaragua								
1 VII 2009 (ESDJ)								
Chinandega	...	...	...	...	*106 635*	...	...	...
León	...	...	...	...	*156 049*	...	...	...
MANAGUA	...	...	...	...	*985 143*	...	...	...
Masaya	...	...	...	...	*110 491*	...	...	...
Tipitapa	...	...	...	...	*105 773*	...	...	...
Panama								
1 VII 2017 (ESDF)								
CIUDAD DE PANAMÁ	477 328[26]	227 308[26]	250 020[26]	98	1 086 788[26]	531 715[26]	555 073[26]	288
San Miguelito	364 962[26]	178 427[26]	186 535[26]	50	...	...	...	...
Puerto Rico - Porto Rico								
1 VII 2016 (ESDJ)								
Bayamón	184 374[27]	87 165[27]	97 209[27]	71	...	...	...	...
Caguas	132 164[27]	61 484[27]	70 680[27]	94	...	...	...	...
Carolina	158 457[27]	72 547[27]	85 910[27]	73	...	...	...	...

8. Population of capital cities and cities of 100 000 or more inhabitants: latest available year, 1998 - 2017
Population des capitales et des villes de 100 000 habitants ou plus : dernière année disponible, 1998 - 2017 (continued - suite)

Continent, country or area, date, code[a] and city / Continent, pays ou zone, date, code[a] et ville	City proper - Ville proprement dite				Urban agglomeration - Agglomération urbaine			
	Population			Surface area - Superficie (km²)	Population			Surface area - Superficie (km²)
	Both sexes - Les deux sexes	Male - Masculin	Female - Féminin		Both sexes - Les deux sexes	Male - Masculin	Female - Féminin	
AMERICA, NORTH - AMÉRIQUE DU NORD								
Puerto Rico - Porto Rico								
1 VII 2016 (ESDJ)								
Ponce	145 278[27]	69 855[27]	75 423[27]	184	...	...	...	...
SAN JUAN	347 052[27]	158 826[27]	188 226[27]	77	...	...	...	...
Saint Lucia - Sainte-Lucie[4]								
10 V 2010* (CDJC)								
CASTRIES	4 173	2 044	2 129	...				
Saint Pierre and Miquelon - Saint Pierre-et-Miquelon								
19 I 2006 (CDFC)								
SAINT-PIERRE	5 509	...		...				
Trinidad and Tobago - Trinité-et-Tobago								
9 I 2011 (CDJC)								
PORT-OF-SPAIN	37 074	18 008	19 066	12	...	...	...	...
Turks and Caicos Islands - Îles Turques et Caïques								
25 I 2012* (CDJC)								
GRAND TURK	4 831	2 325	2 506	...				
United States of America - États-Unis d'Amérique[28]								
1 VII 2016 (ESDJ)								
Abilene (TX)	122 225[29]	...	...	276.3[30]	...	...	...	...
Akron (OH)	197 633[29]	...	...	160.7[30]	...	...	...	...
Albuquerque (NM)	559 277[29]	...	...	487.4[30]	...	...	...	...
Alexandria (VA)	155 810[29]	...	...	39[30]	...	...	...	...
Allentown (PA)	120 443[29]	...	...	45.4[30]	...	...	...	...
Amarillo (TX)	199 582[29]	...	...	262.5[30]	...	...	...	...
Anaheim (CA)	351 043[29]	...	...	129.4[30]	...	...	...	...
Anchorage (AK)	298 192[29]	...	...	4420.1[30]	...	...	...	...
Ann Arbor (MI)	120 782[29]	...	...	72.7[30]	...	...	...	...
Antioch (CA)	110 898[29]	...	...	76.2[30]	...	...	...	...
Arlington (TX)	392 772[29]	...	...	248.2[30]	...	...	...	...
Arvada (CO)	117 453[29]	...	...	100[30]	...	...	...	...
Athens (GA)	123 371[29]	...	...	301.4[30]	...	...	...	...
Atlanta (GA)	472 522[29]	...	...	345.7[30]	...	...	...	...
Augusta (GA)	197 081[29]	...	...	783.4[30]	...	...	...	...
Aurora (CO)	361 710[29]	...	...	397.6[30]	...	...	...	...
Aurora (IL)	201 110[29]	...	...	116.3[30]	...	...	...	...
Austin (TX)	947 890[29]	...	...	810[30]	...	...	...	...
Bakersfield (CA)	376 380[29]	...	...	385.4[30]	...	...	...	...
Baltimore (MD)	614 664[29]	...	...	209.6[30]	...	...	...	...
Baton Rouge (LA)	227 715[29]	...	...	222.5[30]	...	...	...	...
Beaumont (TX)	118 299[29]	...	...	212.8[30]	...	...	...	...
Bellevue (WA)	141 400[29]	...	...	86.7[30]	...	...	...	...
Berkeley (CA)	121 240[29]	...	...	27.1[30]	...	...	...	...
Billings (MT)	110 323[29]	...	...	113.2[30]	...	...	...	...
Birmingham (AL)	212 157[29]	...	...	378.4[30]	...	...	...	...
Boise City (ID)	223 154[29]	...	...	212.6[30]	...	...	...	...
Boston (MA)	673 184[29]	...	...	125.2[30]	...	...	...	...
Boulder (CO)	108 090[29]	...	...	64.3[30]	...	...	...	...
Bridgeport (CT)	145 936[29]	...	...	41.6[30]	...	...	...	...
Broken Arrow (OK)	107 403[29]	...	...	159.9[30]	...	...	...	...
Brownsville (TX)	183 823[29]	...	...	343.1[30]	...	...	...	...
Buffalo (NY)	256 902[29]	...	...	104.6[30]	...	...	...	...
Burbank (CA)	104 447[29]	...	...	44.9[30]	...	...	...	...
Cambridge (MA)	110 651[29]	...	...	16.6[30]	...	...	...	...
Cape Coral (FL)	179 804[29]	...	...	273.5[30]	...	...	...	...
Carlsbad (CA)	113 952[29]	...	...	97.7[30]	...	...	...	...
Carrollton (TX)	133 351[29]	...	...	94[30]	...	...	...	...
Cary (NC)	162 320[29]	...	...	146.3[30]	...	...	...	...
Cedar Rapids (IA)	131 127[29]	...	...	183.3[30]	...	...	...	...
Centennial (CO)	109 932[29]	...	...	76.5[30]	...	...	...	...
Chandler (AZ)	247 477[29]	...	...	168.2[30]	...	...	...	...
Charleston (SC)	134 385[29]	...	...	282.4[30]	...	...	...	...

8. Population of capital cities and cities of 100 000 or more inhabitants: latest available year, 1998 - 2017
Population des capitales et des villes de 100 000 habitants ou plus : dernière année disponible, 1998 - 2017 (continued - suite)

Continent, country or area, date, code[a] and city Continent, pays ou zone, date, code[a] et ville	City proper - Ville proprement dite				Urban agglomeration - Agglomération urbaine			
	Population			Surface area - Superficie (km²)	Population			Surface area - Superficie (km²)
	Both sexes - Les deux sexes	Male - Masculin	Female - Féminin		Both sexes - Les deux sexes	Male - Masculin	Female - Féminin	

AMERICA, NORTH - AMÉRIQUE DU NORD

United States of America - États-Unis d'Amérique[28]
  1 VII 2016 (ESDJ)

Charlotte (NC)	842 051[29]	...	...	790.9[30]	...	...	...	...
Chattanooga (TN)	177 571[29]	...	...	370.6[30]	...	...	...	...
Chesapeake (VA)	237 940[29]	...	...	876.7[30]	...	...	...	...
Chicago (IL)	2 704 958[29]	...	...	588.8[30]	...	...	...	...
Chula Vista (CA)	267 172[29]	...	...	128.5[30]	...	...	...	...
Cincinnati (OH)	298 800[29]	...	...	200.4[30]	...	...	...	...
Clarksville (TN)	150 287[29]	...	...	254.5[30]	...	...	...	...
Clearwater (FL)	114 361[29]	...	...	67[30]	...	...	...	...
Cleveland (OH)	385 809[29]	...	...	201.3[30]	...	...	...	...
Clovis (CA)	106 583[29]	...	...	62.7[30]	...	...	...	...
College Station (TX)	112 141[29]	...	...	132.1[30]	...	...	...	...
Colorado Springs (CO)	465 101[29]	...	...	506.7[30]	...	...	...	...
Columbia (MO)	120 612[29]	...	...	168.3[30]	...	...	...	...
Columbia (SC)	134 309[29]	...	...	345.8[30]	...	...	...	...
Columbus (GA)	197 485[29]	...	...	560.5[30]	...	...	...	...
Columbus (OH)	860 090[29]	...	...	565.8[30]	...	...	...	...
Concord (CA)	128 726[29]	...	...	79.1[30]	...	...	...	...
Coral Springs (FL)	130 059[29]	...	...	61.6[30]	...	...	...	...
Corona (CA)	166 785[29]	...	...	102.2[30]	...	...	...	...
Corpus Christi (TX)	325 733[29]	...	...	452.1[30]	...	...	...	...
Costa Mesa (CA)	112 822[29]	...	...	40.7[30]	...	...	...	...
Dallas (TX)	1 317 929[29]	...	...	882.9[30]	...	...	...	...
Daly City (CA)	106 472[29]	...	...	19.8[30]	...	...	...	...
Davenport (IA)	102 612[29]	...	...	162.9[30]	...	...	...	...
Davie (FL)	101 871[29]	...	...	90.4[30]	...	...	...	...
Dayton (OH)	140 489[29]	...	...	144.2[30]	...	...	...	...
Denton (TX)	133 808[29]	...	...	241.9[30]	...	...	...	...
Denver (CO)	693 060[29]	...	...	397.1[30]	...	...	...	...
Des Moines (IA)	215 472[29]	...	...	230.3[30]	...	...	...	...
Detroit (MI)	672 795[29]	...	...	359.4[30]	...	...	...	...
Downey (CA)	113 267[29]	...	...	32.1[30]	...	...	...	...
Durham (NC)	263 016[29]	...	...	284.3[30]	...	...	...	...
El Cajon (CA)	103 768[29]	...	...	37.5[30]	...	...	...	...
El Monte (CA)	115 807[29]	...	...	24.8[30]	...	...	...	...
El Paso (TX)	683 080[29]	...	...	665[30]	...	...	...	...
Elgin (IL)	112 123[29]	...	...	97[30]	...	...	...	...
Elizabeth (NJ)	128 640[29]	...	...	31.9[30]	...	...	...	...
Elk Grove (CA)	169 743[29]	...	...	109.3[30]	...	...	...	...
Escondido (CA)	151 613[29]	...	...	96[30]	...	...	...	...
Eugene (OR)	166 575[29]	...	...	114.3[30]	...	...	...	...
Evansville (IN)	119 477[29]	...	...	122.6[30]	...	...	...	...
Everett (WA)	109 043[29]	...	...	86.1[30]	...	...	...	...
Fairfield (CA)	114 756[29]	...	...	106[30]	...	...	...	...
Fargo (ND)	120 762[29]	...	...	127.7[30]	...	...	...	...
Fayetteville (NC)	204 759[29]	...	...	382.7[30]	...	...	...	...
Fontana (CA)	209 665[29]	...	...	111.4[30]	...	...	...	...
Fort Collins (CO)	164 207[29]	...	...	144.6[30]	...	...	...	...
Fort Lauderdale (FL)	178 752[29]	...	...	89.7[30]	...	...	...	...
Fort Wayne (IN)	264 488[29]	...	...	286.5[30]	...	...	...	...
Fort Worth (TX)	854 113[29]	...	...	888.1[30]	...	...	...	...
Fremont (CA)	233 136[29]	...	...	200.6[30]	...	...	...	...
Fresno (CA)	522 053[29]	...	...	296.3[30]	...	...	...	...
Frisco (TX)	163 656[29]	...	...	175.3[30]	...	...	...	...
Fullerton (CA)	140 721[29]	...	...	58.1[30]	...	...	...	...
Gainesville (FL)	131 591[29]	...	...	161.4[30]	...	...	...	...
Garden Grove (CA)	174 858[29]	...	...	46.5[30]	...	...	...	...
Garland (TX)	234 943[29]	...	...	147.7[30]	...	...	...	...
Gilbert (AZ)	237 133[29]	...	...	176.1[30]	...	...	...	...
Glendale (AZ)	245 895[29]	...	...	153[30]	...	...	...	...

8. Population of capital cities and cities of 100 000 or more inhabitants: latest available year, 1998 - 2017
Population des capitales et des villes de 100 000 habitants ou plus : dernière année disponible, 1998 - 2017 (continued - suite)

Continent, country or area, date, code[a] and city Continent, pays ou zone, date, code[a] et ville	City proper - Ville proprement dite				Urban agglomeration - Agglomération urbaine			
	Population			Surface area - Superficie (km²)	Population			Surface area - Superficie (km²)
	Both sexes - Les deux sexes	Male - Masculin	Female - Féminin		Both sexes - Les deux sexes	Male - Masculin	Female - Féminin	
AMERICA, NORTH - AMÉRIQUE DU NORD								
United States of America - États-Unis d'Amérique[28]								
1 VII 2016 (ESDJ)								
Glendale (CA)	200 831[29]	...	...	78.8[30]	...	...	...	...
Grand Prairie (TX)	190 682[29]	...	...	187.2[30]	...	...	...	...
Grand Rapids (MI)	196 445[29]	...	...	115.1[30]	...	...	...	...
Greeley (CO)	103 990[29]	...	...	123.9[30]	...	...	...	...
Green Bay (WI)	105 139[29]	...	...	117.7[30]	...	...	...	...
Greensboro (NC)	287 027[29]	...	...	332.3[30]	...	...	...	...
Gresham (OR)	111 523[29]	...	...	60.3[30]	...	...	...	...
Hampton (VA)	135 410[29]	...	...	133.3[30]	...	...	...	...
Hartford (CT)	123 243[29]	...	...	45[30]	...	...	...	...
Hayward (CA)	158 937[29]	...	...	117.9[30]	...	...	...	...
Henderson (NV)	292 969[29]	...	...	271.2[30]	...	...	...	...
Hialeah (FL)	236 387[29]	...	...	55.6[30]	...	...	...	...
High Point City (NC)	111 223[29]	...	...	143[30]	...	...	...	...
Hillsboro (OR)	105 164[29]	...	...	64.7[30]	...	...	...	...
Hollywood (FL)	151 998[29]	...	...	70.6[30]	...	...	...	...
Houston (TX)	2 303 482[29]	...	...	1651.2[30]	...	...	...	...
Huntington Beach (CA)	200 652[29]	...	...	69.8[30]	...	...	...	...
Huntsville (AL)	193 079[29]	...	...	552.6[30]	...	...	...	...
Independence (MO)	117 030[29]	...	...	201.6[30]	...	...	...	...
Indianapolis (IN)	855 164[29]	...	...	936.3[30]	...	...	...	...
Inglewood (CA)	110 654[29]	...	...	23.5[30]	...	...	...	...
Irvine (CA)	266 122[29]	...	...	169.9[30]	...	...	...	...
Irving (TX)	238 289[29]	...	...	173.6[30]	...	...	...	...
Jackson (MS)	169 148[29]	...	...	287.6[30]	...	...	...	...
Jacksonville (FL)	880 619[29]	...	...	1935.9[30]	...	...	...	...
Jersey City (NJ)	264 152[29]	...	...	38.3[30]	...	...	...	...
Joliet (IL)	148 262[29]	...	...	166.9[30]	...	...	...	...
Jurupa Valley (CA)	103 541[29]	...	...	111.2[30]	...	...	...	...
Kansas City (KS)	151 709[29]	...	...	323.3[30]	...	...	...	...
Kansas City (MO)	481 420[29]	...	...	815.8[30]	...	...	...	...
Kent (WA)	127 514[29]	...	...	87.4[30]	...	...	...	...
Killeen (TX)	143 400[29]	...	...	138.7[30]	...	...	...	...
Knoxville (TN)	186 239[29]	...	...	255.2[30]	...	...	...	...
Lafayette (LA)	127 626[29]	...	...	139.4[30]	...	...	...	...
Lakeland (FL)	106 420[29]	...	...	170.7[30]	...	...	...	...
Lakewood (CO)	154 393[29]	...	...	111[30]	...	...	...	...
Lancaster (CA)	160 106[29]	...	...	244.2[30]	...	...	...	...
Lansing (MI)	116 020[29]	...	...	101.3[30]	...	...	...	...
Laredo (TX)	257 156[29]	...	...	261.9[30]	...	...	...	...
Las Cruces (NM)	101 759[29]	...	...	199.3[30]	...	...	...	...
Las Vegas (NV)	632 912[29]	...	...	348[30]	...	...	...	...
League City (TX)	102 010[29]	...	...	132.6[30]	...	...	...	...
Lewisville (TX)	104 659[29]	...	...	95[30]	...	...	...	...
Lexington-Fayette (KY)	318 449[29]	...	...	734.6[30]	...	...	...	...
Lincoln (NE)	280 364[29]	...	...	238.6[30]	...	...	...	...
Little Rock (AR)	198 541[29]	...	...	307.4[30]	...	...	...	...
Long Beach (CA)	470 130[29]	...	...	130.3[30]	...	...	...	...
Los Angeles (CA)	3 976 322[29]	...	...	1214[30]	...	...	...	...
Louisville (KY)	616 261[29]	...	...	841.7[30]	...	...	...	...
Lowell (MA)	110 558[29]	...	...	35.2[30]	...	...	...	...
Lubbock (TX)	252 506[29]	...	...	322.8[30]	...	...	...	...
Macon-Bibb (GA)	152 555[29]	...	...	645.6[30]	...	...	...	...
Madison (WI)	252 551[29]	...	...	199.3[30]	...	...	...	...
Manchester (NH)	110 506[29]	...	...	85.6[30]	...	...	...	...
McAllen (TX)	142 212[29]	...	...	151.1[30]	...	...	...	...
McKinney City (TX)	172 298[29]	...	...	163.1[30]	...	...	...	...
Memphis (TN)	652 717[29]	...	...	822[30]	...	...	...	...
Mesa (AZ)	484 587[29]	...	...	357.1[30]	...	...	...	...
Mesquite (TX)	143 736[29]	...	...	122.3[30]	...	...	...	...

8. Population of capital cities and cities of 100 000 or more inhabitants: latest available year, 1998 - 2017
Population des capitales et des villes de 100 000 habitants ou plus : dernière année disponible, 1998 - 2017 (continued - suite)

Continent, country or area, date, code[a] and city / Continent, pays ou zone, date, code[a] et ville	City proper - Ville proprement dite				Urban agglomeration - Agglomération urbaine			
	Population			Surface area - Superficie (km²)	Population			Surface area - Superficie (km²)
	Both sexes - Les deux sexes	Male - Masculin	Female - Féminin		Both sexes - Les deux sexes	Male - Masculin	Female - Féminin	

AMERICA, NORTH - AMÉRIQUE DU NORD

United States of America - États-Unis d'Amérique[28]
1 VII 2016 (ESDJ)

Miami (FL)	453 579[29]	...	...	93.2[30]	...	...	...	...
Miami Gardens (FL)	113 058[29]	...	...	47.2[30]	...	...	...	...
Midland City (TX)	134 610[29]	...	...	192.6[30]	...	...	...	...
Milwaukee (WI)	595 047[29]	...	...	249.1[30]	...	...	...	...
Minneapolis (MN)	413 651[29]	...	...	139.9[30]	...	...	...	...
Miramar (FL)	138 449[29]	...	...	76.1[30]	...	...	...	...
Mobile (AL)	192 904[29]	...	...	361[30]	...	...	...	...
Modesto (CA)	212 175[29]	...	...	111.3[30]	...	...	...	...
Montgomery (AL)	200 022[29]	...	...	414[30]	...	...	...	...
Moreno Valley (CA)	205 499[29]	...	...	132.8[30]	...	...	...	...
Murfreesboro (TN)	131 947[29]	...	...	144.7[30]	...	...	...	...
Murrieta (CA)	111 674[29]	...	...	87[30]	...	...	...	...
Naperville (IL)	147 122[29]	...	...	100.2[30]	...	...	...	...
Nashville-Davidson (TN)	660 388[29]	...	...	1232.7[30]	...	...	...	...
New Haven (CT)	129 934[29]	...	...	48.4[30]	...	...	...	...
New Orleans (LA)	391 495[29]	...	...	438.8[30]	...	...	...	...
New York (NY)	8 537 673[29]	...	...	780.8[30]	...	...	...	...
Newark (NJ)	281 764[29]	...	...	62.5[30]	...	...	...	...
Newport News (VA)	181 825[29]	...	...	178.9[30]	...	...	...	...
Norfolk (VA)	245 115[29]	...	...	138[30]	...	...	...	...
Norman (OK)	122 180[29]	...	...	463[30]	...	...	...	...
North Charleston (SC)	109 298[29]	...	...	190.8[30]	...	...	...	...
North Las Vegas (NV)	238 702[29]	...	...	253.9[30]	...	...	...	...
Norwalk (CA)	106 178[29]	...	...	25.1[30]	...	...	...	...
Oakland (CA)	420 005[29]	...	...	144.8[30]	...	...	...	...
Oceanside (CA)	175 464[29]	...	...	106.8[30]	...	...	...	...
Odessa (TX)	117 871[29]	...	...	117[30]	...	...	...	...
Oklahoma City (OK)	638 367[29]	...	...	1570.3[30]	...	...	...	...
Olathe (KS)	135 473[29]	...	...	157.6[30]	...	...	...	...
Omaha (NE)	446 970[29]	...	...	345[30]	...	...	...	...
Ontario (CA)	173 212[29]	...	...	129.3[30]	...	...	...	...
Orange (CA)	140 504[29]	...	...	65.7[30]	...	...	...	...
Orlando (FL)	277 173[29]	...	...	272.5[30]	...	...	...	...
Overland Park (KS)	188 966[29]	...	...	194.6[30]	...	...	...	...
Oxnard (CA)	207 906[29]	...	...	69.7[30]	...	...	...	...
Palm Bay City (FL)	110 104[29]	...	...	170.2[30]	...	...	...	...
Palmdale (CA)	157 356[29]	...	...	274.5[30]	...	...	...	...
Pasadena (CA)	142 059[29]	...	...	59.5[30]	...	...	...	...
Pasadena (TX)	153 351[29]	...	...	112.6[30]	...	...	...	...
Paterson (NJ)	147 000[29]	...	...	21.8[30]	...	...	...	...
Pearland (TX)	113 570[29]	...	...	120[30]	...	...	...	...
Pembroke Pines (FL)	168 587[29]	...	...	85.5[30]	...	...	...	...
Peoria (AZ)	164 173[29]	...	...	455[30]	...	...	...	...
Peoria (IL)	114 265[29]	...	...	124.9[30]	...	...	...	...
Philadelphia (PA)	1 567 872[29]	...	...	347.5[30]	...	...	...	...
Phoenix (AZ)	1 615 017[29]	...	...	1340.7[30]	...	...	...	...
Pittsburgh (PA)	303 625[29]	...	...	143.4[30]	...	...	...	...
Plano (TX)	286 057[29]	...	...	185.6[30]	...	...	...	...
Pomona (CA)	152 494[29]	...	...	59.4[30]	...	...	...	...
Pompano Beach (FL)	109 393[29]	...	...	62.3[30]	...	...	...	...
Port St. Lucie (FL)	185 132[29]	...	...	307.9[30]	...	...	...	...
Portland (OR)	639 863[29]	...	...	345.7[30]	...	...	...	...
Providence (RI)	179 219[29]	...	...	47.7[30]	...	...	...	...
Provo (UT)	116 868[29]	...	...	107.9[30]	...	...	...	...
Pueblo (CO)	110 291[29]	...	...	138.8[30]	...	...	...	...
Raleigh (NC)	458 880[29]	...	...	375.7[30]	...	...	...	...
Rancho Cucamonga (CA)	176 534[29]	...	...	103.6[30]	...	...	...	...
Reno (NV)	245 255[29]	...	...	277.9[30]	...	...	...	...
Renton (WA)	100 953[29]	...	...	60.7[30]	...	...	...	...

8. Population of capital cities and cities of 100 000 or more inhabitants: latest available year, 1998 - 2017
Population des capitales et des villes de 100 000 habitants ou plus : dernière année disponible, 1998 - 2017 (continued - suite)

Continent, country or area, date, code[a] and city Continent, pays ou zone, date, code[a] et ville	City proper - Ville proprement dite				Urban agglomeration - Agglomération urbaine			
	Population			Surface area - Superficie (km²)	Population			Surface area - Superficie (km²)
	Both sexes - Les deux sexes	Male - Masculin	Female - Féminin		Both sexes - Les deux sexes	Male - Masculin	Female - Féminin	

AMERICA, NORTH - AMÉRIQUE DU NORD

United States of America - États-Unis d'Amérique[28]
  1 VII 2016 (ESDJ)

Rialto (CA)	103 314[29]	...	...	57.8[30]	...	...	...	...
Richardson (TX)	113 347[29]	...	...	74[30]	...	...	...	...
Richmond (CA)	109 813[29]	...	...	77.8[30]	...	...	...	...
Richmond (VA)	223 170[29]	...	...	154.9[30]	...	...	...	...
Riverside (CA)	324 722[29]	...	...	210.4[30]	...	...	...	...
Rochester (MN)	114 011[29]	...	...	141.3[30]	...	...	...	...
Rochester (NY)	208 880[29]	...	...	92.7[30]	...	...	...	...
Rockford (IL)	147 651[29]	...	...	164.4[30]	...	...	...	...
Roseville (CA)	132 671[29]	...	...	111.3[30]	...	...	...	...
Round Rock (TX)	120 892[29]	...	...	92.1[30]	...	...	...	...
Sacramento (CA)	495 234[29]	...	...	253.6[30]	...	...	...	...
Salem (OR)	167 419[29]	...	...	125.8[30]	...	...	...	...
Salinas (CA)	157 218[29]	...	...	61.2[30]	...	...	...	...
Salt Lake City (UT)	193 744[29]	...	...	288[30]	...	...	...	...
San Angelo (TX)	100 702[29]	...	...	155.3[30]	...	...	...	...
San Antonio (TX)	1 492 510[29]	...	...	1194[30]	...	...	...	...
San Bernardino (CA)	216 239[29]	...	...	159.3[30]	...	...	...	...
San Buenaventura (CA)	109 592[29]	...	...	56.5[30]	...	...	...	...
San Diego (CA)	1 406 630[29]	...	...	842.3[30]	...	...	...	...
San Francisco (CA)	870 887[29]	...	...	121.5[30]	...	...	...	...
San Jose (CA)	1 025 350[29]	...	...	459.7[30]	...	...	...	...
San Mateo (CA)	103 959[29]	...	...	31.4[30]	...	...	...	...
Sandy Springs (GA)	105 703[29]	...	...	97.5[30]	...	...	...	...
Santa Ana (CA)	334 217[29]	...	...	70.3[30]	...	...	...	...
Santa Clara (CA)	125 948[29]	...	...	47.7[30]	...	...	...	...
Santa Clarita (CA)	181 972[29]	...	...	136.6[30]	...	...	...	...
Santa Maria (CA)	106 290[29]	...	...	59[30]	...	...	...	...
Santa Rosa (CA)	175 155[29]	...	...	106.9[30]	...	...	...	...
Savannah (GA)	146 763[29]	...	...	268.3[30]	...	...	...	...
Scottsdale (AZ)	246 645[29]	...	...	476.4[30]	...	...	...	...
Seattle (WA)	704 352[29]	...	...	217.1[30]	...	...	...	...
Shreveport (LA)	194 920[29]	...	...	277.5[30]	...	...	...	...
Simi Valley (CA)	126 327[29]	...	...	107.4[30]	...	...	...	...
Sioux Falls (SD)	174 360[29]	...	...	195.3[30]	...	...	...	...
South Bend (IN)	101 735[29]	...	...	107.2[30]	...	...	...	...
Spokane (WA)	215 973[29]	...	...	178[30]	...	...	...	...
Springfield (IL)	115 715[29]	...	...	155.6[30]	...	...	...	...
Springfield (MA)	154 074[29]	...	...	82.5[30]	...	...	...	...
Springfield (MO)	167 319[29]	...	...	213.2[30]	...	...	...	...
St. Louis (MO)	311 404[29]	...	...	160.5[30]	...	...	...	...
St. Paul (MN)	302 398[29]	...	...	134.6[30]	...	...	...	...
St. Petersburg (FL)	260 999[29]	...	...	159.9[30]	...	...	...	...
Stamford (CT)	129 113[29]	...	...	97.4[30]	...	...	...	...
Sterling Heights (MI)	132 427[29]	...	...	94.6[30]	...	...	...	...
Stockton (CA)	307 072[29]	...	...	159.7[30]	...	...	...	...
Sunnyvale (CA)	152 771[29]	...	...	56.9[30]	...	...	...	...
Surprise (AZ)	132 677[29]	...	...	279.3[30]	...	...	...	...
Syracuse (NY)	143 378[29]	...	...	64.9[30]	...	...	...	...
Tacoma (WA)	211 277[29]	...	...	128.8[30]	...	...	...	...
Tallahassee (FL)	190 894[29]	...	...	260.1[30]	...	...	...	...
Tampa (FL)	377 165[29]	...	...	293.7[30]	...	...	...	...
Temecula (CA)	113 054[29]	...	...	96.5[30]	...	...	...	...
Tempe (AZ)	182 498[29]	...	...	103.5[30]	...	...	...	...
Thornton (CO)	136 703[29]	...	...	92.5[30]	...	...	...	...
Thousand Oaks (CA)	128 888[29]	...	...	142.9[30]	...	...	...	...
Toledo (OH)	278 508[29]	...	...	209.1[30]	...	...	...	...
Topeka (KS)	126 808[29]	...	...	159.2[30]	...	...	...	...
Torrance (CA)	147 195[29]	...	...	53[30]	...	...	...	...
Tucson (AZ)	530 706[29]	...	...	597.8[30]	...	...	...	...

8. Population of capital cities and cities of 100 000 or more inhabitants: latest available year, 1998 - 2017
Population des capitales et des villes de 100 000 habitants ou plus : dernière année disponible, 1998 - 2017 (continued - suite)

Continent, country or area, date, code[a] and city / Continent, pays ou zone, date, code[a] et ville	City proper - Ville proprement dite				Urban agglomeration - Agglomération urbaine			
	Population			Surface area - Superficie (km²)	Population			Surface area - Superficie (km²)
	Both sexes - Les deux sexes	Male - Masculin	Female - Féminin		Both sexes - Les deux sexes	Male - Masculin	Female - Féminin	

AMERICA, NORTH - AMÉRIQUE DU NORD

United States of America - États-Unis d'Amérique[28]
1 VII 2016 (ESDJ)

Tulsa (OK)	403 090[29]	...	...	509.8[30]	...	...	...	...
Tyler (TX)	104 798[29]	...	...	146.7[30]	...	...	...	...
Urban Honolulu (HI)	351 792[29]	...	...	156.8[30]	...	...	...	...
Vallejo (CA)	121 299[29]	...	...	79.4[30]	...	...	...	...
Vancouver (WA)	174 826[29]	...	...	121.6[30]	...	...	...	...
Victorville City (CA)	122 265[29]	...	...	189.9[30]	...	...	...	...
Virginia Beach (VA)	452 602[29]	...	...	633.8[30]	...	...	...	...
Visalia (CA)	131 074[29]	...	...	97.1[30]	...	...	...	...
Vista (CA)	101 659[29]	...	...	48.4[30]	...	...	...	...
Waco (TX)	134 432[29]	...	...	230.6[30]	...	...	...	...
Warren (MI)	135 125[29]	...	...	89.1[30]	...	...	...	...
WASHINGTON (DC)	681 170[29]	...	...	158.4[30]	...	...	...	...
Waterbury (CT)	108 272[29]	...	...	73.9[30]	...	...	...	...
West Covina (CA)	107 847[29]	...	...	41.5[30]	...	...	...	...
West Jordan (UT)	113 699[29]	...	...	83.7[30]	...	...	...	...
West Palm Beach (FL)	108 161[29]	...	...	142.8[30]	...	...	...	...
West Valley City (UT)	136 574[29]	...	...	91.9[30]	...	...	...	...
Westminster (CO)	113 875[29]	...	...	82.2[30]	...	...	...	...
Wichita (KS)	389 902[29]	...	...	415.4[30]	...	...	...	...
Wichita Falls (TX)	104 724[29]	...	...	187[30]	...	...	...	...
Wilmington (NC)	117 525[29]	...	...	133.7[30]	...	...	...	...
Winston-Salem (NC)	242 203[29]	...	...	343.2[30]	...	...	...	...
Worcester (MA)	184 508[29]	...	...	96.8[30]	...	...	...	...
Yonkers (NY)	200 807[29]	...	...	46.7[30]	...	...	...	...

United States Virgin Islands - Îles Vierges américaines[31]
1 IV 2010 (CDJC)

CHARLOTTE AMALIE	10 354	...	...	...	...	...	...	...

AMERICA, SOUTH - AMÉRIQUE DU SUD

Argentina - Argentine[32]
1 VII 2016 (ESDF)

Bahía Blanca-Cerri	...	...	...	...	308 922	148 808	160 114	...
Bariloche	...	...	...	...	158 989	80 341	78 648	...
BUENOS AIRES	...	...	...	...	13 879 707	6 732 655	7 147 052	...
Catamarca	...	...	...	...	213 186	103 592	109 594	...
Comodoro Rivadavia-Rada Tilly	...	...	...	...	218 596	111 629	106 967	...
Concordia	...	...	...	...	161 990	79 065	82 925	...
Córdoba	...	...	...	...	1 525 490	731 552	793 938	...
Corrientes	...	...	...	...	386 379	185 631	200 748	...
Formosa	...	...	...	...	260 788	126 622	134 166	...
La Plata	...	...	...	...	843 851	409 347	434 504	...
La Rioja	...	...	...	...	207 085	101 956	105 129	...
Mar del Plata-Batán	...	...	...	...	641 065	308 438	332 627	...
Mendoza	...	...	...	...	1 094 209	533 737	560 472	...
Neuquén-Plottier	...	...	...	...	314 478	155 618	158 860	...
Paraná	...	...	...	...	276 125	132 139	143 986	...
Posadas	...	...	...	...	358 832	172 792	186 040	...
Rawson-Trelew-Playa Unión	...	...	...	...	139 698	68 235	71 463	...
Resistencia	...	...	...	...	412 445	198 970	213 475	...
Río Cuarto	...	...	...	...	173 807	83 516	90 291	...
Rio Gallegos	...	...	...	...	112 455	56 849	55 606	...
Rosario	...	...	...	...	1 444 436	701 272	743 164	...
Salta	...	...	...	...	634 644	306 877	327 767	...
San Juan	...	...	...	...	520 430	251 730	268 700	...
San Luis - El Chorrillo	...	...	...	...	221 410	108 478	112 932	...
San Nicolás-Villa Constitución	...	...	...	...	190 447	93 127	97 320	...
San Salvador de Jujuy-Palpalá	...	...	...	...	341 634	165 159	176 475	...
Santa Fé	...	...	...	...	534 341	256 803	277 538	...

8. Population of capital cities and cities of 100 000 or more inhabitants: latest available year, 1998 - 2017
Population des capitales et des villes de 100 000 habitants ou plus : dernière année disponible, 1998 - 2017 (continued - suite)

Continent, country or area, date, code[a] and city / Continent, pays ou zone, date, code[a] et ville	City proper - Ville proprement dite				Urban agglomeration - Agglomération urbaine			
	Population			Surface area - Superficie (km²)	Population			Surface area - Superficie (km²)
	Both sexes - Les deux sexes	Male - Masculin	Female - Féminin		Both sexes - Les deux sexes	Male - Masculin	Female - Féminin	
AMERICA, SOUTH - AMÉRIQUE DU SUD								
Argentina - Argentine[32]								
1 VII 2016 (ESDF)								
Santa Rosa-Toay	...	...	...	...	127 055	61 725	65 330	...
Santiago del Estero-La Banda	...	...	...	...	410 083	198 119	211 964	...
Tucumán-Tafí Viejo	...	...	...	...	873 873	420 897	452 976	...
Ushuaia-Río Grande	...	...	...	...	139 989	72 112	67 877	...
Bolivia (Plurinational State of) - Bolivie (État plurinational de)								
1 VII 2010 (ESDF)								
Cochabamba	618 376	294 711	323 666	...	...	...	...	...
El Alto	953 253	463 069	490 184	...	...	...	...	...
LA PAZ	835 361	397 608	437 753	...	...	...	...	...
Oruro	216 724	104 294	112 430	...	...	...	...	...
Potosí	154 693	74 591	80 103	...	...	...	...	...
Sacaba	155 668	75 113	80 555	...	...	...	...	...
Santa Cruz	1 616 063	785 941	830 122	...	...	...	...	...
SUCRE	284 032	137 943	146 090	...	...	...	...	...
Tarija	194 313	94 231	100 082	...	...	...	...	...
Yacuiba	112 096	55 346	56 750	...	...	...	...	...
Brazil - Brésil[33]								
1 VII 2016 (ESDJ)								
Abaeteluba	151 934	...	...	...	...	...	...	...
Açailândia	110 543	...	...	...	...	...	...	...
Aguas Lindas de Goiás	191 499	...	...	...	...	...	...	...
Alagoinhas	155 362	...	...	...	...	...	...	...
Almirante Tamandaré	114 129	...	...	...	...	...	...	...
Altamira	109 938	...	...	...	...	...	...	...
Alvorada	207 392	...	...	...	...	...	...	...
Americana	231 621	...	...	...	...	...	...	...
Ananindeua	510 834	...	...	...	...	...	...	...
Anápolis	370 875	...	...	...	...	...	...	...
Angra dos Reis	191 504	...	...	...	...	...	...	...
Aparecida de Goiania	532 135	...	...	...	...	...	...	...
Apucarana	131 571	...	...	...	...	...	...	...
Aracaju	641 523	...	...	...	...	...	...	...
Araçatuba	193 828	...	...	...	...	...	...	...
Araguaina	173 112	...	...	...	...	...	...	...
Araguario	116 871	...	...	...	...	...	...	...
Arapiraca	232 671	...	...	...	...	...	...	...
Arapongas	116 960	...	...	...	...	...	...	...
Araraquara	228 664	...	...	...	...	...	...	...
Araras	130 102	...	...	...	...	...	...	...
Araruama	124 940	...	...	...	...	...	...	...
Araucária	135 459	...	...	...	...	...	...	...
Araxá	103 287	...	...	...	...	...	...	...
Ariquemes	105 896	...	...	...	...	...	...	...
Assis	102 268	...	...	...	...	...	...	...
Atibaia	138 449	...	...	...	...	...	...	...
Bacabal	103 020	...	...	...	...	...	...	...
Bagé	121 986	...	...	...	...	...	...	...
Balneário Camboriú	131 727	...	...	...	...	...	...	...
Barbacena	135 829	...	...	...	...	...	...	...
Barcarena	118 537	...	...	...	...	...	...	...
Barra Mansa	180 126	...	...	...	...	...	...	...
Barreiras	155 519	...	...	...	...	...	...	...
Barretos	119 948	...	...	...	...	...	...	...
Barueri	264 935	...	...	...	...	...	...	...
Bauru	369 368	...	...	...	...	...	...	...
Belém	1 446 042	...	...	...	...	...	...	...
Belford Roxo	494 141	...	...	...	...	...	...	...
Belo Horizonte	2 513 451	...	...	...	...	...	...	...
Bento Gonçalves	114 203	...	...	...	...	...	...	...
Betim	422 354	...	...	...	...	...	...	...
Birigui	119 536	...	...	...	...	...	...	...
Blumenou	343 715	...	...	...	...	...	...	...

8. Population of capital cities and cities of 100 000 or more inhabitants: latest available year, 1998 - 2017
Population des capitales et des villes de 100 000 habitants ou plus : dernière année disponible, 1998 - 2017 (continued - suite)

Continent, country or area, date, code[a] and city Continent, pays ou zone, date, code[a] et ville	City proper - Ville proprement dite				Urban agglomeration - Agglomération urbaine			
	Population			Surface area - Superficie (km²)	Population			Surface area - Superficie (km²)
	Both sexes - Les deux sexes	Male - Masculin	Female - Féminin		Both sexes - Les deux sexes	Male - Masculin	Female - Féminin	
AMERICA, SOUTH - AMÉRIQUE DU SUD								
Brazil - Brésil[33]								
1 VII 2016 (ESDJ)								
Boa Vista	326 419	...	...	...	...	...	...	...
Botucatu	141 032	...	...	...	...	...	...	...
Bragança	122 881	...	...	...	...	...	...	...
Bragança Paulista	162 435	...	...	...	...	...	...	...
BRASILIA	2 977 216	...	...	...	...	...	...	...
Brusque	125 810	...	...	...	...	...	...	...
Cabo de Santo Agostinho	202 636	...	...	...	...	...	...	...
Cabo Frio	212 289	...	...	...	...	...	...	...
Cachoeirinha	126 666	...	...	...	...	...	...	...
Cachoeiro de Itapemirim	210 325	...	...	...	...	...	...	...
Camacari	292 074	...	...	...	...	...	...	...
Camaragibe	155 228	...	...	...	...	...	...	...
Cambé	104 592	...	...	...	...	...	...	...
Cametá	132 515	...	...	...	...	...	...	...
Campina Grande	407 754	...	...	...	...	...	...	...
Campinas	1 173 370	...	...	...	...	...	...	...
Campo Grande	863 982	...	...	...	...	...	...	...
Campo Largo	125 719	...	...	...	...	...	...	...
Campos dos Goytacazes	487 186	...	...	...	...	...	...	...
Canoas	342 634	...	...	...	...	...	...	...
Caraguatatuba	115 071	...	...	...	...	...	...	...
Carapicuíba	394 465	...	...	...	...	...	...	...
Cariacica	384 621	...	...	...	...	...	...	...
Caruaru	351 686	...	...	...	...	...	...	...
Cascavel	316 226	...	...	...	...	...	...	...
Castanhal	192 571	...	...	...	...	...	...	...
Catalão	100 590	...	...	...	...	...	...	...
Catanduva	120 092	...	...	...	...	...	...	...
Caucaia	358 164	...	...	...	...	...	...	...
Caxias	161 926	...	...	...	...	...	...	...
Caxias do Sul	479 236	...	...	...	...	...	...	...
Chapecó	209 553	...	...	...	...	...	...	...
Codo	120 548	...	...	...	...	...	...	...
Colatina	123 598	...	...	...	...	...	...	...
Colombo	234 941	...	...	...	...	...	...	...
Conselheiro Lafaiete	126 420	...	...	...	...	...	...	...
Contagem	653 800	...	...	...	...	...	...	...
Coronel Fabriciano	109 857	...	...	...	...	...	...	...
Corumbá	109 294	...	...	...	...	...	...	...
Cotia	233 696	...	...	...	...	...	...	...
Crato	129 662	...	...	...	...	...	...	...
Criciúma	209 153	...	...	...	...	...	...	...
Cubatao	127 887	...	...	...	...	...	...	...
Cuiabá	585 367	...	...	...	...	...	...	...
Curitiba	1 893 997	...	...	...	...	...	...	...
Diadema	415 180	...	...	...	...	...	...	...
Divinópolis	232 945	...	...	...	...	...	...	...
Dourados	215 486	...	...	...	...	...	...	...
Duque de Caxias	886 917	...	...	...	...	...	...	...
Embu	264 448	...	...	...	...	...	...	...
Erechim	102 906	...	...	...	...	...	...	...
Eunápolis	114 275	...	...	...	...	...	...	...
Feira de Santana	622 639	...	...	...	...	...	...	...
Ferraz de Vasconcelos	186 808	...	...	...	...	...	...	...
Florianópolis	477 798	...	...	...	...	...	...	...
Formosa	114 036	...	...	...	...	...	...	...
Fortaleza	2 609 716	...	...	...	...	...	...	...
Foz do Iguaçu	263 915	...	...	...	...	...	...	...
Franca	344 704	...	...	...	...	...	...	...
Francisco Morato	169 942	...	...	...	...	...	...	...
Franco da Rocha	147 650	...	...	...	...	...	...	...
Garanhuns	137 810	...	...	...	...	...	...	...
Goiânia	1 448 639	...	...	...	...	...	...	...

8. Population of capital cities and cities of 100 000 or more inhabitants: latest available year, 1998 - 2017
Population des capitales et des villes de 100 000 habitants ou plus : dernière année disponible, 1998 - 2017 (continued - suite)

Continent, country or area, date, code[a] and city / Continent, pays ou zone, date, code[a] et ville	City proper - Ville proprement dite				Urban agglomeration - Agglomération urbaine			
	Population			Surface area - Superficie (km²)	Population			Surface area - Superficie (km²)
	Both sexes - Les deux sexes	Male - Masculin	Female - Féminin		Both sexes - Les deux sexes	Male - Masculin	Female - Féminin	

AMERICA, SOUTH - AMÉRIQUE DU SUD

Brazil - Brésil[33]
  1 VII 2016 (ESDJ)

Governador Valadares	279 665	...	...	...	...	...	...	...
Gravatai	273 742	...	...	...	...	...	...	...
Guarapari	121 506	...	...	...	...	...	...	...
Guarapuava	179 256	...	...	...	...	...	...	...
Guaratinguetá	119 753	...	...	...	...	...	...	...
Guarujá	313 421	...	...	...	...	...	...	...
Guarulhos	1 337 087	...	...	...	...	...	...	...
Hortolandia	219 039	...	...	...	...	...	...	...
Ibirité	175 721	...	...	...	...	...	...	...
Igarassu	113 956	...	...	...	...	...	...	...
Iguatu	102 013	...	...	...	...	...	...	...
Ilhéus	178 210	...	...	...	...	...	...	...
Imperatriz	253 873	...	...	...	...	...	...	...
Indaiatuba	235 367	...	...	...	...	...	...	...
Ipatinga	259 324	...	...	...	...	...	...	...
Itabiraí	118 481	...	...	...	...	...	...	...
Itaboraí	230 786	...	...	...	...	...	...	...
Itabuna	220 386	...	...	...	...	...	...	...
Itaguaí	120 855	...	...	...	...	...	...	...
Itajaí	208 958	...	...	...	...	...	...	...
Itapecerica da Serra	169 103	...	...	...	...	...	...	...
Itapetininga	158 561	...	...	...	...	...	...	...
Itapevi	226 488	...	...	...	...	...	...	...
Itapipoca	126 234	...	...	...	...	...	...	...
Itaquaquecetuba	356 774	...	...	...	...	...	...	...
Itatiba	114 912	...	...	...	...	...	...	...
Itu	168 643	...	...	...	...	...	...	...
Ituiutaba	103 945	...	...	...	...	...	...	...
Itumbiara	101 544	...	...	...	...	...	...	...
Jaboatao dos Guarapes	691 125	...	...	...	...	...	...	...
Jacareí	228 214	...	...	...	...	...	...	...
Jandira	120 177	...	...	...	...	...	...	...
Japeri	100 562	...	...	...	...	...	...	...
Jaraguá do Sul	167 300	...	...	...	...	...	...	...
Jaú	144 828	...	...	...	...	...	...	...
Jequié	161 880	...	...	...	...	...	...	...
Ji-Paraná	131 560	...	...	...	...	...	...	...
Joao Pessoa	801 718	...	...	...	...	...	...	...
Joinville	569 645	...	...	...	...	...	...	...
Juazeiro	220 253	...	...	...	...	...	...	...
Juàzeiro do Norte	268 248	...	...	...	...	...	...	...
Juiz de Fora	559 636	...	...	...	...	...	...	...
Jundiaí	405 740	...	...	...	...	...	...	...
Lagarto	103 188	...	...	...	...	...	...	...
Lages	158 620	...	...	...	...	...	...	...
Lauro de Freitas	194 641	...	...	...	...	...	...	...
Lavras	101 208	...	...	...	...	...	...	...
Leme	100 296	...	...	...	...	...	...	...
Limeira	298 701	...	...	...	...	...	...	...
Linhares	166 491	...	...	...	...	...	...	...
Londrina	553 393	...	...	...	...	...	...	...
Luziânia	196 864	...	...	...	...	...	...	...
Macae	239 471	...	...	...	...	...	...	...
Macapá	465 495	...	...	...	...	...	...	...
Maceió	1 021 709	...	...	...	...	...	...	...
Magé	236 319	...	...	...	...	...	...	...
Manaus	2 094 391	...	...	...	...	...	...	...
Maraba	266 932	...	...	...	...	...	...	...
Maracanau	223 188	...	...	...	...	...	...	...
Maranguape	125 058	...	...	...	...	...	...	...
Maricá	149 876	...	...	...	...	...	...	...
Marília	233 639	...	...	...	...	...	...	...
Maringá	403 063	...	...	...	...	...	...	...

Continent, country or area, date, code[a] and city / Continent, pays ou zone, date, code[a] et ville	City proper - Ville proprement dite				Urban agglomeration - Agglomération urbaine			
	Population			Surface area - Superficie (km²)	Population			Surface area - Superficie (km²)
	Both sexes - Les deux sexes	Male - Masculin	Female - Féminin		Both sexes - Les deux sexes	Male - Masculin	Female - Féminin	

AMERICA, SOUTH - AMÉRIQUE DU SUD

Brazil - Brésil[33]
  1 VII 2016 (ESDJ)

Marituba	125 435	...	...	...	...	...	...	...
Mauá	457 696	...	...	...	...	...	...	...
Mesquita	171 020	...	...	...	...	...	...	...
Moji das Cruzes	429 321	...	...	...	...	...	...	...
Moji-Guaçu	148 327	...	...	...	...	...	...	...
Montes Claros	398 288	...	...	...	...	...	...	...
Mossoró	291 937	...	...	...	...	...	...	...
Muriaé	107 916	...	...	...	...	...	...	...
Natal	877 662	...	...	...	...	...	...	...
Nilópolis	158 319	...	...	...	...	...	...	...
Niterói	497 883	...	...	...	...	...	...	...
Nossa Senhora do Socorro	179 661	...	...	...	...	...	...	...
Nova Friburgo	185 102	...	...	...	...	...	...	...
Nova Iguaçu	797 435	...	...	...	...	...	...	...
Novo Gama	108 410	...	...	...	...	...	...	...
Nôvo Hamburgo	249 113	...	...	...	...	...	...	...
Olinda	390 144	...	...	...	...	...	...	...
Osasco	696 382	...	...	...	...	...	...	...
Ourinhos	111 056	...	...	...	...	...	...	...
Paço do Lumiar	119 915	...	...	...	...	...	...	...
Palhoça	161 395	...	...	...	...	...	...	...
Palmas	279 856	...	...	...	...	...	...	...
Paragominas	108 547	...	...	...	...	...	...	...
Paranaguá	151 829	...	...	...	...	...	...	...
Parauapebas	196 259	...	...	...	...	...	...	...
Parintins	112 716	...	...	...	...	...	...	...
Parnaíba	150 201	...	...	...	...	...	...	...
Parnamirim	248 623	...	...	...	...	...	...	...
Passo Fundo	197 798	...	...	...	...	...	...	...
Passos	113 807	...	...	...	...	...	...	...
Patos	107 067	...	...	...	...	...	...	...
Patos de Minas	149 856	...	...	...	...	...	...	...
Paulínia	100 128	...	...	...	...	...	...	...
Paulista	325 590	...	...	...	...	...	...	...
Paulo Afonso	119 930	...	...	...	...	...	...	...
Pelotas	343 651	...	...	...	...	...	...	...
Petrolina	337 683	...	...	...	...	...	...	...
Petrópolis	298 158	...	...	...	...	...	...	...
Pindamonhangaba	162 327	...	...	...	...	...	...	...
Pinhais	128 256	...	...	...	...	...	...	...
Piracicaba	394 419	...	...	...	...	...	...	...
Piraquara	106 132	...	...	...	...	...	...	...
Poà	114 650	...	...	...	...	...	...	...
Poços de Caldas	164 912	...	...	...	...	...	...	...
Ponta Grossa	341 130	...	...	...	...	...	...	...
Porto Alegre	1 481 019	...	...	...	...	...	...	...
Porto Seguro	147 444	...	...	...	...	...	...	...
Porto Velho	511 219	...	...	...	...	...	...	...
Pouso Alegre	145 535	...	...	...	...	...	...	...
Praia Grande	304 705	...	...	...	...	...	...	...
Presidente Prudente	223 749	...	...	...	...	...	...	...
Queimados	144 525	...	...	...	...	...	...	...
Recife	1 625 583	...	...	...	...	...	...	...
Resende	126 084	...	...	...	...	...	...	...
Ribeirao das Neves	325 846	...	...	...	...	...	...	...
Ribeirao Pires	121 130	...	...	...	...	...	...	...
Ribeirao Prêto	674 405	...	...	...	...	...	...	...
Rio Branco	377 057	...	...	...	...	...	...	...
Rio Claro	201 473	...	...	...	...	...	...	...
Rio das Ostras	136 626	...	...	...	...	...	...	...
Rio de Janeiro	6 498 837	...	...	...	...	...	...	...
Rio Grande	208 641	...	...	...	...	...	...	...
Rio Verde	212 237	...	...	...	...	...	...	...

8. Population of capital cities and cities of 100 000 or more inhabitants: latest available year, 1998 - 2017
Population des capitales et des villes de 100 000 habitants ou plus : dernière année disponible, 1998 - 2017 (continued - suite)

Continent, country or area, date, code[a] and city / Continent, pays ou zone, date, code[a] et ville	City proper - Ville proprement dite				Urban agglomeration - Agglomération urbaine			
	Population			Surface area - Superficie (km²)	Population			Surface area - Superficie (km²)
	Both sexes - Les deux sexes	Male - Masculin	Female - Féminin		Both sexes - Les deux sexes	Male - Masculin	Female - Féminin	

AMERICA, SOUTH - AMÉRIQUE DU SUD

Brazil - Brésil[33]
  1 VII 2016 (ESDJ)

Rondonópolis	218 899	...	...	...	...	...	...	...
Sabára	135 196	...	...	...	...	...	...	...
Salto	115 193	...	...	...	...	...	...	...
Salvador	2 938 092	...	...	...	...	...	...	...
Santa Bárbara D'Oeste	191 024	...	...	...	...	...	...	...
Santa Cruz do Capibaribe	103 660	...	...	...	...	...	...	...
Santa Cruz do Sul	126 775	...	...	...	...	...	...	...
Santa Luzia (Minas Gerais)	217 610	...	...	...	...	...	...	...
Santa Maria	277 309	...	...	...	...	...	...	...
Santa Rita	135 915	...	...	...	...	...	...	...
Santana	113 854	...	...	...	...	...	...	...
Santana de Parnaíba	129 261	...	...	...	...	...	...	...
Santarém	294 447	...	...	...	...	...	...	...
Santo André	712 749	...	...	...	...	...	...	...
Santo Antônio de Jesus	102 469	...	...	...	...	...	...	...
Santos	434 359	...	...	...	...	...	...	...
Sao Bernardo do Campo	822 242	...	...	...	...	...	...	...
Sao Caetano do Sul	158 825	...	...	...	...	...	...	...
Sao Carlo	243 765	...	...	...	...	...	...	...
São Félix do Xingu	120 580	...	...	...	...	...	...	...
Sao Gonçalo	1 044 058	...	...	...	...	...	...	...
Sao Joao de Meriti	460 541	...	...	...	...	...	...	...
Sao José	236 029	...	...	...	...	...	...	...
Sao José de Ribamar	176 008	...	...	...	...	...	...	...
Sao José do Rio Prêto	446 649	...	...	...	...	...	...	...
Sao José dos Campos	695 992	...	...	...	...	...	...	...
Sao José dos Pinhais	302 759	...	...	...	...	...	...	...
Sao Leopoldo	229 678	...	...	...	...	...	...	...
São Lourenço da Mata	111 197	...	...	...	...	...	...	...
Sao Luís	1 082 935	...	...	...	...	...	...	...
São Mateus	126 437	...	...	...	...	...	...	...
Sao Paulo	12 038 175	...	...	...	...	...	...	...
Sao Vicente	357 989	...	...	...	...	...	...	...
Sapucaia do Sul	138 933	...	...	...	...	...	...	...
Senador Canedo	102 947	...	...	...	...	...	...	...
Serra	494 109	...	...	...	...	...	...	...
Sertaozinho	121 412	...	...	...	...	...	...	...
Sete Lagoas	234 221	...	...	...	...	...	...	...
Simoes Filho	134 674	...	...	...	...	...	...	...
Sinop	132 934	...	...	...	...	...	...	...
Sobral	203 682	...	...	...	...	...	...	...
Sorocaba	652 481	...	...	...	...	...	...	...
Sumaré	269 522	...	...	...	...	...	...	...
Susano	288 056	...	...	...	...	...	...	...
Taboao da Serra	275 948	...	...	...	...	...	...	...
Tailândia	100 300	...	...	...	...	...	...	...
Tatuí	117 823	...	...	...	...	...	...	...
Taubaté	305 174	...	...	...	...	...	...	...
Teixeira de Freitas	159 813	...	...	...	...	...	...	...
Teófilo Otoni	141 502	...	...	...	...	...	...	...
Teresina	847 430	...	...	...	...	...	...	...
Teresópolis	174 587	...	...	...	...	...	...	...
Timon	166 295	...	...	...	...	...	...	...
Toledo	133 824	...	...	...	...	...	...	...
Três Lagoas	115 561	...	...	...	...	...	...	...
Trindade	119 385	...	...	...	...	...	...	...
Tubarão	103 674	...	...	...	...	...	...	...
Tucuruí	108 885	...	...	...	...	...	...	...
Ubá	112 186	...	...	...	...	...	...	...
Uberaba	325 279	...	...	...	...	...	...	...
Uberlândia	669 672	...	...	...	...	...	...	...
Umuarama	109 132	...	...	...	...	...	...	...
Uruguaiana	129 720	...	...	...	...	...	...	...

8. Population of capital cities and cities of 100 000 or more inhabitants: latest available year, 1998 - 2017
Population des capitales et des villes de 100 000 habitants ou plus : dernière année disponible, 1998 - 2017 (continued - suite)

Continent, country or area, date, code[a] and city / Continent, pays ou zone, date, code[a] et ville	City proper - Ville proprement dite				Urban agglomeration - Agglomération urbaine			
	Population			Surface area - Superficie (km²)	Population			Surface area - Superficie (km²)
	Both sexes - Les deux sexes	Male - Masculin	Female - Féminin		Both sexes - Les deux sexes	Male - Masculin	Female - Féminin	
AMERICA, SOUTH - AMÉRIQUE DU SUD								
Brazil - Brésil[33]								
1 VII 2016 (ESDJ)								
Valinhos	122 163	...	...	...	...	...	...	...
Valparaíso de Goiás	156 419	...	...	...	...	...	...	...
Varginha	133 384	...	...	...	...	...	...	...
Varzea Grande	271 339	...	...	...	...	...	...	...
Varzea Paulista	117 772	...	...	...	...	...	...	...
Vespasiano	120 510	...	...	...	...	...	...	...
Viamao	252 872	...	...	...	...	...	...	...
Vila Velha	479 664	...	...	...	...	...	...	...
Vitória	359 555	...	...	...	...	...	...	...
Vitória da Conquista	346 069	...	...	...	...	...	...	...
Vitória de Santo Antao	136 706	...	...	...	...	...	...	...
Volta Redonda	263 659	...	...	...	...	...	...	...
Votorantim	118 858	...	...	...	...	...	...	...
Chile - Chili								
1 VII 2017 (ESDF)								
Alto Hospicio	124 877	63 281	61 596	17[34]	...	...	...	...
Antofagasta	388 545	205 983	182 562	44[34]	...	...	...	...
Arica	229 689	114 441	115 248	42[34]	...	...	...	...
Calama	180 283	91 633	88 650	18[34]	...	...	...	...
Chiguallante	101 244	48 160	53 084	34[34]	...	...	...	...
Chillán	159 476	75 030	84 446	33[34]	...	...	...	...
Concepción	220 746	104 151	116 595	56[34]	...	...	...	...
Copiapó	175 162	88 912	86 250	48[34]	...	...	...	...
Coquimbo	216 623	105 602	111 021	42[34]	...	...	...	...
Coronel	109 709	51 462	58 247	25[34]	...	...	...	...
Curicó	102 710	49 371	53 339	21[34]	...	...	...	...
Hualpén	108 803	50 733	58 070	11.9[34]	...	...	...	...
Iquique	196 562	98 599	97 963	22[34]	...	...	...	...
La Serena	205 635	100 151	105 484	66[34]	...	...	...	...
Los Ángeles	128 933	61 836	67 097	27[34]	...	...	...	...
Osorno	139 550	66 890	72 660	32[34]	...	...	...	...
Puente Alto	625 551	308 490	317 061	64[34]	...	...	...	...
Puerto Montt	213 119	106 266	106 853	40[34]	...	...	...	...
Punta Arenas	124 169	61 603	62 566	39[34]	...	...	...	...
Quilpué	172 049	83 317	88 732	38[34]	...	...	...	...
Rancagua	225 563	112 119	113 444	50[34]	...	...	...	...
San Bernardo	296 583	147 549	149 034	52[34]	...	...	...	...
San Pedro de la Paz	139 174	64 934	74 240	49[34]	...	...	...	...
SANTIAGO	5 613 962[35]	2 723 688[35]	2 890 274[35]	843[34]	...	...	...	...
Talca	203 873	97 557	106 316	46[34]	...	...	...	...
Temuco	221 375	105 706	115 669	46[34]	...	...	...	...
Valdivia	143 207	69 519	73 688	42[34]	...	...	...	...
Valparaíso	295 113	147 418	147 695	47[34]	...	...	...	...
Villa Alemana	144 417	70 578	73 839	31[34]	...	...	...	...
Viña del Mar	326 759	157 481	169 278	87[34]	...	...	...	...
Colombia - Colombie								
1 VII 2016 (ESDJ)								
Apartadó	183 716[36]	92 853[36]	90 863[36]	607[23]	...	...	...	...
Armenia (Quindio)	298 199[36]	143 932[36]	154 267[36]	111[23]	...	...	...	...
Barrancabermeja	191 704[36]	94 619[36]	97 085[36]	1274[23]	...	...	...	...
Barranquilla	1 223 616[36]	593 773[36]	629 843[36]	166[23]	...	...	...	...
Bello	464 614[36]	224 833[36]	239 781[36]	151[23]	...	...	...	...
BOGOTÁ, D.C.	7 980 001[36]	3 861 624[36]	4 118 377[36]	1605[23]	...	...	...	...
Bucaramanga	528 269[36]	254 121[36]	274 148[36]	154[23]	...	...	...	...
Buenaventura	407 675[36]	198 261[36]	209 414[36]	6785[23]	...	...	...	...
Cali	2 394 925[36]	1 144 848[36]	1 250 077[36]	552[23]	...	...	...	...
Cartagena	1 013 389[36]	490 036[36]	523 353[36]	559[23]	...	...	...	...
Cartago	132 959[36]	63 949[36]	69 010[36]	260[23]	...	...	...	...
Caucasia	114 902[36]	55 636[36]	59 266[36]	1058[23]	...	...	...	...
Chía	129 652[36]	62 355[36]	67 297[36]	76[23]	...	...	...	...

8. Population of capital cities and cities of 100 000 or more inhabitants: latest available year, 1998 - 2017
Population des capitales et des villes de 100 000 habitants ou plus : dernière année disponible, 1998 - 2017 (continued - suite)

Continent, country or area, date, code[a] and city / Continent, pays ou zone, date, code[a] et ville	City proper - Ville proprement dite				Urban agglomeration - Agglomération urbaine			
	Population			Surface area - Superficie (km²)	Population			Surface area - Superficie (km²)
	Both sexes - Les deux sexes	Male - Masculin	Female - Féminin		Both sexes - Les deux sexes	Male - Masculin	Female - Féminin	

AMERICA, SOUTH - AMÉRIQUE DU SUD

Colombia - Colombie
1 VII 2016 (ESDJ)

Ciénaga (Magdalena)	104 617[36]	52 291[36]	52 326[36]	1366[23]	...	...	...	...
Cúcuta	656 380[36]	317 453[36]	338 927[36]	1098[23]	...	...	...	...
Dosquebradas	200 832[36]	97 789[36]	103 043[36]	80[23]	...	...	...	...
Duitama	113 105[36]	52 101[36]	61 004[36]	229[23]	...	...	...	...
Envigado	227 644[36]	109 645[36]	117 999[36]	51[23]	...	...	...	...
Facatativá	134 522[36]	67 155[36]	67 367[36]	160[23]	...	...	...	...
Florencia	175 407[36]	86 223[36]	89 184[36]	2292[23]	...	...	...	...
Floridablanca	266 049[36]	126 653[36]	139 396[36]	101[23]	...	...	...	...
Fusagasugá	137 164[36]	67 806[36]	69 358[36]	206[23]	...	...	...	...
Girardot	105 701[36]	49 920[36]	55 781[36]	130[23]	...	...	...	...
Girón	185 314[36]	92 433[36]	92 881[36]	681[23]	...	...	...	...
Gudalajara de Buga	115 026[36]	56 361[36]	58 665[36]	873[23]	...	...	...	...
Ibagué	558 805[36]	271 360[36]	287 445[36]	1439[23]	...	...	...	...
Ipiales	141 863[36]	69 925[36]	71 938[36]	1707[23]	...	...	...	...
Itagüí	270 903[36]	132 151[36]	138 752[36]	17[23]	...	...	...	...
Jamundí	122 071[36]	59 328[36]	62 743[36]	603[23]	...	...	...	...
Lorica	119 061[36]	59 550[36]	59 511[36]	890[23]	...	...	...	...
Magangué	123 833[36]	62 639[36]	61 194[36]	1102[23]	...	...	...	...
Maicao	159 675[36]	78 520[36]	81 155[36]	1789[23]	...	...	...	...
Malambo	123 265[36]	62 751[36]	60 514[36]	108[23]	...	...	...	...
Manaure	108 006[36]	53 204[36]	54 802[36]	1643[23]	...	...	...	...
Manizales	397 466[36]	189 446[36]	208 020[36]	477[23]	...	...	...	...
Medellín	2 486 723[36]	1 170 224[36]	1 316 499[36]	387[23]	...	...	...	...
Montería	447 668[36]	217 244[36]	230 424[36]	3043[23]	...	...	...	...
Neiva	344 026[36]	164 582[36]	179 444[36]	1468[23]	...	...	...	...
Palmira	306 706[36]	148 106[36]	158 600[36]	1044[23]	...	...	...	...
Pasto	445 409[36]	215 188[36]	230 221[36]	1131[23]	...	...	...	...
Pereira	472 000[36]	223 658[36]	248 342[36]	702[23]	...	...	...	...
Piedecuesta	152 707[36]	74 232[36]	78 475[36]	481[23]	...	...	...	...
Pitalito	128 263[36]	63 674[36]	64 589[36]	653[23]	...	...	...	...
Popayán	280 054[36]	135 788[36]	144 266[36]	464[23]	...	...	...	...
Quibdo	115 907[36]	58 075[36]	57 832[36]	3075[23]	...	...	...	...
Riohacha	268 712[36]	132 278[36]	136 434[36]	3171[23]	...	...	...	...
Rionegro (Antioquia)	122 231[36]	60 739[36]	61 492[36]	198[23]	...	...	...	...
San Andrés de Tumaco	203 971[36]	101 856[36]	102 115[36]	3778[23]	...	...	...	...
Santa Marta	491 535[36]	240 119[36]	251 416[36]	2369[23]	...	...	...	...
Sincelejo	279 031[36]	137 141[36]	141 890[36]	292[23]	...	...	...	...
Soacha	522 442[36]	257 890[36]	264 552[36]	187[23]	...	...	...	...
Sogamoso	112 790[36]	53 518[36]	59 272[36]	214[23]	...	...	...	...
Soledad	632 183[36]	312 904[36]	319 279[36]	67[23]	...	...	...	...
Tierralta	102 348[36]	51 985[36]	50 363[36]	4728[23]	...	...	...	...
Tuluá	214 095[36]	102 870[36]	111 225[36]	818[23]	...	...	...	...
Tunja	191 924[36]	91 904[36]	100 020[36]	118[23]	...	...	...	...
Turbo	163 525[36]	82 751[36]	80 774[36]	3090[23]	...	...	...	...
Uribia	180 385[36]	88 412[36]	91 973[36]	7904[23]	...	...	...	...
Valledupar	463 219[36]	226 033[36]	237 186[36]	4225[23]	...	...	...	...
Villavicencio	495 227[36]	240 326[36]	254 901[36]	1328[23]	...	...	...	...
Yopal	142 979[36]	71 578[36]	71 401[36]	2532[23]	...	...	...	...
Yumbo	119 932[36]	60 174[36]	59 758[36]	243[23]	...	...	...	...
Zipaquirá	124 376[36]	61 198[36]	63 178[36]	194[23]	...	...	...	...

Ecuador - Équateur[26]
1 VII 2017 (ESDF)

Ambato	177 583	...	...	...	...	...	...	...
Babahoyo	101 476	...	...	...	...	...	...	...
Cuenca	390 205	...	...	...	...	...	...	...
Durán	287 330	...	...	...	...	...	...	...
Esmeraldas	192 748	...	...	...	...	...	...	...
Guayaquil	2 556 951	...	...	...	...	...	...	...
Ibarra	156 683	...	...	...	...	...	...	...
La Libertad	112 282	...	...	...	...	...	...	...

8. Population of capital cities and cities of 100 000 or more inhabitants: latest available year, 1998 - 2017
Population des capitales et des villes de 100 000 habitants ou plus : dernière année disponible, 1998 - 2017 (continued - suite)

Continent, country or area, date, code[a] and city / Continent, pays ou zone, date, code[a] et ville	City proper - Ville proprement dite				Urban agglomeration - Agglomération urbaine			
	Population			Surface area - Superficie (km²)	Population			Surface area - Superficie (km²)
	Both sexes - Les deux sexes	Male - Masculin	Female - Féminin		Both sexes - Les deux sexes	Male - Masculin	Female - Féminin	
AMERICA, SOUTH - AMÉRIQUE DU SUD								
Ecuador - Équateur[26]								
1 VII 2017 (ESDF)								
Loja	220 504	...	...	...	...	...	...	...
Machala	263 259	...	...	...	...	...	...	...
Manta	247 624	...	...	...	...	...	...	...
Milagro	152 336	...	...	...	...	...	...	...
Portoviejo	235 270	...	...	...	...	...	...	...
Quevedo	178 197	...	...	...	...	...	...	...
QUITO	1 792 584	...	...	...	...	...	...	...
Riobamba	166 541	...	...	...	...	...	...	...
Santo Domingo de los Colorados	328 134	...	...	...	...	...	...	...
Falkland Islands (Malvinas) - Îles Falkland (Malvinas)[37]								
15 IV 2012 (CDFC)								
STANLEY	2 108	1 055	1 053	...	...	...	...	...
French Guiana - Guyane française								
1 I 2006 (CDJC)								
CAYENNE	58 004	27 412	30 591	...	75 740	36 484	39 256	...
Guyana								
15 IX 2012* (CDFC)								
GEORGETOWN	24 849	...	...	...	118 368	...	...	...
Paraguay								
1 VII 2014 (ESDF)								
ASUNCIÓN[38]	512 919	236 790	276 129	117	2 887 087	1 402 891	1 484 196	2582
Capiatá	257 116	127 676	129 440	87.7	...	...	...	...
Ciudad del Este	317 525	159 726	157 799	149	...	...	...	...
Fernando de la Mora	200 112	95 174	104 937	21	...	...	...	...
Lambaré	210 725	101 019	109 706	26.8	...	...	...	...
Luque	358 265	175 663	182 602	152.5	...	...	...	...
San Lorenzo	354 283	171 242	183 042	54.2	...	...	...	...
Peru - Pérou[39]								
30 VI 2017 (ESDF)								
Arequipa	885 533	425 989	459 544	...	...	...	...	...
Ayacucho	187 493	92 634	94 859	...	...	...	...	...
Cajamarca	240 755	118 372	122 383	...	...	...	...	...
Chiclayo	611 622	291 431	320 191	...	...	...	...	...
Chimbote	377 085	190 071	187 014	...	...	...	...	...
Chincha Alta	182 463	91 384	91 079	...	...	...	...	...
Cuzco	441 211	214 754	226 457	...	...	...	...	...
Huancayo	372 162	176 672	195 490	...	...	...	...	...
Huánuco	179 266	85 444	93 822	...	...	...	...	...
Huaral	100 659	49 605	51 054	...	...	...	...	...
Huaraz	133 395	65 572	67 823	...	...	...	...	...
Ica	249 234	122 828	126 406	...	...	...	...	...
Iquitos	446 537	225 160	221 377	...	...	...	...	...
Juliaca	287 771	140 013	147 758	...	...	...	...	...
LIMA[40]	10 194 477	4 952 929	5 241 548	...	...	...	...	...
Paita	101 283	50 394	50 889	...	...	...	...	...
Pisco	105 181	53 628	51 553	...	...	...	...	...
Piura	451 829	219 398	232 431	...	...	...	...	...
Pucallpa	211 689	110 460	101 229	...	...	...	...	...
Puno	145 179	70 425	74 754	...	...	...	...	...
Sullana	204 611	99 963	104 648	...	...	...	...	...
Tacna	301 759	153 598	148 161	...	...	...	...	...
Tarapoto	150 466	78 246	72 220	...	...	...	...	...
Trujillo	822 142	399 282	422 860	...	...	...	...	...
Tumbes	114 012	61 973	52 039	...	...	...	...	...
Suriname								
13 VIII 2012 (CDJC)								
PARAMARIBO	240 924	119 439	121 485	182	...	...	...	...
Wanica	118 222	57 776	60 446	443	...	...	...	...
Uruguay[41]								
1 VII 2017 (ESDJ)								
MONTEVIDEO	1 381 228	649 774	731 454	...	...	...	...	...

Continent, country or area, date, code[a] and city Continent, pays ou zone, date, code[a] et ville	City proper - Ville proprement dite				Urban agglomeration - Agglomération urbaine			
	Population			Surface area - Superficie (km²)	Population			Surface area - Superficie (km²)
	Both sexes - Les deux sexes	Male - Masculin	Female - Féminin		Both sexes - Les deux sexes	Male - Masculin	Female - Féminin	

AMERICA, SOUTH - AMÉRIQUE DU SUD

Venezuela (Bolivarian Republic of) - Venezuela (République bolivarienne du)
1 VII 2015 (ESDF)

Anaco(F) (Capital)	140 496	...	...	...	...	...	...	...
Barinas	389 578	...	...	...	...	...	...	...
Barquisimeto	881 127	...	...	...	...	...	...	...
Baruta	358 221	...	...	...	...	...	...	...
Cabimas	293 365	...	...	...	...	...	...	...
Cagua	118 290	...	...	...	...	...	...	...
CARACAS	2 082 130	...	...	...	...	...	...	...
Carora	111 963	...	...	...	...	...	...	...
Carúpano	156 380	...	...	...	...	...	...	...
Ciudad Bolívar	407 452	...	...	...	...	...	...	...
Ciudad Guayana	877 547	...	...	...	...	...	...	...
Ciudad Ojeda	216 489	...	...	...	...	...	...	...
Cua	143 164	...	...	...	...	...	...	...
Cumaná	358 138	...	...	...	...	...	...	...
El Tigre	203 403	...	...	...	...	...	...	...
Guacara	192 536	...	...	...	...	...	...	...
Guanare	160 234	...	...	...	...	...	...	...
Guarenas	247 131	...	...	...	...	...	...	...
Guatire	177 794	...	...	...	...	...	...	...
Los Guayos	173 878	...	...	...	...	...	...	...
Los Teques	216 358	...	...	...	...	...	...	...
Maracaibo	1 653 215	...	...	...	...	...	...	...
Maracay	419 052	...	...	...	...	...	...	...
Maturín	571 276	...	...	...	...	...	...	...
Mérida	248 410	...	...	...	...	...	...	...
Naguanagua	161 658	...	...	...	...	...	...	...
Ocumare Del Tuy	197 952	...	...	...	...	...	...	...
Petare	434 320	...	...	...	...	...	...	...
Pozuelos (F) (Capital)	144 045	...	...	...	...	...	...	...
Puerto Cabello	193 025	...	...	...	...	...	...	...
Punto Fijo	272 239	...	...	...	...	...	...	...
San Cristóbal	282 830	...	...	...	...	...	...	...
San Fernando de Apure	217 590	...	...	...	...	...	...	...
San Francisco	106 763	...	...	...	...	...	...	...
Santa Lucía	133 543	...	...	...	...	...	...	...
Táriba	132 657	...	...	...	...	...	...	...
Tocuyito	186 755	...	...	...	...	...	...	...
Turmero	238 570	...	...	...	...	...	...	...
Valencia	888 109	...	...	...	...	...	...	...
Valera	161 771	...	...	...	...	...	...	...

ASIA - ASIE

Afghanistan
1 VII 2016 (ESDF)

Baghalan Center (Puli Khumry)	110 902	56 839	54 063	...	...	...	...	...
Balkh Center (Mazar- Sharif)	415 053	212 918	202 135	...	...	...	...	...
Herat Center	491 967	249 865	242 102	...	...	...	...	...
KABUL CENTER	3 817 241	1 975 705	1 841 536	...	...	...	...	...
Kandhar Center (Kndhar)	448 262	230 744	217 518	...	...	...	...	...
Kunduz Center	162 168	83 384	78 784	...	...	...	...	...
Nngarhar Center (Jlal Abad)	232 901	119 901	113 000	...	...	...	...	...

Armenia - Arménie
1 VII 2016 (ESDJ)

Gyumri (Leninakan)	116 800	55 280	61 520	...	...	...	...	...
YEREVAN	1 074 751	496 912	577 839	223	...	...	...	...

Azerbaijan - Azerbaïdjan
1 VII 2016 (ESDJ)

BAKU	2 235 814	1 110 998	1 124 816	2150	...	...	...	...
Ganja	330 744	161 226	169 518	110	...	...	...	...
Sumgayit	337 583	166 301	171 282	80	...	...	...	...

8. Population of capital cities and cities of 100 000 or more inhabitants: latest available year, 1998 - 2017
Population des capitales et des villes de 100 000 habitants ou plus : dernière année disponible, 1998 - 2017 (continued - suite)

Continent, country or area, date, code[a] and city Continent, pays ou zone, date, code[a] et ville	City proper - Ville proprement dite				Urban agglomeration - Agglomération urbaine			
	Population			Surface area - Superficie (km²)	Population			Surface area - Superficie (km²)
	Both sexes - Les deux sexes	Male - Masculin	Female - Féminin		Both sexes - Les deux sexes	Male - Masculin	Female - Féminin	
ASIA - ASIE								
Bahrain - Bahreïn								
1 VII 2006 (ESDF)								
MANAMA	176 909	113 503	63 406	30	...	...	...	...
Bangladesh								
15 III 2011 (CDFC)								
Barisal	339 308	174 980	164 328	...	...	...	...	...
Chittagong	2 591 681	1 367 282	1 224 399	...	...	...	...	...
Comilla	296 010	153 523	142 487	...	...	...	...	...
DHAKA	8 906 035	4 931 802	3 974 233	...	...	...	...	...
Khulna	664 728	346 069	318 659	...	...	...	...	...
Mymensingh	389 918	200 053	189 865	...	...	...	...	...
Narayanganj	286 330	148 214	138 116	...	...	...	...	...
Rajshahi	449 756	232 974	216 782	...	...	...	...	...
Saidpur	133 433	68 884	64 549	...	...	...	...	...
Bhutan - Bhoutan								
30 V 2017 (CDFC)								
THIMPHU	114 551	58 996	55 555	26.1	...	...	...	...
Brunei Darussalam - Brunéi Darussalam								
21 VIII 2001 (CDFC)								
BANDAR SERI BEGAWAN	27 285	13 639	13 646	100.4	...	...	...	...
Cambodia - Cambodge[42]								
1 VII 2011 (ESDF)								
Bat Dambang	1 126 345	558 945	567 400	...	...	...	...	...
PHNOM PENH	1 570 791	738 159	832 631	...	...	...	...	...
Seam Reab	999 703	493 184	506 519	...	...	...	...	...
China - Chine[43]								
1 VII 2016 (ESDF)								
BEIJING (PEKING)	...	...	...	...	18 796 000	...	...	...
China, Hong Kong SAR - Chine, Hong Kong RAS								
1 VII 2017 (ESDJ)								
HONG KONG SAR	7 391 700	3 392 500	3 999 200	1106	...	...	...	...
China, Macao SAR - Chine, Macao RAS[44]								
7 VIII 2016 (SSDJ)								
MACAO	650 834	314 018	336 816	...	...	...	...	...
Cyprus - Chypre								
1 I 2017 (ESDJ)								
LEFKOSIA[45]	...	...	...	...	244 200	...	...	...
Lemesos[46]	...	...	...	...	182 600	...	...	...
Democratic People's Republic of Korea - République populaire démocratique de Corée								
1 X 2008 (CDJC)								
Anju	167 646	79 187	88 459	...	...	...	...	...
Chongjin	614 892	292 741	322 151	...	...	...	...	...
Haeju	241 599	116 594	125 005	...	...	...	...	...
Hamhung	614 198	292 058	322 140	...	...	...	...	...
Huichon	136 093	64 547	71 546	...	...	...	...	...
Hyesan	174 015	82 604	91 411	...	...	...	...	...
Jongju	102 659	48 423	54 236	...	...	...	...	...
Kaechon	262 389	124 222	138 167	...	...	...	...	...
Kaesong	192 578	90 653	101 925	...	...	...	...	...
Kanggye	251 971	120 305	131 666	...	...	...	...	...
Kim Chaek	155 284	73 133	82 151	...	...	...	...	...
Kusong	155 181	73 677	81 504	...	...	...	...	...
Nampho	310 864	150 091	160 773	...	...	...	...	...
Phyongsong	236 583	115 817	120 766	...	...	...	...	...
PYONGYANG	2 581 076	1 233 765	1 347 311	...	...	...	...	...
Rason	158 337	74 777	83 560	...	...	...	...	...
Sariwon	271 434	130 181	141 253	...	...	...	...	...
Sinpho	130 951	63 207	67 744	...	...	...	...	...
Sinuiju	334 031	158 139	175 892	...	...	...	...	...
Sunchon	250 738	119 727	131 011	...	...	...	...	...
Tanchon	240 873	113 221	127 652	...	...	...	...	...
Tokchon	210 571	99 655	110 916	...	...	...	...	...
Wonsan	328 467	155 903	172 564	...	...	...	...	...

8. Population of capital cities and cities of 100 000 or more inhabitants: latest available year, 1998 - 2017
Population des capitales et des villes de 100 000 habitants ou plus : dernière année disponible, 1998 - 2017 (continued - suite)

Continent, country or area, date, code[a] and city / Continent, pays ou zone, date, code[a] et ville	City proper - Ville proprement dite				Urban agglomeration - Agglomération urbaine			
	Population			Surface area - Superficie (km²)	Population			Surface area - Superficie (km²)
	Both sexes - Les deux sexes	Male - Masculin	Female - Féminin		Both sexes - Les deux sexes	Male - Masculin	Female - Féminin	
ASIA - ASIE								
Georgia - Géorgie								
1 VII 2016 (ESDJ)								
Batumi	155 000	...	...	...	...	...	...	...
Kutaisi	147 500	...	...	...	...	...	...	...
Rustavi	126 200	...	...	...	...	...	...	...
TBILISI	1 113 800	...	...	...	...	...	...	...
India - Inde								
9 II 2011 (CDFC)								
Abohar	...	...	...	...	145 302	76 984	68 318	...
Achalpur	...	...	...	...	112 311	58 108	54 203	...
Adilabad	...	...	...	...	117 167	59 448	57 719	...
Adityapur	...	...	...	...	174 355	91 664	82 691	...
Adoni	...	...	...	...	184 625	91 736	92 889	...
Agartala	...	...	...	...	400 004	200 132	199 872	...
Agra	...	...	...	...	1 585 704	845 902	739 802	...
Ahmadabad	...	...	...	...	5 633 927	2 968 460	2 665 467	...
Ahmadnagar	...	...	...	...	350 859	178 899	171 960	...
Aizawl	...	...	...	...	293 416	144 913	148 503	...
Ajmer	...	...	...	...	542 321	278 545	263 776	...
Akbarpur	...	...	...	...	111 447	57 330	54 117	...
Akola	...	...	...	...	425 817	217 393	208 424	...
Alandur	...	...	...	...	164 430	82 332	82 098	...
Alappuzha	...	...	...	...	240 991	116 439	124 552	...
Aligarh	...	...	...	...	874 408	461 772	412 636	...
Allahabad	...	...	...	...	1 168 385	630 577	537 808	...
Alwar	...	...	...	...	322 568	170 530	152 038	...
Ambala	...	...	...	...	195 153	102 607	92 546	...
Ambala Sadar	...	...	...	...	104 974	54 680	50 294	...
Ambarnath	...	...	...	...	253 475	132 582	120 893	...
Ambattur	...	...	...	...	466 205	234 923	231 282	...
Ambikapur	...	...	...	...	121 071	62 776	58 295	...
Ambur	...	...	...	...	114 608	56 382	58 226	...
Amravati	...	...	...	...	647 057	329 992	317 065	...
Amreli	...	...	...	...	117 967	59 902	58 065	...
Amritsar	...	...	...	...	1 159 227	615 417	543 810	...
Amroha	...	...	...	...	198 471	103 097	95 374	...
Anand	...	...	...	...	209 410	108 403	101 007	...
Anantapur	...	...	...	...	267 161	133 919	133 242	...
Anantnag	...	...	...	...	150 592	77 712	72 880	...
Arrah	...	...	...	...	261 430	138 804	122 626	...
Asansol	...	...	...	...	563 917	292 387	271 530	...
Ashoknagar Kalyangarh	...	...	...	...	121 592	61 236	60 356	...
Aurangabad (Bihar)	...	...	...	...	102 244	53 542	48 702	...
Aurangabad (Maharashtra)	...	...	...	...	1 175 116	609 206	565 910	...
Avadi	...	...	...	...	345 996	175 658	170 338	...
Azamgarh	...	...	...	...	110 983	57 878	53 105	...
Badlapur	...	...	...	...	174 226	90 365	83 861	...
Bagaha	...	...	...	...	112 634	59 614	53 020	...
Bagalkot	...	...	...	...	111 933	56 378	55 555	...
Bahadurgarh	...	...	...	...	170 767	91 721	79 046	...
Baharampur	...	...	...	...	195 223	100 247	94 976	...
Bahraich	...	...	...	...	186 223	97 653	88 570	...
Baidyabati	...	...	...	...	121 110	62 485	58 625	...
Baleshwar Town	...	...	...	...	144 373	73 721	70 652	...
Ballia	...	...	...	...	104 424	55 459	48 965	...
Bally (Census Town)	...	...	...	...	113 377	58 530	54 847	...
Bally (Municipality)	...	...	...	...	293 373	156 911	136 462	...
Balurghat	...	...	...	...	153 279	76 730	76 549	...
Banda	...	...	...	...	160 473	85 370	75 103	...
Bankura	...	...	...	...	137 386	69 843	67 543	...
Bansberia	...	...	...	...	103 920	53 760	50 160	...
Banswara	...	...	...	...	101 017	51 585	49 432	...
Baran	...	...	...	...	117 992	61 071	56 921	...
Baranagar	...	...	...	...	245 213	126 187	119 026	...
Barasat	...	...	...	...	278 435	140 822	137 613	...

Continent, country or area, date, code[a] and city / Continent, pays ou zone, date, code[a] et ville	City proper - Ville proprement dite				Urban agglomeration - Agglomération urbaine			
	Population			Surface area - Superficie (km²)	Population			Surface area - Superficie (km²)
	Both sexes - Les deux sexes	Male - Masculin	Female - Féminin		Both sexes - Les deux sexes	Male - Masculin	Female - Féminin	
ASIA - ASIE								
India - Inde								
9 II 2011 (CDFC)								
Baraut	...	...	...	...	103 764	55 013	48 751	...
Barddhaman	...	...	...	...	314 265	159 936	154 329	...
Bareilly	...	...	...	...	904 797	477 515	427 282	...
Baripada Town	...	...	...	...	116 849	60 489	56 360	...
Barnala	...	...	...	...	116 449	62 554	53 895	...
Barrackpur	...	...	...	...	152 783	78 349	74 434	...
Barshi	...	...	...	...	118 722	60 801	57 921	...
Basirhat	...	...	...	...	125 254	63 223	62 031	...
Basti	...	...	...	...	114 657	60 095	54 562	...
Batala	...	...	...	...	158 621	83 655	74 966	...
Bathinda	...	...	...	...	285 788	151 524	134 264	...
Beawar	...	...	...	...	151 152	77 616	73 536	...
Begusarai	...	...	...	...	252 008	133 722	118 286	...
Belgaum	...	...	...	...	490 045	246 537	243 508	...
Bellary	...	...	...	...	410 445	206 149	204 296	...
Bettiah	...	...	...	...	132 209	69 529	62 680	...
Betul	...	...	...	...	103 330	52 823	50 507	...
Bhadrak	...	...	...	...	121 338	62 335	59 003	...
Bhadravati	...	...	...	...	151 102	75 009	76 093	...
Bhadreswar	...	...	...	...	101 477	53 330	48 147	...
Bhagalpur	...	...	...	...	400 146	212 813	187 333	...
Bhalswa Jahangir Pur	...	...	...	...	197 148	106 388	90 760	...
Bharatpur	...	...	...	...	252 838	134 040	118 798	...
Bharuch	...	...	...	...	169 007	86 810	82 197	...
Bhatpara	...	...	...	...	386 019	204 539	181 480	...
Bhavnagar	...	...	...	...	605 882	315 429	290 453	...
Bhilai Nagar	...	...	...	...	627 734	323 479	304 255	...
Bhilwara	...	...	...	...	359 483	187 081	172 402	...
Bhimavaram	...	...	...	...	146 961	72 441	74 520	...
Bhind	...	...	...	...	197 585	105 352	92 233	...
Bhiwadi	...	...	...	...	104 921	59 712	45 209	...
Bhiwandi	...	...	...	...	709 665	415 339	294 326	...
Bhiwani	...	...	...	...	196 057	104 026	92 031	...
Bhopal	...	...	...	...	1 798 218	936 168	862 050	...
Bhubaneswar Town	...	...	...	...	885 363	468 043	417 320	...
Bhuj	...	...	...	...	148 834	78 813	70 021	...
Bhusawal	...	...	...	...	187 421	96 147	91 274	...
Bid	...	...	...	...	146 709	75 566	71 143	...
Bidar	...	...	...	...	216 020	111 470	104 550	...
Bidhan Nagar	...	...	...	...	215 514	109 014	106 500	...
Biharsharif	...	...	...	...	297 268	155 216	142 052	...
Bijapur	...	...	...	...	327 427	165 177	162 250	...
Bikaner	...	...	...	...	644 406	338 442	305 964	...
Bilaspur	...	...	...	...	365 579	188 342	177 237	...
Bokaro Steel City	...	...	...	...	414 820	219 646	195 174	...
Bongaon	...	...	...	...	108 864	55 382	53 482	...
Botad	...	...	...	...	130 327	67 675	62 652	...
Brahmapur	...	...	...	...	356 598	185 754	170 844	...
Bruhat Bengaluru Mahanagara Palike (BBMP)	...	...	...	...	8 495 492	4 420 006	4 075 486	...
Budaun	...	...	...	...	159 285	83 176	76 109	...
Bulandshahar	...	...	...	...	230 024	120 275	109 749	...
Bundi	...	...	...	...	104 919	54 485	50 434	...
Burari	...	...	...	...	146 190	78 103	68 087	...
Burhanpur	...	...	...	...	210 886	108 187	102 699	...
Buxar	...	...	...	...	102 861	54 277	48 584	...
Champdani	...	...	...	...	111 251	59 350	51 901	...
Chandannagar	...	...	...	...	166 867	84 009	82 858	...
Chandausi	...	...	...	...	114 383	60 256	54 127	...
Chandigarh	...	...	...	...	970 602	531 051	439 551	...
Chandrapur	...	...	...	...	320 379	164 085	156 294	...
Chapra	...	...	...	...	202 352	106 501	95 851	...
Chas	...	...	...	...	141 640	74 727	66 913	...
Chennai	...	...	...	...	4 646 732	2 335 844	2 310 888	...

Continent, country or area, date, code[a] and city / Continent, pays ou zone, date, code[a] et ville	City proper - Ville proprement dite				Urban agglomeration - Agglomération urbaine			
	Population			Surface area - Superficie (km²)	Population			Surface area - Superficie (km²)
	Both sexes - Les deux sexes	Male - Masculin	Female - Féminin		Both sexes - Les deux sexes	Male - Masculin	Female - Féminin	
ASIA - ASIE								
India - Inde								
9 II 2011 (CDFC)								
Chhatarpur	...	...	...	...	142 128	75 070	67 058	...
Chhindwara	...	...	...	...	175 052	89 396	85 656	...
Chikmagalur	...	...	...	...	118 401	58 702	59 699	...
Chilakaluripet	...	...	...	...	101 398	50 207	51 191	...
Chitradurga	...	...	...	...	145 853	73 020	72 833	...
Chittaurgarh	...	...	...	...	116 406	60 068	56 338	...
Chittoor	...	...	...	...	160 722	80 060	80 662	...
Churu	...	...	...	...	120 157	61 774	58 383	...
Coimbatore	...	...	...	...	1 050 721	526 163	524 558	...
Cuddalore	...	...	...	...	173 636	85 700	87 936	...
Cuttack	...	...	...	...	610 189	316 242	293 947	...
Dabgram	...	...	...	...	119 040	61 078	57 962	...
Dallo Pura	...	...	...	...	154 791	81 262	73 529	...
Damoh	...	...	...	...	139 561	72 869	66 692	...
Darbhanga	...	...	...	...	296 039	155 637	140 402	...
Darjiling	...	...	...	...	118 805	59 187	59 618	...
Datia	...	...	...	...	100 284	52 772	47 512	...
Davanagere	...	...	...	...	434 971	219 776	215 195	...
Deesa	...	...	...	...	111 160	58 657	52 503	...
Dehradun	...	...	...	...	574 840	301 207	273 633	...
Dehri	...	...	...	...	137 231	72 372	64 859	...
Delhi Cantonment	...	...	...	...	110 351	63 757	46 594	...
Delhi Municipal Corporation (DMC)	...	...	...	...	11 034 555	5 882 117	5 152 438	...
Deoghar	...	...	...	...	203 123	107 997	95 126	...
Deoli	...	...	...	...	169 122	90 914	78 208	...
Deoria	...	...	...	...	129 479	67 462	62 017	...
Dewas	...	...	...	...	289 550	150 081	139 469	...
Dhamtari	...	...	...	...	101 677	50 807	50 870	...
Dhanbad	...	...	...	...	1 162 472	614 722	547 750	...
Dharmavaram	...	...	...	...	121 874	62 250	59 624	...
Dhaulpur	...	...	...	...	133 075	71 298	61 777	...
Dhule	...	...	...	...	375 559	193 446	182 113	...
Dibrugarh	...	...	...	...	145 488	75 318	70 170	...
Dimapur	...	...	...	...	122 834	64 300	58 534	...
Dinapur Nizamat	...	...	...	...	182 429	96 875	85 554	...
Dindigul	...	...	...	...	207 327	103 027	104 300	...
Dohad	...	...	...	...	118 846	60 515	58 331	...
Dum Dum	...	...	...	...	114 786	58 566	56 220	...
Durg	...	...	...	...	268 806	136 641	132 165	...
Durgapur	...	...	...	...	566 517	294 255	272 262	...
Eluru	...	...	...	...	218 020	107 511	110 509	...
English Bazar	...	...	...	...	205 521	106 824	98 697	...
Erode	...	...	...	...	157 101	78 222	78 879	...
Etah	...	...	...	...	118 517	62 590	55 927	...
Etawah	...	...	...	...	256 838	135 439	121 399	...
Faizabad	...	...	...	...	165 228	85 620	79 608	...
Faridabad	...	...	...	...	1 414 050	754 542	659 508	...
Farrukhabad-cum-Fatehgarh	...	...	...	...	276 581	145 641	130 940	...
Fatehpur	...	...	...	...	193 193	101 263	91 930	...
Firozabad	...	...	...	...	604 214	319 415	284 799	...
Firozpur	...	...	...	...	110 313	58 451	51 862	...
Gadag-Betigeri	...	...	...	...	172 612	85 920	86 692	...
Gandhidham	...	...	...	...	247 992	131 484	116 508	...
Gandhinagar	...	...	...	...	292 797	153 443	139 354	...
Ganganagar	...	...	...	...	237 780	127 840	109 940	...
Gangapur City	...	...	...	...	119 090	62 829	56 261	...
Gangawati	...	...	...	...	114 642	57 230	57 412	...
Gangtok	...	...	...	...	100 286	52 459	47 827	...
Gaya	...	...	...	...	474 093	250 037	224 056	...
Ghaziabad	...	...	...	...	1 648 643	874 607	774 036	...
Ghazipur	...	...	...	...	121 020	63 513	57 507	...
Giridih	...	...	...	...	114 533	59 966	54 567	...
Godhra	...	...	...	...	143 644	74 230	69 414	...

8. Population of capital cities and cities of 100 000 or more inhabitants: latest available year, 1998 - 2017
Population des capitales et des villes de 100 000 habitants ou plus : dernière année disponible, 1998 - 2017 (continued - suite)

Continent, country or area, date, code[a] and city / Continent, pays ou zone, date, code[a] et ville	City proper - Ville proprement dite				Urban agglomeration - Agglomération urbaine			
	Population			Surface area - Superficie (km²)	Population			Surface area - Superficie (km²)
	Both sexes - Les deux sexes	Male - Masculin	Female - Féminin		Both sexes - Les deux sexes	Male - Masculin	Female - Féminin	
ASIA - ASIE								
India - Inde								
9 II 2011 (CDFC)								
Gokal Pur	...	...	...	...	121 870	64 857	57 013	...
Gonda	...	...	...	...	114 046	59 948	54 098	...
Gondal	...	...	...	...	112 197	58 300	53 897	...
Gondiya	...	...	...	...	132 813	66 500	66 313	...
Gorakhpur	...	...	...	...	673 446	353 907	319 539	...
Greater Hyderabad Municipal Corporation (GHMC)	...	...	...	...	6 993 262	3 576 640	3 416 622	...
Greater Mumbai	...	...	...	...	12 442 373	6 715 931	5 726 442	...
Greater Noida	...	...	...	...	102 054	55 540	46 514	...
Greater Visakhapatnam Municipal Corporation (GVMC)	...	...	...	...	1 728 128	873 599	854 529	...
Gudivada	...	...	...	...	118 167	59 062	59 105	...
Gulbarga	...	...	...	...	543 147	276 552	266 595	...
Guna	...	...	...	...	180 935	94 464	86 471	...
Guntakal	...	...	...	...	126 270	62 851	63 419	...
Guntur	...	...	...	...	670 073	331 435	338 638	...
Gurgaon	...	...	...	...	886 519	480 042	406 477	...
Guwahati	...	...	...	...	962 334	498 450	463 884	...
Gwalior	...	...	...	...	1 054 420	561 165	493 255	...
Habra	...	...	...	...	147 221	74 592	72 629	...
Hajipur	...	...	...	...	147 688	78 047	69 641	...
Haldia	...	...	...	...	200 827	104 841	95 986	...
Haldwani-cum-Kathgodam	...	...	...	...	201 461	105 580	95 881	...
Halisahar	...	...	...	...	124 939	65 467	59 472	...
Hanumangarh	...	...	...	...	150 958	79 709	71 249	...
Haora	...	...	...	...	1 077 075	561 220	515 855	...
Hapur	...	...	...	...	262 983	139 525	123 458	...
Hardoi	...	...	...	...	197 029	103 619	93 410	...
Hardwar	...	...	...	...	231 338	123 455	107 883	...
Hassan	...	...	...	...	155 006	77 051	77 955	...
Hastsal	...	...	...	...	176 877	94 833	82 044	...
Hathras	...	...	...	...	143 020	76 054	66 966	...
Hazaribag	...	...	...	...	142 489	74 132	68 357	...
Hindaun	...	...	...	...	105 452	55 834	49 618	...
Hindupur	...	...	...	...	151 677	76 370	75 307	...
Hinganghat	...	...	...	...	101 805	52 577	49 228	...
Hisar	...	...	...	...	307 024	166 494	140 530	...
Hoshangabad	...	...	...	...	117 988	61 716	56 272	...
Hoshiarpur	...	...	...	...	168 653	88 304	80 349	...
Hospet	...	...	...	...	206 167	102 668	103 499	...
Hosur	...	...	...	...	116 821	59 351	57 470	...
Hubli-Dharwad	...	...	...	...	943 788	474 518	469 270	...
Hugli-Chinsurah	...	...	...	...	179 931	90 217	89 714	...
Ichalkaranji	...	...	...	...	287 353	149 164	138 189	...
Imphal	...	...	...	...	277 196	135 059	142 137	...
Indore	...	...	...	...	1 994 397	1 035 912	958 485	...
Jabalpur	...	...	...	...	1 081 677	559 361	522 316	...
Jagadhri	...	...	...	...	124 894	67 685	57 209	...
Jagdalpur	...	...	...	...	125 463	63 989	61 474	...
Jagtial	...	...	...	...	103 930	51 828	52 102	...
Jaipur	...	...	...	...	3 046 163	1 603 125	1 443 038	...
Jalandhar	...	...	...	...	868 929	460 811	408 118	...
Jalgaon	...	...	...	...	460 228	240 590	219 638	...
Jalna	...	...	...	...	285 577	147 092	138 485	...
Jalpaiguri	...	...	...	...	107 341	53 708	53 633	...
Jamalpur	...	...	...	...	105 434	56 072	49 362	...
Jammu	...	...	...	...	576 198	303 689	272 509	...
Jamnagar	...	...	...	...	600 943	313 214	287 729	...
Jamshedpur	...	...	...	...	677 350	353 212	324 138	...
Jamuria	...	...	...	...	149 220	77 379	71 841	...
Jaunpur	...	...	...	...	180 362	93 718	86 644	...
Jehanabad	...	...	...	...	103 202	54 710	48 492	...
Jetpur Navagadh	...	...	...	...	118 302	62 174	56 128	...

8. Population of capital cities and cities of 100 000 or more inhabitants: latest available year, 1998 - 2017
Population des capitales et des villes de 100 000 habitants ou plus : dernière année disponible, 1998 - 2017 (continued - suite)

Continent, country or area, date, code[a] and city / Continent, pays ou zone, date, code[a] et ville	City proper - Ville proprement dite				Urban agglomeration - Agglomération urbaine			
	Population			Surface area - Superficie (km²)	Population			Surface area - Superficie (km²)
	Both sexes - Les deux sexes	Male - Masculin	Female - Féminin		Both sexes - Les deux sexes	Male - Masculin	Female - Féminin	

ASIA - ASIE

India - Inde
9 II 2011 (CDFC)

Jhansi	...	...	...	...	505 693	265 449	240 244	...
Jhunjhunun	...	...	...	...	118 473	61 548	56 925	...
Jind	...	...	...	...	167 592	89 253	78 339	...
Jodhpur	...	...	...	...	1 056 191	555 371	500 820	...
Jorhat	...	...	...	...	126 736	65 489	61 247	...
Junagadh	...	...	...	...	319 462	163 413	156 049	...
Kadapa	...	...	...	...	344 893	173 314	171 579	...
Kaithal	...	...	...	...	144 915	76 794	68 121	...
Kakinada	...	...	...	...	384 182	188 308	195 874	...
Kalol	...	...	...	...	134 426	70 995	63 431	...
Kalyan Dombivali	...	...	...	...	1 247 327	649 626	597 701	...
Kalyani	...	...	...	...	100 575	50 727	49 848	...
Kamarhati	...	...	...	...	330 211	170 293	159 918	...
Kancheepuram	...	...	...	...	164 384	81 992	82 392	...
Kanchrapara	...	...	...	...	129 576	65 436	64 140	...
Kanhangad	...	...	...	...	125 564	58 564	67 000	...
Kanpur	...	...	...	...	2 768 057	1 490 547	1 277 510	...
Kanpur (Cantonment Board)	...	...	...	...	108 534	58 550	49 984	...
Karaikkudi	...	...	...	...	106 714	53 348	53 366	...
Karawal Nagar	...	...	...	...	224 281	119 951	104 330	...
Karimnagar	...	...	...	...	289 821	146 145	143 676	...
Karnal	...	...	...	...	302 140	159 653	142 487	...
Kasganj	...	...	...	...	101 277	53 552	47 725	...
Kashipur	...	...	...	...	121 623	63 609	58 014	...
Katihar	...	...	...	...	240 838	127 240	113 598	...
Khammam	...	...	...	...	196 283	96 898	99 385	...
Khandwa	...	...	...	...	200 738	102 901	97 837	...
Khanna	...	...	...	...	128 137	67 801	60 336	...
Kharagpur	...	...	...	...	207 604	106 559	101 045	...
Khardaha	...	...	...	...	108 496	54 879	53 617	...
Khargone	...	...	...	...	116 150	59 752	56 398	...
Khora	...	...	...	...	190 005	102 574	87 431	...
Khurja	...	...	...	...	121 207	63 825	57 382	...
Kirari Suleman Nagar	...	...	...	...	283 211	152 348	130 863	...
Kishanganj	...	...	...	...	105 782	55 143	50 639	...
Kishangarh	...	...	...	...	154 886	80 024	74 862	...
Kochi	...	...	...	...	633 553	312 358	321 195	...
Kolar	...	...	...	...	138 462	69 910	68 552	...
Kolhapur	...	...	...	...	549 236	280 366	268 870	...
Kolkata (Calcutta)	...	...	...	...	4 496 694	2 356 766	2 139 928	...
Kollam	...	...	...	...	367 107	177 072	190 035	...
Korba	...	...	...	...	365 253	189 772	175 481	...
Kota	...	...	...	...	1 001 694	528 601	473 093	...
Kozhikode	...	...	...	...	550 440	262 939	287 501	...
Krishnanagar	...	...	...	...	153 062	77 146	75 916	...
Kulti	...	...	...	...	313 809	163 193	150 616	...
Kumbakonam	...	...	...	...	140 156	69 340	70 816	...
Kurichi	...	...	...	...	123 667	61 815	61 852	...
Kurnool	...	...	...	...	457 633	228 148	229 485	...
Lakhimpur	...	...	...	...	151 993	80 523	71 470	...
Lalitpur	...	...	...	...	133 305	69 529	63 776	...
Latur	...	...	...	...	382 940	197 737	185 203	...
Loni	...	...	...	...	516 082	275 025	241 057	...
Lucknow	...	...	...	...	2 817 105	1 460 970	1 356 135	...
Ludhiana	...	...	...	...	1 618 879	874 908	743 971	...
Machilipatnam	...	...	...	...	169 892	83 594	86 298	...
Madanapalle	...	...	...	...	180 180	90 700	89 480	...
Madavaram	...	...	...	...	119 105	59 887	59 218	...
Madhyamgram	...	...	...	...	196 127	98 864	97 263	...
Madurai	...	...	...	...	1 017 865	509 302	508 563	...
Mahbubnagar	...	...	...	...	190 400	96 142	94 258	...
Mahesana	...	...	...	...	190 753	100 558	90 195	...
Maheshtala	...	...	...	...	448 317	229 693	218 624	...

8. Population of capital cities and cities of 100 000 or more inhabitants: latest available year, 1998 - 2017
Population des capitales et des villes de 100 000 habitants ou plus : dernière année disponible, 1998 - 2017 (continued - suite)

Continent, country or area, date, code[a] and city / Continent, pays ou zone, date, code[a] et ville	City proper - Ville proprement dite				Urban agglomeration - Agglomération urbaine			
	Population			Surface area - Superficie (km²)	Population			Surface area - Superficie (km²)
	Both sexes - Les deux sexes	Male - Masculin	Female - Féminin		Both sexes - Les deux sexes	Male - Masculin	Female - Féminin	

ASIA - ASIE

India - Inde

9 II 2011 (CDFC)

Mainpuri	...	...	...	...	136 557	71 274	65 283	...
Malappuram	...	...	...	...	101 386	48 957	52 429	...
Malegaon	...	...	...	...	481 228	244 080	237 148	...
Malerkotla	...	...	...	...	135 424	71 376	64 048	...
Mandoli	...	...	...	...	120 417	64 159	56 258	...
Mandsaur	...	...	...	...	141 667	72 488	69 179	...
Mandya	...	...	...	...	137 358	68 662	68 696	...
Mangalagiri	...	...	...	...	107 197	53 301	53 896	...
Mangalore	...	...	...	...	499 487	247 903	251 584	...
Mango	...	...	...	...	223 805	115 970	107 835	...
Mathura	...	...	...	...	349 909	185 983	163 926	...
Maunath Bhanjan	...	...	...	...	278 745	142 967	135 778	...
Medinipur	...	...	...	...	169 264	84 977	84 287	...
Meerut	...	...	...	...	1 305 429	688 118	617 311	...
Mira Bhayandar	...	...	...	...	809 378	429 260	380 118	...
Miryalaguda	...	...	...	...	104 918	52 565	52 353	...
Mirzapur-cum-Vindhyachal	...	...	...	...	234 871	125 601	109 270	...
Modinagar	...	...	...	...	130 325	69 268	61 057	...
Moga	...	...	...	...	163 397	86 604	76 793	...
Moradabad	...	...	...	...	887 871	464 580	423 291	...
Morena	...	...	...	...	200 482	108 390	92 092	...
Morvi	...	...	...	...	210 451	109 451	101 000	...
Motihari	...	...	...	...	126 158	67 861	58 297	...
Mughalsarai	...	...	...	...	109 650	57 682	51 968	...
Muktsar	...	...	...	...	116 747	61 725	55 022	...
Munger	...	...	...	...	213 303	113 291	100 012	...
Murwara (Katni)	...	...	...	...	221 883	115 348	106 535	...
Mustafabad	...	...	...	...	127 167	66 889	60 278	...
Muzaffarnagar	...	...	...	...	392 768	206 782	185 986	...
Muzaffarpur	...	...	...	...	354 462	187 564	166 898	...
Mysore	...	...	...	...	920 550	461 042	459 508	...
Nabadwip	...	...	...	...	125 543	65 415	60 128	...
Nadiad	...	...	...	...	225 071	115 903	109 168	...
Nagaon	...	...	...	...	121 628	61 642	59 986	...
Nagapattinam	...	...	...	...	102 905	50 793	52 112	...
Nagaur	...	...	...	...	105 218	54 126	51 092	...
Nagda	...	...	...	...	100 039	51 373	48 666	...
Nagercoil	...	...	...	...	224 849	109 938	114 911	...
Nagpur	...	...	...	...	2 405 665	1 225 405	1 180 260	...
Naihati	...	...	...	...	217 900	109 849	108 051	...
Nalgonda	...	...	...	...	154 326	77 320	77 006	...
Nanded Waghala	...	...	...	...	550 439	285 433	265 006	...
Nandurbar	...	...	...	...	111 037	57 412	53 625	...
Nandyal	...	...	...	...	211 424	105 826	105 598	...
Nangloi Jat	...	...	...	...	205 596	110 056	95 540	...
Narasaraopet	...	...	...	...	117 489	59 424	58 065	...
Nashik	...	...	...	...	1 486 053	782 517	703 536	...
Navi Mumbai (New Bombay)	...	...	...	...	1 120 547	610 060	510 487	...
Navi Mumbai Panvel Raigad	...	...	...	...	195 373	107 342	88 031	...
Navsari	...	...	...	...	171 109	88 486	82 623	...
Neemuch	...	...	...	...	128 561	67 890	60 671	...
Nellore	...	...	...	...	547 621	278 787	268 834	...
New Delhi Municipal Council (NDMC)	...	...	...	...	257 803	140 234	117 569	...
Neyveli	...	...	...	...	105 731	53 409	52 322	...
Nizamabad	...	...	...	...	311 152	154 929	156 223	...
Noida	...	...	...	...	637 272	349 397	287 875	...
North Barrackpur	...	...	...	...	132 806	66 924	65 882	...
North Dum Dum	...	...	...	...	249 142	126 279	122 863	...
Ongole	...	...	...	...	208 344	104 646	103 698	...
Orai	...	...	...	...	190 575	101 306	89 269	...
Osmanabad	...	...	...	...	111 825	57 824	54 001	...
Ozhukarai	...	...	...	...	300 104	148 464	151 640	...
Palakkad	...	...	...	...	130 955	63 833	67 122	...

8. Population of capital cities and cities of 100 000 or more inhabitants: latest available year, 1998 - 2017
Population des capitales et des villes de 100 000 habitants ou plus : dernière année disponible, 1998 - 2017 (continued - suite)

Continent, country or area, date, code[a] and city / Continent, pays ou zone, date, code[a] et ville	City proper - Ville proprement dite				Urban agglomeration - Agglomération urbaine			
	Population			Surface area - Superficie (km²)	Population			Surface area - Superficie (km²)
	Both sexes - Les deux sexes	Male - Masculin	Female - Féminin		Both sexes - Les deux sexes	Male - Masculin	Female - Féminin	
ASIA - ASIE								
India - Inde								
9 II 2011 (CDFC)								
Palanpur	...	...	...	...	141 592	74 088	67 504	...
Pali	...	...	...	...	230 075	119 924	110 151	...
Pallavaram	...	...	...	...	233 984	117 405	116 579	...
Palwal	...	...	...	...	131 926	69 997	61 929	...
Panchkula	...	...	...	...	211 355	111 731	99 624	...
Panihati	...	...	...	...	377 347	189 446	187 901	...
Panipat	...	...	...	...	295 970	158 063	137 907	...
Panvel	...	...	...	...	180 020	92 484	87 536	...
Parbhani	...	...	...	...	307 170	156 520	150 650	...
Patan	...	...	...	...	133 737	69 898	63 839	...
Pathankot	...	...	...	...	156 306	82 045	74 261	...
Patiala	...	...	...	...	446 246	236 198	210 048	...
Patna	...	...	...	...	1 684 297	893 445	790 852	...
Pilibhit	...	...	...	...	127 988	67 614	60 374	...
Pimpri Chinchwad	...	...	...	...	1 727 692	942 533	785 159	...
Pithampur	...	...	...	...	126 200	70 250	55 950	...
Porbandar	...	...	...	...	152 760	78 604	74 156	...
Port Blair	...	...	...	...	108 058	57 761	50 297	...
Proddatur	...	...	...	...	163 970	81 874	82 096	...
Puducherry	...	...	...	...	244 377	119 430	124 947	...
Pudukkottai	...	...	...	...	117 630	58 737	58 893	...
Pune	...	...	...	...	3 124 458	1 603 675	1 520 783	...
Puri	...	...	...	...	200 564	104 086	96 478	...
Purnia	...	...	...	...	282 248	148 077	134 171	...
Puruliya	...	...	...	...	121 067	62 351	58 716	...
Rae Bareli	...	...	...	...	191 316	99 903	91 413	...
Raichur	...	...	...	...	234 073	117 657	116 416	...
Raiganj	...	...	...	...	183 612	96 388	87 224	...
Raigarh	...	...	...	...	150 019	76 865	73 154	...
Raipur	...	...	...	...	1 027 264	527 365	499 899	...
Rajahmundry	...	...	...	...	376 333	185 970	190 363	...
Rajapalayam	...	...	...	...	130 442	64 765	65 677	...
Rajarhat Gopalpur	...	...	...	...	402 844	203 911	198 933	...
Rajkot	...	...	...	...	1 323 363	693 473	629 890	...
Rajnandgaon	...	...	...	...	163 114	81 929	81 185	...
Rajpur Sonarpur	...	...	...	...	424 368	215 405	208 963	...
Ramagundam	...	...	...	...	242 979	123 430	119 549	...
Rampur	...	...	...	...	325 313	169 681	155 632	...
Ranchi	...	...	...	...	1 073 427	558 872	514 555	...
Ranibennur	...	...	...	...	106 406	54 040	52 366	...
Raniganj	...	...	...	...	129 441	67 578	61 863	...
Ratlam	...	...	...	...	264 914	134 915	129 999	...
Raurkela Industrial Township	...	...	...	...	216 410	112 897	103 513	...
Raurkela Town	...	...	...	...	320 040	169 095	150 945	...
Rewa	...	...	...	...	235 654	124 012	111 642	...
Rewari	...	...	...	...	143 021	75 764	67 257	...
Rishra	...	...	...	...	124 577	66 606	57 971	...
Robertson Pet	...	...	...	...	162 230	80 375	81 855	...
Rohtak	...	...	...	...	374 292	198 237	176 055	...
Roorkee	...	...	...	...	118 200	63 434	54 766	...
Rudrapur	...	...	...	...	154 554	81 340	73 214	...
S.A.S. Nagar	...	...	...	...	166 864	87 380	79 484	...
Sagar	...	...	...	...	274 556	143 425	131 131	...
Saharanpur	...	...	...	...	705 478	371 740	333 738	...
Saharsa	...	...	...	...	156 540	83 291	73 249	...
Salem	...	...	...	...	829 267	417 317	411 950	...
Sambalpur	...	...	...	...	189 366	97 460	91 906	...
Sambhal	...	...	...	...	220 813	115 767	105 046	...
Sangli-Miraj Kupwad	...	...	...	...	502 793	253 640	249 153	...
Santipur	...	...	...	...	151 777	77 011	74 766	...
Sasaram	...	...	...	...	147 408	77 599	69 809	...
Satara	...	...	...	...	120 195	61 129	59 066	...
Satna	...	...	...	...	282 977	149 415	133 562	...

8. Population of capital cities and cities of 100 000 or more inhabitants: latest available year, 1998 - 2017
Population des capitales et des villes de 100 000 habitants ou plus : dernière année disponible, 1998 - 2017 (continued - suite)

Continent, country or area, date, code[a] and city / Continent, pays ou zone, date, code[a] et ville	City proper - Ville proprement dite				Urban agglomeration - Agglomération urbaine			
	Population			Surface area - Superficie (km²)	Population			Surface area - Superficie (km²)
	Both sexes - Les deux sexes	Male - Masculin	Female - Féminin		Both sexes - Les deux sexes	Male - Masculin	Female - Féminin	

ASIA - ASIE

India - Inde
 9 II 2011 (CDFC)

Sawai Madhopur	...	...	...	...	121 106	63 014	58 092	...
Secunderabad	...	...	...	...	217 910	113 577	104 333	...
Sehore	...	...	...	...	109 118	56 335	52 783	...
Seoni	...	...	...	...	102 343	52 352	49 991	...
Serampore	...	...	...	...	181 842	93 694	88 148	...
Shahjahanpur	...	...	...	...	329 736	173 006	156 730	...
Shamli	...	...	...	...	107 266	57 187	50 079	...
Shikohabad	...	...	...	...	107 404	56 794	50 610	...
Shillong	...	...	...	...	143 229	70 135	73 094	...
Shimla	...	...	...	...	169 578	93 152	76 426	...
Shimoga	...	...	...	...	322 650	162 018	160 632	...
Shivpuri	...	...	...	...	179 977	95 132	84 845	...
Sikar	...	...	...	...	244 497	126 837	117 660	...
Silchar	...	...	...	...	178 865	89 961	88 904	...
Siliguri	...	...	...	...	513 264	263 702	249 562	...
Singrauli	...	...	...	...	220 257	116 867	103 390	...
Sirsa	...	...	...	...	182 534	96 175	86 359	...
Sitapur	...	...	...	...	177 234	92 696	84 538	...
Siwan	...	...	...	...	135 066	70 756	64 310	...
Solapur	...	...	...	...	951 558	481 064	470 494	...
Sonipat	...	...	...	...	289 333	154 407	134 926	...
South Dum Dum	...	...	...	...	403 316	202 214	201 102	...
Srikakulam	...	...	...	...	137 944	68 457	69 487	...
Srinagar	...	...	...	...	1 206 419	631 830	574 589	...
Sujangarh	...	...	...	...	101 523	51 906	49 617	...
Sultan Pur Majra	...	...	...	...	181 554	95 687	85 867	...
Sultanpur	...	...	...	...	107 640	56 420	51 220	...
Surat	...	...	...	...	4 501 610	2 565 803	1 935 807	...
Surendranagar Dudhrej	...	...	...	...	177 851	92 675	85 176	...
Suryapet	...	...	...	...	106 805	52 773	54 032	...
Tadepalligudem	...	...	...	...	104 032	51 438	52 594	...
Tadpatri	...	...	...	...	108 171	54 015	54 156	...
Tambaram	...	...	...	...	174 787	89 060	85 727	...
Tenali	...	...	...	...	164 937	81 427	83 510	...
Thane	...	...	...	...	1 841 488	975 399	866 089	...
Thanesar	...	...	...	...	155 152	83 994	71 158	...
Thanjavur	...	...	...	...	222 943	109 199	113 744	...
Thiruvananthapuram	...	...	...	...	788 271	384 004	404 267	...
Thoothukkudi	...	...	...	...	237 830	118 298	119 532	...
Thrissur	...	...	...	...	315 957	152 296	163 661	...
Tinsukia	...	...	...	...	116 322	62 303	54 019	...
Tiruchirappalli	...	...	...	...	847 387	418 400	428 987	...
Tirunelveli	...	...	...	...	473 637	233 659	239 978	...
Tirupati	...	...	...	...	295 323	150 125	145 198	...
Tiruppur	...	...	...	...	444 352	227 311	217 041	...
Tiruvannamalai	...	...	...	...	145 278	72 406	72 872	...
Tiruvottiyur	...	...	...	...	249 446	125 300	124 146	...
Titagarh	...	...	...	...	116 541	62 735	53 806	...
Tonk	...	...	...	...	165 294	84 806	80 488	...
Tumkur	...	...	...	...	302 143	152 925	149 218	...
Udaipur	...	...	...	...	451 100	233 959	217 141	...
Udgir	...	...	...	...	103 550	54 013	49 537	...
Udupi	...	...	...	...	144 960	71 614	73 346	...
Ujjain	...	...	...	...	515 215	264 871	250 344	...
Ulhasnagar	...	...	...	...	506 098	269 048	237 050	...
Uluberia	...	...	...	...	235 345	120 741	114 604	...
Unnao	...	...	...	...	177 658	93 021	84 637	...
Uttarpara Kotrung	...	...	...	...	159 147	81 410	77 737	...
Vadodara	...	...	...	...	1 752 371	912 721	839 650	...
Valsad	...	...	...	...	139 764	71 400	68 364	...
Vapi	...	...	...	...	163 630	94 105	69 525	...
Varanasi	...	...	...	...	1 198 491	635 140	563 351	...
Vasai-Virar City	...	...	...	...	1 222 390	648 172	574 218	...

Continent, country or area, date, code[a] and city / Continent, pays ou zone, date, code[a] et ville	City proper - Ville proprement dite				Urban agglomeration - Agglomération urbaine			
	Population			Surface area - Superficie (km²)	Population			Surface area - Superficie (km²)
	Both sexes - Les deux sexes	Male - Masculin	Female - Féminin		Both sexes - Les deux sexes	Male - Masculin	Female - Féminin	
ASIA - ASIE								
India - Inde								
9 II 2011 (CDFC)								
Vellore	...	...	...	...	185 803	91 342	94 461	...
Veraval	...	...	...	...	171 121	87 009	84 112	...
Vidisha	...	...	...	...	155 951	81 488	74 463	...
Vijayawada	...	...	...	...	1 143 232	574 794	568 438	...
Vizianagaram	...	...	...	...	228 720	112 290	116 430	...
Warangal	...	...	...	...	704 570	353 309	351 261	...
Wardha	...	...	...	...	106 444	53 697	52 747	...
Yamunanagar	...	...	...	...	217 071	115 663	101 408	...
Yavatmal	...	...	...	...	116 551	58 549	58 002	...
Indonesia - Indonésie								
1 VII 2016 (ESDJ)								
Ambon	444 797	222 350	222 447	359.5	...	...	...	...
Balikpapan	636 012	328 382	307 630	512.3	...	...	...	...
Banda Aceh	259 913	133 728	126 185	61.4	...	...	...	...
Bandar Lampung	1 015 910	511 371	504 539	296	...	...	...	...
Bandjarmasin	692 793	347 005	345 788	72.6	...	...	...	...
Bandung	2 497 938	1 260 204	1 237 734	168.2	...	...	...	...
Batam	1 283 196	654 804	628 392	960.3	...	...	...	...
Bengkulu	368 065	184 887	183 178	144.5	...	...	...	...
Binjai	270 926	135 203	135 723	59.2	...	...	...	...
Bitung	212 409	108 481	103 928	304	...	...	...	...
Blitar	139 995	69 411	70 584	32.6	...	...	...	...
Bogor	1 081 009	548 196	532 813	111.7	...	...	...	...
Cirebon (Tjirebon)	313 325	157 103	156 222	40.2	...	...	...	...
Denpasar	914 279	466 651	447 628	127.8	...	...	...	...
Gorontalo	210 782	103 584	107 198	66	...	...	...	...
JAKARTA	10 374 235	5 202 815	5 171 420	662.3	...	...	...	...
Jambi	591 134	297 036	294 098	205.4	...	...	...	...
Jayapura	293 690	157 710	135 980	950.4	...	...	...	...
Kediri	284 003	141 609	142 394	63.4	...	...	...	...
Madiun	176 099	85 203	90 896	33.9	...	...	...	...
Magelang	121 474	59 766	61 708	18.1	...	...	...	...
Makasar (Ujung Pandang)	1 489 011	737 146	751 865	175.8	...	...	...	...
Malang	861 414	424 811	436 603	145.3	...	...	...	...
Manado	430 133	215 832	214 301	158	...	...	...	...
Mataram	468 509	231 797	236 712	61.3	...	...	...	...
Medan	2 247 425	1 110 000	1 137 425	265	...	...	...	...
Mojokerto	127 279	62 587	64 692	16.5	...	...	...	...
Padang	927 011	463 116	463 895	695	...	...	...	...
Pakalongan	301 870	150 887	150 983	45	...	...	...	...
Pakanbaru	1 091 088	559 917	531 171	632.3	...	...	...	...
Palangkaraya	275 667	141 179	134 488	2400	...	...	...	...
Palembang	1 623 099	813 709	809 390	363.7	...	...	...	...
Pangkal Pinang	204 392	104 927	99 465	118.8	...	...	...	...
Pare Pare	142 097	69 822	72 275	99.3	...	...	...	...
Pasuruan	197 696	97 995	99 701	35.3	...	...	...	...
Pematang Siantar	251 513	122 626	128 887	55.7	...	...	...	...
Pontianak	627 021	312 178	314 843	107.8	...	...	...	...
Probolinggo	233 123	114 822	118 301	56.7	...	...	...	...
Salatiga	188 928	92 426	96 502	53	...	...	...	...
Samarinda	843 446	435 949	407 497	716.5	...	...	...	...
Semarang	1 757 686	861 994	895 692	373.7	...	...	...	...
Sukabumi	323 788	163 891	159 897	49	...	...	...	...
Surabaya	2 874 699	1 420 182	1 454 517	350.5	...	...	...	...
Surakarta	516 102	250 896	265 206	44	...	...	...	...
Tangerang	2 139 891	1 091 787	1 048 104	153.9	...	...	...	...
Tanjung Balai	171 187	86 277	84 910	107.8	...	...	...	...
Tebing Tinggi	160 686	79 379	81 307	31	...	...	...	...
Tegal	248 094	122 817	125 277	34.5	...	...	...	...
Yogyakarta	422 732	206 421	216 311	32.5	...	...	...	...

8. Population of capital cities and cities of 100 000 or more inhabitants: latest available year, 1998 - 2017
Population des capitales et des villes de 100 000 habitants ou plus : dernière année disponible, 1998 - 2017 (continued - suite)

Continent, country or area, date, code[a] and city / Continent, pays ou zone, date, code[a] et ville	City proper - Ville proprement dite				Urban agglomeration - Agglomération urbaine			
	Population			Surface area - Superficie (km²)	Population			Surface area - Superficie (km²)
	Both sexes - Les deux sexes	Male - Masculin	Female - Féminin		Both sexes - Les deux sexes	Male - Masculin	Female - Féminin	

ASIA - ASIE

Iran (Islamic Republic of) - Iran (République islamique d')
24 IX 2016 (CDJC)

Abadan	231 476	115 745	115 731	...	...	...	...	...
Ahar	100 641	50 386	50 255	...	...	...	...	...
Ahwaz	1 184 788	596 774	588 014	...	...	...	...	...
Amol	237 528	118 706	118 822	...	...	...	...	...
Andimeshk	135 116	68 218	66 898	...	...	...	...	...
Andisheh	116 062	58 717	57 345	...	...	...	...	...
Arak	520 944	263 143	257 801	...	...	...	...	...
Ardabil	529 374	269 387	259 987	...	...	...	...	...
Babol	250 217	124 863	125 354	...	...	...	...	...
Bam	127 396	65 128	62 268	...	...	...	...	...
Bandar-e-Abbas	526 648	269 033	257 615	...	...	...	...	...
Bandar-e-Anzali	118 564	58 802	59 762	...	...	...	...	...
Bandar-e-Mahshahr	162 797	81 717	81 080	...	...	...	...	...
Baneh	110 218	55 609	54 609	...	...	...	...	...
Behbahan	122 604	62 124	60 480	...	...	...	...	...
Birjand	203 636	102 399	101 237	...	...	...	...	...
Bojnurd	228 931	114 441	114 490	...	...	...	...	...
Borazjan	110 567	55 675	54 892	...	...	...	...	...
Borujerd	234 997	117 255	117 742	...	...	...	...	...
Bukand	193 501	97 659	95 842	...	...	...	...	...
Bushehr	223 504	115 260	108 244	...	...	...	...	...
Chabahar	106 739	54 657	52 082	...	...	...	...	...
Dezful	264 709	135 925	128 784	...	...	...	...	...
Dorud	121 638	61 395	60 243	...	...	...	...	...
Esfahan	1 961 260	989 168	972 092	...	...	...	...	...
Fardis	181 174	90 573	90 601	...	...	...	...	...
Fasa	110 825	55 650	55 175	...	...	...	...	...
Golestan (Soltanabad)	239 556	123 923	115 633	...	...	...	...	...
Gonbad-e-Kavus	151 910	75 899	76 011	...	...	...	...	...
Gorgan	350 676	174 797	175 879	...	...	...	...	...
Hamadan	554 406	276 455	277 951	...	...	...	...	...
Ilam	194 030	98 276	95 754	...	...	...	...	...
Iranshahr	113 750	58 143	55 607	...	...	...	...	...
Islam Shahr (Qasemabad)	448 129	227 808	220 321	...	...	...	...	...
Izeh	119 399	59 665	59 734	...	...	...	...	...
Jahrom	141 634	73 641	67 993	...	...	...	...	...
Jiroft	130 429	66 874	63 555	...	...	...	...	...
Kamal Shahr	141 669	72 661	69 008	...	...	...	...	...
Karaj	1 592 492	802 398	790 094	...	...	...	...	...
Kashan	304 487	154 100	150 387	...	...	...	...	...
Kashmar	102 282	51 616	50 666	...	...	...	...	...
Kerman	537 718	272 715	265 003	...	...	...	...	...
Kermanshah	946 651	474 073	472 578	...	...	...	...	...
Khomeini shahr	247 128	127 450	119 678	...	...	...	...	...
Khoramabad	373 416	186 481	186 935	...	...	...	...	...
Khoramshahr	133 097	66 113	66 984	...	...	...	...	...
Khoy	198 845	99 712	99 133	...	...	...	...	...
Lahijan	101 073	50 123	50 950	...	...	...	...	...
Mahabad	168 393	84 271	84 122	...	...	...	...	...
Malard	281 027	143 278	137 749	...	...	...	...	...
Malayer	170 237	85 487	84 750	...	...	...	...	...
Marand	130 825	66 671	64 154	...	...	...	...	...
Maraqeh	175 255	87 868	87 387	...	...	...	...	...
Marivan	136 654	69 679	66 975	...	...	...	...	...
Marvadsht	148 858	76 363	72 495	...	...	...	...	...
Mashhad	3 001 184	1 503 824	1 497 360	...	...	...	...	...
Masjed Soleyman	100 497	51 019	49 478	...	...	...	...	...
Miandoab	134 425	68 679	65 746	...	...	...	...	...
Mohammad Shahr	119 418	60 988	58 430	...	...	...	...	...
Najafabad	235 281	118 710	116 571	...	...	...	...	...
Nasim Shahr	200 393	103 371	97 022	...	...	...	...	...
Nazar Abad	119 512	61 074	58 438	...	...	...	...	...

Continent, country or area, date, code[a] and city / Continent, pays ou zone, date, code[a] et ville	City proper - Ville proprement dite				Urban agglomeration - Agglomération urbaine			
	Population			Surface area - Superficie (km²)	Population			Surface area - Superficie (km²)
	Both sexes - Les deux sexes	Male - Masculin	Female - Féminin		Both sexes - Les deux sexes	Male - Masculin	Female - Féminin	

ASIA - ASIE

Iran (Islamic Republic of) - Iran (République islamique d')
24 IX 2016 (CDJC)

Neyshabur	264 375	132 273	132 102	...	...	...	...	...
Orumiyeh	736 224	369 043	367 181	...	...	...	...	...
Pakdasht	236 319	120 459	115 860	...	...	...	...	...
Qaem shahr	204 953	101 999	102 954	...	...	...	...	...
Qarchak	231 075	118 260	112 815	...	...	...	...	...
Qazvin	402 748	203 702	199 046	...	...	...	...	...
Qods	309 605	158 567	151 038	...	...	...	...	...
Qom	1 201 158	609 541	591 617	...	...	...	...	...
Quchan	101 604	51 501	50 103	...	...	...	...	...
Rafsanjan	161 909	83 607	78 302	...	...	...	...	...
Rasht	679 995	336 313	343 682	...	...	...	...	...
Robatkarim	105 393	53 647	51 746	...	...	...	...	...
Sabzewar	243 700	121 667	122 033	...	...	...	...	...
Sanandaj	412 767	208 059	204 708	...	...	...	...	...
Saqez	165 258	82 984	82 274	...	...	...	...	...
Sari	309 820	153 823	155 997	...	...	...	...	...
Saveh	220 762	112 742	108 020	...	...	...	...	...
Semnan	185 129	94 411	90 718	...	...	...	...	...
Shahinshahr	173 329	86 008	87 321	...	...	...	...	...
Shahr-e-Kord	190 441	94 789	95 652	...	...	...	...	...
Shahreza	134 952	68 191	66 761	...	...	...	...	...
Shahriar	309 607	156 085	153 522	...	...	...	...	...
Shahrud	150 129	75 656	74 473	...	...	...	...	...
Shiraz	1 565 572	785 450	780 122	...	...	...	...	...
Shoshtar	101 878	51 762	50 116	...	...	...	...	...
Sirjan	199 704	102 656	97 048	...	...	...	...	...
Tabriz	1 558 693	786 661	772 032	...	...	...	...	...
TEHRAN	8 693 706	4 324 155	4 369 551	...	...	...	...	...
Torbat-e-heydariyeh	140 019	71 603	68 416	...	...	...	...	...
Torbatejam	100 449	50 772	49 677	...	...	...	...	...
Varamin	225 628	114 215	111 413	...	...	...	...	...
Yasooj	134 532	68 427	66 105	...	...	...	...	...
Yazd	529 673	269 732	259 941	...	...	...	...	...
Zabol	134 950	67 691	67 259	...	...	...	...	...
Zahedan	587 730	299 550	288 180	...	...	...	...	...
Zanjan	430 871	217 406	213 465	...	...	...	...	...

Iraq
1 VII 2015 (ESDF)

Abi Gharaq Nahia	108 630	55 009	53 621	191	...	...	...	...
Abna'a Al-Rafidain Nahia	153 712	77 827	75 885	...	...	...	...	...
Abu Al-Khaseeb Qadha Center	215 247	108 228	107 019	1152	...	...	...	...
Abu-Gharib Qadha Center	149 858	76 274	73 584	431	...	...	...	...
Al-Adhamia Qadha Center	286 036	144 825	141 211	29	...	...	...	...
Al-Amara Qadha Center	541 034	270 426	270 608	2862	...	...	...	...
Al-Amirya Nahia	101 119	51 899	49 220	2532	...	...	...	...
Al-Basrah Qadha Center	1 225 793	616 525	609 268	1085	...	...	...	...
Al-Dair Nahia	101 882	50 969	50 913	825	...	...	...	...
Al-Dijail Qadha Center	105 345	53 240	52 105	1286	...	...	...	...
Al-Diwaniya Qadha Center	421 571	212 293	209 278	319	...	...	...	...
Al-Fahama Nahia	619 474	313 651	305 823	90	...	...	...	...
Al-Falluja Qadha Center	321 106	165 111	155 995	478	...	...	...	...
Al-Forat Nahia	379 668	192 233	187 435	...	...	...	...	...
Al-Garma Nahia	129 783	66 577	63 206	1038	...	...	...	...
Al-Gharraf Nahia	118 081	59 318	58 763	623	...	...	...	...
Al-Habbaniya Nahia	133 202	68 366	64 836	714	...	...	...	...
Al-Hamza Qadha Center	128 472	64 739	63 733	600	...	...	...	...
Al-Hartha Nahia	156 391	78 509	77 882	...	...	...	...	...
Al-Hassainya Nahia	147 103	74 383	72 720	334	...	...	...	...
Al-Hawiga Qadha Center	115 910	58 508	57 402	1903	...	...	...	...
Al-Hilla Qadha Center	559 834	282 142	277 692	161	...	...	...	...
Al-Hindiya Qadha Center	113 021	57 001	56 020	134	...	...	...	...
Al-Hur Nahia	231 635	116 740	114 895	...	...	...	...	...

8. Population of capital cities and cities of 100 000 or more inhabitants: latest available year, 1998 - 2017
Population des capitales et des villes de 100 000 habitants ou plus : dernière année disponible, 1998 - 2017 (continued - suite)

Continent, country or area, date, code[a] and city / Continent, pays ou zone, date, code[a] et ville	City proper - Ville proprement dite				Urban agglomeration - Agglomération urbaine			
	Population			Surface area - Superficie (km²)	Population			Surface area - Superficie (km²)
	Both sexes - Les deux sexes	Male - Masculin	Female - Féminin		Both sexes - Les deux sexes	Male - Masculin	Female - Féminin	
ASIA - ASIE								
Iraq								
1 VII 2015 (ESDF)								
Al-Iskandaria Nahia	159 516	80 514	79 002	283	...	...	...	...
Al-Jisr Nahia	159 306	81 464	77 842	153	...	...	...	...
Al-Kadimiya Qadha Center	420 968	213 144	207 824	32	...	...	...	...
Al-Kaim Qadha Center	104 989	53 971	51 018	6460	...	...	...	...
Al-Karkh Qadha Center	113 397	57 415	55 982	...	...	...	...	...
Al-Karrada Al-Sharqia Nahia	318 615	161 321	157 294	49	...	...	...	...
Al-Khalis Qadha Center	139 713	70 624	69 089	1109	...	...	...	...
Al-Kifl Nahia	140 182	71 029	69 153	526	...	...	...	...
Al-Kufa Qadha Center	232 670	116 667	116 003	129	...	...	...	...
Al-Kut Qadha Center	436 673	220 490	216 183	2540	...	...	...	...
Al-Madhatiya Nahia	135 941	68 724	67 217	498	...	...	...	...
Al-Mahawil Qadha Center	116 899	59 181	57 718	608	...	...	...	...
Al-Mamoon Nahia	985 798	499 128	486 670	82	...	...	...	...
Al-Mansour Nahia	434 839	220 167	214 672	119	...	...	...	...
Al-Mashroo Nahia	127 344	64 449	62 895	834	...	...	...	...
Al-Mejar Al-Kabir Qadha Center	108 979	54 373	54 606	506	...	...	...	...
Al-Mosal Qadha Center	1 384 260	708 546	675 714	1783	...	...	...	...
Al-Mounawara Nahia	287 799	145 718	142 081	...	...	...	...	...
Al-Muqdadya Qadha Center	157 593	79 612	77 981	768	...	...	...	...
Al-Najaf Qadha Center	746 180	372 423	373 757	1133	...	...	...	...
Al-Nasir & Al-Salam Nahia	160 606	82 184	78 422	262	...	...	...	...
Al-Nasiriya Qadha Center	537 544	269 480	268 064	1277	...	...	...	...
Al-Noamaniya Qadha Center	111 647	56 363	55 284	946	...	...	...	...
Al-Qasim Nahia	159 420	80 545	78 875	528	...	...	...	...
Al-Qayarra Nahia	129 811	66 129	63 682	686	...	...	...	...
Al-Qurna Qadha Center	136 677	68 704	67 973	1248	...	...	...	...
Al-Ramadi Qadha Center	419 053	215 292	203 761	7829	...	...	...	...
Al-Rifaai Qadha Center	155 478	78 087	77 391	1345	...	...	...	...
Al-Rumaitha Qadha Center	118 011	59 581	58 430	106	...	...	...	...
Al-Rusafa Qadha Center	118 018	59 755	58 263	...	...	...	...	...
Al-Samawa Qadha Center	288 948	145 984	142 964	941	...	...	...	...
Al-Shamal Nahia	158 475	81 035	77 440	...	...	...	...	...
Al-Shattra Qadha Center	239 680	120 266	119 414	384	...	...	...	...
Al-Shirqat Qadha Center	208 586	105 453	103 133	1515	...	...	...	...
Al-Sideeq Al-Akbar Nahia	172 057	87 116	84 941	...	...	...	...	...
Al-Suwaira Qadha Center	142 924	72 148	70 776	1345	...	...	...	...
Al-Taji Nahia	164 894	84 470	80 424	388	...	...	...	...
Al-Wihda Nahia	204 585	104 438	100 147	890	...	...	...	...
Al-Yousifya Nahia	131 507	67 600	63 907	486	...	...	...	...
Al-Zohour Nahia	209 918	106 332	103 586	...	...	...	...	...
Al-Zubair Qadha Center	378 758	190 200	188 558	1134	...	...	...	...
Arbil Qadha Center	787 997	398 450	389 547	2790	...	...	...	...
BAGHDAD	1 211 934[47]	613 625[47]	598 309[47]	111	...	...	...	...
Bakrago Nahia	101 892	51 077	50 815	...	...	...	...	...
Baquba Qadha Center	276 029	138 681	137 348	580	...	...	...	...
Bashiqa Nahia	140 258	71 487	68 771	497	...	...	...	...
Beni Saad Nahia	127 268	64 496	62 772	497	...	...	...	...
Beygee Qadha Center	175 395	88 596	86 799	1188	...	...	...	...
Duhouk Qadha Center	328 113	164 245	163 868	577	...	...	...	...
Kalar Qadha Center	144 235	72 047	72 188	2201	...	...	...	...
Kerbela Qadha Center	514 356	259 193	255 163	2397	...	...	...	...
Kirkuk Qadha Center	938 336	471 419	466 917	1956	...	...	...	...
Mahmudiya Qadha Center	154 741	78 846	75 895	68	...	...	...	...
Qalat Siker Nahia	100 315	50 373	49 942	614	...	...	...	...
Saddat Al-Hindin Nahia	116 247	58 839	57 408	388	...	...	...	...
Sader /1 Qadha Center	130 153	65 899	64 254	...	...	...	...	...
Samarra Qadha Center	203 011	102 444	100 567	4504	...	...	...	...
Shat Al-Arab Qadha Center	136 043	68 413	67 630	1516	...	...	...	...
Sulaimania Qadha Center	651 173	325 147	326 026	3404	...	...	...	...
Suq AL-Shoyolh Qadha Center	126 652	63 493	63 159	285	...	...	...	...
Telafar Qadha Center	206 835	105 780	101 055	3206	...	...	...	...
That Al Salasil Nahia	277 494	140 647	136 847	147	...	...	...	...
Tikrit Qadha Center	182 464	92 119	90 345	991	...	...	...	...

8. Population of capital cities and cities of 100 000 or more inhabitants: latest available year, 1998 - 2017

Population des capitales et des villes de 100 000 habitants ou plus : dernière année disponible, 1998 - 2017 (continued - suite)

Continent, country or area, date, code[a] and city / Continent, pays ou zone, date, code[a] et ville	City proper - Ville proprement dite				Urban agglomeration - Agglomération urbaine			
	Population			Surface area - Superficie (km²)	Population			Surface area - Superficie (km²)
	Both sexes - Les deux sexes	Male - Masculin	Female - Féminin		Both sexes - Les deux sexes	Male - Masculin	Female - Féminin	

ASIA - ASIE

Iraq
1 VII 2015 (ESDF)

Tooz-Khormato Qadha Center	117 458	59 233	58 225	1253	...	...	...	...
Zummar Nahia	128 017	65 210	62 807	1247	...	...	...	...

Israel - Israël
1 VII 2016 (ESDJ)

Ashdod	220 883	107 723	113 159	46	...	...	...	...
Ashqelon	132 557	64 518	68 039	45	...	...	...	...
Bat Yam	128 898	61 353	67 545	8	...	...	...	...
Be'er Sheva	204 707	99 886	104 821	117	...	...	...	...
Bene Beraq	185 882	94 889	90 993	7	...	...	...	...
Bet Shemesh	106 842	53 386	53 456	38	...	...	...	...
Haifa	279 247	134 166	145 081	65	...	...	...	...
Holon	189 836	91 646	98 190	19	...	...	...	...
JERUSALEM[48]	874 186	435 213	438 973	126	...	...	...	...
Netanya	209 390	101 948	107 442	31	...	...	...	...
Petah Tiqwa	233 577	114 235	119 342	36	...	...	...	...
Ramat Gan	153 135	73 192	79 943	16	...	...	...	...
Rehovot	134 199	65 614	68 584	24	...	...	...	...
Rishon Leziyyon	245 648	120 380	125 268	59	...	...	...	...
Tel Aviv-Yafo	435 855	215 747	220 107	52	...	...	...	...

Japan - Japon
1 X 2015 (CDJC)

Abiko	131 606[49]	64 614[49]	66 992[49]	43.2[50]	...	...	...	...
Ageo	225 196[49]	112 157[49]	113 039[49]	45.5[50]	...	...	...	...
Aizuwakamatsu	124 062[49]	59 200[49]	64 862[49]	383[50]	...	...	...	...
Akashi	293 409[49]	141 801[49]	151 608[49]	49.4[50]	...	...	...	...
Akishima	111 539[49]	55 394[49]	56 145[49]	17.3[50]	...	...	...	...
Akita	315 814[49]	148 851[49]	166 963[49]	906.1[50]	...	...	...	...
Amagasaki	452 563[49]	219 059[49]	233 504[49]	50.7[50]	...	...	...	...
Anjo	184 140[49]	94 073[49]	90 067[49]	86.1[50]	...	...	...	...
Aomori	287 648[49]	133 560[49]	154 088[49]	824.6[50]	...	...	...	...
Asahikawa	339 605[49]	156 402[49]	183 203[49]	747.7[50]	...	...	...	...
Asaka	136 299[49]	69 971[49]	66 328[49]	18.3[50]	...	...	...	...
Ashikaga	149 452[49]	73 161[49]	76 291[49]	177.8[50]	...	...	...	...
Atsugi	225 714[49]	116 658[49]	109 056[49]	93.8[50]	...	...	...	...
Beppu	122 138[49]	55 482[49]	66 656[49]	125.3[50]	...	...	...	...
Chiba	971 882[49]	482 840[49]	489 042[49]	271.8[50]	...	...	...	...
Chigasaki	239 348[49]	116 894[49]	122 454[49]	35.7[50]	...	...	...	...
Chikusei	104 573[49]	51 663[49]	52 910[49]	205.3[50]	...	...	...	...
Chikushino	101 081[49]	47 995[49]	53 086[49]	87.7[50]	...	...	...	...
Chofu	229 061[49]	111 921[49]	117 140[49]	21.6[50]	...	...	...	...
Daito	123 217[49]	60 302[49]	62 915[49]	18.3[50]	...	...	...	...
Ebetsu	120 636[49]	57 391[49]	63 245[49]	187.4[50]	...	...	...	...
Ebina	130 190[49]	65 620[49]	64 570[49]	26.6[50]	...	...	...	...
Fuchu	260 274[49]	132 172[49]	128 102[49]	29.4[50]	...	...	...	...
Fuji	248 399[49]	121 901[49]	126 498[49]	245[50]	...	...	...	...
Fujieda	143 605[49]	70 049[49]	73 556[49]	194.1[50]	...	...	...	...
Fujimi	108 102[49]	53 312[49]	54 790[49]	19.8[50]	...	...	...	...
Fujimino	110 970[49]	54 910[49]	56 060[49]	14.6[50]	...	...	...	...
Fujinomiya	130 770[49]	64 281[49]	66 489[49]	389.1[50]	...	...	...	...
Fujisawa	423 894[49]	210 032[49]	213 862[49]	69.6[50]	...	...	...	...
Fukaya	143 811[49]	71 594[49]	72 217[49]	138.4[50]	...	...	...	...
Fukui	265 904[49]	128 892[49]	137 012[49]	536.4[50]	...	...	...	...
Fukuoka	1 538 681[49]	726 666[49]	812 015[49]	343.4[50]	...	...	...	...
Fukushima	294 247[49]	144 690[49]	149 557[49]	767.7[50]	...	...	...	...
Fukuyama	464 811[49]	225 414[49]	239 397[49]	518.1[50]	...	...	...	...
Funabashi	622 890[49]	311 358[49]	311 532[49]	85.6[50]	...	...	...	...
Gifu	406 735[49]	193 760[49]	212 975[49]	203.6[50]	...	...	...	...
Habikino	112 683[49]	53 243[49]	59 440[49]	26.5[50]	...	...	...	...
Hachinohe	231 257[49]	110 493[49]	120 764[49]	305.5[50]	...	...	...	...
Hachioji	577 513[49]	291 238[49]	286 275[49]	186.4[50]	...	...	...	...
Hadano	167 378[49]	85 552[49]	81 826[49]	103.8[50]	...	...	...	...

8. Population of capital cities and cities of 100 000 or more inhabitants: latest available year, 1998 - 2017
Population des capitales et des villes de 100 000 habitants ou plus : dernière année disponible, 1998 - 2017 (continued - suite)

Continent, country or area, date, code[a] and city / Continent, pays ou zone, date, code[a] et ville	City proper - Ville proprement dite				Urban agglomeration - Agglomération urbaine			
	Population			Surface area - Superficie (km²)	Population			Surface area - Superficie (km²)
	Both sexes - Les deux sexes	Male - Masculin	Female - Féminin		Both sexes - Les deux sexes	Male - Masculin	Female - Féminin	

ASIA - ASIE

Japan - Japon
1 X 2015 (CDJC)

Hakodate	265 979[49]	120 376[49]	145 603[49]	677.9[50]	...	...	...	...
Hakusan	109 287[49]	53 085[49]	56 202[49]	754.9[50]	...	...	...	...
Hamamatsu	797 980[49]	395 509[49]	402 471[49]	1558.1[50]	...	...	...	...
Handa	116 908[49]	58 444[49]	58 464[49]	47.4[50]	...	...	...	...
Hatsukaichi	114 906[49]	54 654[49]	60 252[49]	489.5[50]	...	...	...	...
Higashihiroshima	192 907[49]	97 962[49]	94 945[49]	635.2[50]	...	...	...	...
Higashikurume	116 632[49]	56 738[49]	59 894[49]	12.9[50]	...	...	...	...
Higashimurayama	149 956[49]	73 314[49]	76 642[49]	17.1[50]	...	...	...	...
Higashiomi	114 180[49]	56 601[49]	57 579[49]	388.4[50]	...	...	...	...
Higashiosaka	502 784[49]	246 053[49]	256 731[49]	61.8[50]	...	...	...	...
Hikone	113 679[49]	56 090[49]	57 589[49]	196.9[50]	...	...	...	...
Himeji	535 664[49]	258 724[49]	276 940[49]	534.5[50]	...	...	...	...
Hino	186 283[49]	93 349[49]	92 934[49]	27.6[50]	...	...	...	...
Hirakata	404 152[49]	192 816[49]	211 336[49]	65.1[50]	...	...	...	...
Hiratsuka	258 227[49]	129 456[49]	128 771[49]	67.8[50]	...	...	...	...
Hirosaki	177 411[49]	81 367[49]	96 044[49]	524.2[50]	...	...	...	...
Hiroshima	1 194 034[49]	576 850[49]	617 184[49]	906.5[50]	...	...	...	...
Hitachi	185 054[49]	92 595[49]	92 459[49]	225.7[50]	...	...	...	...
Hitachinaka	155 689[49]	78 270[49]	77 419[49]	99.9[50]	...	...	...	...
Hofu	115 942[49]	55 910[49]	60 032[49]	189.4[50]	...	...	...	...
Ibaraki	280 033[49]	135 705[49]	144 328[49]	76.5[50]	...	...	...	...
Ichihara	274 656[49]	141 134[49]	133 522[49]	368.2[50]	...	...	...	...
Ichikawa	481 732[49]	242 652[49]	239 080[49]	57.5[50]	...	...	...	...
Ichinomiya	380 868[49]	185 869[49]	194 999[49]	113.8[50]	...	...	...	...
Ichinoseki	121 583[49]	58 804[49]	62 779[49]	1256.4[50]	...	...	...	...
Iida	101 581[49]	48 443[49]	53 138[49]	658.7[50]	...	...	...	...
Iizuka	129 146[49]	61 249[49]	67 897[49]	214.1[50]	...	...	...	...
Ikeda	103 069[49]	49 372[49]	53 697[49]	22.1[50]	...	...	...	...
Ikoma	118 233[49]	55 972[49]	62 261[49]	53.2[50]	...	...	...	...
Imabari	158 114[49]	74 336[49]	83 778[49]	419.1[50]	...	...	...	...
Inazawa	136 867[49]	67 500[49]	69 367[49]	79.4[50]	...	...	...	...
Iruma	148 390[49]	73 408[49]	74 982[49]	44.7[50]	...	...	...	...
Isahaya	138 078[49]	65 029[49]	73 049[49]	341.8[50]	...	...	...	...
Ise	127 817[49]	60 467[49]	67 350[49]	208.4[50]	...	...	...	...
Isehara	101 514[49]	51 429[49]	50 085[49]	55.6[50]	...	...	...	...
Isesaki	208 814[49]	104 234[49]	104 580[49]	139.4[50]	...	...	...	...
Ishinomaki	147 214[49]	71 826[49]	75 388[49]	554.6[50]	...	...	...	...
Itami	196 883[49]	95 641[49]	101 242[49]	25[50]	...	...	...	...
Iwaki	350 237[49]	172 829[49]	177 408[49]	1232[50]	...	...	...	...
Iwakuni	136 757[49]	64 455[49]	72 302[49]	873.7[50]	...	...	...	...
Iwata	167 210[49]	84 130[49]	83 080[49]	163.5[50]	...	...	...	...
Izumi (Osaka)	186 109[49]	89 868[49]	96 241[49]	85[50]	...	...	...	...
Izumisano	100 966[49]	48 506[49]	52 460[49]	56.5[50]	...	...	...	...
Izumo	171 938[49]	82 707[49]	89 231[49]	624.4[50]	...	...	...	...
Joetsu	196 987[49]	95 990[49]	100 997[49]	973.8[50]	...	...	...	...
Kadoma	123 576[49]	60 620[49]	62 956[49]	12.3[50]	...	...	...	...
Kagoshima	599 814[49]	279 108[49]	320 706[49]	547.6[50]	...	...	...	...
Kakamigahara	144 690[49]	71 167[49]	73 523[49]	87.8[50]	...	...	...	...
Kakegawa	114 602[49]	57 126[49]	57 476[49]	265.7[50]	...	...	...	...
Kakogawa	267 435[49]	131 170[49]	136 265[49]	138.5[50]	...	...	...	...
Kamagaya	108 917[49]	53 490[49]	55 427[49]	21.1[50]	...	...	...	...
Kamakura	173 019[49]	81 664[49]	91 355[49]	39.7[50]	...	...	...	...
Kanazawa	465 699[49]	226 007[49]	239 692[49]	468.6[50]	...	...	...	...
Kanoya	103 608[49]	49 555[49]	54 053[49]	448.2[50]	...	...	...	...
Karatsu	122 785[49]	57 547[49]	65 238[49]	487.6[50]	...	...	...	...
Kariya	149 765[49]	78 456[49]	71 309[49]	50.4[50]	...	...	...	...
Kashihara	124 111[49]	58 888[49]	65 223[49]	39.6[50]	...	...	...	...
Kashiwa	413 954[49]	205 971[49]	207 983[49]	114.7[50]	...	...	...	...
Kasuga	110 743[49]	53 284[49]	57 459[49]	14.2[50]	...	...	...	...

8. Population of capital cities and cities of 100 000 or more inhabitants: latest available year, 1998 - 2017
Population des capitales et des villes de 100 000 habitants ou plus : dernière année disponible, 1998 - 2017 (continued - suite)

Continent, country or area, date, code[a] and city / Continent, pays ou zone, date, code[a] et ville	City proper - Ville proprement dite				Urban agglomeration - Agglomération urbaine			
	Population			Surface area - Superficie (km²)	Population			Surface area - Superficie (km²)
	Both sexes - Les deux sexes	Male - Masculin	Female - Féminin		Both sexes - Les deux sexes	Male - Masculin	Female - Féminin	

ASIA - ASIE

Japan - Japon
1 X 2015 (CDJC)

	Both sexes	Male	Female	Surface area	Both sexes	Male	Female	Surface area
Kasugai	306 508[49]	151 955[49]	154 553[49]	92.8[50]	...	...	...	...
Kasukabe	232 709[49]	114 813[49]	117 896[49]	66[50]	...	...	...	...
Kawachinagano	106 987[49]	50 182[49]	56 805[49]	109.6[50]	...	...	...	...
Kawagoe	350 745[49]	175 559[49]	175 186[49]	109.1[50]	...	...	...	...
Kawaguchi	578 112[49]	292 067[49]	286 045[49]	62[50]	...	...	...	...
Kawanishi	156 375[49]	73 882[49]	82 493[49]	53.4[50]	...	...	...	...
Kawasaki	1 475 213[49]	749 038[49]	726 175[49]	143[50]	...	...	...	...
Kazo	112 229[49]	55 828[49]	56 401[49]	133.3[50]	...	...	...	...
Kirishima	125 857[49]	59 966[49]	65 891[49]	603.2[50]	...	...	...	...
Kiryu	114 714[49]	55 327[49]	59 387[49]	274.5[50]	...	...	...	...
Kisarazu	134 141[49]	67 450[49]	66 691[49]	139[50]	...	...	...	...
Kishiwada	194 911[49]	93 160[49]	101 751[49]	72.7[50]	...	...	...	...
Kitakyushu	961 286[49]	452 682[49]	508 604[49]	492[50]	...	...	...	...
Kitami	121 226[49]	58 020[49]	63 206[49]	1427.4[50]	...	...	...	...
Kobe	1 537 272[49]	726 700[49]	810 572[49]	557[50]	...	...	...	...
Kochi	337 190[49]	157 002[49]	180 188[49]	309[50]	...	...	...	...
Kodaira	190 005[49]	93 777[49]	96 228[49]	20.5[50]	...	...	...	...
Kofu	193 125[49]	94 448[49]	98 677[49]	212.5[50]	...	...	...	...
Koga	140 946[49]	70 354[49]	70 592[49]	123.6[50]	...	...	...	...
Koganei	121 396[49]	60 168[49]	61 228[49]	11.3[50]	...	...	...	...
Kokubunji	122 742[49]	60 274[49]	62 468[49]	11.5[50]	...	...	...	...
Komaki	149 462[49]	75 430[49]	74 032[49]	62.8[50]	...	...	...	...
Komatsu	106 919[49]	51 844[49]	55 075[49]	371.1[50]	...	...	...	...
Konosu	118 072[49]	58 346[49]	59 726[49]	67.4[50]	...	...	...	...
Koriyama	335 444[49]	167 096[49]	168 348[49]	757.2[50]	...	...	...	...
Koshigaya	337 498[49]	167 023[49]	170 475[49]	60.2[50]	...	...	...	...
Kuki	152 311[49]	75 993[49]	76 318[49]	82.4[50]	...	...	...	...
Kumagaya	198 742[49]	99 169[49]	99 573[49]	159.8[50]	...	...	...	...
Kumamoto	740 822[49]	348 470[49]	392 352[49]	390.3[50]	...	...	...	...
Kurashiki	477 118[49]	230 081[49]	247 037[49]	355.6[50]	...	...	...	...
Kure	228 552[49]	110 173[49]	118 379[49]	352.8[50]	...	...	...	...
Kurume	304 552[49]	144 971[49]	159 581[49]	230[50]	...	...	...	...
Kusatsu	137 247[49]	70 129[49]	67 118[49]	67.8[50]	...	...	...	...
Kushiro	174 742[49]	82 185[49]	92 557[49]	1362.9[50]	...	...	...	...
Kuwana	140 303[49]	68 740[49]	71 563[49]	136.7[50]	...	...	...	...
Kyoto	1 475 183[49]	699 748[49]	775 435[49]	827.8[50]	...	...	...	...
Machida	432 348[49]	212 312[49]	220 036[49]	71.8[50]	...	...	...	...
Maebashi	336 154[49]	164 136[49]	172 018[49]	311.6[50]	...	...	...	...
Marugame	110 010[49]	53 183[49]	56 827[49]	111.8[50]	...	...	...	...
Matsubara	120 750[49]	58 096[49]	62 654[49]	16.7[50]	...	...	...	...
Matsudo	483 480[49]	240 928[49]	242 552[49]	61.4[50]	...	...	...	...
Matsue	206 230[49]	99 565[49]	106 665[49]	573[50]	...	...	...	...
Matsumoto	243 293[49]	119 479[49]	123 814[49]	978.5[50]	...	...	...	...
Matsusaka	163 863[49]	78 548[49]	85 315[49]	623.7[50]	...	...	...	...
Matsuyama	514 865[49]	241 656[49]	273 209[49]	429.4[50]	...	...	...	...
Minoh	133 411[49]	63 938[49]	69 473[49]	47.9[50]	...	...	...	...
Misato	136 521[49]	68 950[49]	67 571[49]	30.1[50]	...	...	...	...
Mishima	110 046[49]	53 836[49]	56 210[49]	62[50]	...	...	...	...
Mitaka	186 936[49]	90 641[49]	96 295[49]	16.4[50]	...	...	...	...
Mito	270 783[49]	132 799[49]	137 984[49]	217.3[50]	...	...	...	...
Miyakonojo	165 029[49]	77 521[49]	87 508[49]	653.4[50]	...	...	...	...
Miyazaki	401 138[49]	188 177[49]	212 961[49]	643.7[50]	...	...	...	...
Moriguchi	143 042[49]	68 987[49]	74 055[49]	12.7[50]	...	...	...	...
Morioka	297 631[49]	141 089[49]	156 542[49]	886.5[50]	...	...	...	...
Musashino	144 730[49]	69 475[49]	75 255[49]	11[50]	...	...	...	...
Nagahama	118 193[49]	57 703[49]	60 490[49]	681[50]	...	...	...	...
Nagano	377 598[49]	182 843[49]	194 755[49]	834.8[50]	...	...	...	...
Nagaoka	275 133[49]	134 198[49]	140 935[49]	891.1[50]	...	...	...	...
Nagareyama	174 373[49]	86 249[49]	88 124[49]	35.3[50]	...	...	...	...

8. Population of capital cities and cities of 100 000 or more inhabitants: latest available year, 1998 - 2017
Population des capitales et des villes de 100 000 habitants ou plus : dernière année disponible, 1998 - 2017 (continued - suite)

Continent, country or area, date, code[a] and city / Continent, pays ou zone, date, code[a] et ville	City proper - Ville proprement dite				Urban agglomeration - Agglomération urbaine			
	Population			Surface area - Superficie (km²)	Population			Surface area - Superficie (km²)
	Both sexes - Les deux sexes	Male - Masculin	Female - Féminin		Both sexes - Les deux sexes	Male - Masculin	Female - Féminin	
ASIA - ASIE								
Japan - Japon								
1 X 2015 (CDJC)								
Nagasaki	429 508[49]	198 716[49]	230 792[49]	405.9[50]	...	...	...	...
Nagoya	2 295 638[49]	1 133 640[49]	1 161 998[49]	326.5[50]	...	...	...	...
Naha	319 435[49]	154 685[49]	164 750[49]	39.6[50]	...	...	...	...
Nara	360 310[49]	167 899[49]	192 411[49]	276.9[50]	...	...	...	...
Narashino	167 909[49]	84 323[49]	83 586[49]	21[50]	...	...	...	...
Narita	131 190[49]	65 928[49]	65 262[49]	213.8[50]	...	...	...	...
Nasushiobara	117 146[49]	58 148[49]	58 998[49]	592.7[50]	...	...	...	...
Neyagawa	237 518[49]	115 131[49]	122 387[49]	24.7[50]	...	...	...	...
Niigata	810 157[49]	389 512[49]	420 645[49]	726.5[50]	...	...	...	...
Niihama	119 903[49]	57 551[49]	62 352[49]	234.5[50]	...	...	...	...
Niiza	162 122[49]	80 627[49]	81 495[49]	22.8[50]	...	...	...	...
Nishinomiya	487 850[49]	228 354[49]	259 496[49]	100[50]	...	...	...	...
Nishio	167 990[49]	84 669[49]	83 321[49]	161.2[50]	...	...	...	...
Nishitokyo	200 012[49]	97 830[49]	102 182[49]	15.8[50]	...	...	...	...
Nobeoka	125 159[49]	58 993[49]	66 166[49]	868[50]	...	...	...	...
Noda	153 583[49]	76 541[49]	77 042[49]	103.6[50]	...	...	...	...
Numazu	195 633[49]	95 980[49]	99 653[49]	187[50]	...	...	...	...
Obihiro	169 327[49]	80 994[49]	88 333[49]	619.3[50]	...	...	...	...
Odawara	194 086[49]	94 697[49]	99 389[49]	113.8[50]	...	...	...	...
Ogaki	159 879[49]	77 430[49]	82 449[49]	206.6[50]	...	...	...	...
Oita	478 146[49]	229 844[49]	248 302[49]	502.4[50]	...	...	...	...
Okayama	719 474[49]	345 913[49]	373 561[49]	790[50]	...	...	...	...
Okazaki	381 051[49]	192 771[49]	188 280[49]	387.2[50]	...	...	...	...
Okinawa	139 279[49]	67 522[49]	71 757[49]	49.7[50]	...	...	...	...
Ome	137 381[49]	68 677[49]	68 704[49]	103.3[50]	...	...	...	...
Omuta	117 360[49]	53 859[49]	63 501[49]	81.5[50]	...	...	...	...
Onomichi	138 626[49]	66 292[49]	72 334[49]	285.1[50]	...	...	...	...
Osaka	2 691 185[49]	1 302 562[49]	1 388 623[49]	225.2[50]	...	...	...	...
Osaki	133 391[49]	65 120[49]	68 271[49]	796.8[50]	...	...	...	...
Oshu	119 422[49]	57 377[49]	62 045[49]	993.3[50]	...	...	...	...
Ota	219 807[49]	111 610[49]	108 197[49]	175.5[50]	...	...	...	...
Otaru	121 924[49]	54 985[49]	66 939[49]	243.8[50]	...	...	...	...
Otsu	340 973[49]	164 799[49]	176 174[49]	464.5[50]	...	...	...	...
Oyama	166 760[49]	84 100[49]	82 660[49]	171.8[50]	...	...	...	...
Saga	236 372[49]	111 453[49]	124 919[49]	431.8[50]	...	...	...	...
Sagamihara	720 780[49]	361 060[49]	359 720[49]	328.7[50]	...	...	...	...
Saijo	108 174[49]	51 807[49]	56 367[49]	510[50]	...	...	...	...
Saitama	1 263 979[49]	627 238[49]	636 741[49]	217.4[50]	...	...	...	...
Sakado	101 679[49]	51 307[49]	50 372[49]	41[50]	...	...	...	...
Sakai	839 310[49]	402 379[49]	436 931[49]	209.7[50]	...	...	...	...
Sakata	106 244[49]	50 293[49]	55 951[49]	603[50]	...	...	...	...
Sakura	172 739[49]	84 434[49]	88 305[49]	103.7[50]	...	...	...	...
Sanda	112 691[49]	54 184[49]	58 507[49]	210.3[50]	...	...	...	...
Sano	118 919[49]	58 507[49]	60 412[49]	356[50]	...	...	...	...
Sapporo	1 952 356[49]	910 614[49]	1 041 742[49]	1121.3[50]	...	...	...	...
Sasebo	255 439[49]	120 198[49]	135 241[49]	426.1[50]	...	...	...	...
Sayama	152 405[49]	76 580[49]	75 825[49]	49[50]	...	...	...	...
Sendai	1 082 159[49]	527 170[49]	554 989[49]	786.3[50]	...	...	...	...
Seto	129 046[49]	63 189[49]	65 857[49]	111.4[50]	...	...	...	...
Shimonoseki	268 517[49]	124 722[49]	143 795[49]	715.9[50]	...	...	...	...
Shizuoka	704 989[49]	343 338[49]	361 651[49]	1411.9[50]	...	...	...	...
Shunan	144 842[49]	69 819[49]	75 023[49]	656.3[50]	...	...	...	...
Soka	247 034[49]	125 225[49]	121 809[49]	27.5[50]	...	...	...	...
Suita	374 468[49]	180 669[49]	193 799[49]	36.1[50]	...	...	...	...
Suzuka	196 403[49]	97 500[49]	98 903[49]	194.5[50]	...	...	...	...
Tachikawa	176 295[49]	86 978[49]	89 317[49]	24.4[50]	...	...	...	...
Tajimi	110 441[49]	53 378[49]	57 063[49]	91.3[50]	...	...	...	...
Takamatsu	420 748[49]	205 049[49]	215 699[49]	375.4[50]	...	...	...	...
Takaoka	172 125[49]	82 802[49]	89 323[49]	209.6[50]	...	...	...	...

8. Population of capital cities and cities of 100 000 or more inhabitants: latest available year, 1998 - 2017
Population des capitales et des villes de 100 000 habitants ou plus : dernière année disponible, 1998 - 2017 (continued - suite)

Continent, country or area, date, code[a] and city / Continent, pays ou zone, date, code[a] et ville	City proper - Ville proprement dite				Urban agglomeration - Agglomération urbaine			
	Population			Surface area - Superficie (km²)	Population			Surface area - Superficie (km²)
	Both sexes - Les deux sexes	Male - Masculin	Female - Féminin		Both sexes - Les deux sexes	Male - Masculin	Female - Féminin	
ASIA - ASIE								
Japan - Japon								
1 X 2015 (CDJC)								
Takarazuka	224 903[49]	104 215[49]	120 688[49]	101.8[50]	...	...	...	...
Takasaki	370 884[49]	181 601[49]	189 283[49]	459.2[50]	...	...	...	...
Takatsuki	351 829[49]	168 057[49]	183 772[49]	105.3[50]	...	...	...	...
Tama	146 631[49]	71 762[49]	74 869[49]	21[50]	...	...	...	...
Tochigi	159 211[49]	78 209[49]	81 002[49]	331.5[50]	...	...	...	...
Toda	136 150[49]	69 674[49]	66 476[49]	18.2[50]	...	...	...	...
Tokai	111 944[49]	58 170[49]	53 774[49]	43.4[50]	...	...	...	...
Tokorozawa	340 386[49]	168 205[49]	172 181[49]	72.1[50]	...	...	...	...
Tokushima	258 554[49]	123 014[49]	135 540[49]	191.3[50]	...	...	...	...
TOKYO	9 272 740[51]	4 567 247[51]	4 705 493[51]	626.7[50]	...	...	...	...
Tomakomai	172 737[49]	84 605[49]	88 132[49]	561.6[50]	...	...	...	...
Tondabayashi	113 984[49]	53 693[49]	60 291[49]	39.7[50]	...	...	...	...
Toride	106 570[49]	52 489[49]	54 081[49]	69.9[50]	...	...	...	...
Tottori	193 717[49]	94 151[49]	99 566[49]	765.3[50]	...	...	...	...
Toyama	418 686[49]	203 427[49]	215 259[49]	1241.8[50]	...	...	...	...
Toyohashi	374 765[49]	187 801[49]	186 964[49]	261.9[50]	...	...	...	...
Toyokawa	182 436[49]	90 869[49]	91 567[49]	161.1[50]	...	...	...	...
Toyonaka	395 479[49]	187 319[49]	208 160[49]	36.4[50]	...	...	...	...
Toyota	422 542[49]	222 169[49]	200 373[49]	918.3[50]	...	...	...	...
Tsu	279 886[49]	135 718[49]	144 168[49]	711.1[50]	...	...	...	...
Tsuchiura	140 804[49]	70 101[49]	70 703[49]	122.9[50]	...	...	...	...
Tsukuba	226 963[49]	114 774[49]	112 189[49]	283.7[50]	...	...	...	...
Tsuruoka	129 652[49]	61 761[49]	67 891[49]	1311.5[50]	...	...	...	...
Tsuyama	103 746[49]	49 561[49]	54 185[49]	506.3[50]	...	...	...	...
Ube	169 429[49]	81 133[49]	88 296[49]	286.7[50]	...	...	...	...
Ueda	156 827[49]	76 776[49]	80 051[49]	552[50]	...	...	...	...
Uji	184 678[49]	89 014[49]	95 664[49]	67.5[50]	...	...	...	...
Urasoe	114 232[49]	55 471[49]	58 761[49]	19.5[50]	...	...	...	...
Urayasu	164 024[49]	81 057[49]	82 967[49]	17.3[50]	...	...	...	...
Uruma	118 898[49]	59 409[49]	59 489[49]	87[50]	...	...	...	...
Utsunomiya	518 594[49]	258 960[49]	259 634[49]	416.9[50]	...	...	...	...
Wakayama	364 154[49]	171 215[49]	192 939[49]	208.8[50]	...	...	...	...
Yachiyo	193 152[49]	95 224[49]	97 928[49]	51.4[50]	...	...	...	...
Yaizu	139 462[49]	68 168[49]	71 294[49]	70.3[50]	...	...	...	...
Yamagata	253 832[49]	121 575[49]	132 257[49]	381.3[50]	...	...	...	...
Yamaguchi	197 422[49]	94 245[49]	103 177[49]	1023.2[50]	...	...	...	...
Yamato	232 922[49]	116 714[49]	116 208[49]	27.1[50]	...	...	...	...
Yao	268 800[49]	128 284[49]	140 516[49]	41.7[50]	...	...	...	...
Yatsushiro	127 472[49]	59 221[49]	68 251[49]	681.4[50]	...	...	...	...
Yokkaichi	311 031[49]	154 674[49]	156 357[49]	206.4[50]	...	...	...	...
Yokohama	3 724 844[49]	1 855 985[49]	1 868 859[49]	437.5[50]	...	...	...	...
Yokosuka	406 586[49]	202 775[49]	203 811[49]	100.8[50]	...	...	...	...
Yonago	149 313[49]	70 628[49]	78 685[49]	132.4[50]	...	...	...	...
Zama	128 737[49]	64 478[49]	64 259[49]	17.6[50]	...	...	...	...
Jordan - Jordanie								
31 XII 2017 (ESDF)								
AMMAN	3 850 301	2 061 818	1 788 483	...	...	...	...	...
Aqaba	156 552	89 925	66 627	...	...	...	...	...
Irbid	530 213	276 809	253 404	...	...	...	...	...
Madaba	111 087	59 284	51 803	...	...	...	...	...
Mafraq	111 808	58 508	53 300	...	...	...	...	...
Mukhayyam Al-Za'tary	119 298	59 391	59 907	...	...	...	...	...
Ramtha	164 211	85 675	78 536	...	...	...	...	...
Russiefa	498 446	265 773	232 673	...	...	...	...	...
Salt	105 336	54 941	50 395	...	...	...	...	...
Zarqa	669 878	350 397	319 481	...	...	...	...	...
Kazakhstan								
1 VII 2017 (ESDF)								
Aktau	182 495[52]	88 367[52]	94 128[52]	30[53]	...	...	...	...
Aktobe	413 918[52]	194 211[52]	219 707[52]	230[53]	...	...	...	...

8. Population of capital cities and cities of 100 000 or more inhabitants: latest available year, 1998 - 2017
Population des capitales et des villes de 100 000 habitants ou plus : dernière année disponible, 1998 - 2017 (continued - suite)

Continent, country or area, date, code[a] and city / Continent, pays ou zone, date, code[a] et ville	City proper - Ville proprement dite Population Both sexes - Les deux sexes	Male - Masculin	Female - Féminin	Surface area - Superficie (km²)	Urban agglomeration - Agglomération urbaine Population Both sexes - Les deux sexes	Male - Masculin	Female - Féminin	Surface area - Superficie (km²)
ASIA - ASIE								
Kazakhstan								
1 VII 2017 (ESDF)								
Almaty	1 776 650[52]	811 504[52]	965 146[52]	70[53]	...	...	...	...
ASTANA	1 001 634[52]	482 406[52]	519 228[52]	80[53]	...	...	...	...
Atirau	235 314[52]	111 990[52]	123 324[52]	350[53]	...	...	...	...
Ekibastuz	133 947[52]	63 798[52]	70 149[52]	1890[53]	...	...	...	...
Karaganda	500 826[52]	229 954[52]	270 872[52]	50[53]	...	...	...	...
Koktshetau	145 927[52]	67 578[52]	78 349[52]	40[53]	...	...	...	...
Kustanai	237 478[52]	106 783[52]	130 695[52]	740[53]	...	...	...	...
Kyzylorda	234 736[52]	114 046[52]	120 690[52]	240[53]	...	...	...	...
Pavlodar	335 272[52]	151 816[52]	183 456[52]	60[53]	...	...	...	...
Petropavlovsk (Severo- Kazakhstanskaya oblast)	216 442[52]	97 424[52]	119 018[52]	20[53]	...	...	...	...
Rudni	115 586[52]	54 066[52]	61 520[52]	20[53]	...	...	...	...
Semipalatinsk	320 397[52]	149 054[52]	171 343[52]	2781[53]	...	...	...	...
Shimkent	932 235[52]	448 552[52]	483 683[52]	120[53]	...	...	...	...
Taldykorgan	144 504[52]	67 042[52]	77 462[52]	40[53]	...	...	...	...
Taraz	358 806[52]	168 760[52]	190 046[52]	20[53]	...	...	...	...
Temirtau	178 662[52]	83 130[52]	95 532[52]	30[53]	...	...	...	...
Turkestan	160 746[52]	80 482[52]	80 264[52]	740[53]	...	...	...	...
Uralsk	236 082[52]	107 585[52]	128 497[52]	70[53]	...	...	...	...
Ust-Kamenogorsk	326 498[52]	147 450[52]	179 048[52]	54[53]	...	...	...	...
Kuwait - Koweït								
1 VII 2010 (ESDF)								
Farwanyiah	101 867	68 326	33 541	...	...	...	...	...
Hawalli	127 982	84 506	43 477	...	...	...	...	...
Jaleeb Al-Shuykh	219 629	180 786	38 843	...	...	...	...	...
Salmiya	177 009	103 119	73 890	...	...	...	...	...
South Kheetan	113 426	104 655	8 770	...	...	...	...	...
Kyrgyzstan - Kirghizstan[54]								
1 VII 2017 (ESDJ)								
BISHKEK	976 734	456 400	520 334	...	991 257	463 566	527 691	...
Osh	256 763	123 228	133 535	...	285 372	137 889	147 483	...
Lao People's Democratic Republic - République démocratique populaire lao[55]								
1 VII 2014 (ESDJ)								
VIENTIANE	...	...	...	...	828 494	414 217	414 277	...
Lebanon - Liban[56]								
1 X 2011 (SSDF)								
BEIRUT	...	...	...	...	363 033	179 737	183 296	...
Malaysia - Malaisie[57]								
1 VII 2017 (ESDJ)								
Alor Setar	132 800	...	...	...	...	...	...	...
Bintulu Townland	136 800	...	...	...	...	...	...	...
Georgetown	222 200	...	...	...	...	...	...	...
Kajang dan Sungai Chua	111 200	...	...	...	...	...	...	...
Klang	287 500	...	...	...	...	...	...	...
Kota Kinabalu	244 700	...	...	...	...	...	...	...
KUALA LUMPUR	1 808 400	...	...	...	...	...	...	...
Kuala Terengganu	237 000	...	...	...	...	...	...	...
Kuantan	405 800	...	...	...	...	...	...	...
Kuching "Bandaraya Kuching Utara dan Selatan"	153 700	...	...	...	...	...	...	...
Majlis Perbandaran Ipoh	478 600	...	...	...	...	...	...	...
MB Johor Bahru (Johor Bahru)	502 900	...	...	...	...	...	...	...
Miri Townland	151 500	...	...	...	...	...	...	...
MP Kota Bharu	319 600	...	...	...	...	...	...	...
Petaling Jaya	211 700	...	...	...	...	...	...	...
Sandakan	196 500	...	...	...	...	...	...	...
Selayang Baru	180 600	...	...	...	...	...	...	...
Seremban	371 000	...	...	...	...	...	...	...
Shah Alam	189 000	...	...	...	...	...	...	...
Sibu "Majlis Perbandaran Sibu"	188 000	...	...	...	...	...	...	...
Subang Jaya	205 000	...	...	...	...	...	...	...

8. Population of capital cities and cities of 100 000 or more inhabitants: latest available year, 1998 - 2017
Population des capitales et des villes de 100 000 habitants ou plus : dernière année disponible, 1998 - 2017 (continued - suite)

Continent, country or area, date, code[a] and city / Continent, pays ou zone, date, code[a] et ville	City proper - Ville proprement dite				Urban agglomeration - Agglomération urbaine			
	Population			Surface area - Superficie (km²)	Population			Surface area - Superficie (km²)
	Both sexes - Les deux sexes	Male - Masculin	Female - Féminin		Both sexes - Les deux sexes	Male - Masculin	Female - Féminin	
ASIA - ASIE								
Malaysia - Malaisie[57]								
1 VII 2017 (ESDJ)								
Sungai Petani	196 500	...	...	...	...	...	...	...
Taiping	238 900	...	...	...	...	...	...	...
Tawau	142 900	...	...	...	...	...	...	...
Maldives								
1 VII 2017 (ESDF)								
MALÉ	142 909	71 326	71 582	...	...	...	...	...
Mongolia - Mongolie								
1 VII 2017 (ESDF)								
Bayan-Olgii	101 388	50 673	50 715	46	...	...	...	...
Darkhan-Uul	102 975	50 640	52 335	3	...	...	...	...
Hovsgol	130 471	64 867	65 604	101	...	...	...	...
Orkhon	102 893	50 443	52 450	1	...	...	...	...
Ovorhangay	114 127	56 881	57 246	63	...	...	...	...
Selenge	108 559	55 054	53 505	41	...	...	...	...
ULAANBAATAR	1 451 710	698 357	753 353	5	...	...	...	...
Myanmar								
29 III 2014 (CDFC)								
Bago	...	...	...	...	491 434	235 529	255 905	...
Dawei	...	...	...	...	125 605	60 044	65 561	...
Hpa-an	...	...	...	...	421 575	203 910	217 665	...
Loikaw	...	...	...	...	128 401	63 109	65 292	...
Magway	...	...	...	...	289 247	135 103	154 144	...
Mandalay	...	...	...	...	1 225 546	598 429	627 117	...
Mawlamyine	...	...	...	...	289 388	139 026	150 362	...
Monywa	...	...	...	...	372 095	171 951	200 144	...
Myitkyina	...	...	...	...	306 949	148 485	158 464	...
NAY PYI TAW[58]	...	...	...	...	1 160 242	565 155	595 087	...
Pathein	...	...	...	...	287 071	137 663	149 408	...
Sittway	...	...	...	...	147 899	70 470	77 429	...
Taunggyi	...	...	...	...	381 639	185 954	195 685	...
Yangon	...	...	...	...	5 211 431	2 466 918	2 744 513	...
Nepal - Népal								
22 VI 2011 (CDJC)								
Bharatpur	147 777	74 205	73 572	...	...	...	...	...
Bhimdutta	106 666	53 098	53 568	...	...	...	...	...
Biratnagar	204 949	104 935	100 014	...	...	...	...	...
Birgunj	139 068	75 382	63 686	...	...	...	...	...
Butwal	120 982	60 870	60 112	...	...	...	...	...
Dhangadhi	104 047	53 237	50 810	...	...	...	...	...
Dharan	119 915	57 562	62 353	...	...	...	...	...
KATHMANDU	1 003 285	533 127	470 158	...	...	...	...	...
Lalitpur	226 728	117 932	108 796	...	...	...	...	...
Pokhara	264 991	133 318	131 673	...	...	...	...	...
Oman[59]								
1 VII 2017 (ESDF)								
Al Buraymi	106 786	71 687	35 099	...	...	...	...	...
Al Mudaybi	117 691	74 493	43 198	...	...	...	...	...
Al Rustaq	121 587	70 356	51 231	...	...	...	...	...
As Seeb	404 279	251 296	152 983	...	...	...	...	...
As Suwayq	179 189	110 105	69 084	...	...	...	...	...
Barka	146 596	93 278	53 318	...	...	...	...	...
Bawshar	394 631	316 118	78 513	...	...	...	...	...
Ibri	165 354	100 562	64 792	...	...	...	...	...
Jaalan Bani Bu Ali	100 506	63 163	37 343	...	...	...	...	...
MUSCAT	290 873	217 435	73 438	...	...	...	...	...
Mutrah	237 731	181 800	55 931	...	...	...	...	...
Nizwa	123 396	74 260	49 136	...	...	...	...	...
Saham	147 775	89 832	57 943	...	...	...	...	...
Salalah	374 582	273 069	101 513	...	...	...	...	...
Sohar	231 102	154 418	76 684	...	...	...	...	...
Sur	121 088	76 305	44 783	...	...	...	...	...

8. Population of capital cities and cities of 100 000 or more inhabitants: latest available year, 1998 - 2017
Population des capitales et des villes de 100 000 habitants ou plus : dernière année disponible, 1998 - 2017 (continued - suite)

Continent, country or area, date, code[a] and city / Continent, pays ou zone, date, code[a] et ville	City proper - Ville proprement dite				Urban agglomeration - Agglomération urbaine			
	Population			Surface area - Superficie (km²)	Population			Surface area - Superficie (km²)
	Both sexes - Les deux sexes	Male - Masculin	Female - Féminin		Both sexes - Les deux sexes	Male - Masculin	Female - Féminin	
ASIA - ASIE								
Pakistan								
15 III 2017* (CDFC)								
Faisalabad (Lyallpur)	3 203 846	...	...	...	...	...	...	...
Gujranwala	2 027 001	...	...	...	...	...	...	...
Hyderabad	1 732 693	...	...	...	...	...	...	...
ISLAMABAD	1 014 825	...	...	...	...	...	...	...
Karachi	14 910 352	...	...	...	...	...	...	...
Lahore	11 126 285	...	...	...	...	...	...	...
Multan	1 871 843	...	...	...	...	...	...	...
Peshawar	1 970 042	...	...	...	...	...	...	...
Quetta	1 001 205	...	...	...	...	...	...	...
Rawalpindi	2 098 231	...	...	...	...	...	...	...
Philippines								
1 VIII 2015 (CDJC)								
Angeles	411 634	...	...	...	...	...	...	...
Bacolod	561 875	...	...	...	...	...	...	...
Baguio	345 366	...	...	...	...	...	...	...
Butuan	337 063	...	...	...	...	...	...	...
Cagayan de Oro	675 950	...	...	...	...	...	...	...
Caloocan	1 583 978	...	...	...	...	...	...	...
Cebu	922 611	...	...	...	...	...	...	...
Cotabato	299 438	...	...	...	...	...	...	...
Davao	1 632 991	...	...	...	...	...	...	...
General Santos	594 446	...	...	...	...	...	...	...
Iligan	342 618	...	...	...	...	...	...	...
Iloilo	447 992	...	...	...	...	...	...	...
Isabela	112 788	...	...	...	...	...	...	...
Lapu-Lapu	408 112	...	...	...	...	...	...	...
Las Piñas	588 894	...	...	...	...	...	...	...
Lucena City	266 248	...	...	...	...	...	...	...
Makati	582 602	...	...	...	...	...	...	...
Malabon	365 525	...	...	...	...	...	...	...
Mandaluyong	386 276	...	...	...	...	...	...	...
Mandaue	362 654	...	...	...	...	...	...	...
MANILA	1 780 148	...	...	...	...	...	...	...
Marikina	450 741	...	...	...	...	...	...	...
Muntinlupa	504 509	...	...	...	...	...	...	...
Navotas	249 463	...	...	...	...	...	...	...
Olongapo	233 040	...	...	...	...	...	...	...
Paranaque	665 822	...	...	...	...	...	...	...
Pasay	416 522	...	...	...	...	...	...	...
Pasig	755 300	...	...	...	...	...	...	...
Puerto Princesa	255 116	...	...	...	...	...	...	...
Quezon City	2 936 116	...	...	...	...	...	...	...
San Juan	122 180	...	...	...	...	...	...	...
Tacloban	242 089	...	...	...	...	...	...	...
Taguig	804 915	...	...	...	...	...	...	...
Valenzuela	620 422	...	...	...	...	...	...	...
Zamboanga	861 799	...	...	...	...	...	...	...
Qatar								
21 IV 2010 (CDFC)								
Al-Khoor	193 983	181 005	12 978	...	...	...	...	...
Al-Rayyan	455 623	301 842	153 781	...	...	...	...	...
Al-Wakrah	141 222	114 698	26 524	...	...	...	...	...
DOHA	796 947	610 817	186 130	...	...	...	...	...
Republic of Korea - République de Corée								
1 VII 2017 (ESDJ)								
Busan (Pusan)	3 428 923	1 688 567	1 740 356	769.9[53]	...	...	...	...
Daegu (Taegu)	2 465 268	1 226 252	1 239 016	883.6[53]	...	...	...	...
Daejeon (Taejon)	1 531 256	768 766	762 490	539.3[53]	...	...	...	...
Gwangju (Kwangchu)	1 500 977	748 034	752 943	501.2[53]	...	...	...	...
Incheon	2 923 047	1 470 976	1 452 071	1062.6[53]	...	...	...	...
Jeju (Cheju)	634 161	320 174	313 987	1849.1[53]	...	...	...	...
Sejong	275 594	138 558	137 036	464.9[53]	...	...	...	...

8. Population of capital cities and cities of 100 000 or more inhabitants: latest available year, 1998 - 2017
Population des capitales et des villes de 100 000 habitants ou plus : dernière année disponible, 1998 - 2017 (continued - suite)

Continent, country or area, date, code[a] and city Continent, pays ou zone, date, code[a] et ville	City proper - Ville proprement dite				Urban agglomeration - Agglomération urbaine			
	Population			Surface area - Superficie (km²)	Population			Surface area - Superficie (km²)
	Both sexes - Les deux sexes	Male - Masculin	Female - Féminin		Both sexes - Les deux sexes	Male - Masculin	Female - Féminin	
ASIA - ASIE								
Republic of Korea - République de Corée								
1 VII 2017 (ESDJ)								
SEOUL	9 776 305	4 785 234	4 991 071	605.2[53]	...	...	...	...
Ulsan	1 165 646	605 925	559 721	1060.8[53]	...	...	...	...
Saudi Arabia - Arabie saoudite								
27 IV 2010 (CDFC)								
Abha	236 157	136 118	100 039	...	...	...	...	...
Ad-Dammam	903 312	546 924	356 388	...	...	...	...	...
Al-Hawiyah	148 151	78 735	69 416	...	...	...	...	...
Al-Hufuf	660 788	361 672	299 116	...	...	...	...	...
Al-Jubayl	337 778	237 912	99 866	...	...	...	...	...
Al-Khubar	219 679	131 646	88 033	...	...	...	...	...
Al-Madinah	1 100 093	608 720	491 373	...	...	...	...	...
Al-Qatif	118 327	66 504	51 823	...	...	...	...	...
Al-Qurrayyat	116 162	63 412	52 750	...	...	...	...	...
Al-Seeh	234 607	131 391	103 216	...	...	...	...	...
Ar'ar	167 057	90 771	76 286	...	...	...	...	...
Ath-Thuqbah	238 066	149 691	88 375	...	...	...	...	...
At-Ta'if	579 970	306 682	273 288	...	...	...	...	...
Buraydah	467 410	268 604	198 806	...	...	...	...	...
Dhahran	120 521	68 746	51 775	...	...	...	...	...
Hafar al-Batin	271 642	148 396	123 246	...	...	...	...	...
Ha'il	310 897	170 882	140 015	...	...	...	...	...
Jiddah	3 430 697	1 996 716	1 433 981	...	...	...	...	...
Jizan	127 743	76 987	50 756	...	...	...	...	...
Khamis Mushayt	430 828	245 756	185 072	...	...	...	...	...
Makkah	1 534 731	861 737	672 994	...	...	...	...	...
Najran (Aba as-Suud)	298 288	166 143	132 145	...	...	...	...	...
RIYADH	5 188 286	3 059 287	2 128 999	...	...	...	...	...
Sekaka	150 257	84 881	65 376	...	...	...	...	...
Tabuk	512 629	281 672	230 957	...	...	...	...	...
Unayzah	152 895	86 385	66 510	...	...	...	...	...
Yanbu al-Bahr	233 236	140 897	92 339	...	...	...	...	...
Singapore - Singapour								
30 VI 2017 (ESDJ)								
SINGAPORE	5 612 253[60]	...	...	720[61]	...	...	...	...
Sri Lanka[62]								
17 VII 2001 (CDFC)								
COLOMBO	647 100	346 366	300 734	...	...	...	...	...
Dehiwala-Mount Lavinia	210 546	105 522	105 024	...	...	...	...	...
Kandy	109 343	54 288	55 055	...	...	...	...	...
Moratuwa	177 563	87 313	90 250	...	...	...	...	...
Negombo	121 701	60 947	60 754	...	...	...	...	...
Sri Jayawardanapura Kotte	116 366	59 993	56 373	...	...	...	...	...
State of Palestine - État de Palestine								
1 VII 2016 (ESDF)								
EAST JERUSALEM - JÉRUSALEM-EST[63]	264 937	...	...	...	...	...	...	...
Gaza	583 870	...	...	...	...	...	...	...
Hebron	215 452	...	...	...	...	...	...	...
Jabalya	171 642	...	...	...	...	...	...	...
Khan Yunis	185 250	...	...	...	...	...	...	...
Nablus	153 061	...	...	...	...	...	...	...
Rafah	164 000	...	...	...	...	...	...	...
Syrian Arab Republic - République arabe syrienne								
1 VII 2008 (ESDF)								
Aleppo	4 450 000	2 292 000	2 158 000	...	...	...	...	...
Al-Hasakeh	1 392 000	701 000	691 000	...	...	...	...	...
Al-Raqqah	865 000	456 000	409 000	...	...	...	...	...
Al-Sweida	349 000	171 000	178 000	...	...	...	...	...
DAMASCUS	1 680 000	857 000	823 000	...	...	...	...	...
Damasus rural	2 529 000	1 302 000	1 227 000	...	...	...	...	...
Deir El-Zor	1 111 000	563 000	548 000	...	...	...	...	...
Dra'a	930 000	472 000	458 000	...	...	...	...	...
Hama	1 508 000	768 000	740 000	...	...	...	...	...
Homs	1 667 000	852 000	815 000	...	...	...	...	...

Continent, country or area, date, code[a] and city / Continent, pays ou zone, date, code[a] et ville	City proper - Ville proprement dite				Urban agglomeration - Agglomération urbaine			
	Population			Surface area - Superficie (km²)	Population			Surface area - Superficie (km²)
	Both sexes - Les deux sexes	Male - Masculin	Female - Féminin		Both sexes - Les deux sexes	Male - Masculin	Female - Féminin	
ASIA - ASIE								
Syrian Arab Republic - République arabe syrienne								
1 VII 2008 (ESDF)								
Idleb	1 376 000	704 000	672 000	...	...	...	...	...
Lattakia	951 000	480 000	471 000	...	...	...	...	...
Tartous	756 000	383 000	373 000	...	...	...	...	...
Tajikistan - Tadjikistan								
1 VII 2016 (ESDF)								
DUSHANBE	809 429	422 635	386 794	...	...	...	...	...
Thailand - Thaïlande								
1 IX 2010 (CDJC)								
Ang Thong	...	...	...	...	109 207	51 540	57 667	...
BANGKOK	...	...	...	...	8 305 218	4 032 586	4 272 632	1569
Buri Ram	...	...	...	...	375 999	181 546	194 453	...
Chachoengsao	...	...	...	...	206 250	101 475	104 775	...
Chai Nat	...	...	...	...	205 456	97 373	108 083	...
Chaiyaphum	...	...	...	...	205 112	99 280	105 832	...
Chanthaburi	...	...	...	...	243 126	118 221	124 905	...
Chiang Mai	...	...	...	...	967 020	466 145	500 875	...
Chiang Rai	...	...	...	...	455 732	220 391	235 341	...
Chon Buri	...	...	...	...	1 158 989	575 208	583 781	...
Chumphon	...	...	...	...	147 912	75 339	72 573	...
Kalasin	...	...	...	...	428 940	208 863	220 077	...
Kamphaeng Phet	...	...	...	...	211 774	101 456	110 318	...
Kanchanaburi	...	...	...	...	292 521	143 986	148 535	...
Khon Kaen	...	...	...	...	703 123	339 011	364 112	...
Lampang	...	...	...	...	372 463	180 360	192 103	...
Lamphun	...	...	...	...	262 832	126 662	136 170	...
Loei	...	...	...	...	164 180	81 302	82 878	...
Lop Buri	...	...	...	...	235 827	118 964	116 863	...
Maha Sarakham	...	...	...	...	153 740	72 143	81 597	...
Mukdahan	...	...	...	...	180 600	89 190	91 410	...
Nakhon Pathom	...	...	...	...	339 736	166 150	173 586	...
Nakhon Phanom	...	...	...	...	123 720	59 683	64 037	...
Nakhon Ratchasima	...	...	...	...	653 075	316 329	336 746	...
Nakhon Sawan	...	...	...	...	225 903	107 298	118 605	...
Nakhon Si Thammarat	...	...	...	...	265 606	127 460	138 146	...
Narathiwat	...	...	...	...	133 718	64 616	69 102	...
Nong Bua Lam Phu	...	...	...	...	203 142	98 164	104 978	...
Nong Khai	...	...	...	...	232 798	113 989	118 809	...
Nonthaburi	...	...	...	...	797 739	383 826	413 913	...
Pathum Thani	...	...	...	...	757 175	358 679	398 496	...
Pattani	...	...	...	...	104 617	51 305	53 312	...
Phatthalung	...	...	...	...	244 783	117 039	127 744	...
Phayao	...	...	...	...	221 062	106 657	114 405	...
Phetchabun	...	...	...	...	172 275	82 257	90 018	...
Phetchaburi	...	...	...	...	175 675	83 735	91 940	...
Phichit	...	...	...	...	131 283	62 446	68 837	...
Phitsanulok	...	...	...	...	201 466	93 098	108 368	...
Phra Nakhon Si Ayutthaya	...	...	...	...	365 736	173 280	192 456	...
Phrae	...	...	...	...	156 099	75 175	80 924	...
Phuket	...	...	...	...	358 159	175 144	183 015	...
Prachuap Khiri Khan	...	...	...	...	177 011	87 525	89 486	...
Ranong	...	...	...	...	123 596	62 090	61 506	...
Ratchaburi	...	...	...	...	317 886	149 460	168 426	...
Rayong	...	...	...	...	445 939	224 068	221 871	...
Roi Et	...	...	...	...	365 113	176 648	188 465	...
Sa Kaeo	...	...	...	...	135 536	66 447	69 089	...
Sakon Nakhon	...	...	...	...	315 788	153 785	162 003	...
Samut Prakan	...	...	...	...	1 082 993	527 487	555 506	...
Samut Sakhon	...	...	...	...	479 186	237 778	241 408	...
Saraburi	...	...	...	...	239 281	114 885	124 396	...
Si Sa Ket	...	...	...	...	160 508	77 363	83 145	...
Songkhla	...	...	...	...	800 970	382 828	418 142	...
Sukhothai	...	...	...	...	166 782	79 139	87 643	...
Suphan Buri	...	...	...	...	228 496	108 666	119 830	...

8. Population of capital cities and cities of 100 000 or more inhabitants: latest available year, 1998 - 2017
Population des capitales et des villes de 100 000 habitants ou plus : dernière année disponible, 1998 - 2017 (continued - suite)

Continent, country or area, date, code[a] and city / Continent, pays ou zone, date, code[a] et ville	City proper - Ville proprement dite				Urban agglomeration - Agglomération urbaine			
	Population			Surface area - Superficie (km²)	Population			Surface area - Superficie (km²)
	Both sexes - Les deux sexes	Male - Masculin	Female - Féminin		Both sexes - Les deux sexes	Male - Masculin	Female - Féminin	
ASIA - ASIE								
Thailand - Thaïlande								
1 IX 2010 (CDJC)								
Surat Thani	...	...	...	...	410 984	198 909	212 075	...
Surin	...	...	...	...	153 159	73 082	80 077	...
Tak	...	...	...	...	146 769	70 754	76 015	...
Trat	...	...	...	...	110 398	52 309	58 089	...
Ubon Ratchathani	...	...	...	...	411 954	198 655	213 299	...
Udon Thani	...	...	...	...	483 057	232 326	250 731	...
Uttaradit	...	...	...	...	151 047	72 244	78 803	...
Yala	...	...	...	...	119 744	58 041	61 703	...
Yasothon	...	...	...	...	127 173	63 885	63 288	...
Timor-Leste[64]								
11 VII 2015* (CDFC)								
DILI	222 323	114 792	107 531	...	...	...	...	...
Turkey - Turquie[65]								
31 XII 2016 (ESDJ)								
Adana	...	...	...	...	2 201 670	1 101 340	1 100 330	...
Adıyaman	245 446	123 283	122 163	...	...	...	...	...
Afyonkarahisar	224 968	111 274	113 694	...	...	...	...	...
Ağrı	117 213	60 635	56 578	...	...	...	...	...
Aksaray	213 088	105 563	107 525	...	...	...	...	...
Amasya	104 629	51 697	52 932	...	...	...	...	...
ANKARA	...	...	...	...	5 346 518	2 653 431	2 693 087	...
Antalya	...	...	...	...	2 328 555	1 174 936	1 153 619	...
Aydın	...	...	...	...	1 068 260	533 004	535 256	...
Balıkesir	...	...	...	...	1 196 176	596 896	599 280	...
Batman	402 189	202 874	199 315	...	...	...	...	...
Bingöl	111 364	56 770	54 594	...	...	...	...	...
Bolu	163 018	80 282	82 736	...	...	...	...	...
Bursa	...	...	...	...	2 901 396	1 454 059	1 447 337	...
Çanakkale	126 062	61 732	64 330	...	...	...	...	...
Cizre	112 919	57 078	55 841	...	...	...	...	...
Çorum	259 205	128 523	130 682	...	...	...	...	...
Denizli	...	...	...	...	1 005 687	500 398	505 289	...
Diyarbakir	...	...	...	...	1 673 119	844 011	829 108	...
Düzce	162 897	80 745	82 152	...	...	...	...	...
Edirne	160 233	80 582	79 651	...	...	...	...	...
Elazığ	374 319	186 101	188 218	...	...	...	...	...
Ereğli	115 987	57 594	58 393	...	...	...	...	...
Erzurum	...	...	...	...	762 021	381 138	380 883	...
Eskişehir	...	...	...	...	844 842	421 580	423 262	...
Gaziantep	...	...	...	...	1 974 244	998 926	975 318	...
Giresun	107 953	53 053	54 900	...	...	...	...	...
Hatay	...	...	...	...	1 555 165	780 854	774 311	...
Isparta	220 322	109 770	110 552	...	...	...	...	...
İstanbul	...	...	...	...	14 804 116	7 424 390	7 379 726	...
İzmir	...	...	...	...	4 223 545	2 104 632	2 118 913	...
Kahramanmaraş	...	...	...	...	1 112 634	565 816	546 818	...
Karabük	118 373	58 693	59 680	...	...	...	...	...
Karaman	156 056	76 952	79 104	...	...	...	...	...
Kastamonu	114 131	56 137	57 994	...	...	...	...	...
Kayseri	...	...	...	...	1 358 980	681 269	677 711	...
Kırıkkale	194 675	96 881	97 794	...	...	...	...	...
Kırşehir	130 915	65 691	65 224	...	...	...	...	...
Kocaeli	...	...	...	...	1 830 772	927 157	903 615	...
Konya	...	...	...	...	2 161 303	1 073 631	1 087 672	...
Kütahya	240 814	119 979	120 835	...	...	...	...	...
Lüleburgaz	114 698	58 104	56 594	...	...	...	...	...
Malatya	...	...	...	...	781 305	389 572	391 733	...
Manisa	...	...	...	...	1 396 945	701 094	695 851	...
Mardin	...	...	...	...	796 237	400 475	395 762	...
Mersin	...	...	...	...	1 773 852	885 583	888 269	...
Muğla	...	...	...	...	923 773	470 404	453 369	...
Nevşehir	102 997	50 222	52 775	...	...	...	...	...
Niğde	137 194	70 551	66 643	...	...	...	...	...

8. Population of capital cities and cities of 100 000 or more inhabitants: latest available year, 1998 - 2017
Population des capitales et des villes de 100 000 habitants ou plus : dernière année disponible, 1998 - 2017 (continued - suite)

Continent, country or area, date, code[a] and city / Continent, pays ou zone, date, code[a] et ville	City proper - Ville proprement dite				Urban agglomeration - Agglomération urbaine			
	Population			Surface area - Superficie (km²)	Population			Surface area - Superficie (km²)
	Both sexes - Les deux sexes	Male - Masculin	Female - Féminin		Both sexes - Les deux sexes	Male - Masculin	Female - Féminin	
ASIA - ASIE								
Turkey - Turquie[65]								
31 XII 2016 (ESDJ)								
Ordu	...	...	...	...	750 588	376 243	374 345	...
Osmaniye	229 406	115 137	114 269	...	...	...	...	...
Rize	114 838	56 276	58 562	...	...	...	...	...
Sakarya	...	...	...	...	976 948	490 935	486 013	...
Samsun	...	...	...	...	1 295 927	640 699	655 228	...
Şanlıurfa	...	...	...	...	1 940 627	976 938	963 689	...
Siirt	147 271	76 356	70 915	...				...
Sivas	335 943	165 764	170 179	...	...	...	...	...
Tekirdağ	...	...	...	...	972 875	499 819	473 056	...
Tokat	148 149	72 341	75 808	...				...
Trabzon	...	...	...	...	779 379	385 009	394 370	...
Uşak	206 234	103 787	102 447	...	...	...	...	...
Van	...	...	...	...	1 100 190	561 592	538 598	...
Yalova	116 615	57 590	59 025	...	...	...	...	...
Zonguldak	108 180	52 918	55 262	...	...	...	...	...
United Arab Emirates - Émirats arabes unis								
1 VII 2002 (ESDF)								
ABU DHABI	527 000	359 000	168 000	...	...	...	...	...
Ajman	205 000	122 000	83 000	...	...	...	...	...
Al-Ayn	328 000	215 000	113 000	...	...	...	...	...
Al-Sharjah	488 000	317 000	171 000	...	...	...	...	...
Dubai	1 089 000	759 000	330 000	...	...	...	...	...
Uzbekistan - Ouzbékistan[66]								
1 I 2016 (ESDJ)								
Almalyk	...	...	...	...	124 352	60 446	63 906	...
Andizhan	416 243	208 259	207 984	...	...	...	...	...
Angren	...	...	...	...	180 449	89 859	90 590	...
Bukhara	274 721	135 729	138 992	...	...	...	...	...
Chirchik	...	...	...	...	151 764	74 507	77 257	...
Fergana	271 013	134 082	136 931	...	...	...	...	...
Jizzax	167 369	83 644	83 725	...	...	...	...	...
Karshi	260 712	130 127	130 585	...	...	...	...	...
Kokand	...	...	...	...	239 861	116 898	122 963	...
Margilan	...	...	...	...	222 078	111 196	110 882	...
Namangan	493 336	253 467	239 869	...	...	...	...	...
Navoi	133 526	68 043	65 483	...	...	...	...	...
Nukus	303 683	149 473	154 210	...	...	...	...	...
Samarkand	519 231	250 535	268 696	...	...	...	...	...
Shahrisabz	...	...	...	...	103 527	52 644	50 883	...
TASHKENT	2 393 176	1 165 610	1 227 566	...	...	...	...	...
Termez	140 165	69 025	71 140	...	...	...	...	...
Urgentch	138 640	69 706	68 934	...	...	...	...	...
Yemen - Yémen								
1 VII 2009* (ESDF)								
Adan	684 322	...	...	...	684 322	...	...	...
SANA'A	1 976 286	...	...	...	2 022 867	...	...	...
EUROPE								
Åland Islands - Îles d'Åland								
1 VII 2017 (ESDJ)								
MARIEHAMN	11 621[24]	5 583[24]	6 038[24]	12	...	...	...	...
Albania - Albanie								
1 X 2011 (CDJC)								
Durrës	113 249	56 511	56 738	...	...	...	...	...
TIRANA	418 495	203 239	215 256	...	...	...	...	...
Andorra - Andorre[24]								
1 VII 2011 (ESDJ)								
ANDORRA LA VELLA	...	...	...	...	22 205	11 056	11 149	...

8. Population of capital cities and cities of 100 000 or more inhabitants: latest available year, 1998 - 2017
Population des capitales et des villes de 100 000 habitants ou plus : dernière année disponible, 1998 - 2017 (continued - suite)

Continent, country or area, date, code[a] and city / Continent, pays ou zone, date, code[a] et ville	City proper - Ville proprement dite				Urban agglomeration - Agglomération urbaine			
	Population			Surface area - Superficie (km²)	Population			Surface area - Superficie (km²)
	Both sexes - Les deux sexes	Male - Masculin	Female - Féminin		Both sexes - Les deux sexes	Male - Masculin	Female - Féminin	
EUROPE								
Austria - Autriche								
1 I 2017 (ESDJ)								
Graz	283 869	139 418	144 451	...	...	...	...	...
Innsbruck	132 236	64 471	67 765	...	...	...	...	...
Linz	203 012	98 157	104 855	...	...	...	...	...
Salzburg	152 367	73 063	79 304	...	...	...	...	...
WIEN	1 867 582	909 124	958 458	...	...	...	...	...
Belarus - Bélarus								
1 I 2017 (ESDJ)								
Baranovichi	179 439	81 421	98 018	85	...	...	...	...
Bobruisk	217 940	101 759	116 181	96	...	...	...	...
Borisov	143 287	67 250	76 037	46	...	...	...	...
Brest	343 985	158 983	185 002	146	...	...	...	...
Gomel	...	...	...	...	535 229	243 894	291 335	140
Grodno	368 710	167 443	201 267	142	...	...	...	...
Lida	101 165	47 328	53 837	...	...	...	...	...
MINSK	1 974 819	898 977	1 075 842	348	...	...	...	...
Mogilev	380 440	174 680	205 760	119	...	...	...	...
Mozir	111 801	53 029	58 772	44	...	...	...	...
Novopolotsk	...	...	...	...	108 176	51 585	56 591	48
Orsha	115 938	53 280	62 658	...	...	...	...	...
Pinsk	138 202	63 617	74 585	47	...	...	...	...
Soligorsk	106 839	49 970	56 869	15	...	...	...	...
Vitebsk	...	...	...	...	377 595	167 279	210 316	125
Belgium - Belgique								
1 I 2011 (CDJC)								
Anderlecht	108 940	53 707	55 233	18	...	...	...	...
Antwerpen (Anvers)	498 473	247 192	251 281	205	718 730	354 576	364 154	394
Brugge	117 260	56 952	60 308	138	117 260	56 952	60 308	138
BRUXELLES (BRUSSEL)	174 383	90 317	84 066	33	1 550 299[67]	754 208[67]	796 091[67]	573[67]
Charleroi	204 150	99 221	104 929	102	291 806	141 106	150 700	199
Gent (Gand)	248 358	122 457	125 901	156	280 151	137 980	142 171	207
Liège (Luik)	195 965	96 509	99 456	69	491 767	238 134	253 633	367
Namur	110 175	53 019	57 156	176	110 175	53 019	57 156	176
Schaerbeek	127 525	63 020	64 505	8	...	...	...	...
Bulgaria - Bulgarie								
1 I 2017 (ESDJ)								
Burgas	202 766	96 717	106 049	...	...	...	...	...
Plovdiv	343 424	163 208	180 216	...	...	...	...	...
Ruse	144 936	70 367	74 569	...	...	...	...	...
SOFIA	1 236 047	590 336	645 711	...	...	...	...	...
Stara Zagora	136 781	65 636	71 145	...	...	...	...	...
Varna	335 177	162 170	173 007	...	...	...	...	...
Croatia - Croatie								
1 IV 2011 (CDJC)								
Osijek	108 048	50 357	57 691	174	...	...	...	...
Rijeka	128 624	60 951	67 673	43	...	...	...	...
Split	178 102	84 477	93 625	79	...	...	...	...
ZAGREB	790 017	369 339	420 678	641	...	...	...	...
Czechia - Tchéquie								
1 I 2017 (ESDJ)								
Brno	377 973	182 549	195 424	226[30]	...	...	...	...
Liberec	103 853	50 212	53 641	105[30]	...	...	...	...
Olomouc	100 378	47 473	52 905	101[30]	...	...	...	...
Ostrava	291 634	141 268	150 366	205[30]	...	...	...	...
Plzen	170 548	82 946	87 602	133[30]	...	...	...	...
PRAHA	1 280 508	621 565	658 943	485[30]	...	...	...	...
Denmark - Danemark[68]								
1 VII 2017 (ESDJ)								
Ålborg	211 684[24]	106 646[24]	105 038[24]	1137.3	...	...	...	...
Århus	336 411[24]	165 599[24]	170 812[24]	467.9	...	...	...	...
Esbjerg	115 932[24]	58 121[24]	57 811[24]	795	...	...	...	...
Frederiksberg	104 641[24]	49 601[24]	55 040[24]	8.7	...	...	...	...
KOBENHAVN	605 366[24]	299 235[24]	306 131[24]	86.4	...	...	...	...

8. Population of capital cities and cities of 100 000 or more inhabitants: latest available year, 1998 - 2017
Population des capitales et des villes de 100 000 habitants ou plus : dernière année disponible, 1998 - 2017 (continued - suite)

	City proper - Ville proprement dite				Urban agglomeration - Agglomération urbaine			
Continent, country or area, date, code[a] and city / Continent, pays ou zone, date, code[a] et ville	Population			Surface area - Superficie (km²)	Population			Surface area - Superficie (km²)
	Both sexes - Les deux sexes	Male - Masculin	Female - Féminin		Both sexes - Les deux sexes	Male - Masculin	Female - Féminin	
EUROPE								
Denmark - Danemark[68]								
1 VII 2017 (ESDJ)								
Odense	200 703[24]	99 049[24]	101 654[24]	305.6	...	...	...	...
Vejle	113 720[24]	56 941[24]	56 779[24]	1058.4	...	...	...	...
Estonia - Estonie								
1 I 2017 (ESDJ)								
TALLINN	426 538	191 558	234 980	158	...	...	...	...
Faeroe Islands - Îles Féroé								
1 VII 2017 (ESDJ)								
TÓRSHAVN	13 083	6 515	6 568	6[69]	19 249	9 672	9 577	15[70]
Finland - Finlande[71]								
1 VII 2016 (ESDJ)								
Espoo	272 193[24]	134 943[24]	137 250[24]	312.3	...	...	...	...
HELSINKI	631 695[24]	299 081[24]	332 614[24]	214.2	...	...	...	...
Jyvaskyla	138 109[24]	67 730[24]	70 379[24]	1171	...	...	...	...
Kuopio	117 331[24]	57 118[24]	60 213[24]	3241	...	...	...	...
Lahti	119 098[24]	57 236[24]	61 862[24]	459.5	...	...	...	...
Oulu	199 526[24]	99 451[24]	100 075[24]	3031.9	...	...	...	...
Tampere	226 696[24]	109 867[24]	116 830[24]	524.9	...	...	...	...
Turku	186 756[24]	88 956[24]	97 800[24]	245.7	...	...	...	...
Vantaa	216 973[24]	107 097[24]	109 877[24]	238.4	...	...	...	...
France								
1 I 2010 (CDJS)								
Aix-en-Provence	141 438[72]	65 940[72]	75 498[72]	186.1	...	...	...	...
Amiens	133 448[72]	63 030[72]	70 418[72]	49.5	162 718	77 241	85 477	137.3
Angers	147 571[72]	67 521[72]	80 050[72]	42.7	215 887	100 353	115 534	188.6
Argenteuil	103 125[72]	50 356[72]	52 769[72]	17.2	...	...	...	...
Besançon	116 914[72]	54 937[72]	61 977[72]	65.1	135 050	63 788	71 262	122.4
Bordeaux	239 157[72]	111 452[72]	127 705[72]	49.4	843 425	400 423	443 002	1172.8
Boulogne-Billancourt	114 205[72]	53 038[72]	61 167[72]	6.2	...	...	...	...
Brest	141 303[72]	68 083[72]	73 220[72]	49.5	199 852	96 845	103 007	199.4
Caen	108 954[72]	50 828[72]	58 126[72]	25.7	196 743	93 132	103 611	141.9
Clermont-Ferrand	139 860[72]	65 886[72]	73 974[72]	42.7	260 681	123 262	137 419	180.8
Dijon	151 212[72]	71 041[72]	80 171[72]	40.4	237 117	112 013	125 104	166
Grenoble	155 637[72]	75 558[72]	80 079[72]	18.1	496 951	241 872	255 079	512.3
Le Havre	175 497[72]	82 703[72]	92 794[72]	47	241 037	114 634	126 403	194.9
Le Mans	142 626[72]	66 979[72]	75 647[72]	34.8	207 658	98 772	108 886	294.3
Lille	227 560[72]	108 257[72]	119 303[72]	78	1 018 356	486 736	531 620	442.5
Limoges	139 150[72]	64 643[72]	74 507[72]	47.9	186 499	87 294	99 205	236.3
Lyon	484 344[72]	226 203[72]	258 141[72]	52.8	1 551 108	741 745	809 363	1177.8
Marseille	850 726[72]	400 977[72]	449 749[72]	240.6	1 559 789[73]	741 799[73]	817 990[73]	1731.9
Metz	120 738[72]	58 537[72]	62 201[72]	41.9	288 940	140 573	148 367	306.9
Montpellier	257 351[72]	119 967[72]	137 384[72]	56.9	390 962	184 812	206 150	310
Montreuil	102 770[72]	51 166[72]	51 604[72]	8.9	...	...	...	...
Mulhouse	109 588[72]	52 989[72]	56 599[72]	22.2	242 353	117 380	124 973	239.1
Nancy	105 421[72]	49 278[72]	56 143[72]	15	286 215	135 585	150 630	245.9
Nantes	284 970[72]	134 873[72]	150 097[72]	65.2	591 461	282 368	309 093	537.7
Nice	343 304[72]	159 260[72]	184 044[72]	71.9	941 777	443 854	497 923	743.6
Nîmes	142 205[72]	66 302[72]	75 903[72]	161.9	175 503	82 457	93 046	265.8
Orléans	114 167[72]	54 609[72]	59 558[72]	27.5	269 724	130 085	139 639	289.5
PARIS	2 243 833[72]	1 057 233[72]	1 186 600[72]	105.4	10 460 118[74]	5 037 278[74]	5 422 840[74]	2844.8
Perpignan	117 419[72]	54 431[72]	62 988[72]	68.1	190 668	89 358	101 310	217.5
Reims	179 992[72]	84 862[72]	95 130[72]	46.9	208 639	98 645	109 994	94.3
Rennes	207 178[72]	97 794[72]	109 384[72]	50.4	310 672	148 841	161 831	284.4
Rouen	110 933[72]	52 383[72]	58 550[72]	21.4	463 748	219 416	244 332	453.2
Saint-Denis	106 785[72]	53 787[72]	52 998[72]	12.4	...	...	...	...
Saint-Étienne	171 260[72]	80 545[72]	90 715[72]	80	371 281	176 464	194 817	418.7
Strasbourg	271 782[72]	128 478[72]	143 304[72]	78.3	449 931	214 580	235 351	240.2
Toulon	164 532[72]	77 464[72]	87 068[72]	42.8	557 802	264 944	292 858	763.7
Toulouse	441 802[72]	213 198[72]	228 604[72]	118.3	879 683	427 944	451 739	811.6
Tours	134 817[72]	61 897[72]	72 920[72]	34.7	346 105	163 682	182 423	663.7
Villeurbanne	145 150[72]	70 377[72]	74 773[72]	14.5	...	...	...	...

Continent, country or area, date, code[a] and city / Continent, pays ou zone, date, code[a] et ville	City proper - Ville proprement dite				Urban agglomeration - Agglomération urbaine			
	Population			Surface area - Superficie (km²)	Population			Surface area - Superficie (km²)
	Both sexes - Les deux sexes	Male - Masculin	Female - Féminin		Both sexes - Les deux sexes	Male - Masculin	Female - Féminin	
EUROPE								
Germany - Allemagne								
1 I 2016 (ESDJ)								
Aachen	245 885[1]	127 613[1]	118 272[1]	160.9	...	...	...	...
Augsburg	286 374[1]	140 323[1]	146 051[1]	146.9	...	...	...	...
Bergisch Gladbach	111 366[1]	53 479[1]	57 887[1]	83.1	...	...	...	...
BERLIN	3 520 031[1]	1 726 533[1]	1 793 498[1]	891.7	...	...	...	...
Bielefeld	333 090[1]	161 148[1]	171 942[1]	258.8	...	...	...	...
Bochum	364 742[1]	177 427[1]	187 315[1]	145.7	...	...	...	...
Bonn	318 809[1]	151 954[1]	166 855[1]	141.1	...	...	...	...
Bottrop	117 143[1]	57 004[1]	60 139[1]	100.6	...	...	...	...
Braunschweig	251 364[1]	125 001[1]	126 363[1]	192.2	...	...	...	...
Bremen	557 464[1]	274 119[1]	283 345[1]	326.2	...	...	...	...
Bremerhaven	114 025[1]	56 776[1]	57 249[1]	93.7	...	...	...	...
Chemnitz	248 645[1]	122 748[1]	125 897[1]	221.1	...	...	...	...
Darmstadt	155 353[1]	78 915[1]	76 438[1]	122.1	...	...	...	...
Dortmund	586 181[1]	287 846[1]	298 335[1]	280.7	...	...	...	...
Dresden	543 825[1]	270 410[1]	273 415[1]	328.5	...	...	...	...
Duisburg	491 231[1]	241 417[1]	249 814[1]	232.8	...	...	...	...
Düsseldorf	612 178[1]	295 896[1]	316 282[1]	217.4	...	...	...	...
Erfurt	210 118[1]	102 259[1]	107 859[1]	269.9	...	...	...	...
Erlangen	108 336[1]	53 454[1]	54 882[1]	77	...	...	...	...
Essen	582 624[1]	282 565[1]	300 059[1]	210.3	...	...	...	...
Frankfurt am Main	732 688[1]	362 515[1]	370 173[1]	248.3	...	...	...	...
Freiburg im Breisgau	226 393[1]	107 913[1]	118 480[1]	153.1	...	...	...	...
Fürth	124 171[1]	60 669[1]	63 502[1]	63.4	...	...	...	...
Gelsenkirchen	260 368[1]	129 267[1]	131 101[1]	104.9	...	...	...	...
Göttingen	118 914[1]	57 732[1]	61 182[1]	116.9	...	...	...	...
Hagen	189 044[1]	92 207[1]	96 837[1]	160.5	...	...	...	...
Halle (Saale)	236 991[1]	114 581[1]	122 410[1]	135	...	...	...	...
Hamburg	1 787 408[1]	873 062[1]	914 346[1]	755.3	...	...	...	...
Hamm	179 397[1]	88 166[1]	91 231[1]	226.4	...	...	...	...
Hannover	532 163[1]	259 749[1]	272 414[1]	204.1	...	...	...	...
Heidelberg	156 267[1]	74 954[1]	81 313[1]	108.8	...	...	...	...
Heilbronn	122 567[1]	61 268[1]	61 299[1]	99.9	...	...	...	...
Herne	155 851[1]	75 940[1]	79 911[1]	51.4	...	...	...	...
Hildesheim	101 667[1]	48 291[1]	53 376[1]	92.2	...	...	...	...
Ingolstadt	132 438[1]	66 825[1]	65 613[1]	133.4	...	...	...	...
Jena	109 527[1]	54 467[1]	55 060[1]	114.8	...	...	...	...
Karlsruhe	307 755[1]	156 686[1]	151 069[1]	173.5	...	...	...	...
Kassel	197 984[1]	96 659[1]	101 325[1]	106.8	...	...	...	...
Kiel	246 306[1]	119 835[1]	126 471[1]	118.7	...	...	...	...
Koblenz	112 586[1]	54 391[1]	58 195[1]	105.2	...	...	...	...
Köln	1 060 582[1]	516 976[1]	543 606[1]	405	...	...	...	...
Krefeld	225 144[1]	109 487[1]	115 657[1]	137.8	...	...	...	...
Leipzig	560 472[1]	274 414[1]	286 058[1]	297.8	...	...	...	...
Leverkusen	163 487[1]	79 590[1]	83 897[1]	78.9	...	...	...	...
Lübeck	216 253[1]	103 683[1]	112 570[1]	214.2	...	...	...	...
Ludwigshafen am Rhein	164 718[1]	81 590[1]	83 128[1]	77.6	...	...	...	...
Magdeburg	235 723[1]	115 810[1]	119 913[1]	201	...	...	...	...
Mainz	209 779[1]	101 620[1]	108 159[1]	97.7	...	...	...	...
Mannheim	305 780[1]	152 868[1]	152 912[1]	145	...	...	...	...
Moers	104 529[1]	50 973[1]	53 556[1]	67.7	...	...	...	...
Mönchengladbach	259 996[1]	127 512[1]	132 484[1]	170.5	...	...	...	...
Mülheim an der Ruhr	169 278[1]	81 461[1]	87 817[1]	91.3	...	...	...	...
München	1 450 381[1]	707 150[1]	743 231[1]	310.7	...	...	...	...
Münster (Westf.)	310 039[1]	148 447[1]	161 592[1]	303.3	...	...	...	...
Neuss	155 414[1]	75 929[1]	79 485[1]	99.5	...	...	...	...
Nürnberg	509 975[1]	247 931[1]	262 044[1]	186.4	...	...	...	...
Oberhausen	210 934[1]	103 284[1]	107 650[1]	77.1	...	...	...	...
Offenbach am Main	123 734[1]	61 609[1]	62 125[1]	44.9	...	...	...	...
Oldenburg (Oldenburg)	163 830[1]	78 259[1]	85 571[1]	103	...	...	...	...

Continent, country or area, date, code[a] and city / Continent, pays ou zone, date, code[a] et ville	City proper - Ville proprement dite				Urban agglomeration - Agglomération urbaine			
	Population			Surface area - Superficie (km²)	Population			Surface area - Superficie (km²)
	Both sexes - Les deux sexes	Male - Masculin	Female - Féminin		Both sexes - Les deux sexes	Male - Masculin	Female - Féminin	
EUROPE								
Germany - Allemagne								
1 I 2016 (ESDJ)								
Osnabrück	162 403[1]	78 275[1]	84 128[1]	119.8	...	...	...	...
Paderborn	148 126[1]	73 680[1]	74 446[1]	179.6	...	...	...	...
Pforzheim	122 247[1]	59 901[1]	62 346[1]	98	...	...	...	...
Potsdam	167 745[1]	80 854[1]	86 891[1]	188.3	...	...	...	...
Recklinghausen	114 330[1]	55 697[1]	58 633[1]	66.5	...	...	...	...
Regensburg	145 465[1]	69 969[1]	75 496[1]	80.7	...	...	...	...
Remscheid	109 499[1]	53 725[1]	55 774[1]	74.5	...	...	...	...
Reutlingen	114 310[1]	56 398[1]	57 912[1]	87.1	...	...	...	...
Rostock	206 011[1]	101 078[1]	104 933[1]	181.3	...	...	...	...
Saarbrücken	178 151[1]	87 985[1]	90 166[1]	167.1	...	...	...	...
Salzgitter	101 079[1]	49 898[1]	51 181[1]	223.9	...	...	...	...
Siegen	102 355[1]	49 925[1]	52 430[1]	114.7	...	...	...	...
Solingen	158 726[1]	76 948[1]	81 778[1]	89.5	...	...	...	...
Stuttgart	623 738[1]	310 492[1]	313 246[1]	207.4	...	...	...	...
Trier	114 914[1]	57 510[1]	57 404[1]	117.1	...	...	...	...
Ulm	122 636[1]	60 400[1]	62 236[1]	118.7	...	...	...	...
Wiesbaden	276 218[1]	131 901[1]	144 317[1]	203.9	...	...	...	...
Wolfsburg	124 045[1]	61 581[1]	62 464[1]	204.1	...	...	...	...
Wuppertal	350 046[1]	170 822[1]	179 224[1]	168.4	...	...	...	...
Würzburg	124 873[1]	59 159[1]	65 714[1]	87.6	...	...	...	...
Gibraltar								
31 XII 2015 (ESDF)								
GIBRALTAR	33 573[75]	16 938[75]	16 635[75]	6	...	...	...	...
Greece - Grèce								
9 V 2011 (CDFC)								
ATHINAI	664 046	315 210	348 836	...	...	...	...	...
Calithèa	100 641	46 782	53 859	...	...	...	...	...
Iraclion	140 730	68 024	72 706	...	...	...	...	...
Larissa	144 651	70 797	73 854	...	...	...	...	...
Patrai	167 446	81 114	86 332	...	...	...	...	...
Pésterion	139 981	68 563	71 418	...	...	...	...	...
Pireas	163 688	78 200	85 488	...	...	...	...	...
Thessaloniki	315 196	143 813	171 383	...	...	...	...	...
Guernsey - Guernesey								
31 III 2015 (CDJC)								
ST. PETER PORT	18 599	...	...	...	...	...	...	...
Holy See - Saint-Siège[76]								
21 VI 2012 (ESDF)								
VATICAN CITY	451	...	...	...	...	...	...	...
Hungary - Hongrie								
1 VII 2016 (ESDJ)								
BUDAPEST	1 756 056	814 705	941 351	525.1	2 587 904	1 215 675	1 372 229	2538.4
Debrecen	202 520	94 515	108 005	461.7	266 212	125 965	140 247	1081.8
Györ	129 435	61 168	68 267	174.6	231 802	112 285	119 517	1607
Kecskemét	111 269	52 258	59 011	322.6	133 020	63 021	70 000	666.1
Miskolc	157 639	73 120	84 519	236.7	248 129	116 922	131 207	982.3
Nyiregyhaza	117 874	54 861	63 013	274.5	147 868	69 548	78 320	554.2
Pécs	145 011	66 334	78 677	162.8	180 349	83 758	96 591	671.3
Szeged	161 879	74 287	87 592	281	204 601	95 419	109 182	804.5
Iceland - Islande								
1 VII 2016 (ESDJ)								
REYKJAVIK	122 853[77]	61 252[77]	61 602[77]	274	215 249[78]	107 420[78]	107 829[78]	1044[79]
Ireland - Irlande								
1 IV 2016 (ESDJ)								
Cork	124 391	61 255	63 136	...	...	...	...	...
DUBLIN	544 107	267 319	276 788	...	...	...	...	...
Isle of Man - Île de Man								
23 IV 2006 (CDJC)								
DOUGLAS	26 218	13 000	13 218	...	...	...	...	...

Continent, country or area, date, code[a] and city / Continent, pays ou zone, date, code[a] et ville	City proper - Ville proprement dite				Urban agglomeration - Agglomération urbaine			
	Population			Surface area - Superficie (km²)	Population			Surface area - Superficie (km²)
	Both sexes - Les deux sexes	Male - Masculin	Female - Féminin		Both sexes - Les deux sexes	Male - Masculin	Female - Féminin	
EUROPE								
Italy - Italie								
1 VII 2016 (ESDJ)								
Ancona	100 779	48 070	52 709	125	...	...	...	...
Bari	325 271	156 083	169 189	117	...	...	...	...
Bergamo	119 834	56 156	63 679	40	...	...	...	...
Bologna	387 515	182 507	205 009	141	...	...	...	...
Bolzano	106 696	51 111	55 585	52	...	...	...	...
Brescia	196 575	92 688	103 887	90	...	...	...	...
Cagliari	154 272	71 885	82 387	85	...	...	...	...
Catania	313 976	150 993	162 983	183	...	...	...	...
Ferrara	132 582	62 170	70 413	405	...	...	...	...
Firenze	382 533	179 210	203 323	102	...	...	...	...
Foggia	151 859	73 066	78 793	509	...	...	...	...
Forli	117 930	56 633	61 297	228	...	...	...	...
Genova	585 128	275 386	309 742	240	...	...	...	...
Giugliano in Campania	123 407	61 129	62 278	95	...	...	...	...
Latina	126 068	60 965	65 104	278	...	...	...	...
Livorno	159 068	76 109	82 959	105	...	...	...	...
Messina	237 701	113 874	123 827	214	...	...	...	...
Milano	1 348 707	644 492	704 215	182	...	...	...	...
Modena	184 850	88 234	96 617	183	...	...	...	...
Monza	122 813	58 888	63 926	33	...	...	...	...
Napoli	972 130	464 204	507 926	119	...	...	...	...
Novara	104 332	50 174	54 158	103	...	...	...	...
Padova	210 115	98 682	111 433	93	...	...	...	...
Palermo	674 085	322 153	351 932	161	...	...	...	...
Parma	193 627	92 344	101 283	261	...	...	...	...
Perugia	166 405	79 162	87 244	450	...	...	...	...
Pescara	120 717	56 487	64 230	34	...	...	...	...
Piacenza	102 273	48 645	53 629	118	...	...	...	...
Prato	191 810	92 781	99 029	97	...	...	...	...
Ravenna	159 087	77 096	81 991	654	...	...	...	...
Reggio di Calabria	182 793	87 562	95 232	239	...	...	...	...
Reggio nell'Emilia	171 418	83 305	88 113	231	...	...	...	...
Rimini	148 329	70 936	77 394	136	...	...	...	...
ROMA	2 869 113	1 359 184	1 509 929	1287	...	...	...	...
Salerno	135 056	63 009	72 047	60	...	...	...	...
Sassari	127 529	61 248	66 281	547	...	...	...	...
Siracusa	122 161	59 819	62 343	208	...	...	...	...
Taranto	200 331	95 497	104 834	250	...	...	...	...
Terni	111 478	52 447	59 032	212	...	...	...	...
Torino	888 683	423 081	465 603	130	...	...	...	...
Trento	117 367	56 260	61 107	158	...	...	...	...
Trieste	204 327	97 247	107 080	85	...	...	...	...
Venezia	262 629	124 211	138 418	416	...	...	...	...
Verona	258 059	122 031	136 029	199	...	...	...	...
Vicenza	112 576	53 177	59 399	81	...	...	...	...
Jersey								
11 III 2001 (CDJC)								
ST. HELIER	28 310	13 669	14 641	8.6	...	...	...	...
Latvia - Lettonie								
1 VII 2016 (ESDJ)								
RIGA	640 527	283 765	356 762	304	...	...	...	...
Liechtenstein								
1 VII 2017 (ESDJ)								
VADUZ	5 450	2 650	2 800	17	...	...	...	...
Lithuania - Lituanie								
1 VII 2016 (ESDJ)								
Kaunas	295 269	129 311	165 958	157	...	...	...	...
Klaipeda	152 818	68 715	84 103	98	...	...	...	...
Shauliai	102 097	45 058	57 039	81	...	...	...	...
VILNIUS	544 386	243 745	300 641	401	...	...	...	...
Luxembourg								
1 I 2017 (ESDJ)								
LUXEMBOURG-VILLE	114 303	58 507	55 796	51	...	...	...	...

8. Population of capital cities and cities of 100 000 or more inhabitants: latest available year, 1998 - 2017
Population des capitales et des villes de 100 000 habitants ou plus : dernière année disponible, 1998 - 2017 (continued - suite)

Continent, country or area, date, code[a] and city / Continent, pays ou zone, date, code[a] et ville	City proper - Ville proprement dite				Urban agglomeration - Agglomération urbaine			
	Population			Surface area - Superficie (km²)	Population			Surface area - Superficie (km²)
	Both sexes - Les deux sexes	Male - Masculin	Female - Féminin		Both sexes - Les deux sexes	Male - Masculin	Female - Féminin	

EUROPE

Malta - Malte
1 VII 2016 (ESDJ)

VALLETTA	5 730[80]	2 834[80]	2 896[80]	1	...	...	...	...

Monaco
9 VI 2008 (CDJC)

MONACO	31 109	15 076[81]	15 914[81]	...	...	...	...	...

Montenegro - Monténégro
1 IV 2011 (CDJC)

PODGORICA	185 937	90 614	95 323	1441	...	...	...	...

Netherlands - Pays-Bas
1 I 2015 (ESDJ)

Alkmaar	107 106	52 973	54 133	...	...	...	...	...
Almere	196 932	97 666	99 266	...	...	...	...	...
Alphen aan den	107 396	53 321	54 075	...	...	...	...	...
Amersfoort	152 481	74 967	77 514	...	...	...	...	...
AMSTERDAM	821 752	404 881	416 871	...	...	...	...	...
Apeldoorn	158 099	78 163	79 936	...	...	...	...	...
Arnhem	152 293	75 872	76 421	...	...	...	...	...
Breda	180 937	88 620	92 317	...	...	...	...	...
Delft	101 030	54 035	46 995	...	...	...	...	...
Dordrecht	118 899	58 646	60 253	...	...	...	...	...
Ede	111 575	54 790	56 785	...	...	...	...	...
Eindhoven	223 209	114 034	109 175	...	...	...	...	...
Emmen	107 775	53 399	54 376	...	...	...	...	...
Enschede	158 553	80 411	78 142	...	...	...	...	...
Groningen	200 336	99 657	100 679	...	...	...	...	...
Haarlem	156 645	76 481	80 164	...	...	...	...	...
Haarlemmermeer	144 152	71 642	72 510	...	...	...	...	...
Leeuwarden	107 691	53 264	54 427	...	...	...	...	...
Leiden	121 562	59 084	62 478	...	...	...	...	...
Maastricht	122 397	58 799	63 598	...	...	...	...	...
Nijmegen	170 681	81 934	88 747	...	...	...	...	...
Rotterdam	623 652	307 001	316 651	...	...	...	...	...
s-Gravenhage	514 861	254 187	260 674	...	...	...	...	...
s-Hertogenbosch	150 889	74 424	76 465	...	...	...	...	...
Tilburg	211 648	105 179	106 469	...	...	...	...	...
Utrecht	334 176	162 556	171 620	...	...	...	...	...
Venlo	100 536	49 978	50 558	...	...	...	...	...
Westland	104 302	51 937	52 365	...	...	...	...	...
Zaanstad	151 418	74 778	76 640	...	...	...	...	...
Zoetermeer	124 025	60 554	63 471	...	...	...	...	...
Zwolle	123 861	60 759	63 102	...	...	...	...	...

Norway - Norvège
1 I 2014 (ESDJ)

OSLO	634 293	316 114	318 179	426	...	...	...	...

Poland - Pologne[82]
1 VII 2016 (ESDJ)

Bialystok	293 407[83]	137 908[83]	155 499[83]	102[23]	...	...	...	...
Bielsko-Biala	170 479[83]	80 460[83]	90 019[83]	125[23]	...	...	...	...
Bydgoszcz	354 006[83]	166 712[83]	187 294[83]	176[23]	...	...	...	...
Bytom	168 398[83]	80 446[83]	87 952[83]	69[23]	...	...	...	...
Chorzów	108 640[83]	51 604[83]	57 036[83]	33[23]	...	...	...	...
Czestochowa	225 301[83]	105 759[83]	119 542[83]	160[23]	...	...	...	...
Dabrowa Górnicza	121 409[83]	58 265[83]	63 144[83]	189[23]	...	...	...	...
Elblag	119 308[83]	57 006[83]	62 302[83]	80[23]	...	...	...	...
Gdansk	461 557[83]	219 072[83]	242 485[83]	262[23]	...	...	...	...
Gdynia	244 458[83]	115 653[83]	128 805[83]	135[23]	...	...	...	...
Gliwice	181 310[83]	87 214[83]	94 096[83]	134[23]	...	...	...	...
Gorzów Wielkopolski	122 141[83]	58 034[83]	64 107[83]	86[23]	...	...	...	...
Kalisz	101 307[83]	47 097[83]	54 210[83]	69[23]	...	...	...	...
Katowice	302 397[83]	144 546[83]	157 851[83]	165[23]	...	...	...	...
Kielce	195 942[83]	92 233[83]	103 709[83]	110[23]	...	...	...	...
Koszalin	106 097[83]	50 001[83]	56 096[83]	98[23]	...	...	...	...
Kraków	755 471[83]	352 852[83]	402 619[83]	327[23]	...	...	...	...

8. Population of capital cities and cities of 100 000 or more inhabitants: latest available year, 1998 - 2017
Population des capitales et des villes de 100 000 habitants ou plus : dernière année disponible, 1998 - 2017 (continued - suite)

Continent, country or area, date, code[a] and city / Continent, pays ou zone, date, code[a] et ville	City proper - Ville proprement dite				Urban agglomeration - Agglomération urbaine			
	Population			Surface area - Superficie (km²)	Population			Surface area - Superficie (km²)
	Both sexes - Les deux sexes	Male - Masculin	Female - Féminin		Both sexes - Les deux sexes	Male - Masculin	Female - Féminin	

EUROPE

Poland - Pologne[82]
  1 VII 2016 (ESDJ)

Lódz	696 708[83]	317 520[83]	379 188[83]	293[23]	...	...	...	...
Lublin	342 039[83]	157 574[83]	184 465[83]	147[23]	...	...	...	...
Olsztyn	173 718[83]	81 067[83]	92 651[83]	88[23]	...	...	...	...
Opole	118 303[83]	55 604[83]	62 699[83]	97[23]	...	...	...	...
Plock	120 338[83]	56 827[83]	63 511[83]	88[23]	...	...	...	...
Poznan	540 365[83]	252 357[83]	288 008[83]	262[23]	...	...	...	...
Radom	213 715[83]	101 501[83]	112 214[83]	112[23]	...	...	...	...
Ruda Slaska	138 132[83]	66 848[83]	71 284[83]	78[23]	...	...	...	...
Rybnik	137 800[83]	67 201[83]	70 599[83]	148[23]	...	...	...	...
Rzeszów	183 901[83]	86 919[83]	96 982[83]	117[23]	...	...	...	...
Sosnowiec	204 552[83]	96 809[83]	107 743[83]	91[23]	...	...	...	...
Szczecin	404 461[83]	192 434[83]	212 027[83]	301[23]	...	...	...	...
Tarnów	107 045[83]	50 473[83]	56 572[83]	72[23]	...	...	...	...
Torun	199 469[83]	92 643[83]	106 826[83]	116[23]	...	...	...	...
Tychy	126 807[83]	61 113[83]	65 694[83]	82[23]	...	...	...	...
Walbrzych	113 606[83]	53 509[83]	60 097[83]	85[23]	...	...	...	...
WARSZAWA	1 744 735[83]	802 084[83]	942 651[83]	517[23]	...	...	...	...
Wloclawek	111 086[83]	52 232[83]	58 854[83]	84[23]	...	...	...	...
Wroclaw	632 020[83]	295 898[83]	336 122[83]	293[23]	...	...	...	...
Zabrze	173 682[83]	83 781[83]	89 901[83]	80[23]	...	...	...	...
Zielona Góra	139 136[83]	66 292[83]	72 844[83]	277[23]	...	...	...	...

Portugal
  1 VII 2016 (ESDJ)

Amadora	177 407	82 641	94 766	...	...	...	...	...
LISBOA	504 718	230 855	273 863	...	...	...	...	...
Porto	214 349	96 427	117 923	...	...	...	...	...

Republic of Moldova - République de Moldova
  1 I 2012 (ESDJ)

Balti (Beltsy)	144 507	66 243	78 264	41	...	...	...	...
CHIŞINĂU (KISHINEV)	669 694	311 575	358 119	123	726 075	339 321	386 755	572

Romania - Roumanie
  1 VII 2016 (ESDF)

BUCURESTI	1 835 623	852 004	983 619	240	...	...	...	...

Russian Federation - Fédération de Russie
  1 VII 2012 (ESDJ)

Abakan	168 655	77 052	91 603	...	...	...	...	...
Achinsk	107 943	48 069	59 874	...	109 229	...	...	...
Almetievsk	148 384	69 433	78 951	...	...	...	...	...
Anapa	...	...	...	...	156 928	...	...	...
Angarsk	231 944	105 405	126 539	...	...	...	...	...
Arkhangelsk	350 258	156 523	193 735	...	357 264	...	...	...
Armavir	190 831	87 524	103 307	...	209 742	...	...	...
Artem (Primorskiy Krai)	102 605	49 147	53 458	...	112 102	...	...	...
Arzamas	105 506	47 208	58 298	...	...	...	...	...
Astrakhan	526 363	241 489	284 874	...	...	...	...	...
Balakovo	196 918	88 075	108 843	...	...	...	...	...
Balashikha	228 567	112 191	116 376	...	238 284	...	...	...
Barnaul	625 679	279 300	346 379	...	686 306	...	...	...
Bataisk	115 016	54 477	60 539	...	...	...	...	...
Belgorod	369 815	167 120	202 695	...	...	...	...	...
Belovo	...	...	...	...	132 144	...	...	...
Berezniki	153 806	68 365	85 441	...	...	...	...	...
Biisk	206 327	91 943	114 384	...	215 780	...	...	...
Blagoveshchensk (Amurskaya oblast)	216 691	97 135	119 556	...	222 065	...	...	...
Bor	...	...	...	...	122 201	...	...	...
Bratsk	242 604	109 596	133 008	...	...	...	...	...
Bryansk	411 798	183 540	228 258	...	430 987	...	...	...
Cheboksary	462 669	206 721	255 948	...	473 189	...	...	...
Chelyabinsk	1 149 829	514 456	635 373	...	...	...	...	...
Cherepovets	315 186	142 977	172 209	...	...	...	...	...
Cherkessk	126 884	55 588	71 296	...	...	...	...	...
Chita	329 391	152 092	177 299	...	329 868	...	...	...

8. Population of capital cities and cities of 100 000 or more inhabitants: latest available year, 1998 - 2017
Population des capitales et des villes de 100 000 habitants ou plus : dernière année disponible, 1998 - 2017 (continued - suite)

Continent, country or area, date, code[a] and city / Continent, pays ou zone, date, code[a] et ville	City proper - Ville proprement dite				Urban agglomeration - Agglomération urbaine			
	Population			Surface area - Superficie (km²)	Population			Surface area - Superficie (km²)
	Both sexes - Les deux sexes	Male - Masculin	Female - Féminin		Both sexes - Les deux sexes	Male - Masculin	Female - Féminin	

EUROPE

Russian Federation - Fédération de Russie
1 VII 2012 (ESDJ)

Derbent	119 647	57 527	62 120	...	...	...	...	...
Dimitrovgrad	120 750	55 838	64 912	...	...	...	...	...
Domodedovo	...	...	...	...	142 743	...	...	...
Dzerzhinsk (Nizhegorodskaya oblast)	238 327	105 346	132 981	...	248 649	...	...	...
Ekaterinburg	1 386 909	621 499	765 410	...	1 420 285	...	...	...
Elektrostal	156 136	71 093	85 043	...	...	...	...	...
Elets	107 347	48 757	58 590	...	...	...	...	...
Elista	104 177	47 317	56 860	...	108 753	...	...	...
Engels	210 190	95 953	114 237	...	211 825	...	...	...
Esentuky	101 851	45 327	56 524	...	...	...	...	...
Groznyi	276 524	136 615	139 909	...	...	...	...	...
Hasaviurt	133 188	63 867	69 321	...	...	...	...	...
Irkutsk	601 993	269 003	332 990	...	...	...	...	...
Ivanovo	408 952	180 083	228 869	...	...	...	...	...
Izhevsk	631 182	281 708	349 474	...	...	...	...	...
Kaliningrad (Kaliningradskaya oblast)	437 456	200 849	236 607	...	...	...	...	...
Kaluga	328 871	146 008	182 863	...	344 766	...	...	...
Kamensk-Uralsky	172 639	77 327	95 312	...	174 493	...	...	...
Kamyshin	117 352	53 822	63 530	...	...	...	...	...
Kaspiysk	102 421	49 393	53 028	...	...	...	...	...
Kazan	1 168 745	520 694	648 051	...	...	...	...	...
Kemerovo	538 188	240 431	297 757	...	...	...	...	...
Khabarovsk	589 596	273 949	315 647	...	...	...	...	...
Khimki	218 275	99 122	119 153	...	...	...	...	...
Kirov	480 594	211 205	269 389	...	505 346	...	...	...
Kiselevsk	...	...	...	...	101 180	...	...	...
Kislovodsk	129 313	58 854	70 459	...	136 142	...	...	...
Kolomna	144 838	66 469	78 369	...	...	...	...	...
Komsomolsk-na-Amure	259 081	120 197	138 884	...	...	...	...	...
Kopeysk	139 161	66 142	73 019	...	141 291	...	...	...
Korolev (Moskovskaya oblast)	186 460	84 232	102 228	...	...	...	...	...
Kostroma	270 366	120 622	149 744	...	...	...	...	...
Kovrov	...	...	...	...	346 922	154 144	192 778	...
Krasnodar	773 970	350 519	423 451	...	861 181	...	...	...
Krasnogorsk	125 198	56 432	68 766	...	125 787	...	...	...
Krasnoyarsk	1 006 856	456 171	550 685	...	1 007 654	...	...	...
Kurgan	326 729	146 140	180 589	...	...	...	...	...
Kursk	425 950	189 025	236 925	...	...	...	...	...
Kyzyl	112 659	52 137	60 522	...	...	...	...	...
Leninsk-Kuznetsky	100 073	45 651	54 422	...	102 285	...	...	...
Lipetsk	508 585	230 178	278 407	...	...	...	...	...
Lyubertsy	178 884	80 564	98 320	...	...	...	...	...
Magadan	95 263	45 084	50 179	...	101 933	...	...	...
Magnitogorsk	410 733	186 534	224 199	...	...	...	...	...
Maikop	144 579	64 512	80 067	...	167 281	...	...	...
Makhachkala	575 243	271 687	303 556	...	701 753	...	...	...
Mezhdurechensk	100 278	46 498	53 780	...	102 465	...	...	...
Miass	150 806	67 824	82 982	...	166 205	...	...	...
MOSKVA	11 918 057	5 495 477	6 422 580	...	...	...	...	...
Murmansk	303 754	139 944	163 810	...	...	...	...	...
Murom	113 330	50 293	63 037	...	122 545	...	...	...
Mytishchi	176 825	80 425	96 400	...	185 204	...	...	...
Naberezhnye Tchelny	517 831	237 620	280 211	...	...	...	...	...
Nakhodka	158 649	75 081	83 568	...	159 633	...	...	...
Naltchik	239 230	106 648	132 582	...	265 051	...	...	...
Nazran	100 574	44 126	56 448	...	...	...	...	...
Neftekamsk	123 202	57 271	65 931	...	135 013	...	...	...
Nefteyugansk	125 528	61 635	63 893	...	...	...	...	...
Nevinnomyssk	117 949	53 611	64 338	...	...	...	...	...
Nizhnekamsk	235 179	111 262	123 917	...	235 279	...	...	...
Nizhnevartovsk	261 011	125 937	135 074	...	...	...	...	...
Nizhny Novgorod	1 257 260	552 285	704 975	...	1 266 231	...	...	...
Nizhny Tagil	358 651	162 731	195 920	...	362 185	...	...	...

8. Population of capital cities and cities of 100 000 or more inhabitants: latest available year, 1998 - 2017
Population des capitales et des villes de 100 000 habitants ou plus : dernière année disponible, 1998 - 2017 (continued - suite)

Continent, country or area, date, code[a] and city / Continent, pays ou zone, date, code[a] et ville	City proper - Ville proprement dite				Urban agglomeration - Agglomération urbaine			
	Population			Surface area - Superficie (km²)	Population			Surface area - Superficie (km²)
	Both sexes - Les deux sexes	Male - Masculin	Female - Féminin		Both sexes - Les deux sexes	Male - Masculin	Female - Féminin	
EUROPE								
Russian Federation - Fédération de Russie								
1 VII 2012 (ESDJ)								
Noginsk	101 779	45 741	56 038	...	103 843	...	...	...
Norilsk	177 506	89 198	88 308	...	178 363	...	...	...
Novocheboksarsk	...	...	...	...	124 288	...	...	...
Novocherkassk	171 081	81 921	89 160	...	...	...	...	...
Novokuybishevsk	107 244	48 418	58 826	...	109 521	...	...	...
Novokuznetsk	549 383	247 386	301 997	...	...	...	...	...
Novomoskovsk (Tulskaya oblast)	129 555	57 961	71 594	...	141 893	...	...	...
Novorossiysk	248 857	117 707	131 150	...	305 421	...	...	...
Novoshakhtinsk	110 243	50 410	59 833	...	...	...	...	...
Novosibirsk	1 511 369	694 959	816 410	...	...	...	...	...
Novotroitsk	...	...	...	...	103 061	...	...	...
Novy Urengoy	114 332	59 841	54 491	...	...	...	...	...
Noyabrsk	108 662	53 237	55 425	...	...	...	...	...
Obninsk	105 722	48 323	57 399	...	...	...	...	...
Odintsovo	137 706	63 405	74 301	...	143 848	...	...	...
Oktyabrsky	111 109	51 956	59 153	...	...	...	...	...
Omsk	1 158 627	526 757	631 870	...	...	...	...	...
Orekhovo-Zuevo	121 341	53 443	67 898	...	...	...	...	...
Orel	318 642	139 662	178 980	...	...	...	...	...
Orenburg	555 420	252 906	302 514	...	571 041	...	...	...
Orsk	237 194	106 127	131 067	...	241 327	...	...	...
Penza	519 948	234 270	285 678	...	...	...	...	...
Perm	1 007 272	444 386	562 886	...	1 007 285	...	...	...
Pervouralsk	125 421	56 144	69 277	...	149 796	...	...	...
Petropavlovsk-Kamchatsky	180 702	88 743	91 959	...	...	...	...	...
Petrozavodsk	267 102	118 638	148 464	...	...	...	...	...
Podolsk	200 059	89 931	110 128	...	...	...	...	...
Prokopyevsk	206 023	91 944	114 079	...	...	...	...	...
Pskov	205 062	92 439	112 623	...	...	...	...	...
Pushkino	104 020	46 649	57 371	...	...	...	...	...
Pyatigorsk	144 603	64 578	80 025	...	212 968	...	...	...
Rostov-na-Donu	1 100 091	501 068	599 023	...	...	...	...	...
Rubtsovsk	146 075	69 084	76 991	...	...	...	...	...
Ryazan	526 919	237 791	289 128	...	...	...	...	...
Rybinsk	197 359	87 921	109 438	...	...	...	...	...
Salavat	155 174	72 449	82 725	...	...	...	...	...
Samara (Samarskaya oblast)	1 170 381	522 660	647 721	...	1 170 485	...	...	...
Saransk	298 103	132 543	165 560	...	326 473	...	...	...
Sarapyul	100 362	44 678	55 684	...	...	...	...	...
Saratov	838 321	373 676	464 645	...	...	...	...	...
Sergiev Posad	109 076	48 786	60 290	...	115 858	...	...	...
Serov	...	...	...	...	107 904	...	...	...
Serpukhov	126 729	57 494	69 235	...	...	...	...	...
Severodvinsk	189 313	87 781	101 532	...	190 513	...	...	...
Seversk	109 630	50 705	58 925	...	116 340	...	...	...
Shakhty	238 031	107 544	130 487	...	...	...	...	...
Shchelkovo	111 406	50 812	60 594	...	113 726	...	...	...
Smolensk	330 451	147 446	183 005	...	...	...	...	...
Sochi	364 171	164 632	199 539	...	441 407	...	...	...
St. Petersburg	4 990 602	2 247 375	2 743 227	...	...	...	...	...
Stary Oskol	220 719	100 902	119 817	...	256 790	...	...	...
Stavropol	408 361	187 593	220 768	...	408 560	...	...	...
Sterlitamak	275 087	125 443	149 644	...	...	...	...	...
Surgut	321 062	153 832	167 230	...	...	...	...	...
Syktivkar	239 341	107 945	131 396	...	255 283	...	...	...
Syzran	177 404	79 804	97 600	...	178 205	...	...	...
Taganrog	255 671	114 508	141 163	...	...	...	...	...
Tambov	281 348	126 427	154 921	...	...	...	...	...
Tobolsk	...	...	...	...	101 955	...	...	...
Tolyatti	719 363	331 248	388 115	...	...	...	...	...
Tomsk	543 596	252 173	291 423	...	565 000	...	...	...
Tula	496 656	220 675	275 981	...	...	...	...	...
Tver	407 896	180 459	227 437	...	...	...	...	...

8. Population of capital cities and cities of 100 000 or more inhabitants: latest available year, 1998 - 2017
Population des capitales et des villes de 100 000 habitants ou plus : dernière année disponible, 1998 - 2017 (continued - suite)

Continent, country or area, date, code[a] and city / Continent, pays ou zone, date, code[a] et ville	City proper - Ville proprement dite				Urban agglomeration - Agglomération urbaine			
	Population			Surface area - Superficie (km²)	Population			Surface area - Superficie (km²)
	Both sexes - Les deux sexes	Male - Masculin	Female - Féminin		Both sexes - Les deux sexes	Male - Masculin	Female - Féminin	

EUROPE

Russian Federation - Fédération de Russie
1 VII 2012 (ESDJ)

Tyumen	621 918	288 291	333 627	...	644 799	...	...	...
Ufa	1 075 007	484 893	590 114	...	1 084 420	...	...	...
Uhta	99 680	47 563	52 117	...	121 479	...	...	...
Ulan-Ude	413 850	191 732	222 118	...	...	...	...	...
Ulyanovsk	614 878	278 103	336 775	...	637 637	...	...	...
Ussuriisk	163 465	79 562	83 903	...	189 502	...	...	...
Velikiy Novgorod	219 941	95 446	124 495	...	...	...	...	...
Vladikavkaz (Osetinskaya ASSR)	309 173	139 818	169 355	...	327 448	...	...	...
Vladimir	346 922	154 144	192 778	...	349 525	...	...	...
Vladivostok	598 927	282 260	316 667	...	624 281	...	...	...
Volgodonsk	170 189	78 251	91 938	...	...	...	...	...
Volgograd	1 018 762	460 095	558 667	...	...	...	...	...
Vologda	305 397	135 292	170 105	...	313 679	...	...	...
Volzhsky	320 761	148 339	172 422	...	327 460	...	...	...
Voronezh	997 447	447 484	549 963	...	...	...	...	...
Yakutsk	282 419	132 612	149 807	...	298 926	...	...	...
Yaroslavl	597 161	262 042	335 119	...	...	...	...	...
Yoshkar-Ola	254 987	114 331	140 656	...	265 626	...	...	...
Yuzhno-Sakhalinsk	188 242	89 200	99 042	...	195 104	...	...	...
Zheleznodorozhny	138 814	62 719	76 095	...	...	...	...	...
Zhukovsky	106 555	49 027	57 528	...	...	...	...	...
Zlatoust	172 972	78 071	94 901	...	175 178	...	...	...

San Marino - Saint-Marin
1 VII 2017 (ESDJ)

SAN MARINO	4 109	2 010	2 099	7.1	...	...	...	...

Serbia - Serbie
1 VII 2016 (ESDJ)

BEOGRAD (BELGRADE)	1 374 445[84]	640 737[84]	733 708[84]	716	1 683 962[85]	795 295[85]	888 667[85]	3234[16]
Čačak	72 195[84]	34 412[84]	37 783[84]	36	111 797[85]	54 287[85]	57 510[85]	636[16]
Kragujevac	150 850[84]	72 719[84]	78 131[84]	83	178 368[85]	86 624[85]	91 744[85]	835[16]
Kraljevo	67 142[84]	32 360[84]	34 782[84]	42	120 722[85]	59 284[85]	61 438[85]	1530[16]
Kruševac	57 600[84]	27 364[84]	30 236[84]	11	123 631[85]	60 441[85]	63 190[85]	854[16]
Leskovac	63 964[84]	30 998[84]	32 966[84]	64	138 132[85]	68 691[85]	69 441[85]	1024[16]
Niš	185 987[84]	88 907[84]	97 080[84]	49	257 348[85]	124 881[85]	132 467[85]	597[16]
Novi Pazar	71 497[84]	35 258[84]	36 239[84]	15	104 674[85]	52 061[85]	52 613[85]	742[16]
Novi Sad	289 128[84]	135 383[84]	153 745[84]	164	353 525[85]	167 414[85]	186 111[85]	612[16]
Pancevo	89 281[84]	42 854[84]	46 427[84]	263	120 871[85]	58 810[85]	62 061[85]	756[16]
Šabac	53 155[84]	24 892[84]	28 263[84]	31	112 414[85]	54 904[85]	57 510[85]	798[16]
Smederevo	62 993[84]	30 445[84]	32 548[84]	42	104 987[85]	51 748[85]	53 239[85]	484[16]
Subotica	103 985[84]	49 456[84]	54 529[84]	205	138 331[85]	66 483[85]	71 848[85]	1007[16]
Zrenjanin	74 459[84]	35 434[84]	39 025[84]	193	118 699[85]	57 692[85]	61 007[85]	1326[16]

Slovakia - Slovaquie
1 VII 2016 (ESDJ)

BRATISLAVA	424 428	199 016	225 412	368[53]	...	...	...	...
Kosice	239 171	114 672	124 499	237[53]	...	...	...	...

Slovenia - Slovénie
1 VII 2016 (ESDJ)

LJUBLJANA	279 631	134 584	145 047	164	281 487	135 528	145 959	171
Maribor	94 370	46 084	48 286	41	107 895	52 761	55 134	99

Spain - Espagne[33]
1 VII 2016 (ESDJ)

A Coruña	244 038	113 292	130 746	37.8	...	...	...	...
Albacete	172 621	84 436	88 185	1127	...	...	...	...
Alcalá de Henares	195 108	95 442	99 666	87.7	...	...	...	...
Alcobendas	114 102	54 918	59 184	45	...	...	...	...
Alcorcón	167 747	81 125	86 622	33.7	...	...	...	...
Algeciras	120 867	59 678	61 189	85.8	...	...	...	...
Alicante/Alacant	330 256	160 259	169 997	201.3	...	...	...	...
Almería	194 952	94 787	100 165	295.7	...	...	...	...
Badajoz	150 244	72 883	77 361	1440.4	...	...	...	...
Badalona	215 741	106 258	109 483	20.9	...	...	...	...
Barakaldo	100 169	48 398	51 771	25.1	...	...	...	...

8. Population of capital cities and cities of 100 000 or more inhabitants: latest available year, 1998 - 2017
Population des capitales et des villes de 100 000 habitants ou plus : dernière année disponible, 1998 - 2017 (continued - suite)

Continent, country or area, date, code[a] and city / Continent, pays ou zone, date, code[a] et ville	City proper - Ville proprement dite				Urban agglomeration - Agglomération urbaine			
	Population			Surface area - Superficie (km²)	Population			Surface area - Superficie (km²)
	Both sexes - Les deux sexes	Male - Masculin	Female - Féminin		Both sexes - Les deux sexes	Male - Masculin	Female - Féminin	
EUROPE								
Spain - Espagne[33]								
1 VII 2016 (ESDJ)								
Barcelona	1 614 777	764 056	850 721	98.2	...	...	...	...
Bilbao	345 116	162 651	182 465	41.4	...	...	...	...
Burgos	176 115	83 838	92 277	107.1	...	...	...	...
Cádiz	118 483	56 143	62 340	12.3	...	...	...	...
Cartagena	214 468	107 166	107 302	558.1	...	...	...	...
Castellón de la Plana/Castelló de la Plana	170 244	82 492	87 752	108.8	...	...	...	...
Córdoba	326 262	156 718	169 544	1255.2	...	...	...	...
Donostia/San Sebastián	186 217	87 596	98 621	60.9	...	...	...	...
Dos Hermanas	132 203	65 152	67 051	160.3	...	...	...	...
Elche/Elx	228 167	113 084	115 083	326.4	...	...	...	...
Fuenlabrada	194 420	96 243	98 177	39.4	...	...	...	...
Getafe	177 473	86 960	90 513	78.4	...	...	...	...
Gijón	272 893	128 655	144 238	181.7	...	...	...	...
Granada	233 764	108 366	125 398	81.1	...	...	...	...
Huelva	145 291	69 834	75 457	151.3	...	...	...	...
Jaén	114 448	55 053	59 395	424.3	...	...	...	...
Jerez de la Frontera	212 872	104 193	108 679	1188.1	...	...	...	...
Las Palmas de Gran Canaria	378 324	183 348	194 976	101.9	...	...	...	...
Leganés	187 446	91 290	96 156	43.1	...	...	...	...
León	125 754	57 033	68 721	39	...	...	...	...
L'Hospitalet de Llobregat	256 076	123 974	132 102	13.3	...	...	...	...
Lleida	137 735	68 069	69 666	212	...	...	...	...
Logroño	150 927	71 746	79 181	78.9	...	...	...	...
MADRID	3 174 261	1 476 386	1 697 875	605.8	...	...	...	...
Málaga	569 005	273 675	295 330	395.1	...	...	...	...
Marbella	140 958	68 088	72 870	117.1	...	...	...	...
Mataró	125 822	62 436	63 386	22.3	...	...	...	...
Móstoles	206 101	100 694	105 407	45.4	...	...	...	...
Murcia	442 123	216 041	226 082	886	...	...	...	...
Ourense	105 764	48 206	57 558	84.6	...	...	...	...
Oviedo	220 434	102 169	118 265	186.7	...	...	...	...
Palma de Mallorca	404 720	197 026	207 694	209	...	...	...	...
Pamplona/Iruña	196 394	93 168	103 226	25.1	...	...	...	...
Parla	125 279	62 464	62 815	24.5	...	...	...	...
Reus	103 369	49 996	53 373	53	...	...	...	...
Sabadell	209 088	101 747	107 341	37.5	...	...	...	...
Salamanca	144 692	65 859	78 833	39.3	...	...	...	...
San Cristóbal de La Laguna	153 383	74 433	78 950	102.5	...	...	...	...
Santa Coloma de Gramenet	117 375	58 370	59 005	7.1	...	...	...	...
Santa Cruz de Tenerife	203 638	97 263	106 375	150.4	...	...	...	...
Santander	172 303	79 504	92 799	36.1	...	...	...	...
Sevilla	690 000	327 514	362 486	141.3	...	...	...	...
Tarragona	131 300	63 869	67 431	55	...	...	...	...
Telde	102 084	50 393	51 691	100.3	...	...	...	...
Terrassa	215 774	106 218	109 556	70.3	...	...	...	...
Torrejón de Ardoz	127 497	62 936	64 561	32.6	...	...	...	...
Valencia	789 004	376 221	412 783	136.7	...	...	...	...
Valladolid	300 795	141 499	159 296	197.4	...	...	...	...
Vigo	292 901	138 889	154 012	109.1	...	...	...	...
Vitoria-Gasteiz	245 805	119 981	125 824	276.8	...	...	...	...
Zaragoza	663 023	317 987	345 036	973.8	...	...	...	...
Sweden - Suède								
1 VII 2007 (ESDJ)								
Göteborg	491 630	242 916	248 714	449	...	...	...	...
Helsingborg	124 188	60 672	63 516	346	...	...	...	...
Jönköping	122 952	60 462	62 490	1485	...	...	...	...
Linköping	139 474	70 239	69 235	1431	...	...	...	...
Malmö	278 523	135 997	142 526	154	...	...	...	...
Norrköping	126 072	62 323	63 749	1491	...	...	...	...
Orebro	129 703	63 123	66 581	1371	...	...	...	...
STOCKHOLM	789 024	384 243	404 781	187	...	...	...	...
Umeå	111 503	55 549	55 955	2316	...	...	...	...

8. Population of capital cities and cities of 100 000 or more inhabitants: latest available year, 1998 - 2017
Population des capitales et des villes de 100 000 habitants ou plus : dernière année disponible, 1998 - 2017 (continued - suite)

Continent, country or area, date, code[a] and city / Continent, pays ou zone, date, code[a] et ville	City proper - Ville proprement dite				Urban agglomeration - Agglomération urbaine			
	Population			Surface area - Superficie (km²)	Population			Surface area - Superficie (km²)
	Both sexes - Les deux sexes	Male - Masculin	Female - Féminin		Both sexes - Les deux sexes	Male - Masculin	Female - Féminin	
EUROPE								
Sweden - Suède								
1 VII 2007 (ESDJ)								
Uppsala	186 364	91 149	95 215	2465	...	...	...	...
Västerås	133 324	66 056	67 269	956	...	...	...	...
Switzerland - Suisse								
1 I 2017 (ESDJ)								
Baden-Brugg	30 426	15 366	15 060	19.5	110 347[86]	55 076[86]	55 271[86]	91.6[86]
Bâle	171 017	82 865	88 152	23.9	545 326[86]	266 454[86]	278 872[86]	695.9[86]
BERNE	133 115	64 167	68 948	51.6	415 485[86]	202 262[86]	213 223[86]	780.6[86]
Fribourg	38 829	19 315	19 514	9.3	108 998[86]	54 354[86]	54 644[86]	229[86]
Genève	198 979	95 686	103 293	15.9	585 400[86]	284 339[86]	301 061[86]	536.5[86]
Lausanne	137 810	66 525	71 285	41.4	415 620[86]	204 006[86]	211 614[86]	772.6[86]
Lugano	63 932	30 868	33 064	76	151 708[86]	73 785[86]	77 923[86]	303.9[86]
Luzern	81 592	39 267	42 325	29.1	228 321[86]	112 362[86]	115 959[86]	290.5[86]
St. Gallen	75 481	36 841	38 640	39.4	166 421[86]	82 193[86]	84 228[86]	318.6[86]
Winterthur	109 775	53 830	55 945	68.1	140 227[86]	69 057[86]	71 170[86]	148.5[86]
Zug	29 804	15 082	14 722	21.6	129 062[86]	65 297[86]	63 765[86]	225.8[86]
Zürich	402 762	200 536	202 226	87.9	1 354 140[86]	674 775[86]	679 365[86]	1305.1[86]
TFYR of Macedonia - L'ex-R. y. de Macédoine								
1 VII 2016 (ESDJ)								
SKOPJE	546 824	267 738	279 086	...	...	...	...	...
Ukraine								
1 I 2017 (ESDJ)								
Alchevsk	108 754	49 859	58 895	...	...	...	...	...
Berdyansk	113 354	50 093	63 261	...	116 416	51 555	64 861	...
Bila Tserkva	203 816	94 075	109 741	...	...	...	...	...
Cherkasy	279 074	127 449	151 625	...	279 972	127 923	152 049	...
Chernihiv	285 821	131 285	154 536	...	...	...	...	...
Chernivtsi	262 276	120 248	142 028	...	...	...	...	...
Dnepropetrovsk	966 400	439 549	526 851	...	968 811	440 721	528 090	...
Dniprodzerzhynsk	236 694	106 410	130 284	...	243 643	109 547	134 096	...
Donets'k	918 536	406 250	512 286	...	934 413	413 463	520 950	...
Enakievo (Yenakievo)	79 660	35 319	44 341	...	107 773	47 970	59 803	...
Gorlivka	245 746	110 092	135 654	...	262 473	117 595	144 878	...
Ivano-Frankivsk	230 507	108 022	122 485	...	251 760	117 642	134 118	...
Kharkiv	1 419 469	658 110	761 359	...	...	...	...	...
Kherson	289 697	130 015	159 682	...	326 978	147 474	179 504	...
Khmelnitsky (Hmilnyk)	265 693	122 535	143 158	...	...	...	...	...
Kirovograd	226 491	102 887	123 604	...	234 537	106 547	127 990	...
Kramatorsk	157 175	69 979	87 196	...	190 288	85 392	104 896	...
Krasny Lutch	81 343	37 657	43 686	...	121 592	56 510	65 082	...
Krementchug	221 345	100 410	120 935	...	...	...	...	...
Krivoy Rog	634 780	285 421	349 359	...	637 550	286 822	350 728	...
KYIV	2 884 453	1 334 408	1 550 045	...	...	...	...	...
Lugansk	409 895	182 356	227 539	...	435 828	194 638	241 190	...
Luts'k	213 950	96 373	117 577	...	...	...	...	...
Lviv	721 301	337 327	383 974	...	750 632	351 125	399 507	...
Lysychansk	99 598	44 882	54 716	...	114 436	51 634	62 802	...
Makijivka	345 685	155 606	190 079	...	383 454	173 112	210 342	...
Mariupol	446 103	202 582	243 521	...	467 552	212 610	254 942	...
Melitopol	154 839	70 039	84 800	...	...	...	...	...
Nikolaev	486 267	220 844	265 423	...	...	...	...	...
Nikopol	115 943	51 555	64 388	...	...	...	...	...
Odessa	993 120	464 431	528 689	...	...	...	...	...
Pavlograd	108 685	49 768	58 917	...	...	...	...	...
Poltava	284 942	131 571	153 371	...	...	...	...	...
Rivne	243 934	111 964	131 970	...	...	...	...	...
Sievierodonetsk	106 513	47 265	59 248	...	116 795	52 176	64 619	...
Slovyansk	111 084	48 276	62 808	...	114 260	49 740	64 520	...
Sumy	264 753	119 288	145 465	...	267 666	120 696	146 970	...
Ternopil	216 384	100 016	116 368	...	...	...	...	...
Uzhhorod	112 447	52 217	60 230	...	...	...	...	...
Vinnitsa	370 834	169 761	201 073	...	...	...	...	...

8. Population of capital cities and cities of 100 000 or more inhabitants: latest available year, 1998 - 2017
Population des capitales et des villes de 100 000 habitants ou plus : dernière année disponible, 1998 - 2017 (continued - suite)

Continent, country or area, date, code[a] and city / Continent, pays ou zone, date, code[a] et ville	City proper - Ville proprement dite				Urban agglomeration - Agglomération urbaine			
	Population			Surface area - Superficie (km²)	Population			Surface area - Superficie (km²)
	Both sexes - Les deux sexes	Male - Masculin	Female - Féminin		Both sexes - Les deux sexes	Male - Masculin	Female - Féminin	
EUROPE								
Ukraine								
1 I 2017 (ESDJ)								
Zaporozhye	746 749	337 378	409 371	...	...	...	...	...
Zhytomyr	266 106	122 713	143 393	...	...	...	...	...
United Kingdom of Great Britain and Northern Ireland - Royaume-Uni de Grande-Bretagne et d'Irlande du Nord[87]								
27 III 2011 (CDJC)								
Aberdeen	207 932	102 858	105 078	...	...	...	...	...
Belfast	280 211	134 693	145 518	...	...	...	...	...
Birmingham	1 085 810	534 038	551 772	...	...	...	...	...
Bolton	194 189	95 924	98 265	...	...	...	...	...
Bournemouth	187 503	93 390	94 113	...	...	...	...	...
Bradford	349 561	173 024	176 537	...	...	...	...	...
Brighton and Hove	229 700	115 245	114 455	...	...	...	...	...
Bristol	535 907	265 968	269 939	...	...	...	...	...
Cardiff	335 145	164 427	170 718	...	...	...	...	...
Coventry	325 949	162 069	163 880	...	...	...	...	...
Derby	255 394	126 402	128 992	...	...	...	...	...
Edinburgh	482 005	234 608	247 397	...	...	...	...	...
Glasgow[88]	1 209 143	580 857	628 286	...	...	...	...	...
Kingston-upon-Hull	284 321	141 905	142 416	...	...	...	...	...
Leeds	474 632	233 488	241 144	...	...	...	...	...
Leicester	443 760	218 722	225 038	...	...	...	...	...
Liverpool	552 267	271 342	280 925	...	...	...	...	...
LONDON[89]	8 135 667	4 015 297	4 120 370	...	...	...	...	...
Luton	211 228	105 905	105 323	...	...	...	...	...
Manchester	510 746	256 984	253 762	...	...	...	...	...
Newcastle-upon-Tyne	268 064	134 375	133 689	...	...	...	...	...
Northampton	215 173	105 617	109 556	...	...	...	...	...
Nottingham	289 301	145 855	143 446	...	...	...	...	...
Plymouth	234 982	116 444	118 538	...	...	...	...	...
Portsmouth	238 137	119 369	118 768	...	...	...	...	...
Reading	218 705	109 236	109 469	...	...	...	...	...
Sheffield	518 090	255 755	262 335	...	...	...	...	...
Southampton	253 651	127 630	126 021	...	...	...	...	...
Stoke-on-Trent	270 726	134 642	136 084	...	...	...	...	...
Wolverhampton	210 319	104 047	106 272	...	...	...	...	...
OCEANIA - OCÉANIE								
American Samoa - Samoas américaines[31]								
1 IV 2010 (CDJC)								
PAGO PAGO	3 656	...	...	...	...	...	...	...
Australia - Australie								
9 VIII 2016 (CDJC)								
Adelaide	1 165 632[90]	569 694[90]	595 939[90]	2246.2	...	...	...	...
Brisbane	2 054 614[90]	1 009 029[90]	1 045 588[90]	5326.7	...	...	...	...
Cairns	144 730[90]	71 170[90]	73 558[90]	254.1	...	...	...	...
CANBERRA[90]	395 790	194 879	200 914	...	...	...	...	...
Canberra-Queanbeyan	432 138[90]	213 052[90]	219 091[90]	499.3	...	...	...	...
Central Coast	307 742[90]	148 587[90]	159 149[90]	566.4	...	...	...	...
Darwin	118 456[90]	62 041[90]	56 416[90]	374.4	...	...	...	...
Geelong	157 104[90]	75 635[90]	81 462[90]	1329	...	...	...	...
Gold Coast[90]	540 559	262 469	278 089	...	...	...	...	...
Gold Coast-Tweed Heads	600 335[90]	291 006[90]	309 328[90]	1405	...	...	...	...
Greater Adelaide	...	...	...	...	1 295 714[90]	633 888[90]	661 823[90]	3259.8
Greater Brisbane	...	...	...	...	2 270 800[90]	1 117 452[90]	1 153 351[90]	15842
Greater Darwin	...	...	...	...	136 828[90]	71 889[90]	64 939[90]	3163.9
Greater Hobart	...	...	...	...	222 356[90]	107 930[90]	114 422[90]	1695.4
Greater Melbourne	...	...	...	...	4 485 211[90]	2 199 597[90]	2 285 616[90]	9992.5
Greater Perth	...	...	...	...	1 943 858[90]	963 536[90]	980 326[90]	6416.2
Greater Sydney	...	...	...	...	4 823 991[90]	2 376 766[90]	2 447 221[90]	12368.2

8. Population of capital cities and cities of 100 000 or more inhabitants: latest available year, 1998 - 2017
Population des capitales et des villes de 100 000 habitants ou plus : dernière année disponible, 1998 - 2017 (continued - suite)

Continent, country or area, date, code[a] and city / Continent, pays ou zone, date, code[a] et ville	City proper - Ville proprement dite				Urban agglomeration - Agglomération urbaine			
	Population			Surface area - Superficie (km²)	Population			Surface area - Superficie (km²)
	Both sexes - Les deux sexes	Male - Masculin	Female - Féminin		Both sexes - Les deux sexes	Male - Masculin	Female - Féminin	
OCEANIA - OCÉANIE								
Australia - Australie								
9 VIII 2016 (CDJC)								
Hobart	178 009[90]	85 960[90]	92 047[90]	1149.3	...	...	...	...
Melbourne	4 196 198[90]	2 056 095[90]	2 140 106[90]	6189.1	...	...	...	...
Newcastle[90]	322 278	157 923	164 361	...	...	...	...	...
Perth	1 874 578[90]	927 190[90]	947 382[90]	3531.9	...	...	...	...
Sunshine Coast	243 377[90]	116 734[90]	126 642[90]	1633.1	...	...	...	...
Sydney	4 321 535[90]	2 131 038[90]	2 190 497[90]	4196.3	...	...	...	...
Toowoomba	100 032[90]	47 675[90]	52 357[90]	728.6	...	...	...	...
Townsville	168 729[90]	84 003[90]	84 725[90]	693.3	...	...	...	...
Wollongong	261 896[90]	128 813[90]	133 083[90]	572.3	...	...	...	...
Cook Islands - Îles Cook[91]								
1 XII 2016* (CDFC)								
RAROTONGA	13 044	6 372	6 672	...	...	...	...	...
Fiji - Fidji								
16 IX 2007 (CDFC)								
SUVA	74 481	37 032	37 449	...	...	...	...	...
French Polynesia - Polynésie française								
22 VIII 2012 (CDFC)								
PAPEETE	25 763	12 971	12 792	...	...	...	...	...
Guam								
1 VII 2010 (ESDJ)								
AGANA	1 051	625	426	3	...	...	...	...
Kiribati								
7 XI 2015 (CDFC)								
TARAWA	...	...	...	...	63 017	30 416	32 601	...
Marshall Islands - Îles Marshall								
3 IV 2011 (CDFC)								
MAJURO	27 797	...	...	...	...	...	...	...
Micronesia (Federated States of) - Micronésie (États fédérés de)								
1 IV 2000 (CDJC)								
PALIKIR	6 227	...	...	...	...	...	...	...
New Caledonia - Nouvelle-Calédonie								
26 VIII 2014 (CDFC)								
NOUMEA	99 926	49 218	50 708	...	...	...	...	...
New Zealand - Nouvelle-Zélande[92]								
1 VII 2017 (ESDJ)								
Auckland	1 657 200[93]	817 000[93]	840 200[93]	4938	...	...	...	...
Christchurch	381 500[93]	191 500[93]	190 000[93]	1415	...	...	...	...
Dunedin	128 800[93]	62 300[93]	66 500[93]	3287	...	...	...	...
Hamilton	165 400[93]	80 200[93]	85 200[93]	110	...	...	...	...
Lower Hutt	104 700[93]	51 200[93]	53 500[93]	376	...	...	...	...
Napier-Hastings	...	...	...	...	133 000[93]	63 700[93]	69 300[93]	390
Tauranga	131 500[93]	62 900[93]	68 600[93]	134	...	...	...	...
WELLINGTON	212 700[93]	104 500[93]	108 200[93]	290	...	...	...	...
Niue - Nioué								
11 IX 2011 (CDFC)								
ALOFI	639	311	328	...	...	...	...	...
Northern Mariana Islands - Îles Mariannes septentrionales								
1 IV 2010 (CDFC)								
GARAPAN	3 983	1 953	2 030	...	...	...	...	...
Palau - Palaos								
13 IV 2015 (CDJC)								
KOROR	...	...	...	...	11 754	...	...	...
Papua New Guinea - Papouasie-Nouvelle-Guinée								
10 VII 2011 (CDFC)								
PORT MORESBY	364 125	194 834	169 291	...	...	...	...	...
Pitcairn								
31 XII 2013 (CDJC)								
ADAMSTOWN	49	23	26	...	...	...	...	...

Continent, country or area, date, code[a] and city / Continent, pays ou zone, date, code[a] et ville	City proper - Ville proprement dite				Urban agglomeration - Agglomération urbaine			
	Population			Surface area - Superficie (km²)	Population			Surface area - Superficie (km²)
	Both sexes - Les deux sexes	Male - Masculin	Female - Féminin		Both sexes - Les deux sexes	Male - Masculin	Female - Féminin	
OCEANIA - OCÉANIE								
Samoa								
7 XI 2016* (CDFC)								
APIA	35 744	17 933	17 811	...	...	...	...	...
Solomon Islands - Îles Salomon								
22 XI 2009 (CDFC)								
HONIARA	64 609	...	...	...	80 082	...	...	...
Tonga								
30 XI 2016 (CDJC)								
NUKU'ALOFA	...	...	...	...	35 184	17 490	17 694	...
Tuvalu								
4 XI 2012 (CDFC)								
FUNAFUTI	6 152	...	...	...	...	...	...	...
Vanuatu								
16 XI 2009 (CDFC)								
PORT VILA	44 039	...	...	...	...	...	...	...
Wallis and Futuna Islands - Îles Wallis et Futuna								
21 VII 2008 (CDFC)								
META-UTU	1 126	...	...	...	...	...	...	...

FOOTNOTES - NOTES

The capital city of each country is shown in capital letters. Figures in italics are estimates of questionable reliability. For definition of city proper and urban agglomeration, method of evaluation and limitations of data see Technical Notes for this table. - Le nom de la capitale de chaque pays est imprimé en majuscules. Les chiffres en italique sont des estimations dont la fiabilité n'est pas assurée. Pour la définition de la ville proprement dite et de l'agglomération urbaine, et pour les méthodes d'évaluation et les insuffisances de données, voir les notes techniques pour ce tableau.

Italics: estimates which are less reliable. - Italiques : estimations moins sûres.

* Provisional. - Données provisoires.

[a] 'Code' indicates the source of data, as follows:
CDFC - Census, de facto, complete tabulation
CDFS - Census, de facto, sample tabulation
CDJC - Census, de jure, complete tabulation
CDJS - Census, de jure, sample tabulation
SSDF - Sample survey, de facto
SSDJ - Sample survey, de jure
ESDF - Estimates, de facto
ESDJ - Estimates, de jure

Le 'Code' indique la source des données, comme suit :
CDFC - Recensement, population de fait, tabulation complète
CDFS - Recensement, population de fait, tabulation par sondage
CDJC - Recensement, population de droit, tabulation complète
CDJS - Recensement, population de droit, tabulation par sondage
SSDF - Enquête par sondage, population de fait
SSDJ - Enquête par sondage, population de droit
ESDF - Estimations, population de fait
ESDJ - Estimations, population de droit

[1] Data based on the 2011 Census. - Données fondées sur le recensement de 2011.
[2] Data refer to national projections. - Les données se réfèrent aux projections nationales.
[3] Data refer to Total Urban Governorates. - Les données concernent les gouvernorats entièrement urbaines.
[4] Population in households only. - Population dans les ménages seulement.
[5] Data refer to the city proper plus the peri-urban area. - Les données concernent la population de la ville proprement dite et de la zone périurbaine.

[6] Data refer to Maseru Urban Centre. - Les données concernent le centre urbain de Maseru.
[7] Data refer to Greater Monrovia. - Les données concernent la région métropolitaine de Monrovia.
[8] Data refer to the urban commune of Antananarivo. - Pour la commune urbaine de Antananarivo.
[9] Data refer to District de Bamako. - Les données concernent le district de Bamako.
[10] Including nomadic population. - Y compris la population nomade.
[11] Excludes the islands of St. Brandon and Agalega. - Non compris les îles St. Brandon et Agalega.
[12] Data refer to resident household population. Data refer to total resident population, Saint Helenian and other nationalities. - Les données concernent la population des ménages résidente. Les données concernent la population résidente totale, originaire de Sainte-Hélène ou possédant une autre nationalité.
[13] Projections based on the 2002 Population Census. - Projections fondées sur le recensement de la population de 2002.
[14] Data refer to Greater Victoria. - Les données concernent la région métropolitaine de Victoria.
[15] Bloemfontein is the judicial capital, Cape Town is the legislative capital and Pretoria is the administrative capital. - Bloemfontein est la capitale judiciaire, Le Cap est la capitale législative et Pretoria est la capitale administrative.
[16] Data for urban agglomeration refer to communes which are administrative divisions. - Les données pour l'agglomération urbaine se rapportent aux communes qui sont des divisions administrative.
[17] Data for urban agglomeration refer to urban center (municipality). - Les données de l'agglomération urbaine se rapportent au centre urbain (commune).
[18] Comprising the Northern Region (former Saguia el Hamra) and Southern Region (former Rio de Oro). - Comprend la région septentrionale (ancien Saguia-el-Hamra) et la région méridionale (ancien Rio de Oro).
[19] The "City proper" uses the geographic definition of Census Subdivision (CSD): Census subdivision (CSD) is the general term for municipalities (as determined by provincial/territorial legislation) or areas treated as municipal equivalents for statistical purposes. The "Urban Agglomeration" uses the geographic definition of Census Metropolitan Area\Census Agglomeration (CMA\CA). - La ville est délimitée selon la définition géographique de la subdivision pour le recensement, qui est le terme générique utilisé pour désigner les municipalités (telles que définies par la législation provinciale ou territoriale) et les zones considérées comme telles à des fins statistiques. L'agglomération urbaine correspond à la définition géographique de la région métropolitaine ou de l'agglomération pour le recensement.
[20] Preliminary postcensal estimates. Adjusted for census net undercoverage (including adjustment for incompletely enumerated Indian reserves). - Estimations post censitaires préliminaires. Ajusté pour la sous-estimation du recensement (y compris les réservations en Inde incomplètement énumérées).

21 Excluding the institutional population. - Non compris la population dans les institutions.

22 Data refers to "cantons" rather than to cities. - Les données concernent les « cantons », et non les villes.

23 Surface area includes interior waters. - La superficie comprend les eaux intérieures.

24 Population statistics are compiled from registers. - Les statistiques de la population sont compilées à partir des registres.

25 Data refer to Kingston Metropolitan Area. - Données pour la zone métropolitaine de Kingston.

26 Data based on the 2010 Population Census. - Les données sont fondées sur le recensement de la population de 2010.

27 Including armed forces stationed in the area. Postcensal estimates. - Y compris les militaires en garnison sur le territoire. Estimations post censitaires.

28 City refers to a type of incorporated place in 49 states and the District of Columbia, that has an elected government and provides a range of government functions and services. Also included among the cities on this list is Urban Honolulu, Hawaii Census Designated Place (CDP), for which the Census Bureau reports data under agreement with the State of Hawaii (instead of the combined city and county of Honolulu). - Par ville, on entend un lieu doté de la personnalité morale dans 49 États et dans le district de Columbia, qui a un gouvernement élu et fournit tout un ensemble de fonctions et de services publics. Sont également inclus Honolulu, lieu chargé du recensement pour Hawaii, pour lequel le Census Bureau établit les données en accord avec l'État de Hawaii (au lieu de la ville et du comté d'Honolulu).

29 Excluding U.S. Armed Forces overseas and civilian U.S. citizens whose usual place of residence is outside the United States. - Non compris les militaires américains à l'étranger et les civils américains dont le lieu de résidence habituel est en dehors des États-Unis.

30 Excluding inland water. - Exception faite des eaux intérieures.

31 Including armed forces stationed in the area. - Y compris les militaires en garnison sur le territoire.

32 Projections based on the 2010 Population and Housing Census. - Projections fondées sur le recensement 2010 de la population et des logements.

33 Data refer to municipalities, which may contain an urban centre as well as rural areas. - Pour municipios qui peuvent comprendre un centre urbain et aussi une zone rurale.

34 Excluding interior waters. - Eaux intérieures non comprises.

35 Data exclude the population of the cities of Puente Alto and San Bernardo. - Les données ne comprennent pas la population des villes de Puente Alto et de San Bernardo.

36 Data are revised projections taking into consideration also the results of the 2005 census. - Les données sont des projections révisées tenant compte également des résultats du recensement de 2005.

37 Data excludes "temporary visitors". - Données n'incluant pas les « visiteurs temporaires ».

38 The Metropolitan Area of Asunción is made up of Asunción and the 19 Central Department districts. - La zone métropolitaine d'Asunción est composée d'Asunción et de 19 districts du Département central.

39 Estimates or projections based on the 2007 Population Census. - Estimations ou projections fondées sur le recensement de la population de 2007.

40 Data refer to the Province of Lima and the Constitutional Province of Callao. - Les données concernent la province de Lima et la province constitutionnelle de Callao.

41 Data refer to national projections. Data refer to the department of Montevideo. - Les données se réfèrent aux projections nationales. Les données concernent le département de Montevideo.

42 Excluding foreign diplomatic personnel and their dependants. Data based on the 2008 Population Census. - Non compris le personnel diplomatique étranger et les membres de leur famille les accompagnant. Données fondées sur le recensement de population de 2008.

43 Data refer only to the population in urban areas of Beijing. - Les données ne concernent que la population des zones urbaines de Beijing.

44 Population by-census is conducted between two population censuses, adopting a sampling method to select 29,421 housing units in Macao for enumeration, with the unit of observation being the individuals residing in the selected housing units. - Aux fins du recensement partiel de la population, conduit entre deux recensements, la méthode d'échantillonnage adoptée a permis de sélectionner 29 421 unités d'habitation à Macao, l'unité d'observation étant les personnes qui y résident.

45 The urban agglomeration of Lefkosia is composed of Lefkosia municipality, Agios Dometios, Egkomi, Strovolos, Aglangia, Lakatameia, Anthoupoli, Latsia and Geri. - L'agglomération urbaine de Lefkosia est composée de la municipalité de Lefkosia et Agios Dometios, Egkomi, Strovolos, Aglangia, Lakatameia, Anthoupoli, Latsia et Geri.

46 The urban agglomeration of Lemesos is composed of Lemesos municipality, Mesa Geitonia, Agios Athanasios, Germasogeia, Pano Polemidia, Ypsonas and Kato Polemidia. - L'agglomération de Lemesos comprend la municipalité du même nom, ainsi que Mesa Geitonia, Agios Athanasios, Germasogeia, Pano Polemidia, Ypsonas et Kato Polemidia.

47 Data refer to "Baghdad Al-Jedeeda Nahia" - Les données concernent le district Al-Jadeeda de Bagdad (Baghdad Al-Jedeeda Nahiya).

48 Designation and data provided by Israel. The position of the United Nations on the question of Jerusalem is contained in General Assembly resolution 181 (II) and subsequent resolutions of the General Assembly and the Security Council concerning this question. Including East Jerusalem. - Appelation de données fournies par Israel. La position des Nations Unies concernant la question de Jérusalem est décrite dans la resolution 181 (II) de l'Assemblée générale et résolutions ultérieures de l'Assemblée générale et du Conseil de sécurité sur cette question. Y compris Jérusalem-Est.

49 Excluding diplomatic personnel outside the country and foreign military and civilian personnel and their dependants stationed in the area. - Non compris le personnel diplomatique hors du pays ni les militaires et agents civils étrangers en poste sur le territoire et les membres de leur famille les accompagnant.

50 Land areas are based on the "Municipalities Area Statistics of Japan, 2015" published by the Geospatial Information Authority of Japan, Ministry of Land, Infrastructure, Transport and Tourism. - Les zones terrestres sont déterminées selon les statistiques relatives aux municipalités du Japon en 2015, publiées par l'Autorité japonaise d'information géospatiale du Ministère de l'aménagement foncier, des infrastructures, des transports et du tourisme.

51 Excluding diplomatic personnel outside the country and foreign military and civilian personnel and their dependants stationed in the area. Data for Tokyo refer to 23 ku (wards) of Tokyo. - Non compris le personnel diplomatique hors du pays ni les militaires et agents civils étrangers en poste sur le territoire et les membres de leur famille les accompagnant. Données relatives à Tokyo concernant 23 ku (arrondissements de la ville).

52 Data refer to resident population. Recalculated population estimates taking into account late registration of births and deaths until May 2017. - Les données concernent la population résidente. Réestimation du nombre d'habitants compte tenu de l'enregistrement tardif des naissances et des décès jusqu'en mai 2017.

53 Land area includes inland water. - La zone terrestre comprend les eaux intérieures.

54 Data refer to annual average population. - Les données correspondent à la population annuelle moyenne.

55 Based on the results of the 2005 Population and Housing Census. - Données fondées sur les résultats du recensement de la population et de l'habitat de 2005.

56 Source: Living conditions of household survey, October 2011 to September 2012. - Source: Enquête sur les conditions de vie des ménages, octobre 2011 à septembre 2012.

57 Estimates based on the adjusted results of the Population and Housing Census of 2010. - Les estimations sont fondée sur les résultats ajustées du recensement de la population et de l'habitat de 2010.

58 Including population from all eight townships. - Y compris la population des huit municipalités.

59 Data refer to registered population data from Royal Oman Police. - Les données portent sur la population enregistrée par la police royale de l'Oman.

60 Data refer to total population, which comprises Singapore residents and non-residents. Data exclude residents who have been away from Singapore for a continuous period of 12 months or longer as at the reference date. - Les données se rapportent à la population totale composé des résidents de Singapour et les non résidents. Non compris les résidents hors de Singapour pour une période ininterrompue de 12 mois ou plus avant de la date de référence.

61 The land area of Singapore comprises the mainland and other islands. - La superficie terrestre de Singapour comprend l'île principale et les autres îles.

62 The Population and Housing Census 2001 did not cover the whole area of the country due to the security problems; data refer to the 18 districts for which the census was completed only (in three districts it was not possible to conduct the census at all and in four districts it was partially conducted). - Le recensement de la population et du logement de 2001 n'a pas été réalisé sur la superficie totale du pays à cause de problèmes de sécurité; les données ne concernent que les 18 districts entièrement recensés (3 districts n'ont pas été recensés du tout, et 4 ont été recensés en partie).

63 Designation and data provided by the State of Palestine. The position of the United Nations on the question of Jerusalem is contained in General Assembly resolution 181 (II) and subsequent resolutions of the General Assembly and the Security Council concerning this question. - Appelation de données fournies par l'État de Palestine. La position des Nations Unies concernant la question de Jérusalem est décrite dans la résolution 181 (II) de l'Assemblée générale et résolutions ultérieures de l'Assemblée générale et du Conseil de sécurité sur cette question.

[64] Data refer to urban area of municipality of Dili. - Les données se réfèrent à la zone urbaine de la municipalité de Dili.

[65] Data based on Address Based Population Registration System. - Les données sont basées sur le registre national de la population basé sur l'adresse.

[66] Data refer to resident population. - Les données concernent la population résidente.

[67] Data include Anderlecht and Schaerbeek. - Les données comprennent Anderlecht et Schaerbeek.

[68] Excluding Faeroe Islands and Greenland shown separately, if available. - Non compris les Iles Féroé et le Groenland, qui font l'objet de rubriques distinctes, si disponible.

[69] Land area refers to built over area. - Partie du territoire désigne une zone bâtie.

[70] Urban Agglomeration refers to Tórshavn, Hoyvík, Argir and Hvítanes. Land area refers to built over area. - Agglomération urbaine fait référence à Tórshavn, Hoyvík, Argir et Hvitanes. Partie du territoire désigne une zone bâtie.

[71] Excluding Åland Islands. - Non compris les Îles d'Åland.

[72] City proper refers to commune or municipality. - La ville proprement dite se rapporte à la commune ou à la municipalité.

[73] The city of Aix-en-Provence is part of the urban agglomeration of Marseille. - La ville d'Aix-en-Provence fait partie de l'agglomération urbaine de Marseille.

[74] The communes of Argenteuil, Boulogne-Billancourt and Montreuil are parts of the urban agglomeration of Paris. - Les communes de Argenteuil, Boulogne-Billancourt et Montreuil font partie de l'agglomération urbaine de Paris.

[75] Excluding military personnel, visitors and transients. - Non compris les militaires, ni les visiteurs et transients.

[76] Data refer to the Vatican City State. - Les données se rapportent à l'Etat de la Cité du Vatican.

[77] Data refer to registered resident population. - Les données concernent la population enregistrée résidente.

[78] The urban agglomeration of the capital area includes the following communes: Bessastaðahreppur, Garðabær, Hafnarfjörður, Kjósarhreppur, Kópavogur, Mosfellsbær, Reykjavík, Seltjarnarnes. Data refer to registered resident population. - L'agglomération urbaine de la capitale comprend les communes suivantes : Bessastaðahreppur, Garðabær, Hafnarfjörður, Kjósarhreppur, Kópavogur, Mosfellsbær ,Reykjavík, Seltjarnarnes. Les données concernent la population enregistrée résidente.

[79] The urban agglomeration of the capital area includes the following communes: Bessastaðahreppur, Garðabær, Hafnarfjörður, Kjósarhreppur, Kópavogur, Mosfellsbær ,Reykjavík, Seltjarnarnes. - L'agglomération urbaine de la capitale comprend les communes suivantes : Bessastaðahreppur, Garðabær, Hafnarfjörður, Kjósarhreppur, Kópavogur, Mosfellsbær ,Reykjavík, Seltjarnarnes.

[80] Including civilian nationals temporarily outside the country. - Y compris les civils nationaux temporairement hors du pays.

[81] Figures for male and female population do not add up to the figure for total population, because they exclude 119 persons of unknown sex. - Les chiffres relatifs à la population masculine et féminine ne correspondent pas au chiffre de la population totale, parce que l'on en a exclu 119 personnes de sexe inconnu.

[82] City is defined as an administratively separated area entitled to civil (municipal) rights. - Une ville est définie comme une zone administrativement distincte dotée de droits municipaux.

[83] Data refer to usually resident population. - Les données concernent la population habituellement résidente.

[84] Excludes data for Kosovo and Metohia. - Sans les données pour le Kosovo et Metohie.

[85] Excludes data for Kosovo and Metohia. Data for urban agglomeration refer to communes which are administrative divisions. - Sans les données pour le Kosovo et Metohie. Les données pour l'agglomération urbaine se rapportent aux communes qui sont des divisions administrative.

[86] From 2015, urban refers to urban centers and areas under the influence of urban centers. - A partir de 2015, le territoire urbain inclut l'espace des centres urbains ainsi que l'espace sous influence des centres urbains.

[87] Excluding Channel Islands (Guernsey and Jersey) and Isle of Man, shown separately, if available. - Non compris les îles Anglo-Normandes (Guernesey et Jersey) et l'île de Man, qui font l'objet de rubriques distinctes, si disponible.

[88] Data refer to Greater Glasgow. - Les données concernent la région métropolitaine de Glasgow.

[89] Data refer to Greater London. - Les données concernent la région métropolitaine de London.

[90] These data have been randomly rounded to protect confidentiality. Individual figures may not add up to totals, and values for the same data may vary in different tables. Data based on the Australian Statistical Geography Standard (ASGS). The populations for Greater Sydney, Melbourne, Brisbane, Perth, Adelaide, Hobart and Darwin are based on the 'Greater Capital City Statistical Area (GCCSA)' level. All other cities are based on the 'Significant Urban Areas (SUA) statistical area' level. - Ces données ont été arrondies de façon aléatoire afin d'en préserver la confidentialité. La somme de certains chiffres peut ne pas correspondre aux totaux indiqués et les valeurs des mêmes données peuvent varier d'un tableau à un autre. Chiffres estimatifs basés sur la norme géographique australienne de statistique (Australian Statistical Geography Standard - ASGS). Les chiffres de population pour la région métropolitaine de Sydney, Melbourne, Brisbane, Perth, Adelaide, Hobart et Darwin sont basés sur le niveau de division statistique des grandes capitales régionales (Greater Capital City Statistical Area - GCCSA). Pour toutes les autres villes, les chiffres sont basés sur le niveau de division statistique des grandes zones urbaines (Significant Urban Areas - SUA).

[91] Excluding Niue, shown separately, which is part of Cook Islands, but because of remoteness is administered separately. - Non compris Nioué, qui fait l'objet d'une rubrique distincte et qui fait partie des îles Cook, mais qui, en raison de son éloignement, est administrée séparément.

[92] 1. Land area excludes inlet, inland water and oceanic areas. 2. A city is a territorial authority which is a distinct entity, is predominantly urban in character, has a minimum population of 50,000 and is a major centre of activity within its parent region. 3. Urban agglomerations refer to main urban areas that are centres with populations of 30,000 or more. City proper: due to the establishment of new Auckland council in 2011, amalgamating former Auckland cities, including Manukau city, North Shore city, and Waktakere city, separate population estimates for these cities are not available. Napier-Hastings consist of two separate territorial authorities. Napier is a city, while Hastings is a district based on the New Zealand Standard Areas Classification. - 1. La superficie terrestre ne comprend pas les bras de mer, eaux intérieures et zones océaniques. 2. Une ville est une entité territoriale distincte à caractère essentiellement urbain, comptant au minimum 50 000 habitants et constitue un pôle qui rayonne sur toute la région environnante. 3. Les agglomérations urbaines sont des établissements humains importants comptant 30 000 habitants ou plus. La ville : avec la création de la nouvelle agglomération d'Auckland en 2011, qui regroupe également Manukau, North Shore et Waktakere, il n'y a plus d'estimations démographiques distinctes pour ces différentes villes. Napier-Hastings comprend deux entités territoriales. Napier est une ville, et Hastings est un district selon les critères du classement néozélandais des zones.

[93] Because of rounding, totals are not in all cases the sum of the respective components. - Les chiffres étant arrondis, les totaux ne correspondent pas toujours rigoureusement à la somme des composants respectifs.

Table 9 - *Demographic Yearbook 2017*

Table 9 presents live births and crude birth rates by urban/rural residence for as many years as possible between 2013 and 2017.

Description of variables: Live birth is defined as the complete expulsion or extraction from its mother of a product of conception, irrespective of the duration of pregnancy, which after such separation, breathes or shows any other evidence of life such as beating of the heart, pulsation of the umbilical cord, or definite movements of voluntary muscles, whether or not the umbilical cord has been cut or the placenta is attached; each product of such a birth is considered live-born[1].

Statistics on the number of live births are obtained from civil registers unless otherwise noted. For those countries or areas where civil registration statistics on live births are considered reliable the birth rates shown have been calculated on the basis of registered live births.

For certain countries, there is a discrepancy between the total number of live births shown in this table and those shown in subsequent tables for the same year. Usually this discrepancy arises because the total number of live births occurring in a given year is revised but not the remaining tabulations.

Rate computation: Crude birth rates are the annual number of live births per 1 000 mid-year population.

Rates by urban/rural residence are the annual number of live births, in the appropriate urban or rural category, per 1 000 corresponding mid-year population. Rates are calculated only for data considered complete, that is, coded with a "C" and for estimates and live births statistics for the 12 month period prior to the census date, coded with a "|". These rates are calculated by the Statistics Division of the United Nations based on the appropriate reference population (for example: total population, nationals only, etc.) if known and available. If the reference population is not known or unavailable, the total population is used to calculate the rates. Therefore, if the population that is used to calculate the rates is different from the correct reference population, the rates presented might under- or overstate the true situation in a country or area.

Rates presented in this table are limited to those countries or areas having a minimum number of 30 live births in a given year.

Reliability of data: Each country or area has been asked to indicate the estimated completeness of the live births recorded in its civil register. These national assessments are indicated by the quality codes "C" and "U" that appear in the first column of this table.

"C" indicates that the data are estimated to be virtually complete, that is, representing at least 90 per cent of the live births occurring each year, whereas "U" indicates that data are estimated to be incomplete, that is, representing less than 90 per cent of the live births occurring each year. A third code "..." indicates that no information was provided regarding completeness.

Data from civil registers that are reported as incomplete or of unknown completeness (coded "U" or "...") are considered unreliable. They appear in italics in this table and rates are not calculated for these data.

These quality codes apply only to data from civil registers. If data from other sources are presented, the symbol "|" is shown instead of the quality code. For more information about the quality of vital statistics data in general, and the information available on the basis of the completeness estimates in particular, see section 4.2 of the Technical Notes.

Limitations: Statistics on live births are subject to the same qualifications as have been set forth for vital statistics in general and birth statistics in particular as discussed in section 4 of the Technical Notes.

The reliability of data, an indication of which is described above, is an important factor in considering the limitations. In addition, some live births are tabulated by date of registration and not by date of occurrence; these have been indicated by a plus sign "+". Whenever the lag between the date of occurrence and date of registration is prolonged and, therefore, a large proportion of the live birth registrations are delayed, birth statistics for any given year may be seriously affected.

Another factor that limits international comparability is the practice of some countries or areas not to include in live birth statistics infants who were born alive but died before the registration of the birth or within the first 24 hours of life, thus underestimating the total number of life births. Statistics of this type are footnoted.

In addition, it should be noted that rates are affected also by the quality and limitations of the population estimates that are used in their computation. The problems of under-enumeration or over-enumeration and, to some extent, the differences in definition of total population have been discussed in section 3 of the Technical Notes dealing with population data in general, and specific information pertaining to individual countries or areas is given in the footnotes to table 3.

The rates estimated from the results of sample surveys are subject to possibilities of considerable error as a result of omissions in reporting of births, or as a result of erroneous reporting of births that occurred outside the reference period. However, rates estimated from sample surveys have the advantage of the availability of a built-in and strictly corresponding population base.

It should be emphasized that crude birth rates - like crude death, marriage and divorce rates - may be seriously affected by the age-sex structure of the populations to which they relate. Nevertheless, they do provide a simple measure of the level of and changes in fertility.

The urban/rural classification of birth may refer to the residence of mother or the place of delivery, according to the national practice and it is provided by each country or area. In addition, the comparability of data by urban/rural residence is affected by the national definition of urban and rural used in tabulating these data. It is assumed, in the absence of specific information to the contrary, that the definitions of urban and rural used in connection with the national population census were also used in the compilation of the vital statistics for each country or area. However, it cannot be ruled out that, for a given country or area, different definitions of urban and rural are used for the vital statistics data and the population census data respectively. When known, the definitions of urban used in national population census are presented at the end of the technical notes to table 6. As discussed in detail in the technical notes to table 6, these definitions vary considerably from one area or country to another. Urban/rural differentials in vital rates may also be affected by whether the vital events have been tabulated in terms of place of occurrence or place of usual residence. This problem is discussed in more detail in section 4.1.4.1 of the Technical notes.

Earlier data: Live births have been shown in each issue of the *Demographic Yearbook*. Information on the years and specific topics covered is presented in the Historical Index.

NOTES

[1] *Principles and Recommendations for a Vital Statistics System Revision 3,* Sales No. E.13.XVII.10, United Nations, New York, 2014.

Tableau 9 – Annuaire démographique 2017

Le tableau 9 présente des données sur les naissances vivantes et les taux bruts de natalité selon le lieu de résidence (zone urbaine ou rurale) pour le plus grand nombre d'années possible entre 2013 et 2017.

Description des variables : La naissance vivante est l'expulsion ou l'extraction complète du corps de la mère, indépendamment de la durée de gestation, d'un produit de la conception qui, après cette séparation, respire ou manifeste tout autre signe de vie, tel que battement de cœur, pulsation du cordon ombilical ou contraction effective d'un muscle soumis à l'action de la volonté, que le cordon ombilical ait été coupé ou non et que le placenta soit ou non demeuré attaché ; tout produit d'une telle naissance est considéré comme « enfant né vivant »[1].

Sauf indication contraire, les statistiques relatives au nombre de naissances vivantes sont établies sur la base des registres de l'état civil. Pour les pays ou zones où les statistiques obtenues auprès des services de l'état civil sont jugées sûres, les taux de natalité indiqués ont été calculés par la Division de statistique de l'ONU d'après les naissances vivantes enregistrées.

Pour quelques pays il y a une discordance entre le nombre total des naissances présenté dans ce tableau et ceux présentés après pour la même année. Habituellement ces différences apparaissent lorsque le nombre total des naissances pour une certaine année a été révisé alors que les autres tabulations ne l'ont pas été.

Calcul des taux : Les taux bruts de natalité représentent le nombre annuel de naissances vivantes pour 1 000 habitants au milieu de l'année.

Les taux selon le lieu de résidence (zone urbaine ou rurale) représentent le nombre annuel de naissances vivantes, classées selon la catégorie urbaine ou rurale appropriée pour 1 000 habitants au milieu de l'année. Les taux ont été calculés seulement pour les données considérées complètes, c'est-à-dire celles associées au code « C », ainsi que pour les estimations et les statistiques des naissances vivantes dans la periode des douze mois précédante la date de recensement associées au code « I ». Ces taux sont calculés par la division de statistique des Nations Unies sur la base de la population de référence adéquate (par exemple : population totale, nationaux seulement, etc.) si connue et disponible. Si la population de référence n'est pas connue ou n'est pas disponible, la population totale est utilisée pour calculer les taux. Par conséquent, si la population utilisée pour calculer les taux est différente de la population de référence adéquate, les taux présentés sont susceptibles de sous ou sur estimer la situation réelle d'un pays ou d'un territoire.

Les taux présentés dans ce tableau se rapportent seulement aux pays ou zones où l'on a enregistré un nombre minimal de 30 naissances vivantes au cours d'une année donnée.

Fiabilité des données : Il a été demandé à chaque pays ou zone d'indiquer le degré estimatif de complétude des données sur les naissances vivantes figurant dans ses registres d'état civil. Ces évaluations nationales sont signalées par les codes de qualité "C" et "U" qui apparaissent dans la deuxième colonne du tableau.

La lettre "C" indique que les données sont jugées à peu près complètes, c'est-à-dire qu'elles représentent au moins 90 p. 100 des naissances vivantes survenues chaque année ; la lettre "U" signifie que les données sont jugées incomplètes, c'est-à-dire qu'elles représentent moins de 90 p. 100 des naissances vivantes survenues chaque année. Un troisième code, "...", indique qu'aucun renseignement n'a été communiqué quant à la complétude des données.

Les données provenant des registres de l'état civil qui sont déclarées incomplètes ou dont le degré de complétude n'est pas connu (code "U" ou "...") sont jugées douteuses. Elles apparaissent en italique dans le tableau. Les taux pour ces données ne sont pas calculés.

Les codes de qualité ne s'appliquent qu'aux données provenant des registres de l'état civil. Si l'on présente des données autres que celles de l'état civil, le signe "I" est utilisé à la place du code de qualité. Pour plus de précisions sur la qualité des données reposant sur les statistiques de l'état civil en général et les estimations de complétude en particulier, voir la section 4.2 des Notes techniques.

Insuffisance des données : Les statistiques concernant les naissances vivantes appellent toutes les réserves qui ont été formulées à propos des statistiques de l'état civil en général et des statistiques des naissances en particulier (voir la section 4 des Notes techniques).

La fiabilité des données, au sujet de laquelle des indications ont été fournies plus haut, est un facteur important. Il faut également tenir compte du fait que, dans certains cas, les données relatives aux naissances vivantes sont exploitées selon la date de l'enregistrement et non selon la date de l'événement ; ces cas ont été signalés par le signe '+'. Chaque fois que le décalage entre l'événement et son enregistrement est grand et qu'une forte proportion des naissances vivantes fait l'objet d'un enregistrement tardif, les statistiques des naissances vivantes pour une année donnée peuvent être considérablement faussées.

Un autre facteur qui nuit à la comparabilité internationale est la pratique de certains pays ou zones qui consiste à ne pas inclure dans les statistiques des naissances vivantes les enfants nés vivants mais décédés avant l'enregistrement de leur naissance ou dans les 24 heures qui ont suivi la naissance, pratique qui conduit à sous-estimer le nombre total de naissances vivantes. Lorsque ce facteur a joué, cela a été signalé en note à la fin du tableau.

La qualité et les limitations des estimations concernant la population ont également une incidence sur le calcul des taux. Les problèmes liés au sur-dénombrement ou au sous-dénombrement et, dans une certaine mesure, aux différences dans la définition de la population totale ont été abordés à la section 3 des Notes techniques relative aux données sur la population en général et des précisions sur certains pays ou zones sont données dans les notes se rapportant au tableau 3.

Les taux estimatifs fondés sur les résultats d'enquêtes par sondage comportent des possibilités d'erreurs considérables dues soit à des omissions dans les déclarations, soit au fait que l'on a déclaré à tort des naissances survenues en réalité hors de la période considérée. Toutefois, les taux estimatifs fondés sur les résultats d'enquêtes par sondage présentent un gros avantage : le chiffre de population utilisé comme base est, par définition, rigoureusement correspondant.

Il faut souligner que les taux bruts de natalité, de même que les taux bruts de mortalité, de nuptialité et de divortialité, peuvent varier très sensiblement selon la structure par âge et par sexe de la population à laquelle ils se rapportent. Ils offrent néanmoins un moyen simple de mesurer le niveau et l'évolution de la natalité.

La classification des naissances selon le lieu de résidence (zone urbaine ou rurale) peut se rapporter au lieu de résidence de la mère ou au lieu d'occurrence et correspond à celle indiquée par chaque pays ou zone. En outre, la comparabilité des données selon le lieu de résidence (zone urbaine ou rurale) peut être limitée par les définitions nationales des termes « urbain » et « rural » utilisées pour la mise en tableaux de ces données. En l'absence d'indications contraires, on a supposé que les mêmes définitions avaient servi pour le recensement national de la population et pour l'établissement des statistiques de l'état civil pour chaque pays ou zone. Toutefois, il n'est pas exclu que, pour une zone ou un pays donné, des définitions différentes aient été retenues. Les définitions du terme « urbain » utilisées pour les recensements nationaux de population ont été présentées à la fin des notes techniques du tableau 6 lorsqu'elles étaient connues. Comme on l'a précisé dans les notes techniques relatives au tableau 6, ces définitions varient considérablement d'un pays ou d'une zone à l'autre. La différence entre ces taux pour les zones urbaines et rurales pourra aussi être faussée selon que les faits d'état civil auront été classés d'après le lieu de l'événement ou le lieu de résidence habituel. Ce problème est examiné plus en détail à la section 4.1.4.1 des Notes techniques.

Données publiées antérieurement : Les différentes éditions de l'*Annuaire démographique* contiennent des données sur les naissances vivantes. Pour plus de précisions concernant les années et les sujets pour lesquels des données ont été publiées, se reporter à l'index historique.

NOTES
[1] *Principes et recommandations pour un système de statistique de l'état civil, troisième révision*, numéro de vente : E.13.XVII.10, publication des Nations Unies, New York, 2014.

9. Live births and crude birth rates, by urban/rural residence: 2013 - 2017
Naissances vivantes et taux bruts de natalité selon la résidence, urbaine/rurale : 2013 - 2017

Continent, country or area, and urban/rural residence / Continent, pays ou zone et résidence, urbaine/rurale	Code[a]	Number - Nombre					Rate - Taux				
		2013	2014	2015	2016	2017	2013	2014	2015	2016	2017
AFRICA - AFRIQUE											
Algeria - Algérie[1]											
Total	C	962 722	1 014 248	1 040 285	1 066 823	...	25.1	25.9	26.0	26.1	...
Angola[2]											
Total	I	...	1 152 490	...	...	...	...	44.5	...	...	...
Urban - Urbaine	I	...	670 605	...	...	...	...	41.3	...	...	...
Rural - Rurale	I	...	481 884	...	...	...	...	49.9	...	...	...
Botswana[3]											
Total	U	44 794	41 741	46 765	49 984	...	...	...	...	...	...
Burundi[4]											
Total	+U	248 395	253 698	266 820	...	...	...	...	...	...	...
Côte d'Ivoire[2]											
Total	I	...	841 081	...	...	...	...	37.0	...	...	...
Urban - Urbaine	I	...	354 285	...	...	...	...	31.0	...	...	...
Rural - Rurale	I	...	486 796	...	...	...	...	43.2	...	...	...
Egypt - Égypte											
Total	+C	2 621 902	2 720 495	2 685 276	2 600 173	2 557 440	31.0	31.3	30.2	28.6	26.9
Urban - Urbaine	+C	1 186 887	1 228 275	1 224 729	1 241 469	1 292 661	32.8	33.1	32.2	31.9	32.0
Rural - Rurale	+C	1 435 015	1 492 220	1 460 547	1 358 704	1 264 779	29.6	30.0	28.7	26.1	23.1
Ghana[5]											
Total	+U	463 409	...	...	...	...	...	...	...	...	...
Guinea - Guinée											
Total	+U	205 658	...	...	...	...	...	...	...	...	...
Total[6]	I	...	440 340	...	...	...	...	41.5	...	...	...
Kenya											
Total	U	870 599	954 254	950 224	948 351	...	...	...	...	...	...
Lesotho											
Total	+U	...	...	...	9 655	...	...	...	...	...	...
Mauritania - Mauritanie[7]											
Total[8]	I	114 420	...	...	...	...	32.3	...	...	...	...
Urban - Urbaine	I	54 392	...	...	...	...	...	...	...	...	...
Rural - Rurale	I	58 008	...	...	...	...	...	...	...	...	...
Mauritius - Maurice[9]											
Total	+C	13 488	13 283	12 640	12 948	13 385	10.7	10.5	10.0	10.2	10.6
Urban - Urbaine	+C	5 059	5 158	5 150	5 302	5 303	9.7	10.0	10.0	10.3	10.3
Rural - Rurale	+C	8 429	8 125	7 490	7 646	8 082	11.4	10.9	10.1	10.2	10.8
Mayotte											
Total	C	...	7 306	8 997	9 496	9 762	...	32.4	38.3	38.9	38.4
Mozambique[10]											
Total	U	746 185	794 718	...	...	...	...	...	...	...	...
Reunion - Réunion[11]											
Total	C	...	14 095	14 011	13 742	13 708	...	16.6	16.4	16.0	15.9
Saint Helena ex. dep. - Sainte-Hélène sans dép.											
Total	C	35	48	40	35	36	8.3	10.9	8.9	7.5	...
Sao Tome and Principe - Sao Tomé-et-Principe											
Total	C	4 856	4 939	5 022	5 105	5 190	26.6	26.6	26.5	26.4	26.3
Senegal - Sénégal[12]											
Total	I	478 898	...	...	...	...	35.5	...	...	...	...
Seychelles											
Total	+C	1 566	1 557	1 592	1 645	1 651	17.4	17.0	17.0	17.4	17.2
Sierra Leone[13]											
Total	+U	229 947	...	...	...	...	...	...	...	...	...
South Africa - Afrique du Sud											
Total	U	1 012 808	1 008 740	952 242	...	...	...	...	...	...	...
Total	C	...	...	...	876 435	...	...	...	...	15.7	...
Tunisia - Tunisie											
Total	C	222 962	225 887	222 534	219 441	209 236	20.5	20.5	20.0	19.4	18.3
AMERICA, NORTH - AMÉRIQUE DU NORD											
Anguilla											
Total	+C	165	151	165	135	145	11.9	10.6	11.2	9.0	...
Aruba											
Total	C	1 346	1 376	1 244	1 259	1 202	12.7	12.8	11.4	11.4	10.8

9. Live births and crude birth rates, by urban/rural residence: 2013 - 2017
Naissances vivantes et taux bruts de natalité selon la résidence, urbaine/rurale : 2013 - 2017 (continued - suite)

Continent, country or area, and urban/rural residence — Continent, pays ou zone et résidence, urbaine/rurale	Co-de[a]	Number - Nombre					Rate - Taux				
		2013	2014	2015	2016	2017	2013	2014	2015	2016	2017

AMERICA, NORTH - AMÉRIQUE DU NORD

Bahamas											
Total	+U	4 330	*4 155	*4 253	*4 093	*4 017	...	...	...	...	...
Barbados - Barbade											
Total	+C	3 020	2 902	...	...	...	10.9	10.5	...	...	...
Belize											
Total	U	7 264	7 318	7 456	7 200	...	...	...	...	...	...
Urban - Urbaine	U	3 002	2 952	3 075	2 863	...	...	...	...	...	...
Rural - Rurale	U	4 227	4 339	4 353	4 301	...	...	...	...	...	...
Bermuda - Bermudes[14]											
Total	C	648	574	583	591	*576	10.5	9.3	9.4	9.6	*9.3
British Virgin Islands - Îles Vierges britanniques											
Total	C	277	280	266	...	...	9.7	...	9.1	...	...
Canada[15]											
Total	C	380 323	384 100	382 392	383 102	376 291	10.8	10.8	10.7	10.6	10.3
Cayman Islands - Îles Caïmanes											
Total	C	705	711	649	660	625	12.5	12.5	11.0	10.8	9.9
Costa Rica											
Total	C	70 550	71 793[16]	71 819	70 004	*68 816	15.0	15.0	14.9	14.3	*13.9
Urban - Urbaine	C	24 883	41 631[16]	49 744	48 392	*47 273	7.3	12.0	14.2	13.6	*13.2
Rural - Rurale	C	45 667	30 162[16]	22 075	21 612	*21 543	35.6	23.2	16.7	16.2	*15.9
Cuba											
Total	C	125 880	122 643	125 064	116 872	114 971	11.2	10.9	11.1	10.4	10.2
Urban - Urbaine	C	98 894	96 930	99 434	93 565	...	11.5	11.2	11.5	10.8	...
Rural - Rurale	C	26 986	25 713	25 630	23 307	...	10.4	9.9	9.9	9.0	...
Curaçao											
Total	C	1 962	1 963	1 877	1 789	1 548	12.8	12.6	11.9	11.2	9.7
Dominica - Dominique											
Total	+C	931	858	...	...	...	13.1	12.0	...	...	...
Dominican Republic - République dominicaine[17]											
Total	U	159 785	161 306	157 422	139 583	...	...	...	...	...	...
Urban - Urbaine	U	132 706	137 036	135 056	120 717	...	...	...	...	...	...
Rural - Rurale	U	25 793	23 743	21 885	18 392	...	...	...	...	...	...
El Salvador[18]											
Total	C	109 617	108 903	109 617	...	...	17.4	17.2	17.0	...	...
Urban - Urbaine	C	68 432	62 372	...	...	...	16.5	...	...	...	...
Rural - Rurale	C	41 185	46 531	...	...	...	19.3	...	...	...	...
Greenland - Groenland											
Total	C	820	805	854	830	853	14.5	14.3	15.2	14.8	15.2
Urban - Urbaine	C	697	703	719	699	734	14.5	14.6	14.9	14.4	15.1
Rural - Rurale	C	123	102	135	131	119	14.9	12.7	17.2	16.9	15.6
Grenada - Grenade											
Total	+C	1 838	1 750	...	...	...	16.9	16.0	...	...	...
Guadeloupe[11]											
Total	C	5 069	5 001	4 714	4 653	4 126	12.6	12.5	11.9	11.8	10.5
Guatemala											
Total	C	387 342	386 195	391 425	390 382	...	25.1	24.4	24.2	...	...
Jamaica - Jamaïque											
Total	C	36 746	36 996	37 900	36 160	34 169	13.5	13.6	13.9	13.3	12.5
Martinique[11]											
Total	C	4 130	4 367	3 972	3 782	3 640	10.7	11.4	10.4	10.0	9.7
Mexico - Mexique											
Total	C	2 168 933[19]	2 129 825[19]	2 096 274[19]	*2 293 708	...	18.3	17.8	17.3	*18.8	...
Urban - Urbaine[20]	C	1 523 223	1 563 395	1 540 464	...	...	17.8	18.0	17.6	...	...
Rural - Rurale[20]	C	483 583	464 897	442 539	...	...	14.8	14.1	13.3	...	...
Montserrat											
Total	C	41	50	48	46	...	8.3	10.0	9.6	9.1	...
Nicaragua											
Total	+U	...	...	...	137 772	...	...	...	...	...	...
Urban - Urbaine	+U	...	...	...	71 668	...	...	...	...	...	...
Rural - Rurale	+U	...	...	...	66 104	...	...	...	...	...	...
Panama											
Total	C	73 804	75 183	*75 901	*75 184	*74 832	19.2	19.2	*19.1	*18.6	*18.3
Urban - Urbaine	C	47 901	49 006	*48 960	*47 818	...	18.6	18.5	*18.1	*17.2	...
Rural - Rurale	C	25 903	26 177	*26 941	*27 366	...	20.4	20.6	*21.3	*21.6	...

9. Live births and crude birth rates, by urban/rural residence: 2013 - 2017
Naissances vivantes et taux bruts de natalité selon la résidence, urbaine/rurale : 2013 - 2017 (continued - suite)

Continent, country or area, and urban/rural residence / Continent, pays ou zone et résidence, urbaine/rurale	Code[a]	Number - Nombre					Rate - Taux				
		2013	2014	2015	2016	2017	2013	2014	2015	2016	2017
AMERICA, NORTH - AMÉRIQUE DU NORD											
Puerto Rico - Porto Rico											
Total	C	36 580	34 503	31 241	28 344	24 370	10.2	9.8	9.0	8.3	7.3
Urban - Urbaine	C	19 792	19 014[17]	18 995	18 210	16 348	...	...	...	...	...
Rural - Rurale	C	16 788	15 469[17]	12 246	10 134	8 022	...	...	...	...	...
Saint Kitts and Nevis - Saint-Kitts-et-Nevis											
Total	+C	547	641	...	...	...	...	...	...	...	...
Saint Vincent and the Grenadines - Saint-Vincent-et-les Grenadines											
Total	C	1 738	1 841	...	...	...	15.8	16.7	...	...	...
Sint Maarten (Dutch part) - Saint-Martin (partie néerlandaise)[21]											
Total	+C	511	...	...	...	...	14.0	...	...	...	...
Trinidad and Tobago - Trinité-et-Tobago											
Total	C	*18 823	*18 729	*18 062	...	...	*14.0	*13.9	*13.4	...	...
Turks and Caicos Islands - Îles Turques et Caïques											
Total	C	502	437	437	518	...	14.9	12.4	11.9	13.7	...
United States of America - États-Unis d'Amérique											
Total	C	3 932 181	3 988 076	3 978 497	...	...	12.4	12.5	12.4	...	...
AMERICA, SOUTH - AMÉRIQUE DU SUD											
Argentina - Argentine											
Total	C	754 603	777 012	770 040	728 035	...	17.9	18.2	17.9	16.7	...
Bolivia (Plurinational State of) - Bolivie (État plurinational de)											
Total	U	149 832	153 016	...	...	...	...	...	...	...	...
Total	+U	...	...	277 498	...	...	...	...	...	...	...
Brazil - Brésil											
Total[22]	U	2 832 590	2 913 121	...	...	...	...	...	...	...	...
Total	+C	...	...	2 952 969	2 903 933	...	...	...	14.4	14.1	...
Chile - Chili											
Total	C	242 005	250 997	244 670	*232 616	...	13.8	14.1	13.6	*12.8	...
Urban - Urbaine	C	220 276	228 458	222 438	...	...	14.4	14.7	14.1	...	...
Rural - Rurale	C	21 729	22 539	22 232	...	...	9.6	10.0	9.8	...	...
Colombia - Colombie											
Total	U	658 835	669 137	660 999	647 521	...	...	...	...	...	...
Urban - Urbaine[17]	U	517 470	530 841	526 365	514 829	...	...	...	...	...	...
Rural - Rurale[17]	U	140 632	137 856	134 215	132 183	...	...	...	...	...	...
Ecuador - Équateur[23]											
Total	U	277 620	278 460	283 313	*266 464	...	...	...	...	...	...
Urban - Urbaine	U	225 806	222 212	222 575	*209 341	...	...	...	...	...	...
Rural - Rurale	U	51 814	56 248	60 738	*57 123	...	...	...	...	...	...
French Guiana - Guyane française[11]											
Total	C	6 474	6 591	6 806	7 270	8 057	26.5	26.1	26.4	27.7	29.4
Paraguay											
Total	+U	114 619	116 592	132 241	128 117	...	...	...	...	...	...
Peru - Pérou[24]											
Total	+U	475 349	492 008	529 029	*522 269	*482 914	...	...	...	...	...
Urban - Urbaine	+U	...	...	384 757	...	...	...	...	...	...	...
Rural - Rurale	+U	...	...	144 272	...	...	...	...	...	...	...
Suriname											
Total	C	10 012	10 407	10 148	9 910	...	18.2	18.6	17.9	17.2	...
Urban - Urbaine	C	6 792	6 898	6 683	6 561	...	...	...	...	...	...
Rural - Rurale	C	3 220	3 509	3 465	3 349	...	...	...	...	...	...
Uruguay											
Total	C	48 681	48 368	48 926	47 058	...	14.2	14.0	14.1	13.5	...

Continent, country or area, and urban/rural residence / Continent, pays ou zone et résidence, urbaine/rurale	Code[a]	Number - Nombre					Rate - Taux				
		2013	2014	2015	2016	2017	2013	2014	2015	2016	2017
AMERICA, SOUTH - AMÉRIQUE DU SUD											
Venezuela (Bolivarian Republic of) - Venezuela (République bolivarienne du)											
Total	U	597 902	597 773	600 875	642 644	*561 603	...	...	...	...	...
ASIA - ASIE											
Armenia - Arménie											
Total	C	*41 790	43 031	41 763	40 592	37 700	*13.8	14.3	13.9	13.6	12.7
Urban - Urbaine	C	...	...	27 124	26 474	...	...	...	14.2	13.9	...
Rural - Rurale	C	...	...	14 639	14 118	...	...	...	13.4	13.0	...
Azerbaijan - Azerbaïdjan[25]											
Total	+C	172 671	170 503	166 210	159 464	...	18.3	17.9	17.2	16.3	...
Urban - Urbaine	+C	86 429	81 822	81 149	76 954	...	...	16.1	15.8	14.9	...
Rural - Rurale	+C	86 242	88 681	85 061	82 510	...	...	19.9	18.8	18.0	...
Bahrain - Bahreïn[26]											
Total	C	19 995	20 931	20 983	20 714	...	16.0	15.9	15.3	14.5	...
Brunei Darussalam - Brunéi Darussalam											
Total	+C	6 680	6 891	6 699	6 437	...	16.6	16.9	16.2	15.4	...
China - Chine[27]											
Total	I	16 400 000	16 870 000	16 550 000	...	...	12.1	12.4	12.1	...	...
China, Hong Kong SAR - Chine, Hong Kong RAS											
Total	C	57 084	62 305	59 878	60 856	56 548	8.0	8.6	8.2	8.3	7.7
China, Macao SAR - Chine, Macao RAS											
Total	C	6 571	7 360	7 055	7 146	6 529	11.1	11.8	11.0	11.1	10.0
Cyprus - Chypre[28]											
Total	C	9 341	9 258	9 170	9 455	*9 229	10.8	10.9	10.8	11.1	*10.7
Georgia - Géorgie											
Total	C	57 878	60 635	59 249	56 569	53 293	12.9	16.3	15.9	15.2	14.3
Urban - Urbaine	C	...	...	33 898	32 227	...	...	...	15.9	15.1	...
Rural - Rurale	C	...	...	25 351	24 342	...	...	...	15.9	15.3	...
India - Inde[29]											
Total	I	...	...	...	...	...	21.4	21.0	20.8	20.4	...
Urban - Urbaine	I	...	...	...	...	...	17.3	17.4	17.3	17.0	...
Rural - Rurale	I	...	...	...	...	...	22.9	22.7	22.4	22.1	...
Iran (Islamic Republic of) - Iran (République islamique d')[30]											
Total	+C	1 471 834	1 534 362	1 570 219	1 528 053	...	19.1	19.7	19.9	19.2	...
Urban - Urbaine	+C	1 131 566	1 178 921	1 208 142	1 176 032	...	20.4	20.9	21.1	20.2	...
Rural - Rurale	+C	340 268	355 441	362 077	352 021	...	15.9	16.6	16.9	16.4	...
Iraq											
Total	U	*1 077 645	...	...	...	...	...	...	...	...	...
Israel - Israël[31]											
Total	C	171 444	176 427	178 723	181 405	*183 656	21.3	21.5	21.3	21.2	*21.1
Urban - Urbaine	C	155 127	160 223	162 225	164 561	...	21.1	21.4	21.2	21.1	...
Rural - Rurale	C	16 317	16 204	16 498	16 844	...	23.6	22.7	22.4	22.5	...
Japan - Japon[32]											
Total	C	1 029 816[17]	1 003 539[17]	1 005 677[17]	976 978[17]	*946 060	8.1	7.9	7.9	7.7	*7.5
Urban - Urbaine[33]	C	948 589	926 229	928 962	902 855	...	...	...	...	...	...
Rural - Rurale[33]	C	81 173	77 245	76 662	74 058	...	...	...	...	...	...
Jordan - Jordanie[34]											
Total	C	178 143	188 902	198 018	197 789	...	22.0	21.5	20.7	20.2	...
Kazakhstan											
Total	C	387 256	399 309	398 458	400 694	390 262	22.7	23.1	22.7	22.5	21.6
Urban - Urbaine	C	209 383	222 821	225 808	229 731	226 847	22.4	23.1	22.7	22.6	21.9
Rural - Rurale	C	177 873	176 488	172 650	170 963	163 415	23.2	23.1	22.7	22.3	21.2
Kuwait - Koweït											
Total	C	59 426	61 313	59 271	58 797	...	17.3	16.3	14.9	14.4	...

9. Live births and crude birth rates, by urban/rural residence: 2013 - 2017
Naissances vivantes et taux bruts de natalité selon la résidence, urbaine/rurale : 2013 - 2017 (continued - suite)

Continent, country or area, and urban/rural residence / Continent, pays ou zone et résidence, urbaine/rurale	Code[a]	Number - Nombre					Rate - Taux				
		2013	2014	2015	2016	2017	2013	2014	2015	2016	2017
ASIA - ASIE											
Kyrgyzstan - Kirghizstan											
Total	C	155 520	161 813	163 452	158 160	153 620	27.2	27.7	27.4	26.0	24.8
Urban - Urbaine	C	53 855	55 463	52 477	51 610	52 829	28.0	28.2	26.1	25.2	25.2
Rural - Rurale	C	101 665	106 350	110 975	106 550	100 791	26.8	27.5	28.1	26.5	24.6
Lebanon - Liban											
Total	C	95 246	104 872	...	...	...	...	...	...	...	...
Malaysia - Malaisie											
Total	C	503 914	528 612	521 136	508 203	...	16.7	17.2	16.7	16.1	...
Urban - Urbaine	C	344 410	357 848	350 677	342 253	...	15.6	15.8	15.1	14.5	...
Rural - Rurale	C	159 504	170 764	170 459	165 950	...	19.5	21.1	21.3	20.9	...
Maldives[35]											
Total	C	7 153	7 245	6 986	6 756	...	21.3	21.2	20.3	19.3	...
Urban - Urbaine	C	4 698[36]	4 521[36]	2 404[17]	2 431[17]	...	...	...	18.0	17.6	...
Rural - Rurale	C	2 439[36]	2 378[36]	4 211[17]	3 996[17]	...	...	...	20.0	18.8	...
Mongolia - Mongolie											
Total	+C	79 780	82 839	82 130	79 920	75 321	27.5	28.0	27.1	25.9	23.9
Urban - Urbaine	+C	57 069	56 148	60 861	55 161	51 912	29.1	28.2	29.8	26.0	24.3
Rural - Rurale	+C	22 711	26 691	21 269	24 759	23 409	24.2	27.5	21.6	25.6	23.2
Myanmar											
Total	+U	835 595[37]	736 369[38]	739 152[38]	...	...	...	...	...	...	...
Urban - Urbaine	+U	333 075[37]	227 119[38]	233 206[38]	...	...	...	...	...	...	...
Rural - Rurale	+U	502 520[37]	509 250[38]	505 946[38]	...	...	...	...	...	...	...
Oman											
Total[39]	U	79 417	82 981	86 286	88 346	...	...	...	...	...	...
Total	C	...	...	...	...	90 371	...	...	...	...	19.8
Philippines											
Total	C	1 761 602	1 748 857	1 744 767	1 731 289	...	17.9	17.5	17.2	16.8	...
Qatar											
Total	C	23 708	25 443	26 622	26 816	*25 906	11.8	11.5	10.9	10.2	*9.5
Urban - Urbaine	C	23 708	25 443	26 622	26 816	...	11.8	11.5	10.9	10.2	...
Republic of Korea - République de Corée[40]											
Total	C	436 455	435 435	438 420	406 243	357 771	8.6	8.6	8.6	7.9	7.0
Urban - Urbaine	C	365 381[17]	364 615[17]	367 143	...	...	8.9	8.8	8.8	...	...
Rural - Rurale	C	71 070[17]	70 818[17]	71 277	...	...	7.6	7.5	7.5	...	...
Saudi Arabia - Arabie saoudite[41]											
Total	I	501 583	514 325	449 149	447 040	404 909	16.9	17.0	14.5	14.1	12.4
Singapore - Singapour											
Total	C	39 720	42 232	42 185	41 251	39 615	10.3	10.9	10.8	10.5	10.0
Sri Lanka											
Total	+C	365 762	*349 715	*334 821	331 073	326 052	17.8	*16.8	*16.0	15.6	15.2
Urban - Urbaine	+C	258 823	...	...	...	...	...	...	...	...	...
Rural - Rurale	+C	106 939	...	...	...	...	...	...	...	...	...
State of Palestine - État de Palestine[42]											
Total	U	127 454	128 073	124 331	...	...	...	...	...	...	...
Tajikistan - Tadjikistan[43]											
Total	U	209 417	229 460	237 541	230 044	...	...	...	...	...	...
Urban - Urbaine	U	50 508	54 878	53 034	51 042	...	...	...	...	...	...
Rural - Rurale	U	158 909	174 582	184 507	179 002	...	...	...	...	...	...
Thailand - Thaïlande											
Total	+U	782 129	776 370	738 930	704 058	...	...	...	...	...	...
Timor-Leste[44]											
Total	I	...	...	36 202	...	...	...	...	30.6	...	...
Turkey - Turquie											
Total	C	1 295 987	1 348 413	1 333 329	1 309 771	*1 291 055	16.9	17.4	16.9	16.4	*16.1
United Arab Emirates - Émirats arabes unis[45]											
Total	...	93 539	95 860	97 328	...	...	...	...	...	...	...
Uzbekistan - Ouzbékistan											
Total	+C	679 519	718 036	734 141	726 170	715 519	22.5	23.3	23.5	23.0	22.3
Urban - Urbaine	+C	310 481	326 231	325 660	...	...	20.1	20.8	20.5	...	...
Rural - Rurale	+C	369 038	391 805	408 481	...	...	25.0	25.9	26.5	...	...
Yemen - Yémen[46]											
Total	U	425 165	...	...	...	...	...	...	...	...	...

Continent, country or area, and urban/rural residence / Continent, pays ou zone et résidence, urbaine/rurale	Code[a]	Number - Nombre					Rate - Taux				
		2013	2014	2015	2016	2017	2013	2014	2015	2016	2017
EUROPE											
Åland Islands - Îles d'Åland											
Total	C	287	282	275	293	*282	10.0	9.8	9.5	10.1	*9.6
Urban - Urbaine	C	104	98	97	112	*110	9.1	8.6	8.5	9.7	*9.5
Rural - Rurale	C	183	184	178	181	*172	10.6	10.6	10.2	10.3	*9.7
Albania - Albanie											
Total	C	35 750	35 760	33 221	31 733	30 869	12.3	12.4	11.5	11.0	10.7
Andorra - Andorre											
Total	C	637	639	659	634	...	9.1	9.1	9.3	8.8	...
Austria - Autriche											
Total	C	79 330	81 722	84 381[47]	87 675[47]	*87 633[47]	9.4	9.6	9.8	10.0	*10.0
Belarus - Bélarus											
Total	C	117 997	118 534	119 028	117 779	102 556	12.5	12.5	12.5	12.4	10.8
Urban - Urbaine	C	90 436	91 704	91 870	91 005	...	12.5	12.6	12.5	12.3	...
Rural - Rurale	C	27 561	26 830	27 158	26 774	...	12.4	12.3	12.7	12.7	...
Belgium - Belgique[48]											
Total	C	125 606	125 014	122 274	121 896	119 690	11.2	11.1	10.8	10.8	10.5
Urban - Urbaine	C	123 881	123 346	120 591	...	...	...	...	...	...	...
Rural - Rurale	C	1 725	1 668	1 683	...	...	...	...	...	...	...
Bosnia and Herzegovina - Bosnie-Herzégovine											
Total	C	31 103	29 247	28 906	29 276	29 158	8.8	8.3	8.2	8.3	8.3
Bulgaria - Bulgarie											
Total	C	66 578	67 585	65 950	64 984	63 955	9.2	9.4	9.2	9.1	9.0
Urban - Urbaine	C	...	50 704	49 486	48 733	...	...	9.6	9.4	9.3	...
Rural - Rurale	C	...	16 881	16 464	16 251	...	...	8.7	8.5	8.5	...
Croatia - Croatie											
Total	C	39 939	39 566	37 503	37 537	36 556	9.4	9.3	8.9	9.0	8.9
Urban - Urbaine	C	22 796	22 894	21 802	21 645	...	...	...	...	...	...
Rural - Rurale	C	17 143	16 672	15 701	15 892	...	...	...	...	...	...
Czechia - Tchéquie											
Total	C	106 751	109 860	110 764	112 663	114 405	10.2	10.4	10.5	10.7	10.8
Urban - Urbaine	C	78 469	80 841	81 413	82 912	...	10.2	10.5	10.6	10.7	...
Rural - Rurale	C	28 282	29 019	29 351	29 751	...	10.0	10.2	10.3	10.5	...
Denmark - Danemark[49]											
Total	C	55 873	56 870	58 205	61 614	61 397	10.0	10.1	10.3	10.8	10.7
Estonia - Estonie											
Total	C	13 531	13 551	13 907	14 053	13 784	10.3	10.3	10.6	10.7	10.5
Urban - Urbaine	C	9 286	9 452	9 553[17]	9 566	...	10.3	10.5	10.6	10.6	...
Rural - Rurale	C	4 245	4 099	4 353[17]	4 487	...	10.2	9.8	10.5	10.8	...
Faeroe Islands - Îles Féroé											
Total	C	624	636	605	676	655	12.9	13.1	12.4	13.7	13.0
Urban - Urbaine	C	237	265	227	275	247	13.0	14.4	12.2	14.5	12.8
Rural - Rurale	C	387	371	378	401	408	12.9	12.3	12.5	13.1	13.2
Finland - Finlande											
Total	C	57 847[50]	56 950[50]	55 197[50]	52 521[50]	50 321	10.7	10.5	10.1	9.6	9.1
Urban - Urbaine[50]	C	41 386	41 103	40 711	38 853	...	11.1	10.9	10.6	10.0	...
Rural - Rurale[50]	C	16 461	15 847	14 486	13 668	...	9.8	9.5	9.0	8.6	...
France											
Total	C	781 621	781 167	760 421	744 697	*730 700	12.2	12.2	11.8	11.5	*11.3
Urban - Urbaine[51]	C	623 522	625 957	611 062	601 770	...	...	...	...	...	...
Rural - Rurale[51]	C	156 358	153 342	147 304	140 951	...	...	...	...	...	...
Germany - Allemagne											
Total	C	682 069	714 927	737 575	792 137	*785 234	8.5	8.8	9.0	9.6	*9.5
Gibraltar[52]											
Total	+C	426	488	492	...	...	13.0	14.7	14.7	...	...
Greece - Grèce											
Total	C	94 134	92 149	91 847	92 898	*88 523	8.6	8.5	8.5	8.6	*8.2
Urban - Urbaine	C	64 616	62 785	63 283	64 223	...	...	...	...	...	...
Rural - Rurale	C	29 518	29 364	28 564	28 675	...	...	...	...	...	...
Guernsey - Guernesey											
Total	C	667	627	620	654	...	10.6	10.1	10.0	10.5	...
Hungary - Hongrie											
Total[53]	C	89 524[54]	93 281[55]	92 135[55]	95 361[55]	94 646[55]	9.0	9.5	9.4	9.7	9.7
Urban - Urbaine	C	61 996[54]	65 095[55]	63 961[55]	65 866[56]	...	9.0	9.4	9.2	9.5	...
Rural - Rurale	C	27 511[54]	28 166[55]	28 153[55]	29 495[56]	...	9.1	9.7	9.7	10.2	...

9. Live births and crude birth rates, by urban/rural residence: 2013 - 2017
Naissances vivantes et taux bruts de natalité selon la résidence, urbaine/rurale : 2013 - 2017 (continued - suite)

Continent, country or area, and urban/rural residence — Continent, pays ou zone et résidence, urbaine/rurale	Code[a]	Number - Nombre					Rate - Taux				
		2013	2014	2015	2016	2017	2013	2014	2015	2016	2017
EUROPE											
Iceland - Islande											
Total	C	4 326	4 375	4 129	4 034	4 071	13.4	13.4	12.5	12.0	11.9
Urban - Urbaine	C	4 131	4 164	3 924	3 617	...	13.6	13.6	12.7	11.5	...
Rural - Rurale	C	195	211	205	169	...	9.5	10.2	9.8	7.9	...
Ireland - Irlande											
Total	+C	68 930	67 285	65 537	63 836	62 084	14.9	14.4	13.9	13.4	12.9
Isle of Man - Île de Man											
Total	+C	859	805	785	758	753	10.0	9.3	9.0	8.9	9.0
Italy - Italie											
Total	+C	514 308	...	...	...	...	8.5	...	...	...	...
Total	C	...	502 596	485 780	473 438	458 151	...	8.3	8.0	7.8	7.6
Jersey[19]											
Total	+C	1 029	985	1 021	...	...	9.8	9.9	...	...	...
Latvia - Lettonie											
Total	C	20 596	21 746	21 979	21 968	20 828	10.2	10.9	11.1	11.2	10.7
Urban - Urbaine	C	14 184	15 094	15 099	15 154	...	10.4	11.2	11.2	11.3	...
Rural - Rurale	C	6 412	6 652	6 880	6 814	...	9.9	10.4	10.9	10.9	...
Liechtenstein											
Total	C	339	372	325	378	*338	9.2	10.0	8.7	10.0	*8.9
Lithuania - Lituanie											
Total	C	29 885	30 369	31 475	30 623	28 696	10.1	10.4	10.8	10.7	10.1
Urban - Urbaine	C	20 195	20 989	21 589	21 256	...	10.2	10.7	11.1	11.0	...
Rural - Rurale	C	9 690	9 380	9 886	9 367	...	9.9	9.7	10.4	10.0	...
Luxembourg											
Total	C	6 115	6 070	6 115	6 050	6 174	11.3	10.9	10.7	10.4	10.4
Malta - Malte											
Total	C	4 032	4 191	4 325	4 476	4 319	9.5	9.8	10.0	9.8	9.2
Monaco[57]											
Total	C	992	974	1 067	938	...	26.8	26.4	28.4	24.6	...
Montenegro - Monténégro											
Total	C	7 475	7 529	7 386	7 569	7 432	12.0	12.1	11.9	12.2	11.9
Netherlands - Pays-Bas[58]											
Total	C	171 341	175 181	170 510	172 520	*169 200	10.2	10.4	10.1	10.1	*9.9
Norway - Norvège											
Total	C	58 878	58 976	58 815	58 890	56 633	11.6	11.5	11.3	11.3	10.7
Poland - Pologne											
Total	C	369 576	375 160	369 308	382 257	401 982	9.7	9.9	9.7	10.1	10.6
Urban - Urbaine	C	213 749	217 699	217 391	226 296	...	9.3	9.5	9.5	9.9	...
Rural - Rurale	C	155 827	157 461	151 917	155 961	...	10.4	10.5	10.1	10.3	...
Portugal[19]											
Total	C	82 787	82 367	85 500	87 126	86 154	7.9	7.9	8.3	8.4	8.4
Republic of Moldova - République de Moldova[59]											
Total	C	37 871	38 616	38 610	37 394	34 060	10.6	12.9	...	...	...
Urban - Urbaine	C	...	14 060	13 555	13 359	12 392	...	12.3	...	...	...
Rural - Rurale	C	...	24 556	25 055	24 035	21 668	...	13.2	...	...	...
Romania - Roumanie											
Total	C	182 313	198 740	197 491	200 009	*189 474	9.1	10.0	10.0	10.1	*9.7
Urban - Urbaine	C	98 351	109 093	108 744	...	...	9.1	10.2	10.2	...	...
Rural - Rurale	C	83 962	89 647	88 747	...	...	9.1	9.8	9.7	...	...
Russian Federation - Fédération de Russie[25]											
Total	C	1 895 822	...	...	...	...	13.2	...	...	...	...
San Marino - Saint-Marin											
Total	C	320	296	269	262	228	9.6	8.8	8.0	7.7	6.6
Serbia - Serbie[60]											
Total	+C	65 554	66 461	65 657	64 734	64 894	9.1	9.3	9.3	9.2	9.2
Urban - Urbaine	+C	45 657	46 036	45 640	44 794	...	10.7	10.8	10.7	10.5	...
Rural - Rurale	+C	19 897	20 425	20 017	19 940	...	6.9	7.1	7.1	7.1	...
Slovakia - Slovaquie											
Total	C	54 823	55 033	55 602	57 557	57 969	10.1	10.2	10.3	10.6	10.7
Urban - Urbaine	C	28 692	28 379	29 082	29 719	...	9.8	9.7	10.0	10.2	...
Rural - Rurale	C	26 131	26 654	26 520	27 838	...	10.5	10.7	10.6	11.1	...
Slovenia - Slovénie											
Total	C	21 111	21 165	20 641	20 345	20 241	10.3	10.3	10.0	9.9	9.8
Urban - Urbaine	C	10 698	10 707	10 871	10 765	...	10.2	10.2	9.8	9.7	...
Rural - Rurale	C	10 413	10 458	9 770	9 580	...	10.3	10.3	10.2	10.0	...

Continent, country or area, and urban/rural residence / Continent, pays ou zone et résidence, urbaine/rurale	Code[a]	Number - Nombre					Rate - Taux				
		2013	2014	2015	2016	2017	2013	2014	2015	2016	2017
EUROPE											
Spain - Espagne											
Total	C	424 440	426 076	418 432	408 734	*390 024	9.1	9.2	9.0	8.8	*8.4
Sweden - Suède											
Total	C	113 593	114 907	114 870	117 425	*115 416	11.8	11.9	11.7	11.8	*11.5
Switzerland - Suisse											
Total	C	82 731	85 287	86 559	87 883	87 381	10.2	10.4	10.5	10.5	10.3
Urban - Urbaine	C	62 250	64 109	74 039[61]	75 327	...	10.4	10.6	10.6	10.6	...
Rural - Rurale	C	20 481	21 178	12 520[61]	12 556	...	9.6	9.8	9.7	9.7	...
TFYR of Macedonia - L'ex-R. y. de Macédoine											
Total	C	23 138	23 596	23 075	23 002	21 754	11.2	11.4	11.1	11.1	10.5
Urban - Urbaine	C	13 259	13 764	13 357	13 536	...	...	...	...	...	...
Rural - Rurale	C	9 879	9 832	9 718	9 466	...	...	...	...	...	...
Ukraine[62]											
Total	+C	503 657	465 882[63]	411 781[63]	397 037[63]	363 987[63]	11.1	10.8	9.6	9.3	8.6
Urban - Urbaine	+C	330 284	304 190[63]	266 082[63]	258 688[63]	...	...	...	...	...	...
Rural - Rurale	+C	173 373	161 692[63]	145 699[63]	138 349[63]	...	...	...	...	...	...
United Kingdom of Great Britain and Northern Ireland - Royaume-Uni de Grande-Bretagne et d'Irlande du Nord[64]											
Total	C	778 358	775 908	776 746	774 386	*755 043	12.1	12.0	11.9	11.8	*11.4
OCEANIA - OCÉANIE											
American Samoa - Samoas américaines											
Total	C	1 161	1 084	...	...	...	18.5	17.5	...	...	...
Australia - Australie											
Total	C	308 065	299 697	305 377	311 104	...	13.3	12.8	12.8	12.8	...
Urban - Urbaine[65]	C	209 397	204 990	208 466	215 561	...	10.5	10.1	10.1	10.3	...
Rural - Rurale[65]	C	97 521	93 175	94 562	93 466	...	30.2	28.7	29.1	28.6	...
Cook Islands - Îles Cook[66]											
Total	+C	256	204	*205	...	...	13.8	11.0	*11.0	...	...
Fiji - Fidji											
Total	+C	18 633	18 251	...	...	...	21.6	21.1	...	...	...
French Polynesia - Polynésie française											
Total	C	4 203	4 161	3 888	...	...	15.6	15.3	14.3	...	...
Guam[67]											
Total	C	3 329	3 396	3 367	3 433	3 292	20.8	21.1	20.8	21.1	20.1
Nauru											
Total	C	320	...	...	...	...	...	...	...	...	...
New Caledonia - Nouvelle-Calédonie											
Total	C	4 373	4 370	4 191	4 234	...	16.6	16.3	15.4	15.4	...
New Zealand - Nouvelle-Zélande[68]											
Total	+C	58 716	57 243	61 038	59 427[69]	59 610[69]	13.2	12.7	13.3	12.7	12.4
Urban - Urbaine[17]	+C	51 480	50 355	53 205	51 849[69]	51 876[69]	13.5	13.0	13.4	12.8	12.5
Rural - Rurale[17]	+C	7 227	6 873	7 827	7 572[69]	7 728[69]	11.6	11.0	12.3	11.9	11.9
Northern Mariana Islands - Îles Mariannes septentrionales[70]											
Total	U	1 057	1 057	...	...	...	...	...	...	...	...
Palau - Palaos											
Total	C	229	241	242	213	221	13.0	13.7	13.7	12.0	12.4
Pitcairn											
Total	C	-	...	...	...	...	...	...	...	...	...
Samoa											
Total	+U	4 631	8 493	8 207	9 379	...	...	...	...	...	...

FOOTNOTES - NOTES

Italics: data from civil registers which are incomplete or of unknown completeness. - Italiques : données incomplètes ou dont le degré d'exactitude n'est pas connu, provenant des registres de l'état civil.

* Provisional. - Données provisoires.

a 'Code' indicates the source of data, as follows:
C - Civil registration, estimated over 90% complete
U - Civil registration, estimated less than 90% complete
| - Other source, estimated reliable
+ - Data tabulated by date of registration rather than occurence
... - Information not available

Le 'Code' indique la source des données, comme suit :
C - Registres de l'état civil considérés complets à 90 p. 100 au moins
U - Registres de l'état civil qui ne sont pas considérés complets à 90 p. 100 au moins
| - Autre source, considérée pas douteuses
+ - Données exploitées selon la date de l'enregistrement et non la date de l'événement
... - Information pas disponible

[1] Excluding live-born infants who died before their birth was registered. Data refer to Algerian population only. - Non compris les enfants nés vivants décédés avant l'enregistrement de leur naissance. Les données ne concernent que la population algérienne.

[2] Data refer to the 12 months preceding the census in May. - Les données se rapportent aux 12 mois précédant le recensement de mai.

[3] Source: Vital Statistics Report 2016. - Source: Vital Statistics Report 2016.

[4] Data refer only to events recorded in hospitals and health centres. - Ces données ne concernent que les faits d'état civil enregistrés dans les hôpitaux et les centres de santé uniquement.

[5] The coverage of registration is estimated at 66 per cent. - Le degré de complétude de l'enregistrement est évalué à 66 pour cent.

[6] Adjusted number of births in households referring to the 12 months preceding the census in March. - Le nombre ajusté de naissances vivantes des ménages ordinaires se rapportent aux 12 mois précédant le recensement de mars.

[7] Data refer to the 12 months preceding the census in March. - Les données se rapportent aux 12 mois précédant le recensement de mars.

[8] Including nomadic population. - Y compris la population nomade.

[9] Excludes the islands of St. Brandon and Agalega. - Non compris les îles St. Brandon et Agalega.

[10] Source: Ministry of Health, National Directorate of Planning and Cooperation. - Source : Ministère de la santé, Direction nationale de la planification et de la coopération.

[11] Excluding live-born infants who died before their birth was registered. - Non compris les enfants nés vivants décédés avant l'enregistrement de leur naissance.

[12] Based on estimates and projections from 'Agence Nationale de la Statistique et de la Démographie'. - Données fondées sur des estimations et des projections provenant de l'Agence Nationale de la Statistique et de la Démographie.

[13] Source: National Office of Births and Deaths. - Source : Le bureau national des naissances et des décès.

[14] Excluding non-residents and foreign service personnel and their dependants. - À l'exclusion des non-résidents et du personnel diplomatique et de leurs charges de famille.

[15] Including Canadian residents temporarily in the United States, but excluding United States residents temporarily in Canada. - Y compris les résidents canadiens se trouvant temporairement aux Etats-Unis, mais ne comprenant pas les résidents des Etats-Unis se trouvant temporairement au Canada.

[16] Definition of urban and rural distribution changed from the year 2014. - La définition de la répartition urbaine et rurale a changé depuis 2014.

[17] The total number may include 'Unknown residence', but the categories urban and rural do not. - Le nombre total peut inclure les personnes dont la résidence n'est pas connue, à l'inverse des catégories de population urbaine et rurale.

[18] Excluding children born in the country of non-resident mothers. - Exceptés les enfants nés dans le pays des mères non-résidentes.

[19] Data refer to births to resident mothers. - Ces données concernent les enfants nés de mères résidentes.

[20] Data refer to births to resident mothers. The total number may include 'Unknown residence', but the categories urban and rural do not. - Ces données concernent les enfants nés de mères résidentes. Le nombre total peut inclure les personnes dont la résidence n'est pas connue, à l'inverse des catégories de population urbaine et rurale.

[21] Source: Population Registry and STAT/CBS estimates. - Source: Le registre de la population et les estimations du STAT/CBS.

[22] Including births abroad and births of unknown residence of mother. - Y compris les naissances à l'étranger et les naissances pour lesquelles le lieu de résidence de la mère est inconnu.

[23] Excludes nomadic Indian tribes. - Non compris les tribus d'Indiens nomades.

[24] Source: Reports of the Ministry of Health. - Source : Rapports du Ministère de la Santé.

[25] Excluding infants born alive of less than 28 weeks' gestation, of less than 1 000 g in weight and 35 cm in length, who die within seven days of birth. - Non compris les enfants nés vivants après moins de 28 semaines de gestations, pesant moins de 1 000 g, mesurant moins de 35 cm et décédés dans les sept jours qui ont suivi leur naissance.

[26] Sources: Births and Deaths National Registration System database, and medical records of government hospitals. - Les sources: Les bases de données des << Births and Deaths National Registration System >> et les dossiers médicaux des hôpitaux du gouvernement.

[27] For statistical purposes, the data for China do not include those for the Hong Kong Special Administrative Region (Hong Kong SAR), Macao Special Administrative Region (Macao SAR) and Taiwan province of China. Data have been estimated on the basis of the annual National Sample Survey on Population Changes. - Pour la présentation des statistiques, les données pour la Chine ne comprennent pas la Région Administrative Spéciale de Hong Kong (Hong Kong RAS), la Région Administrative Spéciale de Macao (Macao RAS) et Taïwan province de Chine. Les données ont été estimées sur la base de l'enquête annuelle "National Sample Survey on Population Changes".

[28] Data refer to government controlled areas. - Les données se rapportent aux zones contrôlées par le Gouvernement.

[29] Includes data for the Indian-held part of Jammu and Kashmir, the final status of which has not yet been determined. Rates were obtained by the Sample Registration System of India, which is a large demographic survey. - Y compris les données pour la partie du Jammu et du Cachemire occupée par l'Inde dont le statut définitif n'a pas encore été déterminé. Les taux ont été obtenus par le Système de l'enregistrement par échantillon de l'Inde qui est une large enquête démographique.

[30] Data refer to the Iranian Year which begins on 21 March and ends on 20 March of the following year. - Les données concernent l'année iranienne, qui commence le 21 mars et se termine le 20 mars de l'année suivante.

[31] Includes data for East Jerusalem and Israeli residents in certain other territories under occupation by Israeli military forces since June 1967. - Y compris les données pour Jérusalem-Est et les résidents israéliens dans certains autres territoires occupés depuis 1967 par les forces armées israéliennes.

[32] Data refer to Japanese nationals in Japan only. - Les données se raportent aux nationaux japonais au Japon seulement.

[33] The total number may include 'Unknown residence', but the categories urban and rural do not. Urban and rural distribution refers to the residence of the child. - Le nombre total peut inclure les personnes dont la résidence n'est pas connue, à l'inverse des catégories de population urbaine et rurale. La répartition urbain/rural se réfère au domicile de l'enfant.

[34] Excluding data for Jordanian territory under occupation since June 1967 by Israeli military forces. Excluding foreigners, including registered Palestinian refugees. - Non compris les données pour le territoire jordanien occupé depuis juin 1967 par les forces armées israéliennes. Non compris les étrangers, mais y compris les réfugiés de Palestine enregistrés.

[35] Data do not include foreigners. - Les données sur les etrangers ne sont pas inclus.

[36] Excluding births occurred abroad. - Hormis les naissances intervenues à l'étranger.

[37] Source: "Department of Public Health" - Source : << Le Service de la santé publique >>

[38] Data are from Vital Registration System (VRS). - Les données proviennent du système d'enregistrement des faits d'état civil.

[39] Data from Births and Deaths Notification System (Ministry of Health and all health care providers). - Les données proviennent du système de notification des naissances et des décès (Ministère de la santé et tous prestataires de soins de santé).

[40] Data refer to residence of child. Excluding alien armed forces, civilian aliens employed by armed forces, and foreign diplomatic personnel and their dependants. - Les données correspondent à la résidence de l'enfant. Non compris les militaires étrangers, les civils étrangers employés par les forces armées ni le personnel diplomatique étranger et les membres de leur famille les accompagnant.

[41] Data refer to Saudi Arabian nationals only. Survey based estimates. - Les données ne concernent que les ressortissants saoudiens. Estimations basées sur des enquêtes.

42 Source: Palestinian Central Bureau of Statistics, Population Register, updated version 22/02/2016. - Source: Bureau central de statistique palestinien, registre de la population, version actualisée jusqu'au 22/02/2016.

43 Excluding infants born alive of less than 28 weeks' gestation, of less than 1 000 g in weight and 35 cm in length, who die within seven days of birth. Data have been adjusted for under-registration. - Non compris les enfants nés vivants après moins de 28 semaines de gestations, pesant moins de 1 000 g, mesurant moins de 35 cm et décédés dans les sept jours qui ont suivi leur naissance. Y compris un ajustement pour sous-enregistrement.

44 Data refer to the 12 months preceding the census in July. - Les données se rapportent aux 12 mois précédant le recensement de juillet.

45 The registration of births and deaths is conducted by the Ministry of Health. An estimate of completeness is not provided. - L'enregistrement des naissances et des décès est mené par le Ministère de la Santé. Le degré estimatif de complétude n'est pas fourni.

46 Including Non-Yemeni births. - Y compris les naissances non-yéménites.

47 Including births occurring abroad of mothers with residence in Austria. - Y compris les naissances survenues à l'étranger des mères avec résidence en Autriche.

48 Including armed forces stationed outside the country, but excluding alien armed forces stationed in the area. - Y compris les militaires nationaux hors du pays, mais non compris les militaires étrangers en garnison sur le territoire.

49 Excluding Faeroe Islands and Greenland shown separately, if available. - Non compris les Iles Féroé et le Groenland, qui font l'objet de rubriques distinctes, si disponible.

50 Excluding Åland Islands. - Non compris les Îles d'Åland.

51 Data for urban and rural exclude events corresponding to nationals residing outside the country, which may be included in the total. - Les données relatives à les categories urbaine et rurale n'englobent pas les faits d'état civil qui concernent les nationaux se trouvant à l'étranger, lesquels faits peuvent être inclus au total.

52 Including live births by military personnel and their dependants. - Y compris les naissances vivantes parmi les membres du personnel militaire et leurs personnes à charge.

53 Data include the live births of women with unknown residence and homeless. - Les données incluent les enfants nés vivants de femmes dont la résidence n'est pas connue et de femmes sans domicile fixe.

54 Till 2012 data refer to all live births occurred in Hungary. From 2013 data include the live births of women with Hungarian usual residence regardless of whether the live birth occurred in Hungary or in a foreign country, and do not include the live births of women with foreign country usual residence. - Jusqu'en 2012 les données concernent toutes les naissances vivantes survenues en Hongrie. À partir de 2013, les données concernent les enfants nés vivants de femmes dont la résidence habituelle est en Hongrie, que la naissance vivante ait eu lieu en Hongrie ou dans un pays étranger, et ne comprennent pas les enfants nés vivants de femmes dont la résidence habituelle est dans un pays étranger.

55 Data include the live births of women with Hungarian usual residence regardless of whether the live birth occurred in Hungary or in a foreign country, and do not include the live births of women with foreign country usual residence. - Les données concernent les enfants nés vivants de femmes dont la résidence habituelle est en Hongrie, que la naissance vivante ait eu lieu en Hongrie ou dans un pays étranger, et ne comprennent pas les enfants nés vivants de femmes dont la résidence habituelle est dans un pays étranger.

56 Data include the live births of women with Hungarian usual residence regardless of whether the live birth occurred in Hungary or in a foreign country, and do not include the live births of women with foreign country usual residence. Data include the live births of women with unknown residence and homeless. - Les données concernent les enfants nés vivants de femmes dont la résidence habituelle est en Hongrie, que la naissance vivante ait eu lieu en Hongrie ou dans un pays étranger, et ne comprennent pas les enfants nés vivants de femmes dont la résidence habituelle est dans un pays étranger. Les données incluent les enfants nés vivants de femmes dont la résidence n'est pas connue et de femmes sans domicile fixe.

57 Source: City Hall, Civil Status Registry Office, resident and non-resident births. - Source : La mairie, Bureau de l'État Civil, toutes les naissances.

58 Including residents outside the country if listed in a Netherlands population register. - Englobe les résidents se trouvant à l'étranger à condition qu'ils soient inscrits sur le registre de population des Pays-Bas.

59 Excluding Transnistria and the municipality of Bender. - Les données ne tiennent pas compte de l'information sur la Transnistria et la municipalité de Bender.

60 Excludes data for Kosovo and Metohia. - Sans les données pour le Kosovo et Metohie.

61 From 2015, urban refers to urban centers and areas under the influence of urban centers. - A partir de 2015, le territoire urbain inclut l'espace des centres urbains ainsi que l'espace sous influence des centres urbains.

62 Data refer to births with weight 500g and more (if weight is unknown - with length 25 centimeters and more, or with gestation during 22 weeks or more). - Données concernant les nouveau-nés de 500 grammes ou plus (si le poids est inconnu – de 25 centimètres de long ou plus, ou après une grossesse de 22 semaines ou plus).

63 The Government of Ukraine has informed the United Nations that it is not in a position to provide statistical data concerning the Autonomous Republic of Crimea and the city of Sevastopol. - Le gouvernement Ukrainien a informé l'ONU qu'il n'est pas en mesure de fournir des données statistiques concernant la République autonome de Crimée et la ville de Sébastopol.

64 Excluding Channel Islands (Guernsey and Jersey) and Isle of Man, shown separately. Data tabulated by date of occurrence for England and Wales, and by date of registration for Northern Ireland and Scotland. - Non compris les îles Anglo-Normandes (Guernesey et Jersey) et l'Île de Man, qui font l'objet de rubriques distinctes, si disponible. Données exploitées selon la date de l'événement pour l'Angleterre et le pays de Galles, et selon la date de l'enregistrement pour l'Irlande du Nord et l'Ecosse.

65 Urban refers to Greater Capital City Statistical Areas, and rural refers to other areas within the state or territory. Data for urban and rural figures do not add up to the total because they exclude the events occurred in Migratory, Special Purpose and Other Territories. - Urbain renvoie aux zones statistiques de la capitale métropolitaine, et rural aux autres zones de l'État ou territoire. La somme des chiffres des catégories « en zone urbaine » et « en zone rurale » ne correspond pas au total du fait qu'en sont exclus les événements qui ont eu lieu dans les territoires de migration, les territoires à destination spéciale et autres territoires.

66 Excluding Niue, shown separately, which is part of Cook Islands, but because of remoteness is administered separately. - Non compris Nioué, qui fait l'objet d'une rubrique distincte et qui fait partie des îles Cook, mais qui, en raison de son éloignement, est administrée séparément.

67 Including United States military personnel, their dependants and contract employees. - Y compris les militaires des Etats-Unis, les membres de leur famille les accompagnant et les agents contractuels des Etats-Unis.

68 Random rounding to base 3 is applied in this table as a confidentiality measure. - Les chiffres sont arrondis à la base 3 de manière aléatoire, pour des raisons de confidentialité.

69 Data refers to births registered in the country to mothers resident in the country. - Les données se rapportent aux naissances enregistrées dans le pays pour lesquelles la mère réside dans le pays.

70 Source: Commonwealth Health Center - Vital Statistics Office - Source : Centre de Santé du Commonwealth - Bureau des statistiques d'État civil

Table 10 - *Demographic Yearbook 2017*

Table 10 presents live births by age of mother and sex of the child, general fertility rate, and age-specific fertility rates for the latest available year between 2008 and 2017.

Description of variables: Age is defined as age at last birthday, that is, the difference between the date of birth and the date of the occurrence of the event, expressed in completed solar years. The age classification used in this table is the following: under 15 years, 5-year age groups through 45-49 years, and 50 years and over. A different classification may appear as provided by the reporting country or area.

Rate computation: Age-specific fertility rates are the annual number of births to women in each age group per 1 000 female population in the same age group. These rates are calculated by the Statistics Division of the United Nations.

Since relatively few births occur to women below 15 or above 50 years of age, age-specific fertility rates for women under 20 years of age and for those 45 years of age or over are computed on the female population aged 15-19 and 45-49, respectively. Similarly, the rate for women of "All ages" is based on all live births irrespective of age of mother and is computed on the female population aged 15-49 years. This rate for "All ages" is known as the general fertility rate. The age-specific fertility rates for age groups of women below 15 or 50 and above years of age are not calculated.

Births to mothers of unknown age are distributed proportionately across the age groups, by the Statistics Division of the United Nations, in accordance with the distribution of births by age of mother prior to the calculation of the rates.

The population used in computing the rates is the estimated or enumerated distribution of females by age. First priority was given to the estimated population and second priority to the enumerated population, i.e. to census returns of the year to which the births referred.

Rates presented in this table are limited to those for countries or areas having at least a total of 100 live births in a given year.

Reliability of data: Data from civil registers of live births which are reported as incomplete (less than 90 per cent completeness) or of unknown completeness are considered unreliable and are set in *italics* rather than in roman type. Rates are not computed if the data on live births from civil registers are reported as incomplete (less than 90 per cent completeness) or of unknown completeness. Table 9 and the technical notes for that table provide more detailed information on the completeness of live-birth registration. For more information about the quality of vital statistics data in general, see section 4.2 of the Technical Notes.

Limitations: Statistics on live births by age of mother are subject to the same qualifications as have been set forth for vital statistics in general and birth statistics in particular as discussed in section 4 of the Technical Notes. These include differences in the completeness of registration, the method used to determine age of mother and the quality of the reported information relating to age of mother.

The reliability of the data described above, is an important factor in considering the limitations. In addition, some live births are tabulated by date of registration and not by date of occurrence; these are indicated in the table by a plus sign "+". Whenever the lag between the date of occurrence and date of registration is prolonged and, therefore, a large proportion of the live birth registrations are delayed, birth statistics for any given year may be seriously affected. For example, the age of the mother will almost always refer to the date of registration rather than to the date of birth of the child. Hence, in those countries or areas where registration of births is delayed, possibly for years, statistics on births by age of mother should be used with caution.

Another factor which limits international comparability is the practice of some countries or areas of not including in live birth statistics infants who were born alive but died before the registration of the birth or within the first 24 hours of life, thus underestimating the total number of live births. Statistics of this type are footnoted.

Because these statistics are classified according to age, they are subject to the limitations with respect to accuracy of age reporting similar to those already discussed in connection with section 3.1.3 of the Technical Notes. The factors influencing the accuracy of reporting may be somewhat dissimilar in vital statistics (because of the differences in the method of taking a census and registering a birth) but, in general, the same errors can be observed. The absence of frequencies in the unknown age group does not necessarily indicate completely accurate reporting and tabulation of the age item. It is often an indication that the unknowns have been eliminated by assigning ages to them before tabulation, or by proportionate distribution after tabulation.

On the other hand, large frequencies in the unknown age category may indicate that a large proportion of the births are born outside of wedlock, the records for which tend to be incomplete so far as characteristics of the parents are concerned.

Another limitation of age reporting may result from calculating age of mother at birth of child (or at time of registration) from year of birth rather than from day, month and year of birth. Information on this factor is given in footnotes when known.

In few countries, data by age refer to deliveries rather than to live births causing under-enumeration in the event of a multiple birth. This practice leads to lack of strict comparability, both among countries or areas relying on this practice and between data shown in this table and table 9.

Rates shown in this table are subject to the same limitations that affect the corresponding statistics on live births. In cases of rates based on births tabulated by date of registration and not by date of occurrence; the effect of including delayed registration on the distribution of births by age of mother may be noted in the age-specific fertility rates for women at older ages. In some cases, high age-specific rates for women aged 45 years and over may reflect age of mother at registration of birth and not fertility at these older ages.

Earlier data: Live births and live-birth rates by age of mother (i.e. age-specific fertility rates), have been shown for the latest available year in each issue of the Yearbook. Information on the years and specific topics covered is presented in the Historical Index.

Tableau 10 – *Annuaire démographique 2017*

Le tableau 10 présente les données les plus récentes disponibles pour la période 2008 - 2017 sur les naissances vivantes selon l'âge de la mère et le sexe de l'enfant, le taux de fécondité et les taux de fécondité par âge.

Description des variables : l'âge désigne l'âge au dernier anniversaire, c'est-à-dire la différence entre la date de naissance et la date de l'événement exprimée en années solaires révolues. La classification par âge utilisée dans ce tableau comprend les catégories suivantes : moins de 15 ans, groupes quinquennaux jusqu'à 45-49 ans, 50 ans et plus, et âge inconnu. Des groupes d'âge différents sont parfois utilisés lorsque les pays ou territoires ont fourni les données dans une autre classification.

Les taux de fécondité par âge représentent le nombre annuel de naissances vivantes intervenues dans un groupe d'âge donné pour 1 000 femmes du groupe d'âge. Ces taux ont été calculés par la Division de statistique de l'ONU.

Étant donné que le nombre de naissances parmi les femmes de moins de 15 ans ou de plus de 50 ans est relativement peu élevé, les taux de fécondité par âge parmi les femmes âgées de moins de 20 ans et celles de 45 ans et plus ont été calculés sur la base des populations féminines âgées de 15 à 19 ans et de 45 à 49 ans, respectivement. De même, le taux pour les femmes de « tous âges » est fondé sur la totalité des naissances vivantes, indépendamment de l'âge de la mère et ce chiffre est rapporté à l'effectif de la population féminine âgée de 15 à 49 ans. Ce taux « tous âges » est le taux global de fécondité ou simplement taux de fécondité. Les taux de fécondité parmi les femmes âgées de moins de 15 ans ou celles de 50 ans et plus n'ont pas été calculés.

Les naissances pour lesquelles l'âge de la mère était inconnu ont été réparties par la Division de statistique de l'ONU, avant le calcul des taux, suivant les proportions observées pour celles où l'âge de la mère était connu.

Les chiffres de population utilisés pour le calcul des taux proviennent de dénombrements ou de répartitions estimatives de la population féminine selon l'âge. On a utilisé de préférence les estimations de la population; à défaut, on s'est contenté des données censitaires se rapportant à l'année des naissances.

Les taux présentés dans ce tableau ne concernent que les pays ou zones où l'on a enregistré un total d'au moins 100 naissances vivantes dans une année donnée.

Fiabilité des données : les données sur les naissances vivantes provenant des registres de l'état civil qui sont déclarées incomplètes (degré de complétude inférieur à 90 p. 100) ou dont le degré de complétude n'est pas connu, sont jugées douteuses et apparaissent en italique et non en caractères romains. On a choisi de ne pas faire figurer des taux calculés à partir de données sur les naissances vivantes issues de registres de l'état civil qui sont déclarées incomplètes (degré de complétude inférieur à 90 p. 100) ou dont le degré de complétude n'est pas connu. Le tableau 9 et les notes techniques qui s'y rapportent présentent des renseignements plus détaillés sur le degré de complétude de l'enregistrement des naissances vivantes. Pour plus de précisions sur la qualité des statistiques de l'état civil en général, voir la section 4.2 des Notes techniques.

Insuffisance des données : les statistiques relatives aux naissances vivantes selon l'âge de la mère appellent toutes les réserves qui ont été formulées à propos des statistiques de l'état civil en général et des statistiques de naissances en particulier (voir la section 4 des Notes techniques). Ceci inclut les différences de complétude d'enregistrement des faits d'état civil, de méthode pour déterminer l'âge de la mère et de qualité d'information concernant l'âge de la mère.

La fiabilité des données, au sujet de laquelle des indications ont été données plus haut, est un facteur important. Il faut également tenir compte du fait que, dans certains cas, les données relatives aux naissances vivantes sont exploitées selon la date de l'enregistrement et non la date de l'événement ; ces cas ont été signalés dans le tableau par le signe '+'. Chaque fois que le décalage entre l'événement et son enregistrement est grand et qu'une forte proportion des naissances vivantes fait l'objet d'un enregistrement tardif, les statistiques des naissances vivantes pour une année donnée peuvent être considérablement faussées. Par exemple, l'âge de la mère représente presque toujours son âge à la date de l'enregistrement et non à la date de la naissance de l'enfant. Ainsi, dans les pays ou zones où l'enregistrement des naissances est tardif, le retard atteignant parfois plusieurs années, il faut utiliser avec prudence les statistiques concernant les naissances selon l'âge de la mère.

Un autre facteur qui nuit à la comparabilité internationale est la pratique de certains pays ou zones qui consiste à ne pas inclure dans les statistiques des naissances vivantes les enfants nés vivants mais décédés avant l'enregistrement de leur naissance ou dans les 24 heures qui ont suivi la naissance, pratique qui conduit à sous-estimer le nombre total de naissances vivantes. Quand pareil facteur a joué, cela a été signalé en note à la fin du tableau.

Étant donné que les statistiques du tableau 10 sont classées selon l'âge, elles appellent les mêmes réserves concernant l'exactitude des déclarations d'âge que celles formulées à la section 3.1.3 des Notes techniques. Dans le cas des statistiques de l'état civil, les facteurs qui interviennent à cet égard sont parfois différents, étant donné que le recensement de la population et l'enregistrement des naissances se font par des méthodes différentes, mais, d'une manière générale, les erreurs observées seront les mêmes. Si aucun nombre ne figure dans la rangée réservée aux âges inconnus, cela ne signifie pas nécessairement que les déclarations d'âge et l'exploitation des données par âge ont été tout à fait exactes. C'est souvent une indication que l'on a attribué un âge aux personnes d'âge inconnu avant l'exploitation des données ou qu'elles ont été réparties proportionnellement entre les différents groupes après cette opération.

À l'inverse, lorsque le nombre des personnes d'âge inconnu est important, cela peut signifier que la proportion de naissances parmi les mères célibataires est élevée, étant donné qu'en pareil cas l'acte de naissance ne contient pas tous les renseignements concernant les parents.

Les déclarations par âge peuvent comporter des distorsions, du fait que l'âge de la mère au moment de la naissance d'un enfant (ou de la déclaration de naissance) est donné par année de naissance et non par date exacte (jour, mois et année).

Dans quelques pays, la classification par âges se réfère aux accouchements, et non aux naissances vivantes, ce qui conduit à un sous-dénombrement en cas de naissances gémellaires. Cette pratique nuit à la comparabilité des données, à la fois entre pays ou zones qui recourent à cette méthode et entre les données présentées dans le tableau 10 et celles du tableau 9.

Les taux présentés dans ce tableau sont sujets aux mêmes limitations qui affectent les statistiques correspondantes de naissances vivantes. Dans le cas des taux basés sur des naissances par date d'enregistrement et non par date d'occurrence, l'effet peut être visible sur les taux de fécondité par âge des femmes aux âges plus élevés. Dans certains cas, les taux de fécondité des femmes de plus de 45 ans peuvent refléter l'âge de la mère à l'enregistrement plus que la fécondité à ces âges.

Données publiées antérieurement : les différentes éditions de l'*Annuaire démographique* regroupent les dernières statistiques dont on disposait à l'époque sur les naissances vivantes selon l'âge de la mère et les taux des naissances vivantes selon l'âge de la mère (taux de fécondité par âge). Pour plus de précisions concernant les années pour lesquels des données ont été publiées, se reporter à l'index historique.

10. Live births by age of mother and sex of child, general and age-specific fertility rates: latest available year, 2008 - 2017
Naissances vivantes selon l'âge de la mère et le sexe de l'enfant, taux de fécondité et taux de fécondité par âge : dernière année disponible, 2008 - 2017

Continent, country or area, year, code[a] and age of mother (in years) Continent, pays ou zone, année, code[a] et âge de la mère (en années)	Number - Nombre			Rate Taux
	Total	Male Masculin	Female Féminin	

AFRICA - AFRIQUE

Botswana
2014 (U)[1]
Total	41 741	21 142	20 599	..
0 - 14	30	13	17	..
15 - 19	3 839	1 949	1 890	..
20 - 24	11 268	5 752	5 516	..
25 - 29	10 767	5 441	5 326	...
30 - 34	9 047	4 575	4 472	...
35 - 39	4 813	2 434	2 379	...
40 - 44	1 475	728	747	...
45 - 49	128	63	65	...
50 +	12	5	7	...
Unknown - Inconnu	362	182	180	..

2016 (U)[2]
Total	49 984	...	...	..
10 - 14	35	...	...	..
15 - 19	4 678	...	...	..
20 - 24	13 776	...	...	..
25 - 29	12 383	...	...	..
30 - 34	10 510	...	...	..
35 - 39	5 916	...	...	..
40 - 44	1 895	...	...	..
45 - 49	125	...	...	..
50 +	13	...	...	..
Unknown - Inconnu	653	...	...	..

Côte d'Ivoire
2014 (|)
Total	841 081	426 128	414 953	154.0
0 - 14	3 653	1 875	1 778	..
15 - 19	77 375	39 411	37 964	74.5
20 - 24	192 965	97 499	95 466	178.1
25 - 29	221 215	112 113	109 102	210.1
30 - 34	183 792	92 806	90 986	213.2
35 - 39	105 637	53 532	52 105	171.7
40 - 44	40 638	20 721	19 917	91.0
45 +	15 806	8 171	7 635	43.7

Egypt - Égypte
2012 (+C)
Total	2 629 769	1 343 402	1 286 367	121.1
0 - 19	71 275	36 022	35 253	23.8
20 - 24	1 298 851	665 452	633 399	403.8
25 - 29	399 915	201 967	197 948	127.5
30 - 34	223 307	111 754	111 553	86.0
35 - 39	83 362	41 121	42 241	41.3
40 - 44	21 510	11 229	10 281	12.2
45 +	3 802	2 233	1 569	2.3
Unknown - Inconnu	527 747	273 624	254 123	..

Ghana[3]
2010 (|)
Total	623 700	306 159	317 541	98.1
0 - 14	917	381	536	..
15 - 19	40 307	19 067	21 240	31.0
20 - 24	126 417	61 277	65 140	103.4
25 - 29	167 306	82 741	84 565	151.1
30 - 34	130 724	64 600	66 124	147.1
35 - 39	92 751	46 285	46 466	124.6
40 - 44	41 898	20 783	21 115	68.3
45 - 49	14 742	7 071	7 671	30.4
50 +	8 638	3 954	4 684	..

Guinea - Guinée[4]
2014 (|)
Total	416 607	204 309	212 298	161.9
0 - 14	3 494	1 728	1 766	..
15 - 19	62 085	30 684	31 401	105.6
20 - 24	96 498	47 687	48 811	194.3

Guinea - Guinée[4]
2014 (|)
25 - 29	101 210	49 832	51 378	227.6
30 - 34	72 323	35 456	36 867	204.4
35 - 39	44 261	21 594	22 667	155.4
40 - 44	21 347	10 144	11 203	90.0
45 - 49	9 266	4 348	4 918	54.9
50 +	6 123	2 839	3 284	..

Kenya
2009 (U)
Total	691 312	354 154	337 158	...
0 - 14	3 877	2 019	1 858	...
15 - 19	89 664	45 562	44 102	...
20 - 24	221 828	113 572	108 256	...
25 - 29	174 571	89 674	84 897	...
30 - 34	103 940	53 395	50 545	...
35 - 39	49 527	25 424	24 103	...
40 - 44	13 231	6 713	6 518	...
45 - 49	2 165	1 097	1 068	...
50 +	823	423	400	...
Unknown - Inconnu	31 686	16 275	15 411	...

2012 (U)[5]
Total	754 429	...	...	...
0 - 14	3 047	...	...	...
15 - 19	90 928	...	...	...
20 - 24	234 290	...	...	...
25 - 29	204 221	...	...	...
30 - 34	122 883	...	...	...
35 - 39	64 386	...	...	...
40 - 44	16 674	...	...	...
45 - 49	2 975	...	...	...
50 +	560	...	...	...
Unknown - Inconnu	14 462	...	...	...

Lesotho
2012 (+U)
Total	1 718	...	...	...
10 - 14	97	...	...	...
15 - 19	96	...	...	...
20 - 24	378	...	...	...
25 - 29	506	...	...	...
30 - 34	409	...	...	...
35 - 39	183	...	...	...
40 - 44	42	...	...	...
45 +	7	...	...	...

Liberia - Libéria[6]
2008 (|)
Total	63 171	33 511	29 660	73.1
12 - 14	304	157	147	..
15 - 19	6 973	3 668	3 305	37.4
20 - 24	16 181	8 486	7 695	89.4
25 - 29	14 915	8 017	6 898	98.9
30 - 34	10 277	5 433	4 844	91.5
35 - 39	8 336	4 374	3 962	79.8
40 - 44	3 961	2 138	1 823	53.5
45 - 49	2 224	1 238	986	40.5

Libya - Libye[7]
2009 (+U)
Total	134 682	...	...	...
0 - 19	733	...	...	...
20 - 24	7 067	...	...	...
25 - 29	17 792	...	...	...
30 - 34	18 491	...	...	...
35 - 39	9 801	...	...	...
40 - 44	3 334	...	...	...

10. Live births by age of mother and sex of child, general and age-specific fertility rates: latest available year, 2008 - 2017
Naissances vivantes selon l'âge de la mère et le sexe de l'enfant, taux de fécondité et taux de fécondité par âge : dernière année disponible, 2008 - 2017 (continued - suite)

Continent, country or area, year, code[a] and age of mother (in years) / Continent, pays ou zone, année, code[a] et âge de la mère (en années)	Number - Nombre			Rate Taux
	Total	Male Masculin	Female Féminin	

AFRICA - AFRIQUE

	Total	Male Masculin	Female Féminin	Rate Taux
Libya - Libye[7]				
2009 (+U)				
45 +	409	...	...	...
Unknown - Inconnu	77 055	...	...	..
Malawi[8]				
2008 (I)				
Total	516 629	247 753	268 876	160.1
12 - 14	1 621	751	870	..
15 - 19	70 737	34 137	36 600	101.2
20 - 24	169 406	81 379	88 027	284.1
25 - 29	130 331	62 810	67 521	241.6
30 - 34	79 232	37 758	41 474	153.2
35 - 39	43 747	20 776	22 971	116.8
40 - 44	15 956	7 553	8 403	57.8
45 - 49	5 599	2 589	3 010	25.0
Mali[9]				
2009 (I)				
Total	666 216	324 862	341 354	208.9
12 - 14	34 953	17 432	17 521	..
15 - 19	97 788	47 793	49 995	124.8
20 - 24	138 189	67 575	70 614	225.7
25 - 29	140 359	68 914	71 445	256.8
30 - 34	108 467	52 837	55 630	253.5
35 - 39	74 059	35 667	38 392	226.6
40 - 44	45 402	21 748	23 654	164.9
45 +	26 999	12 896	14 103	124.3
Mauritania - Mauritanie[10]				
2013 (I)				
Total	114 420	...	...	137.6
15 - 19	14 258	...	...	77.0
20 - 24	34 153	...	...	216.2
25 - 29	31 533	...	...	232.3
30 - 34	20 082	...	...	176.6
35 - 39	10 479	...	...	109.9
40 - 44	3 421	...	...	43.2
45 - 49	493	...	...	7.6
Mauritius - Maurice[11]				
2017 (+C)				
Total	13 385	6 809	6 576	41.8
10 - 14	32	18	14	..
15 - 19	1 133	581	552	23.8
20 - 24	2 793	1 422	1 371	57.2
25 - 29	4 110	2 094	2 016	89.5
30 - 34	3 126	1 589	1 537	74.8
35 - 39	1 733	871	862	35.0
40 - 44	346	175	171	8.1
45 - 49	25	10	15	♦0.6
50 +	4	1	3	..
Unknown - Inconnu	83	48	35	..
Namibia - Namibie[12]				
2011 (I)				
Total	61 523	30 560	30 963	110.8
0 - 14	873	443	430	..
15 - 19	7 593	3 723	3 870	62.5
20 - 24	16 655	8 235	8 420	152.3
25 - 29	14 296	7 109	7 187	157.7
30 - 34	11 017	5 632	5 385	145.3
35 - 39	7 237	3 531	3 706	113.0
40 - 44	2 982	1 451	1 531	58.4
45 +	870	436	434	20.2
Saint Helena ex. dep. - Sainte-Hélène sans dép.				
2014 (C)				
Total	48	25	23	...
0 - 14	-	-	-	..

	Total	Male Masculin	Female Féminin	Rate Taux
Saint Helena ex. dep. - Sainte-Hélène sans dép.				
2014 (C)				
15 - 19	8	6	2	...
20 - 24	6	2	4	...
25 - 29	8	5	3	...
30 - 34	19	8	11	...
35 - 39	5	3	2	...
40 - 44	2	1	1	...
45 - 49	-	-	-	...
50 +	-	-	-	...
Unknown - Inconnu	-	-	-	...
Seychelles				
2015 (+C)				
Total	1 592	814	778	66.2
0 - 14	5	3	2	..
15 - 19	187	89	98	69.9
20 - 24	420	211	209	136.0
25 - 29	406	209	197	130.7
30 - 34	325	176	149	78.7
35 - 39	189	99	90	50.0
40 - 44	56	25	31	15.3
45 - 49	4	2	2	♦1.1
50 +	-	-	-	..
2017 (+C)				
Total	1 651	...	...	77.3
0 - 14	3	...	...	..
15 - 19	201	...	...	98.9
20 - 24	458	...	...	307.0
25 - 29	429	...	...	165.6
30 - 34	316	...	...	95.5
35 - 39	190	...	...	42.1
40 - 44	51	...	...	15.3
45 +	3	...	...	♦0.7
South Africa - Afrique du Sud				
2016 (C)				
Total	876 435	442 301	434 134	57.4
0 - 14	1 444	...	...	..
10 - 14	1 444	748	696	..
15 - 19	107 730	54 395	53 335	44.5
20 - 24	225 847	114 144	111 703	85.2
25 - 29	226 996	114 553	112 443	83.5
30 - 34	184 962	93 288	91 674	79.5
35 - 39	97 218	49 024	48 194	48.3
40 - 44	29 298	14 717	14 581	17.5
45 - 49	1 932	958	974	1.3
50 +	110	55	55	..
Unknown - Inconnu	898	419	479	..
Tunisia - Tunisie				
2016 (C)				
Total	219 441	...	...	...
15 - 19	1 948	...	...	...
20 - 24	18 400	...	...	...
25 - 29	39 120	...	...	...
30 - 34	40 213	...	...	...
35 - 39	23 442	...	...	...
40 - 44	6 277	...	...	...
45 +	345	...	...	...
Unknown - Inconnu	89 697	...	...	...
Zambia - Zambie[13]				
2010 (I)				
Total	442 998	224 756	218 242	141.4
12 - 14	921	470	451	..
15 - 19	58 999	29 701	29 298	75.4
20 - 24	128 270	65 048	63 222	200.0

10. Live births by age of mother and sex of child, general and age-specific fertility rates: latest available year, 2008 - 2017
Naissances vivantes selon l'âge de la mère et le sexe de l'enfant, taux de fécondité et taux de fécondité par âge : dernière année disponible, 2008 - 2017 (continued - suite)

Continent, country or area, year, code[a] and age of mother (in years) / Continent, pays ou zone, année, code[a] et âge de la mère (en années)	Total	Male Masculin	Female Féminin	Rate Taux
AFRICA - AFRIQUE				
Zambia - Zambie[13]				
2010 (|)				
25 - 29	114 701	58 366	56 335	205.1
30 - 34	74 066	37 666	36 400	178.4
35 - 39	45 452	23 072	22 380	139.5
40 - 44	16 150	8 181	7 969	72.5
45 - 49	4 439	2 252	2 187	23.7
AMERICA, NORTH - AMÉRIQUE DU NORD				
Aruba				
2017 (C)				
Total	1 202	642	560	45.6
10 - 14	1	1	-	..
15 - 19	94	50	44	26.1
20 - 24	300	154	146	93.7
25 - 29	338	180	158	104.0
30 - 34	274	143	131	76.3
35 - 39	156	94	62	39.4
40 - 44	35	19	16	8.6
45 - 49	4	1	3	♦0.8
Bahamas				
2012 (+U)				
Total	4 469	2 279	2 187	...
0 - 14	4	2	2	..
15 - 19	497	261	236	...
20 - 24	1 028	524	504	...
25 - 29	1 123	580	543	...
30 - 34	972	496	476	...
35 - 39	632	318	314	...
40 - 44	193	91	102	...
45 - 49	15	5	10	...
50 +	1	1	-	..
Unknown - Inconnu	1	1	-	..
Belize				
2016 (U)				
Total	7 200	3 615	3 585	...
0 - 14	20	11	9	...
15 - 19	1 337	653	684	...
20 - 24	2 323	1 171	1 152	...
25 - 29	1 780	924	856	...
30 - 34	1 054	524	530	...
35 - 39	543	260	283	...
40 - 44	129	65	64	...
45 - 49	14	7	7	...
50 +	-	-	-	...
Unknown - Inconnu	-	-	-	..
Bermuda - Bermudes[14]				
2016 (C)				
Total	591	303	288	43.1
0 - 14	-	-	-	..
15 - 19	12	7	5	♦8.2
20 - 24	57	30	27	36.1
25 - 29	131	68	63	70.1
30 - 34	193	101	92	92.3
35 - 39	149	75	74	70.1
40 - 44	46	20	26	21.3
45 - 49	3	2	1	♦1.2
50 +	-	-	-	..
British Virgin Islands - Îles Vierges britanniques				
2015 (C)				
Total	266	...	...	...
13 - 19	22	...	...	...

Continent, country or area, year, code[a] and age of mother (in years) / Continent, pays ou zone, année, code[a] et âge de la mère (en années)	Total	Male Masculin	Female Féminin	Rate Taux
AMERICA, NORTH - AMÉRIQUE DU NORD				
British Virgin Islands - Îles Vierges britanniques				
2015 (C)				
20 - 24	54	...	...	...
25 - 29	64	...	...	...
30 - 34	64	...	...	...
35 - 39	45	...	...	...
40 +	15	...	...	...
Unknown - Inconnu	2	...	...	...
Canada[15]				
2009 (C)				
Total	380 863	195 445	185 418	46.0
0 - 14	104	52	52	..
15 - 19	15 534	7 997	7 537	14.1
20 - 24	57 778	29 564	28 214	51.2
25 - 29	116 878	60 099	56 779	100.7
30 - 34	120 734	62 132	58 602	107.0
35 - 39	57 733	29 493	28 240	50.6
40 - 44	11 364	5 720	5 644	9.2
45 - 49	605	316	289	0.4
Unknown - Inconnu[16]	133	72	61	..
2016 (C)				
Total	383 102	...	...	46.0
10 - 14	62	...	...	..
15 - 19	8 459	...	...	8.4
20 - 24	45 143	...	...	37.6
25 - 29	109 544	...	...	87.6
30 - 34	136 593	...	...	107.6
35 - 39	68 906	...	...	56.0
40 - 44	13 506	...	...	11.5
45 - 49	834	...	...	0.7
Unknown - Inconnu[16]	55	...	...	..
Cayman Islands - Îles Caïmanes				
2014 (C)				
Total	710	...	...	...
15 - 19	35	...	...	...
20 - 24	129	...	...	...
25 - 29	140	...	...	...
30 - 34	210	...	...	...
35 - 39	142	...	...	...
40 - 44	51	...	...	...
45 - 49	3	...	...	...
Costa Rica				
2017* (C)				
Total	68 816	35 431	33 385	52.3
10 - 14	301	175	126	..
15 - 19	9 849	5 068	4 781	46.7
20 - 24	18 390	9 480	8 910	89.5
25 - 29	17 943	9 300	8 643	90.3
30 - 34	13 969	7 122	6 847	70.9
35 - 39	6 789	3 455	3 334	38.8
40 - 44	1 468	777	691	8.9
45 - 49	76	38	38	0.5
50 +	3	-	3	..
Unknown - Inconnu	28	16	12	..
Cuba				
2016 (C)				
Total	116 872	60 918	55 954	42.9
0 - 14	377	193	184	..
15 - 19	16 725	8 630	8 095	48.9
20 - 24	33 918	17 556	16 362	96.8
25 - 29	35 597	18 687	16 910	90.1
30 - 34	19 841	10 432	9 409	57.2
35 - 39	7 977	4 153	3 824	24.9

10. Live births by age of mother and sex of child, general and age-specific fertility rates: latest available year, 2008 - 2017
Naissances vivantes selon l'âge de la mère et le sexe de l'enfant, taux de fécondité et taux de fécondité par âge : dernière année disponible, 2008 - 2017 (continued - suite)

Continent, country or area, year, code[a] and age of mother (in years) / Continent, pays ou zone, année, code[a] et âge de la mère (en années)	Total	Male Masculin	Female Féminin	Rate Taux
AMERICA, NORTH - AMÉRIQUE DU NORD				
Cuba				
2016 (C)				
40 - 44	2 271	1 178	1 093	4.9
45 - 49	113	57	56	0.2
50 +	43	26	17	..
Unknown - Inconnu	10	6	4	..
Curaçao				
2016 (C)				
Total	1 789	901	888	47.8
0 - 14	4	2	2	..
15 - 19	113	64	49	22.9
20 - 24	417	202	215	91.6
25 - 29	465	233	232	98.2
30 - 34	421	211	210	82.8
35 - 39	255	136	119	49.9
40 - 44	65	33	32	11.2
45 - 49	6	2	4	♦0.9
50 +	-	-	-	..
Unknown - Inconnu	43	18	25	..
2017 (C)				
Total	1 548	...	...	41.6
0 - 19	115	...	...	23.9
20 - 24	341	...	...	75.3
25 - 29	413	...	...	87.6
30 - 34	386	...	...	75.3
35 - 39	203	...	...	39.4
40 +	50	...	...	4.2
Unknown - Inconnu	40	...	...	..
Dominican Republic - République dominicaine				
2016 (U)				
Total	139 583	71 871	67 712	...
10 - 14	604	324	280	..
15 - 19	22 326	11 535	10 791	...
20 - 24	41 553	21 476	20 077	...
25 - 29	36 571	18 794	17 777	...
30 - 34	22 682	11 675	11 007	...
35 - 39	10 400	5 281	5 119	...
40 - 44	2 056	1 028	1 028	...
45 - 49	178	99	79	...
50 +	62	31	31	..
Unknown - Inconnu	3 151	1 628	1 523	..
El Salvador[17]				
2015 (C)				
Total	109 617	56 757	52 860	58.9
0 - 14	923	466	457	..
15 - 19	23 452	12 226	11 226	67.2
20 - 24	32 224	16 716	15 508	94.1
25 - 29	24 090	12 451	11 639	82.7
30 - 34	17 103	8 802	8 301	68.5
35 - 39	8 891	4 564	4 327	39.2
40 - 44	2 333	1 205	1 128	11.1
45 - 49	171	96	75	0.9
50 +	45	17	28	..
Unknown - Inconnu	385	214	171	..
Greenland - Groenland				
2017 (C)				
Total	853	448	405	65.1
10 - 14	-	-	-	..
15 - 19	72	39	33	37.9
20 - 24	213	109	104	99.8
25 - 29	272	146	126	120.7
30 - 34	204	103	101	101.7
35 - 39	81	46	35	47.8

Continent, country or area, year, code[a] and age of mother (in years) / Continent, pays ou zone, année, code[a] et âge de la mère (en années)	Total	Male Masculin	Female Féminin	Rate Taux
AMERICA, NORTH - AMÉRIQUE DU NORD				
Greenland - Groenland				
2017 (C)				
40 - 44	11	5	6	♦8.3
45 - 49	-	-	-	..
Grenada - Grenade				
2014 (+C)				
Total	1 750	900	850	62.8
10 - 14	4	1	3	..
15 - 19	169	91	78	35.9
20 - 24	481	252	229	101.2
25 - 29	500	257	243	103.1
30 - 34	351	179	172	88.9
35 - 39	166	85	81	52.3
40 - 44	50	24	26	16.8
45 - 49	5	2	3	♦1.6
Unknown - Inconnu	24	9	15	..
Guatemala				
2011 (C)				
Total	373 692	189 724	183 968	102.4
0 - 14	2 841	1 426	1 415	..
15 - 19	75 175	38 415	36 760	92.4
20 - 24	108 949	55 558	53 391	157.0
25 - 29	85 914	43 599	42 315	142.0
30 - 34	58 050	29 264	28 786	113.4
35 - 39	30 892	15 540	15 352	73.8
40 - 44	10 220	5 136	5 084	30.5
45 - 49	1 176	573	603	4.4
50 +	290	127	163	..
Unknown - Inconnu	185	86	99	..
2016 (C)				
Total	390 382	...	...	...
10 - 14	2 138	...	...	...
15 - 19	71 903	...	...	...
20 - 24	118 747	...	...	...
25 - 29	91 918	...	...	...
30 - 34	61 247	...	...	...
35 - 39	33 894	...	...	...
40 - 44	9 687	...	...	...
45 - 49	682	...	...	...
50 +	65	...	...	...
Unknown - Inconnu	101	...	...	...
Honduras				
2012 (+U)				
Total	196 119	...	...	...
0 - 14	1 571	...	...	...
15 - 19	41 882	...	...	...
20 - 24	56 501	...	...	...
25 - 29	43 429	...	...	...
30 - 34	28 675	...	...	...
35 - 39	14 730	...	...	...
40 - 44	4 791	...	...	...
45 - 49	575	...	...	...
50 +	471	...	...	...
Unknown - Inconnu	3 494	...	...	...
Jamaica - Jamaïque[18]				
2011 (I)				
Total	49 676	23 949[19]	23 339[19]	66.0
15 - 19	6 167	3 034[19]	2 884[19]	50.5
20 - 24	13 977	6 852[19]	6 451[19]	129.9
25 - 29	12 348	5 923[19]	5 900[19]	108.7
30 - 34	8 746	4 182[19]	4 145[19]	73.9
35 - 39	6 001	2 816[19]	2 875[19]	48.9
40 - 44	2 109	1 014[19]	956[19]	21.2
45 - 49	328	128[19]	128[19]	4.8

10. Live births by age of mother and sex of child, general and age-specific fertility rates: latest available year, 2008 - 2017
Naissances vivantes selon l'âge de la mère et le sexe de l'enfant, taux de fécondité et taux de fécondité par âge : dernière année disponible, 2008 - 2017 (continued - suite)

Continent, country or area, year, code[a] and age of mother (in years) / Continent, pays ou zone, année, code[a] et âge de la mère (en années)	Total	Male Masculin	Female Féminin	Rate Taux
AMERICA, NORTH - AMÉRIQUE DU NORD				
Mexico - Mexique[20]				
2015 (C)				
Total	2 096 274	1 068 348[19]	1 027 913[19]	62.8
10 - 14	7 204	3 678[19]	3 526[19]	..
15 - 19	360 457	184 688[19]	175 765[19]	65.4
20 - 24	635 796	324 826[19]	310 967[19]	117.9
25 - 29	520 558	265 023[19]	255 532[19]	103.2
30 - 34	352 681	178 858[19]	173 821[19]	73.8
35 - 39	169 705	86 021[19]	83 683[19]	37.0
40 - 44	41 512	21 098[19]	20 414[19]	9.8
45 - 49	2 723	1 357[19]	1 366[19]	0.7
50 +	450	196[19]	254[19]	..
Unknown - Inconnu	5 188	2 603[19]	2 585[19]	..
Montserrat				
2016 (C)				
Total	46	23	23	...
0 - 14	-	-	-	..
15 - 19	2	-	2	...
20 - 24	10	5	5	...
25 - 29	11	7	4	...
30 - 34	11	6	5	...
35 - 39	8	4	4	...
40 - 44	4	1	3	...
45 - 49	-	-	-	..
50 +	-	-	-	..
Nicaragua				
2010 (+U)				
Total	132 165	68 726	63 439	...
0 - 14	1 539	793	746	..
15 - 19	33 963	17 752	16 211	...
20 - 24	38 897	20 181	18 716	...
25 - 29	30 273	15 790	14 483	...
30 - 34	17 301	8 942	8 359	...
35 - 39	8 010	4 156	3 854	...
40 - 44	1 943	992	951	...
45 - 49	209	105	104	...
50 +	30	15	15	...
Panama				
2016* (C)				
Total	75 184	38 996	36 188	72.2
10 - 14	506	268	238	..
15 - 19	13 519	7 108	6 411	78.8
20 - 24	21 113	10 922	10 191	130.8
25 - 29	17 942	9 292	8 650	115.8
30 - 34	13 263	6 868	6 395	88.8
35 - 39	6 968	3 596	3 372	48.7
40 - 44	1 752	882	870	12.8
45 - 49	94	49	45	0.8
50 +	11	5	6	..
Unknown - Inconnu	16	6	10	..
Puerto Rico - Porto Rico				
2017 (C)				
Total	24 370	12 539	11 831	..
10 - 14	27	13	14	..
15 - 19	2 652	1 352	1 300	..
20 - 24	7 999	4 128	3 871	..
25 - 29	6 670	3 421	3 249	...
30 - 34	4 327	2 267	2 060	...
35 - 39	2 171	1 090	1 081	...
40 - 44	504	257	247	...
45 - 49	19	10	9	...
50 +	1	1	-	...

Continent, country or area, year, code[a] and age of mother (in years) / Continent, pays ou zone, année, code[a] et âge de la mère (en années)	Total	Male Masculin	Female Féminin	Rate Taux
AMERICA, NORTH - AMÉRIQUE DU NORD				
Saint Vincent and the Grenadines - Saint-Vincent-et-les Grenadines				
2014 (C)				
Total	1 841	912	929	65.9
0 - 14	10	4	6	..
15 - 19	312	162	150	64.1
20 - 24	476	240	236	111.7
25 - 29	426	194	232	103.9
30 - 34	332	170	162	83.3
35 - 39	214	113	101	57.5
40 - 44	67	27	40	19.8
45 - 49	4	2	2	♦1.1
50 +	-	-	-	..
Unknown - Inconnu	-	-	-	..
Trinidad and Tobago - Trinité-et-Tobago				
2009 (C)				
Total	17 949	9 067	8 882	...
0 - 14	24	10	14	..
15 - 19	1 961	961	1 000	...
20 - 24	5 029	2 620	2 409	...
25 - 29	5 258	2 606	2 652	...
30 - 34	3 422	1 715	1 707	...
35 - 39	1 763	910	853	...
40 - 44	432	218	214	...
45 - 49	31	13	18	...
50 +	3	1	2	..
Unknown - Inconnu	26	13	13	..
Turks and Caicos Islands - Îles Turques et Caïques				
2016 (C)				
Total	518	272	246	44.7
0 - 14	-	-	-	..
15 - 19	31	17	14	27.3
20 - 24	79	47	32	58.8
25 - 29	117	55	62	73.6
30 - 34	141	77	64	77.5
35 - 39	116	54	62	57.4
40 - 44	26	19	7	♦13.9
45 - 49	-	-	-	..
50 +	-	-	-	..
Unknown - Inconnu	8	3	5	..
United States of America - États-Unis d'Amérique				
2015 (C)				
Total	3 978 497	2 036 161	1 942 336	53.7
0 - 14	2 500	1 265	1 235	..
15 - 19	229 715	118 021	111 694	22.3
20 - 24	850 509	435 461	415 048	76.8
25 - 29	1 152 311	589 719	562 592	104.3
30 - 34	1 094 693	560 429	534 264	101.5
35 - 39	527 996	269 784	258 212	51.8
40 - 44	111 848	56 922	54 926	11.0
45 - 49	8 171	4 172	3 999	0.8
50 +	754	388	366	..
Unknown - Inconnu	-	-	-	..

10. Live births by age of mother and sex of child, general and age-specific fertility rates: latest available year, 2008 - 2017
Naissances vivantes selon l'âge de la mère et le sexe de l'enfant, taux de fécondité et taux de fécondité par âge : dernière année disponible, 2008 - 2017 (continued - suite)

Continent, country or area, year, code[a] and age of mother (in years) / Continent, pays ou zone, année, code[a] et âge de la mère (en années)	Total	Number - Nombre Male Masculin	Number - Nombre Female Féminin	Rate Taux
AMERICA, SOUTH - AMÉRIQUE DU SUD				
Argentina - Argentine				
2016 (C)				
Total	728 035	374 921[19]	352 877[19]	66.2
0 - 14	2 419	1 255[19]	1 161[19]	..
15 - 19	96 905	50 190[19]	46 696[19]	56.4
20 - 24	178 069	91 783[19]	86 229[19]	101.6
25 - 29	170 356	87 901[19]	82 408[19]	101.4
30 - 34	149 478	76 686[19]	72 750[19]	94.4
35 - 39	96 943	49 621[19]	47 299[19]	61.8
40 +	27 215	13 977[19]	13 228[19]	10.5
Unknown - Inconnu	6 650	3 508[19]	3 106[19]	..
Brazil - Brésil				
2016 (C)				
Total	2 803 080	1 435 631[19]	1 367 157[19]	49.9
0 - 14	20 991	10 790[19]	10 198[19]	..
15 - 19	456 140	234 758[19]	221 337[19]	54.3
20 - 24	704 866	361 286[19]	343 512[19]	84.0
25 - 29	668 741	342 911[19]	325 780[19]	79.1
30 - 34	561 136	286 979[19]	274 115[19]	63.8
35 - 39	303 329	154 510[19]	148 794[19]	37.3
40 - 44	71 208	35 987[19]	35 216[19]	9.9
45 - 49	4 265	2 135[19]	2 130[19]	0.6
50 +	343	170[19]	173[19]	..
Unknown - Inconnu	12 061	6 105[19]	5 902[19]	..
Chile - Chili				
2015 (C)				
Total	244 670	124 713[19]	119 936[19]	52.5
10 - 14	717	365[19]	351[19]	..
15 - 19	25 448	12 980[19]	12 465[19]	39.3
20 - 24	54 261	27 746[19]	26 511[19]	75.7
25 - 29	63 210	32 318[19]	30 889[19]	85.3
30 - 34	57 373	29 123[19]	28 245[19]	85.1
35 - 39	33 596	17 013[19]	16 579[19]	54.1
40 - 44	9 545	4 889[19]	4 655[19]	15.3
45 - 49	491	264[19]	227[19]	0.8
50 +	13	8[19]	5[19]	..
Unknown - Inconnu	16	7[19]	9[19]	..
Colombia - Colombie				
2016 (U)				
Total	647 521	332 824[19]	314 617[19]	...
10 - 14	5 551	2 892[19]	2 657[19]	..
15 - 19	130 235	67 241[19]	62 983[19]	...
20 - 24	188 578	96 775[19]	91 781[19]	...
25 - 29	151 065	77 897[19]	73 147[19]	...
30 - 34	103 968	53 224[19]	50 731[19]	...
35 - 39	53 945	27 553[19]	26 384[19]	...
40 - 44	12 849	6 575[19]	6 271[19]	...
45 - 49	1 052	514[19]	538[19]	...
50 +	156	85[19]	71[19]	..
Unknown - Inconnu	122	68[19]	54[19]	..
Ecuador - Équateur[21]				
2016* (U)				
Total	266 464	135 868	130 596	...
10 - 14	2 115	1 085	1 030	..
15 - 19	51 763	26 398	25 365	...
20 - 24	71 439	36 569	34 870	...
25 - 29	62 072	31 701	30 371	...
30 - 34	46 698	23 791	22 907	...
35 - 39	25 097	12 655	12 442	...
40 - 44	6 739	3 402	3 337	...
45 - 49	494	247	247	...
50 +	-	-	-	..
Unknown - Inconnu	47	20	27	..
AMERICA, SOUTH - AMÉRIQUE DU SUD				
Guyana[3]				
2012 (|)				
Total	13 023	...	...	65.5
15 - 19	2 082	...	...	49.5
20 - 24	3 939	...	...	123.4
25 - 29	2 918	...	...	109.8
30 - 34	2 304	...	...	85.3
35 - 39	1 347	...	...	51.8
40 - 44	397	...	...	16.7
45 - 49	36	...	...	1.7
Paraguay				
2008 (+U)				
Total	99 674	51 066	48 608	...
0 - 14	538	269	269	..
15 - 19	20 188	10 404	9 784	..
20 - 24	28 246	14 396	13 850	..
25 - 29	23 863	12 261	11 602	..
30 - 34	14 721	7 480	7 241	..
35 - 39	8 899	4 600	4 299	..
40 - 44	2 819	1 440	1 379	..
45 - 49	250	134	116	..
50 +	2	2	-	..
Unknown - Inconnu	148	80	68	..
2016 (+U)[22]				
Total	122 336	...	...	...
10 - 14	215	...	...	..
15 - 19	15 391	...	...	...
20 - 24	32 373	...	...	...
25 - 29	30 646	...	...	...
30 - 34	22 502	...	...	...
35 - 39	11 900	...	...	...
40 - 44	3 863	...	...	...
45 - 49	776	...	...	...
50 +	253	...	...	...
Unknown - Inconnu	4 417	...	...	...
Peru - Pérou[23]				
2016* (+U)				
Total	522 266	267 339	254 927	...
10 - 14	1 385	727	658	..
15 - 19	62 634	32 046	30 588	...
20 - 24	128 303	65 922	62 381	...
25 - 29	125 321	64 037	61 284	...
30 - 34	106 661	54 634	52 027	...
35 - 39	70 334	35 883	34 451	...
40 - 44	25 411	12 941	12 470	...
45 - 49	2 124	1 097	1 027	...
50 +	92	51	41	..
Unknown - Inconnu	1	1	-	..
Suriname				
2016 (C)				
Total	9 910	5 167	4 743	67.0
10 - 14	42	...	...	..
15 - 19	1 408	...	...	59.6
20 - 24	2 486	...	...	108.0
25 - 29	2 533	...	...	113.3
30 - 34	2 059	...	...	96.3
35 - 39	1 088	...	...	53.6
40 - 44	276	...	...	14.4
45 - 49	18	...	...	♦1.0
50 +	-	...	...	..
Unknown - Inconnu	-	...	...	..
Uruguay				
2016 (C)				
Total	47 058	24 247[19]	22 806[19]	55.1
10 - 14	120	57[19]	63[19]	..

10. Live births by age of mother and sex of child, general and age-specific fertility rates: latest available year, 2008 - 2017
Naissances vivantes selon l'âge de la mère et le sexe de l'enfant, taux de fécondité et taux de fécondité par âge : dernière année disponible, 2008 - 2017 (continued - suite)

Continent, country or area, year, code[a] and age of mother (in years) — Continent, pays ou zone, année, code[a] et âge de la mère (en années)	Number - Nombre Total	Male Masculin	Female Féminin	Rate Taux
AMERICA, SOUTH - AMÉRIQUE DU SUD				
Uruguay				
2016 (C)				
15 - 19	6 578	3 409[19]	3 168[19]	50.3
20 - 24	11 267	5 755[19]	5 511[19]	85.7
25 - 29	10 764	5 532[19]	5 229[19]	86.3
30 - 34	10 294	5 346[19]	4 948[19]	86.2
35 - 39	6 368	3 266[19]	3 102[19]	51.7
40 - 44	1 568	821[19]	747[19]	13.5
45 - 49	90	56[19]	34[19]	0.8
50 +	3	2[19]	1[19]	..
Unknown - Inconnu	6	3[19]	3[19]	..
Venezuela (Bolivarian Republic of) - Venezuela (République bolivarienne du)				
2017* (U)				
Total	561 603	289 524	272 079	...
10 - 14	4 132	2 144	1 988	..
15 - 19	103 657	53 567	50 090	...
20 - 24	160 944	83 140	77 804	...
25 - 29	135 963	69 797	66 166	...
30 - 34	91 809	47 219	44 590	...
35 - 39	47 323	24 468	22 855	...
40 - 44	12 363	6 276	6 087	...
45 - 49	1 213	645	568	...
50 +	285	149	136	...
Unknown - Inconnu	3 914	2 119	1 795	..
ASIA - ASIE				
Armenia - Arménie				
2016 (C)				
Total	40 592	21 445	19 147	52.7
0 - 14	4	3	1	..
15 - 19	1 986	1 050	936	24.0
20 - 24	12 936	6 761	6 175	114.7
25 - 29	14 468	7 707	6 761	101.5
30 - 34	7 942	4 169	3 773	58.9
35 - 39	2 721	1 462	1 259	24.6
40 - 44	490	270	220	5.1
45 - 49	41	21	20	0.4
50 +	4	2	2	..
Unknown - Inconnu	-	-	-	..
Azerbaijan - Azerbaïdjan[24]				
2016 (+C)				
Total	159 464	84 909	74 555	59.9
0 - 14	-	-	-	..
15 - 19	16 894	8 776	8 118	52.8
20 - 24	63 779	33 524	30 255	153.8
25 - 29	48 736	26 251	22 485	102.9
30 - 34	21 248	11 627	9 621	49.0
35 - 39	7 233	3 927	3 306	20.0
40 - 44	1 406	715	691	4.4
45 - 49	139	69	70	0.4
50 +	29	20	9	..
Unknown - Inconnu	-	-	-	..
Bahrain - Bahreïn[25]				
2014 (C)				
Total	20 931	10 785	10 146	69.3
0 - 14	-	-	-	..
15 - 19	521	281	240	14.7
20 - 24	4 370	2 254	2 116	100.5
25 - 29	6 572	3 340	3 232	115.3
30 - 34	5 497	2 868	2 629	102.1
35 - 39	3 084	1 586	1 498	67.2

Continent, country or area, year, code[a] and age of mother (in years) — Continent, pays ou zone, année, code[a] et âge de la mère (en années)	Number - Nombre Total	Male Masculin	Female Féminin	Rate Taux
ASIA - ASIE				
Bahrain - Bahreïn[25]				
2014 (C)				
40 - 44	781	404	377	22.4
45 - 49	93	45	48	2.9
50 +	9	5	4	..
Unknown - Inconnu	4	2	2	..
2016 (C)				
Total	20 714	...	...	64.7
10 - 14	2	...	...	..
15 - 19	502	...	...	13.7
20 - 24	4 027	...	...	92.9
25 - 29	6 684	...	...	111.3
30 - 34	5 628	...	...	97.1
35 - 39	2 969	...	...	59.0
40 - 44	805	...	...	20.3
45 - 49	82	...	...	2.6
50 +	13	...	...	..
Unknown - Inconnu	2	...	...	..
Bangladesh				
2010 (U)				
Total	2 868 494	1 451 664	1 416 831	...
15 - 19	404 570	209 615	194 955	...
20 - 24	1 055 194	527 993	527 201	...
25 - 29	762 338	383 627	378 710	...
30 - 34	389 547	199 767	189 780	...
35 - 39	192 438	97 826	94 613	...
40 - 44	49 380	25 206	24 174	...
45 +	15 027	7 630	7 397	...
Brunei Darussalam - Brunéi Darussalam				
2016 (+C)				
Total	6 437	3 382	3 055	54.5
10 - 14	3	1	2	..
15 - 19	170	101	69	9.7
20 - 24	920	495	425	49.8
25 - 29	2 101	1 109	992	114.2
30 - 34	1 896	973	923	107.8
35 - 39	1 064	558	506	63.8
40 - 44	269	142	127	17.4
45 - 49	12	3	9	◆0.9
50 +	2	-	2	..
Unknown - Inconnu	-	-	-	..
China, Hong Kong SAR - Chine, Hong Kong RAS				
2017 (C)				
Total	56 548	29 234[19]	27 312[19]	28.1
10 - 14	2	1[19]	-[19]	..
15 - 19	391	214	177	2.6
20 - 24	3 504	1 775	1 729	15.7
25 - 29	12 647	6 568	6 079	45.9
30 - 34	22 093	11 438[19]	10 654[19]	64.8
35 - 39	14 616	7 538	7 078	41.5
40 - 44	3 099	1 598	1 501	9.2
45 - 49	181	92	89	0.5
50 +	15	10	5	..
Unknown - Inconnu	-	-	-	..
China, Macao SAR - Chine, Macao RAS				
2017 (C)				
Total	6 529	3 382	3 147	...
0 - 24	611	302	309	...
25 - 29	2 455	1 288	1 167	...
30 - 34	2 317	1 168	1 149	...
35 - 39	903	489	414	...
40 +	243	135	108	...

10. Live births by age of mother and sex of child, general and age-specific fertility rates: latest available year, 2008 - 2017
Naissances vivantes selon l'âge de la mère et le sexe de l'enfant, taux de fécondité et taux de fécondité par âge : dernière année disponible, 2008 - 2017 (continued - suite)

Continent, country or area, year, code[a] and age of mother (in years) — Continent, pays ou zone, année, code[a] et âge de la mère (en années)	Total	Male Masculin	Female Féminin	Rate Taux
ASIA - ASIE				
Cyprus - Chypre[26]				
2016 (C)				
Total	9 455	4 887	4 568	42.8
0 - 14	-	-	-	..
15 - 19	150	78	72	5.8
20 - 24	876	433	443	26.8
25 - 29	2 617	1 342	1 275	73.1
30 - 34	3 622	1 895	1 727	102.3
35 - 39	1 809	937	872	54.5
40 - 44	335	179	156	11.2
45 - 49	38	22	16	1.3
50 +	8	1	7	..
Unknown - Inconnu	-	-	-	..
Democratic People's Republic of Korea - République populaire démocratique de Corée[13]				
2008 (I)				
Total	345 630	176 399	169 231	53.3
15 - 19	633	330	303	0.6
20 - 24	52 214	26 657	25 557	58.0
25 - 29	178 032	90 850	87 182	209.5
30 - 34	90 973	46 224	44 749	110.0
35 - 39	20 275	10 505	9 770	18.5
40 - 44	3 202	1 673	1 529	3.2
45 - 49	301	160	141	0.4
Georgia - Géorgie				
2016 (C)				
Total	56 569	28 887	27 682	65.4
0 - 14	19	8	11	..
0 - 19	4 467	...	...	43.6
10 - 14	19	8	11	..
15 - 19	4 448	2 294	2 154	43.5
20 - 24	15 650	7 977	7 666	134.6
25 - 29	17 613	9 014	8 580	127.1
30 - 34	11 706	5 962	5 744	86.5
35 - 39	5 539	2 815	2 724	43.8
40 - 44	1 386	701	685	11.2
45 +	208	...	...	1.7
45 - 49	183	92	91	1.5
50 +	25	10	15	..
Unknown - Inconnu	26	14	12	..
2017 (C)				
Total	53 293	...	...	62.0
0 - 19	3 614	...	...	35.8
20 - 24	13 834	...	...	123.5
25 - 29	17 350	...	...	125.4
30 - 34	11 496	...	...	84.5
35 - 39	5 581	...	...	44.2
40 - 44	1 285	...	...	10.4
45 +	133	...	...	1.1
Indonesia - Indonésie[27]				
2010 (I)				
Total	6 028 921	...	...	92.5
0 - 14	1 054	...	...	..
15 - 19	344 318	...	...	33.5
20 - 24	1 435 265	...	...	143.5
25 - 29	1 787 802	...	...	167.4
30 - 34	1 352 605	...	...	136.9
35 - 39	776 985	...	...	84.8
40 - 44	254 427	...	...	31.0
45 - 49	57 924	...	...	8.3
50 +	18 541	...	...	

Continent, country or area, year, code[a] and age of mother (in years) — Continent, pays ou zone, année, code[a] et âge de la mère (en années)	Total	Male Masculin	Female Féminin	Rate Taux
ASIA - ASIE				
Iran (Islamic Republic of) - Iran (République islamique d')[28]				
2016 (+C)				
Total	1 487 873	765 507	722 366	64.6
10 - 14	1 556	780	776	..
15 - 19	90 717	46 597	44 120	32.8
20 - 24	301 501	154 823	146 678	93.3
25 - 29	454 131	233 366	220 765	108.9
30 - 34	394 421	203 070	191 351	92.3
35 - 39	191 232	98 561	92 671	56.0
40 - 44	42 307	21 819	20 488	15.8
45 - 49	3 080	1 580	1 500	1.3
50 +	284	147	137	..
Unknown - Inconnu	8 644	4 764	3 880	..
Israel - Israël[29]				
2016 (C)				
Total	181 405	93 364	88 041	90.9
10 - 14	1	1	-	..
15 - 19	2 952	1 564	1 388	9.0
20 - 24	32 003	16 360	15 643	106.1
25 - 29	52 930	27 312	25 618	179.4
30 - 34	53 559	27 589	25 970	183.4
35 - 39	30 505	15 671	14 834	108.6
40 - 44	8 444	4 357	4 087	31.5
45 - 49	732	381	351	3.2
50 +	94	45	49	..
Unknown - Inconnu	185	84	101	..
Japan - Japon[30]				
2016 (C)				
Total	976 978	501 880	475 098	37.5
0 - 14	46	28	18	..
10 - 14	46	28	18	..
15 - 19	11 049	5 699	5 350	3.7
20 - 24	82 169	42 151	40 018	27.5
25 - 29	250 639	128 804	121 835	79.7
30 - 34	354 911	182 633	172 278	98.8
35 - 39	223 287	114 541	108 746	55.3
40 - 44	53 474	27 296	26 178	11.1
45 - 49	1 350	698	652	0.3
50 +	51	28	23	..
Unknown - Inconnu	2	2	-	..
Kazakhstan				
2017 (C)				
Total	390 262	201 756	188 506	85.9
10 - 14	13	4	9	..
15 - 19	13 534	7 032	6 502	24.9
20 - 24	103 138	53 519	49 619	159.0
25 - 29	129 270	66 710	62 560	159.4
30 - 34	89 023	45 980	43 043	118.2
35 - 39	44 108	22 776	21 332	69.2
40 - 44	10 668	5 470	5 198	18.0
45 - 49	463	244	219	0.8
50 +	37	18	19	..
Unknown - Inconnu	8	3	5	..
Kuwait - Koweït				
2016 (C)				
Total	58 797	30 245	28 552	60.4
15 - 19	633	319	314	6.7
20 - 24	8 219	4 294	3 925	98.4
25 - 29	17 397	9 039	8 358	138.5
30 - 34	16 343	8 337	8 006	94.7
35 - 39	9 021	4 578	4 443	56.8
40 - 44	2 551	1 305	1 246	16.1

10. Live births by age of mother and sex of child, general and age-specific fertility rates: latest available year, 2008 - 2017
Naissances vivantes selon l'âge de la mère et le sexe de l'enfant, taux de fécondité et taux de fécondité par âge : dernière année disponible, 2008 - 2017 (continued - suite)

Continent, country or area, year, code[a] and age of mother (in years) — Continent, pays ou zone, année, code[a] et âge de la mère (en années)	Total	Male Masculin	Female Féminin	Rate Taux
ASIA - ASIE				
Kuwait - Koweït				
2016 (C)				
45 +	207	100	107	1.9
Unknown - Inconnu	4 426	2 273	2 153	..
Kyrgyzstan - Kirghizstan				
2017 (C)				
Total	153 620	78 967	74 653	96.7
10 - 14	2	-	2	..
15 - 19	8 261	4 196	4 065	33.9
20 - 24	51 059	26 260	24 799	187.5
25 - 29	47 515	24 406	23 109	165.0
30 - 34	29 613	15 196	14 417	118.5
35 - 39	13 587	7 044	6 543	69.5
40 - 44	3 270	1 698	1 572	18.9
45 - 49	195	106	89	1.2
50 +	8	4	4	..
Unknown - Inconnu	110	57	53	..
Malaysia - Malaisie				
2016 (C)				
Total	508 203	262 755	245 448	59.1
0 - 14	172	87	85	..
15 - 19	13 847	7 103	6 744	10.0
20 - 24	72 129	37 336	34 793	46.8
25 - 29	164 325	85 214	79 111	110.5
30 - 34	158 620	82 012	76 608	119.8
35 - 39	78 441	40 451	37 990	74.2
40 - 44	18 789	9 605	9 184	20.2
45 - 49	1 390	694	696	1.6
50 +	64	35	29	..
Unknown - Inconnu	426	218	208	..
Maldives[31]				
2016 (C)				
Total	6 756	3 390	3 366	68.2
0 - 14	1	-	1	..
15 - 19	134	68	66	9.8
20 - 24	1 514	788	726	90.7
25 - 29	2 393	1 196	1 197	125.3
30 - 34	1 770	876	894	102.0
35 - 39	751	362	389	59.1
40 - 44	170	91	79	16.6
45 - 49	13	6	7	♦1.4
50 +	1	-	1	..
Unknown - Inconnu	9	3	6	..
Mongolia - Mongolie				
2017 (+C)				
Total	75 321	38 958	36 363	87.1
10 - 14	64	35	29	..
15 - 19	3 475	1 799	1 676	30.1
20 - 24	18 028	9 336	8 692	145.7
25 - 29	23 919	12 392	11 527	153.4
30 - 34	17 611	9 222	8 389	125.6
35 - 39	9 759	4 942	4 817	80.4
40 - 44	2 344	1 162	1 182	21.0
45 - 49	118	69	49	1.2
50 +	3	1	2	..
Myanmar[32]				
2015 (+U)				
Total	739 152	381 555	357 597	...
10 - 14	61	32	29	..
15 - 19	41 487	21 638	19 849	...
20 - 24	175 652	90 353	85 299	...
25 - 29	204 863	105 547	99 316	...
30 - 34	164 214	84 801	79 413	...
35 - 39	95 072	49 199	45 873	...
40 - 44	31 037	16 129	14 908	...
ASIA - ASIE				
Myanmar[32]				
2015 (+U)				
45 - 49	3 514	1 823	1 691	...
50 +	106	55	51	...
Unknown - Inconnu	23 146	11 978	11 168	..
Oman				
2017 (C)				
Total	90 371	46 063	44 308	99.0
10 - 14	6	3	3	..
15 - 19	1 480	720	760	12.9
20 - 24	13 970	7 093	6 877	98.8
25 - 29	28 402	14 487	13 915	151.9
30 - 34	26 164	13 499	12 665	147.7
35 - 39	15 327	7 706	7 621	112.2
40 - 44	4 566	2 336	2 230	48.5
45 - 49	430	205	225	7.0
50 +	26	14	12	..
Philippines				
2016 (C)				
Total	1 731 289	903 694	827 595	64.9
10 - 14	1 903	963	940	..
15 - 19	201 182	105 167	96 015	40.9
20 - 24	487 763	255 196	232 567	102.6
25 - 29	444 205	232 003	212 202	105.5
30 - 34	322 878	168 599	154 279	87.0
35 - 39	196 493	102 085	94 408	58.8
40 - 44	64 960	33 472	31 488	21.8
45 - 49	6 622	3 403	3 219	2.5
50 +	387	201	186	..
Unknown - Inconnu	4 896	2 605	2 291	..
Qatar				
2016 (C)				
Total	26 816	13 591	13 225	65.2
10 - 14	-	...	...	..
15 - 19	353	187	166	10.3
20 - 24	3 468	1 750	1 718	77.8
25 - 29	8 551	4 354	4 197	97.4
30 - 34	8 754	4 400	4 354	97.2
35 - 39	4 383	2 248	2 135	60.9
40 - 44	1 198	605	593	24.1
45 - 49	101	43	58	3.1
50 +	8	4	4	..
Republic of Korea - République de Corée[33]				
2015 (C)				
Total	438 420	224 906	213 514	34.4
0 - 14	16	6	10	..
15 - 19	2 211	1 171	1 040	1.4
20 - 24	20 514	10 490	10 024	12.6
25 - 29	94 622	48 802	45 820	61.5
30 - 34	216 252	110 509	105 743	116.5
35 - 39	92 081	47 424	44 657	48.8
40 - 44	12 138	6 231	5 907	5.7
45 - 49	335	169	166	0.2
50 +	14	4	10	..
Unknown - Inconnu	237	100	137	..
2017 (C)				
Total	357 771	...	...	28.6
0 - 14	6	...	...	..
15 - 19	1 520	...	...	1.1
20 - 24	15 768	...	...	9.6
25 - 29	74 026	...	...	46.9
30 - 34	161 045	...	...	96.6
35 - 39	92 645	...	...	47.1
40 - 44	12 202	...	...	6.1

10. Live births by age of mother and sex of child, general and age-specific fertility rates: latest available year, 2008 - 2017
Naissances vivantes selon l'âge de la mère et le sexe de l'enfant, taux de fécondité et taux de fécondité par âge : dernière année disponible, 2008 - 2017 (continued - suite)

Continent, country or area, year, code[a] and age of mother (in years) / Continent, pays ou zone, année, code[a] et âge de la mère (en années)	Number - Nombre			Rate Taux
	Total	Male Masculin	Female Féminin	

ASIA - ASIE

Republic of Korea - République de Corée[33]
2017 (C)

45 - 49	373	...	...	0.2
50 +	9	...	...	..
Unknown - Inconnu	177	...	...	..

Saudi Arabia - Arabie saoudite[9]
2010 (I)

Total	527 461	275 189	252 272	73.2
15 - 19	10 641	4 761	5 880	8.7
20 - 24	68 573	34 423	34 150	54.8
25 - 29	149 707	79 425	70 282	111.9
30 - 34	135 203	89 860	45 343	116.8
35 - 39	108 609	33 195	75 414	112.5
40 - 44	41 602	24 758	16 844	59.7
45 - 49	10 603	7 361	3 242	18.8
50 +	2 523	1 406	1 117	..

Singapore - Singapour
2017 (C)

Total	39 615	20 408	19 207	39.2
10 - 14	8	4	4	..
15 - 19	302	163	139	2.7
20 - 24	2 011	1 016	995	15.8
25 - 29	10 216	5 326	4 890	69.1
30 - 34	16 214	8 267	7 947	110.3
35 - 39	9 063	4 715	4 348	57.3
40 - 44	1 707	871	836	10.6
45 - 49	88	44	44	0.6
50 +	6	2	4	..
Unknown - Inconnu	-	-	-	..

Sri Lanka
2013 (+C)

Total	365 762	...	...	68.0
0 - 14	94	...	...	..
10 - 14	94	...	...	..
15 - 19	16 777	...	...	20.0
20 - 24	73 641	...	...	94.8
25 - 29	112 466	...	...	139.5
30 - 34	104 838	...	...	123.5
35 - 39	46 082	...	...	63.0
40 - 44	10 787	...	...	15.2
45 +	1 077	...	...	1.6
45 - 49	1 017	...	...	1.5
50 +	60	...	...	..

Tajikistan - Tadjikistan[34]
2016 (U)

Total	230 044	...	...	...
10 - 14	-	...	...	..
15 - 19	17 122	...	...	...
20 - 24	99 401	...	...	...
25 - 29	68 011	...	...	...
30 - 34	31 932	...	...	...
35 - 39	10 731	...	...	...
40 - 44	2 046	...	...	...
45 - 49	134	...	...	...
50 +	1	...	...	...
Unknown - Inconnu	666	...	...	...

Thailand - Thaïlande
2011 (+U)

Total	795 031	409 699	385 332	...
0 - 14	3 415	1 793	1 622	..
15 - 19	129 321	66 645	62 676	...
20 - 24	186 942	96 371	90 571	...
25 - 29	204 684	105 355	99 329	...

Continent, country or area, year, code[a] and age of mother (in years) / Continent, pays ou zone, année, code[a] et âge de la mère (en années)	Number - Nombre			Rate Taux
	Total	Male Masculin	Female Féminin	

ASIA - ASIE

Thailand - Thaïlande
2011 (+U)

30 - 34	167 671	86 515	81 156	...
35 - 39	80 348	41 311	39 037	...
40 - 44	20 089	10 251	9 838	...
45 - 49	1 293	653	640	...
50 +	73	30	43	..
Unknown - Inconnu	1 195	775	420	..

Turkey - Turquie
2016 (C)

Total	1 309 771	672 508	637 263	62.7
0 - 14	234	121	113	..
15 - 19	75 265	38 934	36 331	23.5
20 - 24	308 306	158 485	149 821	99.6
25 - 29	405 585	208 057	197 528	132.8
30 - 34	313 395	160 975	152 420	101.4
35 - 39	161 862	82 769	79 093	50.6
40 - 44	33 053	16 886	16 167	11.9
45 - 49	2 339	1 213	1 126	1.0
50 +	471	242	229	..
Unknown - Inconnu	9 261	4 826	4 435	..

Uzbekistan - Ouzbékistan
2015 (+C)

Total	734 141	382 666	351 475	84.6
0 - 14	-	-	-	..
15 - 19	33 035	16 885	16 150	23.8
20 - 24	309 746	159 890	149 856	194.8
25 - 29	247 500	129 252	118 248	162.4
30 - 34	110 819	58 658	52 161	86.1
35 - 39	29 332	15 961	13 371	27.2
40 - 44	3 560	1 939	1 621	3.7
45 - 49	134	70	64	0.2
50 +	15	11	4	..

EUROPE

Åland Islands - Îles d'Åland
2016 (C)

Total	293	148	145	49.5
10 - 14	-	-	-	..
15 - 19	4	3	1	♦5.4
20 - 24	32	16	16	47.7
25 - 29	98	53	45	121.7
30 - 34	102	48	54	118.9
35 - 39	47	25	22	54.2
40 - 44	8	1	7	♦8.7
45 - 49	2	2	-	♦1.9
50 +	-	-	-	..

Albania - Albanie
2016 (C)

Total	31 733	16 401	15 332	45.8
0 - 14	20	11	9	..
15 - 19	1 932	1 009	923	17.3
20 - 24	9 156	4 616	4 540	74.1
25 - 29	11 188	5 800	5 388	107.1
30 - 34	6 551	3 441	3 110	74.7
35 - 39	2 392	1 279	1 113	29.5
40 - 44	430	212	218	5.0
45 - 49	19	7	12	♦0.2
50 +	2		2	..
Unknown - Inconnu	43	26	17	..

10. Live births by age of mother and sex of child, general and age-specific fertility rates: latest available year, 2008 - 2017
Naissances vivantes selon l'âge de la mère et le sexe de l'enfant, taux de fécondité et taux de fécondité par âge : dernière année disponible, 2008 - 2017 (continued - suite)

Continent, country or area, year, code[a] and age of mother (in years) / Continent, pays ou zone, année, code[a] et âge de la mère (en années)	Total	Male Masculin	Female Féminin	Rate Taux
EUROPE				
Andorra - Andorre				
2015 (C)				
Total	659	336	323	...
0 - 14	1	1	-	..
15 - 19	5	4	1	...
20 - 24	32	15	17	...
25 - 29	123	58	65	...
30 - 34	253	140	113	...
35 - 39	198	89	109	...
40 - 44	40	26	14	...
45 - 49	5	2	3	...
50 +	1	-	1	..
Unknown - Inconnu	1	1	-	..
Austria - Autriche[35]				
2016 (C)				
Total	87 675	45 051	42 624	44.0
0 - 14	8	5	3	..
15 - 19	1 585	790	795	7.2
20 - 24	11 422	5 882	5 540	42.5
25 - 29	25 867	13 393	12 474	89.0
30 - 34	29 844	15 296	14 548	101.1
35 - 39	15 434	7 934	7 500	55.2
40 - 44	3 291	1 624	1 667	11.1
45 - 49	198	116	82	0.6
50 +	26	11	15	..
Belarus - Bélarus				
2016 (C)				
Total	117 779	...	...	52.1
0 - 14	11	...	...	..
15 - 19	3 550	...	...	16.0
20 - 24	24 562	...	...	88.0
25 - 29	42 419	...	...	116.1
30 - 34	31 927	...	...	84.4
35 - 39	13 000	...	...	37.7
40 - 44	2 207	...	...	6.5
45 - 49	77	...	...	0.2
50 +	1	...	...	..
Unknown - Inconnu	25	...	...	..
Belgium - Belgique[36]				
2016 (C)				
Total	121 896	62 428	59 468	48.7
0 - 14	16	8	8	..
15 - 19	1 888	983	905	6.2
20 - 24	13 766	7 110	6 656	41.3
25 - 29	40 763	20 911	19 852	112.4
30 - 34	41 291	21 018	20 273	114.8
35 - 39	18 753	9 599	9 154	51.3
40 - 44	3 821	1 987	1 834	10.5
45 - 49	266	130	136	0.7
50 +	25	17	8	..
Unknown - Inconnu	1 307	665	642	..
Bosnia and Herzegovina - Bosnie-Herzégovine				
2010 (C)				
Total	33 528	17 277	16 251	35.2
12 - 14	8	6	2	..
15 - 19	1 792	950	842	13.5
20 - 24	8 293	4 282	4 011	59.4
25 - 29	11 690	5 949	5 741	86.2
30 - 34	7 985	4 144	3 841	66.8
35 - 39	3 027	1 560	1 467	24.3
40 - 44	557	287	270	3.9
45 - 49	30	14	16	0.2
50 +	1	-	1	..
Unknown - Inconnu	145	85	60	..

Continent, country or area, year, code[a] and age of mother (in years) / Continent, pays ou zone, année, code[a] et âge de la mère (en années)	Total	Male Masculin	Female Féminin	Rate Taux
EUROPE				
Bulgaria - Bulgarie				
2016 (C)				
Total	64 984	33 375	31 609	41.9
0 - 14	259	136	123	..
15 - 19	5 772	3 011	2 761	38.2
20 - 24	12 341	6 338	6 003	70.3
25 - 29	20 315	10 419	9 896	88.5
30 - 34	16 530	8 469	8 061	71.2
35 - 39	7 837	4 023	3 814	31.2
40 - 44	1 731	886	845	6.6
45 - 49	181	86	95	0.7
50 +	17	7	10	..
Unknown - Inconnu	1	-	1	..
Croatia - Croatie				
2016 (C)				
Total	37 537	19 072	18 465	41.0
0 - 14	5	5	-	..
15 - 19	1 081	563	518	9.6
20 - 24	5 128	2 569	2 559	43.3
25 - 29	10 946	5 585	5 361	86.6
30 - 34	12 779	6 507	6 272	92.0
35 - 39	6 331	3 184	3 147	44.5
40 - 44	1 208	632	576	8.8
45 - 49	53	24	29	0.4
50 +	4	3	1	..
Unknown - Inconnu	2	-	2	..
Czechia - Tchéquie				
2016 (C)				
Total	112 663	57 837	54 826	47.0
0 - 14	14	6	8	..
15 - 19	2 623	1 304	1 319	11.8
20 - 24	13 792	7 069	6 723	49.4
25 - 29	33 408	17 270	16 138	99.4
30 - 34	38 862	19 855	19 007	109.2
35 - 39	20 015	10 309	9 706	47.6
40 - 44	3 780	1 937	1 843	8.7
45 - 49	160	81	79	0.5
50 +	9	6	3	..
Denmark - Danemark[37]				
2016 (C)				
Total	61 614	31 781	29 833	48.7
0 - 14	-	-	-	..
15 - 19	602	321	281	3.5
20 - 24	6 649	3 436	3 213	35.3
25 - 29	20 635	10 642	9 993	114.4
30 - 34	20 816	10 762	10 054	129.6
35 - 39	10 535	5 421	5 114	61.4
40 - 44	2 259	1 131	1 128	11.5
45 - 49	111	63	48	0.6
50 +	7	5	2	..
Estonia - Estonie				
2016 (C)				
Total	14 053	7 365	6 688	48.6
0 - 14	5	2	3	..
15 - 19	305	175	130	10.5
20 - 24	1 697	897	800	48.0
25 - 29	4 725	2 466	2 259	101.2
30 - 34	4 373	2 283	2 090	95.4
35 - 39	2 298	1 198	1 100	52.4
40 - 44	623	333	290	13.9
45 - 49	23	10	13	◆0.5
50 +	4	1	3	..

10. Live births by age of mother and sex of child, general and age-specific fertility rates: latest available year, 2008 - 2017
Naissances vivantes selon l'âge de la mère et le sexe de l'enfant, taux de fécondité et taux de fécondité par âge : dernière année disponible, 2008 - 2017 (continued - suite)

Continent, country or area, year, code[a] and age of mother (in years) / Continent, pays ou zone, année, code[a] et âge de la mère (en années)	Total	Male Masculin	Female Féminin	Rate Taux
EUROPE				
Faeroe Islands - Îles Féroé				
2017 (C)				
Total	655	303	352	64.7
10 - 14	-	-	-	..
15 - 19	18	8	10	♦10.7
20 - 24	108	44	64	77.7
25 - 29	218	111	107	169.1
30 - 34	177	77	100	139.8
35 - 39	105	50	55	71.6
40 - 44	28	12	16	♦18.9
45 - 49	1	1	-	♦0.6
50 +	-	-	-	..
Finland - Finlande				
2016 (C)				
Total	52 814	26 812	26 002	46.3
0 - 14	1	1	-	..
15 - 19	804	424	380	5.5
20 - 24	7 118	3 629	3 489	43.4
25 - 29	15 515	7 867	7 648	92.7
30 - 34	17 647	8 842	8 805	102.6
35 - 39	9 385	4 810	4 575	56.1
40 - 44	2 202	1 164	1 038	14.2
45 - 49	131	69	62	0.8
50 +	11	6	5	..
France[38]				
2012 (C)				
Total	790 290	404 774	385 516	55.6
12 - 14	147	73	74	..
15 - 19	17 512	8 954	8 558	9.4
20 - 24	111 364	57 130	54 234	58.2
25 - 29	253 800	130 005	123 795	131.0
30 - 34	255 606	130 913	124 693	127.2
35 - 39	121 563	62 225	59 338	59.1
40 - 44	28 620	14 598	14 022	12.9
45 - 49	1 557	818	739	0.7
50 +	121	58	63	..
Germany - Allemagne				
2016 (C)				
Total	792 137	405 584	386 553	45.6
0 - 14	170	79	91	..
15 - 19	18 334	9 327	9 007	9.2
20 - 24	85 571	43 705	41 866	39.3
25 - 29	224 557	115 249	109 308	87.0
30 - 34	276 999	142 033	134 966	109.6
35 - 39	153 719	78 555	75 164	62.3
40 - 44	29 517	14 989	14 528	12.2
45 - 49	1 712	868	844	0.5
50 +	153	78	75	..
Unknown - Inconnu	1 405	701	704	..
Gibraltar[39]				
2015 (+C)				
Total	492	258	234	...
0 - 19	8	3	5	...
20 - 24	69	40	29	...
25 - 29	125	63	62	...
30 - 34	171	94	77	...
35 - 39	96	47	49	...
40 +	23	11	12	...
Greece - Grèce				
2016 (C)				
Total	92 898	47 882	45 016	38.6
0 - 14	77	38	39	..
15 - 19	2 416	1 231	1 185	9.2
20 - 24	7 644	3 986	3 658	28.1
25 - 29	20 292	10 498	9 794	68.8
EUROPE				
Greece - Grèce				
2016 (C)				
30 - 34	33 842	17 510	16 332	98.8
35 - 39	22 510	11 538	10 972	56.1
40 - 44	5 258	2 666	2 592	12.8
45 - 49	744	352	392	1.8
50 +	115	63	52	..
Unknown - Inconnu	-	-	-	..
Hungary - Hongrie[40]				
2016 (C)				
Total	95 361	48 959	46 402	42.0
0 - 14	75	39	36	..
15 - 19	6 021	3 125	2 896	24.8
20 - 24	13 792	7 134	6 658	46.8
25 - 29	24 156	12 453	11 703	80.6
30 - 34	28 531	14 544	13 987	94.1
35 - 39	18 360	9 343	9 017	47.9
40 - 44	4 274	2 241	2 033	10.7
45 - 49	147	77	70	0.4
50 +	5	3	2	..
Iceland - Islande				
2015 (C)				
Total	4 129	2 119	2 010	53.1
0 - 14	-	-	-	..
15 - 19	87	38	49	8.0
20 - 24	660	335	325	54.4
25 - 29	1 341	698	643	115.7
30 - 34	1 213	613	600	107.1
35 - 39	677	367	310	62.1
40 - 44	140	63	77	13.2
45 - 49	11	5	6	♦1.1
50 +	-	-	-	..
Unknown - Inconnu	-	-	-	..
2017 (C)				
Total	4 071	...	...	51.7
10 - 14	-	...	...	..
15 - 19	65	...	...	6.0
20 - 24	601	...	...	49.4
25 - 29	1 363	...	...	111.7
30 - 34	1 221	...	...	108.7
35 - 39	659	...	...	58.5
40 - 44	148	...	...	13.6
45 - 49	12	...	...	♦1.2
50 +	2	...	...	..
Ireland - Irlande				
2016 (+C)				
Total	63 836	32 707	31 129	54.8
0 - 14	2	2	-	..
15 - 19	1 099	551	548	7.4
20 - 24	5 217	2 713	2 504	38.5
25 - 29	11 357	5 863	5 494	75.3
30 - 34	23 011	11 799	11 212	123.6
35 - 39	18 772	9 549	9 223	94.4
40 - 44	4 078	2 083	1 995	22.6
45 - 49	287	141	146	1.8
50 +	13	6	7	..
Isle of Man - Île de Man[9]				
2016 (I)				
Total	731	...	...	41.4
10 - 14	1	...	...	..
15 - 19	23	...	...	♦10.1
20 - 24	111	...	...	51.2
25 - 29	178	...	...	81.1
30 - 34	238	...	...	100.9
35 - 39	146	...	...	58.4

10. Live births by age of mother and sex of child, general and age-specific fertility rates: latest available year, 2008 - 2017
Naissances vivantes selon l'âge de la mère et le sexe de l'enfant, taux de fécondité et taux de fécondité par âge : dernière année disponible, 2008 - 2017 (continued - suite)

Continent, country or area, year, code[a] and age of mother (in years) / Continent, pays ou zone, année, code[a] et âge de la mère (en années)	Number - Nombre			Rate Taux
	Total	Male Masculin	Female Féminin	

EUROPE

Isle of Man - Île de Man[9]				
2016 (|)				
40 - 44	33	...	...	11.4
45 - 49	1	...	...	♦0.3
50 +	-	...	...	..
Italy - Italie				
2016 (C)				
Total	473 438	243 080	230 358	36.3
0 - 14	11	4	7	..
15 - 19	6 739	3 488	3 251	4.8
20 - 24	40 600	20 842	19 758	27.8
25 - 29	105 946	54 653	51 293	66.2
30 - 34	159 891	82 183	77 708	91.9
35 - 39	119 743	61 330	58 413	59.9
40 - 44	37 024	18 896	18 128	15.6
45 - 49	3 152	1 537	1 615	1.3
50 +	332	147	185	..
Latvia - Lettonie				
2016 (C)				
Total	21 968	11 385	10 583	51.1
0 - 14	4	2	2	..
15 - 19	646	309	337	15.4
20 - 24	3 369	1 774	1 595	64.3
25 - 29	7 249	3 759	3 490	106.8
30 - 34	6 494	3 359	3 135	96.4
35 - 39	3 324	1 730	1 594	52.8
40 - 44	826	426	400	12.2
45 - 49	45	21	24	0.6
50 +	3	2	1	..
Unknown - Inconnu	8	3	5	..
Liechtenstein				
2015 (C)				
Total	325	177	148	37.2
0 - 14	-	-	-	..
15 - 19	4	1	3	♦3.6
20 - 24	27	17	10	♦24.5
25 - 29	88	48	40	78.4
30 - 34	121	67	54	106.0
35 - 39	68	34	34	56.9
40 - 44	13	8	5	♦9.1
45 - 49	3	2	1	♦1.8
50 +	1	-	1	..
Unknown - Inconnu	-	-	-	..
Lithuania - Lituanie				
2016 (C)				
Total	30 623	15 847	14 776	47.6
0 - 14	6	5	1	..
15 - 19	1 016	531	485	13.3
20 - 24	4 706	2 397	2 309	51.0
25 - 29	10 901	5 571	5 330	115.5
30 - 34	9 290	4 897	4 393	105.3
35 - 39	3 820	1 986	1 834	44.6
40 - 44	840	436	404	8.6
45 - 49	37	21	16	0.3
50 +	-	-	-	..
Unknown - Inconnu	7	3	4	..
Luxembourg				
2016 (C)				
Total	6 050	3 077	2 973	42.6
0 - 14	-	-	-	..
15 - 19	79	40	39	4.9
20 - 24	499	264	235	28.7
25 - 29	1 460	743	717	71.6
30 - 34	2 233	1 132	1 101	101.1
35 - 39	1 409	698	711	63.6

EUROPE

Luxembourg				
2016 (C)				
40 - 44	334	181	153	15.5
45 - 49	24	11	13	♦1.1
50 +	1	1	-	..
Unknown - Inconnu	11	7	4	..
Malta - Malte				
2016 (C)				
Total	4 476	2 365	2 111	42.9
0 - 14	3	1	2	..
15 - 19	146	78	68	12.6
20 - 24	499	261	238	34.2
25 - 29	1 279	699	580	73.7
30 - 34	1 602	819	783	95.0
35 - 39	798	431	367	49.6
40 - 44	140	73	67	9.4
45 - 49	9	3	6	♦0.7
50 +	-	-	-	..
Unknown - Inconnu	-	-	-	..
Montenegro - Monténégro				
2016 (C)				
Total	7 569	3 850	3 719	51.6
0 - 14	3	2	1	..
10 - 14	3	...	...	10.0
15 - 19	195	94	101	10.0
20 - 24	1 211	621	590	63.1
25 - 29	2 405	1 230	1 175	120.9
30 - 34	2 217	1 140	1 077	100.4
35 - 39	1 078	533	545	50.1
40 - 44	227	110	117	11.0
45 - 49	14	7	7	♦0.7
50 +	3	2	1	..
Unknown - Inconnu	216	111	105	..
Netherlands - Pays-Bas[41]				
2016 (C)				
Total	172 520	88 587	83 933	45.8
0 - 14	-	-	-	..
15 - 19	1 492	791	701	3.0
20 - 24	14 805	7 695	7 110	28.2
25 - 29	52 996	27 381	25 615	100.0
30 - 34	66 101	33 801	32 300	130.6
35 - 39	31 266	15 912	15 354	61.9
40 - 44	5 557	2 846	2 711	9.9
45 - 49	285	150	135	0.4
50 +	18	11	7	..
Norway - Norvège				
2016 (C)				
Total	58 890	30 386	28 504	49.0
0 - 14	1	-	1	..
15 - 19	612	327	285	3.9
20 - 24	6 556	3 401	3 155	39.6
25 - 29	19 241	9 920	9 321	107.3
30 - 34	20 418	10 675	9 743	119.4
35 - 39	9 836	4 969	4 867	59.1
40 - 44	2 077	1 013	1 064	11.7
45 - 49	133	75	58	0.7
50 +	16	6	10	..
Poland - Pologne				
2016 (C)				
Total	382 257	196 221	186 036	42.6
0 - 14	48	20	28	..
15 - 19	11 272	5 813	5 459	12.0
20 - 24	55 770	28 643	27 127	48.6
25 - 29	126 651	65 105	61 546	93.7
30 - 34	126 194	64 716	61 478	81.8

10. Live births by age of mother and sex of child, general and age-specific fertility rates: latest available year, 2008 - 2017
Naissances vivantes selon l'âge de la mère et le sexe de l'enfant, taux de fécondité et taux de fécondité par âge : dernière année disponible, 2008 - 2017 (continued - suite)

Continent, country or area, year, code[a] and age of mother (in years) / Continent, pays ou zone, année, code[a] et âge de la mère (en années)	Number - Nombre			Rate Taux
	Total	Male Masculin	Female Féminin	
EUROPE				
Poland - Pologne				
2016 (C)				
35 - 39	52 316	26 752	25 564	35.2
40 - 44	9 658	5 006	4 652	7.2
45 - 49	344	163	181	0.3
50 +	4	3	1	..
Unknown - Inconnu	-	-	-	..
Portugal[20]				
2016 (C)				
Total	87 126	44 789	42 337	37.1
0 - 14	43	23	20	..
15 - 19	2 165	1 107	1 058	7.9
20 - 24	8 955	4 708	4 247	33.5
25 - 29	18 783	9 665	9 118	67.8
30 - 34	29 769	15 312	14 457	92.6
35 - 39	21 765	11 132	10 633	56.1
40 - 44	5 354	2 710	2 644	12.7
45 - 49	276	126	150	0.7
50 +	16	6	10	..
Unknown - Inconnu	-	-	-	..
Republic of Moldova - République de Moldova[42]				
2016 (C)				
Total	37 394	19 304	18 090	...
0 - 14	10	4	6	..
15 - 19	2 676	1 363	1 313	...
20 - 24	10 476	5 423	5 053	...
25 - 29	12 582	6 491	6 091	...
30 - 34	7 980	4 127	3 853	...
35 - 39	3 122	1 598	1 524	...
40 - 44	528	290	238	...
45 - 49	18	6	12	...
50 +	2	2	-	..
2017 (C)				
Total	34 060	...	...	...
0 - 19	2 318	...	...	...
20 - 24	9 018	...	...	...
25 - 29	11 164	...	...	...
30 - 34	7 771	...	...	...
35 - 39	3 159	...	...	...
40 - 44	600	...	...	...
45 - 49	29	...	...	...
50 +	-	...	...	..
Unknown - Inconnu	1	...	...	..
Romania - Roumanie				
2016 (C)				
Total	200 009	102 597	97 412	43.4
0 - 14	700	368	332	..
15 - 19	19 192	9 755	9 437	36.5
20 - 24	37 259	19 233	18 026	72.2
25 - 29	63 719	32 793	30 926	100.1
30 - 34	49 270	25 165	24 105	78.5
35 - 39	24 629	12 612	12 017	33.0
40 - 44	4 985	2 535	2 450	6.7
45 - 49	251	135	116	0.3
50 +	4	1	3	..
Unknown - Inconnu	-	-	-	..
Russian Federation - Fédération de Russie[24]				
2011 (C)				
Total	1 796 629	923 804	872 825	48.3
12 - 14	351	174	177	..
15 - 19	103 533	53 162	50 371	25.2
20 - 24	510 184	262 085	248 099	85.1
25 - 29	603 791	311 250	292 541	101.2

Continent, country or area, year, code[a] and age of mother (in years) / Continent, pays ou zone, année, code[a] et âge de la mère (en années)	Number - Nombre			Rate Taux
	Total	Male Masculin	Female Féminin	
EUROPE				
Russian Federation - Fédération de Russie[24]				
2011 (C)				
30 - 34	379 884	195 518	184 366	68.6
35 - 39	165 364	84 832	80 532	31.8
40 - 44	30 221	15 168	15 053	6.3
45 - 49	1 481	680	801	0.3
50 +	138	65	73	..
Unknown - Inconnu	1 682	870	812	..
San Marino - Saint-Marin				
2014 (C)				
Total	281	138	143	35.6
0 - 14	-	-	-	..
15 - 19	-	-	-	..
20 - 24	17	9	8	♦23.5
25 - 29	68	37	31	85.2
30 - 34	94	44	50	90.1
35 - 39	77	33	44	55.8
40 - 44	23	15	8	♦15.1
45 - 49	2	-	2	♦1.2
50 +	-	-	-	..
Serbia - Serbie[43]				
2016 (+C)				
Total	64 734	33 477	31 257	41.7
0 - 14	49	27	22	..
15 - 19	2 625	1 299	1 326	15.4
20 - 24	11 385	5 937	5 448	57.6
25 - 29	19 850	10 200	9 650	91.6
30 - 34	19 432	10 029	9 403	82.1
35 - 39	9 302	4 933	4 369	38.1
40 - 44	1 740	879	861	7.1
45 - 49	91	39	52	0.4
50 +	8	4	4	..
Unknown - Inconnu	252	130	122	..
Slovakia - Slovaquie				
2016 (C)				
Total	57 557	29 479	28 078	43.7
0 - 14	48	24	24	..
15 - 19	3 592	1 831	1 761	26.2
20 - 24	8 946	4 638	4 308	53.6
25 - 29	17 194	8 751	8 443	87.6
30 - 34	17 800	9 166	8 634	84.1
35 - 39	8 429	4 298	4 131	38.1
40 - 44	1 483	741	742	7.1
45 - 49	61	27	34	0.3
50 +	4	3	1	..
Slovenia - Slovénie				
2016 (C)				
Total	20 345	10 366	9 979	45.9
0 - 14	2	1	1	..
15 - 19	188	112	76	4.1
20 - 24	2 012	1 021	991	40.2
25 - 29	6 707	3 388	3 319	110.1
30 - 34	7 350	3 791	3 559	108.1
35 - 39	3 387	1 708	1 679	45.4
40 - 44	665	328	337	9.2
45 - 49	33	17	16	0.5
50 +	1	-	1	..
Spain - Espagne				
2016 (C)				
Total	408 734	210 091	198 643	38.3
0 - 14	110	59	51	..
15 - 19	7 843	4 095	3 748	7.4
20 - 24	28 541	14 688	13 853	25.6
25 - 29	72 368	37 261	35 107	56.5

10. Live births by age of mother and sex of child, general and age-specific fertility rates: latest available year, 2008 - 2017
Naissances vivantes selon l'âge de la mère et le sexe de l'enfant, taux de fécondité et taux de fécondité par âge : dernière année disponible, 2008 - 2017 (continued - suite)

Continent, country or area, year, code[a] and age of mother (in years) / Continent, pays ou zone, année, code[a] et âge de la mère (en années)	Number - Nombre			Rate Taux
	Total	Male Masculin	Female Féminin	

Continent, country or area, year, code[a] and age of mother (in years) / Continent, pays ou zone, année, code[a] et âge de la mère (en années)	Number - Nombre			Rate Taux
	Total	Male Masculin	Female Féminin	

EUROPE

Spain - Espagne
2016 (C)

30 - 34	141 470	72 776	68 694	91.3
35 - 39	124 054	63 602	60 452	65.4
40 - 44	31 867	16 341	15 526	16.5
45 - 49	2 348	1 204	1 144	1.3
50 +	133	65	68	..

Sweden - Suède
2016 (C)

Total	117 425	60 199	57 226	54.4
0 - 14	7	2	5	..
15 - 19	1 120	577	543	4.4
20 - 24	13 526	7 015	6 511	43.1
25 - 29	37 937	19 403	18 534	111.6
30 - 34	38 968	19 921	19 047	127.4
35 - 39	20 764	10 636	10 128	69.3
40 - 44	4 792	2 471	2 321	15.0
45 - 49	289	161	128	0.9
50 +	21	13	8	..
Unknown - Inconnu	1	-	1	..

Switzerland - Suisse
2016 (C)

Total	87 883	44 932	42 951	45.5
0 - 14	1	-	1	..
15 - 19	605	313	292	2.8
20 - 24	6 633	3 359	3 274	27.3
25 - 29	22 191	11 383	10 808	80.0
30 - 34	33 691	17 288	16 403	115.5
35 - 39	20 149	10 228	9 921	70.2
40 - 44	4 296	2 206	2 090	14.7
45 - 49	292	144	148	0.9
50 +	25	11	14	..

TFYR of Macedonia - L'ex-R. y. de Macédoine
2016 (C)

Total	23 002	11 868	11 134	44.8
0 - 14	26	12	14	..
15 - 19	978	483	495	16.0
20 - 24	4 646	2 414	2 232	64.3
25 - 29	7 833	3 998	3 835	100.2
30 - 34	6 539	3 436	3 103	81.7
35 - 39	2 529	1 289	1 240	33.1
40 - 44	416	218	198	5.6
45 - 49	20	7	13	♦0.3
50 +	3	2	1	..
Unknown - Inconnu	12	9	3	..

Ukraine[44]
2016 (+C)

Total	397 037	...	...	39.0
0 - 14	177	...	...	..
15 - 19	21 755	...	...	23.2
20 - 24	99 830	...	...	81.6
25 - 29	132 510	...	...	82.3
30 - 34	93 748	...	...	53.1
35 - 39	39 563	...	...	24.8
40 - 44	8 210	...	...	5.2
45 - 49	528	...	...	0.4
50 +	94	...	...	..
Unknown - Inconnu	622	...	...	..

EUROPE

United Kingdom of Great Britain and Northern Ireland - Royaume-Uni de Grande-Bretagne et d'Irlande du Nord[45]
2016 (C)

Total	774 386	397 481	376 905	52.0
0 - 14	109	53	56	..
15 - 19	25 109	12 992	12 117	13.7
20 - 24	113 944	58 665	55 279	54.7
25 - 29	217 688	111 631	106 057	97.4
30 - 34	245 653	126 040	119 613	111.2
35 - 39	139 097	71 423	67 674	66.3
40 - 44	30 306	15 435	14 871	14.4
45 - 49	2 213	1 109	1 104	0.9
50 +	251	125	126	..
Unknown - Inconnu	16	8	8	..

OCEANIA - OCÉANIE

American Samoa - Samoas américaines
2014 (C)

Total	1 084	...	...	...
0 - 14	-	...	...	..
15 - 19	117	...	...	...
20 - 24	291	...	...	...
25 - 29	288	...	...	...
30 - 34	207	...	...	...
35 - 39	135	...	...	...
40 - 44	43	...	...	...
45 - 49	3	...	...	...
50 +	-	...	...	...

Australia - Australie[46]
2016 (C)

Total	311 104	159 537	151 567	53.6
10 - 14	54	33	21	..
15 - 19	7 505	3 827	3 678	10.4
20 - 24	37 022	18 903	18 119	44.6
25 - 29	83 504	43 013	40 491	91.9
30 - 34	111 397	57 106	54 291	123.4
35 - 39	57 958	29 675	28 283	71.9
40 - 44	12 501	6 382	6 119	15.3
45 - 49	949	492	457	1.2
50 +	75	33	42	..
Unknown - Inconnu	139	73	66	..

Cook Islands - Îles Cook[47]
2015* (+C)

Total	205	...	...	...
0 - 19	24	...	...	...
20 - 24	63	...	...	...
25 - 29	47	...	...	...
30 - 34	38	...	...	...
35 - 39	21	...	...	...
40 - 44	12	...	...	...
45 +	-	...	...	...

Fiji - Fidji
2008 (+C)

Total	17 199	...	...	76.6
0 - 14	3	...	...	..
15 - 19	1 057	...	...	27.5
20 - 24	5 180	...	...	135.3
25 - 29	5 688	...	...	157.8
30 - 34	3 227	...	...	103.4

10. Live births by age of mother and sex of child, general and age-specific fertility rates: latest available year, 2008 - 2017
Naissances vivantes selon l'âge de la mère et le sexe de l'enfant, taux de fécondité et taux de fécondité par âge : dernière année disponible, 2008 - 2017 (continued - suite)

Continent, country or area, year, code[a] and age of mother (in years) / Continent, pays ou zone, année, code[a] et âge de la mère (en années)	Number - Nombre			Rate Taux
	Total	Male Masculin	Female Féminin	

OCEANIA - OCÉANIE

Fiji - Fidji
2008 (+C)
35 - 39	1 488	...	...	53.0
40 - 44	509	...	...	18.6
45 - 49	34	...	...	1.4
50 +	-	...	...	..
Unknown - Inconnu	13	...	...	..

French Polynesia - Polynésie française
2014 (C)
Total	4 161	...	...	...
15 - 19	454	...	...	...
20 - 24	1 079	...	...	...
25 - 29	1 075	...	...	...
30 - 34	888	...	...	...
35 - 39	485	...	...	...
40 - 44	166	...	...	...
45 +	14	...	...	...

Guam[48]
2016 (C)
Total	3 433	1 794	1 639	86.6
0 - 14	1	-	1	..
15 - 19	256	138	118	37.6
20 - 24	946	494	452	144.3
25 - 29	940	487	453	155.9
30 - 34	785	421	364	149.4
35 - 39	396	203	193	81.3
40 - 44	102	49	53	20.3
45 - 49	6	2	4	♦1.2
50 +	-	-	-	..
Unknown - Inconnu	1	-	1	..
2017 (C)
Total	3 292	...	...	82.5
10 - 14	-	...	...	..
15 - 19	275	...	...	39.9
20 - 24	830	...	...	126.7
25 - 29	958	...	...	156.5
30 - 34	733	...	...	136.8
35 - 39	389	...	...	80.1
40 - 44	98	...	...	20.0
45 - 49	8	...	...	♦1.5
50 +	-	...	...	..
Unknown - Inconnu	1	...	...	..

Nauru
2011 (C)
Total	370	190	180	...
15 - 19	40	22	18	...
20 - 24	126	69	57	...
25 - 29	111	57	54	...
30 - 34	55	22	33	...
35 - 39	33	17	16	...
40 - 44	5	3	2	...
45 - 49	-	-	-	...

New Caledonia - Nouvelle-Calédonie
2015 (C)
Total	4 191	...	...	...
0 - 19	197	...	...	...
20 - 24	888	...	...	...
25 - 29	1 148	...	...	...
30 - 34	1 046	...	...	...
35 - 39	671	...	...	...
40 - 44	233	...	...	...
45 - 49	6	...	...	...
50 +	2	...	...	...

Continent, country or area, year, code[a] and age of mother (in years) / Continent, pays ou zone, année, code[a] et âge de la mère (en années)	Number - Nombre			Rate Taux
	Total	Male Masculin	Female Féminin	

OCEANIA - OCÉANIE

New Zealand - Nouvelle-Zélande[49]
2017 (+C)
Total	59 610	30 588	29 022	52.5
10 - 14	18	12	3	..
15 - 19	2 301	1 200	1 098	14.9
20 - 24	9 387	4 818	4 569	55.2
25 - 29	16 734	8 574	8 163	93.7
30 - 34	18 795	9 567	9 225	117.0
35 - 39	9 933	5 154	4 779	66.8
40 - 44	2 292	1 185	1 107	14.9
45 +	150	78	72	0.9
Unknown - Inconnu	45	24	18	..

Niue - Nioué[50]
2009 (C)
Total	31	...	...	...
0 - 14	-	...	...	...
15 - 19	1	...	...	...
20 - 24	9	...	...	...
25 - 29	12	...	...	...
30 - 34	6	...	...	...
35 - 39	1	...	...	...
40 - 44	1	...	...	...
45 +	1	...	...	...

Palau - Palaos
2017 (C)
Total	221	112	109	...
15 - 19	18	8	10	...
20 - 24	60	32	28	...
25 - 29	47	18	29	...
30 - 34	51	25	26	...
35 - 39	35	21	14	...
40 - 44	9	8	1	...
45 - 49	1	-	1	...

Samoa[51]
2011 (I)
Total	5 703	3 055	2 648	133.8
15 - 19	369	209	160	39.2
20 - 24	1 557	831	726	218.3
25 - 29	1 471	793	678	238.6
30 - 34	1 154	603	551	206.1
35 - 39	741	398	343	144.1
40 - 44	338	180	158	69.9
45 - 49	73	41	32	16.9

Tokelau - Tokélaou[52]
2011 (I)
Total	16	...	...	...
0 - 14	-	...	...	...
15 - 19	1	...	...	...
20 - 24	6	...	...	...
25 - 29	4	...	...	...
30 - 34	4	...	...	...
35 - 39	1	...	...	...

Wallis and Futuna Islands - Îles Wallis et Futuna
2008 (C)
Total	185	...	...	...
0 - 14	-	...	...	...
15 - 19	9	...	...	...
20 - 24	38	...	...	...
25 - 29	53	...	...	...
30 - 34	51	...	...	...
35 - 39	29	...	...	...
40 - 44	5	...	...	...
45 +	-	...	...	...

FOOTNOTES - NOTES

♦ Rates based on 30 or fewer births. - Taux basés sur 30 naissances ou moins.

* Provisional. - Données provisoires.

a 'Code' indicates the source of data, as follows:
C - Civil registration, estimated over 90% complete
U - Civil registration, estimated less than 90% complete
| - Other source, estimated reliable
+ - Data tabulated by date of registration rather than occurrence
... Information not available

Le 'Code' indique la source des données, comme suit :
C - Registres de l'état civil considérés complets à 90 p. 100 au moins
U - Registres de l'état civil qui ne sont pas considérés complets à 90 p. 100 au moins
| - Autre source, considérée fiable
+ - Données exploitées selon la date de l'enregistrement et non la date de l'événement
... Information non disponible

[1] Source: Vital Statistics Report 2014. - Source: Vital Statistics Report 2014.
[2] Source: Vital Statistics Report 2016. - Source: Vital Statistics Report 2016.
[3] Data refer to the 12 months preceding the census in September. - Les données se rapportent aux 12 mois précédant le recensement de septembre.
[4] Unadjusted number of births in households referring to the 12 months preceding the census in March. - Le nombre non ajusté de naissances vivantes des ménages ordinaires se rapportent aux 12 mois précédant le recensement de mars.
[5] Unrevised data. - Les données n'ont pas été révisées.
[6] Data refer to the 12 months preceding the census in March. - Les données se rapportent aux 12 mois précédant le recensement de mars.
[7] Data refer to Libyan nationals only. - Les données se raportent aux nationaux libyens seulement.
[8] Data refer to the 12 months preceding the census in June. - Les données se raportent aux 12 mois précédant le recensement de juin.
[9] Data refer to the 12 months preceding the census in April. - Les données se rapportent aux douze mois précédant le recensement d'avril.
[10] Data refer to the 12 months preceding the census in March. Including nomadic population. - Les données se rapportent aux 12 mois précédant le recensement de mars. Y compris la population nomade.
[11] Excludes the islands of St. Brandon and Agalega. - Non compris les îles St. Brandon et Agalega.
[12] Data refer to the 12 months preceding the census in August. - Les données se rapportent aux 12 mois précédant le recensement d'août.
[13] Data refer to the 12 months preceding the census in October. - Les données se rapportent aux 12 mois précédant le recensement de octobre.
[14] Excluding non-residents and foreign service personnel and their dependants. - À l'exclusion des non-résidents et du personnel diplomatique et de leurs charges de famille.
[15] Including Canadian residents temporarily in the United States, but excluding United States residents temporarily in Canada. - Y compris les résidents canadiens se trouvant temporairement aux Etats-Unis, mais ne comprenant pas les résidents des Etats-Unis se trouvant temporairement au Canada.
[16] For confidentiality reasons, live births to mothers aged 50 and over and the adopted children with no information on their birth mother are included in 'age of mother Unknown'. - Pour des raisons de confidentialité, on a classé dans la catégorie « âge de la mère Inconnu» les naissances vivantes concernant des femmes âgées de plus de 50 ans et les enfants adoptés nés de mères sur lesquelles on ne dispose pas d'information.
[17] Excluding children born in the country of non-resident mothers. - Exceptés les enfants nés dans le pays des mères non-résidentes.
[18] Data refer to period from 1 January 2010 to 3 April 2011. Data refer to population in private households. - Les données concernent la période du 1 janvier 2010 au 3 avril 2011. Les données portent sur la population des ménages privés.
[19] Figures for male and female may not add up to the total, since they do not include the category "Unknown". - La somme des chiffres indiqués pour les sexes masculin et féminin peut n'être pas égale au total parce qu'elle n'inclut pas la catégorie " inconnue ".
[20] Data refer to births to resident mothers. - Ces données concernent les enfants nés de mères résidentes.
[21] Excludes nomadic Indian tribes. - Non compris les tribus d'Indiens nomades.

[22] Reason for discrepancy between these figures and corresponding figures shown elsewhere not ascertained. - On ne sait pas comment s'explique la divergence entre ces chiffres et les chiffres correspondants indiqués ailleurs.
[23] Source: Reports of the Ministry of Health. - Source : Rapports du Ministère de la Santé.
[24] Excluding infants born alive of less than 28 weeks' gestation, of less than 1 000 g in weight and 35 cm in length, who die within seven days of birth. - Non compris les enfants nés vivants après moins de 28 semaines de gestations, pesant moins de 1 000 g, mesurant moins de 35 cm et décédés dans les sept jours qui ont suivi leur naissance.
[25] Sources: Births and Deaths National Registration System database, and medical records of government hospitals. - Les sources: Les bases de données des << Births and Deaths National Registration System >> et les dossiers médicaux des hôpitaux du gouvernement.
[26] Data refer to government controlled areas. - Les données se rapportent aux zones contrôlées par le Gouvernement.
[27] Data are from 1 January 2009 to 1 May 2010. - Les données vont du 1er janvier 2009 au 1er mai 2010.
[28] Data refer to current birth data; excluding delayed birth registrations. Data refer to the Iranian Year which begins on 21 March and ends on 20 March of the following year. - Les données se rapportent aux naissances actuelles; les déclarations tardives des naissances ne sont pas compris. Les données concernent l'année iranienne, qui commence le 21 mars et se termine le 20 mars de l'année suivante.
[29] Includes data for East Jerusalem and Israeli residents in certain other territories under occupation by Israeli military forces since June 1967. - Y compris les données pour Jérusalem-Est et les résidents israéliens dans certains autres territoires occupés depuis 1967 par les forces armées israéliennes.
[30] Data refer to Japanese nationals in Japan only. - Les données se raportent aux nationaux japonais au Japon seulement.
[31] Data do not include foreigners. - Les données sur les etrangers ne sont pas inclus.
[32] Data are from Vital Registration System (VRS). - Les données proviennent du système d'enregistrement des faits d'état civil.
[33] Excluding alien armed forces, civilian aliens employed by armed forces, and foreign diplomatic personnel and their dependants. - Non compris les militaires étrangers, les civils étrangers employés par les forces armées ni le personnel diplomatique étranger et les membres de leur famille les accompagnant.
[34] Excluding infants born alive of less than 28 weeks' gestation, of less than 1 000 g in weight and 35 cm in length, who die within seven days of birth. Data have been adjusted for under-registration. - Non compris les enfants nés vivants après moins de 28 semaines de gestation, pesant moins de 1 000 g, mesurant moins de 35 cm et décédés dans les sept jours qui ont suivi leur naissance. Y compris un ajustement pour sous-enregistrement.
[35] Including births occurring abroad of mothers with residence in Austria. - Y compris les naissances survenues à l'étranger des mères avec résidence en Autriche.
[36] Including armed forces stationed outside the country, but excluding alien armed forces stationed in the area. - Y compris les militaires nationaux hors du pays, mais non compris les militaires étrangers en garnison sur le territoire.
[37] Excluding Faeroe Islands and Greenland shown separately, if available. - Non compris les Iles Féroé et le Groenland, qui font l'objet de rubriques distinctes, si disponible.
[38] Including armed forces stationed outside the country. - Y compris les militaires nationaux hors du pays.
[39] Including live births by military personnel and their dependants. - Y compris les naissances vivantes parmi les membres du personnel militaire et leurs personnes à charge.
[40] Data include the live births of women with unknown residence and homeless. Data include the live births of women with Hungarian usual residence regardless of whether the live birth occurred in Hungary or in a foreign country, and do not include the live births of women with foreign country usual residence. - Les données incluent les enfants nés vivants de femmes dont la résidence n'est pas connue et de femmes sans domicile fixe. Les données concernent les enfants nés vivants de femmes dont la résidence habituelle est en Hongrie, que la naissance vivante ait eu lieu en Hongrie ou dans un pays étranger, et ne comprennent pas les enfants nés vivants de femmes dont la résidence habituelle est dans un pays étranger.
[41] Including residents outside the country if listed in a Netherlands population register. - Englobe les résidents se trouvant à l'étranger à condition qu'ils soient inscrits sur le registre de population des Pays-Bas.
[42] Excluding Transnistria and the municipality of Bender. - Les données ne tiennent pas compte de l'information sur la Transnistria et la municipalité de Bender.

⁴³ Excludes data for Kosovo and Metohia. - Sans les données pour le Kosovo et Metohie.

⁴⁴ Data refer to births with weight 500g and more (if weight is unknown - with length 25 centimeters and more, or with gestation during 22 weeks or more). The Government of Ukraine has informed the United Nations that it is not in a position to provide statistical data concerning the Autonomous Republic of Crimea and the city of Sevastopol. - Données concernant les nouveau-nés de 500 grammes ou plus (si le poids est inconnu – de 25 centimètres de long ou plus, ou après une grossesse de 22 semaines ou plus). Le gouvernement Ukrainien a informé l'ONU qu'il n'est pas en mesure de fournir des données statistiques concernant la République autonome de Crimée et la ville de Sébastopol.

⁴⁵ Excluding Channel Islands (Guernsey and Jersey) and Isle of Man, shown separately, if available. Data tabulated by date of occurrence for England and Wales, and by date of registration for Northern Ireland and Scotland. - Non compris les îles Anglo-Normandes (Guernesey et Jersey) et l'île de Man, qui font l'objet de rubriques distinctes, si disponible. Données exploitées selon la date de l'événement pour l'Angleterre et le pays de Galles, et selon la date de l'enregistrement pour l'Irlande du Nord et l'Ecosse.

⁴⁶ Data for certain cells suppressed by national statistical office for confidentiality reasons. - Les données pour certaines cases ont été supprimées par le bureau national de statistiques pour des raisons de confidentialité.

⁴⁷ Excluding Niue, shown separately, which is part of Cook Islands, but because of remoteness is administered separately. - Non compris Nioué, qui fait l'objet d'une rubrique distincte et qui fait partie des îles Cook, mais qui, en raison de son éloignement, est administrée séparément.

⁴⁸ Including United States military personnel, their dependants and contract employees. - Y compris les militaires des Etats-Unis, les membres de leur famille les accompagnant et les agents contractuels des Etats-Unis.

⁴⁹ Random rounding to base 3 is applied in this table as a confidentiality measure. Data refers to births registered in the country to mothers resident in the country. - Les chiffres sont arrondis à la base 3 de manière aléatoire, pour des raisons de confidentialité. Les données se rapportent aux naissances enregistrées dans le pays pour lesquelles la mère réside dans le pays.

⁵⁰ Includes children born in New Zealand to women resident in Niue who chose to travel to New Zealand to give birth. - Y compris les enfants nés en Nouvelle-Zélande de femmes résidant à Nioué qui ont choisi de se rendre en Nouvelle-Zélande pour accoucher.

⁵¹ Data refer to the 12 months preceding the census in November. - Données se rapportant aux 12 mois précédant le recensement de novembre.

⁵² Data refer to usually resident population present on census night. Data refer to the 12 months preceding the census in October. - Les données concernent la population habituellement résidente présente la nuit du recensement. Les données se rapportent aux 12 mois précédant le recensement de octobre.

Table 11 - *Demographic Yearbook 2017*

Table 11 presents live births by age of father and live birth rates by age of father for the latest available year between 2008 and 2017.

Description of variables: Age is defined as age at last birthday, that is, the difference between the date of birth and the date of the occurrence of the event, expressed in completed solar years. The age classification used in this table is the following: under 20 years, 5-year age groups through 60-64 years, 65 years and over, and age unknown. A different classification may appear as provided by reporting country or area.

Rate computation: Live-birth rates specific to age of father are the annual number of births to a man in each age group per 1 000 male population in the same age group. These rates are calculated by the Statistics Division of the United Nations.

Since relatively few births occur to men below 15 or above 59 years of age, birth rates for men under 20 years of age and for those 55 years of age or over are computed on the male population aged 15-19 and 55-59, respectively. Similarly, the rate for men of "All ages" is based on all live births irrespective of age of father, and it is computed on the male population aged 15-59 years.

Births to fathers of unknown age are distributed proportionately across the age groups, by the Statistics Division of the United Nations, in accordance with the distribution of births by age of father prior to the calculation of the rates.

The population used in computing the rates is the estimated or enumerated distribution of males by age. First priority is given to the estimated population and second priority to the enumerated population, i.e. to census returns of the year to which the births refer.

Rates presented in this table are limited to those for countries or areas having at least a total of 100 live births in a given year.

Reliability of data: Data from civil registers of live births which are reported as incomplete (less than 90 per cent completeness) or of unknown completeness are considered unreliable and are set in *italics* rather than in roman type. Rates are not computed if the data on live births from civil registers are reported as incomplete (less than 90 per cent completeness) or of unknown completeness. Table 9 and the technical notes for that table provide more detailed information on the completeness of birth registration. For more information about the quality of vital statistics data in general, see section 4.2 of the Technical Notes.

Limitations: Statistics on live births by age of father are subject to the same qualifications as have been set forth for vital statistics in general and birth statistics in particular as discussed in section 4 of the Technical Notes. These include differences in the completeness of registration, the method used to determine age of father and the quality of the reported information relating to age of father.

The reliability of the data described above, is an important factor in considering the limitations. In addition, some live births are tabulated by date of registration and not by date of occurrence; these are indicated in the table by a plus sign "+". Whenever the lag between the date of occurrence and date of registration is prolonged and, therefore, a large proportion of the live-birth registrations are delayed, birth statistics for any given year may be seriously affected. For example, the age of the father will almost always refer to the date of registration rather than to the date of birth of the child. Hence, in those countries or areas where registration of births is delayed, possibly for years, statistics on births by age of father should be used with caution.

Another factor which limits international comparability is the practice of some countries or areas of not including in live birth statistics infants who were born alive but died before the registration of the birth or within the first 24 hours of life, thus underestimating the total number of live births. Statistics of this type are footnoted.

Because these statistics are classified according to age, they are subject to the limitations with respect to accuracy of age reporting similar to those already discussed in connection with section 3.1.3 of the Technical Notes. The factors influencing the accuracy of reporting may be somewhat dissimilar in vital statistics (because of the differences in the method of taking a census and registering a birth) but, in general, the same errors can be observed. The absence of frequencies in the unknown age group does not necessarily indicate completely accurate reporting and tabulation of the age item. It is often an indication that the unknowns have been eliminated by assigning ages to them before tabulation, or by proportionate distribution after tabulation.

On the other hand, large frequencies in the unknown age category may indicate that a large proportion of the births are born outside of wedlock, the records for which tend to be incomplete so far as characteristics of the parents are concerned.

Another limitation of age reporting may result from calculating age of father at birth of child (or at time of registration) from year of birth rather than from day, month and year of birth. Information on this factor is given in footnotes when known.

In few countries, data by age refer to deliveries rather than to live births causing under-enumeration in the event of a multiple birth. This practice leads to lack of strict comparability, both among countries or areas relying on this practice and between data shown in this table and table 9.

Rates shown in this table are subject to the same limitations that affect the corresponding statistics on live births. In cases of rates based on births tabulated by date of registration and not by date of occurrence; the effect of including delayed registration on the distribution of births by age of father may be noted in the age-specific fertility rates for men at older ages. In some cases, high age-specific rates for men aged 55 years and over may reflect age of father at registration of birth and not fertility at these older ages.

Earlier data: Live births and live birth rates by age of father have been shown in previous issues of the *Demographic Yearbook*. Information on the specific years is presented in the Historical Index.

Tableau 11 – *Annuaire démographique 2017*

Le tableau 11 présente les données les plus récentes disponibles pour la période 2008 - 2017 sur les naissances vivantes selon l'âge du père et les taux des naissances vivantes selon l'âge du père.

Description des variables : l'âge désigne l'âge au dernier anniversaire, c'est-à-dire la différence entre la date de naissance et la date de l'événement exprimée en années solaires révolues. La classification par âge utilisée dans ce tableau comprend les catégories suivantes : moins de 20 ans, groupes quinquennaux jusqu'à 60-64 ans, 65 ans et plus, et âge inconnu. Des groupes d'âge différents sont parfois utilisés lorsque les pays ou territoires ont fourni les données dans une autre classification.

Les taux de natalité selon l'âge du père représentent le nombre annuel de naissances vivantes intervenues dans un groupe d'âge donné pour 1 000 hommes du groupe d'âge. Ces taux ont été calculés par la Division de statistique de l'ONU.

Étant donné que le nombre de naissances parmi les hommes de moins de 15 ans ou de plus de 59 ans est relativement peu élevé, les taux de natalité parmi les hommes âgées de moins de 20 ans et celles de 55 ans et plus ont été calculés sur la base des populations masculines âgées de 15 à 19 ans et de 55 à 59 ans, respectivement. De même, le taux pour les hommes de « tous âges » est fondé sur la totalité des naissances vivantes, indépendamment de l'âge du père et ce chiffre est rapporté à l'effectif de la population masculine âgée de 15 à 59 ans.

Les naissances pour lesquelles l'âge du père était inconnu ont été réparties par la Division de statistique de l'ONU, avant le calcul des taux, suivant les proportions observées pour celles où l'âge du père était connu.

Les chiffres de population utilisés pour le calcul des taux proviennent de dénombrements ou de répartitions estimatives de la population masculine selon l'âge. On a utilisé de préférence les estimations de la population; à défaut, on s'est contenté des données censitaires se rapportant à l'année des naissances.

Les taux présentés dans ce tableau ne concernent que les pays ou zones où l'on a enregistré un total d'au moins 100 naissances vivantes dans une année donnée.

Fiabilité des données : les données sur les naissances vivantes provenant des registres de l'état civil qui sont déclarées incomplètes (degré de complétude inférieur à 90 p. 100) ou dont le degré de complétude n'est pas connu sont jugées douteuses et apparaissent en italique et non en caractères romains. On a choisi de ne pas faire figurer dans le tableau 11 des taux calculés à partir de données sur les naissances vivantes issues de registres de l'état civil qui sont déclarées incomplètes (degré de complétude inférieur à 90 p. 100) ou dont le degré de complétude n'est pas connu. Le tableau 9 et les notes techniques qui s'y rapportent présentent des renseignements plus détaillés sur le degré de complétude de l'enregistrement des naissances vivantes. Pour plus de précisions sur la qualité des statistiques de l'état civil en général, voir la section 4.2 des Notes techniques.

Insuffisance des données : les statistiques relatives aux naissances vivantes selon l'âge du père appellent toutes les réserves qui ont été formulées à propos des statistiques de l'état civil en général et des statistiques de naissances en particulier (voir la section 4 des Notes techniques). Ceci inclut les différences de complétude d'enregistrement des faits d'état civil, de méthode pour déterminer l'âge du père et de qualité d'information concernant l'âge du père.

La fiabilité des données, au sujet de laquelle des indications ont été données plus haut, est un facteur important. Il faut également tenir compte du fait que, dans certains cas, les données relatives aux naissances vivantes sont exploitées selon la date de l'enregistrement et non la date de l'événement ; ces cas ont été signalés dans le tableau par le signe '+'. Chaque fois que le décalage entre l'événement et son enregistrement est grand et qu'une forte proportion des naissances vivantes fait l'objet d'un enregistrement tardif, les statistiques des naissances vivantes pour une année donnée peuvent être considérablement faussées. Par exemple, l'âge du père représente presque toujours son âge à la date de l'enregistrement et non à la date de la naissance de l'enfant. Ainsi, dans les pays ou zones où l'enregistrement des naissances est tardif, le retard atteignant parfois plusieurs années, il faut utiliser avec prudence les statistiques concernant les naissances selon l'âge du père.

Un autre facteur qui nuit à la comparabilité internationale est la pratique de certains pays ou zones qui consiste à ne pas inclure dans les statistiques des naissances vivantes les enfants nés vivants mais décédés avant l'enregistrement de leur naissance ou dans les 24 heures qui ont suivi la naissance, pratique qui conduit à sous-estimer le nombre total de naissances vivantes. Quand pareil facteur a joué, cela a été signalé en note à la fin du tableau.

Étant donné que les statistiques du tableau 11 sont classées selon l'âge, elles appellent les mêmes réserves concernant l'exactitude des déclarations d'âge que celles formulées à la section 3.1.3 des Notes techniques. Dans le cas des statistiques de l'état civil, les facteurs qui interviennent à cet égard sont parfois différents, étant donné que le recensement de la population et l'enregistrement des naissances se font par des méthodes différentes, mais, d'une manière générale, les erreurs observées seront les mêmes. Si aucun nombre ne figure dans la rangée réservée aux âges inconnus, cela ne signifie pas nécessairement que les déclarations d'âge et l'exploitation des données par âge ont été tout à fait exactes. C'est souvent une indication que l'on a attribué un âge aux personnes d'âge inconnu avant l'exploitation des données ou qu'elles ont été réparties proportionnellement entre les différents groupes après cette opération.

À l'inverse, lorsque le nombre des personnes d'âge inconnu est important, cela peut signifier que la proportion de naissances parmi les parents célibataires est élevée, étant donné qu'en pareil cas l'acte de naissance ne contient pas tous les renseignements concernant les parents.

Les déclarations par âge peuvent comporter des distorsions, du fait que l'âge du père au moment de la naissance d'un enfant (ou de la déclaration de naissance) est donné par année de naissance et non par date exacte (jour, mois et année).

Dans quelques pays, la classification par âges se réfère aux accouchements, et non aux naissances vivantes, ce qui conduit à un sous-dénombrement en cas de naissances gémellaires. Cette pratique nuit à la comparabilité des données, à la fois entre pays ou zones qui recourent à cette méthode et entre les données présentées dans le tableau 11 et celles du tableau 9.

Les taux présentés dans ce tableau, sont sujets aux mêmes limitations qui affectent les statistiques correspondantes de naissances vivantes. Dans le cas des taux basés sur des naissances par date d'enregistrement et non par date d'occurrence, l'effet peut être visible sur les taux de fécondité par âge des hommes aux âges plus élevés. Dans certains cas, les taux de fécondité des hommes de plus de 55 ans peuvent refléter l'âge du père à l'enregistrement plus que la fécondité à ces âges.

Données publiées antérieurement : Les données sur les naissances vivantes selon l'âge du père et les taux des naissances vivantes selon l'âge du père ont été publié antérieurement dans l'*Annuaire démographique*. Pour plus de précisions concernant les années pour lesquels des données ont été publiées, se reporter à l'index historique.

11. Live births and live birth rates by age of father: latest available year, 2008 - 2017
Naissances vivantes et taux de natalité selon l'âge du père : dernière année disponible, 2008 - 2017

Continent, country or area, year, code[a] and age of father (in years) / Continent, pays ou zone, année, code[a] et âge du père (en années)	Number - Nombre Both sexes Les deux sexes	Rate Taux
AFRICA - AFRIQUE		
Egypt - Égypte		
2012 (+C)		
Total	2 629 769	101.6
0 - 19	4 700	1.2
20 - 24	119 826	28.3
25 - 29	1 489 063	364.7
30 - 34	502 329	150.1
35 - 39	288 404	111.4
40 - 44	134 381	59.4
45 - 49	60 206	29.0
50 - 54	19 391	10.6
55 - 59	6 333	4.2
60 +	5 136	..
Mauritius - Maurice[1]		
2017 (+C)		
Total	13 385	32.2
0 - 19	213	4.5
20 - 24	1 381	29.4
25 - 29	2 810	61.9
30 - 34	3 421	84.0
35 - 39	3 036	62.4
40 - 44	1 246	29.6
45 - 49	431	10.6
50 - 54	143	3.2
55 - 59	36	0.9
60 - 64	14	..
65 +	7	..
Unknown - Inconnu	647	..
South Africa - Afrique du Sud		
2016 (C)		
Total	876 435	51.3
0 - 19	4 502	4.7
20 - 24	35 319	33.8
25 - 29	72 871	66.8
30 - 34	93 538	106.1
35 - 39	69 193	90.6
40 - 44	41 377	65.3
45 - 49	17 105	32.4
50 - 54	6 369	14.7
55 - 59	2 340	6.6
60 - 64	844	..
Unknown - Inconnu	532 977	..
AMERICA, NORTH - AMÉRIQUE DU NORD		
Bahamas		
2014* (+U)		
Total	4 196	...
0 - 19	63	...
20 - 24	576	...
25 - 29	742	...
30 - 34	815	...
35 - 39	659	...
40 - 44	388	...
45 - 49	167	...
50 - 54	60	...
55 - 59	23	...
60 - 64	5	..
65 +	6	..
Unknown - Inconnu	692	..
Canada[2]		
2009 (C)		
Total	380 863	35.1
0 - 19	4 918	4.5
20 - 24	29 959	26.5
25 - 29	84 206	75.0

Continent, country or area, year, code[a] and age of father (in years) / Continent, pays ou zone, année, code[a] et âge du père (en années)	Number - Nombre Both sexes Les deux sexes	Rate Taux
AMERICA, NORTH - AMÉRIQUE DU NORD		
Canada[2]		
2009 (C)		
30 - 34	117 201	109.5
35 - 39	79 126	72.1
40 - 44	31 813	26.9
45 - 49	9 913	7.5
50 - 54	2 642	2.2
55 - 59	683	0.7
60 - 64	200	..
65 +	77	..
Unknown - Inconnu	20 125	
Costa Rica		
2017* (C)		
Total	68 816	45.3
0 - 19	1 084	7.8
20 - 24	6 046	43.7
25 - 29	9 333	77.0
30 - 34	9 817	86.7
35 - 39	6 529	63.1
40 - 44	3 038	32.5
45 - 49	1 234	14.1
50 - 54	538	5.7
55 - 59	189	2.2
60 - 64	81	..
65 +	6 291	..
Unknown - Inconnu	24 636	..
Cuba		
2016 (C)		
Total	116 872	32.3
0 - 19	2 566	8.1
20 - 24	17 335	53.0
25 - 29	29 997	81.5
30 - 34	22 579	71.0
35 - 39	13 030	45.2
40 - 44	9 312	23.1
45 - 49	4 690	10.9
50 - 54	1 923	4.6
55 - 59	449	1.6
60 - 64	165	..
65 +	113	..
Unknown - Inconnu	14 713	..
Dominican Republic - République dominicaine		
2016 (U)		
Total	139 583	...
0 - 19	3 277	...
20 - 24	23 323	...
25 - 29	31 907	...
30 - 34	27 351	...
35 - 39	17 776	...
40 - 44	9 075	...
45 - 49	4 576	...
50 +	3 754	...
Unknown - Inconnu	18 544	..
El Salvador[3]		
2014 (C)		
Total	108 903	62.6
0 - 19	6 884	22.6
20 - 24	22 522	84.4
25 - 29	22 722	115.0
30 - 34	18 048	114.4
35 - 39	12 219	84.6
40 - 44	6 345	47.2
45 - 49	2 957	25.3
50 - 54	1 360	13.7
55 - 59	666	7.9
60 - 64	309	

11. Live births and live birth rates by age of father: latest available year, 2008 - 2017
Naissances vivantes et taux de natalité selon l'âge du père : dernière année disponible, 2008 - 2017 (continued - suite)

Continent, country or area, year, code[a] and age of father (in years) / Continent, pays ou zone, année, code[a] et âge du père (en années)	Number - Nombre Both sexes Les deux sexes	Rate Taux
AMERICA, NORTH - AMÉRIQUE DU NORD		
El Salvador[3]		
2014 (C)		
65 +	199	..
Unknown - Inconnu	14 672	..
Greenland - Groenland		
2008 (C)		
Total	834	...
0 - 19	25	...
20 - 24	109	...
25 - 29	169	...
30 - 34	150	...
35 - 39	112	...
40 - 44	91	...
45 - 49	35	...
50 - 54	9	...
55 - 59	1	...
60 +	-	..
Unknown - Inconnu	133	..
Guatemala		
2016 (C)		
Total	390 382	...
0 - 19	19 482	...
20 - 24	86 609	...
25 - 29	86 999	...
30 - 34	65 396	...
35 - 39	42 972	...
40 - 44	21 537	...
45 - 49	8 592	...
50 +	6 438	...
Unknown - Inconnu	52 357	...
Mexico - Mexique[4]		
2015 (C)		
Total	2 096 274	57.6
0 - 19	131 021	25.5
20 - 24	476 794	98.9
25 - 29	494 282	114.9
30 - 34	396 268	100.5
35 - 39	237 323	63.4
40 - 44	111 077	31.8
45 - 49	40 417	13.1
50 - 54	15 730	6.1
55 - 59	6 577	3.1
60 - 64	2 558	..
65 +	1 554	..
Unknown - Inconnu	182 673	..
Panama		
2016* (C)		
Total	75 184	60.0
0 - 19	2 833	22.4
20 - 24	10 888	92.3
25 - 29	12 852	114.6
30 - 34	11 624	107.8
35 - 39	7 697	74.7
40 - 44	4 199	43.1
45 - 49	1 869	21.3
50 - 54	855	11.4
55 - 59	269	4.4
60 - 64	124	..
65 +	92	..
Unknown - Inconnu	21 882	..
Puerto Rico - Porto Rico		
2017 (C)		
Total	24 370	...
0 - 19	945	...
20 - 24	5 585	...
25 - 29	6 299	...
30 - 34	4 896	...

Continent, country or area, year, code[a] and age of father (in years) / Continent, pays ou zone, année, code[a] et âge du père (en années)	Number - Nombre Both sexes Les deux sexes	Rate Taux
AMERICA, NORTH - AMÉRIQUE DU NORD		
Puerto Rico - Porto Rico		
2017 (C)		
35 - 39	3 057	...
40 - 44	1 331	...
45 - 49	493	...
50 - 54	215	...
55 - 59	72	...
60 - 64	22	...
65 +	31	...
Unknown - Inconnu	1 424	..
Trinidad and Tobago - Trinité-et-Tobago		
2009 (C)		
Total	17 949	...
0 - 19	389	...
20 - 24	3 027	...
25 - 29	4 916	...
30 - 34	4 149	...
35 - 39	2 682	...
40 - 44	1 416	...
45 - 49	730	...
50 - 54	259	...
55 - 59	73	...
60 +	51	...
Unknown - Inconnu	257	..
United States of America - États-Unis d'Amérique		
2015 (C)		
Total	3 978 497	41.1
0 - 19	78 966	8.3
20 - 24	477 664	46.6
25 - 29	866 460	86.4
30 - 34	1 031 310	107.7
35 - 39	648 051	72.5
40 - 44	263 377	29.9
45 - 49	89 921	9.9
50 - 54	29 105	3.0
55 +	12 911	1.4
Unknown - Inconnu	480 732	..
AMERICA, SOUTH - AMÉRIQUE DU SUD		
Chile - Chili		
2015 (C)		
Total	244 670	41.9
0 - 19	10 927	17.8
20 - 24	37 842	56.0
25 - 29	52 737	76.6
30 - 34	53 644	86.4
35 - 39	37 515	66.2
40 - 44	19 185	34.1
45 - 49	6 885	12.1
50 +	3 541	3.5
Unknown - Inconnu	22 394	..
Colombia - Colombie		
2016 (U)		
Total	647 521	...
0 - 19	39 497	...
20 - 24	146 571	...
25 - 29	162 214	...
30 - 34	131 977	...
35 - 39	82 070	...
40 - 44	37 761	...
45 - 49	15 596	...
50 - 54	6 859	...
55 - 59	2 078	...
60 - 64	834	...

11. Live births and live birth rates by age of father: latest available year, 2008 - 2017
Naissances vivantes et taux de natalité selon l'âge du père : dernière année disponible, 2008 - 2017 (continued - suite)

Continent, country or area, year, code[a] and age of father (in years) / Continent, pays ou zone, année, code[a] et âge du père (en années)	Number - Nombre — Both sexes Les deux sexes	Rate Taux
AMERICA, SOUTH - AMÉRIQUE DU SUD		
Colombia - Colombie		
2016 (U)		
65 +	363	..
Unknown - Inconnu	21 701	..
Ecuador - Équateur		
2011 (+U)		
Total	229 780	...
0 - 19	4 219	...
20 - 24	16 514	...
25 - 29	17 040	...
30 - 34	14 115	...
35 - 39	8 339	...
40 - 44	4 405	...
45 - 49	1 864	...
50 - 54	719	...
55 - 59	274	...
60 - 64	104	..
65 +	94	..
Unknown - Inconnu	162 093	..
Uruguay		
2016 (C)		
Total	47 058	45.1
0 - 19	1 186	13.2
20 - 24	4 945	55.3
25 - 29	6 628	79.1
30 - 34	7 810	98.7
35 - 39	6 191	78.0
40 - 44	2 777	37.2
45 - 49	1 024	15.2
50 - 54	386	5.9
55 - 59	138	2.2
60 - 64	45	..
65 +	25	..
Unknown - Inconnu	15 903	..
Venezuela (Bolivarian Republic of) - Venezuela (République bolivarienne du)		
2017* (U)		
Total	561 603	...
0 - 19	25 980	...
20 - 24	96 972	...
25 - 29	111 372	...
30 - 34	94 154	...
35 - 39	61 871	...
40 - 44	32 363	...
45 - 49	16 005	...
50 - 54	6 995	...
55 - 59	2 824	...
60 - 64	1 135	..
65 +	596	..
Unknown - Inconnu	111 336	..
ASIA - ASIE		
Azerbaijan - Azerbaïdjan[5]		
2016 (+C)		
Total	151 420	46.5
0 - 19	353	1.0
20 - 24	20 910	47.2
25 - 29	60 916	129.8
30 - 34	42 261	100.4
35 - 39	17 908	49.9
40 - 44	6 367	21.3
45 - 49	1 938	6.2
50 - 54	542	1.7
55 +	225	0.8

Continent, country or area, year, code[a] and age of father (in years) / Continent, pays ou zone, année, code[a] et âge du père (en années)	Number - Nombre — Both sexes Les deux sexes	Rate Taux
ASIA - ASIE		
Bahrain - Bahreïn[6]		
2016 (C)		
Total	20 714	29.3
0 - 19	34	0.9
20 - 24	1 255	18.9
25 - 29	4 769	35.6
30 - 34	5 987	42.0
35 - 39	4 559	43.1
40 - 44	2 495	31.0
45 - 49	1 006	16.3
50 - 54	379	8.6
55 - 59	150	4.7
60 - 64	23	..
65 +	53	..
Unknown - Inconnu	4	..
Brunei Darussalam - Brunéi Darussalam		
2016 (+C)		
Total	6 437	43.3
0 - 19	22	♦1.2
20 - 24	352	18.3
25 - 29	1 595	79.6
30 - 34	1 940	107.3
35 - 39	1 274	76.4
40 - 44	559	37.9
45 - 49	188	14.7
50 - 54	52	4.8
55 +	42	4.7
Unknown - Inconnu	413	..
China, Hong Kong SAR - Chine, Hong Kong RAS		
2017 (C)		
Total	56 548	26.5
0 - 19	99	0.6
20 - 24	1 676	7.8
25 - 29	7 985	35.3
30 - 34	17 940	79.7
35 - 39	16 340	72.1
40 - 44	7 268	31.7
45 - 49	2 596	11.0
50 - 54	1 022	3.7
55 - 59	464	1.5
60 - 64	154	..
65 +	55	..
Unknown - Inconnu	949	..
China, Macao SAR - Chine, Macao RAS		
2017 (C)		
Total	6 529	...
0 - 24	213	...
25 - 29	1 724	...
30 - 34	2 338	...
35 - 39	1 229	...
40 - 44	532	...
45 +	427	...
Unknown - Inconnu	66	..
Cyprus - Chypre[7]		
2016 (C)		
Total	9 455	36.5
0 - 19	30	1.2
20 - 24	348	10.8
25 - 29	1 731	49.6
30 - 34	3 400	106.2
35 - 39	2 472	86.6
40 - 44	889	35.4
45 - 49	308	12.2
50 +	139	2.7
Unknown - Inconnu	138	..

11. Live births and live birth rates by age of father: latest available year, 2008 - 2017
Naissances vivantes et taux de natalité selon l'âge du père : dernière année disponible, 2008 - 2017 (continued - suite)

Continent, country or area, year, code[a] and age of father (in years) / Continent, pays ou zone, année, code[a] et âge du père (en années)	Number - Nombre — Both sexes Les deux sexes	Rate Taux	Continent, country or area, year, code[a] and age of father (in years) / Continent, pays ou zone, année, code[a] et âge du père (en années)	Number - Nombre — Both sexes Les deux sexes	Rate Taux
ASIA - ASIE			**ASIA - ASIE**		
Georgia - Géorgie			**Kyrgyzstan - Kirghizstan**		
2016 (C)			2016 (C)		
Total	56 569	51.1	50 - 54	713	5.7
0 - 19	569	5.1	55 - 59	215	2.0
20 - 24	8 640	72.2	60 - 64	47	..
25 - 29	16 650	121.9	65 +	26	..
30 - 34	14 105	107.3	Unknown - Inconnu	15 928	..
35 - 39	8 738	72.8	**Malaysia - Malaisie**		
40 - 44	4 421	38.0	2016 (C)		
45 - 49	1 529	13.7	Total	508 203	46.6
50 - 54	394	3.3	0 - 19	2 231	1.6
55 +	154	1.3	20 - 24	30 353	18.6
Unknown - Inconnu	1 369	..	25 - 29	124 484	76.2
Israel - Israël[8]			30 - 34	158 970	112.5
2016 (C)			35 - 39	100 250	88.7
Total	181 405	75.6	40 - 44	45 744	48.3
0 - 19	368	1.1	45 - 49	16 587	19.8
20 - 24	14 949	49.1	50 - 54	5 437	7.0
25 - 29	40 404	138.5	55 - 59	1 891	2.9
30 - 34	54 877	193.5	60 - 64	540	..
35 - 39	40 164	149.1	65 +	220	..
40 - 44	18 338	71.6	Unknown - Inconnu	21 496	..
45 - 49	4 995	23.0	**Maldives[10]**		
50 - 54	1 257	6.5	2016 (C)		
55 - 59	414	2.3	Total	6 756	59.1
60 - 64	160	..	0 - 19	1	♦0.1
65 +	52	..	20 - 24	410	23.8
Unknown - Inconnu	5 427	..	25 - 29	1 892	99.7
Japan - Japon[9]			30 - 34	2 038	122.3
2016 (C)			35 - 39	1 262	102.3
Total	954 576	27.5	40 - 44	658	66.5
0 - 19	3 904	1.3	45 - 49	279	31.4
20 - 24	52 016	16.5	50 - 54	73	9.3
25 - 29	193 913	59.0	55 - 59	28	♦4.3
30 - 34	318 916	86.1	60 - 64	8	..
35 - 39	239 785	57.8	65 +	-	..
40 - 44	108 934	22.0	Unknown - Inconnu	107	..
45 - 49	28 720	6.3	**Oman**		
50 - 54	6 137	1.5	2017 (C)		
55 - 59	1 559	0.4	Total	90 371	38.1
60 - 64	480	..	0 - 19	40	0.3
65 +	212	..	20 - 24	3 737	15.0
Kazakhstan			25 - 29	20 505	39.7
2017 (C)			30 - 34	26 538	54.9
Total	390 262	72.6	35 - 39	19 274	55.6
0 - 19	1 229	2.3	40 - 44	9 893	43.7
20 - 24	42 943	69.3	45 - 49	3 808	23.8
25 - 29	119 110	162.3	50 - 54	1 407	13.8
30 - 34	101 053	148.7	55 - 59	643	9.2
35 - 39	58 052	102.0	60 - 64	253	..
40 - 44	27 260	53.5	65 +	274	..
45 - 49	7 490	16.0	Unknown - Inconnu	3 999	..
50 - 54	1 702	3.9	**Philippines**		
55 - 59	433	1.1	2016 (C)		
60 - 64	121	..	Total	1 731 289	54.4
65 +	35	..	0 - 19	52 070	10.8
Unknown - Inconnu	30 834	..	20 - 24	327 477	71.7
Kyrgyzstan - Kirghizstan			25 - 29	421 840	105.4
2016 (C)			30 - 34	350 258	100.3
Total	158 160	86.0	35 - 39	240 212	75.8
0 - 19	413	1.8	40 - 44	121 795	43.2
20 - 24	18 791	72.3	45 - 49	51 496	20.4
25 - 29	49 641	189.4	50 - 54	17 712	8.2
30 - 34	37 790	176.0	55 - 59	6 565	3.8
35 - 39	21 462	125.6	60 - 64	2 639	..
40 - 44	10 116	68.4	65 +	1 709	..
45 - 49	3 018	22.0	Unknown - Inconnu	137 552	..

11. Live births and live birth rates by age of father: latest available year, 2008 - 2017
Naissances vivantes et taux de natalité selon l'âge du père : dernière année disponible, 2008 - 2017 (continued - suite)

Continent, country or area, year, code[a] and age of father (in years) / Continent, pays ou zone, année, code[a] et âge du père (en années)	Number - Nombre — Both sexes Les deux sexes	Rate Taux
ASIA - ASIE		
Qatar		
2016 (C)		
Total	26 816	15.3
0 - 19	8	♦0.1
20 - 24	845	3.7
25 - 29	4 613	12.3
30 - 34	8 528	24.4
35 - 39	7 038	26.9
40 - 44	3 559	18.0
45 - 49	1 403	10.1
50 +	822	5.8
Republic of Korea - République de Corée[11]		
2015 (C)		
Total	438 420	24.5
0 - 19	614	0.4
20 - 24	6 786	3.7
25 - 29	45 153	26.4
30 - 34	187 484	94.0
35 - 39	140 994	71.1
40 - 44	43 404	19.5
45 - 49	7 854	3.6
50 - 54	1 285	0.6
55 - 59	274	0.1
60 - 64	49	..
65 +	17	..
Unknown - Inconnu	4 506	..
Singapore - Singapour		
2017 (C)		
Total	39 615	31.1
0 - 19	84	0.7
20 - 24	835	6.4
25 - 29	5 989	42.5
30 - 34	13 758	105.1
35 - 39	11 677	82.7
40 - 44	4 732	31.8
45 - 49	1 431	9.8
50 - 54	469	3.0
55 - 59	141	0.9
60 - 64	42	..
65 +	10	..
Unknown - Inconnu	447	..
Tajikistan - Tadjikistan[12]		
2016 (U)		
Total	230 044	...
0 - 19	569	...
20 - 24	44 011	...
25 - 29	90 755	...
30 - 34	51 752	...
35 - 39	21 924	...
40 - 44	7 937	...
45 - 49	2 444	...
50 - 54	773	...
55 - 59	393	...
60 - 64	172	..
65 +	88	..
Unknown - Inconnu	9 226	..
Turkey - Turquie		
2016 (C)		
Total	1 309 771	50.8
0 - 19	7 153	2.1
20 - 24	110 639	34.4
25 - 29	367 480	117.1
30 - 34	403 372	127.4
35 - 39	266 020	82.0
40 - 44	103 823	37.0
45 - 49	27 694	11.6
50 - 54	7 957	3.4

Continent, country or area, year, code[a] and age of father (in years) / Continent, pays ou zone, année, code[a] et âge du père (en années)	Number - Nombre — Both sexes Les deux sexes	Rate Taux
ASIA - ASIE		
Turkey - Turquie		
2016 (C)		
55 - 59	1 812	1.0
60 - 64	817	..
65 +	433	..
Unknown - Inconnu	12 571	..
Uzbekistan - Ouzbékistan[13]		
2015 (+C)		
Total	672 996	66.2
0 - 19	1 241	0.9
20 - 24	104 638	63.5
25 - 29	304 347	195.0
30 - 34	178 532	137.9
35 - 39	64 178	59.7
40 - 44	15 532	16.2
45 - 49	2 988	3.7
50 - 54	889	1.2
55 - 59	378	0.6
60 - 64	55	..
65 +	218	..
EUROPE		
Åland Islands - Îles d'Åland		
2012 (C)		
Total	292	35.4
0 - 19	-	-
20 - 24	20	♦25.1
25 - 29	57	76.1
30 - 34	83	100.3
35 - 39	77	87.8
40 - 44	25	♦27.3
45 - 49	10	♦10.2
50 - 54	2	♦2.2
55 - 59	1	♦1.1
60 - 64	-	..
65 +	-	..
Unknown - Inconnu	17	..
Albania - Albanie		
2016 (U)		
Total	31 733	...
0 - 19	80	...
20 - 24	1 638	...
25 - 29	8 362	...
30 - 34	11 079	...
35 - 39	6 372	...
40 - 44	2 613	...
45 - 49	800	...
50 - 54	169	...
55 - 59	48	...
60 - 64	12	...
65 +	3	..
Unknown - Inconnu	557	..
Andorra - Andorre		
2015 (C)		
Total	659	...
0 - 19	3	...
20 - 24	18	...
25 - 29	70	...
30 - 34	203	...
35 - 39	202	...
40 - 44	104	...
45 - 49	23	...
50 - 54	11	...
55 - 59	4	...
60 - 64	3	..

11. Live births and live birth rates by age of father: latest available year, 2008 - 2017
Naissances vivantes et taux de natalité selon l'âge du père : dernière année disponible, 2008 - 2017 (continued - suite)

Continent, country or area, year, code[a] and age of father (in years) / Continent, pays ou zone, année, code[a] et âge du père (en années)	Number - Nombre Both sexes Les deux sexes	Rate Taux
EUROPE		
Andorra - Andorre		
2015 (C)		
65 +	-	..
Unknown - Inconnu	18	..
Austria - Autriche[14]		
2016 (C)		
Total	50 712	18.7
0 - 19	53	0.2
20 - 24	2 113	7.4
25 - 29	9 758	32.2
30 - 34	16 857	55.8
35 - 39	13 156	46.2
40 - 44	5 844	19.9
45 - 49	2 093	6.0
50 - 54	575	1.6
55 - 59	173	0.6
60 - 64	63	..
65 +	27	..
Belarus - Bélarus[13]		
2016 (C)		
Total	102 143	35.0
0 - 19	584	2.5
20 - 24	12 034	40.9
25 - 29	34 791	90.4
30 - 34	31 549	81.3
35 - 39	15 739	46.2
40 - 44	5 392	17.0
45 - 49	1 495	4.9
50 - 54	387	1.2
55 +	172	0.5
Belgium - Belgique		
2014 (C)		
Total	125 014	37.3
0 - 19	532	1.7
20 - 24	6 420	18.9
25 - 29	27 224	79.5
30 - 34	41 459	116.9
35 - 39	25 524	72.7
40 - 44	11 502	30.7
45 - 49	4 559	11.7
50 - 54	1 602	4.1
55 - 59	502	1.4
60 - 64	153	..
65 +	64	..
Unknown - Inconnu	5 473	..
Bosnia and Herzegovina - Bosnie-Herzégovine		
2010 (C)		
Total	33 528	28.0
0 - 19	99	0.7
20 - 24	3 174	23.3
25 - 29	9 300	75.0
30 - 34	10 238	90.1
35 - 39	5 624	49.2
40 - 44	2 203	16.5
45 - 49	672	4.8
50 - 54	150	1.2
55 - 59	29	0.3
60 - 64	9	..
65 +	4	..
Unknown - Inconnu	2 026	..
Bulgaria - Bulgarie		
2016 (C)		
Total	64 984	30.5
0 - 19	698	5.0
20 - 24	5 090	31.4
25 - 29	13 993	66.1
30 - 34	17 593	80.8

Continent, country or area, year, code[a] and age of father (in years) / Continent, pays ou zone, année, code[a] et âge du père (en années)	Number - Nombre Both sexes Les deux sexes	Rate Taux
EUROPE		
Bulgaria - Bulgarie		
2016 (C)		
35 - 39	12 202	52.1
40 - 44	5 006	20.8
45 - 49	1 336	5.9
50 - 54	336	1.6
55 - 59	117	0.6
60 - 64	45	..
65 +	10	..
Unknown - Inconnu	8 558	..
Croatia - Croatie		
2016 (C)		
Total	37 537	30.4
0 - 19	275	2.4
20 - 24	2 309	18.9
25 - 29	7 718	59.9
30 - 34	12 758	90.3
35 - 39	9 064	62.8
40 - 44	3 404	24.7
45 - 49	1 054	7.8
50 - 54	285	2.0
55 - 59	64	0.4
60 - 64	18	..
65 +	1	..
Unknown - Inconnu	587	..
Czechia - Tchéquie		
2016 (C)		
Total	112 663	35.3
0 - 19	429	2.0
20 - 24	5 877	21.7
25 - 29	20 355	62.5
30 - 34	34 228	97.9
35 - 39	27 410	66.4
40 - 44	11 560	27.1
45 - 49	2 993	9.0
50 - 54	962	3.0
55 - 59	304	1.0
60 - 64	123	..
65 +	46	..
Unknown - Inconnu	8 376	..
Denmark - Danemark[15]		
2016 (C)		
Total	61 614	36.4
0 - 19	91	0.6
20 - 24	2 839	15.7
25 - 29	13 808	80.3
30 - 34	19 554	128.7
35 - 39	12 834	80.6
40 - 44	5 143	28.6
45 - 49	1 444	7.8
50 - 54	448	2.4
55 - 59	134	0.8
60 - 64	32	..
65 +	14	..
Unknown - Inconnu	5 273	..
Estonia - Estonie		
2016 (C)		
Total	14 053	36.4
0 - 19	75	2.5
20 - 24	847	23.7
25 - 29	3 438	69.9
30 - 34	4 233	90.0
35 - 39	2 918	65.7
40 - 44	1 390	31.4
45 - 49	430	10.4
50 - 54	120	3.0
55 - 59	50	1.3

Continent, country or area, year, code[a] and age of father (in years) / Continent, pays ou zone, année, code[a] et âge du père (en années)	Number - Nombre Both sexes Les deux sexes	Rate Taux
EUROPE		
Estonia - Estonie		
2016 (C)		
60 - 64	14	..
65 +	-	..
Unknown - Inconnu	538	..
Faeroe Islands - Îles Féroé		
2017 (C)		
Total	655	44.1
0 - 19	5	♦2.9
20 - 24	49	31.9
25 - 29	153	104.9
30 - 34	170	126.3
35 - 39	143	99.7
40 - 44	65	40.5
45 - 49	22	♦13.9
50 - 54	4	♦2.3
55 - 59	1	♦0.7
60 - 64	-	..
65 +	-	..
Unknown - Inconnu	43	..
Finland - Finlande[16]		
2016 (C)		
Total	52 521	33.5
0 - 19	298	2.0
20 - 24	3 878	23.5
25 - 29	11 357	67.1
30 - 34	16 837	95.7
35 - 39	11 341	66.6
40 - 44	4 528	28.8
45 - 49	1 517	9.1
50 - 54	493	2.7
55 - 59	158	0.9
60 - 64	43	..
65 +	14	..
Unknown - Inconnu	2 057	..
France		
2016 (C)		
Total	744 697	40.7
0 - 19	2 471	1.3
20 - 24	36 311	19.9
25 - 29	155 476	81.3
30 - 34	244 419	122.9
35 - 39	178 704	88.7
40 - 44	81 868	38.4
45 - 49	30 131	13.8
50 - 54	10 436	4.8
55 - 59	3 588	1.7
60 - 64	1 187	..
65 +	106	..
Germany - Allemagne		
2015 (C)		
Total	737 575	29.9
0 - 19	2 243	1.1
20 - 24	32 100	14.4
25 - 29	131 482	51.6
30 - 34	225 083	92.2
35 - 39	175 580	76.6
40 - 44	80 879	33.7
45 - 49	30 309	9.7
50 - 54	8 600	2.6
55 - 59	2 256	0.8
60 - 64	625	..
65 +	303	..
Unknown - Inconnu	48 115	..

Continent, country or area, year, code[a] and age of father (in years) / Continent, pays ou zone, année, code[a] et âge du père (en années)	Number - Nombre Both sexes Les deux sexes	Rate Taux
EUROPE		
Greece - Grèce		
2016 (C)		
Total	92 898	30.0
0 - 19	188	0.7
20 - 24	1 747	6.6
25 - 29	9 517	34.5
30 - 34	27 011	83.0
35 - 39	28 680	76.3
40 - 44	13 689	36.6
45 - 49	4 651	12.4
50 - 54	1 123	3.4
55 - 59	322	1.0
60 - 64	94	..
65 +	16	..
Unknown - Inconnu	5 860	..
Hungary - Hongrie[17]		
2016 (C)		
Total	95 361	32.4
0 - 19	1 165	5.2
20 - 24	6 116	22.7
25 - 29	14 237	51.5
30 - 34	23 339	85.7
35 - 39	22 882	67.5
40 - 44	10 732	30.5
45 - 49	3 012	9.9
50 - 54	783	3.1
55 - 59	225	0.9
60 - 64	85	..
65 +	25	..
Unknown - Inconnu	12 760	..
Iceland - Islande		
2017 (C)		
Total	4 071	38.7
0 - 19	29	♦2.7
20 - 24	338	26.6
25 - 29	1 071	81.2
30 - 34	1 193	100.8
35 - 39	836	71.8
40 - 44	351	31.5
45 - 49	110	10.8
50 - 54	34	3.2
55 - 59	10	♦1.0
60 - 64	3	..
65 +	4	..
Unknown - Inconnu	92	..
Italy - Italie		
2016 (C)		
Total	473 438	26.8
0 - 19	1 295	0.9
20 - 24	13 464	9.4
25 - 29	54 874	36.2
30 - 34	121 882	75.5
35 - 39	131 227	71.3
40 - 44	76 886	35.6
45 - 49	25 225	11.3
50 - 54	6 915	3.2
55 - 59	1 777	1.0
60 - 64	445	..
65 +	204	..
Unknown - Inconnu	39 244	..
Latvia - Lettonie		
2016 (C)		
Total	21 968	38.8
0 - 19	146	3.4
20 - 24	1 771	32.9
25 - 29	5 830	83.9
30 - 34	6 576	96.3

Continent, country or area, year, code[a] and age of father (in years) Continent, pays ou zone, année, code[a] et âge du père (en années)	Number - Nombre Both sexes Les deux sexes	Rate Taux	Continent, country or area, year, code[a] and age of father (in years) Continent, pays ou zone, année, code[a] et âge du père (en années)	Number - Nombre Both sexes Les deux sexes	Rate Taux
EUROPE			**EUROPE**		
Latvia - Lettonie			Montenegro - Monténégro		
2016 (C)			2009 (C)		
35 - 39	4 076	66.8	60 - 64	1	..
40 - 44	1 892	29.6	65 +	6	..
45 - 49	638	10.2	Unknown - Inconnu	935	..
50 - 54	222	3.5	Netherlands - Pays-Bas[18]		
55 - 59	79	1.2	2014 (C)		
60 - 64	23	..	Total	175 181	34.8
65 +	16	..	0 - 19	333	0.7
Unknown - Inconnu	699	..	20 - 24	6 226	12.1
Lithuania - Lituanie			25 - 29	33 346	66.4
2016 (C)			30 - 34	60 729	125.6
Total	30 623	36.2	35 - 39	41 980	87.5
0 - 19	169	2.2	40 - 44	17 247	30.0
20 - 24	2 284	24.5	45 - 49	5 280	8.5
25 - 29	8 481	88.0	50 - 54	1 495	2.5
30 - 34	10 133	115.7	55 - 59	403	0.7
35 - 39	5 454	66.8	60 - 64	97	..
40 - 44	2 029	23.0	65 +	56	..
45 - 49	625	6.6	Unknown - Inconnu	7 989	..
50 - 54	194	2.0	Norway - Norvège		
55 - 59	58	0.6	2012 (C)		
60 - 64	19	..	Total	60 255	38.8
65 +	2	..	0 - 19	271	1.7
Unknown - Inconnu	1 175	..	20 - 24	3 931	23.9
Luxembourg			25 - 29	13 332	83.2
2016 (C)			30 - 34	19 068	116.9
Total	6 050	32.0	35 - 39	13 188	76.5
0 - 19	23	♦1.4	40 - 44	5 590	30.1
20 - 24	237	13.6	45 - 49	1 822	10.3
25 - 29	961	46.0	50 - 54	524	3.3
30 - 34	1 933	89.2	55 - 59	176	1.2
35 - 39	1 638	75.2	60 - 64	47	..
40 - 44	718	32.9	65 +	9	..
45 - 49	242	10.6	Unknown - Inconnu	2 297	..
50 - 54	89	4.0	Poland - Pologne		
55 - 59	30	1.6	2016 (C)		
60 - 64	13	..	Total	382 257	32.5
65 +	1	..	0 - 19	1 575	1.6
Unknown - Inconnu	165	..	20 - 24	26 632	23.1
Malta - Malte			25 - 29	96 032	70.5
2016 (C)			30 - 34	135 909	87.8
Total	4 476	31.3	35 - 39	75 239	50.8
0 - 19	30	2.5	40 - 44	25 750	19.3
20 - 24	239	15.6	45 - 49	6 205	5.5
25 - 29	839	46.7	50 - 54	1 752	1.6
30 - 34	1 554	86.7	55 - 59	588	0.5
35 - 39	1 083	64.0	60 - 64	185	..
40 - 44	408	26.8	65 +	58	..
45 - 49	98	7.4	Unknown - Inconnu	12 332	..
50 - 54	29	2.1	Portugal[4]		
55 - 59	14	♦0.9	2016 (C)		
60 - 64	7	..	Total	87 126	29.6
65 +	1	..	0 - 19	805	2.9
Unknown - Inconnu	174	..	20 - 24	5 268	19.5
Montenegro - Monténégro			25 - 29	14 093	51.6
2009 (C)			30 - 34	26 515	88.0
Total	8 642	43.2	35 - 39	24 164	68.5
0 - 19	32	1.5	40 - 44	10 716	28.1
20 - 24	616	27.3	45 - 49	3 033	8.5
25 - 29	2 011	90.0	50 - 54	831	2.3
30 - 34	2 268	113.7	55 - 59	283	0.9
35 - 39	1 574	85.9	60 - 64	86	..
40 - 44	800	43.7	65 +	35	..
45 - 49	287	14.9	Unknown - Inconnu	1 297	..
50 - 54	89	4.6			
55 - 59	23	♦1.3			

11. Live births and live birth rates by age of father: latest available year, 2008 - 2017
Naissances vivantes et taux de natalité selon l'âge du père : dernière année disponible, 2008 - 2017 (continued - suite)

Continent, country or area, year, code[a] and age of father (in years) / Continent, pays ou zone, année, code[a] et âge du père (en années)	Number - Nombre — Both sexes / Les deux sexes	Rate / Taux
EUROPE		
Republic of Moldova - République de Moldova[19]		
2012 (C)		
Total	39 435	32.8
0 - 19	269	2.3
20 - 24	6 290	41.0
25 - 29	13 306	84.1
30 - 34	8 980	67.6
35 - 39	4 561	40.4
40 - 44	1 640	16.5
45 - 49	446	4.4
50 - 54	142	1.2
55 - 59	31	0.3
60 - 64	14	..
65 +	3	..
Unknown - Inconnu	3 753	..
Romania - Roumanie		
2015 (C)		
Total	197 491	32.3
0 - 19	2 805	5.4
20 - 24	16 811	31.4
25 - 29	50 170	74.6
30 - 34	57 254	89.7
35 - 39	38 786	52.4
40 - 44	13 777	18.9
45 - 49	4 165	5.5
50 - 54	869	1.7
55 - 59	316	0.5
60 - 64	87	..
65 +	24	..
Unknown - Inconnu	12 427	..
Russian Federation - Fédération de Russie[20]		
2012 (C)		
Total	1 902 084	41.9
0 - 19	12 731	3.9
20 - 24	256 939	51.4
25 - 29	564 777	103.0
30 - 34	431 851	88.4
35 - 39	245 613	55.2
40 - 44	102 880	25.6
45 - 49	33 963	8.4
50 - 54	11 671	2.5
55 - 59	3 196	0.8
60 +	1 203	..
Unknown - Inconnu	237 260	..
San Marino - Saint-Marin		
2017 (C)		
Total	228	22.4
0 - 19	-	-
20 - 24	4	♦5.1
25 - 29	17	♦21.8
30 - 34	64	72.2
35 - 39	73	67.7
40 - 44	44	32.2
45 - 49	16	♦10.9
50 - 54	2	♦1.4
55 - 59	1	♦0.8
60 - 64	-	..
65 +	-	..
Unknown - Inconnu	7	..
Serbia - Serbie[21]		
2016 (+C)		
Total	64 734	31.2
0 - 19	369	2.2
20 - 24	4 180	21.8
25 - 29	13 742	66.0
30 - 34	20 432	90.7
35 - 39	13 514	58.5
EUROPE		
Serbia - Serbie[21]		
2016 (+C)		
40 - 44	4 983	22.1
45 - 49	1 395	6.6
50 - 54	373	1.8
55 - 59	117	0.5
60 - 64	33	..
65 +	10	..
Unknown - Inconnu	5 586	..
Slovakia - Slovaquie		
2016 (C)		
Total	57 557	33.1
0 - 19	450	3.6
20 - 24	3 501	23.3
25 - 29	10 572	60.3
30 - 34	17 040	88.9
35 - 39	12 069	59.9
40 - 44	4 358	23.3
45 - 49	1 060	6.9
50 - 54	277	1.8
55 - 59	98	0.6
60 - 64	36	..
65 +	11	..
Unknown - Inconnu	8 085	..
Slovenia - Slovénie		
2016 (C)		
Total	20 345	32.2
0 - 19	55	1.1
20 - 24	840	16.1
25 - 29	4 553	70.6
30 - 34	7 232	98.4
35 - 39	5 001	61.5
40 - 44	1 746	22.4
45 - 49	456	6.1
50 - 54	121	1.6
55 - 59	26	♦0.4
60 - 64	11	..
65 +	3	..
Unknown - Inconnu	301	..
Spain - Espagne		
2016 (C)		
Total	408 734	28.8
0 - 19	2 159	2.0
20 - 24	13 300	11.7
25 - 29	44 027	35.1
30 - 34	114 301	75.5
35 - 39	137 085	72.0
40 - 44	64 590	33.1
45 - 49	17 444	9.5
50 - 54	4 305	2.6
55 - 59	1 108	0.8
60 - 64	345	..
65 +	100	..
Unknown - Inconnu	9 970	..
Sweden - Suède		
2012 (C)		
Total	113 177	40.2
0 - 19	443	1.5
20 - 24	7 043	21.2
25 - 29	23 661	77.8
30 - 34	36 139	122.1
35 - 39	26 932	86.6
40 - 44	11 433	35.6
45 - 49	4 023	12.0
50 - 54	1 169	4.0
55 - 59	404	1.4
60 - 64	116	..

11. Live births and live birth rates by age of father: latest available year, 2008 - 2017
Naissances vivantes et taux de natalité selon l'âge du père : dernière année disponible, 2008 - 2017 (continued - suite)

Continent, country or area, year, code[a] and age of father (in years) / Continent, pays ou zone, année, code[a] et âge du père (en années)	Number - Nombre / Both sexes Les deux sexes	Rate Taux
EUROPE		
Sweden - Suède		
2012 (C)		
65 +	52	..
Unknown - Inconnu	1 762	..
Switzerland - Suisse[13]		
2016 (C)		
Total	66 598	25.7
0 - 19	8	-
20 - 24	1 080	4.3
25 - 29	9 300	32.8
30 - 34	22 567	75.8
35 - 39	20 026	68.5
40 - 44	9 163	30.8
45 - 49	3 065	9.3
50 - 54	966	2.9
55 - 59	283	1.0
60 - 64	92	..
65 +	48	..
TFYR of Macedonia - L'ex-R. y. de Macédoine		
2016 (C)		
Total	23 002	33.9
0 - 19	142	2.3
20 - 24	1 797	24.5
25 - 29	6 041	76.2
30 - 34	7 705	95.9
35 - 39	4 508	58.3
40 - 44	1 415	19.5
45 - 49	341	4.9
50 - 54	81	1.2
55 - 59	19	◆0.3
60 - 64	7	..
65 +	2	..
Unknown - Inconnu	944	..
Ukraine[22]		
2016 (+C)		
Total	397 037	30.7
0 - 19	2 951	3.4
20 - 24	47 925	41.7
25 - 29	114 428	76.7
30 - 34	100 800	62.7
35 - 39	54 118	38.6
40 - 44	22 303	16.9
45 - 49	6 928	5.8
50 - 54	1 991	1.6
55 - 59	902	0.7
Unknown - Inconnu	44 691	..
United Kingdom of Great Britain and Northern Ireland - Royaume-Uni de Grande-Bretagne et d'Irlande du Nord[23]		
2016 (C)		
Total	774 386	40.2
0 - 19	8 897	4.9
20 - 24	64 400	31.1
25 - 29	160 571	74.4
30 - 34	224 485	107.8
35 - 39	166 950	84.7
40 - 44	72 578	37.0
45 - 49	25 524	11.8

Continent, country or area, year, code[a] and age of father (in years) / Continent, pays ou zone, année, code[a] et âge du père (en années)	Number - Nombre / Both sexes Les deux sexes	Rate Taux
EUROPE		
United Kingdom of Great Britain and Northern Ireland - Royaume-Uni de Grande-Bretagne et d'Irlande du Nord[23]		
2016 (C)		
50 - 54	7 993	3.7
55 - 59	2 400	1.3
60 - 64	667	..
65 +	274	..
Unknown - Inconnu	39 647	..
OCEANIA - OCÉANIE		
Australia - Australie		
2016 (C)		
Total	311 104	42.6
0 - 19	2 995	4.1
20 - 24	21 162	25.3
25 - 29	59 401	67.5
30 - 34	103 004	119.3
35 - 39	71 501	92.2
40 - 44	29 223	37.4
45 - 49	9 335	12.3
50 - 54	2 765	3.7
55 - 59	974	1.4
60 - 64	322	..
65 +	167	..
Unknown - Inconnu[24]	10 255	..
New Caledonia - Nouvelle-Calédonie		
2015 (C)		
Total	4 191	...
0 - 19	49	...
20 - 24	433	...
25 - 29	798	...
30 - 34	968	...
35 - 39	728	...
40 - 44	436	...
45 - 49	131	...
50 - 54	43	...
55 - 59	13	...
60 +	4	...
Unknown - Inconnu	588	...
New Zealand - Nouvelle-Zélande[25]		
2017 (+C)		
Total	59 610	42.1
0 - 19	1 209	7.8
20 - 24	6 201	35.2
25 - 29	12 741	73.4
30 - 34	17 295	118.9
35 - 39	11 694	89.4
40 - 44	4 944	36.8
45 - 49	1 704	11.6
50 - 54	522	3.6
55 - 59	174	1.2
60 - 64	51	..
65 +	24	..
Unknown - Inconnu	3 057	..

FOOTNOTES - NOTES

◆ Rates based on 30 or fewer births. - Taux basés sur 30 naissances ou moins.

* Provisional. - Données provisoires.

[a] 'Code' indicates the source of data, as follows:
C - Civil registration, estimated over 90% complete

U - Civil registration, estimated less than 90% complete
| - Other source, estimated reliable
+ - Data tabulated by date of registration rather than occurrence
... Information not available

Le 'Code' indique la source des données, comme suit :
C - Registres de l'état civil considérés complets à 90 p. 100 au moins
U - Registres de l'état civil qui ne sont pas considérés complets à 90 p. 100 au

moins

| - Autre source, considérée fiable

+ - Données exploitées selon la date de l'enregistrement et non la date de l'événement

... Information non disponible

[1] Excludes the islands of St. Brandon and Agalega. - Non compris les îles St. Brandon et Agalega.

[2] Including Canadian residents temporarily in the United States, but excluding United States residents temporarily in Canada. - Y compris les résidents canadiens se trouvant temporairement aux Etats-Unis, mais ne comprenant pas les résidents des Etats-Unis se trouvant temporairement au Canada.

[3] Excluding children born in the country of non-resident mothers. - Exceptés les enfants nés dans le pays des mères non-résidentes.

[4] Data refer to births to resident mothers. - Ces données concernent les enfants nés de mères résidentes.

[5] Excluding infants born alive of less than 28 weeks' gestation, of less than 1 000 g in weight and 35 cm in length, who die within seven days of birth. Excluding newborns registered by application of mothers. - Non compris les enfants nés vivants après moins de 28 semaines de gestations, pesant moins de 1 000 g, mesurant moins de 35 cm et décédés dans les sept jours qui ont suivi leur naissance. Exception faite des nouveau-nés qui ont été enregistrés à la demande des mères.

[6] Sources: Births and Deaths National Registration System database, and medical records of government hospitals. - Les sources: Les bases de données des << Births and Deaths National Registration System >> et les dossiers médicaux des hôpitaux du gouvernement.

[7] Data refer to government controlled areas. - Les données se rapportent aux zones contrôlées par le Gouvernement.

[8] Includes data for East Jerusalem and Israeli residents in certain other territories under occupation by Israeli military forces since June 1967. - Y compris les données pour Jérusalem-Est et les résidents israéliens dans certains autres territoires occupés depuis 1967 par les forces armées israéliennes.

[9] Data refer to live births in Japan only. Data refer to live births in wedlock only. - Les données se raportent aux nationaux japonais au Japon seulement. Les données ne concernent que les naissances vivantes de parents mariés.

[10] Data do not include foreigners. - Les données sur les etrangers ne sont pas inclus.

[11] Excluding alien armed forces, civilian aliens employed by armed forces, and foreign diplomatic personnel and their dependants. - Non compris les militaires étrangers, les civils étrangers employés par les forces armées ni le personnel diplomatique étranger et les membres de leur famille les accompagnant.

[12] Excluding infants born alive of less than 28 weeks' gestation, of less than 1 000 g in weight and 35 cm in length, who die within seven days of birth. Data have been adjusted for under-registration. - Non compris les enfants nés vivants après moins de 28 semaines de gestations, pesant moins de 1 000 g, mesurant moins de 35 cm et décédés dans les sept jours qui ont suivi leur naissance. Y compris un ajustement pour sous-enregistrement.

[13] Data refer to live births in wedlock only. - Les données ne concernent que les naissances vivantes de parents mariés.

[14] Data refer to live births in wedlock only. Including births occurring abroad of mothers with residence in Austria. - Les données ne concernent que les naissances vivantes de parents mariés. Y compris les naissances survenues à l'étranger des mères avec résidence en Autriche.

[15] Excluding Faeroe Islands and Greenland shown separately, if available. - Non compris les Iles Féroé et le Groenland, qui font l'objet de rubriques distinctes, si disponible.

[16] Excluding Åland Islands. - Non compris les Îles d'Åland.

[17] Data include the live births of women with Hungarian usual residence regardless of whether the live birth occurred in Hungary or in a foreign country, and do not include the live births of women with foreign country usual residence. Data include the live births of women with unknown residence and homeless. - Les données concernent les enfants nés vivants de femmes dont la résidence habituelle est en Hongrie, que la naissance vivante ait eu lieu en Hongrie ou dans un pays étranger, et ne comprennent pas les enfants nés vivants de femmes dont la résidence habituelle est dans un pays étranger. Les données incluent les enfants nés vivants de femmes dont la résidence n'est pas connue et de femmes sans domicile fixe.

[18] Including residents outside the country if listed in a Netherlands population register. - Englobe les résidents se trouvant à l'étranger à condition qu'ils soient inscrits sur le registre de population des Pays-Bas.

[19] Excluding Transnistria and the municipality of Bender. - Les données ne tiennent pas compte de l'information sur la Transnistrie et la municipalité de Bender.

[20] Excluding infants born alive of less than 28 weeks' gestation, of less than 1 000 g in weight and 35 cm in length, who die within seven days of birth. - Non compris les enfants nés vivants après moins de 28 semaines de gestations, pesant moins de 1 000 g, mesurant moins de 35 cm et décédés dans les sept jours qui ont suivi leur naissance.

[21] Excludes data for Kosovo and Metohia. - Sans les données pour le Kosovo et Metohie.

[22] Data refer to births with weight 500g and more (if weight is unknown - with length 25 centimeters and more, or with gestation during 22 weeks or more). The Government of Ukraine has informed the United Nations that it is not in a position to provide statistical data concerning the Autonomous Republic of Crimea and the city of Sevastopol. - Données concernant les nouveau-nés de 500 grammes ou plus (si le poids est inconnu – de 25 centimètres de long ou plus, ou après une grossesse de 22 semaines ou plus). Le gouvernement Ukrainien a informé l'ONU qu'il n'est pas en mesure de fournir des données statistiques concernant la République autonome de Crimée et la ville de Sébastopol.

[23] Excluding Channel Islands (Guernsey and Jersey) and Isle of Man, shown separately, if available. Data tabulated by date of occurrence for England and Wales, and by date of registration for Northern Ireland and Scotland. - Non compris les îles Anglo-Normandes (Guernesey et Jersey) et l'île de Man, qui font l'objet de rubriques distinctes, si disponible. Données exploitées selon la date de l'événement pour l'Angleterre et le pays de Galles, et selon la date de l'enregistrement pour l'Irlande du Nord et l'Ecosse.

[24] Data includes births born in wedlock for which age of father is unknown and births born out of wedlock not acknowledged by the father for which therefore age of father is unknown. - Les données se rapportent aux enfants légitimes pour lesquels l'âge du père n'est pas connu et aux naissances hors mariage non reconnues par le père et pour lesquelles l'âge du père n'est par conséquent pas connu.

[25] Random rounding to base 3 is applied in this table as a confidentiality measure. Data refers to births registered in the country to mothers resident in the country. - Les chiffres sont arrondis à la base 3 de manière aléatoire, pour des raisons de confidentialité. Les données se rapportent aux naissances enregistrées dans le pays pour lesquelles la mère réside dans le pays.

Table 12 - *Demographic Yearbook 2017*

Table 12 presents late foetal deaths and late foetal-death ratios by urban/rural residence for as many years as possible between 2013 and 2017.

Description of variables: Late foetal deaths are foetal deaths[1] of 28 or more completed weeks of gestation. Foetal deaths of unknown gestational age are included with those 28 or more weeks.

Statistics on the number of late foetal deaths are obtained from civil registers unless otherwise noted.

The urban/rural classification of late foetal deaths is as provided by each country or area; it is presumed to be based on the national census definitions of urban population that have been set forth at the end of the technical notes for table 6.

Ratio computation: Late foetal-death ratios are the annual number of late foetal deaths per 1 000 live births (as shown in table 9) in the same year. The live-birth base was adopted because it is assumed to be more comparable from one country or area to another than the sum of live births and foetal deaths.

Ratios by urban/rural residence are the annual number of late foetal deaths, in the appropriate urban or rural category, per 1 000 corresponding live births (as shown in table 9). These ratios are calculated by the United Nations Statistics Division.

Ratios presented in this table are limited to those for countries or areas and urban/rural areas having at least a total of 30 late foetal deaths in a given year.

Reliability of data: Each country or area is asked to indicate the estimated completeness of the late foetal deaths recorded in its civil register. These national assessments are indicated by the quality codes "C", "U" and "..." that appear in the first column of this table.

"C" indicates that the data are estimated to be virtually complete, that is, representing at least 90 per cent of the late foetal deaths occurring each year, while "U" indicates that data are estimated to be incomplete, that is, representing less than 90 per cent of the late foetal deaths occurring each year. The code "..." indicates that no information was provided regarding completeness.

Data from civil registers which are reported as incomplete or of unknown completeness (coded "U" or "...") are considered unreliable. They appear in italics in this table. Ratios are not computed for data so coded.

For more information about the quality of vital statistics data in general, see section 4.2 of the Technical Notes.

Limitations: Statistics on late foetal deaths are subject to the same qualifications as have been set forth for vital statistics in general and foetal-death statistics in particular as discussed in section 4 of the Technical Notes.

The reliability of the data is a very important factor. Of all vital statistics, the registration of foetal deaths is probably the most incomplete.

Variation in the definition of foetal deaths, and in particular late foetal deaths, also limits international comparability. The criterion of 28 or more completed weeks of gestation to distinguish late foetal deaths is not universally used; some countries or areas use different durations of gestation or other criteria such as size of the foetus. In addition, the difficulty of accurately determining gestational age further reduces comparability. However, to promote comparability, late foetal deaths shown in this table are restricted to those of at least 28 or more completed weeks of gestation. Wherever this is not possible, a footnote is provided.

Late foetal-death ratios are subject to the limitations of the data on live births with which they have been calculated. These have been set forth in the technical notes for table 9.

It must be pointed out that when late foetal deaths and live births are both under registered, the resulting ratios may be of reasonable magnitude. For the countries or areas where live-birth registration is poorest, the late foetal-death ratios may be the largest, effectively masking the completeness of the base data. For this reason, possible variations in birth-registration completeness as well as the reported completeness of late foetal deaths must always be borne in mind in evaluating late foetal-death ratios.

Finally, it may be noted that the counting of live-born infants as late foetal deaths, because they died before the registration of the birth or within the first 24 hours of life, has the effect of inflating the late foetal-death ratios unduly by decreasing the birth denominator and increasing the foetal-death numerator. This factor should not be overlooked in using data from this table.

The comparability of data by urban/rural residence is affected by the national definitions of urban and rural used in tabulating these data. It is assumed, in the absence of specific information to the contrary, that the definitions of urban and rural used in connection with the national population census were also used in the compilation of the vital statistics for each country or area. However, it cannot be excluded that, for a given country or area, different definitions of urban and rural are used for the vital statistics data and the population census data respectively. When known, the definitions of urban used in national population censuses are presented at the end of the technical notes for table 6. As discussed in detail in the technical notes for table 6, these definitions vary considerably from one country or area to another.

Urban/rural differentials in late foetal death ratios may also be affected by whether the late foetal deaths and live births have been tabulated in terms of place of occurrence or place of usual residence. This problem is discussed in more detail in section 4.1.4.1 of the Introduction.

Earlier data: Late foetal deaths and late foetal-death ratios have been shown in each issue of the Demographic Yearbook beginning with the 1951 issue. A special topic CD on natality published in 2001 presents the data for all available years from 1990 to 1998. For more information on specific topics, and years for which data are reported, readers should consult the Historical Index.

NOTES

[1] For definition, see section 4.1.1 of the Introduction.

Tableau 12 – *Annuaire démographique 2017*

Le tableau 12 présente des données sur les morts fœtales tardives et les rapports de mortinatalité selon le lieu de résidence (zone urbaine ou rurale) pour le plus grand nombre d'années possible entre 2013 et 2017.

Description des variables : Par mort fœtale tardive, on entend le décès d'un fœtus[1] survenu après 28 semaines complètes de gestation au moins. Les morts fœtales pour lesquelles la durée de la période de gestation n'est pas connue sont comprises dans cette catégorie.

Sauf indication contraire, les statistiques du nombre de morts fœtales tardives sont établies sur la base des registres de l'état civil.

La classification des morts fœtales tardives selon le lieu de résidence (zone urbaine ou rurale) est celle qui a été communiquée par chaque pays ou zone ; on part du principe qu'elle repose sur les définitions de la population urbaine utilisées pour les recensements nationaux, telles qu'elles sont reproduites à la fin des notes techniques du tableau 6.

Calcul des rapports : les rapports de mortinatalité représentent le nombre annuel de morts fœtales tardives pour 1 000 naissances vivantes (telles qu'elles sont présentées au tableau 9) survenues pendant la même année. On a pris pour base de calcul les naissances vivantes parce que l'on pense qu'elles sont plus facilement comparables d'un pays ou d'une zone à l'autre que la somme des naissances vivantes et des morts fœtales.

Les rapports selon le lieu de résidence (zone urbaine ou rurale) représentent le nombre annuel de morts fœtales tardives, classées selon la catégorie urbaine ou rurale appropriée pour 1 000 naissances vivantes (telles qu'elles sont présentées au tableau 9) survenues parmi la population correspondante. Ces rapports ont été calculés par la Division des statistiques de l'Organisation des Nations Unies.

Les rapports présentés dans le tableau 12 ne concernent que les pays ou zones où l'on a enregistré un total d'au moins 30 morts fœtales tardives pendant une année donnée.

Fiabilité des données : il a été demandé à chaque pays ou zone d'indiquer le degré estimatif de complétude des données sur les morts fœtales tardives figurant dans ses registres d'état civil. Ces évaluations nationales sont signalées par les codes de qualité "C", "U" et "…" qui apparaissent dans la deuxième colonne du tableau.

La lettre "C" indique que les données sont jugées à peu près complètes, c'est-à-dire qu'elles représentent au moins 90 p. 100 des morts fœtales tardives survenues chaque année ; la lettre "U" signifie que les données sont jugées incomplètes, c'est-à-dire qu'elles représentent moins de 90 p.100 des morts fœtales tardives survenues chaque année. Le code "…" indique qu'aucun renseignement n'a été communiqué quant à la complétude des données.

Les données provenant des registres de l'état civil qui sont déclarées incomplètes ou dont le degré de complétude n'est pas connu (code "U" ou "…") sont jugées douteuses. Elles apparaissent en italique dans le tableau ; les rapports, dans ces cas, n'ont pas été calculés.

Pour plus de précisions sur la qualité des données reposant sur les statistiques de l'état civil en général, voir la section 4.2 des Notes techniques.

Insuffisance des données : les statistiques des morts fœtales tardives appellent toutes les réserves qui ont été formulées à propos des statistiques de l'état civil en général et des statistiques concernant les morts fœtales en particulier (voir la section 4 des Notes techniques).

La fiabilité des données est un facteur très important. Les statistiques concernant les morts fœtales sont probablement les moins complètes de toutes les statistiques de l'état civil.

L'hétérogénéité des définitions de la mort fœtale et, en particulier, de la mort fœtale tardive nuit aussi à la comparabilité internationale des données. Le critère des 28 semaines complètes de gestation au moins n'est pas universellement utilisé ; certains pays ou zones retiennent des critères différents pour la durée de la période de gestation ou d'autres critères tels que la taille du fœtus. De surcroît, la comparabilité est rendue malaisée par le fait qu'il est difficile d'établir avec précision l'âge gestationnel. Pour faciliter les comparaisons, les morts fœtales tardives considérées ici sont exclusivement celles qui sont survenues au terme de 28 semaines de gestation au moins. Les exceptions sont signalées en note.

Les rapports de mortinatalité appellent en outre toutes les réserves qui ont été formulées à propos des statistiques des naissances vivantes qui ont servi à leur calcul (voir à ce sujet les notes techniques relatives au tableau 9).

En ce qui concerne le calcul des rapports, il convient de noter que, si l'enregistrement des morts fœtales tardives et celui des naissances vivantes sont loin d'être exhaustifs, les rapports de mortinatalité peuvent être raisonnables. C'est parfois pour les pays ou zones où l'enregistrement des naissances vivantes laisse le plus à désirer que les rapports de mortinatalité sont les plus élevés, ce qui masque le caractère incomplet des données de base. Aussi, pour porter un jugement sur la qualité des rapports de mortinatalité, il ne faut jamais oublier que la complétude de l'enregistrement des naissances comme celle de l'enregistrement des morts fœtales tardives peuvent varier sensiblement.

Enfin, on notera que l'inclusion parmi les morts fœtales tardives des décès d'enfants nés vivants qui sont décédés avant l'enregistrement de leur naissance ou dans les 24 heures qui ont suivi la naissance conduit à des rapports de mortinatalité exagérés parce que le dénominateur (nombre de naissances) se trouve alors diminué et le numérateur (morts fœtales) augmenté. Il importe de ne pas négliger ce facteur lorsque l'on utilise les données du tableau 12.

La comparabilité des données selon le lieu de résidence (zone urbaine ou rurale) peut être limitée par les définitions nationales des termes « urbain » et « rural » utilisées pour la mise en tableaux de ces données. En l'absence d'indications contraires, on a supposé que les mêmes définitions avaient servi pour le recensement national de la population et pour l'établissement des statistiques de l'état civil pour chaque pays ou zone. Toutefois, il n'est pas exclu que, pour une zone ou un pays donné, des définitions différentes aient été retenues. Les définitions du terme « urbain » utilisées pour les recensements nationaux de population ont été présentées à la fin des notes techniques du tableau 6 lorsqu'elles étaient connues. Comme on l'a précisé dans les notes techniques relatives au tableau 6, ces définitions varient considérablement d'un pays ou d'une zone à l'autre.

La différence entre les rapports de mortinatalité pour les zones urbaines et rurales pourra aussi être faussée selon que les morts fœtales tardives et les naissances vivantes auront été classées d'après le lieu de l'événement ou le lieu de résidence habituel. Ce problème est examiné plus en détail à la section 4.1.4.1 des Notes techniques.

Données publiées antérieurement : les éditions de l'*Annuaire démographique* parues à partir de 1951 contiennent des statistiques concernant les morts fœtales tardives et les rapports de mortinatalité. Un CD-ROM sur la natalité paru en 2001 présente les données pour toutes les années disponibles de 1990 à 1998. Pour plus de précisions concernant les années et les sujets pour lesquels des données ont été publiées, se reporter à l'index.

NOTE

[1] Pour la définition, voir la section 4.1.1 de l'Introduction.

12. Late foetal deaths and late foetal death ratios, by urban/rural residence: 2013 - 2017
Morts foetales tardives et rapports de mortinatalité, selon la résidence, urbaine/rurale : 2013 - 2017

Continent, country or area, and urban/rural residence / Continent, pays ou zone et résidence, urbaine/rurale	Co-de[a]	Number - Nombre					Ratio - Rapport				
		2013	2014	2015	2016	2017	2013	2014	2015	2016	2017
AFRICA - AFRIQUE											
Algeria - Algérie											
Total	+U	15 009	15 077	14 620	14 236	...	...	...	...	...	...
Burundi[1]											
Total	+U	2 141	...	...	...	...	...	...	...	...	...
Mauritius - Maurice[2]											
Total	+C	117	138	125	127	135	8.7	10.4	9.9	9.8	10.1
Urban - Urbaine	+C	46	54	54	52	53	9.1	10.5	10.5	9.8	10.0
Rural - Rurale	+C	71	84	71	75	82	8.4	10.3	9.5	9.8	10.1
Sierra Leone[3]											
Total	+U	1 958	...	...	...	...	...	...	...	...	...
South Africa - Afrique du Sud											
Total	...	15 098	15 157	14 341	11 961	...	...	...	...	...	...
AMERICA, NORTH - AMÉRIQUE DU NORD											
Bahamas[4]											
Total	+C	61	...	...	...	...	15.5	...	...	...	...
Belize											
Total	U	51	66	55	54	...	...	...	...	...	...
Urban - Urbaine	U	20	24	24	21	...	...	...	...	...	...
Rural - Rurale	U	31	42	31	33	...	...	...	...	...	...
Bermuda - Bermudes											
Total	C	3[5]	1	2	4[5]	-[5]	...	...	...	...	...
Canada[6]											
Total	C	1 077	1 140	1 078	1 068	1 073	2.8	3.0	2.8	2.8	2.9
Costa Rica											
Total	C	327	319	326	314	*276	4.6	4.4	4.5	4.5	*4.0
Urban - Urbaine	C	108	176	208	198	*164	4.3	4.2	4.2	4.1	*3.5
Rural - Rurale	C	219	143	118	116	*112	4.8	4.7	5.3	5.4	*5.2
Cuba[7]											
Total	C	1 273	1 135	1 190	1 251	1 331	10.1	9.3	9.5	10.7	11.6
Dominican Republic - République dominicaine											
Total	U	1 886	1 528	...	...	...	...	...	...	...	...
Guatemala[8]											
Total	C	3 344	3 236	3 121	3 161	...	8.6	8.4	8.0	8.1	...
Mexico - Mexique[9]											
Total	+U	9 911	9 755	9 685	9 068	...	...	...	...	...	...
Urban - Urbaine[10]	+U	7 249	7 287	7 005	6 623	...	...	...	...	...	...
Rural - Rurale[10]	+U	2 472	2 325	2 407	2 151	...	...	...	...	...	...
Montserrat											
Total	C	-	2	1	-	...	...	...	...	...	...
Panama											
Total	U	370	423	*436	*373	...	...	...	...	...	...
Puerto Rico - Porto Rico[8]											
Total	C	417	417	358	311	257	11.4	12.1	11.5	11.0	10.5
Urban - Urbaine	C	257[10]	239[10]	205[10]	165	146	13.0	12.6	10.8	9.1	8.9
Rural - Rurale	C	156[10]	151[10]	130[10]	146	111	9.3	9.8	10.6	14.4	13.8
Saint Vincent and the Grenadines - Saint-Vincent-et-les Grenadines											
Total	C	23	...	...	...	...	...	...	...	...	...
United States of America - États-Unis d'Amérique											
Total	C	11 721	11 311	11 354	...	...	3.0	2.8	2.9	...	...
AMERICA, SOUTH - AMÉRIQUE DU SUD											
Argentina - Argentine											
Total	C	3 809	4 043	3 785	3 782	...	5.0	5.2	4.9	5.2	...
Brazil - Brésil											
Total	U	25 744[8]	25 748[8]	26 654[8]	16 224	...	...	...	...	...	...

Continent, country or area, and urban/rural residence / Continent, pays ou zone et résidence, urbaine/rurale	Co-de[a]	Number - Nombre					Ratio - Rapport				
		2013	2014	2015	2016	2017	2013	2014	2015	2016	2017
AMERICA, SOUTH - AMÉRIQUE DU SUD											
Chile - Chili[11]											
Total	C	1 262	1 254	2 028	...	...	5.2	5.0	8.3	...	...
Urban - Urbaine	C	1 149	1 126	1 835	...	...	5.2	4.9	8.2	...	...
Rural - Rurale	C	113	128	193	...	...	5.2	5.7	8.7	...	...
Colombia - Colombie											
Total	U	5 518	5 591	5 935	5 728	...	...	...	...	...	...
Urban - Urbaine[10]	U	4 061	4 160	4 477	4 327	...	...	...	...	...	...
Rural - Rurale[10]	U	1 417	1 387	1 406	1 354	...	...	...	...	...	...
Ecuador - Équateur[12]											
Total	...	974	932	1 028	1 001	...	...	...	...	...	...
Urban - Urbaine	...	816	771	849	822	...	...	...	...	...	...
Rural - Rurale	...	158	161	179	179	...	...	...	...	...	...
Uruguay											
Total	C	202	229	199	183	...	4.1	4.7	4.1	3.9	...
Venezuela (Bolivarian Republic of) - Venezuela (République bolivarienne du)											
Total	...	2 400	2 895	2 483	3 028	2 107	...	...	...	...	...
ASIA - ASIE											
Armenia - Arménie											
Total	C	...	746	796	699	...	...	17.3	19.1	17.2	...
Urban - Urbaine	C	...	...	509	431	...	...	...	18.8	16.3	...
Rural - Rurale	C	...	...	287	268	...	...	...	19.6	19.0	...
Azerbaijan - Azerbaïdjan											
Total	+C	643	764	904	920	...	3.7	4.5	5.4	5.8	...
Bahrain - Bahreïn[13]											
Total	...	106	132	...	...	...	...	...	...	...	...
Brunei Darussalam - Brunéi Darussalam											
Total	+C	44	...	...	...	...	6.6	...	...	...	...
China, Hong Kong SAR - Chine, Hong Kong RAS											
Total	...	119	167	150	180	139	...	...	...	...	...
China, Macao SAR - Chine, Macao RAS											
Total	C	10	12	6	11	12	...	...	...	...	...
Georgia - Géorgie											
Total	C	567	640	589	558	...	9.8	10.6	9.9	9.9	...
Urban - Urbaine	C	309	336	321	310	...	...	...	9.5	9.6	...
Rural - Rurale	C	258	304	268	248	...	...	...	10.6	10.2	...
Israel - Israël[14]											
Total	C	603	601	...	...	...	3.5	3.4	...	...	...
Urban - Urbaine[10]	C	535	537	...	...	...	3.4	3.4	...	...	...
Rural - Rurale[10]	C	61	57	...	...	...	3.7	3.5	...	...	...
Japan - Japon[15]											
Total	C	1 897	1 790	1 830	1 699	...	1.8	1.8	1.8	1.7	...
Urban - Urbaine	C	1 747	1 657	1 695	1 584	...	1.8	1.8	1.8	1.8	...
Rural - Rurale	C	149	131	134	114	...	1.8	1.7	1.7	1.5	...
Kazakhstan											
Total	C	2 357	2 507	2 344	2 382	2 321	6.1	6.3	5.9	5.9	5.9
Urban - Urbaine	C	1 210	1 325	1 268	1 251	1 247	5.8	5.9	5.6	5.4	5.5
Rural - Rurale	C	1 147	1 182	1 076	1 131	1 074	6.4	6.7	6.2	6.6	6.6
Kuwait - Koweït											
Total	C	352	433	405	220	...	5.9	7.1	6.8	3.7	...
Kyrgyzstan - Kirghizstan											
Total	C	1 549	1 555	1 484	*1 423	1 387	10.0	9.6	9.1	*9.0	9.0
Urban - Urbaine[16]	C	1 142	1 147	1 080	*1 006	1 039	21.2	20.7	20.6	*19.5	19.7
Rural - Rurale[16]	C	407	408	404	*417	348	4.0	3.8	3.6	*3.9	3.5
Malaysia - Malaisie											
Total	C	2 188	2 277	2 325	...	...	4.3	4.3	4.5	...	...
Urban - Urbaine	C	1 425	1 484	1 507	...	...	4.1	4.1	4.3	...	...
Rural - Rurale	C	763	793	818	...	...	4.8	4.6	4.8	...	...

12. Late foetal deaths and late foetal death ratios, by urban/rural residence: 2013 - 2017
Morts foetales tardives et rapports de mortinatalité, selon la résidence, urbaine/rurale : 2013 - 2017 (continued - suite)

Continent, country or area, and urban/rural residence / Continent, pays ou zone et résidence, urbaine/rurale	Code[a]	Number - Nombre					Ratio - Rapport				
		2013	2014	2015	2016	2017	2013	2014	2015	2016	2017
ASIA - ASIE											
Maldives[8]											
Total	...	51	37	47	41	...	...	...	...	...	...
Urban - Urbaine	...	31	27	12	16	...	...	...	...	...	...
Rural - Rurale	...	20	10	35	25	...	...	...	...	...	...
Mongolia - Mongolie											
Total	+C	...	...	557	484	451	...	...	6.8	6.1	6.0
Myanmar											
Total	+U	11 718[17]	5 687[18]	10 270[18]	...	...	...	...	...	...	...
Urban - Urbaine	+U	4 898[17]	2 332[18]	5 163[18]	...	...	...	...	...	...	...
Rural - Rurale	+U	6 820[17]	3 355[18]	5 107[18]	...	...	...	...	...	...	...
Oman											
Total[19]	U	279	335	...	403	...	...	...	...	...	...
Total	C	...	...	...	...	266	...	...	...	...	2.9
Philippines											
Total	...	4 013	4 148	4 151	...	...	...	...	...	...	...
Republic of Korea - République de Corée[20]											
Total	C	931	897	836	...	...	2.1	2.1	1.9	...	...
Urban - Urbaine[10]	C	697	611	695	...	...	1.9	1.7	1.9	...	...
Rural - Rurale[10]	C	126	135	119	...	...	1.8	1.9	1.7	...	...
Singapore - Singapour											
Total	+C	80	86	90	89	99	2.0	2.0	2.1	2.2	2.5
Sri Lanka											
Total	+U	939	708	715	959	1 039	...	...	...	...	...
Tajikistan - Tadjikistan											
Total	U	2 234	2 265	2 346	2 326	...	...	...	...	...	...
Urban - Urbaine	U	1 301	951	1 701	1 819	...	...	...	...	...	...
Rural - Rurale	U	933	1 314	645	507	...	...	...	...	...	...
Uzbekistan - Ouzbékistan											
Total	+C	4 122	5 768	6 636	...	...	6.1	8.0	9.0	...	...
Urban - Urbaine	+C	2 537	3 383	3 653	...	...	8.2	10.4	11.2	...	...
Rural - Rurale	+C	1 585	2 385	2 983	...	...	4.3	6.1	7.3	...	...
EUROPE											
Åland Islands - Îles d'Åland											
Total	C	-	-	*-	1	...	...	...	...	...	...
Urban - Urbaine	C	-	-	*-	...	...	...	...	...	...	...
Rural - Rurale	C	-	-	*-	...	...	...	...	...	...	...
Albania - Albanie											
Total	C	...	...	...	61	...	...	...	...	1.9	...
Andorra - Andorre											
Total	C	-	-	1	...	...	...	...	...	...	...
Austria - Autriche[8]											
Total	C	272	273	281	290	...	3.4	3.3	3.3	3.3	...
Belarus - Bélarus											
Total	C	260	256	271	282	...	2.2	2.2	2.3	2.4	...
Urban - Urbaine	C	185	196	192	207	...	2.0	2.1	2.1	2.3	...
Rural - Rurale	C	75	60	79	75	...	2.7	2.2	2.9	2.8	...
Belgium - Belgique											
Total	C	571	596	...	...	...	4.5	4.8	...	...	...
Urban - Urbaine	C	569	588	...	...	...	4.6	4.8	...	...	...
Rural - Rurale	C	2	8	...	...	...	...	...	...	...	...
Bulgaria - Bulgarie[8]											
Total	C	483	498	420	462	...	7.3	7.4	6.4	7.1	...
Urban - Urbaine	C	...	338	284	333	...	...	6.7	5.7	6.8	...
Rural - Rurale	C	...	160	136	129	...	...	9.5	8.3	7.9	...
Croatia - Croatie[21]											
Total	C	144	150	163	169	...	3.6	3.8	4.3	4.5	...
Urban - Urbaine	C	75	77	91	97	...	3.3	3.4	4.2	4.5	...
Rural - Rurale	C	69	73	72	72	...	4.0	4.4	4.6	4.5	...
Czechia - Tchéquie[22]											
Total	C	264	296	296	296	...	2.5	2.7	2.7	2.6	...
Urban - Urbaine	C	198	210	224	215	...	2.5	2.6	2.8	2.6	...
Rural - Rurale	C	66	86	72	81	...	2.3	3.0	2.5	2.7	...

12. Late foetal deaths and late foetal death ratios, by urban/rural residence: 2013 - 2017
Morts foetales tardives et rapports de mortinatalité, selon la résidence, urbaine/rurale : 2013 - 2017 (continued - suite)

Continent, country or area, and urban/rural residence / Continent, pays ou zone et résidence, urbaine/rurale	Code[a]	Number - Nombre					Ratio - Rapport				
		2013	2014	2015	2016	2017	2013	2014	2015	2016	2017
EUROPE											
Denmark - Danemark[23]											
Total	C	219	234	...	237	...	3.9	4.1	...	3.8	...
Estonia - Estonie											
Total	C	30	38	19	38	...	2.2	2.8	...	2.7	...
Urban - Urbaine	C	20	28	14	30	...	...	...	...	3.1	...
Rural - Rurale	C	10	10	5	8	...	...	...	...	...	...
Faeroe Islands - Îles Féroé											
Total	C	-	-	3	2	...	...	...	...	...	...
Urban - Urbaine	C	-	-	...	...	...	...	...	...	...	...
Rural - Rurale	C	-	-	...	...	...	...	...	...	...	...
Finland - Finlande[24]											
Total	C	106	115	115	116	...	1.8	2.0	2.1	2.2	...
Urban - Urbaine	C	81	83	77	86	...	2.0	2.0	1.9	2.2	...
Rural - Rurale	C	25	32	38	30	...	...	2.0	2.6	2.2	...
Germany - Allemagne											
Total	C	2 556	2 597	2 787	...	...	3.7	3.6	3.8	...	...
Greece - Grèce											
Total	C	298	296	272	283	...	3.2	3.2	3.0	3.0	...
Urban - Urbaine	C	212	200	182	182	...	3.3	3.2	2.9	2.8	...
Rural - Rurale	C	86	96	90	101	...	2.9	3.3	3.2	3.5	...
Hungary - Hongrie[25]											
Total	C	392	421	408	410	...	4.4	4.5	4.4	4.3	...
Urban - Urbaine[26]	C	229	274	265	250	...	3.7	4.2	4.1	3.8	...
Rural - Rurale[26]	C	158	143	138	156	...	5.7	5.1	4.9	5.3	...
Iceland - Islande											
Total	C	4	11	8	10	7	...	...	...	...	...
Urban - Urbaine	C	4	11	8	9	...	...	...	...	...	...
Rural - Rurale	C	-	-	-	1	...	...	...	...	...	...
Ireland - Irlande[27]											
Total	C	190	164	...	...	...	2.8	2.4	...	...	...
Italy - Italie											
Total	C	*1 262	1 364	1 305	1 308	...	*2.5	2.7	2.7	2.8	...
Latvia - Lettonie											
Total	C	81	83	72	88	...	3.9	3.8	3.3	4.0	...
Lithuania - Lituanie[21]											
Total	C	143	139	126	130	...	4.8	4.6	4.0	4.2	...
Urban - Urbaine	C	87	96	88	86	...	4.3	4.6	4.1	4.0	...
Rural - Rurale	C	56	43	38	44	...	5.8	4.6	3.8	4.7	...
Luxembourg											
Total	C	33	30	50	36	37	5.4	4.9	8.2	6.0	6.0
Malta - Malte[21]											
Total	C	16	26	...	...	...	...	...	...	...	...
Netherlands - Pays-Bas[28]											
Total	C	401	487	500	493	...	2.3	2.8	2.9	2.9	...
Norway - Norvège											
Total	C	171	217	174	183	139	2.9	3.7	3.0	3.1	2.5
Poland - Pologne											
Total	C	1 016	928	...	...	...	2.7	2.5	...	...	...
Portugal[29]											
Total	C	180	214	216	214	...	2.2	2.6	2.5	2.5	...
Romania - Roumanie[8]											
Total	C	771	782	735	732	...	4.2	3.9	3.7	3.7	...
Urban - Urbaine	C	325	373	340	...	...	3.3	3.4	3.1	...	...
Rural - Rurale	C	446	409	395	...	...	5.3	4.6	4.5	...	...
San Marino - Saint-Marin											
Total	C	1	-	-	2	-	...	...	...	...	...
Serbia - Serbie[30]											
Total	+C	307	348	388	377	...	4.7	5.2	5.9	5.8	...
Urban - Urbaine	+C	170	242	261	258	...	3.7	5.3	5.7	5.8	...
Rural - Rurale	+C	137	106	127	119	...	6.9	5.2	6.3	6.0	...
Slovakia - Slovaquie[31]											
Total	C	163	166	184	160	...	3.0	3.0	3.3	2.8	...
Urban - Urbaine	C	72	76	85	74	...	2.5	2.7	2.9	2.5	...
Rural - Rurale	C	91	90	99	86	...	3.5	3.4	3.7	3.1	...
Slovenia - Slovénie											
Total	C	62	47	55	67	...	2.9	2.2	2.7	3.3	...

Continent, country or area, and urban/rural residence / Continent, pays ou zone et résidence, urbaine/rurale	Code[a]	Number - Nombre					Ratio - Rapport				
		2013	2014	2015	2016	2017	2013	2014	2015	2016	2017
EUROPE											
Spain - Espagne											
Total	C	1 091	1 320	1 287	1 295[8]	...	2.6	3.1	3.1	3.2	...
Sweden - Suède											
Total	C	441	456	429	414	...	3.9	4.0	3.7	3.5	...
Switzerland - Suisse[8]											
Total	C	402	368	357	371	...	4.9	4.3	4.1	4.2	...
Urban - Urbaine	C	310	262	314[32]	317	...	5.0	4.1	4.2	4.2	...
Rural - Rurale	C	92	106	43[32]	54	...	4.5	5.0	3.4	4.3	...
TFYR of Macedonia - L'ex-R. y. de Macédoine											
Total	C	196	171	185	197	...	8.5	7.2	8.0	8.6	...
Urban - Urbaine	C	123	106	110	116	...	9.3	7.7	8.2	8.6	...
Rural - Rurale	C	73	65	75	81	...	7.4	6.6	7.7	8.6	...
Ukraine											
Total	+C	4 030	3 656[33]	3 318[33]	2 244[33]	...	8.0	7.8	8.1	5.7	...
Urban - Urbaine	+C	2 536	2 316[33]	2 035[33]	1 387[33]	...	7.7	7.6	7.6	5.4	...
Rural - Rurale	+C	1 494	1 340[33]	1 283[33]	857[33]	...	8.6	8.3	8.8	6.2	...
United Kingdom of Great Britain and Northern Ireland - Royaume-Uni de Grande-Bretagne et d'Irlande du Nord[34]											
Total	C	3 628	3 563	3 434	3 430	...	4.7	4.6	4.4	4.4	...
OCEANIA - OCÉANIE											
Australia - Australie[35]											
Total	C	237	293	330	*334	...	0.8	1.0	1.1	*1.1	...
Urban - Urbaine	C	124	171	198	*231	...	0.6	0.8	0.9	*1.1	...
Rural - Rurale	C	70	103	111	*90	...	0.7	1.1	1.2	*1.0	...
Guam											
Total	C	42[8]	36[8]	45[8]	44[36]	43[36]	12.6	10.6	13.4	12.8	13.1
New Zealand - Nouvelle-Zélande[37]											
Total	+C	141	147	117	144	141	2.4	2.6	1.9	2.4	2.4
Urban - Urbaine	+C	126	123	105	123	117	2.4	2.4	2.0	2.4	2.3
Rural - Rurale	+C	15	21	12	21	21	...	...	...	...	...
Palau - Palaos											
Total	C	2	3[38]	4[38]	7[38]	2[38]	...	...	...	...	...

FOOTNOTES - NOTES

Italics: data from civil registers which are incomplete or of unknown completeness. - Italiques : données incomplètes ou dont le degré d'exactitude n'est pas connu, provenant des registres de l'état civil.

* Provisional. - Données provisoires.

a 'Code' indicates the source of data, as follows:
C - Civil registration, estimated over 90% complete
U - Civil registration, estimated less than 90% complete
| - Other source, estimated reliable
+ - Data tabulated by date of registration rather than occurence
... - Information not available

Le 'Code' indique la source des données, comme suit :
C - Registres de l'état civil considérés complets à 90 p. 100 au moins
U - Registres de l'état civil qui ne sont pas considérés complets à 90 p. 100 au moins
| - Autre source, considérée pas douteuses
+ - Données exploitées selon la date de l'enregistrement et non la date de l'événement
... - Information pas disponible

1 Data refer only to events recorded in hospitals and health centres. - Ces données ne concernent que les faits d'état civil enregistrés dans les hôpitaux et les centres de santé uniquement.
2 Excludes the islands of St. Brandon and Agalega. - Non compris les îles St. Brandon et Agalega.
3 Source: National Office of Births and Deaths. - Source : Le bureau national des naissances et des décès.
4 Data refer to the death of a foetus at least 22 completed weeks of gestation. - Les données concernent le décès d'un fœtus après 22 semaines de gestation au moins.
5 Source: Bermuda Hospitals Board (BHB). -
6 Including Canadian residents temporarily in the United States, but excluding United States residents temporarily in Canada. - Y compris les résidents canadiens se trouvant temporairement aux Etats-Unis, mais ne comprenant pas les résidents des Etats-Unis se trouvant temporairement au Canada.
7 Late foetal death is indicated by the fact that the foetus is at least 500 g or more in weight. - Les décès foetaux tardifs sont caractérisés par le fait que le foetus pèse au moins 500 g.
8 Data refer to total foetal deaths. - Y compris toutes les morts foetales.
9 Data refer to resident population only. - Pour la population résidante seulement.
10 The total number may include 'Unknown residence', but the categories urban and rural do not. - Le nombre total peut inclure les personnes dont la résidence n'est pas connue, à l'inverse des catégories de population urbaine et rurale.

11 Late foetal death is indicated by the fact that the foetus is at least 22 completed weeks of gestational age. - Les décès intra-utérins tardifs sont définis comme survenant après 22 semaines au moins de gestation.

12 Excludes nomadic Indian tribes. - Non compris les tribus d'Indiens nomades.

13 Sources: Births and Deaths National Registration System database, and medical records of government hospitals. - Les sources: Les bases de données des << Births and Deaths National Registration System >> et les dossiers médicaux des hôpitaux du gouvernement.

14 Includes data for East Jerusalem and Israeli residents in certain other territories under occupation by Israeli military forces since June 1967. - Y compris les données pour Jérusalem-Est et les résidents israéliens dans certains autres territoires occupés depuis 1967 par les forces armées israéliennes.

15 Data refer to Japanese nationals in Japan only. The total number may include 'Unknown residence', but the categories urban and rural do not. Data exclude unknown duration of pregnancy. - Les données se raportent aux nationaux japonais au Japon seulement. Le nombre total peut inclure les personnes dont la résidence n'est pas connue, à l'inverse des catégories de population urbaine et rurale. Exception faite des grossesses dont la durée n'est pas connue.

16 Urban and rural figures refer to the late foetal deaths collected based on the location of the medical facilities, regardless of the mothers' permanent residence location. - Les chiffres urbains et ruraux concernent les décès tardifs du fœtus recueillis sur la base de l'emplacement des établissements médicaux, indépendamment du lieu de résidence permanente des mères.

17 Data are from Health Management Information System (HMIS). Including still births. - Les données proviennent de Système d'information de gestion de la santé (HMIS). Les données comprennent les mortinaissances.

18 Data are from Vital Registration System (VRS). - Les données proviennent du système d'enregistrement des faits d'état civil.

19 Data from Births and Deaths Notification System (Ministry of Health and all health care providers). - Les données proviennent du système de notification des naissances et des décès (Ministère de la santé et tous prestataires de soins de santé).

20 Excluding alien armed forces, civilian aliens employed by armed forces, and foreign diplomatic personnel and their dependants. - Non compris les militaires étrangers, les civils étrangers employés par les forces armées ni le personnel diplomatique étranger et les membres de leur famille les accompagnant.

21 Late foetal death is defined as an infant born without any signs of life, weighing at least 500 g, after duration of pregnancy of at least 22 weeks. - On dit qu'il y a mort intra-utérine tardive lorsqu'un enfant pesant au minimum 500 g naît sans donner aucun signe de vie au terme d'une grossesse qui a duré au moins 22 semaines.

22 Since 1 April 2012, a stillborn child is defined in guidelines for filling in a death certificate as a child fully expelled or removed out of the mother's body, not showing any sign of life and whose birth weight is 500 g or more. If the weight is not possible to determine then duration of pregnancy must be 22 weeks or more. If the duration of pregnancy is not possible to determine, the foetus length must be 25 cm or more. - Depuis le 1er avril 2012, un enfant mort-né est défini dans les directives relatives à l'établissement du certificat de décès comme un enfant complètement expulsé par la mère ou retiré de son corps, ne montrant aucun signe de vie et ayant atteint un poids de 500 g. S'il est impossible d'en déterminer le poids, la durée de gestation doit être au moins de 22 semaines. S'il est impossible de déterminer la durée de gestation, la longueur du fœtus doit être au moins de 25 cm.

23 Excluding Faeroe Islands and Greenland shown separately, if available. - Non compris les Iles Féroé et le Groenland, qui font l'objet de rubriques distinctes, si disponible.

24 Excluding Åland Islands. - Non compris les Îles d'Åland.

25 Late foetal death is indicated by the fact that the foetus is at least 24 completed weeks of gestation (it was 28 weeks until 1996) and does not show any sign of life after the separation from its mother; the foetus has to be 30 cm or more in length or 500 g or more in weight if its gestational age cannot be determined. - Pour qu'il y ait mort foetale tardive, il faut que le décès d'un foetus survienne après 24 semaines complètes de gestation au moins (28 semaines jusqu'en 1996), que le foetus n'ait pas donné signe de vie après avoir été séparé de la mère, qu'il mesure 30 cm au moins ou pèse 500 g si la durée de la période de gestation n'est pas connue.

26 The urban and rural categories do not include the data of foreigners, persons of unknown residence and the homeless, whereas the total category includes them. - Les chiffres portant sur la population urbaine et rurale n' incluent pas les données relatives aux étrangers, aux personnes dont la résidence n'est pas connue et aux personnes sans domicile fixe, à l'inverse, le total les inclut.

27 Data refer to events registered within one year of occurrence. - Les données portent sur des événements enregistrés dans l'année pendant laquelle ils sont survenus.

28 Including residents outside the country if listed in a Netherlands population register. - Englobe les résidents se trouvant à l'étranger à condition qu'ils soient inscrits sur le registre de population des Pays-Bas.

29 Data refer to usually resident population. - Les données concernent la population habituellement résidente.

30 Data refer to total foetal deaths. Excludes data for Kosovo and Metohia. - Y compris toutes les morts foetales. Sans les données pour le Kosovo et Metohie.

31 Including foetal deaths of at least 1 000 g in weight or 28 weeks of gestation. - Y compris les morts de fœtus pesant au moins 1 000 g ou après 28 semaines de gestation.

32 From 2015, urban refers to urban centers and areas under the influence of urban centers. - A partir de 2015, le territoire urbain inclut l'espace des centres urbains ainsi que l'espace sous influence des centres urbains.

33 The Government of Ukraine has informed the United Nations that it is not in a position to provide statistical data concerning the Autonomous Republic of Crimea and the city of Sevastopol. - Le gouvernement Ukrainien a informé l'ONU qu'il n'est pas en mesure de fournir des données statistiques concernant la République autonome de Crimée et la ville de Sébastopol.

34 Excluding Channel Islands (Guernsey and Jersey) and Isle of Man, shown separately, if available. - Non compris les îles Anglo-Normandes (Guernesey et Jersey) et l'île de Man, qui font l'objet de rubriques distinctes, si disponible.

35 Late foetal death include deaths of foetuses of 28 weeks or more of gestation and with a birth weight of at least 400 grams. Data exclude foetal deaths for which the period of gestation and birthweight was not stated on the Medical Certificate of Cause of Perinatal Death. - La mortalité foetale tardive recouvre les décès de foetus de 28 semaines ou plus pesant au moins 400 grammes à la naissance. Les données ne tiennent pas compte des décès intra-utérins pour lesquels la période de gestation et le poids à la naissance n'étaient pas indiqués sur le certificat médical faisant état de la cause du décès périnatal.

36 Including United States military personnel, their dependants and contract employees. - Y compris les militaires des Etats-Unis, les membres de leur famille les accompagnant et les agents contractuels des Etats-Unis.

37 The total number may include 'Unknown residence', but the categories urban and rural do not. Data refer to resident population only. Random rounding to base 3 is applied in this table as a confidentiality measure. - Le nombre total peut inclure les personnes dont la résidence n'est pas connue, à l'inverse des catégories de population urbaine et rurale. Pour la population résidante seulement. Les chiffres sont arrondis à la base 3 de manière aléatoire, pour des raisons de confidentialité.

38 Data includes abortions. - Les données comprennnent les avortement.

Table 13 - *Demographic Yearbook 2017*

Table 13 presents legally induced abortions for as many years as available between 2008 and 2017.

Description of variables: There are two major categories of abortion: spontaneous and induced. Induced abortions are those initiated by deliberate action undertaken with the intention of terminating pregnancy; all other abortions are considered spontaneous.

The induction of abortion is subject to governmental regulation in most, if not all, countries or areas. This regulation varies from complete prohibition in some countries or areas to abortion on request, with services provided by governmental health authorities, in others. More generally, governments have attempted to define the conditions under which a pregnancy may lawfully be terminated and have established procedures for authorizing abortion in individual cases.

Information on abortion policies is collected by the United Nations Population Division and published in the *Abortion Policies and Reproductive Health around the World*[1].

Reliability of data: Unlike data on live births and foetal deaths, which are generally collected through systems of vital registration, data on abortion are collected from a variety of sources. Because of this, the quality specification on the completeness of civil registers, which is presented for other tables, does not appear here.

Limitations: With regard to the collection of information on abortions, a variety of sources are used, but hospital records are the most common source of information. This implies that most cases that have no contact with hospitals are missed. Data from other sources are probably also incomplete. The data in the present table are limited to legally induced abortions, which, by their nature, might be assumed to be more complete than data on all induced abortions.

Earlier data: Legally induced abortions have been shown previously in all issues of the *Demographic Yearbook* since the twenty-third issue. For more information on specific topics and years for which data are reported, readers should consult the Historical Index.

NOTES

[1] United Nations, Department of Economic and Social Affairs, Population Division (2014). *Abortion Policies and Reproductive Health around the World* (United Nations publication, Sales No. E.14.XIII.11).

Tableau 13 – *Annuaire démographique 2017*

Le tableau 13 présente les données disponibles, relatives aux avortements provoqués légalement, entre 2008 et 2017.

Description des variables : l'avortement peut être spontané ou provoqué. L'avortement provoqué est celui qui résulte de manœuvres délibérées, entreprises afin d'interrompre la grossesse ; tous les autres avortements sont considérés comme spontanés.

L'interruption délibérée de la grossesse fait l'objet d'une réglementation officielle dans la plupart des pays ou zones, sinon dans tous. Cette réglementation va de l'interdiction totale à l'autorisation de l'avortement sur demande, pratiqué par des services de santé publique. Le plus souvent, les gouvernements se sont efforcés de définir les circonstances dans lesquelles la grossesse peut être interrompue licitement et de fixer une procédure d'autorisation.

La Division de la population des Nations Unies collecte des informations sur les politiques en matière d'avortement et les publient dans *Abortion Policies and Reproductive Health around the World*[1].

Fiabilité des données : à la différence des données sur les naissances vivantes et les morts fœtales, qui proviennent généralement des registres d'état civil, les données sur l'avortement sont tirées de sources diverses. Aussi ne trouve-t-on pas ici une évaluation de la qualité des données semblable à celle qui indique, pour les autres tableaux, le degré d'exhaustivité des données de l'état civil.

Insuffisance des données : en ce qui concerne les renseignements sur l'avortement, un grand nombre de sources sont utilisées, les relevés hospitaliers restant cependant la source la plus commune. Il s'ensuit que la plupart des cas qui ne passent pas par les hôpitaux sont ignorés. Il faut aussi tenir compte du fait que les données provenant d'autres sources sont probablement incomplètes. Les données du tableau 13 se limitent aux avortements provoqués pour raisons légales dont on peut supposer, en raison de leur nature même, que les statistiques sont plus complètes que les données concernant l'ensemble des avortements provoqués.

Données publiées antérieurement : des statistiques concernant les avortements provoqués pour raisons légales sont publiées dans *l'Annuaire démographique* depuis la vingt-troisième édition. Pour plus de précisions concernant les années et les sujets pour lesquels des données ont été publiées, se reporter à l'index historique.

NOTES

[1] United Nations, Department of Economic and Social Affairs, Population Division (2014). *Abortion Policies and Reproductive Health around the World* (United Nations publication, Sales No. E.14.XIII.11).

13. Legally induced abortions: 2008 - 2017
Avortements provoqués légalement : 2008 - 2017

Continent and country or area Continent et pays ou zone	Number - Nombre									
	2008	**2009**	**2010**	**2011**	**2012**	**2013**	**2014**	**2015**	**2016**	**2017**
AFRICA - AFRIQUE										
Burundi[1]	...	6 329	6 272	3 547	3 630	3 152	...	...	...	...
Reunion - Réunion	4 564	4 402	4 349	4 508	4 280	...	...	...	...	...
Seychelles	453	471	556	579	533	515	549	478	509	521
AMERICA, NORTH - AMÉRIQUE DU NORD										
Bermuda - Bermudes[2]	273	290	275	268	271	270	239	227	226	231
Costa Rica[3]	8 733[4]	7 848	7 697	7 882	7 405	7 283	*7 137	...	...	...
Cuba	74 905	84 724	71 398	83 943	83 682	84 373	85 782	91 500	85 445	...
Dominican Republic - République dominicaine	26 318	22 828	22 551	25 284	26 303	26 180	25 999	...	...	...
Greenland - Groenland	899	799	858	743	784	875	865	...	...	...
Mexico - Mexique[5]	764	867	*986	1 041	294	271	301	411	394	...
United States of America - États-Unis d'Amérique[6]	825 564	...	...	...	...	...	...	...	...	...
AMERICA, SOUTH - AMÉRIQUE DU SUD										
Colombia - Colombie	49	69	82	120	212	633	876	3 002	1 588[7]	...
Ecuador - Équateur[8]	...	...	...	...	41 712	40 256	35 719	31 302	30 410	...
Paraguay	...	...	...	...	4 353	...	...	...	...	...
ASIA - ASIE										
Armenia - Arménie	12 469	13 797	...	...	...	...	11 892	11 104	11 458	...
Azerbaijan - Azerbaïdjan	25 247	24 554	26 799	27 787	31 037	27 892	27 220	27 452	34 569	...
Bahrain - Bahreïn[9]	2 575	2 394	2 525	2 452	2 463	...	...	...	...	...
China, Hong Kong SAR - Chine, Hong Kong RAS	13 199	12 028	11 231	11 864	11 298	10 653	10 359	9 890	9 481	8 780
Georgia - Géorgie	22 062	24 311	25 585	30 590	39 225	37 018	33 469	33 377	29 641	...
Israel - Israël[10]	19 638	19 849	19 575	18 974	18 822	18 263	18 646	18 510	...	...
Japan - Japon	242 326	226 878	212 694[11]	202 106	196 639	186 253	181 905	176 388	168 015	...
Kazakhstan	123 992	113 320	106 074	95 288	95 654	84 265	83 709	81 440	78 857	80 328
Kyrgyzstan - Kirghizstan[12]	20 800	22 088	21 675	23 728	23 547	21 673	24 456	22 084	20 783	19 486
Mongolia - Mongolie	10 688	12 602	12 492	17 504	18 473	15 628	18 145	18 168	18 316	17 530
Singapore - Singapour	12 222	12 318	12 082	11 940	10 624	9 282	8 515	7 942	7 217	6 815
Tajikistan - Tadjikistan	18 481	19 470	19 510	17 503	16 618	15 984	17 347	16 864	14 957	...
Uzbekistan - Ouzbékistan	41 758	45 968	40 651	38 809	37 634	38 546	41 352	40 201	...	...
EUROPE										
Åland Islands - Îles d'Åland	67	68	70	73	60	70	66	69	76	...
Albania - Albanie	8 335	8 139	6 919	7 042	6 755	6 442	5 572	5 619	1 206	...
Belarus - Bélarus	42 197	35 967	33 262	32 031	28 628	31 206	29 797	29 217	27 467	...
Belgium - Belgique	18 595	18 870	19 095	19 578	...	...	...	...	...	...
Bulgaria - Bulgarie	36 593	33 733	31 548	31 716	29 992	29 505	28 145	27 782	26 412	...
Croatia - Croatie	4 497	4 450	4 043	4 347	3 571	3 161	3 020	3 002	2 520	...
Czechia - Tchéquie	25 760	24 636	23 998	24 055	23 032	22 714	21 893	20 403	20 406	...
Denmark - Danemark[13]	16 586	16 664	16 596	16 085	16 220	15 986	15 440	15 325	...	...
Estonia - Estonie[14]	8 409	7 542	7 068	6 668	6 056	5 777	6 901	4 889	6 248	...
Faeroe Islands - Îles Féroé	37	51	33	33	34	23	30	21	26	...
Finland - Finlande[15]	10 414	10 437	10 231	10 622	10 177	10 060	9 714	9 372	9 311	...
France[16]	208 003	208 662	211 248	206 888	205 300	214 649	210 483	202 165	...	...
Germany - Allemagne	114 484	110 694	110 431	108 867	106 815	102 802	99 715	99 237	98 721	...
Hungary - Hongrie	44 089	43 181	40 449	38 443	36 118	34 891	32 663	31 176	30 439	28 496
Iceland - Islande	959	981	977	970	980	963	951	921	1 021	...
Italy - Italie	118 891[17]	114 793[18]	112 463[19]	110 041[19]	103 191[20]	100 342	95 400	87 369	84 874	...
Latvia - Lettonie	10 425	8 881	7 443	7 089	6 197	5 557	5 318	4 802	4 366	...
Lithuania - Lituanie	9 031	8 024	6 989	6 205	6 033	5 353	5 231	4 735	4 502	...
Montenegro - Monténégro	...	...	...	...	...	...	943	980	763	...
Norway - Norvège	16 054	15 774	15 735	15 343	...	...	...	...	...	...

13. Legally induced abortions: 2008 - 2017
Avortements provoqués légalement : 2008 - 2017 (continued - suite)

Continent and country or area Continent et pays ou zone	Number - Nombre									
	2008	2009	2010	2011	2012	2013	2014	2015	2016	2017
EUROPE										
Poland - Pologne[21]	506	538	644	669	752	745	970	1 040	1 098	...
Portugal	18 607	19 848	20 137	20 480	19 156	18 281	16 762	16 652	*15 959	...
Republic of Moldova - République de Moldova	15 900	14 634	14 785	15 710	14 838	...	...	...	...	...
Romania - Roumanie	127 907	116 060	101 915	103 386	87 975	86 432	78 371	70 885	63 518	...
Russian Federation - Fédération de Russie	1 385 600	1 292 389	1 186 108	1 124 880	1 063 982	1 012 399	...	...	...	...
Serbia - Serbie[22]	19 535	18 215	17 466	15 963	15 301	13 650	12 923	12 242	11 093	...
Slovakia - Slovaquie	13 394	13 240	12 582	11 789	11 214	11 105	10 582	10 058	9 390	...
Slovenia - Slovénie	4 946	4 653	4 328	4 263	4 106	4 011	4 060	3 682	3 736	...
Spain - Espagne	115 812	111 482	113 031	118 359	112 390	...	94 796	94 188	...	...
Sweden - Suède	38 053	37 524	37 693	37 750	37 366	...	36 629	38 071	38 177	36 616
Switzerland - Suisse[23]	10 310	10 187	10 650	10 715	10 531	10 177	10 016	10 088	10 085	...
TFYR of Macedonia - L'ex-R. y. de Macédoine	5 900	5 648	5 078	5 324	5 387	4 983	4 738	4 587	4 251	...
Ukraine	217 413	194 845	176 774	169 131	153 147	147 736	116 104[24]	...	...	...
United Kingdom of Great Britain and Northern Ireland - Royaume-Uni de Grande-Bretagne et d'Irlande du Nord[25]	216 062	208 854	209 048	208 636	203 419[26]	...	...	...	197 659	...
OCEANIA - OCÉANIE										
Guam[27]	327	266	269	295	275	213	209	263	289	239
New Zealand - Nouvelle-Zélande	17 940	17 550	16 630	15 863	14 745	14 073	13 137	13 155	12 823	13 285

FOOTNOTES - NOTES

Italics: estimates which are less reliable. - Italiques : estimations moins sûres.

* Provisional. - Données provisoires.

[1] Data refer only to events recorded in hospitals and health centres. - Ces données ne concernent que les faits d'état civil enregistrés dans les hôpitaux et les centres de santé uniquement.

[2] Source: Bermuda Hospitals Board (BHB). -

[3] Excluding abortions performed in private hospitals. - Non comprises les interruptions volontaires de grossesse effectuées dans des hôpitaux privés.

[4] Number of women who report having had a previous abortion when registering a newborn. - Nombre des femmes qui ont signalé d'avoir eu un avortement avant la naissance de l'enfant enregistré.

[5] Data refer to 'Therapeutic Abortions'. According to Mexican law, only induced abortions, prescribed by medical reasons or induced because of pregnancy coming from sexual aggression, are considered as legal; data refer only to the former. Refers to residence of the mother. To calculate the total number of abortions, only foetal deaths of less than 20 weeks of gestation were considered. Excluding abortions in the country by women with usual residence outside of the country. - Les données se rapportent aux « interruptions volontaires de grossesse pour des motifs thérapeutiques ». D'après la loi mexicaine, seuls sont considérés légaux les avortements déclenchés pour des raisons médicales ou parce que la grossesse est le résultat d'une agression sexuelle; les données se réfèrent seulement à la première. Correspond à la résidence de la mère. Seuls les morts fœtales survenues à moins de 20 semaines de gestation ont été prises en compte aux fins du calcul du nombre total d'avortements. Hors avortements dans le pays par des femmes avec résidence habituelle en dehors du pays.

[6] Includes areas that reported abortion counts every year during the period of analysis. Excludes states that did not report abortion numbers: Alaska(1998-2002), California (1997-2008), Louisiana (2005), Maryland (2006-2008), New Hampshire (1998-2008), Oklahoma (1998-1999), and West Virginia (2003-2004). - Sont couvertes les régions qui ont indiqué le nombre annuel d'avortements pour la période analysée. Ne sont pas couverts les États qui n'ont pas fourni de chiffres : l'Alaska (1998-2002), la Californie (1997-2008), la Louisiane (2005), le Maryland (2006-2008), le New Hampshire (1998-2008), l'Oklahoma (1998-1999) et la Virginie occidentale (2003-2004).

[7] Affected by underreporting since, by law, legally induced abortions are not reported directly to the civil registry. - Font l'objet d'une sous-déclaration, toutes les interruptions volontaires de grossesse pratiquées légalement n'étant pas déclarées dans la mesure où la loi n'impose pas de les inscrire directement au registre civil.

[8] Data refer to abortions registered in hospitals due to pregnancy complications. - Les données renvoient aux avortements enregistrés dans les hôpitaux du fait des complications de la grossesse.

[9] Data refer to spontaneous abortions and miscarriages. - Données se rapportant aux avortements spontanés et fausses couches.

[10] Includes data for East Jerusalem and Israeli residents in certain other territories under occupation by Israeli military forces since June 1967. Data refer to applications to commissions for termination of pregnancy and not to authorizations. - Y compris les données pour Jérusalem-Est et les résidents israéliens dans certains autres territoires occupés depuis 1967 par les forces armées israéliennes. Les données relatives aux avortements provoqués légalement se rapportent aux demandes d'autorisation et non aux autorisations elles-mêmes.

[11] Excluding data of cities and towns in the jurisdiction of Sousou Public Health and Welfare Office of Fukushima Prefecture due to the impact of the Great East Japan Earthquake. - Ne sont pas incluses les données relatives aux agglomérations relevant du bureau de la santé publique et des services sociaux de Sousou dans la préfecture de Fukushima, en raison des conséquences du grand séisme dans l'est du Japon.

[12] Based on administrative reporting of the Ministry of Health. - Les données reposent sur les rapports administratifs du Ministère de la santé.

[13] Excluding Faeroe Islands and Greenland shown separately, if available. - Non compris les Îles Féroé et le Groenland, qui font l'objet de rubriques distinctes, si disponible.

[14] Data refer to resident population only. - Pour la population résidante seulement.

[15] Excluding Åland Islands. - Non compris les Îles d'Åland.

[16] Data refer to women between 15 and 49 years of age. - Le total se rapporte uniquement aux femmes dont l'âge est compris entre 15 et 49 ans.

[17] Data are incomplete for Campania, Calabria, Sicilia and Sardegna regions. - Les données sont incomplètes pour les régions de Campanie, de Calabrie, de Sicile et de Sardaigne.

[18] Data are incomplete for Abruzzo, Campania, Basilicata, Sicilia and Sardegna regions. - Données incomplètes pour les régions des Abruzzes, de Campanie, de Basilicate, de Sicile et de Sardaigne.

[19] Data are incomplete for Umbria, Campania and Sicilia regions. - Les données sont incomplètes pour l'Ombrie, la Campanie et la Sicile.

[20] Data are incomplete for Umbria, Abruzzo, Campania, Puglia and Sicilia regions. - Les données sont incomplètes pour les régions d'Ombrie, des Abruzzes, de Campanie, des Pouilles et de Sicile.

[21] Based on hospital and polyclinic records. - D'après les registres des hôpitaux et des polycliniques.

[22] Excludes data for Kosovo and Metohia. - Sans les données pour le Kosovo et Metohia.

[23] Data refer to termination of pregnancy for women who are Switzerland residents. - Les données portent sur les interruptions de grossesse pratiquées sur des femmes qui résident en Suisse.

[24] The Government of Ukraine has informed the United Nations that it is not in a position to provide statistical data concerning the Autonomous Republic of Crimea and the city of Sevastopol. - Le gouvernement Ukrainien a informé l'ONU qu'il n'est pas en mesure de fournir des données statistiques concernant la République autonome de Crimée et la ville de Sébastopol.

[25] Excluding Northern Ireland. Excluding Channel Islands (Guernsey and Jersey) and Isle of Man, shown separately, if available. - Non compris l'Irlande du Nord. Non compris les îles Anglo-Normandes (Guernesey et Jersey) et l'île de Man, qui font l'objet de rubriques distinctes, si disponible.

[26] Including provisional data for Scotland. - Y compris les données provisoires pour l'Écosse.

[27] Including United States military personnel, their dependants and contract employees. - Y compris les militaires des Etats-Unis, les membres de leur famille les accompagnant et les agents contractuels des Etats-Unis.

Table 14 - Demographic Yearbook 2017

Table 14 presents legally induced abortions by age and number of previous live births of women for the latest available year between 2008 and 2017.

Description of variables: Age is defined as age at last birthday, that is, the difference between the date of birth and the date of the occurrence of the event, expressed in complete solar years. The age classification used in this table is the following: under 15 years, 5-year age groups through 45-49 years and 50 years and over.

Except where otherwise indicated, eight categories are used in classifying the number of previous live births: 0 through 5, 6 or more live births, and, if required, number of live births unknown.

Information on abortion policies is collected by the United Nations Population Division and published in the *Abortion Policies and Reproductive Health around the World*[1].

Reliability of data: Unlike data on live births and foetal deaths, which are generally collected through systems of vital registration, data on abortion are collected from a variety of sources. Because of this, the quality specification on the completeness of civil registers, which is presented for other tables, does not appear here.

Limitations: With regard to the collection of information on abortions, a variety of sources are used, but hospital records are the most common source of information. This implies that most cases that have no contact with hospitals are missed. Data from other sources are probably also incomplete. The data in the present table are limited to legally induced abortions, which, by their nature, might be assumed to be more complete than data on all induced abortions.

In addition, deficiencies in the reporting of age and number of previous live births of the woman, differences in the method used for obtaining the age of the woman, and the proportion of abortions for which age or previous live births of the woman are unknown must all be taken into account in using these data.

Earlier data: Legally induced abortions by age and previous live births of women have been shown previously in most issues of the *Demographic Yearbook* since the twenty-third issue. For more information on specific topics and years for which data are reported, readers should consult the Historical Index.

NOTES

[1] United Nations, Department of Economic and Social Affairs, Population Division (2014). *Abortion Policies and Reproductive Health around the World* (United Nations publication, Sales No. E.14.XIII.11).

Tableau 14 – *Annuaire démographique 2017*

Le tableau 14 présente les données les plus récentes disponibles entre 2008 et 2017 sur les avortements provoqués pour des raisons légales, selon l'âge de la mère et le nombre de naissances vivantes précédentes.

Description des variables : L'âge considéré est l'âge au dernier anniversaire, c'est-à-dire la différence entre la date de naissance et la date de l'avortement, exprimée en années solaires révolues. La classification par âge utilisée dans le tableau 14 est la suivante : moins de 15 ans, groupes quinquennaux jusqu'à 45-49 ans, 50 ans et plus, et âge inconnu.

Sauf indication contraire, les naissances vivantes antérieures sont classées dans les huit catégories suivantes: 0 à 5 naissances vivantes, 6 naissances vivantes ou plus et, le cas échéant, nombre de naissances vivantes inconnu.

La Division de la population des Nations Unies collecte des informations sur les politiques en matière d'avortement et les publient dans *Abortion Policies and Reproductive Health around the World*[1].

Fiabilité des données : à la différence des données sur les naissances vivantes et les morts fœtales, qui proviennent généralement des registres d'état civil, les données sur l'avortement sont tirées de sources diverses. Aussi ne trouve-t-on pas ici une évaluation de la qualité des données semblable à celle qui indique, pour les autres tableaux, le degré d'exhaustivité des données de l'état civil.

Insuffisance des données : en ce qui concerne les renseignements sur l'avortement, un grand nombre de sources sont utilisées, les relevés hospitaliers restant cependant la source la plus commune. Il s'ensuit que la plupart des cas qui ne passent pas par les hôpitaux sont ignorés. Il faut aussi tenir compte du fait que les données provenant d'autres sources sont probablement incomplètes. Les données du tableau 14 se limitent aux avortements provoqués pour raisons légales dont on peut supposer, en raison de leur nature même, que les statistiques sont plus complètes que les données concernant l'ensemble des avortements provoqués.

En outre, on doit tenir compte, lorsque l'on utilise ces données, des erreurs de déclaration de l'âge de la mère et du nombre des naissances vivantes précédentes, de l'hétérogénéité des méthodes de calcul de l'âge de la mère et de la proportion d'avortements pour lesquels l'âge de la mère ou le nombre des naissances vivantes ne sont pas connus.

Données publiées antérieurement : Depuis la vingt-troisième édition, la plupart des éditions de l'*Annuaire démographique* contiennent des statistiques concernant les avortements provoqués pour raisons légales, selon l'âge de la mère et le nombre de naissances vivantes antérieures. Pour plus de précisions concernant les années et les sujets pour lesquels des données ont été publiées, se reporter à l'index historique.

NOTES

[1] United Nations, Department of Economic and Social Affairs, Population Division (2014). *Abortion Policies and Reproductive Health around the World* (United Nations publication, Sales No. E.14.XIII.11).

14. Legally induced abortions by age and number of previous live births of women: latest available year, 2008 - 2017
Avortements provoqués légalement selon l'âge de la femme et selon le nombre des naissances vivantes précédentes : dernière année disponible, 2008 - 2017

Continent, country or area, year and age — Continent, pays ou zone, année et âge	Number of previous live births — Nombre des naissances vivantes précédentes								
	Total	0	1	2	3	4	5	6+	Unknown - Inconnu

AFRICA - AFRIQUE

Seychelles
2017

Total	521	...	...	...	...	...	...	...	...
10 - 14	10	...	...	...	...	...	...	...	...
15 - 19	83	...	...	...	...	...	...	...	...
20 - 24	121	...	...	...	...	...	...	...	...
25 - 29	106	...	...	...	...	...	...	...	...
30 - 34	90	...	...	...	...	...	...	...	...
35 - 39	67	...	...	...	...	...	...	...	...
40 - 44	43	...	...	...	...	...	...	...	...
45 - 49	1	...	...	...	...	...	...	...	...

AMERICA, NORTH - AMÉRIQUE DU NORD

Bermuda - Bermudes[1]
2017

Total	231	...	...	...	...	...	...	...	231
0 - 14	-	...	...	...	...	...	...	...	-
15 - 19	11	...	...	...	...	...	...	...	11
20 - 24	47	...	...	...	...	...	...	...	47
25 - 29	69	...	...	...	...	...	...	...	69
30 - 34	61	...	...	...	...	...	...	...	61
35 - 39	33	...	...	...	...	...	...	...	33
40 - 44	9	...	...	...	...	...	...	...	9
45 - 49	1	...	...	...	...	...	...	...	1
50 +	-	...	...	...	...	...	...	...	-
Unknown - Inconnu	-	...	...	...	...	...	...	...	-

Costa Rica[2]
2009

Total	7 848	...	...	...	...	...	...	...	...
10 - 14	68	...	...	...	...	...	...	...	...
15 - 19	1 275	...	...	...	...	...	...	...	...
20 - 44	6 437	...	...	...	...	...	...	...	...
45 +	68	...	...	...	...	...	...	...	...

Cuba
2016

Total	85 445	...	...	...	...	...	...	...	...
0 - 14	1 374	...	...	...	...	...	...	...	...
15 - 19	19 638	...	...	...	...	...	...	...	...
20 - 34	56 028	...	...	...	...	...	...	...	...
35 - 49	8 405	...	...	...	...	...	...	...	...
Unknown - Inconnu	-	...	...	...	...	...	...	...	...

Mexico - Mexique[3]
2016

Total	394	108	116	81	34	7	2	1	45
0 - 14	1	-	-	-	-	-	-	-	1
15 - 19	50	35	6	2	-	-	-	-	7
20 - 24	80	23	35	7	-	1	-	-	14
25 - 29	96	20	27	28	9	1	1	-	10
30 - 34	80	15	28	21	7	1	-	1	7
35 - 39	59	10	13	16	12	4	1	-	3
40 - 44	18	3	6	5	2	-	-	-	2
45 - 49	3	1	-	-	2	-	-	-	-
50 +	-	-	-	-	-	-	-	-	-
Unknown - Inconnu	7	1	1	2	2	-	-	-	1

AMERICA, SOUTH - AMÉRIQUE DU SUD

Colombia - Colombie[4]
2016

Total	1 588	750	462	233	89	27	13	14	...
0 - 14	54	53	1	-	-	-	-	-	...
15 - 19	305	237	64	4	-	-	-	-	...
20 - 24	456	237	152	52	13	-	1	1	...
25 - 29	345	133	107	65	31	7	1	1	...
30 - 34	207	54	77	50	14	4	3	5	...

14. Legally induced abortions by age and number of previous live births of women: latest available year, 2008 - 2017
Avortments provoqués légalement selon l'âge de la femme et selon le nombre des naissances vivantes précédentes : dernière année disponible, 2008 - 2017 (continued - suite)

Continent, country or area, year and age Continent, pays ou zone, année et âge	Total	0	1	2	3	4	5	6+	Unknown - Inconnu
AMERICA, SOUTH - AMÉRIQUE DU SUD									
Colombia - Colombie[4]									
2016									
35 - 39	139	26	41	36	20	7	5	4	...
40 - 44	69	9	16	21	9	8	4	2	...
45 - 49	7	-	1	3	2	-	-	1	...
50 +	-	-	-	-	-	-	-	-	...
Unknown - Inconnu	6	1	3	2	-	-	-	-	...
Ecuador - Équateur[5]									
2016									
Total	30 410	...	...	...	...	...	...	...	...
0 - 14	277	...	...	...	...	...	...	...	...
15 - 19	4 406	...	...	...	...	...	...	...	...
20 - 24	7 066	...	...	...	...	...	...	...	...
25 - 29	6 747	...	...	...	...	...	...	...	...
30 - 34	5 706	...	...	...	...	...	...	...	...
35 - 39	4 023	...	...	...	...	...	...	...	...
40 - 44	1 864	...	...	...	...	...	...	...	...
45 - 49	306	...	...	...	...	...	...	...	...
50 +	15	...	...	...	...	...	...	...	...
ASIA - ASIE									
Armenia - Arménie									
2014									
Total	11 892	...	...	...	...	...	...	...	...
0 - 14	1	...	...	...	...	...	...	...	...
15 - 29	490	...	...	...	...	...	...	...	...
30 - 44	9 251	...	...	...	...	...	...	...	...
45 +	2 150	...	...	...	...	...	...	...	...
Azerbaijan - Azerbaïdjan									
2016									
Total	34 569	...	...	...	...	...	...	...	...
0 - 14	-	...	...	...	...	...	...	...	...
15 - 19	1 261	...	...	...	...	...	...	...	...
20 - 24	7 773	...	...	...	...	...	...	...	...
25 - 29	11 289	...	...	...	...	...	...	...	...
30 - 34	8 930	...	...	...	...	...	...	...	...
35 - 39	5 267	...	...	...	...	...	...	...	...
40 +	49	...	...	...	...	...	...	...	...
China, Hong Kong SAR - Chine, Hong Kong RAS									
2017									
Total	8 780	4 470	1 793	2 041	394	62	13	7	...
0 - 14	17	17	-	-	-	-	-	-	...
15 - 19	488	462	25	1	-	-	-	-	...
20 - 24	1 678	1 444	167	59	8	-	-	-	...
25 - 29	1 783	1 199	303	238	38	4	-	1	...
30 - 34	1 995	790	544	561	82	16	1	1	...
35 - 39	1 885	424	492	757	173	30	6	3	...
40 - 44	838	118	241	380	81	11	5	2	...
45 - 49	94	16	21	43	12	1	1	-	...
50 +	2	-	-	2	-	-	-	-	...
Georgia - Géorgie									
2016									
Total	29 641	...	...	...	...	...	...	...	...
0 - 14	19	...	...	...	...	...	...	...	...
15 - 19	932	...	...	...	...	...	...	...	...
20 - 24	6 032	...	...	...	...	...	...	...	...
25 - 29	8 513	...	...	...	...	...	...	...	...
30 - 34	7 708	...	...	...	...	...	...	...	...
35 - 39	4 743	...	...	...	...	...	...	...	...
40 - 44	1 568	...	...	...	...	...	...	...	...
45 - 49	121	...	...	...	...	...	...	...	...
50 +	5	...	...	...	...	...	...	...	...

14. Legally induced abortions by age and number of previous live births of women: latest available year, 2008 - 2017
Avortments provoqués légalement selon l'âge de la femme et selon le nombre des naissances vivantes précédentes : dernière année disponible, 2008 - 2017 (continued - suite)

Continent, country or area, year and age / Continent, pays ou zone, année et âge	Number of previous live births / Nombre des naissances vivantes précédentes								
	Total	0	1	2	3	4	5	6+	Unknown - Inconnu
ASIA - ASIE									
Israel - Israël[6]									
2015									
Total	18 510	7 790	2 620	3 669	2 696	1 077	375	283	...
0 - 14	34	34	-	-	-	-	-	-	...
15 - 19	1 715	1 633	61	15	5	1	-	-	...
20 - 24	3 502	2 754	421	244	66	12	5	-	...
25 - 29	3 850	1 904	737	687	363	113	36	10	...
30 - 34	3 837	903	764	1 107	659	265	95	44	...
35 - 39	3 468	380	426	1 063	974	384	138	103	...
40 - 44	1 901	164	188	506	559	277	90	117	...
45 - 49	195	16	23	45	67	25	11	8	...
50 +	8	2	-	2	3	-	-	1	...
Japan - Japon									
2016									
Total	168 015	...	...	...	...	...	...	...	...
0 - 14	220	...	...	...	...	...	...	...	...
15 - 19	14 446	...	...	...	...	...	...	...	...
20 - 24	38 561	...	...	...	...	...	...	...	...
25 - 29	33 050	...	...	...	...	...	...	...	...
30 - 34	34 256	...	...	...	...	...	...	...	...
35 - 39	30 307	...	...	...	...	...	...	...	...
40 - 44	15 782	...	...	...	...	...	...	...	...
45 - 49	1 352	...	...	...	...	...	...	...	...
50 +	14	...	...	...	...	...	...	...	...
Unknown - Inconnu	27	...	...	...	...	...	...	...	...
Kyrgyzstan - Kirghizstan[7]									
2008									
Total	20 800	...	...	...	...	...	...	...	...
0 - 14	1	...	...	...	...	...	...	...	...
15 - 19	1 814	...	...	...	...	...	...	...	...
20 - 24	5 018	...	...	...	...	...	...	...	...
25 - 29	5 462	...	...	...	...	...	...	...	...
30 - 34	4 598	...	...	...	...	...	...	...	...
35 - 39	2 776	...	...	...	...	...	...	...	...
40 - 44	1 019	...	...	...	...	...	...	...	...
45 +	112	...	...	...	...	...	...	...	...
Mongolia - Mongolie									
2017									
Total	17 530	...	...	...	...	...	...	...	...
0 - 19	921	...	...	...	...	...	...	...	...
20 - 24	2 950	...	...	...	...	...	...	...	...
25 - 29	4 918	...	...	...	...	...	...	...	...
30 - 34	4 408	...	...	...	...	...	...	...	...
35 - 39	2 815	...	...	...	...	...	...	...	...
40 - 44	1 375	...	...	...	...	...	...	...	...
45 - 49	139	...	...	...	...	...	...	...	...
50 +	4	...	...	...	...	...	...	...	...
Singapore - Singapour									
2017									
Total	6 815	2 990	1 344	1 700	537	^244	...	...	-
0 - 24	1 357	1 133	142	63	13	^6	...	...	-
25 - 29	1 627	1 007	308	213	62	^37	...	...	-
30 - 34	1 674	543	433	498	132	^68	...	...	-
35 - 39	1 492	243	330	630	213	^76	...	...	-
40 - 44	605	58	119	267	108	^53	...	...	-
45 +	60	6	12	29	9	^4	...	...	-
Unknown - Inconnu	-	-	-	-	-	^-	...	...	-
Tajikistan - Tadjikistan									
2016									
Total	14 957	...	...	...	...	...	...	...	...
0 - 14	-	...	...	...	...	...	...	...	...
15 - 17	162	...	...	...	...	...	...	...	...
18 - 19	1 166	...	...	...	...	...	...	...	...
20 - 34	10 408	...	...	...	...	...	...	...	...
35 +	3 221	...	...	...	...	...	...	...	...
Uzbekistan - Ouzbékistan									
2015									
Total	40 201	6 356	...	...	...	...	...	...	33 845
0 - 14	4	4	...	...	...	...	...	...	-

14. Legally induced abortions by age and number of previous live births of women: latest available year, 2008 - 2017
Avortments provoqués légalement selon l'âge de la femme et selon le nombre des naissances vivantes précédentes : dernière année disponible, 2008 - 2017 (continued - suite)

Continent, country or area, year and age / Continent, pays ou zone, année et âge	Number of previous live births / Nombre des naissances vivantes précédentes								
	Total	0	1	2	3	4	5	6+	Unknown - Inconnu
ASIA - ASIE									
Uzbekistan - Ouzbékistan									
2015									
15 - 19	617	285	...	...	...	...	...	...	332
20 - 34	31 627	5 624	...	...	...	...	...	...	26 003
35 - 49	7 953	443	...	...	...	...	...	...	7 510
50 +	-	-	...	...	...	...	...	...	-
EUROPE									
Åland Islands - Îles d'Åland									
2012									
Total	60	31	12	10	5	-	2	-	...
0 - 14	-	-	-	-	-	-	-	-	...
15 - 19	9	9	-	-	-	-	-	-	...
20 - 24	15	11	3	1	-	-	-	-	...
25 - 29	17	6	4	4	1	-	2	-	...
30 - 34	7	2	1	3	1	-	-	-	...
35 - 39	7	1	3	1	2	-	-	-	...
40 - 44	5	2	1	1	1	-	-	-	...
45 - 49	-	-	-	-	-	-	-	-	...
50 +	-	-	-	-	-	-	-	-	...
2016									
Total	76	...	...	...	...	...	...	...	...
0 - 14	-	...	...	...	...	...	...	...	...
15 - 19	8	...	...	...	...	...	...	...	...
20 - 24	20	...	...	...	...	...	...	...	...
25 - 29	21	...	...	...	...	...	...	...	...
30 - 34	13	...	...	...	...	...	...	...	...
35 - 39	12	...	...	...	...	...	...	...	...
40 - 44	2	...	...	...	...	...	...	...	...
45 - 49	-	...	...	...	...	...	...	...	...
50 +	-	...	...	...	...	...	...	...	...
Albania - Albanie									
2016									
Total	1 206	203	165	321	138	42	10	7	320
0 - 14	1	1	-	-	-	-	-	-	-
15 - 19	31	22	6	3	-	-	-	-	-
20 - 24	140	85	31	21	2	1	-	-	-
25 - 29	211	59	53	75	20	3	-	1	-
30 - 34	200	22	36	87	41	13	1	-	-
35 - 39	199	10	28	84	53	16	5	3	-
40 - 44	87	2	10	41	20	8	3	3	-
45 - 49	13	2	-	9	-	1	1	-	-
50 +	-	-	-	-	-	-	-	-	-
Unknown - Inconnu	324	-	1	1	2	-	-	-	320
Belarus - Bélarus									
2016									
Total	27 467	...	...	...	...	...	...	...	...
0 - 14	9	...	...	...	...	...	...	...	...
15 - 19	1 190	...	...	...	...	...	...	...	...
20 - 24	4 444	...	...	...	...	...	...	...	...
25 - 29	6 816	...	...	...	...	...	...	...	...
30 - 34	8 192	...	...	...	...	...	...	...	...
35 - 39	4 659	...	...	...	...	...	...	...	...
40 - 44	1 952	...	...	...	...	...	...	...	...
45 - 49	205	...	...	...	...	...	...	...	...
50 +	-	...	...	...	...	...	...	...	...
Belgium - Belgique									
2011									
Total	19 578	9 145	4 266	3 698	1 636	581	174	78	...
0 - 14	87	86	1	-	-	-	-	-	...
15 - 19	2 575	2 339	207	28	1	-	-	-	...
20 - 24	5 027	3 430	1 070	425	87	12	3	-	...
25 - 29	4 688	1 992	1 249	983	332	104	20	8	...
30 - 34	3 745	863	997	1 131	512	176	46	20	...
35 - 39	2 454	349	538	796	483	184	70	34	...
40 - 44	923	78	188	308	207	99	30	13	...

14. Legally induced abortions by age and number of previous live births of women: latest available year, 2008 - 2017
Avortements provoqués légalement selon l'âge de la femme et selon le nombre des naissances vivantes précédentes : dernière année disponible, 2008 - 2017 (continued - suite)

Continent, country or area, year and age Continent, pays ou zone, année et âge	Total	Number of previous live births Nombre des naissances vivantes précédentes								
		0	1	2	3	4	5	6+	Unknown - Inconnu
EUROPE									
Belgium - Belgique									
2011									
45 - 49	78	7	16	27	14	6	5	3	...
50 +	1	1	-	-	-	-	-	-	...
Bulgaria - Bulgarie									
2016									
Total	26 412	...	...	...	...	...	...	...	...
0 - 14	98	...	...	...	...	...	...	...	...
15 - 19	2 110	...	...	...	...	...	...	...	...
20 - 24	4 821	...	...	...	...	...	...	...	...
25 - 29	6 877	...	...	...	...	...	...	...	...
30 - 34	6 167	...	...	...	...	...	...	...	...
35 - 39	4 616	...	...	...	...	...	...	...	...
40 - 44	1 588	...	...	...	...	...	...	...	...
45 - 49	112	...	...	...	...	...	...	...	...
50 +	23	...	...	...	...	...	...	...	...
Croatia - Croatie									
2016									
Total	2 520	860	479	740	290	68	43	30	10
0 - 14	-	-	-	-	-	-	-	-	-
15 - 19	180	158	17	2	-	-	-	-	3
20 - 24	365	254	65	32	8	4	1	-	1
25 - 29	496	174	109	121	56	16	10	7	3
30 - 34	628	124	143	231	94	16	13	4	3
35 - 39	571	102	101	242	79	22	12	13	-
40 - 44	258	45	41	106	45	8	7	6	-
45 - 49	19	1	3	6	7	2	-	-	-
50 +	1	1	-	-	-	-	-	-	-
Unknown - Inconnu	2	1	-	-	1	-	-	-	-
Czechia - Tchéquie									
2016									
Total	20 406	5 915	5 270	6 522	1 867	531	167	134	...
0 - 14	34	34	-	-	-	-	-	-	...
15 - 19	1 266	1 049	186	27	3	-	-	1	...
20 - 24	3 375	1 887	914	448	89	28	9	-	...
25 - 29	4 327	1 568	1 295	1 024	299	93	32	16	...
30 - 34	4 455	856	1 316	1 643	430	127	42	41	...
35 - 39	4 430	376	1 083	2 104	624	158	48	37	...
40 - 44	2 350	140	442	1 189	386	119	35	39	...
45 - 49	168	4	34	87	36	6	1	-	...
50 +	1	1	-	-	-	-	-	-	...
Denmark - Danemark[8]									
2014									
Total	15 097	...	...	...	...	...	...	...	...
0 - 19	2 051	...	...	...	...	...	...	...	...
20 - 24	4 023	...	...	...	...	...	...	...	...
25 - 29	3 324	...	...	...	...	...	...	...	...
30 - 34	2 609	...	...	...	...	...	...	...	...
35 - 39	2 045	...	...	...	...	...	...	...	...
40 - 44	967	...	...	...	...	...	...	...	...
45 +	78	...	...	...	...	...	...	...	...
Estonia - Estonie[9]									
2016									
Total	6 248	1 881	1 858	1 737	549	150	35	34	4
0 - 14	20	20	-	-	-	-	-	-	-
15 - 19	433	371	58	3	-	-	-	-	1
20 - 24	1 019	552	330	118	16	3	-	-	-
25 - 29	1 500	502	522	389	66	14	4	2	1
30 - 34	1 452	258	484	510	141	42	9	6	2
35 - 39	1 178	122	317	461	189	57	16	16	-
40 - 44	582	49	141	232	121	27	5	7	-
45 - 49	63	7	6	24	15	7	1	3	-
50 +	1	-	-	-	1	-	-	-	-
Faeroe Islands - Îles Féroé									
2016									
Total	26	...	...	...	...	...	...	...	...
0 - 14	-	...	...	...	...	...	...	...	...
15 - 19	3	...	...	...	...	...	...	...	...
20 - 24	6	...	...	...	...	...	...	...	...

14. Legally induced abortions by age and number of previous live births of women: latest available year, 2008 - 2017
Avortments provoqués légalement selon l'âge de la femme et selon le nombre des naissances vivantes précédentes : dernière année disponible, 2008 - 2017 (continued - suite)

Continent, country or area, year and age / Continent, pays ou zone, année et âge	Number of previous live births / Nombre des naissances vivantes précédentes								
	Total	0	1	2	3	4	5	6+	Unknown - Inconnu
EUROPE									
Faeroe Islands - Îles Féroé									
2016									
25 - 29	7	...	...	...	...	...	...	...	...
30 - 34	3	...	...	...	...	...	...	...	...
35 - 39	6	...	...	...	...	...	...	...	...
40 - 44	-	...	...	...	...	...	...	...	...
45 - 49	1	...	...	...	...	...	...	...	...
50 +	-	...	...	...	...	...	...	...	...
Finland - Finlande									
2016									
Total	9 387	4 572	1 742	1 808	807	287	85	44	42
0 - 14	23	23	-	-	-	-	-	-	-
15 - 19	1 126	1 043	69	7	-	-	-	-	7
20 - 24	2 440	1 801	440	166	20	5	-	-	8
25 - 29	2 235	1 019	525	471	168	33	4	2	13
30 - 34	1 781	440	369	542	280	99	32	9	10
35 - 39	1 266	191	226	447	250	100	30	20	2
40 - 44	472	51	99	168	80	46	15	11	2
45 - 49	44	4	14	7	9	4	4	2	-
50 +	-	-	-	-	-	-	-	-	-
France[10]									
2009									
Total[11]	208 290	...	...	...	...	...	...	...	...
15 - 19	29 004	...	...	...	...	...	...	...	...
20 - 24	52 360	...	...	...	...	...	...	...	...
25 - 29	46 237	...	...	...	...	...	...	...	...
30 - 34	36 351	...	...	...	...	...	...	...	...
35 - 39	30 125	...	...	...	...	...	...	...	...
40 - 44	12 805	...	...	...	...	...	...	...	...
45 - 49	1 408	...	...	...	...	...	...	...	...
Germany - Allemagne									
2016									
Total	98 721	38 506	24 259	22 863	8 895	2 724	931	543	...
0 - 14	330	330	-	-	-	-	-	-	...
15 - 19	7 735	6 904	708	119	4	-	-	-	...
20 - 24	19 797	12 430	4 714	2 028	480	108	18	19	...
25 - 29	24 365	9 851	6 839	5 155	1 832	496	144	48	...
30 - 34	22 341	5 439	6 163	6 816	2 649	838	284	152	...
35 - 39	16 790	2 643	4 131	6 016	2 634	861	311	194	...
40 - 44	6 673	816	1 558	2 463	1 175	388	158	115	...
45 - 49	677	90	145	261	118	33	16	14	...
50 +	13	3	1	5	3	-	-	1	...
Hungary - Hongrie									
2013									
Total	34 891	9 707	8 781	8 536	4 632	1 821	808	606	-
0 - 14	168	165	3	-	-	-	-	-	-
15 - 19	4 423	3 395	869	132	25	2	-	-	-
20 - 24	7 335	3 135	2 182	1 309	542	134	28	5	-
25 - 29	6 935	1 622	1 902	1 692	1 007	450	173	89	-
30 - 34	6 839	837	1 737	2 032	1 229	520	277	207	-
35 - 39	6 624	451	1 528	2 331	1 325	521	240	228	-
40 - 44	2 406	94	526	976	470	184	86	70	-
45 - 49	160	8	34	63	34	10	4	7	-
50 +	1	-	-	1	-	-	-	-	-
Unknown - Inconnu	-	-	-	-	-	-	-	-	-
2014									
Total	32 663	...	...	...	...	...	...	...	...
0 - 14	161	...	...	...	...	...	...	...	...
15 - 19	4 245	...	...	...	...	...	...	...	...
20 - 24	7 109	...	...	...	...	...	...	...	...
25 - 29	6 562	...	...	...	...	...	...	...	...
30 - 34	6 035	...	...	...	...	...	...	...	...
35 - 39	6 066	...	...	...	...	...	...	...	...
40 - 44	2 325	...	...	...	...	...	...	...	...
45 - 49	157	...	...	...	...	...	...	...	...
50 +	3	...	...	...	...	...	...	...	...
Unknown - Inconnu	-	...	...	...	...	...	...	...	...

14. Legally induced abortions by age and number of previous live births of women: latest available year, 2008 - 2017
Avortments provoqués légalement selon l'âge de la femme et selon le nombre des naissances vivantes précédentes : dernière année disponible, 2008 - 2017 (continued - suite)

Continent, country or area, year and age / Continent, pays ou zone, année et âge	Number of previous live births / Nombre des naissances vivantes précédentes								
	Total	0	1	2	3	4	5	6+	Unknown - Inconnu
EUROPE									
Iceland - Islande									
2011									
Total	969	415	249	186	83	29	5	2	-
0 - 14	2	2	-	-	-	-	-	-	-
15 - 19	174	155	16	3	-	-	-	-	-
20 - 24	289	182	84	21	2	-	-	-	-
25 - 29	187	46	73	52	10	6	-	-	-
30 - 34	169	25	40	56	36	11	1	-	-
35 - 39	109	5	29	45	20	9	1	-	-
40 - 44	35	-	7	8	12	3	3	2	-
45 - 49	4	-	-	1	3	-	-	-	-
50 +	-	-	-	-	-	-	-	-	-
Unknown - Inconnu	-	-	-	-	-	-	-	-	-
Italy - Italie									
2016									
Total	84 874	32 598	19 733	21 772	6 907	1 450	352	148	1 914
0 - 14	165	156	-	-	-	-	-	-	9
15 - 19	6 275	5 415	486	73	11	5	-	-	285
20 - 24	14 675	9 882	2 960	1 136	225	26	3	7	436
25 - 29	17 314	7 436	4 510	3 709	984	186	37	24	428
30 - 34	18 188	4 937	4 857	5 689	1 852	391	79	34	349
35 - 39	17 724	3 103	4 433	6 875	2 343	499	151	60	260
40 - 44	9 562	1 513	2 248	3 910	1 360	308	72	21	130
45 - 49	911	136	225	367	127	34	10	1	11
50 +	30	10	6	8	3	1	-	1	1
Unknown - Inconnu	30	10	8	5	2	-	-	-	5
Latvia - Lettonie									
2016									
Total	4 366	...	...	...	...	...	...	...	...
0 - 14	4	...	...	...	...	...	...	...	...
15 - 19	268	...	...	...	...	...	...	...	...
20 - 24	751	...	...	...	...	...	...	...	...
25 - 29	1 102	...	...	...	...	...	...	...	...
30 - 34	990	...	...	...	...	...	...	...	...
35 - 39	813	...	...	...	...	...	...	...	...
40 - 44	403	...	...	...	...	...	...	...	...
45 - 49	35	...	...	...	...	...	...	...	...
50 +	-	...	...	...	...	...	...	...	...
Unknown - Inconnu	-	...	...	...	...	...	...	...	...
Lithuania - Lituanie									
2016									
Total	4 502	...	...	...	...	...	...	...	4 502
0 - 14	1	...	...	...	...	...	...	...	1
15 - 19	249	...	...	...	...	...	...	...	249
20 - 24	784	...	...	...	...	...	...	...	784
25 - 29	1 012	...	...	...	...	...	...	...	1 012
30 - 34	1 040	...	...	...	...	...	...	...	1 040
35 - 39	896	...	...	...	...	...	...	...	896
40 - 44	460	...	...	...	...	...	...	...	460
45 - 49	60	...	...	...	...	...	...	...	60
Unknown - Inconnu	-	...	...	...	...	...	...	...	-
Poland - Pologne[12]									
2016									
Total	1 098	...	...	...	...	...	...	...	...
0 - 19	72	...	...	...	...	...	...	...	...
20 - 24	86	...	...	...	...	...	...	...	...
25 - 29	247	...	...	...	...	...	...	...	...
30 - 34	315	...	...	...	...	...	...	...	...
35 +	378	...	...	...	...	...	...	...	...
Portugal									
2016									
Total	15 959	6 871	4 666	3 225	899	223	50	25	-
0 - 14	39	39	-	-	-	-	-	-	-
15 - 19	1 595	1 500	87	6	-	1	-	1	-
20 - 24	3 667	2 500	932	201	28	4	1	1	-
25 - 29	3 440	1 469	1 221	574	138	30	4	4	-
30 - 34	3 109	777	1 113	881	265	58	11	4	-
35 - 39	2 688	425	875	1 000	290	72	17	9	-
40 - 44	1 349	146	417	537	171	55	17	6	-

14. Legally induced abortions by age and number of previous live births of women: latest available year, 2008 - 2017
Avortments provoqués légalement selon l'âge de la femme et selon le nombre des naissances vivantes précédentes : dernière année disponible, 2008 - 2017 (continued - suite)

Continent, country or area, year and age / Continent, pays ou zone, année et âge	Total	Number of previous live births / Nombre des naissances vivantes précédentes							Unknown - Inconnu
		0	1	2	3	4	5	6+	

EUROPE

Portugal
2016

45 - 49	48	3	15	22	6	2	-	-	-
50 +	2	-	1	1	-	-	-	...	-
Unknown - Inconnu	22	12	5	3	1	1	-	-	-

Republic of Moldova - République de Moldova
2012

Total	14 838	...	...	...	...	...	...	...	...
0 - 14	9	...	...	...	...	...	...	...	...
15 - 19	1 383	...	...	...	...	...	...	...	...
Unknown - Inconnu	13 446	...	...	...	...	...	...	...	...

Romania - Roumanie
2016

Total	63 518	...	...	...	...	...	...	...	...
0 - 14	412	...	...	...	...	...	...	...	...
15 - 19	5 955	...	...	...	...	...	...	...	...
20 - 24	11 876	...	...	...	...	...	...	...	...
25 - 29	15 385	...	...	...	...	...	...	...	...
30 - 34	13 395	...	...	...	...	...	...	...	...
35 - 39	11 182	...	...	...	...	...	...	...	...
40 - 44	4 815	...	...	...	...	...	...	...	...
45 - 49	477	...	...	...	...	...	...	...	...
50 +	21	...	...	...	...	...	...	...	...

Russian Federation - Fédération de Russie
2013

Total	1 012 399	...	...	...	...	...	...	...	...
0 - 14	474	...	...	...	...	...	...	...	...
15 - 19	47 732	...	...	...	...	...	...	...	...
20 - 24	203 802	...	...	...	...	...	...	...	...
25 - 29	285 859	...	...	...	...	...	...	...	...
30 - 34	242 437	...	...	...	...	...	...	...	...
35 - 39	165 856	...	...	...	...	...	...	...	...
40 - 44	61 059	...	...	...	...	...	...	...	...
45 - 49	5 029	...	...	...	...	...	...	...	...
50 +	151	...	...	...	...	...	...	...	...

Serbia - Serbie[13]
2008

Total	22 867	6 601	4 346	8 509	2 437	663	198	113	-
0 - 14	9	6	1	2	-	-	-	-	-
15 - 19	975	808	124	35	7	1	-	-	-
20 - 24	3 427	1 823	848	570	122	52	9	3	-
25 - 29	5 117	1 510	1 173	1 757	479	141	47	10	-
30 - 34	5 953	1 240	1 114	2 569	719	212	62	37	-
35 - 39	4 929	806	768	2 354	730	170	59	42	-
40 - 44	2 174	363	279	1 072	347	76	17	20	-
45 - 49	266	40	34	146	31	10	4	1	-
50 +	16	5	4	4	2	1	-	-	-
Unknown - Inconnu	1	-	1	-	-	-	-	-	-

Slovakia - Slovaquie
2016

Total	9 390	2 944	2 663	2 401	826	285	98	173	...
0 - 14	20	19	1	-	-	-	-	-	...
15 - 19	630	501	98	25	5	1	-	-	...
20 - 24	1 504	786	405	223	69	16	4	1	...
25 - 29	1 998	772	593	401	143	52	16	21	...
30 - 34	2 297	571	723	646	199	76	30	52	...
35 - 39	1 945	233	614	694	236	83	31	54	...
40 - 44	925	57	216	381	158	55	15	43	...
45 - 49	68	4	13	30	16	1	2	2	...
50 +	3	1	-	1	-	1	-	-	...

Slovenia - Slovénie
2016

Total	3 736	1 215	809	1 193	318	82	27	16	76
0 - 14	-	-	-	-	-	-	-	-	-
15 - 19	219	197	12	1	3	-	-	-	6
20 - 24	554	408	87	31	8	2	-	-	18
25 - 29	757	332	203	160	23	12	5	2	20
30 - 34	948	160	239	399	92	23	11	7	17

14. Legally induced abortions by age and number of previous live births of women: latest available year, 2008 - 2017
Avortments provoqués légalement selon l'âge de la femme et selon le nombre des naissances vivantes précédentes :
dernière année disponible, 2008 - 2017 (continued - suite)

Continent, country or area, year and age / Continent, pays ou zone, année et âge	Number of previous live births / Nombre des naissances vivantes précédentes								
	Total	0	1	2	3	4	5	6+	Unknown - Inconnu
EUROPE									
Slovenia - Slovénie									
2016									
35 - 39	870	91	187	410	131	30	7	3	11
40 - 44	354	27	78	171	56	15	2	2	3
45 - 49	33	-	3	20	5	-	2	2	1
50 +	1	-	-	1	-	-	-	-	-
Unknown - Inconnu	-	-	-	-	-	-	-	-	-
Spain - Espagne									
2015									
Total	94 188	42 187	25 051	19 197	5 574	^1 525	...	...	654
0 - 14	371	366	5	-	-	^-	...	...	-
15 - 19	9 641	8 652	874	95	16	^4	...	...	-
20 - 24	19 063	12 979	4 460	1 322	249	^41	...	...	12
25 - 29	20 156	9 233	6 073	3 588	970	^212	...	...	80
30 - 34	20 473	6 433	6 318	5 506	1 623	^433	...	...	160
35 - 39	17 117	3 425	5 213	5 887	1 808	^537	...	...	247
40 +	6 745	1 011	1 970	2 544	813	^270	...	...	137
Unknown - Inconnu	622	88	138	255	95	^28	...	...	18
Sweden - Suède[14]									
2010									
Total	37 693	19 435	6 240	7 203	2 993	814	264	137	607
0 - 14	191	178	4	1	-	-	-	-	8
15 - 19	6 199	5 826	214	14	2	-	-	-	143
20 - 24	10 068	7 708	1 587	480	76	5	2	2	208
25 - 29	7 495	3 558	1 838	1 476	385	79	28	10	121
30 - 34	6 124	1 424	1 336	2 113	884	208	77	18	64
35 - 39	5 073	572	862	2 073	1 053	318	88	62	45
40 - 44	2 248	137	353	948	524	174	58	39	15
45 - 49	238	11	33	85	66	27	10	4	2
50 +	56	20	13	13	3	3	1	2	1
Unknown - Inconnu	1	1	-	-	-	-	-	-	-
Switzerland - Suisse[15]									
2016									
Total	10 085	1 947	752	761	266	92	...	...	6 267
0 - 14	8	3	-	-	-	-	...	...	5
15 - 19	724	300	10	1	-	-	...	...	413
20 - 24	2 011	636	113	29	4	1	...	...	1 228
25 - 29	2 334	512	201	152	35	5	...	...	1 429
30 - 34	2 253	286	210	229	92	30	...	...	1 406
35 - 39	1 802	153	142	225	79	30	...	...	1 173
40 - 44	851	50	70	111	53	24	...	...	543
45 - 49	89	3	5	14	3	1	...	...	63
50 +	8	2	-	-	-	-	...	...	6
Unknown - Inconnu	5	2	1	-	-	1	...	...	1
Ukraine[16]									
2014									
Total	116 104	...	...	...	...	...	...	...	...
0 - 14	51	...	...	...	...	...	...	...	...
15 - 19	6 229	...	...	...	...	...	...	...	...
20 - 34	85 575	...	...	...	...	...	...	...	...
35 +	24 249	...	...	...	...	...	...	...	...
United Kingdom of Great Britain and Northern Ireland - Royaume-Uni de Grande-Bretagne et d'Irlande du Nord[17]									
2016									
Total	197 659	...	...	...	...	...	...	...	...
0 - 14	492	...	...	...	...	...	...	...	...
15 - 19	25 761	...	...	...	...	...	...	...	...
20 - 24	53 834	...	...	...	...	...	...	...	...
25 - 29	49 248	...	...	...	...	...	...	...	...
30 - 34	36 146	...	...	...	...	...	...	...	...
35 - 39	23 219	...	...	...	...	...	...	...	...
40 - 44	8 181	...	...	...	...	...	...	...	...
45 - 49	749	...	...	...	...	...	...	...	...
50 +	29	...	...	...	...	...	...	...	...
Unknown - Inconnu	-	...	...	...	...	...	...	...	...

14. Legally induced abortions by age and number of previous live births of women: latest available year, 2008 - 2017
Avortments provoqués légalement selon l'âge de la femme et selon le nombre des naissances vivantes précédentes : dernière année disponible, 2008 - 2017 (continued - suite)

Continent, country or area, year and age / Continent, pays ou zone, année et âge	Total	\multicolumn{9}{c}{Number of previous live births / Nombre des naissances vivantes précédentes}
		0	1	2	3	4	5	6+	Unknown - Inconnu

OCEANIA - OCÉANIE

Continent, country or area, year and age	Total	0	1	2	3	4	5	6+	Unknown - Inconnu
Guam									
2015									
Total	263	...	...	...	...	...	...	...	...
0 - 14	-	...	...	...	...	...	...	...	...
15 - 19	20	...	...	...	...	...	...	...	...
20 - 24	89	...	...	...	...	...	...	...	...
25 - 29	60	...	...	...	...	...	...	...	...
30 - 34	52	...	...	...	...	...	...	...	...
35 - 39	27	...	...	...	...	...	...	...	...
40 - 44	12	...	...	...	...	...	...	...	...
45 - 49	2	...	...	...	...	...	...	...	...
50 +	-	...	...	...	...	...	...	...	...
Unknown - Inconnu	1	...	...	...	...	...	...	...	...
New Zealand - Nouvelle-Zélande									
2015									
Total	13 155	5 665	2 715	2 728	1 264	473	193	117	...
0 - 14	32	32	-	-	-	-	-	-	...
15 - 19	1 635	1 393	208	31	3	-	-	-	...
20 - 24	3 777	2 257	891	470	129	27	3	-	...
25 - 29	3 256	1 183	764	744	376	129	44	16	...
30 - 34	2 309	521	483	712	344	149	63	37	...
35 - 39	1 483	210	261	510	280	117	60	45	...
40 - 44	598	59	94	238	121	48	21	17	...
45 +	65	10	14	23	11	3	2	2	...
2017									
Total	13 285	5 656	2 706	^4 923	...	...	...	...	...
0 - 14	30	...	...	...	...	...	...	...	...
15 - 19	1 414	...	...	...	...	...	...	...	...
20 - 24	3 599	...	...	...	...	...	...	...	...
25 - 29	3 632	...	...	...	...	...	...	...	...
30 - 34	2 419	...	...	...	...	...	...	...	...
35 - 39	1 562	...	...	...	...	...	...	...	...
40 - 44	584	...	...	...	...	...	...	...	...
45 +	45	...	...	...	...	...	...	...	...

FOOTNOTES - NOTES

Italics: estimates which are less reliable. - Italiques : estimations moins sûres.

* Provisional. - Données provisoires.

^ Indicates an open-ended group, for example 4+. - indique un groupe d'âge ouvert, par exemple 4 ou plus.

[1] Source: Bermuda Hospitals Board (BHB). -

[2] Excluding abortions performed in private hospitals. - Non comprises les interruptions volontaires de grossesse effectuées dans des hôpitaux privés.

[3] Refers to residence of the mother. To calculate the total number of abortions, only foetal deaths of less than 20 weeks of gestation were considered. Data refer to 'Therapeutic Abortions'. According to Mexican law, only induced abortions, prescribed by medical reasons or induced because of pregnancy coming from sexual aggression, are considered as legal; data refer only to the former. Excluding abortions in the country by women with usual residence outside of the country. - Correspond à la résidence de la mère. Seuls les morts fœtales survenues à moins de 20 semaines de gestation ont été prises en compte aux fins du calcul du nombre total d'avortements. Les données se rapportent aux « interruptions volontaires de grossesse pour des motifs thérapeutiques ». D'après la loi mexicaine, seuls sont considérés légaux les avortements déclenchés pour des raisons médicales ou parce que la grossesse est le résultat d'une agression sexuelle; les données se réfèrent seulement à la première. Hors avortements dans le pays par des femmes avec résidence habituelle en dehors du pays.

[4] Affected by underreporting since, by law, legally induced abortions are not reported directly to the civil registry. - Font l'objet d'une sous-déclaration, toutes les interruptions volontaires de grossesse pratiquées légalement n'étant pas déclarées dans la mesure où la loi n'impose pas de les inscrire directement au registre civil.

[5] Data refer to abortions registered in hospitals due to pregnancy complications. - Les données renvoient aux avortements enregistrés dans les hôpitaux du fait des complications de la grossesse.

[6] Data refer to applications to commissions for termination of pregnancy and not to authorizations. Includes data for East Jerusalem and Israeli residents in certain other territories under occupation by Israeli military forces since June 1967. - Les données relatives aux avortements provoqués légalement se rapportent aux demandes d'autorisation et non aux autorisations elles-mêmes. Y compris les données pour Jérusalem-Est et les résidents israéliens dans certains autres territoires occupés depuis 1967 par les forces armées israéliennes.

[7] Based on administrative reporting of the Ministry of Health. - Les données reposent sur les rapports administratifs du Ministère de la santé.

[8] Excluding Faeroe Islands and Greenland shown separately, if available. Unrevised data. - Non compris les Iles Féroé et le Groenland, qui font l'objet de rubriques distinctes, si disponible. Les données n'ont pas été révisées.

[9] Data refer to resident population only. - Pour la population résidante seulement.

[10] Unrevised data. - Les données n'ont pas été révisées.

[11] Data refer to women between 15 and 49 years of age. - Le total se rapporte uniquement aux femmes dont l'âge est compris entre 15 et 49 ans.

[12] Based on hospital and polyclinic records. - D'après les registres des hôpitaux et des policliniques.

[13] Excludes data for Kosovo and Metohia. Data refer to institutions included in the Health Institutions Network Plan in the Republic of Serbia. - Sans les données pour le Kosovo et Metohie. Les données se rapportent aux institutions membres du "Health Institutions Network Plan" de la République de Serbie.

[14] Data refer to abortions by previous deliveries of mother rather than previous live births of mother. - Avortements selon les accouchements précédents de la mère plutôt que selon les naissances vivantes de la mère.

[15] Data refer to termination of pregnancy for women who are Switzerland residents. - Les données portent sur les interruptions de grossesse pratiquées sur des femmes qui résident en Suisse.

Table 15 - *Demographic Yearbook 2017*

Table 15 presents infant deaths and infant mortality rates by urban/rural residence for as many years as possible between 2013 and 2017.

Description of variables: Infant deaths are deaths of live-born infants under one year of age.

Statistics on the number of infant deaths are obtained from civil registers unless otherwise noted. Infant mortality rates are, in most instances, calculated from data on registered infant deaths and registered live births for a country or area where civil registration is considered reliable (that is, with an estimated completeness of 90 per cent or more).

The urban/rural classification of infant deaths is that provided by each reporting country or area; it is presumed to be based on the national census definitions of urban population that have been set forth at the end of the technical notes of table 6.

Rate computation: Infant mortality rates are the annual number of deaths of infants under one year of age per 1 000 live births (as shown in table 9) in the same year.

Rates by urban/rural residence are the annual number of infant deaths, in the appropriate urban or rural category, per 1 000 corresponding live births (as shown in table 9). These rates have been calculated by the United Nations Statistics Division.

Rates presented in this table have been limited to those countries or areas having at least a total of 30 infant deaths in a given year and for which the quality code is represented by a "C" or a symbol "|".

Reliability of data: Each country or area has been asked to indicate the estimated completeness of the infant deaths recorded in its civil register. These national assessments are indicated by the quality codes "C", "U" and "|" that appear in the first column of this table.

"C" indicates that the data are estimated to be virtually complete, that is, representing at least 90 per cent of the infant deaths occurring each year, while "U" indicates that data are estimated to be incomplete that is, representing less than 90 per cent of the infant deaths occurring each year. The code "|" indicates that the source of data is not civil registration, but it is still considered reliable. The code "..." indicates that no information was provided regarding completeness.

Data from civil registers that are reported as incomplete or of unknown completeness (coded "U" or "...") are considered unreliable. They appear in italics in this table; rates are not computed for data so coded.

Limitations: Statistics on infant deaths are subject to the same qualifications as have been set forth for vital statistics and particularly for death statistics discussed in section 4 of the Technical Notes.

The reliability of the data, an indication of which is described above, is an important factor in considering the limitations. In addition, some infant deaths are tabulated by date of registration and not by date of occurrence; these have been indicated by a plus sign "+". Whenever the lag between the date of occurrence and date of registration is prolonged and, therefore, a large proportion of the infant-death registrations are delayed, infant-death statistics for any given year may be seriously affected.

Another factor that limits international comparability is the practice of some countries or areas not to include in infant-death statistics infants who were born alive but died before the registration of the birth or within the first 24 hours of life, thus underestimating the total number of infant deaths. Statistics of this type are footnoted.

The method of reckoning age at death for infants may also introduce non-comparability. If year alone, rather than completed minutes, hours, days and months elapsed since birth, is used to calculate age at time of death, many of the infants who died during the eleventh month of life and some of those who died at younger ages will be classified as having completed one year of age and thus be excluded. The effect would be to underestimate the number of infant deaths. Information on this factor is given in footnotes when known. Reckoning of infant age is further discussed in the technical notes for table 16.

In addition, infant mortality rates are subject to the limitations of the data on live births that have been used as denominators for these rates. These have been set forth in the technical notes for table 9.

Because the two components of the infant mortality rate, infant deaths in the numerator and live births in the denominator, are both obtained from systems of civil registration, the limitations which affect live birth statistics are very similar to those which have been mentioned above in connection with the infant death statistics. It is important to consider the reliability of the data (the completeness of registration) and the method of tabulation (by date of occurrence or by date of registration) of live birth statistics as well as infant death statistics, both of which are used to calculate infant mortality rates. The quality code and use of italics to indicate unreliable data presented in this table refer only to infant deaths. Similarly, the indication of the basis of tabulation (the use of the symbol "+" to indicate data tabulated by date of registration) presented in this table also refers only to infant deaths. Table 9 provides the corresponding information for live births.

If the registration of infant deaths is more complete than the registration of live births, then infant mortality rates would be biased upwards. If, however, the registration of live births is more complete than registration of infant deaths, infant mortality rates would be biased downwards.

Infant mortality rates may be seriously affected by the practice of some countries or areas of not considering infants that were born alive but died before the registration of the birth or within the first 24 hours of life as live birth and subsequently infant death. Although this practice results in both the number of infant deaths in the numerator and the number of live births in the denominator being underestimated, its impact is greater on the numerator of the infant mortality rate. As a result, this practice causes infant mortality rates to be biased downwards.

Infant mortality rates will also be underestimated if the method of reckoning age at death results in an underestimation of the number of infant deaths. This point has been discussed above.

Because of all these factors care should be taken in comparing infant mortality rates.

With respect to the method of calculating infant mortality rates used in this table, it should be noted that no adjustment was made to take account of the fact that a proportion of the infant deaths that occur during a given year are deaths of infants that were born during the preceding year and hence are not taken from the universe of births used to compute the rates. However, unless the number of live births or infant deaths is changing rapidly, the error involved is insignificant.

The comparability of data by urban/rural residence is affected by the national definitions of urban and rural used in tabulating these data. It is assumed, in the absence of specific information to the contrary, that the definitions of urban and rural used in connection with the national population census were also used in the compilation of the vital statistics for each country or area. However, it cannot be denied that, for some countries or areas, different definitions of urban and rural may be used for the vital statistics data and the population census data respectively. When known, the definitions of urban used in national population censuses are presented at the end of the technical notes for table 6. As discussed in detail in the technical notes for table 6, these definitions vary considerably from one country or area to another.

Urban/rural differentials in infant mortality rates may also be affected by whether the infant deaths and live births have been tabulated in terms of place of occurrence or place of usual residence. This problem is discussed in more detail in section 4.1.4.1 of the Technical Notes.

Earlier data: Infant deaths and infant mortality rates have been shown in previous issues of the *Demographic Yearbook*. For more information on specific topics and years for which data are reported, readers should consult the Historical Index.

Tableau 15 – *Annuaire démographique 2017*

Le tableau 15 présente des données sur les décès d'enfants de moins d'un an et les taux de mortalité infantile selon le lieu de résidence (zone urbaine ou rurale) pour le plus grand nombre d'années possible entre 2013 et 2017.

Description des variables : les chiffres se rapportent aux décès d'enfants de moins d'un an.

Sauf indication contraire, les statistiques concernant le nombre de décès d'enfants de moins d'un an sont établies à partir des registres de l'état civil. Dans la plupart des cas, les taux de mortalité infantile sont calculés à partir des données relatives aux décès enregistrés d'enfants de moins d'un an et aux naissances vivantes enregistrées dans un pays ou une zone lorsque les registres de l'état civil sont jugés fiables (exhaustivité estimée à 90 p. 100 ou plus).

La classification des décès d'enfants de moins d'un an selon le lieu de résidence (zone urbaine ou rurale) est celle qui a été communiquée par chaque pays ou zone ; on part du principe qu'elle repose sur les définitions de la population urbaine utilisées pour les recensements nationaux, telles qu'elles sont reproduites à la fin des notes techniques du tableau 6.

Calcul des taux : Les taux de mortalité infantile représentent le nombre annuel de décès d'enfants de moins d'un an pour 1 000 naissances vivantes (présentées dans le tableau 9) survenues pendant la même année.

Les taux selon le lieu de résidence (zone urbaine ou rurale) représentent le nombre annuel de décès d'enfants de moins d'un an, classés selon la catégorie urbaine ou rurale appropriée pour 1 000 naissances vivantes survenues parmi la population correspondante (présentées dans le tableau 9). Ces taux ont été calculés par la Division des statistiques de l'Organisation des Nations Unies.

Les taux présentés dans ce tableau se rapportent seulement aux pays ou zones où l'on a enregistré au moins un total de 30 décès d'enfants de moins d'un an au cours d'une année donnée et pour lesquels le code de qualité est soit "C" ou "|".

Fiabilité des données : il a été demandé à chaque pays ou zone d'indiquer le degré estimatif de complétude des données sur les décès d'enfants de moins d'un an figurant dans ses registres d'état civil. Ces évaluations nationales sont signalées par les codes de qualité "C", "U" et "|" qui apparaissent dans la deuxième colonne du tableau.

La lettre "C" indique que les données sont jugées à peu près complètes, c'est-à-dire qu'elles représentent au moins 90 p. 100 des décès d'enfants de moins d'un an survenus chaque année ; la lettre "U" signifie que les données sont jugées incomplètes, c'est-à-dire qu'elles représentent moins de 90 p.100 des décès d'enfants de moins d'un an survenus chaque année. Le symbole '|' indique que la source des données n'est pas un registre de l'état civil, mais est quand même considérée fiable. Le code "..." dénote qu'aucun renseignement n'a été communiqué quant à la complétude des données.

Les données provenant des registres de l'état civil qui sont déclarées incomplètes ou dont le degré de complétude n'est pas connu (code "U" ou "...") sont jugées douteuses. Elles apparaissent en italique dans le tableau ; les taux, dans ces cas là, n'ont pas été calculés.

Insuffisance des données : les statistiques des décès d'enfants de moins d'un an appellent toutes les réserves qui ont été formulées à propos des statistiques de l'état civil en général et des statistiques concernant les décès en particulier (voir la section 4 des notes techniques).

La fiabilité des données, au sujet de laquelle des indications ont été fournies plus haut, est un facteur important. Il faut également tenir compte du fait que, dans certains cas, les données relatives aux décès d'enfants de moins d'un an sont exploitées selon la date de l'enregistrement et non la date de l'événement ; ces cas ont été signalés par le signe "+". Chaque fois que le décalage entre l'événement et son enregistrement est grand et qu'une forte proportion des décès d'enfants de moins d'un an fait l'objet d'un enregistrement tardif, les statistiques des décès d'enfants de moins d'un an pour une année donnée peuvent être considérablement faussées.

Un autre facteur qui nuit à la comparabilité internationale est la pratique de certains pays ou zones qui consiste à ne pas inclure dans les statistiques des décès d'enfants de moins d'un an les enfants nés vivants mais décédés avant l'enregistrement de leur naissance ou dans les 24 heures qui ont suivi la naissance, pratique qui conduit à sous-estimer le nombre total de décès d'enfants de moins d'un an. Quand pareil facteur a joué, cela a été signalé en note.

Les méthodes appliquées pour calculer l'âge au moment du décès peuvent également nuire à la comparabilité des données. Si l'on utilise à cet effet l'année seulement, et non pas les minutes, heures, jours et mois qui se sont écoulés depuis la naissance, de nombreux enfants décédés au cours du onzième mois qui a suivi leur naissance et certains enfants décédés encore plus jeunes seront classés comme décédés à un an révolu et donc exclus des données. Cette pratique conduit à sous-estimer le nombre de décès d'enfants de moins d'un an. Les renseignements dont on dispose sur ce facteur apparaissent en note à la fin du tableau. La question du calcul de l'âge au moment du décès est examinée plus en détail dans les notes techniques se rapportant au tableau 16.

Les taux de mortalité infantile appellent en outre toutes les réserves qui ont été formulées à propos des statistiques des naissances vivantes qui ont servi à leur calcul (voir à ce sujet les notes techniques relatives au tableau 9).

Les deux composantes du taux de mortalité infantile - décès d'enfants de moins d'un an au numérateur et naissances vivantes au dénominateur - étant obtenues à partir des registres de l'état civil, les statistiques des naissances vivantes appellent des réserves presque identiques à celles qui ont été formulées plus haut à propos des statistiques des décès d'enfants de moins d'un an. Il importe de prendre en considération la fiabilité des données (complétude de l'enregistrement) et le mode d'exploitation (selon la date de l'événement ou selon la date de l'enregistrement) dans le cas des statistiques des naissances vivantes tout comme dans le cas de celles des décès d'enfants de moins d'un an, puisque les unes et les autres servent au calcul des taux de mortalité infantile. Dans le tableau 15, le code de qualité et l'emploi de caractères italiques pour signaler les données moins sûres ne concernent que les décès d'enfants de moins d'un an. L'indication du mode d'exploitation des données (emploi du signe "+" pour signaler les données exploitées selon la date de l'enregistrement) ne porte là aussi que sur les décès d'enfants de moins d'un an. Le tableau 9 contient les renseignements correspondants pour les naissances vivantes.

Si l'enregistrement des décès d'enfants de moins d'un an est plus complet que l'enregistrement des naissances vivantes, les taux de mortalité infantile seront entachés d'une erreur par excès. En revanche, si l'enregistrement des naissances vivantes est plus complet que l'enregistrement des décès d'enfants de moins d'un an, les taux de mortalité infantile seront entachés d'une erreur par défaut.

Les taux de mortalité infantile peuvent être gravement faussés par la pratique de certains pays ou zones qui consiste à ne pas classer dans les naissances vivantes et ensuite dans les décès d'enfants de moins d'un an les enfants nés vivants mais décédés soit avant l'enregistrement de leur naissance, soit dans les 24 heures qui ont suivi la naissance. Cette pratique conduit à sous-estimer aussi bien le nombre des décès d'enfants de moins d'un an, qui constitue le numérateur, que le nombre des naissances vivantes, qui constitue le dénominateur, mais c'est pour le numérateur du taux de mortalité infantile que la distorsion est la plus marquée. Ce système a pour effet d'introduire une erreur par défaut dans les taux de mortalité infantile.

Les taux de mortalité infantile seront également sous-estimés si la méthode utilisée pour calculer l'âge au moment du décès conduit à sous-estimer le nombre de décès d'enfants de moins d'un an. Cette question a été examinée plus haut.

Tous ces facteurs sont importants et il faut donc en tenir compte lorsque l'on compare les taux de mortalité infantile.

En ce qui concerne la méthode de calcul des taux de mortalité infantile utilisée dans le tableau, il convient de noter qu'il n'a pas été tenu compte du fait qu'une partie des décès survenus pendant une année donnée sont des décès d'enfants nés l'année précédente et ne correspondent donc pas à l'ensemble des naissances utilisé pour le calcul des taux. Toutefois, l'erreur n'est pas grave, à moins que le nombre des naissances vivantes ou des décès d'enfants de moins d'un an ne varie rapidement.

La comparabilité des données selon le lieu de résidence (zone urbaine ou rurale) peut être limitée par les définitions nationales des termes « urbain » et « rural » utilisées pour la mise en tableaux de ces données. En l'absence d'indications contraires, on a supposé que les mêmes définitions avaient servi pour le recensement national de la population et pour l'établissement des statistiques de l'état civil pour chaque pays ou zone. Toutefois, il n'est pas exclu que, pour une zone ou un pays donné, des définitions différentes aient été retenues. Les définitions du terme « urbain » utilisées pour les recensements nationaux de population ont été présentées à la fin des notes techniques du tableau 6 lorsqu'elles étaient connues. Comme on l'a précisé dans les notes techniques relatives au tableau 6, ces définitions varient considérablement d'un pays ou d'une zone à l'autre.

La différence entre les taux de mortalité infantile pour les zones urbaines et rurales pourra aussi être faussée selon que les décès d'enfants de moins d'un an et les naissances vivantes auront été classés d'après le lieu de l'événement ou le lieu de résidence habituel. Ce problème est examiné plus en détail à la section 4.1.4.1 des Notes techniques.

Données publiées antérieurement : des statistiques concernant les décès d'enfants de moins d'un an et les taux de mortalité infantile ont déjà été présentées dans des éditions antérieures de l'*Annuaire démographique*. Pour plus de précisions concernant les années et les sujets pour lesquels des données ont été publiées, se reporter à l'index historique.

15. Infant deaths and infant mortality rates, by urban/rural residence: 2013 - 2017
Décès d'enfants de moins d'un an et taux de mortalité infantile, selon la résidence, urbaine/rurale : 2013 - 2017

Continent, country or area, and urban/rural residence / Continent, pays ou zone et résidence, urbaine/rurale	Code[a]	Number - Nombre					Rate - Taux				
		2013	2014	2015	2016	2017	2013	2014	2015	2016	2017
AFRICA - AFRIQUE											
Algeria - Algérie[1]											
Total	U	21 586	22 282	23 150	22 271	...	...	...	...	...	...
Angola[2]											
Total	I	...	45 627	...	...	...	...	39.6	...	...	...
Urban - Urbaine	I	...	22 825	...	...	...	...	34.0	...	...	...
Rural - Rurale	I	...	22 801	...	...	...	...	47.3	...	...	...
Botswana[3]											
Total	U	960	1 045	1 012	1 041	...	...	...	...	...	...
Côte d'Ivoire[2]											
Total	I	...	44 530	...	...	...	...	52.9	...	...	...
Egypt - Égypte											
Total	C	38 753	39 679	42 050	39 301	38 685	14.8	14.6	15.7	15.1	15.1
Urban - Urbaine	C	22 605	23 952	25 528	24 370	24 674	19.0	19.5	20.8	19.6	19.1
Rural - Rurale	C	16 148	15 727	16 522	14 931	14 011	11.3	10.5	11.3	11.0	11.1
Guinea - Guinée[4]											
Total	I	...	30 907	...	...	...	...	70.2	...	...	...
Kenya											
Total	U	20 888	18 672	15 861	13 839		...	...	...	...	...
Mauritius - Maurice[5]											
Total	+C	165	194	173	154	164	12.2	14.6	13.7	11.9	12.3
Urban - Urbaine	+C	67	72	81	57	57	13.2	14.0	15.7	10.8	10.7
Rural - Rurale	+C	98	122	92	97	107	11.6	15.0	12.3	12.7	13.2
Saint Helena ex. dep. - Sainte-Hélène sans dép.											
Total	C	-	1	...	...	...	...	...	...	...	...
Seychelles											
Total	+C	29	17	17	...	18	...	...	...	...	...
Sierra Leone[6]											
Total	+U	2 276	...	...	...	...	...	...	...	...	...
South Africa - Afrique du Sud											
Total	U	26 841	26 785	24 994	20 649		...	...	...	...	...
AMERICA, NORTH - AMÉRIQUE DU NORD											
Anguilla											
Total	+C	3	...	...	...	...	...	...	...	...	...
Aruba											
Total	+C	5	5	6	5	6	...	...	...	...	...
Bahamas											
Total	+C	51	*85	*82	*70	*72	11.8	*20.5	*19.3	*17.1	*17.9
Belize											
Total	U	129	91	127	103		...	...	...	...	...
Urban - Urbaine	U	55	30	58	44		...	...	...	...	...
Rural - Rurale	U	74	61	69	59		...	...	...	...	...
Bermuda - Bermudes											
Total	C	1	2	2	2		...	...	...	...	...
Canada[7]											
Total	C	1 884	1 794	1 737	1 741	...	5.0	4.7	4.5	4.5	...
Costa Rica											
Total	C	612	575	557	555	*548	8.7	8.0	7.8	7.9	*8.0
Urban - Urbaine	C	291	362	404	422	*381	11.7	8.7	8.1	8.7	*8.1
Rural - Rurale	C	321	213	153	133	*167	7.0	7.1	6.9	6.2	*7.8
Cuba											
Total	C	525	514	535	497	465	4.2	4.2	4.3	4.3	4.0
Urban - Urbaine	C	440	413	429	419	...	4.4	4.3	4.3	4.5	...
Rural - Rurale	C	85	101	106	78	...	3.1	3.9	4.1	3.3	...
Curaçao											
Total	C	15	24	20	20	16	...	...	...	...	...
Dominican Republic - République dominicaine											
Total	U	659	844	926	800		...	...	...	...	...
Urban - Urbaine[8]	U	549	714	779	705		...	...	...	...	...
Rural - Rurale[8]	U	39	55	35	52		...	...	...	...	...

15. Infant deaths and infant mortality rates, by urban/rural residence: 2013 - 2017
Décès d'enfants de moins d'un an et taux de mortalité infantile, selon la résidence, urbaine/rurale : 2013 - 2017 (continued - suite)

Continent, country or area, and urban/rural residence / Continent, pays ou zone et résidence, urbaine/rurale	Code[a]	Number - Nombre					Rate - Taux				
		2013	2014	2015	2016	2017	2013	2014	2015	2016	2017
AMERICA, NORTH - AMÉRIQUE DU NORD											
El Salvador[9]											
Total	C	859	876	...	...	...	7.8	8.0	...	...	...
Urban - Urbaine	C	...	569	...	...	...	...	9.1	...	...	...
Rural - Rurale	C	...	307	...	...	...	...	6.6	...	...	...
Greenland - Groenland											
Total	C	7	6	9	6	6	...	...	...	...	...
Urban - Urbaine	C	7	5	9	6	6	...	...	...	...	...
Rural - Rurale	C	-	1	-	-	-	...	...	...	...	...
Grenada - Grenade											
Total	+C	32	33	...	...	...	17.4	18.9	...	...	...
Guatemala											
Total	C	7 221	7 342	8 202	8 366	...	18.6	19.0	21.0	21.4	...
Mexico - Mexique[10]											
Total	+C	27 802	26 385	26 045	24 722	...	12.8	12.4	12.4	10.8	...
Urban - Urbaine[8]	+C	21 079	19 987	19 753	18 766	...	13.8	12.8	12.8	...	...
Rural - Rurale[8]	+C	6 041	5 870	5 832	5 593	...	12.5	12.6	13.2	...	...
Montserrat											
Total	C	-	-	3	-	...	...	...	...	...	...
Panama											
Total	U	1 106	...	...	...	...	...	...	...	...	...
Urban - Urbaine	U	682	...	...	...	...	...	...	...	...	...
Rural - Rurale	U	424	...	...	...	...	...	...	...	...	...
Total	C	...	1 036	935	*1 046	...	...	13.8	12.3	*13.9	...
Urban - Urbaine	C	...	585	543	*556	...	...	11.9	11.1	*11.6	...
Rural - Rurale	C	...	451	392	*490	...	...	17.2	14.6	*17.9	...
Puerto Rico - Porto Rico											
Total	C	270	242	222	222	172	7.4	7.0	7.1	7.8	7.1
Urban - Urbaine	C	164	141	124	122	100	8.3	7.4	6.5	6.7	6.1
Rural - Rurale	C	106	101	98	100	72	6.3	6.5	8.0	9.9	9.0
Saint Vincent and the Grenadines - Saint-Vincent-et-les Grenadines											
Total	C	32	29	...	...	...	18.4	...	...	...	...
Trinidad and Tobago - Trinité-et-Tobago											
Total	C	*326	...	...	...	...	*17.3	...	...	...	...
Turks and Caicos Islands - Îles Turques et Caïques											
Total	C	12	2	...	...	...	...	...	...	...	...
United States of America - États-Unis d'Amérique											
Total	C	23 440	23 215	23 455	...	...	6.0	5.8	5.9	...	...
AMERICA, SOUTH - AMÉRIQUE DU SUD											
Argentina - Argentine											
Total	C	8 174	8 202	7 445	7 093	...	10.8	10.6	9.7	9.7	...
Brazil - Brésil											
Total[11]	U	31 944	31 679	...	...	...	...	...	...	...	...
Total	+C	...	...	31 238	30 541	...	...	...	10.6	10.5	...
Chile - Chili											
Total	C	1 692	1 825	1 683	...	...	7.0	7.3	6.9	...	...
Urban - Urbaine	C	1 540	1 604	1 506	...	...	7.0	7.0	6.8	...	...
Rural - Rurale	C	152	221	177	...	...	7.0	9.8	8.0	...	...
Colombia - Colombie											
Total	U	7 618	7 589	7 244	7 220	...	...	...	...	...	...
Urban - Urbaine[8]	U	5 578	5 642	5 384	5 365	...	...	...	...	...	...
Rural - Rurale[8]	U	1 974	1 873	1 799	1 800	...	...	...	...	...	...
Ecuador - Équateur[12]											
Total	U	2 928	2 821	2 979	3 042	...	...	...	...	...	...
Urban - Urbaine	U	2 455	2 308	2 483	2 482	...	...	...	...	...	...
Rural - Rurale	U	473	513	496	560	...	...	...	...	...	...
Paraguay											
Total	+U	...	468	...	485	...	...	...	...	...	...

15. Infant deaths and infant mortality rates, by urban/rural residence: 2013 - 2017
Décès d'enfants de moins d'un an et taux de mortalité infantile, selon la résidence, urbaine/rurale : 2013 - 2017 (continued - suite)

Continent, country or area, and urban/rural residence / Continent, pays ou zone et résidence, urbaine/rurale	Code[a]	Number - Nombre					Rate - Taux				
		2013	2014	2015	2016	2017	2013	2014	2015	2016	2017
AMERICA, SOUTH - AMÉRIQUE DU SUD											
Peru - Pérou[13]											
Total	+U	4 548	4 243	3 852	*3 616	...	...	...	...	...	...
Suriname											
Total	C	168	163	149	170	...	16.8	15.7	14.7	17.2	...
Urban - Urbaine	C	118	117	101	131	...	17.4	17.0	15.1	20.0	...
Rural - Rurale	C	50	46	48	39	...	15.5	13.1	13.9	11.6	...
Uruguay											
Total	C	430	376	367	376	...	8.8	7.8	7.5	8.0	...
Venezuela (Bolivarian Republic of) - Venezuela (République bolivarienne du)											
Total	C	7 630	8 396	9 276	11 783	11 082	12.8	14.0	15.4	18.3	19.7
ASIA - ASIE											
Armenia - Arménie[14]											
Total	C	...	376	370	352	...	...	8.7	8.9	8.7	...
Urban - Urbaine	C	...	...	233	201	...	...	...	8.6	7.6	...
Rural - Rurale	C	...	...	137	151	...	...	...	9.4	10.7	...
Azerbaijan - Azerbaïdjan[14]											
Total	+C	1 862	1 655	2 033	1 666	...	10.8	9.7	12.2	10.4	...
Urban - Urbaine	+C	1 459	1 324	1 602	1 380	...	16.9	16.2	19.7	17.9	...
Rural - Rurale	+C	403	331	431	286	...	4.7	3.7	5.1	3.5	...
Bahrain - Bahreïn[15]											
Total	C	141	218	156	109	...	7.1	10.4	7.4	5.3	...
Brunei Darussalam - Brunéi Darussalam											
Total	+C	51	51	58	52	...	7.6	7.4	8.7	8.1	...
China, Hong Kong SAR - Chine, Hong Kong RAS											
Total	C	100	103	85	109	97	1.8	1.7	1.4	1.8	1.7
China, Macao SAR - Chine, Macao RAS											
Total	C	13	15	11	...	...	...	...	...	...	...
Total[16]	I	...	...	...	12	...	...	...	...	...	...
Cyprus - Chypre[17]											
Total	C	15	19	25	25	...	...	...	...	...	...
Georgia - Géorgie[14]											
Total	C	640	578	507	507	512	11.1	9.5	8.6	9.0	9.6
Urban - Urbaine	C	...	...	259	253	...	...	...	7.6	7.9	...
Rural - Rurale	C	...	...	248	254	...	...	...	9.8	10.4	...
India - Inde[18]											
Total	I	...	...	...	...	...	40.0	39.0	37.0	34.0	...
Urban - Urbaine	I	...	...	...	...	...	27.0	26.0	25.0	23.0	...
Rural - Rurale	I	...	...	...	...	...	44.0	43.0	41.0	38.0	...
Iran (Islamic Republic of) - Iran (République islamique d')[19]											
Total	+C	8 015	7 430	...	8 261	...	5.4	4.8	...	5.4	...
Urban - Urbaine	+C	5 993	5 590	...	6 115	...	5.3	4.7	...	5.2	...
Rural - Rurale	+C	2 022	1 840	...	2 146	...	5.9	5.2	...	6.1	...
Israel - Israël[20]											
Total	C	539	548	563	568	553	3.1	3.1	3.2	3.1	3.0
Urban - Urbaine[8]	C	469	494	496	490	498	3.0	3.1	3.1	3.0	...
Rural - Rurale[8]	C	69	53	63	78	55	4.2	3.3	3.8	4.6	...
Japan - Japon[21]											
Total	C	2 185	2 080	1 916	1 928	...	2.1	2.1	1.9	2.0	...
Urban - Urbaine	C	2 019	1 891	1 754	1 768	...	2.1	2.0	1.9	2.0	...
Rural - Rurale	C	163	187	161	158	...	2.0	2.4	2.1	2.1	...
Kazakhstan											
Total	C	4 400	3 907	3 751	3 438	3 109	11.4	9.8	9.4	8.6	8.0
Urban - Urbaine	C	2 394	2 222	2 177	1 936	1 700	11.4	10.0	9.6	8.4	7.5
Rural - Rurale	C	2 006	1 685	1 574	1 502	1 409	11.3	9.5	9.1	8.8	8.6
Kuwait - Koweït											
Total	C	453	456	456	448	...	7.6	7.4	7.7	7.6	...

15. Infant deaths and infant mortality rates, by urban/rural residence: 2013 - 2017
Décès d'enfants de moins d'un an et taux de mortalité infantile, selon la résidence, urbaine/rurale : 2013 - 2017 (continued - suite)

Continent, country or area, and urban/rural residence / Continent, pays ou zone et résidence, urbaine/rurale	Code[a]	Number - Nombre					Rate - Taux				
		2013	2014	2015	2016	2017	2013	2014	2015	2016	2017
ASIA - ASIE											
Kyrgyzstan - Kirghizstan											
Total	C	3 093	3 268	2 945	2 621	2 401	19.9	20.2	18.0	16.6	15.6
Urban - Urbaine	C	1 886	2 099	1 853	1 586	1 586	35.0	37.8	35.3	30.7	30.0
Rural - Rurale	C	1 207	1 169	1 092	1 035	815	11.9	11.0	9.8	9.7	8.1
Malaysia - Malaisie											
Total	C	3 199	3 543	3 582	3 390	...	6.3	6.7	6.9	6.7	...
Urban - Urbaine	C	2 101	2 313	2 301	2 186	...	6.1	6.5	6.6	6.4	...
Rural - Rurale	C	1 098	1 230	1 281	1 204	...	6.9	7.2	7.5	7.3	...
Maldives[22]											
Total	C	46	59	63	53	...	6.4	8.1	9.0	7.8	...
Urban - Urbaine	C	24[23]	15[23]	8[8]	35[8]	...	...	...	...	14.4	...
Rural - Rurale	C	19[23]	33[23]	17[8]	14[8]	...	...	13.9	...	...	...
Mongolia - Mongolie											
Total	+C	1 166	1 251	1 234	1 315	1 009	14.6	15.1	15.0	16.5	13.4
Myanmar											
Total	+U	*11 516*[24]	*9 386*[25]	*9 849*[25]	...	...	...	...	...	...	...
Urban - Urbaine	+U	*6 840*[24]	*5 806*[25]	*6 256*[25]	...	...	...	...	...	...	...
Rural - Rurale	+U	*4 676*[24]	*3 580*[25]	*3 593*[25]	...	...	...	...	...	...	...
Oman											
Total[26]	U	*772*	*645*	*818*	*816*	...	...	...	...	...	...
Total	C	...	...	...	...	850	...	...	...	...	9.4
Philippines											
Total	C	21 992	21 572	20 750	21 874	...	12.5	12.3	11.9	12.6	...
Qatar											
Total	C	158	168	197	161	...	6.7	6.6	7.4	6.0	...
Urban - Urbaine	C	158	168	197	161	...	6.7	6.6	7.4	6.0	...
Republic of Korea - République de Corée[27]											
Total	C	1 305	1 305	1 190	...	1 000	3.0	3.0	2.7	...	2.8
Urban - Urbaine	C	1 098[8]	1 063	1 010	...	...	3.0	2.9	2.8	...	...
Rural - Rurale	C	203[8]	242	180	...	...	2.9	3.4	2.5	...	...
Saudi Arabia - Arabie saoudite[28]											
Total	I	...	...	...	5 084	...	...	...	...	11.4	...
Singapore - Singapour											
Total	+C	94	83	84	101	94	2.4	2.0	2.0	2.4	2.4
Sri Lanka											
Total	+C	3 043	2 799	2 845	...	...	8.3	8.0	8.5	...	...
Urban - Urbaine	+C	2 604	...	...	...	...	10.1	...	...	...	...
Rural - Rurale	+C	439	...	...	...	...	4.1	...	...	...	...
State of Palestine - État de Palestine[29]											
Total	U	*845*	*800*	*852*	...	...	...	...	...	...	...
Tajikistan - Tadjikistan[14]											
Total	U	*3 622*	*3 273*	*3 082*	*2 725*	...	...	...	...	...	...
Urban - Urbaine	U	*1 817*	*1 515*	*1 617*	*1 479*	...	...	...	...	...	...
Rural - Rurale	U	*1 805*	*1 758*	*1 465*	*1 246*	...	...	...	...	...	...
Thailand - Thaïlande											
Total	+U	*4 755*	*4 615*	*4 221*	*4 233*	...	...	...	...	...	...
Turkey - Turquie[30]											
Total	C	14 027	14 938	13 654	13 036	...	10.8	11.1	10.2	10.0	...
Uzbekistan - Ouzbékistan[14]											
Total	+C	6 569	7 688	8 320	...	...	9.7	10.7	11.3	...	...
Urban - Urbaine	+C	3 881	4 312	4 494	...	...	12.5	13.2	13.8	...	...
Rural - Rurale	+C	2 688	3 376	3 826	...	...	7.3	8.6	9.4	...	...
EUROPE											
Åland Islands - Îles d'Åland											
Total	C	-	-	-	1		...	...	...	...	...
Urban - Urbaine	C	-	-	-	-		...	...	...	...	...
Rural - Rurale	C	-	-	-	1		...	...	...	...	...
Albania - Albanie											
Total	C	282	281	233	277	...	7.9	7.9	7.0	8.7	...

15. Infant deaths and infant mortality rates, by urban/rural residence: 2013 - 2017
Décès d'enfants de moins d'un an et taux de mortalité infantile, selon la résidence, urbaine/rurale : 2013 - 2017 (continued - suite)

Continent, country or area, and urban/rural residence / Continent, pays ou zone et résidence, urbaine/rurale	Co-de[a]	Number - Nombre					Rate - Taux				
		2013	2014	2015	2016	2017	2013	2014	2015	2016	2017
EUROPE											
Andorra - Andorre											
Total	C	1	2	-	...	...	...	...	...	...	...
Austria - Autriche											
Total	C	245	249	259	269	...	3.1	3.0	3.1	3.1	...
Belarus - Bélarus											
Total	C	407	409	352	373	...	3.4	3.5	3.0	3.2	...
Urban - Urbaine	C	291	291	254	288	...	3.2	3.2	2.8	3.2	...
Rural - Rurale	C	116	118	98	85	...	4.2	4.4	3.6	3.2	...
Belgium - Belgique[31]											
Total	C	436	423	400	387	...	3.5	3.4	3.3	3.2	...
Urban - Urbaine	C	432	420	396	...	...	3.5	3.4	3.3	...	...
Rural - Rurale	C	4	3	4	...	...	...	...	...	...	...
Bosnia and Herzegovina - Bosnie-Herzégovine											
Total	C	161	140	174	152	183	5.2	4.8	6.0	5.2	6.3
Bulgaria - Bulgarie											
Total	C	489	517	434	423	...	7.3	7.6	6.6	6.5	...
Urban - Urbaine	C	...	340	255	285	...	...	6.7	5.2	5.8	...
Rural - Rurale	C	...	177	179	138	...	...	10.5	10.9	8.5	...
Croatia - Croatie											
Total	C	162	199	154	161	...	4.1	5.0	4.1	4.3	...
Urban - Urbaine	C	82	101	91	82	...	3.6	4.4	4.2	3.8	...
Rural - Rurale	C	80	98	63	79	...	4.7	5.9	4.0	5.0	...
Czechia - Tchéquie											
Total	C	265	263	272	317	...	2.5	2.4	2.5	2.8	...
Urban - Urbaine	C	193	197	193	231	...	2.5	2.4	2.4	2.8	...
Rural - Rurale	C	72	66	79	86	...	2.5	2.3	2.7	2.9	...
Denmark - Danemark[32]											
Total	C	195	229	216	194	...	3.5	4.0	3.7	3.1	...
Estonia - Estonie											
Total	C	28	36	35	33	...	...	2.7	2.5	2.3	...
Urban - Urbaine	C	18	24	24	24	...	...	...	...	...	...
Rural - Rurale	C	10	12	11	9	...	...	...	...	...	...
Faeroe Islands - Îles Féroé											
Total	C	-	4	-	3	6	...	...	...	...	...
Urban - Urbaine	C	-	1	-	1	2	...	...	...	...	...
Rural - Rurale	C	-	3	-	2	4	...	...	...	...	...
Finland - Finlande[33]											
Total	C	102	124	97	99	...	1.8	2.2	1.8	1.9	...
Urban - Urbaine	C	65	93	66	72	...	1.6	2.3	1.6	1.9	...
Rural - Rurale	C	37	31	31	27	...	2.2	2.0	2.1	...	...
France											
Total	C	2 710	2 598	2 655	2 577	...	3.5	3.3	3.5	3.5	...
Urban - Urbaine[34]	C	2 233	2 138	2 219	2 165	...	3.6	3.4	3.6	3.6	...
Rural - Rurale[34]	C	457	441	408	386	...	2.9	2.9	2.8	2.7	...
Germany - Allemagne											
Total	C	2 250	2 284	2 405	2 700	...	3.3	3.2	3.3	3.4	...
Gibraltar											
Total	+C	-	...	...	...	...	...	...	...	...	...
Greece - Grèce											
Total	C	347	346	364	387	...	3.7	3.8	4.0	4.2	...
Urban - Urbaine	C	...	242	254	254	...	...	3.9	4.0	4.0	...
Rural - Rurale	C	...	104	110	133	...	...	3.5	3.9	4.6	...
Hungary - Hongrie											
Total	C	448[35]	418[37]	383[37]	368[37]	332[37]	5.0	4.5	4.2	3.9	3.5
Urban - Urbaine[36]	C	273[35]	274[37]	242[37]	231[37]	...	4.4	4.2	3.8	3.5	...
Rural - Rurale[36]	C	175[35]	144[37]	140[37]	136[37]	...	6.4	5.1	5.0	4.6	...
Iceland - Islande											
Total	C	8	9	9	3	11	...	...	...	...	...
Urban - Urbaine	C	8	9	8	3	...	...	...	...	...	...
Rural - Rurale	C	-	-	1	-	...	...	...	...	...	...
Ireland - Irlande											
Total	+C	243	224	224	208	174	3.5	3.3	3.4	3.3	2.8
Isle of Man - Île de Man[38]											
Total	I	...	...	...	2	...	...	...	...	...	...
Italy - Italie											
Total	C	1 493	1 523	1 398	1 427	...	2.9	3.0	2.9	3.0	...

15. Infant deaths and infant mortality rates, by urban/rural residence: 2013 - 2017
Décès d'enfants de moins d'un an et taux de mortalité infantile, selon la résidence, urbaine/rurale : 2013 - 2017 (continued - suite)

Continent, country or area, and urban/rural residence / Continent, pays ou zone et résidence, urbaine/rurale	Co-de[a]	Number - Nombre					Rate - Taux				
		2013	2014	2015	2016	2017	2013	2014	2015	2016	2017
EUROPE											
Latvia - Lettonie											
Total	C	91	83	90	81	...	4.4	3.8	4.1	3.7	...
Urban - Urbaine	C	55	53	59	53	...	3.9	3.5	3.9	3.5	...
Rural - Rurale	C	36	30	31	28	...	5.6	4.5	4.5	...	...
Liechtenstein											
Total	C	2	1	2	1	...	...	...	...	...	...
Lithuania - Lituanie											
Total	C	110	118	132	139	...	3.7	3.9	4.2	4.5	...
Urban - Urbaine	C	63	69	92	96	...	3.1	3.3	4.3	4.5	...
Rural - Rurale	C	47	49	40	43	...	4.9	5.2	4.0	4.6	...
Luxembourg											
Total	C	24	17	17	23	20	...	...	...	...	...
Malta - Malte											
Total	C	27	21	25	33		...	...	...	7.4	...
Montenegro - Monténégro											
Total	C	33	37	16	26	...	4.4	4.9	...	...	...
Netherlands - Pays-Bas[39]											
Total	C	645	630	561	597	...	3.8	3.6	3.3	3.5	...
Norway - Norvège[40]											
Total	C	140	139	133	128	...	2.4	2.4	2.3	2.2	...
Poland - Pologne											
Total	C	1 684	1 583	1 476	1 522	...	4.6	4.2	4.0	4.0	...
Urban - Urbaine	C	928	885	859	876	...	4.3	4.1	4.0	3.9	...
Rural - Rurale	C	756	698	617	646	...	4.9	4.4	4.1	4.1	...
Portugal[41]											
Total	C	243	236	250	282	...	2.9	2.9	2.9	3.2	...
Republic of Moldova - République de Moldova[42]											
Total	C	359	372	375	353	330	9.5	9.6	9.7	9.4	9.7
Urban - Urbaine	C	...	...	141	131	107	...	...	10.4	9.8	8.6
Rural - Rurale	C	...	...	234	222	223	...	...	9.3	9.2	10.3
Romania - Roumanie											
Total	C	1 677	1 632	1 500	1 398	...	9.2	8.2	7.6	7.0	...
Urban - Urbaine	C	738	651	648	...	...	7.5	6.0	6.0	...	...
Rural - Rurale	C	939	981	852	...	...	11.2	10.9	9.6	...	...
San Marino - Saint-Marin											
Total	C	1	1	-	1	-	...	...	...	...	...
Serbia - Serbie[43]											
Total	+C	413	381	346	348	...	6.3	5.7	5.3	5.4	...
Urban - Urbaine	+C	281	268	258	265	...	6.2	5.8	5.7	5.9	...
Rural - Rurale	+C	132	113	88	83	...	6.6	5.5	4.4	4.2	...
Slovakia - Slovaquie											
Total	C	301	318	285	311	...	5.5	5.8	5.1	5.4	...
Urban - Urbaine	C	138	160	117	133	...	4.8	5.6	4.0	4.5	...
Rural - Rurale	C	163	158	168	178	...	6.2	5.9	6.3	6.4	...
Slovenia - Slovénie											
Total	C	62	39	33	41	...	2.9	1.8	1.6	2.0	...
Urban - Urbaine	C	37	19	17	15	...	3.5	...	...	...	...
Rural - Rurale	C	25	20	16	26	...	...	...	...	...	...
Spain - Espagne											
Total	C	1 149	1 202	1 117	1 097	...	2.7	2.8	2.7	2.7	...
Sweden - Suède											
Total	C	306	251	282	292	...	2.7	2.2	2.5	2.5	...
Switzerland - Suisse											
Total	C	320	331	340	316	...	3.9	3.9	3.9	3.6	...
Urban - Urbaine	C	258	256	282[44]	279	...	4.1	4.0	3.8	3.7	...
Rural - Rurale	C	62	75	58[44]	37	...	3.0	3.5	4.6	2.9	...
TFYR of Macedonia - L'ex-R. y. de Macédoine											
Total	C	237	233	198	273	...	10.2	9.9	8.6	11.9	...
Urban - Urbaine	C	131	144	116	153	...	9.9	10.5	8.7	11.3	...
Rural - Rurale	C	106	89	82	120	...	10.7	9.1	8.4	12.7	...
Ukraine[45]											
Total	+C	4 030	3 656[46]	3 318[46]	2 955[46]	...	8.0	7.8	8.1	7.4	...
Urban - Urbaine	+C	2 536	2 316[46]	2 035[46]	1 788[46]	...	7.7	7.6	7.6	6.9	...
Rural - Rurale	+C	1 494	1 340[46]	1 283[46]	1 167[46]	...	8.6	8.3	8.8	8.4	...

15. Infant deaths and infant mortality rates, by urban/rural residence: 2013 - 2017

Décès d'enfants de moins d'un an et taux de mortalité infantile, selon la résidence, urbaine/rurale : 2013 - 2017 (continued - suite)

Continent, country or area, and urban/rural residence / Continent, pays ou zone et résidence, urbaine/rurale	Co-de[a]	Number - Nombre					Rate - Taux				
		2013	2014	2015	2016	2017	2013	2014	2015	2016	2017
EUROPE											
United Kingdom of Great Britain and Northern Ireland - Royaume-Uni de Grande-Bretagne et d'Irlande du Nord[47]											
Total	+C	3 030	2 990	3 005	2 976	...	3.9	3.9	3.9	3.8	...
OCEANIA - OCÉANIE											
American Samoa - Samoas américaines											
Total	C	5	9	...	...	...	...	...	...	...	...
Australia - Australie											
Total	C	1 094	1 012	991	970	...	3.6	3.4	3.2	3.1	...
Urban - Urbaine[48]	C	658	617	606	630	...	3.1	3.0	2.9	2.9	...
Rural - Rurale[48]	C	412	380	361	326	...	4.2	4.1	3.8	3.5	...
Cook Islands - Îles Cook[49]											
Total	+C	-	-	-	...	...	...	...	...	...	...
Fiji - Fidji											
Total	+C	353	141	...	...	...	18.9	7.7	...	...	...
French Polynesia - Polynésie française											
Total	C	37	28	29	...	...	8.8	...	...	...	...
Guam[50]											
Total	C	31	28	47	37	28	9.3	...	14.0	10.8	...
New Caledonia - Nouvelle-Calédonie											
Total	C	19	23	25	...	...	...	...	...	...	...
New Zealand - Nouvelle-Zélande[51]											
Total	+C	261	327	249	213[52]	228[52]	4.4	5.7	4.1	3.6	3.8
Urban - Urbaine[8]	+C	222	288	216	189[52]	198[52]	4.3	5.7	4.1	3.6	3.8
Rural - Rurale[8]	+C	33	24	30	18[52]	27[52]	4.6	...	3.8	...	...
Northern Mariana Islands - Îles Mariannes septentrionales[53]											
Total	U	*8*	*7*	...	...	...	...	...	...	...	...
Palau - Palaos											
Total	C	7	3	4	-	5	...	...	...	...	...

FOOTNOTES - NOTES

Italics: data from civil registers which are incomplete or of unknown completeness. - Italiques : données incomplètes ou dont le degré d'exactitude n'est pas connu, provenant des registres de l'état civil.

* Provisional. - Données provisoires.

[a] 'Code' indicates the source of data, as follows:
C - Civil registration, estimated over 90% complete
U - Civil registration, estimated less than 90% complete
| - Other source, estimated reliable
+ - Data tabulated by date of registration rather than occurence
... - Information not available

Le 'Code' indique la source des données, comme suit :
C - Registres de l'état civil considérés complets à 90 p. 100 au moins
U - Registres de l'état civil qui ne sont pas considérés complets à 90 p. 100 au moins
| - Autre source, considérée pas douteuses
+ - Données exploitées selon la date de l'enregistrement et non la date de l'événement
... - Information pas disponible

[1] Excluding live-born infants who died before their birth was registered. Data refer to Algerian population only. - Non compris les enfants nés vivants décédés avant l'enregistrement de leur naissance. Les données ne concernent que la population algérienne.
[2] Data refer to the 12 months preceding the census in May. - Les données se rapportent aux 12 mois précédant le recensement de mai.
[3] Source: Vital Statistics Report 2016. - Source: Vital Statistics Report 2016.
[4] Adjusted number of infant deaths in households referring to the 12 months preceding the census in March. - Le nombre ajusté de décès d'enfants des ménages ordinaires se rapportent aux 12 mois précédant le recensement de mars.
[5] Excludes the islands of St. Brandon and Agalega. - Non compris les îles St. Brandon et Agalega.
[6] Source: National Office of Births and Deaths. - Source : Le bureau national des naissances et des décès.
[7] Including Canadian residents temporarily in the United States, but excluding United States residents temporarily in Canada. - Y compris les résidents canadiens se trouvant temporairement aux Etats-Unis, mais ne comprenant pas les résidents des Etats-Unis se trouvant temporairement au Canada.
[8] The total number may include 'Unknown residence', but the categories urban and rural do not. - Le nombre total peut inclure les personnes dont la résidence n'est pas connue, à l'inverse des catégories de population urbaine et rurale.
[9] Excluding infant deaths to mothers living abroad. - Exception faite des décès d'enfants en bas âge survenus lorsque la mère résidait à l'étranger.

[10] Data refer to resident population only. - Pour la population résidante seulement.

[11] Including deaths abroad and deaths of unknown residence of mother. - Y compris décès à l'étranger et décès de nourrissons nés de mères dont le lieu de résidence n'est pas connu.

[12] Excludes nomadic Indian tribes. - Non compris les tribus d'Indiens nomades.

[13] Source: Reports of the Ministry of Health. - Source : Rapports du Ministère de la Santé.

[14] Excluding infants born alive of less than 28 weeks' gestation, of less than 1 000 g in weight and 35 cm in length, who die within seven days of birth. - Non compris les enfants nés vivants après moins de 28 semaines de gestations, pesant moins de 1 000 g, mesurant moins de 35 cm et décédés dans les sept jours qui ont suivi leur naissance.

[15] Deaths include deaths among some visitors. Sources: Births and Deaths National Registration System database, and medical records of government hospitals. - Les décès comprennent des décès parmi certains visiteurs. Les sources: Les bases de données des << Births and Deaths National Registration System >> et les dossiers médicaux des hôpitaux du gouvernement.

[16] Data refer to the 12 months preceding the census in August. - Les données se rapportent aux 12 mois précédant le recensement d'août.

[17] Data refer to government controlled areas. - Les données se rapportent aux zones contrôlées par le Gouvernement.

[18] Rates were obtained by the Sample Registration System of India, which is a large demographic survey. Includes data for the Indian-held part of Jammu and Kashmir, the final status of which has not yet been determined. - Les taux ont été obtenus par le Système de l'enregistrement par échantillon de l'Inde qui est une large enquête démographique. Y compris les données pour la partie du Jammu et du Cachemire occupée par l'Inde dont le statut définitif n'a pas encore été déterminé.

[19] Data refer to the Iranian Year which begins on 21 March and ends on 20 March of the following year. - Les données concernent l'année iranienne, qui commence le 21 mars et se termine le 20 mars de l'année suivante.

[20] Includes data for East Jerusalem and Israeli residents in certain other territories under occupation by Israeli military forces since June 1967. Including deaths abroad of Israeli residents who were out of the country for less than a year. - Y compris les données pour Jérusalem-Est et les résidents israéliens dans certains autres territoires occupés depuis 1967 par les forces armées israéliennes. Y compris les décès à l'étranger de résidents israéliens qui ont quitté le pays depuis moins d'un an.

[21] Data refer to Japanese nationals in Japan only. The total number may include 'Unknown residence', but the categories urban and rural do not. - Les données se raportent aux nationaux japonais au Japon seulement. Le nombre total peut inclure les personnes dont la résidence n'est pas connue, à l'inverse des catégories de population urbaine et rurale.

[22] Data do not include foreigners. - Les données sur les etrangers ne sont pas inclus.

[23] Excluding deaths occurred abroad. - Hormis les décès à l'étranger.

[24] Source: "Department of Public Health" - Source : << Le Service de la santé publique >>

[25] Data are from Vital Registration System (VRS). - Les données proviennent du système d'enregistrement des faits d'état civil.

[26] Data from Births and Deaths Notification System (Ministry of Health and all health care providers). - Les données proviennent du système de notification des naissances et des décès (Ministère de la santé et tous prestataires de soins de santé).

[27] Excluding alien armed forces, civilian aliens employed by armed forces, and foreign diplomatic personnel and their dependants. - Non compris les militaires étrangers, les civils étrangers employés par les forces armées ni le personnel diplomatique étranger et les membres de leur famille les accompagnant.

[28] Survey based estimates. Data refer to Saudi Arabian nationals only. - Estimations basées sur des enquêtes. Les données ne concernent que les ressortissants saoudiens.

[29] Source: Palestinian Central Bureau of Statistics, Population Register, updated version 22/02/2016. - Source: Bureau central de statistique palestinien, registre de la population, version actualisée jusqu'au 22/02/2016.

[30] Data from MERNIS (Central Population Administrative System). - Données de MERNIS (Système central de données démographiques).

[31] Including armed forces stationed outside the country, but excluding alien armed forces stationed in the area. - Y compris les militaires nationaux hors du pays, mais non compris les militaires étrangers en garnison sur le territoire.

[32] Excluding Faeroe Islands and Greenland shown separately, if available. - Non compris les Iles Féroé et le Groenland, qui font l'objet de rubriques distinctes, si disponible.

[33] Excluding Åland Islands. - Non compris les Îles d'Åland.

[34] Data for urban and rural exclude events corresponding to nationals residing outside the country, which may be included in the total. - Les données relatives à les categories urbaine et rurale n'englobent pas les faits d'état civil qui concernent les nationaux se trouvant à l'étranger, lesquels faits peuvent être inclus au total.

[35] Till 2012 data refer to all infant deaths occurred in Hungary. From 2013 data include the deceased infants with Hungarian usual residence regardless of whether the death occurred in Hungary or in a foreign country, and do not include the deceased infants with foreign country usual residence. - Jusqu'en 2012 les données concernent tous les décès de nourrissons survenus en Hongrie. À partir de 2013, les données comprennent les nourrissons décédés alors que leur résidence habituelle était en Hongrie, que le décès ait eu lieu en Hongrie ou dans un pays étranger, et ne comprennent pas les nourrissons décédés dont la résidence habituelle était dans un pays étranger.

[36] The urban and rural categories do not include the data of foreigners, persons of unknown residence and the homeless, whereas the total category includes them. - Les chiffres portant sur la population urbaine et rurale n' incluent pas les données relatives aux étrangers, aux personnes dont la résidence n'est pas connue et aux personnes sans domicile fixe, à l'inverse, le total les inclut.

[37] Data include the deceased infants with Hungarian usual residence regardless of whether the death occurred in Hungary or in a foreign country, and do not include the deceased infants with foreign country usual residence. - Les données comprennent les nourrissons décédés alors que leur résidence habituelle était en Hongrie, que le décès ait eu lieu en Hongrie ou dans un pays étranger, et ne comprennent pas les nourrissons décédés dont la residence habituelle était dans un pays étranger.

[38] Data refer to the 12 months preceding the census in April. - Les données se rapportent aux douze mois précédant le recensement d'avril.

[39] Including residents outside the country if listed in a Netherlands population register. - Y compris les résidents se trouvant à l'étranger à condition qu'ils soient inscrits sur le registre de population des Pays-Bas.

[40] Including residents temporarily outside the country. - Y compris les résidents se trouvant temporairement hors du pays.

[41] Data refer to usually resident population. - Les données concernent la population habituellement résidente.

[42] Excluding Transnistria and the municipality of Bender. - Les données ne tiennent pas compte de l'information sur la Transnistria et la municipalité de Bender.

[43] Excludes data for Kosovo and Metohia. - Sans les données pour le Kosovo et Metohie.

[44] From 2015, urban refers to urban centers and areas under the influence of urban centers. - A partir de 2015, le territoire urbain inclut l'espace des centres urbains ainsi que l'espace sous influence des centres urbains.

[45] Data includes deaths resulting from births with weight 500 g and more (if weight is unknown - with length 25 cm and more, or with gestation during 22 weeks or more). - Y compris les décès de nouveau-nés de 500 g ou plus (si le poids est inconnu – de 25 cm de long ou plus, ou après une grossesse de 22 semaines ou plus).

[46] The Government of Ukraine has informed the United Nations that it is not in a position to provide statistical data concerning the Autonomous Republic of Crimea and the city of Sevastopol. - Le gouvernement Ukrainien a informé l'ONU qu'il n'est pas en mesure de fournir des données statistiques concernant la République autonome de Crimée et la ville de Sébastopol.

[47] Excluding Channel Islands (Guernsey and Jersey) and Isle of Man, shown separately, if available. - Non compris les îles Anglo-Normandes (Guernesey et Jersey) et l'Île de Man, qui font l'objet de rubriques distinctes, si disponible.

[48] Urban refers to Greater Capital City Statistical Areas, and rural refers to other areas within the state or territory. Data for urban and rural figures do not add up to the total because they exclude the events occurred in Migratory, Special Purpose and Other Territories. - Urbain renvoie aux zones statistiques de la capitale métropolitaine, et rural aux autres zones de l'État ou territoire. La somme des chiffres des catégories « en zone urbaine » et « en zone rurale » ne correspond pas au total du fait qu'en sont exclus les événements qui ont eu lieu dans les territoires de migration, les territoires à destination spéciale et autres territoires.

[49] Excluding Niue, shown separately, which is part of Cook Islands, but because of remoteness is administered separately. - Non compris Nioué, qui fait l'objet d'une rubrique distincte et qui fait partie des îles Cook, mais qui, en raison de son éloignement, est administrée séparément.

[50] Including United States military personnel, their dependants and contract employees. - Y compris les militaires des Etats-Unis, les membres de leur famille les accompagnant et les agents contractuels des Etats-Unis.

[51] Random rounding to base 3 is applied in this table as a confidentiality measure. - Les chiffres sont arrondis à la base 3 de manière aléatoire, pour des raisons de confidentialité.

[52] Data refer to deaths of residents only. - Les données renvoient aux décès de résidents uniquement.

[53] Source: U.S. National Center for Health Statistics, National Vital Statistics Reports (NVSR). - Source : US National Center for Health Statistics, National Vital Statistics Reports (NVSR).

Table 16 - *Demographic Yearbook 2017*

Table 16 presents infant deaths and infant mortality rates by age and sex for latest available year between 2008 and 2017.

Description of variables: Age is defined as hours, days and months of life completed, based on the difference between the hour, day, month and year of birth and the hour, day, month and year of death. The age classification used in this table is as follows: Main categories are "under 1 day", "1-6 days", "7-27 days" and "28 days – 11 months". Additional subcategories are shown within "7-27 days" and "28 days to 11 months" wherever available.

Rate computation: Infant mortality rates by age and sex are the annual number of infant deaths that occurred in a specific age-sex group per 1 000 live births of the corresponding sex. These rates have been calculated by the Statistics Division of the United Nations Department of Economic and Social Affairs. The denominator for all these rates, regardless of age of infant at death, is the total number of live births by sex.

Infant deaths of unknown age are included only in the rate for under one year of age. Infant deaths of unknown sex are included in the rate for the total and, hence, these rates, should agree with the infant mortality rates shown in table 15. Discrepancies are explained in footnotes.

Rates presented in this table have been limited to those countries or areas having at least a total of 100 deaths in a given year. Moreover, rates specific for individual sub-categories based on 30 or fewer infant deaths are identified by the symbol "♦".

Reliability of data: Data from civil registers of infant deaths which are reported as incomplete (less than 90 percent completeness) or of unknown completeness are considered unreliable and are set in italics rather than in roman type. Rates on these data are not computed. Table 15 and its technical notes provide more detailed information on the completeness of infant death registration. For more information about the quality of vital statistics, and the information available on their completeness, see section 4.2 of the Technical Notes.

Limitations: Statistics on infant deaths by age and sex are subject to the same qualifications as have been set forth for vital statistics and particularly for death statistics discussed in section 4 of the Technical Notes.

The reliability of the data, an indication of which is described above, is an important factor in considering the limitations. In addition, some infant deaths are tabulated by date of registration and not by date of occurrence; these have been indicated by a plus sign "+". Whenever the lag between the date of occurrence and date of registration is prolonged and, therefore, a large proportion of the infant-death registrations are delayed, infant-death statistics for any given year may be seriously affected.

Another factor that limits international comparability is the practice of some countries or areas of not including in infant-death statistics infants who were born alive but died before the registration of the birth or within the first 24 hours of life, thus underestimating the total number of infant deaths. Statistics of this type are footnoted. In this table, this practice may contribute to the lack of comparability among deaths under one year, under 28 days, under one week and under one day.

Variation in the method of reckoning age at the time of death may also introduce non-comparability. Although it is to some degree a limiting factor throughout the age span, it is an especially important consideration with respect to deaths at ages under one day and under one week (early neonatal deaths) and under 28 days (neonatal deaths). As noted above, the recommended method of reckoning infant age at death is to calculate duration of life in minutes, hours and days, as appropriate. This gives age in completed units of time. In some countries or areas, however, infant age is calculated to the nearest day only, that is, age at death for an infant is the difference between the day, month and year of birth and the day, month and year of death. The result of this procedure is to classify as deaths at age one day, many deaths of infants that occurred before the infants had completed 24 hours of life. The under-one-day class is thus understated while the frequency in the 1-6-day age group is inflated.

A special limitation on comparability of neonatal (under 28 days) deaths is the variation in the classification of infant age used. Some countries or areas continue to report infant age in calendar, rather than lunar month (4-week or 28-day) periods. This failure to tabulate infant deaths under 4 weeks of age in terms of completed days introduces another source of variation between countries or areas. Deaths classified as occurring under one month usually connote deaths within any one calendar month; these frequencies are not strictly comparable with those referring to deaths within 4 weeks or 27 completed days.

In addition, infant mortality rates by age and sex are subject to the limitations of the data on live births with which they have been calculated. These have been set forth in the technical notes for table 9. These limitations have also been discussed in the technical notes for table 15.

In addition, it should be noted that infant mortality rates by age are affected by the problems related to the practice of excluding infants who were born alive but died before the registration of the birth or within the first 24 hours of life from both infant-death and live-birth statistics and the problems related to the reckoning of infant age at death. These factors, which have been described above, may affect certain age groups more than others. In so far as the numbers of infant deaths for the various age groups are underestimated or overestimated, the corresponding rates for the various age groups will also be underestimated or overestimated. The youngest age groups are more likely to be underestimated than other age groups; the youngest age group (under one day) is likely to be the most seriously affected.

Earlier data: Infant deaths and infant mortality rates by age and sex have been shown in previous issues of the *Demographic Yearbook*. For information on specific years covered, readers should consult the Historical Index.

Tableau 16 – *Annuaire démographique 2017*

Le tableau 16 présente les données les plus récentes disponible, entre 2008 et 2017, sur les décès d'enfants de moins d'un an et les taux de mortalité infantile selon l'âge et le sexe.

Description des variables : l'âge est exprimé en heures, jours et mois révolus et est calculé en retranchant la date de la naissance (heure, jour, mois et année) de celle du décès (heure, jour, mois et année). Les tranches d'âge utilisées dans ce tableau se présentent comme suit : les catégories principales sont « moins d'un jour », « 1-6 jours », « 7-27 jours » et « 28 jours à 11 mois ». Des sous-catégories additionnelles pour « 7-27 jours » et « 28 jours à 11 mois » sont présentées lorsque disponibles.

Calcul des taux : les taux de mortalité infantile selon l'âge et le sexe représentent le nombre annuel de décès d'enfants de moins d'un an intervenu dans un groupe d'âge donné parmi la population de sexe masculin ou féminin pour 1 000 naissances vivantes survenues parmi la population du même sexe. Ces taux ont été calculés par la Division de statistique du Département des affaires économiques et sociales de l'Organisation des Nations Unies. Le dénominateur de tous ces taux, quel que soit l'âge de l'enfant au moment du décès, est le nombre total de naissances vivantes selon le sexe.

Il n'est tenu compte des décès d'enfants d'âge « inconnu » que pour le calcul du taux relatif à l'ensemble des décès de moins d'un an. Étant donné que les décès d'enfants de sexe inconnu sont compris dans le numérateur des taux concernant le total, les chiffres obtenus devraient concorder avec les taux de mortalité infantile du tableau 15. Les divergences sont expliquées en note.

Les taux présentés dans le tableau 16 ne concernent que les pays ou zones où l'on a enregistré un total d'au moins 100 décès au cours d'une année donnée. Les taux relatifs à des sous-catégories qui sont fondées sur un nombre égal ou inférieur à 30 décès d'enfants âgés de moins d'un an sont signalés par le signe "♦".

Fiabilité des données : les données relatives aux décès d'enfants de moins d'un an provenant de registres de l'état civil qui sont déclarées incomplètes (degré de complétude inférieur à 90 p.100) ou dont le degré de complétude n'est pas connu sont jugées douteuses et apparaissent en italique et non en caractères romains. Les taux à partir de ces données n'ont pas été calculés. Le tableau 15 et les notes techniques se rapportant à ce tableau comportent des renseignements plus détaillés sur le degré de complétude de l'enregistrement des décès d'enfants de moins d'un an. Pour plus de précisions sur la qualité des données reposant sur les statistiques de l'état civil en général et les estimations de complétude en particulier, voir la section 4.2 des Notes techniques.

Insuffisance des données : les statistiques des décès d'enfants de moins d'un an selon l'âge et le sexe appellent toutes les réserves qui ont été formulées à propos des statistiques de l'état civil en général et des statistiques concernant les décès en particulier (voir la section 4 des Notes techniques).

La fiabilité des données, au sujet de laquelle des indications ont été fournies plus haut, est un facteur important. Il faut également tenir compte du fait que, dans certains cas, les données relatives aux décès d'enfants de moins d'un an sont exploitées selon la date de l'enregistrement et non la date de l'événement ; ces cas ont été signalés par le signe "+". Chaque fois que le décalage entre l'événement et son enregistrement est grand et qu'une forte proportion des décès d'enfants de moins d'un an fait l'objet d'un enregistrement tardif, les statistiques des décès d'enfants de moins d'un an pour une année donnée peuvent être considérablement faussées.

Un autre facteur qui nuit à la comparabilité internationale est la pratique de certains pays ou zones qui consiste à ne pas inclure dans les statistiques des décès d'enfants de moins d'un an les enfants nés vivants mais décédés soit avant l'enregistrement de leur naissance, soit dans les 24 heures qui ont suivi la naissance, pratique qui conduit à sous-estimer le nombre total de décès d'enfants de moins d'un an. Quand pareil facteur a joué, cela a été signalé en note. Dans le tableau 16 en particulier, ce système peut limiter la comparabilité des données concernant les décès d'enfants de moins d'un an, de moins de 28 jours, de moins d'une semaine et de moins d'un jour.

Le manque d'uniformité des méthodes suivies pour calculer l'âge au moment du décès nuit également à la comparabilité des données. Ce facteur influe dans une certaine mesure sur les données relatives à la mortalité à tous les âges, mais il a des répercussions particulièrement marquées sur les statistiques des décès de moins d'un jour et de moins d'une semaine (mortalité néo-natale précoce) et de moins de 28 jours (mortalité néo-natale). Comme on l'a dit, l'âge d'un enfant de moins d'un an à son décès est calculé, selon la méthode recommandée, en évaluant la durée de vie en minutes, heures et jours, selon le cas. L'âge est ainsi exprimé en unités de temps révolues. Toutefois, dans certains pays ou zones, l'âge de ces enfants est ramené au jour le plus proche en retranchant la date de la naissance (jour, mois et année) de celle du décès (jour, mois et année). Il s'ensuit que de nombreux décès survenus dans les vingt-quatre heures qui suivent la naissance sont classés comme décès d'un jour. Dans ces conditions, les données concernant les décès de moins d'un jour sont entachées d'une erreur par défaut et celles qui se rapportent aux décès de 1 à 6 jours d'une erreur par excès.

La comparabilité des données relatives à la mortalité néo-natale (moins de 28 jours) est influencée par un facteur spécial : l'hétérogénéité de la classification par âge utilisée pour les enfants de moins d'un an. Dans un certain nombre de pays ou zones, on continue d'utiliser le mois civil au lieu du mois lunaire (4 semaines ou 28 jours).

Lorsque les données relatives aux décès de moins de 4 semaines ne sont pas exploitées sur la base de l'âge en jours révolus, il existe une nouvelle cause de non-comparabilité internationale. Les décès de moins d'un mois sont généralement ceux qui se produisent au cours d'un mois civil ; les taux calculés sur la base de ces données ne sont pas strictement comparables à ceux qui sont établis à partir des données concernant les décès survenus dans les 4 semaines ou 27 jours révolus qui suivent la naissance.

Les taux de mortalité infantile selon l'âge et le sexe appellent en outre toutes les réserves qui ont été formulées à propos des statistiques des naissances vivantes qui ont servi à leur calcul (voir à ce sujet les notes techniques relatives au tableau 9). Ces insuffisances ont également été examinées dans les notes techniques relatives au tableau 15.

Il convient de signaler aussi que les taux de mortalité infantile selon l'âge peuvent être gravement faussés par la pratique qui consiste à ne pas classer dans les naissances vivantes et ensuite dans les décès d'enfants de moins d'un an les enfants nés vivants mais décédés soit avant l'enregistrement de leur naissance, soit dans les 24 heures qui ont suivi la naissance, et par les problèmes que pose le calcul de l'âge de l'enfant au moment du décès. Ces facteurs, qui ont été décrits plus haut, peuvent fausser les statistiques concernant certains groupes d'âge plus que d'autres. Si le nombre des décès d'enfants de moins d'un an pour chaque groupe d'âge est sous-estimé ou surestimé, les taux correspondants pour chacun de ces groupes d'âge seront eux aussi sous-estimés ou surestimés. Les risques de sous-estimation sont plus grands pour les groupes les plus jeunes ; c'est pour le groupe d'âge le plus jeune de tous (moins d'un jour) que les données risquent de comporter les plus grosses erreurs.

Données publiées antérieurement : des statistiques des décès d'enfants de moins d'un an et des taux de mortalité infantile selon l'âge et le sexe ont déjà été présentées dans des éditions antérieures de l'Annuaire démographique. Pour plus de précisions concernant les années pour lesquelles ces données ont été publiées, se reporter à l'index historique.

16. Infant deaths and infant mortality rates by age and sex: latest available year, 2008 - 2017
Décès d'enfants de moins d'un an et taux de mortalité infantile selon l'âge et le sexe : dernière année disponible, 2008 - 2017

Continent, country or area, year, code[a] and age Continent, pays ou zone, année, code[a] et âge	Number - Nombre			Rate - Taux		
	Both sexes Les deux sexes	Male Masculin	Female Féminin	Both sexes Les deux sexes	Male Masculin	Female Féminin
AFRICA - AFRIQUE						
Cabo Verde						
2008 (C)						
Total..	316	...	...	24.9	...	...
Less than 7 days - Moins de 7 jours..........................	160	...	...	12.6	...	...
7 - 27 days - 7 - 27 jours	52	...	...	4.1	...	...
28 days - 11 months - 28 jours - 11 mois................	104	...	...	8.2	...	...
Egypt - Égypte						
2017 (C)						
Total..	38 685	...	...	15.1	...	...
1 - 6 days - 1 - 6 jours	7 454	...	...	2.9	...	...
7 - 27 days - 7 - 27 jours	10 325	...	...	4.0	...	...
7 - 13 days - 7 - 13 jours	5 165	...	...	2.0	...	...
14 - 20 days - 14 - 20 jours	3 222	...	...	1.3	...	...
21 - 27 days - 21 - 27 jours	1 938	...	...	0.8	...	...
28 days - 11 months - 28 jours - 11 mois................	20 906	...	...	8.2	...	...
28 days - less than 2 months - 28 jours - moins de 2 mois	5 334	...	...	2.1	...	...
2 months - 2 mois	3 644	...	...	1.4	...	...
3 months - 3 mois	2 580	...	...	1.0	...	...
4 months - 4 mois	2 153	...	...	0.8	...	...
5 months - 5 mois	1 698	...	...	0.7	...	...
6 months - 6 mois	1 424	...	...	0.6	...	...
7 months - 7 mois	1 138	...	...	0.4	...	...
8 months - 8 mois	965	...	...	0.4	...	...
9 months - 9 mois	767	...	...	0.3	...	...
10 months - 10 mois	671	...	...	0.3	...	...
11 months - 11 mois	532	...	...	0.2	...	...
Mauritius - Maurice[1]						
2017 (+C)						
Total..	164	98	66	12.3	14.4	10.0
Less than 1 day - Moins de 1 jour	20	11	9	♦1.5	♦1.6	♦1.4
1 - 6 days - 1 - 6 jours	70	47	23	5.2	6.9	♦3.5
7 - 27 days - 7 - 27 jours	30	16	14	2.2	♦2.3	♦2.1
7 - 13 days - 7 - 13 jours	16	7	9	♦1.2	♦1.0	♦1.4
14 - 20 days - 14 - 20 jours	12	7	5	♦0.9	♦1.0	♦0.8
21 - 27 days - 21 - 27 jours	2	2	-	♦0.1	♦0.3	-
28 days - 11 months - 28 jours - 11 mois................	44	24	20	3.3	♦3.5	♦3.0
28 days - less than 2 months - 28 jours - moins de 2 mois	17	11	6	♦1.3	♦1.6	♦0.9
2 months - 2 mois	9	5	4	♦0.7	♦0.7	♦0.6
3 months - 3 mois	5	4	1	♦0.4	♦0.6	♦0.2
4 months - 4 mois	3	1	2	♦0.2	♦0.1	♦0.3
5 months - 5 mois	1	-	1	♦0.1	-	♦0.1
6 months - 6 mois	4	1	3	♦0.3	♦0.1	♦0.5
7 months - 7 mois	1	1	-	♦0.1	♦0.1	-
8 months - 8 mois	2	1	1	♦0.1	♦0.1	♦0.2
9 months - 9 mois	1	-	1	♦0.1	-	♦0.2
10 months - 10 mois	-	-	-	-	-	-
11 months - 11 mois	1	-	1	♦0.1	-	♦0.2
Saint Helena ex. dep. - Sainte-Hélène sans dép.						
2014 (C)						
Total..	1	-	1	...	...	...
Less than 1 day - Moins de 1 jour	-	-	-	...	...	...
1 - 6 days - 1 - 6 jours	1	-	1	...	...	...
7 - 27 days - 7 - 27 jours	-	-	-	...	...	...
7 - 13 days - 7 - 13 jours	-	-	-	...	...	...
14 - 20 days - 14 - 20 jours	-	-	-	...	...	...
21 - 27 days - 21 - 27 jours	-	-	-	...	...	...
28 days - 11 months - 28 jours - 11 mois................	-	-	-	...	...	...
28 days - less than 2 months - 28 jours - moins de 2 mois	-	-	-	...	...	...
2 months - 2 mois	-	-	-	...	...	...
3 months - 3 mois	-	-	-	...	...	...
4 months - 4 mois	-	-	-	...	...	...
5 months - 5 mois	-	-	-	...	...	...
6 months - 6 mois	-	-	-	...	...	...
7 months - 7 mois	-	-	-	...	...	...
8 months - 8 mois	-	-	-	...	...	...
9 months - 9 mois	-	-	-	...	...	...
10 months - 10 mois	-	-	-	...	...	...
11 months - 11 mois	-	-	-	...	...	...

16. Infant deaths and infant mortality rates by age and sex: latest available year, 2008 - 2017
Décès d'enfants de moins d'un an et taux de mortalité infantile selon l'âge et le sexe : dernière année disponible, 2008 - 2017 (continued - suite)

Continent, country or area, year, code[a] and age / Continent, pays ou zone, année, code[a] et âge	Number - Nombre			Rate - Taux		
	Both sexes Les deux sexes	Male Masculin	Female Féminin	Both sexes Les deux sexes	Male Masculin	Female Féminin
AFRICA - AFRIQUE						
South Africa - Afrique du Sud						
2016 (U)						
Total..	20 649	10 963[2]	9 284[2]	...	...	...
Less than 1 day - Moins de 1 jour	2 363	1 265[2]	978[2]	...	...	...
1 - 6 days - 1 - 6 jours	4 109	2 266[2]	1 735[2]	...	...	...
7 - 27 days - 7 - 27 jours	2 709	1 401[2]	1 249[2]	...	...	...
7 - 13 days - 7 - 13 jours	1 315	666[2]	624[2]	...	...	...
14 - 20 days - 14 - 20 jours	769	406[2]	342[2]	...	...	...
21 - 27 days - 21 - 27 jours	625	329[2]	283[2]	...	...	...
28 days - 11 months - 28 jours - 11 mois............	11 468	6 031[2]	5 322[2]	...	...	...
28 days - less than 2 months - 28 jours - moins de 2 mois	2 403	1 269[2]	1 104[2]	...	...	...
2 months - 2 mois	1 701	887[2]	792[2]	...	...	...
3 months - 3 mois	1 512	746[2]	754[2]	...	...	...
4 months - 4 mois	1 107	594[2]	501[2]	...	...	...
5 months - 5 mois	875	476[2]	393[2]	...	...	...
6 months - 6 mois	821	438[2]	376[2]	...	...	...
7 months - 7 mois	732	398[2]	328[2]	...	...	...
8 months - 8 mois	650	343[2]	303[2]	...	...	...
9 months - 9 mois	615	323[2]	288[2]	...	...	...
10 months - 10 mois	546	279[2]	258[2]	...	...	...
11 months - 11 mois	506	278[2]	225[2]	...	...	...
AMERICA, NORTH - AMÉRIQUE DU NORD						
Aruba						
2017 (+C)						
Total..	6	4	2	...	...	...
Less than 1 day - Moins de 1 jour	3	1	2	...	...	...
1 - 6 days - 1 - 6 jours	1	1	-	...	...	...
7 - 27 days - 7 - 27 jours	-	-	-	...	...	...
7 - 13 days - 7 - 13 jours	-	-	-	...	...	...
14 - 20 days - 14 - 20 jours	-	-	-	...	...	...
21 - 27 days - 21 - 27 jours	-	-	-	...	...	...
28 days - 11 months - 28 jours - 11 mois............	2	2	-	...	...	...
28 days - less than 2 months - 28 jours - moins de 2 mois	-	-	-	...	...	...
2 months - 2 mois	-	-	-	...	...	...
3 months - 3 mois	2	2	-	...	...	...
4 months - 4 mois	-	-	-	...	...	...
5 months - 5 mois	-	-	-	...	...	...
6 months - 6 mois	-	-	-	...	...	...
7 months - 7 mois	-	-	-	...	...	...
8 months - 8 mois	-	-	-	...	...	...
9 months - 9 mois	-	-	-	...	...	...
10 months - 10 mois	-	-	-	...	...	...
11 months - 11 mois	-	-	-	...	...	...
Bahamas						
2012 (+C)						
Total..	57	26	31	...	...	...
Less than 1 day - Moins de 1 jour	-	-	-	...	...	...
1 - 6 days - 1 - 6 jours	18	10	8	...	...	...
7 - 27 days - 7 - 27 jours	19	8	11	...	...	...
7 - 13 days - 7 - 13 jours	16	6	10	...	...	...
14 - 20 days - 14 - 20 jours	2	1	1	...	...	...
21 - 27 days - 21 - 27 jours	1	1	-	...	...	...
28 days - 11 months - 28 jours - 11 mois............	20	8	12	...	...	...
28 days - less than 2 months - 28 jours - moins de 2 mois	9	5	4	...	...	...
2 months - 2 mois	3	1	2	...	...	...
3 months - 3 mois	2	1	1	...	...	...
4 months - 4 mois	3	-	3	...	...	...
5 months - 5 mois	-	-	-	...	...	...
6 months - 6 mois	-	-	-	...	...	...
7 months - 7 mois	1	-	1	...	...	...
8 months - 8 mois	1	1	-	...	...	...
9 months - 9 mois	1	-	1	...	...	...

16. Infant deaths and infant mortality rates by age and sex: latest available year, 2008 - 2017
Décès d'enfants de moins d'un an et taux de mortalité infantile selon l'âge et le sexe : dernière année disponible, 2008 - 2017 (continued - suite)

Continent, country or area, year, code[a] and age Continent, pays ou zone, année, code[a] et âge	Number - Nombre			Rate - Taux		
	Both sexes Les deux sexes	Male Masculin	Female Féminin	Both sexes Les deux sexes	Male Masculin	Female Féminin
AMERICA, NORTH - AMÉRIQUE DU NORD						
Bahamas						
2012 (+C)						
10 months - 10 mois	-	-	-	...	...	...
11 months - 11 mois	-	-	-	...	...	...
Belize						
2016 (U)						
Total	103	61	42	...	...	...
Less than 1 day - Moins de 1 jour	29	14	15	...	...	...
1 - 6 days - 1 - 6 jours	36	26	10	...	...	...
7 - 27 days - 7 - 27 jours	15	8	7	...	...	...
7 - 13 days - 7 - 13 jours	2	1	1	...	...	...
14 - 20 days - 14 - 20 jours	5	2	3	...	...	...
21 - 27 days - 21 - 27 jours	8	5	3	...	...	...
28 days - 11 months - 28 jours - 11 mois	23	13	10	...	...	...
28 days - less than 2 months - 28 jours - moins de 2 mois	1	-	1	...	...	...
2 months - 2 mois	4	2	2	...	...	...
3 months - 3 mois	7	4	3	...	...	...
4 months - 4 mois	3	3	-	...	...	...
5 months - 5 mois	2	1	1	...	...	...
6 months - 6 mois	2	1	1	...	...	...
7 months - 7 mois	1	1	-	...	...	...
8 months - 8 mois	-	-	-	...	...	...
9 months - 9 mois	3	1	2	...	...	...
10 months - 10 mois	-	-	-	...	...	...
11 months - 11 mois	-	-	-	...	...	...
Bermuda - Bermudes						
2016 (C)						
Total	2	2	-	...	...	...
Less than 1 day - Moins de 1 jour	2	2	-	...	...	...
1 - 6 days - 1 - 6 jours	-	-	-	...	...	...
7 - 27 days - 7 - 27 jours	-	-	-	...	...	...
7 - 13 days - 7 - 13 jours	-	-	-	...	...	...
14 - 20 days - 14 - 20 jours	-	-	-	...	...	...
21 - 27 days - 21 - 27 jours	-	-	-	...	...	...
28 days - 11 months - 28 jours - 11 mois	-	-	-	...	...	...
28 days - less than 2 months - 28 jours - moins de 2 mois	-	-	-	...	...	...
2 months - 2 mois	-	-	-	...	...	...
3 months - 3 mois	-	-	-	...	...	...
4 months - 4 mois	-	-	-	...	...	...
5 months - 5 mois	-	-	-	...	...	...
6 months - 6 mois	-	-	-	...	...	...
7 months - 7 mois	-	-	-	...	...	...
8 months - 8 mois	-	-	-	...	...	...
9 months - 9 mois	-	-	-	...	...	...
10 months - 10 mois	-	-	-	...	...	...
11 months - 11 mois	-	-	-	...	...	...
Canada[3]						
2015 (C)						
Total	1 737	937	800	4.5	4.8	4.3
Less than 1 day - Moins de 1 jour	950	499	451	2.5	2.5	2.4
1 - 6 days - 1 - 6 jours	203	119	84	0.5	0.6	0.5
7 - 27 days - 7 - 27 jours	200	103	97	0.5	0.5	0.5
7 - 13 days - 7 - 13 jours	94	55	39	0.2	0.3	0.2
14 - 20 days - 14 - 20 jours	55	28	27	0.1	♦0.1	♦0.1
21 - 27 days - 21 - 27 jours	51	20	31	0.1	♦0.1	0.2
28 days - 11 months - 28 jours - 11 mois	454	259	195	1.2	1.3	1.0
28 days - less than 2 months - 28 jours - moins de 2 mois	185	109	76	0.5	0.6	0.4
2 months - 2 mois	70	43	27	0.2	0.2	♦0.1
3 months - 3 mois	59	37	22	0.2	0.2	♦0.1
4 months - 4 mois	27	15	12	♦0.1	♦0.1	♦0.1
5 months - 5 mois	33	16	17	0.1	♦0.1	♦0.1
6 months - 6 mois	25	10	15	♦0.1	♦0.1	♦0.1
7 months - 7 mois	15	8	7	-	-	-
8 months - 8 mois	17	8	9	-	-	-
9 months - 9 mois	8	6	2	-	-	-
10 months - 10 mois	8	5	3	-	-	-
11 months - 11 mois	7	2	5	-	-	-

16. Infant deaths and infant mortality rates by age and sex: latest available year, 2008 - 2017
Décès d'enfants de moins d'un an et taux de mortalité infantile selon l'âge et le sexe : dernière année disponible, 2008 - 2017 (continued - suite)

Continent, country or area, year, code[a] and age / Continent, pays ou zone, année, code[a] et âge	Number - Nombre			Rate - Taux		
	Both sexes Les deux sexes	Male Masculin	Female Féminin	Both sexes Les deux sexes	Male Masculin	Female Féminin
AMERICA, NORTH - AMÉRIQUE DU NORD						
Costa Rica						
2017* (C)						
Total	548	286	262	8.0	8.1	7.8
Less than 1 day - Moins de 1 jour	151	71	80	2.2	2.0	2.4
1 - 6 days - 1 - 6 jours	164	93	71	2.4	2.6	2.1
7 - 27 days - 7 - 27 jours	108	59	49	1.6	1.7	1.5
7 - 13 days - 7 - 13 jours	53	32	21	0.8	0.9	♦0.6
14 - 20 days - 14 - 20 jours	35	15	20	0.5	♦0.4	♦0.6
21 - 27 days - 21 - 27 jours	20	12	8	♦0.3	♦0.3	♦0.2
28 days - 11 months - 28 jours - 11 mois	125	63	62	1.8	1.8	1.9
28 days - less than 2 months - 28 jours - moins de 2 mois	44	24	20	0.6	♦0.7	♦0.6
2 months - 2 mois	25	14	11	♦0.4	♦0.4	♦0.3
3 months - 3 mois	10	4	6	♦0.1	♦0.1	♦0.2
4 months - 4 mois	6	1	5	♦0.1	-	♦0.1
5 months - 5 mois	9	4	5	♦0.1	♦0.1	♦0.1
6 months - 6 mois	7	4	3	♦0.1	♦0.1	♦0.1
7 months - 7 mois	6	2	4	♦0.1	♦0.1	♦0.1
8 months - 8 mois	3	2	1	-	♦0.1	-
9 months - 9 mois	8	5	3	♦0.1	♦0.1	♦0.1
10 months - 10 mois	3	2	1	-	♦0.1	-
11 months - 11 mois	4	1	3	♦0.1	-	♦0.1
Cuba						
2016 (C)						
Total	497	277	220	4.3	4.5	3.9
Less than 1 day - Moins de 1 jour	57	31	26	0.5	0.5	♦0.5
1 - 6 days - 1 - 6 jours	129	69	60	1.1	1.1	1.1
7 - 27 days - 7 - 27 jours	92	52	40	0.8	0.9	0.7
7 - 13 days - 7 - 13 jours	35	26	9	0.3	♦0.4	♦0.2
14 - 20 days - 14 - 20 jours	29	13	16	♦0.2	♦0.2	♦0.3
21 - 27 days - 21 - 27 jours	28	13	15	♦0.2	♦0.2	♦0.3
28 days - 11 months - 28 jours - 11 mois	219	125	94	1.9	2.1	1.7
28 days - less than 2 months - 28 jours - moins de 2 mois	55	29	26	0.5	♦0.5	♦0.5
2 months - 2 mois	41	24	17	0.4	♦0.4	♦0.3
3 months - 3 mois	31	18	13	0.3	♦0.3	♦0.2
4 months - 4 mois	19	10	9	♦0.2	♦0.2	♦0.2
5 months - 5 mois	16	8	8	♦0.1	♦0.1	♦0.1
6 months - 6 mois	14	8	6	♦0.1	♦0.1	♦0.1
7 months - 7 mois	6	6	-	♦0.1	♦0.1	-
8 months - 8 mois	10	7	3	♦0.1	♦0.1	♦0.1
9 months - 9 mois	13	7	6	♦0.1	♦0.1	♦0.1
10 months - 10 mois	6	4	2	♦0.1	♦0.1	-
11 months - 11 mois	8	4	4	♦0.1	♦0.1	♦0.1
Curaçao						
2016 (C)						
Total	20	11	9	...	...	...
Less than 1 day - Moins de 1 jour	7	3	4	...	...	...
1 - 6 days - 1 - 6 jours	3	1	2	...	...	...
7 - 27 days - 7 - 27 jours	7	5	2	...	...	...
7 - 13 days - 7 - 13 jours	6	4	2	...	...	...
14 - 20 days - 14 - 20 jours	1	1	-	...	...	...
21 - 27 days - 21 - 27 jours	-	-	-	...	...	...
28 days - 11 months - 28 jours - 11 mois	39	20	19	...	...	...
28 days - less than 2 months - 28 jours - moins de 2 mois	1	-	1	...	...	...
2 months - 2 mois	18	9	9	...	...	...
3 months - 3 mois	20	11	9	...	...	...
4 months - 4 mois	-	-	-	...	...	...
5 months - 5 mois	-	-	-	...	...	...
6 months - 6 mois	-	-	-	...	...	...
7 months - 7 mois	-	-	-	...	...	...
8 months - 8 mois	-	-	-	...	...	...
9 months - 9 mois	-	-	-	...	...	...
10 months - 10 mois	-	-	-	...	...	...
11 months - 11 mois	-	-	-	...	...	...
Dominican Republic - République dominicaine						
2016 (U)						
Total	800	443	357	...	...	...
Less than 1 day - Moins de 1 jour	143	76	67	...	...	...
1 - 6 days - 1 - 6 jours	221	127	94	...	...	...

16. Infant deaths and infant mortality rates by age and sex: latest available year, 2008 - 2017
Décès d'enfants de moins d'un an et taux de mortalité infantile selon l'âge et le sexe : dernière année disponible, 2008 - 2017 (continued - suite)

Continent, country or area, year, code[a] and age / Continent, pays ou zone, année, code[a] et âge	Number - Nombre			Rate - Taux		
	Both sexes Les deux sexes	Male Masculin	Female Féminin	Both sexes Les deux sexes	Male Masculin	Female Féminin
AMERICA, NORTH - AMÉRIQUE DU NORD						
Dominican Republic - République dominicaine						
2016 (U)						
7 - 27 days - 7 - 27 jours	140	77	63	...	...	...
7 - 13 days - 7 - 13 jours	85	44	41	...	...	...
14 - 20 days - 14 - 20 jours	37	22	15	...	...	...
21 - 27 days - 21 - 27 jours	18	11	7	...	...	...
28 days - 11 months - 28 jours - 11 mois	294	162	132	...	...	...
28 days - less than 2 months - 28 jours - moins de 2 mois	81	44	37	...	...	...
2 months - 2 mois	42	24	18	...	...	...
3 months - 3 mois	30	17	13	...	...	...
4 months - 4 mois	26	13	13	...	...	...
5 months - 5 mois	27	16	11	...	...	...
6 months - 6 mois	23	13	10	...	...	...
7 months - 7 mois	21	12	9	...	...	...
8 months - 8 mois	13	6	7	...	...	...
9 months - 9 mois	12	5	7	...	...	...
10 months - 10 mois	11	6	5	...	...	...
11 months - 11 mois	8	6	2	...	...	...
Unknown - Inconnu	2	1	1	...	...	...
El Salvador[4]						
2014 (C)						
Total	876	491	385	8.0	8.8	7.3
Less than 1 day - Moins de 1 jour	158	90	68	1.5	1.6	1.3
1 - 6 days - 1 - 6 jours	163	91	72	1.5	1.6	1.4
7 - 27 days - 7 - 27 jours	141	78	63	1.3	1.4	1.2
7 - 13 days - 7 - 13 jours	65	32	33	0.6	0.6	0.6
14 - 20 days - 14 - 20 jours	42	24	18	0.4	♦0.4	♦0.3
21 - 27 days - 21 - 27 jours	34	22	12	0.3	♦0.4	♦0.2
28 days - 11 months - 28 jours - 11 mois	414	232	182	3.8	4.1	3.4
28 days - less than 2 months - 28 jours - moins de 2 mois	97	49	48	0.9	0.9	0.9
2 months - 2 mois	56	33	23	0.5	0.6	♦0.4
3 months - 3 mois	44	28	16	0.4	♦0.5	♦0.3
4 months - 4 mois	35	23	12	0.3	♦0.4	♦0.2
5 months - 5 mois	26	16	10	♦0.2	♦0.3	♦0.2
6 months - 6 mois	38	27	11	0.3	♦0.5	♦0.2
7 months - 7 mois	28	13	15	♦0.3	♦0.2	♦0.3
8 months - 8 mois	20	10	10	♦0.2	♦0.2	♦0.2
9 months - 9 mois	21	9	12	♦0.2	♦0.2	♦0.2
10 months - 10 mois	21	9	12	♦0.2	♦0.2	♦0.2
11 months - 11 mois	28	15	13	♦0.3	♦0.3	♦0.2
Grenada - Grenade						
2014 (+C)						
Total	33	21	12	...	...	...
Less than 1 day - Moins de 1 jour	18	11	7	...	...	...
1 - 6 days - 1 - 6 jours	6	4	2	...	...	...
7 - 27 days - 7 - 27 jours	3	1	2	...	...	...
28 days - 11 months - 28 jours - 11 mois	6	5	1	...	...	...
28 days - 3 months - 28 jours - 3 mois	2	1	1	...	...	...
4 - 6 months - 4 - 6 mois	1	1	-	...	...	...
7 - 11 months - 7 - 11 mois	3	3	-	...	...	...
Guatemala						
2016 (C)						
Total	8 366	4 750	3 616	21.4	23.9	18.8
Less than 1 day - Moins de 1 jour	421	221	200	1.1	1.1	1.0
1 - 6 days - 1 - 6 jours	2 217	1 304	913	5.7	6.6	4.8
7 - 27 days - 7 - 27 jours	1 486	847	639	3.8	4.3	3.3
7 - 13 days - 7 - 13 jours	768	439	329	2.0	2.2	1.7
14 - 27 days - 14 - 27 jours	718	408	310	1.8	2.1	1.6
28 days - 11 months - 28 jours - 11 mois	4 242	2 378	1 864	10.9	12.0	9.7
28 days - less than 2 months - 28 jours - moins de 2 mois	1 665	935	730	4.3	4.7	3.8
2 - 11 months - 2 - 11 mois	2 577	1 443	1 134	6.6	7.3	5.9
Mexico - Mexique[5]						
2016 (+C)						
Total	24 722	13 811[2]	10 765[2]	10.8	...	...
Less than 1 day - Moins de 1 jour	4 577	2 485[2]	2 026[2]	2.0	...	...
1 - 6 days - 1 - 6 jours	6 194	3 595[2]	2 550[2]	2.7	...	...
7 - 27 days - 7 - 27 jours	4 601	2 600[2]	1 985[2]	2.0	...	...
7 - 13 days - 7 - 13 jours	2 493	1 418[2]	1 066[2]	1.1	...	...

16. Infant deaths and infant mortality rates by age and sex: latest available year, 2008 - 2017
Décès d'enfants de moins d'un an et taux de mortalité infantile selon l'âge et le sexe : dernière année disponible, 2008 - 2017 (continued - suite)

Continent, country or area, year, code[a] and age Continent, pays ou zone, année, code[a] et âge	Number - Nombre			Rate - Taux		
	Both sexes Les deux sexes	Male Masculin	Female Féminin	Both sexes Les deux sexes	Male Masculin	Female Féminin
AMERICA, NORTH - AMÉRIQUE DU NORD						
Mexico - Mexique[5]						
2016 (+C)						
14 - 20 days - 14 - 20 jours	1 241	710[2]	528[2]	0.5	...	...
21 - 27 days - 21 - 27 jours	867	472[2]	391[2]	0.4	...	...
28 days - 11 months - 28 jours - 11 mois	9 345	5 129[2]	4 202[2]	4.1	...	...
28 days - less than 2 months - 28 jours - moins de 2 mois	2 726	1 508[2]	1 211[2]	1.2	...	...
2 months - 2 mois	1 602	908[2]	692[2]	0.7	...	...
3 months - 3 mois	1 119	627[2]	489[2]	0.5	...	...
4 months - 4 mois	860	470[2]	389[2]	0.4	...	...
5 months - 5 mois	691	379[2]	312[2]	0.3	...	...
6 months - 6 mois	546	275[2]	271[2]	0.2	...	...
7 months - 7 mois	427	229[2]	198[2]	0.2	...	...
8 months - 8 mois	415	219[2]	195[2]	0.2	...	...
9 months - 9 mois	350	180[2]	170[2]	0.2	...	...
10 months - 10 mois	320	184[2]	136[2]	0.1	...	...
11 months - 11 mois	289	150[2]	139[2]	0.1	...	...
Unknown - Inconnu	5	2[2]	2[2]	-	...	...
Montserrat						
2016 (C)						
Total	-	-	-	...	...	...
Less than 1 day - Moins de 1 jour	-	-	-	...	...	...
1 - 6 days - 1 - 6 jours	-	-	-	...	...	...
7 - 27 days - 7 - 27 jours	-	-	-	...	...	...
28 days - 11 months - 28 jours - 11 mois	-	-	-	...	...	...
Nicaragua						
2008 (+U)						
Total	1 932	1 123	809	...	...	...
Less than 1 day - Moins de 1 jour	386	219	167	...	...	...
1 - 6 days - 1 - 6 jours	664	418	246	...	...	...
7 - 27 days - 7 - 27 jours	277	151	126	...	...	...
7 - 13 days - 7 - 13 jours	156	89	67	...	...	...
14 - 20 days - 14 - 20 jours	74	41	33	...	...	...
21 - 27 days - 21 - 27 jours	47	21	26	...	...	...
28 days - 11 months - 28 jours - 11 mois	591	326	265	...	...	...
28 days - less than 2 months - 28 jours - moins de 2 mois	169	86	83	...	...	...
2 months - 2 mois	116	74	42	...	...	...
3 months - 3 mois	66	38	28	...	...	...
4 months - 4 mois	49	29	20	...	...	...
5 months - 5 mois	45	22	23	...	...	...
6 months - 6 mois	27	13	14	...	...	...
7 months - 7 mois	36	18	18	...	...	...
8 months - 8 mois	27	17	10	...	...	...
9 months - 9 mois	18	8	10	...	...	...
10 months - 10 mois	21	9	12	...	...	...
11 months - 11 mois	17	12	5	...	...	...
Panama						
2016* (C)						
Total	1 046	567	479	13.9	14.5	13.2
Less than 1 day - Moins de 1 jour	131	66	65	1.7	1.7	1.8
1 - 6 days - 1 - 6 jours	261	145	116	3.5	3.7	3.2
7 - 27 days - 7 - 27 jours	189	114	75	2.5	2.9	2.1
7 - 13 days - 7 - 13 jours	87	56	31	1.2	1.4	0.9
14 - 20 days - 14 - 20 jours	53	32	21	0.7	0.8	+0.6
21 - 27 days - 21 - 27 jours	49	26	23	0.7	+0.7	+0.6
28 days - 11 months - 28 jours - 11 mois	465	242	223	6.2	6.2	6.2
28 days - less than 2 months - 28 jours - moins de 2 mois	133	79	54	1.8	2.0	1.5
2 months - 2 mois	74	45	29	1.0	1.2	+0.8
3 months - 3 mois	46	23	23	0.6	+0.6	+0.6
4 months - 4 mois	40	22	18	0.5	+0.6	+0.5
5 months - 5 mois	27	9	18	+0.4	+0.2	+0.5
6 months - 6 mois	28	13	15	+0.4	+0.3	+0.4
7 months - 7 mois	17	6	11	+0.2	+0.2	+0.3
8 months - 8 mois	27	9	18	+0.4	+0.2	+0.5
9 months - 9 mois	22	9	13	+0.3	+0.2	+0.4
10 months - 10 mois	23	13	10	+0.3	+0.3	+0.3
11 months - 11 mois	28	14	14	+0.4	+0.4	+0.4

16. Infant deaths and infant mortality rates by age and sex: latest available year, 2008 - 2017
Décès d'enfants de moins d'un an et taux de mortalité infantile selon l'âge et le sexe : dernière année disponible, 2008 - 2017 (continued - suite)

Continent, country or area, year, code[a] and age / Continent, pays ou zone, année, code[a] et âge	Number - Nombre			Rate - Taux		
	Both sexes Les deux sexes	Male Masculin	Female Féminin	Both sexes Les deux sexes	Male Masculin	Female Féminin
AMERICA, NORTH - AMÉRIQUE DU NORD						
Puerto Rico - Porto Rico						
2017 (C)						
Total	172	101	71	7.1	8.1	6.0
Less than 1 day - Moins de 1 jour	29	13	16	♦1.2	♦1.0	♦1.4
1 - 6 days - 1 - 6 jours	54	34	20	2.2	2.7	♦1.7
7 - 27 days - 7 - 27 jours	38	20	18	1.6	♦1.6	♦1.5
7 - 13 days - 7 - 13 jours	23	10	13	♦0.9	♦0.8	♦1.1
14 - 20 days - 14 - 20 jours	7	4	3	♦0.3	♦0.3	♦0.3
21 - 27 days - 21 - 27 jours	8	6	2	♦0.3	♦0.5	♦0.2
28 days - 11 months - 28 jours - 11 mois	51	34	17	2.1	2.7	♦1.4
28 days - less than 2 months - 28 jours - moins de 2 mois	13	9	4	♦0.5	♦0.7	♦0.3
2 months - 2 mois	9	7	2	♦0.4	♦0.6	♦0.2
3 months - 3 mois	6	4	2	♦0.2	♦0.3	♦0.2
4 months - 4 mois	7	2	5	♦0.3	♦0.2	♦0.4
5 months - 5 mois	6	4	2	♦0.2	♦0.3	♦0.2
6 months - 6 mois	2	2	-	♦0.1	♦0.2	-
7 months - 7 mois	2	2	-	♦0.1	♦0.2	-
8 months - 8 mois	2	1	1	♦0.1	♦0.1	♦0.1
9 months - 9 mois	1	1	-	-	♦0.1	-
10 months - 10 mois	3	2	1	♦0.1	♦0.2	♦0.1
11 months - 11 mois	-	-	-	-	-	-
Saint Vincent and the Grenadines - Saint-Vincent-et-les Grenadines						
2014 (C)						
Total	29	19	10	...	...	...
Less than 1 day - Moins de 1 jour	3	3	-	...	...	...
1 - 6 days - 1 - 6 jours	8	6	2	...	...	...
7 - 27 days - 7 - 27 jours	9	4	5	...	...	...
7 - 13 days - 7 - 13 jours	6	4	2	...	...	...
14 - 20 days - 14 - 20 jours	3	-	3	...	...	...
21 - 27 days - 21 - 27 jours	-	-	-	...	...	...
28 days - 11 months - 28 jours - 11 mois	9	6	3	...	...	...
28 days - less than 2 months - 28 jours - moins de 2 mois	4	2	2	...	...	...
2 months - 2 mois	1	-	1	...	...	...
3 months - 3 mois	1	1	-	...	...	...
4 months - 4 mois	2	2	-	...	...	...
5 months - 5 mois	-	-	-	...	...	...
6 months - 6 mois	-	-	-	...	...	...
7 months - 7 mois	1	1	-	...	...	...
8 months - 8 mois	-	-	-	...	...	...
9 months - 9 mois	-	-	-	...	...	...
10 months - 10 mois	-	-	-	...	...	...
11 months - 11 mois	-	-	-	...	...	...
Trinidad and Tobago - Trinité-et-Tobago						
2012* (C)						
Total	213	103	110	11.4	10.9	11.9
Less than 1 day - Moins de 1 jour	43	16	27	2.3	♦1.7	♦2.9
1 - 6 days - 1 - 6 jours	60	29	31	3.2	♦3.1	3.3
7 - 27 days - 7 - 27 jours	37	19	18	2.0	♦2.0	♦1.9
7 - 13 days - 7 - 13 jours	18	10	8	♦1.0	♦1.1	♦0.9
14 - 20 days - 14 - 20 jours	13	7	6	♦0.7	♦0.7	♦0.6
21 - 27 days - 21 - 27 jours	6	2	4	♦0.3	♦0.2	♦0.4
28 days - 11 months - 28 jours - 11 mois	73	39	34	3.9	4.1	3.7
28 days - less than 2 months - 28 jours - moins de 2 mois	36	16	20	1.9	♦1.7	♦2.2
2 - 11 months - 2 - 11 mois	37	23	14	2.0	♦2.4	♦1.5
United States of America - États-Unis d'Amérique						
2015 (C)						
Total	23 455	13 008	10 447	5.9	6.4	5.4
Less than 1 day - Moins de 1 jour	9 479	5 226	4 253	2.4	2.6	2.2
1 - 6 days - 1 - 6 jours	3 088	1 733	1 355	0.8	0.9	0.7
7 - 27 days - 7 - 27 jours	3 085	1 632	1 453	0.8	0.8	0.7
7 - 13 days - 7 - 13 jours	1 442	765	677	0.4	0.4	0.3
14 - 20 days - 14 - 20 jours	950	500	450	0.2	0.2	0.2
21 - 27 days - 21 - 27 jours	693	367	326	0.2	0.2	0.2
28 days - 11 months - 28 jours - 11 mois	7 803	4 417	3 386	2.0	2.2	1.7
28 days - less than 2 months - 28 jours - moins de 2 mois	2 050	1 105	945	0.5	0.5	0.5
2 months - 2 mois	1 462	838	624	0.4	0.4	0.3
3 months - 3 mois	1 144	681	463	0.3	0.3	0.2
4 months - 4 mois	826	489	337	0.2	0.2	0.2

Continent, country or area, year, code[a] and age Continent, pays ou zone, année, code[a] et âge	Number - Nombre			Rate - Taux		
	Both sexes Les deux sexes	Male Masculin	Female Féminin	Both sexes Les deux sexes	Male Masculin	Female Féminin
AMERICA, NORTH - AMÉRIQUE DU NORD						
United States of America - États-Unis d'Amérique						
2015 (C)						
5 months - 5 mois	623	371	252	0.2	0.2	0.1
6 months - 6 mois	460	252	208	0.1	0.1	0.1
7 months - 7 mois	344	210	134	0.1	0.1	0.1
8 months - 8 mois	286	159	127	0.1	0.1	0.1
9 months - 9 mois	239	123	116	0.1	0.1	0.1
10 months - 10 mois	184	98	86	-	-	-
11 months - 11 mois	185	91	94	-	-	-
AMERICA, SOUTH - AMÉRIQUE DU SUD						
Brazil - Brésil						
2016 (+C)						
Total	30 541	16 971[2]	13 494[2]	10.5	11.4	9.5
Less than 1 day - Moins de 1 jour	6 563	...	...	2.3	...	...
Less than 7 days - Moins de 7 jours[2]	...	8 684	6 679	...	5.8	4.7
1 - 6 days - 1 - 6 jours	8 867	...	...	3.1	...	...
7 - 27 days - 7 - 27 jours	5 276	2 933[2]	2 339[2]	1.8	2.0	1.7
7 - 13 days - 7 - 13 jours	2 786	...	...	1.0	...	...
14 - 20 days - 14 - 20 jours	1 510	...	...	0.5	...	...
21 - 27 days - 21 - 27 jours	980	...	...	0.3	...	...
28 days - 11 months - 28 jours - 11 mois	9 835	5 354	4 476	3.4	3.6	3.2
28 days - less than 2 months - 28 jours - moins de 2 mois	3 019	1 663[2]	1 356[2]	1.0	1.1	1.0
2 months - 2 mois	1 656	...	...	0.6	...	...
2 - 11 months - 2 - 11 mois[2]	...	3 691	3 120	...	2.5	2.2
3 months - 3 mois	1 095	...	...	0.4	...	...
4 months - 4 mois	847	...	...	0.3	...	...
5 months - 5 mois	717	...	...	0.2	...	...
6 months - 6 mois	598	...	...	0.2	...	...
7 months - 7 mois	479	...	...	0.2	...	...
8 months - 8 mois	463	...	...	0.2	...	...
9 months - 9 mois	350	...	...	0.1	...	...
10 months - 10 mois	320	...	...	0.1	...	...
11 months - 11 mois	291	...	...	0.1	...	...
Chile - Chili						
2015 (C)						
Total	1 683	943[6]	721[6]	6.9	7.6	6.0
Less than 1 day - Moins de 1 jour	662	385[6]	262[6]	2.7	3.1	2.2
1 - 6 days - 1 - 6 jours	323	186[6]	134[6]	1.3	1.5	1.1
7 - 27 days - 7 - 27 jours	265	141[6]	123[6]	1.1	1.1	1.0
7 - 13 days - 7 - 13 jours	132	69[6]	62[6]	0.5	0.6	0.5
14 - 20 days - 14 - 20 jours	75	40[6]	35[6]	0.3	0.3	0.3
21 - 27 days - 21 - 27 jours	58	32[6]	26[6]	0.2	0.3	♦0.2
28 days - 11 months - 28 jours - 11 mois	433	231[6]	202[6]	1.8	1.9	1.7
28 days - less than 2 months - 28 jours - moins de 2 mois	141	81[6]	60[6]	0.6	0.6	0.5
2 months - 2 mois	60	31[6]	29[6]	0.2	0.2	♦0.2
3 months - 3 mois	51	26[6]	25[6]	0.2	♦0.2	♦0.2
4 months - 4 mois	45	29[6]	16[6]	0.2	♦0.2	♦0.1
5 months - 5 mois	25	13[6]	12[6]	♦0.1	♦0.1	♦0.1
6 months - 6 mois	29	14[6]	15[6]	♦0.1	♦0.1	♦0.1
7 months - 7 mois	25	9[6]	16[6]	♦0.1	♦0.1	♦0.1
8 months - 8 mois	21	8[6]	13[6]	♦0.1	♦0.1	♦0.1
9 months - 9 mois	15	9[6]	6[6]	♦0.1	♦0.1	♦0.1
10 months - 10 mois	8	4[6]	4[6]	-	-	-
11 months - 11 mois	13	7[6]	6[6]	♦0.1	♦0.1	♦0.1
Colombia - Colombie						
2016 (U)						
Total	7 220	4 074[6]	3 144[6]	...	...	...
Less than 1 day - Moins de 1 jour	1 418	787[6]	631[6]	...	...	...
1 - 6 days - 1 - 6 jours	1 655	971[6]	682[6]	...	...	...
7 - 27 days - 7 - 27 jours	1 439	817[6]	622[6]	...	...	...
7 - 13 days - 7 - 13 jours	791	455[6]	336[6]	...	...	...
14 - 20 days - 14 - 20 jours	397	219[6]	178[6]	...	...	...
21 - 27 days - 21 - 27 jours	251	143[6]	108[6]	...	...	...

16. Infant deaths and infant mortality rates by age and sex: latest available year, 2008 - 2017

Décès d'enfants de moins d'un an et taux de mortalité infantile selon l'âge et le sexe : dernière année disponible, 2008 - 2017 (continued - suite)

Continent, country or area, year, code[a] and age — Continent, pays ou zone, année, code[a] et âge	Number - Nombre			Rate - Taux		
	Both sexes Les deux sexes	Male Masculin	Female Féminin	Both sexes Les deux sexes	Male Masculin	Female Féminin
AMERICA, SOUTH - AMÉRIQUE DU SUD						
Colombia - Colombie						
2016 (U)						
28 days - 11 months - 28 jours - 11 mois..............................	2 707	1 498[6]	1 209[6]	...	...	...
28 days - less than 2 months - 28 jours - moins de 2 mois	665	371[6]	294[6]	...	...	...
2 months - 2 mois...	455	262[6]	193[6]	...	...	...
3 months - 3 mois...	307	169[6]	138[6]	...	...	...
4 months - 4 mois...	270	143[6]	127[6]	...	...	...
5 months - 5 mois...	211	114[6]	97[6]	...	...	...
6 months - 6 mois...	179	89[6]	90[6]	...	...	...
7 months - 7 mois...	153	94[6]	59[6]	...	...	...
8 months - 8 mois...	133	77[6]	56[6]	...	...	...
9 months - 9 mois...	106	57[6]	49[6]	...	...	...
10 months - 10 mois...	116	60[6]	56[6]	...	...	...
11 months - 11 mois...	112	62[6]	50[6]	...	...	...
Unknown - Inconnu	1	1[6]	_[6]	...	...	...
Ecuador - Équateur[7]						
2016 (U)						
Total..	3 042	1 677	1 365	...	...	...
Less than 1 day - Moins de 1 jour	403	205	198	...	...	...
1 - 6 days - 1 - 6 jours	778	464	314	...	...	...
7 - 27 days - 7 - 27 jours	556	308	248	...	...	...
7 - 13 days - 7 - 13 jours	269	148	121	...	...	...
14 - 20 days - 14 - 20 jours	163	100	63	...	...	...
21 - 27 days - 21 - 27 jours	124	60	64	...	...	...
28 days - 11 months - 28 jours - 11 mois..............................	1 305	700	605	...	...	...
28 days - less than 2 months - 28 jours - moins de 2 mois	422	237	185	...	...	...
2 months - 2 mois...	214	118	96	...	...	...
3 months - 3 mois...	123	67	56	...	...	...
4 months - 4 mois...	105	52	53	...	...	...
5 months - 5 mois...	113	56	57	...	...	...
6 months - 6 mois...	70	35	35	...	...	...
7 months - 7 mois...	53	33	20	...	...	...
8 months - 8 mois...	50	23	27	...	...	...
9 months - 9 mois...	70	38	32	...	...	...
10 months - 10 mois...	48	24	24	...	...	...
11 months - 11 mois...	37	17	20	...	...	...
Peru - Pérou[8]						
2016* (+U)						
Total..	3 616	2 048	1 568	...	...	...
Less than 1 day - Moins de 1 jour	592	335	257	...	...	...
1 - 6 days - 1 - 6 jours	886	526	360	...	...	...
7 - 27 days - 7 - 27 jours	553	303	250	...	...	...
7 - 13 days - 7 - 13 jours	286	157	129	...	...	...
14 - 20 days - 14 - 20 jours	145	80	65	...	...	...
21 - 27 days - 21 - 27 jours	122	66	56	...	...	...
28 days - 11 months - 28 jours - 11 mois..............................	1 583	884	699	...	...	...
28 days - less than 2 months - 28 jours - moins de 2 mois	371	203	168	...	...	...
2 months - 2 mois...	295	154	141	...	...	...
3 months - 3 mois...	208	124	84	...	...	...
4 months - 4 mois...	128	66	62	...	...	...
5 months - 5 mois...	114	69	45	...	...	...
6 months - 6 mois...	92	55	37	...	...	...
7 months - 7 mois...	75	41	34	...	...	...
8 months - 8 mois...	81	42	39	...	...	...
9 months - 9 mois...	96	58	38	...	...	...
10 months - 10 mois...	62	33	29	...	...	...
11 months - 11 mois...	61	39	22	...	...	...
Unknown - Inconnu	2	-	2	...	...	...
Uruguay						
2016 (C)						
Total..	376	219[2]	156[2]	8.0	9.0	6.8
Less than 7 days - Moins de 7 jours.....................................	184	112[2]	71[2]	3.9	4.6	3.1
7 - 27 days - 7 - 27 jours	68	40[2]	28[2]	1.4	1.6	♦1.2
28 days - less than 2 months - 28 jours - moins de 2 mois	124	67[2]	57[2]	2.6	2.8	2.5

16. Infant deaths and infant mortality rates by age and sex: latest available year, 2008 - 2017
Décès d'enfants de moins d'un an et taux de mortalité infantile selon l'âge et le sexe : dernière année disponible, 2008 - 2017 (continued - suite)

Continent, country or area, year, code[a] and age / Continent, pays ou zone, année, code[a] et âge	Number - Nombre			Rate - Taux		
	Both sexes Les deux sexes	Male Masculin	Female Féminin	Both sexes Les deux sexes	Male Masculin	Female Féminin
ASIA - ASIE						
Armenia - Arménie[9]						
2016 (C)						
Total	352	213	139	8.7	9.9	7.3
Less than 1 day - Moins de 1 jour	45	25	20	1.1	♦1.2	♦1.0
1 - 6 days - 1 - 6 jours	124	79	45	3.1	3.7	2.4
7 - 27 days - 7 - 27 jours	80	48	32	2.0	2.2	1.7
7 - 13 days - 7 - 13 jours	46	29	17	1.1	♦1.4	♦0.9
14 - 20 days - 14 - 20 jours	18	10	8	♦0.4	♦0.5	♦0.4
21 - 27 days - 21 - 27 jours	16	9	7	♦0.4	♦0.4	♦0.4
28 days - 11 months - 28 jours - 11 mois	103	61	42	2.5	2.8	2.2
28 days - less than 2 months - 28 jours - moins de 2 mois	33	21	12	0.8	♦1.0	♦0.6
2 months - 2 mois	20	12	8	♦0.5	♦0.6	♦0.4
3 months - 3 mois	10	6	4	♦0.2	♦0.3	♦0.2
4 months - 4 mois	6	3	3	♦0.1	♦0.1	♦0.2
5 months - 5 mois	8	6	2	♦0.2	♦0.3	♦0.1
6 months - 6 mois	4	3	1	♦0.1	♦0.1	♦0.1
7 months - 7 mois	6	4	2	♦0.1	♦0.2	♦0.1
8 months - 8 mois	6	3	3	♦0.1	♦0.1	♦0.2
9 months - 9 mois	3	1	2	♦0.1	-	♦0.1
10 months - 10 mois	4	1	3	♦0.1	-	♦0.2
11 months - 11 mois	3	1	2	♦0.1	-	♦0.1
Azerbaijan - Azerbaïdjan[9]						
2016 (+C)						
Total	1 666	999	667	10.4	11.8	8.9
Less than 1 day - Moins de 1 jour	238	131	107	1.5	1.5	1.4
1 - 6 days - 1 - 6 jours	484	312	172	3.0	3.7	2.3
7 - 27 days - 7 - 27 jours	150	87	63	0.9	1.0	0.8
7 - 13 days - 7 - 13 jours	89	58	31	0.6	0.7	0.4
14 - 20 days - 14 - 20 jours	33	21	12	0.2	♦0.2	♦0.2
21 - 27 days - 21 - 27 jours	28	8	20	♦0.2	♦0.1	♦0.3
28 days - 11 months - 28 jours - 11 mois	794	469	325	5.0	5.5	4.4
28 days - less than 2 months - 28 jours - moins de 2 mois	144	102	42	0.9	1.2	0.6
2 months - 2 mois	78	51	27	0.5	0.6	♦0.4
3 months - 3 mois	98	54	44	0.6	0.6	0.6
4 months - 4 mois	77	41	36	0.5	0.5	0.5
5 months - 5 mois	75	32	43	0.5	0.4	0.6
6 months - 6 mois	59	32	27	0.4	0.4	♦0.4
7 months - 7 mois	72	46	26	0.5	0.5	♦0.3
8 months - 8 mois	80	49	31	0.5	0.6	0.4
9 months - 9 mois	49	30	19	0.3	0.4	♦0.3
10 months - 10 mois	52	27	25	0.3	♦0.3	♦0.3
11 months - 11 mois	10	5	5	♦0.1	♦0.1	♦0.1
Bahrain - Bahreïn[10]						
2014 (C)						
Total	218	113	105	10.4	10.5	10.3
Less than 1 day - Moins de 1 jour	25	12	13	♦1.2	♦1.1	♦1.3
1 - 6 days - 1 - 6 jours	55	34	21	2.6	3.2	♦2.1
7 - 27 days - 7 - 27 jours	23	15	8	♦1.1	♦1.4	♦0.8
7 - 13 days - 7 - 13 jours	8	6	2	♦0.4	♦0.6	♦0.2
14 - 20 days - 14 - 20 jours	7	4	3	♦0.3	♦0.4	♦0.3
21 - 27 days - 21 - 27 jours	8	5	3	♦0.4	♦0.5	♦0.3
28 days - 11 months - 28 jours - 11 mois	80	36	44	3.8	3.3	4.3
28 days - less than 2 months - 28 jours - moins de 2 mois	34	11	23	1.6	♦1.0	♦2.3
2 months - 2 mois	12	5	7	♦0.6	♦0.5	♦0.7
3 months - 3 mois	6	4	2	♦0.3	♦0.4	♦0.2
4 months - 4 mois	8	5	3	♦0.4	♦0.5	♦0.3
5 months - 5 mois	8	5	3	♦0.4	♦0.5	♦0.3
6 months - 6 mois	5	1	4	♦0.2	♦0.1	♦0.4
7 months - 7 mois	3	2	1	♦0.1	♦0.2	♦0.1
8 months - 8 mois	1	1	-	-	♦0.1	-
9 months - 9 mois	1	1	-	-	♦0.1	-
10 months - 10 mois	1	-	1	-	-	♦0.1
11 months - 11 mois	1	1	-	-	♦0.1	-
Unknown - Inconnu	35	16	19	1.7	♦1.5	♦1.9
Bangladesh						
2010 (U)						
Total	104 591	55 178	49 413	...	...	...
1 - 6 days - 1 - 6 jours	56 108	30 276	25 832	...	...	...

16. Infant deaths and infant mortality rates by age and sex: latest available year, 2008 - 2017
Décès d'enfants de moins d'un an et taux de mortalité infantile selon l'âge et le sexe : dernière année disponible, 2008 - 2017 (continued - suite)

Continent, country or area, year, code[a] and age / Continent, pays ou zone, année, code[a] et âge	Number - Nombre			Rate - Taux		
	Both sexes Les deux sexes	Male Masculin	Female Féminin	Both sexes Les deux sexes	Male Masculin	Female Féminin
ASIA - ASIE						
Bangladesh						
2010 (U)						
7 - 27 days - 7 - 27 jours	17 576	9 234	8 342	...	...	...
7 - 13 days - 7 - 13 jours	8 488	4 491	3 997	...	...	...
14 - 20 days - 14 - 20 jours	4 845	2 546	2 299	...	...	...
21 - 27 days - 21 - 27 jours	4 243	2 197	2 046	...	...	...
28 days - 11 months - 28 jours - 11 mois	30 907	15 668	15 239	...	...	...
28 days - less than 2 months - 28 jours - moins de 2 mois	7 377	3 906	3 471	...	...	...
2 months - 2 mois	5 234	2 674	2 560	...	...	...
3 months - 3 mois	4 381	2 248	2 133	...	...	...
4 months - 4 mois	2 628	1 333	1 295	...	...	...
5 months - 5 mois	1 188	606	582	...	...	...
6 months - 6 mois	2 123	1 050	1 073	...	...	...
7 months - 7 mois	1 361	669	692	...	...	...
8 months - 8 mois	1 905	918	987	...	...	...
9 months - 9 mois	1 420	696	724	...	...	...
10 months - 10 mois	1 188	566	622	...	...	...
11 months - 11 mois	2 102	1 002	1 100	...	...	...
China, Hong Kong SAR - Chine, Hong Kong RAS						
2017 (C)						
Total	97	50	47	...	...	...
Less than 1 day - Moins de 1 jour	12	4	8	...	...	...
1 - 6 days - 1 - 6 jours	25	10	15	...	...	...
7 - 27 days - 7 - 27 jours	29	18	11	...	...	...
7 - 13 days - 7 - 13 jours	11	6	5	...	...	...
14 - 20 days - 14 - 20 jours	11	8	3	...	...	...
21 - 27 days - 21 - 27 jours	7	4	3	...	...	...
28 days - 11 months - 28 jours - 11 mois	31	18	13	...	...	...
28 days - less than 2 months - 28 jours - moins de 2 mois	7	3	4	...	...	...
2 months - 2 mois	3	2	1	...	...	...
3 months - 3 mois	5	3	2	...	...	...
4 months - 4 mois	2	1	1	...	...	...
5 months - 5 mois	2	1	1	...	...	...
6 months - 6 mois	4	1	3	...	...	...
7 months - 7 mois	1	1	-	...	...	...
8 months - 8 mois	4	4	-	...	...	...
9 months - 9 mois	2	2	-	...	...	...
10 months - 10 mois	1	-	1	...	...	...
11 months - 11 mois	-	-	-	...	...	...
China, Macao SAR - Chine, Macao RAS						
2010 (C)						
Total	15	7	8	...	...	...
Less than 1 day - Moins de 1 jour	7	3	4	...	...	...
1 - 6 days - 1 - 6 jours	4	2	2	...	...	...
7 - 27 days - 7 - 27 jours	2	1	1	...	...	...
7 - 13 days - 7 - 13 jours	-	-	-	...	...	...
14 - 20 days - 14 - 20 jours	1	-	1	...	...	...
21 - 27 days - 21 - 27 jours	1	1	-	...	...	...
28 days - 11 months - 28 jours - 11 mois	2	1	1	...	...	...
28 days - less than 2 months - 28 jours - moins de 2 mois	1	-	1	...	...	...
2 months - 2 mois	-	-	-	...	...	...
3 months - 3 mois	-	-	-	...	...	...
4 months - 4 mois	1	1	-	...	...	...
5 months - 5 mois	-	-	-	...	...	...
6 months - 6 mois	-	-	-	...	...	...
7 months - 7 mois	-	-	-	...	...	...
8 months - 8 mois	-	-	-	...	...	...
9 months - 9 mois	-	-	-	...	...	...
10 months - 10 mois	-	-	-	...	...	...
11 months - 11 mois	-	-	-	...	...	...
Cyprus - Chypre[11]						
2011 (C)						
Total	30	18	12	...	...	...
Less than 1 day - Moins de 1 jour	10	6	4	...	...	...
1 - 6 days - 1 - 6 jours	8	4	4	...	...	...
7 - 27 days - 7 - 27 jours	3	2	1	...	...	...
28 days - 11 months - 28 jours - 11 mois	9	6	3	...	...	...

16. Infant deaths and infant mortality rates by age and sex: latest available year, 2008 - 2017

Décès d'enfants de moins d'un an et taux de mortalité infantile selon l'âge et le sexe : dernière année disponible, 2008 - 2017 (continued - suite)

Continent, country or area, year, code[a] and age / Continent, pays ou zone, année, code[a] et âge	Number - Nombre			Rate - Taux		
	Both sexes Les deux sexes	Male Masculin	Female Féminin	Both sexes Les deux sexes	Male Masculin	Female Féminin
ASIA - ASIE						
Georgia - Géorgie[9]						
2016 (C)						
Total	507	292	215	9.0	10.1	7.8
Less than 1 day - Moins de 1 jour	88	53	35	1.6	1.8	1.3
1 - 6 days - 1 - 6 jours	143	84	59	2.5	2.9	2.1
7 - 27 days - 7 - 27 jours	125	75	50	2.2	2.6	1.8
7 - 13 days - 7 - 13 jours	67	44	23	1.2	1.5	♦0.8
14 - 20 days - 14 - 20 jours	37	17	20	0.7	♦0.6	♦0.7
21 - 27 days - 21 - 27 jours	21	14	7	♦0.4	♦0.5	♦0.3
28 days - 11 months - 28 jours - 11 mois	151	80	71	2.7	2.8	2.6
28 days - less than 2 months - 28 jours - moins de 2 mois	10	6	4	♦0.2	♦0.2	♦0.1
2 months - 2 mois	42	22	20	0.7	♦0.8	♦0.7
3 months - 3 mois	18	13	5	♦0.3	♦0.5	♦0.2
4 months - 4 mois	11	4	7	♦0.2	♦0.1	♦0.3
5 months - 5 mois	9	2	7	♦0.2	♦0.1	♦0.3
6 months - 6 mois	15	6	9	♦0.3	♦0.2	♦0.3
7 months - 7 mois	9	5	4	♦0.2	♦0.2	♦0.1
8 months - 8 mois	9	6	3	♦0.2	♦0.2	♦0.1
9 months - 9 mois	11	7	4	♦0.2	♦0.2	♦0.1
10 months - 10 mois	7	3	4	♦0.1	♦0.1	♦0.1
11 months - 11 mois	10	6	4	♦0.2	♦0.2	♦0.1
Israel - Israël[12]						
2017 (C)						
Total	553	303[2]	250[2]	3.0	...	...
Less than 1 day - Moins de 1 jour	109	62[2]	47[2]	0.6	...	...
1 - 6 days - 1 - 6 jours	153	99[2]	54[2]	0.8	...	...
7 - 27 days - 7 - 27 jours	92	43[2]	49[2]	0.5	...	...
7 - 13 days - 7 - 13 jours	47	20[2]	27[2]	0.3	...	...
14 - 20 days - 14 - 20 jours	27	13[2]	14[2]	♦0.1	...	...
21 - 27 days - 21 - 27 jours	18	10[2]	8[2]	♦0.1	...	...
28 days - 11 months - 28 jours - 11 mois	199	99[2]	100[2]	1.1	...	...
28 days - less than 2 months - 28 jours - moins de 2 mois	57	31[2]	26[2]	0.3	...	...
2 months - 2 mois	31	18[2]	13[2]	0.2	...	...
3 months - 3 mois	19	10[2]	9[2]	♦0.1	...	...
4 months - 4 mois	22	7[2]	15[2]	♦0.1	...	...
5 months - 5 mois	9	5[2]	4[2]	-	...	...
6 months - 6 mois	12	3[2]	9[2]	♦0.1	...	...
7 months - 7 mois	18	8[2]	10[2]	♦0.1	...	...
8 months - 8 mois	7	5[2]	2[2]	-	...	...
9 months - 9 mois	10	5[2]	5[2]	♦0.1	...	...
10 months - 10 mois	10	5[2]	5[2]	♦0.1	...	...
11 months - 11 mois	4	2[2]	2[2]	-	...	...
Japan - Japon[13]						
2016 (C)						
Total	1 928	980	948	2.0	2.0	2.0
Less than 1 day - Moins de 1 jour	441	233	208	0.5	0.5	0.4
1 - 6 days - 1 - 6 jours	235	113	122	0.2	0.2	0.3
7 - 27 days - 7 - 27 jours	198	101	97	0.2	0.2	0.2
7 - 13 days - 7 - 13 jours	93	49	44	0.1	0.1	0.1
14 - 20 days - 14 - 20 jours	56	27	29	0.1	♦0.1	♦0.1
21 - 27 days - 21 - 27 jours	49	25	24	0.1	-	♦0.1
28 days - 11 months - 28 jours - 11 mois	1 054	533	521	1.1	1.1	1.1
28 days - less than 2 months - 28 jours - moins de 2 mois	227	113	114	0.2	0.2	0.2
2 months - 2 mois	148	73	75	0.2	0.1	0.2
3 months - 3 mois	119	60	59	0.1	0.1	0.1
4 months - 4 mois	100	42	58	0.1	0.1	0.1
5 months - 5 mois	111	61	50	0.1	0.1	0.1
6 months - 6 mois	84	48	36	0.1	0.1	0.1
7 months - 7 mois	71	35	36	0.1	0.1	0.1
8 months - 8 mois	65	38	27	0.1	0.1	♦0.1
9 months - 9 mois	47	21	26	-	-	♦0.1
10 months - 10 mois	36	21	15	-	-	-
11 months - 11 mois	46	21	25	-	-	♦0.1
Kazakhstan						
2014 (C)						
Total	3 907	2 216	1 691	9.8	10.8	8.7
Less than 1 day - Moins de 1 jour	315	170	145	0.8	0.8	0.7

16. Infant deaths and infant mortality rates by age and sex: latest available year, 2008 - 2017
Décès d'enfants de moins d'un an et taux de mortalité infantile selon l'âge et le sexe : dernière année disponible, 2008 - 2017 (continued - suite)

Continent, country or area, year, code[a] and age / Continent, pays ou zone, année, code[a] et âge	Number - Nombre			Rate - Taux		
	Both sexes Les deux sexes	Male Masculin	Female Féminin	Both sexes Les deux sexes	Male Masculin	Female Féminin
ASIA - ASIE						
Kazakhstan						
2014 (C)						
1 - 6 days - 1 - 6 jours	1 200	709	491	3.0	3.4	2.5
7 - 27 days - 7 - 27 jours	835	461	374	2.1	2.2	1.9
7 - 13 days - 7 - 13 jours	471	256	215	1.2	1.2	1.1
14 - 20 days - 14 - 20 jours	225	129	96	0.6	0.6	0.5
21 - 27 days - 21 - 27 jours	139	76	63	0.3	0.4	0.3
28 days - 11 months - 28 jours - 11 mois	1 557	876	681	3.9	4.3	3.5
28 days - less than 2 months - 28 jours - moins de 2 mois	500	289	211	1.3	1.4	1.1
2 months - 2 mois	228	135	93	0.6	0.7	0.5
3 months - 3 mois	161	91	70	0.4	0.4	0.4
4 months - 4 mois	141	78	63	0.4	0.4	0.3
5 months - 5 mois	117	63	54	0.3	0.3	0.3
6 months - 6 mois	95	51	44	0.2	0.2	0.2
7 months - 7 mois	92	43	49	0.2	0.2	0.3
8 months - 8 mois	67	41	26	0.2	0.2	◆0.1
9 months - 9 mois	67	38	29	0.2	0.2	◆0.1
10 months - 10 mois	44	24	20	0.1	◆0.1	◆0.1
11 months - 11 mois	45	23	22	0.1	◆0.1	◆0.1
Kuwait - Koweït						
2016 (C)						
Total	448	263	185	7.6	8.7	6.5
Less than 1 day - Moins de 1 jour	90	55	35	1.5	1.8	1.2
1 - 6 days - 1 - 6 jours	86	53	33	1.5	1.8	1.2
7 - 27 days - 7 - 27 jours	94	53	41	1.6	1.8	1.4
7 - 13 days - 7 - 13 jours	44	29	15	0.7	◆1.0	◆0.5
14 - 20 days - 14 - 20 jours	27	15	12	◆0.5	◆0.5	◆0.4
21 - 27 days - 21 - 27 jours	23	9	14	◆0.4	◆0.3	◆0.5
28 days - 11 months - 28 jours - 11 mois	178	102	76	3.0	3.4	2.7
28 days - less than 2 months - 28 jours - moins de 2 mois	60	36	24	1.0	1.2	◆0.8
2 months - 2 mois	36	24	12	0.6	0.8	◆0.4
3 months - 3 mois	24	14	10	◆0.4	◆0.5	◆0.4
4 months - 4 mois	13	7	6	◆0.2	◆0.2	◆0.2
5 months - 5 mois	15	8	7	◆0.3	◆0.3	◆0.2
6 months - 6 mois	3	1	2	◆0.1	-	◆0.1
7 months - 7 mois	7	3	4	◆0.1	◆0.1	◆0.1
8 months - 8 mois	5	1	4	◆0.1	-	◆0.1
9 months - 9 mois	6	2	4	◆0.1	◆0.1	◆0.1
10 months - 10 mois	6	4	2	◆0.1	◆0.1	◆0.1
11 months - 11 mois	3	2	1	◆0.1	◆0.1	-
Kyrgyzstan - Kirghizstan						
2017 (C)						
Total	2 401	1 340	1 061	15.6	17.0	14.2
Less than 1 day - Moins de 1 jour	558	320	238	3.6	4.1	3.2
1 - 6 days - 1 - 6 jours	992	567	425	6.5	7.2	5.7
7 - 27 days - 7 - 27 jours	262	147	115	1.7	1.9	1.5
7 - 13 days - 7 - 13 jours	167	97	70	1.1	1.2	0.9
14 - 20 days - 14 - 20 jours	63	32	31	0.4	0.4	0.4
21 - 27 days - 21 - 27 jours	32	18	14	0.2	◆0.2	◆0.2
28 days - 11 months - 28 jours - 11 mois	589	306	283	3.8	3.9	3.8
28 days - less than 2 months - 28 jours - moins de 2 mois	143	66	77	0.9	0.8	1.0
2 months - 2 mois	68	36	32	0.4	0.5	0.4
3 months - 3 mois	66	40	26	0.4	0.5	◆0.3
4 months - 4 mois	55	30	25	0.4	0.4	◆0.3
5 months - 5 mois	63	32	31	0.4	0.4	0.4
6 months - 6 mois	35	15	20	0.2	◆0.2	◆0.3
7 months - 7 mois	49	19	30	0.3	◆0.2	0.4
8 months - 8 mois	33	19	14	0.2	◆0.2	◆0.2
9 months - 9 mois	27	16	11	◆0.2	◆0.2	◆0.1
10 months - 10 mois	27	17	10	◆0.2	◆0.2	◆0.1
11 months - 11 mois	23	16	7	◆0.1	◆0.2	◆0.1
Maldives[14]						
2016 (C)						
Total	53	21	32	...	...	...
Less than 1 day - Moins de 1 jour	13	3	10	...	...	...
1 - 6 days - 1 - 6 jours	15	6	9	...	...	...
7 - 27 days - 7 - 27 jours	8	3	5	...	...	...
7 - 13 days - 7 - 13 jours	3	2	1	...	...	...

Continent, country or area, year, code[a] and age Continent, pays ou zone, année, code[a] et âge	Number - Nombre			Rate - Taux		
	Both sexes Les deux sexes	Male Masculin	Female Féminin	Both sexes Les deux sexes	Male Masculin	Female Féminin
ASIA - ASIE						
Maldives[14]						
2016 (C)						
14 - 20 days - 14 - 20 jours	4	1	3	...	...	...
21 - 27 days - 21 - 27 jours	1	-	1	...	...	...
28 days - 11 months - 28 jours - 11 mois............	17	9	8	...	...	...
28 days - less than 2 months - 28 jours - moins de 2 mois	8	4	4	...	...	...
2 months - 2 mois	-	-	-	...	...	...
3 months - 3 mois	1	-	1	...	...	...
4 months - 4 mois	1	1	-	...	...	...
5 months - 5 mois	2	1	1	...	...	...
6 months - 6 mois	2	1	1	...	...	...
7 months - 7 mois	2	2	-	...	...	...
8 months - 8 mois	-	-	-	...	...	...
9 months - 9 mois	-	-	-	...	...	...
10 months - 10 mois	1	-	1	...	...	...
11 months - 11 mois	-	-	-	...	...	...
Mongolia - Mongolie						
2017 (+C)						
Total................	1 009	572	437	13.4	14.7	12.0
1 - 6 days - 1 - 6 jours	475	282	193	6.3	7.2	5.3
7 - 27 days - 7 - 27 jours	172	94	78	2.3	2.4	2.1
28 days - 11 months - 28 jours - 11 mois............	362	196	166	4.8	5.0	4.6
Myanmar[15]						
2015 (+U)						
Total................	*9 849*	*5 468*	*4 381*	...	...	...
Less than 1 day - Moins de 1 jour	*410*	*217*	*193*	...	...	...
1 - 6 days - 1 - 6 jours	*4 452*	*2 517*	*1 935*	...	...	...
7 - 27 days - 7 - 27 jours	*1 525*	*826*	*699*	...	...	...
7 - 13 days - 7 - 13 jours	*843*	*463*	*380*	...	...	...
14 - 20 days - 14 - 20 jours	*381*	*203*	*178*	...	...	...
21 - 27 days - 21 - 27 jours	*301*	*160*	*141*	...	...	...
28 days - 11 months - 28 jours - 11 mois............	*3 458*	*1 907*	*1 551*	...	...	...
28 days - less than 2 months - 28 jours - moins de 2 mois	*786*	*441*	*345*	...	...	...
2 months - 2 mois	*611*	*337*	*274*	...	...	...
3 months - 3 mois	*427*	*250*	*177*	...	...	...
4 months - 4 mois	*277*	*152*	*125*	...	...	...
5 months - 5 mois	*241*	*138*	*103*	...	...	...
6 months - 6 mois	*244*	*129*	*115*	...	...	...
7 months - 7 mois	*186*	*103*	*83*	...	...	...
8 months - 8 mois	*212*	*109*	*103*	...	...	...
9 months - 9 mois	*176*	*84*	*92*	...	...	...
10 months - 10 mois	*135*	*73*	*62*	...	...	...
11 months - 11 mois	*163*	*91*	*72*	...	...	...
Unknown - Inconnu	*4*	*1*	*3*	...	...	...
Oman						
2017 (C)						
Total................	850	450	400	9.4	9.7	9.1
Less than 1 day - Moins de 1 jour	250	130	120	2.8	2.8	2.7
1 - 6 days - 1 - 6 jours	184	96	88	2.0	2.1	2.0
7 - 27 days - 7 - 27 jours	126	71	55	1.4	1.5	1.2
7 - 13 days - 7 - 13 jours	56	29	27	0.6	◆0.6	◆0.6
14 - 20 days - 14 - 20 jours	34	17	17	0.4	◆0.4	◆0.4
21 - 27 days - 21 - 27 jours	36	25	11	0.4	◆0.5	◆0.2
28 days - 11 months - 28 jours - 11 mois............	290	153	137	3.2	3.3	3.1
28 days - less than 2 months - 28 jours - moins de 2 mois	59	37	22	0.7	0.8	◆0.5
2 months - 2 mois	38	18	20	0.4	◆0.4	◆0.5
3 months - 3 mois	33	16	17	0.4	◆0.3	◆0.4
4 months - 4 mois	33	16	17	0.4	◆0.3	◆0.4
5 months - 5 mois	27	12	15	◆0.3	◆0.3	◆0.3
6 months - 6 mois	20	13	7	◆0.2	◆0.3	◆0.2
7 months - 7 mois	20	10	10	◆0.2	◆0.2	◆0.2
8 months - 8 mois	15	7	8	◆0.2	◆0.2	◆0.2
9 months - 9 mois	12	5	7	◆0.1	◆0.1	◆0.2
10 months - 10 mois	17	8	9	◆0.2	◆0.2	◆0.2
11 months - 11 mois	16	11	5	◆0.2	◆0.2	◆0.1

Continent, country or area, year, code[a] and age / Continent, pays ou zone, année, code[a] et âge	Number - Nombre			Rate - Taux		
	Both sexes Les deux sexes	Male Masculin	Female Féminin	Both sexes Les deux sexes	Male Masculin	Female Féminin
ASIA - ASIE						
Philippines						
2016 (C)						
Total	21 874	12 566	9 308	12.6	13.9	11.2
Less than 1 day - Moins de 1 jour	2 964	1 651	1 313	1.7	1.8	1.6
1 - 6 days - 1 - 6 jours	5 836	3 520	2 316	3.4	3.9	2.8
7 - 27 days - 7 - 27 jours	2 773	1 626	1 147	1.6	1.8	1.4
7 - 13 days - 7 - 13 jours	1 416	822	594	0.8	0.9	0.7
14 - 20 days - 14 - 20 jours	742	452	290	0.4	0.5	0.4
21 - 27 days - 21 - 27 jours	615	352	263	0.4	0.4	0.3
28 days - 11 months - 28 jours - 11 mois	10 301	5 769	4 532	5.9	6.4	5.5
28 days - less than 2 months - 28 jours - moins de 2 mois	2 396	1 377	1 019	1.4	1.5	1.2
2 months - 2 mois	1 284	731	553	0.7	0.8	0.7
3 months - 3 mois	1 074	608	466	0.6	0.7	0.6
4 months - 4 mois	952	523	429	0.5	0.6	0.5
5 months - 5 mois	899	499	400	0.5	0.6	0.5
6 months - 6 mois	794	447	347	0.5	0.5	0.4
7 months - 7 mois	690	392	298	0.4	0.4	0.4
8 months - 8 mois	656	369	287	0.4	0.4	0.3
9 months - 9 mois	566	306	260	0.3	0.3	0.3
10 months - 10 mois	499	265	234	0.3	0.3	0.3
11 months - 11 mois	491	252	239	0.3	0.3	0.3
Qatar						
2016 (C)						
Total	161	82	79	6.0	6.0	6.0
Less than 1 day - Moins de 1 jour	21	13	8	♦0.8	♦1.0	♦0.6
1 - 6 days - 1 - 6 jours	43	17	26	1.6	♦1.3	♦2.0
7 - 27 days - 7 - 27 jours	20	11	9	♦0.7	♦0.8	♦0.7
7 - 13 days - 7 - 13 jours	10	5	5	♦0.4	♦0.4	♦0.4
14 - 20 days - 14 - 20 jours	6	3	3	♦0.2	♦0.2	♦0.2
21 - 27 days - 21 - 27 jours	4	3	1	♦0.1	♦0.2	♦0.1
28 days - 11 months - 28 jours - 11 mois	77	41	36	2.9	3.0	2.7
28 days - less than 2 months - 28 jours - moins de 2 mois	15	7	8	♦0.6	♦0.5	♦0.6
2 months - 2 mois	20	14	6	♦0.7	♦1.0	♦0.5
3 months - 3 mois	8	1	7	♦0.3	♦0.1	♦0.5
4 months - 4 mois	3	1	2	♦0.1	♦0.1	♦0.2
5 months - 5 mois	10	8	2	♦0.4	♦0.6	♦0.2
6 months - 6 mois	7	2	5	♦0.3	♦0.1	♦0.4
7 months - 7 mois	2	-	2	♦0.1	-	♦0.2
8 months - 8 mois	4	3	1	♦0.1	♦0.2	♦0.1
9 months - 9 mois	2	-	2	♦0.1	-	♦0.2
10 months - 10 mois	5	4	1	♦0.2	♦0.3	♦0.1
11 months - 11 mois	1	1	-	-	♦0.1	-
Republic of Korea - République de Corée[16]						
2015 (C)						
Total	1 190	655	535	2.7	2.9	2.5
Less than 1 day - Moins de 1 jour	189	96	93	0.4	0.4	0.4
1 - 6 days - 1 - 6 jours	266	152	114	0.6	0.7	0.5
7 - 27 days - 7 - 27 jours	222	126	96	0.5	0.6	0.4
7 - 13 days - 7 - 13 jours	115	63	52	0.3	0.3	0.2
14 - 20 days - 14 - 20 jours	68	38	30	0.2	0.2	0.1
21 - 27 days - 21 - 27 jours	39	25	14	0.1	♦0.1	♦0.1
28 days - 11 months - 28 jours - 11 mois	513	281	232	1.2	1.2	1.1
28 days - less than 2 months - 28 jours - moins de 2 mois	149	80	69	0.3	0.4	0.3
2 months - 2 mois	92	55	37	0.2	0.2	0.2
3 months - 3 mois	61	28	33	0.1	♦0.1	0.2
4 months - 4 mois	48	29	19	0.1	♦0.1	♦0.1
5 months - 5 mois	42	22	20	0.1	♦0.1	♦0.1
6 months - 6 mois	26	15	11	♦0.1	♦0.1	♦0.1
7 months - 7 mois	16	8	8	-	-	-
8 months - 8 mois	23	12	11	♦0.1	♦0.1	♦0.1
9 months - 9 mois	21	11	10	-	-	-
10 months - 10 mois	20	13	7	-	♦0.1	-
11 months - 11 mois	15	8	7	-	-	-
Singapore - Singapour						
2017 (+C)						
Total	94	44	50	...	...	...
Less than 1 day - Moins de 1 jour	15	6	9	...	...	...
1 - 6 days - 1 - 6 jours	20	9	11	...	...	...

16. Infant deaths and infant mortality rates by age and sex: latest available year, 2008 - 2017
Décès d'enfants de moins d'un an et taux de mortalité infantile selon l'âge et le sexe : dernière année disponible, 2008 - 2017 (continued - suite)

Continent, country or area, year, code[a] and age / Continent, pays ou zone, année, code[a] et âge	Number - Nombre			Rate - Taux		
	Both sexes Les deux sexes	Male Masculin	Female Féminin	Both sexes Les deux sexes	Male Masculin	Female Féminin
ASIA - ASIE						
Singapore - Singapour						
2017 (+C)						
7 - 27 days - 7 - 27 jours	13	4	9	...	...	...
7 - 13 days - 7 - 13 jours	6	1	5	...	...	...
14 - 20 days - 14 - 20 jours	3	2	1	...	...	...
21 - 27 days - 21 - 27 jours	4	1	3	...	...	...
28 days - 11 months - 28 jours - 11 mois	46	25	21	...	...	...
28 days - less than 2 months - 28 jours - moins de 2 mois	12	6	6	...	...	...
2 months - 2 mois	6	5	1	...	...	...
3 months - 3 mois	8	5	3	...	...	...
4 months - 4 mois	2	-	2	...	...	...
5 months - 5 mois	3	2	1	...	...	...
6 months - 6 mois	5	2	3	...	...	...
7 months - 7 mois	5	2	3	...	...	...
8 months - 8 mois	-	-	-	...	...	...
9 months - 9 mois	4	3	1	...	...	...
10 months - 10 mois	-	-	-	...	...	...
11 months - 11 mois	1	-	1	...	...	...
Tajikistan - Tadjikistan[17]						
2016 (U)						
Total	2 729	1 621	1 108	...	...	...
Less than 1 day - Moins de 1 jour	625	361	264	...	...	...
1 - 6 days - 1 - 6 jours	1 013	616	397	...	...	...
7 - 27 days - 7 - 27 jours	250	177	73	...	...	...
7 - 13 days - 7 - 13 jours	152	113	39	...	...	...
14 - 20 days - 14 - 20 jours	63	42	21	...	...	...
21 - 27 days - 21 - 27 jours	35	22	13	...	...	...
28 days - 11 months - 28 jours - 11 mois	841	467	374	...	...	...
Thailand - Thaïlande						
2016 (+U)						
Total	4 233	2 360	1 873	...	...	...
Less than 1 day - Moins de 1 jour	340	168	172	...	...	...
1 - 6 days - 1 - 6 jours	1 171	666	505	...	...	...
7 - 27 days - 7 - 27 jours	1 384	789	595	...	...	...
7 - 13 days - 7 - 13 jours	450	274	176	...	...	...
14 - 20 days - 14 - 20 jours	238	134	104	...	...	...
21 - 27 days - 21 - 27 jours	165	93	72	...	...	...
28 days - 11 months - 28 jours - 11 mois	1 869	1 035	844	...	...	...
28 days - less than 2 months - 28 jours - moins de 2 mois	531	288	243	...	...	...
2 months - 2 mois	303	172	131	...	...	...
3 months - 3 mois	239	126	113	...	...	...
4 months - 4 mois	179	96	83	...	...	...
5 months - 5 mois	126	75	51	...	...	...
6 months - 6 mois	98	53	45	...	...	...
7 months - 7 mois	87	59	38	...	...	...
8 months - 8 mois	90	50	40	...	...	...
9 months - 9 mois	78	42	36	...	...	...
10 months - 10 mois	74	34	40	...	...	...
11 months - 11 mois	64	40	24	...	...	...
Turkey - Turquie[18]						
2016 (C)						
Total	13 036	7 069	5 967	10.0	10.5	9.4
Less than 1 day - Moins de 1 jour	1 773	982	791	1.4	1.5	1.2
1 - 6 days - 1 - 6 jours	3 913	2 180	1 733	3.0	3.2	2.7
7 - 27 days - 7 - 27 jours	2 647	1 426	1 221	2.0	2.1	1.9
7 - 13 days - 7 - 13 jours	1 395	755	640	1.1	1.1	1.0
14 - 20 days - 14 - 20 jours	753	396	357	0.6	0.6	0.6
21 - 27 days - 21 - 27 jours	499	275	224	0.4	0.4	0.4
28 days - 11 months - 28 jours - 11 mois	4 703	2 481	2 222	3.6	3.7	3.5
28 days - less than 2 months - 28 jours - moins de 2 mois	1 304	720	584	1.0	1.1	0.9
2 months - 2 mois	774	395	379	0.6	0.6	0.6
3 months - 3 mois	525	273	252	0.4	0.4	0.4
4 months - 4 mois	449	247	202	0.3	0.4	0.3
5 months - 5 mois	352	177	175	0.3	0.3	0.3
6 months - 6 mois	314	165	149	0.2	0.2	0.2
7 months - 7 mois	245	123	122	0.2	0.2	0.2
8 months - 8 mois	227	117	110	0.2	0.2	0.2
9 months - 9 mois	175	94	81	0.1	0.1	0.1

16. Infant deaths and infant mortality rates by age and sex: latest available year, 2008 - 2017
Décès d'enfants de moins d'un an et taux de mortalité infantile selon l'âge et le sexe : dernière année disponible, 2008 - 2017 (continued - suite)

Continent, country or area, year, code[a] and age / Continent, pays ou zone, année, code[a] et âge	Number - Nombre			Rate - Taux		
	Both sexes Les deux sexes	Male Masculin	Female Féminin	Both sexes Les deux sexes	Male Masculin	Female Féminin
ASIA - ASIE						
Turkey - Turquie[18]						
2016 (C)						
10 months - 10 mois	191	98	93	0.1	0.1	0.1
11 months - 11 mois	147	72	75	0.1	0.1	0.1
Uzbekistan - Ouzbékistan[9]						
2015 (+C)						
Total	8 320	4 906	3 414	11.3	12.8	9.7
Less than 1 day - Moins de 1 jour	1 314	777	537	1.8	2.0	1.5
1 - 6 days - 1 - 6 jours	3 252	1 974	1 278	4.4	5.2	3.6
7 - 27 days - 7 - 27 jours	1 215	710	505	1.7	1.9	1.4
7 - 13 days - 7 - 13 jours	763	455	308	1.0	1.2	0.9
14 - 20 days - 14 - 20 jours	275	156	119	0.4	0.4	0.3
21 - 27 days - 21 - 27 jours	177	99	78	0.2	0.3	0.2
28 days - 11 months - 28 jours - 11 mois	2 539	1 445	1 094	3.5	3.8	3.1
28 days - less than 2 months - 28 jours - moins de 2 mois	688	448	240	0.9	1.2	0.7
2 months - 2 mois	346	196	150	0.5	0.5	0.4
3 months - 3 mois	261	136	125	0.4	0.4	0.4
4 months - 4 mois	245	127	118	0.3	0.3	0.3
5 months - 5 mois	212	119	93	0.3	0.3	0.3
6 months - 6 mois	165	87	78	0.2	0.2	0.2
7 months - 7 mois	176	90	86	0.2	0.2	0.2
8 months - 8 mois	155	80	75	0.2	0.2	0.2
9 months - 9 mois	109	54	55	0.1	0.1	0.2
10 months - 10 mois	105	57	48	0.1	0.1	0.1
11 months - 11 mois	77	51	26	0.1	0.1	◆0.1
EUROPE						
Åland Islands - Îles d'Åland						
2016 (C)						
Total	1	1	-	...	...	...
Less than 1 day - Moins de 1 jour	-	-	-	...	...	...
1 - 6 days - 1 - 6 jours	-	-	-	...	...	...
7 - 27 days - 7 - 27 jours	1	1	-	...	...	...
7 - 13 days - 7 - 13 jours	1	1	-	...	...	...
14 - 20 days - 14 - 20 jours	-	-	-	...	...	...
21 - 27 days - 21 - 27 jours	-	-	-	...	...	...
28 days - 11 months - 28 jours - 11 mois	-	-	-	...	...	...
28 days - less than 2 months - 28 jours - moins de 2 mois	-	-	-	...	...	...
2 - 11 months - 2 - 11 mois	-	-	-	...	...	...
Albania - Albanie						
2016 (C)						
Total	277	146	131	8.7	8.9	8.5
Less than 1 day - Moins de 1 jour	121	61	60	3.8	3.7	3.9
1 - 6 days - 1 - 6 jours	59	34	25	1.9	2.1	◆1.6
7 - 27 days - 7 - 27 jours	38	24	14	1.2	◆1.5	◆0.9
7 - 13 days - 7 - 13 jours	18	13	5	◆0.6	◆0.8	◆0.3
14 - 20 days - 14 - 20 jours	9	6	3	◆0.3	◆0.4	◆0.2
21 - 27 days - 21 - 27 jours	11	5	6	◆0.3	◆0.3	◆0.4
28 days - 11 months - 28 jours - 11 mois	59	27	32	1.9	◆1.6	2.1
28 days - less than 2 months - 28 jours - moins de 2 mois	18	11	7	◆0.6	◆0.7	◆0.5
2 months - 2 mois	9	3	6	◆0.3	◆0.2	◆0.4
3 months - 3 mois	9	4	5	◆0.3	◆0.2	◆0.3
4 months - 4 mois	8	3	5	◆0.3	◆0.2	◆0.3
5 months - 5 mois	4	1	3	◆0.1	◆0.1	◆0.2
6 months - 6 mois	3	2	1	◆0.1	◆0.1	◆0.1
7 months - 7 mois	2	-	2	◆0.1	-	◆0.1
8 months - 8 mois	2	1	1	◆0.1	◆0.1	◆0.1
9 months - 9 mois	2	-	2	◆0.1	-	◆0.1
10 months - 10 mois	1	1	-	-	◆0.1	-
11 months - 11 mois	1	1	-	-	◆0.1	-
Andorra - Andorre						
2009 (C)						
Total	1	-	1	...	...	...
Less than 1 day - Moins de 1 jour	-	-	-	...	...	...
1 - 6 days - 1 - 6 jours	1	-	1	...	...	...

Continent, country or area, year, code[a] and age Continent, pays ou zone, année, code[a] et âge	Number - Nombre			Rate - Taux		
	Both sexes Les deux sexes	Male Masculin	Female Féminin	Both sexes Les deux sexes	Male Masculin	Female Féminin
EUROPE						
Andorra - Andorre						
2009 (C)						
7 - 27 days - 7 - 27 jours	-	-	-	...	...	...
28 days - 11 months - 28 jours - 11 mois	-	-	-	...	...	...
Austria - Autriche						
2016 (C)						
Total	269	152	117	3.1	3.4	2.7
Less than 1 day - Moins de 1 jour	115	66	49	1.3	1.5	1.1
1 - 6 days - 1 - 6 jours	48	25	23	0.5	♦0.6	♦0.5
7 - 27 days - 7 - 27 jours	40	19	21	0.5	♦0.4	♦0.5
7 - 13 days - 7 - 13 jours	15	6	9	♦0.2	♦0.1	♦0.2
14 - 20 days - 14 - 20 jours	13	8	5	♦0.1	♦0.2	♦0.1
21 - 27 days - 21 - 27 jours	12	5	7	♦0.1	♦0.1	♦0.2
28 days - 11 months - 28 jours - 11 mois	63	40	23	0.7	0.9	♦0.5
28 days - less than 2 months - 28 jours - moins de 2 mois	12	8	4	♦0.1	♦0.2	♦0.1
2 months - 2 mois	12	8	4	♦0.1	♦0.2	♦0.1
3 months - 3 mois	9	5	4	♦0.1	♦0.1	♦0.1
4 months - 4 mois	4	2	2	-	-	-
5 months - 5 mois	5	2	3	♦0.1	-	♦0.1
6 months - 6 mois	6	4	2	♦0.1	♦0.1	-
7 months - 7 mois	5	4	1	♦0.1	♦0.1	-
8 months - 8 mois	3	2	1	-	-	-
9 months - 9 mois	1	-	1	-	-	-
10 months - 10 mois	4	3	1	-	♦0.1	-
11 months - 11 mois	2	2	-	-	-	-
Belarus - Bélarus						
2016 (C)						
Total	373	206	167	3.2	3.4	2.9
Less than 1 day - Moins de 1 jour	33	23	10	0.3	♦0.4	♦0.2
1 - 6 days - 1 - 6 jours	73	36	37	0.6	0.6	0.6
7 - 27 days - 7 - 27 jours	80	42	38	0.7	0.7	0.7
7 - 13 days - 7 - 13 jours	24	9	15	♦0.2	♦0.1	♦0.3
14 - 20 days - 14 - 20 jours	32	20	12	0.3	♦0.3	♦0.2
21 - 27 days - 21 - 27 jours	24	13	11	♦0.2	♦0.2	♦0.2
28 days - 11 months - 28 jours - 11 mois	187	105	82	1.6	1.7	1.4
28 days - less than 2 months - 28 jours - moins de 2 mois	64	34	30	0.5	0.6	0.5
2 months - 2 mois	37	22	15	0.3	♦0.4	♦0.3
3 months - 3 mois	25	11	14	♦0.2	♦0.2	♦0.2
4 months - 4 mois	12	5	7	♦0.1	♦0.1	♦0.1
5 months - 5 mois	9	7	2	♦0.1	♦0.1	-
6 months - 6 mois	5	4	1	-	♦0.1	-
7 months - 7 mois	10	6	4	♦0.1	♦0.1	♦0.1
8 months - 8 mois	9	5	4	♦0.1	♦0.1	♦0.1
9 months - 9 mois	9	9	-	♦0.1	♦0.1	-
10 months - 10 mois	3	1	2	-	-	-
11 months - 11 mois	4	1	3	-	-	♦0.1
Belgium - Belgique[19]						
2014 (C)						
Total	423	247	176	3.4	3.8	2.9
Less than 1 day - Moins de 1 jour	115	61	54	0.9	1.0	0.9
1 - 6 days - 1 - 6 jours	91	58	33	0.7	0.9	0.5
7 - 27 days - 7 - 27 jours	79	39	40	0.6	0.6	0.7
7 - 13 days - 7 - 13 jours	40	21	19	0.3	♦0.3	♦0.3
14 - 20 days - 14 - 20 jours	25	11	14	♦0.2	♦0.2	♦0.2
21 - 27 days - 21 - 27 jours	14	7	7	♦0.1	♦0.1	♦0.1
28 days - 11 months - 28 jours - 11 mois	138	89	49	1.1	1.4	0.8
28 days - less than 2 months - 28 jours - moins de 2 mois	42	25	17	0.3	♦0.4	♦0.3
2 months - 2 mois	23	17	6	♦0.2	♦0.3	♦0.1
3 months - 3 mois	13	9	4	♦0.1	♦0.1	♦0.1
4 months - 4 mois	15	12	3	♦0.1	♦0.2	-
5 months - 5 mois	11	7	4	♦0.1	♦0.1	♦0.1
6 months - 6 mois	8	3	5	♦0.1	-	♦0.1
7 months - 7 mois	9	8	1	♦0.1	♦0.1	-
8 months - 8 mois	7	4	3	♦0.1	♦0.1	-
9 months - 9 mois	2	2	-	-	-	-
10 months - 10 mois	5	1	4	-	-	♦0.1
11 months - 11 mois	3	1	2	-	-	-

16. Infant deaths and infant mortality rates by age and sex: latest available year, 2008 - 2017
Décès d'enfants de moins d'un an et taux de mortalité infantile selon l'âge et le sexe : dernière année disponible, 2008 - 2017 (continued - suite)

Continent, country or area, year, code[a] and age / Continent, pays ou zone, année, code[a] et âge	Number - Nombre			Rate - Taux		
	Both sexes Les deux sexes	Male Masculin	Female Féminin	Both sexes Les deux sexes	Male Masculin	Female Féminin
EUROPE						
Bosnia and Herzegovina - Bosnie-Herzégovine						
2010 (C)						
Total	216	125	91	6.4	7.2	5.6
Less than 1 day - Moins de 1 jour	74	43	31	2.2	2.5	1.9
1 - 6 days - 1 - 6 jours	89	56	33	2.7	3.2	2.0
7 - 27 days - 7 - 27 jours	19	13	6	♦0.6	♦0.8	♦0.4
7 - 13 days - 7 - 13 jours	10	6	4	♦0.3	♦0.3	♦0.2
14 - 20 days - 14 - 20 jours	6	6	-	♦0.2	♦0.3	-
21 - 27 days - 21 - 27 jours	3	1	2	♦0.1	♦0.1	♦0.1
28 days - 11 months - 28 jours - 11 mois	34	13	21	1.0	♦0.8	♦1.3
28 days - less than 2 months - 28 jours - moins de 2 mois	5	2	3	♦0.1	♦0.1	♦0.2
2 months - 2 mois	10	6	4	♦0.3	♦0.3	♦0.2
3 months - 3 mois	1	-	1	-	-	♦0.1
4 months - 4 mois	5	2	3	♦0.1	♦0.1	♦0.2
5 months - 5 mois	3	1	2	♦0.1	♦0.1	♦0.1
6 months - 6 mois	3	1	2	♦0.1	♦0.1	♦0.1
7 months - 7 mois	-	-	-	-	-	-
8 months - 8 mois	1	-	1	-	-	♦0.1
9 months - 9 mois	4	-	4	♦0.1	-	♦0.2
10 months - 10 mois	1	1	-	-	♦0.1	-
11 months - 11 mois	1	-	1	-	-	♦0.1
Bulgaria - Bulgarie						
2016 (C)						
Total	423	258	165	6.5	7.7	5.2
Less than 1 day - Moins de 1 jour	77	48	29	1.2	1.4	♦0.9
1 - 6 days - 1 - 6 jours	105	70	35	1.6	2.1	1.1
7 - 27 days - 7 - 27 jours	71	39	32	1.1	1.2	1.0
7 - 13 days - 7 - 13 jours	27	15	12	♦0.4	♦0.4	♦0.4
14 - 20 days - 14 - 20 jours	21	13	8	♦0.3	♦0.4	♦0.3
21 - 27 days - 21 - 27 jours	23	11	12	♦0.4	♦0.3	♦0.4
28 days - 11 months - 28 jours - 11 mois	170	101	69	2.6	3.0	2.2
28 days - less than 2 months - 28 jours - moins de 2 mois	45	26	19	0.7	♦0.8	♦0.6
2 months - 2 mois	31	18	13	0.5	♦0.5	♦0.4
3 months - 3 mois	27	19	8	♦0.4	♦0.6	♦0.3
4 months - 4 mois	13	6	7	♦0.2	♦0.2	♦0.2
5 months - 5 mois	17	13	4	♦0.3	♦0.4	♦0.1
6 months - 6 mois	11	6	5	♦0.2	♦0.2	♦0.2
7 months - 7 mois	11	7	4	♦0.2	♦0.2	♦0.1
8 months - 8 mois	5	1	4	♦0.1	-	♦0.1
9 months - 9 mois	3	1	2	-	-	♦0.1
10 months - 10 mois	3	2	1	-	♦0.1	-
11 months - 11 mois	4	2	2	♦0.1	♦0.1	♦0.1
Croatia - Croatie						
2016 (C)						
Total	161	82	79	4.3	4.3	4.3
Less than 1 day - Moins de 1 jour	47	27	20	1.3	♦1.4	♦1.1
1 - 6 days - 1 - 6 jours	33	18	15	0.9	♦0.9	♦0.8
7 - 27 days - 7 - 27 jours	31	15	16	0.8	♦0.8	♦0.9
7 - 13 days - 7 - 13 jours	15	6	9	♦0.4	♦0.3	♦0.5
14 - 20 days - 14 - 20 jours	9	3	6	♦0.2	♦0.2	♦0.3
21 - 27 days - 21 - 27 jours	7	6	1	♦0.2	♦0.3	♦0.1
28 days - 11 months - 28 jours - 11 mois	50	22	28	1.3	♦1.2	♦1.5
28 days - less than 2 months - 28 jours - moins de 2 mois	17	10	7	♦0.5	♦0.5	♦0.4
2 months - 2 mois	6	-	6	♦0.2	-	♦0.3
3 months - 3 mois	5	5	-	♦0.1	♦0.3	-
4 months - 4 mois	3	1	2	♦0.1	♦0.1	♦0.1
5 months - 5 mois	2	-	2	♦0.1	-	♦0.1
6 months - 6 mois	4	2	2	♦0.1	♦0.1	♦0.1
7 months - 7 mois	-	-	-	-	-	-
8 months - 8 mois	4	2	2	♦0.1	♦0.1	♦0.1
9 months - 9 mois	4	1	3	♦0.1	♦0.1	♦0.2
10 months - 10 mois	5	1	4	♦0.1	♦0.1	♦0.2
11 months - 11 mois	-	-	-	-	-	-
Czechia - Tchéquie						
2016 (C)						
Total	317	182	135	2.8	3.1	2.5
Less than 1 day - Moins de 1 jour	56	37	19	0.5	0.6	♦0.3
1 - 6 days - 1 - 6 jours	77	46	31	0.7	0.8	0.6

Continent, country or area, year, code[a] and age Continent, pays ou zone, année, code[a] et âge	Number - Nombre			Rate - Taux		
	Both sexes Les deux sexes	Male Masculin	Female Féminin	Both sexes Les deux sexes	Male Masculin	Female Féminin
EUROPE						
Czechia - Tchéquie						
2016 (C)						
7 - 27 days - 7 - 27 jours	59	26	33	0.5	♦0.4	0.6
7 - 13 days - 7 - 13 jours	30	14	16	0.3	♦0.2	♦0.3
14 - 20 days - 14 - 20 jours	19	8	11	♦0.2	♦0.1	♦0.2
21 - 27 days - 21 - 27 jours	10	4	6	♦0.1	♦0.1	♦0.1
28 days - 11 months - 28 jours - 11 mois	125	73	52	1.1	1.3	0.9
28 days - less than 2 months - 28 jours - moins de 2 mois	44	26	18	0.4	♦0.4	♦0.3
2 months - 2 mois	14	6	8	♦0.1	♦0.1	♦0.1
3 months - 3 mois	16	12	4	♦0.1	♦0.2	♦0.1
4 months - 4 mois	14	10	4	♦0.1	♦0.2	♦0.1
5 months - 5 mois	10	6	4	♦0.1	♦0.1	♦0.1
6 months - 6 mois	7	2	5	♦0.1	-	♦0.1
7 months - 7 mois	5	2	3	-	-	♦0.1
8 months - 8 mois	5	3	2	-	♦0.1	-
9 months - 9 mois	3	2	1	-	-	-
10 months - 10 mois	6	3	3	♦0.1	♦0.1	♦0.1
11 months - 11 mois	1	1	-	-	-	-
Denmark - Danemark[20]						
2016 (C)						
Total	194	114	80	3.1	3.6	2.7
Less than 1 day - Moins de 1 jour	102	64	38	1.7	2.0	1.3
1 - 6 days - 1 - 6 jours	39	19	20	0.6	♦0.6	♦0.7
7 - 27 days - 7 - 27 jours	18	8	10	♦0.3	♦0.3	♦0.3
7 - 13 days - 7 - 13 jours	8	2	6	♦0.1	♦0.1	♦0.2
14 - 20 days - 14 - 20 jours	5	2	3	♦0.1	♦0.1	♦0.1
21 - 27 days - 21 - 27 jours	5	4	1	♦0.1	♦0.1	-
28 days - 11 months - 28 jours - 11 mois	35	23	12	0.6	♦0.7	♦0.4
28 days - less than 2 months - 28 jours - moins de 2 mois	13	7	6	♦0.2	♦0.2	♦0.2
2 months - 2 mois	4	3	1	♦0.1	♦0.1	-
3 months - 3 mois	4	2	2	♦0.1	♦0.1	♦0.1
4 months - 4 mois	3	3	-	-	♦0.1	-
5 months - 5 mois	-	-	-	-	-	-
6 months - 6 mois	2	1	1	-	-	-
7 months - 7 mois	-	-	-	-	-	-
8 months - 8 mois	-	-	-	-	-	-
9 months - 9 mois	3	3	-	-	♦0.1	-
10 months - 10 mois	4	3	1	♦0.1	♦0.1	-
11 months - 11 mois	2	1	1	-	-	-
Estonia - Estonie						
2016 (C)						
Total	33	22	11	...	...	...
Less than 1 day - Moins de 1 jour	2	1	1	...	...	...
1 - 6 days - 1 - 6 jours	8	7	1	...	...	...
7 - 27 days - 7 - 27 jours	9	6	3	...	...	...
7 - 13 days - 7 - 13 jours	3	2	1	...	...	...
14 - 20 days - 14 - 20 jours	1	-	1	...	...	...
21 - 27 days - 21 - 27 jours	5	4	1	...	...	...
28 days - 11 months - 28 jours - 11 mois	14	8	6	...	...	...
28 days - less than 2 months - 28 jours - moins de 2 mois	2	2	-	...	...	...
2 months - 2 mois	2	1	1	...	...	...
3 months - 3 mois	3	1	2	...	...	...
4 months - 4 mois	1	1	-	...	...	...
5 months - 5 mois	-	-	-	...	...	...
6 months - 6 mois	1	-	1	...	...	...
7 months - 7 mois	3	1	2	...	...	...
8 months - 8 mois	-	-	-	...	...	...
9 months - 9 mois	1	1	-	...	...	...
10 months - 10 mois	-	-	-	...	...	...
11 months - 11 mois	1	1	-	...	...	...
Faeroe Islands - Îles Féroé[21]						
2017 (C)						
Total	7	2	5	...	...	...
Less than 1 day - Moins de 1 jour	3	1	2	...	...	...
1 - 6 days - 1 - 6 jours	1	1	-	...	...	...
7 - 27 days - 7 - 27 jours	-	-	-	...	...	...
7 - 13 days - 7 - 13 jours	-	-	-	...	...	...
14 - 20 days - 14 - 20 jours	-	-	-	...	...	...

Continent, country or area, year, code[a] and age / Continent, pays ou zone, année, code[a] et âge	Number - Nombre			Rate - Taux		
	Both sexes Les deux sexes	Male Masculin	Female Féminin	Both sexes Les deux sexes	Male Masculin	Female Féminin
EUROPE						
Faeroe Islands - Îles Féroé[21]						
2017 (C)						
21 - 27 days - 21 - 27 jours	-	-	-	...	...	...
28 days - 11 months - 28 jours - 11 mois	3	-	3	...	...	...
28 days - less than 2 months - 28 jours - moins de 2 mois	3	-	3	...	...	...
2 months - 2 mois	-	-	-	...	...	...
3 months - 3 mois	-	-	-	...	...	...
4 months - 4 mois	-	-	-	...	...	...
5 months - 5 mois	-	-	-	...	...	...
6 months - 6 mois	-	-	-	...	...	...
7 months - 7 mois	-	-	-	...	...	...
8 months - 8 mois	-	-	-	...	...	...
9 months - 9 mois	-	-	-	...	...	...
10 months - 10 mois	-	-	-	...	...	...
11 months - 11 mois	-	-	-	...	...	...
Finland - Finlande[22]						
2016 (C)						
Total	99	58	41	...	...	...
Less than 1 day - Moins de 1 jour	28	12	16	...	...	...
1 - 6 days - 1 - 6 jours	24	17	7	...	...	...
7 - 27 days - 7 - 27 jours	13	8	5	...	...	...
7 - 13 days - 7 - 13 jours	2	1	1	...	...	...
14 - 20 days - 14 - 20 jours	4	3	1	...	...	...
21 - 27 days - 21 - 27 jours	7	4	3	...	...	...
28 days - 11 months - 28 jours - 11 mois	34	21	13	...	...	...
28 days - less than 2 months - 28 jours - moins de 2 mois	2	-	2	...	...	...
2 months - 2 mois	10	6	4	...	...	...
3 months - 3 mois	5	4	1	...	...	...
4 months - 4 mois	3	2	1	...	...	...
5 months - 5 mois	3	3	-	...	...	...
6 months - 6 mois	2	1	1	...	...	...
7 months - 7 mois	3	2	1	...	...	...
8 months - 8 mois	2	1	1	...	...	...
9 months - 9 mois	1	1	-	...	...	...
10 months - 10 mois	2	-	2	...	...	...
11 months - 11 mois	1	1	-	...	...	...
France						
2016 (C)						
Total	2 577	1 448	1 129	3.5	3.8	3.1
Less than 1 day - Moins de 1 jour	689	376	313	0.9	1.0	0.9
1 - 6 days - 1 - 6 jours	601	349	252	0.8	0.9	0.7
7 - 27 days - 7 - 27 jours	531	303	228	0.7	0.8	0.6
7 - 13 days - 7 - 13 jours	292	164	128	0.4	0.4	0.4
14 - 20 days - 14 - 20 jours	136	76	60	0.2	0.2	0.2
21 - 27 days - 21 - 27 jours	103	63	40	0.1	0.2	0.1
28 days - 11 months - 28 jours - 11 mois	756	420	336	1.0	1.1	0.9
28 days - less than 2 months - 28 jours - moins de 2 mois	222	113	109	0.3	0.3	0.3
2 months - 2 mois	118	68	50	0.2	0.2	0.1
3 months - 3 mois	101	59	42	0.1	0.2	0.1
4 months - 4 mois	64	39	25	0.1	0.1	♦0.1
5 months - 5 mois	59	38	21	0.1	0.1	♦0.1
6 months - 6 mois	45	22	23	0.1	♦0.1	♦0.1
7 months - 7 mois	35	17	18	-	-	-
8 months - 8 mois	36	22	14	-	♦0.1	-
9 months - 9 mois	29	17	12	-	-	-
10 months - 10 mois	24	13	11	-	-	-
11 months - 11 mois	23	12	11	-	-	-
Germany - Allemagne						
2016 (C)						
Total	2 700	1 495	1 205	3.4	3.7	3.1
Less than 1 day - Moins de 1 jour	974	524	450	1.2	1.3	1.2
1 - 6 days - 1 - 6 jours	544	306	238	0.7	0.8	0.6
7 - 27 days - 7 - 27 jours	402	214	188	0.5	0.5	0.5
28 days - 11 months - 28 jours - 11 mois	780	451	329	1.0	1.1	0.9
Greece - Grèce						
2016 (C)						
Total	387	237	150	4.2	4.9	3.3
Less than 1 day - Moins de 1 jour	76	45	31	0.8	0.9	0.7

16. Infant deaths and infant mortality rates by age and sex: latest available year, 2008 - 2017
Décès d'enfants de moins d'un an et taux de mortalité infantile selon l'âge et le sexe : dernière année disponible, 2008 - 2017 (continued - suite)

Continent, country or area, year, code[a] and age / Continent, pays ou zone, année, code[a] et âge	Number - Nombre			Rate - Taux		
	Both sexes Les deux sexes	Male Masculin	Female Féminin	Both sexes Les deux sexes	Male Masculin	Female Féminin
EUROPE						
Greece - Grèce						
2016 (C)						
1 - 6 days - 1 - 6 jours	90	58	32	1.0	1.2	0.7
7 - 27 days - 7 - 27 jours	95	59	36	1.0	1.2	0.8
7 - 13 days - 7 - 13 jours	53	30	23	0.6	0.6	◆0.5
14 - 20 days - 14 - 20 jours	27	18	9	◆0.3	◆0.4	◆0.2
21 - 27 days - 21 - 27 jours	15	11	4	◆0.2	◆0.2	◆0.1
28 days - 11 months - 28 jours - 11 mois	124	75	49	1.3	1.6	1.1
28 days - less than 2 months - 28 jours - moins de 2 mois	47	31	16	0.5	0.6	◆0.4
2 months - 2 mois	20	13	7	◆0.2	◆0.3	◆0.2
3 months - 3 mois	13	9	4	◆0.1	◆0.2	◆0.1
4 months - 4 mois	8	3	5	◆0.1	◆0.1	◆0.1
5 months - 5 mois	13	7	6	◆0.1	◆0.1	◆0.1
6 months - 6 mois	5	1	4	◆0.1	-	◆0.1
7 months - 7 mois	5	5	-	◆0.1	◆0.1	-
8 months - 8 mois	4	2	2	-	-	-
9 months - 9 mois	3	1	2	-	-	-
10 months - 10 mois	4	3	1	-	◆0.1	-
11 months - 11 mois	2	-	2	-	-	-
Unknown - Inconnu	2	-	2	-	-	-
Hungary - Hongrie[23]						
2016 (C)						
Total	368	203	165	3.9	4.1	3.6
Less than 1 day - Moins de 1 jour	80	46	34	0.8	0.9	0.7
1 - 6 days - 1 - 6 jours	67	41	26	0.7	0.8	◆0.6
7 - 27 days - 7 - 27 jours	92	48	44	1.0	1.0	0.9
7 - 13 days - 7 - 13 jours	55	30	25	0.6	0.6	◆0.5
14 - 20 days - 14 - 20 jours	19	10	9	◆0.2	◆0.2	◆0.2
21 - 27 days - 21 - 27 jours	18	8	10	◆0.2	◆0.2	◆0.2
28 days - 11 months - 28 jours - 11 mois	129	68	61	1.4	1.4	1.3
28 days - less than 2 months - 28 jours - moins de 2 mois	40	19	21	0.4	◆0.4	◆0.5
2 months - 2 mois	19	13	6	◆0.2	◆0.3	◆0.1
3 months - 3 mois	21	7	14	◆0.2	◆0.1	◆0.3
4 months - 4 mois	12	7	5	◆0.1	◆0.1	◆0.1
5 months - 5 mois	8	5	3	◆0.1	◆0.1	◆0.1
6 months - 6 mois	5	3	2	◆0.1	◆0.1	-
7 months - 7 mois	7	3	4	◆0.1	◆0.1	◆0.1
8 months - 8 mois	4	4	-	-	◆0.1	-
9 months - 9 mois	6	2	4	◆0.1	-	◆0.1
10 months - 10 mois	4	2	2	-	-	-
11 months - 11 mois	3	3	-	-	◆0.1	-
Iceland - Islande						
2016 (C)						
Total	3	2	1	...	...	...
Less than 1 day - Moins de 1 jour	-	-	-	...	...	...
1 - 6 days - 1 - 6 jours	-	-	-	...	...	...
7 - 27 days - 7 - 27 jours	2	1	1	...	...	...
7 - 13 days - 7 - 13 jours	1	-	1	...	...	...
14 - 20 days - 14 - 20 jours	1	1	-	...	...	...
21 - 27 days - 21 - 27 jours	-	-	-	...	...	...
28 days - 11 months - 28 jours - 11 mois	1	1	-	...	...	...
28 days - less than 2 months - 28 jours - moins de 2 mois	-	-	-	...	...	...
2 months - 2 mois	-	-	-	...	...	...
3 months - 3 mois	-	-	-	...	...	...
4 months - 4 mois	-	-	-	...	...	...
5 months - 5 mois	1	1	-	...	...	...
6 months - 6 mois	-	-	-	...	...	...
7 months - 7 mois	-	-	-	...	...	...
8 months - 8 mois	-	-	-	...	...	...
9 months - 9 mois	-	-	-	...	...	...
10 months - 10 mois	-	-	-	...	...	...
11 months - 11 mois	-	-	-	...	...	...
Ireland - Irlande						
2011 (+C)						
Total	262	150	112	3.5	4.0	3.1
Less than 1 day - Moins de 1 jour	88	43	45	1.2	1.1	1.2
1 - 6 days - 1 - 6 jours	59	38	21	0.8	1.0	◆0.6

16. Infant deaths and infant mortality rates by age and sex: latest available year, 2008 - 2017
Décès d'enfants de moins d'un an et taux de mortalité infantile selon l'âge et le sexe : dernière année disponible, 2008 - 2017 (continued - suite)

Continent, country or area, year, code[a] and age / Continent, pays ou zone, année, code[a] et âge	Number - Nombre			Rate - Taux		
	Both sexes Les deux sexes	Male Masculin	Female Féminin	Both sexes Les deux sexes	Male Masculin	Female Féminin
EUROPE						
Ireland - Irlande						
2011 (+C)						
7 - 27 days - 7 - 27 jours	41	30	11	0.6	0.8	♦0.3
7 - 13 days - 7 - 13 jours	18	13	5	♦0.2	♦0.3	♦0.1
14 - 20 days - 14 - 20 jours	17	13	4	♦0.2	♦0.3	♦0.1
21 - 27 days - 21 - 27 jours	6	4	2	♦0.1	♦0.1	♦0.1
28 days - 11 months - 28 jours - 11 mois	74	39	35	1.0	1.0	1.0
28 days - less than 2 months - 28 jours - moins de 2 mois	20	12	8	♦0.3	♦0.3	♦0.2
2 months - 2 mois	17	7	10	♦0.2	♦0.2	♦0.3
3 months - 3 mois	11	4	7	♦0.1	♦0.1	♦0.2
4 months - 4 mois	5	5	-	♦0.1	♦0.1	-
5 months - 5 mois	6	3	3	♦0.1	♦0.1	♦0.1
6 months - 6 mois	3	1	2	-	-	♦0.1
7 months - 7 mois	2	1	1	-	-	-
8 months - 8 mois	1	-	1	-	-	-
9 months - 9 mois	4	3	1	♦0.1	♦0.1	-
10 months - 10 mois	4	2	2	♦0.1	♦0.1	♦0.1
11 months - 11 mois	1	1	-	-	-	-
Italy - Italie						
2013 (C)						
Total	1 493	864	629	2.9	3.3	2.5
Less than 1 day - Moins de 1 jour	268	153	115	0.5	0.6	0.5
1 - 6 days - 1 - 6 jours	447	279	168	0.9	1.1	0.7
7 - 27 days - 7 - 27 jours	311	175	136	0.6	0.7	0.5
7 - 13 days - 7 - 13 jours	151	87	64	0.3	0.3	0.3
14 - 20 days - 14 - 20 jours	92	47	45	0.2	0.2	0.2
21 - 27 days - 21 - 27 jours	68	41	27	0.1	0.2	♦0.1
28 days - 11 months - 28 jours - 11 mois	467	257	210	0.9	1.0	0.8
28 days - less than 2 months - 28 jours - moins de 2 mois	149	90	59	0.3	0.3	0.2
2 months - 2 mois	69	31	38	0.1	0.1	0.2
3 months - 3 mois	50	20	30	0.1	♦0.1	0.1
4 months - 4 mois	44	26	18	0.1	♦0.1	♦0.1
5 months - 5 mois	35	21	14	0.1	♦0.1	♦0.1
6 months - 6 mois	33	21	12	0.1	♦0.1	-
7 months - 7 mois	27	10	17	♦0.1	-	♦0.1
8 months - 8 mois	20	16	4	-	♦0.1	-
9 months - 9 mois	18	11	7	-	-	-
10 months - 10 mois	13	6	7	-	-	-
11 months - 11 mois	9	5	4	-	-	-
Latvia - Lettonie						
2016 (C)						
Total	81	38	43	...	...	...
Less than 1 day - Moins de 1 jour	19	5	14	...	...	...
1 - 6 days - 1 - 6 jours	19	11	8	...	...	...
7 - 27 days - 7 - 27 jours	17	8	9	...	...	...
7 - 13 days - 7 - 13 jours	8	3	5	...	...	...
14 - 20 days - 14 - 20 jours	5	3	2	...	...	...
21 - 27 days - 21 - 27 jours	4	2	2	...	...	...
28 days - 11 months - 28 jours - 11 mois	26	14	12	...	...	...
28 days - less than 2 months - 28 jours - moins de 2 mois	9	5	4	...	...	...
2 months - 2 mois	1	1	-	...	...	...
3 months - 3 mois	3	2	1	...	...	...
4 months - 4 mois	1	-	1	...	...	...
5 months - 5 mois	2	2	-	...	...	...
6 months - 6 mois	1	1	-	...	...	...
7 months - 7 mois	4	2	2	...	...	...
8 months - 8 mois	3	1	2	...	...	...
9 months - 9 mois	1	-	1	...	...	...
10 months - 10 mois	-	-	-	...	...	...
11 months - 11 mois	1	-	1	...	...	...
Liechtenstein						
2015 (C)						
Total	2	2	-	...	...	...
1 - 6 days - 1 - 6 jours	2	2	-	...	...	...
Lithuania - Lituanie						
2016 (C)						
Total	139	69	70	4.5	4.4	4.7
Less than 1 day - Moins de 1 jour	24	13	11	♦0.8	♦0.8	♦0.7

Continent, country or area, year, code[a] and age / Continent, pays ou zone, année, code[a] et âge	Number - Nombre			Rate - Taux		
	Both sexes Les deux sexes	Male Masculin	Female Féminin	Both sexes Les deux sexes	Male Masculin	Female Féminin
EUROPE						
Lithuania - Lituanie						
2016 (C)						
1 - 6 days - 1 - 6 jours	26	14	12	♦0.8	♦0.9	♦0.8
7 - 27 days - 7 - 27 jours	26	14	12	♦0.8	♦0.9	♦0.8
7 - 13 days - 7 - 13 jours	15	10	5	♦0.5	♦0.6	♦0.3
14 - 20 days - 14 - 20 jours	5	2	3	♦0.2	♦0.1	♦0.2
21 - 27 days - 21 - 27 jours	6	2	4	♦0.2	♦0.1	♦0.3
28 days - 11 months - 28 jours - 11 mois	63	28	35	2.1	♦1.8	2.4
28 days - less than 2 months - 28 jours - moins de 2 mois	19	9	10	♦0.6	♦0.6	♦0.7
2 months - 2 mois	6	5	1	♦0.2	♦0.3	♦0.1
3 months - 3 mois	6	2	4	♦0.2	♦0.1	♦0.3
4 months - 4 mois	8	3	5	♦0.3	♦0.2	♦0.3
5 months - 5 mois	5	3	2	♦0.2	♦0.2	♦0.1
6 months - 6 mois	3	2	1	♦0.1	♦0.1	♦0.1
7 months - 7 mois	6	1	5	♦0.2	♦0.1	♦0.3
8 months - 8 mois	2	-	2	♦0.1	-	♦0.1
9 months - 9 mois	3	1	2	♦0.1	♦0.1	♦0.1
10 months - 10 mois	4	2	2	♦0.1	♦0.1	♦0.1
11 months - 11 mois	1	-	1	-	-	♦0.1
Luxembourg						
2016 (C)						
Total	23	16	7	...	...	...
Less than 1 day - Moins de 1 jour	8	7	1	...	...	...
1 - 6 days - 1 - 6 jours	5	4	1	...	...	...
7 - 27 days - 7 - 27 jours	5	3	2	...	...	...
7 - 13 days - 7 - 13 jours	4	2	2	...	...	...
14 - 20 days - 14 - 20 jours	-	-	-	...	...	...
21 - 27 days - 21 - 27 jours	1	1	-	...	...	...
28 days - 11 months - 28 jours - 11 mois	5	2	3	...	...	...
28 days - less than 2 months - 28 jours - moins de 2 mois	2	1	1	...	...	...
2 months - 2 mois	2	-	2	...	...	...
3 months - 3 mois	-	-	-	...	...	...
4 months - 4 mois	-	-	-	...	...	...
5 months - 5 mois	-	-	-	...	...	...
6 months - 6 mois	-	-	-	...	...	...
7 months - 7 mois	-	-	-	...	...	...
8 months - 8 mois	-	-	-	...	...	...
9 months - 9 mois	1	1	-	...	...	...
10 months - 10 mois	-	-	-	...	...	...
11 months - 11 mois	-	-	-	...	...	...
Malta - Malte						
2016 (C)						
Total	33	20	13	...	...	...
Less than 1 day - Moins de 1 jour	9	6	3	...	...	...
1 - 6 days - 1 - 6 jours	12	4	8	...	...	...
7 - 27 days - 7 - 27 jours	3	2	1	...	...	...
7 - 13 days - 7 - 13 jours	3	2	1	...	...	...
14 - 20 days - 14 - 20 jours	-	-	-	...	...	...
21 - 27 days - 21 - 27 jours	-	-	-	...	...	...
28 days - 11 months - 28 jours - 11 mois	9	8	1	...	...	...
28 days - less than 2 months - 28 jours - moins de 2 mois	6	6	-	...	...	...
2 months - 2 mois	1	1	-	...	...	...
3 months - 3 mois	-	-	-	...	...	...
4 months - 4 mois	1	-	1	...	...	...
5 months - 5 mois	1	1	-	...	...	...
6 months - 6 mois	-	-	-	...	...	...
7 months - 7 mois	-	-	-	...	...	...
8 months - 8 mois	-	-	-	...	...	...
9 months - 9 mois	-	-	-	...	...	...
10 months - 10 mois	-	-	-	...	...	...
11 months - 11 mois	-	-	-	...	...	...
Montenegro - Monténégro						
2016 (C)						
Total	26	11	15	...	...	...
Less than 1 day - Moins de 1 jour	2	-	2	...	...	...
1 - 6 days - 1 - 6 jours	8	3	5	...	...	...
7 - 27 days - 7 - 27 jours	5	3	2	...	...	...
7 - 13 days - 7 - 13 jours	3	2	1	...	...	...

16. Infant deaths and infant mortality rates by age and sex: latest available year, 2008 - 2017
Décès d'enfants de moins d'un an et taux de mortalité infantile selon l'âge et le sexe : dernière année disponible, 2008 - 2017 (continued - suite)

Continent, country or area, year, code[a] and age Continent, pays ou zone, année, code[a] et âge	Number - Nombre			Rate - Taux		
	Both sexes Les deux sexes	Male Masculin	Female Féminin	Both sexes Les deux sexes	Male Masculin	Female Féminin
EUROPE						
Montenegro - Monténégro						
2016 (C)						
14 - 20 days - 14 - 20 jours	1	1	-	...	...	...
21 - 27 days - 21 - 27 jours	1	-	1	...	...	...
28 days - 11 months - 28 jours - 11 mois	11	5	6	...	...	...
28 days - less than 2 months - 28 jours - moins de 2 mois	3	1	2	...	...	...
2 months - 2 mois	-	-	-	...	...	...
3 months - 3 mois	2	1	1	...	...	...
4 months - 4 mois	-	-	-	...	...	...
5 months - 5 mois	1	-	1	...	...	...
6 months - 6 mois	-	-	-	...	...	...
7 months - 7 mois	2	2	-	...	...	...
8 months - 8 mois	3	1	2	...	...	...
9 months - 9 mois	-	-	-	...	...	...
10 months - 10 mois	-	-	-	...	...	...
11 months - 11 mois	-	-	-	...	...	...
Netherlands - Pays-Bas[24]						
2016 (C)						
Total	597	323	274	3.5	3.6	3.3
Less than 1 day - Moins de 1 jour	191	105	86	1.1	1.2	1.0
1 - 6 days - 1 - 6 jours	149	77	72	0.9	0.9	0.9
7 - 27 days - 7 - 27 jours	104	65	39	0.6	0.7	0.5
28 days - 11 months - 28 jours - 11 mois	153	76	77	0.9	0.9	0.9
Norway - Norvège[25]						
2016 (C)						
Total	128	71	57	2.2	2.3	2.0
Less than 1 day - Moins de 1 jour	28	13	15	♦0.5	♦0.4	♦0.5
1 - 6 days - 1 - 6 jours	34	19	15	0.6	♦0.6	♦0.5
7 - 27 days - 7 - 27 jours	31	20	11	0.5	♦0.7	♦0.4
28 days - 11 months - 28 jours - 11 mois	35	19	16	0.6	♦0.6	♦0.6
Poland - Pologne						
2016 (C)						
Total	1 522	868	654	4.0	4.4	3.5
Less than 1 day - Moins de 1 jour	431	256	175	1.1	1.3	0.9
1 - 6 days - 1 - 6 jours	363	204	159	0.9	1.0	0.9
7 - 27 days - 7 - 27 jours	300	158	142	0.8	0.8	0.8
7 - 13 days - 7 - 13 jours	147	79	68	0.4	0.4	0.4
14 - 20 days - 14 - 20 jours	86	43	43	0.2	0.2	0.2
21 - 27 days - 21 - 27 jours	67	36	31	0.2	0.2	0.2
28 days - 11 months - 28 jours - 11 mois	428	250	178	1.1	1.3	1.0
28 days - less than 2 months - 28 jours - moins de 2 mois	139	76	63	0.4	0.4	0.3
2 months - 2 mois	67	42	25	0.2	0.2	♦0.1
3 months - 3 mois	58	35	23	0.2	0.2	♦0.1
4 months - 4 mois	32	19	13	0.1	♦0.1	♦0.1
5 months - 5 mois	21	13	8	♦0.1	♦0.1	-
6 months - 6 mois	25	12	13	♦0.1	♦0.1	♦0.1
7 months - 7 mois	20	16	4	♦0.1	♦0.1	-
8 months - 8 mois	26	16	10	♦0.1	♦0.1	♦0.1
9 months - 9 mois	11	6	5	-	-	-
10 months - 10 mois	17	8	9	-	-	-
11 months - 11 mois	12	7	5	-	-	-
Portugal[26]						
2016 (C)						
Total	282	165	117	3.2	3.7	2.8
Less than 1 day - Moins de 1 jour	55	29	26	0.6	♦0.6	♦0.6
1 - 6 days - 1 - 6 jours	74	49	25	0.8	1.1	♦0.6
7 - 27 days - 7 - 27 jours	73	36	37	0.8	0.8	0.9
7 - 13 days - 7 - 13 jours	42	18	24	0.5	♦0.4	♦0.6
14 - 20 days - 14 - 20 jours	18	10	8	♦0.2	♦0.2	♦0.2
21 - 27 days - 21 - 27 jours	13	8	5	♦0.1	♦0.2	♦0.1
28 days - 11 months - 28 jours - 11 mois	80	51	29	0.9	1.1	♦0.7
28 days - less than 2 months - 28 jours - moins de 2 mois	26	17	9	♦0.3	♦0.4	♦0.2
2 months - 2 mois	8	4	4	♦0.1	♦0.1	♦0.1
3 months - 3 mois	5	3	2	♦0.1	♦0.1	-
4 months - 4 mois	10	8	2	♦0.1	♦0.2	-
5 months - 5 mois	12	8	4	♦0.1	♦0.2	♦0.1
6 months - 6 mois	4	3	1	-	♦0.1	-
7 months - 7 mois	3	1	2	-	-	-

16. Infant deaths and infant mortality rates by age and sex: latest available year, 2008 - 2017
Décès d'enfants de moins d'un an et taux de mortalité infantile selon l'âge et le sexe : dernière année disponible, 2008 - 2017 (continued - suite)

Continent, country or area, year, code[a] and age Continent, pays ou zone, année, code[a] et âge	Number - Nombre			Rate - Taux		
	Both sexes Les deux sexes	Male Masculin	Female Féminin	Both sexes Les deux sexes	Male Masculin	Female Féminin
EUROPE						
Portugal[26]						
2016 (C)						
8 months - 8 mois	6	2	4	♦0.1	-	♦0.1
9 months - 9 mois	2	2	-	-	-	-
10 months - 10 mois	2	2	-	-	-	-
11 months - 11 mois	2	1	1	-	-	-
Republic of Moldova - République de Moldova[27]						
2016 (C)						
Total	353	204	149	9.4	10.6	8.2
Less than 1 day - Moins de 1 jour	75	41	34	2.0	2.1	1.9
1 - 6 days - 1 - 6 jours	94	59	35	2.5	3.1	1.9
7 - 27 days - 7 - 27 jours	73	42	31	2.0	2.2	1.7
28 days - 11 months - 28 jours - 11 mois	111	62	49	3.0	3.2	2.7
Romania - Roumanie						
2016 (C)						
Total	1 398	813	585	7.0	7.9	6.0
Less than 1 day - Moins de 1 jour	178	91	87	0.9	0.9	0.9
1 - 6 days - 1 - 6 jours	345	208	137	1.7	2.0	1.4
7 - 27 days - 7 - 27 jours	254	148	106	1.3	1.4	1.1
28 days - 11 months - 28 jours - 11 mois	621	366	255	3.1	3.6	2.6
Russian Federation - Fédération de Russie[9]						
2012 (C)						
Total	16 306	9 219	7 087	8.6	9.4	7.7
Less than 1 day - Moins de 1 jour	1 897	1 009	888	1.0	1.0	1.0
1 - 6 days - 1 - 6 jours	5 072	2 961	2 111	2.7	3.0	2.3
7 - 27 days - 7 - 27 jours	3 438	1 958	1 480	1.8	2.0	1.6
7 - 13 days - 7 - 13 jours	1 798	1 020	778	0.9	1.0	0.8
14 - 20 days - 14 - 20 jours	952	560	392	0.5	0.6	0.4
21 - 27 days - 21 - 27 jours	688	378	310	0.4	0.4	0.3
28 days - 11 months - 28 jours - 11 mois	5 898	3 290	2 608	3.1	3.4	2.8
28 days - less than 2 months - 28 jours - moins de 2 mois	2 063	1 166	897	1.1	1.2	1.0
2 months - 2 mois	942	525	417	0.5	0.5	0.5
3 months - 3 mois	691	372	319	0.4	0.4	0.3
4 months - 4 mois	562	333	229	0.3	0.3	0.2
5 months - 5 mois	417	221	196	0.2	0.2	0.2
6 months - 6 mois	334	184	150	0.2	0.2	0.2
7 months - 7 mois	252	139	113	0.1	0.1	0.1
8 months - 8 mois	219	127	92	0.1	0.1	0.1
9 months - 9 mois	172	86	86	0.1	0.1	0.1
10 months - 10 mois	134	74	60	0.1	0.1	0.1
11 months - 11 mois	112	63	49	0.1	0.1	0.1
Unknown - Inconnu	1	1	-	-	-	-
San Marino - Saint-Marin						
2014 (C)						
Total	1	1	-	...	...	...
Less than 1 day - Moins de 1 jour	-	-	-	...	...	...
1 - 6 days - 1 - 6 jours	-	-	-	...	...	...
7 - 27 days - 7 - 27 jours	-	-	-	...	...	...
28 days - 11 months - 28 jours - 11 mois	1	1	-	...	...	...
Serbia - Serbie[28]						
2016 (+C)						
Total	348	210	138	5.4	6.3	4.4
Less than 1 day - Moins de 1 jour	85	49	36	1.3	1.5	1.2
1 - 6 days - 1 - 6 jours	102	65	37	1.6	1.9	1.2
7 - 27 days - 7 - 27 jours	70	41	29	1.1	1.2	♦0.9
7 - 13 days - 7 - 13 jours	39	26	13	0.6	♦0.8	♦0.4
14 - 20 days - 14 - 20 jours	22	10	12	♦0.3	♦0.3	♦0.4
21 - 27 days - 21 - 27 jours	9	5	4	♦0.1	♦0.1	♦0.1
28 days - 11 months - 28 jours - 11 mois	91	55	36	1.4	1.6	1.2
28 days - less than 2 months - 28 jours - moins de 2 mois	32	17	15	0.5	♦0.5	♦0.5
2 months - 2 mois	15	8	7	♦0.2	♦0.2	♦0.2
3 months - 3 mois	9	7	2	♦0.1	♦0.2	♦0.1
4 months - 4 mois	9	7	2	♦0.1	♦0.2	♦0.1
5 months - 5 mois	3	2	1	-	♦0.1	-
6 months - 6 mois	5	4	1	♦0.1	♦0.1	-
7 months - 7 mois	4	2	2	♦0.1	♦0.1	♦0.1
8 months - 8 mois	3	1	2	-	-	♦0.1
9 months - 9 mois	5	3	2	♦0.1	♦0.1	♦0.1

16. Infant deaths and infant mortality rates by age and sex: latest available year, 2008 - 2017
Décès d'enfants de moins d'un an et taux de mortalité infantile selon l'âge et le sexe : dernière année disponible, 2008 - 2017 (continued - suite)

Continent, country or area, year, code[a] and age / Continent, pays ou zone, année, code[a] et âge	Number - Nombre			Rate - Taux		
	Both sexes Les deux sexes	Male Masculin	Female Féminin	Both sexes Les deux sexes	Male Masculin	Female Féminin
EUROPE						
Serbia - Serbie[28]						
2016 (+C)						
10 months - 10 mois	3	1	2	-	-	◆0.1
11 months - 11 mois	3	3	-	-	◆0.1	-
Slovakia - Slovaquie						
2016 (C)						
Total	311	179	132	5.4	6.1	4.7
Less than 1 day - Moins de 1 jour	51	28	23	0.9	◆0.9	◆0.8
1 - 6 days - 1 - 6 jours	43	23	20	0.7	◆0.8	◆0.7
7 - 27 days - 7 - 27 jours	71	39	32	1.2	1.3	1.1
7 - 13 days - 7 - 13 jours	40	21	19	0.7	◆0.7	◆0.7
14 - 20 days - 14 - 20 jours	20	13	7	◆0.3	◆0.4	◆0.2
21 - 27 days - 21 - 27 jours	11	5	6	◆0.2	◆0.2	◆0.2
28 days - 11 months - 28 jours - 11 mois	146	89	57	2.5	3.0	2.0
28 days - less than 2 months - 28 jours - moins de 2 mois	42	30	12	0.7	1.0	◆0.4
2 months - 2 mois	29	21	8	◆0.5	◆0.7	◆0.3
3 months - 3 mois	22	12	10	◆0.4	◆0.4	◆0.4
4 months - 4 mois	12	6	6	◆0.2	◆0.2	◆0.2
5 months - 5 mois	7	4	3	◆0.1	◆0.1	◆0.1
6 months - 6 mois	13	7	6	◆0.2	◆0.2	◆0.2
7 months - 7 mois	6	3	3	◆0.1	◆0.1	◆0.1
8 months - 8 mois	3	1	2	◆0.1	-	◆0.1
9 months - 9 mois	6	3	3	◆0.1	◆0.1	◆0.1
10 months - 10 mois	5	2	3	◆0.1	◆0.1	◆0.1
11 months - 11 mois	1	-	1	-		
Slovenia - Slovénie						
2016 (C)						
Total	41	20	21	...	...	...
Less than 1 day - Moins de 1 jour	12	5	7	...	...	...
1 - 6 days - 1 - 6 jours	6	3	3	...	...	...
7 - 27 days - 7 - 27 jours	10	6	4	...	...	...
28 days - 11 months - 28 jours - 11 mois	13	6	...	...	...	...
28 days - less than 2 months - 28 jours - moins de 2 mois	7	3	4	...	...	...
2 months - 2 mois	1	-	1	...	...	...
3 months - 3 mois	2	1	1	...	...	...
4 months - 4 mois	2	2	...	...	...	...
5 months - 5 mois	-	-	...	...	...	...
6 months - 6 mois	1	-	...	...	...	...
7 months - 7 mois	-	-	...	...	...	...
8 months - 8 mois	-	-	...	...	...	...
9 months - 9 mois	-	-	...	...	...	...
10 months - 10 mois	-	-	...	...	...	...
11 months - 11 mois	-	-	...	...	...	...
Spain - Espagne						
2016 (C)						
Total	1 097	641	456	2.7	3.1	2.3
Less than 1 day - Moins de 1 jour	235	136	99	0.6	0.6	0.5
1 - 6 days - 1 - 6 jours	288	176	112	0.7	0.8	0.6
7 - 27 days - 7 - 27 jours	234	143	91	0.6	0.7	0.5
7 - 13 days - 7 - 13 jours	133	82	51	0.3	0.4	0.3
14 - 20 days - 14 - 20 jours	65	40	25	0.2	0.2	◆0.1
21 - 27 days - 21 - 27 jours	36	21	15	0.1	◆0.1	◆0.1
28 days - 11 months - 28 jours - 11 mois	340	186	154	0.8	0.9	0.8
28 days - less than 2 months - 28 jours - moins de 2 mois	106	54	52	0.3	0.3	0.3
2 months - 2 mois	51	27	24	0.1	◆0.1	◆0.1
3 months - 3 mois	38	15	23	0.1	◆0.1	◆0.1
4 months - 4 mois	30	18	12	0.1	◆0.1	◆0.1
5 months - 5 mois	26	16	10	◆0.1	◆0.1	◆0.1
6 months - 6 mois	20	13	7	-	◆0.1	-
7 months - 7 mois	16	11	5	-	◆0.1	-
8 months - 8 mois	11	7	4	-	-	-
9 months - 9 mois	14	10	4	-	-	-
10 months - 10 mois	15	8	7	-	-	-
11 months - 11 mois	13	7	6	-	-	-
Sweden - Suède						
2016 (C)						
Total	292	157	135	2.5	2.6	2.4
Less than 1 day - Moins de 1 jour	70	37	33	0.6	0.6	0.6

16. Infant deaths and infant mortality rates by age and sex: latest available year, 2008 - 2017
Décès d'enfants de moins d'un an et taux de mortalité infantile selon l'âge et le sexe : dernière année disponible, 2008 - 2017 (continued - suite)

Continent, country or area, year, code[a] and age Continent, pays ou zone, année, code[a] et âge	Number - Nombre			Rate - Taux		
	Both sexes Les deux sexes	Male Masculin	Female Féminin	Both sexes Les deux sexes	Male Masculin	Female Féminin
EUROPE						
Sweden - Suède						
2016 (C)						
1 - 6 days - 1 - 6 jours	64	36	28	0.5	0.6	♦0.5
7 - 27 days - 7 - 27 jours	48	26	22	0.4	♦0.4	♦0.4
28 days - 11 months - 28 jours - 11 mois	110	58	52	0.9	1.0	0.9
Switzerland - Suisse						
2016 (C)						
Total	316	154	162	3.6	3.4	3.8
Less than 1 day - Moins de 1 jour	178	82	96	2.0	1.8	2.2
1 - 6 days - 1 - 6 jours	44	22	22	0.5	♦0.5	♦0.5
7 - 27 days - 7 - 27 jours	42	21	21	0.5	♦0.5	♦0.5
7 - 13 days - 7 - 13 jours	25	11	14	♦0.3	♦0.2	♦0.3
14 - 20 days - 14 - 20 jours	8	5	3	♦0.1	♦0.1	♦0.1
21 - 27 days - 21 - 27 jours	9	5	4	♦0.1	♦0.1	♦0.1
28 days - 11 months - 28 jours - 11 mois	52	29	23	0.6	♦0.6	♦0.5
28 days - less than 2 months - 28 jours - moins de 2 mois	9	3	6	♦0.1	♦0.1	♦0.1
2 months - 2 mois	12	6	6	♦0.1	♦0.1	♦0.1
3 months - 3 mois	7	6	1	♦0.1	♦0.1	-
4 months - 4 mois	8	3	5	♦0.1	♦0.1	♦0.1
5 months - 5 mois	3	3	-	-	♦0.1	-
6 months - 6 mois	4	4	-	-	♦0.1	-
7 months - 7 mois	4	3	1	-	♦0.1	-
8 months - 8 mois	1	1	-	-	-	-
9 months - 9 mois	3	-	3	-	-	♦0.1
10 months - 10 mois	1	-	1	-	-	-
11 months - 11 mois	-	-	-	-	-	-
TFYR of Macedonia - L'ex-R. y. de Macédoine						
2016 (C)						
Total	273	140	133	11.9	11.8	11.9
Less than 1 day - Moins de 1 jour	65	31	34	2.8	2.6	3.1
1 - 6 days - 1 - 6 jours	109	56	53	4.7	4.7	4.8
7 - 27 days - 7 - 27 jours	60	32	28	2.6	2.7	♦2.5
7 - 13 days - 7 - 13 jours	41	18	23	1.8	♦1.5	♦2.1
14 - 20 days - 14 - 20 jours	14	9	5	♦0.6	♦0.8	♦0.4
21 - 27 days - 21 - 27 jours	5	5	-	♦0.2	♦0.4	-
28 days - 11 months - 28 jours - 11 mois	39	21	18	1.7	♦1.8	♦1.6
28 days - less than 2 months - 28 jours - moins de 2 mois	18	7	11	♦0.8	♦0.6	♦1.0
2 months - 2 mois	7	5	2	♦0.3	♦0.4	♦0.2
3 months - 3 mois	4	4	-	♦0.2	♦0.3	-
4 months - 4 mois	2	1	1	♦0.1	♦0.1	♦0.1
5 months - 5 mois	4	2	2	♦0.2	♦0.2	♦0.2
6 months - 6 mois	2	1	1	♦0.1	♦0.1	♦0.1
7 months - 7 mois	-	-	-	-	-	-
8 months - 8 mois	1	-	1	-	-	♦0.1
9 months - 9 mois	1	1	-	-	♦0.1	-
10 months - 10 mois	-	-	-	-	-	-
11 months - 11 mois	-	-	-	-	-	-
Ukraine[29]						
2016 (+C)						
Total	2 955	1 703	1 252	7.4	8.3	6.5
Less than 1 day - Moins de 1 jour	410	222	188	1.0	1.1	1.0
1 - 6 days - 1 - 6 jours	802	472	330	2.0	2.3	1.7
7 - 27 days - 7 - 27 jours	618	375	243	1.6	1.8	1.3
7 - 13 days - 7 - 13 jours	317	196	121	0.8	1.0	0.6
14 - 20 days - 14 - 20 jours	171	103	68	0.4	0.5	0.4
21 - 27 days - 21 - 27 jours	130	76	54	0.3	0.4	0.3
28 days - 11 months - 28 jours - 11 mois	1 125	634	491	2.8	3.1	2.6
28 days - less than 2 months - 28 jours - moins de 2 mois	344	198	146	0.9	1.0	0.8
2 months - 2 mois	197	112	85	0.5	0.5	0.4
3 months - 3 mois	138	86	52	0.3	0.4	0.3
4 months - 4 mois	125	73	52	0.3	0.4	0.3
5 months - 5 mois	72	34	38	0.2	0.2	0.2
6 months - 6 mois	65	35	30	0.2	0.2	0.2
7 months - 7 mois	41	22	19	0.1	♦0.1	♦0.1
8 months - 8 mois	50	29	21	0.1	♦0.1	♦0.1
9 months - 9 mois	30	13	17	0.1	♦0.1	♦0.1
10 months - 10 mois	35	17	18	0.1	♦0.1	♦0.1
11 months - 11 mois	28	15	13	♦0.1	♦0.1	♦0.1

16. Infant deaths and infant mortality rates by age and sex: latest available year, 2008 - 2017

Décès d'enfants de moins d'un an et taux de mortalité infantile selon l'âge et le sexe : dernière année disponible, 2008 - 2017 (continued - suite)

Continent, country or area, year, code[a] and age / Continent, pays ou zone, année, code[a] et âge	Number - Nombre			Rate - Taux		
	Both sexes Les deux sexes	Male Masculin	Female Féminin	Both sexes Les deux sexes	Male Masculin	Female Féminin
EUROPE						
United Kingdom of Great Britain and Northern Ireland - Royaume-Uni de Grande-Bretagne et d'Irlande du Nord[30]						
2016 (+C)						
Total	2 976	1 639	1 337	3.8	4.1	3.5
Less than 1 day - Moins de 1 jour	1 074	606	468	1.4	1.5	1.2
1 - 6 days - 1 - 6 jours	612	324	288	0.8	0.8	0.8
7 - 27 days - 7 - 27 jours	438	240	198	0.6	0.6	0.5
7 - 13 days - 7 - 13 jours	227	125	102	0.3	0.3	0.3
14 - 20 days - 14 - 20 jours	109	61	48	0.1	0.2	0.1
21 - 27 days - 21 - 27 jours	102	54	48	0.1	0.1	0.1
28 days - 11 months - 28 jours - 11 mois	852	469	383	1.1	1.2	1.0
28 days - less than 2 months - 28 jours - moins de 2 mois	276	152	124	0.4	0.4	0.3
2 months - 2 mois	139	71	68	0.2	0.2	0.2
3 months - 3 mois	97	55	42	0.1	0.1	0.1
4 months - 4 mois	94	50	44	0.1	0.1	0.1
5 months - 5 mois	45	25	20	0.1	♦0.1	♦0.1
6 months - 6 mois	48	27	21	0.1	♦0.1	♦0.1
7 months - 7 mois	42	27	15	0.1	♦0.1	-
8 months - 8 mois	40	26	14	0.1	♦0.1	-
9 months - 9 mois	29	16	13	-	-	-
10 months - 10 mois	25	14	11	-	-	-
11 months - 11 mois	17	6	11	-	-	-
OCEANIA - OCÉANIE						
Australia - Australie[31]						
2016 (C)						
Total	970	543	427	3.1	3.4	2.8
Less than 1 day - Moins de 1 jour	433	240	193	1.4	1.5	1.3
1 - 6 days - 1 - 6 jours	148	92	56	0.5	0.6	0.4
7 - 27 days - 7 - 27 jours	119	63	56	0.4	0.4	0.4
7 - 13 days - 7 - 13 jours	57	34	23	0.2	0.2	♦0.2
14 - 20 days - 14 - 20 jours	35	14	21	0.1	♦0.1	♦0.1
21 - 27 days - 21 - 27 jours	27	15	12	♦0.1	♦0.1	♦0.1
28 days - 11 months - 28 jours - 11 mois	270	146	121	0.9	0.9	0.8
28 days - less than 2 months - 28 jours - moins de 2 mois	78	45	33	0.3	0.3	0.2
2 months - 2 mois	52	23	29	0.2	♦0.1	♦0.2
3 months - 3 mois	34	21	13	0.1	♦0.1	♦0.1
4 months - 4 mois	28	17	11	♦0.1	♦0.1	♦0.1
5 months - 5 mois	19	8	11	♦0.1	♦0.1	♦0.1
6 months - 6 mois	9	3	6	-	-	-
7 months - 7 mois	13	7	6	-	-	-
8 months - 8 mois	10	2	6	-	-	-
9 months - 9 mois	11	7	2	-	-	-
10 months - 10 mois	8	7	1	-	-	-
11 months - 11 mois	8	6	3	-	-	-
French Polynesia - Polynésie française						
2008 (C)						
Total	23	...	...	...	...	...
Less than 7 days - Moins de 7 jours	14	...	...	...	...	...
7 - 27 days - 7 - 27 jours	-	...	...	...	...	...
28 days - 11 months - 28 jours - 11 mois	9	...	...	...	...	...
Guam[32]						
2015 (C)						
Total	47	23	24	...	...	...
Less than 1 day - Moins de 1 jour	10	4	6	...	...	...
1 - 6 days - 1 - 6 jours	16	9	7	...	...	...
7 - 27 days - 7 - 27 jours	7	1	6	...	...	...
7 - 13 days - 7 - 13 jours	2	-	2	...	...	...
14 - 20 days - 14 - 20 jours	4	1	3	...	...	...
21 - 27 days - 21 - 27 jours	1	-	1	...	...	...
28 days - 11 months - 28 jours - 11 mois	14	9	5	...	...	...
28 days - less than 2 months - 28 jours - moins de 2 mois	2	2	-	...	...	...
2 months - 2 mois	3	3	-	...	...	...
3 months - 3 mois	3	-	3	...	...	...
4 months - 4 mois	-	-	-	...	...	...
5 months - 5 mois	-	-	-	...	...	...

Continent, country or area, year, code[a] and age Continent, pays ou zone, année, code[a] et âge	Number - Nombre			Rate - Taux		
	Both sexes Les deux sexes	Male Masculin	Female Féminin	Both sexes Les deux sexes	Male Masculin	Female Féminin
OCEANIA - OCÉANIE						
Guam[32]						
2015 (C)						
6 months - 6 mois	2	1	1	...	...	...
7 months - 7 mois	-	-	-	...	...	...
8 months - 8 mois	2	2	-	...	...	...
9 months - 9 mois	1	1	-	...	...	...
10 months - 10 mois	1	-	1	...	...	...
11 months - 11 mois	-	-	-	...	...	...
New Caledonia - Nouvelle-Calédonie						
2015 (C)						
Total	25	18	7	...	...	...
Less than 1 day - Moins de 1 jour	4	3	1	...	...	...
1 - 6 days - 1 - 6 jours	5	4	1	...	...	...
7 - 27 days - 7 - 27 jours	7	5	2	...	...	...
7 - 13 days - 7 - 13 jours	5	4	1	...	...	...
14 - 20 days - 14 - 20 jours	2	1	1	...	...	...
21 - 27 days - 21 - 27 jours	-	-	-	...	...	...
28 days - 11 months - 28 jours - 11 mois	9	6	3	...	...	...
28 days - less than 2 months - 28 jours - moins de 2 mois	3	1	2	...	...	...
2 - 11 months - 2 - 11 mois	6	5	1	...	...	...
New Zealand - Nouvelle-Zélande[33]						
2017 (+C)						
Total	228	123	108	3.8	4.0	3.7
Less than 1 day - Moins de 1 jour	81	45	36	1.4	1.5	1.2
1 - 6 days - 1 - 6 jours	33	15	18	0.6	+0.5	+0.6
7 - 27 days - 7 - 27 jours	33	18	15	0.6	+0.6	+0.5
7 - 13 days - 7 - 13 jours	12	3	6	+0.2	+0.1	+0.2
14 - 20 days - 14 - 20 jours	9	6	3	+0.2	+0.2	+0.1
21 - 27 days - 21 - 27 jours	9	6	3	+0.2	+0.2	+0.1
28 days - 11 months - 28 jours - 11 mois	81	36	36	1.4	1.2	1.2
28 days - less than 2 months - 28 jours - moins de 2 mois	15	3	9	+0.3	+0.1	+0.3
2 months - 2 mois	15	9	6	+0.3	+0.3	+0.2
3 months - 3 mois	9	3	3	+0.2	+0.1	+0.1
4 months - 4 mois	12	6	6	+0.2	+0.2	+0.2
5 months - 5 mois	12	6	3	+0.2	+0.2	+0.1
6 months - 6 mois	6	-	3	+0.1	-	+0.1
7 months - 7 mois	-	-	-	...	...	...
8 months - 8 mois	3	3	-	+0.1	+0.1	-
9 months - 9 mois	3	3	3	+0.1	+0.1	+0.1
10 months - 10 mois	3	3	3	+0.1	+0.1	+0.1
11 months - 11 mois	3	3	-	+0.1	-	-

FOOTNOTES - NOTES

Italics: data from civil registers which are incomplete or of unknown completeness. - Italiques : données incomplètes ou dont le degré d'exactitude n'est pas connu, provenant des registres de l'état civil.

+ Rates based on 30 or fewer infant deaths. - Taux basés sur 30 décès d'enfants ou moins.

* Provisional. - Données provisoires.

[a] 'Code' indicates the source of data, as follows:
C - Civil registration, estimated over 90% complete
U - Civil registration, estimated less than 90% complete
| - Other source, estimated reliable
+ - Data tabulated by date of registration rather than occurence
... - Information not available

Le 'Code' indique la source des données, comme suit :
C - Registres de l'état civil considérés complets à 90 p. 100 au moins
U - Registres de l'état civil qui ne sont pas considérés complets à 90 p. 100 au moins
| - Autre source, considérée pas douteuses
+ - Données exploitées selon la date de l'enregistrement et non la date de l'événement

... - Information pas disponible

[1] Excludes the islands of St. Brandon and Agalega. - Non compris les îles St. Brandon et Agalega.
[2] Data for male and female categories may exclude infant deaths of unknown sex. - Les données pour les catégories hommes et femmes peuvent exclure décès d'enfant de sexe inconnu.
[3] Including Canadian residents temporarily in the United States, but excluding United States residents temporarily in Canada. - Y compris les résidents canadiens se trouvant temporairement aux Etats-Unis, mais ne comprenant pas les résidents des Etats-Unis se trouvant temporairement au Canada.
[4] Excluding infant deaths to mothers living abroad. - Exception faite des décès d'enfants en bas âge survenus lorsque la mère résidait à l'étranger.
[5] Data refer to resident population only. - Pour la population résidante seulement.
[6] Figures for male and female may not add up to the total, since they do not include the category "Unknown". - La somme des chiffres indiqués pour les sexes masculin et féminin peut n'être pas égale au total parce qu'elle n'inclut pas la catégorie " inconnue ".
[7] Excludes nomadic Indian tribes. - Non compris les tribus d'Indiens nomades.
[8] Source: Reports of the Ministry of Health. - Source : Rapports du Ministère de la Santé.
[9] Excluding infants born alive of less than 28 weeks' gestation, of less than 1 000 g in weight and 35 cm in length, who die within seven days of birth. - Non compris les enfants nés vivants après moins de 28 semaines de gestation,

pesant moins de 1 000 g, mesurant moins de 35 cm et décédés dans les sept jours qui ont suivi leur naissance.

[10] Deaths include deaths among some visitors. Sources: Births and Deaths National Registration System database, and medical records of government hospitals. - Les décès comprennent des décès parmi certains visiteurs. Les sources: Les bases de données des << Births and Deaths National Registration System >> et les dossiers médicaux des hôpitaux du gouvernement.

[11] Data refer to government controlled areas. - Les données se rapportent aux zones contrôlées par le Gouvernement.

[12] Includes data for East Jerusalem and Israeli residents in certain other territories under occupation by Israeli military forces since June 1967. Including deaths abroad of Israeli residents who were out of the country for less than a year. - Y compris les données pour Jérusalem-Est et les résidents israéliens dans certains autres territoires occupés depuis 1967 par les forces armées israéliennes. Y compris les décès à l'étranger de résidents israéliens qui ont quitté le pays depuis moins d'un an.

[13] Data refer to Japanese nationals in Japan only. - Les données se raportent aux nationaux japonais au Japon seulement.

[14] Data do not include foreigners. - Les données sur les etrangers ne sont pas inclus.

[15] Data are from Vital Registration System (VRS). - Les données proviennent du système d'enregistrement des faits d'état civil.

[16] Excluding alien armed forces, civilian aliens employed by armed forces, and foreign diplomatic personnel and their dependants. - Non compris les militaires étrangers, les civils étrangers employés par les forces armées ni le personnel diplomatique étranger et les membres de leur famille les accompagnant.

[17] Excluding infants born alive of less than 28 weeks' gestation, of less than 1 000 g in weight and 35 cm in length, who die within seven days of birth. As reported by the country. Reasons for discrepancy with other tables not ascertained. - Non compris les enfants nés vivants après moins de 28 semaines de gestations, pesant moins de 1 000 g, mesurant moins de 35 cm et décédés dans les sept jours qui ont suivi leur naissance. Comme indiqué par le pays. L'on ne connaît pas la raison des écarts avec d'autres tableaux.

[18] Data from MERNIS (Central Population Administrative System). - Données de MERNIS (Système central de données démographiques).

[19] Including armed forces stationed outside the country, but excluding alien armed forces stationed in the area. - Y compris les militaires nationaux hors du pays, mais non compris les militaires étrangers en garnison sur le territoire.

[20] Excluding Faeroe Islands and Greenland shown separately, if available. - Non compris les Iles Féroé et le Groenland, qui font l'objet de rubriques distinctes, si disponible.

[21] Discrepancy with other tables occurs due to later corrections in the population registers. - Les divergences avec d'autres tables sont dues à des corrections apportées ultérieurement aux registres de population.

[22] Excluding Åland Islands. - Non compris les Îles d'Åland.

[23] Data include the deceased infants with Hungarian usual residence regardless of whether the death occurred in Hungary or in a foreign country, and do not include the deceased infants with foreign country usual residence. - Les données comprennent les nourrissons décédés alors que leur résidence habituelle était en Hongrie, que le décès ait eu lieu en Hongrie ou dans un pays étranger, et ne comprennent pas les nourrissons décédés dont la residence habituelle était dans un pays étranger.

[24] Including residents outside the country if listed in a Netherlands population register. - Englobe les résidents se trouvant à l'étranger à condition qu'ils soient inscrits sur le registre de population des Pays-Bas.

[25] Including residents temporarily outside the country. - Y compris les résidents se trouvant temporairement hors du pays.

[26] Data refer to usually resident population. - Les données concernent la population habituellement résidente.

[27] Excluding Transnistria and the municipality of Bender. - Les données ne tiennent pas compte de l'information sur la Transnistria et la municipalité de Bender.

[28] Excludes data for Kosovo and Metohia. - Sans les données pour le Kosovo et Metohie.

[29] Data includes deaths resulting from births with weight 500 g and more (if weight is unknown - with length 25 cm and more, or with gestation during 22 weeks or more). The Government of Ukraine has informed the United Nations that it is not in a position to provide statistical data concerning the Autonomous Republic of Crimea and the city of Sevastopol. - Y compris les décès de nouveau-nés de 500 g ou plus (si le poids est inconnu – de 25 cm de long ou plus, ou après une grossesse de 22 semaines ou plus). Le gouvernement Ukrainien a informé l'ONU qu'il n'est pas en mesure de fournir des données statistiques concernant la République autonome de Crimée et la ville de Sébastopol.

[30] Excluding Channel Islands (Guernsey and Jersey) and Isle of Man, shown separately, if available. - Non compris les îles Anglo-Normandes (Guernesey et Jersey) et l'île de Man, qui font l'objet de rubriques distinctes, si disponible.

[31] Data for certain cells suppressed by national statistical office for confidentiality reasons. - Les données pour certaines cases ont été supprimées par le bureau national de statistiques pour des raisons de confidentialité.

[32] Including United States military personnel, their dependants and contract employees. - Y compris les militaires des Etats-Unis, les membres de leur famille les accompagnant et les agents contractuels des Etats-Unis.

[33] Data refer to deaths of residents only. Random rounding to base 3 is applied in this table as a confidentiality measure. - Les données renvoient aux décès de résidents uniquement. Les chiffres sont arrondis à la base 3 de manière aléatoire, pour des raisons de confidentialité.

Table 17 - *Demographic Yearbook 2017*

Table 17 presents maternal deaths and maternal mortality ratios for as many years available between 2007 and 2016.

Description of variables: Maternal deaths are defined for the purposes of the Demographic Yearbook as those caused by deliveries and complications of pregnancy, childbirth and the puerperium, within 42 days of termination of pregnancy. They are usually defined as deaths coded "38-41" for ICD-9 Basic Tabulation List or as deaths coded "A34", "O00-O95", "O98-O99" for ICD-10, respectively[1]. However, data for ICD-10 shown in this table include deaths due to "O96" and "O97" which refer to deaths from any obstetric cause occurring more than 42 days but less than one year after delivery and death from sequelae of direct obstetric causes occurring one year or more after delivery.

For further information on the definition of maternal mortality from the tenth revisions of the *International Statistical Classification of Diseases and Related Health Problems*[2], see also section 4.3 of the Technical Notes.

Statistics on maternal death presented in this table are provided by the World Health Organisation. They are limited to countries or areas that meet the criterion that cause-of-death statistics are either classified by or convertible to the ninth or tenth revisions mentioned above. Data that are classified by the tenth revision are set in bold in the table.

Ratios computation: Maternal mortality ratios are the annual number of maternal deaths per 100 000 live births (table 9) in the same year. These ratios have been calculated by the Statistics Division of the United Nations Department of Economic and Social Affairs. If maternal mortality data are considered incomplete, or if live birth data for the year are not available, no ratio has been calculated. Ratios based on 30 or fewer maternal deaths are identified by the symbol "♦".

Reliability of data: Countries and areas that have incomplete (less than 90 per cent completeness) or of unknown completeness of cause of deaths data coverage are considered to provide unreliable data, which are set in *italics* rather than in roman type. Ratios on these data are not computed. Information on completeness is normally provided by the World Health Organisation. When this is not the case, information on completeness is set to coincide with that of table 18. The reliability of data for the completeness of cause of death provided by the World Health Organisation[3] may differ from the reliability of data for the total number of reported deaths. Therefore, there are cases when the quality code in table 18 does not correspond with the typeface used in this table.

Territorial composition as set in Section 2.2 of "Technical Notes on the Statistical Tables", including or excluding certain population of a country refers only to the denominator.

Limitations: Statistics on maternal deaths are subject to the same qualifications that have been set forth for vital statistics in general and death statistics in particular as discussed in section 4 of the Technical Notes. The reliability of the data, an indication of which is described above, is an important factor in considering the limitations. In addition, maternal-death statistics are subject to all the qualifications relating to cause-of-death statistics. These have been set forth in section 4 of the Technical Notes.

Maternal mortality ratios are subject to the limitations of the data on live births with which they have been calculated. These have been set forth in the technical notes for table 9. Specific information pertaining to individual countries or areas is given in the footnotes to table 9.

The calculation of the maternal mortality ratios based on the total number of live births approximates the risk of dying from complications of pregnancy, childbirth or puerperium. Ideally this rate should be based on the number of women exposed to the risk of pregnancy, in other words, the number of women conceiving. Since it is impossible to know how many women have conceived, the total number of live births is used in calculating this rate.

Earlier data: Maternal deaths and maternal mortality ratios have been shown in previous issues of the *Demographic Yearbook*. For information on specific years covered, the reader should consult the Index.

It should however be noted that in issues prior to 1975, maternal mortality rates were calculated using the female population rather than live births for the denominators. Therefore, maternal mortality ratios published since 1975 are not comparable to the earlier maternal death rates.

NOTES

[1] Except for Belarus, Russian Federation, Seychelles, Turkmenistan and Ukraine, where A34 and O95 are excluded.

[2] *International Statistical Classification of Diseases and Related Health Problems*, Tenth Revision, Volume 2, World Health Organization, Geneva, 1992. The publication is available online at: http://www.who.int/classifications/icd/en/

[3] For more information on specific method used for countries, see "Mathers CD, Bernard C, Iburg KM, Inoue M, Ma Fat D, Shibuya K et al. *Global burden of disease in 2002: data sources, methods and results.* Geneva, World Health Organization, 2003 (GPE Discussion Paper No. 54).

Tableau 17 – Annuaire démographique 2017

Le tableau 17 présente des statistiques et des taux de mortalité liée à la maternité pour les années disponibles entre 2007 et 2016.

Description des variables : aux fins de l'*Annuaire démographique*, les décès liés à la maternité sont ceux entraînés par l'accouchement ou les complications de la grossesse, de l'accouchement et des suites de couches dans un délai de 42 jours après la terminaison de la grossesse. Ils sont généralement associés aux codes 38 à 41 dans le cas de la liste de base pour la mise en tableaux de la CIM-9 et aux codes A34, O00 à O95 et O98 et O99 dans le cas de la CIM-10[1]. Les statistiques associées à des codes correspondant à la CIM-10 englobent des décès de type O96 et O97, qui désignent les décès liés à des causes obstétriques se produisant après 42 jours mais moins d'un an après l'accouchement et les décès entraînés par les séquelles de complications obstétriques directes qui se produisent un an ou plus après l'accouchement.

Pour plus de précisions concernant les définitions de la mortalité liée à la maternité dans la dixième révision de la *Classification statistique internationale des maladies et des problèmes de santé connexes*[2], se reporter également à la section 4.3 des Notes techniques.

Les statistiques de mortalité liée à la maternité présentées dans le tableau 17 émanent de l'Organisation mondiale de la santé. Elles ne se rapportent qu'aux pays ou zones qui répondent aux critères selon lesquels les statistiques relatives à la cause des décès sont conformes à la liste de la neuvième ou de la dixième révision de la CIM ou peuvent être aisément comparées aux catégories de cette liste. Les données conformes à la dixième révision sont indiquées en gras dans le tableau.

Calcul des taux : les taux de mortalité maternelle représentent le nombre annuel de décès dus à la maternité pour 100 000 naissances vivantes (données du tableau 9) de la même année. Ces taux ont été calculés par la Division de statistique du Département des affaires économiques et sociales de l'Organisation des Nations Unies. Si les données des décès dus à la maternité sont incomplètes ou si les naissances vivantes pour l'année ne sont pas disponibles, les taux ne sont pas calculés. Les taux fondés sur 30 décès liés à la maternité ou moins sont signalés par le signe "♦".

Fiabilité des données : les statistiques relatives aux pays et aux zones pour lesquels la couverture des données concernant les causes de décès est incomplète (mois de 90 pour cent) ou dont le degré de complétude n'est pas connue sont jugés douteuses et apparaissent en *italique* et non en caractères romains. Les taux correspondant ne sont pas calculés. L'information sur la complétude est normalement fournie par l'Organisation Mondiale de la Santé. Si ce n'est pas le cas, l'information sur la complétude est reprise de tableau 18. La fiabilité des données relatives aux causes de décès fournie par l'Organisation Mondiale de la Santé[3] peut différer de la fiabilité des données relatives au nombre de décès enregistrés. En conséquence, il peut apparaitre de différences entre les codes de fiabilité du tableau 18 et du présent tableau.

La composition territoriale est définie dans la Section 2.2 des "Notes Techniques sur les tableaux statistiques". L'inclusion ou l'exclusion de certaines populations d'un pays ne concerne que le dénominateur.

Insuffisance des données : les statistiques de la mortalité liée à la maternité appellent toutes les réserves qui ont été formulées à propos des statistiques de l'état civil en général et des statistiques relatives à la mortalité en particulier (voir la section 4 des Notes techniques). La fiabilité des données, au sujet de laquelle des indications ont été fournies plus haut, est un facteur important. En outre, les statistiques de la mortalité liée à la maternité appellent les mêmes réserves que celles exposées à la section 4 des Notes techniques en ce qui concerne les statistiques des causes de décès.

Les taux de mortalité maternelle appellent également toutes les réserves formulées à propos des statistiques des naissances vivantes qui ont servi à leur calcul (voir à ce sujet les notes techniques relatives au tableau 9). Des précisions sur certains pays ou zones sont données dans les notes se rapportant au tableau 9.

En prenant le nombre total des naissances vivantes comme base pour le calcul des taux de mortalité maternelle, on obtient une mesure approximative de la probabilité de décès dus aux complications de la grossesse, de l'accouchement et des suites de couches. Idéalement, ces taux devraient être calculés sur la base du nombre de femmes exposées aux risques liés à la grossesse, c'est-à-dire sur la base du nombre de femmes qui conçoivent. Étant donné qu'il est impossible de connaître le nombre de femmes ayant conçu, c'est le nombre total de naissances vivantes que l'on utilise pour calculer ces taux.

Données publiées antérieurement : des statistiques concernant les décès liés à la maternité (nombre de décès et taux) ont déjà été présentées dans des éditions antérieures de l'*Annuaire démographique*. Pour plus de précisions concernant les années pour lesquelles ces données ont été publiées, se reporter à l'index.

Il faut souligner que, avant 1975, les taux de mortalité maternelle étaient calculés sur la base de la population féminine et non sur celle du nombre de naissances vivantes. Ils ne sont donc pas comparables à ceux qui figurent dans les éditions de l'*Annuaire démographique* parues après 1975.

NOTES

[1] Sauf pour Bélarus, Fédération de Russie, Seychelles, Turkménistan et Ukraine où A34 et O95 sont exclus.
[2] *Classification statistique internationale des maladies et des problèmes de santé connexes*, dixième révision, volume 2. Genève, Organisation mondiale de la santé, 1992.
[3] Pour plus d'information sur les méthodes spécifiques utilisées pour les pays, voir "Mathers CD, Bernard C, Iburg KM, Inoue M, Ma Fat D, Shibuya K et al. *Global burden of disease in 2002: data sources, methods and results*. Geneva, World Health Organization, 2003 (GPE Discussion Paper No. 54).

17. Maternal deaths and maternal mortality ratios: 2007 - 2016
Mortalité liée à la maternité, nombre de décès et taux : 2007 - 2016

Continent and country or area Continent et pays ou zone	Co-de[a]	2007	2008	2009	2010	2011	2012	2013	2014	2015	2016
AFRICA - AFRIQUE											
Cabo Verde											
Number - Nombre	C					5	1	...	...	...	...
Egypt - Égypte											
Number - Nombre	C	567	449	579	519	550	531	503	497	410	...
Rate - Taux	C	29.1	21.9	26.1	23.0	22.5	20.2	19.2	18.3	15.3	...
Mauritius - Maurice											
Number - Nombre	+C	6	6	10	4	5	9	9	7	4	6
Rate - Taux	+C	♦35.2	♦36.6	♦65.2	♦26.7	♦34.0	♦62.1	♦66.7	♦52.7	♦31.6	♦46.3
Mayotte											
Number - Nombre	C	...	...	...	...	-	1	1	2	...	...
Rate - Taux	C	...	...	...	...	...	...	...	♦27.4	...	...
Morocco - Maroc											
Number - Nombre	U	...	74	...	65	98	93	62	77	...	...
Reunion - Réunion											
Number - Nombre	...	...	2	1	1	5	2	2	2	...	...
Seychelles											
Number - Nombre	+C	-	1	1	2	-	-	-	-	3	...
Rate - Taux	+C	-	♦64.7	♦63.3	♦133.0	-	-	-	-	♦188.4	...
South Africa - Afrique du Sud											
Number - Nombre	C	1 762	1 808	1 880	1 658	1 260	1 050	946	1 027	942	...
Rate - Taux	C	163.8	165.2	182.2	162.3	122.5	102.7	93.4	101.8	98.9	...
Tunisia - Tunisie											
Number - Nombre	U	...	...	...	...	...	...	28	...	...	...
AMERICA, NORTH - AMÉRIQUE DU NORD											
Anguilla											
Number - Nombre	...	...	1	-	1	-	-	-	-	-	-
Antigua and Barbuda - Antigua-et-Barbuda											
Number - Nombre	+U	1	-	-	...	...	1	-	-	-	-
Aruba											
Number - Nombre	...	-	-	-	-	2	-	-	-	-	...
Bahamas											
Number - Nombre	...	...	3[1]	7[1]	5[1]	-[1]	3[2]	3[2]	...	...	...
Rate - Taux	...	...	♦58.5	♦139.2	♦101.7	-	...	...	...	...	...
Barbados - Barbade											
Number - Nombre	...	...	2[3]	-[3]	-[3]	2[3]	1[4]	1[4]	...	...	...
Rate - Taux	...	...	♦56.4	-	-	♦60.9	...	...	...	...	...
Belize											
Number - Nombre	...	2[3]	2[3]	4[3]	4[3]	-[3]	2[4]	-[4]	-[4]	-[4]	...
Rate - Taux	...	♦28.4	♦28.1	♦53.9	♦55.3	-	...	...	...	...	...
Bermuda - Bermudes											
Number - Nombre	...	-	-	-	-	-	-	-	-	-	...
British Virgin Islands - Îles Vierges britanniques											
Number - Nombre	...	...	-	-	-	...	-	-	-	-	...
Canada											
Number - Nombre	C	24	34	29	24	18	22	23	...	...	...
Rate - Taux	C	♦6.5	9.0	♦7.6	♦6.4	♦4.8	♦5.8	♦6.0	...	...	...
Cayman Islands - Îles Caïmanes											
Number - Nombre	...	...	-	-	-	...	...	-	...	...	...
Costa Rica											
Number - Nombre	...	10[2]	20[2]	10[1]	14[1]	17[1]	22[2]	10[2]	21[2]	...	...
Rate - Taux	...	...	...	♦13.3	♦19.7	♦23.1	...	...	...	...	...
Cuba											
Number - Nombre	C	42	57	66	61	61	55	56	50	58	...
Rate - Taux	C	37.3	46.5	50.8	47.8	45.8	43.8	44.5	40.8	46.4	...
Dominica - Dominique											
Number - Nombre	+C	-	1	-	2	-	-	-	-	-	...
Rate - Taux	+C	-	♦103.7	-	♦214.4	-	-	-	-	...	...
Dominican Republic - République dominicaine											
Number - Nombre	U	...	...	56	37	188	177	215	...	...	...

Continent and country or area / Continent et pays ou zone	Code[a]	2007	2008	2009	2010	2011	2012	2013	2014	2015	2016
AMERICA, NORTH - AMÉRIQUE DU NORD											
El Salvador											
Number - Nombre	...	17[2]	18[2]	14[2]	19[2]	16[2]	17[1]	39[1]	52[1]	...	...
Rate - Taux	...	...	...	...	...	...	♦15.3	35.6	47.7	...	...
Grenada - Grenade											
Number - Nombre	...	_[4]	_[3]	_[3]	_[3]	_[3]	2[3]	1[3]	_[3]	_[3]	2[3]
Rate - Taux	...	...	-	-	-	-	♦120.4	♦54.4	-	...	...
Guadeloupe											
Number - Nombre	...	...	2	1	1	-	4	1	-	...	...
Guatemala											
Number - Nombre	...	310[4]	328[4]	346[4]	355[3]	315[3]	356[3]	318[3]	291[3]	298[3]	...
Rate - Taux	...	...	...	...	98.1	84.3	91.6	82.1	75.4	76.1	...
Honduras											
Number - Nombre	+U	...	...	...	28	47	31	37	...	...	...
Jamaica - Jamaïque											
Number - Nombre	...	...	...	...	28	28	...	...	...	...	...
Martinique											
Number - Nombre	...	...	1	2	-	2	1	3	-	...	...
Mexico - Mexique											
Number - Nombre	+C	1 122	1 135	1 230	1 030	1 027	1 036	969	995	905	...
Rate - Taux	+C	51.3	50.6	54.6	47.5	45.4	47.3	44.7	46.7	43.2	...
Montserrat											
Number - Nombre	...	...	-	-	-	-	-	-	-	-	-
Nicaragua											
Number - Nombre	+U	...	69	78	80	71	72	71	53	59	...
Panama											
Number - Nombre	+C	40[1]	41[1]	29[1]	41[1]	59[1]	49	41	44	40	...
Rate - Taux	+C	59.4	59.6	♦42.4	60.3	80.5	64.9	55.6	58.5	52.7	...
Puerto Rico - Porto Rico											
Number - Nombre	...	...	6	10	6	5	1	2	3	15	...
Saint Kitts and Nevis - Saint-Kitts-et-Nevis											
Number - Nombre	+U	-	1	-	-	1	1	...	-	-	...
Saint Lucia - Sainte-Lucie											
Number - Nombre	...	...	1[3]	...	3[4]	1[4]	1[3]	1[3]	2[3]	...	...
Rate - Taux	...	...	♦45.2	...	...	...	♦47.6	...	...	...	...
Saint Pierre and Miquelon - Saint Pierre-et-Miquelon											
Number - Nombre	...	...	-	-	-	...	...	...	...	...	...
Saint Vincent and the Grenadines - Saint-Vincent-et-les Grenadines											
Number - Nombre	...	-	2[1]	_[1]	2[1]	1[1]	_[1]	2[1]	1[1]	_[1]	...
Rate - Taux	...	...	♦105.2	-	♦112.1	♦58.0	-	♦115.1	♦54.3	...	...
Trinidad and Tobago - Trinité-et-Tobago											
Number - Nombre	U	...	11	...	...	...	...	...	...	...	...
Turks and Caicos Islands - Îles Turques et Caïques											
Number - Nombre	...	...	-	1	...	...	-	...	-	...	...
United States of America - États-Unis d'Amérique											
Number - Nombre	C	766	795	962	825	931	990	1 138	1 123	1 140	...
Rate - Taux	C	17.7	18.7	23.3	20.6	23.5	25.0	28.9	28.2	28.7	...
United States Virgin Islands - Îles Vierges américaines											
Number - Nombre	...	...	...	-	-	-	-	...	...	-	...
AMERICA, SOUTH - AMÉRIQUE DU SUD											
Argentina - Argentine											
Number - Nombre	+C	332	319	422	331	318	280	274	307	333	...
Rate - Taux	+C	47.4	42.8	56.6	43.8	42.0	37.9	36.3	39.5	43.2	...

Continent and country or area / Continent et pays ou zone	Code[a]	2007	2008	2009	2010	2011	2012	2013	2014	2015	2016
AMERICA, SOUTH - AMÉRIQUE DU SUD											
Brazil - Brésil											
Number - Nombre	...	1 613[4]	1 641[3]	1 884[3]	1 728[3]	1 680[3]	1 647[3]	1 788[3]	1 889[3]	1 896[3]	...
Rate - Taux	...	...	58.8	68.4	62.6	59.5	58.2	63.1	64.8	64.2	...
Chile - Chili											
Number - Nombre	C	42	36	43	46	46	54	52	56	56	...
Rate - Taux	C	17.5	14.6	17.0	18.4	18.6	22.2	21.5	22.3	22.9	...
Colombia - Colombie											
Number - Nombre	...	503[3]	433[3]	496[3]	474[3]	459[3]	452[4]	381[4]	491[4]	476[4]	...
Rate - Taux	...	70.9	60.5	70.9	72.4	69.0	...	...	...	...	...
Ecuador - Équateur											
Number - Nombre	U	176	162	208	202	239	202	158	169	183	...
French Guiana - Guyane française											
Number - Nombre	...	...	4	1	3	-	2	1	3	...	...
Guyana											
Number - Nombre	...	...	16[4]	9[4]	20[4]	14[4]	14[3]	9[3]	...	...	...
Paraguay											
Number - Nombre	+U	...	117	128	100	94	91	100	71	...	...
Peru - Pérou											
Number - Nombre	+U	155	192	163	137	148	126	97	112	110	...
Suriname											
Number - Nombre	...	...	9[3]	11[3]	6[3]	7[3]	2[4]	11[4]	7[4]	...	...
Rate - Taux	...	...	✦89.1	✦112.3	✦61.8	✦72.1	...	...	...	...	...
Uruguay											
Number - Nombre	C	...	6	11	2	...	5	9	9	11	...
Rate - Taux	C	...	✦12.7	✦23.3	✦4.2	...	✦10.4	✦18.5	✦18.6	✦22.5	...
Venezuela (Bolivarian Republic of) - Venezuela (République bolivarienne du)											
Number - Nombre	...	332[3]	377[3]	434[3]	412[3]	436[3]	416[4]	410[4]	...	...	...
Rate - Taux	...	54.0	64.8	73.1	69.7	70.9	...	...	...	...	...
ASIA - ASIE											
Armenia - Arménie											
Number - Nombre	...	...	16[4]	12[4]	4[4]	6[4]	5[3]	9[3]	8[3]	7[3]	14[3]
Rate - Taux	...	...	...	...	...	...	✦11.8	✦21.5	✦18.6	✦16.8	✦34.5
Azerbaijan - Azerbaïdjan											
Number - Nombre	C	30	...	...	...	...	...	...	...	...	...
Rate - Taux	C	✦19.7	...	...	...	...	...	...	...	...	...
Bahrain - Bahreïn											
Number - Nombre	...	3[3]	3[3]	3[4]	1[4]	2[4]	2[3]	4[3]	2[3]	...	...
Rate - Taux	...	✦18.7	✦17.6	...	...	...	✦10.5	✦20.0	✦9.6	...	...
Brunei Darussalam - Brunéi Darussalam											
Number - Nombre	...	1[1]	-[1]	1[1]	1[2]	-[2]	3[1]	1[1]	-[1]	2[1]	...
Rate - Taux	...	✦15.8	-	✦15.1	...	...	✦43.4	✦15.0	-	✦29.9	...
China, Hong Kong SAR - Chine, Hong Kong RAS											
Number - Nombre	...	1	2	2	1	1	2	-	2	1	...
Cyprus - Chypre											
Number - Nombre	U	-	1	-	1	-	-	1	2	-	-
Georgia - Géorgie											
Number - Nombre	C	2	...	32	13	21	12	16	18	19	...
Rate - Taux	C	✦4.1	...	50.5	✦20.8	✦36.2	✦21.0	✦27.6	✦29.7	✦32.1	...
Iran (Islamic Republic of) - Iran (République islamique d')											
Number - Nombre	U	...	...	...	...	...	...	113	104	111	...
Iraq											
Number - Nombre	U	...	62	...	...	...	...	...	...	...	...
Israel - Israël											
Number - Nombre	C	7	8	5	7	2	9	14	10	7	...
Rate - Taux	C	✦4.6	✦5.1	✦3.1	✦4.2	✦1.2	✦5.3	✦8.2	✦5.7	✦3.9	...
Japan - Japon											
Number - Nombre	C	39	41	61	49	43	50	41	33	44	...
Rate - Taux	C	3.6	3.8	5.7	4.6	4.1	4.8	4.0	3.3	4.4	...

Continent and country or area / Continent et pays ou zone	Code[a]	2007	2008	2009	2010	2011	2012	2013	2014	2015	2016
ASIA - ASIE											
Jordan - Jordanie											
Number - Nombre	U	...	*25*	*26*	*46*	*34*	*44*	...	...	...	...
Kazakhstan											
Number - Nombre	...	107[4]	86[3]	94[3]	65[3]	48[3]	*41[4]*	*41[4]*	*37[4]*	*35[4]*	
Rate - Taux	...	...	24.1	26.4	17.7	12.9	...	...	...	...	
Kuwait - Koweït											
Number - Nombre	...	-[3]	5[3]	7[3]	3[3]	6[3]	*1[4]*	*4[4]*	*7[4]*	...	...
Rate - Taux	...	-	♦9.2	♦12.4	♦5.2	♦10.3	...	...	...	...	...
Kyrgyzstan - Kirghizstan											
Number - Nombre	...	64[4]	70[3]	86[3]	75[3]	81[3]	76[3]	56[3]	81[3]	63[3]	...
Rate - Taux	...	...	55.0	63.5	51.3	54.1	49.1	36.0	50.1	38.5	...
Malaysia - Malaisie											
Number - Nombre	U	...	*133*	...	...	...	*122*	*108*	*119*	...	...
Maldives											
Number - Nombre	...	2[1]	*4[2]*	...	*7[2]*	*4[2]*	...	...	...	...	...
Rate - Taux	...	♦30.4	...	...	...	...	...	...	...	...	...
Mongolia - Mongolie											
Number - Nombre	U	...	...	...	...	...	...	...	...	...	*38*
Oman											
Number - Nombre	U	...	...	*3*	*6*	...	...	...	-	...	...
Philippines											
Number - Nombre	U	...	*1 731*	...	*1 718*	*1 465*	...	...	...	...	...
Qatar											
Number - Nombre	...	5[3]	2[3]	4[3]	*2[4]*	*1[4]*	*1[4]*	-[4]	*1[4]*	*3[4]*	-[4]
Rate - Taux	...	♦31.9	♦11.6	♦21.8	...	...	...	...	...	...	...
Republic of Korea - République de Corée											
Number - Nombre	C	...	39	48	75	85	56	51	48	42	...
Rate - Taux	C	...	8.4	10.8	16.0	18.0	11.6	11.7	11.0	9.6	...
Saudi Arabia - Arabie saoudite											
Number - Nombre	U	...	...	*54*	...	...	*45*	...	...	...	...
Singapore - Singapour											
Number - Nombre	+U	...	*2*	-	*1*	*2*	*1*	-	-	*3*	...
Syrian Arab Republic - République arabe syrienne											
Number - Nombre	+C	...	...	...	*23*	...	...	...	...	...	...
Rate - Taux	+C	...	...	...	♦2.6	...	...	...	...	...	...
Tajikistan - Tadjikistan											
Number - Nombre	U	...	...	...	...	...	...	...	...	...	*18*
Thailand - Thaïlande											
Number - Nombre	+U	...	...	...	*78*	*71*	*141*	*166*	*166*	*167*	*177*
Turkey - Turquie											
Number - Nombre	+U	...	...	*37*	*46*	*58*	*55*	*302*	*273*	*220*	...
Turkmenistan - Turkménistan											
Number - Nombre	U	...	...	...	...	...	*7*	*9*	*4*	*5*	...
United Arab Emirates - Émirats arabes unis											
Number - Nombre	+U	...	*1*	*2*	*4*	...	...	...	...	...	...
Uzbekistan - Ouzbékistan											
Number - Nombre	C	...	...	...	...	...	103	120	131	...	...
Rate - Taux	C	...	...	...	...	...	16.5	17.7	18.2	...	...
EUROPE											
Andorra - Andorre											
Number - Nombre	C	...	...	...	...	...	-	...	-	-	...
Austria - Autriche											
Number - Nombre	C	3	2	2	1	2	1	1	7	4	5
Rate - Taux	C	♦3.9	♦2.6	♦2.6	♦1.3	♦2.6	♦1.3	♦1.3	♦8.6	♦4.7	♦5.7
Belarus - Bélarus											
Number - Nombre	C	7	3	1	1	1	...	-	1	...	...
Rate - Taux	C	♦6.8	♦2.8	♦0.9	♦0.9	♦0.9	...	-	♦0.8	...	...
Belgium - Belgique											
Number - Nombre	C	...	7	6	8	9	5	3	6	4	...
Rate - Taux	C	...	♦5.5	♦4.7	♦6.1	♦7.0	♦3.9	♦2.4	♦4.8	♦3.3	...
Bosnia and Herzegovina - Bosnie-Herzégovine											
Number - Nombre	...	...	...	...	...	*2[4]*	...	...	-[3]	...	...

17. Maternal deaths and maternal mortality ratios: 2007 - 2016
Mortalité liée à la maternité, nombre de décès et taux : 2007 - 2016 (continued - suite)

Continent and country or area / Continent et pays ou zone	Code[a]	2007	2008	2009	2010	2011	2012	2013	2014	2015	2016
EUROPE											
Bulgaria - Bulgarie											
Number - Nombre	C	8	5	4	6	2	3	8	5	...	...
Rate - Taux	C	◆10.6	◆6.4	◆4.9	◆7.9	◆2.8	◆4.3	◆12.0	◆7.4	...	...
Croatia - Croatie											
Number - Nombre	C	6	3	6	4	4	3	2	1	1	1
Rate - Taux	C	◆14.3	◆6.9	◆13.5	◆9.2	◆9.7	◆7.2	◆5.0	◆2.5	◆2.7	◆2.7
Czechia - Tchéquie											
Number - Nombre	C	3	7	3	3	2	6	1	4	2	1
Rate - Taux	C	◆2.6	◆5.9	◆2.5	◆2.6	◆1.8	◆5.5	◆0.9	◆3.6	◆1.8	◆0.9
Denmark - Danemark											
Number - Nombre	C	...	4	4	-	2	-	1	3	-	...
Rate - Taux	C	...	◆6.2	◆6.4	-	◆3.4	-	◆1.8	◆5.3	-	...
Estonia - Estonie											
Number - Nombre	C	-	-	-	1	1	1	1	-	-	...
Rate - Taux	C	-	-	-	◆6.3	◆6.8	◆7.1	◆7.4	-	-	...
Finland - Finlande											
Number - Nombre	C	1	5	1	3	-	2	1	3	2	...
Rate - Taux	C	◆1.7	◆8.4	◆1.7	◆4.9	-	◆3.4	◆1.7	◆5.3	◆3.6	...
France											
Number - Nombre	C	60	52	75	68	45	44	38	37	...	...
Rate - Taux	C	7.6	6.5	9.5	8.5	5.7	5.6	4.9	4.7	...	...
Germany - Allemagne											
Number - Nombre	C	28	36	35	37	32	31	29	29	24	...
Rate - Taux	C	◆4.1	5.3	5.3	5.5	4.8	4.6	◆4.3	◆4.1	◆3.3	...
Greece - Grèce											
Number - Nombre	C	2	-	4	6	4	1	-	4	5	...
Rate - Taux	C	◆1.8	-	◆3.4	◆5.2	◆3.8	◆1.0	-	◆4.3	◆5.4	...
Hungary - Hongrie											
Number - Nombre	C	8	17	18	14	9	9	13	6	5	11
Rate - Taux	C	◆8.2	◆17.1	◆18.7	◆15.5	◆10.2	◆10.0	◆14.5	◆6.4	◆5.4	◆11.5
Iceland - Islande											
Number - Nombre	C	-	-	-	...	...	-	-	-	-	-
Ireland - Irlande											
Number - Nombre	+C	1	3	3	3	2	2	3	1	...	...
Rate - Taux	+C	◆1.4	◆4.0	◆4.0	◆4.0	◆2.7	◆2.8	◆4.4	◆1.5	...	...
Italy - Italie											
Number - Nombre	C	13	13	19	16	14	11	14	6	16	...
Rate - Taux	C	◆2.3	◆2.3	◆3.3	◆2.8	◆2.6	◆2.1	◆2.7	◆1.2	◆3.3	...
Latvia - Lettonie											
Number - Nombre	+C	6	2	7	4	-	4	2	2	12	...
Rate - Taux	+C	◆25.0	◆8.2	◆31.8	◆20.2	-	◆20.1	◆9.7	◆9.2	◆54.6	...
Lithuania - Lituanie											
Number - Nombre	+C	2	3	-	2	2	3	2	1	3	2
Rate - Taux	+C	◆6.7	◆9.5	-	◆6.5	◆6.6	◆9.8	◆6.7	◆3.3	◆9.5	◆6.5
Luxembourg											
Number - Nombre	+C	1	1	-	1	-	1	1	-	-	...
Rate - Taux	+C	◆18.3	◆17.9	-	◆17.0	-	◆16.6	◆16.4	-	-	...
Malta - Malte											
Number - Nombre	+C	-	1	-	1	-	-	-	-	-	...
Rate - Taux	+C	-	◆24.9	-	◆25.7	-	-	-	-	-	...
Montenegro - Monténégro											
Number - Nombre	C	1	-	...	...	...	...	...	...	...	...
Rate - Taux	C	◆12.8	-	...	...	...	...	...	...	...	...
Netherlands - Pays-Bas											
Number - Nombre	+C	9	8	9	4	3	6	5	5	6	6
Rate - Taux	+C	◆5.0	◆4.3	◆4.9	◆2.2	◆1.7	◆3.4	◆2.9	◆2.9	◆3.5	◆3.5
Norway - Norvège											
Number - Nombre	+C	4	3	1	3	3	-	2	2	-	...
Rate - Taux	+C	◆6.8	◆5.0	◆1.6	◆4.9	◆5.0	-	◆3.4	◆3.4	-	...
Poland - Pologne											
Number - Nombre	C	11	19	8	9	9	4	7	8	6	...
Rate - Taux	C	◆2.8	◆4.6	◆1.9	◆2.2	◆2.3	◆1.0	◆1.9	◆2.1	◆1.6	...
Portugal											
Number - Nombre	+C	5	4	7	8	5	4	5	6	...	...
Rate - Taux	+C	◆4.9	◆3.8	◆7.0	◆7.9	◆5.2	◆4.5	◆6.0	◆7.3	...	...
Republic of Moldova - République de Moldova											
Number - Nombre	...	7[1]	17[1]	7[1]	18[1]	6[1]	12[2]	6[2]	7[2]	12[2]	7[2]
Rate - Taux	...	◆18.4	◆43.6	◆17.2	◆44.5	◆15.3	...	...	...	...	...

17. Maternal deaths and maternal mortality ratios: 2007 - 2016
Mortalité liée à la maternité, nombre de décès et taux : 2007 - 2016 (continued - suite)

Continent and country or area / Continent et pays ou zone	Code[a]	2007	2008	2009	2010	2011	2012	2013	2014	2015	2016
EUROPE											
Romania - Roumanie											
Number - Nombre	+C	33	30	47	51	50	23	27	24	27	17
Rate - Taux	+C	15.4	♦13.5	21.1	24.0	25.5	♦11.4	♦14.8	♦12.1	♦13.7	♦8.5
Russian Federation - Fédération de Russie											
Number - Nombre	+C	356	359	388	298	291	221	216	...	...	...
Rate - Taux	+C	22.1	20.9	22.0	16.7	16.2	11.6	11.4	...	...	...
San Marino - Saint-Marin											
Number - Nombre	+C	...	...	...	...	...	-	-	-	-	...
Serbia - Serbie											
Number - Nombre	...	-[2]	4[2]	6[2]	12[1]	7[1]	10[1]	9[1]	8[1]	8[1]	...
Rate - Taux	...	...	...	...	♦17.6	♦10.7	♦14.9	♦13.7	♦12.0	♦12.2	...
Slovakia - Slovaquie											
Number - Nombre	C	-	2	6	-	...	3	1	2	...	...
Rate - Taux	C	-	♦3.5	♦9.8	-	...	♦5.4	♦1.8	♦3.6	...	...
Slovenia - Slovénie											
Number - Nombre	C	3	2	1	-	...	1	1	2	1	...
Rate - Taux	C	♦15.1	♦9.2	♦4.6	-	...	♦4.6	♦4.7	♦9.4	♦4.8	...
Spain - Espagne											
Number - Nombre	C	13	24	17	20	14	10	18	9	15	...
Rate - Taux	C	♦2.6	♦4.6	♦3.4	♦4.1	♦3.0	♦2.2	♦4.2	♦2.1	♦3.6	...
Sweden - Suède											
Number - Nombre	C	2	6	6	3	1	5	7	4	1	3
Rate - Taux	C	♦1.9	♦5.5	♦5.4	♦2.6	♦0.9	♦4.4	♦6.2	♦3.5	♦0.9	♦2.6
Switzerland - Suisse											
Number - Nombre	C	1	8	3	3	3	7	2	5	6	...
Rate - Taux	C	♦1.3	♦10.4	♦3.8	♦3.7	♦3.7	♦8.5	♦2.4	♦5.9	♦6.9	...
TFYR of Macedonia - L'ex-R. y. de Macédoine											
Number - Nombre	...	-	-[3]	1[3]	2[3]	...	1[3]	1[3]	...	...	...
Rate - Taux	...	...	-	♦4.2	♦8.2	...	♦4.2	♦4.3	...	...	...
Ukraine											
Number - Nombre	+C	...	79	129	116	85	66	...	69	60	...
Rate - Taux	+C	...	15.5	25.2	23.3	16.9	12.7	...	14.8	14.6	...
United Kingdom of Great Britain and Northern Ireland - Royaume-Uni de Grande-Bretagne et d'Irlande du Nord											
Number - Nombre	+C	56	49	74	40	53	51	50	52	35	...
Rate - Taux	+C	7.3	6.2	9.4	5.0	6.6	6.3	6.4	6.7	4.5	...
OCEANIA - OCÉANIE											
Australia - Australie											
Number - Nombre	C	...	6	9	12	12	16	6	12	8	...
Rate - Taux	C	...	♦2.0	♦3.0	♦4.0	♦4.0	♦5.2	♦1.9	♦4.0	♦2.6	...
Fiji - Fidji											
Number - Nombre	+C	...	...	5	...	4	8	...	...	...	...
Rate - Taux	+C	...	...	♦27.5	...	♦20.5	♦43.4	...	...	...	...
New Zealand - Nouvelle-Zélande											
Number - Nombre	+C	13	7	11	6	7	7	10	...	...	...
Rate - Taux	+C	♦20.3	♦10.9	♦17.6	♦9.4	♦11.4	♦11.4	♦17.0	...	...	...

FOOTNOTES - NOTES

Data in bold refer to maternal deaths based on ICD-10 Classification, otherwise data refer to maternal deaths based on ICD-9 Classification. - Les données en typographie gras se rapportent aux décès maternelles basées sur la classification CIM-10, autrement les données se rapportent aux décès maternelles basées sur la classification CIM-9.

Italics: data from civil registers which are incomplete or of unknown completeness. - Italiques : données incomplètes ou dont le degré d'exactitude n'est pas connu, provenant des registres de l'état civil.

* Provisional. - Données provisoires.

♦ Rates based on 30 or fewer deaths. - Taux basés sur 30 décès ou moins.

a 'Code' indicates the source of data, as follows:
   C - Civil registration, estimated over 90% complete
   U - Civil registration, estimated less than 90% complete
   | - Other source, estimated reliable
   + - Data tabulated by date of registration rather than occurence
   ... - Information not available

Le 'Code' indique la source des données, comme suit :

C - Registres de l'état civil considérés complèts à 90 p. 100 au moins
U - Registres de l'état civil qui ne sont pas considérés complèts à 90 p. 100 au moins
| - Autre source, considérée pas douteuses
+ - Données exploitées selon la date de l'enregistrement et non la date de l'événement
... - Information pas disponible

[1] The code is +C. - Le code est +C.
[2] The code is +U. - Le code est +U.
[3] The code is C. - Le code est C.
[4] The code is U. - Le code est U.

Table 18 - *Demographic Yearbook 2017*

Table 18 presents deaths and crude death rates by urban/rural residence for as many years as possible between 2013 and 2017.

Description of variables: Death is defined as the permanent disappearance of all evidence of life at any time after live birth has taken place (post-natal cessation of vital functions without capability of resuscitation).

Statistics on the number of deaths are obtained from civil registers unless otherwise noted. For those countries or areas where civil registration statistics on deaths are considered reliable (estimated completeness of 90 per cent or more), the death rates shown have been calculated on the basis of registered deaths.

The urban/rural classification of deaths is that provided by each country or area; it is presumed to be based on the national census definitions of urban population that have been set forth at the end of the technical notes for table 6.

For certain countries, there is a discrepancy between the total number of deaths shown in this table and those shown in subsequent tables for the same year. Usually this discrepancy arises because the total number of deaths occurring in a given year is revised although the remaining tabulations are not.

Rate computation: Crude death rates are the annual number of deaths per 1 000 mid-year population.

Rates by urban/rural residence are the annual number of deaths, in the appropriate urban or rural category, per 1 000 corresponding mid-year population. These rates are calculated by the Statistics Division of the United Nations based on the appropriate reference population (for example: total population, nationals only etc.) if known and available. If the reference population is not known or unavailable, the total population is used to calculate the rates. Therefore, if the population that is used to calculate the rates is different from the correct reference population, the rates presented might under- or overstate the true situation in a country or area.

Rates presented in this table are limited to those countries or areas with a minimum number of 30 deaths in a given year.

Reliability of data: Each country or area has been asked to indicate the estimated completeness of the deaths recorded in its civil register. These national assessments are indicated by the quality codes "C", "U" and "|" that appear in the first column of this table. "C" indicates that the data are estimated to be virtually complete, that is, representing at least 90 per cent of the deaths occurring each year, while "U" indicates that data are estimated to be incomplete that is, representing less than 90 per cent of the deaths occurring each year. The code "|" indicates that the source of data is different than civil registration and is explained by a footnote. The code "..." indicates that no information was provided regarding completeness or no assessment has been done in the country.

Data from civil registers that are reported as incomplete or of unknown completeness (code "U" or "...") are considered unreliable. They appear in italics in this table; rates based on these data are not computed.

Limitations: Statistics on deaths are subject to the same qualifications as have been set forth for vital statistics and particularly for death statistics discussed in section 4 of the Introduction.

The reliability of the data, an indication of which is described above, is an important factor in considering the limitations. In addition, some deaths are tabulated by date of registration and not by date of occurrence; these have been indicated with a plus sign "+". Whenever the lag between the date of occurrence and date of registration is prolonged and, therefore, a large proportion of the death registrations are delayed, death statistics for any given year may be seriously affected. However, delays in the registration of deaths are less common and shorter than in the registration of live births.

International comparability in mortality statistics may also be affected by the exclusion of deaths of infants who were born alive but died before the registration of the birth or within the first 24 hours of life. Statistics of this type are footnoted.

In addition, it should be noted that rates are affected also by the quality and limitations of the population estimates that are used in their computation. The problems of under-enumeration or over-enumeration and, to some extent, the differences in definition of total population have been discussed in section 3 of the Introduction dealing generally with population data. Specific information pertaining to individual countries or areas is given in the footnotes to table 3.

It should be emphasized that crude death rates -- like other crude rates, such as of birth, marriage and divorce -- may be seriously affected by the age-sex structure of the populations to which they relate. Nevertheless, they do provide a simple measure of the level and changes in mortality.

The comparability of data by urban/rural residence is affected by the national definitions of urban and rural used in tabulating these data. It is assumed, in the absence of specific information to the contrary, that the definitions of urban and rural used in connection with the national population census were also used in the compilation of the vital statistics for each country or area. However, it cannot be excluded that, for a given country or area, different definitions of urban and rural are used for the vital statistics data and the population census data respectively. When known, the definitions of urban used in national population censuses are presented at the end of the technical notes for table 6. As discussed in detail in the technical notes for table 6, these definitions vary considerably from one country or area to another.

Earlier data: Deaths and crude death rates have been presented in each issue of the Demographic Yearbook. For information on specific years covered, the reader should consult the Historical Index.

Tableau 18 – *Annuaire démographique 2017*

Le tableau 18 présente le nombre des décès et les taux bruts de mortalité selon le lieu de résidence (zone urbaine ou rurale) pour le plus grand nombre d'années possible entre 2013 et 2017.

Description des variables : Le décès est défini comme la disparition permanente de tout signe de vie à un moment quelconque postérieur à la naissance vivante (cessation des fonctions vitales après la naissance sans possibilité de réanimation).

Sauf indication contraire, les statistiques relatives au nombre de décès sont établies sur la base des registres d'état civil. Pour les pays ou zones où les données concernant l'enregistrement des décès par les services de l'état civil sont jugées sûres (complétude estimée à 90 p. 100 ou plus), les taux de mortalité ont été calculés d'après les décès enregistrés.

La répartition des décès entre zones urbaines et zones rurales est celle qui a été communiquée par chaque pays ou zone ; on part du principe qu'elle repose sur les définitions de la population urbaine utilisées pour les recensements nationaux, qui sont reproduites à la fin des notes techniques du tableau 6.

Pour quelques pays il y a une discordance entre le nombre total des décès présenté dans ce tableau et ceux présentés après pour la même année. Habituellement ces différences apparaissent lorsque le nombre total des décès pour une certaine année a été révisé alors que les autres tabulations ne l'ont pas été.

Calcul des taux : Les taux bruts de mortalité représentent le nombre annuel de décès pour 1 000 habitants en milieu d'année.

Les taux selon le lieu de résidence (zone urbaine ou rurale) représentent le nombre annuel de décès, classés selon la catégorie urbaine ou rurale appropriée, pour 1 000 habitants en milieu d'année. Ces taux sont calculés par la division de statistique des Nations Unies sur la base de la population de référence adéquate (par exemple : population totale, nationaux seulement, etc.) si connue et disponible. Si la population de référence n'est pas connue ou n'est pas disponible, la population totale est utilisée pour calculer les taux. Par conséquent, si la population utilisée pour calculer les taux est différente de la population de référence adéquate, les taux présentés sont susceptibles de sous ou sur estimer la situation réelle d'un pays ou d'un territoire.

Les taux présentés dans ce tableau se rapportent seulement aux pays ou zones où l'on a enregistré un nombre minimal de 30 décès au cours d'une année donnée.

Fiabilité des données : Il a été demandé à chaque pays ou zone d'indiquer le degré estimatif de complétude des données sur les décès d'enfants de moins d'un an figurant dans ses registres d'état civil. Ces évaluations nationales sont signalées par les codes de qualité "C", "U" et "I" qui apparaissent dans la deuxième colonne du tableau.

La lettre "C" indique que les données sont jugées à peu près complètes, c'est-à-dire qu'elles représentent au moins 90 p. 100 des décès survenus chaque année ; la lettre "U" signifie que les données sont jugées incomplètes, c'est-à-dire qu'elles représentent moins de 90 p.100 des décès survenus chaque année. Le symbole "I" indique que la source des données n'est pas un registre de l'état civil ; le symbole, dans ce cas, est accompagné par une note explicative. Le code "..." dénote qu'aucun renseignement n'a été communiqué quant à la complétude des données.

Les données provenant des registres de l'état civil qui sont déclarées incomplètes ou dont le degré de complétude n'est pas connu (code "U" ou "...") sont jugées douteuses. Elles apparaissent en italique dans le présent tableau et les taux correspondants n'ont pas été calculés.

Insuffisance des données : Les statistiques relatives à la mortalité appellent les mêmes réserves que celles qui ont été formulées à propos des statistiques de l'état civil en général et des statistiques relatives aux décès en particulier (voir la section 4 des Notes techniques).

La fiabilité des données, au sujet de laquelle des indications ont été fournies plus haut, est un facteur important. Il faut également tenir compte du fait que, dans certains cas, les décès sont classés par date d'enregistrement et non par date d'occurrence ; ces cas ont été signalés par le signe "+". Chaque fois que le décalage entre le décès et son enregistrement est grand et qu'une forte proportion des décès fait l'objet d'un enregistrement tardif, les statistiques relatives aux décès survenus pendant l'année peuvent être considérablement faussées.

En règle générale, toutefois, les décès sont enregistrés beaucoup plus rapidement que les naissances vivantes, et les retards prolongés sont rares.

Un autre facteur qui nuit à la comparabilité internationale est la pratique qui consiste à ne pas inclure dans les statistiques de la mortalité les enfants nés vivants mais décédés avant l'enregistrement de leur naissance ou dans les 24 heures qui ont suivi la naissance. Quand pareil facteur a joué, cela a été signalé en note à la fin du tableau.

Il convient de noter par ailleurs que l'exactitude des taux dépend également de la qualité et des limitations des estimations de la population qui sont utilisées pour leur calcul. Le problème des erreurs par excès ou par défaut commises lors du dénombrement et, dans une certaine mesure, le problème de l'hétérogénéité des définitions de la population totale ont été examinés à la section 3 de l'Introduction, relative à la population en général ; des indications concernant certains pays ou zones sont données en note à la fin du tableau 3.

Il faut souligner que les taux bruts de mortalité, de même que les taux bruts de natalité, de nuptialité et de divortialité, peuvent varier très sensiblement selon la composition par âge et par sexe de la population à laquelle ils se rapportent. Ils offrent néanmoins un moyen simple de mesurer le niveau et l'évolution de la mortalité.

La comparabilité des données selon le lieu de résidence (zone urbaine ou rurale) peut être limitée par les définitions nationales des termes « urbain » et « rural » utilisées pour le classement de ces données. En l'absence d'indications contraires, on a supposé que les mêmes définitions avaient servi pour le recensement national de la population et pour l'établissement des statistiques de l'état civil pour chaque pays ou zone. Toutefois, il n'est pas exclu que, pour une zone ou un pays donné, des définitions différentes aient été retenues. Les définitions du terme « urbain » utilisées pour les recensements nationaux de population ont été présentées à la fin du tableau 6 lorsqu'elles étaient connues. Comme on l'a précisé dans les notes techniques relatives au tableau 6, ces définitions varient considérablement d'un pays ou d'une zone à l'autre.

Données publiées antérieurement : les différentes éditions de l'*Annuaire démographique* contiennent des statistiques des décès et des taux bruts de mortalité. Pour plus de précisions concernant les années pour lesquelles ces données ont été publiées, se reporter à l'index historique.

18. Deaths and crude death rates, by urban/rural residence: 2013 - 2017
Décès et taux bruts de mortalité, selon la résidence, urbaine/rurale : 2013 - 2017

Continent, country or area, and urban/rural residence — Continent, pays ou zone et résidence, urbaine/rurale	Code[a]	Number - Nombre					Rate - Taux				
		2013	2014	2015	2016	2017	2013	2014	2015	2016	2017
AFRICA - AFRIQUE											
Algeria - Algérie[1]											
Total	U	168 136	173 781	182 570	180 404	...	...	...	...	...	...
Angola[2]											
Total	I	...	239 252	...	...	...	...	9.2	...	...	...
Urban - Urbaine	I	...	135 698	...	...	...	...	8.4	...	...	...
Rural - Rurale	I	...	103 553	...	...	...	...	10.7	...	...	...
Botswana[3]											
Total	U	11 967	12 177	13 030	12 825	...	...	...	...	...	...
Côte d'Ivoire[2]											
Total	I	...	248 930	...	...	...	...	11.0	...	...	...
Egypt - Égypte											
Total	C	511 183	531 864	573 879	556 148	547 208	6.0	6.1	6.5	6.1	5.7
Urban - Urbaine	C	285 611	299 490	324 422	319 409	319 980	7.9	8.1	8.5	8.2	7.9
Rural - Rurale	C	225 572	232 374	249 457	236 739	227 228	4.7	4.7	4.9	4.5	4.1
Ghana[4]											
Total	+U	51 466	...	...	...	...	...	...	...	...	...
Guinea - Guinée[5]											
Total	I	...	119 969	...	...	...	...	11.3	...	...	...
Kenya											
Total	U	194 332	198 611	200 205	189 930	...	...	...	...	...	...
Lesotho											
Total	+U	...	...	...	13 768	...	...	...	...	...	...
Mauritius - Maurice[6]											
Total	+C	9 440	9 682	9 747	10 174	10 140	7.5	7.7	7.7	8.1	8.0
Urban - Urbaine	+C	4 189	4 203	4 454	4 658	4 560	8.1	8.1	8.6	9.0	8.9
Rural - Rurale	+C	5 251	5 479	5 293	5 516	5 580	7.1	7.4	7.1	7.4	7.4
Mayotte											
Total	C	...	590	636	705	735	...	2.6	2.7	2.9	2.9
Reunion - Réunion											
Total	C	...	4 355	4 531	4 689	4 673	...	5.1	5.3	5.5	5.4
Saint Helena ex. dep. - Sainte-Hélène sans dép.											
Total	C	55	61	55	45	58	13.1	13.9	12.3	9.7	...
Sao Tome and Principe - Sao Tomé-et-Principe											
Total	C	1 267	1 243	1 226	1 212	1 202	6.9	6.7	6.5	6.3	6.1
Senegal - Sénégal[7]											
Total	I	136 460	...	...	...	...	10.1	...	...	...	...
Seychelles											
Total	+C	717	725	703	747	748	8.0	7.9	7.5	7.9	7.8
Sierra Leone[8]											
Total	+U	19 403	...	...	...	...	...	...	...	...	...
South Africa - Afrique du Sud											
Total	U	477 163	476 891	473 266	456 612	...	...	...	...	...	...
Tunisia - Tunisie											
Total	U	61 730	62 785	65 743	62 601	67 447	...	...	...	...	...
AMERICA, NORTH - AMÉRIQUE DU NORD											
Anguilla[9]											
Total	+C	68	59	61	*83	...	4.9	4.1	4.1	*5.5	...
Aruba											
Total	C	560	643	679	781	707	5.3	6.0	6.2	7.1	6.4
Bahamas											
Total	+C	2 065	*2 132	*2 243	*2 288	*2 372	5.7	*5.9	*6.1	*6.1	*6.3
Barbados - Barbade											
Total	+C	2 276	2 580	...	...	...	8.2	9.3	...	...	...
Belize											
Total	U	1 637	1 620	1 772	1 796	...	...	...	...	...	...
Urban - Urbaine	U	873	906	910	958	...	...	...	...	...	...
Rural - Rurale	U	764	714	862	838	...	...	...	...	...	...
Bermuda - Bermudes[10]											
Total	C	471	480	478	492	*481	7.6	7.8	7.7	8.0	*7.8

497

18. Deaths and crude death rates, by urban/rural residence: 2013 - 2017
Décès et taux bruts de mortalité, selon la résidence, urbaine/rurale : 2013 - 2017 (continued - suite)

Continent, country or area, and urban/rural residence / Continent, pays ou zone et résidence, urbaine/rurale	Code[a]	Number - Nombre					Rate - Taux				
		2013	2014	2015	2016	2017	2013	2014	2015	2016	2017
AMERICA, NORTH - AMÉRIQUE DU NORD											
British Virgin Islands - Îles Vierges britanniques											
Total	C	113	111	136	...	...	4.0	...	4.7	...	...
Canada[11]											
Total	C	252 338	258 821	264 333	267 213	...	7.2	7.3	7.4	7.4	...
Cayman Islands - Îles Caïmanes[12]											
Total	C	182	163	170	193	216	3.2	2.9	2.9	3.2	3.4
Costa Rica											
Total	C	19 647	20 553	21 039	22 603	*23 251	4.2	4.3	4.4	4.6	*4.7
Urban - Urbaine	C	9 891	14 481[13]	17 103	17 988	*17 879	2.9	4.2	4.9	5.1	*5.0
Rural - Rurale	C	9 756	6 072[13]	3 936	4 615	*5 372	7.6	4.7	3.0	3.4	*4.0
Cuba											
Total	C	92 273	96 330	99 691	99 388	106 941	8.2	8.6	8.9	8.8	9.5
Urban - Urbaine	C	78 107	81 866	84 365	84 574	...	9.1	9.5	9.8	9.8	...
Rural - Rurale	C	14 166	14 464	15 326	14 814	...	5.5	5.6	5.9	5.7	...
Curaçao											
Total	C	1 250	1 370	1 398	1 482	1 420	8.1	8.8	8.8	9.3	8.9
Dominica - Dominique											
Total	+C	630	590	...	...	...	8.8	8.2	...	...	...
Dominican Republic - République dominicaine											
Total	U	36 025	40 466	40 948	42 199	...	...	...	...	...	...
Urban - Urbaine[14]	U	28 255	32 674	33 206	34 925	...	...	...	...	...	...
Rural - Rurale[14]	U	7 139	7 364	7 107	6 952	...	...	...	...	...	...
El Salvador											
Total	C	34 212	37 461	...	...	...	5.4	5.9	...	...	...
Urban - Urbaine	C	22 638	24 617	...	...	...	5.4	...	...	...	...
Rural - Rurale	C	11 574	12 844	...	...	...	5.4	...	...	...	...
Greenland - Groenland											
Total	C	444	461	472	487	499	7.9	8.2	8.4	8.7	8.9
Urban - Urbaine	C	379	388	407	408	428	7.9	8.0	8.4	8.4	8.8
Rural - Rurale	C	65	73	65	79	71	7.9	9.1	8.3	10.2	9.3
Grenada - Grenade											
Total	+C	822	958	...	...	...	7.6	8.8	...	...	...
Guadeloupe[15]											
Total	C	2 951	3 290	2 906	3 227	3 121	7.4	8.2	7.3	8.2	8.0
Guatemala											
Total	C	76 639	77 807	80 876	82 565	...	5.0	4.9	5.0	...	...
Jamaica - Jamaïque											
Total	U	17 350[16]	18 320	19 249	19 761	18 879	...	...	...	...	...
Martinique[15]											
Total	C	...	3 319	3 057	3 284	3 217	...	8.6	8.0	8.7	8.6
Mexico - Mexique[17]											
Total	+C	622 495	632 587	654 593	684 437	...	5.3	5.3	5.4	5.6	...
Urban - Urbaine[14]	+C	472 158	482 499	496 737	520 912	...	5.5	5.6	5.7	5.9	...
Rural - Rurale[14]	+C	139 522	140 144	147 354	153 699	...	4.3	4.3	4.4	4.6	...
Montserrat											
Total	C	45	32	49	43	...	9.1	6.4	9.8	8.5	...
Nicaragua											
Total	+U	...	...	...	23 205	...	...	...	...	...	...
Urban - Urbaine	+U	...	...	...	15 198	...	...	...	...	...	...
Rural - Rurale	+U	...	...	...	8 007	...	...	...	...	...	...
Panama											
Total	U	17 767	...	...	...	...	...	...	...	...	...
Urban - Urbaine	U	12 546	...	...	...	...	...	...	...	...	...
Rural - Rurale	U	5 221	...	...	...	...	...	...	...	...	...
Total	C	...	18 171	18 182	*18 882	*18 388	...	4.6	4.6	*4.7	*4.5
Urban - Urbaine	C	...	12 379	12 265	*12 617	...	...	4.7	4.5	*4.6	...
Rural - Rurale	C	...	5 792	5 917	*6 265	...	...	4.6	4.7	*5.0	...
Puerto Rico - Porto Rico											
Total	C	29 416	30 333	28 409	29 649	30 977	8.2	8.6	8.2	8.7	9.3
Urban - Urbaine[14]	C	16 429	16 952	14 824	15 038	15 586	...	...	...	...	...
Rural - Rurale[14]	C	12 822	13 155	13 099	14 019	14 590	...	...	...	...	...
Saint Kitts and Nevis - Saint-Kitts-et-Nevis											
Total	+C	348	411	...	...	...	...	...	...	...	...

18. Deaths and crude death rates, by urban/rural residence: 2013 - 2017
Décès et taux bruts de mortalité, selon la résidence, urbaine/rurale : 2013 - 2017 (continued - suite)

Continent, country or area, and urban/rural residence / Continent, pays ou zone et résidence, urbaine/rurale	Code[a]	Number - Nombre					Rate - Taux				
		2013	2014	2015	2016	2017	2013	2014	2015	2016	2017
AMERICA, NORTH - AMÉRIQUE DU NORD											
Saint Vincent and the Grenadines - Saint-Vincent-et-les Grenadines											
Total	C	926	1 006	...	...	...	8.4	9.1	...	...	...
Sint Maarten (Dutch part) - Saint-Martin (partie néerlandaise)[18]											
Total	+C	171	...	...	...	...	4.7	...	...	...	...
Trinidad and Tobago - Trinité-et-Tobago											
Total	C	*10 661	*11 461	*11 240	...	...	*8.0	*8.5	*8.3	...	...
Turks and Caicos Islands - Îles Turques et Caïques[19]											
Total	C	101	76	...	...	...	3.0	2.2	...	...	...
United States of America - États-Unis d'Amérique											
Total	C	2 596 993	2 626 418	2 712 630	...	...	8.2	8.2	8.5		
AMERICA, SOUTH - AMÉRIQUE DU SUD											
Argentina - Argentine											
Total	C	326 197	325 539	333 407	352 992	...	7.7	7.6	7.7	8.1	...
Brazil - Brésil[20]											
Total	U	1 180 796	...	...	...	...	...	...	...	...	...
Total	+C	...	1 194 164	1 231 400	1 274 630	...	...	5.9	6.0	6.2	...
Chile - Chili											
Total	C	99 770	101 960	103 327	*104 026	...	5.7	5.7	5.7	*5.7	...
Urban - Urbaine	C	86 887	88 055	89 935	...	...	5.7	5.7	5.7	...	...
Rural - Rurale	C	12 883	13 905	13 392	...	...	5.7	6.2	5.9	...	...
Colombia - Colombie											
Total	U	203 071	210 051	219 472	223 078	...	...	...	...	...	...
Urban - Urbaine[14]	U	161 992	168 236	177 609	179 379	...	...	...	...	...	...
Rural - Rurale[14]	U	38 362	39 128	39 828	41 536	...	...	...	...	...	...
Ecuador - Équateur[21]											
Total	U	63 104	62 981	64 790	67 506	...	...	...	...	...	...
Urban - Urbaine	U	49 912	48 867	49 839	52 213	...	...	...	...	...	...
Rural - Rurale	U	13 192	14 114	14 951	15 293	...	...	...	...	...	...
French Guiana - Guyane française[15]											
Total	C	767	786	834	901	964	3.1	3.1	3.2	3.4	3.5
Guyana											
Total	+C	5 195	5 268	4 922	5 109	4 909	7.0	7.1	6.6	6.9	6.6
Paraguay											
Total	+U	24 193	22 625	24 885	27 243	...	...	...	...	...	...
Urban - Urbaine[22]	+U	17 354	15 940	...	...	...	...	...	...	...	...
Rural - Rurale[22]	+U	6 742	6 579	...	...	...	...	...	...	...	...
Peru - Pérou[23]											
Total	+U	94 394	96 460	96 240	*97 897	...	...	...	...	...	...
Suriname											
Total	C	3 557	3 738	3 663	3 591	...	6.5	6.7	6.5	6.2	...
Urban - Urbaine	C	2 371	2 519	2 536	2 489	...	...	...	...	...	...
Rural - Rurale	C	1 186	1 219	1 127	1 102	...	...	...	...	...	...
Uruguay											
Total	C	32 698	32 122	32 967	34 273	...	9.5	9.3	9.5	9.8	...
Venezuela (Bolivarian Republic of) - Venezuela (République bolivarienne du)											
Total	C	147 901	159 239	163 712	185 697	181 297	5.0	5.3	5.4	6.0	5.8

18. Deaths and crude death rates, by urban/rural residence: 2013 - 2017
Décès et taux bruts de mortalité, selon la résidence, urbaine/rurale : 2013 - 2017 (continued - suite)

Continent, country or area, and urban/rural residence / Continent, pays ou zone et résidence, urbaine/rurale	Co-de[a]	Number - Nombre					Rate - Taux				
		2013	2014	2015	2016	2017	2013	2014	2015	2016	2017
ASIA - ASIE											
Armenia - Arménie[24]											
Total	C	*27 196	27 714	27 878	28 226	27 157	*9.0	9.2	9.3	9.4	9.1
Urban - Urbaine	C	...	...	17 743	18 257	...	...	...	9.3	9.6	...
Rural - Rurale	C	...	...	10 135	9 969	...	...	...	9.3	9.2	...
Azerbaijan - Azerbaïdjan[24]											
Total	+C	54 383	55 648	54 697	56 648	...	5.8	5.8	5.7	5.8	...
Urban - Urbaine	+C	28 863	29 988	29 628	31 385	...	...	5.9	5.8	6.1	...
Rural - Rurale	+C	25 520	25 660	25 069	25 263	...	...	5.7	5.5	5.5	...
Bahrain - Bahreïn[25]											
Total	C	2 588	2 805	2 787	2 858	...	2.1	2.1	2.0	2.0	...
Brunei Darussalam - Brunéi Darussalam											
Total	+C	1 398	1 470	1 547	1 632		3.5	3.6	3.8	3.9	...
China - Chine[26]											
Total	I	9 720 000	9 770 000	9 750 000	...	...	7.2	7.2	7.1	...	...
China, Hong Kong SAR - Chine, Hong Kong RAS											
Total	C	43 397	45 087	46 108	46 905	46 829	6.0	6.2	6.3	6.4	6.3
China, Macao SAR - Chine, Macao RAS											
Total	C	1 920	1 939	2 002	2 248	2 120	3.2	3.1	3.1	3.5	3.2
Cyprus - Chypre[27]											
Total	C	5 141	5 424	5 859	5 471	*5 997	6.0	6.4	6.9	6.4	*7.0
Georgia - Géorgie[24]											
Total	C	48 553	49 087	49 121	50 771	47 822	10.8	13.2	13.2	13.7	12.8
Urban - Urbaine	C	...	...	26 139	26 788	...	...	...	12.3	12.6	...
Rural - Rurale	C	...	...	22 982	23 983	...	...	...	14.4	15.1	...
India - Inde[28]											
Total	I	...	...	...	...	...	7.0	6.7	6.5	6.4	...
Urban - Urbaine	I	...	...	...	...	...	5.6	5.5	5.4	5.4	...
Rural - Rurale	I	...	...	...	...	...	7.5	7.3	7.1	6.9	...
Iran (Islamic Republic of) - Iran (République islamique d')[29]											
Total	+C	372 279	446 333	374 827	369 751	...	4.8	5.7	4.8	4.6	...
Urban - Urbaine	+C	285 117[14]	302 184	280 765	274 870[14]	...	5.1	5.4	4.9	4.7	...
Rural - Rurale	+C	87 063[14]	144 149	94 062	94 788[14]	...	4.1	6.7	4.4	4.4	...
Iraq											
Total	U	*189 118	...				...	...	...	...	...
Israel - Israël[30]											
Total	C	41 683	42 457	44 507	44 204	44 423	5.2	5.2	5.3	5.2	5.1
Urban - Urbaine[14]	C	39 184	39 912	41 775	41 525	41 744	5.3	5.3	5.5	5.3	...
Rural - Rurale[14]	C	2 494	2 533	2 723	2 673	2 677	3.6	3.6	3.7	3.6	...
Japan - Japon[31]											
Total	C	1 268 436[14]	1 273 004[14]	1 290 444[14]	1 307 748[14]	*1 340 433	10.0	10.0	10.1	10.3	*10.6
Urban - Urbaine[14]	C	1 124 417	1 130 587	1 147 467	1 162 734	...	...	...	...	...	...
Rural - Rurale[14]	C	142 556	141 084	141 799	143 801	...	...	...	...	...	...
Jordan - Jordanie[32]											
Total	U	23 898	25 782	26 640	27 608	27 516	...	...	...	...	...
Kazakhstan											
Total	U	136 368	132 287	130 811	131 231	129 009	...	...	...	...	...
Urban - Urbaine	U	78 764	77 803	77 319	78 001	76 522	...	...	...	...	...
Rural - Rurale	U	57 604	54 484	53 492	53 230	52 487	...	...	...	...	...
Kuwait - Koweït											
Total	C	5 909	6 031	6 481	6 338	...	1.7	1.6	1.6	1.6	...
Kyrgyzstan - Kirghizstan											
Total	C	34 880	35 564	34 808	33 475	33 166	6.1	6.1	5.8	5.5	5.4
Urban - Urbaine	C	12 507	12 802	12 294	11 664	11 647	6.5	6.5	6.1	5.7	5.6
Rural - Rurale	C	22 373	22 762	22 514	21 811	21 519	5.9	5.9	5.7	5.4	5.2
Lebanon - Liban											
Total	C	24 013	27 020	...	...	...	...	...	...	...	...
Malaysia - Malaisie											
Total	C	142 202	150 318	155 786	162 201	...	4.7	4.9	5.0	5.1	...
Urban - Urbaine	C	90 855	97 989	101 309	104 817	...	4.1	4.3	4.4	4.4	...
Rural - Rurale	C	51 347	52 329	54 477	57 384	...	6.3	6.5	6.8	7.2	...

Continent, country or area, and urban/rural residence / Continent, pays ou zone et résidence, urbaine/rurale	Code[a]	Number - Nombre					Rate - Taux				
		2013	2014	2015	2016	2017	2013	2014	2015	2016	2017
ASIA - ASIE											
Maldives[33]											
Total	C	1 120	1 143	1 130	1 226	...	3.3	3.3	3.3	3.5	...
Urban - Urbaine	C	513[34]	546[34]	260[14]	263[14]	...	...	...	1.9	1.9	...
Rural - Rurale	C	607[34]	492[34]	744[14]	846[14]	...	...	...	3.5	4.0	...
Mongolia - Mongolie											
Total	+C	17 247	16 521	17 620	17 763	17 357	5.9	5.6	5.8	5.8	5.5
Urban - Urbaine	+C	11 182	11 406	11 753	11 182	11 425	5.7	5.7	5.8	5.3	5.3
Rural - Rurale	+C	6 065	5 115	5 867	6 581	5 932	6.5	5.3	6.0	6.8	5.9
Myanmar											
Total	+U	257 216[35]	213 085[36]	225 526[36]	...	...	...	...	...	...	...
Urban - Urbaine	+U	119 823[35]	96 697[36]	102 923[36]	...	...	...	...	...	...	...
Rural - Rurale	+U	137 393[35]	116 388[36]	122 603[36]	...	...	...	...	...	...	...
Oman											
Total	U	7 669[37]	7 819[37]	8 167[37]	8 196[37]	8 861	...	...	...	...	...
Philippines											
Total	C	531 280	551 716	560 605	582 183	...	5.4	5.5	5.5	5.6	...
Qatar											
Total	C	2 133	2 366	2 317	2 347	*2 294	1.1	1.1	1.0	0.9	*0.8
Urban - Urbaine	C	...	2 366	2 317	2 347	...	...	1.1	1.0	0.9	...
Republic of Korea - République de Corée[38]											
Total	C	266 257	267 692	275 895	280 827	285 534	5.3	5.3	5.4	5.5	5.6
Urban - Urbaine[14]	C	182 888	184 631	189 851	...	...	4.4	4.5	4.6	...	...
Rural - Rurale[14]	C	83 360	83 055	86 038	...	...	9.0	8.9	9.1	...	...
Saudi Arabia - Arabie saoudite											
Total[39]	...	106 521	...	...	...	...	...	...	...	...	...
Total[40]	I	...	...	69 206[41]	58 097[42]	58 915[42]	...	...	2.2	1.8	1.8
Singapore - Singapour											
Total	+C	18 938	19 393	19 862	20 017	20 905	4.9	5.0	5.1	5.1	5.3
Sri Lanka											
Total	+C	127 183	*127 758	*131 614	130 765	139 822	6.2	*6.2	*6.3	6.2	6.5
Urban - Urbaine	+C	54 041	...	...	...	...	...	...	...	...	...
Rural - Rurale	+C	73 142	...	...	...	...	...	...	...	...	...
State of Palestine - État de Palestine[43]											
Total	U	11 188	13 390	11 908	...	...	...	...	...	...	...
Tajikistan - Tadjikistan[24]											
Total	U	31 706	32 879	33 563	34 134	...	...	...	...	...	...
Urban - Urbaine	U	10 091	9 830	9 959	9 944	...	...	...	...	...	...
Rural - Rurale	U	21 615	23 049	23 604	24 190	...	...	...	...	...	...
Thailand - Thaïlande											
Total	+U	438 648	448 601	456 391	480 434	468 911	...	...	...	...	...
Timor-Leste[44]											
Total	I	...	...	9 209	...	...	...	...	7.8	...	...
Turkey - Turquie											
Total	C	373 041[45]	390 944[45]	405 202[45]	422 135[45]	*425 781	4.9	5.0	5.1	5.3	*5.3
United Arab Emirates - Émirats arabes unis[46]											
Total	...	8 015	8 265	8 755	...	...	...	...	...	...	...
Uzbekistan - Ouzbékistan[24]											
Total	+C	145 672	149 761	152 035	154 791	160 723	4.8	4.9	4.9	4.9	5.0
Urban - Urbaine	+C	79 478	81 991	81 094	...	...	5.1	5.2	5.1	...	...
Rural - Rurale	+C	66 194	67 770	70 941	...	...	4.5	4.5	4.6	...	...
Yemen - Yémen[47]											
Total	U	35 066	...	...	...	...	...	...	...	...	...
EUROPE											
Åland Islands - Îles d'Åland											
Total	C	269	251	285	297	*251	9.4	8.7	9.8	10.2	*8.6
Urban - Urbaine	C	115	104	114	120	*123	10.1	9.1	9.9	10.4	*10.6
Rural - Rurale	C	154	147	171	177	*128	8.9	8.5	9.8	10.1	*7.2
Albania - Albanie											
Total	C	20 442	20 656	22 422	21 388	22 232	7.1	7.1	7.8	7.4	7.7

18. Deaths and crude death rates, by urban/rural residence: 2013 - 2017
Décès et taux bruts de mortalité, selon la résidence, urbaine/rurale : 2013 - 2017 (continued - suite)

Continent, country or area, and urban/rural residence / Continent, pays ou zone et résidence, urbaine/rurale	Code[a]	Number - Nombre					Rate - Taux				
		2013	2014	2015	2016	2017	2013	2014	2015	2016	2017
EUROPE											
Andorra - Andorre											
Total	C	239	276	282	310	...	3.4	3.9	4.0	4.3	...
Austria - Autriche[48]											
Total	C	79 526	78 252	83 073	80 669	*83 270	9.4	9.2	9.6	9.2	*9.5
Belarus - Bélarus											
Total	C	125 326	121 542	120 026	119 379	119 311	13.2	12.8	12.6	12.6	12.6
Urban - Urbaine	C	75 275	74 236	73 563	73 599	...	10.4	10.2	10.0	10.0	...
Rural - Rurale	C	50 051	47 306	46 463	45 780	...	22.6	21.8	21.7	21.6	...
Belgium - Belgique[49]											
Total	C	109 334	104 755	110 541	108 097	109 666	9.8	9.3	9.8	9.5	9.6
Urban - Urbaine	C	107 829	103 223	108 942	...	...	...	...	...	...	...
Rural - Rurale	C	1 505	1 532	1 599	...	...	...	...	...	...	...
Bosnia and Herzegovina - Bosnie-Herzégovine											
Total	C	35 837	34 824	37 070	35 530	36 336	10.1	9.9	10.5	10.1	10.4
Bulgaria - Bulgarie											
Total	C	104 345	108 952	110 117	107 580	109 791	14.4	15.1	15.3	15.1	15.5
Urban - Urbaine	C	...	67 008	67 749	67 192	...	...	12.7	12.9	12.9	...
Rural - Rurale	C	...	41 944	42 368	40 388	...	...	21.6	21.9	21.1	...
Croatia - Croatie											
Total	C	50 386	50 839	54 205	51 542	53 477	11.8	12.0	12.9	12.3	12.9
Urban - Urbaine	C	25 464	26 230	28 365	27 000	...	...	...	...	...	...
Rural - Rurale	C	24 922	24 609	25 840	24 542	...	...	...	...	...	...
Czechia - Tchéquie											
Total	C	109 160	105 665	111 173	107 750	111 443	10.4	10.0	10.5	10.2	10.5
Urban - Urbaine	C	79 923	77 826	81 854	79 384	...	10.4	10.1	10.6	10.3	...
Rural - Rurale	C	29 237	27 839	29 319	28 366	...	10.3	9.8	10.3	10.0	...
Denmark - Danemark[50]											
Total	C	52 471	51 340	52 555	52 824	53 261	9.4	9.1	9.3	9.2	9.2
Estonia - Estonie											
Total	C	15 244	15 484	15 243	15 392	15 543	11.6	11.8	11.6	11.7	11.8
Urban - Urbaine	C	10 044	10 464	10 491[14]	10 539[14]	...	11.2	11.7	11.7	11.7	...
Rural - Rurale	C	5 200	5 020	4 744[14]	4 836[14]	...	12.4	12.0	11.4	11.7	...
Faeroe Islands - Îles Féroé											
Total	C	361	394	376	381	446	7.5	8.1	7.7	7.7	8.9
Urban - Urbaine	C	119	130	102	124	157	6.5	7.1	5.5	6.5	8.2
Rural - Rurale	C	242	264	274	257	289	8.0	8.8	9.1	8.4	9.3
Finland - Finlande											
Total	C	51 203[51]	51 935[51]	52 207[51]	53 626[51]	53 722	9.5	9.6	9.6	9.8	9.8
Urban - Urbaine[51]	C	31 777	32 260	32 941	33 949	...	8.5	8.6	8.6	8.7	...
Rural - Rurale[51]	C	19 426	19 675	19 266	19 677	...	11.6	11.8	12.0	12.4	...
France											
Total	C	558 408	547 003	581 770	581 073	*593 400	8.7	8.5	9.0	9.0	*9.1
Urban - Urbaine[52]	C	422 803	414 410	441 398	441 334	...	...	...	...	...	...
Rural - Rurale[52]	C	133 734	130 755	138 220	137 674	...	...	...	...	...	...
Germany - Allemagne											
Total	C	893 825	868 356	925 200	910 902	*933 000	11.1	10.7	11.3	11.1	*11.3
Gibraltar[53]											
Total	+C	230	248	235	...	...	7.0	7.5	7.0	...	...
Greece - Grèce											
Total	C	111 794	113 740	121 183	118 785	124 530	10.2	10.4	11.2	11.0	11.6
Urban - Urbaine	C	62 919	63 724	67 843	67 121	...	...	...	...	...	...
Rural - Rurale	C	48 875	50 016	53 340	51 664	...	...	...	...	...	...
Guernsey - Guernesey											
Total	C	556	526	560	536	...	8.9	8.4	9.0	8.6	...
Hungary - Hongrie											
Total	C	126 677[54]	126 294[56]	131 575[56]	127 098[56]	131 877[56]	12.8	12.8	13.4	13.0	13.5
Urban - Urbaine[55]	C	85 164[54]	85 796[56]	89 692[56]	86 815[56]	...	12.4	12.3	12.9	12.6	...
Rural - Rurale[55]	C	41 383[54]	40 331[56]	41 717[56]	40 130[56]	...	13.7	13.8	14.4	13.8	...
Iceland - Islande											
Total	C	2 154	2 049	2 178	2 309	2 239	6.7	6.3	6.6	6.9	6.5
Urban - Urbaine	C	1 980	1 936	2 009	2 038	...	6.5	6.3	6.5	6.5	...
Rural - Rurale	C	174	113	169	183	...	8.4	5.4	8.1	8.6	...
Ireland - Irlande											
Total	+C	30 018	29 188	30 064	30 390	30 484	6.5	6.3	6.4	6.4	6.3
Isle of Man - Île de Man											
Total	+C	792	787	...	852	837	9.2	9.1	...	10.0	10.0

18. Deaths and crude death rates, by urban/rural residence: 2013 - 2017
Décès et taux bruts de mortalité, selon la résidence, urbaine/rurale : 2013 - 2017 (continued - suite)

Continent, country or area, and urban/rural residence / Continent, pays ou zone et résidence, urbaine/rurale	Code[a]	Number - Nombre					Rate - Taux				
		2013	2014	2015	2016	2017	2013	2014	2015	2016	2017
EUROPE											
Italy - Italie											
Total	C	600 744	598 364	647 571	615 261	649 061	10.0	9.8	10.7	10.1	10.7
Jersey											
Total	+C	717	700	756	...	...	...	6.9	7.4	...	...
Latvia - Lettonie											
Total	C	28 691	28 466	28 478	28 580	28 757	14.3	14.3	14.4	14.6	14.8
Urban - Urbaine	C	18 764	18 847	18 884	18 877	...	13.8	13.9	14.0	14.1	...
Rural - Rurale	C	9 927	9 619	9 594	9 701	...	15.3	15.0	15.2	15.6	...
Liechtenstein											
Total	C	246	268	252	271	*249	6.7	7.2	6.7	7.2	*6.6
Lithuania - Lituanie											
Total	C	41 511	40 252	41 776	41 106	40 142	14.0	13.7	14.4	14.3	14.2
Urban - Urbaine	C	25 403	24 823	25 850	25 817	...	12.8	12.6	13.2	13.4	...
Rural - Rurale	C	16 108	15 429	15 926	15 289	...	16.5	16.0	16.7	16.2	...
Luxembourg											
Total	C	3 822	3 841	3 983	3 967	4 263	7.0	6.9	7.0	6.8	7.1
Malta - Malte											
Total	C	3 236	3 270	3 442	3 342	3 571	7.6	7.7	8.0	7.3	7.6
Monaco[57]											
Total	C	567	524	595	503	...	15.3	14.2	15.8	13.2	...
Montenegro - Monténégro											
Total	C	5 917	6 014	6 329	6 464	6 523	9.5	9.7	10.2	10.4	10.5
Netherlands - Pays-Bas[58]											
Total	C	141 245	139 223	147 134	148 997	*150 027	8.4	8.3	8.7	8.7	*8.8
Norway - Norvège[59]											
Total	C	41 131	40 369	40 676	40 726	40 774	8.1	7.9	7.8	7.8	7.7
Poland - Pologne											
Total	C	387 312	376 467	394 921	388 009	402 852	10.2	9.9	10.4	10.2	10.6
Urban - Urbaine	C	235 097	229 697	242 067	236 749	...	10.2	10.0	10.6	10.4	...
Rural - Rurale	C	152 215	146 770	152 854	151 260	...	10.1	9.7	10.1	10.0	...
Portugal[60]											
Total	C	106 554	104 843	108 539	110 573	109 586	10.2	10.1	10.5	10.7	10.6
Republic of Moldova - République de Moldova[61]											
Total	C	38 060	39 494	39 906	38 489	36 768	10.7	13.2	...	...	...
Urban - Urbaine	C	...	...	...	12 766	12 473	...	...	...	...	...
Rural - Rurale	C	...	...	...	25 723	24 295	...	...	...	...	...
Romania - Roumanie											
Total	C	246 967	254 965	261 294	257 215	*260 599	12.4	12.8	13.2	13.1	*13.3
Urban - Urbaine	C	114 091	118 040	121 616	...	...	10.6	11.0	11.4	...	...
Rural - Rurale	C	132 876	136 925	139 678	...	...	14.4	14.9	15.3	...	...
Russian Federation - Fédération de Russie[24]											
Total	C	1 871 809	...	...	...	...	13.0	...	...	...	...
San Marino - Saint-Marin											
Total	C	247	252	235	253	278	7.4	7.5	6.9	7.4	8.1
Serbia - Serbie[62]											
Total	+C	100 300	101 247	103 678	100 834	103 722	14.0	14.2	14.6	14.3	14.8
Urban - Urbaine	+C	53 169	53 932	56 161	54 902	...	12.4	12.6	13.2	12.9	...
Rural - Rurale	+C	47 131	47 315	47 517	45 932	...	16.3	16.5	16.8	16.4	...
Slovakia - Slovaquie											
Total	C	52 089	51 346	53 826	52 351	53 914	9.6	9.5	9.9	9.6	9.9
Urban - Urbaine	C	26 482	26 198	27 254	27 070	...	9.0	9.0	9.3	9.3	...
Rural - Rurale	C	25 607	25 148	26 572	25 281	...	10.3	10.1	10.6	10.1	...
Slovenia - Slovénie											
Total	C	19 334	18 886	19 834	19 689	20 509	9.4	9.2	9.6	9.5	9.9
Urban - Urbaine	C	9 268	9 103	10 098	9 890	...	8.8	8.7	9.1	8.9	...
Rural - Rurale	C	10 066	9 783	9 736	9 799	...	10.0	9.7	10.2	10.2	...
Spain - Espagne											
Total	C	388 600	393 734	420 408	408 231	*421 269	8.3	8.5	9.1	8.8	*9.1
Sweden - Suède											
Total	C	90 402	88 976	90 907	90 982	*91 972	9.4	9.2	9.3	9.2	*9.1
Switzerland - Suisse											
Total	C	64 961	63 938	67 606	64 964	66 971	8.0	7.8	8.2	7.8	7.9
Urban - Urbaine	C	47 654	47 089	56 647[63]	54 293	...	8.0	7.8	8.1	7.7	...
Rural - Rurale	C	17 307	16 849	10 959[63]	10 671	...	8.1	7.8	8.5	8.2	...

18. Deaths and crude death rates, by urban/rural residence: 2013 - 2017
Décès et taux bruts de mortalité, selon la résidence, urbaine/rurale : 2013 - 2017 (continued - suite)

Continent, country or area, and urban/rural residence / Continent, pays ou zone et résidence, urbaine/rurale	Co-de[a]	Number - Nombre					Rate - Taux				
		2013	2014	2015	2016	2017	2013	2014	2015	2016	2017
EUROPE											
TFYR of Macedonia - L'ex-R. y. de Macédoine											
Total	C	19 208	19 718	20 461	20 417	20 318	9.3	9.5	9.9	9.9	9.8
Urban - Urbaine	C	11 539	11 944	12 462	12 438	...	...	...	...	...	...
Rural - Rurale	C	7 669	7 774	7 999	7 983	...	...	...	...	...	...
Ukraine[64]											
Total	+C	662 368	632 296[65]	594 796[65]	583 631[65]	574 123[65]	14.6	14.7	13.9	13.7	13.6
Urban - Urbaine	+C	412 553	391 739[65]	358 749[65]	354 634[65]	...	...	...	...	...	...
Rural - Rurale	+C	249 815	240 557[65]	236 047[65]	228 997[65]	...	...	...	...	...	...
United Kingdom of Great Britain and Northern Ireland - Royaume-Uni de Grande-Bretagne et d'Irlande du Nord[66]											
Total	+C	574 945	568 840	601 272	595 655	*607 172	9.0	8.8	9.2	9.1	*9.2
OCEANIA - OCÉANIE											
American Samoa - Samoas américaines											
Total	C	270	259	...	...	...	4.3	4.2	...	...	...
Australia - Australie											
Total	C	147 678	153 580	159 052	158 504	...	6.4	6.5	6.7	6.5	...
Urban - Urbaine[67]	C	87 845	91 129	94 156	93 337	...	4.4	4.5	4.6	4.5	...
Rural - Rurale[67]	C	59 257	61 892	64 388	64 638	...	18.4	19.1	19.8	19.8	...
Cook Islands - Îles Cook[68]											
Total	+C	115	113	*102	...	...	6.2	6.1	*5.5	...	...
Fiji - Fidji											
Total	+C	6 488	5 801	...	...	...	7.5	6.7	...	...	...
French Polynesia - Polynésie française											
Total	C	1 441	1 427	1 394	...	...	5.3	5.3	5.1	...	...
Guam[69]											
Total	C	904	952	1 009	1 022	1 008	5.6	5.9	6.2	6.3	6.2
Nauru											
Total	C	95	...	...	...	...	...	...	...	...	...
New Caledonia - Nouvelle-Calédonie											
Total	C	1 374	1 406	1 465	1 580	...	5.2	5.2	5.4	5.8	...
New Zealand - Nouvelle-Zélande[70]											
Total	+C	29 568	31 065	31 608	31 179[71]	33 339[71]	6.7	6.9	6.9	6.6	7.0
Urban - Urbaine[14]	+C	26 523	27 930	28 455	27 912[71]	29 913[71]	6.9	7.2	7.2	6.9	7.2
Rural - Rurale[14]	+C	3 021	3 099	3 132	3 246[71]	3 411[71]	4.8	5.0	4.9	5.1	5.3
Norfolk Island - Île Norfolk[72]											
Total	+C	11	13	11	...	...	...	...	...	...	...
Northern Mariana Islands - Îles Mariannes septentrionales[73]											
Total	U	200	220	...	...	...	...	...	...	...	...
Palau - Palaos											
Total	C	192	167	136	175	183	10.9	9.5	7.7	9.9	10.3
Samoa											
Total	+U	876	884	1 124	2 034	...	...	...	...	...	...

FOOTNOTES - NOTES

Italics: data from civil registers which are incomplete or of unknown completeness. - Italiques : données incomplètes ou dont le degré d'exactitude n'est pas connu, provenant des registres de l'état civil.

* Provisional. - Données provisoires.

[a] 'Code' indicates the source of data, as follows:
C - Civil registration, estimated over 90% complete
U - Civil registration, estimated less than 90% complete
| - Other source, estimated reliable
+ - Data tabulated by date of registration rather than occurence
... - Information not available

Le 'Code' indique la source des données, comme suit :
C - Registres de l'état civil considérés complets à 90 p. 100 au moins
U - Registres de l'état civil qui ne sont pas considérés complets à 90 p. 100 au

moins

| - Autre source, considérée pas douteuses

+ - Données exploitées selon la date de l'enregistrement et non la date de l'événement

... - Information pas disponible

[1] Excluding live-born infants who died before their birth was registered. Data refer to Algerian population only. - Non compris les enfants nés vivants décédés avant l'enregistrement de leur naissance. Les données ne concernent que la population algérienne.

[2] Data refer to the 12 months preceding the census in May. - Les données se rapportent aux 12 mois précédant le recensement de mai.

[3] Source: Vital Statistics Report 2016. - Source: Vital Statistics Report 2016.

[4] The coverage of registration is estimated at 26 per cent. - Le degré de complétude de l'enregistrement est évalué à 26 pour cent.

[5] Adjusted number of deaths in households referring to the 12 months preceding the census in March. - Le nombre ajusté de décès des ménages ordinaires se rapportent aux 12 mois précédant le recensement de mars.

[6] Excludes the islands of St. Brandon and Agalega. - Non compris les îles St. Brandon et Agalega.

[7] Based on estimates and projections from 'Agence Nationale de la Statistique et de la Démographie'. - Données fondées sur des estimations et des projections provenant de l'Agence Nationale de la Statistique et de la Démographie.

[8] Source: National Office of Births and Deaths. - Source : Le bureau national des naissances et des décès.

[9] Excluding visitors. - Ne comprend pas les visiteurs.

[10] Excluding non-residents and foreign service personnel and their dependants. - À l'exclusion des non-résidents et du personnel diplomatique et de leurs charges de famille.

[11] Including Canadian residents temporarily in the United States, but excluding United States residents temporarily in Canada. - Y compris les résidents canadiens se trouvant temporairement aux Etats-Unis, mais ne comprenant pas les résidents des Etats-Unis se trouvant temporairement au Canada.

[12] Total includes resident deaths outside of the islands but buried in the islands. - Le total comprend les décès de résidents hors des îles mais inhumés dans les îles.

[13] Definition of urban and rural distribution changed from the year 2014. - La définition de la répartition urbaine et rurale a changé depuis 2014.

[14] The total number may include 'Unknown residence', but the categories urban and rural do not. - Le nombre total peut inclure les personnes dont la résidence n'est pas connue, à l'inverse des catégories de population urbaine et rurale.

[15] Excluding live-born infants who died before their birth was registered. - Non compris les enfants nés vivants décédés avant l'enregistrement de leur naissance.

[16] Data have been adjusted for undercoverage of infant deaths and sudden and violent deaths. - Ajusté pour la sous-estimation de la mortalité infantile, du nombre de morts soudaines et de morts violentes.

[17] Data refer to resident population only. - Pour la population résidante seulement.

[18] Source: Population Registry and STAT/CBS estimates. - Source: Le registre de la population et les estimations du STAT/CBS.

[19] Excluding deaths of persons living abroad. - Exception faite des personnes décédées à l'étranger.

[20] Including deaths abroad and deaths of unknown place of residence. - Y compris décès à l'étranger et décès dont le lieu de résidence n'est pas connu.

[21] Excludes nomadic Indian tribes. - Non compris les tribus d'Indiens nomades.

[22] Data for urban and rural exclude deaths of unknown residence. - Les données pur la résidence urbaine et rurale non comprent pas les décès dont on ignore la résidence.

[23] Source: Reports of the Ministry of Health. - Source : Rapports du Ministère de la Santé.

[24] Excluding infants born alive of less than 28 weeks' gestation, of less than 1 000 g in weight and 35 cm in length, who die within seven days of birth. - Non compris les enfants nés vivants après moins de 28 semaines de gestations, pesant moins de 1 000 g, mesurant moins de 35 cm et décédés dans les sept jours qui ont suivi leur naissance.

[25] Sources: Births and Deaths National Registration System database, and medical records of government hospitals. - Les sources: Les bases de données des << Births and Deaths National Registration System >> et les dossiers médicaux des hôpitaux du gouvernement.

[26] For statistical purposes, the data for China do not include those for the Hong Kong Special Administrative Region (Hong Kong SAR), Macao Special Administrative Region (Macao SAR) and Taiwan province of China. Data have been estimated on the basis of the annual National Sample Survey on Population Changes. - Pour la présentation des statistiques, les données pour la Chine ne comprennent pas la Région Administrative Spéciale de Hong Kong (Hong Kong RAS), la Région Administrative Spéciale de Macao (Macao RAS) et Taïwan province de Chine. Les données ont été estimées sur la base de l'enquête annuelle "National Sample Survey on Population Changes".

[27] Data refer to government controlled areas. Data refer to deaths of residents only. - Les données se rapportent aux zones contrôlées par le Gouvernement. Les données renvoient aux décès de résidents uniquement.

[28] Includes data for the Indian-held part of Jammu and Kashmir, the final status of which has not yet been determined. Rates were obtained by the Sample Registration System of India, which is a large demographic survey. - Y compris les données pour la partie du Jammu et du Cachemire occupée par l'Inde dont le statut définitif n'a pas encore été déterminé. Les taux ont été obtenus par le Système de l'enregistrement par échantillon de l'Inde qui est une large enquête démographique.

[29] Data refer to the Iranian Year which begins on 21 March and ends on 20 March of the following year. - Les données concernent l'année iranienne, qui commence le 21 mars et se termine le 20 mars de l'année suivante.

[30] Including deaths abroad of Israeli residents who were out of the country for less than a year. Includes data for East Jerusalem and Israeli residents in certain other territories under occupation by Israeli military forces since June 1967. - Y compris les décès à l'étranger de résidents israéliens qui ont quitté le pays depuis moins d'un an. Y compris les données pour Jérusalem-Est et les résidents israéliens dans certains autres territoires occupés depuis 1967 par les forces armées israéliennes.

[31] Data refer to Japanese nationals in Japan only. - Les données se raportent aux nationaux japonais au Japon seulement.

[32] Excluding data for Jordanian territory under occupation since June 1967 by Israeli military forces. Excluding foreigners, including registered Palestinian refugees. - Non compris les données pour le territoire jordanien occupé depuis juin 1967 par les forces armées israéliennes. Non compris les étrangers, mais y compris les réfugiés de Palestine enregistrés.

[33] Data do not include foreigners. - Les données sur les etrangers ne sont pas inclus.

[34] Data by the place of occurrence of death, not by the residence of deceased. Excluding deaths occurred abroad. - Données classées selon le lieu du décès, et non selon le lieu de résidence de la personne décédée. Hormis les décès à l'étranger.

[35] Source: "Department of Public Health" - Source : << Le Service de la santé publique >>

[36] Data are from Vital Registration System (VRS). - Les données proviennent du système d'enregistrement des faits d'état civil.

[37] Data from Births and Deaths Notification System (Ministry of Health and all health care providers). - Les données proviennent du système de notification des naissances et des décès (Ministère de la santé et tous prestataires de soins de santé).

[38] Excluding alien armed forces, civilian aliens employed by armed forces, and foreign diplomatic personnel and their dependants. - Non compris les militaires étrangers, les civils étrangers employés par les forces armées ni le personnel diplomatique étranger et les membres de leur famille les accompagnant.

[39] Projections based on the final results of the 2004 Population and Housing Census. - Projections basées sur les résultats définitifs du recensement de la population et de l'habitat de 2004.

[40] Data refer to Saudi Arabian nationals only. - Les données ne concernent que les ressortissants saoudiens.

[41] Based on 2010 population census and 2016 demographic survey. - D'après le recensement de la population de 2010 et l'enquête démographique de 2016.

[42] Survey based estimates. - Estimations basées sur des enquêtes.

[43] Source: Palestinian Central Bureau of Statistics, Population Register, updated version 22/02/2016. - Source: Bureau central de statistique palestinien, registre de la population, version actualisée jusqu'au 22/02/2016.

[44] Data refer to the 12 months preceding the census in July. - Les données se rapportent aux 12 mois précédant le recensement de juillet.

[45] Data from MERNIS (Central Population Administrative System). - Données de MERNIS (Système central de données démographiques).

[46] The registration of births and deaths is conducted by the Ministry of Health. An estimate of completeness is not provided. - L'enregistrement des naissances et des décès est mené par le Ministère de la Santé. Le degré estimatif de complétude n'est pas fourni.

[47] Including Non-Yemeni deaths. - Y compris les décès non-yéménites.

[48] Including deaths of nationals abroad. - Y compris les décès des nationaux survenus à l'étranger.

[49] Including armed forces stationed outside the country, but excluding alien armed forces stationed in the area. - Y compris les militaires nationaux hors du pays, mais non compris les militaires étrangers en garnison sur le territoire.

[50] Excluding Faeroe Islands and Greenland shown separately, if available. - Non compris les Iles Féroé et le Groenland, qui font l'objet de rubriques distinctes, si disponible.

[51] Excluding Åland Islands. - Non compris les Îles d'Åland.

[52] Data for urban and rural exclude events corresponding to nationals residing outside the country, which may be included in the total. - Les données relatives à les categories urbaine et rurale n'englobent pas les faits d'état civil qui concernent les nationaux se trouvant à l'étranger, lesquels faits peuvent être inclus au total.

[53] Excluding armed forces. - Non compris les militaires en garnison.

[54] Till 2012 data refer to all deaths occurred in Hungary. From 2013 data include the deceased persons with Hungarian usual residence regardless of whether the death occurred in Hungary or in a foreign country, and do not include the deceased persons with foreign country usual residence. - Jusqu'en 2012 les données concernent tous les décès survenus en Hongrie. À partir de 2013, les données comprennent les décès de personnes dont la résidence habituelle était en Hongrie, que le décès ait eu lieu en Hongrie ou dans un pays étranger, et ne comprennent pas les décès de personnes dont la residence habituelle était dans un pays étranger.

[55] The urban and rural categories do not include the data of foreigners, persons of unknown residence and the homeless, whereas the total category includes them. - Les chiffres portant sur la population urbaine et rurale n' incluent pas les données relatives aux étrangers, aux personnes dont la résidence n'est pas connue et aux personnes sans domicile fixe, à l'inverse, le total les inclut.

[56] Data include the deceased persons with Hungarian usual residence regardless of whether the death occurred in Hungary or in a foreign country, and do not include the deceased persons with foreign country usual residence. - Les données comprennent tous les décès survenus alors que leur résidence habituelle était en Hongrie, que le décès ait eu lieu en Hongrie ou dans un pays étranger, et ne comprennent pas les décès des personnes dont la residence habituelle était dans un pays étranger.

[57] Including still births. Source: City Hall, Civil Status Registry Office, resident and non-resident deaths. - Les données comprennent les mortinaissances. Source : La mairie, Bureau de l'État Civil, toutes les décès.

[58] Including residents outside the country if listed in a Netherlands population register. - Englobe les résidents se trouvant à l'étranger à condition qu'ils soient inscrits sur le registre de population des Pays-Bas.

[59] Including residents temporarily outside the country. - Y compris les résidents se trouvant temporairement hors du pays.

[60] Data refer to usually resident population. - Les données concernent la population habituellement résidente.

[61] Excluding Transnistria and the municipality of Bender. - Les données ne tiennent pas compte de l'information sur la Transnistria et la municipalité de Bender.

[62] Excludes data for Kosovo and Metohia. - Sans les données pour le Kosovo et Metohie.

[63] From 2015, urban refers to urban centers and areas under the influence of urban centers. - A partir de 2015, le territoire urbain inclut l'espace des centres urbains ainsi que l'espace sous influence des centres urbains.

[64] Data includes deaths resulting from births with weight 500 g and more (if weight is unknown - with length 25 cm and more, or with gestation during 22 weeks or more). - Y compris les décès de nouveau-nés de 500 g ou plus (si le poids est inconnu – de 25 cm de long ou plus, ou après une grossesse de 22 semaines ou plus).

[65] The Government of Ukraine has informed the United Nations that it is not in a position to provide statistical data concerning the Autonomous Republic of Crimea and the city of Sevastopol. - Le gouvernement Ukrainien a informé l'ONU qu'il n'est pas en mesure de fournir des données statistiques concernant la République autonome de Crimée et la ville de Sébastopol.

[66] Excluding Channel Islands (Guernsey and Jersey) and Isle of Man, shown separately, if available. - Non compris les îles Anglo-Normandes (Guernesey et Jersey) et l'île de Man, qui font l'objet de rubriques distinctes, si disponible.

[67] Data for urban and rural figures do not add up to the total because they exclude the events occurred in Migratory, Special Purpose and Other Territories. Urban refers to Greater Capital City Statistical Areas, and rural refers to other areas within the state or territory. - La somme des chiffres des catégories « en zone urbaine » et « en zone rurale » ne correspond pas au total du fait qu'en sont exclus les événements qui ont eu lieu dans les territoires de migration, les territoires à destination spéciale et autres territoires. Urbain renvoie aux zones statistiques de la capitale métropolitaine, et rural aux autres zones de l'État ou territoire.

[68] Excluding Niue, shown separately, which is part of Cook Islands, but because of remoteness is administered separately. - Non compris Nioué, qui fait l'objet d'une rubrique distincte et qui fait partie des îles Cook, mais qui, en raison de son éloignement, est administrée séparément.

[69] Including United States military personnel, their dependants and contract employees. - Y compris les militaires des Etats-Unis, les membres de leur famille les accompagnant et les agents contractuels des Etats-Unis.

[70] Random rounding to base 3 is applied in this table as a confidentiality measure. - Les chiffres sont arrondis à la base 3 de manière aléatoire, pour des raisons de confidentialité.

[71] Data refer to deaths of residents only. - Les données renvoient aux décès de résidents uniquement.

[72] Data cover the period from 1 July of the previous year to 30 June of the present year. - Pour la période allant du 1er juillet de l'année précédente au 30 juin de l'année en cours.

[73] Source: Commonwealth Health Center - Vital Statistics Office - Source : Centre de Santé du Commonwealth - Bureau des statistiques d'État civil

Table 19 - *Demographic Yearbook 2017*

Table 19 presents deaths by age and sex and age-specific death rates by sex for the latest available year between 2008 and 2017.

Description of variables: Age is defined as age at last birthday, that is, the difference between the date of birth and the date of the occurrence of the event, expressed in completed solar years. The age classification used in this table is the following: under 1 year, 1-4 years, 5-year age groups through 95-99 years, and 100 years or over.

Rate computation: Age-specific death rates by sex are the annual number of deaths in each age-sex group per 1 000 population in the same age-sex group. These rates are calculated by the Statistics Division of the United Nations.

Deaths at unknown age and the population of unknown age are excluded from age-specific rate calculations but are part of the death rate for all ages combined.

Death rates for infants under one year of age in this table differ from the infant mortality rates shown elsewhere, because the latter are computed per 1 000 live births rather than per 1 000 population.

The population used in computing the rates is the estimated or the enumerated population by age and sex reported to United Nations Statistics Division. First priority is given to an estimate and second priority to census returns of the year to which the deaths refer.

Rates presented in this table have been limited to those countries or areas having at least a total of 100 deaths in a given year. Moreover, rates specific for individual sub-categories that are based on 30 or fewer deaths are identified by the symbol "♦".

Reliability of data: Data from civil registers of deaths that are reported as incomplete (less than 90 per cent completeness) or of unknown completeness are considered unreliable and are set in italics rather than in roman type. Table 18 and the technical notes for that table provide more detailed information on the completeness of death registration. For more information about the quality of vital statistics data in general and the information available on the basis of the completeness estimates in particular, see section 4.2 of the Introduction.

Rates are not computed if data from civil registers of deaths are reported as incomplete (less than 90 per cent completeness) or of unknown completeness, and therefore deemed unreliable.

Limitations: Statistics on deaths by age and sex are subject to the same qualifications as are set forth for vital statistics and particularly for death statistics discussed in section 4 of the Introduction.

The reliability of the data is an important factor in considering the limitations. In addition, some deaths are tabulated by date of registration and not by date of occurrence; these have been indicated by a plus sign "+". Whenever the lag between the date of occurrence and date of registration is prolonged and, therefore, a large proportion of the death registrations are delayed, death statistics for any given year may be seriously affected. However, delays in the registration of deaths are less common and shorter than in the registration of live births.

International comparability in mortality statistics may also be affected by the exclusion of deaths of infants who were born alive but died before the registration of the birth or within the first 24 hours of life. Statistics of this type are footnoted.

Because these statistics are classified according to age, they are subject to the limitations with respect to accuracy of age reporting similar to those already discussed in connection with section 3.1.3 of the Introduction. The factors influencing the accuracy of reporting may be somewhat dissimilar in vital statistics (because of the differences in the method of taking a census and registering a death) but, in general, the same errors can be observed.

The absence of data in the unknown age group does not necessarily indicate completely accurate reporting and tabulation of the age item. It is often an indication that the unknowns have been eliminated by assigning ages to them before tabulation, or by proportionate distribution after tabulation.

International comparability of statistics on deaths by age is also affected by the use of different methods to determine age at death. If age is obtained from an item that simply requests age at death in completed years or is derived from information on year of birth and death rather than from information on complete date (day, month and year) of birth and death, the number of deaths classified in the under-one-year age group will tend to be reduced and the number of deaths in the next age group will tend to be somewhat increased. A similar bias may affect other age groups but its impact is usually negligible. Information on this factor is given in the footnotes when known.

Limitations of rates: Rates shown in this table are subject to the same limitations that affect the corresponding data and are set forth in the technical notes for table 18. These include differences in the completeness of registration, the treatment of infants who were born alive but died before the registration of their birth or within the first 24 hours of life, the method used to determine age at death and the quality of the reported information relating to age at death. In addition, some rates are based on deaths tabulated by date of registration and not by date of occurrence; these have been indicated with a plus sign "+".

The problem of obtaining precise correspondence between deaths (numerator) and population (denominator) as regards the inclusion or exclusion of armed forces, refugees, displaced persons and other special groups is particularly difficult where age-specific death rates are concerned. Even when deaths and population do correspond conceptually, comparability of the rates may be affected by abnormal conditions such as absence from the country or area of large numbers of young men in the military forces or working abroad as temporary workers. Death rates may appear high in the younger ages, simply because a large section of the able-bodied members of the age group, whose death rates under normal conditions might be less than the average for persons of their age, is not included. Therefore, care should be exercised in using these rates for comparative purposes.

Also, in a number of cases the rates shown here for all ages combined differ from crude death rates shown elsewhere, because in this table they are computed on the population for which an appropriate age-sex distribution was available, while the crude death rates shown elsewhere may utilize a different total population. The population by age and sex might refer to a census date within the year rather than to the mid-point, or it might be more or less inclusive as regards ethnic groups, armed forces and so forth. In a few instances, the difference is attributable to the fact that the rates in this table were computed on the mean population whereas the corresponding rates in other tables were computed on an estimate for 1 July.

Earlier data: Age-specific deaths and death rates by sex have been shown for the latest available year in each issue of the Yearbook since the 1955 issue. For information on specific years covered, the reader should consult the Historical Index.

Tableau 19 – *Annuaire démographique 2017*

Le tableau 19 présente les données disponibles les plus récentes, entre 2008 et 2017, sur les décès et les taux de mortalité selon l'âge et le sexe.

Description des variables : L'âge considéré est l'âge au dernier anniversaire, c'est-à-dire la différence entre la date de naissance et la date du décès, exprimée en années solaires révolues. La classification par âge est la suivante : moins d'un an, 1 à 4 ans, groupes quinquennaux jusqu'à 95-99 ans et 100 ans et plus.

Calcul des taux : les taux de mortalité selon l'âge et le sexe représentent le nombre annuel de décès survenus pour chaque sexe et chaque groupe d'âge pour 1 000 personnes du même groupe. Ces taux ont été calculés par la Division de statistique de l'ONU.

On n'a pas tenu compte des décès à un âge inconnu ni de la population d'âge inconnu, sauf dans les taux de mortalité pour tous les âges combinés.

Il convient de noter que, dans ce tableau, les taux de mortalité des groupes de moins d'un an sont différents des taux de mortalité infantile qui figurent dans d'autres tableaux, ces derniers ayant été établis pour 1 000 naissances vivantes et non pour 1 000 habitants.

Les chiffres de population utilisés pour le calcul des taux proviennent de dénombrements ou de répartitions estimatives de la population selon l'âge et le sexe. On a utilisé de préférence les estimations de la population; à défaut, on s'est contenté des données censitaires se rapportant à l'année des décès.

Les taux présentés dans ce tableau ne se rapportent qu'aux pays ou zones où l'on a enregistré un total d'au moins 100 décès pendant l'année. Les taux relatifs à des sous-catégories, qui sont fondés sur 30 décès ou moins, sont signalés par le signe "♦".

Fiabilité des données : Les données sur les décès issues des registres d'état civil qui sont déclarées incomplètes (degré d'exhaustivité inférieur à 90 p.100) ou dont le degré d'exhaustivité n'est pas connu sont jugées douteuses et apparaissent en italique et non en caractères romains. Le tableau 18 et les notes techniques s'y rapportant présentent des renseignements plus détaillés sur le degré d'exhaustivité de l'enregistrement des décès. Pour plus de précisions sur la qualité des statistiques de l'état civil en général et le degré de complétude en particulier, voir la section 4.2 de l'Introduction.

On a choisi de ne pas faire figurer dans le tableau 19 des taux calculés à partir de données sur les décès issues de registres d'état civil qui sont déclarées incomplètes (degré d'exhaustivité inférieur à 90 p. 100) ou dont le degré d'exhaustivité n'est pas connu.

Insuffisance des données : Les statistiques des décès selon l'âge et le sexe appellent les mêmes réserves que les statistiques de l'état civil en général et les statistiques relatives à la mortalité en particulier (voir la section 4 de l'Introduction).

La fiabilité des données est un facteur important. Il faut également tenir compte du fait que, dans certains cas, les données relatives aux décès sont classées par date d'enregistrement et non par date d'occurrence ; ces cas ont été signalés par le signe "+". Chaque fois que le décalage entre le décès et son enregistrement est grand et qu'une forte proportion des décès fait l'objet d'un enregistrement tardif, les statistiques des décès de l'année peuvent être considérablement faussées. En règle générale, toutefois, les décès sont enregistrés beaucoup plus rapidement que les naissances vivantes, et les retards prolongés sont rares.

Un autre facteur qui nuit à la comparabilité internationale est la pratique de certains pays ou zones qui consiste à ne pas inclure dans les statistiques des décès les enfants nés vivants mais décédés avant l'enregistrement de leur naissance ou dans les 24 heures qui ont suivi la naissance, pratique qui conduit à sous-évaluer le nombre de décès à moins d'un an. Quand pareil facteur a joué, cela a été signalé en note à la fin du tableau.

Étant donné que les statistiques relatives à la mortalité sont classées selon l'âge, elles appellent les mêmes réserves concernant l'exactitude des déclarations d'âge que celles qui ont été formulées à la section 3.1.3 des Introduction. Dans le cas des données d'état civil, les facteurs qui interviennent à cet égard sont parfois un peu différents, du fait que le recensement et l'enregistrement des décès se font par des méthodes différentes, mais, d'une manière générale, les erreurs observées sont les mêmes.

Si aucun nombre ne figure dans la rangée réservée aux âges inconnus, cela ne signifie pas nécessairement que les déclarations d'âge et le classement par âge sont tout à fait exacts. C'est souvent une indication que l'on a attribué un âge aux personnes d'âge inconnu avant l'exploitation des données ou qu'elles ont été réparties proportionnellement entre les différents groupes après cette opération.

Le manque d'uniformité des méthodes suivies pour obtenir l'âge au moment du décès nuit également à la comparabilité internationale des données. Si l'âge est connu, soit d'après la réponse à une simple question sur l'âge du décès en années révolues, soit d'après l'année de la naissance et l'année du décès, et non d'après des renseignements concernant la date exacte (jour, mois et année) de la naissance et du décès, le nombre de décès classés dans la catégorie « moins d'un an » sera entaché d'une erreur par défaut et le chiffre figurant dans la catégorie suivante d'une erreur par excès.

Les données pour les autres groupes d'âge pourront être entachées d'une distorsion analogue, mais les répercussions seront généralement négligeables. Les imperfections, lorsqu'elles étaient connues, ont été signalées en note à la fin du tableau.

Insuffisance des taux : les taux présentés dans le tableau 19 appellent les mêmes réserves que celles formulées à propos des fréquences correspondantes (voir à ce sujet les notes techniques se rapportant au tableau 18). Leurs imperfections tiennent notamment aux différences d'exhaustivité de l'enregistrement, au classement des enfants nés vivants mais décédés avant l'enregistrement de leur naissance ou dans les 24 heures qui ont suivi la naissance, à la méthode utilisée pour obtenir l'âge au moment du décès, et à la qualité des déclarations concernant l'âge au moment du décès. En outre, dans certains cas, les données relatives aux décès sont classées par date d'enregistrement et non par date de l'événement ; ces cas ont été signalés par le signe "+".

S'agissant des taux de mortalité par âge, il est particulièrement difficile d'établir une correspondance exacte entre les décès (numérateur) et la population (dénominateur) du fait de l'inclusion ou de l'exclusion des militaires, des réfugiés, des personnes déplacées et d'autres groupes spéciaux. Il convient d'ajouter que, même lorsque population et décès correspondent, la comparabilité des taux peut être compromise par des conditions anormales telles que l'absence du pays ou de la zone d'un grand nombre de jeunes gens qui sont sous les drapeaux ou qui travaillent à l'étranger comme travailleurs temporaires. Il arrive ainsi que les taux de mortalité paraissent élevés parmi les groupes les plus jeunes simplement parce que l'on en a exclu un grand nombre d'individus en bonne santé pour lesquels le taux de mortalité pourrait être, dans des conditions normales, inférieur à la moyenne observée pour les personnes du même âge. Par conséquent, il importe d'être prudent quand on les utilise ces taux de mortalité dans des comparaisons.

De même, les taux indiqués pour tous les âges combinés diffèrent dans plusieurs cas des taux bruts de mortalité qui figurent dans d'autres tableaux, parce qu'ils se rapportent à une population pour laquelle on disposait d'une répartition par âge et par sexe appropriée, tandis que les taux bruts de mortalité indiqués ailleurs peuvent avoir été calculés sur la base d'un chiffre de population totale différent. Ainsi, il est possible que les chiffres de population par âge et par sexe proviennent d'un recensement effectué dans le courant de l'année et non au milieu de l'année, et qu'ils se différencient des autres chiffres de population en excluant ou en incluant certains groupes ethniques, les militaires, etc. Quelquefois, la différence tient à ce que les taux du tableau 19 ont été calculés sur la base de la population moyenne, alors que les taux correspondants des autres tableaux reposent sur une estimation au 1er juillet.

Données publiées antérieurement : Les éditions de l'*Annuaire démographique* parues depuis 1955 présentent les statistiques les plus récentes dont on disposait à l'époque sur les décès selon l'âge et le sexe et sur les taux de mortalité selon l'âge et le sexe. Pour plus de précisions concernant les années pour lesquelles ces données ont été publiées, se reporter à l'index historique.

19. Deaths by age and sex and age-specific death rates by sex: latest available year, 2008 - 2017
Décès et taux de mortalité selon l'âge et le sexe : dernière année disponible, 2008 - 2017

Continent, country or area, date, code[a] and age (in years) / Continent, pays ou zone, date, code[a] et âge (en années)	Number - Nombre			Rate - Taux		
	Both sexes Les deux sexes	Male Masculin	Female Féminin	Both sexes Les deux sexes	Male Masculin	Female Féminin
AFRICA - AFRIQUE						
Algeria - Algérie[1]						
2016 (U)						
Total	180 404	92 981	87 423	...	...	...
0	22 271	12 157	10 114	...	...	...
1 - 4	2 986	1 581	1 406	...	...	...
5 - 9	1 458	795	664	...	...	...
10 - 14	1 066	570	495	...	...	...
15 - 19	1 610	1 008	601	...	...	...
20 - 24	2 440	1 630	810	...	...	...
25 - 29	2 741	1 710	1 031	...	...	...
30 - 34	3 362	1 892	1 470	...	...	...
35 - 39	3 685	1 957	1 728	...	...	...
40 - 44	4 206	2 134	2 071	...	...	...
45 - 49	5 321	2 711	2 611	...	...	...
50 - 54	6 817	3 651	3 166	...	...	...
55 - 59	8 144	4 457	3 687	...	...	...
60 - 64	11 005	6 279	4 726	...	...	...
65 - 69	11 794	6 649	5 145	...	...	...
70 - 74	12 746	6 905	5 841	...	...	...
75 - 79	18 197	9 162	9 035	...	...	...
80 - 84	22 572	10 897	11 675	...	...	...
85 +	37 984	16 836	21 147	...	...	...
Botswana[2]						
2016 (U)						
Total	12 825	6 661	6 164	...	...	...
0	1 041	574	467	...	...	...
1 - 4	241	137	104	...	...	...
5 - 9	86	50	36	...	...	...
10 - 14	93	59	34	...	...	...
15 - 19	169	97	72	...	...	...
20 - 24	376	191	185	...	...	...
25 - 29	497	271	226	...	...	...
30 - 34	759	382	377	...	...	...
35 - 39	855	459	396	...	...	...
40 - 44	802	453	349	...	...	...
45 - 49	661	385	276	...	...	...
50 - 54	694	373	321	...	...	...
55 - 59	748	433	315	...	...	...
60 - 64	731	424	307	...	...	...
65 - 69	738	434	304	...	...	...
70 - 74	687	370	317	...	...	...
75 - 79	797	419	378	...	...	...
80 - 84	844	415	429	...	...	...
85 +	1 984	720	1 264	...	...	...
Unknown - Inconnu	22	15	7	..	..	..
Congo[3]						
2009 (+U)						
Total	7 554	...	...	...	...	...
0 - 4	2 150	...	...	...	...	...
5 - 14	2 905	...	...	...	...	...
15 - 59	292	...	...	...	...	...
60 +	2 207	...	...	...	...	...
Egypt - Égypte						
2017 (C)						
Total	547 208	300 898	246 310	5.7	6.1	5.3
0	38 685	20 964	17 721	14.9	15.6	14.0
1 - 4	11 184	6 046	5 138	1.1	1.1	1.0
5 - 9	4 599	2 720	1 879	0.4	0.5	0.4
10 - 14	3 788	2 448	1 340	0.4	0.5	0.3
15 - 19	6 292	4 305	1 987	0.7	0.9	0.5
20 - 24	6 565	4 637	1 928	0.8	1.1	0.5
25 - 29	7 201	4 862	2 339	0.9	1.2	0.6
30 - 34	8 695	5 646	3 049	1.2	1.5	0.8
35 - 39	10 005	6 393	3 612	1.5	1.9	1.1
40 - 44	12 343	7 758	4 585	2.4	2.9	1.8
45 - 49	17 557	11 229	6 328	4.0	4.9	3.0
50 - 54	32 080	20 586	11 494	8.0	10.0	5.9

Continent, country or area, date, code[a] and age (in years) / Continent, pays ou zone, date, code[a] et âge (en annèes)	Number - Nombre			Rate - Taux		
	Both sexes Les deux sexes	Male Masculin	Female Féminin	Both sexes Les deux sexes	Male Masculin	Female Féminin
AFRICA - AFRIQUE						
Egypt - Égypte						
2017 (C)						
55 - 59	45 493	28 810	16 683	13.9	16.7	10.7
60 - 64	59 405	36 007	23 398	22.3	25.3	18.9
65 - 69	67 018	37 985	29 033	38.8	40.1	37.2
70 - 74	61 623	32 111	29 512	60.4	60.2	60.6
75 +	154 675	68 391	86 284	166.2	142.8	191.1
75 - 79	56 925	27 754	29 171	...	...	...
80 - 84	47 982	21 385	26 597	...	...	...
85 +	49 768	19 252	30 516	...	...	...
Ghana[4]						
2010 (|)						
Total	163 534	84 214	79 320	6.6	7.0	6.3
0	28 068	15 807	12 261	38.4	42.7	34.0
1 - 4	17 868	9 424	8 444	6.7	6.9	6.4
5 - 9	6 275	3 437	2 838	2.0	2.2	1.8
10 - 14	3 641	1 587	2 054	1.2	1.1	1.4
15 - 19	4 399	1 752	2 647	1.7	1.3	2.0
20 - 24	5 467	2 117	3 350	2.4	1.9	2.7
25 - 29	6 325	2 516	3 809	3.1	2.7	3.4
30 - 34	8 218	3 397	4 821	4.9	4.3	5.4
35 - 39	8 215	3 579	4 636	5.8	5.3	6.2
40 - 44	8 855	4 141	4 714	7.5	7.2	7.7
45 - 49	7 573	3 715	3 858	8.1	8.2	8.0
50 - 54	8 577	4 376	4 201	10.3	11.1	9.6
55 - 59	5 656	3 564	2 092	10.8	13.8	7.9
60 - 64	7 159	4 418	2 741	15.0	19.5	11.0
65 - 69	5 670	3 360	2 310	19.3	24.7	14.7
70 - 74	8 443	5 096	3 347	24.0	34.1	16.6
75 - 79	6 197	3 599	2 598	30.1	40.4	22.2
80 - 84	6 543	3 346	3 197	41.1	53.7	33.1
85 - 89	4 436	2 166	2 270	53.4	65.8	45.3
90 - 94	3 650	1 797	1 853	71.5	94.6	57.8
95 +	2 299	1 020	1 279	99.3	116.6	88.9
Guinea - Guinée[5]						
2014 (|)						
Total	129 896	70 815	59 081	12.3	13.9	10.9
0	36 556	20 751	15 805	112.1	125.9	97.9
1 - 4	21 083	11 308	9 775	14.7	15.6	13.7
5 - 9	5 661	3 128	2 533	3.3	3.6	3.0
10 - 14	3 237	1 821	1 416	2.6	2.9	2.3
15 - 19	3 585	1 630	1 955	3.2	3.1	3.3
20 - 24	3 775	1 806	1 969	4.2	4.4	4.0
25 - 29	4 350	1 934	2 416	5.6	5.7	5.4
30 - 34	4 366	2 077	2 289	6.9	7.5	6.5
35 - 39	3 909	1 986	1 923	7.6	8.7	6.8
40 - 44	4 168	2 226	1 942	9.5	11.1	8.2
45 - 49	3 567	2 063	1 504	10.9	12.9	8.9
50 - 54	4 461	2 562	1 899	15.0	17.5	12.5
55 - 59	2 963	1 857	1 106	14.0	16.2	11.4
60 - 64	4 659	2 695	1 964	22.8	25.6	19.8
65 - 69	3 490	2 070	1 420	27.4	30.4	23.9
70 - 74	5 181	2 884	2 297	44.4	50.7	38.4
75 - 79	3 461	2 029	1 432	54.2	59.8	47.9
80 - 84	4 300	2 248	2 052	84.3	91.1	78.0
85 - 89	2 350	1 297	1 053	113.4	120.2	106.0
90 - 94	1 673	929	744	142.4	165.0	121.6
95 +	3 101	1 514	1 587	259.3	264.8	254.2
95 - 99	1 886	963	923	...	...	...
100 +	1 215	551	664	...	...	...
Kenya[6]						
2011 (U)						
Total	174 487	96 026	78 461	...	...	...
0	23 167	12 119	11 048	...	...	...
1 - 4	12 129	6 530	5 599	...	...	...
5 - 14	9 145	4 949	4 196	...	...	...
15 - 24	11 961	5 931	6 030	...	...	...

19. Deaths by age and sex and age-specific death rates by sex: latest available year, 2008 - 2017
Décès et taux de mortalité selon l'âge et le sexe : dernière année disponible, 2008 - 2017 (continued - suite)

Continent, country or area, date, code[a] and age (in years) / Continent, pays ou zone, date, code[a] et âge (en années)	Number - Nombre			Rate - Taux		
	Both sexes Les deux sexes	Male Masculin	Female Féminin	Both sexes Les deux sexes	Male Masculin	Female Féminin
AFRICA - AFRIQUE						
Kenya[6]						
2011 (U)						
25 - 34	21 054	11 329	9 725	...	...	...
35 - 44	21 605	12 382	9 223	...	...	...
45 - 54	18 606	11 124	7 482	...	...	...
55 - 74	29 686	17 525	12 161	...	...	...
75 +	27 134	14 137	12 997	...	...	...
Lesotho						
2010 (+U)						
Total	7 864	4 154	3 710	...	...	...
0 - 4	271	147	124	...	...	...
5 - 9	69	34	35	...	...	...
10 - 14	67	43	24	...	...	...
15 - 19	112	50	62	...	...	...
20 - 24	237	106	131	...	...	...
25 - 29	477	199	278	...	...	...
30 - 34	727	347	380	...	...	...
35 - 39	732	383	349	...	...	...
40 - 44	675	376	299	...	...	...
45 - 49	583	337	246	...	...	...
50 - 54	627	406	221	...	...	...
55 - 59	550	363	187	...	...	...
60 - 64	484	302	182	...	...	...
65 - 69	388	234	154	...	...	...
70 - 74	502	256	246	...	...	...
75 - 79	481	227	254	...	...	...
80 - 84	384	153	231	...	...	...
85 +	441	158	283	...	...	...
Unknown - Inconnu	57	33	24	..	..	..
Malawi[7]						
2008 (|)						
Total	135 865	70 991	64 874	10.0	10.6	9.4
0 - 4	56 721	29 832	26 889	20.9	21.9	20.0
0	30 508	16 606	13 902	50.9	54.9	46.9
1 - 4	26 213	13 226	12 987	12.4	12.5	12.4
5 - 9	6 413	3 350	3 063	2.8	2.9	2.7
10 - 14	5 333	3 071	2 262	3.5	4.1	2.9
15 - 19	4 266	1 863	2 403	3.1	2.7	3.4
20 - 24	7 188	3 038	4 150	6.1	5.1	7.0
25 - 29	7 903	3 405	4 498	7.6	6.8	8.3
30 - 34	9 042	4 280	4 762	9.7	10.4	9.2
35 - 39	7 200	3 813	3 387	9.7	10.3	9.0
40 - 44	6 004	3 410	2 594	10.8	12.2	9.4
45 - 49	4 275	2 436	1 839	9.7	11.3	8.2
50 - 54	3 414	2 092	1 322	10.7	13.3	8.2
55 +	18 106	10 401	7 705	34.1	40.9	27.9
55 - 59	2 447	1 523	924	...	...	...
60 - 64	2 978	1 827	1 151	...	...	...
65 - 69	2 314	1 372	942	...	...	...
70 - 74	2 871	1 665	1 206	...	...	...
75 - 79	2 149	1 254	895	...	...	...
80 - 84	2 151	1 138	1 013	...	...	...
85 +	3 196	1 622	1 574	...	...	...
Mali[8]						
2009 (|)						
Total	62 371	34 387	27 984	4.3	4.8	3.8
0 - 4	29 336	16 098	13 238	11.2	12.1	10.2
5 - 9	3 486	1 933	1 553	1.5	1.6	1.3
10 - 14	1 598	914	684	0.9	1.0	0.8
15 - 19	1 638	777	861	1.1	1.1	1.1
20 - 24	1 570	712	858	1.4	1.3	1.4
25 - 29	1 618	752	866	1.6	1.7	1.6
30 - 34	1 729	839	890	2.1	2.2	2.1
35 - 39	1 604	798	806	2.5	2.5	2.5
40 - 44	1 547	858	689	2.8	3.2	2.5
45 - 49	1 462	890	572	3.3	3.9	2.6
50 - 54	1 527	884	643	4.0	4.7	3.3

19. Deaths by age and sex and age-specific death rates by sex: latest available year, 2008 - 2017
Décès et taux de mortalité selon l'âge et le sexe : dernière année disponible, 2008 - 2017 (continued - suite)

Continent, country or area, date, code[a] and age (in years) Continent, pays ou zone, date, code[a] et âge (en années)	Number - Nombre			Rate - Taux		
	Both sexes Les deux sexes	Male Masculin	Female Féminin	Both sexes Les deux sexes	Male Masculin	Female Féminin
AFRICA - AFRIQUE						
Mali[8]						
2009 (I)						
55 - 59	1 544	954	590	5.5	6.4	4.4
60 - 64	1 960	1 201	759	7.8	9.4	6.1
65 - 69	1 958	1 152	806	11.8	13.0	10.5
70 - 74	2 093	1 198	895	15.7	17.8	13.5
75 - 79	1 891	1 113	778	24.5	27.2	21.5
80 +	3 372	1 836	1 536	39.4	43.7	35.2
Unknown - Inconnu	2 438	1 478	960	..	..	..
Mauritius - Maurice[9]						
2017 (+C)						
Total	10 140	5 572	4 568	8.0	8.9	7.1
0	164	98	66	12.7	14.8	10.5
1 - 4	29	17	12	♦0.5	♦0.6	♦0.5
5 - 9	13	7	6	♦0.2	♦0.2	♦0.2
10 - 14	17	10	7	♦0.2	♦0.2	♦0.2
15 - 19	53	35	18	0.5	0.7	♦0.4
20 - 24	91	59	32	0.9	1.2	0.7
25 - 29	121	84	37	1.3	1.8	0.8
30 - 34	135	88	47	1.6	2.1	1.1
35 - 39	214	143	71	2.1	2.8	1.4
40 - 44	277	182	95	3.2	4.1	2.2
45 - 49	368	241	127	4.4	5.7	3.0
50 - 54	718	496	222	7.6	10.5	4.7
55 - 59	834	542	292	9.9	13.1	6.8
60 - 64	1 035	677	358	14.5	19.8	9.7
65 - 69	1 232	723	509	22.2	28.3	17.1
70 - 74	1 083	567	516	33.0	40.0	27.7
75 - 79	1 050	540	510	50.8	63.5	41.9
80 - 84	1 045	480	565	76.6	93.5	66.4
85 +	1 661	583	1 078	163.5	187.0	153.1
85 - 89	854	317	537	...	...	...
90 - 94	590	216	374	...	...	...
95 - 99	179	43	136	...	...	...
100 +	38	7	31	...	...	...
Namibia - Namibie[10]						
2011 (I)						
Total	22 668	12 491	10 177	10.7	12.2	9.3
0	2 685	1 411	1 274	41.9	44.1	39.6
1 - 4	1 346	719	627	6.1	6.5	5.7
5 - 9	447	255	192	1.9	2.1	1.6
10 - 14	384	212	172	1.6	1.7	1.4
15 - 19	577	298	279	2.4	2.5	2.3
20 - 24	918	537	381	4.3	5.1	3.5
25 - 29	1 233	645	588	7.0	7.4	6.5
30 - 34	1 591	890	701	10.7	12.1	9.2
35 - 39	1 487	873	614	11.9	14.3	9.6
40 - 44	1 323	807	516	13.5	17.2	10.1
45 - 49	1 140	698	442	14.2	18.6	10.3
50 - 54	917	535	382	14.9	19.5	11.2
55 - 59	891	562	329	18.6	26.1	12.5
60 - 64	994	584	410	24.4	31.7	18.3
65 - 69	766	424	342	24.6	32.3	19.0
70 - 74	739	424	315	30.7	41.3	22.8
75 - 79	682	382	300	39.5	54.5	29.3
80 - 84	792	402	390	55.3	76.2	43.1
85 - 89	638	282	356	68.6	90.2	57.6
90 - 94	549	234	315	80.6	98.4	71.1
95 +	1 003	403	600	178.7	228.6	155.8
Unknown - Inconnu	1 566	914	652	..	..	..
Niger						
2011 (+U)						
Total	*6 761*	...	...	...	...	...
0	*236*	...	...	...	...	...
1 - 4	*329*	...	...	...	...	...
5 - 9	*120*	...	...	...	...	...
10 - 14	*81*	...	...	...	...	...

Continent, country or area, date, code[a] and age (in years) / Continent, pays ou zone, date, code[a] et âge (en années)	Number - Nombre			Rate - Taux		
	Both sexes Les deux sexes	Male Masculin	Female Féminin	Both sexes Les deux sexes	Male Masculin	Female Féminin
AFRICA - AFRIQUE						
Niger						
2011 (+U)						
15 - 19	147	...	...	...	...	...
20 - 24	242	...	...	...	...	...
25 - 29	319	...	...	...	...	...
30 - 34	378	...	...	...	...	...
35 - 39	414	...	...	...	...	...
40 - 44	470	...	...	...	...	...
45 - 49	485	...	...	...	...	...
50 - 54	495	...	...	...	...	...
55 - 59	443	...	...	...	...	...
60 - 64	541	...	...	...	...	...
65 - 69	443	...	...	...	...	...
70 - 74	517	...	...	...	...	...
75 - 79	347	...	...	...	...	...
80 - 84	298	...	...	...	...	...
85 - 89	112	...	...	...	...	...
90 - 94	90	...	...	...	...	...
95 - 99	26	...	...	...	...	...
100 +	53	...	...	...	...	...
Unknown - Inconnu	175	...	...	..	..	..
Republic of South Sudan - République de Soudan du Sud[11]						
2008 (|)						
Total	165 898	88 797	77 101	19.8	20.5	19.1
0 - 4	84 891	41 528	43 363	61.6	57.1	66.6
0	29 217	12 384	16 833	...	...	...
1 - 4	55 674	29 144	26 530	...	...	...
5 - 9	22 571	12 351	10 220	17.3	17.8	16.7
10 - 14	12 487	6 785	5 702	11.7	11.8	11.6
15 - 19	11 665	6 297	5 368	13.0	13.5	12.5
20 - 24	9 256	5 556	3 700	12.5	15.3	9.7
25 - 29	6 022	4 063	1 959	8.6	12.1	5.4
30 - 34	4 496	2 634	1 862	8.3	10.1	6.7
35 - 39	3 046	2 237	809	6.4	9.3	3.4
40 - 44	2 627	1 605	1 022	7.7	9.2	6.1
45 - 49	1 656	993	663	6.0	6.6	5.2
50 - 54	1 513	977	536	7.6	9.3	5.8
55 - 59	946	618	328	7.7	9.1	6.1
60 - 64	1 094	668	426	9.4	10.4	8.3
65 - 69	908	528	380	12.4	12.7	12.0
70 - 74	1 036	766	270	17.5	22.1	11.0
75 - 79	487	415	72	17.0	24.1	6.3
80 - 84	493	277	216	20.5	19.7	21.5
85 - 89	355	229	126	33.4	35.2	30.6
90 - 94	177	110	67	25.3	25.9	24.4
95 +	172	160	12	26.8	44.7	♦4.2
Saint Helena ex. dep. - Sainte-Hélène sans dép.						
2014 (C)						
Total	61	36	25	...	...	...
0	1	-	1	...	...	...
1 - 4	-	-	-	...	...	...
5 - 9	-	-	-	...	...	...
10 - 14	-	-	-	...	...	...
15 - 19	-	-	-	...	...	...
20 - 24	-	-	-	...	...	...
25 - 29	1	1	-	...	...	...
30 - 34	-	-	-	...	...	...
35 - 39	-	-	-	...	...	...
40 - 44	-	-	-	...	...	...
45 - 49	1	1	-	...	...	...
50 - 54	-	-	-	...	...	...
55 - 59	4	2	2	...	...	...
60 - 64	7	5	2	...	...	...
65 - 69	7	5	2	...	...	...
70 - 74	9	6	3	...	...	...
75 - 79	7	6	1	...	...	...

19. Deaths by age and sex and age-specific death rates by sex: latest available year, 2008 - 2017
Décès et taux de mortalité selon l'âge et le sexe : dernière année disponible, 2008 - 2017 (continued - suite)

Continent, country or area, date, code[a] and age (in years) Continent, pays ou zone, date, code[a] et âge (en années)	Number - Nombre			Rate - Taux		
	Both sexes Les deux sexes	Male Masculin	Female Féminin	Both sexes Les deux sexes	Male Masculin	Female Féminin
AFRICA - AFRIQUE						
Saint Helena ex. dep. - Sainte-Hélène sans dép.						
2014 (C)						
80 - 84	7	4	3	...	...	...
85 - 89	8	4	4	...	...	...
90 - 94	4	1	3	...	...	...
95 - 99	5	1	4	...	...	...
100 +	-	-	-	...	...	...
Sao Tome and Principe - Sao Tomé-et-Principe[12]						
2012 (|)						
Total	1 287	735	552	7.2	8.3	6.1
0	132	82	50	23.1	27.8	18.0
1 - 4	69	41	29	3.1	3.7	◆2.6
5 - 9	18	5	13	◆0.7	◆0.4	◆1.0
10 - 14	29	20	10	◆1.4	◆1.9	◆0.9
15 - 19	29	23	6	◆1.6	◆2.5	◆0.7
20 - 24	54	36	18	3.4	4.5	◆2.3
25 - 29	39	26	13	2.6	◆3.5	◆1.7
30 - 34	41	31	10	3.3	5.0	◆1.6
35 - 39	61	41	20	6.3	8.4	◆4.1
40 - 44	51	34	17	6.5	8.6	◆4.4
45 - 49	49	24	25	7.8	◆7.9	◆7.7
50 - 54	77	44	33	14.4	16.9	12.0
55 - 59	52	21	31	13.6	◆11.6	15.4
60 - 64	86	59	27	32.3	44.1	◆20.4
65 - 69	60	33	27	31.2	35.9	◆26.8
70 - 74	102	60	42	54.3	70.6	40.9
75 - 79	103	51	52	73.0	83.7	64.8
80 +	234	104	130	170.1	198.1	152.8
Seychelles						
2017 (+C)						
Total	748	426	322	7.8	8.7	6.8
0	18	10	8	◆11.1	◆12.1	◆10.1
1 - 4	4	2	2	◆0.7	◆0.6	◆0.7
5 - 9	3	1	2	◆0.5	◆0.3	◆0.6
10 - 14	2	2	-	◆0.4	◆0.8	-
15 - 19	2	2	-	◆0.5	◆1.0	-
20 - 24	16	10	6	◆4.3	◆4.5	◆4.0
25 - 29	11	6	5	◆1.8	◆1.8	◆1.9
30 - 34	12	8	4	◆1.5	◆1.7	◆1.2
35 - 39	15	8	7	◆1.6	◆1.7	◆1.6
40 - 44	22	17	5	◆3.2	◆4.8	◆1.5
45 - 49	39	30	9	4.6	◆6.9	◆2.2
50 - 54	57	39	18	8.3	13.0	◆4.7
55 - 59	53	40	13	6.3	9.6	◆3.1
60 - 64	51	35	16	8.8	12.1	◆5.5
65 - 69	63	46	17	16.3	23.9	◆8.8
70 - 74	68	42	26	32.6	42.2	◆23.8
75 - 79	88	50	38	57.6	82.9	41.1
80 - 84	85	36	49	85.5	114.3	72.2
85 +	139	42	97	180.8	269.2	158.2
Sierra Leone[13]						
2013 (+U)						
Total	19 403	9 982	9 421	...	...	...
0	2 276	1 151	1 125	...	...	...
1 - 4	2 413	1 168	1 245	...	...	...
5 - 14	2 904	1 447	1 457	...	...	...
15 +	11 810	6 216	5 594	...	...	...
South Africa - Afrique du Sud						
2016 (U)						
Total	456 612	240 001[14]	214 988[14]	...	...	...
0	20 649	10 963[14]	9 284[14]	...	...	...
1 - 4	7 008	3 686[14]	3 281[14]	...	...	...
5 - 9	2 965	1 672[14]	1 287[14]	...	...	...
10 - 14	3 083	1 781[14]	1 298[14]	...	...	...
15 - 19	6 821	4 019[14]	2 781[14]	...	...	...
20 - 24	13 708	8 272[14]	5 375[14]	...	...	...
25 - 29	22 209	12 851[14]	9 238[14]	...	...	...

19. Deaths by age and sex and age-specific death rates by sex: latest available year, 2008 - 2017
Décès et taux de mortalité selon l'âge et le sexe : dernière année disponible, 2008 - 2017 (continued - suite)

Continent, country or area, date, code[a] and age (in years) / Continent, pays ou zone, date, code[a] et âge (en années)	Number - Nombre			Rate - Taux		
	Both sexes Les deux sexes	Male Masculin	Female Féminin	Both sexes Les deux sexes	Male Masculin	Female Féminin

AFRICA - AFRIQUE

South Africa - Afrique du Sud
2016 (U)

30 - 34	28 519	16 597[14]	11 769[14]	...	...	...
35 - 39	28 244	16 535[14]	11 558[14]	...	...	...
40 - 44	29 290	17 270[14]	11 898[14]	...	...	...
45 - 49	28 635	16 890[14]	11 656[14]	...	...	...
50 - 54	31 618	18 470[14]	13 093[14]	...	...	...
55 - 59	33 917	19 796[14]	14 055[14]	...	...	...
60 - 64	36 372	20 689[14]	15 633[14]	...	...	...
65 - 69	35 684	19 486[14]	16 168[14]	...	...	...
70 - 74	31 418	15 753[14]	15 632[14]	...	...	...
75 - 79	32 210	14 361[14]	17 829[14]	...	...	...
80 - 84	25 323	9 280[14]	16 031[14]	...	...	...
85 - 89	21 280	6 736[14]	14 525[14]	...	...	...
90 - 94	10 508	2 975[14]	7 527[14]	...	...	...
95 - 99	5 114	1 211[14]	3 897[14]	...	...	...
100 +	1 325	304[14]	1 018[14]	...	...	...
Unknown - Inconnu	712	404[14]	155[14]	..	..	..

Zambia - Zambie[15]
2010 (|)

Total	164 385	87 693	76 692	12.6	13.6	11.6
0	35 103	18 953	16 150	79.7	86.1	73.2
1 - 4	28 943	15 297	13 646	16.0	17.0	15.0
5 - 9	8 405	4 519	3 886	4.4	4.7	4.0
10 - 14	4 836	2 550	2 286	2.7	2.9	2.6
15 - 19	5 856	2 821	3 035	3.8	3.8	3.9
20 - 24	7 967	3 746	4 221	6.7	6.8	6.6
25 - 29	10 471	5 112	5 359	9.9	10.3	9.6
30 - 34	11 305	5 986	5 319	13.5	14.1	12.8
35 - 39	9 972	5 698	4 274	14.6	16.0	13.1
40 - 44	7 336	4 334	3 002	15.5	17.3	13.5
45 - 49	6 021	3 603	2 418	16.0	19.1	12.9
50 - 54	4 770	2 687	2 083	16.7	19.4	14.3
55 - 59	3 546	2 056	1 490	18.3	21.3	15.3
60 - 64	3 929	2 146	1 783	23.3	27.4	19.8
65 - 69	3 363	1 732	1 631	27.4	30.5	24.7
70 - 74	4 084	2 138	1 946	43.8	48.7	39.4
75 +	8 478	4 315	4 163	65.1	67.1	63.2

AMERICA, NORTH - AMÉRIQUE DU NORD

Anguilla[16]
2013 (+C)[6]

Total	72	43	29	...	...	...
0	3	2	1	...	...	...
1 - 4	-	-	-	...	...	...
5 - 9	-	-	-	...	...	...
10 - 14	-	-	-	...	...	...
15 - 19	2	2	-	...	...	...
20 - 24	1	1	-	...	...	...
25 - 29	2	2	-	...	...	...
30 - 34	-	-	-	...	...	...
35 - 39	2	1	1	...	...	...
40 - 44	-	-	-	...	...	...
45 - 49	1	1	-	...	...	...
50 - 54	5	3	2	...	...	...
55 - 59	5	3	2	...	...	...
60 - 64	3	3	-	...	...	...
65 - 69	7	3	4	...	...	...
70 - 74	4	3	1	...	...	...
75 - 79	9	5	4	...	...	...
80 - 84	8	5	3	...	...	...
85 +	20	9	11	...	...	...

19. Deaths by age and sex and age-specific death rates by sex: latest available year, 2008 - 2017
Décès et taux de mortalité selon l'âge et le sexe : dernière année disponible, 2008 - 2017 (continued - suite)

Continent, country or area, date, code[a] and age (in years) / Continent, pays ou zone, date, code[a] et âge (en années)	Number - Nombre			Rate - Taux		
	Both sexes Les deux sexes	Male Masculin	Female Féminin	Both sexes Les deux sexes	Male Masculin	Female Féminin
AMERICA, NORTH - AMÉRIQUE DU NORD						
Anguilla[16]						
2015 (+C)						
Total	61	...	...	...	...	...
0 - 4	5	...	...	...	...	...
5 - 14	-	...	...	...	...	...
15 - 29	3	...	...	...	...	...
30 - 44	5	...	...	...	...	...
45 - 59	8	...	...	...	...	...
60 - 64	-	...	...	...	...	...
65 - 69	1	...	...	...	...	...
70 - 74	6	...	...	...	...	...
75 - 79	8	...	...	...	...	...
80 - 84	8	...	...	...	...	...
85 +	15	...	...	...	...	...
Aruba						
2017 (C)						
Total	707	353	354	6.4	6.7	6.1
0	6	4	2	♦4.8	♦6.1	♦3.4
1 - 4	-	-	-	-	-	-
5 - 9	2	2	-	♦0.3	♦0.6	-
10 - 14	-	-	-	-	-	-
15 - 19	1	-	1	♦0.1	-	♦0.3
20 - 24	3	2	1	♦0.5	♦0.6	♦0.3
25 - 29	3	3	-	♦0.5	♦0.9	-
30 - 34	4	2	2	♦0.6	♦0.6	♦0.6
35 - 39	6	2	4	♦0.8	♦0.6	♦1.0
40 - 44	11	5	6	♦1.5	♦1.4	♦1.5
45 - 49	19	11	8	♦2.2	♦2.8	♦1.7
50 - 54	19	14	5	♦2.1	♦3.3	♦1.0
55 - 59	47	24	23	5.3	♦5.9	♦4.9
60 - 64	66	32	34	9.2	9.8	8.6
65 - 69	69	40	29	12.8	16.4	♦9.8
70 - 74	75	45	30	20.0	27.8	♦14.0
75 - 79	106	49	57	40.5	43.9	37.9
80 - 84	112	55	57	69.2	94.1	55.1
85 - 89	96	44	52	115.4	143.1	99.1
90 - 94	39	14	25	155.1	♦203.4	♦136.9
95 +	23	5	18	♦253.0	♦192.9	♦277.0
Bahamas						
2012 (+C)						
Total	1 995	1 094	901	5.5	6.2	4.9
0	57	26	31	8.6	♦7.6	9.7
1 - 4	18	10	8	♦0.7	♦0.8	♦0.7
5 - 9	9	5	4	♦0.3	♦0.3	♦0.3
10 - 14	8	6	2	♦0.3	♦0.4	♦0.1
15 - 19	27	17	10	♦0.9	♦1.1	♦0.6
20 - 24	57	42	15	1.9	2.9	♦1.0
25 - 29	49	42	7	1.8	3.2	♦0.5
30 - 34	72	52	20	2.8	4.1	♦1.5
35 - 39	84	47	37	3.1	3.5	2.6
40 - 44	100	58	42	3.6	4.4	2.9
45 - 49	130	72	58	4.9	5.6	4.2
50 - 54	159	84	75	6.8	7.5	6.2
55 - 59	147	94	53	8.5	11.4	5.9
60 - 64	149	83	66	12.2	14.5	10.2
65 - 69	147	87	60	16.1	21.0	12.1
70 - 74	183	96	87	27.6	32.9	23.5
75 - 79	176	93	83	43.0	54.4	34.9
80 - 84	170	81	89	98.0	154.6	74.0
85 - 89	116	61	55	143.7	279.8	91.5
90 +	137	38	99	259.0	351.9	222.0
90 - 94	90	30	60	...	...	...
95 - 99	36	6	30	...	...	...
100 +	11	2	9	...	...	...

Continent, country or area, date, code[a] and age (in years) / Continent, pays ou zone, date, code[a] et âge (en années)	Number - Nombre			Rate - Taux		
	Both sexes Les deux sexes	Male Masculin	Female Féminin	Both sexes Les deux sexes	Male Masculin	Female Féminin
AMERICA, NORTH - AMÉRIQUE DU NORD						
Belize						
2016 (U)						
Total	1 796	1 120	676	...	...	...
0	103	61	42	...	...	...
1 - 4	18	11	7	...	...	...
5 - 9	10	5	5	...	...	...
10 - 14	11	8	3	...	...	...
15 - 19	45	31	14	...	...	...
20 - 24	65	52	13	...	...	...
25 - 29	73	57	16	...	...	...
30 - 34	99	69	30	...	...	...
35 - 39	78	57	21	...	...	...
40 - 44	91	67	24	...	...	...
45 - 49	94	56	38	...	...	...
50 - 54	110	63	47	...	...	...
55 - 59	130	81	49	...	...	...
60 - 64	121	74	47	...	...	...
65 - 69	123	78	45	...	...	...
70 - 74	124	85	39	...	...	...
75 - 79	139	68	71	...	...	...
80 - 84	140	82	58	...	...	...
85 - 89	129	72	57	...	...	...
90 - 94	64	28	36	...	...	...
95 - 99	25	15	10	...	...	...
100 +	4	-	4	...	...	...
Bermuda - Bermudes[17]						
2016 (C)						
Total	492	266	226	8.0	9.0	7.0
0	2	2	-	♦3.2	♦6.4	-
1 - 4	-	-	-	-	-	-
5 - 9	1	-	1	♦0.3	-	♦0.6
10 - 14	1	-	1	♦0.3	-	♦0.7
15 - 19	3	2	1	♦1.0	♦1.4	♦0.7
20 - 24	4	4	-	♦1.3	♦2.8	-
25 - 29	4	2	2	♦1.1	♦1.2	♦1.1
30 - 34	6	4	2	♦1.5	♦2.0	♦1.0
35 - 39	7	6	1	♦1.6	♦2.8	♦0.5
40 - 44	7	4	3	♦1.6	♦1.8	♦1.4
45 - 49	6	4	2	♦1.3	♦1.7	♦0.8
50 - 54	18	14	4	♦3.3	♦5.2	♦1.4
55 - 59	31	15	16	6.0	♦6.4	♦5.7
60 - 64	41	33	8	9.5	16.5	♦3.5
65 - 69	39	25	14	11.3	♦15.5	♦7.6
70 - 74	50	33	17	18.3	26.8	♦11.3
75 - 79	58	36	22	31.1	45.7	♦20.4
80 - 84	62	30	32	43.3	♦51.5	37.6
85 +	152	52	100	139.1	162.0	129.5
85 - 89	62	30	32	...	...	...
90 - 94	64	19	45	...	...	...
95 - 99	22	3	19	...	...	...
100 +	4	-	4	...	...	...
Canada[18]						
2015 (C)						
Total	264 333	133 441	130 892	7.4	7.5	7.2
0	1 737	937	800	4.5	4.7	4.2
1 - 4	289	172	117	0.2	0.2	0.2
5 - 9	167	90	77	0.1	0.1	0.1
10 - 14	219	119	100	0.1	0.1	0.1
15 - 19	700	457	243	0.3	0.4	0.2
20 - 24	1 273	897	376	0.5	0.7	0.3
25 - 29	1 502	1 061	441	0.6	0.9	0.4
30 - 34	1 708	1 131	577	0.7	0.9	0.5
35 - 39	1 936	1 238	698	0.8	1.0	0.6
40 - 44	2 829	1 735	1 094	1.2	1.5	0.9
45 - 49	4 394	2 727	1 667	1.8	2.2	1.4
50 - 54	8 213	4 887	3 326	3.0	3.5	2.4
55 - 59	12 377	7 456	4 921	4.8	5.7	3.8

Continent, country or area, date, code[a] and age (in years)	Number - Nombre			Rate - Taux		
Continent, pays ou zone, date, code[a] et âge (en années)	Both sexes Les deux sexes	Male Masculin	Female Féminin	Both sexes Les deux sexes	Male Masculin	Female Féminin
AMERICA, NORTH - AMÉRIQUE DU NORD						
Canada[18]						
2015 (C)						
60 - 64	16 728	10 021	6 707	7.5	9.1	5.9
65 - 69	21 496	12 788	8 708	11.2	13.7	8.9
70 - 74	24 689	14 242	10 447	18.0	21.8	14.5
75 - 79	29 259	16 341	12 918	29.3	35.8	23.8
80 - 84	38 860	20 196	18 664	52.2	63.1	43.9
85 - 89	43 505	20 006	23 499	90.9	110.8	78.8
90 - 94	35 177	12 750	22 427	158.2	187.0	145.4
95 - 99	14 026	3 623	10 403	278.2	341.5	261.4
100 +	3 249	567	2 682	467.4	679.0	438.5
Cayman Islands - Îles Caïmanes						
2017 (C)						
Total	216	114	102	3.4	3.5	3.3
0 - 14	10	7	3	♦0.9	♦1.2	♦0.6
15 - 19	1	1	-	...	...	...
20 - 24	2	2	-	...	...	...
25 - 29	1	-	1	...	...	...
30 - 34	4	3	1	...	...	...
35 - 39	5	3	2	...	...	...
40 - 49	13	9	4	...	...	...
50 - 59	20	13	7	...	...	...
60 - 69	39	22	17	...	...	...
70 - 79	37	19	18	...	...	...
80 - 89	55	27	28	...	...	...
90 +	29	8	21	...	...	...
Costa Rica						
2017* (C)						
Total	23 251	13 098	10 153	4.7	5.4	4.0
0 - 4	661	353	308	2.2	2.3	2.0
0	548	286	262	...	...	...
1 - 4	113	67	46	...	...	...
5 - 9	61	33	28	0.2	0.2	♦0.2
10 - 14	70	34	36	0.2	0.2	0.2
15 - 19	220	166	54	0.5	0.8	0.3
20 - 24	449	376	73	1.1	1.7	0.4
25 - 29	486	382	104	1.3	2.0	0.5
30 - 34	497	364	133	1.3	2.1	0.7
35 - 39	519	368	151	1.5	2.3	0.9
40 - 44	580	357	223	1.9	2.5	1.4
45 - 49	718	443	275	2.4	3.2	1.7
50 - 54	994	623	371	3.2	4.3	2.2
55 - 59	1 402	856	546	5.0	6.4	3.8
60 - 64	1 677	1 029	648	7.2	9.5	5.1
65 - 69	1 898	1 112	786	10.8	13.4	8.5
70 - 74	2 110	1 227	883	16.2	22.1	11.8
75 - 79	2 438	1 374	1 064	25.3	27.0	23.4
80 - 84	2 741	1 395	1 346	46.2	49.5	43.2
85 - 89	2 765	1 341	1 424	74.9	83.0	68.6
90 - 94	1 850	819	1 031	113.2	133.0	101.2
95 +	1 107	442	665	193.7	187.1	198.4
95 - 99	876	357	519	...	...	...
100 +	231	85	146	...	...	...
Unknown - Inconnu	8	4	4	..	..	..
Cuba						
2016 (C)						
Total	99 388	54 284	45 104	8.8	9.7	8.0
0	497	277	220	4.1	4.4	3.8
1 - 4	147	72	75	0.3	0.3	0.3
5 - 9	129	76	53	0.2	0.2	0.2
10 - 14	143	93	50	0.2	0.3	0.2
15 - 19	282	182	100	0.4	0.5	0.3
20 - 24	366	240	126	0.5	0.6	0.4
25 - 29	585	412	173	0.7	1.0	0.4
30 - 34	663	436	227	0.9	1.2	0.7
35 - 39	797	505	292	1.2	1.5	0.9
40 - 44	1 617	1 045	572	1.8	2.3	1.2

Continent, country or area, date, code[a] and age (in years) Continent, pays ou zone, date, code[a] et âge (en années)	Number - Nombre			Rate - Taux		
	Both sexes Les deux sexes	Male Masculin	Female Féminin	Both sexes Les deux sexes	Male Masculin	Female Féminin
AMERICA, NORTH - AMÉRIQUE DU NORD						
Cuba						
2016 (C)						
45 - 49	2 756	1 783	973	2.8	3.6	1.9
50 - 54	4 618	2 952	1 666	4.7	6.1	3.3
55 - 59	5 375	3 333	2 042	8.0	10.2	5.9
60 - 64	7 000	4 194	2 806	11.8	14.7	9.1
65 - 69	9 497	5 586	3 911	18.3	22.6	14.5
70 - 74	11 674	6 803	4 871	28.1	34.7	22.1
75 - 79	13 196	7 297	5 899	43.4	51.7	36.2
80 - 84	13 735	7 095	6 640	72.4	82.9	63.8
85 +	26 286	11 879	14 407	146.8	158.0	138.8
85 - 89	12 501	6 055	6 446	...	...	...
90 - 94	8 642	3 788	4 854	...	...	...
95 - 99	3 925	1 601	2 324	...	...	...
100 +	1 218	435	783	...	...	...
Unknown - Inconnu	25	24	1	..	..	..
Curaçao						
2017 (C)						
Total	1 420	748	672	8.9	10.2	7.7
0	16	...	...	♦9.7	...	...
1 - 19	6	...	...	♦0.2	...	...
20 - 24	6	...	...	♦0.6	...	...
25 - 29	13	...	...	♦1.4	...	...
30 - 34	7	...	...	♦0.7	...	...
35 - 39	10	...	...	♦1.1	...	...
40 - 44	12	...	...	♦1.2	...	...
45 - 49	28	...	...	♦2.4	...	...
50 - 54	54	...	...	4.2	...	...
55 - 59	74	...	...	6.0	...	...
60 - 64	108	...	...	10.3	...	...
65 - 69	126	...	...	14.0	...	...
70 - 74	190	...	...	27.4	...	...
75 - 79	207	...	...	45.1	...	...
80 - 84	228	...	...	72.4	...	...
85 - 89	164	...	...	100.7	...	...
90 - 94	115	...	...	174.1	...	...
95 - 99	47	...	...	253.4	...	...
100 +	9	...	...	♦225.0	...	...
Dominican Republic - République dominicaine						
2016 (U)						
Total	42 199	25 061	17 138	...	...	...
0	800	443	357	...	...	...
1 - 4	227	123	104	...	...	...
5 - 9	156	99	57	...	...	...
10 - 14	189	111	78	...	...	...
15 - 19	647	502	145	...	...	...
20 - 24	1 116	836	280	...	...	...
25 - 29	1 097	831	266	...	...	...
30 - 34	1 016	704	312	...	...	...
35 - 39	1 267	838	429	...	...	...
40 - 44	1 508	1 007	501	...	...	...
45 - 49	1 915	1 241	674	...	...	...
50 - 54	2 334	1 477	857	...	...	...
55 - 59	2 630	1 682	948	...	...	...
60 - 64	3 180	1 943	1 237	...	...	...
65 - 69	3 706	2 235	1 471	...	...	...
70 - 74	3 861	2 347	1 514	...	...	...
75 - 79	4 230	2 406	1 824	...	...	...
80 - 84	4 436	2 283	2 153	...	...	...
85 - 89	3 867	1 995	1 872	...	...	...
90 - 94	2 109	1 026	1 083	...	...	...
95 +	1 401	663	738	...	...	...
Unknown - Inconnu	507	269	238	..	..	..
El Salvador						
2014 (C)						
Total	37 461	21 326	16 135	5.9	7.2	4.8
0	876	491	385	7.0	7.7	6.3

Continent, country or area, date, code[a] and age (in years) Continent, pays ou zone, date, code[a] et âge (en années)	Number - Nombre			Rate - Taux		
	Both sexes Les deux sexes	Male Masculin	Female Féminin	Both sexes Les deux sexes	Male Masculin	Female Féminin
AMERICA, NORTH - AMÉRIQUE DU NORD						
El Salvador						
2014 (C)						
1 - 4	240	131	109	0.5	0.5	0.5
5 - 9	125	66	59	0.2	0.2	0.2
10 - 14	250	160	90	0.4	0.5	0.3
15 - 19	983	813	170	1.4	2.3	0.5
20 - 24	1 139	926	213	1.8	3.0	0.6
25 - 29	1 047	869	178	2.1	3.8	0.6
30 - 34	1 249	1 015	234	2.9	5.6	1.0
35 - 39	1 348	1 061	287	3.5	6.4	1.3
40 - 44	1 313	942	371	3.6	6.1	1.8
45 - 49	1 492	985	507	4.7	7.3	2.8
50 - 54	1 669	1 022	647	6.3	8.9	4.2
55 - 59	1 991	1 129	862	8.9	11.6	6.8
60 - 64	2 302	1 275	1 027	12.1	15.4	9.6
65 - 69	2 678	1 398	1 280	17.1	20.4	14.6
70 - 74	3 107	1 644	1 463	24.7	29.7	20.8
75 - 79	3 687	1 826	1 861	38.6	44.0	34.4
80 +	11 965	5 573	6 392	109.6	120.9	101.3
80 - 84	4 057	1 977	2 080	...	...	...
85 - 89	3 853	1 851	2 002	...	...	...
90 - 94	2 642	1 186	1 456	...	...	...
95 +	1 413	559	854	...	...	...
Greenland - Groenland						
2017 (C)						
Total	499	276	223	8.9	9.3	8.4
0	6	5	1	♦7.1	♦11.3	♦2.5
1 - 4	1	-	1	♦0.3	-	♦0.7
5 - 9	5	3	2	♦1.3	♦1.5	♦1.1
10 - 14	1	-	1	♦0.3	-	♦0.5
15 - 19	10	9	1	♦2.6	♦4.7	♦0.5
20 - 24	6	5	1	♦1.4	♦2.3	♦0.5
25 - 29	11	5	6	♦2.4	♦2.1	♦2.7
30 - 34	8	3	5	♦1.9	♦1.4	♦2.5
35 - 39	7	4	3	♦2.0	♦2.1	♦1.8
40 - 44	9	5	4	♦3.0	♦3.0	♦3.0
45 - 49	6	3	3	♦1.5	♦1.4	♦1.7
50 - 54	32	21	11	6.2	♦7.6	♦4.6
55 - 59	28	20	8	♦6.5	♦8.3	♦4.2
60 - 64	64	39	25	21.1	23.0	♦18.7
65 - 69	71	42	29	38.2	38.2	♦38.1
70 - 74	79	43	36	58.4	57.1	60.0
75 - 79	66	35	31	84.0	89.7	78.3
80 - 84	44	18	26	120.5	♦113.2	♦126.2
85 - 89	37	14	23	237.2	♦280.0	♦217.0
90 - 94	6	2	4	♦206.9	♦222.2	♦200.0
95 +	2	-	2	♦666.7	-	♦1000.0
Grenada - Grenade						
2014 (+C)						
Total	958	514	444	8.8	9.3	8.2
0 - 4	35	23	12	4.1	♦5.2	♦2.9
0	33	21	12	...	...	...
1 - 4	2	2	-	...	...	...
5 - 9	1	-	1	♦0.1	-	♦0.3
10 - 14	5	3	2	♦0.7	♦0.8	♦0.5
15 - 19	4	3	1	♦0.4	♦0.6	♦0.2
20 - 24	14	8	6	♦1.4	♦1.6	♦1.2
25 - 29	12	8	4	♦1.2	♦1.6	♦0.8
30 - 34	16	10	6	♦2.0	♦2.4	♦1.5
35 - 39	17	8	9	♦2.6	♦2.4	♦2.8
40 - 44	19	11	8	♦3.0	♦3.3	♦2.7
45 - 49	25	16	9	♦3.9	♦4.9	♦2.9
50 - 54	58	39	19	8.7	11.4	♦5.9
55 - 59	57	32	25	9.8	10.7	♦9.0
60 - 64	64	43	21	15.1	19.8	♦10.2
65 - 69	64	39	25	19.8	24.4	♦15.3
70 +	567	271	296	67.2	75.0	61.3

Continent, country or area, date, code[a] and age (in years) / Continent, pays ou zone, date, code[a] et âge (en années)	Number - Nombre			Rate - Taux		
	Both sexes Les deux sexes	Male Masculin	Female Féminin	Both sexes Les deux sexes	Male Masculin	Female Féminin
AMERICA, NORTH - AMÉRIQUE DU NORD						
Grenada - Grenade						
2014 (+C)						
70 - 74	85	50	35	...	...	...
75 - 79	114	67	47	...	...	...
80 - 84	127	59	68	...	...	...
85 - 89	122	58	64	...	...	...
90 - 94	71	22	49	...	...	...
95 - 99	32	12	20	...	...	...
100 +	16	3	13	...	...	...
Guatemala						
2016 (C)						
Total	82 565	46 267	36 298	...	...	...
0	8 366	4 750	3 616	...	...	...
1 - 4	2 662	1 414	1 248	...	...	...
5 - 9	694	388	306	...	...	...
10 - 14	848	477	371	...	...	...
15 - 19	2 362	1 616	746	...	...	...
20 - 24	2 947	2 221	726	...	...	...
25 - 29	2 699	2 009	690	...	...	...
30 - 34	2 739	1 966	773	...	...	...
35 - 39	3 037	2 082	955	...	...	...
40 - 44	2 982	1 944	1 038	...	...	...
45 - 49	3 215	1 957	1 258	...	...	...
50 - 54	3 730	2 116	1 614	...	...	...
55 - 59	4 683	2 506	2 177	...	...	...
60 - 64	5 218	2 696	2 522	...	...	...
65 - 69	5 760	2 928	2 832	...	...	...
70 - 74	5 793	3 015	2 778	...	...	...
75 - 79	6 420	3 224	3 196	...	...	...
80 - 84	6 770	3 366	3 404	...	...	...
85 - 89	6 363	3 152	3 211	...	...	...
90 - 94	3 534	1 609	1 925	...	...	...
95 +	1 278	548	730	...	...	...
Unknown - Inconnu	465	283	182	..	..	..
Jamaica - Jamaïque[19]						
2011 (|)						
Total	21 001	10 061[14]	8 618[14]	7.8	7.6	6.3
0 - 4	361	187[14]	163[14]	1.6	1.7	1.5
5 - 9	118	53[14]	61[14]	0.5	0.4	0.5
10 - 14	128	74[14]	54[14]	0.5	0.5	0.4
15 - 19	382	288[14]	90[14]	1.5	2.3	0.7
20 - 24	521	423[14]	92[14]	2.5	4.2	0.9
25 - 29	515	367[14]	136[14]	2.4	3.6	1.2
30 - 34	451	304[14]	134[14]	2.0	2.9	1.1
35 - 39	557	319[14]	224[14]	2.4	3.0	1.8
40 - 44	609	329[14]	268[14]	3.1	3.3	2.7
45 - 49	631	324[14]	299[14]	4.7	4.8	4.4
50 - 54	749	418[14]	320[14]	6.4	6.8	5.7
55 - 59	702	367[14]	319[14]	8.1	8.1	7.8
60 - 64	1 003	501[14]	482[14]	14.6	14.9	13.7
65 - 69	1 031	554[14]	448[14]	15.7	17.5	13.2
70 - 74	1 343	700[14]	610[14]	22.4	24.6	19.3
75 +	9 932	4 853[14]	4 918[14]	94.6	115.9	77.9
75 - 79	1 567	805[14]	722[14]	...	...	...
80 - 84	1 721	876[14]	806[14]	...	...	...
85 - 89	3 057	1 259[14]	1 798[14]	...	...	...
90 +	3 505	1 913[14]	1 592[14]	...	...	...
Unknown - Inconnu	1 968	-[14]	-[14]	..	..	..
Mexico - Mexique[20]						
2016 (+C)						
Total	684 437	381 848[14]	302 167[14]	5.6	6.4	4.8
0	24 722	13 811[14]	10 765[14]	11.2	12.2	10.0
1 - 4	5 068	2 716[14]	2 349[14]	0.6	0.6	0.5
5 - 9	2 509	1 409[14]	1 100[14]	0.2	0.2	0.2
10 - 14	3 242	1 896[14]	1 346[14]	0.3	0.3	0.2
15 - 19	8 462	6 038[14]	2 424[14]	0.8	1.1	0.4

19. Deaths by age and sex and age-specific death rates by sex: latest available year, 2008 - 2017
Décès et taux de mortalité selon l'âge et le sexe : dernière année disponible, 2008 - 2017 (continued - suite)

Continent, country or area, date, code[a] and age (in years) / Continent, pays ou zone, date, code[a] et âge (en années)	Number - Nombre			Rate - Taux		
	Both sexes Les deux sexes	Male Masculin	Female Féminin	Both sexes Les deux sexes	Male Masculin	Female Féminin
AMERICA, NORTH - AMÉRIQUE DU NORD						
Mexico - Mexique[20]						
2016 (+C)						
20 - 24	13 499	10 371[14]	3 126[14]	1.3	1.9	0.6
25 - 29	14 357	10 923[14]	3 432[14]	1.5	2.3	0.7
30 - 34	15 476	11 564[14]	3 912[14]	1.7	2.7	0.8
35 - 39	18 648	13 399[14]	5 245[14]	2.1	3.3	1.1
40 - 44	23 788	16 329[14]	7 454[14]	2.9	4.2	1.7
45 - 49	28 341	18 379[14]	9 960[14]	3.9	5.3	2.6
50 - 54	36 632	22 520[14]	14 110[14]	6.0	7.8	4.4
55 - 59	45 487	26 878[14]	18 607[14]	9.0	11.3	7.0
60 - 64	52 641	29 969[14]	22 670[14]	13.2	16.0	10.8
65 - 69	58 009	32 315[14]	25 694[14]	19.5	23.2	16.3
70 - 74	63 565	34 292[14]	29 271[14]	29.3	34.1	25.1
75 - 79	69 469	36 253[14]	33 215[14]	45.8	52.6	40.2
80 - 84	72 138	35 721[14]	36 416[14]	73.4	81.5	66.9
85 - 89	63 261	28 969[14]	34 291[14]	115.1	122.3	109.7
90 - 94	41 388	17 661[14]	23 726[14]	170.1	176.2	165.8
95 - 99	16 106	6 192[14]	9 914[14]	202.7	198.7	205.2
100 +	4 360	1 551[14]	2 809[14]	219.8	211.5	224.6
Unknown - Inconnu	3 269	2 692[14]	331[14]	..	..	..
Montserrat						
2016 (C)						
Total	43	26	17	...	...	...
0	-	-	-	...	...	...
1 - 4	-	-	-	...	...	...
5 - 9	-	-	-	...	...	...
10 - 14	-	-	-	...	...	...
15 - 19	-	-	-	...	...	...
20 - 24	1	-	1	...	...	...
25 - 29	1	1	-	...	...	...
30 - 34	-	-	-	...	...	...
35 - 39	-	-	-	...	...	...
40 - 44	-	-	-	...	...	...
45 - 49	-	-	-	...	...	...
50 - 54	1	-	1	...	...	...
55 - 59	-	-	-	...	...	...
60 - 64	3	2	1	...	...	...
65 - 69	7	4	3	...	...	...
70 - 74	7	7	-	...	...	...
75 - 79	1	1	-	...	...	...
80 - 84	8	3	5	...	...	...
85 - 89	5	4	1	...	...	...
90 +	9	4	5	...	...	...
Nicaragua						
2010 (+U)						
Total	19 944	11 416	8 528	...	...	...
0	1 891	1 077	814	...	...	...
1 - 4	252	155	97	...	...	...
5 - 9	155	86	69	...	...	...
10 - 14	182	95	87	...	...	...
15 - 19	458	313	145	...	...	...
20 - 24	564	428	136	...	...	...
25 - 29	672	514	158	...	...	...
30 - 34	615	458	157	...	...	...
35 - 39	697	491	206	...	...	...
40 - 44	758	495	263	...	...	...
45 - 49	843	540	303	...	...	...
50 - 54	997	594	403	...	...	...
55 - 59	1 166	693	473	...	...	...
60 - 64	1 258	704	554	...	...	...
65 - 69	1 385	787	598	...	...	...
70 - 74	1 584	863	721	...	...	...
75 - 79	1 740	931	809	...	...	...
80 +	4 727	2 192	2 535	...	...	...

Continent, country or area, date, code[a] and age (in years) / Continent, pays ou zone, date, code[a] et âge (en années)	Number - Nombre			Rate - Taux		
	Both sexes Les deux sexes	Male Masculin	Female Féminin	Both sexes Les deux sexes	Male Masculin	Female Féminin
AMERICA, NORTH - AMÉRIQUE DU NORD						
Panama						
2016* (C)						
Total	18 882	10 859	8 023	4.7	5.4	4.0
0	1 046	567	479	14.1	14.9	13.2
1 - 4	291	162	129	1.0	1.1	0.9
5 - 9	90	47	43	0.2	0.3	0.2
10 - 14	105	60	45	0.3	0.3	0.3
15 - 19	267	185	82	0.8	1.0	0.5
20 - 24	346	274	72	1.1	1.6	0.4
25 - 29	417	307	110	1.3	1.9	0.7
30 - 34	394	271	123	1.3	1.8	0.8
35 - 39	423	275	148	1.5	1.9	1.0
40 - 44	482	294	188	1.8	2.1	1.4
45 - 49	620	394	226	2.5	3.2	1.8
50 - 54	757	475	282	3.6	4.5	2.6
55 - 59	969	597	372	5.5	6.9	4.2
60 - 64	1 144	713	431	8.4	10.7	6.1
65 - 69	1 413	863	550	13.4	17.1	10.1
70 - 74	1 676	1 019	657	21.1	27.1	15.7
75 - 79	1 902	1 132	770	33.4	42.8	25.2
80 - 84	2 024	1 124	900	54.2	66.6	44.0
85 - 89	1 987	995	992	92.8	106.2	82.4
90 - 94	1 483	695	788	148.1	165.0	135.8
95 - 99	791	309	482	230.1	222.8	235.1
100 +	225	80	145	352.7	321.3	372.8
Unknown - Inconnu	30	21	9	..	..	..
Puerto Rico - Porto Rico						
2017 (C)						
Total	30 977	16 847	14 130	...	...	...
0	172	101	71	...	...	...
1 - 4	23	13	10	...	...	...
5 - 9	16	8	8	...	...	...
10 - 14	12	4	8	...	...	...
15 - 19	105	79	26	...	...	...
20 - 24	292	245	47	...	...	...
25 - 29	321	267	54	...	...	...
30 - 34	343	277	66	...	...	...
35 - 39	413	312	101	...	...	...
40 - 44	523	382	141	...	...	...
45 - 49	704	470	234	...	...	...
50 - 54	1 081	726	355	...	...	...
55 - 59	1 536	1 016	520	...	...	...
60 - 64	1 905	1 225	680	...	...	...
65 - 69	2 683	1 707	976	...	...	...
70 - 74	3 383	1 949	1 434	...	...	...
75 - 79	3 847	2 190	1 657	...	...	...
80 - 84	4 367	2 143	2 224	...	...	...
85 - 89	4 203	1 877	2 326	...	...	...
90 - 94	3 190	1 230	1 960	...	...	...
95 - 99	1 450	509	941	...	...	...
100 +	404	114	290	...	...	...
Unknown - Inconnu	4	3	1	..	..	..
Saint Vincent and the Grenadines - Saint-Vincent-et-les Grenadines[21]						
2013 (C)						
Total	928	514	414	8.5	9.2	7.7
0	32	20	12	20.4	+25.5	+15.3
1 - 4	2	1	1	+0.3	+0.3	+0.3
5 - 9	3	3	-	+0.4	+0.7	-
10 - 14	4	3	1	+0.4	+0.6	+0.2
15 - 19	10	7	3	+1.0	+1.4	+0.6
20 - 24	10	7	3	+1.2	+1.6	+0.7
25 - 29	21	13	8	+2.5	+3.1	+2.0
30 - 34	29	16	13	+3.7	+4.1	+3.3
35 - 39	31	19	12	4.1	+4.9	+3.2
40 - 44	26	14	12	+3.6	+3.7	+3.5
45 - 49	45	30	15	6.0	+7.8	+4.2

19. Deaths by age and sex and age-specific death rates by sex: latest available year, 2008 - 2017
Décès et taux de mortalité selon l'âge et le sexe : dernière année disponible, 2008 - 2017 (continued - suite)

Continent, country or area, date, code[a] and age (in years) / Continent, pays ou zone, date, code[a] et âge (en années)	Number - Nombre			Rate - Taux		
	Both sexes Les deux sexes	Male Masculin	Female Féminin	Both sexes Les deux sexes	Male Masculin	Female Féminin
AMERICA, NORTH - AMÉRIQUE DU NORD						
Saint Vincent and the Grenadines - Saint-Vincent-et-les Grenadines[21]						
2013 (C)						
50 - 54	52	33	19	7.9	9.6	♦6.1
55 - 59	62	37	25	12.3	14.0	♦10.5
60 - 64	49	31	18	12.8	15.7	♦9.7
65 - 69	72	44	28	25.3	30.2	♦20.2
70 - 74	87	53	34	34.3	41.3	27.1
75 - 79	114	66	48	57.6	68.5	47.2
80 - 84	101	51	50	69.9	76.8	64.0
85 +	174	62	112	145.8	129.0	157.1
85 - 89	90	33	57	...	...	...
90 - 94	53	20	33	...	...	...
95 - 99	23	8	15	...	...	...
100 +	8	1	7	...	...	...
Unknown - Inconnu	4	4	-	..	..	..
Trinidad and Tobago - Trinité-et-Tobago						
2011* (C)						
Total	9 435	5 441	3 994	7.1	8.2	6.0
0	252	150	102	15.0	17.4	12.5
1 - 4	33	20	13	0.4	♦0.5	♦0.3
5 - 9	22	12	10	♦0.2	♦0.3	♦0.2
10 - 14	26	13	13	♦0.3	♦0.3	♦0.3
15 - 19	93	70	23	0.9	1.4	♦0.5
20 - 24	183	153	30	1.6	2.7	♦0.5
25 - 29	230	163	67	1.9	2.6	1.1
30 - 34	229	163	66	2.2	3.0	1.3
35 - 39	232	139	93	2.5	3.0	2.0
40 - 44	281	173	108	3.3	4.0	2.5
45 - 49	443	273	170	4.6	5.6	3.6
50 - 54	607	382	225	7.0	8.7	5.2
55 - 59	737	456	281	10.1	12.4	7.7
60 - 64	841	524	317	14.3	17.7	10.9
65 - 69	948	572	376	21.2	26.5	16.3
70 - 74	988	586	402	32.6	41.3	25.0
75 - 79	939	518	421	45.3	55.8	36.7
80 - 84	868	426	442	68.5	79.5	60.4
85 +	1 475	642	833	138.3	159.8	125.3
Unknown - Inconnu	8	6	2	..	..	..
United States of America - États-Unis d'Amérique						
2015 (C)						
Total	2 712 630	1 373 404	1 339 226	8.4	8.7	8.2
0	23 455	13 008	10 447	5.9	6.4	5.4
1 - 4	3 965	2 281	1 684	0.2	0.3	0.2
5 - 9	2 402	1 377	1 025	0.1	0.1	0.1
10 - 14	3 009	1 776	1 233	0.1	0.2	0.1
15 - 19	10 186	7 187	2 999	0.5	0.7	0.3
20 - 24	20 308	15 159	5 149	0.9	1.3	0.5
25 - 29	23 898	17 173	6 725	1.1	1.5	0.6
30 - 34	27 619	18 608	9 011	1.3	1.7	0.8
35 - 39	31 417	20 190	11 227	1.5	2.0	1.1
40 - 44	41 671	25 480	16 191	2.1	2.5	1.6
45 - 49	64 377	38 807	25 570	3.1	3.8	2.4
50 - 54	110 117	66 740	43 377	4.9	6.1	3.8
55 - 59	159 589	97 172	62 417	7.3	9.2	5.6
60 - 64	198 196	120 454	77 742	10.4	13.2	7.8
65 - 69	235 482	137 630	97 852	14.7	18.1	11.6
70 - 74	259 534	144 717	114 817	22.6	27.3	18.6
75 - 79	290 405	153 719	136 686	35.7	42.6	30.3
80 - 84	347 161	170 127	177 034	59.9	70.5	52.3
85 - 89	390 747	168 932	221 815	101.1	117.1	91.6
90 - 94	313 796	112 676	201 120	169.5	191.3	159.4
95 - 99	127 628	35 157	92 471	257.9	274.7	252.0
100 +	27 530	4 939	22 591	357.7	327.3	365.0
Unknown - Inconnu	138	95	43	..	..	..

19. Deaths by age and sex and age-specific death rates by sex: latest available year, 2008 - 2017
Décès et taux de mortalité selon l'âge et le sexe : dernière année disponible, 2008 - 2017 (continued - suite)

Continent, country or area, date, code[a] and age (in years) Continent, pays ou zone, date, code[a] et âge (en années)	Number - Nombre			Rate - Taux		
	Both sexes Les deux sexes	Male Masculin	Female Féminin	Both sexes Les deux sexes	Male Masculin	Female Féminin

AMERICA, SOUTH - AMÉRIQUE DU SUD

Argentina - Argentine
2016 (C)
Total	352 992	181 339[14]	171 408[14]	8.1	8.5	7.7
0 - 4	8 443	4 766[14]	3 652[14]	2.2	2.5	2.0
0	7 093	4 015[14]	3 057[14]	...	...	...
1 - 4	1 350	751[14]	595[14]	...	...	...
5 - 9	698	406[14]	292[14]	0.2	0.2	0.2
10 - 14	836	467[14]	366[14]	0.2	0.3	0.2
15 - 19	2 604	1 843[14]	757[14]	0.7	1.0	0.4
20 - 24	3 420	2 518[14]	896[14]	1.0	1.4	0.5
25 - 29	3 475	2 472[14]	1 001[14]	1.0	1.5	0.6
30 - 34	3 763	2 506[14]	1 254[14]	1.2	1.6	0.8
35 - 39	4 849	3 042[14]	1 805[14]	1.5	2.0	1.1
40 - 44	5 846	3 620[14]	2 223[14]	2.1	2.6	1.6
45 - 49	7 944	4 881[14]	3 060[14]	3.4	4.2	2.5
50 - 54	11 601	7 180[14]	4 414[14]	5.3	6.8	3.9
55 - 59	17 285	10 892[14]	6 384[14]	8.6	11.3	6.1
60 - 64	24 722	15 236[14]	9 467[14]	13.7	17.9	9.9
65 - 69	31 879	19 656[14]	12 206[14]	20.7	27.9	14.6
70 - 74	37 410	22 170[14]	15 204[14]	31.3	42.5	22.6
75 - 79	42 530	22 939[14]	19 574[14]	48.7	64.9	37.7
80 - 84	48 827	23 140[14]	25 669[14]	81.6	105.9	67.5
85 +	95 070	32 502[14]	62 526[14]	175.8	204.1	164.0
Unknown - Inconnu	1 790	1 103[14]	658[14]	..	..	..

Bolivia (Plurinational State of) - Bolivie (État plurinational de)[22]
2012 (|)
Total	127 050	59 027	68 023	12.6	11.8	13.5
0	5 363	2 406	2 957	26.6	23.4	29.9
1 - 4	6 695	3 085	3 610	7.5	6.8	8.3
5 - 9	2 531	1 183	1 348	2.5	2.3	2.8
10 - 14	1 961	827	1 134	1.8	1.5	2.1
15 - 19	3 699	1 460	2 239	3.3	2.6	4.1
20 - 24	4 767	1 618	3 149	4.9	3.3	6.5
25 - 29	4 089	1 393	2 696	5.0	3.4	6.6
30 - 34	4 323	1 556	2 767	5.7	4.2	7.3
35 - 39	4 670	1 868	2 802	7.4	6.0	8.7
40 - 44	4 597	1 849	2 748	8.4	6.8	10.0
45 - 49	5 769	2 483	3 286	12.5	10.9	14.0
50 - 54	6 298	2 849	3 449	15.6	14.3	16.9
55 - 59	6 851	2 946	3 905	21.1	18.5	23.7
60 - 64	9 105	4 256	4 849	32.5	31.7	33.3
65 - 69	9 801	4 792	5 009	47.9	48.8	47.1
70 - 74	9 701	4 649	5 052	63.6	64.7	62.7
75 - 79	9 798	4 756	5 042	98.7	105.7	92.9
80 - 84	11 190	5 952	5 238	138.0	172.7	112.3
85 - 89	8 493	4 674	3 819	224.0	294.3	173.3
90 - 94	3 927	2 332	1 595	267.8	388.9	184.0
95 +	3 422	2 093	1 329	415.6	633.3	269.6

Brazil - Brésil
2016 (+C)
Total	1 274 630[23]	716 874[14]	557 358[14]	6.2	7.0	5.3
0	30 541[23]	16 971[14]	13 494[14]	10.7	11.7	9.7
1 - 4	5 786[23]	3 132[14]	2 650[14]	0.5	0.5	0.5
5 - 9	3 123[23]	1 754[14]	1 369[14]	0.2	0.2	0.2
10 - 14	4 598[23]	2 832[14]	1 764[14]	0.3	0.3	0.2
15 - 19	20 453[23]	16 842[14]	3 607[14]	1.2	1.9	0.4
20 - 24	26 835[23]	22 300[14]	4 532[14]	1.6	2.6	0.5
25 - 29	26 184[23]	20 640[14]	5 539[14]	1.5	2.4	0.7
30 - 34	28 968[23]	21 270[14]	7 693[14]	1.6	2.4	0.9
35 - 39	33 714[23]	23 095[14]	10 614[14]	2.1	2.9	1.3
40 - 44	39 010[23]	25 488[14]	13 518[14]	2.7	3.6	1.9
45 - 49	51 379[23]	32 886[14]	18 487[14]	4.0	5.2	2.8
50 - 54	68 419[23]	43 254[14]	25 154[14]	5.8	7.5	4.1
55 - 59	86 357[23]	53 963[14]	32 387[14]	8.5	11.2	6.1

19. Deaths by age and sex and age-specific death rates by sex: latest available year, 2008 - 2017
Décès et taux de mortalité selon l'âge et le sexe : dernière année disponible, 2008 - 2017 (continued - suite)

Continent, country or area, date, code[a] and age (in years) Continent, pays ou zone, date, code[a] et âge (en années)	Number - Nombre			Rate - Taux		
	Both sexes Les deux sexes	Male Masculin	Female Féminin	Both sexes Les deux sexes	Male Masculin	Female Féminin
AMERICA, SOUTH - AMÉRIQUE DU SUD						
Brazil - Brésil						
2016 (+C)						
60 - 64	102 515[23]	62 689[14]	39 815[14]	12.7	16.5	9.3
65 - 69	115 606[23]	68 250[14]	47 349[14]	18.9	24.4	14.3
70 - 74	122 960[23]	69 504[14]	53 450[14]	28.9	37.0	22.4
75 - 79	136 983[23]	72 096[14]	64 875[14]	45.6	57.2	37.2
80 - 84	136 606[23]	65 474[14]	71 119[14]	73.1	88.5	62.9
85 - 89	121 214[23]	51 664[14]	69 540[14]	119.7	137.6	109.1
90 +	109 870	40 145	69 693	190.9	216.4	178.7
90 - 94	72 719[23]	27 781[14]	44 936[14]	...	...	...
95 - 99	28 510[23]	9 697[14]	18 800[14]	...	...	...
100 +	8 641[23]	2 667[14]	5 957[14]	...	...	...
Unknown - Inconnu	3 509[23]	2 625[14]	709[14]	..	..	..
Chile - Chili						
2015 (C)						
Total	103 327	54 693[14]	48 615[14]	5.7	6.1	5.3
0	1 683	943[14]	721[14]	6.8	7.4	5.9
1 - 4	254	127[14]	127[14]	0.3	0.3	0.3
5 - 9	183	95[14]	88[14]	0.1	0.2	0.1
10 - 14	205	109[14]	96[14]	0.2	0.2	0.2
15 - 19	621	449[14]	172[14]	0.5	0.7	0.3
20 - 24	871	659[14]	212[14]	0.6	0.9	0.3
25 - 29	1 098	828[14]	270[14]	0.7	1.1	0.4
30 - 34	1 114	823[14]	291[14]	0.8	1.2	0.4
35 - 39	1 423	943[14]	480[14]	1.1	1.5	0.8
40 - 44	2 044	1 348[14]	696[14]	1.6	2.2	1.1
45 - 49	2 959	1 889[14]	1 070[14]	2.4	3.0	1.7
50 - 54	4 495	2 891[14]	1 604[14]	3.7	4.8	2.6
55 - 59	5 825	3 634[14]	2 191[14]	5.5	7.1	4.1
60 - 64	7 118	4 430[14]	2 688[14]	8.7	11.2	6.3
65 - 69	9 079	5 485[14]	3 594[14]	14.1	18.2	10.6
70 - 74	10 987	6 457[14]	4 530[14]	22.5	29.3	16.9
75 - 79	12 309	6 703[14]	5 606[14]	35.9	46.1	28.4
80 +	41 059	16 880[14]	24 179[14]	106.7	125.4	96.6
80 - 84	14 149	6 972[14]	7 177[14]	...	...	...
85 - 89	14 058	5 937[14]	8 121[14]	...	...	...
90 - 94	8 664	2 949[14]	5 715[14]	...	...	...
95 - 99	3 383	864[14]	2 519[14]	...	...	...
100 +	805	158[14]	647[14]	...	...	...
Colombia - Colombie						
2016 (U)						
Total	223 078	123 806[14]	99 242[14]	...	...	...
0	7 220	4 074[14]	3 144[14]	...	...	...
1 - 4	1 625	869[14]	756[14]	...	...	...
5 - 9	874	480[14]	394[14]	...	...	...
10 - 14	1 079	607[14]	472[14]	...	...	...
15 - 19	3 830	2 901[14]	929[14]	...	...	...
20 - 24	5 554	4 520[14]	1 031[14]	...	...	...
25 - 29	5 393	4 232[14]	1 160[14]	...	...	...
30 - 34	5 331	3 978[14]	1 352[14]	...	...	...
35 - 39	5 199	3 583[14]	1 614[14]	...	...	...
40 - 44	5 443	3 471[14]	1 969[14]	...	...	...
45 - 49	6 951	4 112[14]	2 838[14]	...	...	...
50 - 54	9 274	5 335[14]	3 938[14]	...	...	...
55 - 59	12 253	7 225[14]	5 028[14]	...	...	...
60 - 64	15 109	8 770[14]	6 338[14]	...	...	...
65 - 69	17 532	10 157[14]	7 375[14]	...	...	...
70 - 74	20 343	11 522[14]	8 821[14]	...	...	...
75 - 79	24 981	13 517[14]	11 464[14]	...	...	...
80 - 84	27 212	13 479[14]	13 733[14]	...	...	...
85 - 89	25 415	11 826[14]	13 589[14]	...	...	...
90 - 94	14 902	6 222[14]	8 680[14]	...	...	...
95 - 99	5 947	2 263[14]	3 684[14]	...	...	...

19. Deaths by age and sex and age-specific death rates by sex: latest available year, 2008 - 2017
Décès et taux de mortalité selon l'âge et le sexe : dernière année disponible, 2008 - 2017 (continued - suite)

Continent, country or area, date, code[a] and age (in years) Continent, pays ou zone, date, code[a] et âge (en années)	Number - Nombre			Rate - Taux		
	Both sexes Les deux sexes	Male Masculin	Female Féminin	Both sexes Les deux sexes	Male Masculin	Female Féminin
AMERICA, SOUTH - AMÉRIQUE DU SUD						
Colombia - Colombie						
2016 (U)						
100 +	1 397	484[14]	913[14]	...	...	...
Unknown - Inconnu	214	179[14]	20[14]	..	..	..
Ecuador - Équateur[24]						
2016 (U)						
Total	67 506	36 905	30 601	...	...	...
0	3 042	1 677	1 365	...	...	...
1 - 4	802	456	346	...	...	...
5 - 9	514	295	219	...	...	...
10 - 14	514	288	226	...	...	...
15 - 19	1 114	727	387	...	...	...
20 - 24	1 516	1 140	376	...	...	...
25 - 29	1 528	1 101	427	...	...	...
30 - 34	1 667	1 169	498	...	...	...
35 - 39	1 734	1 154	580	...	...	...
40 - 44	1 805	1 133	672	...	...	...
45 - 49	2 156	1 283	873	...	...	...
50 - 54	2 818	1 648	1 170	...	...	...
55 - 59	3 512	2 025	1 487	...	...	...
60 - 64	4 383	2 446	1 937	...	...	...
65 - 69	4 947	2 710	2 237	...	...	...
70 - 74	5 548	3 069	2 479	...	...	...
75 - 79	6 396	3 492	2 904	...	...	...
80 - 84	7 408	3 878	3 530	...	...	...
85 - 89	7 441	3 632	3 809	...	...	...
90 - 94	5 500	2 403	3 097	...	...	...
95 - 99	2 416	934	1 482	...	...	...
100 +	743	244	499	...	...	...
Unknown - Inconnu	2	1	1	..	..	..
Paraguay						
2016 (+U)						
Total	27 243	15 413[14]	11 807[14]	...	...	...
0	485	273[14]	211[14]	...	...	...
1 - 4	172	95[14]	77[14]	...	...	...
5 - 9	127	72[14]	55[14]	...	...	...
10 - 14	178	110[14]	68[14]	...	...	...
15 - 19	469	335[14]	134[14]	...	...	...
20 - 24	571	415[14]	156[14]	...	...	...
25 - 29	536	374[14]	162[14]	...	...	...
30 - 34	559	375[14]	183[14]	...	...	...
35 - 39	606	389[14]	217[14]	...	...	...
40 - 44	698	445[14]	253[14]	...	...	...
45 - 49	991	629[14]	361[14]	...	...	...
50 - 54	1 400	880[14]	520[14]	...	...	...
55 - 59	1 726	1 096[14]	629[14]	...	...	...
60 - 64	2 078	1 296[14]	779[14]	...	...	...
65 - 69	2 381	1 416[14]	963[14]	...	...	...
70 - 74	2 732	1 588[14]	1 137[14]	...	...	...
75 - 79	3 155	1 764[14]	1 389[14]	...	...	...
80 - 84	2 807	1 418[14]	1 389[14]	...	...	...
85 +	5 550	2 432[14]	3 115[14]	...	...	...
Unknown - Inconnu	22	11[14]	9[14]	..	..	..
Peru - Pérou[25]						
2016* (+U)						
Total	97 897	52 463	45 434	...	...	...
0	3 616	2 048	1 568	...	...	...
1 - 4	1 215	673	542	...	...	...
5 - 9	685	382	303	...	...	...
10 - 14	618	314	304	...	...	...
15 - 19	1 175	726	449	...	...	...
20 - 24	1 673	1 139	534	...	...	...
25 - 29	1 841	1 290	551	...	...	...
30 - 34	2 047	1 317	730	...	...	...
35 - 39	2 283	1 454	829	...	...	...
40 - 44	2 651	1 583	1 068	...	...	...

19. Deaths by age and sex and age-specific death rates by sex: latest available year, 2008 - 2017
Décès et taux de mortalité selon l'âge et le sexe : dernière année disponible, 2008 - 2017 (continued - suite)

Continent, country or area, date, code[a] and age (in years) Continent, pays ou zone, date, code[a] et âge (en années)	Number - Nombre			Rate - Taux		
	Both sexes Les deux sexes	Male Masculin	Female Féminin	Both sexes Les deux sexes	Male Masculin	Female Féminin

AMERICA, SOUTH - AMÉRIQUE DU SUD

Peru - Pérou[25]
2016* (+U)

45 - 49	3 366	1 943	1 423	...	...	...
50 - 54	4 075	2 251	1 824	...	...	...
55 - 59	4 969	2 776	2 193	...	...	...
60 - 64	6 155	3 408	2 747	...	...	...
65 - 69	7 269	3 989	3 280	...	...	...
70 - 74	8 440	4 609	3 831	...	...	...
75 - 79	10 307	5 523	4 784	...	...	...
80 - 84	12 287	6 399	5 888	...	...	...
85 - 89	11 689	5 697	5 992	...	...	...
90 - 94	7 386	3 298	4 088	...	...	...
95 - 99	3 076	1 213	1 863	...	...	...
100 +	726	244	482	...	...	...
Unknown - Inconnu	348	187	161	..	..	..

Suriname
2016 (C)

Total	3 591	2 017	1 574	6.2	7.0	5.5
0	170	97	73	17.2	18.8	15.4
1 - 4	21	12	9	◆0.5	◆0.5	◆0.4
5 - 9	17	7	10	◆0.3	◆0.3	◆0.4
10 - 14	11	5	6	◆0.2	◆0.2	◆0.3
15 - 19	45	25	20	0.9	◆1.0	◆0.8
20 - 24	56	35	21	1.2	1.5	◆0.9
25 - 29	78	53	25	1.7	2.4	◆1.1
30 - 34	99	59	40	2.3	2.8	1.9
35 - 39	101	63	38	2.5	3.1	1.9
40 - 44	122	74	48	3.2	3.9	2.5
45 - 49	160	104	56	4.4	5.7	3.1
50 - 54	257	166	91	8.0	10.4	5.6
55 - 59	311	198	113	11.3	14.7	8.1
60 - 64	308	205	103	14.0	19.4	9.0
65 - 69	294	165	129	18.0	21.7	14.7
70 - 74	345	186	159	28.7	34.2	24.2
75 - 79	385	184	201	47.9	52.5	44.4
80 +	811	379	432	102.0	115.9	92.3
80 - 84	376	186	190	...	...	...
85 - 89	262	133	129	...	...	...
90 - 94	119	42	77	...	...	...
95 - 99	45	15	30	...	...	...
100 +	9	3	6	...	...	...

Uruguay
2016 (C)

Total	34 273	17 212[14]	17 050[14]	9.8	10.2	9.5
0	376	219[14]	156[14]	8.2	9.4	7.0
1 - 4	52	34[14]	18[14]	0.3	0.4	◆0.2
5 - 9	33	18[14]	15[14]	0.1	◆0.1	◆0.1
10 - 14	36	24[14]	12[14]	0.1	◆0.2	◆0.1
15 - 19	169	129[14]	40[14]	0.6	0.9	0.3
20 - 24	268	200[14]	68[14]	1.0	1.5	0.5
25 - 29	246	196[14]	50[14]	1.0	1.5	0.4
30 - 34	276	193[14]	83[14]	1.2	1.6	0.7
35 - 39	347	210[14]	137[14]	1.4	1.8	1.1
40 - 44	446	287[14]	159[14]	1.9	2.5	1.4
45 - 49	591	366[14]	225[14]	2.8	3.6	2.1
50 - 54	1 039	688[14]	351[14]	5.1	7.0	3.3
55 - 59	1 506	930[14]	576[14]	7.7	10.0	5.6
60 - 64	2 268	1 425[14]	842[14]	13.4	18.1	9.3
65 - 69	2 764	1 789[14]	975[14]	19.5	28.0	12.5
70 - 74	3 527	2 100[14]	1 427[14]	29.9	41.5	21.2
75 - 79	4 291	2 301[14]	1 990[14]	45.9	62.0	35.3
80 - 84	5 244	2 467[14]	2 776[14]	74.9	98.6	61.7
85 - 89	5 429	2 086[14]	3 340[14]	125.4	153.3	112.5
90 +	5 082	1 438[14]	3 644[14]	225.5	242.1	219.6
90 - 94	3 498	1 090[14]	2 408[14]	...	...	...

Continent, country or area, date, code[a] and age (in years)	Number - Nombre			Rate - Taux		
Continent, pays ou zone, date, code[a] et âge (en années)	Both sexes Les deux sexes	Male Masculin	Female Féminin	Both sexes Les deux sexes	Male Masculin	Female Féminin
AMERICA, SOUTH - AMÉRIQUE DU SUD						
Uruguay						
2016 (C)						
95 +	1 584	348[14]	1 236[14]	...	...	...
Unknown - Inconnu	283	112[14]	166[14]	..	..	..
Venezuela (Bolivarian Republic of) - Venezuela (République bolivarienne du)						
2016 (C)						
Total	185 697	113 747	71 950	...	...	...
0	11 783	6 897	4 886	...	...	...
1 - 4	1 759	938	821	...	...	...
5 - 9	820	472	348	...	...	...
10 - 14	1 072	661	411	...	...	...
15 - 19	5 434	4 630	804	...	...	...
20 - 24	9 136	8 076	1 060	...	...	...
25 - 29	7 532	6 396	1 136	...	...	...
30 - 34	6 074	4 723	1 351	...	...	...
35 - 39	5 660	4 002	1 658	...	...	...
40 - 44	5 602	3 738	1 864	...	...	...
45 - 49	6 640	4 345	2 295	...	...	...
50 - 54	8 797	5 498	3 299	...	...	...
55 - 59	11 256	7 095	4 161	...	...	...
60 - 64	14 011	8 619	5 392	...	...	...
65 - 69	15 006	9 169	5 837	...	...	...
70 - 74	15 095	9 069	6 026	...	...	...
75 - 79	15 995	9 081	6 914	...	...	...
80 - 84	16 360	8 527	7 833	...	...	...
85 - 89	14 716	6 785	7 931	...	...	...
90 - 94	8 748	3 539	5 209	...	...	...
95 - 99	3 366	1 214	2 152	...	...	...
100 +	835	273	562	...	...	...
ASIA - ASIE						
Armenia - Arménie						
2016 (C)						
Total	28 226	14 536	13 690	9.4	10.2	8.7
0	352	213	139	8.6	9.9	7.2
1 - 4	56	33	23	0.3	0.4	◆0.3
5 - 9	45	28	17	0.2	◆0.3	◆0.2
10 - 14	31	19	12	0.2	◆0.2	◆0.1
15 - 19	138	127	11	0.8	1.4	◆0.1
20 - 24	137	107	30	0.6	1.0	◆0.3
25 - 29	170	119	51	0.6	0.9	0.4
30 - 34	201	139	62	0.8	1.1	0.5
35 - 39	255	174	81	1.2	1.7	0.7
40 - 44	398	280	118	2.2	3.4	1.2
45 - 49	620	429	191	3.7	5.6	2.1
50 - 54	1 264	901	363	6.3	10.0	3.3
55 - 59	2 063	1 415	648	9.5	14.5	5.4
60 - 64	2 446	1 583	863	15.1	22.4	9.5
65 - 69	2 500	1 519	981	22.5	32.6	15.2
70 - 74	2 028	1 086	942	36.0	47.8	28.1
75 - 79	5 363	2 530	2 833	61.8	76.4	52.8
80 - 84	4 785	2 041	2 744	95.5	106.8	88.6
85 +	5 374	1 793	3 581	195.6	184.5	201.6
85 - 89	3 957	1 450	2 507	...	...	...
90 - 94	1 152	287	865	...	...	...
95 - 99	198	37	161	...	...	...
100 +	67	19	48	...	...	...
Azerbaijan - Azerbaïdjan[26]						
2016 (+C)						
Total	56 648	29 924	26 724	5.8	6.2	5.5
0	1 666	999	667	10.2	11.5	8.8
1 - 4	426	260	166	0.6	0.7	0.5
5 - 9	229	134	95	0.3	0.3	0.3
10 - 14	174	104	70	0.3	0.3	0.2

Continent, country or area, date, code[a] and age (in years) / Continent, pays ou zone, date, code[a] et âge (en années)	Number - Nombre			Rate - Taux		
	Both sexes Les deux sexes	Male Masculin	Female Féminin	Both sexes Les deux sexes	Male Masculin	Female Féminin
ASIA - ASIE						
Azerbaijan - Azerbaïdjan[26]						
2016 (+C)						
15 - 19	363	250	113	0.5	0.7	0.4
20 - 24	581	393	188	0.7	0.9	0.5
25 - 29	587	401	186	0.6	0.9	0.4
30 - 34	645	419	226	0.8	1.0	0.5
35 - 39	774	545	229	1.1	1.5	0.6
40 - 44	1 178	814	364	1.9	2.7	1.1
45 - 49	1 955	1 299	656	3.0	4.2	1.9
50 - 54	3 464	2 312	1 152	5.3	7.4	3.3
55 - 59	5 010	3 247	1 763	8.4	11.4	5.7
60 - 64	5 357	3 337	2 020	14.6	19.5	10.2
65 - 69	5 264	3 099	2 165	22.7	29.8	16.9
70 - 74	3 874	2 010	1 864	36.8	45.1	30.7
75 - 79	9 180	4 160	5 020	62.7	70.0	57.7
80 - 84	8 616	3 597	5 019	106.5	111.2	103.3
85 - 89	5 109	1 964	3 145	156.1	152.6	158.4
90 - 94	1 569	490	1 079	195.8	168.1	211.7
95 - 99	419	69	350	156.2	89.4	183.2
100 +	208	21	187	318.0	♦172.1	351.5
Bahrain - Bahreïn[27]						
2016 (C)						
Total	2 858	1 682	1 176	2.0	1.9	2.2
0 - 4	136	63	73	1.3	1.2	1.5
0	109	53	56	...	...	...
1 - 4	27	10	17	...	...	...
5 - 9	17	7	10	♦0.2	♦0.1	♦0.2
10 - 14	13	7	6	♦0.2	♦0.2	♦0.1
15 - 19	27	18	9	♦0.4	♦0.5	♦0.2
20 - 24	59	47	12	0.5	0.7	♦0.3
25 - 29	78	63	15	0.4	0.5	♦0.2
30 - 34	90	71	19	0.4	0.5	♦0.3
35 - 39	110	84	26	0.7	0.8	♦0.5
40 - 44	124	88	36	1.0	1.1	0.9
45 - 49	160	105	55	1.7	1.7	1.7
50 - 54	181	123	58	2.5	2.8	2.1
55 - 59	239	165	74	4.6	5.2	3.7
60 - 64	259	149	110	8.8	8.5	9.2
65 - 69	239	148	91	15.8	17.0	14.2
70 - 74	238	121	117	27.0	26.8	27.2
75 +	888	423	465	69.8	70.8	68.9
Brunei Darussalam - Brunéi Darussalam						
2016 (+C)						
Total	1 632	890	742	3.9	4.2	3.7
0	52	25	27	13.4	♦12.0	♦15.0
1 - 4	13	9	4	♦0.5	♦0.7	♦0.3
5 - 9	9	6	3	♦0.3	♦0.4	♦0.2
10 - 14	8	6	2	♦0.2	♦0.3	♦0.1
15 - 19	10	6	4	♦0.3	♦0.3	♦0.2
20 - 24	19	15	4	♦0.5	♦0.7	♦0.2
25 - 29	33	18	15	0.8	♦0.8	♦0.8
30 - 34	39	25	14	1.1	♦1.3	♦0.8
35 - 39	57	38	19	1.7	2.1	♦1.1
40 - 44	72	45	27	2.3	2.9	♦1.8
45 - 49	100	60	40	3.6	4.4	2.9
50 - 54	125	85	40	5.4	7.3	3.5
55 - 59	149	85	64	7.7	9.0	6.5
60 - 64	137	68	69	9.4	9.6	9.2
65 - 69	137	74	63	15.3	17.4	13.4
70 - 74	153	77	76	30.0	30.4	29.7
75 - 79	157	76	81	41.5	43.8	39.6
80 - 84	180	86	94	81.6	88.3	76.3
85 - 89	113	58	55	111.3	116.5	106.4
90 - 94	48	23	25	121.2	♦125.0	♦117.9
95 - 99	19	5	14	♦153.2	♦78.1	♦233.3
100 +	2	-	2	♦80.0	-	♦133.3

Continent, country or area, date, code[a] and age (in years)	Number - Nombre			Rate - Taux		
Continent, pays ou zone, date, code[a] et âge (en années)	Both sexes Les deux sexes	Male Masculin	Female Féminin	Both sexes Les deux sexes	Male Masculin	Female Féminin
ASIA - ASIE						
China - Chine[28]						
2010 (|)						
Total	7 421 990	4 293 783	3 128 207	5.6	6.3	4.8
0	60 217	32 026	28 191	4.4	4.3	4.5
1 - 4	39 591	23 119	16 472	0.6	0.7	0.6
5 - 9	21 183	13 621	7 562	0.3	0.4	0.2
10 - 14	23 088	15 243	7 845	0.3	0.4	0.2
15 - 19	40 469	28 088	12 381	0.4	0.5	0.3
20 - 24	62 552	43 738	18 814	0.5	0.7	0.3
25 - 29	60 661	42 497	18 164	0.6	0.8	0.4
30 - 34	79 960	55 804	24 156	0.8	1.1	0.5
35 - 39	140 531	98 382	42 149	1.2	1.6	0.7
40 - 44	216 353	149 111	67 242	1.7	2.3	1.1
45 - 49	262 531	179 446	83 085	2.5	3.3	1.6
50 - 54	337 397	226 888	110 509	4.3	5.6	2.9
55 - 59	494 339	324 817	169 522	6.1	7.9	4.2
60 - 64	586 160	377 069	209 091	10.0	12.6	7.3
65 - 69	695 662	435 007	260 655	16.9	21.0	12.8
70 - 74	999 653	599 394	400 259	30.3	36.5	24.2
75 - 79	1 162 694	657 140	505 554	48.7	58.3	40.2
80 - 84	1 081 704	553 704	528 000	80.9	93.6	70.8
85 - 89	686 462	306 678	379 784	121.9	139.4	110.7
90 - 94	279 569	104 048	175 521	177.1	196.0	167.6
95 - 99	74 729	23 292	51 437	202.0	197.9	203.9
100 +	16 485	4 671	11 814	458.8	527.7	436.2
China, Hong Kong SAR - Chine, Hong Kong RAS						
2017 (C)						
Total	46 829	25 982[14]	20 846[14]	6.3	7.7	5.2
0	97	50	47	1.8	1.8	1.8
1 - 4	26	15	11	♦0.1	♦0.1	♦0.1
5 - 9	24	18	6	♦0.1	♦0.1	-
10 - 14	25	15	10	♦0.1	♦0.1	♦0.1
15 - 19	62	45	17	0.2	0.3	♦0.1
20 - 24	117	71	46	0.3	0.3	0.2
25 - 29	162	104	58	0.3	0.5	0.2
30 - 34	199	115	84	0.3	0.5	0.2
35 - 39	351	211	140	0.6	0.9	0.4
40 - 44	534	314	220	0.9	1.3	0.7
45 - 49	882	491	391	1.5	2.1	1.2
50 - 54	1 532	903	629	2.4	3.2	1.8
55 - 59	2 317	1 521	796	3.7	5.0	2.5
60 - 64	3 041	2 033	1 008	5.8	7.9	3.8
65 - 69	3 723	2 489	1 234	9.0	12.2	5.9
70 - 74	3 620	2 456	1 164	14.5	19.7	9.3
75 - 79	4 978	3 268	1 710	25.1	33.4	17.1
80 - 84	7 374	4 294	3 080	43.0	56.1	32.5
85 +	17 707	7 526	10 181	96.7	118.7	85.1
Unknown - Inconnu	58	43[14]	14[14]	..	..	..
China, Macao SAR - Chine, Macao RAS						
2017 (C)						
Total	2 120	1 252	868	...	...	...
0 - 19	25	12	13	...	...	...
20 - 24	16	13	3	...	...	...
25 - 29	12	8	4	...	...	...
30 - 34	20	17	3	...	...	...
35 - 39	19	14	5	...	...	...
40 - 44	34	26	8	...	...	...
45 - 49	49	31	18	...	...	...
50 - 54	94	69	25	...	...	...
55 - 59	153	107	46	...	...	...
60 - 64	225	147	78	...	...	...
65 - 69	235	176	59	...	...	...
70 - 74	188	135	53	...	...	...
75 - 79	166	119	47	...	...	...
80 - 84	247	137	110	...	...	...
85 +	637	241	396	...	...	...

19. Deaths by age and sex and age-specific death rates by sex: latest available year, 2008 - 2017
Décès et taux de mortalité selon l'âge et le sexe : dernière année disponible, 2008 - 2017 (continued - suite)

Continent, country or area, date, code[a] and age (in years) Continent, pays ou zone, date, code[a] et âge (en années)	Number - Nombre			Rate - Taux		
	Both sexes Les deux sexes	Male Masculin	Female Féminin	Both sexes Les deux sexes	Male Masculin	Female Féminin

ASIA - ASIE

Cyprus - Chypre[29]
2016 (C)

Total	5 471	2 926	2 545	6.4	7.1	5.8
0	25	15	10	◆2.7	◆3.1	◆2.3
1 - 4	2	-	2	◆0.1	-	◆0.1
5 - 9	6	4	2	◆0.1	◆0.2	◆0.1
10 - 14	4	2	2	◆0.1	◆0.1	◆0.1
15 - 19	12	10	2	◆0.2	◆0.4	◆0.1
20 - 24	16	13	3	◆0.2	◆0.4	◆0.1
25 - 29	14	10	4	◆0.2	◆0.3	◆0.1
30 - 34	20	15	5	◆0.3	◆0.5	◆0.1
35 - 39	35	28	7	0.6	◆1.0	◆0.2
40 - 44	46	30	16	0.8	◆1.2	◆0.5
45 - 49	84	55	29	1.6	2.1	◆1.0
50 - 54	126	77	49	2.3	2.9	1.7
55 - 59	205	145	60	4.0	5.7	2.3
60 - 64	261	165	96	5.7	7.3	4.1
65 - 69	392	252	140	9.0	12.0	6.3
70 - 74	515	326	189	16.3	21.8	11.3
75 - 79	762	453	309	30.4	39.1	23.0
80 - 84	974	530	444	59.8	76.5	47.4
85 - 89	1 017	446	571	123.5	135.2	115.7
90 - 94	668	259	409	216.9	235.5	206.6
95 - 99	245	79	166	522.4	506.4	530.4
100 +	42	12	30	446.8	◆240.0	◆681.8

Democratic People's Republic of Korea - République populaire démocratique de Corée[15]
2008 (|)

Total	216 616	112 827	103 789	9.0	9.6	8.4
0	6 686	3 593	3 093	19.6	20.6	18.5
1 - 4	2 552	1 372	1 180	1.9	2.0	1.8
5 - 9	1 680	960	720	0.9	1.0	0.8
10 - 14	1 614	869	745	0.8	0.8	0.8
15 - 19	2 426	1 348	1 078	1.2	1.3	1.1
20 - 24	3 171	1 922	1 249	1.7	2.0	1.4
25 - 29	3 528	2 160	1 368	2.0	2.4	1.6
30 - 34	3 907	2 424	1 483	2.3	2.8	1.8
35 - 39	5 792	3 655	2 137	2.6	3.3	1.9
40 - 44	6 312	3 907	2 405	3.1	3.9	2.4
45 - 49	6 468	3 915	2 553	4.1	5.1	3.2
50 - 54	7 630	4 715	2 915	5.8	7.4	4.3
55 - 59	11 295	7 113	4 182	12.5	16.8	8.7
60 - 64	26 360	16 815	9 545	24.9	35.3	16.4
65 - 69	34 068	22 281	11 787	37.3	58.7	22.1
70 - 74	34 093	18 886	15 207	51.5	82.7	35.0
75 - 79	28 690	10 991	17 699	85.5	138.7	69.1
80 +	30 344	5 901	24 443	163.8	238.8	152.3

Georgia - Géorgie[26]
2017 (C)

Total	47 822	24 423	23 399	12.9	13.7	12.1
0	512	278	234	9.1	9.7	8.5
1 - 4	82	49	33	0.4	0.4	0.3
5 - 9	55	34	21	0.2	0.3	◆0.2
10 - 14	57	37	20	0.3	0.3	◆0.2
15 - 19	103	67	36	0.5	0.6	0.4
20 - 24	202	162	40	0.9	1.4	0.4
25 - 29	298	238	60	1.1	1.7	0.4
30 - 34	315	234	81	1.2	1.7	0.6
35 - 39	521	415	106	2.1	3.4	0.8
40 - 44	809	620	189	3.3	5.2	1.5
45 - 49	1 159	865	294	4.9	7.6	2.4
50 - 54	1 814	1 343	471	7.1	11.2	3.5
55 - 59	2 899	2 105	794	11.2	17.8	5.7
60 - 64	3 439	2 315	1 124	15.6	23.9	9.1
65 - 69	4 346	2 795	1 551	24.0	37.1	14.7
70 - 74	3 702	2 119	1 583	37.1	54.5	26.0
75 - 79	8 541	4 054	4 487	62.1	81.7	51.0

534

19. Deaths by age and sex and age-specific death rates by sex: latest available year, 2008 - 2017
Décès et taux de mortalité selon l'âge et le sexe : dernière année disponible, 2008 - 2017 (continued - suite)

Continent, country or area, date, code[a] and age (in years) / Continent, pays ou zone, date, code[a] et âge (en années)	Number - Nombre			Rate - Taux		
	Both sexes Les deux sexes	Male Masculin	Female Féminin	Both sexes Les deux sexes	Male Masculin	Female Féminin
ASIA - ASIE						
Georgia - Géorgie[26]						
2017 (C)						
80 - 84	8 558	3 523	5 035	114.9	136.0	103.6
85 +	10 410	3 170	7 240	231.8	249.6	224.8
Indonesia - Indonésie[30]						
2010 (I)						
Total	1 236 154	687 976	548 178	5.2	5.8	4.6
0	106 846	61 546	45 300	24.3	27.2	21.2
1 - 4	37 689	20 958	16 731	2.1	2.2	1.9
5 - 9	19 409	10 807	8 602	0.8	0.9	0.8
10 - 14	15 382	9 029	6 353	0.7	0.8	0.6
15 - 19	23 642	14 948	8 694	1.1	1.4	0.8
20 - 24	27 089	16 020	11 069	1.4	1.6	1.1
25 - 29	31 020	17 855	13 165	1.5	1.7	1.2
30 - 34	31 290	17 168	14 122	1.6	1.7	1.4
35 - 39	38 257	20 382	17 875	2.1	2.2	1.9
40 - 44	49 757	26 901	22 856	3.0	3.2	2.8
45 - 49	65 139	36 351	28 788	4.6	5.2	4.1
50 - 54	89 078	51 820	37 258	7.7	8.8	6.5
55 - 59	86 308	53 355	32 953	10.2	12.1	8.1
60 - 64	105 991	62 663	43 328	17.5	21.4	13.8
65 - 69	107 730	62 508	45 222	23.0	28.1	18.3
70 - 74	138 235	76 159	62 076	40.0	49.7	32.2
75 - 79	92 062	49 343	42 719	46.5	58.6	37.6
80 - 84	86 057	42 547	43 510	75.3	88.4	65.8
85 +	85 173	37 616	47 557	119.4	133.2	110.3
Iran (Islamic Republic of) - Iran (République islamique d')[31]						
2016 (+U)						
Total	347 987	198 480	149 507	...	...	...
0	8 261	4 485	3 776	...	...	...
1 - 4	3 643	1 994	1 649	...	...	...
5 - 9	2 280	1 268	1 012	...	...	...
10 - 14	2 155	1 220	935	...	...	...
15 - 19	4 340	3 068	1 272	...	...	...
20 - 24	6 026	4 431	1 595	...	...	...
25 - 29	7 928	5 405	2 523	...	...	...
30 - 34	8 977	6 002	2 975	...	...	...
35 - 39	8 789	6 000	2 789	...	...	...
40 - 44	8 685	5 904	2 781	...	...	...
45 - 49	10 986	7 344	3 642	...	...	...
50 - 54	14 174	9 460	4 714	...	...	...
55 - 59	19 902	12 956	6 946	...	...	...
60 - 64	24 007	14 631	9 376	...	...	...
65 - 69	25 292	14 236	11 056	...	...	...
70 - 74	28 691	15 752	12 939	...	...	...
75 +	158 424	81 323	77 101	...	...	...
Unknown - Inconnu	5 427	3 001	2 426	...	..	...
Israel - Israël[32]						
2017 (C)						
Total	44 423	22 565	21 858	...	...	...
0	553	303	250	...	...	...
1 - 4	138	77	61	...	...	...
5 - 9	77	39	38	...	...	...
10 - 14	63	41	22	...	...	...
15 - 19	173	125	48	...	...	...
20 - 24	198	141	57	...	...	...
25 - 29	199	138	61	...	...	...
30 - 34	280	189	91	...	...	...
35 - 39	304	179	125	...	...	...
40 - 44	501	298	203	...	...	...
45 - 49	689	452	237	...	...	...
50 - 54	1 005	656	349	...	...	...
55 - 59	1 599	1 003	596	...	...	...
60 - 64	2 327	1 409	918	...	...	...
65 - 69	3 471	2 076	1 395	...	...	...
70 - 74	3 816	2 239	1 577	...	...	...

19. Deaths by age and sex and age-specific death rates by sex: latest available year, 2008 - 2017
Décès et taux de mortalité selon l'âge et le sexe : dernière année disponible, 2008 - 2017 (continued - suite)

Continent, country or area, date, code[a] and age (in years) / Continent, pays ou zone, date, code[a] et âge (en années)	Number - Nombre			Rate - Taux		
	Both sexes Les deux sexes	Male Masculin	Female Féminin	Both sexes Les deux sexes	Male Masculin	Female Féminin
ASIA - ASIE						
Israel - Israël[32]						
2017 (C)						
75 - 79	4 963	2 690	2 273	...	...	...
80 - 84	6 831	3 397	3 434	...	...	...
85 - 89	7 966	3 505	4 461	...	...	...
90 - 94	6 404	2 510	3 894	...	...	...
95 - 99	2 365	935	1 430	...	...	...
100 +	493	158	335	...	...	...
Unknown - Inconnu	8	5	3	..	..	..
Japan - Japon[33]						
2016 (C)						
Total	1 307 748	674 733	633 015	10.3	10.9	9.7
0 - 4	2 618	1 351	1 267	0.5	0.5	0.5
0	1 928	980	948			
1 - 4	690	371	319	...	...	...
5 - 9	391	229	162	0.1	0.1	0.1
10 - 14	440	254	186	0.1	0.1	0.1
15 - 19	1 166	816	350	0.2	0.3	0.1
20 - 24	2 083	1 471	612	0.3	0.5	0.2
25 - 29	2 479	1 713	766	0.4	0.5	0.2
30 - 34	3 354	2 226	1 128	0.5	0.6	0.3
35 - 39	5 193	3 282	1 911	0.6	0.8	0.5
40 - 44	9 263	5 835	3 428	0.9	1.2	0.7
45 - 49	13 923	8 888	5 035	1.5	1.9	1.1
50 - 54	19 480	12 526	6 954	2.5	3.1	1.8
55 - 59	28 331	19 068	9 263	3.8	5.1	2.4
60 - 64	48 223	33 464	14 759	5.9	8.3	3.5
65 - 69	93 505	65 077	28 428	9.1	13.1	5.4
70 - 74	107 826	72 534	35 292	14.6	21.0	8.9
75 - 79	153 008	97 102	55 906	23.7	33.9	15.6
80 - 84	223 763	127 978	95 785	43.4	61.5	31.2
85 - 89	260 536	124 528	136 008	80.2	112.3	63.6
90 - 94	209 379	70 767	138 612	143.4	190.2	127.4
95 - 99	95 935	21 273	74 662	252.5	317.5	238.5
100 +	26 427	4 015	22 412	400.4	446.1	393.2
Unknown - Inconnu	425	336	89	..	..	..
Kazakhstan						
2017 (U)						
Total	129 009	69 104	59 905	...	...	...
0	3 109	1 771	1 338	...	...	...
1 - 4	888	498	390	...	...	...
5 - 9	497	280	217	...	...	...
10 - 14	391	237	154	...	...	...
15 - 19	677	441	236	...	...	...
20 - 24	1 213	879	334	...	...	...
25 - 29	1 884	1 378	506	...	...	...
30 - 34	2 658	1 934	724	...	...	...
35 - 39	3 584	2 565	1 019	...	...	...
40 - 44	4 519	3 193	1 326	...	...	...
45 - 49	5 655	3 951	1 704	...	...	...
50 - 54	7 553	5 192	2 361	...	...	...
55 - 59	10 750	7 186	3 564	...	...	...
60 - 64	12 368	8 024	4 344	...	...	...
65 - 69	13 963	8 341	5 622	...	...	...
70 - 74	9 550	5 255	4 295	...	...	...
75 - 79	18 676	8 377	10 299	...	...	...
80 - 84	14 289	5 405	8 884	...	...	...
85 - 89	10 629	2 944	7 685	...	...	...
90 - 94	4 979	1 040	3 939	...	...	...
95 - 99	970	181	789	...	...	...
100 +	197	22	175	...	...	...
Unknown - Inconnu	10	10	-	..	..	..
Kuwait - Koweït						
2016 (C)						
Total	6 338	3 944	2 394	1.6	1.6	1.5
0	448	263	185	7.4	8.2	6.5
1 - 4	86	43	43	0.3	0.3	0.4

19. Deaths by age and sex and age-specific death rates by sex: latest available year, 2008 - 2017
Décès et taux de mortalité selon l'âge et le sexe : dernière année disponible, 2008 - 2017 (continued - suite)

Continent, country or area, date, code[a] and age (in years) Continent, pays ou zone, date, code[a] et âge (en années)	Number - Nombre			Rate - Taux		
	Both sexes Les deux sexes	Male Masculin	Female Féminin	Both sexes Les deux sexes	Male Masculin	Female Féminin
ASIA - ASIE						
Kuwait - Koweït						
2016 (C)						
5 - 9	51	36	15	0.2	0.2	♦0.1
10 - 14	57	33	24	0.2	0.2	♦0.2
15 - 19	83	65	18	0.4	0.5	♦0.2
20 - 24	152	127	25	0.8	1.1	♦0.3
25 - 29	178	145	33	0.6	0.9	0.2
30 - 34	197	153	44	0.4	0.5	0.2
35 - 39	253	191	62	0.5	0.6	0.4
40 - 44	327	260	67	0.6	0.8	0.4
45 - 49	429	329	100	1.2	1.4	0.9
50 - 54	444	346	98	1.8	2.1	1.2
55 - 59	488	343	145	3.0	3.1	2.9
60 - 64	488	329	159	5.1	5.1	5.1
65 - 69	501	262	239	10.0	8.3	12.9
70 - 74	513	270	243	20.2	18.7	22.2
75 - 79	551	279	272	37.4	33.4	42.6
80 +	948	412	536	76.3	61.7	93.3
80 - 84	451	197	254	...	...	...
85 - 89	312	144	168	...	...	...
90 - 94	132	52	80	...	...	...
95 +	53	19	34	...	...	...
Unknown - Inconnu	144	58	86	..	..	..
Kyrgyzstan - Kirghizstan						
2017 (C)						
Total	33 166	18 632	14 534	5.4	6.1	4.6
0	2 401	1 340	1 061	15.6	17.0	14.2
1 - 4	459	275	184	0.7	0.9	0.6
5 - 9	202	138	64	0.3	0.4	0.2
10 - 14	196	128	68	0.4	0.5	0.3
15 - 19	282	182	100	0.6	0.7	0.4
20 - 24	433	295	138	0.8	1.0	0.5
25 - 29	579	401	178	1.0	1.4	0.6
30 - 34	796	567	229	1.6	2.3	0.9
35 - 39	931	654	277	2.4	3.3	1.4
40 - 44	1 234	865	369	3.6	5.2	2.1
45 - 49	1 618	1 125	493	5.1	7.3	3.0
50 - 54	2 141	1 492	649	7.4	10.8	4.2
55 - 59	2 863	1 915	948	10.8	15.6	6.7
60 - 64	3 066	1 934	1 132	17.2	24.4	11.5
65 - 69	3 005	1 720	1 285	25.5	34.8	18.8
70 - 74	1 793	989	804	36.0	49.3	27.0
75 - 79	3 735	1 761	1 974	67.5	84.2	57.4
80 - 84	3 352	1 464	1 888	103.1	130.0	88.9
85 - 89	2 744	997	1 747	158.1	171.5	151.4
90 - 94	1 023	329	694	153.0	125.6	170.6
95 - 99	238	53	185	149.1	105.0	169.6
100 +	73	6	67	211.0	♦44.4	317.5
Unknown - Inconnu	2	2	-	..	..	..
Malaysia - Malaisie						
2016 (C)						
Total	162 201	93 698	68 503	5.1	5.7	4.5
0	3 390	1 862	1 528	6.3	6.7	5.9
1 - 4	743	398	345	0.4	0.4	0.3
5 - 9	578	338	240	0.2	0.3	0.2
10 - 14	733	486	247	0.3	0.4	0.2
15 - 19	2 032	1 611	421	0.7	1.1	0.3
20 - 24	2 466	1 860	606	0.8	1.1	0.4
25 - 29	2 340	1 680	660	0.7	1.0	0.4
30 - 34	3 242	2 240	1 002	1.2	1.5	0.8
35 - 39	3 974	2 755	1 219	1.8	2.3	1.2
40 - 44	5 228	3 573	1 655	2.7	3.6	1.8
45 - 49	7 133	4 810	2 323	4.1	5.5	2.7
50 - 54	10 353	6 798	3 555	6.5	8.4	4.6
55 - 59	13 630	8 682	4 948	10.1	12.7	7.5
60 - 64	16 122	10 129	5 993	15.5	19.3	11.6
65 - 69	17 650	10 685	6 965	22.5	27.5	17.5

19. Deaths by age and sex and age-specific death rates by sex: latest available year, 2008 - 2017
Décès et taux de mortalité selon l'âge et le sexe : dernière année disponible, 2008 - 2017 (continued - suite)

Continent, country or area, date, code[a] and age (in years) / Continent, pays ou zone, date, code[a] et âge (en années)	Number - Nombre			Rate - Taux		
	Both sexes Les deux sexes	Male Masculin	Female Féminin	Both sexes Les deux sexes	Male Masculin	Female Féminin
ASIA - ASIE						
Malaysia - Malaisie						
2016 (C)						
70 - 74	17 758	10 436	7 322	36.2	43.7	29.1
75 - 79	19 405	10 431	8 974	58.6	66.6	51.4
80 - 84	16 944	7 858	9 086	100.9	100.6	101.3
85 - 89	11 249	4 505	6 744	133.1	116.2	147.5
90 - 94	5 201	1 927	3 274	157.7	122.2	190.2
95 +	2 030	634	1 396	94.8	58.7	131.6
Maldives[34]						
2016 (C)						
Total	1 226	658	568	3.5	3.7	3.3
0	53	21	32	6.8	◆5.2	8.5
1 - 4	10	5	5	◆0.3	◆0.3	◆0.4
5 - 9	6	3	3	◆0.2	◆0.2	◆0.3
10 - 14	9	8	1	◆0.3	◆0.6	◆0.1
15 - 19	15	9	6	◆0.5	◆0.6	◆0.4
20 - 24	13	9	4	◆0.4	◆0.5	◆0.2
25 - 29	14	9	5	◆0.4	◆0.5	◆0.3
30 - 34	17	9	8	◆0.5	◆0.5	◆0.5
35 - 39	16	7	9	◆0.6	◆0.6	◆0.7
40 - 44	17	9	8	◆0.8	◆0.9	◆0.8
45 - 49	34	21	13	1.9	◆2.3	◆1.4
50 - 54	39	20	19	2.5	◆2.5	◆2.4
55 - 59	73	44	29	5.6	6.6	◆4.6
60 - 64	51	28	23	6.4	◆6.7	◆6.1
65 - 69	70	42	28	14.5	17.0	◆11.9
70 - 74	150	84	66	33.0	36.9	29.1
75 - 79	232	113	119	57.5	54.9	60.3
80 +	407	217	190	126.7	117.1	139.8
80 - 84	218	118	100	...	...	...
85 - 89	119	64	55	...	...	...
90 - 94	53	28	25	...	...	...
95 - 99	13	5	8	...	...	...
100 +	4	2	2	...	...	...
Mongolia - Mongolie						
2017 (+C)						
Total	17 357	10 571	6 786	5.5	6.8	4.2
0	1 009	572	437	13.0	14.3	11.6
1 - 4	228	120	108	0.7	0.7	0.7
5 - 9	126	83	43	0.4	0.5	0.3
10 - 14	96	58	38	0.4	0.5	0.3
15 - 19	183	122	61	0.8	1.0	0.5
20 - 24	271	192	79	1.1	1.5	0.6
25 - 29	373	264	109	1.2	1.7	0.7
30 - 34	543	390	153	1.9	2.8	1.1
35 - 39	703	530	173	2.9	4.5	1.4
40 - 44	985	775	210	4.6	7.4	1.9
45 - 49	1 246	911	335	6.8	10.4	3.5
50 - 54	1 635	1 160	475	10.2	15.6	5.5
55 - 59	1 845	1 268	577	14.8	22.7	8.4
60 - 64	1 593	1 028	565	20.7	30.9	12.9
65 - 69	1 346	742	604	29.6	39.8	22.5
70 - 74	1 260	687	573	40.5	54.2	31.1
75 - 79	1 445	739	706	62.3	78.0	51.5
80 - 84	1 172	508	664	94.7	116.3	82.8
85 - 89	759	282	477	136.1	170.5	121.6
90 - 94	361	101	260	210.1	227.0	204.2
95 - 99	144	36	108	305.1	480.0	272.0
100 +	34	3	31	430.4	◆250.0	462.7
Myanmar[35]						
2015 (+U)						
Total	225 526	132 606	92 920	...	...	...
0	9 849	5 468	4 381	...	...	...
1 - 4	2 110	1 116	994	...	...	...
5 - 9	1 968	1 073	895	...	...	...
10 - 14	1 751	946	805	...	...	...
15 - 19	3 068	1 903	1 165	...	...	...

Continent, country or area, date, code[a] and age (in years)	Number - Nombre			Rate - Taux		
Continent, pays ou zone, date, code[a] et âge (en années)	Both sexes Les deux sexes	Male Masculin	Female Féminin	Both sexes Les deux sexes	Male Masculin	Female Féminin
ASIA - ASIE						
Myanmar[35]						
2015 (+U)						
20 - 24	4 287	2 886	1 401	...	...	...
25 - 29	5 985	4 352	1 633	...	...	...
30 - 34	9 378	7 202	2 176	...	...	...
35 - 39	11 832	9 095	2 737	...	...	...
40 - 44	12 878	9 816	3 062	...	...	...
45 - 49	14 687	10 672	4 015	...	...	...
50 - 54	15 404	10 377	5 027	...	...	...
55 - 59	16 637	10 564	6 073	...	...	...
60 - 64	17 769	10 496	7 273	...	...	...
65 - 69	19 154	10 651	8 503	...	...	...
70 - 74	17 550	9 144	8 406	...	...	...
75 - 79	20 269	9 954	10 315	...	...	...
80 - 84	18 736	8 217	10 519	...	...	...
85 +	21 945	8 485	13 460	...	...	...
Unknown - Inconnu	269	189	80	..	..	...
Oman						
2017 (U)						
Total	8 861	5 619	3 242	...	...	...
0	850	450	400	...	...	...
1 - 4	178	104	74	...	...	...
5 - 9	97	50	47	...	...	...
10 - 14	89	50	39	...	...	...
15 - 19	115	80	35	...	...	...
20 - 24	255	212	43	...	...	...
25 - 29	333	275	58	...	...	...
30 - 34	384	304	80	...	...	...
35 - 39	352	272	80	...	...	...
40 - 44	352	277	75	...	...	...
45 - 49	344	279	65	...	...	...
50 - 54	419	315	104	...	...	...
55 - 59	553	388	165	...	...	...
60 - 64	575	366	209	...	...	...
65 - 69	688	384	304	...	...	...
70 - 74	835	459	376	...	...	...
75 - 79	899	499	400	...	...	...
80 - 84	736	431	305	...	...	...
85 - 89	455	250	205	...	...	...
90 - 94	208	108	100	...	...	...
95 - 99	96	47	49	...	...	...
100 +	48	19	29	...	...	...
Philippines						
2016 (C)						
Total	582 183	334 678	247 505	5.6	6.4	4.8
0 - 4	31 004	17 471	13 533	2.7	3.0	2.4
0	21 874	12 566	9 308	...	...	...
1 - 4	9 130	4 905	4 225	...	...	...
5 - 9	5 395	2 944	2 451	0.5	0.5	0.5
10 - 14	4 637	2 708	1 929	0.4	0.5	0.4
15 - 19	7 922	5 121	2 801	0.8	1.0	0.6
20 - 24	11 583	8 043	3 540	1.2	1.6	0.7
25 - 29	13 641	9 765	3 876	1.6	2.2	0.9
30 - 34	15 659	10 957	4 702	2.1	2.9	1.3
35 - 39	19 439	13 190	6 249	2.9	3.8	1.9
40 - 44	23 348	15 500	7 848	3.9	5.1	2.6
45 - 49	31 066	20 549	10 517	5.7	7.5	3.9
50 - 54	38 786	25 329	13 457	8.3	10.8	5.8
55 - 59	45 860	29 879	15 981	12.0	15.8	8.3
60 - 64	53 206	34 113	19 093	18.4	24.4	12.8
65 - 69	57 687	35 595	22 092	27.8	37.1	19.8
70 - 74	55 132	31 660	23 472	41.5	55.0	31.1
75 - 79	56 419	29 107	27 312	63.4	81.5	51.3
80 +	111 110	42 548	68 562	137.0	146.8	131.6
80 - 84	50 596	22 055	28 541	...	...	...
85 - 89	34 942	12 913	22 029	...	...	...
90 - 94	18 077	5 453	12 624	...	...	...

19. Deaths by age and sex and age-specific death rates by sex: latest available year, 2008 - 2017
Décès et taux de mortalité selon l'âge et le sexe : dernière année disponible, 2008 - 2017 (continued - suite)

Continent, country or area, date, code[a] and age (in years) / Continent, pays ou zone, date, code[a] et âge (en années)	Number - Nombre			Rate - Taux		
	Both sexes Les deux sexes	Male Masculin	Female Féminin	Both sexes Les deux sexes	Male Masculin	Female Féminin
ASIA - ASIE						
Philippines						
2016 (C)						
95 +	7 495	2 127	5 368	...	...	...
Unknown - Inconnu	289	199	90	..	..	..
Qatar						
2016 (C)						
Total	2 347	1 747	600	0.9	0.9	0.9
0	161	82	79	6.0	6.0	6.1
1 - 4	29	16	13	♦0.3	♦0.3	♦0.2
5 - 9	22	11	11	♦0.2	♦0.2	♦0.2
10 - 14	17	13	4	♦0.2	♦0.3	♦0.1
15 - 19	34	27	7	0.4	♦0.5	♦0.2
20 - 24	114	106	8	0.4	0.5	♦0.2
25 - 29	152	140	12	0.3	0.4	♦0.1
30 - 34	166	138	28	0.4	0.4	♦0.3
35 - 39	170	146	24	0.5	0.6	♦0.3
40 - 44	136	113	23	0.5	0.6	♦0.5
45 - 49	181	155	26	1.0	1.1	♦0.8
50 - 54	158	132	26	1.5	1.5	♦1.2
55 - 59	189	151	38	2.7	2.7	2.6
60 - 64	171	115	56	5.2	4.7	6.7
65 - 69	151	103	48	10.3	10.0	11.1
70 - 74	144	86	58	21.4	21.0	21.8
75 - 79	114	74	40	28.6	33.1	22.9
80 +	237	138	99	71.5	81.5	61.0
80 - 84	135	77	58	...	...	...
85 - 89	55	32	23	...	...	...
90 - 94	29	19	10	...	...	...
95 +	18	10	8	...	...	...
Unknown - Inconnu	1	1	-	..	..	..
Republic of Korea - République de Corée[36]						
2017 (C)						
Total	285 534	154 328	131 206	5.6	6.0	5.1
0	1 000	569	431	2.4	2.7	2.2
1 - 4	261	139	122	0.1	0.2	0.1
5 - 9	210	134	76	0.1	0.1	0.1
10 - 14	197	115	82	0.1	0.1	0.1
15 - 19	626	424	202	0.2	0.3	0.1
20 - 24	1 087	750	337	0.3	0.4	0.2
25 - 29	1 384	953	431	0.4	0.5	0.3
30 - 34	1 849	1 153	696	0.5	0.6	0.4
35 - 39	3 062	1 983	1 079	0.8	0.9	0.5
40 - 44	4 680	3 089	1 591	1.1	1.5	0.8
45 - 49	8 022	5 647	2 375	1.8	2.5	1.1
50 - 54	11 260	8 296	2 964	2.7	3.9	1.4
55 - 59	16 431	12 359	4 072	3.9	5.9	1.9
60 - 64	17 721	13 059	4 662	5.6	8.4	2.9
65 - 69	19 942	14 172	5 770	8.7	12.9	4.9
70 - 74	26 828	17 571	9 257	15.3	21.9	9.7
75 - 79	43 132	25 446	17 686	28.9	41.0	20.2
80 - 84	50 618	24 679	25 939	54.3	75.0	43.1
85 - 89	42 481	15 111	27 370	99.5	129.8	88.2
90 - 94	24 706	6 634	18 072	177.0	211.2	167.0
95 - 99	8 329	1 777	6 552	267.8	283.4	263.9
100 +	1 667	252	1 415	469.4	499.0	464.5
Unknown - Inconnu	41	16	25	..	..	..
Saudi Arabia - Arabie saoudite[37]						
2016 (I)						
Total	58 097	35 497	22 600	1.8	1.9	1.7
0 - 4	5 084	2 273	2 811	1.9	1.7	2.1
5 - 9	1 033	577	456	0.4	0.4	0.3
10 - 14	2 125	1 206	919	0.9	1.0	0.8
15 - 19	1 487	1 368	119	0.7	1.2	0.1
20 - 24	4 859	3 146	1 713	2.0	2.4	1.5
25 - 29	3 926	2 673	1 253	1.3	1.6	0.9
30 - 34	2 106	1 582	524	0.7	0.9	0.4
35 - 39	3 232	2 207	1 025	1.0	1.0	0.8

19. Deaths by age and sex and age-specific death rates by sex: latest available year, 2008 - 2017
Décès et taux de mortalité selon l'âge et le sexe : dernière année disponible, 2008 - 2017 (continued - suite)

Continent, country or area, date, code[a] and age (in years) / Continent, pays ou zone, date, code[a] et âge (en années)	Number - Nombre			Rate - Taux		
	Both sexes Les deux sexes	Male Masculin	Female Féminin	Both sexes Les deux sexes	Male Masculin	Female Féminin
ASIA - ASIE						
Saudi Arabia - Arabie saoudite[37]						
2016 (|)						
40 - 44	2 714	2 027	687	0.9	1.0	0.6
45 - 49	2 629	1 233	1 396	1.2	0.8	1.8
50 - 54	3 031	2 571	460	1.9	2.4	0.9
55 - 59	3 901	2 404	1 497	3.6	3.3	4.0
60 - 64	2 895	1 844	1 051	4.0	4.1	3.8
65 - 69	2 547	1 181	1 366	6.3	5.4	7.4
70 - 74	4 186	2 922	1 264	15.5	20.7	9.8
75 - 79	1 846	709	1 137	11.5	8.3	14.9
80 + ...	10 496	5 574	4 922	54.6	58.1	51.1
80 - 84	4 678	1 900	2 778	...	...	...
85 + ...	5 818	3 674	2 144	...	...	...
Singapore - Singapour						
2017 (+C)						
Total	20 905	11 363	9 542	5.3	5.8	4.7
0 - 4	116	54	62	0.6	0.6	0.7
0	94	44	50	...	...	...
1 - 4	22	10	12	...	...	...
5 - 9	13	8	5	♦0.1	♦0.1	♦0.1
10 - 14	25	12	13	♦0.1	♦0.1	♦0.1
15 - 19	55	37	18	0.2	0.3	♦0.2
20 - 24	94	67	27	0.4	0.5	♦0.2
25 - 29	139	99	40	0.5	0.7	0.3
30 - 34	148	100	48	0.5	0.8	0.3
35 - 39	205	135	70	0.7	0.9	0.4
40 - 44	325	222	103	1.0	1.5	0.6
45 - 49	492	304	188	1.6	2.1	1.2
50 - 54	869	541	328	2.8	3.5	2.1
55 - 59	1 232	759	473	4.1	5.0	3.1
60 - 64	1 739	1 116	623	6.6	8.5	4.7
65 - 69	2 121	1 346	775	10.4	13.5	7.4
70 - 74	2 139	1 365	774	17.9	24.2	12.3
75 - 79	2 764	1 567	1 197	30.1	38.7	23.3
80 - 84	3 013	1 511	1 502	55.4	67.5	47.0
85 + ...	5 416	2 120	3 296	115.4	133.0	106.3
85 - 89	2 843	1 249	1 594	...	...	...
90 - 94	1 682	641	1 041	...	...	...
95 - 99	702	190	512	...	...	...
100 + ...	189	40	149	...	...	...
Sri Lanka						
2013 (+C)						
Total	127 183	72 410	54 773	6.2	7.3	5.2
0 - 4	3 573	2 022	1 551	2.0	2.3	1.8
0	3 043	1 712	1 331	...	...	...
1 - 4	530	310	220	...	...	...
5 - 9	395	220	175	0.2	0.2	0.2
10 - 14	446	263	183	0.3	0.3	0.2
15 - 19	1 021	680	341	0.6	0.8	0.4
20 - 24	1 377	950	427	0.9	1.3	0.5
25 - 29	1 395	984	411	0.9	1.3	0.5
30 - 34	1 713	1 200	513	1.0	1.5	0.6
35 - 39	1 981	1 419	562	1.4	2.1	0.8
40 - 44	2 728	1 880	848	2.0	2.8	1.2
45 - 49	4 438	3 104	1 334	3.4	5.0	2.0
50 - 54	6 770	4 681	2 089	5.5	8.0	3.2
55 - 59	8 576	5 818	2 758	8.0	11.5	4.9
60 - 64	11 459	7 452	4 007	12.4	17.4	8.1
65 - 69	13 617	8 327	5 290	21.4	29.0	15.2
70 - 74	14 993	8 508	6 485	36.3	46.7	28.1
75 - 79	16 137	8 284	7 853	56.4	71.4	46.2
80 + ...	36 480	16 562	19 918	135.1	154.8	121.5
80 - 84	15 980	7 671	8 309	...	...	...
85 - 89	12 427	5 605	6 822	...	...	...
90 - 94	5 516	2 306	3 210	...	...	...
95 - 99	2 081	807	1 274	...	...	...

19. Deaths by age and sex and age-specific death rates by sex: latest available year, 2008 - 2017
Décès et taux de mortalité selon l'âge et le sexe : dernière année disponible, 2008 - 2017 (continued - suite)

Continent, country or area, date, code[a] and age (in years) / Continent, pays ou zone, date, code[a] et âge (en années)	Number - Nombre			Rate - Taux		
	Both sexes Les deux sexes	Male Masculin	Female Féminin	Both sexes Les deux sexes	Male Masculin	Female Féminin
ASIA - ASIE						
Sri Lanka						
2013 (+C)						
100 +	476	173	303	...	...	...
Unknown - Inconnu	84	56	28	..		..
State of Palestine - État de Palestine[38]						
2015 (U)						
Total	11 908	6 424	5 484	...	...	...
0	852	457	395	...	...	...
1 - 4	333	172	161	...	...	...
5 - 9	139	85	54	...	...	...
10 - 14	94	66	28	...	...	...
15 - 19	197	144	53	...	...	...
20 - 24	243	186	57	...	...	...
25 - 29	157	108	49	...	...	...
30 - 34	162	102	60	...	...	...
35 - 39	218	145	73	...	...	...
40 - 44	249	160	89	...	...	...
45 - 49	344	205	139	...	...	...
50 - 54	575	356	219	...	...	...
55 - 59	774	481	293	...	...	...
60 - 64	907	553	354	...	...	...
65 - 69	1 109	612	497	...	...	...
70 - 74	1 216	589	627	...	...	...
75 - 79	1 414	675	739	...	...	...
80 - 84	1 309	611	698	...	...	...
85 - 89	980	443	537	...	...	...
90 - 94	426	180	246	...	...	...
95 - 99	142	61	81	...	...	...
100 +	68	33	35	...	...	...
Tajikistan - Tadjikistan[26]						
2016 (U)						
Total	34 134	19 072	15 062	...	...	...
0	2 729	1 621	1 108	...	...	...
1 - 4	606	321	285	...	...	...
5 - 9	231	130	101	...	...	...
10 - 14	223	135	88	...	...	...
15 - 19	378	226	152	...	...	...
20 - 24	563	357	206	...	...	...
25 - 29	710	407	303	...	...	...
30 - 34	733	434	299	...	...	...
35 - 39	793	498	295	...	...	...
40 - 44	987	613	374	...	...	...
45 - 49	1 270	766	504	...	...	...
50 - 54	1 715	1 024	691	...	...	...
55 - 59	2 587	1 530	1 057	...	...	...
60 - 64	2 843	1 628	1 215	...	...	...
65 - 69	3 140	1 712	1 428	...	...	...
70 - 74	2 542	1 539	1 003	...	...	...
75 - 79	4 408	2 428	1 980	...	...	...
80 - 84	3 826	1 918	1 908	...	...	...
85 - 89	2 559	1 273	1 286	...	...	...
90 - 94	895	387	508	...	...	...
95 - 99	273	90	183	...	...	...
100 +	73	10	63	...	...	...
Unknown - Inconnu	50	25	25	..		..
Thailand - Thaïlande[39]						
2016 (+U)						
Total	469 085	265 439	203 646	...	...	...
0	4 233	2 360	1 873	...	...	...
1 - 4	1 627	976	651	...	...	...
5 - 9	1 225	726	499	...	...	...
10 - 14	1 856	1 197	659	...	...	...
15 - 19	4 953	3 793	1 160	...	...	...
20 - 24	5 697	4 400	1 297	...	...	...
25 - 29	6 214	4 718	1 496	...	...	...
30 - 34	8 662	6 512	2 150	...	...	...
35 - 39	13 424	9 882	3 542	...	...	...

Continent, country or area, date, code[a] and age (in years) Continent, pays ou zone, date, code[a] et âge (en années)	Number - Nombre			Rate - Taux		
	Both sexes Les deux sexes	Male Masculin	Female Féminin	Both sexes Les deux sexes	Male Masculin	Female Féminin
ASIA - ASIE						
Thailand - Thaïlande[39]						
2016 (+U)						
40 - 44	18 282	13 395	4 887	...	...	...
45 - 49	24 131	16 806	7 325	...	...	...
50 - 54	30 478	20 509	9 969	...	...	...
55 - 59	35 171	22 996	12 175	...	...	...
60 - 64	39 411	24 348	15 063	...	...	...
65 - 69	42 972	25 136	17 836	...	...	...
70 +	230 742	107 681	123 061	...	...	...
Unknown - Inconnu	7	4	3	..	..	..
Turkey - Turquie[40]						
2016 (C)						
Total	422 135	231 200	190 935	5.3	5.8	4.8
0	13 036	7 069	5 967	10.4	11.0	9.7
1 - 4	2 806	1 514	1 292	0.5	0.6	0.5
5 - 9	1 419	842	577	0.2	0.3	0.2
10 - 14	1 514	921	593	0.2	0.3	0.2
15 - 19	3 200	2 343	857	0.5	0.7	0.3
20 - 24	3 745	2 871	874	0.6	0.9	0.3
25 - 29	3 757	2 827	930	0.6	0.9	0.3
30 - 34	4 013	2 848	1 165	0.6	0.9	0.4
35 - 39	5 219	3 439	1 780	0.8	1.1	0.6
40 - 44	6 909	4 474	2 435	1.2	1.6	0.9
45 - 49	9 608	6 371	3 237	2.0	2.6	1.4
50 - 54	16 824	11 477	5 347	3.5	4.8	2.3
55 - 59	22 029	15 228	6 801	5.9	8.2	3.7
60 - 64	32 712	22 109	10 603	9.8	13.5	6.2
65 - 69	38 826	24 775	14 051	16.1	21.9	11.0
70 - 74	46 389	27 307	19 082	27.6	35.8	20.8
75 - 79	57 672	30 294	27 378	48.0	59.1	39.7
80 - 84	68 042	33 472	34 570	84.1	99.6	73.1
85 - 89	54 156	21 530	32 626	134.8	158.0	122.9
90 - 94	24 122	8 121	16 001	198.1	236.9	182.9
95 - 99	4 864	1 174	3 690	265.2	308.8	253.9
100 +	1 273	194	1 079	243.3	287.8	236.7
Uzbekistan - Ouzbékistan[26]						
2015 (+C)						
Total	152 035	83 051	68 984	4.9	5.3	4.4
0	8 320	4 906	3 414	11.9	13.5	10.2
1 - 4	2 482	1 389	1 093	1.0	1.0	0.9
5 - 9	951	587	364	0.3	0.4	0.2
10 - 14	926	553	373	0.4	0.4	0.3
15 - 19	1 767	1 024	743	0.6	0.7	0.5
20 - 24	2 515	1 498	1 017	0.8	0.9	0.6
25 - 29	3 033	1 913	1 120	1.0	1.2	0.7
30 - 34	3 308	2 094	1 214	1.3	1.6	0.9
35 - 39	4 039	2 595	1 444	1.9	2.4	1.3
40 - 44	4 881	3 175	1 706	2.5	3.3	1.8
45 - 49	6 444	4 065	2 379	3.9	5.1	2.8
50 - 54	9 571	5 975	3 596	6.0	7.8	4.4
55 - 59	13 015	8 107	4 908	10.2	13.2	7.4
60 - 64	14 102	8 298	5 804	16.9	21.0	13.2
65 - 69	12 940	7 241	5 699	27.7	33.5	22.8
70 - 74	12 364	6 771	5 593	44.5	52.1	37.8
75 - 79	19 560	9 743	9 817	71.1	81.9	62.8
80 - 84	15 514	6 969	8 545	120.7	141.7	107.7
85 +	16 113	6 002	10 111	123.7	127.2	121.8
Unknown - Inconnu	190	146	44	..	..	..
EUROPE						
Åland Islands - Îles d'Åland						
2016 (C)						
Total	297	152	145	10.2	10.5	9.9
0	1	1	-	♦3.5	♦6.8	-
1 - 4	-	-	-	-	-	-

Continent, country or area, date, code[a] and age (in years) Continent, pays ou zone, date, code[a] et âge (en années)	Number - Nombre			Rate - Taux		
	Both sexes Les deux sexes	Male Masculin	Female Féminin	Both sexes Les deux sexes	Male Masculin	Female Féminin
EUROPE						
Åland Islands - Îles d'Åland						
2016 (C)						
5 - 9	-	-	-	-	-	-
10 - 14	-	-	-	-	-	-
15 - 19	1	1	-	♦0.6	♦1.2	-
20 - 24	-	-	-	-	-	-
25 - 29	2	1	1	♦1.2	♦1.1	♦1.2
30 - 34	3	2	1	♦1.7	♦2.3	♦1.2
35 - 39	3	2	1	♦1.7	♦2.2	♦1.2
40 - 44	2	1	1	♦1.1	♦1.0	♦1.1
45 - 49	6	3	3	♦2.9	♦2.9	♦2.9
50 - 54	4	3	1	♦1.9	♦2.9	♦1.0
55 - 59	8	6	2	♦4.1	♦6.5	♦2.0
60 - 64	13	8	5	♦6.4	♦8.2	♦4.7
65 - 69	26	17	9	♦13.2	♦17.5	♦9.1
70 - 74	24	16	8	♦15.2	♦20.0	♦10.3
75 - 79	34	17	17	32.7	♦33.7	♦31.7
80 - 84	40	22	18	52.2	♦66.1	♦41.5
85 - 89	61	33	28	130.3	180.3	♦98.2
90 - 94	50	14	36	227.3	♦237.3	223.6
95 - 99	16	5	11	♦290.9	♦625.0	♦234.0
100 +	3	-	3	♦600.0	-	♦750.0
Albania - Albanie						
2016 (C)						
Total	21 388	11 283	10 105	7.4	7.7	7.1
0	277	146	131	8.6	8.7	8.5
1 - 4	48	23	25	0.4	♦0.3	♦0.4
5 - 9	28	17	11	♦0.2	♦0.2	♦0.1
10 - 14	46	25	21	0.2	♦0.2	♦0.2
15 - 19	88	47	41	0.4	0.4	0.4
20 - 24	88	57	31	0.3	0.4	0.3
25 - 29	118	78	40	0.5	0.6	0.4
30 - 34	116	77	39	0.6	0.8	0.4
35 - 39	176	114	62	1.1	1.4	0.8
40 - 44	230	149	81	1.4	1.8	0.9
45 - 49	398	255	143	2.1	2.8	1.5
50 - 54	609	409	200	3.0	4.1	2.0
55 - 59	970	657	313	4.9	6.7	3.1
60 - 64	1 256	804	452	7.8	10.1	5.6
65 - 69	1 610	1 031	579	12.9	16.7	9.1
70 - 74	2 261	1 342	919	23.0	27.6	18.5
75 - 79	3 674	2 015	1 659	44.9	51.2	39.1
80 - 84	4 050	2 102	1 948	89.1	98.2	81.0
85 +	5 345	1 935	3 410	238.5	213.4	255.6
85 - 89	3 127	1 333	1 794	...	...	...
90 - 94	1 456	451	1 005	...	...	...
95 - 99	575	129	446	...	...	...
100 +	187	22	165	...	...	...
Andorra - Andorre						
2015 (C)						
Total	282	151	131	...	...	...
0	-	-	-	...	...	...
1 - 4	-	-	-	...	...	...
5 - 9	1	1	-	...	...	...
10 - 14	-	-	-	...	...	...
15 - 19	-	-	-	...	...	...
20 - 24	1	1	-	...	...	...
25 - 29	1	-	1	...	...	...
30 - 34	2	1	1	...	...	...
35 - 39	5	2	3	...	...	...
40 - 44	4	3	1	...	...	...
45 - 49	1	1	-	...	...	...
50 - 54	15	6	9	...	...	...
55 - 59	14	10	4	...	...	...
60 - 64	11	9	2	...	...	...
65 - 69	27	22	5	...	...	...
70 - 74	17	11	6	...	...	...

19. Deaths by age and sex and age-specific death rates by sex: latest available year, 2008 - 2017
Décès et taux de mortalité selon l'âge et le sexe : dernière année disponible, 2008 - 2017 (continued - suite)

Continent, country or area, date, code[a] and age (in years) / Continent, pays ou zone, date, code[a] et âge (en années)	Number - Nombre			Rate - Taux		
	Both sexes Les deux sexes	Male Masculin	Female Féminin	Both sexes Les deux sexes	Male Masculin	Female Féminin
EUROPE						
Andorra - Andorre						
2015 (C)						
75 - 79	30	16	14	...	...	...
80 - 84	41	22	19	...	...	...
85 - 89	55	24	31	...	...	...
90 - 94	41	17	24	...	...	...
95 - 99	13	4	9	...	...	...
100 +	3	1	2	...	...	...
Austria - Autriche[41]						
2016 (C)						
Total	80 669	39 022	41 647	9.2	9.1	9.4
0	269	152	117	3.2	3.5	2.8
1 - 4	50	30	20	0.1	♦0.2	♦0.1
5 - 9	34	16	18	0.1	♦0.1	♦0.1
10 - 14	33	14	19	0.1	♦0.1	♦0.1
15 - 19	138	92	46	0.3	0.4	0.2
20 - 24	197	152	45	0.4	0.5	0.2
25 - 29	226	160	66	0.4	0.5	0.2
30 - 34	308	215	93	0.5	0.7	0.3
35 - 39	369	239	130	0.7	0.8	0.5
40 - 44	616	380	236	1.0	1.3	0.8
45 - 49	1 202	783	419	1.7	2.3	1.2
50 - 54	2 016	1 281	735	2.8	3.6	2.1
55 - 59	3 064	1 992	1 072	5.0	6.6	3.5
60 - 64	3 977	2 576	1 401	8.0	10.8	5.5
65 - 69	5 932	3 757	2 175	13.2	17.7	9.2
70 - 74	7 448	4 482	2 966	19.6	25.9	14.4
75 - 79	10 377	5 921	4 456	29.3	38.0	22.5
80 - 84	11 810	5 841	5 969	56.0	69.8	46.9
85 - 89	15 421	6 362	9 059	107.7	128.9	96.6
90 - 94	12 833	3 582	9 251	198.9	223.4	190.8
95 - 99	3 752	884	2 868	315.3	375.3	300.5
100 +	597	111	486	489.7	598.4	470.2
Belarus - Bélarus						
2016 (C)						
Total	119 379	59 315	60 064	12.6	13.4	11.8
0	373	206	167	3.1	3.4	2.9
1 - 4	112	72	40	0.2	0.3	0.2
5 - 9	80	48	32	0.2	0.2	0.1
10 - 14	61	33	28	0.1	0.1	♦0.1
15 - 19	177	114	63	0.4	0.5	0.3
20 - 24	374	305	69	0.7	1.0	0.2
25 - 29	707	545	162	0.9	1.4	0.4
30 - 34	1 178	878	300	1.5	2.3	0.8
35 - 39	1 691	1 240	451	2.5	3.6	1.3
40 - 44	2 312	1 706	606	3.5	5.4	1.8
45 - 49	3 382	2 515	867	5.3	8.3	2.6
50 - 54	5 528	4 115	1 413	7.9	12.6	3.8
55 - 59	8 542	6 119	2 423	11.6	18.4	6.0
60 - 64	10 384	7 393	2 991	17.5	29.6	8.7
65 - 69	11 777	7 755	4 022	25.1	42.1	14.1
70 - 74	9 416	5 207	4 209	36.9	58.8	25.2
75 - 79	17 908	8 088	9 820	56.7	86.2	44.3
80 - 84	18 310	6 366	11 944	95.0	129.9	83.1
85 - 89	17 534	4 756	12 778	156.7	190.8	146.9
90 - 94	7 874	1 534	6 340	235.8	255.7	231.5
95 - 99	1 399	274	1 125	317.6	365.8	307.7
100 +	260	46	214	301.4	351.1	292.5
Belgium - Belgique[42]						
2016 (C)						
Total	108 097	53 326	54 771	9.5	9.6	9.5
0	387	247	140	3.2	4.0	2.3
1 - 4	77	32	45	0.2	0.1	0.2
5 - 9	64	41	23	0.1	0.1	♦0.1
10 - 14	43	29	14	0.1	♦0.1	-
15 - 19	151	100	51	0.2	0.3	0.2
20 - 24	265	199	66	0.4	0.6	0.2

19. Deaths by age and sex and age-specific death rates by sex: latest available year, 2008 - 2017
Décès et taux de mortalité selon l'âge et le sexe : dernière année disponible, 2008 - 2017 (continued - suite)

Continent, country or area, date, code[a] and age (in years) Continent, pays ou zone, date, code[a] et âge (en années)	Number - Nombre			Rate - Taux		
	Both sexes Les deux sexes	Male Masculin	Female Féminin	Both sexes Les deux sexes	Male Masculin	Female Féminin
EUROPE						
Belgium - Belgique[42]						
2016 (C)						
25 - 29	356	245	111	0.5	0.7	0.3
30 - 34	456	313	143	0.6	0.9	0.4
35 - 39	601	400	201	0.8	1.1	0.5
40 - 44	950	627	323	1.3	1.7	0.9
45 - 49	1 577	951	626	2.0	2.4	1.6
50 - 54	2 666	1 620	1 046	3.3	3.9	2.6
55 - 59	4 006	2 522	1 484	5.2	6.6	3.9
60 - 64	5 862	3 688	2 174	8.6	11.0	6.3
65 - 69	7 799	4 980	2 819	12.8	16.9	9.0
70 - 74	8 820	5 423	3 397	19.2	25.2	13.9
75 - 79	12 328	7 115	5 213	31.9	41.9	24.1
80 - 84	18 073	9 154	8 919	56.9	71.8	46.9
85 - 89	21 611	9 037	12 574	106.4	128.9	94.5
90 - 94	16 169	5 299	10 870	191.8	225.0	178.9
95 - 99	4 994	1 174	3 820	311.2	342.0	302.9
100 +	842	130	712	466.0	493.4	461.3
Bosnia and Herzegovina - Bosnie-Herzégovine						
2010 (C)						
Total	35 118	17 900	17 218	9.1	9.5	8.8
0 - 4	252	143	109	1.5	1.7	1.3
0	216	125	91	6.5	7.3	5.6
1 - 4	36	18	18	0.3	♦0.3	♦0.3
5 - 9	28	19	9	♦0.1	♦0.2	♦0.1
10 - 14	27	14	13	♦0.1	♦0.1	♦0.1
15 - 19	84	58	26	0.3	0.4	♦0.2
20 - 24	120	92	28	0.4	0.6	♦0.2
25 - 29	165	130	35	0.6	1.0	0.3
30 - 34	160	109	51	0.7	0.9	0.4
35 - 39	254	180	74	1.0	1.5	0.6
40 - 44	432	265	167	1.5	1.9	1.2
45 - 49	844	553	291	2.7	3.7	1.9
50 - 54	1 465	980	485	5.5	7.2	3.7
55 - 59	2 141	1 429	712	9.2	13.6	5.6
60 - 64	2 610	1 647	963	14.3	19.1	10.0
65 - 69	3 390	2 032	1 358	16.8	22.6	12.1
70 - 74	6 045	3 199	2 846	32.8	38.8	27.9
75 - 79	6 948	3 344	3 604	57.7	66.1	51.6
80 - 84	6 006	2 440	3 566	125.3	124.5	125.9
85 +	4 119	1 254	2 865	164.3	175.6	159.9
85 - 89	3 105	966	2 139	...	...	...
90 - 94	737	210	527	...	...	...
95 - 99	245	69	176	...	...	...
100 +	32	9	23	...	...	...
Unknown - Inconnu	28	12	16	..	..	..
Bulgaria - Bulgarie						
2016 (C)						
Total	107 580	56 122	51 458	15.1	16.2	14.0
0	423	258	165	6.5	7.7	5.2
1 - 4	68	33	35	0.3	0.2	0.3
5 - 9	56	29	27	0.2	♦0.2	♦0.2
10 - 14	56	37	19	0.2	0.2	♦0.1
15 - 19	141	96	45	0.5	0.6	0.3
20 - 24	217	167	50	0.6	0.9	0.3
25 - 29	335	234	101	0.7	1.0	0.4
30 - 34	474	331	143	1.0	1.3	0.6
35 - 39	804	585	219	1.5	2.2	0.9
40 - 44	1 323	916	407	2.5	3.3	1.6
45 - 49	2 251	1 524	727	4.4	5.9	2.9
50 - 54	3 420	2 392	1 028	7.2	10.0	4.3
55 - 59	5 607	3 898	1 709	11.4	16.2	6.8
60 - 64	8 261	5 622	2 639	16.7	24.5	10.0
65 - 69	11 295	7 373	3 922	23.1	34.4	14.3
70 - 74	12 460	7 264	5 196	33.8	47.6	24.1
75 - 79	15 148	7 557	7 591	55.1	71.1	45.0
80 - 84	19 635	8 497	11 138	95.5	113.3	85.2

Continent, country or area, date, code[a] and age (in years) Continent, pays ou zone, date, code[a] et âge (en années)	Number - Nombre			Rate - Taux		
	Both sexes Les deux sexes	Male Masculin	Female Féminin	Both sexes Les deux sexes	Male Masculin	Female Féminin
EUROPE						
Bulgaria - Bulgarie						
2016 (C)						
85 - 89	16 114	6 128	9 986	165.9	182.0	157.4
90 - 94	7 928	2 680	5 248	274.9	293.4	266.3
95 - 99	1 387	436	951	395.2	413.5	387.4
100 +	177	65	112	607.2	718.2	557.2
Croatia - Croatie						
2016 (C)						
Total	51 542	25 344	26 198	12.3	12.6	12.1
0	161	82	79	4.4	4.4	4.4
1 - 4	22	14	8	◆0.1	◆0.2	◆0.1
5 - 9	23	14	9	◆0.1	◆0.1	◆0.1
10 - 14	21	15	6	◆0.1	◆0.1	◆0.1
15 - 19	70	58	12	0.3	0.5	◆0.1
20 - 24	98	78	20	0.4	0.6	◆0.2
25 - 29	115	86	29	0.4	0.7	◆0.2
30 - 34	170	125	45	0.6	0.9	0.3
35 - 39	246	171	75	0.9	1.2	0.5
40 - 44	397	284	113	1.4	2.0	0.8
45 - 49	696	485	211	2.5	3.5	1.5
50 - 54	1 308	919	389	4.4	6.3	2.6
55 - 59	2 261	1 599	662	7.4	10.8	4.2
60 - 64	3 529	2 459	1 070	11.9	17.3	7.0
65 - 69	4 530	2 955	1 575	18.0	25.9	11.4
70 - 74	4 901	2 904	1 997	27.5	38.7	19.4
75 - 79	8 032	4 171	3 861	45.9	60.8	36.2
80 - 84	10 623	4 444	6 179	84.7	102.3	75.3
85 - 89	8 970	3 134	5 836	149.8	174.4	139.3
90 - 94	4 342	1 120	3 222	248.0	278.7	238.9
95 - 99	914	199	715	379.6	429.8	367.6
100 +	113	28	85	634.8	◆777.8	598.6
Czechia - Tchéquie						
2016 (C)						
Total	107 750	54 880	52 870	10.2	10.6	9.8
0	317	182	135	2.8	3.2	2.5
1 - 4	72	37	35	0.2	0.2	0.2
5 - 9	43	24	19	0.1	◆0.1	◆0.1
10 - 14	51	26	25	0.1	◆0.1	◆0.1
15 - 19	129	88	41	0.3	0.4	0.2
20 - 24	268	208	60	0.5	0.7	0.2
25 - 29	345	247	98	0.5	0.7	0.3
30 - 34	455	313	142	0.6	0.8	0.4
35 - 39	772	515	257	0.9	1.2	0.6
40 - 44	1 215	815	400	1.4	1.8	0.9
45 - 49	1 707	1 148	559	2.4	3.2	1.6
50 - 54	2 639	1 788	851	3.8	5.1	2.5
55 - 59	4 322	2 956	1 366	6.7	9.3	4.2
60 - 64	7 749	5 269	2 480	10.8	15.3	6.7
65 - 69	11 918	7 740	4 178	17.2	24.2	11.2
70 - 74	13 616	8 217	5 399	26.5	36.8	18.6
75 - 79	13 695	7 384	6 311	41.3	55.2	31.9
80 - 84	16 806	7 546	9 260	72.9	90.5	62.9
85 - 89	18 245	6 636	11 609	133.3	155.1	123.4
90 - 94	10 900	3 160	7 740	226.9	259.9	215.7
95 - 99	2 202	532	1 670	340.2	400.2	324.7
100 +	284	49	235	397.8	292.5	430.0
Denmark - Danemark[43]						
2016 (C)						
Total	52 824	26 416	26 408	9.2	9.3	9.2
0	194	114	80	3.2	3.7	2.7
1 - 4	34	21	13	0.1	◆0.2	◆0.1
5 - 9	29	13	16	◆0.1	◆0.1	◆0.1
10 - 14	19	11	8	◆0.1	◆0.1	-
15 - 19	58	28	30	0.2	◆0.2	◆0.2
20 - 24	137	88	49	0.4	0.4	0.3
25 - 29	143	97	46	0.4	0.5	0.3
30 - 34	149	99	50	0.5	0.6	0.3

Continent, country or area, date, code[a] and age (in years) / Continent, pays ou zone, date, code[a] et âge (en années)	Number - Nombre			Rate - Taux		
	Both sexes Les deux sexes	Male Masculin	Female Féminin	Both sexes Les deux sexes	Male Masculin	Female Féminin
EUROPE						
Denmark - Danemark[43]						
2016 (C)						
35 - 39	238	154	84	0.7	0.9	0.5
40 - 44	412	266	146	1.1	1.4	0.7
45 - 49	751	471	280	1.9	2.3	1.4
50 - 54	1 306	777	529	3.2	3.7	2.6
55 - 59	2 073	1 290	783	5.7	7.1	4.3
60 - 64	3 104	1 863	1 241	9.2	11.2	7.3
65 - 69	4 574	2 745	1 829	13.5	16.6	10.6
70 - 74	6 274	3 665	2 609	20.6	25.0	16.6
75 - 79	6 857	3 745	3 112	34.8	41.3	29.3
80 - 84	8 094	4 095	3 999	63.3	75.1	54.5
85 - 89	8 466	3 772	4 694	112.9	135.2	99.7
90 - 94	6 628	2 333	4 295	194.5	235.1	177.8
95 - 99	2 758	687	2 071	313.9	363.5	300.4
100 +	526	82	444	484.3	539.5	475.4
Estonia - Estonie						
2016 (C)						
Total	15 392	7 335	8 057	11.7	11.9	11.5
0	33	22	11	2.3	♦3.0	♦1.6
1 - 4	7	3	4	♦0.1	♦0.1	♦0.1
5 - 9	11	6	5	♦0.1	♦0.2	♦0.1
10 - 14	8	5	3	♦0.1	♦0.1	♦0.1
15 - 19	30	14	16	♦0.5	♦0.5	♦0.6
20 - 24	61	40	21	0.8	1.1	♦0.6
25 - 29	85	62	23	0.9	1.2	♦0.5
30 - 34	130	92	38	1.4	1.9	0.8
35 - 39	162	112	50	1.8	2.4	1.1
40 - 44	193	148	45	2.1	3.2	1.0
45 - 49	290	215	75	3.3	5.0	1.7
50 - 54	468	343	125	5.4	8.3	2.8
55 - 59	778	549	229	8.7	13.4	4.8
60 - 64	1 074	751	323	12.9	20.5	6.9
65 - 69	1 368	907	461	18.3	29.8	10.4
70 - 74	1 410	830	580	26.4	41.6	17.3
75 - 79	2 164	1 114	1 050	38.7	61.5	27.8
80 - 84	2 480	973	1 507	67.4	94.0	57.0
85 - 89	2 700	778	1 922	120.2	146.9	111.9
90 - 94	1 506	312	1 194	195.5	226.9	188.7
95 - 99	380	56	324	340.8	384.9	334.2
100 +	54	3	51	426.9	♦193.5	459.5
Faeroe Islands - Îles Féroé						
2017 (C)						
Total	446	228	218	8.9	8.8	9.0
0	6	2	4	♦8.6	♦6.0	♦11.0
1 - 4	-	-	-	-	-	-
5 - 9	-	-	-	-	-	-
10 - 14	-	-	-	-	-	-
15 - 19	-	-	-	-	-	-
20 - 24	1	1	-	♦0.3	♦0.6	-
25 - 29	1	-	1	♦0.4	-	♦0.8
30 - 34	-	-	-	-	-	-
35 - 39	-	-	-	-	-	-
40 - 44	1	1	-	♦0.3	♦0.6	-
45 - 49	2	2	-	♦0.6	♦1.2	-
50 - 54	12	8	4	♦3.5	♦4.4	♦2.5
55 - 59	17	11	6	♦5.5	♦7.0	♦3.9
60 - 64	22	14	8	♦7.7	♦9.5	♦5.8
65 - 69	38	26	12	13.9	♦18.6	♦8.9
70 - 74	37	26	11	16.9	♦22.3	♦10.7
75 - 79	53	24	29	33.7	♦30.8	♦36.5
80 - 84	73	50	23	68.7	103.3	♦39.8
85 - 89	77	35	42	107.2	124.6	96.1
90 - 94	65	18	47	200.6	♦204.5	199.2
95 - 99	38	10	28	584.6	♦588.2	♦583.3
100 +	3	-	3	♦272.7	-	♦333.3

19. Deaths by age and sex and age-specific death rates by sex: latest available year, 2008 - 2017
Décès et taux de mortalité selon l'âge et le sexe : dernière année disponible, 2008 - 2017 (continued - suite)

Continent, country or area, date, code[a] and age (in years) / Continent, pays ou zone, date, code[a] et âge (en années)	Number - Nombre			Rate - Taux		
	Both sexes Les deux sexes	Male Masculin	Female Féminin	Both sexes Les deux sexes	Male Masculin	Female Féminin
EUROPE						
Finland - Finlande						
2016 (C)						
Total	53 923	26 922	27 001	9.9	10.0	9.7
0	100	59	41	1.8	2.1	1.5
1 - 4	23	11	12	◆0.1	◆0.1	◆0.1
5 - 9	29	15	14	◆0.1	◆0.1	◆0.1
10 - 14	30	16	14	◆0.1	◆0.1	◆0.1
15 - 19	81	53	28	0.3	0.3	◆0.2
20 - 24	170	116	54	0.5	0.7	0.3
25 - 29	206	153	53	0.6	0.9	0.3
30 - 34	238	174	64	0.7	1.0	0.4
35 - 39	312	234	78	0.9	1.3	0.5
40 - 44	386	281	105	1.2	1.7	0.7
45 - 49	696	477	219	2.0	2.7	1.3
50 - 54	1 242	868	374	3.3	4.6	2.0
55 - 59	1 810	1 222	588	5.0	6.8	3.2
60 - 64	3 038	2 033	1 005	8.2	11.3	5.3
65 - 69	4 643	3 084	1 559	12.3	17.0	8.0
70 - 74	5 093	3 167	1 926	19.1	25.6	13.5
75 - 79	6 438	3 678	2 760	31.6	41.8	23.9
80 - 84	8 306	4 203	4 103	57.7	74.4	46.9
85 - 89	10 536	4 230	6 306	111.9	138.0	99.4
90 - 94	7 556	2 239	5 317	199.7	235.9	187.5
95 - 99	2 618	549	2 069	345.5	386.8	336.0
100 +	372	60	312	475.7	491.8	472.7
France[44]						
2012 (C)						
Total	559 227	281 468	277 759	8.8	9.1	8.5
0 - 4	3 174	1 788	1 386	0.8	0.9	0.7
0	2 643	1 479	1 164	3.4	3.8	3.1
1 - 4	531	309	222	0.2	0.2	0.1
5 - 9	298	162	136	0.1	0.1	0.1
10 - 14	365	199	166	0.1	0.1	0.1
15 - 19	1 032	729	303	0.3	0.4	0.2
20 - 24	1 751	1 301	450	0.5	0.7	0.2
25 - 29	2 003	1 468	535	0.5	0.8	0.3
30 - 34	2 485	1 753	732	0.6	0.9	0.4
35 - 39	3 724	2 489	1 235	0.9	1.2	0.6
40 - 44	6 509	4 355	2 154	1.5	2.0	1.0
45 - 49	10 827	7 067	3 760	2.5	3.3	1.7
50 - 54	16 881	11 249	5 632	4.0	5.4	2.6
55 - 59	24 454	16 710	7 744	6.0	8.5	3.7
60 - 64	33 129	22 684	10 445	8.2	11.7	5.0
65 - 69	33 793	22 651	11 142	11.2	15.7	7.0
70 - 74	38 076	24 317	13 759	16.4	23.0	10.9
75 - 79	59 955	34 915	25 040	27.2	37.4	19.8
80 - 84	90 672	46 166	44 506	49.7	66.1	39.6
85 - 89	111 079	46 643	64 436	94.4	121.3	81.3
90 - 94	79 942	26 749	53 193	167.7	206.8	153.2
95 - 99	29 993	6 755	23 238	306.8	362.7	293.7
100 +	9 085	1 318	7 767	466.5	474.1	465.3
Germany - Allemagne						
2016 (C)						
Total	910 902	448 305	462 597	11.1	11.0	11.1
0	2 700	1 495	1 205	3.5	3.8	3.2
1 - 4	457	262	195	0.2	0.2	0.1
5 - 9	315	187	128	0.1	0.1	0.1
10 - 14	327	177	150	0.1	0.1	0.1
15 - 19	992	670	322	0.2	0.3	0.2
20 - 24	1 445	1 079	366	0.3	0.5	0.2
25 - 29	1 934	1 369	565	0.4	0.5	0.2
30 - 34	2 690	1 809	881	0.5	0.7	0.3
35 - 39	3 716	2 484	1 232	0.7	1.0	0.5
40 - 44	5 852	3 777	2 075	1.2	1.5	0.9
45 - 49	12 793	8 143	4 650	2.0	2.5	1.5
50 - 54	23 588	15 303	8 285	3.4	4.3	2.4
55 - 59	35 433	23 030	12 403	5.8	7.5	4.0

19. Deaths by age and sex and age-specific death rates by sex: latest available year, 2008 - 2017
Décès et taux de mortalité selon l'âge et le sexe : dernière année disponible, 2008 - 2017 (continued - suite)

Continent, country or area, date, code[a] and age (in years) Continent, pays ou zone, date, code[a] et âge (en années)	Number - Nombre			Rate - Taux		
	Both sexes Les deux sexes	Male Masculin	Female Féminin	Both sexes Les deux sexes	Male Masculin	Female Féminin
EUROPE						
Germany - Allemagne						
2016 (C)						
60 - 64	47 456	30 738	16 718	9.1	12.0	6.2
65 - 69	60 804	38 577	22 227	13.7	18.1	9.6
70 - 74	78 459	47 844	30 615	20.6	26.9	15.0
75 - 79	138 768	79 961	58 807	32.2	41.9	24.5
80 - 84	155 874	78 388	77 486	59.7	74.0	50.0
85 - 89	171 109	70 241	100 868	114.7	137.2	102.9
90 - 94	121 831	33 902	87 929	203.2	231.7	193.9
95 - 99	37 754	7 962	29 792	319.1	362.3	309.2
100 +	6 605	907	5 698	416.6	368.8	425.4
Greece - Grèce						
2016 (C)						
Total	118 785	60 530	58 255	11.0	11.6	10.5
0	387	237	150	4.2	5.0	3.3
1 - 4	75	41	34	0.2	0.2	0.2
5 - 9	57	34	23	0.1	0.1	♦0.1
10 - 14	46	27	19	0.1	♦0.1	♦0.1
15 - 19	130	92	38	0.2	0.3	0.1
20 - 24	225	165	60	0.4	0.6	0.2
25 - 29	265	198	67	0.4	0.7	0.2
30 - 34	411	282	129	0.6	0.8	0.4
35 - 39	624	435	189	0.8	1.1	0.5
40 - 44	979	627	352	1.2	1.6	0.9
45 - 49	1 657	1 092	565	2.0	2.7	1.3
50 - 54	2 572	1 712	860	3.5	4.8	2.2
55 - 59	3 848	2 611	1 237	5.4	7.7	3.3
60 - 64	5 318	3 620	1 698	8.2	11.7	5.0
65 - 69	7 204	4 775	2 429	11.8	16.6	7.5
70 - 74	9 054	5 807	3 247	17.8	24.7	11.9
75 - 79	14 973	8 480	6 493	31.4	40.7	24.2
80 - 84	23 444	11 562	11 882	60.9	71.8	53.1
85 - 89	26 433	11 262	15 171	119.1	124.9	115.1
90 - 94	15 474	5 662	9 812	195.7	185.1	202.4
95 - 99	4 641	1 542	3 099	237.2	197.0	264.0
100 +	968	267	701	140.6	106.9	159.9
Hungary - Hongrie[45]						
2016 (C)						
Total	127 098	62 673	64 425	13.0	13.4	12.6
0	368	203	165	3.9	4.2	3.6
1 - 4	74	45	29	0.2	0.2	♦0.2
5 - 9	38	22	16	0.1	♦0.1	♦0.1
10 - 14	63	41	22	0.1	0.2	♦0.1
15 - 19	145	107	38	0.3	0.4	0.2
20 - 24	233	165	68	0.4	0.5	0.2
25 - 29	294	215	79	0.5	0.7	0.3
30 - 34	412	277	135	0.7	0.9	0.4
35 - 39	817	530	287	1.1	1.4	0.7
40 - 44	1 409	931	478	1.8	2.3	1.2
45 - 49	2 538	1 758	780	3.6	5.0	2.2
50 - 54	4 090	2 834	1 256	7.0	9.8	4.2
55 - 59	7 484	5 048	2 436	11.7	16.8	7.2
60 - 64	12 342	8 074	4 268	16.9	24.5	10.7
65 - 69	13 609	8 553	5 056	23.2	33.9	15.1
70 - 74	14 617	8 344	6 273	32.0	45.5	22.9
75 - 79	17 003	8 105	8 898	49.4	66.6	40.0
80 - 84	19 848	7 934	11 914	84.4	106.7	74.0
85 - 89	18 280	6 011	12 269	140.8	165.0	131.3
90 - 94	10 552	2 816	7 736	222.6	248.7	214.5
95 - 99	2 533	596	1 937	280.0	280.1	280.0
100 +	349	64	285	224.1	132.2	265.6
Iceland - Islande						
2017 (C)						
Total	2 239	1 124	1 115	6.6	6.6	6.7
0	11	5	6	♦2.7	♦2.4	♦3.0
1 - 4	3	-	3	♦0.2	-	♦0.3
5 - 9	2	-	2	♦0.1	-	♦0.2

Continent, country or area, date, code[a] and age (in years) / Continent, pays ou zone, date, code[a] et âge (en années)	Number - Nombre			Rate - Taux		
	Both sexes Les deux sexes	Male Masculin	Female Féminin	Both sexes Les deux sexes	Male Masculin	Female Féminin
EUROPE						
Iceland - Islande						
2017 (C)						
10 - 14	3	3	-	♦0.1	♦0.3	-
15 - 19	5	3	2	♦0.2	♦0.3	♦0.2
20 - 24	10	8	2	♦0.4	♦0.6	♦0.2
25 - 29	12	10	2	♦0.5	♦0.7	♦0.2
30 - 34	22	17	5	♦0.9	♦1.4	♦0.4
35 - 39	23	18	5	♦1.0	♦1.5	♦0.4
40 - 44	14	11	3	♦0.6	♦1.0	♦0.3
45 - 49	27	18	9	♦1.3	♦1.7	♦0.9
50 - 54	55	38	17	2.5	3.5	♦1.5
55 - 59	84	57	27	4.0	5.3	♦2.6
60 - 64	96	53	43	5.1	5.6	4.6
65 - 69	141	88	53	9.1	11.2	6.9
70 - 74	203	122	81	17.2	20.9	13.6
75 - 79	250	128	122	31.9	34.3	29.8
80 - 84	390	205	185	63.7	75.0	54.6
85 - 89	436	189	247	105.9	113.8	100.6
90 - 94	308	113	195	188.3	212.0	176.8
95 +	144	38	106	364.6	351.9	369.3
Ireland - Irlande						
2017 (+C)						
Total	30 484	15 497	14 987	6.4	6.5	6.2
0	174	90	84	2.8	2.8	2.7
1 - 4	28	19	9	♦0.1	♦0.1	♦0.1
5 - 9	23	10	13	♦0.1	♦0.1	♦0.1
10 - 14	22	14	8	♦0.1	♦0.1	♦0.1
15 - 19	76	48	28	0.2	0.3	♦0.2
20 - 24	99	79	20	0.4	0.6	♦0.1
25 - 29	128	92	36	0.4	0.6	0.2
30 - 34	178	116	62	0.5	0.7	0.3
35 - 39	289	190	99	0.7	1.0	0.5
40 - 44	390	249	141	1.1	1.4	0.8
45 - 49	527	318	209	1.6	1.9	1.3
50 - 54	785	490	295	2.6	3.3	1.9
55 - 59	1 119	686	433	4.1	5.1	3.2
60 - 64	1 620	945	675	6.7	7.9	5.6
65 - 69	2 220	1 353	867	10.5	12.9	8.2
70 - 74	3 144	1 836	1 308	18.8	22.4	15.4
75 - 79	3 976	2 306	1 670	34.2	42.1	27.1
80 - 84	5 018	2 616	2 402	60.7	72.6	51.6
85 +	10 668	4 040	6 628	152.6	166.2	145.3
Isle of Man - Île de Man[8]						
2016 (I)						
Total	870	437	433	10.4	10.6	10.3
0	2	-	2	♦2.5	-	♦5.3
1 - 4	1	1	-	♦0.3	♦0.6	-
5 - 9	-	-	-	-	-	-
10 - 14	3	2	1	♦0.7	♦0.9	♦0.5
15 - 19	1	1	-	♦0.2	♦0.4	-
20 - 24	3	2	1	♦0.7	♦0.9	♦0.5
25 - 29	3	3	-	♦0.7	♦1.4	-
30 - 34	5	3	2	♦1.1	♦1.4	♦0.8
35 - 39	5	4	1	♦1.0	♦1.7	♦0.4
40 - 44	8	6	2	♦1.4	♦2.2	♦0.7
45 - 49	11	7	4	♦1.7	♦2.2	♦1.2
50 - 54	22	15	7	♦3.3	♦4.5	♦2.1
55 - 59	28	16	12	♦4.8	♦5.5	♦4.0
60 - 64	36	23	13	7.0	♦8.8	♦5.1
65 - 69	60	38	22	11.0	14.0	♦8.1
70 - 74	85	50	35	20.2	24.1	16.4
75 - 79	126	78	48	39.9	51.0	29.5
80 - 84	128	64	64	60.1	66.8	54.7
85 - 89	153	67	86	110.9	128.4	100.2
90 - 94	118	38	80	174.8	188.1	169.1
95 - 99	58	15	43	308.5	♦283.0	318.5
100 +	14	4	10	♦560.0	♦400.0	♦666.7

19. Deaths by age and sex and age-specific death rates by sex: latest available year, 2008 - 2017
Décès et taux de mortalité selon l'âge et le sexe : dernière année disponible, 2008 - 2017 (continued - suite)

Continent, country or area, date, code[a] and age (in years) Continent, pays ou zone, date, code[a] et âge (en années)	Number - Nombre			Rate - Taux		
	Both sexes Les deux sexes	Male Masculin	Female Féminin	Both sexes Les deux sexes	Male Masculin	Female Féminin
EUROPE						
Italy - Italie						
2016 (C)						
Total	615 261	295 775	319 486	10.1	10.0	10.2
0	1 339	738	601	2.8	3.0	2.6
1 - 4	224	116	108	0.1	0.1	0.1
5 - 9	219	121	98	0.1	0.1	0.1
10 - 14	262	156	106	0.1	0.1	0.1
15 - 19	569	410	159	0.2	0.3	0.1
20 - 24	874	623	251	0.3	0.4	0.2
25 - 29	1 024	706	318	0.3	0.4	0.2
30 - 34	1 365	939	426	0.4	0.5	0.2
35 - 39	2 237	1 384	853	0.6	0.7	0.4
40 - 44	4 153	2 586	1 567	0.9	1.1	0.7
45 - 49	7 103	4 294	2 809	1.4	1.8	1.1
50 - 54	11 646	7 173	4 473	2.4	3.0	1.8
55 - 59	16 173	10 156	6 017	3.9	5.0	2.8
60 - 64	22 398	14 223	8 175	6.1	8.0	4.3
65 - 69	36 488	23 017	13 471	10.0	13.2	7.1
70 - 74	47 379	29 018	18 361	16.2	21.4	11.7
75 - 79	76 350	44 047	32 303	27.4	35.7	20.8
80 - 84	107 560	54 945	52 615	52.1	65.9	42.8
85 - 89	132 045	56 622	75 423	99.9	123.7	87.3
90 - 94	103 969	34 432	69 537	182.4	218.9	168.5
95 - 99	33 649	8 614	25 035	285.1	335.3	271.2
100 +	8 235	1 455	6 780	452.5	484.8	446.2
Latvia - Lettonie						
2016 (C)						
Total	28 580	13 522	15 058	14.6	15.0	14.2
0 - 4	106	51	55	1.0	0.9	1.1
0	81	38	43	3.7	3.3	4.1
1 - 4	25	13	12	♦0.3	♦0.3	♦0.3
5 - 9	13	5	8	♦0.1	♦0.1	♦0.2
10 - 14	15	8	7	♦0.2	♦0.2	♦0.2
15 - 19	42	31	11	0.5	0.7	♦0.3
20 - 24	93	72	21	0.9	1.3	♦0.4
25 - 29	181	146	35	1.3	2.0	0.5
30 - 34	224	185	39	1.6	2.6	0.6
35 - 39	316	243	73	2.5	3.9	1.2
40 - 44	510	386	124	3.8	5.9	1.8
45 - 49	683	462	221	5.1	7.2	3.2
50 - 54	1 020	736	284	7.4	11.3	3.9
55 - 59	1 644	1 130	514	11.4	17.3	6.5
60 - 64	1 987	1 362	625	16.2	26.1	8.8
65 - 69	2 513	1 603	910	23.0	37.4	13.8
70 - 74	3 018	1 693	1 325	33.9	54.1	22.9
75 - 79	4 252	1 960	2 292	47.5	69.3	37.4
80 - 84	4 414	1 641	2 773	79.9	109.9	68.8
85 - 89	4 574	1 241	3 333	141.6	165.7	134.3
90 - 94	2 388	463	1 925	225.9	270.4	217.3
95 - 99	511	90	421	361.6	393.0	355.6
100 +	74	12	62	468.4	♦571.4	452.6
Unknown - Inconnu	2	2	-	..	..	..
Liechtenstein						
2016 (C)						
Total	271	142	129	7.2	7.6	6.8
0	1	-	1	♦3.1	-	♦6.7
1 - 4	-	-	-	-	-	-
5 - 9	-	-	-	-	-	-
10 - 14	-	-	-	-	-	-
15 - 19	2	-	2	♦0.9	-	♦1.8
20 - 24	1	1	-	♦0.4	♦0.9	-
25 - 29	-	-	-	-	-	-
30 - 34	1	-	1	♦0.4	-	♦0.9
35 - 39	3	1	2	♦1.2	♦0.8	♦1.6
40 - 44	-	-	-	-	-	-
45 - 49	4	1	3	♦1.2	♦0.6	♦1.8
50 - 54	4	2	2	♦1.3	♦1.3	♦1.2

Continent, country or area, date, codeᵃ and age (in years) / Continent, pays ou zone, date, codeᵃ et âge (en années)	Number - Nombre			Rate - Taux		
	Both sexes Les deux sexes	Male Masculin	Female Féminin	Both sexes Les deux sexes	Male Masculin	Female Féminin
EUROPE						
Liechtenstein						
2016 (C)						
55 - 59	14	7	7	♦4.9	♦5.0	♦4.9
60 - 64	20	14	6	♦8.5	♦12.0	♦5.1
65 - 69	30	15	15	♦14.2	♦14.1	♦14.2
70 - 74	36	24	12	21.6	♦29.4	♦14.1
75 - 79	30	21	9	♦26.5	♦39.9	♦14.9
80 - 84	33	15	18	48.4	♦56.8	♦43.1
85 - 89	45	26	19	113.1	♦184.4	♦73.9
90 - 94	35	12	23	204.7	♦315.8	♦172.9
95 - 99	10	2	8	♦344.8	♦222.2	♦400.0
100 +	2	1	1	♦333.3	♦333.3	♦333.3
Lithuania - Lituanie						
2016 (C)						
Total	41 106	20 328	20 778	14.3	15.4	13.4
0	139	69	70	4.5	4.3	4.7
1 - 4	27	16	11	♦0.2	♦0.3	♦0.2
5 - 9	14	5	9	♦0.1	♦0.1	♦0.1
10 - 14	26	19	7	♦0.2	♦0.3	♦0.1
15 - 19	66	49	17	0.4	0.6	♦0.2
20 - 24	130	108	22	0.7	1.1	♦0.2
25 - 29	220	178	42	1.1	1.8	0.4
30 - 34	334	262	72	1.9	2.9	0.8
35 - 39	458	358	100	2.7	4.2	1.2
40 - 44	739	584	155	3.9	6.4	1.6
45 - 49	1 162	857	305	5.7	8.8	2.8
50 - 54	1 702	1 238	464	7.8	12.1	4.0
55 - 59	2 436	1 759	677	11.1	17.7	5.6
60 - 64	2 856	1 998	858	16.6	27.1	8.7
65 - 69	3 349	2 151	1 198	22.5	36.6	13.3
70 - 74	4 050	2 347	1 703	31.9	51.5	20.9
75 - 79	5 457	2 717	2 740	45.6	69.3	34.1
80 - 84	6 564	2 526	4 038	75.4	100.3	65.2
85 - 89	6 725	2 075	4 650	138.6	166.1	129.1
90 - 94	3 650	804	2 846	232.4	263.5	224.8
95 - 99	818	165	653	361.6	412.5	350.7
100 +	184	43	141	576.8	558.4	582.6
Luxembourg						
2016 (C)						
Total	3 967	2 040	1 927	6.9	7.1	6.7
0	23	16	7	♦3.8	♦5.1	♦2.4
1 - 4	5	2	3	♦0.2	♦0.2	♦0.2
5 - 9	-	-	-	-	-	-
10 - 14	1	-	1	-	-	♦0.1
15 - 19	6	5	1	♦0.2	♦0.3	♦0.1
20 - 24	8	4	4	♦0.2	♦0.2	♦0.2
25 - 29	12	9	3	♦0.3	♦0.4	♦0.1
30 - 34	17	13	4	♦0.4	♦0.6	♦0.2
35 - 39	20	12	8	♦0.4	♦0.5	♦0.4
40 - 44	45	23	22	1.0	♦1.0	♦1.0
45 - 49	70	46	24	1.5	2.0	♦1.1
50 - 54	112	78	34	2.6	3.4	1.6
55 - 59	192	133	59	5.2	7.0	3.3
60 - 64	213	146	67	7.1	9.7	4.6
65 - 69	299	195	104	12.1	15.8	8.4
70 - 74	357	213	144	19.2	24.0	14.8
75 - 79	429	258	171	27.2	37.1	19.4
80 - 84	654	338	316	54.8	69.3	44.7
85 - 89	785	344	441	102.1	130.8	87.1
90 - 94	509	160	349	190.7	252.0	171.6
95 - 99	179	41	138	384.1	398.1	380.2
100 +	31	4	27	476.9	♦266.7	♦540.0
Malta - Malte						
2016 (C)						
Total	3 342	1 644	1 698	7.3	7.2	7.5
0	33	20	13	7.2	♦8.5	♦5.9
1 - 4	2	1	1	♦0.1	♦0.1	♦0.1

Continent, country or area, date, code[a] and age (in years) Continent, pays ou zone, date, code[a] et âge (en années)	Number - Nombre			Rate - Taux		
	Both sexes Les deux sexes	Male Masculin	Female Féminin	Both sexes Les deux sexes	Male Masculin	Female Féminin
EUROPE						
Malta - Malte						
2016 (C)						
5 - 9	1	1	-	-	♦0.1	-
10 - 14	1	-	1	-	-	♦0.1
15 - 19	8	4	4	♦0.3	♦0.3	♦0.3
20 - 24	5	3	2	♦0.2	♦0.2	♦0.1
25 - 34	22	16	6	♦0.3	♦0.4	♦0.2
25 - 29	11	10	1	♦0.3	♦0.5	♦0.1
30 - 34	11	6	5	♦0.3	♦0.3	♦0.3
35 - 44	57	37	20	0.9	1.1	♦0.6
35 - 39	35	20	15	1.0	♦1.1	♦0.9
40 - 44	22	17	5	♦0.7	♦1.1	♦0.3
45 - 54	133	88	45	2.4	3.1	1.7
45 - 49	47	27	20	1.8	♦2.0	♦1.5
50 - 54	86	61	25	3.0	4.2	♦1.8
55 - 64	309	191	118	5.1	6.3	3.9
55 - 59	132	81	51	4.2	5.2	3.3
60 - 64	177	110	67	6.1	7.6	4.6
65 - 74	673	394	279	13.0	15.8	10.4
65 - 69	306	181	125	10.2	12.3	8.1
70 - 74	367	213	154	16.9	20.6	13.5
75 - 79	401	217	184	27.4	33.5	22.5
80 - 84	599	266	333	57.2	64.3	52.6
85 - 89	549	236	313	101.0	125.5	88.1
90 - 94	404	130	274	196.0	206.3	191.5
95 - 99	125	36	89	268.2	283.5	262.5
100 +	20	4	16	♦303.0	♦222.2	♦333.3
Montenegro - Monténégro						
2016 (C)						
Total	6 464	3 385	3 079	10.4	11.0	9.8
0	26	11	15	♦3.5	♦2.8	♦4.2
1 - 4	3	2	1	♦0.1	♦0.1	♦0.1
5 - 9	6	2	4	♦0.2	♦0.1	♦0.2
10 - 14	5	3	2	♦0.1	♦0.1	♦0.1
15 - 19	12	6	6	♦0.3	♦0.3	♦0.3
20 - 24	15	13	2	♦0.4	♦0.6	♦0.1
25 - 29	27	20	7	♦0.6	♦0.9	♦0.3
30 - 34	29	20	9	♦0.6	♦0.8	♦0.4
35 - 39	46	30	16	1.0	♦1.4	♦0.7
40 - 44	67	39	28	1.6	1.9	♦1.3
45 - 49	105	71	34	2.6	3.6	1.7
50 - 54	213	150	63	5.0	7.2	2.9
55 - 59	375	245	130	8.9	11.7	6.1
60 - 64	534	351	183	13.5	18.3	9.0
65 - 69	722	444	278	23.2	31.5	16.3
70 - 74	665	362	303	34.7	44.8	27.3
75 - 79	1 145	581	564	58.2	71.6	48.7
80 - 84	1 120	490	630	100.6	108.8	95.2
85 +	1 349	545	804	211.5	220.6	205.7
Netherlands - Pays-Bas[46]						
2016 (C)						
Total	148 997	72 180	76 817	8.8	8.6	9.0
0	597	323	274	3.5	3.7	3.3
1 - 4	106	65	41	0.2	0.2	0.1
5 - 9	55	25	30	0.1	♦0.1	♦0.1
10 - 14	79	42	37	0.1	0.1	0.1
15 - 19	183	116	67	0.2	0.2	0.1
20 - 24	315	211	104	0.3	0.4	0.2
25 - 29	366	230	136	0.3	0.4	0.3
30 - 34	480	294	186	0.5	0.6	0.4
35 - 39	608	334	274	0.6	0.7	0.5
40 - 44	1 098	657	441	1.0	1.2	0.8
45 - 49	2 043	1 155	888	1.6	1.8	1.4
50 - 54	3 625	1 966	1 659	2.8	3.1	2.6
55 - 59	5 564	3 097	2 467	4.8	5.3	4.2
60 - 64	8 058	4 732	3 326	7.6	9.0	6.3
65 - 69	12 444	7 363	5 081	11.9	14.2	9.6

19. Deaths by age and sex and age-specific death rates by sex: latest available year, 2008 - 2017
Décès et taux de mortalité selon l'âge et le sexe : dernière année disponible, 2008 - 2017 (continued - suite)

Continent, country or area, date, code[a] and age (in years) / Continent, pays ou zone, date, code[a] et âge (en années)	Number - Nombre			Rate - Taux		
	Both sexes Les deux sexes	Male Masculin	Female Féminin	Both sexes Les deux sexes	Male Masculin	Female Féminin

EUROPE

Netherlands - Pays-Bas[46]
2016 (C)

70 - 74	14 675	8 718	5 957	20.1	24.7	15.8
75 - 79	18 383	10 447	7 936	32.8	40.6	26.2
80 - 84	24 330	12 556	11 774	61.6	77.0	50.8
85 - 89	27 338	11 586	15 752	116.7	141.7	103.3
90 - 94	20 382	6 482	13 900	210.2	245.8	196.9
95 - 99	7 237	1 635	5 602	354.2	390.9	344.7
100 +	1 031	146	885	490.7	532.8	484.4

Norway - Norvège[47]
2016 (C)

Total	40 726	19 683	21 043	7.8	7.5	8.1
0	128	71	57	2.2	2.3	2.0
1 - 4	25	10	15	♦0.1	♦0.1	♦0.1
5 - 9	12	6	6	-	-	-
10 - 14	30	20	10	♦0.1	♦0.1	♦0.1
15 - 19	84	51	33	0.3	0.3	0.2
20 - 24	119	81	38	0.3	0.5	0.2
25 - 29	160	113	47	0.4	0.6	0.3
30 - 34	204	145	59	0.6	0.8	0.3
35 - 39	236	161	75	0.7	0.9	0.5
40 - 44	330	208	122	0.9	1.1	0.7
45 - 49	540	346	194	1.4	1.8	1.1
50 - 54	865	527	338	2.5	2.9	2.0
55 - 59	1 271	760	511	4.0	4.7	3.3
60 - 64	1 940	1 170	770	6.6	7.9	5.3
65 - 69	3 068	1 836	1 232	11.1	13.3	8.9
70 - 74	3 792	2 259	1 533	17.1	21.0	13.5
75 - 79	4 384	2 398	1 986	29.9	35.6	25.0
80 - 84	5 882	2 993	2 889	56.3	68.0	47.8
85 - 89	7 619	3 396	4 223	106.1	128.7	93.0
90 - 94	6 714	2 315	4 399	193.9	224.7	180.8
95 - 99	2 855	734	2 121	328.1	392.7	310.5
100 +	468	83	385	496.8	544.3	487.7

Poland - Pologne
2016 (C)

Total	388 009	202 150	185 859	10.2	11.0	9.5
0	1 522	868	654	4.2	4.6	3.7
1 - 4	239	140	99	0.2	0.2	0.1
5 - 9	192	110	82	0.1	0.1	0.1
10 - 14	201	123	78	0.1	0.1	0.1
15 - 19	677	489	188	0.4	0.5	0.2
20 - 24	1 311	1 065	246	0.6	0.9	0.2
25 - 29	1 828	1 459	369	0.7	1.0	0.3
30 - 34	2 863	2 239	624	0.9	1.4	0.4
35 - 39	4 004	3 059	945	1.3	2.0	0.6
40 - 44	5 595	4 162	1 433	2.1	3.0	1.1
45 - 49	8 159	6 021	2 138	3.5	5.2	1.9
50 - 54	13 420	9 664	3 756	5.7	8.3	3.2
55 - 59	24 994	17 598	7 396	9.1	13.2	5.2
60 - 64	36 760	24 858	11 902	13.5	19.6	8.2
65 - 69	42 721	27 699	15 022	19.3	28.1	12.2
70 - 74	33 870	20 126	13 744	27.1	38.7	18.8
75 - 79	45 852	24 305	21 547	40.6	57.3	30.5
80 - 84	58 783	25 851	32 932	67.9	88.9	57.3
85 - 89	60 013	20 751	39 262	117.6	139.4	108.6
90 - 94	35 209	9 370	25 839	193.8	216.6	186.6
95 - 99	8 333	1 926	6 407	294.4	316.0	288.5
100 +	1 463	267	1 196	283.7	253.8	291.4

Portugal[48]
2016 (C)

Total	110 573	55 626	54 947	10.7	11.4	10.1
0	282	165	117	3.3	3.7	2.8
1 - 4	52	29	23	0.2	♦0.2	♦0.1
5 - 9	30	15	15	♦0.1	♦0.1	♦0.1
10 - 14	50	30	20	0.1	♦0.1	♦0.1
15 - 19	128	82	46	0.2	0.3	0.2

19. Deaths by age and sex and age-specific death rates by sex: latest available year, 2008 - 2017

Décès et taux de mortalité selon l'âge et le sexe : dernière année disponible, 2008 - 2017 (continued - suite)

Continent, country or area, date, code[a] and age (in years) Continent, pays ou zone, date, code[a] et âge (en années)	Number - Nombre			Rate - Taux		
	Both sexes Les deux sexes	Male Masculin	Female Féminin	Both sexes Les deux sexes	Male Masculin	Female Féminin
EUROPE						
Portugal[48]						
2016 (C)						
20 - 24	182	139	43	0.3	0.5	0.2
25 - 29	207	165	42	0.4	0.6	0.2
30 - 34	260	171	89	0.4	0.6	0.3
35 - 39	582	351	231	0.8	1.0	0.6
40 - 44	1 127	739	388	1.4	1.9	0.9
45 - 49	1 711	1 149	562	2.3	3.2	1.4
50 - 54	2 839	1 987	852	3.7	5.5	2.1
55 - 59	3 926	2 753	1 173	5.5	8.2	3.1
60 - 64	5 195	3 594	1 601	8.0	11.8	4.6
65 - 69	6 923	4 601	2 322	11.5	16.7	7.2
70 - 74	9 150	5 584	3 566	18.1	25.2	12.6
75 - 79	13 847	7 860	5 987	32.2	43.6	23.9
80 - 84	20 168	10 053	10 115	58.6	75.6	47.9
85 - 89	22 237	9 380	12 857	115.6	144.9	100.7
90 - 94	15 633	5 265	10 368	231.8	279.9	213.2
95 - 99	5 094	1 352	3 742	331.5	333.7	330.3
100 +	950	162	788	221.7	105.6	286.5
Republic of Moldova - République de Moldova[49]						
2017 (C)						
Total	36 768	19 247	17 521	...	...	...
0	330	189	141	...	...	...
1 - 4	57	27	30	...	...	...
5 - 9	41	19	22	...	...	...
10 - 14	47	29	18	...	...	...
15 - 19	74	52	22	...	...	...
20 - 24	139	116	23	...	...	...
25 - 29	270	206	64	...	...	...
30 - 34	408	310	98	...	...	...
35 - 39	550	417	133	...	...	...
40 - 44	852	601	251	...	...	...
45 - 49	1 154	820	334	...	...	...
50 - 54	1 767	1 278	489	...	...	...
55 - 59	3 096	2 131	965	...	...	...
60 - 64	4 043	2 656	1 387	...	...	...
65 - 69	4 793	2 894	1 899	...	...	...
70 - 74	3 240	1 629	1 611	...	...	...
75 - 79	5 205	2 287	2 918	...	...	...
80 - 84	5 004	1 890	3 114	...	...	...
85 - 89	3 846	1 231	2 615	...	...	...
90 - 94	1 490	371	1 119	...	...	...
95 - 99	321	77	244	...	...	...
100 +	28	5	23	...	...	...
Unknown - Inconnu	13	12	1	..	..	..
Romania - Roumanie						
2016 (C)						
Total	257 215	134 495	122 720	13.1	14.0	12.2
0	1 398	813	585	7.1	8.0	6.1
1 - 4	270	147	123	0.4	0.4	0.3
5 - 9	182	103	79	0.2	0.2	0.2
10 - 14	236	142	94	0.2	0.3	0.2
15 - 19	434	297	137	0.4	0.5	0.3
20 - 24	565	420	145	0.5	0.8	0.3
25 - 29	926	676	250	0.7	1.0	0.4
30 - 34	1 090	769	321	0.8	1.1	0.5
35 - 39	2 128	1 494	634	1.4	1.9	0.9
40 - 44	3 739	2 640	1 099	2.5	3.4	1.5
45 - 49	7 096	5 139	1 957	4.2	6.0	2.4
50 - 54	7 743	5 608	2 135	7.3	10.5	4.1
55 - 59	14 865	10 651	4 214	11.5	17.0	6.3
60 - 64	21 668	14 673	6 995	16.0	23.5	9.6
65 - 69	24 841	15 743	9 098	22.1	31.6	14.5
70 - 74	25 602	14 717	10 885	33.4	46.0	24.4
75 - 79	38 936	19 362	19 574	53.6	69.4	43.7
80 - 84	45 770	19 698	26 072	91.4	108.1	81.9
85 - 89	37 577	14 228	23 349	149.8	164.5	142.0

Continent, country or area, date, code[a] and age (in years) Continent, pays ou zone, date, code[a] et âge (en années)	Number - Nombre			Rate - Taux		
	Both sexes Les deux sexes	Male Masculin	Female Féminin	Both sexes Les deux sexes	Male Masculin	Female Féminin
EUROPE						
Romania - Roumanie						
2016 (C)						
90 - 94	18 352	6 089	12 263	220.8	224.2	219.2
95 - 99	3 324	955	2 369	225.2	218.4	228.0
100 +	473	131	342	279.6	263.6	286.2
Russian Federation - Fédération de Russie[26]						
2011 (C)						
Total	1 925 720	997 494	928 226	13.5	15.1	12.1
0 - 4	16 465	9 472	6 993	2.1	2.3	1.8
0	13 168	7 572	5 596	8.0	9.0	7.0
1 - 4	3 297	1 900	1 397	0.5	0.6	0.5
5 - 9	1 972	1 160	812	0.3	0.3	0.2
10 - 14	2 006	1 249	757	0.3	0.4	0.2
15 - 19	6 656	4 634	2 022	0.8	1.1	0.5
20 - 24	18 666	14 374	4 292	1.5	2.3	0.7
25 - 29	32 160	24 684	7 476	2.7	4.1	1.3
30 - 34	45 451	34 852	10 599	4.1	6.4	1.9
35 - 39	50 630	38 270	12 360	5.0	7.7	2.4
40 - 44	55 007	40 708	14 299	6.0	9.1	3.0
45 - 49	81 813	60 225	21 588	7.7	12.0	3.8
50 - 54	124 961	89 971	34 990	10.9	17.1	5.6
55 - 59	156 587	108 205	48 382	15.6	24.9	8.5
60 - 64	177 990	118 728	59 262	22.7	36.6	12.9
65 - 69	111 156	66 246	44 910	27.8	44.4	17.9
70 - 74	263 633	136 875	126 758	40.8	62.8	29.6
75 - 79	232 616	99 250	133 366	65.5	92.9	53.7
80 - 84	290 314	94 614	195 700	101.1	129.8	91.4
85 - 89	172 178	35 533	136 645	166.8	187.8	162.0
90 - 94	56 714	9 585	47 129	244.6	241.3	245.3
95 - 99	18 647	2 652	15 995	320.7	294.4	325.5
100 +	2 562	320	2 242	352.6	232.1	380.8
Unknown - Inconnu	7 536	5 887	1 649	..	..	..
San Marino - Saint-Marin						
2014 (C)						
Total	252	128	124	7.5	7.8	7.2
0	1	1	-	♦3.1	♦5.6	-
1 - 4	-	-	-	-	-	-
5 - 9	-	-	-	-	-	-
10 - 14	-	-	-	-	-	-
15 - 19	1	-	1	♦0.6	-	♦1.3
20 - 24	1	1	-	♦0.7	♦1.3	-
25 - 29	-	-	-	-	-	-
30 - 34	-	-	-	-	-	-
35 - 39	-	-	-	-	-	-
40 - 44	1	1	-	♦0.3	♦0.7	-
45 - 49	2	1	1	♦0.6	♦0.7	♦0.6
50 - 54	5	3	2	♦1.8	♦2.2	♦1.4
55 - 59	4	2	2	♦1.8	♦1.9	♦1.8
60 - 64	11	6	5	♦5.7	♦6.4	♦5.1
65 - 69	13	9	4	♦7.7	♦11.0	♦4.5
70 - 74	16	12	4	♦11.2	♦17.5	♦5.4
75 - 79	23	17	6	♦19.6	♦30.8	♦9.6
80 - 84	47	23	24	50.7	♦59.0	♦44.7
85 - 89	60	32	28	112.8	172.0	♦80.9
90 - 94	45	15	30	160.1	♦185.2	♦150.0
95 - 99	15	4	11	♦263.2	♦363.6	♦239.1
100 +	7	1	6	♦777.8	♦1000.0	♦750.0
Serbia - Serbie[50]						
2016 (+C)						
Total	100 834	50 708	50 126	14.3	14.8	13.8
0	348	210	138	5.4	6.3	4.4
1 - 4	46	23	23	0.2	♦0.2	♦0.2
5 - 9	35	22	13	0.1	♦0.1	♦0.1
10 - 14	43	22	21	0.1	♦0.1	♦0.1
15 - 19	118	84	34	0.3	0.5	0.2
20 - 24	179	135	44	0.4	0.6	0.2
25 - 29	249	167	82	0.6	0.7	0.4

19. Deaths by age and sex and age-specific death rates by sex: latest available year, 2008 - 2017
Décès et taux de mortalité selon l'âge et le sexe : dernière année disponible, 2008 - 2017 (continued - suite)

Continent, country or area, date, code[a] and age (in years) / Continent, pays ou zone, date, code[a] et âge (en années)	Number - Nombre			Rate - Taux		
	Both sexes Les deux sexes	Male Masculin	Female Féminin	Both sexes Les deux sexes	Male Masculin	Female Féminin
EUROPE						
Serbia - Serbie[50]						
2016 (+C)						
30 - 34	386	269	117	0.8	1.1	0.5
35 - 39	542	346	196	1.1	1.4	0.8
40 - 44	932	590	342	1.9	2.4	1.4
45 - 49	1 543	961	582	3.3	4.2	2.5
50 - 54	2 801	1 797	1 004	5.9	7.7	4.1
55 - 59	4 870	3 239	1 631	9.6	13.3	6.2
60 - 64	8 458	5 539	2 919	15.1	20.9	9.9
65 - 69	10 730	6 651	4 079	22.5	30.5	15.8
70 - 74	10 403	5 788	4 615	35.5	45.4	27.8
75 - 79	16 327	7 901	8 426	58.7	68.8	51.6
80 - 84	20 715	8 858	11 857	108.1	118.3	101.6
85 - 89	15 404	5 867	9 537	179.0	186.1	174.9
90 - 94	5 792	1 946	3 846	249.4	249.8	249.2
95 - 99	846	271	575	207.5	206.4	208.0
100 +	67	22	45	156.2	♦154.9	156.8
Slovakia - Slovaquie						
2016 (C)						
Total	52 351	26 764	25 587	9.6	10.1	9.2
0	311	179	132	5.4	6.1	4.7
1 - 4	45	28	17	0.2	♦0.2	♦0.2
5 - 9	35	17	18	0.1	♦0.1	♦0.1
10 - 14	32	18	14	0.1	♦0.1	♦0.1
15 - 19	90	62	28	0.3	0.4	♦0.2
20 - 24	175	126	49	0.5	0.7	0.3
25 - 29	212	153	59	0.5	0.8	0.3
30 - 34	327	214	113	0.8	1.0	0.5
35 - 39	518	363	155	1.1	1.5	0.7
40 - 44	810	567	243	1.9	2.6	1.2
45 - 49	1 113	783	330	3.1	4.4	1.9
50 - 54	1 938	1 348	590	5.3	7.4	3.2
55 - 59	3 121	2 225	896	8.4	12.4	4.7
60 - 64	4 912	3 392	1 520	13.5	19.9	7.8
65 - 69	5 711	3 684	2 027	19.8	28.9	12.6
70 - 74	5 613	3 223	2 390	28.8	41.1	20.5
75 - 79	6 643	3 365	3 278	46.2	64.6	35.7
80 - 84	7 976	3 188	4 788	81.8	100.8	72.6
85 - 89	7 572	2 446	5 126	144.1	163.0	136.6
90 - 94	4 265	1 180	3 085	232.1	253.1	224.9
95 - 99	836	189	647	261.7	218.4	277.8
100 +	96	14	82	115.5	♦46.7	154.3
Slovenia - Slovénie						
2016 (C)						
Total	19 689	9 673	10 016	9.5	9.4	9.6
0	41	20	21	2.0	♦1.9	♦2.1
1 - 4	13	6	7	♦0.2	♦0.1	♦0.2
5 - 9	4	1	3	-	-	♦0.1
10 - 14	10	9	1	♦0.1	♦0.2	-
15 - 19	39	25	14	0.4	♦0.5	♦0.3
20 - 24	51	43	8	0.5	0.8	♦0.2
25 - 29	55	43	12	0.4	0.7	♦0.2
30 - 34	85	61	24	0.6	0.8	♦0.4
35 - 39	120	90	30	0.8	1.1	♦0.4
40 - 44	142	95	47	0.9	1.2	0.6
45 - 49	280	196	84	1.9	2.6	1.2
50 - 54	546	385	161	3.5	4.9	2.1
55 - 59	865	603	262	5.8	8.0	3.5
60 - 64	1 315	910	405	9.1	12.5	5.6
65 - 69	1 567	1 075	492	13.1	18.6	7.9
70 - 74	1 745	1 072	673	20.5	28.2	14.3
75 - 79	2 422	1 385	1 037	31.6	43.3	23.2
80 - 84	3 490	1 626	1 864	61.5	80.1	51.2
85 - 89	3 818	1 333	2 485	115.3	139.1	105.7
90 - 94	2 380	586	1 794	198.9	231.3	190.2
95 - 99	620	97	523	332.8	283.6	343.9
100 +	81	12	69	387.6	♦387.1	387.6

19. Deaths by age and sex and age-specific death rates by sex: latest available year, 2008 - 2017
Décès et taux de mortalité selon l'âge et le sexe : dernière année disponible, 2008 - 2017 (continued - suite)

Continent, country or area, date, code[a] and age (in years) / Continent, pays ou zone, date, code[a] et âge (en années)	Number - Nombre			Rate - Taux		
	Both sexes Les deux sexes	Male Masculin	Female Féminin	Both sexes Les deux sexes	Male Masculin	Female Féminin
EUROPE						
Spain - Espagne						
2016 (C)						
Total	408 231	207 346	200 885	8.8	9.1	8.5
0	1 097	641	456	2.6	3.0	2.2
1 - 4	239	129	110	0.1	0.1	0.1
5 - 9	172	103	69	0.1	0.1	0.1
10 - 14	175	103	72	0.1	0.1	0.1
15 - 19	376	246	130	0.2	0.2	0.1
20 - 24	531	376	155	0.2	0.3	0.1
25 - 29	717	495	222	0.3	0.4	0.2
30 - 34	1 168	810	358	0.4	0.5	0.2
35 - 39	2 015	1 274	741	0.5	0.7	0.4
40 - 44	3 499	2 246	1 253	0.9	1.1	0.7
45 - 49	6 037	3 929	2 108	1.6	2.1	1.1
50 - 54	10 129	6 751	3 378	2.9	3.9	1.9
55 - 59	14 019	9 520	4 499	4.6	6.3	2.9
60 - 64	17 788	12 333	5 455	6.9	9.9	4.1
65 - 69	23 786	16 358	7 428	10.1	14.6	6.0
70 - 74	31 278	20 676	10 602	15.8	22.6	10.0
75 - 79	42 214	25 530	16 684	26.6	36.9	18.7
80 - 84	71 677	37 743	33 934	50.1	65.2	39.8
85 - 89	86 456	37 837	48 619	97.2	119.8	84.8
90 - 94	66 387	23 208	43 179	178.9	209.0	166.0
95 - 99	23 652	6 132	17 520	280.9	303.1	273.9
100 +	4 819	906	3 913	292.7	241.1	308.0
Sweden - Suède						
2016 (C)						
Total	90 982	44 421	46 561	9.2	8.9	9.4
0	292	157	135	2.5	2.6	2.4
1 - 4	60	31	29	0.1	0.1	♦0.1
5 - 9	49	27	22	0.1	♦0.1	♦0.1
10 - 14	45	18	27	0.1	♦0.1	♦0.1
15 - 19	104	74	30	0.2	0.3	♦0.1
20 - 24	248	172	76	0.4	0.5	0.2
25 - 29	346	257	89	0.5	0.7	0.3
30 - 34	365	258	107	0.6	0.8	0.3
35 - 39	397	271	126	0.6	0.9	0.4
40 - 44	578	365	213	0.9	1.1	0.7
45 - 49	946	577	369	1.4	1.7	1.1
50 - 54	1 470	900	570	2.2	2.7	1.8
55 - 59	2 226	1 321	905	3.8	4.5	3.1
60 - 64	3 744	2 258	1 486	6.7	8.1	5.3
65 - 69	6 234	3 744	2 490	10.7	13.1	8.5
70 - 74	9 277	5 410	3 867	17.7	21.0	14.4
75 - 79	10 671	6 063	4 608	30.4	36.9	24.7
80 - 84	13 950	7 234	6 716	56.9	68.5	48.1
85 - 89	17 481	7 754	9 727	107.6	127.1	95.9
90 - 94	15 260	5 555	9 705	201.3	233.3	186.7
95 - 99	6 258	1 790	4 468	329.1	387.6	310.4
100 +	981	185	796	506.1	571.9	492.9
Switzerland - Suisse						
2016 (C)						
Total	64 964	31 283	33 681	7.8	7.6	8.0
0	316	154	162	3.7	3.5	3.9
1 - 4	31	14	17	0.1	♦0.1	♦0.1
5 - 9	21	10	11	♦0.1	-	♦0.1
10 - 14	37	20	17	0.1	♦0.1	♦0.1
15 - 19	76	47	29	0.2	0.2	♦0.1
20 - 24	150	110	40	0.3	0.4	0.2
25 - 29	194	134	60	0.3	0.5	0.2
30 - 34	224	136	88	0.4	0.5	0.3
35 - 39	297	183	114	0.5	0.6	0.4
40 - 44	482	294	188	0.8	1.0	0.6
45 - 49	841	496	345	1.3	1.5	1.1
50 - 54	1 485	950	535	2.3	2.8	1.6
55 - 59	2 067	1 288	779	3.7	4.6	2.8
60 - 64	2 836	1 788	1 048	6.0	7.7	4.4

19. Deaths by age and sex and age-specific death rates by sex: latest available year, 2008 - 2017
Décès et taux de mortalité selon l'âge et le sexe : dernière année disponible, 2008 - 2017 (continued - suite)

Continent, country or area, date, code[a] and age (in years)	Number - Nombre			Rate - Taux		
Continent, pays ou zone, date, code[a] et âge (en années)	Both sexes Les deux sexes	Male Masculin	Female Féminin	Both sexes Les deux sexes	Male Masculin	Female Féminin

EUROPE

Switzerland - Suisse
2016 (C)

65 - 69	4 128	2 530	1 598	9.5	12.1	7.1
70 - 74	5 674	3 402	2 272	15.3	19.4	11.6
75 - 79	6 947	3 881	3 066	25.4	32.0	20.2
80 - 84	10 522	5 341	5 181	49.7	61.8	41.4
85 - 89	13 111	5 615	7 496	98.3	119.9	86.6
90 - 94	10 787	3 713	7 074	185.5	220.8	171.2
95 - 99	3 969	1 019	2 950	323.6	359.3	312.9
100 +	769	158	611	492.3	544.8	480.3

TFYR of Macedonia - L'ex-R. y. de Macédoine
2016 (C)

Total	20 417	10 744	9 673	9.9	10.3	9.4
0	273	140	133	12.0	11.9	12.1
1 - 4	28	18	10	♦0.3	♦0.4	♦0.2
5 - 9	15	11	4	♦0.1	♦0.2	♦0.1
10 - 14	22	11	11	♦0.2	♦0.2	♦0.2
15 - 19	40	28	12	0.3	♦0.4	♦0.2
20 - 24	48	34	14	0.3	0.4	♦0.2
25 - 29	82	56	26	0.5	0.7	♦0.3
30 - 34	95	68	27	0.6	0.8	♦0.3
35 - 39	148	91	57	0.9	1.1	0.7
40 - 44	260	182	78	1.7	2.4	1.1
45 - 49	377	232	145	2.6	3.2	2.0
50 - 54	692	450	242	4.8	6.3	3.4
55 - 59	1 143	784	359	8.3	11.4	5.2
60 - 64	1 728	1 122	606	13.9	18.4	9.6
65 - 69	2 177	1 278	899	21.7	27.5	16.7
70 - 74	2 458	1 345	1 113	35.3	42.9	29.1
75 - 79	3 343	1 632	1 711	63.1	70.6	57.3
80 - 84	3 979	1 785	2 194	118.3	127.3	111.9
85 - 89	2 464	1 045	1 419	207.0	227.0	194.4
90 - 94	888	367	521	341.3	385.1	315.9
95 - 99	141	61	80	138.0	208.9	109.6
100 +	16	4	12	...	...	...

Ukraine[51]
2016 (+C)

Total	583 631	285 896	297 735	13.7	14.5	13.0
0	2 955	1 703	1 252	7.4	8.2	6.4
1 - 4	655	366	289	0.4	0.4	0.3
5 - 9	377	217	160	0.2	0.2	0.1
10 - 14	392	244	148	0.2	0.2	0.2
15 - 19	1 022	724	298	0.5	0.7	0.3
20 - 24	2 096	1 606	490	0.8	1.2	0.4
25 - 29	4 384	3 332	1 052	1.3	2.0	0.7
30 - 34	7 490	5 633	1 857	2.1	3.1	1.1
35 - 39	10 663	7 933	2 730	3.4	5.0	1.7
40 - 44	13 911	10 207	3 704	4.6	6.9	2.4
45 - 49	17 265	12 464	4 801	6.1	9.2	3.2
50 - 54	25 114	18 154	6 960	8.4	13.3	4.3
55 - 59	37 292	26 020	11 272	11.9	18.8	6.4
60 - 64	48 188	32 340	15 848	18.1	29.3	10.2
65 - 69	57 452	34 723	22 729	25.9	40.4	16.8
70 - 74	52 444	27 070	25 374	39.4	59.3	29.0
75 - 79	107 271	46 773	60 498	60.9	85.0	50.0
80 - 84	75 398	26 857	48 541	94.1	114.2	85.7
85 - 89	77 853	21 410	56 443	151.0	164.0	146.6
90 - 94	34 654	6 902	27 752	220.6	195.2	227.9
95 - 99	5 892	1 042	4 850	215.1	133.2	247.8
100 +	863	176	687	129.6	89.8	146.1

United Kingdom of Great Britain and Northern Ireland - Royaume-Uni de Grande-Bretagne et d'Irlande du Nord[52]
2016 (+C)

Total	595 655	292 072	303 583	9.1	9.0	9.1
0	2 976	1 639	1 337	3.8	4.1	3.5
1 - 4	486	257	229	0.2	0.2	0.1

Continent, country or area, date, code[a] and age (in years) Continent, pays ou zone, date, code[a] et âge (en années)	Number - Nombre			Rate - Taux		
	Both sexes Les deux sexes	Male Masculin	Female Féminin	Both sexes Les deux sexes	Male Masculin	Female Féminin
EUROPE						
United Kingdom of Great Britain and Northern Ireland - Royaume-Uni de Grande-Bretagne et d'Irlande du Nord[52]						
2016 (+C)						
5 - 9	274	158	116	0.1	0.1	0.1
10 - 14	315	178	137	0.1	0.1	0.1
15 - 19	883	585	298	0.2	0.3	0.2
20 - 24	1 602	1 129	473	0.4	0.5	0.2
25 - 29	2 143	1 484	659	0.5	0.7	0.3
30 - 34	2 966	1 920	1 046	0.7	0.9	0.5
35 - 39	3 811	2 398	1 413	0.9	1.2	0.7
40 - 44	6 203	3 888	2 315	1.5	1.9	1.1
45 - 49	9 921	5 999	3 922	2.2	2.6	1.7
50 - 54	14 715	8 688	6 027	3.2	3.8	2.6
55 - 59	20 222	11 835	8 387	5.0	5.9	4.1
60 - 64	27 837	16 491	11 346	7.9	9.5	6.3
65 - 69	44 339	26 124	18 215	12.4	15.0	9.9
70 - 74	56 234	32 211	24 023	19.5	23.4	15.9
75 - 79	73 358	40 346	33 012	33.9	40.6	28.2
80 - 84	96 170	49 003	47 167	59.8	70.5	51.6
85 - 89	107 966	47 589	60 377	108.7	125.0	98.6
90 - 94	83 296	30 065	53 231	186.8	210.7	175.5
95 - 99	33 427	8 935	24 492	308.7	343.3	297.7
100 +	6 511	1 150	5 361	438.5	482.8	430.0
OCEANIA - OCÉANIE						
American Samoa - Samoas américaines						
2014 (C)						
Total	259	142	117	...	...	...
0	9	4	5	...	...	...
1 - 4	2	-	2	...	...	...
5 - 9	1	-	1	...	...	...
10 - 14	1	1	-	...	...	...
15 - 19	3	1	2	...	...	...
20 - 24	4	2	2	...	...	...
25 - 29	3	2	1	...	...	...
30 - 34	7	6	1	...	...	...
35 - 39	7	6	1	...	...	...
40 - 44	11	5	6	...	...	...
45 - 49	16	5	11	...	...	...
50 - 54	23	11	12	...	...	...
55 - 59	19	11	8	...	...	...
60 - 64	27	14	13	...	...	...
65 - 69	28	19	9	...	...	...
70 - 74	35	23	12	...	...	...
75 - 79	22	14	8	...	...	...
80 - 84	21	14	7	...	...	...
85 +	20	4	16	...	...	...
Australia - Australie[53]						
2016 (C)						
Total	158 504	81 867	76 637	6.5	6.8	6.3
0	970	543	427	3.1	3.3	2.8
1 - 4	191	111	80	0.2	0.2	0.1
5 - 9	113	69	44	0.1	0.1	0.1
10 - 14	133	80	53	0.1	0.1	0.1
15 - 19	410	283	127	0.3	0.4	0.2
20 - 24	728	531	197	0.4	0.6	0.2
25 - 29	866	596	270	0.5	0.7	0.3
30 - 34	1 135	740	395	0.6	0.8	0.4
35 - 39	1 372	895	477	0.9	1.1	0.6
40 - 44	2 070	1 291	779	1.3	1.6	0.9
45 - 49	2 858	1 749	1 109	1.8	2.2	1.4
50 - 54	4 174	2 561	1 613	2.7	3.4	2.0
55 - 59	5 948	3 660	2 288	4.0	5.1	3.0
60 - 64	7 839	4 872	2 967	6.0	7.6	4.4

19. Deaths by age and sex and age-specific death rates by sex: latest available year, 2008 - 2017
Décès et taux de mortalité selon l'âge et le sexe : dernière année disponible, 2008 - 2017 (continued - suite)

Continent, country or area, date, code[a] and age (in years) / Continent, pays ou zone, date, code[a] et âge (en années)	Number - Nombre			Rate - Taux		
	Both sexes Les deux sexes	Male Masculin	Female Féminin	Both sexes Les deux sexes	Male Masculin	Female Féminin
OCEANIA - OCÉANIE						
Australia - Australie[53]						
2016 (C)						
65 - 69	10 964	6 764	4 200	9.2	11.5	6.9
70 - 74	13 753	8 411	5 342	15.4	19.2	11.8
75 - 79	17 622	10 252	7 370	27.1	33.3	21.5
80 - 84	23 166	12 513	10 653	50.9	61.8	42.2
85 - 89	29 166	13 878	15 288	95.5	113.3	83.5
90 - 94	23 974	9 000	14 974	171.1	192.2	160.5
95 - 99	9 232	2 678	6 554	274.4	290.3	268.4
100 +	1 816	387	1 429	515.0	525.1	512.4
Unknown - Inconnu	3	3	3	..	..	..
Cook Islands - Îles Cook[54]						
2009 (+C)						
Total	67	37	30	...	...	...
0	2	1	1	...	...	...
1 - 4	1	1	-	...	...	...
5 - 9	-	-	-	...	...	...
10 - 14	-	-	-	...	...	...
15 - 19	3	2	1	...	...	...
20 - 24	3	3	-	...	...	...
25 - 29	1	1	-	...	...	...
30 - 34	2	1	1	...	...	...
35 - 39	4	3	1	...	...	...
40 - 44	-	-	-	...	...	...
45 - 49	2	1	1	...	...	...
50 - 54	3	1	2	...	...	...
55 - 59	1	1	-	...	...	...
60 - 64	6	3	3	...	...	...
65 - 69	8	4	4	...	...	...
70 - 74	9	1	8	...	...	...
75 - 79	8	5	3	...	...	...
80 +	14	9	5	...	...	...
Fiji - Fidji						
2008 (+C)						
Total	6 471	3 519	2 952	7.7	8.2	7.2
0	319	180	139	18.9	20.4	17.3
1 - 4	128	70	58	1.9	2.0	1.8
5 - 9	45	29	16	0.6	♦0.7	♦0.4
10 - 14	42	25	17	0.5	♦0.6	♦0.4
15 - 19	70	34	36	0.9	0.8	0.9
20 - 24	104	64	40	1.3	1.6	1.0
25 - 29	124	65	59	1.7	1.7	1.6
30 - 34	120	61	59	1.9	1.8	1.9
35 - 39	183	114	69	3.2	3.9	2.5
40 - 44	296	168	128	5.3	5.9	4.7
45 - 49	446	279	167	8.8	10.7	6.7
50 - 54	549	344	205	13.2	16.3	10.0
55 - 59	663	381	282	20.5	23.3	17.6
60 - 64	737	409	328	29.9	33.5	26.3
65 - 69	718	385	333	40.4	44.8	36.3
70 - 74	621	303	318	57.2	59.1	55.5
75 +	1 306	608	698	103.5	108.7	99.3
75 - 79	564	290	274	...	...	...
80 - 84	360	156	204	...	...	...
85 - 89	246	113	133	...	...	...
90 - 94	71	27	44	...	...	...
95 +	65	22	43	...	...	...
Guam[55]						
2016 (C)						
Total	1 022	584[14]	437[14]	6.3	7.1	5.4
0	45	29[14]	16[14]	16.7	♦20.9	♦12.2
1 - 4	9	6[14]	3[14]	♦0.8	♦1.1	♦0.6
5 - 9	3	1[14]	2[14]	♦0.2	♦0.1	♦0.3
10 - 14	7	2[14]	5[14]	♦0.5	♦0.3	♦0.8
15 - 19	14	6[14]	8[14]	♦1.0	♦0.8	♦1.2
20 - 24	13	12[14]	1[14]	♦1.0	♦1.7	♦0.2
25 - 29	19	14[14]	5[14]	♦1.6	♦2.3	♦0.8

19. Deaths by age and sex and age-specific death rates by sex: latest available year, 2008 - 2017
Décès et taux de mortalité selon l'âge et le sexe : dernière année disponible, 2008 - 2017 (continued - suite)

Continent, country or area, date, code[a] and age (in years) / Continent, pays ou zone, date, code[a] et âge (en années)	Number - Nombre			Rate - Taux		
	Both sexes Les deux sexes	Male Masculin	Female Féminin	Both sexes Les deux sexes	Male Masculin	Female Féminin
OCEANIA - OCÉANIE						
Guam[55]						
2016 (C)						
30 - 34	25	16[14]	9[14]	♦2.4	♦3.0	♦1.7
35 - 39	31	23[14]	8[14]	3.2	♦4.7	♦1.6
40 - 44	37	24[14]	13[14]	3.6	♦4.7	♦2.6
45 - 49	50	27[14]	23[14]	4.7	♦4.9	♦4.5
50 - 54	72	49[14]	23[14]	7.0	9.2	♦4.6
55 - 59	92	64[14]	28[14]	10.7	14.5	♦6.6
60 - 64	100	59[14]	41[14]	14.3	16.8	11.7
65 - 69	121	76[14]	45[14]	21.0	27.0	15.3
70 - 74	84	47[14]	37[14]	23.5	27.5	19.8
75 - 79	96	39[14]	57[14]	34.2	31.7	36.2
80 - 84	96	48[14]	48[14]	55.0	70.3	45.1
85 - 89	77	33[14]	44[14]	95.5	107.5	88.2
90 - 94	24	8[14]	16[14]	♦84.5	♦89.9	♦82.1
95 - 99	4	1[14]	3[14]	♦59.7	♦66.7	♦57.7
100 +	2	-[14]	2[14]	♦285.7	-	♦333.3
Unknown - Inconnu	1	-[14]	-[14]	..	..	..
Kiribati[56]						
2011 (U)						
Total	481	279	202	...	...	...
0 - 4	132	75	57	...	...	...
5 - 19	14	10	4	...	...	...
20 - 29	34	24	10	...	...	...
30 - 39	28	15	13	...	...	...
40 - 49	60	37	23	...	...	...
50 - 59	74	42	32	...	...	...
60 - 69	54	34	20	...	...	...
70 +	85	42	43	...	...	...
Nauru						
2011 (C)						
Total	75	41	34	...	...	...
0	10	5	5	...	...	...
1 - 4	1	1	-	...	...	...
5 - 9	-	-	-	...	...	...
10 - 14	1	1	-	...	...	...
15 - 19	-	-	-	...	...	...
20 - 24	2	2	-	...	...	...
25 - 29	5	1	4	...	...	...
30 - 34	4	1	3	...	...	...
35 - 39	2	1	1	...	...	...
40 - 44	2	2	-	...	...	...
45 - 49	6	3	3	...	...	...
50 - 54	15	7	8	...	...	...
55 - 59	9	7	2	...	...	...
60 - 64	6	2	4	...	...	...
65 - 69	4	2	2	...	...	...
70 +	8	6	2	...	...	...
New Caledonia - Nouvelle-Calédonie						
2015 (C)						
Total	1 465	853	612	...	...	...
0	25	18	7	...	...	...
1 - 4	7	4	3	...	...	...
5 - 9	2	-	2	...	...	...
10 - 14	6	4	2	...	...	...
15 - 19	19	13	6	...	...	...
20 - 24	26	22	4	...	...	...
25 - 29	19	17	2	...	...	...
30 - 34	32	23	9	...	...	...
35 - 39	24	21	3	...	...	...
40 - 44	58	45	13	...	...	...
45 - 49	58	41	17	...	...	...
50 - 54	77	48	29	...	...	...
55 - 59	83	46	37	...	...	...
60 - 64	120	76	44	...	...	...
65 - 69	144	95	49	...	...	...

Continent, country or area, date, code[a] and age (in years) / Continent, pays ou zone, date, code[a] et âge (en années)	Number - Nombre			Rate - Taux		
	Both sexes Les deux sexes	Male Masculin	Female Féminin	Both sexes Les deux sexes	Male Masculin	Female Féminin
OCEANIA - OCÉANIE						
New Caledonia - Nouvelle-Calédonie						
2015 (C)						
70 - 74	154	91	63	...	...	...
75 - 79	177	94	83	...	...	...
80 - 84	167	83	84	...	...	...
85 - 89	144	66	78	...	...	...
90 - 94	76	29	47	...	...	...
95 +	47	17	30	...	...	...
New Zealand - Nouvelle-Zélande[57]						
2017 (+C)						
Total	33 342	16 848	16 494	7.0	7.1	6.7
0	228	120	108	3.8	3.9	3.6
1 - 4	45	30	18	0.2	♦0.2	♦0.2
5 - 9	30	15	15	♦0.1	♦0.1	♦0.1
10 - 14	33	21	12	0.1	♦0.1	♦0.1
15 - 19	129	81	48	0.4	0.5	0.3
20 - 24	207	144	66	0.6	0.8	0.4
25 - 29	219	156	60	0.6	0.9	0.3
30 - 34	216	135	78	0.7	0.9	0.5
35 - 39	261	156	105	0.9	1.1	0.7
40 - 44	351	234	117	1.2	1.7	0.8
45 - 49	630	369	258	2.0	2.4	1.5
50 - 54	945	549	396	3.0	3.6	2.4
55 - 59	1 344	768	579	4.4	5.2	3.7
60 - 64	1 824	1 077	747	6.9	8.4	5.5
65 - 69	2 451	1 422	1 032	10.4	12.4	8.6
70 - 74	3 129	1 761	1 368	17.3	20.1	14.6
75 - 79	4 125	2 280	1 845	30.5	35.9	25.7
80 - 84	4 866	2 538	2 325	56.4	65.7	48.9
85 - 89	5 874	2 742	3 129	106.5	120.4	96.7
90 +	6 432	2 250	4 185	213.8	227.0	207.5
90 - 94	4 416	1 671	2 745	...	...	...
95 - 99	1 731	501	1 230	...	...	...
100 +	285	78	210	...	...	...
Niue - Nioué[58]						
2009 (C)						
Total	12	6	6	...	...	...
0	-	-	-	...	...	...
1 - 4	-	-	-	...	...	...
5 - 9	-	-	-	...	...	...
10 - 14	-	-	-	...	...	...
15 - 19	-	-	-	...	...	...
20 - 24	-	-	-	...	...	...
25 - 29	-	-	-	...	...	...
30 - 34	-	-	-	...	...	...
35 - 39	-	-	-	...	...	...
40 - 44	-	-	-	...	...	...
45 - 49	-	-	-	...	...	...
50 - 54	-	-	-	...	...	...
55 - 59	2	2	-	...	...	...
60 - 64	-	-	-	...	...	...
65 - 69	-	-	-	...	...	...
70 - 74	1	-	1	...	...	...
75 - 79	1	1	-	...	...	...
80 +	8	3	5	...	...	...
Palau - Palaos						
2017 (C)						
Total	183	111	72	...	...	...
0	5	4	1	...	...	...
1 - 14	3	2	1	...	...	...
15 - 24	5	2	3	...	...	...
25 - 44	23	18	5	...	...	...
45 - 64	67	50	17	...	...	...
65 +	80	35	45	...	...	...

19. Deaths by age and sex and age-specific death rates by sex: latest available year, 2008 - 2017
Décès et taux de mortalité selon l'âge et le sexe : dernière année disponible, 2008 - 2017 (continued - suite)

Continent, country or area, date, code[a] and age (in years) Continent, pays ou zone, date, code[a] et âge (en années)	Number - Nombre			Rate - Taux		
	Both sexes Les deux sexes	Male Masculin	Female Féminin	Both sexes Les deux sexes	Male Masculin	Female Féminin
OCEANIA - OCÉANIE						
Samoa[22]						
2011 (|)						
Total........................	812	427	385	4.3	4.4	4.2
0 - 4	92	58	34	3.4	4.2	2.6
0	78	51	27	...	...	...
1 - 4	14	7	7	...	...	...
5 - 9	4	1	3	♦0.2	♦0.1	♦0.3
10 - 14	2	-	2	♦0.1	-	♦0.2
15 - 19	10	7	3	♦0.5	♦0.7	♦0.3
20 - 24	12	5	7	♦0.8	♦0.6	♦1.0
25 - 29	10	8	2	♦0.8	♦1.2	♦0.3
30 - 34	6	4	2	♦0.5	♦0.7	♦0.4
35 - 39	20	8	12	♦1.8	♦1.4	♦2.3
40 - 44	19	12	7	♦1.8	♦2.1	♦1.4
45 - 49	38	20	18	4.3	♦4.4	♦4.2
50 - 54	48	28	20	6.3	♦7.1	♦5.5
55 - 59	49	22	27	8.3	♦7.3	♦9.3
60 - 64	69	37	32	17.3	18.5	16.2
65 - 69	76	36	40	22.5	22.4	22.6
70 - 74	101	59	42	39.5	49.7	30.7
75 + ...	250	120	130	74.5	92.2	63.4
75 - 79	80	45	35	...	...	...
80 - 84	84	37	47	...	...	...
85 - 89	62	30	32	...	...	...
90 - 94	17	6	11	...	...	...
95 - 99	7	2	5	...	...	...
100 + ...	-	-	-	...	...	...
Unknown - Inconnu	6	2	4	...	...	...
Wallis and Futuna Islands - Îles Wallis et Futuna						
2008 (C)						
Total.....................	90	51	39	...	...	...
0 - 4	1	1	-	...	...	...
5 - 9	-	-	-	...	...	...
10 - 14	1	1	-	...	...	...
15 - 19	2	1	1	...	...	...
20 - 24	4	3	1	...	...	...
25 - 29	4	4	-	...	...	...
30 - 34	3	3	-	...	...	...
35 - 39	2	1	1	...	...	...
40 - 44	-	-	-	...	...	...
45 - 49	2	1	1	...	...	...
50 - 54	2	1	1	...	...	...
55 - 59	4	2	2	...	...	...
60 - 64	5	4	1	...	...	...
65 - 69	12	8	4	...	...	...
70 - 74	15	9	6	...	...	...
75 - 79	13	4	9	...	...	...
80 - 84	11	4	7	...	...	...
85 - 89	5	3	2	...	...	...
90 - 94	4	1	3	...	...	...
95 - 99	-	-	-	...	...	...
100 + ...	-	-	-	...	...	...

FOOTNOTES - NOTES

♦ Rates based on 30 or fewer deaths. - Taux basés sur 30 décès ou moins.

Italics: estimates which are less reliable. - Italiques : estimations moins sûres.

ˉ Provisional. - Données provisoires.

[a] 'Code' indicates the source of data, as follows:
C - Civil registration, estimated over 90% complete
U - Civil registration, estimated less than 90% complete
\| - Other source, estimated reliable
+ - Data tabulated by date of registration rather than occurence

... - Information not available

Le 'Code' indique la source des données, comme suit :
C - Registres de l'état civil considérés complets à 90 p. 100 au moins
U - Registres de l'état civil qui ne sont pas considérés complets à 90 p. 100 au moins
\| - Autre source, considérée pas douteuses
+ - Données exploitées selon la date de l'enregistrement et non la date de l'événement
... - Information pas disponible

¹ Excluding live-born infants who died before their birth was registered. Data refer to Algerian population only. - Non compris les enfants nés vivants décédés avant l'enregistrement de leur naissance. Les données ne concernent que la population algérienne.

² Source: Vital Statistics Report 2016. - Source: Vital Statistics Report 2016.

³ Data from civil registration centres of Brazzaville, Dolisie, Nkayi, Mossendijo and Ouesso communes. - Données issues des centres d'enregistrement des faits d'état-civil des communes de Brazzaville, Dolisie, Nkayi, Mossendijo et Ouesso.

⁴ Data refer to the 12 months preceding the census in September. - Les données se rapportent aux 12 mois précédant le recensement de septembre.

⁵ Unadjusted number of deaths in households referring to the 12 months preceding the census in March. - Le nombre non ajusté de décès des ménages ordinaires se rapportent aux 12 mois précédant le recensement de mars.

⁶ Unrevised data. - Les données n'ont pas été révisées.

⁷ Data refer to the 12 months preceding the census in June. - Les données se raportent aux 12 mois précédant le recensement de juin.

⁸ Data refer to the 12 months preceding the census in April. - Les données se rapportent aux douze mois précédant le recensement d'avril.

⁹ Excludes the islands of St. Brandon and Agalega. - Non compris les îles St. Brandon et Agalega.

¹⁰ Data refer to the 12 months preceding the census in August. - Les données se rapportent aux 12 mois précédant le recensement d'août.

¹¹ Data refer to the 12 months preceding the census in April. The figures in this table are derived from survey data. They are representative only of private households, internally displaced persons, refugees and nomads, and do not include cattle camps, institutional households, homeless people or overnight travelers. - Les données se rapportent aux douze mois précédant le recensement d'avril. Les chiffres de ce tableau proviennent de données d'enquête. Ils représentent exclusivement les ménages privés et les déplacés, réfugiés et nomades; ils ne comprennent ni les personnes se trouvant dans des camps pastoraux et des établissements collectifs, ni les sans-abri, ni les voyageurs.

¹² Data refer to the 12 months preceding the census in May. - Les données se rapportent aux 12 mois précédant le recensement de mai.

¹³ Source: National Office of Births and Deaths. - Source : Le bureau national des naissances et des décès.

¹⁴ Figures for male and female may not add up to the total, since they do not include the category "Unknown". - La somme des chiffres indiqués pour les sexes masculin et féminin peut n'être pas égale au total parce qu'elle n'inclut pas la catégorie " inconnue ".

¹⁵ Data refer to the 12 months preceding the census in October. - Les données se rapportent aux 12 mois précédant le recensement de octobre.

¹⁶ Excluding visitors. - Ne comprend pas les visiteurs.

¹⁷ Excluding non-residents and foreign service personnel and their dependants. - À l'exclusion des non-résidents et du personnel diplomatique et de leurs charges de famille.

¹⁸ Including Canadian residents temporarily in the United States, but excluding United States residents temporarily in Canada. - Y compris les résidents canadiens se trouvant temporairement aux Etats-Unis, mais ne comprenant pas les résidents des Etats-Unis se trouvant temporairement au Canada.

¹⁹ Data refer to population in private households. Data refer to period from 1 January 2010 to 3 April 2011. - Les données portent sur la population des ménages privés. Les données concernent la période du 1 janvier 2010 au 3 avril 2011.

²⁰ Data refer to resident population only. - Pour la population résidante seulement.

²¹ Data refer to resident and non resident deaths that occurred in Saint Vincent and the Grenadines. - Les données concernent les décès de résidents et de non-résidents survenus à St Vincent-et-les-Grenadines.

²² Data refer to the 12 months preceding the census in November. - Données se rapportant aux 12 mois précédant le recensement de novembre.

²³ Including deaths abroad and deaths of unknown place of residence. - Y compris décès à l'étranger et décès dont le lieu de résidence n'est pas connu.

²⁴ Excludes nomadic Indian tribes. - Non compris les tribus d'Indiens nomades.

²⁵ Source: Reports of the Ministry of Health. - Source : Rapports du Ministère de la Santé.

²⁶ Excluding infants born alive of less than 28 weeks' gestation, of less than 1 000 g in weight and 35 cm in length, who die within seven days of birth. - Non compris les enfants nés vivants après moins de 28 semaines de gestations, pesant moins de 1 000 g, mesurant moins de 35 cm et décédés dans les sept jours qui ont suivi leur naissance.

²⁷ Sources: Births and Deaths National Registration System database, and medical records of government hospitals. - Les sources: Les bases de données des << Births and Deaths National Registration System >> et les dossiers médicaux des hôpitaux du gouvernement.

²⁸ For statistical purposes, the data for China do not include those for the Hong Kong Special Administrative Region (Hong Kong SAR), Macao Special Administrative Region (Macao SAR) and Taiwan province of China. Data refer to the 12 months preceding the census in November. - Pour la présentation des statistiques, les données pour la Chine ne comprennent pas la Région Administrative Spéciale de Hong Kong (Hong Kong RAS), la Région Administrative Spéciale de Macao (Macao RAS) et Taïwan province de Chine. Données se rapportant aux 12 mois précédant le recensement de novembre.

²⁹ Data refer to government controlled areas. Data refer to deaths of residents only. - Les données se rapportent aux zones contrôlées par le Gouvernement. Les données renvoient aux décès de résidents uniquement.

³⁰ Data are from 1 January 2009 to 1 May 2010. - Les données vont du 1er janvier 2009 au 1er mai 2010.

³¹ Data refer to the Iranian Year which begins on 21 March and ends on 20 March of the following year. Data refer to current deaths; excluding delayed registrations. - Les données concernent l'année iranienne, qui commence le 21 mars et se termine le 20 mars de l'année suivante. Les données se rapportent aux décès actuels; les déclarations tardives des décès ne sont pas compris.

³² Includes data for East Jerusalem and Israeli residents in certain other territories under occupation by Israeli military forces since June 1967. Including deaths abroad of Israeli residents who were out of the country for less than a year. - Y compris les données pour Jérusalem-Est et les résidents israéliens dans certains autres territoires occupés depuis 1967 par les forces armées israéliennes. Y compris les décès à l'étranger de résidents israéliens qui ont quitté le pays depuis moins d'un an.

³³ Data refer to Japanese nationals in Japan only. - Les données se raportent aux nationaux japonais au Japon seulement.

³⁴ Data do not include foreigners. - Les données sur les etrangers ne sont pas inclus.

³⁵ Data are from Vital Registration System (VRS). - Les données proviennent du système d'enregistrement des faits d'état civil.

³⁶ Excluding alien armed forces, civilian aliens employed by armed forces, and foreign diplomatic personnel and their dependants. - Non compris les militaires étrangers, les civils étrangers employés par les forces armées ni le personnel diplomatique étranger et les membres de leur famille les accompagnant.

³⁷ Data refer to Saudi Arabian nationals only. Based on 2010 population census and 2016 demographic survey. - Les données ne concernent que les ressortissants saoudiens. D'après le recensement de la population de 2010 et l'enquête démographique de 2016.

³⁸ Source: Palestinian Central Bureau of Statistics, Population Register, updated version 22/02/2016. - Source: Bureau central de statistique palestinien, registre de la population, version actualisée jusqu'au 22/02/2016.

³⁹ Figures for this table vary from other tables because of a different source. - Les chiffres figurant dans ce tableau ne correspondent pas à ceux d'autres tableaux parce que des sources différentes ont été utilisées.

⁴⁰ Data from MERNIS (Central Population Administrative System). - Données de MERNIS (Système central de données démographiques).

⁴¹ Including deaths of nationals abroad. - Y compris les décès des nationaux survenus à l'étranger.

⁴² Including armed forces stationed outside the country, but excluding alien armed forces stationed in the area. - Y compris les militaires nationaux hors du pays, mais non compris les militaires étrangers en garnison sur le territoire.

⁴³ Excluding Faeroe Islands and Greenland shown separately, if available. - Non compris les îles Féroé et le Groenland, qui font l'objet de rubriques distinctes, si disponible.

⁴⁴ Including armed forces stationed outside the country. - Y compris les militaires nationaux hors du pays.

⁴⁵ Data include the deceased persons with Hungarian usual residence regardless of whether the death occurred in Hungary or in a foreign country, and do not include the deceased persons with foreign country usual residence. - Les données comprennent tous les décès survenus alors que leur résidence habituelle était en Hongrie, que le décès ait eu lieu en Hongrie ou dans un pays étranger, et ne comprennent pas les décès des personnes dont la residence habituelle était dans un pays étranger.

⁴⁶ Including residents outside the country if listed in a Netherlands population register. - Englobe les résidents se trouvant à l'étranger à condition qu'ils soient inscrits sur le registre de population des Pays-Bas.

⁴⁷ Including residents temporarily outside the country. - Y compris les résidents se trouvant temporairement hors du pays.

⁴⁸ Data refer to usually resident population. - Les données concernent la population habituellement résidente.

⁴⁹ Excluding Transnistria and the municipality of Bender. - Les données ne tiennent pas compte de l'information sur la Transnistria et la municipalité de Bender.

⁵⁰ Excludes data for Kosovo and Metohia. - Sans les données pour le Kosovo et Metohie.

51   Data includes deaths resulting from births with weight 500 g and more (if weight is unknown - with length 25 cm and more, or with gestation during 22 weeks or more).   The Government of Ukraine has informed the United Nations that it is not in a position to provide statistical data concerning the Autonomous Republic of Crimea and the city of Sevastopol. - Y compris les décès de nouveau-nés de 500 g ou plus (si le poids est inconnu – de 25 cm de long ou plus, ou après une grossesse de 22 semaines ou plus).   Le gouvernement Ukrainien a informé l'ONU qu'il n'est pas en mesure de fournir des données statistiques concernant la République autonome de Crimée et la ville de Sébastopol.

52   Excluding Channel Islands (Guernesey and Jersey) and Isle of Man, shown separately, if available. - Non compris les îles Anglo-Normandes (Guernesey et Jersey) et l'île de Man, qui font l'objet de rubriques distinctes, si disponible.

53   Data for certain cells suppressed by national statistical office for confidentiality reasons. - Les données pour certaines cases ont été supprimées par le bureau national de statistiques pour des raisons de confidentialité.

54   Excluding Niue, shown separately, which is part of Cook Islands, but because of remoteness is administered separately.   Unrevised data. - Non compris Nioué, qui fait l'objet d'une rubrique distincte et qui fait partie des îles Cook, mais qui, en raison de son éloignement, est administrée séparément.   Les données n'ont pas été révisées.

55   Including United States military personnel, their dependants and contract employees. - Y compris les militaires des Etats-Unis, les membres de leur famille les accompagnant et les agents contractuels des Etats-Unis.

56   Excluding deaths of unknown age or sex. - Les données ne comprennent pas les décès d'âge ou de sexe inconnus.

57   Data refer to deaths of residents only.   Random rounding to base 3 is applied in this table as a confidentiality measure. - Les données renvoient aux décès de résidents uniquement.   Les chiffres sont arrondis à la base 3 de manière aléatoire, pour des raisons de confidentialité.

58   Includes deaths occurred in New Zealand but buried in Niue and deaths occurred in Niue but buried elsewhere. - Y compris les personnes décédées en Nouvelle-Zélande qui sont enterrées à Nioué et les personnes décédées à Nioué qui sont enterrées ailleurs.

Table 20 – *Demographic Yearbook 2017*

Table 20 presents deaths and death rates by cause and sex for the two latest available years between 2012 and 2016.

Description of variables: Causes of death are all those diseases, morbid conditions or injuries which either resulted in or contributed to death and the circumstances of the accident or violence which produced any such injuries.[1]

The underlying cause of death, rather than direct or intermediate antecedent cause, is the one recommended as the main cause for tabulation of mortality statistics. It is defined as (a) the disease or injury which initiated the train of events leading directly to death, or (b) the circumstances of the accident or violence which produced the fatal injury.[1]

Statistics on deaths by cause presented in this table are provided by the World Health Organisation. They are limited to countries or areas that meet the criterion that cause-of-death statistics are classified to the ninth or tenth revisions of the International Classification of Diseases (ICD-9 or ICD-10). Data that are classified by the tenth revision are set in bold in the table.

Rate computation: Rates are the annual number of deaths in each cause group by sex reported for the year per 100 000 corresponding mid-year population. For certain causes, the population that more nearly approximates the population at risk is used as denominator, as specified below:
- rates for malignant neoplasm of female breast and malignant neoplasm of cervix uteri are computed per 100 000 female population 15 years and over;
- rates for hyperplasia of prostate are computed per 100 000 male population 50 years and over; and
- rates for direct and indirect obstetric causes, and rates for conditions originating in the perinatal period are computed per 100 000 total live births in the same year.

Rates presented in this table have been limited to those countries or areas having a total of at least 1 000 deaths from all causes in a given year. In certain cases death rates by cause have not been calculated because the population data needed for the denominator are not available (no data on population at risk are available). Moreover, rates based on 30 or fewer deaths shown in this table are identified by the symbol (♦).

Reliability of data: Countries and areas that have incomplete (less than 90 per cent completeness) or of unknown completeness of cause of deaths data coverage are considered unreliable and are set in *italics* rather than in roman type. Rates on these data are not computed. Information on completeness is normally provided by the World Health Organisation, when this is not the case, information on completeness is set to coincide with that of Table 18. Similarly, the reliability of data for the completeness of cause of death is provided by the World Health Organisation and it may differ from the reliability of data for the total number of reported deaths. Therefore, there are cases when the quality code in table 18 does not correspond with the typeface used in this table.

Territorial composition as set in Section 2.2 of "Technical Notes on the Statistical Tables", including or excluding certain population of a country refers only to the denominator.

Limitations: Statistics on deaths by cause are subject to the same qualifications as have been set forth for vital statistics in general and death statistics in particular as discussed in section 4 of the Technical Notes.

In considering cause-of-death statistics it is important to take account of the differences among countries or areas in the quality, availability, and efficiency of medical services, certification procedures, and coding practices. When a death is registered and reported for statistical purposes, the cause of death if available will be stated in the death registration form. This statement of cause may have several sources: (1) If the death has been followed by an autopsy, presumably the "true" cause will have been discovered; (2) If an autopsy is not performed but the decedent was treated prior to death by a medical attendant, the reported cause of death will reflect the opinion of that physician based on observation of the patient while he or she was alive; and (3) If, on the other hand, the decedent has died without medical attendance, the body

---

NOTES

[1] *International Statistical Classification of Diseases and Related Health Problems*, Tenth Revision, Volume 2, World Health Organization, Geneva, 1992

may be examined (without autopsy) by a physician who, aided by the questioning of persons who saw the patient before death, may come to a decision as to the probable cause of death. These three possible sources of information on cause of death constitute in general three degrees of decreasing accuracy in reporting.

Serious difficulties of comparability may stem also from differences in the form of death certificate being used, an increasing tendency to enter more than one cause of death on the certificate and diversity in the principles by which the primary or underlying cause is selected for statistical use when more than one is entered.

Differences in terminology used to identify the same disease also result in lack of comparability in statistics. These differences may arise in the same language in various parts of one country or area, but they are particularly troublesome between different languages.

Coding problems, and problems in interpretation of rules, arise constantly in using the various revisions of the International Statistical Classification of Diseases and Related Health Problems. Lack of uniformity between countries or areas in these interpretations and in adapting rules to national needs, results in a lack of comparability that can be observed in the statistics. It is particularly evident in causes that are coded differently according to the age of the decedent, such as pneumonia, diarrhoeal diseases and others. Changing interpretations and new rules can also introduce disparities into the time series for one country or area. Hence, large increases or decreases in deaths reported from specified diseases should be examined carefully for possible explanations in terms of coding practice, before they are accepted as changes in mortality.

Further limitations of statistics by cause of death result from the periodic revision of the International Classification of Diseases. Data might not be comparable among countries or areas if different revisions of the Classification were used. Similarly, comparison over time for one country or area is not appropriate if different revisions were applied in the country. For a correspondence between ICD-10 and ICD-9, please see table 20-1 below.

In addition to the qualifications explained in footnotes, particular care must be taken in using distributions with relatively large numbers of deaths attributed to ill-defined causes. Large frequencies in this category may indicate that cause of death among whole segments of the population has been undiagnosed, and the distribution of known causes in such cases is likely to be quite unrepresentative of the situation as a whole.

The possibility of error being introduced by the exclusion of deaths of infants who were born alive but died before the registration of the birth or within the first 24 hours of life should not be overlooked. These infant deaths are incorrectly classified as late foetal deaths. In several countries or areas, tabulation procedures have been devised to separate these pseudo-late-foetal deaths from true late foetal deaths and to incorporate them into the total deaths, but even in these cases there is no way of knowing the cause of death.

In addition, it should be noted that rates are affected also by the quality and limitations of the population at risk that are used in their computation. The problems of under-enumeration or over-enumeration and, to some extent, the differences in definition of population and live births have been discussed in section 3 of the Technical Notes dealing with population data in general and section 4 with vital statistics, respectively, Specific information pertaining to individual countries or areas is given in the footnotes to table 3 on total population and to table 9 on live births.

Earlier data: Deaths and death rates by cause have been shown annually since the 1951 issue of the *Demographic Yearbook* and every other year since the 2000 issue. For information on specific years covered, readers should consult the Historical Index.

Table 20-1. Tabulation list for ICD-9 and ICD-10 data for presentation in the Demographic Yearbook

Disease	ICD-10	ICD-9 Basic Tabulation List
All causes	**A00-Y89**	**01-56**
Certain infectious and parasitic diseases	**A00-A33, A35-B99**	**01-07, 184**
Intestinal infectious diseases	A00-A09	01
Tuberculosis	A15-A19	02
Tetanus[1]	A33, A35	037
Diphtheria	A36	033
Whooping cough	A37	034
Meningococcal infection	A39	036
Septicaemia	A40-A41	038
Acute poliomyelitis	A80	040
Measles	B05	042
Viral hepatitis	B15-B19	046
Human immunodeficiency virus [HIV] disease	B20-B24	184
Malaria	B50-B54	052
Neoplasms	**C00-D48**	**08-17**
Malignant neoplasms	**C00-C97**	**08-14**
Malignant neoplasm of lip, oral cavity and pharynx	C00-C14	08
Malignant neoplasm of oesophagus	C15	090
Malignant neoplasm of stomach	C16	091
Malignant neoplasm of colon, rectosigmoid junction, rectum, anus and anal canal	C18-C21	093-094
Malignant neoplasm of liver and intrahepatic bile ducts	C22	095
Malignant neoplasm of pancreas	C25	096
Malignant neoplasm of trachea, bronchus and lung	C33-C34	101
Malignant neoplasm of **female** breast	C50	113
Malignant neoplasm of cervix uteri	C53	120
Malignant neoplasm of prostate	C61	124
Malignant neoplasm of lymphoid, haematopoietic and related tissue	C81-C96	14
Disorders of the blood and blood-forming organs and certain disorders involving the immune mechanism	**D50-D89**	**20**
Anaemias	D50-D64	200
Endocrine, nutritional and metabolic diseases	**E00-E88**	**18-19, minus 184**
Diabetes mellitus	E10-E14	181
Malnutrition	E40-E46	190-192
Mental and behavioural disorders	**F01-F99**	**21**
Diseases of the nervous system	**G00-G98**	**22**
Diseases of the circulatory system	**I00-I99**	**25-30**
Acute rheumatic fever and chronic rheumatic heart diseases	I01-I09	25
Hypertensive diseases	I10-I13	26
Ischaemic heart diseases	I20-I25	27
Cerebrovascular diseases	I60-I69	29
Diseases of arteries, arterioles and capillaries	I70-I79	300-302
Diseases of the respiratory system	**J00-J98**	**31-32**
Influenza	J10-J11	322

Table 20-1. Tabulation list for ICD-9 and ICD-10 data for presentation in the Demographic Yearbook

Disease	ICD-10	ICD-9 Basic Tabulation List
Pneumonia	J12-J18	321
Chronic lower respiratory diseases	J40-J47	323-325
Diseases of the digestive system	**K00-K92**	**33-34**
Gastric and duodenal ulcer	K25-K27	341
Diseases of the liver	K70-K76	347
Diseases of the musculoskeletal system and connective tissue	**M00-M99**	**43**
Diseases of the genitourinary system	**N00-N98**	**35-37**
Disorders of kidney and ureter	N00-N28	350-351
Hyperplasia of prostate	N40	360
Pregnancy, childbirth and the puerperium	**O00-O99, A34**	**38-41**
Pregnancy with abortive outcome	O00-O07	38
Other direct obstetric causes[1]	O10-092, O95, A34	39
Indirect obstetric causes	O98-O99	40
Certain conditions originating in the perinatal period	**P00-P96**	**45**
Congenital malformations, deformations and chromosomal abnormalities	**Q00-Q99**	**44**
Symptoms, signs and abnormal clinical and laboratory findings, not elsewhere classified	**R00-R99**	**46**
All other diseases	**H00-H95, L00-L98**	**23-24, 42**
External causes	**V01-Y89**	**E47-E56**
Accidents	**V01-X59**	**E47-E53**
Transport accidents	V01-V99	E47
Falls	W00-W19	E50
Accidental drowning and submersion	W65-W74	E521
Exposure to smoke, fire and flames	X00-X09	E51
Accidental poisoning by and exposure to noxious substances	X40-X49	E48
Intentional self-harm	**X60-X84**	**E54**
Assault	**X85-Y09**	**E55**
All other external causes	**Y10-Y89**	**E56**

[1] In ICD-10 obstetrical tetanus is classified to A34 but in this table it is included with "Other direct obstetric causes", except for Belarus, Russian Federation, Seychelles, Turkmenistan and Ukraine, where obstetrical tetanus is included in "Tetanus" and "Other direct obstetric causes" excludes A34 and O95.

Tableau 20 - *Annuaire démographique 2017*

Le tableau 20 présente la statistique des décès par cause et sexe pour les deux dernières années entre 2012 et 2016.

Description des variables : les causes des décès sont toutes les maladies, états morbides ou traumatismes qui ont abouti ou contribué au décès et les circonstances de l'accident ou de la violence qui ont entraîné ces traumatismes[1].

La cause initiale de décès, plutôt que la cause directe du décès, est recommandée pour les statistiques de la mortalité. La cause initiale de décès est définie comme : a) la maladie ou le traumatisme qui a déclenché l'évolution morbide conduisant directement au décès ; b) les circonstances de l'accident ou de la violence qui ont entraîné le traumatisme mortel[1].

Les statistiques sur les décès classés en fonction de la cause qui les a provoqués émanent de l'Organisation mondiale de la santé. Elles ne portent que sur les pays ou les zones dans lesquels les statistiques relatives à la cause des décès sont conformes à la liste de la neuvième ou de la dixième révision de la *Classification statistique internationale des maladies* (CIM-9 ou CIM-10). Les données conformes à la liste de la dixième révision sont indiquées en caractères gras dans le tableau.

Calcul des taux : les taux représentent le nombre annuel de décès signalés dans chaque groupe, pour l'année, dans une population de 100 000 habitants en milieu d'année.

Les taux relatifs à certaines catégories de causes correspondent aux populations les plus semblables à la population exposée comme spécifié ci-dessous :
- les taux correspondant aux catégories « tumeur maligne du sein chez la femme » et « tumeur maligne du col de l'utérus » sont calculés sur une population de 100 000 femmes de 15 ans ou plus.
- les taux correspondant à la catégorie « tumeur maligne de la prostate » sont calculés sur une population de 100 000 personnes de sexe masculin âgées de 50 ans ou plus, et
- les taux pour les catégories « décès maternels directs », « décès maternels indirects » et « affections dont l'origine se situe dans la période périnatale » sont calculés sur 100 000 naissances vivantes dans la même année.

Les taux figurant dans ce tableau ne concernent que les pays ou zones où l'on a relevé au moins 1 000 décès, toutes causes confondues, dans l'année. Dans certains cas, on n'a pas calculé les taux de mortalité selon la cause car l'on ne disposait pas des informations sur la population qui étaient nécessaires pour déterminer le dénominateur (pas d'informations sur la population exposée au risque). De plus, les taux calculés sur la base de 30 décès ou moins, qui sont indiqués dans le tableau, sont signalés par le signe '♦'.

Fiabilité des données : les statistiques relatives aux pays et aux zones pour lesquels la couverture des données concernant les causes de décès est incomplète (mois de 90 pour cent) ou dont le degré de complétude n'est pas connue sont jugés douteuses et apparaissent en *italique* et non en caractères romains. Les taux correspondant ne sont pas calculés. L'information sur la complétude est normalement fournie par l'Organisation Mondiale de la Santé. Si ce n'est pas le cas, l'information sur la complétude est reprise de tableau 18. De même, la fiabilité des données relatives aux causes de décès est fournie par l'Organisation Mondiale de la Santé et peut différer de la fiabilité des données relatives au nombre de décès enregistrés. En conséquence, il peut apparaitre de différences entre les codes de fiabilité du tableau 18 et du présent tableau.

La composition territoriale est définie dans la Section 2.2 des "Notes Techniques sur les tableaux statistiques". L'inclusion ou l'exclusion de certaines populations d'un pays ne concerne que le dénominateur.

Insuffisance des données : les statistiques des décès selon la cause appellent les mêmes réserves que celles qui ont été formulées à propos des statistiques de l'état civil en général et des statistiques relatives aux décès en particulier (voir la section 4 des Notes techniques).

Lorsque l'on étudie les statistiques des causes des décès, il importe de prendre en considération les disparités existant entre pays ou zones du point de vue de la qualité, de la disponibilité et de l'efficacité des services médicaux, ainsi que des méthodes d'établissement des certificats de décès et des procédés de codage. Lorsqu'un décès est enregistré et déclaré aux fins de statistiques, le bulletin établi doit mentionner la cause du décès si elle est connue. Or la déclaration de la cause peut émaner de plusieurs sources : 1) si le décès a été suivi d'une autopsie, il est probable qu'on en aura décelé la cause « véritable » ; 2) s'il n'y a pas eu d'autopsie mais que le défunt a reçu, avant sa mort, les soins d'un médecin, la déclaration de la cause du décès reflétera l'opinion de ce médecin fondée sur l'observation du malade alors qu'il vivait encore ; 3) si, au contraire, le défunt est mort sans avoir reçu de soins médicaux, il se peut qu'un médecin examine le corps (sans qu'il soit fait d'autopsie), auquel cas il pourra, en questionnant les personnes qui ont vu le défunt avant sa mort, se former une opinion sur la cause probable du décès. À ces trois sources de renseignements possibles correspondent généralement trois degrés décroissants d'exactitude des données.

La comparabilité est aussi parfois très difficile à assurer par suite des différences existant dans la forme des certificats de décès utilisés, de la tendance croissante à indiquer plus d'une cause de décès sur le certificat et de la diversité des principes régissant le choix de la cause principale ou initiale à retenir dans les statistiques quand le certificat indique plus d'une cause.

Les différences entre les termes utilisés pour désigner une même maladie compromettent aussi la comparabilité des statistiques. On en rencontre parfois d'une région à l'autre dans un même pays ou une même zone où toute la population parle la même langue, mais elles sont particulièrement gênantes lorsque plusieurs langues interviennent.

En outre, des problèmes de codage et d'interprétation des règles se posent constamment lorsque l'on utilise les diverses révisions de la *Classification statistique internationale des maladies et des problèmes de santé connexes*. Les pays ou zones n'interprètent pas ces règles de manière uniforme et ne les adaptent pas de la même façon à leurs besoins ; la comparabilité s'en ressent comme le montrent les statistiques. Cela est particulièrement vrai pour les causes comme la pneumonie et les maladies diarrhéiques et autres, qui sont codées différemment selon l'âge du défunt. Les changements d'interprétation et l'adoption de nouvelles règles peuvent aussi introduire des divergences dans les séries chronologiques d'un même pays ou d'une même zone. En conséquence, il convient d'examiner attentivement les cas où le nombre de décès attribués à des maladies déterminées s'accroît ou diminue fortement, pour s'assurer, avant de conclure à une évolution de la mortalité, que le changement n'est pas dû à la méthode de codage.

D'autres irrégularités statistiques résultent des révisions périodiques de la *Classification statistique internationale des maladies*. Il est possible que les données ne soient pas comparables d'un pays ou d'une zone à un autre si différentes révisions de la classification ont été utilisées. De même, il n'est pas possible de comparer les données dans le temps pour un même pays ou zone lorsque différentes révisions y ont été utilisées. Pour une correspondance entre CIM-10 et CIM-9, veuillez voir le tableau 20-2 ci-dessous.

Outre les réserves expliquées dans les notes, il faut interpréter avec circonspection les répartitions comportant un nombre relativement élevé de décès attribués à des causes mal définies. Si les chiffres donnés pour cette catégorie sont importants, c'est peut-être parce que les décès survenus parmi des pans entiers de la population n'ont fait l'objet d'aucun diagnostic ; en pareil cas, il est probable que la répartition des causes connues est loin de donner une vue exacte de la situation d'ensemble.

Il ne faut pas négliger non plus le risque d'erreur que peut présenter l'exclusion des enfants nés vivants mais décédés avant l'enregistrement de leur naissance ou dans les 24 heures qui ont suivi la naissance. Ces décès sont classés à tort dans les morts fœtales tardives. Dans plusieurs pays ou zones, les méthodes d'exploitation permettent de différencier ces pseudo-morts fœtales tardives des morts fœtales tardives véritables et de les ajouter au nombre total des décès, mais, là encore, il est impossible de connaître la cause du décès.

De plus, il convient de noter que les taux sont également fonction de la qualité de l'évaluation de la population à risque et des caractéristiques de celle-ci dont il est tenu compte dans leur calcul. Les problèmes du sous-enregistrement et du sur-enregistrement et, à un certain degré, les différences entre les définitions de la population et des naissances vivantes ont été examinés, respectivement, à la section 3 des Notes techniques, qui traite des données démographiques en général, et à la section 4, qui traite des statistiques de l'état civil. Des informations sur certains pays ou certaines zones sont données dans les notes du tableau 3, relatif à la population totale, et dans celles du tableau 9, relatif aux naissances vivantes.

Données antérieures : Le nombre des décès et les taux de mortalité par cause ont été publiés chaque année dans les éditions de l'*Annuaire démographique* 1951 à 2000, et tous les deux ans depuis. Pour obtenir ces informations pour une année donnée, les lecteurs doivent se reporter à l'index historique.

Tableau 20-2. Liste de tabulation pour les données CIM-9 et CIM-10 pour la présentation dans l'annuaire démographique

Maladie	CIM-10	CIM-9 (Liste de base pour la mise en tableaux)
Toutes causes	**A00-Y89**	**01-56**
Certaines maladies infectieuses et parasitaires	**A00-A33, A35-B99**	**01-07, 184**
Maladies infectieuses intestinales	A00-A09	01
Tuberculose	A15-A19	02
Tétanos[2]	A33, A35	037
Diphtérie	A36	033
Coqueluche	A37	034
Infection à méningocoques	A39	036
Septicémie	A40-A41	038
Poliomyélite aiguë	A80	040
Rougeole	B05	042
Hépatite virale	B15-B19	046
Maladies dues au virus de l'immunodéficience humaine (VIH)	B20-B24	184
Malaria	B50-B54	052
Tumeurs	**C00-D48**	**08-17**
Tumeurs malignes	**C00-C97**	**08-14**
Tumeur maligne de la lèvre, de la cavité buccale et du pharynx	C00-C14	08
Tumeur maligne de l'oesophage	C15	090
Tumeur maligne de l'estomac	C16	091
sigmoïdienne, du rectum, de l'anus et du canal anal	C18-C21	093-094
Tumeur maligne du foie et des voies bilaires intrahépatiques	C22	095
Tumeur maligne du pancréas	C25	096
Tumeur maligne de la trachée, des bronches et du poumon	C33-C34	101
Tumeur maligne du sein chez la femme	C50	113
Tumeur maligne du col de l'utérus	C53	120
Tumeur maligne de la prostate	C61	124
Tumeurs malignes primitives ou présumées primitives des tissus lymphoïde, hématopoïétique et apparentés	C81-C96	14
Maladies du sang et des organes hématopoïétiques et certains troubles du système immunitaire	**D50-D89**	**20**
Anémies	D50-D64	200
Maladies endocriniennes, nutritionnelles et métaboliques	**E00-E88**	**18-19, minus 184**
Diabète sucré	E10-E14	181
Malnutrition	E40-E46	190-192
Troubles mentaux et du comportement	**F01-F99**	**21**
Maladies du système nerveux	**G00-G98**	**22**
Maladies de l'appareil circulatoire	**I00-I99**	**25-30**
Rhumatisme articularie aigu et cardiopathies rhumatismales chroniques	I01-I09	25
Maladies hypertensives	I10-I13	26
Cardiopathies ischémiques	I20-I25	27
Maladies cérébrovasculaires	I60-I69	29
Maladies des artères, artérioles et capillaires	I70-I79	300-302
Maladies de l'appareil respiratoire	**J00-J98**	**31-32**

Tableau 20-2. Liste de tabulation pour les données CIM-9 et CIM-10 pour la présentation dans l'annuaire démographique

Maladie	CIM-10	CIM-9 (Liste de base pour la mise en tableaux)
Grippe	J10-J11	322
Pneumopathies	J12-J18	321
Maladies chroniques des voies respiratoires inférieures	J40-J47	323-325
Maladies de l'appareil digestif	**K00-K92**	**33-34**
Ulcère de l'estomac et du duodénum	K25-K27	341
Maladies du foie	K70-K76	347
Maladies du système ostéo-articularie, des muscles et du tissu conjonctif	**M00-M99**	**43**
Maladies de l'appareil génito-urinaire	**N00-N98**	**35-37**
Affections du rein et de l'uretère	N00-N28	350-351
Hyperplasie de la prostate	N40	360
Grossesse, accouchement et puerpéralité	**O00-O99, A34**	**38-41**
Grossesse se terminant par un avortement	O00-O07	38
Autres décès maternels directs[2]	O10-092, O95, A34	39
Décès maternels indirects	O98-O99	40
Certaines affections dont l'origine se situe dans la période périnatale	**P00-P96**	**45**
Malformations congénitales et anomalies chromosomiques	**Q00-Q99**	**44**
Symptômes, signes et résultats anormaux d'examens cliniques et de laboratoire, non classés ailleurs	**R00-R99**	**46**
Toutes autres maladies	**H00-H95, L00-L98**	**23-24, 42**
Causes externes	**V01-Y89**	**E47-E56**
Accidents	**V01-X59**	**E47-E53**
Accidents de transport	V01-V99	E47
Chutes	W00-W19	E50
Noyade et submersion accidentelles	W65-W74	E521
Exposition à la fumée, au feu et aux flammes	X00-X09	E51
Intoxication accidentelle par des substances nocives et exposition à ces substances	X40-X49	E48
Lésions auto-infligées	**X60-X84**	**E54**
Agresssions	**X85-Y09**	**E55**
Toutes autres causes externes	**Y10-Y89**	**E56**

NOTES

[1] *Classification statistique internationale des maladies et des problèmes de santé connexes*, dixième révision, volume 2. Genève, Organisation mondiale de la santé, 1992.

[2] Dans la Classification internationale des maladies (CIM-10), le tétanos obstétrique est classé à la rubrique A34 mais, dans ce tableau, il est inclus dans les « Autres causes obstétriques directes », sauf pour Bélarus, Fédération de Russie, Seychelles, Turkménistan et Ukraine où le tétanos obstétrique est inclus dans « Tétanos » et « Autres causes obstétriques directes » exclut A34 et O95.

20. Death and death rates by cause and sex: 2012 - 2016
Décès et taux de mortalité par cause et sexe : 2012 - 2016

Cause of death — Cause de décès	Cabo Verde 2012 (C)				Egypt - Égypte 2014 (C)			
	Male — Masculin		Female — Féminin		Male — Masculin		Female — Féminin	
	Number Nombre	Rate Taux	Number Nombre	Rate Taux	Number Nombre	Rate Taux	Number Nombre	Rate Taux
TOTAL	1 477	587.5	1 287	505.5	293 313	662.1	238 551	561.2
Certain infectious and parasitic diseases — Certaines maladies infectieuses et parasitaires								
Total	102	40.6	96	37.7	10 536	23.8	7 829	18.4
Intestinal infectious diseases — Maladies infectieuses intestinales	9	♦3.6	16	♦6.3	1 940	4.4	2 079	4.9
Tuberculosis — Tuberculose	11	♦4.4	6	♦2.4	171	0.4	62	0.1
Tetanus — Tétanos	-	-	-	-	51	0.1	8	♦0.0
Diphtheria — Diphtérie	-	-	-	-	-	-	-	-
Whooping cough — Coqueluche	-	-	-	-	-	-	-	-
Meningococcal infection — Infection à méningocoques	-	-	-	-	18	♦0.0	8	♦0.0
Septicaemia — Septicémie	28	♦11.1	43	16.9	2 201	5.0	1 938	4.6
Acute poliomyelitis — Poliomyélite aiguë	-	-	-	-	7	♦0.0	6	♦0.0
Measles — Rougeole	-	-	-	-	9	♦0.0	7	♦0.0
Viral hepatitis — Hépatite virale	3	♦1.2	2	♦0.8	4 619	10.4	2 651	6.2
Human immunodeficiency virus [HIV] disease — Maladies dues au virus de l'immunodéficience humaine (VIH)	51	20.3	28	♦11.0	9	♦0.0	8	♦0.0
Malaria — Paludisme	-	-	1	♦0.4	3	♦0.0	1	♦0.0
Neoplasms — Tumeurs	202	80.4	183	71.9	19 589	44.2	15 746	37.0
Malignant neoplasms — Tumeurs malignes								
Total	202	80.4	180	70.7	18 547	41.9	14 317	33.7
Malignant neoplasm of lip, oral cavity and pharynx — Tumeur maligne de la lèvre, de la cavité buccale et du pharynx	8	♦3.2	4	♦1.6	235	0.5	156	0.4
Malignant neoplasm of oesophagus — Tumeur maligne de l'oesophage	28	♦11.1	7	♦2.7	215	0.5	112	0.3
Malignant neoplasm of stomach — Tumeur maligne de l'estomac	32	12.7	20	♦7.9	919	2.1	802	1.9
Malignant neoplasm of colon, rectosigmoid junction, rectum, anus and anal canal — Tumeur maligne du côlon, de la jonction recto-sigmoïdienne, du rectum, de l'anus et du canal anal	8	♦3.2	8	♦3.1	928	2.1	791	1.9
Malignant neoplasm of liver and intrahepatic bile ducts — Tumeur maligne du foie et des voies bilaires intrahépatiques	14	♦5.6	18	♦7.1	4 952	11.2	2 284	5.4
Malignant neoplasm of pancreas — Tumeur maligne du pancréas	6	♦2.4	14	♦5.5	765	1.7	423	1.0
Malignant neoplasm of trachea, bronchus and lung — Tumeur maligne de la trachée, des bronches et du poumon	19	♦7.6	13	♦5.1	2 347	5.3	1 115	2.6
Malignant neoplasm of female breast — Tumeur maligne du sein chez la femme	..	..	13	♦7.3	..	..	2 503	8.5
Malignant neoplasm of cervix uteri — Tumeur maligne du col de l'utérus	..	..	20	♦11.3	..	..	156	0.5
Malignant neoplasm of prostate — Tumeur maligne de la prostate	46	156.7	..	..	750	11.7	..	..
Malignant neoplasm of lymphoid, haematopoietic and related tissue — Tumeurs malignes primitives ou présumées primitives des tissus lymphoïde, hématopoïétique et apparentés	10	♦4.0	15	♦5.9	1 927	4.3	1 556	3.7
Disorders of the blood and blood-forming organs and certain disorders involving the immune mechanism — Maladies du sang et des organes hématopoïétiques et certains troubles du système immunitaire								
Total	6	♦2.4	8	♦3.1	2 858	6.5	2 711	6.4
Anaemias — Anémies	5	♦2.0	7	♦2.7	439	1.0	515	1.2
Endocrine, nutritional and metabolic diseases — Maladies endocriniennes, nutritionnelles et métaboliques								
Total	37	14.7	51	20.0	11 551	26.1	13 311	31.3
Diabetes mellitus — Diabète sucré	27	♦10.7	46	18.1	9 240	20.9	10 598	24.9
Malnutrition — Malnutrition	4	♦1.6	2	♦0.8	119	0.3	109	0.3
Mental and behavioural disorders — Troubles mentaux et du comportement	72	28.6	14	♦5.5	532	1.2	362	0.9
Diseases of the nervous system — Maladies du système nerveux	25	♦9.9	14	♦5.5	3 166	7.1	2 978	7.0
Diseases of the circulatory system — Maladies de l'appareil circulatoire								
Total	306	121.7	385	151.2	134 419	303.4	119 592	281.3
Acute rheumatic fever and chronic rheumatic heart diseases — Rhumatisme articularie aigu et cardiopathies rhumatismales chroniques	1	♦0.4	-	-	1 199	2.7	1 215	2.9
Hypertensive diseases — Maladies hypertensives	18	♦7.2	35	13.7	16 008	36.1	16 064	37.8
Ischaemic heart disease — Cardiopathie ischémique	54	21.5	70	27.5	12 866	29.0	9 651	22.7
Cerebrovascular disease — Maladie cérébrovasculaire	146	58.1	156	61.3	21 652	48.9	19 575	46.0

20. Death and death rates by cause and sex: 2012 - 2016
Décès et taux de mortalité par cause et sexe : 2012 - 2016

	Cabo Verde				Egypt - Égypte			
	2012 (C)				2014 (C)			
Cause of death — Cause de décès	Male — Masculin		Female — Féminin		Male — Masculin		Female — Féminin	
	Number Nombre	Rate Taux	Number Nombre	Rate Taux	Number Nombre	Rate Taux	Number Nombre	Rate Taux
Diseases of arteries, arterioles and capillaries — Maladies des artères, artérioles et capillaires	4	♦1.6	4	♦1.6	13 862	31.3	12 763	30.0
Diseases of the respiratory system — Maladies de l'appareil respiratoire								
Total	149	59.3	111	43.6	21 965	49.6	18 704	44.0
Influenza — Grippe	-	-	-	-	16	♦0.0	10	♦0.0
Pneumonia — Pneumopathies	96	38.2	67	26.3	8 319	18.8	7 487	17.6
Chronic lower respiratory diseases — Maladies chroniques des voies respiratoires inférieures	14	♦5.6	11	♦4.3	2 582	5.8	1 920	4.5
Diseases of the digestive system — Maladies de l'appareil digestif								
Total	52	20.7	36	14.1	36 094	81.5	22 396	52.7
Gastric and duodenal ulcer — Ulcère de l'estomac et du duodénum	1	♦0.4	3	♦1.2	178	0.4	132	0.3
Diseases of the liver — Maladies du foie	28	♦11.1	18	♦7.1	34 202	77.2	21 022	49.5
Diseases of the musculoskeletal system and connective tissue — Maladies du système ostéo-articularie, des muscles et du tissu conjonctif	-	-	3	♦1.2	117	0.3	197	0.5
Diseases of the genitourinary system — Maladies de l'appareil génito-urinaire								
Total	34	13.5	27	♦10.6	11 464	25.9	9 221	21.7
Disorders of kidney and ureter — Affections du rein et de l'uretère	26	♦10.3	24	♦9.4	11 316	25.5	9 138	21.5
Hyperplasia of prostate — Hyperplasie de la prostate	3	♦10.2	..	..	77	1.2	..	..
Pregnancy, childbirth and the puerperium — Grossesse, accouchement et puerpéralité								
Total	..	..	1	...	..	..	497	18.3
Pregnancy with abortive outcome — Grossesse se terminant par un avortement	..	..	-	...	..	..	14	♦0.5
Other direct obstetric causes — Autres décès maternels directs	..	..	1	...	..	..	464	17.1
Indirect obstetric causes — Décès maternels indirects	..	..	-	...	..	..	6	♦0.2
Certain conditions originating in the perinatal period — Certaines affections dont l'origine se situe dans la période périnatale	133	...	110	...	2 796	201.1	2 035	153.0
Congenital malformations, deformations and chromosomal abnormalities — Malformations congénitales et anomalies chromosomiques	25	...	10	...	4 628	332.8	4 026	302.7
Symptoms, signs and abnormal clinical and laboratory findings, not elsewhere classified — Symptômes, signes et résultats anormaux d'examens cliniques et de laboratoire, non classés ailleurs	123	48.9	179	70.3	16 465	37.2	14 252	33.5
All other diseases — Toutes autres maladies	1	♦0.4	1	♦0.4	175	0.4	277	0.7
External causes — Causes externes								
Total	210	83.5	58	22.8	16 958	38.3	4 417	10.4
Accidents								
Total	35	13.9	11	♦4.3	14 569	32.9	3 504	8.2
Transport accidents — Accidents de transport	1	♦0.4	1	♦0.4	9 024	20.4	1 976	4.6
Falls — Chutes	-	-	-	-	1 418	3.2	463	1.1
Accidental drowning and submersion — Noyade et submersion accidentelles	25	♦9.9	6	♦2.4	1 648	3.7	292	0.7
Exposure to smoke, fire and flames — Exposition à la fumée, au feu et aux flammes	-	-	-	-	320	0.7	278	0.7
Accidental poisoning by and exposure to noxious substances — Intoxication accidentelle par des substances nocives et exposition à ces substances	-	-	-	-	70	0.2	58	0.1
Intentional self-harm — Lésions auto-infligées	37	14.7	8	♦3.1	71	0.2	17	♦0.0
Assault — Agresssions	45	17.9	10	♦3.9	195	0.4	34	0.1
All other external causes — Toutes autres causes externes	93	37.0	29	♦11.4	2 123	4.8	862	2.0

Cause of death — Cause de décès	Egypt - Égypte 2015 (C)				Mauritius - Maurice 2015 (+C)			
	Male — Masculin		Female — Féminin		Male — Masculin		Female — Féminin	
	Number Nombre	Rate Taux	Number Nombre	Rate Taux	Number Nombre	Rate Taux	Number Nombre	Rate Taux
TOTAL	313 392	690.6	260 487	597.7	5 306	849.3	4 190	656.9
Certain infectious and parasitic diseases — Certaines maladies infectieuses et parasitaires								
Total	11 172	24.6	8 779	20.1	149	23.8	64	10.0
Intestinal infectious diseases — Maladies infectieuses intestinales	2 020	4.5	2 282	5.2	6	+1.0	8	+1.3
Tuberculosis — Tuberculose	231	0.5	89	0.2	10	+1.6	4	+0.6
Tetanus — Tétanos	55	0.1	20	+0.0	-	-	-	-
Diphtheria — Diphtérie	-	-	-	-	-	-	-	-
Whooping cough — Coqueluche	-	-	1	+0.0	-	-	-	-
Meningococcal infection — Infection à méningocoques	11	+0.0	11	+0.0	-	-	-	-
Septicaemia — Septicémie	2 558	5.6	2 412	5.5	36	5.8	38	6.0
Acute poliomyelitis — Poliomyélite aiguë	7	+0.0	3	+0.0	-	-	-	-
Measles — Rougeole	5	+0.0	8	+0.0	-	-	-	-
Viral hepatitis — Hépatite virale	5 116	11.3	3 139	7.2	12	+1.9	3	+0.5
Human immunodeficiency virus [HIV] disease — Maladies dues au virus de l'immunodéficience humaine (VIH)	8	+0.0	6	+0.0	77	12.3	9	+1.4
Malaria — Paludisme	-	-	2	+0.0	-	-	-	-
Neoplasms — Tumeurs	18 894	41.6	15 839	36.3	637	102.0	627	98.3
Malignant neoplasms — Tumeurs malignes								
Total	17 855	39.3	14 531	33.3	610	97.6	596	93.4
Malignant neoplasm of lip, oral cavity and pharynx — Tumeur maligne de la lèvre, de la cavité buccale et du pharynx	222	0.5	164	0.4	35	5.6	13	+2.0
Malignant neoplasm of oesophagus — Tumeur maligne de l'oesophage	199	0.4	104	0.2	19	+3.0	3	+0.5
Malignant neoplasm of stomach — Tumeur maligne de l'estomac	883	1.9	802	1.8	52	8.3	36	5.6
Malignant neoplasm of colon, rectosigmoid junction, rectum, anus and anal canal — Tumeur maligne du côlon, de la jonction recto-sigmoïdienne, du rectum, de l'anus et du canal anal	894	2.0	788	1.8	77	12.3	57	8.9
Malignant neoplasm of liver and intrahepatic bile ducts — Tumeur maligne du foie et des voies bilaires intrahépatiques	4 599	10.1	2 186	5.0	31	5.0	19	+3.0
Malignant neoplasm of pancreas — Tumeur maligne du pancréas	724	1.6	433	1.0	34	5.4	19	+3.0
Malignant neoplasm of trachea, bronchus and lung — Tumeur maligne de la trachée, des bronches et du poumon	2 437	5.4	1 148	2.6	109	17.4	55	8.6
Malignant neoplasm of female breast — Tumeur maligne du sein chez la femme	..	..	2 646	8.7	..	..	177	34.3
Malignant neoplasm of cervix uteri — Tumeur maligne du col de l'utérus	..	..	166	0.5	..	..	33	6.4
Malignant neoplasm of prostate — Tumeur maligne de la prostate	793	11.4	..	..	65	38.4	..	..
Malignant neoplasm of lymphoid, haematopoietic and related tissue — Tumeurs malignes primitives ou présumées primitives des tissus lymphoïde, hématopoïétique et apparentés	1 794	4.0	1 530	3.5	57	9.1	32	5.0
Disorders of the blood and blood-forming organs and certain disorders involving the immune mechanism — Maladies du sang et des organes hématopoïétiques et certains troubles du système immunitaire								
Total	3 257	7.2	2 961	6.8	23	+3.7	25	+3.9
Anaemias — Anémies	492	1.1	537	1.2	17	+2.7	23	+3.6
Endocrine, nutritional and metabolic diseases — Maladies endocriniennes, nutritionnelles et métaboliques								
Total	6 285	13.9	7 147	16.4	1 220	195.3	1 126	176.5
Diabetes mellitus — Diabète sucré	3 898	8.6	4 544	10.4	1 189	190.3	1 096	171.8
Malnutrition — Malnutrition	98	0.2	82	0.2	6	+1.0	9	+1.4
Mental and behavioural disorders — Troubles mentaux et du comportement	316	0.7	272	0.6	67	10.7	5	+0.8
Diseases of the nervous system — Maladies du système nerveux	3 179	7.0	3 095	7.1	99	15.8	61	9.6
Diseases of the circulatory system — Maladies de l'appareil circulatoire								
Total	143 366	315.9	126 163	289.5	1 724	275.9	1 460	228.9
Acute rheumatic fever and chronic rheumatic heart diseases — Rhumatisme articularie aigu et cardiopathies rhumatismales chroniques	914	2.0	914	2.1	2	+0.3	2	+0.3
Hypertensive diseases — Maladies hypertensives	21 922	48.3	22 007	50.5	205	32.8	238	37.3
Ischaemic heart disease — Cardiopathie ischémique	17 640	38.9	13 474	30.9	671	107.4	528	82.8
Cerebrovascular disease — Maladie cérébrovasculaire	20 020	44.1	17 185	39.4	456	73.0	357	56.0

	Egypt - Égypte				Mauritius - Maurice			
	2015 (C)				2015 (+C)			
Cause of death — Cause de décès	Male — Masculin		Female — Féminin		Male — Masculin		Female — Féminin	
	Number Nombre	Rate Taux	Number Nombre	Rate Taux	Number Nombre	Rate Taux	Number Nombre	Rate Taux
Diseases of arteries, arterioles and capillaries — Maladies des artères, artérioles et capillaires	12 762	28.1	12 024	27.6	9	٠1.4	7	٠1.1
Diseases of the respiratory system — Maladies de l'appareil respiratoire								
Total	22 710	50.0	19 410	44.5	525	84.0	347	54.4
Influenza — Grippe	7	٠0.0	6	٠0.0	-	-	1	٠0.2
Pneumonia — Pneumopathies	8 653	19.1	7 835	18.0	144	23.0	103	16.1
Chronic lower respiratory diseases — Maladies chroniques des voies respiratoires inférieures	2 606	5.7	1 884	4.3	117	18.7	58	9.1
Diseases of the digestive system — Maladies de l'appareil digestif								
Total	34 943	77.0	22 664	52.0	229	36.7	97	15.2
Gastric and duodenal ulcer — Ulcère de l'estomac et du duodénum	216	0.5	166	0.4	7	٠1.1	6	٠0.9
Diseases of the liver — Maladies du foie	32 991	72.7	21 317	48.9	133	21.3	35	5.5
Diseases of the musculoskeletal system and connective tissue — Maladies du système ostéo-articularie, des muscles et du tissu conjonctif	99	0.2	149	0.3	3	٠0.5	27	٠4.2
Diseases of the genitourinary system — Maladies de l'appareil génito-urinaire								
Total	12 338	27.2	9 901	22.7	77	12.3	62	9.7
Disorders of kidney and ureter — Affections du rein et de l'uretère	12 137	26.7	9 793	22.5	57	9.1	45	7.1
Hyperplasia of prostate — Hyperplasie de la prostate	116	1.7	..	..	3	٠1.8	..	..
Pregnancy, childbirth and the puerperium — Grossesse, accouchement et puerpéralité								
Total	..	..	410	15.3	..	..	4	٠31.6
Pregnancy with abortive outcome — Grossesse se terminant par un avortement	..	..	13	٠0.5	..	..	1	٠7.9
Other direct obstetric causes — Autres décès maternels directs	..	..	385	14.3	..	..	2	٠15.8
Indirect obstetric causes — Décès maternels indirects	..	..	3	٠0.1	..	..	1	٠7.9
Certain conditions originating in the perinatal period — Certaines affections dont l'origine se situe dans la période périnatale	2 375	173.0	1 852	141.1	49	747.3	54	887.7
Congenital malformations, deformations and chromosomal abnormalities — Malformations congénitales et anomalies chromosomiques	4 209	306.7	3 690	281.1	23	٠350.8	15	٠246.6
Symptoms, signs and abnormal clinical and laboratory findings, not elsewhere classified — Symptômes, signes et résultats anormaux d'examens cliniques et de laboratoire, non classés ailleurs	33 817	74.5	32 844	75.4	77	12.3	77	12.1
All other diseases — Toutes autres maladies	204	0.4	348	0.8	19	٠3.0	20	٠3.1
External causes — Causes externes								
Total	16 228	35.8	4 963	11.4	385	61.6	119	18.7
Accidents								
Total	10 659	23.5	2 779	6.4	256	41.0	59	9.3
Transport accidents — Accidents de transport	6 648	14.7	1 563	3.6	142	22.7	25	٠3.9
Falls — Chutes	986	2.2	325	0.7	47	7.5	13	٠2.0
Accidental drowning and submersion — Noyade et submersion accidentelles	1 360	3.0	255	0.6	36	5.8	3	٠0.5
Exposure to smoke, fire and flames — Exposition à la fumée, au feu et aux flammes	175	0.4	144	0.3	8	٠1.3	6	٠0.9
Accidental poisoning by and exposure to noxious substances — Intoxication accidentelle par des substances nocives et exposition à ces substances	62	0.1	49	0.1	7	٠1.1	5	٠0.8
Intentional self-harm — Lésions auto-infligées	35	0.1	14	٠0.0	78	12.5	26	٠4.1
Assault — Agresssions	121	0.3	25	٠0.1	23	٠3.7	7	٠1.1
All other external causes — Toutes autres causes externes	5 413	11.9	2 145	4.9	28	٠4.5	27	٠4.2

Cause of death — Cause de décès	Mauritius - Maurice				Mayotte			
	2016 (+C)				2013 (C)		2014 (C)	
	Male — Masculin		Female — Féminin		Male — Masculin	Female — Féminin	Male — Masculin	Female — Féminin
	Number Nombre	Rate Taux	Number Nombre	Rate Taux	Number Nombre	Number Nombre	Number Nombre	Number Nombre
TOTAL	5 460	873.3	4 460	698.8	248	166	330	258
Certain infectious and parasitic diseases — Certaines maladies infectieuses et parasitaires								
Total	170	27.2	75	11.8	7	3	6	10
Intestinal infectious diseases — Maladies infectieuses intestinales	10	♦1.6	6	♦0.9	1	-	3	2
Tuberculosis — Tuberculose	11	♦1.8	5	♦0.8	-	-	-	1
Tetanus — Tétanos	-	-	-	-	-	-	-	-
Diphtheria — Diphtérie	-	-	-	-	-	-	-	-
Whooping cough — Coqueluche	-	-	-	-	-	-	-	-
Meningococcal infection — Infection à méningocoques	-	-	-	-	-	-	-	-
Septicaemia — Septicémie	33	5.3	35	5.5	2	2	2	5
Acute poliomyelitis — Poliomyélite aiguë	-	-	-	-	-	-	-	-
Measles — Rougeole	-	-	-	-	-	-	-	-
Viral hepatitis — Hépatite virale	12	♦1.9	1	♦0.2	1	-	1	-
Human immunodeficiency virus [HIV] disease — Maladies dues au virus de l'immunodéficience humaine (VIH)	99	15.8	25	♦3.9	-	-	-	-
Malaria — Paludisme	-	-	-	-	-	-	-	-
Neoplasms — Tumeurs	594	95.0	672	105.3	43	27	48	41
Malignant neoplasms — Tumeurs malignes								
Total	567	90.7	637	99.8	40	26	46	39
Malignant neoplasm of lip, oral cavity and pharynx — Tumeur maligne de la lèvre, de la cavité buccale et du pharynx	36	5.8	13	♦2.0	-	1	-	-
Malignant neoplasm of oesophagus — Tumeur maligne de l'oesophage	16	♦2.6	9	♦1.4	-	-	-	1
Malignant neoplasm of stomach — Tumeur maligne de l'estomac	40	6.4	31	4.9	1	1	3	3
Malignant neoplasm of colon, rectosigmoid junction, rectum, anus and anal canal — Tumeur maligne du côlon, de la jonction recto-sigmoïdienne, du rectum, de l'anus et du canal anal	76	12.2	80	12.5	1	1	-	-
Malignant neoplasm of liver and intrahepatic bile ducts — Tumeur maligne du foie et des voies bilaires intrahépatiques	23	♦3.7	26	♦4.1	6	1	6	3
Malignant neoplasm of pancreas — Tumeur maligne du pancréas	34	5.4	20	♦3.1	5	2	2	-
Malignant neoplasm of trachea, bronchus and lung — Tumeur maligne de la trachée, des bronches et du poumon	123	19.7	32	5.0	1	2	5	1
Malignant neoplasm of female breast — Tumeur maligne du sein chez la femme	..	..	176	33.8	..	5	..	9
Malignant neoplasm of cervix uteri — Tumeur maligne du col de l'utérus	..	..	26	♦5.0	..	3	..	5
Malignant neoplasm of prostate — Tumeur maligne de la prostate	59	33.7	..	..	9	..	11	..
Malignant neoplasm of lymphoid, haematopoietic and related tissue — Tumeurs malignes primitives ou présumées primitives des tissus lymphoïde, hématopoïétique et apparentés	51	8.2	54	8.5	8	2	7	1
Disorders of the blood and blood-forming organs and certain disorders involving the immune mechanism — Maladies du sang et des organes hématopoïétiques et certains troubles du système immunitaire								
Total	33	5.3	35	5.5	1	-	5	1
Anaemias — Anémies	19	♦3.0	29	♦4.5	1	-	4	1
Endocrine, nutritional and metabolic diseases — Maladies endocriniennes, nutritionnelles et métaboliques								
Total	1 285	205.5	1 108	173.6	13	17	16	16
Diabetes mellitus — Diabète sucré	1 251	200.1	1 078	168.9	9	11	15	11
Malnutrition — Malnutrition	2	♦0.3	4	♦0.6	1	-	-	-
Mental and behavioural disorders — Troubles mentaux et du comportement	70	11.2	8	♦1.3	3	-	2	3
Diseases of the nervous system — Maladies du système nerveux	109	17.4	55	8.6	12	6	14	4
Diseases of the circulatory system — Maladies de l'appareil circulatoire								
Total	1 817	290.6	1 673	262.1	52	34	75	56
Acute rheumatic fever and chronic rheumatic heart diseases — Rhumatisme articularie aigu et cardiopathies rhumatismales chroniques	5	♦0.8	11	♦1.7	2	1	-	-
Hypertensive diseases — Maladies hypertensives	220	35.2	289	45.3	9	5	7	12
Ischaemic heart disease — Cardiopathie ischémique	658	105.2	485	76.0	7	1	11	5

	Mauritius - Maurice				Mayotte			
	2016 (+C)				2013 (C)		2014 (C)	
Cause of death — Cause de décès	Male — Masculin		Female — Féminin		Male — Masculin	Female — Féminin	Male — Masculin	Female — Féminin
	Number Nombre	Rate Taux	Number Nombre	Rate Taux	Number Nombre	Number Nombre	Number Nombre	Number Nombre
Cerebrovascular disease — Maladie cérébrovasculaire....................	523	83.7	470	73.6	15	13	31	16
Diseases of arteries, arterioles and capillaries — Maladies des artères, artérioles et capillaires	14	♦2.2	7	♦1.1	3	1	3	1
Diseases of the respiratory system — Maladies de l'appareil respiratoire								
Total............	490	78.4	392	61.4	9	9	14	15
Influenza — Grippe.........	-	-	-	-	-	-	-	1
Pneumonia — Pneumopathies..........	113	18.1	95	14.9	1	1	4	5
Chronic lower respiratory diseases — Maladies chroniques des voies respiratoires inférieures	94	15.0	65	10.2	3	7	3	4
Diseases of the digestive system — Maladies de l'appareil digestif								
Total............	245	39.2	102	16.0	6	-	10	2
Gastric and duodenal ulcer — Ulcère de l'estomac et du duodénum.............	12	♦1.9	8	♦1.3	1	-	-	-
Diseases of the liver — Maladies du foie.........	135	21.6	34	5.3	3	-	6	1
Diseases of the musculoskeletal system and connective tissue — Maladies du système ostéo-articularie, des muscles et du tissu conjonctif	5	♦0.8	14	♦2.2	-	-	1	3
Diseases of the genitourinary system — Maladies de l'appareil génito-urinaire								
Total............	87	13.9	71	11.1	4	2	5	-
Disorders of kidney and ureter — Affections du rein et de l'uretère	50	8.0	54	8.5	2	1	2	-
Hyperplasia of prostate — Hyperplasie de la prostate...........	3	♦1.7	..	..	1	..	-	..
Pregnancy, childbirth and the puerperium — Grossesse, accouchement et puerpéralité								
Total............	..	..	6	♦46.3	..	1	..	2
Pregnancy with abortive outcome — Grossesse se terminant par un avortement	..	..	3	♦23.2	..	-	..	-
Other direct obstetric causes — Autres décès maternels directs	..	..	3	♦23.2	..	1	..	2
Indirect obstetric causes — Décès maternels indirects	..	..	-	-	..	..	..	-
Certain conditions originating in the perinatal period — Certaines affections dont l'origine se situe dans la période périnatale	43	651.8	39	614.1	11	12	15	11
Congenital malformations, deformations and chromosomal abnormalities — Malformations congénitales et anomalies chromosomiques	29	♦439.6	24	♦377.9	6	4	11	13
Symptoms, signs and abnormal clinical and laboratory findings, not elsewhere classified — Symptômes, signes et résultats anormaux d'examens cliniques et de laboratoire, non classés ailleurs	62	9.9	62	9.7	59	41	78	64
All other diseases — Toutes autres maladies.............	22	♦3.5	26	♦4.1	3	2	-	-
External causes — Causes externes								
Total............	399	63.8	98	15.4	19	8	30	17
Accidents								
Total............	279	44.6	51	8.0	13	6	28	17
Transport accidents — Accidents de transport.............	152	24.3	13	♦2.0	2	-	4	3
Falls — Chutes	46	7.4	10	♦1.6	-	-	2	1
Accidental drowning and submersion — Noyade et submersion accidentelles.........	33	5.3	10	♦1.6	4	1	12	4
Exposure to smoke, fire and flames — Exposition à la fumée, au feu et aux flammes............	11	♦1.8	12	♦1.9	1	2	2	2
Accidental poisoning by and exposure to noxious substances — Intoxication accidentelle par des substances nocives et exposition à ces substances	14	♦2.2	3	♦0.5	1	1	-	-
Intentional self-harm — Lésions auto-infligées.............	83	13.3	15	♦2.4	3	-	1	-
Assault — Agresssions.........	11	♦1.8	9	♦1.4	1	-	-	-
All other external causes — Toutes autres causes externes	26	♦4.2	23	♦3.6	2	2	1	-

20. Death and death rates by cause and sex: 2012 - 2016
Décès et taux de mortalité par cause et sexe : 2012 - 2016 (continued - suite)

Cause of death — Cause de décès	Morocco - Maroc 2013 (U) Male — Masculin Number Nombre	Morocco - Maroc 2013 (U) Female — Féminin Number Nombre	Morocco - Maroc 2014 (U) Male — Masculin Number Nombre	Morocco - Maroc 2014 (U) Female — Féminin Number Nombre	Reunion - Réunion 2013 (...) Male — Masculin Number Nombre	Reunion - Réunion 2013 (...) Female — Féminin Number Nombre	Reunion - Réunion 2014 (...) Male — Masculin Number Nombre	Reunion - Réunion 2014 (...) Female — Féminin Number Nombre
TOTAL	26 513	20 522	29 382	23 062	2 330	1 923	2 403	1 946
Certain infectious and parasitic diseases — Certaines maladies infectieuses et parasitaires								
Total	882	588	1 147	764	48	42	48	30
Intestinal infectious diseases — Maladies infectieuses intestinales	49	43	52	64	12	10	10	6
Tuberculosis — Tuberculose	337	141	406	157	2	-	2	2
Tetanus — Tétanos	13	-	14	3	-	-	-	-
Diphtheria — Diphtérie	-	-	-	-	-	-	-	-
Whooping cough — Coqueluche	-	-	-	1	-	-	-	-
Meningococcal infection — Infection à méningocoques	2	1	2	1	-	-	-	-
Septicaemia — Septicémie	333	275	466	370	20	23	20	13
Acute poliomyelitis — Poliomyélite aiguë	-	-	-	-	-	-	-	-
Measles — Rougeole	-	-	-	-	-	-	-	-
Viral hepatitis — Hépatite virale	81	84	94	109	5	3	2	2
Human immunodeficiency virus [HIV] disease — Maladies dues au virus de l'immunodéficience humaine (VIH)	19	14	27	13	3	1	4	-
Malaria — Paludisme	-	-	1	1	-	-	-	-
Neoplasms — Tumeurs	3 301	2 294	3 599	2 534	609	390	730	488
Malignant neoplasms — Tumeurs malignes								
Total	3 209	2 238	3 410	2 363	593	374	713	470
Malignant neoplasm of lip, oral cavity and pharynx — Tumeur maligne de la lèvre, de la cavité buccale et du pharynx	76	30	78	41	38	1	42	3
Malignant neoplasm of oesophagus — Tumeur maligne de l'oesophage	28	27	30	19	40	1	36	6
Malignant neoplasm of stomach — Tumeur maligne de l'estomac	200	148	209	126	39	25	42	27
Malignant neoplasm of colon, rectosigmoid junction, rectum, anus and anal canal — Tumeur maligne du côlon, de la jonction recto-sigmoïdienne, du rectum, de l'anus et du canal anal	159	120	146	146	58	52	59	57
Malignant neoplasm of liver and intrahepatic bile ducts — Tumeur maligne du foie et des voies bilaires intrahépatiques	144	117	163	137	41	21	43	29
Malignant neoplasm of pancreas — Tumeur maligne du pancréas	141	85	139	91	19	18	37	31
Malignant neoplasm of trachea, bronchus and lung — Tumeur maligne de la trachée, des bronches et du poumon	856	153	832	145	135	27	153	48
Malignant neoplasm of female breast — Tumeur maligne du sein chez la femme	..	425	..	385	..	62	..	80
Malignant neoplasm of cervix uteri — Tumeur maligne du col de l'utérus	..	80	..	102	..	16	..	11
Malignant neoplasm of prostate — Tumeur maligne de la prostate	310	..	336	..	49	..	78	..
Malignant neoplasm of lymphoid, haematopoietic and related tissue — Tumeurs malignes primitives ou présumées primitives des tissus lymphoïde, hématopoïétique et apparentés	236	145	274	181	43	31	49	36
Disorders of the blood and blood-forming organs and certain disorders involving the immune mechanism — Maladies du sang et des organes hématopoïétiques et certains troubles du système immunitaire								
Total	165	135	160	151	6	9	10	8
Anaemias — Anémies	121	105	116	100	4	4	5	5
Endocrine, nutritional and metabolic diseases — Maladies endocriniennes, nutritionnelles et métaboliques								
Total	1 487	1 593	1 479	1 538	127	152	125	173
Diabetes mellitus — Diabète sucré	1 325	1 469	1 325	1 395	101	113	99	135
Malnutrition — Malnutrition	3	4	6	-	8	11	5	12
Mental and behavioural disorders — Troubles mentaux et du comportement	68	46	84	54	82	41	81	79
Diseases of the nervous system — Maladies du système nerveux	499	458	485	440	72	94	81	100
Diseases of the circulatory system — Maladies de l'appareil circulatoire								
Total	4 582	3 771	6 288	5 274	506	544	522	496
Acute rheumatic fever and chronic rheumatic heart diseases — Rhumatisme articularie aigu et cardiopathies rhumatismales chroniques	44	36	45	31	2	12	1	8
Hypertensive diseases — Maladies hypertensives	431	581	342	487	38	58	45	58
Ischaemic heart disease — Cardiopathie ischémique	491	201	538	269	159	123	182	115

20. Death and death rates by cause and sex: 2012 - 2016
Décès et taux de mortalité par cause et sexe : 2012 - 2016 (continued - suite)

Cause of death — Cause de décès	Morocco - Maroc 2013 (U) Male — Masculin Number Nombre	2013 (U) Female — Féminin Number Nombre	2014 (U) Male — Masculin Number Nombre	2014 (U) Female — Féminin Number Nombre	Reunion - Réunion 2013 (...) Male — Masculin Number Nombre	2013 (...) Female — Féminin Number Nombre	2014 (...) Male — Masculin Number Nombre	2014 (...) Female — Féminin Number Nombre
Cerebrovascular disease — Maladie cérébrovasculaire	1 051	971	1 223	1 191	145	173	141	137
Diseases of arteries, arterioles and capillaries — Maladies des artères, artérioles et capillaires	56	21	65	32	24	19	24	22
Diseases of the respiratory system — Maladies de l'appareil respiratoire								
Total	1 364	769	1 652	905	160	132	182	129
Influenza — Grippe	4	1	7	6	5	6	5	10
Pneumonia — Pneumopathies	548	269	579	265	35	38	43	37
Chronic lower respiratory diseases — Maladies chroniques des voies respiratoires inférieures	340	168	382	184	69	34	70	30
Diseases of the digestive system — Maladies de l'appareil digestif								
Total	674	532	757	586	125	76	114	76
Gastric and duodenal ulcer — Ulcère de l'estomac et du duodénum	32	13	29	17	5	2	6	2
Diseases of the liver — Maladies du foie	267	200	303	255	69	40	63	31
Diseases of the musculoskeletal system and connective tissue — Maladies du système ostéo-articularie, des muscles et du tissu conjonctif	32	29	36	48	8	16	11	16
Diseases of the genitourinary system — Maladies de l'appareil génito-urinaire								
Total	787	541	810	529	31	38	40	32
Disorders of kidney and ureter — Affections du rein et de l'uretère	642	515	646	497	26	31	35	28
Hyperplasia of prostate — Hyperplasie de la prostate	22	..	29	..	-	..	-	..
Pregnancy, childbirth and the puerperium — Grossesse, accouchement et puerpéralité								
Total	..	62	..	77	..	2	..	2
Pregnancy with abortive outcome — Grossesse se terminant par un avortement	..	2	..	1	..	-	..	-
Other direct obstetric causes — Autres décès maternels directs	..	56	..	75	..	1	..	2
Indirect obstetric causes — Décès maternels indirects	..	4	..	1	..	1	..	-
Certain conditions originating in the perinatal period — Certaines affections dont l'origine se situe dans la période périnatale	2 094	1 446	2 307	1 713	26	19	25	32
Congenital malformations, deformations and chromosomal abnormalities — Malformations congénitales et anomalies chromosomiques	342	291	376	273	7	17	14	20
Symptoms, signs and abnormal clinical and laboratory findings, not elsewhere classified — Symptômes, signes et résultats anormaux d'examens cliniques et de laboratoire, non classés ailleurs	7 776	7 251	7 572	7 402	281	265	188	172
All other diseases — Toutes autres maladies	15	17	24	20	2	4	1	6
External causes — Causes externes								
Total	2 445	699	2 606	754	240	82	231	87
Accidents								
Total	2 170	582	2 414	684	141	59	151	68
Transport accidents — Accidents de transport	756	170	720	167	31	5	49	6
Falls — Chutes	94	26	106	38	25	11	22	13
Accidental drowning and submersion — Noyade et submersion accidentelles	185	35	255	55	8	3	8	4
Exposure to smoke, fire and flames — Exposition à la fumée, au feu et aux flammes	34	7	27	17	7	3	2	1
Accidental poisoning by and exposure to noxious substances — Intoxication accidentelle par des substances nocives et exposition à ces substances	43	38	52	51	22	8	15	9
Intentional self-harm — Lésions auto-infligées	114	44	82	36	76	16	68	14
Assault — Agresssions	65	16	98	24	9	3	8	2
All other external causes — Toutes autres causes externes	96	57	12	10	14	4	4	3

20. Death and death rates by cause and sex: 2012 - 2016
Décès et taux de mortalité par cause et sexe : 2012 - 2016 (continued - suite)

	Seychelles				South Africa - Afrique du Sud			
Cause of death — Cause de décès	2014 (+C)		2015 (+C)		2014 (C)			
	Male — Masculin	Female — Féminin	Male — Masculin	Female — Féminin	Male — Masculin		Female — Féminin	
	Number Nombre	Number Nombre	Number Nombre	Number Nombre	Number Nombre	Rate Taux	Number Nombre	Rate Taux
TOTAL	425	300	401	302	236 613	893.6	214 826	776.5
Certain infectious and parasitic diseases — Certaines maladies infectieuses et parasitaires								
Total	50	32	28	19	52 412	197.9	45 980	166.2
Intestinal infectious diseases — Maladies infectieuses intestinales	1	2	1	2	6 795	25.7	7 607	27.5
Tuberculosis — Tuberculose	-	-	1	-	22 545	85.1	15 174	54.8
Tetanus — Tétanos............	-	-	-	-	7	٭0.0	4	٭0.0
Diphtheria — Diphtérie............	-	-	-	-	-	-	-	-
Whooping cough — Coqueluche	-	-	-	-	2	٭0.0	-	-
Meningococcal infection — Infection à méningocoques	-	-	-	-	23	٭0.1	34	0.1
Septicaemia — Septicémie	26	23	18	14	2 452	9.3	3 066	11.1
Acute poliomyelitis — Poliomyélite aiguë	-	-	-	-	-	-	-	-
Measles — Rougeole............	-	-	-	-	1	٭0.0	3	٭0.0
Viral hepatitis — Hépatite virale............	1	-	2	-	166	0.6	113	0.4
Human immunodeficiency virus [HIV] disease — Maladies dues au virus de l'immunodéficience humaine (VIH)............	9	6	3	2	11 160	42.1	10 685	38.6
Malaria — Paludisme............	-	-	-	-	227	0.9	156	0.6
Neoplasms — Tumeurs	69	56	88	63	19 319	73.0	19 776	71.5
Malignant neoplasms — Tumeurs malignes								
Total	69	56	87	62	18 668	70.5	19 098	69.0
Malignant neoplasm of lip, oral cavity and pharynx — Tumeur maligne de la lèvre, de la cavité buccale et du pharynx	11	1	12	2	737	2.8	297	1.1
Malignant neoplasm of oesophagus — Tumeur maligne de l'oesophage	2	-	3	2	1 683	6.4	1 089	3.9
Malignant neoplasm of stomach — Tumeur maligne de l'estomac	2	4	2	2	631	2.4	471	1.7
Malignant neoplasm of colon, rectosigmoid junction, rectum, anus and anal canal — Tumeur maligne du côlon, de la jonction recto-sigmoïdienne, du rectum, de l'anus et du canal anal	11	13	8	11	1 239	4.7	1 142	4.1
Malignant neoplasm of liver and intrahepatic bile ducts — Tumeur maligne du foie et des voies bilaires intrahépatiques	6	2	4	2	983	3.7	581	2.1
Malignant neoplasm of pancreas — Tumeur maligne du pancréas............	3	1	2	2	671	2.5	659	2.4
Malignant neoplasm of trachea, bronchus and lung — Tumeur maligne de la trachée, des bronches et du poumon	7	3	8	3	3 522	13.3	1 720	6.2
Malignant neoplasm of female breast — Tumeur maligne du sein chez la femme	..	10		9			3 122	15.9
Malignant neoplasm of cervix uteri — Tumeur maligne du col de l'utérus.........	..	7		6	..		3 444	17.6
Malignant neoplasm of prostate — Tumeur maligne de la prostate	15	..	22	..	2 729	70.5	..	..
Malignant neoplasm of lymphoid, haematopoietic and related tissue — Tumeurs malignes primitives ou présumées primitives des tissus lymphoïde, hématopoïétique et apparentés	...	...	...	...	1 532	5.8	1 316	4.8
Disorders of the blood and blood-forming organs and certain disorders involving the immune mechanism — Maladies du sang et des organes hématopoïétiques et certains troubles du système immunitaire								
Total	6	9	1	3	4 466	16.9	5 100	18.4
Anaemias — Anémies	5	8	1	3	868	3.3	1 258	4.5
Endocrine, nutritional and metabolic diseases — Maladies endocriniennes, nutritionnelles et métaboliques								
Total	9	9	8	7	12 137	45.8	17 465	63.1
Diabetes mellitus — Diabète sucré............	8	9	5	5	8 914	33.7	13 819	49.9
Malnutrition — Malnutrition	-	-	2	1	1 006	3.8	858	3.1
Mental and behavioural disorders — Troubles mentaux et du comportement	1	1	4	1	900	3.4	1 091	3.9
Diseases of the nervous system — Maladies du système nerveux............	3	3	3	7	5 722	21.6	4 520	16.3
Diseases of the circulatory system — Maladies de l'appareil circulatoire								
Total	108	94	118	98	35 140	132.7	42 985	155.4
Acute rheumatic fever and chronic rheumatic heart diseases — Rhumatisme articularie aigu et cardiopathies rhumatismales chroniques	2	1	1	-	122	0.5	203	0.7
Hypertensive diseases — Maladies hypertensives............	20	38	20	26	6 670	25.2	11 081	40.1
Ischaemic heart disease — Cardiopathie ischémique............	24	12	16	15	6 200	23.4	4 696	17.0

20. Death and death rates by cause and sex: 2012 - 2016
Décès et taux de mortalité par cause et sexe : 2012 - 2016 (continued - suite)

	Seychelles				South Africa - Afrique du Sud			
Cause of death — Cause de décès	2014 (+C)		2015 (+C)		2014 (C)			
	Male — Masculin	Female — Féminin	Male — Masculin	Female — Féminin	Male — Masculin		Female — Féminin	
	Number Nombre	Number Nombre	Number Nombre	Number Nombre	Number Nombre	Rate Taux	Number Nombre	Rate Taux
Cerebrovascular disease — Maladie cérébrovasculaire..............	24	8	32	26	9 908	37.4	13 149	47.5
Diseases of arteries, arterioles and capillaries — Maladies des artères, artérioles et capillaires	...	...	...	...	840	3.2	606	2.2
Diseases of the respiratory system — Maladies de l'appareil respiratoire								
Total	54	41	44	40	24 576	92.8	20 649	74.6
Influenza — Grippe.........	-	-	-	-	192	0.7	280	1.0
Pneumonia — Pneumopathies	36	29	33	34	11 011	41.6	10 459	37.8
Chronic lower respiratory diseases — Maladies chroniques des voies respiratoires inférieures	12	4	7	3	7 300	27.6	4 785	17.3
Diseases of the digestive system — Maladies de l'appareil digestif								
Total	37	17	19	23	6 358	24.0	5 537	20.0
Gastric and duodenal ulcer — Ulcère de l'estomac et du duodénum...............	4	1	3	-	766	2.9	720	2.6
Diseases of the liver — Maladies du foie.........	16	8	11	11	2 390	9.0	1 770	6.4
Diseases of the musculoskeletal system and connective tissue — Maladies du système ostéo-articulaire, des muscles et du tissu conjonctif	-	-	-	-	597	2.3	1 020	3.7
Diseases of the genitourinary system — Maladies de l'appareil génito-urinaire								
Total	30	17	20	18	4 534	17.1	4 220	15.3
Disorders of kidney and ureter — Affections du rein et de l'uretère	...	...	...	...	4 101	15.5	3 776	13.6
Hyperplasia of prostate — Hyperplasie de la prostate.........	...	..	...	...	156	4.0	..	..
Pregnancy, childbirth and the puerperium — Grossesse, accouchement et puerpéralité								
Total	..	-	..	3	..	..	1 027	101.8
Pregnancy with abortive outcome — Grossesse se terminant par un avortement	..	-	..	-	..	..	103	10.2
Other direct obstetric causes — Autres décès maternels directs	..	-	..	-	..	..	612	60.7
Indirect obstetric causes — Décès maternels indirects	..	-	..	3	..	..	312	30.9
Certain conditions originating in the perinatal period — Certaines affections dont l'origine se situe dans la période périnatale	8	3	3	5	5 041	991.2	4 035	806.8
Congenital malformations, deformations and chromosomal abnormalities — Malformations congénitales et anomalies chromosomiques	6	-	2	3	1 127	221.6	967	193.3
Symptoms, signs and abnormal clinical and laboratory findings, not elsewhere classified — Symptômes, signes et résultats anormaux d'examens cliniques et de laboratoire, non classés ailleurs	9	4	9	8	27 614	104.3	28 937	104.6
All other diseases — Toutes autres maladies.........	1	2	3	3	363	1.4	500	1.8
External causes — Causes externes								
Total	34	12	51	1	36 307	137.1	11 017	39.8
Accidents								
Total	...	...	...	...	23 998	90.6	7 736	28.0
Transport accidents — Accidents de transport.........	8	4	13	-	4 393	16.6	1 504	5.4
Falls — Chutes	2	-	6	-	129	0.5	54	0.2
Accidental drowning and submersion — Noyade et submersion accidentelles.........	8	4	19	-	1 225	4.6	343	1.2
Exposure to smoke, fire and flames — Exposition à la fumée, au feu et aux flammes.........	3	-	-	-	1 416	5.3	854	3.1
Accidental poisoning by and exposure to noxious substances — Intoxication accidentelle par des substances nocives et exposition à ces substances	-	-	-	-	477	1.8	382	1.4
Intentional self-harm — Lésions auto-infligées.........	2	2	6	1	461	1.7	121	0.4
Assault — Agresssions.........	6	2	1	-	4 670	17.6	601	2.2
All other external causes — Toutes autres causes externes	...	...	...	-	7 178	27.1	2 559	9.2

20. Death and death rates by cause and sex: 2012 - 2016
Décès et taux de mortalité par cause et sexe : 2012 - 2016 (continued - suite)

Cause of death — Cause de décès	South Africa - Afrique du Sud				Tunisia - Tunisie		Anguilla	
	2015 (C)				2013 (U)		2015 (...)	
	Male — Masculin		Female — Féminin		Male — Masculin	Female — Féminin	Male — Masculin	Female — Féminin
	Number Nombre	Rate Taux	Number Nombre	Rate Taux	Number Nombre	Number Nombre	Number Nombre	Number Nombre
TOTAL	241 156	895.7	217 087	772.8	*12 439*	*9 446*	*43*	*22*
Certain infectious and parasitic diseases — Certaines maladies infectieuses et parasitaires								
Total	48 081	178.6	41 274	146.9	*411*	*273*	*2*	*2*
Intestinal infectious diseases — Maladies infectieuses intestinales	4 615	17.1	5 292	18.8	*22*	*18*	*-*	*1*
Tuberculosis — Tuberculose	20 111	74.7	12 811	45.6	*53*	*11*	*-*	*-*
Tetanus — Tétanos	8	♦0.0	4	♦0.0	*2*	*-*	*-*	*-*
Diphtheria — Diphtérie...	2	♦0.0	-	-	*-*	*-*	*-*	*-*
Whooping cough — Coqueluche	4	♦0.0	4	♦0.0	*1*	*5*	*-*	*-*
Meningococcal infection — Infection à méningocoques.............................	9	♦0.0	15	♦0.1	*1*	*1*	*-*	*-*
Septicaemia — Septicémie..	2 324	8.6	2 722	9.7	*231*	*181*	*1*	*-*
Acute poliomyelitis — Poliomyélite aiguë	2	♦0.0	-	-	*-*	*-*	*-*	*-*
Measles — Rougeole...	2	♦0.0	4	♦0.0	*1*	*-*	*-*	*-*
Viral hepatitis — Hépatite virale..	187	0.7	129	0.5	*52*	*20*	*-*	*-*
Human immunodeficiency virus [HIV] disease — Maladies dues au virus de l'immunodéficience humaine (VIH)	11 275	41.9	10 545	37.5	*3*	*4*	*-*	*-*
Malaria — Paludisme..	211	0.8	119	0.4	*-*	*-*	*-*	*-*
Neoplasms — Tumeurs	20 710	76.9	21 032	74.9	*2 164*	*1 294*	*7*	*5*
Malignant neoplasms — Tumeurs malignes								
Total	20 065	74.5	20 339	72.4	*2 073*	*1 240*	*7*	*5*
Malignant neoplasm of lip, oral cavity and pharynx — Tumeur maligne de la lèvre, de la cavité buccale et du pharynx	700	2.6	336	1.2	*64*	*29*	*1*	*-*
Malignant neoplasm of oesophagus — Tumeur maligne de l'oesophage	1 696	6.3	1 112	4.0	*14*	*6*	*-*	*-*
Malignant neoplasm of stomach — Tumeur maligne de l'estomac	749	2.8	512	1.8	*91*	*59*	*-*	*1*
Malignant neoplasm of colon, rectosigmoid junction, rectum, anus and anal canal — Tumeur maligne du côlon, de la jonction recto-sigmoïdienne, du rectum, de l'anus et du canal anal	1 338	5.0	1 244	4.4	*147*	*132*	*-*	*1*
Malignant neoplasm of liver and intrahepatic bile ducts — Tumeur maligne du foie et des voies bilaires intrahépatiques	1 114	4.1	721	2.6	*101*	*90*	*-*	*-*
Malignant neoplasm of pancreas — Tumeur maligne du pancréas..................	750	2.8	725	2.6	*91*	*55*	*-*	*-*
Malignant neoplasm of trachea, bronchus and lung — Tumeur maligne de la trachée, des bronches et du poumon	3 746	13.9	1 852	6.6	*703*	*112*	*2*	*-*
Malignant neoplasm of female breast — Tumeur maligne du sein chez la femme	..	..	3 297	...	..	*255*	..	*2*
Malignant neoplasm of cervix uteri — Tumeur maligne du col de l'utérus.........	..	..	3 619	...	..	*11*	..	..
Malignant neoplasm of prostate — Tumeur maligne de la prostate	3 033	...	..	..	*219*	..	*2*	..
Malignant neoplasm of lymphoid, haematopoietic and related tissue — Tumeurs malignes primitives ou présumées primitives des tissus lymphoïde, hématopoïétique et apparentés..	1 724	6.4	1 316	4.7	*141*	*108*	*-*	*-*
Disorders of the blood and blood-forming organs and certain disorders involving the immune mechanism — Maladies du sang et des organes hématopoïétiques et certains troubles du système immunitaire								
Total	6 143	22.8	6 749	24.0	*52*	*49*	*-*	*-*
Anaemias — Anémies	815	3.0	1 203	4.3	*31*	*27*	*-*	*-*
Endocrine, nutritional and metabolic diseases — Maladies endocriniennes, nutritionnelles et métaboliques								
Total	12 722	47.3	18 848	67.1	*972*	*1 010*	*2*	*3*
Diabetes mellitus — Diabète sucré...	9 657	35.9	15 396	54.8	*840*	*865*	*1*	*3*
Malnutrition — Malnutrition	961	3.6	799	2.8	*6*	*8*	*-*	*-*
Mental and behavioural disorders — Troubles mentaux et du comportement	940	3.5	956	3.4	*66*	*38*	*1*	*-*
Diseases of the nervous system — Maladies du système nerveux..................	6 030	22.4	4 672	16.6	*284*	*212*	*-*	*4*
Diseases of the circulatory system — Maladies de l'appareil circulatoire								
Total	36 653	136.1	44 988	160.2	*3 001*	*2 716*	*19*	*6*
Acute rheumatic fever and chronic rheumatic heart diseases — Rhumatisme articularie aigu et cardiopathies rhumatismales chroniques	111	0.4	203	0.7	*9*	*19*	*-*	*-*
Hypertensive diseases — Maladies hypertensives...............................	7 342	27.3	12 078	43.0	*188*	*258*	*1*	*2*
Ischaemic heart disease — Cardiopathie ischémique	6 944	25.8	5 280	18.8	*819*	*500*	*8*	*3*

20. Death and death rates by cause and sex: 2012 - 2016
Décès et taux de mortalité par cause et sexe : 2012 - 2016 (continued - suite)

Cause of death — Cause de décès	South Africa - Afrique du Sud				Tunisia - Tunisie		Anguilla	
	2015 (C)				2013 (U)		2015 (...)	
	Male — Masculin		Female — Féminin		Male — Masculin	Female — Féminin	Male — Masculin	Female — Féminin
	Number Nombre	Rate Taux	Number Nombre	Rate Taux	Number Nombre	Number Nombre	Number Nombre	Number Nombre
Cerebrovascular disease — Maladie cérébrovasculaire....................	9 696	36.0	13 146	46.8	1 117	1 066	1	-
Diseases of arteries, arterioles and capillaries — Maladies des artères, artérioles et capillaires	831	3.1	591	2.1	39	15	1	-
Diseases of the respiratory system — Maladies de l'appareil respiratoire								
Total	24 267	90.1	19 891	70.8	847	463	-	1
Influenza — Grippe	215	0.8	226	0.8	19	16	-	-
Pneumonia — Pneumopathies	10 290	38.2	9 736	34.7	209	153	-	1
Chronic lower respiratory diseases — Maladies chroniques des voies respiratoires inférieures	7 691	28.6	4 948	17.6	343	116	-	-
Diseases of the digestive system — Maladies de l'appareil digestif								
Total	6 513	24.2	5 599	19.9	366	320	1	-
Gastric and duodenal ulcer — Ulcère de l'estomac et du duodénum.................	792	2.9	736	2.6	16	12	-	-
Diseases of the liver — Maladies du foie..	2 466	9.2	1 695	6.0	109	101	-	-
Diseases of the musculoskeletal system and connective tissue — Maladies du système ostéo-articulaire, des muscles et du tissu conjonctif	623	2.3	1 040	3.7	20	30	-	-
Diseases of the genitourinary system — Maladies de l'appareil génito-urinaire								
Total	4 666	17.3	4 341	15.5	245	223	1	1
Disorders of kidney and ureter — Affections du rein et de l'uretère	4 163	15.5	3 891	13.9	208	214	1	-
Hyperplasia of prostate — Hyperplasie de la prostate........................	174	...	..	..	13	..	-	-
Pregnancy, childbirth and the puerperium — Grossesse, accouchement et puerpéralité								
Total	..	..	942	98.9	..	28	-	-
Pregnancy with abortive outcome — Grossesse se terminant par un avortement	..	..	110	11.6	..	1	-	-
Other direct obstetric causes — Autres décès maternels directs	..	..	586	61.5	..	27	-	-
Indirect obstetric causes — Décès maternels indirects	..	..	246	25.8	..	-	-	-
Certain conditions originating in the perinatal period — Certaines affections dont l'origine se situe dans la période périnatale	5 081	1 059.6	4 108	869.0	669	502	1	-
Congenital malformations, deformations and chromosomal abnormalities — Malformations congénitales et anomalies chromosomiques	1 131	235.9	1 063	224.9	310	209	-	-
Symptoms, signs and abnormal clinical and laboratory findings, not elsewhere classified — Symptômes, signes et résultats anormaux d'examens cliniques et de laboratoire, non classés ailleurs	27 726	103.0	29 232	104.1	2 151	1 673	-	-
All other diseases — Toutes autres maladies	568	2.1	837	3.0	36	54	1	-
External causes — Causes externes								
Total	39 302	146.0	11 515	41.0	845	352	8	-
Accidents								
Total	29 141	108.2	8 834	31.4	326	75	7	-
Transport accidents — Accidents de transport	4 680	17.4	1 588	5.7	250	48	-	-
Falls — Chutes	139	0.5	72	0.3	8	4	-	-
Accidental drowning and submersion — Noyade et submersion accidentelles..	1 125	4.2	278	1.0	31	7	3	-
Exposure to smoke, fire and flames — Exposition à la fumée, au feu et aux flammes	1 441	5.4	894	3.2	3	-	-	-
Accidental poisoning by and exposure to noxious substances — Intoxication accidentelle par des substances nocives et exposition à ces substances	548	2.0	384	1.4	7	6	-	-
Intentional self-harm — Lésions auto-infligées	377	1.4	105	0.4	9	2	-	-
Assault — Agresssions	6 353	23.6	801	2.9	10	-	-	-
All other external causes — Toutes autres causes externes	3 431	12.7	1 775	6.3	500	275	1	-

20. Death and death rates by cause and sex: 2012 - 2016
Décès et taux de mortalité par cause et sexe : 2012 - 2016 (continued - suite)

Cause of death — Cause de décès	Anguilla 2016 (...)		Antigua and Barbuda - Antigua-et-Barbuda 2014 (+U)		2015 (+U)		Aruba 2014 (...)	
	Male — Masculin	Female — Féminin	Male — Masculin	Female — Féminin	Male — Masculin	Female — Féminin	Male — Masculin	Female — Féminin
	Number Nombre	Number Nombre	Number Nombre	Number Nombre	Number Nombre	Number Nombre	Number Nombre	Number Nombre
TOTAL	*53*	*37*	*325*	*255*	*283*	*245*	*335*	*307*
Certain infectious and parasitic diseases — Certaines maladies infectieuses et parasitaires								
Total	-	-	19	19	16	11	12	4
Intestinal infectious diseases — Maladies infectieuses intestinales	-	-	1	-	-	1	-	1
Tuberculosis — Tuberculose	-	-	-	-	-	-	-	-
Tetanus — Tétanos	-	-	-	-	-	-	-	-
Diphtheria — Diphtérie	-	-	-	-	-	-	-	-
Whooping cough — Coqueluche	-	-	-	-	-	-	-	-
Meningococcal infection — Infection à méningocoques	-	-	-	-	-	-	-	-
Septicaemia — Septicémie	-	-	10	16	14	10	9	3
Acute poliomyelitis — Poliomyélite aiguë	-	-	-	-	-	-	-	-
Measles — Rougeole	-	-	-	-	-	-	-	-
Viral hepatitis — Hépatite virale	-	-	-	-	-	-	-	-
Human immunodeficiency virus [HIV] disease — Maladies dues au virus de l'immunodéficience humaine (VIH)	-	-	7	3	1	-	2	-
Malaria — Paludisme	-	-	-	-	-	-	-	-
Neoplasms — Tumeurs	*10*	*8*	*76*	*57*	*47*	*46*	*81*	*84*
Malignant neoplasms — Tumeurs malignes								
Total	*10*	*5*	*75*	*56*	*47*	*43*	*79*	*83*
Malignant neoplasm of lip, oral cavity and pharynx — Tumeur maligne de la lèvre, de la cavité buccale et du pharynx	-	-	1	-	-	-	3	*1*
Malignant neoplasm of oesophagus — Tumeur maligne de l'oesophage	-	-	1	-	-	-	-	*2*
Malignant neoplasm of stomach — Tumeur maligne de l'estomac	-	-	8	2	4	2	9	*4*
Malignant neoplasm of colon, rectosigmoid junction, rectum, anus and anal canal — Tumeur maligne du côlon, de la jonction recto-sigmoïdienne, du rectum, de l'anus et du canal anal	*1*	-	8	8	4	6	5	*16*
Malignant neoplasm of liver and intrahepatic bile ducts — Tumeur maligne du foie et des voies bilaires intrahépatiques	-	-	1	4	4	4	5	*4*
Malignant neoplasm of pancreas — Tumeur maligne du pancréas	-	-	3	1	2	1	2	*7*
Malignant neoplasm of trachea, bronchus and lung — Tumeur maligne de la trachée, des bronches et du poumon	*1*	-	1	2	2	-	12	*7*
Malignant neoplasm of female breast — Tumeur maligne du sein chez la femme	..	*1*	..	15	..	12	..	*15*
Malignant neoplasm of cervix uteri — Tumeur maligne du col de l'utérus	..	*1*	..	3	..	4	..	*1*
Malignant neoplasm of prostate — Tumeur maligne de la prostate	*4*	..	35	..	17	..	17	..
Malignant neoplasm of lymphoid, haematopoietic and related tissue — Tumeurs malignes primitives ou présumées primitives des tissus lymphoïde, hématopoïétique et apparentés	-	-	4	5	2	3	5	*5*
Disorders of the blood and blood-forming organs and certain disorders involving the immune mechanism — Maladies du sang et des organes hématopoïétiques et certains troubles du système immunitaire								
Total	*1*	*1*	3	3	10	3	2	*1*
Anaemias — Anémies	*1*	*1*	2	1	9	2	-	-
Endocrine, nutritional and metabolic diseases — Maladies endocriniennes, nutritionnelles et métaboliques								
Total	*6*	*4*	29	27	27	31	21	*27*
Diabetes mellitus — Diabète sucré	*5*	*4*	25	20	18	24	16	*21*
Malnutrition — Malnutrition	-	-	1	4	-	-	1	*1*
Mental and behavioural disorders — Troubles mentaux et du comportement	*3*	-	3	-	4	-	4	*1*
Diseases of the nervous system — Maladies du système nerveux	*3*	*2*	5	6	8	7	18	*24*
Diseases of the circulatory system — Maladies de l'appareil circulatoire								
Total	*15*	*15*	108	103	94	86	109	*95*
Acute rheumatic fever and chronic rheumatic heart diseases — Rhumatisme articularie aigu et cardiopathies rhumatismales chroniques	-	-	-	-	-	-	-	*1*
Hypertensive diseases — Maladies hypertensives	*5*	*2*	20	22	23	29	4	*6*
Ischaemic heart disease — Cardiopathie ischémique	*4*	*4*	29	20	32	12	36	*17*

Cause of death — Cause de décès	Anguilla 2016 (...)		Antigua and Barbuda - Antigua-et-Barbuda 2014 (+U)		2015 (+U)		Aruba 2014 (...)	
	Male — Masculin Number Nombre	Female — Féminin Number Nombre	Male — Masculin Number Nombre	Female — Féminin Number Nombre	Male — Masculin Number Nombre	Female — Féminin Number Nombre	Male — Masculin Number Nombre	Female — Féminin Number Nombre
Cerebrovascular disease — Maladie cérébrovasculaire	-	3	27	30	14	26	23	33
Diseases of arteries, arterioles and capillaries — Maladies des artères, artérioles et capillaires	1	-	5	5	4	2	1	3
Diseases of the respiratory system — Maladies de l'appareil respiratoire								
Total	2	2	24	15	25	24	27	15
Influenza — Grippe	-	-	-	-	-	-	2	1
Pneumonia — Pneumopathies	1	1	7	2	6	5	11	8
Chronic lower respiratory diseases — Maladies chroniques des voies respiratoires inférieures	1	-	2	1	1	5	3	3
Diseases of the digestive system — Maladies de l'appareil digestif								
Total	2	-	11	6	5	8	18	16
Gastric and duodenal ulcer — Ulcère de l'estomac et du duodénum	1	-	-	-	-	-	-	-
Diseases of the liver — Maladies du foie	1	-	6	3	3	3	8	8
Diseases of the musculoskeletal system and connective tissue — Maladies du système ostéo-articularie, des muscles et du tissu conjonctif	-	-	3	2	-	4	-	1
Diseases of the genitourinary system — Maladies de l'appareil génito-urinaire								
Total	-	1	8	5	15	6	11	8
Disorders of kidney and ureter — Affections du rein et de l'uretère	-	-	5	4	9	2	9	8
Hyperplasia of prostate — Hyperplasie de la prostate	-	..	1	..	1	..	-	..
Pregnancy, childbirth and the puerperium — Grossesse, accouchement et puerpéralité								
Total	..	-	..	-	..	-	..	-
Pregnancy with abortive outcome — Grossesse se terminant par un avortement	..	-	..	-	..	-	..	-
Other direct obstetric causes — Autres décès maternels directs	..	-	..	-	..	-	..	-
Indirect obstetric causes — Décès maternels indirects	..	-	..	-	..	-	..	-
Certain conditions originating in the perinatal period — Certaines affections dont l'origine se situe dans la période périnatale	-	-	2	1	2	3	-	1
Congenital malformations, deformations and chromosomal abnormalities — Malformations congénitales et anomalies chromosomiques	-	2	3	-	2	3	3	2
Symptoms, signs and abnormal clinical and laboratory findings, not elsewhere classified — Symptômes, signes et résultats anormaux d'examens cliniques et de laboratoire, non classés ailleurs	-	1	1	-	3	-	6	15
All other diseases — Toutes autres maladies	-	1	4	5	4	4	1	3
External causes — Causes externes								
Total	11	-	26	6	21	9	22	10
Accidents								
Total	10	-	24	6	17	5	16	5
Transport accidents — Accidents de transport	4	-	-	-	-	-	6	1
Falls — Chutes	1	-	-	-	-	-	1	1
Accidental drowning and submersion — Noyade et submersion accidentelles	3	-	1	-	-	-	4	3
Exposure to smoke, fire and flames — Exposition à la fumée, au feu et aux flammes	-	-	1	-	-	-	1	-
Accidental poisoning by and exposure to noxious substances — Intoxication accidentelle par des substances nocives et exposition à ces substances	-	-	2	1	-	-	1	-
Intentional self-harm — Lésions auto-infligées	-	-	-	-	-	1	3	2
Assault — Agresssions	-	-	-	-	-	-	2	-
All other external causes — Toutes autres causes externes	1	-	2	-	4	3	1	3

Cause of death — Cause de décès	Aruba		Bahamas				Barbados - Barbade	
	2015 (...)		2012 (+U)		2013 (+U)		2012 (U)	
	Male — Masculin	Female — Féminin	Male — Masculin	Female — Féminin	Male — Masculin	Female — Féminin	Male — Masculin	Female — Féminin
	Number Nombre	Number Nombre	Number Nombre	Number Nombre	Number Nombre	Number Nombre	Number Nombre	Number Nombre
TOTAL	382	311	1 091	902	1 138	927	1 159	1 167
Certain infectious and parasitic diseases — Certaines maladies infectieuses et parasitaires								
Total	15	8	83	81	97	92	56	55
Intestinal infectious diseases — Maladies infectieuses intestinales	-	1	1	1	2	1	2	4
Tuberculosis — Tuberculose	2	-	-	1	1	1	-	-
Tetanus — Tétanos	-	-	-	-	-	-	-	-
Diphtheria — Diphtérie........	-	-	-	-	-	-	-	-
Whooping cough — Coqueluche	-	-	-	-	-	-	-	-
Meningococcal infection — Infection à méningocoques	-	-	-	-	-	-	-	-
Septicaemia — Septicémie	7	3	18	30	29	29	41	40
Acute poliomyelitis — Poliomyélite aiguë	-	-	-	-	-	-	-	-
Measles — Rougeole	-	-	-	-	-	-	-	1
Viral hepatitis — Hépatite virale........	1	-	-	-	-	-	-	1
Human immunodeficiency virus [HIV] disease — Maladies dues au virus de l'immunodéficience humaine (VIH)	4	-	60	49	61	59	2	1
Malaria — Paludisme........	-	-	-	-	-	-	-	-
Neoplasms — Tumeurs	85	77	196	186	194	217	280	236
Malignant neoplasms — Tumeurs malignes								
Total	81	75	190	179	187	211	273	229
Malignant neoplasm of lip, oral cavity and pharynx — Tumeur maligne de la lèvre, de la cavité buccale et du pharynx	4	-	8	4	5	1	12	-
Malignant neoplasm of oesophagus — Tumeur maligne de l'oesophage	2	-	7	-	5	2	6	3
Malignant neoplasm of stomach — Tumeur maligne de l'estomac	1	1	5	3	11	11	13	5
Malignant neoplasm of colon, rectosigmoid junction, rectum, anus and anal canal — Tumeur maligne du côlon, de la jonction recto-sigmoïdienne, du rectum, de l'anus et du canal anal	11	9	20	13	30	23	36	22
Malignant neoplasm of liver and intrahepatic bile ducts — Tumeur maligne du foie et des voies bilaires intrahépatiques	1	3	11	3	6	2	5	4
Malignant neoplasm of pancreas — Tumeur maligne du pancréas........	3	4	4	4	8	2	16	11
Malignant neoplasm of trachea, bronchus and lung — Tumeur maligne de la trachée, des bronches et du poumon	14	6	16	8	14	10	22	10
Malignant neoplasm of female breast — Tumeur maligne du sein chez la femme	..	21	..	53	..	63	..	63
Malignant neoplasm of cervix uteri — Tumeur maligne du col de l'utérus........	..	2	..	17	..	23	..	10
Malignant neoplasm of prostate — Tumeur maligne de la prostate	13	..	62	..	43	..	92	..
Malignant neoplasm of lymphoid, haematopoietic and related tissue — Tumeurs malignes primitives ou présumées primitives des tissus lymphoïde, hématopoïétique et apparentés........	14	7	16	19	18	14	27	27
Disorders of the blood and blood-forming organs and certain disorders involving the immune mechanism — Maladies du sang et des organes hématopoïétiques et certains troubles du système immunitaire								
Total	4	-	6	9	10	6	14	13
Anaemias — Anémies	1	-	4	7	10	5	6	8
Endocrine, nutritional and metabolic diseases — Maladies endocriniennes, nutritionnelles et métaboliques								
Total	18	31	78	80	74	84	102	137
Diabetes mellitus — Diabète sucré........	16	26	55	54	46	56	73	112
Malnutrition — Malnutrition	1	1	1	2	6	6	-	-
Mental and behavioural disorders — Troubles mentaux et du comportement	5	1	14	2	6	1	21	37
Diseases of the nervous system — Maladies du système nerveux	13	22	18	25	33	25	39	29
Diseases of the circulatory system — Maladies de l'appareil circulatoire								
Total	126	99	313	302	345	277	310	369
Acute rheumatic fever and chronic rheumatic heart diseases — Rhumatisme articularie aigu et cardiopathies rhumatismales chroniques	1	-	-	2	-	1	-	-
Hypertensive diseases — Maladies hypertensives........	10	5	65	88	79	71	45	53
Ischaemic heart disease — Cardiopathie ischémique........	34	27	107	70	121	76	79	89

Cause of death — Cause de décès	Aruba 2015 (...) Male — Masculin Number Nombre	Aruba 2015 (...) Female — Féminin Number Nombre	Bahamas 2012 (+U) Male — Masculin Number Nombre	Bahamas 2012 (+U) Female — Féminin Number Nombre	Bahamas 2013 (+U) Male — Masculin Number Nombre	Bahamas 2013 (+U) Female — Féminin Number Nombre	Barbados - Barbade 2012 (U) Male — Masculin Number Nombre	Barbados - Barbade 2012 (U) Female — Féminin Number Nombre
Cerebrovascular disease — Maladie cérébrovasculaire	37	31	76	75	72	74	103	126
Diseases of arteries, arterioles and capillaries — Maladies des artères, artérioles et capillaires	5	1	3	7	3	6	9	13
Diseases of the respiratory system — Maladies de l'appareil respiratoire								
Total	25	16	58	65	47	47	108	112
Influenza — Grippe	1	1	-	-	-	-	-	-
Pneumonia — Pneumopathies	12	11	26	47	22	26	44	46
Chronic lower respiratory diseases — Maladies chroniques des voies respiratoires inférieures	7	3	15	6	10	2	12	7
Diseases of the digestive system — Maladies de l'appareil digestif								
Total	21	18	52	36	54	37	48	35
Gastric and duodenal ulcer — Ulcère de l'estomac et du duodénum	1	1	6	2	6	2	6	3
Diseases of the liver — Maladies du foie	11	6	21	15	25	20	20	3
Diseases of the musculoskeletal system and connective tissue — Maladies du système ostéo-articularie, des muscles et du tissu conjonctif	1	6	3	10	9	13	5	12
Diseases of the genitourinary system — Maladies de l'appareil génito-urinaire								
Total	13	4	31	19	27	31	54	46
Disorders of kidney and ureter — Affections du rein et de l'uretère	10	2	25	10	11	15	22	18
Hyperplasia of prostate — Hyperplasie de la prostate	-	..	4	..	4	..	11	..
Pregnancy, childbirth and the puerperium — Grossesse, accouchement et puerpéralité								
Total	..	-	..	3	..	3	..	1
Pregnancy with abortive outcome — Grossesse se terminant par un avortement	..	-	..	2	..	-	..	1
Other direct obstetric causes — Autres décès maternels directs	..	-	..	1	..	1	..	-
Indirect obstetric causes — Décès maternels indirects	..	-	..	-	..	2	..	-
Certain conditions originating in the perinatal period — Certaines affections dont l'origine se situe dans la période périnatale	1	-	15	14	11	11	13	6
Congenital malformations, deformations and chromosomal abnormalities — Malformations congénitales et anomalies chromosomiques	5	1	7	4	6	9	9	7
Symptoms, signs and abnormal clinical and laboratory findings, not elsewhere classified — Symptômes, signes et résultats anormaux d'examens cliniques et de laboratoire, non classés ailleurs	18	17	18	12	13	14	17	10
All other diseases — Toutes autres maladies	1	4	4	14	4	11	8	22
External causes — Causes externes								
Total	31	7	195	40	208	49	75	40
Accidents								
Total	19	5	67	24	81	28	21	21
Transport accidents — Accidents de transport	9	4	35	14	40	15	12	9
Falls — Chutes	-	-	6	1	4	1	2	1
Accidental drowning and submersion — Noyade et submersion accidentelles	2	1	16	3	20	5	-	-
Exposure to smoke, fire and flames — Exposition à la fumée, au feu et aux flammes	-	-	1	-	5	-	-	-
Accidental poisoning by and exposure to noxious substances — Intoxication accidentelle par des substances nocives et exposition à ces substances	1	-	-	-	-	-	2	-
Intentional self-harm — Lésions auto-infligées	7	2	4	1	4	1	-	-
Assault — Agresssions	2	-	116	13	113	12	-	-
All other external causes — Toutes autres causes externes	3	-	8	2	10	8	54	19

Cause of death — Cause de décès	Barbados - Barbade 2013 (U) Male — Masculin Number Nombre	Barbados - Barbade 2013 (U) Female — Féminin Number Nombre	Barbados - Barbade 2014 (U) Male — Masculin Number Nombre	Barbados - Barbade 2014 (U) Female — Féminin Number Nombre	Belize 2015 (U) Male — Masculin Number Nombre	Belize 2015 (U) Female — Féminin Number Nombre	Bermuda - Bermudes 2014 (...) Male — Masculin Number Nombre	Bermuda - Bermudes 2014 (...) Female — Féminin Number Nombre
TOTAL	1 216	1 272	943	644	1 095	677	248	236
Certain infectious and parasitic diseases — Certaines maladies infectieuses et parasitaires								
Total	76	61	86	48	103	52	4	3
Intestinal infectious diseases — Maladies infectieuses intestinales	1	3	2	1	5	3	-	-
Tuberculosis — Tuberculose	1	1	3	1	6	2	-	-
Tetanus — Tétanos	-	-	-	-	-	-	-	-
Diphtheria — Diphtérie	-	-	-	-	-	-	-	-
Whooping cough — Coqueluche	-	-	-	-	-	-	-	-
Meningococcal infection — Infection à méningocoques	-	-	-	-	-	-	-	-
Septicaemia — Septicémie	54	42	13	10	14	8	3	2
Acute poliomyelitis — Poliomyélite aiguë	-	-	-	-	-	-	-	-
Measles — Rougeole	-	-	-	-	-	-	-	-
Viral hepatitis — Hépatite virale	2	-	-	-	-	1	-	-
Human immunodeficiency virus [HIV] disease — Maladies dues au virus de l'immunodéficience humaine (VIH)	2	1	66	35	77	37	-	1
Malaria — Paludisme	-	-	-	-	-	-	-	-
Neoplasms — Tumeurs	278	280	82	104	121	99	83	65
Malignant neoplasms — Tumeurs malignes								
Total	270	263	78	97	115	91	82	65
Malignant neoplasm of lip, oral cavity and pharynx — Tumeur maligne de la lèvre, de la cavité buccale et du pharynx	7	1	1	1	4	-	4	1
Malignant neoplasm of oesophagus — Tumeur maligne de l'oesophage	-	3	2	-	3	-	1	-
Malignant neoplasm of stomach — Tumeur maligne de l'estomac	10	5	7	2	9	7	1	-
Malignant neoplasm of colon, rectosigmoid junction, rectum, anus and anal canal — Tumeur maligne du côlon, de la jonction recto-sigmoïdienne, du rectum, de l'anus et du canal anal	38	40	5	8	10	8	8	6
Malignant neoplasm of liver and intrahepatic bile ducts — Tumeur maligne du foie et des voies bilaires intrahépatiques	5	9	9	4	16	5	3	2
Malignant neoplasm of pancreas — Tumeur maligne du pancréas	19	12	2	4	-	3	4	7
Malignant neoplasm of trachea, bronchus and lung — Tumeur maligne de la trachée, des bronches et du poumon	16	11	12	3	17	9	21	7
Malignant neoplasm of female breast — Tumeur maligne du sein chez la femme	..	54	..	18	..	17	..	8
Malignant neoplasm of cervix uteri — Tumeur maligne du col de l'utérus	..	28	..	17	..	13	..	-
Malignant neoplasm of prostate — Tumeur maligne de la prostate	97	..	16	..	30	..	21	..
Malignant neoplasm of lymphoid, haematopoietic and related tissue — Tumeurs malignes primitives ou présumées primitives des tissus lymphoïde, hématopoïétique et apparentés	26	31	6	5	8	4	3	5
Disorders of the blood and blood-forming organs and certain disorders involving the immune mechanism — Maladies du sang et des organes hématopoïétiques et certains troubles du système immunitaire								
Total	9	9	13	4	7	4	1	1
Anaemias — Anémies	6	8	10	3	7	4	-	1
Endocrine, nutritional and metabolic diseases — Maladies endocriniennes, nutritionnelles et métaboliques								
Total	117	163	76	105	92	107	12	13
Diabetes mellitus — Diabète sucré	87	132	59	89	80	98	9	10
Malnutrition — Malnutrition	-	-	12	5	2	3	-	-
Mental and behavioural disorders — Troubles mentaux et du comportement	15	36	8	-	5	1	1	3
Diseases of the nervous system — Maladies du système nerveux	31	24	18	18	22	16	18	25
Diseases of the circulatory system — Maladies de l'appareil circulatoire								
Total	350	395	199	169	213	184	85	101
Acute rheumatic fever and chronic rheumatic heart diseases — Rhumatisme articularie aigu et cardiopathies rhumatismales chroniques	-	2	-	2	-	-	-	-
Hypertensive diseases — Maladies hypertensives	33	59	42	47	28	38	2	12
Ischaemic heart disease — Cardiopathie ischémique	101	101	70	28	76	52	39	44

Cause of death — Cause de décès	Barbados - Barbade 2013 (U)		Belize 2014 (U)		Belize 2015 (U)		Bermuda - Bermudes 2014 (...)	
	Male — Masculin Number Nombre	Female — Féminin Number Nombre	Male — Masculin Number Nombre	Female — Féminin Number Nombre	Male — Masculin Number Nombre	Female — Féminin Number Nombre	Male — Masculin Number Nombre	Female — Féminin Number Nombre
Cerebrovascular disease — Maladie cérébrovasculaire....................	107	140	43	56	61	38	17	18
Diseases of arteries, arterioles and capillaries — Maladies des artères, artérioles et capillaires	13	8	3	6	5	2	11	8
Diseases of the respiratory system — Maladies de l'appareil respiratoire								
Total	98	104	89	56	119	66	12	9
Influenza — Grippe	1	-	-	-	-	1	-	-
Pneumonia — Pneumopathies..	36	43	37	37	50	42	-	2
Chronic lower respiratory diseases — Maladies chroniques des voies respiratoires inférieures	19	9	25	9	36	8	5	3
Diseases of the digestive system — Maladies de l'appareil digestif								
Total	45	44	50	37	66	33	4	4
Gastric and duodenal ulcer — Ulcère de l'estomac et du duodénum................	5	7	2	-	1	-	-	-
Diseases of the liver — Maladies du foie..................................	18	9	35	18	44	16	4	1
Diseases of the musculoskeletal system and connective tissue — Maladies du système ostéo-articularie, des muscles et du tissu conjonctif	5	12	2	9	1	4	-	3
Diseases of the genitourinary system — Maladies de l'appareil génito-urinaire								
Total	49	44	19	20	22	16	6	4
Disorders of kidney and ureter — Affections du rein et de l'uretère	18	23	13	10	20	8	6	3
Hyperplasia of prostate — Hyperplasie de la prostate.........................	9	..	3	..	1	..	-	..
Pregnancy, childbirth and the puerperium — Grossesse, accouchement et puerpéralité								
Total	..	1	..	-	..	-	..	-
Pregnancy with abortive outcome — Grossesse se terminant par un avortement	..	-	..	-	..	-	..	-
Other direct obstetric causes — Autres décès maternels directs	..	1	..	-	..	-	..	-
Indirect obstetric causes — Décès maternels indirects	..	-	..	-	..	-	..	-
Certain conditions originating in the perinatal period — Certaines affections dont l'origine se situe dans la période périnatale	9	6	29	20	40	35	2	-
Congenital malformations, deformations and chromosomal abnormalities — Malformations congénitales et anomalies chromosomiques	10	14	14	12	19	15	-	-
Symptoms, signs and abnormal clinical and laboratory findings, not elsewhere classified — Symptômes, signes et résultats anormaux d'examens cliniques et de laboratoire, non classés ailleurs	26	8	9	3	15	4	-	-
All other diseases — Toutes autres maladies................................	23	33	-	3	1	2	-	-
External causes — Causes externes								
Total	75	38	249	36	249	39	20	5
Accidents								
Total	25	17	127	14	124	24	16	2
Transport accidents — Accidents de transport	14	2	76	8	74	14	13	1
Falls — Chutes	4	-	2	1	10	3	-	-
Accidental drowning and submersion — Noyade et submersion accidentelles..	-	-	24	1	20	2	3	1
Exposure to smoke, fire and flames — Exposition à la fumée, au feu et aux flammes	-	-	1	-	1	1	-	-
Accidental poisoning by and exposure to noxious substances — Intoxication accidentelle par des substances nocives et exposition à ces substances	-	-	4	-	2	3	-	-
Intentional self-harm — Lésions auto-infligées..............................	-	-	18	6	22	4	1	-
Assault — Agresssions	1	-	102	12	103	10	3	1
All other external causes — Toutes autres causes externes	49	21	2	4	-	1	-	2

Cause of death — Cause de décès	Bermuda - Bermudes		Canada			
	2015 (...)		2012 (C)			
	Male — Masculin	Female — Féminin	Male — Masculin		Female — Féminin	
	Number Nombre	Number Nombre	Number Nombre	Rate Taux	Number Nombre	Rate Taux
TOTAL	249	217	124 235	721.1	122 361	698.3
Certain infectious and parasitic diseases — Certaines maladies infectieuses et parasitaires						
Total	10	3	2 761	16.0	3 019	17.2
Intestinal infectious diseases — Maladies infectieuses intestinales	-	-	695	4.0	1 014	5.8
Tuberculosis — Tuberculose	-	-	48	0.3	20	+0.1
Tetanus — Tétanos	-	-	-	-	-	-
Diphtheria — Diphtérie	-	-	-	-	-	-
Whooping cough — Coqueluche	-	-	1	+0.0	2	+0.0
Meningococcal infection — Infection à méningocoques	-	-	4	+0.0	10	+0.1
Septicaemia — Septicémie	6	2	1 173	6.8	1 438	8.2
Acute poliomyelitis — Poliomyélite aiguë	-	-	-	-	-	-
Measles — Rougeole	-	-	-	-	-	-
Viral hepatitis — Hépatite virale	-	-	354	2.1	171	1.0
Human immunodeficiency virus [HIV] disease — Maladies dues au virus de l'immunodéficience humaine (VIH)	2	-	206	1.2	70	0.4
Malaria — Paludisme	-	-	3	+0.0	-	-
Neoplasms — Tumeurs	67	63	39 846	231.3	35 988	205.4
Malignant neoplasms — Tumeurs malignes						
Total	66	61	39 080	226.8	35 281	201.3
Malignant neoplasm of lip, oral cavity and pharynx — Tumeur maligne de la lèvre, de la cavité buccale et du pharynx	2	2	787	4.6	335	1.9
Malignant neoplasm of oesophagus — Tumeur maligne de l'oesophage	-	-	1 394	8.1	430	2.5
Malignant neoplasm of stomach — Tumeur maligne de l'estomac	2	-	1 137	6.6	726	4.1
Malignant neoplasm of colon, rectosigmoid junction, rectum, anus and anal canal — Tumeur maligne du côlon, de la jonction recto-sigmoïdienne, du rectum, de l'anus et du canal anal	5	12	4 381	25.4	3 730	21.3
Malignant neoplasm of liver and intrahepatic bile ducts — Tumeur maligne du foie et des voies bilaires intrahépatiques	4	2	1 637	9.5	891	5.1
Malignant neoplasm of pancreas — Tumeur maligne du pancréas	3	7	2 078	12.1	2 190	12.5
Malignant neoplasm of trachea, bronchus and lung — Tumeur maligne de la trachée, des bronches et du poumon	18	7	10 718	62.2	8 986	51.3
Malignant neoplasm of female breast — Tumeur maligne du sein chez la femme	..	7	..	..	4 977	33.6
Malignant neoplasm of cervix uteri — Tumeur maligne du col de l'utérus	..	4	..	..	443	3.0
Malignant neoplasm of prostate — Tumeur maligne de la prostate	9	..	3 708	63.0	..	..
Malignant neoplasm of lymphoid, haematopoietic and related tissue — Tumeurs malignes primitives ou présumées primitives des tissus lymphoïde, hématopoïétique et apparentés	5	5	3 855	22.4	3 036	17.3
Disorders of the blood and blood-forming organs and certain disorders involving the immune mechanism — Maladies du sang et des organes hématopoïétiques et certains troubles du système immunitaire						
Total	4	1	386	2.2	493	2.8
Anaemias — Anémies	2	1	189	1.1	288	1.6
Endocrine, nutritional and metabolic diseases — Maladies endocriniennes, nutritionnelles et métaboliques						
Total	12	20	4 915	28.5	4 682	26.7
Diabetes mellitus — Diabète sucré	9	18	3 702	21.5	3 291	18.8
Malnutrition — Malnutrition	1	-	62	0.4	106	0.6
Mental and behavioural disorders — Troubles mentaux et du comportement	2	1	5 481	31.8	9 497	54.2
Diseases of the nervous system — Maladies du système nerveux	19	23	5 284	30.7	7 199	41.1
Diseases of the circulatory system — Maladies de l'appareil circulatoire						
Total	95	75	33 774	196.0	33 178	189.3
Acute rheumatic fever and chronic rheumatic heart diseases — Rhumatisme articularie aigu et cardiopathies rhumatismales chroniques	-	-	165	1.0	300	1.7
Hypertensive diseases — Maladies hypertensives	6	6	1 025	5.9	1 596	9.1
Ischaemic heart disease — Cardiopathie ischémique	47	23	19 166	111.3	14 707	83.9
Cerebrovascular disease — Maladie cérébrovasculaire	16	16	5 581	32.4	7 593	43.3
Diseases of arteries, arterioles and capillaries — Maladies des artères, artérioles et capillaires	4	4	1 633	9.5	1 508	8.6

20. Death and death rates by cause and sex: 2012 - 2016
Décès et taux de mortalité par cause et sexe : 2012 - 2016 (continued - suite)

Cause of death — Cause de décès	Bermuda - Bermudes 2015 (...)		Canada 2012 (C)			
	Male — Masculin	Female — Féminin	Male — Masculin		Female — Féminin	
	Number Nombre	Number Nombre	Number Nombre	Rate Taux	Number Nombre	Rate Taux
Diseases of the respiratory system — Maladies de l'appareil respiratoire						
Total	12	11	11 253	65.3	10 886	62.1
Influenza — Grippe	-	-	147	0.9	255	1.5
Pneumonia — Pneumopathies	4	3	2 435	14.1	2 852	16.3
Chronic lower respiratory diseases — Maladies chroniques des voies respiratoires inférieures	2	3	5 683	33.0	5 447	31.1
Diseases of the digestive system — Maladies de l'appareil digestif						
Total	4	5	5 025	29.2	4 833	27.6
Gastric and duodenal ulcer — Ulcère de l'estomac et du duodénum	-	-	215	1.2	195	1.1
Diseases of the liver — Maladies du foie	2	1	2 162	12.5	1 273	7.3
Diseases of the musculoskeletal system and connective tissue — Maladies du système ostéo-articularie, des muscles et du tissu conjonctif	1	3	490	2.8	1 038	5.9
Diseases of the genitourinary system — Maladies de l'appareil génito-urinaire						
Total	6	2	2 343	13.6	2 729	15.6
Disorders of kidney and ureter — Affections du rein et de l'uretère	6	2	1 747	10.1	1 888	10.8
Hyperplasia of prostate — Hyperplasie de la prostate	-	..	112	1.9	..	..
Pregnancy, childbirth and the puerperium — Grossesse, accouchement et puerpéralité						
Total	..	-	..	..	22	✦5.8
Pregnancy with abortive outcome — Grossesse se terminant par un avortement	..	-	..	..	1	✦0.3
Other direct obstetric causes — Autres décès maternels directs	..	-	..	..	10	✦2.6
Indirect obstetric causes — Décès maternels indirects	..	-	..	..	8	✦2.1
Certain conditions originating in the perinatal period — Certaines affections dont l'origine se situe dans la période périnatale	2	1	580	295.2	500	269.7
Congenital malformations, deformations and chromosomal abnormalities — Malformations congénitales et anomalies chromosomiques	-	-	499	254.0	491	264.8
Symptoms, signs and abnormal clinical and laboratory findings, not elsewhere classified — Symptômes, signes et résultats anormaux d'examens cliniques et de laboratoire, non classés ailleurs	-	4	1 070	6.2	1 261	7.2
All other diseases — Toutes autres maladies	-	1	175	1.0	254	1.4
External causes — Causes externes						
Total	15	4	10 353	60.1	6 291	35.9
Accidents						
Total	13	4	6 322	36.7	4 762	27.2
Transport accidents — Accidents de transport	7	1	1 805	10.5	719	4.1
Falls — Chutes	1	2	2 041	11.8	2 454	14.0
Accidental drowning and submersion — Noyade et submersion accidentelles	3	-	244	1.4	65	0.4
Exposure to smoke, fire and flames — Exposition à la fumée, au feu et aux flammes	1	-	108	0.6	76	0.4
Accidental poisoning by and exposure to noxious substances — Intoxication accidentelle par des substances nocives et exposition à ces substances	-	1	1 186	6.9	593	3.4
Intentional self-harm — Lésions auto-infligées	-	-	2 970	17.2	954	5.4
Assault — Agresssions	1	-	356	2.1	132	0.8
All other external causes — Toutes autres causes externes	1	-	705	4.1	443	2.5

Cause of death — Cause de décès	Canada 2013 (C) Male — Masculin Number Nombre	Canada 2013 (C) Male — Masculin Rate Taux	Canada 2013 (C) Female — Féminin Number Nombre	Canada 2013 (C) Female — Féminin Rate Taux	Cayman Islands - Îles Caïmanes 2013 (...) Male — Masculin Number Nombre	Cayman Islands - Îles Caïmanes 2013 (...) Female — Féminin Number Nombre	Costa Rica 2013 (+U) Male — Masculin Number Nombre	Costa Rica 2013 (+U) Female — Féminin Number Nombre
TOTAL	126 973	728.5	125 365	707.4	81	89	10 906	8 459
Certain infectious and parasitic diseases — Certaines maladies infectieuses et parasitaires								
Total	2 372	13.6	2 516	14.2	2	3	248	132
Intestinal infectious diseases — Maladies infectieuses intestinales	453	2.6	755	4.3	-	-	46	54
Tuberculosis — Tuberculose	57	0.3	25	♦0.1	-	-	27	5
Tetanus — Tétanos	-	-	-	-	-	-	-	-
Diphtheria — Diphtérie	-	-	-	-	-	-	-	-
Whooping cough — Coqueluche	-	-	1	♦0.0	-	-	1	-
Meningococcal infection — Infection à méningocoques	6	♦0.0	4	♦0.0	-	-	-	-
Septicaemia — Septicémie	1 070	6.1	1 219	6.9	2	1	19	16
Acute poliomyelitis — Poliomyélite aiguë	-	-	-	-	-	-	-	-
Measles — Rougeole	-	-	1	♦0.0	-	-	-	-
Viral hepatitis — Hépatite virale	353	2.0	187	1.1	-	-	6	-
Human immunodeficiency virus [HIV] disease — Maladies dues au virus de l'immunodéficience humaine (VIH)	189	1.1	52	0.3	-	2	106	27
Malaria — Paludisme	-	-	-	-	-	-	-	-
Neoplasms — Tumeurs	40 166	230.4	36 477	205.8	28	21	2 548	2 119
Malignant neoplasms — Tumeurs malignes								
Total	39 384	226.0	35 728	201.6	28	20	2 389	2 029
Malignant neoplasm of lip, oral cavity and pharynx — Tumeur maligne de la lèvre, de la cavité buccale et du pharynx	933	5.4	411	2.3	1	-	58	18
Malignant neoplasm of oesophagus — Tumeur maligne de l'oesophage	1 455	8.3	450	2.5	1	-	41	14
Malignant neoplasm of stomach — Tumeur maligne de l'estomac	1 160	6.7	773	4.4	-	2	373	226
Malignant neoplasm of colon, rectosigmoid junction, rectum, anus and anal canal — Tumeur maligne du côlon, de la jonction recto-sigmoïdienne, du rectum, de l'anus et du canal anal	4 495	25.8	3 954	22.3	3	2	228	231
Malignant neoplasm of liver and intrahepatic bile ducts — Tumeur maligne du foie et des voies bilaires intrahépatiques	1 685	9.7	1 018	5.7	2	-	165	103
Malignant neoplasm of pancreas — Tumeur maligne du pancréas	2 324	13.3	2 227	12.6	-	3	94	127
Malignant neoplasm of trachea, bronchus and lung — Tumeur maligne de la trachée, des bronches et du poumon	10 426	59.8	9 219	52.0	6	1	192	92
Malignant neoplasm of female breast — Tumeur maligne du sein chez la femme	..	..	5 004	33.4	..	3	..	342
Malignant neoplasm of cervix uteri — Tumeur maligne du col de l'utérus	..	..	399	2.7	..	-	..	131
Malignant neoplasm of prostate — Tumeur maligne de la prostate	3 947	64.8	..	..	5	..	401	..
Malignant neoplasm of lymphoid, haematopoietic and related tissue — Tumeurs malignes primitives ou présumées primitives des tissus lymphoïde, hématopoïétique et apparentés	3 925	22.5	3 054	17.2	3	1	258	222
Disorders of the blood and blood-forming organs and certain disorders involving the immune mechanism — Maladies du sang et des organes hématopoïétiques et certains troubles du système immunitaire								
Total	423	2.4	498	2.8	-	1	35	39
Anaemias — Anémies	230	1.3	275	1.6	-	1	23	28
Endocrine, nutritional and metabolic diseases — Maladies endocriniennes, nutritionnelles et métaboliques								
Total	4 989	28.6	4 684	26.4	3	9	382	455
Diabetes mellitus — Diabète sucré	3 786	21.7	3 259	18.4	2	6	333	377
Malnutrition — Malnutrition	64	0.4	100	0.6	-	1	13	18
Mental and behavioural disorders — Troubles mentaux et du comportement	6 422	36.8	10 581	59.7	-	1	124	182
Diseases of the nervous system — Maladies du système nerveux	5 441	31.2	7 313	41.3	1	3	265	240
Diseases of the circulatory system — Maladies de l'appareil circulatoire								
Total	34 443	197.6	33 988	191.8	22	29	2 941	2 612
Acute rheumatic fever and chronic rheumatic heart diseases — Rhumatisme articularie aigu et cardiopathies rhumatismales chroniques	186	1.1	381	2.1	-	-	21	27
Hypertensive diseases — Maladies hypertensives	1 321	7.6	1 893	10.7	7	11	291	314
Ischaemic heart disease — Cardiopathie ischémique	19 340	111.0	14 544	82.1	6	5	1 541	1 123

20. Death and death rates by cause and sex: 2012 - 2016
Décès et taux de mortalité par cause et sexe : 2012 - 2016 (continued - suite)

	Canada				Cayman Islands - Îles Caïmanes		Costa Rica	
Cause of death — Cause de décès	2013 (C)				2013 (...)		2013 (+U)	
	Male — Masculin		Female — Féminin		Male — Masculin	Female — Féminin	Male — Masculin	Female — Féminin
	Number Nombre	Rate Taux	Number Nombre	Rate Taux	Number Nombre	Number Nombre	Number Nombre	Number Nombre
Cerebrovascular disease — Maladie cérébrovasculaire..................................	5 543	31.8	7 857	44.3	4	3	608	669
Diseases of arteries, arterioles and capillaries — Maladies des artères, artérioles et capillaires	1 689	9.7	1 560	8.8	4	2	92	43
Diseases of the respiratory system — Maladies de l'appareil respiratoire								
Total	11 654	66.9	11 551	65.2	7	10	889	788
Influenza — Grippe	364	2.1	530	3.0	-	-	3	3
Pneumonia — Pneumopathies	2 622	15.0	3 022	17.1	2	7	281	219
Chronic lower respiratory diseases — Maladies chroniques des voies respiratoires inférieures	6 030	34.6	5 946	33.6	3	1	426	384
Diseases of the digestive system — Maladies de l'appareil digestif								
Total	5 265	30.2	5 091	28.7	-	1	800	621
Gastric and duodenal ulcer — Ulcère de l'estomac et du duodénum.................	244	1.4	216	1.2	-	-	41	18
Diseases of the liver — Maladies du foie...........................	2 287	13.1	1 334	7.5	-	-	443	255
Diseases of the musculoskeletal system and connective tissue — Maladies du système ostéo-articularie, des muscles et du tissu conjonctif	569	3.3	1 141	6.4	-	-	52	131
Diseases of the genitourinary system — Maladies de l'appareil génito-urinaire								
Total	2 242	12.9	2 549	14.4	1	4	320	240
Disorders of kidney and ureter — Affections du rein et de l'uretère	1 598	9.2	1 718	9.7	-	2	271	156
Hyperplasia of prostate — Hyperplasie de la prostate...........................	111	1.8	..	..	-	..	7	..
Pregnancy, childbirth and the puerperium — Grossesse, accouchement et puerpéralité								
Total...........................	..	..	23	♦6.0	..	-	..	10
Pregnancy with abortive outcome — Grossesse se terminant par un avortement	..	..	5	♦1.3	..	-	..	-
Other direct obstetric causes — Autres décès maternels directs	..	..	12	♦3.2	..	-	..	6
Indirect obstetric causes — Décès maternels indirects...........................	..	..	5	♦1.3	..	-	..	4
Certain conditions originating in the perinatal period — Certaines affections dont l'origine se situe dans la période périnatale	628	321.7	497	268.4	1	1	169	139
Congenital malformations, deformations and chromosomal abnormalities — Malformations congénitales et anomalies chromosomiques	519	265.9	476	257.1	-	-	131	106
Symptoms, signs and abnormal clinical and laboratory findings, not elsewhere classified — Symptômes, signes et résultats anormaux d'examens cliniques et de laboratoire, non classés ailleurs	1 112	6.4	1 285	7.3	2	3	360	189
All other diseases — Toutes autres maladies...........................	207	1.2	327	1.8	-	1	42	43
External causes — Causes externes								
Total	10 521	60.4	6 368	35.9	14	2	1 600	413
Accidents								
Total...........................	6 416	36.8	4 833	27.3	7	2	909	298
Transport accidents — Accidents de transport...........................	1 659	9.5	721	4.1	3	1	493	108
Falls — Chutes...........................	2 187	12.5	2 483	14.0	-	1	71	15
Accidental drowning and submersion — Noyade et submersion accidentelles...........................	224	1.3	68	0.4	4	-	87	15
Exposure to smoke, fire and flames — Exposition à la fumée, au feu et aux flammes	137	0.8	106	0.6	-	-	9	6
Accidental poisoning by and exposure to noxious substances — Intoxication accidentelle par des substances nocives et exposition à ces substances	1 248	7.2	580	3.3	-	-	37	7
Intentional self-harm — Lésions auto-infligées...........................	3 038	17.4	1 012	5.7	1	-	273	39
Assault — Agresssions...........................	311	1.8	127	0.7	5	-	336	32
All other external causes — Toutes autres causes externes...........................	756	4.3	396	2.2	1	-	82	44

20. Death and death rates by cause and sex: 2012 - 2016
Décès et taux de mortalité par cause et sexe : 2012 - 2016 (continued - suite)

Cause of death — Cause de décès	Costa Rica 2014 (+U) Male — Masculin Number Nombre	Costa Rica 2014 (+U) Female — Féminin Number Nombre	Cuba 2014 (C) Male — Masculin Number Nombre	Cuba 2014 (C) Male — Masculin Rate Taux	Cuba 2014 (C) Female — Féminin Number Nombre	Cuba 2014 (C) Female — Féminin Rate Taux
TOTAL	11 497	8 793	51 918	927.9	44 412	789.0
Certain infectious and parasitic diseases — Certaines maladies infectieuses et parasitaires						
Total	238	153	745	13.3	459	8.2
Intestinal infectious diseases — Maladies infectieuses intestinales	52	61	145	2.6	173	3.1
Tuberculosis — Tuberculose	26	15	25	+0.4	6	+0.1
Tetanus — Tétanos	-	-	-	-	-	-
Diphtheria — Diphtérie	-	-	-		-	
Whooping cough — Coqueluche	-	-	-		-	
Meningococcal infection — Infection à méningocoques	-	-	2	+0.0	1	+0.0
Septicaemia — Septicémie	17	20	60	1.1	66	1.2
Acute poliomyelitis — Poliomyélite aiguë	-	-	-	-	-	-
Measles — Rougeole	-	-	-		-	
Viral hepatitis — Hépatite virale	4	-	98	1.8	95	1.7
Human immunodeficiency virus [HIV] disease — Maladies dues au virus de l'immunodéficience humaine (VIH)	117	35	310	5.5	63	1.1
Malaria — Paludisme	-	-	2	+0.0	-	-
Neoplasms — Tumeurs	2 608	2 184	13 945	249.2	10 451	185.7
Malignant neoplasms — Tumeurs malignes						
Total	2 481	2 061	13 667	244.3	10 181	180.9
Malignant neoplasm of lip, oral cavity and pharynx — Tumeur maligne de la lèvre, de la cavité buccale et du pharynx	72	19	634	11.3	183	3.3
Malignant neoplasm of oesophagus — Tumeur maligne de l'oesophage	37	14	700	12.5	141	2.5
Malignant neoplasm of stomach — Tumeur maligne de l'estomac	388	224	538	9.6	353	6.3
Malignant neoplasm of colon, rectosigmoid junction, rectum, anus and anal canal — Tumeur maligne du côlon, de la jonction recto-sigmoïdienne, du rectum, de l'anus et du canal anal	266	216	1 065	19.0	1 403	24.9
Malignant neoplasm of liver and intrahepatic bile ducts — Tumeur maligne du foie et des voies bilaires intrahépatiques	148	116	415	7.4	359	6.4
Malignant neoplasm of pancreas — Tumeur maligne du pancréas	91	122	423	7.6	447	7.9
Malignant neoplasm of trachea, bronchus and lung — Tumeur maligne de la trachée, des bronches et du poumon	179	105	3 450	61.7	2 004	35.6
Malignant neoplasm of female breast — Tumeur maligne du sein chez la femme	..	328	..	..	1 541	32.7
Malignant neoplasm of cervix uteri — Tumeur maligne du col de l'utérus	..	125	..	..	485	10.3
Malignant neoplasm of prostate — Tumeur maligne de la prostate	405	..	2 844	164.3	..	..
Malignant neoplasm of lymphoid, haematopoietic and related tissue — Tumeurs malignes primitives ou présumées primitives des tissus lymphoïde, hématopoïétique et apparentés	286	203	827	14.8	739	13.1
Disorders of the blood and blood-forming organs and certain disorders involving the immune mechanism — Maladies du sang et des organes hématopoïétiques et certains troubles du système immunitaire						
Total	40	37	101	1.8	112	2.0
Anaemias — Anémies	25	24	73	1.3	91	1.6
Endocrine, nutritional and metabolic diseases — Maladies endocriniennes, nutritionnelles et métaboliques						
Total	388	435	998	17.8	1 523	27.1
Diabetes mellitus — Diabète sucré	330	381	898	16.0	1 376	24.4
Malnutrition — Malnutrition	12	10	22	+0.4	19	+0.3
Mental and behavioural disorders — Troubles mentaux et du comportement	126	153	2 308	41.2	2 666	47.4
Diseases of the nervous system — Maladies du système nerveux	289	267	845	15.1	725	12.9
Diseases of the circulatory system — Maladies de l'appareil circulatoire						
Total	3 262	2 706	18 928	338.3	17 499	310.9
Acute rheumatic fever and chronic rheumatic heart diseases — Rhumatisme articularie aigu et cardiopathies rhumatismales chroniques	16	25	53	0.9	72	1.3
Hypertensive diseases — Maladies hypertensives	301	349	1 682	30.1	1 708	30.3
Ischaemic heart disease — Cardiopathie ischémique	1 778	1 191	8 615	154.0	7 665	136.2
Cerebrovascular disease — Maladie cérébrovasculaire	676	682	4 700	84.0	4 624	82.1
Diseases of arteries, arterioles and capillaries — Maladies des artères, artérioles et capillaires	74	55	1 447	25.9	1 349	24.0

Cause of death — Cause de décès	Costa Rica 2014 (+U)		Cuba 2014 (C)			
	Male — Masculin	Female — Féminin	Male — Masculin		Female — Féminin	
	Number Nombre	Number Nombre	Number Nombre	Rate Taux	Number Nombre	Rate Taux
Diseases of the respiratory system — Maladies de l'appareil respiratoire						
Total	990	856	5 344	95.5	4 811	85.5
Influenza — Grippe	5	2	1	+0.0	-	-
Pneumonia — Pneumopathies	353	233	3 065	54.8	2 808	49.9
Chronic lower respiratory diseases — Maladies chroniques des voies respiratoires inférieures	448	424	2 121	37.9	1 856	33.0
Diseases of the digestive system — Maladies de l'appareil digestif						
Total	836	631	2 313	41.3	1 520	27.0
Gastric and duodenal ulcer — Ulcère de l'estomac et du duodénum	46	21	238	4.3	141	2.5
Diseases of the liver — Maladies du foie	459	255	1 161	20.7	384	6.8
Diseases of the musculoskeletal system and connective tissue — Maladies du système ostéo-articularie, des muscles et du tissu conjonctif	50	139	225	4.0	436	7.7
Diseases of the genitourinary system — Maladies de l'appareil génito-urinaire						
Total	393	292	540	9.7	447	7.9
Disorders of kidney and ureter — Affections du rein et de l'uretère	316	189	417	7.5	360	6.4
Hyperplasia of prostate — Hyperplasie de la prostate	6	..	44	2.5	..	..
Pregnancy, childbirth and the puerperium — Grossesse, accouchement et puerpéralité						
Total	..	21	..	..	50	40.8
Pregnancy with abortive outcome — Grossesse se terminant par un avortement	..	1	..	..	5	+4.1
Other direct obstetric causes — Autres décès maternels directs	..	12	..	..	23	+18.8
Indirect obstetric causes — Décès maternels indirects	..	8	..	..	15	+12.2
Certain conditions originating in the perinatal period — Certaines affections dont l'origine se situe dans la période périnatale	143	128	166	262.2	111	187.1
Congenital malformations, deformations and chromosomal abnormalities — Malformations congénitales et anomalies chromosomiques	144	119	225	355.3	162	273.1
Symptoms, signs and abnormal clinical and laboratory findings, not elsewhere classified — Symptômes, signes et résultats anormaux d'examens cliniques et de laboratoire, non classés ailleurs	244	132	445	8.0	275	4.9
All other diseases — Toutes autres maladies	42	51	109	1.9	129	2.3
External causes — Causes externes						
Total	1 704	489	4 681	83.7	3 036	53.9
Accidents						
Total	1 005	357	2 507	44.8	1 554	27.6
Transport accidents — Accidents de transport	551	103	818	14.6	189	3.4
Falls — Chutes	61	13	1 069	19.1	1 233	21.9
Accidental drowning and submersion — Noyade et submersion accidentelles	95	15	215	3.8	18	+0.3
Exposure to smoke, fire and flames — Exposition à la fumée, au feu et aux flammes	11	4	23	+0.4	16	+0.3
Accidental poisoning by and exposure to noxious substances — Intoxication accidentelle par des substances nocives et exposition à ces substances	49	6	73	1.3	14	+0.2
Intentional self-harm — Lésions auto-infligées	223	45	1 147	20.5	306	5.4
Assault — Agresssions	394	49	443	7.9	156	2.8
All other external causes — Toutes autres causes externes	82	38	584	10.4	1 020	18.1

20. Death and death rates by cause and sex: 2012 - 2016
Décès et taux de mortalité par cause et sexe : 2012 - 2016 (continued - suite)

Cause of death — Cause de décès	Cuba 2015 (C)				Dominica - Dominique 2014 (+C)		2015 (+C)	
	Male — Masculin		Female — Féminin		Male — Masculin	Female — Féminin	Male — Masculin	Female — Féminin
	Number Nombre	Rate Taux	Number Nombre	Rate Taux	Number Nombre	Number Nombre	Number Nombre	Number Nombre
TOTAL	53 812	960.8	45 879	813.8	318	296	381	280
Certain infectious and parasitic diseases — Certaines maladies infectieuses et parasitaires								
Total	708	12.6	364	6.5	12	17	10	11
Intestinal infectious diseases — Maladies infectieuses intestinales	93	1.7	108	1.9	3	1	2	2
Tuberculosis — Tuberculose	27	♦0.5	9	♦0.2	-	-	-	-
Tetanus — Tétanos	-	-	-	-	-	-	-	-
Diphtheria — Diphtérie	-	-	-	-	-	-	-	-
Whooping cough — Coqueluche	-	-	-	-	-	-	-	-
Meningococcal infection — Infection à méningocoques	2	♦0.0	2	♦0.0	-	-	-	-
Septicaemia — Septicémie	45	0.8	48	0.9	3	13	5	6
Acute poliomyelitis — Poliomyélite aiguë	-	-	-	-	-	-	-	-
Measles — Rougeole	-	-	-	-	-	-	-	-
Viral hepatitis — Hépatite virale	86	1.5	81	1.4	-	-	-	-
Human immunodeficiency virus [HIV] disease — Maladies dues au virus de l'immunodéficience humaine (VIH)	374	6.7	73	1.3	2	-	1	1
Malaria — Paludisme	-	-	-	-	-	-	-	-
Neoplasms — Tumeurs	14 540	259.6	10 419	184.8	61	46	91	45
Malignant neoplasms — Tumeurs malignes								
Total	14 190	253.4	10 143	179.9	60	42	82	43
Malignant neoplasm of lip, oral cavity and pharynx — Tumeur maligne de la lèvre, de la cavité buccale et du pharynx	615	11.0	172	3.1	1	-	3	-
Malignant neoplasm of oesophagus — Tumeur maligne de l'oesophage	671	12.0	117	2.1	1	-	2	-
Malignant neoplasm of stomach — Tumeur maligne de l'estomac	555	9.9	346	6.1	2	5	3	3
Malignant neoplasm of colon, rectosigmoid junction, rectum, anus and anal canal — Tumeur maligne du côlon, de la jonction recto-sigmoïdienne, du rectum, de l'anus et du canal anal	1 145	20.4	1 462	25.9	3	8	5	4
Malignant neoplasm of liver and intrahepatic bile ducts — Tumeur maligne du foie et des voies bilaires intrahépatiques	409	7.3	341	6.0	2	4	2	4
Malignant neoplasm of pancreas — Tumeur maligne du pancréas	437	7.8	424	7.5	1	2	5	3
Malignant neoplasm of trachea, bronchus and lung — Tumeur maligne de la trachée, des bronches et du poumon	3 539	63.2	1 984	35.2	6	2	6	3
Malignant neoplasm of female breast — Tumeur maligne du sein chez la femme	..	..	1 557	32.9	..	6	..	8
Malignant neoplasm of cervix uteri — Tumeur maligne du col de l'utérus	..	..	479	10.1	..	2	..	1
Malignant neoplasm of prostate — Tumeur maligne de la prostate	2 954	165.4	..	..	25	..	39	..
Malignant neoplasm of lymphoid, haematopoietic and related tissue — Tumeurs malignes primitives ou présumées primitives des tissus lymphoïde, hématopoïétique et apparentés	909	16.2	654	11.6	10	3	7	6
Disorders of the blood and blood-forming organs and certain disorders involving the immune mechanism — Maladies du sang et des organes hématopoïétiques et certains troubles du système immunitaire								
Total	107	1.9	95	1.7	9	3	12	5
Anaemias — Anémies	74	1.3	74	1.3	5	3	8	3
Endocrine, nutritional and metabolic diseases — Maladies endocriniennes, nutritionnelles et métaboliques								
Total	1 067	19.1	1 560	27.7	12	20	20	32
Diabetes mellitus — Diabète sucré	950	17.0	1 402	24.9	10	18	16	28
Malnutrition — Malnutrition	26	♦0.5	18	♦0.3	1	1	4	1
Mental and behavioural disorders — Troubles mentaux et du comportement	2 486	44.4	2 835	50.3	-	-	3	3
Diseases of the nervous system — Maladies du système nerveux	959	17.1	871	15.4	8	3	8	7
Diseases of the circulatory system — Maladies de l'appareil circulatoire								
Total	19 252	343.7	17 900	317.5	129	136	117	103
Acute rheumatic fever and chronic rheumatic heart diseases — Rhumatisme articularie aigu et cardiopathies rhumatismales chroniques	52	0.9	99	1.8	-	1	1	2
Hypertensive diseases — Maladies hypertensives	1 807	32.3	1 696	30.1	24	28	26	24
Ischaemic heart disease — Cardiopathie ischémique	9 034	161.3	7 988	141.7	11	18	21	16

Cause of death — Cause de décès	Cuba 2015 (C)				Dominica - Dominique 2014 (+C)		2015 (+C)	
	Male — Masculin		Female — Féminin		Male — Masculin	Female — Féminin	Male — Masculin	Female — Féminin
	Number Nombre	Rate Taux	Number Nombre	Rate Taux	Number Nombre	Number Nombre	Number Nombre	Number Nombre
Cerebrovascular disease — Maladie cérébrovasculaire...................	4 644	82.9	4 676	82.9	36	33	23	27
Diseases of arteries, arterioles and capillaries — Maladies des artères, artérioles et capillaires	1 433	25.6	1 370	24.3	3	3	3	3
Diseases of the respiratory system — Maladies de l'appareil respiratoire								
Total	5 820	103.9	5 423	96.2	20	14	28	14
Influenza — Grippe	7	♦0.1	4	♦0.1	-	-	-	-
Pneumonia — Pneumopathies	3 324	59.3	3 282	58.2	11	4	15	7
Chronic lower respiratory diseases — Maladies chroniques des voies respiratoires inférieures	2 302	41.1	1 990	35.3	2	2	6	5
Diseases of the digestive system — Maladies de l'appareil digestif								
Total	2 337	41.7	1 477	26.2	5	9	8	12
Gastric and duodenal ulcer — Ulcère de l'estomac et du duodénum................	211	3.8	121	2.1	-	-	2	-
Diseases of the liver — Maladies du foie..	1 247	22.3	357	6.3	2	5	2	3
Diseases of the musculoskeletal system and connective tissue — Maladies du système ostéo-articularie, des muscles et du tissu conjonctif	254	4.5	492	8.7	2	-	1	2
Diseases of the genitourinary system — Maladies de l'appareil génito-urinaire								
Total	612	10.9	493	8.7	1	2	9	1
Disorders of kidney and ureter — Affections du rein et de l'uretère	450	8.0	378	6.7	1	1	4	1
Hyperplasia of prostate — Hyperplasie de la prostate..........................	69	3.9	..	..	-	..	2	..
Pregnancy, childbirth and the puerperium — Grossesse, accouchement et puerpéralité								
Total	..	..	58	46.4	..	-	..	-
Pregnancy with abortive outcome — Grossesse se terminant par un avortement	..	..	4	♦3.2	..	-	..	-
Other direct obstetric causes — Autres décès maternels directs	..	..	26	♦20.8	..	-	..	-
Indirect obstetric causes — Décès maternels indirects	..	..	22	♦17.6	..	-	..	-
Certain conditions originating in the perinatal period — Certaines affections dont l'origine se situe dans la période périnatale	163	251.1	121	201.1	16	18	13	7
Congenital malformations, deformations and chromosomal abnormalities — Malformations congénitales et anomalies chromosomiques	196	302.0	185	307.5	3	1	3	6
Symptoms, signs and abnormal clinical and laboratory findings, not elsewhere classified — Symptômes, signes et résultats anormaux d'examens cliniques et de laboratoire, non classés ailleurs	449	8.0	265	4.7	11	8	19	16
All other diseases — Toutes autres maladies..	106	1.9	144	2.6	3	11	1	3
External causes — Causes externes								
Total	4 756	84.9	3 177	56.4	26	8	38	13
Accidents								
Total	2 517	44.9	1 774	31.5	16	5	23	10
Transport accidents — Accidents de transport	833	14.9	215	3.8	4	2	7	2
Falls — Chutes	1 085	19.4	1 402	24.9	1	-	1	-
Accidental drowning and submersion — Noyade et submersion accidentelles...	182	3.2	18	♦0.3	1	-	2	-
Exposure to smoke, fire and flames — Exposition à la fumée, au feu et aux flammes...	41	0.7	14	♦0.2	-	-	-	1
Accidental poisoning by and exposure to noxious substances — Intoxication accidentelle par des substances nocives et exposition à ces substances	68	1.2	14	♦0.2	-	-	-	1
Intentional self-harm — Lésions auto-infligées.......................................	1 211	21.6	298	5.3	3	-	4	1
Assault — Agresssions...	478	8.5	138	2.4	6	2	9	2
All other external causes — Toutes autres causes externes	550	9.8	967	17.2	1	1	2	-

20. Death and death rates by cause and sex: 2012 - 2016
Décès et taux de mortalité par cause et sexe : 2012 - 2016 (continued - suite)

Cause of death — Cause de décès	Dominican Republic - République dominicaine				El Salvador			
	2012 (U)		2013 (U)		2013 (+C)			
	Male — Masculin	Female — Féminin	Male — Masculin	Female — Féminin	Male — Masculin		Female — Féminin	
	Number Nombre	Number Nombre	Number Nombre	Number Nombre	Number Nombre	Rate Taux	Number Nombre	Rate Taux
TOTAL	*20 805*	*15 233*	*22 166*	*15 417*	18 945	641.7	15 302	458.6
Certain infectious and parasitic diseases — Certaines maladies infectieuses et parasitaires								
Total	*1 080*	*784*	*1 056*	*745*	773	26.2	620	18.6
Intestinal infectious diseases — Maladies infectieuses intestinales	*85*	*86*	*61*	*69*	59	2.0	44	1.3
Tuberculosis — Tuberculose	*198*	*100*	*184*	*80*	34	1.2	21	+0.6
Tetanus — Tétanos	*21*	*3*	*12*	*1*	1	+0.0	-	-
Diphtheria — Diphtérie	-	-	-	-	-	-	-	-
Whooping cough — Coqueluche	-	-	-	*2*	1	+0.0	1	+0.0
Meningococcal infection — Infection à méningocoques	*7*	*2*	*5*	*2*	-	-	-	-
Septicaemia — Septicémie	*284*	*273*	*198*	*156*	422	14.3	424	12.7
Acute poliomyelitis — Poliomyélite aiguë	-	-	-	-	-	-	-	-
Measles — Rougeole	-	-	-	-	-	-	-	-
Viral hepatitis — Hépatite virale	*19*	*15*	*114*	*97*	5	+0.2	5	+0.1
Human immunodeficiency virus [HIV] disease — Maladies dues au virus de l'immunodéficience humaine (VIH)	*339*	*221*	*350*	*269*	215	7.3	98	2.9
Malaria — Paludisme	*2*	*2*	*4*	-	-	-	-	-
Neoplasms — Tumeurs	*2 414*	*2 058*	*2 653*	*2 247*	1 633	55.3	2 178	65.3
Malignant neoplasms — Tumeurs malignes								
Total	*2 331*	*1 965*	*2 544*	*2 118*	1 628	55.1	2 167	64.9
Malignant neoplasm of lip, oral cavity and pharynx — Tumeur maligne de la lèvre, de la cavité buccale et du pharynx	*136*	*72*	*112*	*56*	35	1.2	31	0.9
Malignant neoplasm of oesophagus — Tumeur maligne de l'oesophage	*49*	*24*	*45*	*19*	44	1.5	16	+0.5
Malignant neoplasm of stomach — Tumeur maligne de l'estomac	*135*	*98*	*149*	*110*	247	8.4	214	6.4
Malignant neoplasm of colon, rectosigmoid junction, rectum, anus and anal canal — Tumeur maligne du côlon, de la jonction recto-sigmoïdienne, du rectum, de l'anus et du canal anal	*159*	*158*	*172*	*166*	82	2.8	116	3.5
Malignant neoplasm of liver and intrahepatic bile ducts — Tumeur maligne du foie et des voies bilaires intrahépatiques	*159*	*146*	*175*	*137*	130	4.4	183	5.5
Malignant neoplasm of pancreas — Tumeur maligne du pancréas	*108*	*86*	*123*	*100*	60	2.0	67	2.0
Malignant neoplasm of trachea, bronchus and lung — Tumeur maligne de la trachée, des bronches et du poumon	*292*	*216*	*324*	*220*	139	4.7	120	3.6
Malignant neoplasm of female breast — Tumeur maligne du sein chez la femme	..	*360*	..	*442*	..	...	189	...
Malignant neoplasm of cervix uteri — Tumeur maligne du col de l'utérus	..	*217*	..	*214*	..	...	215	...
Malignant neoplasm of prostate — Tumeur maligne de la prostate	*764*	..	*813*	..	231	...	..	..
Malignant neoplasm of lymphoid, haematopoietic and related tissue — Tumeurs malignes primitives ou présumées primitives des tissus lymphoïde, hématopoïétique et apparentés	*182*	*134*	*206*	*176*	175	5.9	173	5.2
Disorders of the blood and blood-forming organs and certain disorders involving the immune mechanism — Maladies du sang et des organes hématopoïétiques et certains troubles du système immunitaire								
Total	*96*	*108*	*114*	*89*	78	2.6	71	2.1
Anaemias — Anémies	*59*	*69*	*85*	*65*	61	2.1	55	1.6
Endocrine, nutritional and metabolic diseases — Maladies endocriniennes, nutritionnelles et métaboliques								
Total	*750*	*826*	*845*	*956*	927	31.4	1 362	40.8
Diabetes mellitus — Diabète sucré	*666*	*743*	*752*	*869*	766	25.9	1 214	36.4
Malnutrition — Malnutrition	*37*	*29*	*27*	*27*	101	3.4	67	2.0
Mental and behavioural disorders — Troubles mentaux et du comportement	*47*	*27*	*25*	*30*	448	15.2	15	+0.4
Diseases of the nervous system — Maladies du système nerveux	*262*	*217*	*237*	*243*	359	12.2	383	11.5
Diseases of the circulatory system — Maladies de l'appareil circulatoire								
Total	*6 591*	*5 547*	*6 344*	*5 554*	2 699	91.4	2 888	86.6
Acute rheumatic fever and chronic rheumatic heart diseases — Rhumatisme articulaire aigu et cardiopathies rhumatismales chroniques	*8*	*16*	*15*	*18*	2	+0.1	4	+0.1
Hypertensive diseases — Maladies hypertensives	*754*	*773*	*834*	*881*	259	8.8	319	9.6
Ischaemic heart disease — Cardiopathie ischémique	*2 921*	*2 343*	*2 790*	*2 253*	1 121	38.0	1 067	32.0

20. Death and death rates by cause and sex: 2012 - 2016
Décès et taux de mortalité par cause et sexe : 2012 - 2016 (continued - suite)

Cause of death — Cause de décès	Dominican Republic - République dominicaine				El Salvador			
	2012 (U)		2013 (U)		2013 (+C)			
	Male — Masculin	Female — Féminin	Male — Masculin	Female — Féminin	Male — Masculin		Female — Féminin	
	Number Nombre	Number Nombre	Number Nombre	Number Nombre	Number Nombre	Rate Taux	Number Nombre	Rate Taux
Cerebrovascular disease — Maladie cérébrovasculaire....................	1 947	1 562	1 851	1 611	467	15.8	530	15.9
Diseases of arteries, arterioles and capillaries — Maladies des artères, artérioles et capillaires	51	46	75	57	27	+0.9	21	+0.6
Diseases of the respiratory system — Maladies de l'appareil respiratoire								
Total	1 724	1 472	1 392	1 278	1 299	44.0	1 365	40.9
Influenza — Grippe	5	5	2	6	1	+0.0	2	+0.1
Pneumonia — Pneumopathies	551	537	467	471	724	24.5	658	19.7
Chronic lower respiratory diseases — Maladies chroniques des voies respiratoires inférieures	335	228	309	250	251	8.5	391	11.7
Diseases of the digestive system — Maladies de l'appareil digestif								
Total	757	516	690	496	980	33.2	711	21.3
Gastric and duodenal ulcer — Ulcère de l'estomac et du duodénum.................	84	56	91	46	54	1.8	62	1.9
Diseases of the liver — Maladies du foie................................	410	249	312	211	622	21.1	357	10.7
Diseases of the musculoskeletal system and connective tissue — Maladies du système ostéo-articulaire, des muscles et du tissu conjonctif	25	49	30	55	33	1.1	75	2.2
Diseases of the genitourinary system — Maladies de l'appareil génito-urinaire								
Total	300	194	314	186	2 107	71.4	936	28.1
Disorders of kidney and ureter — Affections du rein et de l'uretère	272	186	285	172	1 984	67.2	849	25.4
Hyperplasia of prostate — Hyperplasie de la prostate....................	16	..	13	..	39	....	..	..
Pregnancy, childbirth and the puerperium — Grossesse, accouchement et puerpéralité								
Total	..	177	..	215	..	..	39	35.6
Pregnancy with abortive outcome — Grossesse se terminant par un avortement	..	15	..	21	..	..	1	+0.9
Other direct obstetric causes — Autres décès maternels directs....................	..	122	..	129	..	..	37	33.8
Indirect obstetric causes — Décès maternels indirects	..	40	..	51	..	..	1	+0.9
Certain conditions originating in the perinatal period — Certaines affections dont l'origine se situe dans la période périnatale	1 514	1 365	1 721	1 400	257	452.8	178	336.7
Congenital malformations, deformations and chromosomal abnormalities — Malformations congénitales et anomalies chromosomiques	393	328	294	231	155	273.1	107	202.4
Symptoms, signs and abnormal clinical and laboratory findings, not elsewhere classified — Symptômes, signes et résultats anormaux d'examens cliniques et de laboratoire, non classés ailleurs	1 043	806	723	668	3 360	113.8	3 690	110.6
All other diseases — Toutes autres maladies........................	4	4	33	36	40	1.4	55	1.6
External causes — Causes externes								
Total	3 805	755	5 695	988	3 797	128.6	629	18.9
Accidents								
Total	1 663	339	2 710	526	1 347	45.6	324	9.7
Transport accidents — Accidents de transport	1 400	230	2 012	327	775	26.3	181	5.4
Falls — Chutes	20	9	25	13	155	5.3	70	2.1
Accidental drowning and submersion — Noyade et submersion accidentelles	22	6	157	30	178	6.0	27	+0.8
Exposure to smoke, fire and flames — Exposition à la fumée, au feu et aux flammes	11	10	22	17	10	+0.3	9	+0.3
Accidental poisoning by and exposure to noxious substances — Intoxication accidentelle par des substances nocives et exposition à ces substances	4	-	62	23	172	5.8	11	+0.3
Intentional self-harm — Lésions auto-infligées	213	43	369	77	389	13.2	98	2.9
Assault — Agresssions	1 130	123	1 881	172	1 977	67.0	187	5.6
All other external causes — Toutes autres causes externes	799	250	735	213	84	2.8	20	+0.6

20. Death and death rates by cause and sex: 2012 - 2016
Décès et taux de mortalité par cause et sexe : 2012 - 2016 (continued - suite)

Cause of death — Cause de décès	El Salvador				Grenada - Grenade			
	2014 (+C)				2015 (C)		2016 (C)	
	Male — Masculin		Female — Féminin		Male — Masculin	Female — Féminin	Male — Masculin	Female — Féminin
	Number Nombre	Rate Taux	Number Nombre	Rate Taux	Number Nombre	Number Nombre	Number Nombre	Number Nombre
TOTAL	21 335	719.0	16 139	480.2	483	386	497	402
Certain infectious and parasitic diseases — Certaines maladies infectieuses et parasitaires								
Total	999	33.7	821	24.4	15	9	9	9
Intestinal infectious diseases — Maladies infectieuses intestinales	64	2.2	52	1.5	3	-	-	-
Tuberculosis — Tuberculose	49	1.7	15	♦0.4	2	-	-	-
Tetanus — Tétanos	1	♦0.0	-	-	-	-	-	-
Diphtheria — Diphtérie...................	-	-	1	♦0.0	-	-	-	-
Whooping cough — Coqueluche	-	-	-	-	-	-	-	-
Meningococcal infection — Infection à méningocoques ...	1	♦0.0	-	-	-	-	-	-
Septicaemia — Septicémie	622	21.0	644	19.2	6	5	1	6
Acute poliomyelitis — Poliomyélite aiguë	-	-	-	-	-	-	-	-
Measles — Rougeole....................	-	-	-	-	-	-	-	-
Viral hepatitis — Hépatite virale	3	♦0.1	-	-	-	-	-	1
Human immunodeficiency virus [HIV] disease — Maladies dues au virus de l'immunodéficience humaine (VIH)...................	206	6.9	76	2.3	3	2	3	1
Malaria — Paludisme......................	-	-	1	♦0.0	-	-	-	-
Neoplasms — Tumeurs	1 660	55.9	2 087	62.1	90	81	128	72
Malignant neoplasms — Tumeurs malignes								
Total	1 648	55.5	2 071	61.6	86	78	125	70
Malignant neoplasm of lip, oral cavity and pharynx — Tumeur maligne de la lèvre, de la cavité buccale et du pharynx	43	1.4	28	♦0.8	5	2	6	1
Malignant neoplasm of oesophagus — Tumeur maligne de l'oesophage	31	1.0	20	♦0.6	4	-	10	-
Malignant neoplasm of stomach — Tumeur maligne de l'estomac	258	8.7	229	6.8	2	3	7	3
Malignant neoplasm of colon, rectosigmoid junction, rectum, anus and anal canal — Tumeur maligne du côlon, de la jonction recto-sigmoïdienne, du rectum, de l'anus et du canal anal	95	3.2	131	3.9	5	11	8	5
Malignant neoplasm of liver and intrahepatic bile ducts — Tumeur maligne du foie et des voies bilaires intrahépatiques	115	3.9	145	4.3	4	1	3	1
Malignant neoplasm of pancreas — Tumeur maligne du pancréas....................	73	2.5	70	2.1	3	1	5	1
Malignant neoplasm of trachea, bronchus and lung — Tumeur maligne de la trachée, des bronches et du poumon	123	4.1	122	3.6	6	2	15	9
Malignant neoplasm of female breast — Tumeur maligne du sein chez la femme	..	..	196	7.9	..	18	..	23
Malignant neoplasm of cervix uteri — Tumeur maligne du col de l'utérus.........	..	..	198	8.0	..	8	..	4
Malignant neoplasm of prostate — Tumeur maligne de la prostate	241	47.7	..	..	32	..	37	..
Malignant neoplasm of lymphoid, haematopoietic and related tissue — Tumeurs malignes primitives ou présumées primitives des tissus lymphoïde, hématopoïétique et apparentés.....................	190	6.4	170	5.1	7	7	12	7
Disorders of the blood and blood-forming organs and certain disorders involving the immune mechanism — Maladies du sang et des organes hématopoïétiques et certains troubles du système immunitaire								
Total	86	2.9	95	2.8	8	5	6	7
Anaemias — Anémies	64	2.2	70	2.1	4	4	4	6
Endocrine, nutritional and metabolic diseases — Maladies endocriniennes, nutritionnelles et métaboliques								
Total	876	29.5	1 311	39.0	62	53	57	61
Diabetes mellitus — Diabète sucré....................	779	26.3	1 181	35.1	49	42	42	46
Malnutrition — Malnutrition	62	2.1	79	2.4	5	-	6	1
Mental and behavioural disorders — Troubles mentaux et du comportement	518	17.5	34	1.0	3	1	7	4
Diseases of the nervous system — Maladies du système nerveux.................	363	12.2	327	9.7	6	7	5	5
Diseases of the circulatory system — Maladies de l'appareil circulatoire								
Total	2 853	96.1	2 956	88.0	155	116	159	155
Acute rheumatic fever and chronic rheumatic heart diseases — Rhumatisme articularie aigu et cardiopathies rhumatismales chroniques	1	♦0.0	3	♦0.1	-	1	-	2
Hypertensive diseases — Maladies hypertensives...........................	338	11.4	397	11.8	24	20	22	16
Ischaemic heart disease — Cardiopathie ischémique...........................	1 217	41.0	1 043	31.0	43	23	74	58

Cause of death — Cause de décès	El Salvador 2014 (+C)				Grenada - Grenade 2015 (C)		2016 (C)	
	Male — Masculin		Female — Féminin		Male — Masculin	Female — Féminin	Male — Masculin	Female — Féminin
	Number Nombre	Rate Taux	Number Nombre	Rate Taux	Number Nombre	Number Nombre	Number Nombre	Number Nombre
Cerebrovascular disease — Maladie cérébrovasculaire	495	16.7	566	16.8	43	33	34	36
Diseases of arteries, arterioles and capillaries — Maladies des artères, artérioles et capillaires	20	♦0.7	24	♦0.7	21	13	10	10
Diseases of the respiratory system — Maladies de l'appareil respiratoire								
Total	1 639	55.2	1 473	43.8	34	39	30	30
Influenza — Grippe	-	-	1	♦0.0	1	1	-	-
Pneumonia — Pneumopathies	941	31.7	796	23.7	20	26	20	22
Chronic lower respiratory diseases — Maladies chroniques des voies respiratoires inférieures	274	9.2	287	8.5	5	3	5	4
Diseases of the digestive system — Maladies de l'appareil digestif								
Total	1 048	35.3	757	22.5	28	10	19	12
Gastric and duodenal ulcer — Ulcère de l'estomac et du duodénum	59	2.0	71	2.1	5	1	5	-
Diseases of the liver — Maladies du foie	677	22.8	391	11.6	10	2	10	5
Diseases of the musculoskeletal system and connective tissue — Maladies du système ostéo-articularie, des muscles et du tissu conjonctif	24	♦0.8	69	2.1	2	4	1	3
Diseases of the genitourinary system — Maladies de l'appareil génito-urinaire								
Total	2 230	75.2	994	29.6	13	14	12	6
Disorders of kidney and ureter — Affections du rein et de l'uretère	2 114	71.2	922	27.4	7	11	8	5
Hyperplasia of prostate — Hyperplasie de la prostate	44	8.7	..	..	3	..	2	..
Pregnancy, childbirth and the puerperium — Grossesse, accouchement et puerpéralité								
Total	..	..	52	47.7	..	-	..	2
Pregnancy with abortive outcome — Grossesse se terminant par un avortement	..	..	2	♦1.8	..	-	..	-
Other direct obstetric causes — Autres décès maternels directs	..	..	34	31.2	..	-	..	2
Indirect obstetric causes — Décès maternels indirects	..	..	16	♦14.7	..	-	..	-
Certain conditions originating in the perinatal period — Certaines affections dont l'origine se situe dans la période périnatale	199	355.8	163	307.7	14	5	11	10
Congenital malformations, deformations and chromosomal abnormalities — Malformations congénitales et anomalies chromosomiques	125	223.5	117	220.9	4	2	2	3
Symptoms, signs and abnormal clinical and laboratory findings, not elsewhere classified — Symptômes, signes et résultats anormaux d'examens cliniques et de laboratoire, non classés ailleurs	3 875	130.6	4 062	120.9	4	12	2	3
All other diseases — Toutes autres maladies	33	1.1	41	1.2	-	14	7	10
External causes — Causes externes								
Total	4 807	162.0	780	23.2	45	14	42	10
Accidents								
Total	1 377	46.4	351	10.4	40	12	35	9
Transport accidents — Accidents de transport	809	27.3	208	6.2	9	2	10	-
Falls — Chutes	174	5.9	86	2.6	8	2	1	-
Accidental drowning and submersion — Noyade et submersion accidentelles	150	5.1	17	♦0.5	2	-	5	1
Exposure to smoke, fire and flames — Exposition à la fumée, au feu et aux flammes	13	♦0.4	4	♦0.1	-	-	1	-
Accidental poisoning by and exposure to noxious substances — Intoxication accidentelle par des substances nocives et exposition à ces substances	136	4.6	10	♦0.3	1	1	-	-
Intentional self-harm — Lésions auto-infligées	278	9.4	108	3.2	-	-	-	-
Assault — Agresssions	3 051	102.8	293	8.7	4	-	7	-
All other external causes — Toutes autres causes externes	101	3.4	28	♦0.8	1	2	-	1

20. Death and death rates by cause and sex: 2012 - 2016
Décès et taux de mortalité par cause et sexe : 2012 - 2016 (continued - suite)

Cause of death — Cause de décès	Guadeloupe				Guatemala			
	2013 (...)		2014 (...)		2014 (C)			
	Male — Masculin	Female — Féminin	Male — Masculin	Female — Féminin	Male — Masculin		Female — Féminin	
	Number Nombre	Number Nombre	Number Nombre	Number Nombre	Number Nombre	Rate Taux	Number Nombre	Rate Taux
TOTAL	*1 618*	*1 324*	*1 766*	*1 513*	**42 693**	**527.9**	**33 116**	**429.0**
Certain infectious and parasitic diseases — Certaines maladies infectieuses et parasitaires								
Total	*52*	*40*	*88*	*67*	2 453	30.3	1 991	25.8
Intestinal infectious diseases — Maladies infectieuses intestinales	*7*	*5*	*5*	*3*	1 161	14.4	1 005	13.0
Tuberculosis — Tuberculose	-	*1*	-	-	197	2.4	109	1.4
Tetanus — Tétanos	-	-	-	-	4	+0.0	1	+0.0
Diphtheria — Diphtérie	-	-	-	-	-	-	-	-
Whooping cough — Coqueluche	-	-	-	-	8	+0.1	2	+0.0
Meningococcal infection — Infection à méningocoques	-	-	-	-	2	+0.0	-	-
Septicaemia — Septicémie	*24*	*20*	*26*	*19*	607	7.5	599	7.8
Acute poliomyelitis — Poliomyélite aiguë	-	*1*	-	-	-	-	-	-
Measles — Rougeole	-	-	-	-	-	-	-	-
Viral hepatitis — Hépatite virale	*3*	*3*	-	*1*	29	+0.4	19	+0.2
Human immunodeficiency virus [HIV] disease — Maladies dues au virus de l'immunodéficience humaine (VIH)	*6*	*3*	*12*	*2*	311	3.8	154	2.0
Malaria — Paludisme	-	-	-	-	3	+0.0	-	-
Neoplasms — Tumeurs	*400*	*291*	*389*	*324*	3 591	44.4	4 367	56.6
Malignant neoplasms — Tumeurs malignes								
Total	*386*	*281*	*376*	*302*	3 333	41.2	4 161	53.9
Malignant neoplasm of lip, oral cavity and pharynx — Tumeur maligne de la lèvre, de la cavité buccale et du pharynx	*12*	*3*	*13*	-	65	0.8	52	0.7
Malignant neoplasm of oesophagus — Tumeur maligne de l'oesophage	*21*	*3*	*17*	-	71	0.9	35	0.5
Malignant neoplasm of stomach — Tumeur maligne de l'estomac	*32*	*19*	*35*	*19*	601	7.4	794	10.3
Malignant neoplasm of colon, rectosigmoid junction, rectum, anus and anal canal — Tumeur maligne du côlon, de la jonction recto-sigmoïdienne, du rectum, de l'anus et du canal anal	*41*	*28*	*48*	*35*	144	1.8	162	2.1
Malignant neoplasm of liver and intrahepatic bile ducts — Tumeur maligne du foie et des voies bilaires intrahépatiques	*12*	*13*	*20*	*8*	576	7.1	733	9.5
Malignant neoplasm of pancreas — Tumeur maligne du pancréas	*31*	*26*	*26*	*34*	73	0.9	95	1.2
Malignant neoplasm of trachea, bronchus and lung — Tumeur maligne de la trachée, des bronches et du poumon	*31*	*17*	*43*	*14*	195	2.4	167	2.2
Malignant neoplasm of female breast — Tumeur maligne du sein chez la femme	*..*	*53*	*..*	*62*	..	..	280	5.6
Malignant neoplasm of cervix uteri — Tumeur maligne du col de l'utérus	*..*	*8*	*..*	*4*	..	..	449	9.0
Malignant neoplasm of prostate — Tumeur maligne de la prostate	*102*	*..*	*79*	*..*	624	72.7	..	..
Malignant neoplasm of lymphoid, haematopoietic and related tissue — Tumeurs malignes primitives ou présumées primitives des tissus lymphoïde, hématopoïétique et apparentés	*37*	*39*	*34*	*26*	322	4.0	284	3.7
Disorders of the blood and blood-forming organs and certain disorders involving the immune mechanism — Maladies du sang et des organes hématopoïétiques et certains troubles du système immunitaire								
Total	*6*	*14*	*9*	*5*	337	4.2	363	4.7
Anaemias — Anémies	*3*	*11*	*4*	*4*	211	2.6	239	3.1
Endocrine, nutritional and metabolic diseases — Maladies endocriniennes, nutritionnelles et métaboliques								
Total	*74*	*105*	*113*	*149*	3 351	41.4	4 512	58.5
Diabetes mellitus — Diabète sucré	*48*	*73*	*75*	*119*	2 427	30.0	3 489	45.2
Malnutrition — Malnutrition	*12*	*10*	*8*	*11*	649	8.0	765	9.9
Mental and behavioural disorders — Troubles mentaux et du comportement	*54*	*20*	*61*	*35*	402	5.0	40	0.5
Diseases of the nervous system — Maladies du système nerveux	*84*	*76*	*95*	*84*	748	9.2	637	8.3
Diseases of the circulatory system — Maladies de l'appareil circulatoire								
Total	*345*	*365*	*390*	*389*	6 329	78.3	6 204	80.4
Acute rheumatic fever and chronic rheumatic heart diseases — Rhumatisme articularie aigu et cardiopathies rhumatismales chroniques	*1*	*4*	*3*	*2*	7	+0.1	14	+0.2
Hypertensive diseases — Maladies hypertensives	*42*	*60*	*47*	*67*	477	5.9	598	7.7
Ischaemic heart disease — Cardiopathie ischémique	*48*	*50*	*55*	*47*	2 922	36.1	2 507	32.5

	Guadeloupe				Guatemala			
	2013 (...)		2014 (...)		2014 (C)			
Cause of death — Cause de décès	Male — Masculin	Female — Féminin	Male — Masculin	Female — Féminin	Male — Masculin		Female — Féminin	
	Number Nombre	Number Nombre	Number Nombre	Number Nombre	Number Nombre	Rate Taux	Number Nombre	Rate Taux
Cerebrovascular disease — Maladie cérébrovasculaire....................	121	130	123	124	1 639	20.3	1 665	21.6
Diseases of arteries, arterioles and capillaries — Maladies des artères, artérioles et capillaires	23	7	19	25	58	0.7	65	0.8
Diseases of the respiratory system — Maladies de l'appareil respiratoire								
Total	72	54	90	75	4 772	59.0	4 211	54.6
Influenza — Grippe	1	4	1	3	1	♦0.0	4	♦0.1
Pneumonia — Pneumopathies	30	19	37	26	3 597	44.5	3 222	41.7
Chronic lower respiratory diseases — Maladies chroniques des voies respiratoires inférieures	19	9	20	11	538	6.7	547	7.1
Diseases of the digestive system — Maladies de l'appareil digestif								
Total	70	63	89	69	3 741	46.3	2 307	29.9
Gastric and duodenal ulcer — Ulcère de l'estomac et du duodénum................	4	3	4	4	303	3.7	344	4.5
Diseases of the liver — Maladies du foie...................................	31	13	44	14	2 384	29.5	1 084	14.0
Diseases of the musculoskeletal system and connective tissue — Maladies du système ostéo-articulaire, des muscles et du tissu conjonctif	9	10	8	15	82	1.0	180	2.3
Diseases of the genitourinary system — Maladies de l'appareil génito-urinaire								
Total	30	27	26	25	1 912	23.6	1 482	19.2
Disorders of kidney and ureter — Affections du rein et de l'uretère	21	22	18	21	1 727	21.4	1 400	18.1
Hyperplasia of prostate — Hyperplasie de la prostate..........................	-	..	1	..	110	12.8	..	..
Pregnancy, childbirth and the puerperium — Grossesse, accouchement et puerpéralité								
Total	..	1	..	-	..	..	291	75.4
Pregnancy with abortive outcome — Grossesse se terminant par un avortement	..	-	..	-	..	..	18	♦4.7
Other direct obstetric causes — Autres décès maternels directs	..	1	..	-	..	..	237	61.4
Indirect obstetric causes — Décès maternels indirects.............................	..	-	..	..	..	..	36	9.3
Certain conditions originating in the perinatal period — Certaines affections dont l'origine se situe dans la période périnatale	16	11	13	9	1 753	891.3	1 295	683.3
Congenital malformations, deformations and chromosomal abnormalities — Malformations congénitales et anomalies chromosomiques	17	6	3	8	771	392.0	678	357.8
Symptoms, signs and abnormal clinical and laboratory findings, not elsewhere classified — Symptômes, signes et résultats anormaux d'examens cliniques et de laboratoire, non classés ailleurs	208	187	220	192	2 450	30.3	2 405	31.2
All other diseases — Toutes autres maladies................................	9	6	5	9	23	♦0.3	29	♦0.4
External causes — Causes externes								
Total	172	48	167	58	9 978	123.4	2 124	27.5
Accidents								
Total	108	38	127	44	6 035	74.6	1 389	18.0
Transport accidents — Accidents de transport	44	4	39	11	1 013	12.5	207	2.7
Falls — Chutes	9	10	17	12	3	♦0.0	2	♦0.0
Accidental drowning and submersion — Noyade et submersion accidentelles..	13	-	13	1	281	3.5	62	0.8
Exposure to smoke, fire and flames — Exposition à la fumée, au feu et aux flammes..	-	1	2	2	80	1.0	32	0.4
Accidental poisoning by and exposure to noxious substances — Intoxication accidentelle par des substances nocives et exposition à ces substances	5	4	9	2	793	9.8	168	2.2
Intentional self-harm — Lésions auto-infligées.............................	33	6	17	8	357	4.4	156	2.0
Assault — Agresssions...	13	-	6	2	3 571	44.2	564	7.3
All other external causes — Toutes autres causes externes	18	4	17	4	15	♦0.2	15	♦0.2

20. Death and death rates by cause and sex: 2012 - 2016
Décès et taux de mortalité par cause et sexe : 2012 - 2016 (continued - suite)

Cause of death — Cause de décès	Guatemala 2015 (C)				Honduras 2012 (+U)		Honduras 2013 (+U)	
	Male — Masculin		Female — Féminin		Male — Masculin	Female — Féminin	Male — Masculin	Female — Féminin
	Number Nombre	Rate Taux	Number Nombre	Rate Taux	Number Nombre	Number Nombre	Number Nombre	Number Nombre
TOTAL	44 457	537.4	34 585	437.6	*3 140*	*2 885*	*3 430*	*3 047*
Certain infectious and parasitic diseases — Certaines maladies infectieuses et parasitaires								
Total	2 189	26.5	1 828	23.1	*266*	*218*	*260*	*217*
Intestinal infectious diseases — Maladies infectieuses intestinales	1 047	12.7	1 033	13.1	*41*	*48*	*37*	*30*
Tuberculosis — Tuberculose	199	2.4	106	1.3	*46*	*36*	*52*	*33*
Tetanus — Tétanos	4	♦0.0	1	♦0.0	*1*	*1*	*1*	*3*
Diphtheria — Diphtérie	-	-	-	-	*-*	*-*	*-*	*-*
Whooping cough — Coqueluche	16	♦0.2	7	♦0.1	*6*	*8*	*2*	*6*
Meningococcal infection — Infection à méningocoques	1	♦0.0	-	-	*-*	*-*	*-*	*-*
Septicaemia — Septicémie	448	5.4	418	5.3	*37*	*34*	*45*	*45*
Acute poliomyelitis — Poliomyélite aiguë	-	-	-	-	*-*	*-*	*-*	*-*
Measles — Rougeole	-	-	-	-	*-*	*-*	*-*	*-*
Viral hepatitis — Hépatite virale	25	♦0.3	17	♦0.2	*3*	*1*	*3*	*4*
Human immunodeficiency virus [HIV] disease — Maladies dues au virus de l'immunodéficience humaine (VIH)	272	3.3	112	1.4	*99*	*66*	*86*	*65*
Malaria — Paludisme	3	♦0.0	2	♦0.0	*-*	*2*	*-*	*1*
Neoplasms — Tumeurs	3 655	44.2	4 346	55.0	*212*	*319*	*240*	*259*
Malignant neoplasms — Tumeurs malignes								
Total	3 382	40.9	4 063	51.4	*186*	*284*	*216*	*233*
Malignant neoplasm of lip, oral cavity and pharynx — Tumeur maligne de la lèvre, de la cavité buccale et du pharynx	59	0.7	40	0.5	*2*	*1*	*1*	*4*
Malignant neoplasm of oesophagus — Tumeur maligne de l'oesophage	61	0.7	43	0.5	*2*	*2*	*5*	*-*
Malignant neoplasm of stomach — Tumeur maligne de l'estomac	622	7.5	692	8.8	*30*	*25*	*25*	*19*
Malignant neoplasm of colon, rectosigmoid junction, rectum, anus and anal canal — Tumeur maligne du côlon, de la jonction recto-sigmoïdienne, du rectum, de l'anus et du canal anal	119	1.4	170	2.2	*4*	*13*	*11*	*14*
Malignant neoplasm of liver and intrahepatic bile ducts — Tumeur maligne du foie et des voies bilaires intrahépatiques	628	7.6	701	8.9	*15*	*16*	*8*	*13*
Malignant neoplasm of pancreas — Tumeur maligne du pancréas	95	1.1	121	1.5	*4*	*8*	*1*	*6*
Malignant neoplasm of trachea, bronchus and lung — Tumeur maligne de la trachée, des bronches et du poumon	195	2.4	146	1.8	*19*	*16*	*26*	*15*
Malignant neoplasm of female breast — Tumeur maligne du sein chez la femme	..	..	348	6.8	*..*	*14*	*..*	*17*
Malignant neoplasm of cervix uteri — Tumeur maligne du col de l'utérus	..	..	370	7.2	*..*	*47*	*..*	*33*
Malignant neoplasm of prostate — Tumeur maligne de la prostate	588	66.8	..	..	*8*	*..*	*21*	*..*
Malignant neoplasm of lymphoid, haematopoietic and related tissue — Tumeurs malignes primitives ou présumées primitives des tissus lymphoïde, hématopoïétique et apparentés	365	4.4	302	3.8	*45*	*61*	*57*	*48*
Disorders of the blood and blood-forming organs and certain disorders involving the immune mechanism — Maladies du sang et des organes hématopoïétiques et certains troubles du système immunitaire								
Total	364	4.4	374	4.7	*37*	*35*	*27*	*29*
Anaemias — Anémies	216	2.6	250	3.2	*24*	*26*	*18*	*24*
Endocrine, nutritional and metabolic diseases — Maladies endocriniennes, nutritionnelles et métaboliques								
Total	3 356	40.6	4 535	57.4	*222*	*395*	*224*	*356*
Diabetes mellitus — Diabète sucré	2 421	29.3	3 503	44.3	*182*	*342*	*176*	*321*
Malnutrition — Malnutrition	513	6.2	570	7.2	*28*	*32*	*36*	*23*
Mental and behavioural disorders — Troubles mentaux et du comportement	564	6.8	114	1.4	*25*	*2*	*20*	*4*
Diseases of the nervous system — Maladies du système nerveux	851	10.3	715	9.0	*54*	*43*	*66*	*63*
Diseases of the circulatory system — Maladies de l'appareil circulatoire								
Total	6 312	76.3	6 269	79.3	*515*	*563*	*553*	*590*
Acute rheumatic fever and chronic rheumatic heart diseases — Rhumatisme articularie aigu et cardiopathies rhumatismales chroniques	8	♦0.1	9	♦0.1	*6*	*6*	*7*	*12*
Hypertensive diseases — Maladies hypertensives	515	6.2	687	8.7	*87*	*86*	*83*	*104*
Ischaemic heart disease — Cardiopathie ischémique	2 956	35.7	2 623	33.2	*129*	*134*	*135*	*151*

608

20. Death and death rates by cause and sex: 2012 - 2016
Décès et taux de mortalité par cause et sexe : 2012 - 2016 (continued - suite)

Cause of death — Cause de décès	Guatemala 2015 (C) Male — Masculin Number Nombre	Rate Taux	Female — Féminin Number Nombre	Rate Taux	Honduras 2012 (+U) Male — Masculin Number Nombre	Female — Féminin Number Nombre	2013 (+U) Male — Masculin Number Nombre	Female — Féminin Number Nombre
Cerebrovascular disease — Maladie cérébrovasculaire	1 570	19.0	1 634	20.7	188	200	194	226
Diseases of arteries, arterioles and capillaries — Maladies des artères, artérioles et capillaires	57	0.7	54	0.7	8	15	16	10
Diseases of the respiratory system — Maladies de l'appareil respiratoire								
Total	5 172	62.5	4 386	55.5	263	276	305	319
Influenza — Grippe	5	♦0.1	4	♦0.1	-	-	1	2
Pneumonia — Pneumopathies	3 745	45.3	3 164	40.0	126	105	141	143
Chronic lower respiratory diseases — Maladies chroniques des voies respiratoires inférieures	648	7.8	586	7.4	90	121	115	127
Diseases of the digestive system — Maladies de l'appareil digestif								
Total	3 839	46.4	2 341	29.6	240	179	267	215
Gastric and duodenal ulcer — Ulcère de l'estomac et du duodénum	261	3.2	300	3.8	6	5	5	6
Diseases of the liver — Maladies du foie	2 484	30.0	1 145	14.5	169	85	156	98
Diseases of the musculoskeletal system and connective tissue — Maladies du système ostéo-articularie, des muscles et du tissu conjonctif	126	1.5	239	3.0	8	23	7	26
Diseases of the genitourinary system — Maladies de l'appareil génito-urinaire								
Total	1 845	22.3	1 466	18.5	74	61	85	65
Disorders of kidney and ureter — Affections du rein et de l'uretère	1 624	19.6	1 328	16.8	53	53	58	52
Hyperplasia of prostate — Hyperplasie de la prostate	95	10.8	..	..	14	..	16	..
Pregnancy, childbirth and the puerperium — Grossesse, accouchement et puerpéralité								
Total	..	..	298	76.1	..	31	..	37
Pregnancy with abortive outcome — Grossesse se terminant par un avortement	..	..	16	♦4.1	..	2	..	2
Other direct obstetric causes — Autres décès maternels directs	..	..	263	67.2	..	26	..	30
Indirect obstetric causes — Décès maternels indirects	..	..	19	♦4.9	..	3	..	5
Certain conditions originating in the perinatal period — Certaines affections dont l'origine se situe dans la période périnatale	1 798	904.7	1 299	674.2	559	379	706	496
Congenital malformations, deformations and chromosomal abnormalities — Malformations congénitales et anomalies chromosomiques	705	354.7	627	325.4	195	195	190	205
Symptoms, signs and abnormal clinical and laboratory findings, not elsewhere classified — Symptômes, signes et résultats anormaux d'examens cliniques et de laboratoire, non classés ailleurs	3 704	44.8	3 527	44.6	23	22	23	34
All other diseases — Toutes autres maladies	106	1.3	129	1.6	19	19	8	10
External causes — Causes externes								
Total	9 871	119.3	2 092	26.5	428	125	449	122
Accidents								
Total	6 026	72.8	1 373	17.4	249	70	202	61
Transport accidents — Accidents de transport	996	12.0	193	2.4	63	16	83	28
Falls — Chutes	8	♦0.1	1	♦0.0	25	15	24	6
Accidental drowning and submersion — Noyade et submersion accidentelles	270	3.3	34	0.4	1	-	1	-
Exposure to smoke, fire and flames — Exposition à la fumée, au feu et aux flammes	68	0.8	52	0.7	3	2	3	3
Accidental poisoning by and exposure to noxious substances — Intoxication accidentelle par des substances nocives et exposition à ces substances	765	9.2	155	2.0	38	11	5	1
Intentional self-harm — Lésions auto-infligées	352	4.3	144	1.8	77	34	63	31
Assault — Agresssions	3 478	42.0	558	7.1	75	7	127	12
All other external causes — Toutes autres causes externes	15	♦0.2	17	♦0.2	27	14	57	18

Cause of death — Cause de décès	Martinique				Mexico - Mexique			
	2013 (...)		2014 (...)		2014 (+C)			
	Male — Masculin	Female — Féminin	Male — Masculin	Female — Féminin	Male — Masculin		Female — Féminin	
	Number Nombre	Number Nombre	Number Nombre	Number Nombre	Number Nombre	Rate Taux	Number Nombre	Rate Taux
TOTAL	1 515	1 381	1 674	1 640	342 763	586.6	275 070	448.9
Certain infectious and parasitic diseases — Certaines maladies infectieuses et parasitaires								
Total	40	36	74	89	10 018	17.1	6 454	10.5
Intestinal infectious diseases — Maladies infectieuses intestinales	3	2	1	6	1 626	2.8	1 755	2.9
Tuberculosis — Tuberculose	-	-	2	-	1 513	2.6	657	1.1
Tetanus — Tétanos	-	-	-	-	6	✦0.0	1	✦0.0
Diphtheria — Diphtérie	-	-	-	-	-	-	-	-
Whooping cough — Coqueluche	-	-	-	-	8	✦0.0	14	✦0.0
Meningococcal infection — Infection à méningocoques	-	-	-	1	1	✦0.0	-	-
Septicaemia — Septicémie	20	25	27	22	1 844	3.2	1 865	3.0
Acute poliomyelitis — Poliomyélite aiguë	-	-	-	-	-	-	-	-
Measles — Rougeole	-	-	-	-	-	-	-	-
Viral hepatitis — Hépatite virale	1	1	-	2	448	0.8	678	1.1
Human immunodeficiency virus [HIV] disease — Maladies dues au virus de l'immunodéficience humaine (VIH)	6	3	4	2	3 854	6.6	909	1.5
Malaria — Paludisme	-	-	1	-	-	-	-	-
Neoplasms — Tumeurs	472	353	452	374	39 808	68.1	41 475	67.7
Malignant neoplasms — Tumeurs malignes								
Total	443	334	434	350	37 047	63.4	38 605	63.0
Malignant neoplasm of lip, oral cavity and pharynx — Tumeur maligne de la lèvre, de la cavité buccale et du pharynx	13	1	18	1	758	1.3	415	0.7
Malignant neoplasm of oesophagus — Tumeur maligne de l'oesophage	8	5	11	1	776	1.3	242	0.4
Malignant neoplasm of stomach — Tumeur maligne de l'estomac	38	15	35	32	3 010	5.2	2 711	4.4
Malignant neoplasm of colon, rectosigmoid junction, rectum, anus and anal canal — Tumeur maligne du côlon, de la jonction recto-sigmoïdienne, du rectum, de l'anus et du canal anal	49	48	50	39	2 792	4.8	2 522	4.1
Malignant neoplasm of liver and intrahepatic bile ducts — Tumeur maligne du foie et des voies bilaires intrahépatiques	19	10	16	18	2 917	5.0	3 079	5.0
Malignant neoplasm of pancreas — Tumeur maligne du pancréas	32	31	26	22	1 889	3.2	2 099	3.4
Malignant neoplasm of trachea, bronchus and lung — Tumeur maligne de la trachée, des bronches et du poumon	41	30	32	24	4 159	7.1	2 447	4.0
Malignant neoplasm of female breast — Tumeur maligne du sein chez la femme	..	65	..	62	..	..	5 895	13.1
Malignant neoplasm of cervix uteri — Tumeur maligne du col de l'utérus	..	3	..	6	..	..	3 987	8.9
Malignant neoplasm of prostate — Tumeur maligne de la prostate	123	..	111	..	6 152	59.3	..	..
Malignant neoplasm of lymphoid, haematopoietic and related tissue — Tumeurs malignes primitives ou présumées primitives des tissus lymphoïde, hématopoïétique et apparentés	42	27	44	41	4 658	8.0	3 796	6.2
Disorders of the blood and blood-forming organs and certain disorders involving the immune mechanism — Maladies du sang et des organes hématopoïétiques et certains troubles du système immunitaire								
Total	5	7	5	14	2 282	3.9	2 432	4.0
Anaemias — Anémies	5	4	3	10	1 702	2.9	1 845	3.0
Endocrine, nutritional and metabolic diseases — Maladies endocriniennes, nutritionnelles et métaboliques								
Total	89	115	108	138	52 416	89.7	54 937	89.7
Diabetes mellitus — Diabète sucré	56	79	65	94	44 820	76.7	47 160	77.0
Malnutrition — Malnutrition	11	14	13	11	3 481	6.0	3 567	5.8
Mental and behavioural disorders — Troubles mentaux et du comportement	48	27	50	27	4 048	6.9	1 225	2.0
Diseases of the nervous system — Maladies du système nerveux	100	107	119	141	5 756	9.9	4 825	7.9
Diseases of the circulatory system — Maladies de l'appareil circulatoire								
Total	326	373	380	438	79 910	136.7	74 656	121.8
Acute rheumatic fever and chronic rheumatic heart diseases — Rhumatisme articularie aigu et cardiopathies rhumatismales chroniques	3	8	4	7	254	0.4	532	0.9
Hypertensive diseases — Maladies hypertensives	39	49	34	68	9 741	16.7	12 253	20.0
Ischaemic heart disease — Cardiopathie ischémique	59	35	62	40	44 877	76.8	35 285	57.6

20. Death and death rates by cause and sex: 2012 - 2016
Décès et taux de mortalité par cause et sexe : 2012 - 2016 (continued - suite)

Cause of death — Cause de décès	Martinique				Mexico - Mexique			
	2013 (...)		2014 (...)		2014 (+C)			
	Male — Masculin	Female — Féminin	Male — Masculin	Female — Féminin	Male — Masculin		Female — Féminin	
	Number Nombre	Number Nombre	Number Nombre	Number Nombre	Number Nombre	Rate Taux	Number Nombre	Rate Taux
Cerebrovascular disease — Maladie cérébrovasculaire....................................	100	116	115	131	15 650	26.8	16 721	27.3
Diseases of arteries, arterioles and capillaries — Maladies des artères, artérioles et capillaires	16	20	26	31	1 039	1.8	974	1.6
Diseases of the respiratory system — Maladies de l'appareil respiratoire								
Total	73	64	80	69	29 725	50.9	24 810	40.5
Influenza — Grippe	4	7	2	-	120	0.2	87	0.1
Pneumonia — Pneumopathies	27	19	37	27	10 767	18.4	8 509	13.9
Chronic lower respiratory diseases — Maladies chroniques des voies respiratoires inférieures	19	10	12	8	12 945	22.2	11 260	18.4
Diseases of the digestive system — Maladies de l'appareil digestif								
Total	65	58	71	57	36 135	61.8	21 784	35.5
Gastric and duodenal ulcer — Ulcère de l'estomac et du duodénum...................	6	1	3	5	1 216	2.1	1 103	1.8
Diseases of the liver — Maladies du foie.......	18	10	17	6	24 094	41.2	9 598	15.7
Diseases of the musculoskeletal system and connective tissue — Maladies du système ostéo-articularie, des muscles et du tissu conjonctif	11	13	6	9	1 627	2.8	3 091	5.0
Diseases of the genitourinary system — Maladies de l'appareil génito-urinaire								
Total	21	22	37	34	11 097	19.0	9 572	15.6
Disorders of kidney and ureter — Affections du rein et de l'uretère	12	16	22	28	8 096	13.9	6 689	10.9
Hyperplasia of prostate — Hyperplasie de la prostate..	1	..	-	..	763	7.4	..	..
Pregnancy, childbirth and the puerperium — Grossesse, accouchement et puerpéralité								
Total	..	3	..	-	..	..	995	46.7
Pregnancy with abortive outcome — Grossesse se terminant par un avortement	..	-	..	-	..	..	81	3.8
Other direct obstetric causes — Autres décès maternels directs	..	3	..	-	..	..	513	24.1
Indirect obstetric causes — Décès maternels indirects	..	-	..	-	..	..	281	13.2
Certain conditions originating in the perinatal period — Certaines affections dont l'origine se situe dans la période périnatale	8	5	8	8	7 472	687.7	5 455	522.9
Congenital malformations, deformations and chromosomal abnormalities — Malformations congénitales et anomalies chromosomiques	9	9	9	8	5 057	465.4	4 382	420.0
Symptoms, signs and abnormal clinical and laboratory findings, not elsewhere classified — Symptômes, signes et résultats anormaux d'examens cliniques et de laboratoire, non classés ailleurs	126	134	122	153	5 046	8.6	4 873	8.0
All other diseases — Toutes autres maladies	7	8	4	17	1 120	1.9	1 588	2.6
External causes — Causes externes								
Total	115	47	149	64	51 246	87.7	12 516	20.4
Accidents								
Total	83	34	107	53	25 752	44.1	7 894	12.9
Transport accidents — Accidents de transport	23	2	22	1	12 833	22.0	3 246	5.3
Falls — Chutes	10	6	18	13	2 077	3.6	544	0.9
Accidental drowning and submersion — Noyade et submersion accidentelles...................................	9	4	11	1	1 750	3.0	272	0.4
Exposure to smoke, fire and flames — Exposition à la fumée, au feu et aux flammes..	2	2	2	2	334	0.6	130	0.2
Accidental poisoning by and exposure to noxious substances — Intoxication accidentelle par des substances nocives et exposition à ces substances	5	5	9	7	777	1.3	228	0.4
Intentional self-harm — Lésions auto-infligées..	18	9	25	7	4 984	8.5	1 231	2.0
Assault — Agresssions...............................	6	-	4	1	16 684	28.6	2 289	3.7
All other external causes — Toutes autres causes externes	8	4	13	3	3 826	6.5	1 102	1.8

	Mexico - Mexique				Montserrat			
	2015 (+C)				2015 (...)		2016 (...)	
Cause of death — Cause de décès	Male — Masculin		Female — Féminin		Male — Masculin	Female — Féminin	Male — Masculin	Female — Féminin
	Number Nombre	Rate Taux	Number Nombre	Rate Taux	Number Nombre	Number Nombre	Number Nombre	Number Nombre
TOTAL	355 112	601.4	285 498	460.8	*27*	*22*	*26*	*17*
Certain infectious and parasitic diseases — Certaines maladies infectieuses et parasitaires								
Total	9 816	16.6	6 177	10.0	-	-	2	-
Intestinal infectious diseases — Maladies infectieuses intestinales	1 739	2.9	1 961	3.2	-	-	1	-
Tuberculosis — Tuberculose	1 485	2.5	598	1.0	-	-	-	-
Tetanus — Tétanos	10	♦0.0	-	-	-	-	-	-
Diphtheria — Diphtérie..............	-	-	-	-	-	-	-	-
Whooping cough — Coqueluche	14	♦0.0	22	♦0.0	-	-	-	-
Meningococcal infection — Infection à méningocoques	4	♦0.0	3	♦0.0	-	-	-	-
Septicaemia — Septicémie	1 452	2.5	1 411	2.3	-	-	-	-
Acute poliomyelitis — Poliomyélite aiguë	-	-	-	-	-	-	-	-
Measles — Rougeole	-	-	-	-	-	-	-	-
Viral hepatitis — Hépatite virale	488	0.8	634	1.0	-	-	-	-
Human immunodeficiency virus [HIV] disease — Maladies dues au virus de l'immunodéficience humaine (VIH)..............	3 837	6.5	905	1.5	-	-	-	-
Malaria — Paludisme..............	2	♦0.0	1	♦0.0	-	-	-	-
Neoplasms — Tumeurs	40 904	69.3	42 710	68.9	*3*	*4*	*5*	-
Malignant neoplasms — Tumeurs malignes								
Total	38 131	64.6	39 878	64.4	*3*	*4*	*5*	-
Malignant neoplasm of lip, oral cavity and pharynx — Tumeur maligne de la lèvre, de la cavité buccale et du pharynx	746	1.3	425	0.7	-	-	-	-
Malignant neoplasm of oesophagus — Tumeur maligne de l'oesophage	825	1.4	243	0.4	-	-	-	-
Malignant neoplasm of stomach — Tumeur maligne de l'estomac	3 193	5.4	2 749	4.4	*1*	-	-	-
Malignant neoplasm of colon, rectosigmoid junction, rectum, anus and anal canal — Tumeur maligne du côlon, de la jonction recto-sigmoïdienne, du rectum, de l'anus et du canal anal..............	3 037	5.1	2 739	4.4	-	*1*	-	-
Malignant neoplasm of liver and intrahepatic bile ducts — Tumeur maligne du foie et des voies bilaires intrahépatiques	3 026	5.1	3 179	5.1	-	-	*1*	-
Malignant neoplasm of pancreas — Tumeur maligne du pancréas..............	1 917	3.2	2 197	3.5	-	-	-	-
Malignant neoplasm of trachea, bronchus and lung — Tumeur maligne de la trachée, des bronches et du poumon	4 230	7.2	2 539	4.1	-	-	*1*	-
Malignant neoplasm of female breast — Tumeur maligne du sein chez la femme	..	..	6 169	13.5	..	*1*	..	-
Malignant neoplasm of cervix uteri — Tumeur maligne du col de l'utérus..........	..	..	3 899	8.5	..	-	..	-
Malignant neoplasm of prostate — Tumeur maligne de la prostate	6 309	58.9	..	..	*2*	..	*2*	..
Malignant neoplasm of lymphoid, haematopoietic and related tissue — Tumeurs malignes primitives ou présumées primitives des tissus lymphoïde, hématopoïétique et apparentés..............	4 694	7.9	3 754	6.1	-	-	*1*	-
Disorders of the blood and blood-forming organs and certain disorders involving the immune mechanism — Maladies du sang et des organes hématopoïétiques et certains troubles du système immunitaire								
Total	2 302	3.9	2 342	3.8	-	*1*	-	-
Anaemias — Anémies	1 688	2.9	1 772	2.9	-	*1*	-	-
Endocrine, nutritional and metabolic diseases — Maladies endocriniennes, nutritionnelles et métaboliques								
Total	54 486	92.3	57 737	93.2	*5*	*6*	*5*	*2*
Diabetes mellitus — Diabète sucré..............	46 882	79.4	49 626	80.1	*5*	*6*	*5*	*2*
Malnutrition — Malnutrition	3 322	5.6	3 542	5.7	-	-	-	-
Mental and behavioural disorders — Troubles mentaux et du comportement	3 878	6.6	1 321	2.1	-	-	-	-
Diseases of the nervous system — Maladies du système nerveux..............	6 118	10.4	5 016	8.1	-	*1*	-	-
Diseases of the circulatory system — Maladies de l'appareil circulatoire								
Total	84 585	143.3	78 439	126.6	*11*	*7*	*13*	*8*
Acute rheumatic fever and chronic rheumatic heart diseases — Rhumatisme articularie aigu et cardiopathies rhumatismales chroniques	244	0.4	510	0.8	-	-	-	-
Hypertensive diseases — Maladies hypertensives..............	10 171	17.2	12 583	20.3	*3*	*4*	*4*	*3*
Ischaemic heart disease — Cardiopathie ischémique	48 016	81.3	37 945	61.2	*3*	*2*	*5*	*1*

Cause of death — Cause de décès	Mexico - Mexique				Montserrat			
	2015 (+C)				2015 (...)		2016 (...)	
	Male — Masculin		Female — Féminin		Male — Masculin	Female — Féminin	Male — Masculin	Female — Féminin
	Number Nombre	Rate Taux	Number Nombre	Rate Taux	Number Nombre	Number Nombre	Number Nombre	Number Nombre
Cerebrovascular disease — Maladie cérébrovasculaire	16 150	27.4	17 259	27.9	3	-	1	1
Diseases of arteries, arterioles and capillaries — Maladies des artères, artérioles et capillaires	1 154	2.0	1 042	1.7	1	-	-	-
Diseases of the respiratory system — Maladies de l'appareil respiratoire								
Total	29 281	49.6	24 891	40.2	4	1	-	2
Influenza — Grippe	28	+0.0	37	0.1	-	1	-	-
Pneumonia — Pneumopathies	10 169	17.2	8 220	13.3	-	-	-	-
Chronic lower respiratory diseases — Maladies chroniques des voies respiratoires inférieures	13 544	22.9	11 880	19.2	1	-	-	1
Diseases of the digestive system — Maladies de l'appareil digestif								
Total	38 511	65.2	23 167	37.4	-	-	-	3
Gastric and duodenal ulcer — Ulcère de l'estomac et du duodénum	1 275	2.2	1 067	1.7	-	-	-	-
Diseases of the liver — Maladies du foie	25 159	42.6	9 766	15.8	-	-	-	-
Diseases of the musculoskeletal system and connective tissue — Maladies du système ostéo-articularie, des muscles et du tissu conjonctif	1 498	2.5	3 000	4.8	-	-	-	-
Diseases of the genitourinary system — Maladies de l'appareil génito-urinaire								
Total	11 671	19.8	10 405	16.8	-	1	1	1
Disorders of kidney and ureter — Affections du rein et de l'uretère	8 402	14.2	7 131	11.5	-	1	1	1
Hyperplasia of prostate — Hyperplasie de la prostate	789	7.4	..	..	-	..	-	..
Pregnancy, childbirth and the puerperium — Grossesse, accouchement et puerpéralité								
Total	..	..	905	43.2	..	-	..	-
Pregnancy with abortive outcome — Grossesse se terminant par un avortement	..	..	72	3.4	..	-	..	-
Other direct obstetric causes — Autres décès maternels directs	..	..	477	22.8	..	-	..	-
Indirect obstetric causes — Décès maternels indirects	..	..	229	10.9	..	-	..	-
Certain conditions originating in the perinatal period — Certaines affections dont l'origine se situe dans la période périnatale	7 353	688.3	5 540	539.0	2	1	-	-
Congenital malformations, deformations and chromosomal abnormalities — Malformations congénitales et anomalies chromosomiques	4 926	461.1	4 320	420.3	-	-	-	-
Symptoms, signs and abnormal clinical and laboratory findings, not elsewhere classified — Symptômes, signes et résultats anormaux d'examens cliniques et de laboratoire, non classés ailleurs	5 323	9.0	5 107	8.2	-	-	-	1
All other diseases — Toutes autres maladies	1 240	2.1	1 620	2.6	-	-	-	-
External causes — Causes externes								
Total	53 220	90.1	12 801	20.7	2	-	-	-
Accidents								
Total	26 968	45.7	8 159	13.2	2	-	-	-
Transport accidents — Accidents de transport	12 883	21.8	3 346	5.4	1	-	-	-
Falls — Chutes	2 116	3.6	543	0.9	-	-	-	-
Accidental drowning and submersion — Noyade et submersion accidentelles	1 766	3.0	307	0.5	1	-	-	-
Exposure to smoke, fire and flames — Exposition à la fumée, au feu et aux flammes	358	0.6	162	0.3	-	-	-	-
Accidental poisoning by and exposure to noxious substances — Intoxication accidentelle par des substances nocives et exposition à ces substances	917	1.6	256	0.4	-	-	-	-
Intentional self-harm — Lésions auto-infligées	5 031	8.5	1 251	2.0	-	-	-	-
Assault — Agresssions	17 620	29.8	2 277	3.7	-	-	-	-
All other external causes — Toutes autres causes externes	3 601	6.1	1 114	1.8	-	-	-	-

20. Death and death rates by cause and sex: 2012 - 2016
Décès et taux de mortalité par cause et sexe : 2012 - 2016 (continued - suite)

	Nicaragua				Panama			
Cause of death — Cause de décès	2014 (+U)		2015 (+U)		2014 (+C)			
	Male — Masculin	Female — Féminin	Male — Masculin	Female — Féminin	Male — Masculin		Female — Féminin	
	Number Nombre	Number Nombre	Number Nombre	Number Nombre	Number Nombre	Rate Taux	Number Nombre	Rate Taux
TOTAL	*12 613*	*9 825*	*12 516*	*9 837*	*10 442*	*531.4*	*7 729*	*396.7*
Certain infectious and parasitic diseases — Certaines maladies infectieuses et parasitaires								
Total	*420*	*235*	*470*	*259*	*786*	*40.0*	*438*	*22.5*
Intestinal infectious diseases — Maladies infectieuses intestinales	*50*	*41*	*61*	*54*	*103*	*5.2*	*79*	*4.1*
Tuberculosis — Tuberculose	*67*	*37*	*92*	*38*	*121*	*6.2*	*80*	*4.1*
Tetanus — Tétanos	-	-	*1*	-	-	-	*1*	*♦0.1*
Diphtheria — Diphtérie	-	-	-	-	-	-	-	-
Whooping cough — Coqueluche	-	-	-	-	-	-	*1*	*♦0.1*
Meningococcal infection — Infection à méningocoques	*1*	-	-	*1*	*1*	*♦0.1*	-	-
Septicaemia — Septicémie	*97*	*77*	*108*	*89*	*144*	*7.3*	*141*	*7.2*
Acute poliomyelitis — Poliomyélite aiguë	-	-	-	-	-	-	-	-
Measles — Rougeole	-	-	-	-	-	-	-	-
Viral hepatitis — Hépatite virale	*6*	*2*	*7*	*3*	*4*	*♦0.2*	*3*	*♦0.2*
Human immunodeficiency virus [HIV] disease — Maladies dues au virus de l'immunodéficience humaine (VIH)	*179*	*67*	*169*	*50*	*373*	*19.0*	*111*	*5.7*
Malaria — Paludisme	*1*	-	*1*	*1*	-	-	-	-
Neoplasms — Tumeurs	*1 317*	*1 609*	*1 365*	*1 533*	*1 652*	*84.1*	*1 473*	*75.6*
Malignant neoplasms — Tumeurs malignes								
Total	*1 272*	*1 548*	*1 300*	*1 470*	*1 566*	*79.7*	*1 396*	*71.7*
Malignant neoplasm of lip, oral cavity and pharynx — Tumeur maligne de la lèvre, de la cavité buccale et du pharynx	*30*	*19*	*21*	*15*	*58*	*3.0*	*17*	*♦0.9*
Malignant neoplasm of oesophagus — Tumeur maligne de l'oesophage	*17*	*6*	*12*	*4*	*27*	*♦1.4*	*8*	*♦0.4*
Malignant neoplasm of stomach — Tumeur maligne de l'estomac	*176*	*146*	*169*	*105*	*197*	*10.0*	*112*	*5.7*
Malignant neoplasm of colon, rectosigmoid junction, rectum, anus and anal canal — Tumeur maligne du côlon, de la jonction recto-sigmoïdienne, du rectum, de l'anus et du canal anal	*68*	*117*	*84*	*114*	*156*	*7.9*	*144*	*7.4*
Malignant neoplasm of liver and intrahepatic bile ducts — Tumeur maligne du foie et des voies bilaires intrahépatiques	*163*	*153*	*158*	*135*	*78*	*4.0*	*72*	*3.7*
Malignant neoplasm of pancreas — Tumeur maligne du pancréas	*52*	*63*	*50*	*65*	*66*	*3.4*	*46*	*2.4*
Malignant neoplasm of trachea, bronchus and lung — Tumeur maligne de la trachée, des bronches et du poumon	*97*	*85*	*110*	*83*	*179*	*9.1*	*100*	*5.1*
Malignant neoplasm of female breast — Tumeur maligne du sein chez la femme	*..*	*186*	*..*	*197*	*..*	*..*	*212*	*15.0*
Malignant neoplasm of cervix uteri — Tumeur maligne du col de l'utérus	*..*	*276*	*..*	*240*			*166*	*11.7*
Malignant neoplasm of prostate — Tumeur maligne de la prostate	*212*	*..*	*217*	*..*	*305*	*81.0*	*..*	*..*
Malignant neoplasm of lymphoid, haematopoietic and related tissue — Tumeurs malignes primitives ou présumées primitives des tissus lymphoïde, hématopoïétique et apparentés	*164*	*150*	*189*	*143*	*149*	*7.6*	*113*	*5.8*
Disorders of the blood and blood-forming organs and certain disorders involving the immune mechanism — Maladies du sang et des organes hématopoïétiques et certains troubles du système immunitaire								
Total	*58*	*58*	*75*	*52*	*75*	*3.8*	*47*	*2.4*
Anaemias — Anémies	*47*	*41*	*46*	*35*	*63*	*3.2*	*37*	*1.9*
Endocrine, nutritional and metabolic diseases — Maladies endocriniennes, nutritionnelles et métaboliques								
Total	*887*	*1 184*	*928*	*1 184*	*690*	*35.1*	*816*	*41.9*
Diabetes mellitus — Diabète sucré	*790*	*1 100*	*846*	*1 083*	*529*	*26.9*	*684*	*35.1*
Malnutrition — Malnutrition	*70*	*49*	*49*	*69*	*62*	*3.2*	*54*	*2.8*
Mental and behavioural disorders — Troubles mentaux et du comportement	*303*	*17*	*264*	*23*	*34*	*1.7*	*23*	*♦1.2*
Diseases of the nervous system — Maladies du système nerveux	*185*	*163*	*185*	*149*	*261*	*13.3*	*286*	*14.7*
Diseases of the circulatory system — Maladies de l'appareil circulatoire								
Total	*3 143*	*3 222*	*3 098*	*3 148*	*2 883*	*146.7*	*2 187*	*112.3*
Acute rheumatic fever and chronic rheumatic heart diseases — Rhumatisme articularie aigu et cardiopathies rhumatismales chroniques	*7*	*5*	*2*	*11*	*4*	*♦0.2*	*6*	*♦0.3*
Hypertensive diseases — Maladies hypertensives	*466*	*471*	*521*	*538*	*336*	*17.1*	*309*	*15.9*
Ischaemic heart disease — Cardiopathie ischémique	*1 670*	*1 630*	*1 598*	*1 522*	*1 041*	*53.0*	*689*	*35.4*

20. Death and death rates by cause and sex: 2012 - 2016
Décès et taux de mortalité par cause et sexe : 2012 - 2016 (continued - suite)

Cause of death — Cause de décès	Nicaragua				Panama			
	2014 (+U)		2015 (+U)		2014 (+C)			
	Male — Masculin	Female — Féminin	Male — Masculin	Female — Féminin	Male — Masculin		Female — Féminin	
	Number Nombre	Number Nombre	Number Nombre	Number Nombre	Number Nombre	Rate Taux	Number Nombre	Rate Taux
Cerebrovascular disease — Maladie cérébrovasculaire.........................	647	729	582	680	868	44.2	689	35.4
Diseases of arteries, arterioles and capillaries — Maladies des artères, artérioles et capillaires	23	21	21	23	57	2.9	40	2.1
Diseases of the respiratory system — Maladies de l'appareil respiratoire								
Total	861	777	960	889	950	48.3	865	44.4
Influenza — Grippe.........	-	-	-	-	5	+0.3	10	+0.5
Pneumonia — Pneumopathies	325	275	399	360	352	17.9	321	16.5
Chronic lower respiratory diseases — Maladies chroniques des voies respiratoires inférieures	427	392	402	395	289	14.7	259	13.3
Diseases of the digestive system — Maladies de l'appareil digestif								
Total	1 252	658	1 209	660	441	22.4	330	16.9
Gastric and duodenal ulcer — Ulcère de l'estomac et du duodénum.................	44	28	42	21	15	+0.8	9	+0.5
Diseases of the liver — Maladies du foie.........	952	362	942	405	201	10.2	114	5.9
Diseases of the musculoskeletal system and connective tissue — Maladies du système ostéo-articulaire, des muscles et du tissu conjonctif	26	83	31	80	22	+1.1	42	2.2
Diseases of the genitourinary system — Maladies de l'appareil génito-urinaire								
Total	1 183	468	1 200	458	354	18.0	225	11.5
Disorders of kidney and ureter — Affections du rein et de l'uretère	1 149	448	1 150	433	284	14.5	187	9.6
Hyperplasia of prostate — Hyperplasie de la prostate.........	18	..	23	..	18	+4.8	..	..
Pregnancy, childbirth and the puerperium — Grossesse, accouchement et puerpéralité								
Total	..	53	..	59	..	..	44	58.5
Pregnancy with abortive outcome — Grossesse se terminant par un avortement	..	4	..	5	..	..	1	+1.3
Other direct obstetric causes — Autres décès maternels directs	..	45	..	48	..	..	34	45.2
Indirect obstetric causes — Décès maternels indirects.........	..	4	..	6	..	..	9	+12.0
Certain conditions originating in the perinatal period — Certaines affections dont l'origine se situe dans la période périnatale	723	458	693	481	239	619.6	186	508.0
Congenital malformations, deformations and chromosomal abnormalities — Malformations congénitales et anomalies chromosomiques	268	220	306	222	212	549.6	168	458.9
Symptoms, signs and abnormal clinical and laboratory findings, not elsewhere classified — Symptômes, signes et résultats anormaux d'examens cliniques et de laboratoire, non classés ailleurs	138	164	187	214	297	15.1	271	13.9
All other diseases — Toutes autres maladies.........	26	43	45	54	37	1.9	53	2.7
External causes — Causes externes								
Total	1 823	413	1 500	372	1 509	76.8	275	14.1
Accidents								
Total	1 131	260	970	228	675	34.3	192	9.9
Transport accidents — Accidents de transport.........	633	90	534	75	385	19.6	92	4.7
Falls — Chutes	78	62	97	66	93	4.7	34	1.7
Accidental drowning and submersion — Noyade et submersion accidentelles.........	143	9	108	21	91	4.6	22	+1.1
Exposure to smoke, fire and flames — Exposition à la fumée, au feu et aux flammes.........	8	3	5	5	9	+0.5	6	+0.3
Accidental poisoning by and exposure to noxious substances — Intoxication accidentelle par des substances nocives et exposition à ces substances	30	10	32	5	6	+0.3	2	+0.1
Intentional self-harm — Lésions auto-infligées.........	241	70	230	85	127	6.5	20	+1.0
Assault — Agressions.........	350	61	221	24	587	29.9	40	2.1
All other external causes — Toutes autres causes externes	101	22	79	35	120	6.1	23	+1.2

Cause of death — Cause de décès	Panama				Puerto Rico - Porto Rico			
	2015 (+C)				2014 (...)		2015 (...)	
	Male — Masculin		Female — Féminin		Male — Masculin	Female — Féminin	Male — Masculin	Female — Féminin
	Number Nombre	Rate Taux	Number Nombre	Rate Taux	Number Nombre	Number Nombre	Number Nombre	Number Nombre
TOTAL	10 402	521.2	7 780	393.0	16 279	13 873	15 152	12 932
Certain infectious and parasitic diseases — Certaines maladies infectieuses et parasitaires								
Total	740	37.1	382	19.3	791	596	640	511
Intestinal infectious diseases — Maladies infectieuses intestinales	64	3.2	64	3.2	23	20	18	15
Tuberculosis — Tuberculose	122	6.1	85	4.3	6	4	3	3
Tetanus — Tétanos....................	-	-	-	-	1	-	-	-
Diphtheria — Diphtérie....................	-	-	-	-	-	-	-	-
Whooping cough — Coqueluche	-	-	-	-	-	1	-	-
Meningococcal infection — Infection à méningocoques	1	+0.1	-	-	1	1	-	-
Septicaemia — Septicémie	99	5.0	88	4.4	434	430	339	382
Acute poliomyelitis — Poliomyélite aiguë	-	-	-	-	-	-	-	-
Measles — Rougeole....................	-	-	-	-	-	-	-	-
Viral hepatitis — Hépatite virale....................	7	+0.4	1	+0.1	60	17	72	14
Human immunodeficiency virus [HIV] disease — Maladies dues au virus de l'immunodéficience humaine (VIH)....................	414	20.7	124	6.3	175	66	144	53
Malaria — Paludisme....................	-	-	-	-	-	-	-	-
Neoplasms — Tumeurs	1 736	87.0	1 498	75.7	3 097	2 457	2 953	2 371
Malignant neoplasms — Tumeurs malignes								
Total	1 641	82.2	1 404	70.9	3 012	2 378	2 860	2 299
Malignant neoplasm of lip, oral cavity and pharynx — Tumeur maligne de la lèvre, de la cavité buccale et du pharynx	45	2.3	15	+0.8	82	22	119	26
Malignant neoplasm of oesophagus — Tumeur maligne de l'oesophage	35	1.8	12	+0.6	97	21	81	22
Malignant neoplasm of stomach — Tumeur maligne de l'estomac	203	10.2	118	6.0	138	86	126	93
Malignant neoplasm of colon, rectosigmoid junction, rectum, anus and anal canal — Tumeur maligne du côlon, de la jonction recto-sigmoïdienne, du rectum, de l'anus et du canal anal....................	147	7.4	123	6.2	419	332	357	299
Malignant neoplasm of liver and intrahepatic bile ducts — Tumeur maligne du foie et des voies biliaires intrahépatiques	96	4.8	97	4.9	186	115	233	118
Malignant neoplasm of pancreas — Tumeur maligne du pancréas....................	57	2.9	50	2.5	164	131	166	155
Malignant neoplasm of trachea, bronchus and lung — Tumeur maligne de la trachée, des bronches et du poumon	188	9.4	120	6.1	412	227	376	216
Malignant neoplasm of female breast — Tumeur maligne du sein chez la femme	..	..	211	14.6	..	454	..	432
Malignant neoplasm of cervix uteri — Tumeur maligne du col de l'utérus.........	..	..	161	11.1	..	50	..	50
Malignant neoplasm of prostate — Tumeur maligne de la prostate	333	85.2	..	..	509	..	483	..
Malignant neoplasm of lymphoid, haematopoietic and related tissue — Tumeurs malignes primitives ou présumées primitives des tissus lymphoïde, hématopoïétique et apparentés....................	161	8.1	119	6.0	282	224	268	223
Disorders of the blood and blood-forming organs and certain disorders involving the immune mechanism — Maladies du sang et des organes hématopoïétiques et certains troubles du système immunitaire								
Total	67	3.4	71	3.6	168	171	144	173
Anaemias — Anémies	52	2.6	63	3.2	101	115	93	119
Endocrine, nutritional and metabolic diseases — Maladies endocriniennes, nutritionnelles et métaboliques								
Total	748	37.5	838	42.3	2 021	1 996	1 769	1 819
Diabetes mellitus — Diabète sucré	614	30.8	699	35.3	1 658	1 612	1 464	1 462
Malnutrition — Malnutrition	66	3.3	68	3.4	40	32	34	32
Mental and behavioural disorders — Troubles mentaux et du comportement	67	3.4	34	1.7	379	311	229	207
Diseases of the nervous system — Maladies du système nerveux....................	276	13.8	299	15.1	1 024	1 501	1 019	1 591
Diseases of the circulatory system — Maladies de l'appareil circulatoire								
Total	2 864	143.5	2 311	116.7	3 825	3 513	3 688	3 253
Acute rheumatic fever and chronic rheumatic heart diseases — Rhumatisme articularie aigu et cardiopathies rhumatismales chroniques	8	+0.4	15	+0.8	9	11	11	14
Hypertensive diseases — Maladies hypertensives....................	416	20.8	393	19.9	610	673	520	568
Ischaemic heart disease — Cardiopathie ischémique....................	885	44.3	606	30.6	1 792	1 417	1 837	1 378

20. Death and death rates by cause and sex: 2012 - 2016
Décès et taux de mortalité par cause et sexe : 2012 - 2016 (continued - suite)

	Panama				Puerto Rico - Porto Rico			
	2015 (+C)				2014 (...)		2015 (...)	
Cause of death — Cause de décès	Male — Masculin		Female — Féminin		Male — Masculin	Female — Féminin	Male — Masculin	Female — Féminin
	Number Nombre	Rate Taux	Number Nombre	Rate Taux	Number Nombre	Number Nombre	Number Nombre	Number Nombre
Cerebrovascular disease — Maladie cérébrovasculaire.........	827	41.4	699	35.3	657	685	632	666
Diseases of arteries, arterioles and capillaries — Maladies des artères, artérioles et capillaires	86	4.3	56	2.8	93	74	80	64
Diseases of the respiratory system — Maladies de l'appareil respiratoire								
Total	815	40.8	766	38.7	1 323	1 241	1 172	1 104
Influenza — Grippe	3	✦0.2	3	✦0.2	15	21	23	15
Pneumonia — Pneumopathies	289	14.5	243	12.3	400	377	301	293
Chronic lower respiratory diseases — Maladies chroniques des voies respiratoires inférieures	264	13.2	251	12.7	543	487	513	501
Diseases of the digestive system — Maladies de l'appareil digestif								
Total	488	24.5	327	16.5	735	539	718	459
Gastric and duodenal ulcer — Ulcère de l'estomac et du duodénum.........	13	✦0.7	10	✦0.5	19	13	9	7
Diseases of the liver — Maladies du foie.........	233	11.7	142	7.2	460	229	466	220
Diseases of the musculoskeletal system and connective tissue — Maladies du système ostéo-articularie, des muscles et du tissu conjonctif	22	✦1.1	52	2.6	49	127	62	112
Diseases of the genitourinary system — Maladies de l'appareil génito-urinaire								
Total	412	20.6	244	12.3	722	677	646	551
Disorders of kidney and ureter — Affections du rein et de l'uretère	356	17.8	200	10.1	616	533	542	423
Hyperplasia of prostate — Hyperplasie de la prostate.........	20	✦5.1	..	..	6	..	5	..
Pregnancy, childbirth and the puerperium — Grossesse, accouchement et puerpéralité								
Total	..	..	40	52.7	..	3	..	15
Pregnancy with abortive outcome — Grossesse se terminant par un avortement	..	..	3	✦4.0	..	-	..	1
Other direct obstetric causes — Autres décès maternels directs	..	..	32	42.2	..	3	..	8
Indirect obstetric causes — Décès maternels indirects	..	..	5	✦6.6	..	-	..	2
Certain conditions originating in the perinatal period — Certaines affections dont l'origine se situe dans la période périnatale	231	592.9	154	416.9	78	56	59	49
Congenital malformations, deformations and chromosomal abnormalities — Malformations congénitales et anomalies chromosomiques	179	459.4	170	460.2	52	38	47	31
Symptoms, signs and abnormal clinical and laboratory findings, not elsewhere classified — Symptômes, signes et résultats anormaux d'examens cliniques et de laboratoire, non classés ailleurs	415	20.8	297	15.0	330	164	416	167
All other diseases — Toutes autres maladies.........	37	1.9	47	2.4	108	133	92	141
External causes — Causes externes								
Total	1 305	65.4	250	12.6	1 577	350	1 498	378
Accidents								
Total	643	32.2	152	7.7	719	218	658	234
Transport accidents — Accidents de transport	387	19.4	89	4.5	274	59	290	72
Falls — Chutes	74	3.7	27	✦1.4	118	29	176	78
Accidental drowning and submersion — Noyade et submersion accidentelles.........	87	4.4	17	✦0.9	27	2	23	8
Exposure to smoke, fire and flames — Exposition à la fumée, au feu et aux flammes.........	9	✦0.5	1	✦0.1	6	-	6	3
Accidental poisoning by and exposure to noxious substances — Intoxication accidentelle par des substances nocives et exposition à ces substances	3	✦0.2	1	✦0.1	52	13	24	4
Intentional self-harm — Lésions auto-infligées.........	91	4.6	19	✦1.0	188	32	201	25
Assault — Agresssions.........	416	20.8	52	2.6	626	52	547	39
All other external causes — Toutes autres causes externes	155	7.8	27	✦1.4	44	48	92	80

20. Death and death rates by cause and sex: 2012 - 2016
Décès et taux de mortalité par cause et sexe : 2012 - 2016 (continued - suite)

Cause of death — Cause de décès	Saint Kitts and Nevis - Saint-Kitts-et-Nevis				Saint Lucia - Sainte-Lucie			
	2014 (+U)		2015 (+U)		2013 (C)			
	Male — Masculin	Female — Féminin	Male — Masculin	Female — Féminin	Male — Masculin		Female — Féminin	
	Number Nombre	Number Nombre	Number Nombre	Number Nombre	Number Nombre	Rate Taux	Number Nombre	Rate Taux
TOTAL	234	178	209	162	605	713.7	488	566.4
Certain infectious and parasitic diseases — Certaines maladies infectieuses et parasitaires								
Total	3	1	2	-	26	♦30.7	20	♦23.2
Intestinal infectious diseases — Maladies infectieuses intestinales	-	1	-	-	4	♦4.7	1	♦1.2
Tuberculosis — Tuberculose	-	-	-	-	4	♦4.7	1	♦1.2
Tetanus — Tétanos	-	-	-	-	-	-	-	-
Diphtheria — Diphtérie...........	-	-	-	-	-	-	-	-
Whooping cough — Coqueluche	-	-	-	-	-	-	-	-
Meningococcal infection — Infection à méningocoques...........	-	-	-	-	-	-	-	-
Septicaemia — Septicémie...........	-	-	-	-	14	♦16.5	14	♦16.2
Acute poliomyelitis — Poliomyélite aiguë	-	-	-	-	-	-	-	-
Measles — Rougeole...........	-	-	-	-	-	-	-	-
Viral hepatitis — Hépatite virale...........	-	-	-	-	-	-	-	-
Human immunodeficiency virus [HIV] disease — Maladies dues au virus de l'immunodéficience humaine (VIH)...........	1	-	1	-	-	-	1	♦1.2
Malaria — Paludisme...........	-	-	-	-	-	-	-	-
Neoplasms — Tumeurs	32	37	47	40	104	122.7	89	103.3
Malignant neoplasms — Tumeurs malignes								
Total	32	37	47	39	101	119.1	84	97.5
Malignant neoplasm of lip, oral cavity and pharynx — Tumeur maligne de la lèvre, de la cavité buccale et du pharynx	-	-	2	1	5	♦5.9	-	-
Malignant neoplasm of oesophagus — Tumeur maligne de l'oesophage	1	-	-	-	3	♦3.5	1	♦1.2
Malignant neoplasm of stomach — Tumeur maligne de l'estomac	1	2	1	-	8	♦9.4	6	♦7.0
Malignant neoplasm of colon, rectosigmoid junction, rectum, anus and anal canal — Tumeur maligne du côlon, de la jonction recto-sigmoïdienne, du rectum, de l'anus et du canal anal	2	5	6	6	8	♦9.4	4	♦4.6
Malignant neoplasm of liver and intrahepatic bile ducts — Tumeur maligne du foie et des voies bilaires intrahépatiques	3	1	5	-	2	♦2.4	1	♦1.2
Malignant neoplasm of pancreas — Tumeur maligne du pancréas...........	2	2	4	4	1	♦1.2	4	♦4.6
Malignant neoplasm of trachea, bronchus and lung — Tumeur maligne de la trachée, des bronches et du poumon	-	1	2	5	14	♦16.5	3	♦3.5
Malignant neoplasm of female breast — Tumeur maligne du sein chez la femme	..	9	..	10	..	..	16	...
Malignant neoplasm of cervix uteri — Tumeur maligne du col de l'utérus...........	..	4	..	..	..	..	11	...
Malignant neoplasm of prostate — Tumeur maligne de la prostate	15	..	13	..	32	...	..	..
Malignant neoplasm of lymphoid, haematopoietic and related tissue — Tumeurs malignes primitives ou présumées primitives des tissus lymphoïde, hématopoïétique et apparentés...........	2	1	1	3	11	♦13.0	12	♦13.9
Disorders of the blood and blood-forming organs and certain disorders involving the immune mechanism — Maladies du sang et des organes hématopoïétiques et certains troubles du système immunitaire								
Total	-	-	-	-	12	♦14.2	3	♦3.5
Anaemias — Anémies	-	-	-	-	7	♦8.3	3	♦3.5
Endocrine, nutritional and metabolic diseases — Maladies endocriniennes, nutritionnelles et métaboliques								
Total	21	34	17	19	48	56.6	52	60.4
Diabetes mellitus — Diabète sucré...........	15	29	15	18	36	42.5	38	44.1
Malnutrition — Malnutrition	-	1	-	1	1	♦1.2	-	-
Mental and behavioural disorders — Troubles mentaux et du comportement	6	-	3	-	2	♦2.4	-	-
Diseases of the nervous system — Maladies du système nerveux...........	7	7	4	5	12	♦14.2	3	♦3.5
Diseases of the circulatory system — Maladies de l'appareil circulatoire								
Total	72	64	64	70	178	210.0	218	253.0
Acute rheumatic fever and chronic rheumatic heart diseases — Rhumatisme articularie aigu et cardiopathies rhumatismales chroniques	-	-	-	-	1	♦1.2	3	♦3.5
Hypertensive diseases — Maladies hypertensives...........	21	13	17	11	22	♦26.0	48	55.7
Ischaemic heart disease — Cardiopathie ischémique...........	23	14	17	13	39	46.0	36	41.8

Cause of death — Cause de décès	Saint Kitts and Nevis - Saint-Kitts-et-Nevis				Saint Lucia - Sainte-Lucie			
	2014 (+U)		2015 (+U)		2013 (C)			
	Male — Masculin	Female — Féminin	Male — Masculin	Female — Féminin	Male — Masculin		Female — Féminin	
	Number Nombre	Number Nombre	Number Nombre	Number Nombre	Number Nombre	Rate Taux	Number Nombre	Rate Taux
Cerebrovascular disease — Maladie cérébrovasculaire	11	24	19	29	64	75.5	79	91.7
Diseases of arteries, arterioles and capillaries — Maladies des artères, artérioles et capillaires	1	2	4	2	6	♦7.1	8	♦9.3
Diseases of the respiratory system — Maladies de l'appareil respiratoire								
Total	11	5	7	5	37	43.6	27	♦31.3
Influenza — Grippe	-	-	-	-	-	-	-	-
Pneumonia — Pneumopathies	-	-	-	-	6	♦7.1	8	♦9.3
Chronic lower respiratory diseases — Maladies chroniques des voies respiratoires inférieures	-	2	1	1	21	♦24.8	4	♦4.6
Diseases of the digestive system — Maladies de l'appareil digestif								
Total	15	7	8	1	35	41.3	16	♦18.6
Gastric and duodenal ulcer — Ulcère de l'estomac et du duodénum	2	-	1	-	7	♦8.3	2	♦2.3
Diseases of the liver — Maladies du foie	4	5	6	-	16	♦18.9	5	♦5.8
Diseases of the musculoskeletal system and connective tissue — Maladies du système ostéo-articularie, des muscles et du tissu conjonctif	1	-	-	2	4	♦4.7	3	♦3.5
Diseases of the genitourinary system — Maladies de l'appareil génito-urinaire								
Total	13	8	6	3	19	♦22.4	8	♦9.3
Disorders of kidney and ureter — Affections du rein et de l'uretère	5	7	4	3	9	♦10.6	4	♦4.6
Hyperplasia of prostate — Hyperplasie de la prostate	2	..	-	..	4	...	..	...
Pregnancy, childbirth and the puerperium — Grossesse, accouchement et puerpéralité								
Total	..	-	..	-	..	...	1	...
Pregnancy with abortive outcome — Grossesse se terminant par un avortement	..	-	..	-	..	...	-	...
Other direct obstetric causes — Autres décès maternels directs	..	-	..	-	..	...	1	...
Indirect obstetric causes — Décès maternels indirects	..	-	..	-	..	...	-	...
Certain conditions originating in the perinatal period — Certaines affections dont l'origine se situe dans la période périnatale	2	6	5	7	12	...	9	...
Congenital malformations, deformations and chromosomal abnormalities — Malformations congénitales et anomalies chromosomiques	5	1	2	3	4	...	2	...
Symptoms, signs and abnormal clinical and laboratory findings, not elsewhere classified — Symptômes, signes et résultats anormaux d'examens cliniques et de laboratoire, non classés ailleurs	6	2	1	-	10	♦11.8	12	♦13.9
All other diseases — Toutes autres maladies	-	1	-	1	5	♦5.9	3	♦3.5
External causes — Causes externes								
Total	40	5	43	6	97	114.4	22	♦25.5
Accidents								
Total	21	3	14	4	54	63.7	15	♦17.4
Transport accidents — Accidents de transport	10	1	6	1	26	♦30.7	5	♦5.8
Falls — Chutes	3	-	-	2	3	♦3.5	-	-
Accidental drowning and submersion — Noyade et submersion accidentelles	2	1	-	-	9	♦10.6	1	♦1.2
Exposure to smoke, fire and flames — Exposition à la fumée, au feu et aux flammes	1	-	-	-	-	-	1	♦1.2
Accidental poisoning by and exposure to noxious substances — Intoxication accidentelle par des substances nocives et exposition à ces substances	-	1	1	1	3	♦3.5	-	-
Intentional self-harm — Lésions auto-infligées	-	-	-	-	13	♦15.3	1	♦1.2
Assault — Agressions	19	1	23	-	28	♦33.0	5	♦5.8
All other external causes — Toutes autres causes externes	-	1	6	2	2	♦2.4	1	♦1.2

Cause of death — Cause de décès	Saint Lucia - Sainte-Lucie 2014 (C)				Saint Vincent and the Grenadines - Saint-Vincent-et-les Grenadines 2014 (+C)		2015 (+C)	
	Male — Masculin		Female — Féminin		Male — Masculin	Female — Féminin	Male — Masculin	Female — Féminin
	Number Nombre	Rate Taux	Number Nombre	Rate Taux	Number Nombre	Number Nombre	Number Nombre	Number Nombre
TOTAL	727	848.9	572	657.6	559	436	507	372
Certain infectious and parasitic diseases — Certaines maladies infectieuses et parasitaires								
Total	28	♦32.7	24	♦27.6	37	38	27	26
Intestinal infectious diseases — Maladies infectieuses intestinales	1	♦1.2	-	-	4	1	1	3
Tuberculosis — Tuberculose	3	♦3.5	-	-	2	1	1	-
Tetanus — Tétanos	-	-	-	-	-	-	-	-
Diphtheria — Diphtérie	-	-	-	-	-	-	-	-
Whooping cough — Coqueluche	-	-	-	-	-	-	-	-
Meningococcal infection — Infection à méningocoques	-	-	-	-	-	-	-	-
Septicaemia — Septicémie	13	♦15.2	11	♦12.6	8	20	6	14
Acute poliomyelitis — Poliomyélite aiguë	-	-	-	-	-	-	-	-
Measles — Rougeole	-	-	-	-	-	-	-	-
Viral hepatitis — Hépatite virale	-	-	-	-	-	-	-	-
Human immunodeficiency virus [HIV] disease — Maladies dues au virus de l'immunodéficience humaine (VIH)	1	♦1.2	1	♦1.1	14	11	16	5
Malaria — Paludisme	-	-	-	-	-	-	-	-
Neoplasms — Tumeurs	147	171.7	102	117.3	96	69	112	73
Malignant neoplasms — Tumeurs malignes								
Total	143	167.0	97	111.5	91	69	110	72
Malignant neoplasm of lip, oral cavity and pharynx — Tumeur maligne de la lèvre, de la cavité buccale et du pharynx	8	♦9.3	1	♦1.1	2	2	2	-
Malignant neoplasm of oesophagus — Tumeur maligne de l'oesophage	5	♦5.8	1	♦1.1	4	-	3	-
Malignant neoplasm of stomach — Tumeur maligne de l'estomac	12	♦14.0	7	♦8.0	9	5	8	3
Malignant neoplasm of colon, rectosigmoid junction, rectum, anus and anal canal — Tumeur maligne du côlon, de la jonction recto-sigmoïdienne, du rectum, de l'anus et du canal anal	11	♦12.8	13	♦14.9	6	6	9	3
Malignant neoplasm of liver and intrahepatic bile ducts — Tumeur maligne du foie et des voies bilaires intrahépatiques	4	♦4.7	4	♦4.6	1	-	8	4
Malignant neoplasm of pancreas — Tumeur maligne du pancréas	7	♦8.2	4	♦4.6	4	4	1	4
Malignant neoplasm of trachea, bronchus and lung — Tumeur maligne de la trachée, des bronches et du poumon	12	♦14.0	2	♦2.3	1	3	7	4
Malignant neoplasm of female breast — Tumeur maligne du sein chez la femme	..	..	14	...	..	16	..	14
Malignant neoplasm of cervix uteri — Tumeur maligne du col de l'utérus	..	..	10	...	..	11	..	7
Malignant neoplasm of prostate — Tumeur maligne de la prostate	42	...	..	..	35	..	51	..
Malignant neoplasm of lymphoid, haematopoietic and related tissue — Tumeurs malignes primitives ou présumées primitives des tissus lymphoïde, hématopoïétique et apparentés	11	♦12.8	6	♦6.9	9	4	3	6
Disorders of the blood and blood-forming organs and certain disorders involving the immune mechanism — Maladies du sang et des organes hématopoïétiques et certains troubles du système immunitaire								
Total	9	♦10.5	7	♦8.0	5	4	6	5
Anaemias — Anémies	6	♦7.0	5	♦5.7	3	3	5	4
Endocrine, nutritional and metabolic diseases — Maladies endocriniennes, nutritionnelles et métaboliques								
Total	50	58.4	93	106.9	58	72	40	37
Diabetes mellitus — Diabète sucré	44	51.4	78	89.7	48	61	34	34
Malnutrition — Malnutrition	1	♦1.2	2	♦2.3	5	2	2	-
Mental and behavioural disorders — Troubles mentaux et du comportement	3	♦3.5	1	♦1.1	4	2	1	-
Diseases of the nervous system — Maladies du système nerveux	10	♦11.7	11	♦12.6	10	2	8	8
Diseases of the circulatory system — Maladies de l'appareil circulatoire								
Total	214	249.9	196	225.3	199	188	149	134
Acute rheumatic fever and chronic rheumatic heart diseases — Rhumatisme articularie aigu et cardiopathies rhumatismales chroniques	-	-	2	♦2.3	3	-	1	-
Hypertensive diseases — Maladies hypertensives	37	43.2	49	56.3	39	47	18	33
Ischaemic heart disease — Cardiopathie ischémique	50	58.4	32	36.8	64	71	49	42

Cause of death — Cause de décès	Saint Lucia - Sainte-Lucie 2014 (C)				Saint Vincent and the Grenadines - Saint-Vincent-et-les Grenadines 2014 (+C)		2015 (+C)	
	Male — Masculin		Female — Féminin		Male — Masculin	Female — Féminin	Male — Masculin	Female — Féminin
	Number Nombre	Rate Taux	Number Nombre	Rate Taux	Number Nombre	Number Nombre	Number Nombre	Number Nombre
Cerebrovascular disease — Maladie cérébrovasculaire	61	71.2	62	71.3	65	44	42	37
Diseases of arteries, arterioles and capillaries — Maladies des artères, artérioles et capillaires	7	♦8.2	6	♦6.9	3	1	4	3
Diseases of the respiratory system — Maladies de l'appareil respiratoire								
Total	68	79.4	33	37.9	34	18	38	29
Influenza — Grippe	-	-	-	-				
Pneumonia — Pneumopathies	16	♦18.7	10	♦11.5	14	15	17	16
Chronic lower respiratory diseases — Maladies chroniques des voies respiratoires inférieures	36	42.0	10	♦11.5	12	2	7	4
Diseases of the digestive system — Maladies de l'appareil digestif								
Total	39	45.5	27	♦31.0	23	9	20	12
Gastric and duodenal ulcer — Ulcère de l'estomac et du duodénum	4	♦4.7	2	♦2.3	4	-	3	-
Diseases of the liver — Maladies du foie	21	♦24.5	10	♦11.5	10	2	6	2
Diseases of the musculoskeletal system and connective tissue — Maladies du système ostéo-articulaire, des muscles et du tissu conjonctif	3	♦3.5	5	♦5.7	1	5	2	4
Diseases of the genitourinary system — Maladies de l'appareil génito-urinaire								
Total	21	♦24.5	11	♦12.6	7	3	10	9
Disorders of kidney and ureter — Affections du rein et de l'uretère	11	♦12.8	6	♦6.9	5	1	6	7
Hyperplasia of prostate — Hyperplasie de la prostate	3	...	..	..	1	...	1	..
Pregnancy, childbirth and the puerperium — Grossesse, accouchement et puerpéralité								
Total	..	..	2	...	...	1	..	-
Pregnancy with abortive outcome — Grossesse se terminant par un avortement	..	..	-	...	...	-	..	-
Other direct obstetric causes — Autres décès maternels directs	..	..	2	...	...	1	..	-
Indirect obstetric causes — Décès maternels indirects	..	..	-	...	...	-	..	-
Certain conditions originating in the perinatal period — Certaines affections dont l'origine se situe dans la période périnatale	16	...	9	...	11	5	7	6
Congenital malformations, deformations and chromosomal abnormalities — Malformations congénitales et anomalies chromosomiques	7	...	1	...	5	5	5	2
Symptoms, signs and abnormal clinical and laboratory findings, not elsewhere classified — Symptômes, signes et résultats anormaux d'examens cliniques et de laboratoire, non classés ailleurs	10	♦11.7	18	♦20.7	4	4	14	6
All other diseases — Toutes autres maladies	6	♦7.0	14	♦16.1	-	4	7	7
External causes — Causes externes								
Total	96	112.1	18	♦20.7	65	7	61	14
Accidents								
Total	48	56.0	8	♦9.2	24	4	37	8
Transport accidents — Accidents de transport	21	♦24.5	1	♦1.1	11	1	18	6
Falls — Chutes	-	-	-	-	4	1	5	-
Accidental drowning and submersion — Noyade et submersion accidentelles	13	♦15.2	-	-	4	1	6	-
Exposure to smoke, fire and flames — Exposition à la fumée, au feu et aux flammes	-	-	-	-	3	-	-	1
Accidental poisoning by and exposure to noxious substances — Intoxication accidentelle par des substances nocives et exposition à ces substances	4	♦4.7	-	-	-	-	2	-
Intentional self-harm — Lésions auto-infligées	11	♦12.8	3	♦3.4	2	-	2	1
Assault — Agresssions	34	39.7	-	-	36	3	21	4
All other external causes — Toutes autres causes externes	3	♦3.5	7	♦8.0	3	-	1	1

Cause of death — Cause de décès	Turks and Caicos Islands - Îles Turques et Caïques 2013 (...) Male — Masculin Number Nombre	Female — Féminin Number Nombre	2014 (...) Male — Masculin Number Nombre	Female — Féminin Number Nombre	United States of America - États-Unis d'Amérique 2014 (C) Male — Masculin Number Nombre	Rate Taux	Female — Féminin Number Nombre	Rate Taux
TOTAL	53	45	52	25	1 328 239	847.2	1 298 179	802.4
Certain infectious and parasitic diseases — Certaines maladies infectieuses et parasitaires								
Total	2	-	1	-	36 131	23.0	34 282	21.2
Intestinal infectious diseases — Maladies infectieuses intestinales	1	-	-	-	3 944	2.5	5 886	3.6
Tuberculosis — Tuberculose	-	-	-	-	315	0.2	178	0.1
Tetanus — Tétanos	-	-	-	-	-	-	1	♦0.0
Diphtheria — Diphtérie	-	-	-	-	-	-	-	-
Whooping cough — Coqueluche	-	-	-	-	9	♦0.0	5	♦0.0
Meningococcal infection — Infection à méningocoques	-	-	-	-	23	♦0.0	20	♦0.0
Septicaemia — Septicémie	-	-	-	-	18 333	11.7	20 607	12.7
Acute poliomyelitis — Poliomyélite aiguë	-	-	-	-	-	-	-	-
Measles — Rougeole	-	-	-	-	-	-	-	-
Viral hepatitis — Hépatite virale	1	-	-	-	5 314	3.4	2 767	1.7
Human immunodeficiency virus [HIV] disease — Maladies dues au virus de l'immunodéficience humaine (VIH)	-	-	1	-	4 938	3.1	1 783	1.1
Malaria — Paludisme	-	-	-	-	4	♦0.0	4	♦0.0
Neoplasms — Tumeurs	6	10	7	3	319 836	204.0	287 958	178.0
Malignant neoplasms — Tumeurs malignes								
Total	6	10	7	3	311 309	198.6	280 418	173.3
Malignant neoplasm of lip, oral cavity and pharynx — Tumeur maligne de la lèvre, de la cavité buccale et du pharynx	-	-	-	-	6 769	4.3	2 636	1.6
Malignant neoplasm of oesophagus — Tumeur maligne de l'oesophage	-	1	-	-	11 953	7.6	2 982	1.8
Malignant neoplasm of stomach — Tumeur maligne de l'estomac	-	-	1	-	6 786	4.3	4 525	2.8
Malignant neoplasm of colon, rectosigmoid junction, rectum, anus and anal canal — Tumeur maligne du côlon, de la jonction recto-sigmoïdienne, du rectum, de l'anus et du canal anal	-	2	-	-	27 303	17.4	24 931	15.4
Malignant neoplasm of liver and intrahepatic bile ducts — Tumeur maligne du foie et des voies bilaires intrahépatiques	1	-	-	-	16 623	10.6	8 075	5.0
Malignant neoplasm of pancreas — Tumeur maligne du pancréas	-	-	1	-	20 755	13.2	19 664	12.2
Malignant neoplasm of trachea, bronchus and lung — Tumeur maligne de la trachée, des bronches et du poumon	1	1	2	1	84 910	54.2	70 700	43.7
Malignant neoplasm of female breast — Tumeur maligne du sein chez la femme	..	2	..	-	..	..	41 213	...
Malignant neoplasm of cervix uteri — Tumeur maligne du col de l'utérus	..	1	..	1	..	..	4 115	...
Malignant neoplasm of prostate — Tumeur maligne de la prostate	2	..	1	..	28 344	...	..	..
Malignant neoplasm of lymphoid, haematopoietic and related tissue — Tumeurs malignes primitives ou présumées primitives des tissus lymphoïde, hématopoïétique et apparentés	1	1	-	1	32 293	20.6	25 271	15.6
Disorders of the blood and blood-forming organs and certain disorders involving the immune mechanism — Maladies du sang et des organes hématopoïétiques et certains troubles du système immunitaire								
Total	-	-	-	1	4 785	3.1	5 903	3.6
Anaemias — Anémies	-	-	-	-	2 196	1.4	3 023	1.9
Endocrine, nutritional and metabolic diseases — Maladies endocriniennes, nutritionnelles et métaboliques								
Total	4	5	2	4	58 332	37.2	54 405	33.6
Diabetes mellitus — Diabète sucré	3	4	2	3	41 111	26.2	35 377	21.9
Malnutrition — Malnutrition	-	-	-	-	1 556	1.0	2 377	1.5
Mental and behavioural disorders — Troubles mentaux et du comportement	1	2	-	-	53 793	34.3	97 255	60.1
Diseases of the nervous system — Maladies du système nerveux	-	-	2	2	66 890	42.7	98 544	60.9
Diseases of the circulatory system — Maladies de l'appareil circulatoire								
Total	19	12	18	11	408 739	260.7	399 021	246.6
Acute rheumatic fever and chronic rheumatic heart diseases — Rhumatisme articularie aigu et cardiopathies rhumatismales chroniques	-	-	-	-	1 083	0.7	2 198	1.4
Hypertensive diseases — Maladies hypertensives	1	1	2	1	34 681	22.1	38 651	23.9
Ischaemic heart disease — Cardiopathie ischémique	13	6	11	5	207 412	132.3	157 181	97.2

20. Death and death rates by cause and sex: 2012 - 2016
Décès et taux de mortalité par cause et sexe : 2012 - 2016 (continued - suite)

Cause of death — Cause de décès	Turks and Caicos Islands - Îles Turques et Caïques 2013 (...) Male — Masculin Number Nombre	Female — Féminin Number Nombre	2014 (...) Male — Masculin Number Nombre	Female — Féminin Number Nombre	United States of America - États-Unis d'Amérique 2014 (C) Male — Masculin Number Nombre	Rate Taux	Female — Féminin Number Nombre	Rate Taux
Cerebrovascular disease — Maladie cérébrovasculaire	2	3	1	3	55 471	35.4	77 632	48.0
Diseases of arteries, arterioles and capillaries — Maladies des artères, artérioles et capillaires	1	-	1	2	12 933	8.2	12 622	7.8
Diseases of the respiratory system — Maladies de l'appareil respiratoire								
Total	1	2	5	1	125 697	80.2	132 636	82.0
Influenza — Grippe	-	-	-	-	1 918	1.2	2 010	1.2
Pneumonia — Pneumopathies	-	1	4	1	24 313	15.5	26 309	16.3
Chronic lower respiratory diseases — Maladies chroniques des voies respiratoires inférieures	1	1	-	-	69 456	44.3	77 645	48.0
Diseases of the digestive system — Maladies de l'appareil digestif								
Total	2	-	2	1	53 682	34.2	47 307	29.2
Gastric and duodenal ulcer — Ulcère de l'estomac et du duodénum	-	-	-	-	1 565	1.0	1 441	0.9
Diseases of the liver — Maladies du foie	-	-	1	-	31 304	20.0	19 377	12.0
Diseases of the musculoskeletal system and connective tissue — Maladies du système ostéo-articularie, des muscles et du tissu conjonctif	-	-	-	-	4 762	3.0	8 582	5.3
Diseases of the genitourinary system — Maladies de l'appareil génito-urinaire								
Total	-	2	1	-	31 587	20.1	34 578	21.4
Disorders of kidney and ureter — Affections du rein et de l'uretère	-	1	1	-	26 526	16.9	26 120	16.1
Hyperplasia of prostate — Hyperplasie de la prostate	-	..	-	..	547	...		..
Pregnancy, childbirth and the puerperium — Grossesse, accouchement et puerpéralité								
Total	..	-	..	-	..	..	1 123	28.2
Pregnancy with abortive outcome — Grossesse se terminant par un avortement	..	-	..	-	..	..	28	♦0.7
Other direct obstetric causes — Autres décès maternels directs	..	-	..	-	..	..	536	13.4
Indirect obstetric causes — Décès maternels indirects	..	-	..	-	..	..	292	7.3
Certain conditions originating in the perinatal period — Certaines affections dont l'origine se situe dans la période périnatale	1	1	-	-	6 702	328.4	5 194	266.7
Congenital malformations, deformations and chromosomal abnormalities — Malformations congénitales et anomalies chromosomiques	1	-	-	-	4 991	244.6	4 618	237.1
Symptoms, signs and abnormal clinical and laboratory findings, not elsewhere classified — Symptômes, signes et résultats anormaux d'examens cliniques et de laboratoire, non classés ailleurs	-	-	5	1	14 689	9.4	17 553	10.8
All other diseases — Toutes autres maladies	-	1	-	-	1 982	1.3	2 565	1.6
External causes — Causes externes								
Total	16	10	9	1	135 641	86.5	66 655	41.2
Accidents								
Total	13	8	4	1	84 256	53.7	50 004	30.9
Transport accidents — Accidents de transport	12	6	3	-	26 650	17.0	10 545	6.5
Falls — Chutes	-	-	-	-	16 029	10.2	15 930	9.8
Accidental drowning and submersion — Noyade et submersion accidentelles	1	2	1	1	2 640	1.7	766	0.5
Exposure to smoke, fire and flames — Exposition à la fumée, au feu et aux flammes	-	-	-	-	1 627	1.0	1 074	0.7
Accidental poisoning by and exposure to noxious substances — Intoxication accidentelle par des substances nocives et exposition à ces substances	-	-	-	-	27 225	17.4	14 807	9.2
Intentional self-harm — Lésions auto-infligées	-	-	1	-	33 059	21.1	9 645	6.0
Assault — Agresssions	3	1	2	-	12 279	7.8	3 283	2.0
All other external causes — Toutes autres causes externes	-	1	2	-	6 047	3.9	3 723	2.3

20. Death and death rates by cause and sex: 2012 - 2016
Décès et taux de mortalité par cause et sexe : 2012 - 2016 (continued - suite)

Cause of death — Cause de décès	United States of America - États-Unis d'Amérique 2015 (C)				United States Virgin Islands - Îles Vierges américaines 2012 (...)		2015 (...)	
	Male — Masculin		Female — Féminin		Male — Masculin	Female — Féminin	Male — Masculin	Female — Féminin
	Number Nombre	Rate Taux	Number Nombre	Rate Taux	Number Nombre	Number Nombre	Number Nombre	Number Nombre
TOTAL	1 373 404	869.5	1 339 226	821.9	*432*	*291*	*384*	*271*
Certain infectious and parasitic diseases — Certaines maladies infectieuses et parasitaires								
Total	37 156	23.5	34 934	21.4	*18*	*9*	*13*	*11*
Intestinal infectious diseases — Maladies infectieuses intestinales	4 070	2.6	6 061	3.7	-	-	*1*	*1*
Tuberculosis — Tuberculose	307	0.2	163	0.1	-	-	-	-
Tetanus — Tétanos	1	✦0.0	2	✦0.0	-	-	-	-
Diphtheria — Diphtérie....................................	-	-	-	-	-	-	-	-
Whooping cough — Coqueluche	4	✦0.0	3	✦0.0	-	-	-	-
Meningococcal infection — Infection à méningocoques ...	20	✦0.0	20	✦0.0	-	-	-	-
Septicaemia — Septicémie	19 385	12.3	21 388	13.1	*12*	*4*	*6*	*6*
Acute poliomyelitis — Poliomyélite aiguë	-	-	-	-	-	-	-	-
Measles — Rougeole......................................	-	-	-	-	-	-	-	-
Viral hepatitis — Hépatite virale.......................	4 977	3.2	2 484	1.5	-	-	*1*	-
Human immunodeficiency virus [HIV] disease — Maladies dues au virus de l'immunodéficience humaine (VIH)	4 796	3.0	1 669	1.0	*5*	*4*	*4*	*3*
Malaria — Paludisme......................................	6	✦0.0	2	✦0.0	-	-	-	-
Neoplasms — Tumeurs	322 487	204.2	289 774	177.8	*91*	*66*	*81*	*53*
Malignant neoplasms — Tumeurs malignes								
Total	313 833	198.7	282 122	173.1	*88*	*66*	*78*	*53*
Malignant neoplasm of lip, oral cavity and pharynx — Tumeur maligne de la lèvre, de la cavité buccale et du pharynx ...	6 882	4.4	2 872	1.8	*2*	*1*	*1*	*2*
Malignant neoplasm of oesophagus — Tumeur maligne de l'oesophage	12 187	7.7	3 025	1.9	*2*	*3*	*1*	*5*
Malignant neoplasm of stomach — Tumeur maligne de l'estomac	6 754	4.3	4 577	2.8	*6*	*3*	*2*	-
Malignant neoplasm of colon, rectosigmoid junction, rectum, anus and anal canal — Tumeur maligne du côlon, de la jonction recto-sigmoïdienne, du rectum, de l'anus et du canal anal...	27 805	17.6	25 371	15.6	*13*	*6*	*8*	*5*
Malignant neoplasm of liver and intrahepatic bile ducts — Tumeur maligne du foie et des voies bilaires intrahépatiques ...	17 414	11.0	8 347	5.1	*2*	*3*	*1*	-
Malignant neoplasm of pancreas — Tumeur maligne du pancréas...................	21 392	13.5	20 223	12.4	*4*	*3*	*1*	*2*
Malignant neoplasm of trachea, bronchus and lung — Tumeur maligne de la trachée, des bronches et du poumon ...	83 700	53.0	70 119	43.0	*11*	*6*	*10*	*10*
Malignant neoplasm of female breast — Tumeur maligne du sein chez la femme	..	..	41 524	31.1		*17*		*11*
Malignant neoplasm of cervix uteri — Tumeur maligne du col de l'utérus.........	..	..	4 175	3.1		*2*	..	*1*
Malignant neoplasm of prostate — Tumeur maligne de la prostate	28 848	55.7	..	..	*25*	..	*22*	..
Malignant neoplasm of lymphoid, haematopoietic and related tissue — Tumeurs malignes primitives ou présumées primitives des tissus lymphoïde, hématopoïétique et apparentés	32 345	20.5	24 405	15.0	*4*	*5*	*10*	*5*
Disorders of the blood and blood-forming organs and certain disorders involving the immune mechanism — Maladies du sang et des organes hématopoïétiques et certains troubles du système immunitaire								
Total	4 896	3.1	5 749	3.5	*2*	*1*	-	-
Anaemias — Anémies	2 253	1.4	2 997	1.8	*1*	-	-	-
Endocrine, nutritional and metabolic diseases — Maladies endocriniennes, nutritionnelles et métaboliques								
Total	61 694	39.1	56 838	34.9	*24*	*22*	*23*	*19*
Diabetes mellitus — Diabète sucré....................	43 123	27.3	36 412	22.3	*23*	*17*	*21*	*16*
Malnutrition — Malnutrition	1 870	1.2	3 140	1.9	-	*1*	*1*	-
Mental and behavioural disorders — Troubles mentaux et du comportement	49 564	31.4	87 092	53.5	*15*	*9*	*16*	*7*
Diseases of the nervous system — Maladies du système nerveux..................	76 012	48.1	114 500	70.3	*18*	*18*	*16*	*22*
Diseases of the circulatory system — Maladies de l'appareil circulatoire								
Total	422 345	267.4	414 181	254.2	*108*	*101*	*114*	*101*
Acute rheumatic fever and chronic rheumatic heart diseases — Rhumatisme articularie aigu et cardiopathies rhumatismales chroniques ...	1 119	0.7	2 253	1.4	-	*1*	-	-
Hypertensive diseases — Maladies hypertensives.......	37 098	23.5	41 756	25.6	*19*	*35*	*24*	*32*
Ischaemic heart disease — Cardiopathie ischémique ...	209 298	132.5	157 503	96.7	*47*	*28*	*43*	*22*

20. Death and death rates by cause and sex: 2012 - 2016
Décès et taux de mortalité par cause et sexe : 2012 - 2016 (continued - suite)

Cause of death — Cause de décès	United States of America - États-Unis d'Amérique 2015 (C)				United States Virgin Islands - Îles Vierges américaines			
	Male — Masculin		Female — Féminin		2012 (...)		2015 (...)	
					Male — Masculin	Female — Féminin	Male — Masculin	Female — Féminin
	Number Nombre	Rate Taux	Number Nombre	Rate Taux	Number Nombre	Number Nombre	Number Nombre	Number Nombre
Cerebrovascular disease — Maladie cérébrovasculaire............	58 288	36.9	82 035	50.3	15	16	20	22
Diseases of arteries, arterioles and capillaries — Maladies des artères, artérioles et capillaires	12 887	8.2	12 772	7.8	1	3	4	1
Diseases of the respiratory system — Maladies de l'appareil respiratoire								
Total	130 590	82.7	140 639	86.3	18	12	13	11
Influenza — Grippe..........	2 125	1.3	3 110	1.9	-	-	-	-
Pneumonia — Pneumopathies..........	24 766	15.7	27 045	16.6	4	2	4	2
Chronic lower respiratory diseases — Maladies chroniques des voies respiratoires inférieures	72 498	45.9	82 543	50.7	5	6	5	5
Diseases of the digestive system — Maladies de l'appareil digestif								
Total	55 376	35.1	49 268	30.2	20	8	14	7
Gastric and duodenal ulcer — Ulcère de l'estomac et du duodénum..........	1 543	1.0	1 470	0.9	1	-	1	-
Diseases of the liver — Maladies du foie..........	32 342	20.5	20 524	12.6	16	3	8	5
Diseases of the musculoskeletal system and connective tissue — Maladies du système ostéo-articularie, des muscles et du tissu conjonctif	4 890	3.1	8 779	5.4	3	3	1	2
Diseases of the genitourinary system — Maladies de l'appareil génito-urinaire								
Total	33 450	21.2	35 923	22.0	8	5	6	10
Disorders of kidney and ureter — Affections du rein et de l'uretère	28 018	17.7	27 203	16.7	6	5	4	9
Hyperplasia of prostate — Hyperplasie de la prostate..........	571	1.1	..	..	1	..	-	..
Pregnancy, childbirth and the puerperium — Grossesse, accouchement et puerpéralité								
Total	..	..	1 140	28.7	..	-	..	-
Pregnancy with abortive outcome — Grossesse se terminant par un avortement	..	..	19	♦0.5	..	-	..	-
Other direct obstetric causes — Autres décès maternels directs	..	..	547	13.7	..	-	..	-
Indirect obstetric causes — Décès maternels indirects	..	..	266	6.7	..	-	..	-
Certain conditions originating in the perinatal period — Certaines affections dont l'origine se situe dans la période périnatale	6 494	318.9	5 221	268.8	3	2	-	-
Congenital malformations, deformations and chromosomal abnormalities — Malformations congénitales et anomalies chromosomiques	5 316	261.1	4 701	242.0	2	-	1	-
Symptoms, signs and abnormal clinical and laboratory findings, not elsewhere classified — Symptômes, signes et résultats anormaux d'examens cliniques et de laboratoire, non classés ailleurs	14 917	9.4	17 130	10.5	16	20	20	18
All other diseases — Toutes autres maladies..........	2 121	1.3	2 764	1.7	1	-	1	1
External causes — Causes externes								
Total	146 096	92.5	70 593	43.3	85	15	65	9
Accidents								
Total	91 633	58.0	53 084	32.6	26	9	20	6
Transport accidents — Accidents de transport..........	28 482	18.0	11 193	6.9	12	5	11	2
Falls — Chutes..........	16 881	10.7	16 500	10.1	-	-	1	1
Accidental drowning and submersion — Noyade et submersion accidentelles	2 716	1.7	886	0.5	7	-	4	2
Exposure to smoke, fire and flames — Exposition à la fumée, au feu et aux flammes..........	1 586	1.0	1 060	0.7	1	2	-	-
Accidental poisoning by and exposure to noxious substances — Intoxication accidentelle par des substances nocives et exposition à ces substances	31 436	19.9	16 042	9.8	-	1	-	1
Intentional self-harm — Lésions auto-infligées..........	33 959	21.5	10 186	6.3	6	4	3	-
Assault — Agresssions..........	14 051	8.9	3 474	2.1	49	2	40	3
All other external causes — Toutes autres causes externes	6 453	4.1	3 849	2.4	4	-	2	-

20. Death and death rates by cause and sex: 2012 - 2016
Décès et taux de mortalité par cause et sexe : 2012 - 2016 (continued - suite)

Argentina - Argentine

Cause of death — Cause de décès	2014 (+C)				2015 (+C)			
	Male — Masculin		Female — Féminin		Male — Masculin		Female — Féminin	
	Number Nombre	Rate Taux	Number Nombre	Rate Taux	Number Nombre	Rate Taux	Number Nombre	Rate Taux
TOTAL	166 178	795.3	155 523	714.3	170 333	806.1	160 074	727.6
Certain infectious and parasitic diseases — Certaines maladies infectieuses et parasitaires								
Total	7 356	35.2	6 984	32.1	6 789	32.1	6 679	30.4
Intestinal infectious diseases — Maladies infectieuses intestinales	181	0.9	256	1.2	225	1.1	283	1.3
Tuberculosis — Tuberculose	380	1.8	184	0.8	406	1.9	193	0.9
Tetanus — Tétanos	2	◆0.0	2	◆0.0	5	◆0.0	1	◆0.0
Diphtheria — Diphtérie	-	-	-	-	-	-	-	-
Whooping cough — Coqueluche	1	◆0.0	3	◆0.0	7	◆0.0	4	◆0.0
Meningococcal infection — Infection à méningocoques	9	◆0.0	15	◆0.1	9	◆0.0	11	◆0.0
Septicaemia — Septicémie	5 188	24.8	5 604	25.7	4 448	21.0	5 181	23.5
Acute poliomyelitis — Poliomyélite aiguë	-	-	-	-	-	-	-	-
Measles — Rougeole	-	-	-	-	-	-	-	-
Viral hepatitis — Hépatite virale	82	0.4	69	0.3	97	0.5	95	0.4
Human immunodeficiency virus [HIV] disease — Maladies dues au virus de l'immunodéficience humaine (VIH)	965	4.6	495	2.3	1 054	5.0	483	2.2
Malaria — Paludisme	-	-	-	-	1	◆0.0	-	-
Neoplasms — Tumeurs	32 758	156.8	30 267	139.0	33 918	160.5	31 112	141.4
Malignant neoplasms — Tumeurs malignes								
Total	31 399	150.3	29 002	133.2	32 444	153.5	29 751	135.2
Malignant neoplasm of lip, oral cavity and pharynx — Tumeur maligne de la lèvre, de la cavité buccale et du pharynx	627	3.0	277	1.3	607	2.9	273	1.2
Malignant neoplasm of oesophagus — Tumeur maligne de l'oesophage	1 201	5.7	568	2.6	1 163	5.5	574	2.6
Malignant neoplasm of stomach — Tumeur maligne de l'estomac	1 855	8.9	1 009	4.6	1 939	9.2	1 072	4.9
Malignant neoplasm of colon, rectosigmoid junction, rectum, anus and anal canal — Tumeur maligne du côlon, de la jonction recto-sigmoïdienne, du rectum, de l'anus et du canal anal	3 902	18.7	3 387	15.6	4 067	19.2	3 487	15.8
Malignant neoplasm of liver and intrahepatic bile ducts — Tumeur maligne du foie et des voies bilaires intrahépatiques	1 042	5.0	784	3.6	1 164	5.5	839	3.8
Malignant neoplasm of pancreas — Tumeur maligne du pancréas	1 921	9.2	2 125	9.8	1 989	9.4	2 253	10.2
Malignant neoplasm of trachea, bronchus and lung — Tumeur maligne de la trachée, des bronches et du poumon	6 264	30.0	3 020	13.9	6 595	31.2	3 131	14.2
Malignant neoplasm of female breast — Tumeur maligne du sein chez la femme	..	..	5 622	34.0	..	..	5 932	35.5
Malignant neoplasm of cervix uteri — Tumeur maligne du col de l'utérus	..	..	1 104	6.7	..	..	1 108	6.6
Malignant neoplasm of prostate — Tumeur maligne de la prostate	3 683	78.9	...	..	3 819	80.4	...	..
Malignant neoplasm of lymphoid, haematopoietic and related tissue — Tumeurs malignes primitives ou présumées primitives des tissus lymphoïde, hématopoïétique et apparentés	2 182	10.4	1 820	8.4	2 331	11.0	1 883	8.6
Disorders of the blood and blood-forming organs and certain disorders involving the immune mechanism — Maladies du sang et des organes hématopoïétiques et certains troubles du système immunitaire								
Total	563	2.7	761	3.5	605	2.9	756	3.4
Anaemias — Anémies	334	1.6	529	2.4	379	1.8	531	2.4
Endocrine, nutritional and metabolic diseases — Maladies endocriniennes, nutritionnelles et métaboliques								
Total	5 407	25.9	5 772	26.5	6 091	28.8	6 427	29.2
Diabetes mellitus — Diabète sucré	4 144	19.8	3 977	18.3	4 742	22.4	4 414	20.1
Malnutrition — Malnutrition	373	1.8	388	1.8	377	1.8	496	2.3
Mental and behavioural disorders — Troubles mentaux et du comportement	1 141	5.5	1 501	6.9	1 108	5.2	1 413	6.4
Diseases of the nervous system — Maladies du système nerveux	2 196	10.5	2 506	11.5	2 382	11.3	2 879	13.1
Diseases of the circulatory system — Maladies de l'appareil circulatoire								
Total	45 031	215.5	46 094	211.7	47 123	223.0	48 279	219.4
Acute rheumatic fever and chronic rheumatic heart diseases — Rhumatisme articulaire aigu et cardiopathies rhumatismales chroniques	45	0.2	97	0.4	63	0.3	95	0.4
Hypertensive diseases — Maladies hypertensives	2 666	12.8	3 486	16.0	3 538	16.7	4 642	21.1
Ischaemic heart disease — Cardiopathie ischémique	11 687	55.9	8 122	37.3	12 739	60.3	9 179	41.7
Cerebrovascular disease — Maladie cérébrovasculaire	9 540	45.7	10 132	46.5	10 194	48.2	10 557	48.0

Argentina - Argentine

Cause of death — Cause de décès	2014 (+C)				2015 (+C)			
	Male — Masculin		Female — Féminin		Male — Masculin		Female — Féminin	
	Number Nombre	Rate Taux	Number Nombre	Rate Taux	Number Nombre	Rate Taux	Number Nombre	Rate Taux
Diseases of arteries, arterioles and capillaries — Maladies des artères, artérioles et capillaires	1 301	6.2	821	3.8	1 415	6.7	976	4.4
Diseases of the respiratory system — Maladies de l'appareil respiratoire								
Total	25 937	124.1	27 748	127.4	27 083	128.2	29 453	133.9
Influenza — Grippe	-	-	3	+0.0	5	+0.0	6	+0.0
Pneumonia — Pneumopathies	11 413	54.6	12 940	59.4	12 869	60.9	14 749	67.0
Chronic lower respiratory diseases — Maladies chroniques des voies respiratoires inférieures	3 926	18.8	2 485	11.4	4 531	21.4	3 096	14.1
Diseases of the digestive system — Maladies de l'appareil digestif								
Total	8 681	41.5	5 984	27.5	9 702	45.9	6 497	29.5
Gastric and duodenal ulcer — Ulcère de l'estomac et du duodénum	207	1.0	170	0.8	264	1.2	203	0.9
Diseases of the liver — Maladies du foie	4 063	19.4	1 423	6.5	4 508	21.3	1 501	6.8
Diseases of the musculoskeletal system and connective tissue — Maladies du système ostéo-articularie, des muscles et du tissu conjonctif	334	1.6	734	3.4	354	1.7	767	3.5
Diseases of the genitourinary system — Maladies de l'appareil génito-urinaire								
Total	5 648	27.0	6 102	28.0	6 268	29.7	6 560	29.8
Disorders of kidney and ureter — Affections du rein et de l'uretère	4 341	20.8	4 181	19.2	4 732	22.4	4 295	19.5
Hyperplasia of prostate — Hyperplasie de la prostate	42	0.9	..	..	51	1.1	..	..
Pregnancy, childbirth and the puerperium — Grossesse, accouchement et puerpéralité								
Total	..	..	307	39.5	..	..	333	43.2
Pregnancy with abortive outcome — Grossesse se terminant par un avortement	..	..	43	5.5	..	..	54	7.0
Other direct obstetric causes — Autres décès maternels directs	..	..	176	22.7	..	..	158	20.5
Indirect obstetric causes — Décès maternels indirects	..	..	64	8.2	..	..	81	10.5
Certain conditions originating in the perinatal period — Certaines affections dont l'origine se situe dans la période périnatale	2 355	588.5	1 702	451.9	2 117	534.9	1 544	412.7
Congenital malformations, deformations and chromosomal abnormalities — Malformations congénitales et anomalies chromosomiques	1 441	360.1	1 340	355.8	1 345	339.9	1 242	332.0
Symptoms, signs and abnormal clinical and laboratory findings, not elsewhere classified — Symptômes, signes et résultats anormaux d'examens cliniques et de laboratoire, non classés ailleurs	11 515	55.1	11 485	52.7	9 824	46.5	9 508	43.2
All other diseases — Toutes autres maladies	687	3.3	1 157	5.3	874	4.1	1 451	6.6
External causes — Causes externes								
Total	15 128	72.4	5 079	23.3	14 750	69.8	5 174	23.5
Accidents								
Total	7 631	36.5	2 980	13.7	7 518	35.6	3 108	14.1
Transport accidents — Accidents de transport	4 091	19.6	1 134	5.2	3 888	18.4	998	4.5
Falls — Chutes	195	0.9	121	0.6	231	1.1	113	0.5
Accidental drowning and submersion — Noyade et submersion accidentelles	331	1.6	68	0.3	323	1.5	64	0.3
Exposure to smoke, fire and flames — Exposition à la fumée, au feu et aux flammes	207	1.0	107	0.5	181	0.9	86	0.4
Accidental poisoning by and exposure to noxious substances — Intoxication accidentelle par des substances nocives et exposition à ces substances	191	0.9	103	0.5	174	0.8	80	0.4
Intentional self-harm — Lésions auto-infligées	2 560	12.3	688	3.2	2 492	11.8	608	2.8
Assault — Agresssions	2 012	9.6	307	1.4	1 950	9.2	303	1.4
All other external causes — Toutes autres causes externes	2 925	14.0	1 104	5.1	2 790	13.2	1 155	5.2

20. Death and death rates by cause and sex: 2012 - 2016
Décès et taux de mortalité par cause et sexe : 2012 - 2016 (continued - suite)

Brazil - Brésil

Cause of death — Cause de décès	2014 (C)				2015 (C)			
	Male — Masculin		Female — Féminin		Male — Masculin		Female — Féminin	
	Number Nombre	Rate Taux	Number Nombre	Rate Taux	Number Nombre	Rate Taux	Number Nombre	Rate Taux
TOTAL	693 922	692.8	532 362	518.8	709 117	702.4	554 383	535.7
Certain infectious and parasitic diseases — Certaines maladies infectieuses et parasitaires								
Total	29 808	29.8	22 338	21.8	30 994	30.7	24 020	23.2
Intestinal infectious diseases — Maladies infectieuses intestinales	1 904	1.9	2 404	2.3	1 971	2.0	2 401	2.3
Tuberculosis — Tuberculose	3 330	3.3	1 134	1.1	3 437	3.4	1 171	1.1
Tetanus — Tétanos	64	0.1	18	◆0.0	67	0.1	21	◆0.0
Diphtheria — Diphtérie..........	-	-	4	◆0.0	4	◆0.0	-	-
Whooping cough — Coqueluche	44	0.0	89	0.1	20	◆0.0	22	◆0.0
Meningococcal infection — Infection à méningocoques	144	0.1	113	0.1	106	0.1	104	0.1
Septicaemia — Septicémie..........	8 209	8.2	8 643	8.4	8 956	8.9	9 637	9.3
Acute poliomyelitis — Poliomyélite aiguë	-	-	-	-	-	-	-	-
Measles — Rougeole..........	-	-	-	-	-	-	-	-
Viral hepatitis — Hépatite virale..........	1 805	1.8	1 077	1.0	1 695	1.7	1 116	1.1
Human immunodeficiency virus [HIV] disease — Maladies dues au virus de l'immunodéficience humaine (VIH)..........	8 413	8.4	4 158	4.1	8 384	8.3	4 280	4.1
Malaria — Paludisme..........	22	◆0.0	14	◆0.0	20	◆0.0	15	◆0.0
Neoplasms — Tumeurs	107 308	107.1	94 636	92.2	111 105	110.1	98 662	95.3
Malignant neoplasms — Tumeurs malignes								
Total	105 426	105.3	92 853	90.5	109 230	108.2	96 755	93.5
Malignant neoplasm of lip, oral cavity and pharynx — Tumeur maligne de la lèvre, de la cavité buccale et du pharynx	5 766	5.8	1 601	1.6	6 146	6.1	1 528	1.5
Malignant neoplasm of oesophagus — Tumeur maligne de l'oesophage	6 275	6.3	1 823	1.8	6 525	6.5	1 876	1.8
Malignant neoplasm of stomach — Tumeur maligne de l'estomac ...	9 021	9.0	5 005	4.9	9 132	9.0	5 132	5.0
Malignant neoplasm of colon, rectosigmoid junction, rectum, anus and anal canal — Tumeur maligne du côlon, de la jonction recto-sigmoïdienne, du rectum, de l'anus et du canal anal..........	7 864	7.9	8 457	8.2	8 163	8.1	8 533	8.2
Malignant neoplasm of liver and intrahepatic bile ducts — Tumeur maligne du foie et des voies bilaires intrahépatiques	5 234	5.2	3 931	3.8	5 647	5.6	4 063	3.9
Malignant neoplasm of pancreas — Tumeur maligne du pancréas..........	4 476	4.5	4 415	4.3	4 654	4.6	4 808	4.6
Malignant neoplasm of trachea, bronchus and lung — Tumeur maligne de la trachée, des bronches et du poumon..........	15 127	15.1	10 299	10.0	15 514	15.4	10 978	10.6
Malignant neoplasm of female breast — Tumeur maligne du sein chez la femme..........	..	..	14 622	18.5	..	..	15 403	19.2
Malignant neoplasm of cervix uteri — Tumeur maligne du col de l'utérus........	..	..	5 448	6.9	..	..	5 727	7.1
Malignant neoplasm of prostate — Tumeur maligne de la prostate	14 161	70.0	..	..	14 484	69.2	..	..
Malignant neoplasm of lymphoid, haematopoietic and related tissue — Tumeurs malignes primitives ou présumées primitives des tissus lymphoïde, hématopoïétique et apparentés..........	7 629	7.6	6 533	6.4	7 940	7.9	6 791	6.6
Disorders of the blood and blood-forming organs and certain disorders involving the immune mechanism — Maladies du sang et des organes hématopoïétiques et certains troubles du système immunitaire								
Total	2 970	3.0	3 124	3.0	3 218	3.2	3 272	3.2
Anaemias — Anémies	2 034	2.0	2 048	2.0	2 171	2.2	2 180	2.1
Endocrine, nutritional and metabolic diseases — Maladies endocriniennes, nutritionnelles et métaboliques								
Total	33 589	33.5	40 360	39.3	34 677	34.3	41 551	40.1
Diabetes mellitus — Diabète sucré..........	25 761	25.7	32 102	31.3	26 800	26.5	32 836	31.7
Malnutrition — Malnutrition	3 323	3.3	2 982	2.9	3 213	3.2	3 025	2.9
Mental and behavioural disorders — Troubles mentaux et du comportement	8 810	8.8	3 495	3.4	8 911	8.8	3 513	3.4
Diseases of the nervous system — Maladies du système nerveux..........	14 772	14.7	17 585	17.1	15 668	15.5	19 048	18.4
Diseases of the circulatory system — Maladies de l'appareil circulatoire								
Total	178 337	178.1	161 956	157.8	182 529	180.8	167 018	161.4
Acute rheumatic fever and chronic rheumatic heart diseases — Rhumatisme articulaire aigu et cardiopathies rhumatismales chroniques	759	0.8	1 263	1.2	749	0.7	1 300	1.3
Hypertensive diseases — Maladies hypertensives..........	21 380	21.3	24 384	23.8	21 893	21.7	25 387	24.5
Ischaemic heart disease — Cardiopathie ischémique	62 940	62.8	44 952	43.8	65 224	64.6	46 625	45.1
Cerebrovascular disease — Maladie cérébrovasculaire..........	49 830	49.8	49 434	48.2	50 251	49.8	50 252	48.6

20. Death and death rates by cause and sex: 2012 - 2016
Décès et taux de mortalité par cause et sexe : 2012 - 2016 (continued - suite)

Brazil - Brésil

Cause of death — Cause de décès	2014 (C)				2015 (C)			
	Male — Masculin		Female — Féminin		Male — Masculin		Female — Féminin	
	Number Nombre	Rate Taux	Number Nombre	Rate Taux	Number Nombre	Rate Taux	Number Nombre	Rate Taux
Diseases of arteries, arterioles and capillaries — Maladies des artères, artérioles et capillaires	6 874	6.9	5 535	5.4	6 947	6.9	5 806	5.6
Diseases of the respiratory system — Maladies de l'appareil respiratoire								
Total	71 562	71.4	67 406	65.7	76 283	75.6	73 219	70.7
Influenza — Grippe	150	0.1	129	0.1	115	0.1	139	0.1
Pneumonia — Pneumopathies	34 833	34.8	36 045	35.1	37 793	37.4	39 518	38.2
Chronic lower respiratory diseases — Maladies chroniques des voies respiratoires inférieures	23 531	23.5	18 679	18.2	24 671	24.4	20 472	19.8
Diseases of the digestive system — Maladies de l'appareil digestif								
Total	39 046	39.0	23 722	23.1	39 965	39.6	24 259	23.4
Gastric and duodenal ulcer — Ulcère de l'estomac et du duodénum	1 986	2.0	1 185	1.2	2 014	2.0	1 260	1.2
Diseases of the liver — Maladies du foie	20 330	20.3	6 030	5.9	20 543	20.3	5 944	5.7
Diseases of the musculoskeletal system and connective tissue — Maladies du système ostéo-articularie, des muscles et du tissu conjonctif	1 912	1.9	3 412	3.3	1 986	2.0	3 393	3.3
Diseases of the genitourinary system — Maladies de l'appareil génito-urinaire								
Total	15 700	15.7	16 790	16.4	17 691	17.5	18 851	18.2
Disorders of kidney and ureter — Affections du rein et de l'uretère	9 240	9.2	8 067	7.9	10 071	10.0	8 828	8.5
Hyperplasia of prostate — Hyperplasie de la prostate	698	3.5	..	..	754	3.6	..	..
Pregnancy, childbirth and the puerperium — Grossesse, accouchement et puerpéralité								
Total	..	..	1 889	64.8	..	..	1 896	64.2
Pregnancy with abortive outcome — Grossesse se terminant par un avortement	..	..	121	4.2	..	..	121	4.1
Other direct obstetric causes — Autres décès maternels directs	..	..	1 100	37.8	..	..	1 119	37.9
Indirect obstetric causes — Décès maternels indirects	..	..	484	16.6	..	..	466	15.8
Certain conditions originating in the perinatal period — Certaines affections dont l'origine se situe dans la période périnatale	12 643	846.5	9 757	687.5	12 476	825.1	9 610	667.0
Congenital malformations, deformations and chromosomal abnormalities — Malformations congénitales et anomalies chromosomiques	5 788	387.5	5 155	363.3	5 654	373.9	5 222	362.5
Symptoms, signs and abnormal clinical and laboratory findings, not elsewhere classified — Symptômes, signes et résultats anormaux d'examens cliniques et de laboratoire, non classés ailleurs	40 437	40.4	30 597	29.8	40 721	40.3	30 854	29.8
All other diseases — Toutes autres maladies	1 924	1.9	2 549	2.5	2 295	2.3	2 842	2.7
External causes — Causes externes								
Total	129 316	129.1	27 591	26.9	124 944	123.8	27 153	26.2
Accidents								
Total	57 314	57.2	17 259	16.8	53 481	53.0	16 612	16.1
Transport accidents — Accidents de transport	36 764	36.7	8 044	7.8	32 590	32.3	6 937	6.7
Falls — Chutes	7 804	7.8	5 519	5.4	8 058	8.0	5 839	5.6
Accidental drowning and submersion — Noyade et submersion accidentelles	4 635	4.6	667	0.7	4 618	4.6	604	0.6
Exposure to smoke, fire and flames — Exposition à la fumée, au feu et aux flammes	693	0.7	334	0.3	590	0.6	343	0.3
Accidental poisoning by and exposure to noxious substances — Intoxication accidentelle par des substances nocives et exposition à ces substances	898	0.9	257	0.3	920	0.9	277	0.3
Intentional self-harm — Lésions auto-infligées	8 419	8.4	2 233	2.2	8 780	8.7	2 396	2.3
Assault — Agresssions	54 736	54.6	4 832	4.7	53 424	52.9	4 616	4.5
All other external causes — Toutes autres causes externes	8 847	8.8	3 267	3.2	9 259	9.2	3 529	3.4

Chile - Chili

Cause of death — Cause de décès	2014 (C)				2015 (C)			
	Male — Masculin		Female — Féminin		Male — Masculin		Female — Féminin	
	Number Nombre	Rate Taux	Number Nombre	Rate Taux	Number Nombre	Rate Taux	Number Nombre	Rate Taux
TOTAL	53 975	612.0	47 968	533.0	54 693	613.7	48 615	534.6
Certain infectious and parasitic diseases — Certaines maladies infectieuses et parasitaires								
Total	1 500	17.0	1 099	12.2	1 462	16.4	1 111	12.2
Intestinal infectious diseases — Maladies infectieuses intestinales	207	2.3	253	2.8	170	1.9	229	2.5
Tuberculosis — Tuberculose	150	1.7	61	0.7	175	2.0	70	0.8
Tetanus — Tétanos.................	2	♦0.0	1	♦0.0	-	-	-	-
Diphtheria — Diphtérie.................	-	-	-	-	-	-	-	-
Whooping cough — Coqueluche	4	♦0.0	12	♦0.1	8	♦0.1	2	♦0.0
Meningococcal infection — Infection à méningocoques.................	20	♦0.2	14	♦0.2	12	♦0.1	23	♦0.3
Septicaemia — Septicémie.................	329	3.7	415	4.6	317	3.6	400	4.4
Acute poliomyelitis — Poliomyélite aiguë	-	-	-	-	-	-	-	-
Measles — Rougeole.................	-	-	-	-	-	-	-	-
Viral hepatitis — Hépatite virale.................	66	0.7	41	0.5	26	♦0.3	41	0.5
Human immunodeficiency virus [HIV] disease — Maladies dues au virus de l'immunodéficience humaine (VIH).................	424	4.8	82	0.9	451	5.1	77	0.8
Malaria — Paludisme.................	-	-	-	-	-	-	-	-
Neoplasms — Tumeurs	13 634	154.6	12 408	137.9	14 045	157.6	12 821	141.0
Malignant neoplasms — Tumeurs malignes								
Total	13 134	148.9	11 878	132.0	13 503	151.5	12 261	134.8
Malignant neoplasm of lip, oral cavity and pharynx — Tumeur maligne de la lèvre, de la cavité buccale et du pharynx	151	1.7	69	0.8	158	1.8	90	1.0
Malignant neoplasm of oesophagus — Tumeur maligne de l'oesophage	376	4.3	274	3.0	387	4.3	275	3.0
Malignant neoplasm of stomach — Tumeur maligne de l'estomac	2 184	24.8	1 081	12.0	2 247	25.2	1 123	12.3
Malignant neoplasm of colon, rectosigmoid junction, rectum, anus and anal canal — Tumeur maligne du côlon, de la jonction recto-sigmoïdienne, du rectum, de l'anus et du canal anal.................	1 205	13.7	1 232	13.7	1 253	14.1	1 313	14.4
Malignant neoplasm of liver and intrahepatic bile ducts — Tumeur maligne du foie et des voies bilaires intrahépatiques	635	7.2	585	6.5	690	7.7	580	6.4
Malignant neoplasm of pancreas — Tumeur maligne du pancréas..................	629	7.1	696	7.7	640	7.2	709	7.8
Malignant neoplasm of trachea, bronchus and lung — Tumeur maligne de la trachée, des bronches et du poumon	1 828	20.7	1 227	13.6	1 845	20.7	1 262	13.9
Malignant neoplasm of female breast — Tumeur maligne du sein chez la femme	..	..	1 422	19.7	..	..	1 511	20.7
Malignant neoplasm of cervix uteri — Tumeur maligne du col de l'utérus..........	..	..	539	7.5	..	..	620	8.5
Malignant neoplasm of prostate — Tumeur maligne de la prostate	2 054	91.9	..	..	2 097	90.6	..	..
Malignant neoplasm of lymphoid, haematopoietic and related tissue — Tumeurs malignes primitives ou présumées primitives des tissus lymphoïde, hématopoïétique et apparentés.................	1 054	12.0	884	9.8	1 021	11.5	935	10.3
Disorders of the blood and blood-forming organs and certain disorders involving the immune mechanism — Maladies du sang et des organes hématopoïétiques et certains troubles du système immunitaire								
Total	213	2.4	287	3.2	214	2.4	274	3.0
Anaemias — Anémies	151	1.7	222	2.5	156	1.8	220	2.4
Endocrine, nutritional and metabolic diseases — Maladies endocriniennes, nutritionnelles et métaboliques								
Total	2 422	27.5	2 766	30.7	2 784	31.2	3 074	33.8
Diabetes mellitus — Diabète sucré.................	1 988	22.5	2 197	24.4	2 260	25.4	2 466	27.1
Malnutrition — Malnutrition	196	2.2	208	2.3	250	2.8	212	2.3
Mental and behavioural disorders — Troubles mentaux et du comportement	708	8.0	1 128	12.5	722	8.1	939	10.3
Diseases of the nervous system — Maladies du système nerveux.................	1 611	18.3	1 973	21.9	1 665	18.7	2 131	23.4
Diseases of the circulatory system — Maladies de l'appareil circulatoire								
Total	14 177	160.7	13 887	154.3	14 231	159.7	14 090	154.9
Acute rheumatic fever and chronic rheumatic heart diseases — Rhumatisme articularie aigu et cardiopathies rhumatismales chroniques	48	0.5	94	1.0	42	0.5	66	0.7
Hypertensive diseases — Maladies hypertensives.................	2 279	25.8	3 397	37.7	2 336	26.2	3 494	38.4
Ischaemic heart disease — Cardiopathie ischémique.................	4 954	56.2	3 148	35.0	5 097	57.2	3 294	36.2
Cerebrovascular disease — Maladie cérébrovasculaire.................	4 236	48.0	4 367	48.5	4 077	45.7	4 403	48.4

Chile - Chili

Cause of death — Cause de décès	2014 (C)				2015 (C)			
	Male — Masculin		Female — Féminin		Male — Masculin		Female — Féminin	
	Number Nombre	Rate Taux	Number Nombre	Rate Taux	Number Nombre	Rate Taux	Number Nombre	Rate Taux
Diseases of arteries, arterioles and capillaries — Maladies des artères, artérioles et capillaires	500	5.7	418	4.6	488	5.5	396	4.4
Diseases of the respiratory system — Maladies de l'appareil respiratoire								
Total	5 283	59.9	5 165	57.4	5 019	56.3	4 916	54.1
Influenza — Grippe..	13	♦0.1	15	♦0.2	28	♦0.3	36	0.4
Pneumonia — Pneumopathies................................	2 063	23.4	2 169	24.1	1 615	18.1	1 650	18.1
Chronic lower respiratory diseases — Maladies chroniques des voies respiratoires inférieures	1 665	18.9	1 558	17.3	1 799	20.2	1 649	18.1
Diseases of the digestive system — Maladies de l'appareil digestif								
Total	4 628	52.5	2 841	31.6	4 801	53.9	2 865	31.5
Gastric and duodenal ulcer — Ulcère de l'estomac et du duodénum................	118	1.3	63	0.7	122	1.4	76	0.8
Diseases of the liver — Maladies du foie....................	3 090	35.0	1 242	13.8	3 248	36.4	1 277	14.0
Diseases of the musculoskeletal system and connective tissue — Maladies du système ostéo-articularie, des muscles et du tissu conjonctif	163	1.8	407	4.5	154	1.7	430	4.7
Diseases of the genitourinary system — Maladies de l'appareil génito-urinaire								
Total	1 406	15.9	1 667	18.5	1 460	16.4	1 665	18.3
Disorders of kidney and ureter — Affections du rein et de l'uretère	961	10.9	1 028	11.4	993	11.1	1 023	11.2
Hyperplasia of prostate — Hyperplasie de la prostate..............	41	1.8	..	..	57	2.5	..	..
Pregnancy, childbirth and the puerperium — Grossesse, accouchement et puerpéralité								
Total	..	..	56	22.3	..	..	56	22.9
Pregnancy with abortive outcome — Grossesse se terminant par un avortement	..	..	4	♦1.6	..	..	9	♦3.7
Other direct obstetric causes — Autres décès maternels directs	..	..	16	♦6.4	..	..	17	♦6.9
Indirect obstetric causes — Décès maternels indirects	..	..	14	♦5.6	..	..	12	♦4.9
Certain conditions originating in the perinatal period — Certaines affections dont l'origine se situe dans la période périnatale	477	372.1	365	297.2	469	376.1	335	279.3
Congenital malformations, deformations and chromosomal abnormalities — Malformations congénitales et anomalies chromosomiques	487	379.9	484	394.1	492	394.5	422	351.9
Symptoms, signs and abnormal clinical and laboratory findings, not elsewhere classified — Symptômes, signes et résultats anormaux d'examens cliniques et de laboratoire, non classés ailleurs	1 252	14.2	1 366	15.2	1 085	12.2	1 240	13.6
All other diseases — Toutes autres maladies..............	132	1.5	205	2.3	183	2.1	285	3.1
External causes — Causes externes								
Total	5 882	66.7	1 864	20.7	5 907	66.3	1 961	21.6
Accidents								
Total	3 587	40.7	1 385	15.4	3 628	40.7	1 432	15.7
Transport accidents — Accidents de transport..............	1 635	18.5	421	4.7	1 590	17.8	442	4.9
Falls — Chutes..	402	4.6	476	5.3	356	4.0	472	5.2
Accidental drowning and submersion — Noyade et submersion accidentelles..............	286	3.2	36	0.4	288	3.2	55	0.6
Exposure to smoke, fire and flames — Exposition à la fumée, au feu et aux flammes...........	212	2.4	126	1.4	173	1.9	91	1.0
Accidental poisoning by and exposure to noxious substances — Intoxication accidentelle par des substances nocives et exposition à ces substances	165	1.9	44	0.5	184	2.1	58	0.6
Intentional self-harm — Lésions auto-infligées..............	1 475	16.7	314	3.5	1 459	16.4	378	4.2
Assault — Agresssions..	732	8.3	102	1.1	692	7.8	94	1.0
All other external causes — Toutes autres causes externes	88	1.0	63	0.7	128	1.4	57	0.6

Cause of death — Cause de décès	Colombia - Colombie				Ecuador - Équateur			
	2014 (U)		2015 (U)		2014 (U)		2015 (U)	
	Male — Masculin	Female — Féminin	Male — Masculin	Female — Féminin	Male — Masculin	Female — Féminin	Male — Masculin	Female — Féminin
	Number Nombre	Number Nombre	Number Nombre	Number Nombre	Number Nombre	Number Nombre	Number Nombre	Number Nombre
TOTAL	116 379	93 649	121 395	98 037	34 778	28 203	35 577	29 213
Certain infectious and parasitic diseases — Certaines maladies infectieuses et parasitaires								
Total	3 926	2 209	4 004	2 238	1 301	716	1 259	707
Intestinal infectious diseases — Maladies infectieuses intestinales	267	347	295	368	63	74	69	86
Tuberculosis — Tuberculose	665	283	685	273	277	138	287	145
Tetanus — Tétanos	19	5	13	7	2	1	5	1
Diphtheria — Diphtérie	-	-	-	-	-	-	-	-
Whooping cough — Coqueluche	7	4	10	7	1	-	-	-
Meningococcal infection — Infection à méningocoques	4	5	10	9	2	2	2	-
Septicaemia — Septicémie	517	520	477	517	237	223	177	202
Acute poliomyelitis — Poliomyélite aiguë	-	-	-	-	2	1	-	-
Measles — Rougeole	-	-	-	-	-	-	-	-
Viral hepatitis — Hépatite virale	52	59	69	55	13	14	12	11
Human immunodeficiency virus [HIV] disease — Maladies dues au virus de l'immunodéficience humaine (VIH)	1 812	566	1 859	589	626	202	607	190
Malaria — Paludisme	7	11	9	17	-	-	-	-
Neoplasms — Tumeurs	20 266	21 035	20 955	21 601	5 008	5 379	5 224	5 520
Malignant neoplasms — Tumeurs malignes								
Total	18 717	19 493	19 383	20 036	4 669	5 038	4 940	5 218
Malignant neoplasm of lip, oral cavity and pharynx — Tumeur maligne de la lèvre, de la cavité buccale et du pharynx	363	258	391	277	54	48	75	64
Malignant neoplasm of oesophagus — Tumeur maligne de l'oesophage	448	232	479	211	82	28	89	24
Malignant neoplasm of stomach — Tumeur maligne de l'estomac	3 058	1 972	3 136	1 975	887	698	821	682
Malignant neoplasm of colon, rectosigmoid junction, rectum, anus and anal canal — Tumeur maligne du côlon, de la jonction recto-sigmoïdienne, du rectum, de l'anus et du canal anal	1 527	1 672	1 602	1 793	310	368	339	396
Malignant neoplasm of liver and intrahepatic bile ducts — Tumeur maligne du foie et des voies biliaires intrahépatiques	864	935	911	916	320	330	334	376
Malignant neoplasm of pancreas — Tumeur maligne du pancréas	717	871	772	953	138	194	181	205
Malignant neoplasm of trachea, bronchus and lung — Tumeur maligne de la trachée, des bronches et du poumon	2 620	1 853	2 654	1 981	384	333	407	304
Malignant neoplasm of female breast — Tumeur maligne du sein chez la femme	..	2 773	..	2 865	..	520	..	551
Malignant neoplasm of cervix uteri — Tumeur maligne du col de l'utérus	..	1 633	..	1 629	..	371	..	445
Malignant neoplasm of prostate — Tumeur maligne de la prostate	2 852	..	2 888	..	833	..	931	..
Malignant neoplasm of lymphoid, haematopoietic and related tissue — Tumeurs malignes primitives ou présumées primitives des tissus lymphoïde, hématopoïétique et apparentés	1 938	1 730	2 173	1 799	587	492	647	537
Disorders of the blood and blood-forming organs and certain disorders involving the immune mechanism — Maladies du sang et des organes hématopoïétiques et certains troubles du système immunitaire								
Total	394	423	410	399	252	252	275	295
Anaemias — Anémies	197	227	197	196	192	206	214	238
Endocrine, nutritional and metabolic diseases — Maladies endocriniennes, nutritionnelles et métaboliques								
Total	4 178	5 297	4 539	5 411	2 461	2 864	2 460	3 034
Diabetes mellitus — Diabète sucré	3 082	4 052	3 378	4 172	2 030	2 371	2 046	2 520
Malnutrition — Malnutrition	767	787	841	773	230	298	228	268
Mental and behavioural disorders — Troubles mentaux et du comportement	185	243	257	343	120	74	88	55
Diseases of the nervous system — Maladies du système nerveux	1 765	1 461	1 994	1 756	641	573	680	669
Diseases of the circulatory system — Maladies de l'appareil circulatoire								
Total	34 047	32 052	35 844	34 017	7 585	6 951	7 940	7 186
Acute rheumatic fever and chronic rheumatic heart diseases — Rhumatisme articularie aigu et cardiopathies rhumatismales chroniques	18	25	17	32	34	69	38	61
Hypertensive diseases — Maladies hypertensives	3 733	4 093	4 178	4 537	1 698	1 874	1 742	1 738
Ischaemic heart disease — Cardiopathie ischémique	18 899	15 554	19 660	16 537	2 643	1 787	3 006	2 058

Cause of death — Cause de décès	Colombia - Colombie 2014 (U) Male — Masculin Number Nombre	2014 (U) Female — Féminin Number Nombre	2015 (U) Male — Masculin Number Nombre	2015 (U) Female — Féminin Number Nombre	Ecuador - Équateur 2014 (U) Male — Masculin Number Nombre	2014 (U) Female — Féminin Number Nombre	2015 (U) Male — Masculin Number Nombre	2015 (U) Female — Féminin Number Nombre
Cerebrovascular disease — Maladie cérébrovasculaire	6 595	7 750	6 955	8 174	1 886	1 891	1 993	2 112
Diseases of arteries, arterioles and capillaries — Maladies des artères, artérioles et capillaires	1 167	728	1 197	731	156	113	145	111
Diseases of the respiratory system — Maladies de l'appareil respiratoire								
Total	12 263	11 774	13 204	12 623	3 286	2 934	3 291	2 932
Influenza — Grippe	11	7	15	14	21	21	9	21
Pneumonia — Pneumopathies	3 481	3 462	4 287	4 247	1 656	1 720	1 615	1 622
Chronic lower respiratory diseases — Maladies chroniques des voies respiratoires inférieures	6 475	6 218	6 840	6 573	956	700	956	730
Diseases of the digestive system — Maladies de l'appareil digestif								
Total	5 197	4 749	5 497	5 024	2 254	1 687	2 453	1 851
Gastric and duodenal ulcer — Ulcère de l'estomac et du duodénum	366	300	405	301	122	101	97	90
Diseases of the liver — Maladies du foie	1 647	1 072	1 736	1 131	1 231	807	1 383	875
Diseases of the musculoskeletal system and connective tissue — Maladies du système ostéo-articularie, des muscles et du tissu conjonctif	623	1 534	621	1 490	101	283	111	296
Diseases of the genitourinary system — Maladies de l'appareil génito-urinaire								
Total	3 431	2 899	3 937	3 361	1 002	810	1 092	834
Disorders of kidney and ureter — Affections du rein et de l'uretère	2 256	1 669	2 566	1 881	871	693	877	695
Hyperplasia of prostate — Hyperplasie de la prostate	298	..	293	..	67	..	92	..
Pregnancy, childbirth and the puerperium — Grossesse, accouchement et puerpéralité								
Total	..	491	..	476	..	169	..	183
Pregnancy with abortive outcome — Grossesse se terminant par un avortement	..	27	..	24	..	24	..	13
Other direct obstetric causes — Autres décès maternels directs	..	214	..	220	..	104	..	110
Indirect obstetric causes — Décès maternels indirects	..	116	..	111	..	38	..	27
Certain conditions originating in the perinatal period — Certaines affections dont l'origine se situe dans la période périnatale	2 301	1 697	2 242	1 569	775	555	825	646
Congenital malformations, deformations and chromosomal abnormalities — Malformations congénitales et anomalies chromosomiques	1 331	1 123	1 337	1 126	435	415	540	463
Symptoms, signs and abnormal clinical and laboratory findings, not elsewhere classified — Symptômes, signes et résultats anormaux d'examens cliniques et de laboratoire, non classés ailleurs	2 219	1 755	2 246	1 639	3 010	2 692	2 900	2 657
All other diseases — Toutes autres maladies	461	639	478	628	52	71	75	93
External causes — Causes externes								
Total	23 792	4 268	23 830	4 336	6 495	1 778	6 364	1 792
Accidents								
Total	8 543	2 167	9 083	2 178	4 036	1 119	4 293	1 182
Transport accidents — Accidents de transport	5 502	1 310	6 009	1 340	2 590	652	2 525	584
Falls — Chutes	914	361	974	330	289	85	379	104
Accidental drowning and submersion — Noyade et submersion accidentelles	646	134	648	118	229	67	323	81
Exposure to smoke, fire and flames — Exposition à la fumée, au feu et aux flammes	78	40	71	36	55	22	57	23
Accidental poisoning by and exposure to noxious substances — Intoxication accidentelle par des substances nocives et exposition à ces substances	119	27	110	26	139	34	107	29
Intentional self-harm — Lésions auto-infligées	1 764	372	1 863	484	567	167	807	266
Assault — Agresssions	11 731	1 153	11 312	1 048	905	140	826	155
All other external causes — Toutes autres causes externes	1 754	576	1 572	626	987	352	438	189

20. Death and death rates by cause and sex: 2012 - 2016
Décès et taux de mortalité par cause et sexe : 2012 - 2016 (continued - suite)

	French Guiana - Guyane française				Guyana			
	2013 (...)		2014 (...)		2012 (C)			
Cause of death — Cause de décès	Male — Masculin	Female — Féminin	Male — Masculin	Female — Féminin	Male — Masculin		Female — Féminin	
	Number Nombre	Number Nombre	Number Nombre	Number Nombre	Number Nombre	Rate Taux	Number Nombre	Rate Taux
TOTAL	441	321	457	323	3 208	863.0	2 340	624.0
Certain infectious and parasitic diseases — Certaines maladies infectieuses et parasitaires								
Total	28	21	16	21	366	98.5	221	58.9
Intestinal infectious diseases — Maladies infectieuses intestinales	2	2	1	1	31	8.3	13	✦3.5
Tuberculosis — Tuberculose	1	1	2	1	82	22.1	25	✦6.7
Tetanus — Tétanos	-	-	-	-	-	-	-	-
Diphtheria — Diphtérie	-	-	-	-	-	-	-	-
Whooping cough — Coqueluche	-	-	-	-	-	-	-	-
Meningococcal infection — Infection à méningocoques	-	-	-	-	-	-	-	-
Septicaemia — Septicémie	5	4	5	5	64	17.2	52	13.9
Acute poliomyelitis — Poliomyélite aiguë	-	-	-	-	-	-	-	-
Measles — Rougeole	-	-	-	-	-	-	-	-
Viral hepatitis — Hépatite virale	-	-	-	-	4	✦1.1	2	✦0.5
Human immunodeficiency virus [HIV] disease — Maladies dues au virus de l'immunodéficience humaine (VIH)	15	8	8	11	148	39.8	110	29.3
Malaria — Paludisme	-	-	-	-	26	✦7.0	10	✦2.7
Neoplasms — Tumeurs	76	53	84	70	200	53.8	271	72.3
Malignant neoplasms — Tumeurs malignes								
Total	71	50	81	66	190	51.1	263	70.1
Malignant neoplasm of lip, oral cavity and pharynx — Tumeur maligne de la lèvre, de la cavité buccale et du pharynx	2	1	4	-	6	✦1.6	2	✦0.5
Malignant neoplasm of oesophagus — Tumeur maligne de l'oesophage	-	-	3	1	3	✦0.8	2	✦0.5
Malignant neoplasm of stomach — Tumeur maligne de l'estomac	4	-	4	5	7	✦1.9	5	✦1.3
Malignant neoplasm of colon, rectosigmoid junction, rectum, anus and anal canal — Tumeur maligne du côlon, de la jonction recto-sigmoïdienne, du rectum, de l'anus et du canal anal	7	3	7	8	9	✦2.4	12	✦3.2
Malignant neoplasm of liver and intrahepatic bile ducts — Tumeur maligne du foie et des voies bilaires intrahépatiques	5	-	6	2	8	✦2.2	13	✦3.5
Malignant neoplasm of pancreas — Tumeur maligne du pancréas	5	4	4	1	4	✦1.1	8	✦2.1
Malignant neoplasm of trachea, bronchus and lung — Tumeur maligne de la trachée, des bronches et du poumon	9	3	14	5	4	✦1.1	4	✦1.1
Malignant neoplasm of female breast — Tumeur maligne du sein chez la femme	..	12	..	11	..	..	35	13.2
Malignant neoplasm of cervix uteri — Tumeur maligne du col de l'utérus	..	2	..	6	..	..	46	17.4
Malignant neoplasm of prostate — Tumeur maligne de la prostate	7	..	14	..	62	102.1	..	..
Malignant neoplasm of lymphoid, haematopoietic and related tissue — Tumeurs malignes primitives ou présumées primitives des tissus lymphoïde, hématopoïétique et apparentés	8	7	11	9	21	✦5.6	14	✦3.7
Disorders of the blood and blood-forming organs and certain disorders involving the immune mechanism — Maladies du sang et des organes hématopoïétiques et certains troubles du système immunitaire								
Total	1	3	3	3	58	15.6	53	14.1
Anaemias — Anémies	-	3	2	2	53	14.3	44	11.7
Endocrine, nutritional and metabolic diseases — Maladies endocriniennes, nutritionnelles et métaboliques								
Total	24	18	15	17	258	69.4	314	83.7
Diabetes mellitus — Diabète sucré	17	15	8	11	193	51.9	250	66.7
Malnutrition — Malnutrition	3	1	-	1	12	✦3.2	6	✦1.6
Mental and behavioural disorders — Troubles mentaux et du comportement	11	7	11	6	3	✦0.8	2	✦0.5
Diseases of the nervous system — Maladies du système nerveux	14	10	10	10	47	12.6	28	✦7.5
Diseases of the circulatory system — Maladies de l'appareil circulatoire								
Total	66	67	76	68	1 099	295.6	952	253.9
Acute rheumatic fever and chronic rheumatic heart diseases — Rhumatisme articularie aigu et cardiopathies rhumatismales chroniques	1	1	1	3	1	✦0.3	4	✦1.1
Hypertensive diseases — Maladies hypertensives	3	17	9	11	219	58.9	193	51.5
Ischaemic heart disease — Cardiopathie ischémique	7	7	15	9	373	100.3	261	69.6

Cause of death — Cause de décès	French Guiana - Guyane française				Guyana			
	2013 (...)		2014 (...)		2012 (C)			
	Male — Masculin	Female — Féminin	Male — Masculin	Female — Féminin	Male — Masculin		Female — Féminin	
	Number Nombre	Number Nombre	Number Nombre	Number Nombre	Number Nombre	Rate Taux	Number Nombre	Rate Taux
Cerebrovascular disease — Maladie cérébrovasculaire	31	21	29	19	280	75.3	279	74.4
Diseases of arteries, arterioles and capillaries — Maladies des artères, artérioles et capillaires	1	-	3	1	23	♦6.2	13	♦3.5
Diseases of the respiratory system — Maladies de l'appareil respiratoire								
Total	19	10	18	11	164	44.1	107	28.5
Influenza — Grippe	1	-	-	-	-	-	-	-
Pneumonia — Pneumopathies	6	3	8	3	87	23.4	73	19.5
Chronic lower respiratory diseases — Maladies chroniques des voies respiratoires inférieures	4	2	6	3	44	11.8	14	♦3.7
Diseases of the digestive system — Maladies de l'appareil digestif								
Total	21	15	21	5	220	59.2	89	23.7
Gastric and duodenal ulcer — Ulcère de l'estomac et du duodénum	-	-	2	-	27	♦7.3	8	♦2.1
Diseases of the liver — Maladies du foie	14	9	8	1	138	37.1	47	12.5
Diseases of the musculoskeletal system and connective tissue — Maladies du système ostéo-articularie, des muscles et du tissu conjonctif	4	3	2	2	3	♦0.8	3	♦0.8
Diseases of the genitourinary system — Maladies de l'appareil génito-urinaire								
Total	11	6	10	6	57	15.3	50	13.3
Disorders of kidney and ureter — Affections du rein et de l'uretère	5	6	9	4	43	11.6	48	12.8
Hyperplasia of prostate — Hyperplasie de la prostate	-	..	-	..	5	♦8.2	..	..
Pregnancy, childbirth and the puerperium — Grossesse, accouchement et puerpéralité								
Total	..	1	..	3	..	...	14	...
Pregnancy with abortive outcome — Grossesse se terminant par un avortement	..	-	..	1	..	...	-	...
Other direct obstetric causes — Autres décès maternels directs	..	1	..	2	..	...	12	...
Indirect obstetric causes — Décès maternels indirects	..	-	..	1	..	...	2	...
Certain conditions originating in the perinatal period — Certaines affections dont l'origine se situe dans la période périnatale	10	13	9	11	70	...	46	...
Congenital malformations, deformations and chromosomal abnormalities — Malformations congénitales et anomalies chromosomiques	6	6	7	7	19	...	15	...
Symptoms, signs and abnormal clinical and laboratory findings, not elsewhere classified — Symptômes, signes et résultats anormaux d'examens cliniques et de laboratoire, non classés ailleurs	83	59	99	62	31	8.3	22	♦5.9
All other diseases — Toutes autres maladies	-	2	-	1	1	♦0.3	1	♦0.3
External causes — Causes externes								
Total	67	27	76	20	612	164.6	152	40.5
Accidents								
Total	42	19	50	14	299	80.4	58	15.5
Transport accidents — Accidents de transport	14	4	20	4	107	28.8	13	♦3.5
Falls — Chutes	2	2	3	-	4	♦1.1	2	♦0.5
Accidental drowning and submersion — Noyade et submersion accidentelles	8	-	10	2	91	24.5	15	♦4.0
Exposure to smoke, fire and flames — Exposition à la fumée, au feu et aux flammes	-	2	1	-	3	♦0.8	3	♦0.8
Accidental poisoning by and exposure to noxious substances — Intoxication accidentelle par des substances nocives et exposition à ces substances	2	-	4	1	2	♦0.5	3	♦0.8
Intentional self-harm — Lésions auto-infligées	14	5	11	4	156	42.0	50	13.3
Assault — Agressions	5	1	4	1	71	19.1	13	♦3.5
All other external causes — Toutes autres causes externes	6	2	11	2	86	23.1	31	8.3

20. Death and death rates by cause and sex: 2012 - 2016
Décès et taux de mortalité par cause et sexe : 2012 - 2016 (continued - suite)

	Guyana				Paraguay			
	2013 (C)				2013 (+U)		2014 (+U)	
Cause of death — Cause de décès	Male — Masculin		Female — Féminin		Male — Masculin	Female — Féminin	Male — Masculin	Female — Féminin
	Number Nombre	Rate Taux	Number Nombre	Rate Taux	Number Nombre	Number Nombre	Number Nombre	Number Nombre
TOTAL	3 076	827.8	2 289	611.0	*15 445*	*12 242*	*15 203*	*11 763*
Certain infectious and parasitic diseases — Certaines maladies infectieuses et parasitaires								
Total	332	89.3	175	46.7	*800*	*551*	*572*	*324*
Intestinal infectious diseases — Maladies infectieuses intestinales	25	♦6.7	19	♦5.1	*48*	*43*	*48*	*43*
Tuberculosis — Tuberculose	81	21.8	26	♦6.9	*123*	*28*	*115*	*34*
Tetanus — Tétanos	-	-	-	-	*1*	*-*	*4*	*1*
Diphtheria — Diphtérie	-	-	-	-	*-*	*-*	*-*	*-*
Whooping cough — Coqueluche	-	-	-	-	*2*	*2*	*1*	*1*
Meningococcal infection — Infection à méningocoques	-	-	-	-	*-*	*-*	*2*	*1*
Septicaemia — Septicémie	56	15.1	60	16.0	*162*	*157*	*123*	*120*
Acute poliomyelitis — Poliomyélite aiguë	-	-	-	-	*-*	*-*	*-*	*-*
Measles — Rougeole...	-	-	-	-	*-*	*-*	*-*	*-*
Viral hepatitis — Hépatite virale	-	-	-	-	*5*	*6*	*3*	*4*
Human immunodeficiency virus [HIV] disease — Maladies dues au virus de l'immunodéficience humaine (VIH)..	129	34.7	59	15.7	*143*	*70*	*165*	*71*
Malaria — Paludisme...	29	♦7.8	2	♦0.5	*-*	*-*	*-*	*-*
Neoplasms — Tumeurs	206	55.4	281	75.0	*2 107*	*1 934*	*2 135*	*1 926*
Malignant neoplasms — Tumeurs malignes								
Total	187	50.3	266	71.0	*1 938*	*1 782*	*1 956*	*1 785*
Malignant neoplasm of lip, oral cavity and pharynx — Tumeur maligne de la lèvre, de la cavité buccale et du pharynx	8	♦2.2	3	♦0.8	*77*	*17*	*70*	*11*
Malignant neoplasm of oesophagus — Tumeur maligne de l'oesophage	1	♦0.3	3	♦0.8	*89*	*26*	*101*	*16*
Malignant neoplasm of stomach — Tumeur maligne de l'estomac	11	♦3.0	13	♦3.5	*119*	*83*	*139*	*78*
Malignant neoplasm of colon, rectosigmoid junction, rectum, anus and anal canal — Tumeur maligne du côlon, de la jonction recto-sigmoïdienne, du rectum, de l'anus et du canal anal...	11	♦3.0	19	♦5.1	*147*	*152*	*159*	*157*
Malignant neoplasm of liver and intrahepatic bile ducts — Tumeur maligne du foie et des voies bilaires intrahépatiques	9	♦2.4	8	♦2.1	*75*	*46*	*70*	*52*
Malignant neoplasm of pancreas — Tumeur maligne du pancréas.................	11	♦3.0	6	♦1.6	*82*	*81*	*99*	*83*
Malignant neoplasm of trachea, bronchus and lung — Tumeur maligne de la trachée, des bronches et du poumon	26	♦7.0	11	♦2.9	*401*	*103*	*368*	*105*
Malignant neoplasm of female breast — Tumeur maligne du sein chez la femme	..	..	59	...	*..*	*324*	*..*	*346*
Malignant neoplasm of cervix uteri — Tumeur maligne du col de l'utérus.........	..	..	37	...	*..*	*278*	*..*	*269*
Malignant neoplasm of prostate — Tumeur maligne de la prostate	51	...	..	..	*301*	*..*	*303*	*..*
Malignant neoplasm of lymphoid, haematopoietic and related tissue — Tumeurs malignes primitives ou présumées primitives des tissus lymphoïde, hématopoïétique et apparentés	16	♦4.3	10	♦2.7	*181*	*140*	*186*	*128*
Disorders of the blood and blood-forming organs and certain disorders involving the immune mechanism — Maladies du sang et des organes hématopoïétiques et certains troubles du système immunitaire								
Total	33	8.9	51	13.6	*84*	*77*	*96*	*83*
Anaemias — Anémies	32	8.6	46	12.3	*63*	*57*	*71*	*52*
Endocrine, nutritional and metabolic diseases — Maladies endocriniennes, nutritionnelles et métaboliques								
Total	261	70.2	280	74.7	*1 167*	*1 597*	*1 240*	*1 592*
Diabetes mellitus — Diabète sucré...	210	56.5	235	62.7	*917*	*1 301*	*952*	*1 274*
Malnutrition — Malnutrition	16	♦4.3	8	♦2.1	*142*	*123*	*144*	*132*
Mental and behavioural disorders — Troubles mentaux et du comportement	1	♦0.3	2	♦0.5	*200*	*47*	*279*	*41*
Diseases of the nervous system — Maladies du système nerveux.................	56	15.1	40	10.7	*228*	*215*	*216*	*185*
Diseases of the circulatory system — Maladies de l'appareil circulatoire								
Total	966	260.0	936	249.8	*3 845*	*3 506*	*3 608*	*3 171*
Acute rheumatic fever and chronic rheumatic heart diseases — Rhumatisme articulaire aigu et cardiopathies rhumatismales chroniques	9	♦2.4	5	♦1.3	*12*	*21*	*16*	*20*
Hypertensive diseases — Maladies hypertensives................................	141	37.9	193	51.5	*565*	*634*	*560*	*553*
Ischaemic heart disease — Cardiopathie ischémique	354	95.3	251	67.0	*1 519*	*1 048*	*1 377*	*901*

Cause of death — Cause de décès	Guyana 2013 (C) Male — Masculin Number Nombre	Guyana 2013 (C) Male — Masculin Rate Taux	Guyana 2013 (C) Female — Féminin Number Nombre	Guyana 2013 (C) Female — Féminin Rate Taux	Paraguay 2013 (+U) Male — Masculin Number Nombre	Paraguay 2013 (+U) Female — Féminin Number Nombre	Paraguay 2014 (+U) Male — Masculin Number Nombre	Paraguay 2014 (+U) Female — Féminin Number Nombre
Cerebrovascular disease — Maladie cérébrovasculaire	262	70.5	290	77.4	1 053	1 118	943	1 045
Diseases of arteries, arterioles and capillaries — Maladies des artères, artérioles et capillaires	14	♦3.8	18	♦4.8	74	64	88	58
Diseases of the respiratory system — Maladies de l'appareil respiratoire								
Total	199	53.6	117	31.2	987	712	953	714
Influenza — Grippe	-	-	1	♦0.3	20	27	12	14
Pneumonia — Pneumopathies	83	22.3	72	19.2	361	349	313	329
Chronic lower respiratory diseases — Maladies chroniques des voies respiratoires inférieures	66	17.8	14	♦3.7	373	163	419	154
Diseases of the digestive system — Maladies de l'appareil digestif								
Total	184	49.5	114	30.4	693	424	721	486
Gastric and duodenal ulcer — Ulcère de l'estomac et du duodénum	20	♦5.4	9	♦2.4	35	19	26	29
Diseases of the liver — Maladies du foie	113	30.4	56	14.9	296	78	338	84
Diseases of the musculoskeletal system and connective tissue — Maladies du système ostéo-articulaire, des muscles et du tissu conjonctif	3	♦0.8	1	♦0.3	65	123	63	127
Diseases of the genitourinary system — Maladies de l'appareil génito-urinaire								
Total	75	20.2	41	10.9	451	347	520	378
Disorders of kidney and ureter — Affections du rein et de l'uretère	61	16.4	37	9.9	361	288	421	285
Hyperplasia of prostate — Hyperplasie de la prostate	2	...	..	...	33	..	33	..
Pregnancy, childbirth and the puerperium — Grossesse, accouchement et puerpéralité								
Total	..	..	9	...	..	100	..	71
Pregnancy with abortive outcome — Grossesse se terminant par un avortement	..	..	2		..	20	..	15
Other direct obstetric causes — Autres décès maternels directs	..	..	7		..	51	..	45
Indirect obstetric causes — Décès maternels indirects	..	..	-		..	29	..	11
Certain conditions originating in the perinatal period — Certaines affections dont l'origine se situe dans la période périnatale	69	...	41	...	482	363	478	367
Congenital malformations, deformations and chromosomal abnormalities — Malformations congénitales et anomalies chromosomiques	25	...	19	...	267	226	310	231
Symptoms, signs and abnormal clinical and laboratory findings, not elsewhere classified — Symptômes, signes et résultats anormaux d'examens cliniques et de laboratoire, non classés ailleurs	27	♦7.3	15	♦4.0	1 628	1 359	1 547	1 342
All other diseases — Toutes autres maladies	-	-	1	♦0.3	34	40	29	40
External causes — Causes externes								
Total	639	172.0	166	44.3	2 407	621	2 436	685
Accidents								
Total	247	66.5	61	16.3	1 602	456	1 535	447
Transport accidents — Accidents de transport	108	29.1	12	♦3.2	1 012	199	943	178
Falls — Chutes	4	♦1.1	4	♦1.1	62	21	47	19
Accidental drowning and submersion — Noyade et submersion accidentelles	79	21.3	10	♦2.7	147	28	140	23
Exposure to smoke, fire and flames — Exposition à la fumée, au feu et aux flammes	8	♦2.2	10	♦2.7	24	10	27	9
Accidental poisoning by and exposure to noxious substances — Intoxication accidentelle par des substances nocives et exposition à ces substances	-	-	-	-	17	9	20	6
Intentional self-harm — Lésions auto-infligées	160	43.1	50	13.3	250	74	271	112
Assault — Agresssions	110	29.6	24	♦6.4	477	60	491	59
All other external causes — Toutes autres causes externes	122	32.8	31	8.3	78	31	139	67

	Peru - Pérou				Suriname			
Cause of death — Cause de décès	2014 (+U)		2015 (+U)		2013 (U)		2014 (U)	
	Male — Masculin	Female — Féminin	Male — Masculin	Female — Féminin	Male — Masculin	Female — Féminin	Male — Masculin	Female — Féminin
	Number Nombre	Number Nombre	Number Nombre	Number Nombre	Number Nombre	Number Nombre	Number Nombre	Number Nombre
TOTAL	51 785	44 674	51 597	44 643	1 807	1 339	1 792	1 356
Certain infectious and parasitic diseases — Certaines maladies infectieuses et parasitaires								
Total	5 290	4 728	4 018	3 077	114	84	127	98
Intestinal infectious diseases — Maladies infectieuses intestinales	194	196	345	357	4	9	3	5
Tuberculosis — Tuberculose	838	416	951	424	4	1	9	1
Tetanus — Tétanos	7	4	3	1	-	-	-	-
Diphtheria — Diphtérie	-	-	-	-	-	-	-	-
Whooping cough — Coqueluche	1	-	1	2	-	-	-	3
Meningococcal infection — Infection à méningocoques	-	-	1	-	-	-	-	1
Septicaemia — Septicémie	3 479	3 803	7	4	26	19	29	36
Acute poliomyelitis — Poliomyélite aiguë	-	-	-	-	-	-	-	-
Measles — Rougeole	-	-	-	-	-	-	-	-
Viral hepatitis — Hépatite virale	31	23	36	22	8	6	4	5
Human immunodeficiency virus [HIV] disease — Maladies dues au virus de l'immunodéficience humaine (VIH)	605	208	661	210	56	39	61	35
Malaria — Paludisme	2	1	-	-	-	1	-	-
Neoplasms — Tumeurs	9 261	10 144	9 275	10 076	239	223	240	195
Malignant neoplasms — Tumeurs malignes								
Total	9 260	10 144	9 275	10 076	237	220	239	193
Malignant neoplasm of lip, oral cavity and pharynx — Tumeur maligne de la lèvre, de la cavité buccale et du pharynx	126	107	146	134	11	2	12	4
Malignant neoplasm of oesophagus — Tumeur maligne de l'oesophage	138	62	149	64	1	-	4	1
Malignant neoplasm of stomach — Tumeur maligne de l'estomac	1 594	1 398	1 509	1 386	9	4	12	5
Malignant neoplasm of colon, rectosigmoid junction, rectum, anus and anal canal — Tumeur maligne du côlon, de la jonction recto-sigmoïdienne, du rectum, de l'anus et du canal anal	560	723	645	663	33	31	21	17
Malignant neoplasm of liver and intrahepatic bile ducts — Tumeur maligne du foie et des voies biliaires intrahépatiques	642	717	634	698	15	12	21	8
Malignant neoplasm of pancreas — Tumeur maligne du pancréas.............	407	452	401	425	12	10	6	7
Malignant neoplasm of trachea, bronchus and lung — Tumeur maligne de la trachée, des bronches et du poumon	956	848	923	822	40	24	46	18
Malignant neoplasm of female breast — Tumeur maligne du sein chez la femme	..	1 034	..	995	..	33	..	37
Malignant neoplasm of cervix uteri — Tumeur maligne du col de l'utérus.........	..	994	..	990	..	23	..	34
Malignant neoplasm of prostate — Tumeur maligne de la prostate	1 485	..	1 498	..	52	..	46	..
Malignant neoplasm of lymphoid, haematopoietic and related tissue — Tumeurs malignes primitives ou présumées primitives des tissus lymphoïde, hématopoïétique et apparentés.............	1 113	889	1 187	937	22	19	20	18
Disorders of the blood and blood-forming organs and certain disorders involving the immune mechanism — Maladies du sang et des organes hématopoïétiques et certains troubles du système immunitaire								
Total	85	98	96	123	6	2	2	8
Anaemias — Anémies	85	98	91	119	3	2	2	6
Endocrine, nutritional and metabolic diseases — Maladies endocriniennes, nutritionnelles et métaboliques								
Total	2 055	2 235	2 347	2 633	97	115	93	117
Diabetes mellitus — Diabète sucré	1 811	1 940	1 926	2 106	89	109	83	109
Malnutrition — Malnutrition	201	246	406	494	2	1	1	1
Mental and behavioural disorders — Troubles mentaux et du comportement	-	-	-	-	10	2	8	2
Diseases of the nervous system — Maladies du système nerveux.............	222	146	239	166	26	16	32	15
Diseases of the circulatory system — Maladies de l'appareil circulatoire								
Total	9 292	8 649	8 868	8 498	517	351	528	398
Acute rheumatic fever and chronic rheumatic heart diseases — Rhumatisme articularie aigu et cardiopathies rhumatismales chroniques	27	43	39	55	1	-	-	1
Hypertensive diseases — Maladies hypertensives.............	1 918	1 922	1 840	1 839	45	30	47	43
Ischaemic heart disease — Cardiopathie ischémique.............	2 611	1 976	1 896	1 469	175	76	159	89

Cause of death — Cause de décès	Peru - Pérou				Suriname			
	2014 (+U)		2015 (+U)		2013 (U)		2014 (U)	
	Male — Masculin	Female — Féminin	Male — Masculin	Female — Féminin	Male — Masculin	Female — Féminin	Male — Masculin	Female — Féminin
	Number Nombre	Number Nombre	Number Nombre	Number Nombre	Number Nombre	Number Nombre	Number Nombre	Number Nombre
Cerebrovascular disease — Maladie cérébrovasculaire....................	2 049	2 054	2 307	2 239	192	159	189	161
Diseases of arteries, arterioles and capillaries — Maladies des artères, artérioles et capillaires	123	120	138	110	13	6	20	3
Diseases of the respiratory system — Maladies de l'appareil respiratoire								
Total	10 500	9 774	10 681	10 033	115	80	126	76
Influenza — Grippe...................	9	3	16	5	2	-	-	-
Pneumonia — Pneumopathies...................	6 942	6 522	6 555	6 346	70	56	79	48
Chronic lower respiratory diseases — Maladies chroniques des voies respiratoires inférieures	984	930	1 220	1 172	26	10	25	12
Diseases of the digestive system — Maladies de l'appareil digestif								
Total	3 656	2 643	4 127	2 930	90	56	94	49
Gastric and duodenal ulcer — Ulcère de l'estomac et du duodénum...................	167	141	125	127	12	3	10	3
Diseases of the liver — Maladies du foie...................	2 297	1 393	2 479	1 479	39	18	34	12
Diseases of the musculoskeletal system and connective tissue — Maladies du système ostéo-articularie, des muscles et du tissu conjonctif	-	-	-	-	5	7	5	11
Diseases of the genitourinary system — Maladies de l'appareil génito-urinaire								
Total	2 275	1 958	2 695	2 618	62	48	59	49
Disorders of kidney and ureter — Affections du rein et de l'uretère	2 055	1 948	2 479	2 617	42	30	39	29
Hyperplasia of prostate — Hyperplasie de la prostate...................	170	..	173	..	1	..	-	..
Pregnancy, childbirth and the puerperium — Grossesse, accouchement et puerpéralité								
Total	..	112	..	110	..	11	..	7
Pregnancy with abortive outcome — Grossesse se terminant par un avortement	..	5	..	10	..	-	..	1
Other direct obstetric causes — Autres décès maternels directs	..	105	..	97	..	8	..	4
Indirect obstetric causes — Décès maternels indirects	..	2	..	3	..	3	..	2
Certain conditions originating in the perinatal period — Certaines affections dont l'origine se situe dans la période périnatale	1 078	770	1 021	723	74	42	55	48
Congenital malformations, deformations and chromosomal abnormalities — Malformations congénitales et anomalies chromosomiques	678	596	630	578	15	19	17	12
Symptoms, signs and abnormal clinical and laboratory findings, not elsewhere classified — Symptômes, signes et résultats anormaux d'examens cliniques et de laboratoire, non classés ailleurs	65	31	185	102	151	178	149	157
All other diseases — Toutes autres maladies...................	-	-	-	-	14	17	12	24
External causes — Causes externes								
Total	7 328	2 790	7 415	2 976	272	88	245	90
Accidents								
Total	6 001	2 361	6 209	2 634	122	28	114	35
Transport accidents — Accidents de transport	1 902	603	1 973	699	45	12	54	17
Falls — Chutes	135	33	146	35	3	1	9	3
Accidental drowning and submersion — Noyade et submersion accidentelles...................	258	56	263	85	26	5	22	2
Exposure to smoke, fire and flames — Exposition à la fumée, au feu et aux flammes	75	43	57	39	4	1	3	4
Accidental poisoning by and exposure to noxious substances — Intoxication accidentelle par des substances nocives et exposition à ces substances	209	87	222	61	1	1	2	1
Intentional self-harm — Lésions auto-infligées...................	264	138	169	95	98	35	94	36
Assault — Agresssions...................	693	151	779	138	26	8	23	12
All other external causes — Toutes autres causes externes	370	140	258	109	26	17	14	7

20. Death and death rates by cause and sex: 2012 - 2016
Décès et taux de mortalité par cause et sexe : 2012 - 2016 (continued - suite)

Uruguay

Cause of death — Cause de décès	2014 (C)				2015 (C)			
	Male — Masculin		Female — Féminin		Male — Masculin		Female — Féminin	
	Number Nombre	Rate Taux	Number Nombre	Rate Taux	Number Nombre	Rate Taux	Number Nombre	Rate Taux
TOTAL	16 362	979.7	15 748	882.9	16 528	985.5	16 429	917.9
Certain infectious and parasitic diseases — Certaines maladies infectieuses et parasitaires								
Total	358	21.4	306	17.2	374	22.3	268	15.0
Intestinal infectious diseases — Maladies infectieuses intestinales	57	3.4	88	4.9	63	3.8	88	4.9
Tuberculosis — Tuberculose	41	2.5	17	◆1.0	55	3.3	18	◆1.0
Tetanus — Tétanos	-	-	-	-	-	-	-	-
Diphtheria — Diphtérie	-	-	-	-	-	-	-	-
Whooping cough — Coqueluche	1	◆0.1	-	-	2	◆0.1	-	-
Meningococcal infection — Infection à méningocoques	2	◆0.1	-	-	1	◆0.1	1	◆0.1
Septicaemia — Septicémie	96	5.7	121	6.8	88	5.2	92	5.1
Acute poliomyelitis — Poliomyélite aiguë	-	-	-	-	-	-	-	-
Measles — Rougeole	-	-	-	-	-	-	-	-
Viral hepatitis — Hépatite virale	2	◆0.1	2	◆0.1	4	◆0.2	-	-
Human immunodeficiency virus [HIV] disease — Maladies dues au virus de l'immunodéficience humaine (VIH)	125	7.5	50	2.8	130	7.8	40	2.2
Malaria — Paludisme	-	-	-	-	1	◆0.1	-	-
Neoplasms — Tumeurs	4 453	266.6	3 599	201.8	4 373	260.7	3 757	209.9
Malignant neoplasms — Tumeurs malignes								
Total	4 332	259.4	3 436	192.6	4 233	252.4	3 609	201.6
Malignant neoplasm of lip, oral cavity and pharynx — Tumeur maligne de la lèvre, de la cavité buccale et du pharynx	99	5.9	33	1.9	104	6.2	36	2.0
Malignant neoplasm of oesophagus — Tumeur maligne de l'oesophage	133	8.0	59	3.3	166	9.9	66	3.7
Malignant neoplasm of stomach — Tumeur maligne de l'estomac	255	15.3	150	8.4	236	14.1	159	8.9
Malignant neoplasm of colon, rectosigmoid junction, rectum, anus and anal canal — Tumeur maligne du côlon, de la jonction recto-sigmoïdienne, du rectum, de l'anus et du canal anal	443	26.5	465	26.1	487	29.0	493	27.5
Malignant neoplasm of liver and intrahepatic bile ducts — Tumeur maligne du foie et des voies bilaires intrahépatiques	94	5.6	47	2.6	69	4.1	59	3.3
Malignant neoplasm of pancreas — Tumeur maligne du pancréas	255	15.3	295	16.5	267	15.9	307	17.2
Malignant neoplasm of trachea, bronchus and lung — Tumeur maligne de la trachée, des bronches et du poumon	1 006	60.2	325	18.2	963	57.4	354	19.8
Malignant neoplasm of female breast — Tumeur maligne du sein chez la femme	..	..	616	43.2	..	..	662	46.1
Malignant neoplasm of cervix uteri — Tumeur maligne du col de l'utérus	..	..	87	6.1	..	..	81	5.6
Malignant neoplasm of prostate — Tumeur maligne de la prostate	568	124.4	..	..	551	119.3	..	..
Malignant neoplasm of lymphoid, haematopoietic and related tissue — Tumeurs malignes primitives ou présumées primitives des tissus lymphoïde, hématopoïétique et apparentés	314	18.8	241	13.5	307	18.3	255	14.2
Disorders of the blood and blood-forming organs and certain disorders involving the immune mechanism — Maladies du sang et des organes hématopoïétiques et certains troubles du système immunitaire								
Total	68	4.1	106	5.9	64	3.8	119	6.6
Anaemias — Anémies	47	2.8	75	4.2	39	2.3	87	4.9
Endocrine, nutritional and metabolic diseases — Maladies endocriniennes, nutritionnelles et métaboliques								
Total	545	32.6	675	37.8	558	33.3	685	38.3
Diabetes mellitus — Diabète sucré	409	24.5	439	24.6	423	25.2	444	24.8
Malnutrition — Malnutrition	29	◆1.7	33	1.9	38	2.3	42	2.3
Mental and behavioural disorders — Troubles mentaux et du comportement	268	16.0	448	25.1	297	17.7	500	27.9
Diseases of the nervous system — Maladies du système nerveux	485	29.0	695	39.0	530	31.6	678	37.9
Diseases of the circulatory system — Maladies de l'appareil circulatoire								
Total	4 040	241.9	4 621	259.1	4 254	253.6	5 015	280.2
Acute rheumatic fever and chronic rheumatic heart diseases — Rhumatisme articularie aigu et cardiopathies rhumatismales chroniques	13	◆0.8	17	◆1.0	13	◆0.8	23	◆1.3
Hypertensive diseases — Maladies hypertensives	295	17.7	426	23.9	321	19.1	537	30.0
Ischaemic heart disease — Cardiopathie ischémique	1 288	77.1	988	55.4	1 333	79.5	1 040	58.1
Cerebrovascular disease — Maladie cérébrovasculaire	1 002	60.0	1 450	81.3	1 070	63.8	1 526	85.3

Uruguay

Cause of death — Cause de décès	2014 (C)				2015 (C)			
	Male — Masculin		Female — Féminin		Male — Masculin		Female — Féminin	
	Number Nombre	Rate Taux	Number Nombre	Rate Taux	Number Nombre	Rate Taux	Number Nombre	Rate Taux
Diseases of arteries, arterioles and capillaries — Maladies des artères, artérioles et capillaires	239	14.3	203	11.4	227	13.5	189	10.6
Diseases of the respiratory system — Maladies de l'appareil respiratoire								
Total	1 587	95.0	1 530	85.8	1 750	104.3	1 664	93.0
Influenza — Grippe......	1	♦0.1	2	♦0.1	-	-	3	♦0.2
Pneumonia — Pneumopathies......	464	27.8	621	34.8	483	28.8	619	34.6
Chronic lower respiratory diseases — Maladies chroniques des voies respiratoires inférieures	709	42.5	343	19.2	871	51.9	437	24.4
Diseases of the digestive system — Maladies de l'appareil digestif								
Total	683	40.9	625	35.0	643	38.3	634	35.4
Gastric and duodenal ulcer — Ulcère de l'estomac et du duodénum......	24	♦1.4	17	♦1.0	27	♦1.6	24	♦1.3
Diseases of the liver — Maladies du foie......	249	14.9	78	4.4	239	14.3	75	4.2
Diseases of the musculoskeletal system and connective tissue — Maladies du système ostéo-articulaire, des muscles et du tissu conjonctif	106	6.3	178	10.0	74	4.4	181	10.1
Diseases of the genitourinary system — Maladies de l'appareil génito-urinaire								
Total	500	29.9	543	30.4	433	25.8	530	29.6
Disorders of kidney and ureter — Affections du rein et de l'uretère	345	20.7	346	19.4	302	18.0	265	14.8
Hyperplasia of prostate — Hyperplasie de la prostate......	10	♦2.2	..	..	17	♦3.7	..	..
Pregnancy, childbirth and the puerperium — Grossesse, accouchement et puerpéralité								
Total	..	..	9	♦18.6	..	..	11	♦22.5
Pregnancy with abortive outcome — Grossesse se terminant par un avortement	..	..	1	♦2.1	..	..	-	-
Other direct obstetric causes — Autres décès maternels directs......	..	..	5	♦10.3	..	..	6	♦12.3
Indirect obstetric causes — Décès maternels indirects......	..	..	3	♦6.2	..	..	5	♦10.2
Certain conditions originating in the perinatal period — Certaines affections dont l'origine se situe dans la période périnatale	104	419.3	65	276.0	102	406.2	65	273.0
Congenital malformations, deformations and chromosomal abnormalities — Malformations congénitales et anomalies chromosomiques	85	342.7	67	284.5	93	370.4	75	315.0
Symptoms, signs and abnormal clinical and laboratory findings, not elsewhere classified — Symptômes, signes et résultats anormaux d'examens cliniques et de laboratoire, non classés ailleurs	1 371	82.1	1 453	81.5	1 276	76.1	1 444	80.7
All other diseases — Toutes autres maladies......	51	3.1	100	5.6	33	2.0	86	4.8
External causes — Causes externes								
Total	1 658	99.3	728	40.8	1 674	99.8	717	40.1
Accidents								
Total	932	55.8	503	28.2	863	51.5	474	26.5
Transport accidents — Accidents de transport......	396	23.7	99	5.6	365	21.8	113	6.3
Falls — Chutes......	26	♦1.6	18	♦1.0	37	2.2	11	♦0.6
Accidental drowning and submersion — Noyade et submersion accidentelles......	69	4.1	18	♦1.0	58	3.5	7	♦0.4
Exposure to smoke, fire and flames — Exposition à la fumée, au feu et aux flammes......	22	♦1.3	13	♦0.7	26	♦1.6	17	♦0.9
Accidental poisoning by and exposure to noxious substances — Intoxication accidentelle par des substances nocives et exposition à ces substances	16	♦1.0	13	♦0.7	12	♦0.7	14	♦0.8
Intentional self-harm — Lésions auto-infligées......	466	27.9	135	7.6	510	30.4	132	7.4
Assault — Agresssions......	185	11.1	36	2.0	220	13.1	38	2.1
All other external causes — Toutes autres causes externes	75	4.5	54	3.0	81	4.8	73	4.1

Cause of death — Cause de décès	Venezuela (Bolivarian Republic of) - Venezuela (République bolivarienne du)				Armenia - Arménie			
	2012 (U)		2013 (U)		2015 (C)			
	Male — Masculin	Female — Féminin	Male — Masculin	Female — Féminin	Male — Masculin		Female — Féminin	
	Number Nombre	Number Nombre	Number Nombre	Number Nombre	Number Nombre	Rate Taux	Number Nombre	Rate Taux
TOTAL	91 034	57 053	91 259	58 617	14 302	993.8	13 576	863.9
Certain infectious and parasitic diseases — Certaines maladies infectieuses et parasitaires								
Total	3 738	2 180	3 673	2 224	223	15.5	85	5.4
Intestinal infectious diseases — Maladies infectieuses intestinales	504	506	492	525	6	♦0.4	3	♦0.2
Tuberculosis — Tuberculose	407	201	457	220	57	4.0	7	♦0.4
Tetanus — Tétanos	11	1	6	1	-	-	-	-
Diphtheria — Diphtérie	-	-	-	-	-	-	-	-
Whooping cough — Coqueluche	23	17	15	9	-	-	-	-
Meningococcal infection — Infection à méningocoques	14	15	13	7	-	-	2	♦0.1
Septicaemia — Septicémie	382	396	465	470	19	♦1.3	16	♦1.0
Acute poliomyelitis — Poliomyélite aiguë	-	-	-	-	-	-	-	-
Measles — Rougeole	-	-	-	-	-	-	-	-
Viral hepatitis — Hépatite virale	52	27	36	23	87	6.0	16	♦1.0
Human immunodeficiency virus [HIV] disease — Maladies dues au virus de l'immunodéficience humaine (VIH)	1 603	558	1 535	518	25	♦1.7	8	♦0.5
Malaria — Paludisme	7	3	24	14	-	-	-	-
Neoplasms — Tumeurs	12 749	12 360	12 898	12 556	3 371	234.2	2 732	173.9
Malignant neoplasms — Tumeurs malignes								
Total	11 490	11 327	11 665	11 451	3 360	233.5	2 709	172.4
Malignant neoplasm of lip, oral cavity and pharynx — Tumeur maligne de la lèvre, de la cavité buccale et du pharynx	333	119	305	136	45	3.1	9	♦0.6
Malignant neoplasm of oesophagus — Tumeur maligne de l'oesophage	253	68	249	80	36	2.5	13	♦0.8
Malignant neoplasm of stomach — Tumeur maligne de l'estomac	1 113	822	1 082	709	305	21.2	203	12.9
Malignant neoplasm of colon, rectosigmoid junction, rectum, anus and anal canal — Tumeur maligne du côlon, de la jonction recto-sigmoïdienne, du rectum, de l'anus et du canal anal	756	801	837	896	221	15.4	286	18.2
Malignant neoplasm of liver and intrahepatic bile ducts — Tumeur maligne du foie et des voies bilaires intrahépatiques	494	437	490	418	246	17.1	178	11.3
Malignant neoplasm of pancreas — Tumeur maligne du pancréas	451	462	469	486	174	12.1	170	10.8
Malignant neoplasm of trachea, bronchus and lung — Tumeur maligne de la trachée, des bronches et du poumon	2 039	1 366	1 999	1 414	1 020	70.9	222	14.1
Malignant neoplasm of female breast — Tumeur maligne du sein chez la femme	..	2 067	..	2 062	..	..	568	43.7
Malignant neoplasm of cervix uteri — Tumeur maligne du col de l'utérus	..	1 321	..	1 386	..	..	73	5.6
Malignant neoplasm of prostate — Tumeur maligne de la prostate	2 419	..	2 438	..	304	77.9	..	..
Malignant neoplasm of lymphoid, haematopoietic and related tissue — Tumeurs malignes primitives ou présumées primitives des tissus lymphoïde, hématopoïétique et apparentés	1 048	925	1 081	865	153	10.6	116	7.4
Disorders of the blood and blood-forming organs and certain disorders involving the immune mechanism — Maladies du sang et des organes hématopoïétiques et certains troubles du système immunitaire								
Total	200	182	250	218	10	♦0.7	5	♦0.3
Anaemias — Anémies	138	106	171	151	4	♦0.3	5	♦0.3
Endocrine, nutritional and metabolic diseases — Maladies endocriniennes, nutritionnelles et métaboliques								
Total	5 686	5 719	6 291	6 106	496	34.5	827	52.6
Diabetes mellitus — Diabète sucré	5 202	5 328	5 819	5 640	475	33.0	801	51.0
Malnutrition — Malnutrition	255	171	242	215	1	♦0.1	1	♦0.1
Mental and behavioural disorders — Troubles mentaux et du comportement	81	20	7	4	6	♦0.4	8	♦0.5
Diseases of the nervous system — Maladies du système nerveux	1 260	1 018	1 247	1 139	67	4.7	51	3.2
Diseases of the circulatory system — Maladies de l'appareil circulatoire								
Total	25 115	19 718	25 333	19 872	6 164	428.3	6 653	423.4
Acute rheumatic fever and chronic rheumatic heart diseases — Rhumatisme articularie aigu et cardiopathies rhumatismales chroniques	37	47	50	70	38	2.6	117	7.4
Hypertensive diseases — Maladies hypertensives	2 628	2 615	2 867	2 822	273	19.0	425	27.0
Ischaemic heart disease — Cardiopathie ischémique	14 332	9 262	14 646	9 440	4 181	290.5	3 937	250.5

Cause of death — Cause de décès	Venezuela (Bolivarian Republic of) - Venezuela (République bolivarienne du)				Armenia - Arménie			
	2012 (U)		2013 (U)		2015 (C)			
	Male — Masculin	Female — Féminin	Male — Masculin	Female — Féminin	Male — Masculin		Female — Féminin	
	Number Nombre	Number Nombre	Number Nombre	Number Nombre	Number Nombre	Rate Taux	Number Nombre	Rate Taux
Cerebrovascular disease — Maladie cérébrovasculaire..................	5 759	5 551	5 617	5 546	1 000	69.5	1 428	90.9
Diseases of arteries, arterioles and capillaries — Maladies des artères, artérioles et capillaires	416	341	375	324	389	27.0	422	26.9
Diseases of the respiratory system — Maladies de l'appareil respiratoire								
Total	5 180	4 649	5 628	5 166	1 041	72.3	1 085	69.0
Influenza — Grippe.........................	4	7	8	5	-	-	2	٭0.1
Pneumonia — Pneumopathies.........................	2 019	1 750	2 295	2 093	311	21.6	351	22.3
Chronic lower respiratory diseases — Maladies chroniques des voies respiratoires inférieures	2 190	1 926	2 265	2 068	623	43.3	626	39.8
Diseases of the digestive system — Maladies de l'appareil digestif								
Total	3 837	2 010	4 039	2 159	870	60.5	782	49.8
Gastric and duodenal ulcer — Ulcère de l'estomac et du duodénum..........	245	165	216	156	134	9.3	116	7.4
Diseases of the liver — Maladies du foie..................	2 337	571	2 479	619	541	37.6	409	26.0
Diseases of the musculoskeletal system and connective tissue — Maladies du système ostéo-articularie, des muscles et du tissu conjonctif	108	393	101	437	25	٭1.7	39	2.5
Diseases of the genitourinary system — Maladies de l'appareil génito-urinaire								
Total	1 438	1 044	1 563	1 131	432	30.0	409	26.0
Disorders of kidney and ureter — Affections du rein et de l'uretère	1 128	840	1 255	917	344	23.9	402	25.6
Hyperplasia of prostate — Hyperplasie de la prostate..................	148	..	132	..	83	21.3	..	..
Pregnancy, childbirth and the puerperium — Grossesse, accouchement et puerpéralité								
Total	..	416	..	410	..	..	7	٭16.8
Pregnancy with abortive outcome — Grossesse se terminant par un avortement	..	35	..	27	..	..	1	٭2.4
Other direct obstetric causes — Autres décès maternels directs	..	235	..	234	..	..	3	٭7.2
Indirect obstetric causes — Décès maternels indirects	..	143	..	148	..	..	3	٭7.2
Certain conditions originating in the perinatal period — Certaines affections dont l'origine se situe dans la période périnatale	3 189	2 256	3 033	2 243	86	388.6	69	351.5
Congenital malformations, deformations and chromosomal abnormalities — Malformations congénitales et anomalies chromosomiques	1 353	1 119	1 329	1 097	250	1 129.5	151	769.2
Symptoms, signs and abnormal clinical and laboratory findings, not elsewhere classified — Symptômes, signes et résultats anormaux d'examens cliniques et de laboratoire, non classés ailleurs	413	335	287	347	259	18.0	300	19.1
All other diseases — Toutes autres maladies.........................	5	8	6	13	13	٭0.9	7	٭0.4
External causes — Causes externes								
Total	26 682	3 626	25 574	3 495	989	68.7	366	23.3
Accidents								
Total	7 875	1 990	7 764	1 931	383	26.6	91	5.8
Transport accidents — Accidents de transport.........................	5 796	1 206	5 872	1 195	256	17.8	63	4.0
Falls — Chutes.........................	421	254	447	227	9	٭0.6	1	٭0.1
Accidental drowning and submersion — Noyade et submersion accidentelles.........................	369	79	343	77	22	٭1.5	1	٭0.1
Exposure to smoke, fire and flames — Exposition à la fumée, au feu et aux flammes.........................	110	31	71	47	3	٭0.2	2	٭0.1
Accidental poisoning by and exposure to noxious substances — Intoxication accidentelle par des substances nocives et exposition à ces substances.........................	82	51	74	35	10	٭0.7	3	٭0.2
Intentional self-harm — Lésions auto-infligées.........................	600	129	500	116	55	3.8	19	٭1.2
Assault — Agresssions.........................	9 362	583	8 351	493	25	٭1.7	13	٭0.8
All other external causes — Toutes autres causes externes..................	8 845	924	8 959	955	526	36.5	243	15.5

Cause of death — Cause de décès	Armenia - Arménie 2016 (C) Male — Masculin Number Nombre	Rate Taux	Female — Féminin Number Nombre	Rate Taux	Bahrain - Bahreïn 2013 (C) Male — Masculin Number Nombre	Rate Taux	Female — Féminin Number Nombre	Rate Taux
TOTAL	14 536	1 020.9	13 690	872.8	1 549	196.5	1 020	219.4
Certain infectious and parasitic diseases — Certaines maladies infectieuses et parasitaires								
Total	175	12.3	66	4.2	23	٭2.9	26	٭5.6
Intestinal infectious diseases — Maladies infectieuses intestinales	3	٭0.2	4	٭0.3	1	٭0.1	1	٭0.2
Tuberculosis — Tuberculose	46	3.2	9	٭0.6	3	٭0.4	2	٭0.4
Tetanus — Tétanos	-	-	-	-	-	-	-	-
Diphtheria — Diphtérie	-	-	-	-	-	-	-	-
Whooping cough — Coqueluche	-	-	-	-	-	-	-	-
Meningococcal infection — Infection à méningocoques	-	-	-	-	-	-	-	-
Septicaemia — Septicémie	15	٭1.1	12	٭0.8	3	٭0.4	11	٭2.4
Acute poliomyelitis — Poliomyélite aiguë	-	-	-	-	-	-	-	-
Measles — Rougeole	-	-	-	-	-	-	-	-
Viral hepatitis — Hépatite virale	74	5.2	13	٭0.8	7	٭0.9	6	٭1.3
Human immunodeficiency virus [HIV] disease — Maladies dues au virus de l'immunodéficience humaine (VIH)	21	٭1.5	8	٭0.5	5	٭0.6	3	٭0.6
Malaria — Paludisme	-	-	-	-	1	٭0.1	-	-
Neoplasms — Tumeurs	3 208	225.3	2 487	158.6	116	14.7	121	26.0
Malignant neoplasms — Tumeurs malignes								
Total	3 197	224.5	2 465	157.2	113	14.3	115	24.7
Malignant neoplasm of lip, oral cavity and pharynx — Tumeur maligne de la lèvre, de la cavité buccale et du pharynx	38	2.7	12	٭0.8	8	٭1.0	2	٭0.4
Malignant neoplasm of oesophagus — Tumeur maligne de l'oesophage	34	2.4	20	٭1.3	2	٭0.3	1	٭0.2
Malignant neoplasm of stomach — Tumeur maligne de l'estomac	303	21.3	162	10.3	5	٭0.6	8	٭1.7
Malignant neoplasm of colon, rectosigmoid junction, rectum, anus and anal canal — Tumeur maligne du côlon, de la jonction recto-sigmoïdienne, du rectum, de l'anus et du canal anal	209	14.7	253	16.1	12	٭1.5	5	٭1.1
Malignant neoplasm of liver and intrahepatic bile ducts — Tumeur maligne du foie et des voies bilaires intrahépatiques	209	14.7	166	10.6	2	٭0.3	5	٭1.1
Malignant neoplasm of pancreas — Tumeur maligne du pancréas	190	13.3	171	10.9	5	٭0.6	2	٭0.4
Malignant neoplasm of trachea, bronchus and lung — Tumeur maligne de la trachée, des bronches et du poumon	975	68.5	195	12.4	22	٭2.8	13	٭2.8
Malignant neoplasm of female breast — Tumeur maligne du sein chez la femme	..	..	464	35.9	..	..	44	12.7
Malignant neoplasm of cervix uteri — Tumeur maligne du col de l'utérus	..	..	59	4.6	..	..	2	٭0.6
Malignant neoplasm of prostate — Tumeur maligne de la prostate	267	68.4	..	..	9	٭9.6	..	..
Malignant neoplasm of lymphoid, haematopoietic and related tissue — Tumeurs malignes primitives ou présumées primitives des tissus lymphoïde, hématopoïétique et apparentés	140	9.8	106	6.8	21	٭2.7	13	٭2.8
Disorders of the blood and blood-forming organs and certain disorders involving the immune mechanism — Maladies du sang et des organes hématopoïétiques et certains troubles du système immunitaire								
Total	14	٭1.0	13	٭0.8	24	٭3.0	16	٭3.4
Anaemias — Anémies	11	٭0.8	11	٭0.7	19	٭2.4	13	٭2.8
Endocrine, nutritional and metabolic diseases — Maladies endocriniennes, nutritionnelles et métaboliques								
Total	460	32.3	747	47.6	229	29.0	220	47.3
Diabetes mellitus — Diabète sucré	450	31.6	721	46.0	197	25.0	188	40.4
Malnutrition — Malnutrition	-	-	2	٭0.1	-	-	-	-
Mental and behavioural disorders — Troubles mentaux et du comportement	3	٭0.2	2	٭0.1	8	٭1.0	5	٭1.1
Diseases of the nervous system — Maladies du système nerveux	79	5.5	76	4.8	31	3.9	20	٭4.3
Diseases of the circulatory system — Maladies de l'appareil circulatoire								
Total	6 521	458.0	7 049	449.4	550	69.8	289	62.2
Acute rheumatic fever and chronic rheumatic heart diseases — Rhumatisme articulaire aigu et cardiopathies rhumatismales chroniques	44	3.1	85	5.4	2	٭0.3	4	٭0.9
Hypertensive diseases — Maladies hypertensives	241	16.9	389	24.8	104	13.2	94	20.2
Ischaemic heart disease — Cardiopathie ischémique	4 405	309.4	4 200	267.8	65	8.2	36	7.7
Cerebrovascular disease — Maladie cérébrovasculaire	1 054	74.0	1 407	89.7	52	6.6	38	8.2

Cause of death — Cause de décès	Armenia - Arménie				Bahrain - Bahreïn			
	2016 (C)				2013 (C)			
	Male — Masculin		Female — Féminin		Male — Masculin		Female — Féminin	
	Number Nombre	Rate Taux	Number Nombre	Rate Taux	Number Nombre	Rate Taux	Number Nombre	Rate Taux
Diseases of arteries, arterioles and capillaries — Maladies des artères, artérioles et capillaires	372	26.1	486	31.0	3	✦0.4	-	-
Diseases of the respiratory system — Maladies de l'appareil respiratoire								
Total	1 079	75.8	1 069	68.2	61	7.7	36	7.7
Influenza — Grippe	4	✦0.3	4	✦0.3	1	✦0.1	1	✦0.2
Pneumonia — Pneumopathies	393	27.6	437	27.9	21	✦2.7	13	✦2.8
Chronic lower respiratory diseases — Maladies chroniques des voies respiratoires inférieures	582	40.9	539	34.4	18	✦2.3	14	✦3.0
Diseases of the digestive system — Maladies de l'appareil digestif								
Total	988	69.4	855	54.5	34	4.3	26	✦5.6
Gastric and duodenal ulcer — Ulcère de l'estomac et du duodénum	134	9.4	129	8.2	2	✦0.3	2	✦0.4
Diseases of the liver — Maladies du foie	667	46.8	505	32.2	20	✦2.5	10	✦2.2
Diseases of the musculoskeletal system and connective tissue — Maladies du système ostéo-articularie, des muscles et du tissu conjonctif	14	✦1.0	28	✦1.8	7	✦0.9	7	✦1.5
Diseases of the genitourinary system — Maladies de l'appareil génito-urinaire								
Total	448	31.5	422	26.9	41	5.2	38	8.2
Disorders of kidney and ureter — Affections du rein et de l'uretère	377	26.5	411	26.2	35	4.4	25	✦5.4
Hyperplasia of prostate — Hyperplasie de la prostate	65	16.7	..	..	2	✦2.1	..	..
Pregnancy, childbirth and the puerperium — Grossesse, accouchement et puerpéralité								
Total	..	..	14	✦34.5	..	..	4	✦20.0
Pregnancy with abortive outcome — Grossesse se terminant par un avortement	..	..	2	✦4.9	..	..	1	✦5.0
Other direct obstetric causes — Autres décès maternels directs	..	..	8	✦19.7	..	..	1	✦5.0
Indirect obstetric causes — Décès maternels indirects	..	..	4	✦9.9	..	..	2	✦10.0
Certain conditions originating in the perinatal period — Certaines affections dont l'origine se situe dans la période périnatale	96	447.7	56	292.5	29	✦283.0	20	✦205.2
Congenital malformations, deformations and chromosomal abnormalities — Malformations congénitales et anomalies chromosomiques	226	1 053.9	174	908.8	22	✦214.7	24	✦246.2
Symptoms, signs and abnormal clinical and laboratory findings, not elsewhere classified — Symptômes, signes et résultats anormaux d'examens cliniques et de laboratoire, non classés ailleurs	246	17.3	302	19.3	186	23.6	117	25.2
All other diseases — Toutes autres maladies	18	✦1.3	6	✦0.4	7	✦0.9	5	✦1.1
External causes — Causes externes								
Total	961	67.5	324	20.7	181	23.0	46	9.9
Accidents								
Total	290	20.4	83	5.3	125	15.9	29	✦6.2
Transport accidents — Accidents de transport	168	11.8	53	3.4	68	8.6	18	✦3.9
Falls — Chutes	10	✦0.7	5	✦0.3	9	✦1.1	2	✦0.4
Accidental drowning and submersion — Noyade et submersion accidentelles	12	✦0.8	1	✦0.1	15	✦1.9	3	✦0.6
Exposure to smoke, fire and flames — Exposition à la fumée, au feu et aux flammes	7	✦0.5	-	-	18	✦2.3	2	✦0.4
Accidental poisoning by and exposure to noxious substances — Intoxication accidentelle par des substances nocives et exposition à ces substances	6	✦0.4	3	✦0.2	-	-	-	-
Intentional self-harm — Lésions auto-infligées	53	3.7	14	✦0.9	5	✦0.6	-	-
Assault — Agresssions	26	✦1.8	8	✦0.5	3	✦0.4	2	✦0.4
All other external causes — Toutes autres causes externes	592	41.6	219	14.0	48	6.1	15	✦3.2

20. Death and death rates by cause and sex: 2012 - 2016
Décès et taux de mortalité par cause et sexe : 2012 - 2016 (continued - suite)

Cause of death — Cause de décès	Bahrain - Bahreïn 2014 (C)				Brunei Darussalam - Brunéi Darussalam 2014 (+C)			
	Male — Masculin		Female — Féminin		Male — Masculin		Female — Féminin	
	Number Nombre	Rate Taux	Number Nombre	Rate Taux	Number Nombre	Rate Taux	Number Nombre	Rate Taux
TOTAL	1 638	203.1	1 057	208.0	833	397.2	637	321.9
Certain infectious and parasitic diseases — Certaines maladies infectieuses et parasitaires								
Total	40	5.0	21	٭4.1	56	26.7	29	٭14.7
Intestinal infectious diseases — Maladies infectieuses intestinales	2	٭0.2	1	٭0.2	2	٭1.0	1	٭0.5
Tuberculosis — Tuberculose	6	٭0.7	-	-	7	٭3.3	7	٭3.5
Tetanus — Tétanos	-	-	-	-	-	-	-	-
Diphtheria — Diphtérie	-	-	-	-	-	-	-	-
Whooping cough — Coqueluche	-	-	-	-	-	-	-	-
Meningococcal infection — Infection à méningocoques	-	-	-	-	-	-	-	-
Septicaemia — Septicémie	8	٭1.0	12	٭2.4	28	٭13.4	14	٭7.1
Acute poliomyelitis — Poliomyélite aiguë	-	-	-	-	-	-	-	-
Measles — Rougeole	-	-	-	-	-	-	-	-
Viral hepatitis — Hépatite virale	15	٭1.9	6	٭1.2	4	٭1.9	1	٭0.5
Human immunodeficiency virus [HIV] disease — Maladies dues au virus de l'immunodéficience humaine (VIH)	8	٭1.0			1	٭0.5	-	-
Malaria — Paludisme	-	-	-	-	-	-	-	-
Neoplasms — Tumeurs	146	18.1	146	28.7	147	70.1	168	84.9
Malignant neoplasms — Tumeurs malignes								
Total	140	17.4	139	27.4	138	65.8	160	80.8
Malignant neoplasm of lip, oral cavity and pharynx — Tumeur maligne de la lèvre, de la cavité buccale et du pharynx	3	٭0.4	2	٭0.4	6	٭2.9	4	٭2.0
Malignant neoplasm of oesophagus — Tumeur maligne de l'oesophage	2	٭0.2	-	-	2	٭1.0	1	٭0.5
Malignant neoplasm of stomach — Tumeur maligne de l'estomac	10	٭1.2	3	٭0.6	11	٭5.2	10	٭5.1
Malignant neoplasm of colon, rectosigmoid junction, rectum, anus and anal canal — Tumeur maligne du côlon, de la jonction recto-sigmoïdienne, du rectum, de l'anus et du canal anal	22	٭2.7	13	٭2.6	16	٭7.6	19	٭9.6
Malignant neoplasm of liver and intrahepatic bile ducts — Tumeur maligne du foie et des voies bilaires intrahépatiques	5	٭0.6	4	٭0.8	17	٭8.1	6	٭3.0
Malignant neoplasm of pancreas — Tumeur maligne du pancréas	9	٭1.1	8	٭1.6	4	٭1.9	3	٭1.5
Malignant neoplasm of trachea, bronchus and lung — Tumeur maligne de la trachée, des bronches et du poumon	23	٭2.9	5	٭1.0	37	17.6	25	٭12.6
Malignant neoplasm of female breast — Tumeur maligne du sein chez la femme	..	..	43	11.4	..	..	29	٭19.3
Malignant neoplasm of cervix uteri — Tumeur maligne du col de l'utérus	..	..	5	٭1.3	..	..	11	٭7.3
Malignant neoplasm of prostate — Tumeur maligne de la prostate	16	٭14.1	..	..	12	٭34.8	..	..
Malignant neoplasm of lymphoid, haematopoietic and related tissue — Tumeurs malignes primitives ou présumées primitives des tissus lymphoïde, hématopoïétique et apparentés	12	٭1.5	7	٭1.4	18	٭8.6	17	٭8.6
Disorders of the blood and blood-forming organs and certain disorders involving the immune mechanism — Maladies du sang et des organes hématopoïétiques et certains troubles du système immunitaire								
Total	23	٭2.9	23	٭4.5	4	٭1.9	7	٭3.5
Anaemias — Anémies	18	٭2.2	19	٭3.7	2	٭1.0	1	٭0.5
Endocrine, nutritional and metabolic diseases — Maladies endocriniennes, nutritionnelles et métaboliques								
Total	295	36.6	235	46.3	96	45.8	70	35.4
Diabetes mellitus — Diabète sucré	270	33.5	204	40.2	84	40.1	57	28.8
Malnutrition — Malnutrition	-	-	-	-	-	-	-	-
Mental and behavioural disorders — Troubles mentaux et du comportement	9	٭1.1	7	٭1.4	3	٭1.4	3	٭1.5
Diseases of the nervous system — Maladies du système nerveux	28	٭3.5	19	٭3.7	19	٭9.1	14	٭7.1
Diseases of the circulatory system — Maladies de l'appareil circulatoire								
Total	595	73.8	270	53.1	263	125.4	145	73.3
Acute rheumatic fever and chronic rheumatic heart diseases — Rhumatisme articularie aigu et cardiopathies rhumatismales chroniques	2	٭0.2	8	٭1.6	-	-	1	٭0.5
Hypertensive diseases — Maladies hypertensives	113	14.0	80	15.7	32	15.3	32	16.2
Ischaemic heart disease — Cardiopathie ischémique	62	7.7	24	٭4.7	134	63.9	43	21.7
Cerebrovascular disease — Maladie cérébrovasculaire	50	6.2	31	6.1	51	24.3	52	26.3

Cause of death — Cause de décès	Bahrain - Bahreïn 2014 (C) Male — Masculin Number Nombre	Rate Taux	Female — Féminin Number Nombre	Rate Taux	Brunei Darussalam - Brunéi Darussalam 2014 (+C) Male — Masculin Number Nombre	Rate Taux	Female — Féminin Number Nombre	Rate Taux
Diseases of arteries, arterioles and capillaries — Maladies des artères, artérioles et capillaires	3	♦0.4	4	♦0.8	9	♦4.3	-	-
Diseases of the respiratory system — Maladies de l'appareil respiratoire								
Total	46	5.7	37	7.3	78	37.2	69	34.9
Influenza — Grippe	-	-	-	-	-	-	-	-
Pneumonia — Pneumopathies	15	♦1.9	13	♦2.6	33	15.7	30	♦15.2
Chronic lower respiratory diseases — Maladies chroniques des voies respiratoires inférieures	17	♦2.1	13	♦2.6	29	♦13.8	25	♦12.6
Diseases of the digestive system — Maladies de l'appareil digestif								
Total	34	4.2	19	♦3.7	23	♦11.0	15	♦7.6
Gastric and duodenal ulcer — Ulcère de l'estomac et du duodénum	3	♦0.4	1	♦0.2	2	♦1.0	-	-
Diseases of the liver — Maladies du foie	19	♦2.4	7	♦1.4	7	♦3.3	5	♦2.5
Diseases of the musculoskeletal system and connective tissue — Maladies du système ostéo-articularie, des muscles et du tissu conjonctif	6	♦0.7	8	♦1.6	4	♦1.9	9	♦4.5
Diseases of the genitourinary system — Maladies de l'appareil génito-urinaire								
Total	33	4.1	23	♦4.5	20	♦9.5	20	♦10.1
Disorders of kidney and ureter — Affections du rein et de l'uretère	22	♦2.7	16	♦3.1	14	♦6.7	13	♦6.6
Hyperplasia of prostate — Hyperplasie de la prostate	2	♦1.8	..	..	3	♦8.7	..	..
Pregnancy, childbirth and the puerperium — Grossesse, accouchement et puerpéralité								
Total	..	..	2	♦9.6	..	..	-	-
Pregnancy with abortive outcome — Grossesse se terminant par un avortement	..	..	1	♦4.8	..	..	-	-
Other direct obstetric causes — Autres décès maternels directs	..	..	1	♦4.8	..	..	-	-
Indirect obstetric causes — Décès maternels indirects	..	..	-	-	..	..	-	-
Certain conditions originating in the perinatal period — Certaines affections dont l'origine se situe dans la période périnatale	43	398.7	34	335.1	14	♦390.5	10	♦302.5
Congenital malformations, deformations and chromosomal abnormalities — Malformations congénitales et anomalies chromosomiques	32	296.7	33	325.3	13	♦362.6	9	♦272.2
Symptoms, signs and abnormal clinical and laboratory findings, not elsewhere classified — Symptômes, signes et résultats anormaux d'examens cliniques et de laboratoire, non classés ailleurs	125	15.5	140	27.6	29	♦13.8	39	19.7
All other diseases — Toutes autres maladies	9	♦1.1	4	♦0.8	2	♦1.0	10	♦5.1
External causes — Causes externes								
Total	174	21.6	36	7.1	62	29.6	20	♦10.1
Accidents								
Total	129	16.0	27	♦5.3	49	23.4	12	♦6.1
Transport accidents — Accidents de transport	64	7.9	14	♦2.8	23	♦11.0	5	♦2.5
Falls — Chutes	12	♦1.5	2	♦0.4	8	♦3.8	-	-
Accidental drowning and submersion — Noyade et submersion accidentelles	7	♦0.9	-	-	6	♦2.9	1	♦0.5
Exposure to smoke, fire and flames — Exposition à la fumée, au feu et aux flammes	8	♦1.0	4	♦0.8	2	♦1.0	2	♦1.0
Accidental poisoning by and exposure to noxious substances — Intoxication accidentelle par des substances nocives et exposition à ces substances	-	-	-	-	2	♦1.0	-	-
Intentional self-harm — Lésions auto-infligées	8	♦1.0	1	♦0.2	3	♦1.4	2	♦1.0
Assault — Agresssions	7	♦0.9	-	-	-	-	1	♦0.5
All other external causes — Toutes autres causes externes	30	♦3.7	8	♦1.6	10	♦4.8	5	♦2.5

20. Death and death rates by cause and sex: 2012 - 2016
Décès et taux de mortalité par cause et sexe : 2012 - 2016 (continued - suite)

Cause of death — Cause de décès	Brunei Darussalam - Brunéi Darussalam 2015 (+C) Male — Masculin Number Nombre	Rate Taux	Female — Féminin Number Nombre	Rate Taux	China, Hong Kong SAR - Chine, Hong Kong RAS 2014 (...) Male — Masculin Number Nombre	Female — Féminin Number Nombre	2015 (...) Male — Masculin Number Nombre	Female — Féminin Number Nombre
TOTAL	830	391.7	717	357.6	25 378	20 328	25 810	20 943
Certain infectious and parasitic diseases — Certaines maladies infectieuses et parasitaires								
Total	56	26.4	36	18.0	663	667	696	586
Intestinal infectious diseases — Maladies infectieuses intestinales	1	+0.5	-	-	29	36	22	37
Tuberculosis — Tuberculose	8	+3.8	6	+3.0	131	56	142	25
Tetanus — Tétanos..........	-	-	-	-	-	-	-	-
Diphtheria — Diphtérie..........	-	-	-	-	-	-	-	-
Whooping cough — Coqueluche	-	-	-	-	-	-	-	-
Meningococcal infection — Infection à méningocoques	-	-	-	-	-	-	1	-
Septicaemia — Septicémie	25	+11.8	26	+13.0	383	501	424	467
Acute poliomyelitis — Poliomyélite aiguë	-	-	-	-	-	-	-	-
Measles — Rougeole..........	-	-	-	-	-	-	-	-
Viral hepatitis — Hépatite virale	11	+5.2	2	+1.0	58	20	25	6
Human immunodeficiency virus [HIV] disease — Maladies dues au virus de l'immunodéficience humaine (VIH)..........	1	+0.5	1	+0.5	18	2	20	5
Malaria — Paludisme..........	-	-	-	-	1	-	-	-
Neoplasms — Tumeurs	142	67.0	181	90.3	8 380	5 747	8 540	6 098
Malignant neoplasms — Tumeurs malignes								
Total..........	137	64.7	175	87.3	8 223	5 580	8 345	5 971
Malignant neoplasm of lip, oral cavity and pharynx — Tumeur maligne de la lèvre, de la cavité buccale et du pharynx	11	+5.2	3	+1.5	387	134	415	129
Malignant neoplasm of oesophagus — Tumeur maligne de l'oesophage	4	+1.9	-	-	254	73	242	57
Malignant neoplasm of stomach — Tumeur maligne de l'estomac	3	+1.4	7	+3.5	394	263	410	259
Malignant neoplasm of colon, rectosigmoid junction, rectum, anus and anal canal — Tumeur maligne du côlon, de la jonction recto-sigmoïdienne, du rectum, de l'anus et du canal anal..........	15	+7.1	28	+14.0	1 139	895	1 177	896
Malignant neoplasm of liver and intrahepatic bile ducts — Tumeur maligne du foie et des voies bilaires intrahépatiques	21	+9.9	7	+3.5	1 149	436	1 139	432
Malignant neoplasm of pancreas — Tumeur maligne du pancréas..........	5	+2.4	6	+3.0	328	248	345	346
Malignant neoplasm of trachea, bronchus and lung — Tumeur maligne de la trachée, des bronches et du poumon..........	26	+12.3	26	+13.0	2 537	1 329	2 604	1 427
Malignant neoplasm of female breast — Tumeur maligne du sein chez la femme	..		33	21.6	..	604	..	637
Malignant neoplasm of cervix uteri — Tumeur maligne du col de l'utérus..........	..	..	8	+5.2	..	131	..	169
Malignant neoplasm of prostate — Tumeur maligne de la prostate	9	+24.5	..	..	398	..	404	..
Malignant neoplasm of lymphoid, haematopoietic and related tissue — Tumeurs malignes primitives ou présumées primitives des tissus lymphoïde, hématopoïétique et apparentés..........	19	+9.0	12	+6.0	490	331	468	395
Disorders of the blood and blood-forming organs and certain disorders involving the immune mechanism — Maladies du sang et des organes hématopoïétiques et certains troubles du système immunitaire								
Total	6	+2.8	11	+5.5	46	60	46	53
Anaemias — Anémies	4	+1.9	3	+1.5	22	39	22	27
Endocrine, nutritional and metabolic diseases — Maladies endocriniennes, nutritionnelles et métaboliques								
Total	93	43.9	85	42.4	244	279	293	324
Diabetes mellitus — Diabète sucré..........	82	38.7	65	32.4	186	204	241	251
Malnutrition — Malnutrition	-	-	1	+0.5	5	2	8	2
Mental and behavioural disorders — Troubles mentaux et du comportement	14	+6.6	9	+4.5	451	671	463	695
Diseases of the nervous system — Maladies du système nerveux..........	28	+13.2	16	+8.0	217	182	205	206
Diseases of the circulatory system — Maladies de l'appareil circulatoire								
Total	167	78.8	139	69.3	5 615	4 832	5 409	4 696
Acute rheumatic fever and chronic rheumatic heart diseases — Rhumatisme articularie aigu et cardiopathies rhumatismales chroniques	-	-	3	+1.5	29	59	20	56
Hypertensive diseases — Maladies hypertensives..........	30	+14.2	24	+12.0	362	433	335	394
Ischaemic heart disease — Cardiopathie ischémique..........	69	32.6	36	18.0	2 515	1 778	2 406	1 717

20. Death and death rates by cause and sex: 2012 - 2016
Décès et taux de mortalité par cause et sexe : 2012 - 2016 (continued - suite)

Cause of death — Cause de décès	Brunei Darussalam - Brunéi Darussalam 2015 (+C)				China, Hong Kong SAR - Chine, Hong Kong RAS			
	Male — Masculin		Female — Féminin		2014 (...)		2015 (...)	
					Male — Masculin	Female — Féminin	Male — Masculin	Female — Féminin
	Number Nombre	Rate Taux	Number Nombre	Rate Taux	Number Nombre	Number Nombre	Number Nombre	Number Nombre
Cerebrovascular disease — Maladie cérébrovasculaire	40	18.9	42	20.9	1 717	1 619	1 671	1 588
Diseases of arteries, arterioles and capillaries — Maladies des artères, artérioles et capillaires	7	♦3.3	8	♦4.0	268	153	299	152
Diseases of the respiratory system — Maladies de l'appareil respiratoire								
Total	66	31.1	93	46.4	5 711	4 200	6 038	4 594
Influenza — Grippe	-	-	-	-	32	17	105	118
Pneumonia — Pneumopathies	33	15.6	42	20.9	4 038	3 464	4 223	3 781
Chronic lower respiratory diseases — Maladies chroniques des voies respiratoires inférieures	19	♦9.0	34	17.0	1 310	432	1 275	385
Diseases of the digestive system — Maladies de l'appareil digestif								
Total	25	♦11.8	17	♦8.5	821	743	881	691
Gastric and duodenal ulcer — Ulcère de l'estomac et du duodénum	1	♦0.5	1	♦0.5	55	44	66	39
Diseases of the liver — Maladies du foie	10	♦4.7	6	♦3.0	315	179	311	157
Diseases of the musculoskeletal system and connective tissue — Maladies du système ostéo-articularie, des muscles et du tissu conjonctif	6	♦2.8	4	♦2.0	75	98	74	87
Diseases of the genitourinary system — Maladies de l'appareil génito-urinaire								
Total	15	♦7.1	20	♦10.0	1 038	1 199	1 056	1 210
Disorders of kidney and ureter — Affections du rein et de l'uretère	10	♦4.7	16	♦8.0	830	906	841	874
Hyperplasia of prostate — Hyperplasie de la prostate	3	♦8.2	..	..	4	..	7	..
Pregnancy, childbirth and the puerperium — Grossesse, accouchement et puerpéralité								
Total	..	..	2	♦29.9	..	2	..	1
Pregnancy with abortive outcome — Grossesse se terminant par un avortement	..	..	1	♦14.9	..	-	..	1
Other direct obstetric causes — Autres décès maternels directs	..	..	1	♦14.9	..	2	..	-
Indirect obstetric causes — Décès maternels indirects	..	..	-	-	..	-	..	-
Certain conditions originating in the perinatal period — Certaines affections dont l'origine se situe dans la période périnatale	15	♦425.9	12	♦377.7	20	24	21	16
Congenital malformations, deformations and chromosomal abnormalities — Malformations congénitales et anomalies chromosomiques	21	♦596.3	13	♦409.2	23	38	29	36
Symptoms, signs and abnormal clinical and laboratory findings, not elsewhere classified — Symptômes, signes et résultats anormaux d'examens cliniques et de laboratoire, non classés ailleurs	37	17.5	38	19.0	792	813	713	824
All other diseases — Toutes autres maladies	5	♦2.4	6	♦3.0	107	114	67	112
External causes — Causes externes								
Total	76	35.9	35	17.5	1 175	659	1 279	714
Accidents								
Total	66	31.1	26	♦13.0	539	253	603	313
Transport accidents — Accidents de transport	26	♦12.3	8	♦4.0	91	36	77	33
Falls — Chutes	5	♦2.4	2	♦1.0	166	75	211	116
Accidental drowning and submersion — Noyade et submersion accidentelles	15	♦7.1	2	♦1.0	22	10	32	16
Exposure to smoke, fire and flames — Exposition à la fumée, au feu et aux flammes	-	-	1	♦0.5	1	3	5	5
Accidental poisoning by and exposure to noxious substances — Intoxication accidentelle par des substances nocives et exposition à ces substances	1	♦0.5	3	♦1.5	113	27	115	23
Intentional self-harm — Lésions auto-infligées	5	♦2.4	2	♦1.0	563	363	628	363
Assault — Agresssions	2	♦0.9	-	-	6	7	13	9
All other external causes — Toutes autres causes externes	3	♦1.4	7	♦3.5	67	36	35	29

	Cyprus - Chypre				Georgia - Géorgie			
Cause of death — Cause de décès	2015 (U)		2016 (U)		2014 (C)			
	Male — Masculin	Female — Féminin	Male — Masculin	Female — Féminin	Male — Masculin		Female — Féminin	
	Number Nombre	Number Nombre	Number Nombre	Number Nombre	Number Nombre	Rate Taux	Number Nombre	Rate Taux
TOTAL	3 138	2 850	3 012	2 575	24 851	1 401.7	24 236	1 248.7
Certain infectious and parasitic diseases — Certaines maladies infectieuses et parasitaires								
Total	72	74	62	70	419	23.6	135	7.0
Intestinal infectious diseases — Maladies infectieuses intestinales	21	17	12	26	9	٭0.5	5	٭0.3
Tuberculosis — Tuberculose	1	-	1	-	88	5.0	23	٭1.2
Tetanus — Tétanos	-	-	-	-	-	-	-	-
Diphtheria — Diphtérie	-	-	-	-	-	-	-	-
Whooping cough — Coqueluche	-	-	-	-	-	-	-	-
Meningococcal infection — Infection à méningocoques	-	1	-	-	3	٭0.2	1	٭0.1
Septicaemia — Septicémie	38	50	34	37	33	1.9	22	٭1.1
Acute poliomyelitis — Poliomyélite aiguë	-	-	-	-	-	-	-	-
Measles — Rougeole	-	-	-	-	-	-	-	-
Viral hepatitis — Hépatite virale	4	1	5	1	205	11.6	48	2.5
Human immunodeficiency virus [HIV] disease — Maladies dues au virus de l'immunodéficience humaine (VIH)	4	-	1	-	37	2.1	8	٭0.4
Malaria — Paludisme	-	-	-	-	-	-	-	-
Neoplasms — Tumeurs	791	592	778	546	3 132	176.7	2 493	128.4
Malignant neoplasms — Tumeurs malignes								
Total	769	566	758	522	2 992	168.8	2 381	122.7
Malignant neoplasm of lip, oral cavity and pharynx — Tumeur maligne de la lèvre, de la cavité buccale et du pharynx	12	5	14	6	104	5.9	25	٭1.3
Malignant neoplasm of oesophagus — Tumeur maligne de l'oesophage	6	1	7	1	47	2.7	19	٭1.0
Malignant neoplasm of stomach — Tumeur maligne de l'estomac	43	18	31	28	289	16.3	190	9.8
Malignant neoplasm of colon, rectosigmoid junction, rectum, anus and anal canal — Tumeur maligne du côlon, de la jonction recto-sigmoïdienne, du rectum, de l'anus et du canal anal	61	54	74	42	175	9.9	165	8.5
Malignant neoplasm of liver and intrahepatic bile ducts — Tumeur maligne du foie et des voies bilaires intrahépatiques	34	17	29	21	188	10.6	137	7.1
Malignant neoplasm of pancreas — Tumeur maligne du pancréas	50	35	46	36	114	6.4	105	5.4
Malignant neoplasm of trachea, bronchus and lung — Tumeur maligne de la trachée, des bronches et du poumon	183	53	197	62	780	44.0	136	7.0
Malignant neoplasm of female breast — Tumeur maligne du sein chez la femme	..	113	..	106	..	...	515	...
Malignant neoplasm of cervix uteri — Tumeur maligne du col de l'utérus	..	14	..	13	..	...	158	...
Malignant neoplasm of prostate — Tumeur maligne de la prostate	100	..	90	..	235	...	..	...
Malignant neoplasm of lymphoid, haematopoietic and related tissue — Tumeurs malignes primitives ou présumées primitives des tissus lymphoïde, hématopoïétique et apparentés	71	74	70	46	181	10.2	172	8.9
Disorders of the blood and blood-forming organs and certain disorders involving the immune mechanism — Maladies du sang et des organes hématopoïétiques et certains troubles du système immunitaire								
Total	17	16	22	25	112	6.3	130	6.7
Anaemias — Anémies	8	9	12	15	76	4.3	94	4.8
Endocrine, nutritional and metabolic diseases — Maladies endocriniennes, nutritionnelles et métaboliques								
Total	219	232	207	178	495	27.9	632	32.6
Diabetes mellitus — Diabète sucré	186	189	178	133	461	26.0	576	29.7
Malnutrition — Malnutrition	2	1	2	1	3	٭0.2	2	٭0.1
Mental and behavioural disorders — Troubles mentaux et du comportement	50	100	54	108	47	2.7	49	2.5
Diseases of the nervous system — Maladies du système nerveux	107	128	107	116	310	17.5	289	14.9
Diseases of the circulatory system — Maladies de l'appareil circulatoire								
Total	1 058	1 025	981	871	9 680	546.0	10 939	563.6
Acute rheumatic fever and chronic rheumatic heart diseases — Rhumatisme articularie aigu et cardiopathies rhumatismales chroniques	9	19	11	22	55	3.1	75	3.9
Hypertensive diseases — Maladies hypertensives	85	131	55	118	1 296	73.1	1 875	96.6
Ischaemic heart disease — Cardiopathie ischémique	426	243	443	203	2 943	166.0	3 043	156.8

Cause of death — Cause de décès	Cyprus - Chypre				Georgia - Géorgie			
	2015 (U)		2016 (U)		2014 (C)			
	Male — Masculin	Female — Féminin	Male — Masculin	Female — Féminin	Male — Masculin		Female — Féminin	
	Number Nombre	Number Nombre	Number Nombre	Number Nombre	Number Nombre	Rate Taux	Number Nombre	Rate Taux
Cerebrovascular disease — Maladie cérébrovasculaire	170	206	163	200	2 592	146.2	3 153	162.4
Diseases of arteries, arterioles and capillaries — Maladies des artères, artérioles et capillaires	51	27	45	17	159	9.0	114	5.9
Diseases of the respiratory system — Maladies de l'appareil respiratoire								
Total	313	237	276	220	767	43.3	574	29.6
Influenza — Grippe	2	-	1	1	5	♦0.3	4	♦0.2
Pneumonia — Pneumopathies	31	39	34	30	256	14.4	225	11.6
Chronic lower respiratory diseases — Maladies chroniques des voies respiratoires inférieures	94	40	96	56	198	11.2	101	5.2
Diseases of the digestive system — Maladies de l'appareil digestif								
Total	100	94	112	82	875	49.4	470	24.2
Gastric and duodenal ulcer — Ulcère de l'estomac et du duodénum	2	4	9	3	75	4.2	45	2.3
Diseases of the liver — Maladies du foie	40	16	38	12	476	26.8	127	6.5
Diseases of the musculoskeletal system and connective tissue — Maladies du système ostéo-articularie, des muscles et du tissu conjonctif	10	18	8	18	21	♦1.2	45	2.3
Diseases of the genitourinary system — Maladies de l'appareil génito-urinaire								
Total	114	103	98	104	284	16.0	243	12.5
Disorders of kidney and ureter — Affections du rein et de l'uretère	68	58	57	49	247	13.9	224	11.5
Hyperplasia of prostate — Hyperplasie de la prostate	5	..	4	..	15	...	..	..
Pregnancy, childbirth and the puerperium — Grossesse, accouchement et puerpéralité								
Total	..	-	..	-	..	..	18	♦29.7
Pregnancy with abortive outcome — Grossesse se terminant par un avortement	..	-	..	-	..	..	2	♦3.3
Other direct obstetric causes — Autres décès maternels directs	..	-	..	-	..	..	13	♦21.4
Indirect obstetric causes — Décès maternels indirects	..	-	..	-	..	..	3	♦4.9
Certain conditions originating in the perinatal period — Certaines affections dont l'origine se situe dans la période périnatale	9	9	12	7	217	692.7	171	583.4
Congenital malformations, deformations and chromosomal abnormalities — Malformations congénitales et anomalies chromosomiques	7	8	11	8	79	252.2	74	252.5
Symptoms, signs and abnormal clinical and laboratory findings, not elsewhere classified — Symptômes, signes et résultats anormaux d'examens cliniques et de laboratoire, non classés ailleurs	79	100	69	98	6 998	394.7	7 424	382.5
All other diseases — Toutes autres maladies	8	13	11	25	15	♦0.8	16	♦0.8
External causes — Causes externes								
Total	184	101	204	99	1 400	79.0	534	27.5
Accidents								
Total	134	84	155	81	1 051	59.3	432	22.3
Transport accidents — Accidents de transport	49	26	47	16	473	26.7	153	7.9
Falls — Chutes	16	6	28	12	92	5.2	91	4.7
Accidental drowning and submersion — Noyade et submersion accidentelles	9	3	17	5	38	2.1	11	♦0.6
Exposure to smoke, fire and flames — Exposition à la fumée, au feu et aux flammes	1	4	1	1	62	3.5	19	♦1.0
Accidental poisoning by and exposure to noxious substances — Intoxication accidentelle par des substances nocives et exposition à ces substances	11	1	12	5	23	♦1.3	14	♦0.7
Intentional self-harm — Lésions auto-infligées	31	9	31	5	153	8.6	36	1.9
Assault — Agresssions	10	3	7	5	59	3.3	26	♦1.3
All other external causes — Toutes autres causes externes	9	5	11	8	137	7.7	40	2.1

Cause of death — Cause de décès	Georgia - Géorgie 2015 (C)				Iran (Islamic Republic of) - Iran (République islamique d')			
	Male — Masculin		Female — Féminin		2014 (U)		2015 (U)	
					Male — Masculin	Female — Féminin	Male — Masculin	Female — Féminin
	Number Nombre	Rate Taux	Number Nombre	Rate Taux	Number Nombre	Number Nombre	Number Nombre	Number Nombre
TOTAL	25 198	1 418.6	23 923	1 232.6	158 106	114 405	189 429	137 716
Certain infectious and parasitic diseases — Certaines maladies infectieuses et parasitaires								
Total	357	20.1	155	8.0	2 765	1 937	3 601	2 356
Intestinal infectious diseases — Maladies infectieuses intestinales	6	♦0.3	10	♦0.5	233	202	462	380
Tuberculosis — Tuberculose	50	2.8	17	♦0.9	295	184	478	314
Tetanus — Tétanos	-	-	1	♦0.1	3	-	3	1
Diphtheria — Diphtérie	-	-	-	-	-	1	-	-
Whooping cough — Coqueluche	-	-	-	-	-	1	1	1
Meningococcal infection — Infection à méningocoques	-	-	-	-	29	28	155	106
Septicaemia — Septicémie	41	2.3	29	♦1.5	795	692	604	490
Acute poliomyelitis — Poliomyélite aiguë	-	-	-	-	2	-	9	3
Measles — Rougeole	-	-	1	♦0.1	-	-	3	-
Viral hepatitis — Hépatite virale	210	11.8	60	3.1	474	155	644	197
Human immunodeficiency virus [HIV] disease — Maladies dues au virus de l'immunodéficience humaine (VIH)	29	♦1.6	10	♦0.5	213	39	263	71
Malaria — Paludisme	-	-	-	-	2	1	2	-
Neoplasms — Tumeurs	3 462	194.9	2 786	143.5	22 719	15 599	28 838	20 083
Malignant neoplasms — Tumeurs malignes								
Total	3 329	187.4	2 660	137.1	21 406	14 463	27 491	19 078
Malignant neoplasm of lip, oral cavity and pharynx — Tumeur maligne de la lèvre, de la cavité buccale et du pharynx	143	8.1	32	1.6	191	164	292	212
Malignant neoplasm of oesophagus — Tumeur maligne de l'oesophage	46	2.6	19	♦1.0	862	653	1 005	719
Malignant neoplasm of stomach — Tumeur maligne de l'estomac	261	14.7	219	11.3	4 194	2 188	4 841	2 451
Malignant neoplasm of colon, rectosigmoid junction, rectum, anus and anal canal — Tumeur maligne du côlon, de la jonction recto-sigmoïdienne, du rectum, de l'anus et du canal anal	227	12.8	197	10.2	1 438	1 053	1 923	1 418
Malignant neoplasm of liver and intrahepatic bile ducts — Tumeur maligne du foie et des voies bilaires intrahépatiques	204	11.5	135	7.0	1 534	1 113	1 619	1 182
Malignant neoplasm of pancreas — Tumeur maligne du pancréas	103	5.8	81	4.2	698	449	1 031	675
Malignant neoplasm of trachea, bronchus and lung — Tumeur maligne de la trachée, des bronches et du poumon	866	48.8	150	7.7	3 101	1 366	3 529	1 511
Malignant neoplasm of female breast — Tumeur maligne du sein chez la femme	..	..	600	37.3	..	1 825	..	2 793
Malignant neoplasm of cervix uteri — Tumeur maligne du col de l'utérus	..	..	162	10.1	..	131	..	184
Malignant neoplasm of prostate — Tumeur maligne de la prostate	279	52.4	..	..	1 851	..	2 586	..
Malignant neoplasm of lymphoid, haematopoietic and related tissue — Tumeurs malignes primitives ou présumées primitives des tissus lymphoïde, hématopoïétique et apparentés	185	10.4	160	8.2	2 296	1 451	3 270	2 065
Disorders of the blood and blood-forming organs and certain disorders involving the immune mechanism — Maladies du sang et des organes hématopoïétiques et certains troubles du système immunitaire								
Total	161	9.1	162	8.3	590	494	909	744
Anaemias — Anémies	119	6.7	121	6.2	274	219	394	362
Endocrine, nutritional and metabolic diseases — Maladies endocriniennes, nutritionnelles et métaboliques								
Total	455	25.6	637	32.8	5 045	6 273	8 604	9 816
Diabetes mellitus — Diabète sucré	415	23.4	573	29.5	4 377	5 609	7 361	8 710
Malnutrition — Malnutrition	1	♦0.1	2	♦0.1	50	44	67	75
Mental and behavioural disorders — Troubles mentaux et du comportement	42	2.4	35	1.8	1 310	704	1 154	624
Diseases of the nervous system — Maladies du système nerveux	312	17.6	252	13.0	2 655	2 304	3 994	3 389
Diseases of the circulatory system — Maladies de l'appareil circulatoire								
Total	9 621	541.6	11 294	581.9	62 655	52 599	74 071	61 690
Acute rheumatic fever and chronic rheumatic heart diseases — Rhumatisme articularie aigu et cardiopathies rhumatismales chroniques	112	6.3	179	9.2	324	321	684	655
Hypertensive diseases — Maladies hypertensives	1 100	61.9	1 786	92.0	8 991	9 143	10 069	10 359
Ischaemic heart disease — Cardiopathie ischémique	2 413	135.8	2 467	127.1	26 718	19 915	29 259	21 677

Cause of death — Cause de décès	Georgia - Géorgie 2015 (C)				Iran (Islamic Republic of) - Iran (République islamique d')			
	Male — Masculin		Female — Féminin		2014 (U)		2015 (U)	
					Male — Masculin	Female — Féminin	Male — Masculin	Female — Féminin
	Number Nombre	Rate Taux	Number Nombre	Rate Taux	Number Nombre	Number Nombre	Number Nombre	Number Nombre
Cerebrovascular disease — Maladie cérébrovasculaire..................................	2 889	162.6	3 412	175.8	11 983	11 260	14 265	13 137
Diseases of arteries, arterioles and capillaries — Maladies des artères, artérioles et capillaires	310	17.5	512	26.4	2 366	1 809	2 540	2 014
Diseases of the respiratory system — Maladies de l'appareil respiratoire								
Total	1 002	56.4	801	41.3	9 258	6 612	12 145	8 770
Influenza — Grippe..	3	⬩0.2	1	⬩0.1	32	31	241	208
Pneumonia — Pneumopathies..............................	408	23.0	399	20.6	2 412	1 828	3 275	2 560
Chronic lower respiratory diseases — Maladies chroniques des voies respiratoires inférieures	198	11.1	120	6.2	3 397	2 226	4 242	2 705
Diseases of the digestive system — Maladies de l'appareil digestif								
Total	885	49.8	543	28.0	3 841	2 809	4 553	3 339
Gastric and duodenal ulcer — Ulcère de l'estomac et du duodénum................	77	4.3	53	2.7	336	211	375	213
Diseases of the liver — Maladies du foie..........	485	27.3	156	8.0	1 331	831	1 674	1 059
Diseases of the musculoskeletal system and connective tissue — Maladies du système ostéo-articulaire, des muscles et du tissu conjonctif	15	⬩0.8	42	2.2	368	439	826	851
Diseases of the genitourinary system — Maladies de l'appareil génito-urinaire								
Total	280	15.8	188	9.7	2 884	2 235	4 832	3 503
Disorders of kidney and ureter — Affections du rein et de l'uretère	235	13.2	159	8.2	2 507	2 038	4 411	3 201
Hyperplasia of prostate — Hyperplasie de la prostate.............	11	⬩2.1	..	..	48	..	86	..
Pregnancy, childbirth and the puerperium — Grossesse, accouchement et puerpéralité								
Total	..	..	19	⬩32.1	..	104	..	111
Pregnancy with abortive outcome — Grossesse se terminant par un avortement	..	..	-	-	..	13	..	25
Other direct obstetric causes — Autres décès maternels directs	..	..	11	⬩18.6	..	64	..	65
Indirect obstetric causes — Décès maternels indirects	..	..	8	⬩13.5	..	15	..	17
Certain conditions originating in the perinatal period — Certaines affections dont l'origine se situe dans la période périnatale	189	611.6	156	550.3	5 491	4 572	6 093	4 994
Congenital malformations, deformations and chromosomal abnormalities — Malformations congénitales et anomalies chromosomiques	75	242.7	77	271.6	2 764	2 342	2 667	2 179
Symptoms, signs and abnormal clinical and laboratory findings, not elsewhere classified — Symptômes, signes et résultats anormaux d'examens cliniques et de laboratoire, non classés ailleurs	7 055	397.2	6 331	326.2	10 898	7 575	10 808	6 842
All other diseases — Toutes autres maladies	31	1.7	31	1.6	352	385	577	643
External causes — Causes externes								
Total	1 256	70.7	414	21.3	24 503	7 419	25 754	7 781
Accidents								
Total	915	51.5	325	16.7	18 503	5 573	19 450	5 988
Transport accidents — Accidents de transport	491	27.6	155	8.0	11 709	3 399	11 595	3 359
Falls — Chutes	122	6.9	47	2.4	1 003	362	839	325
Accidental drowning and submersion — Noyade et submersion accidentelles	72	4.1	21	⬩1.1	593	123	615	149
Exposure to smoke, fire and flames — Exposition à la fumée, au feu et aux flammes	52	2.9	30	⬩1.5	435	385	468	364
Accidental poisoning by and exposure to noxious substances — Intoxication accidentelle par des substances nocives et exposition à ces substances	13	⬩0.7	10	⬩0.5	1 087	296	1 105	318
Intentional self-harm — Lésions auto-infligées.................	138	7.8	48	2.5	1 695	793	1 669	706
Assault — Agresssions.................................	59	3.3	9	⬩0.5	1 710	224	697	157
All other external causes — Toutes autres causes externes	144	8.1	32	1.6	2 595	829	3 938	930

Israel - Israël

Cause of death — Cause de décès	2014 (C)				2015 (C)			
	Male — Masculin		Female — Féminin		Male — Masculin		Female — Féminin	
	Number Nombre	Rate Taux	Number Nombre	Rate Taux	Number Nombre	Rate Taux	Number Nombre	Rate Taux
TOTAL	21 024	516.5	21 146	510.1	22 334	537.7	21 932	518.9
Certain infectious and parasitic diseases — Certaines maladies infectieuses et parasitaires								
Total	1 132	27.8	1 208	29.1	1 222	29.4	1 318	31.2
Intestinal infectious diseases — Maladies infectieuses intestinales	96	2.4	124	3.0	84	2.0	129	3.1
Tuberculosis — Tuberculose	2	♦0.0	6	♦0.1	7	♦0.2	7	♦0.2
Tetanus — Tétanos	-	-	-	-	-	-	-	-
Diphtheria — Diphtérie	-	-	-	-	-	-	-	-
Whooping cough — Coqueluche	-	-	1	♦0.0	-	-	3	♦0.1
Meningococcal infection — Infection à méningocoques	1	♦0.0	2	♦0.0	1	♦0.0	1	♦0.0
Septicaemia — Septicémie	885	21.7	979	23.6	982	23.6	1 069	25.3
Acute poliomyelitis — Poliomyélite aiguë	-	-	-	-	-	-	-	-
Measles — Rougeole	-	-	-	-	-	-	-	-
Viral hepatitis — Hépatite virale	57	1.4	33	0.8	41	1.0	36	0.9
Human immunodeficiency virus [HIV] disease — Maladies dues au virus de l'immunodéficience humaine (VIH)	18	♦0.4	9	♦0.2	16	♦0.4	14	♦0.3
Malaria — Paludisme	-	-	-	-	-	-	-	-
Neoplasms — Tumeurs	5 621	138.1	5 572	134.4	5 861	141.1	5 534	130.9
Malignant neoplasms — Tumeurs malignes								
Total	5 511	135.4	5 420	130.7	5 719	137.7	5 398	127.7
Malignant neoplasm of lip, oral cavity and pharynx — Tumeur maligne de la lèvre, de la cavité buccale et du pharynx	58	1.4	46	1.1	77	1.9	49	1.2
Malignant neoplasm of oesophagus — Tumeur maligne de l'oesophage	71	1.7	49	1.2	81	2.0	44	1.0
Malignant neoplasm of stomach — Tumeur maligne de l'estomac	277	6.8	189	4.6	283	6.8	211	5.0
Malignant neoplasm of colon, rectosigmoid junction, rectum, anus and anal canal — Tumeur maligne du côlon, de la jonction recto-sigmoïdienne, du rectum, de l'anus et du canal anal	635	15.6	611	14.7	664	16.0	633	15.0
Malignant neoplasm of liver and intrahepatic bile ducts — Tumeur maligne du foie et des voies bilaires intrahépatiques	201	4.9	147	3.5	196	4.7	150	3.5
Malignant neoplasm of pancreas — Tumeur maligne du pancréas	446	11.0	457	11.0	497	12.0	454	10.7
Malignant neoplasm of trachea, bronchus and lung — Tumeur maligne de la trachée, des bronches et du poumon	1 282	31.5	667	16.1	1 258	30.3	666	15.8
Malignant neoplasm of female breast — Tumeur maligne du sein chez la femme	..	..	1 017	33.7	..	..	1 026	33.4
Malignant neoplasm of cervix uteri — Tumeur maligne du col de l'utérus	..	..	95	3.2	..	..	78	2.5
Malignant neoplasm of prostate — Tumeur maligne de la prostate	444	47.5	..	..	466	48.6	..	..
Malignant neoplasm of lymphoid, haematopoietic and related tissue — Tumeurs malignes primitives ou présumées primitives des tissus lymphoïde, hématopoïétique et apparentés	668	16.4	595	14.4	654	15.7	557	13.2
Disorders of the blood and blood-forming organs and certain disorders involving the immune mechanism — Maladies du sang et des organes hématopoïétiques et certains troubles du système immunitaire								
Total	148	3.6	171	4.1	110	2.6	175	4.1
Anaemias — Anémies	94	2.3	111	2.7	56	1.3	131	3.1
Endocrine, nutritional and metabolic diseases — Maladies endocriniennes, nutritionnelles et métaboliques								
Total	1 406	34.5	1 728	41.7	1 588	38.2	1 790	42.3
Diabetes mellitus — Diabète sucré	1 096	26.9	1 276	30.8	1 224	29.5	1 300	30.8
Malnutrition — Malnutrition	11	♦0.3	18	♦0.4	9	♦0.2	10	♦0.2
Mental and behavioural disorders — Troubles mentaux et du comportement	550	13.5	808	19.5	665	16.0	911	21.6
Diseases of the nervous system — Maladies du système nerveux	722	17.7	907	21.9	769	18.5	845	20.0
Diseases of the circulatory system — Maladies de l'appareil circulatoire								
Total	4 826	118.6	5 262	126.9	5 117	123.2	5 283	125.0
Acute rheumatic fever and chronic rheumatic heart diseases — Rhumatisme articulaire aigu et cardiopathies rhumatismales chroniques	45	1.1	93	2.2	53	1.3	102	2.4
Hypertensive diseases — Maladies hypertensives	351	8.6	537	13.0	391	9.4	552	13.1
Ischaemic heart disease — Cardiopathie ischémique	2 103	51.7	1 763	42.5	2 218	53.4	1 697	40.1
Cerebrovascular disease — Maladie cérébrovasculaire	1 050	25.8	1 311	31.6	1 098	26.4	1 356	32.1

Israel - Israël

Cause of death — Cause de décès	2014 (C)				2015 (C)			
	Male — Masculin		Female — Féminin		Male — Masculin		Female — Féminin	
	Number Nombre	Rate Taux	Number Nombre	Rate Taux	Number Nombre	Rate Taux	Number Nombre	Rate Taux
Diseases of arteries, arterioles and capillaries — Maladies des artères, artérioles et capillaires	203	5.0	148	3.6	240	5.8	160	3.8
Diseases of the respiratory system — Maladies de l'appareil respiratoire								
Total	1 759	43.2	1 652	39.9	1 861	44.8	1 813	42.9
Influenza — Grippe	6	+0.1	8	+0.2	19	+0.5	9	+0.2
Pneumonia — Pneumopathies	522	12.8	492	11.9	584	14.1	632	15.0
Chronic lower respiratory diseases — Maladies chroniques des voies respiratoires inférieures	715	17.6	581	14.0	728	17.5	609	14.4
Diseases of the digestive system — Maladies de l'appareil digestif								
Total	710	17.4	694	16.7	716	17.2	771	18.2
Gastric and duodenal ulcer — Ulcère de l'estomac et du duodénum	23	+0.6	15	+0.4	18	+0.4	18	+0.4
Diseases of the liver — Maladies du foie	225	5.5	154	3.7	219	5.3	195	4.6
Diseases of the musculoskeletal system and connective tissue — Maladies du système ostéo-articularie, des muscles et du tissu conjonctif	147	3.6	190	4.6	146	3.5	224	5.3
Diseases of the genitourinary system — Maladies de l'appareil génito-urinaire								
Total	1 032	25.4	1 014	24.5	1 100	26.5	1 093	25.9
Disorders of kidney and ureter — Affections du rein et de l'uretère	804	19.8	737	17.8	882	21.2	808	19.1
Hyperplasia of prostate — Hyperplasie de la prostate	12	+1.3	..	..	9	+0.9	..	..
Pregnancy, childbirth and the puerperium — Grossesse, accouchement et puerpéralité								
Total	..	..	10	+5.7	..	..	7	+3.9
Pregnancy with abortive outcome — Grossesse se terminant par un avortement	..	..	-	-	..	..	-	-
Other direct obstetric causes — Autres décès maternels directs	..	..	5	+2.8	..	..	5	+2.8
Indirect obstetric causes — Décès maternels indirects	..	..	-	-	..	..	2	+1.1
Certain conditions originating in the perinatal period — Certaines affections dont l'origine se situe dans la période périnatale	127	139.9	114	133.1	145	157.8	106	122.1
Congenital malformations, deformations and chromosomal abnormalities — Malformations congénitales et anomalies chromosomiques	139	153.1	113	131.9	144	156.7	137	157.8
Symptoms, signs and abnormal clinical and laboratory findings, not elsewhere classified — Symptômes, signes et résultats anormaux d'examens cliniques et de laboratoire, non classés ailleurs	1 308	32.1	885	21.3	1 491	35.9	1 079	25.5
All other diseases — Toutes autres maladies	201	4.9	263	6.3	214	5.2	244	5.8
External causes — Causes externes								
Total	1 196	29.4	555	13.4	1 185	28.5	602	14.2
Accidents								
Total	619	15.2	373	9.0	690	16.6	413	9.8
Transport accidents — Accidents de transport	240	5.9	82	2.0	276	6.6	102	2.4
Falls — Chutes	82	2.0	46	1.1	78	1.9	60	1.4
Accidental drowning and submersion — Noyade et submersion accidentelles	37	0.9	12	+0.3	30	+0.7	4	+0.1
Exposure to smoke, fire and flames — Exposition à la fumée, au feu et aux flammes	23	+0.6	14	+0.3	11	+0.3	9	+0.2
Accidental poisoning by and exposure to noxious substances — Intoxication accidentelle par des substances nocives et exposition à ces substances	1	+0.0	-	-	2	+0.0	1	+0.0
Intentional self-harm — Lésions auto-infligées	294	7.2	86	2.1	269	6.5	73	1.7
Assault — Agresssions	104	2.6	26	+0.6	109	2.6	27	+0.6
All other external causes — Toutes autres causes externes	179	4.4	70	1.7	117	2.8	89	2.1

20. Death and death rates by cause and sex: 2012 - 2016
Décès et taux de mortalité par cause et sexe : 2012 - 2016 (continued - suite)

Japan - Japon

Cause of death — Cause de décès	2014 (C)				2015 (C)			
	Male — Masculin		Female — Féminin		Male — Masculin		Female — Féminin	
	Number Nombre	Rate Taux	Number Nombre	Rate Taux	Number Nombre	Rate Taux	Number Nombre	Rate Taux
TOTAL	660 334	1 066.7	612 670	937.2	666 707	1 078.0	623 737	955.3
Certain infectious and parasitic diseases — Certaines maladies infectieuses et parasitaires								
Total	12 321	19.9	13 248	20.3	12 307	19.9	12 933	19.8
Intestinal infectious diseases — Maladies infectieuses intestinales	1 048	1.7	1 369	2.1	1 036	1.7	1 296	2.0
Tuberculosis — Tuberculose	1 251	2.0	849	1.3	1 169	1.9	787	1.2
Tetanus — Tétanos	5	♦0.0	4	♦0.0	7	♦0.0	2	♦0.0
Diphtheria — Diphtérie............................	-	-	-	-	-	-	-	-
Whooping cough — Coqueluche	1	♦0.0	-	-	-	-	1	♦0.0
Meningococcal infection — Infection à méningocoques	-	-	-	-	-	-	-	-
Septicaemia — Septicémie........................	5 339	8.6	5 940	9.1	5 485	8.9	5 872	9.0
Acute poliomyelitis — Poliomyélite aiguë	-	-	-	-	-	-	-	-
Measles — Rougeole..............................	-	-	1	♦0.0	-	-	-	-
Viral hepatitis — Hépatite virale	2 151	3.5	2 596	4.0	2 024	3.3	2 490	3.8
Human immunodeficiency virus [HIV] disease — Maladies dues au virus de l'immunodéficience humaine (VIH).................	40	0.1	5	♦0.0	50	0.1	6	♦0.0
Malaria — Paludisme..............................	-	-	-	-	1	♦0.0	-	-
Neoplasms — Tumeurs	224 140	362.1	155 007	237.1	225 469	364.6	156 236	239.3
Malignant neoplasms — Tumeurs malignes								
Total	218 402	352.8	149 712	229.0	219 510	354.9	150 843	231.0
Malignant neoplasm of lip, oral cavity and pharynx — Tumeur maligne de la lèvre, de la cavité buccale et du pharynx	5 268	8.5	2 147	3.3	5 258	8.5	2 122	3.2
Malignant neoplasm of oesophagus — Tumeur maligne de l'oesophage	9 629	15.6	1 947	3.0	9 774	15.8	1 965	3.0
Malignant neoplasm of stomach — Tumeur maligne de l'estomac	31 483	50.9	16 420	25.1	30 809	49.8	15 870	24.3
Malignant neoplasm of colon, rectosigmoid junction, rectum, anus and anal canal — Tumeur maligne du côlon, de la jonction recto-sigmoïdienne, du rectum, de l'anus et du canal anal.................	26 390	42.6	22 507	34.4	27 027	43.7	23 083	35.4
Malignant neoplasm of liver and intrahepatic bile ducts — Tumeur maligne du foie et des voies biliaires intrahépatiques.........	19 208	31.0	10 335	15.8	19 008	30.7	9 881	15.1
Malignant neoplasm of pancreas — Tumeur maligne du pancréas..................	16 411	26.5	15 305	23.4	16 186	26.2	15 680	24.0
Malignant neoplasm of trachea, bronchus and lung — Tumeur maligne de la trachée, des bronches et du poumon........	52 505	84.8	20 891	32.0	53 208	86.0	21 170	32.4
Malignant neoplasm of female breast — Tumeur maligne du sein chez la femme	..	..	13 240	23.1	..	..	13 584	23.7
Malignant neoplasm of cervix uteri — Tumeur maligne du col de l'utérus........	..	..	2 902	5.1	..	..	2 813	4.9
Malignant neoplasm of prostate — Tumeur maligne de la prostate	11 507	43.8	..	..	11 326	42.8	..	..
Malignant neoplasm of lymphoid, haematopoietic and related tissue — Tumeurs malignes primitives ou présumées primitives des tissus lymphoïde, hématopoïétique et apparentés.................	13 561	21.9	10 363	15.9	13 806	22.3	10 835	16.6
Disorders of the blood and blood-forming organs and certain disorders involving the immune mechanism — Maladies du sang et des organes hématopoïétiques et certains troubles du système immunitaire								
Total	1 846	3.0	2 429	3.7	1 907	3.1	2 394	3.7
Anaemias — Anémies	749	1.2	1 177	1.8	778	1.3	1 216	1.9
Endocrine, nutritional and metabolic diseases — Maladies endocriniennes, nutritionnelles et métaboliques								
Total	10 561	17.1	10 504	16.1	10 497	17.0	10 446	16.0
Diabetes mellitus — Diabète sucré................	7 265	11.7	6 404	9.8	7 125	11.5	6 202	9.5
Malnutrition — Malnutrition	822	1.3	875	1.3	747	1.2	831	1.3
Mental and behavioural disorders — Troubles mentaux et du comportement	3 979	6.4	8 705	13.3	4 088	6.6	9 102	13.9
Diseases of the nervous system — Maladies du système nerveux..................	13 032	21.1	15 352	23.5	13 843	22.4	17 068	26.1
Diseases of the circulatory system — Maladies de l'appareil circulatoire								
Total	161 804	261.4	179 956	275.3	160 339	259.2	178 754	273.8
Acute rheumatic fever and chronic rheumatic heart diseases — Rhumatisme articulaire aigu et cardiopathies rhumatismales chroniques	724	1.2	1 596	2.4	744	1.2	1 591	2.4
Hypertensive diseases — Maladies hypertensives......	2 637	4.3	4 295	6.6	2 605	4.2	4 121	6.3
Ischaemic heart disease — Cardiopathie ischémique....	41 920	67.7	31 965	48.9	41 076	66.4	30 597	46.9
Cerebrovascular disease — Maladie cérébrovasculaire....	54 995	88.8	59 212	90.6	53 576	86.6	58 397	89.4

Japan - Japon

Cause of death — Cause de décès	2014 (C)				2015 (C)			
	Male — Masculin		Female — Féminin		Male — Masculin		Female — Féminin	
	Number Nombre	Rate Taux	Number Nombre	Rate Taux	Number Nombre	Rate Taux	Number Nombre	Rate Taux
Diseases of arteries, arterioles and capillaries — Maladies des artères, artérioles et capillaires	10 166	16.4	9 835	15.0	10 212	16.5	10 317	15.8
Diseases of the respiratory system — Maladies de l'appareil respiratoire								
Total	115 235	186.1	87 393	133.7	118 495	191.6	89 905	137.7
Influenza — Grippe	559	0.9	571	0.9	1 068	1.7	1 194	1.8
Pneumonia — Pneumopathies	64 780	104.6	54 870	83.9	65 609	106.1	55 344	84.8
Chronic lower respiratory diseases — Maladies chroniques des voies respiratoires inférieures	14 069	22.7	5 004	7.7	13 680	22.1	5 002	7.7
Diseases of the digestive system — Maladies de l'appareil digestif								
Total	25 134	40.6	22 845	34.9	25 354	41.0	22 962	35.2
Gastric and duodenal ulcer — Ulcère de l'estomac et du duodénum	1 609	2.6	1 186	1.8	1 511	2.4	1 155	1.8
Diseases of the liver — Maladies du foie	10 031	16.2	5 661	8.7	10 016	16.2	5 643	8.6
Diseases of the musculoskeletal system and connective tissue — Maladies du système ostéo-articulaire, des muscles et du tissu conjonctif	2 294	3.7	3 698	5.7	2 308	3.7	3 792	5.8
Diseases of the genitourinary system — Maladies de l'appareil génito-urinaire								
Total	16 283	26.3	20 474	31.3	16 439	26.6	20 626	31.6
Disorders of kidney and ureter — Affections du rein et de l'uretère	14 060	22.7	16 431	25.1	14 185	22.9	16 413	25.1
Hyperplasia of prostate — Hyperplasie de la prostate	100	0.4	..	..	97	0.4	..	..
Pregnancy, childbirth and the puerperium — Grossesse, accouchement et puerpéralité								
Total	..	..	33	3.3	..	..	44	4.4
Pregnancy with abortive outcome — Grossesse se terminant par un avortement	..	..	-	-	..	..	1	♦0.1
Other direct obstetric causes — Autres décès maternels directs	..	..	19	♦1.9	..	..	30	♦3.0
Indirect obstetric causes — Décès maternels indirects	..	..	9	♦0.9	..	..	8	♦0.8
Certain conditions originating in the perinatal period — Certaines affections dont l'origine se situe dans la période périnatale	269	52.2	263	53.9	279	54.1	218	44.5
Congenital malformations, deformations and chromosomal abnormalities — Malformations congénitales et anomalies chromosomiques	993	192.6	1 049	215.0	926	179.6	1 096	223.6
Symptoms, signs and abnormal clinical and laboratory findings, not elsewhere classified — Symptômes, signes et résultats anormaux d'examens cliniques et de laboratoire, non classés ailleurs	28 916	46.7	64 044	98.0	31 873	51.5	71 173	109.0
All other diseases — Toutes autres maladies	650	1.0	998	1.5	622	1.0	1 044	1.6
External causes — Causes externes								
Total	42 877	69.3	26 672	40.8	41 961	67.8	25 944	39.7
Accidents								
Total	22 562	36.4	16 467	25.2	22 121	35.8	16 185	24.8
Transport accidents — Accidents de transport	3 923	6.3	1 794	2.7	3 886	6.3	1 760	2.7
Falls — Chutes	4 520	7.3	3 426	5.2	4 461	7.2	3 531	5.4
Accidental drowning and submersion — Noyade et submersion accidentelles	3 879	6.3	3 629	5.6	3 911	6.3	3 573	5.5
Exposure to smoke, fire and flames — Exposition à la fumée, au feu et aux flammes	666	1.1	420	0.6	567	0.9	373	0.6
Accidental poisoning by and exposure to noxious substances — Intoxication accidentelle par des substances nocives et exposition à ces substances	419	0.7	258	0.4	382	0.6	230	0.4
Intentional self-harm — Lésions auto-infligées	16 875	27.3	7 542	11.5	16 202	26.2	6 950	10.6
Assault — Agresssions	181	0.3	176	0.3	138	0.2	176	0.3
All other external causes — Toutes autres causes externes	3 259	5.3	2 487	3.8	3 500	5.7	2 633	4.0

Cause of death — Cause de décès	Jordan - Jordanie		Kazakhstan				Kuwait - Koweït	
	2012 (U)		2014 (U)		2015 (U)		2013 (U)	
	Male — Masculin	Female — Féminin	Male — Masculin	Female — Féminin	Male — Masculin	Female — Féminin	Male — Masculin	Female — Féminin
	Number Nombre	Number Nombre	Number Nombre	Number Nombre	Number Nombre	Number Nombre	Number Nombre	Number Nombre
TOTAL	10 027	7 530	71 929	59 966	71 389	59 640	3 753	2 156
Certain infectious and parasitic diseases — Certaines maladies infectieuses et parasitaires								
Total	206	178	1 056	551	988	520	122	128
Intestinal infectious diseases — Maladies infectieuses intestinales	8	12	19	16	28	34	3	3
Tuberculosis — Tuberculose	10	2	621	231	514	170	5	2
Tetanus — Tétanos	-	-	-	-	-	-	-	-
Diphtheria — Diphtérie	-	-	-	-	-	1	-	-
Whooping cough — Coqueluche	-	-	-	-	-	-	-	-
Meningococcal infection — Infection à méningocoques	-	-	16	13	16	10	1	-
Septicaemia — Septicémie	152	139	150	142	128	137	105	115
Acute poliomyelitis — Poliomyélite aiguë	-	-	-	1	-	-	-	-
Measles — Rougeole	-	-	-	-	-	1	-	-
Viral hepatitis — Hépatite virale	32	22	29	22	26	25	6	5
Human immunodeficiency virus [HIV] disease — Maladies dues au virus de l'immunodéficience humaine (VIH)	1	-	140	41	154	63	-	-
Malaria — Paludisme	-	-	-	-	-	-	-	-
Neoplasms — Tumeurs	1 539	1 306	8 828	7 567	8 745	7 708	425	367
Malignant neoplasms — Tumeurs malignes								
Total	1 436	1 215	8 680	7 429	8 592	7 552	417	363
Malignant neoplasm of lip, oral cavity and pharynx — Tumeur maligne de la lèvre, de la cavité buccale et du pharynx	59	16	338	157	359	178	7	4
Malignant neoplasm of oesophagus — Tumeur maligne de l'oesophage	15	6	533	378	530	399	7	3
Malignant neoplasm of stomach — Tumeur maligne de l'estomac	71	56	1 303	702	1 267	674	15	8
Malignant neoplasm of colon, rectosigmoid junction, rectum, anus and anal canal — Tumeur maligne du côlon, de la jonction recto-sigmoïdienne, du rectum, de l'anus et du canal anal	155	149	767	806	783	812	59	32
Malignant neoplasm of liver and intrahepatic bile ducts — Tumeur maligne du foie et des voies bilaires intrahépatiques	52	39	477	254	436	296	37	17
Malignant neoplasm of pancreas — Tumeur maligne du pancréas	77	46	473	392	445	377	24	25
Malignant neoplasm of trachea, bronchus and lung — Tumeur maligne de la trachée, des bronches et du poumon	353	85	2 234	530	2 202	515	71	24
Malignant neoplasm of female breast — Tumeur maligne du sein chez la femme	..	298	..	1 252	..	1 290	..	87
Malignant neoplasm of cervix uteri — Tumeur maligne du col de l'utérus	..	16	..	630	..	630	..	4
Malignant neoplasm of prostate — Tumeur maligne de la prostate	111	..	347	..	370	..	24	..
Malignant neoplasm of lymphoid, haematopoietic and related tissue — Tumeurs malignes primitives ou présumées primitives des tissus lymphoïde, hématopoïétique et apparentés	213	149	441	368	444	382	49	35
Disorders of the blood and blood-forming organs and certain disorders involving the immune mechanism — Maladies du sang et des organes hématopoïétiques et certains troubles du système immunitaire								
Total	35	31	71	98	80	92	4	14
Anaemias — Anémies	7	8	35	50	41	59	2	8
Endocrine, nutritional and metabolic diseases — Maladies endocriniennes, nutritionnelles et métaboliques								
Total	722	676	963	1 763	1 410	2 519	71	98
Diabetes mellitus — Diabète sucré	662	610	873	1 584	1 323	2 349	57	81
Malnutrition — Malnutrition	1	-	24	45	25	39	-	-
Mental and behavioural disorders — Troubles mentaux et du comportement	8	7	404	724	565	1 144	1	1
Diseases of the nervous system — Maladies du système nerveux	195	139	4 897	6 268	4 503	6 335	30	22
Diseases of the circulatory system — Maladies de l'appareil circulatoire								
Total	3 672	2 764	19 042	16 801	18 145	15 844	1 737	754
Acute rheumatic fever and chronic rheumatic heart diseases — Rhumatisme articularie aigu et cardiopathies rhumatismales chroniques	9	9	109	189	115	165	1	1
Hypertensive diseases — Maladies hypertensives	932	935	574	615	645	610	64	67
Ischaemic heart disease — Cardiopathie ischémique	1 364	646	7 269	5 759	7 218	5 355	865	216

Cause of death — Cause de décès	Jordan - Jordanie 2012 (U)		Kazakhstan 2014 (U)		2015 (U)		Kuwait - Koweït 2013 (U)	
	Male — Masculin	Female — Féminin	Male — Masculin	Female — Féminin	Male — Masculin	Female — Féminin	Male — Masculin	Female — Féminin
	Number Nombre	Number Nombre	Number Nombre	Number Nombre	Number Nombre	Number Nombre	Number Nombre	Number Nombre
Cerebrovascular disease — Maladie cérébrovasculaire	811	785	6 076	6 882	5 804	6 787	250	156
Diseases of arteries, arterioles and capillaries — Maladies des artères, artérioles et capillaires	49	17	886	988	790	893	13	2
Diseases of the respiratory system — Maladies de l'appareil respiratoire								
Total	628	402	9 112	7 462	10 127	8 294	288	259
Influenza — Grippe	-	-	10	4	5	3	1	3
Pneumonia — Pneumopathies	292	240	1 974	1 256	2 367	1 733	238	226
Chronic lower respiratory diseases — Maladies chroniques des voies respiratoires inférieures	219	84	6 549	5 765	7 199	6 127	21	10
Diseases of the digestive system — Maladies de l'appareil digestif								
Total	295	228	7 519	5 980	7 421	5 602	85	68
Gastric and duodenal ulcer — Ulcère de l'estomac et du duodénum	24	12	462	241	449	253	6	1
Diseases of the liver — Maladies du foie	120	86	5 859	4 697	5 686	4 285	39	27
Diseases of the musculoskeletal system and connective tissue — Maladies du système ostéo-articulaire, des muscles et du tissu conjonctif	16	33	201	637	491	1 362	2	11
Diseases of the genitourinary system — Maladies de l'appareil génito-urinaire								
Total	266	278	1 928	2 153	2 447	2 352	42	67
Disorders of kidney and ureter — Affections du rein et de l'uretère	248	254	1 513	2 127	1 657	2 321	23	44
Hyperplasia of prostate — Hyperplasie de la prostate	1	..	378		689		..	-
Pregnancy, childbirth and the puerperium — Grossesse, accouchement et puerpéralité								
Total	..	44	..	37	..	35	..	4
Pregnancy with abortive outcome — Grossesse se terminant par un avortement	..	-	..	2	..	-	..	1
Other direct obstetric causes — Autres décès maternels directs	..	43	..	24	..	19	..	3
Indirect obstetric causes — Décès maternels indirects	..	1	..	11	..	16	..	-
Certain conditions originating in the perinatal period — Certaines affections dont l'origine se situe dans la période périnatale	547	411	1 252	910	1 174	814	121	88
Congenital malformations, deformations and chromosomal abnormalities — Malformations congénitales et anomalies chromosomiques	377	371	621	536	611	537	101	102
Symptoms, signs and abnormal clinical and laboratory findings, not elsewhere classified — Symptômes, signes et résultats anormaux d'examens cliniques et de laboratoire, non classés ailleurs	275	237	4 151	5 099	3 312	3 246	38	35
All other diseases — Toutes autres maladies	12	14	61	67	62	76	-	2
External causes — Causes externes								
Total	1 234	411	11 823	3 313	11 308	3 160	686	136
Accidents								
Total	787	248	6 827	2 131	6 288	1 906	557	101
Transport accidents — Accidents de transport	520	149	2 109	702	1 970	674	404	60
Falls — Chutes	51	13	530	181	509	145	52	8
Accidental drowning and submersion — Noyade et submersion accidentelles	39	7	652	157	650	138	24	2
Exposure to smoke, fire and flames — Exposition à la fumée, au feu et aux flammes	65	41	273	94	235	87	11	14
Accidental poisoning by and exposure to noxious substances — Intoxication accidentelle par des substances nocives et exposition à ces substances	13	9	1 442	453	1 265	398	9	3
Intentional self-harm — Lésions auto-infligées	23	8	2 560	563	2 343	530	29	15
Assault — Agresssions	96	20	796	226	814	232	18	-
All other external causes — Toutes autres causes externes	328	135	1 640	393	1 863	492	82	20

20. Death and death rates by cause and sex: 2012 - 2016
Décès et taux de mortalité par cause et sexe : 2012 - 2016 (continued - suite)

Cause of death — Cause de décès	Kuwait - Koweït 2014 (U)		Kyrgyzstan - Kirghizstan 2014 (C)			
	Male — Masculin	Female — Féminin	Male — Masculin		Female — Féminin	
	Number Nombre	Number Nombre	Number Nombre	Rate Taux	Number Nombre	Rate Taux
TOTAL	**3 810**	**2 221**	**20 006**	**693.0**	**15 545**	**527.1**
Certain infectious and parasitic diseases — Certaines maladies infectieuses et parasitaires						
Total	187	188	618	21.4	298	10.1
Intestinal infectious diseases — Maladies infectieuses intestinales	2	1	55	1.9	51	1.7
Tuberculosis — Tuberculose	4	4	372	12.9	138	4.7
Tetanus — Tétanos	1	-	-	-	-	-
Diphtheria — Diphtérie	-	-	-	-	-	-
Whooping cough — Coqueluche	-	-	-	-	-	-
Meningococcal infection — Infection à méningocoques	-	-	7	♦0.2	3	♦0.1
Septicaemia — Septicémie	165	179	14	♦0.5	15	♦0.5
Acute poliomyelitis — Poliomyélite aiguë	-	-	-	-	-	-
Measles — Rougeole	-	-	-	-	-	-
Viral hepatitis — Hépatite virale	12	2	32	1.1	24	♦0.8
Human immunodeficiency virus [HIV] disease — Maladies dues au virus de l'immunodéficience humaine (VIH)	1	1	92	3.2	38	1.3
Malaria — Paludisme	-	-	-	-	-	-
Neoplasms — Tumeurs	**436**	**412**	**1 991**	**69.0**	**1 762**	**59.7**
Malignant neoplasms — Tumeurs malignes						
Total	412	386	1 964	68.0	1 736	58.9
Malignant neoplasm of lip, oral cavity and pharynx — Tumeur maligne de la lèvre, de la cavité buccale et du pharynx	10	4	75	2.6	35	1.2
Malignant neoplasm of oesophagus — Tumeur maligne de l'oesophage	7	2	86	3.0	55	1.9
Malignant neoplasm of stomach — Tumeur maligne de l'estomac	18	13	448	15.5	220	7.5
Malignant neoplasm of colon, rectosigmoid junction, rectum, anus and anal canal — Tumeur maligne du côlon, de la jonction recto-sigmoïdienne, du rectum, de l'anus et du canal anal	45	33	108	3.7	109	3.7
Malignant neoplasm of liver and intrahepatic bile ducts — Tumeur maligne du foie et des voies bilaires intrahépatiques	24	12	169	5.9	129	4.4
Malignant neoplasm of pancreas — Tumeur maligne du pancréas	29	17	94	3.3	79	2.7
Malignant neoplasm of trachea, bronchus and lung — Tumeur maligne de la trachée, des bronches et du poumon	85	25	398	13.8	98	3.3
Malignant neoplasm of female breast — Tumeur maligne du sein chez la femme		121	..	..	266	12.9
Malignant neoplasm of cervix uteri — Tumeur maligne du col de l'utérus		7	..	..	209	10.2
Malignant neoplasm of prostate — Tumeur maligne de la prostate	32	..	70	17.2	..	..
Malignant neoplasm of lymphoid, haematopoietic and related tissue — Tumeurs malignes primitives ou présumées primitives des tissus lymphoïde, hématopoïétique et apparentés	62	32	101	3.5	88	3.0
Disorders of the blood and blood-forming organs and certain disorders involving the immune mechanism — Maladies du sang et des organes hématopoïétiques et certains troubles du système immunitaire						
Total	12	13	25	♦0.9	20	♦0.7
Anaemias — Anémies	6	9	17	♦0.6	11	♦0.4
Endocrine, nutritional and metabolic diseases — Maladies endocriniennes, nutritionnelles et métaboliques						
Total	83	76	204	7.1	240	8.1
Diabetes mellitus — Diabète sucré	68	59	194	6.7	224	7.6
Malnutrition — Malnutrition	-	-	2	♦0.1	-	-
Mental and behavioural disorders — Troubles mentaux et du comportement	**3**	**3**	**29**	**♦1.0**	**16**	**♦0.5**
Diseases of the nervous system — Maladies du système nerveux	**33**	**35**	**325**	**11.3**	**220**	**7.5**
Diseases of the circulatory system — Maladies de l'appareil circulatoire						
Total	1 579	694	9 171	317.7	8 738	296.3
Acute rheumatic fever and chronic rheumatic heart diseases — Rhumatisme articularie aigu et cardiopathies rhumatismales chroniques	3	-	82	2.8	92	3.1
Hypertensive diseases — Maladies hypertensives	64	77	277	9.6	233	7.9
Ischaemic heart disease — Cardiopathie ischémique	1 085	228	5 648	195.7	5 783	196.1
Cerebrovascular disease — Maladie cérébrovasculaire	248	164	2 486	86.1	2 334	79.1
Diseases of arteries, arterioles and capillaries — Maladies des artères, artérioles et capillaires	11	3	85	2.9	66	2.2

20. Death and death rates by cause and sex: 2012 - 2016
Décès et taux de mortalité par cause et sexe : 2012 - 2016 (continued - suite)

Cause of death — Cause de décès	Kuwait - Koweït 2014 (U)		Kyrgyzstan - Kirghizstan 2014 (C)			
	Male — Masculin	Female — Féminin	Male — Masculin		Female — Féminin	
	Number Nombre	Number Nombre	Number Nombre	Rate Taux	Number Nombre	Rate Taux
Diseases of the respiratory system — Maladies de l'appareil respiratoire						
Total	280	297	1 281	44.4	911	30.9
Influenza — Grippe	5	1	22	٠0.8	19	٠0.6
Pneumonia — Pneumopathies	236	251	376	13.0	261	8.9
Chronic lower respiratory diseases — Maladies chroniques des voies respiratoires inférieures	15	15	790	27.4	572	19.4
Diseases of the digestive system — Maladies de l'appareil digestif						
Total	64	62	1 553	53.8	784	26.6
Gastric and duodenal ulcer — Ulcère de l'estomac et du duodénum	5	-	57	2.0	19	٠0.6
Diseases of the liver — Maladies du foie	23	16	1 339	46.4	663	22.5
Diseases of the musculoskeletal system and connective tissue — Maladies du système ostéo-articularie, des muscles et du tissu conjonctif	1	10	24	٠0.8	66	2.2
Diseases of the genitourinary system — Maladies de l'appareil génito-urinaire						
Total	48	48	276	9.6	223	7.6
Disorders of kidney and ureter — Affections du rein et de l'uretère	24	23	266	9.2	219	7.4
Hyperplasia of prostate — Hyperplasie de la prostate	-	..	9	٠2.2	..	..
Pregnancy, childbirth and the puerperium — Grossesse, accouchement et puerpéralité						
Total	..	7	..	..	81	50.1
Pregnancy with abortive outcome — Grossesse se terminant par un avortement	..	1	..	..	2	٠1.2
Other direct obstetric causes — Autres décès maternels directs	..	6	..	..	58	35.8
Indirect obstetric causes — Décès maternels indirects	..	-	..	..	21	٠13.0
Certain conditions originating in the perinatal period — Certaines affections dont l'origine se situe dans la période périnatale	139	96	1 391	1 669.1	1 103	1 405.6
Congenital malformations, deformations and chromosomal abnormalities — Malformations congénitales et anomalies chromosomiques	119	102	153	183.6	137	174.6
Symptoms, signs and abnormal clinical and laboratory findings, not elsewhere classified — Symptômes, signes et résultats anormaux d'examens cliniques et de laboratoire, non classés ailleurs	55	32	560	19.4	230	7.8
All other diseases — Toutes autres maladies	3	-	7	٠0.2	7	٠0.2
External causes — Causes externes						
Total	768	146	2 398	83.1	709	24.0
Accidents						
Total	620	104	1 625	56.3	489	16.6
Transport accidents — Accidents de transport	434	69	674	23.3	216	7.3
Falls — Chutes	73	11	79	2.7	14	٠0.5
Accidental drowning and submersion — Noyade et submersion accidentelles	13	3	151	5.2	46	1.6
Exposure to smoke, fire and flames — Exposition à la fumée, au feu et aux flammes	26	7	46	1.6	12	٠0.4
Accidental poisoning by and exposure to noxious substances — Intoxication accidentelle par des substances nocives et exposition à ces substances	19	3	315	10.9	86	2.9
Intentional self-harm — Lésions auto-infligées	52	19	358	12.4	103	3.5
Assault — Agresssions	20	11	152	5.3	53	1.8
All other external causes — Toutes autres causes externes	76	12	263	9.1	64	2.2

20. Death and death rates by cause and sex: 2012 - 2016
Décès et taux de mortalité par cause et sexe : 2012 - 2016 (continued - suite)

	Kyrgyzstan - Kirghizstan				Malaysia - Malaisie			
Cause of death — Cause de décès	2015 (C)				2013 (U)		2014 (U)	
	Male — Masculin		Female — Féminin		Male — Masculin	Female — Féminin	Male — Masculin	Female — Féminin
	Number Nombre	Rate Taux	Number Nombre	Rate Taux	Number Nombre	Number Nombre	Number Nombre	Number Nombre
TOTAL	19 376	657.1	15 433	513.0	46 229	27 918	47 871	29 494
Certain infectious and parasitic diseases — Certaines maladies infectieuses et parasitaires								
Total	591	20.0	295	9.8	4 240	2 668	4 475	2 877
Intestinal infectious diseases — Maladies infectieuses intestinales	60	2.0	54	1.8	83	72	126	131
Tuberculosis — Tuberculose	324	11.0	129	4.3	479	192	536	189
Tetanus — Tétanos..	1	◆0.0	-		5	-	3	1
Diphtheria — Diphtérie..	-		-		-	-	-	-
Whooping cough — Coqueluche	-		-		-	-	-	1
Meningococcal infection — Infection à méningocoques	7	◆0.2	11	◆0.4	3	2	1	6
Septicaemia — Septicémie..	16	◆0.5	10	◆0.3	2 602	2 009	2 627	2 071
Acute poliomyelitis — Poliomyélite aiguë	-		-		-	-	-	-
Measles — Rougeole..	1	◆0.0	2	◆0.1	-	-	-	1
Viral hepatitis — Hépatite virale..	39	1.3	19	◆0.6	109	27	124	45
Human immunodeficiency virus [HIV] disease — Maladies dues au virus de l'immunodéficience humaine (VIH)................................	89	3.0	27	◆0.9	362	66	380	56
Malaria — Paludisme..	-		-		4	4	5	1
Neoplasms — Tumeurs	1 970	66.8	1 871	62.2	5 332	4 809	5 646	5 151
Malignant neoplasms — Tumeurs malignes								
Total	1 938	65.7	1 839	61.1	5 099	4 569	5 347	4 871
Malignant neoplasm of lip, oral cavity and pharynx — Tumeur maligne de la lèvre, de la cavité buccale et du pharynx	76	2.6	45	1.5	331	123	315	154
Malignant neoplasm of oesophagus — Tumeur maligne de l'oesophage	80	2.7	47	1.6	91	29	87	31
Malignant neoplasm of stomach — Tumeur maligne de l'estomac	473	16.0	225	7.5	190	126	208	142
Malignant neoplasm of colon, rectosigmoid junction, rectum, anus and anal canal — Tumeur maligne du côlon, de la jonction recto-sigmoïdienne, du rectum, de l'anus et du canal anal.........	112	3.8	131	4.4	533	364	515	407
Malignant neoplasm of liver and intrahepatic bile ducts — Tumeur maligne du foie et des voies bilaires intrahépatiques	190	6.4	125	4.2	684	217	665	244
Malignant neoplasm of pancreas — Tumeur maligne du pancréas...................	88	3.0	77	2.6	202	128	202	137
Malignant neoplasm of trachea, bronchus and lung — Tumeur maligne de la trachée, des bronches et du poumon	341	11.6	112	3.7	1 255	561	1 220	521
Malignant neoplasm of female breast — Tumeur maligne du sein chez la femme	..	..	258	12.3	..	1 028	..	1 060
Malignant neoplasm of cervix uteri — Tumeur maligne du col de l'utérus.........	..	..	259	12.4	..	261	..	253
Malignant neoplasm of prostate — Tumeur maligne de la prostate	65	15.4	..	..	194	..	252	..
Malignant neoplasm of lymphoid, haematopoietic and related tissue — Tumeurs malignes primitives ou présumées primitives des tissus lymphoïde, hématopoïétique et apparentés..........................	117	4.0	75	2.5	610	408	677	466
Disorders of the blood and blood-forming organs and certain disorders involving the immune mechanism — Maladies du sang et des organes hématopoïétiques et certains troubles du système immunitaire								
Total	27	◆0.9	17	◆0.6	304	241	296	258
Anaemias — Anémies	15	◆0.5	12	◆0.4	85	79	82	91
Endocrine, nutritional and metabolic diseases — Maladies endocriniennes, nutritionnelles et métaboliques								
Total	168	5.7	225	7.5	547	517	574	620
Diabetes mellitus — Diabète sucré...	153	5.2	206	6.8	220	230	198	269
Malnutrition — Malnutrition	5	◆0.2	5	◆0.2	6	5	3	2
Mental and behavioural disorders — Troubles mentaux et du comportement	23	◆0.8	19	◆0.6	12	2	15	2
Diseases of the nervous system — Maladies du système nerveux..............	319	10.8	190	6.3	607	428	701	433
Diseases of the circulatory system — Maladies de l'appareil circulatoire								
Total	8 951	303.5	8 745	290.7	12 862	7 171	13 537	7 451
Acute rheumatic fever and chronic rheumatic heart diseases — Rhumatisme articularie aigu et cardiopathies rhumatismales chroniques	85	2.9	92	3.1	43	44	45	39
Hypertensive diseases — Maladies hypertensives..........................	255	8.6	237	7.9	393	216	433	299
Ischaemic heart disease — Cardiopathie ischémique............................	5 589	189.5	5 826	193.7	7 016	3 153	7 295	3 137

Cause of death — Cause de décès	Kyrgyzstan - Kirghizstan 2015 (C)				Malaysia - Malaisie 2013 (U)		2014 (U)	
	Male — Masculin		Female — Féminin		Male — Masculin	Female — Féminin	Male — Masculin	Female — Féminin
	Number Nombre	Rate Taux	Number Nombre	Rate Taux	Number Nombre	Number Nombre	Number Nombre	Number Nombre
Cerebrovascular disease — Maladie cérébrovasculaire	2 322	78.7	2 231	74.2	2 979	2 177	3 170	2 304
Diseases of arteries, arterioles and capillaries — Maladies des artères, artérioles et capillaires	123	4.2	93	3.1	314	160	309	142
Diseases of the respiratory system — Maladies de l'appareil respiratoire								
Total	1 039	35.2	800	26.6	7 894	5 449	8 062	5 695
Influenza — Grippe	11	♦0.4	12	♦0.4	-	1	-	-
Pneumonia — Pneumopathies	293	9.9	215	7.1	5 344	3 798	5 333	3 917
Chronic lower respiratory diseases — Maladies chroniques des voies respiratoires inférieures	669	22.7	526	17.5	836	379	834	385
Diseases of the digestive system — Maladies de l'appareil digestif								
Total	1 462	49.6	832	27.7	2 033	935	2 136	1 044
Gastric and duodenal ulcer — Ulcère de l'estomac et du duodénum	54	1.8	29	♦1.0	170	91	162	83
Diseases of the liver — Maladies du foie	1 252	42.5	691	23.0	986	341	1 028	367
Diseases of the musculoskeletal system and connective tissue — Maladies du système ostéo-articularie, des muscles et du tissu conjonctif	26	♦0.9	58	1.9	274	263	332	332
Diseases of the genitourinary system — Maladies de l'appareil génito-urinaire								
Total	291	9.9	193	6.4	1 452	1 466	1 623	1 648
Disorders of kidney and ureter — Affections du rein et de l'uretère	285	9.7	189	6.3	1 073	892	1 136	958
Hyperplasia of prostate — Hyperplasie de la prostate	4	♦1.0	..	..	1	..	1	..
Pregnancy, childbirth and the puerperium — Grossesse, accouchement et puerpéralité								
Total	..	..	63	38.5	..	108	..	119
Pregnancy with abortive outcome — Grossesse se terminant par un avortement	..	..	3	♦1.8	..	12	..	18
Other direct obstetric causes — Autres décès maternels directs	..	..	49	30.0	..	69	..	76
Indirect obstetric causes — Décès maternels indirects	..	..	11	♦6.7	..	27	..	25
Certain conditions originating in the perinatal period — Certaines affections dont l'origine se situe dans la période périnatale	1 265	1 494.4	959	1 217.0	717	511	713	506
Congenital malformations, deformations and chromosomal abnormalities — Malformations congénitales et anomalies chromosomiques	181	213.8	164	208.1	551	434	575	481
Symptoms, signs and abnormal clinical and laboratory findings, not elsewhere classified — Symptômes, signes et résultats anormaux d'examens cliniques et de laboratoire, non classés ailleurs	700	23.7	241	8.0	1 739	927	1 675	897
All other diseases — Toutes autres maladies	10	♦0.3	6	♦0.2	385	406	434	456
External causes — Causes externes								
Total	2 353	79.8	755	25.1	7 280	1 583	7 077	1 524
Accidents								
Total	1 630	55.3	552	18.3	4 424	885	4 453	886
Transport accidents — Accidents de transport	681	23.1	249	8.3	3 852	686	3 636	668
Falls — Chutes	59	2.0	20	♦0.7	85	33	89	22
Accidental drowning and submersion — Noyade et submersion accidentelles	174	5.9	51	1.7	92	23	347	63
Exposure to smoke, fire and flames — Exposition à la fumée, au feu et aux flammes	16	♦0.5	11	♦0.4	3	3	6	4
Accidental poisoning by and exposure to noxious substances — Intoxication accidentelle par des substances nocives et exposition à ces substances	338	11.5	81	2.7	31	12	35	9
Intentional self-harm — Lésions auto-infligées	327	11.1	90	3.0	17	5	19	2
Assault — Agresssions	158	5.4	55	1.8	108	25	116	16
All other external causes — Toutes autres causes externes	238	8.1	58	1.9	2 731	668	2 489	620

Cause of death — Cause de décès	Mongolia - Mongolie		Oman		Qatar			
	2016 (U)		2014 (U)		2015 (U)		2016 (U)	
	Male — Masculin	Female — Féminin	Male — Masculin	Female — Féminin	Male — Masculin	Female — Féminin	Male — Masculin	Female — Féminin
	Number Nombre	Number Nombre	Number Nombre	Number Nombre	Number Nombre	Number Nombre	Number Nombre	Number Nombre
TOTAL	9 662	6 520	4 943	2 866	1 610	575	1 647	560
Certain infectious and parasitic diseases — Certaines maladies infectieuses et parasitaires								
Total	289	181	248	151	25	18	17	14
Intestinal infectious diseases — Maladies infectieuses intestinales	-	-	12	4	-	-	2	2
Tuberculosis — Tuberculose	174	100	6	3	2	2	-	-
Tetanus — Tétanos	-	-	-	-	-	-	-	-
Diphtheria — Diphtérie	-	-	-	-	-	-	-	-
Whooping cough — Coqueluche	-	-	-	-	-	-	-	-
Meningococcal infection — Infection à méningocoques	1	-	2	1	-	-	-	1
Septicaemia — Septicémie	7	9	199	125	15	9	5	2
Acute poliomyelitis — Poliomyélite aiguë	-	-	-	-	-	-	-	-
Measles — Rougeole	75	56	-	-	-	1	-	-
Viral hepatitis — Hépatite virale	4	1	10	9	5	5	4	4
Human immunodeficiency virus [HIV] disease — Maladies dues au virus de l'immunodéficience humaine (VIH)	6	1	3	1	-	-	-	-
Malaria — Paludisme	1	-	-	1	-	-	-	2
Neoplasms — Tumeurs	2 309	1 838	213	170	159	114	170	120
Malignant neoplasms — Tumeurs malignes								
Total	2 293	1 823	202	159	157	114	168	117
Malignant neoplasm of lip, oral cavity and pharynx — Tumeur maligne de la lèvre, de la cavité buccale et du pharynx	41	20	7	7	9	-	5	3
Malignant neoplasm of oesophagus — Tumeur maligne de l'oesophage	157	107	3	2	2	-	3	-
Malignant neoplasm of stomach — Tumeur maligne de l'estomac	458	250	26	6	11	5	6	4
Malignant neoplasm of colon, rectosigmoid junction, rectum, anus and anal canal — Tumeur maligne du côlon, de la jonction recto-sigmoïdienne, du rectum, de l'anus et du canal anal	53	60	8	20	17	10	29	7
Malignant neoplasm of liver and intrahepatic bile ducts — Tumeur maligne du foie et des voies bilaires intrahépatiques	942	799	22	10	26	11	23	10
Malignant neoplasm of pancreas — Tumeur maligne du pancréas	81	54	5	6	6	4	10	6
Malignant neoplasm of trachea, bronchus and lung — Tumeur maligne de la trachée, des bronches et du poumon	287	67	19	8	23	12	14	4
Malignant neoplasm of female breast — Tumeur maligne du sein chez la femme	..	48	..	25	..	41	..	39
Malignant neoplasm of cervix uteri — Tumeur maligne du col de l'utérus	..	130	..	1	..	3	..	2
Malignant neoplasm of prostate — Tumeur maligne de la prostate	27	..	15	..	10	..	5	..
Malignant neoplasm of lymphoid, haematopoietic and related tissue — Tumeurs malignes primitives ou présumées primitives des tissus lymphoïde, hématopoïétique et apparentés	52	54	35	20	16	4	32	8
Disorders of the blood and blood-forming organs and certain disorders involving the immune mechanism — Maladies du sang et des organes hématopoïétiques et certains troubles du système immunitaire								
Total	3	12	44	38	1	3	2	4
Anaemias — Anémies	2	8	29	15	-	1	1	1
Endocrine, nutritional and metabolic diseases — Maladies endocriniennes, nutritionnelles et métaboliques								
Total	104	100	254	185	82	55	73	36
Diabetes mellitus — Diabète sucré	84	83	208	145	70	50	62	28
Malnutrition — Malnutrition	2	-	3	1	1	-	-	-
Mental and behavioural disorders — Troubles mentaux et du comportement	9	9	11	4	-	-	-	-
Diseases of the nervous system — Maladies du système nerveux	180	130	72	37	17	8	21	11
Diseases of the circulatory system — Maladies de l'appareil circulatoire								
Total	3 120	2 274	1 112	713	267	90	579	143
Acute rheumatic fever and chronic rheumatic heart diseases — Rhumatisme articularie aigu et cardiopathies rhumatismales chroniques	26	25	2	5	2	2	2	-
Hypertensive diseases — Maladies hypertensives	77	94	176	154	46	32	42	24
Ischaemic heart disease — Cardiopathie ischémique	1 497	982	237	117	100	21	167	30

Cause of death — Cause de décès	Mongolia - Mongolie 2016 (U)		Oman 2014 (U)		Qatar 2015 (U)		Qatar 2016 (U)	
	Male — Masculin Number Nombre	Female — Féminin Number Nombre	Male — Masculin Number Nombre	Female — Féminin Number Nombre	Male — Masculin Number Nombre	Female — Féminin Number Nombre	Male — Masculin Number Nombre	Female — Féminin Number Nombre
Cerebrovascular disease — Maladie cérébrovasculaire	1 128	891	192	121	42	14	78	25
Diseases of arteries, arterioles and capillaries — Maladies des artères, artérioles et capillaires	56	59	11	4	2	-	9	1
Diseases of the respiratory system — Maladies de l'appareil respiratoire								
Total	403	294	260	184	108	54	171	50
Influenza — Grippe	5	3	1	1	-	1	1	-
Pneumonia — Pneumopathies	248	182	90	70	38	12	46	14
Chronic lower respiratory diseases — Maladies chroniques des voies respiratoires inférieures	96	83	34	16	4	3	13	7
Diseases of the digestive system — Maladies de l'appareil digestif								
Total	643	557	109	48	34	16	39	16
Gastric and duodenal ulcer — Ulcère de l'estomac et du duodénum	56	31	8	1	-	-	1	-
Diseases of the liver — Maladies du foie	414	390	69	18	21	6	20	7
Diseases of the musculoskeletal system and connective tissue — Maladies du système ostéo-articularie, des muscles et du tissu conjonctif	16	36	9	11	-	1	1	-
Diseases of the genitourinary system — Maladies de l'appareil génito-urinaire								
Total	129	117	118	86	33	26	41	37
Disorders of kidney and ureter — Affections du rein et de l'uretère	118	108	84	63	31	25	39	33
Hyperplasia of prostate — Hyperplasie de la prostate	2	..	2	..	-	..	-	..
Pregnancy, childbirth and the puerperium — Grossesse, accouchement et puerpéralité								
Total	..	38	..	-	..	3	..	-
Pregnancy with abortive outcome — Grossesse se terminant par un avortement	..	3	..	-	..	-	..	-
Other direct obstetric causes — Autres décès maternels directs	..	21	..	-	..	2	..	-
Indirect obstetric causes — Décès maternels indirects	..	14	..	-	..	-	..	-
Certain conditions originating in the perinatal period — Certaines affections dont l'origine se situe dans la période périnatale	342	242	153	134	38	39	23	27
Congenital malformations, deformations and chromosomal abnormalities — Malformations congénitales et anomalies chromosomiques	118	101	72	65	41	38	33	34
Symptoms, signs and abnormal clinical and laboratory findings, not elsewhere classified — Symptômes, signes et résultats anormaux d'examens cliniques et de laboratoire, non classés ailleurs	52	83	1 619	879	430	58	97	31
All other diseases — Toutes autres maladies	14	10	30	24	5	2	3	-
External causes — Causes externes								
Total	1 931	498	619	137	370	50	377	37
Accidents								
Total	1 309	372	380	64	298	37	308	28
Transport accidents — Accidents de transport	365	119	321	54	205	30	186	10
Falls — Chutes	109	55	19	2	32	1	29	-
Accidental drowning and submersion — Noyade et submersion accidentelles	119	16	26	3	13	2	13	5
Exposure to smoke, fire and flames — Exposition à la fumée, au feu et aux flammes	27	12	5	3	5	1	19	3
Accidental poisoning by and exposure to noxious substances — Intoxication accidentelle par des substances nocives et exposition à ces substances	424	87	1	-	8	3	3	1
Intentional self-harm — Lésions auto-infligées	387	63	6	-	57	9	63	7
Assault — Agresssions	155	42	1	-	1	1	3	1
All other external causes — Toutes autres causes externes	80	21	232	73	14	3	3	1

20. Death and death rates by cause and sex: 2012 - 2016
Décès et taux de mortalité par cause et sexe : 2012 - 2016 (continued - suite)

Republic of Korea - République de Corée

Cause of death — Cause de décès	2014 (C)				2015 (C)			
	Male — Masculin		Female — Féminin		Male — Masculin		Female — Féminin	
	Number Nombre	Rate Taux	Number Nombre	Rate Taux	Number Nombre	Rate Taux	Number Nombre	Rate Taux
TOTAL	147 321	580.6	120 371	474.1	150 449	591.0	125 446	492.1
Certain infectious and parasitic diseases — Certaines maladies infectieuses et parasitaires								
Total	3 688	14.5	3 224	12.7	3 754	14.7	3 541	13.9
Intestinal infectious diseases — Maladies infectieuses intestinales	244	1.0	424	1.7	250	1.0	420	1.6
Tuberculosis — Tuberculose	1 480	5.8	825	3.2	1 390	5.5	819	3.2
Tetanus — Tétanos	1	♦0.0	2	♦0.0	-	-	2	♦0.0
Diphtheria — Diphtérie	-	-	-	-	-	-	-	-
Whooping cough — Coqueluche	-	-	-	-	-	-	-	-
Meningococcal infection — Infection à méningocoques	-	-	-	-	1	♦0.0	-	-
Septicaemia — Septicémie	1 091	4.3	1 412	5.6	1 300	5.1	1 745	6.8
Acute poliomyelitis — Poliomyélite aiguë	-	-	1	♦0.0	-	-	-	-
Measles — Rougeole	-	-	-	-	-	-	-	-
Viral hepatitis — Hépatite virale	414	1.6	306	1.2	359	1.4	308	1.2
Human immunodeficiency virus [HIV] disease — Maladies dues au virus de l'immunodéficience humaine (VIH)	106	0.4	15	♦0.1	100	0.4	4	♦0.0
Malaria — Paludisme	6	♦0.0	1	♦0.0	-	-	-	-
Neoplasms — Tumeurs	48 552	191.3	29 350	115.6	48 428	190.2	29 853	117.1
Malignant neoplasms — Tumeurs malignes								
Total	47 869	188.7	28 742	113.2	47 678	187.3	29 177	114.4
Malignant neoplasm of lip, oral cavity and pharynx — Tumeur maligne de la lèvre, de la cavité buccale et du pharynx	824	3.2	273	1.1	884	3.5	286	1.1
Malignant neoplasm of oesophagus — Tumeur maligne de l'oesophage	1 407	5.5	133	0.5	1 401	5.5	130	0.5
Malignant neoplasm of stomach — Tumeur maligne de l'estomac	5 767	22.7	3 150	12.4	5 507	21.6	3 019	11.8
Malignant neoplasm of colon, rectosigmoid junction, rectum, anus and anal canal — Tumeur maligne du côlon, de la jonction recto-sigmoïdienne, du rectum, de l'anus et du canal anal	4 791	18.9	3 606	14.2	4 731	18.6	3 649	14.3
Malignant neoplasm of liver and intrahepatic bile ducts — Tumeur maligne du foie et des voies bilaires intrahépatiques	8 616	34.0	2 950	11.6	8 382	32.9	2 929	11.5
Malignant neoplasm of pancreas — Tumeur maligne du pancréas	2 752	10.8	2 364	9.3	2 908	11.4	2 531	9.9
Malignant neoplasm of trachea, bronchus and lung — Tumeur maligne de la trachée, des bronches et du poumon	12 785	50.4	4 655	18.3	12 677	49.8	4 722	18.5
Malignant neoplasm of female breast — Tumeur maligne du sein chez la femme	..	..	2 254	10.3	..	..	2 338	10.6
Malignant neoplasm of cervix uteri — Tumeur maligne du col de l'utérus	..	..	960	4.4	..	..	967	4.4
Malignant neoplasm of prostate — Tumeur maligne de la prostate	1 667	21.1	..	..	1 700	20.8	..	..
Malignant neoplasm of lymphoid, haematopoietic and related tissue — Tumeurs malignes primitives ou présumées primitives des tissus lymphoïde, hématopoïétique et apparentés	2 388	9.4	1 865	7.3	2 537	10.0	1 905	7.5
Disorders of the blood and blood-forming organs and certain disorders involving the immune mechanism — Maladies du sang et des organes hématopoïétiques et certains troubles du système immunitaire								
Total	283	1.1	354	1.4	322	1.3	402	1.6
Anaemias — Anémies	166	0.7	248	1.0	193	0.8	261	1.0
Endocrine, nutritional and metabolic diseases — Maladies endocriniennes, nutritionnelles et métaboliques								
Total	5 836	23.0	5 775	22.7	5 812	22.8	5 847	22.9
Diabetes mellitus — Diabète sucré	5 283	20.8	5 243	20.7	5 250	20.6	5 308	20.8
Malnutrition — Malnutrition	29	♦0.1	28	♦0.1	43	0.2	34	0.1
Mental and behavioural disorders — Troubles mentaux et du comportement	2 080	8.2	3 016	11.9	2 241	8.8	3 108	12.2
Diseases of the nervous system — Maladies du système nerveux	4 089	16.1	5 878	23.2	4 318	17.0	6 415	25.2
Diseases of the circulatory system — Maladies de l'appareil circulatoire								
Total	27 503	108.4	30 312	119.4	28 199	110.8	31 345	123.0
Acute rheumatic fever and chronic rheumatic heart diseases — Rhumatisme articulaire aigu et cardiopathies rhumatismales chroniques	42	0.2	117	0.5	53	0.2	113	0.4
Hypertensive diseases — Maladies hypertensives	1 517	6.0	3 544	14.0	1 505	5.9	3 545	13.9
Ischaemic heart disease — Cardiopathie ischémique	7 481	29.5	6 703	26.4	7 827	30.7	6 897	27.1
Cerebrovascular disease — Maladie cérébrovasculaire	11 827	46.6	12 659	49.9	11 793	46.3	12 662	49.7

Republic of Korea - République de Corée

Cause of death — Cause de décès	2014 (C)				2015 (C)			
	Male — Masculin		Female — Féminin		Male — Masculin		Female — Féminin	
	Number Nombre	Rate Taux	Number Nombre	Rate Taux	Number Nombre	Rate Taux	Number Nombre	Rate Taux
Diseases of arteries, arterioles and capillaries — Maladies des artères, artérioles et capillaires	750	3.0	605	2.4	781	3.1	618	2.4
Diseases of the respiratory system — Maladies de l'appareil respiratoire								
Total	13 541	53.4	10 618	41.8	15 484	60.8	12 288	48.2
Influenza — Grippe	46	0.2	51	0.2	90	0.4	95	0.4
Pneumonia — Pneumopathies	6 120	24.1	5 901	23.2	7 582	29.8	7 136	28.0
Chronic lower respiratory diseases — Maladies chroniques des voies respiratoires inférieures	4 496	17.7	2 675	10.5	4 705	18.5	2 833	11.1
Diseases of the digestive system — Maladies de l'appareil digestif								
Total	7 284	28.7	4 067	16.0	7 428	29.2	4 280	16.8
Gastric and duodenal ulcer — Ulcère de l'estomac et du duodénum	280	1.1	245	1.0	257	1.0	247	1.0
Diseases of the liver — Maladies du foie	5 045	19.9	1 590	6.3	5 183	20.4	1 664	6.5
Diseases of the musculoskeletal system and connective tissue — Maladies du système ostéo-articularie, des muscles et du tissu conjonctif	525	2.1	1 034	4.1	502	2.0	989	3.9
Diseases of the genitourinary system — Maladies de l'appareil génito-urinaire								
Total	2 739	10.8	3 095	12.2	3 017	11.9	3 529	13.8
Disorders of kidney and ureter — Affections du rein et de l'uretère	2 453	9.7	2 468	9.7	2 721	10.7	2 825	11.1
Hyperplasia of prostate — Hyperplasie de la prostate	46	0.6	..	..	53	0.6	..	..
Pregnancy, childbirth and the puerperium — Grossesse, accouchement et puerpéralité								
Total	..	..	48	11.0	..	..	42	9.6
Pregnancy with abortive outcome — Grossesse se terminant par un avortement	..	..	2	♦0.5	..	..	-	-
Other direct obstetric causes — Autres décès maternels directs	..	..	37	8.5	..	..	36	8.2
Indirect obstetric causes — Décès maternels indirects	..	..	9	♦2.1	..	..	2	♦0.5
Certain conditions originating in the perinatal period — Certaines affections dont l'origine se situe dans la période périnatale	389	174.2	307	144.8	353	157.0	278	130.2
Congenital malformations, deformations and chromosomal abnormalities — Malformations congénitales et anomalies chromosomiques	236	105.7	235	110.8	223	99.2	210	98.4
Symptoms, signs and abnormal clinical and laboratory findings, not elsewhere classified — Symptômes, signes et résultats anormaux d'examens cliniques et de laboratoire, non classés ailleurs	10 408	41.0	13 392	52.7	10 562	41.5	13 834	54.3
All other diseases — Toutes autres maladies	173	0.7	312	1.2	183	0.7	290	1.1
External causes — Causes externes								
Total	19 995	78.8	9 354	36.8	19 600	77.0	9 184	36.0
Accidents								
Total	8 350	32.9	4 126	16.3	8 262	32.5	4 118	16.2
Transport accidents — Accidents de transport	4 182	16.5	1 518	6.0	4 052	15.9	1 487	5.8
Falls — Chutes	1 689	6.7	593	2.3	1 702	6.7	618	2.4
Accidental drowning and submersion — Noyade et submersion accidentelles	440	1.7	124	0.5	440	1.7	149	0.6
Exposure to smoke, fire and flames — Exposition à la fumée, au feu et aux flammes	214	0.8	109	0.4	178	0.7	91	0.4
Accidental poisoning by and exposure to noxious substances — Intoxication accidentelle par des substances nocives et exposition à ces substances	130	0.5	79	0.3	148	0.6	65	0.3
Intentional self-harm — Lésions auto-infligées	9 736	38.4	4 100	16.1	9 559	37.5	3 954	15.5
Assault — Agresssions	261	1.0	250	1.0	267	1.0	252	1.0
All other external causes — Toutes autres causes externes	1 648	6.5	878	3.5	1 512	5.9	860	3.4

20. Death and death rates by cause and sex: 2012 - 2016
Décès et taux de mortalité par cause et sexe : 2012 - 2016 (continued - suite)

Cause of death — Cause de décès	Saudi Arabia - Arabie saoudite 2012 (U) Male — Masculin Number Nombre	Saudi Arabia - Arabie saoudite 2012 (U) Female — Féminin Number Nombre	Singapore - Singapour 2014 (+U) Male — Masculin Number Nombre	Singapore - Singapour 2014 (+U) Female — Féminin Number Nombre	Singapore - Singapour 2015 (+U) Male — Masculin Number Nombre	Singapore - Singapour 2015 (+U) Female — Féminin Number Nombre	Tajikistan - Tadjikistan 2016 (U) Male — Masculin Number Nombre	Tajikistan - Tadjikistan 2016 (U) Female — Féminin Number Nombre
TOTAL	29 994	15 642	9 802	8 434	10 042	8 598	19 068	15 058
Certain infectious and parasitic diseases — Certaines maladies infectieuses et parasitaires								
Total	808	614	130	65	109	70	415	356
Intestinal infectious diseases — Maladies infectieuses intestinales	66	54	13	20	15	24	114	109
Tuberculosis — Tuberculose	135	127	41	14	27	12	227	187
Tetanus — Tétanos	5	1	-	-	-	-	-	-
Diphtheria — Diphtérie	-	-	-	-	-	-	-	-
Whooping cough — Coqueluche	-	1	-	-	-	1	-	-
Meningococcal infection — Infection à méningocoques	-	-	-	-	-	-	5	8
Septicaemia — Septicémie	449	348	16	19	23	18	12	9
Acute poliomyelitis — Poliomyélite aiguë	-	-	-	-	-	-	-	-
Measles — Rougeole	1	-	-	-	-	-	-	-
Viral hepatitis — Hépatite virale	45	23	1	-	2	-	40	27
Human immunodeficiency virus [HIV] disease — Maladies dues au virus de l'immunodéficience humaine (VIH)	84	50	46	1	29	3	-	-
Malaria — Paludisme	9	1	-	-	-	-	-	-
Neoplasms — Tumeurs	1 094	936	3 038	2 470	3 097	2 594	1 405	1 372
Malignant neoplasms — Tumeurs malignes								
Total	1 091	935	2 997	2 431	3 054	2 559	1 397	1 366
Malignant neoplasm of lip, oral cavity and pharynx — Tumeur maligne de la lèvre, de la cavité buccale et du pharynx	26	23	180	68	174	41	36	35
Malignant neoplasm of oesophagus — Tumeur maligne de l'oesophage	16	17	70	21	80	25	70	44
Malignant neoplasm of stomach — Tumeur maligne de l'estomac	48	43	164	130	159	148	421	296
Malignant neoplasm of colon, rectosigmoid junction, rectum, anus and anal canal — Tumeur maligne du côlon, de la jonction recto-sigmoïdienne, du rectum, de l'anus et du canal anal	107	67	405	377	449	400	83	41
Malignant neoplasm of liver and intrahepatic bile ducts — Tumeur maligne du foie et des voies bilaires intrahépatiques	175	88	393	165	388	152	101	97
Malignant neoplasm of pancreas — Tumeur maligne du pancréas	46	31	164	127	193	161	32	28
Malignant neoplasm of trachea, bronchus and lung — Tumeur maligne de la trachée, des bronches et du poumon	113	51	828	398	826	435	127	77
Malignant neoplasm of female breast — Tumeur maligne du sein chez la femme	..	149	..	411	..	424	..	194
Malignant neoplasm of cervix uteri — Tumeur maligne du col de l'utérus	..	10	..	77	..	70	..	98
Malignant neoplasm of prostate — Tumeur maligne de la prostate	51	..	173	..	172	..	30	..
Malignant neoplasm of lymphoid, haematopoietic and related tissue — Tumeurs malignes primitives ou présumées primitives des tissus lymphoïde, hématopoïétique et apparentés	121	95	192	144	191	150	93	68
Disorders of the blood and blood-forming organs and certain disorders involving the immune mechanism — Maladies du sang et des organes hématopoïétiques et certains troubles du système immunitaire								
Total	135	133	10	8	2	3	60	71
Anaemias — Anémies	83	79	5	2	1	3	36	50
Endocrine, nutritional and metabolic diseases — Maladies endocriniennes, nutritionnelles et métaboliques								
Total	668	531	124	161	120	141	713	694
Diabetes mellitus — Diabète sucré	546	404	114	154	110	132	711	694
Malnutrition — Malnutrition	16	8	-	-	-	-	-	-
Mental and behavioural disorders — Troubles mentaux et du comportement	2	1	-	1	1	-	48	22
Diseases of the nervous system — Maladies du système nerveux	287	228	72	64	115	75	512	308
Diseases of the circulatory system — Maladies de l'appareil circulatoire								
Total	4 854	3 362	3 064	2 540	3 164	2 508	8 972	7 173
Acute rheumatic fever and chronic rheumatic heart diseases — Rhumatisme articularie aigu et cardiopathies rhumatismales chroniques	9	9	9	19	7	15	11	14
Hypertensive diseases — Maladies hypertensives	726	638	351	312	414	308	2 034	1 924
Ischaemic heart disease — Cardiopathie ischémique	1 385	693	1 741	1 151	1 896	1 203	2 902	2 171

Cause of death — Cause de décès	Saudi Arabia - Arabie saoudite 2012 (U) Male — Masculin Number Nombre	Saudi Arabia - Arabie saoudite 2012 (U) Female — Féminin Number Nombre	Singapore - Singapour 2014 (+U) Male — Masculin Number Nombre	Singapore - Singapour 2014 (+U) Female — Féminin Number Nombre	Singapore - Singapour 2015 (+U) Male — Masculin Number Nombre	Singapore - Singapour 2015 (+U) Female — Féminin Number Nombre	Tajikistan - Tadjikistan 2016 (U) Male — Masculin Number Nombre	Tajikistan - Tadjikistan 2016 (U) Female — Féminin Number Nombre
Cerebrovascular disease — Maladie cérébrovasculaire	1 350	1 055	714	823	580	685	1 877	1 430
Diseases of arteries, arterioles and capillaries — Maladies des artères, artérioles et capillaires	18	7	102	80	97	90	868	810
Diseases of the respiratory system — Maladies de l'appareil respiratoire								
Total	1 093	833	2 133	1 944	2 235	2 059	1 010	801
Influenza — Grippe	1	-	-	-	1	-	6	12
Pneumonia — Pneumopathies	625	444	1 754	1 803	1 852	1 909	232	176
Chronic lower respiratory diseases — Maladies chroniques des voies respiratoires inférieures	204	160	325	105	324	118	318	252
Diseases of the digestive system — Maladies de l'appareil digestif								
Total	542	300	241	210	221	225	865	609
Gastric and duodenal ulcer — Ulcère de l'estomac et du duodénum	17	12	24	10	23	12	39	31
Diseases of the liver — Maladies du foie	406	204	105	68	101	71	731	498
Diseases of the musculoskeletal system and connective tissue — Maladies du système ostéo-articularie, des muscles et du tissu conjonctif	2	22	39	38	41	46	25	21
Diseases of the genitourinary system — Maladies de l'appareil génito-urinaire								
Total	928	630	333	596	334	560	447	382
Disorders of kidney and ureter — Affections du rein et de l'uretère	882	594	183	236	208	263	419	381
Hyperplasia of prostate — Hyperplasie de la prostate	-	..	-	..	-	..	21	..
Pregnancy, childbirth and the puerperium — Grossesse, accouchement et puerpéralité								
Total	..	45	..	-	..	3	..	18
Pregnancy with abortive outcome — Grossesse se terminant par un avortement	..	1	..	-	..	1	..	1
Other direct obstetric causes — Autres décès maternels directs	..	42	..	-	..	2	..	17
Indirect obstetric causes — Décès maternels indirects	..	1	..	-	..	-	..	-
Certain conditions originating in the perinatal period — Certaines affections dont l'origine se situe dans la période périnatale	2 055	1 567	18	20	20	5	792	553
Congenital malformations, deformations and chromosomal abnormalities — Malformations congénitales et anomalies chromosomiques	667	577	25	18	28	23	612	397
Symptoms, signs and abnormal clinical and laboratory findings, not elsewhere classified — Symptômes, signes et résultats anormaux d'examens cliniques et de laboratoire, non classés ailleurs	9 127	4 554	26	22	34	28	2 149	1 970
All other diseases — Toutes autres maladies	108	73	45	73	36	74	2	1
External causes — Causes externes								
Total	7 624	1 236	504	204	485	184	1 041	310
Accidents								
Total	2 788	386	213	83	239	61	696	176
Transport accidents — Accidents de transport	2 426	318	102	26	96	24	304	74
Falls — Chutes	165	24	71	40	104	22	75	16
Accidental drowning and submersion — Noyade et submersion accidentelles	10	3	5	-	5	1	175	51
Exposure to smoke, fire and flames — Exposition à la fumée, au feu et aux flammes	-	-	2	1	4	1	31	8
Accidental poisoning by and exposure to noxious substances — Intoxication accidentelle par des substances nocives et exposition à ces substances	-	-	7	2	11	6	-	-
Intentional self-harm — Lésions auto-infligées	59	17	250	105	218	111	154	82
Assault — Agresssions	-	-	4	5	11	4	60	17
All other external causes — Toutes autres causes externes	4 777	833	37	11	17	8	131	35

20. Death and death rates by cause and sex: 2012 - 2016
Décès et taux de mortalité par cause et sexe : 2012 - 2016 (continued - suite)

Cause of death — Cause de décès	Thailand - Thaïlande				Turkey - Turquie			
	2015 (+U)		2016 (+U)		2014 (+U)		2015 (+U)	
	Male — Masculin	Female — Féminin	Male — Masculin	Female — Féminin	Male — Masculin	Female — Féminin	Male — Masculin	Female — Féminin
	Number Nombre	Number Nombre	Number Nombre	Number Nombre	Number Nombre	Number Nombre	Number Nombre	Number Nombre
TOTAL	252 302	193 662	265 439	203 646	208 856	174 747	215 977	180 994
Certain infectious and parasitic diseases — Certaines maladies infectieuses et parasitaires								
Total	24 512	18 646	21 828	15 437	3 656	3 176	4 307	4 021
Intestinal infectious diseases — Maladies infectieuses intestinales	964	922	1 135	1 098	271	325	244	342
Tuberculosis — Tuberculose	4 374	1 710	4 475	1 632	242	125	273	139
Tetanus — Tétanos	20	17	22	14	3	3	6	5
Diphtheria — Diphtérie..	3	4	4	1	-	-	-	-
Whooping cough — Coqueluche	-	-	-	-	1	1	-	-
Meningococcal infection — Infection à méningocoques	1	2	5	-	11	9	9	10
Septicaemia — Septicémie	13 678	12 672	11 191	9 909	2 027	2 037	2 876	2 827
Acute poliomyelitis — Poliomyélite aiguë	-	-	-	-	-	1	1	1
Measles — Rougeole..	-	-	2	-	1	2	1	2
Viral hepatitis — Hépatite virale	649	277	683	308	481	327	383	324
Human immunodeficiency virus [HIV] disease — Maladies dues au virus de l'immunodéficience humaine (VIH)...	3 478	1 978	3 203	1 751	66	12	71	20
Malaria — Paludisme...	23	10	20	6	-	-	2	1
Neoplasms — Tumeurs	42 598	31 340	44 490	33 076	50 798	27 276	51 256	27 903
Malignant neoplasms — Tumeurs malignes								
Total	42 312	31 036	43 966	32 538	49 885	26 590	50 275	27 188
Malignant neoplasm of lip, oral cavity and pharynx — Tumeur maligne de la lèvre, de la cavité buccale et du pharynx	1 983	963	2 183	972	548	285	569	275
Malignant neoplasm of oesophagus — Tumeur maligne de l'oesophage	1 420	219	1 512	213	493	333	471	346
Malignant neoplasm of stomach — Tumeur maligne de l'estomac	1 048	822	1 136	935	4 518	2 350	4 394	2 305
Malignant neoplasm of colon, rectosigmoid junction, rectum, anus and anal canal — Tumeur maligne du côlon, de la jonction recto-sigmoïdienne, du rectum, de l'anus et du canal anal	2 293	1 811	2 540	2 018	3 905	2 918	4 060	2 907
Malignant neoplasm of liver and intrahepatic bile ducts — Tumeur maligne du foie et des voies bilaires intrahépatiques	11 569	4 806	12 086	4 984	1 870	1 010	1 913	1 125
Malignant neoplasm of pancreas — Tumeur maligne du pancréas..................	640	564	631	611	2 532	1 813	2 667	1 904
Malignant neoplasm of trachea, bronchus and lung — Tumeur maligne de la trachée, des bronches et du poumon	8 530	4 546	8 726	4 688	19 228	3 348	19 466	3 531
Malignant neoplasm of female breast — Tumeur maligne du sein chez la femme	..	3 752	..	4 099	..	3 750	..	3 876
Malignant neoplasm of cervix uteri — Tumeur maligne du col de l'utérus..........	..	2 195	..	2 193	..	483	..	473
Malignant neoplasm of prostate — Tumeur maligne de la prostate	1 303	..	1 404	..	3 592	..	3 515	..
Malignant neoplasm of lymphoid, haematopoietic and related tissue — Tumeurs malignes primitives ou présumées primitives des tissus lymphoïde, hématopoïétique et apparentés...	1 940	1 536	2 248	1 908	3 798	2 598	3 769	2 599
Disorders of the blood and blood-forming organs and certain disorders involving the immune mechanism — Maladies du sang et des organes hématopoïétiques et certains troubles du système immunitaire								
Total	466	470	467	579	659	700	639	655
Anaemias — Anémies	261	258	289	326	260	325	311	329
Endocrine, nutritional and metabolic diseases — Maladies endocriniennes, nutritionnelles et métaboliques								
Total	6 084	8 467	6 709	9 177	8 264	11 166	8 386	11 417
Diabetes mellitus — Diabète sucré	5 096	7 525	6 006	8 481	6 612	8 942	6 810	9 158
Malnutrition — Malnutrition	128	151	140	136	245	372	228	407
Mental and behavioural disorders — Troubles mentaux et du comportement	1 085	165	1 201	194	252	289	288	283
Diseases of the nervous system — Maladies du système nerveux...............	4 090	5 853	4 935	7 007	7 603	9 006	8 591	10 514
Diseases of the circulatory system — Maladies de l'appareil circulatoire								
Total	34 697	27 173	39 358	30 339	75 604	78 044	79 216	79 975
Acute rheumatic fever and chronic rheumatic heart diseases — Rhumatisme articularie aigu et cardiopathies rhumatismales chroniques	68	129	92	200	100	198	162	301
Hypertensive diseases — Maladies hypertensives............................	3 811	4 074	3 830	4 100	6 533	10 936	5 664	9 334
Ischaemic heart disease — Cardiopathie ischémique................................	11 557	7 860	12 634	8 374	35 105	26 184	36 902	27 789

Cause of death — Cause de décès	Thailand - Thaïlande				Turkey - Turquie			
	2015 (+U)		2016 (+U)		2014 (+U)		2015 (+U)	
	Male — Masculin	Female — Féminin	Male — Masculin	Female — Féminin	Male — Masculin	Female — Féminin	Male — Masculin	Female — Féminin
	Number Nombre	Number Nombre	Number Nombre	Number Nombre	Number Nombre	Number Nombre	Number Nombre	Number Nombre
Cerebrovascular disease — Maladie cérébrovasculaire	16 004	12 142	18 273	13 412	16 803	20 913	17 442	21 206
Diseases of arteries, arterioles and capillaries — Maladies des artères, artérioles et capillaires	760	523	916	614	1 583	896	1 796	965
Diseases of the respiratory system — Maladies de l'appareil respiratoire								
Total	24 437	15 522	25 891	16 197	23 738	16 854	25 593	18 227
Influenza — Grippe	18	23	35	37	55	68	102	103
Pneumonia — Pneumopathies	15 985	11 392	16 551	11 919	5 112	4 765	6 523	6 172
Chronic lower respiratory diseases — Maladies chroniques des voies respiratoires inférieures	6 347	2 415	7 300	2 670	16 047	9 783	16 521	9 755
Diseases of the digestive system — Maladies de l'appareil digestif								
Total	12 636	5 872	14 039	6 364	5 212	4 776	5 242	4 861
Gastric and duodenal ulcer — Ulcère de l'estomac et du duodénum	381	237	400	286	287	234	310	226
Diseases of the liver — Maladies du foie	7 532	2 840	8 564	3 203	2 015	1 499	2 132	1 549
Diseases of the musculoskeletal system and connective tissue — Maladies du système ostéo-articularie, des muscles et du tissu conjonctif	1 072	1 316	1 326	1 703	393	748	433	723
Diseases of the genitourinary system — Maladies de l'appareil génito-urinaire								
Total	10 013	11 145	11 421	12 732	6 027	5 958	6 755	6 684
Disorders of kidney and ureter — Affections du rein et de l'uretère	8 966	9 564	10 116	10 690	5 277	5 345	5 977	6 041
Hyperplasia of prostate — Hyperplasie de la prostate	147	..	141	..	245	..	247	..
Pregnancy, childbirth and the puerperium — Grossesse, accouchement et puerpéralité								
Total	..	167	..	177	..	273	..	220
Pregnancy with abortive outcome — Grossesse se terminant par un avortement	..	14	..	15	..	-	..	2
Other direct obstetric causes — Autres décès maternels directs	..	105	..	118	..	160	..	101
Indirect obstetric causes — Décès maternels indirects	..	47	..	44	..	107	..	115
Certain conditions originating in the perinatal period — Certaines affections dont l'origine se situe dans la période périnatale	1 370	967	1 271	922	4 512	3 468	4 565	3 518
Congenital malformations, deformations and chromosomal abnormalities — Malformations congénitales et anomalies chromosomiques	854	756	881	809	2 908	2 513	2 988	2 611
Symptoms, signs and abnormal clinical and laboratory findings, not elsewhere classified — Symptômes, signes et résultats anormaux d'examens cliniques et de laboratoire, non classés ailleurs	56 758	56 454	59 294	59 349	4 674	4 587	4 192	3 711
All other diseases — Toutes autres maladies	1 158	1 204	1 082	1 272	132	185	88	176
External causes — Causes externes								
Total	30 472	8 145	31 246	8 312	14 424	5 728	13 438	5 495
Accidents								
Total	18 223	5 076	19 055	5 180	11 098	4 752	10 907	4 695
Transport accidents — Accidents de transport	11 463	3 053	12 215	3 259	4 888	1 527	5 079	1 628
Falls — Chutes	1 545	568	1 341	435	2 061	2 014	2 163	1 959
Accidental drowning and submersion — Noyade et submersion accidentelles	2 636	614	2 850	650	605	157	577	172
Exposure to smoke, fire and flames — Exposition à la fumée, au feu et aux flammes	176	97	193	98	181	113	149	106
Accidental poisoning by and exposure to noxious substances — Intoxication accidentelle par des substances nocives et exposition à ces substances	27	22	38	20	898	237	600	217
Intentional self-harm — Lésions auto-infligées	3 366	839	3 283	848	1 209	408	1 135	397
Assault — Agresssions	1 867	302	1 494	279	991	209	869	213
All other external causes — Toutes autres causes externes	7 016	1 928	7 414	2 005	1 126	359	527	190

Cause of death — Cause de décès	Turkmenistan - Turkménistan 2014 (U) Male — Masculin Number Nombre	2014 (U) Female — Féminin Number Nombre	2015 (U) Male — Masculin Number Nombre	2015 (U) Female — Féminin Number Nombre	Uzbekistan - Ouzbékistan 2013 (C) Male — Masculin Number Nombre	Male — Masculin Rate Taux	Female — Féminin Number Nombre	Female — Féminin Rate Taux
TOTAL	*18 079*	*13 672*	*18 112*	*14 135*	*78 794*	*520.2*	*66 878*	*443.0*
Certain infectious and parasitic diseases — Certaines maladies infectieuses et parasitaires								
Total	513	294	496	226	1 936	12.8	1 056	7.0
Intestinal infectious diseases — Maladies infectieuses intestinales	20	22	30	33	35	0.2	45	0.3
Tuberculosis — Tuberculose	322	151	324	104	1 221	8.1	567	3.8
Tetanus — Tétanos	9	3	2	1	-	-	-	-
Diphtheria — Diphtérie	-	-	-	-	1	◆0.0	-	-
Whooping cough — Coqueluche	-	-	-	-	-	-	-	-
Meningococcal infection — Infection à méningocoques	2	2	2	6	20	◆0.1	16	◆0.1
Septicaemia — Septicémie	80	65	64	46	285	1.9	212	1.4
Acute poliomyelitis — Poliomyélite aiguë	-	-	-	-	-	-	-	-
Measles — Rougeole	-	-	-	-	-	-	-	-
Viral hepatitis — Hépatite virale	44	16	46	21	193	1.3	123	0.8
Human immunodeficiency virus [HIV] disease — Maladies dues au virus de l'immunodéficience humaine (VIH)	-	-	-	-	152	1.0	69	0.5
Malaria — Paludisme	-	-	-	-	-	-	-	-
Neoplasms — Tumeurs	*1 264*	*1 311*	*1 324*	*1 367*	*5 485*	*36.2*	*5 950*	*39.4*
Malignant neoplasms — Tumeurs malignes								
Total	1 245	1 299	1 309	1 359	5 464	36.1	5 923	39.2
Malignant neoplasm of lip, oral cavity and pharynx — Tumeur maligne de la lèvre, de la cavité buccale et du pharynx	79	42	63	33	274	1.8	205	1.4
Malignant neoplasm of oesophagus — Tumeur maligne de l'oesophage	115	109	129	119	292	1.9	266	1.8
Malignant neoplasm of stomach — Tumeur maligne de l'estomac	160	80	187	102	978	6.5	637	4.2
Malignant neoplasm of colon, rectosigmoid junction, rectum, anus and anal canal — Tumeur maligne du côlon, de la jonction recto-sigmoïdienne, du rectum, de l'anus et du canal anal	55	47	52	62	339	2.2	296	2.0
Malignant neoplasm of liver and intrahepatic bile ducts — Tumeur maligne du foie et des voies biliaires intrahépatiques	104	62	107	72	438	2.9	320	2.1
Malignant neoplasm of pancreas — Tumeur maligne du pancréas	39	29	53	42	167	1.1	159	1.1
Malignant neoplasm of trachea, bronchus and lung — Tumeur maligne de la trachée, des bronches et du poumon	203	68	201	65	918	6.1	347	2.3
Malignant neoplasm of female breast — Tumeur maligne du sein chez la femme	..	270	..	243	..	..	1 220	11.1
Malignant neoplasm of cervix uteri — Tumeur maligne du col de l'utérus	..	166	..	133	..	..	621	5.7
Malignant neoplasm of prostate — Tumeur maligne de la prostate	38	..	32	..	126	5.9	..	..
Malignant neoplasm of lymphoid, haematopoietic and related tissue — Tumeurs malignes primitives ou présumées primitives des tissus lymphoïde, hématopoïétique et apparentés	...	...	...	...	506	3.3	381	2.5
Disorders of the blood and blood-forming organs and certain disorders involving the immune mechanism — Maladies du sang et des organes hématopoïétiques et certains troubles du système immunitaire								
Total	32	29	22	23	114	0.8	160	1.1
Anaemias — Anémies	12	11	6	11	83	0.5	135	0.9
Endocrine, nutritional and metabolic diseases — Maladies endocriniennes, nutritionnelles et métaboliques								
Total	252	371	294	387	2 193	14.5	2 334	15.5
Diabetes mellitus — Diabète sucré	241	363	291	375	2 170	14.3	2 303	15.3
Malnutrition — Malnutrition	-	-	-	-	-	-	1	◆0.0
Mental and behavioural disorders — Troubles mentaux et du comportement	*14*	*9*	*16*	*7*	*9*	*◆0.1*	*2*	*◆0.0*
Diseases of the nervous system — Maladies du système nerveux	*186*	*149*	*208*	*165*	*1 572*	*10.4*	*1 190*	*7.9*
Diseases of the circulatory system — Maladies de l'appareil circulatoire								
Total	7 720	6 614	7 654	6 710	46 060	304.1	42 720	283.0
Acute rheumatic fever and chronic rheumatic heart diseases — Rhumatisme articularie aigu et cardiopathies rhumatismales chroniques	26	53	32	44	243	1.6	328	2.2
Hypertensive diseases — Maladies hypertensives	1 198	1 102	1 140	964	9 217	60.8	8 897	58.9
Ischaemic heart disease — Cardiopathie ischémique	3 760	3 199	3 838	3 394	23 044	152.1	20 769	137.6

Cause of death — Cause de décès	Turkmenistan - Turkménistan				Uzbekistan - Ouzbékistan			
	2014 (U)		2015 (U)		2013 (C)			
	Male — Masculin	Female — Féminin	Male — Masculin	Female — Féminin	Male — Masculin		Female — Féminin	
	Number Nombre	Number Nombre	Number Nombre	Number Nombre	Number Nombre	Rate Taux	Number Nombre	Rate Taux
Cerebrovascular disease — Maladie cérébrovasculaire	2 127	1 827	2 183	1 910	7 479	49.4	6 762	44.8
Diseases of arteries, arterioles and capillaries — Maladies des artères, artérioles et capillaires	...	...	...	...	1 744	11.5	2 301	15.2
Diseases of the respiratory system — Maladies de l'appareil respiratoire								
Total	1 102	811	1 066	880	4 689	31.0	3 697	24.5
Influenza — Grippe	-	4	2	4	170	1.1	155	1.0
Pneumonia — Pneumopathies	452	335	482	387	1 925	12.7	1 495	9.9
Chronic lower respiratory diseases — Maladies chroniques des voies respiratoires inférieures	100	75	103	87	961	6.3	792	5.2
Diseases of the digestive system — Maladies de l'appareil digestif								
Total	1 523	805	1 581	868	4 825	31.9	3 496	23.2
Gastric and duodenal ulcer — Ulcère de l'estomac et du duodénum	84	25	83	31	331	2.2	186	1.2
Diseases of the liver — Maladies du foie	1 287	681	1 381	731	4 052	26.7	2 996	19.8
Diseases of the musculoskeletal system and connective tissue — Maladies du système ostéo-articularie, des muscles et du tissu conjonctif	16	36	11	24	77	0.5	146	1.0
Diseases of the genitourinary system — Maladies de l'appareil génito-urinaire								
Total	254	196	229	166	1 521	10.0	1 258	8.3
Disorders of kidney and ureter — Affections du rein et de l'uretère	...	...	...	...	1 462	9.7	1 245	8.2
Hyperplasia of prostate — Hyperplasie de la prostate	...	..	...	..	40	1.9	..	..
Pregnancy, childbirth and the puerperium — Grossesse, accouchement et puerpéralité								
Total	..	4	..	5	..	..	120	17.7
Pregnancy with abortive outcome — Grossesse se terminant par un avortement	..	1	..	-	..	..	2	♦0.3
Other direct obstetric causes — Autres décès maternels directs	..	3	..	5	..	..	107	15.7
Indirect obstetric causes — Décès maternels indirects	..	-	..	-	..	..	7	♦1.0
Certain conditions originating in the perinatal period — Certaines affections dont l'origine se situe dans la période périnatale	907	579	912	643	2 014	570.6	1 277	391.1
Congenital malformations, deformations and chromosomal abnormalities — Malformations congénitales et anomalies chromosomiques	460	331	444	351	348	98.6	259	79.3
Symptoms, signs and abnormal clinical and laboratory findings, not elsewhere classified — Symptômes, signes et résultats anormaux d'examens cliniques et de laboratoire, non classés ailleurs	2 925	1 865	2 943	1 970	903	6.0	771	5.1
All other diseases — Toutes autres maladies	3	2	4	2	7	♦0.0	10	♦0.1
External causes — Causes externes								
Total	908	266	908	341	7 041	46.5	2 432	16.1
Accidents								
Total	...	...	...	...	4 861	32.1	1 516	10.0
Transport accidents — Accidents de transport	115	29	98	33	2 132	14.1	563	3.7
Falls — Chutes	36	2	37	9	268	1.8	50	0.3
Accidental drowning and submersion — Noyade et submersion accidentelles	62	16	61	16	661	4.4	255	1.7
Exposure to smoke, fire and flames — Exposition à la fumée, au feu et aux flammes	43	26	20	20	184	1.2	144	1.0
Accidental poisoning by and exposure to noxious substances — Intoxication accidentelle par des substances nocives et exposition à ces substances	44	23	39	30	256	1.7	105	0.7
Intentional self-harm — Lésions auto-infligées	92	44	92	41	1 322	8.7	628	4.2
Assault — Agresssions	71	18	50	13	374	2.5	123	0.8
All other external causes — Toutes autres causes externes	...	...	...	...	484	3.2	165	1.1

20. Death and death rates by cause and sex: 2012 - 2016
Décès et taux de mortalité par cause et sexe : 2012 - 2016 (continued - suite)

Cause of death — Cause de décès	Uzbekistan - Ouzbékistan 2014 (C)				Andorra - Andorre			
	Male — Masculin		Female — Féminin		2014 (C)		2015 (C)	
					Male — Masculin	Female — Féminin	Male — Masculin	Female — Féminin
	Number Nombre	Rate Taux	Number Nombre	Rate Taux	Number Nombre	Number Nombre	Number Nombre	Number Nombre
TOTAL	81 465	528.5	68 296	445.1	168	108	150	132
Certain infectious and parasitic diseases — Certaines maladies infectieuses et parasitaires								
Total	1 987	12.9	1 066	6.9	-	2	5	4
Intestinal infectious diseases — Maladies infectieuses intestinales	58	0.4	43	0.3	-	-	-	-
Tuberculosis — Tuberculose	1 253	8.1	569	3.7	-	-	-	-
Tetanus — Tétanos	-	-	-	-	-	-	-	-
Diphtheria — Diphtérie	-	-	-	-	-	-	-	-
Whooping cough — Coqueluche	-	-	-	-	-	-	-	-
Meningococcal infection — Infection à méningocoques	16	◆0.1	14	◆0.1	-	-	-	-
Septicaemia — Septicémie	278	1.8	216	1.4	-	1	1	1
Acute poliomyelitis — Poliomyélite aiguë	-	-	-	-	-	-	-	-
Measles — Rougeole	1	◆0.0	1	◆0.0	-	-	-	-
Viral hepatitis — Hépatite virale	139	0.9	103	0.7	-	1	1	-
Human immunodeficiency virus [HIV] disease — Maladies dues au virus de l'immunodéficience humaine (VIH)	212	1.4	97	0.6	-	-	2	1
Malaria — Paludisme	-	-	-	-	-	-	-	-
Neoplasms — Tumeurs	6 004	38.9	6 309	41.1	76	36	54	34
Malignant neoplasms — Tumeurs malignes								
Total	5 970	38.7	6 253	40.8	75	36	52	34
Malignant neoplasm of lip, oral cavity and pharynx — Tumeur maligne de la lèvre, de la cavité buccale et du pharynx	327	2.1	196	1.3	1	1	1	-
Malignant neoplasm of oesophagus — Tumeur maligne de l'oesophage	336	2.2	282	1.8	3	-	4	-
Malignant neoplasm of stomach — Tumeur maligne de l'estomac	978	6.3	671	4.4	3	-	2	3
Malignant neoplasm of colon, rectosigmoid junction, rectum, anus and anal canal — Tumeur maligne du côlon, de la jonction recto-sigmoïdienne, du rectum, de l'anus et du canal anal	374	2.4	304	2.0	5	6	10	1
Malignant neoplasm of liver and intrahepatic bile ducts — Tumeur maligne du foie et des voies bilaires intrahépatiques	503	3.3	394	2.6	9	1	-	1
Malignant neoplasm of pancreas — Tumeur maligne du pancréas	183	1.2	167	1.1	3	2	2	1
Malignant neoplasm of trachea, bronchus and lung — Tumeur maligne de la trachée, des bronches et du poumon	916	5.9	353	2.3	23	1	13	8
Malignant neoplasm of female breast — Tumeur maligne du sein chez la femme	..	..	1 226	11.0	..	5	..	5
Malignant neoplasm of cervix uteri — Tumeur maligne du col de l'utérus	..	..	626	5.6	..	2	..	1
Malignant neoplasm of prostate — Tumeur maligne de la prostate	167	7.4	..	..	3	..	3	..
Malignant neoplasm of lymphoid, haematopoietic and related tissue — Tumeurs malignes primitives ou présumées primitives des tissus lymphoïde, hématopoïétique et apparentés	496	3.2	387	2.5	...	...	...	...
Disorders of the blood and blood-forming organs and certain disorders involving the immune mechanism — Maladies du sang et des organes hématopoïétiques et certains troubles du système immunitaire								
Total	167	1.1	163	1.1	2	-	-	-
Anaemias — Anémies	125	0.8	134	0.9	-	-	-	-
Endocrine, nutritional and metabolic diseases — Maladies endocriniennes, nutritionnelles et métaboliques								
Total	2 387	15.5	2 466	16.1	1	-	-	2
Diabetes mellitus — Diabète sucré	2 356	15.3	2 419	15.8	1	-	-	-
Malnutrition — Malnutrition	4	◆0.0	4	◆0.0	-	-	-	-
Mental and behavioural disorders — Troubles mentaux et du comportement	26	◆0.2	12	◆0.1	2	7	11	14
Diseases of the nervous system — Maladies du système nerveux	1 581	10.3	1 051	6.9	1	3	2	9
Diseases of the circulatory system — Maladies de l'appareil circulatoire								
Total	47 415	307.6	43 442	283.1	32	30	32	33
Acute rheumatic fever and chronic rheumatic heart diseases — Rhumatisme articularie aigu et cardiopathies rhumatismales chroniques	231	1.5	336	2.2	-	-	-	1
Hypertensive diseases — Maladies hypertensives	10 292	66.8	9 827	64.0	6	9	4	8
Ischaemic heart disease — Cardiopathie ischémique	22 300	144.7	19 592	127.7	9	8	12	5

Cause of death — Cause de décès	Uzbekistan - Ouzbékistan				Andorra - Andorre			
	2014 (C)				2014 (C)		2015 (C)	
	Male — Masculin		Female — Féminin		Male — Masculin	Female — Féminin	Male — Masculin	Female — Féminin
	Number Nombre	Rate Taux	Number Nombre	Rate Taux	Number Nombre	Number Nombre	Number Nombre	Number Nombre
Cerebrovascular disease — Maladie cérébrovasculaire	7 588	49.2	6 673	43.5	5	4	8	6
Diseases of arteries, arterioles and capillaries — Maladies des artères, artérioles et capillaires	1 783	11.6	2 350	15.3	...	...	...	...
Diseases of the respiratory system — Maladies de l'appareil respiratoire								
Total	4 166	27.0	3 287	21.4	15	13	14	13
Influenza — Grippe	101	0.7	110	0.7	-	1	-	-
Pneumonia — Pneumopathies	1 905	12.4	1 461	9.5	4	2	1	5
Chronic lower respiratory diseases — Maladies chroniques des voies respiratoires inférieures	902	5.9	725	4.7	4	4	5	3
Diseases of the digestive system — Maladies de l'appareil digestif								
Total	5 032	32.6	3 679	24.0	5	3	9	4
Gastric and duodenal ulcer — Ulcère de l'estomac et du duodénum	354	2.3	183	1.2	-	-	-	-
Diseases of the liver — Maladies du foie	4 192	27.2	3 115	20.3	3	1	2	2
Diseases of the musculoskeletal system and connective tissue — Maladies du système ostéo-articularie, des muscles et du tissu conjonctif	60	0.4	105	0.7	-	-	-	1
Diseases of the genitourinary system — Maladies de l'appareil génito-urinaire								
Total	1 500	9.7	1 177	7.7	2	1	4	2
Disorders of kidney and ureter — Affections du rein et de l'uretère	1 430	9.3	1 158	7.5	...	...	...	...
Hyperplasia of prostate — Hyperplasie de la prostate	36	1.6	..	..	...	...	...	...
Pregnancy, childbirth and the puerperium — Grossesse, accouchement et puerpéralité								
Total	..	..	131	18.2	..	-	..	-
Pregnancy with abortive outcome — Grossesse se terminant par un avortement	..	..	4	♦0.6	..	-	..	-
Other direct obstetric causes — Autres décès maternels directs	..	..	109	15.2	..	-	..	-
Indirect obstetric causes — Décès maternels indirects	..	..	17	♦2.4	..	-	..	-
Certain conditions originating in the perinatal period — Certaines affections dont l'origine se situe dans la période périnatale	2 439	653.4	1 764	511.7	1	1	-	-
Congenital malformations, deformations and chromosomal abnormalities — Malformations congénitales et anomalies chromosomiques	475	127.3	371	107.6	1	-	-	1
Symptoms, signs and abnormal clinical and laboratory findings, not elsewhere classified — Symptômes, signes et résultats anormaux d'examens cliniques et de laboratoire, non classés ailleurs	1 262	8.2	994	6.5	22	6	9	5
All other diseases — Toutes autres maladies	16	♦0.1	19	♦0.1	-	-	-	-
External causes — Causes externes								
Total	6 948	45.1	2 260	14.7	8	6	10	10
Accidents								
Total	4 720	30.6	1 315	8.6	...	...	...	...
Transport accidents — Accidents de transport	2 048	13.3	494	3.2	2	2	1	1
Falls — Chutes	234	1.5	45	0.3	3	3	5	6
Accidental drowning and submersion — Noyade et submersion accidentelles	624	4.0	205	1.3	-	-	-	-
Exposure to smoke, fire and flames — Exposition à la fumée, au feu et aux flammes	200	1.3	122	0.8	-	-	-	-
Accidental poisoning by and exposure to noxious substances — Intoxication accidentelle par des substances nocives et exposition à ces substances	276	1.8	102	0.7	-	-	-	-
Intentional self-harm — Lésions auto-infligées	1 408	9.1	690	4.5	3	1	3	2
Assault — Agresssions	309	2.0	107	0.7	-	-	-	-
All other external causes — Toutes autres causes externes	511	3.3	148	1.0	...	...	...	...

Austria - Autriche

Cause of death — Cause de décès	2015 (C)				2016 (C)			
	Male — Masculin		Female — Féminin		Male — Masculin		Female — Féminin	
	Number Nombre	Rate Taux	Number Nombre	Rate Taux	Number Nombre	Rate Taux	Number Nombre	Rate Taux
TOTAL	39 860	950.2	43 213	986.3	39 022	914.9	41 647	941.2
Certain infectious and parasitic diseases — Certaines maladies infectieuses et parasitaires								
Total	408	9.7	430	9.8	398	9.3	469	10.6
Intestinal infectious diseases — Maladies infectieuses intestinales	41	1.0	53	1.2	52	1.2	87	2.0
Tuberculosis — Tuberculose	30	♦0.7	16	♦0.4	22	♦0.5	9	♦0.2
Tetanus — Tétanos	-	-	2	♦0.0	-	-	-	-
Diphtheria — Diphtérie	-	-	-	-	-	-	-	-
Whooping cough — Coqueluche	-	-	-	-	1	♦0.0	-	-
Meningococcal infection — Infection à méningocoques	2	♦0.0	-	-	1	♦0.0	2	♦0.0
Septicaemia — Septicémie	89	2.1	90	2.1	116	2.7	121	2.7
Acute poliomyelitis — Poliomyélite aiguë	-	-	-	-	1	♦0.0	-	-
Measles — Rougeole	-	-	-	-	-	-	-	-
Viral hepatitis — Hépatite virale	112	2.7	148	3.4	76	1.8	105	2.4
Human immunodeficiency virus [HIV] disease — Maladies dues au virus de l'immunodéficience humaine (VIH)	30	♦0.7	11	♦0.3	28	♦0.7	7	♦0.2
Malaria — Paludisme	1	♦0.0	-	-	-	-	-	-
Neoplasms — Tumeurs	11 235	267.8	9 747	222.5	11 119	260.7	9 799	221.5
Malignant neoplasms — Tumeurs malignes								
Total	10 946	260.9	9 403	214.6	10 763	252.3	9 419	212.9
Malignant neoplasm of lip, oral cavity and pharynx — Tumeur maligne de la lèvre, de la cavité buccale et du pharynx	372	8.9	153	3.5	447	10.5	135	3.1
Malignant neoplasm of oesophagus — Tumeur maligne de l'oesophage	267	6.4	67	1.5	277	6.5	97	2.2
Malignant neoplasm of stomach — Tumeur maligne de l'estomac	462	11.0	363	8.3	425	10.0	353	8.0
Malignant neoplasm of colon, rectosigmoid junction, rectum, anus and anal canal — Tumeur maligne du côlon, de la jonction recto-sigmoïdienne, du rectum, de l'anus et du canal anal	1 145	27.3	899	20.5	1 215	28.5	908	20.5
Malignant neoplasm of liver and intrahepatic bile ducts — Tumeur maligne du foie et des voies bilaires intrahépatiques	630	15.0	287	6.6	596	14.0	211	4.8
Malignant neoplasm of pancreas — Tumeur maligne du pancréas	866	20.6	805	18.4	787	18.5	891	20.1
Malignant neoplasm of trachea, bronchus and lung — Tumeur maligne de la trachée, des bronches et du poumon	2 396	57.1	1 493	34.1	2 415	56.6	1 534	34.7
Malignant neoplasm of female breast — Tumeur maligne du sein chez la femme	..	..	1 568	41.4	..	..	1 588	41.6
Malignant neoplasm of cervix uteri — Tumeur maligne du col de l'utérus	..	..	139	3.7	..	..	138	3.6
Malignant neoplasm of prostate — Tumeur maligne de la prostate	1 128	73.4	..	..	1 225	77.8	..	..
Malignant neoplasm of lymphoid, haematopoietic and related tissue — Tumeurs malignes primitives ou présumées primitives des tissus lymphoïde, hématopoïétique et apparentés	881	21.0	795	18.1	978	22.9	847	19.1
Disorders of the blood and blood-forming organs and certain disorders involving the immune mechanism — Maladies du sang et des organes hématopoïétiques et certains troubles du système immunitaire								
Total	91	2.2	119	2.7	84	2.0	115	2.6
Anaemias — Anémies	42	1.0	78	1.8	38	0.9	63	1.4
Endocrine, nutritional and metabolic diseases — Maladies endocriniennes, nutritionnelles et métaboliques								
Total	1 961	46.7	2 274	51.9	1 987	46.6	2 162	48.9
Diabetes mellitus — Diabète sucré	1 577	37.6	1 886	43.0	1 521	35.7	1 779	40.2
Malnutrition — Malnutrition	-	-	1	♦0.0	-	-	1	♦0.0
Mental and behavioural disorders — Troubles mentaux et du comportement	851	20.3	921	21.0	943	22.1	1 158	26.2
Diseases of the nervous system — Maladies du système nerveux	1 244	29.7	1 619	37.0	1 249	29.3	1 615	36.5
Diseases of the circulatory system — Maladies de l'appareil circulatoire								
Total	15 053	358.8	20 484	467.5	14 352	336.5	18 896	427.1
Acute rheumatic fever and chronic rheumatic heart diseases — Rhumatisme articularie aigu et cardiopathies rhumatismales chroniques	100	2.4	192	4.4	98	2.3	181	4.1
Hypertensive diseases — Maladies hypertensives	1 581	37.7	3 528	80.5	1 513	35.5	3 284	74.2
Ischaemic heart disease — Cardiopathie ischémique	7 375	175.8	7 530	171.9	7 062	165.6	7 002	158.2
Cerebrovascular disease — Maladie cérébrovasculaire	2 031	48.4	3 147	71.8	1 852	43.4	2 760	62.4

Austria - Autriche

Cause of death — Cause de décès	2015 (C)				2016 (C)			
	Male — Masculin		Female — Féminin		Male — Masculin		Female — Féminin	
	Number Nombre	Rate Taux	Number Nombre	Rate Taux	Number Nombre	Rate Taux	Number Nombre	Rate Taux
Diseases of arteries, arterioles and capillaries — Maladies des artères, artérioles et capillaires	569	13.6	674	15.4	558	13.1	671	15.2
Diseases of the respiratory system — Maladies de l'appareil respiratoire								
Total	2 410	57.4	2 054	46.9	2 319	54.4	2 016	45.6
Influenza — Grippe	35	0.8	26	♦0.6	22	♦0.5	16	♦0.4
Pneumonia — Pneumopathies	425	10.1	511	11.7	424	9.9	518	11.7
Chronic lower respiratory diseases — Maladies chroniques des voies respiratoires inférieures	1 649	39.3	1 298	29.6	1 584	37.1	1 248	28.2
Diseases of the digestive system — Maladies de l'appareil digestif								
Total	1 612	38.4	1 243	28.4	1 659	38.9	1 197	27.1
Gastric and duodenal ulcer — Ulcère de l'estomac et du duodénum	66	1.6	84	1.9	87	2.0	78	1.8
Diseases of the liver — Maladies du foie	1 098	26.2	458	10.5	1 076	25.2	436	9.9
Diseases of the musculoskeletal system and connective tissue — Maladies du système ostéo-articularie, des muscles et du tissu conjonctif	78	1.9	189	4.3	106	2.5	212	4.8
Diseases of the genitourinary system — Maladies de l'appareil génito-urinaire								
Total	671	16.0	1 034	23.6	696	16.3	1 043	23.6
Disorders of kidney and ureter — Affections du rein et de l'uretère	576	13.7	869	19.8	575	13.5	843	19.1
Hyperplasia of prostate — Hyperplasie de la prostate	7	♦0.5	..	..	11	♦0.7	..	..
Pregnancy, childbirth and the puerperium — Grossesse, accouchement et puerpéralité								
Total	..	..	4	♦4.7	..	..	5	♦5.7
Pregnancy with abortive outcome — Grossesse se terminant par un avortement	..	..	-	-	..	..	-	-
Other direct obstetric causes — Autres décès maternels directs	..	..	2	♦2.4	..	..	4	♦4.6
Indirect obstetric causes — Décès maternels indirects	..	..	2	♦2.4	..	..	1	♦1.1
Certain conditions originating in the perinatal period — Certaines affections dont l'origine se situe dans la période périnatale	81	185.8	54	132.4	73	162.0	62	145.5
Congenital malformations, deformations and chromosomal abnormalities — Malformations congénitales et anomalies chromosomiques	133	305.0	123	301.6	145	321.9	120	281.5
Symptoms, signs and abnormal clinical and laboratory findings, not elsewhere classified — Symptômes, signes et résultats anormaux d'examens cliniques et de laboratoire, non classés ailleurs	1 207	28.8	1 162	26.5	1 270	29.8	1 108	25.0
All other diseases — Toutes autres maladies	14	♦0.3	42	1.0	25	♦0.6	54	1.2
External causes — Causes externes								
Total	2 811	67.0	1 714	39.1	2 597	60.9	1 616	36.5
Accidents								
Total	1 448	34.5	1 155	26.4	1 326	31.1	1 063	24.0
Transport accidents — Accidents de transport	355	8.5	120	2.7	307	7.2	116	2.6
Falls — Chutes	470	11.2	422	9.6	442	10.4	408	9.2
Accidental drowning and submersion — Noyade et submersion accidentelles	28	♦0.7	11	♦0.3	32	0.8	8	♦0.2
Exposure to smoke, fire and flames — Exposition à la fumée, au feu et aux flammes	16	♦0.4	19	♦0.4	15	♦0.4	15	♦0.3
Accidental poisoning by and exposure to noxious substances — Intoxication accidentelle par des substances nocives et exposition à ces substances	22	♦0.5	8	♦0.2	14	♦0.3	10	♦0.2
Intentional self-harm — Lésions auto-infligées	960	22.9	289	6.6	904	21.2	294	6.6
Assault — Agresssions	20	♦0.5	30	♦0.7	17	♦0.4	26	♦0.6
All other external causes — Toutes autres causes externes	383	9.1	240	5.5	350	8.2	233	5.3

Belarus - Bélarus

Cause of death — Cause de décès	2013 (C)				2014 (C)			
	Male — Masculin		Female — Féminin		Male — Masculin		Female — Féminin	
	Number Nombre	Rate Taux	Number Nombre	Rate Taux	Number Nombre	Rate Taux	Number Nombre	Rate Taux
TOTAL	63 012	1 432.3	62 314	1 229.9	61 274	1 390.9	60 268	1 188.9
Certain infectious and parasitic diseases — Certaines maladies infectieuses et parasitaires								
Total	720	16.4	245	4.8	661	15.0	232	4.6
Intestinal infectious diseases — Maladies infectieuses intestinales	3	♦0.1	3	♦0.1	2	♦0.0	5	♦0.1
Tuberculosis — Tuberculose	460	10.5	87	1.7	383	8.7	62	1.2
Tetanus — Tétanos	-	-	-	-	-	-	-	-
Diphtheria — Diphtérie	-	-	-	-	-	-	-	-
Whooping cough — Coqueluche	-	-	-	-	-	-	-	-
Meningococcal infection — Infection à méningocoques	9	♦0.2	4	♦0.1	3	♦0.1	6	♦0.1
Septicaemia — Septicémie	36	0.8	26	♦0.5	31	0.7	23	♦0.5
Acute poliomyelitis — Poliomyélite aiguë	-	-	-	-	-	-	-	-
Measles — Rougeole	-	-	-	-	-	-	-	-
Viral hepatitis — Hépatite virale	13	♦0.3	5	♦0.1	23	♦0.5	8	♦0.2
Human immunodeficiency virus [HIV] disease — Maladies dues au virus de l'immunodéficience humaine (VIH)	161	3.7	79	1.6	179	4.1	96	1.9
Malaria — Paludisme	-	-	-	-	-	-	-	-
Neoplasms — Tumeurs	9 976	226.8	7 344	144.9	10 156	230.5	7 171	141.5
Malignant neoplasms — Tumeurs malignes								
Total	9 851	223.9	7 212	142.3	10 050	228.1	7 018	138.4
Malignant neoplasm of lip, oral cavity and pharynx — Tumeur maligne de la lèvre, de la cavité buccale et du pharynx	661	15.0	69	1.4	706	16.0	88	1.7
Malignant neoplasm of oesophagus — Tumeur maligne de l'oesophage	358	8.1	47	0.9	351	8.0	40	0.8
Malignant neoplasm of stomach — Tumeur maligne de l'estomac	1 171	26.6	768	15.2	1 124	25.5	719	14.2
Malignant neoplasm of colon, rectosigmoid junction, rectum, anus and anal canal — Tumeur maligne du côlon, de la jonction recto-sigmoïdienne, du rectum, de l'anus et du canal anal	1 094	24.9	1 186	23.4	1 089	24.7	1 107	21.8
Malignant neoplasm of liver and intrahepatic bile ducts — Tumeur maligne du foie et des voies bilaires intrahépatiques	224	5.1	107	2.1	213	4.8	114	2.2
Malignant neoplasm of pancreas — Tumeur maligne du pancréas	443	10.1	401	7.9	510	11.6	409	8.1
Malignant neoplasm of trachea, bronchus and lung — Tumeur maligne de la trachée, des bronches et du poumon	2 477	56.3	339	6.7	2 550	57.9	339	6.7
Malignant neoplasm of female breast — Tumeur maligne du sein chez la femme	..	..	1 169	...	..	..	1 106	25.5
Malignant neoplasm of cervix uteri — Tumeur maligne du col de l'utérus	..	..	321	...	..	..	318	7.3
Malignant neoplasm of prostate — Tumeur maligne de la prostate	745	...	..	..	799	60.0	..	..
Malignant neoplasm of lymphoid, haematopoietic and related tissue — Tumeurs malignes primitives ou présumées primitives des tissus lymphoïde, hématopoïétique et apparentés	...	...	...	...	...	...	...	...
Disorders of the blood and blood-forming organs and certain disorders involving the immune mechanism — Maladies du sang et des organes hématopoïétiques et certains troubles du système immunitaire								
Total	29	♦0.7	32	0.6	34	0.8	34	0.7
Anaemias — Anémies	11	♦0.3	11	♦0.2	7	♦0.2	19	♦0.4
Endocrine, nutritional and metabolic diseases — Maladies endocriniennes, nutritionnelles et métaboliques								
Total	132	3.0	165	3.3	131	3.0	154	3.0
Diabetes mellitus — Diabète sucré	82	1.9	114	2.3	84	1.9	110	2.2
Malnutrition — Malnutrition	3	♦0.1	3	♦0.1	2	♦0.0	2	♦0.0
Mental and behavioural disorders — Troubles mentaux et du comportement	828	18.8	670	13.2	831	18.9	883	17.4
Diseases of the nervous system — Maladies du système nerveux	895	20.3	964	19.0	1 094	24.8	1 299	25.6
Diseases of the circulatory system — Maladies de l'appareil circulatoire								
Total	32 437	737.3	33 771	666.5	32 671	741.6	34 802	686.5
Acute rheumatic fever and chronic rheumatic heart diseases — Rhumatisme articularie aigu et cardiopathies rhumatismales chroniques	117	2.7	173	3.4	107	2.4	158	3.1
Hypertensive diseases — Maladies hypertensives	101	2.3	84	1.7	92	2.1	59	1.2
Ischaemic heart disease — Cardiopathie ischémique	23 586	536.1	24 032	474.3	24 096	547.0	24 881	490.8
Cerebrovascular disease — Maladie cérébrovasculaire	6 064	137.8	7 913	156.2	5 810	131.9	7 904	155.9

20. Death and death rates by cause and sex: 2012 - 2016
Décès et taux de mortalité par cause et sexe : 2012 - 2016 (continued - suite)

Belarus - Bélarus

Cause of death — Cause de décès	2013 (C)				2014 (C)			
	Male — Masculin		Female — Féminin		Male — Masculin		Female — Féminin	
	Number Nombre	Rate Taux	Number Nombre	Rate Taux	Number Nombre	Rate Taux	Number Nombre	Rate Taux
Diseases of arteries, arterioles and capillaries — Maladies des artères, artérioles et capillaires	...	...	...	...	...	...	...	...
Diseases of the respiratory system — Maladies de l'appareil respiratoire								
Total	1 707	38.8	431	8.5	1 508	34.2	357	7.0
Influenza — Grippe	3	♦0.1	-	-	-	-	4	♦0.1
Pneumonia — Pneumopathies	551	12.5	110	2.2	468	10.6	81	1.6
Chronic lower respiratory diseases — Maladies chroniques des voies respiratoires inférieures	978	22.2	265	5.2	868	19.7	222	4.4
Diseases of the digestive system — Maladies de l'appareil digestif								
Total	2 432	55.3	1 744	34.4	2 235	50.7	1 646	32.5
Gastric and duodenal ulcer — Ulcère de l'estomac et du duodénum...............	136	3.1	73	1.4	132	3.0	65	1.3
Diseases of the liver — Maladies du foie...............	1 431	32.5	906	17.9	1 302	29.6	815	16.1
Diseases of the musculoskeletal system and connective tissue — Maladies du système ostéo-articularie, des muscles et du tissu conjonctif	39	0.9	112	2.2	51	1.2	88	1.7
Diseases of the genitourinary system — Maladies de l'appareil génito-urinaire								
Total	395	9.0	329	6.5	340	7.7	324	6.4
Disorders of kidney and ureter — Affections du rein et de l'uretère	...	...	...	...	...	...	...	...
Hyperplasia of prostate — Hyperplasie de la prostate...............	...	...	...	...	...	...	...	...
Pregnancy, childbirth and the puerperium — Grossesse, accouchement et puerpéralité								
Total	..	..	-	-	..	..	1	♦0.8
Pregnancy with abortive outcome — Grossesse se terminant par un avortement	..	..	-	-	..	..	-	-
Other direct obstetric causes — Autres décès maternels directs...............	..	..	-	-	..	..	-	-
Indirect obstetric causes — Décès maternels indirects	..	..	-	-	..	..	-	-
Certain conditions originating in the perinatal period — Certaines affections dont l'origine se situe dans la période périnatale	107	176.1	76	132.8	107	174.6	72	125.7
Congenital malformations, deformations and chromosomal abnormalities — Malformations congénitales et anomalies chromosomiques	136	223.8	110	192.2	140	228.5	113	197.4
Symptoms, signs and abnormal clinical and laboratory findings, not elsewhere classified — Symptômes, signes et résultats anormaux d'examens cliniques et de laboratoire, non classés ailleurs	4 931	112.1	14 037	277.0	3 693	83.8	10 949	216.0
All other diseases — Toutes autres maladies...............	42	1.0	34	0.7	34	0.8	47	0.9
External causes — Causes externes								
Total	8 206	186.5	2 250	44.4	7 588	172.3	2 096	41.3
Accidents								
Total	...	...	...	...	...	...	...	...
Transport accidents — Accidents de transport...............	832	18.9	286	5.6	747	17.0	255	5.0
Falls — Chutes	616	14.0	224	4.4	531	12.1	173	3.4
Accidental drowning and submersion — Noyade et submersion accidentelles...............	493	11.2	83	1.6	535	12.1	94	1.9
Exposure to smoke, fire and flames — Exposition à la fumée, au feu et aux flammes...............	521	11.8	183	3.6	569	12.9	211	4.2
Accidental poisoning by and exposure to noxious substances — Intoxication accidentelle par des substances nocives et exposition à ces substances	1 584	36.0	421	8.3	1 388	31.5	367	7.2
Intentional self-harm — Lésions auto-infligées...............	1 569	35.7	334	6.6	1 466	33.3	276	5.4
Assault — Agresssions...............	290	6.6	106	2.1	238	5.4	118	2.3
All other external causes — Toutes autres causes externes	...	...	...	...	...	...	...	...

20. Death and death rates by cause and sex: 2012 - 2016
Décès et taux de mortalité par cause et sexe : 2012 - 2016 (continued - suite)

Belgium - Belgique

Cause of death — Cause de décès	2014 (C)				2015 (C)			
	Male — Masculin		Female — Féminin		Male — Masculin		Female — Féminin	
	Number Nombre	Rate Taux	Number Nombre	Rate Taux	Number Nombre	Rate Taux	Number Nombre	Rate Taux
TOTAL	51 579	934.0	53 176	931.4	53 631	965.8	56 910	992.8
Certain infectious and parasitic diseases — Certaines maladies infectieuses et parasitaires								
Total	1 176	21.3	1 334	23.4	1 006	18.1	1 319	23.0
Intestinal infectious diseases — Maladies infectieuses intestinales	124	2.2	216	3.8	162	2.9	298	5.2
Tuberculosis — Tuberculose	18	+0.3	5	+0.1	17	+0.3	14	+0.2
Tetanus — Tétanos	-	-	-	-	-	-	-	-
Diphtheria — Diphtérie	-	-	-	-	-	-	-	-
Whooping cough — Coqueluche	1	+0.0	-	-	1	+0.0	1	+0.0
Meningococcal infection — Infection à méningocoques	1	+0.0	1	+0.0	3	+0.1	3	+0.1
Septicaemia — Septicémie	623	11.3	684	12.0	413	7.4	471	8.2
Acute poliomyelitis — Poliomyélite aiguë	-	-	-	-	-	-	-	-
Measles — Rougeole	-	-	-	-	-	-	-	-
Viral hepatitis — Hépatite virale	32	0.6	39	0.7	35	0.6	35	0.6
Human immunodeficiency virus [HIV] disease — Maladies dues au virus de l'immunodéficience humaine (VIH)	22	+0.4	13	+0.2	20	+0.4	9	+0.2
Malaria — Paludisme	1	+0.0	2	+0.0	1	+0.0	-	-
Neoplasms — Tumeurs	15 805	286.2	12 719	222.8	15 864	285.7	12 743	222.3
Malignant neoplasms — Tumeurs malignes								
Total	15 048	272.5	11 993	210.1	15 112	272.2	12 043	210.1
Malignant neoplasm of lip, oral cavity and pharynx — Tumeur maligne de la lèvre, de la cavité buccale et du pharynx	455	8.2	144	2.5	424	7.6	162	2.8
Malignant neoplasm of oesophagus — Tumeur maligne de l'oesophage	563	10.2	209	3.7	554	10.0	201	3.5
Malignant neoplasm of stomach — Tumeur maligne de l'estomac	468	8.5	276	4.8	472	8.5	268	4.7
Malignant neoplasm of colon, rectosigmoid junction, rectum, anus and anal canal — Tumeur maligne du côlon, de la jonction recto-sigmoïdienne, du rectum, de l'anus et du canal anal	1 457	26.4	1 331	23.3	1 545	27.8	1 300	22.7
Malignant neoplasm of liver and intrahepatic bile ducts — Tumeur maligne du foie et des voies bilaires intrahépatiques	547	9.9	342	6.0	600	10.8	336	5.9
Malignant neoplasm of pancreas — Tumeur maligne du pancréas	788	14.3	859	15.0	815	14.7	895	15.6
Malignant neoplasm of trachea, bronchus and lung — Tumeur maligne de la trachée, des bronches et du poumon	4 603	83.4	1 924	33.7	4 338	78.1	1 936	33.8
Malignant neoplasm of female breast — Tumeur maligne du sein chez la femme	..	..	2 238	46.9	..	..	2 167	45.2
Malignant neoplasm of cervix uteri — Tumeur maligne du col de l'utérus	..	..	157	3.3	..	..	161	3.4
Malignant neoplasm of prostate — Tumeur maligne de la prostate	1 430	72.5	..	..	1 532	76.4	..	..
Malignant neoplasm of lymphoid, haematopoietic and related tissue — Tumeurs malignes primitives ou présumées primitives des tissus lymphoïde, hématopoïétique et apparentés	1 223	22.1	1 044	18.3	1 233	22.2	1 131	19.7
Disorders of the blood and blood-forming organs and certain disorders involving the immune mechanism — Maladies du sang et des organes hématopoïétiques et certains troubles du système immunitaire								
Total	161	2.9	210	3.7	162	2.9	211	3.7
Anaemias — Anémies	76	1.4	133	2.3	84	1.5	140	2.4
Endocrine, nutritional and metabolic diseases — Maladies endocriniennes, nutritionnelles et métaboliques								
Total	1 126	20.4	1 623	28.4	1 107	19.9	1 666	29.1
Diabetes mellitus — Diabète sucré	671	12.2	864	15.1	670	12.1	836	14.6
Malnutrition — Malnutrition	75	1.4	157	2.8	76	1.4	194	3.4
Mental and behavioural disorders — Troubles mentaux et du comportement	1 711	31.0	2 900	50.8	2 004	36.1	3 355	58.5
Diseases of the nervous system — Maladies du système nerveux	2 082	37.7	3 005	52.6	2 398	43.2	3 193	55.7
Diseases of the circulatory system — Maladies de l'appareil circulatoire								
Total	13 673	247.6	16 291	285.4	14 158	255.0	17 184	299.8
Acute rheumatic fever and chronic rheumatic heart diseases — Rhumatisme articularie aigu et cardiopathies rhumatismales chroniques	75	1.4	205	3.6	96	1.7	184	3.2
Hypertensive diseases — Maladies hypertensives	312	5.6	615	10.8	326	5.9	708	12.4
Ischaemic heart disease — Cardiopathie ischémique	4 497	81.4	3 212	56.3	4 528	81.5	3 317	57.9
Cerebrovascular disease — Maladie cérébrovasculaire	2 795	50.6	4 006	70.2	2 732	49.2	4 140	72.2

20. Death and death rates by cause and sex: 2012 - 2016
Décès et taux de mortalité par cause et sexe : 2012 - 2016 (continued - suite)

Belgium - Belgique

Cause of death — Cause de décès	2014 (C)				2015 (C)			
	Male — Masculin		Female — Féminin		Male — Masculin		Female — Féminin	
	Number Nombre	Rate Taux	Number Nombre	Rate Taux	Number Nombre	Rate Taux	Number Nombre	Rate Taux
Diseases of arteries, arterioles and capillaries — Maladies des artères, artérioles et capillaires	711	12.9	550	9.6	776	14.0	585	10.2
Diseases of the respiratory system — Maladies de l'appareil respiratoire								
Total	5 400	97.8	4 745	83.1	6 133	110.4	5 715	99.7
Influenza — Grippe	20	♦0.4	29	♦0.5	89	1.6	219	3.8
Pneumonia — Pneumopathies	1 610	29.2	1 759	30.8	1 955	35.2	2 165	37.8
Chronic lower respiratory diseases — Maladies chroniques des voies respiratoires inférieures	2 556	46.3	1 708	29.9	2 728	49.1	1 949	34.0
Diseases of the digestive system — Maladies de l'appareil digestif								
Total	2 203	39.9	2 143	37.5	2 377	42.8	2 387	41.6
Gastric and duodenal ulcer — Ulcère de l'estomac et du duodénum	90	1.6	95	1.7	90	1.6	101	1.8
Diseases of the liver — Maladies du foie	941	17.0	530	9.3	993	17.9	580	10.1
Diseases of the musculoskeletal system and connective tissue — Maladies du système ostéo-articularie, des muscles et du tissu conjonctif	190	3.4	351	6.1	225	4.1	402	7.0
Diseases of the genitourinary system — Maladies de l'appareil génito-urinaire								
Total	1 101	19.9	1 435	25.1	1 174	21.1	1 679	29.3
Disorders of kidney and ureter — Affections du rein et de l'uretère	857	15.5	1 057	18.5	897	16.2	1 231	21.5
Hyperplasia of prostate — Hyperplasie de la prostate	11	♦0.6	..	..	20	♦1.0	..	..
Pregnancy, childbirth and the puerperium — Grossesse, accouchement et puerpéralité								
Total	..	..	6	♦4.8	..	..	4	♦3.3
Pregnancy with abortive outcome — Grossesse se terminant par un avortement	..	..	1	♦0.8	..	..	-	-
Other direct obstetric causes — Autres décès maternels directs	..	..	5	♦4.0	..	..	4	♦3.3
Indirect obstetric causes — Décès maternels indirects	..	..	-	-	..	..	-	-
Certain conditions originating in the perinatal period — Certaines affections dont l'origine se situe dans la période périnatale	120	187.0	100	164.4	111	177.4	87	145.7
Congenital malformations, deformations and chromosomal abnormalities — Malformations congénitales et anomalies chromosomiques	134	208.8	111	182.4	107	171.0	107	179.2
Symptoms, signs and abnormal clinical and laboratory findings, not elsewhere classified — Symptômes, signes et résultats anormaux d'examens cliniques et de laboratoire, non classés ailleurs	2 708	49.0	3 268	57.2	2 793	50.3	3 684	64.3
All other diseases — Toutes autres maladies	75	1.4	215	3.8	87	1.6	210	3.7
External causes — Causes externes								
Total	3 914	70.9	2 720	47.6	3 925	70.7	2 964	51.7
Accidents								
Total	2 170	39.3	1 905	33.4	2 258	40.7	2 178	38.0
Transport accidents — Accidents de transport	536	9.7	163	2.9	502	9.0	191	3.3
Falls — Chutes	711	12.9	798	14.0	726	13.1	892	15.6
Accidental drowning and submersion — Noyade et submersion accidentelles	46	0.8	14	♦0.2	74	1.3	18	♦0.3
Exposure to smoke, fire and flames — Exposition à la fumée, au feu et aux flammes	46	0.8	25	♦0.4	38	0.7	36	0.6
Accidental poisoning by and exposure to noxious substances — Intoxication accidentelle par des substances nocives et exposition à ces substances	146	2.6	80	1.4	155	2.8	83	1.4
Intentional self-harm — Lésions auto-infligées	1 338	24.2	560	9.8	1 314	23.7	552	9.6
Assault — Agresssions	70	1.3	44	0.8	65	1.2	54	0.9
All other external causes — Toutes autres causes externes	336	6.1	211	3.7	288	5.2	180	3.1

Cause of death — Cause de décès	Bosnia and Herzegovina - Bosnie-Herzégovine				Bulgaria - Bulgarie			
	2014 (C)				2013 (C)			
	Male — Masculin		Female — Féminin		Male — Masculin		Female — Féminin	
	Number Nombre	Rate Taux	Number Nombre	Rate Taux	Number Nombre	Rate Taux	Number Nombre	Rate Taux
TOTAL	18 360	...	17 620	...	54 827	1 551.3	49 518	1 327.7
Certain infectious and parasitic diseases — Certaines maladies infectieuses et parasitaires								
Total	168	...	126	...	320	9.1	198	5.3
Intestinal infectious diseases — Maladies infectieuses intestinales	5	...	8	...	11	♦0.3	14	♦0.4
Tuberculosis — Tuberculose	74	...	35	...	117	3.3	32	0.9
Tetanus — Tétanos	-	...	-	...	1	♦0.0	-	-
Diphtheria — Diphtérie	-	...	-	...	-	-	-	-
Whooping cough — Coqueluche	-	...	-	...	-	-	-	-
Meningococcal infection — Infection à méningocoques	-	...	2	...	2	♦0.1	2	♦0.1
Septicaemia — Septicémie	48	...	58	...	138	3.9	114	3.1
Acute poliomyelitis — Poliomyélite aiguë	-	...	-	...	-	-	-	-
Measles — Rougeole	-	...	-	...	-	-	-	-
Viral hepatitis — Hépatite virale	23	...	15	...	9	♦0.3	7	♦0.2
Human immunodeficiency virus [HIV] disease — Maladies dues au virus de l'immunodéficience humaine (VIH)	1	...	1	...	5	♦0.1	3	♦0.1
Malaria — Paludisme	-	...	-	...	1	♦0.0	-	-
Neoplasms — Tumeurs	4 569	...	3 252	...	10 934	309.4	7 340	196.8
Malignant neoplasms — Tumeurs malignes								
Total	4 531	...	3 231	...	10 842	306.8	7 273	195.0
Malignant neoplasm of lip, oral cavity and pharynx — Tumeur maligne de la lèvre, de la cavité buccale et du pharynx	106	...	26	...	375	10.6	87	2.3
Malignant neoplasm of oesophagus — Tumeur maligne de l'oesophage	77	...	16	...	159	4.5	40	1.1
Malignant neoplasm of stomach — Tumeur maligne de l'estomac	315	...	196	...	780	22.1	478	12.8
Malignant neoplasm of colon, rectosigmoid junction, rectum, anus and anal canal — Tumeur maligne du côlon, de la jonction recto-sigmoïdienne, du rectum, de l'anus et du canal anal	527	...	382	...	1 549	43.8	1 041	27.9
Malignant neoplasm of liver and intrahepatic bile ducts — Tumeur maligne du foie et des voies bilaires intrahépatiques	212	...	181	...	427	12.1	234	6.3
Malignant neoplasm of pancreas — Tumeur maligne du pancréas	234	...	203	...	654	18.5	437	11.7
Malignant neoplasm of trachea, bronchus and lung — Tumeur maligne de la trachée, des bronches et du poumon	1 468	...	390	...	2 959	83.7	665	17.8
Malignant neoplasm of female breast — Tumeur maligne du sein chez la femme	..		520	...	..		1 274	...
Malignant neoplasm of cervix uteri — Tumeur maligne du col de l'utérus	..		107	...			352	...
Malignant neoplasm of prostate — Tumeur maligne de la prostate	383	...	..		994	...	..	
Malignant neoplasm of lymphoid, haematopoietic and related tissue — Tumeurs malignes primitives ou présumées primitives des tissus lymphoïde, hématopoïétique et apparentés	189	...	161	...	528	14.9	432	11.6
Disorders of the blood and blood-forming organs and certain disorders involving the immune mechanism — Maladies du sang et des organes hématopoïétiques et certains troubles du système immunitaire								
Total	14	...	26	...	74	2.1	69	1.9
Anaemias — Anémies	8	...	20	...	46	1.3	43	1.2
Endocrine, nutritional and metabolic diseases — Maladies endocriniennes, nutritionnelles et métaboliques								
Total	925	...	1 342	...	632	17.9	814	21.8
Diabetes mellitus — Diabète sucré	907	...	1 324	...	609	17.2	784	21.0
Malnutrition — Malnutrition	1	...	-	...	1	♦0.0	1	♦0.0
Mental and behavioural disorders — Troubles mentaux et du comportement	130	...	65	...	41	1.2	41	1.1
Diseases of the nervous system — Maladies du système nerveux	198	...	185	...	491	13.9	468	12.5
Diseases of the circulatory system — Maladies de l'appareil circulatoire								
Total	8 320	...	9 586	...	33 094	936.4	34 816	933.5
Acute rheumatic fever and chronic rheumatic heart diseases — Rhumatisme articularie aigu et cardiopathies rhumatismales chroniques	11	...	5	...	30	♦0.8	40	1.1
Hypertensive diseases — Maladies hypertensives	529	...	801	...	3 396	96.1	4 007	107.4
Ischaemic heart disease — Cardiopathie ischémique	2 082	...	1 800	...	6 944	196.5	5 734	153.7
Cerebrovascular disease — Maladie cérébrovasculaire	1 893	...	2 293	...	9 316	263.6	11 147	298.9

Cause of death — Cause de décès	Bosnia and Herzegovina - Bosnie-Herzégovine				Bulgaria - Bulgarie			
	2014 (C)				2013 (C)			
	Male — Masculin		Female — Féminin		Male — Masculin		Female — Féminin	
	Number Nombre	Rate Taux	Number Nombre	Rate Taux	Number Nombre	Rate Taux	Number Nombre	Rate Taux
Diseases of arteries, arterioles and capillaries — Maladies des artères, artérioles et capillaires	317	...	379	...	1 290	36.5	1 556	41.7
Diseases of the respiratory system — Maladies de l'appareil respiratoire								
Total	822	...	549	.:.	2 158	61.1	1 354	36.3
Influenza — Grippe	1	...	2	...	5	٭0.1	5	٭0.1
Pneumonia — Pneumopathies	77	...	82	...	727	20.6	559	15.0
Chronic lower respiratory diseases — Maladies chroniques des voies respiratoires inférieures	532	...	291	...	910	25.7	449	12.0
Diseases of the digestive system — Maladies de l'appareil digestif								
Total	544	...	403	...	2 367	67.0	1 262	33.8
Gastric and duodenal ulcer — Ulcère de l'estomac et du duodénum	36	...	42	...	176	5.0	104	2.8
Diseases of the liver — Maladies du foie	305	...	101	...	1 364	38.6	414	11.1
Diseases of the musculoskeletal system and connective tissue — Maladies du système ostéo-articularie, des muscles et du tissu conjonctif	16	...	44	...	18	٭0.5	22	٭0.6
Diseases of the genitourinary system — Maladies de l'appareil génito-urinaire								
Total	259	...	273	...	734	20.8	555	14.9
Disorders of kidney and ureter — Affections du rein et de l'uretère	243	...	269	...	719	20.3	551	14.8
Hyperplasia of prostate — Hyperplasie de la prostate	7	...	..		7	...	..	..
Pregnancy, childbirth and the puerperium — Grossesse, accouchement et puerpéralité								
Total	..	..	..		-		8	٭12.0
Pregnancy with abortive outcome — Grossesse se terminant par un avortement	..	..	..		-		-	-
Other direct obstetric causes — Autres décès maternels directs	..	..	..		-		8	٭12.0
Indirect obstetric causes — Décès maternels indirects	..	..	..		-		-	-
Certain conditions originating in the perinatal period — Certaines affections dont l'origine se situe dans la période périnatale	42	277.6	44	311.6	136	399.5	102	313.5
Congenital malformations, deformations and chromosomal abnormalities — Malformations congénitales et anomalies chromosomiques	20	٭132.2	28	٭198.3	102	299.6	54	166.0
Symptoms, signs and abnormal clinical and laboratory findings, not elsewhere classified — Symptômes, signes et résultats anormaux d'examens cliniques et de laboratoire, non classés ailleurs	1 512	...	1 432	...	1 556	44.0	1 775	47.6
All other diseases — Toutes autres maladies	16	...	21	...	17	٭0.5	28	٭0.8
External causes — Causes externes								
Total	805	...	244	...	2 153	60.9	612	16.4
Accidents								
Total	448	...	138	...	1 328	37.6	390	10.5
Transport accidents — Accidents de transport	196	...	48	...	458	13.0	125	3.4
Falls — Chutes	26	...	6	...	269	7.6	100	2.7
Accidental drowning and submersion — Noyade et submersion accidentelles	45	...	17	...	97	2.7	18	٭0.5
Exposure to smoke, fire and flames — Exposition à la fumée, au feu et aux flammes	16	...	8	...	54	1.5	37	1.0
Accidental poisoning by and exposure to noxious substances — Intoxication accidentelle par des substances nocives et exposition à ces substances	7	...	5	...	72	2.0	27	٭0.7
Intentional self-harm — Lésions auto-infligées	243	...	70	...	572	16.2	148	4.0
Assault — Agresssions	34	...	12	...	59	1.7	31	0.8
All other external causes — Toutes autres causes externes	80	...	24	...	194	5.5	43	1.2

20. Death and death rates by cause and sex: 2012 - 2016
Décès et taux de mortalité par cause et sexe : 2012 - 2016 (continued - suite)

Cause of death — Cause de décès	Bulgaria - Bulgarie 2014 (C)				Croatia - Croatie 2015 (C)			
	Male — Masculin		Female — Féminin		Male — Masculin		Female — Féminin	
	Number Nombre	Rate Taux	Number Nombre	Rate Taux	Number Nombre	Rate Taux	Number Nombre	Rate Taux
TOTAL	56 630	1 611.8	52 322	1 410.1	26 414	1 295.3	27 791	1 271.3
Certain infectious and parasitic diseases — Certaines maladies infectieuses et parasitaires								
Total	285	8.1	173	4.7	207	10.2	178	8.1
Intestinal infectious diseases — Maladies infectieuses intestinales	13	٭0.4	16	٭0.4	14	٭0.7	27	٭1.2
Tuberculosis — Tuberculose	95	2.7	28	٭0.8	25	٭1.2	21	٭1.0
Tetanus — Tétanos	-	-	-	-	-	-	-	-
Diphtheria — Diphtérie	-	-	-	-	-	-	-	-
Whooping cough — Coqueluche	-	-	1	٭0.0	-	-	-	-
Meningococcal infection — Infection à méningocoques	4	٭0.1	2	٭0.1	1	٭0.0	2	٭0.1
Septicaemia — Septicémie	101	2.9	79	2.1	101	5.0	98	4.5
Acute poliomyelitis — Poliomyélite aiguë	-	-	-	-	-	-	-	-
Measles — Rougeole	-	-	-	-	-	-	-	-
Viral hepatitis — Hépatite virale	21	٭0.6	14	٭0.4	45	2.2	15	٭0.7
Human immunodeficiency virus [HIV] disease — Maladies dues au virus de l'immunodéficience humaine (VIH)	12	٭0.3	4	٭0.1	9	٭0.4	1	٭0.0
Malaria — Paludisme	-	-	1	٭0.0	-	-	-	-
Neoplasms — Tumeurs	10 552	300.3	7 561	203.8	8 175	400.9	6 115	279.7
Malignant neoplasms — Tumeurs malignes								
Total	10 476	298.2	7 494	202.0	8 030	393.8	5 982	273.6
Malignant neoplasm of lip, oral cavity and pharynx — Tumeur maligne de la lèvre, de la cavité buccale et du pharynx	327	9.3	92	2.5	274	13.4	68	3.1
Malignant neoplasm of oesophagus — Tumeur maligne de l'oesophage	146	4.2	28	٭0.8	140	6.9	40	1.8
Malignant neoplasm of stomach — Tumeur maligne de l'estomac	718	20.4	441	11.9	478	23.4	323	14.8
Malignant neoplasm of colon, rectosigmoid junction, rectum, anus and anal canal — Tumeur maligne du côlon, de la jonction recto-sigmoïdienne, du rectum, de l'anus et du canal anal	1 508	42.9	1 052	28.4	1 202	58.9	854	39.1
Malignant neoplasm of liver and intrahepatic bile ducts — Tumeur maligne du foie et des voies bilaires intrahépatiques	424	12.1	255	6.9	331	16.2	163	7.5
Malignant neoplasm of pancreas — Tumeur maligne du pancréas	624	17.8	520	14.0	363	17.8	399	18.3
Malignant neoplasm of trachea, bronchus and lung — Tumeur maligne de la trachée, des bronches et du poumon	2 746	78.2	739	19.9	2 101	103.0	720	32.9
Malignant neoplasm of female breast — Tumeur maligne du sein chez la femme	..	..	1 343	41.6	..	..	1 038	55.1
Malignant neoplasm of cervix uteri — Tumeur maligne du col de l'utérus	..	..	349	10.8	..	..	111	5.9
Malignant neoplasm of prostate — Tumeur maligne de la prostate	949	72.5	..	..	824	109.2	..	..
Malignant neoplasm of lymphoid, haematopoietic and related tissue — Tumeurs malignes primitives ou présumées primitives des tissus lymphoïde, hématopoïétique et apparentés	510	14.5	380	10.2	531	26.0	470	21.5
Disorders of the blood and blood-forming organs and certain disorders involving the immune mechanism — Maladies du sang et des organes hématopoïétiques et certains troubles du système immunitaire								
Total	87	2.5	69	1.9	12	٭0.6	13	٭0.6
Anaemias — Anémies	61	1.7	49	1.3	6	٭0.3	6	٭0.3
Endocrine, nutritional and metabolic diseases — Maladies endocriniennes, nutritionnelles et métaboliques								
Total	659	18.8	883	23.8	708	34.7	991	45.3
Diabetes mellitus — Diabète sucré	644	18.3	853	23.0	692	33.9	965	44.1
Malnutrition — Malnutrition	2	٭0.1	-	-	-	-	-	-
Mental and behavioural disorders — Troubles mentaux et du comportement	47	1.3	29	٭0.8	530	26.0	812	37.1
Diseases of the nervous system — Maladies du système nerveux	562	16.0	494	13.3	543	26.6	586	26.8
Diseases of the circulatory system — Maladies de l'appareil circulatoire								
Total	34 727	988.4	37 032	998.0	11 007	539.8	14 687	671.8
Acute rheumatic fever and chronic rheumatic heart diseases — Rhumatisme articularie aigu et cardiopathies rhumatismales chroniques	35	1.0	49	1.3	62	3.0	105	4.8
Hypertensive diseases — Maladies hypertensives	3 164	90.1	3 840	103.5	645	31.6	1 345	61.5
Ischaemic heart disease — Cardiopathie ischémique	6 831	194.4	5 821	156.9	5 190	254.5	6 319	289.1
Cerebrovascular disease — Maladie cérébrovasculaire	10 355	294.7	12 157	327.6	3 134	153.7	4 299	196.7

Cause of death — Cause de décès	Bulgaria - Bulgarie 2014 (C)				Croatia - Croatie 2015 (C)			
	Male — Masculin		Female — Féminin		Male — Masculin		Female — Féminin	
	Number Nombre	Rate Taux	Number Nombre	Rate Taux	Number Nombre	Rate Taux	Number Nombre	Rate Taux
Diseases of arteries, arterioles and capillaries — Maladies des artères, artérioles et capillaires	1 154	32.8	1 454	39.2	501	24.6	638	29.2
Diseases of the respiratory system — Maladies de l'appareil respiratoire								
Total	2 420	68.9	1 515	40.8	1 520	74.5	1 143	52.3
Influenza — Grippe....................	14	♦0.4	7	♦0.2	20	♦1.0	22	♦1.0
Pneumonia — Pneumopathies	855	24.3	621	16.7	288	14.1	270	12.4
Chronic lower respiratory diseases — Maladies chroniques des voies respiratoires inférieures	909	25.9	442	11.9	1 142	56.0	799	36.5
Diseases of the digestive system — Maladies de l'appareil digestif								
Total	2 567	73.1	1 286	34.7	1 279	62.7	886	40.5
Gastric and duodenal ulcer — Ulcère de l'estomac et du duodénum....................	194	5.5	96	2.6	84	4.1	105	4.8
Diseases of the liver — Maladies du foie....................	1 476	42.0	430	11.6	747	36.6	252	11.5
Diseases of the musculoskeletal system and connective tissue — Maladies du système ostéo-articularie, des muscles et du tissu conjonctif	23	♦0.7	32	0.9	22	♦1.1	109	5.0
Diseases of the genitourinary system — Maladies de l'appareil génito-urinaire								
Total	741	21.1	609	16.4	458	22.5	614	28.1
Disorders of kidney and ureter — Affections du rein et de l'uretère	714	20.3	599	16.1	286	14.0	372	17.0
Hyperplasia of prostate — Hyperplasie de la prostate....................	17	♦1.3	..	..	39	5.2	..	..
Pregnancy, childbirth and the puerperium — Grossesse, accouchement et puerpéralité								
Total	..	..	5	♦7.4	..	..	1	♦2.7
Pregnancy with abortive outcome — Grossesse se terminant par un avortement	..	..	-	-	..	..	..	..
Other direct obstetric causes — Autres décès maternels directs	..	..	5	♦7.4	..	..	1	♦2.7
Indirect obstetric causes — Décès maternels indirects	..	..	-	-	..	..	..	..
Certain conditions originating in the perinatal period — Certaines affections dont l'origine se situe dans la période périnatale	149	429.0	113	344.0	53	273.5	41	226.2
Congenital malformations, deformations and chromosomal abnormalities — Malformations congénitales et anomalies chromosomiques	64	184.3	60	182.6	56	289.0	58	320.0
Symptoms, signs and abnormal clinical and laboratory findings, not elsewhere classified — Symptômes, signes et résultats anormaux d'examens cliniques et de laboratoire, non classés ailleurs	1 550	44.1	1 661	44.8	173	8.5	329	15.0
All other diseases — Toutes autres maladies....................	25	♦0.7	27	♦0.7	4	♦0.2	7	♦0.3
External causes — Causes externes								
Total	2 172	61.8	773	20.8	1 667	81.7	1 221	55.9
Accidents								
Total	1 352	38.5	489	13.2	1 078	52.9	953	43.6
Transport accidents — Accidents de transport	483	13.7	156	4.2	338	16.6	94	4.3
Falls — Chutes	277	7.9	141	3.8	438	21.5	722	33.0
Accidental drowning and submersion — Noyade et submersion accidentelles	117	3.3	39	1.1	72	3.5	24	♦1.1
Exposure to smoke, fire and flames — Exposition à la fumée, au feu et aux flammes	50	1.4	27	♦0.7	26	♦1.3	14	♦0.6
Accidental poisoning by and exposure to noxious substances — Intoxication accidentelle par des substances nocives et exposition à ces substances	65	1.9	20	♦0.5	74	3.6	20	♦0.9
Intentional self-harm — Lésions auto-infligées....................	551	15.7	171	4.6	542	26.6	197	9.0
Assault — Agresssions....................	64	1.8	32	0.9	19	♦0.9	18	♦0.8
All other external causes — Toutes autres causes externes	205	5.8	81	2.2	28	♦1.4	53	2.4

Cause of death — Cause de décès	Croatia - Croatie 2016 (C)				Czechia - Tchéquie 2015 (C)			
	Male — Masculin		Female — Féminin		Male — Masculin		Female — Féminin	
	Number Nombre	Rate Taux	Number Nombre	Rate Taux	Number Nombre	Rate Taux	Number Nombre	Rate Taux
TOTAL	25 344	1 252.9	26 198	1 208.5	55 934	1 079.8	55 239	1 030.1
Certain infectious and parasitic diseases — Certaines maladies infectieuses et parasitaires								
Total	241	11.9	216	10.0	928	17.9	1 050	19.6
Intestinal infectious diseases — Maladies infectieuses intestinales	23	✦1.1	40	1.8	107	2.1	178	3.3
Tuberculosis — Tuberculose	39	1.9	19	✦0.9	32	0.6	14	✦0.3
Tetanus — Tétanos	-	-	1	✦0.0	-	-	-	-
Diphtheria — Diphtérie	-	-	-	-	-	-	-	-
Whooping cough — Coqueluche	1	✦0.0	-	-	-	-	-	-
Meningococcal infection — Infection à méningocoques	2	✦0.1	1	✦0.0	3	✦0.1	1	✦0.0
Septicaemia — Septicémie	103	5.1	136	6.3	643	12.4	752	14.0
Acute poliomyelitis — Poliomyélite aiguë	-	-	-	-	-	-	-	-
Measles — Rougeole	-	-	-	-	-	-	-	-
Viral hepatitis — Hépatite virale	61	3.0	14	✦0.6	20	✦0.4	13	✦0.2
Human immunodeficiency virus [HIV] disease — Maladies dues au virus de l'immunodéficience humaine (VIH)	6	✦0.3	-	-	9	✦0.2	1	✦0.0
Malaria — Paludisme	-	-	-	-	-	-	-	-
Neoplasms — Tumeurs	8 236	407.2	6 124	282.5	15 105	291.6	12 302	229.4
Malignant neoplasms — Tumeurs malignes								
Total	8 099	400.4	5 966	275.2	14 826	286.2	12 026	224.3
Malignant neoplasm of lip, oral cavity and pharynx — Tumeur maligne de la lèvre, de la cavité buccale et du pharynx	272	13.4	64	3.0	553	10.7	190	3.5
Malignant neoplasm of oesophagus — Tumeur maligne de l'oesophage	163	8.1	34	1.6	443	8.6	83	1.5
Malignant neoplasm of stomach — Tumeur maligne de l'estomac	449	22.2	308	14.2	590	11.4	450	8.4
Malignant neoplasm of colon, rectosigmoid junction, rectum, anus and anal canal — Tumeur maligne du côlon, de la jonction recto-sigmoïdienne, du rectum, de l'anus et du canal anal	1 273	62.9	896	41.3	2 091	40.4	1 491	27.8
Malignant neoplasm of liver and intrahepatic bile ducts — Tumeur maligne du foie et des voies bilaires intrahépatiques	376	18.6	159	7.3	514	9.9	304	5.7
Malignant neoplasm of pancreas — Tumeur maligne du pancréas	377	18.6	380	17.5	1 038	20.0	982	18.3
Malignant neoplasm of trachea, bronchus and lung — Tumeur maligne de la trachée, des bronches et du poumon	2 122	104.9	744	34.3	3 568	68.9	1 693	31.6
Malignant neoplasm of female breast — Tumeur maligne du sein chez la femme	..	..	990	52.9	..	..	1 609	35.1
Malignant neoplasm of cervix uteri — Tumeur maligne du col de l'utérus	..	..	115	6.1	..	..	354	7.7
Malignant neoplasm of prostate — Tumeur maligne de la prostate	769	101.4	..	..	1 327	73.7	..	..
Malignant neoplasm of lymphoid, haematopoietic and related tissue — Tumeurs malignes primitives ou présumées primitives des tissus lymphoïde, hématopoïétique et apparentés	483	23.9	445	20.5	943	18.2	881	16.4
Disorders of the blood and blood-forming organs and certain disorders involving the immune mechanism — Maladies du sang et des organes hématopoïétiques et certains troubles du système immunitaire								
Total	18	✦0.9	27	✦1.2	103	2.0	134	2.5
Anaemias — Anémies	4	✦0.2	13	✦0.6	33	0.6	63	1.2
Endocrine, nutritional and metabolic diseases — Maladies endocriniennes, nutritionnelles et métaboliques								
Total	793	39.2	1 153	53.2	1 977	38.2	2 514	46.9
Diabetes mellitus — Diabète sucré	770	38.1	1 119	51.6	1 689	32.6	2 039	38.0
Malnutrition — Malnutrition	-	-	-	-	89	1.7	133	2.5
Mental and behavioural disorders — Troubles mentaux et du comportement	436	21.6	653	30.1	602	11.6	889	16.6
Diseases of the nervous system — Maladies du système nerveux	512	25.3	599	27.6	1 341	25.9	1 678	31.3
Diseases of the circulatory system — Maladies de l'appareil circulatoire								
Total	10 054	497.0	13 136	605.9	23 425	452.2	27 544	513.6
Acute rheumatic fever and chronic rheumatic heart diseases — Rhumatisme articularie aigu et cardiopathies rhumatismales chroniques	50	2.5	89	4.1	113	2.2	174	3.2
Hypertensive diseases — Maladies hypertensives	515	25.5	982	45.3	1 172	22.6	1 745	32.5
Ischaemic heart disease — Cardiopathie ischémique	4 835	239.0	5 561	256.5	12 777	246.6	13 882	258.9
Cerebrovascular disease — Maladie cérébrovasculaire	2 724	134.7	3 870	178.5	3 929	75.8	5 657	105.5

20. Death and death rates by cause and sex: 2012 - 2016
Décès et taux de mortalité par cause et sexe : 2012 - 2016 (continued - suite)

Cause of death — Cause de décès	Croatia - Croatie				Czechia - Tchéquie			
	2016 (C)				2015 (C)			
	Male — Masculin		Female — Féminin		Male — Masculin		Female — Féminin	
	Number Nombre	Rate Taux	Number Nombre	Rate Taux	Number Nombre	Rate Taux	Number Nombre	Rate Taux
Diseases of arteries, arterioles and capillaries — Maladies des artères, artérioles et capillaires	497	24.6	666	30.7	1 126	21.7	1 324	24.7
Diseases of the respiratory system — Maladies de l'appareil respiratoire								
Total	1 392	68.8	1 048	48.3	4 115	79.4	3 363	62.7
Influenza — Grippe...............	12	♦0.6	7	♦0.3	46	0.9	79	1.5
Pneumonia — Pneumopathies	309	15.3	269	12.4	1 356	26.2	1 308	24.4
Chronic lower respiratory diseases — Maladies chroniques des voies respiratoires inférieures	1 008	49.8	727	33.5	2 186	42.2	1 547	28.8
Diseases of the digestive system — Maladies de l'appareil digestif								
Total	1 228	60.7	845	39.0	2 626	50.7	2 033	37.9
Gastric and duodenal ulcer — Ulcère de l'estomac et du duodénum...............	97	4.8	83	3.8	265	5.1	170	3.2
Diseases of the liver — Maladies du foie...............	723	35.7	246	11.3	1 445	27.9	713	13.3
Diseases of the musculoskeletal system and connective tissue — Maladies du système ostéo-articularie, des muscles et du tissu conjonctif	17	♦0.8	120	5.5	93	1.8	148	2.8
Diseases of the genitourinary system — Maladies de l'appareil génito-urinaire								
Total	507	25.1	766	35.3	623	12.0	789	14.7
Disorders of kidney and ureter — Affections du rein et de l'uretère	351	17.4	510	23.5	450	8.7	525	9.8
Hyperplasia of prostate — Hyperplasie de la prostate...............	42	5.5	..	..	27	♦1.5	..	..
Pregnancy, childbirth and the puerperium — Grossesse, accouchement et puerpéralité								
Total	..	..	1	♦2.7	..	..	2	♦1.8
Pregnancy with abortive outcome — Grossesse se terminant par un avortement	..	..	-	-	..	..	-	-
Other direct obstetric causes — Autres décès maternels directs	..	..	1	♦2.7	..	..	2	♦1.8
Indirect obstetric causes — Décès maternels indirects	..	..	-	-	..	..	-	-
Certain conditions originating in the perinatal period — Certaines affections dont l'origine se situe dans la période périnatale	40	209.7	35	189.5	94	165.4	57	105.7
Congenital malformations, deformations and chromosomal abnormalities — Malformations congénitales et anomalies chromosomiques	55	288.4	48	260.0	78	137.3	78	144.6
Symptoms, signs and abnormal clinical and laboratory findings, not elsewhere classified — Symptômes, signes et résultats anormaux d'examens cliniques et de laboratoire, non classés ailleurs	150	7.4	250	11.5	852	16.4	633	11.8
All other diseases — Toutes autres maladies	3	♦0.1	5	♦0.2	69	1.3	116	2.2
External causes — Causes externes								
Total	1 662	82.2	1 172	54.1	3 903	75.3	1 909	35.6
Accidents								
Total	1 066	52.7	900	41.5	2 478	47.8	1 440	26.9
Transport accidents — Accidents de transport	314	15.5	76	3.5	635	12.3	176	3.3
Falls — Chutes	439	21.7	657	30.3	383	7.4	214	4.0
Accidental drowning and submersion — Noyade et submersion accidentelles...............	68	3.4	25	♦1.2	137	2.6	29	♦0.5
Exposure to smoke, fire and flames — Exposition à la fumée, au feu et aux flammes...............	17	♦0.8	7	♦0.3	34	0.7	20	♦0.4
Accidental poisoning by and exposure to noxious substances — Intoxication accidentelle par des substances nocives et exposition à ces substances	61	3.0	25	♦1.2	291	5.6	135	2.5
Intentional self-harm — Lésions auto-infligées...............	515	25.5	168	7.7	1 130	21.8	254	4.7
Assault — Agressions...............	30	♦1.5	21	♦1.0	55	1.1	34	0.6
All other external causes — Toutes autres causes externes	51	2.5	83	3.8	240	4.6	181	3.4

20. Death and death rates by cause and sex: 2012 - 2016
Décès et taux de mortalité par cause et sexe : 2012 - 2016 (continued - suite)

Cause of death — Cause de décès	Czechia - Tchéquie 2016 (C) Male — Masculin Number Nombre	Rate Taux	Female — Féminin Number Nombre	Rate Taux	Denmark - Danemark 2014 (C) Male — Masculin Number Nombre	Rate Taux	Female — Féminin Number Nombre	Rate Taux
TOTAL	54 880	1 058.2	52 870	985.0	25 458	909.2	25 535	899.2
Certain infectious and parasitic diseases — Certaines maladies infectieuses et parasitaires								
Total	980	18.9	1 054	19.6	381	13.6	501	17.6
Intestinal infectious diseases — Maladies infectieuses intestinales	105	2.0	158	2.9	72	2.6	131	4.6
Tuberculosis — Tuberculose	31	0.6	9	◆0.2	9	◆0.3	3	◆0.1
Tetanus — Tétanos	-	-	-	-	-	-	-	-
Diphtheria — Diphtérie	-	-	-	-	-	-	-	-
Whooping cough — Coqueluche	-	-	1	◆0.0	-	-	-	-
Meningococcal infection — Infection à méningocoques	5	◆0.1	5	◆0.1	1	◆0.0	2	◆0.1
Septicaemia — Septicémie	716	13.8	738	13.7	148	5.3	183	6.4
Acute poliomyelitis — Poliomyélite aiguë	1	◆0.0	1	◆0.0	2	◆0.1	1	◆0.0
Measles — Rougeole	-	-	-	-	-	-	-	-
Viral hepatitis — Hépatite virale	17	◆0.3	13	◆0.2	17	◆0.6	11	◆0.4
Human immunodeficiency virus [HIV] disease — Maladies dues au virus de l'immunodéficience humaine (VIH)	11	◆0.2	6	◆0.1	11	◆0.4	5	◆0.2
Malaria — Paludisme	3	◆0.1	-	-	-	-	-	-
Neoplasms — Tumeurs	15 385	296.6	12 421	231.4	8 205	293.0	7 405	260.8
Malignant neoplasms — Tumeurs malignes								
Total	15 095	291.1	12 166	226.7	8 050	287.5	7 254	255.4
Malignant neoplasm of lip, oral cavity and pharynx — Tumeur maligne de la lèvre, de la cavité buccale et du pharynx	542	10.5	214	4.0	252	9.0	96	3.4
Malignant neoplasm of oesophagus — Tumeur maligne de l'oesophage	416	8.0	100	1.9	292	10.4	105	3.7
Malignant neoplasm of stomach — Tumeur maligne de l'estomac	599	11.5	399	7.4	247	8.8	168	5.9
Malignant neoplasm of colon, rectosigmoid junction, rectum, anus and anal canal — Tumeur maligne du côlon, de la jonction recto-sigmoïdienne, du rectum, de l'anus et du canal anal	2 105	40.6	1 404	26.2	950	33.9	800	28.2
Malignant neoplasm of liver and intrahepatic bile ducts — Tumeur maligne du foie et des voies bilaires intrahépatiques	515	9.9	314	5.9	310	11.1	152	5.4
Malignant neoplasm of pancreas — Tumeur maligne du pancréas	1 058	20.4	1 020	19.0	455	16.3	512	18.0
Malignant neoplasm of trachea, bronchus and lung — Tumeur maligne de la trachée, des bronches et du poumon	3 618	69.8	1 715	32.0	1 970	70.4	1 746	61.5
Malignant neoplasm of female breast — Tumeur maligne du sein chez la femme	..	..	1 685	36.8	..	..	1 115	47.1
Malignant neoplasm of cervix uteri — Tumeur maligne du col de l'utérus	..	..	314	6.9	..	..	97	4.1
Malignant neoplasm of prostate — Tumeur maligne de la prostate	1 421	78.1	..	..	1 142	112.7	..	..
Malignant neoplasm of lymphoid, haematopoietic and related tissue — Tumeurs malignes primitives ou présumées primitives des tissus lymphoïde, hématopoïétique et apparentés	1 010	19.5	888	16.5	590	21.1	442	15.6
Disorders of the blood and blood-forming organs and certain disorders involving the immune mechanism — Maladies du sang et des organes hématopoïétiques et certains troubles du système immunitaire								
Total	93	1.8	135	2.5	109	3.9	109	3.8
Anaemias — Anémies	32	0.6	61	1.1	65	2.3	77	2.7
Endocrine, nutritional and metabolic diseases — Maladies endocriniennes, nutritionnelles et métaboliques								
Total	1 995	38.5	2 526	47.1	904	32.3	789	27.8
Diabetes mellitus — Diabète sucré	1 701	32.8	2 065	38.5	746	26.6	547	19.3
Malnutrition — Malnutrition	75	1.4	132	2.5	4	◆0.1	3	◆0.1
Mental and behavioural disorders — Troubles mentaux et du comportement	591	11.4	819	15.3	1 327	47.4	1 788	63.0
Diseases of the nervous system — Maladies du système nerveux	1 432	27.6	1 724	32.1	924	33.0	1 119	39.4
Diseases of the circulatory system — Maladies de l'appareil circulatoire								
Total	22 257	429.1	25 354	472.4	6 109	218.2	6 000	211.3
Acute rheumatic fever and chronic rheumatic heart diseases — Rhumatisme articulaire aigu et cardiopathies rhumatismales chroniques	113	2.2	174	3.2	35	1.3	49	1.7
Hypertensive diseases — Maladies hypertensives	1 178	22.7	1 779	33.1	355	12.7	481	16.9
Ischaemic heart disease — Cardiopathie ischémique	11 787	227.3	11 961	222.8	2 201	78.6	1 632	57.5
Cerebrovascular disease — Maladie cérébrovasculaire	3 707	71.5	5 088	94.8	1 434	51.2	1 832	64.5

Cause of death — Cause de décès	Czechia - Tchéquie				Denmark - Danemark			
	2016 (C)				2014 (C)			
	Male — Masculin		Female — Féminin		Male — Masculin		Female — Féminin	
	Number Nombre	Rate Taux	Number Nombre	Rate Taux	Number Nombre	Rate Taux	Number Nombre	Rate Taux
Diseases of arteries, arterioles and capillaries — Maladies des artères, artérioles et capillaires	1 086	20.9	1 226	22.8	460	16.4	393	13.8
Diseases of the respiratory system — Maladies de l'appareil respiratoire								
Total	3 984	76.8	3 144	58.6	2 641	94.3	2 881	101.4
Influenza — Grippe..	64	1.2	47	0.9	6	♦0.2	7	♦0.2
Pneumonia — Pneumopathies............................	1 455	28.1	1 323	24.6	748	26.7	808	28.5
Chronic lower respiratory diseases — Maladies chroniques des voies respiratoires inférieures	1 956	37.7	1 358	25.3	1 558	55.6	1 805	63.6
Diseases of the digestive system — Maladies de l'appareil digestif								
Total	2 552	49.2	1 960	36.5	1 107	39.5	1 062	37.4
Gastric and duodenal ulcer — Ulcère de l'estomac et du duodénum................	240	4.6	181	3.4	82	2.9	135	4.8
Diseases of the liver — Maladies du foie........	1 392	26.8	719	13.4	520	18.6	269	9.5
Diseases of the musculoskeletal system and connective tissue — Maladies du système ostéo-articularie, des muscles et du tissu conjonctif	86	1.7	107	2.0	120	4.3	241	8.5
Diseases of the genitourinary system — Maladies de l'appareil génito-urinaire								
Total	684	13.2	852	15.9	390	13.9	398	14.0
Disorders of kidney and ureter — Affections du rein et de l'uretère	508	9.8	578	10.8	244	8.7	219	7.7
Hyperplasia of prostate — Hyperplasie de la prostate...........................	21	♦1.2	..	..	23	♦2.3	..	..
Pregnancy, childbirth and the puerperium — Grossesse, accouchement et puerpéralité								
Total	..	..	1	♦0.9	..	..	3	♦5.3
Pregnancy with abortive outcome — Grossesse se terminant par un avortement	..	..	-	-	..	..	1	♦1.8
Other direct obstetric causes — Autres décès maternels directs.....................	..	..	1	♦0.9	..	..	2	♦3.5
Indirect obstetric causes — Décès maternels indirects	..	..	-	-	..	..	-	-
Certain conditions originating in the perinatal period — Certaines affections dont l'origine se situe dans la période périnatale	118	204.0	76	138.6	66	225.6	49	177.4
Congenital malformations, deformations and chromosomal abnormalities — Malformations congénitales et anomalies chromosomiques	87	150.4	78	142.3	85	290.6	67	242.6
Symptoms, signs and abnormal clinical and laboratory findings, not elsewhere classified — Symptômes, signes et résultats anormaux d'examens cliniques et de laboratoire, non classés ailleurs	908	17.5	664	12.4	1 809	64.6	2 312	81.4
All other diseases — Toutes autres maladies................	61	1.2	111	2.1	22	♦0.8	31	1.1
External causes — Causes externes								
Total	3 667	70.7	1 844	34.4	1 259	45.0	780	27.5
Accidents								
Total	2 260	43.6	1 371	25.5	731	26.1	577	20.3
Transport accidents — Accidents de transport	536	10.3	179	3.3	163	5.8	47	1.7
Falls — Chutes	359	6.9	203	3.8	227	8.1	268	9.4
Accidental drowning and submersion — Noyade et submersion accidentelles..	114	2.2	29	♦0.5	32	1.1	2	♦0.1
Exposure to smoke, fire and flames — Exposition à la fumée, au feu et aux flammes...	31	0.6	22	♦0.4	39	1.4	18	♦0.6
Accidental poisoning by and exposure to noxious substances — Intoxication accidentelle par des substances nocives et exposition à ces substances	324	6.2	140	2.6	134	4.8	59	2.1
Intentional self-harm — Lésions auto-infligées..................................	1 059	20.4	257	4.8	469	16.8	160	5.6
Assault — Agresssions	27	♦0.5	26	♦0.5	19	♦0.7	19	♦0.7
All other external causes — Toutes autres causes externes	321	6.2	190	3.5	40	1.4	24	♦0.8

20. Death and death rates by cause and sex: 2012 - 2016
Décès et taux de mortalité par cause et sexe : 2012 - 2016 (continued - suite)

Cause of death — Cause de décès	Denmark - Danemark 2015 (C)				Estonia - Estonie 2014 (C)			
	Male — Masculin		Female — Féminin		Male — Masculin		Female — Féminin	
	Number Nombre	Rate Taux	Number Nombre	Rate Taux	Number Nombre	Rate Taux	Number Nombre	Rate Taux
TOTAL	26 047	922.8	26 177	916.6	7 465	1 214.0	8 005	1 142.1
Certain infectious and parasitic diseases — Certaines maladies infectieuses et parasitaires								
Total	408	14.5	528	18.5	68	11.1	59	8.4
Intestinal infectious diseases — Maladies infectieuses intestinales	53	1.9	112	3.9	-	-	-	-
Tuberculosis — Tuberculose	10	♦0.4	6	♦0.2	13	♦2.1	9	♦1.3
Tetanus — Tétanos	-	-	-	-	-	-	-	-
Diphtheria — Diphtérie	-	-	-	-	-	-	-	-
Whooping cough — Coqueluche	-	-	-	-	-	-	-	-
Meningococcal infection — Infection à méningocoques	-	-	1	♦0.0	-	-	-	-
Septicaemia — Septicémie	178	6.3	244	8.5	5	♦0.8	15	♦2.1
Acute poliomyelitis — Poliomyélite aiguë	-	-	-	-	-	-	-	-
Measles — Rougeole	2	♦0.1	-	-	-	-	-	-
Viral hepatitis — Hépatite virale	11	♦0.4	7	♦0.2	3	♦0.5	8	♦1.1
Human immunodeficiency virus [HIV] disease — Maladies dues au virus de l'immunodéficience humaine (VIH)	9	♦0.3	4	♦0.1	36	5.9	11	♦1.6
Malaria — Paludisme	-	-	1	♦0.0	-	-	-	-
Neoplasms — Tumeurs	8 284	293.5	7 430	260.2	2 060	335.0	1 827	260.7
Malignant neoplasms — Tumeurs malignes								
Total	8 125	287.9	7 275	254.7	2 021	328.7	1 790	255.4
Malignant neoplasm of lip, oral cavity and pharynx — Tumeur maligne de la lèvre, de la cavité buccale et du pharynx	241	8.5	99	3.5	78	12.7	15	♦2.1
Malignant neoplasm of oesophagus — Tumeur maligne de l'oesophage	299	10.6	97	3.4	56	9.1	17	♦2.4
Malignant neoplasm of stomach — Tumeur maligne de l'estomac	246	8.7	131	4.6	170	27.6	139	19.8
Malignant neoplasm of colon, rectosigmoid junction, rectum, anus and anal canal — Tumeur maligne du côlon, de la jonction recto-sigmoïdienne, du rectum, de l'anus et du canal anal	960	34.0	876	30.7	215	35.0	240	34.2
Malignant neoplasm of liver and intrahepatic bile ducts — Tumeur maligne du foie et des voies bilaires intrahépatiques	276	9.8	164	5.7	42	6.8	41	5.8
Malignant neoplasm of pancreas — Tumeur maligne du pancréas	481	17.0	480	16.8	107	17.4	144	20.5
Malignant neoplasm of trachea, bronchus and lung — Tumeur maligne de la trachée, des bronches et du poumon	1 894	67.1	1 788	62.6	533	86.7	182	26.0
Malignant neoplasm of female breast — Tumeur maligne du sein chez la femme	..	..	1 069	44.8	..	..	251	41.8
Malignant neoplasm of cervix uteri — Tumeur maligne du col de l'utérus	..	..	97	4.1	..	..	66	11.0
Malignant neoplasm of prostate — Tumeur maligne de la prostate	1 170	113.4	..	..	271	134.9	..	..
Malignant neoplasm of lymphoid, haematopoietic and related tissue — Tumeurs malignes primitives ou présumées primitives des tissus lymphoïde, hématopoïétique et apparentés	623	22.1	472	16.5	135	22.0	156	22.3
Disorders of the blood and blood-forming organs and certain disorders involving the immune mechanism — Maladies du sang et des organes hématopoïétiques et certains troubles du système immunitaire								
Total	109	3.9	142	5.0	8	♦1.3	10	♦1.4
Anaemias — Anémies	64	2.3	109	3.8	5	♦0.8	7	♦1.0
Endocrine, nutritional and metabolic diseases — Maladies endocriniennes, nutritionnelles et métaboliques								
Total	887	31.4	841	29.4	59	9.6	108	15.4
Diabetes mellitus — Diabète sucré	741	26.3	611	21.4	53	8.6	97	13.8
Malnutrition — Malnutrition	4	♦0.1	7	♦0.2	-	-	-	-
Mental and behavioural disorders — Troubles mentaux et du comportement	1 515	53.7	1 920	67.2	71	11.5	36	5.1
Diseases of the nervous system — Maladies du système nerveux	1 019	36.1	1 237	43.3	147	23.9	136	19.4
Diseases of the circulatory system — Maladies de l'appareil circulatoire								
Total	6 289	222.8	6 215	217.6	3 342	543.5	4 908	700.2
Acute rheumatic fever and chronic rheumatic heart diseases — Rhumatisme articularie aigu et cardiopathies rhumatismales chroniques	32	1.1	42	1.5	5	♦0.8	13	♦1.9
Hypertensive diseases — Maladies hypertensives	426	15.1	536	18.8	877	142.6	1 727	246.4
Ischaemic heart disease — Cardiopathie ischémique	2 174	77.0	1 605	56.2	1 495	243.1	1 909	272.4
Cerebrovascular disease — Maladie cérébrovasculaire	1 500	53.1	1 890	66.2	363	59.0	581	82.9

Cause of death — Cause de décès	Denmark - Danemark				Estonia - Estonie			
	2015 (C)				2014 (C)			
	Male — Masculin		Female — Féminin		Male — Masculin		Female — Féminin	
	Number Nombre	Rate Taux	Number Nombre	Rate Taux	Number Nombre	Rate Taux	Number Nombre	Rate Taux
Diseases of arteries, arterioles and capillaries — Maladies des artères, artérioles et capillaires	473	16.8	412	14.4	117	19.0	138	19.7
Diseases of the respiratory system — Maladies de l'appareil respiratoire								
Total	2 813	99.7	3 032	106.2	372	60.5	178	25.4
Influenza — Grippe............	13	♦0.5	8	♦0.3	11	♦1.8	4	♦0.6
Pneumonia — Pneumopathies	830	29.4	915	32.0	158	25.7	94	13.4
Chronic lower respiratory diseases — Maladies chroniques des voies respiratoires inférieures	1 663	58.9	1 839	64.4	174	28.3	62	8.8
Diseases of the digestive system — Maladies de l'appareil digestif								
Total	1 098	38.9	976	34.2	339	55.1	245	35.0
Gastric and duodenal ulcer — Ulcère de l'estomac et du duodénum............	111	3.9	122	4.3	32	5.2	28	♦4.0
Diseases of the liver — Maladies du foie............	496	17.6	220	7.7	198	32.2	78	11.1
Diseases of the musculoskeletal system and connective tissue — Maladies du système ostéo-articularie, des muscles et du tissu conjonctif	124	4.4	239	8.4	13	♦2.1	26	♦3.7
Diseases of the genitourinary system — Maladies de l'appareil génito-urinaire								
Total	396	14.0	399	14.0	52	8.5	68	9.7
Disorders of kidney and ureter — Affections du rein et de l'uretère	243	8.6	225	7.9	35	5.7	54	7.7
Hyperplasia of prostate — Hyperplasie de la prostate............	23	♦2.2	..	..	5	♦2.5	..	..
Pregnancy, childbirth and the puerperium — Grossesse, accouchement et puerpéralité								
Total	..	..	-	-	..	..	-	-
Pregnancy with abortive outcome — Grossesse se terminant par un avortement	..	..	-	-	..	..	-	-
Other direct obstetric causes — Autres décès maternels directs	..	..	-	-	..	..	-	-
Indirect obstetric causes — Décès maternels indirects	..	..	-	-	..	..	-	-
Certain conditions originating in the perinatal period — Certaines affections dont l'origine se situe dans la période périnatale	63	211.1	55	194.0	7	♦101.1	6	♦90.5
Congenital malformations, deformations and chromosomal abnormalities — Malformations congénitales et anomalies chromosomiques	67	224.5	63	222.2	17	♦245.6	12	♦181.0
Symptoms, signs and abnormal clinical and laboratory findings, not elsewhere classified — Symptômes, signes et résultats anormaux d'examens cliniques et de laboratoire, non classés ailleurs	1 789	63.4	2 305	80.7	152	24.7	158	22.5
All other diseases — Toutes autres maladies............	27	♦1.0	34	1.2	4	♦0.7	7	♦1.0
External causes — Causes externes								
Total	1 159	41.1	761	26.6	754	122.6	221	31.5
Accidents								
Total	702	24.9	551	19.3	492	80.0	152	21.7
Transport accidents — Accidents de transport............	152	5.4	56	2.0	64	10.4	28	♦4.0
Falls — Chutes	207	7.3	256	9.0	71	11.5	30	♦4.3
Accidental drowning and submersion — Noyade et submersion accidentelles............	19	♦0.7	6	♦0.2	54	8.8	11	♦1.6
Exposure to smoke, fire and flames — Exposition à la fumée, au feu et aux flammes	43	1.5	15	♦0.5	33	5.4	11	♦1.6
Accidental poisoning by and exposure to noxious substances — Intoxication accidentelle par des substances nocives et exposition à ces substances	122	4.3	51	1.8	188	30.6	49	7.0
Intentional self-harm — Lésions auto-infligées............	390	13.8	174	6.1	193	31.4	48	6.8
Assault — Agresssions	21	♦0.7	12	♦0.4	33	5.4	9	♦1.3
All other external causes — Toutes autres causes externes	46	1.6	24	♦0.8	36	5.9	12	♦1.7

Cause of death — Cause de décès	Estonia - Estonie 2015 (C)				Finland - Finlande 2014 (C)			
	Male — Masculin		Female — Féminin		Male — Masculin		Female — Féminin	
	Number Nombre	Rate Taux	Number Nombre	Rate Taux	Number Nombre	Rate Taux	Number Nombre	Rate Taux
TOTAL	7 217	1 174.7	8 026	1 148.4	25 864	964.9	26 545	958.0
Certain infectious and parasitic diseases — Certaines maladies infectieuses et parasitaires								
Total	70	11.4	43	6.2	139	5.2	171	6.2
Intestinal infectious diseases — Maladies infectieuses intestinales	1	♦0.2	1	♦0.1	6	♦0.2	11	♦0.4
Tuberculosis — Tuberculose	12	♦2.0	4	♦0.6	12	♦0.4	8	♦0.3
Tetanus — Tétanos	-	-	-	-	-	-	-	-
Diphtheria — Diphtérie	-	-	-	-	-	-	-	-
Whooping cough — Coqueluche	-	-	-	-	1	♦0.0	-	-
Meningococcal infection — Infection à méningocoques	-	-	-	-	1	♦0.0	1	♦0.0
Septicaemia — Septicémie	9	♦1.5	16	♦2.3	63	2.4	83	3.0
Acute poliomyelitis — Poliomyélite aiguë	-	-	-	-	-	-	-	-
Measles — Rougeole	-	-	-	-	-	-	-	-
Viral hepatitis — Hépatite virale	4	♦0.7	2	♦0.3	4	♦0.1	5	♦0.2
Human immunodeficiency virus [HIV] disease — Maladies dues au virus de l'immunodéficience humaine (VIH)	33	5.4	11	♦1.6	-	-	3	♦0.1
Malaria — Paludisme	-	-	-	-	-	-	-	-
Neoplasms — Tumeurs	2 077	338.1	1 825	261.1	6 476	241.6	5 794	209.1
Malignant neoplasms — Tumeurs malignes								
Total	2 049	333.5	1 767	252.8	6 318	235.7	5 602	202.2
Malignant neoplasm of lip, oral cavity and pharynx — Tumeur maligne de la lèvre, de la cavité buccale et du pharynx	77	12.5	16	♦2.3	143	5.3	74	2.7
Malignant neoplasm of oesophagus — Tumeur maligne de l'oesophage	60	9.8	10	♦1.4	185	6.9	89	3.2
Malignant neoplasm of stomach — Tumeur maligne de l'estomac	149	24.3	127	18.2	244	9.1	169	6.1
Malignant neoplasm of colon, rectosigmoid junction, rectum, anus and anal canal — Tumeur maligne du côlon, de la jonction recto-sigmoïdienne, du rectum, de l'anus et du canal anal	222	36.1	249	35.6	646	24.1	583	21.0
Malignant neoplasm of liver and intrahepatic bile ducts — Tumeur maligne du foie et des voies bilaires intrahépatiques	66	10.7	36	5.2	303	11.3	186	6.7
Malignant neoplasm of pancreas — Tumeur maligne du pancréas	110	17.9	128	18.3	535	20.0	545	19.7
Malignant neoplasm of trachea, bronchus and lung — Tumeur maligne de la trachée, des bronches et du poumon	506	82.4	166	23.8	1 381	51.5	771	27.8
Malignant neoplasm of female breast — Tumeur maligne du sein chez la femme	..	..	240	40.2	..	..	813	34.8
Malignant neoplasm of cervix uteri — Tumeur maligne du col de l'utérus	..	..	59	9.9	..	..	53	2.3
Malignant neoplasm of prostate — Tumeur maligne de la prostate	292	143.9	..	..	859	84.9	..	..
Malignant neoplasm of lymphoid, haematopoietic and related tissue — Tumeurs malignes primitives ou présumées primitives des tissus lymphoïde, hématopoïétique et apparentés	149	24.3	168	24.0	604	22.5	578	20.9
Disorders of the blood and blood-forming organs and certain disorders involving the immune mechanism — Maladies du sang et des organes hématopoïétiques et certains troubles du système immunitaire								
Total	7	♦1.1	19	♦2.7	35	1.3	29	♦1.0
Anaemias — Anémies	4	♦0.7	12	♦1.7	13	♦0.5	12	♦0.4
Endocrine, nutritional and metabolic diseases — Maladies endocriniennes, nutritionnelles et métaboliques								
Total	58	9.4	100	14.3	352	13.1	327	11.8
Diabetes mellitus — Diabète sucré	53	8.6	84	12.0	270	10.1	228	8.2
Malnutrition — Malnutrition	-	-	1	♦0.1	1	♦0.0	-	-
Mental and behavioural disorders — Troubles mentaux et du comportement	68	11.1	34	4.9	853	31.8	1 472	53.1
Diseases of the nervous system — Maladies du système nerveux	149	24.3	175	25.0	2 805	104.6	5 111	184.5
Diseases of the circulatory system — Maladies de l'appareil circulatoire								
Total	3 157	513.8	4 808	688.0	9 496	354.3	10 147	366.2
Acute rheumatic fever and chronic rheumatic heart diseases — Rhumatisme articulaire aigu et cardiopathies rhumatismales chroniques	2	♦0.3	14	♦2.0	8	♦0.3	17	♦0.6
Hypertensive diseases — Maladies hypertensives	901	146.6	1 829	261.7	518	19.3	1 061	38.3
Ischaemic heart disease — Cardiopathie ischémique	1 373	223.5	1 802	257.8	5 532	206.4	4 805	173.4
Cerebrovascular disease — Maladie cérébrovasculaire	341	55.5	501	71.7	1 786	66.6	2 642	95.3

Cause of death — Cause de décès	Estonia - Estonie 2015 (C)				Finland - Finlande 2014 (C)			
	Male — Masculin		Female — Féminin		Male — Masculin		Female — Féminin	
	Number Nombre	Rate Taux	Number Nombre	Rate Taux	Number Nombre	Rate Taux	Number Nombre	Rate Taux
Diseases of arteries, arterioles and capillaries — Maladies des artères, artérioles et capillaires	112	18.2	98	14.0	550	20.5	472	17.0
Diseases of the respiratory system — Maladies de l'appareil respiratoire								
Total	329	53.5	204	29.2	1 149	42.9	688	24.8
Influenza — Grippe	7	♦1.1	6	♦0.9	9	♦0.3	17	♦0.6
Pneumonia — Pneumopathies	142	23.1	107	15.3	99	3.7	81	2.9
Chronic lower respiratory diseases — Maladies chroniques des voies respiratoires inférieures	157	25.6	73	10.4	813	30.3	443	16.0
Diseases of the digestive system — Maladies de l'appareil digestif								
Total	340	55.3	280	40.1	1 478	55.1	951	34.3
Gastric and duodenal ulcer — Ulcère de l'estomac et du duodénum	31	5.0	27	♦3.9	94	3.5	51	1.8
Diseases of the liver — Maladies du foie	210	34.2	110	15.7	904	33.7	335	12.1
Diseases of the musculoskeletal system and connective tissue — Maladies du système ostéo-articularie, des muscles et du tissu conjonctif	19	♦3.1	24	♦3.4	72	2.7	133	4.8
Diseases of the genitourinary system — Maladies de l'appareil génito-urinaire								
Total	61	9.9	70	10.0	141	5.3	174	6.3
Disorders of kidney and ureter — Affections du rein et de l'uretère	38	6.2	53	7.6	124	4.6	149	5.4
Hyperplasia of prostate — Hyperplasie de la prostate	14	♦6.9	..	..	9	♦0.9	..	..
Pregnancy, childbirth and the puerperium — Grossesse, accouchement et puerpéralité								
Total	..	..	-	-	..	..	3	♦5.3
Pregnancy with abortive outcome — Grossesse se terminant par un avortement	..	..	-	-	..	..	-	-
Other direct obstetric causes — Autres décès maternels directs	..	..	-	-	..	..	2	♦3.5
Indirect obstetric causes — Décès maternels indirects	..	..	-	-	..	..	1	♦1.8
Certain conditions originating in the perinatal period — Certaines affections dont l'origine se situe dans la période périnatale	9	♦125.5	7	♦103.9	20	♦68.7	26	♦93.4
Congenital malformations, deformations and chromosomal abnormalities — Malformations congénitales et anomalies chromosomiques	9	♦125.5	11	♦163.3	87	298.7	90	323.4
Symptoms, signs and abnormal clinical and laboratory findings, not elsewhere classified — Symptômes, signes et résultats anormaux d'examens cliniques et de laboratoire, non classés ailleurs	199	32.4	206	29.5	426	15.9	259	9.3
All other diseases — Toutes autres maladies	9	♦1.5	13	♦1.9	17	♦0.6	11	♦0.4
External causes — Causes externes								
Total	656	106.8	207	29.6	2 318	86.5	1 159	41.8
Accidents								
Total	430	70.0	151	21.6	1 525	56.9	874	31.5
Transport accidents — Accidents de transport	53	8.6	32	4.6	232	8.7	69	2.5
Falls — Chutes	83	13.5	33	4.7	587	21.9	554	20.0
Accidental drowning and submersion — Noyade et submersion accidentelles	27	♦4.4	8	♦1.1	87	3.2	28	♦1.0
Exposure to smoke, fire and flames — Exposition à la fumée, au feu et aux flammes	33	5.4	19	♦2.7	50	1.9	20	♦0.7
Accidental poisoning by and exposure to noxious substances — Intoxication accidentelle par des substances nocives et exposition à ces substances	168	27.3	37	5.3	383	14.3	110	4.0
Intentional self-harm — Lésions auto-infligées	159	25.9	36	5.2	595	22.2	188	6.8
Assault — Agresssions	32	5.2	10	♦1.4	48	1.8	27	♦1.0
All other external causes — Toutes autres causes externes	35	5.7	10	♦1.4	150	5.6	70	2.5

20. Death and death rates by cause and sex: 2012 - 2016
Décès et taux de mortalité par cause et sexe : 2012 - 2016 (continued - suite)

Cause of death — Cause de décès	Finland - Finlande 2015 (C)				France 2013 (C)			
	Male — Masculin		Female — Féminin		Male — Masculin		Female — Féminin	
	Number Nombre	Rate Taux	Number Nombre	Rate Taux	Number Nombre	Rate Taux	Number Nombre	Rate Taux
TOTAL	**25 884**	**961.6**	**26 418**	**950.3**	**279 954**	**907.0**	**276 077**	**840.9**
Certain infectious and parasitic diseases — Certaines maladies infectieuses et parasitaires								
Total	132	4.9	126	4.5	5 086	16.5	5 574	17.0
Intestinal infectious diseases — Maladies infectieuses intestinales	12	✦0.4	11	✦0.4	766	2.5	1 195	3.6
Tuberculosis — Tuberculose	10	✦0.4	8	✦0.3	124	0.4	75	0.2
Tetanus — Tétanos	-	-	-	-	-	-	1	✦0.0
Diphtheria — Diphtérie	-	-	-	-	1	✦0.0	-	-
Whooping cough — Coqueluche	-	-	-	-	2	✦0.0	8	✦0.0
Meningococcal infection — Infection à méningocoques	-	-	4	✦0.1	9	✦0.0	14	✦0.0
Septicaemia — Septicémie	68	2.5	53	1.9	2 551	8.3	2 647	8.1
Acute poliomyelitis — Poliomyélite aiguë	-	-	-	-	-	-	-	-
Measles — Rougeole	-	-	-	-	-	-	-	-
Viral hepatitis — Hépatite virale	4	✦0.1	2	✦0.1	337	1.1	274	0.8
Human immunodeficiency virus [HIV] disease — Maladies dues au virus de l'immunodéficience humaine (VIH)	-	-	-	-	320	1.0	129	0.4
Malaria — Paludisme	1	✦0.0	-	-	10	✦0.0	2	✦0.0
Neoplasms — Tumeurs	**6 623**	**246.0**	**5 858**	**210.7**	**92 045**	**298.2**	**67 673**	**206.1**
Malignant neoplasms — Tumeurs malignes								
Total	6 481	240.8	5 687	204.6	88 516	286.8	64 255	195.7
Malignant neoplasm of lip, oral cavity and pharynx — Tumeur maligne de la lèvre, de la cavité buccale et du pharynx	134	5.0	98	3.5	3 021	9.8	819	2.5
Malignant neoplasm of oesophagus — Tumeur maligne de l'oesophage	168	6.2	65	2.3	2 877	9.3	775	2.4
Malignant neoplasm of stomach — Tumeur maligne de l'estomac	249	9.3	192	6.9	2 985	9.7	1 680	5.1
Malignant neoplasm of colon, rectosigmoid junction, rectum, anus and anal canal — Tumeur maligne du côlon, de la jonction recto-sigmoïdienne, du rectum, de l'anus et du canal anal	654	24.3	557	20.0	9 044	29.3	7 882	24.0
Malignant neoplasm of liver and intrahepatic bile ducts — Tumeur maligne du foie et des voies bilaires intrahépatiques	321	11.9	188	6.8	5 911	19.2	2 209	6.7
Malignant neoplasm of pancreas — Tumeur maligne du pancréas	540	20.1	597	21.5	5 143	16.7	4 974	15.1
Malignant neoplasm of trachea, bronchus and lung — Tumeur maligne de la trachée, des bronches et du poumon	1 458	54.2	776	27.9	22 190	71.9	8 021	24.4
Malignant neoplasm of female breast — Tumeur maligne du sein chez la femme	..	..	816	34.8	..	..	11 678	...
Malignant neoplasm of cervix uteri — Tumeur maligne du col de l'utérus	..	..	63	2.7	..	..	749	...
Malignant neoplasm of prostate — Tumeur maligne de la prostate	898	87.6	..	..	8 590	...	..	..
Malignant neoplasm of lymphoid, haematopoietic and related tissue — Tumeurs malignes primitives ou présumées primitives des tissus lymphoïde, hématopoïétique et apparentés	636	23.6	529	19.0	7 379	23.9	6 207	18.9
Disorders of the blood and blood-forming organs and certain disorders involving the immune mechanism — Maladies du sang et des organes hématopoïétiques et certains troubles du système immunitaire								
Total	34	1.3	52	1.9	900	2.9	1 134	3.5
Anaemias — Anémies	14	✦0.5	12	✦0.4	466	1.5	708	2.2
Endocrine, nutritional and metabolic diseases — Maladies endocriniennes, nutritionnelles et métaboliques								
Total	326	12.1	311	11.2	8 608	27.9	10 869	33.1
Diabetes mellitus — Diabète sucré	251	9.3	232	8.3	5 450	17.7	5 720	17.4
Malnutrition — Malnutrition	3	✦0.1	7	✦0.3	1 017	3.3	1 975	6.0
Mental and behavioural disorders — Troubles mentaux et du comportement	**841**	**31.2**	**1 512**	**54.4**	**9 038**	**29.3**	**13 140**	**40.0**
Diseases of the nervous system — Maladies du système nerveux	**3 036**	**112.8**	**5 263**	**189.3**	**13 455**	**43.6**	**21 522**	**65.6**
Diseases of the circulatory system — Maladies de l'appareil circulatoire								
Total	9 528	354.0	9 907	356.4	64 213	208.0	74 681	227.5
Acute rheumatic fever and chronic rheumatic heart diseases — Rhumatisme articularie aigu et cardiopathies rhumatismales chroniques	10	✦0.4	27	✦1.0	614	2.0	1 034	3.1
Hypertensive diseases — Maladies hypertensives	613	22.8	1 150	41.4	3 424	11.1	6 415	19.5
Ischaemic heart disease — Cardiopathie ischémique	5 549	206.1	4 660	167.6	19 439	63.0	13 990	42.6
Cerebrovascular disease — Maladie cérébrovasculaire	1 800	66.9	2 499	89.9	13 074	42.4	18 525	56.4

Cause of death — Cause de décès	Finland - Finlande 2015 (C)				France 2013 (C)			
	Male — Masculin		Female — Féminin		Male — Masculin		Female — Féminin	
	Number Nombre	Rate Taux	Number Nombre	Rate Taux	Number Nombre	Rate Taux	Number Nombre	Rate Taux
Diseases of arteries, arterioles and capillaries — Maladies des artères, artérioles et capillaires	494	18.4	495	17.8	4 206	13.6	3 393	10.3
Diseases of the respiratory system — Maladies de l'appareil respiratoire								
Total	1 158	43.0	782	28.1	18 994	61.5	17 836	54.3
Influenza — Grippe	52	1.9	66	2.4	240	0.8	357	1.1
Pneumonia — Pneumopathies	63	2.3	80	2.9	5 589	18.1	6 218	18.9
Chronic lower respiratory diseases — Maladies chroniques des voies respiratoires inférieures	819	30.4	490	17.6	6 183	20.0	4 136	12.6
Diseases of the digestive system — Maladies de l'appareil digestif								
Total	1 331	49.4	895	32.2	12 062	39.1	10 383	31.6
Gastric and duodenal ulcer — Ulcère de l'estomac et du duodénum	91	3.4	54	1.9	398	1.3	422	1.3
Diseases of the liver — Maladies du foie	787	29.2	331	11.9	5 347	17.3	2 420	7.4
Diseases of the musculoskeletal system and connective tissue — Maladies du système ostéo-articularie, des muscles et du tissu conjonctif	65	2.4	145	5.2	1 551	5.0	2 479	7.6
Diseases of the genitourinary system — Maladies de l'appareil génito-urinaire								
Total	132	4.9	150	5.4	4 322	14.0	4 412	13.4
Disorders of kidney and ureter — Affections du rein et de l'uretère	108	4.0	133	4.8	3 278	10.6	3 484	10.6
Hyperplasia of prostate — Hyperplasie de la prostate	9	◆0.9	..	..	71		..	..
Pregnancy, childbirth and the puerperium — Grossesse, accouchement et puerpéralité								
Total	..	..	2	◆3.6	..	..	38	4.9
Pregnancy with abortive outcome — Grossesse se terminant par un avortement	..	..	-	-	..	..	2	◆0.3
Other direct obstetric causes — Autres décès maternels directs	..	..	2	◆3.6	..	..	30	◆3.8
Indirect obstetric causes — Décès maternels indirects	..	..	-	-	..	..	6	◆0.8
Certain conditions originating in the perinatal period — Certaines affections dont l'origine se situe dans la période périnatale	24	◆84.7	29	◆107.9	778	194.4	627	164.4
Congenital malformations, deformations and chromosomal abnormalities — Malformations congénitales et anomalies chromosomiques	87	307.1	75	279.1	791	197.7	709	185.9
Symptoms, signs and abnormal clinical and laboratory findings, not elsewhere classified — Symptômes, signes et résultats anormaux d'examens cliniques et de laboratoire, non classés ailleurs	333	12.4	218	7.8	26 323	85.3	29 560	90.0
All other diseases — Toutes autres maladies	14	◆0.5	16	◆0.6	467	1.5	852	2.6
External causes — Causes externes								
Total	2 220	82.5	1 077	38.7	21 321	69.1	14 588	44.4
Accidents								
Total	1 484	55.1	845	30.4	12 864	41.7	11 382	34.7
Transport accidents — Accidents de transport	222	8.2	74	2.7	2 317	7.5	701	2.1
Falls — Chutes	605	22.5	538	19.4	3 146	10.2	3 400	10.4
Accidental drowning and submersion — Noyade et submersion accidentelles	92	3.4	19	◆0.7	644	2.1	310	0.9
Exposure to smoke, fire and flames — Exposition à la fumée, au feu et aux flammes	44	1.6	17	◆0.6	234	0.8	164	0.5
Accidental poisoning by and exposure to noxious substances — Intoxication accidentelle par des substances nocives et exposition à ces substances	361	13.4	120	4.3	1 104	3.6	885	2.7
Intentional self-harm — Lésions auto-infligées	556	20.7	173	6.2	7 217	23.4	2 372	7.2
Assault — Agresssions	52	1.9	16	◆0.6	245	0.8	150	0.5
All other external causes — Toutes autres causes externes	128	4.8	43	1.5	995	3.2	684	2.1

Cause of death — Cause de décès	France 2014 (C)				Germany - Allemagne 2014 (C)			
	Male — Masculin		Female — Féminin		Male — Masculin		Female — Féminin	
	Number Nombre	Rate Taux	Number Nombre	Rate Taux	Number Nombre	Rate Taux	Number Nombre	Rate Taux
TOTAL	274 169	883.7	270 449	819.5	422 223	1 067.4	446 133	1 082.6
Certain infectious and parasitic diseases — Certaines maladies infectieuses et parasitaires								
Total	4 929	15.9	5 297	16.1	8 350	21.1	9 637	23.4
Intestinal infectious diseases — Maladies infectieuses intestinales	625	2.0	973	2.9	1 904	4.8	3 277	8.0
Tuberculosis — Tuberculose	146	0.5	108	0.3	146	0.4	115	0.3
Tetanus — Tétanos	2	◆0.0	-	-	1	◆0.0	1	◆0.0
Diphtheria — Diphtérie	1	◆0.0	1	◆0.0	-	-	-	-
Whooping cough — Coqueluche	2	◆0.0	1	◆0.0	-	-	1	◆0.0
Meningococcal infection — Infection à méningocoques	17	◆0.1	7	◆0.0	11	◆0.0	19	◆0.0
Septicaemia — Septicémie	2 573	8.3	2 708	8.2	4 325	10.9	4 194	10.2
Acute poliomyelitis — Poliomyélite aiguë	-	-	-	-	-	-	1	◆0.0
Measles — Rougeole	-	-	1	◆0.0	1	◆0.0	-	-
Viral hepatitis — Hépatite virale	320	1.0	249	0.8	448	1.1	406	1.0
Human immunodeficiency virus [HIV] disease — Maladies dues au virus de l'immunodéficience humaine (VIH)	271	0.9	88	0.3	305	0.8	83	0.2
Malaria — Paludisme	6	◆0.0	7	◆0.0	4	◆0.0	1	◆0.0
Neoplasms — Tumeurs	93 633	301.8	69 577	210.8	125 120	316.3	105 651	256.4
Malignant neoplasms — Tumeurs malignes								
Total	90 073	290.3	66 114	200.3	121 766	307.8	101 992	247.5
Malignant neoplasm of lip, oral cavity and pharynx — Tumeur maligne de la lèvre, de la cavité buccale et du pharynx	3 022	9.7	849	2.6	4 095	10.4	1 353	3.3
Malignant neoplasm of oesophagus — Tumeur maligne de l'oesophage	2 931	9.4	825	2.5	4 107	10.4	1 236	3.0
Malignant neoplasm of stomach — Tumeur maligne de l'estomac	2 961	9.5	1 617	4.9	5 545	14.0	4 065	9.9
Malignant neoplasm of colon, rectosigmoid junction, rectum, anus and anal canal — Tumeur maligne du côlon, de la jonction recto-sigmoïdienne, du rectum, de l'anus et du canal anal	9 021	29.1	7 852	23.8	13 580	34.3	11 932	29.0
Malignant neoplasm of liver and intrahepatic bile ducts — Tumeur maligne du foie et des voies bilaires intrahépatiques	5 998	19.3	2 226	6.7	5 246	13.3	2 440	5.9
Malignant neoplasm of pancreas — Tumeur maligne du pancréas	5 336	17.2	5 035	15.3	8 231	20.8	8 384	20.3
Malignant neoplasm of trachea, bronchus and lung — Tumeur maligne de la trachée, des bronches et du poumon	22 509	72.6	8 904	27.0	29 560	74.7	15 524	37.7
Malignant neoplasm of female breast — Tumeur maligne du sein chez la femme	..	..	11 950	43.9	..	..	17 670	49.0
Malignant neoplasm of cervix uteri — Tumeur maligne du col de l'utérus	..	..	734	2.7	..	..	1 506	4.2
Malignant neoplasm of prostate — Tumeur maligne de la prostate	8 423	77.3	..	..	13 704	86.1	..	..
Malignant neoplasm of lymphoid, haematopoietic and related tissue — Tumeurs malignes primitives ou présumées primitives des tissus lymphoïde, hématopoïétique et apparentés	7 477	24.1	6 279	19.0	10 009	25.3	8 600	20.9
Disorders of the blood and blood-forming organs and certain disorders involving the immune mechanism — Maladies du sang et des organes hématopoïétiques et certains troubles du système immunitaire								
Total	862	2.8	1 115	3.4	1 198	3.0	1 733	4.2
Anaemias — Anémies	428	1.4	683	2.1	480	1.2	895	2.2
Endocrine, nutritional and metabolic diseases — Maladies endocriniennes, nutritionnelles et métaboliques								
Total	8 433	27.2	10 272	31.1	12 646	32.0	16 624	40.3
Diabetes mellitus — Diabète sucré	5 359	17.3	5 464	16.6	9 941	25.1	12 702	30.8
Malnutrition — Malnutrition	1 035	3.3	1 870	5.7	91	0.2	178	0.4
Mental and behavioural disorders — Troubles mentaux et du comportement	8 880	28.6	13 217	40.0	13 974	35.3	21 961	53.3
Diseases of the nervous system — Maladies du système nerveux	13 145	42.4	20 929	63.4	12 636	31.9	13 222	32.1
Diseases of the circulatory system — Maladies de l'appareil circulatoire								
Total	62 878	202.7	73 312	222.1	148 538	375.5	189 518	459.9
Acute rheumatic fever and chronic rheumatic heart diseases — Rhumatisme articularie aigu et cardiopathies rhumatismales chroniques	495	1.6	994	3.0	1 022	2.6	2 089	5.1
Hypertensive diseases — Maladies hypertensives	3 317	10.7	6 519	19.8	11 311	28.6	25 865	62.8
Ischaemic heart disease — Cardiopathie ischémique	19 061	61.4	13 666	41.4	64 467	163.0	56 699	137.6
Cerebrovascular disease — Maladie cérébrovasculaire	12 515	40.3	18 217	55.2	22 012	55.6	33 220	80.6

20. Death and death rates by cause and sex: 2012 - 2016
Décès et taux de mortalité par cause et sexe : 2012 - 2016 (continued - suite)

Cause of death — Cause de décès	France 2014 (C)				Germany - Allemagne 2014 (C)			
	Male — Masculin		Female — Féminin		Male — Masculin		Female — Féminin	
	Number Nombre	Rate Taux	Number Nombre	Rate Taux	Number Nombre	Rate Taux	Number Nombre	Rate Taux
Diseases of arteries, arterioles and capillaries — Maladies des artères, artérioles et capillaires	4 210	13.6	3 293	10.0	8 256	20.9	9 621	23.3
Diseases of the respiratory system — Maladies de l'appareil respiratoire								
Total	17 965	57.9	16 795	50.9	31 744	80.2	26 860	65.2
Influenza — Grippe	112	0.4	116	0.4	33	0.1	34	0.1
Pneumonia — Pneumopathies	5 129	16.5	5 715	17.3	8 474	21.4	8 237	20.0
Chronic lower respiratory diseases — Maladies chroniques des voies respiratoires inférieures	5 780	18.6	3 916	11.9	17 086	43.2	13 402	32.5
Diseases of the digestive system — Maladies de l'appareil digestif								
Total	12 183	39.3	10 187	30.9	19 993	50.5	18 544	45.0
Gastric and duodenal ulcer — Ulcère de l'estomac et du duodénum	417	1.3	395	1.2	1 025	2.6	1 194	2.9
Diseases of the liver — Maladies du foie	5 381	17.3	2 279	6.9	9 590	24.2	5 154	12.5
Diseases of the musculoskeletal system and connective tissue — Maladies du système ostéo-articularie, des muscles et du tissu conjonctif	1 560	5.0	2 394	7.3	1 175	3.0	2 142	5.2
Diseases of the genitourinary system — Maladies de l'appareil génito-urinaire								
Total	4 312	13.9	4 703	14.3	9 779	24.7	12 468	30.3
Disorders of kidney and ureter — Affections du rein et de l'uretère	3 195	10.3	3 687	11.2	7 441	18.8	9 366	22.7
Hyperplasia of prostate — Hyperplasie de la prostate	62	0.6	..	..	145	0.9	..	..
Pregnancy, childbirth and the puerperium — Grossesse, accouchement et puerpéralité								
Total	..	..	37	4.7	..	..	29	♦4.1
Pregnancy with abortive outcome — Grossesse se terminant par un avortement	..	..	2	♦0.3	..	..	2	♦0.3
Other direct obstetric causes — Autres décès maternels directs	..	..	34	4.4	..	..	23	♦3.2
Indirect obstetric causes — Décès maternels indirects	..	..	1	♦0.1	..	..	4	♦0.6
Certain conditions originating in the perinatal period — Certaines affections dont l'origine se situe dans la période périnatale	764	191.3	607	158.9	704	191.9	533	153.1
Congenital malformations, deformations and chromosomal abnormalities — Malformations congénitales et anomalies chromosomiques	733	183.6	704	184.3	866	236.1	799	229.5
Symptoms, signs and abnormal clinical and laboratory findings, not elsewhere classified — Symptômes, signes et résultats anormaux d'examens cliniques et de laboratoire, non classés ailleurs	22 583	72.8	26 339	79.8	14 130	35.7	11 669	28.3
All other diseases — Toutes autres maladies	393	1.3	764	2.3	525	1.3	921	2.2
External causes — Causes externes								
Total	20 916	67.4	14 200	43.0	20 845	52.7	13 822	33.5
Accidents								
Total	12 923	41.7	11 192	33.9	11 294	28.6	9 634	23.4
Transport accidents — Accidents de transport	2 300	7.4	756	2.3	2 796	7.1	927	2.2
Falls — Chutes	3 167	10.2	3 481	10.5	5 363	13.6	6 219	15.1
Accidental drowning and submersion — Noyade et submersion accidentelles	566	1.8	253	0.8	287	0.7	102	0.2
Exposure to smoke, fire and flames — Exposition à la fumée, au feu et aux flammes	213	0.7	141	0.4	214	0.5	133	0.3
Accidental poisoning by and exposure to noxious substances — Intoxication accidentelle par des substances nocives et exposition à ces substances	1 138	3.7	830	2.5	476	1.2	176	0.4
Intentional self-harm — Lésions auto-infligées	6 659	21.5	2 216	6.7	7 624	19.3	2 585	6.3
Assault — Agresssions	184	0.6	100	0.3	174	0.4	194	0.5
All other external causes — Toutes autres causes externes	1 150	3.7	692	2.1	1 753	4.4	1 409	3.4

20. Death and death rates by cause and sex: 2012 - 2016
Décès et taux de mortalité par cause et sexe : 2012 - 2016 (continued - suite)

Cause of death — Cause de décès	Germany - Allemagne 2015 (C)				Greece - Grèce 2014 (C)			
	Male — Masculin		Female — Féminin		Male — Masculin		Female — Féminin	
	Number Nombre	Rate Taux	Number Nombre	Rate Taux	Number Nombre	Rate Taux	Number Nombre	Rate Taux
TOTAL	449 512	1 128.4	475 688	1 150.1	58 546	1 104.3	55 194	985.2
Certain infectious and parasitic diseases — Certaines maladies infectieuses et parasitaires								
Total	9 271	23.3	10 672	25.8	1 496	28.2	2 019	36.0
Intestinal infectious diseases — Maladies infectieuses intestinales	2 217	5.6	3 550	8.6	12	✦0.2	24	✦0.4
Tuberculosis — Tuberculose	162	0.4	99	0.2	36	0.7	16	✦0.3
Tetanus — Tétanos	-	-	-	-	1	✦0.0	1	✦0.0
Diphtheria — Diphtérie	1	✦0.0	-	-	-	-	-	-
Whooping cough — Coqueluche	-	-	-	-	-	-	-	-
Meningococcal infection — Infection à méningocoques	16	✦0.0	16	✦0.0	1	✦0.0	-	-
Septicaemia — Septicémie	4 634	11.6	4 681	11.3	1 268	23.9	1 848	33.0
Acute poliomyelitis — Poliomyélite aiguë	-	-	1	✦0.0	-	-	-	-
Measles — Rougeole	2	✦0.0	1	✦0.0	-	-	1	✦0.0
Viral hepatitis — Hépatite virale	527	1.3	411	1.0	66	1.2	48	0.9
Human immunodeficiency virus [HIV] disease — Maladies dues au virus de l'immunodéficience humaine (VIH)	306	0.8	64	0.2	37	0.7	7	✦0.1
Malaria — Paludisme	3	✦0.0	2	✦0.0	-	-	-	-
Neoplasms — Tumeurs	126 407	317.3	107 345	259.5	18 036	340.2	11 475	204.8
Malignant neoplasms — Tumeurs malignes								
Total	122 916	308.6	103 421	250.0	17 813	336.0	11 273	201.2
Malignant neoplasm of lip, oral cavity and pharynx — Tumeur maligne de la lèvre, de la cavité buccale et du pharynx	4 086	10.3	1 378	3.3	250	4.7	124	2.2
Malignant neoplasm of oesophagus — Tumeur maligne de l'oesophage	4 269	10.7	1 238	3.0	165	3.1	52	0.9
Malignant neoplasm of stomach — Tumeur maligne de l'estomac	5 429	13.6	3 829	9.3	803	15.1	497	8.9
Malignant neoplasm of colon, rectosigmoid junction, rectum, anus and anal canal — Tumeur maligne du côlon, de la jonction recto-sigmoïdienne, du rectum, de l'anus et du canal anal	13 649	34.3	11 769	28.5	1 553	29.3	1 197	21.4
Malignant neoplasm of liver and intrahepatic bile ducts — Tumeur maligne du foie et des voies bilaires intrahépatiques	5 231	13.1	2 611	6.3	967	18.2	484	8.6
Malignant neoplasm of pancreas — Tumeur maligne du pancréas	8 497	21.3	8 659	20.9	928	17.5	835	14.9
Malignant neoplasm of trachea, bronchus and lung — Tumeur maligne de la trachée, des bronches et du poumon	29 378	73.7	15 881	38.4	5 726	108.0	1 354	24.2
Malignant neoplasm of female breast — Tumeur maligne du sein chez la femme	..	..	18 136	50.2	..	..	1 992	...
Malignant neoplasm of cervix uteri — Tumeur maligne du col de l'utérus	..	..	1 541	4.3	..	..	142	...
Malignant neoplasm of prostate — Tumeur maligne de la prostate	13 900	85.5	..	...	1 698	...	..	...
Malignant neoplasm of lymphoid, haematopoietic and related tissue — Tumeurs malignes primitives ou présumées primitives des tissus lymphoïde, hématopoïétique et apparentés	10 266	25.8	8 660	20.9	1 339	25.3	1 014	18.1
Disorders of the blood and blood-forming organs and certain disorders involving the immune mechanism — Maladies du sang et des organes hématopoïétiques et certains troubles du système immunitaire								
Total	1 432	3.6	1 903	4.6	122	2.3	159	2.8
Anaemias — Anémies	555	1.4	1 014	2.5	63	1.2	91	1.6
Endocrine, nutritional and metabolic diseases — Maladies endocriniennes, nutritionnelles et métaboliques								
Total	14 084	35.4	18 390	44.5	985	18.6	967	17.3
Diabetes mellitus — Diabète sucré	10 871	27.3	13 529	32.7	856	16.1	811	14.5
Malnutrition — Malnutrition	135	0.3	312	0.8	1	✦0.0	-	-
Mental and behavioural disorders — Troubles mentaux et du comportement	17 263	43.3	27 327	66.1	226	4.3	439	7.8
Diseases of the nervous system — Maladies du système nerveux	14 368	36.1	14 745	35.6	1 245	23.5	1 278	22.8
Diseases of the circulatory system — Maladies de l'appareil circulatoire								
Total	157 996	396.6	198 620	480.2	21 347	402.7	23 800	424.8
Acute rheumatic fever and chronic rheumatic heart diseases — Rhumatisme articulaire aigu et cardiopathies rhumatismales chroniques	1 157	2.9	2 263	5.5	44	0.8	94	1.7
Hypertensive diseases — Maladies hypertensives	12 921	32.4	28 842	69.7	1 634	30.8	1 764	31.5
Ischaemic heart disease — Cardiopathie ischémique	68 464	171.9	59 766	144.5	7 413	139.8	4 787	85.4
Cerebrovascular disease — Maladie cérébrovasculaire	23 398	58.7	33 584	81.2	5 864	110.6	8 415	150.2

20. Death and death rates by cause and sex: 2012 - 2016
Décès et taux de mortalité par cause et sexe : 2012 - 2016 (continued - suite)

Cause of death — Cause de décès	Germany - Allemagne 2015 (C)				Greece - Grèce 2014 (C)			
	Male — Masculin		Female — Féminin		Male — Masculin		Female — Féminin	
	Number Nombre	Rate Taux	Number Nombre	Rate Taux	Number Nombre	Rate Taux	Number Nombre	Rate Taux
Diseases of arteries, arterioles and capillaries — Maladies des artères, artérioles et capillaires	7 011	17.6	8 220	19.9	686	12.9	379	6.8
Diseases of the respiratory system — Maladies de l'appareil respiratoire								
Total	36 600	91.9	31 700	76.6	6 442	121.5	6 309	112.6
Influenza — Grippe	264	0.7	306	0.7	48	0.9	36	0.6
Pneumonia — Pneumopathies	10 216	25.6	9 957	24.1	545	10.3	492	8.8
Chronic lower respiratory diseases — Maladies chroniques des voies respiratoires inférieures	19 270	48.4	15 825	38.3	1 704	32.1	1 125	20.1
Diseases of the digestive system — Maladies de l'appareil digestif								
Total	20 689	51.9	19 155	46.3	1 775	33.5	1 520	27.1
Gastric and duodenal ulcer — Ulcère de l'estomac et du duodénum	1 103	2.8	1 296	3.1	221	4.2	229	4.1
Diseases of the liver — Maladies du foie	9 964	25.0	5 226	12.6	725	13.7	290	5.2
Diseases of the musculoskeletal system and connective tissue — Maladies du système ostéo-articularie, des muscles et du tissu conjonctif	1 366	3.4	2 405	5.8	83	1.6	148	2.6
Diseases of the genitourinary system — Maladies de l'appareil génito-urinaire								
Total	10 864	27.3	14 035	33.9	1 217	23.0	1 574	28.1
Disorders of kidney and ureter — Affections du rein et de l'uretère	8 350	21.0	10 698	25.9	991	18.7	1 153	20.6
Hyperplasia of prostate — Hyperplasie de la prostate	186	1.1	..	..	1	...	..	..
Pregnancy, childbirth and the puerperium — Grossesse, accouchement et puerpéralité								
Total	..	..	24	♦3.3	...	...	4	♦4.3
Pregnancy with abortive outcome — Grossesse se terminant par un avortement	..	..	1	♦0.1	...	...	1	♦1.1
Other direct obstetric causes — Autres décès maternels directs	..	..	19	♦2.6	...	...	3	♦3.3
Indirect obstetric causes — Décès maternels indirects	..	..	3	♦0.4	...	...	-	-
Certain conditions originating in the perinatal period — Certaines affections dont l'origine se situe dans la période périnatale	709	187.3	611	170.1	112	236.4	78	174.2
Congenital malformations, deformations and chromosomal abnormalities — Malformations congénitales et anomalies chromosomiques	931	246.0	885	246.5	82	173.1	73	163.1
Symptoms, signs and abnormal clinical and laboratory findings, not elsewhere classified — Symptômes, signes et résultats anormaux d'examens cliniques et de laboratoire, non classés ailleurs	15 378	38.6	12 059	29.2	2 777	52.4	4 332	77.3
All other diseases — Toutes autres maladies	563	1.4	907	2.2	15	♦0.3	51	0.9
External causes — Causes externes								
Total	21 591	54.2	14 905	36.0	2 586	48.8	968	17.3
Accidents								
Total	12 083	30.3	10 538	25.5	1 742	32.9	658	11.7
Transport accidents — Accidents de transport	2 758	6.9	930	2.2	822	15.5	203	3.6
Falls — Chutes	6 027	15.1	6 840	16.5	246	4.6	175	3.1
Accidental drowning and submersion — Noyade et submersion accidentelles	316	0.8	128	0.3	255	4.8	94	1.7
Exposure to smoke, fire and flames — Exposition à la fumée, au feu et aux flammes	206	0.5	137	0.3	26	♦0.5	30	♦0.5
Accidental poisoning by and exposure to noxious substances — Intoxication accidentelle par des substances nocives et exposition à ces substances	510	1.3	190	0.5	153	2.9	31	0.6
Intentional self-harm — Lésions auto-infligées	7 397	18.6	2 681	6.5	450	8.5	115	2.1
Assault — Agresssions	214	0.5	219	0.5	91	1.7	30	♦0.5
All other external causes — Toutes autres causes externes	1 897	4.8	1 467	3.5	303	5.7	165	2.9

Cause of death — Cause de décès	Greece - Grèce 2015 (C) Male — Masculin Number Nombre	Rate Taux	Female — Féminin Number Nombre	Rate Taux	Hungary - Hongrie 2015 (C) Male — Masculin Number Nombre	Rate Taux	Female — Féminin Number Nombre	Rate Taux
TOTAL	61 950	1 175.9	59 535	1 065.1	63 545	1 354.3	68 152	1 323.1
Certain infectious and parasitic diseases — Certaines maladies infectieuses et parasitaires								
Total	1 580	30.0	2 356	42.1	401	8.5	481	9.3
Intestinal infectious diseases — Maladies infectieuses intestinales	10	♦0.2	26	♦0.5	141	3.0	243	4.7
Tuberculosis — Tuberculose	25	♦0.5	17	♦0.3	48	1.0	14	♦0.3
Tetanus — Tétanos	-	-	-	-	-	-	2	♦0.0
Diphtheria — Diphtérie	-	-	-	-	-	-	-	-
Whooping cough — Coqueluche	-	-	-	-	-	-	-	-
Meningococcal infection — Infection à méningocoques	-	-	1	♦0.0	3	♦0.1	6	♦0.1
Septicaemia — Septicémie	1 392	26.4	2 218	39.7	23	♦0.5	24	♦0.5
Acute poliomyelitis — Poliomyélite aiguë	-	-	-	-	-	-	-	-
Measles — Rougeole	-	-	-	-	-	-	-	-
Viral hepatitis — Hépatite virale	53	1.0	25	♦0.4	93	2.0	111	2.2
Human immunodeficiency virus [HIV] disease — Maladies dues au virus de l'immunodéficience humaine (VIH)	34	0.6	5	♦0.1	10	♦0.2	1	♦0.0
Malaria — Paludisme	-	-	-	-	1	♦0.0	-	-
Neoplasms — Tumeurs	18 438	350.0	11 814	211.4	17 895	381.4	15 426	299.5
Malignant neoplasms — Tumeurs malignes								
Total	18 132	344.2	11 554	206.7	17 655	376.3	15 137	293.9
Malignant neoplasm of lip, oral cavity and pharynx — Tumeur maligne de la lèvre, de la cavité buccale et du pharynx	250	4.7	121	2.2	1 167	24.9	305	5.9
Malignant neoplasm of oesophagus — Tumeur maligne de l'oesophage	158	3.0	29	♦0.5	464	9.9	113	2.2
Malignant neoplasm of stomach — Tumeur maligne de l'estomac	842	16.0	515	9.2	853	18.2	647	12.6
Malignant neoplasm of colon, rectosigmoid junction, rectum, anus and anal canal — Tumeur maligne du côlon, de la jonction recto-sigmoïdienne, du rectum, de l'anus et du canal anal	1 583	30.0	1 222	21.9	2 825	60.2	2 183	42.4
Malignant neoplasm of liver and intrahepatic bile ducts — Tumeur maligne du foie et des voies bilaires intrahépatiques	1 036	19.7	522	9.3	565	12.0	297	5.8
Malignant neoplasm of pancreas — Tumeur maligne du pancréas	1 011	19.2	848	15.2	946	20.2	1 032	20.0
Malignant neoplasm of trachea, bronchus and lung — Tumeur maligne de la trachée, des bronches et du poumon	5 745	109.0	1 413	25.3	5 356	114.1	3 397	65.9
Malignant neoplasm of female breast — Tumeur maligne du sein chez la femme	..	..	2 117	43.9	..	..	2 220	49.8
Malignant neoplasm of cervix uteri — Tumeur maligne du col de l'utérus	..	..	139	2.9	..	..	476	10.7
Malignant neoplasm of prostate — Tumeur maligne de la prostate	1 763	88.2	..	..	1 258	78.9	..	..
Malignant neoplasm of lymphoid, haematopoietic and related tissue — Tumeurs malignes primitives ou présumées primitives des tissus lymphoïde, hématopoïétique et apparentés	1 232	23.4	1 023	18.3	969	20.7	948	18.4
Disorders of the blood and blood-forming organs and certain disorders involving the immune mechanism — Maladies du sang et des organes hématopoïétiques et certains troubles du système immunitaire								
Total	88	1.7	151	2.7	56	1.2	105	2.0
Anaemias — Anémies	44	0.8	75	1.3	24	♦0.5	57	1.1
Endocrine, nutritional and metabolic diseases — Maladies endocriniennes, nutritionnelles et métaboliques								
Total	1 029	19.5	1 007	18.0	1 366	29.1	1 764	34.2
Diabetes mellitus — Diabète sucré	914	17.3	866	15.5	1 224	26.1	1 547	30.0
Malnutrition — Malnutrition	1	♦0.0	1	♦0.0	7	♦0.1	8	♦0.2
Mental and behavioural disorders — Troubles mentaux et du comportement	460	8.7	699	12.5	1 340	28.6	2 217	43.0
Diseases of the nervous system — Maladies du système nerveux	1 455	27.6	1 508	27.0	953	20.3	1 054	20.5
Diseases of the circulatory system — Maladies de l'appareil circulatoire								
Total	22 140	420.2	24 272	434.2	28 313	603.4	37 180	721.8
Acute rheumatic fever and chronic rheumatic heart diseases — Rhumatisme articulaire aigu et cardiopathies rhumatismales chroniques	33	0.6	65	1.2	89	1.9	200	3.9
Hypertensive diseases — Maladies hypertensives	1 735	32.9	2 087	37.3	3 063	65.3	5 607	108.9
Ischaemic heart disease — Cardiopathie ischémique	7 519	142.7	4 777	85.5	14 600	311.2	18 407	357.4
Cerebrovascular disease — Maladie cérébrovasculaire	6 088	115.6	8 357	149.5	5 448	116.1	7 052	136.9

Cause of death — Cause de décès	Greece - Grèce 2015 (C)				Hungary - Hongrie 2015 (C)			
	Male — Masculin		Female — Féminin		Male — Masculin		Female — Féminin	
	Number Nombre	Rate Taux	Number Nombre	Rate Taux	Number Nombre	Rate Taux	Number Nombre	Rate Taux
Diseases of arteries, arterioles and capillaries — Maladies des artères, artérioles et capillaires	822	15.6	444	7.9	1 479	31.5	1 942	37.7
Diseases of the respiratory system — Maladies de l'appareil respiratoire								
Total	7 238	137.4	7 597	135.9	4 547	96.9	3 956	76.8
Influenza — Grippe	21	♦0.4	22	♦0.4	14	♦0.3	13	♦0.3
Pneumonia — Pneumopathies	599	11.4	551	9.9	554	11.8	589	11.4
Chronic lower respiratory diseases — Maladies chroniques des voies respiratoires inférieures	2 043	38.8	1 443	25.8	3 522	75.1	2 984	57.9
Diseases of the digestive system — Maladies de l'appareil digestif								
Total	1 765	33.5	1 546	27.7	3 761	80.2	2 601	50.5
Gastric and duodenal ulcer — Ulcère de l'estomac et du duodénum	279	5.3	255	4.6	383	8.2	362	7.0
Diseases of the liver — Maladies du foie	656	12.5	290	5.2	2 371	50.5	935	18.2
Diseases of the musculoskeletal system and connective tissue — Maladies du système ostéo-articularie, des muscles et du tissu conjonctif	74	1.4	159	2.8	145	3.1	317	6.2
Diseases of the genitourinary system — Maladies de l'appareil génito-urinaire								
Total	1 633	31.0	2 030	36.3	434	9.2	583	11.3
Disorders of kidney and ureter — Affections du rein et de l'uretère	1 319	25.0	1 432	25.6	240	5.1	402	7.8
Hyperplasia of prostate — Hyperplasie de la prostate	-		..	..	93	5.8	..	..
Pregnancy, childbirth and the puerperium — Grossesse, accouchement et puerpéralité								
Total	..	..	5	♦5.4	..	..	5	♦5.4
Pregnancy with abortive outcome — Grossesse se terminant par un avortement	..	..	-	-	..	..	-	-
Other direct obstetric causes — Autres décès maternels directs	..	..	4	♦4.4	..	..	3	♦3.3
Indirect obstetric causes — Décès maternels indirects	..	..	1	♦1.1	..	..	2	♦2.2
Certain conditions originating in the perinatal period — Certaines affections dont l'origine se situe dans la période périnatale	102	215.7	93	208.7	125	264.0	90	201.0
Congenital malformations, deformations and chromosomal abnormalities — Malformations congénitales et anomalies chromosomiques	108	228.4	74	166.1	169	356.9	138	308.1
Symptoms, signs and abnormal clinical and laboratory findings, not elsewhere classified — Symptômes, signes et résultats anormaux d'examens cliniques et de laboratoire, non classés ailleurs	2 916	55.3	4 850	86.8	94	2.0	94	1.8
All other diseases — Toutes autres maladies	19	♦0.4	32	0.6	36	0.8	72	1.4
External causes — Causes externes								
Total	2 905	55.1	1 342	24.0	3 910	83.3	2 069	40.2
Accidents								
Total	2 156	40.9	996	17.8	2 270	48.4	1 441	28.0
Transport accidents — Accidents de transport	935	17.7	322	5.8	654	13.9	218	4.2
Falls — Chutes	312	5.9	272	4.9	905	19.3	933	18.1
Accidental drowning and submersion — Noyade et submersion accidentelles	239	4.5	111	2.0	121	2.6	31	0.6
Exposure to smoke, fire and flames — Exposition à la fumée, au feu et aux flammes	41	0.8	46	0.8	59	1.3	21	♦0.4
Accidental poisoning by and exposure to noxious substances — Intoxication accidentelle par des substances nocives et exposition à ces substances	236	4.5	48	0.9	75	1.6	15	♦0.3
Intentional self-harm — Lésions auto-infligées	422	8.0	107	1.9	1 391	29.6	479	9.3
Assault — Agresssions	68	1.3	31	0.6	67	1.4	55	1.1
All other external causes — Toutes autres causes externes	259	4.9	208	3.7	182	3.9	94	1.8

Cause of death — Cause de décès	Hungary - Hongrie 2016 (C)				Iceland - Islande 2015 (C)			
	Male — Masculin		Female — Féminin		Male — Masculin		Female — Féminin	
	Number Nombre	Rate Taux	Number Nombre	Rate Taux	Number Nombre	Rate Taux	Number Nombre	Rate Taux
TOTAL	62 658	1 338.3	64 395	1 254.7	1 065	644.7	1 117	681.5
Certain infectious and parasitic diseases — Certaines maladies infectieuses et parasitaires								
Total	349	7.5	411	8.0	12	♦7.3	12	♦7.3
Intestinal infectious diseases — Maladies infectieuses intestinales	111	2.4	206	4.0	2	♦1.2	4	♦2.4
Tuberculosis — Tuberculose	36	0.8	12	♦0.2	-	-	2	♦1.2
Tetanus — Tétanos	1	♦0.0	4	♦0.1	-	-	-	-
Diphtheria — Diphtérie	-	-	-	-	-	-	-	-
Whooping cough — Coqueluche	-	-	-	-	-	-	-	-
Meningococcal infection — Infection à méningocoques	4	♦0.1	4	♦0.1	-	-	-	-
Septicaemia — Septicémie	38	0.8	36	0.7	6	♦3.6	5	♦3.1
Acute poliomyelitis — Poliomyélite aiguë	-	-	-	-	-	-	-	-
Measles — Rougeole	-	-	-	-	-	-	-	-
Viral hepatitis — Hépatite virale	88	1.9	88	1.7	2	♦1.2	1	♦0.6
Human immunodeficiency virus [HIV] disease — Maladies dues au virus de l'immunodéficience humaine (VIH)	8	♦0.2	1	♦0.0	-	-	-	-
Malaria — Paludisme	1	♦0.0	1	♦0.0	-	-	-	-
Neoplasms — Tumeurs	18 335	391.6	15 283	297.8	311	188.3	299	182.4
Malignant neoplasms — Tumeurs malignes								
Total	18 020	384.9	14 967	291.6	306	185.2	295	180.0
Malignant neoplasm of lip, oral cavity and pharynx — Tumeur maligne de la lèvre, de la cavité buccale et du pharynx	1 122	24.0	273	5.3	5	♦3.0	2	♦1.2
Malignant neoplasm of oesophagus — Tumeur maligne de l'oesophage	471	10.1	87	1.7	9	♦5.4	5	♦3.1
Malignant neoplasm of stomach — Tumeur maligne de l'estomac	930	19.9	649	12.6	11	♦6.7	12	♦7.3
Malignant neoplasm of colon, rectosigmoid junction, rectum, anus and anal canal — Tumeur maligne du côlon, de la jonction recto-sigmoïdienne, du rectum, de l'anus et du canal anal	2 845	60.8	2 214	43.1	40	24.2	30	♦18.3
Malignant neoplasm of liver and intrahepatic bile ducts — Tumeur maligne du foie et des voies bilaires intrahépatiques	581	12.4	269	5.2	10	♦6.1	9	♦5.5
Malignant neoplasm of pancreas — Tumeur maligne du pancréas	1 056	22.6	1 122	21.9	25	♦15.1	28	♦17.1
Malignant neoplasm of trachea, bronchus and lung — Tumeur maligne de la trachée, des bronches et du poumon	5 542	118.4	3 341	65.1	48	29.1	69	42.1
Malignant neoplasm of female breast — Tumeur maligne du sein chez la femme	..	..	2 223	50.1	..	..	55	42.0
Malignant neoplasm of cervix uteri — Tumeur maligne du col de l'utérus	..	..	396	8.9	..	..	4	♦3.1
Malignant neoplasm of prostate — Tumeur maligne de la prostate	1 301	81.4	..	..	56	110.2	..	..
Malignant neoplasm of lymphoid, haematopoietic and related tissue — Tumeurs malignes primitives ou présumées primitives des tissus lymphoïde, hématopoïétique et apparentés	914	19.5	873	17.0	35	21.2	14	♦8.5
Disorders of the blood and blood-forming organs and certain disorders involving the immune mechanism — Maladies du sang et des organes hématopoïétiques et certains troubles du système immunitaire								
Total	72	1.5	107	2.1	1	♦0.6	4	♦2.4
Anaemias — Anémies	35	0.7	62	1.2	1	♦0.6	1	♦0.6
Endocrine, nutritional and metabolic diseases — Maladies endocriniennes, nutritionnelles et métaboliques								
Total	1 420	30.3	1 725	33.6	21	♦12.7	14	♦8.5
Diabetes mellitus — Diabète sucré	1 265	27.0	1 521	29.6	15	♦9.1	8	♦4.9
Malnutrition — Malnutrition	7	♦0.1	5	♦0.1	1	♦0.6	1	♦0.6
Mental and behavioural disorders — Troubles mentaux et du comportement	1 292	27.6	2 072	40.4	33	20.0	46	28.1
Diseases of the nervous system — Maladies du système nerveux	936	20.0	981	19.1	88	53.3	125	76.3
Diseases of the circulatory system — Maladies de l'appareil circulatoire								
Total	27 919	596.3	34 927	680.6	383	231.9	362	220.8
Acute rheumatic fever and chronic rheumatic heart diseases — Rhumatisme articularie aigu et cardiopathies rhumatismales chroniques	66	1.4	196	3.8	1	♦0.6	1	♦0.6
Hypertensive diseases — Maladies hypertensives	3 370	72.0	5 902	115.0	3	♦1.8	22	♦13.4
Ischaemic heart disease — Cardiopathie ischémique	14 454	308.7	16 830	327.9	194	117.4	120	73.2
Cerebrovascular disease — Maladie cérébrovasculaire	4 713	100.7	5 988	116.7	66	40.0	88	53.7

20. Death and death rates by cause and sex: 2012 - 2016
Décès et taux de mortalité par cause et sexe : 2012 - 2016 (continued - suite)

	Hungary - Hongrie				Iceland - Islande			
Cause of death — Cause de décès	2016 (C)				2015 (C)			
	Male — Masculin		Female — Féminin		Male — Masculin		Female — Féminin	
	Number Nombre	Rate Taux	Number Nombre	Rate Taux	Number Nombre	Rate Taux	Number Nombre	Rate Taux
Diseases of arteries, arterioles and capillaries — Maladies des artères, artérioles et capillaires	1 475	31.5	1 748	34.1	18	♦10.9	9	♦5.5
Diseases of the respiratory system — Maladies de l'appareil respiratoire								
Total	3 920	83.7	3 285	64.0	65	39.3	101	61.6
Influenza — Grippe	8	♦0.2	-	-	1	♦0.6	3	♦1.8
Pneumonia — Pneumopathies	499	10.7	499	9.7	23	♦13.9	33	20.1
Chronic lower respiratory diseases — Maladies chroniques des voies respiratoires inférieures	3 061	65.4	2 494	48.6	32	19.4	55	33.6
Diseases of the digestive system — Maladies de l'appareil digestif								
Total	3 646	77.9	2 556	49.8	34	20.6	45	27.5
Gastric and duodenal ulcer — Ulcère de l'estomac et du duodénum	361	7.7	347	6.8	3	♦1.8	1	♦0.6
Diseases of the liver — Maladies du foie	2 284	48.8	893	17.4	7	♦4.2	7	♦4.3
Diseases of the musculoskeletal system and connective tissue — Maladies du système ostéo-articularie, des muscles et du tissu conjonctif	113	2.4	283	5.5	3	♦1.8	10	♦6.1
Diseases of the genitourinary system — Maladies de l'appareil génito-urinaire								
Total	417	8.9	420	8.2	15	♦9.1	17	♦10.4
Disorders of kidney and ureter — Affections du rein et de l'uretère	193	4.1	280	5.5	12	♦7.3	13	♦7.9
Hyperplasia of prostate — Hyperplasie de la prostate	127	7.9	..	..	1	♦2.0	..	..
Pregnancy, childbirth and the puerperium — Grossesse, accouchement et puerpéralité								
Total	..	..	11	♦11.5	..	..	-	-
Pregnancy with abortive outcome — Grossesse se terminant par un avortement	..	..	-	-	..	..	-	-
Other direct obstetric causes — Autres décès maternels directs	..	..	9	♦9.4	..	..	-	-
Indirect obstetric causes — Décès maternels indirects	..	..	2	♦2.1	..	..	-	-
Certain conditions originating in the perinatal period — Certaines affections dont l'origine se situe dans la période périnatale	107	218.6	90	194.0	1	♦47.2	4	♦199.0
Congenital malformations, deformations and chromosomal abnormalities — Malformations congénitales et anomalies chromosomiques	169	345.2	124	267.2	4	♦188.8	3	♦149.3
Symptoms, signs and abnormal clinical and laboratory findings, not elsewhere classified — Symptômes, signes et résultats anormaux d'examens cliniques et de laboratoire, non classés ailleurs	106	2.3	127	2.5	11	♦6.7	18	♦11.0
All other diseases — Toutes autres maladies	59	1.3	92	1.8	2	♦1.2	2	♦1.2
External causes — Causes externes								
Total	3 798	81.1	1 901	37.0	81	49.0	55	33.6
Accidents								
Total	2 266	48.4	1 334	26.0	42	25.4	38	23.2
Transport accidents — Accidents de transport	666	14.2	195	3.8	14	♦8.5	2	♦1.2
Falls — Chutes	898	19.2	806	15.7	8	♦4.8	7	♦4.3
Accidental drowning and submersion — Noyade et submersion accidentelles	98	2.1	27	♦0.5	1	♦0.6	-	-
Exposure to smoke, fire and flames — Exposition à la fumée, au feu et aux flammes	58	1.2	43	0.8	-	-	-	-
Accidental poisoning by and exposure to noxious substances — Intoxication accidentelle par des substances nocives et exposition à ces substances	77	1.6	27	♦0.5	5	♦3.0	11	♦6.7
Intentional self-harm — Lésions auto-infligées	1 316	28.1	446	8.7	29	♦17.6	11	♦6.7
Assault — Agresssions	60	1.3	39	0.8	3	♦1.8	-	-
All other external causes — Toutes autres causes externes	156	3.3	82	1.6	7	♦4.2	6	♦3.7

Cause of death — Cause de décès	Iceland - Islande 2016 (C)				Ireland - Irlande 2013 (+C)			
	Male — Masculin		Female — Féminin		Male — Masculin		Female — Féminin	
	Number Nombre	Rate Taux	Number Nombre	Rate Taux	Number Nombre	Rate Taux	Number Nombre	Rate Taux
TOTAL	1 197	715.6	1 113	673.5	14 958	655.1	14 546	625.3
Certain infectious and parasitic diseases — Certaines maladies infectieuses et parasitaires								
Total	11	♦6.6	5	♦3.0	119	5.2	126	5.4
Intestinal infectious diseases — Maladies infectieuses intestinales	2	♦1.2	1	♦0.6	14	♦0.6	30	♦1.3
Tuberculosis — Tuberculose	-	-	-	-	12	♦0.5	5	♦0.2
Tetanus — Tétanos	-	-	-	-	-	-	-	-
Diphtheria — Diphtérie	-	-	-	-	-	-	-	-
Whooping cough — Coqueluche	-	-	-	-	-	-	-	-
Meningococcal infection — Infection à méningocoques	-	-	-	-	2	♦0.1	1	♦0.0
Septicaemia — Septicémie	3	♦1.8	4	♦2.4	42	1.8	49	2.1
Acute poliomyelitis — Poliomyélite aiguë	-	-	-	-	-	-	1	♦0.0
Measles — Rougeole	-	-	-	-	-	-	-	-
Viral hepatitis — Hépatite virale	-	-	-	-	20	♦0.9	7	♦0.3
Human immunodeficiency virus [HIV] disease — Maladies dues au virus de l'immunodéficience humaine (VIH)	-	-	-	-	7	♦0.3	3	♦0.1
Malaria — Paludisme	-	-	-	-	-	-	-	-
Neoplasms — Tumeurs	350	209.2	332	200.9	4 742	207.7	4 219	181.4
Malignant neoplasms — Tumeurs malignes								
Total	347	207.4	328	198.5	4 606	201.7	4 119	177.1
Malignant neoplasm of lip, oral cavity and pharynx — Tumeur maligne de la lèvre, de la cavité buccale et du pharynx	5	♦3.0	6	♦3.6	117	5.1	46	2.0
Malignant neoplasm of oesophagus — Tumeur maligne de l'oesophage	13	♦7.8	8	♦4.8	258	11.3	114	4.9
Malignant neoplasm of stomach — Tumeur maligne de l'estomac	5	♦3.0	11	♦6.7	179	7.8	119	5.1
Malignant neoplasm of colon, rectosigmoid junction, rectum, anus and anal canal — Tumeur maligne du côlon, de la jonction recto-sigmoïdienne, du rectum, de l'anus et du canal anal	40	23.9	34	20.6	592	25.9	440	18.9
Malignant neoplasm of liver and intrahepatic bile ducts — Tumeur maligne du foie et des voies bilaires intrahépatiques	15	♦9.0	5	♦3.0	184	8.1	122	5.2
Malignant neoplasm of pancreas — Tumeur maligne du pancréas	29	♦17.3	21	♦12.7	237	10.4	258	11.1
Malignant neoplasm of trachea, bronchus and lung — Tumeur maligne de la trachée, des bronches et du poumon	73	43.6	82	49.6	1 074	47.0	757	32.5
Malignant neoplasm of female breast — Tumeur maligne du sein chez la femme	..	..	51	38.4	..	..	704	...
Malignant neoplasm of cervix uteri — Tumeur maligne du col de l'utérus	..	..	2	♦1.5	..	..	76	...
Malignant neoplasm of prostate — Tumeur maligne de la prostate	64	122.8	...	...	499	...	..	..
Malignant neoplasm of lymphoid, haematopoietic and related tissue — Tumeurs malignes primitives ou présumées primitives des tissus lymphoïde, hématopoïétique et apparentés	30	♦17.9	17	♦10.3	382	16.7	340	14.6
Disorders of the blood and blood-forming organs and certain disorders involving the immune mechanism — Maladies du sang et des organes hématopoïétiques et certains troubles du système immunitaire								
Total	5	♦3.0	6	♦3.6	36	1.6	66	2.8
Anaemias — Anémies	3	♦1.8	5	♦3.0	17	♦0.7	39	1.7
Endocrine, nutritional and metabolic diseases — Maladies endocriniennes, nutritionnelles et métaboliques								
Total	33	19.7	15	♦9.1	385	16.9	369	15.9
Diabetes mellitus — Diabète sucré	23	♦13.8	9	♦5.4	320	14.0	253	10.9
Malnutrition — Malnutrition	2	♦1.2	3	♦1.8	-	-	2	♦0.1
Mental and behavioural disorders — Troubles mentaux et du comportement	30	♦17.9	36	21.8	387	16.9	820	35.2
Diseases of the nervous system — Maladies du système nerveux	102	61.0	155	93.8	602	26.4	776	33.4
Diseases of the circulatory system — Maladies de l'appareil circulatoire								
Total	401	239.7	337	203.9	4 791	209.8	4 682	201.3
Acute rheumatic fever and chronic rheumatic heart diseases — Rhumatisme articularie aigu et cardiopathies rhumatismales chroniques	-	-	1	♦0.6	18	♦0.8	33	1.4
Hypertensive diseases — Maladies hypertensives	18	♦10.8	29	♦17.5	117	5.1	191	8.2
Ischaemic heart disease — Cardiopathie ischémique	196	117.2	110	66.6	2 707	118.5	1 935	83.2
Cerebrovascular disease — Maladie cérébrovasculaire	61	36.5	68	41.1	803	35.2	1 156	49.7

20. Death and death rates by cause and sex: 2012 - 2016
Décès et taux de mortalité par cause et sexe : 2012 - 2016 (continued - suite)

	Iceland - Islande 2016 (C)				Ireland - Irlande 2013 (+C)			
Cause of death — Cause de décès	Male — Masculin		Female — Féminin		Male — Masculin		Female — Féminin	
	Number Nombre	Rate Taux	Number Nombre	Rate Taux	Number Nombre	Rate Taux	Number Nombre	Rate Taux
Diseases of arteries, arterioles and capillaries — Maladies des artères, artérioles et capillaires	13	♦7.8	12	♦7.3	268	11.7	227	9.8
Diseases of the respiratory system — Maladies de l'appareil respiratoire								
Total	84	50.2	105	63.5	1 685	73.8	1 819	78.2
Influenza — Grippe	-	-	3	♦1.8	6	♦0.3	10	♦0.4
Pneumonia — Pneumopathies	30	♦17.9	35	21.2	410	18.0	573	24.6
Chronic lower respiratory diseases — Maladies chroniques des voies respiratoires inférieures	44	26.3	59	35.7	808	35.4	849	36.5
Diseases of the digestive system — Maladies de l'appareil digestif								
Total	27	♦16.1	29	♦17.5	533	23.3	536	23.0
Gastric and duodenal ulcer — Ulcère de l'estomac et du duodénum	1	♦0.6	1	♦0.6	31	1.4	33	1.4
Diseases of the liver — Maladies du foie	5	♦3.0	7	♦4.2	239	10.5	127	5.5
Diseases of the musculoskeletal system and connective tissue — Maladies du système ostéo-articulaire, des muscles et du tissu conjonctif	5	♦3.0	8	♦4.8	60	2.6	160	6.9
Diseases of the genitourinary system — Maladies de l'appareil génito-urinaire								
Total	14	♦8.4	17	♦10.3	309	13.5	324	13.9
Disorders of kidney and ureter — Affections du rein et de l'uretère	9	♦5.4	11	♦6.7	264	11.6	210	9.0
Hyperplasia of prostate — Hyperplasie de la prostate	1	♦1.9	..	..	7	...	..	..
Pregnancy, childbirth and the puerperium — Grossesse, accouchement et puerpéralité								
Total	..	..	-	-	..	..	3	♦4.4
Pregnancy with abortive outcome — Grossesse se terminant par un avortement	..	..	-	-	..	..	-	-
Other direct obstetric causes — Autres décès maternels directs	..	..	-	-	..	..	2	♦2.9
Indirect obstetric causes — Décès maternels indirects	..	..	-	-	..	..	1	♦1.5
Certain conditions originating in the perinatal period — Certaines affections dont l'origine se situe dans la période périnatale	1	♦49.0	-	-	64	181.4	43	127.8
Congenital malformations, deformations and chromosomal abnormalities — Malformations congénitales et anomalies chromosomiques	2	♦97.9	5	♦251.0	114	323.2	82	243.6
Symptoms, signs and abnormal clinical and laboratory findings, not elsewhere classified — Symptômes, signes et résultats anormaux d'examens cliniques et de laboratoire, non classés ailleurs	15	♦9.0	14	♦8.5	46	2.0	61	2.6
All other diseases — Toutes autres maladies	1	♦0.6	2	♦1.2	21	♦0.9	33	1.4
External causes — Causes externes								
Total	116	69.3	47	28.4	1 064	46.6	427	18.4
Accidents								
Total	67	40.1	41	24.8	596	26.1	302	13.0
Transport accidents — Accidents de transport	16	♦9.6	6	♦3.6	128	5.6	39	1.7
Falls — Chutes	12	♦7.2	9	♦5.4	103	4.5	94	4.0
Accidental drowning and submersion — Noyade et submersion accidentelles	5	♦3.0	-	-	44	1.9	7	♦0.3
Exposure to smoke, fire and flames — Exposition à la fumée, au feu et aux flammes	1	♦0.6	-	-	13	♦0.6	12	♦0.5
Accidental poisoning by and exposure to noxious substances — Intoxication accidentelle par des substances nocives et exposition à ces substances	14	♦8.4	5	♦3.0	203	8.9	79	3.4
Intentional self-harm — Lésions auto-infligées	36	21.5	4	♦2.4	391	17.1	96	4.1
Assault — Agresssions	-	-	1	♦0.6	22	♦1.0	4	♦0.2
All other external causes — Toutes autres causes externes	13	♦7.8	1	♦0.6	55	2.4	25	♦1.1

Cause of death — Cause de décès	Ireland - Irlande 2014 (+C)				Italy - Italie 2014 (C)			
	Male — Masculin		Female — Féminin		Male — Masculin		Female — Féminin	
	Number Nombre	Rate Taux	Number Nombre	Rate Taux	Number Nombre	Rate Taux	Number Nombre	Rate Taux
TOTAL	14 897	648.9	14 355	612.9	289 800	982.9	308 870	986.9
Certain infectious and parasitic diseases — Certaines maladies infectieuses et parasitaires								
Total	131	5.7	165	7.0	6 378	21.6	6 839	21.9
Intestinal infectious diseases — Maladies infectieuses intestinales	15	♦0.7	38	1.6	323	1.1	508	1.6
Tuberculosis — Tuberculose	6	♦0.3	9	♦0.4	139	0.5	90	0.3
Tetanus — Tétanos	-	-	-	-	3	♦0.0	6	♦0.0
Diphtheria — Diphtérie	-	-	-	-	-	-	-	-
Whooping cough — Coqueluche	-	-	-	-	1	♦0.0	-	-
Meningococcal infection — Infection à méningocoques	-	-	2	♦0.1	9	♦0.0	10	♦0.0
Septicaemia — Septicémie	56	2.4	85	3.6	3 536	12.0	4 100	13.1
Acute poliomyelitis — Poliomyélite aiguë	-	-	-	-	-	-	-	-
Measles — Rougeole	-	-	-	-	-	-	-	-
Viral hepatitis — Hépatite virale	16	♦0.7	8	♦0.3	1 328	4.5	1 491	4.8
Human immunodeficiency virus [HIV] disease — Maladies dues au virus de l'immunodéficience humaine (VIH)	7	♦0.3	1	♦0.0	561	1.9	161	0.5
Malaria — Paludisme	1	♦0.0	-	-	3	♦0.0	-	-
Neoplasms — Tumeurs	4 840	210.8	4 380	187.0	99 415	337.2	77 892	248.9
Malignant neoplasms — Tumeurs malignes								
Total	4 724	205.8	4 298	183.5	94 933	322.0	74 165	237.0
Malignant neoplasm of lip, oral cavity and pharynx — Tumeur maligne de la lèvre, de la cavité buccale et du pharynx	116	5.1	51	2.2	2 011	6.8	906	2.9
Malignant neoplasm of oesophagus — Tumeur maligne de l'oesophage	270	11.8	114	4.9	1 359	4.6	466	1.5
Malignant neoplasm of stomach — Tumeur maligne de l'estomac	225	9.8	144	6.1	5 703	19.3	3 854	12.3
Malignant neoplasm of colon, rectosigmoid junction, rectum, anus and anal canal — Tumeur maligne du côlon, de la jonction recto-sigmoïdienne, du rectum, de l'anus et du canal anal	555	24.2	432	18.4	10 104	34.3	8 567	27.4
Malignant neoplasm of liver and intrahepatic bile ducts — Tumeur maligne du foie et des voies bilaires intrahépatiques	187	8.1	139	5.9	6 576	22.3	3 339	10.7
Malignant neoplasm of pancreas — Tumeur maligne du pancréas	274	11.9	240	10.2	5 410	18.3	5 776	18.5
Malignant neoplasm of trachea, bronchus and lung — Tumeur maligne de la trachée, des bronches et du poumon	1 062	46.3	872	37.2	24 177	82.0	9 209	29.4
Malignant neoplasm of female breast — Tumeur maligne du sein chez la femme	..	..	735	...	..	..	12 201	44.8
Malignant neoplasm of cervix uteri — Tumeur maligne du col de l'utérus	..	..	96	...	..	..	459	1.7
Malignant neoplasm of prostate — Tumeur maligne de la prostate	540	...	..	..	7 174	62.1	..	..
Malignant neoplasm of lymphoid, haematopoietic and related tissue — Tumeurs malignes primitives ou présumées primitives des tissus lymphoïde, hématopoïétique et apparentés	433	18.9	292	12.5	7 955	27.0	6 824	21.8
Disorders of the blood and blood-forming organs and certain disorders involving the immune mechanism — Maladies du sang et des organes hématopoïétiques et certains troubles du système immunitaire								
Total	38	1.7	51	2.2	1 127	3.8	1 711	5.5
Anaemias — Anémies	16	♦0.7	26	♦1.1	728	2.5	1 244	4.0
Endocrine, nutritional and metabolic diseases — Maladies endocriniennes, nutritionnelles et métaboliques								
Total	361	15.7	319	13.6	11 296	38.3	14 829	47.4
Diabetes mellitus — Diabète sucré	271	11.8	211	9.0	8 858	30.0	11 325	36.2
Malnutrition — Malnutrition	1	♦0.0	1	♦0.0	168	0.6	336	1.1
Mental and behavioural disorders — Troubles mentaux et du comportement	473	20.6	879	37.5	5 952	20.2	11 645	37.2
Diseases of the nervous system — Maladies du système nerveux	657	28.6	763	32.6	10 324	35.0	14 091	45.0
Diseases of the circulatory system — Maladies de l'appareil circulatoire								
Total	4 448	193.7	4 404	188.0	96 066	325.8	124 127	396.6
Acute rheumatic fever and chronic rheumatic heart diseases — Rhumatisme articularie aigu et cardiopathies rhumatismales chroniques	22	♦1.0	36	1.5	651	2.2	1 445	4.6
Hypertensive diseases — Maladies hypertensives	98	4.3	183	7.8	10 597	35.9	20 086	64.2
Ischaemic heart disease — Cardiopathie ischémique	2 498	108.8	1 785	76.2	35 714	121.1	33 939	108.4
Cerebrovascular disease — Maladie cérébrovasculaire	752	32.8	1 100	47.0	22 609	76.7	34 621	110.6

20. Death and death rates by cause and sex: 2012 - 2016
Décès et taux de mortalité par cause et sexe : 2012 - 2016 (continued - suite)

Cause of death — Cause de décès	Ireland - Irlande 2014 (+C)				Italy - Italie 2014 (C)			
	Male — Masculin		Female — Féminin		Male — Masculin		Female — Féminin	
	Number Nombre	Rate Taux	Number Nombre	Rate Taux	Number Nombre	Rate Taux	Number Nombre	Rate Taux
Diseases of arteries, arterioles and capillaries — Maladies des artères, artérioles et capillaires	222	9.7	223	9.5	3 995	13.5	3 270	10.4
Diseases of the respiratory system — Maladies de l'appareil respiratoire								
Total	1 713	74.6	1 779	76.0	22 532	76.4	19 011	60.7
Influenza — Grippe	12	♦0.5	17	♦0.7	93	0.3	166	0.5
Pneumonia — Pneumopathies	439	19.1	564	24.1	4 429	15.0	4 712	15.1
Chronic lower respiratory diseases — Maladies chroniques des voies respiratoires inférieures	773	33.7	778	33.2	12 035	40.8	8 199	26.2
Diseases of the digestive system — Maladies de l'appareil digestif								
Total	549	23.9	490	20.9	11 120	37.7	11 452	36.6
Gastric and duodenal ulcer — Ulcère de l'estomac et du duodénum	35	1.5	39	1.7	309	1.0	314	1.0
Diseases of the liver — Maladies du foie	222	9.7	98	4.2	4 767	16.2	2 966	9.5
Diseases of the musculoskeletal system and connective tissue — Maladies du système ostéo-articularie, des muscles et du tissu conjonctif	70	3.0	164	7.0	959	3.3	2 164	6.9
Diseases of the genitourinary system — Maladies de l'appareil génito-urinaire								
Total	299	13.0	315	13.5	5 623	19.1	6 404	20.5
Disorders of kidney and ureter — Affections du rein et de l'uretère	221	9.6	197	8.4	4 664	15.8	5 379	17.2
Hyperplasia of prostate — Hyperplasie de la prostate	18	...	..	..	184	1.6	..	..
Pregnancy, childbirth and the puerperium — Grossesse, accouchement et puerpéralité								
Total	..	..	1	♦1.5	..	..	6	♦1.2
Pregnancy with abortive outcome — Grossesse se terminant par un avortement	..	..	..	..	..	..	2	♦0.4
Other direct obstetric causes — Autres décès maternels directs	..	..	1	♦1.5	..	..	4	♦0.8
Indirect obstetric causes — Décès maternels indirects	..	..	-	-	..	..	-	-
Certain conditions originating in the perinatal period — Certaines affections dont l'origine se situe dans la période périnatale	54	155.7	46	141.1	499	193.0	401	164.3
Congenital malformations, deformations and chromosomal abnormalities — Malformations congénitales et anomalies chromosomiques	100	288.4	75	230.0	680	263.0	596	244.2
Symptoms, signs and abnormal clinical and laboratory findings, not elsewhere classified — Symptômes, signes et résultats anormaux d'examens cliniques et de laboratoire, non classés ailleurs	44	1.9	53	2.3	4 221	14.3	7 266	23.2
All other diseases — Toutes autres maladies	23	♦1.0	38	1.6	374	1.3	782	2.5
External causes — Causes externes								
Total	1 097	47.8	433	18.5	13 234	44.9	9 654	30.8
Accidents								
Total	621	27.0	323	13.8	9 187	31.2	7 569	24.2
Transport accidents — Accidents de transport	121	5.3	48	2.0	2 884	9.8	838	2.7
Falls — Chutes	145	6.3	121	5.2	1 938	6.6	1 748	5.6
Accidental drowning and submersion — Noyade et submersion accidentelles	44	1.9	10	♦0.4	269	0.9	67	0.2
Exposure to smoke, fire and flames — Exposition à la fumée, au feu et aux flammes	18	♦0.8	15	♦0.6	131	0.4	86	0.3
Accidental poisoning by and exposure to noxious substances — Intoxication accidentelle par des substances nocives et exposition à ces substances	181	7.9	69	2.9	345	1.2	134	0.4
Intentional self-harm — Lésions auto-infligées	399	17.4	87	3.7	3 214	10.9	931	3.0
Assault — Agresssions	27	♦1.2	5	♦0.2	259	0.9	119	0.4
All other external causes — Toutes autres causes externes	50	2.2	18	♦0.8	574	1.9	1 035	3.3

Cause of death — Cause de décès	Italy - Italie				Latvia - Lettonie			
	2015 (C)				2014 (+C)			
	Male — Masculin		Female — Féminin		Male — Masculin		Female — Féminin	
	Number Nombre	Rate Taux	Number Nombre	Rate Taux	Number Nombre	Rate Taux	Number Nombre	Rate Taux
TOTAL	307 392	1 042.0	338 656	1 082.2	13 557	1 483.1	14 644	1 356.4
Certain infectious and parasitic diseases — Certaines maladies infectieuses et parasitaires								
Total	7 408	25.1	8 402	26.8	184	20.1	105	9.7
Intestinal infectious diseases — Maladies infectieuses intestinales	379	1.3	609	1.9	1	♦0.1	3	♦0.3
Tuberculosis — Tuberculose	161	0.5	112	0.4	37	4.0	10	♦0.9
Tetanus — Tétanos	5	♦0.0	14	♦0.0	-	-	-	-
Diphtheria — Diphtérie	-	-	-	-	-	-	1	♦0.1
Whooping cough — Coqueluche	-	-	2	♦0.0	-	-	-	-
Meningococcal infection — Infection à méningocoques	6	♦0.0	10	♦0.0	-	-	-	-
Septicaemia — Septicémie	4 385	14.9	5 344	17.1	15	♦1.6	18	♦1.7
Acute poliomyelitis — Poliomyélite aiguë	-	-	-	-	-	-	-	-
Measles — Rougeole	-	-	1	♦0.0	-	-	-	-
Viral hepatitis — Hépatite virale	1 354	4.6	1 531	4.9	28	♦3.1	18	♦1.7
Human immunodeficiency virus [HIV] disease — Maladies dues au virus de l'immunodéficience humaine (VIH)	536	1.8	168	0.5	70	7.7	32	3.0
Malaria — Paludisme	2	♦0.0	-	-	-	-	-	-
Neoplasms — Tumeurs	99 437	337.1	79 443	253.9	3 273	358.0	2 807	260.0
Malignant neoplasms — Tumeurs malignes								
Total	94 870	321.6	75 469	241.2	3 233	353.7	2 739	253.7
Malignant neoplasm of lip, oral cavity and pharynx — Tumeur maligne de la lèvre, de la cavité buccale et du pharynx	1 899	6.4	990	3.2	154	16.8	37	3.4
Malignant neoplasm of oesophagus — Tumeur maligne de l'oesophage	1 359	4.6	485	1.5	113	12.4	20	♦1.9
Malignant neoplasm of stomach — Tumeur maligne de l'estomac	5 491	18.6	3 933	12.6	252	27.6	202	18.7
Malignant neoplasm of colon, rectosigmoid junction, rectum, anus and anal canal — Tumeur maligne du côlon, de la jonction recto-sigmoïdienne, du rectum, de l'anus et du canal anal	10 110	34.3	8 869	28.3	336	36.8	353	32.7
Malignant neoplasm of liver and intrahepatic bile ducts — Tumeur maligne du foie et des voies biliaires intrahépatiques	6 369	21.6	3 333	10.7	85	9.3	65	6.0
Malignant neoplasm of pancreas — Tumeur maligne du pancréas	5 555	18.8	5 945	19.0	173	18.9	202	18.7
Malignant neoplasm of trachea, bronchus and lung — Tumeur maligne de la trachée, des bronches et du poumon	24 405	82.7	9 570	30.6	760	83.1	186	17.2
Malignant neoplasm of female breast — Tumeur maligne du sein chez la femme	..	..	12 312	...	..	..	439	46.9
Malignant neoplasm of cervix uteri — Tumeur maligne du col de l'utérus	..	..	442	...	..	..	111	11.9
Malignant neoplasm of prostate — Tumeur maligne de la prostate	7 214	...	..	..	409	132.7	..	..
Malignant neoplasm of lymphoid, haematopoietic and related tissue — Tumeurs malignes primitives ou présumées primitives des tissus lymphoïde, hématopoïétique et apparentés	8 091	27.4	6 721	21.5	195	21.3	238	22.0
Disorders of the blood and blood-forming organs and certain disorders involving the immune mechanism — Maladies du sang et des organes hématopoïétiques et certains troubles du système immunitaire								
Total	1 229	4.2	1 909	6.1	16	♦1.8	24	♦2.2
Anaemias — Anémies	808	2.7	1 377	4.4	10	♦1.1	15	♦1.4
Endocrine, nutritional and metabolic diseases — Maladies endocriniennes, nutritionnelles et métaboliques								
Total	12 646	42.9	16 612	53.1	187	20.5	342	31.7
Diabetes mellitus — Diabète sucré	9 882	33.5	12 364	39.5	178	19.5	326	30.2
Malnutrition — Malnutrition	205	0.7	376	1.2	1	♦0.1	1	♦0.1
Mental and behavioural disorders — Troubles mentaux et du comportement	6 946	23.5	14 451	46.2	145	15.9	161	14.9
Diseases of the nervous system — Maladies du système nerveux	11 918	40.4	16 220	51.8	150	16.4	156	14.4
Diseases of the circulatory system — Maladies de l'appareil circulatoire								
Total	103 247	350.0	136 267	435.4	6 699	732.8	9 372	868.1
Acute rheumatic fever and chronic rheumatic heart diseases — Rhumatisme articulaire aigu et cardiopathies rhumatismales chroniques	696	2.4	1 547	4.9	9	♦1.0	40	3.7
Hypertensive diseases — Maladies hypertensives	11 838	40.1	22 929	73.3	374	40.9	703	65.1
Ischaemic heart disease — Cardiopathie ischémique	37 366	126.7	35 806	114.4	3 551	388.5	4 536	420.1
Cerebrovascular disease — Maladie cérébrovasculaire	24 342	82.5	37 442	119.6	1 717	187.8	3 157	292.4

Cause of death — Cause de décès	Italy - Italie 2015 (C)				Latvia - Lettonie 2014 (+C)			
	Male — Masculin		Female — Féminin		Male — Masculin		Female — Féminin	
	Number Nombre	Rate Taux	Number Nombre	Rate Taux	Number Nombre	Rate Taux	Number Nombre	Rate Taux
Diseases of arteries, arterioles and capillaries — Maladies des artères, artérioles et capillaires	4 056	13.7	3 444	11.0	202	22.1	228	21.1
Diseases of the respiratory system — Maladies de l'appareil respiratoire								
Total	25 512	86.5	23 006	73.5	476	52.1	220	20.4
Influenza — Grippe	196	0.7	378	1.2	-	-	2	♦0.2
Pneumonia — Pneumopathies	5 491	18.6	6 141	19.6	220	24.1	126	11.7
Chronic lower respiratory diseases — Maladies chroniques des voies respiratoires inférieures	12 953	43.9	9 545	30.5	218	23.8	64	5.9
Diseases of the digestive system — Maladies de l'appareil digestif								
Total	11 419	38.7	11 867	37.9	529	57.9	460	42.6
Gastric and duodenal ulcer — Ulcère de l'estomac et du duodénum	356	1.2	326	1.0	66	7.2	75	6.9
Diseases of the liver — Maladies du foie	4 668	15.8	2 944	9.4	249	27.2	164	15.2
Diseases of the musculoskeletal system and connective tissue — Maladies du système ostéo-articularie, des muscles et du tissu conjonctif	980	3.3	2 492	8.0	25	♦2.7	46	4.3
Diseases of the genitourinary system — Maladies de l'appareil génito-urinaire								
Total	6 315	21.4	7 303	23.3	186	20.3	188	17.4
Disorders of kidney and ureter — Affections du rein et de l'uretère	5 125	17.4	5 963	19.1	113	12.4	152	14.1
Hyperplasia of prostate — Hyperplasie de la prostate	258	...	..	..	46	14.9	..	..
Pregnancy, childbirth and the puerperium — Grossesse, accouchement et puerpéralité								
Total	..	..	16	♦3.3	..	..	2	♦9.2
Pregnancy with abortive outcome — Grossesse se terminant par un avortement	..	..	1	♦0.2	..	..	-	-
Other direct obstetric causes — Autres décès maternels directs	..	..	15	♦3.1	..	..	1	♦4.6
Indirect obstetric causes — Décès maternels indirects	..	..	-	-	..	..	1	♦4.6
Certain conditions originating in the perinatal period — Certaines affections dont l'origine se situe dans la période périnatale	464	185.6	393	166.6	26	♦231.5	16	♦152.1
Congenital malformations, deformations and chromosomal abnormalities — Malformations congénitales et anomalies chromosomiques	753	301.3	641	271.8	27	♦240.4	20	♦190.2
Symptoms, signs and abnormal clinical and laboratory findings, not elsewhere classified — Symptômes, signes et résultats anormaux d'examens cliniques et de laboratoire, non classés ailleurs	4 964	16.8	8 512	27.2	191	20.9	215	19.9
All other diseases — Toutes autres maladies	439	1.5	909	2.9	24	♦2.6	59	5.5
External causes — Causes externes								
Total	13 715	46.5	10 213	32.6	1 419	155.2	451	41.8
Accidents								
Total	9 688	32.8	8 088	25.8	863	94.4	283	26.2
Transport accidents — Accidents de transport	2 970	10.1	783	2.5	182	19.9	58	5.4
Falls — Chutes	2 105	7.1	1 853	5.9	115	12.6	62	5.7
Accidental drowning and submersion — Noyade et submersion accidentelles	283	1.0	77	0.2	152	16.6	30	♦2.8
Exposure to smoke, fire and flames — Exposition à la fumée, au feu et aux flammes	136	0.5	95	0.3	73	8.0	37	3.4
Accidental poisoning by and exposure to noxious substances — Intoxication accidentelle par des substances nocives et exposition à ces substances	345	1.2	167	0.5	121	13.2	29	♦2.7
Intentional self-harm — Lésions auto-infligées	3 104	10.5	884	2.8	311	34.0	71	6.6
Assault — Agresssions	280	0.9	112	0.4	97	10.6	40	3.7
All other external causes — Toutes autres causes externes	643	2.2	1 129	3.6	148	16.2	57	5.3

Cause of death — Cause de décès	Latvia - Lettonie 2015 (+C)				Lithuania - Lituanie 2015 (+C)			
	Male — Masculin		Female — Féminin		Male — Masculin		Female — Féminin	
	Number Nombre	Rate Taux	Number Nombre	Rate Taux	Number Nombre	Rate Taux	Number Nombre	Rate Taux
TOTAL	13 164	1 444.7	15 021	1 397.4	20 529	1 534.4	21 247	1 355.9
Certain infectious and parasitic diseases — Certaines maladies infectieuses et parasitaires								
Total	203	22.3	106	9.9	428	32.0	307	19.6
Intestinal infectious diseases — Maladies infectieuses intestinales	2	+0.2	5	+0.5	7	+0.5	10	+0.6
Tuberculosis — Tuberculose	73	8.0	14	+1.3	146	10.9	40	2.6
Tetanus — Tétanos	-	-	-	-	-	-	-	-
Diphtheria — Diphtérie	1	+0.1	-	-	-	-	-	-
Whooping cough — Coqueluche	-	-	-	-	-	-	1	+0.1
Meningococcal infection — Infection à méningocoques	-	-	-	-	-	-	6	+0.4
Septicaemia — Septicémie	10	+1.1	20	+1.9	227	17.0	218	13.9
Acute poliomyelitis — Poliomyélite aiguë	-	-	-	-	-	-	-	-
Measles — Rougeole	-	-	-	-	-	-	-	-
Viral hepatitis — Hépatite virale	36	4.0	18	+1.7	19	+1.4	11	+0.7
Human immunodeficiency virus [HIV] disease — Maladies dues au virus de l'immunodéficience humaine (VIH)	59	6.5	27	+2.5	14	+1.0	2	+0.1
Malaria — Paludisme	-	-	-	-	1	+0.1	-	-
Neoplasms — Tumeurs	3 093	339.4	2 898	269.6	4 714	352.3	3 783	241.4
Malignant neoplasms — Tumeurs malignes								
Total	3 044	334.1	2 832	263.5	4 640	346.8	3 708	236.6
Malignant neoplasm of lip, oral cavity and pharynx — Tumeur maligne de la lèvre, de la cavité buccale et du pharynx	148	16.2	36	3.3	236	17.6	60	3.8
Malignant neoplasm of oesophagus — Tumeur maligne de l'oesophage	106	11.6	21	+2.0	172	12.9	31	2.0
Malignant neoplasm of stomach — Tumeur maligne de l'estomac	278	30.5	194	18.0	414	30.9	269	17.2
Malignant neoplasm of colon, rectosigmoid junction, rectum, anus and anal canal — Tumeur maligne du côlon, de la jonction recto-sigmoïdienne, du rectum, de l'anus et du canal anal	311	34.1	392	36.5	509	38.0	474	30.2
Malignant neoplasm of liver and intrahepatic bile ducts — Tumeur maligne du foie et des voies bilaires intrahépatiques	80	8.8	54	5.0	125	9.3	85	5.4
Malignant neoplasm of pancreas — Tumeur maligne du pancréas	170	18.7	202	18.8	227	17.0	243	15.5
Malignant neoplasm of trachea, bronchus and lung — Tumeur maligne de la trachée, des bronches et du poumon	674	74.0	217	20.2	1 098	82.1	246	15.7
Malignant neoplasm of female breast — Tumeur maligne du sein chez la femme	..	..	445	47.9	..	..	571	42.0
Malignant neoplasm of cervix uteri — Tumeur maligne du col de l'utérus	..	..	117	12.6	..	..	206	15.1
Malignant neoplasm of prostate — Tumeur maligne de la prostate	392	126.9	..	..	544	118.5	..	..
Malignant neoplasm of lymphoid, haematopoietic and related tissue — Tumeurs malignes primitives ou présumées primitives des tissus lymphoïde, hématopoïétique et apparentés	171	18.8	206	19.2	265	19.8	278	17.7
Disorders of the blood and blood-forming organs and certain disorders involving the immune mechanism — Maladies du sang et des organes hématopoïétiques et certains troubles du système immunitaire								
Total	12	+1.3	16	+1.5	20	+1.5	23	+1.5
Anaemias — Anémies	6	+0.7	11	+1.0	11	+0.8	12	+0.8
Endocrine, nutritional and metabolic diseases — Maladies endocriniennes, nutritionnelles et métaboliques								
Total	191	21.0	315	29.3	164	12.3	191	12.2
Diabetes mellitus — Diabète sucré	182	20.0	290	27.0	140	10.5	178	11.4
Malnutrition — Malnutrition	-	-	-	-	1	+0.1	2	+0.1
Mental and behavioural disorders — Troubles mentaux et du comportement	200	21.9	209	19.4	54	4.0	68	4.3
Diseases of the nervous system — Maladies du système nerveux	171	18.8	203	18.9	292	21.8	297	19.0
Diseases of the circulatory system — Maladies de l'appareil circulatoire								
Total	6 573	721.4	9 562	889.6	9 753	729.0	13 836	883.0
Acute rheumatic fever and chronic rheumatic heart diseases — Rhumatisme articulaire aigu et cardiopathies rhumatismales chroniques	13	+1.4	25	+2.3	27	+2.0	57	3.6
Hypertensive diseases — Maladies hypertensives	334	36.7	740	68.8	268	20.0	374	23.9
Ischaemic heart disease — Cardiopathie ischémique	3 498	383.9	4 536	422.0	6 492	485.2	9 074	579.1
Cerebrovascular disease — Maladie cérébrovasculaire	1 730	189.9	3 379	314.4	1 986	148.4	3 708	236.6

Cause of death — Cause de décès	Latvia - Lettonie 2015 (+C)				Lithuania - Lituanie 2015 (+C)			
	Male — Masculin		Female — Féminin		Male — Masculin		Female — Féminin	
	Number Nombre	Rate Taux	Number Nombre	Rate Taux	Number Nombre	Rate Taux	Number Nombre	Rate Taux
Diseases of arteries, arterioles and capillaries — Maladies des artères, artérioles et capillaires	179	19.6	233	21.7	257	19.2	177	11.3
Diseases of the respiratory system — Maladies de l'appareil respiratoire								
Total	475	52.1	237	22.0	891	66.6	466	29.7
Influenza — Grippe	10	♦1.1	10	♦0.9	1	♦0.1	3	♦0.2
Pneumonia — Pneumopathies	209	22.9	130	12.1	335	25.0	220	14.0
Chronic lower respiratory diseases — Maladies chroniques des voies respiratoires inférieures	208	22.8	82	7.6	497	37.1	216	13.8
Diseases of the digestive system — Maladies de l'appareil digestif								
Total	506	55.5	509	47.4	1 120	83.7	978	62.4
Gastric and duodenal ulcer — Ulcère de l'estomac et du duodénum	49	5.4	77	7.2	168	12.6	135	8.6
Diseases of the liver — Maladies du foie	267	29.3	155	14.4	547	40.9	326	20.8
Diseases of the musculoskeletal system and connective tissue — Maladies du système ostéo-articulaire, des muscles et du tissu conjonctif	38	4.2	54	5.0	38	2.8	46	2.9
Diseases of the genitourinary system — Maladies de l'appareil génito-urinaire								
Total	165	18.1	224	20.8	168	12.6	189	12.1
Disorders of kidney and ureter — Affections du rein et de l'uretère	116	12.7	189	17.6	124	9.3	164	10.5
Hyperplasia of prostate — Hyperplasie de la prostate	32	10.4	..	..	18	♦3.9	..	..
Pregnancy, childbirth and the puerperium — Grossesse, accouchement et puerpéralité								
Total	..	..	12	♦54.6	..	..	3	♦9.5
Pregnancy with abortive outcome — Grossesse se terminant par un avortement	..	..	-	-	..	..	-	-
Other direct obstetric causes — Autres décès maternels directs	..	..	9	♦40.9	..	..	3	♦9.5
Indirect obstetric causes — Décès maternels indirects	..	..	3	♦13.6	..	..	-	-
Certain conditions originating in the perinatal period — Certaines affections dont l'origine se situe dans la période périnatale	26	♦227.2	17	♦161.3	29	♦179.0	17	♦111.3
Congenital malformations, deformations and chromosomal abnormalities — Malformations congénitales et anomalies chromosomiques	29	♦253.5	23	♦218.3	45	277.8	37	242.2
Symptoms, signs and abnormal clinical and laboratory findings, not elsewhere classified — Symptômes, signes et résultats anormaux d'examens cliniques et de laboratoire, non classés ailleurs	141	15.5	165	15.4	398	29.7	181	11.6
All other diseases — Toutes autres maladies	22	♦2.4	36	3.3	13	♦1.0	20	♦1.3
External causes — Causes externes								
Total	1 319	144.8	435	40.5	2 402	179.5	805	51.4
Accidents								
Total	787	86.4	266	24.7	1 325	99.0	513	32.7
Transport accidents — Accidents de transport	164	18.0	54	5.0	221	16.5	86	5.5
Falls — Chutes	132	14.5	74	6.9	255	19.1	139	8.9
Accidental drowning and submersion — Noyade et submersion accidentelles	94	10.3	25	♦2.3	109	8.1	37	2.4
Exposure to smoke, fire and flames — Exposition à la fumée, au feu et aux flammes	67	7.4	35	3.3	37	2.8	21	♦1.3
Accidental poisoning by and exposure to noxious substances — Intoxication accidentelle par des substances nocives et exposition à ces substances	125	13.7	26	♦2.4	376	28.1	106	6.8
Intentional self-harm — Lésions auto-infligées	305	33.5	81	7.5	727	54.3	169	10.8
Assault — Agresssions	69	7.6	30	♦2.8	81	6.1	40	2.6
All other external causes — Toutes autres causes externes	158	17.3	58	5.4	269	20.1	83	5.3

20. Death and death rates by cause and sex: 2012 - 2016
Décès et taux de mortalité par cause et sexe : 2012 - 2016 (continued - suite)

Cause of death — Cause de décès	Lithuania - Lituanie 2016 (+C)				Luxembourg 2014 (+C)			
	Male — Masculin		Female — Féminin		Male — Masculin		Female — Féminin	
	Number Nombre	Rate Taux	Number Nombre	Rate Taux	Number Nombre	Rate Taux	Number Nombre	Rate Taux
TOTAL	20 327	1 528.8	20 779	1 332.9	1 919	697.5	1 786	650.5
Certain infectious and parasitic diseases — Certaines maladies infectieuses et parasitaires								
Total	448	33.7	352	22.6	25	♦9.1	28	♦10.2
Intestinal infectious diseases — Maladies infectieuses intestinales	16	♦1.2	16	♦1.0	-	-	-	-
Tuberculosis — Tuberculose	138	10.4	36	2.3	1	♦0.4	-	-
Tetanus — Tétanos	1	♦0.1	-	-	-	-	-	-
Diphtheria — Diphtérie	-	-	-	-	-	-	-	-
Whooping cough — Coqueluche	-	-	-	-	-	-	-	-
Meningococcal infection — Infection à méningocoques	3	♦0.2	4	♦0.3	-	-	1	♦0.4
Septicaemia — Septicémie	218	16.4	238	15.3	13	♦4.7	19	♦6.9
Acute poliomyelitis — Poliomyélite aiguë	-	-	-	-	-	-	-	-
Measles — Rougeole	-	-	-	-	-	-	-	-
Viral hepatitis — Hépatite virale	19	♦1.4	13	♦0.8	4	♦1.5	2	♦0.7
Human immunodeficiency virus [HIV] disease — Maladies dues au virus de l'immunodéficience humaine (VIH)	27	♦2.0	6	♦0.4	3	♦1.1	-	-
Malaria — Paludisme	-	-	-	-	-	-	-	-
Neoplasms — Tumeurs	4 600	346.0	3 745	240.2	651	236.6	480	174.8
Malignant neoplasms — Tumeurs malignes								
Total	4 525	340.3	3 672	235.5	635	230.8	460	167.5
Malignant neoplasm of lip, oral cavity and pharynx — Tumeur maligne de la lèvre, de la cavité buccale et du pharynx	227	17.1	56	3.6	17	♦6.2	4	♦1.5
Malignant neoplasm of oesophagus — Tumeur maligne de l'oesophage	149	11.2	30	♦1.9	22	♦8.0	4	♦1.5
Malignant neoplasm of stomach — Tumeur maligne de l'estomac	395	29.7	267	17.1	31	11.3	19	♦6.9
Malignant neoplasm of colon, rectosigmoid junction, rectum, anus and anal canal — Tumeur maligne du côlon, de la jonction recto-sigmoïdienne, du rectum, de l'anus et du canal anal	432	32.5	489	31.4	66	24.0	40	14.6
Malignant neoplasm of liver and intrahepatic bile ducts — Tumeur maligne du foie et des voies bilaires intrahépatiques	147	11.1	79	5.1	32	11.6	12	♦4.4
Malignant neoplasm of pancreas — Tumeur maligne du pancréas	220	16.5	272	17.4	49	17.8	45	16.4
Malignant neoplasm of trachea, bronchus and lung — Tumeur maligne de la trachée, des bronches et du poumon	1 031	77.5	262	16.8	171	62.2	82	29.9
Malignant neoplasm of female breast — Tumeur maligne du sein chez la femme	..	..	512	37.9	..	..	85	37.0
Malignant neoplasm of cervix uteri — Tumeur maligne du col de l'utérus	..	..	187	13.8	..	..	8	♦3.5
Malignant neoplasm of prostate — Tumeur maligne de la prostate	561	122.0	..	..	48	55.5	..	..
Malignant neoplasm of lymphoid, haematopoietic and related tissue — Tumeurs malignes primitives ou présumées primitives des tissus lymphoïde, hématopoïétique et apparentés	272	20.5	315	20.2	46	16.7	40	14.6
Disorders of the blood and blood-forming organs and certain disorders involving the immune mechanism — Maladies du sang et des organes hématopoïétiques et certains troubles du système immunitaire								
Total	13	♦1.0	13	♦0.8	6	♦2.2	10	♦3.6
Anaemias — Anémies	7	♦0.5	8	♦0.5	4	♦1.5	5	♦1.8
Endocrine, nutritional and metabolic diseases — Maladies endocriniennes, nutritionnelles et métaboliques								
Total	151	11.4	188	12.1	61	22.2	64	23.3
Diabetes mellitus — Diabète sucré	138	10.4	169	10.8	51	18.5	43	15.7
Malnutrition — Malnutrition	2	♦0.2	1	♦0.1	-	-	9	♦3.3
Mental and behavioural disorders — Troubles mentaux et du comportement	58	4.4	101	6.5	79	28.7	106	38.6
Diseases of the nervous system — Maladies du système nerveux	289	21.7	319	20.5	72	26.2	80	29.1
Diseases of the circulatory system — Maladies de l'appareil circulatoire								
Total	9 717	730.8	13 386	858.7	543	197.4	620	225.8
Acute rheumatic fever and chronic rheumatic heart diseases — Rhumatisme articularie aigu et cardiopathies rhumatismales chroniques	35	2.6	49	3.1	6	♦2.2	10	♦3.6
Hypertensive diseases — Maladies hypertensives	230	17.3	395	25.3	13	♦4.7	38	13.8
Ischaemic heart disease — Cardiopathie ischémique	6 476	487.1	8 718	559.2	205	74.5	119	43.3
Cerebrovascular disease — Maladie cérébrovasculaire	2 032	152.8	3 566	228.7	85	30.9	139	50.6

Cause of death — Cause de décès	Lithuania - Lituanie				Luxembourg			
	2016 (+C)				2014 (+C)			
	Male — Masculin		Female — Féminin		Male — Masculin		Female — Féminin	
	Number Nombre	Rate Taux	Number Nombre	Rate Taux	Number Nombre	Rate Taux	Number Nombre	Rate Taux
Diseases of arteries, arterioles and capillaries — Maladies des artères, artérioles et capillaires	224	16.8	179	11.5	29	♦10.5	25	♦9.1
Diseases of the respiratory system — Maladies de l'appareil respiratoire								
Total	836	62.9	456	29.3	132	48.0	125	45.5
Influenza — Grippe	17	♦1.3	11	♦0.7	-	-	2	♦0.7
Pneumonia — Pneumopathies	346	26.0	226	14.5	33	12.0	33	12.0
Chronic lower respiratory diseases — Maladies chroniques des voies respiratoires inférieures	421	31.7	182	11.7	65	23.6	63	22.9
Diseases of the digestive system — Maladies de l'appareil digestif								
Total	1 223	92.0	942	60.4	98	35.6	73	26.6
Gastric and duodenal ulcer — Ulcère de l'estomac et du duodénum	182	13.7	137	8.8	1	♦0.4	4	♦1.5
Diseases of the liver — Maladies du foie	596	44.8	306	19.6	52	18.9	19	♦6.9
Diseases of the musculoskeletal system and connective tissue — Maladies du système ostéo-articulaire, des muscles et du tissu conjonctif	40	3.0	56	3.6	6	♦2.2	12	♦4.4
Diseases of the genitourinary system — Maladies de l'appareil génito-urinaire								
Total	174	13.1	220	14.1	42	15.3	37	13.5
Disorders of kidney and ureter — Affections du rein et de l'uretère	134	10.1	194	12.4	31	11.3	33	12.0
Hyperplasia of prostate — Hyperplasie de la prostate	14	♦3.0	..	..	1	♦1.2	..	..
Pregnancy, childbirth and the puerperium — Grossesse, accouchement et puerpéralité								
Total	..	..	2	♦6.5	..	..	-	-
Pregnancy with abortive outcome — Grossesse se terminant par un avortement	..	..	-	-	..	..	-	-
Other direct obstetric causes — Autres décès maternels directs	..	..	2	♦6.5	..	..	-	-
Indirect obstetric causes — Décès maternels indirects	..	..	-	-	..	..	-	-
Certain conditions originating in the perinatal period — Certaines affections dont l'origine se situe dans la période périnatale	24	♦151.4	18	♦121.8	4	♦127.4	6	♦204.7
Congenital malformations, deformations and chromosomal abnormalities — Malformations congénitales et anomalies chromosomiques	39	246.1	39	263.9	5	♦159.3	2	♦68.2
Symptoms, signs and abnormal clinical and laboratory findings, not elsewhere classified — Symptômes, signes et résultats anormaux d'examens cliniques et de laboratoire, non classés ailleurs	381	28.7	167	10.7	47	17.1	47	17.1
All other diseases — Toutes autres maladies	16	♦1.2	31	2.0	2	♦0.7	2	♦0.7
External causes — Causes externes								
Total	2 318	174.3	744	47.7	146	53.1	94	34.2
Accidents								
Total	1 279	96.2	486	31.2	77	28.0	62	22.6
Transport accidents — Accidents de transport	185	13.9	61	3.9	23	♦8.4	6	♦2.2
Falls — Chutes	251	18.9	150	9.6	24	♦8.7	28	♦10.2
Accidental drowning and submersion — Noyade et submersion accidentelles	156	11.7	34	2.2	-	-	1	♦0.4
Exposure to smoke, fire and flames — Exposition à la fumée, au feu et aux flammes	24	♦1.8	13	♦0.8	1	♦0.4	2	♦0.7
Accidental poisoning by and exposure to noxious substances — Intoxication accidentelle par des substances nocives et exposition à ces substances	324	24.4	95	6.1	6	♦2.2	2	♦0.7
Intentional self-harm — Lésions auto-infligées	694	52.2	129	8.3	52	18.9	15	♦5.5
Assault — Agresssions	70	5.3	30	♦1.9	2	♦0.7	2	♦0.7
All other external causes — Toutes autres causes externes	275	20.7	99	6.4	15	♦5.5	15	♦5.5

Cause of death — Cause de décès	Luxembourg				Malta - Malte			
	2015 (+C)				2014 (+C)			
	Male — Masculin		Female — Féminin		Male — Masculin		Female — Féminin	
	Number Nombre	Rate Taux	Number Nombre	Rate Taux	Number Nombre	Rate Taux	Number Nombre	Rate Taux
TOTAL	1 869	662.8	1 970	701.1	1 655	774.8	1 615	755.3
Certain infectious and parasitic diseases — Certaines maladies infectieuses et parasitaires								
Total	35	12.4	33	11.7	13	♦6.1	12	♦5.6
Intestinal infectious diseases — Maladies infectieuses intestinales	2	♦0.7	1	♦0.4	-	-	-	-
Tuberculosis — Tuberculose	1	♦0.4	-	-	1	♦0.5	-	-
Tetanus — Tétanos	-	-	-	-	-	-	-	-
Diphtheria — Diphtérie............	-	-	-	-	-	-	-	-
Whooping cough — Coqueluche	-	-	-	-	-	-	-	-
Meningococcal infection — Infection à méningocoques	-	-	-	-	-	-	-	-
Septicaemia — Septicémie	22	♦7.8	27	♦9.6	9	♦4.2	8	♦3.7
Acute poliomyelitis — Poliomyélite aiguë	-	-	-	-	-	-	-	-
Measles — Rougeole............	-	-	-	-	-	-	-	-
Viral hepatitis — Hépatite virale............	3	♦1.1	-	-	1	♦0.5	2	♦0.9
Human immunodeficiency virus [HIV] disease — Maladies dues au virus de l'immunodéficience humaine (VIH)............	4	♦1.4	-	-	2	♦0.9	1	♦0.5
Malaria — Paludisme............	-	-	-	-	-	-	-	-
Neoplasms — Tumeurs	561	199.0	519	184.7	532	249.1	401	187.5
Malignant neoplasms — Tumeurs malignes								
Total	535	189.7	499	177.6	523	244.8	389	181.9
Malignant neoplasm of lip, oral cavity and pharynx — Tumeur maligne de la lèvre, de la cavité buccale et du pharynx	10	♦3.5	7	♦2.5	17	♦8.0	10	♦4.7
Malignant neoplasm of oesophagus — Tumeur maligne de l'oesophage	12	♦4.3	7	♦2.5	20	♦9.4	5	♦2.3
Malignant neoplasm of stomach — Tumeur maligne de l'estomac	15	♦5.3	16	♦5.7	27	♦12.6	14	♦6.5
Malignant neoplasm of colon, rectosigmoid junction, rectum, anus and anal canal — Tumeur maligne du côlon, de la jonction recto-sigmoïdienne, du rectum, de l'anus et du canal anal............	56	19.9	58	20.6	60	28.1	46	21.5
Malignant neoplasm of liver and intrahepatic bile ducts — Tumeur maligne du foie et des voies bilaires intrahépatiques	31	11.0	12	♦4.3	16	♦7.5	10	♦4.7
Malignant neoplasm of pancreas — Tumeur maligne du pancréas............	27	♦9.6	34	12.1	47	22.0	41	19.2
Malignant neoplasm of trachea, bronchus and lung — Tumeur maligne de la trachée, des bronches et du poumon	145	51.4	79	28.1	142	66.5	28	♦13.1
Malignant neoplasm of female breast — Tumeur maligne du sein chez la femme	..	..	93	39.0	..	..	75	40.8
Malignant neoplasm of cervix uteri — Tumeur maligne du col de l'utérus.........	..	..	10	♦4.2	..	..	4	♦2.2
Malignant neoplasm of prostate — Tumeur maligne de la prostate............	55	60.0	..	..	43	54.5	..	..
Malignant neoplasm of lymphoid, haematopoietic and related tissue — Tumeurs malignes primitives ou présumées primitives des tissus lymphoïde, hématopoïétique et apparentés............	56	19.9	44	15.7	35	16.4	32	15.0
Disorders of the blood and blood-forming organs and certain disorders involving the immune mechanism — Maladies du sang et des organes hématopoïétiques et certains troubles du système immunitaire								
Total	12	♦4.3	8	♦2.8	2	♦0.9	6	♦2.8
Anaemias — Anémies	6	♦2.1	5	♦1.8	2	♦0.9	3	♦1.4
Endocrine, nutritional and metabolic diseases — Maladies endocriniennes, nutritionnelles et métaboliques								
Total	52	18.4	69	24.6	85	39.8	87	40.7
Diabetes mellitus — Diabète sucré............	41	14.5	42	14.9	80	37.5	77	36.0
Malnutrition — Malnutrition	4	♦1.4	7	♦2.5	-	-	1	♦0.5
Mental and behavioural disorders — Troubles mentaux et du comportement	94	33.3	136	48.4	46	21.5	93	43.5
Diseases of the nervous system — Maladies du système nerveux	81	28.7	102	36.3	34	15.9	42	19.6
Diseases of the circulatory system — Maladies de l'appareil circulatoire								
Total	536	190.1	626	222.8	577	270.1	654	305.9
Acute rheumatic fever and chronic rheumatic heart diseases — Rhumatisme articularie aigu et cardiopathies rhumatismales chroniques	7	♦2.5	9	♦3.2	-	-	4	♦1.9
Hypertensive diseases — Maladies hypertensives............	18	♦6.4	52	18.5	13	♦6.1	19	♦8.9
Ischaemic heart disease — Cardiopathie ischémique............	184	65.3	124	44.1	352	164.8	337	157.6
Cerebrovascular disease — Maladie cérébrovasculaire............	104	36.9	127	45.2	116	54.3	160	74.8

	Luxembourg				Malta - Malte			
	2015 (+C)				2014 (+C)			
Cause of death — Cause de décès	Male — Masculin		Female — Féminin		Male — Masculin		Female — Féminin	
	Number Nombre	Rate Taux	Number Nombre	Rate Taux	Number Nombre	Rate Taux	Number Nombre	Rate Taux
Diseases of arteries, arterioles and capillaries — Maladies des artères, artérioles et capillaires	36	12.8	22	♦7.8	22	♦10.3	13	♦6.1
Diseases of the respiratory system — Maladies de l'appareil respiratoire								
Total	148	52.5	171	60.9	171	80.1	140	65.5
Influenza — Grippe	4	♦1.4	4	♦1.4	-	-	-	-
Pneumonia — Pneumopathies	38	13.5	47	16.7	51	23.9	57	26.7
Chronic lower respiratory diseases — Maladies chroniques des voies respiratoires inférieures	79	28.0	83	29.5	74	34.6	24	♦11.2
Diseases of the digestive system — Maladies de l'appareil digestif								
Total	78	27.7	88	31.3	53	24.8	61	28.5
Gastric and duodenal ulcer — Ulcère de l'estomac et du duodénum	1	♦0.4	8	♦2.8	3	♦1.4	4	♦1.9
Diseases of the liver — Maladies du foie	38	13.5	27	♦9.6	23	♦10.8	4	♦1.9
Diseases of the musculoskeletal system and connective tissue — Maladies du système ostéo-articularie, des muscles et du tissu conjonctif	8	♦2.8	18	♦6.4	8	♦3.7	12	♦5.6
Diseases of the genitourinary system — Maladies de l'appareil génito-urinaire								
Total	36	12.8	36	12.8	28	♦13.1	35	16.4
Disorders of kidney and ureter — Affections du rein et de l'uretère	31	11.0	26	♦9.3	14	♦6.6	16	♦7.5
Hyperplasia of prostate — Hyperplasie de la prostate	1	♦1.1	..	..	3	♦3.8	..	...
Pregnancy, childbirth and the puerperium — Grossesse, accouchement et puerpéralité								
Total	..	..	-	-	..	..	-	-
Pregnancy with abortive outcome — Grossesse se terminant par un avortement	..	..	-	-	..	..	-	-
Other direct obstetric causes — Autres décès maternels directs	..	..	-	-	..	..	-	-
Indirect obstetric causes — Décès maternels indirects	..	..	-	-	..	..	-	-
Certain conditions originating in the perinatal period — Certaines affections dont l'origine se situe dans la période périnatale	3	♦94.7	1	♦33.9	6	♦269.9	7	♦355.7
Congenital malformations, deformations and chromosomal abnormalities — Malformations congénitales et anomalies chromosomiques	6	♦189.4	2	♦67.9	10	♦449.8	4	♦203.3
Symptoms, signs and abnormal clinical and laboratory findings, not elsewhere classified — Symptômes, signes et résultats anormaux d'examens cliniques et de laboratoire, non classés ailleurs	52	18.4	65	23.1	9	♦4.2	11	♦5.1
All other diseases — Toutes autres maladies	1	♦0.4	3	♦1.1	6	♦2.8	18	♦8.4
External causes — Causes externes								
Total	166	58.9	93	33.1	75	35.1	32	15.0
Accidents								
Total	87	30.9	62	22.1	42	19.7	25	♦11.7
Transport accidents — Accidents de transport	20	♦7.1	5	♦1.8	7	♦3.3	4	♦1.9
Falls — Chutes	29	♦10.3	24	♦8.5	23	♦10.8	18	♦8.4
Accidental drowning and submersion — Noyade et submersion accidentelles	3	♦1.1	1	♦0.4	2	♦0.9	-	-
Exposure to smoke, fire and flames — Exposition à la fumée, au feu et aux flammes	-	-	2	♦0.7	-	-	-	-
Accidental poisoning by and exposure to noxious substances — Intoxication accidentelle par des substances nocives et exposition à ces substances	6	♦2.1	6	♦2.1	4	♦1.9	-	-
Intentional self-harm — Lésions auto-infligées	45	16.0	19	♦6.8	27	♦12.6	5	♦2.3
Assault — Agresssions	3	♦1.1	2	♦0.7	4	♦1.9	-	-
All other external causes — Toutes autres causes externes	31	11.0	10	♦3.6	2	♦0.9	2	♦0.9

Cause of death — Cause de décès	Malta - Malte 2015 (+C)				Netherlands - Pays-Bas 2015 (+C)			
	Male — Masculin		Female — Féminin		Male — Masculin		Female — Féminin	
	Number Nombre	Rate Taux	Number Nombre	Rate Taux	Number Nombre	Rate Taux	Number Nombre	Rate Taux
TOTAL	1 734	802.1	1 709	792.1	71 029	848.3	76 105	892.4
Certain infectious and parasitic diseases — Certaines maladies infectieuses et parasitaires								
Total	9	♦4.2	13	♦6.0	1 675	20.0	1 818	21.3
Intestinal infectious diseases — Maladies infectieuses intestinales	-	-	2	♦0.9	212	2.5	344	4.0
Tuberculosis — Tuberculose	1	♦0.5	-	-	7	♦0.1	9	♦0.1
Tetanus — Tétanos	-	-	-	-	-	-	-	-
Diphtheria — Diphtérie	-	-	-	-	-	-	-	-
Whooping cough — Coqueluche	-	-	-	-	-	-	1	♦0.0
Meningococcal infection — Infection à méningocoques	-	-	-	-	1	♦0.0	3	♦0.0
Septicaemia — Septicémie	5	♦2.3	8	♦3.7	991	11.8	933	10.9
Acute poliomyelitis — Poliomyélite aiguë	-	-	-	-	-	-	-	-
Measles — Rougeole	-	-	-	-	-	-	-	-
Viral hepatitis — Hépatite virale	-	-	-	-	42	0.5	14	♦0.2
Human immunodeficiency virus [HIV] disease — Maladies dues au virus de l'immunodéficience humaine (VIH)	2	♦0.9	1	♦0.5	30	♦0.4	3	♦0.0
Malaria — Paludisme	-	-	-	-	-	-	-	-
Neoplasms — Tumeurs	510	235.9	427	197.9	24 661	294.5	21 057	246.9
Malignant neoplasms — Tumeurs malignes								
Total	502	232.2	413	191.4	23 901	285.5	20 225	237.2
Malignant neoplasm of lip, oral cavity and pharynx — Tumeur maligne de la lèvre, de la cavité buccale et du pharynx	17	♦7.9	8	♦3.7	430	5.1	224	2.6
Malignant neoplasm of oesophagus — Tumeur maligne de l'oesophage	12	♦5.6	5	♦2.3	1 342	16.0	471	5.5
Malignant neoplasm of stomach — Tumeur maligne de l'estomac	17	♦7.9	17	♦7.9	824	9.8	466	5.5
Malignant neoplasm of colon, rectosigmoid junction, rectum, anus and anal canal — Tumeur maligne du côlon, de la jonction recto-sigmoïdienne, du rectum, de l'anus et du canal anal	67	31.0	55	25.5	2 778	33.2	2 373	27.8
Malignant neoplasm of liver and intrahepatic bile ducts — Tumeur maligne du foie et des voies bilaires intrahépatiques	15	♦6.9	9	♦4.2	609	7.3	340	4.0
Malignant neoplasm of pancreas — Tumeur maligne du pancréas	50	23.1	33	15.3	1 363	16.3	1 331	15.6
Malignant neoplasm of trachea, bronchus and lung — Tumeur maligne de la trachée, des bronches et du poumon	148	68.5	41	19.0	6 141	73.3	4 279	50.2
Malignant neoplasm of female breast — Tumeur maligne du sein chez la femme	..	..	81	43.6	..	..	3 271	45.8
Malignant neoplasm of cervix uteri — Tumeur maligne du col de l'utérus	..	..	5	♦2.7	..	..	207	2.9
Malignant neoplasm of prostate — Tumeur maligne de la prostate	39	48.6	..	..	2 641	85.2	..	..
Malignant neoplasm of lymphoid, haematopoietic and related tissue — Tumeurs malignes primitives ou présumées primitives des tissus lymphoïde, hématopoïétique et apparentés	38	17.6	33	15.3	1 928	23.0	1 529	17.9
Disorders of the blood and blood-forming organs and certain disorders involving the immune mechanism — Maladies du sang et des organes hématopoïétiques et certains troubles du système immunitaire								
Total	1	♦0.5	6	♦2.8	222	2.7	266	3.1
Anaemias — Anémies	1	♦0.5	3	♦1.4	142	1.7	196	2.3
Endocrine, nutritional and metabolic diseases — Maladies endocriniennes, nutritionnelles et métaboliques								
Total	101	46.7	83	38.5	1 638	19.6	2 004	23.5
Diabetes mellitus — Diabète sucré	95	43.9	78	36.2	1 306	15.6	1 524	17.9
Malnutrition — Malnutrition	-	-	1	♦0.5	4	♦0.0	13	♦0.2
Mental and behavioural disorders — Troubles mentaux et du comportement	41	19.0	98	45.4	3 833	45.8	7 544	88.5
Diseases of the nervous system — Maladies du système nerveux	49	22.7	50	23.2	3 321	39.7	4 282	50.2
Diseases of the circulatory system — Maladies de l'appareil circulatoire								
Total	643	297.4	691	320.3	18 543	221.5	20 757	243.4
Acute rheumatic fever and chronic rheumatic heart diseases — Rhumatisme articulaire aigu et cardiopathies rhumatismales chroniques	-	-	2	♦0.9	69	0.8	153	1.8
Hypertensive diseases — Maladies hypertensives	14	♦6.5	33	15.3	528	6.3	935	11.0
Ischaemic heart disease — Cardiopathie ischémique	380	175.8	352	163.2	5 292	63.2	3 690	43.3
Cerebrovascular disease — Maladie cérébrovasculaire	126	58.3	153	70.9	3 968	47.4	5 641	66.1

20. Death and death rates by cause and sex: 2012 - 2016
Décès et taux de mortalité par cause et sexe : 2012 - 2016 (continued - suite)

Cause of death — Cause de décès	Malta - Malte 2015 (+C) Male — Masculin Number Nombre	Rate Taux	Female — Féminin Number Nombre	Rate Taux	Netherlands - Pays-Bas 2015 (+C) Male — Masculin Number Nombre	Rate Taux	Female — Féminin Number Nombre	Rate Taux
Diseases of arteries, arterioles and capillaries — Maladies des artères, artérioles et capillaires	19	♦8.8	19	♦8.8	1 568	18.7	1 150	13.5
Diseases of the respiratory system — Maladies de l'appareil respiratoire								
Total	190	87.9	158	73.2	6 319	75.5	6 358	74.6
Influenza — Grippe..........................	-	-	-	-	143	1.7	229	2.7
Pneumonia — Pneumopathies..............	43	19.9	55	25.5	1 517	18.1	1 847	21.7
Chronic lower respiratory diseases — Maladies chroniques des voies respiratoires inférieures	77	35.6	22	♦10.2	3 688	44.0	3 378	39.6
Diseases of the digestive system — Maladies de l'appareil digestif								
Total	44	20.4	54	25.0	2 145	25.6	2 392	28.0
Gastric and duodenal ulcer — Ulcère de l'estomac et du duodénum.................	2	♦0.9	4	♦1.9	68	0.8	66	0.8
Diseases of the liver — Maladies du foie..............	14	♦6.5	4	♦1.9	631	7.5	436	5.1
Diseases of the musculoskeletal system and connective tissue — Maladies du système ostéo-articularie, des muscles et du tissu conjonctif	5	♦2.3	11	♦5.1	350	4.2	709	8.3
Diseases of the genitourinary system — Maladies de l'appareil génito-urinaire								
Total	35	16.2	49	22.7	1 482	17.7	1 865	21.9
Disorders of kidney and ureter — Affections du rein et de l'uretère	14	♦6.5	23	♦10.7	991	11.8	1 130	13.3
Hyperplasia of prostate — Hyperplasie de la prostate..............	3	♦3.7	..	..	39	1.3	..	..
Pregnancy, childbirth and the puerperium — Grossesse, accouchement et puerpéralité								
Total	..	..	-	-	..	..	6	♦3.5
Pregnancy with abortive outcome — Grossesse se terminant par un avortement	..	..	-	-	..	..	-	-
Other direct obstetric causes — Autres décès maternels directs	..	..	-	-	..	..	5	♦2.9
Indirect obstetric causes — Décès maternels indirects	..	..	-	-	..	..	1	♦0.6
Certain conditions originating in the perinatal period — Certaines affections dont l'origine se situe dans la période périnatale	9	♦407.6	3	♦141.7	186	212.7	148	178.1
Congenital malformations, deformations and chromosomal abnormalities — Malformations congénitales et anomalies chromosomiques	5	♦226.4	10	♦472.4	208	237.9	223	268.4
Symptoms, signs and abnormal clinical and laboratory findings, not elsewhere classified — Symptômes, signes et résultats anormaux d'examens cliniques et de laboratoire, non classés ailleurs	5	♦2.3	10	♦4.6	2 486	29.7	3 051	35.8
All other diseases — Toutes autres maladies................	8	♦3.7	11	♦5.1	111	1.3	233	2.7
External causes — Causes externes								
Total	79	36.5	35	16.2	3 849	46.0	3 392	39.8
Accidents								
Total	49	22.7	26	♦12.1	2 224	26.6	2 387	28.0
Transport accidents — Accidents de transport	9	♦4.2	3	♦1.4	476	5.7	154	1.8
Falls — Chutes	19	♦8.8	16	♦7.4	1 200	14.3	1 639	19.2
Accidental drowning and submersion — Noyade et submersion accidentelles..............	2	♦0.9	1	♦0.5	64	0.8	19	♦0.2
Exposure to smoke, fire and flames — Exposition à la fumée, au feu et aux flammes	-	-	-	-	18	♦0.2	21	♦0.2
Accidental poisoning by and exposure to noxious substances — Intoxication accidentelle par des substances nocives et exposition à ces substances	7	♦3.2	1	♦0.5	125	1.5	41	0.5
Intentional self-harm — Lésions auto-infligées	27	♦12.5	7	♦3.2	1 280	15.3	591	6.9
Assault — Agresssions..............	2	♦0.9	1	♦0.5	62	0.7	42	0.5
All other external causes — Toutes autres causes externes	1	♦0.5	1	♦0.5	283	3.4	372	4.4

20. Death and death rates by cause and sex: 2012 - 2016
Décès et taux de mortalité par cause et sexe : 2012 - 2016 (continued - suite)

Cause of death — Cause de décès	Netherlands - Pays-Bas 2016 (+C)				Norway - Norvège 2014 (+C)			
	Male — Masculin		Female — Féminin		Male — Masculin		Female — Féminin	
	Number Nombre	Rate Taux	Number Nombre	Rate Taux	Number Nombre	Rate Taux	Number Nombre	Rate Taux
TOTAL	72 180	857.5	76 817	897.2	19 685	766.8	20 659	813.0
Certain infectious and parasitic diseases — Certaines maladies infectieuses et parasitaires								
Total	1 444	17.2	1 610	18.8	411	16.0	503	19.8
Intestinal infectious diseases — Maladies infectieuses intestinales	207	2.5	307	3.6	44	1.7	67	2.6
Tuberculosis — Tuberculose	8	♦0.1	7	♦0.1	4	♦0.2	1	♦0.0
Tetanus — Tétanos	-	-	-	-	1	♦0.0	-	-
Diphtheria — Diphtérie	-	-	-	-	-	-	-	-
Whooping cough — Coqueluche	1	♦0.0	1	♦0.0	1	♦0.0	-	-
Meningococcal infection — Infection à méningocoques	2	♦0.0	4	♦0.0	-	-	-	-
Septicaemia — Septicémie	786	9.3	768	9.0	168	6.5	173	6.8
Acute poliomyelitis — Poliomyélite aiguë	-	-	-	-	-	-	-	-
Measles — Rougeole	-	-	-	-	-	-	-	-
Viral hepatitis — Hépatite virale	25	♦0.3	17	♦0.2	13	♦0.5	5	♦0.2
Human immunodeficiency virus [HIV] disease — Maladies dues au virus de l'immunodéficience humaine (VIH)	27	♦0.3	15	♦0.2	8	♦0.3	3	♦0.1
Malaria — Paludisme	2	♦0.0	1	♦0.0	-	-	-	-
Neoplasms — Tumeurs	25 350	301.2	21 626	252.6	5 889	229.4	5 199	204.6
Malignant neoplasms — Tumeurs malignes								
Total	24 542	291.6	20 737	242.2	5 766	224.6	5 075	199.7
Malignant neoplasm of lip, oral cavity and pharynx — Tumeur maligne de la lèvre, de la cavité buccale et du pharynx	435	5.2	242	2.8	69	2.7	41	1.6
Malignant neoplasm of oesophagus — Tumeur maligne de l'oesophage	1 392	16.5	477	5.6	170	6.6	56	2.2
Malignant neoplasm of stomach — Tumeur maligne de l'estomac	758	9.0	481	5.6	179	7.0	122	4.8
Malignant neoplasm of colon, rectosigmoid junction, rectum, anus and anal canal — Tumeur maligne du côlon, de la jonction recto-sigmoïdienne, du rectum, de l'anus et du canal anal	2 769	32.9	2 438	28.5	784	30.5	780	30.7
Malignant neoplasm of liver and intrahepatic bile ducts — Tumeur maligne du foie et des voies bilaires intrahépatiques	678	8.1	418	4.9	120	4.7	84	3.3
Malignant neoplasm of pancreas — Tumeur maligne du pancréas	1 417	16.8	1 413	16.5	349	13.6	364	14.3
Malignant neoplasm of trachea, bronchus and lung — Tumeur maligne de la trachée, des bronches et du poumon	6 300	74.8	4 391	51.3	1 198	46.7	960	37.8
Malignant neoplasm of female breast — Tumeur maligne du sein chez la femme	..	..	3 150	43.8	..	..	663	...
Malignant neoplasm of cervix uteri — Tumeur maligne du col de l'utérus	..	..	229	3.2	..	..	63	...
Malignant neoplasm of prostate — Tumeur maligne de la prostate	2 770	87.6	..	..	1 093	...	..	..
Malignant neoplasm of lymphoid, haematopoietic and related tissue — Tumeurs malignes primitives ou présumées primitives des tissus lymphoïde, hématopoïétique et apparentés	2 075	24.7	1 546	18.1	457	17.8	414	16.3
Disorders of the blood and blood-forming organs and certain disorders involving the immune mechanism — Maladies du sang et des organes hématopoïétiques et certains troubles du système immunitaire								
Total	243	2.9	268	3.1	72	2.8	82	3.2
Anaemias — Anémies	147	1.7	209	2.4	36	1.4	54	2.1
Endocrine, nutritional and metabolic diseases — Maladies endocriniennes, nutritionnelles et métaboliques								
Total	1 700	20.2	1 911	22.3	425	16.6	520	20.5
Diabetes mellitus — Diabète sucré	1 381	16.4	1 510	17.6	307	12.0	307	12.1
Malnutrition — Malnutrition	-	-	10	♦0.1	29	♦1.1	66	2.6
Mental and behavioural disorders — Troubles mentaux et du comportement	4 173	49.6	7 784	90.9	847	33.0	1 570	61.8
Diseases of the nervous system — Maladies du système nerveux	3 680	43.7	4 674	54.6	841	32.8	1 094	43.1
Diseases of the circulatory system — Maladies de l'appareil circulatoire								
Total	18 148	215.6	20 499	239.4	5 477	213.4	6 239	245.5
Acute rheumatic fever and chronic rheumatic heart diseases — Rhumatisme articularie aigu et cardiopathies rhumatismales chroniques	66	0.8	160	1.9	18	♦0.7	37	1.5
Hypertensive diseases — Maladies hypertensives	526	6.2	905	10.6	180	7.0	301	11.8
Ischaemic heart disease — Cardiopathie ischémique	5 065	60.2	3 575	41.8	2 220	86.5	1 872	73.7
Cerebrovascular disease — Maladie cérébrovasculaire	3 931	46.7	5 576	65.1	1 114	43.4	1 591	62.6

20. Death and death rates by cause and sex: 2012 - 2016
Décès et taux de mortalité par cause et sexe : 2012 - 2016 (continued - suite)

Cause of death — Cause de décès	Netherlands - Pays-Bas 2016 (+C)				Norway - Norvège 2014 (+C)			
	Male — Masculin		Female — Féminin		Male — Masculin		Female — Féminin	
	Number Nombre	Rate Taux	Number Nombre	Rate Taux	Number Nombre	Rate Taux	Number Nombre	Rate Taux
Diseases of arteries, arterioles and capillaries — Maladies des artères, artérioles et capillaires	1 552	18.4	1 145	13.4	350	13.6	279	11.0
Diseases of the respiratory system — Maladies de l'appareil respiratoire								
Total	6 055	71.9	5 929	69.2	1 865	72.7	1 885	74.2
Influenza — Grippe	157	1.9	183	2.1	19	◆0.7	21	◆0.8
Pneumonia — Pneumopathies	1 489	17.7	1 641	19.2	575	22.4	691	27.2
Chronic lower respiratory diseases — Maladies chroniques des voies respiratoires inférieures	3 438	40.8	3 258	38.1	1 028	40.0	1 013	39.9
Diseases of the digestive system — Maladies de l'appareil digestif								
Total	2 207	26.2	2 442	28.5	581	22.6	629	24.8
Gastric and duodenal ulcer — Ulcère de l'estomac et du duodénum	60	0.7	76	0.9	64	2.5	75	3.0
Diseases of the liver — Maladies du foie	672	8.0	454	5.3	141	5.5	83	3.3
Diseases of the musculoskeletal system and connective tissue — Maladies du système ostéo-articulaire, des muscles et du tissu conjonctif	376	4.5	773	9.0	104	4.1	162	6.4
Diseases of the genitourinary system — Maladies de l'appareil génito-urinaire								
Total	1 444	17.2	1 766	20.6	399	15.5	409	16.1
Disorders of kidney and ureter — Affections du rein et de l'uretère	922	11.0	1 052	12.3	239	9.3	224	8.8
Hyperplasia of prostate — Hyperplasie de la prostate	32	1.0	..	..	36	...	..	..
Pregnancy, childbirth and the puerperium — Grossesse, accouchement et puerpéralité								
Total	..	..	6	◆3.5	..	..	2	◆3.4
Pregnancy with abortive outcome — Grossesse se terminant par un avortement	..	..	-	-	..	..	-	-
Other direct obstetric causes — Autres décès maternels directs	..	..	6	◆3.5	..	..	2	◆3.4
Indirect obstetric causes — Décès maternels indirects	..	..	-	-	..	..	-	-
Certain conditions originating in the perinatal period — Certaines affections dont l'origine se situe dans la période périnatale	193	217.9	160	190.6	39	128.6	40	139.6
Congenital malformations, deformations and chromosomal abnormalities — Malformations congénitales et anomalies chromosomiques	220	248.3	221	263.3	65	214.4	53	185.0
Symptoms, signs and abnormal clinical and laboratory findings, not elsewhere classified — Symptômes, signes et résultats anormaux d'examens cliniques et de laboratoire, non classés ailleurs	2 779	33.0	3 309	38.6	1 087	42.3	1 162	45.7
All other diseases — Toutes autres maladies	92	1.1	184	2.1	36	1.4	82	3.2
External causes — Causes externes								
Total	4 068	48.3	3 646	42.6	1 547	60.3	1 028	40.5
Accidents								
Total	2 466	29.3	2 610	30.5	1 101	42.9	854	33.6
Transport accidents — Accidents de transport	474	5.6	182	2.1	148	5.8	38	1.5
Falls — Chutes	1 389	16.5	1 914	22.4	275	10.7	250	9.8
Accidental drowning and submersion — Noyade et submersion accidentelles	65	0.8	21	◆0.2	62	2.4	12	◆0.5
Exposure to smoke, fire and flames — Exposition à la fumée, au feu et aux flammes	27	◆0.3	15	◆0.2	27	◆1.1	21	◆0.8
Accidental poisoning by and exposure to noxious substances — Intoxication accidentelle par des substances nocives et exposition à ces substances	148	1.8	39	0.5	244	9.5	92	3.6
Intentional self-harm — Lésions auto-infligées	1 279	15.2	614	7.2	401	15.6	147	5.8
Assault — Agressions	63	0.7	32	0.4	22	◆0.9	9	◆0.4
All other external causes — Toutes autres causes externes	260	3.1	390	4.6	23	◆0.9	18	◆0.7

Cause of death — Cause de décès	Norway - Norvège 2015 (+C)				Poland - Pologne 2014 (C)			
	Male — Masculin		Female — Féminin		Male — Masculin		Female — Féminin	
	Number Nombre	Rate Taux	Number Nombre	Rate Taux	Number Nombre	Rate Taux	Number Nombre	Rate Taux
TOTAL	19 695	757.7	20 991	817.6	195 791	1 063.9	180 676	921.2
Certain infectious and parasitic diseases — Certaines maladies infectieuses et parasitaires								
Total	424	16.3	520	20.3	1 102	6.0	821	4.2
Intestinal infectious diseases — Maladies infectieuses intestinales	60	2.3	78	3.0	164	0.9	258	1.3
Tuberculosis — Tuberculose	2	+0.1	1	+0.0	413	2.2	113	0.6
Tetanus — Tétanos	-	-	-	-	-	-	2	+0.0
Diphtheria — Diphtérie	-	-	-	-	-	-	-	-
Whooping cough — Coqueluche	-	-	1	+0.0	-	-	-	-
Meningococcal infection — Infection à méningocoques	1	+0.0	1	+0.0	1	+0.0	4	+0.0
Septicaemia — Septicémie	155	6.0	163	6.3	139	0.8	170	0.9
Acute poliomyelitis — Poliomyélite aiguë	-	-	-	-	-	-	-	-
Measles — Rougeole	-	-	-	-	-	-	-	-
Viral hepatitis — Hépatite virale	13	+0.5	5	+0.2	183	1.0	138	0.7
Human immunodeficiency virus [HIV] disease — Maladies dues au virus de l'immunodéficience humaine (VIH)	4	+0.2	5	+0.2	93	0.5	32	0.2
Malaria — Paludisme	-	-	-	-	1	+0.0	-	-
Neoplasms — Tumeurs	5 956	229.1	5 095	198.5	55 255	300.2	45 074	229.8
Malignant neoplasms — Tumeurs malignes								
Total	5 821	224.0	4 941	192.5	52 688	286.3	42 873	218.6
Malignant neoplasm of lip, oral cavity and pharynx — Tumeur maligne de la lèvre, de la cavité buccale et du pharynx	112	4.3	54	2.1	2 004	10.9	671	3.4
Malignant neoplasm of oesophagus — Tumeur maligne de l'oesophage	160	6.2	56	2.2	1 171	6.4	344	1.8
Malignant neoplasm of stomach — Tumeur maligne de l'estomac	204	7.8	121	4.7	3 379	18.4	1 874	9.6
Malignant neoplasm of colon, rectosigmoid junction, rectum, anus and anal canal — Tumeur maligne du côlon, de la jonction recto-sigmoïdienne, du rectum, de l'anus et du canal anal	811	31.2	779	30.3	6 423	34.9	4 988	25.4
Malignant neoplasm of liver and intrahepatic bile ducts — Tumeur maligne du foie et des voies bilaires intrahépatiques	166	6.4	96	3.7	1 084	5.9	840	4.3
Malignant neoplasm of pancreas — Tumeur maligne du pancréas	376	14.5	385	15.0	2 464	13.4	2 519	12.8
Malignant neoplasm of trachea, bronchus and lung — Tumeur maligne de la trachée, des bronches et du poumon	1 191	45.8	984	38.3	15 847	86.1	7 363	37.5
Malignant neoplasm of female breast — Tumeur maligne du sein chez la femme	..	..	585	27.7	..	..	5 975	...
Malignant neoplasm of cervix uteri — Tumeur maligne du col de l'utérus	..	..	79	3.7	..	..	1 628	...
Malignant neoplasm of prostate — Tumeur maligne de la prostate	1 045	122.0	..	..	4 440	...	..	..
Malignant neoplasm of lymphoid, haematopoietic and related tissue — Tumeurs malignes primitives ou présumées primitives des tissus lymphoïde, hématopoïétique et apparentés	526	20.2	408	15.9	3 269	17.8	2 805	14.3
Disorders of the blood and blood-forming organs and certain disorders involving the immune mechanism — Maladies du sang et des organes hématopoïétiques et certains troubles du système immunitaire								
Total	46	1.8	87	3.4	101	0.5	111	0.6
Anaemias — Anémies	25	+1.0	60	2.3	40	0.2	47	0.2
Endocrine, nutritional and metabolic diseases — Maladies endocriniennes, nutritionnelles et métaboliques								
Total	460	17.7	510	19.9	3 150	17.1	4 056	20.7
Diabetes mellitus — Diabète sucré	319	12.3	285	11.1	2 965	16.1	3 821	19.5
Malnutrition — Malnutrition	38	1.5	91	3.5	80	0.4	87	0.4
Mental and behavioural disorders — Troubles mentaux et du comportement	827	31.8	1 803	70.2	1 176	6.4	314	1.6
Diseases of the nervous system — Maladies du système nerveux	823	31.7	1 082	42.1	2 339	12.7	2 851	14.5
Diseases of the circulatory system — Maladies de l'appareil circulatoire								
Total	5 436	209.1	6 177	240.6	78 817	428.3	90 917	463.5
Acute rheumatic fever and chronic rheumatic heart diseases — Rhumatisme articularie aigu et cardiopathies rhumatismales chroniques	18	+0.7	52	2.0	286	1.6	454	2.3
Hypertensive diseases — Maladies hypertensives	145	5.6	298	11.6	1 669	9.1	2 269	11.6
Ischaemic heart disease — Cardiopathie ischémique	2 301	88.5	1 913	74.5	21 044	114.3	17 494	89.2
Cerebrovascular disease — Maladie cérébrovasculaire	1 110	42.7	1 513	58.9	13 365	72.6	17 644	90.0

Cause of death — Cause de décès	Norway - Norvège 2015 (+C)				Poland - Pologne 2014 (C)			
	Male — Masculin		Female — Féminin		Male — Masculin		Female — Féminin	
	Number Nombre	Rate Taux	Number Nombre	Rate Taux	Number Nombre	Rate Taux	Number Nombre	Rate Taux
Diseases of arteries, arterioles and capillaries — Maladies des artères, artérioles et capillaires	372	14.3	317	12.3	14 050	76.3	23 881	121.8
Diseases of the respiratory system — Maladies de l'appareil respiratoire								
Total	2 069	79.6	2 155	83.9	11 611	63.1	8 760	44.7
Influenza — Grippe	58	2.2	66	2.6	7	+0.0	4	+0.0
Pneumonia — Pneumopathies	675	26.0	809	31.5	6 491	35.3	5 759	29.4
Chronic lower respiratory diseases — Maladies chroniques des voies respiratoires inférieures	1 097	42.2	1 104	43.0	4 174	22.7	2 264	11.5
Diseases of the digestive system — Maladies de l'appareil digestif								
Total	607	23.4	664	25.9	8 729	47.4	6 669	34.0
Gastric and duodenal ulcer — Ulcère de l'estomac et du duodénum	76	2.9	69	2.7	1 246	6.8	1 021	5.2
Diseases of the liver — Maladies du foie	160	6.2	103	4.0	4 504	24.5	2 077	10.6
Diseases of the musculoskeletal system and connective tissue — Maladies du système ostéo-articulaire, des muscles et du tissu conjonctif	112	4.3	202	7.9	157	0.9	431	2.2
Diseases of the genitourinary system — Maladies de l'appareil génito-urinaire								
Total	385	14.8	412	16.0	1 329	7.2	1 516	7.7
Disorders of kidney and ureter — Affections du rein et de l'uretère	233	9.0	249	9.7	991	5.4	1 073	5.5
Hyperplasia of prostate — Hyperplasie de la prostate	22	+2.6	..	..	25	...	..	..
Pregnancy, childbirth and the puerperium — Grossesse, accouchement et puerpéralité								
Total	..	..	-	-	..	..	8	+2.1
Pregnancy with abortive outcome — Grossesse se terminant par un avortement	..	..	-	-	..	..	1	+0.3
Other direct obstetric causes — Autres décès maternels directs	..	..	-	-	..	..	7	+1.9
Indirect obstetric causes — Décès maternels indirects	..	..	-	-	..	..	-	-
Certain conditions originating in the perinatal period — Certaines affections dont l'origine se situe dans la période périnatale	41	135.6	26	+91.0	457	236.7	348	191.1
Congenital malformations, deformations and chromosomal abnormalities — Malformations congénitales et anomalies chromosomiques	58	191.8	60	210.0	446	231.0	432	237.3
Symptoms, signs and abnormal clinical and laboratory findings, not elsewhere classified — Symptômes, signes et résultats anormaux d'examens cliniques et de laboratoire, non classés ailleurs	1 011	38.9	1 102	42.9	14 829	80.6	13 049	66.5
All other diseases — Toutes autres maladies	38	1.5	64	2.5	94	0.5	118	0.6
External causes — Causes externes								
Total	1 402	53.9	1 032	40.2	16 199	88.0	5 201	26.5
Accidents								
Total	974	37.5	806	31.4	9 073	49.3	3 740	19.1
Transport accidents — Accidents de transport	127	4.9	34	1.3	2 965	16.1	872	4.4
Falls — Chutes	377	14.5	438	17.1	2 655	14.4	2 063	10.5
Accidental drowning and submersion — Noyade et submersion accidentelles	38	1.5	9	+0.4	648	3.5	108	0.6
Exposure to smoke, fire and flames — Exposition à la fumée, au feu et aux flammes	23	+0.9	17	+0.7	372	2.0	115	0.6
Accidental poisoning by and exposure to noxious substances — Intoxication accidentelle par des substances nocives et exposition à ces substances	225	8.7	95	3.7	1 028	5.6	192	1.0
Intentional self-harm — Lésions auto-infligées	399	15.4	190	7.4	5 122	27.8	811	4.1
Assault — Agresssions	9	+0.3	12	+0.5	247	1.3	89	0.5
All other external causes — Toutes autres causes externes	20	+0.8	24	+0.9	1 757	9.5	561	2.9

20. Death and death rates by cause and sex: 2012 - 2016
Décès et taux de mortalité par cause et sexe : 2012 - 2016 (continued - suite)

Cause of death — Cause de décès	Poland - Pologne 2015 (C)				Portugal 2013 (+C)			
	Male — Masculin		Female — Féminin		Male — Masculin		Female — Féminin	
	Number Nombre	Rate Taux	Number Nombre	Rate Taux	Number Nombre	Rate Taux	Number Nombre	Rate Taux
TOTAL	204 469	1 111.4	190 452	971.3	54 406	1 093.2	52 469	957.4
Certain infectious and parasitic diseases — Certaines maladies infectieuses et parasitaires								
Total	1 098	6.0	817	4.2	1 307	26.3	1 131	20.6
Intestinal infectious diseases — Maladies infectieuses intestinales	205	1.1	343	1.7	72	1.4	157	2.9
Tuberculosis — Tuberculose	420	2.3	117	0.6	91	1.8	27	+0.5
Tetanus — Tétanos	1	+0.0	3	+0.0	-	-	-	-
Diphtheria — Diphtérie	-	-	-	-	-	-	-	-
Whooping cough — Coqueluche	-	-	-	-	1	+0.0	1	+0.0
Meningococcal infection — Infection à méningocoques	7	+0.0	5	+0.0	1	+0.0	4	+0.1
Septicaemia — Septicémie	85	0.5	95	0.5	527	10.6	679	12.4
Acute poliomyelitis — Poliomyélite aiguë	-	-	-	-	-	-	-	-
Measles — Rougeole	-	-	-	-	-	-	-	-
Viral hepatitis — Hépatite virale	192	1.0	128	0.7	97	1.9	43	0.8
Human immunodeficiency virus [HIV] disease — Maladies dues au virus de l'immunodéficience humaine (VIH)	107	0.6	36	0.2	359	7.2	99	1.8
Malaria — Paludisme	-	-	-	-	4	+0.1	-	-
Neoplasms — Tumeurs	58 233	316.5	47 241	240.9	15 746	316.4	10 661	194.5
Malignant neoplasms — Tumeurs malignes								
Total	55 662	302.6	44 939	229.2	15 463	310.7	10 457	190.8
Malignant neoplasm of lip, oral cavity and pharynx — Tumeur maligne de la lèvre, de la cavité buccale et du pharynx	2 117	11.5	676	3.4	568	11.4	128	2.3
Malignant neoplasm of oesophagus — Tumeur maligne de l'oesophage	1 167	6.3	316	1.6	485	9.7	59	1.1
Malignant neoplasm of stomach — Tumeur maligne de l'estomac	3 419	18.6	1 860	9.5	1 350	27.1	916	16.7
Malignant neoplasm of colon, rectosigmoid junction, rectum, anus and anal canal — Tumeur maligne du côlon, de la jonction recto-sigmoïdienne, du rectum, de l'anus et du canal anal	6 827	37.1	5 332	27.2	2 237	44.9	1 611	29.4
Malignant neoplasm of liver and intrahepatic bile ducts — Tumeur maligne du foie et des voies bilaires intrahépatiques	1 124	6.1	907	4.6	726	14.6	311	5.7
Malignant neoplasm of pancreas — Tumeur maligne du pancréas	2 469	13.4	2 440	12.4	732	14.7	644	11.8
Malignant neoplasm of trachea, bronchus and lung — Tumeur maligne de la trachée, des bronches et du poumon	16 261	88.4	7 484	38.2	3 153	63.4	857	15.6
Malignant neoplasm of female breast — Tumeur maligne du sein chez la femme	..	..	6 319	37.6	..	..	1 646	34.8
Malignant neoplasm of cervix uteri — Tumeur maligne du col de l'utérus	..	..	1 585	9.4	..	..	205	4.3
Malignant neoplasm of prostate — Tumeur maligne de la prostate	4 876	79.8	..	..	1 717	93.5	..	..
Malignant neoplasm of lymphoid, haematopoietic and related tissue — Tumeurs malignes primitives ou présumées primitives des tissus lymphoïde, hématopoïétique et apparentés	3 278	17.8	2 933	15.0	1 202	24.2	1 001	18.3
Disorders of the blood and blood-forming organs and certain disorders involving the immune mechanism — Maladies du sang et des organes hématopoïétiques et certains troubles du système immunitaire								
Total	90	0.5	111	0.6	212	4.3	244	4.5
Anaemias — Anémies	32	0.2	44	0.2	125	2.5	170	3.1
Endocrine, nutritional and metabolic diseases — Maladies endocriniennes, nutritionnelles et métaboliques								
Total	3 663	19.9	4 971	25.4	2 393	48.1	3 382	61.7
Diabetes mellitus — Diabète sucré	3 516	19.1	4 733	24.1	1 910	38.4	2 638	48.1
Malnutrition — Malnutrition	46	0.3	73	0.4	28	+0.6	42	0.8
Mental and behavioural disorders — Troubles mentaux et du comportement	1 785	9.7	433	2.2	887	17.8	1 336	24.4
Diseases of the nervous system — Maladies du système nerveux	2 448	13.3	2 989	15.2	1 596	32.1	1 931	35.2
Diseases of the circulatory system — Maladies de l'appareil circulatoire								
Total	83 288	452.7	97 055	495.0	13 981	280.9	17 547	320.2
Acute rheumatic fever and chronic rheumatic heart diseases — Rhumatisme articularie aigu et cardiopathies rhumatismales chroniques	272	1.5	413	2.1	61	1.2	126	2.3
Hypertensive diseases — Maladies hypertensives	1 781	9.7	2 647	13.5	836	16.8	1 458	26.6
Ischaemic heart disease — Cardiopathie ischémique	21 335	116.0	18 024	91.9	3 711	74.6	3 225	58.8
Cerebrovascular disease — Maladie cérébrovasculaire	13 168	71.6	17 307	88.3	5 362	107.7	6 911	126.1

Cause of death — Cause de décès	Poland - Pologne 2015 (C)				Portugal 2013 (+C)			
	Male — Masculin		Female — Féminin		Male — Masculin		Female — Féminin	
	Number Nombre	Rate Taux	Number Nombre	Rate Taux	Number Nombre	Rate Taux	Number Nombre	Rate Taux
Diseases of arteries, arterioles and capillaries — Maladies des artères, artérioles et capillaires	12 682	68.9	21 307	108.7	739	14.8	889	16.2
Diseases of the respiratory system — Maladies de l'appareil respiratoire								
Total	13 390	72.8	10 889	55.5	6 565	131.9	6 062	110.6
Influenza — Grippe	9	+0.0	8	+0.0	10	+0.2	15	+0.3
Pneumonia — Pneumopathies	7 618	41.4	7 071	36.1	2 988	60.0	2 947	53.8
Chronic lower respiratory diseases — Maladies chroniques des voies respiratoires inférieures	4 506	24.5	2 729	13.9	1 715	34.5	1 005	18.3
Diseases of the digestive system — Maladies de l'appareil digestif								
Total	8 557	46.5	6 201	31.6	2 578	51.8	2 005	36.6
Gastric and duodenal ulcer — Ulcère de l'estomac et du duodénum	1 193	6.5	1 051	5.4	141	2.8	108	2.0
Diseases of the liver — Maladies du foie	4 672	25.4	2 060	10.5	1 208	24.3	407	7.4
Diseases of the musculoskeletal system and connective tissue — Maladies du système ostéo-articulaire, des muscles et du tissu conjonctif	148	0.8	386	2.0	155	3.1	236	4.3
Diseases of the genitourinary system — Maladies de l'appareil génito-urinaire								
Total	1 398	7.6	1 628	8.3	1 301	26.1	1 629	29.7
Disorders of kidney and ureter — Affections du rein et de l'uretère	1 029	5.6	1 087	5.5	787	15.8	862	15.7
Hyperplasia of prostate — Hyperplasie de la prostate	27	+0.4	..	..	41	2.2	..	..
Pregnancy, childbirth and the puerperium — Grossesse, accouchement et puerpéralité								
Total	..	..	6	+1.6	..	..	5	+6.0
Pregnancy with abortive outcome — Grossesse se terminant par un avortement	..	..	2	+0.5	..	..	-	-
Other direct obstetric causes — Autres décès maternels directs	..	..	4	+1.1	..	..	4	+4.8
Indirect obstetric causes — Décès maternels indirects	..	..	-	-	..	..	1	+1.2
Certain conditions originating in the perinatal period — Certaines affections dont l'origine se situe dans la période périnatale	469	247.3	314	174.8	88	208.4	52	128.2
Congenital malformations, deformations and chromosomal abnormalities — Malformations congénitales et anomalies chromosomiques	442	233.0	390	217.1	85	201.3	75	184.9
Symptoms, signs and abnormal clinical and laboratory findings, not elsewhere classified — Symptômes, signes et résultats anormaux d'examens cliniques et de laboratoire, non classés ailleurs	14 515	78.9	11 886	60.6	4 655	93.5	4 703	85.8
All other diseases — Toutes autres maladies	105	0.6	148	0.8	35	0.7	65	1.2
External causes — Causes externes								
Total	14 840	80.7	4 987	25.4	2 822	56.7	1 405	25.6
Accidents								
Total	8 364	45.5	3 665	18.7	1 366	27.4	661	12.1
Transport accidents — Accidents de transport	2 723	14.8	802	4.1	599	12.0	168	3.1
Falls — Chutes	2 421	13.2	2 086	10.6	322	6.5	211	3.9
Accidental drowning and submersion — Noyade et submersion accidentelles	641	3.5	104	0.5	58	1.2	23	+0.4
Exposure to smoke, fire and flames — Exposition à la fumée, au feu et aux flammes	356	1.9	121	0.6	38	0.8	19	+0.3
Accidental poisoning by and exposure to noxious substances — Intoxication accidentelle par des substances nocives et exposition à ces substances	975	5.3	198	1.0	30	+0.6	20	+0.4
Intentional self-harm — Lésions auto-infligées	4 695	25.5	722	3.7	812	16.3	241	4.4
Assault — Agresssions	205	1.1	88	0.4	62	1.2	35	0.6
All other external causes — Toutes autres causes externes	1 576	8.6	512	2.6	582	11.7	468	8.5

20. Death and death rates by cause and sex: 2012 - 2016
Décès et taux de mortalité par cause et sexe : 2012 - 2016 (continued - suite)

Cause of death — Cause de décès	Portugal 2014 (+C)				Republic of Moldova - République de Moldova			
					2015 (+U)		2016 (+U)	
	Male — Masculin		Female — Féminin		Male — Masculin	Female — Féminin	Male — Masculin	Female — Féminin
	Number Nombre	Rate Taux	Number Nombre	Rate Taux	Number Nombre	Number Nombre	Number Nombre	Number Nombre
TOTAL	53 498	1 082.8	51 721	947.2	20 951	18 955	20 411	18 076
Certain infectious and parasitic diseases — Certaines maladies infectieuses et parasitaires								
Total	1 206	24.4	1 014	18.6	319	119	301	126
Intestinal infectious diseases — Maladies infectieuses intestinales	79	1.6	135	2.5	2	3	2	4
Tuberculosis — Tuberculose	87	1.8	26	✦0.5	223	48	203	39
Tetanus — Tétanos	-	-	1	✦0.0	-	-	-	-
Diphtheria — Diphtérie.............................	-	-	-	-	-	-	-	-
Whooping cough — Coqueluche	-	-	-	-	-	-	-	-
Meningococcal infection — Infection à méningocoques	2	✦0.0	1	✦0.0	3	4	7	5
Septicaemia — Septicémie	431	8.7	570	10.4	15	13	18	15
Acute poliomyelitis — Poliomyélite aiguë	-	-	-	-	-	-	-	-
Measles — Rougeole..............................	-	-	-	-	-	-	-	-
Viral hepatitis — Hépatite virale..................	105	2.1	53	1.0	4	4	6	2
Human immunodeficiency virus [HIV] disease — Maladies dues au virus de l'immunodéficience humaine (VIH)	317	6.4	102	1.9	58	30	51	39
Malaria — Paludisme...............................	5	✦0.1	1	✦0.0	-	-	-	-
Neoplasms — Tumeurs	15 934	322.5	10 808	197.9	3 546	2 568	3 639	2 587
Malignant neoplasms — Tumeurs malignes								
Total	15 649	316.7	10 571	193.6	3 513	2 533	3 606	2 556
Malignant neoplasm of lip, oral cavity and pharynx — Tumeur maligne de la lèvre, de la cavité buccale et du pharynx	584	11.8	110	2.0	263	33	278	34
Malignant neoplasm of oesophagus — Tumeur maligne de l'oesophage	482	9.8	83	1.5	65	13	83	6
Malignant neoplasm of stomach — Tumeur maligne de l'estomac	1 382	28.0	911	16.7	302	167	293	155
Malignant neoplasm of colon, rectosigmoid junction, rectum, anus and anal canal — Tumeur maligne du côlon, de la jonction recto-sigmoïdienne, du rectum, de l'anus et du canal anal	2 200	44.5	1 608	29.4	468	357	481	396
Malignant neoplasm of liver and intrahepatic bile ducts — Tumeur maligne du foie et des voies bilaires intrahépatiques	777	15.7	313	5.7	298	168	314	167
Malignant neoplasm of pancreas — Tumeur maligne du pancréas..................	742	15.0	620	11.4	195	155	198	159
Malignant neoplasm of trachea, bronchus and lung — Tumeur maligne de la trachée, des bronches et du poumon	3 084	62.4	853	15.6	776	184	820	179
Malignant neoplasm of female breast — Tumeur maligne du sein chez la femme	..	..	1 664	35.2	..	524	..	515
Malignant neoplasm of cervix uteri — Tumeur maligne du col de l'utérus.........	..	..	210	4.4	..	149	..	151
Malignant neoplasm of prostate — Tumeur maligne de la prostate	1 791	96.5	..	..	213	..	229	..
Malignant neoplasm of lymphoid, haematopoietic and related tissue — Tumeurs malignes primitives ou présumées primitives des tissus lymphoïde, hématopoïétique et apparentés..................	1 190	24.1	1 029	18.8	169	146	184	164
Disorders of the blood and blood-forming organs and certain disorders involving the immune mechanism — Maladies du sang et des organes hématopoïétiques et certains troubles du système immunitaire								
Total	217	4.4	250	4.6	17	9	7	12
Anaemias — Anémies	137	2.8	176	3.2	7	6	3	9
Endocrine, nutritional and metabolic diseases — Maladies endocriniennes, nutritionnelles et métaboliques								
Total	2 331	47.2	3 166	58.0	182	234	170	252
Diabetes mellitus — Diabète sucré................	1 853	37.5	2 422	44.4	179	230	164	246
Malnutrition — Malnutrition	28	✦0.6	31	0.6	-	-	1	-
Mental and behavioural disorders — Troubles mentaux et du comportement	1 082	21.9	1 557	28.5	146	35	88	22
Diseases of the nervous system — Maladies du système nerveux...............	1 618	32.7	1 932	35.4	251	116	215	107
Diseases of the circulatory system — Maladies de l'appareil circulatoire								
Total	14 574	295.0	17 712	324.4	10 453	12 584	10 137	11 789
Acute rheumatic fever and chronic rheumatic heart diseases — Rhumatisme articularie aigu et cardiopathies rhumatismales chroniques	70	1.4	131	2.4	28	41	25	48
Hypertensive diseases — Maladies hypertensives..................	846	17.1	1 539	28.2	733	1 179	796	1 320
Ischaemic heart disease — Cardiopathie ischémique...............................	4 178	84.6	3 278	60.0	6 464	7 816	6 160	7 026

20. Death and death rates by cause and sex: 2012 - 2016
Décès et taux de mortalité par cause et sexe : 2012 - 2016 (continued - suite)

Cause of death — Cause de décès	Portugal				Republic of Moldova - République de Moldova			
	2014 (+C)				2015 (+U)		2016 (+U)	
	Male — Masculin		Female — Féminin		Male — Masculin	Female — Féminin	Male — Masculin	Female — Féminin
	Number Nombre	Rate Taux	Number Nombre	Rate Taux	Number Nombre	Number Nombre	Number Nombre	Number Nombre
Cerebrovascular disease — Maladie cérébrovasculaire....................	5 117	103.6	6 691	122.5	2 641	3 198	2 575	3 078
Diseases of arteries, arterioles and capillaries — Maladies des artères, artérioles et capillaires	767	15.5	834	15.3	145	103	154	133
Diseases of the respiratory system — Maladies de l'appareil respiratoire								
Total	6 308	127.7	5 856	107.2	1 290	544	1 187	514
Influenza — Grippe...........	11	♦0.2	13	♦0.2	10	4	5	11
Pneumonia — Pneumopathies	2 813	56.9	2 816	51.6	697	228	662	220
Chronic lower respiratory diseases — Maladies chroniques des voies respiratoires inférieures	1 726	34.9	1 030	18.9	497	285	462	260
Diseases of the digestive system — Maladies de l'appareil digestif								
Total	2 619	53.0	1 985	36.4	2 004	1 763	2 002	1 695
Gastric and duodenal ulcer — Ulcère de l'estomac et du duodénum............	112	2.3	99	1.8	161	51	151	51
Diseases of the liver — Maladies du foie............	1 194	24.2	346	6.3	1 517	1 475	1 509	1 381
Diseases of the musculoskeletal system and connective tissue — Maladies du système ostéo-articularie, des muscles et du tissu conjonctif	161	3.3	246	4.5	13	17	15	20
Diseases of the genitourinary system — Maladies de l'appareil génito-urinaire								
Total	1 216	24.6	1 666	30.5	160	137	139	131
Disorders of kidney and ureter — Affections du rein et de l'uretère	710	14.4	829	15.2	140	130	122	128
Hyperplasia of prostate — Hyperplasie de la prostate............	43	2.3	..	..	12	..	12	..
Pregnancy, childbirth and the puerperium — Grossesse, accouchement et puerpéralité								
Total	..	..	6	♦7.3	..	12	..	7
Pregnancy with abortive outcome — Grossesse se terminant par un avortement	..	..	-	-	..	1	..	1
Other direct obstetric causes — Autres décès maternels directs	..	..	3	♦3.6	..	3	..	3
Indirect obstetric causes — Décès maternels indirects	..	..	3	♦3.6	..	8	..	3
Certain conditions originating in the perinatal period — Certaines affections dont l'origine se situe dans la période périnatale	83	195.6	61	152.7	102	74	99	61
Congenital malformations, deformations and chromosomal abnormalities — Malformations congénitales et anomalies chromosomiques	97	228.6	68	170.3	84	51	66	66
Symptoms, signs and abnormal clinical and laboratory findings, not elsewhere classified — Symptômes, signes et résultats anormaux d'examens cliniques et de laboratoire, non classés ailleurs	2 836	57.4	3 640	66.7	220	81	211	74
All other diseases — Toutes autres maladies	65	1.3	87	1.6	12	21	22	21
External causes — Causes externes								
Total	3 151	63.8	1 667	30.5	2 152	590	2 113	592
Accidents								
Total	1 545	31.3	811	14.9	1 463	409	1 400	439
Transport accidents — Accidents de transport	653	13.2	162	3.0	305	67	263	83
Falls — Chutes	371	7.5	247	4.5	123	32	135	30
Accidental drowning and submersion — Noyade et submersion accidentelles	58	1.2	20	♦0.4	157	24	140	35
Exposure to smoke, fire and flames — Exposition à la fumée, au feu et aux flammes	25	♦0.5	23	♦0.4	37	17	36	24
Accidental poisoning by and exposure to noxious substances — Intoxication accidentelle par des substances nocives et exposition à ces substances	53	1.1	21	♦0.4	285	106	238	81
Intentional self-harm — Lésions auto-infligées...........	925	18.7	298	5.5	464	92	462	84
Assault — Agresssions...........	52	1.1	57	1.0	116	60	134	41
All other external causes — Toutes autres causes externes	629	12.7	501	9.2	109	29	117	28

20. Death and death rates by cause and sex: 2012 - 2016
Décès et taux de mortalité par cause et sexe : 2012 - 2016 (continued - suite)

Romania - Roumanie

Cause of death — Cause de décès	2015 (+C)				2016 (+C)			
	Male — Masculin		Female — Féminin		Male — Masculin		Female — Féminin	
	Number Nombre	Rate Taux	Number Nombre	Rate Taux	Number Nombre	Rate Taux	Number Nombre	Rate Taux
TOTAL	135 886	1 403.7	125 408	1 236.9	134 495	1 396.9	122 720	1 217.7
Certain infectious and parasitic diseases — Certaines maladies infectieuses et parasitaires								
Total	1 745	18.0	992	9.8	1 916	19.9	1 215	12.1
Intestinal infectious diseases — Maladies infectieuses intestinales	83	0.9	91	0.9	80	0.8	100	1.0
Tuberculosis — Tuberculose	838	8.7	220	2.2	788	8.2	184	1.8
Tetanus — Tétanos	1	♦0.0	3	♦0.0	-	-	2	♦0.0
Diphtheria — Diphtérie	-	-	-	-	-	-	-	-
Whooping cough — Coqueluche	-	-	-	-	-	-	-	-
Meningococcal infection — Infection à méningocoques	7	♦0.1	5	♦0.0	9	♦0.1	3	♦0.0
Septicaemia — Septicémie	590	6.1	510	5.0	796	8.3	723	7.2
Acute poliomyelitis — Poliomyélite aiguë	-	-	1	♦0.0	-	-	1	♦0.0
Measles — Rougeole	-	-	-	-	1	♦0.0	3	♦0.0
Viral hepatitis — Hépatite virale	39	0.4	44	0.4	35	0.4	61	0.6
Human immunodeficiency virus [HIV] disease — Maladies dues au virus de l'immunodéficience humaine (VIH)	133	1.4	56	0.6	147	1.5	72	0.7
Malaria — Paludisme	4	♦0.0	-	-	-	-	-	-
Neoplasms — Tumeurs	30 316	313.2	20 999	207.1	30 690	318.7	21 096	209.3
Malignant neoplasms — Tumeurs malignes								
Total	30 156	311.5	20 868	205.8	30 525	317.0	20 989	208.3
Malignant neoplasm of lip, oral cavity and pharynx — Tumeur maligne de la lèvre, de la cavité buccale et du pharynx	1 869	19.3	305	3.0	1 831	19.0	273	2.7
Malignant neoplasm of oesophagus — Tumeur maligne de l'oesophage	572	5.9	128	1.3	635	6.6	123	1.2
Malignant neoplasm of stomach — Tumeur maligne de l'estomac	2 230	23.0	1 125	11.1	2 219	23.0	1 139	11.3
Malignant neoplasm of colon, rectosigmoid junction, rectum, anus and anal canal — Tumeur maligne du côlon, de la jonction recto-sigmoïdienne, du rectum, de l'anus et du canal anal	3 595	37.1	2 532	25.0	3 825	39.7	2 593	25.7
Malignant neoplasm of liver and intrahepatic bile ducts — Tumeur maligne du foie et des voies biliaires intrahépatiques	1 967	20.3	1 092	10.8	1 997	20.7	1 124	11.2
Malignant neoplasm of pancreas — Tumeur maligne du pancréas	1 578	16.3	1 286	12.7	1 584	16.5	1 299	12.9
Malignant neoplasm of trachea, bronchus and lung — Tumeur maligne de la trachée, des bronches et du poumon	8 058	83.2	2 303	22.7	7 904	82.1	2 324	23.1
Malignant neoplasm of female breast — Tumeur maligne du sein chez la femme	..	..	3 433	39.7	..	..	3 460	40.3
Malignant neoplasm of cervix uteri — Tumeur maligne du col de l'utérus	..	..	1 644	19.0	..	..	1 590	18.5
Malignant neoplasm of prostate — Tumeur maligne de la prostate	2 198	68.8	..	..	2 332	73.3	..	..
Malignant neoplasm of lymphoid, haematopoietic and related tissue — Tumeurs malignes primitives ou présumées primitives des tissus lymphoïde, hématopoïétique et apparentés	1 417	14.6	1 120	11.0	1 362	14.1	1 163	11.5
Disorders of the blood and blood-forming organs and certain disorders involving the immune mechanism — Maladies du sang et des organes hématopoïétiques et certains troubles du système immunitaire								
Total	57	0.6	65	0.6	79	0.8	86	0.9
Anaemias — Anémies	34	0.4	39	0.4	42	0.4	50	0.5
Endocrine, nutritional and metabolic diseases — Maladies endocriniennes, nutritionnelles et métaboliques								
Total	1 257	13.0	1 411	13.9	1 350	14.0	1 551	15.4
Diabetes mellitus — Diabète sucré	1 182	12.2	1 328	13.1	1 239	12.9	1 441	14.3
Malnutrition — Malnutrition	51	0.5	48	0.5	81	0.8	63	0.6
Mental and behavioural disorders — Troubles mentaux et du comportement	147	1.5	65	0.6	166	1.7	75	0.7
Diseases of the nervous system — Maladies du système nerveux	1 640	16.9	2 100	20.7	1 694	17.6	2 226	22.1
Diseases of the circulatory system — Maladies de l'appareil circulatoire								
Total	71 237	735.9	82 673	815.4	69 122	717.9	79 443	788.3
Acute rheumatic fever and chronic rheumatic heart diseases — Rhumatisme articulaire aigu et cardiopathies rhumatismales chroniques	153	1.6	201	2.0	157	1.6	224	2.2
Hypertensive diseases — Maladies hypertensives	12 561	129.8	18 144	178.9	12 051	125.2	17 062	169.3
Ischaemic heart disease — Cardiopathie ischémique	26 066	269.3	26 643	262.8	24 801	257.6	24 920	247.3
Cerebrovascular disease — Maladie cérébrovasculaire	19 763	204.2	24 542	242.1	19 073	198.1	23 802	236.2

20. Death and death rates by cause and sex: 2012 - 2016
Décès et taux de mortalité par cause et sexe : 2012 - 2016 (continued - suite)

Romania - Roumanie

Cause of death — Cause de décès	2015 (+C)				2016 (+C)			
	Male — Masculin		Female — Féminin		Male — Masculin		Female — Féminin	
	Number Nombre	Rate Taux	Number Nombre	Rate Taux	Number Nombre	Rate Taux	Number Nombre	Rate Taux
Diseases of arteries, arterioles and capillaries — Maladies des artères, artérioles et capillaires	4 836	50.0	6 655	65.6	4 686	48.7	6 357	63.1
Diseases of the respiratory system — Maladies de l'appareil respiratoire								
Total	9 146	94.5	5 856	57.8	8 924	92.7	5 629	55.9
Influenza — Grippe...........	12	♦0.1	13	♦0.1	26	♦0.3	31	0.3
Pneumonia — Pneumopathies...........	3 957	40.9	2 844	28.0	3 834	39.8	2 743	27.2
Chronic lower respiratory diseases — Maladies chroniques des voies respiratoires inférieures	4 114	42.5	2 191	21.6	3 921	40.7	1 994	19.8
Diseases of the digestive system — Maladies de l'appareil digestif								
Total	8 663	89.5	5 718	56.4	8 782	91.2	5 728	56.8
Gastric and duodenal ulcer — Ulcère de l'estomac et du duodénum...........	306	3.2	167	1.6	314	3.3	205	2.0
Diseases of the liver — Maladies du foie...........	6 135	63.4	3 636	35.9	6 206	64.5	3 678	36.5
Diseases of the musculoskeletal system and connective tissue — Maladies du système ostéo-articularie, des muscles et du tissu conjonctif	20	♦0.2	25	♦0.2	23	♦0.2	26	♦0.3
Diseases of the genitourinary system — Maladies de l'appareil génito-urinaire								
Total	1 823	18.8	1 633	16.1	1 878	19.5	1 746	17.3
Disorders of kidney and ureter — Affections du rein et de l'uretère	1 681	17.4	1 579	15.6	1 737	18.0	1 704	16.9
Hyperplasia of prostate — Hyperplasie de la prostate...........	113	3.5	..	..	117	3.7	..	..
Pregnancy, childbirth and the puerperium — Grossesse, accouchement et puerpéralité								
Total	..	..	27	♦13.7	..	..	17	♦8.5
Pregnancy with abortive outcome — Grossesse se terminant par un avortement	..	..	5	♦2.5	..	..	-	-
Other direct obstetric causes — Autres décès maternels directs...........	..	..	13	♦6.6	..	..	10	♦5.0
Indirect obstetric causes — Décès maternels indirects...........	..	..	9	♦4.6	..	..	7	♦3.5
Certain conditions originating in the perinatal period — Certaines affections dont l'origine se situe dans la période périnatale	317	311.3	230	240.4	288	280.7	211	216.6
Congenital malformations, deformations and chromosomal abnormalities — Malformations congénitales et anomalies chromosomiques	233	228.8	192	200.7	217	211.5	180	184.8
Symptoms, signs and abnormal clinical and laboratory findings, not elsewhere classified — Symptômes, signes et résultats anormaux d'examens cliniques et de laboratoire, non classés ailleurs	1 629	16.8	1 123	11.1	1 730	18.0	1 136	11.3
All other diseases — Toutes autres maladies...........	37	0.4	47	0.5	41	0.4	43	0.4
External causes — Causes externes								
Total	7 619	78.7	2 252	22.2	7 595	78.9	2 312	22.9
Accidents								
Total	5 278	54.5	1 710	16.9	5 476	56.9	1 817	18.0
Transport accidents — Accidents de transport...........	1 723	17.8	561	5.5	1 757	18.2	593	5.9
Falls — Chutes	990	10.2	301	3.0	1 069	11.1	348	3.5
Accidental drowning and submersion — Noyade et submersion accidentelles...........	504	5.2	134	1.3	465	4.8	132	1.3
Exposure to smoke, fire and flames — Exposition à la fumée, au feu et aux flammes	234	2.4	148	1.5	222	2.3	145	1.4
Accidental poisoning by and exposure to noxious substances — Intoxication accidentelle par des substances nocives et exposition à ces substances	493	5.1	224	2.2	519	5.4	187	1.9
Intentional self-harm — Lésions auto-infligées...........	1 886	19.5	342	3.4	1 651	17.1	318	3.2
Assault — Agresssions...........	196	2.0	105	1.0	209	2.2	94	0.9
All other external causes — Toutes autres causes externes	259	2.7	95	0.9	259	2.7	83	0.8

20. Death and death rates by cause and sex: 2012 - 2016
Décès et taux de mortalité par cause et sexe : 2012 - 2016 (continued - suite)

Russian Federation - Fédération de Russie

Cause of death — Cause de décès	2012 (+C)				2013 (+C)		
	Male — Masculin		Female — Féminin		Male — Masculin	Female — Féminin	
	Number Nombre	Rate Taux	Number Nombre	Rate Taux	Number Nombre	Number Nombre	Rate Taux
TOTAL	977 254	1 474.8	929 081	1 207.6	954 390	917 419	...
Certain infectious and parasitic diseases — Certaines maladies infectieuses et parasitaires							
Total	23 583	35.6	8 501	11.0	23 000	8 807	...
Intestinal infectious diseases — Maladies infectieuses intestinales	190	0.3	161	0.2	166	175	...
Tuberculosis — Tuberculose	14 352	21.7	3 614	4.7	12 728	3 462	...
Tetanus — Tétanos	6	+0.0	6	+0.0	4	4	...
Diphtheria — Diphtérie	-	-	-	-	-	1	...
Whooping cough — Coqueluche	2	+0.0	4	+0.0	-	-	...
Meningococcal infection — Infection à méningocoques	135	0.2	125	0.2	129	115	...
Septicaemia — Septicémie	1 094	1.7	867	1.1	1 078	789	...
Acute poliomyelitis — Poliomyélite aiguë	3	+0.0	-	-	1	2	...
Measles — Rougeole	2	+0.0	1	+0.0	-	1	...
Viral hepatitis — Hépatite virale	774	1.2	504	0.7	797	501	...
Human immunodeficiency virus [HIV] disease — Maladies dues au virus de l'immunodéficience humaine (VIH)	6 360	9.6	2 615	3.4	7 440	3 171	...
Malaria — Paludisme	1	+0.0	-	-	1	1	...
Neoplasms — Tumeurs	154 613	233.3	136 267	177.1	155 002	136 773	...
Malignant neoplasms — Tumeurs malignes							
Total	153 291	231.3	134 498	174.8	153 668	134 968	...
Malignant neoplasm of lip, oral cavity and pharynx — Tumeur maligne de la lèvre, de la cavité buccale et du pharynx	7 467	11.3	1 765	2.3	7 622	1 823	...
Malignant neoplasm of oesophagus — Tumeur maligne de l'oesophage	5 096	7.7	1 400	1.8	5 242	1 320	...
Malignant neoplasm of stomach — Tumeur maligne de l'estomac	18 319	27.6	13 610	17.7	17 960	13 509	...
Malignant neoplasm of colon, rectosigmoid junction, rectum, anus and anal canal — Tumeur maligne du côlon, de la jonction recto-sigmoïdienne, du rectum, de l'anus et du canal anal	17 369	26.2	21 390	27.8	17 476	21 276	...
Malignant neoplasm of liver and intrahepatic bile ducts — Tumeur maligne du foie et des voies bilaires intrahépatiques	4 786	7.2	3 859	5.0	4 974	3 951	...
Malignant neoplasm of pancreas — Tumeur maligne du pancréas	8 214	12.4	7 971	10.4	8 095	8 022	...
Malignant neoplasm of trachea, bronchus and lung — Tumeur maligne de la trachée, des bronches et du poumon	41 066	62.0	8 842	11.5	41 123	8 945	...
Malignant neoplasm of female breast — Tumeur maligne du sein chez la femme	..	..	22 936	34.8	..	22 890	...
Malignant neoplasm of cervix uteri — Tumeur maligne du col de l'utérus	..	..	6 340	9.6	..	6 522	...
Malignant neoplasm of prostate — Tumeur maligne de la prostate	10 861	56.9	..	..	11 111	..	...
Malignant neoplasm of lymphoid, haematopoietic and related tissue — Tumeurs malignes primitives ou présumées primitives des tissus lymphoïde, hématopoïétique et apparentés	...	...	...	...	...	...	...
Disorders of the blood and blood-forming organs and certain disorders involving the immune mechanism — Maladies du sang et des organes hématopoïétiques et certains troubles du système immunitaire							
Total	452	0.7	656	0.9	525	719	...
Anaemias — Anémies	252	0.4	396	0.5	300	464	...
Endocrine, nutritional and metabolic diseases — Maladies endocriniennes, nutritionnelles et métaboliques							
Total	3 490	5.3	8 114	10.5	4 235	9 716	...
Diabetes mellitus — Diabète sucré	3 051	4.6	7 490	9.7	3 790	9 095	...
Malnutrition — Malnutrition	87	0.1	69	0.1	52	82	...
Mental and behavioural disorders — Troubles mentaux et du comportement	3 288	5.0	1 786	2.3	3 344	2 349	...
Diseases of the nervous system — Maladies du système nerveux	10 037	15.1	8 537	11.1	11 353	11 434	...
Diseases of the circulatory system — Maladies de l'appareil circulatoire							
Total	473 584	714.7	582 008	756.5	449 983	551 816	...
Acute rheumatic fever and chronic rheumatic heart diseases — Rhumatisme articularie aigu et cardiopathies rhumatismales chroniques	1 064	1.6	2 074	2.7	927	1 946	...
Hypertensive diseases — Maladies hypertensives	9 860	14.9	14 879	19.3	8 581	13 116	...
Ischaemic heart disease — Cardiopathie ischémique	263 646	397.9	299 311	389.0	248 332	281 493	...
Cerebrovascular disease — Maladie cérébrovasculaire	124 294	187.6	198 709	258.3	119 745	190 785	...

Russian Federation - Fédération de Russie

Cause of death — Cause de décès	2012 (+C)				2013 (+C)		
	Male — Masculin		Female — Féminin		Male — Masculin	Female — Féminin	
	Number Nombre	Rate Taux	Number Nombre	Rate Taux	Number Nombre	Number Nombre	Rate Taux
Diseases of arteries, arterioles and capillaries — Maladies des artères, artérioles et capillaires	...	...	...	...	...	...	...
Diseases of the respiratory system — Maladies de l'appareil respiratoire							
Total	49 199	74.2	21 594	28.1	50 368	23 700	...
Influenza — Grippe	33	0.0	33	0.0	153	114	...
Pneumonia — Pneumopathies	25 393	38.3	11 028	14.3	25 956	12 316	...
Chronic lower respiratory diseases — Maladies chroniques des voies respiratoires inférieures	20 364	30.7	8 905	11.6	20 983	9 500	...
Diseases of the digestive system — Maladies de l'appareil digestif							
Total	49 823	75.2	39 044	50.7	49 063	39 368	...
Gastric and duodenal ulcer — Ulcère de l'estomac et du duodénum	5 337	8.1	3 473	4.5	5 250	3 690	...
Diseases of the liver — Maladies du foie	27 902	42.1	19 377	25.2	26 895	18 894	...
Diseases of the musculoskeletal system and connective tissue — Maladies du système ostéo-articularie, des muscles et du tissu conjonctif	586	0.9	1 151	1.5	601	1 200	...
Diseases of the genitourinary system — Maladies de l'appareil génito-urinaire							
Total	5 548	8.4	6 024	7.8	5 861	6 517	...
Disorders of kidney and ureter — Affections du rein et de l'uretère	...	...	...	...	...	...	...
Hyperplasia of prostate — Hyperplasie de la prostate	...	...	..	...	...	..	...
Pregnancy, childbirth and the puerperium — Grossesse, accouchement et puerpéralité							
Total	..	..	221	11.6	..	216	11.4
Pregnancy with abortive outcome — Grossesse se terminant par un avortement	..	..	28	٠1.5	..	17	٠0.9
Other direct obstetric causes — Autres décès maternels directs	..	..	140	7.4	..	151	8.0
Indirect obstetric causes — Décès maternels indirects	..	..	51	2.7	..	47	2.5
Certain conditions originating in the perinatal period — Certaines affections dont l'origine se situe dans la période périnatale	5 179	529.3	3 903	422.6	4 882	3 562	...
Congenital malformations, deformations and chromosomal abnormalities — Malformations congénitales et anomalies chromosomiques	2 830	289.2	2 416	261.6	2 746	2 249	...
Symptoms, signs and abnormal clinical and laboratory findings, not elsewhere classified — Symptômes, signes et résultats anormaux d'examens cliniques et de laboratoire, non classés ailleurs	44 925	67.8	63 060	82.0	48 988	75 877	...
All other diseases — Toutes autres maladies	1 013	1.5	1 129	1.5	995	1 207	...
External causes — Causes externes							
Total	149 104	225.0	44 670	58.1	143 444	41 909	...
Accidents							
Total	...	...	...	...	...	...	...
Transport accidents — Accidents de transport	22 076	33.3	7 826	10.2	21 510	7 425	...
Falls — Chutes	6 222	9.4	2 513	3.3	6 215	2 655	...
Accidental drowning and submersion — Noyade et submersion accidentelles	6 873	10.4	1 265	1.6	6 330	1 120	...
Exposure to smoke, fire and flames — Exposition à la fumée, au feu et aux flammes	5 084	7.7	2 201	2.9	4 493	1 882	...
Accidental poisoning by and exposure to noxious substances — Intoxication accidentelle par des substances nocives et exposition à ces substances	22 161	33.4	6 226	8.1	21 475	5 796	...
Intentional self-harm — Lésions auto-infligées	24 275	36.6	5 460	7.1	23 794	4 985	...
Assault — Agresssions	11 673	17.6	3 735	4.9	11 037	3 390	...
All other external causes — Toutes autres causes externes	...	...	...	...	...	...	...

Cause of death — Cause de décès	San Marino - Saint-Marin				Serbia - Serbie			
	2014 (+C)		2015 (+C)		2014 (+C)			
	Male — Masculin	Female — Féminin	Male — Masculin	Female — Féminin	Male — Masculin		Female — Féminin	
	Number Nombre	Number Nombre	Number Nombre	Number Nombre	Number Nombre	Rate Taux	Number Nombre	Rate Taux
TOTAL	100	98	97	84	51 010	1 465.9	50 237	1 370.0
Certain infectious and parasitic diseases — Certaines maladies infectieuses et parasitaires								
Total	-	-	-	-	305	8.8	250	6.8
Intestinal infectious diseases — Maladies infectieuses intestinales	-	-	-	-	52	1.5	84	2.3
Tuberculosis — Tuberculose	-	-	-	-	54	1.6	33	0.9
Tetanus — Tétanos	-	-	-	-	-	-	-	-
Diphtheria — Diphtérie..	-	-	-	-	-	-	-	-
Whooping cough — Coqueluche	-	-	-	-	-	-	-	-
Meningococcal infection — Infection à méningocoques	-	-	-	-	-	-	1	+0.0
Septicaemia — Septicémie	-	-	-	-	120	3.4	83	2.3
Acute poliomyelitis — Poliomyélite aiguë	-	-	-	-	-	-	-	-
Measles — Rougeole...	-	-	-	-	-	-	-	-
Viral hepatitis — Hépatite virale...................................	-	-	-	-	28	+0.8	13	+0.4
Human immunodeficiency virus [HIV] disease — Maladies dues au virus de l'immunodéficience humaine (VIH)	-	-	-	-	11	+0.3	1	+0.0
Malaria — Paludisme..	-	-	-	-	-.	-	-	-
Neoplasms — Tumeurs	37	25	33	24	12 374	355.6	9 432	257.2
Malignant neoplasms — Tumeurs malignes								
Total	35	25	32	22	12 117	348.2	9 205	251.0
Malignant neoplasm of lip, oral cavity and pharynx — Tumeur maligne de la lèvre, de la cavité buccale et du pharynx	4	-	-	-	401	11.5	110	3.0
Malignant neoplasm of oesophagus — Tumeur maligne de l'oesophage	-	-	1	-	203	5.8	50	1.4
Malignant neoplasm of stomach — Tumeur maligne de l'estomac	4	4	1	2	618	17.8	339	9.2
Malignant neoplasm of colon, rectosigmoid junction, rectum, anus and anal canal — Tumeur maligne du côlon, de la jonction recto-sigmoïdienne, du rectum, de l'anus et du canal anal	7	2	3	5	1 545	44.4	1 050	28.6
Malignant neoplasm of liver and intrahepatic bile ducts — Tumeur maligne du foie et des voies bilaires intrahépatiques	-	-	2	-	455	13.1	279	7.6
Malignant neoplasm of pancreas — Tumeur maligne du pancréas...............	2	-	2	2	573	16.5	483	13.2
Malignant neoplasm of trachea, bronchus and lung — Tumeur maligne de la trachée, des bronches et du poumon	6	3	6	3	3 798	109.1	1 427	38.9
Malignant neoplasm of female breast — Tumeur maligne du sein chez la femme	..	5	..	3	...	...	1 648	...
Malignant neoplasm of cervix uteri — Tumeur maligne du col de l'utérus.........	..	-	..	-	..	..	415	...
Malignant neoplasm of prostate — Tumeur maligne de la prostate	3	..	2	..	977	...	..	..
Malignant neoplasm of lymphoid, haematopoietic and related tissue — Tumeurs malignes primitives ou présumées primitives des tissus lymphoïde, hématopoïétique et apparentés.............................	...	...	...	...	667	19.2	534	14.6
Disorders of the blood and blood-forming organs and certain disorders involving the immune mechanism — Maladies du sang et des organes hématopoïétiques et certains troubles du système immunitaire								
Total	-	-	-	-	93	2.7	158	4.3
Anaemias — Anémies	-	-	-	-	53	1.5	101	2.8
Endocrine, nutritional and metabolic diseases — Maladies endocriniennes, nutritionnelles et métaboliques								
Total	4	3	6	5	1 138	32.7	1 505	41.0
Diabetes mellitus — Diabète sucré.................................	4	3	5	5	1 096	31.5	1 417	38.6
Malnutrition — Malnutrition	-	-	-	-	7	+0.2	5	+0.1
Mental and behavioural disorders — Troubles mentaux et du comportement	2	2	2	3	606	17.4	697	19.0
Diseases of the nervous system — Maladies du système nerveux.................	6	8	5	9	812	23.3	960	26.2
Diseases of the circulatory system — Maladies de l'appareil circulatoire								
Total	33	41	29	22	24 691	709.5	29 302	799.1
Acute rheumatic fever and chronic rheumatic heart diseases — Rhumatisme articularie aigu et cardiopathies rhumatismales chroniques	-	-	-	-	34	1.0	47	1.3
Hypertensive diseases — Maladies hypertensives.............................	-	8	1	1	2 292	65.9	3 431	93.6
Ischaemic heart disease — Cardiopathie ischémique.............................	9	5	6	2	5 382	154.7	4 589	125.1

	San Marino - Saint-Marin				Serbia - Serbie			
	2014 (+C)		2015 (+C)		2014 (+C)			
	Male — Masculin	Female — Féminin	Male — Masculin	Female — Féminin	Male — Masculin		Female — Féminin	
Cause of death — Cause de décès	Number Nombre	Number Nombre	Number Nombre	Number Nombre	Number Nombre	Rate Taux	Number Nombre	Rate Taux
Cerebrovascular disease — Maladie cérébrovasculaire...................	4	7	4	8	5 477	157.4	6 842	186.6
Diseases of arteries, arterioles and capillaries — Maladies des artères, artérioles et capillaires	...	...	...	...	1 159	33.3	1 461	39.8
Diseases of the respiratory system — Maladies de l'appareil respiratoire								
Total	6	7	6	6	2 877	82.7	2 192	59.8
Influenza — Grippe	-	-	-	-	3	♦0.1	3	♦0.1
Pneumonia — Pneumopathies	1	1	-	1	553	15.9	449	12.2
Chronic lower respiratory diseases — Maladies chroniques des voies respiratoires inférieures	3	4	4	5	1 517	43.6	982	26.8
Diseases of the digestive system — Maladies de l'appareil digestif								
Total	3	3	2	6	1 922	55.2	1 429	39.0
Gastric and duodenal ulcer — Ulcère de l'estomac et du duodénum...........	1	-	-	-	282	8.1	232	6.3
Diseases of the liver — Maladies du foie...........................	1	-	2	1	674	19.4	188	5.1
Diseases of the musculoskeletal system and connective tissue — Maladies du système ostéo-articularie, des muscles et du tissu conjonctif	-	-	-	-	32	0.9	109	3.0
Diseases of the genitourinary system — Maladies de l'appareil génito-urinaire								
Total	2	1	1	2	1 153	33.1	901	24.6
Disorders of kidney and ureter — Affections du rein et de l'uretère	...	...	...	...	1 081	31.1	881	24.0
Hyperplasia of prostate — Hyperplasie de la prostate.................	...	..	...	..	30	...	..	..
Pregnancy, childbirth and the puerperium — Grossesse, accouchement et puerpéralité								
Total	..	-	..	-	..	..	8	♦12.0
Pregnancy with abortive outcome — Grossesse se terminant par un avortement	..	-	..	-	..	..	-	-
Other direct obstetric causes — Autres décès maternels directs	..	-	..	-	..	..	5	♦7.5
Indirect obstetric causes — Décès maternels indirects	..	-	..	-	..	..	3	♦4.5
Certain conditions originating in the perinatal period — Certaines affections dont l'origine se situe dans la période périnatale	1	-	-	-	158	460.3	94	292.5
Congenital malformations, deformations and chromosomal abnormalities — Malformations congénitales et anomalies chromosomiques	-	-	-	-	61	177.7	59	183.6
Symptoms, signs and abnormal clinical and laboratory findings, not elsewhere classified — Symptômes, signes et résultats anormaux d'examens cliniques et de laboratoire, non classés ailleurs	1	2	1	3	2 494	71.7	2 255	61.5
All other diseases — Toutes autres maladies........................	-	-	-	-	47	1.4	58	1.6
External causes — Causes externes								
Total	5	6	12	4	2 247	64.6	828	22.6
Accidents								
Total	...	...	...	...	1 052	30.2	400	10.9
Transport accidents — Accidents de transport	1	-	3	-	418	12.0	111	3.0
Falls — Chutes	1	2	4	1	241	6.9	134	3.7
Accidental drowning and submersion — Noyade et submersion accidentelles	-	-	-	-	56	1.6	17	♦0.5
Exposure to smoke, fire and flames — Exposition à la fumée, au feu et aux flammes	-	-	-	-	37	1.1	19	♦0.5
Accidental poisoning by and exposure to noxious substances — Intoxication accidentelle par des substances nocives et exposition à ces substances	-	-	-	-	31	0.9	15	♦0.4
Intentional self-harm — Lésions auto-infligées..............................	-	1	5	1	857	24.6	277	7.6
Assault — Agresssions	-	-	-	-	82	2.4	32	0.9
All other external causes — Toutes autres causes externes	...	...	...	...	256	7.4	119	3.2

Cause of death — Cause de décès	Serbia - Serbie 2015 (+C)				Slovakia - Slovaquie 2013 (C)			
	Male — Masculin		Female — Féminin		Male — Masculin		Female — Féminin	
	Number Nombre	Rate Taux	Number Nombre	Rate Taux	Number Nombre	Rate Taux	Number Nombre	Rate Taux
TOTAL	52 145	1 505.2	51 533	1 411.9	26 863	1 019.1	25 221	908.9
Certain infectious and parasitic diseases — Certaines maladies infectieuses et parasitaires								
Total	316	9.1	276	7.6	166	6.3	167	6.0
Intestinal infectious diseases — Maladies infectieuses intestinales	74	2.1	104	2.8	12	♦0.5	12	♦0.4
Tuberculosis — Tuberculose	43	1.2	27	♦0.7	14	♦0.5	5	♦0.2
Tetanus — Tétanos	1	♦0.0	3	♦0.1	-	-	-	-
Diphtheria — Diphtérie	-	-	-	-	-	-	-	-
Whooping cough — Coqueluche	-	-	-	-	-	-	-	-
Meningococcal infection — Infection à méningocoques	1	♦0.0	-	-	3	♦0.1	-	-
Septicaemia — Septicémie	127	3.7	94	2.6	107	4.1	121	4.4
Acute poliomyelitis — Poliomyélite aiguë	-	-	-	-	-	-	-	-
Measles — Rougeole	-	-	-	-	-	-	-	-
Viral hepatitis — Hépatite virale	25	♦0.7	20	♦0.5	9	♦0.3	7	♦0.3
Human immunodeficiency virus [HIV] disease — Maladies dues au virus de l'immunodéficience humaine (VIH)	23	♦0.7	1	♦0.0	2	♦0.1	-	-
Malaria — Paludisme	-	-	1	♦0.0	1	♦0.0	1	♦0.0
Neoplasms — Tumeurs	12 640	364.9	9 225	252.7	7 755	294.2	5 708	205.7
Malignant neoplasms — Tumeurs malignes								
Total	12 377	357.3	8 998	246.5	7 725	293.1	5 652	203.7
Malignant neoplasm of lip, oral cavity and pharynx — Tumeur maligne de la lèvre, de la cavité buccale et du pharynx	404	11.7	97	2.7	598	22.7	92	3.3
Malignant neoplasm of oesophagus — Tumeur maligne de l'oesophage	212	6.1	59	1.6	245	9.3	32	1.2
Malignant neoplasm of stomach — Tumeur maligne de l'estomac	587	16.9	316	8.7	426	16.2	268	9.7
Malignant neoplasm of colon, rectosigmoid junction, rectum, anus and anal canal — Tumeur maligne du côlon, de la jonction recto-sigmoïdienne, du rectum, de l'anus et du canal anal	1 594	46.0	1 000	27.4	1 255	47.6	836	30.1
Malignant neoplasm of liver and intrahepatic bile ducts — Tumeur maligne du foie et des voies bilaires intrahépatiques	434	12.5	310	8.5	272	10.3	140	5.0
Malignant neoplasm of pancreas — Tumeur maligne du pancréas	618	17.8	516	14.1	381	14.5	335	12.1
Malignant neoplasm of trachea, bronchus and lung — Tumeur maligne de la trachée, des bronches et du poumon	3 815	110.1	1 449	39.7	1 684	63.9	547	19.7
Malignant neoplasm of female breast — Tumeur maligne du sein chez la femme	..	..	1 693	53.7	..	..	973	...
Malignant neoplasm of cervix uteri — Tumeur maligne du col de l'utérus	..	..	424	13.4	..	..	240	...
Malignant neoplasm of prostate — Tumeur maligne de la prostate	1 073	81.3	..	..	626	...	..	..
Malignant neoplasm of lymphoid, haematopoietic and related tissue — Tumeurs malignes primitives ou présumées primitives des tissus lymphoïde, hématopoïétique et apparentés	651	18.8	499	13.7	535	20.3	457	16.5
Disorders of the blood and blood-forming organs and certain disorders involving the immune mechanism — Maladies du sang et des organes hématopoïétiques et certains troubles du système immunitaire								
Total	96	2.8	135	3.7	25	♦0.9	35	1.3
Anaemias — Anémies	59	1.7	90	2.5	9	♦0.3	10	♦0.4
Endocrine, nutritional and metabolic diseases — Maladies endocriniennes, nutritionnelles et métaboliques								
Total	1 385	40.0	1 768	48.4	422	16.0	546	19.7
Diabetes mellitus — Diabète sucré	1 336	38.6	1 691	46.3	350	13.3	442	15.9
Malnutrition — Malnutrition	3	♦0.1	3	♦0.1	16	♦0.6	12	♦0.4
Mental and behavioural disorders — Troubles mentaux et du comportement	652	18.8	812	22.2	289	11.0	436	15.7
Diseases of the nervous system — Maladies du système nerveux	999	28.8	1 140	31.2	440	16.7	486	17.5
Diseases of the circulatory system — Maladies de l'appareil circulatoire								
Total	24 690	712.7	29 686	813.3	10 989	416.9	13 139	473.5
Acute rheumatic fever and chronic rheumatic heart diseases — Rhumatisme articularie aigu et cardiopathies rhumatismales chroniques	23	♦0.7	40	1.1	31	1.2	69	2.5
Hypertensive diseases — Maladies hypertensives	2 395	69.1	3 609	98.9	608	23.1	737	26.6
Ischaemic heart disease — Cardiopathie ischémique	5 131	148.1	4 436	121.5	6 466	245.3	7 904	284.8
Cerebrovascular disease — Maladie cérébrovasculaire	5 502	158.8	7 047	193.1	2 236	84.8	2 803	101.0

Cause of death — Cause de décès	Serbia - Serbie 2015 (+C)				Slovakia - Slovaquie 2013 (C)			
	Male — Masculin		Female — Féminin		Male — Masculin		Female — Féminin	
	Number Nombre	Rate Taux	Number Nombre	Rate Taux	Number Nombre	Rate Taux	Number Nombre	Rate Taux
Diseases of arteries, arterioles and capillaries — Maladies des artères, artérioles et capillaires	1 149	33.2	1 444	39.6	270	10.2	200	7.2
Diseases of the respiratory system — Maladies de l'appareil respiratoire								
Total	3 250	93.8	2 311	63.3	1 712	64.9	1 320	47.6
Influenza — Grippe	22	♦0.6	13	♦0.4	8	♦0.3	6	♦0.2
Pneumonia — Pneumopathies	774	22.3	589	16.1	984	37.3	864	31.1
Chronic lower respiratory diseases — Maladies chroniques des voies respiratoires inférieures	1 658	47.9	1 065	29.2	554	21.0	309	11.1
Diseases of the digestive system — Maladies de l'appareil digestif								
Total	1 892	54.6	1 494	40.9	1 705	64.7	1 138	41.0
Gastric and duodenal ulcer — Ulcère de l'estomac et du duodénum	281	8.1	251	6.9	139	5.3	99	3.6
Diseases of the liver — Maladies du foie	646	18.6	181	5.0	1 064	40.4	424	15.3
Diseases of the musculoskeletal system and connective tissue — Maladies du système ostéo-articulaire, des muscles et du tissu conjonctif	38	1.1	117	3.2	22	♦0.8	54	1.9
Diseases of the genitourinary system — Maladies de l'appareil génito-urinaire								
Total	1 198	34.6	1 113	30.5	328	12.4	427	15.4
Disorders of kidney and ureter — Affections du rein et de l'uretère	1 131	32.6	1 073	29.4	268	10.2	350	12.6
Hyperplasia of prostate — Hyperplasie de la prostate	33	2.5	..	..	7	...	..	..
Pregnancy, childbirth and the puerperium — Grossesse, accouchement et puerpéralité								
Total	..	..	8	♦12.2	..	..	1	♦1.8
Pregnancy with abortive outcome — Grossesse se terminant par un avortement	..	..	-	-	..	..	1	♦1.8
Other direct obstetric causes — Autres décès maternels directs	..	..	2	♦3.0	..	..	-	-
Indirect obstetric causes — Décès maternels indirects	..	..	6	♦9.1	..	..	-	-
Certain conditions originating in the perinatal period — Certaines affections dont l'origine se situe dans la période périnatale	124	364.7	100	315.9	80	285.0	47	175.7
Congenital malformations, deformations and chromosomal abnormalities — Malformations congénitales et anomalies chromosomiques	50	147.0	48	151.6	78	277.9	100	373.8
Symptoms, signs and abnormal clinical and laboratory findings, not elsewhere classified — Symptômes, signes et résultats anormaux d'examens cliniques et de laboratoire, non classés ailleurs	2 569	74.2	2 386	65.4	545	20.7	630	22.7
All other diseases — Toutes autres maladies	44	1.3	60	1.6	53	2.0	102	3.7
External causes — Causes externes								
Total	2 202	63.6	854	23.4	2 254	85.5	885	31.9
Accidents								
Total	1 099	31.7	413	11.3	1 508	57.2	723	26.1
Transport accidents — Accidents de transport	437	12.6	123	3.4	279	10.6	88	3.2
Falls — Chutes	248	7.2	142	3.9	689	26.1	500	18.0
Accidental drowning and submersion — Noyade et submersion accidentelles	62	1.8	21	♦0.6	113	4.3	31	1.1
Exposure to smoke, fire and flames — Exposition à la fumée, au feu et aux flammes	50	1.4	22	♦0.6	25	♦0.9	6	♦0.2
Accidental poisoning by and exposure to noxious substances — Intoxication accidentelle par des substances nocives et exposition à ces substances	27	♦0.8	11	♦0.3	111	4.2	36	1.3
Intentional self-harm — Lésions auto-infligées	794	22.9	269	7.4	533	20.2	83	3.0
Assault — Agresssions	64	1.8	38	1.0	37	1.4	30	♦1.1
All other external causes — Toutes autres causes externes	245	7.1	134	3.7	176	6.7	49	1.8

Cause of death — Cause de décès	Slovakia - Slovaquie 2014 (C)				Slovenia - Slovénie 2014 (C)			
	Male — Masculin		Female — Féminin		Male — Masculin		Female — Féminin	
	Number Nombre	Rate Taux	Number Nombre	Rate Taux	Number Nombre	Rate Taux	Number Nombre	Rate Taux
TOTAL	26 498	1 004.1	24 847	894.8	9 208	901.5	9 678	930.4
Certain infectious and parasitic diseases — Certaines maladies infectieuses et parasitaires								
Total	168	6.4	200	7.2	67	6.6	79	7.6
Intestinal infectious diseases — Maladies infectieuses intestinales	21	♦0.8	28	♦1.0	4	♦0.4	2	♦0.2
Tuberculosis — Tuberculose	21	♦0.8	11	♦0.4	10	♦1.0	3	♦0.3
Tetanus — Tétanos	-	-	-	-	-	-	1	♦0.1
Diphtheria — Diphtérie	-	-	-	-	-	-	-	-
Whooping cough — Coqueluche	1	♦0.0	-	-	-	-	-	-
Meningococcal infection — Infection à méningocoques	4	♦0.2	4	♦0.1	-	-	1	♦0.1
Septicaemia — Septicémie	92	3.5	121	4.4	32	3.1	59	5.7
Acute poliomyelitis — Poliomyélite aiguë	-	-	-	-	-	-	-	-
Measles — Rougeole	-	-	-	-	-	-	-	-
Viral hepatitis — Hépatite virale	11	♦0.4	10	♦0.4	3	♦0.3	4	♦0.4
Human immunodeficiency virus [HIV] disease — Maladies dues au virus de l'immunodéficience humaine (VIH)	1	♦0.0	-	-	4	♦0.4	-	-
Malaria — Paludisme	-	-	-	-	-	-	-	-
Neoplasms — Tumeurs	7 650	289.9	5 978	215.3	3 284	321.5	2 606	250.5
Malignant neoplasms — Tumeurs malignes								
Total	7 616	288.6	5 927	213.4	3 270	320.1	2 575	247.5
Malignant neoplasm of lip, oral cavity and pharynx — Tumeur maligne de la lèvre, de la cavité buccale et du pharynx	554	21.0	89	3.2	131	12.8	18	♦1.7
Malignant neoplasm of oesophagus — Tumeur maligne de l'oesophage	251	9.5	37	1.3	73	7.1	12	♦1.2
Malignant neoplasm of stomach — Tumeur maligne de l'estomac	371	14.1	285	10.3	213	20.9	144	13.8
Malignant neoplasm of colon, rectosigmoid junction, rectum, anus and anal canal — Tumeur maligne du côlon, de la jonction recto-sigmoïdienne, du rectum, de l'anus et du canal anal	1 133	42.9	856	30.8	421	41.2	315	30.3
Malignant neoplasm of liver and intrahepatic bile ducts — Tumeur maligne du foie et des voies bilaires intrahépatiques	278	10.5	149	5.4	142	13.9	88	8.5
Malignant neoplasm of pancreas — Tumeur maligne du pancréas	428	16.2	394	14.2	211	20.7	162	15.6
Malignant neoplasm of trachea, bronchus and lung — Tumeur maligne de la trachée, des bronches et du poumon	1 607	60.9	567	20.4	777	76.1	392	37.7
Malignant neoplasm of female breast — Tumeur maligne du sein chez la femme	..	..	898	..	..	..	377	42.2
Malignant neoplasm of cervix uteri — Tumeur maligne du col de l'utérus	..	..	228	...	..	..	49	5.5
Malignant neoplasm of prostate — Tumeur maligne de la prostate	738	...	..	..	362	96.8	..	..
Malignant neoplasm of lymphoid, haematopoietic and related tissue — Tumeurs malignes primitives ou présumées primitives des tissus lymphoïde, hématopoïétique et apparentés	507	19.2	513	18.5	274	26.8	247	23.7
Disorders of the blood and blood-forming organs and certain disorders involving the immune mechanism — Maladies du sang et des organes hématopoïétiques et certains troubles du système immunitaire								
Total	24	♦0.9	30	♦1.1	8	♦0.8	10	♦1.0
Anaemias — Anémies	7	♦0.3	12	♦0.4	-	-	1	♦0.1
Endocrine, nutritional and metabolic diseases — Maladies endocriniennes, nutritionnelles et métaboliques								
Total	451	17.1	583	21.0	162	15.9	196	18.8
Diabetes mellitus — Diabète sucré	392	14.9	503	18.1	129	12.6	160	15.4
Malnutrition — Malnutrition	14	♦0.5	18	♦0.6	-	-	-	-
Mental and behavioural disorders — Troubles mentaux et du comportement	405	15.3	542	19.5	168	16.4	33	3.2
Diseases of the nervous system — Maladies du système nerveux	527	20.0	620	22.3	169	16.5	222	21.3
Diseases of the circulatory system — Maladies de l'appareil circulatoire								
Total	10 540	399.4	12 349	444.7	3 070	300.6	4 684	450.3
Acute rheumatic fever and chronic rheumatic heart diseases — Rhumatisme articulaire aigu et cardiopathies rhumatismales chroniques	30	♦1.1	54	1.9	30	♦2.9	67	6.4
Hypertensive diseases — Maladies hypertensives	534	20.2	778	28.0	211	20.7	541	52.0
Ischaemic heart disease — Cardiopathie ischémique	6 138	232.6	7 200	259.3	1 049	102.7	816	78.4
Cerebrovascular disease — Maladie cérébrovasculaire	2 358	89.3	2 829	101.9	773	75.7	1 171	112.6

20. Death and death rates by cause and sex: 2012 - 2016
Décès et taux de mortalité par cause et sexe : 2012 - 2016 (continued - suite)

Cause of death — Cause de décès	Slovakia - Slovaquie 2014 (C)				Slovenia - Slovénie 2014 (C)			
	Male — Masculin		Female — Féminin		Male — Masculin		Female — Féminin	
	Number Nombre	Rate Taux	Number Nombre	Rate Taux	Number Nombre	Rate Taux	Number Nombre	Rate Taux
Diseases of arteries, arterioles and capillaries — Maladies des artères, artérioles et capillaires	246	9.3	239	8.6	164	16.1	213	20.5
Diseases of the respiratory system — Maladies de l'appareil respiratoire								
Total	1 578	59.8	1 150	41.4	576	56.4	576	55.4
Influenza — Grippe	1	♦0.0	-	-	4	♦0.4	6	♦0.6
Pneumonia — Pneumopathies	860	32.6	717	25.8	252	24.7	329	31.6
Chronic lower respiratory diseases — Maladies chroniques des voies respiratoires inférieures	574	21.8	310	11.2	243	23.8	142	13.7
Diseases of the digestive system — Maladies de l'appareil digestif								
Total	1 734	65.7	1 158	41.7	548	53.7	425	40.9
Gastric and duodenal ulcer — Ulcère de l'estomac et du duodénum	124	4.7	108	3.9	26	♦2.5	32	3.1
Diseases of the liver — Maladies du foie	1 113	42.2	409	14.7	365	35.7	134	12.9
Diseases of the musculoskeletal system and connective tissue — Maladies du système ostéo-articularie, des muscles et du tissu conjonctif	29	♦1.1	51	1.8	25	♦2.4	59	5.7
Diseases of the genitourinary system — Maladies de l'appareil génito-urinaire								
Total	367	13.9	441	15.9	98	9.6	158	15.2
Disorders of kidney and ureter — Affections du rein et de l'uretère	300	11.4	351	12.6	77	7.5	89	8.6
Hyperplasia of prostate — Hyperplasie de la prostate	7	...	..	..	1	♦0.3	..	..
Pregnancy, childbirth and the puerperium — Grossesse, accouchement et puerpéralité								
Total	..	..	2	♦3.6	..	..	2	♦9.4
Pregnancy with abortive outcome — Grossesse se terminant par un avortement	..	..	1	♦1.8	..	..	1	♦4.7
Other direct obstetric causes — Autres décès maternels directs	..	..	1	♦1.8	..	..	1	♦4.7
Indirect obstetric causes — Décès maternels indirects	..	..	-	-	..	..	-	-
Certain conditions originating in the perinatal period — Certaines affections dont l'origine se situe dans la période périnatale	78	277.6	63	233.9	15	♦137.3	10	♦97.7
Congenital malformations, deformations and chromosomal abnormalities — Malformations congénitales et anomalies chromosomiques	101	359.4	69	256.2	20	♦183.0	19	♦185.6
Symptoms, signs and abnormal clinical and laboratory findings, not elsewhere classified — Symptômes, signes et résultats anormaux d'examens cliniques et de laboratoire, non classés ailleurs	553	21.0	571	20.6	207	20.3	129	12.4
All other diseases — Toutes autres maladies	71	2.7	96	3.5	5	♦0.5	9	♦0.9
External causes — Causes externes								
Total	2 222	84.2	944	34.0	786	77.0	461	44.3
Accidents								
Total	1 228	46.5	543	19.6	393	38.5	345	33.2
Transport accidents — Accidents de transport	316	12.0	112	4.0	96	9.4	33	3.2
Falls — Chutes	426	16.1	305	11.0	181	17.7	270	26.0
Accidental drowning and submersion — Noyade et submersion accidentelles	103	3.9	26	♦0.9	16	♦1.6	4	♦0.4
Exposure to smoke, fire and flames — Exposition à la fumée, au feu et aux flammes	14	♦0.5	6	♦0.2	6	♦0.6	6	♦0.6
Accidental poisoning by and exposure to noxious substances — Intoxication accidentelle par des substances nocives et exposition à ces substances	118	4.5	31	1.1	31	3.0	8	♦0.8
Intentional self-harm — Lésions auto-infligées	471	17.8	82	3.0	325	31.8	63	6.1
Assault — Agresssions	29	♦1.1	18	♦0.6	10	♦1.0	10	♦1.0
All other external causes — Toutes autres causes externes	494	18.7	301	10.8	58	5.7	43	4.1

20. Death and death rates by cause and sex: 2012 - 2016
Décès et taux de mortalité par cause et sexe : 2012 - 2016 (continued - suite)

	Slovenia - Slovénie 2015 (C)				Spain - Espagne 2014 (C)			
	Male — Masculin		Female — Féminin		Male — Masculin		Female — Féminin	
Cause of death — Cause de décès	Number Nombre	Rate Taux	Number Nombre	Rate Taux	Number Nombre	Rate Taux	Number Nombre	Rate Taux
TOTAL	9 739	952.4	10 095	970.2	201 571	882.1	194 259	822.1
Certain infectious and parasitic diseases — Certaines maladies infectieuses et parasitaires								
Total	56	5.5	96	9.2	3 263	14.3	3 245	13.7
Intestinal infectious diseases — Maladies infectieuses intestinales	1	♦0.1	6	♦0.6	278	1.2	475	2.0
Tuberculosis — Tuberculose	4	♦0.4	4	♦0.4	150	0.7	66	0.3
Tetanus — Tétanos	-	-	1	♦0.1	-	-	1	♦0.0
Diphtheria — Diphtérie	-	-	-	-	-	-	-	-
Whooping cough — Coqueluche	-	-	-	-	3	♦0.0	2	♦0.0
Meningococcal infection — Infection à méningocoques	1	♦0.1	-	-	4	♦0.0	4	♦0.0
Septicaemia — Septicémie	32	3.1	66	6.3	1 482	6.5	1 775	7.5
Acute poliomyelitis — Poliomyélite aiguë	-	-	-	-	-	-	-	-
Measles — Rougeole	-	-	-	-	-	-	-	-
Viral hepatitis — Hépatite virale	-	-	2	♦0.2	488	2.1	431	1.8
Human immunodeficiency virus [HIV] disease — Maladies dues au virus de l'immunodéficience humaine (VIH)	2	♦0.2	-	-	531	2.3	169	0.7
Malaria — Paludisme	-	-	-	-	3	♦0.0	-	-
Neoplasms — Tumeurs	3 471	339.4	2 737	263.0	67 278	294.4	43 000	182.0
Malignant neoplasms — Tumeurs malignes								
Total	3 443	336.7	2 713	260.7	65 163	285.2	41 106	174.0
Malignant neoplasm of lip, oral cavity and pharynx — Tumeur maligne de la lèvre, de la cavité buccale et du pharynx	122	11.9	24	♦2.3	1 769	7.7	571	2.4
Malignant neoplasm of oesophagus — Tumeur maligne de l'oesophage	72	7.0	14	♦1.3	1 545	6.8	289	1.2
Malignant neoplasm of stomach — Tumeur maligne de l'estomac	211	20.6	128	12.3	3 334	14.6	2 200	9.3
Malignant neoplasm of colon, rectosigmoid junction, rectum, anus and anal canal — Tumeur maligne du côlon, de la jonction recto-sigmoïdienne, du rectum, de l'anus et du canal anal	449	43.9	329	31.6	9 260	40.5	6 216	26.3
Malignant neoplasm of liver and intrahepatic bile ducts — Tumeur maligne du foie et des voies bilaires intrahépatiques	156	15.3	93	8.9	3 401	14.9	1 654	7.0
Malignant neoplasm of pancreas — Tumeur maligne du pancréas	185	18.1	182	17.5	3 199	14.0	3 088	13.1
Malignant neoplasm of trachea, bronchus and lung — Tumeur maligne de la trachée, des bronches et du poumon	836	81.8	356	34.2	17 212	75.3	4 058	17.2
Malignant neoplasm of female breast — Tumeur maligne du sein chez la femme	..	..	428	48.0	..	..	6 231	...
Malignant neoplasm of cervix uteri — Tumeur maligne du col de l'utérus	..	..	49	5.5	..	..	590	...
Malignant neoplasm of prostate — Tumeur maligne de la prostate	404	106.3	..	..	5 863	...	..	..
Malignant neoplasm of lymphoid, haematopoietic and related tissue — Tumeurs malignes primitives ou présumées primitives des tissus lymphoïde, hématopoïétique et apparentés	268	26.2	276	26.5	4 536	19.8	3 781	16.0
Disorders of the blood and blood-forming organs and certain disorders involving the immune mechanism — Maladies du sang et des organes hématopoïétiques et certains troubles du système immunitaire								
Total	10	♦1.0	10	♦1.0	781	3.4	1 003	4.2
Anaemias — Anémies	2	♦0.2	1	♦0.1	445	1.9	698	3.0
Endocrine, nutritional and metabolic diseases — Maladies endocriniennes, nutritionnelles et métaboliques								
Total	186	18.2	200	19.2	5 431	23.8	7 582	32.1
Diabetes mellitus — Diabète sucré	159	15.5	169	16.2	4 100	17.9	5 525	23.4
Malnutrition — Malnutrition	-	-	1	♦0.1	90	0.4	97	0.4
Mental and behavioural disorders — Troubles mentaux et du comportement	222	21.7	50	4.8	6 343	27.8	12 363	52.3
Diseases of the nervous system — Maladies du système nerveux	186	18.2	234	22.5	8 907	39.0	14 466	61.2
Diseases of the circulatory system — Maladies de l'appareil circulatoire								
Total	3 184	311.4	4 798	461.1	53 581	234.5	63 812	270.1
Acute rheumatic fever and chronic rheumatic heart diseases — Rhumatisme articularie aigu et cardiopathies rhumatismales chroniques	30	♦2.9	50	4.8	482	2.1	1 186	5.0
Hypertensive diseases — Maladies hypertensives	213	20.8	522	50.2	3 699	16.2	7 874	33.3
Ischaemic heart disease — Cardiopathie ischémique	1 153	112.8	923	88.7	19 101	83.6	13 463	57.0
Cerebrovascular disease — Maladie cérébrovasculaire	776	75.9	1 189	114.3	11 573	50.6	16 006	67.7

20. Death and death rates by cause and sex: 2012 - 2016
Décès et taux de mortalité par cause et sexe : 2012 - 2016 (continued - suite)

Cause of death — Cause de décès	Slovenia - Slovénie 2015 (C)				Spain - Espagne 2014 (C)			
	Male — Masculin		Female — Féminin		Male — Masculin		Female — Féminin	
	Number Nombre	Rate Taux	Number Nombre	Rate Taux	Number Nombre	Rate Taux	Number Nombre	Rate Taux
Diseases of arteries, arterioles and capillaries — Maladies des artères, artérioles et capillaires	154	15.1	227	21.8	2 908	12.7	2 123	9.0
Diseases of the respiratory system — Maladies de l'appareil respiratoire								
Total	631	61.7	675	64.9	24 906	109.0	18 935	80.1
Influenza — Grippe	3	♦0.3	6	♦0.6	199	0.9	181	0.8
Pneumonia — Pneumopathies	293	28.7	380	36.5	4 357	19.1	4 088	17.3
Chronic lower respiratory diseases — Maladies chroniques des voies respiratoires inférieures	241	23.6	174	16.7	11 434	50.0	4 112	17.4
Diseases of the digestive system — Maladies de l'appareil digestif								
Total	479	46.8	392	37.7	10 071	44.1	9 314	39.4
Gastric and duodenal ulcer — Ulcère de l'estomac et du duodénum	20	♦2.0	29	♦2.8	211	0.9	200	0.8
Diseases of the liver — Maladies du foie	309	30.2	113	10.9	3 823	16.7	1 630	6.9
Diseases of the musculoskeletal system and connective tissue — Maladies du système ostéo-articularie, des muscles et du tissu conjonctif	18	♦1.8	54	5.2	1 268	5.5	2 411	10.2
Diseases of the genitourinary system — Maladies de l'appareil génito-urinaire								
Total	123	12.0	188	18.1	5 050	22.1	6 480	27.4
Disorders of kidney and ureter — Affections du rein et de l'uretère	84	8.2	106	10.2	3 283	14.4	3 794	16.1
Hyperplasia of prostate — Hyperplasie de la prostate	-	-	..	..	183	....	..	..
Pregnancy, childbirth and the puerperium — Grossesse, accouchement et puerpéralité								
Total	..	..	1	♦4.8	..	..	9	♦2.1
Pregnancy with abortive outcome — Grossesse se terminant par un avortement	..	..	-	-	..	..	1	♦0.2
Other direct obstetric causes — Autres décès maternels directs	..	..	1	♦4.8	..	..	8	♦1.9
Indirect obstetric causes — Décès maternels indirects	..	..	-	-	..	..	-	-
Certain conditions originating in the perinatal period — Certaines affections dont l'origine se situe dans la période périnatale	10	♦94.3	8	♦79.7	446	202.7	332	161.1
Congenital malformations, deformations and chromosomal abnormalities — Malformations congénitales et anomalies chromosomiques	13	♦122.6	13	♦129.5	430	195.4	398	193.2
Symptoms, signs and abnormal clinical and laboratory findings, not elsewhere classified — Symptômes, signes et résultats anormaux d'examens cliniques et de laboratoire, non classés ailleurs	247	24.2	132	12.7	3 981	17.4	4 502	19.1
All other diseases — Toutes autres maladies	8	♦0.8	7	♦0.7	447	2.0	892	3.8
External causes — Causes externes								
Total	895	87.5	500	48.1	9 388	41.1	5 515	23.3
Accidents								
Total	453	44.3	348	33.4	6 028	26.4	4 258	18.0
Transport accidents — Accidents de transport	111	10.9	31	3.0	1 608	7.0	465	2.0
Falls — Chutes	218	21.3	273	26.2	1 433	6.3	1 316	5.6
Accidental drowning and submersion — Noyade et submersion accidentelles	13	♦1.3	8	♦0.8	335	1.5	99	0.4
Exposure to smoke, fire and flames — Exposition à la fumée, au feu et aux flammes	10	♦1.0	-	-	112	0.5	61	0.3
Accidental poisoning by and exposure to noxious substances — Intoxication accidentelle par des substances nocives et exposition à ces substances	38	3.7	13	♦1.2	625	2.7	296	1.3
Intentional self-harm — Lésions auto-infligées	332	32.5	90	8.6	2 938	12.9	972	4.1
Assault — Agresssions	6	♦0.6	7	♦0.7	201	0.9	116	0.5
All other external causes — Toutes autres causes externes	104	10.2	55	5.3	221	1.0	169	0.7

Cause of death — Cause de décès	Spain - Espagne 2015 (C)				Sweden - Suède 2015 (C)			
	Male — Masculin		Female — Féminin		Male — Masculin		Female — Féminin	
	Number Nombre	Rate Taux	Number Nombre	Rate Taux	Number Nombre	Rate Taux	Number Nombre	Rate Taux
TOTAL	213 309	934.8	209 259	885.6	44 542	908.7	46 460	948.6
Certain infectious and parasitic diseases — Certaines maladies infectieuses et parasitaires								
Total	3 748	16.4	3 819	16.2	1 149	23.4	1 156	23.6
Intestinal infectious diseases — Maladies infectieuses intestinales	337	1.5	558	2.4	107	2.2	144	2.9
Tuberculosis — Tuberculose	117	0.5	61	0.3	6	♦0.1	6	♦0.1
Tetanus — Tétanos	1	♦0.0	-	-	-	-	-	-
Diphtheria — Diphtérie..	1	♦0.0	-	-	-	-	-	-
Whooping cough — Coqueluche	4	♦0.0	4	♦0.0	-	-	-	-
Meningococcal infection — Infection à méningocoques	8	♦0.0	7	♦0.0	1	♦0.0	2	♦0.0
Septicaemia — Septicémie	1 856	8.1	2 326	9.8	594	12.1	538	11.0
Acute poliomyelitis — Poliomyélite aiguë	-	-	-	-	-	-	-	-
Measles — Rougeole	-	-	-	-	-	-	-	-
Viral hepatitis — Hépatite virale	503	2.2	403	1.7	50	1.0	28	♦0.6
Human immunodeficiency virus [HIV] disease — Maladies dues au virus de l'immunodéficience humaine (VIH)	513	2.2	120	0.5	13	♦0.3	2	♦0.0
Malaria — Paludisme..	5	♦0.0	-	-	1	♦0.0	1	♦0.0
Neoplasms — Tumeurs	67 723	296.8	43 658	184.8	12 232	249.6	11 223	229.2
Malignant neoplasms — Tumeurs malignes								
Total	65 483	287.0	41 712	176.5	11 731	239.3	10 691	218.3
Malignant neoplasm of lip, oral cavity and pharynx — Tumeur maligne de la lèvre, de la cavité buccale et du pharynx	1 733	7.6	592	2.5	221	4.5	117	2.4
Malignant neoplasm of oesophagus — Tumeur maligne de l'oesophage	1 626	7.1	305	1.3	331	6.8	113	2.3
Malignant neoplasm of stomach — Tumeur maligne de l'estomac	3 331	14.6	2 175	9.2	348	7.1	219	4.5
Malignant neoplasm of colon, rectosigmoid junction, rectum, anus and anal canal — Tumeur maligne du côlon, de la jonction recto-sigmoïdienne, du rectum, de l'anus et du canal anal	9 094	39.9	6 286	26.6	1 473	30.1	1 307	26.7
Malignant neoplasm of liver and intrahepatic bile ducts — Tumeur maligne du foie et des voies bilaires intrahépatiques	3 455	15.1	1 589	6.7	451	9.2	238	4.9
Malignant neoplasm of pancreas — Tumeur maligne du pancréas...................	3 311	14.5	3 095	13.1	872	17.8	940	19.2
Malignant neoplasm of trachea, bronchus and lung — Tumeur maligne de la trachée, des bronches et du poumon	17 259	75.6	4 366	18.5	1 813	37.0	1 813	37.0
Malignant neoplasm of female breast — Tumeur maligne du sein chez la femme	..	..	6 235	30.8	..	..	1 423	34.9
Malignant neoplasm of cervix uteri — Tumeur maligne du col de l'utérus	..	..	659	3.3	..	..	163	4.0
Malignant neoplasm of prostate — Tumeur maligne de la prostate	5 757	70.5	..	..	2 357	132.5	..	..
Malignant neoplasm of lymphoid, haematopoietic and related tissue — Tumeurs malignes primitives ou présumées primitives des tissus lymphoïde, hématopoïétique et apparentés.................	4 589	20.1	3 865	16.4	1 019	20.8	924	18.9
Disorders of the blood and blood-forming organs and certain disorders involving the immune mechanism — Maladies du sang et des organes hématopoïétiques et certains troubles du système immunitaire								
Total	869	3.8	1 159	4.9	141	2.9	172	3.5
Anaemias — Anémies	524	2.3	809	3.4	73	1.5	111	2.3
Endocrine, nutritional and metabolic diseases — Maladies endocriniennes, nutritionnelles et métaboliques								
Total	5 953	26.1	8 112	34.3	1 286	26.2	1 250	25.5
Diabetes mellitus — Diabète sucré................................	4 421	19.4	5 760	24.4	1 065	21.7	965	19.7
Malnutrition — Malnutrition	122	0.5	139	0.6	32	0.7	50	1.0
Mental and behavioural disorders — Troubles mentaux et du comportement	7 182	31.5	14 151	59.9	2 178	44.4	4 052	82.7
Diseases of the nervous system — Maladies du système nerveux................	9 879	43.3	15 938	67.4	1 923	39.2	2 603	53.1
Diseases of the circulatory system — Maladies de l'appareil circulatoire								
Total	56 461	247.4	67 736	286.7	15 583	317.9	16 416	335.2
Acute rheumatic fever and chronic rheumatic heart diseases — Rhumatisme articulaire aigu et cardiopathies rhumatismales chroniques	504	2.2	1 217	5.2	43	0.9	77	1.6
Hypertensive diseases — Maladies hypertensives...............	4 052	17.8	8 623	36.5	882	18.0	1 509	30.8
Ischaemic heart disease — Cardiopathie ischémique............	19 563	85.7	14 206	60.1	6 818	139.1	5 303	108.3
Cerebrovascular disease — Maladie cérébrovasculaire............	12 077	52.9	16 357	69.2	2 724	55.6	3 451	70.5

Cause of death — Cause de décès	Spain - Espagne 2015 (C)				Sweden - Suède 2015 (C)			
	Male — Masculin		Female — Féminin		Male — Masculin		Female — Féminin	
	Number Nombre	Rate Taux	Number Nombre	Rate Taux	Number Nombre	Rate Taux	Number Nombre	Rate Taux
Diseases of arteries, arterioles and capillaries — Maladies des artères, artérioles et capillaires	2 952	12.9	2 007	8.5	916	18.7	840	17.2
Diseases of the respiratory system — Maladies de l'appareil respiratoire								
Total	28 930	126.8	22 918	97.0	3 062	62.5	3 339	68.2
Influenza — Grippe	211	0.9	263	1.1	144	2.9	174	3.6
Pneumonia — Pneumopathies	5 229	22.9	4 980	21.1	1 035	21.1	987	20.2
Chronic lower respiratory diseases — Maladies chroniques des voies respiratoires inférieures	12 375	54.2	4 389	18.6	1 318	26.9	1 700	34.7
Diseases of the digestive system — Maladies de l'appareil digestif								
Total	10 633	46.6	9 727	41.2	1 450	29.6	1 411	28.8
Gastric and duodenal ulcer — Ulcère de l'estomac et du duodénum	267	1.2	196	0.8	138	2.8	145	3.0
Diseases of the liver — Maladies du foie	3 970	17.4	1 652	7.0	511	10.4	288	5.9
Diseases of the musculoskeletal system and connective tissue — Maladies du système ostéo-articulaire, des muscles et du tissu conjonctif	1 366	6.0	2 782	11.8	145	3.0	310	6.3
Diseases of the genitourinary system — Maladies de l'appareil génito-urinaire								
Total	5 313	23.3	6 856	29.0	647	13.2	598	12.2
Disorders of kidney and ureter — Affections du rein et de l'uretère	3 267	14.3	3 846	16.3	432	8.8	423	8.6
Hyperplasia of prostate — Hyperplasie de la prostate	174	2.1	..	..	49	2.8	..	..
Pregnancy, childbirth and the puerperium — Grossesse, accouchement et puerpéralité								
Total	..	..	15	+3.6	..	..	1	+0.9
Pregnancy with abortive outcome — Grossesse se terminant par un avortement	..	..	2	+0.5	..	..	1	+0.9
Other direct obstetric causes — Autres décès maternels directs	..	..	12	+2.9	..	..	-	-
Indirect obstetric causes — Décès maternels indirects	..	..	1	+0.2	..	..	-	-
Certain conditions originating in the perinatal period — Certaines affections dont l'origine se situe dans la période périnatale	380	176.3	294	144.9	91	152.9	55	99.3
Congenital malformations, deformations and chromosomal abnormalities — Malformations congénitales et anomalies chromosomiques	405	187.9	397	195.6	108	181.5	98	177.0
Symptoms, signs and abnormal clinical and laboratory findings, not elsewhere classified — Symptômes, signes et résultats anormaux d'examens cliniques et de laboratoire, non classés ailleurs	4 590	20.1	4 914	20.8	1 223	25.0	1 796	36.7
All other diseases — Toutes autres maladies	534	2.3	1 047	4.4	73	1.5	116	2.4
External causes — Causes externes								
Total	9 343	40.9	5 736	24.3	3 251	66.3	1 864	38.1
Accidents								
Total	6 280	27.5	4 547	19.2	1 979	40.4	1 291	26.4
Transport accidents — Accidents de transport	1 620	7.1	477	2.0	234	4.8	69	1.4
Falls — Chutes	1 432	6.3	1 351	5.7	582	11.9	474	9.7
Accidental drowning and submersion — Noyade et submersion accidentelles	334	1.5	96	0.4	71	1.4	23	+0.5
Exposure to smoke, fire and flames — Exposition à la fumée, au feu et aux flammes	95	0.4	62	0.3	47	1.0	26	+0.5
Accidental poisoning by and exposure to noxious substances — Intoxication accidentelle par des substances nocives et exposition à ces substances	532	2.3	307	1.3	459	9.4	129	2.6
Intentional self-harm — Lésions auto-infligées	2 680	11.7	922	3.9	848	17.3	331	6.8
Assault — Agresssions	164	0.7	121	0.5	72	1.5	26	+0.5
All other external causes — Toutes autres causes externes	219	1.0	146	0.6	352	7.2	216	4.4

20. Death and death rates by cause and sex: 2012 - 2016
Décès et taux de mortalité par cause et sexe : 2012 - 2016 (continued - suite)

Cause of death — Cause de décès	Sweden - Suède 2016 (C)				Switzerland - Suisse 2014 (C)			
	Male — Masculin		Female — Féminin		Male — Masculin		Female — Féminin	
	Number Nombre	Rate Taux	Number Nombre	Rate Taux	Number Nombre	Rate Taux	Number Nombre	Rate Taux
TOTAL	44 485	894.7	46 586	941.0	30 896	768.2	32 967	800.6
Certain infectious and parasitic diseases — Certaines maladies infectieuses et parasitaires								
Total	961	19.3	1 064	21.5	395	9.8	357	8.7
Intestinal infectious diseases — Maladies infectieuses intestinales	99	2.0	167	3.4	57	1.4	72	1.7
Tuberculosis — Tuberculose	12	♦0.2	4	♦0.1	6	♦0.1	3	♦0.1
Tetanus — Tétanos	-	-	-	-	-	-	-	-
Diphtheria — Diphtérie.............	-	-	1	♦0.0	-	-	-	-
Whooping cough — Coqueluche	-	-	-	-	-	-	-	-
Meningococcal infection — Infection à méningocoques	3	♦0.1	2	♦0.0	2	♦0.0	2	♦0.0
Septicaemia — Septicémie.............	409	8.2	366	7.4	96	2.4	88	2.1
Acute poliomyelitis — Poliomyélite aiguë	-	-	-	-	-	-	-	-
Measles — Rougeole.............	-	-	-	-	-	-	-	-
Viral hepatitis — Hépatite virale.............	38	0.8	18	♦0.4	13	♦0.3	10	♦0.2
Human immunodeficiency virus [HIV] disease — Maladies dues au virus de l'immunodéficience humaine (VIH).............	10	♦0.2	3	♦0.1	29	♦0.7	12	♦0.3
Malaria — Paludisme.............	-	-	-	-	1	♦0.0	-	-
Neoplasms — Tumeurs	12 335	248.1	11 176	225.7	9 570	237.9	7 773	188.8
Malignant neoplasms — Tumeurs malignes								
Total	11 842	238.2	10 676	215.6	9 297	231.1	7 468	181.4
Malignant neoplasm of lip, oral cavity and pharynx — Tumeur maligne de la lèvre, de la cavité buccale et du pharynx	238	4.8	114	2.3	268	6.7	109	2.6
Malignant neoplasm of oesophagus — Tumeur maligne de l'oesophage	384	7.7	142	2.9	364	9.1	111	2.7
Malignant neoplasm of stomach — Tumeur maligne de l'estomac	329	6.6	248	5.0	343	8.5	215	5.2
Malignant neoplasm of colon, rectosigmoid junction, rectum, anus and anal canal — Tumeur maligne du côlon, de la jonction recto-sigmoïdienne, du rectum, de l'anus et du canal anal.............	1 421	28.6	1 354	27.3	950	23.6	784	19.0
Malignant neoplasm of liver and intrahepatic bile ducts — Tumeur maligne du foie et des voies bilaires intrahépatiques	487	9.8	245	4.9	477	11.9	235	5.7
Malignant neoplasm of pancreas — Tumeur maligne du pancréas.............	839	16.9	901	18.2	611	15.2	591	14.4
Malignant neoplasm of trachea, bronchus and lung — Tumeur maligne de la trachée, des bronches et du poumon	1 855	37.3	1 827	36.9	2 015	50.1	1 184	28.8
Malignant neoplasm of female breast — Tumeur maligne du sein chez la femme	..	..	1 391	33.9	..	..	1 336	...
Malignant neoplasm of cervix uteri — Tumeur maligne du col de l'utérus.............	..	..	135	3.3	..	..	63	...
Malignant neoplasm of prostate — Tumeur maligne de la prostate	2 347	129.7	..	..	1 331	...	..	..
Malignant neoplasm of lymphoid, haematopoietic and related tissue — Tumeurs malignes primitives ou présumées primitives des tissus lymphoïde, hématopoïétique et apparentés.............	1 123	22.6	866	17.5	820	20.4	663	16.1
Disorders of the blood and blood-forming organs and certain disorders involving the immune mechanism — Maladies du sang et des organes hématopoïétiques et certains troubles du système immunitaire								
Total	138	2.8	181	3.7	60	1.5	102	2.5
Anaemias — Anémies	66	1.3	118	2.4	35	0.9	71	1.7
Endocrine, nutritional and metabolic diseases — Maladies endocriniennes, nutritionnelles et métaboliques								
Total	1 359	27.3	1 254	25.3	758	18.8	863	21.0
Diabetes mellitus — Diabète sucré.............	1 116	22.4	930	18.8	582	14.5	632	15.3
Malnutrition — Malnutrition	37	0.7	60	1.2	13	♦0.3	43	1.0
Mental and behavioural disorders — Troubles mentaux et du comportement	2 325	46.8	4 164	84.1	1 670	41.5	3 216	78.1
Diseases of the nervous system — Maladies du système nerveux.............	2 201	44.3	2 810	56.8	1 491	37.1	1 880	45.7
Diseases of the circulatory system — Maladies de l'appareil circulatoire								
Total	15 231	306.3	16 385	330.9	9 483	235.8	11 488	279.0
Acute rheumatic fever and chronic rheumatic heart diseases — Rhumatisme articularie aigu et cardiopathies rhumatismales chroniques	38	0.8	76	1.5	37	0.9	58	1.4
Hypertensive diseases — Maladies hypertensives.............	878	17.7	1 626	32.8	1 016	25.3	2 016	49.0
Ischaemic heart disease — Cardiopathie ischémique.............	6 552	131.8	5 050	102.0	3 944	98.1	3 380	82.1
Cerebrovascular disease — Maladie cérébrovasculaire.............	2 705	54.4	3 403	68.7	1 321	32.8	2 131	51.8

20. Death and death rates by cause and sex: 2012 - 2016
Décès et taux de mortalité par cause et sexe : 2012 - 2016 (continued - suite)

Cause of death — Cause de décès	Sweden - Suède 2016 (C)				Switzerland - Suisse 2014 (C)			
	Male — Masculin		Female — Féminin		Male — Masculin		Female — Féminin	
	Number Nombre	Rate Taux	Number Nombre	Rate Taux	Number Nombre	Rate Taux	Number Nombre	Rate Taux
Diseases of arteries, arterioles and capillaries — Maladies des artères, artérioles et capillaires	863	17.4	841	17.0	570	14.2	465	11.3
Diseases of the respiratory system — Maladies de l'appareil respiratoire								
Total	2 993	60.2	3 258	65.8	1 965	48.9	1 869	45.4
Influenza — Grippe	115	2.3	111	2.2	18	٠0.4	22	٠0.5
Pneumonia — Pneumopathies	929	18.7	885	17.9	512	12.7	608	14.8
Chronic lower respiratory diseases — Maladies chroniques des voies respiratoires inférieures	1 338	26.9	1 837	37.1	1 033	25.7	913	22.2
Diseases of the digestive system — Maladies de l'appareil digestif								
Total	1 493	30.0	1 424	28.8	1 197	29.8	1 294	31.4
Gastric and duodenal ulcer — Ulcère de l'estomac et du duodénum	138	2.8	126	2.5	49	1.2	56	1.4
Diseases of the liver — Maladies du foie	551	11.1	337	6.8	457	11.4	254	6.2
Diseases of the musculoskeletal system and connective tissue — Maladies du système ostéo-articularie, des muscles et du tissu conjonctif	159	3.2	339	6.8	209	5.2	434	10.5
Diseases of the genitourinary system — Maladies de l'appareil génito-urinaire								
Total	630	12.7	604	12.2	480	11.9	561	13.6
Disorders of kidney and ureter — Affections du rein et de l'uretère	443	8.9	438	8.8	300	7.5	353	8.6
Hyperplasia of prostate — Hyperplasie de la prostate	31	1.7	..	..	28	...	..	..
Pregnancy, childbirth and the puerperium — Grossesse, accouchement et puerpéralité								
Total	..	..	3	٠2.6	..	..	5	٠5.9
Pregnancy with abortive outcome — Grossesse se terminant par un avortement	..	..	-	-	..	..	1	٠1.2
Other direct obstetric causes — Autres décès maternels directs	..	..	2	٠1.7	..	..	1	٠1.2
Indirect obstetric causes — Décès maternels indirects	..	..	1	٠0.9	..	..	1	٠1.2
Certain conditions originating in the perinatal period — Certaines affections dont l'origine se situe dans la période périnatale	83	137.9	65	113.6	109	248.6	69	166.5
Congenital malformations, deformations and chromosomal abnormalities — Malformations congénitales et anomalies chromosomiques	138	229.2	140	244.6	149	339.8	134	323.4
Symptoms, signs and abnormal clinical and laboratory findings, not elsewhere classified — Symptômes, signes et résultats anormaux d'examens cliniques et de laboratoire, non classés ailleurs	1 320	26.5	1 782	36.0	1 201	29.9	1 287	31.3
All other diseases — Toutes autres maladies	74	1.5	115	2.3	37	0.9	61	1.5
External causes — Causes externes								
Total	3 045	61.2	1 822	36.8	2 122	52.8	1 574	38.2
Accidents								
Total	1 871	37.6	1 261	25.5	1 293	32.1	1 230	29.9
Transport accidents — Accidents de transport	226	4.5	65	1.3	209	5.2	71	1.7
Falls — Chutes	535	10.8	484	9.8	765	19.0	986	23.9
Accidental drowning and submersion — Noyade et submersion accidentelles	90	1.8	19	٠0.4	30	٠0.7	16	٠0.4
Exposure to smoke, fire and flames — Exposition à la fumée, au feu et aux flammes	31	0.6	21	٠0.4	8	٠0.2	8	٠0.2
Accidental poisoning by and exposure to noxious substances — Intoxication accidentelle par des substances nocives et exposition à ces substances	420	8.4	122	2.5	110	2.7	38	0.9
Intentional self-harm — Lésions auto-infligées	783	15.7	351	7.1	754	18.7	274	6.7
Assault — Agresssions	62	1.2	24	٠0.5	12	٠0.3	21	٠0.5
All other external causes — Toutes autres causes externes	329	6.6	186	3.8	63	1.6	49	1.2

20. Death and death rates by cause and sex: 2012 - 2016
Décès et taux de mortalité par cause et sexe : 2012 - 2016 (continued - suite)

	Switzerland - Suisse				TFYR of Macedonia - L'ex-R. y. de Macédoine			
	2015 (C)				2012 (C)			
	Male — Masculin		Female — Féminin		Male — Masculin		Female — Féminin	
Cause of death — Cause de décès	Number Nombre	Rate Taux	Number Nombre	Rate Taux	Number Nombre	Rate Taux	Number Nombre	Rate Taux
TOTAL	32 646	801.3	34 960	839.6	10 523	1 019.1	9 611	934.5
Certain infectious and parasitic diseases — Certaines maladies infectieuses et parasitaires								
Total	397	9.7	431	10.4	49	4.7	27	✦2.6
Intestinal infectious diseases — Maladies infectieuses intestinales	54	1.3	110	2.6	4	✦0.4	1	✦0.1
Tuberculosis — Tuberculose	8	✦0.2	4	✦0.1	16	✦1.5	6	✦0.6
Tetanus — Tétanos	-	-	1	✦0.0	-	-	-	-
Diphtheria — Diphtérie..........	-	-	-	-	-	-	-	-
Whooping cough — Coqueluche	1	✦0.0	-	-	-	-	-	-
Meningococcal infection — Infection à méningocoques..........	3	✦0.1	5	✦0.1	-	-	1	✦0.1
Septicaemia — Septicémie..........	109	2.7	105	2.5	17	✦1.6	14	✦1.4
Acute poliomyelitis — Poliomyélite aiguë	-	-	-	-	-	-	-	-
Measles — Rougeole..........	-	-	-	-	-	-	-	-
Viral hepatitis — Hépatite virale..........	15	✦0.4	8	✦0.2	8	✦0.8	2	✦0.2
Human immunodeficiency virus [HIV] disease — Maladies dues au virus de l'immunodéficience humaine (VIH)	29	✦0.7	6	✦0.1	-	-	-	-
Malaria — Paludisme..........	-	-	-	-	-	-	-	-
Neoplasms — Tumeurs	9 834	241.4	7 974	191.5	2 237	216.7	1 452	141.2
Malignant neoplasms — Tumeurs malignes								
Total	9 571	234.9	7 690	184.7	2 229	215.9	1 444	140.4
Malignant neoplasm of lip, oral cavity and pharynx — Tumeur maligne de la lèvre, de la cavité buccale et du pharynx	293	7.2	121	2.9	37	3.6	12	✦1.2
Malignant neoplasm of oesophagus — Tumeur maligne de l'oesophage	343	8.4	112	2.7	31	3.0	7	✦0.7
Malignant neoplasm of stomach — Tumeur maligne de l'estomac	332	8.1	198	4.8	219	21.2	118	11.5
Malignant neoplasm of colon, rectosigmoid junction, rectum, anus and anal canal — Tumeur maligne du côlon, de la jonction recto-sigmoïdienne, du rectum, de l'anus et du canal anal	976	24.0	792	19.0	220	21.3	163	15.8
Malignant neoplasm of liver and intrahepatic bile ducts — Tumeur maligne du foie et des voies bilaires intrahépatiques	532	13.1	223	5.4	118	11.4	80	7.8
Malignant neoplasm of pancreas — Tumeur maligne du pancréas..........	605	14.9	668	16.0	106	10.3	81	7.9
Malignant neoplasm of trachea, bronchus and lung — Tumeur maligne de la trachée, des bronches et du poumon..........	2 056	50.5	1 186	28.5	654	63.3	148	14.4
Malignant neoplasm of female breast — Tumeur maligne du sein chez la femme	..	..	1 424	39.9	..	..	285	...
Malignant neoplasm of cervix uteri — Tumeur maligne du col de l'utérus..........	..	..	75	2.1	..	..	39	...
Malignant neoplasm of prostate — Tumeur maligne de la prostate	1 356	92.1	..	..	190	...	..	..
Malignant neoplasm of lymphoid, haematopoietic and related tissue — Tumeurs malignes primitives ou présumées primitives des tissus lymphoïde, hématopoïétique et apparentés..........	873	21.4	737	17.7	84	8.1	69	6.7
Disorders of the blood and blood-forming organs and certain disorders involving the immune mechanism — Maladies du sang et des organes hématopoïétiques et certains troubles du système immunitaire								
Total	100	2.5	96	2.3	6	✦0.6	2	✦0.2
Anaemias — Anémies	56	1.4	58	1.4	4	✦0.4	1	✦0.1
Endocrine, nutritional and metabolic diseases — Maladies endocriniennes, nutritionnelles et métaboliques								
Total	834	20.5	963	23.1	362	35.1	491	47.7
Diabetes mellitus — Diabète sucré..........	631	15.5	685	16.5	361	35.0	489	47.5
Malnutrition — Malnutrition	25	✦0.6	59	1.4	-	-	1	✦0.1
Mental and behavioural disorders — Troubles mentaux et du comportement	1 820	44.7	3 661	87.9	10	✦1.0	-	-
Diseases of the nervous system — Maladies du système nerveux..........	1 640	40.3	2 024	48.6	116	11.2	102	9.9
Diseases of the circulatory system — Maladies de l'appareil circulatoire								
Total	9 715	238.5	11 878	285.3	5 738	555.7	6 188	601.6
Acute rheumatic fever and chronic rheumatic heart diseases — Rhumatisme articularie aigu et cardiopathies rhumatismales chroniques	21	✦0.5	47	1.1	5	✦0.5	4	✦0.4
Hypertensive diseases — Maladies hypertensives..........	1 030	25.3	2 119	50.9	365	35.3	479	46.6
Ischaemic heart disease — Cardiopathie ischémique..........	4 001	98.2	3 372	81.0	1 049	101.6	704	68.4
Cerebrovascular disease — Maladie cérébrovasculaire..........	1 455	35.7	2 113	50.7	1 728	167.4	2 137	207.8

Cause of death — Cause de décès	Switzerland - Suisse 2015 (C)				TFYR of Macedonia - L'ex-R. y. de Macédoine 2012 (C)			
	Male — Masculin		Female — Féminin		Male — Masculin		Female — Féminin	
	Number Nombre	Rate Taux	Number Nombre	Rate Taux	Number Nombre	Rate Taux	Number Nombre	Rate Taux
Diseases of arteries, arterioles and capillaries — Maladies des artères, artérioles et capillaires	502	12.3	455	10.9	163	15.8	189	18.4
Diseases of the respiratory system — Maladies de l'appareil respiratoire								
Total	2 315	56.8	2 299	55.2	476	46.1	319	31.0
Influenza — Grippe	74	1.8	145	3.5	-	-	-	-
Pneumonia — Pneumopathies	664	16.3	805	19.3	62	6.0	39	3.8
Chronic lower respiratory diseases — Maladies chroniques des voies respiratoires inférieures	1 145	28.1	979	23.5	298	28.9	169	16.4
Diseases of the digestive system — Maladies de l'appareil digestif								
Total	1 228	30.1	1 250	30.0	236	22.9	154	15.0
Gastric and duodenal ulcer — Ulcère de l'estomac et du duodénum	68	1.7	49	1.2	30	♦2.9	16	♦1.6
Diseases of the liver — Maladies du foie	474	11.6	261	6.3	128	12.4	46	4.5
Diseases of the musculoskeletal system and connective tissue — Maladies du système ostéo-articularie, des muscles et du tissu conjonctif	224	5.5	453	10.9	1	♦0.1	4	♦0.4
Diseases of the genitourinary system — Maladies de l'appareil génito-urinaire								
Total	557	13.7	623	15.0	193	18.7	113	11.0
Disorders of kidney and ureter — Affections du rein et de l'uretère	356	8.7	384	9.2	191	18.5	112	10.9
Hyperplasia of prostate — Hyperplasie de la prostate	26	♦1.8	..	..	2	...	..	..
Pregnancy, childbirth and the puerperium — Grossesse, accouchement et puerpéralité								
Total	..	..	6	♦6.9	..	..	1	♦4.2
Pregnancy with abortive outcome — Grossesse se terminant par un avortement	..	..	-	-	..	..	-	-
Other direct obstetric causes — Autres décès maternels directs	..	..	3	♦3.5	..	..	1	♦4.2
Indirect obstetric causes — Décès maternels indirects	..	..	3	♦3.5	..	..	-	-
Certain conditions originating in the perinatal period — Certaines affections dont l'origine se situe dans la période périnatale	96	215.0	80	190.9	94	767.8	82	724.1
Congenital malformations, deformations and chromosomal abnormalities — Malformations congénitales et anomalies chromosomiques	154	344.9	132	315.0	7	♦57.2	9	♦79.5
Symptoms, signs and abnormal clinical and laboratory findings, not elsewhere classified — Symptômes, signes et résultats anormaux d'examens cliniques et de laboratoire, non classés ailleurs	1 382	33.9	1 468	35.3	573	55.5	508	49.4
All other diseases — Toutes autres maladies	51	1.3	94	2.3	-	-	-	-
External causes — Causes externes								
Total	2 299	56.4	1 528	36.7	425	41.2	159	15.5
Accidents								
Total	1 419	34.8	1 179	28.3	273	26.4	99	9.6
Transport accidents — Accidents de transport	231	5.7	70	1.7	81	7.8	20	♦1.9
Falls — Chutes	805	19.8	930	22.3	32	3.1	28	♦2.7
Accidental drowning and submersion — Noyade et submersion accidentelles	48	1.2	12	♦0.3	15	♦1.5	6	♦0.6
Exposure to smoke, fire and flames — Exposition à la fumée, au feu et aux flammes	19	♦0.5	3	♦0.1	5	♦0.5	4	♦0.4
Accidental poisoning by and exposure to noxious substances — Intoxication accidentelle par des substances nocives et exposition à ces substances	113	2.8	48	1.2	8	♦0.8	2	♦0.2
Intentional self-harm — Lésions auto-infligées	792	19.4	279	6.7	120	11.6	52	5.1
Assault — Agresssions	26	♦0.6	21	♦0.5	27	♦2.6	7	♦0.7
All other external causes — Toutes autres causes externes	62	1.5	49	1.2	5	♦0.5	1	♦0.1

20. Death and death rates by cause and sex: 2012 - 2016
Décès et taux de mortalité par cause et sexe : 2012 - 2016 (continued - suite)

Cause of death — Cause de décès	TFYR of Macedonia - L'ex-R. y. de Macédoine 2013 (C)				Ukraine 2014 (+C)			
	Male — Masculin		Female — Féminin		Male — Masculin		Female — Féminin	
	Number Nombre	Rate Taux	Number Nombre	Rate Taux	Number Nombre	Rate Taux	Number Nombre	Rate Taux
TOTAL	10 136	981.1	9 072	881.5	310 671	1 477.7	321 625	1 318.0
Certain infectious and parasitic diseases — Certaines maladies infectieuses et parasitaires								
Total	32	3.1	18	٭1.7	8 005	38.1	2 969	12.2
Intestinal infectious diseases — Maladies infectieuses intestinales	-	-	-	-	12	٭0.1	18	٭0.1
Tuberculosis — Tuberculose	14	٭1.4	5	٭0.5	4 326	20.6	914	3.7
Tetanos — Tétanos	-	-	-	-	3	٭0.0	2	٭0.0
Diphtheria — Diphtérie	-	-	-	-	1	٭0.0	1	٭0.0
Whooping cough — Coqueluche	-	-	-	-	1	٭0.0		
Meningococcal infection — Infection à méningocoques	2	٭0.2	1	٭0.1	28	٭0.1	32	0.1
Septicaemia — Septicémie	11	٭1.1	9	٭0.9	207	1.0	179	0.7
Acute poliomyelitis — Poliomyélite aiguë	-	-	-	-	-	-	-	-
Measles — Rougeole	-	-	-	-	-	-	-	-
Viral hepatitis — Hépatite virale	3	٭0.3	2	٭0.2	149	0.7	103	0.4
Human immunodeficiency virus [HIV] disease — Maladies dues au virus de l'immunodéficience humaine (VIH)	1	٭0.1	-	-	2 880	13.7	1 519	6.2
Malaria — Paludisme	-	-	-	-	3	٭0.0	-	-
Neoplasms — Tumeurs	2 195	212.5	1 459	141.8	46 545	221.4	37 349	153.1
Malignant neoplasms — Tumeurs malignes								
Total	2 188	211.8	1 452	141.1	46 194	219.7	36 887	151.2
Malignant neoplasm of lip, oral cavity and pharynx — Tumeur maligne de la lèvre, de la cavité buccale et du pharynx	44	4.3	14	٭1.4	3 179	15.1	456	1.9
Malignant neoplasm of oesophagus — Tumeur maligne de l'oesophage	23	٭2.2	7	٭0.7	1 381	6.6	165	0.7
Malignant neoplasm of stomach — Tumeur maligne de l'estomac	198	19.2	109	10.6	4 860	23.1	3 051	12.5
Malignant neoplasm of colon, rectosigmoid junction, rectum, anus and anal canal — Tumeur maligne du côlon, de la jonction recto-sigmoïdienne, du rectum, de l'anus et du canal anal	235	22.7	183	17.8	5 771	27.4	5 733	23.5
Malignant neoplasm of liver and intrahepatic bile ducts — Tumeur maligne du foie et des voies bilaires intrahépatiques	108	10.5	70	6.8	992	4.7	706	2.9
Malignant neoplasm of pancreas — Tumeur maligne du pancréas	122	11.8	85	8.3	2 486	11.8	2 072	8.5
Malignant neoplasm of trachea, bronchus and lung — Tumeur maligne de la trachée, des bronches et du poumon	689	66.7	159	15.4	10 959	52.1	2 284	9.4
Malignant neoplasm of female breast — Tumeur maligne du sein chez la femme	..	..	272	...	..	..	7 275	...
Malignant neoplasm of cervix uteri — Tumeur maligne du col de l'utérus	..	..	36	...	..	..	2 102	..
Malignant neoplasm of prostate — Tumeur maligne de la prostate	203	...	..	..	3 715	...	..	..
Malignant neoplasm of lymphoid, haematopoietic and related tissue — Tumeurs malignes primitives ou présumées primitives des tissus lymphoïde, hématopoïétique et apparentés	87	8.4	76	7.4	...	...	...	...
Disorders of the blood and blood-forming organs and certain disorders involving the immune mechanism — Maladies du sang et des organes hématopoïétiques et certains troubles du système immunitaire								
Total	4	٭0.4	8	٭0.8	117	0.6	124	0.5
Anaemias — Anémies	3	٭0.3	6	٭0.6	47	0.2	59	0.2
Endocrine, nutritional and metabolic diseases — Maladies endocriniennes, nutritionnelles et métaboliques								
Total	347	33.6	492	47.8	923	4.4	1 299	5.3
Diabetes mellitus — Diabète sucré	345	33.4	491	47.7	780	3.7	1 168	4.8
Malnutrition — Malnutrition	1	٭0.1	-	-	22	٭0.1	15	٭0.1
Mental and behavioural disorders — Troubles mentaux et du comportement	14	٭1.4	7	٭0.7	1 082	5.1	527	2.2
Diseases of the nervous system — Maladies du système nerveux	118	11.4	106	10.3	3 528	16.8	2 354	9.6
Diseases of the circulatory system — Maladies de l'appareil circulatoire								
Total	5 469	529.4	5 632	547.2	183 219	871.5	242 388	993.3
Acute rheumatic fever and chronic rheumatic heart diseases — Rhumatisme articularie aigu et cardiopathies rhumatismales chroniques	6	٭0.6	6	٭0.6	345	1.6	494	2.0
Hypertensive diseases — Maladies hypertensives	430	41.6	566	55.0	356	1.7	222	0.9
Ischaemic heart disease — Cardiopathie ischémique	989	95.7	598	58.1	126 762	602.9	164 683	674.9
Cerebrovascular disease — Maladie cérébrovasculaire	1 746	169.0	1 855	180.2	35 465	168.7	52 425	214.8

Cause of death — Cause de décès	TFYR of Macedonia - L'ex-R. y. de Macédoine				Ukraine			
	2013 (C)				2014 (+C)			
	Male — Masculin		Female — Féminin		Male — Masculin		Female — Féminin	
	Number Nombre	Rate Taux	Number Nombre	Rate Taux	Number Nombre	Rate Taux	Number Nombre	Rate Taux
Diseases of arteries, arterioles and capillaries — Maladies des artères, artérioles et capillaires	140	13.6	165	16.0	...	...	...	...
Diseases of the respiratory system — Maladies de l'appareil respiratoire								
Total	365	35.3	300	29.2	10 619	50.5	4 191	17.2
Influenza — Grippe	-	-	1	♦0.1	7	♦0.0	7	♦0.0
Pneumonia — Pneumopathies	33	3.2	37	3.6	3 713	17.7	1 270	5.2
Chronic lower respiratory diseases — Maladies chroniques des voies respiratoires inférieures	222	21.5	147	14.3	5 816	27.7	2 532	10.4
Diseases of the digestive system — Maladies de l'appareil digestif								
Total	247	23.9	134	13.0	15 759	75.0	9 466	38.8
Gastric and duodenal ulcer — Ulcère de l'estomac et du duodénum	20	♦1.9	10	♦1.0	1 086	5.2	616	2.5
Diseases of the liver — Maladies du foie	138	13.4	50	4.9	11 021	52.4	5 766	23.6
Diseases of the musculoskeletal system and connective tissue — Maladies du système ostéo-articularie, des muscles et du tissu conjonctif	-	-	7	♦0.7	201	1.0	318	1.3
Diseases of the genitourinary system — Maladies de l'appareil génito-urinaire								
Total	162	15.7	118	11.5	1 414	6.7	1 281	5.2
Disorders of kidney and ureter — Affections du rein et de l'uretère	159	15.4	118	11.5	...	...	...	...
Hyperplasia of prostate — Hyperplasie de la prostate	2	...	..	..	...	...	...	...
Pregnancy, childbirth and the puerperium — Grossesse, accouchement et puerpéralité								
Total	..	..	1	♦4.3	..	..	69	14.8
Pregnancy with abortive outcome — Grossesse se terminant par un avortement	..	..	-	-	..	..	3	♦0.6
Other direct obstetric causes — Autres décès maternels directs	..	..	1	♦4.3	..	..	41	8.8
Indirect obstetric causes — Décès maternels indirects	..	..	-	-	..	..	24	♦5.2
Certain conditions originating in the perinatal period — Certaines affections dont l'origine se situe dans la période périnatale	95	785.6	78	706.2	1 159	482.8	799	353.8
Congenital malformations, deformations and chromosomal abnormalities — Malformations congénitales et anomalies chromosomiques	14	♦115.8	15	♦135.8	800	333.3	713	315.7
Symptoms, signs and abnormal clinical and laboratory findings, not elsewhere classified — Symptômes, signes et résultats anormaux d'examens cliniques et de laboratoire, non classés ailleurs	664	64.3	553	53.7	5 236	24.9	9 163	37.6
All other diseases — Toutes autres maladies	2	♦0.2	-	-	253	1.2	291	1.2
External causes — Causes externes								
Total	408	39.5	144	14.0	31 811	151.3	8 324	34.1
Accidents								
Total	257	24.9	104	10.1	...	...	...	...
Transport accidents — Accidents de transport	108	10.5	37	3.6	3 947	18.8	1 217	5.0
Falls — Chutes	25	♦2.4	22	♦2.1	1 646	7.8	505	2.1
Accidental drowning and submersion — Noyade et submersion accidentelles	12	♦1.2	5	♦0.5	1 921	9.1	322	1.3
Exposure to smoke, fire and flames — Exposition à la fumée, au feu et aux flammes	9	♦0.9	3	♦0.3	1 004	4.8	429	1.8
Accidental poisoning by and exposure to noxious substances — Intoxication accidentelle par des substances nocives et exposition à ces substances	10	♦1.0	4	♦0.4	4 173	19.8	1 070	4.4
Intentional self-harm — Lésions auto-infligées	136	13.2	34	3.3	6 414	30.5	1 556	6.4
Assault — Agresssions	12	♦1.2	6	♦0.6	2 124	10.1	721	3.0
All other external causes — Toutes autres causes externes	3	♦0.3	-	-	...	...	...	...

Cause of death — Cause de décès	Ukraine				United Kingdom of Great Britain and Northern Ireland - Royaume-Uni de Grande-Bretagne et d'Irlande du Nord			
	2015 (+C)				2014 (+C)			
	Male — Masculin		Female — Féminin		Male — Masculin		Female — Féminin	
	Number Nombre	Rate Taux	Number Nombre	Rate Taux	Number Nombre	Rate Taux	Number Nombre	Rate Taux
TOTAL	291 561	1 466.1	303 235	1 316.0	278 455	879.8	291 886	893.7
Certain infectious and parasitic diseases — Certaines maladies infectieuses et parasitaires								
Total	7 218	36.3	2 682	11.6	2 767	8.7	3 289	10.1
Intestinal infectious diseases — Maladies infectieuses intestinales	17	+0.1	11	+0.0	526	1.7	925	2.8
Tuberculosis — Tuberculose	3 765	18.9	837	3.6	171	0.5	139	0.4
Tetanus — Tétanos	2	+0.0	1	+0.0	-	-	1	+0.0
Diphtheria — Diphtérie	-	-	-	-	-	-	-	-
Whooping cough — Coqueluche	2	+0.0	-	-	3	+0.0	4	+0.0
Meningococcal infection — Infection à méningocoques	36	0.2	24	+0.1	27	+0.1	19	+0.1
Septicaemia — Septicémie	218	1.1	192	0.8	1 202	3.8	1 626	5.0
Acute poliomyelitis — Poliomyélite aiguë	-	-	-	-	-	-	-	-
Measles — Rougeole	-	-	-	-	-	-	-	-
Viral hepatitis — Hépatite virale	159	0.8	114	0.5	195	0.6	92	0.3
Human immunodeficiency virus [HIV] disease — Maladies dues au virus de l'immunodéficience humaine (VIH)	2 669	13.4	1 363	5.9	139	0.4	39	0.1
Malaria — Paludisme	4	+0.0	-	-	1	+0.0	1	+0.0
Neoplasms — Tumeurs	44 518	223.9	35 012	151.9	88 664	280.2	78 915	241.6
Malignant neoplasms — Tumeurs malignes								
Total	44 148	222.0	34 602	150.2	86 731	274.0	77 063	236.0
Malignant neoplasm of lip, oral cavity and pharynx — Tumeur maligne de la lèvre, de la cavité buccale et du pharynx	3 111	15.6	428	1.9	1 852	5.9	892	2.7
Malignant neoplasm of oesophagus — Tumeur maligne de l'oesophage	1 390	7.0	173	0.8	5 218	16.5	2 580	7.9
Malignant neoplasm of stomach — Tumeur maligne de l'estomac	4 389	22.1	2 707	11.7	2 922	9.2	1 665	5.1
Malignant neoplasm of colon, rectosigmoid junction, rectum, anus and anal canal — Tumeur maligne du côlon, de la jonction recto-sigmoïdienne, du rectum, de l'anus et du canal anal	5 653	28.4	5 268	22.9	8 725	27.6	7 563	23.2
Malignant neoplasm of liver and intrahepatic bile ducts — Tumeur maligne du foie et des voies bilaires intrahépatiques	925	4.7	655	2.8	3 069	9.7	2 042	6.3
Malignant neoplasm of pancreas — Tumeur maligne du pancréas	2 356	11.8	1 920	8.3	4 433	14.0	4 401	13.5
Malignant neoplasm of trachea, bronchus and lung — Tumeur maligne de la trachée, des bronches et du poumon	10 264	51.6	2 109	9.2	19 600	61.9	16 360	50.1
Malignant neoplasm of female breast — Tumeur maligne du sein chez la femme	..	..	6 832	34.4	..	..	11 384	...
Malignant neoplasm of cervix uteri — Tumeur maligne du col de l'utérus	..	..	1 922	9.7	..	..	893	...
Malignant neoplasm of prostate — Tumeur maligne de la prostate	3 644	59.7	..	..	11 301	...	..	..
Malignant neoplasm of lymphoid, haematopoietic and related tissue — Tumeurs malignes primitives ou présumées primitives des tissus lymphoïde, hématopoïétique et apparentés	...	...	...	...	7 189	22.7	5 668	17.4
Disorders of the blood and blood-forming organs and certain disorders involving the immune mechanism — Maladies du sang et des organes hématopoïétiques et certains troubles du système immunitaire								
Total	129	0.6	115	0.5	539	1.7	542	1.7
Anaemias — Anémies	40	0.2	62	0.3	177	0.6	251	0.8
Endocrine, nutritional and metabolic diseases — Maladies endocriniennes, nutritionnelles et métaboliques								
Total	923	4.6	1 246	5.4	4 036	12.8	4 452	13.6
Diabetes mellitus — Diabète sucré	809	4.1	1 096	4.8	3 016	9.5	3 293	10.1
Malnutrition — Malnutrition	21	+0.1	16	+0.1	32	0.1	64	0.2
Mental and behavioural disorders — Troubles mentaux et du comportement	853	4.3	452	2.0	15 889	50.2	30 313	92.8
Diseases of the nervous system — Maladies du système nerveux	2 884	14.5	1 980	8.6	12 176	38.5	15 663	48.0
Diseases of the circulatory system — Maladies de l'appareil circulatoire								
Total	175 080	880.4	229 471	995.9	78 243	247.2	76 402	233.9
Acute rheumatic fever and chronic rheumatic heart diseases — Rhumatisme articularie aigu et cardiopathies rhumatismales chroniques	287	1.4	453	2.0	319	1.0	618	1.9
Hypertensive diseases — Maladies hypertensives	336	1.7	184	0.8	2 742	8.7	3 973	12.2
Ischaemic heart disease — Cardiopathie ischémique	121 276	609.8	157 438	683.3	41 365	130.7	27 798	85.1
Cerebrovascular disease — Maladie cérébrovasculaire	32 961	165.7	46 814	203.2	16 219	51.2	23 061	70.6

20. Death and death rates by cause and sex: 2012 - 2016
Décès et taux de mortalité par cause et sexe : 2012 - 2016 (continued - suite)

	Ukraine				United Kingdom of Great Britain and Northern Ireland - Royaume-Uni de Grande-Bretagne et d'Irlande du Nord			
Cause of death — Cause de décès	2015 (+C)				2014 (+C)			
	Male — Masculin		Female — Féminin		Male — Masculin		Female — Féminin	
	Number Nombre	Rate Taux	Number Nombre	Rate Taux	Number Nombre	Rate Taux	Number Nombre	Rate Taux
Diseases of arteries, arterioles and capillaries — Maladies des artères, artérioles et capillaires	...	...	...	...	5 135	16.2	4 422	13.5
Diseases of the respiratory system — Maladies de l'appareil respiratoire								
Total	9 970	50.1	3 981	17.3	36 346	114.8	38 942	119.2
Influenza — Grippe	12	+0.1	9	+0.0	52	0.2	51	0.2
Pneumonia — Pneumopathies	3 656	18.4	1 298	5.6	12 278	38.8	15 526	47.5
Chronic lower respiratory diseases — Maladies chroniques des voies respiratoires inférieures	5 347	26.9	2 328	10.1	16 399	51.8	16 595	50.8
Diseases of the digestive system — Maladies de l'appareil digestif								
Total	14 108	70.9	8 710	37.8	13 694	43.3	14 179	43.4
Gastric and duodenal ulcer — Ulcère de l'estomac et du duodénum	1 126	5.7	628	2.7	1 133	3.6	927	2.8
Diseases of the liver — Maladies du foie...............	9 529	47.9	5 174	22.5	5 503	17.4	3 363	10.3
Diseases of the musculoskeletal system and connective tissue — Maladies du système ostéo-articularie, des muscles et du tissu conjonctif	182	0.9	297	1.3	1 391	4.4	2 874	8.8
Diseases of the genitourinary system — Maladies de l'appareil génito-urinaire								
Total	1 327	6.7	1 242	5.4	4 256	13.4	6 043	18.5
Disorders of kidney and ureter — Affections du rein et de l'uretère	...	...	...	...	1 892	6.0	2 433	7.4
Hyperplasia of prostate — Hyperplasie de la prostate...............	...	...	..	..	181	...		..
Pregnancy, childbirth and the puerperium — Grossesse, accouchement et puerpéralité								
Total	...	..	60	14.6	..	..	52	6.7
Pregnancy with abortive outcome — Grossesse se terminant par un avortement	..	..	3	+0.7	..	..	3	+0.4
Other direct obstetric causes — Autres décès maternels directs	..	..	30	+7.3	..	..	30	+3.9
Indirect obstetric causes — Décès maternels indirects	..	..	27	+6.6	..	..	18	+2.3
Certain conditions originating in the perinatal period — Certaines affections dont l'origine se situe dans la période périnatale	978	459.5	752	378.0	916	230.1	714	189.0
Congenital malformations, deformations and chromosomal abnormalities — Malformations congénitales et anomalies chromosomiques	809	380.1	634	318.7	1 086	272.8	1 019	269.7
Symptoms, signs and abnormal clinical and laboratory findings, not elsewhere classified — Symptômes, signes et résultats anormaux d'examens cliniques et de laboratoire, non classés ailleurs	5 057	25.4	9 074	39.4	3 312	10.5	8 521	26.1
All other diseases — Toutes autres maladies...............	234	1.2	249	1.1	706	2.2	1 272	3.9
External causes — Causes externes								
Total	27 291	137.2	7 278	31.6	14 434	45.6	8 694	26.6
Accidents								
Total	...	...	...	...	9 106	28.8	6 630	20.3
Transport accidents — Accidents de transport...............	3 662	18.4	1 145	5.0	1 512	4.8	486	1.5
Falls — Chutes	1 551	7.8	470	2.0	2 650	8.4	2 857	8.7
Accidental drowning and submersion — Noyade et submersion accidentelles...............	1 669	8.4	296	1.3	204	0.6	66	0.2
Exposure to smoke, fire and flames — Exposition à la fumée, au feu et aux flammes...............	886	4.5	440	1.9	146	0.5	117	0.4
Accidental poisoning by and exposure to noxious substances — Intoxication accidentelle par des substances nocives et exposition à ces substances	3 552	17.9	797	3.5	2 447	7.7	985	3.0
Intentional self-harm — Lésions auto-infligées...............	6 149	30.9	1 426	6.2	3 716	11.7	1 071	3.3
Assault — Agresssions...............	1 510	7.6	601	2.6	81	0.3	48	0.1
All other external causes — Toutes autres causes externes	...	...	...	...	1 531	4.8	945	2.9

20. Death and death rates by cause and sex: 2012 - 2016
Décès et taux de mortalité par cause et sexe : 2012 - 2016 (continued - suite)

Cause of death — Cause de décès	United Kingdom of Great Britain and Northern Ireland - Royaume-Uni de Grande-Bretagne et d'Irlande du Nord 2015 (+C)				Australia - Australie 2014 (C)			
	Male — Masculin		Female — Féminin		Male — Masculin		Female — Féminin	
	Number Nombre	Rate Taux	Number Nombre	Rate Taux	Number Nombre	Rate Taux	Number Nombre	Rate Taux
TOTAL	292 707	916.2	310 074	941.7	78 341	670.8	75 239	636.3
Certain infectious and parasitic diseases — Certaines maladies infectieuses et parasitaires								
Total	3 075	9.6	3 649	11.1	1 411	12.1	1 321	11.2
Intestinal infectious diseases — Maladies infectieuses intestinales	526	1.6	1 036	3.1	116	1.0	158	1.3
Tuberculosis — Tuberculose	179	0.6	116	0.4	29	+0.2	14	+0.1
Tetanus — Tétanos.	-		-		-		-	
Diphtheria — Diphtérie.	-		-		-		-	
Whooping cough — Coqueluche	4	+0.0	2	+0.0	2	+0.0	2	+0.0
Meningococcal infection — Infection à méningocoques	42	0.1	29	+0.1	2	+0.0	5	+0.0
Septicaemia — Septicémie.	1 406	4.4	1 838	5.6	784	6.7	869	7.3
Acute poliomyelitis — Poliomyélite aiguë	-		-		-		-	
Measles — Rougeole.	-		-		-		-	
Viral hepatitis — Hépatite virale.	236	0.7	101	0.3	203	1.7	86	0.7
Human immunodeficiency virus [HIV] disease — Maladies dues au virus de l'immunodéficience humaine (VIH).	125	0.4	56	0.2	54	0.5	2	+0.0
Malaria — Paludisme.	5	+0.0	2	+0.0	-		-	
Neoplasms — Tumeurs	89 669	280.7	78 939	239.7	24 995	214.0	19 742	167.0
Malignant neoplasms — Tumeurs malignes								
Total	87 676	274.4	77 102	234.2	24 357	208.5	19 195	162.3
Malignant neoplasm of lip, oral cavity and pharynx — Tumeur maligne de la lèvre, de la cavité buccale et du pharynx	1 927	6.0	913	2.8	552	4.7	229	1.9
Malignant neoplasm of oesophagus — Tumeur maligne de l'oesophage	5 466	17.1	2 494	7.6	869	7.4	329	2.8
Malignant neoplasm of stomach — Tumeur maligne de l'estomac	2 817	8.8	1 581	4.8	705	6.0	433	3.7
Malignant neoplasm of colon, rectosigmoid junction, rectum, anus and anal canal — Tumeur maligne du côlon, de la jonction recto-sigmoïdienne, du rectum, de l'anus et du canal anal.	8 873	27.8	7 589	23.0	2 280	19.5	1 890	16.0
Malignant neoplasm of liver and intrahepatic bile ducts — Tumeur maligne du foie et des voies bilaires intrahépatiques	3 091	9.7	2 088	6.3	1 131	9.7	601	5.1
Malignant neoplasm of pancreas — Tumeur maligne du pancréas.	4 469	14.0	4 472	13.6	1 292	11.1	1 255	10.6
Malignant neoplasm of trachea, bronchus and lung — Tumeur maligne de la trachée, des bronches et du poumon.	19 200	60.1	16 357	49.7	4 947	42.4	3 304	27.9
Malignant neoplasm of female breast — Tumeur maligne du sein chez la femme.	..	..	11 470	42.0	..	..	2 814	29.2
Malignant neoplasm of cervix uteri — Tumeur maligne du col de l'utérus.	..	..	855	3.1	..	..	223	2.3
Malignant neoplasm of prostate — Tumeur maligne de la prostate	11 827	106.9	..	..	3 102	83.7	..	..
Malignant neoplasm of lymphoid, haematopoietic and related tissue — Tumeurs malignes primitives ou présumées primitives des tissus lymphoïde, hématopoïétique et apparentés.	7 403	23.2	5 721	17.4	2 413	20.7	1 862	15.7
Disorders of the blood and blood-forming organs and certain disorders involving the immune mechanism — Maladies du sang et des organes hématopoïétiques et certains troubles du système immunitaire								
Total	584	1.8	706	2.1	249	2.1	286	2.4
Anaemias — Anémies	208	0.7	335	1.0	105	0.9	149	1.3
Endocrine, nutritional and metabolic diseases — Maladies endocriniennes, nutritionnelles et métaboliques								
Total	4 367	13.7	4 622	14.0	3 112	26.6	3 101	26.2
Diabetes mellitus — Diabète sucré.	3 238	10.1	3 321	10.1	2 215	19.0	2 138	18.1
Malnutrition — Malnutrition	37	0.1	66	0.2	52	0.4	44	0.4
Mental and behavioural disorders — Troubles mentaux et du comportement	18 483	57.9	35 590	108.1	3 269	28.0	5 734	48.5
Diseases of the nervous system — Maladies du système nerveux	14 070	44.0	18 462	56.1	3 795	32.5	4 323	36.6
Diseases of the circulatory system — Maladies de l'appareil circulatoire								
Total	80 108	250.8	78 053	237.0	21 643	185.3	23 411	198.0
Acute rheumatic fever and chronic rheumatic heart diseases — Rhumatisme articularie aigu et cardiopathies rhumatismales chroniques	310	1.0	624	1.9	120	1.0	257	2.2
Hypertensive diseases — Maladies hypertensives.	2 979	9.3	4 146	12.6	797	6.8	1 428	12.1
Ischaemic heart disease — Cardiopathie ischémique.	41 955	131.3	27 828	84.5	11 098	95.0	9 091	76.9
Cerebrovascular disease — Maladie cérébrovasculaire.	16 560	51.8	23 612	71.7	4 270	36.6	6 474	54.7

20. Death and death rates by cause and sex: 2012 - 2016
Décès et taux de mortalité par cause et sexe : 2012 - 2016 (continued - suite)

Cause of death — Cause de décès	United Kingdom of Great Britain and Northern Ireland - Royaume-Uni de Grande-Bretagne et d'Irlande du Nord				Australia - Australie			
	2015 (+C)				2014 (C)			
	Male — Masculin		Female — Féminin		Male — Masculin		Female — Féminin	
	Number Nombre	Rate Taux	Number Nombre	Rate Taux	Number Nombre	Rate Taux	Number Nombre	Rate Taux
Diseases of arteries, arterioles and capillaries — Maladies des artères, artérioles et capillaires	5 097	16.0	4 382	13.3	973	8.3	866	7.3
Diseases of the respiratory system — Maladies de l'appareil respiratoire								
Total	40 693	127.4	44 752	135.9	7 179	61.5	6 609	55.9
Influenza — Grippe	164	0.5	210	0.6	116	1.0	126	1.1
Pneumonia — Pneumopathies	14 315	44.8	18 018	54.7	1 180	10.1	1 437	12.2
Chronic lower respiratory diseases — Maladies chroniques des voies respiratoires inférieures	17 925	56.1	18 682	56.7	4 167	35.7	3 649	30.9
Diseases of the digestive system — Maladies de l'appareil digestif								
Total	14 008	43.8	14 801	44.9	2 815	24.1	2 670	22.6
Gastric and duodenal ulcer — Ulcère de l'estomac et du duodénum	1 129	3.5	966	2.9	130	1.1	134	1.1
Diseases of the liver — Maladies du foie	5 623	17.6	3 631	11.0	1 230	10.5	526	4.4
Diseases of the musculoskeletal system and connective tissue — Maladies du système ostéo-articularie, des muscles et du tissu conjonctif	1 539	4.8	3 021	9.2	421	3.6	816	6.9
Diseases of the genitourinary system — Maladies de l'appareil génito-urinaire								
Total	4 737	14.8	6 151	18.7	1 427	12.2	1 815	15.3
Disorders of kidney and ureter — Affections du rein et de l'uretère	2 121	6.6	2 561	7.8	1 062	9.1	1 256	10.6
Hyperplasia of prostate — Hyperplasie de la prostate	170	1.5	..	..	58	1.6	..	...
Pregnancy, childbirth and the puerperium — Grossesse, accouchement et puerpéralité								
Total	..	..	35	4.5	..	..	12	+4.0
Pregnancy with abortive outcome — Grossesse se terminant par un avortement	..	..	1	+0.1	..	..	1	+0.3
Other direct obstetric causes — Autres décès maternels directs	..	..	22	+2.8	..	..	10	+3.3
Indirect obstetric causes — Décès maternels indirects	..	..	12	+1.5	..	..	1	+0.3
Certain conditions originating in the perinatal period — Certaines affections dont l'origine se situe dans la période périnatale	943	236.5	676	178.8	286	186.2	257	175.9
Congenital malformations, deformations and chromosomal abnormalities — Malformations congénitales et anomalies chromosomiques	1 128	282.9	907	240.0	315	205.1	302	206.7
Symptoms, signs and abnormal clinical and laboratory findings, not elsewhere classified — Symptômes, signes et résultats anormaux d'examens cliniques et de laboratoire, non classés ailleurs	3 450	10.8	9 145	27.8	791	6.8	853	7.2
All other diseases — Toutes autres maladies	741	2.3	1 411	4.3	217	1.9	288	2.4
External causes — Causes externes								
Total	15 112	47.3	9 154	27.8	6 416	54.9	3 699	31.3
Accidents								
Total	9 752	30.5	6 991	21.2	3 719	31.8	2 671	22.6
Transport accidents — Accidents de transport	1 407	4.4	446	1.4	1 026	8.8	382	3.2
Falls — Chutes	3 103	9.7	3 282	10.0	1 109	9.5	1 235	10.4
Accidental drowning and submersion — Noyade et submersion accidentelles	195	0.6	70	0.2	152	1.3	40	0.3
Exposure to smoke, fire and flames — Exposition à la fumée, au feu et aux flammes	155	0.5	101	0.3	37	0.3	21	+0.2
Accidental poisoning by and exposure to noxious substances — Intoxication accidentelle par des substances nocives et exposition à ces substances	2 757	8.6	1 064	3.2	832	7.1	419	3.5
Intentional self-harm — Lésions auto-infligées	3 732	11.7	1 178	3.6	2 179	18.7	709	6.0
Assault — Agresssions	73	0.2	47	0.1	158	1.4	90	0.8
All other external causes — Toutes autres causes externes	1 555	4.9	938	2.8	360	3.1	229	1.9

20. Death and death rates by cause and sex: 2012 - 2016
Décès et taux de mortalité par cause et sexe : 2012 - 2016 (continued - suite)

Cause of death — Cause de décès	Australia - Australie				Fiji - Fidji			
	2015 (C)				2012 (+C)			
	Male — Masculin		Female — Féminin		Male — Masculin		Female — Féminin	
	Number Nombre	Rate Taux	Number Nombre	Rate Taux	Number Nombre	Rate Taux	Number Nombre	Rate Taux
TOTAL	81 330	686.9	77 722	647.1	3 757	...	3 009	...
Certain infectious and parasitic diseases — Certaines maladies infectieuses et parasitaires								
Total	1 452	12.3	1 391	11.6	213	...	150	...
Intestinal infectious diseases — Maladies infectieuses intestinales	101	0.9	190	1.6	73	...	43	...
Tuberculosis — Tuberculose	26	♦0.2	22	♦0.2	22	...	13	...
Tetanus — Tétanos	-	-	-	-	-		-	
Diphtheria — Diphtérie	-	-	-	-	-		-	
Whooping cough — Coqueluche	2	♦0.0	1	♦0.0	-		-	
Meningococcal infection — Infection à méningocoques	3	♦0.0	8	♦0.1	-		-	
Septicaemia — Septicémie	855	7.2	859	7.2	65	...	63	...
Acute poliomyelitis — Poliomyélite aiguë	-	-	-	-	-		-	
Measles — Rougeole	-	-	-	-	-		-	
Viral hepatitis — Hépatite virale	198	1.7	85	0.7	4	...	4	...
Human immunodeficiency virus [HIV] disease — Maladies dues au virus de l'immunodéficience humaine (VIH)	39	0.3	5	♦0.0	2	...	3	...
Malaria — Paludisme	-	-	-	-	-		-	
Neoplasms — Tumeurs	26 123	220.6	20 428	170.1	275	...	425	...
Malignant neoplasms — Tumeurs malignes								
Total	25 445	214.9	19 845	165.2	247	...	399	...
Malignant neoplasm of lip, oral cavity and pharynx — Tumeur maligne de la lèvre, de la cavité buccale et du pharynx	641	5.4	254	2.1	7	...	5	...
Malignant neoplasm of oesophagus — Tumeur maligne de l'oesophage	949	8.0	380	3.2	6	...	3	...
Malignant neoplasm of stomach — Tumeur maligne de l'estomac	711	6.0	439	3.7	11	...	4	...
Malignant neoplasm of colon, rectosigmoid junction, rectum, anus and anal canal — Tumeur maligne du côlon, de la jonction recto-sigmoïdienne, du rectum, de l'anus et du canal anal	2 394	20.2	2 039	17.0	19	...	24	...
Malignant neoplasm of liver and intrahepatic bile ducts — Tumeur maligne du foie et des voies bilaires intrahépatiques	1 222	10.3	598	5.0	35	...	20	...
Malignant neoplasm of pancreas — Tumeur maligne du pancréas	1 433	12.1	1 327	11.0	8	...	2	...
Malignant neoplasm of trachea, bronchus and lung — Tumeur maligne de la trachée, des bronches et du poumon	4 989	42.1	3 477	29.0	21	...	12	...
Malignant neoplasm of female breast — Tumeur maligne du sein chez la femme	..	..	2 939	30.1	..	..	114	...
Malignant neoplasm of cervix uteri — Tumeur maligne du col de l'utérus	..	..	230	2.4	..	..	76	...
Malignant neoplasm of prostate — Tumeur maligne de la prostate	3 195	84.5	..	..	41	...	..	..
Malignant neoplasm of lymphoid, haematopoietic and related tissue — Tumeurs malignes primitives ou présumées primitives des tissus lymphoïde, hématopoïétique et apparentés	2 531	21.4	1 881	15.7	42	...	28	...
Disorders of the blood and blood-forming organs and certain disorders involving the immune mechanism — Maladies du sang et des organes hématopoïétiques et certains troubles du système immunitaire								
Total	237	2.0	285	2.4	34	...	38	...
Anaemias — Anémies	108	0.9	156	1.3	22	...	26	...
Endocrine, nutritional and metabolic diseases — Maladies endocriniennes, nutritionnelles et métaboliques								
Total	3 379	28.5	3 259	27.1	778	...	785	...
Diabetes mellitus — Diabète sucré	2 463	20.8	2 199	18.3	712	...	740	...
Malnutrition — Malnutrition	46	0.4	49	0.4	5	...	6	...
Mental and behavioural disorders — Troubles mentaux et du comportement	3 598	30.4	5 997	49.9	1	...	2	...
Diseases of the nervous system — Maladies du système nerveux	3 901	32.9	4 559	38.0	60	...	39	...
Diseases of the circulatory system — Maladies de l'appareil circulatoire								
Total	21 937	185.3	23 455	195.3	1 405	...	859	...
Acute rheumatic fever and chronic rheumatic heart diseases — Rhumatisme articularie aigu et cardiopathies rhumatismales chroniques	156	1.3	262	2.2	25	...	24	...
Hypertensive diseases — Maladies hypertensives	826	7.0	1 459	12.1	480	...	408	...
Ischaemic heart disease — Cardiopathie ischémique	11 075	93.5	8 702	72.5	585	...	169	...
Cerebrovascular disease — Maladie cérébrovasculaire	4 363	36.8	6 506	54.2	76	...	76	...

Cause of death — Cause de décès	Australia - Australie 2015 (C)				Fiji - Fidji 2012 (+C)			
	Male — Masculin		Female — Féminin		Male — Masculin		Female — Féminin	
	Number Nombre	Rate Taux	Number Nombre	Rate Taux	Number Nombre	Rate Taux	Number Nombre	Rate Taux
Diseases of arteries, arterioles and capillaries — Maladies des artères, artérioles et capillaires	998	8.4	895	7.5	18	...	10	...
Diseases of the respiratory system — Maladies de l'appareil respiratoire								
Total	7 214	60.9	7 100	59.1	223	...	171	...
Influenza — Grippe	122	1.0	160	1.3	-	...	-	...
Pneumonia — Pneumopathies	1 186	10.0	1 567	13.0	56	...	50	...
Chronic lower respiratory diseases — Maladies chroniques des voies respiratoires inférieures	4 103	34.7	3 888	32.4	140	...	88	...
Diseases of the digestive system — Maladies de l'appareil digestif								
Total	2 831	23.9	2 836	23.6	105	...	52	...
Gastric and duodenal ulcer — Ulcère de l'estomac et du duodénum...............	128	1.1	114	0.9	16	...	5	...
Diseases of the liver — Maladies du foie...............	1 235	10.4	622	5.2	27	...	15	...
Diseases of the musculoskeletal system and connective tissue — Maladies du système ostéo-articularie, des muscles et du tissu conjonctif	452	3.8	850	7.1	26	...	40	...
Diseases of the genitourinary system — Maladies de l'appareil génito-urinaire								
Total	1 624	13.7	1 911	15.9	124	...	72	...
Disorders of kidney and ureter — Affections du rein et de l'uretère	1 234	10.4	1 338	11.1	103	...	58	...
Hyperplasia of prostate — Hyperplasie de la prostate...............	58	1.5	..	..	13	...	..	...
Pregnancy, childbirth and the puerperium — Grossesse, accouchement et puerpéralité								
Total	..	..	8	♦2.6	..	..	8	♦43.4
Pregnancy with abortive outcome — Grossesse se terminant par un avortement	..	..	1	♦0.3	..	..	1	♦5.4
Other direct obstetric causes — Autres décès maternels directs	..	..	7	♦2.3	..	..	7	♦38.0
Indirect obstetric causes — Décès maternels indirects	..	..	-	-	..	..	-	-
Certain conditions originating in the perinatal period — Certaines affections dont l'origine se situe dans la période périnatale	294	187.2	252	169.9	61	641.6	66	739.4
Congenital malformations, deformations and chromosomal abnormalities — Malformations congénitales et anomalies chromosomiques	315	200.5	266	179.4	65	683.6	42	470.5
Symptoms, signs and abnormal clinical and laboratory findings, not elsewhere classified — Symptômes, signes et résultats anormaux d'examens cliniques et de laboratoire, non classés ailleurs	1 041	8.8	945	7.9	116	...	131	...
All other diseases — Toutes autres maladies...............	203	1.7	336	2.8	27	...	18	...
External causes — Causes externes								
Total	6 729	56.8	3 844	32.0	244	...	111	...
Accidents								
Total	3 878	32.8	2 784	23.2	150	...	74	...
Transport accidents — Accidents de transport	1 015	8.6	368	3.1	34	...	12	...
Falls — Chutes	1 154	9.7	1 320	11.0	8	...	2	...
Accidental drowning and submersion — Noyade et submersion accidentelles...............	142	1.2	42	0.3	51	...	16	...
Exposure to smoke, fire and flames — Exposition à la fumée, au feu et aux flammes...............	37	0.3	20	♦0.2	15	...	14	...
Accidental poisoning by and exposure to noxious substances — Intoxication accidentelle par des substances nocives et exposition à ces substances	823	7.0	369	3.1	1	...	-	...
Intentional self-harm — Lésions auto-infligées...............	2 292	19.4	735	6.1	24	...	10	...
Assault — Agresssions...............	179	1.5	86	0.7	10	...	2	...
All other external causes — Toutes autres causes externes	380	3.2	239	2.0	60	...	25	...

New Zealand - Nouvelle-Zélande

Cause of death — Cause de décès	2012 (+C)				2013 (+C)			
	Male — Masculin		Female — Féminin		Male — Masculin		Female — Féminin	
	Number Nombre	Rate Taux	Number Nombre	Rate Taux	Number Nombre	Rate Taux	Number Nombre	Rate Taux
TOTAL	15 148	702.9	15 129	671.5	14 996	690.4	14 640	645.0
Certain infectious and parasitic diseases — Certaines maladies infectieuses et parasitaires								
Total	145	6.7	169	7.5	145	6.7	157	6.9
Intestinal infectious diseases — Maladies infectieuses intestinales	37	1.7	59	2.6	15	♦0.7	47	2.1
Tuberculosis — Tuberculose	4	♦0.2	-	-	4	♦0.2	1	♦0.0
Tetanus — Tétanos	-	-	-	-	-	-	-	-
Diphtheria — Diphtérie	-	-	-	-	-	-	-	-
Whooping cough — Coqueluche	-	-	2	♦0.1	2	♦0.1	-	-
Meningococcal infection — Infection à méningocoques	-	-	4	♦0.2	2	♦0.1	1	♦0.0
Septicaemia — Septicémie	43	2.0	67	3.0	60	2.8	71	3.1
Acute poliomyelitis — Poliomyélite aiguë	-	-	-	-	-	-	-	-
Measles — Rougeole	-	-	-	-	-	-	-	-
Viral hepatitis — Hépatite virale	31	1.4	8	♦0.4	27	♦1.2	13	♦0.6
Human immunodeficiency virus [HIV] disease — Maladies dues au virus de l'immunodéficience humaine (VIH)	8	♦0.4	3	♦0.1	8	♦0.4	1	♦0.0
Malaria — Paludisme	-	-	-	-	1	♦0.0	-	-
Neoplasms — Tumeurs	4 767	221.2	4 216	187.1	4 853	223.4	4 288	188.9
Malignant neoplasms — Tumeurs malignes								
Total	4 671	216.8	4 120	182.9	4 741	218.3	4 195	184.8
Malignant neoplasm of lip, oral cavity and pharynx — Tumeur maligne de la lèvre, de la cavité buccale et du pharynx	74	3.4	41	1.8	87	4.0	49	2.2
Malignant neoplasm of oesophagus — Tumeur maligne de l'oesophage	161	7.5	66	2.9	170	7.8	79	3.5
Malignant neoplasm of stomach — Tumeur maligne de l'estomac	178	8.3	123	5.5	177	8.1	105	4.6
Malignant neoplasm of colon, rectosigmoid junction, rectum, anus and anal canal — Tumeur maligne du côlon, de la jonction recto-sigmoïdienne, du rectum, de l'anus et du canal anal	664	30.8	619	27.5	659	30.3	593	26.1
Malignant neoplasm of liver and intrahepatic bile ducts — Tumeur maligne du foie et des voies bilaires intrahépatiques	154	7.1	82	3.6	177	8.1	75	3.3
Malignant neoplasm of pancreas — Tumeur maligne du pancréas	229	10.6	234	10.4	215	9.9	248	10.9
Malignant neoplasm of trachea, bronchus and lung — Tumeur maligne de la trachée, des bronches et du poumon	891	41.3	737	32.7	864	39.8	792	34.9
Malignant neoplasm of female breast — Tumeur maligne du sein chez la femme	..	..	617	34.0	..	..	633	34.6
Malignant neoplasm of cervix uteri — Tumeur maligne du col de l'utérus	..	..	56	3.1	..	..	54	3.0
Malignant neoplasm of prostate — Tumeur maligne de la prostate	607	90.2	..	..	647	93.7	..	..
Malignant neoplasm of lymphoid, haematopoietic and related tissue — Tumeurs malignes primitives ou présumées primitives des tissus lymphoïde, hématopoïétique et apparentés	463	21.5	348	15.4	499	23.0	340	15.0
Disorders of the blood and blood-forming organs and certain disorders involving the immune mechanism — Maladies du sang et des organes hématopoïétiques et certains troubles du système immunitaire								
Total	31	1.4	30	♦1.3	26	♦1.2	36	1.6
Anaemias — Anémies	15	♦0.7	17	♦0.8	11	♦0.5	14	♦0.6
Endocrine, nutritional and metabolic diseases — Maladies endocriniennes, nutritionnelles et métaboliques								
Total	551	25.6	512	22.7	563	25.9	452	19.9
Diabetes mellitus — Diabète sucré	430	20.0	377	16.7	437	20.1	356	15.7
Malnutrition — Malnutrition	5	♦0.2	5	♦0.2	4	♦0.2	2	♦0.1
Mental and behavioural disorders — Troubles mentaux et du comportement	447	20.7	859	38.1	505	23.2	941	41.5
Diseases of the nervous system — Maladies du système nerveux	617	28.6	699	31.0	568	26.1	650	28.6
Diseases of the circulatory system — Maladies de l'appareil circulatoire								
Total	5 023	233.1	5 336	236.8	4 875	224.4	4 891	215.5
Acute rheumatic fever and chronic rheumatic heart diseases — Rhumatisme articularie aigu et cardiopathies rhumatismales chroniques	46	2.1	69	3.1	50	2.3	78	3.4
Hypertensive diseases — Maladies hypertensives	144	6.7	200	8.9	165	7.6	242	10.7
Ischaemic heart disease — Cardiopathie ischémique	2 953	137.0	2 387	105.9	2 813	129.5	2 217	97.7
Cerebrovascular disease — Maladie cérébrovasculaire	968	44.9	1 643	72.9	938	43.2	1 378	60.7

20. Death and death rates by cause and sex: 2012 - 2016
Décès et taux de mortalité par cause et sexe : 2012 - 2016 (continued - suite)

New Zealand - Nouvelle-Zélande

Cause of death — Cause de décès	2012 (+C)				2013 (+C)			
	Male — Masculin		Female — Féminin		Male — Masculin		Female — Féminin	
	Number Nombre	Rate Taux	Number Nombre	Rate Taux	Number Nombre	Rate Taux	Number Nombre	Rate Taux
Diseases of arteries, arterioles and capillaries — Maladies des artères, artérioles et capillaires	230	10.7	220	9.8	216	9.9	208	9.2
Diseases of the respiratory system — Maladies de l'appareil respiratoire								
Total	**1 369**	**63.5**	**1 452**	**64.4**	**1 332**	**61.3**	**1 384**	**61.0**
Influenza — Grippe...	**16**	*♦0.7*	**23**	*♦1.0*	**3**	*♦0.1*	**12**	*♦0.5*
Pneumonia — Pneumopathies..............................	**284**	**13.2**	**394**	**17.5**	**251**	**11.6**	**379**	**16.7**
Chronic lower respiratory diseases — Maladies chroniques des voies respiratoires inférieures	**851**	**39.5**	**865**	**38.4**	**859**	**39.5**	**822**	**36.2**
Diseases of the digestive system — Maladies de l'appareil digestif								
Total	**430**	**20.0**	**481**	**21.3**	**430**	**19.8**	**503**	**22.2**
Gastric and duodenal ulcer — Ulcère de l'estomac et du duodénum................	**38**	**1.8**	**29**	*♦1.3*	**27**	*♦1.2*	**22**	*♦1.0*
Diseases of the liver — Maladies du foie...............	**104**	**4.8**	**68**	**3.0**	**92**	**4.2**	**62**	**2.7**
Diseases of the musculoskeletal system and connective tissue — Maladies du système ostéo-articularie, des muscles et du tissu conjonctif	**80**	**3.7**	**160**	**7.1**	**77**	**3.5**	**143**	**6.3**
Diseases of the genitourinary system — Maladies de l'appareil génito-urinaire								
Total	**215**	**10.0**	**217**	**9.6**	**207**	**9.5**	**234**	**10.3**
Disorders of kidney and ureter — Affections du rein et de l'uretère	**140**	**6.5**	**128**	**5.7**	**143**	**6.6**	**128**	**5.6**
Hyperplasia of prostate — Hyperplasie de la prostate.............	**25**	*♦3.7*	..	..	**16**	*♦2.3*	..	..
Pregnancy, childbirth and the puerperium — Grossesse, accouchement et puerpéralité								
Total	..	..	**7**	*♦11.4*	..	..	**10**	*♦17.0*
Pregnancy with abortive outcome — Grossesse se terminant par un avortement	..	..	-	-	..	..	**1**	*♦1.7*
Other direct obstetric causes — Autres décès maternels directs	..	..	**2**	*♦3.3*	..	..	**4**	*♦6.8*
Indirect obstetric causes — Décès maternels indirects	..	..	**5**	*♦8.2*	..	..	**5**	*♦8.5*
Certain conditions originating in the perinatal period — Certaines affections dont l'origine se situe dans la période périnatale	**78**	**249.7**	**70**	**233.8**	**88**	**292.0**	**64**	**223.9**
Congenital malformations, deformations and chromosomal abnormalities — Malformations congénitales et anomalies chromosomiques	**96**	**307.3**	**64**	**213.8**	**83**	**275.4**	**72**	**251.9**
Symptoms, signs and abnormal clinical and laboratory findings, not elsewhere classified — Symptômes, signes et résultats anormaux d'examens cliniques et de laboratoire, non classés ailleurs	**47**	**2.2**	**89**	**4.0**	**75**	**3.5**	**91**	**4.0**
All other diseases — Toutes autres maladies............	**37**	**1.7**	**68**	**3.0**	**38**	**1.7**	**81**	**3.6**
External causes — Causes externes								
Total	**1 215**	**56.4**	**700**	**31.1**	**1 131**	**52.1**	**643**	**28.3**
Accidents								
Total	**723**	**33.5**	**492**	**21.8**	**668**	**30.8**	**439**	**19.3**
Transport accidents — Accidents de transport.............	**305**	**14.2**	**100**	**4.4**	**250**	**11.5**	**86**	**3.8**
Falls — Chutes	**226**	**10.5**	**290**	**12.9**	**217**	**10.0**	**259**	**11.4**
Accidental drowning and submersion — Noyade et submersion accidentelles..........	**38**	**1.8**	**9**	*♦0.4*	**47**	**2.2**	**12**	*♦0.5*
Exposure to smoke, fire and flames — Exposition à la fumée, au feu et aux flammes..........	**10**	*♦0.5*	**5**	*♦0.2*	**14**	*♦0.6*	**8**	*♦0.4*
Accidental poisoning by and exposure to noxious substances — Intoxication accidentelle par des substances nocives et exposition à ces substances	**62**	**2.9**	**41**	**1.8**	**60**	**2.8**	**28**	*♦1.2*
Intentional self-harm — Lésions auto-infligées.............	**404**	**18.7**	**145**	**6.4**	**366**	**16.8**	**147**	**6.5**
Assault — Agresssions..	**31**	**1.4**	**25**	*♦1.1*	**40**	**1.8**	**14**	*♦0.6*
All other external causes — Toutes autres causes externes............	**57**	**2.6**	**38**	**1.7**	**57**	**2.6**	**43**	**1.9**

FOOTNOTES — NOTES

Data in bold refer to deaths based on ICD-10 Classification, otherwise data refer to deaths based on ICD-9 Classification. - Les données en typographie gras se rapportent aux décès basées sur la classification CIM-10, autrement les données se rapportent aux décès basées sur la classification CIM-9.

Italics: data from civil registers that are incomplete or of unknown completeness. — Italiques : données incomplètes ou dont le degré d'exactitude n'est pas connu provenant des registres de l'état civil.

Table 21 - *Demographic Yearbook 2017*

Table 21 presents the life tables' probabilities of dying in the five year interval following specified ages ($_5q_x$), for each sex, for the latest available year between 2003 and 2017. The probabilities are multiplied by a thousand, that is, the values presented in the table are 1000*$_5q_x$.

Male and female probabilities of dying are shown separately for selected ages beginning at birth and proceeding at every fifth age thereafter up to age 100.

The values presented in the table are derived by the United Nations Statistics Division from the official complete life tables reported by the countries or areas.

Data are shown with one decimal regardless of the number of digits provided in the original computation.

The life table is a statistical device for summarizing the mortality experience of a population, from which the probability of dying, survivorship and expectation of life can be calculated. It is based on the assumption that the theoretical cohort is subject, throughout its existence, to the age-specific mortality rates observed at a particular time. Thus, levels of mortality prevailing at the time a life table is constructed are assumed to remain unchanged into the future until all members of the cohort have died.

Reliability of data: The values shown in this table are derived from official complete life tables. It is assumed that, if necessary, the basic data (population and deaths classified by age and sex) have been adjusted for deficiencies before their use in constructing the complete life tables.

Limitations: The life tables' probabilities of dying are subject to the same qualifications as have been set forth for population statistics in general and death statistics in particular, as discussed in sections 3 and 4, respectively, of the Technical Notes. They must be interpreted strictly using the underlying assumption that surviving cohorts are subjected to the same age-specific mortality rates of the period to which the life table refers.

Earlier data: The life tables' probabilities of dying at specified ages, for each sex, have been shown in previous issues of the *Demographic Yearbook*. For information on specific years covered, the reader should consult the Historical Index.

Tableau 21 – *Annuaire démographique 2017*

Le tableau 21 donne les probabilités de décès dans l'intervalle de cinq ans que suit l'âge spécifié ($_5q_x$), pour chaque sexe, pour la dernière année disponible entre 2003 et 2017. Les probabilités sont multipliées par mille, c'est-à-dire que les valeurs indiquées dans le tableau sont égales à 1000*$_5q_x$.

Les probabilités de décès sont indiquées séparément pour les hommes et les femmes pour différents âges, depuis la naissance puis tous les cinq ans jusqu'à 100 ans.

Les chiffres indiqués dans ce tableau ont été calculés par la Division de statistique de l'Organisation des Nations Unies à partir des tables de mortalité complètes communiquées par les pays ou zones.

Les données sont arrondies à la première décimale, indépendamment du nombre de décimales qui figurent dans le calcul initial.

La table de mortalité est un moyen statistique que s'utilise pour donner un aperçu complet de la mortalité d'une population incluant les probabilités de décès et l'espérance de vie à chaque âge. Les tables de mortalité reposent sur l'hypothèse que chaque cohorte théoriquement distinguée connaît, pendant toute son existence, les taux de mortalité par âge observé à un moment donné. Les taux de mortalité correspondant à l'époque à laquelle sont calculées les tables de mortalité sont ainsi censés demeurer inchangées dans l'avenir jusqu'au décès de tous les membres de la cohorte.

Fiabilité des donnés : Les chiffres indiqués dans ce tableau ont été calculés à partir des tables officielles de mortalité complètes. En ce qui concerne les chiffres extraits de tables officielles de mortalité, on part du principe que les données de base (effectif de la population et nombre de décès selon l'âge et le sexe) ont été ajustées, en tant que de besoin, avant de servir à l'établissement de la table de mortalité.

Insuffisance des données : Les probabilités de décès appellent les mêmes réserves que celles qui ont été formulées à propos des statistiques de la population en général et des statistiques de mortalité en particulier (voir les sections 3 et 4 des Notes techniques). Lorsque l'on interprète les données, il ne faut jamais perdre de vue que, par hypothèse, les cohortes de survivants sont soumises, pour chaque âge, aux conditions de mortalité de la période visée par la table de mortalité.

Données publiées antérieurement : Les probabilités de décès pour chaque sexe figuraient déjà dans des éditions antérieures de *l'Annuaire démographique*. Pour plus de précisions concernant les années pour lesquelles ces données ont été publiées, se reporter à l'index historique.

21. Probability of dying in the five year interval following specified age (5qx), by sex, latest available year: 2003 - 2017
Probabilité de décès dans l'intervalle de cinq ans qui suit un âge donné (5qx), par sexe, dernière année disponible : 2003 - 2017

Continent, country or area and date / Continent, pays ou zone et date	0	5	10	15	20	25	30	35	40	45	50	55	60	65	70	75	80	85	90	95	100
AFRICA - AFRIQUE																					
Republic of South Sudan - République de Soudan du Sud																					
2010																					
Male - Hommes	130.6	14.1	10.8	18.5	25.6	27.0	28.8	33.1	40.1	51.8	70.0	98.7	143.7	213.2	316.6	457.7	624.2	785.1	907.0	...	...
Female - Femmes	111.9	13.7	10.7	18.4	25.9	27.8	30.2	35.2	43.3	56.8	78.0	111.6	164.6	245.8	362.8	513.5	678.3	826.7	931.7	...	...
AMERICA, NORTH - AMÉRIQUE DU NORD																					
Canada																					
2013 - 2015																					
Male - Hommes	5.7	0.4	0.6	2.0	3.5	3.9	4.4	5.0	7.4	11.6	17.8	27.5	43.1	68.3	109.1	174.9	278.8	434.8	636.9	818.0	921.5
Female - Femmes	5.0	0.4	0.6	1.1	1.5	1.8	2.3	2.9	4.7	7.6	11.6	17.7	27.6	44.2	72.2	120.1	202.0	337.7	537.7	752.8	893.0
Costa Rica																					
2017																					
Male - Hommes	8.7	0.7	1.2	3.5	5.9	6.8	7.6	8.9	11.5	16.0	23.1	33.8	51.8	81.0	124.5	195.3	291.1	418.7	582.4	756.4	*1000
Female - Femmes	7.1	0.5	0.8	1.4	1.5	1.9	2.5	3.4	5.0	8.0	12.1	19.8	31.4	51.3	82.1	136.6	230.0	363.4	531.2	718.7	*1000
Cuba																					
2011 - 2013																					
Male - Hommes	6.0	1.0	1.3	2.4	3.5	4.5	5.7	7.3	10.5	17.5	29.3	44.9	67.2	100.5	148.8	223.2	334.7	477.3	602.9	645.4	*1000
Female - Femmes	5.6	0.9	0.9	1.4	1.9	2.4	3.0	4.1	6.5	11.0	18.7	29.3	44.6	67.0	104.8	168.7	270.2	421.1	577.7	655.4	*1000
Curaçao																					
2016																					
Male - Hommes	9.6	0.4	0.5	2.1	5.8	7.2	7.2	8.9	11.0	15.4	28.1	49.3	69.2	103.7	158.6	226.0	359.1	525.1	701.4	841.0	...
Female - Femmes	14.6	0.3	0.2	0.7	1.8	2.5	2.9	3.9	6.2	8.9	12.1	19.1	33.3	53.2	83.1	148.5	257.1	388.1	571.7	776.1	...
Dominican Republic - République dominicaine																					
2010 - 2015																					
Male - Hommes	33.8	1.5	2.2	6.6	12.0	13.8	15.2	17.5	21.3	28.4	42.9	61.1	86.0	127.0	178.3	282.0	*1000	...	...	...	...
Female - Femmes	25.6	1.4	1.5	2.8	4.8	6.6	8.4	10.7	14.3	19.4	30.9	45.6	64.3	98.8	145.1	253.9	*1000	...	...	...	...
Greenland - Groenland																					
2009 - 2013																					
Male - Hommes	15.4	0.5	2.8	15.7	22.9	16.2	14.3	13.6	18.4	25.9	35.9	72.3	87.1	167.8	303.9	470.3	648.6	758.8	...	...	...
Female - Femmes	7.0	0.5	2.7	10.3	8.0	2.5	6.9	10.8	9.1	20.1	26.0	50.6	83.8	147.4	209.0	326.2	565.3	731.9	970.6	...	...
Jamaica - Jamaïque																					
2006																					
Male - Hommes	31.7	2.8	2.5	4.5	6.5	6.5	7.0	9.4	14.5	23.2	37.5	60.5	96.9	153.2	236.8	353.8	502.7	667.6	817.2	921.8	*1000
Female - Femmes	18.0	1.3	1.1	1.7	2.6	3.4	4.3	5.9	8.7	13.9	22.8	38.0	63.2	104.5	169.8	268.2	405.3	574.1	747.0	883.6	*1000
Martinique																					
2007																					
Male - Hommes	11.6	1.0	1.1	4.2	8.8	7.5	8.8	8.5	10.4	13.5	26.7	28.9	42.2	87.6	122.7	202.9	325.3	532.7	663.7	834.4	*1000
Female - Femmes	7.8	0.4	0.7	0.6	2.1	2.9	4.6	4.1	4.8	5.3	11.3	14.8	28.6	45.6	76.8	135.3	216.7	362.2	508.4	810.4	*1000
Mexico - Mexique																					
2005																					
Male - Hommes	21.6	1.7	2.2	4.3	7.4	9.9	12.0	15.1	20.3	28.7	41.3	59.9	86.6	124.3	176.5	246.8	337.7	448.7	574.2	702.2	*1000
Female - Femmes	17.4	1.3	1.2	1.8	2.4	3.1	4.3	6.4	9.9	15.4	23.9	37.2	57.5	88.4	134.4	201.1	293.6	414.1	557.1	705.8	*1000
Panama[1]																					
2016																					
Male - Hommes	21.4	1.9	2.4	7.0	12.5	14.1	13.0	12.5	14.2	18.9	27.1	39.9	59.2	87.7	128.9	187.3	267.1	371.2	497.7	636.7	*1000
Female - Femmes	16.1	1.3	1.4	2.3	3.3	4.3	5.2	6.4	8.3	11.2	16.0	23.9	36.7	57.2	89.6	139.8	214.8	321.0	459.8	619.7	*1000
Puerto Rico - Porto Rico																					
2015 - 2017																					
Male - Hommes	8.1	0.5	0.5	3.5	9.8	11.1	12.7	13.6	15.8	21.5	33.2	47.3	62.6	87.0	120.1	177.9	266.8	*1000	...	...	...
Female - Femmes	7.1	0.6	0.4	1.0	1.6	2.5	3.4	4.7	6.7	9.6	14.6	21.6	30.6	44.7	72.0	117.2	200.8	*1000	...	...	...
United States of America - États-Unis d'Amérique																					
2014																					
Male - Hommes	7.4	0.6	0.8	3.1	6.1	7.0	7.9	9.3	12.2	18.8	29.8	45.1	63.7	86.6	130.0	198.4	311.2	481.1	670.9	828.2	*1000
Female - Femmes	6.2	0.5	0.6	1.3	2.2	2.9	3.8	5.4	7.9	12.1	18.9	27.3	38.4	56.6	89.8	145.1	239.4	390.6	588.0	774.4	*1000

21. Probability of dying in the five year interval following specified age (5qx), by sex, latest available year: 2003 - 2017
Probabilité de décès dans l'intervalle de cinq ans qui suit un âge donné (5qx), par sexe, dernière année disponible : 2003 - 2017 (continued - suite)

Continent, country or area and date / Continent, pays ou zone et date	0	5	10	15	20	25	30	35	40	45	50	55	60	65	70	75	80	85	90	95	100
AMERICA, SOUTH - AMÉRIQUE DU SUD																					
Argentina - Argentine 2008 - 2010																					
Male - Hommes	15.8	1.3	1.8	5.3	7.5	7.9	8.1	10.0	14.5	22.1	37.3	59.5	89.5	133.8	194.0	289.6	431.2	568.1	692.6	804.3	*1000
Female - Femmes	13.0	1.0	1.2	2.2	2.6	3.1	4.0	5.7	8.4	13.2	20.4	31.0	45.5	68.2	105.9	175.1	309.8	460.7	614.6	762.3	*1000
Bolivia (Plurinational State of) - Bolivie (État plurinational de)[2] 2016 - 2017																					
Male - Hommes	44.2	5.3	4.1	8.9	13.6	14.2	16.1	18.9	24.3	30.8	41.6	57.2	83.1	117.2	167.4	233.2	329.5	416.5	609.4	*1000	...
Female - Femmes	34.5	3.5	2.4	4.7	5.3	5.9	7.4	9.9	14.4	20.0	27.8	39.3	57.6	84.3	119.8	165.8	236.7	317.6	487.2	*1000	...
Brazil - Brésil 2015																					
Male - Hommes	17.4	1.5	1.9	8.2	12.5	12.6	13.5	15.7	20.2	28.1	40.3	56.8	79.0	114.1	168.7	246.7	*1000	...	...	...	...
Female - Femmes	14.7	1.1	1.2	2.2	2.8	3.5	4.7	6.4	9.6	14.8	21.7	31.6	46.7	71.9	112.3	173.9	*1000	...	...	...	...
Chile - Chili 2014																					
Male - Hommes	8.5	0.8	0.9	2.4	4.3	5.5	6.4	8.1	10.9	15.9	23.5	35.8	56.7	89.9	141.1	212.3	366.8	514.5	...	...	...
Female - Femmes	8.2	0.6	0.7	1.1	1.5	1.8	2.4	3.5	5.2	8.0	12.7	20.3	32.7	53.0	85.7	136.9	249.3	383.1	...	...	...
Ecuador - Équateur[3] 2010 - 2017																					
Male - Hommes	21.7	0.9	1.1	3.1	4.6	6.6	9.7	10.9	13.1	19.4	28.9	42.2	67.5	103.3	163.0	251.4	380.5	549.7	722.2	853.7	*1000
Female - Femmes	18.6	0.9	0.9	1.8	2.2	2.7	2.9	3.9	6.1	9.0	13.7	20.6	32.6	54.4	96.6	177.4	312.9	496.7	688.4	841.1	*1000
French Guiana - Guyane française 2007																					
Male - Hommes	16.3	1.5	2.1	4.9	7.7	8.1	10.0	14.0	17.2	29.4	16.0	32.3	52.4	79.5	135.5	261.3	306.7	474.0	733.7	...	...
Female - Femmes	15.1	1.9	1.3	1.4	1.2	3.0	4.6	4.2	11.9	11.0	10.4	11.6	26.7	85.4	77.4	203.8	253.1	321.1	434.3	...	...
Uruguay 2004																					
Male - Hommes	20.0	1.3	1.3	3.5	5.8	6.8	7.2	9.0	12.8	21.2	36.4	62.2	95.4	145.2	204.6	305.7	430.5	610.5	776.7	862.5	*1000
Female - Femmes	15.5	1.0	1.1	1.6	1.9	2.7	3.8	5.2	7.9	12.5	19.4	30.5	41.2	63.4	97.2	177.7	292.9	472.0	654.3	820.5	*1000
ASIA - ASIE																					
Armenia - Arménie 2015 - 2016																					
Male - Hommes	11.2	1.5	1.1	4.6	5.4	4.6	5.9	8.4	16.7	26.8	44.9	68.0	105.3	154.2	204.1	314.6	427.7	640.7	819.5	921.4	...
Female - Femmes	8.9	1.0	0.8	0.8	1.4	1.3	2.1	3.8	6.4	10.8	15.8	26.2	44.4	75.7	121.2	219.8	372.2	610.3	951.9	940.3	...
Azerbaijan - Azerbaïdjan 2016																					
Male - Hommes	14.4	1.7	1.6	3.4	4.4	4.3	5.0	7.7	13.5	20.7	36.4	56.6	95.8	142.5	204.4	297.0	436.0	559.6	548.9	334.6	...
Female - Femmes	10.8	1.4	1.2	1.8	2.2	2.0	2.6	3.2	5.7	9.6	16.5	28.4	51.2	83.0	142.3	251.6	417.5	575.1	669.0	646.9	...
China, Hong Kong SAR - Chine, Hong Kong RAS 2017																					
Male - Hommes	2.3	0.5	0.6	1.3	1.7	2.1	2.7	4.4	6.7	10.2	15.7	24.6	38.6	59.8	95.7	154.7	247.5	373.5	535.2	715.8	*1000
Female - Femmes	2.0	0.2	0.4	0.6	1.0	1.1	1.2	1.9	3.3	5.9	8.9	12.5	18.9	29.2	46.5	82.0	151.4	258.6	414.0	610.1	*1000
China, Macao SAR - Chine, Macao RAS 2002 - 2005																					
Male - Hommes	7.2	0.6	0.4	1.7	3.9	5.4	6.2	7.6	9.0	13.6	17.8	25.8	43.1	72.1	128.9	239.9	369.5	574.4	841.2	991.4	*1000
Female - Femmes	5.2	0.4	0.2	0.9	1.5	1.9	2.3	3.8	4.7	5.9	7.4	10.9	19.3	33.3	70.4	186.2	317.0	485.2	717.3	923.7	*1000
Israel - Israël[4] 2012 - 2016																					
Male - Hommes	4.3	0.5	0.7	1.6	2.6	2.7	2.9	3.8	6.1	10.4	17.4	27.4	42.3	67.1	110.0	181.4	291.7	441.8	612.3	767.8	*1000
Female - Femmes	3.7	0.4	0.5	0.7	0.9	1.1	1.5	2.2	3.7	6.1	9.7	15.1	23.7	39.5	70.4	129.2	233.0	393.0	591.1	775.7	*1000
Japan - Japon[5] 2015																					
Male - Hommes	2.9	0.5	0.5	1.3	2.5	2.7	3.2	4.1	6.2	10.0	16.2	25.7	41.2	65.8	100.6	160.7	278.5	450.1	652.9	810.7	...
Female - Femmes	2.5	0.4	0.4	0.7	1.0	1.3	1.7	2.4	3.7	5.8	8.9	12.3	18.0	27.3	43.9	77.2	150.4	286.0	501.4	728.1	...

21. Probability of dying in the five year interval following specified age (5qx), by sex, latest available year: 2003 - 2017
Probabilité de décès dans l'intervalle de cinq ans qui suit un âge donné (5qx), par sexe, dernière année disponible :
2003 - 2017 (continued - suite)

Continent, country or area and date / Continent, pays ou zone et date	Age (in years) - Age (en années)																				
	0	5	10	15	20	25	30	35	40	45	50	55	60	65	70	75	80	85	90	95	100
ASIA - ASIE																					
Kazakhstan																					
2016																					
Male - Hommes	12.0	1.7	2.5	3.7	5.7	9.0	14.0	21.4	32.2	47.4	68.4	96.6	134.0	182.4	243.7	319.3	409.7	513.1	624.7	736.1	...
Female - Femmes	9.6	1.2	1.1	1.6	2.6	4.0	5.5	7.4	10.1	14.5	21.9	34.7	56.3	92.3	150.4	239.9	368.4	533.0	710.3	859.4	...
Kyrgyzstan - Kirghizstan																					
2016																					
Male - Hommes	20.9	1.9	2.3	3.2	5.1	7.3	10.9	18.5	26.6	35.7	49.8	75.6	119.3	169.1	365.1	542.3	677.0	734.3	813.7	880.6	*1000
Female - Femmes	18.4	0.9	1.4	2.5	2.8	3.1	4.5	7.3	11.1	14.0	20.8	36.0	60.4	92.0	162.1	277.6	469.6	596.6	685.9	794.8	*1000
Qatar																					
2006																					
Male - Hommes	10.2	0.8	1.8	9.4	8.9	6.5	5.6	6.6	7.1	9.0	16.1	22.1	42.2	88.0	167.5	248.6	376.7	*1000	...	...	...
Female - Femmes	9.0	1.3	0.9	2.2	1.4	2.4	1.2	1.8	3.8	6.7	9.8	22.1	76.0	120.2	253.6	354.1	348.3	*1000	...	...	...
Republic of Korea - République de Corée																					
2016																					
Male - Hommes	3.8	0.5	0.5	1.4	2.0	2.8	3.6	4.9	8.1	13.0	20.5	30.0	44.0	66.5	111.3	199.3	331.3	496.3	672.3	822.1	*1000
Female - Femmes	3.1	0.4	0.3	0.8	1.2	1.5	2.2	3.0	4.0	5.5	7.8	11.0	16.1	26.1	49.5	102.9	206.9	374.7	580.0	769.4	*1000
Singapore - Singapour[6]																					
2017																					
Male - Hommes	2.8	0.4	0.7	1.3	1.5	1.8	2.3	3.3	5.6	9.0	15.8	25.6	41.1	66.1	110.3	179.0	288.2	443.7	627.6	802.5	*1000
Female - Femmes	2.9	0.3	0.4	0.7	0.8	1.0	1.2	1.8	3.3	5.6	9.5	14.9	22.4	35.5	60.0	113.5	204.9	340.2	517.6	708.8	*1000
Turkey - Turquie																					
2014 - 2016																					
Male - Hommes	13.8	1.3	1.6	3.3	4.1	4.0	4.2	5.2	8.1	14.0	24.7	42.2	68.2	106.6	169.1	259.6	390.3	558.6	710.8	806.6	*1000
Female - Femmes	12.2	1.0	1.0	1.3	1.4	1.5	1.9	2.8	4.5	7.2	11.6	19.1	32.2	55.9	103.3	182.8	305.2	465.0	621.1	718.1	*1000
EUROPE																					
Austria - Autriche																					
2016																					
Male - Hommes	4.1	0.4	0.3	1.9	2.7	2.6	3.5	4.2	6.4	11.2	17.8	32.6	53.0	83.9	121.6	178.6	299.1	489.3	692.7	884.4	...
Female - Femmes	3.2	0.4	0.5	1.0	0.8	1.1	1.6	2.3	3.9	6.0	10.4	17.3	27.2	44.4	69.0	109.9	210.8	391.3	633.5	824.2	...
Belarus - Bélarus																					
2016																					
Male - Hommes	4.6	1.2	0.6	2.6	4.9	7.0	11.3	18.2	26.6	40.9	60.6	89.4	138.2	188.1	257.7	359.5	483.7	623.0	761.8	878.1	...
Female - Femmes	3.6	0.5	0.7	1.3	1.4	2.1	4.1	6.5	8.9	13.1	18.9	29.1	42.6	68.6	113.9	206.6	346.2	532.1	737.6	903.6	...
Belgium - Belgique[7]																					
2015																					
Male - Hommes	4.2	0.5	0.4	1.4	3.2	3.0	4.0	5.4	7.7	12.4	20.1	35.5	55.2	81.7	122.3	193.8	315.6	506.2	717.7	872.7	*1000
Female - Femmes	3.6	0.4	0.5	0.8	1.1	1.3	2.0	2.8	4.9	8.3	12.6	21.3	33.1	44.8	71.3	119.0	222.4	406.4	643.5	832.8	*1000
Bulgaria - Bulgarie																					
2014 - 2016																					
Male - Hommes	8.4	1.2	1.2	3.2	4.4	5.0	6.9	10.5	16.1	29.2	50.3	77.2	115.5	157.8	214.6	308.0	449.4	622.0	797.5	887.4	...
Female - Femmes	7.1	0.8	0.8	1.4	2.0	2.2	3.1	4.7	8.6	13.7	22.1	33.1	47.6	70.1	117.0	208.4	370.3	570.0	759.8	877.9	...
Czechia - Tchéquie																					
2016																					
Male - Hommes	3.8	0.4	0.5	1.8	3.6	3.7	4.1	5.8	8.8	15.8	25.8	44.2	74.7	114.3	169.0	248.1	363.2	509.0	674.7	830.6	...
Female - Femmes	3.1	0.3	0.5	1.0	1.1	1.5	2.0	3.1	4.6	8.0	12.5	20.9	32.5	54.3	89.8	151.9	266.7	435.5	655.9	864.8	...
Denmark - Danemark[8]																					
2015 - 2016																					
Male - Hommes	4.6	0.3	0.4	0.8	2.3	2.8	2.7	4.2	7.1	12.8	20.4	34.1	54.6	77.9	121.4	191.6	324.6	507.9	710.7	857.0	...
Female - Femmes	3.4	0.4	0.2	0.7	0.9	0.9	1.5	2.7	3.9	6.8	12.4	21.4	35.4	50.4	82.1	135.7	247.6	397.5	611.4	800.5	...
Estonia - Estonie																					
2016																					
Male - Hommes	3.4	0.8	0.8	2.3	5.4	6.0	9.4	12.1	15.9	24.9	40.3	64.6	97.7	139.3	187.2	266.8	379.6	536.1	713.3	887.9	*1000
Female - Femmes	1.9	0.7	0.5	2.8	3.0	2.4	4.1	5.7	5.0	8.5	13.9	23.7	33.8	51.0	82.3	130.6	251.8	437.9	629.0	843.2	*1000
Faeroe Islands - Îles Féroé																					
2016 - 2017																					
Male - Hommes	2.8	0.0	0.0	0.0	6.2	0.0	0.0	0.0	0.0	6.4	17.2	22.0	31.2	77.0	116.7	149.3	380.5	489.4	725.4	...	...
Female - Femmes	6.0	0.0	0.0	2.9	0.0	3.5	0.0	3.3	0.0	0.0	15.5	19.2	31.8	39.5	46.9	158.0	199.9	371.4	616.5	892.6	...

21. Probability of dying in the five year interval following specified age (5qx), by sex, latest available year: 2003 - 2017
Probabilité de décès dans l'intervalle de cinq ans qui suit un âge donné (5qx), par sexe, dernière année disponible : 2003 - 2017 (continued - suite)

Continent, country or area and date / Continent, pays ou zone et date	0	5	10	15	20	25	30	35	40	45	50	55	60	65	70	75	80	85	90	95	100

EUROPE

Finland - Finlande[9]
2016
Male - Hommes	2.5	0.5	0.5	1.7	3.4	4.3	4.7	6.5	8.6	13.5	22.9	33.0	54.6	81.3	122.3	190.7	316.3	514.3	719.4	863.5	...
Female - Femmes	2.0	0.5	0.5	1.0	1.6	1.6	1.8	2.3	3.3	6.3	10.0	15.8	26.1	38.9	66.6	113.8	211.5	402.0	628.7	842.3	...

France[7]
2012 - 2015
Male - Hommes	4.5	0.5	0.5	1.6	2.9	3.5	4.4	5.8	8.8	14.5	22.5	37.1	53.9	72.1	101.4	154.3	259.8	433.8	646.9	825.2	...
Female - Femmes	3.8	0.3	0.4	0.8	1.1	1.2	1.6	2.7	4.4	7.5	11.8	17.3	23.9	32.8	51.0	84.9	160.5	312.7	539.3	764.8	...

Germany - Allemagne
2013 - 2015
Male - Hommes	4.2	0.4	0.4	1.5	2.3	2.6	3.5	4.8	7.4	12.9	22.9	38.2	59.2	85.8	126.1	198.4	334.8	518.8	724.9	868.7	...
Female - Femmes	3.6	0.3	0.4	0.8	1.0	1.1	1.7	2.6	4.2	7.3	12.7	20.1	30.7	46.9	70.1	123.7	238.9	426.5	657.8	828.6	...

Greece - Grèce
2016
Male - Hommes	5.8	0.6	0.6	1.7	2.8	3.3	4.0	5.4	7.9	13.8	24.1	38.4	57.2	81.6	120.3	190.8	315.9	463.9	611.3	767.4	...
Female - Femmes	3.9	0.4	0.5	0.8	0.9	1.1	1.8	2.7	4.3	6.8	10.4	16.0	23.5	38.3	67.2	133.7	269.8	437.9	591.9	753.6	...

Hungary - Hongrie
2016
Male - Hommes	5.2	0.4	0.8	1.9	2.9	3.3	4.6	6.5	11.5	24.7	49.0	79.0	116.3	156.7	204.2	293.0	413.5	616.8	858.9	986.5	...
Female - Femmes	4.3	0.4	0.4	0.8	1.0	1.4	2.2	3.6	6.1	11.2	20.9	34.7	52.1	73.4	107.6	186.4	311.5	541.6	834.4	987.0	...

Iceland - Islande
2015 - 2016
Male - Hommes	2.8	0.2	0.7	3.0	1.7	3.7	5.1	5.9	5.8	8.1	11.5	23.2	26.2	57.4	109.5	151.5	295.4	530.6	739.5	854.1	...
Female - Femmes	2.2	0.2	0.2	0.7	1.2	0.9	1.1	1.6	4.0	4.9	10.0	16.9	27.1	44.2	80.2	126.9	234.5	390.3	652.3	814.5	...

Ireland - Irlande
2005 - 2007
Male - Hommes	4.9	0.6	0.8	3.6	5.4	4.7	5.1	5.7	8.6	13.3	21.1	33.3	54.5	88.7	148.8	247.0	395.4	567.3	730.3	919.0	...
Female - Femmes	4.5	0.4	0.7	1.6	1.5	1.6	2.0	3.0	5.2	9.2	13.6	21.3	33.8	53.6	90.1	153.4	284.4	460.3	643.4	800.7	...

Italy - Italie
2016
Male - Hommes	3.8	0.4	0.5	1.5	2.1	2.3	2.8	3.9	5.8	9.5	15.1	25.4	40.2	64.9	104.4	167.1	289.4	474.2	686.4	834.7	...
Female - Femmes	3.3	0.3	0.4	0.6	0.8	1.0	1.3	2.3	3.5	5.8	9.2	14.3	21.7	35.1	58.6	101.4	199.3	366.2	591.4	770.5	...

Latvia - Lettonie
2006
Male - Hommes	10.5	1.4	1.6	3.0	6.2	11.3	18.6	28.3	40.6	56.3	76.6	104.3	143.2	199.8	282.1	397.7	547.0	712.6	...	...	...
Female - Femmes	12.7	1.3	1.2	1.5	2.2	3.2	4.8	7.3	11.2	17.3	26.7	41.0	63.0	96.1	145.1	215.5	312.2	436.5	...	...	...

Lithuania - Lituanie
2016
Male - Hommes	5.3	0.3	1.4	2.7	5.3	8.3	14.2	21.1	31.1	42.4	58.3	85.3	127.2	170.7	224.9	297.9	398.1	586.3	759.7	888.6	*1000
Female - Femmes	5.4	0.6	0.5	0.9	1.2	2.2	3.7	5.9	8.0	13.7	19.8	27.6	43.1	65.1	98.8	158.6	282.6	489.0	700.4	849.7	*1000

Luxembourg
2014 - 2016
Male - Hommes	2.8	0.5	0.6	1.7	1.6	2.0	2.9	4.2	6.5	9.7	17.6	30.1	47.5	72.2	116.6	181.0	299.1	509.0	694.9	*1000	...
Female - Femmes	2.0	0.1	0.4	0.5	0.8	0.6	1.1	1.5	4.2	5.5	7.5	15.7	25.6	42.7	70.3	109.6	205.6	370.1	579.7	*1000	...

Malta - Malte
2012
Male - Hommes	5.6	0.5	0.4	0.4	2.3	2.2	5.4	4.8	6.1	12.6	14.8	26.8	46.3	77.4	112.0	220.3	378.6	640.6	887.5	975.9	*1000
Female - Femmes	6.0	0.6	0.9	0.8	0.0	2.0	2.7	1.8	5.6	4.5	11.8	13.5	27.6	41.3	67.7	130.5	273.1	474.9	737.6	853.6	*1000

Netherlands - Pays-Bas
2009
Male - Hommes	4.8	0.5	0.6	1.4	2.3	2.4	3.0	4.1	6.6	10.7	18.7	30.3	49.9	79.1	132.1	225.2	363.5	539.8	738.0	...	...
Female - Femmes	4.1	0.4	0.5	0.8	1.0	1.3	1.7	2.9	5.0	8.9	15.0	21.5	32.5	47.8	76.4	136.1	249.6	428.5	644.7	...	...

Norway - Norvège
2012
Male - Hommes	3.3	0.4	0.6	1.5	3.2	3.3	4.2	4.9	6.0	9.5	17.2	26.3	45.2	70.3	111.2	192.3	335.0	513.3	727.7	859.1	...
Female - Femmes	2.7	0.4	0.6	0.8	1.0	1.2	1.4	2.4	3.9	6.7	10.6	17.1	28.2	46.4	75.5	127.0	232.7	402.3	640.0	837.9	...

Poland - Pologne
2016
Male - Hommes	5.2	0.5	0.7	2.4	4.4	5.1	6.7	9.6	15.1	25.0	40.3	63.0	93.5	130.4	178.0	252.4	361.7	495.9	642.1	780.4	...
Female - Femmes	4.1	0.4	0.4	1.0	1.1	1.3	1.9	3.1	5.2	9.1	15.4	25.3	39.8	59.6	88.1	143.8	252.0	407.5	586.6	758.4	...

Portugal
2014 - 2016
Male - Hommes	4.2	0.4	0.6	1.5	2.4	2.9	3.4	5.3	9.9	17.1	26.7	40.0	54.9	79.1	120.7	194.6	336.4	638.0	862.9	970.5	...
Female - Femmes	2.8	0.4	0.4	0.7	1.0	1.0	1.6	2.6	4.6	7.1	10.7	15.0	22.9	35.7	60.7	112.5	234.1	519.8	790.4	948.5	...

21. Probability of dying in the five year interval following specified age (5qx), by sex, latest available year: 2003 - 2017
Probabilité de décès dans l'intervalle de cinq ans qui suit un âge donné (5qx), par sexe, dernière année disponible : 2003 - 2017 (continued - suite)

Continent, country or area and date / Continent, pays ou zone et date	0	5	10	15	20	25	30	35	40	45	50	55	60	65	70	75	80	85	90	95	100
EUROPE																					
Republic of Moldova - République de Moldova 2012																					
Male - Hommes	12.2	1.4	2.0	4.4	5.6	7.1	11.3	19.8	30.9	50.0	71.2	102.2	157.9	176.7	292.1	388.4	503.1	558.6	*1000	...	...
Female - Femmes	12.1	1.1	1.2	1.6	1.8	2.4	3.6	8.1	10.6	16.1	26.8	44.1	78.0	103.1	191.4	289.0	418.9	550.8	*1000	...	...
Romania - Roumanie 2013 - 2015																					
Male - Hommes	11.0	1.1	1.3	2.7	3.9	4.2	5.3	8.2	15.1	27.4	46.7	74.6	106.9	147.3	207.7	299.1	425.8	575.0	718.1	837.7	...
Female - Femmes	8.7	0.7	0.7	1.3	1.3	1.8	2.2	3.7	6.2	10.9	18.9	29.5	45.1	70.2	116.4	206.2	351.7	524.6	694.3	833.7	...
Russian Federation - Fédération de Russie 2012																					
Male - Hommes	11.6	1.7	1.8	5.4	11.6	19.0	30.3	36.8	42.1	56.4	77.9	110.6	155.6	193.8	273.2	361.6	481.9	577.2	694.9	771.0	*1000
Female - Femmes	9.5	1.1	1.2	2.5	3.4	5.6	9.0	11.6	14.3	18.9	26.2	39.5	57.7	84.1	137.1	230.5	372.9	543.1	716.4	825.0	*1000
San Marino - Saint-Marin 2017																					
Male - Hommes	2.5	0.0	0.0	1.9	2.7	1.9	0.5	2.4	3.2	4.1	11.1	20.6	29.4	49.1	76.1	153.8	285.3	430.4	655.9	933.0	...
Female - Femmes	2.7	0.0	0.0	1.3	0.0	0.0	0.5	0.8	3.7	5.0	6.2	11.3	14.0	27.7	45.6	74.0	170.1	341.0	564.7	821.0	...
Serbia - Serbie[10] 2010 - 2012																					
Male - Hommes	8.1	0.5	0.9	2.4	3.7	4.7	6.4	8.2	13.3	25.5	44.0	69.0	101.6	145.8	216.4	334.2	492.1	676.0	856.4	973.0	...
Female - Femmes	6.5	0.6	0.9	1.1	1.5	2.0	2.6	4.3	7.4	12.8	21.1	33.3	50.4	82.2	147.2	265.6	432.9	632.3	840.3	975.2	...
Slovakia - Slovaquie 2016																					
Male - Hommes	7.0	0.6	0.7	2.2	3.6	3.7	4.8	7.8	12.8	21.9	36.3	60.0	95.4	135.2	188.7	279.5	403.0	570.0	750.7	900.7	...
Female - Femmes	5.3	0.6	0.6	1.0	1.4	1.5	2.6	3.6	5.7	9.6	15.5	23.6	38.7	61.9	98.6	165.7	309.4	508.3	753.3	938.6	...
Slovenia - Slovénie 2015 - 2016																					
Male - Hommes	2.4	0.3	0.9	2.2	3.1	3.3	3.9	5.3	8.4	13.2	25.7	40.2	63.6	89.3	140.9	207.2	357.7	522.6	699.9	762.5	...
Female - Femmes	1.8	0.5	0.3	0.6	1.4	0.6	1.9	2.3	3.7	7.1	11.2	17.5	29.0	46.3	68.8	120.9	236.2	421.4	661.8	806.5	...
Spain - Espagne 2016																					
Male - Hommes	3.6	0.4	0.4	1.1	1.6	1.9	2.7	3.3	5.6	10.4	19.3	30.7	47.7	70.3	105.9	171.6	279.6	453.2	651.1	761.9	*1000
Female - Femmes	2.8	0.3	0.3	0.6	0.7	0.9	1.2	2.0	3.2	5.7	9.6	14.2	20.2	29.6	48.4	91.0	181.2	349.7	568.0	738.9	*1000
Sweden - Suède 2012																					
Male - Hommes	3.5	0.4	0.5	1.4	3.2	3.6	3.2	3.8	5.4	9.2	15.2	25.0	40.8	65.6	109.3	186.3	322.6	519.0	727.6	886.1	...
Female - Femmes	2.7	0.3	0.5	0.9	1.1	1.1	1.6	2.8	3.4	6.4	11.0	16.2	26.3	45.6	71.4	126.8	229.8	416.2	644.1	827.2	...
Switzerland - Suisse 2016																					
Male - Hommes	3.7	0.2	0.4	1.0	2.1	2.4	2.3	2.9	4.9	8.1	13.2	22.5	37.9	59.0	90.5	150.2	265.7	459.2	682.0	839.2	...
Female - Femmes	4.2	0.2	0.4	0.7	0.8	1.0	1.5	2.1	3.1	4.9	8.4	13.9	22.1	34.3	55.5	98.5	187.4	353.3	591.8	806.7	...
TFYR of Macedonia - L'ex-R. y. de Macédoine 2015																					
Male - Hommes	11.7	1.0	0.9	2.1	2.4	3.2	3.6	5.4	10.3	18.1	33.0	54.6	87.6	129.6	199.3	304.9	484.5	688.6	865.0	...	...
Female - Femmes	10.6	0.7	0.8	0.9	1.1	1.3	2.0	3.7	5.5	9.7	17.2	27.8	46.9	81.0	138.5	259.2	448.0	665.0	806.5	...	...
Ukraine[11] 2016																					
Male - Hommes	9.7	1.0	1.3	3.9	6.6	10.5	16.7	26.8	36.3	48.9	68.8	97.9	149.0	200.2	274.6	378.9	492.0	612.7	713.4	801.4	...
Female - Femmes	7.8	0.8	0.9	1.7	2.1	3.4	5.6	9.1	12.7	17.2	23.1	34.7	54.3	88.6	144.5	244.3	392.8	572.3	757.3	903.9	...
United Kingdom of Great Britain and Northern Ireland - Royaume-Uni de Grande-Bretagne et d'Irlande du Nord[12] 2014 - 2016																					
Male - Hommes	4.9	0.4	0.5	1.5	2.6	3.2	4.3	5.9	9.0	12.9	18.8	29.4	47.2	71.0	115.4	186.6	306.8	483.9	680.0	834.4	...
Female - Femmes	4.1	0.3	0.4	0.9	1.1	1.5	2.3	3.5	5.4	8.2	12.7	19.8	31.0	47.1	78.9	132.9	235.2	401.2	608.2	788.3	...

Age (in years) - Age (en années)

21. Probability of dying in the five year interval following specified age (5qx), by sex, latest available year: 2003 - 2017
Probabilité de décès dans l'intervalle de cinq ans qui suit un âge donné (5qx), par sexe, dernière année disponible :
2003 - 2017 (continued - suite)

Continent, country or area and date / Continent, pays ou zone et date	0	5	10	15	20	25	30	35	40	45	50	55	60	65	70	75	80	85	90	95	100
OCEANIA - OCÉANIE																					
Australia - Australie																					
2014 - 2016																					
Male - Hommes	4.3	0.4	0.5	1.9	3.0	3.4	4.4	5.9	8.2	11.7	17.5	26.3	39.2	59.5	96.2	160.2	274.2	450.4	648.9	803.0	...
Female - Femmes	3.9	0.4	0.5	1.0	1.2	1.5	2.1	3.1	4.7	7.1	10.7	15.8	23.2	36.3	61.0	106.9	196.3	357.8	579.4	776.3	...
New Zealand - Nouvelle-Zélande																					
2012 - 2014																					
Male - Hommes	5.9	0.7	0.9	3.2	4.1	4.0	4.2	5.6	7.6	11.6	17.6	26.2	40.3	65.4	108.3	176.2	298.2	485.4	667.7	822.5	*1000
Female - Femmes	4.9	0.5	0.7	1.5	1.6	1.5	2.3	3.2	5.1	8.0	12.5	17.9	28.2	43.2	71.4	126.3	219.4	391.0	615.3	807.3	*1000

FOOTNOTES - NOTES

* Open-ended group (e.g. 80 years or over). - Groupe d'âge ouvert (par exemple, 80 ans ou plus).

[1] Excluding Indian jungle population. - Non compris les Indiens de la jungle.

[2] Data refer to the 12 months from 30 June 2016 to 30 June 2017. - Les données font référence aux douze mois de 30 juin 2016 à 30 juin 2017.

[3] Data based on the 2010 Population Census. Excludes nomadic Indian tribes. - Les données sont fondées sur le recensement de la population de 2010. Non compris les tribus d'Indiens nomades.

[4] Includes data for East Jerusalem and Israeli residents in certain other territories under occupation by Israeli military forces since June 1967. - Y compris les données pour Jérusalem-Est et les résidents israéliens dans certains autres territoires occupés depuis 1967 par les forces armées israéliennes.

[5] Data refer to Japanese nationals in Japan only. - Les données se raportent aux nationaux japonais au Japon seulement.

[6] Provisional data. Data refer to resident population which comprises Singapore citizens and permanent residents. - Données provisoires. Les données se rapportent à la population résidente composé des citoyens de Singapour et des résidents permanents.

[7] Provisional data. - Données provisoires.

[8] Excluding Faeroe Islands and Greenland shown separately, if available. - Non compris les Iles Féroé et le Groenland, qui font l'objet de rubriques distinctes, si disponible.

[9] Excluding Åland Islands. - Non compris les Îles d'Åland.

[10] Excludes data for Kosovo and Metohia. - Sans les données pour le Kosovo et Metohie.

[11] The Government of Ukraine has informed the United Nations that it is not in a position to provide statistical data concerning the Autonomous Republic of Crimea and the city of Sevastopol. - Le gouvernement Ukrainien a informé l'ONU qu'il n'est pas en mesure de fournir des données statistiques concernant la République autonome de Crimée et la ville de Sébastopol.

[12] Excluding Channel Islands (Guernsey and Jersey) and Isle of Man, shown separately, if available. - Non compris les îles Anglo-Normandes (Guernesey et Jersey) et l'île de Man, qui font l'objet de rubriques distinctes, si disponible.

Table 22 - Demographic Yearbook 2017

Table 22 presents life expectancy at specified ages for each sex, for the latest available year between 1998 and 2017.

Description of variables: Life expectancy at age x, e_x, is defined as the average number of years of life remaining to persons who have reached age x if they continue to be subject to the mortality conditions of the period indicated in the life table.

Male and female life expectancy values are shown separately at selected ages beginning at birth and proceeding at every fifth age thereafter up to age 100.

The table shows life expectancy derived from a complete or abridged life table as reported by the country or area.

Data are shown with one decimal regardless of the number of digits provided in the original computation.

The life table is a statistical device for summarizing the mortality experience of a population, from which the probability of dying, survivorship and life expectancy can be calculated. It is based on the assumption that the theoretical cohort is subject, throughout its existence, to the age-specific mortality rates observed at a particular time period. Thus, levels of mortality prevailing at the time a life table is constructed are assumed to remain unchanged into the future until all members of the cohort have died.

Reliability of data: The values shown in this table come from official life tables. It is assumed that, if necessary, the basic data (population and deaths classified by age and sex) have been adjusted for deficiencies before their use in constructing the life tables.

Limitations: Life expectancy values are subject to the same qualifications as have been set forth for population statistics in general and death statistics in particular, as discussed in sections 3 and 4, respectively, of the Technical Notes. They must be interpreted strictly using the underlying assumption that surviving cohorts are subjected to the same age-specific mortality rates of the period to which the life table refers.

Earlier data: Life expectancy values at specified ages for each sex have been shown in previous issues of the *Demographic Yearbook*. For information on specific years covered, the reader should consult the Historical Index.

Tableau 22 – *Annuaire démographique 2017*

Le tableau 22 présente les espérances de vie à des âges déterminés, pour chaque sexe, pour la dernière année disponible entre 1998 et 2017.

Description des variables : L'espérance de vie à l'âge x, e_x, se définit comme le nombre moyen d'années restant à vivre aux hommes et aux femmes qui ont atteint l'âge x, à supposer qu'ils continuent de connaître les mêmes conditions de mortalité observées pendant la période sur laquelle porte la table de mortalité.

Les chiffres sont présentés séparément pour chaque sexe à partir de la naissance et puis tous les cinq ans jusqu'à 100 ans.

Dans le tableau figurent les espérances de vie calculées selon les tables de mortalité complètes ou abrégées communiquées par les pays et les zones.

Les données sont arrondies à la première décimale, indépendamment du nombre de décimales qui figurent dans le calcul initial.

La table de mortalité est un moyen statistique que s'utilise pour donner un aperçu complet de la mortalité d'une population incluant les probabilités de décès et l'espérance de vie à chaque âge. Les tables de mortalité reposent sur l'hypothèse que chaque cohorte théoriquement distinguée connaît, pendant toute son existence, les taux de mortalité par âge observé à un moment donné. Les taux de mortalité correspondant à l'époque à laquelle sont calculées les tables de mortalité sont ainsi censés demeurer inchangées dans l'avenir jusqu'au décès de tous les membres de la cohorte.

Fiabilité des donnés : Les chiffres figurant dans ce tableau proviennent de tables officielles de mortalité. En ce qui concerne les chiffres extraits de tables officielles de mortalité, on part du principe que les données de base (effectif de la population et nombre de décès selon l'âge et le sexe) ont été ajustées, en tant que de besoin, avant de servir à l'établissement de la table de mortalité.

Insuffisance des données : les espérances de vie appellent les mêmes réserves que celles qui ont été formulées à propos des statistiques de la population en général et des statistiques de mortalité en particulier (voir les sections 3 et 4 des Notes techniques). Lorsque l'on interprète les données, il ne faut jamais perdre de vue que, par hypothèse, les cohortes de survivants sont soumises, pour chaque âge, aux conditions de mortalité de la période visée par la table de mortalité.

Données publiées antérieurement : les espérances de vie à des âges déterminés pour chaque sexe figuraient déjà dans des éditions antérieures de *l'Annuaire démographique*. Pour plus de précisions concernant les années pour lesquelles ces données ont été publiées, se reporter à l'index historique.

Continent, country or area and date / Continent, pays ou zone et date	Age (in years) - Age (en années)																				
	0	5	10	15	20	25	30	35	40	45	50	55	60	65	70	75	80	85	90	95	100

AFRICA - AFRIQUE

	0	5	10	15	20	25	30	35	40	45	50	55	60	65	70	75	80	85	90	95	100
Algeria - Algérie[1] 2016																					
Male - Hommes	77.1	74.2	69.3	64.4	59.6	54.9	50.1	45.4	40.7	36.0	31.4	27.0	22.7	18.8	15.1	11.7	8.8	6.5	...	...	...
Female - Femmes	78.2	75.1	70.2	65.3	60.5	55.6	50.7	45.9	41.2	36.5	31.9	27.4	23.0	18.9	14.9	11.2	7.9	5.3	...	...	...
Benin - Bénin[2] 2002																					
Male - Hommes	57.2	63.4	59.1	54.7	50.2	45.9	41.8	37.8	33.8	30.0	26.2	22.7	19.4	16.2	13.2	10.6	8.1	5.5	3.8	...	...
Female - Femmes	61.3	65.4	61.2	56.7	52.3	48.1	43.9	39.9	36.0	32.1	28.3	24.6	21.2	18.0	14.2	10.8	7.7	4.8	2.9	...	...
Botswana[3] 2016																					
Male - Hommes	64.9	62.0	57.4	52.6	48.1	43.9	40.3	37.3	34.4	31.7	28.4	24.9	21.3	17.7	14.1	10.4	6.7	...	...	...	...
Female - Femmes	65.9	62.8	58.1	53.3	48.6	44.1	39.8	36.0	32.5	29.2	25.7	22.3	19.0	15.6	12.4	9.1	5.8	...	...	...	...
Burkina Faso[4] 2006																					
Male - Hommes	55.8	60.0	55.9	51.3	46.9	42.8	38.6	34.5	30.5	26.6	22.8	19.3	16.0	12.9	10.3	8.1	6.2	4.8	...	...	...
Female - Femmes	57.5	61.6	57.6	53.1	48.6	44.4	40.2	36.1	32.0	28.0	24.1	20.3	16.8	13.5	10.7	8.4	6.4	4.9	...	...	...
Burundi 2008																					
Male - Hommes	46.0	49.7	46.5	42.5	39.0	35.8	32.4	28.9	25.4	21.9	18.6	15.3	12.3	9.5	7.2	5.2	3.8	...	...	...	...
Female - Femmes	51.8	55.4	52.1	47.9	44.0	40.3	36.7	33.0	29.2	25.4	21.5	17.8	14.2	11.0	8.3	6.0	4.4	...	...	...	...
2017																					
Male - Hommes	56.9	...	...	...	...	...	...	...	...	...	...	...	...	...	...	...	...	...	...	...	...
Female - Femmes	61.3	...	...	...	...	...	...	...	...	...	...	...	...	...	...	...	...	...	...	...	...
Côte d'Ivoire 2016																					
Male - Hommes	54.9	...	...	...	...	...	...	...	...	...	...	...	...	...	...	...	...	...	...	...	...
Female - Femmes	57.5	...	...	...	...	...	...	...	...	...	...	...	...	...	...	...	...	...	...	...	...
Djibouti[5] 2002																					
Male - Hommes	51.8	...	...	...	...	...	...	...	...	...	...	...	...	...	...	...	...	...	...	...	...
Female - Femmes	54.1	...	...	...	...	...	...	...	...	...	...	...	...	...	...	...	...	...	...	...	...
Egypt - Égypte 2016																					
Male - Hommes	70.5	67.0	62.1	57.2	52.4	47.5	42.7	37.9	33.1	28.5	24.1	20.1	16.3	12.8	9.5	6.6	3.6	...	...	...	...
Female - Femmes	73.3	69.6	64.7	59.7	54.8	49.9	44.9	40.0	35.1	30.3	25.6	21.1	16.9	12.9	9.3	6.0	2.4	...	...	...	...
Equatorial Guinea - Guinée équatoriale 2001																					
Male - Hommes	...	...	...	...	...	...	...	...	...	...	...	...	...	...	...	...	...	...	...	...	...
Female - Femmes	59.3	...	...	...	...	...	...	...	...	...	...	...	...	...	...	...	...	...	...	...	...
Eswatini 2007																					
Male - Hommes	42.2	44.9	40.5	36.0	31.5	27.5	24.9	23.3	22.1	20.9	19.1	17.4	15.4	13.6	10.9	8.9	...	...	...	...	...
Female - Femmes	43.1	48.2	43.9	39.3	35.0	32.3	30.9	30.3	29.5	27.6	25.1	22.7	19.5	16.8	13.5	10.5	...	...	...	...	...
Ghana 2005																					
Male - Hommes	58.3	...	...	...	...	...	...	...	...	...	...	...	...	...	...	...	...	...	...	...	...
Female - Femmes	62.0	...	...	...	...	...	...	...	...	...	...	...	...	...	...	...	...	...	...	...	...
Guinea - Guinée 2014[6]																					
Male - Hommes	57.4	62.5	58.3	53.9	49.5	45.3	41.2	37.2	33.3	29.6	25.9	22.3	18.7	15.1	11.8	8.4	5.0	...	...	...	...
Female - Femmes	60.4	65.5	61.1	56.6	52.3	48.0	43.9	39.9	35.8	31.8	27.8	23.9	19.8	16.1	12.3	8.8	5.0	...	...	...	...
2017																					
Male - Hommes	58.4	...	...	...	...	...	...	...	...	...	...	...	...	...	...	...	...	...	...	...	...
Female - Femmes	61.4	...	...	...	...	...	...	...	...	...	...	...	...	...	...	...	...	...	...	...	...
Guinea-Bissau - Guinée-Bissau 2008 - 2009																					
Male - Hommes	49.2	49.8	45.3	41.0	36.8	32.8	29.3	26.2	23.3	20.7	18.0	15.5	13.1	11.2	9.4	8.0	6.8	...	...	...	...
Female - Femmes	51.2	50.1	45.7	41.5	37.8	34.4	31.3	28.4	25.6	22.9	20.0	17.4	14.9	12.8	10.6	8.8	7.1	...	...	...	...
2014																					
Male - Hommes	51.2	...	...	...	...	...	...	...	...	...	...	...	...	...	...	...	...	...	...	...	...
Female - Femmes	53.6	...	...	...	...	...	...	...	...	...	...	...	...	...	...	...	...	...	...	...	...
Kenya[2] 2009																					
Male - Hommes	57.8	58.1	53.9	49.7	45.3	41.0	36.9	33.3	30.2	27.1	23.9	20.4	16.7	13.2	10.0	7.0	4.0	...	...	...	...
Female - Femmes	60.7	60.1	55.8	51.4	46.9	42.6	38.7	35.7	33.0	29.8	26.2	22.3	18.3	14.5	11.0	7.7	4.7	...	...	...	...

22. Life expectancy at specified ages for each sex: latest available year, 1998 - 2017
Espérance de vie à un âge donné pour chaque sexe : dernière année disponible, 1998 - 2017 (continued - suite)

Continent, country or area and date / Continent, pays ou zone et date	0	5	10	15	20	25	30	35	40	45	50	55	60	65	70	75	80	85	90	95	100
AFRICA - AFRIQUE																					
Lesotho																					
2006[7]																					
Male - Hommes	39.8	40.4	36.0	31.5	27.2	23.6	20.9	19.2	18.2	17.3	16.4	14.9	13.2	11.3	9.4	7.4	5.3	2.9	...	...	...
Female - Femmes	42.9	42.7	38.4	33.8	29.6	26.3	24.2	23.2	22.8	22.3	21.5	20.2	18.6	16.7	14.5	12.1	9.6	7.4	...	...	...
2011																					
Male - Hommes	39.4	...	...	...	...	...	...	...	...	...	...	...	...	...	...	...	...	...	...	...	...
Female - Femmes	45.3	...	...	...	...	...	...	...	...	...	...	...	...	...	...	...	...	...	...	...	...
Malawi																					
2008																					
Male - Hommes	47.4	...	...	...	...	...	...	...	...	...	...	...	...	...	...	...	...	...	...	...	...
Female - Femmes	50.6	...	...	...	...	...	...	...	...	...	...	...	...	...	...	...	...	...	...	...	...
Mauritania - Mauritanie																					
2013																					
Male - Hommes	58.3	61.5	57.5	53.0	48.7	44.6	40.5	36.4	32.2	28.2	24.2	20.4	16.8	13.5	10.5	8.0	6.0	...	...	...	...
Female - Femmes	61.8	63.8	59.8	55.3	50.9	46.6	42.4	38.1	33.9	29.8	25.6	21.7	17.8	14.3	11.2	8.5	6.4	...	...	...	...
Mauritius - Maurice[8]																					
2015 - 2017																					
Male - Hommes	71.3	67.4	62.4	57.5	52.7	48.0	43.4	38.9	34.4	30.2	26.0	22.2	18.5	15.3	12.2	9.6	7.3	5.4	...	...	...
Female - Femmes	77.9	73.9	68.9	64.0	59.1	54.3	49.5	44.7	40.0	35.4	30.9	26.5	22.4	18.5	14.9	11.7	9.0	6.6	...	...	...
Mayotte																					
2015																					
Male - Hommes	75.3	...	...	...	56.7	...	...	...	37.8	...	...	...	20.5	...							
Female - Femmes	77.2	...	...	...	58.4	...	...	...	39.0	...	...	...	20.9	...							
Morocco - Maroc																					
2013																					
Male - Hommes	72.4	...	...	...	...	...	...	...	...	...	...	...	...	...	...	...	...	...	...	...	...
Female - Femmes	75.1	...	...	...	...	...	...	...	...	...	...	...	...	...	...	...	...	...	...	...	...
Mozambique																					
2014																					
Male - Hommes	50.2	54.0	50.0	45.6	41.6	37.7	33.9	30.1	26.5	22.9	19.6	16.4	13.5	10.9	8.7	6.8	5.0	...	...	...	...
Female - Femmes	55.4	59.0	54.8	50.3	46.1	42.1	38.1	34.1	30.2	26.3	22.5	19.0	15.7	12.7	10.0	7.7	5.8	...	...	...	...
2016																					
Male - Hommes	52.0	...	...	...	...	...	...	...	...	...	...	...	...	...	...	...	...	...	...	...	...
Female - Femmes	56.2	...	...	...	...	...	...	...	...	...	...	...	...	...	...	...	...	...	...	...	...
Namibia - Namibie																					
2011																					
Male - Hommes	53.3	52.4	48.0	43.4	39.0	35.1	31.5	28.6	25.8	23.2	20.6	17.7	15.1	12.6	9.8	7.4	5.6	...	...	...	...
Female - Femmes	60.5	59.6	55.1	50.5	46.1	42.0	38.4	35.2	32.0	28.7	25.2	21.6	17.9	14.5	11.3	8.6	6.5	...	...	...	...
Republic of South Sudan - République de Soudan du Sud																					
2010																					
Male - Hommes	54.4	57.4	53.2	48.8	44.6	40.7	36.8	32.8	28.9	25.0	21.2	17.6	14.2	11.2	8.5	6.3	4.5	3.2	2.2	1.5	...
Female - Femmes	54.5	56.2	51.9	47.5	43.3	39.4	35.4	31.5	27.5	23.7	19.9	16.4	13.1	10.2	7.7	5.6	4.1	2.9	2.0	1.4	...
Reunion - Réunion																					
2015																					
Male - Hommes	77.1	...	...	...	58.1	...	...	...	39.3	...	...	...	21.8	...							
Female - Femmes	83.6	...	...	...	64.3	...	...	...	44.8	...	...	...	26.2	...							
Rwanda																					
2002																					
Male - Hommes	48.4	58.4	54.4	49.9	45.6	41.6	37.5	33.5	29.4	25.4	21.6	17.9	14.5	11.4	8.6	6.3	4.6	...	...	...	...
Female - Femmes	53.8	63.1	58.8	54.3	49.9	45.7	41.4	37.2	32.9	28.7	24.5	20.4	16.5	12.9	9.8	7.1	5.1	...	...	...	...
2012[9]																					
Male - Hommes	62.6	...	...	...	...	...	...	...	...	...	...	...	...	...	...	...	...	...	...	...	...
Female - Femmes	66.2	...	...	...	...	...	...	...	...	...	...	...	...	...	...	...	...	...	...	...	...
Saint Helena ex. dep. - Sainte-Hélène sans dép.[10]																					
2003 - 2012																					
Male - Hommes	72.0	68.1	63.4	...	53.9	...	44.2	...	35.5	...	27.1	...	19.3	...	12.5	...	7.2	...	...	...	...
Female - Femmes	79.7	75.3	70.3	...	60.3	...	51.0	...	41.8	...	32.0	...	23.0	...	15.5	...	8.6	...	...	...	...

Continent, country or area and date / Continent, pays ou zone et date	\multicolumn{21}{c}{Age (in years) - Age (en années)}																				
	0	5	10	15	20	25	30	35	40	45	50	55	60	65	70	75	80	85	90	95	100
AFRICA - AFRIQUE																					
Sao Tome and Principe - Sao Tomé-et-Principe																					
2011 - 2012																					
Male - Hommes	62.1	59.5	54.6	50.1	45.8	41.6	37.5	33.4	29.6	25.8	22.1	18.4	15.2	12.0	9.8	7.4	5.0	...	...	...	...
Female - Femmes	68.7	65.9	61.2	56.5	51.8	47.1	42.5	38.0	33.5	29.3	25.3	21.7	18.2	14.9	11.8	9.0	6.6	...	...	...	...
Senegal - Sénégal[11]																					
2013																					
Male - Hommes	63.2	...	...	...	...	...	...	...	...	...	...	...	...	...	...	...	...	...	...	...	...
Female - Femmes	66.5	...	...	...	...	...	...	...	...	...	...	...	...	...	...	...	...	...	...	...	...
Seychelles																					
2007																					
Male - Hommes	68.9	65.0	60.2	55.3	50.5	45.9	41.6	37.0	32.7	28.7	24.4	20.9	17.1	14.1	11.0	9.0	7.4	...	...	...	...
Female - Femmes	77.7	73.3	68.5	63.5	58.5	53.7	48.9	44.3	39.5	35.3	31.0	26.4	22.2	18.5	15.1	12.1	9.2	...	...	...	...
2017																					
Male - Hommes	70.3	...	...	...	...	...	...	...	...	...	...	...	...	...	...	...	...	...	...	...	...
Female - Femmes	78.5	...	...	...	...	...	...	...	...	...	...	...	...	...	...	...	...	...	...	...	...
Sierra Leone																					
2004																					
Male - Hommes	47.5	...	...	...	...	...	...	...	...	...	...	...	...	...	...	...	...	...	...	...	...
Female - Femmes	49.4	...	...	...	...	...	...	...	...	...	...	...	...	...	...	...	...	...	...	...	...
South Africa - Afrique du Sud																					
2014																					
Male - Hommes	59.1	...	...	...	...	...	...	...	...	...	...	...	...	...	...	...	...	...	...	...	...
Female - Femmes	63.1	...	...	...	...	...	...	...	...	...	...	...	...	...	...	...	...	...	...	...	...
Sudan - Soudan																					
2008																					
Male - Hommes	58.1	...	...	...	...	...	...	...	...	...	...	...	...	...	...	...	...	...	...	...	...
Female - Femmes	61.4	...	...	...	...	...	...	...	...	...	...	...	...	...	...	...	...	...	...	...	...
Tunisia - Tunisie																					
2015																					
Male - Hommes	74.5	...	...	...	...	...	...	...	...	...	...	...	...	...	...	...	...	...	...	...	...
Female - Femmes	77.8	...	...	...	...	...	...	...	...	...	...	...	...	...	...	...	...	...	...	...	...
Uganda - Ouganda																					
2002[12]																					
Male - Hommes	48.8	53.0	49.2	44.8	40.5	36.6	33.6	31.0	28.4	25.8	23.2	20.4	17.2	14.4	11.6	9.2	6.7	4.1	...	...	...
Female - Femmes	52.0	56.0	52.1	47.6	43.3	39.6	36.7	34.2	31.5	28.6	25.6	22.3	18.9	15.7	12.6	9.9	7.0	4.2	...	...	...
2014[13]																					
Male - Hommes	62.2	...	...	...	...	...	...	...	...	...	...	...	...	...	...	...	...	...	...	...	...
Female - Femmes	64.2	...	...	...	...	...	...	...	...	...	...	...	...	...	...	...	...	...	...	...	...
Zimbabwe																					
2001 - 2002																					
Male - Hommes	45.8	44.2	40.0	35.4	30.9	26.8	23.8	22.1	21.8	21.3	20.4	19.2	17.7	15.7	13.7	11.4	9.5	7.5	6.2	5.2	...
Female - Femmes	50.3	48.6	44.2	39.7	35.3	32.1	30.4	30.1	30.2	29.0	27.6	25.3	22.9	20.2	17.6	14.8	12.2	9.9	8.1	7.3	...
2012																					
Male - Hommes	57.4	...	...	...	...	...	...	...	...	...	...	...	...	...	...	...	...	...	...	...	...
Female - Femmes	64.0	...	...	...	...	...	...	...	...	...	...	...	...	...	...	...	...	...	...	...	...
AMERICA, NORTH - AMÉRIQUE DU NORD																					
Anguilla																					
2000 - 2002																					
Male - Hommes	76.5	72.1	67.1	62.1	57.3	53.1	48.4	43.7	39.4	34.7	30.2	25.4	21.1	16.5	12.7	10.0	8.0	6.9	...	...	...
Female - Femmes	81.1	76.4	71.4	66.4	61.4	57.1	52.7	47.7	42.7	38.3	33.5	28.7	24.0	19.4	15.3	10.8	8.3	7.6	...	...	...
Antigua and Barbuda - Antigua-et-Barbuda																					
2010																					
Male - Hommes	74.0	...	...	...	...	...	...	...	...	...	...	...	...	...	...	...	...	...	...	...	...
Female - Femmes	79.7	...	...	...	...	...	...	...	...	...	...	...	...	...	...	...	...	...	...	...	...
Aruba																					
2010 - 2011																					
Male - Hommes	73.9	69.4	64.4	59.5	54.6	50.0	45.4	40.8	36.3	31.7	27.3	23.1	19.1	15.3	12.3	9.4	7.3	5.0	3.5	2.7	...
Female - Femmes	79.8	76.2	71.2	66.2	61.3	56.4	51.5	46.6	42.0	37.3	32.6	27.9	23.8	19.7	16.0	12.5	9.5	6.8	5.0	3.8	...

Continent, country or area and date / Continent, pays ou zone et date	0	5	10	15	20	25	30	35	40	45	50	55	60	65	70	75	80	85	90	95	100
AMERICA, NORTH - AMÉRIQUE DU NORD																					
Bahamas																					
1999 - 2001																					
Male - Hommes	69.9	...	...	...	...	...	...	...	...	...	...	...	...	...	...	...	...	...	...	...	...
Female - Femmes	76.4	...	...	...	...	...	...	...	...	...	...	...	...	...	...	...	...	...	...	...	...
Bermuda - Bermudes																					
2017																					
Male - Hommes	77.7	73.0	68.0	63.1	58.3	53.7	49.2	44.6	39.9	35.3	30.8	26.3	22.0	18.0	14.3	10.9	7.8	5.1	...	...	...
Female - Femmes	85.4	80.5	75.5	70.5	65.6	60.6	55.7	50.7	45.8	41.0	36.2	31.5	27.0	22.5	18.3	14.2	10.8	7.7	...	...	...
British Virgin Islands - Îles Vierges britanniques																					
2004																					
Male - Hommes	69.9	...	...	...	...	...	...	...	...	...	...	...	...	...	...	...	...	...	...	...	...
Female - Femmes	78.5	...	...	...	...	...	...	...	...	...	...	...	...	...	...	...	...	...	...	...	...
Canada																					
2013 - 2015																					
Male - Hommes	79.8	75.3	70.3	65.4	60.5	55.7	50.9	46.1	41.3	36.6	32.0	27.6	23.3	19.2	15.4	12.0	8.9	6.4	4.4	3.0	2.1
Female - Femmes	83.9	79.3	74.4	69.4	64.5	59.6	54.7	49.8	44.9	40.1	35.4	30.8	26.3	22.0	17.9	14.1	10.6	7.6	5.2	3.5	2.4
Cayman Islands - Îles Caïmanes[14]																					
2010																					
Male - Hommes	79.8	75.5	70.5	65.6	61.1	56.8	52.2	47.4	42.5	37.6	32.9	28.3	23.9	19.6	15.2	11.6	8.9	6.2	5.0	3.6	2.5
Female - Femmes	84.7	80.1	75.1	70.1	65.1	60.3	55.3	50.4	45.4	40.5	35.7	30.8	26.1	21.5	17.0	13.2	9.8	7.2	4.9	3.8	2.5
Costa Rica																					
2017																					
Male - Hommes	77.6	73.3	68.4	63.5	58.7	54.0	49.3	44.7	40.1	35.5	31.0	26.7	22.6	18.6	15.1	11.8	9.1	6.7	4.8	3.3	...
Female - Femmes	82.7	78.3	73.4	68.4	63.5	58.6	53.7	48.9	44.0	39.2	34.5	29.9	25.5	21.2	17.2	13.5	10.2	7.5	5.3	3.6	...
Cuba																					
2011 - 2013																					
Male - Hommes	76.5	72.0	67.0	62.1	57.3	52.5	47.7	42.9	38.2	33.6	29.2	25.0	21.0	17.3	14.0	11.0	8.4	6.3	4.9	3.8	2.0
Female - Femmes	80.4	75.9	71.0	66.0	61.1	56.2	51.4	46.5	41.7	36.9	32.3	27.9	23.6	19.6	15.8	12.4	9.4	6.9	5.1	3.8	2.1
Curaçao																					
2016																					
Male - Hommes	74.9	71.1	66.2	61.2	56.3	51.6	47.0	42.3	37.7	33.0	28.5	24.3	20.4	16.7	13.3	10.4	7.6	5.5	3.9	2.8	2.4
Female - Femmes	81.0	77.7	72.7	67.7	62.8	57.9	53.0	48.2	43.3	38.6	33.9	29.3	24.8	20.6	16.6	12.8	9.6	7.0	4.9	3.3	2.2
2015 - 2017																					
Male - Hommes	74.7	...	...	...	...	...	...	...	...	...	...	...	...	...	...	...	...	...	...	...	...
Female - Femmes	81.5	...	...	...	...	...	...	...	...	...	...	...	...	...	...	...	...	...	...	...	...
Dominica - Dominique																					
2008																					
Male - Hommes	73.8	...	...	...	...	...	...	...	...	...	...	...	...	...	...	...	...	...	...	...	...
Female - Femmes	78.2	...	...	...	...	...	...	...	...	...	...	...	...	...	...	...	...	...	...	...	...
Dominican Republic - République dominicaine																					
2010 - 2015																					
Male - Hommes	70.0	67.5	62.6	57.7	53.0	48.7	44.3	40.0	35.6	31.3	27.2	23.3	19.6	16.2	13.2	10.5	8.6	...	...	...	...
Female - Femmes	74.8	71.8	66.9	62.0	57.1	52.4	47.7	43.1	38.5	34.1	29.7	25.5	21.6	17.9	14.6	11.7	9.7	...	...	...	...
El Salvador[15]																					
2000 - 2005																					
Male - Hommes	65.4	62.6	57.8	52.9	48.7	45.0	41.5	37.8	34.1	30.4	26.8	23.3	20.0	16.7	13.8	11.1	9.0	...	...	...	...
Female - Femmes	74.9	72.0	67.1	62.3	57.5	52.9	48.2	43.6	39.0	34.6	30.3	26.1	22.1	18.4	15.0	12.0	9.6	...	...	...	...
Greenland - Groenland																					
2010 - 2014																					
Male - Hommes	69.1	65.4	60.4	55.5	51.1	47.3	42.9	38.5	34.0	29.6	25.3	21.0	17.1	13.4	10.2	7.8	6.0	4.7	3.2	4.0	...
Female - Femmes	73.7	69.3	64.4	59.5	54.9	50.5	45.7	40.9	36.4	31.7	27.2	22.7	18.5	14.8	11.7	8.8	6.3	4.5	3.3	3.1	...
Guadeloupe																					
2015																					
Male - Hommes	77.0	...	...	...	58.2	...	...	...	40.4	...	...	...	23.5	...	...	...	...	...	...	...	...
Female - Femmes	84.8	...	...	...	65.6	...	...	...	46.1	...	...	...	27.4	...	...	...	...	...	...	...	...
Guatemala																					
1995 - 2000																					
Male - Hommes	61.4	60.6	56.0	51.2	46.8	42.7	38.8	34.9	31.2	27.4	23.7	20.1	16.8	13.6	10.7	8.2	6.1	...	...	...	...
Female - Femmes	67.2	66.2	62.6	56.9	52.3	47.7	43.3	38.9	34.6	30.4	26.3	22.3	18.6	15.2	12.0	9.2	6.9	...	...	...	...

Continent, country or area and date / Continent, pays ou zone et date	0	5	10	15	20	25	30	35	40	45	50	55	60	65	70	75	80	85	90	95	100
AMERICA, NORTH - AMÉRIQUE DU NORD																					
2010 - 2015																					
Male - Hommes	67.9	...	...	...	...	...	...	...	...	...	...	...	...	...	...	...	...	...	...	...	...
Female - Femmes	75.0	...	...	...	...	...	...	...	...	...	...	...	...	...	...	...	...	...	...	...	...
Jamaica - Jamaïque																					
2006																					
Male - Hommes	69.7	67.0	62.2	57.3	52.6	47.9	43.2	38.5	33.8	29.3	24.9	20.8	16.9	13.5	10.4	7.8	5.8	4.1	2.9	2.1	1.5
Female - Femmes	75.2	71.6	66.7	61.7	56.8	52.0	47.1	42.3	37.6	32.9	28.3	23.9	19.7	15.9	12.4	9.4	6.9	5.0	3.5	2.4	1.7
Martinique																					
2015																					
Male - Hommes	79.4	...	...	...	60.1	...	...	...	41.7	...	...	...	24.1	...	...	...	...	...	...	...	...
Female - Femmes	84.7	...	...	...	65.4	...	...	...	45.9	...	...	...	27.4	...	...	...	...	...	...	...	...
Mexico - Mexique																					
2008																					
Male - Hommes	72.8	69.2	64.3	59.4	54.7	50.0	45.5	40.9	36.5	32.1	27.9	23.9	20.2	16.8	13.7	11.0	8.7	6.6	4.9	3.5	2.6
Female - Femmes	77.5	73.8	68.9	63.9	59.0	54.2	49.3	44.5	39.7	35.1	30.6	26.2	22.1	18.3	14.8	11.7	9.0	6.8	4.9	3.5	2.6
2015																					
Male - Hommes	72.3	...	...	...	...	...	...	...	...	...	...	...	...	...	...	...	...	...	...	...	...
Female - Femmes	77.7	...	...	...	...	...	...	...	...	...	...	...	...	...	...	...	...	...	...	...	...
Nicaragua																					
2005 - 2010																					
Male - Hommes	63.4	61.1	56.5	51.8	47.9	44.2	40.5	36.5	32.5	28.6	24.9	21.3	17.7	14.6	11.6	9.0	6.5		...	...	...
Female - Femmes	68.9	66.2	61.4	56.7	52.1	47.6	43.0	38.5	34.1	29.8	25.7	21.9	18.1	14.9	11.8	9.3	6.9		...	...	...
Panama[16]																					
2016																					
Male - Hommes	75.0	71.6	66.8	61.9	57.3	53.0	48.8	44.4	39.9	35.4	31.1	26.9	22.9	19.1	15.7	12.7	10.0	7.7	5.8	4.2	2.5
Female - Femmes	81.1	77.4	72.5	67.6	62.7	57.9	53.2	48.4	43.7	39.1	34.5	30.0	25.7	21.6	17.7	14.2	11.1	8.4	6.1	4.3	2.5
Puerto Rico - Porto Rico																					
2015 - 2017																					
Male - Hommes	76.6	72.3	67.3	62.3	57.5	53.1	48.6	44.2	39.8	35.4	31.1	27.1	23.3	19.7	16.3	13.2	10.5	8.4	...	...	...
Female - Femmes	84.4	80.0	75.1	70.1	65.2	60.3	55.4	50.6	45.8	41.1	36.5	32.0	27.6	23.4	19.4	15.7	12.4	9.8	...	...	...
Saint Kitts and Nevis - Saint-Kitts-et-Nevis																					
1998																					
Male - Hommes	68.2	65.0	60.1	55.3	50.5	45.8	41.1	36.5	32.7	28.5	24.3	20.6	16.6	13.3	11.0	9.1	6.6	4.7	3.4	2.2	0.4
Female - Femmes	70.7	67.5	62.5	57.6	52.7	48.0	43.4	38.8	34.4	29.8	25.4	21.3	17.6	14.3	11.3	8.9	6.3	4.6	3.3	2.2	0.4
Saint Lucia - Sainte-Lucie																					
2005																					
Male - Hommes	69.9	66.4	61.5	56.6	52.0	47.4	43.1	38.6	34.3	30.1	25.9	21.7	17.9	14.7	11.8	9.0	7.2	5.2	...	...	...
Female - Femmes	75.7	72.2	67.3	62.4	57.5	52.6	47.8	43.2	38.4	33.8	29.2	25.0	20.8	17.2	13.8	10.4	7.7	4.8	...	...	...
2012																					
Male - Hommes	75.3	...	...	...	...	...	...	...	...	...	...	...	...	...	...	...	...	...	...	...	...
Female - Femmes	82.5	...	...	...	...	...	...	...	...	...	...	...	...	...	...	...	...	...	...	...	...
Saint Vincent and the Grenadines - Saint-Vincent-et-les Grenadines																					
2016																					
Male - Hommes	71.0	66.8	62.1	57.3	52.8	48.3	43.8	39.5	35.1	30.9	26.5	22.7	19.6	16.7	14.7	11.7	9.0	6.5	...	...	...
Female - Femmes	75.2	71.1	66.3	61.4	56.5	51.8	47.1	42.5	38.0	33.5	29.0	25.1	21.4	17.9	14.7	11.5	9.2	6.6	...	...	...
Sint Maarten (Dutch part) - Saint-Martin (partie néerlandaise)																					
2011 - 2012																					
Male - Hommes	69.2	65.5	60.6	55.7	51.0	46.9	42.5	38.2	33.9	29.5	25.3	21.2	17.6	13.8	10.4	7.4	5.2	4.0	...	...	...
Female - Femmes	77.1	72.3	67.4	62.6	57.8	52.8	48.0	43.1	38.2	33.5	28.6	24.0	19.4	14.9	11.5	8.1	5.0	1.8	...	...	...
Trinidad and Tobago - Trinité-et-Tobago[2]																					
2011																					
Male - Hommes	71.4	67.6	62.7	57.8	53.2	49.0	44.7	40.4	36.0	31.7	27.5	23.5	19.6	16.2	12.9	10.2	7.9	6.0	...	...	...
Female - Femmes	77.8	74.1	69.2	64.2	59.4	54.6	49.9	45.3	40.6	36.2	31.7	27.5	23.3	19.4	15.9	12.6	9.7	7.6	...	...	...

Continent, country or area and date / Continent, pays ou zone et date	0	5	10	15	20	25	30	35	40	45	50	55	60	65	70	75	80	85	90	95	100
AMERICA, NORTH - AMÉRIQUE DU NORD																					
Turks and Caicos Islands - Îles Turques et Caïques																					
2001																					
Male - Hommes	79.0	75.3	70.3	65.3	60.3	55.8	50.8	46.0	41.2	37.1	33.0	28.4	24.3	20.8	17.5	12.5	7.5	4.1	...	...	...
Female - Femmes	77.4	72.5	67.5	62.5	57.5	52.9	48.2	43.4	38.6	33.8	29.6	25.0	20.0	17.0	13.2	11.7	10.3	8.8	...	...	...
2012																					
Male - Hommes	75.8	...	...	...	...	...	...	...	...	...	...	...	...	...	...	...	...	...	...	...	...
Female - Femmes	77.8	...	...	...	...	...	...	...	...	...	...	...	...	...	...	...	...	...	...	...	...
United States of America - États-Unis d'Amérique																					
2014																					
Male - Hommes	76.4	72.0	67.0	62.1	57.3	52.6	48.0	43.3	38.7	34.2	29.8	25.6	21.7	18.0	14.4	11.2	8.3	5.9	4.1	2.9	2.1
Female - Femmes	81.2	76.7	71.7	66.8	61.9	57.0	52.1	47.3	42.6	37.9	33.3	28.9	24.7	20.5	16.6	13.0	9.7	7.0	4.8	3.3	2.3
2015																					
Male - Hommes	76.3	...	...	...	...	...	...	...	...	...	...	...	...	...	...	...	...	...	...	...	...
Female - Femmes	81.2	...	...	...	...	...	...	...	...	...	...	...	...	...	...	...	...	...	...	...	...
AMERICA, SOUTH - AMÉRIQUE DU SUD																					
Argentina - Argentine																					
2008 - 2010																					
Male - Hommes	72.1	68.2	63.3	58.4	53.7	49.1	44.5	39.8	35.2	30.7	26.3	22.2	18.5	15.0	11.9	9.2	6.9	5.2	4.0	3.1	2.6
Female - Femmes	78.8	74.8	69.9	65.0	60.1	55.3	50.5	45.6	40.9	36.2	31.7	27.3	23.1	19.0	15.2	11.7	8.6	6.3	4.7	3.5	2.9
2015[17]																					
Male - Hommes	73.7	...	...	...	...	...	...	...	...	...	...	...	...	...	...	...	...	...	...	...	...
Female - Femmes	80.3	...	...	...	...	...	...	...	...	...	...	...	...	...	...	...	...	...	...	...	...
Bolivia (Plurinational State of) - Bolivie (État plurinational de)[18]																					
2016 - 2017																					
Male - Hommes	69.1	67.3	62.6	57.9	53.4	49.1	44.7	40.4	36.2	32.0	27.9	24.0	20.3	16.9	13.8	11.1	8.7	6.8	4.9	3.7	...
Female - Femmes	75.9	73.6	68.9	64.0	59.3	54.6	50.0	45.3	40.7	36.3	32.0	27.8	23.8	20.1	16.8	13.7	10.9	8.5	6.3	4.8	...
Brazil - Brésil																					
2015																					
Male - Hommes	71.9	68.2	63.3	58.4	53.9	49.5	45.1	40.7	36.3	32.0	27.9	23.9	20.2	16.7	13.5	10.7	8.4	...	...	...	...
Female - Femmes	79.1	75.3	70.4	65.4	60.6	55.7	50.9	46.2	41.4	36.8	32.3	28.0	23.8	19.8	16.2	12.9	10.1	...	...	...	...
Chile - Chili																					
2015																					
Male - Hommes	77.1	72.7	67.7	62.8	57.9	53.2	48.4	43.7	39.1	34.5	30.0	25.6	21.5	17.6	14.0	10.8	8.0	5.9	4.5	3.5	2.8
Female - Femmes	82.7	78.4	73.4	68.5	63.6	58.6	53.7	48.9	44.0	39.3	34.6	30.0	25.6	21.3	17.3	13.6	10.3	7.8	5.9	4.5	3.5
Colombia - Colombie																					
2010 - 2015																					
Male - Hommes	72.1	68.9	64.0	59.1	54.5	50.1	45.7	41.3	36.8	32.3	27.9	23.7	19.7	16.0	12.7	9.8	7.4	...	...	...	...
Female - Femmes	78.5	74.9	70.0	65.1	60.2	55.4	50.6	45.8	41.0	36.3	31.7	27.2	22.9	18.8	15.0	11.6	8.7	...	...	...	...
Ecuador - Équateur[19]																					
2010 - 2017																					
Male - Hommes	73.9	70.5	65.6	60.6	55.8	51.1	46.4	41.8	37.3	32.7	28.3	24.1	20.0	16.3	12.8	9.8	7.3	5.2	3.6	2.4	0.5
Female - Femmes	79.5	76.0	71.1	66.2	61.3	56.4	51.5	46.7	41.9	37.1	32.4	27.8	23.4	19.1	15.0	11.3	8.2	5.7	3.9	2.5	0.5
French Guiana - Guyane française																					
2015																					
Male - Hommes	76.4	...	...	...	58.0	...	...	...	39.5	...	...	...	22.0	...	...	...	...	...	...	...	...
Female - Femmes	82.0	...	...	...	63.0	...	...	...	43.6	...	...	...	25.3	...	...	...	...	...	...	...	...
Paraguay																					
2005 - 2010																					
Male - Hommes	69.7	...	...	...	...	...	...	...	...	...	...	...	...	...	...	...	...	...	...	...	...
Female - Femmes	73.9	...	...	...	...	...	...	...	...	...	...	...	...	...	...	...	...	...	...	...	...
Peru - Pérou																					
2010 - 2015																					
Male - Hommes	71.5	69.0	64.3	59.4	54.7	50.0	45.5	40.9	36.4	32.0	27.7	23.6	19.8	16.2	13.0	10.1	7.7	...	...	...	...
Female - Femmes	76.8	73.8	69.0	64.1	59.3	54.5	49.7	45.0	40.3	35.7	31.2	26.9	22.7	18.7	15.0	11.7	8.8	...	...	...	...

22. Life expectancy at specified ages for each sex: latest available year, 1998 - 2017
Espérance de vie à un âge donné pour chaque sexe : dernière année disponible, 1998 - 2017 (continued - suite)

Continent, country or area and date / Continent, pays ou zone et date	0	5	10	15	20	25	30	35	40	45	50	55	60	65	70	75	80	85	90	95	100
AMERICA, SOUTH - AMÉRIQUE DU SUD																					
Suriname																					
2013 - 2015																					
Male - Hommes	70.1	66.5	61.6	56.8	52.1	47.5	42.9	38.5	34.1	29.9	25.9	22.2	18.5	14.9	11.7	8.6	5.9	4.0	...	...	...
Female - Femmes	75.3	71.5	66.6	61.7	57.0	52.2	47.6	42.9	38.4	33.8	29.4	25.2	21.1	17.1	13.3	9.8	6.6	4.3	...	...	...
Uruguay																					
2010																					
Male - Hommes	72.8	68.5	63.6	58.7	54.0	49.4	44.8	40.2	35.6	31.0	26.6	22.4	18.6	15.1	12.0	9.3	7.0	5.2	4.0	...	...
Female - Femmes	80.0	75.6	70.7	65.8	60.9	56.1	51.2	46.4	41.6	36.9	32.3	27.9	23.6	19.5	15.6	12.0	8.9	6.4	4.5	...	...
2016																					
Male - Hommes	73.8	...	...	...	...	...	...	...	...	...	...	...	...	...	...	...	...	...	...	...	...
Female - Femmes	80.6	...	...	...	...	...	...	...	...	...	...	...	...	...	...	...	...	...	...	...	...
Venezuela (Bolivarian Republic of) - Venezuela (République bolivarienne du)																					
1995 - 2000																					
Male - Hommes	68.6	66.6	61.8	56.9	52.3	47.8	43.3	38.8	34.3	29.9	25.6	21.6	17.9	14.5	11.4	8.6	5.9	...	...	...	...
Female - Femmes	74.5	72.1	67.2	62.3	57.5	52.6	47.8	43.1	38.4	33.7	29.2	24.9	20.8	16.9	13.3	9.9	6.9	...	...	...	...
2016[20]																					
Male - Hommes	72.3	...	...	...	...	...	...	...	...	...	...	...	...	...	...	...	...	...	...	...	...
Female - Femmes	78.4	...	...	...	...	...	...	...	...	...	...	...	...	...	...	...	...	...	...	...	...
ASIA - ASIE																					
Afghanistan																					
2004																					
Male - Hommes	45.0	...	...	...	...	...	...	...	...	...	...	...	...	...	...	...	...	...	...	...	...
Female - Femmes	44.0	...	...	...	...	...	...	...	...	...	...	...	...	...	...	...	...	...	...	...	...
Armenia - Arménie																					
2015 - 2016																					
Male - Hommes	71.6	67.4	62.5	57.5	52.8	48.1	43.3	38.5	33.8	29.4	25.1	21.2	17.5	14.3	11.4	8.6	6.4	4.4	2.9	2.2	0.7
Female - Femmes	78.3	74.0	69.1	64.1	59.2	54.3	49.3	44.4	39.6	34.8	30.2	25.6	21.2	17.1	13.3	9.7	6.7	4.2	2.0	1.6	0.5
Azerbaijan - Azerbaïdjan																					
2016																					
Male - Hommes	72.8	68.9	64.0	59.1	54.3	49.5	44.7	39.9	35.2	30.7	26.2	22.1	18.3	14.9	12.0	9.4	7.2	6.0	5.4	4.7	0.9
Female - Femmes	77.5	73.4	68.5	63.6	58.7	53.8	48.9	44.0	39.1	34.4	29.7	25.1	20.8	16.7	13.0	9.7	7.1	5.4	4.3	3.6	0.9
Bahrain - Bahreïn																					
2001																					
Male - Hommes	73.2	69.3	64.4	59.5	54.7	49.9	45.2	40.4	35.6	30.9	26.4	22.0	17.8	14.1	11.3	9.5	...	...	...	...	...
Female - Femmes	76.2	72.0	67.1	62.1	57.2	52.3	47.4	42.5	37.7	32.9	28.2	23.7	19.6	15.9	12.9	10.9	...	...	...	...	...
2010 - 2015																					
Male - Hommes	75.8	...	...	...	...	...	...	...	...	...	...	...	...	...	...	...	...	...	...	...	...
Female - Femmes	77.4	...	...	...	...	...	...	...	...	...	...	...	...	...	...	...	...	...	...	...	...
Bangladesh																					
2011																					
Male - Hommes	67.9	65.5	60.8	56.1	51.3	46.5	41.8	37.1	32.6	28.2	24.1	20.2	16.6	13.2	10.0	6.7	4.4	...	...	...	...
Female - Femmes	70.3	67.8	63.1	58.3	53.6	48.8	44.0	39.3	34.7	30.1	25.6	21.4	17.4	13.8	10.3	6.7	5.6	...	...	...	...
2016[21]																					
Male - Hommes	70.3	...	...	...	...	...	...	...	...	...	...	...	...	...	...	...	...	...	...	...	...
Female - Femmes	72.9	...	...	...	...	...	...	...	...	...	...	...	...	...	...	...	...	...	...	...	...
Bhutan - Bhoutan																					
2005																					
Male - Hommes	65.7	...	...	...	...	...	...	...	...	...	...	...	...	...	...	...	...	...	...	...	...
Female - Femmes	66.9	...	...	...	...	...	...	...	...	...	...	...	...	...	...	...	...	...	...	...	...
Brunei Darussalam - Brunéi Darussalam																					
2016																					
Male - Hommes	80.5	...	...	...	...	...	...	...	...	...	...	...	...	...	...	...	...	...	...	...	...
Female - Femmes	80.8	...	...	...	...	...	...	...	...	...	...	...	...	...	...	...	...	...	...	...	...
China - Chine[22]																					
2010																					
Male - Hommes	66.8	...	...	...	...	...	...	...	...	...	...	...	...	...	...	...	...	...	...	...	...
Female - Femmes	70.5	...	...	...	...	...	...	...	...	...	...	...	...	...	...	...	...	...	...	...	...

22. Life expectancy at specified ages for each sex: latest available year, 1998 - 2017
Espérance de vie à un âge donné pour chaque sexe : dernière année disponible, 1998 - 2017 (continued - suite)

Continent, country or area and date / Continent, pays ou zone et date	0	5	10	15	20	25	30	35	40	45	50	55	60	65	70	75	80	85	90	95	100
ASIA - ASIE																					
China, Hong Kong SAR - Chine, Hong Kong RAS																					
2017																					
Male - Hommes	81.9	77.1	72.1	67.2	62.3	57.4	52.5	47.6	42.8	38.1	33.4	28.9	24.6	20.5	16.6	13.1	10.0	7.4	5.3	3.7	2.5
Female - Femmes	87.6	82.8	77.8	72.8	67.9	63.0	58.0	53.1	48.2	43.3	38.6	33.9	29.3	24.8	20.5	16.3	12.6	9.3	6.7	4.6	3.0
China, Macao SAR - Chine, Macao RAS																					
2012 - 2015																					
Male - Hommes	79.9	75.2	70.3	65.3	60.4	55.6	50.7	45.9	41.2	36.6	32.0	27.6	23.4	19.3	15.5	12.1	9.2	7.3	...	...	...
Female - Femmes	86.3	81.5	76.5	71.6	66.6	61.8	56.8	51.9	47.1	42.2	37.5	32.9	28.3	23.8	19.4	15.5	12.2	9.6	...	...	...
2013 - 2016																					
Male - Hommes	80.3	...	...	...	...	...	...	...	...	...	...	...	...	...	...	...	...	...	...	...	...
Female - Femmes	86.4	...	...	...	...	...	...	...	...	...	...	...	...	...	...	...	...	...	...	...	...
Cyprus - Chypre[23]																					
2013																					
Male - Hommes	80.0	75.1	70.2	65.3	60.4	55.5	50.7	45.8	41.0	36.3	31.6	27.0	22.6	18.5	14.7	11.2	8.2	5.9	...	...	...
Female - Femmes	84.8	79.8	74.9	69.9	64.9	60.0	55.0	50.1	45.2	40.3	35.4	30.6	25.9	21.4	17.2	13.1	9.5	6.6	...	...	...
2016																					
Male - Hommes	80.3	...	...	...	...	...	...	...	...	...	...	...	...	...	...	...	...	...	...	...	...
Female - Femmes	84.7	...	...	...	...	...	...	...	...	...	...	...	...	...	...	...	...	...	...	...	...
Democratic People's Republic of Korea - République populaire démocratique de Corée																					
2008																					
Male - Hommes	65.6	...	...	...	...	...	...	...	...	...	...	...	...	...	...	...	...	...	...	...	...
Female - Femmes	72.7	...	...	...	...	...	...	...	...	...	...	...	...	...	...	...	...	...	...	...	...
Georgia - Géorgie																					
2016																					
Male - Hommes	68.2	64.1	59.1	54.2	49.4	44.7	40.1	35.6	31.2	27.0	23.0	19.4	16.0	12.9	10.1	7.6	5.5	3.7	...	...	...
Female - Femmes	77.1	72.8	67.9	62.9	58.0	53.2	48.3	43.5	38.7	33.9	29.3	24.8	20.6	16.5	12.7	9.3	6.5	4.4	...	...	...
India - Inde[24]																					
2012 - 2016																					
Male - Hommes	67.4	65.5	60.8	56.0	51.2	46.6	42.0	37.5	33.1	28.8	24.7	20.8	17.3	14.0	11.0	8.4	6.1	4.5	...	...	...
Female - Femmes	70.2	68.9	64.1	59.3	54.6	49.9	45.2	40.6	35.9	31.4	26.9	22.9	18.9	15.3	12.1	9.3	6.7	4.8	...	...	...
Indonesia - Indonésie																					
2012																					
Male - Hommes	67.7	...	...	...	...	...	...	...	...	...	...	...	...	...	...	...	...				
Female - Femmes	71.7	...	...	...	...	...	...	...	...	...	...	...	...	...	...	...	...				
Iran (Islamic Republic of) - Iran (République islamique d')[25]																					
2016																					
Male - Hommes	72.5	...	...	...	...	...	...	...	...	...	...	...	...	...	...	...	...	...	...	...	...
Female - Femmes	75.5	...	...	...	...	...	...	...	...	...	...	...	...	...	...	...	...	...	...	...	...
Israel - Israël[26]																					
2012 - 2016																					
Male - Hommes	80.2	75.6	70.6	65.7	60.8	55.9	51.1	46.2	41.4	36.6	32.0	27.5	23.2	19.1	15.3	11.8	8.9	6.5	4.6	3.3	2.4
Female - Femmes	84.0	79.3	74.3	69.3	64.4	59.4	54.5	49.6	44.7	39.8	35.1	30.4	25.8	21.4	17.1	13.2	9.8	6.9	4.8	3.3	2.3
Japan - Japon[27]																					
2016																					
Male - Hommes	81.0	76.2	71.2	66.3	61.3	56.5	51.6	46.8	42.0	37.2	32.5	28.0	23.7	19.6	15.7	12.1	8.9	6.3	4.3	2.9	1.9
Female - Femmes	87.1	82.4	77.4	72.4	67.5	62.5	57.6	52.7	47.8	43.0	38.2	33.5	28.9	24.4	20.0	15.8	11.8	8.4	5.6	3.7	2.5
Jordan - Jordanie[28]																					
2012																					
Male - Hommes	72.7	69.1	64.2	59.3	54.4	49.6	44.8	40.0	35.2	30.5	26.0	21.7	17.8	14.2	10.9	8.2	6.0	...	...	...	...
Female - Femmes	76.7	73.1	68.1	63.2	58.2	53.3	48.4	43.6	38.7	33.9	29.3	24.7	20.3	16.2	12.4	9.2	6.8	...	...	...	...
2016																					
Male - Hommes	72.8	...	...	...	...	...	...	...	...	...	...	...	...	...	...	...	...	...	...	...	...
Female - Femmes	74.2	...	...	...	...	...	...	...	...	...	...	...	...	...	...	...	...	...	...	...	...
Kazakhstan																					
2017																					
Male - Hommes	68.7	64.5	59.6	54.7	49.9	45.2	40.6	36.1	31.8	27.6	23.6	19.8	16.3	13.2	10.6	8.3	6.5	5.1	4.6	4.6	3.0
Female - Femmes	76.9	72.6	67.7	62.8	57.9	53.1	48.2	43.4	38.8	34.2	29.7	25.3	21.0	17.1	13.4	10.0	7.2	4.8	3.4	2.5	1.9

22. Life expectancy at specified ages for each sex: latest available year, 1998 - 2017
Espérance de vie à un âge donné pour chaque sexe : dernière année disponible, 1998 - 2017 (continued - suite)

Continent, country or area and date / Continent, pays ou zone et date	Age (in years) - Age (en années)																				
	0	5	10	15	20	25	30	35	40	45	50	55	60	65	70	75	80	85	90	95	100
ASIA - ASIE																					
Kuwait - Koweït																					
2016																					
Male - Hommes	81.0	...	...	...	...	...	...	...	...	...	...	...	...	...	...	...	...	...	...	...	...
Female - Femmes	80.5	...	...	...	...	...	...	...	...	...	...	...	...	...	...	...	...	...	...	...	...
Kyrgyzstan - Kirghizstan																					
2016																					
Male - Hommes	67.0	63.5	58.6	53.7	48.9	44.1	39.4	34.8	30.4	26.2	22.1	18.1	14.3	10.9	7.6	5.5	4.2	3.6	3.0	2.4	1.9
Female - Femmes	75.1	71.5	66.5	61.6	56.8	51.9	47.1	42.3	37.6	33.0	28.4	23.9	19.7	15.8	12.2	9.0	6.4	4.9	4.0	3.0	1.8
Lao People's Democratic Republic - République démocratique populaire lao[29]																					
2015																					
Male - Hommes	61.8	...	...	...	...	...	...	...	...	...	...	...	...	...	...	...	...	...	...	...	...
Female - Femmes	65.2	...	...	...	...	...	...	...	...	...	...	...	...	...	...	...	...	...	...	...	...
Malaysia - Malaisie																					
2017																					
Male - Hommes	72.7	68.2	63.3	58.4	53.7	49.0	44.2	39.5	34.9	30.5	26.2	22.2	18.4	15.0	11.7	8.7	6.2	...	...	...	...
Female - Femmes	77.4	72.9	68.0	63.1	58.2	53.3	48.4	43.6	38.8	34.2	29.6	25.2	21.0	17.1	13.4	9.9	7.0	...	...	...	...
Maldives																					
2015																					
Male - Hommes	73.1	69.0	64.0	59.1	54.3	49.4	44.6	39.7	34.8	29.9	25.2	20.7	16.2	11.9	7.9	4.7	...	...	...	...	...
Female - Femmes	74.6	70.3	65.4	60.5	55.6	50.7	45.7	40.7	35.8	31.0	26.1	21.4	16.7	12.2	7.8	4.4	...	...	...	...	...
2016																					
Male - Hommes	73.0	...	...	...	...	...	...	...	...	...	...	...	...	...	...	...	...	...	...	...	...
Female - Femmes	74.7	...	...	...	...	...	...	...	...	...	...	...	...	...	...	...	...	...	...	...	...
Mongolia - Mongolie																					
2017																					
Male - Hommes	65.9	62.5	57.7	52.9	48.2	43.6	39.1	34.8	30.7	26.8	23.2	20.0	17.2	14.6	12.4	...	...	...	...	...	...
Female - Femmes	75.4	72.0	67.1	62.2	57.4	52.6	47.8	43.1	38.5	34.0	29.7	25.6	21.8	18.3	15.3	...	...	...	...	...	...
Myanmar[30]																					
2015																					
Male - Hommes	59.7	59.4	54.9	50.2	45.6	41.1	37.0	33.2	29.7	26.3	23.0	19.6	16.4	13.3	10.6	8.0	6.0	4.6	...	...	...
Female - Femmes	69.3	68.6	64.0	59.3	54.5	49.8	45.2	40.6	36.1	31.7	27.3	23.1	19.2	15.5	12.2	9.1	6.5	5.0	...	...	...
Nepal - Népal																					
2011																					
Male - Hommes	65.4	...	...	...	...	...	...	...	...	...	...	...	...	...	...	...	...	...	...	...	...
Female - Femmes	67.9	...	...	...	...	...	...	...	...	...	...	...	...	...	...	...	...	...	...	...	...
Oman																					
2013																					
Male - Hommes	74.8	70.9	66.0	61.1	56.4	51.8	47.1	42.4	37.6	33.0	28.5	24.3	20.4	16.9	13.6	10.4	...	...	...	...	...
Female - Femmes	78.5	74.3	69.4	64.4	59.5	54.6	49.7	44.8	39.9	35.1	30.5	25.9	21.6	17.5	13.8	10.2	...	...	...	...	...
2017[31]																					
Male - Hommes	74.8	...	...	...	...	...	...	...	...	...	...	...	...	...	...	...	...	...	...	...	...
Female - Femmes	79.2	...	...	...	...	...	...	...	...	...	...	...	...	...	...	...	...	...	...	...	...
Pakistan[32]																					
2007																					
Male - Hommes	63.6	65.3	60.7	55.9	51.3	46.7	42.2	37.7	33.3	29.0	25.0	21.3	18.1	15.2	12.7	10.8	9.2	7.3	...	...	...
Female - Femmes	67.6	68.6	64.1	59.5	54.9	50.3	45.7	41.1	36.5	32.1	27.7	23.5	19.6	16.2	13.4	10.9	8.6	6.1	...	...	...
Qatar																					
2015																					
Male - Hommes	77.5	73.1	68.2	63.3	58.9	54.5	49.8	45.1	40.4	35.6	31.2	26.9	22.9	22.3	18.6	15.2	12.3	...	...	...	...
Female - Femmes	82.1	77.8	72.8	67.9	62.9	57.9	53.1	48.2	43.3	38.5	33.8	29.3	25.0	21.3	18.2	16.5	14.9	...	...	...	...
2016																					
Male - Hommes	78.9	...	...	...	...	...	...	...	...	...	...	...	...	...	...	...	...	...	...	...	...
Female - Femmes	82.3	...	...	...	...	...	...	...	...	...	...	...	...	...	...	...	...	...	...	...	...
Republic of Korea - République de Corée																					
2016																					
Male - Hommes	79.3	74.6	69.6	64.7	59.8	54.9	50.0	45.2	40.4	35.7	31.1	26.7	22.5	18.4	14.5	11.0	8.1	5.8	4.1	2.9	...
Female - Femmes	85.4	80.7	75.7	70.7	65.8	60.9	55.9	51.1	46.2	41.4	36.6	31.9	27.2	22.6	18.1	13.9	10.2	7.1	4.9	3.3	...

22. Life expectancy at specified ages for each sex: latest available year, 1998 - 2017
Espérance de vie à un âge donné pour chaque sexe : dernière année disponible, 1998 - 2017 (continued - suite)

Continent, country or area and date / Continent, pays ou zone et date	\multicolumn{21}{c}{Age (in years) - Age (en années)}
	0	5	10	15	20	25	30	35	40	45	50	55	60	65	70	75	80	85	90	95	100
ASIA - ASIE																					
Saudi Arabia - Arabie saoudite[33]																					
2016																					
Male - Hommes	73.5	...	...	...	...	...	...	...	...	...	...	...	...	...	...	...	...	...	...	...	...
Female - Femmes	74.8	...	...	...	...	...	...	...	...	...	...	...	...	...	...	...	...	...	...	...	...
Singapore - Singapour[34]																					
2017																					
Male - Hommes	80.7	76.0	71.0	66.0	61.1	56.2	51.3	46.4	41.6	36.8	32.1	27.6	23.2	19.1	15.3	11.8	8.8	6.4	4.5	3.1	2.1
Female - Femmes	85.2	80.5	75.5	70.5	65.6	60.6	55.7	50.8	45.8	41.0	36.2	31.5	27.0	22.5	18.3	14.2	10.7	7.8	5.5	3.8	2.6
Sri Lanka																					
2000 - 2002																					
Male - Hommes	68.8	...	...	...	...	...	...	...	...	...	...	...	...	...	...	...	...	...	...	...	...
Female - Femmes	77.2	...	...	...	...	...	...	...	...	...	...	...	...	...	...	...	...	...	...	...	...
State of Palestine - État de Palestine																					
2001																					
Male - Hommes	70.5	67.5	62.7	57.8	53.1	48.4	43.6	38.9	34.2	29.6	25.2	21.1	17.2	13.8	10.7	8.1	6.1	...	...	...	...
Female - Femmes	73.6	70.3	65.5	60.5	55.7	50.9	46.1	41.3	36.6	32.0	27.5	23.2	19.0	15.2	11.7	8.8	6.4	...	...	...	...
2016																					
Male - Hommes	72.1	...	...	...	...	...	...	...	...	...	...	...	...	...	...	...	...	...	...	...	...
Female - Femmes	75.2	...	...	...	...	...	...	...	...	...	...	...	...	...	...	...	...	...	...	...	...
Tajikistan - Tadjikistan																					
2008																					
Male - Hommes	69.7	67.9	63.0	58.1	53.3	48.5	43.7	39.1	34.6	30.1	25.7	21.6	17.9	14.7	12.2	10.4	9.2	...	...	...	...
Female - Femmes	74.8	72.5	67.6	62.7	57.8	52.9	48.1	43.4	38.6	33.9	29.4	25.0	21.0	17.5	14.7	12.5	11.1	...	...	...	...
2016																					
Male - Hommes	71.9	...	...	...	...	...	...	...	...	...	...	...	...	...	...	...	...	...	...	...	...
Female - Femmes	75.7	...	...	...	...	...	...	...	...	...	...	...	...	...	...	...	...	...	...	...	...
Thailand - Thaïlande																					
2005 - 2006																					
Male - Hommes	69.9	...	...	...	...	...	...	...	...	...	...	...	...	...	...	...	...	...	...	...	...
Female - Femmes	77.6	...	...	...	...	...	...	...	...	...	...	...	...	...	...	...	...	...	...	...	...
Turkey - Turquie																					
2014 - 2016																					
Male - Hommes	75.3	71.3	66.4	61.5	56.7	51.9	47.1	42.3	37.5	32.8	28.2	23.9	19.8	16.1	12.7	9.7	7.2	5.2	3.9	3.2	3.2
Female - Femmes	80.7	76.7	71.8	66.8	61.9	57.0	52.1	47.2	42.3	37.5	32.7	28.1	23.6	19.3	15.3	11.7	8.7	6.4	4.9	4.1	4.3
United Arab Emirates - Émirats arabes unis																					
2006																					
Male - Hommes	76.7	72.5	67.6	62.7	57.9	53.1	48.3	43.5	38.7	33.9	29.3	24.8	20.7	16.9	13.8	11.3	10.2	...	...	...	...
Female - Femmes	78.8	74.5	69.5	64.6	59.7	54.8	49.8	44.9	40.0	35.2	30.4	25.8	21.6	18.0	15.4	14.0	14.5	...	...	...	...
Uzbekistan - Ouzbékistan																					
2015																					
Male - Hommes	71.2	67.4	62.5	57.7	52.8	48.1	43.4	38.7	34.1	29.7	25.4	21.3	17.5	14.2	11.4	9.0	7.4	7.7	...	...	...
Female - Femmes	76.0	72.1	67.1	62.2	57.4	52.6	47.8	43.0	38.2	33.6	29.0	24.6	20.4	16.6	13.4	10.6	8.6	8.2	...	...	...
2017																					
Male - Hommes	71.3	...	...	...	...	...	...	...	...	...	...	...	...	...	...	...	...	...	...	...	...
Female - Femmes	76.1	...	...	...	...	...	...	...	...	...	...	...	...	...	...	...	...	...	...	...	...
Viet Nam																					
2016																					
Male - Hommes	70.8	67.8	63.0	58.2	53.4	48.7	43.9	39.2	34.6	30.1	25.8	21.9	18.3	15.0	12.3	10.0	8.3	...	...	...	...
Female - Femmes	76.1	72.3	67.3	62.4	57.5	52.6	47.8	42.9	38.2	33.5	29.0	24.7	20.6	16.9	13.6	11.0	8.9	...	...	...	...
Yemen - Yémen																					
2004																					
Male - Hommes	60.2	...	...	...	...	...	...	...	...	...	...	...	...	...	...	...	...	...	...	...	...
Female - Femmes	62.0	...	...	...	...	...	...	...	...	...	...	...	...	...	...	...	...	...	...	...	...
EUROPE																					
Åland Islands - Îles d'Åland																					
2016																					
Male - Hommes	78.5	74.0	69.0	64.0	59.4	54.4	49.7	45.2	40.7	35.9	31.2	26.8	22.5	18.4	14.5	11.1	7.8	4.9	3.2	1.5	1.0
Female - Femmes	83.6	78.6	73.6	68.6	63.6	58.6	54.0	49.3	44.6	39.8	35.4	30.4	25.8	21.4	17.2	13.0	9.8	6.6	3.8	2.7	1.2

Continent, country or area and date / Continent, pays ou zone et date	Age (in years) - Age (en années)																				
	0	5	10	15	20	25	30	35	40	45	50	55	60	65	70	75	80	85	90	95	100
EUROPE																					
Albania - Albanie																					
2016																					
Male - Hommes	77.0	72.8	67.9	63.0	58.1	53.2	48.4	43.5	38.8	34.2	29.6	25.2	20.9	16.9	13.2	9.7	6.9	4.7	...	...	...
Female - Femmes	80.1	75.9	70.9	66.0	61.1	56.2	51.3	46.4	41.6	36.7	32.0	27.3	22.7	18.3	14.0	10.1	6.8	3.9	...	...	...
Austria - Autriche																					
2016																					
Male - Hommes	79.1	74.5	69.5	64.5	59.6	54.8	49.9	45.1	40.3	35.5	30.9	26.4	22.2	18.3	14.7	11.4	8.3	5.7	3.8	2.5	...
Female - Femmes	84.0	79.2	74.3	69.3	64.4	59.4	54.5	49.6	44.7	39.8	35.1	30.4	25.9	21.5	17.4	13.5	9.8	6.7	4.4	3.0	...
Belarus - Bélarus																					
2016																					
Male - Hommes	68.9	64.3	59.3	54.4	49.5	44.7	40.0	35.5	31.1	26.8	22.9	19.2	15.8	12.9	10.3	8.0	6.1	4.6	3.4	2.4	1.7
Female - Femmes	79.0	74.3	69.3	64.3	59.4	54.5	49.6	44.8	40.1	35.4	30.9	26.4	22.1	18.0	14.1	10.6	7.6	5.3	3.5	2.3	1.4
Belgium - Belgique[9]																					
2015																					
Male - Hommes	78.5	73.9	68.9	63.9	59.0	54.2	49.4	44.6	39.8	35.1	30.5	26.0	21.9	18.0	14.4	11.0	8.1	5.6	3.8	2.6	1.8
Female - Femmes	83.1	78.4	73.5	68.5	63.6	58.6	53.7	48.8	43.9	39.1	34.4	29.9	25.4	21.2	17.1	13.2	9.6	6.6	4.3	2.9	1.9
Bosnia and Herzegovina - Bosnie-Herzégovine																					
2003																					
Male - Hommes	71.3	...	...	...	...	...	...	...	...	...	...	...	...	...	...	...	...	...	...	...	...
Female - Femmes	76.7	...	...	...	...	...	...	...	...	...	...	...	...	...	...	...	...	...	...	...	...
Bulgaria - Bulgarie																					
2014 - 2016																					
Male - Hommes	71.2	66.8	61.9	57.0	52.2	47.4	42.6	37.9	33.2	28.7	24.5	20.7	17.2	14.1	11.2	8.6	6.3	4.5	3.1	2.0	0.5
Female - Femmes	78.2	73.7	68.8	63.8	58.9	54.0	49.2	44.3	39.5	34.8	30.3	25.9	21.7	17.6	13.8	10.2	7.2	4.9	3.3	2.1	0.5
Croatia - Croatie																					
2014																					
Male - Hommes	74.7	...	...	...	...	...	...	...	...	...	...	...	...	...	...	...	...	...	...	...	...
Female - Femmes	81.0	...	...	...	...	...	...	...	...	...	...	...	...	...	...	...	...	...	...	...	...
Czechia - Tchéquie																					
2016																					
Male - Hommes	76.2	71.5	66.5	61.6	56.7	51.9	47.0	42.2	37.5	32.8	28.2	23.9	19.9	16.3	13.1	10.2	7.7	5.7	4.1	2.8	1.9
Female - Femmes	82.1	77.3	72.3	67.4	62.4	57.5	52.6	47.7	42.8	38.0	33.3	28.7	24.2	19.9	15.9	12.2	9.0	6.3	4.1	2.6	1.6
Denmark - Danemark[35]																					
2015 - 2016																					
Male - Hommes	78.8	74.2	69.2	64.2	59.3	54.4	49.6	44.7	39.9	35.1	30.6	26.1	22.0	18.1	14.4	11.0	8.0	5.6	3.8	2.6	...
Female - Femmes	82.8	78.1	73.1	68.2	63.2	58.3	53.3	48.4	43.5	38.7	33.9	29.3	24.9	20.7	16.7	12.9	9.5	6.8	4.6	3.1	...
Estonia - Estonie																					
2016																					
Male - Hommes	73.2	68.4	63.5	58.5	53.6	48.9	44.2	39.6	35.0	30.6	26.3	22.3	18.6	15.4	12.4	9.7	7.4	5.4	3.8	2.5	1.6
Female - Femmes	81.9	77.1	72.1	67.1	62.3	57.5	52.6	47.8	43.1	38.3	33.6	29.0	24.7	20.5	16.4	12.6	9.1	6.3	4.3	2.8	1.8
Faeroe Islands - Îles Féroé																					
2016 - 2017																					
Male - Hommes	80.9	76.1	71.1	66.1	61.1	56.4	51.4	46.4	41.4	36.4	31.7	27.2	22.7	18.3	14.7	11.2	7.7	6.2	4.3	3.3	2.0
Female - Femmes	83.7	79.2	74.2	69.2	64.4	59.4	54.6	49.6	44.8	39.8	34.8	30.3	25.8	21.6	17.4	13.1	10.1	7.0	4.5	2.3	2.0
Finland - Finlande[36]																					
2016																					
Male - Hommes	78.4	73.6	68.7	63.7	58.8	54.0	49.2	44.4	39.7	35.0	30.5	26.1	21.9	18.0	14.4	11.0	8.0	5.5	3.7	2.5	1.7
Female - Femmes	84.1	79.3	74.3	69.4	64.4	59.5	54.6	49.7	44.8	40.0	35.2	30.5	26.0	21.6	17.4	13.4	9.8	6.7	4.4	2.8	1.9
France[9]																					
2012 - 2015																					
Male - Hommes	79.1	74.4	69.4	64.5	59.6	54.8	49.9	45.2	40.4	35.8	31.3	27.0	22.9	19.1	15.5	12.0	8.8	6.1	4.1	2.9	2.3
Female - Femmes	85.1	80.5	75.5	70.5	65.6	60.6	55.7	50.8	45.9	41.1	36.4	31.9	27.4	23.0	18.7	14.6	10.8	7.5	5.0	3.2	2.2
Germany - Allemagne																					
2013 - 2015																					
Male - Hommes	78.2	73.5	68.5	63.6	58.7	53.8	48.9	44.1	39.3	34.6	30.0	25.6	21.5	17.7	14.1	10.8	7.8	5.4	3.7	2.6	1.8
Female - Femmes	83.1	78.4	73.4	68.4	63.5	58.5	53.6	48.7	43.8	39.0	34.2	29.6	25.2	20.9	16.8	12.9	9.3	6.4	4.2	2.9	2.0
Gibraltar																					
2001																					
Male - Hommes	78.5	73.5	68.5	63.5	58.5	53.5	...	43.5	...	33.9	...	25.8	...	17.9	...	11.3	...	...	...	...	...
Female - Femmes	83.3	79.5	75.0	70.0	65.0	60.0	...	50.3	...	40.3	...	30.3	...	20.6	...	13.7	...	...	...	...	...

22. Life expectancy at specified ages for each sex: latest available year, 1998 - 2017
Espérance de vie à un âge donné pour chaque sexe : dernière année disponible, 1998 - 2017 (continued - suite)

Continent, country or area and date / Continent, pays ou zone et date	0	5	10	15	20	25	30	35	40	45	50	55	60	65	70	75	80	85	90	95	100
EUROPE																					
Greece - Grèce																					
2016																					
Male - Hommes	78.4	73.9	68.9	64.0	59.1	54.2	49.4	44.6	39.8	35.1	30.6	26.3	22.2	18.4	14.8	11.5	8.5	6.3	4.6	3.3	2.3
Female - Femmes	83.4	78.7	73.7	68.8	63.8	58.9	54.0	49.0	44.2	39.4	34.6	29.9	25.4	20.9	16.7	12.7	9.2	6.6	4.8	3.4	2.3
Hungary - Hongrie																					
2016																					
Male - Hommes	72.4	67.8	62.8	57.9	53.0	48.1	43.3	38.5	33.7	29.1	24.7	20.9	17.4	14.4	11.6	8.9	6.6	4.4	2.7	1.5	0.6
Female - Femmes	79.2	74.6	69.6	64.6	59.7	54.7	49.8	44.9	40.1	35.3	30.6	26.2	22.1	18.2	14.4	10.8	7.7	5.0	2.9	1.5	0.6
Iceland - Islande																					
2015 - 2016																					
Male - Hommes	80.7	75.9	70.9	66.0	61.2	56.3	51.5	46.7	42.0	37.2	32.5	27.8	23.4	19.0	15.0	11.5	8.1	5.4	3.6	2.5	1.5
Female - Femmes	83.7	78.9	73.9	68.9	64.0	59.0	54.1	49.1	44.2	39.4	34.6	29.9	25.4	21.0	16.8	13.1	9.6	6.7	4.3	2.8	1.5
Ireland - Irlande																					
2005 - 2007																					
Male - Hommes	76.8	72.2	67.2	62.3	57.5	52.8	48.0	43.3	38.5	33.8	29.2	24.8	20.6	16.6	13.0	9.8	7.1	5.1	3.6	2.6	1.9
Female - Femmes	81.6	76.9	72.0	67.0	62.1	57.2	52.3	47.4	42.5	37.7	33.1	28.5	24.0	19.8	15.8	12.1	8.8	6.2	4.3	3.1	2.1
2014[9]																					
Male - Hommes	79.3	...	...	...	...	...	...	...	...	...	...	...	...	...	...	...	...	...	...	...	...
Female - Femmes	83.5	...	...	...	...	...	...	...	...	...	...	...	...	...	...	...	...	...	...	...	...
Italy - Italie																					
2016																					
Male - Hommes	80.6	75.9	70.9	65.9	61.0	56.1	51.3	46.4	41.6	36.8	32.1	27.6	23.2	19.1	15.2	11.7	8.5	5.9	4.0	2.8	1.9
Female - Femmes	85.0	80.3	75.4	70.4	65.4	60.5	55.5	50.6	45.7	40.9	36.1	31.4	26.8	22.3	18.1	14.0	10.3	7.2	4.8	3.3	2.2
Latvia - Lettonie																					
2016																					
Male - Hommes	69.8	65.1	60.1	55.1	50.3	45.6	41.1	36.6	32.2	28.1	24.1	20.3	16.9	13.9	11.3	9.0	6.7	4.9	3.4	...	...
Female - Femmes	79.4	74.8	69.9	64.9	60.0	55.1	50.3	45.4	40.7	36.0	31.5	27.1	22.9	18.8	15.0	11.5	8.3	5.7	4.0	...	...
Lithuania - Lituanie																					
2016																					
Male - Hommes	69.5	64.9	59.9	55.0	50.1	45.4	40.7	36.3	32.0	27.9	24.0	20.4	17.0	14.1	11.5	9.1	6.9	4.9	3.4	2.3	1.8
Female - Femmes	80.0	75.4	70.5	65.5	60.6	55.6	50.8	45.9	41.2	36.5	32.0	27.6	23.3	19.2	15.4	11.7	8.5	5.7	3.9	2.6	1.7
Luxembourg																					
2014 - 2016																					
Male - Hommes	84.6	79.8	74.8	69.8	64.9	59.9	54.9	50.0	45.1	40.3	35.5	30.7	26.2	21.8	17.6	13.8	10.1	7.0	4.6	...	...
Female - Femmes	85.4	80.6	75.6	70.6	65.7	60.7	55.8	50.8	45.9	41.1	36.3	31.5	27.0	22.6	18.4	14.5	10.9	7.8	5.2	...	...
Malta - Malte																					
2016																					
Male - Hommes	80.6	76.3	71.4	66.4	61.5	56.5	51.7	46.8	42.0	37.2	32.6	28.2	23.9	19.7	15.8	12.2	9.0	...	...	...	...
Female - Femmes	84.4	79.9	74.9	70.0	65.1	60.1	55.2	50.2	45.5	40.5	35.8	31.1	26.6	22.1	18.0	14.1	10.4	...	...	...	...
Netherlands - Pays-Bas																					
2009																					
Male - Hommes	78.5	73.8	68.8	63.9	59.0	54.1	49.2	44.4	39.5	34.8	30.1	25.6	21.4	17.3	13.6	10.3	7.5	5.3	3.6	2.6	...
Female - Femmes	82.7	77.8	72.8	67.9	62.9	58.0	53.1	48.2	43.3	38.5	33.8	29.3	24.9	20.6	16.5	12.7	9.2	6.4	4.3	2.9	...
2014																					
Male - Hommes	80.0	...	...	...	...	...	...	...	...	...	...	...	...	...	...	...	...	...	...	...	...
Female - Femmes	83.5	...	...	...	...	...	...	...	...	...	...	...	...	...	...	...	...	...	...	...	...
Norway - Norvège																					
2012																					
Male - Hommes	79.4	74.7	69.7	64.8	59.8	55.0	50.2	45.4	40.6	35.8	31.2	26.7	22.3	18.2	14.4	10.9	7.8	5.5	3.7	2.6	2.3
Female - Femmes	83.4	78.6	73.7	68.7	63.8	58.8	53.9	49.0	44.1	39.2	34.5	29.8	25.3	21.0	16.9	13.0	9.5	6.6	4.3	2.8	1.9
2014																					
Male - Hommes	80.1	...	...	...	...	...	...	...	...	...	...	...	...	...	...	...	...	...	...	...	...
Female - Femmes	84.2	...	...	...	...	...	...	...	...	...	...	...	...	...	...	...	...	...	...	...	...
Poland - Pologne																					
2016																					
Male - Hommes	73.9	69.3	64.4	59.4	54.5	49.8	45.0	40.3	35.7	31.2	26.9	22.9	19.3	16.0	13.0	10.3	7.9	5.9	4.4	3.2	2.4
Female - Femmes	81.9	77.3	72.3	67.3	62.4	57.5	52.5	47.6	42.8	38.0	33.3	28.8	24.5	20.4	16.5	12.8	9.5	6.9	4.9	3.4	2.4
Portugal																					
2014 - 2016																					
Male - Hommes	77.6	72.9	68.0	63.0	58.1	53.2	48.4	43.5	38.8	34.1	29.7	25.4	21.4	17.4	13.7	10.2	7.1	4.3	2.6	1.7	1.1
Female - Femmes	83.3	78.6	73.6	68.6	63.7	58.7	53.8	48.9	44.0	39.2	34.4	29.8	25.2	20.7	16.4	12.3	8.5	5.3	3.2	1.9	1.2

Continent, country or area and date / Continent, pays ou zone et date	Age (in years) - Age (en années)																				
	0	5	10	15	20	25	30	35	40	45	50	55	60	65	70	75	80	85	90	95	100
EUROPE																					
Republic of Moldova - République de Moldova[37]																					
2012																					
Male - Hommes	67.2	63.1	58.1	53.3	48.5	43.7	39.0	34.5	30.1	26.0	22.2	18.7	15.5	13.0	10.2	8.4	7.1	6.9	7.8	...	...
Female - Femmes	75.0	70.9	66.0	61.0	56.1	51.2	46.4	41.5	36.8	32.2	27.7	23.4	19.3	15.7	12.2	9.5	7.4	5.9	5.3	...	...
Romania - Roumanie																					
2013 - 2015																					
Male - Hommes	71.9	67.7	62.8	57.9	53.0	48.2	43.4	38.6	33.9	29.4	25.2	21.3	17.8	14.6	11.7	9.0	6.8	5.1	3.7	2.8	2.1
Female - Femmes	78.9	74.6	69.6	64.7	59.8	54.8	49.9	45.1	40.2	35.4	30.8	26.3	22.1	18.0	14.1	10.6	7.7	5.5	3.9	2.8	2.0
Russian Federation - Fédération de Russie																					
2012																					
Male - Hommes	64.6	60.3	55.4	50.5	45.8	41.3	37.0	33.1	29.3	25.4	21.8	18.4	15.4	12.8	10.2	8.1	6.4	5.1	4.0	3.0	1.4
Female - Femmes	75.9	71.6	66.7	61.7	56.9	52.1	47.3	42.8	38.2	33.7	29.3	25.1	21.0	17.1	13.4	10.2	7.4	5.3	3.8	2.8	1.8
San Marino - Saint-Marin																					
2017																					
Male - Hommes	82.7	77.9	72.9	67.9	63.0	58.2	53.3	48.3	43.4	38.5	33.7	29.0	24.6	20.2	16.1	12.2	8.9	6.4	4.2	2.2	...
Female - Femmes	86.8	82.0	77.0	72.0	67.1	62.1	57.1	52.2	47.2	42.4	37.6	32.8	28.1	23.5	19.1	14.8	10.8	7.4	4.8	2.7	...
Serbia - Serbie[38]																					
2016																					
Male - Hommes	72.7	68.2	63.3	58.3	53.5	48.6	43.8	39.0	34.3	29.7	25.3	21.3	17.6	14.3	11.2	8.5	6.1	4.3	...	...	...
Female - Femmes	77.8	73.2	68.3	63.3	58.3	53.4	48.5	43.6	38.8	34.0	29.4	25.0	20.7	16.7	12.9	9.4	6.6	4.5	...	...	...
Slovakia - Slovaquie																					
2016																					
Male - Hommes	73.7	69.2	64.3	59.3	54.4	49.6	44.8	40.0	35.3	30.7	26.3	22.2	18.5	15.1	12.1	9.3	7.0	5.0	3.4	2.3	1.5
Female - Femmes	80.4	75.8	70.9	65.9	61.0	56.1	51.2	46.3	41.4	36.7	32.0	27.4	23.0	18.9	14.9	11.3	8.0	5.4	3.4	2.0	1.2
Slovenia - Slovénie																					
2015 - 2016																					
Male - Hommes	77.6	72.8	67.8	62.9	58.0	53.2	48.3	43.5	38.7	34.0	29.5	25.2	21.1	17.4	13.8	10.6	7.7	5.5	4.0	2.9	2.0
Female - Femmes	83.5	78.7	73.7	68.7	63.8	58.8	53.9	49.0	44.1	39.2	34.5	29.9	25.3	21.0	16.9	13.0	9.4	6.4	4.2	3.0	2.1
Spain - Espagne																					
2016																					
Male - Hommes	80.3	75.6	70.6	65.7	60.7	55.8	50.9	46.0	41.2	36.4	31.8	27.3	23.1	19.1	15.4	11.9	8.8	6.2	4.3	3.2	1.9
Female - Femmes	85.8	81.1	76.1	71.1	66.2	61.2	56.3	51.3	46.4	41.6	36.8	32.1	27.5	23.1	18.7	14.5	10.7	7.4	5.0	3.4	2.1
Sweden - Suède																					
2012																					
Male - Hommes	79.9	75.1	70.2	65.2	60.3	55.5	50.7	45.8	41.0	36.2	31.5	27.0	22.6	18.4	14.5	11.0	7.9	5.4	3.6	2.4	1.6
Female - Femmes	83.5	78.8	73.8	68.8	63.9	59.0	54.0	49.1	44.2	39.4	34.6	30.0	25.4	21.0	16.9	13.0	9.5	6.5	4.3	2.9	1.9
2014																					
Male - Hommes	80.4	...	...	...	...	...	...	...	...	...	...	...	...	...	...	...	...	...	...	...	...
Female - Femmes	84.2	...	...	...	...	...	...	...	...	...	...	...	...	...	...	...	...	...	...	...	...
Switzerland - Suisse																					
2016																					
Male - Hommes	81.5	76.8	71.9	66.9	61.9	57.1	52.2	47.3	42.4	37.6	32.9	28.3	23.9	19.8	15.8	12.1	8.8	6.0	4.0	2.8	1.9
Female - Femmes	85.3	80.6	75.6	70.7	65.7	60.8	55.8	50.9	46.0	41.1	36.3	31.6	27.0	22.6	18.3	14.2	10.4	7.2	4.7	3.1	2.2
TFYR of Macedonia - L'ex-R. y. de Macédoine																					
2015																					
Male - Hommes	73.4	69.3	64.4	59.4	54.6	49.7	44.8	40.0	35.2	30.5	26.0	21.8	17.9	14.4	11.2	8.3	5.8	3.9	2.6	2.4	...
Female - Femmes	77.4	73.2	68.3	63.3	58.4	53.5	48.5	43.6	38.8	34.0	29.3	24.7	20.4	16.2	12.4	9.0	6.2	4.2	2.9	2.7	...
Ukraine[39]																					
2016																					
Male - Hommes	66.7	62.4	57.4	52.5	47.7	43.0	38.4	34.0	29.9	25.9	22.1	18.6	15.3	12.5	10.0	7.9	6.1	4.8	3.8	3.0	2.1
Female - Femmes	76.5	72.1	67.1	62.2	57.3	52.4	47.6	42.8	38.2	33.6	29.2	24.8	20.6	16.6	13.0	9.7	7.0	5.0	3.4	2.3	1.5
United Kingdom of Great Britain and Northern Ireland - Royaume-Uni de Grande-Bretagne et d'Irlande du Nord[40]																					
2014 - 2016																					
Male - Hommes	79.2	74.6	69.6	64.6	59.7	54.9	50.0	45.2	40.5	35.8	31.3	26.8	22.6	18.5	14.8	11.3	8.3	5.9	4.0	2.8	2.1
Female - Femmes	82.9	78.2	73.2	68.3	63.3	58.4	53.5	48.6	43.7	39.0	34.3	29.7	25.2	20.9	16.8	13.1	9.7	6.8	4.6	3.2	2.2

22. Life expectancy at specified ages for each sex: latest available year, 1998 - 2017
Espérance de vie à un âge donné pour chaque sexe : dernière année disponible, 1998 - 2017 (continued - suite)

Continent, country or area and date / Continent, pays ou zone et date	0	5	10	15	20	25	30	35	40	45	50	55	60	65	70	75	80	85	90	95	100
OCEANIA - OCÉANIE																					
American Samoa - Samoas américaines																					
2011																					
Male - Hommes	71.1	66.8	61.9	57.0	52.2	47.4	42.6	38.0	33.5	29.1	25.3	21.4	18.0	14.6	11.7	9.6	...	...	...	...	...
Female - Femmes	77.8	73.3	68.3	63.4	58.5	53.6	48.9	44.4	39.6	35.0	30.6	26.5	22.8	19.2	16.1	13.8	...	...	...	...	...
Australia - Australie																					
2014 - 2016																					
Male - Hommes	80.5	75.8	70.8	65.9	61.0	56.2	51.3	46.6	41.8	37.1	32.6	28.1	23.8	19.6	15.7	12.1	8.9	6.2	4.3	3.0	2.1
Female - Femmes	84.6	79.9	74.9	70.0	65.0	60.1	55.2	50.3	45.4	40.6	35.9	31.3	26.7	22.3	18.0	14.0	10.4	7.3	4.9	3.3	2.3
Cook Islands - Îles Cook[41]																					
2006																					
Male - Hommes	69.5	66.0	61.3	56.5	52.0	47.4	42.8	38.1	33.6	29.1	24.8	20.9	17.5	14.3	11.4	9.0	7.3	...	...	...	...
Female - Femmes	76.2	72.4	67.4	62.4	57.4	52.7	48.0	43.2	38.4	33.6	29.1	24.7	20.4	16.4	12.6	9.5	6.9	...	...	...	...
Fiji - Fidji																					
2007																					
Male - Hommes	65.3	...	...	...	...	...	...	...	...	...	...	...	...	...	...	...	...	...	...	...	...
Female - Femmes	69.6	...	...	...	...	...	...	...	...	...	...	...	...	...	...	...	...	...	...	...	...
French Polynesia - Polynésie française																					
2012																					
Male - Hommes	73.3	69.6	64.6	59.8	55.0	50.3	45.7	41.0	36.2	31.6	27.1	22.7	18.3	14.8	11.4	8.5	6.5	4.7	...	...	...
Female - Femmes	78.2	73.8	68.8	63.9	59.1	54.1	49.3	44.5	39.7	35.0	30.4	26.1	22.0	17.9	14.2	10.6	7.6	5.0	...	...	...
2015																					
Male - Hommes	74.4	...	...	...	...	...	...	...	...	...	...	...	...	...	...	...	...	...	...	...	...
Female - Femmes	78.1	...	...	...	...	...	...	...	...	...	...	...	...	...	...	...	...	...	...	...	...
Guam																					
2017																					
Male - Hommes	73.6	...	...	...	...	...	...	...	...	...	...	...	...	...	...	...	...	...	...	...	...
Female - Femmes	78.6	...	...	...	...	...	...	...	...	...	...	...	...	...	...	...	...	...	...	...	...
Kiribati																					
2005																					
Male - Hommes	58.9	58.2	53.6	48.9	44.4	40.0	35.6	31.3	27.1	23.1	19.4	16.0	13.0	10.4	8.3	6.6	5.3	4.2	...	...	...
Female - Femmes	63.1	62.6	57.9	53.1	48.6	44.1	39.7	35.4	31.2	27.1	23.2	19.5	16.1	13.1	10.4	8.1	6.2	4.7	...	...	...
Marshall Islands - Îles Marshall																					
2004																					
Male - Hommes	67.0	...	...	...	...	...	...	...	...	...	...	...	...	...	...	...	...	...	...	...	...
Female - Femmes	70.6	...	...	...	...	...	...	...	...	...	...	...	...	...	...	...	...	...	...	...	...
Micronesia (Federated States of) - Micronésie (États fédérés de)																					
2000																					
Male - Hommes	66.5	...	...	...	...	...	...	...	...	...	...	...	...	...	...	...	...	...	...	...	...
Female - Femmes	67.5	...	...	...	...	...	...	...	...	...	...	...	...	...	...	...	...	...	...	...	...
Nauru[42]																					
2011																					
Male - Hommes	56.8	...	...	...	...	...	...	...	...	...	...	...	...	...	...	...	...	...	...	...	...
Female - Femmes	62.7	...	...	...	...	...	...	...	...	...	...	...	...	...	...	...	...	...	...	...	...
New Caledonia - Nouvelle-Calédonie																					
2012																					
Male - Hommes	74.0	69.4	64.6	59.7	55.3	51.1	46.7	42.0	37.3	32.9	28.5	...	20.1	...	13.1	...	7.5	...	...	...	...
Female - Femmes	80.4	75.7	70.8	65.8	61.0	56.0	51.1	46.2	41.5	36.7	32.1	...	23.5	...	15.2	...	8.9	...	...	...	...
New Zealand - Nouvelle-Zélande																					
2015 - 2017																					
Male - Hommes	80.0	75.4	70.5	65.5	60.7	55.9	51.1	46.3	41.6	36.9	32.3	27.8	23.5	19.4	15.5	11.9	8.8	6.2	4.4	...	...
Female - Femmes	83.4	78.8	73.8	68.9	64.0	59.1	54.2	49.3	44.5	39.7	35.0	30.4	25.9	21.5	17.3	13.5	9.9	7.0	4.8	...	...
Niue - Nioué																					
2007 - 2011																					
Male - Hommes	70.1	...	...	...	...	...	...	...	...	...	...	...	...	...	...	...	...	...	...	...	...
Female - Femmes	76.3	...	...	...	...	...	...	...	...	...	...	...	...	...	...	...	...	...	...	...	...

Continent, country or area and date / Continent, pays ou zone et date	0	5	10	15	20	25	30	35	40	45	50	55	60	65	70	75	80	85	90	95	100

Age (in years) - Age (en années)

OCEANIA - OCÉANIE

Northern Mariana Islands - Îles Mariannes septentrionales

2009

	0	5	10	15	20	25	30	35	40	45	50	55	60	65	70	75	80	85	90	95	100
Male - Hommes	74.5	...	...	...	...	...	...	...	...	...	...	...	...	...	...	...	...	...	...	...	...
Female - Femmes	79.9	...	...	...	...	...	...	...	...	...	...	...	...	...	...	...	...	...	...	...	...

Palau - Palaos

2005

Male - Hommes	66.3	...	...	...	...	...	...	...	...	...	...	...	...	...	...	...	...	...	...	...	...
Female - Femmes	72.1	...	...	...	...	...	...	...	...	...	...	...	...	...	...	...	...	...	...	...	...

Papua New Guinea - Papouasie-Nouvelle-Guinée

2000

Male - Hommes	53.7	54.1	50.2	45.7	41.6	37.7	33.7	29.8	25.9	22.1	18.5	15.0	11.9	9.2	6.9	5.0	3.6	2.6	1.7	0.6	...
Female - Femmes	54.8	54.7	50.8	46.3	42.1	38.1	34.1	30.1	26.2	22.3	18.6	15.2	12.0	9.2	6.8	5.0	3.6	2.5	1.6	0.6	...

Samoa

2006

Male - Hommes	71.5	...	...	...	...	...	...	...	...	...	...	...	...	...	...	...	...	...	...	...	...
Female - Femmes	74.2	...	...	...	...	...	...	...	...	...	...	...	...	...	...	...	...	...	...	...	...

Solomon Islands - Îles Salomon

2009

Male - Hommes	66.2	...	...	...	...	...	...	...	...	...	...	...	...	...	...	...	...	...	...	...	...
Female - Femmes	73.1	...	...	...	...	...	...	...	...	...	...	...	...	...	...	...	...	...	...	...	...

Tonga

2006

Male - Hommes	67.3	64.1	59.3	54.5	49.9	45.4	40.7	36.2	31.6	27.2	23.4	19.4	15.9	13.0	9.4	6.3	4.0	...	...	...	...
Female - Femmes	73.0	69.3	64.6	59.8	55.0	50.1	45.2	40.4	35.7	31.3	27.1	23.0	19.0	15.3	11.6	8.6	6.1	...	...	...	...

2010

Male - Hommes	65.0	...	...	...	...	...	...	...	...	...	...	...	...	...	...	...	...	...	...	...	...
Female - Femmes	69.0	...	...	...	...	...	...	...	...	...	...	...	...	...	...	...	...	...	...	...	...

Tuvalu

1997 - 2002

Male - Hommes	61.7	59.5	54.8	50.0	45.2	40.6	35.9	32.1	28.0	24.1	20.0	17.1	13.7	10.8	9.0	6.9	5.4	...	...	...	...
Female - Femmes	65.1	62.6	57.7	53.7	50.0	45.3	40.9	36.6	32.2	28.1	23.8	20.3	16.9	13.2	10.6	7.9	6.4	...	...	...	...

Vanuatu[43]

2009

Male - Hommes	69.6	66.4	61.6	56.8	52.1	47.5	42.8	38.1	33.5	29.0	24.7	20.6	16.8	13.4	10.4	7.9	6.0	...	...	...	...
Female - Femmes	72.7	69.3	64.5	59.5	54.7	49.9	45.1	40.3	35.5	30.8	26.3	22.0	18.0	14.4	11.2	8.5	6.4	...	...	...	...

Wallis and Futuna Islands - Îles Wallis et Futuna

2003

Male - Hommes	73.1	...	...	...	...	...	...	...	...	...	...	...	...	...	...	...	...	...	...	...	...
Female - Femmes	75.5	...	...	...	...	...	...	...	...	...	...	...	...	...	...	...	...	...	...	...	...

FOOTNOTES - NOTES

[1] Data refer to Algerian population only. - Les données ne concernent que la population algérienne.

[2] Based on the results of the Population Census. - D'après les résultats du recensement de la population.

[3] Source: Botswana Population Projections 2011-2026. - Source: Botswana Population Projections 2011-2026.

[4] Based on the results of the 2006 Population and Housing Census. - Données fondées sur les résultats du recensement de la population et de l'habitat de 2006.

[5] Source: Department of Statistics and Demographic Studies (DISED); 2002 EDAM-IS2 and 2002 EDSF/PAPFAM surveys - Source : Direction de la Statistique et des Etudes Démographiques (DISED); 2002 Enquête Djiboutienne auprès des Ménages (EDAM-IS2) et 2002 Enquête Djiboutienne sur la Sante de la Famille (EDSF/PAPFAM - 2002)

[6] Based on underlying data of the Population and Housing Census 2014. - Données fondées sur le recensement de la population de 2014.

[7] Data refer to the 12 months preceding the census in April. - Les données se rapportent aux douze mois précédant le recensement d'avril.

[8] Excludes the islands of St. Brandon and Agalega. - Non compris les îles St. Brandon et Agalega.

[9] Provisional data. - Données provisoires.

[10] Data refer to Saint Helenian resident population. - Pour la population résidante de Sainte-Hélène.

[11] Data refer to the 12 months preceding the census in November. - Données se rapportent aux 12 mois précédant le recensement de novembre.

[12] Based on underlying data of the 2002 Population Census. - Données fondées sur le recensement de la population de 2002.

[13] Based on the results of the 2014 Population Census. Provisional data. - D'après les résultats du recensement de la population de 2014. Données provisoires.

[14] Data are based on a small number of deaths. - Les données sont basées sur un nombre limité de décès.

15 Data refer to projections based on the 1992 Population Census. - Les données se réfèrent aux projections basées sur le recensement de la population de 1992.

16 Excluding Indian jungle population. - Non compris les Indiens de la jungle.

17 Data refer to national projections. - Les données se réfèrent aux projections nationales.

18 Data refer to the 12 months from 30 June 2016 to 30 June 2017. - Les données font référence aux douze mois de 30 juin 2016 à 30 juin 2017.

19 Data based on the 2010 Population Census. Excludes nomadic Indian tribes. - Les données sont fondées sur le recensement de la population de 2010. Non compris les tribus d'Indiens nomades.

20 Based on the results of the 2011 Population Census. - Basé sur les résultats du recencement de la population de 2011.

21 Source: Sample vital registration system of Bangladesh - Source : << Sample Vital Registration System >> du Bangladesh.

22 For statistical purposes, the data for China do not include those for the Hong Kong Special Administrative Region (Hong Kong SAR), Macao Special Administrative Region (Macao SAR) and Taiwan province of China. - Pour la présentation des statistiques, les données pour la Chine ne comprennent pas la Région Administrative Spéciale de Hong Kong (Hong Kong RAS), la Région Administrative Spéciale de Macao (Macao RAS) et Taïwan province de Chine.

23 Data refer to government controlled areas. - Les données se rapportent aux zones contrôlées par le Gouvernement.

24 Includes data for the Indian-held part of Jammu and Kashmir, the final status of which has not yet been determined. - Y compris les données pour la partie du Jammu et du Cachemire occupée par l'Inde dont le statut définitif n'a pas encore été déterminé.

25 Data refer to the Iranian Year which begins on 21 March and ends on 20 March of the following year. - Les données concernent l'année iranienne, qui commence le 21 mars et se termine le 20 mars de l'année suivante.

26 Includes data for East Jerusalem and Israeli residents in certain other territories under occupation by Israeli military forces since June 1967. - Y compris les données pour Jérusalem-Est et les résidents israéliens dans certains autres territoires occupés depuis 1967 par les forces armées israéliennes.

27 Data refer to Japanese nationals in Japan only. - Les données se raportent aux nationaux japonais au Japon seulement.

28 Excluding data for Jordanian territory under occupation since June 1967 by Israeli military forces. Excluding foreigners, including registered Palestinian refugees. - Non compris les données pour le territoire jordanien occupé depuis juin 1967 par les forces armées israéliennes. Non compris les étrangers, mais y compris les réfugiés de Palestine enregistrés.

29 Based on underlying data of the 2015 census. - Données fondées sur celles extraites du recensement de 2015.

30 Based on Vital Registration System (VRS). - Système d'enregistrement des faits d'état civil.

31 Data refer to Omani citizen only. - Les données concernent les citoyens d'Oman uniquement.

32 Excluding data for the Pakistan-held part of Jammu and Kashmir, the final status of which has not yet been determined. Based on the results of the Pakistan Demographic Survey. - Non compris les données concernant la partie du Jammu et Cachemire occupée par le Pakistan dont le statut définitif n'a pas été déterminé. Données extraites de l'enquête démographique effectuée par le Pakistan.

33 Data refer to Saudi Arabian nationals only. - Les données ne concernent que les ressortissants saoudiens.

34 Data refer to resident population which comprises Singapore citizens and permanent residents. Provisional data. - Les données se rapportent à la population résidente composé des citoyens de Singapour et des résidents permanents. Données provisoires.

35 Excluding Faeroe Islands and Greenland shown separately, if available. - Non compris les Iles Féroé et le Groenland, qui font l'objet de rubriques distinctes, si disponible.

36 Excluding Åland Islands. - Non compris les Îles d'Åland.

37 Excluding Transnistria and the municipality of Bender. - Les données ne tiennent pas compte de l'information sur la Transnistria et la municipalité de Bender.

38 Excludes data for Kosovo and Metohia. - Sans les données pour le Kosovo et Metohie.

39 The Government of Ukraine has informed the United Nations that it is not in a position to provide statistical data concerning the Autonomous Republic of Crimea and the city of Sevastopol. - Le gouvernement Ukrainien a informé l'ONU qu'il n'est pas en mesure de fournir des données statistiques concernant la République autonome de Crimée et la ville de Sébastopol.

40 Excluding Channel Islands (Guernsey and Jersey) and Isle of Man, shown separately, if available. - Non compris les îles Anglo-Normandes (Guernesey et Jersey) et l'île de Man, qui font l'objet de rubriques distinctes, si disponible.

41 Excluding Niue, shown separately, which is part of Cook Islands, but because of remoteness is administered separately. - Non compris Nioué, qui fait l'objet d'une rubrique distincte et qui fait partie des îles Cook, mais qui, en raison de son éloignement, est administrée séparément.

42 Data refer to the 12 months preceding the census in October. - Les données se rapportent aux 12 mois précédant le recensement de octobre.

43 Based on underlying data of the 2009 census. - Données fondées sur celles extraites du recensement de 2009.

Table 23 - *Demographic Yearbook 2017*

Table 23 presents the number of marriages and crude marriage rates by urban/rural residence for every year with available data between 2013 and 2017.

Description of variables: Marriage is defined as the act, ceremony or process by which the legal relationship of spouses is constituted. The legality of the union may be established by civil, religious or other means as recognized by the laws of each country[1].

Marriage statistics in this table, therefore, include both first marriages and remarriages after divorce, widowhood or annulment. They do not, unless otherwise noted, include resumption of marriage ties after legal separation. These statistics refer to the number of marriages performed, and not to the number of persons marrying.

Statistics shown are obtained from civil registers of marriage. Exceptions, such as data from church registers, are identified in footnotes.

The urban/rural classification of marriages is that provided by each country or area; it is presumed to be based on the national census definitions of urban population which have been set forth at the end of the notes for table 6.

For certain countries, there is a discrepancy between the total number of marriages shown in this table and those shown in subsequent tables for the same year. Usually this discrepancy arises because the total number of marriages occurring in a given year is revised although the remaining tabulations are not.

Rate computation: Crude marriage rates are the annual number of marriages per 1 000 mid-year population. Rates by urban/rural residence are the annual number of marriages, in the appropriate urban or rural category, per 1 000 corresponding mid-year population. Rates presented in this table have been limited to those for countries or areas having at least a total of 30 marriages in a given year. These rates are calculated by the Statistics Division of the United Nations based on the appropriate reference population (for example: total population, nationals only, etc.) if known and available. If the reference population is not known or unavailable the total population is used to calculate the rates. Therefore, if the population that is used to calculate the rates is different from the correct reference population, the rates presented might under- or overstate the true situation in a country or area.

Reliability of data: Each country or area has been asked to indicate the estimated completeness of the number of marriages recorded in its civil register. These national assessments are indicated by the quality codes "C" and "U" that appear in the first column of this table.

"C" indicates that the data are estimated to be virtually complete, that is, representing at least 90 per cent of the marriages occurring each year, while "U" indicates that data are estimated to be incomplete, that is representing less than 90 per cent of the marriages occurring each year. The code "..." indicates that no information was provided regarding completeness.

Data from civil registers which are reported as incomplete or of unknown completeness (coded "U" or "...") are considered unreliable. They appear in italics in this table; rates are not computed for these data.

These quality codes apply only to data from civil registers. For more information about the quality of vital statistics data in general, see section 4.2 of the Technical Notes.

Limitations: Statistics on marriages are subject to the same qualifications that have been set forth for vital statistics in general and marriage statistics in particular as discussed in section 4 of the Technical Notes.

The fact that marriage is a legal event, unlike birth and death that are biological events, has implications for international comparability of data. Marriage has been defined, for statistical purposes, in terms of the laws of individual countries or areas. These laws vary throughout the world. In addition, comparability is further limited because some countries or areas compile statistics only for civil marriages although religious marriages may also be legally recognized; in other countries or areas, the only available records are church registers and, therefore, the statistics may not reflect marriages that are civil marriages only.

Because in many countries or areas marriage is a civil legal contract which, to establish its legality, must be celebrated before a civil officer, it follows that for these countries or areas registration would tend to be almost automatic at the time of, or immediately following, the marriage ceremony. This factor should be kept in mind when considering the reliability of data, described above. For this reason the practice of tabulating data by date of registration does not generally pose serious problems of comparability as it does in the case of birth and death statistics.

As indicators of family formation, the statistics on the number of marriages presented in this table are bound to be deficient to the extent that they do not include either customary unions, which are not registered even though they are considered legal and binding under customary law, or consensual unions (also known as extra-legal or de facto unions). In general, lower marriage rates over a period of years are an indication of higher incidence of customary or consensual unions.

In addition, rates are affected also by the quality and limitations of the population estimates that are used in their computation. The problems of under-enumeration or over-enumeration and, to some extent, the differences in definition of total population have been discussed in section 3 of the Technical Notes dealing with population data in general, and specific information pertaining to individual countries or areas is given in the footnotes to table 3.

Strict correspondence between the numerator of the rate and the denominator is not always obtained; for example, marriages among civilian and military segments of the population may be related to civilian population. The effect of this may be to increase the rates, but, in most cases, this effect is negligible.

It should be emphasized that crude marriage rates like crude birth, death and divorce rates, may be seriously affected by the age-sex-marital structure of the population to which they relate. Crude marriage rates do, however, provide a simple measure of the level and changes in marriage.

The comparability of data by urban/rural residence is affected by the national definitions of urban and rural used in tabulating these data. It is assumed, in the absence of specific information to the contrary, that the definitions of urban and rural used in connection with the national population census were also used in the compilation of the vital statistics for each country or area. However, it cannot be excluded that, for a given country or area, different definitions of urban and rural are used for the vital statistics data and the population census data respectively. When known, the definitions of urban in national population censuses are presented at the end of the technical notes for table 6. As discussed in detail in the notes, these definitions vary considerably from one country or area to another.

In addition to problems of comparability, marriage rates classified by urban/rural residence are also subject to certain special types of bias. If, when calculating marriage rates, different definitions of urban are used in connection with the vital events and the population data, and if this results in a net difference between the numerator and denominator of the rate in the population at risk, then the marriage rates would be biased. Urban/rural differentials in marriage rates may also be affected by whether the vital events have been tabulated in terms of place of occurrence or place of usual residence. This problem is discussed in more detail in section 4.1.4.1 of the Technical Notes.

Earlier data: Marriages and crude marriage rates have been shown in each issue of the *Demographic Yearbook*. For more information on specific topics, and years for which data are reported, readers should consult the Historical Index.

NOTES

[1] *Principles and Recommendations for a Vital Statistics System Revision 3,* Sales No. E.13.XVII.10, United Nations, New York, 2014.

Tableau 23 – *Annuaire démographique 2017*

Le tableau 23 présente des données sur les mariages et les taux bruts de nuptialité selon le lieu de résidence (zone urbaine ou rurale) pour les années où l'information est disponible entre 2013 et 2017.

Description des variables : le mariage désigne l'acte, la cérémonie ou la procédure qui établit un rapport légal entre les époux. L'union peut être rendue légale par une procédure civile ou religieuse, ou par toute autre procédure, conformément à la législation du pays[1].

Les statistiques de la nuptialité présentées dans ce tableau comprennent donc les premiers mariages et les remariages faisant suite à un divorce, un veuvage ou une annulation. Toutefois, sauf indication contraire, elles ne comprennent pas les unions reconstituées après une séparation légale. Ces statistiques se rapportent au nombre de mariages célébrés, non au nombre de personnes qui se marient.

Les statistiques présentées reposent sur l'enregistrement des mariages par les services de l'état civil. Les exceptions (données provenant des registres des églises, par exemple) font l'objet d'une note à la fin du tableau.

La classification des mariages selon le lieu de résidence (zone urbaine ou rurale) est celle qui a été communiquée par chaque pays ou zone ; on part du principe qu'elle repose sur les définitions de la population urbaine utilisées pour les recensements nationaux telles qu'elles sont reproduites à la fin des notes se rapportant au tableau 6.

Pour quelques pays il y a une discordance entre le nombre total de mariages présenté dans ce tableau et ceux présentés après pour la même année. Habituellement ces différences apparaissent lorsque le nombre total des mariages pour une certaine année a été révisé alors que les autres tabulations ne l'ont pas été.

Calcul des taux : les taux bruts de nuptialité représentent le nombre annuel de mariages pour 1 000 habitants au milieu de l'année. Les taux selon le lieu de résidence (zone urbaine ou rurale) représentent le nombre annuel de mariages, classés selon la catégorie urbaine ou rurale appropriée, pour 1 000 habitants au milieu de l'année. Les taux de ce tableau ne se rapportent qu'aux pays ou zones où l'on a enregistré un total d'au moins 30 mariages pendant une année donnée. Ces taux sont calculés par la division de statistique des Nations Unies sur la base de la population de référence adéquate (par exemple : population totale, nationaux seulement, etc.) si connue et disponible. Si la population de référence n'est pas connue ou n'est pas disponible, la population totale est utilisée pour calculer les taux. Par conséquent, si la population utilisée pour calculer les taux est différente de la population de référence adéquate, les taux présentés sont susceptibles de sous ou sur estimer la situation réelle d'un pays ou d'un territoire.

Fiabilité des données : il a été demandé à chaque pays ou zone d'indiquer le degré estimatif de complétude des données sur les mariages figurant dans ses registres d'état civil. Ces évaluations nationales sont signalées par les codes de qualité "C" et "U" qui apparaissent dans la deuxième colonne du tableau.

La lettre "C" indique que les données sont jugées à peu près complètes, c'est-à-dire qu'elles représentent au moins 90 p. 100 des mariages survenus chaque année ; la lettre "U" signale que les données sont jugées incomplètes, c'est-à-dire qu'elles représentent moins de 90 p. 100 des mariages survenus chaque année. Le code "..." indique qu'aucun renseignement n'a été communiqué quant à la complétude des données.

Les données issues des registres de l'état civil qui sont déclarées incomplètes ou dont le degré de complétude n'est pas connu (code "U" ou "...") sont jugées douteuses. Elles apparaissent en italique dans le tableau et les taux correspondants n'ont pas été calculés.

Les codes de qualité ne s'appliquent qu'aux données provenant des registres de l'état civil. Pour plus de précisions sur la qualité des données reposant sur les statistiques de l'état civil en général, voir la section 4.2 des Notes techniques.

Insuffisance des données : les statistiques relatives aux mariages appellent les mêmes réserves que celles qui ont été formulées à propos des statistiques de l'état civil en général et des statistiques concernant la nuptialité en particulier (voir la section 4 des Notes techniques).

Le fait que le mariage soit un acte juridique, à la différence de la naissance et du décès, qui sont des faits biologiques, a des répercussions sur la comparabilité internationale des données. Aux fins de la statistique, le mariage est défini par la législation de chaque pays ou zone. Cette législation varie d'un pays à l'autre. La comparabilité est limitée en outre du fait que certains pays ou zones ne réunissent des statistiques que pour les mariages civils, bien que les mariages religieux y soient également reconnus par la loi ; dans d'autres, les seuls relevés disponibles sont les registres des églises et, en conséquence, les statistiques peuvent ne pas rendre compte des mariages exclusivement civils.

Étant donné que, dans de nombreux pays ou zones, le mariage est un contrat juridique civil qui, pour être légal, doit être conclu devant un officier d'état civil, il s'ensuit que dans ces pays ou zones l'enregistrement se fait à peu près systématiquement au moment de la cérémonie ou immédiatement après. Il faut tenir compte de cet élément lorsque l'on évalue la fiabilité des données, dont il est question plus haut. C'est pourquoi la pratique consistant à exploiter les données selon la date de l'enregistrement ne pose généralement pas les graves problèmes de comparabilité auxquels on se heurte dans le cas des statistiques concernant les naissances et les décès.

Les statistiques relatives au nombre des mariages présentées dans ce tableau donnent une idée forcément trompeuse de la formation des familles, dans la mesure où elles ne tiennent compte ni des mariages coutumiers, qui ne sont pas enregistrés bien qu'ils soient considérés comme légaux et créateurs d'obligations en vertu du droit coutumier, ni des unions consensuelles (appelées également unions non légalisées ou unions de fait). En général, une diminution du taux de nuptialité pendant un certain nombre d'années indique une augmentation des mariages coutumiers ou des unions consensuelles.

L'exactitude des taux dépend également de la qualité et des insuffisances des estimations de population qui sont utilisées pour leur calcul. Le problème des erreurs par excès ou par défaut commises lors du dénombrement et, dans une certaine mesure, le problème de l'hétérogénéité des définitions de la population totale ont été examinés à la section 3 des Notes techniques relative à la population en général ; des indications concernant les différents pays ou zones sont données en note à la fin du tableau 3.

Il n'a pas toujours été possible d'obtenir une correspondance rigoureuse entre le numérateur et le dénominateur pour le calcul des taux. Par exemple, les mariages parmi la population civile et les militaires sont parfois rapportés à la population civile. Cela peut avoir pour effet d'accroître les taux, mais, dans la plupart des cas, il est probable que la différence sera négligeable.

Il faut souligner que les taux bruts de nuptialité, de même que les taux bruts de natalité, de mortalité et de divortialité, peuvent varier sensiblement selon la structure par âge et par sexe de la population à laquelle ils se rapportent. Les taux bruts de nuptialité offrent néanmoins un moyen simple de mesurer la fréquence et l'évolution des mariages.

La comparabilité des données selon le lieu de résidence (zone urbaine ou rurale) peut être limitée par les définitions nationales des termes « urbain » et « rural » utilisées pour le classement de ces données. En l'absence d'indications contraires, on a supposé que les mêmes définitions avaient servi pour le recensement national de la population et pour l'établissement des statistiques de l'état civil pour chaque pays ou zone. Toutefois, il n'est pas exclu que, pour une zone ou un pays donné, des définitions différentes aient été retenues. Les définitions du terme « urbain » utilisées pour les recensements nationaux de population ont été présentées à la fin des notes techniques du tableau 6 lorsqu'elles étaient connues. Comme on l'a précisé dans les notes techniques relatives au tableau 6, ces définitions varient considérablement d'un pays ou d'une zone à l'autre.

Outre les problèmes de comparabilité, les taux de nuptialité classés selon le lieu de résidence (zone urbaine ou rurale) sont également sujets à des distorsions particulières. Si l'on utilise des définitions différentes du terme « urbain » pour classer les faits d'état civil et les données relatives à la population lors du calcul des taux et qu'il en résulte une différence nette entre le numérateur et le dénominateur pour le taux de la population exposée au risque, les taux de nuptialité s'en trouveront faussés. La différence entre ces taux pour les zones urbaines et rurales pourra aussi être faussée selon que les faits d'état civil auront été classés d'après le lieu où ils se sont produits ou d'après le lieu de résidence habituel. Ce problème est examiné plus en détail à la section 4.1.4.1 des Notes techniques.

Données publiées antérieurement : les différentes éditions de *l'Annuaire démographique* regroupent des données sur le nombre des mariages. Pour plus de précisions concernant les années et les sujets pour lesquels des données ont été publiées, se reporter à l'index historique.

NOTE

[1] *Principes et recommandations pour un système de statistique de l'état civil, troisième révision,* numéro de vente : E.13.XVII.10, publication des Nations Unies, New York, 2014.

23. Marriages and crude marriage rates, by urban/rural residence: 2013 - 2017
Mariages et taux bruts de nuptialité, selon la résidence, urbaine/rurale : 2013 - 2017

Continent, country or area, and urban/rural residence / Continent, pays ou zone et résidence, urbaine/rurale	Code[a]	Number - Nombre					Rate - Taux				
		2013	2014	2015	2016	2017	2013	2014	2015	2016	2017
AFRICA - AFRIQUE											
Algeria - Algérie[1]											
Total	...	387 947	386 422	369 074	356 600	...	...	...	...	...	...
Botswana[2]											
Total	+U	5 333	5 591	6 677	6 051	...	...	...	...	...	...
Côte d'Ivoire											
Total	...	...	...	25 689	26 678	...	...	...	...	...	...
Urban - Urbaine	...	...	...	23 750	25 189	...	...	...	...	...	...
Rural - Rurale	...	...	...	1 939	1 489	...	...	...	...	...	...
Egypt - Égypte											
Total	+C	909 350	953 137	969 399[3]	938 526[3]	912 606	10.7	11.0	10.9	10.3	9.6
Urban - Urbaine	+C	371 995	384 799	409 906[3]	370 411[3]	356 634	10.3	10.4	10.8	9.5	8.8
Rural - Rurale	+C	537 355	568 338	559 493[3]	568 115[3]	555 972	11.1	11.4	11.0	10.9	10.2
Lesotho											
Total	+U	4 552	...	...	...	...	...	...	...	...	...
Mauritius - Maurice[4]											
Total	+C	9 575	9 959	9 709	10 042	9 757	7.6	7.9	7.7	7.9	7.7
Urban - Urbaine	+C	2 902	3 216	3 194	3 224	3 186	5.6	6.2	6.2	6.2	6.2
Rural - Rurale	+C	6 673	6 743	6 515	6 818	6 571	9.0	9.1	8.7	9.1	8.8
Mayotte											
Total	C	...	467	346	346	...	...	2.1	1.5	1.4	...
Reunion - Réunion											
Total	C	2 791	2 771	2 827	2 882	...	3.3	3.3	3.3	3.4	...
Saint Helena ex. dep. - Sainte-Hélène sans dép.											
Total	C	8	7	...	...	...	...	...	...	...	...
Seychelles[5]											
Total	+C	1 708	1 655	1 845	2 147	2 821	19.0	18.1	19.7	22.7	29.4
South Africa - Afrique du Sud											
Total	...	158 642	150 852	138 627	139 512	...	...	...	...	...	...
Sudan - Soudan											
Total	U	...	...	158 051	...	...	...	...	...	...	...
Tunisia - Tunisie											
Total	...	110 119	108 843	108 453	99 281	94 131	...	...	...	...	...
AMERICA, NORTH - AMÉRIQUE DU NORD											
Anguilla[6]											
Total	C	42	64	40	64	64	3.0	4.5	2.7	4.2	...
Aruba											
Total	C	523	617	696	639	537	4.9	5.7	6.4	5.8	4.8
Bahamas											
Total	+C	2 122	*3 964[7]	*3 829[7]	*3 950[7]	*3 574[7]	5.9	*10.9	*10.4	*10.6	*9.5
Barbados - Barbade											
Total	+C	1 829	1 855	...	...	...	6.6	6.7	...	...	...
Bermuda - Bermudes											
Total	C	471	477	509	450	...	7.6	7.7	8.2	7.3	...
Cayman Islands - Îles Caïmanes[8]											
Total	+C	527	452	468	493	513	9.4	7.9	7.9	8.1	8.1
Costa Rica[9]											
Total	C	25 725	25 909	26 512	26 718	*25 501	5.5	5.4	5.5	5.5	*5.2
Urban - Urbaine	C	12 229	17 905	21 258	21 565	*20 129	3.6	5.2	6.1	6.1	*5.6
Rural - Rurale	C	13 496	8 004	5 254	5 153	*5 372	10.5	6.1	4.0	3.9	*4.0
Cuba[10]											
Total	C	61 449	63 954	61 902	61 903	53 684	5.5	5.7	5.5	5.5	4.8
Urban - Urbaine	C	56 462	58 137	57 600	57 596	...	6.6	6.7	6.7	6.7	...
Rural - Rurale	C	4 987	5 817	4 302	4 307	...	1.9	2.2	1.7	1.7	...
Curaçao[11]											
Total	C	665	696	703	695	729	4.3	4.5	4.4	4.4	4.6
Dominican Republic - République dominicaine											
Total	+C	45 163	47 235	50 158	52 896	...	4.6	4.8	5.0	5.3	...
Grenada - Grenade											
Total	+C	566	618	...	...	...	5.2	5.7	...	...	...

Continent, country or area, and urban/rural residence / Continent, pays ou zone et résidence, urbaine/rurale	Code[a]	Number - Nombre					Rate - Taux				
		2013	2014	2015	2016	2017	2013	2014	2015	2016	2017
AMERICA, NORTH - AMÉRIQUE DU NORD											
Guadeloupe											
Total	C	1 136	1 198	1 172	1 185	...	2.8	3.0	3.0	3.0	...
Guatemala											
Total	C	80 750	79 496	79 177	69 613	...	5.2	5.0	4.9	...	...
Jamaica - Jamaïque											
Total	+C	18 835	18 699	18 373	17 609	17 411	6.9	6.9	6.7	6.5	6.4
Martinique											
Total	C	1 017	968	1 017	1 067	...	2.6	2.5	2.7	2.8	...
Mexico - Mexique[12]											
Total	+C	583 264	577 713	558 022	543 749	...	4.9	4.8	4.6	4.4	...
Urban - Urbaine[13]	+C	418 686	420 856	416 507	411 481	...	4.9	4.8	4.7	4.6	...
Rural - Rurale[13]	+C	114 574	119 600	108 675	100 862	...	3.5	3.6	3.3	3.0	...
Montserrat											
Total	C	18	14	14	10	...	...	...	...	...	...
Nicaragua											
Total	+U	25 082	31 145	26 628	22 097	...	...	...	...	...	...
Panama[9]											
Total	C	13 213	12 869	*14 341	*14 233	...	3.4	3.3	*3.6	*3.5	...
Urban - Urbaine	C	10 535	10 443	*11 824	*11 730	...	4.1	4.0	*4.4	*4.2	...
Rural - Rurale	C	2 678	2 426	*2 517	*2 503	...	2.1	1.9	*2.0	*2.0	...
Puerto Rico - Porto Rico											
Total	C	17 010	16 702	17 002	15 907	12 793	4.7	4.7	4.9	4.7	3.8
Saint Vincent and the Grenadines - Saint-Vincent-et-les Grenadines											
Total	C	511	526	574	...	...	4.6	4.8	5.2	...	...
Sint Maarten (Dutch part) - Saint-Martin (partie néerlandaise)											
Total	+C	230	...	...	...	...	6.3	...	...	...	...
Trinidad and Tobago - Trinité-et-Tobago											
Total	C	*8 017	...	...	...	...	*6.0	...	...	...	...
United States of America - États-Unis d'Amérique											
Total	C	2 081 301[14]	2 140 272[14]	2 221 579	...	...	6.6	6.7	6.9	...	...
AMERICA, SOUTH - AMÉRIQUE DU SUD											
Argentina - Argentine											
Total	C	123 810	119 266	118 809	119 334	...	2.9	2.8	2.8	2.7	...
Bolivia (Plurinational State of) - Bolivie (État plurinational de)											
Total	+U	42 016	60 105	39 942	...	...	...	...	...	...	...
Brazil - Brésil[12]											
Total	+U	1 052 477	1 106 440	1 137 348	1 095 535	...	...	...	...	...	...
Chile - Chili											
Total	+C	61 446	64 868	61 744	62 464	...	3.5	3.6	3.4	3.4	...
Urban - Urbaine[15]	+C	56 758	59 858	56 984	57 413	...	3.7	3.8	3.6	3.6	...
Rural - Rurale[15]	+C	4 688	5 010	4 760	5 051	...	2.1	2.2	2.1	2.2	...
Ecuador - Équateur[16]											
Total	U	53 986	60 328	60 636	57 738	...	...	...	...	...	...
Urban - Urbaine[15]	U	44 721	50 434	50 425	47 322	...	...	...	...	...	...
Rural - Rurale[15]	U	9 265	9 894	10 211	10 416	...	...	...	...	...	...
French Guiana - Guyane française											
Total	C	540	573	590	631	...	2.2	2.3	2.3	2.4	...
Guyana[17]											
Total	C	4 667	4 679	4 744	4 445	3 990	6.3	6.3	6.4	6.0	5.4
Paraguay											
Total	U	19 076	19 527	19 504	19 440	...	...	...	...	...	...
Peru - Pérou[18]											
Total	+C	89 763	95 770	86 191	94 094	*78 164	2.9	3.1	2.8	3.0	*2.5

23. Marriages and crude marriage rates, by urban/rural residence: 2013 - 2017
Mariages et taux bruts de nuptialité, selon la résidence, urbaine/rurale : 2013 - 2017 (continued - suite)

Continent, country or area, and urban/rural residence / Continent, pays ou zone et résidence, urbaine/rurale	Code[a]	Number - Nombre					Rate - Taux				
		2013	2014	2015	2016	2017	2013	2014	2015	2016	2017
AMERICA, SOUTH - AMÉRIQUE DU SUD											
Suriname											
Total	C	2 190	2 143	2 010	2 125	...	4.0	3.8	3.5	3.7	...
Uruguay											
Total	C	10 034	10 226	9 501	9 820	...	2.9	3.0	2.7	2.8	...
Venezuela (Bolivarian Republic of) - Venezuela (République bolivarienne du)											
Total	C	99 065	94 519	91 688	84 349	77 062	3.3	3.1	3.0	2.7	2.5
ASIA - ASIE											
Armenia - Arménie											
Total	+C	...	18 912	17 603	16 294	...	...	6.3	5.9	5.4	...
Urban - Urbaine	+C	...	...	11 836	11 113	...	...	...	6.2	5.8	...
Rural - Rurale	+C	...	...	5 767	5 181	...	...	...	5.3	4.8	...
Azerbaijan - Azerbaïdjan											
Total	+C	86 852	84 912	68 773	66 771	...	9.2	8.9	7.1	6.8	...
Urban - Urbaine	+C	46 324	43 608	36 623	36 739	...	...	8.6	7.1	7.1	...
Rural - Rurale	+C	40 528	41 304	32 150	30 032	...	...	9.3	7.1	6.6	...
Bahrain - Bahreïn											
Total	...	7 463	7 673	6 953	7 019	6 691	...	...	...	...	...
Brunei Darussalam - Brunéi Darussalam											
Total	+C	2 741	2 992	2 750	2 532		6.8	7.3	6.7	6.1	
China, Hong Kong SAR - Chine, Hong Kong RAS											
Total	C	55 274	56 454	51 609	50 008	51 817	7.7	7.8	7.1	6.8	7.0
China, Macao SAR - Chine, Macao RAS											
Total	+C	4 153	4 085	3 719	3 891	3 883	7.0	6.6	5.8	6.0	5.9
Cyprus - Chypre[19]											
Total	C	5 493	5 378	6 092	6 375	...	6.4	6.3	7.2	7.5	...
Georgia - Géorgie											
Total	C	34 693	31 526	29 157	25 101	23 684	7.7	8.5	7.8	6.7	6.4
Urban - Urbaine[15]	C	18 903	18 363	17 127	14 961	...	...	...	8.1	7.0	...
Rural - Rurale[15]	C	15 790	13 163	12 030	10 140	...	...	...	7.6	6.4	...
Indonesia - Indonésie											
Total	U	2 210 046	2 110 776	1 958 394	...	...	...	...	...	...	...
Iran (Islamic Republic of) - Iran (République islamique d')[20]											
Total	+C	774 513	724 324	685 352	704 716	...	10.1	9.3	8.7	8.8	...
Urban - Urbaine	+C	...	...	562 671	616 042	...	...	...	9.8	10.6	...
Rural - Rurale	+C	...	...	122 681	88 674	...	...	...	5.7	4.1	...
Israel - Israël[21]											
Total	C	52 705	50 797	53 579	52 809	...	6.5	6.2	6.4	6.2	...
Urban - Urbaine[22]	C	47 506	45 729	48 236	47 651	...	6.4	6.1	6.3	6.1	...
Rural - Rurale[22]	C	3 951	3 715	3 936	3 828	...	5.7	5.2	5.3	5.1	...
Japan - Japon[23]											
Total	+C	660 613	643 749	635 156	620 531	...	5.2	5.1	5.0	4.9	...
Urban - Urbaine[15]	+C	613 648	598 792	590 947	578 265	...	...	...	...	...	...
Rural - Rurale[15]	+C	46 965	44 957	44 209	42 266	...	...	...	...	...	...
Jordan - Jordanie[24]											
Total	+C	70 965	81 209	81 373	81 343	77 700	8.7	9.2	8.5	8.3	7.7
Kazakhstan											
Total	+C	168 447	159 328	148 769	141 702	141 791	9.9	9.2	8.5	8.0	7.9
Urban - Urbaine	+C	107 508	105 172	98 927	94 672	96 865	11.5	10.9	10.0	9.3	9.4
Rural - Rurale	+C	60 939	54 156	49 842	47 030	44 926	7.9	7.1	6.6	6.1	5.8
Kuwait - Koweït											
Total	C	15 118	15 086	15 412	14 693	13 932	4.4	4.0	3.9	3.6	3.5
Kyrgyzstan - Kirghizstan											
Total	C	53 578	54 942	52 043	47 837	43 350	9.4	9.4	8.7	7.9	7.0
Urban - Urbaine	C	17 329	17 150	15 875	15 990	16 274	9.0	8.7	7.9	7.8	7.8
Rural - Rurale	C	36 249	37 792	36 168	31 847	27 076	9.5	9.8	9.2	7.9	6.6

23. Marriages and crude marriage rates, by urban/rural residence: 2013 - 2017
Mariages et taux bruts de nuptialité, selon la résidence, urbaine/rurale : 2013 - 2017 (continued - suite)

Continent, country or area, and urban/rural residence / Continent, pays ou zone et résidence, urbaine/rurale	Co-de[a]	Number - Nombre					Rate - Taux				
		2013	2014	2015	2016	2017	2013	2014	2015	2016	2017
ASIA - ASIE											
Lebanon - Liban											
Total	C	38 737	41 049	...	...	...	...	...	...	...	...
Maldives											
Total	...	...	...	5 763	5 488	...	...	...	...	...	...
Urban - Urbaine	...	...	...	2 610	2 527	...	...	...	...	...	...
Rural - Rurale	...	...	...	3 153	2 961	...	...	...	...	...	...
Mongolia - Mongolie											
Total	+C	15 785	17 332	17 586	16 778	20 470	5.4	5.8	5.8	5.4	6.5
Urban - Urbaine	+C	10 613	12 075	12 506	11 915	14 617	5.4	6.1	6.1	5.6	6.8
Rural - Rurale	+C	5 172	5 257	5 080	4 863	5 853	5.5	5.4	5.2	5.0	5.8
Oman											
Total	U	28 515	28 152	25 659	...	...	...	...	...	...	...
Philippines											
Total	U	442 900	429 723	439 424	419 268	...	...	...	...	...	...
Qatar											
Total	C	3 619	3 674	3 724	3 830	3 718	1.8	1.7	1.5	1.5	1.4
Urban - Urbaine	C	...	3 674	3 724	3 830	3 718	...	1.7	1.5	1.5	1.4
Republic of Korea - République de Corée[25]											
Total	+C	322 807	305 507	302 828	281 635	264 455	6.4	6.0	5.9	5.5	5.1
Urban - Urbaine[22]	+C	263 992	248 965	247 486	229 747	...	6.4	6.0	6.0	5.5	...
Rural - Rurale[22]	+C	50 906	48 818	48 638	46 792	...	5.5	5.2	5.1	4.9	...
Singapore - Singapour[26]											
Total	+C	26 254	28 407	28 322	27 971	28 212	6.8	7.3	7.3	7.1	7.1
Sri Lanka											
Total	+U	*180 760	*175 728	*175 939	*173 990	*169 365	...	...	...	...	...
State of Palestine - État de Palestine											
Total	C	42 698	43 732	50 438	49 930	...	9.7	9.6	10.8	10.4	...
Tajikistan - Tadjikistan											
Total	+C	96 989	95 537	76 956	72 499	...	12.0	11.6	9.1	8.4	...
Urban - Urbaine	+C	25 306	25 757	19 810	18 378	...	11.8	11.7	8.9	8.1	...
Rural - Rurale	+C	71 683	69 780	57 146	54 121	...	12.1	11.5	9.2	8.5	...
Thailand - Thaïlande											
Total	U	295 519	296 258	304 392	307 746	297 501	...	...	...	...	...
Turkey - Turquie[27]											
Total	C	600 138	599 704	602 982	594 493	...	7.8	7.7	7.7	7.4	...
United Arab Emirates - Émirats arabes unis											
Total	...	16 441	16 917	16 248	...	...	...	...	...	...	...
Uzbekistan - Ouzbékistan											
Total	+C	304 859	296 055	287 582	275 048	306 197	10.1	9.6	9.2	8.7	9.5
Urban - Urbaine	+C	140 958	136 707	131 216	125 820	138 681	9.1	8.7	8.3	7.9	8.5
Rural - Rurale	+C	163 901	159 348	156 366	149 228	167 516	11.1	10.5	10.1	9.6	10.6
EUROPE											
Åland Islands - Îles d'Åland											
Total	C	118	115	118	123	*116	4.1	4.0	4.1	4.2	*4.0
Urban - Urbaine	C	46	53	49	49	*50	4.0	4.6	4.3	4.3	*4.3
Rural - Rurale	C	72	62	69	74	*66	4.2	3.6	3.9	4.2	*3.7
Albania - Albanie											
Total	C	23 820	...	...	...	...	8.2	...	...	...	...
Total	U	...	...	24 997	22 562	...	...	...	...	...	...
Andorra - Andorre											
Total	C	291	271	285	295	320	4.2	3.9	4.0	4.1	...
Austria - Autriche											
Total	C	36 140[28]	37 458[28]	44 502[29]	44 890[29]	44 981[29]	4.3	4.4	5.2	5.1	5.1
Belarus - Bélarus											
Total	C	87 127	83 942	82 030	64 536	66 215	9.2	8.9	8.6	6.8	7.0
Urban - Urbaine	C	71 702	69 649	68 305	53 819	...	9.9	9.5	9.3	7.3	...
Rural - Rurale	C	15 425	14 293	13 725	10 717	...	7.0	6.6	6.4	5.1	...
Belgium - Belgique[30]											
Total	C	37 854	39 879	40 049	44 725	44 319	3.4	3.6	3.5	3.9	3.9
Urban - Urbaine	C	37 332	39 332	39 500	...	...	...	...	...	...	...
Rural - Rurale	C	522	547	549	...	...	...	...	...	...	...

23. Marriages and crude marriage rates, by urban/rural residence: 2013 - 2017
Mariages et taux bruts de nuptialité, selon la résidence, urbaine/rurale : 2013 - 2017 (continued - suite)

Continent, country or area, and urban/rural residence / Continent, pays ou zone et résidence, urbaine/rurale	Code[a]	Number - Nombre					Rate - Taux				
		2013	2014	2015	2016	2017	2013	2014	2015	2016	2017
EUROPE											
Bosnia and Herzegovina - Bosnie-Herzégovine											
Total	C	18 387	18 409	19 680	19 233	19 617	5.2	5.2	5.6	5.5	5.6
Bulgaria - Bulgarie[31]											
Total	C	21 943	24 596	27 720	26 803	28 593	3.0	3.4	3.9	3.8	4.0
Urban - Urbaine	C	...	18 756	20 795	19 977	21 536	...	3.6	4.0	3.8	...
Rural - Rurale	C	...	5 840	6 925	6 826	7 057	...	3.0	3.6	3.6	...
Croatia - Croatie[9]											
Total	C	19 169	19 501	19 834	20 467	...	4.5	4.6	4.7	4.9	...
Urban - Urbaine	C	10 691	10 924	10 937	11 287	...	...	...	...	...	...
Rural - Rurale	C	8 478	8 577	8 897	9 180	...	...	...	...	...	...
Czechia - Tchéquie[9]											
Total	C	43 499	45 575	48 191	50 768	*52 567	4.1	4.3	4.6	4.8	*5.0
Urban - Urbaine	C	31 976	33 356	35 192	37 207	...	4.2	4.3	4.6	4.8	...
Rural - Rurale	C	11 523	12 219	12 999	13 561	...	4.1	4.3	4.6	4.8	...
Denmark - Danemark[32]											
Total	C	27 503	28 331	28 853	30 767	31 777	4.9	5.0	5.1	5.4	5.5
Estonia - Estonie											
Total	C	5 630	6 220	6 815	6 360	6 447	4.3	4.7	5.2	4.8	4.9
Urban - Urbaine[33]	C	3 963	4 232	4 660	4 214	...	4.4	4.7	5.2	4.7	...
Rural - Rurale[33]	C	1 368	1 496	1 733	1 748	...	3.3	3.6	4.2	4.2	...
Faeroe Islands - Îles Féroé											
Total	C	259	250	268	268	275	5.4	5.2	5.5	5.4	5.5
Finland - Finlande[34]											
Total	C	25 001	24 347	24 590	24 341	...	4.6	4.5	4.5	4.5	...
Urban - Urbaine	C	18 856	18 485	18 838	18 676	...	5.1	4.9	4.9	4.8	...
Rural - Rurale	C	6 145	5 862	5 752	5 665	...	3.7	3.5	3.6	3.6	...
France[12]											
Total	C	233 108	235 315	230 364	226 614	...	3.7	3.7	3.6	3.5	...
Urban - Urbaine[35]	C	181 513	182 905	179 606	177 747	...	...	...	...	...	...
Rural - Rurale[35]	C	49 361	49 824	48 118	46 219	...	...	...	...	...	...
Germany - Allemagne											
Total	C	373 655	385 952	400 115	410 426	407 466	4.6	4.8	4.9	5.0	4.9
Gibraltar[8]											
Total	+C	195	204	195	...	...	6.0	6.2	5.8	...	...
Greece - Grèce											
Total	C	51 256	53 105	53 672	49 632	50 138	4.7	4.9	5.0	4.6	4.7
Urban - Urbaine	C	...	37 743	37 870	35 268	...	...	...	...	...	...
Rural - Rurale	C	...	15 362	15 802	14 364	...	...	...	...	...	...
Hungary - Hongrie[10]											
Total	C	36 986	38 780	46 137	51 805	50 572	3.7	3.9	4.7	5.3	5.2
Urban - Urbaine[36]	C	27 189	28 854	33 144	36 422	...	4.0	4.2	4.8	5.3	...
Rural - Rurale[36]	C	9 424	9 538	12 492	14 810	...	3.1	3.3	4.3	5.1	...
Ireland - Irlande											
Total	+C	20 680	22 045	22 116[12]	22 626[12]	22 021[12]	4.5	4.7	4.7	4.8	4.6
Isle of Man - Île de Man											
Total	+C	231	197	199	240	247	2.7	2.3	2.3	2.8	2.9
Italy - Italie											
Total	C	194 057	189 765	194 377	203 258	...	3.2	3.1	3.2	3.4	...
Latvia - Lettonie[9]											
Total	C	11 436	12 515	13 617	13 002	13 150	5.7	6.3	6.9	6.6	6.8
Liechtenstein[9]											
Total	C	211	208	205	198	229	5.7	5.6	5.5	5.3	6.0
Lithuania - Lituanie											
Total	C	20 469	22 142	21 987	21 347	21 186	6.9	7.6	7.6	7.4	7.5
Urban - Urbaine	C	14 166	15 250	15 219	14 914	...	7.1	7.7	7.8	7.7	...
Rural - Rurale	C	6 303	6 892	6 768	6 433	...	6.5	7.2	7.1	6.8	...
Luxembourg[8]											
Total	C	1 722	1 657	2 052[12]	1 884[12]	1 908[12]	3.2	3.0	3.6	3.2	3.2
Malta - Malte											
Total	C	2 578	2 871	3 002	3 034	...	6.1	6.7	7.0	6.7	...
Montenegro - Monténégro											
Total	C	3 847	3 527	3 837	3 178	...	6.2	5.7	6.2	5.1	...
Netherlands - Pays-Bas[37]											
Total	C	64 549[38]	65 333[38]	64 308	65 249	64 402	3.8	3.9	3.8	3.8	3.8
Norway - Norvège[12]											
Total	C	23 916	23 462	23 227	23 672	22 444	4.7	4.6	4.5	4.5	4.3

Continent, country or area, and urban/rural residence / Continent, pays ou zone et résidence, urbaine/rurale	Code[a]	Number - Nombre					Rate - Taux				
		2013	2014	2015	2016	2017	2013	2014	2015	2016	2017
EUROPE											
Poland - Pologne											
Total	C	180 396	188 488	188 832	193 455	192 576	4.7	5.0	5.0	5.1	5.1
Urban - Urbaine	C	105 734	110 030	111 246	114 612	...	4.6	4.8	4.9	5.0	...
Rural - Rurale	C	74 662	78 458	77 586	78 843	...	5.0	5.2	5.2	5.2	...
Portugal[39]											
Total	C	31 998	31 478	32 393	32 399	33 634	3.1	3.0	3.1	3.1	3.3
Republic of Moldova - République de Moldova											
Total	C	24 449	25 624	24 709	21 992	20 924	6.9	8.5	...	...	...
Urban - Urbaine	C	12 523	13 376	12 919	11 233	10 980	...	11.7	...	...	...
Rural - Rurale	C	11 926	12 248	11 790	10 759	9 944	...	6.6	...	...	...
Romania - Roumanie											
Total	C	107 507	118 075	125 454	133 183	142 613	5.4	5.9	6.3	6.8	7.3
Urban - Urbaine	C	68 985	76 833	80 975	84 226	91 212	6.4	7.2	7.6	8.0	...
Rural - Rurale	C	38 522	41 242	44 479	48 957	51 401	4.2	4.5	4.9	5.4	...
Russian Federation - Fédération de Russie[40]											
Total	C	1 225 501	...	...	...	...	8.5	...	...	...	...
San Marino - Saint-Marin[41]											
Total	C	221	187	182	181	159[42]	6.6	5.6	5.4	5.3	4.6
Serbia - Serbie[43]											
Total	+C	36 209	36 429	36 949[44]	35 921[44]	...	5.1	5.1	5.2	5.1	...
Urban - Urbaine	+C	23 573	23 718	24 521[44]	23 554[44]	...	5.5	5.6	5.7	5.5	...
Rural - Rurale	+C	12 636	12 711	12 428[44]	12 367[44]	...	4.4	4.4	4.4	4.4	...
Slovakia - Slovaquie[9]											
Total	C	25 491	26 737	28 775	29 897	31 309	4.7	4.9	5.3	5.5	5.8
Urban - Urbaine	C	14 491	15 280	16 443	16 793	17 588	4.9	5.2	5.6	5.7	...
Rural - Rurale	C	11 000	11 457	12 332	13 104	13 721	4.4	4.6	4.9	5.2	...
Slovenia - Slovénie											
Total	C	6 254[45]	6 571[45]	6 449[45]	6 667[45]	6 481	3.0	3.2	3.1	3.2	3.1
Urban - Urbaine[45]	C	3 295	3 365	3 418	3 665	...	3.1	3.2	3.1	3.3	...
Rural - Rurale[45]	C	2 959	3 206	3 031	3 002	...	2.9	3.2	3.2	3.1	...
Spain - Espagne											
Total	C	151 433	160 256	166 651	173 049	*171 454	3.3	3.4	3.6	3.7	*3.7
Sweden - Suède[12]											
Total	C	51 554	53 051	52 314	53 817	52 497	5.4	5.5	5.3	5.4	5.2
Switzerland - Suisse											
Total	C	39 794[46]	41 891[46]	41 437[46]	41 646[46]	40 599	4.9	5.1	5.0	5.0	4.8
Urban - Urbaine[46]	C	30 455	32 019	35 758[47]	35 995	...	5.1	5.3	5.1	5.1	...
Rural - Rurale[46]	C	9 339	9 872	5 679[47]	5 651	...	4.4	4.6	4.4	4.4	...
TFYR of Macedonia - L'ex-R. y. de Macédoine											
Total	C	13 982	13 813	14 186	13 199	13 781	6.8	6.7	6.9	6.4	6.6
Urban - Urbaine	C	7 759	7 782	8 168	7 328	...	...	...	...	...	...
Rural - Rurale	C	6 223	6 031	6 018	5 871	...	...	...	...	...	...
Ukraine											
Total	+C	304 232	294 962[48]	299 038[48]	229 453[48]	...	6.7	6.9	7.0	5.4	...
Urban - Urbaine	+C	235 108	224 539[48]	222 747[48]	172 663[48]	...	...	...	...	...	...
Rural - Rurale	+C	69 124	70 423[48]	76 291[48]	56 790[48]	...	...	...	...	...	...
United Kingdom of Great Britain and Northern Ireland - Royaume-Uni de Grande-Bretagne et d'Irlande du Nord[49]											
Total	C	276 527	289 841	283 559	...	...	4.3	4.5	4.4	...	...
OCEANIA - OCÉANIE											
American Samoa - Samoas américaines											
Total	C	186	217	...	...	...	3.0	3.5	...	...	...
Australia - Australie											
Total	+C	118 962	121 197	113 595	118 401	...	5.1	5.2	4.8	4.9	...
Cook Islands - Îles Cook[50]											
Total	+C	843	746	720	...	...	45.3	40.1	38.5	...	...

Continent, country or area, and urban/rural residence / Continent, pays ou zone et résidence, urbaine/rurale	Code[a]	Number - Nombre					Rate - Taux				
		2013	2014	2015	2016	2017	2013	2014	2015	2016	2017
OCEANIA - OCÉANIE											
Fiji - Fidji											
Total	+C	8 639	8 501	...	...	...	10.0	9.8	...	...	...
French Polynesia - Polynésie française											
Total	C	1 474	1 480	1 456	...	...	5.5	5.5	5.3	...	...
Guam[51]											
Total	C	1 462	1 463	1 348[12]	1 185[12]	1 244[12]	9.1	9.1	8.3	7.3	7.6
New Caledonia - Nouvelle-Calédonie											
Total	C	926	971	983[12]	894[12]	...	3.5	3.6	3.6	3.3	...
New Zealand - Nouvelle-Zélande[12]											
Total	+C	19 237[9]	20 125[52]	19 947[53]	20 235[53]	*20 685[53]	4.3	4.5	4.3	4.3	*4.3
Norfolk Island - Île Norfolk[54]											
Total	+C	19	15	24	...	...	...	...	...	...	...
Samoa											
Total	U	...	...	865	...	...	...	...	...	...	...

FOOTNOTES - NOTES

Italics: data from civil registers which are incomplete or of unknown completeness. - Italiques : données incomplètes ou dont le degré d'exactitude n'est pas connu, provenant des registres de l'état civil.

* Provisional. - Données provisoires.

a 'Code' indicates the source of data, as follows:
C - Civil registration, estimated over 90% complete
U - Civil registration, estimated less than 90% complete
| - Other source, estimated reliable
+ - Data tabulated by date of registration rather than occurence
... - Information not available

Le 'Code' indique la source des données, comme suit :
C - Registres de l'état civil considérés complets à 90 p. 100 au moins
U - Registres de l'état civil qui ne sont pas considérés complets à 90 p. 100 au moins
| - Autre source, considérée pas douteuses
+ - Données exploitées selon la date de l'enregistrement et non la date de l'événement
... - Information pas disponible

1 Data refer to Algerian population only. - Les données ne concernent que la population algérienne.
2 Source: Vital Statistics Report 2016. - Source: Vital Statistics Report 2016.
3 Including marriages resumed after 'revocable divorce' (among Moslem population), which approximates legal separation. - Y compris les unions reconstituées après un 'divorce révocable' (parmi la population musulmane), qui est à peu près l'équivalent d'une séparation légale.
4 Excludes the islands of St. Brandon and Agalega. - Non compris les îles St. Brandon et Agalega.
5 Including visitors. - Y compris les visiteurs.
6 Excluding visitors. - Ne comprend pas les visiteurs.
7 Including non-residents. - Y compris les non-résidents.
8 Data refer to marriages where one or both partners are residents. - Les données portent sur les mariages pour lesquels l'un des deux partenaires ou les deux sont résidents.
9 Data refer to marriages by residence of the groom. - Les données concernent les mariages selon la résidence du marié.
10 Marriages registered by residence of bride. - Les mariages sont enregistrés selon le lieu de résidence de la mariée.
11 Data refers to the number of marriages of which at least one of the partners is a resident of Curacao. - Les données concernent le nombre de mariages dont au moins l'un des partenaires est un résident de Curaçao.
12 Including same sex marriages. - Y compris les mariages entre personnes du même sexe.

13 The total number may include 'Unknown residence', but the categories urban and rural do not. Urban and rural distribution refers to the usual residence of the bride. - Le nombre total peut inclure les personnes dont la résidence n'est pas connue, à l'inverse des catégories de population urbaine et rurale. La répartition entre résidence urbaine et résidence rurale fait référence au lieu de résidence habituel de la mariée.
14 Excluding data for Georgia, one of the states of the United States of America. - À l'exclusion des données pour la Géorgie, l'un des États des États-Unis d'Amérique.
15 Urban and rural residence refers to the place of usual residence of groom. - Le lieu de résidence (zone urbaine ou zone rurale) correspond au lieu de résidence habituel du marié.
16 Excludes nomadic Indian tribes. - Non compris les tribus d'Indiens nomades.
17 Excluding Amerindians. - Non compris les Amérindiens.
18 Data are compiled from the National Registers of Identification and Civil Status (RENIEC). - Les données sont rédigées à partir des Registres Nationaux d'Identification et d'État Civil (RENIEC).
19 Data refer to marriages of residents only. Data refer to government controlled areas. - Les données ne portent que sur les mariages de résidents. Les données se rapportent aux zones contrôlées par le Gouvernement.
20 Data refer to the Iranian Year which begins on 21 March and ends on 20 March of the following year. - Les données concernent l'année iranienne, qui commence le 21 mars et se termine le 20 mars de l'année suivante.
21 Includes data for East Jerusalem and Israeli residents in certain other territories under occupation by Israeli military forces since June 1967. - Y compris les données pour Jérusalem-Est et les résidents israéliens dans certains autres territoires occupés depuis 1967 par les forces armées israéliennes.
22 The total number may include 'Unknown residence', but the categories urban and rural do not. Urban and rural residence refers to the place of usual residence of groom. - Le nombre total peut inclure les personnes dont la résidence n'est pas connue, à l'inverse des catégories de population urbaine et rurale. Le lieu de résidence (zone urbaine ou zone rurale) correspond au lieu de résidence habituel du marié.
23 Data refer to Japanese nationals in Japan only. - Les données se raportent aux nationaux japonais au Japon seulement.
24 Excluding data for Jordanian territory under occupation since June 1967 by Israeli military forces. Excluding foreigners, including registered Palestinian refugees. - Non compris les données pour le territoire jordanien occupé depuis juin 1967 par les forces armées israéliennes. Non compris les étrangers, mais y compris les réfugiés de Palestine enregistrés.
25 Excluding alien armed forces, civilian aliens employed by armed forces, and foreign diplomatic personnel and their dependants. - Non compris les militaires étrangers, les civils étrangers employés par les forces armées ni le personnel diplomatique étranger et les membres de leur famille les accompagnant.
26 Excluding marriages previously officiated outside Singapore or under religious and customary rites. Data comprise civil marriages registered under the Women's Charter and Muslim marriages registered under the Administration of Muslim Law Act. - Ne comprend pas les mariages prononcés ailleurs qu'à

Singapour ni les mariages religieux ou coutumiers. Les données comprennent les mariages civils enregistrés en vertu de la Charte des droits de la femme, ainsi que les mariages musulmans enregistrés en vertu de la loi sur l'administration du droit islamique.

[27] Data from MERNIS (Central Population Administrative System). - Données de MERNIS (Système central de données démographiques).

[28] Excluding marriages of aliens temporarily in the area. - Non compris les mariages d'étrangers temporairement dans la région.

[29] Excluding marriages of aliens temporarily in the area, but including marriages abroad of persons with residence in Austria. - Non compris les mariages d'étrangers temporairement dans la région, mais y compris des mariages à l'étranger de personnes ayant leur résidence en Autriche.

[30] Including armed forces stationed outside the country and alien armed forces in the area, if the marriage is performed by local authority. Including same sex marriages. - Y compris les militaires nationaux hors du pays et les militaires étrangers en garnison sur le territoire, si le mariage a été célébré par l'autorité locale. Y compris les mariages entre personnes du même sexe.

[31] Including nationals outside the country, but excluding foreigners in the country. - Y compris les nationaux à l'étranger, mais non compris les étrangers sur le territoire.

[32] Excluding Faeroe Islands and Greenland shown separately, if available. - Non compris les Iles Féroé et le Groenland, qui font l'objet de rubriques distinctes, si disponible.

[33] The difference between 'Total' and the sum of urban and rural is due to the unknown place of residence of grooms and to grooms living outside the country. Urban and rural residence refers to the place of usual residence of groom. - La différence entre le « Total » et la somme des chiffres urbains et ruraux s'explique par le fait que la résidence du marié n'est pas toujours connue ou est située à l'étranger. Le lieu de résidence (zone urbaine ou zone rurale) correspond au lieu de résidence habituel du marié.

[34] Urban and rural distribution refers to the usual residence of the bride. Excluding Åland Islands. - La répartition entre résidence urbaine et résidence rurale fait référence au lieu de résidence habituel de la mariée. Non compris les Îles d'Åland.

[35] Data for urban and rural exclude events corresponding to nationals residing outside the country, which may be included in the total. - Les données relatives à les categories urbaine et rurale n'englobent pas les faits d'état civil qui concernent les nationaux se trouvant à l'étranger, lesquels faits peuvent être inclus au total.

[36] The urban and rural categories do not include the data of foreigners, persons of unknown residence and the homeless, whereas the total category includes them. - Les chiffres portant sur la population urbaine et rurale n' incluent pas les données relatives aux étrangers, aux personnes dont la résidence n'est pas connue et aux personnes sans domicile fixe, à l'inverse, le total les inclut.

[37] Marriages of couples of which at least one partner is recorded in a Dutch municipal register, irrespective of the country where the marriage was performed. Including same sex marriages. - Correspond aux mariages pour lesquels au moins l'un des partenaires est inscrit sur un registre municipal néerlandais, quel que soit le pays dans lequel le mariage est célébré. Y compris les mariages entre personnes du même sexe.

[38] Data exclude registered partnerships. - Les données ne comprennent pas les partenariats d'un pacte civil enregistrés.

[39] Marriages registered by place of occurrence of marriage. Including same sex marriages. - Mariages enregistrés en fonction du lieu de l'événement. Y compris les mariages entre personnes du même sexe.

[40] Data refer to population 15 years of age or more. - Les données concernent la population âgée de 15 ans ou plus.

[41] Includes civil and religious marriages as well as not specified. - Englobe les mariages civils et religieux et ceux pour lesquels rien n'a été indiqué.

[42] If either the groom or the bride (or both) is (are) resident in San Marino, their marriage is included in these data, independently of the place of occurrence of marriage. - Si l'un ou les deux époux résident à Saint-Marin, leur mariage est compris dans ces données, quel que soit le lieu où a été conclu le mariage.

[43] Excludes data for Kosovo and Metohia. - Sans les données pour le Kosovo et Metohie.

[44] Residence refers to residence of groom. - La catégorie « résidence » correspond au lieu de résidence du jeune marié.

[45] Data refer to residence of groom or bride before marriage. - Données relatives au lieu de résidence du marié ou de la mariée avant le mariage.

[46] Data based on the residence of groom if he has permanent address in the country, otherwise, based on the residence of bride. If neither partner is a permanent resident, the marriage is not included in the official statistics. - Les données sont fondées sur la résidence du marié si celui-ci a une adresse permanente dans le pays, sinon elles sont fondées sur la résidence de la mariée. Si aucun des deux partenaires n'est un résident permanent, le mariage n'apparaît pas dans les statistiques officielles.

[47] From 2015, urban refers to urban centers and areas under the influence of urban centers. - A partir de 2015, le territoire urbain inclut l'espace des centres urbains ainsi que l'espace sous influence des centres urbains.

[48] The Government of Ukraine has informed the United Nations that it is not in a position to provide statistical data concerning the Autonomous Republic of Crimea and the city of Sevastopol. - Le gouvernement Ukrainien a informé l'ONU qu'il n'est pas en mesure de fournir des données statistiques concernant la République autonome de Crimée et la ville de Sébastopol.

[49] Excluding Channel Islands (Guernsey and Jersey) and Isle of Man, shown separately, if available. Data tabulated by date of occurrence for England and Wales, and by date of registration for Northern Ireland and Scotland. - Non compris les îles Anglo-Normandes (Guernesey et Jersey) et l'île de Man, qui font l'objet de rubriques distinctes, si disponible. Données exploitées selon la date de l'événement pour l'Angleterre et le pays de Galles, et selon la date de l'enregistrement pour l'Irlande du Nord et l'Ecosse.

[50] Including non-residents. Excluding Niue, shown separately, which is part of Cook Islands, but because of remoteness is administered separately. - Y compris les non-résidents. Non compris Nioué, qui fait l'objet d'une rubrique distincte et qui fait partie des îles Cook, mais qui, en raison de son éloignement, est administrée séparément.

[51] Including United States military personnel, their dependants and contract employees. - Y compris les militaires des Etats-Unis, les membres de leur famille les accompagnant et les agents contractuels des Etats-Unis.

[52] Data refer to marriages and civil unions by residence of 'partner 2'. - Les données concernent les mariages et les unions civiles selon la résidence du « partenaire 2 ».

[53] Data refer to marriages and civil unions by residence of 'partner 2'. Data have been randomly rounded. - Les données concernent les mariages et les unions civiles selon la résidence du « partenaire 2 ». Ces données ont été arrondies de façon aléatoire.

[54] Data cover the period from 1 July of the previous year to 30 June of the present year. - Pour la période allant du 1er juillet de l'année précédente au 30 juin de l'année en cours.

Table 24 - *Demographic Yearbook 2017*

Table 24 presents the marriages cross-classified by age of groom and age of bride for the latest available year between 2008 and 2017.

Description of variables: Marriage is defined as the act, ceremony or process by which the legal relationship of spouses is constituted. The legality of the union may be established by civil, religious or other means as recognized by the laws of each country[1].

Marriage statistics in this table, therefore, include both first marriages and remarriages after divorce, widowhood or annulment. They do not, unless otherwise noted, include resumption of marriage ties after legal separation. These statistics refer to the number of marriages performed, and not to the number of persons marrying.

Age is defined as age at last birthday, that is, the difference between the date of birth and the date of the occurrence of the event, expressed in completed solar years. The age classification used for brides in this table is the following: under 15 years, 5-year age groups through 90-94, and 95 years and over, depending on the availability of data. Age classification for grooms is restricted to: under 15 years, 5-year age groups from 15 to 59, and 60 years and over.

In an effort to provide interpretation of these statistics, countries or areas providing data on marriages by age of groom and bride have been requested to specify "the minimum legal age at which marriage can take place with and without parental consent". This information is presented in the table 24-1 below.

Reliability of data: Data from civil registers of marriages that are reported as incomplete (less than 90 per cent completeness) or of unknown completeness are considered unreliable and are set in *italics* rather than in roman type. Table 23 and the technical notes for that table provide more detailed information on the completeness of marriage registration. For more information about the quality of vital statistics data in general, see Section 4.2 of the Technical Notes.

Limitations: Statistics on marriages by age of groom and age of bride are subject to the same qualifications as have been set forth for vital statistics in general and marriage statistics in particular as discussed in Section 4 of the Technical Notes.

The fact that marriage is a legal event, unlike birth and death that are biological events, has implications for international comparability of data. Marriage has been defined, for statistical purposes, in terms of the laws of individual countries or areas. These laws vary throughout the world. In addition, comparability is further limited because some countries or areas compile statistics only for civil marriages although religious marriages may also be legally recognized; in other countries or areas, the only available records are church registers and, therefore, the statistics may not reflect marriages that are civil marriages only.

Because in many countries or areas marriage is a civil legal contract which, to establish its legality, must be celebrated before a civil officer, it follows that for these countries or areas registration would tend to be almost automatic at the time of, or immediately following, the marriage ceremony. This factor should be kept in mind when considering the reliability of data, described above.

Because these statistics are classified according to age, they are subject to the limitations with respect to accuracy of age reporting similar to those already discussed in connection with Section 3.1.3 of the Technical Notes. It is probable that biases are less pronounced in marriage statistics, because information is obtained from the persons concerned and since marriage is a legal act, the participants are likely to give correct information. However, in some countries or areas, there appears to be a concentration of marriages at the legal minimum age for marriage and at the age at which valid marriage may be contracted without parental consent, indicating perhaps an overstatement in some cases to comply with the law.

Aside from the possibility of age misreporting, it should be noted that marriage patterns at younger ages, that is, for ages up to 24 years, are influenced to a large extent by laws regarding the minimum age for marriage.

Factors that may influence age reporting, particularly at older ages include an inclination to understate the age of the bride in order that it may be equal to or less than that of the groom.

The absence of data in the unknown age group does not necessarily indicate completely accurate reporting and tabulation of the age item. It is sometimes an indication that the unknowns have been eliminated by assigning ages to them before tabulation, or by proportionate distribution after tabulation.

Another age-reporting factor that must be kept in mind in using these data is the variation that may result from calculating age at marriage from year of birth rather than from day, month and year of birth. Information on this factor is given in footnotes when known.

Earlier data: Marriages by age of groom and age of bride have been shown for the latest available year in most issues of the *Demographic Yearbook*. Data cross-classified by age of groom and bride have been presented in previous issues featuring marriage and divorce statistics. For information on the specific topics and the years covered, readers should consult the Historical Index.

24-1 Minimum legal age at which marriage can take place

Country or area	With parental consent		Without parental consent	
	Groom	Bride	Groom	Bride
Africa				
Botswana	18	18	21	21
Burkina Faso[2]	18	15	20	17
Burundi[5]			21	18
Cameroon[3]	18	15	21	18
Egypt	18	18		
Ghana			18	18
Guinea	25	18		
Liberia	16	16	21	18
Libya[4]	18	18		
Malawi[5]			18	18
Mauritius	16	16	18	18
Morocco[5]			18	18
Namibia	18	18	21	21
Saint Helena ex. Dep.	16	16	21	21
Senegal	Under 18	Under 18	18	18
Seychelles	16	16	18	18
Sierra Leone[5]			18	18
South Africa[6]	Under 18	Under 18	18	18
Swaziland	18	18	21	21
Uganda[5, 7]			18	18
Zimbabwe	16	16	18	18
America, North				
Anguilla	16	16	18	18
Aruba[8]	16	16	18	18
Bermuda	16	16	18	18
Canada[9]	16	16	18	18
Cayman Islands	16	16	18	18
Costa Rica	15	15	18	18
Cuba	16	14	18	16

Country or area	With parental consent		Without parental consent	
	Groom	Bride	Groom	Bride
Curaçao	16	16	18	18
Dominican Republic	16	15	18	18
El Salvador	Under 18	Under 18	18	18
Greenland[5]			18	18
Jamaica	16	16	18	18
Mexico[10]	Under 18	Under 18	18	18
Montserrat[11]	16	16	18	18
Panama	16	14	18	18
Puerto Rico	17	17	21	21
Saint Vincent and the Grenadines			18	18
Trinidad and Tobago[12]	Under 18	Under 18	18	18
America, South				
Bolivia (Plurinational State of)[13]	16	14	18	18
Brazil	16	16	18	18
Chile	16	16	18	18
Colombia	14	14	18	18
Ecuador	14	12	18	18
Suriname	17	15	21	21
Uruguay	16	16	18	18
Venezuela (Bolivarian Republic of)	14	12	18	18
Asia				
Armenia			18	17
Azerbaijan	18	17		
Bahrain			15	
Cambodia			18	18
China, Hong Kong SAR	16	16	21	21
China, Macao SAR	16	16	18	18
Cyprus	16	16	18	18
Georgia	16	16	18	18
Indonesia			19	16
Iran (Islamic Republic of)	18	15		
Israel[5]			18	18
Japan	18	16	20	20
Jordan	18	18		
Kazakhstan	16	16	18	17
Kyrgyzstan[5]			16	16
Malaysia[14]	18	16 and 18	18 and 21	18 and 21
Mongolia			18	18

Country or area	With parental consent		Without parental consent	
	Groom	Bride	Groom	Bride
Nepal	18	18	20	20
Oman[5]			18	18
Philippines	18	18	22	22
Republic of Korea	18	18	19	19
Singapore[15]	Under 21	Under 21	21	21
State of Palestine[16]		14.5	15.5	
Tajikistan	17	17	18	18
Turkey	16	16	18	18
Uzbekistan	18	17		
Europe				
Åland Islands[19]			18	18
Albania			18	18
Austria[17]	16	16	18	18
Belarus	15	15	18	18
Belgium			18	18
Bosnia and Herzegovina			18	18
Bulgaria	16	16	18	18
Croatia	16	16	18	18
Czechia[18]	16	16	18	18
Denmark	15	15	18	18
Estonia	15	15	18	18
Faeroe Islands[5]			18	18
Finland[19]			18	18
France[5]			18	18
Germany[20]	16	16	18	18
Gibraltar	16	16	18	18
Greece[21]			18	18
Hungary	16	16	18	18
Iceland	No limit	No limit	18	18
Ireland[5, 22]			18	18
Isle of Man	16	16	18	18
Italy	16	16	18	18
Jersey	16	16	18	18
Latvia	16	16	18	18
Liechtenstein[17]			18	18
Lithuania[23]	15	15	18	18
Luxembourg			18	18
Malta			16	16
Montenegro	16	16	18	18
Netherlands	16	16	18	18

Country or area	With parental consent		Without parental consent	
	Groom	Bride	Groom	Bride
Norway	16	16	18	18
Poland[24]			18	18
Portugal	16	16	18	18
Republic of Moldova			18	16
Romania[25]	16	16	18	18
Russian Federation	16	16	18	18
Serbia[26]	16	16	18	18
Slovakia			16	16
Slovenia	15	15	18	18
Spain	14	14	18	18
Sweden[27]			18	18
Switzerland			18	18
TFYR of Macedonia	16	16	18	18
Ukraine[17]	16	16	18	18
United Kingdom of Great Britain and Northern Ireland	16	16	18	18
Oceania				
Australia[28]	16	16	18	18
Cook Islands	16	16	21	21
Guam[29]	17	17	18	18
New Caledonia			18	18
New Zealand	16	16	18	18

NOTES

[1] *Principles and Recommendations for a Vital Statistics System Revision 3,* Sales No. E.13.XVII.10, United Nations, New York, 2014.

[2] In addition, an age waiver may be granted by a civil court for a serious reason from 15 years for women and 18 years for men.

[3] Marriages can be exceptionally authorised by the President of the Republic for brides who are at least 13 years old without parental consent.

[4] According to the Islamic law, marriage requires parental consent. Consent of the bride herself, as well as the guardian's consent are fundamental in the marriage contract. Young men usually choose the consent of the parents. Minimum age at marriage is usually 18 years. According to the law, marriage is not restricted to individuals over the age of 18 years.

[5] The minimum legal age at which marriage can take place is the same with or without parental consent.

[6] Marriages under the age of 18 can be performed with parental consent or with judicial permission if parental consent has been unreasonably refused. Additionally, boys under the age of 18 and girls under the age of 16 may also be required to seek the consent of the Minister of Home Affairs.

[7] As reported by Uganda Bureau of Statistics, marriages with or without parental consent may occur much earlier than 18 years of age.

[8] The legal minimum marriage age is 18, with two exceptions: if the persons concerned are older than 16 and the woman is pregnant or has given birth or the Minister of Security and Justice grants a dispensation based on their request.

[9] Marriage is under provincial and territory legislations. Without parental consent, the minimum legal age at which marriage can take place is 18 years of age in all provinces and territories in Canada except in British Columbia, Newfoundland and Labrador, Nova Scotia, Nunavut, and Yukon where the minimum legal age is 19 years. With parental consent, the minimum legal age is 16 years in all provinces except in Northwest Territories, Nunavut, and Yukon. With parental consent, in Northwest Territories, and Yukon the minimum legal age is 15 years whereas in Nunavut, the minimum legal age is 18 years.

[10] Each of the 31 Federal States and the Federal District has its own civil code for marriage. Marriages under 18 require parental consent. Additionally, in the Federal District and in the states of Guanajuato, Morelos, Puebla and San Luis Potosí the minimum age with parental consent is 16 for both bride and groom and in the states of Michoacán, Nayarit, Sinaloa and Sonora the minimum age with parental consent is 14 for the bride and 16 for the groom.

[11] Consent can be given by a guardian or a person who has custody of the child wishing to marry. Also, the Governor has discretion to permit persons as young as 15 years and 1 day old to marry, if he thinks that getting married is in the best interest of the persons who are intending to marry and the persons in this instance must have also received the necessary consent.

[12] With parental consent, age for marriage is 14 years for males and 12 years for females in a civil marriage; 16 years for males and 12 years for females in a Muslim marriage; 18 years for males and 14 years for females in a Hindu marriage; and 18 years for males and 16 for females in Orisa marriage.

[13] Grooms younger than 16 and brides younger than 14 need court authorization.

[14] For marriage with parental consent, it is 18 years of age for males whereas it is 18 years of age for non-Muslim females and 16 years of age for Muslim females. Without parental consent, it is 21 years of age for non-Muslims and 18 years of age for Muslims.

[15] Specified minimum legal marriage age refers to marriages contracted under the Women's Charter. For Muslim marriages under the Administration of Muslim Law Act, no marriage shall be solemnised when either party is below the age of 18 years. Notwithstanding that, Muslim women below the age of 18 years who have attained the age of puberty may be married under the Administration of the Muslim Law Act.

[16] The legal marriage age for females is 14 years, 6 months and 22 days. There must be parental consent (father or brother if the father is dead). The legal marriage age for males is 15 years, 6 months and 21 days. Parental consent is not required.

[17] Persons less than 18 years old need a decision of the court.

[18] The court may, for important reasons, allow the marriage of a minor over 16 years.

[19] Persons less than 18 years old need the permission of the Ministry of Justice.

[20] Marriage at 16-17 years of age requires that the other spouse be an adult (18 years or older) and an exemption from the requirement of majority by a competent family court.

[21] Under some conditions (e.g. pregnancy) the marriage can take place without age restrictions.

[22] An exemption on the minimum age can be granted by court order if granting of such an exemption is in the best interests of the parties to the intended marriage and good reasons for the application can be demonstrated.

[23] In addition to parental consent, persons less than 18 years old need judicial approval. In case of pregnancy, marriage can be allowed below 15 years of age.

[24] Females can marry at the age of 16 or 17 years with parental and court consent.

[25] Marriage for persons under 18 years requires parental consent, a medical certificate and the agreement by the local family court.

[26] Marriage is not allowed for persons below the age of 18; only the court may, for good cause, permit marriage to a minor who has attained the age of 16 years of age, and attained physical and mental maturity to exercise the rights and responsibilities of marriage. Parental consent is not required.

[27] With parental consent, no limit but authorities must approve; without parental consent, 18 years of age for Swedish citizens.

[28] Persons 16 or 17 years old need the court approval.

[29] Under 18, both a court order and parent or legal guardian consent are needed.

Tableau 24 – *Annuaire démographique 2017*

Le tableau 24 présente des statistiques concernant les mariages classés selon l'âge de l'époux et selon l'âge de l'épouse pour les années où les données sont disponibles entre 2008 et 2017.

Description des variables : le mariage désigne l'acte, la cérémonie ou la procédure qui établit un rapport légal entre les époux. L'union peut être rendue légale par une procédure civile ou religieuse, ou par toute autre procédure, conformément à la législation du pays[1].

Les statistiques de la nuptialité présentées dans ce tableau comprennent donc les premiers mariages et les remariages faisant suite à un divorce, un veuvage ou une annulation. Toutefois, sauf indication contraire, elles ne comprennent pas les unions reconstituées après une séparation légale. Ces statistiques se rapportent au nombre de mariages célébrés, non au nombre de personnes qui se marient.

L'âge désigne l'âge au dernier anniversaire, c'est-à-dire la différence entre la date de naissance et la date de l'événement, exprimée en années solaires révolues. Le classement par âge pour l'épouse utilisé dans ce tableau comprend les groupes suivants : moins de 15 ans, groupes quinquennaux jusqu'à 90-94 ans, et 95 ans et plus, selon la disponibilité des données. Le classement par âge pour l'époux est : moins de 15 ans, groupes quinquennal de 15 jusqu' à 59 ans et 60 ans et plus.

Dans un effort de fournir l'interprétation de ces statistiques, les pays ou les zones fournissant des données sur les mariages par l'âge de l'épouse et de par l'âge de l'époux ont été demandés d'indiquer « l'âge légal minimum avec auquel le mariage peut avoir lieu avec et sans consentement parental ». Cette information est présentée dans le tableau 24-1 ci-dessous.

Fiabilité des données : les données sur les mariages issues des registres de l'état civil qui sont déclarées incomplètes (degré de complétude inférieur à 90 p. 100) ou dont le degré de complétude n'est pas connu sont jugées douteuses et apparaissent en italique et non en caractères romains. Le tableau 23 et les notes techniques s'y rapportant présentent des renseignements plus détaillés sur le degré de complétude de l'enregistrement des mariages. Pour plus de précisions sur la qualité des données reposant sur les statistiques de l'état civil en général, voir la section 4.2 des notes techniques.

Insuffisance des données : les statistiques des mariages selon l'âge de l'époux et selon l'âge de l'épouse appellent les mêmes réserves que celles formulées à propos des statistiques de l'état civil en général et des statistiques de la nuptialité en particulier (voir la section 4 des Notes techniques).

Le fait que le mariage soit un acte juridique, à la différence de la naissance et du décès, qui sont des faits biologiques, a des répercussions sur la comparabilité internationale des données. Aux fins de la statistique, le mariage est défini par la législation de chaque pays ou zone. Cette législation varie d'un pays à l'autre. La comparabilité est limitée en outre du fait que certains pays et zones ne réunissent des statistiques que pour les mariages civils, bien que les mariages religieux y soient également reconnus par la loi ; dans d'autres, les seuls relevés disponibles sont les registres des églises et, en conséquence, les statistiques peuvent ne pas rendre compte des mariages exclusivement civils.

Le mariage étant, dans de nombreux pays ou zones, un contrat juridique civil qui, pour être légal, doit être conclu devant un officier d'état civil, il s'ensuit que, dans ces pays ou zones, l'enregistrement se fait à peu près systématiquement au moment de la cérémonie ou immédiatement après. Il faut tenir compte de cet élément lorsque l'on évalue la fiabilité des données, dont il est question plus haut.

Étant donné que ces statistiques sont classées selon l'âge, elles appellent les mêmes réserves concernant l'exactitude des déclarations d'âge que celles dont il a déjà été question à la section 3.1.3 des Notes techniques. Il est probable que les statistiques de la nuptialité sont moins faussées par ce genre d'erreur, car les renseignements sont donnés par les intéressés eux-mêmes, et, comme le mariage est un acte juridique, il y a toutes chances que leurs déclarations soient exactes. Toutefois, dans certains pays ou zones, il semble y avoir une concentration de mariages à l'âge minimal légal de nubilité ainsi qu'à l'âge auquel le mariage peut être valablement contracté sans le consentement des parents, ce qui peut indiquer que certains déclarants se vieillissent pour se conformer à la loi.

Outre la possibilité d'erreurs dans les déclarations d'âge, il convient de noter que la législation fixant l'âge minimal de nubilité influe notablement sur les caractéristiques de la nuptialité pour les premiers âges, c'est-à-dire jusqu'à 24 ans.

Parmi les facteurs pouvant exercer une influence sur les déclarations d'âge, en particulier celles qui sont faites par des personnes plus âgées, il faut citer la tendance à diminuer l'âge de l'épouse de façon qu'il soit égal ou inférieur à celui de l'époux.

Si aucun nombre ne figure dans la rangée réservée aux âges inconnus, cela ne signifie pas nécessairement que les déclarations d'âge et l'exploitation des données par âge aient été tout à fait exactes. C'est parfois une indication que l'on a attribué un âge aux personnes d'âge inconnu avant l'exploitation des données ou qu'elles ont été réparties proportionnellement entre les différents groupes après cette opération.

Il importe de ne pas oublier non plus, lorsque l'on utilisera ces données, que l'on calcule parfois l'âge des conjoints au moment du mariage sur la base de l'année de naissance seulement et non d'après la date exacte (jour, mois et année) de naissance. Des renseignements à ce sujet sont donnés en note chaque fois que possible.

Donnés publiées antérieurement : on trouve dans la plupart des éditions de l'*Annuaire démographique* des statistiques concernant les mariages selon l'âge de l'époux et selon l'âge de l'épouse qui ont été établies à partir des données les plus récentes dont on disposait à l'époque. Des données croisant l'âge des époux ont été présentées dans des éditions antérieurs, plus particulièrement consacrées aux statistiques de la nuptialité et de la divortialité. Pour plus de précisions concernant les années et les sujets pour lesquels des données ont été publiées, se reporter à l'index historique.

24-1 L'âge légal minimum auquel le mariage peut avoir lieu

Pays ou zone	Avec consentement parental		Sans consentement parental	
	Epoux	Epouse	Epoux	Epouse
Afrique				
Afrique du Sud[2]	Moins de 18	Moins de 18	18	18
Botswana	18	18	21	21
Burkina Faso[3]	18	15	20	17
Burundi[6]			21	18
Cameroun[4]	18	15	21	18
Egypte	18	18		
Ghana			18	18
Guinée	25	18		
Libéria	16	16	21	18
Libye[5]	18	18		
Malawi[6]			18	18
Maurice	16	16	18	18
Maroc[6]			18	18
Namibie	18	18	21	21
Ouganda[6, 7]			18	18
Sainte-Hélène sans dép.	16	16	21	21
Sénégal	Moins de 18	Moins de 18	18	18
Seychelles	16	16	18	18
Sierra Leone[6]			18	18
Swaziland	18	18	21	21
Zimbabwe	16	16	18	18
Amérique du Nord				

Pays ou zone	Avec consentement parental		Sans consentement parental	
	Epoux	Epouse	Epoux	Epouse
Anguilla	16	16	18	18
Aruba[8]	16	16	18	18
Bermudes	16	16	18	18
Canada[9]	16	16	18	18
Costa Rica	15	15	18	18
Cuba	16	14	18	18
Curaçao	16	16	18	18
El Salvador	Moins de 18	Moins de 18	18	18
Groenland[6]			18	18
Îles Caïmanes	16	16	18	18
Jamaïque	16	16	18	18
Mexique[10]	Moins de 18	Moins de 18	18	18
Montserrat[11]	16	16	18	18
Panama	16	14	18	18
Porto Rico	17	17	21	21
République dominicaine	16	15	18	18
Saint-Vincent-et-les Grenadines			18	18
Trinité-et-Tobago[12]	Moins de 18	Moins de 18	18	18
Amérique du Sud				
Bolivie (État plurinational de)[13]	16	14	18	18
Brésil	16	16	18	18
Chili	16	16	18	18
Colombie	14	14	18	18
Equateur	14	12	18	18
Suriname	17	15	21	21
Uruguay	16	16	18	18
Venezuela (République bolivarienne du)	14	12	18	18
Asie				
Arménie			18	17
Azerbaïdjan	18	17		
Bahreïn			15	
Cambodge			18	18
Chine, Hong Kong RAS	16	16	21	21
Chine, Macao RAS	16	16	18	18
Chypre	16	16	18	18
État de Palestine[14]		14.5	15.5	

Pays ou zone	Avec consentement parental		Sans consentement parental	
	Epoux	*Epouse*	*Epoux*	*Epouse*
Géorgie	16	16	18	18
Indonésie			19	16
Iran (République islamique d')	18	15		
Israël[6]			18	18
Japon	18	16	20	20
Jordanie	18	18		
Kazakhstan	16	16	18	17
Kirghizistan[6]			16	16
Malaisie[15]	18	16 et 18	18 et 21	18 et 21
Mongolie			18	18
Népal	18	18	20	20
Oman[6]			18	18
Ouzbékistan	18	17		
Philippines	18	18	22	22
République de Corée	18	18	19	19
Singapour[16]	Moins de 21	Moins de 21	21	21
Tadjikistan	17	17	18	18
Turquie	16	16	18	18
Europe				
Albanie			18	18
Allemagne[17]	16	16	18	18
Autriche[18]	16	16	18	18
Bélarus	15	15	18	18
Belgique			18	18
Bosnie-Herzégovine			18	18
Bulgarie	16	16	18	18
Croatie	16	16	18	18
Danemark	15	15	18	18
Espagne	14	14	18	18
Estonie	15	15	18	18
Fédération de Russie	16	16	18	18
Finlande[19]			18	18
France[6]			18	18
Gibraltar	16	16	18	18
Grèce[20]			18	18
Hongrie	16	16	18	18
Île de Man	16	16	18	18
Îles d'Åland[19]			18	18

Pays ou zone	Avec consentement parental		Sans consentement parental	
	Epoux	Epouse	Epoux	Epouse
Îles Féroé[6]			18	18
Irlande[6, 21]			18	18
Islande	Pas de limites	Pas de limites	18	18
Italie	16	16	18	18
Jersey	16	16	18	18
L'ex-R. y. de Macédoine	16	16	18	18
Lettonie	16	16	18	18
Liechtenstein[18]			18	18
Lituanie[22]	15	15	18	18
Luxembourg			18	18
Malte			16	16
Monténégro	16	16	18	18
Norvège	16	16	18	18
Pays-Bas	16	16	18	18
Pologne[23]			18	18
Portugal	16	16	18	18
République de Moldova			18	16
Roumanie[24]	16	16	18	18
Royaume-Uni de Grande-Bretagne et d'Irlande du Nord	16	16	18	18
Serbie[25]	16	16	18	18
Slovaquie			16	16
Slovénie	15	15	18	18
Suède[26]			18	18
Suisse			18	18
Tchéquie[27]	16	16	18	18
Ukraine[18]	16	16	18	18
Océanie				
Australie[28]	16	16	18	18
Guam[29]	17	17	18	18
Îles Cook	16	16	21	21
Nouvelle-Calédonie			18	18
Nouvelle-Zélande	16	16	18	18

NOTES

[1] *Principes et recommandations pour un système de statistique de l'état civil, troisième révision,* numéro de vente : E.13.XVII.10, publication des Nations Unies, New York, 2014.

² Il est possible de se marier avant 18 ans avec consentement parental, ou autorisation judiciaire si le consentement parental a été refusé sans motif raisonnable. De plus, les garçons âgés de moins de 18 ans et les filles âgées de moins de 16 ans peuvent être également tenus de demander le consentement du Ministère de l'intérieur.

³ De plus, une dispense d'âge peut être accordée par un tribunal civil pour motif grave à partir de 15 ans pour les femmes et de 18 ans pour les hommes.

⁴ Par ailleurs, à défaut d'avoir l'âge requis pour se marier avec l'aval des parents, la jeune fille peut exceptionnellement être autorisée par le Président de la République à se marier à 13 ans.

⁵ Conformément à la loi islamique, le mariage requiert le consentement parental. Le consentement de la mariée, elle-même ainsi que le consentement du tuteur sont fondamentaux dans le contrat de mariage. Les jeunes hommes choisissent habituellement le consentement des parents. L'âge minimum du mariage est généralement 18 ans. Conformément à la loi, le mariage n'est pas limité aux individus âgés de plus de 18 ans.

⁶ L'âge minimum légal du mariage est le même avec ou sans le consentement parental.

⁷ Tel que le signale l'"Uganda Bureau of Statistics", les mariages avec ou sans le consentement parental peuvent se produire beaucoup plus tôt que 18 ans.

⁸ L'âge minimum légal du mariage est 18 ans, avec deux exceptions : si les personnes en cause ont plus de 16 ans et la femme est enceinte ou a accouché, ou si le Ministre de la sécurité et de la justice leur a accordé une dispense sur leur demande.

⁹ Le mariage est en vertu des législations provinciales et territoriales. Sans le consentement des parents, l'âge minimum légal du mariage est de 18 ans dans toutes les provinces et territoires du Canada sauf en Colombie-Britannique, Terre-Neuve-et-Labrador, la Nouvelle-Écosse, du Nunavut et du Yukon, où l'âge minimum légal est de 19 ans. Avec le consentement des parents, l'âge minimum légal est de 16 ans dans toutes les provinces sauf dans les Territoires du Nord-Ouest, Nunavut et Yukon. Avec le consentement des parents, dans les Territoires du Nord-Ouest et le Yukon l'âge minimum légal est de 15 ans alors que dans le Nunavut, l'âge minimum légal est de 18 ans.

¹⁰ Chacun des 31 Etats fédéraux et du District fédéral a son propre code civil pour le mariage. Avant 18 ans, il faut le consentement parental pour pouvoir se marier. De plus, dans le District fédéral et les États de Guanajuato, Morelos, Puebla et San Luis Potosí l'âge minimum, avec consentement parental, est de 16 ans pour le fiancé et la fiancée, et dans les États de Michoacán, Nayarit, Sinaloa et Sonora, l'âge minimum avec consentement parental est de 14 ans pour la fiancée et 16 ans pour le fiancé.

¹¹ Le consentement peut être donné par un tuteur ou une personne qui a la garde de l'enfant qui souhaitent se marier. En outre, le gouverneur a la faculté de permettre aux personnes âgées d'au moins 15 ans et 1 jour de se marier, s'il pense que le mariage est dans le meilleur intérêt des personnes qui ont l'intention de s'unir et que les personnes concernées aient également reçu le consentement nécessaire.

¹² Avec l'âge du le consentement parental, l'âge minimum du mariage pour se marier est de 14 ans pour les hommes et de 12 ans pour les femmes pour un mariage civil ; de 16 ans pour les hommes et de 12 ans pour les femmes pour un mariage musulman ; de 18 ans pour les hommes et de 14 ans pour les femmes pour un mariage hindou, et de 18 ans pour les hommes et de 16 pour les femmes pour un mariage orisa.

¹³ Il est nécessaire d'avoir une autorisation judiciaire pour se marier avant 16 ans pour les hommes et avant 14 ans pour les femmes.

¹⁴ L'âge légal du mariage pour les femmes est de 14 ans, 6 mois et 22 jours. Le consentement parental (du père ou du frère si le père est mort) est requis. L'âge légal du mariage pour les hommes est de 15 ans, 6 mois et 21 jours. Le consentement parental n'est pas nécessaire.

¹⁵ Pour le mariage avec le consentement parental, il est de 18 ans pour les hommes alors qu'il est de 18 ans pour les femmes non-musulmanes et il est de 16 ans pour les femmes musulmanes. Sans le consentement parental, il est de 21 ans pour les non-musulmans et de 18 ans pour les musulmans.

¹⁶ L'âge minimum légal du mariage spécifié correspond à des mariages contractés en vertu de la Charte des femmes. Pour les mariages musulmans sous l'administration de la « Loi sur le Droit Musulman », aucun mariage ne doit être célébré lorsque l'une des parties est en dessous de l'âge de 18 ans. Néanmoins, les femmes musulmanes en dessous de l'âge de 18 ans qui ont atteint l'âge de la puberté peuvent être mariées dans le cadre de l'administration de la « Loi sur le Droit Musulman ».

¹⁷ Le mariage à 16-17 ans exige que l'autre conjoint soit un adulte (18 ans ou plus) ainsi qu'une exemption de l'obligation de la majorité par un juge aux affaires familiales.

¹⁸ Les personnes âgées de moins de 18 ans doivent obtenir l'autorisation de la justice.

¹⁹ Les personnes âgées de moins de 18 ans doivent obtenir l'autorisation du ministère de la justice.

²⁰ Dans certaines conditions (par exemple la grossesse), le mariage peut avoir lieu sans restriction d'âge.

²¹ Une exemption sur l'âge minimum peut être accordée par ordonnance du tribunal si l'octroi d'une telle exemption est dans le meilleur intérêt des parties ayant l'intention de se marier et si la demande est appuyée par de bonnes raisons.

²² En plus du consentement parental, les personnes de moins de 18 ans doivent obtenir l'approbation judiciaire. En cas de grossesse, le mariage peut être autorisé en dessous de 15 ans.

²³ Les femmes peuvent se marier à l'âge de 16 ou 17 ans avec les autorisations des parents et du tribunal.

[24] Le mariage avant 18 ans exige le consentement parental, un certificat médical et l'autorisation du tribunal local de famille.

[25] Il n'est pas permis de se marier avant 18 ans ; seul le tribunal peut, pour un motif valable, y autoriser une personne mineure ayant atteint l'âge de 16 ans et parvenue à la maturité physique et mentale voulue pour exercer les droits et les responsabilités du mariage. Le consentement parental n'est pas requis.

[26] Avec le consentement des parents, aucune limite mais les autorités doivent approuver. Sans le consentement parental, l'âge minimum légal du mariage est de 18 ans pour les citoyens suédois.

[27] Il est possible de se marier de 16 ans par autorisation judiciaire pour des raisons importantes.

[28] Les personnes âgées 16 ou 17 ans doivent obtenir l'autorisation du tribunal.

[29] Le mariage avant 18 ans exige le consentement parental ou de personne qui a la garde de mineur, et l'autorisation du tribunal.

24. Marriages by age of groom and by age of bride: latest available year, 2008 - 2017
Mariages selon l'âge de l'époux et selon l'âge de l'épouse : dernière année disponible, 2008 - 2017

Continent, country or area, year, code[a] and age of bride / Continent, pays ou zone, date, code[a] et âge de l'épouse	Total	0-14	15-19	20-24	25-29	30-34	35-39	40-44	45-49	50-54	55-59	60+	Unknown Inconnu
AFRICA - AFRIQUE													
Botswana[1]													
2014 (+U)													
Total	5 591	-	-	59	572	1 389	1 275	847	540	329	235	345	...
0 - 14	-	-	-	-	-	-	-	-	-	-	-	-	...
15 - 19	9	-	-	2	6	-	1	-	-	-	-	-	...
20 - 24	401	-	-	39	166	119	53	13	8	3	-	-	...
25 - 29	1 407	-	-	14	325	626	303	84	37	9	6	3	...
30 - 34	1 631	-	-	3	63	552	565	264	111	35	24	14	...
35 - 39	965	-	-	1	10	71	274	322	179	72	23	13	...
40 - 44	499	-	-	-	2	13	63	133	136	89	40	23	...
45 - 49	266	-	-	-	-	3	10	26	55	79	50	43	...
50 - 54	206	-	-	-	-	4	4	5	12	38	70	73	...
55 - 59	91	-	-	-	-	-	2	-	2	3	18	66	...
60 - 64	56	-	-	-	-	1	-	-	-	1	4	50	...
65 +	60	-	-	-	-	-	-	-	-	-	-	60	...
Egypt - Égypte													
2017 (+C)													
Total	912 606	11 898	168 833	380 721	191 823	63 605	30 354	19 854	14 851	11 035	7 302	12 330	...
0 - 14	270 030	7 319	85 729	129 287	41 233	4 958	785	289	163	97	49	121	...
15 - 19	343 095	3 485	72 733	175 825	72 642	13 020	2 806	1 056	643	401	196	288	...
20 - 24	146 595	738	7 721	63 589	48 305	15 988	5 207	2 330	1 228	735	370	384	...
25 - 29	68 241	198	1 561	8 620	22 751	17 646	8 038	4 026	2 436	1 425	836	704	...
30 - 34	36 485	66	491	1 976	4 842	8 909	7 908	5 021	3 169	1 958	1 091	1 054	...
35 - 39	20 915	21	202	586	1 231	2 143	4 222	4 529	3 142	2 162	1 293	1 384	...
40 - 44	11 455	33	126	288	411	602	946	1 958	2 557	1 839	1 233	1 462	...
45 - 49	6 585	6	80	169	163	186	299	454	1 173	1 616	1 115	1 324	...
50 - 54	2 916	4	28	71	56	52	70	119	243	636	714	923	...
55 - 59	1 352	6	15	43	35	29	27	22	56	111	332	676	...
60 - 64	508	3	12	16	12	5	10	17	13	22	53	345	...
65 - 69	222	3	6	6	4	3	3	5	-	11	9	172	...
70 - 74	624	4	55	118	76	37	22	19	23	16	6	248	...
75 +	3 583	12	74	127	62	27	11	9	5	6	5	3 245	...
Lesotho													
2013 (+U)													
Total	4 552	...	11	370	1 402	1 133	635	325	225	175	99	162	15
15 - 19	188	...	9	101	56	15	7	-	-	-	-	-	-
20 - 24	1 230	...	2	235	673	237	55	10	6	8	2	1	1
25 - 29	1 502	...	-	28	611	597	165	55	21	11	7	7	-
30 - 34	792	...	-	6	51	246	289	109	49	24	9	9	-
35 - 39	370	...	-	-	3	28	103	106	65	34	19	11	1
40 - 44	173	...	-	-	1	1	8	38	57	39	14	15	-
45 - 49	116	...	-	-	-	2	2	6	24	50	22	10	-
50 - 54	40	...	-	-	-	-	1	-	2	8	17	12	-
55 - 59	23	...	-	-	-	-	-	-	1	-	7	15	-
60 - 64	11	...	-	-	-	-	-	-	-	1	2	8	-
65 +	91	...	-	-	6	7	3	1	-	-	-	74	-
Unknown - Inconnu	16	...	-	-	1	-	2	-	-	-	-	-	13
Mauritius - Maurice[2]													
2017 (+C)													
Total	9 757	-	86	1 056	3 028	2 204	1 340	717	452	365	243	264	2
0 - 14	-	-	-	-	-	-	-	-	-	-	-	-	-
15 - 19	578	-	67	282	163	39	17	6	4	-	-	-	-
20 - 24	2 216	-	19	575	1 079	377	130	26	5	4	-	1	-
25 - 29	3 232	-	-	156	1 527	1 036	366	100	21	14	6	5	1
30 - 34	1 499	-	-	26	199	585	423	166	52	32	11	5	-
35 - 39	891	-	-	15	45	124	287	223	127	41	15	14	-
40 - 44	493	-	-	1	7	24	79	140	109	77	38	18	-
45 - 49	358	-	-	-	6	12	26	44	89	103	46	32	-
50 - 54	244	-	-	1	2	6	10	10	34	69	67	45	-
55 - 59	150	-	-	-	-	-	-	2	8	20	52	68	-
60 - 64	66	-	-	-	-	-	1	-	3	5	6	51	-
65 - 69	14	-	-	-	-	-	-	-	-	-	1	13	-
70 - 74	12	-	-	-	-	1	-	-	-	-	1	10	-
75 +	2	-	-	-	-	-	-	-	-	-	-	2	-
Unknown - Inconnu	2	-	-	-	-	1	-	-	-	-	-	-	1

24. Marriages by age of groom and by age of bride: latest available year, 2008 - 2017
Mariages selon l'âge de l'époux et selon l'âge de l'épouse : dernière année disponible, 2008 - 2017 (continued - suite)

Continent, pays ou zone, date, code[a] et âge de l'épouse	Total	0-14	15-19	20-24	25-29	30-34	35-39	40-44	45-49	50-54	55-59	60+	Unknown Inconnu
AFRICA - AFRIQUE													
Reunion - Réunion													
2008 (C)													
Total	3 149	-	15	338	787	681	514	306	185	150	62	111	...
0 - 14	1	-	1	-	-	-	-	-	-	-	-	-	...
15 - 19	91	-	8	45	26	7	2	2	1	-	-	-	...
20 - 24	679	-	4	235	296	99	28	13	3	-	1	-	...
25 - 29	858	-	2	42	391	264	117	30	7	4	1	-	...
30 - 34	584	-	-	12	52	232	185	56	29	10	4	4	...
35 - 39	384	-	-	3	16	55	134	106	38	25	4	3	...
40 - 44	234	-	-	-	4	16	34	77	49	28	13	13	...
45 - 49	144	-	-	1	1	7	11	18	34	40	18	14	...
50 - 54	94	-	-	-	1	1	3	4	19	30	12	24	...
55 - 59	39	-	-	-	-	-	-	-	3	10	7	19	...
60 - 64	16	-	-	-	-	-	-	-	2	2	1	11	...
65 - 69	16	-	-	-	-	-	-	-	-	1	1	14	...
70 - 74	7	-	-	-	-	-	-	-	-	-	-	7	...
75 +	2	-	-	-	-	-	-	-	-	-	-	2	...
Saint Helena ex. dep. -													
Sainte-Hélène sans dép.													
2012 (C)													
Total	12	-	-	-	1	3	-	2	5	-	-	1	...
0 - 14	-	-	-	-	-	-	-	-	-	-	-	-	...
15 - 19	-	-	-	-	-	-	-	-	-	-	-	-	...
20 - 24	-	-	-	-	-	-	-	-	-	-	-	-	...
25 - 29	2	-	-	-	1	1	-	-	-	-	-	-	...
30 - 34	2	-	-	-	-	1	-	1	-	-	-	-	...
35 - 39	3	-	-	-	-	1	-	-	2	-	-	-	...
40 - 44	2	-	-	-	-	-	-	1	1	-	-	-	...
45 - 49	1	-	-	-	-	-	-	-	1	-	-	-	...
50 - 54	1	-	-	-	-	-	-	-	1	-	-	-	...
55 - 59	1	-	-	-	-	-	-	-	-	-	-	1	...
60 - 64	-	-	-	-	-	-	-	-	-	-	-	-	...
65 - 69	-	-	-	-	-	-	-	-	-	-	-	-	...
70 - 74	-	-	-	-	-	-	-	-	-	-	-	-	...
75 +	-	-	-	-	-	-	-	-	-	-	-	-	...
Seychelles[3]													
2017 (+C)													
Total	2 821	...	3	95	484	755	556	325	224	195	184[t]	...	...
15 - 19	20	...	1	8	4	5	1	-	-	1	-[t]	...	...
20 - 24	188	...	-	41	73	33	25	9	1	2	4[t]	...	...
25 - 29	765	...	1	31	267	281	101	52	12	15	5[t]	...	...
30 - 34	811	...	-	10	99	326	217	75	52	18	14[t]	...	...
35 - 39	488	...	-	2	28	74	164	112	51	29	28[t]	...	...
40 - 44	228	...	-	3	9	25	33	59	49	23	27[t]	...	...
45 - 49	165	...	-	-	2	8	12	13	39	60	31[t]	...	...
50 - 54	96	...	-	-	2	3	3	5	18	32	33[t]	...	...
55 +	60	...	1	-	-	-	-	-	2	15	42[t]	...	...
South Africa - Afrique du Sud													
2015 (...)													
Total	138 627	-	107	5 940	25 345	32 021	25 027	18 288	11 917	7 976	5 133	6 870	3
0 - 14	-	-	-	-	-	-	-	-	-	-	-	-	-
15 - 19	1 056	-	48	487	345	111	35	17	6	2	3	2	-
20 - 24	17 052	-	51	3 902	8 082	3 405	1 064	348	120	42	22	16	-
25 - 29	37 355	-	5	1 213	13 536	14 276	5 460	1 854	639	229	86	57	-
30 - 34	32 390	-	3	247	2 681	11 551	10 537	4 702	1 685	608	235	141	-
35 - 39	19 702	-	-	57	537	2 062	6 083	6 301	2 779	1 158	456	269	-
40 - 44	12 844	-	-	23	119	463	1 419	3 865	3 732	1 815	824	584	-
45 - 49	8 048	-	-	9	35	117	342	918	2 213	2 336	1 207	871	-
50 - 54	4 854	-	-	1	8	30	64	219	586	1 359	1 316	1 270	1
55 - 59	2 627	-	-	1	-	5	13	44	122	340	743	1 358	1
60 - 64	1 421	-	-	-	1	1	5	14	26	67	180	1 127	-
65 - 69	708	-	-	-	1	-	1	4	8	13	47	634	-
70 - 74	335	-	-	-	-	-	-	1	-	5	11	318	-
75 +	233	-	-	-	-	-	2	1	1	2	3	223	1
Unknown - Inconnu	2	-	-	-	-	-	2	-	-	-	-	-	-

Continent, pays ou zone, date, code[a] et âge de l'épouse	Total	0-14	15-19	20-24	25-29	30-34	35-39	40-44	45-49	50-54	55-59	60+	Unknown Inconnu
AFRICA - AFRIQUE													
2016 (...)													
Total	139 512	...	105[f]	5 430	24 626	32 104	24 859	18 828	12 335	8 585	5 424	7 214	2
0 - 19	1 050	...	...	...	...	...	...	...	...	...	...	...	...
20 - 24	15 487	...	...	...	...	...	...	...	...	...	...	...	...
25 - 29	36 775	...	...	...	...	...	...	...	...	...	...	...	...
30 - 34	32 921	...	...	...	...	...	...	...	...	...	...	...	...
35 - 39	20 456	...	...	...	...	...	...	...	...	...	...	...	...
40 - 44	13 546	...	...	...	...	...	...	...	...	...	...	...	...
45 - 49	8 255	...	...	...	...	...	...	...	...	...	...	...	...
50 - 54	5 315	...	...	...	...	...	...	...	...	...	...	...	...
55 - 59	2 833	...	...	...	...	...	...	...	...	...	...	...	...
60 - 64	1 593	...	...	...	...	...	...	...	...	...	...	...	...
65 - 69	738	...	...	...	...	...	...	...	...	...	...	...	...
70 +	543	...	...	...	...	...	...	...	...	...	...	...	...
Tunisia - Tunisie													
2016 (...)													
Total	99 281	...	196[f]	4 892	25 279	33 007	18 016	7 557	3 463	2 349	1 361	3 080	81
0 - 19	5 684	...	...	...	...	...	...	...	...	...	...	...	...
20 - 24	25 503	...	...	...	...	...	...	...	...	...	...	...	...
25 - 29	34 004	...	...	...	...	...	...	...	...	...	...	...	...
30 - 34	17 288	...	...	...	...	...	...	...	...	...	...	...	...
35 - 39	8 084	...	...	...	...	...	...	...	...	...	...	...	...
40 - 44	4 187	...	...	...	...	...	...	...	...	...	...	...	...
45 - 49	2 444	...	...	...	...	...	...	...	...	...	...	...	...
50 +	2 053	...	...	...	...	...	...	...	...	...	...	...	...
Unknown - Inconnu	34	...	...	...	...	...	...	...	...	...	...	...	...
AMERICA, NORTH - AMÉRIQUE DU NORD													
Anguilla[4]													
2013 (C)													
Total	42	4	9	9	4	4	4	1	-	1	...	...	6
0 - 14	5	2	2	-	-	-	1	-	-	-	...	...	-
15 - 19	12	1	5	3	3	-	-	-	-	-	...	...	-
20 - 24	9	-	1	5	1	1	1	-	-	-	...	...	-
25 - 29	5	1	1	1	-	2	-	-	-	-	...	...	-
30 - 34	3	-	-	-	-	-	2	1	-	1	...	...	-
35 - 39	2	-	-	-	-	1	-	-	-	1	...	...	-
40 - 44	-	-	-	-	-	-	-	-	-	-	...	...	-
45 - 49	-	-	-	-	-	-	-	-	-	-	...	...	-
50 - 54	-	-	-	-	-	-	-	-	-	-	...	...	-
Unknown - Inconnu	6	-	-	-	-	-	-	-	-	-	...	...	6
Aruba													
2017 (C)													
Total	537	-	11	58	126	100	72	50	52	32	16	19	1
0 - 14	-	-	-	-	-	-	-	-	-	-	-	-	-
15 - 19	3	-	1	2	-	-	-	-	-	-	-	-	-
20 - 24	45	-	6	19	9	6	2	3	-	-	-	-	-
25 - 29	94	-	3	23	47	11	7	3	-	-	-	-	-
30 - 34	80	-	1	6	33	24	9	3	1	3	-	-	-
35 - 39	85	-	-	4	18	30	20	6	5	1	-	-	1
40 - 44	71	-	-	2	9	13	21	12	12	1	-	1	-
45 - 49	54	-	-	1	7	9	7	7	15	6	1	1	-
50 - 54	48	-	-	1	2	4	4	10	13	9	3	2	-
55 - 59	21	-	-	-	1	1	-	3	5	7	4	-	-
60 - 64	21	-	-	-	-	2	2	3	1	2	5	6	-
65 - 69	10	-	-	-	-	-	-	-	-	3	2	5	-
70 - 74	4	-	-	-	-	-	-	-	-	-	1	3	-
75 +	1	-	-	-	-	-	-	-	-	-	-	1	-
Bahamas													
2013 (+C)													
Total	2 122	...	...	...	104	472	498	325	223	163	106	226	5
25 - 29	171	...	...	...	24	64	39	16	3	5	-	20	-
30 - 34	543	...	...	...	27	202	161	62	42	13	12	24	-
35 - 39	391	...	...	...	9	61	131	87	48	24	12	18	1

24. Marriages by age of groom and by age of bride: latest available year, 2008 - 2017
Mariages selon l'âge de l'époux et selon l'âge de l'épouse : dernière année disponible, 2008 - 2017 (continued - suite)

Continent, country or area, year, codeª and age of bride / Continent, pays ou zone, date, codeª et âge de l'épouse	Total	0-14	15-19	20-24	25-29	30-34	35-39	40-44	45-49	50-54	55-59	60+	Unknown Inconnu
AMERICA, NORTH - AMÉRIQUE DU NORD													
Bahamas													
2013													
40 - 44	249	...	...	...	5	21	53	70	50	28	9	13	-
45 - 49	219	...	...	...	5	24	33	28	38	44	23	24	-
50 - 54	192	...	...	...	6	21	28	26	22	38	21	30	-
55 - 59	133	...	...	...	6	17	20	17	9	6	18	39	1
60 +	216	...	...	...	22	62	33	17	10	4	11	56	1
Unknown - Inconnu	8	...	...	...	-	-	-	2	1	1	-	2	2
Bermuda - Bermudes													
2016 (C)													
Total	450	-	-	11	68	99	77	52	50	32	31	30	...
0 - 14	-	-	-	-	-	-	-	-	-	-	-	-	...
15 - 19	1	-	-	1	-	-	-	-	-	-	-	-	...
20 - 24	16	-	-	5	8	2	1	-	-	-	-	-	...
25 - 29	87	-	-	5	36	28	14	3	-	1	-	-	...
30 - 34	115	-	-	-	18	47	32	12	3	2	1	-	...
35 - 39	67	-	-	-	4	17	15	15	13	2	-	1	...
40 - 44	55	-	-	-	2	4	11	12	16	6	2	2	...
45 - 49	45	-	-	-	-	1	3	7	13	10	8	3	...
50 - 54	26	-	-	-	-	-	1	-	2	7	10	6	...
55 - 59	24	-	-	-	-	-	-	2	3	4	9	6	...
60 - 64	4	-	-	-	-	-	-	-	-	-	1	3	...
65 - 69	7	-	-	-	-	-	-	1	-	-	-	6	...
70 - 74	2	-	-	-	-	-	-	-	-	-	-	2	...
75 +	1	-	-	-	-	-	-	-	-	-	-	1	...
Costa Rica⁵													
2017* (C)													
Total	25 501	-	224	2 791	5 931	5 621	3 532	2 228	1 561	1 232	865	1 457	59
0 - 14	-	-	-	-	-	-	-	-	-	-	-	-	-
15 - 19	989	-	108	501	242	85	22	13	8	5	-	3	2
20 - 24	4 777	-	88	1 513	1 892	833	250	110	45	17	11	14	4
25 - 29	6 619	-	15	533	2 658	2 104	783	287	121	56	30	24	8
30 - 34	4 901	-	5	163	803	1 786	1 166	519	207	134	55	61	2
35 - 39	2 964	-	6	51	222	549	871	584	325	173	93	87	3
40 - 44	1 833	-	1	20	76	174	282	453	385	224	101	115	2
45 - 49	1 226	-	1	7	18	54	110	170	281	269	150	163	3
50 - 54	927	-	-	2	8	15	32	53	135	218	226	237	1
55 - 59	552	-	-	-	2	5	8	25	38	94	132	247	1
60 - 64	314	-	-	-	1	1	5	7	5	29	42	224	-
65 - 69	176	-	-	-	-	1	-	2	1	7	18	147	-
70 - 74	91	-	-	-	-	1	-	-	1	3	4	82	-
75 +	54	-	-	-	-	-	-	-	2	1	1	50	-
Unknown - Inconnu	78	-	-	1	9	13	3	5	7	2	2	3	33
Cuba⁶													
2016 (C)													
Total	61 903	-	898	6 324	11 510	9 707	6 547	7 136	6 217	5 141	2 926	5 496	1
0 - 14	38	-	7	16	7	5	2	1	-	-	-	-	-
15 - 19	3 861	-	535	1 657	1 048	367	85	61	46	28	15	19	-
20 - 24	10 074	-	230	2 804	3 747	1 737	685	388	212	126	50	95	-
25 - 29	12 453	-	60	1 110	4 183	3 419	1 625	1 043	503	271	105	134	-
30 - 34	8 532	-	27	379	1 366	2 357	1 672	1 360	728	348	121	174	-
35 - 39	5 635	-	11	137	487	873	1 152	1 297	870	455	179	174	-
40 - 44	6 019	-	5	79	300	460	708	1 495	1 424	918	341	288	1
45 - 49	5 451	-	12	50	182	234	373	884	1 378	1 275	529	534	-
50 - 54	4 612	-	6	52	94	156	157	431	696	1 185	830	1 005	-
55 - 59	2 282	-	-	16	39	50	42	108	221	358	500	948	-
60 - 64	1 423	-	2	12	21	22	25	28	77	114	189	933	-
65 - 69	836	-	1	3	13	9	7	21	33	42	39	668	-
70 - 74	402	-	1	3	9	9	3	10	13	9	15	330	-
75 +	282	-	1	6	13	8	11	9	15	12	13	194	-
Unknown - Inconnu	3	-	-	-	1	1	-	-	1	-	-	-	-
Curaçao⁷													
2016 (C)													
Total	695	-	1	35	104	108	116	73	70	63	55	59	11
0 - 14	-	-	-	-	-	-	-	-	-	-	-	-	-
15 - 19	9	-	1	5	1	-	1	1	-	-	-	-	-

24. Marriages by age of groom and by age of bride: latest available year, 2008 - 2017
Mariages selon l'âge de l'époux et selon l'âge de l'épouse : dernière année disponible, 2008 - 2017 (continued - suite)

Continent, country or area, year, code[a] and age of bride / Continent, pays ou zone, date, code[a] et âge de l'épouse	Total	\multicolumn{12}{c}{Age of groom - - âge de l'époux}
		0-14	15-19	20-24	25-29	30-34	35-39	40-44	45-49	50-54	55-59	60+	Unknown Inconnu
AMERICA, NORTH - AMÉRIQUE DU NORD													
Curaçao[7]													
2016													
20 - 24	82	-	-	20	36	9	9	5	3	-	-	-	-
25 - 29	141	-	-	9	46	35	33	8	6	2	2	-	-
30 - 34	133	-	-	1	18	50	23	16	16	2	4	3	-
35 - 39	75	-	-	-	2	9	26	15	10	8	3	2	-
40 - 44	70	-	-	-	1	3	12	21	13	13	5	2	-
45 - 49	57	-	-	-	-	2	9	5	14	13	8	6	-
50 - 54	60	-	-	-	-	-	1	1	8	19	21	10	-
55 - 59	31	-	-	-	-	-	2	1	-	3	10	15	-
60 - 64	11	-	-	-	-	-	-	-	-	2	1	8	-
65 - 69	10	-	-	-	-	-	-	-	-	1	1	8	-
70 - 74	3	-	-	-	-	-	-	-	-	-	-	3	-
75 +	2	-	-	-	-	-	-	-	-	-	-	2	-
Unknown - Inconnu	11	-	-	-	-	-	-	-	-	-	-	-	11
Dominican Republic - République dominicaine													
2016 (+C)													
Total	52 896	-	519	6 339	10 445	8 672	7 061	5 651	4 612	9 238	359[t]	...	...
0 - 14	-	-	-	-	-	-	-	-	-	-	-[t]	...	...
15 - 19	2 274	-	195	1 058	566	233	93	49	29	50	1[t]	...	...
20 - 24	10 511	-	174	3 300	3 796	1 577	735	361	223	335	10[t]	...	...
25 - 29	11 189	-	64	1 148	3 862	2 936	1 441	746	434	548	10[t]	...	...
30 - 34	8 062	-	25	387	1 134	2 219	1 939	1 030	573	750	5[t]	...	...
35 - 39	6 511	-	25	189	512	919	1 540	1 465	849	1 010	2[t]	...	...
40 - 44	5 014	-	10	118	282	392	713	1 129	1 102	1 264	4[t]	...	...
45 - 49	3 698	-	8	52	137	220	336	473	788	1 678	6[t]	...	...
50 - 54	5 174	-	10	47	127	161	249	390	605	3 579	6[t]	...	...
55 +	463	-	8	40	29	15	15	8	9	24	315[t]	...	...
El Salvador[8]													
2012 (...)													
Total	29 267	-	1 098	6 586	6 762	5 101	3 026	2 078	1 528	989	671	1 294	134
0 - 14	37	-	10	16	6	3	2	-	-	-	-	-	-
15 - 19	3 670	-	544	1 856	787	250	113	53	25	12	5	9	16
20 - 24	8 329	-	414	3 407	2 652	1 113	374	176	90	37	12	19	35
25 - 29	6 227	-	80	933	2 304	1 713	647	264	153	70	27	23	13
30 - 34	4 049	-	16	230	704	1 360	902	414	223	82	47	53	18
35 - 39	2 433	-	14	69	179	436	654	509	272	134	74	84	8
40 - 44	1 604	-	4	25	58	118	208	410	348	175	107	149	2
45 - 49	1 144	-	2	6	18	54	80	174	290	234	125	157	4
50 - 54	633	-	-	3	6	15	16	43	84	162	140	164	-
55 - 59	403	-	1	1	1	6	5	10	23	61	89	206	-
60 - 64	242	-	1	-	1	2	2	10	10	12	26	177	1
65 +	279	-	2	1	-	2	3	3	3	7	13	245	-
Unknown - Inconnu	217	-	10	39	46	29	20	12	7	3	6	8	37
Grenada - Grenade													
2014 (+C)													
Total	618	...	-	33	119	128	114	65	48	50	34	26	1
15 - 19	3	...	-	3	-	-	-	-	-	-	-	-	-
20 - 24	82	...	-	18	32	23	6	2	-	1	-	-	-
25 - 29	150	...	-	8	63	46	18	5	3	4	1	2	-
30 - 34	135	...	-	3	17	39	40	20	6	5	4	1	-
35 - 39	87	...	-	1	6	12	31	18	8	5	5	1	-
40 - 44	59	...	-	-	1	5	12	15	16	7	2	1	-
45 - 49	42	...	-	-	-	2	5	3	9	13	7	3	-
50 - 54	31	...	-	-	-	-	1	2	5	14	7	2	-
55 - 59	11	...	-	-	-	-	1	-	-	-	4	6	-
60 - 64	8	...	-	-	-	1	-	-	-	1	2	4	-
65 +	9	...	-	-	-	-	-	-	1	-	2	6	-
Unknown - Inconnu	1	...	-	-	-	-	-	-	-	-	-	-	1
Guatemala													
2016 (C)													
Total	69 613	...	3 770	22 309	17 775	9 964	5 310	3 047	2 002	1 483	1 170	2 775	8
15 - 19	10 278	...	1 955	6 003	1 714	391	128	35	29	10	6	6	1
20 - 24	25 405	...	1 567	12 810	7 847	2 188	616	202	87	39	23	25	1

24. Marriages by age of groom and by age of bride: latest available year, 2008 - 2017
Mariages selon l'âge de l'époux et selon l'âge de l'épouse : dernière année disponible, 2008 - 2017 (continued - suite)

Continent, pays ou zone, date, code[a] et âge de l'épouse	Total	0-14	15-19	20-24	25-29	30-34	35-39	40-44	45-49	50-54	55-59	60+	Unknown Inconnu
AMERICA, NORTH - AMÉRIQUE DU NORD													
Guatemala													
2016													
25 - 29	14 915	...	188	2 798	6 294	3 787	1 151	354	162	78	39	62	2
30 - 34	7 674	...	44	556	1 491	2 705	1 687	637	269	124	72	89	-
35 - 39	4 196	...	12	107	327	696	1 288	952	396	182	99	137	-
40 - 44	2 273	...	-	21	69	145	321	594	530	272	135	185	1
45 - 49	1 513	...	-	10	20	34	84	201	367	390	180	226	1
50 - 54	1 089	...	2	3	9	9	23	55	123	279	282	304	-
55 - 59	868	...	-	-	2	6	7	14	31	69	239	499	1
60 - 64	602	...	-	-	1	1	4	-	8	26	66	496	-
65 +	792	...	-	-	-	1	-	3	-	14	29	745	-
Unknown - Inconnu	8	...	2	1	1	1	1	-	-	-	-	1	1
Mexico - Mexique[g]													
2016 (+C)													
Total	543 749	7	25 460	138 026	145 372	91 485	49 201	29 962	19 140	13 386	10 330	20 599	781
0 - 14	212	6	99	80	17	8	-	1	-	1	-	-	-
15 - 19	68 132	1	16 660	37 524	10 197	2 494	784	246	115	40	31	29	11
20 - 24	160 887	-	7 558	78 028	53 135	15 031	4 406	1 607	597	266	110	127	22
25 - 29	135 801	-	887	17 920	64 673	35 134	10 882	3 731	1 445	577	281	249	22
30 - 34	73 128	-	179	3 269	13 504	29 154	16 032	6 354	2 490	1 118	502	501	25
35 - 39	38 367	-	45	808	2 809	7 200	12 044	8 110	3 702	1 741	923	976	9
40 - 44	23 942	-	13	240	704	1 750	3 601	6 783	4 995	2 707	1 448	1 695	6
45 - 49	15 808	-	7	62	191	492	1 031	2 236	4 081	3 250	1 982	2 475	1
50 - 54	10 956	-	-	22	55	117	283	601	1 221	2 621	2 540	3 494	2
55 - 59	7 159	-	4	7	8	39	66	175	317	740	1 765	4 034	4
60 - 64	4 343	-	-	5	6	4	21	59	109	229	539	3 370	1
65 - 69	2 194	-	-	2	1	4	10	16	32	50	143	1 934	2
70 - 74	1 104	-	-	-	-	-	2	10	10	23	48	1 009	2
75 +	735	-	-	2	3	3	-	6	7	10	13	690	1
Unknown - Inconnu	981	-	8	57	69	55	39	27	19	13	5	16	673
Montserrat													
2016 (C)													
Total	10	-	-	1	3	2	1	-	-	-	2	1	...
0 - 14	-	-	-	-	-	-	-	-	-	-	-	-	...
15 - 19	-	-	-	-	-	-	-	-	-	-	-	-	...
20 - 24	2	-	-	1	1	-	-	-	-	-	-	-	...
25 - 29	2	-	-	-	1	-	-	-	-	-	1	-	...
30 - 34	3	-	-	-	1	1	1	-	-	-	-	-	...
35 - 39	1	-	-	-	-	1	-	-	-	-	-	-	...
40 - 44	-	-	-	-	-	-	-	-	-	-	-	-	...
45 - 49	-	-	-	-	-	-	-	-	-	-	-	-	...
50 - 54	-	-	-	-	-	-	-	-	-	-	-	-	...
55 - 59	-	-	-	-	-	-	-	-	-	-	-	-	...
60 - 64	2	-	-	-	-	-	-	-	-	-	1	1	...
65 - 69	-	-	-	-	-	-	-	-	-	-	-	-	...
70 - 74	-	-	-	-	-	-	-	-	-	-	-	-	...
75 +	-	-	-	-	-	-	-	-	-	-	-	-	...
Panama[5]													
2016* (C)													
Total	14 233	-	112	1 565	3 009	2 746	1 901	2 320[n]	...	1 124[o]	...	965	491
0 - 14	-	-	-	-	-	-	-	-[n]	...	-[o]	...	-	-
15 - 19	465	-	53	231	111	37	12	2[n]	...	-[o]	...	1	18
20 - 24	2 462	-	39	875	926	346	116	84[n]	...	10[o]	...	6	60
25 - 29	3 232	-	13	291	1 300	952	373	203[n]	...	31[o]	...	4	65
30 - 34	2 505	-	2	80	404	891	580	390[n]	...	73[o]	...	27	58
35 - 39	1 669	-	1	23	132	298	456	576[n]	...	123[o]	...	25	35
40 - 49	1 900	-	1	11	40	114	251	796[n]	...	426[o]	...	211	50
50 - 59	888	-	1	-	2	10	22	129[n]	...	343[o]	...	360	21
60 - 69	316	-	-	-	1	-	2	14[n]	...	55[o]	...	236	8
70 +	74	-	-	-	-	-	-	1[n]	...	4[o]	...	68	1
Unknown - Inconnu	722	-	2	54	93	98	89	125[n]	...	59[o]	...	27	175
Puerto Rico - Porto Rico													
2017 (C)													
Total	12 793	-	222	1 973	2 725	2 021	1 441	1 174	964	804	547	915	7
0 - 14	-	-	-	-	-	-	-	-	-	-	-	-	-

Continent, pays ou zone, date, code[a] et âge de l'épouse	Total	0-14	15-19	20-24	25-29	30-34	35-39	40-44	45-49	50-54	55-59	60+	Unknown Inconnu
AMERICA, NORTH - AMÉRIQUE DU NORD													
Puerto Rico - Porto Rico													
2017													
15 - 19	323	-	97	180	34	10	2	-	-	-	-	-	-
20 - 24	2 185	-	100	1 179	650	175	57	9	11	3	1	-	-
25 - 29	2 708	-	22	462	1 345	553	201	82	24	14	4	1	-
30 - 34	1 969	-	-	105	454	753	372	171	71	27	7	9	-
35 - 39	1 528	-	-	28	161	348	443	304	132	67	23	22	-
40 - 44	1 144	-	-	14	48	115	232	326	214	108	55	32	-
45 - 49	940	-	1	3	19	43	89	180	272	191	86	56	-
50 - 54	750	-	-	1	9	13	37	69	134	206	142	139	-
55 - 59	490	-	2	-	4	5	6	19	60	110	112	172	-
60 - 64	359	-	-	1	1	3	2	6	31	52	66	197	-
65 - 69	177	-	-	-	-	2	-	4	8	11	26	126	-
70 - 74	126	-	-	-	-	-	-	3	2	9	13	99	-
75 +	87	-	-	-	-	1	-	1	5	6	12	62	-
Unknown - Inconnu	7	-	-	-	-	-	-	-	-	-	-	-	7
Saint Vincent and the Grenadines - Saint-Vincent-et-les Grenadines													
2015 (C)													
Total	572	-	-	26	83	113	84	76	48	60	32	50	...
0 - 14	-	-	-	-	-	-	-	-	-	-	-	-	...
15 - 19	5	-	-	1	1	1	1	-	-	-	-	1	...
20 - 24	60	-	-	14	27	11	5	2	1	-	-	-	...
25 - 29	130	-	-	10	39	42	27	8	2	1	-	1	...
30 - 34	98	-	-	-	6	37	23	17	6	7	1	1	...
35 - 39	91	-	-	1	7	10	21	26	10	10	5	1	...
40 - 44	68	-	-	-	2	8	3	15	15	15	6	4	...
45 - 49	51	-	-	-	-	3	3	3	12	15	3	12	...
50 - 54	31	-	-	-	1	1	1	3	1	8	10	6	...
55 - 59	17	-	-	-	-	-	-	-	-	3	4	10	...
60 - 64	15	-	-	-	-	-	-	2	1	1	2	9	...
65 - 69	3	-	-	-	-	-	-	-	-	-	-	3	...
70 - 74	3	-	-	-	-	-	-	-	-	-	1	2	...
75 +	-	-	-	-	-	-	-	-	-	-	-	-	...
Trinidad and Tobago - Trinité-et-Tobago													
2013* (C)													
Total	8 017	-	86	826	2 111	1 787	1 091	699	502	377	231	305	2
0 - 14	5	-	2	2	1	-	-	-	-	-	-	-	-
15 - 19	374	-	48	180	91	39	10	4	2	-	-	-	-
20 - 24	1 432	-	24	389	627	233	80	43	21	8	5	2	-
25 - 29	2 406	-	7	179	1 028	760	243	106	43	27	9	3	1
30 - 34	1 526	-	5	46	244	531	385	160	80	39	19	16	1
35 - 39	889	-	-	22	76	142	243	192	102	61	28	23	-
40 - 44	545	-	-	4	29	54	83	119	120	74	35	27	-
45 - 49	363	-	-	1	10	20	26	54	90	83	35	44	-
50 - 54	217	-	-	-	3	5	12	18	30	53	50	46	-
55 - 59	150	-	-	1	-	2	8	3	10	25	32	69	-
60 - 64	61	-	-	-	1	1	1	-	1	6	11	40	-
65 +	47	-	-	1	-	-	-	-	3	1	7	35	-
Unknown - Inconnu	2	-	-	1	1	-	-	-	-	-	-	-	...
Turks and Caicos Islands - Îles Turques et Caïques													
2008 (C)													
Total	486	...	-	20	110	114	94	63	51	17	10	7	...
15 - 19	2	...	...	...	...	...	...	...	...	...	...	...	...
20 - 24	47	...	...	...	...	...	...	...	...	...	...	...	...
25 - 29	134	...	...	...	...	...	...	...	...	...	...	...	...
30 - 34	127	...	...	...	...	...	...	...	...	...	...	...	...
35 - 39	94	...	...	...	...	...	...	...	...	...	...	...	...
40 - 44	37	...	...	...	...	...	...	...	...	...	...	...	...
45 - 49	26	...	...	...	...	...	...	...	...	...	...	...	...
50 - 54	12	...	...	...	...	...	...	...	...	...	...	...	...
55 - 59	6	...	...	...	...	...	...	...	...	...	...	...	...

24. Marriages by age of groom and by age of bride: latest available year, 2008 - 2017
Mariages selon l'âge de l'époux et selon l'âge de l'épouse : dernière année disponible, 2008 - 2017 (continued - suite)

Continent, pays ou zone, date, code[a] et âge de l'épouse	Total	0-14	15-19	20-24	25-29	30-34	35-39	40-44	45-49	50-54	55-59	60+	Unknown Inconnu
AMERICA, NORTH - AMÉRIQUE DU NORD													
Turks and Caicos Islands - Îles Turques et Caïques													
2008													
60 - 64	-	...	...	...	...	...	...	...	...	...	...	...	...
65 +	1	...	...	...	...	...	...	...	...	...	...	...	...
AMERICA, SOUTH - AMÉRIQUE DU SUD													
Bolivia (Plurinational State of) - Bolivie (État plurinational de)													
2012 (U)													
Total	34 542	...	...	...	...	...	...	...	...	...	1 864[t]	...	11
15 - 24	11 851	...	...	...	...	...	...	...	...	...	...	...	...
25 - 34	16 113	...	...	...	...	...	...	...	...	...	...	...	...
35 - 44	3 944	...	...	...	...	...	...	...	...	...	...	...	...
45 - 54	1 335	...	...	...	...	...	...	...	...	...	...	...	...
55 +	1 247	...	...	...	...	...	...	...	...	...	...	...	...
Unknown - Inconnu	52	...	...	...	...	...	...	...	...	...	...	...	...
Brazil - Brésil[9]													
2016 (+U)													
Total	1095535	4	28 428	193 925	264 937	218 883	139 723	85 605	57 245	40 267	26 139	39 779	600
0 - 14	244	2	124	91	19	4	2	1	1	-	-	-	-
15 - 19	109 474	1	18 204	59 632	21 976	6 495	2 049	688	242	111	36	40	-
20 - 24	244 453	1	7 668	93 913	92 279	33 652	10 971	3 627	1 362	597	216	167	-
25 - 29	255 195	-	1 631	27 982	102 240	78 493	28 918	9 430	3 744	1 651	636	466	4
30 - 34	187 138	-	529	8 336	34 079	66 853	45 469	18 332	7 693	3 338	1 402	1 098	9
35 - 39	117 530	-	175	2 702	10 153	23 132	33 732	24 722	12 107	5 976	2 645	2 183	3
40 - 44	70 281	-	59	850	2 834	6 879	12 226	17 399	14 334	8 143	3 958	3 599	-
45 - 49	47 214	-	19	263	934	2 409	4 290	7 485	10 881	9 604	5 580	5 748	1
50 - 54	30 761	-	14	81	279	688	1 510	2 795	4 688	7 073	6 169	7 464	-
55 - 59	16 464	-	4	34	86	182	387	781	1 519	2 520	3 650	7 301	-
60 - 64	8 804	-	-	25	30	62	107	226	463	872	1 273	5 746	-
65 +	7 361	-	1	11	18	30	57	116	210	381	573	5 963	1
Unknown - Inconnu	616	-	-	5	10	4	5	3	1	1	1	4	582
Chile - Chili													
2015 (+C)													
Total	61 744	-	1 423	9 550	17 368	12 639	6 703	4 430	3 382	2 529	1 696	2 024	...
0 - 14	-	-	-	-	-	-	-	-	-	-	-	-	...
15 - 19	384	-	214	134	28	6	2	-	-	-	-	-	...
20 - 24	6 368	-	784	3 733	1 459	280	82	22	4	3	-	1	...
25 - 29	15 277	-	295	4 017	8 361	2 039	417	113	25	6	4	-	...
30 - 34	14 014	-	73	1 169	5 361	5 649	1 307	336	79	30	10	-	...
35 - 39	8 094	-	38	336	1 442	3 002	2 221	735	245	60	11	4	...
40 - 44	5 221	-	13	112	481	1 072	1 512	1 290	500	178	44	19	...
45 - 49	3 534	-	4	31	153	358	668	959	838	360	119	44	...
50 - 54	2 821	-	2	13	52	134	281	540	807	625	250	117	...
55 - 59	2 137	-	-	4	20	55	124	255	451	561	414	253	...
60 - 64	1 543	-	-	1	8	28	45	107	233	345	371	405	...
65 - 69	1 117	-	-	-	2	9	27	45	127	206	266	435	...
70 - 74	597	-	-	-	1	1	13	19	46	93	119	305	...
75 +	637	-	-	-	-	6	4	9	27	62	88	441	...
Ecuador - Équateur[10]													
2016 (U)													
Total	57 738	-	1 568	12 337	15 833	10 689	6 161	3 450	2 422	1 722	1 215	2 341	...
0 - 14	-	-	-	-	-	-	-	-	-	-	-	-	...
15 - 19	5 235	-	901	2 934	983	297	72	30	7	6	3	2	...
20 - 24	16 263	-	577	7 218	5 918	1 760	530	158	60	22	7	13	...
25 - 29	15 118	-	69	1 734	6 948	4 244	1 446	418	149	59	31	20	...
30 - 34	8 336	-	13	332	1 519	3 223	1 968	750	290	138	54	49	...
35 - 39	4 807	-	5	84	346	907	1 533	1 009	513	232	91	87	...
40 - 44	2 763	-	2	20	79	180	426	730	620	342	202	162	...
45 - 49	2 022	-	1	12	25	51	132	262	524	490	253	272	...
50 - 54	1 285	-	-	2	9	25	43	61	200	303	284	358	...
55 - 59	819	-	-	1	2	1	10	24	44	95	202	440	...

Continent, country or area, year, code[a] and age of bride / Continent, pays ou zone, date, code[a] et âge de l'épouse	Total	0-14	15-19	20-24	25-29	30-34	35-39	40-44	45-49	50-54	55-59	60+	Unknown Inconnu
AMERICA, SOUTH - AMÉRIQUE DU SUD													
Ecuador - Équateur[10]													
2016													
60 - 64	483	-	-	-	2	1	-	4	8	27	60	381	...
65 - 69	297	-	-	-	2	-	-	3	5	7	21	259	...
70 - 74	153	-	-	-	-	-	1	1	1	1	3	146	...
75 +	157	-	-	-	-	-	-	-	1	-	4	152	...
Paraguay													
2014 (U)													
Total	19 527	-	522	4 026	5 754	4 204	1 953	1 143	687	472	279	481	6
0 - 14	6	-	2	1	3	-	-	-	-	-	-	-	-
15 - 19	2 725	-	373	1 359	659	224	68	24	7	7	2	2	-
20 - 24	5 192	-	119	1 962	2 002	788	192	74	27	15	3	9	1
25 - 29	5 035	-	21	527	2 250	1 541	441	147	57	23	12	16	-
30 - 34	3 249	-	4	120	687	1 227	669	310	112	64	24	31	1
35 - 39	1 355	-	3	35	102	284	396	285	142	66	17	25	-
40 - 44	725	-	-	13	32	78	123	187	158	69	22	43	-
45 - 49	496	-	-	3	15	40	43	65	116	115	60	39	-
50 - 54	322	-	-	3	2	14	14	32	46	68	72	71	-
55 - 59	181	-	-	1	1	5	2	11	15	32	37	77	-
60 - 64	110	-	-	-	-	1	2	4	3	6	19	75	-
65 - 69	66	-	-	-	-	2	1	2	3	4	10	44	-
70 - 74	30	-	-	1	-	-	-	1	1	1	1	25	-
75 +	27	-	-	-	-	-	1	-	-	2	-	24	-
Unknown - Inconnu	8	-	-	1	1	-	1	1	-	-	-	-	4
2016 (U)													
Total	19 440	-	465	3 786	5 646	4 048	2 268	1 187	693	487	315	542	3
0 - 14	-	...	...	...	...	...	...	...	...	...	...	...	...
15 - 19	2 323	...	...	...	...	...	...	...	...	...	...	...	...
20 - 24	4 994	...	...	...	...	...	...	...	...	...	...	...	...
25 - 29	5 167	...	...	...	...	...	...	...	...	...	...	...	...
30 - 34	3 197	...	...	...	...	...	...	...	...	...	...	...	...
35 - 39	1 640	...	...	...	...	...	...	...	...	...	...	...	...
40 - 44	823	...	...	...	...	...	...	...	...	...	...	...	...
45 - 49	511	...	...	...	...	...	...	...	...	...	...	...	...
50 - 54	332	...	...	...	...	...	...	...	...	...	...	...	...
55 - 59	186	...	...	...	...	...	...	...	...	...	...	...	...
60 - 64	117	...	...	...	...	...	...	...	...	...	...	...	...
65 - 69	74	...	...	...	...	...	...	...	...	...	...	...	...
70 - 74	38	...	...	...	...	...	...	...	...	...	...	...	...
75 +	31	...	...	...	...	...	...	...	...	...	...	...	...
Unknown - Inconnu	7	...	...	...	...	...	...	...	...	...	...	...	...
Peru - Pérou[11,12]													
2015 (+C)													
Total	31 888	-	235	3 004	7 519	7 818	5 369	3 109	1 846	1 131	667	1 190	...
0 - 14	-	-	-	-	-	-	-	-	-	-	-	-	...
15 - 19	800	-	136	402	211	38	7	6	-	-	-	-	...
20 - 24	4 889	-	79	1 806	1 996	667	239	80	15	7	-	-	...
25 - 29	8 964	-	16	653	3 939	2 907	1 013	284	88	34	4	26	...
30 - 34	7 565	-	3	104	1 114	3 308	1 971	675	242	83	25	40	...
35 - 39	4 289	-	1	30	192	748	1 629	1 028	404	132	68	57	...
40 - 44	2 333	-	-	6	45	128	397	775	545	278	87	72	...
45 - 49	1 386	-	-	3	10	15	89	198	416	342	171	142	...
50 - 54	729	-	-	-	3	4	13	43	102	193	175	196	...
55 - 59	432	-	-	-	3	1	-	6	21	48	114	239	...
60 +	501	-	-	-	6	2	11	14	13	14	23	418	...
Venezuela (Bolivarian Republic of) - Venezuela (République bolivarienne du)													
2016 (C)													
Total	84 349	2	1 718	15 084	22 936	16 410	10 357	6 625	4 328	2 720	1 791	2 378	...
0 - 14	72	-	25	33	8	2	3	-	1	-	-	-	...
15 - 19	6 605	1	1 040	3 454	1 403	433	158	53	27	17	9	10	...
20 - 24	20 630	-	459	8 472	7 872	2 441	825	309	157	46	25	24	...
25 - 29	22 412	1	114	2 333	10 214	6 150	2 204	803	352	134	55	52	...
30 - 34	13 919	-	44	533	2 475	5 155	3 193	1 447	603	261	115	93	...
35 - 39	8 483	-	21	154	648	1 538	2 657	1 805	927	418	171	144	...

Continent, country or area, year, code[a] and age of bride / Continent, pays ou zone, date, code[a] et âge de l'épouse	Total	0-14	15-19	20-24	25-29	30-34	35-39	40-44	45-49	50-54	55-59	60+	Unknown Inconnu
AMERICA, SOUTH - AMÉRIQUE DU SUD													
Venezuela (Bolivarian Republic of) - Venezuela (République bolivarienne du)													
2016													
40 - 44	5 044	-	7	49	200	464	895	1 425	1 000	537	253	214	...
45 - 49	3 227	-	4	24	71	152	295	514	848	629	380	310	...
50 - 54	1 855	-	2	9	20	39	86	192	291	448	389	379	...
55 - 59	1 035	-	1	8	10	16	18	47	77	160	252	446	...
60 - 64	606	-	-	6	5	5	8	17	31	49	104	381	...
65 - 69	252	-	1	3	2	4	7	8	7	11	30	179	...
70 - 74	120	-	-	4	5	1	3	1	6	5	5	90	...
75 +	89	-	-	2	3	10	5	4	1	5	3	56	...
ASIA - ASIE													
Armenia - Arménie													
2016 (+C)													
Total	16 294	...	49	2 633	6 419	3 770	1 540	756	412	281	191	243	...
15 - 19	911	...	30	374	423	82	2	-	-	-	-	-	...
20 - 24	6 351	...	14	1 965	3 282	969	108	9	3	1	-	-	...
25 - 29	4 911	...	4	242	2 416	1 717	447	61	15	7	-	2	...
30 - 34	2 050	...	-	30	234	847	624	229	54	22	9	1	...
35 - 39	986	...	-	10	40	114	303	311	137	43	20	8	...
40 - 44	464	...	-	8	13	25	46	118	134	76	31	13	...
45 - 49	219	...	1	1	5	9	7	20	50	73	34	19	...
50 - 54	157	...	-	3	1	5	3	4	14	37	56	34	...
55 - 59	127	...	-	-	5	1	-	3	4	16	32	66	...
60 +	118	...	-	-	-	1	-	1	1	6	9	100	...
Azerbaijan - Azerbaïdjan													
2016 (+C)													
Total	66 771	...	385	17 692	29 260	10 896	3 716	1 923	1 093	703	464	639	...
15 - 19	15 380	...	243	6 313	7 294	1 431	92	5	2	-	-	-	...
20 - 24	29 435	...	123	9 851	14 714	4 050	593	82	19	3	-	-	...
25 - 29	12 629	...	14	1 341	6 265	3 491	1 120	303	71	17	5	2	...
30 - 34	4 567	...	4	140	804	1 561	1 165	601	212	58	13	9	...
35 - 39	2 113	...	-	35	134	293	556	556	327	130	57	25	...
40 - 44	1 142	...	1	6	36	45	147	281	258	192	108	68	...
45 - 49	666	...	-	3	9	16	28	69	157	182	92	110	...
50 - 54	437	...	-	1	2	6	10	23	35	93	118	149	...
55 - 59	261	...	-	1	-	2	5	3	11	24	62	153	...
60 +	141	...	-	1	2	1	-	-	1	4	9	123	...
Bahrain - Bahreïn													
2017 (...)													
Total	6 691	...	155	1 896	2 562	976	386	232	166	318[s]	...	...	...
0 - 14	8	...	2	3	2	-	1	-	-	_[s]	...	...	...
15 - 19	1 115	...	127	677	270	30	5	2	-	4[s]	...	...	...
20 - 24	2 768	...	24	1 085	1 400	200	25	15	13	6[s]	...	...	...
25 - 29	1 524	...	1	101	779	467	110	33	19	14[s]	...	...	...
30 - 34	619	...	1	23	90	217	150	52	40	46[s]	...	...	...
35 - 39	314	...	-	3	15	46	76	83	33	58[s]	...	...	...
40 - 44	148	...	-	2	3	10	13	39	41	40[s]	...	...	...
45 - 49	97	...	-	2	2	5	6	7	18	57[s]	...	...	...
50 +	98	...	-	-	1	1	-	1	2	93[s]	...	...	...
Brunei Darussalam - Brunéi Darussalam													
2016 (+C)													
Total	2 532	-	39	401	1 078	519	241	102	49	33	28	42	...
0 - 14	-	...	...	...	...	...	...	...	...	...	...	...	...
15 - 19	146	...	...	...	...	...	...	...	...	...	...	...	...
20 - 24	624	...	...	...	...	...	...	...	...	...	...	...	...
25 - 29	1 063	...	...	...	...	...	...	...	...	...	...	...	...
30 - 34	379	...	...	...	...	...	...	...	...	...	...	...	...
35 - 39	151	...	...	...	...	...	...	...	...	...	...	...	...
40 - 44	89	...	...	...	...	...	...	...	...	...	...	...	...

Continent, country or area, year, code[a] and age of bride / Continent, pays ou zone, date, code[a] et âge de l'épouse	Total	0-14	15-19	20-24	25-29	30-34	35-39	40-44	45-49	50-54	55-59	60+	Unknown Inconnu
ASIA - ASIE													
Brunei Darussalam - Brunéi Darussalam													
2016													
45 - 49	37	...	...	...	...	...	...	...	...	...	...	...	...
50 - 54	19	...	...	...	...	...	...	...	...	...	...	...	...
55 - 59	13	...	...	...	...	...	...	...	...	...	...	...	...
60 - 64	6	...	...	...	...	...	...	...	...	...	...	...	...
65 - 69	3	...	...	...	...	...	...	...	...	...	...	...	...
70 +	2	...	...	...	...	...	...	...	...	...	...	...	...
China, Hong Kong SAR - Chine, Hong Kong RAS													
2017 (C)													
Total	51 817	-	116	2 812	12 202	14 258	7 603	4 648	3 195	2 373	1 915	2 695	...
0 - 14	-	-	-	-	-	-	-	-	-	-	-	-	...
15 - 19	361	-	57	191	69	34	6	1	1	1	1	-	...
20 - 24	5 239	-	41	1 831	2 059	835	281	86	54	24	15	13	...
25 - 29	16 790	-	14	617	7 987	5 506	1 588	565	263	121	77	52	...
30 - 34	13 669	-	2	109	1 697	6 547	3 014	1 153	516	309	193	129	...
35 - 39	6 384	-	1	40	252	1 011	2 050	1 366	698	425	277	264	...
40 - 44	3 910	-	1	15	85	217	473	975	789	498	410	447	...
45 - 49	2 685	-	-	7	42	85	144	363	617	505	371	551	...
50 - 54	1 568	-	-	2	8	17	34	112	196	353	350	496	...
55 - 59	667	-	-	-	2	4	9	20	42	111	163	316	...
60 - 64	321	-	-	-	1	1	3	5	15	17	48	231	...
65 - 69	141	-	-	-	-	1	1	2	3	8	9	117	...
70 - 74	40	-	-	-	-	-	-	-	-	1	-	39	...
75 +	42	-	-	-	-	-	-	-	1	-	1	40	...
China, Macao SAR - Chine, Macao RAS													
2009 (+C)													
Total	3 035	-	18	608	1 023	697	286	157	98	68	39	41	...
0 - 14	-	-	-	-	-	-	-	-	-	-	-	-	...
15 - 19	66	-	5	40	17	3	1	-	-	-	-	-	...
20 - 24	993	-	12	445	353	125	36	14	5	3	-	-	...
25 - 29	1 166	-	1	109	575	313	94	42	13	11	7	1	...
30 - 34	444	-	-	10	62	212	83	33	25	12	5	2	...
35 - 39	195	-	-	4	9	30	62	41	26	8	8	7	...
40 - 44	72	-	-	-	5	8	9	17	12	9	6	6	...
45 - 49	58	-	-	-	1	4	1	7	16	14	8	7	...
50 - 54	20	-	-	-	1	2	-	3	1	9	2	2	...
55 - 59	11	-	-	-	-	-	-	-	-	1	2	8	...
60 - 64	4	-	-	-	-	-	-	-	-	1	1	2	...
65 - 69	1	-	-	-	-	-	-	-	-	-	-	1	...
70 +	5	-	-	-	-	-	-	-	-	-	-	5	...
2015 (+C)													
Total	3 719	...	...	418[g]	...	...	...	...	392[r]	...	...	...	...
0 - 24	861	...	...	...	...	...	...	...	...	...	...	...	...
25 - 34	2 317	...	...	...	...	...	...	...	...	...	...	...	...
35 - 44	348	...	...	...	...	...	...	...	...	...	...	...	...
45 +	193	...	...	...	...	...	...	...	...	...	...	...	...
Cyprus - Chypre[13,14]													
2016 (C)													
Total	6 375	-	59	687	1 952	1 933	792	322	199	142	106	164	19
0 - 14	-	-	-	-	-	-	-	-	-	-	-	-	-
15 - 19	168	-	15	87	48	12	5	1	-	-	-	-	-
20 - 24	838	-	20	298	371	111	31	5	1	1	-	-	-
25 - 29	2 376	-	13	150	1 147	822	188	29	13	8	3	3	-
30 - 34	1 651	-	7	74	287	791	322	88	36	29	9	8	-
35 - 39	692	-	3	47	67	153	186	125	55	23	13	20	-
40 - 44	310	-	-	24	24	31	41	58	47	34	22	29	-
45 - 49	153	-	-	3	7	7	14	14	34	27	21	26	-
50 - 54	78	-	-	2	1	3	3	2	8	14	22	23	-
55 - 59	46	-	1	-	-	-	1	-	4	6	11	23	-
60 +	41	-	-	1	-	2	-	-	1	-	5	32	-
Unknown - Inconnu	22	...	-	1	-	1	1	-	-	-	-	-	19

Continent, country or area, year, code[a] and age of bride / Continent, pays ou zone, date, code[a] et âge de l'épouse	Total	0-14	15-19	20-24	25-29	30-34	35-39	40-44	45-49	50-54	55-59	60+	Unknown Inconnu
ASIA - ASIE													
Georgia - Géorgie													
2016 (C)													
Total....................	25 101	...	458[h]	5 695	7 174	4 533	2 919	1 848	1 040	592	386	456	...
16 - 19	2 545	...	...	...	...	...	...	...	...	...	...	...	...
20 - 24	7 978	...	...	...	...	...	...	...	...	...	...	...	...
25 - 29	6 096	...	...	...	...	...	...	...	...	...	...	...	...
30 - 34	3 514	...	...	...	...	...	...	...	...	...	...	...	...
35 - 39	2 204	...	...	...	...	...	...	...	...	...	...	...	...
40 - 44	1 237	...	...	...	...	...	...	...	...	...	...	...	...
45 - 49	673	...	...	...	...	...	...	...	...	...	...	...	...
50 - 54	423	...	...	...	...	...	...	...	...	...	...	...	...
55 - 59	234	...	...	...	...	...	...	...	...	...	...	...	...
60 + ...	197	...	...	...	...	...	...	...	...	...	...	...	...
Iran (Islamic Republic of) - Iran (République islamique d')[15]													
2016 (+C)													
Total....................	704 716	366	28 210	206 221	255 904	124 281	41 283	16 870	9 609	5 923	4 740	11 308	1
0 - 14	39 279	146	6 007	22 340	9 487	1 048	138	63	29	7	7	6	1
15 - 19	197 936	145	17 830	98 927	68 148	11 275	1 137	257	116	45	30	26	-
20 - 24	200 600	55	3 568	67 900	94 186	29 501	4 078	794	278	103	67	70	-
25 - 29	143 073	8	606	13 895	67 250	46 237	10 909	2 475	950	350	188	205	-
30 - 34	69 888	4	139	2 434	13 832	28 915	15 156	5 343	2 166	874	436	589	-
35 - 39	29 252	-	48	597	2 494	6 151	7 848	5 276	3 001	1 540	974	1 323	-
40 - 44	12 322	-	8	102	414	962	1 675	2 130	2 062	1 569	1 265	2 135	-
45 - 49	5 986	-	3	21	76	158	282	457	814	968	932	2 275	-
50 - 54	3 007	-	1	3	14	26	44	63	151	362	554	1 789	-
55 - 59	1 759	-	-	1	3	5	13	10	30	90	229	1 378	-
60 - 64	919	-	-	1	-	1	3	1	10	14	44	845	-
65 - 69	381	-	-	-	-	1	-	-	2	-	12	366	-
70 - 74	180	-	-	-	-	-	-	-	-	1	2	177	-
75 + ...	126	-	-	-	-	1	-	1	-	-	-	124	-
Unknown - Inconnu	8	8	-	-	-	-	-	-	-	-	-	-	-
Israel - Israël[16]													
2016 (C)													
Total....................	52 809	...	2 021	13 140	19 078	10 106	3 433	1 492	770	516	337	620	1 296
15 - 19	6 681	...	1 374	3 468	1 303	212	17	2	3	1	-	-	301
20 - 24	19 198	...	590	8 758	7 360	1 668	245	42	12	4	-	1	518
25 - 29	16 251	...	4	611	9 333	4 915	891	191	44	9	3	-	250
30 - 34	5 604	...	1	47	789	2 784	1 332	396	101	31	7	5	111
35 - 39	1 970	...	-	8	66	307	733	496	191	65	28	17	59
40 - 44	887	...	-	1	6	45	112	251	225	125	57	42	23
45 - 49	487	...	-	2	3	5	10	38	136	140	58	79	16
50 - 54	335	...	-	-	-	3	3	6	27	99	101	87	9
55 - 59	204	...	-	-	-	1	-	3	3	13	58	122	4
60 - 64	121	...	-	-	-	-	-	-	-	2	6	109	4
65 - 69	81	...	-	-	-	-	-	-	-	-	1	79	1
70 - 74	31	...	-	-	-	-	-	-	-	-	2	29	-
75 + ...	15	...	-	-	-	-	-	-	-	-	-	15	-
Unknown - Inconnu	944	...	52	245	218	166	90	67	28	27	16	35	-
Japan - Japon[17]													
2016 (+C)													
Total....................	496 425	-	4 893	51 595	156 407	120 132	72 776	43 234	21 363	10 677	6 031	9 315	2
0 - 14	-	-	-	-	-	-	-	-	-	-	-	-	-
15 - 19	8 921	-	3 628	3 533	969	416	193	87	46	22	19	8	-
20 - 24	76 028	-	1 133	35 307	24 797	9 067	3 560	1 303	467	194	100	100	-
25 - 29	183 655	-	85	10 112	106 310	45 642	14 583	4 664	1 403	483	190	183	-
30 - 34	113 510	-	38	1 970	19 928	51 514	26 001	9 686	2 880	856	354	283	-
35 - 39	59 846	-	7	545	3 637	11 066	22 710	14 270	5 151	1 529	513	418	-
40 - 44	27 647	-	1	101	626	1 994	4 692	10 416	6 009	2 304	843	661	-
45 - 49	12 584	-	1	18	113	368	857	2 279	4 157	2 617	1 249	925	-
50 - 54	6 574	-	-	6	24	57	157	420	1 037	2 152	1 408	1 313	-
55 - 59	3 337	-	-	1	2	6	21	92	172	418	1 086	1 539	-
60 - 64	1 840	-	-	2	-	2	2	10	31	75	190	1 528	-
65 - 69	1 416	-	-	-	1	-	-	6	9	21	67	1 312	-
70 - 74	623	-	-	-	-	-	-	1	-	3	8	611	-

Continent, country or area, year, code[a] and age of bride / Continent, pays ou zone, date, code[a] et âge de l'épouse	Total	0-14	15-19	20-24	25-29	30-34	35-39	40-44	45-49	50-54	55-59	60+	Unknown Inconnu
ASIA - ASIE													
Japan - Japon[17]													
2016													
75 +	442	-	-	-	-	-	-	-	1	3	4	434	-
Unknown - Inconnu	2	-	-	-	-	-	-	-	-	-	-	-	2
Jordan - Jordanie[18]													
2010 (+C)													
Total	62 107	...	16 151	25 559	12 760	4 002	1 795	1 151	437	252[s]	...	...	...
18 - 19	1 262	...	1 017	191	40	11	1	2	-	-[s]	...	...	...
20 - 24	14 272	...	6 768	6 453	835	139	42	20	7	8[s]	...	...	...
25 - 29	25 434	...	6 276	12 608	5 720	633	120	45	16	16[s]	...	...	...
30 - 34	11 523	...	1 603	4 782	3 679	1 153	197	70	25	14[s]	...	...	...
35 - 39	4 064	...	299	1 043	1 434	819	350	92	19	8[s]	...	...	...
40 - 44	2 365	...	99	321	681	647	358	217	35	7[s]	...	...	...
45 - 49	1 139	...	35	81	220	283	249	196	57	18[s]	...	...	...
50 - 54	639	...	14	37	73	152	169	121	53	20[s]	...	...	...
55 - 59	425	...	12	18	35	80	95	107	56	22[s]	...	...	...
60 - 64	318	...	11	7	21	40	66	97	39	37[s]	...	...	...
65 +	666	...	17	18	22	45	148	184	130	102[s]	...	...	...
Kazakhstan													
2017 (+C)													
Total	141 791	-	2 040	41 972	51 794	21 901	10 247	5 699	3 215	2 078	1 406	1 439	...
0 - 14	-	-	-	-	-	-	-	-	-	-	-	-	...
15 - 19	15 253	-	1 489	9 134	4 003	542	70	13	2	-	-	-	...
20 - 24	63 027	-	491	29 181	27 358	5 045	769	132	31	15	1	4	...
25 - 29	32 163	-	42	3 156	17 131	8 725	2 329	583	129	44	15	9	...
30 - 34	14 590	-	13	406	2 702	5 954	3 598	1 322	397	125	52	21	...
35 - 39	7 648	-	4	72	494	1 328	2 607	1 936	769	290	105	43	...
40 - 44	4 116	-	1	15	77	232	693	1 346	1 006	465	192	89	...
45 - 49	2 161	-	-	2	24	62	146	284	667	564	268	144	...
50 - 54	1 280	-	-	2	3	13	30	66	167	404	351	244	...
55 - 59	862	-	-	2	-	-	3	13	37	136	323	348	...
60 - 64	403	-	-	1	-	-	2	3	9	27	77	284	...
65 - 69	194	-	-	-	-	-	-	-	1	3	18	172	...
70 - 74	52	-	-	-	1	-	-	1	-	3	3	44	...
75 +	41	-	-	1	-	-	-	-	-	2	1	37	...
Unknown - Inconnu	1	-	-	-	1	-	-	-	-	-	-	-	...
Kuwait - Koweït													
2017 (C)													
Total	13 932	-	189	3 426	4 761	2 371	1 266	728	1 191[r]	...	...	...	...
0 - 14	-	-	-	-	-	-	-	-	-[r]	...	...	...	...
15 - 19	1 829	-	127	1 194	424	64	9	4	7[r]	...	...	...	...
20 - 24	4 946	-	55	1 914	2 345	497	87	26	22[r]	...	...	...	...
25 - 29	3 469	-	6	275	1 656	1 004	348	101	79[r]	...	...	...	...
30 - 34	1 687	-	-	28	240	577	423	210	209[r]	...	...	...	...
35 - 39	996	-	1	7	52	161	279	214	282[r]	...	...	...	...
40 - 44	539	-	-	4	26	44	78	116	271[r]	...	...	...	...
45 +	466	-	-	4	18	24	42	57	321[r]	...	...	...	...
Kyrgyzstan - Kirghizstan													
2017 (C)													
Total	43 350	-	408	13 240	17 746	5 913	2 526	1 506	891	456	317	347	...
0 - 14	-	-	-	-	-	-	-	-	-	-	-	-	...
15 - 19	8 283	-	314	4 987	2 774	186	17	4	-	1	-	-	...
20 - 24	20 416	-	87	7 745	10 636	1 700	201	30	11	3	3	-	...
25 - 29	7 888	-	6	449	3 929	2 567	676	201	41	11	3	5	...
30 - 34	3 296	-	1	52	346	1 274	996	428	144	32	16	7	...
35 - 39	1 686	-	-	6	44	155	542	530	274	87	30	18	...
40 - 44	897	-	-	1	16	27	82	264	286	128	61	32	...
45 - 49	400	-	-	-	-	2	11	34	105	120	73	55	...
50 - 54	225	-	-	-	1	2	1	12	20	60	68	61	...
55 - 59	154	-	-	-	-	-	-	1	9	11	52	81	...
60 - 64	63	-	-	-	-	-	-	1	1	2	10	49	...
65 - 69	22	-	-	-	-	-	-	1	-	1	-	20	...
70 - 74	9	-	-	-	-	-	-	-	-	-	1	8	...
75 +	11	-	-	-	-	-	-	-	-	-	-	11	...

Continent, country or area, year, code[a] and age of bride / Continent, pays ou zone, date, code[a] et âge de l'épouse	Total	0-14	15-19	20-24	25-29	30-34	35-39	40-44	45-49	50-54	55-59	60+	Unknown Inconnu
ASIA - ASIE													
Mongolia - Mongolie													
2017 (+C)													
Total..............................	20 470	...	181[j]	4 783	8 275	3 520	1 559	965	635	552[s]	...	...	...
18 - 19..............................	652	...	...	...	...	...	...	...	...	...	...	...	...
20 - 24..............................	6 619	...	...	...	...	...	...	...	...	...	...	...	...
25 - 29..............................	7 390	...	...	...	...	...	...	...	...	...	...	...	...
30 - 34..............................	2 715	...	...	...	...	...	...	...	...	...	...	...	...
35 - 39..............................	1 305	...	...	...	...	...	...	...	...	...	...	...	...
40 - 44..............................	921	...	...	...	...	...	...	...	...	...	...	...	...
45 - 49..............................	493	...	...	...	...	...	...	...	...	...	...	...	...
50 +..............................	375	...	...	...	...	...	...	...	...	...	...	...	...
Philippines[19]													
2016 (U)													
Total..............................	418 906	34	34 877	138 934	137 825	62 283	23 804	9 297	5 206	3 095	1 727	1 784	40
0 - 14..............................	2	1	1	-	-	-	-	-	-	-	-	-	-
15 - 19..............................	8 161	17	4 523	3 133	361	76	34	6	5	3	1	-	2
20 - 24..............................	96 556	11	19 915	60 280	13 933	1 797	417	97	41	19	6	33	7
25 - 29..............................	149 090	4	7 719	54 489	70 979	12 949	2 235	467	126	34	28	52	8
30 - 34..............................	88 311	1	1 769	14 490	37 299	27 979	5 333	980	289	81	44	36	10
35 - 39..............................	37 970	-	549	3 803	9 945	12 691	8 408	1 843	534	142	32	21	2
40 - 44..............................	15 591	-	168	1 210	2 676	3 789	4 066	2 563	815	213	64	27	-
45 - 49..............................	8 274	-	100	626	1 105	1 351	1 621	1 617	1 239	454	104	56	1
50 - 54..............................	5 318	-	43	315	637	710	770	786	949	761	246	100	1
55 - 59..............................	3 818	-	34	263	393	425	407	438	580	649	441	188	-
60 - 64..............................	2 688	-	27	165	237	257	265	250	325	381	393	387	1
65 - 69..............................	1 586	-	14	83	145	139	143	148	178	185	195	356	-
70 - 74..............................	766	-	6	30	60	71	57	60	63	104	79	236	-
75 +..............................	759	-	9	45	50	49	47	42	62	69	94	291	1
Unknown - Inconnu	16	-	-	2	5	-	1	-	-	-	-	1	7
Qatar													
2017 (C)													
Total..............................	3 718	...	40[f]	888	1 370	703	314	158	105	74	29	36	1
0 - 19..............................	462	...	24[f]	259	154	23	-	1	-	1	-	-	-
20 - 24..............................	1 387	...	13[f]	542	641	159	23	4	-	-	1	3	1
25 - 29..............................	971	...	3[f]	70	451	299	90	29	16	7	4	2	-
30 - 34..............................	477	...	-[f]	13	89	166	103	52	35	11	4	4	-
35 - 39..............................	226	...	-[f]	4	27	41	68	42	18	16	7	3	-
40 - 44..............................	109	...	-[f]	-	7	9	20	20	23	16	4	10	-
45 - 49..............................	54	...	-[f]	-	1	5	7	7	10	15	3	6	-
50 - 54..............................	22	...	-[f]	-	-	1	3	3	2	6	3	4	-
55 - 59..............................	9	...	-[f]	-	-	-	-	-	1	2	3	3	-
60 +..............................	1	...	-[f]	-	-	-	-	-	-	-	-	1	-
Republic of Korea - République de Corée[20]													
2017 (+C)													
Total..............................	264 455	-	572	7 823	57 157	98 117	48 186	19 837	12 299	8 303	6 178	5 983	...
0 - 14..............................	-	-	-	-	-	-	-	-	-	-	-	-	...
15 - 19..............................	2 780	-	402	633	309	237	546	478	153	15	7	-	...
20 - 24..............................	20 336	-	144	5 117	7 662	3 919	1 674	1 129	563	98	26	4	...
25 - 29..............................	93 697	-	19	1 724	40 483	41 798	7 456	1 300	634	204	59	20	...
30 - 34..............................	79 861	-	3	275	7 857	46 479	20 866	3 047	885	308	94	47	...
35 - 39..............................	30 564	-	4	63	747	5 131	15 237	6 930	1 767	459	146	80	...
40 - 44..............................	12 680	-	-	11	80	488	2 003	5 300	3 245	1 072	358	123	...
45 - 49..............................	9 605	-	-	-	13	53	347	1 353	3 773	2 693	1 044	329	...
50 - 54..............................	7 087	-	-	-	6	10	51	262	1 030	2 625	2 230	873	...
55 - 59..............................	4 562	-	-	-	-	2	6	31	213	708	1 832	1 770	...
60 - 64..............................	1 960	-	-	-	-	-	-	6	31	101	342	1 480	...
65 - 69..............................	747	-	-	-	-	-	-	1	5	15	33	693	...
70 - 74..............................	382	-	-	-	-	-	-	-	-	5	6	371	...
75 +..............................	194	-	-	-	-	-	-	-	-	-	1	193	...
Singapore - Singapour[21,22]													
2017 (+C)													
Total..............................	28 212	-	58	1 376	10 494	8 102	3 623	1 925	1 047	690	464	433	...
0 - 14..............................	-	-	-	-	-	-	-	-	-	-	-	-	...
15 - 19..............................	204	-	38	104	34	15	6	3	2	1	1	-	...

24. Marriages by age of groom and by age of bride: latest available year, 2008 - 2017
Mariages selon l'âge de l'époux et selon l'âge de l'épouse : dernière année disponible, 2008 - 2017 (continued - suite)

Continent, country or area, year, code[a] and age of bride / Continent, pays ou zone, date, code[a] et âge de l'épouse	Total	0-14	15-19	20-24	25-29	30-34	35-39	40-44	45-49	50-54	55-59	60+	Unknown Inconnu
ASIA - ASIE													
Singapore - Singapour[21,22]													
2017													
20 - 24	3 259	-	16	855	1 667	436	160	67	30	16	7	5	...
25 - 29	13 361	-	3	346	7 636	3 979	875	319	130	45	20	8	...
30 - 34	6 490	-	1	54	967	3 115	1 455	507	196	110	62	23	...
35 - 39	2 595	-	-	10	147	434	910	587	280	93	71	63	...
40 - 44	1 145	-	-	3	27	98	168	342	207	171	77	52	...
45 - 49	623	-	-	3	9	21	42	82	152	138	95	81	...
50 - 54	295	-	-	-	4	3	4	11	39	94	71	69	...
55 - 59	144	-	-	1	3	-	3	6	10	15	47	59	...
60 +	96	-	-	-	-	1	-	1	1	7	13	73	...
State of Palestine - État de Palestine													
2016 (C)													
Total	49 930	...	2 962	20 311	17 505	4 744	1 644	873	603	444	298	546	...
12 - 14	777	...	184	467	117	5	2	-	1	-	1	-	...
15 - 19	20 330	...	2 480	11 481	5 626	650	66	18	6	1	-	2	...
20 - 24	20 213	...	270	7 841	9 131	2 266	471	132	59	25	9	9	...
25 - 29	5 437	...	21	474	2 401	1 379	621	287	137	66	32	19	...
30 - 34	1 628	...	5	29	190	355	336	248	198	113	78	76	...
35 - 39	810	...	1	15	31	62	118	123	109	138	79	134	...
40 - 44	428	...	1	4	6	21	21	54	59	65	59	138	...
45 - 49	180	...	-	-	2	4	4	11	23	22	22	92	...
50 - 54	90	...	-	-	-	2	5	-	11	11	15	46	...
55 - 59	20	...	-	-	-	-	-	-	-	1	2	17	...
60 - 64	11	...	-	-	-	-	-	-	-	2	1	8	...
65 +	6	...	-	-	1	-	-	-	-	-	-	5	...
Tajikistan - Tadjikistan													
2016 (+C)													
Total	72 499	-	2 249	37 750	21 967	4 747	2 243	1 569	889	425	255	317	88
0 - 14	-	-	-	-	-	-	-	-	-	-	-	-	-
15 - 19	31 982	-	2 088	22 040	7 582	246	-	1	-	-	-	-	25
20 - 24	27 761	-	155	15 243	10 900	1 363	61	-	5	-	-	-	34
25 - 29	6 614	-	-	415	3 243	2 046	682	161	58	1	3	-	5
30 - 34	2 967	-	-	-	200	1 037	1 019	427	145	83	35	20	1
35 - 39	1 725	-	-	-	-	45	473	701	265	116	65	60	-
40 - 44	806	-	-	-	-	-	5	269	296	100	56	80	-
45 - 49	329	-	-	-	-	-	-	6	120	94	44	65	-
50 - 54	114	-	-	-	-	-	-	-	-	28	40	46	-
55 - 59	43	-	-	-	-	-	-	-	-	3	11	29	-
60 - 64	9	-	-	-	-	-	-	-	-	-	-	9	-
65 - 69	5	-	-	-	-	-	-	-	-	-	-	5	-
70 - 74	2	-	-	-	-	-	-	-	-	-	-	2	-
75 +	-	-	-	-	-	-	-	-	-	-	-	-	-
Unknown - Inconnu	142	-	6	52	42	10	3	4	-	-	1	1	23
Turkey - Turquie[23]													
2016 (C)													
Total	594 493	-[b]	11 008[h]	144 925	235 986	104 725	43 323	19 724	11 258	8 431	5 331	9 314	468
0 - 15	-	-[b]	-[h]	-	-	-	-	-	-	-	-	-	-
16 - 19	100 233	-[b]	8 157[h]	50 223	34 253	6 414	924	141	34	14	4	2	67
20 - 24	208 954	-[b]	2 412[h]	77 558	98 643	24 992	4 236	713	173	59	18	14	136
25 - 29	153 567	-[b]	241[h]	13 398	86 016	40 690	10 187	2 097	543	194	60	45	96
30 - 34	54 259	-[b]	48[h]	1 465	10 466	22 313	13 105	4 446	1 450	535	194	166	71
35 - 39	28 050	-[b]	16[h]	348	1 867	5 351	9 478	6 032	2 771	1 259	462	418	48
40 - 44	14 161	-[b]	3[h]	50	340	968	2 247	3 681	3 140	2 028	851	824	29
45 - 49	7 618	-[b]	-[h]	13	60	180	400	801	1 725	2 069	1 164	1 197	9
50 - 54	4 847	-[b]	-[h]	-	14	25	59	156	387	1 201	1 297	1 704	4
55 - 59	2 536	-[b]	-[h]	-	1	7	10	20	69	232	642	1 547	8
60 - 64	1 560	-[b]	-[h]	-	1	-	2	7	10	50	154	1 336	-
65 - 69	659	-[b]	-[h]	-	-	-	1	1	6	8	23	620	-
70 - 74	234	-[b]	-[h]	-	-	-	-	-	-	2	1	231	-
75 +	138	-[b]	-[h]	-	-	-	-	-	-	-	1	137	-
Unknown - Inconnu	17 677	-[b]	131[h]	1 870	4 325	3 785	2 674	1 629	950	780	460	1 073	-

Continent, country or area, year, code[a] and age of bride / Continent, pays ou zone, date, code[a] et âge de l'épouse	Total	0-14	15-19	20-24	25-29	30-34	35-39	40-44	45-49	50-54	55-59	60+	Unknown Inconnu
ASIA - ASIE													
Uzbekistan - Ouzbékistan													
2015 (+C)													
Total	287 582	-	3 423	118 392	126 899	20 912	7 721	4 274	2 295	1 523	1 006	1 137	...
0 - 14	-	-	-	-	-	-	-	-	-	-	-	-	...
15 - 19	66 440	-	2 723	40 351	22 554	748	46	12	3	-	-	3	...
20 - 24	163 621	-	663	75 556	80 436	6 239	553	130	24	13	3	4	...
25 - 29	37 484	-	31	2 335	22 761	9 175	2 175	649	232	69	31	26	...
30 - 34	11 363	-	6	125	1 031	4 366	3 389	1 405	540	297	142	62	...
35 - 39	4 600	-	-	20	90	324	1 398	1 430	648	366	196	128	...
40 - 44	2 000	-	-	3	23	50	129	573	537	326	184	175	...
45 - 49	927	-	-	1	3	6	24	62	253	248	162	168	...
50 - 54	667	-	-	1	1	2	4	9	47	167	186	250	...
55 - 59	285	-	-	-	-	1	3	2	8	33	83	155	...
60 - 64	123	-	-	-	-	-	-	1	2	3	18	99	...
65 - 69	49	-	-	-	-	1	-	1	1	1	1	44	...
70 - 74	14	-	-	-	-	-	-	-	-	-	-	14	...
75 +	9	-	-	-	-	-	-	-	-	-	-	9	...
EUROPE													
Åland Islands - Îles d'Åland													
2016 (C)													
Total	123	-	-	3	17	22	26	18	12	13	7	5	...
0 - 14	-	-	-	-	-	-	-	-	-	-	-	-	...
15 - 19	1	-	-	-	1	-	-	-	-	-	-	-	...
20 - 24	10	-	-	3	5	1	1	-	-	-	-	-	...
25 - 29	25	-	-	-	9	11	4	1	-	-	-	-	...
30 - 34	22	-	-	-	1	7	7	4	2	1	-	-	...
35 - 39	23	-	-	-	-	3	12	5	2	1	-	-	...
40 - 44	18	-	-	-	1	-	2	5	3	6	-	1	...
45 - 49	14	-	-	-	-	-	-	3	4	2	4	1	...
50 - 54	6	-	-	-	-	-	-	-	1	3	2	-	...
55 - 59	1	-	-	-	-	-	-	-	-	-	1	-	...
60 - 64	3	-	-	-	-	-	-	-	-	-	-	3	...
65 - 69	-	-	-	-	-	-	-	-	-	-	-	-	...
70 - 74	-	-	-	-	-	-	-	-	-	-	-	-	...
75 +	-	-	-	-	-	-	-	-	-	-	-	-	...
Albania - Albanie													
2016 (U)													
Total	22 562	-	88	2 787	9 051	6 600	2 256	915	408	201	139	117	...
0 - 14	-	-	-	-	-	-	-	-	-	-	-	-	...
15 - 19	3 339	-	48	870	1 807	555	52	6	1	-	-	-	...
20 - 24	9 052	-	30	1 623	4 320	2 578	442	53	5	-	1	-	...
25 - 29	6 342	-	7	204	2 609	2 445	828	211	31	5	2	-	...
30 - 34	2 210	-	2	42	226	888	641	298	80	20	10	3	...
35 - 39	819	-	1	25	45	90	223	228	145	32	19	11	...
40 - 44	427	-	-	9	27	24	43	95	101	74	42	12	...
45 - 49	194	-	-	9	11	12	17	19	33	47	25	21	...
50 - 54	99	-	-	2	4	5	7	5	10	19	27	20	...
55 - 59	50	-	-	2	2	2	2	-	2	3	12	25	...
60 - 64	20	-	-	1	-	1	1	-	-	1	1	15	...
65 - 69	6	-	-	-	-	-	-	-	-	-	-	6	...
70 - 74	3	-	-	-	-	-	-	-	-	-	-	3	...
75 +	1	-	-	-	-	-	-	-	-	-	-	1	...
Andorra - Andorre													
2016 (C)													
Total	295	-	-	18	50	58	62	41	29	20	10	7	...
0 - 14	-	-	-	-	-	-	-	-	-	-	-	-	...
15 - 19	3	-	-	3	-	-	-	-	-	-	-	-	...
20 - 24	30	-	-	11	15	1	2	1	-	-	-	-	...
25 - 29	48	-	-	3	20	17	6	1	1	-	-	-	...
30 - 34	66	-	-	-	10	25	22	3	5	1	-	-	...
35 - 39	63	-	-	1	5	10	23	17	4	2	-	1	...
40 - 44	40	-	-	-	-	3	7	14	8	7	1	-	...
45 - 49	19	-	-	-	-	1	1	4	4	3	5	1	...

Continent, country or area, year, code[a] and age of bride / Continent, pays ou zone, date, code[a] et âge de l'épouse	Total	0-14	15-19	20-24	25-29	30-34	35-39	40-44	45-49	50-54	55-59	60+	Unknown Inconnu
EUROPE													
Andorra - Andorre													
2016													
50 - 54	17	-	-	-	-	1	1	-	7	5	2	1	...
55 - 59	7	-	-	-	-	-	-	1	-	1	2	3	...
60 - 64	2	-	-	-	-	-	-	-	-	1	-	1	...
65 - 69	-	-	-	-	-	-	-	-	-	-	-	-	...
70 - 74	-	-	-	-	-	-	-	-	-	-	-	-	...
75 +	-	-	-	-	-	-	-	-	-	-	-	-	...
Austria - Autriche[24]													
2016 (C)													
Total	44 890	-	143	3 088	8 892	10 754	6 974	4 438	3 693	2 865	1 845	2 198	...
0 - 14	-	-	-	-	-	-	-	-	-	-	-	-	...
15 - 19	636	-	75	389	133	31	5	3	-	-	-	-	...
20 - 24	5 474	-	58	2 043	2 426	673	166	51	35	9	5	8	...
25 - 29	11 362	-	8	498	4 866	4 278	1 169	308	150	44	23	18	...
30 - 34	10 327	-	2	100	1 129	4 619	2 889	969	388	144	50	37	...
35 - 39	5 885	-	-	31	230	908	2 139	1 451	711	253	107	55	...
40 - 44	3 600	-	-	15	67	172	459	1 117	943	530	183	114	...
45 - 49	3 018	-	-	8	27	48	105	382	945	838	392	273	...
50 - 54	2 440	-	-	4	11	20	30	116	411	770	591	487	...
55 - 59	1 268	-	-	-	2	5	8	37	89	222	375	530	...
60 - 64	502	-	-	-	1	-	3	4	17	45	98	334	...
65 - 69	222	-	-	-	-	-	1	-	2	4	16	199	...
70 - 74	107	-	-	-	-	-	-	-	1	6	4	96	...
75 +	49	-	-	-	-	-	-	-	1	-	1	47	...
Belarus - Bélarus													
2016 (C)													
Total	64 536	74[d]	935[j]	15 453	20 814	10 853	5 645	3 478	2 401	1 928	1 409	1 546	...
0 - 17	589	50[d]	158[j]	294	70	14	3	-	-	-	-	-	...
18 - 19	3 492	17[d]	447[j]	2 173	711	118	17	4	2	2	1	-	...
20 - 24	21 748	5[d]	270[j]	10 276	8 974	1 765	353	67	23	10	4	1	...
25 - 29	16 980	2[d]	48[j]	2 219	8 639	4 391	1 193	328	116	30	11	3	...
30 - 34	8 781	-[d]	8[j]	392	1 887	3 288	1 975	817	279	86	34	15	...
35 - 39	4 815	-[d]	4[j]	77	424	998	1 471	1 037	483	211	77	33	...
40 - 44	2 792	-[d]	-[j]	16	87	218	451	840	661	322	129	68	...
45 - 49	1 870	-[d]	-[j]	3	14	50	144	250	587	486	248	88	...
50 - 54	1 419	-[d]	-[j]	1	6	8	29	105	178	525	369	198	...
55 - 59	1 048	-[d]	-[j]	1	1	2	7	21	54	198	398	366	...
60 +	1 002	-[d]	-[j]	1	1	1	2	9	18	58	138	774	...
Belgium - Belgique[25,26]													
2015 (C)													
Total	40 049	-	69	2 350	9 971	8 521	5 515	3 966	3 101	2 588	1 809	2 159	...
0 - 14	-	-	-	-	-	-	-	-	-	-	-	-	...
15 - 19	398	-	34	200	126	27	6	2	3	-	-	-	...
20 - 24	5 029	-	31	1 592	2 483	656	169	50	30	7	8	3	...
25 - 29	11 749	-	2	467	6 197	3 717	897	285	111	47	18	8	...
30 - 34	7 535	-	1	70	888	3 265	2 041	786	287	122	54	21	...
35 - 39	4 901	-	1	10	190	638	1 769	1 307	569	270	94	53	...
40 - 44	3 333	-	-	6	47	155	460	1 062	892	437	187	87	...
45 - 49	2 619	-	-	4	28	43	127	349	801	714	332	221	...
50 - 54	2 166	-	-	1	6	12	31	94	315	721	542	444	...
55 - 59	1 265	-	-	-	4	2	11	23	79	226	422	498	...
60 - 64	610	-	-	-	2	4	3	3	12	35	123	428	...
65 - 69	278	-	-	-	-	1	1	5	-	8	25	238	...
70 - 74	103	-	-	-	-	-	-	-	1	1	3	98	...
75 +	63	-	-	-	-	1	-	-	1	-	1	60	...
Bosnia and Herzegovina - Bosnie-Herzégovine													
2012 (C)													
Total	18 235	-	147	3 617	6 959	3 922	1 571	739	438	259	185	398	...
0 - 14	-	-	-	-	-	-	-	-	-	-	-	-	...
15 - 19	1 885	-	91	1 028	606	122	27	6	2	1	-	2	...
20 - 24	6 191	-	48	2 130	2 958	844	160	36	7	5	2	1	...
25 - 29	5 764	-	8	403	2 936	1 833	431	113	26	10	2	2	...
30 - 34	2 228	-	-	42	405	941	581	172	66	14	2	5	...

Continent, pays ou zone, date, code[a] et âge de l'épouse	Total	0-14	15-19	20-24	25-29	30-34	35-39	40-44	45-49	50-54	55-59	60+	Unknown Inconnu
EUROPE													
Bosnia and Herzegovina - Bosnie-Herzégovine													
2012													
35 - 39	871	-	-	10	35	150	292	240	92	34	14	4	...
40 - 44	437	-	-	1	9	20	56	117	122	60	19	33	...
45 - 49	349	-	-	2	6	6	13	41	85	76	52	68	...
50 - 54	237	-	-	-	2	4	6	10	30	39	52	94	...
55 - 59	136	-	-	-	-	-	2	3	6	17	34	74	...
60 - 64	78	-	-	-	-	2	1	1	-	1	7	66	...
65 - 69	27	-	-	-	-	-	-	-	1	2	1	23	...
70 - 74	18	-	-	-	-	-	-	-	1	-	-	17	...
75 +	9	-	-	-	-	-	-	-	-	-	-	9	...
Unknown - Inconnu	5	-	-	1	2	-	2	-	-	-	-	-	...
Bulgaria - Bulgarie[27]													
2016 (C)													
Total	26 803	-	302	3 352	8 334	6 569	3 536	2 119	1 104	572	350	565	...
0 - 14	-	-	-	-	-	-	-	-	-	-	-	-	...
15 - 19	1 732	-	227	991	405	86	14	5	2	2	-	-	...
20 - 24	6 160	-	71	1 820	3 027	981	208	41	8	4	-	-	...
25 - 29	8 967	-	2	458	4 187	3 181	843	226	48	17	3	2	...
30 - 34	4 538	-	1	64	598	1 895	1 343	454	122	39	12	10	...
35 - 39	2 422	-	1	14	81	348	857	755	245	71	29	21	...
40 - 44	1 466	-	-	2	24	67	230	514	402	140	51	36	...
45 - 49	657	-	-	2	8	11	36	95	208	178	71	48	...
50 - 54	358	-	-	-	3	-	5	22	52	95	94	87	...
55 - 59	214	-	-	-	1	-	-	6	15	21	64	107	...
60 - 64	143	-	-	-	-	-	-	-	2	3	22	116	...
65 - 69	99	-	-	1	-	-	-	-	-	1	2	95	...
70 - 74	34	-	-	-	-	-	-	-	-	1	2	31	...
75 +	13	-	-	-	-	-	-	1	-	-	-	12	...
Croatia - Croatie[5]													
2016 (C)													
Total	20 467	-	109	2 014	6 904	5 872	2 685	1 079	634	409	275	486	...
0 - 14	-	-	-	-	-	-	-	-	-	-	-	-	...
15 - 19	705	-	70	382	183	50	14	3	2	1	-	-	...
20 - 24	4 294	-	36	1 189	2 065	767	180	40	11	4	2	-	...
25 - 29	7 714	-	3	378	3 792	2 630	715	135	38	17	5	1	...
30 - 34	4 274	-	-	55	731	2 020	1 020	303	96	36	9	4	...
35 - 39	1 637	-	-	8	112	336	597	333	158	61	18	14	...
40 - 44	714	-	-	2	17	59	121	192	172	89	39	23	...
45 - 49	423	-	-	-	3	8	32	62	115	106	51	46	...
50 - 54	275	-	-	-	1	6	9	28	73	76	82	-	...
55 - 59	160	-	-	-	-	1	-	1	7	11	51	89	...
60 - 64	136	-	-	-	-	-	-	-	4	9	19	104	...
65 - 69	82	-	-	-	1	-	-	-	1	1	4	75	...
70 - 74	32	-	-	-	-	-	-	-	-	1	-	31	...
75 +	19	-	-	-	-	-	-	-	1	-	1	17	...
Unknown - Inconnu	2	-	-	-	-	-	-	1	1	-	-	-	...
Czechia - Tchéquie[5]													
2016 (C)													
Total	50 768	-	79	2 889	12 876	13 596	8 509	4 833	2 704	2 014	1 285	1 983	...
0 - 14	-	-	-	-	-	-	-	-	-	-	-	-	...
15 - 19	367	-	31	184	100	25	20	3	3	1	-	-	...
20 - 24	6 311	-	38	1 729	2 902	1 121	359	103	35	17	4	3	...
25 - 29	17 718	-	6	736	7 869	6 246	2 058	562	147	59	22	13	...
30 - 34	11 476	-	2	156	1 566	4 907	3 175	1 088	351	159	36	36	...
35 - 39	5 942	-	1	64	340	997	2 079	1 492	557	249	99	64	...
40 - 44	3 481	-	1	12	78	247	625	1 086	776	407	148	101	...
45 - 49	2 148	-	-	7	17	43	149	372	570	553	268	169	...
50 - 54	1 457	-	-	-	3	7	30	99	208	411	360	339	...
55 - 59	850	-	-	-	-	2	10	23	44	113	257	401	...
60 - 64	598	-	-	1	1	-	3	2	13	33	70	475	...
65 - 69	278	-	-	-	-	1	1	2	-	9	14	251	...
70 - 74	99	-	-	-	-	-	-	-	-	3	5	91	...
75 +	43	-	-	-	-	-	1	-	-	-	2	40	...

Continent, country or area, year, code[a] and age of bride / Continent, pays ou zone, date, code[a] et âge de l'épouse	Total	0-14	15-19	20-24	25-29	30-34	35-39	40-44	45-49	50-54	55-59	60+	Unknown Inconnu
EUROPE													
Denmark - Danemark[28]													
2016 (C)													
Total	30 767	-	35	1 414	6 513	6 789	4 468	2 979	2 286	2 100	1 460	2 007	716
0 - 14	-	-	-	-	-	-	-	-	-	-	-	-	-
15 - 19	162	-	14	85	32	12	-	1	1	-	-	-	17
20 - 24	2 832	-	10	918	1 272	339	76	32	12	4	5	1	163
25 - 29	8 266	-	5	280	4 141	2 660	695	168	58	39	8	7	205
30 - 34	6 191	-	-	31	723	2 942	1 662	471	149	68	19	12	114
35 - 39	3 718	-	1	8	105	514	1 485	1 008	314	134	51	17	81
40 - 44	2 399	-	-	3	27	83	322	849	648	278	95	37	57
45 - 49	1 882	-	-	3	5	22	60	221	624	593	224	98	32
50 - 54	1 743	-	-	-	2	7	7	51	284	638	464	268	22
55 - 59	993	-	-	-	-	-	-	12	53	150	362	402	14
60 - 64	601	-	-	-	-	-	-	1	6	36	93	456	9
65 - 69	318	-	-	-	1	-	1	-	2	4	19	291	-
70 - 74	207	-	-	-	-	-	-	-	1	1	9	194	2
75 +	116	-	-	-	-	1	-	-	1	2	2	110	-
Unknown - Inconnu	1 339	-	5	86	205	209	160	165	133	153	109	114	-
Estonia - Estonie													
2016 (C)													
Total	6 360	-	22	471	1 593	1 519	975	569	461	250	172	195	133
0 - 14	-	-	-	-	-	-	-	-	-	-	-	-	-
15 - 19	88	-	10	44	19	5	5	-	1	-	-	-	4
20 - 24	921	-	9	290	429	114	29	4	10	1	1	1	33
25 - 29	1 932	-	-	103	896	626	189	58	17	7	-	-	36
30 - 34	1 331	-	3	18	178	578	358	105	50	14	3	1	23
35 - 39	805	-	-	5	36	138	275	188	103	29	9	6	16
40 - 44	467	-	-	2	13	34	89	131	128	36	17	9	8
45 - 49	322	-	-	-	7	8	15	56	117	67	36	12	4
50 - 54	199	-	-	-	-	2	7	11	25	67	48	36	3
55 - 59	118	-	-	-	-	-	2	6	6	17	41	41	5
60 - 64	56	-	-	-	-	-	-	-	1	7	12	35	1
65 - 69	32	-	-	-	-	-	-	1	-	-	2	29	-
70 - 74	16	-	-	-	-	-	-	-	-	-	-	16	-
75 +	7	-	-	-	-	-	-	-	-	-	-	7	-
Unknown - Inconnu	66	-	-	9	15	14	6	9	3	5	3	2	-
Faeroe Islands - Îles Féroé[29]													
2017 (C)													
Total	215	-	-	19	53	40	32	34	12	10	7	8	...
0 - 14	-	-	-	-	-	-	-	-	-	-	-	-	...
15 - 19	6	-	-	4	2	-	-	-	-	-	-	-	...
20 - 24	38	-	-	15	19	3	-	1	-	-	-	-	...
25 - 29	50	-	-	-	28	15	3	2	-	2	-	-	...
30 - 34	48	-	-	-	3	19	16	10	-	-	-	-	...
35 - 39	30	-	-	-	1	3	11	9	4	1	1	-	...
40 - 44	19	-	-	-	-	-	2	11	5	1	-	-	...
45 - 49	8	-	-	-	-	-	-	1	1	2	3	1	...
50 - 54	8	-	-	-	-	-	-	-	2	4	1	1	...
55 - 59	4	-	-	-	-	-	-	-	-	-	1	3	...
60 - 64	2	-	-	-	-	-	-	-	-	-	1	1	...
65 - 69	1	-	-	-	-	-	-	-	-	-	-	1	...
70 - 74	-	-	-	-	-	-	-	-	-	-	-	-	...
75 +	1	-	-	-	-	-	-	-	-	-	-	1	...
Finland - Finlande[30]													
2016 (C)													
Total	24 341	-	191	1 916	5 404	5 586	3 430	2 197	2 238	1 280	937	1 162	...
0 - 14	-	-	-	-	-	-	-	-	-	-	-	-	...
15 - 19	415	-	115	233	49	12	1	5	-	-	-	-	...
20 - 24	2 920	-	55	1 229	1 189	312	77	33	17	5	2	1	...
25 - 29	6 660	-	14	336	3 275	2 217	590	139	59	21	8	1	...
30 - 34	5 071	-	1	64	673	2 359	1 309	440	158	48	11	8	...
35 - 39	2 848	-	3	26	149	502	1 074	666	286	96	36	10	...
40 - 44	1 816	-	1	13	34	114	273	600	524	179	53	25	...
45 - 49	2 063	-	1	11	20	40	75	246	931	419	227	93	...
50 - 54	1 050	-	-	2	11	18	20	53	190	368	263	125	...
55 - 59	684	-	-	2	1	8	9	11	60	108	230	255	...

Continent, pays ou zone, date, code[a] et âge de l'épouse	Total	0-14	15-19	20-24	25-29	30-34	35-39	40-44	45-49	50-54	55-59	60+	Unknown Inconnu
EUROPE													
Finland - Finlande[30]													
2016													
60 - 64	415	-	-	-	2	4	2	3	10	27	94	273	...
65 - 69	240	-	1	-	-	-	-	1	3	6	11	218	...
70 - 74	108	-	-	-	1	-	-	-	-	2	1	104	...
75 +	51	-	-	-	-	-	-	-	-	1	1	49	...
France[31]													
2016 (C)													
Total	219 549	-	166	9 004	46 926	52 709	33 649	22 808	16 263	13 868	10 339	13 817	...
0 - 14	-	-	-	-	-	-	-	-	-	-	-	-	...
15 - 19	1 366	-	77	623	467	144	42	9	1	2	-	1	...
20 - 24	19 743	-	66	6 083	9 710	2 798	695	228	90	38	16	19	...
25 - 29	57 737	-	17	1 818	29 958	19 397	4 537	1 224	458	191	84	53	...
30 - 34	48 860	-	2	317	5 381	24 038	12 962	3 843	1 435	552	210	120	...
35 - 39	29 564	-	3	111	927	4 647	11 525	7 650	2 860	1 132	435	274	...
40 - 44	19 963	-	-	34	304	1 104	2 823	7 051	4 809	2 350	949	539	...
45 - 49	14 373	-	-	14	115	383	770	2 054	4 379	3 817	1 708	1 133	...
50 - 54	12 179	-	-	3	47	137	207	559	1 729	4 011	3 190	2 296	...
55 - 59	7 843	-	-	1	10	39	60	150	366	1 333	2 631	3 253	...
60 - 64	4 415	-	1	-	4	12	20	32	111	339	836	3 060	...
65 +	3 506	-	-	-	3	10	8	8	25	103	280	3 069	...
Germany - Allemagne													
2015 (C)													
Total	400 115	-	660	20 450	88 623	99 432	58 243	34 353	31 943	27 698	17 978	20 735	...
0 - 14	-	-	-	-	-	-	-	-	-	-	-	-	...
15 - 19	3 551	-	353	1 986	917	194	51	18	19	9	3	1	...
20 - 24	42 750	-	252	13 264	21 255	5 760	1 445	425	205	86	38	20	...
25 - 29	115 844	-	41	4 214	53 466	42 240	11 137	2 888	1 234	424	124	76	...
30 - 34	92 114	-	10	722	10 777	42 625	25 272	8 070	3 016	1 075	360	187	...
35 - 39	45 351	-	3	156	1 656	7 102	16 286	11 562	5 576	2 031	628	351	...
40 - 44	25 477	-	1	65	333	1 090	2 940	7 438	7 807	3 801	1 290	712	...
45 - 49	26 968	-	-	26	147	276	805	2 786	9 129	8 399	3 449	1 951	...
50 - 54	23 812	-	-	11	46	105	244	910	3 835	8 584	6 121	3 956	...
55 - 59	13 259	-	-	6	21	26	45	198	868	2 571	4 449	5 075	...
60 - 64	6 493	-	-	-	3	8	15	46	210	573	1 198	4 440	...
65 - 69	2 558	-	-	-	2	5	-	7	32	122	244	2 146	...
70 - 74	1 155	-	-	-	-	-	2	2	8	16	44	1 083	...
75 +	783	-	-	-	-	1	1	3	4	7	30	737	...
Greece - Grèce													
2016 (C)													
Total	49 632	...	176	1 648	9 428	16 906	11 115	4 995	2 482	1 151	750	981	...
0 - 14	9	...	5	4	-	-	-	-	-	-	-	-	...
15 - 19	781	...	139	339	193	79	21	7	-	1	1	1	...
20 - 24	4 867	...	27	897	2 131	1 266	405	99	31	5	3	3	...
25 - 29	15 158	...	5	319	5 301	6 387	2 369	594	137	31	9	6	...
30 - 34	15 990	...	-	77	1 526	7 576	4 742	1 483	415	116	33	22	...
35 - 39	7 378	...	-	10	238	1 384	2 907	1 764	750	201	79	45	...
40 - 44	2 654	...	-	1	31	178	565	794	621	266	117	81	...
45 - 49	1 349	...	-	1	8	30	84	204	398	286	186	152	...
50 - 54	717	...	-	-	-	6	14	40	100	181	178	198	...
55 - 59	425	...	-	-	-	-	4	8	21	51	118	223	...
60 - 64	180	...	-	-	-	-	3	1	7	12	20	137	...
65 - 69	81	...	-	-	-	-	1	1	1	-	4	74	...
70 - 74	27	...	-	-	-	-	-	-	1	1	1	24	...
75 +	16	...	-	-	-	-	-	-	-	-	1	15	...
Hungary - Hongrie[6]													
2016 (C)													
Total	51 805	-	340	3 348	12 058	13 392	9 525	5 311	2 832	1 622	1 219	2 158	...
0 - 14	-	-	-	-	-	-	-	-	-	-	-	-	...
15 - 19	1 141	-	231	581	212	66	26	11	8	3	2	1	...
20 - 24	7 090	-	83	1 909	3 126	1 305	439	152	53	14	4	5	...
25 - 29	16 259	-	13	666	6 762	5 795	2 206	590	159	40	16	12	...
30 - 34	11 432	-	6	124	1 514	4 735	3 377	1 194	318	106	34	24	...
35 - 39	6 689	-	5	51	339	1 154	2 531	1 679	578	222	86	44	...
40 - 44	3 639	-	1	15	84	268	728	1 213	775	301	137	117	...
45 - 49	2 188	-	-	2	18	58	177	354	684	446	236	213	...

24. Marriages by age of groom and by age of bride: latest available year, 2008 - 2017
Mariages selon l'âge de l'époux et selon l'âge de l'épouse : dernière année disponible, 2008 - 2017 (continued - suite)

Continent, country or area, year, code[a] and age of bride / Continent, pays ou zone, date, code[a] et âge de l'épouse	Total	0-14	15-19	20-24	25-29	30-34	35-39	40-44	45-49	50-54	55-59	60+	Unknown Inconnu
EUROPE													
Hungary - Hongrie[6]													
2016													
50 - 54	1 302	-	1	-	3	7	32	93	187	345	317	317	...
55 - 59	905	-	-	-	-	3	2	20	53	99	271	457	...
60 - 64	711	-	-	-	-	1	4	3	12	38	89	564	...
65 - 69	298	-	-	-	-	-	2	2	4	7	25	258	...
70 - 74	109	-	-	-	-	-	-	-	-	1	-	108	...
75 +	42	-	-	-	-	-	1	-	1	-	2	38	...
Iceland - Islande[32,33]													
2011 (C)													
Total	1 458	-	3	77	302	334	272	161	111	74	64	55	5
0 - 14	-	-	-	-	-	-	-	-	-	-	-	-	-
15 - 19	6	-	-	2	4	-	-	-	-	-	-	-	-
20 - 24	152	-	3	52	69	21	1	3	1	1	-	-	1
25 - 29	371	-	-	19	173	115	44	9	5	3	1	1	1
30 - 34	350	-	-	3	43	157	104	25	9	3	4	1	1
35 - 39	243	-	-	1	7	33	101	62	22	9	6	1	1
40 - 44	113	-	-	-	3	6	14	44	28	11	3	4	-
45 - 49	94	-	-	-	1	-	6	15	36	24	7	4	1
50 - 54	68	-	-	-	-	1	1	2	9	18	25	12	-
55 - 59	30	-	-	-	-	-	1	-	1	4	15	9	-
60 - 64	18	-	-	-	-	-	-	1	-	1	2	14	-
65 - 69	7	-	-	-	-	-	-	-	-	-	1	6	-
70 - 74	2	-	-	-	-	-	-	-	-	-	-	2	-
75 +	1	-	-	-	-	-	-	-	-	-	-	1	-
Unknown - Inconnu	3	-	-	-	2	1	-	-	-	-	-	-	-
Ireland - Irlande													
2012 (+C)													
Total	20 713	...	102	516	4 523	8 245	3 896	1 585	766	452	258	370	...
15 - 19	237	...	80	91	43	17	5	-	-	-	1	-	...
20 - 24	968	...	22	258	457	168	40	13	7	3	-	-	...
25 - 29	6 485	...	-	136	2 944	2 670	578	110	33	10	-	4	...
30 - 34	8 016	...	-	25	930	4 640	1 858	419	102	28	11	3	...
35 - 39	2 827	...	-	5	120	673	1 149	588	200	67	15	10	...
40 - 44	995	...	-	1	20	54	228	331	198	99	40	24	...
45 - 49	542	...	-	-	8	18	29	97	157	120	71	42	...
50 - 54	340	...	-	-	-	3	6	21	53	97	81	79	...
55 - 59	168	...	-	-	1	2	2	4	12	25	33	89	...
60 - 64	89	...	-	-	-	-	1	2	2	3	6	75	...
65 - 69	26	...	-	-	-	-	-	-	1	-	-	25	...
70 - 74	17	...	-	-	-	-	-	-	1	-	-	16	...
75 +	3	...	-	-	-	-	-	-	-	-	-	3	...
Italy - Italie													
2016 (C)													
Total	203 258	...	208	6 142	37 208	58 955	38 161	23 071	13 561	9 456	6 281	10 215	...
15 - 19	1 393	...	97	719	418	114	31	6	5	3	-	-	...
20 - 24	16 082	...	78	3 675	8 000	3 085	830	257	79	41	18	19	...
25 - 29	57 183	...	18	1 340	22 445	23 788	6 867	1 911	477	183	78	76	...
30 - 34	56 031	...	7	279	5 232	26 394	16 199	5 450	1 560	515	178	217	...
35 - 39	28 574	...	3	80	804	4 493	10 739	7 515	2 919	1 219	458	344	...
40 - 44	17 630	...	3	27	190	821	2 740	5 845	4 168	2 162	931	743	...
45 - 49	10 891	...	2	11	63	181	559	1 602	3 052	2 594	1 408	1 419	...
50 - 54	7 618	...	-	10	41	57	145	387	1 033	2 044	1 749	2 152	...
55 - 59	4 292	...	-	-	9	15	32	81	222	544	1 088	2 301	...
60 - 64	2 091	...	-	1	6	4	14	10	32	125	284	1 615	...
65 - 69	881	...	-	-	-	2	2	7	11	19	65	775	...
70 - 74	320	...	-	-	-	1	3	-	2	1	15	298	...
75 +	272	...	-	-	-	-	-	-	1	6	9	256	...
Latvia - Lettonie[5]													
2016 (C)													
Total	13 002	-	191	1 814	4 140	2 579	1 414	957	706	485	317	399	...
0 - 14	-	-	-	-	-	-	-	-	-	-	-	-	-
15 - 19	32	-	22	7	3	-	-	-	-	-	-	-	-
20 - 24	953	-	99	594	201	40	14	3	1	-	1	-	...
25 - 29	3 615	-	53	902	2 128	407	99	21	4	-	1	-	...
30 - 34	3 045	-	13	247	1 322	1 091	264	81	21	4	1	1	...

Continent, country or area, year, code[a] and age of bride / Continent, pays ou zone, date, code[a] et âge de l'épouse	Total	0-14	15-19	20-24	25-29	30-34	35-39	40-44	45-49	50-54	55-59	60+	Unknown Inconnu
EUROPE													
Latvia - Lettonie[5]													
2016													
35 - 39	1 769	-	2	48	351	682	482	154	36	7	6	1	...
40 - 44	1 129	-	1	11	82	242	337	296	123	28	6	3	...
45 - 49	784	-	-	2	29	70	118	220	224	87	31	3	...
50 - 54	620	-	-	2	14	35	61	128	172	145	49	14	...
55 - 59	400	-	1	-	7	8	20	38	79	122	94	31	...
60 - 64	292	-	-	1	2	4	15	11	33	49	78	99	...
65 - 69	166	-	-	-	1	-	3	2	3	29	30	98	...
70 - 74	99	-	-	-	-	-	1	3	7	8	9	71	...
75 +	98	-	-	-	-	-	-	-	3	6	11	78	...
Liechtenstein[5]													
2012 (C)													
Total	185	-	-	8	30	59	33	19	20	10	2	4	...
Lithuania - Lituanie													
2016 (C)													
Total	21 347	-	87	2 290	7 468	4 862	2 369	1 405	1 040	754	483	589	...
0 - 14	-	-	-	-	-	-	-	-	-	-	-	-	...
15 - 19	455	-	55	262	106	21	9	1	1	-	-	-	...
20 - 24	4 472	-	25	1 470	2 274	537	127	25	9	-	1	4	...
25 - 29	7 909	-	3	475	4 328	2 310	576	151	44	17	4	1	...
30 - 34	3 643	-	2	65	606	1 558	889	347	118	42	10	6	...
35 - 39	1 692	-	2	13	120	318	546	381	199	69	29	15	...
40 - 44	1 153	-	-	4	30	91	159	334	285	153	62	35	...
45 - 49	820	-	-	1	4	20	50	126	252	223	96	48	...
50 - 54	562	-	-	-	-	5	10	30	109	186	122	100	...
55 - 59	324	-	-	-	-	2	2	9	21	46	117	127	...
60 - 64	179	-	-	-	-	-	1	1	2	15	30	130	...
65 - 69	91	-	-	-	-	-	-	-	-	2	11	78	...
70 - 74	31	-	-	-	-	-	-	-	-	-	1	30	...
75 +	16	-	-	-	-	-	-	-	-	1	-	15	...
Luxembourg[9,34]													
2016 (C)													
Total	1 884	-	5	85	387	459	267	205	152	146	103	75	...
0 - 14	-	-	-	-	-	-	-	-	-	-	-	-	...
15 - 19	18	-	3	8	5	2	-	-	-	-	-	-	...
20 - 24	158	-	1	53	71	21	7	3	1	1	-	-	...
25 - 29	513	-	1	19	252	170	42	17	6	6	-	-	...
30 - 34	462	-	-	2	48	201	113	60	22	10	4	2	...
35 - 39	240	-	-	2	3	45	72	57	38	15	6	2	...
40 - 44	175	-	-	-	5	13	24	40	45	29	12	7	...
45 - 49	129	-	-	-	2	5	7	20	24	34	24	13	...
50 - 54	116	-	-	1	1	1	2	8	15	39	33	16	...
55 - 59	48	-	-	-	-	1	-	-	1	11	19	16	...
60 - 64	18	-	-	-	-	-	-	-	-	1	4	13	...
65 - 69	3	-	-	-	-	-	-	-	-	-	1	2	...
70 - 74	2	-	-	-	-	-	-	-	-	-	-	2	...
75 +	2	-	-	-	-	-	-	-	-	-	-	2	...
Malta - Malte													
2016 (C)													
Total	3 034	...	3[h]	134	925	907	447	197	156	103	65	96	1
16 - 19	9	...	1[h]	4	3	1	-	-	-	-	-	-	-
20 - 24	362	...	2[h]	76	200	64	14	3	2	-	-	1	-
25 - 29	1 177	...	-[h]	42	603	396	106	20	7	2	-	1	-
30 - 34	725	...	-[h]	8	91	372	178	46	23	5	-	2	-
35 - 39	327	...	-[h]	2	24	62	112	75	31	9	6	5	1
40 - 44	152	...	-[h]	1	2	8	24	36	45	22	9	5	-
45 - 49	116	...	-[h]	1	1	2	8	12	36	29	13	14	-
50 - 54	85	...	-[h]	-	1	-	5	4	11	26	21	17	-
55 - 59	43	...	-[h]	-	-	-	-	-	1	8	14	20	-
60 - 64	18	...	-[h]	-	-	-	-	-	-	1	2	15	-
65 +	17	...	-[h]	-	-	1	-	-	-	-	-	16	-
Unknown - Inconnu	3	...	-[h]	-	-	1	-	1	-	1	-	-	-

24. Marriages by age of groom and by age of bride: latest available year, 2008 - 2017
Mariages selon l'âge de l'époux et selon l'âge de l'épouse : dernière année disponible, 2008 - 2017 (continued - suite)

Continent, country or area, year, code[a] and age of bride / Continent, pays ou zone, date, code[a] et âge de l'épouse	Total	Age of groom - - âge de l'époux											Unknown Inconnu
		0-14	15-19	20-24	25-29	30-34	35-39	40-44	45-49	50-54	55-59	60+	

EUROPE

Montenegro - Monténégro
2009 (C)

Total	3 829	...	26	619	1 371	876	425	232	131	66	31	52	...
0 - 14	-	...	-	-	-	-	-	-	-	-	-	-	...
15 - 19	376	...	15	172	131	41	11	4	1	-	-	1	...
20 - 24	1 268	...	9	358	600	217	53	22	6	2	1	-	...
25 - 29	1 243	...	1	75	549	406	151	47	12	1	1	-	...
30 - 34	517	...	-	8	81	176	135	79	33	5	-	-	...
35 - 39	203	...	-	3	8	32	60	47	33	16	2	2	...
40 - 44	96	...	-	2	1	2	15	25	31	10	7	3	...
45 - 49	55	...	1	1	-	1	-	7	12	15	7	11	...
50 - 54	34	...	-	-	1	1	-	1	1	15	6	9	...
55 - 59	22	...	-	-	-	-	-	-	2	1	5	14	...
60 - 64	8	...	-	-	-	-	-	-	-	1	2	5	...
65 - 69	7	...	-	-	-	-	-	-	-	-	-	7	...
70 - 74	-	...	-	-	-	-	-	-	-	-	-	-	...
75 +	-	...	-	-	-	-	-	-	-	-	-	-	...

Netherlands - Pays-Bas[9,35]
2014 (C)

Total	75 696	...	93	5 415	18 406	18 053	10 388	7 078	5 065	4 156	2 989	4 053	...
15 - 19	707	...	53	359	202	57	17	12	4	2	1	-	...
20 - 24	11 835	...	30	4 051	5 752	1 433	345	130	62	21	3	8	...
25 - 29	22 426	...	7	856	10 426	8 207	1 966	609	201	95	36	23	...
30 - 34	15 494	...	3	105	1 726	7 034	4 306	1 512	478	202	73	55	...
35 - 39	7 942	...	-	24	214	1 050	2 925	2 245	929	329	136	90	...
40 - 44	5 397	...	-	9	53	205	641	1 840	1 499	730	259	161	...
45 - 49	4 147	...	-	8	26	54	137	529	1 325	1 229	503	336	...
50 - 54	3 524	...	-	3	7	8	42	162	427	1 163	1 036	676	...
55 - 59	2 113	...	-	-	-	3	8	31	107	302	702	960	...
60 - 64	1 153	...	-	-	-	2	1	5	27	60	189	869	...
65 - 69	569	...	-	-	-	-	-	2	4	18	44	501	...
70 - 74	251	...	-	-	-	-	-	1	1	4	5	240	...
75 +	138	...	-	-	-	-	-	-	1	1	2	134	...

Norway - Norvège
2012 (C)

Total	24 077	-	38	1 503	5 000	5 362	3 852	2 786	1 989	1 440	1 018	1 089	...
0 - 14	-	-	-	-	-	-	-	-	-	-	-	-	...
15 - 19	352	-	19	164	105	35	14	10	3	1	-	1	...
20 - 24	3 246	-	15	1 069	1 372	457	164	79	51	21	7	11	...
25 - 29	6 632	-	3	226	2 933	2 215	721	289	140	61	25	19	...
30 - 34	5 312	-	-	29	486	2 197	1 503	614	245	129	64	45	...
35 - 39	3 099	-	1	13	82	386	1 128	840	352	154	79	64	...
40 - 44	2 083	-	-	1	19	55	259	718	553	270	128	80	...
45 - 49	1 463	-	-	1	2	10	51	180	477	416	201	125	...
50 - 54	981	-	-	-	1	4	9	48	137	301	291	190	...
55 - 59	505	-	-	-	-	1	2	6	24	74	177	221	...
60 - 64	231	-	-	-	-	1	1	2	5	13	37	172	...
65 - 69	129	-	-	-	-	-	-	-	2	-	8	119	...
70 - 74	28	-	-	-	-	-	-	-	-	-	1	27	...
75 +	15	-	-	-	-	-	-	-	-	-	-	15	...
Unknown - Inconnu	1	-	-	-	-	1	-	-	-	-	-	-	...

Poland - Pologne
2016 (C)

Total	193 455	-	489	25 113	77 976	46 092	18 312	9 044	4 842	3 246	2 887	5 454	...
0 - 14	-	-	-	-	-	-	-	-	-	-	-	-	...
15 - 19	3 161	-	292	1 966	710	145	37	6	3	-	1	1	...
20 - 24	51 124	-	179	18 389	26 276	5 240	796	180	45	9	6	4	...
25 - 29	76 805	-	15	4 221	45 088	21 984	4 175	948	252	77	31	14	...
30 - 34	31 202	-	2	423	4 998	15 423	7 226	2 191	606	206	79	48	...
35 - 39	12 572	-	1	86	759	2 650	4 593	2 801	1 018	388	168	108	...
40 - 44	6 525	-	-	25	122	537	1 167	2 121	1 339	677	334	203	...
45 - 49	3 890	-	-	2	18	91	254	600	1 091	839	535	460	...
50 - 54	2 849	-	-	-	4	18	54	145	346	709	806	767	...
55 - 59	2 169	-	-	1	1	4	7	38	109	227	617	1 165	...
60 - 64	1 690	-	-	-	-	-	2	9	24	89	228	1 338	...
65 - 69	950	-	-	-	-	-	1	5	7	17	66	854	...

24. Marriages by age of groom and by age of bride: latest available year, 2008 - 2017
Mariages selon l'âge de l'époux et selon l'âge de l'épouse : dernière année disponible, 2008 - 2017 (continued - suite)

Continent, country or area, year, code[a] and age of bride / Continent, pays ou zone, date, code[a] et âge de l'épouse	Total	0-14	15-19	20-24	25-29	30-34	35-39	40-44	45-49	50-54	55-59	60+	Unknown Inconnu
EUROPE													
Poland - Pologne													
2016													
70 - 74	307	-	-	-	-	-	-	-	2	3	8	294	...
75 +	211	-	-	-	-	-	-	-	-	5	8	198	...
Portugal[36,37]													
2016 (C)													
Total	32 399	-	88	1 883	7 758	8 534	5 140	2 981	1 890	1 339	964	1 822	...
0 - 14	-	-	-	-	-	-	-	-	-	-	-	-	...
15 - 19	359	-	52	194	82	20	7	2	1	1	-	-	...
20 - 24	3 364	-	32	1 093	1 570	444	137	57	16	6	6	3	...
25 - 29	9 517	-	3	449	4 686	3 213	805	246	68	27	13	7	...
30 - 34	7 964	-	1	105	1 151	3 813	2 028	565	184	60	35	22	...
35 - 39	4 190	-	-	30	207	798	1 513	968	400	159	54	61	...
40 - 44	2 563	-	-	8	48	183	489	778	556	266	131	104	...
45 - 49	1 603	-	-	3	8	38	125	263	446	358	192	170	...
50 - 54	1 161	-	-	-	3	16	27	77	169	311	250	308	...
55 - 59	785	-	-	-	3	7	5	19	38	107	221	385	...
60 - 64	465	-	-	1	-	1	2	5	5	35	46	370	...
65 - 69	265	-	-	-	1	2	1	3	6	7	245	...	
70 - 74	106	-	-	-	-	-	-	4	3	8	91	...	
75 +	57	-	-	-	-	-	-	-	-	1	56	...	
Republic of Moldova - République de Moldova													
2012[38] (C)													
Total	18 565	-	308	7 229	7 959	2 219	583	143	61	37	12	13	1
0 - 14	-	-	-	-	-	-	-	-	-	-	-	-	-
15 - 19	2 706	-	189	1 743	675	83	11	3	1	1	-	-	-
20 - 24	10 091	-	108	4 720	4 452	710	92	5	2	-	2	-	-
25 - 29	4 470	-	9	714	2 535	975	188	39	7	2	-	1	-
30 - 34	938	-	1	41	274	384	191	33	9	4	1	-	-
35 - 39	241	-	-	8	19	64	79	44	17	9	-	1	-
40 - 44	66	-	-	3	4	1	20	17	15	5	1	-	-
45 - 49	25	-	1	-	-	1	1	1	9	10	1	1	-
50 - 54	11	-	-	-	-	-	1	1	1	2	3	3	-
55 - 59	10	-	-	-	-	-	-	-	-	3	3	4	-
60 - 64	5	-	-	-	-	1	-	-	-	1	1	2	-
65 - 69	-												
70 - 74	1	-	-	-	-	-	-	-	-	-	-	1	-
75 +	-	-	-	-	-	-	-	-	-	-	-	-	-
Unknown - Inconnu	1	-	-	-	-	-	-	-	-	-	-	-	1
2017 (C)													
Total	20 924	...	101[f]	4 265	8 151	4 129	1 664	1 569[n]	...	697[o]	...	348	...
0 - 19	1 467	...	...	...	...	...	...	...	...	...	...	...	...
20 - 24	7 962	...	...	...	...	...	...	...	...	...	...	...	...
25 - 29	5 857	...	...	...	...	...	...	...	...	...	...	...	...
30 - 34	2 525	...	...	...	...	...	...	...	...	...	...	...	...
35 - 39	1 277	...	...	...	...	...	...	...	...	...	...	...	...
40 - 49	1 137	...	...	...	...	...	...	...	...	...	...	...	...
50 - 59	490	...	...	...	...	...	...	...	...	...	...	...	...
60 +	209	...	...	...	...	...	...	...	...	...	...	...	...
Romania - Roumanie													
2015 (C)													
Total	125 454	-	468	14 033	47 524	30 209	15 198	7 320	4 358	2 256	1 828	2 260	...
0 - 14	-	-	-	-	-	-	-	-	-	-	-	-	...
15 - 19	7 166	-	278	3 342	2 704	638	152	33	15	2	1	1	...
20 - 24	32 997	-	157	8 227	17 991	5 134	1 162	241	52	18	10	5	...
25 - 29	44 530	-	28	2 127	22 839	14 146	4 079	963	242	56	33	17	...
30 - 34	18 891	-	4	264	3 295	7 932	4 993	1 645	526	131	61	40	...
35 - 39	9 796	-	1	56	551	1 904	3 561	2 231	994	286	123	89	...
40 - 44	5 013	-	-	12	113	355	938	1 555	1 202	462	238	138	...
45 - 49	3 499	-	-	1	22	86	267	538	1 053	751	460	321	...
50 - 54	1 504	-	-	3	5	11	36	83	212	395	428	331	...
55 - 59	1 095	-	-	-	3	2	8	24	47	123	368	520	...
60 - 64	584	-	-	1	1	1	-	7	11	25	88	450	...
65 - 69	233	-	-	-	-	-	2	-	4	5	16	206	...

24. Marriages by age of groom and by age of bride: latest available year, 2008 - 2017
Mariages selon l'âge de l'époux et selon l'âge de l'épouse : dernière année disponible, 2008 - 2017 (continued - suite)

Continent, pays ou zone, date, code[a] et âge de l'épouse	Total	0-14	15-19	20-24	25-29	30-34	35-39	40-44	45-49	50-54	55-59	60+	Unknown Inconnu
EUROPE													
Romania - Roumanie													
2015													
70 - 74	97	-	-	-	-	-	-	-	-	-	2	95	...
75 +	49	-	-	-	-	-	-	-	-	2	-	47	...
Russian Federation - Fédération de Russie													
2012[39] (C)													
Total	1213598	...	15 848	312 104	402 995	191 131	105 357	63 778	43 196	34 745	21 315	23 078	51
15 - 19	81 342	...	9 599	50 495	18 055	2 523	468	130	38	20	7	6	1
20 - 24	425 562	...	5 186	200 558	173 664	35 196	7 918	2 062	620	221	80	54	3
25 - 29	337 474	...	802	50 809	166 737	80 206	26 188	8 444	2 758	1 022	326	182	-
30 - 34	154 765	...	189	8 034	34 743	52 674	34 829	15 241	5 645	2 339	749	318	4
35 - 39	83 803	...	50	1 683	7 769	15 610	25 204	18 450	9 030	4 074	1 366	564	3
40 - 44	45 822	...	17	377	1 571	3 745	7 817	13 055	10 391	5 807	2 044	996	2
45 - 49	31 345	...	1	94	327	880	2 159	4 456	9 684	8 528	3 435	1 778	3
50 - 54	25 096	...	1	37	89	230	606	1 487	3 793	9 098	6 198	3 553	4
55 - 59	14 880	...	1	7	22	46	121	360	985	2 837	5 299	5 202	-
60 +	13 481	...	2	8	16	20	47	91	252	798	1 811	10 424	12
Unknown - Inconnu	28	...	-	2	2	1	-	2	-	1	-	1	19
San Marino - Saint-Marin[40]													
2016 (C)													
Total	181	-	-	3	35	49	38	16	6	3	1	4	26
0 - 14	-	-	-	-	-	-	-	-	-	-	-	-	-
15 - 19	-	-	-	-	-	-	-	-	-	-	-	-	-
20 - 24	9	-	-	2	5	1	-	-	-	-	-	-	1
25 - 29	57	-	-	1	23	22	6	3	-	-	-	-	2
30 - 34	44	-	-	-	6	15	15	3	1	-	-	1	3
35 - 39	30	-	-	-	-	7	13	3	2	-	-	-	5
40 - 44	13	-	-	-	1	2	-	2	2	1	-	-	5
45 - 49	4	-	-	-	-	-	-	1	-	1	-	1	1
50 - 54	5	-	-	-	-	-	-	-	-	-	-	-	5
55 - 59	-	-	-	-	-	-	-	-	-	-	-	-	-
60 - 64	-	-	-	-	-	-	-	-	-	-	-	-	-
65 - 69	1	-	-	-	-	-	-	-	-	-	-	1	-
70 - 74	-	-	-	-	-	-	-	-	-	-	-	-	-
75 +	-	-	-	-	-	-	-	-	-	-	-	-	-
Unknown - Inconnu	18	-	-	-	-	2	4	4	1	1	1	1	4
Serbia - Serbie[41,42]													
2016 (+C)													
Total	35 921	-	217	3 625	10 780	9 960	4 852	2 274	1 314	874	670	1 268	87
0 - 14	-	-	-	-	-	-	-	-	-	-	-	-	-
15 - 19	1 454	-	130	730	422	117	33	13	4	4	-	1	-
20 - 24	7 939	-	74	2 158	3 722	1 505	345	72	22	13	5	9	14
25 - 29	11 779	-	8	603	5 381	4 221	1 182	256	74	22	10	8	14
30 - 34	7 120	-	2	73	1 010	3 327	1 844	557	197	62	19	22	7
35 - 39	3 124	-	-	26	152	604	1 099	735	292	118	60	33	5
40 - 44	1 618	-	-	9	43	114	256	448	352	214	97	79	6
45 - 49	975	-	-	8	10	29	54	121	257	220	125	149	2
50 - 54	801	-	-	1	5	12	13	43	78	170	198	279	2
55 - 59	439	-	-	-	-	-	4	12	18	27	122	255	1
60 - 64	280	-	-	2	1	4	1	5	10	13	18	225	1
65 - 69	160	-	-	1	4	1	-	2	2	4	11	135	-
70 - 74	49	-	-	1	-	-	1	1	-	1	2	43	-
75 +	33	-	1	1	-	-	1	-	1	3	1	25	-
Unknown - Inconnu	150	-	2	12	30	26	19	9	7	3	2	5	35
Slovakia - Slovaquie[5]													
2016 (C)													
Total	29 897	-	451	2 428	8 937	8 553	4 517	2 109	1 017	671	461	753	...
0 - 14	-	-	-	-	-	-	-	-	-	-	-	-	...
15 - 19	991	-	362	452	130	36	5	2	4	-	-	-	...
20 - 24	4 937	-	78	1 423	2 380	812	177	50	13	4	-	-	...
25 - 29	11 340	-	9	447	5 339	4 051	1 167	231	68	13	11	4	...
30 - 34	6 681	-	1	84	900	3 013	1 787	612	165	79	29	11	...
35 - 39	2 793	-	1	17	158	519	1 056	655	229	83	49	26	...
40 - 44	1 330	-	-	2	23	103	252	405	276	158	55	56	...
45 - 49	697	-	-	2	5	15	61	112	186	159	80	77	...

24. Marriages by age of groom and by age of bride: latest available year, 2008 - 2017
Mariages selon l'âge de l'époux et selon l'âge de l'épouse : dernière année disponible, 2008 - 2017 (continued - suite)

Continent, pays ou zone, date, code[a] et âge de l'épouse	Total	0-14	15-19	20-24	25-29	30-34	35-39	40-44	45-49	50-54	55-59	60+	Unknown Inconnu
EUROPE													
Slovakia - Slovaquie[5]													
2016													
50 - 54	489	-	-	1	2	2	8	35	57	130	118	136	...
55 - 59	289	-	-	-	-	-	4	5	19	33	74	154	...
60 - 64	226	-	-	-	-	2	-	2	-	10	36	176	...
65 - 69	79	-	-	-	-	-	-	-	-	2	6	71	...
70 - 74	29	-	-	-	-	-	-	-	-	-	3	26	...
75 +	16	-	-	-	-	-	-	-	-	-	-	16	...
Slovenia - Slovénie[43]													
2016 (C)													
Total	6 667	-	29	412	1 708	1 851	1 169	637	304	244	116	197	...
0 - 14	-	-	-	-	-	-	-	-	-	-	-	-	...
15 - 19	86	-	13	40	23	7	3	-	-	-	-	-	...
20 - 24	782	-	11	250	365	106	35	9	2	2	1	1	...
25 - 29	2 202	-	5	92	1 039	791	209	44	17	4	1	-	...
30 - 34	1 682	-	-	23	222	746	482	155	35	14	3	2	...
35 - 39	873	-	-	4	45	155	325	230	68	30	10	6	...
40 - 44	467	-	-	2	9	34	91	159	93	57	13	9	...
45 - 49	248	-	-	1	5	8	15	29	60	80	26	24	...
50 - 54	154	-	-	-	-	3	8	10	25	42	30	36	...
55 - 59	75	-	-	-	-	1	-	1	2	9	21	41	...
60 - 64	55	-	-	-	-	-	1	-	2	4	8	40	...
65 - 69	28	-	-	-	-	-	-	-	-	2	3	23	...
70 - 74	8	-	-	-	-	-	-	-	-	-	-	8	...
75 +	7	-	-	-	-	-	-	-	-	-	-	7	...
Spain - Espagne[44]													
2016 (C)													
Total	168 765	-	129	2 782	22 663	49 341	39 411	22 645	11 978	7 669	5 026	7 121	...
0 - 14	-	-	-	-	-	-	-	-	-	-	-	-	...
15 - 19	666	-	57	292	204	78	25	6	-	1	3	-	...
20 - 24	6 631	-	43	1 408	3 072	1 420	439	153	50	19	19	8	...
25 - 29	36 639	-	21	733	14 024	15 838	4 428	1 065	313	119	64	34	...
30 - 34	50 707	-	6	233	4 352	25 631	15 160	3 773	975	325	139	113	...
35 - 39	33 447	-	2	78	748	5 300	15 169	8 274	2 436	839	342	259	...
40 - 44	18 348	-	-	28	179	816	3 419	7 137	3 963	1 614	680	512	...
45 - 49	9 903	-	-	6	56	177	597	1 767	3 011	2 232	1 108	949	...
50 - 54	6 335	-	-	3	16	59	126	380	983	1 876	1 453	1 439	...
55 - 59	3 405	-	-	-	8	15	32	70	193	505	943	1 639	...
60 - 64	1 626	-	-	1	1	4	13	17	44	107	225	1 214	...
65 - 69	640	-	-	-	3	2	3	1	6	26	42	557	...
70 - 74	285	-	-	-	-	1	-	1	3	5	5	270	...
75 +	133	-	-	-	-	-	-	1	1	1	3	127	...
Sweden - Suède													
2012 (C)													
Total	50 044	-	69	1 803	7 703	10 419	8 284	5 587	4 328	2 880	2 142	2 688	4 141
0 - 14	-	-	-	-	-	-	-	-	-	-	-	-	-
15 - 19	668	-	33	130	81	26	7	1	1	-	-	1	388
20 - 24	4 680	-	27	1 194	1 729	551	164	63	30	7	4	2	909
25 - 29	11 233	-	5	378	4 640	3 898	1 046	288	123	41	15	12	787
30 - 34	10 932	-	2	71	1 004	4 783	3 106	858	319	104	37	30	618
35 - 39	7 543	-	1	12	183	930	3 005	1 924	666	218	81	54	469
40 - 44	5 154	-	1	10	43	175	732	1 768	1 317	434	192	87	395
45 - 49	3 922	-	-	5	19	42	178	525	1 383	905	407	180	278
50 - 54	2 665	-	-	2	2	7	36	127	395	863	690	383	160
55 - 59	1 595	-	-	1	2	6	5	28	75	242	526	647	63
60 - 64	934	-	-	-	-	1	5	4	16	58	150	657	43
65 - 69	468	-	-	-	-	-	-	1	2	8	36	396	25
70 - 74	160	-	-	-	-	-	-	-	-	-	4	153	3
75 +	90	-	-	-	-	-	-	-	-	1	-	86	3
Switzerland - Suisse[45]													
2016 (C)													
Total	41 646	-	53	2 304	8 836	11 685	7 314	3 682	2 541	2 080	1 357	1 794	...
0 - 14	-	-	-	-	-	-	-	-	-	-	-	-	...
15 - 19	435	-	26	237	133	25	7	6	1	-	-	-	...
20 - 24	4 729	-	24	1 467	2 175	685	229	63	42	29	11	4	...
25 - 29	11 600	-	2	434	4 918	4 285	1 302	354	153	84	37	31	...

Continent, country or area, year, code[a] and age of bride / Continent, pays ou zone, date, code[a] et âge de l'épouse	Total	0-14	15-19	20-24	25-29	30-34	35-39	40-44	45-49	50-54	55-59	60+	Unknown Inconnu
EUROPE													
Switzerland - Suisse[45]													
2016													
30 - 34	11 410	-	1	99	1 256	5 289	3 120	959	371	183	76	56	...
35 - 39	5 775	-	-	39	224	1 081	2 131	1 237	588	273	120	82	...
40 - 44	2 682	-	-	14	68	196	369	702	649	361	182	141	...
45 - 49	1 941	-	-	5	33	66	99	249	489	480	290	230	...
50 - 54	1 560	-	-	9	18	39	40	73	181	473	334	393	...
55 - 59	875	-	-	-	7	7	13	25	55	147	246	375	...
60 - 64	348	-	-	-	4	7	3	7	9	35	44	239	...
65 - 69	170	-	-	-	-	4	1	7	3	12	12	131	...
70 - 74	71	-	-	-	-	-	-	-	-	3	4	64	...
75 +	50	-	-	-	-	1	-	-	-	-	1	48	...
TFYR of Macedonia - L'ex-R. y. de Macédoine													
2016 (C)													
Total	13 199	-	183	2 635	4 896	3 041	1 132	527	304	188	124	169	...
0 - 14	-	-	-	-	-	-	-	-	-	-	-	-	...
15 - 19	1 182	-	119	702	296	48	12	4	-	1	-	-	...
20 - 24	4 447	-	58	1 688	2 082	497	99	20	3	-	-	-	...
25 - 29	4 202	-	2	218	2 199	1 450	267	51	6	5	3	1	...
30 - 34	1 814	-	2	18	273	896	433	143	36	7	2	4	...
35 - 39	671	-	1	4	38	123	238	155	61	32	10	9	...
40 - 44	385	-	1	2	6	18	69	122	96	45	12	14	...
45 - 49	222	-	-	1	1	6	10	28	84	45	23	24	...
50 - 54	138	-	-	1	-	2	2	3	17	40	46	27	...
55 - 59	67	-	-	-	-	1	2	1	-	11	19	33	...
60 - 64	45	-	-	1	1	-	-	-	-	1	8	34	...
65 - 69	17	-	-	-	-	-	-	-	-	-	1	16	...
70 - 74	4	-	-	-	-	-	-	-	-	-	-	4	...
75 +	5	-	-	-	-	-	-	-	1	1	-	3	...
Ukraine[46]													
2016 (+C)													
Total	229 453	-	4 191	55 606	72 835	39 977	20 085	12 521	8 319	6 030	4 320	5 569	...
0 - 14	13	-	5	8	-	-	-	-	-	-	-	-	...
15 - 19	21 747	-	2 538	12 768	5 248	913	188	59	17	9	5	2	...
20 - 24	77 986	-	1 374	34 342	32 071	7 841	1 675	439	154	52	30	8	...
25 - 29	58 067	-	186	6 857	27 717	16 146	4 877	1 481	505	193	77	28	...
30 - 34	29 680	-	61	1 185	6 022	10 974	6 757	2 931	1 106	414	160	70	...
35 - 39	15 757	-	14	281	1 367	3 058	4 584	3 549	1 751	717	290	146	...
40 - 44	9 507	-	9	110	291	803	1 444	2 703	2 188	1 186	509	264	...
45 - 49	6 340	-	4	34	79	172	408	977	1 839	1 557	810	460	...
50 - 54	4 313	-	-	16	24	52	109	295	567	1 350	1 138	762	...
55 - 59	2 870	-	-	2	12	14	35	66	153	412	998	1 178	...
60 +	3 173	-	-	3	4	4	8	21	39	140	303	2 651	...
United Kingdom of Great Britain and Northern Ireland - Royaume-Uni de Grande-Bretagne et d'Irlande du Nord[47,48]													
2015 (C)													
Total	283 559	-	641	15 591	68 340	69 010	39 069	26 215	21 607	17 079	11 057	14 920	30
0 - 14	-	-	-	-	-	-	-	-	-	-	-	-	-
15 - 19	1 768	-	423	899	332	77	21	9	3	2	1	1	-
20 - 24	27 833	-	170	10 300	12 785	3 279	800	269	125	55	24	26	-
25 - 29	83 717	-	38	3 412	43 842	26 748	6 646	1 875	739	271	91	53	2
30 - 34	64 435	-	4	692	9 223	30 902	15 431	5 160	1 977	690	245	110	1
35 - 39	32 355	-	3	196	1 598	6 098	11 433	7 764	3 340	1 270	420	233	-
40 - 44	22 008	-	1	56	370	1 355	3 413	7 156	5 606	2 637	934	480	-
45 - 49	19 234	-	-	25	119	394	952	2 922	6 512	4 998	2 151	1 161	-
50 - 54	14 622	-	-	7	50	114	284	826	2 526	5 039	3 431	2 345	-
55 - 59	8 495	-	1	3	13	28	68	188	593	1 583	2 755	3 263	-
60 - 64	4 377	-	1	-	2	4	13	30	139	400	743	3 045	-
65 - 69	2 661	-	-	-	3	4	5	7	39	97	208	2 298	-
70 - 74	1 243	-	-	-	-	2	1	3	2	27	40	1 168	-
75 +	774	-	-	1	-	1	-	5	6	10	14	737	-
Unknown - Inconnu	37	-	-	-	3	4	2	1	-	-	-	-	27

24. Marriages by age of groom and by age of bride: latest available year, 2008 - 2017
Mariages selon l'âge de l'époux et selon l'âge de l'épouse : dernière année disponible, 2008 - 2017 (continued - suite)

Continent, pays ou zone, date, code[a] et âge de l'épouse	Total	0-14	15-19	20-24	25-29	30-34	35-39	40-44	45-49	50-54	55-59	60+	Unknown Inconnu
OCEANIA - OCÉANIE													
Australia - Australie[49]													
2016 (+C)													
Total	118 401	-	345	10 606	34 873	29 947	14 451	8 535	6 317	4 824	3 584	4 931	...
0 - 14	-	-	-	-	-	-	-	-	-	-	-	-	...
15 - 19	1 297	-	186	704	291	76	16	6	3	3	-	-	...
20 - 24	17 446	-	127	7 358	7 389	1 771	440	165	81	46	33	37	...
25 - 29	40 976	-	24	2 106	22 257	12 365	2 727	795	353	165	93	89	...
30 - 34	26 801	-	10	316	4 204	13 037	6 012	1 924	728	307	154	123	...
35 - 39	11 316	-	-	82	536	2 191	3 947	2 504	1 180	475	227	169	...
40 - 44	7 018	-	-	26	136	362	1 010	2 193	1 726	867	377	313	...
45 - 49	5 143	-	-	4	36	97	221	725	1 512	1 353	717	475	...
50 - 54	3 762	-	-	-	11	32	51	172	552	1 175	1 007	753	...
55 - 59	2 231	-	-	-	4	6	17	45	144	334	735	948	...
60 - 64	1 213	-	-	-	-	4	8	10	26	79	185	896	...
65 - 69	686	-	-	-	-	-	3	-	3	18	45	615	...
70 - 74	314	-	-	-	-	-	-	-	3	3	3	301	...
75 +	202	-	-	-	-	-	-	-	-	-	4	199	...
Fiji - Fidji													
2008 (+C)													
Total	8 180	...	99	1 960	2 932	1 346	741	454	296	158	95	99	...
15 - 19	1 050	...	...	...	...	...	...	...	...	...	...	...	...
20 - 24	3 049	...	...	...	...	...	...	...	...	...	...	...	...
25 - 29	2 024	...	...	...	...	...	...	...	...	...	...	...	...
30 - 34	903	...	...	...	...	...	...	...	...	...	...	...	...
35 - 39	493	...	...	...	...	...	...	...	...	...	...	...	...
40 - 44	310	...	...	...	...	...	...	...	...	...	...	...	...
45 - 49	200	...	...	...	...	...	...	...	...	...	...	...	...
50 - 54	83	...	...	...	...	...	...	...	...	...	...	...	...
55 - 59	44	...	...	...	...	...	...	...	...	...	...	...	...
60 - 64	14	...	...	...	...	...	...	...	...	...	...	...	...
65 +	10	...	...	...	...	...	...	...	...	...	...	...	...
New Caledonia - Nouvelle-Calédonie													
2010 (C)													
Total	908	...	2[f]	62	149	200	171	169[n]	...	90[o]	...	65	-
0 - 19	13	...	1[f]	6	2	2	1	1[n]	...	-[o]	...	-	-
20 - 24	118	...	-[f]	36	51	18	10	2[n]	...	1[o]	...	-	-
25 - 29	194	...	1[f]	16	77	63	20	13[n]	...	3[o]	...	1	-
30 - 34	205	...	-[f]	4	14	94	62	27[n]	...	4[o]	...	-	-
35 - 39	139	...	-[f]	-	3	19	55	52[n]	...	7[o]	...	3	-
40 - 49	150	...	-[f]	-	2	4	22	65[n]	...	41[o]	...	16	-
50 - 59	59	...	-[f]	-	-	-	1	9[n]	...	30[o]	...	19	-
60 +	30	...	-[f]	-	-	-	-	-[n]	...	4[o]	...	26	-
New Zealand - Nouvelle-Zélande[9,50,51]													
2016 (+C)													
Total	20 235	-	60	1 590	5 085	4 728	2 649	1 611	1 365	1 053	822	1 266	...
0 - 14	-	-	-	-	-	-	-	-	-	-	-	-	...
15 - 19	339	-	57	213	45	12	6	-		-	-	-	...
20 - 24	3 459	-	-	1 380	1 605	351	84	24	12	3	3	-	...
25 - 29	6 642	-	-	-	3 438	2 433	516	147	66	24	12	15	...
30 - 34	3 912	-	-	-	-	1 935	1 359	369	162	48	21	15	...
35 - 39	1 758	-	-	-	-	-	684	666	267	84	30	21	...
40 - 44	1 281	-	-	-	-	-	-	405	522	201	87	66	...
45 - 49	1 071	-	-	-	-	-	-	-	327	429	195	117	...
50 - 54	798	-	-	-	-	-	-	-	-	264	330	207	...
55 - 59	477	-	-	-	-	-	-	-	-	-	153	327	...
60 - 64	243	-	-	-	-	-	-	-	-	-	-	246	...
65 - 69	144	-	-	-	-	-	-	-	-	-	-	144	...
70 - 74	69	-	-	-	-	-	-	-	-	-	-	66	...
75 +	51	-	-	-	-	-	-	-	-	-	-	51	...
Niue - Nioué													
2009 (C)													
Total	12	...	-	2	3	4	-	1	1	-	1	-	-
15 - 19	-	...	-	-	-	-	-	-	-	-	-	...	...
20 - 24	-	...	-	-	-	-	-	-	-	-	-	...	...

Continent, country or area, year, code[a] and age of bride / Continent, pays ou zone, date, code[a] et âge de l'épouse	Total	\multicolumn{12}{c}{Age of groom - - âge de l'époux}
		0-14	15-19	20-24	25-29	30-34	35-39	40-44	45-49	50-54	55-59	60+	Unknown Inconnu
OCEANIA - OCÉANIE													
Niue - Nioué													
2009													
25 - 29	3	...	...	...	...	...	...	...	...	...	...	...	...
30 - 34	4	...	...	...	...	...	...	...	...	...	...	...	...
35 - 39	3	...	...	...	...	...	...	...	...	...	...	...	...
40 - 44	-	...	...	...	...	...	...	...	...	...	...	...	...
45 - 49	1	...	...	...	...	...	...	...	...	...	...	...	...
50 - 54	1	...	...	...	...	...	...	...	...	...	...	...	...
55 - 59	-	...	...	...	...	...	...	...	...	...	...	...	...
60 - 64	-	...	...	...	...	...	...	...	...	...	...	...	...
65 +	-	...	...	...	...	...	...	...	...	...	...	...	...
Wallis and Futuna Islands - Îles Wallis et Futuna													
2008 (C)													
Total	53	-	1	14	23	8	3	2	-	2	-	-	-
0 - 14	-	...	...	...	...	...	...	...	...	...	...	...	...
15 - 19	9	...	...	...	...	...	...	...	...	...	...	...	...
20 - 24	18	...	...	...	...	...	...	...	...	...	...	...	...
25 - 29	12	...	...	...	...	...	...	...	...	...	...	...	...
30 - 34	7	...	...	...	...	...	...	...	...	...	...	...	...
35 - 39	5	...	...	...	...	...	...	...	...	...	...	...	...
40 - 44	-	...	...	...	...	...	...	...	...	...	...	...	...
45 - 49	1	...	...	...	...	...	...	...	...	...	...	...	...
50 - 54	-	...	...	...	...	...	...	...	...	...	...	...	...
55 - 59	-	...	...	...	...	...	...	...	...	...	...	...	...
60 - 64	1	...	...	...	...	...	...	...	...	...	...	...	...
65 - 69	-	...	...	...	...	...	...	...	...	...	...	...	...
70 - 74	-	...	...	...	...	...	...	...	...	...	...	...	...
75 +	-	...	...	...	...	...	...	...	...	...	...	...	...

FOOTNOTES - NOTES

Italics: data from civil registers which are incomplete or of unknown completeness. - Italiques : données incomplètes ou dont le degré d'exactitude n'est pas connu, provenant des registres de l'état civil.

* Provisional. - Données provisoires.

[a] 'Code' indicates the source of data, as follows:
C - Civil registration, estimated over 90% complete
U - Civil registration, estimated less than 90% complete
| - Other source, estimated reliable
+ - Data tabulated by date of registration rather than occurence
... - Information not available

Le 'Code' indique la source des données, comme suit :
C - Registres de l'état civil considérés complèts à 90 p. 100 au moins
U - Registres de l'état civil qui ne sont pas considérés complèts à 90 p. 100 au moins
| - Autre source, considérée pas douteuses
+ - Données exploitées selon la date de l'enregistrement et non la date de l'événement
... - Information pas disponible

[b] Refers to 0-15 years of age. - Données se raportent au groupe d'âges 0-15.
[c] Refers to 0-16 years of age. - Données se raportent au groupe d'âges 0-16.
[d] Refers to 0-17 years of age. - Données se raportent au groupe d'âges 0-17.
[e] Refers to 0-18 years of age. - Données se raportent au groupe d'âges 0-18.
[f] Refers to 0-19 years of age. - Données se raportent au groupe d'âges 0-19.
[g] Refers to 0-24 years of age. - Données se raportent au groupe d'âges 0-24.
[h] Refers to 16-19 years of age. - Données se raportent au groupe d'âges 16-19.
[i] Refers to 17-19 years of age. - Données se raportent au groupe d'âges 17-19.
[j] Refers to 18-19 years of age. - Données se raportent au groupe d'âges 18-19.
[k] Refers to 19-24 years of age. - Données se raportent au groupe d'âges 19-24.
[l] Refers to 20-29 years of age. - Données se raportent au groupe d'âges 20-29.

[m] Refers to 30-39 years of age. - Données se raportent au groupe d'âges 30-39.
[n] Refers to 40-49 years of age. - Données se raportent au groupe d'âges 40-49.
[o] Refers to 50-59 years of age. - Données se raportent au groupe d'âges 50-59.
[p] Refers to 35+ years of age. - Données se raportent au groupe d'âges 35+.
[q] Refers to 40+ years of age. - Données se raportent au groupe d'âges 40+.
[r] Refers to 45+ years of age. - Données se raportent au groupe d'âges 45+.
[s] Refers to 50+ years of age. - Données se raportent au groupe d'âges 50+.
[t] Refers to 55+ years of age. - Données se raportent au groupe d'âges 55+.

[1] Source: Vital Statistics Report 2014. - Source: Vital Statistics Report 2014.
[2] Excludes the islands of St. Brandon and Agalega. - Non compris les îles St. Brandon et Agalega.
[3] Including visitors. - Y compris les visiteurs.
[4] Excluding visitors. - Ne comprend pas les visiteurs.
[5] Data refer to marriages by residence of the groom. - Les données concernent les mariages selon la résidence du marié.
[6] Marriages registered by residence of bride. - Les mariages sont enregistrés selon le lieu de résidence de la mariée.
[7] Data refers to the number of marriages of which at least one of the partners is a resident of Curacao. - Les données concernent le nombre de mariages dont au moins l'un des partenaires est un résident de Curaçao.
[8] Including marriages where bride/groom are non-residents. - Y compris les mariages pour lesquels le marié et la mariée sont des non-résidents.
[9] Including same sex marriages. - Y compris les mariages entre personnes du même sexe.
[10] Excludes nomadic Indian tribes. - Non compris les tribus d'Indiens nomades.
[11] Data are compiled from the National Registers of Identification and Civil Status (RENIEC). - Les données sont rédigées à partir des Registres Nationaux d'Identification et d'État Civil (RENIEC).
[12] Data refers to metropolitan Lima and Callao. - Les données font référence à la région métropolitaine de Lima et Callao.
[13] Data refer to marriages of residents only. - Les données ne portent que sur les mariages de résidents.
[14] Data refer to government controlled areas. - Les données se rapportent aux zones contrôlées par le Gouvernement.

[15] Data refer to the Iranian Year which begins on 21 March and ends on 20 March of the following year. - Les données concernent l'année iranienne, qui commence le 21 mars et se termine le 20 mars de l'année suivante.

[16] Includes data for East Jerusalem and Israeli residents in certain other territories under occupation by Israeli military forces since June 1967. - Y compris les données pour Jérusalem-Est et les résidents israéliens dans certains autres territoires occupés depuis 1967 par les forces armées israéliennes.

[17] Data refer to Japanese nationals in Japan only; and to grooms and brides whose marriages occurred and were registered in the same year. - Les données se raportent aux nationaux japonais au Japon seulement; et aux époux et épouses dont le mariage a été célébré et enregistré la même année.

[18] Excluding data for Jordanian territory under occupation since June 1967 by Israeli military forces. Excluding foreigners, including registered Palestinian refugees. - Non compris les données pour le territoire jordanien occupé depuis juin 1967 par les forces armées israéliennes. Non compris les étrangers, mais y compris les réfugiés de Palestine enregistrés.

[19] Excluding marriages by groom and bride that are under "Married" status. - Sauf mariages entre personnes qui ont le statut de « marié(e) ».

[20] Excluding alien armed forces, civilian aliens employed by armed forces, and foreign diplomatic personnel and their dependants. - Non compris les militaires étrangers, les civils étrangers employés par les forces armées ni le personnel diplomatique étranger et les membres de leur famille les accompagnant.

[21] Data comprise civil marriages registered under the Women's Charter and Muslim marriages registered under the Administration of Muslim Law Act. - Les données comprennent les mariages civils enregistrés en vertu de la Charte des droits de la femme, ainsi que les mariages musulmans enregistrés en vertu de la loi sur l'administration du droit islamique.

[22] Excluding marriages previously officiated outside Singapore or under religious and customary rites. - Ne comprend pas les mariages prononcés ailleurs qu'à Singapour ni les mariages religieux ou coutumiers.

[23] Data from MERNIS (Central Population Administrative System). - Données de MERNIS (Système central de données démographiques).

[24] Excluding marriages of aliens temporarily in the area, but including marriages abroad of persons with residence in Austria. - Non compris les mariages d'étrangers temporairement dans la région, mais y compris des mariages à l'étranger de personnes ayant leur résidence en Autriche.

[25] Since 2003, marriage between persons of the same sex is authorized in Belgium, but the sex of spouses is not revealed. In this table, husband is used for first spouse, whereas wife is used for second spouse. - Depuis 2003, le mariage entre personnes de même sexe est autorisé en Belgique, mais le sexe des conjoints n'est pas indiqué. Dans ce tableau, la mention "époux" est utilisée pour le premier conjoint et la mention "épouse" pour le second conjoint.

[26] Including armed forces stationed outside the country and alien armed forces in the area, if the marriage is performed by local authority. - Y compris les militaires nationaux hors du pays et les militaires étrangers en garnison sur le territoire, si le mariage a été célébré par l'autorité locale.

[27] Including nationals outside the country, but excluding foreigners in the country. - Y compris les nationaux à l'étranger, mais non compris les étrangers sur le territoire.

[28] Excluding Faeroe Islands and Greenland shown separately, if available. - Non compris les Iles Féroé et le Groenland, qui font l'objet de rubriques distinctes, si disponible.

[29] As reported by the country. Reasons for discrepancy with other tables not ascertained. - Comme indiqué par le pays. L'on ne connaît pas la raison des écarts avec d'autres tableaux.

[30] Excluding Åland Islands. - Non compris les Îles d'Åland.

[31] Data refer to marriages between persons of different sex. - Les données se rapportent aux mariages entre personnes de sexe différent.

[32] Data for residence abroad are excluded. - Les données relatives aux résidents à l'étranger sont exclues.

[33] Data refer to common residence after marriage. - Données se rapportant à la résidence commune après le mariage.

[34] Data refer to marriages where one or both partners are residents. - Les données portent sur les mariages pour lesquels l'un des deux partenaires ou les deux sont résidents.

[35] Marriages of couples of which at least one partner is recorded in a Dutch municipal register, irrespective of the country where the marriage was performed. - Correspond aux mariages pour lesquels au moins l'un des partenaires est inscrit sur un registre municipal néerlandais, quel que soit le pays dans lequel le mariage est célébré.

[36] Marriages registered by place of occurrence of marriage. - Mariages enregistrés en fonction du lieu de l'événement.

[37] Groom refers to the man for opposite sex marriages, and to spouse 1 as specified in the Civil Register for same sex marriages. Bride refers to the woman for opposite sex marriages, and to spouse 2 as specified in the Civil Register for same sex marriages. - Marié se réfère à l'homme en cas de mariage entre personnes de sexe différent et à l'époux 1 inscrit sur le Registre d'état civil en cas

de mariage entre personnes du même sexe. Mariée se réfère à la femme en cas de mariage entre personnes de sexe différent et à l'époux 2 inscrit sur le Registre d'état civil en cas de mariage entre personnes du même sexe.

[38] Data refer to first marriages only. - Données se rapportent aux premiers mariages seulement.

[39] Data refer to population 15 years of age or more. - Les données concernent la population âgée de 15 ans ou plus.

[40] Includes civil and religious marriages as well as not specified. - Englobe les mariages civils et religieux et ceux pour lesquels rien n'a été indiqué.

[41] Excludes data for Kosovo and Metohia. - Sans les données pour le Kosovo et Metohie.

[42] Residence refers to residence of groom. - La catégorie « résidence » correspond au lieu de résidence du jeune marié.

[43] Data refer to residence of groom or bride before marriage. - Données relatives au lieu de résidence du marié ou de la mariée avant le mariage.

[44] Unrevised data. - Les données n'ont pas été révisées.

[45] Data based on the residence of groom if he has permanent address in the country, otherwise, based on the residence of bride. If neither partner is a permanent resident, the marriage is not included in the official statistics. - Les données sont fondées sur la résidence du marié si celui-ci a une adresse permanente dans le pays, sinon elles sont fondées sur la résidence de la mariée. Si aucun des deux partenaires n'est un résident permanent, le mariage n'apparaît pas dans les statistiques officielles.

[46] The Government of Ukraine has informed the United Nations that it is not in a position to provide statistical data concerning the Autonomous Republic of Crimea and the city of Sevastopol. - Le gouvernement Ukrainien a informé l'ONU qu'il n'est pas en mesure de fournir des données statistiques concernant la République autonome de Crimée et la ville de Sébastopol.

[47] Data tabulated by date of occurrence for England and Wales, and by date of registration for Northern Ireland and Scotland. - Données exploitées selon la date de l'événement pour l'Angleterre et le pays de Galles, et selon la date de l'enregistrement pour l'Irlande du Nord et l'Ecosse.

[48] Excluding Channel Islands (Guernsey and Jersey) and Isle of Man, shown separately, if available. - Non compris les îles Anglo-Normandes (Guernesey et Jersey) et l'île de Man, qui font l'objet de rubriques distinctes, si disponible.

[49] Data for certain cells suppressed by national statistical office for confidentiality reasons. - Les données pour certaines cases ont été supprimées par le bureau national de statistiques pour des raisons de confidentialité.

[50] Data refer to marriages and civil unions by residence of 'partner 2'. - Les données concernent les mariages et les unions civiles selon la résidence du « partenaire 2 ».

[51] Data have been randomly rounded. - Ces données ont été arrondies de façon aléatoire.

Table 25 - *Demographic Yearbook 2017*

Table 25 presents the number of divorces and crude divorce rates for as many years as possible between 2013 and 2017.

Description of variables: Divorce is defined as a final legal dissolution of a marriage, that is, the separation of husband and wife which confers on the parties the right to remarriage under civil, religious and/or other provisions, according to the laws of each country[1].

Unless otherwise noted, divorce statistics exclude legal separations that do not allow remarriage. These statistics refer to the number of divorces granted, and not to the number of persons divorcing.

Divorce statistics are obtained from court records and/or civil registers according to national practice. The actual compilation of these statistics may be the responsibility of the civil registrar, the national statistical office or other government offices.

The urban/rural classification of divorces is that provided by each country or area; it is presumed to be based on the national census definitions of urban population, which have been set forth at the end of the technical notes for table 6.

Rate computation: Crude divorce rates by urban/rural residence are the annual number of divorces per 1 000 mid-year population. Rates presented in this table have been limited to those countries or areas having at least a total of 30 divorces in a given year. These rates are calculated by the Statistics Division of the United Nations based on the appropriate reference population (for example: total population, nationals only etc.) if known and available. If the reference population is not known or unavailable, the total population is used to calculate the rates. Therefore, if the population that is used to calculate the rates is different from the correct reference population, the rates presented might under- or overstate the true situation in a country or area.

Reliability of data: Each country or area has been asked to indicate the estimated completeness of the divorces recorded in its civil register. These national assessments are indicated by the quality codes "C" and "U" that appear in the first column of this table.

"C" indicates that the data are estimated to be virtually complete, that is, representing at least 90 per cent of the divorces that occur each year, while "U" indicates that data are estimated to be incomplete, that is, representing less than 90 per cent of the divorces occurring each year. The code "..." indicates that no information was provided regarding completeness.

Data from civil registers that are reported as incomplete or of unknown completeness (coded "U" or "...") are considered unreliable. They appear in *italics* in this table and the rates were not computed on data so coded. These quality codes apply only to data from civil registers. For more information about the quality of vital statistics data in general, see section 4.2 of the Technical Notes.

Limitations: Statistics on divorces are subject to the same qualifications as have been set forth for vital statistics in general and divorce statistics in particular as discussed in section 4 of the Technical Notes.

Divorce, like marriage, is a legal event, and this has implications for international comparability of data. Divorce has been defined, for statistical purposes, in terms of the laws of individual countries or areas. The laws pertaining to divorce vary considerably from one country or area to another. This variation in the legal provision for divorce also affects the incidence of divorce, which is relatively low in countries or areas where divorce decrees are difficult to obtain.

Since divorces are granted by courts and statistics on divorce refer to the actual divorce decree, effective as of the date of the decree, marked year-to-year fluctuations may reflect court delays and clearances rather than trends in the incidence of divorce. The comparability of divorce statistics may also be affected by tabulation procedures. In some countries or areas annulments and/or legal separations may be included. This practice is more common for countries or areas in which the number of divorces is small. Information on this practice is given in the footnotes when known.

The registration of a divorce in many countries or areas is the responsibility solely of the court or the authority which granted it. Since the registration recording such cases is part of the records of the court proceedings, divorces are likely to be registered soon after the decree is granted. For this reason the practice of tabulating data by date of registration does not generally pose serious problems of comparability as it does in the case of birth and death statistics.

As noted briefly above, the incidence of divorce is affected by the relative ease or difficulty of obtaining a divorce according to the laws of individual countries or areas. The incidence of divorce is also affected by the ability of individuals to meet financial and other costs of the court procedures. Connected with this aspect is the influence of certain religious faiths on the incidence of divorce. For all these reasons, divorce statistics are not strictly comparable as measures of family dissolution by legal means. Furthermore, family dissolution by other than legal means, such as separation, is not measured in statistics for divorce.

For certain countries or areas there is or was no legal provision for divorce in the sense used here, and therefore no data for these countries or areas appear in this table.

In addition, it should be noted that rates are affected also by the quality and limitations of the population estimates that are used in their computation. The problems of under-enumeration or over-enumeration, and to some extent, the differences in definition of total population, have been discussed in section 3 of the Technical Notes dealing with population data in general, and specific information pertaining to individual countries or areas is given in the footnotes to table 3.

As will be seen from the footnotes, strict correspondence between the numerator of the rate and the denominator is not always obtained; for example, divorces among civilian plus military segments of the population may be related to civilian population only. The effect of this may be to increase the rates but, in most cases, the effect is negligible.

As mentioned above, data for some countries or areas may include annulments and/or legal separations. This practice affects the comparability of the crude divorce rates. For example, inclusion of annulments in the numerator of the rates produces a negligible effect on the rates, but inclusion of legal separations may have a measurable effect on the level.

It should be emphasized that crude divorce rates like crude birth, death and marriage rates may be seriously affected by age-sex structure of the populations to which they relate. Like crude marriage rates, they are also affected by the existing distribution of the population by marital status. Nevertheless, crude divorce rates provide a simple measure of the level and changes in divorces.

The comparability of data by urban/rural residence is affected by the national definitions of urban and rural used in tabulating these data. It is assumed, in the absence of specific information to the contrary, that the definitions of urban and rural used in connection with the national population census were also used in the compilation of the vital statistics for each country or area. However, it cannot be excluded that, for a given country or area, different definitions of urban and rural are used for the vital statistics data and the population census data respectively. When known, the definitions of urban in national population censuses are presented at the end of the technical notes for table 6. As discussed in detail in the notes, these definitions vary considerably from one country or area to another.

In addition to problems of comparability, divorce rates classified by urban/rural residence are also subject to certain special types of bias. If, when calculating divorce rates, different definitions of urban are used in connection with the vital events and the population data, and if this results in a net difference between the numerator and denominator of the rate in the population at risk, then the divorce rates would be biased. Urban/rural differentials in divorce rates may also be affected by whether the vital events have been tabulated in terms of place of occurrence or place of usual residence. This problem is discussed in more detail in section 4.1.4.1 of the Technical Notes.

Earlier data: Divorces have been shown in previous issues of the Demographic Yearbook. The earliest data, which were for 1935, appeared in the 1951 issue. For more information on specific topics and years for which data are reported, readers should consult the Historical Index.

NOTES

[1] For definition, please see section 4.1.1 of the Technical Notes.

Tableau 25 – *Annuaire démographique 2017*

Le tableau 25 présente des statistiques concernant les divorces et les taux bruts de divortialité, pour le plus grand nombre d'années possible entre 2013 et 2017.

Description des variables : le divorce est la dissolution légale et définitive des liens du mariage, c'est-à-dire la séparation de l'époux et de l'épouse qui confère aux parties le droit de se remarier civilement ou religieusement, ou selon toute autre procédure, conformément à la législation du pays[1].

Sauf indication contraire, les statistiques de la divortialité n'englobent pas les séparations légales qui excluent un remariage. Ces statistiques se rapportent aux jugements de divorce prononcés, non aux personnes divorcées.

Les statistiques de la divortialité proviennent, selon la pratique suivie par chaque pays, des actes des tribunaux et/ou des registres de l'état civil. L'officier d'état civil, les services nationaux de statistique ou d'autres services gouvernementaux peuvent être chargés d'établir ces statistiques.

La classification des divorces selon le lieu de résidence (zone urbaine ou rurale) est celle qui a été communiquée par chaque pays ou zone ; on part du principe qu'elle repose sur les définitions de la population urbaine utilisées pour les recensements nationaux, qui sont reproduites à la fin des notes techniques du tableau 6.

Calcul des taux : les taux bruts de divortialité selon le lieu de résidence (zone urbaine ou rurale) représentent le nombre annuel de divorces enregistrés pour 1 000 habitants au milieu de l'année. Les taux de ce tableau ne se rapportent qu'aux pays ou zones où l'on a enregistré un total d'au moins 30 divorces pendant une année donnée. Ces taux sont calculés par la division de statistique des Nations Unies sur la base de la population de référence adéquate (par exemple : population totale, nationaux seulement, etc.) si connue et disponible. Si la population de référence n'est pas connue ou n'est pas disponible, la population totale est utilisée pour calculer les taux. Par conséquent, si la population utilisée pour calculer les taux est différente de la population de référence adéquate, les taux présentés sont susceptibles de sous ou sur estimer la situation réelle d'un pays ou d'un territoire.

Fiabilité des données : il a été demandé à chaque pays ou zone d'indiquer le degré estimatif de complétude des données sur les divorces figurant dans ses registres d'état civil. Ces évaluations nationales sont désignées par les codes de qualité "C" et "U" qui apparaissent dans la deuxième colonne du tableau.

La lettre "C" indique que les données sont jugées à peu près complètes, c'est-à-dire qu'elles représentent au moins 90 p. 100 des divorces survenus chaque année ; la lettre "U" signale que les données sont jugées incomplètes, c'est-à-dire qu'elles représentent moins de 90 p. 100 des divorces survenus chaque année. Le code "..." indique qu'aucun renseignement n'a été communiqué quant à la complétude des données.

Les données issues des registres de l'état civil qui sont déclarées incomplètes ou dont le degré de complétude n'est pas connu (code "U" ou "...") sont jugées douteuses. Elles apparaissent en italique dans le tableau et les taux correspondants n'ont pas été calculés. Les codes de qualité ne s'appliquent qu'aux données extraites des registres de l'état civil. Pour plus de précisions sur la qualité des données reposant sur les statistiques de l'état civil en général, voir la section 4.2 des notes techniques.

Insuffisance des données : les statistiques des divorces appellent les mêmes réserves que celles formulées à propos des statistiques de l'état civil en général et des statistiques de divortialité en particulier (voir la section 4 des notes techniques).

Le divorce est, comme le mariage, un acte juridique, et ce fait influe sur la comparabilité internationale des données. Aux fins de la statistique, le divorce est défini par la législation de chaque pays ou zone. La législation sur le divorce varie considérablement d'un pays ou d'une zone à l'autre, ce qui influe aussi sur la fréquence des divorces, laquelle est relativement faible dans les pays ou zones où le jugement de divorce est difficile à obtenir.

Du fait que les divorces sont prononcés par les tribunaux et que les statistiques de la divortialité se rapportent aux jugements de divorce proprement dits, qui prennent effet à la date où ces jugements sont rendus, il se peut que des fluctuations annuelles accusées traduisent le rythme plus ou moins rapide auquel les affaires sont jugées plutôt que l'évolution de la fréquence des divorces. Les méthodes d'exploitation des données peuvent aussi influer sur la comparabilité des statistiques de la divortialité. Dans certains pays ou zones, ces statistiques peuvent comprendre les annulations et/ou les séparations légales. C'est notamment le cas dans les pays ou zones où les divorces sont peu nombreux. Lorsqu'ils sont connus, des renseignements à ce propos sont donnés en note à la fin du tableau.

Étant donné que dans de nombreux pays ou zones, le tribunal ou l'autorité qui a prononcé le divorce est seul habilité à enregistrer cet acte, et, comme l'acte d'enregistrement figure alors sur les registres du tribunal, l'enregistrement suit généralement de peu le jugement. C'est pourquoi la pratique consistant à exploiter les données selon la date de l'enregistrement ne pose généralement pas les graves problèmes de comparabilité auxquels on se heurte dans le cas des statistiques des naissances et des décès.

Comme on l'a brièvement mentionné ci-dessus, la fréquence des divorces est fonction notamment de la facilité relative avec laquelle la législation de chaque pays ou zone permet d'obtenir le divorce. Elle dépend également de la capacité des intéressés à supporter les frais de procédure. Il faut aussi citer l'influence de certaines religions sur la fréquence des divorces. Pour toutes ces raisons, les statistiques de divortialité ne sont pas rigoureusement comparables et ne permettent pas de mesurer exactement la fréquence des dissolutions légales des mariages. De plus, elles ne rendent pas compte des cas de dissolution extrajudiciaire du mariage, comme la séparation.

Dans certains pays ou zones, il n'existe ou il n'existait pas de législation sur le divorce selon l'acception retenue aux fins de ce tableau, si bien que l'on ne dispose pas de données les concernant.

De surcroît, il convient de noter que l'exactitude des taux dépend également de la qualité et des insuffisances des estimations de population qui sont utilisées pour leur calcul. Le problème des erreurs par excès ou par défaut commises lors du dénombrement et, dans une certaine mesure, le problème de l'hétérogénéité des définitions de la population totale ont été examinés à la section 3 des notes techniques, relative à la population en général ; des explications concernant les différents pays ou zones sont données en note à la fin du tableau 3.

Comme on le verra dans les notes, il n'a pas toujours été possible d'obtenir une correspondance rigoureuse entre le numérateur et le dénominateur pour le calcul des taux. Par exemple, les divorces parmi la population civile et les militaires sont parfois rapportés à la population civile seulement. Cela peut avoir pour effet d'accroître les taux, mais, dans la plupart des cas, il est probable que la différence sera négligeable.

Comme indiqué plus haut, les données concernant certains pays ou zones peuvent comprendre les annulations et/ou les séparations légales. Cette pratique influe sur la comparabilité des taux bruts de divortialité. Par exemple, l'inclusion des annulations dans le numérateur a une influence négligeable, mais l'inclusion des séparations légales peut avoir un effet appréciable.

Il faut souligner que les taux bruts de divortialité, de même que les taux bruts de natalité, de mortalité et de nuptialité, peuvent varier sensiblement selon la structure par âge et par sexe. Comme les taux bruts de nuptialité, ils peuvent également varier en raison de la répartition de la population selon l'état matrimonial. Les taux bruts de divortialité offrent néanmoins un moyen simple de mesurer la fréquence et l'évolution des divorces.

La comparabilité des données selon le lieu de résidence (zone urbaine ou rurale) peut être limitée par les définitions nationales des termes « urbain » et « rural » utilisées pour la mise en tableaux de ces données. En l'absence d'indications contraires, on a supposé que les mêmes définitions avaient servi pour le recensement national de la population et pour l'établissement des statistiques de l'état civil pour chaque pays ou zone. Toutefois, il n'est pas exclu que, pour une zone ou un pays donné, des définitions différentes aient été retenues. Les définitions du terme « urbain » utilisées pour les recensements nationaux de population ont été présentées à la fin des notes techniques du tableau 6 lorsqu'elles étaient connues. Comme on l'a précisé dans les notes techniques relatives au tableau 6, ces définitions varient considérablement d'un pays ou d'une zone à l'autre.

Outre les problèmes de comparabilité, les taux de divortialité classés selon le lieu de résidence (zone urbaine ou rurale) sont également sujets à des distorsions particulières. Si l'on utilise des définitions différentes du terme « urbain » pour classer les faits d'état civil et les données relatives à la population lors du calcul des taux et qu'il en résulte une différence nette entre le numérateur et le dénominateur pour le taux de la population exposée au risque, les taux de divortialité s'en trouveront faussés. La différence entre ces taux pour les zones urbaines et rurales pourra aussi être faussée selon que les faits d'état civil auront été classés d'après le lieu de l'événement ou d'après le lieu de résidence habituel. Ce problème est examiné plus en détail à la section 4.1.4.1 des notes techniques.

Données publiées antérieurement : des statistiques concernant les divorces ont déjà été présentées dans des éditions antérieures de l'*Annuaire démographique*. Les plus anciennes, qui portaient sur 1935, ont été publiées dans l'édition de 1951. Pour plus de précisions concernant les années et les sujets pour lesquels des données ont été publiées, se reporter à l'index historique.

NOTE

[1] Pour la définition, voir la section 4.1.1 des Notes techniques.

25. Divorces and crude divorce rates by urban/rural residence: 2013 - 2017
Divorces et taux bruts de divortialité selon la résidence, urbaine/rurale : 2013 - 2017

Continent, country or area, and urban/rural residence Continent, pays ou zone et résidence, urbaine/rurale	Code[a]	Number - Nombre					Rate - Taux				
		2013	2014	2015	2016	2017	2013	2014	2015	2016	2017
AFRICA - AFRIQUE											
Côte d'Ivoire											
Total	...	...	...	...	...	*1 285*	...	...	...	...	...
Egypt - Égypte[1]											
Total	+C	162 583	180 344	199 867	192 079	198 269	1.9	2.1	2.2	2.1	2.1
Urban - Urbaine	+C	91 040	97 953	114 780	105 200	108 224	2.5	2.6	3.0	2.7	2.7
Rural - Rurale	+C	71 543	82 391	85 087	86 879	90 045	1.5	1.7	1.7	1.7	1.6
Lesotho											
Total	+U	...	...	...	*169*		...	...	...	...	...
Urban - Urbaine	+U	...	...	...	*82*		...	...	...	...	...
Rural - Rurale	+U	...	...	...	*87*		...	...	...	...	...
Mauritius - Maurice[2]											
Total	+C	1 584	2 262	2 161	1 910	1 996	1.3	1.8	1.7	1.5	1.6
Mayotte											
Total	C	...	155	139	...	...	...	0.7	0.6	...	...
Reunion - Réunion											
Total	C	...	1 420	1 561	...	...	...	1.7	1.8	...	...
Saint Helena ex. dep. - Sainte-Hélène sans dép.											
Total	C	7	4	...	...	...	...	...	...	...	...
Seychelles											
Total	+C	193	158	149	185	207	2.1	1.7	1.6	2.0	2.2
South Africa - Afrique du Sud											
Total	...	*23 885*	*24 689*	*25 260*	*25 326*		...	...	...	...	...
Sudan - Soudan											
Total	U	...	...	*43 926*	...		...	...	...	...	...
Tunisia - Tunisie											
Total	...	*13 867*	*14 527*	*14 982*	*15 632*		...	...	...	...	...
AMERICA, NORTH - AMÉRIQUE DU NORD											
Aruba											
Total	C	477	468	366	382	378	4.5	4.3	3.4	3.5	3.4
Barbados - Barbade											
Total	+C	459	443	...	...	...	1.7	1.6	...	...	...
Bermuda - Bermudes											
Total	C	165	104	116	120	...	2.7	1.7	1.9	1.9	...
Costa Rica											
Total	+C	13 349	10 864	10 111	13 155	*12 661	2.8	2.3	2.1	2.7	*2.6
Cuba											
Total	C	32 848	32 934	33 174	31 598	32 183	2.9	2.9	3.0	2.8	2.9
Urban - Urbaine	C	30 819	30 906	31 131	29 468	...	3.6	3.6	3.6	3.4	...
Rural - Rurale	C	2 029	2 028	2 043	2 130	...	0.8	0.8	0.8	0.8	...
Curaçao											
Total	C	366	344	375	365	415	2.4	2.2	2.4	2.3	2.6
Dominica - Dominique											
Total	+C	81	80	...	...	...	1.1	1.1	...	...	...
Dominican Republic - République dominicaine											
Total	+C	18 882	19 370	20 352	21 750	...	1.9	2.0	2.0	2.2	...
El Salvador[3]											
Total	...	*6 841*	...	...	...	...	...	...	...	...	...
Urban - Urbaine	...	*6 592*	...	...	...	...	...	...	...	...	...
Rural - Rurale	...	*249*	...	...	...	...	...	...	...	...	...
Grenada - Grenade											
Total	+C	158	119	...	...	...	1.5	1.1	...	...	...
Guadeloupe											
Total	C	806	729	659	...	...	2.0	1.8	1.7	...	...
Guatemala											
Total	C	5 542	5 575	5 726	5 665	...	0.4	0.4	0.4	...	...
Jamaica - Jamaïque											
Total	+C	2 410	1 744	1 734	2 146	3 166	0.9	0.6	0.6	0.8	1.2
Martinique											
Total	C	...	414	369	...	...	...	1.1	1.0	...	...

25. Divorces and crude divorce rates by urban/rural residence: 2013 - 2017
Divorces et taux bruts de divortialité selon la résidence, urbaine/rurale : 2013 - 2017 (continued - suite)

Continent, country or area, and urban/rural residence / Continent, pays ou zone et résidence, urbaine/rurale	Co-de[a]	Number - Nombre					Rate - Taux				
		2013	2014	2015	2016	2017	2013	2014	2015	2016	2017
AMERICA, NORTH - AMÉRIQUE DU NORD											
Mexico - Mexique											
Total	+C	108 727	113 478[6]	123 883[6]	139 807[6]	...	0.9	0.9	1.0	1.1	...
Urban - Urbaine[4]	+C	97 087[5]	101 093[6]	108 804[6]	119 819[6]	...	1.1	1.2	1.2	1.4	...
Rural - Rurale[4]	+C	5 305[5]	5 786[6]	6 305[6]	6 725[6]	...	0.2	0.2	0.2	0.2	...
Nicaragua											
Total	+U	4 998	7 069	7 461	6 363	...	...	...	...	...	...
Panama											
Total	C	4 083	4 336	*4 479	*4 360	...	1.1	1.1	*1.1	*1.1	...
Urban - Urbaine	C	3 453	3 781	*3 806	*3 730	...	1.3	1.4	*1.4	*1.3	...
Rural - Rurale	C	630	555	*673	*630	...	0.5	0.4	*0.5	*0.5	...
Puerto Rico - Porto Rico											
Total	C	12 908	11 776	11 877	10 998	8 515	3.6	3.3	3.4	3.2	2.6
Saint Vincent and the Grenadines - Saint-Vincent-et-les Grenadines											
Total	C	29	39	...	...	...	...	0.4	...	...	...
Sint Maarten (Dutch part) - Saint-Martin (partie néerlandaise)											
Total	+C	99	...	...	...	...	2.7	...	...	...	...
Trinidad and Tobago - Trinité-et-Tobago											
Total	C	*2 468	...	...	...	...	*1.8	...	...	...	...
Turks and Caicos Islands - Îles Turques et Caïques											
Total	C	29	...	...	...	...	...	...	...	...	...
United States of America - États-Unis d'Amérique[7]											
Total	C	832 157	813 862	800 909	...	...	2.6	2.6	2.5	...	...
AMERICA, SOUTH - AMÉRIQUE DU SUD											
Brazil - Brésil											
Total	...	324 921	341 181	328 960	344 526	...	...	...	...	...	...
Ecuador - Équateur[8]											
Total	U	21 122	24 771	25 692	25 648	...	...	...	...	...	...
Urban - Urbaine[9]	U	19 458	22 854	24 021	23 180	...	...	...	...	...	...
Rural - Rurale[9]	U	1 664	1 917	1 671	2 468	...	...	...	...	...	...
French Guiana - Guyane française											
Total	C	216	251	209	...	...	0.9	1.0	0.8	...	...
Peru - Pérou[10]											
Total	+C	14 103	13 598	13 757	*15 109	...	0.5	0.4	0.4	*0.5	...
Suriname[11]											
Total	C	602	778	733	636	...	1.1	1.4	1.3	1.1	...
Venezuela (Bolivarian Republic of) - Venezuela (République bolivarienne du)											
Total	...	31 355	26 127	24 126	21 966	21 178	...	...	...	...	...
ASIA - ASIE											
Armenia - Arménie											
Total	+C	...	4 496	3 670	3 648	...	...	1.5	1.2	1.2	...
Urban - Urbaine	+C	...	...	2 801	2 923	...	...	...	1.5	1.5	...
Rural - Rurale	+C	...	...	869	725	...	...	...	0.8	0.7	...
Azerbaijan - Azerbaïdjan											
Total	+C	11 730	12 088	12 764	13 114	...	1.2	1.3	1.3	1.3	...
Urban - Urbaine	+C	8 451	8 190	8 658	9 173	...	...	1.6	1.7	1.8	...
Rural - Rurale	+C	3 279	3 898	4 106	3 941	...	...	0.9	0.9	0.9	...
Bahrain - Bahreïn											
Total	...	1 824	1 795	1 745	1 749	1 890	...	...	...	...	...

25. Divorces and crude divorce rates by urban/rural residence: 2013 - 2017
Divorces et taux bruts de divortialité selon la résidence, urbaine/rurale : 2013 - 2017 (continued - suite)

Continent, country or area, and urban/rural residence / Continent, pays ou zone et résidence, urbaine/rurale	Code[a]	Number - Nombre 2013	2014	2015	2016	2017	Rate - Taux 2013	2014	2015	2016	2017
ASIA - ASIE											
Brunei Darussalam - Brunéi Darussalam											
Total	+C	502	522	545	566	...	1.2	1.3	1.3	1.4	...
China, Hong Kong SAR - Chine, Hong Kong RAS											
Total	...	22 271	20 019	20 075	17 196	19 394	...	...	...	...	...
China, Macao SAR - Chine, Macao RAS											
Total	+C	1 172	1 308	1 168	1 245	1 479	2.0	2.1	1.8	1.9	2.3
Cyprus - Chypre[12]											
Total	C	1 857	1 884	1 807	1 948	...	2.2	2.2	2.1	2.3	...
Urban - Urbaine[13]	C	1 444	...	...	...	...	...	...	...	...	...
Rural - Rurale[13]	C	333	...	...	...	...	...	...	...	...	...
Georgia - Géorgie											
Total	C	8 089	9 119	9 112	9 539	10 222	1.8	2.4	2.5	2.6	2.7
Urban - Urbaine	C	5 693	6 253	6 320	6 565	...	...	...	3.0	3.1	...
Rural - Rurale	C	2 396	2 866	2 792	2 974	...	...	...	1.8	1.9	...
Indonesia - Indonésie											
Total	U	324 247	344 237	347 256		...	...	...	...	...	...
Iran (Islamic Republic of) - Iran (République islamique d')[14]											
Total	+C	155 369	163 569	163 765	181 049	...	2.0	2.1	2.1	2.3	...
Urban - Urbaine	+C	...	...	146 714	168 774	...	...	...	2.6	2.9	...
Rural - Rurale	+C	...	...	17 051	12 275	...	...	...	0.8	0.6	...
Israel - Israël[15]											
Total	C	14 735	14 430	14 487	14 819	...	1.8	1.8	1.7	1.7	...
Urban - Urbaine[13]	C	13 392	13 166	13 095	13 385	...	1.8	1.8	1.7	1.7	...
Rural - Rurale[13]	C	1 021	929	1 070	1 042	...	1.5	1.3	1.5	1.4	...
Japan - Japon[16]											
Total	+C	231 383	222 107	226 215	216 798	...	1.8	1.7	1.8	1.7	...
Urban - Urbaine	+C	212 844	204 352	208 181	199 561	...	...	...	...	...	...
Rural - Rurale	+C	18 539	17 755	18 034	17 237	...	...	...	...	...	...
Jordan - Jordanie[17]											
Total	+C	18 976	20 911	22 070	21 969	21 210	2.3	2.4	2.3	2.2	2.1
Kazakhstan											
Total	+C	51 482	52 673	53 293	51 993	54 626	3.0	3.0	3.0	2.9	3.0
Urban - Urbaine	+C	38 365	39 433	39 846	38 716	40 774	4.1	4.1	4.0	3.8	3.9
Rural - Rurale	+C	13 117	13 240	13 447	13 277	13 852	1.7	1.7	1.8	1.7	1.8
Kuwait - Koweït											
Total	C	6 904	7 327	7 201	7 223	7 433	2.0	1.9	1.8	1.8	1.8
Kyrgyzstan - Kirghizstan											
Total	C	9 052	9 235	8 588	9 102	9 588	1.6	1.6	1.4	1.5	1.5
Urban - Urbaine	C	5 255	5 324	4 797	5 297	5 302	2.7	2.7	2.4	2.6	2.5
Rural - Rurale	C	3 797	3 911	3 791	3 805	4 286	1.0	1.0	1.0	0.9	1.0
Lebanon - Liban											
Total	+C	6 644	7 206	...	...	...	...	...	...	...	...
Maldives											
Total	...	...	...	3 358	3 417	...	...	...	...	...	...
Urban - Urbaine	...	...	...	1 455	1 496	...	...	...	...	...	...
Rural - Rurale	...	...	...	1 903	1 921	...	...	...	...	...	...
Mongolia - Mongolie											
Total	+C	3 522	3 750	3 873	4 003	3 945	1.2	1.3	1.3	1.3	1.3
Urban - Urbaine	+C	2 978	3 333	3 455	3 501	3 384	1.5	1.7	1.7	1.6	1.6
Rural - Rurale	+C	544	417	418	502	561	0.6	0.4	0.4	0.5	0.6
Oman											
Total	U	3 550	3 622	3 619	...	...	...	...	...	...	...
Qatar											
Total	C	1 325	1 315	1 307	1 151	1 206	0.7	0.6	0.5	0.4	0.4
Urban - Urbaine	C	...	1 315	1 307	1 151	1 206	...	0.6	0.5	0.4	0.4
Republic of Korea - République de Corée[18]											
Total	+C	115 292	115 510	109 153	107 328	106 032	2.3	2.3	2.1	2.1	2.1
Urban - Urbaine[13]	+C	89 793	89 689	84 958	83 872	...	2.2	2.2	2.0	2.0	...
Rural - Rurale[13]	+C	22 218	22 596	21 384	21 504	...	2.4	2.4	2.3	2.3	...
Singapore - Singapour											
Total	+C	7 133	6 861	7 117	7 207	7 207	1.9	1.8	1.8	1.8	1.8

Continent, country or area, and urban/rural residence / Continent, pays ou zone et résidence, urbaine/rurale	Code[a]	Number - Nombre 2013	2014	2015	2016	2017	Rate - Taux 2013	2014	2015	2016	2017
ASIA - ASIE											
State of Palestine - État de Palestine											
Total	C	7 114	7 603	8 179	8 510	...	1.6	1.7	1.7	1.8	...
Tajikistan - Tadjikistan											
Total	+C	7 920	9 037	8 346	8 845	...	1.0	1.1	1.0	1.0	...
Urban - Urbaine	+C	3 264	3 279	3 366	3 557	...	1.5	1.5	1.5	1.6	...
Rural - Rurale	+C	4 656	5 758	4 980	5 288	...	0.8	0.9	0.8	0.8	...
Thailand - Thaïlande											
Total	...	107 031	111 810	117 880	118 539	121 617	...	...	...	...	...
Turkey - Turquie[19]											
Total	C	125 305	130 913	131 830	126 164	...	1.6	1.7	1.7	1.6	...
United Arab Emirates - Émirats arabes unis											
Total	...	4 233	4 809	4 913	...	...	...	...	...	...	...
Uzbekistan - Ouzbékistan											
Total	+C	24 025	28 811	29 647	29 340	31 929	0.8	0.9	0.9	0.9	1.0
Urban - Urbaine	+C	16 524	19 634	19 480	18 605	19 618	1.1	1.3	1.2	1.2	1.2
Rural - Rurale	+C	7 501	9 177	10 167	10 735	12 311	0.5	0.6	0.7	0.7	0.8
EUROPE											
Åland Islands - Îles d'Åland											
Total	C	54	50	77	62	*53	1.9	1.7	2.7	2.1	*1.8
Urban - Urbaine	C	29	20	44	35	*28	...	...	3.8	3.0	...
Rural - Rurale	C	25	30	33	27	*25	...	1.7	1.9	...	...
Albania - Albanie											
Total	C	3 747	4 240	3 761	5 582	...	1.3	1.5	1.3	1.9	...
Austria - Autriche[20]											
Total	C	15 958	16 647	16 351	15 919	16 180	1.9	1.9	1.9	1.8	1.8
Belarus - Bélarus											
Total	C	36 105	34 864	32 984	32 628	32 006	3.8	3.7	3.5	3.4	3.4
Urban - Urbaine	C	31 239	30 436	28 419	28 326	...	4.3	4.2	3.9	3.8	...
Rural - Rurale	C	4 866	4 428	4 565	4 302	...	2.2	2.0	2.1	2.0	...
Belgium - Belgique[21]											
Total	C	24 872	24 310	24 414	23 583	23 059	2.2	2.2	2.2	2.1	2.0
Urban - Urbaine	C	24 603	24 029	24 132	...	...	...	...	...	...	...
Rural - Rurale	C	269	281	282	...	...	...	...	...	...	...
Bosnia and Herzegovina - Bosnie-Herzégovine											
Total	C	1 608	1 655	1 997	1 797	1 961	0.5	0.5	0.6	0.5	0.6
Bulgaria - Bulgarie[22]											
Total	C	10 908	10 584	10 483	10 603	10 411	1.5	1.5	1.5	1.5	1.5
Urban - Urbaine	C	...	8 680	8 629	8 603	8 438	...	1.6	1.6	1.6	...
Rural - Rurale	C	...	1 904	1 854	2 000	1 973	...	1.0	1.0	1.0	...
Croatia - Croatie											
Total	C	5 992	6 570	6 010	7 036	...	1.4	1.6	1.4	1.7	...
Urban - Urbaine	C	4 105	4 585	4 170	4 955	...	...	...	...	...	...
Rural - Rurale	C	1 887	1 985	1 840	2 081	...	...	...	...	...	...
Czechia - Tchéquie											
Total	C	27 895	26 764	26 083	24 996	*25 755	2.7	2.5	2.5	2.4	*2.4
Urban - Urbaine	C	21 882	20 676	19 646	18 569	...	2.8	2.7	2.6	2.4	...
Rural - Rurale	C	6 013	6 088	6 437	6 427	...	2.1	2.2	2.3	2.3	...
Denmark - Danemark[23]											
Total	C	18 875	19 435	16 343	17 222	15 265	3.4	3.4	2.9	3.0	2.6
Estonia - Estonie											
Total	C	3 343	3 218	3 382	3 262	3 323	2.5	2.4	2.6	2.5	2.5
Urban - Urbaine[24]	C	2 275	2 197	2 226	2 143	...	2.5	2.4	2.5	2.4	...
Rural - Rurale[24]	C	888	836	985	908	...	2.1	2.0	2.4	2.2	...
Faeroe Islands - Îles Féroé											
Total	C	76	83	78	52	65	1.6	1.7	1.6	1.1	1.3
Finland - Finlande[25]											
Total	C	13 712	13 632	13 862	13 479	...	2.5	2.5	2.5	2.5	...
Urban - Urbaine	C	10 257	10 229	10 521	10 254	...	2.7	2.7	2.7	2.6	...
Rural - Rurale	C	3 455	3 403	3 341	3 225	...	2.1	2.0	2.1	2.0	...
France											
Total	C	121 849	120 568	120 731	124 768	...	1.9	1.9	1.9	1.9	...

25. Divorces and crude divorce rates by urban/rural residence: 2013 - 2017
Divorces et taux bruts de divortialité selon la résidence, urbaine/rurale : 2013 - 2017 (continued - suite)

Continent, country or area, and urban/rural residence / Continent, pays ou zone et résidence, urbaine/rurale	Code[a]	Number - Nombre					Rate - Taux				
		2013	2014	2015	2016	2017	2013	2014	2015	2016	2017
EUROPE											
Germany - Allemagne											
Total	C	169 833	166 199	163 335	162 397	153 501	2.1	2.1	2.0	2.0	1.9
Gibraltar											
Total	+C	84	72	61	...	...	2.6	2.2	1.8	...	...
Greece - Grèce											
Total	C	16 717	14 427	...	11 013	...	1.5	1.3	...	1.0	...
Hungary - Hongrie[11]											
Total	C	20 209	19 576	20 315	19 552	18 495	2.0	2.0	2.1	2.0	1.9
Urban - Urbaine[26]	C	15 044	14 801	15 168	14 741	...	2.2	2.1	2.2	2.1	...
Rural - Rurale[26]	C	4 928	4 536	4 893	4 540	...	1.6	1.6	1.7	1.6	...
Ireland - Irlande											
Total	+C	2 949	2 629	...	...	...	0.6	0.6	...	...	...
Italy - Italie											
Total	C	52 943	52 355	82 469	99 071	...	0.9	0.9	1.4	1.6	...
Latvia - Lettonie											
Total	C	7 031	6 271	5 151	6 061	5 943	3.5	3.1	2.6	3.1	3.1
Liechtenstein											
Total	C	75	82	98	81	90	2.0	2.2	2.6	2.1	2.4
Lithuania - Lituanie											
Total	C	9 974	9 806	9 371	8 879	8 518	3.4	3.3	3.2	3.1	3.0
Urban - Urbaine	C	6 924	6 831	6 394	6 037	...	3.5	3.5	3.3	3.1	...
Rural - Rurale	C	3 050	2 975	2 977	2 842	...	3.1	3.1	3.1	3.0	...
Luxembourg											
Total	C	1 163	1 453	1 345	1 241	1 192	2.1	2.6	2.4	2.1	2.0
Malta - Malte											
Total	C	338	323	372	371	...	0.8	0.8	0.9	0.8	...
Montenegro - Monténégro											
Total	C	499	584	577	703	...	0.8	0.9	0.9	1.1	...
Netherlands - Pays-Bas[6]											
Total	C	33 636[27]	35 409[27]	34 232[27]	33 414[28]	32 768[28]	2.0	2.1	2.0	2.0	1.9
Norway - Norvège[6]											
Total	C	10 212	9 918	9 793	9 944	9 848	2.0	1.9	1.9	1.9	1.9
Poland - Pologne											
Total	C	66 132	65 761	67 296	63 497	65 257	1.7	1.7	1.8	1.7	1.7
Urban - Urbaine[29]	C	49 342	48 490	48 896	45 904	...	2.1	2.1	2.1	2.0	...
Rural - Rurale[29]	C	16 129	16 632	17 587	16 690	...	1.1	1.1	1.2	1.1	...
Portugal											
Total	C	22 525[30]	21 988[30]	23 377[30]	22 649[30]	21 866	2.2	2.1	2.3	2.2	2.1
Republic of Moldova - République de Moldova											
Total	C	10 775	11 130	11 199	10 605	9 312	3.0	3.7	...	...	...
Urban - Urbaine	C	7 708	7 834	10 915	10 112	8 954	...	6.8	...	...	...
Rural - Rurale	C	3 067	3 296	284	493	358	...	1.8	...	...	...
Romania - Roumanie											
Total	C	28 507	27 188	31 527	30 497	31 147	1.4	1.4	1.6	1.5	1.6
Urban - Urbaine	C	19 594	18 692	21 496	20 485	20 625	1.8	1.7	2.0	1.9	...
Rural - Rurale	C	8 913	8 496	10 031	10 012	10 522	1.0	0.9	1.1	1.1	...
Russian Federation - Fédération de Russie											
Total	C	667 971	...	...	...	...	4.7	...	...	...	...
San Marino - Saint-Marin											
Total	C	54	51	65	83	90	1.6	1.5	1.9	2.4	2.6
Serbia - Serbie[31]											
Total	+C	8 170	7 614	9 381[11]	9 046[11]	...	1.1	1.1	1.3	1.3	...
Urban - Urbaine	+C	5 761	5 322	6 833[11]	6 532[11]	...	1.3	1.2	1.6	1.5	...
Rural - Rurale	+C	2 409	2 292	2 548[11]	2 514[11]	...	0.8	0.8	0.9	0.9	...
Slovakia - Slovaquie											
Total	C	10 946	10 514	9 786	9 286	10 199	2.0	1.9	1.8	1.7	1.9
Urban - Urbaine	C	6 840	6 490	5 945	5 664	6 187	2.3	2.2	2.0	1.9	...
Rural - Rurale	C	4 106	4 024	3 841	3 622	4 012	1.7	1.6	1.5	1.4	...
Slovenia - Slovénie											
Total	C	2 351	2 469	2 432	2 531	2 387	1.1	1.2	1.2	1.2	1.2
Urban - Urbaine	C	1 307	1 399	1 484	1 545	...	1.2	1.3	1.3	1.4	...
Rural - Rurale	C	1 044	1 070	948	986	...	1.0	1.1	1.0	1.0	...
Spain - Espagne											
Total	C	95 427	100 746	96 562	96 824	...	2.0	2.2	2.1	2.1	...

25. Divorces and crude divorce rates by urban/rural residence: 2013 - 2017
Divorces et taux bruts de divortialité selon la résidence, urbaine/rurale : 2013 - 2017 (continued - suite)

Continent, country or area, and urban/rural residence / Continent, pays ou zone et résidence, urbaine/rurale	Co-de[a]	Number - Nombre					Rate - Taux				
		2013	2014	2015	2016	2017	2013	2014	2015	2016	2017
EUROPE											
Sweden - Suède[6]											
Total	C	26 933	26 143	24 876	24 258	24 210	2.8	2.7	2.5	2.4	2.4
Switzerland - Suisse											
Total	U	*17 119*	*16 737*	*16 982*	*17 028*	*15 906*	...	...	...	...	...
Urban - Urbaine	U	*13 123*	*14 397*[32]	...	*14 638*		...	...	...	...	...
Rural - Rurale	U	*3 996*	*2 340*[32]	...	*2 390*		...	...	...	...	...
TFYR of Macedonia - L'ex-R. y. de Macédoine											
Total	C	2 045	2 210	2 200	1 985	1 994	1.0	1.1	1.1	1.0	1.0
Urban - Urbaine	C	1 372	1 472	1 420	1 315		...	...	...	...	...
Rural - Rurale	C	673	738	780	670		...	...	...	...	...
Ukraine											
Total	+C	164 939	130 673[33]	129 373[33]	129 997[33]	...	3.6	3.0	3.0	3.1	...
United Kingdom of Great Britain and Northern Ireland - Royaume-Uni de Grande-Bretagne et d'Irlande du Nord[34]											
Total	C	126 718	122 654	112 411	118 505	...	2.0	1.9	1.7	1.8	...
OCEANIA - OCÉANIE											
American Samoa - Samoas américaines											
Total	C	61	63	...	...	...	1.0	1.0	...	...	...
Australia - Australie											
Total	+C	47 638	46 498	48 517	46 604	...	2.1	2.0	2.0	1.9	...
Guam[35]											
Total	C	720	739	657	647	683	4.5	4.6	4.1	4.0	4.2
New Zealand - Nouvelle-Zélande											
Total	+C	8 279	8 171	8 523[36]	8 169[36]	*8 001[36]	1.9	1.8	1.9	1.7	*1.7

FOOTNOTES - NOTES

Italics: data from civil registers which are incomplete or of unknown completeness. - Italiques : données incomplètes ou dont le degré d'exactitude n'est pas connu, provenant des registres de l'état civil.

* Provisional. - Données provisoires.

a 'Code' indicates the source of data, as follows:
C - Civil registration, estimated over 90% complete
U - Civil registration, estimated less than 90% complete
| - Other source, estimated reliable
+ - Data tabulated by date of registration rather than occurence
... - Information not available

Le 'Code' indique la source des données, comme suit :
C - Registres de l'état civil considérés complèts à 90 p. 100 au moins
U - Registres de l'état civil qui ne sont pas considérés complèts à 90 p. 100 au moins
| - Autre source, considérée pas douteuses
+ - Données exploitées selon la date de l'enregistrement et non la date de l'événement
... - Information pas disponible

1 Including 'revocable divorces' (among Muslim population), which approximate legal separations. - Y compris les 'divorces révocables' (parmi la population musulmane), qui sont plus au moins l'équivalent des séparations légales.
2 Excludes the islands of St. Brandon and Agalega. - Non compris les îles St. Brandon et Agalega.
3 Data refer to the usual residence of the wife and excludes divorces granted in the country of wives living abroad. - Données relatives à la résidence habituelle de l'épouse, sauf cas de divorces prononcés dans les pays d'épouses vivant à l'étranger.
4 The total number may include 'Unknown residence', but the categories urban and rural do not. - Le nombre total peut inclure les personnes dont la résidence n'est pas connue, à l'inverse des catégories de population urbaine et rurale.
5 Urban and rural distribution refers to the usual residence of the wife. - La répartition entre résidence urbaine et résidence rurale fait référence au lieu de résidence habituel de la femme.
6 Including same sex divorces. - Y compris les divorces entre conjoints du même sexe.
7 Excluding data for California, Georgia, Hawaii, Indiana, and Minnesota. - À l'exclusion des données pour la Californie, la Géorgie, Hawaï, l'Indiana et le Minnesota.
8 Excludes nomadic Indian tribes. - Non compris les tribus d'Indiens nomades.
9 Urban and rural residence refers to the place of usual residence of husband. - Le lieu de résidence (zone urbaine ou zone rurale) correspond au lieu de résidence habituel du mari.
10 Data are compiled from the National Registers of Identification and Civil Status (RENIEC). - Les données sont rédigées à partir des Registres Nationaux d'Identification et d'État Civil (RENIEC).
11 Including annulments. - Y compris les annulations.
12 Data refer to government controlled areas. - Les données se rapportent aux zones contrôlées par le Gouvernement.
13 The total number may include 'Unknown residence', but the categories urban and rural do not. Urban and rural residence refers to the place of usual residence of husband. - Le nombre total peut inclure les personnes dont la résidence n'est pas connue, à l'inverse des catégories de population urbaine et rurale. Le lieu de résidence (zone urbaine ou zone rurale) correspond au lieu de résidence habituel du mari.
14 Data refer to the Iranian Year which begins on 21 March and ends on 20 March of the following year. - Les données concernent l'année iranienne, qui commence le 21 mars et se termine le 20 mars de l'année suivante.

15 Includes data for East Jerusalem and Israeli residents in certain other territories under occupation by Israeli military forces since June 1967. - Y compris les données pour Jérusalem-Est et les résidents israéliens dans certains autres territoires occupés depuis 1967 par les forces armées israéliennes.

16 Data refer to Japanese nationals in Japan only. - Les données se raportent aux nationaux japonais au Japon seulement.

17 Excluding data for Jordanian territory under occupation since June 1967 by Israeli military forces. Excluding foreigners, including registered Palestinian refugees. - Non compris les données pour le territoire jordanien occupé depuis juin 1967 par les forces armées israéliennes. Non compris les étrangers, mais y compris les réfugiés de Palestine enregistrés.

18 Excluding alien armed forces, civilian aliens employed by armed forces, and foreign diplomatic personnel and their dependants. - Non compris les militaires étrangers, les civils étrangers employés par les forces armées ni le personnel diplomatique étranger et les membres de leur famille les accompagnant.

19 Data from MERNIS (Central Population Administrative System). - Données de MERNIS (Système central de données démographiques).

20 Excluding divorces of aliens temporarily in the area. - Non compris les divorces d'étrangers temporairement dans la région.

21 Including divorces among armed forces stationed outside the country and alien armed forces in the area. - Y compris les divorces de militaires nationaux hors du pays et les militaires étrangers en garnison sur le territoire.

22 Including nationals outside the country, but excluding foreigners in the country. Including annulments. - Y compris les nationaux à l'étranger, mais non compris les étrangers sur le territoire. Y compris les annulations.

23 Excluding Faeroe Islands and Greenland shown separately, if available. - Non compris les Iles Féroé et le Groenland, qui font l'objet de rubriques distinctes, si disponible.

24 Urban and rural residence refers to the place of usual residence of husband. The difference between 'Total' and the sum of urban and rural is due to the unknown place of residence of husbands and to husbands living outside the country. - Le lieu de résidence (zone urbaine ou zone rurale) correspond au lieu de résidence habituel du mari. La différence entre le « Total » et la somme des chiffres urbains et ruraux s'explique par le fait que la résidence du mari n'est pas toujours connue ou est située à l'étranger.

25 Excluding Åland Islands. Including annulments. - Non compris les Îles d'Åland. Y compris les annulations.

26 The urban and rural categories do not include the data of foreigners, persons of unknown residence and the homeless, whereas the total category includes them. - Les chiffres portant sur la population urbaine et rurale n' incluent pas les données relatives aux étrangers, aux personnes dont la résidence n'est pas connue et aux personnes sans domicile fixe, à l'inverse, le total les inclut.

27 Based on the general office for civil registration. - Données provenant des services généraux d'état civil.

28 Including residents outside the country if listed in a Netherlands population register. - Englobe les résidents se trouvant à l'étranger à condition qu'ils soient inscrits sur le registre de population des Pays-Bas.

29 Data for urban and rural exclude divorces if both persons live abroad. - Les données pour les zones urbaines et rurales excluent le divorce si les deux personnes vivent à l'étranger.

30 Data refer to resident spouses only. - Les données concernent uniquement les conjoints résidents.

31 Excludes data for Kosovo and Metohia. - Sans les données pour le Kosovo et Metohie.

32 From 2014, urban refers to urban centers and areas under the influence of urban centers. - A partir de 2014, le territoire urbain inclut l'espace des centres urbains ainsi que l'espace sous influence des centres urbains.

33 The Government of Ukraine has informed the United Nations that it is not in a position to provide statistical data concerning the Autonomous Republic of Crimea and the city of Sevastopol. - Le gouvernement Ukrainien a informé l'ONU qu'il n'est pas en mesure de fournir des données statistiques concernant la République autonome de Crimée et la ville de Sébastopol.

34 Data tabulated by date of occurrence for England and Wales, and by date of registration for Northern Ireland and Scotland. Excluding Channel Islands (Guernsey and Jersey) and Isle of Man, shown separately, if available. - Données exploitées selon la date de l'événement pour l'Angleterre et le pays de Galles, et selon la date de l'enregistrement pour l'Irlande du Nord et l'Ecosse. Non compris les îles Anglo-Normandes (Guernesey et Jersey) et l'île de Man, qui font l'objet de rubriques distinctes, si disponible.

35 Including United States military personnel, their dependants and contract employees. - Y compris les militaires des Etats-Unis, les membres de leur famille les accompagnant et les agents contractuels des Etats-Unis.

36 Data have been randomly rounded. - Ces données ont été arrondies de façon aléatoire.

Continent and country or area / Continent et pays ou zone	Population estimates (in thousands) - Estimations de population (en milliers)									
	2008	2009	2010	2011	2012	2013	2014	2015	2016	2017

AFRICA - AFRIQUE

	2008	2009	2010	2011	2012	2013	2014	2015	2016	2017
Algeria - Algérie	34 861	35 466	36 118	36 820	37 566	38 339	39 113	39 872	40 606	41 318
Angola	21 759	22 550	23 369	24 219	25 096	25 998	26 920	27 859	28 813	29 784
Benin - Bénin	8 697	8 945	9 199	9 461	9 729	10 004	10 287	10 576	10 872	11 176
Botswana	1 946	1 980	2 015	2 051	2 089	2 129	2 169	2 209	2 250	2 292
Burkina Faso	14 690	15 141	15 605	16 082	16 571	17 073	17 586	18 111	18 646	19 193
Burundi	8 212	8 489	8 767	9 044	9 320	9 600	9 892	10 199	10 524	10 864
Cabo Verde	492	497	502	508	514	520	526	533	540	546
Cameroon - Cameroun	18 907	19 433	19 970	20 520	21 082	21 656	22 240	22 835	23 439	24 054
Central African Republic - République centrafricaine	4 345	4 404	4 449	4 476	4 490	4 500	4 515	4 546	4 595	4 659
Chad - Tchad	11 134	11 503	11 887	12 289	12 705	13 134	13 569	14 009	14 453	14 900
Comoros - Comores	657	673	690	707	724	742	759	777	796	814
Congo	4 115	4 254	4 387	4 513	4 633	4 751	4 871	4 996	5 126	5 261
Côte d'Ivoire	19 498	19 936	20 401	20 895	21 419	21 966	22 531	23 108	23 696	24 295
Democratic Republic of the Congo - République démocratique du Congo	60 374	62 409	64 523	66 714	68 979	71 316	73 723	76 197	78 736	81 340
Djibouti	823	837	851	866	881	897	912	927	942	957
Egypt - Égypte	80 954	82 465	84 108	85 898	87 813	89 807	91 813	93 778	95 689	97 553
Equatorial Guinea - Guinée équatoriale	868	909	951	994	1 039	1 084	1 129	1 175	1 221	1 268
Eritrea - Érythrée	4 233	4 310	4 391	4 475	4 561	4 651	4 746	4 847	4 955	5 069
Eswatini	1 159	1 181	1 203	1 225	1 248	1 271	1 295	1 319	1 343	1 367
Ethiopia - Éthiopie	83 185	85 416	87 703	90 047	92 444	94 888	97 367	99 873	102 403	104 957
Gabon	1 536	1 587	1 640	1 697	1 757	1 817	1 876	1 930	1 980	2 025
Gambia - Gambie	1 589	1 640	1 692	1 746	1 802	1 859	1 918	1 978	2 039	2 101
Ghana	23 299	23 904	24 512	25 122	25 733	26 346	26 963	27 583	28 207	28 834
Guinea - Guinée	10 323	10 557	10 794	11 035	11 281	11 537	11 806	12 092	12 396	12 717
Guinea-Bissau - Guinée-Bissau	1 481	1 517	1 556	1 596	1 638	1 681	1 726	1 771	1 816	1 861
Kenya	39 148	40 237	41 350	42 487	43 647	44 827	46 024	47 236	48 462	49 700
Lesotho	2 000	2 019	2 041	2 064	2 090	2 117	2 146	2 175	2 204	2 233
Liberia - Libéria	3 663	3 812	3 948	4 070	4 182	4 286	4 391	4 500	4 614	4 732
Libya - Libye	6 053	6 121	6 169	6 194	6 198	6 196	6 204	6 235	6 293	6 375
Madagascar	19 996	20 569	21 152	21 744	22 347	22 961	23 590	24 234	24 895	25 571
Malawi	14 271	14 715	15 167	15 628	16 097	16 577	17 069	17 574	18 092	18 622
Mali	14 138	14 607	15 075	15 541	16 007	16 478	16 963	17 468	17 995	18 542
Mauritania - Mauritanie	3 408	3 506	3 610	3 718	3 830	3 946	4 064	4 182	4 301	4 420
Mauritius - Maurice[1]	1 239	1 244	1 248	1 251	1 253	1 255	1 257	1 259	1 262	1 265
Mayotte	196	203	209	215	221	227	234	240	246	253
Morocco - Maroc	31 597	31 990	32 410	32 859	33 334	33 825	34 318	34 803	35 277	35 740
Mozambique	22 847	23 524	24 221	24 939	25 677	26 434	27 212	28 011	28 829	29 669
Namibia - Namibie	2 106	2 137	2 173	2 216	2 264	2 317	2 371	2 426	2 480	2 534
Niger	15 229	15 814	16 426	17 065	17 732	18 426	19 148	19 897	20 673	21 477
Nigeria - Nigéria	150 347	154 402	158 578	162 877	167 297	171 829	176 461	181 182	185 990	190 886
Republic of South Sudan - République de Soudan du Sud	9 263	9 671	10 067	10 449	10 818	11 177	11 531	11 882	12 231	12 576
Reunion - Réunion	816	824	831	837	844	850	857	863	870	877
Rwanda	9 708	9 977	10 247	10 516	10 789	11 065	11 345	11 630	11 918	12 208
Sao Tome and Principe - Sao Tomé-et-Principe	167	171	175	179	183	187	191	196	200	204
Senegal - Sénégal	12 204	12 551	12 916	13 301	13 704	14 120	14 546	14 977	15 412	15 851
Seychelles	91	91	91	92	92	93	93	94	94	95
Sierra Leone	6 165	6 310	6 459	6 612	6 766	6 922	7 079	7 237	7 396	7 557
Somalia - Somalie	11 369	11 708	12 053	12 405	12 764	13 132	13 513	13 908	14 318	14 743
South Africa - Afrique du Sud	50 412	50 971	51 585	52 264	52 998	53 767	54 540	55 291	56 015	56 717
Sudan - Soudan	32 955	33 651	34 386	35 167	35 990	36 850	37 738	38 648	39 579	40 533
Togo	6 162	6 330	6 503	6 679	6 859	7 043	7 229	7 417	7 606	7 798
Tunisia - Tunisie	10 407	10 522	10 640	10 761	10 887	11 015	11 144	11 274	11 403	11 532
Uganda - Ouganda	31 664	32 772	33 915	35 094	36 307	37 554	38 833	40 145	41 488	42 863
United Republic of Tanzania - République Unie de Tanzanie[2]	43 270	44 664	46 099	47 571	49 083	50 637	52 235	53 880	55 572	57 310
Western Sahara - Sahara occidental	469	474	480	488	496	505	515	526	539	553
Zambia - Zambie	13 083	13 456	13 850	14 265	14 700	15 153	15 621	16 101	16 591	17 094
Zimbabwe	13 558	13 811	14 086	14 387	14 711	15 055	15 412	15 777	16 150	16 530

AMERICA, NORTH - AMÉRIQUE DU NORD

	2008	2009	2010	2011	2012	2013	2014	2015	2016	2017
Anguilla	13	14	14	14	14	14	14	15	15	15
Antigua and Barbuda - Antigua-et-Barbuda	92	94	95	96	97	98	99	100	101	102
Aruba	101	101	102	102	103	103	104	104	105	105
Bahamas	349	355	361	367	372	377	382	387	391	395
Barbados - Barbade	277	278	280	281	282	283	283	284	285	286

Continent and country or area / Continent et pays ou zone	Population estimates (in thousands) - Estimations de population (en milliers)									
	2008	2009	2010	2011	2012	2013	2014	2015	2016	2017

AMERICA, NORTH - AMÉRIQUE DU NORD

	2008	2009	2010	2011	2012	2013	2014	2015	2016	2017
Belize	306	314	322	329	337	344	352	359	367	375
Bermuda - Bermudes	65	64	64	64	63	63	62	62	62	61
Bonaire, Saba and Sint Eustatius - Bonaire, Saba et Saint-Eustache	18	20	21	22	23	24	24	25	25	25
British Virgin Islands - Îles Vierges britanniques	26	26	27	28	29	29	30	30	31	31
Canada	33 405	33 790	34 169	34 539	34 901	35 255	35 605	35 950	36 290	36 624
Cayman Islands - Îles Caïmanes	53	54	56	57	58	58	59	60	61	62
Costa Rica	4 430	4 488	4 545	4 600	4 654	4 706	4 758	4 808	4 857	4 906
Cuba	11 310	11 319	11 333	11 355	11 382	11 412	11 440	11 461	11 476	11 485
Curaçao	140	144	148	151	153	155	157	158	159	161
Dominica - Dominique	71	71	71	72	72	72	73	73	74	74
Dominican Republic - République dominicaine	9 637	9 768	9 898	10 027	10 155	10 281	10 406	10 528	10 649	10 767
El Salvador	6 110	6 137	6 165	6 193	6 221	6 251	6 281	6 312	6 345	6 378
Greenland - Groenland	57	57	57	57	56	56	56	56	56	56
Grenada - Grenade	104	104	105	105	105	106	106	107	107	108
Guadeloupe[3]	447	449	451	451	452	451	451	450	450	450
Guatemala	14 006	14 316	14 630	14 949	15 271	15 596	15 924	16 252	16 582	16 914
Haiti - Haïti	9 705	9 853	10 000	10 145	10 289	10 432	10 572	10 711	10 847	10 981
Honduras	7 873	8 035	8 195	8 352	8 506	8 658	8 809	8 961	9 113	9 265
Jamaica - Jamaïque	2 790	2 804	2 817	2 829	2 841	2 852	2 862	2 872	2 881	2 890
Martinique	397	396	395	393	391	389	387	386	385	385
Mexico - Mexique	113 662	115 505	117 319	119 090	120 828	122 536	124 222	125 891	127 540	129 163
Montserrat	5	5	5	5	5	5	5	5	5	5
Nicaragua	5 595	5 667	5 738	5 808	5 877	5 946	6 014	6 082	6 150	6 218
Panama	3 516	3 579	3 643	3 708	3 773	3 838	3 904	3 969	4 034	4 099
Puerto Rico - Porto Rico	3 736	3 726	3 717	3 707	3 698	3 689	3 681	3 674	3 668	3 663
Saint Kitts and Nevis - Saint-Kitts-et-Nevis	50	51	51	52	53	53	54	54	55	55
Saint Lucia - Sainte-Lucie	169	171	173	174	175	176	176	177	178	179
Saint Pierre and Miquelon - Saint Pierre-et-Miquelon	6	6	6	6	6	6	6	6	6	6
Saint Vincent and the Grenadines - Saint-Vincent-et-les Grenadines	109	109	109	109	109	109	109	109	110	110
Sint Maarten (Dutch part) - Saint-Martin (partie néerlandaise)	32	33	33	34	35	36	38	39	40	40
Trinidad and Tobago - Trinité-et-Tobago	1 315	1 322	1 328	1 335	1 342	1 348	1 354	1 360	1 365	1 369
Turks and Caicos Islands - Îles Turques et Caïques	29	30	31	32	32	33	34	34	35	35
United States of America - États-Unis d'Amérique	303 374	306 076	308 641	311 051	313 335	315 537	317 719	319 929	322 180	324 459
United States Virgin Islands - Îles Vierges américaines	107	106	106	106	106	105	105	105	105	105

AMERICA, SOUTH - AMÉRIQUE DU SUD

	2008	2009	2010	2011	2012	2013	2014	2015	2016	2017
Argentina - Argentine	40 382	40 799	41 224	41 657	42 097	42 540	42 982	43 418	43 847	44 271
Bolivia (Plurinational State of) - Bolivie (État plurinational de)	9 600	9 759	9 918	10 078	10 239	10 400	10 562	10 725	10 888	11 052
Brazil - Brésil	192 979	194 896	196 796	198 687	200 561	202 409	204 213	205 962	207 653	209 288
Chile - Chili	16 662	16 829	16 993	17 153	17 310	17 463	17 614	17 763	17 910	18 055
Colombia - Colombie	44 902	45 416	45 918	46 407	46 881	47 343	47 792	48 229	48 653	49 066
Ecuador - Équateur	14 448	14 691	14 935	15 177	15 420	15 662	15 903	16 144	16 385	16 625
Falkland Islands (Malvinas) - Îles Falkland (Malvinas)	3	3	3	3	3	3	3	3	3	3
French Guiana - Guyane française	222	228	234	241	247	255	262	269	276	283
Guyana	746	746	747	749	753	758	763	769	773	778
Paraguay	6 047	6 128	6 210	6 294	6 379	6 466	6 553	6 639	6 725	6 811
Peru - Pérou	28 642	29 002	29 374	29 760	30 159	30 566	30 973	31 377	31 774	32 165
Suriname	515	521	526	532	537	543	548	553	558	563
Uruguay	3 351	3 363	3 374	3 386	3 397	3 408	3 420	3 432	3 444	3 457
Venezuela (Bolivarian Republic of) - Venezuela (République bolivarienne du)	28 142	28 587	29 028	29 463	29 893	30 318	30 738	31 155	31 568	31 977

ASIA - ASIE

	2008	2009	2010	2011	2012	2013	2014	2015	2016	2017
Afghanistan	27 294	28 004	28 803	29 709	30 697	31 732	32 758	33 736	34 656	35 530
Armenia - Arménie	2 908	2 889	2 877	2 876	2 882	2 894	2 906	2 917	2 925	2 930
Azerbaijan - Azerbaïdjan[4]	8 822	8 924	9 032	9 146	9 265	9 385	9 504	9 617	9 725	9 828
Bahrain - Bahreïn	1 115	1 185	1 241	1 278	1 300	1 315	1 336	1 372	1 425	1 493
Bangladesh	148 806	150 455	152 149	153 912	155 727	157 571	159 405	161 201	162 952	164 670
Bhutan - Bhoutan	701	714	728	741	753	765	776	787	798	808
Brunei Darussalam - Brunéi Darussalam	379	384	389	394	400	406	412	418	423	429

Continent and country or area Continent et pays ou zone	Population estimates (in thousands) - Estimations de population (en milliers)									
	2008	2009	2010	2011	2012	2013	2014	2015	2016	2017
ASIA - ASIE										
Cambodia - Cambodge	13 881	14 090	14 309	14 538	14 777	15 023	15 271	15 518	15 762	16 005
China - Chine[5]	1 344 415	1 352 068	1 359 755	1 367 480	1 375 199	1 382 793	1 390 110	1 397 029	1 403 500	1 409 517
China, Hong Kong SAR - Chine, Hong Kong RAS	6 940	6 983	7 025	7 066	7 106	7 149	7 195	7 246	7 303	7 365
China, Macao SAR - Chine, Macao RAS	514	525	537	549	563	576	589	601	612	623
Cyprus - Chypre[6]	1 082	1 098	1 113	1 125	1 135	1 144	1 152	1 161	1 170	1 180
Democratic People's Republic of Korea - République populaire démocratique de Corée	24 335	24 463	24 592	24 722	24 854	24 986	25 116	25 244	25 369	25 491
Georgia - Géorgie[7]	4 341	4 288	4 232	4 171	4 108	4 046	3 992	3 952	3 925	3 912
India - Inde	1 197 147	1 214 270	1 230 981	1 247 236	1 263 066	1 278 562	1 293 859	1 309 054	1 324 171	1 339 180
Indonesia - Indonésie	236 159	239 340	242 524	245 708	248 883	252 032	255 131	258 162	261 115	263 991
Iran (Islamic Republic of) - Iran (République islamique d')	72 846	73 688	74 568	75 492	76 454	77 435	78 411	79 360	80 277	81 163
Iraq	29 111	29 895	30 763	31 727	32 777	33 883	35 006	36 116	37 203	38 275
Israel - Israël	7 097	7 268	7 426	7 569	7 699	7 821	7 941	8 065	8 192	8 322
Japan - Japon	128 551	128 567	128 552	128 505	128 426	128 313	128 163	127 975	127 749	127 484
Jordan - Jordanie	6 490	6 821	7 182	7 575	7 993	8 413	8 809	9 159	9 456	9 702
Kazakhstan	16 001	16 184	16 399	16 647	16 921	17 207	17 488	17 750	17 988	18 204
Kuwait - Koweït	2 652	2 819	2 998	3 191	3 396	3 598	3 782	3 936	4 053	4 137
Kyrgyzstan - Kirghizstan	5 262	5 341	5 422	5 507	5 594	5 684	5 775	5 865	5 956	6 045
Lao People's Democratic Republic - République démocratique populaire lao	6 052	6 152	6 246	6 333	6 415	6 495	6 576	6 664	6 758	6 858
Lebanon - Liban	4 111	4 183	4 337	4 588	4 916	5 276	5 603	5 851	6 007	6 082
Malaysia - Malaisie[8]	27 111	27 605	28 112	28 635	29 170	29 707	30 228	30 723	31 187	31 624
Maldives	345	355	365	375	386	397	408	418	428	436
Mongolia - Mongolie	2 628	2 668	2 713	2 762	2 814	2 869	2 924	2 977	3 027	3 076
Myanmar	49 480	49 801	50 156	50 553	50 987	51 448	51 924	52 404	52 885	53 371
Nepal - Népal	26 476	26 741	27 023	27 327	27 650	27 985	28 323	28 656	28 983	29 305
Oman	2 759	2 883	3 041	3 237	3 465	3 961	4 200	4 425	4 636
Pakistan	163 645	167 050	170 560	174 184	177 912	181 713	185 546	189 381	193 203	197 016
Philippines	90 752	92 221	93 727	95 278	96 867	98 481	100 102	101 716	103 320	104 918
Qatar	1 389	1 591	1 780	1 952	2 110	2 250	2 374	2 482	2 570	2 639
Republic of Korea - République de Corée	49 219	49 379	49 553	49 745	49 952	50 169	50 386	50 594	50 792	50 982
Saudi Arabia - Arabie saoudite	25 941	26 661	27 426	28 238	29 086	29 944	30 777	31 557	32 276	32 938
Singapore - Singapour	4 851	4 966	5 074	5 176	5 271	5 361	5 448	5 535	5 622	5 709
Sri Lanka	19 946	20 075	20 198	20 315	20 425	20 527	20 624	20 714	20 798	20 877
State of Palestine - État de Palestine[9]	3 852	3 958	4 067	4 179	4 295	4 415	4 537	4 663	4 791	4 921
Syrian Arab Republic - République arabe syrienne	20 325	20 825	21 019	20 864	20 421	19 809	19 203	18 735	18 430	18 270
Tajikistan - Tadjikistan	7 310	7 473	7 642	7 816	7 995	8 178	8 363	8 549	8 735	8 921
Thailand - Thaïlande	66 546	66 882	67 209	67 530	67 844	68 143	68 417	68 658	68 864	69 038
Timor-Leste	1 078	1 092	1 110	1 132	1 157	1 184	1 213	1 241	1 269	1 296
Turkey - Turquie	70 440	71 339	72 327	73 409	74 570	75 787	77 031	78 271	79 512	80 745
Turkmenistan - Turkménistan	4 936	5 008	5 087	5 174	5 268	5 366	5 466	5 565	5 663	5 758
United Arab Emirates - Émirats arabes unis	6 894	7 666	8 271	8 672	8 900	9 006	9 071	9 154	9 270	9 400
Uzbekistan - Ouzbékistan	27 716	28 155	28 606	29 068	29 541	30 020	30 500	30 976	31 447	31 911
Viet Nam	86 708	87 565	88 473	89 437	90 452	91 498	92 545	93 572	94 569	95 541
Yemen - Yémen	22 356	22 975	23 607	24 252	24 910	25 576	26 246	26 916	27 584	28 250
EUROPE										
Albania - Albanie	2 992	2 963	2 941	2 927	2 920	2 919	2 921	2 923	2 926	2 930
Andorra - Andorre	84	84	84	84	82	81	79	78	77	77
Austria - Autriche	8 338	8 370	8 410	8 460	8 518	8 578	8 633	8 679	8 712	8 735
Belarus - Bélarus	9 507	9 486	9 473	9 469	9 472	9 479	9 485	9 486	9 480	9 468
Belgium - Belgique	10 779	10 860	10 939	11 013	11 084	11 152	11 219	11 288	11 358	11 429
Bosnia and Herzegovina - Bosnie-Herzégovine	3 764	3 747	3 722	3 689	3 648	3 605	3 566	3 536	3 517	3 507
Bulgaria - Bulgarie	7 510	7 456	7 405	7 356	7 310	7 266	7 222	7 177	7 131	7 085
Croatia - Croatie	4 352	4 341	4 328	4 313	4 297	4 278	4 258	4 236	4 213	4 189
Czechia - Tchéquie	10 424	10 487	10 536	10 569	10 587	10 594	10 599	10 604	10 611	10 618
Denmark - Danemark	5 498	5 526	5 555	5 583	5 611	5 638	5 664	5 689	5 712	5 734
Estonia - Estonie	1 340	1 336	1 332	1 328	1 325	1 322	1 318	1 315	1 312	1 310
Faeroe Islands - Îles Féroé	48	49	49	49	49	49	49	49	49	49
Finland - Finlande[10]	5 320	5 343	5 366	5 389	5 413	5 437	5 460	5 482	5 503	5 523
France	62 330	62 688	63 027	63 344	63 640	63 920	64 191	64 457	64 721	64 980
Germany - Allemagne	81 131	80 966	80 895	80 934	81 066	81 265	81 490	81 708	81 915	82 114
Gibraltar	33	33	33	33	34	34	34	34	34	35
Greece - Grèce	11 420	11 444	11 446	11 423	11 378	11 321	11 265	11 218	11 184	11 160
Holy See - Saint-Siège	1	1	1	1	1	1	1	1	1	1
Hungary - Hongrie	9 991	9 959	9 928	9 898	9 870	9 842	9 813	9 784	9 753	9 722

Annex I: Mid-year population, United Nations estimates: 2008 - 2017
Annexe I : Population au milieu de l'année, estimations des Nations Unies : 2008 - 2017 (continued - suite)

Continent and country or area Continent et pays ou zone	Population estimates (in thousands) - Estimations de population (en milliers)									
	2008	2009	2010	2011	2012	2013	2014	2015	2016	2017

EUROPE

Iceland - Islande	311	316	320	323	326	327	328	330	332	335
Ireland - Irlande	4 490	4 568	4 627	4 663	4 678	4 682	4 686	4 700	4 726	4 762
Isle of Man - Île de Man	79	79	80	81	81	82	83	83	84	84
Italy - Italie	59 502	59 642	59 730	59 760	59 734	59 668	59 586	59 504	59 430	59 360
Latvia - Lettonie	2 172	2 145	2 119	2 092	2 066	2 041	2 016	1 993	1 971	1 950
Liechtenstein	36	36	36	36	37	37	37	37	38	38
Lithuania - Lituanie	3 215	3 169	3 124	3 080	3 037	2 997	2 962	2 932	2 908	2 890
Luxembourg	485	496	508	520	532	545	556	567	576	583
Malta - Malte	412	414	416	418	421	423	426	428	429	431
Monaco	36	37	37	37	38	38	38	38	38	39
Montenegro - Monténégro	621	623	624	625	626	627	628	628	629	629
Netherlands - Pays-Bas	16 569	16 627	16 683	16 737	16 789	16 840	16 889	16 938	16 987	17 036
Norway - Norvège[11]	4 771	4 827	4 886	4 948	5 012	5 077	5 140	5 200	5 255	5 305
Poland - Pologne	38 326	38 325	38 323	38 321	38 317	38 309	38 293	38 265	38 224	38 171
Portugal	10 652	10 661	10 652	10 625	10 582	10 528	10 471	10 418	10 372	10 330
Republic of Moldova - République de Moldova[12]	4 111	4 096	4 084	4 077	4 074	4 072	4 070	4 066	4 060	4 051
Romania - Roumanie	20 821	20 618	20 440	20 293	20 171	20 068	19 973	19 877	19 778	19 679
Russian Federation - Fédération de Russie	143 083	143 093	143 154	143 264	143 421	143 597	143 761	143 888	143 965	143 990
San Marino - Saint-Marin	30	31	31	32	32	32	33	33	33	33
Serbia - Serbie[13]	9 100	9 065	9 030	8 994	8 957	8 920	8 885	8 851	8 820	8 791
Slovakia - Slovaquie	5 399	5 401	5 404	5 410	5 417	5 425	5 433	5 439	5 444	5 448
Slovenia - Slovénie	2 025	2 035	2 045	2 053	2 060	2 066	2 071	2 075	2 078	2 080
Spain - Espagne[14]	45 998	46 476	46 789	46 909	46 857	46 698	46 522	46 398	46 348	46 354
Sweden - Suède	9 237	9 313	9 390	9 466	9 541	9 615	9 689	9 764	9 838	9 911
Switzerland - Suisse	7 646	7 737	7 832	7 930	8 032	8 133	8 230	8 320	8 402	8 476
TFYR of Macedonia - L'ex-R. y. de Macédoine	2 067	2 069	2 071	2 072	2 074	2 076	2 077	2 079	2 081	2 083
Ukraine[15]	46 186	45 994	45 793	45 576	45 349	45 116	44 883	44 658	44 439	44 223
United Kingdom of Great Britain and Northern Ireland - Royaume-Uni de Grande-Bretagne et d'Irlande du Nord	62 076	62 723	63 307	63 812	64 250	64 641	65 016	65 397	65 789	66 182

OCEANIA - OCÉANIE

American Samoa - Samoas américaines	57	56	56	55	55	55	55	56	56	56
Australia - Australie[16]	21 342	21 739	22 120	22 480	22 822	23 151	23 475	23 800	24 126	24 451
Cook Islands - Îles Cook	19	19	19	18	18	18	18	17	17	17
Fiji - Fidji	843	852	860	867	874	880	886	892	899	906
French Polynesia - Polynésie française	263	266	268	270	272	274	275	278	280	283
Guam	159	159	159	160	160	160	161	162	163	164
Kiribati	98	101	103	105	107	109	110	112	114	116
Marshall Islands - Îles Marshall	52	52	52	53	53	53	53	53	53	53
Micronesia (Federated States of) - Micronésie (États fédérés de)	104	104	104	103	104	104	104	104	105	106
Nauru	10	10	10	10	10	11	11	11	11	11
New Caledonia - Nouvelle-Calédonie	244	247	251	255	258	262	265	269	273	276
New Zealand - Nouvelle-Zélande	4 278	4 323	4 370	4 418	4 468	4 518	4 567	4 615	4 661	4 706
Niue - Nioué	2	2	2	2	2	2	2	2	2	2
Northern Mariana Islands - Îles Mariannes septentrionales	57	56	54	54	54	54	54	55	55	55
Palau - Palaos	20	20	20	21	21	21	21	21	22	22
Papua New Guinea - Papouasie-Nouvelle-Guinée	6 787	6 947	7 108	7 269	7 431	7 593	7 756	7 920	8 085	8 251
Samoa	184	185	186	188	189	191	192	194	195	196
Solomon Islands - Îles Salomon	504	516	528	540	552	564	576	587	599	611
Tokelau - Tokélaou	1	1	1	1	1	1	1	1	1	1
Tonga	103	104	104	105	105	105	106	106	107	108
Tuvalu	10	10	11	11	11	11	11	11	11	11
Vanuatu	225	231	236	242	247	253	259	265	270	276
Wallis and Futuna Islands - Îles Wallis et Futuna	14	14	13	13	13	13	12	12	12	12

SOURCE

United Nations, Department of Economic and Social Affairs, Population Division (2017). 2017 Revision of World Population Prospects - Organisation des Nations Unies, Département des affaires économiques et sociales, Division de la population (2017). Perspectives de la population mondiale : La révision de 2017

FOOTNOTES - NOTES

[1] Including Agalega, Rodrigues and Saint Brandon. - Y compris Agalega, Rodrigues et Saint Brandon.

[2] Including Zanzibar. - Y compris le Zanzibar.

[3] Including Saint-Barthélemy and Saint-Martin (French part). - Y compris Saint-Barthélemy et Saint-Martin (partie française).

[4] Including Nagorno-Karabakh. - Y compris le Haut-Karabakh.

[5] For statistical purposes, the data for China do not include Hong Kong and Macao Special Administrative Regions (SAR) of China. - A des fins statistiques, les données pour la Chine ne comprennent pas les Régions Administratives Spéciales (SAR) de Hong Kong et Macao.

[6] Refers to the whole country. - Les données se rapportent au pays en entier.

[7] Including Abkhazia and South Ossetia. - Y compris l'Abkhazie et l'Ossétie du Sud.

[8] Including Sabah and Sarawak. - Y compris le Sabah et le Sarawak.

[9] Including East Jerusalem. - Y compris Jérusalem-Est.

[10] Including Åland Islands. - Y compris les îles Åland.

[11] Including Svalbard and Jan Mayen Islands. - Y compris Svalbard et l'île Jan Mayen.

[12] Including Transnistria. - Y compris la Transnistrie.

[13] Including Kosovo. - Y compris le Kosovo.

[14] Including Canary Islands, Ceuta and Melilla. - Y compris les îles Canaries, Ceuta et Melilla.

[15] Including Crimea. - Y compris la Crimée.

[16] Including Christmas Island, Cocos (Keeling) Islands and Norfolk Island. - Y compris les îles Christmas, Cocos (Keeling) et Norfolk.

Annex II: Vital statistics summary, United Nations estimates: 2015-2020
Annexe II: Aperçu des statistiques de l'état civil, estimations des Nations Unies : 2015-2020

Continent and country or area Continent et pays ou zone	Crude birth rate - Taux bruts de natalité	Crude death rate - Taux bruts de mortalité	Infant mortality rate - Décès d'enfants de moins d'un an	Life expectancy at birth - Espérance de vie à la naissance		Total fertility rate - Indice synthétique de fécondité	Natural increase - Accroissement naturel
				Male - Masculin	Female - Féminin		
AFRICA - AFRIQUE							
Algeria - Algérie	21.6	4.8	23.6	75.2	77.7	2.65	16.9
Angola	41.1	8.4	59.3	59.0	64.7	5.59	32.7
Benin - Bénin	36.4	9.0	61.3	59.8	62.8	4.87	27.4
Botswana	22.8	6.3	28.0	65.5	70.5	2.65	16.6
Burkina Faso	38.2	8.3	54.2	60.1	61.6	5.23	29.9
Burundi	41.5	10.4	68.8	56.1	60.0	5.58	31.1
Cabo Verde	20.6	5.4	19.8	71.0	75.1	2.29	15.2
Cameroon - Cameroun	35.5	9.7	58.2	57.8	59.9	4.60	25.8
Central African Republic - République centrafricaine	35.0	12.9	81.2	51.4	55.3	4.75	22.2
Chad - Tchad	42.6	12.6	80.8	52.1	54.6	5.80	29.9
Comoros - Comores	32.1	7.3	53.1	62.3	65.8	4.24	24.8
Congo	33.7	7.1	39.0	63.6	66.9	4.56	26.6
Côte d'Ivoire	36.4	11.8	57.2	53.0	55.9	4.81	24.6
Democratic Republic of the Congo - République démocratique du Congo	41.4	9.6	64.9	58.7	61.7	5.96	31.8
Djibouti	22.5	8.4	50.7	61.0	64.4	2.76	14.1
Egypt - Égypte	25.0	5.8	15.6	69.5	74.1	3.16	19.2
Equatorial Guinea - Guinée équatoriale	33.4	10.0	61.0	56.8	59.5	4.55	23.4
Eritrea - Érythrée	31.3	6.6	34.7	63.6	68.0	4.03	24.7
Eswatini	28.2	9.3	43.6	55.3	61.4	3.01	18.9
Ethiopia - Éthiopie	31.0	6.6	37.0	64.1	67.9	4.03	24.4
Gabon	28.5	7.4	35.0	65.1	68.4	3.68	21.2
Gambia - Gambie	38.7	7.9	44.9	60.2	63.0	5.32	30.8
Ghana	30.2	7.9	40.4	62.1	64.2	3.89	22.3
Guinea - Guinée	35.2	8.8	51.7	60.3	61.5	4.74	26.5
Guinea-Bissau - Guinée-Bissau	35.6	10.2	69.8	56.3	59.8	4.51	25.5
Kenya	30.7	5.7	34.7	65.0	69.6	3.77	25.0
Lesotho	27.3	12.4	49.3	52.4	56.8	3.01	14.9
Liberia - Libéria	33.8	7.6	46.8	62.2	64.3	4.48	26.2
Libya - Libye	18.8	5.2	20.9	69.5	75.3	2.21	13.6
Madagascar	32.8	6.1	29.7	64.9	68.1	4.11	26.7
Malawi	36.4	7.1	59.2	61.1	66.3	4.49	29.3
Mali	41.8	9.8	65.8	58.0	59.5	5.92	32.0
Mauritania - Mauritanie	33.5	7.8	63.3	61.9	65.0	4.58	25.7
Mauritius - Maurice[1]	10.6	8.3	10.3	71.5	78.5	1.43	2.3
Mayotte	28.3	2.5	3.6	77.3	83.8	3.73	25.8
Morocco - Maroc	19.2	5.1	21.9	74.9	77.3	2.43	14.1
Mozambique	38.4	9.7	64.0	57.0	61.3	5.14	28.7
Namibia - Namibie	28.4	7.0	30.7	62.0	67.9	3.31	21.3
Niger	47.7	9.4	56.9	59.5	61.6	7.15	38.3
Nigeria - Nigéria	38.1	12.0	63.5	53.3	54.9	5.42	26.1
Republic of South Sudan - République de Soudan du Sud	35.4	10.6	65.9	56.5	58.6	4.74	24.8
Reunion - Réunion	14.9	5.9	3.6	77.3	83.8	2.27	9.0
Rwanda	30.1	5.8	37.0	65.4	69.7	3.78	24.3
Sao Tome and Principe - Sao Tomé-et-Principe	33.1	6.5	41.5	64.6	69.0	4.36	26.6
Senegal - Sénégal	34.6	5.7	33.8	65.5	69.5	4.65	28.9
Seychelles	15.4	8.3	8.0	69.6	78.7	2.26	7.1
Sierra Leone	34.2	12.5	79.7	51.7	52.9	4.32	21.7
Somalia - Somalie	42.9	11.0	69.3	55.3	58.7	6.12	31.9
South Africa - Afrique du Sud	20.5	9.5	30.4	60.2	67.3	2.41	11.0
Sudan - Soudan	32.4	7.3	43.9	63.1	66.4	4.43	25.0
Togo	33.3	8.6	49.7	59.7	61.4	4.35	24.7
Tunisia - Tunisie	17.5	6.3	15.6	74.0	78.1	2.15	11.2
Uganda - Ouganda	41.4	8.5	55.0	58.0	62.5	5.46	32.9
United Republic of Tanzania - République Unie de Tanzanie[2]	37.5	6.4	39.1	65.0	68.4	4.92	31.2
Western Sahara - Sahara occidental	20.3	4.9	28.8	68.2	71.9	2.42	15.4
Zambia - Zambie	37.7	7.6	46.3	59.6	65.1	4.90	30.1
Zimbabwe	31.7	7.8	41.3	59.9	63.8	3.63	23.9
AMERICA, NORTH - AMÉRIQUE DU NORD							
Antigua and Barbuda - Antigua-et-Barbuda	16.0	5.8	7.8	74.1	79.0	2.03	10.2
Aruba	11.0	9.0	13.6	73.6	78.4	1.80	2.1
Bahamas	14.1	6.5	8.0	72.8	78.8	1.76	7.6
Barbados - Barbade	11.8	10.9	8.0	73.7	78.5	1.80	0.9

Continent and country or area / Continent et pays ou zone	Crude birth rate - Taux bruts de natalité	Crude death rate - Taux bruts de mortalité	Infant mortality rate - Décès d'enfants de moins d'un an	Life expectancy at birth - Espérance de vie à la naissance		Total fertility rate - Indice synthétique de fécondité	Natural increase - Accroissement naturel
				Male - Masculin	Female - Féminin		
AMERICA, NORTH - AMÉRIQUE DU NORD							
Belize	22.2	5.4	11.6	68.0	73.8	2.46	16.8
Canada	10.5	7.5	4.1	80.7	84.4	1.56	3.0
Costa Rica	14.0	5.0	8.0	77.8	82.5	1.76	8.9
Cuba	10.7	8.1	4.8	78.1	82.0	1.72	2.5
Curaçao	12.5	8.8	9.0	75.5	81.4	2.02	3.6
Dominican Republic - République dominicaine	19.7	6.1	22.1	71.1	77.4	2.38	13.5
El Salvador	18.3	6.8	14.2	69.2	78.2	2.05	11.5
Grenada - Grenade	18.2	7.1	8.4	71.4	76.3	2.07	11.1
Guadeloupe[3]	10.8	8.1	4.8	78.2	84.8	1.92	2.7
Guatemala	24.8	4.8	22.2	70.5	76.9	2.90	20.0
Haiti - Haïti	23.7	8.5	41.9	61.5	65.9	2.85	15.1
Honduras	21.4	4.8	24.3	71.3	76.5	2.42	16.5
Jamaica - Jamaïque	16.4	7.1	13.3	73.8	78.6	1.99	9.3
Martinique	10.9	8.6	5.2	79.2	85.2	1.88	2.3
Mexico - Mexique	17.6	4.9	16.5	75.0	79.8	2.14	12.7
Nicaragua	18.9	4.8	16.6	72.7	78.7	2.16	14.1
Panama	19.0	5.1	13.4	75.4	81.3	2.47	14.0
Puerto Rico - Porto Rico	10.6	8.0	5.4	76.4	83.9	1.47	2.6
Saint Lucia - Sainte-Lucie	11.9	7.5	9.2	73.2	78.5	1.44	4.4
Saint Vincent and the Grenadines - Saint-Vincent-et-les Grenadines	15.1	7.3	14.9	71.2	75.6	1.90	7.8
Trinidad and Tobago - Trinité-et-Tobago	13.0	9.8	22.7	67.4	74.5	1.73	3.2
United States of America - États-Unis d'Amérique	12.7	8.4	5.2	77.3	81.9	1.89	4.3
United States Virgin Islands - Îles Vierges américaines	12.7	8.6	8.4	77.7	82.3	2.19	4.1
AMERICA, SOUTH - AMÉRIQUE DU SUD							
Argentina - Argentine	16.9	7.6	11.9	73.1	80.5	2.27	9.3
Bolivia (Plurinational State of) - Bolivie (État plurinational de)	22.9	7.3	34.9	67.1	72.2	2.83	15.6
Brazil - Brésil	13.8	6.3	13.0	72.2	79.4	1.71	7.5
Chile - Chili	13.1	6.2	6.3	77.3	82.2	1.77	6.9
Colombia - Colombie	14.8	6.1	15.5	71.1	78.3	1.83	8.7
Ecuador - Équateur	19.7	5.1	18.7	74.0	79.4	2.44	14.6
French Guiana - Guyane française	23.5	3.0	9.2	77.3	83.4	3.26	20.5
Guyana	20.3	8.3	30.7	64.5	69.3	2.47	12.0
Paraguay	20.7	5.8	27.6	71.1	75.5	2.45	14.9
Peru - Pérou	18.7	5.7	15.5	72.7	78.0	2.35	13.1
Suriname	17.9	7.4	15.3	68.4	74.9	2.34	10.4
Uruguay	13.9	9.4	11.0	74.1	81.1	1.98	4.5
Venezuela (Bolivarian Republic of) - Venezuela (République bolivarienne du)	18.6	5.7	12.2	70.9	79.0	2.28	12.9
ASIA - ASIE							
Afghanistan	32.3	6.5	51.9	62.9	65.6	4.41	25.7
Armenia - Arménie	12.9	9.7	11.2	71.5	77.9	1.60	3.2
Azerbaijan - Azerbaïdjan[4]	16.7	6.9	28.3	69.1	75.2	2.04	9.8
Bahrain - Bahreïn	14.2	2.4	6.0	76.3	78.2	2.00	11.8
Bangladesh	18.5	5.3	26.5	71.3	74.7	2.07	13.2
Bhutan - Bhoutan	17.8	6.0	24.1	70.4	71.1	2.02	11.8
Brunei Darussalam - Brunéi Darussalam	15.4	3.7	5.6	75.9	79.2	1.85	11.7
Cambodia - Cambodge	22.7	6.0	22.2	67.2	71.5	2.52	16.7
China - Chine[5]	11.6	7.5	10.0	75.0	78.1	1.64	4.1
China, Hong Kong SAR - Chine, Hong Kong RAS	11.1	6.9	1.4	81.2	87.2	1.33	4.2
China, Macao SAR - Chine, Macao RAS	12.2	3.9	2.6	81.1	87.0	1.35	8.3
Cyprus - Chypre[6]	10.6	7.0	3.5	78.6	82.8	1.34	3.6
Democratic People's Republic of Korea - République populaire démocratique de Corée	13.8	9.0	14.2	68.3	75.4	1.89	4.8
Georgia - Géorgie[7]	12.9	13.1	9.4	69.3	77.7	1.97	-0.2
India - Inde	18.7	7.4	34.9	67.4	70.5	2.30	11.4
Indonesia - Indonésie	18.4	7.2	21.3	67.4	71.7	2.32	11.2
Iran (Islamic Republic of) - Iran (République islamique d')	15.6	4.5	12.0	75.1	77.4	1.62	11.1
Iraq	32.5	4.9	27.4	67.8	72.5	4.27	27.6
Israel - Israël	19.6	5.3	2.7	81.0	84.3	2.92	14.3

Continent and country or area Continent et pays ou zone	Crude birth rate - Taux bruts de natalité	Crude death rate - Taux bruts de mortalité	Infant mortality rate - Décès d'enfants de moins d'un an	Life expectancy at birth - Espérance de vie à la naissance		Total fertility rate - Indice synthétique de fécondité	Natural increase - Accroissement naturel
				Male - Masculin	Female - Féminin		
ASIA - ASIE							
Japan - Japon	8.1	10.8	1.9	80.7	87.2	1.48	-2.7
Jordan - Jordanie	25.5	3.8	14.9	72.9	76.3	3.26	21.7
Kazakhstan	20.1	8.9	11.7	65.2	74.9	2.57	11.3
Kuwait - Koweït	15.8	2.9	7.2	74.0	76.2	1.97	13.0
Kyrgyzstan - Kirghizstan	23.9	6.3	16.7	67.1	75.1	2.91	17.6
Lao People's Democratic Republic - République démocratique populaire lao	23.2	6.6	40.0	65.6	68.7	2.62	16.6
Lebanon - Liban	15.4	4.7	8.4	78.3	81.7	1.70	10.7
Malaysia - Malaisie[8]	17.0	5.0	5.5	73.4	77.9	2.01	11.9
Maldives	17.3	3.3	6.6	76.9	79.0	2.03	14.0
Mongolia - Mongolie	22.4	6.4	18.6	65.5	73.8	2.66	16.0
Myanmar	17.6	8.2	41.9	64.4	69.1	2.18	9.3
Nepal - Népal	19.5	6.2	26.2	69.1	72.4	2.08	13.3
Oman	17.2	2.5	7.8	75.7	79.8	2.54	14.8
Pakistan	27.4	7.2	63.9	65.7	67.8	3.38	20.2
Philippines	22.9	6.5	19.5	66.0	72.9	2.88	16.3
Qatar	10.0	1.6	6.3	77.6	80.1	1.88	8.4
Republic of Korea - République de Corée	8.9	6.1	2.4	79.3	85.4	1.32	2.8
Saudi Arabia - Arabie saoudite	19.1	3.6	10.9	73.5	76.6	2.48	15.5
Singapore - Singapour	8.7	5.1	1.8	81.3	85.3	1.26	3.5
Sri Lanka	14.9	7.0	6.8	72.2	78.9	2.03	7.8
State of Palestine - État de Palestine[9]	31.2	3.5	17.8	71.8	75.7	3.91	27.7
Syrian Arab Republic - République arabe syrienne	20.5	5.3	15.5	65.9	77.7	2.84	15.2
Tajikistan - Tadjikistan	27.9	5.1	34.1	68.5	74.4	3.28	22.8
Thailand - Thaïlande	10.0	8.1	9.4	71.9	79.3	1.46	1.9
Timor-Leste	34.4	5.4	34.3	67.6	71.3	5.34	29.0
Turkey - Turquie	15.8	5.8	9.9	72.9	79.3	2.02	10.0
Turkmenistan - Turkménistan	24.0	7.1	43.3	64.5	71.5	2.79	16.9
United Arab Emirates - Émirats arabes unis	9.2	1.7	5.3	76.8	79.0	1.73	7.5
Uzbekistan - Ouzbékistan	20.2	5.9	28.0	68.6	74.3	2.24	14.4
Viet Nam	16.2	5.8	16.6	71.9	81.1	1.95	10.4
Yemen - Yémen	30.7	6.3	42.2	63.8	66.8	3.84	24.3
EUROPE							
Albania - Albanie	11.7	7.7	12.8	76.6	80.6	1.71	4.0
Austria - Autriche	9.7	9.7	2.2	79.5	84.2	1.51	0.1
Belarus - Bélarus	11.8	13.5	3.1	67.5	78.5	1.71	-1.7
Belgium - Belgique	11.4	9.8	2.8	79.0	83.7	1.80	1.6
Bosnia and Herzegovina - Bosnie-Herzégovine	9.2	11.2	6.3	74.7	79.7	1.39	-2.0
Bulgaria - Bulgarie	9.3	15.3	7.2	71.5	78.4	1.58	-6.0
Croatia - Croatie	9.0	12.8	3.3	74.6	81.1	1.45	-3.8
Czechia - Tchéquie	10.1	10.7	2.2	76.0	81.8	1.57	-0.6
Denmark - Danemark	10.7	9.6	3.0	79.0	82.8	1.76	1.1
Estonia - Estonie	10.7	12.2	2.8	73.0	82.0	1.66	-1.5
Finland - Finlande[10]	10.8	9.8	1.6	78.8	84.4	1.78	1.0
France	11.7	9.0	2.8	79.9	85.7	1.97	2.7
Germany - Allemagne	8.9	11.3	2.1	79.0	83.6	1.47	-2.5
Greece - Grèce	7.9	10.9	3.0	79.0	84.0	1.30	-3.0
Hungary - Hongrie	9.0	13.0	4.2	72.5	79.5	1.40	-4.0
Iceland - Islande	13.1	6.5	1.5	81.6	84.4	1.92	6.6
Ireland - Irlande	13.5	6.6	2.0	79.8	83.7	1.98	6.9
Italy - Italie	8.2	10.6	2.3	81.1	85.4	1.49	-2.4
Latvia - Lettonie	10.0	15.1	5.2	69.7	79.4	1.57	-5.1
Lithuania - Lituanie	10.6	14.3	3.7	69.4	80.0	1.66	-3.8
Luxembourg	11.4	7.3	2.9	79.8	84.1	1.59	4.2
Malta - Malte	10.0	8.9	4.1	79.5	82.7	1.48	1.0
Montenegro - Monténégro	11.2	10.0	3.3	74.9	79.6	1.66	1.2
Netherlands - Pays-Bas	10.6	8.7	2.5	80.3	83.8	1.75	1.9
Norway - Norvège[11]	12.0	7.9	1.8	80.5	84.3	1.83	4.1
Poland - Pologne	9.1	10.5	4.0	73.9	81.7	1.29	-1.4
Portugal	7.5	10.8	1.6	78.6	84.3	1.24	-3.3
Republic of Moldova - République de Moldova[12]	10.0	11.7	12.4	67.4	75.9	1.23	-1.7
Romania - Roumanie	9.5	13.0	7.4	72.2	79.1	1.54	-3.4
Russian Federation - Fédération de Russie	12.4	13.6	7.0	65.6	76.8	1.75	-1.3
Serbia - Serbie[13]	10.5	12.8	8.3	72.6	78.2	1.62	-2.2

Continent and country or area Continent et pays ou zone	Crude birth rate - Taux bruts de natalité	Crude death rate - Taux bruts de mortalité	Infant mortality rate - Décès d'enfants de moins d'un an	Life expectancy at birth - Espérance de vie à la naissance		Total fertility rate - Indice synthétique de fécondité	Natural increase - Accroissement naturel
				Male - Masculin	Female - Féminin		
EUROPE							
Slovakia - Slovaquie............................	10.3	10.1	5.1	73.5	80.4	1.46	0.3
Slovenia - Slovénie..............................	10.0	9.9	2.1	78.4	83.9	1.64	0.1
Spain - Espagne[14]...............................	8.5	9.1	2.3	80.6	86.0	1.39	-0.6
Sweden - Suède..................................	12.3	9.1	1.9	81.0	84.4	1.91	3.2
Switzerland - Suisse............................	10.4	8.0	3.4	81.6	85.4	1.55	2.4
TFYR of Macedonia - L'ex-R. y. de Macédoine.....................	11.2	9.9	8.1	73.9	78.0	1.55	1.3
Ukraine[15]...	10.5	14.9	7.2	67.1	76.9	1.56	-4.4
United Kingdom of Great Britain and Northern Ireland - Royaume-Uni de Grande-Bretagne et d'Irlande du Nord	12.1	9.0	3.5	80.0	83.5	1.87	3.1
OCEANIA - OCÉANIE							
Australia - Australie[16]	12.8	6.7	3.1	81.3	85.0	1.83	6.1
Fiji - Fidji	18.9	7.3	13.6	67.6	73.7	2.48	11.6
French Polynesia - Polynésie française	15.1	5.6	5.6	74.9	79.5	1.99	9.5
Guam...	16.6	5.2	8.5	77.5	82.3	2.32	11.4
Kiribati	27.7	7.0	43.0	63.3	69.9	3.58	20.7
Micronesia (Federated States of) - Micronésie (États fédérés de)	23.8	6.2	31.0	68.2	70.6	3.08	17.6
New Caledonia - Nouvelle-Calédonie	15.5	6.8	11.5	74.7	80.2	2.14	8.7
New Zealand - Nouvelle-Zélande	13.1	7.0	3.8	80.5	83.7	1.97	6.2
Papua New Guinea - Papouasie-Nouvelle-Guinée	27.2	7.1	44.9	63.4	68.4	3.59	20.1
Samoa..	24.1	5.0	16.2	72.3	78.6	3.90	19.2
Solomon Islands - Îles Salomon............	27.9	4.7	24.9	69.6	72.8	3.77	23.3
Tonga...	23.4	5.9	19.2	70.2	76.3	3.58	17.5
Vanuatu...	25.4	4.8	21.3	70.3	74.8	3.22	20.6

SOURCE

United Nations, Department of Economic and Social Affairs, Population Division (2017). 2017 Revision of World Population Prospects - Organisation des Nations Unies, Département des affaires économiques et sociales, Division de la population (2017). Perspectives de la population mondiale : La révision de 2017

FOOTNOTES - NOTES

[1] Including Agalega, Rodrigues and Saint Brandon. - Y compris Agalega, Rodrigues et Saint Brandon.
[2] Including Zanzibar. - Y compris le Zanzibar.
[3] Including Saint-Barthélemy and Saint-Martin (French part). - Y compris Saint-Barthélemy et Saint-Martin (partie française).
[4] Including Nagorno-Karabakh. - Y compris le Haut-Karabakh.
[5] For statistical purposes, the data for China do not include Hong Kong and Macao Special Administrative Regions (SAR) of China. - A des fins statistiques, les données pour la Chine ne comprennent pas les Régions Administratives Spéciales (SAR) de Hong Kong et Macao.
[6] Refers to the whole country. - Les données se rapportent au pays en entier.
[7] Including Abkhazia and South Ossetia. - Y compris l'Abkhazie et l'Ossétie du Sud.
[8] Including Sabah and Sarawak. - Y compris le Sabah et le Sarawak.
[9] Including East Jerusalem. - Y compris Jérusalem-Est.
[10] Including Åland Islands. - Y compris les îles Åland.
[11] Including Svalbard and Jan Mayen Islands. - Y compris Svalbard et l'île Jan Mayen.
[12] Including Transnistria. - Y compris la Transnistrie.
[13] Including Kosovo. - Y compris le Kosovo.
[14] Including Canary Islands, Ceuta and Melilla. - Y compris les îles Canaries, Ceuta et Melilla.
[15] Including Crimea. - Y compris la Crimée.
[16] Including Christmas Island, Cocos (Keeling) Islands and Norfolk Island. - Y compris les îles Christmas, Cocos (Keeling) et Norfolk.

Historical index
(See notes at end of index)

Subject-matter	Year of issue	Time coverage		Subject-matter	Year of issue	Time coverage
A				Ageing	*see "Population"*	
Abortions, Legal	1971	Latest		**Annulments**	1958	1948-57
	1972	1964-72			1968	1958-67
	1973	1965-73			1976	1966-75
	1974	1965-74				
	1975	1965-74		**Annulment rates**	1958	1948-57
	1976	1966-75			1968	1958-67
	1977	1967-76			1976	1966-75
	1978	1968-77				
	1979	1969-78		**B**		
	1980	1971-79				
	1981	1972-80		**Bibliography**	1948	1930-48
	1982	1973-81			1949-50	1930-50
	1983	1974-82			1951-1952	1930-51[i]
	1984	1975-83			1953	1900-53
	1985	1976-84			1954	1900-54[i]
	1986	1977-85			1955	1900-55[i]
	1987	1978-86				
	1988	1979-87		**Births**	1948	1932-47
	1989	1980-88			1949-50	1934-49
	1990	1981-89			1951	1935-50
	1991	1982-90			1952	1936-51
	1992	1983-91			1953	1950-52
	1993	1984-92			1954	1938-53
	1994	1985-93			1955	1946-54
	1995	1986-94			1956	1947-55
	1996	1987-95			1957	1948-56
	1997	1988-96			1958	1948-57
	1998	1989-97			1959	1949-58
	1999	1990-98			1960	1950-59
	2000	1991-99			1961	1952-61
	2001	1993-01			1962	1953-62
	2002	1993-02			1963	1954-63
	2003	1994-03			1964	1960-64
	2004	1995-04			1965	1946-65
	2005	1996-05			1966	1957-66
	2006	1997-06			1967	1963-67
	2007	1998-07			1968	1964-68
	2008	1999-08			1969	1950-69
	2009-2010	2001-10			1970	1966-70
	2011	2002-11			1971	1967-71
	2012	2003-12			1972	1968-72
	2013	2004-13			1973	1969-73
	2014	2005-14			1974	1970-74
	2015	2006-15			1975	1956-75
	2016	2007-16			1976	1972-76
	2017	2008-17			1977	1973-77
					1978	1974-78
Abortions, Legal	1971-1975	Latest			1978HS[ii]	1948-78
by age of woman and	1977-1981	Latest			1979	1975-79
number of previous live	1983-2017	Latest			1980	1976-80
births of woman					1981	1962-81

Subject-matter	Year of issue	Time coverage	Subject-matter	Year of issue	Time coverage
	1954	1936-53		1986	1977-85
	1955	Latest		1999CD[iv]	1990-98
	1959	1949-58			
	1965	1955-64	**Births**	1965	Latest
	1969	1963-68	by urban/rural	1967	Latest
	1975	1966-74	residence		
	1981	1972-80		1968	1964-68
	1986	1977-85		1969	1964-68
	1999CD[iv]	1990-98		1970	1966-70
				1971	1967-71
Births	1975	Latest		1972	1968-72
by birth weight	1981	1972-80		1973	1969-73
	1986	1977-85		1974	1970-74
	1999CD[iv]	1990-98		1975	1956-75
				1976	1972-76
Births	1975	Latest		1977	1973-77
by gestational age	1981	1972-80		1978	1974-78
	1986	1977-85		1979	1975-79
	1999CD[iv]	1990-98		1980	1976-80
				1981	1962-81
Births	1959	1949-58		1982	1978-82
by legitimacy status	1965	1955-64		1983	1979-83
	1969	1963-68		1984	1980-84
	1975	1966-74		1985	1981-85
	1981	1972-80		1986	1967-86
	1986	1977-85		1987	1983-87
	1999CD[iv]	1990-98		1988	1984-88
				1989	1985-89
Births	2002	1980-02		1990	1986-90
by month				1991	1987-91
				1992	1983-92
Births	1965	Latest		1993	1989-93
by occupation of father	1969	Latest		1994	1990-94
				1995	1991-95
Births	1959	1949-58		1996	1992-96
by sex	1965	1955-64		1997	1993-97
	1967-1968	Latest		1998	1994-98
	1969	1963-68		1999	1995-99
	1970-1974	Latest		1999CD[iv]	1980-99
	1975	1956-75		2000	1996-00
	1976-1980	Latest		2001	1997-01
	1981	1962-81		2002	1998-02
	1982-1985	Latest		2003	1999-03
	1986	1967-86		2004	2000-04
	1987-1991	Latest		2005	2001-05
	1992	1983-92		2006	2002-06
	1993-1999	Latest		2007	2003-07
	1999CD[iv]	1990-98		2008	2004-08
	2000-2017	Latest		2009-2010	2006-10
				2011	2007-11
Births	1965	Latest		2012	2008-12
by plurality	1969	Latest		2013	2009-13
	1975	Latest		2014	2010-14
	1981	1972-80		2015	2011-15

Subject-matter	Year of issue	Time coverage	Subject-matter	Year of issue	Time coverage
	2016	2012-16	**Births**	1948	1936-47
	2017	2013-17	legitimate, by duration	1949-50	1936-49
			of marriage	1954	1936-53
Births	1965	Latest		1959	1949-58
by urban/rural	1969-1974	Latest		1965	1955-64
residence and age of	1975	1966-74		1969	1963-68
mother				1975	1966-74
	1976-1980	Latest		1981	1972-80
	1981	1972-80		1986	1977-85
	1982-1985	Latest		1999CD[iv]	1990-98
	1986	1977-85			
	1987-1991	Latest	**Birth rates**	1948	1932-47
	1992	1983-92		1949-50	1932-49
	1993-1997	Latest		1951	1905-30[v]
	1997HS[iii]	1948-96			1930-50
	1998-1999	Latest		1952	1920-34[v]
	1999CD[iv]	1990-98			1934-51
	2000-2006	Latest		1953	1920-39[v]
					1940-52
Births	1959	1949-58		1954	1920-39[v]
illegitimate	1965	1955-64			1939-53
	1969	1963-68		1955	1920-34[v]
	1975	1966-74			1946-54
	1981	1972-80		1956	1947-55
	1986	1977-85		1957	1948-56
	1999CD[iv]	1990-98		1958	1948-57
				1959	1920-54[v]
Births	1948	1936-47			1953-58
legitimate	1949-50	1936-49		1960	1950-59
	1954	1936-53		1961	1945-59[v]
	1959	1949-58			1952-61
	1965	1955-64		1962	1945-54[v]
	1969	1963-68			1952-62
	1975	1966-74		1963	1945-59[v]
	1981	1972-80			1954-63
	1986	1977-85		1964	1960-64
	1999CD[iv]	1990-98		1965	1920-64[v]
					1950-65
Births	1959	1949-58		1966	1950-64[v]
legitimate, by age of	1965	1955-64			1957-66
father	1969	1963-68		1967	1963-67
	1975	1966-74		1968	1964-68
	1981	1972-80		1969	1925-69[v]
	1986	1977-85			1954-69
				1970	1966-70
Births	1954	1936-53		1971	1967-71
legitimate, by age of	1959	1949-58		1972	1968-72
mother	1965	1955-64		1973	1969-73
	1969	1963-68		1974	1970-74
	1975	1966-74		1975	1956-75
	1981	1972-80		1976	1972-76
	1986	1977-85		1977	1973-77
				1978	1974-78
				1978HS[ii]	1948-78

Historical index

(See notes at end of index)

Subject-matter	Year of issue	Time coverage	Subject-matter	Year of issue	Time coverage
	1969	1964-68		1976-1980	Latest
	1970	1966-70		1981	1972-80
	1971	1967-71		1982-1985	Latest
	1972	1968-72		1986	1977-85
	1973	1969-73		1987-1991	Latest
	1974	1970-74		1992	1983-92
	1975	1956-75		1993-1997	Latest
	1976	1972-76		1997HS[iii]	1948-96
	1977	1973-77		1998-1999	Latest
	1978	1974-78		1999CD[iv]	1990-98
	1979	1975-79		2000-2006	Latest
	1980	1976-80			
	1981	1962-81	**Birth rates**	1949-50	1947
	1982	1978-82	estimated (for	1956-1977	Latest
	1983	1979-83	continents)		
	1984	1980-84		1978-1979	1970-75
	1985	1981-85		1980-1983	1975-80
	1986	1967-86		1984-1986	1980-85
	1987	1983-87		1987-1992	1985-90
	1988	1984-88		1993-1997	1990-95
	1989	1985-89		1998-2000	1995-00
	1990	1986-90		2001-2005	2000-05
	1991	1987-91		2006-2010	2005-10
	1992	1983-92		2011-2015	2010-15
	1993	1989-93		2016	2015-20
	1994	1990-94		2017	2015-20
	1995	1991-95			
	1996	1992-96	**Birth rates**	1964-1977	Latest
	1997	1993-97	estimated (for macro	1978-1979	1970-75
	1998	1994-98	regions)	1980-1983	1975-80
	1999	1995-99		1984-1986	1980-85
	1999CD[iv]	1985-99		1987-1992	1985-90
	2000	1996-00		1993-1997	1990-95
	2001	1997-01		1998-2000	1995-00
	2002	1998-02		2001-2005	2000-05
	2003	1999-03		2006-2010	2005-10
	2004	2000-04		2011-2015	2010-15
	2005	2001-05		2016	2015-20
	2006	2002-06		2017	2015-20
	2007	2003-07			
	2008	2004-08	**Birth rates**	1949/1950	1947
	2009-2010	2006-10	estimated (for regions)	1956-1977	Latest
	2011	2007-11		1978-1979	1970-75
	2012	2008-12		1980-1983	1975-80
	2013	2009-13		1984-1986	1980-85
	2014	2010-14		1987-1992	1985-90
	2015	2011-15		1993-1997	1990-95
	2016	2012-16		1998-2000	1995-00
	2017	2013-17		2001-2005	2000-05
				2006-2010	2005-10
Birth rates	1965	Latest		2011-2015	2010-15
by urban/rural	1969	Latest		2016	2015-20
residence and age of	1975	1966-74		2017	2015-20
mother					

Subject-matter	Year of issue	Time coverage	Subject-matter	Year of issue	Time coverage
Birth rates..................	1949-50	1947		1986	1977-85
estimated (for the world)	1956-1977	Latest		1997HS[iii]	1948-96
				1999CD[iv]	1980-99
	1978-1979	1970-75			
	1980-1983	1975-80	**Birth ratios**..................	1959	1949-58
	1984-1986	1980-85	illegitimate	1965	1955-64
	1987-1992	1985-90		1969	1963-68
	1993-1997	1990-95		1975	1965-74
	1998-2000	1995-00		1981	1972-80
	2001-2005	2000-05		1986	1977-85
	2006-2010	2005-10			
	2011-2015	2010-15	**C**		
	2016	2015-20			
	2017	2015-20	**Child-woman ratios**	1949-50	1900-50
				1954	1900-52
Birth rates..................	1959	1949-58		1955	1945-54
illegitimate				1959	1935-59
				1963	1955-63
Birth rates..................	1954	1936-53		1965	1945-65
legitimate	1959	1949-58		1969	Latest
	1965	Latest		1975	1966-74
	1969	Latest		1978HS[ii]	1948-77
	1975	Latest		1981	1962-80
	1981	Latest		1986	1967-85
	1986	Latest		1997HS[iii]	1948-96
				1999CD[iv]	1980-99
Birth rates..................	1959	1949-58			
legitimate by age of father	1965	Latest	**Child-woman ratios**	1965	Latest
	1969	Latest	by urban/rural residence	1969	Latest
	1975	Latest			
	1981	Latest			
	1986	Latest	**Children**..........................	1949-50	Latest
			ever born, by age of mother	1954	1930-53
Birth rates..................	1954	1936-53		1955	1945-54
legitimate by age of mother	1959	1949-58		1959	1949-58
	1965	Latest		1963	1955-63
	1969	Latest		1965	1955-65
	1975	Latest		1969	Latest
	1981	Latest		1978HS[ii]	1948-77
	1986	Latest		1997HS[iii]	1948-96
Birth rates..................	1959	1950-57	**Children**..........................	1971	1962-71
legitimate by duration of marriage	1965	Latest	ever born, by age of mother and urban/rural residence	1973	1965-73
	1969	Latest		1975	1965-74
	1975	Latest		1981	1972-80
				1986	1977-85
Birth ratios..................	1949/1950	Latest		1997HS[iii]	1948-96
fertility	1954	Latest			
	1959	1949-58	**Children**..........................	1958	1949-57
	1965	1955-65	involved in divorces	1968	1958-67
	1969	1963-68		1976	1966-75
	1975	1965-74		1982	1972-81
	1978HS[ii]	1948-77		1990	1980-89
	1981	1972-80			

Subject-matter	Year of issue	Time coverage	Subject-matter	Year of issue	Time coverage
Children	1949-50	Latest		1981	1977-81
living, by age of mother	1954	1930-53		1982	1978-82
	1955	1945-54		1983	1979-83
	1959	1949-58		1984	1980-84
	1963	1955-63		1985	1976-85
	1965	1955-65		1986	1982-86
	1968	1955-67		1987	1983-87
	1969	Latest		1988	1984-88
	1978HS[ii]	1948-77		1989	1985-89
	1997HS[iii]	1948-96		1990	1986-90
				1991	1987-91
Children	1971	1962-71		1992	1983-92
living, by age of mother	1973	1965-73		1993	1989-93
and urban/rural	1975	1965-74		1994	1990-94
residence	1981	1972-80		1995	1991-95
	1986	1977-85		1996	1987-96
	1997HS[iii]	1948-96		1997	1993-97
				1997HS[iii]	1948-97
Cities		*see "Population"*		1998	1994-98
				1999	1995-99
D				2000	1996-00
				2001	1997-01
Deaths	1948	1932-47		2002	1998-02
	1949-50	1934-49		2003	1999-03
	1951	1935-50		2004	2000-04
	1952	1936-51		2005	2001-05
	1953	1950-52		2006	2002-06
	1954	1946-53		2007	2003-07
	1955	1946-54		2008	2004-08
	1956	1947-55		2009-2010	2006-10
	1957	1940-56		2011	2007-11
	1958	1948-57		2012	2008-12
	1959	1949-58		2013	2009-13
	1960	1950-59		2014	2010-14
	1961	1952-61		2015	2011-15
	1962	1953-62		2016	2012-16
	1963	1954-63		2017	2013-17
	1964	1960-64			
	1966	1947-66	**Deaths**	1948	1936-47
	1967	1963-67	by age and sex	1951	1936-50
	1968	1964-68		1955-1956	Latest
	1969	1965-69		1957	1948-56
	1970	1966-70		1958-1960	Latest
	1971	1967-71		1961	1955-60
	1972	1968-72		1962-1965	Latest
	1973	1969-73		1966	1961-65
	1974	1965-74		1967-1973	Latest
	1975	1971-75		1974	1965-73
	1976	1972-76		1975-1979	Latest
	1977	1973-77		1978HS[ii]	1948-77
	1978	1974-78		1980	1971-79
	1978HS[ii]	1948-78		1981-1984	Latest
	1979	1975-79		1985	1976-84
	1980	1971-80		1986-1991	Latest

Subject-matter	Year of issue	Time coverage	Subject-matter	Year of issue	Time coverage
	1992	1983-92		1961	Latest
	1993-1995	Latest		1967	Latest
	1996	1987-95		1974	Latest
	1997	Latest		1980	Latest
	1997HS[iii]	1948-96		1985	Latest
	1998-2017	Latest		1991PA[vii]	1960-90
				1996	Latest
Deaths..................................	1967-1973	Latest			
by age and sex and	1974	1965-73	**Deaths**..................................	1967	Latest
urban/rural residence	1975-1979	Latest	by cause, age and sex		
	1980	1971-79	and urban/rural		
	1981-1984	Latest	residence		
	1985	1976-84			
	1986-1991	Latest	**Deaths**..................................	1967	Latest
	1992	1983-92	by cause and sex	1974	Latest
	1993-1995	Latest		1980	Latest
	1996	1987-95		1985	Latest
	1997	Latest		1996	Latest
	1997HS[iii]	1948-96		2006	2002-06
	1998-2006	Latest		2008	2004-08
				2011	2006-10
Deaths..................................	1951	1947-50		2013	2008-12
by cause	1952	1947-51[vi]		2015	2010-14
	1953	Latest		2017	2012-16
	1954	1945-53			
	1955-1956	Latest	**Deaths**..................................	1958	Latest
	1957	1952-56	by marital status, age	1961	Latest
	1958-1960	Latest	and sex	1967	Latest
	1961	1955-60		1974	Latest
	1962-1965	Latest		1980	Latest
	1966	1960-65		1985	Latest
	1967-1973	Latest		1991PA[vii]	1950-90
	1974	1965-73		1996	Latest
	1975-1979	Latest		2003	Latest
	1980	1971-79			
	1981-1984	Latest	**Deaths**..................................	1951	1946-50
	1985	1976-84	by month	1967	1962-66
	1986-1991	Latest		1974	1965-73
	1991PA[vii]	1960-90		1980	1971-79
	1992-1995	Latest		1985	1976-84
	1996	1987-95		2001	1985-00
	1997-2000	Latest		2005	2001-05
	2002	1995-02			
	2004	1995-04	**Deaths**..................................	1957	Latest
	2006	2002-06	by occupation and age,	1961	1957-60
	2008	2004-08	males	1967	1962-66
	2011	2006-10			
	2013	2008-12	**Deaths**..................................	1957	Latest
	2015	2010-14	by type of certification	1974	1965-73
	2017	2012-16	and cause (numbers)	1980	1971-79
				1985	1976-84
Deaths..................................	1951	Latest			
by cause, age and sex	1952	Latest	**Deaths**..................................	1957	Latest
	1957	Latest		1961	1955-60

Historical index

(See notes at end of index)

Subject-matter	Year of issue	Time coverage	Subject-matter	Year of issue	Time coverage
by type of certification and cause (percent)	1966	1960-65		2016	2012-16
				2017	2013-17
	1974	1965-73			
	1980	1971-79	Deaths		*See "Infant deaths"*
	1985	1976-84	of infants (see infant deaths)		
Deaths	1967	Latest			
by urban/rural residence	1968	1964-68	Death rates	1948	1932-47
				1949-50[ii]	1932-49
	1969	1965-69		1951	1905-30[v]
	1970	1966-70			1930-50
	1971	1967-71		1952	1920-34[v]
	1972	1968-72			1934-51
	1973	1969-73		1953	1920-39[v]
	1974	1965-74			1940-52
	1975	1971-75		1954	1920-39[v]
	1976	1972-76			1946-53
	1977	1973-77		1955	1920-34[v]
	1978	1974-78			1946-54
	1979	1975-79		1956	1947-55
	1980	1971-80		1957	1930-56
	1981	1977-81		1958	1948-57
	1982	1978-82		1959	1949-58
	1983	1979-83		1960	1950-59
	1984	1980-84		1961	1945-59[v]
	1985	1976-85			1952-61
	1986	1982-86		1962	1945-54[v]
	1987	1983-87			1952-62
	1988	1984-88		1963	1945-59[v]
	1989	1985-89			1954-63
	1990	1986-90		1964	1960-64
	1991	1987-91		1965	1961-65
	1992	1983-92		1966	1920-64[v]
	1993	1989-93			1951-66
	1994	1990-94		1967	1963-67
	1995	1991-95		1968	1964-68
	1996	1987-96		1969	1965-69
	1997	1993-97		1970	1966-70
	1998	1994-98		1971	1967-71
	1999	1995-99		1972	1968-72
	2000	1996-00		1973	1969-73
	2001	1997-01		1974	1965-74
	2002	1998-02		1975	1971-75
	2003	1999-03		1976	1972-76
	2004	2000-04		1977	1973-77
	2006	2002-06		1978	1974-78
	2007	2003-07		1978HS[ii]	1948-78
	2008	2004-08		1979	1975-79
	2009-2010	2006-10		1980	1971-80
	2011	2007-11		1981	1977-81
	2012	2008-12		1982	1978-82
	2013	2009-13		1983	1979-83
	2014	2010-14		1984	1980-84
	2015	2011-15		1985	1976-85

Subject-matter	Year of issue	Time coverage	Subject-matter	Year of issue	Time coverage
	1986	1982-86		1996	1987-95
	1987	1983-87		1997	Latest
	1988	1984-88		1997HS[iii]	1948-96
	1989	1985-89		1998-2017	Latest
	1990	1986-90			
	1991	1987-91	**Death rates**	1967	Latest
	1992	1983-92	by age and sex and	1972	Latest
	1993	1989-93	urban/rural residence	1974	1965-73
	1994	1990-94		1975-1979	Latest
	1995	1991-95		1980	1971-79
	1996	1987-96		1981-1984	Latest
	1997	1993-97		1985	1976-84
	1997HS[iii]	1948-97		1986-1991	Latest
	1998	1994-98		1991PA[vii]	1950-1990
	1999	1995-99		1992	1983-1992
	2000	1996-00		1993-1995	Latest
	2001	1997-01		1996	1987-95
	2002	1998-02		1997	Latest
	2003	1999-03		1997HS[iii]	1948-96
	2004	2000-04		1998-2006	Latest
	2005	2001-05			
	2006	2002-06	**Death rates**	1951	1947-49
	2007	2003-07	by cause	1952	1947-51[vi]
	2008	2004-08		1953	1947-52
	2009-2010	2006-10		1954	1945-53
	2011	2007-11		1955-1956	Latest
	2012	2008-12		1957	1952-56
	2013	2009-13		1958-1960	Latest
	2014	2010-14		1961	1955-60
	2015	2011-15		1962-1965	Latest
	2016	2012-16		1966	1960-65
	2017	2013-17		1967-1973	Latest
				1974	1965-73
Death rates	1948	1935-47		1975-1979	Latest
by age and sex	1949-50	1936-49		1980	1971-79
	1951	1936-50		1981-1984	Latest
	1952	1936-51		1985	1976-84
	1953	1940-52		1986-1991	Latest
	1954	1946-53		1991PA[vii]	1960-90
	1955-1956	Latest		1992-1995	Latest
	1957	1948-56		1996	1987-95
	1961	1952-60		1997-2000	Latest
	1966	1950-65		2002	1995-02
	1972	Latest		2004	1995-04
	1974	1965-73		2006	2002-06
	1975-1979	Latest		2008	2004-08
	1978HS[ii]	1948-77		2011	2006-10
	1980	1971-79		2013	2008-12
	1981-1984	Latest		2015	2010-14
	1985	1976-84		2017	2012-16
	1986-1991	Latest			
	1991PA[vii]	1950-1990	**Death rates**	1957	Latest
	1992	1983-1992	by cause, age and sex	1961	Latest
	1993-1995	Latest		1991PA[vii]	1960-90

Subject-matter	Year of issue	Time coverage	Subject-matter	Year of issue	Time coverage
				1991	1987-91
Death rates	1967	Latest		1992	1983-92
by cause and sex	1974	Latest		1993	1989-93
	1980	Latest		1994	1990-94
	1985	Latest		1995	1991-95
	1996	Latest		1996	1987-96
	2006	2002-06		1997	1993-97
	2008	2004-08		1998	1994-98
	2011	2006-10		1999	1995-99
	2013	2008-12		1987	1983-87
	2015	2010-14		1988	1984-88
	2017	2012-16		1989	1985-89
				1990	1986-90
Death rates	1961	Latest		1991	1987-91
by marital status, age	1967	Latest		1992	1983-92
and sex	1974	Latest		1993	1989-93
	1980	Latest		1994	1990-94
	1985	Latest		1995	1991-95
	1996	Latest		1996	1987-96
	2003	Latest		1997	1993-97
				1998	1994-98
Death rates	1957	Latest		1999	1995-99
by occupation, age and				2000	1996-00
sex				2001	1997-01
				2002	1998-02
Death rates	1961	Latest		2003	1999-03
by occupation and age,	1967	Latest		2004	2000-04
males				2005	2001-05
				2006	2002-06
Death rates	1967	Latest		2007	2003-07
by urban/rural	1968	1964-68		2008	2004-08
residence				2009-2010	2006-10
	1969	1965-69		2011	2007-11
	1970	1966-70		2012	2008-12
	1971	1967-71		2013	2009-13
	1972	1968-72		2014	2010-14
	1973	1969-73		2015	2011-15
	1974	1965-74		2016	2012-16
	1975	1971-75		2017	2013-17
	1976	1972-76			
	1977	1973-77	**Death rates**	1949-50	1947
	1978	1974-78	estimated (for	1956-1977	Latest
	1979	1975-79	continents)		
	1980	1971-80		1978-1979	1970-75
	1981	1977-81		1980-1983	1975-80
	1982	1978-82		1984-1986	1980-85
	1983	1979-83		1984-1986	1980-85
	1984	1980-84		1987-1992	1985-90
	1985	1976-85		1993-1997	1990-95
	1986	1982-86		1998-2000	1995-00
	1987	1983-87		2001-2005	2000-05
	1988	1984-88		2006-2010	2005-10
	1989	1985-89		2011-2015	2010-15
	1990	1986-90		2016	2015-20

Subject-matter	Year of issue	Time coverage	Subject-matter	Year of issue	Time coverage
	2001	2001		1966	1962-66
	2002	2002		1967	1963-67
	2003	2003		1968	1949-68
	2004	2004		1969	1965-69
	2005	2005		1970	1966-70
	2006	2006		1971	1967-71
	2007	2007		1972	1968-72
	2008	2008		1973	1969-73
	2009-2010	2010		1974	1970-74
	2011	2011		1975	1971-75
	2012	2012		1976	1957-76
	2013	2013		1977	1973-77
	2014	2014		1978	1974-78
	2015	2015		1979	1975-79
	2016	2016		1980	1976-80
	2017	2017		1981	1977-81
				1982	1963-82
Density of population.........	1949-50	1920-49		1983	1979-83
of the world	1952-1999	Latest		1984	1980-84
	2000	2000		1985	1981-85
	2001	2001		1986	1982-86
	2002	2002		1987	1983-87
	2003	2003		1988	1984-88
	2004	2004		1989	1985-89
	2005	2005		1990	1971-90
	2006	2006		1991	1987-91
	2007	2007		1992	1988-92
	2008	2008		1993	1989-93
	2009-2010	2010		1994	1990-94
	2011	2011		1995	1991-95
	2012	2012		1996	1992-96
	2013	2013		1997	1993-97
	2014	2014		1998	1994-98
	2015	2015		1999	1995-99
	2016	2016		2000	1996-00
	2017	2017		2001	1997-01
				2002	1998-02
Disability...........................	*see "Population"*			2003	1999-03
				2004	2000-04
Divorces.............................	1951	1935-50		2005	2001-05
	1952	1936-51		2006	2002-06
	1953	1950-52		2007	2003-07
	1954	1946-53		2008	2004-08
	1955	1946-54		2009-2010	2006-10
	1956	1947-55		2011	2007-11
	1957	1948-56		2012	2008-12
	1958	1940-57		2013	2009-13
	1959	1949-58		2014	2010-14
	1960	1950-59		2015	2011-15
	1961	1952-61		2016	2012-16
	1962	1953-62		2017	2013-17
	1963	1954-63			
	1964	1960-64	**Divorces**	1968	1958-67
	1965	1961-65	by age of husband	1976	1966-75

Subject-matter	Year of issue	Time coverage	Subject-matter	Year of issue	Time coverage
F				1963	1955-63
				1965	1955-65
Fertility rates	1948	1936-47		1969	Latest
general	1949-50	1936-49		1975	1966-74
	1951	1936-50		1978HS[ii]	1948-77
	1952	1936-50		1981	1962-80
	1953	1936-52		1986	1967-85
	1954	1936-53		1997HS[iii]	1948-96
	1955-1956	Latest		1999CD[iv]	1980-99
	1959	1949-58			
	1960-1964	Latest	**Foetal deaths**	1957	1950-56
	1965	1955-64	by period of gestation	1959	1949-58
	1966-1974	Latest		1961	1952-60
	1975	1966-74		1965	5-Latest
	1976-1978	Latest		1966	1956-65
	1978HS[ii]	1948-77		1967-1968	Latest
	1979-1980	Latest		1969	1963-68
	1981	1962-80		1974	1965-73
	1982-1985	Latest		1975	1966-74
	1986	1977-85		1980	1971-79
	1987-1991	Latest		1981	1972-80
	1992	1983-92		1985	1976-84
	1993-1997	Latest		1986	1977-85
	1997HS[iii]	1948-96		1996	1987-95
	1998-2017	Latest		1999CD[iv]	1990-98
Fertility rates	1986	1967-85	**Foetal deaths, late**	1951	1935-50
total	1987-1997	Latest		1952	1936-51
	1997HS[iii]	1948-96		1953	1936-52
	1998	1995-98		1954	1938-53
	1999	1996-99		1955	1946-54
	1999CD[iv]	1980-99		1956	1947-55
	2000	1995-00		1957	1948-56
	2001	1997-01		1958	1948-57
	2002	1998-02		1959	1949-58
	2003	1999-03		1960	1950-59
	2004	2000-04		1961	1952-60
	2005	2001-05		1962	1953-61
	2006	2002-06		1963	1953-62
	2007	2003-07		1964	1959-63
	2008	2004-08		1965	1955-64
	2009-2010	2006-10		1966	1947-65
	2011	2007-11		1967	1962-66
	2012	2008-12		1968	1963-67
	2013	2009-13		1969	1959-68
	2014	2010-14		1970	1965-69
	2015	2011-15		1971	1966-70
	2016	2012-16		1972	1967-71
	2017	2013-17		1973	1968-72
				1974	1965-73
Fertility ratios	1949-50	1900-50		1975	1966-74
	1954	1900-52		1976	1971-75
	1955	1945-54		1977	1972-76
	1959	1935-59		1978	1973-77

Subject-matter	Year of issue	Time coverage	Subject-matter	Year of issue	Time coverage
	1979	1974-78		1986	1977-85
	1980	1971-79			
	1981	1972-80	**Foetal deaths, late**	1957	1950-56
	1982	1977-81	by period of gestation	1959	1949-58
	1983	1978-82		1961	1952-60
	1984	1979-83		1965	5-Latest
	1985	1975-84		1966	1956-65
	1986	1977-85		1967-1968	Latest
	1987	1982-86		1969	1963-68
	1988	1983-87		1974	1965-73
	1989	1984-88		1975	1966-74
	1990	1985-89		1980	1971-79
	1991	1986-90		1981	1972-80
	1992	1987-91		1985	1976-84
	1993	1988-92		1986	1977-85
	1994	1989-93		1996	1987-95
	1995	1990-94			
	1996	1987-95	**Foetal deaths, late**	1961	1952-60
	1997	1992-96	by sex	1965	5 Latest
	1998	1993-97		1969	1963-68
	1999	1994-98		1975	1966-74
	1999CD[iv]	1990-98		1981	1972-80
	2000	1995-99		1986	1977-85
	2001	1997-01			
	2002	1998-02	**Foetal deaths, late**	1971	1966-70
	2003	1999-03	by urban/rural	1972	1967-71
	2004	2000-04	residence	1973	1968-72
	2005	2001-05		1974	1965-73
	2006	2002-06		1975	1966-74
	2007	2003-07		1976	1971-75
	2008	2004-08		1977	1972-76
	2009-2010	2006-10		1978	1973-77
	2011	2007-11		1979	1974-78
	2012	2008-12		1980	1971-79
	2013	2009-13		1981	1972-80
	2014	2010-14		1982	1977-81
	2015	2011-15		1983	1978-82
	2016	2012-16		1984	1979-83
	2017	2013-17		1985	1975-84
				1986	1977-85
Foetal deaths, late	1954	1936-53		1987	1982-86
by age of mother	1959	1949-58		1988	1983-87
	1965	1955-64		1989	1984-88
	1969	1963-68		1990	1985-89
	1975	1966-74		1991	1986-90
	1981	1972-80		1992	1987-91
	1986	1977-85		1993	1988-92
				1994	1989-93
Foetal deaths, late	1954	Latest		1995	1990-94
by age of mother and	1959	1949-58		1996	1987-95
birth order	1965	3-Latest		1997	1992-96
	1969	1963-68		1998	1993-97
	1975	1966-74		1999	1994-98
	1981	1972-80		1999CD[iv]	1990-98

Subject-matter	Year of issue	Time coverage	Subject-matter	Year of issue	Time coverage
				1981	1972-80
Households......................	1987	1975-86		1986	1977-85
population by relationship to householder	1991PA[vii]	Latest		1999CD[iv]	1990-98
			Illegitimate........................	1961	1952-60
			foetal death(s), late	1965	5-Latest
Households......................	1991PA[vii]	Latest		1969	1963-68
by sex and persons 60+				1975	1966-74
				1981	1972-80
Households......................	1955	1945-54		1986	1977-85
population in each type of	1962	1955-62			
	1963	1955-63[vi]	Illegitimate........................	1961	1952-60
	1968	Latest	foetal death ratios, late	1965	5-Latest
	1971	1962-71		1969	1963-68
	1973	1965-73[vi]		1975	1966-74
	1976	Latest		1981	1972-80
	1982	Latest		1986	1977-85
	1987	1975-86			
	1990	1980-89	Illiteracy rates......................		see "Population"
	1995	1985-95			
			Immigrants........................		see "Migration"
I					
			Infant deaths	1948	1932-47
Illegitimacy rates and ratios.....................				1949-50	1934-49
of births	1959	1949-58		1951	1935-50
	1965	1955-64		1952	1936-51
	1969	1963-68		1953	1950-52
	1975	1966-74		1954	1946-53
	1981	1972-80		1955	1946-54
	1986	1977-85		1956	1947-55
	1999CD[iv]	1990-98		1957	1948-56
				1958	1948-57
Illegitimacy rates and ratios.....................	1961	1952-60		1959	1949-58
of foetal deaths, late	1965	5-Latest		1960	1950-59
	1969	1963-68		1961	1952-61
	1975	1966-74		1962	1953-62
	1981	1972-80		1963	1954-63
	1986	1977-85		1964	1960-64
				1965	1961-65
Illegitimate	1959	1949-58		1966	1947-66
birth(s)	1965	1955-64		1967	1963-67
	1969	1963-68		1968	1964-68
	1975	1966-74		1969	1965-69
	1981	1972-80		1970	1966-70
	1986	1977-85		1971	1967-71
	1999CD[iv]	1990-98		1972	1968-72
				1973	1969-73
	see also "Births" and "Foetal deaths, late"			1974	1965-74
				1975	1971-75
				1976	1972-76
Illegitimate	1959	1949-58		1977	1973-77
birth ratios	1965	1955-64		1978	1974-78
	1969	1963-68		1978HS[ii]	1948-78
	1975	1966-74		1979	1975-79

Subject-matter	Year of issue	Time coverage	Subject-matter	Year of issue	Time coverage
	1980	1971-80		1996	1987-95
	1981	1977-81		1997-2004	Latest
	1982	1978-82		2005	1996-05
	1983	1979-83		2006-2017	Latest
	1984	1980-84			
	1985	1976-85	Infant deaths	1967-1973	Latest
	1986	1982-86	by age and sex and	1974	1965-73
	1987	1983-87	urban/rural residence	1975-1979	Latest
	1988	1984-88		1980	1971-79
	1989	1985-89		1981-1984	Latest
	1990	1986-90		1985	1976-84
	1991	1987-91		1986-1991	Latest
	1992	1983-92		1992	1983-92
	1993	1989-93		1993-1995	Latest
	1994	1990-94		1996	1987-95
	1995	1991-95		1997-1999	Latest
	1996	1987-96			
	1997	1993-97	Infant deaths	1967	1962-66
	1997HS[iii]	1948-97	by month	1974	1965-73
	1998	1994-98		1980	1971-79
	1999	1995-99		1985	1976-84
	2000	1996-00			
	2001	1997-01	Infant deaths	1967	Latest
	2002	1998-02	by urban/rural	1968	1964-68
	2003	1999-03	residence		
	2004	2000-04		1969	1965-69
	2005	2001-05		1970	1966-70
	2006	2002-06		1971	1967-71
	2007	2003-07		1972	1968-72
	2008	2004-08		1973	1969-73
	2009-2010	2006-10		1974	1965-74
	2011	2007-11		1975	1971-75
	2012	2008-12		1976	1972-76
	2013	2009-13		1977	1973-77
	2014	2010-14		1978	1974-78
	2015	2011-15		1979	1975-79
	2016	2012-16		1980	1971-80
	2017	2013-17		1981	1977-81
				1982	1978-82
Infant deaths	1948	1936-47		1983	1979-83
by age and sex	1951	1936-49		1984	1980-84
	1957	1948-56		1985	1976-85
	1961	1952-60		1986	1982-86
	1962-1965	Latest		1987	1983-87
	1966	1956-65		1988	1984-88
	1967-1973	Latest		1989	1985-89
	1974	1965-73		1990	1986-90
	1975-1979	Latest		1991	1987-91
	1980	1971-79		1992	1983-92
	1981-1984	Latest		1993	1989-93
	1985	1976-84		1994	1990-94
	1986-1991	Latest		1995	1991-95
	1992	1983-92		1996	1987-96
	1993-1995	Latest		1997	1993-97

Subject-matter	Year of issue	Time coverage	Subject-matter	Year of issue	Time coverage
	1998	1994-98		1975	1971-75
	1999	1995-99		1976	1972-76
	2000	1996-00		1977	1973-77
	2001	1997-01		1978	1974-78
	2002	1998-02		1978HS[ii]	1948-78
	2003	1999-03		1979	1975-79
	2004	2000-04		1980	1971-80
	2005	2001-05		1981	1977-81
	2006	2002-06		1982	1978-82
	2007	2003-07		1983	1979-83
	2008	2004-08		1984	1980-84
	2009-2010	2006-10		1985	1976-85
	2011	2007-11		1986	1982-86
	2012	2008-12		1987	1983-87
	2013	2009-13		1988	1984-88
	2014	2010-14		1989	1985-89
	2015	2011-15		1990	1986-90
	2016	2012-16		1991	1987-91
	2017	2013-17		1992	1983-92
				1993	1989-93
				1994	1990-94
Infant mortality rates	1948	1932-47		1995	1991-95
	1949-50	1932-49		1996	1987-96
	1951	1930-50		1997	1993-97
	1952	1920-34[v]		1997HS[iii]	1948-97
		1934-51		1998	1994-98
	1953	1920-39[v]		1999	1995-99
		1940-52		2000	1996-00
	1954	1920-39[v]		2001	1997-01
		1946-53		2002	1998-02
	1955	1920-34[v]		2003	1999-03
		1946-54		2004	2000-04
	1956	1947-55		2005	2001-05
	1957	1948-56		2006	2002-06
	1958	1948-57		2007	2003-07
	1959	1949-58		2008	2004-08
	1960	1950-59		2009-2010	2006-10
	1961	1945-59[v]		2011	2007-11
		1952-61		2012	2008-12
	1962	1945-54[v]		2013	2009-13
		1952-62		2014	2010-14
	1963	1945-59[v]		2015	2011-15
	1963	1954-63		2016	2012-16
	1964	1960-64		2017	2013-17
	1965	1961-65			
	1966	1920-64[v]			
		1951-66	**Infant mortality rates**..........	1948	1936-47
	1967	1963-67	by age and sex	1951	1936-49
	1968	1964-68		1957	1948-56
	1969	1965-69		1961	1952-60
	1970	1966-70		1966	1956-65
	1971	1967-71		1967	1962-66
	1972	1968-72		1971-1973	Latest
	1973	1969-73		1974	1965-73
	1974	1965-74		1975-1979	Latest

Subject-matter	Year of issue	Time coverage	Subject-matter	Year of issue	Time coverage
	1980	1971-79		1999	1995-99
	1981-1984	Latest		2000	1996-00
	1985	1976-84		2001	1997-01
	1986-1991	Latest		2002	1998-02
	1992	1983-92		2003	1999-03
	1993-1995	Latest		2004	2000-04
	1996	1987-95		2005	2001-05
	1997-2017	Latest		2006	2002-06
				2007	2003-07
Infant mortality rates	1971-1973	Latest		2008	2004-08
by age and sex and	1974	1965-73		2009-2010	2006-10
urban/rural residence	1975-1979	Latest		2011	2007-11
	1980	1971-79		2012	2008-12
	1981-1984	Latest		2013	2009-13
	1985	1976-84		2014	2010-14
	1986-1991	Latest		2015	2011-15
	1992	1983-92		2016	2012-16
	1993-1995	Latest		2017	2013-17
	1996	1987-95			
	1997-1999	Latest	**Intercensal rates of population increase**	1948	1900-48
				1949-50	1900-50
Infant mortality rates	1967	Latest		1951	1900-51
by urban/rural residence	1968	1964-68		1952	1850-1952
				1953	1850-1953
	1969	1965-69		1955	1850-1954
	1970	1966-70		1960	1900-61
	1971	1967-71		1962	1900-62
	1972	1968-72		1964	1955-64
	1973	1969-73		1970	1900-70
	1974	1965-74		1978HS[ii]	1948-78
	1975	1971-75		1997HS[iii]	1948-97
	1976	1972-76			
	1977	1973-77	**International migration**	*see "Migration"*	
	1978	1974-78			
	1979	1975-79	**L**		
	1980	1971-80			
	1981	1977-81	**Late foetal deaths**	*see "Foetal deaths, late"*	
	1982	1978-82			
	1983	1979-83			
	1984	1980-84			
	1985	1976-85	**Life tables**	1959-1973	Latest
	1986	1982-86	life expectancy at birth,	1974	2 latest
	1987	1983-87	by sex	1975-1978	Latest
	1988	1984-88		1978HS[ii]	1948-77
	1989	1985-89		1979	Latest
	1990	1986-90		1980	2 latest
	1991	1987-91		1981-1984	Latest
	1992	1983-92		1985	2 latest
	1993	1989-93		1986-1991	Latest
	1994	1990-94		1991PA[vii]	1950-90
	1995	1991-95		1992-1995	Latest
	1996	1987-96		1996	2 latest
	1997	1993-97		1997	Latest
	1998	1994-98		1997HS[iii]	1948-96

Historical index
(See notes at end of index)

Subject-matter	Year of issue	Time coverage
	1974	1970-74
	1975	1971-75
	1976	1957-76
	1977	1973-77
	1978	1974-78
	1979	1975-79
	1980	1976-80
	1981	1977-81
	1982	1963-82
	1983	1979-83
	1984	1980-84
	1985	1981-85
	1986	1982-86
	1987	1983-87
	1988	1984-88
	1989	1985-89
	1990	1971-90
	1991	1987-91
	1992	1988-92
	1993	1989-93
	1994	1990-94
	1995	1991-95
	1996	1992-96
	1997	1993-97
	1998	1994-98
	1999	1995-99
	2000	1996-00
	2001	1997-01
	2002	1998-02
	2003	1999-03
	2004	2000-04
	2005	2001-05
	2006	2002-06
	2007	2003-07
	2008	2004-08
	2009-2010	2006-10
	2011	2007-11
	2012	2008-12
	2013	2009-13
	2014	2010-14
	2015	2011-15
	2016	2012-16
	2017	2013-17
Marriages............ by age of bride	1948	1936-47
	1949-50	1936-49
	1958	1948-57
	1959-1967	Latest
	1968	1958-67
	1969-1975	Latest
	1976	1966-75
	1977-1981	Latest
	1982	1972-81
	1983-1986	Latest

Subject-matter	Year of issue	Time coverage
	1987	1975-86
	1988-1989	Latest
	1990	1980-1989
	1991-1997	Latest
	1998	1993-97
	1999	1994-98
	2000	1995-99
	2001	1997-01
	2002	1998-02
	2003	1999-03
	2004	2000-04
	2005	2001-05
	2006-2017	Latest
Marriages............ by age of bride and age of groom	1958	1948-57
	1968	Latest
	1976	Latest
	1982	Latest
	1990	Latest
	2006-2017	Latest
Marriages............ by age of bride and previous marital status	1958	1948-57
	1968	Latest
	1976	Latest
	1982	Latest
	1990	Latest
Marriages............ by age of groom	1948	1936-47
	1949-50	1936-49
	1958	1948-57
	1959-1967	Latest
	1968	1958-67
	1969-1975	Latest
	1976	1966-75
	1977-1981	Latest
	1982	1972-81
	1983-1986	Latest
	1987	1975-86
	1988-1989	Latest
	1990	1980-1989
	1990-1997	Latest
	1998	1993-97
	1999	1994-98
	2000	1995-99
	2001	1997-01
	2002	1998-02
	2003	1999-03
	2004	2000-04
	2005	2001-05
	2006-2017	Latest
Marriages............ by age of groom and age of bride	1958	1948-57
	1968	Latest
	1976	Latest

Subject-matter	Year of issue	Time coverage	Subject-matter	Year of issue	Time coverage
	1982	Latest		1979	1975-79
	1990	Latest		1980	1976-80
	2006-2017	Latest		1981	1977-81
				1982	1963-82
Marriages............................	1958	1948-57		1983	1979-83
by age of groom and	1968	Latest		1984	1980-84
previous marital status	1976	Latest		1985	1981-85
	1982	Latest		1986	1982-86
	1990	Latest		1987	1983-87
				1988	1984-88
Marriages............................	1968	1963-67		1989	1985-89
by month				1990	1971-90
				1991	1987-91
Marriages............................	1958	1946-57		1992	1988-92
by previous marital	1968	Latest		1993	1989-93
status of bride and age	1976	Latest		1994	1990-94
	1982	Latest		1995	1991-95
	1990	Latest		1996	1992-96
				1997	1993-97
Marriages............................	1949-50	Latest		1998	1994-98
by previous marital	1958	1948-57		1999	1995-99
status of bride and	1968	1958-67		2000	1996-00
groom				2001	1997-01
	1976	1966-75		2002	1998-02
	1982	1972-81		2003	1999-03
	1990	1980-89		2004	2000-04
				2005	2001-05
Marriages............................	1958	1946-57		2006	2002-06
by previous marital	1968	Latest		2007	2003-07
status of groom and	1976	Latest		2008	2004-08
age				2009-2010	2006-10
	1982	Latest		2011	2007-11
	1990	Latest		2012	2008-12
				2013	2009-13
Marriages............................	1949-50	Latest		2014	2010-14
by previous marital	1958	1948-57		2015	2011-15
status of groom and	1968	1958-67		2016	2012-16
bride				2017	2013-17
	1976	1966-75			
	1982	1972-81	**Marriage, first**....................	1976	Latest
	1990	1980-89	by detailed age of	1982	1972-81
			groom and bride	1990	1980-89
Marriages............................	1968	Latest			
by urban/rural	1969	1965-69	**Marriage rates**	1948	1932-47
residence				1949-50	1932-49
	1970	1966-70		1951	1930-50
	1971	1967-71		1952	1920-34ᵛ
	1972	1968-72			1934-51
	1973	1969-73		1953	1920-39ᵛ
	1974	1970-74			1940-52
	1975	1971-75		1954	1920-39ᵛ
	1976	1957-76			1946-53
	1977	1973-77		1955	1920-34ᵛ
	1978	1974-78			1946-54

Subject-matter	Year of issue	Time coverage	Subject-matter	Year of issue	Time coverage
	1956	1947-55		2009-2010	2006-10
	1957	1948-56		2011	2007-11
	1958	1930-57		2012	2008-12
	1959	1949-58		2013	2009-13
	1960	1950-59		2014	2010-14
	1961	1952-61		2015	2011-15
	1962	1953-62		2016	2012-16
	1963	1954-63		2017	2013-17
	1964	1960-64			
	1965	1956-65	**Marriage rates**	1948	1936-46
	1966	1962-66	by age and sex	1949-50	1936-49
	1967	1963-67		1953	1936-51
	1968	1920-64ᵛ		1954	1936-52
		1953-68		1958	1935-56
	1969	1965-69		1968	1955-67
	1970	1966-70		1976	1966-75
	1971	1967-71		1982	1972-81
	1972	1968-72		1987	1975-86
	1973	1969-73		1990	1980-89
	1974	1970-74			
	1975	1971-75	**Marriage rates**	1958	1935-56
	1976	1957-76	by sex among	1968	1935-67
	1977	1973-77	marriageable	1976	1966-75
	1978	1974-78	population		
	1979	1975-79		1982	1972-81
	1980	1976-80		1990	1980-89
	1981	1977-81			
	1982	1963-82	**Marriage rates**	1968	Latest
	1983	1979-83	by urban/rural	1969	1965-69
	1984	1980-84	residence		
	1985	1981-85		1970	1966-70
	1986	1982-86		1971	1967-71
	1987	1983-87		1972	1968-72
	1988	1984-88		1973	1969-73
	1989	1985-89		1974	1970-74
	1990	1971-90		1975	1971-75
	1991	1987-91		1976	1957-76
	1992	1988-92		1977	1973-77
	1993	1989-93		1978	1974-78
	1994	1990-94		1979	1975-79
	1995	1991-95		1980	1976-80
	1996	1992-96		1981	1977-81
	1997	1993-97		1982	1963-82
	1998	1994-98		1983	1979-83
	1999	1995-99		1984	1980-84
	2000	1996-00		1985	1981-85
	2001	1997-01		1986	1982-86
	2002	1998-02		1987	1983-87
	2003	1999-03		1988	1984-88
	2004	2000-04		1989	1985-89
	2005	2001-05		1990	1971-90
	2006	2002-06		1991	1987-91
	2007	2003-07		1992	1988-92
	2008	2004-08		1993	1989-93

Historical index
(See notes at end of index)

Subject-matter	Year of issue	Time coverage	Subject-matter	Year of issue	Time coverage
	1983	1973-82	**Migration (international) ...**	1948	1936-47
	1984	1974-83	continental and	1977	1967-76
	1985	1975-84	inter-continental		
	1986	1976-85			
	1987	1977-86	**Migration (international) ...**	1970	1963-69
	1988	1978-87	departures	1972	1965-71
	1989	1979-88		1974	1967-73
	1990	1980-89		1976	1969-75
	1991	1981-90		1977	1967-76
	1992	1982-91		1985	1975-84
	1993	1983-92		1989	1979-88
	1994	1984-93		1996	1986-95
	1995	1985-94			
	1996	1986-95	**Migration (international) ...**	1949-50	1945-49
	1997	1987-96	departures, by major	1951	1946-50
	1998	1988-97	categories	1952	1947-51
	1999	1989-98		1954	1948-53
	2000	1991-00		1957	1951-56
	2001	1991-00		1959	1953-58
	2002	1995-02		1962	1956-61
	2003	1995-02		1966	1960-65
	2004	1995-04		1968	1966-67
	2006	1997-06		1977	1967-76
	2007	1997-06		1985	1975-84
	2008	1999-08		1989	1979-88
	2009-2010	1999-08		1996	1986-95
	2011-2012	2001-10			
	2013-2014	2003-12	**Migration (international) ...**	1948	1945-47
	2015-2016	2005-14	emigrants (long term)	1949-50	1946-48
	2017	2007-16	by age and sex	1951	1948-50
				1952	1949-51
Migration (international) ...	1970	1963-69		1954	1950-53
arrivals	1972	1965-71		1957	1953-56
	1974	1967-73		1959	1955-58
	1976	1969-75		1962	1958-61
	1977	1967-76		1966	1960-65
	1985	1975-84		1970	1962-69
	1989	1979-88		1977	1967-76
	1996	1986-95		1989	1975-88
Migration (international) ...	1949-50	1945-49	**Migration (international) ...**	1948	1945-47
arrivals, by major	1951	1946-50	emigrants (long term)	1949-50	1945-48
categories	1952	1947-51	by country or area of	1951	1948-50
	1954	1948-53	intended residence	1952	1949-51
	1957	1951-56		1954	1950-53
	1959	1953-58		1957	1953-56
	1962	1956-61		1959	1956-58
	1966	1960-65		1977	1958-76
	1968	1966-67		1989	1975-88
	1977	1967-76			
	1985	1975-84	**Migration (international) ...**	1948	1945-47
	1989	1979-88	immigrants (long term)	1949-50	1946-48
	1996	1986-95	by age and sex	1951	1948-50
				1952	1949-51

888

Subject-matter	Year of issue	Time coverage	Subject-matter	Year of issue	Time coverage
Neonatal mortality rates....	1971-1973	Latest	Population	1948-1952	Latest
by sex and urban/rural residence	1974	1965-73	by age groups and sex (enumerated)	1953	1950-52
	1975-1979	Latest		1954-1959	Latest[vi]
	1980	1971-79		1960	1940-60
	1981-1984	Latest		1961	Latest
	1985	1976-84		1962	1955-62
	1986-1991	Latest		1963	1955-63
	1992	1983-92		1964	1955-64[vi]
	1993-1995	Latest		1965-1969	Latest
	1996	1987-95		1970	1950-70
	1997	Latest		1971	1962-71
	1997HS[iii]	1948-96		1972	Latest
	1998-1999	Latest		1973	1965-73
				1974-1978	Latest
Net reproduction rates.......	*see "Reproduction rates"*			1978HS[ii]	1948-77
				1979-1991	Latest
Nuptiality..........................	*see "Marriages"*			1991PA[vii]	1950-90
				1992-1997	Latest
				1997HS[iii]	1948-97
				1998-2017	Latest

P

Subject-matter	Year of issue	Time coverage	Subject-matter	Year of issue	Time coverage
Perinatal deaths	1961	1952-60			
	1966	1956-65	Population	1948	1945 & Latest
	1971	1966-70	by age groups and sex (estimated)	1949-50	Latest[vi]
	1974	1965-73		1951-1959	Latest
	1980	1971-79		1960	1940-60
	1985	1976-84		1961-1969	Latest
	1996	1987-95		1970	1950-70
				1971-1997	Latest
Perinatal deaths	1971	1966-70		1997HS[iii]	1948-97
by urban/rural residence	1974	1965-73		1998-2017	Latest
	1980	1971-79	Population	1948	1945 & Latest
	1985	1976-84	by age groups and sex (percentage distribution)	1949-50	Latest[vi]
	1996	1987-95		1951-1952	Latest
Perinatal death ratios	1961	1952-60			
	1966	1956-65	Population	1956	1945-55
	1971	1966-70	by country or area of birth and sex	1963	1955-63
	1974	1965-73		1964	1955-64[vi]
	1980	1971-79		1971	1962-71
	1985	1976-84		1973	1965-73[vi]
	1996	1987-95		*see also "Population, foreign born"*	
Perinatal death ratios	1971	1966-70			
by urban/rural residence	1974	1965-73	Population	1977	Latest
	1980	1971-79	by country or area of birth and sex and age	1983	1974-83
	1985	1976-84		1989	1980-88[vi]
	1996	1987-95		*see also "Population, foreign born"*	
Population			Population	1956	1945-55
ageing, selected indicators	1991PA[vii]	1950-90	by citizenship	1963	1955-63
				1964	1955-64[vi]
				1971	1962-71

Subject-matter	Year of issue	Time coverage	Subject-matter	Year of issue	Time coverage
	1963	1955-63[vi]		1988	1980-88[vi]
	1971	1962-71		1993	1985-93
	1973	1965-73[vi]			
	1979	1970-79[vi]	**Population**	1948-1952	Latest
	1983	1974-83	by sex (enumerated)	1953	1950-52
	1988	1980-88[vi]		1954-1959	Latest
	1993	1985-93		1960	1900-61
				1961	Latest
Population	1948	Latest		1962	1900-62
by marital status, age	1949/50	1926-48		1963	1955-63
and sex	1955	1945-54		1964	1955-64
	1958	1945-57		1965-1969	Latest
	1962	1955-62[vi]		1970	1950-70
	1963	1955-63[vi]		1971	1962-71
	1965	1955-65		1972	Latest
	1968	1955-67		1973	1965-73
	1971	1962-71		1974-1978	Latest
	1973	1965-73[vi]		1978HS[ii]	1948-78
	1976	1966-75		1979-1982	Latest
	1978HS[ii]	1948-77		1983	1974-83
	1982	1972-81		1984-1997	Latest
	1987	1975-86		1997HS[iii]	1948-97
	1990	1980-89		1998-2017	Latest
	1997HS[iii]	1948-96			
	see also "Population, married" and "Population, single"		**Population**	1948	1945 & latest
			by sex (estimated)	1949-50-1959	Latest
				1960	1940-60
Population	1991PA[vii]	Latest		1961-1969	Latest
for persons 60+ and				1970	1950-70
urban/rural				1971	1962-71
				1972	Latest
Population	1948	Latest		1973	1965-73
for persons 60+ and				1974-1997	Latest
urban/rural (percentage				1997HS[iii]	1948-97
distribution)				1998-1999	Latest
				2000	1991-00
				2001	1992-01
Population	1956	1945-55		2002	1993-02
by religion and sex	1963	1955-63		2003	1994-03
	1964	1955-64[vi]		2004	1995-04
	1971	1962-71		2005	1996-05
	1973	1965-73[vi]		2006	1997-06
	1979	1970-79[vi]		2007	1998-07
	1983	1974-83		2008	1999-08
	1988	1980-88[vi]		2009-2010	2001-10
	1993	1985-93		2011	2002-11
				2012	2003-12
Population	1956	1945-55		2013	2004-13
by school attendance,	1963	1955-63		2014	2005-14
age and sex	1964	1955-64[vi]		2015	2006-15
	1971	1962-71		2016	2007-16
	1973	1965-73[vi]		2017	2008-17
	1979	1970-79			
	1983	1974-83			

Subject-matter	Year of issue	Time coverage	Subject-matter	Year of issue	Time coverage
	1970	1950-70	- foreign-born by occupation, age and sex	1994	1985-94
	1972	1962-72			
	1973	1965-73[vi]		*see also "Population by country of birth"*	
	1979	1970-79[vi]			
	1984	1974-84			
	1994	1985-94	- foreign-born by occupation and sex	1977	Latest
- by status, age and sex	1956	1945-55		*see also "Population by country of birth"*	
	1964	1955-64			
	1972	1962-72	- unemployed, by age and sex	1949-50	1946-49
- by status, age and sex and urban/rural residence	1973	1965-73[vi]	**Population**		
	1979	1970-79[vi]	economically inactive by sub-groups and sex	1956	1945-54
	1984	1974-84		1964	1955-64
	1988	1980-88[vi]		1972	1962-72
	1994	1985-94		1973	1965-73[vi]
- by status, industry and sex	1948	Latest		1979	1970-79[vi]
	1949-50	Latest		1984	1974-84[vi]
	1955	1945-54		1988	1980-88[vi]
	1964	1955-64		1994	1985-94
	1972	1962-72			
- by status, industry, and sex and urban/rural residence	1973	1965-73[vi]	**Population** .... elderly, by economic, socio-demographic and urban/rural	1991PA[vii]	1950-90
	1979	1970-79[vi]			
	1984	1974-84			
	1988	1980-88[vi]			
	1994	1985-94	**Population** .... female, by age and duration of marriage	1968	Latest
- by status, occupation and sex	1956	1945-55			
	1964	1955-64			
	1972	1962-72	**Population** .... female, by number of children born alive and age	1949-50	Latest
- by status, occupation and sex and urban/rural residence	1973	1965-73[vi]		1954	1930-53
	1979	1970-79[vi]		1955	1945-54
	1984	1974-84		1959	1949-58
	1988	1980-88[vi]		1963	1955-63
				1965	1955-65
	1994	1985-94		1969	Latest
- female, by marital status and age	1956	1945-55		1971	1962-71
	1964	1955-64		1973	1965-73[vi]
	1968	Latest		1975	1965-74
	1972	1962-72		1978HS[ii]	1948-77
- female, by marital status and age and urban/rural residence	1973	1965-73[vi]		1981	1972-80
	1979	1970-79[vi]		1986	1977-85
	1984	1974-84		1997HS[iii]	1948-96
	1988	1980-88[vi]	**Population** .... female, by number of children living and age	1949-50	Latest
	1994	1985-94		1954	1930-53
				1955	1945-54
	1984	1974-84		1959	1949-58
	1988	1980-88[vi]		1963	1955-63
				1965	1955-65
				1968-1969	Latest

Historical index
(See notes at end of index)

Subject-matter	Year of issue	Time coverage	Subject-matter	Year of issue	Time coverage
	1971	1962-71		1990	1985-90
	1973	1965-73[vi]		1991	1985-91
	1975	1965-74		1992	1985-92
	1978HS[ii]	1948-77		1993	1990-93
	1981	1972-80		1994	1990-94
	1986	1977-85		1995	1990-95
	1997HS[iii]	1948-96		1996	1990-96
				1997	1990-97
Population .... female, in households, by age, sex of householder, size and relationship to householder and urban/rural residence	1987 1995	1975-86 1991-95		1998 1999 2000 2001 2002	1993-98 1995-99 1995-00 1995-01 1995-02
				2003	2000-03
				2004	2000-04
Population .... institutional, by age, sex and urban/rural residence	1987 1995	1875-86 1991-95		2005 2006 2007 2008 2009-2010	2000-05 2000-06 2005-07 2005-08 2005-10
				2011	2005-11
Population .... growth rates (annual average for countries or areas)	1957 1958 1959 1960 1961 1962 1963 1964	1953-56 1953-57 1953-58 1953-59 1953-60 1958-61 1958-62 1958-63		2012 2013 2014 2015 2016 2017	2005-12 2010-13 2010-14 2010-15 2010-16 2010-17
	1965	1958-64	**Population** .... growth rates (annual average for the world, macro-regions (continents) and regions)	1957 1958 1959 1960 1961	1950-56 1950-57 1950-58 1950-59 1950-60
	1966	1958-66			
	1967	1963-67			
	1968	1963-68			
	1969	1963-69			
	1970	1963-70		1962	1950-61
	1971	1963-71		1963	1958-62
	1972	1963-72			1960-62
	1973	1970-73		1964	1958-63
	1974	1970-74			1960-63
	1975	1970-75		1965	1958-64
	1976	1970-76			1960-64
	1977	1970-77		1966	1958-66
	1978	1975-78			1960-66
	1979	1975-79		1967	1960-67
	1980	1975-80			1963-67
	1981	1975-81		1968	1960-68
	1982	1975-82			1963-68
	1983	1980-83		1969	1960-69
	1984	1980-84			1963-69
	1985	1980-85		1970	1963-70
	1986	1980-86			1965-70
	1987	1980-87		1971	1963-71
	1988	1985-88			1965-71
	1989	1985-89		1972	1963-72

Subject-matter	Year of issue	Time coverage	Subject-matter	Year of issue	Time coverage
		1965-72	**Population**	1973	1965-73
	1973	1965-73	illiterate, by sex and	1979	1970-79[vi]
		1970-73	age and urban/rural	1983	1974-83
	1974	1965-74	residence	1988	1980-88[vi]
		1970-74		1993	1985-93
	1975	1965-75			
		1970-75	**Population**	1973	1965-73
	1976	1965-76	illiterate, by sex and	1979	1970-79[vi]
		1970-76	urban/rural residence	1983	1974-83
	1977	1965-77		1988	1980-88[vi]
		1970-77		1993	1985-93
	1978-1979	1970-75			
	1980-1983	1975-80	**Population**	1991PA[vii]	Latest
	1984-1986	1980-85	in collective living		
	1987-1992	1985-90	quarters and homeless		
	1993-1997	1990-95			
	1998-2000	1995-00	**Population**		see "Population by
	2001-2005	2000-05	in households		household type" and
	2006-2010	2005-10			"Households"
	2011-2015	2010-15			
	2016	2015-20	**Population**		see "Population by
	2017	2015-20	in localities		localities" and "Population
					by locality size-classes"
Population	1991PA[vii]	Latest			
homeless by age and			**Population**		see "Population growth
sex			increase rates		rates"
Population	1948	Latest	**Population**		
illiteracy rates by sex	1955	1945-54	literacy rates by sex	1955	1945-54
	1960	1920-60			see also "Population
	1963	1955-63[vi]			illiteracy rates"
	1964	1955-64[vi]			
	1970	1950-70	**Population**	1955	1945-54
			literacy rates by sex		
Population	1973	1965-73	and age		
illiteracy rates by sex	1979	1970-79[vi]			
and urban/rural	1983	1974-83	**Population**	1948	Latest
residence			literate, by sex and age	1955	1945-54
	1988	1980-88[vi]		1963	1955-63
	1993	1985-93		1964	1955-64[vi]
					see also "Population,
Population	1948	Latest			illiterate"
illiterate, by sex	1955	1945-54			
	1960	1920-60	**Population**	1971	1962-71
	1963	1955-63	literate, by sex and age	1973	1965-73[vi]
	1964	1955-64	by urban/rural	1979	1970-74[vi]
	1970	1950-70	residence		
				1983	1974-83
Population	1948	Latest		1988	1980-88[vi]
illiterate, by sex and	1955	1945-54		1993	1985-93
age				1987	1975-86
	1963	1955-63			
	1964	1955-64[vi]	**Population**	1991PA[vii]	1950-90
	1970	1950-70	living arrangements	1995	1985-95

Historical index
(See notes at end of index)

Subject-matter	Year of issue	Time coverage	Subject-matter	Year of issue	Time coverage
	1976	1967-76		1960	1920-59
	1977	1968-77		1961	1920-60
	1978	1969-78		1962	1920-61
	1978HS[ii]	1948-78		1963	1930-62
	1979	1970-79		1964	1930-63
	1980	1971-80		1965	1930-65
	1981	1972-81		1966	1930-66
	1982	1973-82		1967	1930-67
	1983	1974-83		1968	1930-68
	1984	1975-84		1969	1930-69
	1985	1976-85		1970	1950-70
	1986	1977-86		1971	1950-71
	1987	1978-87		1972	1950-72
	1988	1979-88		1973	1950-73
	1989	1980-89		1974	1950-74
	1990	1981-90		1975	1950-75
	1991	1982-91		1976	1950-76
	1992	1983-92		1977	1950-77
	1993	1984-93		1978	1950-78
	1994	1985-94		1979	1950-79
	1995	1986-95		1980	1950-80
	1996	1987-96		1981	1950-81
	1997	1988-97		1982	1950-82
	1997HS[iii]	1948-97		1983	1950-83
	1998	1989-98		1984	1950-84
	1999	1990-99		1985	1950-85
	2000	1991-00		1986	1950-86
	2001	1992-01		1987	1950-87
	2002	1993-02		1988	1950-88
	2003	1994-03		1989	1950-89
	2004	1995-04		1990	1950-90
	2005	1996-05		1991	1950-91
	2006	1997-06		1992	1950-92
	2007	1998-07		1993	1950-93
	2008	1999-08		1994	1950-94
	2009-2010	2001-10		1995	1950-95
	2011	2002-11		1996	1950-96
	2012	2003-12		1997	1950-97
	2013	2004-13		1998-1999	1950-00
	2014	2005-14		2000	1950-00
	2015	2006-15		2001	1950-01
	2016	2007-16		2002	1950-02
	2017	2008-17		2003	1950-03
				2004	1950-04
Population	1949-50	1920-49		2005	1950-05
- of major regions	1951	1950		2006	1950-06
	1952	1920-51		2007	1950-07
	1953	1920-52		2008	1950-08
	1954	1920-53		2009-2010	1950-10
	1955	1920-54		2011	1960-11
	1956	1920-55		2012	1960-12
	1957	1920-56		2013	1960-13
	1958	1920-57		2014	1960-14
	1959	1920-58		2015	1960-15

Subject-matter	Year of issue	Time coverage	Subject-matter	Year of issue	Time coverage
	2016	1960-16		2003	1950-03
	2017	1960-17		2004	1950-04
				2005	1950-05
Population	1949-50	1920-49		2006	1950-06
- of regions	1952	1920-51		2007	1950-07
	1953	1920-52		2008	1950-08
	1954	1920-53		2009-2010	1950-10
	1955	1920-54		2011	1960-11
	1956	1920-55		2012	1960-12
	1957	1920-56		2013	1960-13
	1958	1920-57		2014	1960-14
	1959	1920-58		2015	1960-15
	1960	1920-59		2016	1960-16
	1961	1920-60		2017	1960-17
	1962	1920-61			
	1963	1930-62	**Population**	1949-50	1920-49
	1964	1930-63	- of the world	1951	1950
	1965	1930-65		1952	1920-51
	1966	1930-66		1953	1920-52
	1967	1930-67		1954	1920-53
	1968	1930-68		1955	1920-54
	1969	1930-69		1956	1920-55
	1970	1950-70		1957	1920-56
	1971	1950-71		1958	1920-57
	1972	1950-72		1959	1920-58
	1973	1950-73		1960	1920-59
	1974	1950-74		1961	1920-60
	1975	1950-75		1962	1920-61
	1976	1950-76		1963	1930-62
	1977	1950-77		1964	1930-63
	1978	1950-78		1965	1930-65
	1979	1950-79		1966	1930-66
	1980	1950-80		1967	1930-67
	1981	1950-81		1968	1930-68
	1982	1950-82		1969	1930-69
	1983	1950-83		1970	1950-70
	1984	1950-84		1971	1950-71
	1985	1950-85		1972	1950-72
	1986	1950-86		1973	1950-73
	1987	1950-87		1974	1950-74
	1988	1950-88		1975	1950-75
	1989	1950-89		1976	1950-76
	1990	1950-90		1977	1950-77
	1991	1950-91		1978	1950-78
	1992	1950-92		1979	1950-79
	1993	1950-93		1980	1950-80
	1994	1950-94		1981	1950-81
	1995	1950-95		1982	1950-82
	1996	1950-96		1983	1950-83
	1997	1950-97		1984	1950-84
	1998-1999	1950-00		1985	1950-85
	2000	1950-00		1986	1950-86
	2001	1950-01		1987	1950-87
	2002	1950-02		1988	1950-88

Subject-matter	Year of issue	Time coverage	Subject-matter	Year of issue	Time coverage
	1989	1950-89		1982	1973-82
	1990	1950-90		1983	1974-83
	1991	1950-91		1984	1975-84
	1992	1950-92		1985	1976-85
	1993	1950-93		1986	1977-86
	1994	1950-94		1987	1978-87
	1995	1950-95		1988	1979-88
	1996	1950-96		1989	1980-89
	1997	1950-97		1990	1981-90
	1998-1999	1950-00		1991	1982-91
	2000	1950-00		1992	1983-92
	2001	1950-01		1993	1984-93
	2002	1950-02		1994	1985-94
	2003	1950-03		1995	1986-95
	2004	1950-04		1996	1987-96
	2005	1950-05		1997	1988-97
	2006	1950-06		1998	1989-98
	2007	1950-07		1999	1990-99
	2008	1950-08		2000	1991-00
	2009-2010	1950-10		2001	1992-01
	2011	1960-11		2002	1993-02
	2012	1960-12		2003	1994-03
	2013	1960-13		2004	1995-04
	2014	1960-14		2005	1996-05
	2015	1960-15		2006	1997-06
	2016	1960-16		2007	1998-07
	2017	1960-17		2008	1999-08
				2009-2010	2001-10
Population .... rural residence	*see "Population by urban/rural residence"*			2011	2002-11
				2012	2003-12
				2013	2004-13
Population .... single, by age and sex (numbers)	1960	1920-60		2014	2005-14
	1970	1950-70		2015	2006-15
	see also "Population by marital status"			2016	2007-16
				2017	2008-17
Population .... single, by age and sex (percent)	1949-50	1926-48	- by age and sex (enumerated)	1963	1955-63
	1960	1920-60		1964	1955-64[vi]
	1970	1950-70		1967	Latest
				1970	1950-70
Population .... urban/rural residence:	1968	1964-68		1971	1962-71
	1969	1965-69		1972	Latest
	1970	1950-70		1973	1965-73
	1971	1962-71		1974-1978	Latest
	1972	1968-72		1978HS[ii]	1948-77
	1973	1965-73		1979-1996	Latest
	1974	1966-74		1979-1997	Latest
	1975	1967-75		1997HS[iii]	1948-96
	1976	1967-76		1998-2017	Latest
	1977	1968-77				
	1978	1969-78	- by age and sex (estimated)	1963	Latest
	1979	1970-79		1967	Latest
	1980	1971-80		1970	1950-70
	1981	1972-81		1971-1997	Latest

Subject-matter	Year of issue	Time coverage	Subject-matter	Year of issue	Time coverage
	1997HS[iii]	1948-96		1993	1985-93
	1998-2017	Latest			
			- by major civil divisions	1971	1962-71
- by country or area of birth and sex	1971	1962-71		1973	1965-73[vi]
	1973	1965-73[vi]		1979	1970-79[vi]
				1983	1974-83
- by country or area of birth and sex and age	1977	Latest		1988	1980-88[vi]
				1993	1985-93
- by citizenship and sex	1971	1962-71	- by marital status, age and sex	1971	1962-71
	1973	1965-73[vi]		1973	1965-73[vi]
- by citizenship and sex and age	1977	Latest	- by religion and sex	1971	1962-71
	1983	1974-83		1973	1965-73[vi]
	1989	1980-88		1979	1970-79[vi]
				1983	1974-83
- by ethnic composition and sex	1971	Latest		1988	1980-88[vi]
	1973	1965-73[vi]		1993	1985-93
	1979	1970-79[vi]	- by school attendance, age and sex	1971	1962-71
	1983	1974-83		1973	1965-73[vi]
	1988	1980-88[vi]		1979	1970-79[vi]
	1993	1985-93		1983	1974-83
				1988	1980-88[vi]
- by households, number and size	1968	Latest		1993	1985-93
	1971	1962-71			
	1973	1965-73[vi]	- by sex (numbers)	1948	Latest
	1976	Latest		1952	1900-51
	1982	Latest		1955	1945-54
	1987	1975-86		1960	1920-60
	1990	1980-89		1962	1955-62
	1995	1985-95		1963	1955-63
				1964	1955-64[vi]
	see also "Households"			1967	Latest
				1970	1950-70
- by language and sex	1971	1962-71		1971	1962-71
	1973	1965-73[vi]		1972	Latest
	1979	1970-79[vi]		1973	1965-73
	1983	1974-83		1974	1966-74
	1988	1980-88[vi]		1975	1967-75
	1993	1985-93		1976	1967-76
				1977	1968-77
- by level of education, age and sex	1971	1962-71		1978	1969-78
	1973	1965-73[vi]		1979	1970-79
	1979	1970-79[vi]		1980	1971-80
	1983	1974-83		1981	1972-81
	1988	1980-88[vi]		1982	1973-82
	1993	1985-93		1983	1974-83
				1984	1975-84
- by literacy, age and sex	1971	1962-71		1985	1976-85
	1973	1965-73[vi]		1986	1977-86
	1979	1970-79[vi]		1987	1978-87
	1983	1974-83		1988	1979-88
	1988	1980-88[vi]		1989	1980-89

Historical index
(See notes at end of index)

Subject-matter	Year of issue	Time coverage	Subject-matter	Year of issue	Time coverage
	1990	1981-90		1992	1983-92
	1991	1982-91		1993	1984-93
	1992	1983-92		1994	1985-94
	1993	1984-93		1995	1986-95
	1994	1985-94		1996	1987-96
	1995	1986-95		1997	1988-97
	1996	1987-96		1998	1989-98
	1997	1988-97		1999	1990-99
	1998	1989-98		2000	1991-00
	1999	1990-99		2001	1992-01
	2000	1991-00		2002	1993-02
	2001	1992-01		2003	1994-03
	2002	1993-02		2004	1995-04
	2003	1994-03		2005	1996-05
	2004	1995-04		2006	1997-06
	2005	1996-05		2007	1998-07
	2006	1997-06		2008	1999-08
	2007	1998-07		2009-2010	2001-10
	2008	1999-08		2011	2002-11
	2009-2010	2001-10		2012	2003-12
	2011	2002-11		2013	2004-13
	2012	2003-12		2014	2005-14
	2013	2004-13		2015	2006-15
	2014	2005-14		2016	2007-16
	2015	2006-15		2017	2008-17
	2016	2007-16			
	2017	2008-17	- by single years of age and sex	1971	1962-71
				1973	1965-73[vi]
- by sex (percent)	1948	Latest		1979	1970-79[vi]
	1952	1900-51		1983	1974-83
	1955	1945-54		1993	1985-93
	1960	1920-60			
	1962	1955-62	- female, by number	1971	1962-71
	1970	1950-70	of children born	1973	1965-73[vi]
	1971	1962-71	alive and age	1975	1965-74
	1973	1965-73		1978HS[ii]	1948-77
	1974	1966-74		1981	1972-80
	1975	1967-75		1986	1977-85
	1976	1967-76		1997HS[iii]	1948-96
	1977	1968-77			
	1978	1969-78	- female, by number	1971	1962-71
	1979	1970-79	of children living	1973	1965-73[vi]
	1980	1971-80	and age	1975	1965-74
	1981	1972-81		1978HS[ii]	1948-77
	1982	1973-82		1981	1972-80
	1983	1974-83		1986	1977-85
	1984	1975-84		1997HS[iii]	1948-96
	1985	1976-85			
	1986	1977-86	Post-neonatal deaths..........	1948	1936-47
	1987	1978-87	by sex	1951	1936-50
	1988	1979-88		1957	1948-56
	1989	1980-89		1961	1952-60
	1990	1981-90		1963-1965	Latest
	1991	1982-91		1966	1961-65

Subject-matter	Year of issue	Time coverage	Subject-matter	Year of issue	Time coverage
	1967	1962-66	**Post-neonatal mortality**		
	1968-1973	Latest	**rates**	1971-1973	Latest
	1974	1965-73	by urban/rural	1974	1965-73
	1975-1979	Latest	residence		
	1980	1971-79		1975-1979	Latest
	1981-1984	Latest		1980	1971-79
	1985	1976-84		1981-1984	Latest
	1986-1991	Latest		1985	1976-84
	1992	1983-92		1986-1991	Latest
	1993-1995	Latest		1992	1983-92
	1996	1987-95		1993-1995	Latest
	1997	Latest		1996	1987-95
	1997HS[ii]	1948-96		1997	Latest
	1998-2017	Latest		1997HS[ii]	1948-96
				1998-1999	Latest
Post-neonatal deaths	1971-1973	Latest			
by urban/rural	1974	1965-73	**R**		
residence					
	1975-1979	Latest	**Rates**	see "Annulments", "Births",	
	1980	1971-79		"Deaths", "Divorces",	
	1981-1984	Latest		"Fertility", "Illiteracy",	
	1985	1976-84		"Infant Mortality",	
	1986-1991	Latest		"Intercensal", "Life Tables",	
	1992	1983-92		"Literacy", "Marriages",	
	1993-1995	Latest		"Maternal mortality",	
	1996	1987-95		"Natural increase", "Neo	
	1997	Latest		natal mortality",	
	1997HS[ii]	1948-96		"Population growth", "Post	
	1998-1999	Latest		neo natal mortality" and	
				"Reproduction"	
Post-neonatal mortality					
rates	1948	1936-47	**Ratios**	see "Births", "Child-	
by sex	1951	1936-50		woman", "Fertility",	
	1957	1948-56		"Foetal deaths" and	
	1961	1952-60		"Perinatal mortality"	
	1966	1956-65			
	1967	1962-66	**Refugees, by country or**		
	1968-1973	Latest	**area of destination**	1952	1947-51
	1974	1965-73	repatriated by the		
	1975-1979	Latest	International Refugee		
	1980	1971-79	Organization		
	1981-1984	Latest			
	1985	1976-84	**Refugees, by country or**		
	1986-1991	Latest	**area of destination**	1952	1947-51
	1992	1983-92	resettled by the		
	1993-1995	Latest	International Refugee		
	1996	1987-95	Organization		
	1997	Latest			
	1997HS [ii]	1948-96	**Religion and sex**	see "Population"	
	1998-2017	Latest			
			Reproduction rates,		
			gross and net	1948	1920-47
				1949-50	1900-48
				1954	1920-53
				1965	1930-64
				1969	1963-68

Subject-matter	Year of issue	Time coverage	Subject-matter	Year of issue	Time coverage
	2001	2001		1996	1987-96
	2002	2002			
	2003	2003	- Natality	1949-50	1932-49
	2004	2004		1954	1920-53
	2005	2005		1959	1920-58
	2006	2006		1965	1920-65
	2007	2007		1969	1925-69
	2008	2008		1975	1956-75
	2009-2010	2010		1981	1962-81
	2011	2011		1986	1967-86
	2012	2012		1992	1983-92
	2013	2013		1999CD[iv]	1980-99
	2014	2014			
	2015	2015	- Nuptiality	see Topic "Marriage and Divorce" above	
	2016	2016			
	2017	2017			
Survivors	see "Life tables"		- Population Ageing and the Situation of Elderly Persons	1991PA[vii]	1950-90

T

Subject-matter	Year of issue	Time coverage	Subject-matter	Year of issue	Time coverage
Text	see separate listing in Appendix to this Index		- Population Census:		
			· Economic characteristics	1956	1945-55
				1964	1955-64
Topic of each Demographic Yearbook				1972	1962-72
- Divorce	see Topic "Marriage and Divorce" below			1973	1965-73[vi]
				1979	1970-79[vi]
- General demography	1948	1900-48		1984	1974-84
	1953	1950-53		1988	1980-88[vi]
				1994	1985-94
- Historical supplement	1978HS[ii]	1948-78		2014[viii]	1995-2014
	1997HS[iii]	1948-97	· Educational characteristics	1955	1945-54
- Marriage and Divorce	1958	1930-57		1956	1945-55
	1968	1920-68		1963	1955-63
	1976	1957-76		1964	1955-64[vi]
	1982	1963-82		1971	1962-71
	1990	1971-90		1973	1965-73[vi]
				1979	1970-79[vi]
- Migration (international)	1977	1958-76		1983	1974-83
				1988	1980-88[vi]
	1989	1975-88		1993	1985-93
- Mortality	1951	1905-50	· Ethnic characteristics	1956	1945-55
	1957	1930-56		1963	1955-63
	1961	1945-61		1964	1955-64[vi]
	1966	1920-66		1971	1962-71
	1967	1900-67		1973	1965-73[vi]
	1974	1965-74		1979	1970-79[vi]
	1980	1971-80		1983	1974-83
	1985	1976-85		1988	1980-88[vi]
	1992	1983-92		1993	1985-93
			· Fertility characteristics	1940/50	1900-50
				1954	1900-53

Subject-matter	Year of issue	Time coverage	Subject-matter	Year of issue	Time coverage
	1955	1945-54		1983	1974-83
	1959	1935-59		1987	1975-86
	1963	1955-63		1995	1985-95
	1965	1955-65		2013[viii]	1995-2013
	1969	Latest	· Personal	1955	1945-54
	1971	1962-71	characteristics	1962	1955-62
	1973	1965-73[vi]		1971	1962-71
	1975	1965-75		1973	1965-73[vi]
	1981	1972-81		1979	1970-79[vi]
	1986	1977-86		1983	1974-83
	1992	1983-92		1988	1980-88[vi]
				1993	1985-93
· Geographic	1952	1900-51	- Population trends	1960	1920-60
characteristics	1955	1945-54		1970	1950-70
	1962	1955-62			
	1964	1955-64[vi]			
	1971	1962-71			
	1973	1965-73[vi]			
	1979	1970-79[vi]			
	1983	1974-83			
	1988	1980-88[vi]			
	1993	1985-93			
· Household	1955	1945-54			
characteristics	1962	1955-62			
	1963	1955-63[vi]			
	1971	1962-71			
	1973	1965-73[vi]			
	1976	1966-75			

U

Urban/rural births...............	see "Births"
Urban/rural deaths	see "Deaths"
Urban/rural infant deaths .	see "Infant deaths"
Urban/rural population	see "Population, urban/rural residence"
Urban/rural population by average size of households	see "Households"

APPENDIX

Special text of each Demographic Yearbook

Divorce:

'Uses of Marriage and Divorce Statistics', 1958.

Marriage:

'Uses of Marriage and Divorce Statistics', 1958.

Households:

'Concepts and definitions of households, householder and institutional population', 1987.

Migration:

'Statistics of International Migration', 1977.

Mortality:

'Recent Mortality Trends', 1951.
'Development of Statistics of Causes of Death', 1951.
'Factors in Declining Mortality', 1957.
'Notes on Methods of Evaluating the Reliability of Conventional Mortality Statistics', 1961.
'Recent Trends of Mortality', 1966.
'Mortality Trends among Elderly Persons', 1991PA[vii].

Natality:

'Graphic Presentation of Trends in Fertility', 1959.
'Recent Trends in Birth Rates', 1965.
'Recent Changes in World Fertility', 1969.

Population

'World Population Trends, 1920-1949', 1949-50.
'Urban Trends and Characteristics', 1952.
'Background to the1950 Censuses of Population', 1955.
'The World Demographic Situation', 1956.
'How Well Do We Know the Present Size and Trend of the World's Population?', 1960.
'Notes on Availability of National Population Census Data and Methods of Estimating their Reliability', 1962.
'Availability and Adequacy of Selected Data Obtained from Population Censuses Taken 1955-1963', 1963.
'Availability of Selected Population Census Statistics: 1955-1964', 1964.
'Statistical Concepts and Definitions of Urban and Rural Population', 1967.
'Statistical Concepts and Definitions of Household', 1968.
'How Well Do We Know the Present Size and Trend of the World's Population?', 1970.
'United Nations Recommendations on Topics to be Investigated in a Population Census
Compared with Country Practice in National Censuses taken 1965-1971', 1971.
'Statistical Definitions of Urban Population and their Use in Applied Demography', 1972.
'Dates of National Population and Housing Census carried out during the decade1965-1974', 1974.
'Dates of National Population and/or Housing Censuses taken or anticipated during the decade 1975-1984', 1979.
'Dates of National Population and/or Housing Censuses taken during the decade1965-1974 and
taken or anticipated during the decade 1975-1984', 1983.
'Dates of National Population and/or Housing Censuses taken during the decade1975-1984 and taken or
anticipated during the decade 1985-1994', 1988 and 1993.
'Statistics Concerning the Economically Active Population: An Overview', 1984.
'Disability', 1991PA[vii].
'Population Ageing', 1991PA[vii].
'Special Needs for the Study of Population Ageing and Elderly Persons', 1991PA[vii].

Historical index
(See notes at end of index)

GENERAL NOTES

This cumulative index covers the contents of each of the 68 issues of the Demographic Yearbook. 'Year of issue' stands for the particular issue in which the indicated subject-matter appears. Unless otherwise specified, 'Time coverage' designates the years for which annual statistics are shown in the Demographic Yearbook referred to in 'Year of issue' column. 'Latest' or '2 latest' indicates that data are for latest available year(s) only.

---

[i] Only titles not available for preceding bibliography.
[ii] Historical Supplement to the 30th DYB published in a separate volume in year 1979.
[iii] Historical Supplement to the 49th DYB published in a separate volume (CD-ROM) in year 2000.
[iv] Supplement to the 51st DYB focusing on natality published in a separate volume (CD-ROM) in year 2002.
[v] Five year average rates.
[vi] Only data not available for preceding issue.
[vii] Population ageing published in separate volume.
[viii] Tables published online.

Index historique
(Voir notes à la fin de l'index)

Sujet	Année de l'édition	Période considérée	Sujet	Année de l'édition	Période considérée
				1960	1920-60
				1963	1955-63
A				1964	1955-64 [iii]
				1970	1950-70
Accroissement intercensitaire de la population, taux d'............	1948	1900-48		1971	1962-71
	1949-50	1900-50		1973	1965-73
	1951	1900-51		1979	1970-79 [iii]
	1952	1850-1952		1983	1974-83
	1953	1850-1953		1988	1980-88 [iii]
	1955	1850-1954		1993	1985-93 [iii]
	1960	1900-61			
	1962	1900-62	**Alphabétisme selon le sexe et l'âge, taux d'**	1948	Dernière
	1964	1955-64		1955	1945-54
	1970	1900-70		1971	1962-71
	1978 SR [i]	1948-78		1973	1965-73 [iii]
	1997 SR [ii]	1948-97		1979	1970-79 [iii]
				1983	1974-83
Accroissement naturel, taux d'	1958-1978	Dernière		1988	1980-88 [iii]
	1978 SR [i]	1948-78			
	1979-1997	Dernière	**Alphabètes**........................	*voir: Population*	
	1997 SR [ii]	1948-97			
	1998	1995-98	**Annulations**	1958	1948-57
	1999	1996-99		1968	1958-67
	2000	1995-00		1976	1966-75
	2001	1997-01			
	2002	1998-02	**Annulations, taux**...............	1958	1948-57
	2003	1999-03		1968	1958-67
	2004	2000-04		1976	1966-75
	2005	2001-05			
	2006	2002-06	**Avortements, légaux**	1971	Dernière
	2007	2003-07		1972	1964-72
	2008	2004-08		1973	1965-73
	2009-2010	2006-10		1974	1965-74
	2011	2007-11		1975	1965-74
	2012	2008-12		1976	1965-75
	2013	2009-13		1977	1967-76
	2014	2010-14		1978	1968-77
	2015	2011-15		1979	1969-78
	2016	2012-16		1980	1971-79
	2017	2013-17		1981	1972-80
				1982	1973-81
Activité économique	*voir: Population active*			1983	1974-82
				1984	1975-83
Age	*voir la rubrique appropriée par sujet, p.ex. Immigrants: Mortalité, taux de: Naissances: Population: etc.*			1985	1976-84
				1986	1977-85
				1987	1978-86
				1988	1979-87
Analphabètes	*voir: Population*			1989	1980-88
				1990	1981-89
Alphabétisme selon le sexe, taux d'	1948	Dernière		1992	1983-91
	1955	1945-54		1993	1984-92
				1994	1985-93

Sujet	Année de l'édition	Période considérée
	2006	2002-06
	2007	2003-07
	2008	2004-08
	2009-2010	2006-10
	2011	2007-11
	2012	2008-12
	2013	2009-13
	2014	2010-14
	2015	2011-15
	2016	2012-16
	2017	2013-17
Décès.................................. d'enfants de moins d'un an	*voir: Mortalité infantile*	
Décès.................................. selon l'âge et le sexe	1948	1936-47
	1951	1936-50
	1955-1956	Dernière
	1957	1948-56
	1958-1960	Dernière
	1961	1955-60
	1962-1965	Dernière
	1966	1961-65
	1967-1973	Dernière
	1974	1965-73
	1975-1979	Dernière
	1978 SR [i]	1948-77
	1980	1971-79
	1981-1984	Dernière
	1985	1976-84
	1986-1991	Dernière
	1992	1983-92
	1993-1995	Dernière
	1996	1987-95
	1997	Dernière
	1997SR [ii]	1948-96
	1998-2017	Dernière
Décès.................................. selon l'âge et le sexe et la résidence (urbaine/rurale)	1967-1973	Dernière
	1974	1965-73
	1975-1979	Dernière
	1980	1971-79
	1981-1984	Dernière
	1985	1976-84
	1986-1991	Dernière
	1992	1983-92
	1993-1995	Dernière
	1996	1987-95
	1997	Dernière
	1997SR [ii]	1948-96
	1998-2006	Dernière

Sujet	Année de l'édition	Période considérée
Décès.................................. selon la cause	1951	1947-50
	1952	1947-51 [iii]
	1953	Dernière
	1954	1945-53
	1955-1956	Dernière
	1957	1952-56
	1958-1960	Dernière
	1961	1955-60
	1962-1965	Dernière
	1966	1960-65
	1967-1973	Dernière
	1974	1965-73
	1975-1979	Dernière
	1980	1971-79
	1981-1984	Dernière
	1985	1976-84
	1986-1995	Dernière
	1996	1987-95
	1997-2000	Dernière
	2002	1995-02
	2004	1995-04
	2006	2002-06
	2008	2004-08
	2011	2006-10
	2013	2008-12
	2015	2010-14
	2017	2012-16
Décès.................................. selon la cause, l'âge et le sexe	1951	Dernière
	1952	Dernière [iii]
	1957	Dernière
	1961	Dernière
	1967	Dernière
	1974	Dernière
	1980	Dernière
	1985	Dernière
	1991 VP [v]	1960-90
	1996	Dernière
Décès.................................. selon la cause, l'âge et le sexe et la résidence (urbaine/rurale)	1967	Dernière
Décès.................................. selon la cause et le sexe	1967	Dernière
	1974	Dernière
	1980	Dernière
	1985	Dernière
	1991VP [v]	1960-90
	1996	Dernière
	2006	2002-06
	2008	2004-08

Index historique
(Voir notes à la fin de l'index)

Sujet	Année de l'édition	Période considérée	Sujet	Année de l'édition	Période considérée
	2011	2006-10		2017	2013-17
	2013	2008-12			
	2015	2010-14	**Décès**..................	1958	Dernière
	2017	2012-16	selon l'état	1961	Dernière
			matrimonial, l'âge et le	1967	Dernière
Décès..................	1967	Dernière	sexe		
selon la résidence	1968	1964-68		1974	Dernière
(urbaine/rurale)	1969	1965-69		1980	Dernière
	1970	1966-70		1985	Dernière
	1971	1967-71		1991 VP [v]	1950-90
	1972	1968-72		1996	Dernière
	1973	1969-73		2003	Dernière
	1974	1965-74			
	1975	1971-75	**Décès**..................	1951	1946-50
	1976	1972-76	selon le mois	1967	1962-66
	1977	1973-77		1974	1965-73
	1978	1974-78		1980	1971-79
	1979	1975-79		1985	1976-84
	1980	1971-80		2001	1985-00
	1981	1977-81		2005	2001-05
	1982	1978-82			
	1983	1979-83	**Décès**..................	1957	Dernière
	1984	1980-84	selon la profession et	1961	1957-60
	1985	1976-85	l'âge (sexe masculin)	1967	1962-66
	1986	1982-86			
	1987	1983-87	**Décès**..................	1957	Dernière
	1988	1984-88	selon le type de	1974	1965-73
	1989	1985-89	certification et la cause	1980	1971-79
	1990	1986-90	(nombres)	1985	1976-84
	1991	1987-91			
	1992	1983-92	**Décès**..................	1957	Dernière
	1993	1989-93	selon le type de	1961	1955-60
	1994	1990-94	certification et la cause	1966	1960-65
	1995	1991-95	(pourcentage)	1974	1965-73
	1996	1987-96		1980	1971-79
	1997	1993-97		1985	1976-84
	1998	1994-98			
	1999	1995-99	**Décès, taux de**...................	1948	1932-47
	2001	1997-01		1949-50	1932-49
	2002	1998-02		1951	1905-30 [vi]
	2003	1999-03			1930-50
	2004	2000-04		1952	1920-34 [vi]
	2005	2001-05			1934-51
	2006	2002-06		1953	1920-39 [vi]
	2007	2003-07			1940-52
	2008	2004-08		1954	1920-39 [vi]
	2009-2010	2006-10			1946-53
	2011	2007-11		1955	1920-34 [vi]
	2012	2008-12			1946-54
	2013	2009-13		1956	1947-55
	2014	2010-14		1957	1930-56
	2015	2011-15		1958	1948-57
	2016	2012-16		1959	1949-58

Sujet	Année de l'édition	Période considérée	Sujet	Année de l'édition	Période considérée
	1960	1950-59		2006	2002-06
	1961	1945-59 vi		2007	2003-07
		1952-61		2008	2004-08
	1962	1945-54 vi		2009-2010	2006-10
		1952-62		2011	2007-11
	1963	1945-59 vi		2012	2008-12
		1954-63		2013	2009-13
	1964	1960-64		2014	2010-14
	1965	1961-65		2015	2011-15
	1966	1920-64 vi		2016	2012-16
		1951-66		2017	2013-17
	1967	1963-67			
	1968	1964-68	**Décès, taux de**		*voir: Mortalités infantile*
	1969	1965-69	d'enfants de moins		
	1970	1966-70	d'un an		
	1971	1967-71			
	1972	1968-72	**Décès, taux de**	1949-50	1947
	1973	1969-73	estimatifs, pour les	1956-1977	Dernière
	1974	1965-74	continents	1978-1979	1970-75
	1975	1971-75		1980-1983	1975-80
	1976	1972-76		1984-1986	1980-85
	1977	1973-77		1987-1992	1985-90
	1978	1974-78		1993-1997	1990-95
	1978SR i	1948-78		1998-2000	1995-00
	1979	1975-79		2001-2005	2000-05
	1980	1971-80		2006-2010	2005-10
	1981	1977-81		2011-2015	2010-15
	1982	1978-82		2016	2015-20
	1983	1979-83		2017	2015-20
	1984	1980-84			
	1985	1976-85	**Décès, taux de**	1964-1977	Dernière
	1986	1982-86	estimatifs, pour les	1978-1979	1970-75
	1987	1983-87	grandes régions	1980-1983	1975-80
	1988	1984-88	(continentales)	1984-1986	1980-85
	1989	1985-89		1987-1992	1985-90
	1990	1986-90		1993-1997	1990-95
	1991	1987-91		1998-2000	1995-00
	1992	1983-92		2001-2005	2000-05
	1993	1989-93		2006-2010	2005-10
	1994	1990-94		2011-2015	2010-15
	1995	1991-95		2016	2015-20
	1996	1987-96		2017	2015-20
	1997	1993-97			
	1997SR ii	1948-97	**Décès, taux de**	1949-50	1947
	1998	1994-98	estimatifs, pour les	1956-1977	Dernière
	1999	1995-99	régions	1978-1979	1970-75
	2000	1996-00		1980-1983	1975-80
	2001	1997-01		1984-1986	1980-85
	2002	1998-02		1987-1992	1985-90
	2003	1999-03		1993-1997	1990-95
	2004	2000-04		1998-2000	1995-00
	2005	2001-05		2001-2005	2000-05
				2006-2010	2005-10

Index historique
(Voir notes à la fin de l'index)

Sujet	Année de l'édition	Période considérée	Sujet	Année de l'édition	Période considérée
	2011-2015	2010-15		1985	1976-84
	2016	2015-20		1986-1991	Dernière
	2017	2015-20		1991 VP [v]	1950-90
				1992	1983-92
Décès, taux de	1949-50	1947		1993-1995	Dernière
estimatifs, pour	1956-1977	Dernière		1996	1987-95
l'ensemble du monde	1978-1979	1970-75		1997	Dernière
	1980-1983	1975-80		1997SR [ii]	1948-96
	1984-1986	1980-85		1998-2006	Dernière
	1987-1992	1985-90			
	1993-1997	1990-95	**Décès, taux de**	1951	1947-49
	1998-2000	1995-00	selon la cause	1952	1947-51
	2001-2005	2000-05		1953	1947-52
	2006-2010	2005-10		1954	1945-53
	2011-2015	2010-15		1955-1956	Dernière
	2016	2015-20		1957	1952-56
	2017	2015-20		1958-1960	Dernière
				1961	1955-60
				1962-1965	Dernière
Décès, taux de	1948	1935-47		1966	1960-65
selon l'âge et le sexe	1949-50	1936-49		1967-1973	Dernière
	1951	1936-50		1974	1965-73
	1952	1936-51		1975-1979	Dernière
	1953	1940-52		1980	1971-79 [vi]
	1954	1946-53		1981-1984	Dernière
	1955-1956	Dernière		1985	1976-84
	1957	1948-56		1986-1995	Dernière
	1961	1952-60		1996	1987-95
	1966	1950-65		1997-2000	Dernière
	1967	Dernière		2002	1985-02
	1972	Dernière		2004	1995-04
	1974	1965-73		2006	2002-06
	1975-1978	Dernière		2008	2004-08
	1978SR [i]	1948-77		2011	2006-10
	1979	Dernière		2013	2008-12
	1980	1971-79		2015	2010-14
	1981-1984	Dernière		2017	2012-16
	1985	1976-84			
	1986-1991	Dernière	**Décès, taux de**	1957	Dernière
	1991 VP [v]	1950-90	selon la cause, l'âge et	1961	Dernière
	1992	1983-92	le sexe	1991 VP [v]	1960-90
	1993-1995	Dernière			
	1996	1987-95	**Décès, taux de**	1967	Dernière
	1997	Dernière	selon la cause et le	1974	Dernière
	1997SR [ii]	1948-96	sexe		
	1998-2017	Dernière		1980	Dernière
				1985	Dernière
Décès, taux de	1967	Dernière		1991 VP [v]	1960-90
selon l'âge et le sexe et	1972	Dernière		1996	Dernière
la résidence	1974	1965-73		2006	2002-06
(urbaine/rurale)	1975-1978	Dernière		2008	2004-08
	1979	Dernière		2011	2006-10
	1980	1971-79		2013	2008-12
	1981-1984	Dernière			

Index historique
(Voir notes à la fin de l'index)

Sujet	Année de l'édition	Période considérée	Sujet	Année de l'édition	Période considérée
	2015	2010-14		2000	1996-00
	2017	2012-16		2001	1997-01
				2002	1998-02
Décès, taux de..................	1961	Dernière		2003	1999-03
selon l'état	1967	Dernière		2004	2000-04
matrimonial, l'âge et le	1974	Dernière		2005	2001-05
sexe				2006	2002-06
	1980	Dernière		2007	2003-07
	1985	Dernière		2008	2004-08
	1996	Dernière		2009-2010	2006-10
	2003	Dernière		2011	2007-11
				2012	2008-12
Décès, taux de..................	1957	Dernière		2013	2009-13
selon la profession,				2014	2010-14
l'âge et le sexe				2015	2011-15
				2016	2012-16
Décès, taux de..................	1961	Dernière		2017	2013-17
selon la profession et	1967	Dernière			
l'âge (sexe masculin)			**Densité de population**	1949-50	1920-49
			des continents	1951-1999	Dernière
Décès, taux de..................	1967	Dernière		2001	2001
selon la résidence	1968	1964-68		2002	2002
(urbaine/rurale)	1969	1965-69		2003	2003
	1970	1966-70		2004	2004
	1971	1967-71		2005	2005
	1972	1968-72		2006	2006
	1973	1969-73		2007	2007
	1974	1965-74		2008	2008
	1975	1971-75		2009-2010	2010
	1976	1972-76		2011	2011
	1977	1973-77		2012	2012
	1978	1974-78		2013	2013
	1979	1975-79		2014	2014
	1980	1971-80		2015	2015
	1981	1977-81		2016	2016
	1982	1978-82		2017	2017
	1983	1979-83			
	1984	1980-84	**Densité de population**	1964-1999	Dernière
	1985	1976-85	des grandes régions	2000	2000
	1986	1982-86	(continentales)	2001	2001
	1987	1983-87		2002	2002
	1988	1984-88		2003	2003
	1989	1985-89		2004	2004
	1990	1986-90		2005	2005
	1991	1987-91		2006	2006
	1992	1983-92		2007	2007
	1993	1989-93		2008	2008
	1994	1990-94		2009-2010	2010
	1995	1991-95		2011	2011
	1996	1987-96		2012	2012
	1997	1993-97		2013	2013
	1998	1994-98		2014	2014
	1999	1995-99		2015	2015

Sujet	Année de l'édition	Période considérée	Sujet	Année de l'édition	Période considérée
	1976	1957-76		2013	2009-13
	1977	1973-77		2014	2010-14
	1962	1953-62		2015	2011-15
	1963	1954-63		2016	2012-16
	1964	1960-64		2017	2013-17
	1965	1961-65			
	1966	1962-66	**Divorces**	1968	1958-67
	1967	1963-67	selon l'âge de l'épouse	1976	1966-75
	1968	1949-68		1982	1972-81
	1969	1965-69		1987	1975-86
	1970	1966-70		1990	1980-89
	1971	1967-71			
	1972	1968-72	**Divorces**	1958	1946-57
	1973	1969-73	selon l'âge de l'épouse,	1968	Dernière
	1974	1970-74	classés par âge de	1976	Dernière
	1975	1971-75	l'époux	1982	Dernière
	1976	1957-76		1990	Dernière
	1977	1973-77			
	1978	1974-78	**Divorces**	1968	1958-67
	1979	1975-79	selon l'âge de l'époux	1976	1966-75
	1980	1976-80		1982	1972-81
	1981	1977-81		1987	1975-86
	1982	1963-82		1990	1980-89
	1983	1979-83			
	1984	1980-84	**Divorces**	1958	1948-57
	1985	1981-85	selon la durée du	1968	1958-67
	1986	1982-86	mariage	1976	1966-75
	1987	1983-87		1982	1972-81
	1988	1984-88		1990	1980-89
	1989	1985-89		2007	Dernière
	1990	1971-90		2009-2010	Dernière
	1991	1987-91		2012	Dernière
	1992	1988-92		2014	Dernière
	1993	1989-93		2016	Dernière
	1994	1990-94			
	1995	1991-95	**Divorces**	1958	1946-57
	1996	1992-96	selon la durée du	1968	Dernière
	1997	1993-97	mariage, classés selon	1976	Dernière
	1998	1994-98	l'âge de l'épouse et	1982	Dernière
	1999	1995-99	selon l'âge de l'époux	1990	Dernière
	2000	1996-00			
	2001	1997-01	**Divorces**	1958	1948-57
	2002	1998-02	selon le nombre	1968	1958-67
	2003	1999-03	d'enfants	1976	1966-75
	2004	2000-04		1982	1972-81
	2005	2001-05		2007	Dernière
	2006	2002-06			
	2007	2003-07	**Divorces**	2002	1998-02
	2008	2004-08	selon la résidence	2003	1999-03
	2009-2010	2006-10	(urbaine/rurale)	2004	2000-04
	2011	2007-11		2005	2001-05
	2012	2008-12		2006	2002-06
				2007	2003-07

Index historique
(Voir notes à la fin de l'index)

Sujet	Année de l'édition	Période considérée
	1976	1957-76
	1977	1973-77
	1978	1974-78
	1979	1975-79
	1980	1976-80
	1981	1977-81
	1982	1963-82
	1983	1979-83
	1984	1980-84
	1985	1981-85
	1986	1982-86
	1987	1983-87
	1988	1984-88
	1989	1985-89
	1990	1971-90
	1991	1987-91
	1992	1988-92
	1993	1989-93
	1994	1990-94
	1995	1991-95
	1996	1992-96
	1997	1993-97
	1998	1994-98
	1999	1995-99
	2000	1996-00
	2001	1997-01
	2002	1998-02
	2003	1999-03
	2004	2000-04
	2005	2001-05
	2006	2002-06
	2007	2003-07
	2008	2004-08
	2009-2010	2006-10
	2011	2007-11
	2012	2008-12
	2013	2009-13
	2014	2010-14
	2015	2011-15
	2016	2012-16
	2017	2013-17
Mariages selon l'âge de l'épouse	1948	1936-47
	1949-50	1936-49
	1958	1948-57
	1959-1967	Dernière
	1968	1958-67
	1969-1975	Dernière
	1976	1966-75
	1977-1981	Dernière
	1982	1972-81
	1983-1986	Dernière
	1987	1975-86
	1988-1989	Dernière
	1990	1980-89
	1991-1997	Dernière
	1998	1993-97
	1999	1994-98
	2000	1995-99
	2001	1997-01
	2002	1998-02
	2003	1999-03
	2004	2000-04
	2005	2001-05
	2006-2017	Dernière
Mariages selon l'âge de l'épouse et l'âge de l'époux	1958	1948-57
	1968	Dernière
	1976	Dernière
	1982	Dernière
	1990	Dernière
	2006-2017	Dernière
Mariages selon l'âge de l'épouse et l'état matrimonial antérieur	1958	1948-57
	1968	Dernière
	1976	Dernière
	1982	Dernière
	1990	Dernière
Mariages selon l'âge de l'époux	1948	1936-47
	1949-50	1936-49
	1958	1948-57
	1959-1967	Dernière
	1968	1958-67
	1969-1975	Dernière
	1976	1966-75
	1977-1981	Dernière
	1982	1972-81
	1983-1986	Dernière
	1987	1975-86
	1988-1989	Dernière
	1990	1980-89
	1991-1997	Dernière
	1998	1993-97
	1999	1994-98
	2000	1995-99
	2001	1997-01
	2002	1998-02
	2003	1999-03
	2004	2000-04
	2005	2001-05
	2006-2017	Dernière
Mariages	1958	1948-57
	1968	Dernière

Sujet	Année de l'édition	Période considérée	Sujet	Année de l'édition	Période considérée
	1976	1969-75	**Mortalité fœtale tardive, rapports de**	1951	1935-50
	1977	1967-76		1952	1935-51
	1985	1975-84		1953	1936-52
	1989	1979-88		1954	1938-53
	1996	1986-95		1955	1946-54
				1956	1947-55
Migration internationale	1949-50	1945-49		1957	1948-56
sorties par catégories	1951	1946-50		1958	1948-57
principales	1952	1947-51		1959	1920-54 [vi]
	1954	1948-53			1953-58
	1957	1951-56		1960	1950-59
	1959	1953-58		1961	1945-49 [vi]
	1962	1956-61			1952-60
	1966	1960-65		1962	1945-54 [vi]
	1968	1966-67			1952-61
	1977	1967-76		1963	1945-59 [vi]
	1985	1975-84			1953-62
	1989	1979-88		1964	1959-63
	1996	1986-95		1965	1950-64 [vi]
					1955-64
Mortalité	voir: Décès; Décès, taux de;			1966	1950-64 [vi]
	Enfants de moins d'un an,				1956-65
	décès d'; Mortalité fœtale,			1967	1962-66
	rapports de; Mortalité			1968	1963-67
	infantile, taux de; Mortalité			1969	1950-64 [vi]
	maternelle, taux de; Mortalité			1969	1959-68
	néonatale, taux de; Mortalité			1970	1965-69
	périnatale; Mortalité post-			1971	1966-70
	néonatale, taux de; Mortalité,			1972	1967-71
	tables de; Mortalité, taux de			1973	1968-72
	Morts fœtales; Morts			1974	1965-73
	néonatales; Morts post-			1975	1966-74
	néonatales			1976	1971-75
				1977	1972-76
Mortalité fœtale	voir: Morts fœtales			1978	1973-77
				1979	1974-78
Mortalité fœtale, rapports de	1957	1950-56		1980	1971-79
selon la période de	1959	1949-58		1981	1972-80
gestation	1961	1952-60		1982	1977-81
	1965	5-Dernières		1983	1978-82
	1966	1956-65		1984	1979-83
	1967-1968	Dernière		1985	1975-84
	1969	1963-68		1986	1977-85
	1974	1965-73		1987	1982-86
	1975	1966-74		1988	1983-87
	1980	1971-79		1989	1984-88
	1981	1972-80		1964	1959-63
	1985	1976-84		1990	1985-89
	1986	1977-85		1991	1986-90
	1996	1987-95		1992	1987-91
	1999CD [vii]	1990-98		1993	1988-92
				1994	1989-93
Mortalité fœtale tardive	voir: Morts fœtales tardive				

Sujet	Année de l'édition	Période considérée	Sujet	Année de l'édition	Période considérée
	1996	1987-95		1978	1974-78
	1997	1992-96		1978SR [i]	1948-78
	1998	1993-97		1979	1975-79
	1999	1994-98		1980	1971-80
	1999CD [vii]	1990-98		1981	1977-81
	2000	1995-99		1982	1978-82
	2001	1997-01		1983	1979-83
	2002	1998-02		1984	1980-84
	2003	1999-03		1985	1976-85
	2004	2000-04		1986	1982-86
	2005	2001-05		1987	1983-87
	2006	2002-06		1988	1984-88
	2007	2003-07		1989	1985-89
	2008	2004-08		1990	1986-90
	2009-2010	2006-10		1991	1987-91
	2011	2007-11		1992	1983-92
	2012	2008-12		1993	1989-93
	2013	2009-13		1994	1990-94
	2014	2010-14		1995	1991-95
	2015	2011-15		1996	1987-96
	2016	2012-16		1997	1993-97
	2017	2013-17		1997SR [ii]	1948-97
				1998	1994-98
Mortalité infantile				1999	1995-99
(nombres)	1948	1932-47		2000	1996-00
	1949-50	1934-49		2001	1997-01
	1951	1935-50		2002	1998-02
	1952	1936-51		2003	1999-03
	1953	1950-52		2004	2000-04
	1954	1946-53		2005	2001-05
	1955	1946-54		2006	2002-06
	1956	1947-55		2007	2003-07
	1957	1948-56		2008	2004-08
	1958	1948-57		2009-2010	2006-10
	1959	1949-58		2011	2007-11
	1960	1950-59		2012	2008-12
	1961	1952-61		2013	2009-13
	1962	1953-62		2014	2010-14
	1963	1954-63		2015	2011-15
	1964	1960-64		2016	2012-16
	1965	1961-65		2017	2013-17
	1966	1947-66			
	1967	1963-67	**Mortalité infantile**		
	1968	1964-68	**(nombres)**	1948	1936-47
	1969	1965-69	selon l'âge et le sexe	1951	1936-49
	1970	1966-70		1957	1948-56
	1971	1967-71		1961	1952-60
	1972	1968-72		1962-1965	Dernière
	1973	1969-73		1966	1956-65
	1974	1965-74		1967-1973	Dernière
	1975	1971-75		1974	1965-73
	1976	1972-76		1975-1979	Dernière
	1977	1973-77		1980	1971-79

Sujet	Année de l'édition	Période considérée	Sujet	Année de l'édition	Période considérée
	1981-1984	Dernière		1996	1987-96
	1985	1976-84		1997	1993-97
	1986-1991	Dernière		1998	1994-98
	1992	1983-92		1999	1995-99
	1993-1995	Dernière		2000	1996-00
	1996	1987-95		2001	1997-01
	1997-2004	Dernière		2002	1998-02
	2005	1996-05		2003	1999-03
	2006-2017	Dernière		2004	2000-04
				2005	2001-05
Mortalité infantile				2006	2002-06
(nombres)	1968-1973	Dernière		2007	2003-07
selon l'âge et le sexe et	1974	1965-73		2008	2004-08
la résidence	1975-1979	Dernière		2009-2010	2006-10
(urbaine/rurale)	1980	1971-79		2011	2007-11
	1981-1984	Dernière		2012	2008-12
	1985	1976-84		2013	2009-13
	1986-1991	Dernière		2014	2010-14
	1992	1983-92		2015	2011-15
	1993-1995	Dernière		2016	2012-16
	1996	1987-95		2017	2013-17
	1997-1999	Dernière			
			Mortalité infantile		
			(nombres)	1967	1962-66
Mortalité infantile			selon le mois	1974	1965-73
(nombres)	1967	Dernière		1980	1971-79
selon la résidence	1968	1964-68		1985	1976-84
(urbaine/rurale)	1969	1965-69			
	1970	1966-70	**Mortalité infantile, taux de**	1948	1932-47
	1971	1967-71		1949-50	1932-49
	1972	1968-72		1951	1930-50
	1973	1969-73		1952	1920-34 [vi]
	1974	1965-74			1934-51
	1975	1971-75		1953	1920-39 [vi]
	1976	1972-76			1940-52
	1977	1973-77		1954	1920-39 [vi]
	1978	1974-78			1946-53
	1979	1975-79		1955	1920-34 [vi]
	1980	1971-80			1946-54
	1981	1977-81		1956	1947-55
	1982	1978-82		1957	1948-56
	1983	1979-83		1958	1948-57
	1984	1980-84		1959	1949-58
	1985	1976-85		1960	1950-59
	1986	1982-86		1961	1945-59 [vi]
	1987	1983-87			1952-61
	1988	1984-88		1962	1945-59 [vi]
	1989	1985-89			1952-62
	1990	1986-90		1963	1945-59 [vi]
	1991	1987-91			1954-63
	1992	1983-92		1964	1960-64
	1993	1989-93		1965	1961-65
	1994	1990-94		1966	1920-64 [vi]
	1995	1991-95			

Sujet	Année de l'édition	Période considérée	Sujet	Année de l'édition	Période considérée
		1951-66	**Mortalité infantile, taux de**	1948	1936-47
	1967	1963-67	selon l'âge et le sexe	1951	1936-49
	1968	1964-68		1957	1948-56
	1969	1965-69		1961	1952-60
	1970	1966-70		1966	1956-65
	1971	1967-71		1967	1962-66
	1972	1968-72		1971-1973	Dernière
	1973	1969-73		1974	1965-73
	1974	1965-74		1975-1979	Dernière
	1975	1971-75		1980	1971-79
	1976	1972-76		1981-1984	Dernière
	1977	1973-77		1985	1976-84
	1978	1974-78		1986-1991	Dernière
	1978SR [i]	1948-78		1992	1983-92
	1979	1975-79		1993-1995	Dernière
	1980	1971-80		1996	1987-95
	1981	1977-81		1997-2017	Dernière
	1982	1978-82			
	1983	1979-83	**Mortalité infantile, taux de**	1971-1973	Dernière
	1984	1980-84	selon l'âge et le sexe et	1974	1965-73
	1985	1976-85	la résidence	1975-1979	Dernière
	1986	1982-86	(urbaine/rurale)	1980	1971-79
	1987	1983-87		1981-1984	Dernière
	1988	1984-88		1985	1976-84
	1989	1985-89		1986-1991	Dernière
	1990	1986-90		1992	1983-92
	1991	1987-91		1993-1995	Dernière
	1992	1983-92		1996	1987-95
	1993	1989-93		1997-1999	Dernière
	1994	1990-94			
	1995	1991-95	**Mortalité infantile, taux de**	1967	Dernière
	1996	1987-96	selon la résidence	1968	1964-68
	1997	1993-97	(urbaine/rurale)	1969	1965-69
	1997SR [ii]	1948-97		1970	1966-70
	1998	1994-98		1971	1967-71
	1999	1995-99		1972	1968-72
	2000	1996-00		1973	1969-73
	2001	1997-01		1974	1965-74
	2002	1998-02		1975	1971-75
	2003	1999-03		1976	1972-76
	2004	2000-04		1977	1973-77
	2005	2001-05		1978	1974-78
	2006	2002-06		1979	1975-79
	2007	2003-07		1980	1971-80
	2008	2004-08		1981	1977-81
	2009-2010	2006-10		1982	1978-82
	2011	2007-11		1983	1979-83
	2012	2008-12		1984	1980-84
	2013	2009-13		1985	1976-85
	2014	2010-14		1986	1982-86
	2015	2011-15		1987	1983-87
	2016	2012-16		1988	1984-88
	2017	2013-17			

Index historique
(Voir notes à la fin de l'index)

Sujet	Année de l'édition	Période considérée	Sujet	Année de l'édition	Période considérée
	1968	1963-67		1969	1963-68
	1969	1959-68		1975	1966-74
	1970	1965-69		1981	1972-80
	1971	1966-70		1986	1977-85
	1972	1967-71			
	1973	1968-72	Morts fœtales tardives	1961	1952-60
	1974	1965-73	illégitimes, en	1965	5-Dernières
	1975	1966-74	pourcentage	1969	1963-68
	1976	1971-75		1975	1966-74
	1977	1972-76		1981	1972-80
	1978	1973-77		1986	1977-85
	1979	1974-78			
	1980	1971-79	Morts fœtales tardives	1959	1949-58
	1981	1972-80	légitimes	1965	1955-64
	1982	1977-81		1969	1963-68
	1983	1978-82		1975	1966-74
	1984	1979-83		1981	1972-80
	1985	1975-84		1986	1977-85
	1986	1977-85			
	1987	1982-86	Morts fœtales tardives	1959	1949-58
	1988	1983-87	légitimes selon l'âge de	1965	1955-64
	1989	1984-88	la mère	1969	1963-68
	1990	1985-89		1975	1966-74
	1991	1986-90		1981	1972-80
	1992	1987-91		1986	1977-85
	1993	1988-92			
	1994	1989-93	Morts fœtales tardives	1954	1936-53
	1995	1990-94	selon l'âge de la mère	1959	1949-58
	1996	1987-95		1965	1955-64
	1997	1992-96		1969	1963-68
	1998	1993-97		1975	1966-74
	1999	1994-98		1981	1972-80
	1999CD [vii]	1990-98		1986	1977-85
	2000	1995-99		1999CD [vii]	1990-98
	2001	1997-01			
	2002	1998-02	Morts fœtales tardives	1954	Dernière
	2003	1999-03	selon l'âge de la mère	1959	1949-58
	2004	2000-04	et le rang de naissance	1965	3-Dernières
	2005	2001-05		1969	1963-68
	2006	2002-06		1975	1966-74
	2007	2003-07		1981	1972-80
	2008	2004-08		1986	1977-85
	2009-2010	2006-10		1999CD [vii]	1990-98
	2011	2007-11			
	2012	2008-12	Morts fœtales tardives	1957	1950-56
	2013	2009-13	selon la période de	1959	1949-58
	2014	2010-14	gestation	1961	1952-60
	2015	2011-15		1965	5-Dernières
	2016	2012-16		1966	1956-65
	2017	2013-17		1967-1968	Dernière
				1969	1963-68
Morts fœtales tardives	1961	1952-60		1974	1965-73
illégitimes	1965	5-Dernières		1975	1966-74

Sujet	Année de l'édition	Période considérée
	1980	1971-79
	1981	1972-80
	1985	1976-84
	1986	1977-85
	1996	1987-95
Morts fœtales tardives	1971	1966-70
selon la résidence	1972	1967-71
(urbaine/rurale)	1973	1968-72
	1974	1965-73
	1975	1966-74
	1976	1971-75
	1977	1972-76
	1978	1973-77
	1979	1974-78
	1980	1971-79
	1981	1972-80
	1982	1977-81
	1983	1978-82
	1984	1979-83
	1985	1975-84
	1986	1977-85
	1987	1982-86
	1988	1983-87
	1989	1984-88
	1990	1985-89
	1991	1986-90
	1992	1987-91
	1993	1988-92
	1994	1989-93
	1995	1990-94
	1996	1987-95
	1997	1992-96
	1998	1993-97
	1999	1994-98
	1999CD [vii]	1990-98
	2000	1995-99
	2001	1997-01
	2002	1998-02
	2003	1999-03
	2004	2000-04
	2005	2001-05
	2006	2002-06
	2007	2003-07
	2008	2004-08
	2009-2010	2006-10
	2011	2007-11
	2012	2008-12
	2013	2009-13
	2014	2010-14
	2015	2011-15
	2016	2012-16
	2017	2013-17

Sujet	Année de l'édition	Période considérée
Morts fœtales tardives	1961	1952-60
selon le sexe	1965	5-Dernières
	1969	1963-68
	1975	1966-74
	1981	1972-80
	1986	1977-85
Mortinatalité, rapports de..	*voir: Mortalité fœtale tardive*	
Morts néonatales, selon le sexe	*voir: Mortalité post-néonatale*	
Morts post-néonatales, selon le sexe	*voir: Mortalité post-néonatale*	

N

Sujet	Année de l'édition	Période considérée
Naissances	1948	1932-47
	1949-50	1934-49
	1951	1935-50
	1952	1936-51
	1953	1950-52
	1954	1938-53
	1955	1946-54
	1956	1947-55
	1957	1948-56
	1958	1948-57
	1959	1949-58
	1960	1950-59
	1961	1952-61
	1962	1953-62
	1963	1954-63
	1964	1960-64
	1965	1946-65
	1966	1957-66
	1967	1963-67
	1968	1964-68
	1969	1950-69
	1970	1966-70
	1971	1967-71
	1972	1968-72
	1973	1969-73
	1974	1970-74
	1975	1956-75
	1976	1972-76
	1977	1973-77
	1978	1974-78
	1978SR [i]	1948-78
	1979	1975-79
	1980	1976-80
	1981	1962-81
	1982	1978-82

Index historique
(Voir notes à la fin de l'index)

Sujet	Année de l'édition	Période considérée	Sujet	Année de l'édition	Période considérée
	1998-1999	Dernière	Naissances....................	*voir: légitimes selon la durée du mariage*	
	1999CD [vii]	1990-98			
	2000-2017	Dernière	selon la durée du mariage		
Naissances....................	1949-50	1936-47	**Naissances**....................	2002	1980-02
selon l'âge de la mère et le rang de naissance	1954	Dernière	selon le mois		
	1959	1949-58			
	1965	1955-64	**Naissances**....................	1965	Dernière
	1969	1963-68	selon la profession du père	1969	Dernière
	1975	1966-74			
	1981	1972-80			
	1986	1977-85	**Naissances**....................	1965	Dernière
	1999CD [vii]	1990-98	selon la résidence (urbaine/rurale)	1967	Dernière
				1968	1964-68
Naissances....................	*voir: selon la résidence (urbaine/rurale), ci-dessous*			1969	1964-68
selon l'âge de la mère et la résidence (urbaine/rurale)				1970	1966-70
				1971	1967-71
				1972	1968-72
				1973	1969-73
Naissances....................	1965-1968	Dernière		1974	1970-74
selon l'âge de la mère et le sexe	1969	1963-68		1975	1956-75
	1970-1974	Dernière		1976	1972-76
	1975	1966-74		1977	1973-77
	1976-1978	Dernière		1978	1974-78
	1978SR [i]	1948-77		1979	1975-79
	1979-1980	Dernière		1980	1976-80
	1981	1972-80		1981	1962-81
	1982-1985	Dernière		1982	1978-82
	1986	1977-85		1983	1979-83
	1987-1991	Dernière		1984	1980-84
	1992	1983-92		1985	1981-85
	1993-1997	Dernière		1986	1967-86
	1997SR [ii]	1948-96		1987	1983-87
	1998-1999	Dernière		1988	1984-88
	1999CD [vii]	1990-98		1989	1985-89
	2000-2017	Dernière		1990	1986-90
				1991	1987-91
				1992	1983-92
Naissances....................	1949-50	1942-49		1993	1989-93
selon l'âge du père	1954	1936-53		1994	1990-94
	1959	1949-58		1995	1991-95
	1965	1955-64		1996	1992-96
	1969	1963-68		1997	1993-97
	1975	1966-74		1998	1994-98
	1981	1972-80		1999	1995-99
	1986	1977-85		1999CD [vii]	1980-99
	1999CD [vii]	1990-98		2000	1996-00
	2007-2017	Dernière		2001	1997-01
				2002	1998-02
Naissances....................	1975	Dernière		2003	1999-03
selon la durée de gestation	1981	1972-80		2004	2000-04
	1986	1977-85		2005	2001-05
	1999CD [vii]	1990-98		2006	2002-06

Sujet	Année de l'édition	Période considérée	Sujet	Année de l'édition	Période considérée
				2004	2000-04
Natalité, taux de	1951	1936-49		2005	2001-05
selon le rang de	1952	1936-50		2006	2002-06
naissance	1953	1936-52		2007	2003-07
	1954	1936-53		2008	2004-08
	1955	Dernière		2009-2010	2006-10
	1959	1949-58		2011	2007-11
	1965	1955-64		2012	2008-12
	1969	1963-68		2013	2009-13
	1975	1966-74		2014	2010-14
	1981	1972-80		2015	2011-15
	1986	1977-85		2016	2012-16
	1999CD [vii]	1990-98		2017	2013-17
Natalité, taux de	1965	Dernière	**Natalité, taux de**	1965	Dernière
selon la résidence	1967	Dernière	selon la résidence	1969	Dernière
(urbaine/rurale)	1968	1964-68	(urbaine/rurale) et l'âge	1975	1966-74
	1969	1964-68	de la mère	1976-1980	Dernière
	1970	1966-70		1981	1972-80
	1971	1967-71		1982-1985	Dernière
	1972	1968-72		1986	1977-85
	1973	1969-73		1987-1991	Dernière
	1974	1970-74		1992	1983-92
	1975	1956-75		1993-1997	Dernière
	1976	1972-76		1997SR [ii]	1948-96
	1977	1973-77		1998-1999	Dernière
	1978	1974-78		1999CD [vii]	1990-98
	1979	1975-79		2000-2006	Dernière
	1980	1976-80			
	1981	1962-81	**Nationalité**		*voir: Population*
	1982	1978-82			
	1983	1979-83	**Nuptialité**		*voir: Mariages*
	1984	1980-84			
	1985	1981-85	**Nuptialité, taux de**	1948	1932-47
	1986	1967-86		1949-50	1932-49
	1987	1983-87		1951	1930-50
	1988	1984-88		1952	1920-34 [vi]
	1989	1985-89			1934-51
	1990	1986-90		1953	1920-39 [vi]
	1991	1987-91			1940-52
	1992	1983-92		1954	1920-39 [vi]
	1993	1989-93			1946-53
	1994	1990-94		1955	1920-34 [vi]
	1995	1991-95			1946-54
	1996	1992-96		1956	1947-55
	1997	1993-97		1957	1948-56
	1998	1994-98		1958	1930-57
	1999	1995-99		1959	1949-58
	1999CD [vii]	1985-99		1960	1950-59
	2000	1996-00		1961	1952-61
	2001	1997-01		1962	1953-62
	2002	1998-02		1963	1954-63
	2003	1999-03		1964	1960-64

Index historique
(Voir notes à la fin de l'index)

Sujet	Année de l'édition	Période considérée	Sujet	Année de l'édition	Période considérée
	2008	2005-08		2006-2010	2005-10
	2009-2010	2005-10		2011-2015	2010-15
	2011	2005-11		2016	2015-20
	2012	2005-12		2017	2015-20
	2013	2010-13			
	2014	2010-14	**Population**	1956	1945-55
	2015	2010-15	active:	1967	1955-64
	2016	2010-16	-féminin, selon l'état	1968	Dernière
	2017	2010-17	matrimonial et l'âge	1972	1962-77
Population	1957	1950-56	-féminin, selon l'état	1973	1965-73
accroissement, taux d'	1958	1950-57	matrimonial et l'âge	1979	1970-79
(annuels moyens pour	1959	1950-58	et la résidence	1984	1974-84
le monde, les grandes	1960	1950-59	(urbaine/rurale)	1988	1980-88 [iii]
régions (continentes) et	1961	1950-60			
les régions	1962	1950-61	-née à l'étranger	1984	1974-84
géographiques)	1963	1958-62	selon la profession,	1989	1980-88
		1960-62	l'âge et le sexe		
	1964	1958-63			
		1960-63	-née à l'étranger	1977	Dernière
	1965	1958-64	selon la profession,		
		1960-64	l'âge et le sexe		
	1966	1958-66			
		1960-66	-selon l'âge et le	1955	1945-54
	1967	1960-67	sexe		
		1963-67		1956	1945-55
	1968	1960-68		1964	1955-64
		1963-68		1972	1962-72
	1969	1960-69			
		1963-69	-selon l'âge et le	1973	1965-73 [iii]
	1970	1963-70	sexe et la résidence	1979	1970-79 [iii]
		1965-70	(urbaine/rurale)	1984	1974-84
	1971	1963-71		1988	1980-88 [iii]
		1965-71		1994	1985-94
	1972	1963-72			
		1965-72	-selon l'âge et le	1948	Dernière
	1973	1965-73	sexe en	1949-50	1930-48
		1970-73	pourcentage		
	1974	1965-74		1955	1945-54
		1970-74		1956	1945-55
	1975	1965-75		1964	1955-64
		1970-75		1972	1962-72
	1976	1965-76			
		1970-76	-selon l'âge et le	1973	1965-73 [iii]
	1977	1965-77	sexe en	1979	1970-79 [iii]
		1970-77	pourcentage et la	1984	1974-84
	1978-1979	1970-75	résidence (urbaine/	1988	1980-88 [iii]
	1980-1983	1975-80	rurale)		
	1984-1986	1980-85		1994	1985-94
	1987-1992	1985-90			
	1993-1997	1990-95	-selon la branche	1956	1945-55
	1998-2000	1995-00	d'activité	1964	1955-64
	2001-2005	2000-05	économique, le	1972	1962-72
			sexe, et l'âge		

Sujet	Année de l'édition	Période considérée	Sujet	Année de l'édition	Période considérée
-selon la branche d'activité économique, le sexe, et l'âge et la résidence (urbaine/rurale)	1973 1979 1984 1988	1965-73 [iii] 1970-79 [iii] 1974-84 1980-88 [iii]	-selon la situation dans la profession, la branche d'activité économique et le sexe	1948 1949-50 1955 1964 1972	Dernière Dernière 1945-54 1955-64 1962-72
-selon la branche d'activité économique la situation dans la profession et le sexe	1948 1949-50 1955 1964 1972	Dernière Dernière 1945-54 1955-64 1962-72	-selon la situation dans la profession, la branche d'activité économique et le sexe et la résidence (urbaine/rurale)	1973 1979 1984 1988 1994	1965-73 [iii] 1970-79 [iii] 1974-84 1980-88 [iii] 1985-94
-selon la branche d'activité économique la situation dans la profession et le sexe et la résidence (urbaine/rurale)	1973 1979 1984 1988 1994	1965-73 [iii] 1970-79 1974-84 1980-88 [iii] 1985-94	-selon la situation dans la profession et le sexe et l'âge	1956 1964 1972	1945-55 1955-64 1962-72
-selon l'état matrimonial et l'âge (sexe féminin)	1956 1964 1968 1972	1945-55 1955-64 Dernière 1962-72	-selon la situation dans la profession et le sexe et l'âge et la résidence (urbaine/rurale)	1973 1979 1984 1988 1994	1965-73 [iii] 1970-79 [iii] 1974-84 1980-88 [iii] 1985-94
-selon l'état matrimonial et l'âge (sexe féminin) et la résidence (urbaine/rurale)	1973 1979 1984 1988 1994	1965-73 [iii] 1970-79 [iii] 1974-84 1980-88 [iii] 1985-94	-selon la situation dans la profession, la profession et le sexe	1956 1964 1972	1945-55 1955-64 1962-72
-selon la profession, la l'âge et le sexe	1956 1964 1972	1945-55 1955-64 1962-72			
-selon la profession, l'âge et le sexe et la résidence (urbaine/rurale)	1973 1979 1984 1988	1965-73 [iii] 1970-79 [iii] 1974-84 1980-88 [iii]	-selon la situation dans la profession, la profession et le sexe et la résidence (urbaine/rurale)	1973 1979 1984 1988 1994	1965-73 [iii] 1970-79 [iii] 1974-84 1980-88 [iii] 1985-94
-selon la profession, la situation dans la profession et le sexe	1956 1964 1972	1945-55 1955-64 1962-72	-selon le sexe	1948 1949-50 1955 1956 1960 1963 1964 1970 1972 1973 1979 1984 1988 1994	Dernière 1926-48 1945-54 1945-55 1920-60 1955-63 1955-64 1950-70 1962-72 1965-73 [iii] 1970-79 [iii] 1974-84 1980-88 [iii] 1985-94
-selon la profession, la situation dans la profession et le sexe et la résidence (urbaine/rurale)	1973 1979 1984 1988 1994	1965-73 [iii] 1970-79 [iii] 1974-84 1980-88 [iii] 1985-94	-chômeurs selon l'âge et le sexe	1949-50	1946-49

Index historique
(Voir notes à la fin de l'index)

Sujet	Année de l'édition	Période considérée	Sujet	Année de l'édition	Période considérée
	1969	1960-69	des principales	1962	1955-62
	1970	1950-70	divisions		
	1971	1962-71	administratives		
	1972	1963-72		1963	1955-63 [iii]
	1973	1964-73		1971	1962-71
	1974	1965-74		1973	1965-73 [iii]
	1975	1966-75		1979	1970-79 [iii]
	1976	1967-76		1983	1974-83
	1977	1968-77		1988	1980-88 [iii]
	1978	1969-78		1993	1985-93
	1978SR [i]	1948-78			
	1979	1970-79	**Population**	1949-50	1920-49
	1980	1971-80	des régions	1952	1920-51
	1981	1972-81		1953	1920-52
	1982	1973-82		1954	1920-53
	1983	1974-83		1955	1920-54
	1984	1975-84		1956	1920-55
	1985	1976-85		1957	1920-56
	1986	1977-86		1958	1920-57
	1987	1978-87		1959	1920-58
	1988	1979-88		1960	1920-59
	1989	1980-89		1961	1920-60
	1990	1981-90		1962	1920-61
	1991	1982-91		1963	1930-62
	1992	1983-92		1964	1930-63
	1993	1984-93		1965	1930-65
	1994	1985-94		1966	1930-66
	1995	1986-95		1967	1930-67
	1996	1987-96		1968	1930-68
	1997	1988-97		1969	1930-69
	1997SR [ii]	1948-97		1970	1950-70
	1998	1989-98		1971	1950-71
	1999	1990-99		1972	1950-72
	2000	1991-00		1973	1950-73
	2001	1992-01		1974	1950-74
	2002	1993-02		1975	1950-75
	2003	1994-03		1976	1950-76
	2004	1995-04		1977	1950-77
	2005	1996-05		1978	1950-78
	2006	1997-06		1979	1950-79
	2007	1998-07		1980	1950-80
	2008	1999-08		1981	1950-81
	2009-2010	2001-10		1982	1950-82
	2011	2002-11		1983	1950-83
	2012	2003-12		1984	1950-84
	2013	2004-13		1985	1950-85
	2014	2005-14		1986	1950-86
	2015	2006-15		1987	1950-87
	2016	2007-16		1988	1950-88
	2017	2008-17		1989	1950-89
				1990	1950-90
Population	1952	Dernière		1991	1950-91
	1955	1945-54		1992	1950-92

Index historique
(Voir notes à la fin de l'index)

Sujet	Année de l'édition	Période considérée	Sujet	Année de l'édition	Période considérée
Population	1948	Dernière	**Population**	1977	Dernière
selon l'importance des	1952	Dernière	selon le pays ou zone	1983	1974-83
localités de 20 000	1955	1945-54	de naissance et le sexe	1989	1980-88
habitants et plus	1960	1920-61	et l'âge		
	1962	1955-62			
	1963	1955-63 [iii]	**Population**	1956	1945-55
	1970	1950-70	selon la nationalité	1963	1955-63
	1971	1962-71	juridique et le sexe	1964	1955-64 [iii]
	1973	1965-73 [iii]		1971	1962-71
	1979	1970-79 [iii]		1973	1965-73 [iii]
	1983	1974-83			
	1988	1980-88 [iii]	**Population**	1977	Dernière
	1993	1985-93	selon la nationalité	1983	1974-83
			juridique et le sexe et	1989	1980-88
Population	1948	Dernière	l'âge		
selon l'importance des	1952	Dernière			
localités et le sexe	1955	1945-54	**Population**		voir: des principales divisions
	1962	1955-62	selon les principales		administratives, ci-dessus
	1963	1955-63 [iii]	divisions		
	1971	1962-71	administratives		
	1973	1965-73 [iii]			
	1979	1970-79 [iii]	**Population**	1956	1945-55
	1983	1974-83	selon la religion et le	1963	1955-63
	1988	1980-88 [iii]	sexe	1964	1955-64 [iii]
	1993	1985-93		1971	1962-71
				1973	1965-73 [iii]
Population	1956	1945-55		1979	1970-79 [iii]
selon la langue et le	1963	1955-63		1983	1974-83
sexe				1988	1980-88 [iii]
	1964	1955-64 [iii]		1993	1985-93
	1971	1962-71			
	1973	1965-73 [iii]	**Population**	1968	1964-68
	1979	1970-79 [iii]	selon la résidence	1969	1965-69
	1983	1974-83	(urbaine/rurale)	1970	1950-70
	1988	1980-88 [iii]		1971	1962-71
	1993	1985-93		1972	1968-72
				1973	1965-73
Population	1956	1945-55		1974	1966-74
selon le niveau	1963	1955-63		1975	1967-75
d'instruction, l'âge et le	1964	1955-64 [iii]		1976	1967-76
sexe	1971	1962-71		1977	1968-77
	1973	1965-73 [iii]		1978	1969-78
	1979	1970-79 [iii]		1979	1970-79
	1983	1974-83		1980	1971-80
	1988	1980-88 [iii]		1981	1972-81
	1993	1985-93		1982	1973-82
				1983	1974-83
Population	1956	1945-55		1984	1975-84
selon le pays ou zone	1963	1955-63		1985	1976-85
de naissance et le sexe	1964	1955-64 [iii]		1986	1977-86
	1971	1962-71		1987	1978-87
	1973	1965-73 [iii]		1988	1979-88
				1989	1980-89
				1990	1981-90

Sujet	Année de l'édition	Période considérée	Sujet	Année de l'édition	Période considérée
	1983	1974-83		1993	1985-93
	1993	1985-93			
			-selon la nationalité juridique et le sexe	1971	1962-71
-selon la situation familiale	1991 VP [v]	Dernière		1973	1965-73 [iii]
			-selon la nationalité juridique et le sexe et l'âge	1977	Dernière
-selon l'âge et le sexe: dénombrée	1963	1955-63		1983	1974-83
	1964	1955-64 [iii]		1989	1980-88
	1967	Dernière	-selon le niveau d'instruction, l'âge et le sexe	1971	1962-71
	1970	1950-70		1973	1965-73 [iii]
	1971	1962-71		1979	1970-79 [iii]
	1972	Dernière		1983	1974-83
	1973	1965-73		1988	1980-88 [iii]
	1974-78	Dernière		1993	1985-93
	1978SR [i]	1948-77			
	1979-91	Dernière	-selon le pays ou zone de naissance et le sexe	1971	1962-71
	1991VP [v]	1950-90		1973	1965-73 [iii]
	1992-97	Dernière			
	1997SR [ii]	1948-97			
	1998-2017	Dernière	-selon le pays ou zone de naissance et le sexe et l'âge	1977	Dernière
-selon l'âge et le sexe: estimée	1963	Dernière		1983	1974-83
	1967	Dernière		1989	1980-88
	1970	1950-70	-selon les principales divisions administratives	1971	1962-71
	1971-1997	Dernière		1973	1965-73 [iii]
	1997SR [ii]	1948-97		1979	1970-79 [iii]
	1998-2017	Dernière		1983	1974-83
				1988	1980-88 [iii]
-selon l'alphabétisme, l'âge et le sexe	1971	1962-71		1993	1985-93
	1973	1965-73 [iii]			
	1979	1970-79 [iii]	-selon la religion et le sexe	1971	1962-71
	1983	1974-83		1973	1965-73 [iii]
	1988	1980-88 [iii]		1979	1970-79 [iii]
	1993	1985-93		1983	1974-83
				1988	1980-88 [iii]
-selon la composition ethnique et le sexe	1971	1962-71		1993	1985-93
	1973	1965-73 [iii]			
	1979	1970-79 [iii]	-selon le sexe (nombres)	1948	Dernière
	1983	1974-83		1952	1900-51
	1988	1980-88 [iii]		1955	1945-54
	1993	1985-93		1960	1920-60
	1971	1962-71		1962	1955-62
				1963	1955-63
-selon l'état matrimonial, l'âge et le sexe	1971	1962-71		1964	1955-64 [iii]
	1973	1965-73 [iii]		1967	Dernière
				1970	1950-70
				1971	1962-71
-selon la langue et le sexe	1971	1962-71		1972	Dernière
	1973	1965-73 [iii]		1973	1965-73
	1979	1970-79 [iii]		1974	1966-74
	1983	1974-83		1975	1967-75
	1988	1980-88 [iii]		1976	1967-76
				1977	1968-77

Index historique
(Voir notes à la fin de l'index)

Sujet	Année de l'édition	Période considérée	Sujet	Année de l'édition	Période considérée
	1978	1969-78		1979	1970-79
	1979	1970-79		1980	1971-80
	1980	1971-80		1981	1972-81
	1981	1972-81		1982	1973-82
	1982	1973-82		1983	1974-83
	1983	1974-83		1984	1975-84
	1984	1975-84		1985	1976-85
	1985	1976-85		1986	1977-86
	1986	1977-86		1987	1978-87
	1987	1978-87		1988	1979-88
	1988	1979-88		1989	1980-89
	1989	1980-89		1990	1981-90
	1990	1981-90		1991	1982-91
	1991	1982-91		1992	1983-92
	1992	1983-92		1993	1984-93
	1993	1984-93		1994	1985-94
	1994	1985-94		1995	1986-95
	1995	1986-95		1996	1987-96
	1996	1987-96		1997	1988-97
	1997	1988-97		1998	1989-98
	1998	1989-98		1999	1990-99
	1999	1990-99		2000	1991-00
	2000	1991-00		2001	1992-01
	2001	1992-01		2002	1993-02
	2002	1993-02		2003	1994-03
	2003	1994-03		2004	1995-04
	2004	1995-04		2005	1996-05
	2005	1996-05		2006	1997-06
	2006	1997-06		2007	1998-07
	2007	1998-07		2008	1999-08
	2008	1999-08		2009-2010	2001-10
	2009-2010	2001-10		2011	2002-11
	2011	2002-11		2012	2003-12
	2012	2003-12		2013	2004-13
	2013	2004-13		2014	2005-14
	2014	2005-14		2015	2006-15
	2015	2006-15		2016	2007-16
	2016	2007-16		2017	2008-17
	2017	2008-17			
			Population .... Vieillissement indicateurs divers	1991 VP [v]	1950-90
-selon le sexe (pourcentage)	1948	Dernière			
	1952	1900-51			
	1955	1945-54	**Population** .... Villes		*voir: des villes, ci-dessus*
	1960	1920-60			
	1962	1955-62			
	1970	1950-70	**R**		
	1971	1962-71			
	1973	1965-73	**Rapports**		*voir: Fécondité proportionnelle; Mortalité fœtale (tardive), rapports de; Mortalité périnatale, rapports de; Natalité proportionnelle; Rapports enfants-femmes*
	1974	1966-74			
	1975	1967-75			
	1976	1967-76			
	1977	1968-77			
	1978	1969-78			

Sujet	Année de l'édition	Période considérée	Sujet	Année de l'édition	Période considérée
	1972	1962-72		1971	1962-71
	1973	1965-73 [iii]		1973	1965-73 [iii]
	1979	1970-79 [iii]		1976	1966-75
	1984	1974-84		1983	1974-83
	1988	1980-88 [iii]		1987	1975-86
	1994	1985-94		1995	1985-95
	2014[viii]	1995-2014		2013[viii]	1995-2013
· Caractéristiques ethniques	1956	1945-55	· Caractéristiques relatives à la fécondité	1949-50	1900-50
	1963	1955-63		1954	1900-53
	1964	1955-64 [iii]		1955	1945-54
	1971	1962-71		1959	1935-59
	1973	1965-73 [iii]		1963	1955-63
	1979	1970-79 [iii]		1965	1955-65
	1983	1974-83		1969	Dernière
	1988	1980-88 [iii]		1971	1962-71
	1993	1985-93		1973	1965-73 [iii]
· Caractéristiques géographiques	1952	1900-51		1975	1965-75
	1955	1945-54		1981	1972-81
	1962	1955-62		1986	1977-86
	1964	1955-64 [iii]		1992	1983-92
	1971	1962-71		1999CD [vii]	1980-99
	1973	1965-73 [iii]	-Evolution de la population	1960	1920-60
	1979	1970-79 [iii]		1970	1950-70
	1983	1974-83	-Supplément historique	1978SR [i]	1948-78
	1988	1980-88 [iii]		1997SR [ii]	1948-97
	1993	1985-93	-Vieillissement de la population et situation des personnes âgées	1991VP [v]	1950-90
· Caractéristiques individuelles	1955	1945-54			
	1962	1955-62			
	1971	1962-71			
	1973	1965-73 [iii]	Superficie des continents	1949-50-1999	Dernière
	1979	1970-79 [iii]		2000	2000
	1983	1974-83		2001	2001
	1988	1980-88 [iii]		2002	2002
	1993	1985-93		2003	2003
				2004	2004
· Caractéristiques relatives à l'éducation	1955	1945-54		2005	2005
	1956	1945-55		2006	2006
	1963	1955-63 [iii]		2007	2007
	1964	1955-64		2008	2008
	1971	1962-71		2009-2010	2010
	1973	1965-73 [iii]		2011	2011
	1979	1970-79		2012	2012
	1983	1974-83		2013	2013
	1988	1980-88		2014	2014
	1993	1985-93		2015	2015
				2016	2016
· Caractéristiques relatives aux ménages	1955	1945-54		2017	2017
	1962	1955-62	Superficie des grandes régions	1964-1999	Dernière
	1963	1955-63 [iii]		2000	2000

Index historique
(Voir notes à la fin de l'index)

Sujet	Année de l'édition	Période considérée
(continentales)	2001	2001
	2002	2002
	2003	2003
	2004	2004
	2005	2005
	2006	2006
	2007	2007
	2008	2008
	2009-2010	2010
	2011	2011
	2012	2012
	2013	2013
	2014	2014
	2015	2015
	2016	2016
	2017	2017
Superficie..................... des pays ou zones	1948-2017	Dernière
Superficie..................... des régions	1952-1999	Dernière
	2000	2000
	2001	2001
	2002	2002
	2003	2003
	2004	2004
	2005	2005
	2006	2006
	2007	2007
	2008	2008
	2009-2010	2010
	2011	2011
	2012	2012
	2013	2013
	2014	2014
	2015	2015
	2016	2016
	2017	2017
Superficie..................... du monde	1949-50-1999	Dernière
	2000	2000
	2001	2001
	2004	2004
	2005	2005
	2006	2006
	2007	2007
	2008	2008
	2009-2010	2010
	2011	2011
	2012	2012
	2013	2013

Sujet	Année de l'édition	Période considérée
	2014	2014
	2015	2015
	2016	2016
	2017	2017
Survivants.....................		*voir: Mortalité, tables de*

T

Sujet	Année de l'édition	Période considérée
Tables de mortalité............		*voir: Mortalité, tables de*
Taux.....................		*voir: Accroissement intercensitaire de la population; Accroissement naturel; Alphabétisme; Analphabétisme; Annulation; Divortialité; Fécondité Intercensitaire; Mortalité Infantile, Mortalité maternelle; Mortalité néonatale; Mortalité post-néonatale; Mortalité, tables de; Mortalité; Natalité; Nuptialité; Reproduction; taux bruts et nets de*
Taux bruts de reproduction.....................		*voir: Reproduction*
Taux nets de reproduction.		*voir: Reproduction*
Texte spécial.....................		*voir liste détaillée dans l'Appendice de cet index*

U

Sujet	Année de l'édition	Période considérée
Urbaine/rurale (décès)........		*voir: Décès*
Urbaine/rurale (ménages: dimension moyenne des) ..		*voir: Ménages*
Urbaine/rurale (mortalité infantile)		*voir: Mortalité infantile*
Urbaine/rurale (naissances)		*voir: Naissances*
Urbaine/rurale(population)		*voir: Population selon la résidence (urbaine/rurale)*

V

Sujet	Année de l'édition	Période considérée
Vieillissement.....................		*voir: Population*
Villes...............................		*voir: Population*

APPENDICE

Texte spécial de chaque Annuaire démographique

Divorce:

"Application des statistiques de la nuptialité et de la divortialité", 1958.

Mariage:

"Application des statistiques de la nuptialité et de la divortialité", 1958.

Ménages:

"Concepts et définitions des ménages, du chef de ménage et de la population des collectivités", 1987.

Migration:

"'Statistiques des migrations internationales",1977.

Mortalité:

"Tendances récentes de la mortalité", 1951.
"Développement des statistiques des causes de décès",1951.
"Les facteurs du fléchissement de la mortalité",1957.
"Notes sur les méthodes d'évaluation de la fiabilité des statistiques classiques de la mortalité",1961.
"Mortalité: Tendances récentes",1966.
"Tendances de la mortalité chez les personnes âgées",1991VP ^{v}.

Natalité:

"Présentation graphiques des tendances de la fécondité",1959.

"Taux de natalité: Tendances récentes",1965.

Population: ..

"Tendances démo-graphiques mondiales,1920-1949",1949-50.
"Mouvements d'urbanisation et ses caractéristiques",1952.
"Les recensements de population de 1950",1955.
"Situation démographique mondiale",1956.
"Ce que nous savons de l'état et de l'évolution de la population mondiale",1960.
"Notes sur les statistiques disponibles des recensements nationaux de population et méthodes d'évaluation de leur exactitude",1962.
"Disponibilité et qualité de certaines données statistiques fondées sur les recensements de population effectués entre 1955 et 1963",1963.
"Disponibilité de certaines statistiques fondées sur les recensements de population: 1955-1964",1964.

"Définitions et concepts statistiques de la population urbaine et de la population rurale",1967.
"Application des statistiques de la nuptialité et de la divortialité",1958.
"Ce que nous savons de l'état et de l'évolution de la population mondiale",1970.
"Recommandations de l'Organisation des Nations Unies quant aux sujets sur lesquels doit porter un recensement de population, en regard de la pratique adoptée par les différents pays dans les recensements nationaux effectués de 1965 à 1971",1971.
"Les définitions statistiques de la population urbaine et leurs usages en démographie appliquée",1972.

"Evolution récente de la fécondité dans le monde",1969.
"Dates des recensements nationaux de la population et de l'habitation effectués au cours de la décennie 1965-1974", 1974.

Index historique
(Voir notes à la fin de l'index)

"Dates des recensements nationaux de la population et de l'habitation effectués ou prévus, au cours de la décennie 1975-1984",1979.

"Dates des recensements nationaux de la population et/ou de l'habitation effectués au cours de la décennie 1965-1974 et effectués ou prévus au cours de la décennie1975-1984",1983.

"Définitions et concepts statistiques du ménage",1968.

"Dates des recensements nationaux de la population et/ou de l'habitation effectués au cours de la décennie 1975-1984 et effectués ou prévus au cours de la décennie1985-1994", 1988, 1993.

"Statistiques concernant la population active: un aperçu",1984.

"'Etude du vieillissement et de la situation des personnes âgées: Besoins particuliers",1991VP [v].

"Les incapacités", 1991VP [v].

"Le vieillissement", 1991VP [v].

Notes générales

Cet index alphabétique donne la liste des sujets traités dans chacune de 68 éditions de l'Annuaire démographique. La colonne "Année de l'édition" indique l'édition spécifique dans laquelle le sujet a été traité. Sauf indication contraire, la colonne "Période considérée" désigne les années pour lesquelles les statistiques annuelles apparaissant dans l'Annuaire démographique sont indiquées sous la colonne "Année de l'édition". La rubrique "Dernière" ou " 2-Dernières" indique que les données représentent la ou les dernières années disponibles seulement.

[i] Le Supplément rétrospectif du 30ème Annuaire Démographique fait l'objet d'un tirage spécial publié en 1979.

[ii] Le Supplément rétrospectif du 49ème Annuaire Démographique fait l'objet d'un tirage spécial (CD-ROM) publié en 2000.

[iii] Données non disponibles dans l'édition précédente seulement.

[iv] Titres non disponibles dans la bibliographie précédente seulement.

[v] Vieillissement de la population.

[vi] Taux moyens pour 5 ans.

[vii] Le Supplément du 51 Annuaire Démographique, ayant comme suject la natalité, fait l'objet d'un tirage spécial (CD-ROM) publié en 2002.

[viii] Les tableaux sont publiés en ligne.

SUPPLEMENTAL INDEX OF DATASETS PUBLISHED ONLINE[1]

In recent years, additionally to publishing annually the United Nations *Demographic Yearbook*, several demographic and social datasets are published online via the UNdata portal. UNdata portal is an internet based data service maintained by the Statistics Division of the Department of Economic and Social Affairs of the United Nations. Below is an alphabetical order list of datasets published online as of October 2018. These datasets can be accessed at http://data.un.org/Explorer.aspx?d=POP.

- City population by sex, city and city type
- Deaths by age, sex and urban/rural residence
- Deaths by cause of death, age and sex
- Deaths by month of death
- Deaths by sex and urban/rural residence
- Divorces by urban/rural residence
- Economically active foreign-born population by occupation, age, sex and urban/rural residence
- Employed population by age, sex and industry
- Employed population by age, sex and marital status
- Employed population by occupation, age and sex
- Employed population by status in employment, age and sex
- Employed population by status in employment, industry and sex
- Employed population by status in employment, occupation and sex
- Female population by age, number of children ever born and urban/rural residence
- Female population by age, number of children living and urban/rural residence
- Foreign population (non-citizens) 15 years of age or over by country of citizenship, educational attainment and sex
- Foreign population (non-citizens) by country of citizenship, age and sex
- Foreign-born population 15 years of age or over by country/area of birth, educational attainment and sex
- Foreign-born population by country/area of birth, age and sex
- Households by age and sex of reference person and by size of household
- Households by broad types of living quarters/number of roofless by urban/rural location
- Households by broad types of living quarters/number of roofless for selected cities
- Households by type of household and sex and marital status of head of household or other reference member
- Households by type of household, age and sex of head of household or other reference member
- Households in housing units by type of housing unit and availability of communication technology devices/access to Internet for selected cities
- Households in housing units by type of housing unit and tenure of household for selected cities
- Households in housing units by type of housing unit and urban/rural residence
- Households in housing units by type of housing unit for selected cities
- Households in housing units by type of housing unit, availability of communication technology devices/access to Internet by urban/rural location
- Households in housing units by type of housing unit, tenure of household and urban/rural residence
- Infant deaths by sex and urban/rural residence
- Inflows by purpose of staying abroad and sex
- Inflows by reason for admission and sex
- Legally induced abortions by urban/rural residence of woman
- Live births by age of mother and sex of child
- Live births by birth order and age of mother
- Live births by birth weight and sex of child
- Live births by gestational age
- Live births by month of birth
- Live births by plurality
- Live births by sex and urban/rural residence
- Live births in wedlock by duration of marriage
- Living quarters by broad types and urban/rural location
- Living quarters by broad types for selected cities
- Marriages by urban/rural residence

---

[1] This supplemental index is available only in English.

- Native and foreign-born population by age, sex and urban/rural residence
- Number of departing international migrants by citizenship status, age and sex
- Number of emigrating citizens by future country of usual residence and sex
- Number of incoming foreign migrants by country of citizenship and sex
- Number of incoming international migrants by previous country of usual residence and sex
- Number of incoming migrants by citizenship status, age and sex
- Occupants of housing units by type of housing unit and number of rooms for selected cities
- Occupants of housing units by type of housing unit and urban/rural residence
- Occupants of housing units by type of housing unit for selected cities
- Occupants of housing units by type of housing unit, number of rooms and urban/rural residence
- Occupied housing units by type of housing unit and availability of kitchen for selected cities
- Occupied housing units by type of housing unit and construction material of outer walls for selected cities
- Occupied housing units by type of housing unit and main source of drinking water for selected cities
- Occupied housing units by type of housing unit and main type of fuel used for cooking for selected cities
- Occupied housing units by type of housing unit and main type of solid waste disposal for selected cities
- Occupied housing units by type of housing unit and number of rooms for selected cities
- Occupied housing units by type of housing unit and type of bathing facilities for selected cities
- Occupied housing units by type of housing unit and type of lighting for selected cities
- Occupied housing units by type of housing unit and type of toilet for selected cities
- Occupied housing units by type of housing unit and type of water supply system for selected cities
- Occupied housing units by type of housing unit and urban/rural location
- Occupied housing units by type of housing unit for selected cities
- Occupied housing units by type of housing unit, availability of kitchen and urban/rural location
- Occupied housing units by type of housing unit, construction material of outer walls and urban/rural residence
- Occupied housing units by type of housing unit, main source of drinking water and urban/rural location
- Occupied housing units by type of housing unit, main type of fuel used for cooking and urban/rural location
- Occupied housing units by type of housing unit, main type of solid waste disposal and urban/rural location
- Occupied housing units by type of housing unit, number of rooms and urban/rural location
- Occupied housing units by type of housing unit, type of bathing facilities and urban/rural location
- Occupied housing units by type of housing unit, type of lighting and urban/rural location
- Occupied housing units by type of housing unit, type of toilet and urban/rural location
- Occupied housing units by type of housing unit, type of water supply system and urban/rural location
- Outflows by purpose of going abroad and sex
- Outflows by status at time of departure and sex
- Population 15 years of age and over, by educational attainment, age and sex
- Population 5 to 24 years of age by school attendance, sex and urban/rural residence
- Population by activity status, age, sex and urban/rural residence
- Population by age, sex and urban/rural residence
- Population by broad types of living quarters/number of roofless and sex for selected cities
- Population by broad types of living quarters/number of roofless, sex and urban/rural residence
- Population by citizenship status, age and sex
- Population by language, sex and urban/rural residence
- Population by literacy, age, sex and urban/rural residence
- Population by marital status, age, sex and urban/rural residence
- Population by national and/or ethnic group, sex and urban/rural residence
- Population by religion, sex and urban/rural residence
- Population by sex and urban/rural residence
- Population by type of living quarters, age and sex
- Population in collective living quarters by type of living quarters and sex for selected cities
- Population in collective living quarters by type of living quarters, sex and urban/rural residence
- Population in households by relation to head of household or other reference member and by age and sex
- Population in households by type of household, age and sex
- Population in households by type of household, age and sex of head of household or other reference member
- Population not economically active by functional category, age, sex and urban/rural residence